MW01007092

Presented To

By

On

Your word is like a lamp for my feet
and a light for my path . . .
I will follow your rules forever,
because they make me happy . . .
I love your commands
more than the purest gold.

PSALM 119:105, 111, 127

Holy Bible

New Century Version

The Holy Bible
New Century Version

The EVERYDAY Study Bible

FOR PEOPLE WHO WANT
TO KNOW THE WORD

JOEL B. GREEN, PH.D.
TREMPER LONGMAN III, PH.D.
General Editors

WORD
BIBLES

Dallas • London • Vancouver • Melbourne

The Holy Bible, New Century Version

The Publisher is pleased hereby to grant permission for the *New Century Version* to be quoted or reprinted without prior written permission with the following qualifications: (1) up to and including one thousand (1,000) verses may be quoted, except: (a) the verses being quoted may not comprise as much as 50 percent of the work in which they are quoted, and/or (b) the verses quoted may not comprise an entire book of the Bible when quoted.

Quotations from this Bible may be identified in written form with the abbreviation (NCV) in less formal documents, such as bulletins, newsletters, curriculum, media pieces, posters, transparencies, and where space is limited.

A proper copyright credit line must appear on the title or copyright page of any work quoting from the *New Century Version,* as follows:

"Scriptures quoted from *The Holy Bible, New Century Version,* copyright © 1987, 1988, 1991 by Word Publishing, Dallas, Texas 75234. Used by permission."

Quotations of more than 1,000 verses, or other permission requests, must be approved by Word Publishing in writing in advance of use.

All excerpts used by permission.

The preliminary research and development of the *New Century Version* was done by the World Bible Translation Center, Inc., Fort Worth, TX 76182.

Article entitled "Women" excerpted from *Let Me Be A Woman,* by Elisabeth Elliot, © 1976 by Tyndale House Publishers, Inc. Used by permission. All rights reserved.

Interior illustrations used by permission. Copyright © Lion Publishing. All rights reserved.

Cover art and initial interior design done by The Puckett Group, Atlanta, Georgia.

Typesetting, final interior design, and production done by Koechel Peterson and Associates, Inc., Minneapolis, Minnesota.

Library of Congress Cataloging-in-Publication Data

Bible. English. New Century Version. 1996.

The everyday study Bible: for people who want to know the word/
Joel B. Green and Tremper Longman III, general editors.

p. cm.

Includes Index

ISBN 0-8499-5009-0 (hardcover:alk. paper).

ISBN 0-8499-5290-5 (leatherflex:alk. paper).

I. Green, Joel B., 1956– II. Longman III, Tremper III. Title.

BS195.N353 1996

220.5'208—dc20 96-22917

CIP

96 97 98 99 00 01 RRD 9 8 7 6 5 4 3 2 1

Published by Word Publishing

Contents

Books of the Old Testament

Books of the New Testament

Alphabetical List of Bible Books

New Testament books are in italics.

WHERE DO I FIND...?

Have you ever known what you were looking for but didn't know where to find it in the Bible? A great event? A famous passage? A favorite story? Use this guide to help you find stories you remember but don't know where to find. The descriptions listed here are the common descriptions and are not always exactly the same as the descriptions in the Bible translation.

STORIES AND PEOPLE	SCRIPTURE REFERENCE	PAGE
Abraham	Genesis 11:27-25:11	16
Adam	Genesis 2:4-3:24	6
Beatitudes	Matthew 5:1-12	1125
	Luke 6:20-23	1211
Cain and Abel	Genesis 4:1-24	8
Creation	Genesis 1:1-2:3	5
	Genesis 2:4-25	6
Daniel	Daniel 1-6	1003
David	1 Samuel 16-30	324
	2 Samuel 1-24	343
	1 Chronicles 11-22; 28-29	462
David and Goliath	1 Samuel 17:1-58	324
Deborah	Judges 4	273
Elijah, the prophet	1 Kings 17-19, 21	402
Esther	Esther 1-10	557
Eve	Genesis 2:18-3:24	6
Exodus from Egypt	Exodus 12:31-14:31	82
Fruit of the Spirit	Galatians 5:22-23	1395
Garden of Eden	Genesis 2:4-3:24	6
Golden rule	Matthew 7:12	1128
Good Samaritan	Luke 10:25-37	1221
Great commandment	Matthew 22:34-40	1155
	Mark 12:28-34	1190
	Luke 10:25-28	1221
Great commission	Matthew 28:18-20	1167
Isaac	Genesis 21-27	26
Jacob	Genesis 25:19-33, 35	31
Jesus' life		
Birth	Matthew 1:18-2:12	1119
	Luke 2:1-21	1205
Boyhood	Luke 2:41-52	1206
Baptism	Matthew 3:13-17	1124
	Mark 1:9-11	1171
	Luke 3:21-22	1207
Temptation	Matthew 4:1-11	1124
	Mark 1:12-13	1171
	Luke 4:1-13	1208
Choosing his disciples	Matthew 4:18-22	1124
	Mark 1:16-20	1171
	Luke 5:1-11	1210

PREFACE TO THE NEW CENTURY VERSION

God intended for everyone to be able to understand his Word. Earliest Scriptures were in Hebrew, ideally suited for a barely literate society because of its economy of words, acrostic literary form and poetic parallelism. The New Testament was first written in the simple Greek of everyday life, not in the Latin of Roman courts or the classical Greek of the academies. Even Jesus, the Master Teacher, taught spiritual principles by comparing them to such familiar terms as pearls, seeds, rocks, trees, and sheep. Likewise, the *New Century Version* translates the Scriptures in familiar, everyday words of our times.

The *New Century Version* is a bestselling translation of God's Word from the original Hebrew and Greek languages. Several previous editions of the complete *New Century Version* have been published, such as the *International Children's Bible* (1986); *Time With God* (1991); *The Odyssey Bible* (1994); *The Answer* (1993); and *The Inspirational Study Bible* (1995), among others.

A Trustworthy Translation

Two basic premises guided the translation process of the *New Century Version.* The first concern was that the translation be faithful to the manuscripts in the original languages. A team composed of the World Bible Translation Center and fifty additional, highly qualified and experienced Bible scholars and translators was assembled. The team included people with translation experience on such accepted versions as the *New International Version,* the *New American Standard Bible* and the *New King James Version.* The most recent scholarship and the best available Hebrew and Greek texts were used, principally the third edition of the United Bible Societies' Greek text and the latest edition of the Biblia Hebraica, along with the Septuagint.

A Clear Translation

The second concern was to make the language clear enough for anyone to read the Bible and understand it for himself. In maintaining clear language, several guidelines were followed. Vocabulary choice has been based upon *The Living Word Vocabulary* by Dr. Edgar Dale and Dr. Joseph O'Rourke (Worldbook Childcraft International), which is the standard used by the editors of *The World Book Encyclopedia* to determine appropriate vocabulary. For difficult words which have no simpler synonyms, footnotes and dictionary references are provided. Footnotes appear at the bottom of the page and the dictionary/topical concordance is located at the back of the Bible.

The *New Century Version* aids understanding by putting concepts into natural terms. Modern measurements and geographical locations have been used as much as possible. For instance, terms such as "shekels," "cubits," "omer" and "hin" have been converted to modern equivalents of weights and measures. Where geographical references are identical, the modern name has been used, such as the "Mediterranean Sea" instead of "Great Sea" or "Western Sea." Also, to minimize confusion, the most familiar name for a place is used consistently, instead of using variant names for the same place. "Lake Galilee" is used throughout rather than its variant forms, "Sea of Kinnereth," "Lake Gennesaret" and "Sea of Tiberias."

Ancient customs are often unfamiliar to modern readers. Customs such as shaving a man's beard to shame him or walking between the halves of a dead animal to seal an agreement are meaningless to most people. So these are clarified either in the text or in a footnote.

Since *meanings* of words change with time, care has been taken to avoid potential misunderstandings. Frequently in the Old Testament God tells his people to "devote" something to him, as when he tells the Israelites to devote Jericho and everything in it to him. While we might understand this to mean he is telling them to keep it safe and holy, the exact opposite is true. He is telling them to destroy it totally as an offering to him. The *New Century Version* communicates the idea clearly by translating "devoted," in these situations, as "destroyed as an offering to the Lord."

Rhetorical questions have been stated according to their implied answers. The psalmist's question, "What god is so great as our God?" has been stated more directly as, "No god is as great as our God."

Figures of speech have been translated according to their meanings. For instance, the expression, "the Virgin Daughter of Zion," which is frequently used in the Old Testament, is simply translated "the people of Jerusalem."

Idiomatic expressions of the biblical languages are translated to communicate the same meaning to today's reader that would have been understood by the original audience. For example, the Hebrew idiom "he rested with his fathers" is translated by its corresponding current meaning—"he died."

Obscure terms have been clarified. In the Old Testament God frequently condemns the people for their "high places" and "Asherah poles." The *New Century Version* translates those according to their meanings, which would have been understood by the Hebrews. "High places" is translated "places where gods were worshiped" and "Asherah poles" is translated "Asherah idols."

Gender language has also been translated with a concern for clarity. To avoid the misconception that "man" and "mankind" and "he" are exclusively masculine when they are being used in a generic sense, this translation has chosen to use less ambiguous language, such as "people" and "humans" and "human beings," and has prayerfully attempted throughout to choose gender language that would accurately convey the intent of the original writers. Specifically and exclusively masculine and feminine references in the text have been retained.

Following in the tradition of other English versions, the *New Century Version* indicates the divine name YHWH, the Tetragrammaton, by putting LORD, and sometimes GOD, in capital letters. This is to distinguish it from Adonai, another Hebrew word that is translated Lord.

Every attempt has been made to maintain proper English style, while clarifying concepts and communication. The beauty of the Hebrew parallelism in poetry and the word plays have been retained, and the images of the ancient languages have been captured in equivalent English images wherever possible.

Our Prayer

It is with great humility and prayerfulness that this Bible is presented. We acknowledge the infallibility of God's Word and yet our own human frailty. We pray that God has worked through us as his vessels so that we all might better learn his truth for ourselves and that it might richly grow in our lives. It is to his glory that this Bible is given.

THE PUBLISHER

INTRODUCTION TO THE EVERYDAY STUDY BIBLE

Using the *Holy Bible, New Century Version* as its base text, *The Everyday Study Bible* is a delightful blend of God's inspired Word and insightful writings by biblical scholars that illuminate and explain the two hundred sixty most important themes and ideas of God's message. Combined with dozens of other proven Bible study tools, such as the helpful Dictionary/Concordance, the book you hold in your hands is like an all-in-one biblical reference library.

Browse through its pages, and you'll encounter kings and paupers, heroes and cowards, giants and toddlers. The world's greatest victories and worst defeats share its factual pages. It's every kind of book rolled into one—an intriguing mystery, the greatest happily-ever-after love story ever told, a detailed and accurate historical record, a sensitive book of poetry, a songbook, the most quotable quote book in the world, the most effective how-to book on being a success in today's world, and a biography of the greatest man ever to live. This book is resplendent with physical feats so phenomenal they sound like fiction, verifiable testimonies of actual encounters with angels and demons, puzzling dreams and explosive visions, diabolical plots, and heartwarming tales of simple charity. Is it any wonder that the Bible is the best-selling book of all time?

All of that, plus some distinctive features, help you discover the truth contained in its powerful pages—truth from the dawn of time that still applies to you today. It is the wondrous Book of God.

FEATURES

To enrich your personal study, *The Everyday Study Bible* incorporates some excellent features and tools to enhance your understanding.

Thematic Articles are inserted throughout the Bible text. Each of these two hundred sixty articles explores a vital topic in God's Word—an important theme, Bible character, place, or contemporary issue. These articles have been prepared by a team of more than seventy Bible scholars from a variety of theological backgrounds. The articles illuminate important biblical truths and help you apply those truths to your daily life.

In-Text Notes. In conjunction with the Thematic Articles, explanatory notes about specific points of the articles have been included to give you more in-depth information on that point. These nuggets of information enrich your understanding of historical backgrounds to Bible events, biographical sketches of Bible characters, special cultural aspects, and other helpful concepts.

Section Introductions. The books of the Bible fall into six primary categories. Each of these six sections is preceded in this study Bible by an introduction that describes and explains the type of writing and literature in that section. See the contents page in the front of the book for the locations of these section introductions.

Bible Book Introductions. To help you get started quickly in your study of a particular book of the Bible, *The Everyday Study Bible* provides an introduction to each Bible book written by our team of Bible scholars. The Bible book introduction immediately precedes the respective book to give an overview of that particular book and its importance to the complete Word of God.

How To Study the Bible. This seven-step, practical approach to studying the Bible will help you answer the basic questions you need to grasp about each Bible book or passage you study. The seven-step study approach is carried through this Bible in the introduction of each Bible book where the seven questions are answered.

Where Do I Find? This alphabetical list in the front of your Bible is a quick-reference tool to help you locate favorite Bible people, places, and events. Do you love the story of Stephen, but you don't know where to look for it? Look for "Stephen" on the "Where Do I Find?" list, and you will find the Bible reference location you need.

Bible Dictionary. When you come across a word that's unfamiliar to you during your study, look in the Topical Dictionary/Concordance in the back of this book. You'll likely find a clear definition of the word, along with a pronunciation guide, and a list of other places in the Bible where that word or concept can be found.

Concordance. Perhaps you need to find some additional scriptures on some topic like "God's grace." Find that key word ("grace") in the Topical Dictionary/Concordance in the back of this book, and some passages will be listed where you can read more about that topic.

Chain Reference Study System. At the end of each of the Thematic Articles (see explanation above), you will be referred to the first in a list (or "chain") of scriptures that deal with that topic. A small chain symbol ⚭ will appear at the end of the reading and again at the bottom of that Bible page. For instance, at the end of the article on "Abraham," a chain symbol will appear referring you to the corresponding chain symbol at the bottom of the page where you will see a reference like this:

⚭**Abraham:** For additional scriptures on this topic go to Genesis 11:26–27.

Turn to and read/study the passage in Genesis. At the end of verse 27 will appear the chain symbol again, referring to the next scripture in the chain at the bottom of that page. Continue following the chain of references until they lead you back to the article on "Abraham" where you began.

Note: You can begin following any chain at any point along the chain. If you are reading through Genesis and come to 11:27, you can choose to begin following the chain and follow it until it brings you back to 11:27 where you began. Along the way you will come across the article on "Abraham," who is mentioned in 11:27.

Index to Thematic Articles & One-Year Daily Study Guide. In the back of this Bible you will find a one-year study guide based on the Thematic Articles explained above and their respective chain references. Each week day (Monday – Friday), chose a topic from the Daily Study Guide to use as your personal devotion for that day. Start the devotional with a prayer that God will bless your study of his Word. Read the thematic article you have chosen for that day. Then, follow the scripture chain that begins at the end of that article until you are lead back to the article. Some topics have more references than others. Close your devotional time with a prayer asking God to show you how to apply what you have learned to your own life. When you have completed the day's study, check the small box ❑ in front of that topic in the Daily Study Guide so you will know that you have covered that topic. At the end of one year, you will have studied the two hundred sixty most vital subjects in the Bible.

You will also find these other useful tools and features in this Bible:

- **Charts, Illustrations, and Maps** inserted throughout the text lend visual understanding and at-a-glance coverage of specific concepts, such as the parables of Jesus, or the missionary journeys of Paul the Apostle. For a list of these visual aids, see the Index of Charts, Illustrations, and Maps in the back of this book.
- **An Alphabetical List of Bible Book Names** in the front of this Bible serves as a quick way to find the number of the page on which a particular book begins.
- **Table of Weights and Measurements** in the back of this book is a visualization and explanation of Bible weights and measures in modern terms.
- **Money of Bible Times** in the back of this book depicts typical coins of Bible times and their values.

ACKNOWLEDGMENTS

I would like to thank God for the opportunity and privilege of serving, along with Joel Green, as editor of T*he Everyday Study Bible.* It has been a project that has allowed me to enter deeply into the study of God's Word and the occasion of learning from many insightful people.

In that regard, I would first like to thank the contributors who are listed on the next page. Their careful thinking and writing lessened my workload and instructed me in the truth of the Scriptures.

I would also thank Joel Green, with whom I always enjoy working. It was fun to brainstorm with him and the others at Word Publishing about a new type of reference Bible.

Lastly, but most importantly to me, I would like to thank my wife, Alice, and my three sons—Tremper (IV), Timothy, and Andrew—for their encouragement and support during the long hours it has taken to complete this project.

TREMPER LONGMAN III
GENERAL EDITOR

In addition, we at Word Publishing wish to thank the many talented freelance editors, proofreaders, artists, designers, computer operators, and production personnel who made such valuable and timely contributions to this book. We couldn't have accomplished the project without you.

Our special appreciation to the Puckett Group in Atlanta and Koechel Peterson Design in Minneapolis who added their unique designs both to the exterior and interior of this book, taking it from piles of manuscript to the well organized and useful resource you hold in your hand in a remarkable length of time.

It is our hope and prayer that *The Everyday Study Bible* will touch the hearts and lives of people with the saving message of God's grace on a daily basis. To him alone be the glory, honor, and praise, for he alone is worthy.

THE PUBLISHER

CONTRIBUTORS

General Editors:
Joel B. Green; Tremper Longman III

The individuals named below contributed significantly to *The Everyday Study Bible* through the development and writing of one or more thematic articles and in-text notes included throughout the book. An associate scholar carefully reviewed and evaluated each article, made recommendations for corrections and finalization, and in some cases prepared additional in-text notes. The General Editors examined and/or edited each article as required for accuracy, appropriateness, and helpfulness, including in-text notes. Original articles were contributed by the following people:

Margaret Alter
Jane Bacon
Mark Baker
Robert Banks
Dick Belcher
Jessie Bible
Mark Lau Branson
Michael Brown
Greg Camp
Frank Chan
Michael Christensen
Chuck Colson
Greg Cootsona
Larry Crabb
Melinda Creson
Richard Davis
Brian Dodd
John W. Drane
Elisabeth Elliot
Milton Eng
Peter Enns
M. A. Eschelbach
Douglas Green
Joel Green
Hank Hanegraaff
Steve Harper
Jack Hayford
Carl F. H. Henry
Steve Horine
Evan Howard
Bonnie Howe
Meagan Howland
Don Hudson
Bill Hybels
Karen Jobes
Scott Jones
C. Everett Koop
Tremper Longman III
John MacArthur
Christopher Maitz
Larry Martin
Walter Martin
Stephen Martyn
Dan McCartney
Josh McDowell
Luan Mendel
Don Mills
John Warwick Montgomery
Erika Moore
Daniel Oden
Dana Ortiz
J. I. Packer
Alan Padgett
Margaret Parker
R. Wade Paschal
Steven Pattie
Edward Pauley
Susan Phillips
Wesley Putnam
Russell Rathbun
Bora Lee Reed
Steven Sao-Yuan Lee
Elizabeth Sendek
Gary Smalley
David Stabnow
Charles Stanley
Leslie Stanley-Stevens
Charles Swindoll
Daniel Taylor
John Trent
Michael Wilkins
Michael Williams
Ben Witherington III
Barry Wong

Publisher: David L. Moberg
Editorial Director:
Mary Hollingsworth
Production Manager: Lyn Rose
Book Design/Production:
The Puckett Group, Atlanta
Koechel Peterson, Minneapolis

How To Study the Bible

Studying God's Word—what a privilege! What an exhilirating experience! What an overwhelming thought. . . .

Do you have to be a scholar to understand it? Where do you begin? What process do you use? Can you even hope to figure it out on your own?

Relax! Admittedly at first glance the Bible may be a little intimidating to a new student of the Word. But remember, millions of people have successfully read it for themselves and learned God's will for their lives . . . and you can too.

The whole point to studying the Bible is finding answers to your own personal questions about God, Jesus, salvation, and life. The best way to do that is through a systematic method of study, rather than a random approach. There are many different logical methods of Bible study, each of which you may want to pursue in the exciting days ahead of exploring God's Word. One good method to get you started is simple but revealing. It's what might be called "The Seven Ws" method.

The Seven Ws

In order to best understand the various books and writings in the Bible, it is imperative that you identify the settings, characters, audiences, issues, and reasons for those writings. By applying seven basic questions to each section of Scripture as you begin studying it, you will put everything into perspective and, thus, be able to make the proper application of the teachings in that passage to your own life.

1. *Who wrote this passage or book?* Who is the inspired writer of this portion of Scripture? You can often discover the answer to this question in the opening verses of the book of the Bible in which you're studying. For instance, let's look at the Book of James in the New Testament. Verse one of the first chapter identifies the writer as "James, a servant of God and of the Lord Jesus Christ."

   If the opening verses of the book do not clearly identify the writer, you may wish to refer to the introduction that has been provided for you in *The Everyday Study Bible* immediately preceeding each Bible book.

2. *To whom is the passage or book written?* Once again the opening verses of a book often reveal the intended recipient of the message. Let's look again at the Book of James. The second part of verse one says "to all of God's people who are scattered everywhere in the world." Verse two identifies them further when James calls them "my brothers and sisters." James was evidently writing to his Christian brothers and sisters, who are God's people, all over the world.

   If the opening verses of the book do not clearly identify to whom the passage is addressed, you may wish to check for the answer in the introduction of that book in this study Bible.

3. *Where was it written?* Was the writer living in a palace, like King Solomon, or imprisoned in a rat-infested dungeon, like Paul? Was he in the north or the south? Was he in the desert or the Promised Land? His "where" might have great impact on what he says.

   Searching out the "where" of Bible passages is sometimes easy . . . and sometimes not so easy. Finding the answer to where the writer composed the writing often becomes more apparent as you read farther into the book or passage. For instance, the early verses of the Book of Romans do not reveal where Paul the Apostle was when he wrote the letter to the Christians at Rome. However, because of references to Phoebe of Cenchrea (16:1) and to Gaius, Paul's host (16:23), who was probably a citizen of the city of Corinth, scholars have concluded that Paul was likely in Corinth or Cenchrea when he wrote the letter to the Romans.

   You may also want to know where the recipients to the message were located. Were they in captivity? Were they in Rome or Egypt or Jerusalem? Their "where" may have greatly influenced what the writer said to them.

   Watch for clues to the "where" of the writer and the recipients as you read a book in the Bible. But also feel free to look for that answer quickly in the introduction to the book that has been provided for you in *The Everyday Study Bible.*

4. *When was it written?* What was happening in the world at the time of the writing? What historical events were influencing the writer and the recipients of the message? Were they living in a time of peace or war?

Were they under persecution or enjoying freedom? Was this written before or after Jesus lived?

Like the "where" of a passage, the "when" is not often obvious in the writing itself. It must be deduced from clues in the text. A good example appears in the first verse of the Book of Ezra in the Old Testament. Ezra, the writer, identifies the "when" of his writing as "the first year of Cyrus king of Persia." By checking world history for the dates of Cyrus's reign, scholars have determined that the Book of Ezra was written about 440 B.C.

However, when the dates are less evident from reading the text, you can refer to the scholarly helps provided in the introduction to the book in which you are studying.

5. *WHAT IS THE WRITING ABOUT?* Each book in the Bible is centered around some theme or topic. For instance, the first seventeen books of the Old Testament (Genesis – Esther) are about the history and laws of God's people. The Book of Acts in the New Testament tells the story of how the church of Jesus Christ grew and spread into all the world, while the Book of Psalms (sometimes called "Israel's Songbook") is a collection of Hebrew poetry that was written to be sung by the people.

   The "what" of a passage can be discovered by carefully reading the book or a passage in its complete context. To give additional insight, however, *The Everyday Study Bible* provides six section introductions that slot the various Bible books into broad subject categories, such as "Pastoral Letters." Beyond that, the book introduction itself may give further definition of the book's message.

6. *WHY WAS IT WRITTEN?* Each Bible book was written for a specific purpose as a part of the inspiration of God. Knowing the "why" of a book or passage is critical to understanding its importance. Was it written to record an event for history, such as Esther? Was it written to praise God, like Psalms? Was it written to solve a problem, as Philemon was? Was it written to teach something important, as Galatians teaches about the grace of God?

   For a quick explanation of a book's theme or "why," you may want to refer to the book's introduction in this study Bible. For a more personal discovery, carefully read and study the writing itself within its complete context. As you read, continually ask yourself, "Why is this writing in the Bible? What purpose does it serve?" You'll surprise yourself at how often you'll be able to determine that reason for yourself.

7. *SO WHAT DOES THIS PASSAGE OR BOOK MEAN TO US?* Once you have found answers for the first six questions about a biblical book or passage, say to yourself, "So what?" In other words, "What do all these facts have to do with me personally?" "How can I use the information I've discovered in this passage to improve my life and draw closer to God?" "How do these inspired words from God apply to me and my spiritual life?"

   Of all the seven Ws, the "So what?" is the most important. The words of the Bible can only help you if you apply them daily to your personal life. Without application, they are useless ink on paper. But when you take them into your heart and mind, the words of God transform you from lost to saved, they give you peace in the midst of panic, they create light out of darkness, and they produce heavenly joy from worldly depression.

God's promises are rich and rare, like diamonds dug from the earth. And you find them one at a time by carefully mining his Word. That experience is your life's most delightful search, an adventure to be treasured and enjoyed throughout life. It's an exploration into the very heart of God—the One who gave you life, the One who gave you unmerited love, the One who gave you his only Son, and the One who offers you eternal joy. Pursue his promises daily in *The Everyday Study Bible.*

The Old Testament

INTRODUCTION TO SECTION ONE
GENESIS - ESTHER

THE BOOKS OF OLD TESTAMENT HISTORY AND LAW

GENESIS	NUMBERS	JUDGES	2 SAMUEL	1 CHRONICLES	NEHEMIAH
EXODUS	DEUTERONOMY	RUTH	1 KINGS	2 CHRONICLES	ESTHER
LEVITICUS	JOSHUA	1 SAMUEL	2 KINGS	EZRA	

The very first words of the Bible (Genesis 1:1) plunge us into the past. Indeed, they take us to the very dawn of history even before human beings are created.

The past, history, is very important in the Bible because God reveals himself in the arena where we, his people, live—the arena of space and time. The Bible testifies to us that God does not live somewhere in another dimension separate from his creatures but has entered into the world that he made from nothing.

The fact that the Bible tells us about the time before any human being ever existed just underlines an important characteristic of all biblical history—it is God's revelation to us, not the result of human research. And specifically the Bible is God's revelation of his plan of salvation for the human race.

Why Is the Old Testament Important to Us Today?

The Bible is the story of God's grace. The Bible has a story to tell, and it is told in a wonderfully interesting way, better than any other story we can find. It is a story made up of a number of individual stories. These stories in and of themselves are interesting and show God's power and love, but they all contribute to the one story of the whole Bible, the story of God's providing salvation for his lost and sinful people. This story reaches its climax in the death and resurrection of God's son, Jesus Christ, but one of the wonders of the Old Testament is that its stories of salvation are often anticipations of this, the greatest salvation of all.

The stories of the Old Testament and the Bible in general are not fairy tales or myths. They are true history. That is, the events that they recount took place in real space and real time. They actually happened. They witness to both the ordinary events and miracles that God performed in order to bring about our salvation.

The stories of Old Testament history are peopled with the most fascinating characters. These people perform admirably, like Joseph resisting the temptation of Potiphar's wife (Genesis 39), and miserably (David sleeping with Bathsheba, another man's wife [2 Samuel 11]). The Old Testament stories, according to Paul (1 Corinthians 10:6), were written as examples for us. So besides providing the account of God's history of our salvation, the Old Testament history provides examples for us of both admirable and repulsive behavior.

In a sense, we might think of the history books as sermons. They are not written to provide us with the dry bones of the past, but rather the acts of history are recounted to us in order to draw us to God himself.

Many of the Old Testament history books contain God's laws as well. These combined laws are referred to often in the Bible simply as "the Law." It is important to recognize that law is given in the context of the history of salvation, that is to a people whom God has already saved. Keeping the Law never saved anyone, but those whom God has saved are responsible to respond with gratitude by following the guidance of their heavenly father. The Law of the Old Testament gives Israel that opportunity.

God said, "Let there be light,"

and there was light.

God saw that the light was good,

so he divided the light from the darkness.

God named the light "day"

and the darkness "night."

Genesis 1:3–4

INTRODUCTION TO THE BOOK OF GENESIS

The Beginning of All Things

WHO WROTE THIS BOOK?

Both Jewish and Christian traditions hold that Moses was the author of the Pentateuch (also called the Torah)—the first five books of the Bible, including Genesis.

TO WHOM WAS THIS BOOK WRITTEN?

The Book of Genesis was written for God's people, the people of Israel. The historical events were also recorded as object lessons for believers of all time (see 1 Corinthians 10:11).

WHERE WAS IT WRITTEN?

Genesis was probably written in the desert area where the people of Israel wandered for forty years.

WHEN WAS IT WRITTEN?

Genesis was likely written between 1446 and 1406 B.C., during the forty years that Moses led the people of Israel through the desert.

WHAT IS THE BOOK ABOUT?

This book is a historical record of the beginning of all things. The book is also a record of God's dealings with a people he chose for himself. It covers history from the time of Abraham until the time when Jacob's son, Joseph, became governor over Egypt and Jacob's twelve sons settled in Egypt.

WHY WAS THIS BOOK WRITTEN?

People always need to know their origins and destinations. The Book of Genesis shows the people of Israel that they originated with God—the great Creator of the universe—a dramatic and significant beginning to be sure. God chose them out of all the nations of the world to be his own special people. Genesis also reveals that Israel's destination is Canaan, the Promised Land, which was a fertile land.

SO WHAT DOES THIS BOOK MEAN TO US?

Like God's people of old, Christians today can know that we originated with God, who gives each of us our beginnings, both physically and spiritually. As his new creation, we can be certain that we are both significant and loved. And, like the people of Israel, God has promised us a land to call our own, a marvelous land where we will dwell with him for eternity. Our promised land is called heaven.

SUMMARY:

Genesis means "beginnings," and the book's name informs us of its content and purpose. The book describes the beginning of the universe, the earth, the human race, and perhaps most importantly, the beginning of salvation.

Genesis has three parts to it:

I. The Early History (Genesis 1–11)
II. The Story of the Patriarchs' Struggle with Faith (Genesis 12–36)
III. The Joseph Story (Genesis 37–50)

I. The Early History (Genesis1–11)

The book opens with two chapters which tell the story of God's creation of the world. At the beginning there was nothing, but then God called creation into existence by the power of his word. He spoke, and the universe sprang into being. As he looked at what he created, he judged that what he had made was "good." He took great pleasure in what he made.

Genesis 1 describes God as creating the universe in six days. He could have done it in the blink of an eye, but he chose to take his time and savor the moment. Whether the six days of creation are literal twenty-four hour days is a matter of debate, but it is clear that in the first three days he created three realms, and in the second three days he filled those realms with inhabitants.

Day One	Day Two	Day Three	Day Four	Day Five	Day Six
Light, Dark	Water, Sky	Land, Plants	Sun, Moon, Stars	Fish, Birds	Land Animals Human Beings

The climax of creation took place on the final day when God created Adam and Eve. Their special place in God's creation is illustrated by the fact that they were made from the dust of the ground (thus showing their relationship to the created order) and the breath of God (thus showing their relationship to God).

Sadly, Adam and Eve did not follow God. They sinned against him, causing a break in their relationship with him. They were thrown out of the Garden of Eden, and a life of struggle and pain followed. God, though, graciously presented the hope of salvation right from the start (Genesis 3:15). The next few chapters of Genesis show a pattern of sin, followed by God's judgment, which is softened by his continued grace in their life (Genesis 4–11).

II. The Story of the Patriarchs' Struggle with Faith (Genesis 12–36)

A significant shift takes place with Genesis 12. Until that point, the biblical storyteller had been looking at God's dealings with the entire world, but in Genesis 12 we observe that God will now work through one people, starting with a single individual, Abraham. The second part of the Book of Genesis (Genesis 12–36) is often called the "patriarchal narratives" (stories of the fathers). Here we learn the story of the great promises of land, seed, and blessing given to Abraham, father of the Israelites, and continued in the lives of his descendants, Isaac and Jacob. In these chapters we see how the patriarchs fluctuate between faith and doubt in the promises of God.

III. The Joseph Story (Genesis 37–50)

Joseph, as the son of Jacob, is a descendent of Abraham, and his story is the third and last part of the Book of Genesis (37–50). The emphasis in this last section of Genesis is on how God works things out in the world so that his promises will come true. Not even major obstacles will stand in the way. A famine threatened to destroy Jacob's family, but God used the evil actions of Jacob's brothers in order to put Joseph in a position of authority in Egypt so that he could provide the food that they needed to survive. Joseph recognized God's hand in his life when he told his brothers, "You meant to hurt me, but God turned your evil to good to save the lives of many people, which is being done" (Genesis 50:20).

The three parts of the Book of Genesis each prepare us for the message of the New Testament. Genesis 1–2 teach us about creation and the wonderful relationship between God and human beings in the Garden of Eden. Genesis 3–11 tells us how sin broke that relationship, but it also presents a way of salvation. In Genesis 3:15 God says "I will make you and the woman enemies to each other. Your descendants and her descendants will be enemies. One of her descendants will crush your head, and you will bite his heel." This is the first anticipation of Christ, who will deliver us from the serpent who is Satan (Revelation 16:9). Revelation 21–36 gives Christians an example of the struggle of faith which we endure even today. Just as Abraham sometimes doubted, and sometimes had great faith, so do we. The Abraham story, besides informing us of the agreement between God and Abraham (see "agreement" in the Dictionary/Concordance), gives us encouragement in the midst of our own struggle with faith in this world.

And then finally the Joseph story helps us to see that God can overrule evil for good even in our own day. As a matter of fact, we get an even more dramatic example of this principle in the death and resurrection of Jesus. Those who crucified Jesus did so for evil motives only, but God used their very actions to bring salvation for the lost into the world (Acts 2:22–24).

The Book of Genesis is just the first of five parts of the Torah or Law of Moses. Moses is named because later parts of the Bible attribute the authorship of Genesis, Exodus, Leviticus, Numbers, and Deuteronomy to him.

GENESIS

The Beginning of the World

In the beginning God created the sky and the earth. 2The earth was empty and had no form. Darkness covered the ocean, and God's Spirit was moving over the water.

3Then God said, "Let there be light," and there was light. 4God saw that the light was good, so he divided the light from the darkness. 5God named the light "day" and the darkness "night." Evening passed, and morning came. This was the first day.

6Then God said, "Let there be something to divide the water in two." 7So God made the air and placed some of the water above the air and some below it. 8God named the air "sky." Evening passed, and morning came. This was the second day.

9Then God said, "Let the water under the sky be gathered together so the dry land will appear." And it happened. 10God named the dry land "earth" and the water that was gathered together "seas." God saw that this was good.

11Then God said, "Let the earth produce plants—some to make grain for seeds and others to make fruits with seeds in them. Every seed will produce more of its own kind of plant." And it happened. 12The earth produced plants with grain for seeds and trees that made fruits with seeds in them. Each seed grew its own kind of plant. God saw that all this was good. 13Evening passed, and morning came. This was the third day.

14Then God said, "Let there be lights in the sky to separate day from night. These lights will be used for signs, seasons, days, and years. 15They will be in the sky to give light to the earth." And it happened.

16So God made the two large lights. He made the brighter light to rule the day and made the smaller light to rule the night. He also made the stars. 17God

"God looked at everything he had made, and it was very good" (1:31).

put all these in the sky to shine on the earth, 18to rule over the day and over the night, and to separate the light from the darkness. God saw that all these things were good. 19Evening passed, and morning came. This was the fourth day.

20Then God said, "Let the water be filled with living things, and let birds fly in the air above the earth."

21So God created the large sea animals and every living thing that moves in the sea. The sea is filled with these living things, with each one producing more of its own kind. He also made every bird that flies, and each bird produced more of its own kind. God saw that this was good. 22God blessed them and said, "Have many young ones so that you may grow in number. Fill the water of the seas, and let the birds grow in number on the earth." 23Evening passed, and morning came. This was the fifth day.

24Then God said, "Let the earth be filled with animals, each producing more of its own kind. Let there be tame animals and small crawling animals and wild animals, and let each produce more of its kind." And it happened.

---

1 God existed before creation, but time as we know it did not exist until God created the universe. God is not bound by the moments we experience through the movements of the sun, moon, stars, and earth. We are creatures that live in the middle of time.

1:1 God was in complete control in the creation and formation of the earth. The formless and disorderly mass (verse 2) responded immediately and completely to his every command. Everything God does is good. What God did in his creation work, he is able to do in the lives of people. He can bring peace and order to an unstructured life.

1:1 *In the beginning.* Creation myths from the ancient Near East talk about how the gods themselves are created or born and then shape the world into existence from matter that already is there. Genesis tells us from the start that God was always there and created the world out of nothing by the power of his word.

1:1–11:32 The first eleven chapters of Genesis cover a vast amount of time. It also is a history of the world, not just of a particular people. We should not be surprised if all our questions about the beginning of time are not fully answered, because the Bible is focused on our salvation.

Genesis 1 tells the story of creation of the cosmos. Genesis 2 tells the story again, but this time with an emphasis on the creation of the first human couple, Adam and Eve.

While they enjoy the wonders of God's creation in Eden and close fellowship with him and each other, they still give in to the temptation of the serpent and are cast out of the garden. The rest of the Bible is the account of how God provided for their salvation and dealt with their rebellion. We see how he judges sin but extends his grace in the accounts of Cain's murder of Abel, the sons of God and the daughters of men, the Flood, and the tower of Babel.

1:2 Holy Spirit: John 3:5–8

25So God made the wild animals, the tame animals, and all the small crawling animals to produce more of their own kind. God saw that this was good.

26Then God said, "Let us make human beings in our image and likeness. And let them rule over the fish in the sea and the birds in the sky, over the tame animals, over all the earth, and over all the small crawling animals on the earth."

27So God created human beings in his image. In the image of God he created them. He created them male and female. 28God blessed them and said, "Have many children and grow in number. Fill the earth and be its master. Rule over the fish in the sea and over the birds in the sky and over every living thing that moves on the earth."

29God said, "Look, I have given you all the plants that have grain for seeds and all the trees whose fruits have seeds in them. They will be food for you. 30I have given all the green plants as food for every wild animal, every bird of the air, and every small crawling animal." And it happened. 31God looked at everything he had made, and it was very good. Evening passed, and morning came. This was the sixth day.

The Seventh Day—Rest

2 So the sky, the earth, and all that filled them were finished. 2By the seventh day God finished the work he had been doing, so he rested from all his work. 3God blessed the seventh day and made it a holy day, because on that day he rested from all the work he had done in creating the world.

The First People

4This is the story of the creation of the sky and the earth. When the LORD God first made the earth and the sky, 5there were still no plants on the earth. Nothing was growing in the fields because the LORD God had not yet made it rain on the land. And there was no person to care for the ground, 6but a mist would rise up from the earth and water all the ground.

7Then the LORD God took dust from the ground and formed a man from it. He breathed the breath of life into the man's nose, and the man became a living person. 8Then the LORD God planted a garden in the east, in a place called Eden, and put the man he had formed into it. 9The LORD God caused every beautiful tree and every tree that was good for food to grow out of the ground. In the middle of the garden, God put the tree that gives life and also the tree that gives the knowledge of good and evil.

10A river flowed through Eden and watered the garden. From there the river branched out to become four rivers. 11The first river, named Pishon, flows around the whole land of Havilah, where there is gold. 12The gold of that land is excellent. Bdellium and onyx are also found there. 13The second river, named Gihon, flows around the whole land of Cush. 14The third river, named Tigris, flows out of Assyria toward the east. The fourth river is the Euphrates.

15The LORD God put the man in the garden of Eden to care for it and work it. 16The LORD God commanded him, "You may eat the fruit from any tree in the garden, 17but you must not eat the fruit from the tree which gives the knowledge of good and evil. If you ever eat fruit from that tree, you will die!"

The First Woman

18Then the LORD God said, "It is not good for the man to be alone. I will make a helper who is right for him."

1:26 *in our image.* Human beings are made in the image of God. In the world of the ancient Near East, an image was a representative of something. Thus, human beings are God's representatives in the world. It does not mean we are divine. It does mean we are like God in that we are persons who think, feel, and act.

1:26–27 The concept of "spirituality" is rooted in our being made in the image of God. The image of God describes the essence of our spirituality and our ability to relate to God, others, and ourselves as God intends.

1:26–31 The first pages of the Bible tell us of a God who has entrusted the stewardship of creation to men and women. From the beginning it was God's plan to turn over to humans all that had been created.

1:27 Sexuality: Genesis 2:20

1:27 Divorce: Genesis 2:24

1:27 Family: Matthew 1

1:27 Body/Flesh: Genesis 1:31

1:28 Children: Psalm 127:3–5

1:28 Although prayer is not mentioned in this verse, it reflects the essence of prayer: God in communication and conversation with human beings. The dialogue continues in chapter two. This is God's supreme desire and our great privilege.

1:31 World/Worldly: Matthew 24:14

1:31 Body/Flesh: Genesis 2:7

1:31 Evil: Genesis 3

2:3 Work: Genesis 2:15

2:3 Sabbath: Exodus 23:12

2:7 Human: Genesis 9:6

2:7 Body/Flesh: Genesis 3:24

2:12 *bdellium and onyx.* Bdellium is an expensive, sweet-smelling resin like myrrh, and onyx is a gem.

2:15 Work: Genesis 3:17–19

2:15–17 Man's native moral endowment on the basis of creation, his conscience, was not enough; God supplemented it by positive commandments. Such were the moral laws which were given in Eden by supernatural revelation. Apart from such moral instruction, man could not have clearly discerned the will of God in many of its implications. The principle here is that conscience does not supply its own content as far as God's specific expectations are concerned.

2:17 Obedience: Deuteronomy 18:14–22

2:18 Celibacy: Genesis 9:1

19From the ground God formed every wild animal and every bird in the sky, and he brought them to the man so the man could name them. Whatever the man called each living thing, that became its name. 20The man gave names to all the tame animals, to the birds in the sky, and to all the wild animals. But Adam did not find a helper that was right for him. 21So the LORD God caused the man to sleep very deeply, and while he was asleep, God removed one of the man's ribs. Then God closed up the man's skin at the place where he took the rib. 22The LORD God used the rib from the man to make a woman, and then he brought the woman to the man.

23And the man said,

"Now, this is someone whose bones came
from my bones,
whose body came from my body.
I will call her 'woman,'
because she was taken out of man."

24So a man will leave his father and mother and be united with his wife, and the two will become one body.

25The man and his wife were naked, but they were not ashamed.

The Beginning of Sin

3 Now the snake was the most clever of all the wild animals the LORD God had made. One day the snake said to the woman, "Did God really say that you must not eat fruit from any tree in the garden?"

2The woman answered the snake, "We may eat fruit from the trees in the garden. 3But God told us, 'You must not eat fruit from the tree that is in the middle of the garden. You must not even touch it, or you will die.'"

4But the snake said to the woman, "You will not die. 5God knows that if you eat the fruit from that tree, you will learn about good and evil and you will be like God!"

6The woman saw that the tree was beautiful, that its fruit was good to eat, and that it would make her wise. So she took some of its fruit and ate it. She also gave some of the fruit to her husband, and he ate it.

7Then, it was as if their eyes were opened. They realized they were naked, so they sewed fig leaves together and made something to cover themselves.

8Then they heard the LORD God walking in the garden during the cool part of the day, and the man and his wife hid from the LORD God among the trees in the garden. 9But the LORD God called to the man and said, "Where are you?"

10The man answered, "I heard you walking in the garden, and I was afraid because I was naked, so I hid."

11God asked, "Who told you that you were naked? Did you eat fruit from the tree from which I commanded you not to eat?"

12The man said, "You gave this woman to me and she gave me fruit from the tree, so I ate it."

13Then the LORD God said to the woman, "How could you have done such a thing?"

She answered, "The snake tricked me, so I ate the fruit."

14The LORD God said to the snake,

"Because you did this,
a curse will be put on you.
You will be cursed as no other animal, tame
or wild, will ever be.
You will crawl on your stomach,
and you will eat dust all the days
of your life.

2:20 *Adam.* This is the name of the first man. It also means "humans," including men and women.

2:20 Animals: Exodus 20:10

2:20 Sexuality: Genesis 2:24–25

2:24 Adultery: Leviticus 20:10

2:24 Divorce: Genesis 5:2

2:25 Sexuality: Genesis 3:21

2:25 Homosexuality: Leviticus 18:22

3 Though the term is never used, Genesis 3 tells the story of the origin and basic character of "sin." In the previous chapter God had commanded Adam not to eat of the fruit of the tree of the knowledge of good and evil (Genesis 2:17). In chapter three the snake enters to tempt the woman, encouraging her unbelief ("Did God really say?") and her pride ("if you eat . . . you will be like God"). The woman moved by admiration and desire ("saw that the tree was beautiful . . . and that it would make her wise"), takes the fruit in disobedience to God's command and shares with Adam. The consequences of this act are that they become aware and ashamed before the presence of God, that their life is cursed, and that they are removed from "the tree of life." Yet even in the curse, there is hope of the snake's demise, and there is provision from God ("The Lord God made clothes"). The pattern of temptation, disobedience, curse, and hope is something every person since Adam and Eve both inherits and experiences.

3:6 Wisdom: Exodus 28:3

3:6 Notice some of the similarities between Satan's temptation of Adam and Eve in Genesis 3:6 and what 1 John 2:16 says: (1) Wanting to please our sinful selves/its fruit was good to eat; (2) wanting the sinful things we see/the woman saw the tree was beautiful; (3) being too proud of what we have/it would make her wise. Of course neither the tree, nor the desire to be wise were in themselves sinful, and Eve herself had not yet sinned (until the next sentence in Genesis 3:6). But Satan was able to get Eve to want these things apart from God so that she did act on that desire, and sinned against God.

3:8 Conscience: 1 Samuel 24:5

3:10 Before the Fall, Adam and Eve had nothing to fear. After all, God was with them in an intimate and personal way. They had no need to protect themselves from danger. But after they sinned, they became vulnerable to attack. They also distorted reality and feared danger when none was present. Forever after, fear has become an everyday part of human life. It either drives us away from God as we seek to protect ourselves or into his comforting arms.

3:13 Guilt: Genesis 32:8–12

3:14 Curse: Genesis 3:17

15I will make you and the woman
enemies to each other.
Your descendants and her descendants
will be enemies.
One of her descendants will crush your head,
and you will bite his heel."

16Then God said to the woman,
"I will cause you to have much trouble
when you are pregnant,
and when you give birth to children,
you will have great pain.
You will greatly desire your husband,
but he will rule over you."

17Then God said to the man, "You listened to
what your wife said, and you ate fruit from the
tree from which I commanded you not to eat.
"So I will put a curse on the ground,
and you will have to work very hard
for your food.
In pain you will eat its food
all the days of your life.
18The ground will produce thorns and
weeds for you,
and you will eat the plants of the field.
19You will sweat and work hard
for your food.
Later you will return to the ground,
because you were taken from it.
You are dust,
and when you die, you will return
to the dust."

20The man named his wife Eve, because she is
the mother of everyone who has ever lived.
21The LORD God made clothes from animal
skins for the man and his wife and dressed them.
22Then the LORD God said, "The man has become
like one of us; he knows good and evil. We must
keep him from eating some of the fruit from the
tree of life, or he will live forever." 23So the LORD
God forced the man out of the garden of Eden to
work the ground from which he was taken.
24After God forced the man out of the garden, he
placed angels and a sword of fire that flashed
around in every direction on its eastern border.
This kept people from getting to the tree of life.

The First Family

4 Adam had sexual relations with his wife Eve,
and she became pregnant and gave birth to
Cain. Eve said, "With the LORD's help, I have
given birth to a man." 2After that, Eve gave birth
to Cain's brother Abel. Abel took care of flocks,
and Cain became a farmer.
3Later, Cain brought some food from the ground
as a gift to God. 4Abel brought the best parts from
some of the firstborn of his flock. The LORD accepted
Abel and his gift, 5but he did not accept Cain and his
gift. So Cain became very angry and felt rejected.

3:15 Holy War & Divine Warrior: Genesis 3:24

3:15 God created Adam and Eve and placed them in a beautiful garden where they would live in his presence. He just gave them one command to obey and that was not to eat the fruit of the tree which gives the knowledge of good and evil.

They lived a happy life in the garden until a serpent appeared who talked Eve into eating the forbidden fruit. Eve then convinced Adam to eat and in this way they both rebelled against God and were ejected from the garden.

Who was this serpent who tempted Eve? From the context, we can see that the serpent was a creature who was set against God and his ways, but it is not until we read later scripture that we can be clear as to its identify. The serpent, according to Romans 16:20 and Revelation 12:9, is none other than Satan, God's chief adversary.

3:15 This verse is the first indication that there are only two groups of people in the world. One group is made up of the descendants of the woman who are the followers of God. The second group of people in the world are all those who do not follow God. Jesus is the descendant of the woman who defeats Satan (who made himself appear as a snake to Eve).

3:15 These words are often taken to be the first indication of a promise from God that he would provide salvation from the curse of sin. The predictions of a lesser blow to the descendants of the woman (Christ and godly people) and the greater blow to the serpent (Satan) are references to Satan's partial victories over mankind and God's total victory over Satan at the cross (Romans 16:20; Colossians 2:15; Hebrews 2:14).

3:17 Curse: Genesis 8:21

3:17 Because of the disobedience of Adam and Eve, God placed the world under a curse. Under this curse, the creation has been turned against itself and painfully awaits its renewal like a woman ready to give birth (Romans 8:22). As descendants of Adam and Eve, we also are lawbreakers under God's curse. Christ took God's curse upon himself so that we might live (Galatians 3:13).

3:19 Pride: Job 33:14–30

3:19 Work: Genesis 3:23

3:20 *Eve.* This name sounds like the Hebrew word meaning "alive."

3:20 Eve: Genesis 4:1–2

3:20 Family: Genesis 4:15

3:21 Sacrifice: Genesis 22:8

3:21 Sexuality: Exodus 22:16

3:23 Garden of Eden: Genesis 13:10

3:23 Work: Proverbs 22:29

3:24 Holy War & Divine Warrior: Joshua 5:13–15

3:24 *cherubim.* The cherubim are spiritual creatures who often are pictured as protectors of God's holiness. Here they block people from reentering Eden.

3:24 Body/Flesh: Matthew 10:28

3:24 Evil: Genesis 50:20

4:1 *Cain.* This name sounds like the Hebrew word for "I have given birth."

4:1 God created Adam in such a way that he reflected his image, but Adam, along with his wife Eve, rebelled against God by disobeying him. Adam deserved to die on the spot, but God let him live. He even had children. His firstborn was the notorious Cain. Genesis 4 tells a story that indicates that Adam's descendants are no better than he is. We are all rebels against God.

4:2 Eve: Genesis 4:25

4:3 God's acceptance or rejection of a sacrifice is based upon attitude more than the thing being offered. Unlike Cain, Abel had great respect for God and came to him in faith. The disrespect in Cain's heart is seen in the murder of his brother and his lack of sorrow over sin.

Animals

Genesis 1

What place do animals have in the world?
How do animals help us understand our relationship to God?

Genesis 1:20–25 describes the creation of the animals. God pronounces their creation "good" (Genesis 1:21, 25) and blesses them with the command to increase in number (Genesis 1:22). The sheer delight God has for animals is beautifully expressed in Job 39. In bringing Job to a recognition of the limits of his own knowledge and wisdom, God sets forth the wonders of the animal world. God enjoys the animals he has created and so should we.

Several themes occur in the early chapters of Genesis that are significant throughout the rest of the Bible. First of all, since animals are a part of God's good creation, they should be treated properly. There are numerous examples in Scripture showing God's care for his creatures. God provides their needs (Psalms 104:10–11; 147:9; Matthew 6:26), preserves them (Psalm 36:6), and providentially watches over them (Matthew 10:29; Luke 12:6). A very striking passage demonstrating God's concern for animals is Jonah 4:11. Jonah was angry because God had compassion on the Ninevites and did not destroy them. God asks Jonah: "Then shouldn't I show concern for the great city Nineveh, which has more than one hundred twenty thousand people who do not know right from wrong, and many animals too?" God's compassion included the many animals of Nineveh.

There are also specific commands in the law related to the treatment of animals. They are to benefit from the physical rest that comes with the Sabbath (Exodus 20:10; Deuteronomy 5:14). They should be allowed to eat as they labor (Deuteronomy 25:4). Paul quotes this passage in 1 Corinthians 9:9 and applies the principle to those who preach the gospel: they should expect to earn a living from their work. Proverbs 12:10 summarizes proper treatment of animals by stating, "Good people take care of their animals."

A second major theme in the Bible concerning animals is that animals are not on the same level as people. Humans are made in the image of God and are given rule over the animal world (Genesis 1:27–28; Psalm 8:4–8). Such rule is demonstrated when God brought the animals to Adam in Genesis 2:19–20 for him to name them. Throughout the Bible, God allows animals to be used for the benefit of people. Their labor serves humans, their skins are used for clothing (Genesis 3:21), and their meat is used for food (Genesis 9:2–3). God also gives specific regulations concerning the use of animals in sacrificial offerings (Leviticus 1–7).

The way animals are used teaches us about our relationship to God. The animals brought for sacrifices were not to have anything wrong with them (Leviticus 1:3; 3:1). This regulation ensured that the people brought their best animals to God. It is also picked up in the New Testament as a reference to the perfection of Jesus as the lamb of God (1 Peter 1:19).

There is also a clear difference between animals which are clean and unclean. Detailed analysis of how to tell clean animals from unclean animals is given in Leviticus 11. To eat an unclean animal made a person unclean. God underscores the importance of distinguishing clean from unclean animals by stressing holiness: "Keep yourselves holy for me because I am holy" (Leviticus 11:44). Distinguishing clean from unclean animals served two functions. It set the people of Israel apart from other nations—a major focus of holiness, and it also taught that holiness involved making right distinctions in their decision-making process.

The regulations dealing with clean and unclean animals in Leviticus 11 are no longer binding because of the coming of Jesus Christ. Jesus' statements in Mark 7:14–22 nullified the food regulations. Although early Jewish believers struggled with the removal of these regulations (see Peter's vision in Acts 10:9–16), they were not to be a barrier that hindered taking the gospel to the Gentiles. Neither were the food regulations meant to separate Jewish believers from Gentile believers (Galatians 2:11–16).

Finally, animals are affected by the entrance of sin into the world, but they also benefit when God sends his blessings. They suffer under divine judgments sent upon people by God, such as the flood (Genesis 6–8; see also Joel 1:15, 18–20). But the covenant with Noah after the flood (Gen 9:9–10) is also made with the animals. They benefit when God blesses people. In Isaiah's description of the new heavens and the new earth, one of the ways he sets forth the changed conditions of blessing and peace is by showing animals that are normally enemies living in peace (Isaiah 65:25). Everything God has made, including the animals, looks forward to when God's creation will be set free from ruin (Romans 8:19–21).

Animals: For additional scriptures on this topic go to Genesis 2:19–20.

Environment

Genesis 1:9–25

What does the Bible say about the environment?
Should Christians today be concerned about the environment?

Historically, Christians have taken a stand on the social issues of their time. In recent times it has become apparent that humans are destroying the earth. Christians sometimes wonder if caring for the environment is where they should put their energies. For Christians, the environment can be defined as God's creation. Careful reading of the Bible reveals that God not only created the environment but is in relationship with the environment in many of the same ways God is in relationship with us.

To begin, God created all of the rest of creation as well as creating people. Each time God created something new, God deemed the creation good (Genesis 1:10, 12, 18, 21, 25). In fact, though Genesis 1 makes it clear that humankind is the apex of creation, people are the only thing that God repented having made (Genesis 6:6). The New Testament reiterates the importance of all of creation, stating that all things were created in Christ (John 1:3; Colossians 1:16). And 1 Timothy 4:4 states that everything created by God is good. The value of the environment is further expressed when the Bible talks about the beauty of nature and how important all of God's creation is to him (Psalm 48:2; Matthew 6:28–29). God's commitment to caring for all of creation is expressed through the covenant after the flood (Genesis 9:8–17). Here, God emphasizes that God's agreement is not only with Noah but with all of creation.

Also, Scripture reveals how God relates to nature (see Psalm 104). Psalm 19:1–6 describes how nature reveals God's glory. Job 37:6 and Psalm 107:29 show how nature responds to God's requests. Similarly, the wind and sea were calmed by Jesus' command (Matthew 8:26). Psalm 52:8 describes how a green olive tree trusts in the loving kindness of God. Verses in Isaiah (35:1–2; 55:12) and the Psalms (96:11–12; 98:7–9; 145:9–10) describe nature rejoicing in and praising the Lord.

Another reason supported by Scripture for people caring about the environment is that they are intimately connected to the environment. In Genesis, the Bible explains how people were made "from the dust of the ground," and we are repeatedly reminded that we are part of the earth (Genesis 3:19; 13:16; 18:27; Job 34:15; Psalm 90:3). The earth is seen as a source of life for humans as well as other creatures.

Ecclesiastes 3:18–22 reminds us how close human beings are to the animals. Of course, at this point of the book the speaker is talking about life "under the sun," that is, apart from God. But from his limited view he shows that animals and humans share the same fate. In this passage and from his viewpoint, human beings have no privilege over the animals when it comes to death. Humans and animals both die. Our common mortality should make us humble as we contemplate our relationship to animals and other parts of God's creation.

Of course, it is also true that Jesus teaches that human beings are "worth much more than many sparrows" (Matthew 10:31). That is, human beings are the pinnacle of God's creation. It is also true that the animals were given to human beings as food (Genesis 9:3). But our use of resources must be done wisely.

After all, we have a specific obligation to take care of the Lord's creation (Genesis 1:28). While the earth's resources are here given to human beings as a gift, it is not a gift without responsibility. Unfortunately, this passage is sometimes wrongly used to support the unlimited exploitation of nature. Because we love God, we feel responsible to care for his creation. God states that, "The land really belongs to me.… You are only foreigners and travelers living for a while on my land" (Leviticus 25:23). In Leviticus 25, God explains to Moses that the land needs a time of rest. Similarly, rest is important for God and people (Genesis 2:2; Exodus 31:15; Hebrews 4:1–4). God asserts that if the land were allowed to rest on a regular basis, it would provide ample food for the people. In recent years all over the world, land has been pushed to its limit, to where it can no longer produce. The same is true for fresh water sources. Some have been pushed to where they cannot replenish themselves. From the Bible we can take this basic principle of allowing the land to rest as a means of addressing environmental concerns.

We realize that "the earth belongs to the Lord, and everything in it" (Psalm 24:1a). Through the stories of the great flood (Genesis 7–8), the parting of the Red Sea (Exodus 14), Jonah and the great fish (Jonah 1–4), and the darkness that fell over the earth at the time of Jesus' death (Matthew 27:45), Scripture describes how nature shows God's power. The world belongs to God, and as God's stewards (Matthew 25:14–30) we should take care of it.

Environment: For additional scriptures on this topic go to Job 37:6.

6The LORD asked Cain, "Why are you angry? Why do you look so unhappy? 7If you do things well, I will accept you, but if you do not do them well, sin is ready to attack you. Sin wants you, but you must rule over it."

8Cain said to his brother Abel, "Let's go out into the field." While they were out in the field, Cain attacked his brother Abel and killed him.

9Later, the LORD said to Cain, "Where is your brother Abel?"

Cain answered, "I don't know. Is it my job to take care of my brother?"

10Then the LORD said, "What have you done? Your brother's blood is crying out to me from the ground. 11And now you will be cursed in your work with the ground, the same ground where your brother's blood fell and where your hands killed him. 12You will work the ground, but it will not grow good crops for you anymore, and you will wander around on the earth."

13Then Cain said to the LORD, "This punishment is more than I can stand! 14Today you have forced me to stop working the ground, and now I must hide from you. I must wander around on the earth, and anyone who meets me can kill me."

15The LORD said to Cain, "No! If anyone kills you, I will punish that person seven times more." Then the LORD put a mark on Cain warning anyone who met him not to kill him.

Cain's Family

16So Cain went away from the LORD and lived in the land of Nod, east of Eden. 17He had sexual relations with his wife, and she became pregnant and gave birth to Enoch. At that time Cain was building a city, which he named after his son Enoch. 18Enoch had a son named Irad, Irad had a son named Mehujael, Mehujael had a son named Methushael, and Methushael had a son named Lamech.

19Lamech married two women, Adah and Zillah. 20Adah gave birth to Jabal, who became the first person to live in tents and raise cattle. 21Jabal's brother was Jubal, the first person to play the harp and flute. 22Zillah gave birth to Tubal-Cain, who made tools out of bronze and iron. The sister of Tubal-Cain was Naamah.

23Lamech said to his wives:

"Adah and Zillah, hear my voice!
You wives of Lamech, listen to what I say.
I killed a man for wounding me,
a young man for hitting me.
24If Cain's killer is punished seven times,
then Lamech's killer will be punished
seventy-seven times."

Adam and Eve Have a New Son

25Adam had sexual relations with his wife Eve again, and she gave birth to a son. She named him Seth and said, "God has given me another child. He will take the place of Abel, who was killed by Cain." 26Seth also had a son, and they named him Enosh. At that time people began to pray to the LORD.

Adam's Family History

5 This is the family history of Adam. When God created human beings, he made them in his own likeness. 2He created them male and female, and on that day he blessed them and named them human beings.

3When Adam was 130 years old, he became the father of another son in his likeness and image, and Adam named him Seth. 4After Seth was born, Adam lived 800 years and had other sons and daughters. 5So Adam lived a total of 930 years, and then he died.

6When Seth was 105 years old, he had a son named Enosh. 7After Enosh was born, Seth lived 807 years and had other sons and daughters. 8So Seth lived a total of 912 years, and then he died.

9When Enosh was 90 years old, he had a son named Kenan. 10After Kenan was born, Enosh lived 815 years and had other sons and daughters. 11So Enosh lived a total of 905 years, and then he died.

12When Kenan was 70 years old, he had a son named Mahalalel. 13After Mahalalel was born, Kenan lived 840 years and had other sons and daughters. 14So Kenan lived a total of 910 years, and then he died.

15When Mahalalel was 65 years old, he had a son named Jared. 16After Jared was born, Mahalalel lived 830 years and had other sons and daughters. 17So Mahalalel lived a total of 895 years, and then he died.

18When Jared was 162 years old, he had a son named Enoch. 19After Enoch was born, Jared lived 800 years and had other sons and daughters. 20So Jared lived a total of 962 years, and then he died.

4:12 Road/Way: Genesis 18:19
4:15 Family: Mark 3:21–22
4:15 Murder: Exodus 20:13
4:16 *Nod.* This name sounds like the Hebrew word for "wander."
4:21 Music: Numbers 2:27
4:24 Numbers: Genesis 5:25
4:25 *Seth.* This name sounds like the Hebrew word for "to give."
4:25 Eve: 1 Timothy 2:11–14
4:26 Prayer: Psalm 65:2
5:2 Divorce: Exodus 22:16–17
5:5 Adam: Luke 3:28

21When Enoch was 65 years old, he had a son named Methuselah. 22After Methuselah was born, Enoch walked with God 300 years more and had other sons and daughters. 23So Enoch lived a total of 365 years. 24Enoch walked with God; one day Enoch could not be found, because God took him.

25When Methuselah was 187 years old, he had a son named Lamech. 26After Lamech was born, Methuselah lived 782 years and had other sons and daughters. 27So Methuselah lived a total of 969 years, and then he died.

28When Lamech was 182, he had a son. 29Lamech named his son Noah and said, "He will comfort us in our work, which comes from the ground the LORD has cursed." 30After Noah was born, Lamech lived 595 years and had other sons and daughters. 31So Lamech lived a total of 777 years, and then he died.

32After Noah was 500 years old, he became the father of Shem, Ham, and Japheth.

The Human Race Becomes Evil

6 The number of people on earth began to grow, and daughters were born to them. 2When the sons of God saw that these girls were beautiful, they married any of them they chose. 3The LORD said, "My Spirit will not remain in human beings forever, because they are flesh. They will live only 120 years."

4The Nephilim were on the earth in those days and also later. That was when the sons of God had sexual relations with the daughters of human beings. These women gave birth to children, who became famous and were the mighty warriors of long ago.

5The LORD saw that the human beings on the earth were very wicked and that everything they thought about was evil. 6He was sorry he had made human beings on the earth, and his heart was filled with pain. 7So the LORD said, "I will destroy all human beings that I made on the earth. And I will destroy every animal and everything that crawls on the earth and the birds of the air, because I am sorry I have made them." 8But Noah pleased the LORD.

Noah and the Great Flood

9This is the family history of Noah. Noah was a good man, the most innocent man of his time, and he walked with God. 10He had three sons: Shem, Ham, and Japheth.

11People on earth did what God said was evil, and violence was everywhere. 12When God saw that everyone on the earth did only evil, 13he said to Noah, "Because people have made the earth full of violence, I will destroy all of them from the earth. 14Build a boat of cypress wood for yourself. Make rooms in it and cover it inside and outside with tar. 15This is how big I want you to build the boat: four hundred fifty feet long, seventy-five feet wide, and forty-five feet high. 16Make an opening around the top of the boat that is eighteen inches high from the edge of the roof down. Put a door in the side of the boat. Make an upper, middle, and lower deck in it. 17I will bring a flood of water on the earth to destroy all living things that live under the sky, including everything that has the breath of life. Everything on the earth will die. 18But I will make an agreement with you—you, your sons, your wife, and your sons' wives will all go into the boat. 19Also, you must bring into the boat two of every living thing, male and female. Keep them alive with you. 20Two of every kind of bird, animal, and crawling thing will come to you to be kept alive. 21Also gather some of every kind of food and store it on the boat as food for you and the animals."

22Noah did everything that God commanded him.

The Flood Begins

7 Then the LORD said to Noah, "I have seen that you are the best person among the people of this time, so you and your family can go into the boat. 2Take with you seven pairs, each male with its female, of every kind of clean animal, and take one pair, each male with its female, of every kind of unclean animal. 3Take seven pairs of all the birds of the sky, each male with its female. This will allow all these animals to continue living on the earth after the flood. 4Seven days from now I will send rain on the earth. It will rain forty days

5:25 Numbers: Numbers 1–4
5:29 *Noah.* This name sounds like the Hebrew word for "rest."
5:32 Genealogy: Genesis 10
6:1-2 *daughters . . . the sons of God.* Much debate surrounds the exact identification of these two groups whose intermarriage leads to God's judgment. Perhaps the *daughters of men* are a name for those who are descended from Cain, and *sons of God,* those who are descended from Seth. Thus the sin would be the intermingling of the godly line with the ungodly. Others believe, on the basis of Jude 6, that this passage describes the intermarriage of angels and mortals.
6:7 Earth: Psalm 74:12
6:18 Commitment: Exodus 6:4–5

7 In the first biblical reference to mountains, their dual function as places of judgment and blessing is clear. In the Flood story, the water level only stops rising when it reaches more than twenty feet above the highest mountains, assuring the destruction of all living creatures (Genesis 7:17–24). This affirms the severity and universal scope of God's judgment. Yet when Noah and his family leave the boat on one of the mountains of Ararat, the mountain site becomes a place of worship and blessing. There Noah builds an altar and worships the Lord. God, in turn, promises never again to destroy the earth and all living beings by a flood (Genesis 8:18–9:17).

and forty nights, and I will wipe off from the earth
every living thing that I have made."
5Noah did everything the LORD commanded him.
6Noah was six hundred years old when the
flood came. 7He and his wife and his sons and
their wives went into the boat to escape the waters
of the flood. 8The clean animals, the unclean animals, the birds, and everything that crawls on the
ground 9came to Noah. They went into the boat
in groups of two, male and female, just as God
had commanded Noah. 10Seven days later the
flood started.
11When Noah was six hundred years old, the
flood started. On the seventeenth day of the second month of that year the underground springs
split open, and the clouds in the sky poured out
rain. 12The rain fell on the earth for forty days and
forty nights.
13On that same day Noah and his wife, his sons
Shem, Ham, and Japheth, and their wives went into
the boat. 14They had every kind of wild and tame
animal, every kind of animal that crawls on the
earth, and every kind of bird. 15Every creature that
had the breath of life came to Noah in the boat in
groups of two. 16One male and one female of every
living thing came, just as God had commanded
Noah. Then the LORD closed the door behind them.
17Water flooded the earth for forty days, and as
it rose it lifted the boat off the ground. 18The
water continued to rise, and the boat floated on it
above the earth. 19The water rose so much that
even the highest mountains under the sky were
covered by it. 20It continued to rise until it was
more than twenty feet above the mountains.
21All living things that moved on the earth died.
This included all the birds, tame animals, wild animals, and creatures that swarm on the earth, as well
as all human beings. 22So everything on dry land that
had the breath of life in it died. 23God destroyed
from the earth every living thing that was on the
land—every man, animal, crawling thing, and bird
of the sky. All that was left was Noah and what was
with him in the boat. 24And the waters continued to
cover the earth for one hundred fifty days.⚭

The Flood Ends

8 But God remembered Noah and all the wild
and tame animals with him in the boat. He
made a wind blow over the earth, and the water
went down. 2The underground springs stopped
flowing, and the clouds in the sky stopped pouring
down rain. 3-4The water that covered the earth
began to go down. After one hundred fifty days it
had gone down so much that the boat touched
land again. It came to rest on one of the mountains of Ararat on the seventeenth day of the seventh month. 5The water continued to go down so
that by the first day of the tenth month the tops of
the mountains could be seen.
6Forty days later Noah opened the window he
had made in the boat, and 7he sent out a raven. It
flew here and there until the water had dried up
from the earth. 8Then Noah sent out a dove to
find out if the water had dried up from the

A Stock Dove (left) and a Turtle Dove (right)

ground. 9The dove could not find a place to land
because water still covered the earth, so it came
back to the boat. Noah reached out his hand and
took the bird and brought it back into the boat.
10After seven days Noah again sent out the
dove from the boat, 11and that evening it came
back to him with a fresh olive leaf in its mouth.
Then Noah knew that the ground was almost dry.
12Seven days later he sent the dove out again, but
this time it did not come back.
13When Noah was six hundred and one years
old, in the first day of the first month of that year,
the water was dried up from the land. Noah
removed the covering of the boat and saw that
the land was dry. 14By the twenty-seventh day of
the second month the land was completely dry.
15Then God said to Noah, 16"You and your
wife, your sons, and their wives should go out of
the boat. 17Bring every animal out of the boat
with you—the birds, animals, and everything
that crawls on the earth. Let them have many
young ones so that they might grow in number."
18So Noah went out with his sons, his wife, and
his sons' wives. 19Every animal, everything that
crawls on the earth, and every bird went out of
the boat by families.

⚭**7:24 Water:** Exodus 14:5–31

8:4 *Ararat.* The ancient land of Urartu, an area in Eastern Turkey.

20Then Noah built an altar to the LORD. He took
some of all the clean birds and animals, and he
burned them on the altar as offerings to God.
21The LORD was pleased with these sacrifices and
said to himself, "I will never again curse the
ground because of human beings. Their thoughts
are evil even when they are young, but I will
never again destroy every living thing on the
earth as I did this time.
22"As long as the earth continues,
planting and harvest,
cold and hot,
summer and winter,
day and night
will not stop."

The New Beginning

9 Then God blessed Noah and his sons and said
to them, "Have many children; grow in number and fill the earth. 2Every animal on earth,
every bird in the sky, every animal that crawls on
the ground, and every fish in the sea will respect
and fear you. I have given them to you.
3"Everything that moves, everything that is
alive, is yours for food. Earlier I gave you the
green plants, but now I give you everything for
food. 4But you must not eat meat that still has
blood in it, because blood gives life. 5I will
demand blood for life. I will demand the life of
any animal that kills a person, and I will demand
the life of anyone who takes another person's life.

6"Whoever kills a human being
will be killed by a human being,
because God made humans
in his own image.

7"As for you, Noah, I want you and your family
to have many children, to grow in number on the
earth, and to become many."
8Then God said to Noah and his sons, 9"Now I
am making my agreement with you and your people who will live after you, 10and with every living
thing that is with you—the birds, the tame and
the wild animals, and with everything that came
out of the boat with you—with every living thing
on earth. 11I make this agreement with you: I will
never again destroy all living things by a flood. A
flood will never again destroy the earth."
12And God said, "This is the sign of the agreement between me and you and every living creature that is with you. 13I am putting my rainbow
in the clouds as the sign of the agreement
between me and the earth. 14When I bring clouds
over the earth and a rainbow appears in them, 15I
will remember my agreement between me and
you and every living thing. Floods will never
again destroy all life on the earth. 16When the
rainbow appears in the clouds, I will see it and I
will remember the agreement that continues forever between me and every living thing on the
earth."
17So God said to Noah, "The rainbow is a sign
of the agreement that I made with all living things
on earth."

Noah and His Sons

18The sons of Noah who came out of the boat
with him were Shem, Ham, and Japheth. (Ham
was the father of Canaan.) 19These three men
were Noah's sons, and all the people on earth
came from these three sons.
20Noah became a farmer and planted a vineyard.
21When he drank wine made from his grapes, he
became drunk and lay naked in his tent. 22Ham,
the father of Canaan, looked at his naked father
and told his brothers outside. 23Then Shem and
Japheth got a coat and, carrying it on both their
shoulders, they walked backwards into the tent
and covered their father. They turned their faces
away so that they did not see their father's
nakedness.
24Noah was sleeping because of the wine.
When he woke up and learned what his youngest
son, Ham, had done to him, 25he said,
"May there be a curse on Canaan!

8:21 Curse: Genesis 12:3
9:1 Celibacy: Leviticus 21:7
9:1 Creation/New Creation: Exodus 1:7
9:4 After the Flood, God not only gives plants to his human creatures for food, but for the first time he permits them to eat meat. However, he strictly forbids eating meat with blood still in it. This law is just one of a number that signifies the importance of blood as a symbol of life and shed blood, a symbol of death. Blood is so important to the sacrifices of Israel that special care is taken that it not be treated lightly.
9:6 Whoever assaults another person assaults God. After all, human beings are created in God's image. To degrade another person is to degrade God, and, as this verse points out, to murder another person is an attack upon God and deserves the severest punishment.
9:6 Human: Exodus 20:4–6
9:6 This passage occurs in the context of the agreement God made with Noah after the Flood. That means it was made with the person who was the ancestor of all people, not just the Israelites. For that reason, its provisions apply to all people. Among its provisions, it makes it very clear that murder, the unlawful taking of life, was wrong. After all, each person is created in the image of God. A murderer had to forfeit his own life as punishment. An implication of this is that the killing of a murderer is not murder itself.
9:15 Remembrance means more than simply calling to mind. After all God knows everything. When God remembers his agreement it means he acts on behalf of his people. He acts to save them.
9:15 Memory: Exodus 20:8
9:24 Alcohol: Leviticus 10:9

May he be the lowest slave to his brothers."
[26]Noah also said,
"May the LORD, the God of Shem, be praised!
May Canaan be Shem's slave.
[27]May God give more land to Japheth.
May Japheth live in Shem's tents,
and may Canaan be their slave."
[28]After the flood Noah lived 350 years. [29]He
lived a total of 950 years, and then he died.

Nations Grow and Spread

10 This is the family history of Shem, Ham,
and Japheth, the sons of Noah. After the
flood these three men had sons.

Japheth's Sons

[2]The sons of Japheth were Gomer, Magog,
Madai, Javan, Tubal, Meshech, and Tiras.
[3]The sons of Gomer were Ashkenaz, Riphath,
and Togarmah.
[4]The sons of Javan were Elishah, Tarshish,
Kittim, and Rodanim. [5]Those who lived in the
lands around the Mediterranean Sea came from
these sons of Japheth. All the families grew and
became different nations, each nation with its
own land and its own language.

Ham's Sons

[6]The sons of Ham were Cush, Mizraim, Put,
and Canaan.
[7]The sons of Cush were Seba, Havilah, Sabtah,
Raamah, and Sabteca.
The sons of Raamah were Sheba and Dedan.
[8]Cush also had a descendant named Nimrod,
who became a very powerful man on earth. [9]He
was a great hunter before the LORD, which is why
people say someone is "like Nimrod, a great
hunter before the LORD." [10]At first Nimrod's kingdom covered Babylon, Erech, Akkad, and Calneh
in the land of Babylonia. [11]From there he went
to Assyria, where he built the cities of Nineveh,
Rehoboth Ir, and Calah. [12]He also built Resen,
the great city between Nineveh and Calah.
[13]Mizraim was the father of the Ludites,
Anamites, Lehabites, Naphtuhites, [14]Pathrusites,
Casluhites, and the people of Crete. (The
Philistines came from the Casluhites.)
[15]Canaan was the father of Sidon, his first son,
and of Heth. [16]He was also the father of the
Jebusites, Amorites, Girgashites, [17]Hivites, Arkites,
Sinites, [18]Arvadites, Zemarites, and Hamathites.
The families of the Canaanites scattered. [19]Their
land reached from Sidon to Gerar as far as Gaza,
and then to Sodom, Gomorrah, Admah, and
Zeboiim, as far as Lasha.
[20]All these people were the sons of Ham, and
all these families had their own languages, their
own lands, and their own nations.

Shem's Sons

[21]Shem, Japheth's older brother, also had sons.
One of his descendants was the father of all the
sons of Eber.
[22]The sons of Shem were Elam, Asshur,
Arphaxad, Lud, and Aram.
[23]The sons of Aram were Uz, Hul, Gether, and
Meshech.
[24]Arphaxad was the father of Shelah, who was
the father of Eber. [25]Eber was the father of two
sons—one named Peleg, because the earth was
divided during his life, and the other was named
Joktan.
[26]Joktan was the father of Almodad, Sheleph,
Hazarmaveth, Jerah, [27]Hadoram, Uzal, Diklah,
[28]Obal, Abimael, Sheba, [29]Ophir, Havilah, and
Jobab. All these people were the sons of Joktan.
[30]They lived in the area between Mesha and
Sephar in the hill country in the East.
[31]These are the people from the family of
Shem, arranged by families, languages, countries,
and nations.
[32]This is the list of the families from the sons of
Noah, arranged according to their nations. From
these families came all the nations who spread
across the earth after the flood.

The Languages Confused

11 At this time the whole world spoke one
language, and everyone used the same
words. [2]As people moved from the east, they
found a plain in the land of Babylonia and settled
there.
[3]They said to each other, "Let's make bricks
and bake them to make them hard." So they used
bricks instead of stones, and tar instead of mortar.
[4]Then they said to each other, "Let's build a city
and a tower for ourselves, whose top will reach
high into the sky. We will become famous. Then
we will not be scattered over all the earth."
[5]The LORD came down to see the city and the
tower that the people had built. [6]The LORD said,
"Now, these people are united, all speaking the

10:4 *Kittim.* His descendants were the people of Cyprus.
10:6 *Mizraim.* This is another name for Egypt.
10:10 Babylon: Genesis 11:1–11
10:11 Samaria: Ezekiel 23:49
10:25 *Peleg.* This name sounds like the Hebrew word for "divided."
10:32 Births: Genesis 11:10–12:4
10:32 Genealogy: Genesis 11

same language. This is only the beginning of what they will do. They will be able to do anything they want. 7Come, let us go down and confuse their language so they will not be able to understand each other."

8So the LORD scattered them from there over all the earth, and they stopped building the city. 9The place is called Babel since that is where the LORD confused the language of the whole world. So the LORD caused them to spread out from there over the whole world.

The Story of Shem's Family

10This is the family history of Shem. Two years after the flood, when Shem was 100 years old, his son Arphaxad was born. 11After that, Shem lived 500 years and had other sons and daughters.

12When Arphaxad was 35 years old, his son Shelah was born. 13After that, Arphaxad lived 403 years and had other sons and daughters.

14When Shelah was 30 years old, his son Eber was born. 15After that, Shelah lived 403 years and had other sons and daughters.

16When Eber was 34 years old, his son Peleg was born. 17After that, Eber lived 430 years and had other sons and daughters.

18When Peleg was 30 years old, his son Reu was born. 19After that, Peleg lived 209 years and had other sons and daughters.

20When Reu was 32 years old, his son Serug was born. 21After that, Reu lived 207 years and had other sons and daughters.

22When Serug was 30 years old, his son Nahor was born. 23After that, Serug lived 200 years and had other sons and daughters.

24When Nahor was 29 years old, his son Terah was born. 25After that, Nahor lived 119 years and had other sons and daughters.

26After Terah was 70 years old, his sons Abram, Nahor, and Haran were born.

The Story of Terah's Family

27This is the family history of Terah. Terah was the father of Abram, Nahor, and Haran. Haran was the father of Lot. 28While his father, Terah, was still alive, Haran died in Ur in Babylonia, where he was born. 29Abram and Nahor both married. Abram's wife was named Sarai, and Nahor's wife was named Milcah. She was the daughter of Haran, who was the father of both Milcah and Iscah. 30Sarai was not able to have children.

31Terah took his son Abram, his grandson Lot (Haran's son), and his daughter-in-law Sarai (Abram's wife) and moved out of Ur of Babylonia. They had planned to go to the land of Canaan, but when they reached the city of Haran, they settled there.

32Terah lived to be 205 years old, and then he died in Haran.

Simple mud "beehive" houses at present-day Haran

God Calls Abram

12 The LORD said to Abram, "Leave your country, your relatives, and your father's family, and go to the land I will show you.

2I will make you a great nation,
and I will bless you.
I will make you famous,
and you will be a blessing to others.
3I will bless those who bless you,
and I will place a curse on those who harm you.

11:9 *Babel.* This name sounds like the Hebrew word for "confused."
11:9 Crossing Cultural Boundaries: Genesis 12:1–5
11:9 Tongues: Deuteronomy 28:49
11:11 Babylon: Psalm 137
11:30 Sarah: Genesis 12:11
11:32 Genealogy: Genesis 46

12:1–3 In this passage, God gives Abram a vision for the people of God that will be his descendants. The promise given to Abram has significance beyond Abram and his descendants. This vision from God includes the promise of land, the promise of a great nation, the promise of greatness, and the promise of family members who will follow. Like blessing, a true vision from God has meanings for others, eventually blessing all the generations.

12:1-3 Though the term *agreement* is not used here, these promises to Abram, as well as the demands made upon him, clearly flow from a formal agreement. It is not surprising, therefore, that later passages look at the relationship between Abram and God as an agreement (Genesis 15:18, which is a renewal, or reaffirmation, of the agreement).

12:1–36:40 At this point the biblical story puts on the close focus lens and concentrates on one person from whom will come a nation who will be known as God's people. God will use this nation to bless the rest of the world. It begins with the promise given to Abraham in Genesis 12:1–3 that he will be made into a great and blessed nation. In return God calls Abraham (then known as Abram) to leave his comfortable home in Ur and travel to Canaan.

Once he gets there the struggle of faith begins. In order to be the father of a people, he needs to have a child. He and Sarah grow older and older, and they still have no child. God calls them to trust him to provide even against human odds. Sometimes they fail (Genesis 12:10–20), but at other times Abram is able to rely on God (Genesis 13:1–18 and ultimately Genesis 22:1–24).

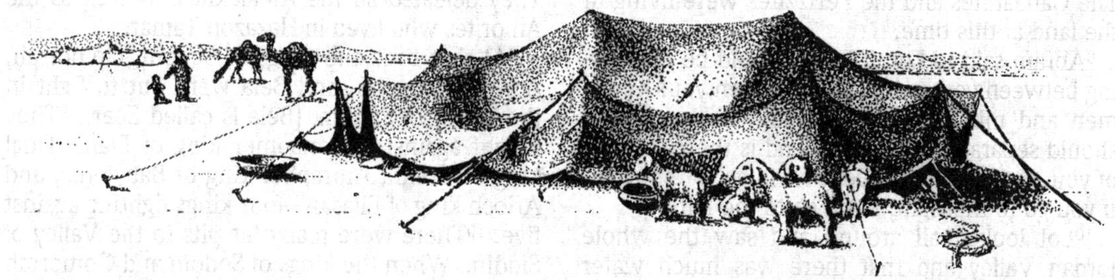

Abraham and his family lived in tents, moving about to find fresh pasture for their flocks.

And all the people on earth
will be blessed through you."∞
4So Abram left Haran as the LORD had told him,
and Lot went with him. At this time Abram was
75 years old.∞ 5He took his wife Sarai, his
nephew Lot, and everything they owned, as well
as all the servants they had gotten in Haran. They
set out from Haran, planning to go to the land of
Canaan, and in time they arrived there.∞
6Abram traveled through that land as far as the
great tree of Moreh at Shechem. The Canaanites
were living in the land at that time. 7The LORD
appeared to Abram and said, "I will give this land
to your descendants." So Abram built an altar
there to the LORD, who had appeared to him.∞
8Then he traveled from Shechem to the mountain
east of Bethel and set up his tent there. Bethel
was to the west, and Ai was to the east. There
Abram built another altar to the LORD and worshiped him. 9After this, he traveled on toward
southern Canaan.

Abram Goes to Egypt

10At this time there was not much food in the
land, so Abram went down to Egypt to live because
there was so little food.∞ 11Just before they arrived
in Egypt, he said to his wife Sarai, "I know you are
a very beautiful woman.∞ 12When the Egyptians
see you, they will say, 'This woman is his wife.'
Then they will kill me but let you live. 13Tell them
you are my sister so that things will go well with
me and I may be allowed to live because of you."
14When Abram came to Egypt, the Egyptians saw
that Sarai was very beautiful.∞ 15The Egyptian
officers saw her and told the king of Egypt how
beautiful she was. They took her to the king's
palace, and 16the king was kind to Abram because
he thought Abram was her brother. He gave
Abram sheep, cattle, male and female donkeys,
male and female servants, and camels.
17But the LORD sent terrible diseases on the
king and all the people in his house because of
Abram's wife Sarai. 18So the king sent for Abram
and said, "What have you done to me? Why didn't
you tell me Sarai was your wife? 19Why did you
say, 'She is my sister' so that I made her my wife?
Now, here is your wife. Take her and leave!" 20Then
the king commanded his men to make Abram
leave Egypt; so Abram and his wife left with
everything they owned.

Abram and Lot Separate

13 So Abram, his wife, and Lot left Egypt, taking
everything they owned, and traveled to
southern Canaan. 2Abram was very rich in cattle,
silver, and gold.
3He left southern Canaan and went back to
Bethel where he had camped before, between
Bethel and Ai, 4and where he had built an altar.
So he worshiped the LORD there.∞
5During this time Lot was traveling with Abram,
and Lot also had flocks, herds, and tents. 6Abram
and Lot had so many animals that the land could
not support both of them together, 7so Abram's

12:3 Too often we interpret God's blessings as being for our own benefit. Abraham was blessed by God, but he was blessed to be a blessing to others. Through God's selection of Abraham, all the nations of the world would come to know the Lord. This is a model for our mission as well—when we receive the goodness of God, we need to share it.

∞**12:3 Curse:** Deuteronomy 21:23

∞**12:3 Gentiles (Non-Jews):** Deuteronomy 7:1–6

∞**12:3 Election (Chosen):** Genesis 15:1–19

∞**12:3 Mission:** Joshua 2

∞**12:4 Births:** Genesis 17:15–21

∞**12:5 Crossing Cultural Boundaries:** Ruth 1–2

∞**12:5 Racism:** Exodus 1:8–14

∞**12:7 Presence of God:** Genesis 13:4

∞**12:10 Famine:** Leviticus 26:14–20

∞**12:11 Sarah:** Genesis 12:14

∞**12:14 Sarah:** Genesis 16:1

∞**13:4 Presence of God:** Genesis 15:17

herdsmen and Lot's herdsmen began to argue.
The Canaanites and the Perizzites were living in
the land at this time.
8Abram said to Lot, "There should be no arguing between you and me, or between your herdsmen and mine, because we are brothers. 9We
should separate. The whole land is there in front
of you. If you go to the left, I will go to the right.
If you go to the right, I will go to the left."
10Lot looked all around and saw the whole
Jordan Valley and that there was much water
there. It was like the LORD's garden, like the land
of Egypt in the direction of Zoar. (This was before
the LORD destroyed Sodom and Gomorrah.)
11So Lot chose to move east and live in the Jordan
Valley. In this way Abram and Lot separated.
12Abram lived in the land of Canaan, but Lot lived
among the cities in the Jordan Valley, very near to
Sodom. 13Now the people of Sodom were very
evil and were always sinning against the LORD.
14After Lot left, the LORD said to Abram, "Look
all around you—to the north and south and east
and west. 15All this land that you see I will give
to you and your descendants forever. 16I will
make your descendants as many as the dust of
the earth. If anyone could count the dust on the
earth, he could count your people. 17Get up!
Walk through all this land because I am now
giving it to you."
18So Abram moved his tents and went to live
near the great trees of Mamre at the city of
Hebron. There he built an altar to the LORD.

Lot Is Captured

14 Now Amraphel was king of Babylonia,
Arioch was king of Ellasar, Kedorlaomer
was king of Elam, and Tidal was king of Goiim. 2All
these kings went to war against several other kings:
Bera king of Sodom, Birsha king of Gomorrah,
Shinab king of Admah, Shemeber king of Zeboiim,
and the king of Bela. (Bela is also called Zoar.)
3These kings who were attacked united their
armies in the Valley of Siddim (now the Dead Sea).
4They had served Kedorlaomer for twelve years,
but in the thirteenth year, they all turned against
him. 5Then in the fourteenth year, Kedorlaomer
and the kings with him came and defeated the
Rephaites in Ashteroth Karnaim, the Zuzites in
Ham, and the Emites in Shaveh Kiriathaim. 6They
also defeated the Horites in the mountains of Edom
to El Paran (near the desert). 7Then they turned
back and went to En Mishpat (that is, Kadesh).
They defeated all the Amalekites, as well as the
Amorites who lived in Hazazon Tamar.
8At that time the kings of Sodom, Gomorrah,
Admah, Zeboiim, and Bela went out to fight in
the Valley of Siddim. (Bela is called Zoar.) 9They
fought against Kedorlaomer king of Elam, Tidal
king of Goiim, Amraphel king of Babylonia, and
Arioch king of Ellasar—four kings fighting against
five. 10There were many tar pits in the Valley of
Siddim. When the kings of Sodom and Gomorrah
and their armies ran away, some of the soldiers
fell into the tar pits, but the others ran away to
the mountains.
11Now Kedorlaomer and his armies took everything the people of Sodom and Gomorrah owned,
including their food. 12They took Lot, Abram's
nephew who was living in Sodom, and everything he owned. Then they left. 13One of the men
who was not captured went to Abram, the
Hebrew, and told him what had happened. At
that time Abram was camped near the great trees
of Mamre the Amorite. Mamre was a brother of
Eshcol and Aner, and they had all made an agreement to help Abram.

Abram Rescues Lot

14When Abram learned that Lot had been captured, he called out his 318 trained men who had
been born in his camp. He led the men and
chased the enemy all the way to the town of Dan.
15That night he divided his men into groups, and
they made a surprise attack against the enemy.
They chased them all the way to Hobah, north of
Damascus. 16Then Abram brought back everything the enemy had stolen, the women and the
other people, and Lot, and everything Lot owned.
17After defeating Kedorlaomer and the kings
who were with him, Abram went home. As he
was returning, the king of Sodom came out to
meet him in the Valley of Shaveh (now called
King's Valley).
18Melchizedek king of Salem brought out bread
and wine. He was a priest for God Most High
19and blessed Abram, saying,

"Abram, may you be blessed by God Most High,
the God who made heaven and earth.
20And we praise God Most High,
who has helped you to defeat your enemies."

Then Abram gave Melchizedek a tenth of everything he had brought back from the battle.

13:10 Garden of Eden: Deuteronomy 11:10–12
14:18 Jerusalem: Joshua 10:1
14:18 Priesthood: Exodus 29:9
14:20 Tithe: Genesis 28:22
14:20 Stewardship: Genesis 28:22

HUMAN

GENESIS 1:26–28

What is meant by the "image of God"? What does it mean to be human? How is our humanity and the image of God related to Christ?

We are created in the image of God. That is the message repeated three times that we learn in Genesis 1:26–27. But what does this mean?

The nature of the divine image in humanity has provoked a number of different answers as we survey church history. Some have suggested that the image of God is manifested in human rationality. Others have proposed moral action, or freedom, or dominion over creation, or even relationality (the ability and need to relate to others). There is some merit to all these suggestions, but we should say that humanity's dominion over creation and ability and need to relate are emphasized in the text of Genesis 1.

In verse 26, directly after creating human beings, God says to "let them rule" over all animals. This dominion means that human beings are to be representatives of God's ultimate rule. In the ancient Near East, kings were in the habit of setting their statue up throughout their kingdom. This signified that even though the king was not physically present in a particular city, he still was sovereign over that area. When a citizen saw that statue or image, he or she was reminded who the king was. In the same way, human beings represent God's presence and sovereignty over the earth. Human dominion reflects God's care for the creation (Psalm 8:4–6).

In Genesis 1:27, creation as male and female implies that human beings of both genders are to relate to one another, with marriage being the most definitive human institution (Genesis 2:24). Both male and female are created in God's image; neither is definitively the human being, but being human is only adequately represented in both sexes. Most importantly, the relational aspect of the image of God is that God can communicate with men and women, as in verses 29–30 where God speaks directly to them. Because human beings are made in God's image, we can enter into a relationship with God. In fact, this relationship with God is the highest call of human beings. As Jesus said, "Love one another as I have loved you" (John 15:12), and he even goes so far as to call his followers "friends" (John 15:15), indicating how intimate this relationship can be.

While the Bible never says that human beings are God, it is still true to say that one aspect of human beings is to reflect divinity. This aspect of humanity is remarkable when considered against the strong denunciation of "graven images" (or idolatry) in Old Testament passages such as Exodus 20:4–6.

Bearing the divine image emphasizes the spiritual dimension of human existence. The second creation account in Genesis 2 balances this emphasis by highlighting the relationship of human beings and the rest of creation: "Then the Lord God took dust from the ground and formed a man from it" (verse 7). Being human thus involves both spiritual and material dimensions; these two aspects form a unity, and to speak of one to the exclusion of the other distorts our humanity.

In the New Testament, the accent falls upon Christ as the image of God and Christ's work in redeeming the image of God in believers. Since God is not directly visible to anyone, human beings have a tendency to worship created things in the form of idols, so that they can worship something they can see (Romans 1:23, 25). Nevertheless, Christ has altered this situation. "No one can see God, but Jesus Christ is exactly like him" (Colossians 1:15). The latter phrase can in fact be literally translated that Christ is "the image of the invisible God." Christ has made God fully visible, and, in case his readers might be confused, Paul writes in 2:9, "All of God lives in Christ fully." This theological affirmation has specific ethical implications: Colossians 3:10 says that believers are becoming "like [literally, "according to the image of"] the One who made you." The metaphor of the church as the body of Christ (as in Ephesians 4:12) gives this ethical dimension of bearing God's image a corporate emphasis. Negatively stated, James 3:9 says that to curse other people and to praise God is unthinkable because "God made [human beings] like himself." Because women and men are made in God's image and likeness, they have dignity and are to be respected.

Finally, bearing the image of God has a future thrust. God will one day bring to fulfillment the image of God in humanity. Christians await Christ's return when Christ's image in us will be fully realized (1 John 3:2). First Corinthians 15:49 states the hope of full redemption: "Just as we were made like the man of earth, we will be made like the man of heaven." That is, we will have resurrection bodies just like his.

There can be no higher calling for human beings than to reflect this image of God in Christ. For in doing so we bring honor to God and show others what he is like.

Human: For additional scriptures on this topic go to Genesis 2:7.

EARTH

GENESIS 2:4

What does the Bible mean by the term earth? From where did it come? What is our responsibility toward the earth? What will eventually happen to the earth?

The term earth refers to the place where all humankind lives. It is separate from the sky where the sun, moon, and stars have their places. The earth, then, includes the ground beneath our feet, the air that we breathe, and the creation around us (see "creation"). The earth was created by God based upon his wisdom (Genesis 1:1; Psalm 146:6; Proverbs 3:19). As God's creation, the earth and all that it contains are "good" (Genesis 1:10, 12, 18, 21, 25).

What is God's relationship to the earth? The earth as God's footstool symbolizes how much greater God is than the earth and the people who live there (Isaiah 66:1). Even though God is much higher than earthly existence, in all of creation the earth is the center of God's concern. As God's creation, the earth belongs to God (Psalm 24:1; Matthew 5:35). He rules over and cares for it in a special way (Colossians 1:16–17). The earth also shows forth the goodness and greatness of God (Psalm 33:5; Isaiah 6:3) as well as his wealth and kindness (Psalms 104:24; 119:64). The earth and its creation also display his everlasting power (Romans 1:20). There is no excuse for a person not to worship the great God of creation.

What is our relationship to the earth? What is our responsibility toward it? The earth supplied the materials God used to make the first human. God created Adam in his very likeness and breathed into him spiritual life (Genesis 2:7). Adam and Eve were, therefore, both physical (earthlike) and spiritual (Godlike). In the final act of creation, God saw human beings as the highest point of his creation—very good (Genesis 1:31). Humans were given the jobs of caring for the earth and overseeing everything that it contains (Genesis 2:5, 20). God expresses his kindness (see "grace") toward his creatures by giving a certain stability and permanence to the earth (Genesis 8:22; Psalms 74:12–17; 104:5–6). As caretakers of God's earth, we are responsible for taking care of it.

If the earth, as God's creation, is good, why does it contain such terrible things as famine and disease (see "famine")? The earth was to be a place where humans would have a special relationship with God. Due to human sin, God at times has used the earth as a means of judgment. Shortly after Adam sinned, the earth was placed under a curse (see "sin," "curse"). It has been ruined, or made worthless, in comparison to what it was originally (Romans 1:20–21). The earth itself underwent certain changes. It changed from being a friend to humans to being a resistant foe. The plentiful garden of Eden has been replaced by weeds, insects, disease, and hard work (Genesis 3:17–19; Romans 8:20). Also, since sin brought death into the world, when we die our bodies return to the earth from which they originally came.

In light of this very bad situation, is there a cure for the condition of the earth? Due to the curse, the earth is still in desperate need of renewal (see "redeem"). Prior to renewal though, God brings judgment to remove that which is evil. God uses the earth twice more as a means of judgment. Both times, he does this to cleanse the world of sin. He brought a flood upon the earth to destroy humankind in the time of Noah (Genesis 6–9). In the future, God will again judge the entire world. This judgment will be more complete than the flood of Noah's day. The earth will be burned up with fire prior to the bringing in of a new heaven and a new earth (Isaiah 65:17; 66:22; 2 Peter 3:10–12; Revelation 21:2). The purpose of the future judgment is to cleanse the earth of all the effects of sin and clear a way for the setting up of God's kingdom on a renewed earth.

What is the relationship between God's work as Creator and as Savior of the earth? God's work as Creator cannot be separated from his role as Savior. This applies to the earth as well as to humans since God created them both. The Bible often pictures God's creative work as the deliverance of creation from the powers of disorder (Psalms 74:12–17; 89:8–14; 104:5–9; Isaiah 40:28–31; 51:9–11). Just as God took total control over these powers in the past, he will some day defeat Satan and all other forces who stand against him (Revelation 20:10). At that time, the earth will be changed and all creation will obey him (Revelation 20:10; 14:7).

How do the future judgment and renewing of earth relate to my life? In light of the seriousness of this judgment, Peter urges Christians to live holy lives—to try to be without sin and without fault. Also, we are to be at peace with God and serve him. At the same time, we are to be happy as we look forward to this time when God will fulfill his promise to give his people a new world where goodness lives (2 Peter 3:11–12).

Earth: For additional scriptures on this topic go to Genesis 6:7.

21The king of Sodom said to Abram, "You may
keep all these things for yourself. Just give me my
people who were captured."
22But Abram said to the king of Sodom, "I
make a promise to the LORD, the God Most
High, who made heaven and earth. 23I promise
that I will not keep anything that is yours. I will
not keep even a thread or a sandal strap so that
you cannot say, 'I made Abram rich.' 24I will
keep nothing but the food my young men have
eaten. But give Aner, Eshcol, and Mamre their
share of what we won, because they went with
me into battle."

God's Agreement with Abram

15 After these things happened, the LORD
spoke his word to Abram in a vision:
"Abram, don't be afraid. I will defend you, and I
will give you a great reward."
2But Abram said, "Lord GOD, what can you give
me? I have no son, so my slave Eliezer from
Damascus will get everything I own after I die."
3Abram said, "Look, you have given me no son,
so a slave born in my house will inherit everything I have."
4Then the LORD spoke his word to Abram: "He
will not be the one to inherit what you have. You
will have a son of your own who will inherit what
you have."
5Then God led Abram outside and said, "Look
at the sky. There are so many stars you cannot
count them. Your descendants also will be too
many to count."
6Abram believed the LORD. And the LORD
accepted Abram's faith, and that faith made him
right with God.
7God said to Abram, "I am the LORD who led
you out of Ur of Babylonia so that I could give you
this land to own."
8But Abram said, "Lord GOD, how can I be sure
that I will own this land?"
9The LORD said to Abram, "Bring me a three-
year-old cow, a three-year-old goat, a three-year-
old male sheep, a dove, and a young pigeon."
10Abram brought them all to God. Then Abram
killed the animals and cut each of them into two
pieces, laying each half opposite the other half.
But he did not cut the birds in half. 11Later, large
birds flew down to eat the animals, but Abram
chased them away.
12As the sun was going down, Abram fell into a
deep sleep. While he was asleep, a very terrible
darkness came. 13Then the LORD said to Abram,
"You can be sure that your descendants will be
strangers and travel in a land they don't own. The
people there will make them slaves and be cruel
to them for four hundred years. 14But I will punish the nation where they are slaves. Then your
descendants will leave that land, taking great
wealth with them. 15And you, Abram, will die in
peace and will be buried at an old age. 16After
your great-great-grandchildren are born, your
people will come to this land again. It will take
that long, because I am not yet going to punish
the Amorites for their evil behavior."
17After the sun went down, it was very dark.
Suddenly a smoking firepot and a blazing torch
passed between the halves of the dead animals.
18So on that day the LORD made an agreement
with Abram and said, "I will give to your descendants the land between the river of Egypt and the
great river Euphrates. 19This is the land of the
Kenites, Kenizzites, Kadmonites, 20Hittites,
Perizzites, Rephaites, 21Amorites, Canaanites,
Girgashites, and Jebusites."

Ishmael Is Born

16 Sarai, Abram's wife, had no children, but
she had a slave girl from Egypt named
Hagar. 2Sarai said to Abram, "Look, the LORD
has not allowed me to have children, so have sexual relations with my slave girl. If she has a child,
maybe I can have my own family through her."
Abram did what Sarai said. 3It was after he had
lived ten years in Canaan that Sarai gave Hagar to
her husband Abram. (Hagar was her slave girl
from Egypt.)

15:1 Vision: Genesis 46:2
15:1 Fear: Genesis 21:17
15:2 *Eliezer of Damascus.* Apparently there was a law at this time which allowed for the servant of the household to inherit the wealth of a childless couple.
15:3 Complaint/Lament/Protest: Judges 15:18
15:6 God promised Abram descendants "too many to count" and a land in which to dwell. Abram's faith put him in the right relationship to God and started the story of God's salvation. Not only would Abram and his descendants be blessed, but all the peoples of the world would be blessed through him (Genesis 12:3). In Romans 4 Paul uses Abram as the example to show that salvation is by faith and not by works.
15:6 Intercession: 1 Kings 17:20–23
15:10 *cut them in two.* This ritual reflects an ancient Near Eastern custom. When two people entered into an important agreement, they would cut animals into two parts and then walk through the halves. This was an oath that they would keep the agreement, and if they failed to do so, then they were calling upon themselves the same fate as the animals.
15:17 Presence of God: Exodus 19:16–19
15:17 *passed . . . animals.* This showed that God sealed the agreement between himself and Abram.
15:19 Election (Chosen): Exodus 4:22
16:1 Sarah: Hebrews 11:11

[4]Abram had sexual relations with Hagar, and she became pregnant. When Hagar learned she was pregnant, she began to treat her mistress Sarai badly. [5]Then Sarai said to Abram, "This is your fault. I gave my slave girl to you, and when she became pregnant, she began to treat me badly. Let the LORD decide who is right—you or me."

[6]But Abram said to Sarai, "You are Hagar's mistress. Do anything you want to her." Then Sarai was hard on Hagar, and Hagar ran away.

[7]The angel of the LORD found Hagar beside a spring of water in the desert, by the road to Shur. [8]The angel said, "Hagar, Sarai's slave girl, where have you come from? Where are you going?"

Hagar answered, "I am running away from my mistress Sarai."

[9]The angel of the LORD said to her, "Go home to your mistress and obey her." [10]The angel also said, "I will give you so many descendants they cannot be counted."

[11]The angel added,

"You are now pregnant,
  and you will have a son.
You will name him Ishmael,
  because the LORD has heard your cries.
[12]Ishmael will be like a wild donkey.
  He will be against everyone,
  and everyone will be against him.
He will attack all his brothers."

[13]The slave girl gave a name to the LORD who spoke to her: "You are 'God who sees me,'" because she said to herself, "Have I really seen God who sees me?" [14]So the well there, between Kadesh and Bered, was called Beer Lahai Roi.

[15]Hagar gave birth to a son for Abram, and Abram named him Ishmael. [16]Abram was eighty-six years old when Hagar gave birth to Ishmael.

Proof of the Agreement

17 When Abram was ninety-nine years old, the LORD appeared to him and said, "I am God Almighty. Obey me and do what is right. [2]I will make an agreement between us, and I will make you the ancestor of many people."

[3]Then Abram bowed facedown on the ground. God said to him, [4]"I am making my agreement with you: I will make you the father of many nations. [5]I am changing your name from Abram to Abraham because I am making you a father of many nations. [6]I will give you many descendants. New nations will be born from you, and kings will come from you. [7]And I will make an agreement between me and you and all your descendants from now on: I will be your God and the God of all your descendants. [8]You live in the land of Canaan now as a stranger, but I will give you and your descendants all this land forever. And I will be the God of your descendants."

[9]Then God said to Abraham, "You and your descendants must keep this agreement from now on. [10]This is my agreement with you and all your descendants, which you must obey: Every male among you must be circumcised. [11]Cut away your foreskin to show that you are prepared to follow the agreement between me and you. [12]From now on when a baby boy is eight days old, you will circumcise him. This includes any boy born among your people or any who is your slave, who is not one of your descendants. [13]Circumcise every baby boy whether he is born in your family or bought as a slave. Your bodies will be marked to show that you are part of my agreement that lasts forever. [14]Any male who is not circumcised will be cut off from his people, because he has broken my agreement."

Isaac—the Promised Son

[15]God said to Abraham, "I will change the name of Sarai, your wife, to Sarah. [16]I will bless her and give her a son, and you will be the father. She will be the mother of many nations. Kings of nations will come from her."

[17]Abraham bowed facedown on the ground and laughed. He said to himself, "Can a man have a child when he is a hundred years old? Can Sarah give birth to a child when she is ninety?" [18]Then Abraham said to God, "Please let Ishmael be the son you promised."

[19]God said, "No, Sarah your wife will have a son, and you will name him Isaac. I will make my agreement with him to be an agreement that continues forever with all his descendants.

[20]"As for Ishmael, I have heard you. I will bless him and give him many descendants. And I will cause their numbers to grow greatly. He will be the father of twelve great leaders, and I will make

---

16:11 *Ishmael.* The Hebrew words for "Ishmael" and "has heard" sound similar.

16:14 Trinity: Exodus 20:3

16:14 Wilderness (Desert): Genesis 21:8–21

16:14 *Beer Lahai Roi.* This means "the well of the Living One who sees me."

16:16 Abortion and Crisis Pregnancy: Luke 10:30–37

17:5 *Abram.* This name means "honored father."

17:5 *Abraham.* The end of the Hebrew word for "Abraham" sounds like the beginning of the Hebrew word for "many."

17:8 Promise: Exodus 6:8

17:15 *Sarai.* An Aramaic name meaning "princess."

17:15 *Sarah.* A Hebrew name meaning "princess."

17:19 *Isaac.* The Hebrew words for "he laughed" (v. 17) and "Isaac" sound the same.

him into a great nation. 21But I will make my agreement with Isaac, the son whom Sarah will have at this same time next year." 22After God finished talking with Abraham, God rose and left him.

23Then Abraham gathered Ishmael, all the males born in his camp, and the slaves he had bought. So that day Abraham circumcised every man and boy in his camp as God had told him to do. 24Abraham was ninety-nine years old when he was circumcised. 25And Ishmael, his son, was thirteen years old when he was circumcised. 26Abraham and his son were circumcised on the same day. 27Also on that day all the men in Abraham's camp were circumcised, including all those born in his camp and all the slaves he had bought from other nations.

The Three Visitors

18 Later, the LORD again appeared to Abraham near the great trees of Mamre. Abraham was sitting at the entrance of his tent during the hottest part of the day. 2He looked up and saw three men standing near him. When Abraham saw them, he ran from his tent to meet them. He bowed facedown on the ground before them 3and said, "Sir, if you think well of me, please stay awhile with me, your servant. 4I will bring some water so all of you can wash your feet. You may rest under the tree, 5and I will get some bread for you so you can regain your strength. Then you may continue your journey."

The three men said, "That is fine. Do as you said."

6Abraham hurried to the tent where Sarah was and said to her, "Hurry, prepare twenty quarts of fine flour, and make it into loaves of bread." 7Then Abraham ran to his herd and took one of his best calves. He gave it to a servant, who hurried to kill it and to prepare it for food. 8Abraham gave the three men the calf that had been cooked and milk curds and milk. While they ate, he stood under the tree near them.

9The men asked Abraham, "Where is your wife Sarah?"

"There, in the tent," said Abraham.

10Then the LORD said, "I will certainly return to you about this time a year from now. At that time your wife Sarah will have a son."

Sarah was listening at the entrance of the tent which was behind him. 11Abraham and Sarah were very old. Since Sarah was past the age when women normally have children, 12she laughed to herself, "My husband and I are too old to have a baby."

13Then the LORD said to Abraham, "Why did Sarah laugh? Why did she say, 'I am too old to have a baby'? 14Is anything too hard for the LORD? No! I will return to you at the right time a year from now, and Sarah will have a son."

15Sarah was afraid, so she lied and said, "I didn't laugh."

But the LORD said, "No. You did laugh."

16Then the men got up to leave and started out toward Sodom. Abraham walked along with them a short time to send them on their way.

Abraham's Bargain with God

17The LORD said, "Should I tell Abraham what I am going to do now? 18Abraham's children will certainly become a great and powerful nation, and all nations on earth will be blessed through him. 19I have chosen him so he would command his children and his descendants to live the way the LORD wants them to, to live right and be fair. Then I, the LORD, will give Abraham what I promised him."

20Then the LORD said, "I have heard many complaints against the people of Sodom and Gomorrah. They are very evil. 21I will go down and see if they are as bad as I have heard. If not, I will know."

22So the men turned and went toward Sodom, but Abraham stood there before the LORD. 23Then Abraham approached him and asked, "Do you plan to destroy the good people along with the evil ones? 24What if there are fifty good people in that city? Will you still destroy it? Surely you will save the city for the fifty good people living there. 25Surely you will not destroy the good people along with the evil ones; then they would be treated the same. You are the judge of all the earth. Won't you do what is right?"

26The LORD said, "If I find fifty good people in the city of Sodom, I will save the whole city because of them."

27Then Abraham said, "Though I am only dust and ashes, I have been brave to speak to the Lord.

17:21 Births: Numbers 3–4

18:1–16 The incident of Abraham's entertaining three men (angels in the form of men) and their announcement of a child to be born to Abraham and Sarah is a wonderful case of God's intervention to overcome a couple's infertility. Sarah's reaction to the news was one of disbelief because she knew they were both too old to have children. The Lord's response is instructive: "Is anything too hard for the Lord?"

18:16 Table Fellowship/Lord's Supper: Exodus 16–17

18:16 Infertility (Childlessness/Barrenness): Genesis 29:31–30:24

18:17–33 This is one of the most passionate and prolonged examples of intercession in the Old Testament. It not only shows the boldness of Abraham, but also the willingness of God to receive heartfelt prayer. Abraham's "dealings" with God are not interpreted as manipulative, but rather as the genuine concerns of a godly man.

18:19 Road/Way: Exodus 13:21

28What if there are only forty-five good people in the city? Will you destroy the whole city for the lack of five good people?"

The LORD said, "If I find forty-five there, I will not destroy the city."

29Again Abraham said to him, "If you find only forty good people there, will you destroy the city?"

The LORD said, "If I find forty, I will not destroy it."

30Then Abraham said, "Lord, please don't be angry with me, but let me ask you this. If you find only thirty good people in the city, will you destroy it?"

He said, "If I find thirty good people there, I will not destroy the city."

31Then Abraham said, "I have been brave to speak to the Lord. But what if there are twenty good people in the city?"

He answered, "If I find twenty there, I will not destroy the city."

32Then Abraham said, "Lord, please don't be angry with me, but let me bother you this one last time. What if you find ten there?"

He said, "If I find ten there, I will not destroy it."

33When the LORD finished speaking to Abraham, he left, and Abraham returned home.

Lot Leaves Sodom

19 The two angels came to Sodom in the evening as Lot was sitting near the city gate. When he saw them, he got up and went to them and bowed facedown on the ground. 2Lot said, "Sirs, please come to my house and spend the night. There you can wash your feet, and then tomorrow you may continue your journey."

The angels answered, "No, we will spend the night in the city's public square."

3But Lot begged them to come, so they agreed and went to his house. Then Lot prepared a meal for them. He baked bread without yeast, and they ate it.

4Before bedtime, men both young and old and from every part of Sodom surrounded Lot's house. 5They called to Lot, "Where are the two men who came to you tonight? Bring them out to us so we can have sexual relations with them."

6Lot went outside to them, closing the door behind him. 7He said, "No, my brothers! Do not do this evil thing. 8Look! I have two daughters who have never slept with a man. I will give them to you, and you may do anything you want with them. But please don't do anything to these men. They have come to my house, and I must protect them."

9The men around the house answered, "Move out of the way!" Then they said to each other, "This man Lot came to our city as a stranger, and now he wants to tell us what to do!" They said to Lot, "We will do worse things to you than to them." They started pushing him back and were ready to break down the door.

10But the two men staying with Lot opened the door, pulled him back inside the house, and then closed the door. 11They struck those outside the door with blindness, so the men, both young and old, could not find the door.

12The two men said to Lot, "Do you have any other relatives in this city? Do you have any sons-in-law, sons, daughters, or any other relatives? If you do, tell them to leave now, 13because we are about to destroy this city. The LORD has heard of all the evil that is here, so he has sent us to destroy it."

14So Lot went out and said to his future sons-in-law who were pledged to marry his daughters, "Hurry and leave this city! The LORD is about to destroy it!" But they thought Lot was joking.

15At dawn the next morning, the angels begged Lot to hurry. They said, "Go! Take your wife and your two daughters with you so you will not be destroyed when the city is punished."

16But Lot delayed. So the two men took the hands of Lot, his wife, and his two daughters and led them safely out of the city. So the LORD was merciful to Lot and his family.∞ 17After they brought them out of the city, one of the men said, "Run for your lives! Don't look back or stop anywhere in the valley. Run to the mountains, or you will be destroyed."

18But Lot said to one of them, "Sir, please don't force me to go so far! 19You have been merciful and kind to me and have saved my life. But I can't run to the mountains. The disaster will catch me, and I will die. 20Look, that little town over there is not too far away. Let me run there. It's really just a little town, and I'll be safe there."

21The angel said to Lot, "Very well, I will allow you to do this also. I will not destroy that town. 22But run there fast, because I cannot destroy Sodom until you are safely in that town." (That town is named Zoar, because it is little.)

Sodom and Gomorrah Are Destroyed

23The sun had already come up when Lot entered Zoar. 24The LORD sent a rain of burning sulfur down

19:1–29 At first glance, it appears that the evil that led to the destruction of Sodom and Gomorrah was the practice of homosexuality. However, God expressed his intent to destroy Sodom and Gomorrah before Lot's visitors arrived at Lot's home. In Genesis 18:20–21 the wickedness of these cities is not named. We should not read this story as suggesting that God has placed a special curse on homosexuals then, even though each form of sin carries its own consequences, including the sin of homosexuality.

∞**19:16 Hospitality:** Genesis 26:26–31

19:22 *Zoar.* This name sounds like the Hebrew word for "little."

from the sky on Sodom and Gomorrah 25and destroyed those cities. He also destroyed the whole Jordan Valley, everyone living in the cities, and even all the plants.

26At that point Lot's wife looked back. When she did, she became a pillar of salt.

27Early the next morning, Abraham got up and went to the place where he had stood before the LORD. 28He looked down toward Sodom and Gomorrah and all the Jordan Valley and saw smoke rising from the land, like smoke from a furnace.

29God destroyed the cities in the valley, but he remembered what Abraham had asked. So God saved Lot's life, but he destroyed the city where Lot had lived.

Lot and His Daughters

30Lot was afraid to continue living in Zoar, so he and his two daughters went to live in the mountains in a cave. 31One day the older daughter said to the younger, "Our father is old. Everywhere on the earth women and men marry, but there are no men around here for us to marry. 32Let's get our father drunk and have sexual relations with him. We can use him to have children and continue our family."

33That night the two girls got their father drunk, and the older daughter went and had sexual relations with him. But Lot did not know when she lay down or when she got up.

34The next day the older daughter said to the younger, "Last night I had sexual relations with my father. Let's get him drunk again tonight so you can go and have sexual relations with him, too. In this way we can use our father to have children to continue our family." 35So that night they got their father drunk again, and the younger daughter went and had sexual relations with him. Again, Lot did not know when she lay down or when she got up.

36So both of Lot's daughters became pregnant by their father. 37The older daughter gave birth to a son and named him Moab. He is the ancestor of all the Moabite people who are still living today. 38The younger daughter also gave birth to a son and named him Ben-Ammi. He is the father of all the Ammonite people who are still living today.

Abraham Tricks Abimelech

20 Abraham left Hebron and traveled to southern Canaan where he stayed awhile between Kadesh and Shur. When he moved to Gerar, 2he told people that his wife Sarah was his sister. Abimelech king of Gerar heard this, so he sent some servants to take her. 3But one night God spoke to Abimelech in a dream and said, "You will die. The woman you took is married."

4But Abimelech had not gone near Sarah, so he said, "Lord, would you destroy an innocent nation? 5Abraham himself told me, 'This woman is my sister,' and she also said, 'He is my brother.' I am innocent. I did not know I was doing anything wrong."

6Then God said to Abimelech in the dream, "Yes, I know you did not realize what you were doing. So I did not allow you to sin against me and touch her. 7Give Abraham his wife back. He is a prophet. He will pray for you, and you will not die. But if you do not give Sarah back, you and all your family will surely die."

8So early the next morning, Abimelech called all his officers and told them everything that had happened in the dream. They were very afraid. 9Then Abimelech called Abraham to him and said, "What have you done to us? What wrong did I do against you? Why did you bring this trouble to my kingdom? You should not have done these things to me. 10What were you thinking that caused you to do this?"

11Then Abraham answered, "I thought no one in this place respected God and that someone would kill me to get Sarah. 12And it is true that she is my sister. She is the daughter of my father, but she is not the daughter of my mother. 13When God told me to leave my father's house and wander in many different places, I told Sarah, 'You must do a special favor for me. Everywhere we go tell people I am your brother.'"

14Then Abimelech gave Abraham some sheep, cattle, and male and female slaves. He also gave Sarah, Abraham's wife, back to him 15and said, "Look around you at my land. You may live anywhere you want."

16Abimelech said to Sarah, "I gave your brother Abraham twenty-five pounds of silver to make up for any wrong that people may think about you. I want everyone to know that you are innocent."

17Then Abraham prayed to God, and God healed Abimelech, his wife, and his servant girls so they could have children. 18The LORD had kept all the women in Abimelech's house from having children as a punishment on Abimelech for taking Abraham's wife Sarah.

19:26 Salt: Numbers 18:19
20:7 Prophet & Prophecy: Exodus 6:28–7:5
20:7 Dreams: Genesis 28:10–16

A Baby for Sarah

21 The Lord cared for Sarah as he had said and did for her what he had promised. 2Sarah became pregnant and gave birth to a son for Abraham in his old age. Everything happened at the time God had said it would. 3Abraham named his son Isaac, the son Sarah gave birth to. 4He circumcised Isaac when he was eight days old as God had commanded.

5Abraham was one hundred years old when his son Isaac was born. 6And Sarah said, "God has made me laugh. Everyone who hears about this will laugh with me. 7No one thought that I would be able to have Abraham's child, but even though Abraham is old I have given him a son."

Hagar and Ishmael Leave

8Isaac grew, and when he became old enough to eat food, Abraham gave a great feast. 9But Sarah saw Ishmael making fun of Isaac. (Ishmael was the son of Abraham by Hagar, Sarah's Egyptian slave.) 10So Sarah said to Abraham, "Throw out this slave woman and her son. Her son should not inherit anything; my son Isaac should receive it all."

11This troubled Abraham very much because Ishmael was also his son. 12But God said to Abraham, "Don't be troubled about the boy and the slave woman. Do whatever Sarah tells you. The descendants I promised you will be from Isaac. 13I will also make the descendants of Ishmael into a great nation because he is your son, too."

14Early the next morning Abraham took some food and a leather bag full of water. He gave them to Hagar and sent her away. Carrying these things and her son, Hagar went and wandered in the desert of Beersheba.

15Later, when all the water was gone from the bag, Hagar put her son under a bush. 16Then she went away a short distance and sat down. She thought, "My son will die, and I cannot watch this happen." She sat there and began to cry.

17God heard the boy crying, and God's angel called to Hagar from heaven. He said, "What is wrong, Hagar? Don't be afraid! God has heard the boy crying there.∞ 18Help him up and take him by the hand. I will make his descendants into a great nation."

19Then God showed Hagar a well of water. So she went to the well and filled her bag with water and gave the boy a drink.

20God was with the boy as he grew up. Ishmael lived in the desert and became an archer. 21He lived in the Desert of Paran, and his mother found a wife for him in Egypt.∞

Abraham's Bargain with Abimelech

22Then Abimelech came with Phicol, the commander of his army, and said to Abraham, "God is with you in everything you do. 23So make a promise to me here before God that you will be fair with me and my children and my descendants. Be kind to me and to this land where you have lived as a stranger—as kind as I have been to you."

24And Abraham said, "I promise." 25Then Abraham complained to Abimelech about Abimelech's servants who had seized a well of water.

26But Abimelech said, "I don't know who did this. You never told me about this before today."

27Then Abraham gave Abimelech some sheep and cattle, and they made an agreement. 28Abraham also put seven female lambs in front of Abimelech.

29Abimelech asked Abraham, "Why did you put these seven female lambs by themselves?"

30Abraham answered, "Accept these lambs from me to prove that you believe I dug this well."

31So that place was called Beersheba because they made a promise to each other there.

32After Abraham and Abimelech made the agreement at Beersheba, Abimelech and Phicol, the commander of his army, went back to the land of the Philistines.

33Abraham planted a tamarisk tree at Beersheba and prayed to the LORD, the God who lives forever. 34And Abraham lived as a stranger in the land of the Philistines for a long time.

God Tests Abraham

22 After these things God tested Abraham's faith. God said to him, "Abraham!"

And he answered, "Here I am."

2Then God said, "Take your only son, Isaac, the son you love, and go to the land of Moriah. Kill him there and offer him as a whole burnt offering on one of the mountains I will tell you about."

3Abraham got up early in the morning and saddled his donkey. He took Isaac and two servants with him. After he cut the wood for the sacrifice, they went to the place God had told them to go. 4On the third day Abraham looked up and saw the place in the distance. 5He said to his servants, "Stay here with the donkey. My son and I will go over there and worship, and then we will come back to you."

21:6 *laugh.* The Hebrew words for "he laughed" and "Isaac" sound the same.

∞**21:17 Fear:** Genesis 43:23

∞**21:21 Wilderness (Desert):** Exodus 14–17

21:31 *Beersheba.* This name means "well of the promise" or "well of seven."

6Abraham took the wood for the sacrifice and
gave it to his son to carry, but he himself took the
knife and the fire. So he and his son went on
together.
7Isaac said to his father Abraham, "Father!"
Abraham answered, "Yes, my son."
Isaac said, "We have the fire and the wood, but
where is the lamb we will burn as a sacrifice?"
8Abraham answered, "God will give us the
lamb for the sacrifice, my son."
So Abraham and his son went on together 9and
came to the place God had told him about.
Abraham built an altar there. He laid the wood on
it and then tied up his son Isaac and laid him on
the wood on the altar. 10Then Abraham took his
knife and was about to kill his son.
11But the angel of the LORD called to him from
heaven and said, "Abraham! Abraham!"
Abraham answered, "Yes."
12The angel said, "Don't kill your son or hurt
him in any way. Now I can see that you trust God
and that you have not kept your son, your only
son, from me."
13Then Abraham looked up and saw a male
sheep caught in a bush by its horns. So Abraham
went and took the sheep and killed it. He offered
it as a whole burnt offering to God, and his son
was saved. 14So Abraham named that place The
LORD Provides. Even today people say, "On the
mountain of the LORD it will be provided."
15The angel of the LORD called to Abraham from
heaven a second time 16and said, "The LORD says,
'Because you did not keep back your son, your
only son, from me, I make you this promise by my
own name: 17I will surely bless you and give you
many descendants. They will be as many as the
stars in the sky and the sand on the seashore, and
they will capture the cities of their enemies.
18Through your descendants all the nations on the
earth will be blessed, because you obeyed me.'"
19Then Abraham returned to his servants. They
all traveled back to Beersheba, and Abraham
stayed there.
20After these things happened, someone told
Abraham: "Your brother Nahor and his wife
Milcah have children now. 21The first son is Uz,
and the second is Buz. The third son is Kemuel
(the father of Aram). 22Then there are Kesed,
Hazo, Pildash, Jidlaph, and Bethuel." 23Bethuel
became the father of Rebekah. Milcah was the
mother of these eight sons, and Nahor, Abraham's
brother, was the father. 24Also Nahor had four

"Then Abraham looked up and saw a male sheep (ram) caught in a bush by its horns" (22:13).

other sons by his slave woman Reumah. Their
names were Tebah, Gaham, Tahash, and Maacah.

Sarah Dies

23 Sarah lived to be one hundred twenty-
seven years old. 2She died in Kiriath Arba
(that is, Hebron) in the land of Canaan. Abraham
was very sad and cried because of her. 3After a
while he got up from the side of his wife's body
and went to talk to the Hittites. He said, 4"I am
only a stranger and a foreigner here. Sell me some
of your land so that I can bury my dead wife."
5The Hittites answered Abraham, 6"Sir, you are
a great leader among us. You may have the best
place we have to bury your dead. You may have
any of our burying places that you want, and none
of us will stop you from burying your dead wife."
7Abraham rose and bowed to the people of the
land, the Hittites. 8He said to them, "If you truly
want to help me bury my dead wife here, speak to
Ephron, the son of Zohar for me. 9Ask him to sell
me the cave of Machpelah at the edge of his field.
I will pay him the full price. You can be the witnesses that I am buying it as a burial place."
10Ephron was sitting among the Hittites at the
city gate. He answered Abraham, 11"No, sir. I will
give you the land and the cave that is in it, with
these people as witnesses. Bury your dead wife."
12Then Abraham bowed down before the Hittites. 13He said to Ephron before all the people,
"Please let me pay you the full price for the field.
Accept my money, and I will bury my dead there."
14Ephron answered Abraham, 15"Sir, the land
is worth ten pounds of silver, but I won't argue

22:8 Sacrifice: Genesis 35:14
22:12 Family: Job 1
23:4 Foreigner (Alien): Exodus 22:21

with you over the price. Take the land, and bury
your dead wife."
16Abraham agreed and paid Ephron in front of
the Hittite witnesses. He weighed out the full
price, ten pounds of silver, and they counted the
weight as the traders normally did.
17-18So Ephron's field in Machpelah, east of
Mamre, was sold. Abraham became the owner of
the field, the cave in it, and all the trees that were
in the field. The sale was made at the city gate,
with the Hittites as witnesses. 19After this,
Abraham buried his wife Sarah in the cave in the
field of Machpelah, near Mamre. (Mamre was
later called Hebron in the land of Canaan.) 20So
Abraham bought the field and the cave in it from
the Hittites to use as a burying place.

A Wife for Isaac

24 Abraham was now very old, and the LORD
had blessed him in every way. 2Abraham
said to his oldest servant, who was in charge of
everything he owned, "Put your hand under my
leg. 3Make a promise to me before the LORD, the
God of heaven and earth. Don't get a wife for my
son from the Canaanite girls who live around
here. 4Instead, go back to my country, to the land
of my relatives, and get a wife for my son Isaac."
5The servant said to him, "What if this woman
does not want to return with me to this land?
Then, should I take your son with me back to
your homeland?"
6Abraham said to him, "No! Don't take my son
back there. 7The LORD, the God of heaven,
brought me from the home of my father and the
land of my relatives. And he promised me, 'I will
give this land to your descendants.' The LORD will
send his angel before you to help you get a wife
for my son there. 8If the girl won't come back
with you, you will be free from this promise. But
you must not take my son back there." 9So the
servant put his hand under his master's leg and
made a promise to Abraham about this.
10The servant took ten of Abraham's camels
and left, carrying with him many different kinds
of beautiful gifts. He went to Northwest Mesopotamia to Nahor's city. 11In the evening, when
the women come out to get water, he made the
camels kneel down at the well outside the city.
12The servant said, "LORD, God of my master
Abraham, allow me to find a wife for his son today.
Please show this kindness to my master Abraham.
13Here I am, standing by the spring, and the girls
from the city are coming out to get water. 14I will
say to one of them, 'Please put your jar down so I
can drink.' Then let her say, 'Drink, and I will also
give water to your camels.' If that happens, I will
know she is the right one for your servant Isaac
and that you have shown kindness to my master."
15Before the servant had finished praying, Rebekah, the daughter of Bethuel, came out of the city.
(Bethuel was the son of Milcah and Nahor,
Abraham's brother.) Rebekah was carrying her
water jar on her shoulder. 16She was very pretty, a
virgin; she had never had sexual relations with a
man. She went down to the spring and filled her jar,
then came back up. 17The servant ran to her and
said, "Please give me a little water from your jar."
18Rebekah said, "Drink, sir." She quickly lowered the jar from her shoulder and gave him a
drink. 19After he finished drinking, Rebekah said,
"I will also pour some water for your camels."
20So she quickly poured all the water from her jar
into the drinking trough for the camels. Then she
kept running to the well until she had given all
the camels enough to drink.
21The servant quietly watched her. He wanted
to be sure the LORD had made his trip successful.
22After the camels had finished drinking, he gave
Rebekah a gold ring weighing one-fifth of an ounce
and two gold arm bracelets weighing about four
ounces each. 23He asked, "Who is your father? Is
there a place in his house for me and my men to
spend the night?"
24Rebekah answered, "My father is Bethuel,
the son of Milcah and Nahor." 25Then she said,
"And, yes, we have straw for your camels and a
place for you to spend the night."
26The servant bowed and worshiped the LORD
27and said, "Blessed is the LORD, the God of my master Abraham. The LORD has been kind and truthful
to him and has led me to my master's relatives."
28Then Rebekah ran and told her mother's family about all these things. 29She had a brother
named Laban, who ran out to Abraham's servant,
who was still at the spring. 30Laban had heard
what she had said and had seen the ring and the
bracelets on his sister's arms. So he ran out to the
well, and there was the man standing by the camels
at the spring. 31Laban said, "Sir, you are welcome
to come in; you don't have to stand outside. I
have prepared the house for you and also a place
for your camels."
32So Abraham's servant went into the house.
After Laban unloaded the camels and gave them
straw and food, he gave water to Abraham's servant so he and the men with him could wash

24:2 *Put . . . leg.* This showed that a person would keep the promise.

Garden of Eden

Genesis 2:8

What is Eden? Does its description have theological/symbolic overtones? Is Eden restored in Revelation 21–22?

The story of humanity began in the garden of Eden. After God created the first man, he gave him the garden as a generous gift. God caused every tree to grow out of the ground in that garden (Genesis 2:9a), and he put the tree of life and the tree of good and evil in the middle of the garden (2:9b).

The garden was watered by a river that flowed through it (Genesis 2:10), and God put the man in the garden "to care for it and work it" (2:15). In other words, Adam was to protect and nurture the garden as a vocation. In this garden, Adam and Eve were to enjoy a paradise free of pain and agonizing labor. By creating Eden, God intended that the first humans live in perfect harmony in a perfect world.

Eden, though, was much more than a paradise for Adam and Eve to enjoy. The garden of Eden was a sacred place that made perfect relationships possible. It was here in the garden that God created Eve from Adam's body (Genesis 2:21), and it was here that God spoke intimately and directly with his children (3:8). They could eat freely from the tree of life—a tree whose fruit gave them eternal life. As far as we can determine, Adam and Eve could have lived eternally in the garden if they had not sinned. The garden, then, was a place very different from our world today—there was no sorrow, no relational strife, no death, and no separation from God.

God gave Adam and Eve one simple command to remember as they lived in Eden. They were never to eat from the tree of the knowledge of good and evil which stood in the middle of the garden. The serpent, which in the ancient Near East represented chaos and death, entered this paradise and tempted Adam and Eve to eat from the tree (Genesis 3:1–7). Even though Adam was there with Eve at the temptation, he was silent. Eve did all the speaking with the serpent. In the end, they both gave way to the serpent's deceitful words and disobeyed God. They ate from the tree of the knowledge of good and evil (3:6). The silence of Adam and the naive innocence of Eve brought sin into the world and ruined their paradise.

It is important to note the results of the first sin—God cast Adam and Eve out of the garden of Eden (Genesis 3:23–24). He cursed the serpent (3:14) and the ground (3:17). Eve would bear children with great pain (3:16), and Adam would work the land with agonizing labor (3:18–19). No longer would the earth be as the garden of Eden. In fact, the earth would be a daily reminder to humanity that they had lost Eden.

After Adam and Eve left the garden, their children became either nomads who wandered the land, farmers who faced the woes of nature, or city dwellers who longed for lush gardens. Never again would men and women enjoy the bliss and innocence that the lush garden brought to their lives.

Though the first humans were expelled from the garden of Eden, their children have never been able to forget Eden. Nor have they been able to return. The writers of the Bible allude to the garden throughout the Bible (Song of Solomon 4:12–15; Isaiah 51:3; Ezekiel 28:13). In later passages, the garden of Eden symbolizes peace and prosperity. Many of these passages speak of humanity's desire to return to the garden.

When we think about the garden of Eden, we should keep the book of Revelation in focus. The story of the Bible begins in a garden but ends in a beautiful new city called the New Jerusalem. Heaven will not be a garden, but a city where the righteous will dwell forever. There are a few hints in the book of Revelation that refer back to the garden of Eden. Revelation 22:2 tells us that a river flows from the throne of God through the middle of the city. On each side of the river there will be the tree of life.

In the Book of Genesis, humanity, after leaving the garden of Eden, arrogantly built the great city of Babel to reach God (11:1–10). But in Revelation, God is the city-builder who lets his people dwell in safety and prosperity. These truths teach us that we cannot reach God by going back to the garden of Eden or building our own cities. The story in Genesis begans tragically with man and woman being expelled from the garden and the tree of life. But it is in the last chapter of Revelation that the dreams and aspirations of humanity are fulfilled. Humanity is no longer cut off from the tree of life, so they can live eternally.

However, each of us yearns for the garden of Eden. And so it should be, for God created the garden as a paradise that resonates with the longing in our hearts. But he has something far greater waiting for us as Christians. We have lost the garden of Genesis, but we have gained the heaven of Revelation. God is a city-builder, and he is building a city for his people. Like Abraham, we are to look for that city which "has real foundations—the city planned and built by God" (Hebrews 11:10).

Garden of Eden: For additional scriptures on this topic go to Genesis 3:23.

LONELINESS

GENESIS 2:18

Are there examples of loneliness in the Bible? Is loneliness more than being alone? What did people in the Bible do about loneliness? What does this say about our loneliness and ability to be alone?

Incidents of loneliness occur in people's lives in both Testaments. From creation, being isolated is recognized as painful and not God's plan for human beings. For example, before Eve is created, God says, "It is not good for the man to be alone. I will make a helper who is right for him" (Genesis 2:18). Many biblical people demonstrate how aloneness becomes loneliness: Joseph (Genesis 37:18–36), King Saul (1 Samuel 28:1–20), and Jesus (Matthew 27:46) all report experiences of loneliness. They also all show an ability to be alone, either for solitude and prayer or for making necessary independent decisions. Both Mary of Bethany, when she chooses a disciple's role unusual for a woman of her time (Luke 10: 39–42), and Mary the mother of Jesus, when she accepts the assignment to be the Messiah's mother (Luke 1:26–38), equally demonstrate an ability to be alone and act independently.

Loneliness is not always the same as being alone. One may feel lonely while alone, but loneliness also persists in a crowd, in a dormitory, in a youth group, or even in a family or a marriage. On the other hand, an individual may choose to be alone as Jesus did for solitude and prayer (Matthew 14:23; Mark 6:46; Luke 6:12). Being alone can provide respite in a busy life. In addition to solitude, being alone represents those moments in life when an individual must make a solitary decision and live with the consequences.

The ability to be alone is a psychological milestone in human development. Infants and small children fear being left alone; they have an intuitive recognition that they are so helpless, they would die if they were abandoned. Small children only gradually learn that Mother will come back when she leaves the room. They often cling to their mothers or fathers when dropped off at church school or day care. Gradually, with maturation and much parental patience, children realize that they are not abandoned when their parents are out of sight.

Adult experience of intense loneliness retains a deep, often secret, life-or-death sense of abandonment. Intense loneliness is so humanly frightening that we usually avoid it at all costs rather than allow ourselves to become aware of it, name it, and experience it. In extreme loneliness some adults cling to others in their lives—parents, friends, sweethearts, spouses, siblings, or children—to ease their frightening feelings. Others try to stop the feelings through using alcohol, taking drugs, or keeping very busy. King Saul tried to avoid his loneliness through using David's music to distract him (1 Samuel 16:14–23). Saul began his reign as a man capable of being alone and making hard decisions, but ended it as a profoundly lonely man desperately trying to control the future (1 Samuel 28:1–20). Avoidance and clinging did not work for King Saul, and they do not work for us either. Loneliness avoided does not go away. In fact, coping with loneliness is part of becoming a mature human being who can make important life decisions.

Jesus' experience of loneliness and abandonment appears more stark. Jesus, who did not deny his feelings, manifests intense and painful loneliness and stress in the garden of Gethsemane (Matthew 26:36–46; Mark 14:32–42; Luke 22:40–46). Rather than distract himself, he shared his distress with his closest friends and asked for their companionship as he dealt with it. Knowing that he faced death, he turned to God asking that the "cup" be removed, but confessed, "But do what you want, not what I want" (Luke 22:42). We know that his friends failed him: they could not or would not endure the feeling; they fell asleep "because of their sadness." We know the cup was not removed, and there is nothing in the text to indicate the Father's showing Jesus the "kindness" shown Joseph. Jesus faced stark abandonment, which he named on the cross (Matthew 27:46), called it what it was, and walked with power and confidence into the arrest, trial, and crucifixion scenes (Matthew 26:47–56; Mark 14:43–52; Luke 22:47–53; John 18:1–11). Jesus' ability to be alone in spite of loneliness clearly empowered him.

Loneliness is a normal part of human life. All children and all adults experience loneliness. Some lonely times occur when we face a decision only we can make, a decision with consequences. Some loneliness occurs when we, like King Saul, try to control the future by worrying about it. If we take people in the Bible as examples, we understand there will be times when we feel very lonely and do not feel God's "kindness" as Joseph did. Nevertheless, we will need to endure the experience, naming it as it is, and do whatever life tasks lie before us. Only much later we might realize that God held and sustained us the entire time. And Jesus has promised never to leave us or forsake us (Matthew 28:20; Hebrews 13:5).

Loneliness: For additional scriptures on this topic go to Genesis 32:22–29.

their feet. 33Then Laban gave the servant food, but the servant said, "I will not eat until I have told you why I came."

So Laban said, "Then tell us."

34He said, "I am Abraham's servant. 35The LORD has greatly blessed my master in everything, and he has become a rich man. The LORD has given him many flocks of sheep, herds of cattle, silver and gold, male and female servants, camels, and horses. 36Sarah, my master's wife, gave birth to a son when she was old, and my master has given everything he owns to that son. 37My master had me make a promise to him and said, 'Don't get a wife for my son from the Canaanite girls who live around here. 38Instead, you must go to my father's people and to my family. There you must get a wife for my son.' 39I said to my master, 'What if the woman will not come back with me?' 40But he said, 'I serve the LORD, who will send his angel with you and will help you. You will get a wife for my son from my family and my father's people. 41Then you will be free from the promise. But if they will not give you a wife for my son, you will be free from this promise.'

42"Today I came to this spring. I said, 'LORD, God of my master Abraham, please make my trip successful. 43I am standing by this spring. I will wait for a young woman to come out to get water, and I will say, "Please give me water from your jar to drink." 44Then let her say, "Drink this water, and I will also get water for your camels." By this I will know the LORD has chosen her for my master's son.'

45"Before I finished my silent prayer, Rebekah came out of the city with her water jar on her shoulder. She went down to the spring and got water. I said to her, 'Please give me a drink.' 46She quickly lowered the jar from her shoulder and said, 'Drink this. I will also get water for your camels.' So I drank, and she gave water to my camels too. 47When I asked her, 'Who is your father?' she answered, 'My father is Bethuel son of Milcah and Nahor.' Then I put the ring in her nose and the bracelets on her arms, 48and I bowed my head and thanked the LORD. I praised the LORD, the God of my master Abraham, because he led me on the right road to get the granddaughter of my master's brother for his son. 49Now, tell me, will you be kind and truthful to my master? And if not, tell me so. Then I will know what I should do."

50Laban and Bethuel answered, "This is clearly from the LORD, and we cannot change what must happen. 51Rebekah is yours. Take her and go. Let her marry your master's son as the LORD has commanded."

52When Abraham's servant heard these words, he bowed facedown on the ground before the LORD. 53Then he gave Rebekah gold and silver jewelry and clothes. He also gave expensive gifts to her brother and mother. 54The servant and the men with him ate and drank and spent the night there. When they got up the next morning, the servant said, "Now let me go back to my master."

55Rebekah's mother and her brother said, "Let Rebekah stay with us at least ten days. After that she may go."

56But the servant said to them, "Do not make me wait, because the LORD has made my trip successful. Now let me go back to my master."

57Rebekah's brother and mother said, "We will call Rebekah and ask her what she wants to do." 58They called her and asked her, "Do you want to go with this man now?"

She said, "Yes, I do."

59So they allowed Rebekah and her nurse to go with Abraham's servant and his men. 60They blessed Rebekah and said,

"Our sister, may you be the mother of thousands of people,
and may your descendants capture the cities of their enemies."

61Then Rebekah and her servant girls got on the camels and followed the servant and his men. So the servant took Rebekah and left.

62At this time Isaac had left Beer Lahai Roi and was living in southern Canaan. 63One evening when he went out to the field to think, he looked up and saw camels coming. 64Rebekah also looked and saw Isaac. Then she jumped down from the camel 65and asked the servant, "Who is that man walking in the field to meet us?"

The servant answered, "That is my master." So Rebekah covered her face with her veil.

66The servant told Isaac everything that had happened. 67Then Isaac brought Rebekah into the tent of Sarah, his mother, and she became his wife. Isaac loved her very much, and so he was comforted after his mother's death.

Abraham's Family

25 Abraham married again, and his new wife was Keturah. 2She gave birth to Zimran, Jokshan, Medan, Midian, Ishbak, and Shuah. 3Jokshan was the father of Sheba and Dedan. Dedan's descendants were the people of Assyria, Letush, and Leum. 4The sons of Midian were Ephah, Epher, Hanoch, Abida, and Eldaah. All these were descendants of Keturah. 5Abraham left everything he owned to Isaac. 6But before Abraham

died, he did give gifts to the sons of his other wives,
then sent them to the East to be away from Isaac.
7Abraham lived to be one hundred seventy-five
years old. 8He breathed his last breath and died at
an old age, after a long and satisfying life. 9His
sons Isaac and Ishmael buried him in the cave of
Machpelah in the field of Ephron east of Mamre.
(Ephron was the son of Zohar the Hittite.) 10So
Abraham was buried with his wife Sarah in the
same field that he had bought from the Hittites.
11After Abraham died, God blessed his son Isaac.
Isaac was now living at Beer Lahai Roi.

12This is the family history of Ishmael, Abraham's
son. (Hagar, Sarah's Egyptian servant, was Ishmael's
mother.) 13These are the names of Ishmael's sons in
the order they were born: Nebaioth, the first son,
then Kedar, Adbeel, Mibsam, 14Mishma, Dumah,
Massa, 15Hadad, Tema, Jetur, Naphish, and
Kedemah. 16These were Ishmael's sons, and these
are the names of the tribal leaders listed according to
their settlements and camps. 17Ishmael lived one
hundred thirty-seven years and then breathed his
last breath and died. 18His descendants lived from
Havilah to Shur, which is east of Egypt stretching
toward Assyria. They often attacked the descendants
of his brothers.

Isaac's Family

19This is the family history of Isaac. Abraham
had a son named Isaac. 20When Isaac was forty
years old, he married Rebekah, who came from
Northwest Mesopotamia. She was Bethuel's
daughter and the sister of Laban the Aramean.

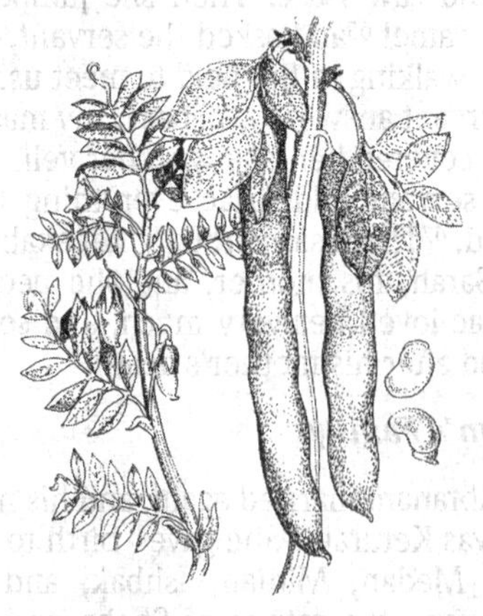

Lentils (left) and beans (right)

21Isaac's wife could not have children, so Isaac
prayed to the LORD for her. The LORD heard
Isaac's prayer, and Rebekah became pregnant.
22While she was pregnant, the babies struggled inside her. She asked, "Why is this happening to me?" Then she went to get an answer
from the LORD.
23The LORD said to her,

"Two nations are in your body,
and two groups of people will be taken
from you.
One group will be stronger than the other,
and the older will serve the younger."

24When the time came, Rebekah gave birth to
twins. 25The first baby was born red. Since his
skin was like a hairy robe, he was named Esau.
26When the second baby was born, he was holding
on to Esau's heel, so that baby was named Jacob.
Isaac was sixty years old when they were born.
27When the boys grew up, Esau became a
skilled hunter. He loved to be out in the fields.
But Jacob was a quiet man and stayed among the
tents. 28Isaac loved Esau because he hunted the
wild animals that Isaac enjoyed eating. But
Rebekah loved Jacob.
29One day Jacob was boiling a pot of vegetable
soup. Esau came in from hunting in the fields, weak
from hunger. 30So Esau said to Jacob, "Let me eat
some of that red soup, because I am weak with
hunger." (That is why people call him Edom.)
31But Jacob said, "You must sell me your rights
as the firstborn son."
32Esau said, "I am almost dead from hunger. If
I die, all of my father's wealth will not help me."
33But Jacob said, "First, promise me that you will
give it to me." So Esau made a promise to Jacob and
sold his part of their father's wealth to Jacob. 34Then
Jacob gave Esau bread and vegetable soup, and he
ate and drank, and then left. So Esau showed how
little he cared about his rights as the firstborn son.

Isaac Lies to Abimelech

26 Now there was a time of hunger in the land,
besides the time of hunger that happened
during Abraham's life. So Isaac went to the town
of Gerar to see Abimelech king of the Philistines.
2The LORD appeared to Isaac and said, "Don't go
down to Egypt, but live in the land where I tell
you to live. 3Stay in this land, and I will be with
you and bless you. I will give you and your

25:18 Abraham: Exodus 3:6
25:25 *Esau.* This name may mean "hairy."
25:26 *Jacob.* This name sounds like the Hebrew word for "heel." "Grabbing someone's heel" is a Hebrew saying for tricking someone.
25:30 *Edom.* This name sounds like the Hebrew word for "red."
25:31 *rights . . . son.* Usually the firstborn son had a high rank in the family. The firstborn son usually became the new head of the family.

descendants all these lands, and I will keep the oath I made to Abraham your father. [4]I will give you many descendants, as hard to count as the stars in the sky, and I will give them all these lands. Through your descendants all the nations on the earth will be blessed. [5]I will do this because your father Abraham obeyed me. He did what I said and obeyed my commands, my teachings, and my rules."

[6]So Isaac stayed in Gerar. [7]His wife Rebekah was very beautiful, and the men of that place asked Isaac about her. Isaac said, "She is my sister," because he was afraid to tell them she was his wife. He thought they might kill him so they could have her.

[8]Isaac lived there a long time. One day as Abimelech king of the Philistines looked out his window, he saw Isaac holding his wife Rebekah tenderly. [9]Abimelech called for Isaac and said, "This woman is your wife. Why did you say she was your sister?"

Isaac said to him, "I was afraid you would kill me so you could have her."

[10]Abimelech said, "What have you done to us? One of our men might have had sexual relations with your wife. Then we would have been guilty of a great sin."

[11]So Abimelech warned everyone, "Anyone who touches this man or his wife will be put to death."

Isaac Becomes Rich

[12]Isaac planted seed in that land, and that year he gathered a great harvest. The LORD blessed him very much, [13]and he became rich. He gathered more wealth until he became a very rich man. [14]He had so many slaves and flocks and herds that the Philistines envied him. [15]So they stopped up all the wells the servants of Isaac's father Abraham had dug. (They had dug them when Abraham was alive.) The Philistines filled those wells with dirt. [16]And Abimelech said to Isaac, "Leave our country because you have become much more powerful than we are."

[17]So Isaac left that place and camped in the Valley of Gerar and lived there. [18]Long before this time Abraham had dug many wells, but after he died, the Philistines filled them with dirt. So Isaac dug those wells again and gave them the same names his father had given them. [19]Isaac's servants dug a well in the valley, from which a spring of water flowed. [20]But the herdsmen of Gerar argued with them and said, "This water is ours." So Isaac named that well Argue because they argued with him. [21]Then his servants dug another well. When the people also argued about it, Isaac named that well Fight. [22]He moved from there and dug another well. No one argued about this one, so he named it Room Enough. Isaac said, "Now the LORD has made room for us, and we will be successful in this land."

[23]From there Isaac went to Beersheba. [24]The LORD appeared to him that night and said, "I am the God of your father Abraham. Don't be afraid, because I am with you. I will bless you and give you many descendants because of my servant Abraham." [25]So Isaac built an altar and worshiped the LORD there. He also made a camp there, and his servants dug a well.

[26]Abimelech came from Gerar to see Isaac. He brought with him Ahuzzath, who advised him, and Phicol, the commander of his army. [27]Isaac asked them, "Why have you come to see me? You were my enemy and forced me to leave your country."

[28]They answered, "Now we know that the LORD is with you. Let us swear an oath to each other. Let us make an agreement with you [29]that since we did not hurt you, you will not hurt us. We were good to you and sent you away in peace. Now the LORD has blessed you."

[30]So Isaac prepared food for them, and they all ate and drank. [31]Early the next morning the men swore an oath to each other. Then Isaac sent them away, and they left in peace.⚭

[32]That day Isaac's servants came and told him about the well they had dug, saying, "We found water in that well." [33]So Isaac named it Shibah and that city is called Beersheba even now.

[34]When Esau was forty years old, he married two Hittite women—Judith daughter of Beeri and Basemath daughter of Elon. [35]These women brought much sorrow to Isaac and Rebekah.

Jacob Tricks Isaac

27 When Isaac was old, his eyesight was poor, so he could not see clearly. One day he called his older son Esau to him and said, "Son."

Esau answered, "Here I am."

[2]Isaac said, "I am old and don't know when I might die. [3]So take your bow and arrows and go hunting in the field for an animal for me to eat. [4]When you prepare the tasty food that I love, bring it to me, and I will eat. Then I will bless you before I die." [5]So Esau went out in the field to hunt.

Rebekah was listening as Isaac said this to his son Esau. [6]She said to her son Jacob, "Listen, I heard your father saying to your brother Esau,

⚭**26:31 Hospitality:** Deuteronomy 10:17–19

26:33 *Shibah.* This name sounds like the Hebrew words for "seven" and "promise."

7'Kill an animal and prepare some tasty food for
me to eat. Then I will bless you in the presence of
the LORD before I die.' 8So obey me, my son, and
do what I tell you. 9Go out to our goats and bring
me two of the best young ones. I will prepare
them just the way your father likes them. 10Then
you will take the food to your father, and he will
bless you before he dies."

11But Jacob said to his mother Rebekah, "My
brother Esau is a hairy man, and I am smooth! 12If
my father touches me, he will know I am not
Esau. Then he will not bless me but will place a
curse on me because I tried to trick him."

13So Rebekah said to him, "If your father puts a
curse on you, I will accept the blame. Just do
what I said and go, get the goats for me."

14So Jacob went out and got two goats and
brought them to his mother, and she cooked them
in the special way Isaac enjoyed. 15She took the
best clothes of her older son Esau that were in the
house and put them on the younger son Jacob.
16She also took the skins of the goats and put them
on Jacob's hands and neck. 17Then she gave Jacob
the tasty food and the bread she had made.

18Jacob went in to his father and said, "Father."
And his father said, "Yes, my son. Who are you?"

19Jacob said to him, "I am Esau, your first son. I
have done what you told me. Now sit up and eat
some meat of the animal I hunted for you. Then
bless me."

20But Isaac asked his son, "How did you find
and kill the animal so quickly?"

Jacob answered, "Because the LORD your God
helped me to find it."

21Then Isaac said to Jacob, "Come near so I can
touch you, my son. Then I will know if you are
really my son Esau."

22So Jacob came near to Isaac his father. Isaac
touched him and said, "Your voice sounds like
Jacob's voice, but your hands are hairy like the
hands of Esau." 23Isaac did not know it was Jacob,
because his hands were hairy like Esau's hands,
so Isaac blessed him. 24Isaac asked, "Are you
really my son Esau?"

Jacob answered, "Yes, I am."

25Then Isaac said, "Bring me the food, and I
will eat it and bless you." So Jacob gave him the
food, and he ate. Jacob gave him wine, and he
drank. 26Then Isaac said to him, "My son, come
near and kiss me." 27So Jacob went to his father
and kissed him. When Isaac smelled Esau's
clothes, he blessed him and said,

"The smell of my son
is like the smell of the field
that the LORD has blessed.
28May God give you plenty of rain
and good soil
so that you will have plenty of grain
and new wine.
29May nations serve you
and peoples bow down to you.
May you be master over your brothers,
and may your mother's sons bow down
to you.
May everyone who curses you be cursed,
and may everyone who blesses you
be blessed."

30Isaac finished blessing Jacob. Then, just as
Jacob left his father Isaac, Esau came in from
hunting. 31He also prepared some tasty food and
brought it to his father. He said, "Father, rise and
eat the food that your son killed for you and then
bless me."

32Isaac asked, "Who are you?"

He answered, "I am your son—your firstborn
son—Esau."

33Then Isaac trembled greatly and said, "Then
who was it that hunted the animals and brought me
food before you came? I ate it, and I blessed him,
and it is too late now to take back my blessing."

34When Esau heard the words of his father, he
let out a loud and bitter cry. He said to his father,
"Bless me—me, too, my father!"

35But Isaac said, "Your brother came and
tricked me. He has taken your blessing."

36Esau said, "Jacob is the right name for him.
He has tricked me these two times. He took away
my share of everything you own, and now he has
taken away my blessing." Then Esau asked,
"Haven't you saved a blessing for me?"

37Isaac answered, "I gave Jacob the power to
be master over you, and all his brothers will be
his servants. And I kept him strong with grain
and new wine. There is nothing left to give you,
my son."

38But Esau continued, "Do you have only one
blessing, Father? Bless me, too, Father!" Then
Esau began to cry out loud.

39Isaac said to him,

"You will live far away from the best land,
far from the rain.
40You will live by using your sword,
and you will be a slave to your brother.
But when you struggle,
you will break free from him."

41After that Esau hated Jacob because of the

27:36 *Jacob.* This name sounds like the Hebrew word for "heel." "Grabbing someone's heel" is a Hebrew saying for tricking someone.

blessing from Isaac. He thought to himself, "My
father will soon die, and I will be sad for him.
Then I will kill Jacob."
42Rebekah heard about Esau's plan to kill Jacob.
So she sent for Jacob and said to him, "Listen, your
brother Esau is comforting himself by planning to
kill you. 43So, my son, do what I say. My brother
Laban is living in Haran. Go to him at once! 44Stay
with him for a while, until your brother is not so
angry. 45In time, your brother will not be angry,
and he will forget what you did to him. Then I will
send a servant to bring you back. I don't want to
lose both of my sons on the same day."
46Then Rebekah said to Isaac, "I am tired of Hittite women. If Jacob marries one of these Hittite
women here in this land, I want to die."

Jacob Searches for a Wife

28 Isaac called Jacob and blessed him and
commanded him, "You must not marry a
Canaanite woman. 2Go to the house of Bethuel,
your mother's father, in Northwest Mesopotamia. Laban, your mother's brother, lives there.
Marry one of his daughters. 3May God Almighty
bless you and give you many children, and may
you become a group of many peoples. 4May he
give you and your descendants the blessing of
Abraham so that you may own the land where
you are now living as a stranger, the land God
gave to Abraham." 5So Isaac sent Jacob to
Northwest Mesopotamia, to Laban the brother of
Rebekah. Bethuel the Aramean was the father of
Laban and Rebekah, and Rebekah was the
mother of Jacob and Esau.
6Esau learned that Isaac had blessed Jacob and
sent him to Northwest Mesopotamia to find a
wife there. He also learned that Isaac had commanded Jacob not to marry a Canaanite woman
7and that Jacob had obeyed his father and mother
and had gone to Northwest Mesopotamia. 8So
Esau saw that his father Isaac did not want his
sons to marry Canaanite women. 9Now Esau
already had wives, but he went to Ishmael son of
Abraham, and he married Mahalath, Ishmael's
daughter. Mahalath was the sister of Nebaioth.

Jacob's Dream at Bethel

10Jacob left Beersheba and set out for Haran.
11When he came to a place, he spent the night
there because the sun had set. He found a stone and
laid his head on it to go to sleep. 12Jacob dreamed
that there was a ladder resting on the earth and
reaching up into heaven, and he saw angels of God
going up and coming down the ladder. 13Then
Jacob saw the LORD standing above the ladder, and
he said, "I am the LORD, the God of Abraham your
grandfather, and the God of Isaac. I will give you
and your descendants the land on which you are
now sleeping. 14Your descendants will be as many
as the dust of the earth. They will spread west and
east, north and south, and all the families of the
earth will be blessed through you and your descendants. 15I am with you and will protect you everywhere you go and will bring you back to this land.
I will not leave you until I have done what I have
promised you."
16Then Jacob woke from his sleep and said,
"Surely the LORD is in this place, but I did not
know it." 17He was afraid and said, "This place
frightens me! It is surely the house of God and the
gate of heaven."
18Jacob rose early in the morning and took the
stone he had slept on and set it up on its end.
Then he poured olive oil on the top of it. 19At
first, the name of that city was Luz, but Jacob
named it Bethel.
20Then Jacob made a promise. He said, "I want
God to be with me and to protect me on this journey. I want him to give me food to eat and clothes
to wear 21so I will be able to return in peace to my
father's house. If the LORD does these things, he
will be my God. 22This stone which I have set up
on its end will be the house of God. And I will
give God one-tenth of all he gives me."

Jacob Arrives in Northwest Mesopotamia

29 Then Jacob continued his journey and
came to the land of the people of the
East. 2He looked and saw a well in the field and
three flocks of sheep lying nearby, because they
drank water from this well. A large stone covered
the mouth of the well. 3When all the flocks would
gather there, the shepherds would roll the stone
away from the well and water the sheep. Then
they would put the stone back in its place.
4Jacob said to the shepherds there, "My brothers, where are you from?"
They answered, "We are from Haran."
5Then Jacob asked, "Do you know Laban,
grandson of Nahor?"
They answered, "We know him."
6Then Jacob asked, "How is he?"

28:16 Dreams: Genesis 31:24
28:18 Stone: Genesis 31:45–54
28:19 *Bethel.* This name means "house of God."
28:22 Tithe: Malachi 3:6–12
28:22 Stewardship: 1 Chronicles 29:11–14

They answered, "He is well. Look, his daughter Rachel is coming now with his sheep."

7Jacob said, "But look, it is still the middle of the day. It is not time for the sheep to be gathered for the night, so give them water and let them go back into the pasture."

8But they said, "We cannot do that until all the flocks are gathered. Then we will roll away the stone from the mouth of the well and water the sheep."

9While Jacob was talking with the shepherds, Rachel came with her father's sheep, because it was her job to care for the sheep. 10When Jacob saw Laban's daughter Rachel and Laban's sheep, he went to the well and rolled the stone from its mouth and watered Laban's sheep. Now Laban was the brother of Rebekah, Jacob's mother. 11Then Jacob kissed Rachel and cried. 12He told her that he was from her father's family and that he was the son of Rebekah. So Rachel ran home and told her father.

13When Laban heard the news about his sister's son Jacob, he ran to meet him. Laban hugged him and kissed him and brought him to his house, where Jacob told Laban everything that had happened.

14Then Laban said, "You are my own flesh and blood."

Jacob Is Tricked

Jacob stayed there a month. 15Then Laban said to Jacob, "You are my relative, but it is not right for you to work for me without pay. What would you like me to pay you?"

16Now Laban had two daughters. The older was Leah, and the younger was Rachel. 17Leah had weak eyes, but Rachel was very beautiful. 18Jacob loved Rachel, so he said to Laban, "Let me marry your younger daughter Rachel. If you will, I will work seven years for you."

19Laban said, "It would be better for her to marry you than someone else, so stay here with me." 20So Jacob worked for Laban seven years so he could marry Rachel. But they seemed like just a few days to him because he loved Rachel very much.

21After seven years Jacob said to Laban, "Give me Rachel so that I may marry her. The time I promised to work for you is over."

22So Laban gave a feast for all the people there. 23That evening he brought his daughter Leah to Jacob, and they had sexual relations. 24(Laban gave his slave girl Zilpah to his daughter to be her servant.) 25In the morning when Jacob saw that he had had sexual relations with Leah, he said to Laban, "What have you done to me? I worked hard for you so that I could marry Rachel! Why did you trick me?"

26Laban said, "In our country we do not allow the younger daughter to marry before the older daughter. 27But complete the full week of the marriage ceremony with Leah, and I will give you Rachel to marry also. But you must serve me another seven years."

28So Jacob did this, and when he had completed the week with Leah, Laban gave him his daughter Rachel as a wife. 29(Laban gave his slave girl Bilhah to his daughter Rachel to be her servant.) 30So Jacob had sexual relations with Rachel also, and Jacob loved Rachel more than Leah. Jacob worked for Laban for another seven years.

Jacob's Family Grows

31When the LORD saw that Jacob loved Rachel more than Leah, he made it possible for Leah to have children, but not Rachel. 32Leah became pregnant and gave birth to a son. She named him Reuben, because she said, "The LORD has seen my troubles. Surely now my husband will love me."

33Leah became pregnant again and gave birth to another son. She named him Simeon and said, "The LORD has heard that I am not loved, so he has given me this son."

34Leah became pregnant again and gave birth to another son. She named him Levi and said, "Now, surely my husband will be close to me, because I have given him three sons."

35Then Leah gave birth to another son. She named him Judah, because she said, "Now I will praise the LORD." Then Leah stopped having children.

30 When Rachel saw that she was not having children for Jacob, she envied her sister Leah. She said to Jacob, "Give me children, or I'll die!" 2Jacob became angry with her and said, "Can I do what only God can do? He is the one who has kept you from having children."

3Then Rachel said, "Here is my slave girl Bilhah. Have sexual relations with her so she can give birth to a child for me. Then I can have my own family through her."

4So Rachel gave Bilhah, her slave girl, to Jacob as a wife, and he had sexual relations with her.

29:32 *Reuben.* This name sounds like the Hebrew word for "he has seen my troubles."

29:33 *Simeon.* This name sounds like the Hebrew word for "has heard."

29:34 *Levi.* This name sounds like the Hebrew word for "be close to."

29:35 *Judah.* This name sounds like the Hebrew word for "praise."

5She became pregnant and gave Jacob a son.
6Rachel said, "God has judged me innocent. He
has listened to my prayer and has given me a
son," so she named him Dan.
7Bilhah became pregnant again and gave Jacob
a second son. 8Rachel said, "I have struggled hard
with my sister, and I have won." So she named
that son Naphtali.
9Leah saw that she had stopped having children, so she gave her slave girl Zilpah to Jacob as
a wife. 10When Zilpah had a son, 11Leah said, "I
am lucky," so she named him Gad. 12Zilpah gave
birth to another son, 13and Leah said, "I am very
happy! Now women will call me happy," so she
named him Asher.
14During the wheat harvest Reuben went into
the field and found some mandrake plants and
brought them to his mother Leah. But Rachel
said to Leah, "Please give me some of your son's
mandrakes."
15Leah answered, "You have already taken
away my husband, and now you are trying to take
away my son's mandrakes."
But Rachel answered, "If you will give me your
son's mandrakes, you may sleep with Jacob
tonight."
16When Jacob came in from the field that night,
Leah went out to meet him. She said, "You will
have sexual relations with me tonight because I
have paid for you with my son's mandrakes." So
Jacob slept with her that night.
17Then God answered Leah's prayer, and she
became pregnant again. She gave birth to a fifth
son 18and said, "God has given me what I paid
for, because I gave my slave girl to my husband."
So Leah named her son Issachar.
19Leah became pregnant again and gave birth
to a sixth son. 20She said, "God has given me a
fine gift. Now surely Jacob will honor me,
because I have given him six sons," so she named
him Zebulun. 21Later Leah gave birth to a daughter and named her Dinah.
22Then God remembered Rachel and answered
her prayer, making it possible for her to have children. 23When she became pregnant and gave
birth to a son, she said, "God has taken away my
shame," 24and she named him Joseph. Rachel said,
"I wish the LORD would give me another son."

Jacob Tricks Laban

25After the birth of Joseph, Jacob said to Laban,
"Now let me go to my own home and country.
26Give me my wives and my children and let me
go. I have earned them by working for you, and
you know that I have served you well."
27Laban said to him, "If I have pleased you,
please stay. I know the LORD has blessed me
because of you. 28Tell me what I should pay you,
and I will give it to you."
29Jacob answered, "You know that I have worked
hard for you, and your flocks have grown while I
cared for them. 30When I came, you had little, but
now you have much. Every time I did something for
you, the LORD blessed you. But when will I be able
to do something for my own family?"
31Laban asked, "Then what should I give you?"
Jacob answered, "I don't want you to give me
anything. Just do this one thing, and I will come
back and take care of your flocks. 32Today let me
go through all your flocks. I will take every speckled or spotted sheep, every black lamb, and every
spotted or speckled goat. That will be my pay.
33In the future you can easily see if I am honest.
When you come to look at my flocks, if I have any
goat that isn't speckled or spotted or any lamb
that isn't black, you will know I stole it."
34Laban answered, "Agreed! We will do what
you ask." 35But that day Laban took away all the
male goats that had streaks or spots, all the speckled
and spotted female goats (all those that had white
on them), and all the black sheep. He told his sons
to watch over them. 36Then he took these animals
to a place that was three days' journey away from
Jacob. Jacob took care of all the flocks that were left.
37So Jacob cut green branches from poplar,
almond, and plane trees and peeled off some of
the bark so that the branches had white stripes
on them. 38He put the branches in front of the
flocks at the watering places. When the animals
came to drink, they also mated there, 39so the
flocks mated in front of the branches. Then the
young that were born were streaked, speckled, or
spotted. 40Jacob separated the young animals
from the others, and he made them face the
streaked and dark animals in Laban's flock. Jacob
kept his animals separate from Laban's. 41When
the stronger animals in the flock were mating,

30:6 *Dan.* This name means "he has judged."
30:8 *Naphtali.* This name sounds like the Hebrew word for "my struggle."
30:11 *Gad.* This name may mean "lucky."
30:13 *Asher.* This name may mean "happy."
30:13 Happiness: Deuteronomy 33:29
30:14 *mandrake.* A plant which was believed to cause a woman to become pregnant.
30:18 *Issachar.* This name sounds like the Hebrew word for "paid for."
30:20 *Zebulun.* This name sounds like the Hebrew word for "honor."
30:24 Infertility (Childlessness/Barrenness): Judges 13:2–25
30:24 *Joseph.* This name sounds like the Hebrew word for "he adds."

Jacob put the branches before their eyes so they would mate near the branches. 42But when the weaker animals mated, Jacob did not put the branches there. So the animals born from the weaker animals were Laban's, and those born from the stronger animals were Jacob's. 43In this way Jacob became very rich. He had large flocks, many male and female servants, camels, and donkeys.

Jacob Runs Away

31 One day Jacob heard Laban's sons talking. They said, "Jacob has taken everything our father owned, and in this way he has become rich." 2Then Jacob noticed that Laban was not as friendly as he had been before. 3The LORD said to Jacob, "Go back to the land where your ancestors lived, and I will be with you."

4So Jacob told Rachel and Leah to meet him in the field where he kept his flocks. 5He said to them, "I have seen that your father is not as friendly with me as he used to be, but the God of my father has been with me. 6You both know that I have worked as hard as I could for your father, 7but he cheated me and changed my pay ten times. But God has not allowed your father to harm me. 8When Laban said, 'You can have all the speckled animals as your pay,' all the animals gave birth to speckled young ones. But when he said, 'You can have all the streaked animals as your pay,' all the flocks gave birth to streaked babies. 9So God has taken the animals away from your father and has given them to me.

10"I had a dream during the season when the flocks were mating. I saw that the only male goats who were mating were streaked, speckled, or spotted. 11The angel of God spoke to me in that dream and said, 'Jacob!' I answered, 'Yes!' 12The angel said, 'Look! Only the streaked, speckled, or spotted male goats are mating. I have seen all the wrong things Laban has been doing to you. 13I am the God who appeared to you at Bethel, where you poured olive oil on the stone you set up on end and where you made a promise to me. Now I want you to leave here and go back to the land where you were born.'"

14Rachel and Leah answered Jacob, "Our father has nothing to give us when he dies. 15He has treated us like strangers. He sold us to you, and then he spent all of the money you paid for us. 16God took all this wealth from our father, and now it belongs to us and our children. So do whatever God has told you to do."

17So Jacob put his children and his wives on camels, 18and they began their journey back to Isaac, his father, in the land of Canaan. All the flocks of animals that Jacob owned walked ahead of them. He carried everything with him that he had gotten while he lived in Northwest Mesopotamia.

19While Laban was gone to cut the wool from his sheep, Rachel stole the idols that belonged to him. 20And Jacob tricked Laban the Aramean by not telling him he was leaving. 21Jacob and his family left quickly, crossed the Euphrates River, and traveled toward the mountains of Gilead.

22Three days later Laban learned that Jacob had run away, 23so he gathered his relatives and began to chase him. After seven days Laban found him in the mountains of Gilead. 24That night God came to Laban the Aramean in a dream and said, "Be careful! Do not say anything to Jacob, good or bad."∞

The Search for the Stolen Idols

25So Laban caught up with Jacob. Now Jacob had made his camp in the mountains, so Laban and his relatives set up their camp in the mountains of Gilead. 26Laban said to Jacob, "What have you done? You cheated me and took my daughters as if you had captured them in a war. 27Why did you run away secretly and trick me? Why didn't you tell me? Then I could have sent you away with joy and singing and with the music of tambourines and harps. 28You did not even let me kiss my grandchildren and my daughters good-bye. You were very foolish to do this! 29I have the power to harm you, but last night the God of your father spoke to me and warned me not to say anything to you, good or bad. 30I know you want to go back to your home, but why did you steal my idols?"

31Jacob answered Laban, "I left without telling you, because I was afraid you would take your daughters away from me. 32If you find anyone here who has taken your idols, that person will be killed! Your relatives will be my witnesses. You may look for anything that belongs to you and take anything that is yours." (Now Jacob did not know that Rachel had stolen Laban's idols.)

33So Laban looked in Jacob's tent, in Leah's tent, and in the tent where the two slave women stayed, but he did not find his idols. When he left Leah's tent, he went into Rachel's tent. 34Rachel had hidden the idols inside her camel's saddle and was sitting on them. Although Laban looked through the whole tent, he did not find them.

∞**31:24 Dreams:** Genesis 37:5–10

31:30 *my god.* The presence of household gods shows that Laban still believed in the many deities of the ancient Near East. Rachel may have stolen them because the one who possessed them would have a claim on the family inheritance, according to ancient Near Eastern custom.

ADAM

GENESIS 2:20

What did Adam do and how does this affect our lives? What is "original sin" and what are its implications? What does it mean for Christ to be the "second Adam"?

The Old Testament teaches that on the sixth day of creation, God created male and female in his image (Genesis 1:26–31). In Genesis 2:4–25, we see a more detailed description of the creation of the first humans. First God created "the man" (Genesis 1:27–28); next he created from one of the man's ribs a "helper" for this man, called "woman" (Genesis 2:20–23). "Adam" is not only a name, but means "man." So, as the first man, "Adam" is a most appropriate name.

Adam was made in God's "image and likeness" (Genesis 1:26). What does it mean that human beings are created in the image of God? The Bible does not spell it out in detail, so we should avoid being dogmatic about it. But we can get a hint from the way that "image" was used in the ancient Near Eastern context in which Genesis was written.

Ancient kings of the Near East, who ruled vast territories, knew that they could not be physically present everywhere in their kingdoms, so they commissioned statues of themselves to be placed in all the major cities of their realms. When people looked at these statues, they were reminded of the authority of the king who ruled them. The statue was not the same as the king, but it represented the king and was due the same glory and honor.

Humanity is to function in the same way. We are dim reflections, rough images of the Creator in ways that his other creatures are not. The startling truth behind the image of God is that we reflect the glory of our heavenly father (Psalm 8). We, as human beings, are like God—certainly not exactly, but we dimly reflect him. God is a person; we are persons. He desires; we desire. He thinks; we think. He feels, wills, and acts; we feel, will, and act.

God commands Adam and Eve not to eat "the fruit from the tree which gives the knowledge of good and evil" (Genesis 2:17). But Adam and Eve are tempted by the serpent to disobey God, and the result is disastrous. (Adam's and Eve's disobedience is often referred to as "the Fall.") Not only are the first parents driven from the garden of paradise, but all their offspring—all humankind—are also affected by this disobedience. This tendency to sin, like the disobedience of Adam and Eve, which is the breaking of their joyous relationship with God, is passed on to their children forever. So now all humans are born with the ability to be separated from God; their relationship to God, like that one lost by Adam and Eve, needs to be restored.

As we read in the following chapters of Genesis, we see that it did not take long for the effects of our first parents' act to make itself known in their children. Cain killed his younger brother Abel out of jealousy (Genesis 4), thus joining in with sin. In fact, things get to the point that God even is "sorry he had made human beings on the earth and his heart was filled with pain" (Genesis 6:6). He then floods the earth and saves only Noah and his family. Yet, even with Noah, who is "a good man, the most innocent man of his time" (Genesis 6:9), sin cannot be avoided: Noah's son commits an indecent act (9:20–28). And in chapter 11, the people became so hostile toward God that they even try to build a tower to heaven in order to become "famous" (11:4).

Throughout the Old Testament we see over and over the results of the broken relationships between humans and God that began with Adam. In fact, the entire Old Testament may be thought of as telling the story of those broken relationships and the steps God takes to restore those relationships. Neither Noah, Abraham, the king (for example, David), nor anyone else could undo what Adam had done. What was needed was a savior, a "new Adam," who could undo Adam's sin and restore God creation back to a whole relationship with him.

There are two New Testament passages in particular that speak of Jesus as the new Adam: Romans 5:12–21 and 1 Corinthians 15:22. Paul explains in some detail what it means for Jesus to be the new Adam. In Romans 5:14, Paul says that Adam was "like the One who was coming in the future." He is, of course, speaking of Christ. Paul is saying that Jesus and Adam are similar. But in what way? This Paul spells out in Romans 5:15–19, especially verses 18–19. Adam disobeyed, and this brought punishment and death to all. Yet Christ's "one good act . . . makes all people right with God." Adam disobeyed in the garden, but Christ was fully obedient to God, even if that meant dying on a cross (Philippians 2:8). In the same way that humanity shares in sin and is guilty (Romans 5:12), now all humanity can share in Christ's grace (verses 15–17).

Adam: For additional scriptures on this topic go to Genesis 5:5.

WOMEN

GENESIS 2:20–25

What is the meaning of womanhood? Is being a woman fundamentally different from being a man? Is there anything inherent in the nature of human beings that says certain tasks or jobs must be done by one sex or the other?

In order to learn what it means to be a woman, we must start with the God who made her. According to Genesis 1:26–27, God made human beings in his own image. But in Genesis 2:18, we are told that for the first time God saw something that was not good. It was not good for the man to be alone. God determined to make a helper who was right for him. And it was after this decision, according to Genesis 2:19, that he brought the animals he had made to Adam to name. It was as though from among them Adam might choose such a helper. He named the animals, "but Adam did not find a helper that was right for him" (2:20). He needed more than the companionship of the animals. He needed a helper, specially designed and prepared to fill that role. It was a woman God gave him—a woman who was right, fit, suitable, entirely appropriate for him, made of his very bones and flesh.

You can't make proper use of a thing unless you know what it was made for, whether it's a safety pin or a sailboat. It is a wonderful thing to be a woman under God's guidance. It's wonderful to know, first of all, that women were *made:* "So God created human beings in his image. In the image of God he created them. He created them male and female" (1:27). And it's wonderful to know that we were made *for* something: "The LORD God used the rib from the man to make a woman, and then he brought the woman to the man" (2:22).

This was the original idea. This is why woman was created. The New Testament refers back clearly and strongly to this purpose: "Man did not come from woman, but woman came from man. And man was not made for woman, but woman was made for man" (1 Corinthians 11:8–9). Some Scriptures are harder to understand, but this one is clear.

It was, in fact, the woman, Eve, who saw the opportunity to be something other than she was meant to be. The serpent convinced her that she could easily "be like God" (Genesis 3:4). So she tried it. We have no way of knowing whether a talk with her husband first might have led to an entirely different ending. Perhaps it might.

But Eve had already tried the fruit. She had not been struck dead (physically). She offered it to her husband. How could he refuse? Eve was undoubtedly a beautiful woman. She was the woman God had given him. She was only testing out what seemed an unnecessary and small rule, and her boldness had been rewarded. She had gotten away with it, and now why shouldn't Adam do the same?

What sort of world might it have been if Eve had refused the serpent's offer and had said to him instead, "Let me not be like God. Let me be what I was made to be. Let me be a woman"?

Women are called to be women. That does not make a woman a different kind of Christian than a man. But being a Christian does make a woman a different kind of woman. Women can accept with joy God's idea of them, and their whole lives are then gifts back to him of all that they are and all that he wants them to be.

It was God who made men and women different, and he did it on purpose. Recent scientific research proves the ancient truth that mankind has always recognized. God created male and female. The male was created to call forth, to lead, to rule. The female was created to respond, to follow, to adapt, to submit. Even if we held to a different theory of origin, the physical structure of the female would tell us that woman was made to receive, to bear, to be acted upon, to complement, to nourish.

We know that this order of rule and submission comes from the nature of God himself. Within the Godhead there is both the just and rightful authority of the Father, and the willing and joyful submission of the Son, as well as the submission of the Holy Spirit to both the Father and the Son.

Womanhood is a call. It's a work to do under God's authority. Women are glad if it means the literal bearing of children. They are thankful as well for all that it means in a much wider sense. Every woman, married or single, who has had children or not, may be part of the willingness to enter into suffering, to receive, to carry, to give life, to nurture, and to care for others—like our example, Mary the virgin.

This is not to deny or belittle the other gifts God has given women. These gifts fit in with the tasks and knowledge of the fact that woman was made for man. The "intellectual" women who feel held back by this idea have not yet understood the biblical meaning of freedom, which is to be what we are created to be.

Women: For additional scriptures on this topic go to Psalm 144:12.

and the children set the speed at which we travel.
I will meet you, my master, in Edom."
15So Esau said, "Then let me leave some of my
people with you."
"No, thank you," said Jacob. "I only want to
please you, my master." 16So that day Esau
started back to Edom. 17But Jacob went to
Succoth, where he built a house for himself and
shelters for his animals. That is why the place was
named Succoth.
18Jacob left Northwest Mesopotamia and
arrived safely at the city of Shechem in the land
of Canaan. There he camped east of the city.
19He bought a part of the field where he had
camped from the sons of Hamor father of
Shechem for one hundred pieces of silver. 20He
built an altar there and named it after God, the
God of Israel.

Dinah Is Attacked

34 At this time Dinah, the daughter of Leah
and Jacob, went out to visit the women of
the land. 2When Shechem son of Hamor the
Hivite, the ruler of the land, saw her, he took her
and forced her to have sexual relations with him.
3Shechem fell in love with Dinah, and he spoke
kindly to her. 4He told his father, Hamor, "Please
get this girl for me so I can marry her."
5Jacob learned how Shechem had disgraced his
daughter, but since his sons were out in the field
with the cattle, Jacob said nothing until they
came home. 6While he waited, Hamor father of
Shechem went to talk with Jacob.
7When Jacob's sons heard what had happened,
they came in from the field. They were very
angry that Shechem had done such a wicked
thing to Israel. It was wrong for him to have sexual relations with Jacob's daughter; a thing like
this should not be done.
8But Hamor talked to Dinah's brothers and
said, "My son Shechem is deeply in love with
Dinah. Please let him marry her. 9Marry our people. Give your women to our men as wives and
take our women for your men as wives. 10You can
live in the same land with us. You will be free to
own land and to trade here."
11Shechem also talked to Jacob and to Dinah's
brothers and said, "Please accept my offer. I will
give anything you ask. 12Ask as much as you want
for the payment for the bride, and I will give it to
you. Just let me marry Dinah."
13Jacob's sons answered Shechem and his
father with lies, because Shechem had disgraced
their sister Dinah. 14The brothers said to them,
"We cannot allow you to marry our sister,
because you are not circumcised. That would be
a disgrace to us. 15But we will allow you to marry
her if you do this one thing: Every man in your
town must be circumcised like us. 16Then your
men can marry our women, and our men can
marry your women, and we will live in your land
and become one people. 17If you refuse to be circumcised, we will take Dinah and leave."
18What they asked seemed fair to Hamor and
Shechem. 19So Shechem quickly went to be circumcised because he loved Jacob's daughter.
Now Shechem was the most respected man in
his family. 20So Hamor and Shechem went to the
gate of their city and spoke to the men of their
city, saying, 21"These people want to be friends
with us. So let them live in our land and trade
here. There is enough land for all of us. Let us
marry their women, and we can let them marry
our women. 22But we must agree to one thing: All
our men must be circumcised as they are. Then
they will agree to live in our land, and we will be
one people. 23If we do this, their cattle and their
animals will belong to us. Let us do what they say,
and they will stay in our land." 24All the people
who had come to the city gate heard this. They
agreed with Hamor and Shechem, and every man
was circumcised.
25Three days later the men who were circumcised were still in pain. Two of Jacob's sons,
Simeon and Levi (Dinah's brothers), took their
swords and made a surprise attack on the city,
killing all the men there. 26They killed Hamor and
his son Shechem and then took Dinah out of
Shechem's house and left. 27Jacob's sons came
upon the dead bodies and stole everything that
was in the city, to pay them back for what
Shechem had done to their sister. 28So the brothers took the flocks, herds, and donkeys, and everything in the city and in the fields. 29They took
every valuable thing the people owned, even their
wives and children and everything in the houses.
30Then Jacob said to Simeon and Levi, "You
have caused me a lot of trouble. Now the
Canaanites and the Perizzites who live in the
land will hate me. Since there are only a few of
us, if they join together to attack us, my people
and I will be destroyed."

33:17 *Succoth.* This name means "shelters."

34:14 God had already commanded his people, the descendants of Abraham, and those who would associate with them to practice circumcision (Genesis 17; see also Exodus 12:43–49). It identified or marked off his people from other peoples and nations. Only by adopting the same practice could the people of Shechem intermarry and become "one people" with Jacob (Genesis 34:16). As it turned out, the suggestion was only a deceitful ruse.

31But the brothers said, "We will not allow our sister to be treated like a prostitute."

Jacob in Bethel

35 God said to Jacob, "Go to the city of Bethel and live there. Make an altar to the God who appeared to you there when you were running away from your brother Esau."

2So Jacob said to his family and to all who were with him, "Put away the foreign gods you have, and make yourselves clean, and change your clothes. 3We will leave here and go to Bethel. There I will build an altar to God, who has helped me during my time of trouble. He has been with me everywhere I have gone." 4So they gave Jacob all the foreign gods they had, and the earrings they were wearing, and he hid them under the great tree near the town of Shechem. 5Then Jacob and his sons left there. But God caused the people in the nearby cities to be afraid, so they did not follow them. 6And Jacob and all the people who were with him went to Luz, which is now called Bethel, in the land of Canaan. 7There Jacob built an altar and named the place Bethel, after God, because God had appeared to him there when he was running from his brother.

8Deborah, Rebekah's nurse, died and was buried under the oak tree at Bethel, so they named that place Oak of Crying.

Jacob's New Name

9When Jacob came back from Northwest Mesopotamia, God appeared to him again and blessed him. 10God said to him, "Your name is Jacob, but you will not be called Jacob any longer. Your new name will be Israel." So he called him Israel. 11God said to him, "I am God Almighty. Have many children and grow in number as a nation. You will be the ancestor of many nations and kings. 12The same land I gave to Abraham and Isaac I will give to you and your descendants." 13Then God left him. 14Jacob set up a stone on edge in that place where God had talked to him, and he poured a drink offering and olive oil on it to make it special for God. 15And Jacob named the place Bethel.

Rachel Dies Giving Birth

16Jacob and his group left Bethel. Before they came to Ephrath, Rachel began giving birth to her baby, 17but she was having much trouble. When Rachel's nurse saw this, she said, "Don't be afraid, Rachel. You are giving birth to another son." 18Rachel gave birth to the son, but she herself died. As she lay dying, she named the boy Son of My Suffering, but Jacob called him Benjamin.

19Rachel was buried on the road to Ephrath, a district of Bethlehem, 20and Jacob set up a rock on her grave to honor her. That rock is still there. 21Then Israel continued his journey and camped just south of Migdal Eder.

22While Israel was there, Reuben had sexual relations with Israel's slave woman Bilhah, and Israel heard about it.

The Family of Israel

Jacob had twelve sons. 23He had six sons by his wife Leah: Reuben, his first son, then Simeon, Levi, Judah, Issachar, and Zebulun.

24He had two sons by his wife Rachel: Joseph and Benjamin.

25He had two sons by Rachel's slave girl Bilhah: Dan and Naphtali.

26And he had two sons by Leah's slave girl Zilpah: Gad and Asher.

These are Jacob's sons who were born in Northwest Mesopotamia.

27Jacob went to his father Isaac at Mamre near Hebron, where Abraham and Isaac had lived. 28Isaac lived one hundred eighty years. 29So Isaac breathed his last breath and died when he was very old, and his sons Esau and Jacob buried him.

Esau's Family

36 This is the family history of Esau (also called Edom). 2Esau married women from the land of Canaan: Adah daughter of Elon the Hittite; and Oholibamah daughter of Anah, the son of Zibeon the Hivite; 3and Basemath, Ishmael's daughter, the sister of Nebaioth.

4Adah gave birth to Eliphaz for Esau. Basemath gave him Reuel, 5and Oholibamah gave him Jeush, Jalam, and Korah. These were Esau's sons who were born in the land of Canaan.

6Esau took his wives, his sons, his daughters, and all the people who lived with him, his herds and other animals, and all the belongings he had gotten in Canaan, and he went to a land away from his brother Jacob. 7Esau's and Jacob's belongings were becoming too many for them to live in the same land. The land where they had lived could not support both of them, because they had

---

35:14 Sacrifice: Leviticus 6:9

35:18 *Benjamin.* This name means "right–hand son" or "favorite son."

35:21 *Israel.* Also called Jacob.

36 The family history of Esau is given in Genesis 36. Although it was through Jacob, Esau's brother, that God worked to fulfill his promises, the family history of Esau is important because of the later history between Esau's descendants, the Edomites, and Jacob's descendants, the Israelites (see Numbers 20:14–21; Deuteronomy 23:7; Obadiah 1:10–12).

too many herds. 8So Esau lived in the mountains
of Edom. (Esau is also named Edom.)
9This is the family history of Esau. He is the
ancestor of the Edomites, who live in the mountains of Edom.
10Esau's sons were Eliphaz, son of Adah and
Esau, and Reuel, son of Basemath and Esau.
11Eliphaz had five sons: Teman, Omar, Zepho,
Gatam, and Kenaz. 12Eliphaz also had a slave
woman named Timna, and Timna and Eliphaz
gave birth to Amalek. These were Esau's grandsons by his wife Adah.
13Reuel had four sons: Nahath, Zerah, Shammah, and Mizzah. These were Esau's grandsons
by his wife Basemath.
14Esau's third wife was Oholibamah the daughter
of Anah. (Anah was the son of Zibeon.) Esau and
Oholibamah gave birth to Jeush, Jalam, and Korah.
15These were the leaders that came from Esau:
Esau's first son was Eliphaz. From him came
these leaders: Teman, Omar, Zepho, Kenaz,
16Korah, Gatam, and Amalek. These were the
leaders that came from Eliphaz in the land of
Edom. They were the grandsons of Adah.
17Esau's son Reuel was the father of these leaders: Nahath, Zerah, Shammah, and Mizzah.
These were the leaders that came from Reuel in
the land of Edom. They were the grandsons of
Esau's wife Basemath.
18Esau's wife Oholibamah gave birth to these
leaders: Jeush, Jalam, and Korah. These are the leaders that came from Esau's wife Oholibamah the
daughter of Anah. 19These were the sons of Esau
(also called Edom), and these were their leaders.
20These were the sons of Seir the Horite, who
were living in the land: Lotan, Shobal, Zibeon,
Anah, 21Dishon, Ezer, and Dishan. These sons of
Seir were the leaders of the Horites in Edom.
22The sons of Lotan were Hori and Homam.
(Timna was Lotan's sister.)
23The sons of Shobal were Alvan, Manahath,
Ebal, Shepho, and Onam.
24The sons of Zibeon were Aiah and Anah. Anah
is the man who found the hot springs in the desert
while he was caring for his father's donkeys.
25The children of Anah were Dishon and Oholibamah daughter of Anah.
26The sons of Dishon were Hemdan, Eshban,
Ithran, and Keran.
27The sons of Ezer were Bilhan, Zaavan, and
Akan.
28The sons of Dishan were Uz and Aran.
29These were the names of the Horite leaders:
Lotan, Shobal, Zibeon, Anah, 30Dishon, Ezer, and
Dishan.
These men were the leaders of the Horite families who lived in the land of Edom.
31These are the kings who ruled in the land of
Edom before the Israelites ever had a king:
32Bela son of Beor was the king of Edom. He
came from the city of Dinhabah.
33When Bela died, Jobab son of Zerah became
king. Jobab was from Bozrah.
34When Jobab died, Husham became king. He
was from the land of the Temanites.
35When Husham died, Hadad son of Bedad,
who had defeated Midian in the country of Moab,
became king. Hadad was from the city of Avith.
36When Hadad died, Samlah became king. He
was from Masrekah.
37When Samlah died, Shaul became king. He
was from Rehoboth on the Euphrates River.
38When Shaul died, Baal-Hanan son of Acbor
became king.
39When Baal-Hanan son of Acbor died, Hadad
became king. He was from the city of Pau. His
wife's name was Mehetabel daughter of Matred,
who was the daughter of Me-Zahab.
40These Edomite leaders, listed by their families and regions, came from Esau. Their names
were Timna, Alvah, Jetheth, 41Oholibamah,
Elah, Pinon, 42Kenaz, Teman, Mibzar, 43Mag-
diel, and Iram. They were the leaders of Edom.
(Esau was the father of the Edomites.) The area
where each of these families lived was named
after that family.

Joseph the Dreamer

37 Jacob lived in the land of Canaan, where
his father had lived. 2This is the family his-
tory of Jacob:
Joseph was a young man, seventeen years old.
He and his brothers, the sons of Bilhah and
Zilpah, his father's wives, cared for the flocks.
Joseph gave his father bad reports about his
brothers. 3Since Joseph was born when his father
Israel was old, Israel loved him more than his
other sons. He made Joseph a special robe with

37:1–50:26 The story of Joseph continues the story of the patriarchs, because, after all, Joseph is the son of Jacob. As happens so often in Genesis, an obstacle arises that threatens the promises of God. At this time, a famine comes on the land that could wipe out the family of God. The last part of Genesis shows how God uses Joseph to provide for the deliverance of his people. Though from a human point of view it looks like events go badly in Joseph's life, God is really working things out so that Joseph is in a position of power and authority in Egypt when the famine hits.

37:3 *Israel.* Also called Jacob.

long sleeves. 4When Joseph's brothers saw that their father loved him more than he loved them, they hated their brother and could not speak to him politely.

5One time Joseph had a dream, and when he told his brothers about it, they hated him even more. 6Joseph said, "Listen to the dream I had. 7We were in the field tying bundles of wheat together. My bundle stood up, and your bundles of wheat gathered around it and bowed down to it."

8His brothers said, "Do you really think you will be king over us? Do you truly think you will rule over us?" His brothers hated him even more because of his dreams and what he had said.

9Then Joseph had another dream, and he told his brothers about it also. He said, "Listen, I had another dream. I saw the sun, moon, and eleven stars bowing down to me."

10Joseph also told his father about this dream, but his father scolded him, saying, "What kind of dream is this? Do you really believe that your mother, your brothers, and I will bow down to you?" 11Joseph's brothers were jealous of him, but his father thought about what all these things could mean.

12One day Joseph's brothers went to Shechem to graze their father's flocks. 13Israel said to Joseph, "Go to Shechem where your brothers are grazing the flocks."

Joseph answered, "I will go."

14His father said, "Go and see if your brothers and the flocks are all right. Then come back and tell me." So Joseph's father sent him from the Valley of Hebron.

When Joseph came to Shechem, 15a man found him wandering in the field and asked him, "What are you looking for?"

16Joseph answered, "I am looking for my brothers. Can you tell me where they are grazing the flocks?"

17The man said, "They have already gone. I heard them say they were going to Dothan." So Joseph went to look for his brothers and found them in Dothan.

Joseph Sold into Slavery

18Joseph's brothers saw him coming from far away. Before he reached them, they made a plan to kill him. 19They said to each other, "Here comes that dreamer. 20Let's kill him and throw his body into one of the wells. We can tell our father that a wild animal killed him. Then we will see what will become of his dreams."

21But Reuben heard their plan and saved Joseph, saying, "Let's not kill him. 22Don't spill any blood. Throw him into this well here in the desert, but don't hurt him!" Reuben planned to save Joseph later and send him back to his father. 23So when Joseph came to his brothers, they pulled off his robe with long sleeves 24and threw him into the well. It was empty, and there was no water in it.

25While Joseph was in the well, the brothers sat down to eat. When they looked up, they saw a group of Ishmaelites traveling from Gilead to Egypt. Their camels were carrying spices, balm, and myrrh.

26Then Judah said to his brothers, "What will we gain if we kill our brother and hide his death? 27Let's sell him to these Ishmaelites. Then we will not be guilty of killing our own brother. After all, he is our brother, our own flesh and blood." And the other brothers agreed. 28So when the Midianite traders came by, the brothers took Joseph out of the well and sold him to the Ishmaelites for eight ounces of silver. And the Ishmaelites took him to Egypt.

29When Reuben came back to the well and Joseph was not there, he tore his clothes to show he was upset. 30Then he went back to his brothers and said, "The boy is not there! What shall I do?" 31The brothers killed a goat and dipped Joseph's robe in its blood. 32Then they brought the long-sleeved robe to their father and said, "We found this robe. Look it over carefully and see if it is your son's robe."

33Jacob looked it over and said, "It is my son's robe! Some savage animal has eaten him. My son Joseph has been torn to pieces!" 34Then Jacob tore his clothes and put on rough cloth to show that he was upset, and he continued to be sad about his son for a long time. 35All of his sons and daughters tried to comfort him, but he could not be comforted. He said, "I will be sad about my son until the day I die." So Jacob cried for his son Joseph.

36Meanwhile the Midianites who had bought Joseph had taken him to Egypt. There they sold him to Potiphar, an officer to the king of Egypt and captain of the palace guard.

Judah and Tamar

38 About that time, Judah left his brothers and went to stay with a man named Hirah in the town of Adullam. 2There Judah met a Canaanite girl, the daughter of a man named Shua, and married her. Judah had sexual relations with her, 3and she became pregnant and gave birth to a son, whom Judah named Er. 4Later she gave birth to another son and named him Onan. 5Still later she had another son and named him Shelah.

37:10 Dreams: Genesis 40:8–17
37:28 Loneliness: Genesis 39:21
37:35 Comfort: Job 2:11
37:36 Joseph: Genesis 39–50

She was at Kezib when this third son was born.
[6]Judah chose a girl named Tamar to be the wife
of his first son Er. [7]But Er, Judah's oldest son, did
what the LORD said was evil, so the LORD killed
him. [8]Then Judah said to Er's brother Onan, "Go
and have sexual relations with your dead
brother's wife. It is your duty to provide children
for your brother in this way."
[9]But Onan knew that the children would not
belong to him, so when he was supposed to have
sexual relations with Tamar he did not complete
the sex act. This made it impossible for Tamar to
become pregnant and for Er to have descendants.
[10]The LORD was displeased by this wicked thing
Onan had done, so the LORD killed Onan also.
[11]Then Judah said to his daughter-in-law Tamar,
"Go back to live in your father's house, and don't
marry until my young son Shelah grows up." Judah
was afraid that Shelah also would die like his brothers. So Tamar returned to her father's home.⚭
[12]After a long time Judah's wife, the daughter
of Shua, died. After Judah had gotten over his sorrow, he went to Timnah to his men who were
cutting the wool from his sheep. His friend Hirah
from Adullam went with him. [13]Tamar learned
that Judah, her father-in-law, was going to Timnah to cut the wool from his sheep. [14]So she took
off the clothes that showed she was a widow and
covered her face with a veil to hide who she was.
Then she sat down by the gate of Enaim on the
road to Timnah. She did this because Judah's
younger son Shelah had grown up, but Judah had
not made plans for her to marry him.
[15]When Judah saw her, he thought she was a
prostitute, because she had covered her face with
a veil. [16]So Judah went to her and said, "Let me
have sexual relations with you." He did not know
that she was Tamar, his daughter-in-law.
She asked, "What will you give me if I let you
have sexual relations with me?"
[17]Judah answered, "I will send you a young
goat from my flock."
She answered, "First give me something to
keep as a deposit until you send the goat."
[18]Judah asked, "What do you want me to give
you as a deposit?"
Tamar answered, "Give me your seal and its
cord, and give me your walking stick." So Judah
gave these things to her. Then Judah and Tamar
had sexual relations, and Tamar became pregnant. [19]When Tamar went home, she took off the
veil that covered her face and put on the clothes
that showed she was a widow.
[20]Judah sent his friend Hirah with the young
goat to find the woman and get back his seal and
the walking stick he had given her, but Hirah
could not find her. [21]He asked some of the people
at the town of Enaim, "Where is the prostitute
who was here by the road?"
They answered, "There has never been a prostitute here."
[22]So he went back to Judah and said, "I could not
find the woman, and the people who lived there
said, 'There has never been a prostitute here.'"
[23]Judah said, "Let her keep the things. I don't
want people to laugh at us. I sent her the goat as
I promised, but you could not find her."
[24]About three months later someone told
Judah, "Tamar, your daughter-in-law, is guilty of
acting like a prostitute, and now she is pregnant."
Then Judah said, "Bring her out and let her be
burned to death."
[25]When the people went to bring Tamar out,
she sent a message to her father-in-law that said,
"The man who owns these things has made me
pregnant. Look at this seal and its cord and this
walking stick, and tell me whose they are."
[26]Judah recognized them and said, "She is more
in the right than I. She did this because I did not give
her to my son Shelah as I promised." And Judah did
not have sexual relations with her again.⚭
[27]When the time came for Tamar to give birth,
there were twins in her body. [28]While she was
giving birth, one baby put his hand out. The
nurse tied a red string on his hand and said, "This
baby came out first." [29]But he pulled his hand
back in, so the other baby was born first. The
nurse said, "So you are able to break out first,"
and they named him Perez. [30]After this, the baby
with the red string on his hand was born, and
they named him Zerah.

38:8 *Go . . . wife.* It was a custom in Israel that if a man died without children, one of his brothers would marry the widow. If a child was born, it would be considered the dead man's child.

⚭**38:11 Ruth:** Deuteronomy 23:3–4

38:18 *seal . . . cord.* A seal was used like a rubber stamp, and people ran a string through it to tie around the neck. They wrote a contract, folded it, put wax or clay on the contract, and pressed the seal onto it as a signature.

38:26 Even though Tamar's husband Er had died, she was still expected to have a son to carry on his name. Custom required that another family member—usually a brother of the dead man—have sexual relations with the widow to produce this child (Deuteronomy 25:5–10). By withholding Shelah from Tamar, Judah improperly avoided his obligation to provide a husband for Er's widow. Tamar, on the other hand, is "more in the right" than Judah because she was so committed to producing a son for her dead husband.

⚭**38:26 The Widow:** Deuteronomy 24:19–22

⚭**38:26 Deborah:** Joshua 2:1–21

38:29 *Perez.* This name means "breaking out."

Joseph Is Sold to Potiphar

39 Now Joseph had been taken down to Egypt. An Egyptian named Potiphar was an officer to the king of Egypt and the captain of the palace guard. He bought Joseph from the Ishmaelites who had brought him down there. 2The LORD was with Joseph, and he became a successful man. He lived in the house of his master, Potiphar the Egyptian.

3Potiphar saw that the LORD was with Joseph and that the LORD made Joseph successful in everything he did. 4So Potiphar was very happy with Joseph and allowed him to be his personal servant. He put Joseph in charge of the house, trusting him with everything he owned. 5When Joseph was put in charge of the house and everything Potiphar owned, the LORD blessed the people in Potiphar's house because of Joseph. And the LORD blessed everything that belonged to Potiphar, both in the house and in the field. 6So Potiphar left Joseph in charge of everything he owned and was not concerned about anything except the food he ate.

Joseph Is Put into Prison

Now Joseph was well built and handsome. 7After some time the wife of Joseph's master began to desire Joseph, and one day she said to him, "Have sexual relations with me."

8But Joseph refused and said to her, "My master trusts me with everything in his house. He has put me in charge of everything he owns. 9There is no one in his house greater than I. He has not kept anything from me except you, because you are his wife. How can I do such an evil thing? It is a sin against God."

10The woman talked to Joseph every day, but he refused to have sexual relations with her or even spend time with her.

11One day Joseph went into the house to do his work as usual and was the only man in the house at that time. 12His master's wife grabbed his coat and said to him, "Come and have sexual relations with me." But Joseph left his coat in her hand and ran out of the house.

13When she saw that Joseph had left his coat in her hands and had run outside, 14she called to the servants in her house and said, "Look! This Hebrew slave was brought here to shame us. He came in and tried to have sexual relations with me, but I screamed. 15My scream scared him and he ran away, but he left his coat with me." 16She kept his coat until her husband came home, 17and she told him the same story. She said, "This Hebrew slave you brought here came in to shame me! 18When he came near me, I screamed. He ran away, but he left his coat."

19When Joseph's master heard what his wife said Joseph had done, he became very angry. 20So Potiphar arrested Joseph and put him into the prison where the king's prisoners were put. And Joseph stayed there in the prison.

21But the LORD was with Joseph and showed him kindness and caused the prison warden to like Joseph. 22The prison warden chose Joseph to take care of all the prisoners, and he was responsible for whatever was done in the prison. 23The warden paid no attention to anything that was in Joseph's care because the LORD was with Joseph and made him successful in everything he did.

Joseph Interprets Two Dreams

40 After these things happened, two of the king's officers displeased the king—the man who served wine to the king and the king's baker. 2The king became angry with his officer who served him wine and his baker, 3so he put them in the prison of the captain of the guard, the same prison where Joseph was kept. 4The captain of the guard put the two prisoners in Joseph's care, and they stayed in prison for some time.

5One night both the king's officer who served him wine and the baker had a dream. Each had his own dream with its own meaning. 6When Joseph came to them the next morning, he saw they were

39:7–23 Perhaps one of the best examples of personal integrity was when Joseph refused to have sexual relations with Potiphar's wife despite her numerous protestations to do so. "How can I do such an evil thing? It is a sin against God" (Genesis 39:9). In the end, the woman tricked Joseph by keeping his coat and using that as evidence for her husband that he had tried to rape her. While unjustly imprisoned, because of his honesty and integrity the Lord showed Joseph kindness and "made him successful in everything he did" (Genesis 39:23). Because it violates a trust, Joseph is clear that adultery is a wrong against Potiphar's husband, and therefore against God and his own conscience.

39:9 Joseph's master's wife here tempts him to sin by offering her body to him while her husband is away. Joseph's reaction is important because it shows the heart of sin. He refuses her advances as an offense not only against his master, but especially against God. Sin is the act of rebelling against God, doing something he does not want us to do or not doing something he does want us to do.

39:21 Loneliness: Exodus 3:1–6

39:23 Success: 1 Samuel 18:14

40:1 *the cupbearer and the baker of the king.* These are actually names of high-level governmental positions in Egypt. They are not lowly servants or slaves.

EVE

GENESIS 2:21

Who is Eve? What does it mean that she was created in God's image? What can we learn from her story about human relationships, especially marriage?

In contemporary society, an array of voices clamor for attention regarding a woman's role in the family, church, and society. Does the biblical account of Eve's creation and her fall into sin provide any guidance for understanding God's design for men and women? Genesis 2:18–25 describes the why, when, and how of Eve's creation. It highlights the unique circumstances surrounding Eve's creation that were glossed over in the earlier, general account of the creation of human beings in Genesis 1:26–28.

While Genesis 1:27 tells us that both male and female reflect God's image, Genesis 2:18–25 shows how each sex does this uniquely. Genesis 1:27 tells us that the creation of male and female human beings was "good." Chapter 2 shows why anything less was "not good." After God created Adam, he said that it was not good for Adam to be alone. God designed human beings to live in a community with others. People cannot fully enjoy life or please God without other people. That is why none of the animals God made could meet Adam's need. Adam was different from the animals; he needed a helper just right for him. Man was created to be satisfied with nothing less than human society.

God's answer to Adam's need for human society was to create a woman. God caused Adam to fall into a deep sleep during which time he formed (literally, "built") Eve from Adam's side (or rib). When God brought the woman to Adam, he immediately and enthusiastically recognized that she was perfectly suitable for him. Adam's encounter with Eve, the first example of human society, is also the first example of the marriage relationship. According to the editorial comment in Genesis 2:24, marriage is built on the foundation of the unity of a man and woman, making the family the foundation of human society.

Who exactly was this woman? Eve was formed from Adam's rib and not the dust. She shared his nature. She was more like than different from him. She was also made as a "helper who was right for him" (verse 20). First, this means that Eve complemented Adam in a way no other created being could. The concept of woman as a "helper" for man is by no means demeaning. The same Hebrew word is most often used of God in his relationship to Israel (Exodus 18:4; Deuteronomy 33:7; Psalm 20:2). The biblical use of "helper" evokes an image of support and self-sacrifice. Second, it means that in some uniquely mysterious way woman was made for man. Eve's formation as a helper to complement Adam occured before the Fall as part of the created order. Before the entrance of sin, God established this hierarchy, suggesting that this hierarchy has a permanent validity in God's economy. They were equal as image bearers, but they carried out their roles in different ways.

The account of Eve's deception by the serpent and her punishment (Genesis 3) provides further insight into some of the realities that women live with today. Whether or not Adam was present during Eve's dialogue with the serpent is unclear. What is certain is that Eve was aware of the prohibition regarding the "tree which gives the knowledge of good and evil" (Genesis 2:17). Furthermore, the serpent got the best of her in an argument pertaining to God's will. This, together with the fact that when God came looking for the couple, he addressed the man, indicates that in a very special way Eve was to be protected by Adam, and without that protection she fell into sin. Both were responsible for their particular sins, yet Adam had to answer to God for both his and Eve's behavior (verses 9–12). In a unique sense, Adam was viewed as Eve's representative before God, so that even though Eve committed the initial sin, Adam was held accountable for the curse pronounced on the entire race (Romans 5:12–21).

The two-pronged punishment meted out to Eve, pain in childbearing and an inordinate desire to rule her husband (Genesis 3:16) takes the viscerally satisfying experiences of a woman's life and twists them into sources of agony. The language used to describe Eve's desire for her husband strongly resembles that used to depict sin's desire to master Cain in Genesis 4:7. The parallel suggests that Eve's desire was not a healthy sexual longing, but rather a sinful urge to dominate and reverse God's hierarchical, created order for marriage. Further, the judgment ("but he will rule over you," Genesis 3:16) serves as a warning to women that their sinful propensity will be met by male domination. This knowledge can help couples prepare themselves for dealing with their own sinful desires in the marriage relationship. The New Testament commands regarding marital relationships bear this out (Ephesians 5:22–33; Colossians 3:18, 19).

Eve: For additional scriptures on this topic go to Genesis 3:20.

MARRIAGE

GENESIS 2:23–25

When does marriage begin? What is marriage?
Is marriage forever? How is marriage used as an image of our relationship with God?

Marriage is an important and crucial institution in the Bible. Its foundation is established as early as Genesis 1 and Revelation 19:6–10 describe our union with Christ as a great wedding feast.

Marriage, after all, unites two human beings in the most intimate and passionate relationship possible. As such, it mirrors on a human level the relationship we enjoy with God. Frequently in the Bible, God's relationship with his people is described as a marriage, both good and bad. Our relationship with our spouse and our relationship with God are the only two relationships that are mutually exclusive, allowing no rivals, and thus the only two relationships where jealousy may be legitimate (see "Jealousy").

God created Adam first, but noted that something seemed to be missing. Adam was lonely, so God created Eve from Adam's very body, showing the fundamental equality between male and female (Genesis 2:19–24). They both were created in the image of God, reflecting God's glory. "So God created human beings in his image. In the image of God he created them. He created them male and female" (Genesis 1:27). Thus, when a man and a woman obey God's command to leave their parents, be united to their spouse, and become one flesh—"So a man will leave his father and mother and be united with his wife, and the two will become one body" (Genesis 2:24)—their union is the merging of two glorious creatures of God.

Genesis 3 tells the story of Adam and Eve's sin. They failed to obey God's command and were thrown out of the garden of Eden. They represented every human being in the test they failed, so their sin affects us all: "Sin came into the world because of what one man did, and with sin came death" (Romans 5:12). All marriages unite not only two glorious creatures of God, but also two sinners. Marriage does not completely solve the problem of loneliness. Intimate relationship between the time of the Fall and the Second Coming is marred by conflicts and strife even in the best marriages.

The Bible recognizes that not every marriage is happy and fulfilling. Nonetheless, it insists that marriage is based on more than emotion. It is a relationship of commitment that should not be entered into lightly and certainly not broken on the basis of a change of feeling. Malachi 2:16 quotes God as saying, "I hate divorce." It is a ripping apart of what God has brought together and what is described as an agreement (covenant) between a man and his wife.

The New Testament, nonetheless, allows for divorce in two specific instances: adultery (Matthew 19:1–12) and desertion by an unbeliever (1 Corinthians 7:15). (For how broadly these exceptions should be interpreted please refer to the article on divorce.)

Though marriage this side of the Fall can be difficult, the Song of Solomon reminds us that marriage can still be a relationship of great joy and can give us glimpses of God's grace. But even in the Song of Solomon the intense love of the man and the woman is subject to misunderstanding and struggle (Song of Solomon 5). A successful marriage is one that is characterized by a forgiving heart and a recognition on the part of both the husband and wife that they need forgiveness as well.

As mentioned, God's relationship with his human creatures is often spoken of as a marriage relationship. Christians know well the teaching of the New Testament that the relationship between a husband and wife is like the relationship between Christ and the church (Ephesians 5:21–33). Already in the Old Testament God is pictured as the husband of Israel, his people. Unfortunately, most often the image is used in negative circumstances; for instance, in Hosea where Hosea's marriage to the promiscuous Gomer represents the fact that Israel had turned away from God and was now worshiping idols (Hosea 1–3; Ezekiel 16; 23). Though the primary meaning of the Song of Solomon focuses on human beings, the frequent use of the marriage metaphor for the divine-human relationship encourages us to read that book too as a poem that expresses the deep love that God has for his people.

Marriage, as such, will no longer be needed in heaven and, according to Jesus in Matthew 22:23–33, will pass away. However, this statement should not be interpreted to mean that heaven will be a somber, passionless place. Rather, the union between God and his creatures, as well as between his creatures, will be so complete, intimate, and passionate that the institution of marriage will no longer be required.

Marriage: For additional scriptures on this topic go to Deuteronomy 20:7.

worried. 7He asked the king's officers who were with him, "Why do you look so unhappy today?"

8The two men answered, "We both had dreams last night, but no one can explain their meaning to us."

Joseph said to them, "God is the only One who can explain the meaning of dreams. Tell me your dreams."

9So the man who served wine to the king told Joseph his dream. He said, "I dreamed I saw a vine, and 10on the vine were three branches. I watched the branches bud and blossom, and then the grapes ripened. 11I was holding the king's cup, so I took the grapes and squeezed the juice into the cup. Then I gave it to the king."

12Then Joseph said, "I will explain the dream to you. The three branches stand for three days. 13Before the end of three days the king will free you, and he will allow you to return to your work. You will serve the king his wine just as you did before. 14But when you are free, remember me. Be kind to me, and tell the king about me so I can get out of this prison. 15I was taken by force from the land of the Hebrews, and I have done nothing here to deserve being put in prison."

16The baker saw that Joseph's explanation of the dream was good, so he said to him, "I also had a dream. I dreamed there were three bread baskets on my head. 17In the top basket were all kinds of baked food for the king, but the birds were eating this food out of the basket on my head."

18Joseph answered, "I will tell you what the dream means. The three baskets stand for three days. 19Before the end of three days, the king will cut off your head! He will hang your body on a pole, and the birds will eat your flesh."

20Three days later, on his birthday, the king gave a feast for all his officers. In front of his officers, he released from prison the chief officer who served his wine and the chief baker. 21The king gave his chief officer who served wine his old position, and once again he put the king's cup of wine into the king's hand. 22But the king hanged the baker on a pole. Everything happened just as Joseph had said it would, 23but the officer who served wine did not remember Joseph. He forgot all about him.

The King's Dreams

41 Two years later the king dreamed he was standing on the bank of the Nile River. 2He saw seven fat and beautiful cows come up out of the river, and they stood there, eating the grass. 3Then seven more cows came up out of the river, but they were thin and ugly. They stood beside the seven beautiful cows on the bank of the Nile. 4The seven thin and ugly cows ate the seven beautiful fat cows. Then the king woke up. 5The king slept again and dreamed a second time. In his dream he saw seven full and good heads of grain growing on one stalk. 6After that, seven more heads of grain sprang up, but they were thin and burned by the hot east wind. 7The thin heads of grain ate the seven full and good heads. Then the king woke up again, and he realized it was only a dream. 8The next morning the king was troubled about these dreams, so he sent for all the magicians and wise men of Egypt. The king told them his dreams, but no one could explain their meaning to him.

9Then the chief officer who served wine to the king said to him, "Now I remember something I promised to do, but I forgot about it. 10There was a time when you were angry with the baker and me, and you put us in prison in the house of the captain of the guard. 11In prison we each had a dream on the same night, and each dream had a different meaning. 12A young Hebrew man, a servant of the captain of the guard, was in the prison with us. When we told him our dreams, he explained their meanings to us. He told each man the meaning of his dream, and 13things happened exactly as he said they would: I was given back my old position, and the baker was hanged."

14So the king called for Joseph. The guards quickly brought him out of the prison, and he shaved, put on clean clothes, and went before the king.

15The king said to Joseph, "I have had a dream, but no one can explain its meaning to me. I have heard that you can explain a dream when someone tells it to you."

16Joseph answered the king, "I am not able to explain the meaning of dreams, but God will do this for the king."

17Then the king said to Joseph, "In my dream I was standing on the bank of the Nile River. 18I saw seven fat and beautiful cows that came up out of the river and ate the grass. 19Then I saw seven more cows come out of the river that were thin and lean and ugly—the worst looking cows I have seen in all the land of Egypt. 20And these thin and ugly cows ate the first seven fat cows, 21but after they had eaten the seven cows, no one could tell

40:17 Dreams: Genesis 41:1–7
41:7 Dreams: Genesis 41:15–16
41:16 Dreams: Numbers 12:6

they had eaten them. They looked just as thin and
ugly as they did in the beginning. Then I woke up.
22"I had another dream. I saw seven full and good
heads of grain growing on one stalk. 23Then seven
more heads of grain sprang up after them, but these
heads were thin and ugly and were burned by the
hot east wind. 24Then the thin heads ate the seven
good heads. I told this dream to the magicians, but
no one could explain its meaning to me."

Joseph Tells the Dreams' Meaning

25Then Joseph said to the king, "Both of these
dreams mean the same thing. God is telling you
what he is about to do. 26The seven good cows
stand for seven years, and the seven good heads
of grain stand for seven years. Both dreams mean
the same thing. 27The seven thin and ugly cows
stand for seven years, and the seven thin heads of
grain burned by the hot east wind stand for seven
years of hunger. 28This will happen as I told you.
God is showing the king what he is about to do.
29You will have seven years of good crops and
plenty to eat in all the land of Egypt. 30But after
those seven years, there will come seven years of
hunger, and all the food that grew in the land of
Egypt will be forgotten. The time of hunger will
eat up the land. 31People will forget what it was
like to have plenty of food, because the hunger
that follows will be so great. 32You had two
dreams which mean the same thing. This shows
that God has firmly decided that this will happen,
and he will make it happen soon.
33"So let the king choose a man who is very wise
and understanding and set him over the land of
Egypt. 34And let the king also appoint officers over
the land, who should take one-fifth of all the food
that is grown during the seven good years. 35They
should gather all the food that is produced during
the good years that are coming, and under the
king's authority they should store the grain in the
cities and guard it. 36That food should be saved to
use during the seven years of hunger that will come
on the land of Egypt. Then the people in Egypt will
not die during the seven years of hunger."

Joseph Is Made Ruler over Egypt

37This seemed like a very good idea to the king,
and all his officers agreed. 38And the king asked
them, "Can we find a better man than Joseph to
take this job? God's spirit is truly in him!"
39So the king said to Joseph, "God has shown
you all this. There is no one as wise and understanding as you are, so 40I will put you in charge
of my palace. All the people will obey your orders,
and only I will be greater than you."
41Then the king said to Joseph, "Look! I have
put you in charge of all the land of Egypt." 42Then
the king took off from his own finger his ring with
the royal seal on it, and he put it on Joseph's finger. He gave Joseph fine linen clothes to wear,
and he put a gold chain around Joseph's neck.
43The king had Joseph ride in the second royal
chariot, and people walked ahead of his chariot
calling, "Bow down!" By doing these things, the
king put Joseph in charge of all of Egypt.

"Then the king took off . . . his ring with the royal seal on it. . . ." (41:42).

44The king said to him, "I am the king, and I say
that no one in all the land of Egypt may lift a hand
or a foot without your permission." 45The king
gave Joseph the name Zaphenath-Paneah. He also
gave Joseph a wife named Asenath, who was the
daughter of Potiphera, priest of On. So Joseph traveled through all the land of Egypt.
46Joseph was thirty years old when he began
serving the king of Egypt. And he left the king's
court and traveled through all the land of Egypt.
47During the seven good years, the crops in the
land grew well. 48And Joseph gathered all the
food which was produced in Egypt during those
seven years of good crops and stored the food in
the cities. In every city he stored grain that had
been grown in the fields around that city.
49Joseph stored much grain, as much as the sand
of the seashore—so much that he could not measure it.

41:31 Seven years of famine may sound far-fetched, but biblical scholars have an actual text of an ancient Egyptian king who wrote, "I was in distress on the Great Throne, and those who are in the palace were in heart's affliction from a very great evil, since the Nile had not come in my time for a *space of seven years.* Grain was scant, fruits were dried up,... The temples were shut up; the sanctuaries held nothing but air. Everything was found empty."

41:36 God used the occasion of coming famine to bring out both Joseph's ability to interpret dreams and his ability to administer the country in storing up food. It was also the occasion of reuniting his family, for his brothers needed to come to Egypt later for food (Genesis 42:1–2). God also used the famine to fulfill Joseph's dreams in Genesis 37.

[50]Joseph's wife was Asenath daughter of Potiphera, the priest of On. Before the years of hunger came, Joseph and Asenath had two sons. [51]Joseph named the first son Manasseh and said, "God has made me forget all the troubles I have had and all my father's family." [52]Joseph named the second son Ephraim and said, "God has given me children in the land of my troubles."

[53]The seven years of good crops came to an end in the land of Egypt. [54]Then the seven years of hunger began, just as Joseph had said. In all the lands people had nothing to eat, but in Egypt there was food. [55]The time of hunger became terrible in all of Egypt, and the people cried to the king for food. He said to all the Egyptians, "Go to Joseph and do whatever he tells you."

[56]The hunger was everywhere in that part of the world. And Joseph opened the storehouses and sold grain to the people of Egypt, because the time of hunger became terrible in Egypt. [57]And all the people in that part of the world came to Joseph in Egypt to buy grain because the hunger was terrible everywhere in that part of the world.

The Dreams Come True

42 Jacob learned that there was grain in Egypt, so he said to his sons, "Why are you just sitting here looking at one another? [2]I have heard that there is grain in Egypt. Go down there and buy grain for us to eat, so that we will live and not die."

[3]So ten of Joseph's brothers went down to buy grain from Egypt. [4]But Jacob did not send Benjamin, Joseph's brother, with them, because he was afraid that something terrible might happen to him. [5]Along with many other people, the sons of Israel went to Egypt to buy grain, because the people in the land of Canaan were also hungry.

[6]Now Joseph was governor over Egypt. He was the one who sold the grain to people who came to buy it. So Joseph's brothers came to him and bowed facedown on the ground before him. [7]When Joseph saw his brothers, he knew who they were, but he acted as if he didn't know them. He asked unkindly, "Where do you come from?"

They answered, "We have come from the land of Canaan to buy food."

[8]Joseph knew they were his brothers, but they did not know who he was. [9]And Joseph remembered his dreams about his brothers bowing to him. He said to them, "You are spies! You came to learn where the nation is weak!"

[10]But his brothers said to him, "No, my master. We come as your servants just to buy food. [11]We are all sons of the same father. We are honest men, not spies."

[12]Then Joseph said to them, "No! You have come to learn where this nation is weak!"

[13]And they said, "We are ten of twelve brothers, sons of the same father, and we live in the land of Canaan. Our youngest brother is there with our father right now, and our other brother is gone."

[14]But Joseph said to them, "I can see I was right! You are spies! [15]But I will give you a way to prove you are telling the truth. As surely as the king lives, you will not leave this place until your youngest brother comes here. [16]One of you must go and get your brother. The rest of you will stay here in prison. We will see if you are telling the truth. If not, as surely as the king lives, you are spies." [17]Then Joseph put them all in prison for three days.

[18]On the third day Joseph said to them, "I am a God-fearing man. Do this and I will let you live: [19]If you are honest men, let one of your brothers stay here in prison while the rest of you go and carry grain back to feed your hungry families. [20]Then bring your youngest brother back here to me. If you do this, I will know you are telling the truth, and you will not die."

The brothers agreed to this. [21]They said to each other, "We are being punished for what we did to our brother. We saw his trouble, and he begged us to save him, but we refused to listen. That is why we are in this trouble now."

[22]Then Reuben said to them, "I told you not to harm the boy, but you refused to listen to me. So now we are being punished for what we did to him."

[23]When Joseph talked to his brothers, he used an interpreter, so they did not know that Joseph understood what they were saying. [24]Then Joseph left them and cried. After a short time he went back and spoke to them. He took Simeon and tied him up while the other brothers watched. [25]Joseph told his servants to fill his brothers' bags with grain and to put the money the brothers had paid for the grain back in their bags. The servants were also to give them what they would need for their trip back home. And the servants did this.

[26]So the brothers put the grain on their donkeys and left. [27]When they stopped for the night, one of the brothers opened his sack to get food for his donkey. Then he saw his money in the top of the sack. [28]He said to the other brothers, "The

41:51 *Manasseh.* This name sounds like the Hebrew word for "made me forget."

41:52 *Ephraim.* This name sounds like the Hebrew word for "given me children."

42:5 *Israel.* Also called Jacob.

money I paid for the grain has been put back.
Here it is in my sack!"
The brothers were very frightened. They said
to each other, "What has God done to us?"

The Brothers Return to Jacob

29The brothers went to their father Jacob in the
land of Canaan and told him everything that had
happened. 30They said, "The master of that land
spoke unkindly to us. He accused us of spying on
his country, 31but we told him that we were honest men, not spies. 32We told him that we were ten
of twelve brothers—sons of one father. We said
that one of our brothers was gone and that our
youngest brother was with our father in Canaan.
33"Then the master of the land said to us, 'Here
is a way I can know you are honest men: Leave
one of your brothers with me, and take grain to
feed your hungry families, and go. 34And bring
your youngest brother to me so I will know you
are not spies but honest men. Then I will give you
back your brother whom you leave with me, and
you can move about freely in our land.'"
35As the brothers emptied their sacks, each of
them found his money in his sack. When they
and their father saw it, they were afraid.
36Their father Jacob said to them, "You are robbing me of all my children. Joseph is gone, Simeon
is gone, and now you want to take Benjamin away,
too. Everything is against me."
37Then Reuben said to his father, "You may put
my two sons to death if I don't bring Benjamin
back to you. Trust him to my care, and I will bring
him back to you."
38But Jacob said, "I will not allow Benjamin to go
with you. His brother is dead, and he is the only son
left from my wife Rachel. I am afraid something
terrible might happen to him during the trip to
Egypt. Then I would be sad until the day I die."

The Brothers Go Back to Egypt

43 Still no food grew in the land of Canaan.
2When Jacob's family had eaten all the
grain they had brought from Egypt, Jacob said to
them, "Go to Egypt again and buy a little more
grain for us to eat."
3But Judah said to Jacob, "The governor of that
country strongly warned us, 'If you don't bring
your brother back with you, you will not be
allowed to see me.' 4If you will send Benjamin
with us, we will go down and buy food for you.
5But if you refuse to send Benjamin, we will not
go. The governor of that country warned us that
we would not see him if we didn't bring
Benjamin with us."
6Israel said, "Why did you tell the man you had
another brother? You have caused me a lot of
trouble."
7The brothers answered, "He questioned us
carefully about ourselves and our family. He
asked us, 'Is your father still alive? Do you have
another brother?' We just answered his questions. How could we know he would ask us to
bring our other brother to him?"
8Then Judah said to his father Jacob, "Send
Benjamin with me, and we will go at once so that
we, you, and our children may live and not die. 9I
will guarantee you that he will be safe, and I will
be personally responsible for him. If I don't bring
him back to you, you can blame me all my life. 10If
we had not wasted all this time, we could have
already made two trips."
11Then their father Jacob said to them, "If it has
to be that way, then do this: Take some of the
best foods in our land in your packs. Give them to
the man as a gift: some balm, some honey, spices,
myrrh, pistachio nuts, and almonds. 12Take twice
as much money with you this time, and take back
the money that was returned to you in your sacks
last time. Maybe it was a mistake. 13And take
Benjamin with you. Now leave and go to the
man. 14I pray that God Almighty will cause the
governor to be merciful to you and that he will
allow Simeon and Benjamin to come back with
you. If I am robbed of my children, then I am
robbed of them!"
15So the brothers took the gifts. They also took
twice as much money as they had taken the first
time, and they took Benjamin. They hurried
down to Egypt and stood before Joseph.
16When Joseph saw Benjamin with them, he
said to the servant in charge of his house, "Bring
those men into my house. Kill an animal and prepare a meal. Those men will eat with me today at
noon." 17The servant did as Joseph told him and
brought the men to Joseph's house.
18The brothers were afraid when they were
brought to Joseph's house and thought, "We
were brought here because of the money that
was put in our sacks on the first trip. He wants
to attack us, make us slaves, and take our donkeys." 19So the brothers went to the servant in
charge of Joseph's house and spoke to him at
the door of the house. 20They said, "Master,
we came here once before to buy food. 21While
we were going home, we stopped for the night

43:6 *Israel.* Also called Jacob.

and when we opened our sacks each of us found all his money in his sack. We brought that money with us to give it back to you. 22And we have brought more money to pay for the food we want to buy this time. We don't know who put that money in our sacks."

23But the servant answered, "It's all right. Don't be afraid. Your God, the God of your father, must have put the money in your sacks. I got the money you paid me for the grain last time." Then the servant brought Simeon out to them.⚭

24The servant led the men into Joseph's house and gave them water, and they washed their feet. Then he gave their donkeys food to eat. 25The men prepared their gift to give to Joseph when he arrived at noon, because they had heard they were going to eat with him there.

26When Joseph came home, the brothers gave him the gift they had brought into the house and bowed down to the ground in front of him. 27Joseph asked them how they were doing. He said, "How is your aged father you told me about? Is he still alive?"

28The brothers answered, "Your servant, our father, is well. He is still alive." And they bowed low before Joseph to show him respect.

29When Joseph saw his brother Benjamin, who had the same mother as he, Joseph asked, "Is this your youngest brother you told me about?" Then he said to Benjamin, "God be good to you, my son!" 30Then Joseph hurried off because he had to hold back the tears when he saw his brother Benjamin. So Joseph went into his room and cried there. 31Then he washed his face and came out. He controlled himself and said, "Serve the meal."

32So they served Joseph at one table, his brothers at another table, and the Egyptians who ate with him at another table. This was because Egyptians did not like Hebrews and never ate with them. 33Joseph's brothers were seated in front of him in order of their ages, from oldest to youngest. They looked at each other because they were so amazed. 34Food from Joseph's table was taken to them, but Benjamin was given five times more food than the others. Joseph's brothers ate and drank freely with him.

Joseph Sets a Trap

44 Then Joseph gave a command to the servant in charge of his house. He said, "Fill the men's sacks with as much grain as they can carry, and put each man's money into his sack with the grain. 2Put my silver cup in the sack of the youngest brother, along with his money for the grain." The servant did what Joseph told him.

3At dawn the brothers were sent away with their donkeys. 4They were not far from the city when Joseph said to the servant in charge of his house, "Go after the men. When you catch up with them, say, 'Why have you paid back evil for good? 5The cup you have stolen is the one my master uses for drinking and for explaining dreams. You have done a very wicked thing!'"

6So the servant caught up with the brothers and said to them what Joseph had told him to say.

7But the brothers said to the servant, "Why do you say these things? We would not do anything like that! 8We brought back to you from the land of Canaan the money we found in our sacks. So surely we would not steal silver or gold from your master's house. 9If you find that silver cup in the sack of one of us, then let him die, and we will be your slaves."

10The servant said, "We will do as you say, but only the man who has taken the cup will become my slave. The rest of you may go free."

11Then every brother quickly lowered his sack to the ground and opened it. 12The servant searched the sacks, going from the oldest brother to the youngest, and found the cup in Benjamin's sack. 13The brothers tore their clothes to show they were afraid. Then they put their sacks back on the donkeys and returned to the city.

14When Judah and his brothers went back to Joseph's house, Joseph was still there, so the brothers bowed facedown on the ground before him. 15Joseph said to them, "What have you done? Didn't you know that a man like me can learn things by signs and dreams?"

16Judah said, "Master, what can we say? And how can we show we are not guilty? God has uncovered our guilt, so all of us will be your slaves, not just Benjamin."

17But Joseph said, "I will not make you all slaves! Only the man who stole the cup will be my slave. The rest of you may go back safely to your father."

18Then Judah went to Joseph and said, "Master, please let me speak plainly to you, and please don't be angry with me. I know that you are as powerful as the king of Egypt himself. 19When we were here before, you asked us, 'Do you have a father or a brother?' 20And we answered you, 'We have an old father. And we have a younger brother, who was born when our father was old. This youngest son's brother is dead, so he is the only one of his mother's children left alive, and our father loves him very much.' 21Then you said

⚭**43:23 Fear:** Deuteronomy 1:17

to us, 'Bring that brother to me. I want to see him.' 22And we said to you, 'That young boy cannot leave his father, because if he leaves him, his father would die.' 23But you said to us, 'If you don't bring your youngest brother, you will not be allowed to see me again.' 24So we went back to our father and told him what you had said.

25"Later, our father said, 'Go again and buy us a little more food.' 26We said to our father, 'We cannot go without our youngest brother. Without our youngest brother, we will not be allowed to see the governor.' 27Then my father said to us, 'You know that my wife Rachel gave me two sons. 28When one son left me, I thought, "Surely he has been torn apart by a wild animal," and I haven't seen him since. 29Now you want to take this son away from me also. But something terrible might happen to him, and I would be miserable until the day I die.' 30Now what will happen if we go home to our father without our youngest brother? He is so important in our father's life that 31when our father sees the young boy is not with us, he will die. And it will be our fault. We will cause the great sorrow that kills our father.

32"I gave my father a guarantee that the young boy would be safe. I said to my father, 'If I don't bring him back to you, you can blame me all my life.' 33So now, please allow me to stay here and be your slave, and let the young boy go back home with his brothers. 34I cannot go back to my father if the boy is not with me. I couldn't stand to see my father that sad."

Joseph Reveals Who He Is

45 Joseph could not control himself in front of his servants any longer, so he cried out, "Have everyone leave me." When only the brothers were left with Joseph, he told them who he was. 2Joseph cried so loudly that the Egyptians heard him, and the people in the king's palace heard about it. 3He said to his brothers, "I am Joseph. Is my father still alive?" But the brothers could not answer him, because they were very afraid of him.

4So Joseph said to them, "Come close to me." When the brothers came close to him, he said to them, "I am your brother Joseph, whom you sold as a slave to go to Egypt. 5Now don't be worried or angry with yourselves because you sold me here. God sent me here ahead of you to save people's lives. 6No food has grown on the land for two years now, and there will be five more years without planting or harvest. 7So God sent me here ahead of you to make sure you have some descendants left on earth and to keep you alive in an amazing way. 8So it was not you who sent me here, but God. God has made me the highest officer of the king of Egypt. I am in charge of his palace, and I am the master of all the land of Egypt.

9"So leave quickly and go to my father. Tell him, 'Your son Joseph says: God has made me master over all Egypt. Come down to me quickly. 10Live in the land of Goshen where you will be near me. Your children, your grandchildren, your flocks and herds, and all that you have will also be near me. 11I will care for you during the next five years of hunger so that you and your family and all that you have will not starve.'

12"Now you can see for yourselves, and so can my brother Benjamin, that the one speaking to you is really Joseph. 13So tell my father about how powerful I have become in Egypt. Tell him about everything you have seen. Now hurry and bring him back to me." 14Then Joseph hugged his brother Benjamin and cried, and Benjamin cried also. 15And Joseph kissed all his brothers and cried as he hugged them. After this, his brothers talked with him.

16When the king of Egypt and his officers learned that Joseph's brothers had come, they were very happy. 17So the king said to Joseph, "Tell your brothers to load their animals and go back to the land of Canaan 18and bring their father and their families back here to me. I will give them the best land in Egypt, and they will eat the best food we have here. 19Tell them to take some wagons from Egypt for their children and their wives and to bring their father back also. 20Tell them not to worry about bringing any of their things with them, because we will give them the best of what we have in Egypt."

21So the sons of Israel did this. Joseph gave them wagons as the king had ordered and food for their trip. 22He gave each brother a change of clothes, but he gave Benjamin five changes of clothes and about seven and one-half pounds of silver. 23Joseph also sent his father ten donkeys loaded with the best things from Egypt and ten female donkeys loaded with grain, bread, and other food for his father on his trip back. 24Then Joseph told his brothers to go. As they were leaving, he said to them, "Don't quarrel on the way home."

25So the brothers left Egypt and went to their father Jacob in the land of Canaan. 26They told

45:1 Self-Control: Ruth
45:7 The Remnant: 2 Kings 19:4
45:8 Guilt: Hosea 14:1–4

him, "Joseph is still alive and is the ruler over all the land of Egypt." Their father was shocked and did not believe them. 27But when the brothers told him everything Joseph had said, and when Jacob saw the wagons Joseph had sent to carry him back to Egypt, he felt better. 28Israel said, "Now I believe you. My son Joseph is still alive, and I will go and see him before I die."

Jacob Goes to Egypt

46 So Israel took all he had and started his trip. He went to Beersheba, where he offered sacrifices to the God of his father Isaac. 2During the night God spoke to Israel in a vision and said, "Jacob, Jacob."

And Jacob answered, "Here I am."

3Then God said, "I am God, the God of your father. Don't be afraid to go to Egypt, because I will make your descendants a great nation there. 4I will go to Egypt with you, and I will bring you out of Egypt again. Joseph's own hands will close your eyes when you die."

5Then Jacob left Beersheba. The sons of Israel loaded their father, their children, and their wives in the wagons the king of Egypt had sent. 6They also took their farm animals and everything they had gotten in Canaan. So Jacob went to Egypt with all his descendants— 7his sons and grandsons, his daughters and granddaughters. He took all his family to Egypt with him.

Jacob's Family

8Now these are the names of the children of Israel who went into Egypt (Jacob and his descendants).

Reuben was Jacob's first son. 9Reuben's sons were Hanoch, Pallu, Hezron, and Carmi.

10Simeon's sons were Jemuel, Jamin, Ohad, Jakin, Zohar, and Shaul (Simeon's son by a Canaanite woman).

11Levi's sons were Gershon, Kohath, and Merari.

12Judah's sons were Er, Onan, Shelah, Perez, and Zerah (but Er and Onan had died in the land of Canaan). Perez's sons were Hezron and Hamul.

13Issachar's sons were Tola, Puah, Jashub, and Shimron.

14Zebulun's sons were Sered, Elon, and Jahleel.

15These are the sons of Leah and Jacob born in Northwest Mesopotamia, in addition to his daughter Dinah. There were thirty-three persons in this part of Jacob's family.

16Gad's sons were Zephon, Haggi, Shuni, Ezbon, Eri, Arodi, and Areli.

17Asher's sons were Imnah, Ishvah, Ishvi, and Beriah, and their sister was Serah. Beriah's sons were Heber and Malkiel.

18These are Jacob's sons by Zilpah, the slave girl whom Laban gave to his daughter Leah. There were sixteen persons in this part of Jacob's family.

19The sons of Jacob's wife Rachel were Joseph and Benjamin. 20In Egypt, Joseph became the father of Manasseh and Ephraim by his wife Asenath, the daughter of Potiphera, priest of On.

21Benjamin's sons were Bela, Beker, Ashbel, Gera, Naaman, Ehi, Rosh, Muppim, Huppim, and Ard.

22These are the sons of Jacob by his wife Rachel. There were fourteen persons in this part of Jacob's family.

23Dan's son was Hushim.

24Naphtali's sons were Jahziel, Guni, Jezer, and Shillem.

25These are Jacob's sons by Bilhah, the slave girl whom Laban gave to his daughter Rachel. There were seven persons in this part of Jacob's family.

26So the total number of Jacob's direct descendants who went to Egypt was sixty-six, not counting the wives of Jacob's sons. 27Joseph had two sons born in Egypt, so the total number in the family of Jacob in Egypt was seventy.

Jacob Arrives in Egypt

28Jacob sent Judah ahead of him to see Joseph in Goshen. When Jacob and his people came into the land of Goshen, 29Joseph prepared his chariot and went to meet his father Israel in Goshen. As soon as Joseph saw his father, he hugged him, and cried there for a long time.

30Then Israel said to Joseph, "Now I am ready to die, because I have seen your face and I know you are still alive."

31Joseph said to his brothers and his father's family, "I will go and tell the king you are here. I will say, 'My brothers and my father's family have left the land of Canaan and have come here to me. 32They are shepherds and take care of farm animals, and they have brought their flocks and their herds and everything they own with them.' 33When the king calls you, he will ask, 'What work do you do?' 34This is what you should tell him: 'We, your servants, have taken care of farm animals all our lives. Our ancestors did the same thing.' Then the king will allow you to settle in the land of Goshen, away from the Egyptians, because they don't like to be near shepherds."

45:28 *Israel.* Also called Jacob.
46:1 *Israel.* See note at 45:28.

46:2 Vision: Nehemiah 2:17–18
46:27 Genealogy: Numbers 26

Jacob Settles in Goshen

47 Joseph went in to the king and said, "My father and my brothers have arrived from Canaan with their flocks and herds and everything they own. They are now in the land of Goshen." [2]Joseph chose five of his brothers to introduce to the king.

[3]The king said to the brothers, "What work do you do?"

And they said to him, "We, your servants, are shepherds, just as our ancestors were." [4]They said to the king, "We have come to live in this land, because there is no grass in the land of Canaan for our animals to eat, and the hunger is terrible there. So please allow us to live in the land of Goshen."

[5]Then the king said to Joseph, "Your father and your brothers have come to you, [6]and you may choose any place in Egypt for them to live. Give your father and your brothers the best land; let them live in the land of Goshen. And if any of them are skilled shepherds, put them in charge of my sheep and cattle."

[7]Then Joseph brought in his father Jacob and introduced him to the king, and Jacob blessed the king.

[8]Then the king said to Jacob, "How old are you?"

[9]Jacob said to him, "My life has been spent wandering from place to place. It has been short and filled with trouble—only one hundred thirty years. My ancestors lived much longer than I." [10]Then Jacob blessed the king and left.

[11]Joseph obeyed the king and gave his father and brothers the best land in Egypt, near the city of Rameses. [12]And Joseph gave his father, his brothers, and everyone who lived with them the food they needed.

Joseph Buys Land for the King

[13]The hunger became worse, and since there was no food anywhere in the land, Egypt and Canaan became very poor. [14]Joseph collected all the money that was to be found in Egypt and Canaan. People paid for the grain they were buying, and he brought that money to the king's palace. [15]After some time, when the people in Egypt and Canaan had no money left, they went to Joseph and said, "Please give us food. Our money is gone, and if we don't eat, we will die here in front of you."

[16]Joseph answered, "Since you have no money, give me your farm animals, and I will give you food in return." [17]So people brought their farm animals to Joseph, and he gave them food in exchange for their horses, sheep, goats, cattle, and donkeys. And he kept them alive by trading food for their farm animals that year.

[18]The next year the people came to Joseph and said, "You know we have no money left, and all our animals belong to you. We have nothing left except our bodies and our land. [19]Surely both we and our land will die here in front of you. Buy us and our land in exchange for food, and we will be slaves to the king, together with our land. Give us seed to plant so that we will live and not die, and the land will not become a desert."

[20]So Joseph bought all the land in Egypt for the king. Every Egyptian sold Joseph his field, because the hunger was very great. So the land became the king's, [21]and Joseph made the people slaves from one end of Egypt to the other. [22]The only land he did not buy was the land the priests owned. They did not need to sell their land because the king paid them for their work. So they had money to buy food.

[23]Joseph said to the people, "Now I have bought you and your land for the king, so I will give you seed and you can plant your fields. [24]At harvest time you must give one-fifth to the king. You may keep four-fifths for yourselves to use as seed for the field and as food for yourselves, your families, and your children."

[25]The people said, "You have saved our lives. If you like, we will become slaves of the king."

[26]So Joseph made a law in Egypt, which continues today: One-fifth of everything from the land belongs to the king. The only land the king did not get was the priests' land.

"Don't Bury Me in Egypt"

[27]The Israelites continued to live in the land of Goshen in Egypt. There they got possessions and had many children and grew in number.

[28]Jacob lived in Egypt seventeen years, so he lived to be one hundred forty-seven years old. [29]When Israel knew he soon would die, he called his son Joseph to him and said to him, "If you love me, put your hand under my leg. Promise me you will not bury me in Egypt. [30]When I die, carry me out of Egypt, and bury me where my ancestors are buried."

Joseph answered, "I will do as you say."

[31]Then Jacob said, "Promise me." And Joseph promised him that he would do this. Then Israel worshiped as he leaned on the top of his walking stick.

47:28 *Jacob.* Also called Israel.

47:29 *put . . . leg.* This showed that a person would keep a promise.

Conflict

Genesis 3

What is conflict? How is conflict resolved? Is all conflict bad?

Conflict on the human level began when Adam and Eve disobeyed God (Genesis 3). The effects of their disobedience were tragic and long-lasting. The harmony of God's good creation was destroyed. Human relationships became broken. Fellowship with God was replaced by hiding from God (verse 10). The first human couple experienced conflict as Adam blamed Eve for what happened (verses 7, 12). The marriage relationship became a battleground (verse 16).

The relationship of the human couple to creation was also destroyed because God's curse on the ground meant humans would have to work hard for their food (verses 17–19). Childbirth became painful (verse 16). Death became a reality (verse 19). Conflict was also promised between the descendants of the woman and the descendants of the snake, who had encouraged Eve to disobey God (verse 15). This promise became the basis for how conflict would eventually be resolved.

It does not matter if conflict is between individuals or nations, the source of conflict resides inside of people. Jesus said that evil thoughts, murder, greed, evil actions, and pride begin in the mind (Mark 7:20–22). James 4 states that fights and arguments come from selfish desires within us. We want things, but we do not have them, so we are jealous of other people and are ready to kill (verses 1–3). Basically such activity is against God. Galatians 5 teaches that the sinful self, which does wrong things like hating, making trouble, being selfish, and causing divisions among people (verse 20), is against the Holy Spirit. Those who do such things will not inherit God's kingdom (verse 21).

Only God can provide a solution for the source of conflict inside a person. Jesus calls certain religious leaders of his day hypocrites because they look good on the outside but the inside is rotten (Matthew 23:25–28). He tells them to clean the inside and then the outside will also be clean. Such radical, internal cleansing comes when a person believes that Jesus died on the cross for their sins. The blood of Jesus takes away our sin (Hebrews 9:26), cleanses us (1 John 1:9), and purifies our consciences (Hebrews 9:14).

This internal cleansing heals our broken relationships. We were once enemies of God, but now we are God's friends through the death of Jesus (Romans 5:10). The divisions caused by our selfishness are replaced by the fruit of the Spirit, which includes love, peace, patience, and self-control (Galatians 5:22–23). Hatred between various groups of people now has a basis for being taken away. The major division between Jewish people and those who were not Jews is destroyed. Christ is "our peace," and he has broken down the wall of hate (Ephesians 2:12–14). We have been sent by God to proclaim this peace (2 Corinthians 5:18–21). The power of the gospel is very evident when people who once hated each other now love each other. Many places in the world need this message that can take away conflict.

Conflict continues to be a part of the experience of the Christian because we are in a spiritual fight. Ephesians 6 tells us to put on the "full armor of God" so that we can "fight against the devil's evil tricks." Jesus warned his followers that the world would hate them just as it hated him (John 15:18–19). We also experience conflict within ourselves as our sinful selves war against the Holy Spirit (Galatians 5:17).

Christians must be on guard that they do not lose this battle. When problems arise that destroy the peace that Christ has won, steps need to be taken to restore it. If someone does something wrong, they should gently be helped to make it right again (Galatians 6:1). Matthew 18:15–17 lays out the proper steps that should be taken when someone sins against you. It is important to keep the matter private at first, only bringing in witnesses as a second step if the conflict cannot be solved. The purpose of all of this is to help that person be your brother or sister again. Only if the person refuses to listen should the matter be taken further (see also 1 Corinthians 5:1–5).

Confession and forgiveness are the steps to remove conflict. If we confess our sins to God he will forgive them (1 John 1:9). Once we have experienced God's forgiveness we should be ready to forgive others who ask to be forgiven (Matthew 18:35).

Conflict will not be completely removed until Jesus comes again. At that point our relationship with God, other people, and all creation will experience the fullness of peace (Romans 8:18–25; Revelation 21:1–4). The conflict we have experienced will fade into insignificance in the presence of Jesus.

Conflict: For additional scriptures on this topic go to Proverbs 27:7.

THE FALL

GENESIS 3

What is meant by "the Fall"? What is the significance of the Fall for Adam and Eve? For Creation? For people today? What impact does the work of Jesus Christ have on the consequences of the Fall?

The term *Fall* sometimes used to describe the first sin. This first sin occurred when Adam and Eve were deceived by the serpent's craftiness into disobeying God's command not to eat the fruit of the tree which gave knowledge of good and evil (Genesis 2:16–17). For the first human pair, the consequences of their disobedience were disastrous. The woman would have trouble and pain in pregnancy and childbirth. She was also placed in a subordinate role to her husband, who would experience hardship, being able to obtain his food from the ground only through hard labor. God had earlier warned the couple that they would experience death if they ate from the forbidden tree, and this death was now realized. Adam and Eve were banished from the Garden of Eden to prevent them from eating from the tree of life. Where no thought or expectation of death had existed for people before, it was now a certain eventual reality for all.

The sin of Adam and Eve not only introduced physical difficulty and death, but also introduced spiritual death, or separation between humanity and God. Adam's sin merited a guilt that both he and all of the following generations that he then represented would have to bear. As a result, everyone born after Adam already carries the guilt of sin and so is separated from any fellowship with God (Romans 5:12–14).

The first sin not only affected humanity as a whole, however, but also affected every person individually. The introduction of sin into God's perfect creation where it had not existed before produced the corruption of death and ruin that penetrates even into our human nature. Sin has so contaminated our natural selves that we are born with an inability to live the kind of life that pleases God and results in fellowship with him (Romans 8:7). Instead, we are controlled by sin, like slaves (Romans 6:17). The sin of Adam and Eve has caused us "to fall" from the lofty position of favor and fellowship with God that humanity once enjoyed to the desperately sinful condition in which we now find ourselves.

It is also important to note that the Fall affected us as whole people. It is not as if only one aspect of our personality is distorted by sin, but every aspect of our being. That means that our intellect, emotions, imagination, desires, will, and body have all experienced the ravages of the first sin.

Left to its own resources, humanity would have no hope of a restored relationship with God (Romans 5:6). God's eyes are too pure to look at evil (Habakkuk 1:13). The inevitable result of sin's presence in us, therefore, would be to separate us from God. But God has provided a remedy for the effects of the Fall upon creation and upon us through Jesus Christ. Jesus led a perfect life in complete obedience to the Father, and so merited none of the guilt that is caused by committing sin. He can therefore pay the penalty for the guilt of sin that we bear so that we can be restored to friendship and fellowship with God (2 Corinthians 5:21). Also, just as the guilt of Adam's sin is attributed to all the following generations of humanity that he represented, Jesus' guiltlessness, or righteousness, is attributed to all those who by faith claim him as their representative. In this way, Jesus is like Adam in that the consequences of his actions are applied to others (Romans 5:18–19) so that "those who are in Christ Jesus are not judged guilty" (Romans 8:1; 2 Corinthians 5:19). In addition, those who trust in Christ have been recreated (2 Corinthians 5:17) as new spiritual persons who are given the Holy Spirit to empower them to live a life pleasing to God (Romans 8:1–17).

This restoration of fellowship between believers and God undoes a major effect of sin's presence in the world. The gift of the Holy Spirit is a guarantee that God will ultimately undo all of sin's effects upon believers (Ephesians 1:14). Even the physical death and decay that believers' bodies experience as a result of the Fall will no longer take place when they receive new, glorious bodies at Christ's return (1 Corinthians 15:35–58). All of creation looks forward to the day when it, too, will be released from sin's corrupting effects to enjoy the same freedom and glory that God's children now enjoy in part (Romans 8:19–23). This total removal of the effects of the Fall upon the world and upon believers is discussed in the Book of Revelation and described as taking place in the new Jerusalem, where "there will be no more death, sadness, crying, or pain, because all the old ways are gone." In their place will be only joyful, intimate friendship with our glorious God (Revelation 21).

The Fall: For additional scriptures on this topic go to Romans 6:17.

Blessings for Manasseh and Ephraim

48 Some time later Joseph learned that his
father was very sick, so he took his two
sons Manasseh and Ephraim and went to his
father. 2When Joseph arrived, someone told
Jacob, "Your son Joseph has come to see you."
Jacob was weak, so he used all his strength and
sat up on his bed.

3Then Jacob said to Joseph, "God Almighty
appeared to me at Luz in the land of Canaan and
blessed me there. 4He said to me, 'I will give you
many children. I will make you the father of many
peoples, and I will give your descendants this land
forever.' 5Your two sons, who were born here in
Egypt before I came, will be counted as my own
sons. Ephraim and Manasseh will be my sons just
as Reuben and Simeon are my sons. 6But if you
have other children, they will be your own, and
their land will be part of the land given to Ephraim
and Manasseh. 7When I came from Northwest
Mesopotamia, Rachel died in the land of Canaan,
as we were traveling toward Ephrath. This made
me very sad, and I buried her there beside the
road to Ephrath." (Today Ephrath is Bethlehem.)

8Then Israel saw Joseph's sons and said, "Who
are these boys?"

9Joseph said to his father, "They are my sons
that God has given me here in Egypt."

Israel said, "Bring your sons to me so I may
bless them."

10At this time Israel's eyesight was bad because
he was old. So Joseph brought the boys close to
him, and Israel kissed the boys and put his arms
around them. 11He said to Joseph, "I thought I
would never see you alive again, and now God
has let me see you and also your children."
12Then Joseph moved his sons off Israel's lap and
bowed facedown to the ground. 13He put Ephraim
on his right side and Manasseh on his left. (So
Ephraim was near Israel's left hand, and Manasseh
was near Israel's right hand.) Joseph brought the
boys close to Israel. 14But Israel crossed his arms
and put his right hand on the head of Ephraim,
who was younger. He put his left hand on the
head of Manasseh, the firstborn son. 15And Israel
blessed Joseph and said,

"My ancestors Abraham and Isaac served
our God,
and like a shepherd God has led me
all my life.
16He was the Angel who saved me from
all my troubles.
Now I pray that he will bless these boys.
May my name be known through these boys,
and may the names of my ancestors Abraham
and Isaac be known through them.
May they have many descendants
on the earth."

17When Joseph saw that his father put his right
hand on Ephraim's head, he didn't like it. So he
took hold of his father's hand, wanting to move it
from Ephraim's head to Manasseh's head.
18Joseph said to his father, "You are doing it
wrong, Father. Manasseh is the firstborn son. Put
your right hand on his head."

19But his father refused and said, "I know, my
son, I know. Manasseh will be great and have
many descendants. But his younger brother will
be greater, and his descendants will be enough to
make a nation."

20So Israel blessed them that day and said,
"When a blessing is given in Israel,
they will say:
'May God make you like Ephraim
and Manasseh.'"
In this way he made Ephraim greater than
Manasseh.

21Then Israel said to Joseph, "Look at me; I am
about to die. But God will be with you and will
take you back to the land of your fathers. 22I have
given you something that I did not give your
brothers—the land of Shechem that I took from
the Amorite people with my sword and my bow."

Jacob Blesses His Sons

49 Then Jacob called his sons to him. He
said, "Come here to me, and I will tell you
what will happen to you in the future.

2"Come together and listen, sons of Jacob.
Listen to Israel, your father."

3"Reuben, my first son, you are my strength.
Your birth showed I could be a father.
You have the highest position among my sons,
and you are the most powerful.
4But you are uncontrolled like water,
so you will no longer lead your brothers.
This is because you got into your father's bed
and shamed me by having sexual relations
with my slave girl.

5"Simeon and Levi are brothers
who used their swords to do violence.
6I will not join their secret talks,
and I will not meet with them to plan evil.

48:2 *Jacob.* Also called Israel.

They killed men because they were angry,
and they crippled oxen just for fun.
7May their anger be cursed, because it is
too violent.
May their violence be cursed, because it is
too cruel.
I will divide them up among the tribes of Jacob
and scatter them through all the tribes
of Israel.

8"Judah, your brothers will praise you.
You will grab your enemies by the neck,
and your brothers will bow down to you.
9Judah is like a young lion.
You have returned from killing, my son.
Like a lion, he stretches out and lies down
to rest,
and no one is brave enough to wake him.
10Kings will come from Judah's family;
someone from Judah will always be
on the throne.
Judah will rule until Shiloh comes,
and the nations will obey him.
11He ties his donkey to a grapevine,
his young donkey to the best branch.
He can afford to use wine to wash his clothes
and the best wine to wash his robes.
12His eyes are dark like the color of wine,
and his teeth are as white as the color of milk.

13"Zebulun will live near the sea.
His shore will be a safe place for ships,
and his land will reach as far as Sidon.

14"Issachar is like a strong donkey
who lies down while carrying his load.
15When he sees his resting place is good
and how pleasant his land is,
he will put his back to the load
and become a slave.

16"Dan will rule his own people
like the other tribes in Israel.
17Dan will be like a snake by the side of the road,
a dangerous snake lying near the path.
That snake bites a horse's leg,
and the rider is thrown off backward.

18"LORD, I wait for your salvation.

19"Robbers will attack Gad,
but he will defeat them and drive them away.

20"Asher's land will grow much good food;
he will grow food fit for a king.

21"Naphtali is like a female deer that runs free,
that has beautiful fawns.

22"Joseph is like a grapevine that produces
much fruit,
a healthy vine watered by a spring,
whose branches grow over the wall.
23Archers attack him violently
and shoot at him angrily,
24but he aims his bow well.
His arms are made strong.
He gets his power from the Mighty God
of Jacob
and his strength from the Shepherd,
the Rock of Israel.
25Your father's God helps you.
God Almighty blesses you.
He blesses you with rain from above,
with water from springs below,
with many babies born to your wives,
and many young ones born to your animals.
26The blessings of your father are greater
than the blessings of the oldest mountains,
greater than the good things of the
long-lasting hills.
May these blessings rest on the head of Joseph,
on the forehead of the one who was
separated from his brothers.

27"Benjamin is like a hungry wolf.
In the morning he eats what he has caught,
and in the evening he divides what he
has taken."⚭

28These are the twelve tribes of Israel, and this
is what their father said to them. He gave each
son the blessing that was right for him. 29Then
Israel gave them a command and said, "I am
about to die. Bury me with my ancestors in the

49:7 *I will scatter them.* Because of the sin that they committed in Genesis 34, Jacob pronounces a curse on Levi and Simeon. It is interesting to chart the future of these two tribes. Simeon entered the land, did not get a separate place to settle, and was soon absorbed into the tribe of Judah. Levi also did not get a separate settlement but became the priestly tribe which lived throughout the land and earned a distinctive reputation. The reason for the difference is given in Exodus 32 where Levi stood up for the Lord against the rebellion of the other tribes.
49:10 This verse may well be a messianic prophecy pointing to the fact that the kingly messiah will come from the tribe of Judah.
⚭**49:27 Prophetic Symbolism:** Numbers 12:6-8
49:28 Jacob's blessing of his sons is a model of what every parent can do for his or her children. Arrange an evening of blessing for your children, perhaps a special meal with some of each child's favorites! Write out a few short sentences for you to read that express your love and appreciation for your child(ren). This would be a good time to lay your hand on the child's shoulder or head while you bless him or her. Individualize your blessing as Jacob did his.

cave in the field of Ephron the Hittite. 30That cave
is in the field of Machpelah east of Mamre in the
land of Canaan. Abraham bought the field and
cave from Ephron the Hittite for a burying place.
31Abraham and Sarah his wife are buried there.
Isaac and Rebekah his wife are buried there, and
I buried my wife Leah there. 32The field and the
cave in it were bought from the Hittite people."
33After Jacob finished talking to his sons, he lay
down. He put his feet back on the bed, took his
last breath, and died.

Jacob's Burial

50 When Jacob died, Joseph hugged his
father and cried over him and kissed him.
2He commanded the doctors who served him to
prepare his father's body, so the doctors prepared
Jacob's body to be buried. 3It took the doctors forty
days to prepare his body (the usual time it took).
And the Egyptians had a time of sorrow for Jacob
that lasted seventy days.

4When this time of sorrow had ended, Joseph
spoke to the king's officers and said, "If you think
well of me, please tell this to the king: 5'When my
father was near death, I made a promise to him
that I would bury him in a cave in the land of
Canaan, in a burial place that he cut out for himself. So please let me go and bury my father, and
then I will return.'"

6The king answered, "Keep your promise. Go
and bury your father."

7So Joseph went to bury his father. All the
king's officers, the older leaders, and all the leading men of Egypt went with Joseph. 8Everyone
who lived with Joseph and his brothers went
with him, as well as everyone who lived with his
father. They left only their children, their flocks,
and their herds in the land of Goshen. 9They
went with Joseph in chariots and on horses. It
was a very large group.

10When they came to the threshing floor of
Atad, near the Jordan River, they cried loudly and
bitterly for his father. Joseph's time of sorrow
continued for seven days. 11The people that lived
in Canaan saw the sadness at the threshing floor
of Atad and said, "Those Egyptians are showing
great sorrow!" So now that place is named Sorrow
of the Egyptians.

12So Jacob's sons did as their father commanded.
13They carried his body to the land of Canaan and
buried it in the cave in the field of Machpelah near
Mamre. Abraham had bought this cave and field
from Ephron the Hittite to use as a burial place.
14After Joseph buried his father, he returned to
Egypt, along with his brothers and everyone who
had gone with him to bury his father.

The Brothers Fear Joseph

15After Jacob died, Joseph's brothers said,
"What if Joseph is still angry with us? We did
many wrong things to him. What if he plans to
pay us back?" 16So they sent a message to Joseph
that said, "Your father gave this command before
he died. 17He said to us, 'You have done wrong and
have sinned and done evil to Joseph. Tell Joseph to
forgive you, his brothers.' So now, Joseph, we beg
you to forgive our wrong. We are the servants of
the God of your father." When Joseph received
the message, he cried.

18And his brothers went to him and bowed low
before him and said, "We are your slaves."

19Then Joseph said to them, "Don't be afraid.
Can I do what only God can do? 20You meant to
hurt me, but God turned your evil into good to
save the lives of many people, which is being
done. 21So don't be afraid. I will take care of
you and your children." So Joseph comforted his
brothers and spoke kind words to them.

22Joseph continued to live in Egypt with all his
father's family. He died when he was one hundred ten years old. 23During Joseph's life Ephraim
had children and grandchildren, and Joseph's son
Manasseh had a son named Makir. Joseph
accepted Makir's children as his own.

The Death of Joseph

24Joseph said to his brothers, "I am about to
die, but God will take care of you. He will lead
you out of this land to the land he promised to
Abraham, Isaac, and Jacob." 25Then Joseph had
the sons of Israel make a promise. He said,
"Promise me that you will carry my bones with
you out of Egypt."

26Joseph died when he was one hundred ten
years old. Doctors prepared his body for burial,
and then they put him in a coffin in Egypt.

50:20 Encouragement: Ecclesiastes 9:10

50:20 Evil: Job 1:6–12

50:20 Joseph recognizes that his brothers and others wanted to hurt him, but he also realizes that God used these very actions to save God's chosen family from death during the famine. God often chooses to bring about salvation by overruling the evil intentions of human beings (see Acts 2:22–24).

50:26 Joseph: Acts 7:9–10

Notes:

INTRODUCTION TO THE BOOK OF

EXODUS

Escape from Egypt

WHO WROTE THIS BOOK?

Both Jewish and Christian traditions hold that Moses was the author of the Pentateuch (also called the Torah), which is the first five books of the Bible, including Exodus.

TO WHOM WAS THIS BOOK WRITTEN?

The Exodus of Israel from Egypt was recorded for Israel. It was also recorded to show God's people of all ages how he rescues and reveals himself to his own.

WHERE WAS IT WRITTEN?

This book was probably written in the desert area where the people of Israel wandered for forty years, led by Moses.

WHEN WAS IT WRITTEN?

Exodus was most likely written between 1446 and 1406 B.C., during Israel's desert wanderings.

WHAT IS THE BOOK ABOUT?

The Book of Exodus continues the story of God's people, which began in Genesis. In this book of their history, God delivered Israel out of captivity in Egypt and took care of them in the years to follow as they wandered in the desert on their way to the land he had promised them. It also tells how God gave his people the Ten Commandments (chapter 20) and established a Meeting Tent (33:7) where he would meet with Moses, Aaron, and other leaders of the nation. The Holy Tent was where the glory of God's presence could be seen in the form of a cloud that covered the Tent (40:34).

WHY WAS THIS BOOK WRITTEN?

Exodus is a great description of God in his many facets: his name, his characteristics, his law, his power, and his desire to be loved, worshipped, and obeyed. Moses wrote this account so that Israel would always remember to follow God. Exodus 15:11 reveals the God of Israel through the eyes of his mighty servant, Moses: "There are no gods like you. You are wonderfully holy, amazingly powerful, a worker of miracles."

SO WHAT DOES THIS BOOK MEAN TO US?

The all-powerful God of Israel is the same today as he was in the days of Moses. He is our mighty God, who loves and cares for us. As he did with his people of Israel, he will instruct and lead us through the deserts of life and protect us until we reach the land he has promised us—heaven. Nothing about God has changed. He remains "wonderfully holy, amazingly powerful, a worker of miracles" (15:11).

SUMMARY:

The Book of Exodus contains some of the most exciting material in the Old Terstament. It begins with the action-packed story of God's freeing the enslaved Israelites from their Egyptian oppressors and starting them off on what turns out to be a forty-year journey to their new home in Palestine. God delivers them from Egypt because he promised their ancestor Abraham (Genesis 12) by a special agreement that they would be his people, and he would take care of them.

The book continues with the awesome appearance of God on Mount Sinai where he presents the Ten Commandments and other related laws to his people, instructing them as to how they are to act if they are to be his people.

The book then concludes with God's command to build the Holy Tent (sometimes called the Tabernacle), which serves as a symbol of his presence with his people while they wander through the desert. The Holy Tent communicates God's message "I am with you" to his hurting people. And indeed this is the overall message of the Book of Exodus—God is present with his people. He will take care of them and lead them in the right direction, if they follow him. The story of the people's worship of the golden calf (Exodus 32–33) indicates that life will be a struggle for God's people, because of their tendency to turn away from the true God and worship gods of their own making.

The Book of Exodus continues the story of the Book of Genesis, though there is a gap of considerable time bertween the end of Genesis and the beginning of Exodus. When Genesis ended, the people of God were a large family, enjoying a good relationship with the Egyptian authorities. Times have changed by the beginning of Exodus. Israel is now a large group of people, and when they leave Egypt, they take on the status of a nation. And, though they are still in Egypt at the beginning of the book, they have been made slaves and do hard labor for their owners.

Moses is the major figure in the book. God uses him to lead his people out of Egypt. God gives his law to his people through Moses, and he tells Moses how his Holy Tent should be constructed.

Though Moses is the major figure of the book, God is at the center of the book. He shows himself to be a great warrior who fights for his people against those who would make them slaves (Exodus 15:3). He is the lawgiver, who guides his people. And he dwells with his people in the form of a cloud, which fills the Most Holy Place of the Holy Tent (40:34–38).

Exodus is the story of God's dramatic rescue of Israel when they were in deep trouble. As such, it is later remembered as a sign that God can save anyone from their problems, no matter how difficult (Psalm 77). It also is a beacon of hope for Israel later in its history when they once again are dominated by a great pagan nation, Babylon (Isaiah 40:3–5; Hosea 2:14–21).

In this way, the Exodus is a pattern for later deliverances. It is, therefore, not surprising that Jesus' life follows the pattern of the Exodus. For instance, he wanders for forty days in the wilderness, struggling with the same temptations as did the Israelites (Matthew 4:1–11). He delivers the law from a mountain (Matthew 5–11). He dies during the week of Passover, the festival of the Exodus, becoming our Passover Lamb. In this way, he shows that he is the fulfillment of the Exodus. He is the one who provides ultimate salvation for his people who have been made slaves, not by a pagan nation, but by Satan.

The deliverance from Egypt, the Law, and the Holy Tent are the three major topics found in this book, and an outline of the book show this:

I. God Saves Israel from Egyptian Slavery (1:1–18:27)
II. God Gives Israel his Law (19:1–24:18)
III. God Commands Israel to Build the Holy Tent (25:1–40:38)

I. God Saves Israel from Egyptian Slavery (1:1–18:27)

Centuries had passed since the end of Genesis. God's people were now a large group, not a family, and instead of being respected in Egypt, they were feared and hated. As a result, the king of Egypt forced the Israelites to work as slaves.

God, though, raised up Moses to save his people from their slavery. He miraculously saved Moses at birth. Later God revealed himself to Moses in order to commission him for the task to come.

Moses, who was raised in Egypt, returns there to confront the Egyptian king and demand the release of his people. The king resists, and God brings a series of plagues on the Egyptians. Finally, the king frees them, but as the trip begins to the Promised Land, the king changes his mind and attacks the Israelites by the Red Sea. With the sea in front and the Egyptian army attacking them from behind, it looks like Israel's fate is sealed. God saves them by the miracle of splitting the sea, allowing them to pass safely to the other side. When the Egyptians try to follow them, God causes the sea to drown them.

Once they cross the Red Sea, the Israelites begin their journey to the Promised Land. Right from the start we see that Israel has very little trust in God. They grumble about water and food.

II. God Gives Israel His Law (19:1–24:18)

After three months the Israelites arrive at Mount Sinai, an imposing mountain in the rugged Desert of Sinai. God reveals himself to his people there in the form of smoke and fire from the top of the mountain. The people found the experience frightening and so asked Moses to talk to God for them. Moses is the first of many prophets who speak to God for the people and speak to the people for God.

God gives his people the Law on Mount Sinai. The Law tells the people how God wants them to behave. It is important to notice that God does not use the Law as a way to enter into a relationship with him. The people of Israel were already his people, but the Law allows them to thank God by their actions. Of course, if they do not keep the Law, then it shows that they really don't love him, and God will break off the relationship.

The Law begins with the Ten Commandments. These are general principles. A whole series of more detailed laws follow the Ten Commandments and are applications of the Ten Commandments to the people of God at that time.

All of this is part of an agreement between God and Israel for which Moses is the messenger. It builds on the previous agreement with Abraham (Genesis 12, 15, and 17).

III. God Commands Israel to Build the Holy Tent (25:1–40:38)

The remainder of the Book of Exodus has to do with worship during the desert wanderings. In the first part (25:1–31:18), God instructs Moses in how to build his place of worship, the Holy Tent. The materials and pattern of the Holy Tent all point to one important truth: a holy God is present in the community.

But while Moses has been up on Mount Sinai, the people of Israel did a horrible thing; they worshiped a golden calf (32:1–33:17). God punishes Israel severly, but thanks to Moses' prayer, he allows them to continue on their way to the Promised Land.

The final few chapters of the Book of Exodus (33:18–40:38) describe the actual construction of the Holy Tent, and the book concludes with a description of God's coming to dwell in the Tent.

EXODUS

Jacob's Family Grows Strong

When Jacob went to Egypt, he took his sons,
and each son took his own family with him.
These are the names of the sons of Israel:
2Reuben, Simeon, Levi, Judah, 3Issachar, Zebulun,
Benjamin, 4Dan, Naphtali, Gad, and Asher. 5There
was a total of seventy people who were descendants
of Jacob. Jacob's son Joseph was already in Egypt.
6Some time later, Joseph and his brothers died,
along with all the people who had lived at that
same time. 7But the people of Israel had many
children, and their number grew greatly. They
became very strong, and the country of Egypt was
filled with them.

Trouble for the People of Israel

8Then a new king began to rule Egypt, who did
not know who Joseph was. 9This king said to his
people, "Look! The people of Israel are too many
and too strong for us to handle! 10If we don't make
plans against them, the number of their people will
grow even more. Then if there is a war, they might
join our enemies and fight us and escape from the
country!"
11So the Egyptians made life hard for the Israelites. They put slave masters over them, who forced
the Israelites to build the cities Pithom and
Rameses as supply centers for the king. 12But the
harder the Egyptians forced the Israelites to work,
the more the Israelites grew in number and
spread out. So the Egyptians became very afraid of
them 13and demanded even more of them. 14They
made their lives bitter. They forced the Israelites
to work hard to make bricks and mortar and to do
all kinds of work in the fields. The Egyptians were
not merciful to them in all their painful work.
15Two Hebrew nurses, named Shiphrah and
Puah, helped the Israelite women give birth to their
babies. The king of Egypt said to the nurses,
16"When you are helping the Hebrew women give
birth to their babies, watch! If the baby is a girl, let
her live, but if it is a boy, kill him!" 17But the nurses
feared God, so they did not do as the king told
them; they let all the boy babies live. 18Then the
king of Egypt sent for the nurses and said, "Why did
you do this? Why did you let the boys live?"

Picture writing (called cuneiform) was invented in Babylonia between 3500 and 3000 B.C. This is a Sumerian stone.

19The nurses said to him, "The Hebrew women
are much stronger than the Egyptian women. They
give birth to their babies before we can get there."
20God was good to the nurses. And the Hebrew
people continued to grow in number, so they
became even stronger. 21Because the nurses
feared God, he gave them families of their own.
22So the king commanded all his people, "Every
time a boy is born to the Hebrews, you must throw
him into the Nile River, but let all the girl babies
live."

Baby Moses

2 Now a man from the family of Levi married a
woman who was also from the family of Levi.
2She became pregnant and gave birth to a son.
When she saw how wonderful the baby was, she
hid him for three months. 3But after three
months she was not able to hide the baby any
longer, so she got a basket made of reeds and covered it with tar so that it would float. She put the
baby in the basket. Then she put the basket
among the tall stalks of grass at the edge of the
Nile River. 4The baby's sister stood a short distance away to see what would happen to him.
5Then the daughter of the king of Egypt came
to the river to take a bath, and her servant girls
were walking beside the river. When she saw

1:1 *Jacob.* Also called Israel.
1:7 Creation/New Creation: Romans 5:15–21
1:14 Racism: Exodus 12:48–49
1:18 Persecution: Daniel 6
2:3 Apart from the Flood story (Genesis 6–9), this is the only mention of an ark in the Old Testament. The picture the Bible seems to be presenting is that Moses' deliverance from the waters of the Nile by an ark is similar to Noah's deliverance from the Flood. Moses' deliverance, as well as the Israelites' deliverance from the waters of the Red Sea (Exodus 14), are both examples of God's punishment of sin and the deliverance of his people.

WORK

2 THESSALONIANS 3:6

Was work a part of God's design for creation, or is it the result of the Fall? What did Jesus say about work? Is there a difference between ordinary and spiritual work?

Productive work is a gift of the Creator who found joy and delight in the work of creation. And he set apart a special day of rest for the human family (Genesis 2:2–3). Sometimes work is tiresome and disliked, and we are tempted to see it as a burden that results from sin in the world (Genesis 3:17–19). The creation account makes it clear, however, that although the tough side of work comes from the Fall, the goodness of created work was a part of God's plan for men and women. So we read, "The LORD God put the man in the garden of Eden to care for it and work it" (Genesis 2:15). The Creator's plan was that we should find useful work for our hands, and so the Bible makes almost 600 references to work.

In Ecclesiastes 5:18 we find a positive statement about the goodness of work: "I have seen what is best for people here on earth. They should eat and drink and enjoy their work." This upbeat sentence shows an understanding of the goodness of work as a part of the plan of creation. Remarks elsewhere in the book appear to go against this, but this is just the cynical style of the author. The attitude of Ecclesiastes 2:4–11, for example, should not be taken as the biblical view of work but rather the negative view of this writer who is frustrated with life (1:2; 2:17). Furthermore, the next chapter talks about a proper time for planting, building, and sewing (3:2–3, 7). In the same way 4:4–8 does not value laziness ("to fold your hands," verse 5). Rather, it makes fun of working all the time just to get things that others have. And it questions the value of putting work over family (compare 4:8 with 4:9).

Proverbs preaches against laziness: "Like a door turning back and forth on its hinges, the lazy person turns over and over in bed" and "Lazy people put their hands in the dish, but they are too tired to lift the food to their mouths" (26:14–15). The lazy are not smart because when they put off needed work, things are made worse (Ecclesiastes 10:18), and the Bible teaches in different words the man-made proverb, "A stitch in time saves nine."

Against a negative attitude toward laziness is placed the positive and desired value of skilled workers (Proverbs 22:29). The prophet Isaiah desires the fulfillment that comes from working with his hands. This desire comes from being frustrated because the people are continually uprooted and taken away from their farming lifestyle. Here the prophet says that useful work will be enjoyed by those who are saved (Isaiah 65:21–23). Perhaps the highest praise of an industrious and hardworking person is given to the hard-to-find "good wife" (Proverbs 31:10–31). She is shown to be good by her thrift, conscientiousness, and diligence about her tasks. Beyond her wisdom, teaching, and respect for the Lord, she is characterized by her wisdom in business dealings, by getting up early to accomplish work for the day, and by working late into the night when necessary. "She does her work with energy, and her arms are strong. She knows that what she makes is good" (31:17–18). "The good wife" is really a model for any hardworking person who claims to respect the Lord (31:30).

Jesus valued common, everyday chores by telling many of his stories about jobs his hearers would spend time doing, such as cleaning the house, fishing, shepherding, planting seeds, and reaping a harvest. In one example, he tells a story about a loyal servant to teach that when we work we use the gifts God has given to us (Matthew 25:14–30). In another story the point is made, "When the master comes and finds the servant doing his work, the servant will be blessed" (Luke 12:43). The meaning is obvious, and the motivation is added, "I tell you the truth, the master will choose that servant to take care of everything he owns" (12:44).

For the Christian there is an added, spiritual part to a productive life. That is the faithful use of spiritual gifts given by the Spirit of God in baptism. Whether one's gift is leadership, service, lending a helping hand, or teaching (see Romans 12:6–11; 1 Corinthians 12), Paul teaches us that we "should truly want to have the spiritual gifts" (1 Corinthians 14:1). This is because when each of us uses these God-given gifts diligently and faithfully we "make the body of Christ stronger." Therefore, "This work must continue until we are all joined together in the same faith and in the same knowledge of the Son of God" (Ephesians 4:12–13). This service for God is as highly valued as proper use of more ordinary gifts, so Paul says, "Do not be lazy but work hard, serving the Lord with all your heart" (Romans 12:11). It is no surprise that one of Paul's favorite descriptions of missionaries is "God's workers, working together" (1 Corinthians 3:9).

The Bible does not value "spiritual work" more than "lowly" labor. One time, Jesus did the work of the lowest servant in the household by washing his disciples' feet. Peter's sharp reaction and unwillingness to let Jesus do this gives us an indication of how socially wrong this must have felt to the disciples and the original readers of this story. It is often noted that Jesus sets a pattern of servant leadership for his disciples, but it should not be overlooked that he does this by valuing a most humble task (John 13:1–17). Peter knew from his three years as Jesus' disciple that he should value ordinary work. Jesus very naturally finds him back at his fishing nets and has to give him a special commission to be set aside for the work of his church (John 21:15–22).

Indeed, it is wrong to value "secular work" more than "spiritual work" or "ministry" in the narrow sense. This makes it seem that the "spiritual work" is sacred and the "secular work" is not. God calls us to do both. Doing the work of a lawyer is as spiritually important as that of a minister. Being a homemaker is as important to God as being a foreign missionary. We have all been given our work by God, and each has its part in building the kingdom.

Whatever we do, Paul reminds us, we must "work the best you can. Work as if you were doing it for the Lord, not for people. Remember that you will receive your reward from the Lord, which he promised to his people. You are serving the Lord Christ" (Colossians 3:23–24). These words are specifically written to slaves, but they apply to every type of honest work.

By knowing Jesus' valuation of work we can better understand three passages which could be misinterpreted to devalue labor. First, the lazy person could misinterpret Matthew 6:25–34 by emphasizing Jesus' words that birds "don't plant or harvest or store food in barns" and that the lilies "don't work or make clothes for themselves." Instead, Jesus is not against industry and hard work, but rather deals with the problem of worry, which he mentions five times in this short passage. He uses the birds and flowers as an example to show "how much more." If it is true for these who do not work, *how much more* is it true for those of greater worth who faithfully do their work. Similarly, a second passage that could be misinterpreted is the brief episode between Jesus, Mary, and Martha in Luke 10:38–42. This, too, should be understood as dealing with Martha's attitude of worry (10:41). It is not a put-down of her work and industry. Rather, Jesus confronts Martha's attitude of worrying about many things. A third passage, Matthew 20:1–16, has been thought of as a Marxist tract nineteen centuries before its time. However, this parable is not about how to run a business or how to treat employee pay. As the opening verse says, it is about what the "kingdom of heaven is like." The story catches people's attention because of how outrageous it sounds. The emphasis is on the equal treatment received by those who have been the people of God and have labored long and those who have recently become a part of God's people. God's generous mercy allows the same promise and benefit of salvation in Christ to all people regardless of how long they have labored in God's vineyard—the mission field.

Paul, by his own personal example, placed a high value on supporting oneself by manual labor. Even though he had a right as a missionary to be financially supported by the Christian churches, he chose to work with his own hands. This kept his missionary motives from being questioned. He could not be charged with being someone who traveled around in order to prey financially on others (1 Corinthians 4:12; 9; 2 Corinthians 2:17; 1 Thessalonians 2:8–10).

Some believers in the church Paul founded in Thessalonica thought his teaching that the Lord could return any time meant they did not need to work any longer (2 Thessalonians 3:6–12). In the strongest possible words he tells them that they are wrong. He also tells them of two consequences to keep them from being lazy. First, the Thessalonians are to stay away from those who take advantage of others by eating their food without earning it (verse 6). Second, they are not to give food to people who won't work: "Anyone who refuses to work should not eat" (verse 10). To these two consequences Paul adds a strong personal appeal: "We command these people and beg them in the Lord Jesus Christ to work quietly and earn their own food" (verse 12).

Part of Paul's reason for such strong words in 2 Thessalonians may have been his concern about their influence on unbelievers who saw the Christians not working. But Paul's value of work is clearly related to God's plan for people in creation. This plan is repeated throughout the Old and New Testaments. God wants us to find and enjoy creative work. And it is always good for us to pray that we may use our gifts to help others and together find joy in God's creation. Whether our works are lowly or toward missionary ends we should stay busy: "Everything you do or say should be done to obey Jesus your Lord. And in all you do, give thanks to God the Father through Jesus" (Colossians 3:17).⚭

⚭**Work:** For additional scriptures on this topic go to Genesis 2:2–3.

the basket in the tall grass, she sent her slave girl to get it. [6]The king's daughter opened the basket and saw the baby boy. He was crying, so she felt sorry for him and said, "This is one of the Hebrew babies."

[7]Then the baby's sister asked the king's daughter, "Would you like me to go and find a Hebrew woman to nurse the baby for you?"

[8]The king's daughter said, "Go!" So the girl went and got the baby's own mother.

[9]The king's daughter said to the woman, "Take this baby and nurse him for me, and I will pay you." So the woman took her baby and nursed him. [10]When the child grew older, the woman took him to the king's daughter, and she adopted the baby as her own son. The king's daughter named him Moses, because she had pulled him out of the water.

Moses Tries to Help

[11]Moses grew and became a man. One day he visited his people and saw that they were forced to work very hard. He saw an Egyptian beating a Hebrew man, one of Moses' own people. [12]Moses looked all around and saw that no one was watching, so he killed the Egyptian and hid his body in the sand.

[13]The next day Moses returned and saw two Hebrew men fighting each other. He said to the one that was in the wrong, "Why are you hitting one of your own people?"

[14]The man answered, "Who made you our ruler and judge? Are you going to kill me as you killed the Egyptian?"

Moses was afraid and thought, "Now everyone knows what I did."

[15]When the king heard what Moses had done, he tried to kill him. But Moses ran away from the king and went to live in the land of Midian. There he sat down near a well.

Moses in Midian

[16]There was a priest in Midian who had seven daughters. His daughters went to that well to get water to fill the water troughs for their father's flock. [17]Some shepherds came and chased the girls away, but Moses defended the girls and watered their flock.

[18]When they went back to their father Reuel, he asked them, "Why have you come home early today?"

[19]The girls answered, "The shepherds chased us away, but an Egyptian defended us. He got water for us and watered our flock."

[20]He asked his daughters, "Where is this man? Why did you leave him? Invite him to eat with us."

[21]Moses agreed to stay with Jethro, and he gave his daughter Zipporah to Moses to be his wife. [22]Zipporah gave birth to a son. Moses named him Gershom, because Moses was a stranger in a land that was not his own.

[23]After a long time, the king of Egypt died. The people of Israel groaned, because they were forced to work very hard. When they cried for help, God heard them. [24]God heard their cries, and he remembered the agreement he had made with Abraham, Isaac, and Jacob. [25]He saw the troubles of the people of Israel, and he was concerned about them.

The Burning Bush

3 One day Moses was taking care of Jethro's flock. (Jethro was the priest of Midian and also Moses' father-in-law.) When Moses led the flock to the west side of the desert, he came to Sinai, the mountain of God. [2]There the angel of the LORD appeared to him in flames of fire coming out of a bush. Moses saw that the bush was on fire, but it was not burning up. [3]So he said, "I will go closer to this strange thing. How can a bush continue burning without burning up?"

[4]When the LORD saw Moses was coming to look at the bush, God called to him from the bush, "Moses, Moses!"

And Moses said, "Here I am."

[5]Then God said, "Do not come any closer. Take off your sandals, because you are standing on holy ground. [6]I am the God of your ancestors—the God of Abraham, the God of Isaac, and the God of Jacob." Moses covered his face because he was afraid to look at God.

[7]The LORD said, "I have seen the troubles my people have suffered in Egypt, and I have heard their cries when the Egyptian slave masters hurt

---

2:10 *Moses.* The name Moses sounds like the Hebrew word for "to pull out."
2:18 *Reuel.* He was also called Jethro.
2:22 *Gershom.* This name sounds like the Hebrew word meaning "a stranger there."
2:24 Agreement: Deuteronomy 4:13
3 The angel of the Lord who appeared to Moses in the burning bush (verse 2) is identified as the Lord who saw Moses coming to the bush and as God who spoke to Moses out of the bush (verse 4). God identifies himself to Moses as "I AM WHO I AM," which Jesus applies to himself (John 8:58). It is likely that appearances of the angel of the Lord are appearances of Jesus before he became human.
3:1 Jethro is another name for Reuel (see 2:18)
3:1 Sinai is a mountain located on what is today known as the Sinai Peninsula. It is between Egypt and the land of Palestine.
3:6 Abraham: Deuteronomy 34:4
3:6 Loneliness: 1 Samuel 16:14–23

them. I am concerned about their pain, 8and I have
come down to save them from the Egyptians. I will
bring them out of that land and lead them to a good
land with lots of room—a fertile land. It is the land
of the Canaanites, Hittites, Amorites, Perizzites,
Hivites, and Jebusites. 9I have heard the cries of
the people of Israel, and I have seen the way the
Egyptians have made life hard for them. 10So now I
am sending you to the king of Egypt. Go! Bring my
people, the Israelites, out of Egypt!"

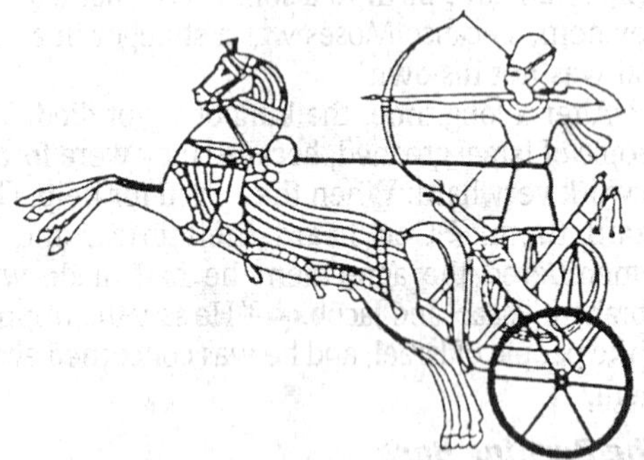

An Egyptian king (pharaoh) in his war chariot

11But Moses said to God, "I am not a great man!
How can I go to the king and lead the Israelites out
of Egypt?"
12God said, "I will be with you. This will be the
proof that I am sending you: After you lead the people out of Egypt, all of you will worship me on this
mountain."
13Moses said to God, "When I go to the Israelites,
I will say to them, 'The God of your fathers sent me
to you.' What if the people say, 'What is his name?'
What should I tell them?"
14Then God said to Moses, "I AM WHO I AM.
When you go to the people of Israel, tell them, 'I
AM sent me to you.'"
15God also said to Moses, "This is what you
should tell the people: 'The LORD is the God of your
ancestors—the God of Abraham, the God of Isaac,
and the God of Jacob. He sent me to you.' This
will always be my name, by which people from
now on will know me.
16"Go and gather the older leaders and tell them
this: 'The LORD, the God of your ancestors Abraham,
Isaac, and Jacob, has appeared to me. He said, I care
about you, and I have seen what has happened to
you in Egypt. 17I promised I would take you out of
your troubles in Egypt. I will lead you to the land of
the Canaanites, Hittites, Amorites, Perizzites,
Hivites, and Jebusites—a fertile land.'
18"The older leaders will listen to you. And
then you and the older leaders of Israel will go to
the king of Egypt and tell him, 'The LORD, the God
of the Hebrews, appeared to us. Let us travel three
days into the desert to offer sacrifices to the LORD
our God.'
19"But I know that the king of Egypt will not let
you go. Only a great power will force him to let you
go, 20so I will use my great power against Egypt. I
will strike Egypt with all the miracles that will
happen in that land. After I do that, he will let you
go. 21I will cause the Egyptians to think well of the
Israelites. So when you leave, they will give gifts to
your people. 22Each woman should ask her
Egyptian neighbor and any Egyptian woman living
in her house for gifts—silver, gold, and clothing.
You should put those gifts on your children when
you leave Egypt. In this way you will take with you
the riches of the Egyptians."

Proof for Moses

4 Then Moses answered, "What if the people of
Israel do not believe me or listen to me?
What if they say, 'The LORD did not appear to
you'?"
2The LORD said to him, "What is that in your
hand?"
Moses answered, "It is my walking stick."
3The LORD said, "Throw it on the ground."
So Moses threw it on the ground, and it became
a snake. Moses ran from the snake, 4but the LORD
said to him, "Reach out and grab the snake by its
tail." When Moses reached out and took hold of
the snake, it again became a stick in his hand. 5The
LORD said, "This is so that the Israelites will believe
that the LORD appeared to you. I am the God of

3:8 *The Canaanites, Hittites, Amorites, Perizzites, Hivites, and Jebusites.* a list of the peoples who lived in the land of Palestine before Israel took it over under Joshua.

3:10 Moses had fled Egypt and sought a hiding place in the wilderness. It was there that God appeared to him and told him that he wanted Moses to return to Egypt to free his fellow Israelites from their hard slavery. This dramatic episode in the life of Moses is the call to his life work.

Today, we may not receive as dramatic a call, but the call is no less real and important. Whether we are a homemaker, engineer, airline pilot, or minister, God has a plan for our careers. Like Moses, we, too, have a place in God's plan of redemption. We should work for the glory of God.

3:14 *I . . . I AM.* The Hebrew words are like the name *"Yahweh."* This Hebrew name for God, usually called "LORD," shows that God always lives and is always with his people.

3:14 Names of God: Exodus 17:14–15
3:15 Freedom: Deuteronomy 5:1–6
3:22 Mediator: See article on page 981.
3:22 Communication: 1 Samuel 3:4

4:2 *walking stick.* Here and elsewhere the biblical story highlights Moses' and Aaron's walking stick. It often is at the center of a miracle. The stick was made of wood, which comes from a tree. Throughout the Old Testament, the tree represents God's presence.

their ancestors, the God of Abraham, the God of
Isaac, and the God of Jacob."
6Then the LORD said to Moses, "Put your hand
inside your coat." So Moses put his hand inside his
coat. When he took it out, it was white with a skin
disease.
7Then he said, "Now put your hand inside your
coat again." So Moses put his hand inside his coat
again. When he took it out, his hand was healthy
again, like the rest of his skin.
8Then the LORD said, "If the people do not
believe you or pay attention to the first miracle,
they may believe you when you show them this
second miracle. 9After these two miracles, if they
still do not believe or listen to you, take some
water from the Nile River and pour it on the dry
ground. The water will become blood when it
touches the ground."
10But Moses said to the LORD, "Please, Lord, I
have never been a skilled speaker. Even now, after
talking to you, I cannot speak well. I speak slowly
and can't find the best words."
11Then the LORD said to him, "Who made a person's mouth? And who makes someone deaf or not
able to speak? Or who gives a person sight or blindness? It is I, the LORD. 12Now go! I will help you
speak, and I will teach you what to say."
13But Moses said, "Please, Lord, send someone
else."
14The LORD became angry with Moses and said,
"Your brother Aaron, from the family of Levi, is a
skilled speaker. He is already coming to meet you,
and he will be happy when he sees you. 15You
will speak to Aaron and tell him what to say. I will
help both of you to speak and will teach you what
to do. 16Aaron will speak to the people for you.
You will tell him what God says, and he will speak
for you. 17Take your walking stick with you, and
use it to do the miracles."

Moses Returns to Egypt

18Moses went back to Jethro, his father-in-law,
and said to him, "Let me go back to my people in
Egypt. I want to see if they are still alive."
Jethro said to Moses, "Go! I wish you well."
19While Moses was still in Midian, the LORD said
to him, "Go back to Egypt, because the men who
wanted to kill you are dead now."
20So Moses took his wife and his sons, put them
on a donkey, and started back to Egypt. He took
with him the walking stick of God.
21The LORD said to Moses, "When you get back
to Egypt, do all the miracles I have given you the
power to do. Show them to the king of Egypt. But
I will make the king very stubborn, and he will not
let the people go. 22Then say to the king, 'This is
what the LORD says: Israel is my firstborn son.
23I told you to let my son go so he may worship
me. But you refused to let Israel go, so I will kill
your firstborn son.'"
24As Moses was on his way to Egypt, he
stopped at a resting place for the night. The LORD
met him there and tried to kill him. 25But
Zipporah took a flint knife and circumcised her
son. Taking the skin, she touched Moses' feet
with it and said to him, "You are a bridegroom of
blood to me." 26She said, "You are a bridegroom
of blood," because she had to circumcise her son.
So the LORD let Moses alone.
27Meanwhile the LORD said to Aaron, "Go out
into the desert to meet Moses." When Aaron
went, he met Moses at Sinai, the mountain of

4:11 God is all-powerful. He gives sight, and he withholds it from certain individuals. To be blind is not a punishment from God, though that was what the disciples thought. Jesus set them straight by saying that God can have other reasons for a person's blindness (John 9:1–5), such as, in this case, the display of God's glory. God can use blindness to develop other gifts that a person has as well.

4:14 God's Anger: Joshua 7:11–12

4:15 God has used many means to express to us his nature and his intent. The Bible is mostly about communication. Moses is charged to be God's vehicle for his message. This message is more than words, but will also be an event which gives birth to a nation. Yet Moses is more than reluctant to become God's spokesman. So God gives Aaron to assist Moses because Aaron is a good speaker.

Good speaking is not enough. God's presence is also necessary if there is to be a clear communication. Without God we tend to get caught up in our messages and meanings. "I will help both of you to speak and will teach you what to do" (Exodus 4:15). Communication uses more than words to convey meaning. Actions, gestures, and events are all a part of communication. Even a walking stick becomes a tool to get a point across (Exodus 4:17). And so God sent Moses off the mountain to communicate his message.

In the incarnation, God himself leaves the mountain to become "God with us." No longer content merely with words, the Word became a human (John 1:14) so that nothing stands between us and his meaning.

4:17 Communication: See article on page 1499.

4:21 This is the first among several passages which indicate that God made the king of Egypt stubborn (Exodus 7:3; 9:12; 10:1, 20, 27; 11:10; 14:4, 8, 17). This, of course, is describing from God's perspective what was also true from a human perspective: that the king himself chose to be stubborn (Exodus 7:13, 14, 22; 8:15, 19, 32; 9:7, 34, 35; 13:15). Presenting the divine side emphasizes God's control and purpose in bringing salvation to many (Romans 9:17–24).

4:21–23 God chose Israel to be his own people. They were like a son to him. In the ancient Near East the firstborn son had a privileged place in the family. Israel is here called God's firstborn son, showing the intimate love and concern which God had for his people.

4:22 Election (Chosen): Deuteronomy 7:6–11

4:24–26 Apparently, Moses had not circumcised his son, which was commanded by God for his people in Genesis 17. The offense was so serious, God sought to take his life. Ritual purity was important when serving the Lord. Circumcision was necessary before partaking of the Passover Feast (Exodus 12: 43–49). Joshua circumcised the entire nation before entering into holy war (Joshua 5). Flint knives were commonly used for circumcision probably because they were sharper than other materials.

God, and kissed him. 28Moses told Aaron everything the LORD had said to him when he sent him to Egypt. He also told him about the miracles which the LORD had commanded him to do.

29Moses and Aaron gathered all the older leaders of the Israelites, 30and Aaron told them everything that the LORD had told Moses. Then Moses did the miracles for all the people to see, 31and the Israelites believed. When they heard that the LORD was concerned about them and had seen their troubles, they bowed down and worshiped him.

Moses and Aaron Before the King

5 After Moses and Aaron talked to the people, they went to the king of Egypt and said, "This is what the LORD, the God of Israel, says: 'Let my people go so they may hold a feast for me in the desert.'"

2But the king of Egypt said, "Who is the LORD? Why should I obey him and let Israel go? I do not know the LORD, and I will not let Israel go."

3Then Aaron and Moses said, "The God of the Hebrews has met with us. Now let us travel three days into the desert to offer sacrifices to the LORD our God. If we don't do this, he may kill us with a disease or in war."

4But the king said to them, "Moses and Aaron, why are you taking the people away from their work? Go back to your jobs! 5There are very many Hebrews, and now you want them to quit working!"

6That same day the king gave a command to the slave masters and foremen. 7He said, "Don't give the people straw to make bricks as you used to do. Let them gather their own straw. 8But they must still make the same number of bricks as they did before. Do not accept fewer. They have become lazy, and that is why they are asking me, 'Let us go to offer sacrifices to our God.' 9Make these people work harder and keep them busy; then they will not have time to listen to the lies of Moses."

10So the slave masters and foremen went to the Israelites and said, "This is what the king says: I will no longer give you straw. 11Go and get your own straw wherever you can find it. But you must make as many bricks as you made before." 12So the people went everywhere in Egypt looking for dry stalks to use for straw. 13The slave masters kept forcing the people to work harder. They said, "You must make just as many bricks as you did when you were given straw." 14The king's slave masters had made the Israelite foremen responsible for the work the people did. The Egyptian slave masters beat these men and asked them, "Why aren't you making as many bricks as you made in the past?"

15Then the Israelite foremen went to the king and complained, "Why are you treating us, your servants, this way? 16You give us no straw, but we are commanded to make bricks. Our slave masters beat us, but it is your own people's fault."

17The king answered, "You are lazy! You don't want to work! That is why you ask to leave here and make sacrifices to the LORD. 18Now, go back to work! We will not give you any straw, but you must make just as many bricks as you did before."

19The Israelite foremen knew they were in trouble, because the king had told them, "You must make just as many bricks each day as you did before." 20As they were leaving the meeting with the king, they met Moses and Aaron, who were waiting for them. 21So they said to Moses and Aaron, "May the LORD punish you. You caused the king and his officers to hate us. You have given them an excuse to kill us."

Moses Complains to God

22Then Moses returned to the LORD and said, "Lord, why have you brought this trouble on your people? Is this why you sent me here? 23I went to the king and said what you told me to say, but ever since that time he has made the people suffer. And you have done nothing to save them."

6 Then the LORD said to Moses, "Now you will see what I will do to the king of Egypt. I will use my great power against him, and he will let my people go. Because of my power, he will force them out of his country."

2Then God said to Moses, "I am the LORD. 3I appeared to Abraham, Isaac, and Jacob by the name God Almighty, but they did not know me by my name, the LORD. 4I also made my agreement with them to give them the land of Canaan. They lived in that land, but it was not their own. 5Now I have heard the cries of the Israelites, whom the Egyptians are treating as slaves, and I remember my agreement. 6So tell the people of Israel that I say to them, 'I am the LORD. I will save you from the hard work the Egyptians force you to do. I will make you free, so you will not be slaves to the Egyptians. I will free you by my great power, and I will punish the Egyptians terribly. 7I will make you my own people, and I will be your God. You will know that I am the LORD your God, the One who saves you from the hard work the Egyptians force you to do. 8I will lead you to the land that I

6:5 Commitment: Leviticus 26:11–13

6:7 Community: Exodus 19:4–6

promised to Abraham, Isaac, and Jacob, and I will
give you that land to own. I am the LORD.'"
9So Moses told this to the Israelites, but they
would not listen to him. They were discouraged,
and their slavery was hard.
10Then the LORD said to Moses, 11"Go tell the
king of Egypt that he must let the Israelites leave
his land."
12But Moses answered, "The Israelites will not
listen to me, so surely the king will not listen to me
either. I am not a good speaker."
13But the LORD spoke to Moses and Aaron and
gave them orders about the Israelites and the king
of Egypt. He commanded them to lead the
Israelites out of Egypt.

Families of Israel

14These are the leaders of the families of Israel:

Israel's first son, Reuben, had four sons: Hanoch,
Pallu, Hezron, and Carmi. These are the family
groups of Reuben.
15Simeon's sons were Jemuel, Jamin, Ohad,
Jakin, Zohar, and Shaul, the son of a Canaanite
woman. These are the family groups of Simeon.
16Levi lived one hundred thirty-seven years.
These are the names of his sons according to their
family history: Gershon, Kohath, and Merari.
17Gershon had two sons, Libni and Shimei,
with their families.
18Kohath lived one hundred thirty-three years.
The sons of Kohath were Amram, Izhar, Hebron,
and Uzziel.
19The sons of Merari were Mahli and Mushi.
These are the family groups of Levi, according to
their family history.
20Amram married his father's sister Jochebed,
who gave birth to Aaron and Moses. Amram lived
one hundred thirty-seven years.
21Izhar's sons were Korah, Nepheg, and Zicri.
22Uzziel's sons were Mishael, Elzaphan, and
Sithri.
23Aaron married Elisheba, the daughter of Amminadab and the sister of Nahshon. Elisheba gave
birth to Nadab, Abihu, Eleazar, and Ithamar.
24The sons of Korah were Assir, Elkanah, and
Abiasaph. These are the family groups of the
Korahites.
25Eleazar son of Aaron married a daughter of
Putiel, and she gave birth to Phinehas.
These are the leaders of the family groups of
the Levites.
26This was the Aaron and Moses to whom the
LORD said, "Lead the people of Israel out of Egypt
by their divisions." 27Aaron and Moses are the
ones who talked to the king of Egypt and told him
to let the Israelites leave Egypt.

God Repeats His Call to Moses

28The LORD spoke to Moses in the land of Egypt
29and said, "I am the LORD. Tell the king of Egypt
everything I tell you."
30But Moses answered, "I am not a good speaker.
The king will not listen to me."

7 The LORD said to Moses, "I have made you like
God to the king of Egypt, and your brother
Aaron will be like a prophet for you. 2Tell Aaron
your brother everything that I command you, and
let him tell the king of Egypt to let the Israelites
leave his country. 3But I will make the king stubborn. I will do many miracles in Egypt, 4but he will
still refuse to listen. So then I will punish Egypt terribly, and I will lead my divisions, my people the
Israelites, out of that land. 5I will punish Egypt with
my power, and I will bring the Israelites out of that
land. Then they will know I am the LORD."
6Moses and Aaron did just as the LORD had commanded them. 7Moses was eighty years old and
Aaron was eighty-three when they spoke to the
king.

Aaron's Walking Stick Becomes a Snake

8The LORD said to Moses and Aaron, 9"Moses,
when the king asks you to do a miracle, tell Aaron
to throw his walking stick down in front of the king,
and it will become a snake."
10So Moses and Aaron went to the king as the
LORD had commanded. Aaron threw his walking
stick down in front of the king and his officers,
and it became a snake.
11So the king called in his wise men and his
magicians, and with their tricks the Egyptian magicians were able to do the same thing. 12They threw
their walking sticks on the ground, and their sticks
became snakes. But Aaron's stick swallowed theirs.
13Still the king was stubborn and refused to listen
to Moses and Aaron, just as the LORD had said.

The Water Becomes Blood

14Then the LORD said to Moses, "The king is
being stubborn and refuses to let the people go.
15In the morning the king will go out to the Nile
River. Go meet him by the edge of the river, and
take with you the walking stick that became a
snake. 16Tell him: The LORD, the God of the
Hebrews, sent me to you. He said, 'Let my people

6:8 Promise: Deuteronomy 28

7:5 Prophet & Prophecy: Deuteronomy 13:1–11

go worship me in the desert.' Until now you have not listened. 17This is what the LORD says: 'This is how you will know that I am the LORD. I will strike the water of the Nile River with this stick in my hand, and the water will change into blood. 18Then the fish in the Nile will die, and the river will begin to stink. The Egyptians will not be able to drink the water from the Nile.'"

19The LORD said to Moses, "Tell Aaron: 'Take the walking stick in your hand and stretch your hand over the rivers, canals, ponds, and pools in Egypt.' The water will become blood everywhere in Egypt, both in wooden buckets and in stone jars."

20So Moses and Aaron did just as the LORD had commanded. In front of the king and his officers, Aaron raised his walking stick and struck the water in the Nile River. So all the water in the Nile changed into blood. 21The fish in the Nile died, and the river began to stink, so the Egyptians could not drink water from it. Blood was everywhere in the land of Egypt.

22Using their tricks, the magicians of Egypt did the same thing. So the king was stubborn and refused to listen to Moses and Aaron, just as the LORD had said. 23The king turned and went into his palace and ignored what Moses and Aaron had done. 24The Egyptians could not drink the water from the Nile, so all of them dug along the bank of the river, looking for water to drink.

The Frogs

25Seven days passed after the LORD changed the Nile River.

8 Then the LORD told Moses, "Go to the king of Egypt and tell him, 'This is what the LORD says: Let my people go to worship me. 2If you refuse, I will punish Egypt with frogs. 3The Nile River will be filled with frogs. They will come up into your palace, into your bedroom, on your bed, into the houses of your officers, and onto your people. They will come into your ovens and into your baking pans. 4The frogs will jump all over you, your people, and your officers.'"

5Then the LORD said to Moses, "Tell Aaron to hold his walking stick in his hand over the rivers, canals, and ponds. Make frogs come up out of the water onto the land of Egypt."

6So Aaron held his hand over all the waters of Egypt, and the frogs came up out of the water and covered the land of Egypt. 7The magicians used their tricks to do the same thing, so even more frogs came up onto the land of Egypt.

8The king called for Moses and Aaron and said, "Pray to the LORD to take the frogs away from me and my people. I will let your people go to offer sacrifices to the LORD."

9Moses said to the king, "Please set the time when I should pray for you, your people, and your officers. Then the frogs will leave you and your houses and will remain only in the Nile."

10The king answered, "Tomorrow."

Moses said, "What you want will happen. By this you will know that there is no one like the LORD our God. 11The frogs will leave you, your houses, your officers, and your people. They will remain only in the Nile."

12After Moses and Aaron left the king, Moses asked the LORD about the frogs he had sent to the king. 13And the LORD did as Moses asked. The frogs died in the houses, in the yards, and in the fields. 14The Egyptians put them in piles, and the whole country began to stink. 15But when the king saw that they were free of the frogs, he became stubborn again. He did not listen to Moses and Aaron, just as the LORD had said.

The Gnats

16Then the Lord said to Moses, "Tell Aaron to raise his walking stick and strike the dust on the ground. Then everywhere in Egypt the dust will change into gnats." 17They did this, and when Aaron raised the walking stick that was in his hand and struck the dust on the ground, everywhere in Egypt the dust changed into gnats. The gnats got on the people and animals. 18Using their tricks, the magicians tried to do the same thing, but they could not make the dust change into gnats. The gnats remained on the people and animals. 19So the magicians told the king that the power of God had done this. But the king was stubborn and refused to listen to them, just as the Lord had said.

The Flies

20The LORD told Moses, "Get up early in the morning, and meet the king of Egypt as he goes out to the river. Tell him, 'This is what the LORD says: Let my people go so they can worship me. 21If you don't let them go, I will send swarms of flies into your houses. The flies will be on you, your officers, and your people. The houses of Egypt will be full of flies, and they will be all over the ground, too. 22But I will not treat the Israelites the same as the Egyptian people. There will not be any flies in the land of Goshen, where my people live. By this you will know that I, the LORD, am in this land. 23I will

8:22 *Goshen.* This territory is in the northeastern section of the Nile Delta. The Egyptians permitted Jacob and his children to live there when they came to Egypt to escape a famine.

treat my people differently from your people. This
miracle will happen tomorrow.'"
24So the LORD did as he had said, and great
swarms of flies came into the king's palace and his
officers' houses. All over Egypt flies were ruining
the land. 25The king called for Moses and Aaron
and told them, "Offer sacrifices to your God here
in this country."
26But Moses said, "It wouldn't be right to do
that, because the Egyptians hate the sacrifices we
offer to the LORD our God. If they see us offering
sacrifices they hate, they will throw stones at us
and kill us. 27Let us make a three-day journey into
the desert. We must offer sacrifices to the LORD our
God there, as the LORD told us to do."
28The king said, "I will let you go so that you
may offer sacrifices to the LORD your God in the
desert, but you must not go very far away. Now go
and pray for me."
29Moses said, "I will leave and pray to the LORD,
and he will take the flies away from you, your officers, and your people tomorrow. But do not try to
trick us again. Do not stop the people from going
to offer sacrifices to the LORD."
30So Moses left the king and prayed to the LORD,
31and the LORD did as he asked. He removed the
flies from the king, his officers, and his people so
that not one fly was left. 32But the king became
stubborn again and did not let the people go.

The Disease on the Farm Animals

9 Then the LORD told Moses, "Go to the king of
Egypt and tell him, 'This is what the LORD,
the God of the Hebrews, says: Let my people go
to worship me. 2If you refuse to let them go and
continue to hold them, 3the LORD will punish you.
He will send a terrible disease on your farm animals that are in the fields. He will cause your
horses, donkeys, camels, cattle, goats, and sheep
to become sick. 4But the LORD will treat Israel's
animals differently from the animals of Egypt.
None of the animals that belong to the Israelites
will die. 5The LORD has set tomorrow as the time
he will do this in the land.'" 6The next day the
LORD did as he promised. All the farm animals in
Egypt died, but none of the animals belonging to
Israelites died. 7The king sent people to see what
had happened to the animals of Israel, and they
found that not one of them had died. But the king
was still stubborn and did not let the people go.

The Boils

8The LORD said to Moses and Aaron, "Fill your
hands with ashes from a furnace. Moses, throw the
ashes into the air in front of the king of Egypt.
9The ashes will spread like dust through all the
land of Egypt. They will cause boils to break out
and become sores on the skin of people and animals everywhere in the land."
10So Moses and Aaron took ashes from a furnace and went and stood before the king. Moses
threw ashes into the air, which caused boils to
break out and become sores on people and animals. 11The magicians could not stand before
Moses, because all the Egyptians had boils, even
the magicians. 12But the LORD made the king stubborn, so he refused to listen to Moses and Aaron,
just as the LORD had said.

The Hail

13Then the LORD said to Moses, "Get up early in
the morning and go to the king of Egypt. Tell him,
'This is what the LORD, the God of the Hebrews,
says: Let my people go to worship me. 14If you
don't, this time I will punish you, your officers,
and your people, with all my power. Then you will
know there is no one in the whole land like me.
15By now I could have used my power and caused
a terrible disease that would have destroyed you
and your people from the earth. 16But I have let
you live for this reason: to show you my power so
that my name will be talked about in all the earth.
17You are still against my people and do not want
to let them go. 18So at this time tomorrow, I will
send a terrible hailstorm, the worst in Egypt since
it became a nation. 19Now send for your animals
and whatever you have in the fields, and bring
them into a safe place. The hail will fall on every
person or animal that is still in the fields. If they
have not been brought in, they will die.'" 20Some
of the king's officers respected the word of the
LORD and hurried to bring their slaves and animals
inside. 21But others ignored the LORD's message
and left their slaves and animals in the fields.
22The LORD told Moses, "Raise your hand
toward the sky. Then the hail will start falling in
all the land of Egypt. It will fall on people, animals,
and on everything that grows in the fields of
Egypt." 23When Moses raised his walking stick
toward the sky, the LORD sent thunder and hail,
and lightning flashed down to the earth. So he
caused hail to fall upon the land of Egypt. 24There
was hail, and lightning flashed as it hailed—the
worst hailstorm in Egypt since it had become a
nation. 25The hail destroyed all the people and animals that were in the fields in all the land of Egypt.
It also destroyed everything that grew in the fields
and broke all the trees in the fields. 26The only
place it did not hail was in the land of Goshen,
where the Israelites lived.

27The king sent for Moses and Aaron and told them, "This time I have sinned. The LORD is in the right, and I and my people are in the wrong. 28Pray to the LORD. We have had enough of God's thunder and hail. I will let you go; you do not have to stay here any longer."

29Moses told the king, "When I leave the city, I will raise my hands to the LORD in prayer, and the thunder and hail will stop. Then you will know that the earth belongs to the LORD. 30But I know that you and your officers do not yet fear the LORD God."

31The flax was in bloom, and the barley had ripened, so these crops were destroyed. 32But both wheat crops ripen later, so they were not destroyed.

33Moses left the king and went outside the city. He raised his hands to the LORD, and the thunder and hail stopped. The rain also stopped falling to the ground. 34When the king saw that the rain, hail, and thunder had stopped, he sinned again, and he and his officers became stubborn. 35So the king became stubborn and refused to let the Israelites go, just as the LORD had said through Moses.

The Locusts

10 The LORD said to Moses, "Go to the king of Egypt. I have made him and his officers stubborn so I could show them my powerful miracles. 2I also did this so you could tell your children and your grandchildren how I was hard on the Egyptians. Tell them about the miracles I did among them so that all of you will know that I am the LORD."

3So Moses and Aaron went to the king and told him, "This is what the LORD, the God of the Hebrews, says: 'How long will you refuse to be sorry for what you have done? Let my people go to worship me. 4If you refuse to let my people go, tomorrow I will bring locusts into your country. 5They will cover the land so that no one will be able to see the ground. They will eat anything that was left from the hailstorm and the leaves from every tree growing in the field. 6They will fill your palaces and all your officers' houses, as well as the houses of all the Egyptians. There will be more locusts than your fathers or ancestors have ever seen—more than there have been since people began living in Egypt.'" Then Moses turned and walked away from the king.

7The king's officers asked him, "How long will this man make trouble for us? Let the Israelites go to worship the LORD their God. Don't you know that Egypt is ruined?"

8So Moses and Aaron were brought back to the king. He said to them, "Go and worship the LORD your God. But tell me, just who is going?"

9Moses answered, "We will go with our young and old people, our sons and daughters, and our flocks and herds, because we are going to have a feast to honor the LORD."

10The king said to them, "The LORD will really have to be with you if ever I let you and all of your children leave Egypt. See, you are planning something evil! 11No! Only the men may go and worship the LORD, which is what you have been asking for." Then the king forced Moses and Aaron out of his palace.

12The LORD told Moses, "Raise your hand over the land of Egypt, and the locusts will come. They will spread all over the land of Egypt and will eat all the plants the hail did not destroy."

13So Moses raised his walking stick over the land of Egypt, and the LORD caused a strong wind to blow from the east. It blew across the land all that day and night, and when morning came, the east wind had brought the locusts. 14Swarms of locusts covered all the land of Egypt and settled everywhere. There were more locusts than ever before or after, 15and they covered the whole land so that it was black. They ate everything that was left after the hail—every plant in the field and all the fruit on the trees. Nothing green was left on any tree or plant anywhere in Egypt.

16The king quickly called for Moses and Aaron. He said, "I have sinned against the LORD your God and against you. 17Now forgive my sin this time. Pray to the LORD your God, and ask him to stop this punishment that kills."

18Moses left the king and prayed to the LORD. 19So the LORD changed the wind. He made a very strong wind blow from the west, and it blew the locusts away into the Red Sea. Not one locust was left anywhere in Egypt. 20But the LORD caused the king to be stubborn again, and he did not let the Israelites go.

The Darkness

21Then the LORD told Moses, "Raise your hand toward the sky, and darkness will cover the land of Egypt. It will be so dark you will be able to feel it." 22Moses raised his hand toward the sky, and total darkness was everywhere in Egypt for three days.

10:2 It is important to keep alive the memory of what God has done. Since only one generation actually was part of the Exodus, future generations were to be taught by their parents so that they might also know God's power. Some of the psalms also speak of retelling God's mighty deeds throughout the generations (Psalms 77, 78, 105, 106).

MURDER

GENESIS 4

What is murder? Is the taking of another life always wrong?

Murder is the unlawful, premeditated killing of another human being. The story of Cain and Abel (Genesis 4) illustrates the biblical stance against the wrongful taking of another life: "You must not murder anyone" (Exodus 20:13). Petty rivalry led Cain to kill his own brother. God asks Cain the convicting question, "Where is your brother Abel?" Cain attempts a feeble evasion with the rhetorical reply, "Is it my job to take care of my brother?" God's implied answer is "Yes, and I am against murder." This prohibition against murder is reiterated again and again throughout the Bible, and may be the most widely shared moral principle across cultures and religions. Human life is a gift of God to be cherished and protected, and so murder is an act against God.

Cain is punished, but his sentence is far more merciful than the biblical prescription of the death penalty for murderers (Genesis 9:6; Numbers 35:16–31). In biblical terms, the killing of a murderer is not itself a violation of the command, and murder does not include all killing. Accidental killing is not murder, and the perpetrator is to be protected from the retaliation of relatives (Numbers 35:22–28). Likewise self-defense and slaying in battle both justify homicide and are not included in what is meant by the crime of murder (Exodus 22:2–3; 2 Samuel 2:18–23). Suicide or "self-murder" is not specifically prohibited in either the Old or New Testament (see, for example, 1 Samuel 31:4–5), but in a long tradition following Augustine (fifth century C.E.) Christians have viewed killing oneself, no matter what the circumstance, as a violation of the sixth commandment.

In light of the repeated commands against murder in the Bible, it is difficult to make sense of the Old Testament stories where God commands his people to annihilate their enemies. For example, Joshua leads the people of Israel in the conquest of Jericho and Ai where all the people—women, youth, the elderly, and animals included!—are slaughtered (Joshua 6–8). While killing in combat may be accepted as justifiable homicide, it is confusing to read that God himself commands the killing of noncombatants (compare Joshua 8:2 and 6:21). In ancient times this practice may not have struck a reader as barbaric since it was a common convention of warfare designed to eliminate heirs who might rise up in vengeance at a later date. Furthermore, from the perspective of God's people, this was an execution of corporate punishment, a group death penalty for an evil people who acted against the God of Israel. This fate for those of Canaan ("the Amorites") is already predicted in Genesis 15:16, although at that time the judgment of God is restrained: "I am not yet going to punish the Amorites for their evil behavior." This explanation may be difficult for a modern reader to accept, but we are left having to trust in the goodness of God to judge rightly in these matters.

Two other explanations for God's summary judgment on the pagan inhabitants of Canaan should be considered. Every member of the family was involved in pagan worship, even among Israelites (Jeremiah 7:18). But more significantly, God wanted to remove every source of future corruption to his people, including all the heinous and immoral practices associated with idol worship (Deuteronomy 20:16–18).

We should not over-generalize and suppose that all the Old Testament stories are bloodthirsty. David, for example, shows great remorse at the covert killing of Abner (2 Samuel 3). By the morality of "eye for an eye" Joab seemed justified in taking Abner's life in exchange for killing Joab's brother Asahel. David had offered peace to Joab and was personally offended at the violation of his word. And so, "David and all the people cried at Abner's grave" (2 Samuel 3:32). Later, David himself is guilty of murdering Bathsheba's husband, but Psalm 51 expresses his deep remorse at this evil, begging God's forgiveness (51:14). Even during this period of wars and bloodletting there remains a moral sense that murder is wrong and human life is sacred.

The New Testament accepts the Old Testament prescriptions against murder (Matthew 19:18; Mark 7:21; Romans 1:29), but the principle of respect for human life is expanded to include matters of the heart, so that even anger toward someone else approximates a violation of the command not to murder. In Matthew 5:21–22, Jesus interprets the sixth command to exclude harboring murderous intentions in one's heart against another, recognized by its twin fruits of anger and name-calling. The early Christians took this expansion very seriously, as can be seen in 1 John: "Do not be like Cain who belonged to the Evil One and killed his brother. And why did he kill him? Because the things Cain did were evil and the things his brother did were good. . . . Everyone who hates a brother or sister is a murderer, and you know that murderers have no eternal life in them" (1 John 3:12, 15).

Murder: For additional scriptures on this topic go to Genesis 4:1–15.

CAIN

GENESIS 4:1–24

Cain has the dubious distinction of being the first murderer. What kind of person would commit such a crime? What lessons can we learn from Cain's crime and its aftermath?

In Genesis 4 Cain and Abel both worship God by bringing him gifts. What is it that makes Abel's gift acceptable and Cain's gift unacceptable? Ostensibly both gifts were tokens of thanksgiving to God. Each son's gift was a product of his livelihood. One possibility is that Abel's gift, which involved a blood sacrifice, shows he was aware of his need for sacrificial cleansing. Cain's bloodless offering showed no such need. The problem with this interpretation is that the system of blood sacrifices to pay for sins did not develop until a later time. Perhaps a better explanation is to be found in the way the text itself describes the two gifts. Whereas Cain brought "some food from the ground," Abel offered "the best parts from some of the firstborn" (Genesis 4:3–4). By offering the best of the first, Abel expresses his heartfelt thanksgiving to God. Cain's offering is rejected by God because it betrays Cain's ingratitude and unbelief. Cain's religious activity was recognized by God to be nothing more than pretentious tokenism. This interpretation is supported by Hebrews 11:4 where Abel's faith is pinpointed as the difference between the two brothers.

The issue is the integrity of the heart. Cain's heart attitude is betrayed in both his countenance and his response to God's rebuke. God emphasizes to Cain the dangers of leaving sin unconfessed and issues a call for Cain to repent (verses 6–7). However, instead of repenting, Cain lashes out in jealous hate and murders his brother. The horrible nature of Cain's crime is highlighted by the six-fold repetition of the word "brother" in verses 8–11.

Cain does not have a right relationship with God and therefore he does not have a right relationship with his brother. This is John's answer to the question as to why Cain killed Abel. Cain's unbelief led him to envy his brother's righteous faith. This jealous hatred issued in murder (1 John 3:12). According to John (verses 13, 14) Cain's envy typifies the attitude of the world towards believers. Because evil and righteousness are diametrically opposed, evil cannot bear the presence of righteousness and seeks to suppress or destroy it. Christians should not be surprised when they are persecuted because of their righteous behavior, but rather should expect this in the course of their contacts and associations with unbelievers (Matthew 5:10).

When questioned by God as to the whereabouts of Abel, Cain compounds his sin by lying (verse 9). After revealing his awareness of Cain's sin, God responds with both punishment and protection. As punishment God curses the ground for Cain absolutely, forcing him to wander, homeless and friendless. When Cain hears his punishment, he is overwhelmed with despair. Out of pure mercy, God protects Cain with a mark (the exact nature of the mark is unclear), allowing him the opportunity to rebuild a godly heritage. Cain's response to God reveals a lack of remorse for his crime, suspicion of God, and restless anxiety born of self-concern. These traits indicate that God's love was not living in him (1 John 1:8; 2:3; 3:17; 3:21).

Despite the technological advancements credited to Cain's progeny, the history of his descendants should serve as a warning against the virulence of an unrepentant heart attitude (verses 16–24). That history ends with the boast of Lamech (verses 23–24). Lamech's words reveal the depths of his sin: godlessness, polygamy, arrogance, revenge, and violence. His words are put at the end of the story of Cain's descendants to show that without repentance people go from bad to worse. Then a new son of Adam, Seth, is introduced. In Seth's birth announcement an echo of God's creation of human beings can be heard (compare Genesis 5:1–3 with Genesis 1:26–27), suggesting that God's intentions for the human race will be accomplished through Seth and not Cain.

In Jude 11, the "way of Cain" is used (along with Balaam and Korah) to characterize the habitual course of the false teachers who had "secretly entered" (Jude 4) the early church. Like Cain, the false teachers associated themselves with the family of God, and, like Cain, their rebellion against God caused disruption and destruction in God's family. Their presence with God's people and their religious pretensions disguise their sins, so that Christians are more likely to follow their bad teachings. The author of Jude warns the church that just as Cain's false worship showed that he was a spiritual child of Satan, Satan's cohorts within the Christian community will exhibit a bad attitude toward God. Believers must recognize the existence of these insidious enemies in the church, guard themselves against the possibility of being led astray, and prepare for trouble when they openly oppose them.

Cain: For additional scriptures on this topic go to Jude 11.

23No one could see anyone else, and no one could go
anywhere for three days. But the Israelites had light
where they lived.
24Again the king of Egypt called for Moses. He
said, "All of you may go and worship the LORD. You
may take your women and children with you, but
you must leave your flocks and herds here."
25Moses said, "You must let us have animals to
use as sacrifices and burnt offerings, because we
have to offer them to the LORD our God. 26So we
must take our animals with us; not a hoof will be
left behind. We have to use some of the animals
to worship the LORD our God. We won't know
exactly what we will need to worship the LORD
until we get there."
27But the LORD made the king stubborn again, so
he refused to let them go. 28Then he told Moses,
"Get out of here, and don't come again! The next
time you see me, you will die."
29Then Moses told the king, "I'll do what you
say. I will not come to see you again."

The Death of the Firstborn

11 Now the LORD had told Moses, "I have one
more way to punish the king and the people
of Egypt. After this, the king will send all of you away
from Egypt. When he does, he will force you to
leave completely. 2Tell the men and women of Israel
to ask their neighbors for things made of silver
and gold." 3The LORD had caused the Egyptians to
respect the Israelites, and both the king's officers
and the Egyptian people considered Moses to be a
great man.
4So Moses said to the king, "This is what the
LORD says: 'About midnight tonight I will go
through all Egypt. 5Every firstborn son in the land
of Egypt will die—from the firstborn son of the
king, who sits on his throne, to the firstborn of
the slave girl grinding grain. Also the firstborn
farm animals will die. 6There will be loud outcries
everywhere in Egypt, worse than any time before
or after this. 7But not even a dog will bark at the
Israelites or their animals.' Then you will know
that the LORD treats Israel differently from Egypt.
8All your officers will come to me. They will bow
facedown to the ground before me and say,
'Leave and take all your people with you.' After
that, I will leave." Then Moses very angrily left
the king.
9The LORD had told Moses, "The king will not
listen to you and Aaron so that I may do many miracles in the land of Egypt." 10Moses and Aaron did
all these great miracles in front of the king. But
the LORD made him stubborn, and the king would
not let the Israelites leave his country.

The First Passover

12 The LORD spoke to Moses and Aaron in the
land of Egypt: 2"This month will be the
beginning of months, the first month of the year
for you. 3Tell the whole community of Israel that on
the tenth day of this month each man must get one
lamb for the people in his house. 4If there are not
enough people in his house to eat a whole lamb, he
must share it with his closest neighbor, considering the number of people. There must be enough
lamb for everyone to eat. 5The lamb must be a one-
year-old male that has nothing wrong with it. This
animal can be either a young sheep or a young
goat. 6Take care of the animals until the fourteenth day of the month. On that day all the people of the community of Israel will kill them in the
evening before dark. 7The people must take some
of the blood and put it on the sides and tops of the
doorframes of the houses where they eat the lambs.
8On this night they must roast the lamb over a fire.
They must eat it with bitter herbs and bread made
without yeast. 9Do not eat the lamb raw or boiled
in water. Roast the whole lamb over a fire—with
its head, legs, and inner organs. 10You must not
leave any of it until morning, but if any of it is left
over until morning, you must burn it with fire.
11"This is the way you must eat it: You must be
fully dressed as if you were going on a trip. You
must have your sandals on and your walking stick
in your hand. You must eat it in a hurry; this is the
LORD's Passover.
12"That night I will go through the land of
Egypt and kill all the firstborn animals and people
in the land of Egypt. I will also punish all the gods
of Egypt. I am the LORD. 13But the blood will be a
sign on the houses where you are. When I see the
blood, I will pass over you. Nothing terrible will
hurt you when I punish the land of Egypt.
14"You are always to remember this day and
celebrate it with a feast to the LORD. Your descendants are to honor the LORD with this feast from
now on. 15For this feast you must eat bread made
without yeast for seven days. On the first day, you
are to remove all the yeast from your houses. No
one should eat any yeast for the full seven days of
the feast, or that person will be cut off from Israel.
16You are to have holy meetings on the first and
last days of the feast. You must not do any work
on these days; the only work you may do is to prepare your meals. 17You must celebrate the Feast

11:10 Growing Old: Exodus 13
12:11 *Passover.* This Israelite festival is still celebrated today by Jewish people and celebrates the night God "passed over" the houses of Israel to enter and kill the firstborn children of the Egyptians.

of Unleavened Bread, because on this very day I brought your divisions of people out of Egypt. So all of your descendants must celebrate this day. This is a law that will last from now on. 18In the first month of the year you are to eat bread made without yeast, from the evening of the fourteenth day until the evening of the twenty-first day. 19For seven days there must not be any yeast in your houses. Anybody who eats yeast during this time, either an Israelite or non-Israelite, must be cut off from the community of Israel. 20During this feast you must not eat anything made with yeast. You must eat only bread made without yeast wherever you live."

21Then Moses called all the older leaders of Israel together and told them, "Get the animals for your families and kill the lamb for the Passover. 22Take a branch of the hyssop plant, dip it into the bowl filled with blood, and then wipe the blood on the sides and tops of the doorframes. No one may leave that house until morning. 23When the LORD goes through Egypt to kill the Egyptians, he will see the blood on the sides and tops of the doorframes, and he will pass over that house. He will not let the one who brings death come into your houses and kill you.

24"You must keep this command as a law for you and your descendants from now on. 25Do this when you go to the land the LORD has promised to give you. 26When your children ask you, 'Why are we doing these things?' 27you will say, 'This is the Passover sacrifice to honor the LORD. When we were in Egypt, the LORD passed over the houses of Israel, and when he killed the Egyptians, he saved our homes.'" Then the people bowed down and worshiped the LORD. 28They did just as the LORD commanded Moses and Aaron.

29At midnight the LORD killed all the firstborn sons in the land of Egypt—from the firstborn of the king who sat on the throne to the firstborn of the prisoner in jail. Also, all the firstborn farm animals died. 30The king, his officers, and all the Egyptians got up during the night because someone had died in every house. So there was a loud outcry everywhere in Egypt.

Israel Leaves Egypt

31During the night the king called for Moses and Aaron and said, "Get up and leave my people. You and your people may do as you have asked; go and worship the LORD. 32Take all of your flocks and herds as you have asked, and go. And also bless me." 33The Egyptians also asked the Israelites to hurry and leave, saying, "If you don't leave, we will all die!"

34So the people took their dough before the yeast was added. They wrapped the bowls for making dough in clothing and carried them on their shoulders. 35The Israelites did what Moses told them to do and asked their Egyptian neighbors for things made of silver and gold and for clothing. 36The LORD caused the Egyptians to think well of them, and the Egyptians gave the people everything they asked for. So the Israelites took rich gifts from them.

37The Israelites traveled from Rameses to Succoth. There were about six hundred thousand men walking, not including the women and children. 38Many other people who were not Israelites went with them, as well as a large number of sheep, goats, and cattle. 39The Israelites used the dough they had brought out of Egypt to bake loaves of bread without yeast. The dough had no yeast in it, because they had been rushed out of Egypt and had no time to get food ready for their trip.

40The people of Israel had lived in Egypt for four hundred thirty years; 41on the very day the four hundred thirty years ended, the LORD's divisions of people left Egypt. 42That night the LORD kept watch to bring them out of Egypt, and so on this same night the Israelites are to keep watch to honor the LORD from now on.

43The LORD told Moses and Aaron, "Here are the rules for Passover: No foreigner is to eat the Passover. 44If someone buys a slave and circumcises him, the slave may eat the Passover. 45But neither a person who lives for a short time in your country nor a hired worker may eat it.

46"The meal must be eaten inside a house; take none of the meat outside the house. Don't break any of the bones. 47The whole community of Israel must take part in this feast. 48A foreigner who lives with you may share in the LORD's Passover if all the males in his house become circumcised. Then, since he will be like a citizen of Israel, he may share in the meal. But a man who is not circumcised may not eat the Passover meal. 49The same rules apply to an Israelite born in the country or to a foreigner living there."

50So all the Israelites did just as the LORD had commanded Moses and Aaron. 51On that same day the LORD led the Israelites out of Egypt by their divisions.

12:26 Instruction: Exodus 13:8
12:49 Circumcision: Joshua 5
12:49 Racism: Exodus 34:12–16
12:51 Celebration: Exodus 15
12:51 Exodus/New Exodus: See article on page 229.

The Law of the Firstborn

13 Then the LORD said to Moses, 2“Give every firstborn male to me. Every firstborn male among the Israelites belongs to me, whether human or animal.”

3Moses said to the people, “Remember this day, the day you left Egypt. You were slaves in that land, but the LORD with his great power brought you out of it. You must not eat bread made with yeast. 4Today, in the month of Abib, you are leaving Egypt. 5The LORD will lead you to the land of the Canaanites, Hittites, Amorites, Hivites, and Jebusites. This is the land he promised your ancestors he would give you, a fertile land. There you must celebrate this feast during the first month of every year. 6For seven days you must eat bread made without yeast, and on the seventh day there will be a feast to honor the LORD. 7So for seven days you must not eat any bread made with yeast. There must be no bread made with yeast anywhere in your land. 8On that day you should tell your son: ‘We are having this feast because of what the LORD did for me when I came out of Egypt.’ 9This feast will help you remember, like a mark on your hand or a reminder on your forehead. This feast will remind you to speak the LORD’s teachings, because the LORD used his great power to bring you out of Egypt. 10So celebrate this feast every year at the right time.

11“And when the LORD takes you into the land of the Canaanites, the land he promised to give you and your ancestors, 12you must give him every firstborn male. Also every firstborn male animal must be given to the LORD. 13Buy back every firstborn donkey by offering a lamb. But if you don’t want to buy the donkey back, then break its neck. You must buy back from the LORD every firstborn of your sons.

14“From now on when your son asks you, ‘What does this mean?’ you will answer, ‘With his great power, the LORD brought us out from Egypt, the land where we were slaves. 15The king of Egypt was stubborn and refused to let us leave. But the LORD killed every firstborn male in Egypt, both human and animal. That is why I sacrifice every firstborn male animal to the LORD, and that is why I buy back each of my firstborn sons from the LORD.’ 16This feast is like a mark on your hand and a reminder on your forehead to help you remember that the LORD brought us out of Egypt with his great power.”

The Way Out of Egypt

17When the king sent the people out of Egypt, God did not lead them on the road through the Philistine country, though that was the shortest way. God said, “If they have to fight, they might change their minds and go back to Egypt.” 18So God led them through the desert toward the Red Sea. The Israelites were dressed for fighting when they left the land of Egypt.

19Moses carried the bones of Joseph with him, because before Joseph died, he had made the Israelites promise to do this. He had said, “When God saves you, remember to carry my bones with you out of Egypt.”

20The Israelites left Succoth and camped at Etham, on the edge of the desert. 21The LORD showed them the way; during the day he went ahead of them in a pillar of cloud, and during the night he was in a pillar of fire to give them light. In this way they could travel during the day or night. 22The pillar of cloud was always with them during the day, and the pillar of fire was always with them at night.

14 Then the LORD said to Moses, 2“Tell the Israelites to turn back to Pi Hahiroth and to camp between Migdol and the Red Sea. Camp across from Baal Zephon, on the shore of the sea. 3The king will think, ‘The Israelites are lost, trapped by the desert.’ 4I will make the king stubborn again so he will chase after them, but I will defeat the king and his army. This will bring honor to me, and the Egyptians will know that I am the LORD.” The Israelites did just as they were told.

The King Chases the Israelites

5When the king of Egypt was told that the Israelites had left, he and his officers changed their minds about them. They said, “What have we done? We have let the Israelites leave. We have lost our slaves!” 6So the king prepared his war chariot and took his army with him. 7He took six hundred of his best chariots, together with all the other chariots of Egypt, each with an officer in it. 8The LORD made the king of Egypt stubborn, so he chased the Israelites, who were leaving victoriously. 9The Egyptians—with all the king’s horses, chariot drivers, and army—chased the Israelites. They caught up with them while they were camped by the Red Sea, near Pi Hahiroth and Baal Zephon.

13:2 *firstborn.* The firstborn son was the favored son, who normally received the major portion of the inheritance and who continued the family name.

13:8 Instruction: Exodus 13:14

13:14 Instruction: Deuteronomy 4:9

13:21 Road/Way: Deuteronomy 1:31

13:22 Growing Old: Exodus 18:15–16

10When the Israelites saw the king and his
army coming after them, they were very frightened
and cried to the LORD for help. 11They said to Moses,
"What have you done to us? Why did you bring us
out of Egypt to die in the desert? There were plenty
of graves for us in Egypt. 12We told you in Egypt,
'Let us alone; we will stay and serve the Egyptians.'
Now we will die in the desert."

13But Moses answered, "Don't be afraid! Stand
still and you will see the LORD save you today. You
will never see these Egyptians again after today.
14You only need to remain calm; the LORD will
fight for you."

15Then the LORD said to Moses, "Why are you
crying out to me? Command the Israelites to start
moving. 16Raise your walking stick and hold it
over the sea so that the sea will split and the people
can cross it on dry land. 17I will make the Egyptians
stubborn so they will chase the Israelites, but I will
be honored when I defeat the king and all of his
chariot drivers and chariots. 18When I defeat the
king, his chariot drivers, and chariots, the Egyptians
will know that I am the LORD."

19Now the angel of God that usually traveled in
front of Israel's army moved behind them. Also,
the pillar of cloud moved from in front of the people and stood behind them. 20So the cloud came
between the Egyptians and the Israelites. This
made it dark for the Egyptians but gave light to
the Israelites. So the cloud kept the two armies
apart all night.

21Then Moses held his hand over the sea. All
that night the LORD drove back the sea with a
strong east wind, making the sea become dry
ground. The water was split, 22and the Israelites
went through the sea on dry land, with a wall of
water on their right and on their left.

23Then all the king's horses, chariots, and chariot drivers followed them into the sea. 24When
morning came, the LORD looked down from the
pillar of cloud and fire at the Egyptian army and
made them panic. 25He kept the wheels of the
chariots from turning, making it hard to drive the
chariots. The Egyptians shouted, "Let's get away
from the Israelites! The LORD is fighting for them
and against Egypt."

26Then the LORD told Moses, "Hold your hand
over the sea so that the water will come back over
the Egyptians, their chariots, and chariot drivers."
27So Moses raised his hand over the sea, and at
dawn the sea returned to its place. The Egyptians
tried to run from it, but the LORD swept them away
into the sea. 28The water returned, covering the
chariots, chariot drivers, and all the king's army
that had followed the Israelites into the sea. Not
one of them survived.

29But the Israelites crossed the sea on dry land,
with a wall of water on their right and on their
left. 30So that day the LORD saved the Israelites from
the Egyptians, and the Israelites saw the Egyptians
lying dead on the seashore. 31When the Israelites
saw the great power the LORD had used against the
Egyptians, they feared the LORD, and they trusted
him and his servant Moses.

The Song of Moses

15 Then Moses and the Israelites sang this
song to the LORD:

"I will sing to the LORD,
because he is worthy of great honor.
He has thrown the horse and its rider
into the sea.
2The LORD gives me strength and makes me sing;
he has saved me.
He is my God,
and I will praise him.
He is the God of my fathers,
and I will honor him.
3The LORD is a warrior;
the LORD is his name.
4The chariots and soldiers of the king
of Egypt
he has thrown into the sea.
The king's best officers
are drowned in the Red Sea.
5The deep waters covered them,
and they sank to the bottom like a rock.
6Your right hand, LORD,
is amazingly strong.
LORD, your right hand
broke the enemy to pieces.
7In your great victory
you destroyed those who were against you.
Your anger destroyed them,
like fire burning straw.
8Just a blast of your breath,
and the waters piled up.
The moving water stood like a wall;
the deep waters became solid in the middle
of the sea.

9"The enemy bragged,
'I'll chase them and catch them.

14:12 Rebellion: Exodus 32:1–6
14:31 Servant of the Lord: Exodus 21:2–6
14:31 Water: Job 36:22–37:13

15:8 Flood: Psalm 66:6
15:8 Images of God: Psalm 36:7–9

I'll take all their riches;
  I'll take all I want.
I'll pull out my sword,
  and my hand will destroy them.'
10But you blew on them with your breath
  and covered them with the sea.
They sank like lead
  in the raging water.

11"Are there any gods like you, LORD?
  There are no gods like you.
  You are wonderfully holy,
  amazingly powerful,
  a worker of miracles.
12You reached out with your right hand,
  and the earth swallowed our enemies.
13You keep your loving promise
  and lead the people you have saved.
With your strength you will guide them
  to your holy place.

14"The other nations will hear this and tremble
    with fear;
  terror will take hold of the Philistines.
15The leaders of the tribes of Edom will be very
    frightened;
  the powerful men of Moab will shake with fear;
  the people of Canaan will lose all their courage.
16Terror and horror will fall on them.
When they see your strength,
  they will be as still as a rock.
They will be still until your people pass by,
    LORD.
  They will be still until the people you have
    taken as your own pass by.
17You will lead your people and place them
  on your very own mountain,
the place that you, LORD, made for yourself to
    live,
  the temple, Lord, that your hands have made.
18The LORD will be king forever!"

19The horses, chariot drivers, and chariots of
the king of Egypt went into the sea, and the LORD
covered them with water from the sea. But the
Israelites walked through the sea on dry land.
20Then Aaron's sister Miriam, a prophetess, took
a tambourine in her hand. All the women followed her, playing tambourines and dancing.
21Miriam told them:

"Sing to the LORD,
  because he is worthy of great honor;
he has thrown the horse and its rider
  into the sea."

Bitter Water Becomes Good

22Moses led the Israelites away from the Red Sea
into the Desert of Shur. They traveled for three
days in the desert but found no water. 23Then they
came to Marah, where there was water, but they
could not drink it because it was too bitter. (That
is why the place was named Marah.) 24The people grumbled to Moses and asked, "What will we
drink?"

25So Moses cried out to the LORD, and the LORD
showed him a tree. When Moses threw the tree
into the water, the water became good to drink.

There the LORD gave the people a rule and a law
to live by, and there he tested their loyalty to him.
26He said, "You must obey the LORD your God and
do what he says is right. If you obey all his commands and keep his rules, I will not bring on you
any of the sicknesses I brought on the Egyptians. I
am the LORD who heals you."

27Then the people traveled to Elim, where there
were twelve springs of water and seventy palm
trees. So the people camped there near the water.

The People Demand Food

16 The whole Israelite community left Elim
and came to the Desert of Sin, which was
between Elim and Sinai; they arrived there on the
fifteenth day of the second month after they had
left Egypt. 2Then the whole Israelite community
grumbled to Moses and Aaron in the desert. 3They
said to them, "It would have been better if the
LORD had killed us in the land of Egypt. There we
had meat to eat and all the food we wanted. But
you have brought us into this desert to starve us
to death."

4Then the LORD said to Moses, "I will cause
food to fall like rain from the sky for all of you.
Every day the people must go out and gather what
they need for that day. I want to see if the people
will do what I teach them. 5On the sixth day of
each week, they are to gather twice as much as
they gather on other days. Then they are to prepare it."

6So Moses and Aaron said to all the Israelites:
"This evening you will know that the LORD is the

15:18 The People of God: Deuteronomy 32:35–40
15:23 *Marah.* This name means "bitter."
15:23 *desert.* Or, more precisely, *wilderness.* The Israelites journey in an area that is rugged and difficult, but is not without vegetation, springs, and oases. We are not to imagine a completely barren sandy area.

15:25 Test/Temptation: Psalm 139:1
15:26 Physical Handicap: Leviticus 19:14
15:27 Exodus/New Exodus: Psalm 77:16–20
15:27 Celebration: Numbers 28:16–29:40

one who brought you out of Egypt. 7Tomorrow morning you will see the glory of the LORD, because he has heard you grumble against him. We are nothing, so you are not grumbling against us, but against the LORD." 8And Moses said, "Each evening the LORD will give you meat to eat, and every morning he will give you all the bread you want, because he has heard you grumble against him. You are not grumbling against Aaron and me, because we are nothing; you are grumbling against the LORD."

9Then Moses said to Aaron, "Speak to the whole community of the Israelites, and say to them, 'Meet together in the presence of the LORD, because he has heard your grumblings.'"

10While Aaron was speaking to the whole community of the Israelites, they looked toward the desert. There the glory of the LORD appeared in a cloud.

11The LORD said to Moses, 12"I have heard the grumblings of the people of Israel. So tell them, 'At twilight you will eat meat, and every morning you will eat all the bread you want. Then you will know I am the LORD your God.'"

13That evening quail came and covered the camp, and in the morning dew lay around the camp. 14When the dew was gone, thin flakes like frost were on the desert ground. 15When the Israelites saw it, they asked each other, "What is it?" because they did not know what it was.

So Moses told them, "This is the bread the LORD has given you to eat. 16The LORD has commanded, 'Each one of you must gather what he needs, about two quarts for every person in your family.'"

17So the people of Israel did this; some people gathered much, and some gathered little. 18Then they measured it. The person who gathered more did not have too much, nor did the person who gathered less have too little. Each person gathered just as much as he needed.

19Moses said to them, "Don't keep any of it to eat the next day." 20But some of the people did not listen to Moses and kept part of it to eat the next morning. It became full of worms and began to stink, so Moses was angry with those people.

21Every morning each person gathered as much food as he needed, but when the sun became hot, it melted away.

22On the sixth day the people gathered twice as much food—four quarts for every person. When all the leaders of the community came and told this to Moses, 23he said to them, "This is what the LORD commanded, because tomorrow is the Sabbath, the LORD's holy day of rest. Bake what you want to bake, and boil what you want to boil

"That evening quail came and covered the camp . . ." (16:13).

today. Save the rest of the food until tomorrow morning."

24So the people saved it until the next morning, as Moses had commanded, and none of it began to stink or have worms in it. 25Moses told the people, "Eat the food you gathered yesterday. Today is a Sabbath, the LORD's day of rest; you will not find any out in the field today. 26You should gather the food for six days, but the seventh day is a Sabbath day. On that day there will not be any food on the ground."

27On the seventh day some of the people went out to gather food, but they couldn't find any. 28Then the LORD said to Moses, "How long will you people refuse to obey my commands and teachings? 29Look, the LORD has made the Sabbath a day of rest for you. So on the sixth day he will give you enough food for two days, but on the seventh day each of you must stay where you are. Do not go anywhere." 30So the people rested on the seventh day.

31The people of Israel called the food manna. It was like small white seeds and tasted like wafers made with honey.

32Then Moses said, "The LORD said, 'Save two quarts of this food for your descendants. Then they can see the food I gave you to eat in the desert when I brought you out of Egypt.'"

33Moses told Aaron, "Take a jar and fill it with two quarts of manna. Then place it before the

16:31 *manna.* This is the name given to the food which God provided for the Israelites during their journey in the desert. It is a Hebrew name and sounds like the question "What is it?" This question continues until today. While some people try to identify it with some known food, this is impossible to prove and most likely we are to understand it as specially made by God for this occasion.

LORD, and save it for your descendants." 34So Aaron did what the LORD had commanded Moses. He put the jar of manna in front of the Agreement to keep it safe. 35The Israelites ate manna for forty years, until they came to the land where they settled—the edge of the land of Canaan. 36The measure they used for the manna was two quarts, or one-tenth of an ephah.

Water from a Rock

17 The whole Israelite community left the Desert of Sin and traveled from place to place, as the LORD commanded. They camped at Rephidim, but there was no water there for the people to drink. 2So they quarreled with Moses and said, "Give us water to drink."

Moses said to them, "Why do you quarrel with me? Why are you testing the LORD?"

3But the people were very thirsty for water, so they grumbled against Moses. They said, "Why did you bring us out of Egypt? Was it to kill us, our children, and our farm animals with thirst?"

4So Moses cried to the LORD, "What can I do with these people? They are almost ready to stone me to death."

5The LORD said to Moses, "Go ahead of the people, and take some of the older leaders of Israel with you. Carry with you the walking stick that you used to strike the Nile River. Now go! 6I will stand in front of you on a rock at Mount Sinai. Hit that rock with the stick, and water will come out of it so that the people can drink." Moses did these things as the older leaders of Israel watched. 7He named that place Massah, because the Israelites tested the LORD when they asked, "Is the LORD with us or not?" He also named it Meribah, because they quarreled.

The Amalekites Fight Israel

8At Rephidim the Amalekites came and fought the Israelites. 9So Moses said to Joshua, "Choose some men and go and fight the Amalekites. Tomorrow I will stand on the top of the hill, holding the walking stick of God in my hands."

10Joshua obeyed Moses and went to fight the Amalekites, while Moses, Aaron, and Hur went to the top of the hill. 11As long as Moses held his hands up, the Israelites would win the fight, but when Moses put his hands down, the Amalekites would win. 12Later, when Moses' arms became tired, the men put a large rock under him, and he sat on it. Then Aaron and Hur held up Moses' hands—Aaron on one side and Hur on the other. They kept his hands steady until the sun went down. 13So Joshua defeated the Amalekites in this battle.

14Then the LORD said to Moses, "Write about this battle in a book so people will remember. And be sure to tell Joshua, because I will completely destroy the Amalekites from the earth."

15Then Moses built an altar and named it The LORD is my Banner. 16Moses said, "I lifted my hands toward the LORD's throne. The LORD will fight against the Amalekites forever."

Jethro Visits Moses

18 Jethro, Moses' father-in-law, was the priest of Midian. He heard about everything that God had done for Moses and his people, the Israelites, and how the LORD had led the Israelites out of Egypt. 2Now Moses had sent his wife Zipporah to Jethro, his father-in-law, 3along with his two sons. The first son was named Gershom, because when he was born, Moses said, "I am a stranger in a foreign country." 4The other son was named Eliezer, because when he was born, Moses said, "The God of my father is my help. He saved me from the king of Egypt."

5So Jethro, Moses' father-in-law, took Moses' wife and his two sons and went to Moses. He was camped in the desert near the mountain of God. 6Jethro had sent a message ahead to Moses that said, "I, Jethro, your father-in-law, am coming to you with your wife and her two sons."

16:34 The "Agreement" is a one-word description of the two stone tablets of the Ten Commandments (Exodus 34:29), which Moses had put into the Ark of the Agreement (Exodus 40:20). Thus, Aaron put the jar of manna also into the Ark in front of the two stone tablets. Later, Aaron's walking stick was also placed in or near the Ark (Numbers 17:10; Hebrews 9:3–4). The expression "before the Lord" in the previous verse emphasizes how the people of Israel understood the Ark as representing God's presence.

16:36 *ephah.* An ephah was a measure that equaled twenty quarts.

17:7 *Massah.* This name is the Hebrew word for "testing."

17:7 *Meribah.* This name is the Hebrew word for "quarrel."

17:7 Apostasy: Exodus 32–33

17:9 This is the first mention of Joshua, Moses' assistant and later leader of Israel, in the Bible. We see him working in the area that would distinguish him during the conquest of the Promised Land—as a warrior. God used him time and again to win victories over Israel's enemies. In this way, he anticipates the coming of Jesus Christ who fights a spiritual battle on our behalf.

17:10 See comment at 4:2.

17:15 Names of God: Job 1:21

17:16 Wilderness (Desert): 1 Kings 19

17:16 Table Fellowship/Lord's Supper: Exodus 24:9–11

17:16 The Lord's promise that he would be at war against the Amalekites from generation to generation is brought against Haman, the enemy of the Persian Jews, many centuries later. In the Book of Esther, Haman is called an Agagite (Esther 3:1, 8:5). Agag was the king of the Amalekites when Saul was the first king of Israel (1 Samuel 15:8). By calling Haman an Agagite, he is labeled for destruction by God under the promise of Exodus 17:16.

18:3 *Gershom.* This name sounds like the Hebrew word for "a stranger there."

18:4 *Eliezer.* This name sounds like the Hebrew words "My God is my help."

7So Moses went out to meet his father-in-law
and bowed down and kissed him. After the two
men asked about each other's health, they went
into Moses' tent. 8Moses told his father-in-law
everything the LORD had done to the king and the
Egyptians to help Israel. He told about all the problems they had faced along the way and how the
LORD had saved them.
9Jethro was very happy to hear all the good things
the LORD had done for Israel when he had saved
them from the Egyptians. 10He said, "Praise the
LORD. He has saved you from the Egyptians and
their king, and he has saved the people from the
power of the Egyptians. 11Now I know the LORD is
greater than all gods, because he did this to those
who looked down on Israel." 12Then Jethro, Moses'
father-in-law, gave a whole burnt offering and other
sacrifices to God. Aaron and all the older leaders of
Israel came to Moses' father-in-law to eat the holy
meal together before God.
13The next day Moses solved disagreements
among the people, and the people stood around
him from morning until night. 14When Moses'
father-in-law saw all that Moses was doing for the
people, he asked, "What is all this you are doing
for the people? Why are you the only one to solve
disagreements? All the people are standing around
you from morning until night!"
15Then Moses said to his father-in-law, "It is
because the people come to me for God's help in
solving their disagreements. 16When people have
a disagreement, they come to me, and I decide
who is right. I tell them God's laws and teachings."
17Moses' father-in-law said to him, "You are
not doing this right. 18You and the people who
come to you will get too tired. This is too much
work for you; you can't do it by yourself. 19Now listen to me, and I will give you some advice. I want
God to be with you. You must speak to God for the
people and tell him about their disagreements.
20Warn them about the laws and teachings, and
teach them the right way to live and what they
should do. 21But choose some capable men from
among the people—men who respect God, who
can be trusted, and who will not change their
decisions for money. Make these men officers
over the people, to rule over groups of thousands,
hundreds, fifties, and tens. 22Let these officers solve
the disagreements among the people all the time.
They can bring the hard cases to you, but they can
decide the simple cases themselves. That will make
it easier for you, because they will share the work
with you. 23If you do this as God commands you,
then you will be able to do your job, and all the people will go home with their disagreements solved."
24So Moses listened to his father-in-law and did
everything he said. 25He chose capable men from
all the Israelites and made them leaders over the
people; they were officers over groups of thousands, hundreds, fifties, and tens. 26These officers
solved disagreements among the people all the
time. They brought the hard cases to Moses, but
they decided the simple cases themselves.
27So Moses sent his father-in-law on his way,
and Jethro went back to his own home.

Israel Camps at Sinai

19 Exactly three months after the Israelites had
left Egypt, they reached the Desert of Sinai.
2When they left Rephidim, they came to the
Desert of Sinai and camped in the desert in front of
the mountain. 3Then Moses went up on the
mountain to God. The LORD called to him from the
mountain and said, "Say this to the family of Jacob,
and tell the people of Israel: 4'Every one of you has
seen what I did to the people of Egypt. You saw
how I carried you out of Egypt, as if on eagle's
wings. And I brought you here to me. 5So now if
you obey me and keep my agreement, you will be
my own possession, chosen from all nations. Even
though the whole earth is mine, 6you will be my
kingdom of priests and a holy nation.' You must
tell the Israelites these words."
7So Moses went down and called the older leaders of the people together. He told them all the
words the LORD had commanded him to say. 8All
the people answered together, "We will do everything he has said." Then Moses took their answer
back to the LORD.
9And the LORD said to Moses, "I will come to
you in a thick cloud and speak to you. The people
will hear me speaking with you and will always
trust you." Then Moses told the LORD what the
people had said.
10The LORD said to Moses, "Go to the people and

18:13 Government: Exodus 18:15–16
18:16 Growing Old: Leviticus 19:32
18:16 Government: Matthew 6:3
19:5 God entered into an agreement with Israel through the leadership of Moses. This agreement recognized that the people of God were no longer simply a family, but a nation. The laws, including the Ten Commandments, are part of the obligations that Israel owed to God for entering into an agreement with him.
19:5–6 God set the nation of Israel apart from all the other nations as the object of his special favor and as those who should serve him. The sacrifices for the removal of their sin (Leviticus 1–8) and the guidelines for living their lives in a way that brought him honor (Exodus 20; Deuteronomy 5) pointed toward the perfect sacrifice of Jesus Christ. His sacrifice on our behalf brings us into God's presence as people who are holy (Colossians 1:22) and frees us from the power of sin so that we may live holy lives in service to God, as he desires (Hebrews 9:14; 1 Peter 1:14–16).
19:6 Community: Exodus 20:21–23:19

BIRTHS

GENESIS 5

Why does the Bible include so many accounts of births? What theological purpose do they serve? What role does barrenness play in birth accounts?

In Genesis 1:28 God tells humans to have children and fill the earth. The early chapters of Genesis describe the beginning of this process. Birth accounts (also called family histories) play a major role. They give historical information and are used to connect historical accounts together. The family history of Adam is given in Genesis 5. It takes one from the events of Adam's family in Genesis 4 to Noah and the flood. Genesis 10 gives the family histories of Noah's three sons: Japheth, Ham, and Shem. These histories demonstrate how families grew, spread over the earth, and formed nations.

Beginning at Genesis 11:10 attention is focused on the family history of Shem. This birth account brings us down to Abram (later called Abraham, 17:5). God begins to work through him and his family to fulfill God's purposes for the world. God told Abraham: "all the people on the earth will be blessed through you" (Genesis 12:3).

Abraham and Sarah must have a son for God to fulfill his promises. However, they are too old to have children. Here is one of the first cases of barrenness recorded in the Bible. The inability to have children brought humiliation and shame to a woman (Genesis 30:22–23). Children were evidence of God's blessing and helped ensure the future well-being of the family (Psalm 127). Many cases of barrenness recorded in Scripture occurred in the lives of Abraham and his descendants (Sarah: Genesis 17:15–21; Rebekah: 25:21; and Rachel: 30:22–23). In the case of Abraham and Sarah, the point is clearly made that through Isaac, the miraculous child of promise born to them in their old age, God would continue his agreement with Abraham. God is able to fulfill his promises, even in seemingly impossible situations. In many of the other cases of barrenness recorded in Scripture, the child that is born to a previously barren mother takes up a special role among the people of God: Samson (Judges 13), Samuel (1 Samuel 1), and John the Baptist (Luke 1).

The rest of the Book of Genesis tells the story of Abraham, Isaac, and Jacob. The family histories are an important part of staging the events. (For Isaac, 25:19–26; for Jacob, 35:23–29, including 46:8–27, which gives the names of Jacob and his descendants who went into Egypt.) These family histories record the line of God's people and demonstrate the fulfillment of God's promises to them.

The birth accounts in Chronicles, Ezra, and Nehemiah are significant because these books speak to the situation of restoration after the captivity. The Temple had been destroyed and the people carried away into exile. When they returned to the land to establish the nation and the worship of God at the Temple, family histories helped solved questions of land inheritance. They also ensured that the right people were in charge of the Temple and sacrifices. The birth accounts in 1 Chronicles 1–9 begin with Adam and conclude with King Saul. Much attention is given to David and his family (chapter 3). Birth accounts of the Levites and the priests are given in chapters 23–24. Both Ezra 2 and Nehemiah 7 give an account of the captives who returned from the exile in Babylon. It was important when restoring the nation that people set up the institutions according to the way God had meant them to be set up, which included using people who had proper family connections to carry out specific functions. People who could not find their family records could not be priests (Ezra 2:62).

The importance of connecting Jesus with the history of the Jewish people is seen in the fact that two of the gospels include a family history of Jesus. He is the one through whom the promises of God will be fulfilled. Luke's family history of Jesus stresses Joseph's side of the family. He begins with Joseph and goes all the way back to Adam. Matthew begins his story with a family history showing descent from Abraham to Mary. He highlights connections with Abraham and David. Jesus was from the right family to receive the throne of David (Luke 1:32–33).

Although family connections were important for people in the Old Testament because God was accomplishing his purposes through the Jewish people, such family connections are no longer significant after the death and resurrection of Jesus. The gospel goes out to everyone regardless of their family background. If a person believes in Jesus they have a spiritual heritage linked to Abraham. As Galatians 3:29 puts it: "You belong to Christ, so you are Abraham's descendants. You will inherit all of God's blessings because of the promise God made to Abraham."

Births: For additional scriptures on this topic go to Genesis 10.

FLOOD

GENESIS 6:9

Why was the story of the Flood important for the Israelites? Does the New Testament place the same importance on the Flood story? Does the story of the flood speak to Christians today?

To grasp the importance of Noah's flood to Genesis and the rest of the Bible, we need to understand the importance of water in the minds of people who lived during the times of the Bible. To the ancients, water was either restorative or destructive. Every society was agrarian, and water was essential for the sustenance of life and happiness. The Egyptians and Babylonians, for example, lived according to the rhythm of the great rivers that flowed through their lands.

But the ancients feared the destructive nature of water, too. To them, the oceans were dangerous places inhabited by dark, mysterious creatures. Thus, people who lived during the time of ancient Israel feared the sea because it represented chaos and uncertainty. They also feared floods. Many of the great cities stood near the banks of rivers such as the Nile and the Euphrates, and the inhabitants lived in fear of being overwhelmed by a flooding river at certain times of the year.

Essentially, water in the ancient world—whether too little or too much—could bring chaos to the lives of the people. Thus worship of pagan deities included prayers that the gods would deliver the people from the chaos of drought or flood.

In its opening chapter, the Bible acknowledges that water can be dreadfully chaotic. Genesis 1 opens with this mention of water: "Darkness covered the ocean, and God's Spirit was moving over the water" (Genesis 1:2). We see that Noah's flood was not the first time the earth was covered by water. Indeed, God began his creative activity when "the earth was empty and had no form" (Genesis 1:2). From this watery wasteland, God created the dry land by separating it from the ocean (Genesis 1:9). It was important that the Hebrews worship a God who had power over the destructive nature of water.

The flood of Genesis 6–9 is a return to the wasteland of Genesis 1. God removed the flood in Genesis 1 to bring life, but now in Genesis 6 he floods the earth in order to destroy. This "second" flood was sent to punish the people who had become so wicked in those days that God was sorry he had even created them (6:5–7). In just a few chapters, humanity had moved from a beautiful, peaceful garden to the devastation of the flood. The people's disobedience had returned death and destruction to the earth.

Not everyone was destroyed though. There was one person who was an exception to the wicked people covering the earth. Genesis 6:8 tells us that "Noah pleased the LORD." God informed Noah that he was going to destroy the earth with a flood but that he would rescue him and his family. God gave specific commands for Noah to build a boat that would carry his family and the pairs of animals safely during the flood (Genesis 6:11–21). Just as he promised, God sent the flood and destroyed every living creature on the earth, saving only Noah, his family, and the animals. Immediately after the floodwaters receded, God put a rainbow in the sky as a sign that he would never again punish humankind by destroying the earth with a flood (9:11).

The flood is important in the Old Testament because it teaches an important truth about God: he is the supreme ruler over chaos who can either punish the wicked with a flood or redeem the faithful out of a flood. In every stage of history, God has chosen his remnant who worship him and love him. Noah, in the lineage of Seth (Genesis 5:3), is the chosen one whom God delivers in the midst of the horrifying flood.

This same significance of the flood is also seen in the New Testament in 2 Peter 2:5. Peter compared the flood story to the destruction of Sodom and Gomorrah as God's certain punishment of wickedness. He also used the flood story to remind Christians that God keeps his promises. The crux of Peter's argument was that God is faithful to punish evildoers, but his mercy will surely save those who worship him. Once again the flood story is a warning to the disobedient but an encouragement to the righteous.

The story of the flood reminds Christians today that God is victorious over all chaos—even the chaos of the serpent: that is, Satan. Rarely though has God removed his people from trials and tribulations such as the flood. Noah had to experience the flood, and in so doing he learned the goodness and faithfulness of God. Just like Noah, we can rest in the truth that God always saves his people from the most terrifying dangers.

Flood: For additional scriptures on this topic go to Exodus 15:8.

have them spend today and tomorrow preparing
themselves. They must wash their clothes 11and be
ready by the day after tomorrow. On that day I, the
LORD, will come down on Mount Sinai, and all the
people will see me. 12But you must set a limit
around the mountain that the people are not to
cross. Tell them not to go up on the mountain and
not to touch the foot of it. Anyone who touches the
mountain must be put to death 13with stones or
shot with arrows. No one is allowed to touch him.
Whether it is a person or an animal, he will not
live. But the trumpet will make a long blast, and
only then may the people go up on the mountain."

14After Moses went down from the mountain to
the people, he made them prepare themselves for
service to God, and they washed their clothes.
15Then Moses said to the people, "Be ready in
three days. Do not have sexual relations during
this time."

16On the morning of the third day, there was
thunder and lightning with a thick cloud on the
mountain. There was a very loud blast from a trumpet, and all the people in the camp trembled.
17Then Moses led the people out of the camp to
meet God, and they stood at the foot of the mountain. 18Mount Sinai was covered with smoke,
because the LORD came down on it in fire. The
smoke rose from the mountain like smoke from a
furnace, and the whole mountain shook wildly.
19The sound from the trumpet became louder.
Then Moses spoke, and the voice of God answered
him.

20When the LORD came down on top of Mount
Sinai, he called Moses to come up to the top of
the mountain, and Moses went up. 21The LORD
said to Moses, "Go down and warn the people
that they must not force their way through to see
me. If they do, many of them will die. 22Even the
priests, who may come near me, must first prepare themselves. If they don't, I, the LORD, will
punish them."

23Moses told the LORD, "The people cannot
come up on Mount Sinai, because you yourself told
us, 'Set a limit around the mountain, and set it
apart as holy.'"

The ram's-horn trumpet was sounded for special occasions and announcements, such as in Exodus 19:13.

24The LORD said to him, "Go down and bring
Aaron up with you, but don't allow the priests or
the people to force their way through. They must
not come up to the LORD, or I will punish them."

25So Moses went down to the people and told
them these things.

The Ten Commandments

20 Then God spoke all these words:
2"I am the LORD your God, who brought
you out of the land of Egypt where you were
slaves.

3"You must not have any other gods except me.

4"You must not make for yourselves an idol
that looks like anything in the sky above or on the
earth below or in the water below the land. 5You
must not worship or serve any idol, because I, the
LORD your God, am a jealous God. If you hate me,
I will punish your children, and even your grandchildren and great-grandchildren. 6But I show
kindness to thousands who love me and obey my
commands.

7"You must not use the name of the LORD your
God thoughtlessly; the LORD will punish anyone
who misuses his name.

8"Remember to keep the Sabbath holy.
9Work and get everything done during six days
each week, 10but the seventh day is a day of rest to
honor the LORD your God. On that day no one may
do any work: not you, your son or daughter, your

19:11 *Mount Sinai.* God often appears on mountains in the Old Testament. In this way God uses the customs of the day to speak to his people since all the nations of the Near East thought that the mountains were the homes of their gods. Mountains symbolize strength and firmness.

19:15 *sexual relations.* Semen is protected by the holiness laws of the Old Testament (see Leviticus 15:16–18). This is not because it is "dirty" and "evil," but because it is important in the fulfillment of the promise of many descendants.

19:19 Presence of God: Exodus 40:34–38

19:25 Mountain: Exodus 34

20:3 Trinity: Exodus 34:14

20:5 Hate: Psalm 25:19

20:6 Human: Romans 1:23–25

20:7 To speak in the name of the Lord is to say that God himself is actually speaking. This verse warns anyone who speaks in the name of the Lord to be careful that they speak meaningfully and not carelessly. The name of God represents the very character of God. Therefore, any use of God's name implies that God's integrity is behind the words or deeds of the person using his name.

20:8 Memory: Deuteronomy 8:18

male or female slaves, your animals, or the foreigners living in your cities. 11The reason is that
in six days the LORD made everything—the sky,
the earth, the sea, and everything in them. On the
seventh day he rested. So the LORD blessed the
Sabbath day and made it holy.
12"Honor your father and your mother so that
you will live a long time in the land that the LORD
your God is going to give you.
13"You must not murder anyone.
14"You must not be guilty of adultery.
15"You must not steal.
16"You must not tell lies about your neighbor.
17"You must not want to take your neighbor's
house. You must not want his wife or his male or
female slaves, or his ox or his donkey, or anything
that belongs to your neighbor."
18When the people heard the thunder and the
trumpet, and when they saw the lightning and the
smoke rising from the mountain, they shook with
fear and stood far away from the mountain. 19Then
they said to Moses, "Speak to us yourself, and we
will listen. But don't let God speak to us, or we will
die."
20Then Moses said to the people, "Don't be
afraid, because God has come to test you. He wants
you to respect him so you will not sin."
21The people stood far away from the mountain
while Moses went near the dark cloud where God
was. 22Then the LORD told Moses to say these things
to the Israelites: "You yourselves have seen that I
talked with you from heaven. 23You must not use
gold or silver to make idols for yourselves; do not
worship these gods in addition to me.
24"Make an altar of dirt for me, and sacrifice on
it your whole burnt offerings and fellowship offerings, your sheep and your cattle. Worship me in
every place that I choose, and I will come and
bless you. 25If you use stones to make an altar for
me, don't use stones that you have shaped with
tools. When you use any tools on them, you make
them unsuitable for use in worship. 26And you
must not go up to my altar on steps, or people will
be able to see under your clothes."

Laws for Living

21 Then God said to Moses, "These are the laws
for living that you will give to the Israelites:
2"If you buy a Hebrew slave, he will serve you
for six years. In the seventh year you are to set
him free, and he will have to pay nothing. 3If he
is not married when he becomes your slave, he
must leave without a wife. But if he is married
when he becomes your slave, he may take his
wife with him. 4If the slave's master gives him a
wife, and she gives birth to sons or daughters,
the woman and her children will belong to the
master. When the slave is set free, only he may
leave.
5"But if the slave says, 'I love my master, my
wife and my children, and I don't want to go free,'
6then the slave's master must take him to God.
The master is to take him to a door or doorframe
and punch a hole through the slave's ear using a
sharp tool. Then the slave will serve that master
all his life.
7"If a man sells his daughter as a slave, the rules
for setting her free are different from the rules for
setting the male slaves free. 8If the master
wanted to marry her but then decided he was not
pleased with her, he must let one of her close relatives buy her back. He has no right to sell her to
foreigners, because he has treated her unfairly. 9If
the man who bought her promises to let the
woman marry his son, he must treat her as a
daughter. 10If the man who bought her marries
another woman, he must not keep his first wife
from having food or clothing or sexual relations.
11If he does not give her these three things, she
may go free, and she owes him no money.

20:10 Animals: Leviticus 11

20:11 Time: Psalm 90:12

20:12 Parenting: Deuteronomy 5:16

20:12 The fourth commandment directs God's people to honor, that is to respect and obey, their parents. The duty to defer to the authority of our parents is placed upon all people. Proper authority, after all, flows from God, so obeying such authority is ultimately obeying God himself.

20:13 The sixth commandment prohibits murder. One may not unlawfully take another person's life. After all, each human being is created in God's image. To murder another is to assault not just the human being, but God himself.

20:13 Murder: Numbers 35:16–31

20:14 The seventh of the Ten Commandments forbids adultery. Sexuality was created by God as the ultimate expression of the oneness of marriage. Sex is something to be enjoyed by married couples alone. Marriage, after all, is a relationship that allows no rivals. God forbids adultery, having sex with someone else's wife or husband, not because sex itself is bad, but because it is reserved for marriage alone.

20:17 Unlike the previous commandments which address outward actions, this tenth commandment goes deeper, addressing the inner thought world as well (see Matthew 5:21–30). This is the only commandment repeated twice in the New Testament (Romans 7:7–11, 13:9).

20:21–23:19 *Laws for Living.* The Laws for Living, also called the Book of the Agreement, contained laws about relationships, about injuries, about property, about fairness and justice, and about the feasts and Sabbath rests in which the people were to remember and celebrate God's goodness. The Law covered all kinds of situations and set up structures for Israelite society so that the people could become a holy nation, displaying God's loving–kindness and justice in such a compelling way that other nations would be drawn to God. The Torah took worship of the all-powerful, transcendent God and put it into everyday practices.

21:6 Servant of the Lord: Leviticus 25:42

21:17 Capital Punishment: Exodus 22:18–20

Laws About Injuries

12“Anyone who hits a person and kills him
must be put to death. 13But if a person kills someone accidentally, God allowed that to happen, so
the person must go to a place I will choose. 14But
if someone plans and murders another person on
purpose, put him to death, even if he has run to
my altar for safety.

15“Anyone who hits his father or his mother
must be put to death.

16“Anyone who kidnaps someone and either
sells him as a slave or still has him when he is
caught must be put to death.

17“Anyone who says cruel things to his father
or mother must be put to death.

18“If two men argue, and one hits the other
with a rock or with his fist, the one who is hurt but
not killed might have to stay in bed. 19Later if he is
able to get up and walk around outside with his
walking stick, the one who hit him is not to be
punished. But he must pay the injured man for the
loss of his time, and he must support the injured
man until he is completely healed.

20“If a man beats his male or female slave with
a stick, and the slave dies on the spot, the owner
must be punished. 21But if the slave gets well after
a day or two, the owner will not be punished since
the slave belongs to him.

22“Suppose two men are fighting and hit a pregnant woman, causing the baby to come out. If
there is no further injury, the man who caused the
accident must pay money—whatever amount the
woman’s husband says and the court allows. 23But
if there is further injury, then the punishment that
must be paid is life for life, 24eye for eye, tooth for
tooth, hand for hand, foot for foot, 25burn for burn,
wound for wound, and bruise for bruise.

26“If a man hits his male or female slave in the
eye, and the eye is blinded, the man is to free the
slave to pay for the eye. 27If a master knocks out a
tooth of his male or female slave, the man is to free
the slave to pay for the tooth.

28“If a man’s bull kills a man or woman, you must
kill that bull by throwing stones at it, and you
should not eat the bull. But the owner of the bull is
not guilty. 29However, suppose the bull has hurt
people in the past and the owner, though warned,
did not keep it in a pen. Then if it kills a man or
woman, the bull must be stoned to death, and the
owner must also be put to death. 30But if the family
of the dead person accepts money, the one who
owned the bull may buy back his life, but he must
pay whatever is demanded. 31Use this same law if
the bull kills a person’s son or daughter. 32If the bull
kills a male or female slave, the owner must pay the
master the price for a new slave, or twelve ounces
of silver, and the bull must also be stoned to death.

33“If a man takes the cover off a pit, or digs a pit
and does not cover it, and another man’s ox or
donkey comes and falls into it, 34the owner of the
pit must pay the owner of the animal for the loss.
The dead animal will belong to the one who pays.

35“If a man’s bull kills another man’s bull, they
must sell the bull that is alive. Both men will get
half of the money and half of the bull that was
killed. 36But if a person’s bull has hurt other animals in the past and the owner did not keep it in
a pen, that owner must pay bull for bull, and the
dead animal is his.

Property Laws

22 “If a man steals a bull or a sheep and kills or
sells it, he must pay back five bulls for the
one bull he stole and four sheep for the one sheep
he stole.

2-4“The robber who is caught must pay back
what he stole. If he owns nothing, he must be sold
as a slave to pay for what he stole. If the stolen animal is found alive with the robber, he must give
the owner two animals for every animal he stole,
whether it was a bull, donkey, or sheep.

“If a thief is killed while breaking into a house
at night, the one who killed him is not guilty of
murder. But if this happens during the day, he is
guilty of murder.

5“If a man lets his farm animal graze in his field
or vineyard, and it wanders into another man’s
field or vineyard, the owner of the animal must pay
back the loss from the best of his crop.

6“Suppose a man starts a fire that spreads
through the thornbushes to his neighbor’s field. If
the fire burns his neighbor’s growing grain or grain
that has been stacked, or if it burns his whole field,
the person who started the fire must pay for what
was burned.

7“Suppose a man gives his neighbor money or
other things to keep for him and those things are
stolen from the neighbor’s house. If the thief is
caught, he must pay back twice as much as he
stole. 8But if the thief is never found, the owner of
the house must make a promise before God that
he has not stolen his neighbor’s things.

9“Suppose two men disagree about who owns
something—whether ox, donkey, sheep, clothing, or something else that is lost. If each says, ‘This
is mine,’ each man must bring his case to God.
God’s judges will decide who is guilty, and that person must pay the other man twice as much as the
object is worth.

10“Suppose a man asks his neighbor to keep his donkey, ox, sheep, or some other animal for him, and that animal dies, gets hurt, or is taken away, without anyone seeing what happened. 11That neighbor must promise before the LORD that he did not harm or kill the other man’s animal, and the owner of the animal must accept his promise made before God. The neighbor does not have to pay the owner for the animal. 12But if the animal was stolen from the neighbor, he must pay the owner for it. 13If wild animals killed it, the neighbor must bring the body as proof, and he will not have to pay for the animal that was killed.

14“If a man borrows an animal from his neighbor, and it gets hurt or dies while the owner is not there, the one who borrowed it must pay the owner for the animal. 15But if the owner is with the animal, the one who borrowed it does not have to pay. If the animal was rented, the rental price covers the loss.

Laws and Relationships

16“Suppose a man finds a woman who is not pledged to be married and has never had sexual relations with a man. If he tricks her into having sexual relations with him, he must give her family the payment to marry her, and she will become his wife. 17But if her father refuses to allow his daughter to marry him, the man must still give the usual payment for a bride who has never had sexual relations.

18“Put to death any woman who does evil magic.

19“Put to death anyone who has sexual relations with an animal.

20“Destroy completely any person who makes a sacrifice to any god except the LORD.

21“Do not cheat or hurt a foreigner, because you were foreigners in the land of Egypt.

22“Do not cheat a widow or an orphan. 23If you do, and they cry out to me for help, I certainly will hear their cry. 24And I will be very angry and kill you in war. Then your wives will become widows, and your children will become orphans.

25“If you lend money to one of my people who is poor, do not treat him as a moneylender would. Charge him nothing for using your money. 26If your neighbor gives you his coat as a promise for the money he owes you, you must give it back to him by sunset, 27because it is the only cover to keep his body warm. He has nothing else to sleep in. If he cries out to me for help, I will listen, because I am merciful.

28“You must not speak against God or curse a leader of your people.

29“Do not hold back your offering from the first of your harvest and the first wine that you make. Also, you must give me your firstborn sons. 30You must do the same with your bulls and your sheep. Let the firstborn males stay with their mothers for seven days, and on the eighth day you must give them to me.

31“You are to be my holy people. You must not eat the meat of any animal that has been killed by wild animals. Instead, give it to the dogs.

Laws About Fairness

23 “You must not tell lies. If you are a witness in court, don’t help a wicked person by telling lies.

2“You must not do wrong just because everyone else is doing it. If you are a witness in court, you must not ruin a fair trial. You must not tell lies just because everyone else is. 3If a poor person is in court, you must not take his side just because he is poor.

4“If you see your enemy’s ox or donkey wandering away, you must return it to him. 5If you see that your enemy’s donkey has fallen because its load is too heavy, do not leave it there. You must help your enemy get the donkey back on its feet.

6“You must not be unfair to a poor person when he is in court. 7You must not lie when you accuse someone in court. Never allow an innocent or honest person to be put to death as punishment, because I will not treat guilty people as if they were innocent.

22:14 Neighbor: Exodus 32:27

22:16 Sexuality: Leviticus 18

22:16 *payment.* In biblical times the husband had to pay his future father-in-law at the time he married his wife. This payment probably paid the father back for the loss of a member of the family who could work to support the family.

22:17 Divorce: Leviticus 18

22:18 Magic: Leviticus 19:26

22:20 Capital Punishment: Exodus 35:2

22:21 Foreigner (Alien): Leviticus 24:22

22:21 The people of Israel were commanded to treat foreigners fairly because they were once foreigners themselves in Egypt. Christians should be especially sensitive to the needs of newly arrived foreigners, for in extending love and friendship in the name of Christ many can be won to him.

22:22 Adoption: Deuteronomy 10:18

22:22 *widow or orphan.* In ancient biblical society the widow and orphan who did not have husband or father to protect them were in a very dangerous position. God here protects them by law.

22:27 Debt/Loan: Deuteronomy 15:7–8

22:28 Citizen: Deuteronomy 1:17

22:31 Crime: Deuteronomy 19:15

23:3, 6 In many places in the Bible, God commands his people to help the poor. However, in these two laws God warns his people not to let a person’s poverty distort the judgment in a legal case. The people of God should neither favor nor despise the poor; they should render their judgments fairly without regard for one’s wealth or lack of it.

8"You must not accept money from a person who wants you to lie in court, because such money will not let you see what is right. Such money makes good people tell lies.

9"You must not mistreat a foreigner. You know how it feels to be a foreigner, because you were foreigners in Egypt.

Laws for the Sabbath

10"For six years you are to plant and harvest crops on your land. 11Then during the seventh year, do not plow or plant your land. If any food grows there, allow the poor people to have it, and let the wild animals eat what is left. You should do the same with your vineyards and your orchards of olive trees.

12"You should work six days a week, but on the seventh day you must rest. This lets your ox and your donkey rest, and it also lets the slave born in your house and the foreigner be refreshed.

13"Be sure to do all that I have said to you. You must not even say the names of other gods; those names must not come out of your mouth.

Three Yearly Feasts

14"Three times each year you must hold a feast to honor me. 15You must celebrate the Feast of Unleavened Bread in the way I commanded you. For seven days you must eat bread that is made without yeast at the set time during the month of Abib, the month when you came out of Egypt. No one is to come to worship me without bringing an offering.

16"You must celebrate the Feast of Weeks. Offer to God the first things you harvest from the crops you planted in your fields.

"You must celebrate the Feast of Shelters in the fall, when you gather all the crops from your fields.

17"So three times during every year all your males must come to worship the LORD God.

18"You must not offer animal blood along with anything that has yeast in it.

"You must not save any of the fat from the sacrifice for the next day.

19"You must bring the best of the firstfruits of your land to the Holy Tent of the LORD your God.

"You must not cook a young goat in its mother's milk.

God Will Help Israel

20"I am sending an angel ahead of you, who will protect you as you travel. He will lead you to the place I have prepared. 21Pay attention to the angel and obey him. Do not turn against him; he will not forgive such turning against him because my power is in him. 22If you listen carefully to all he says and do everything that I tell you, I will be an enemy to your enemies. I will fight all who fight against you. 23My angel will go ahead of you and take you into the land of the Amorites, Hittites, Perizzites, Canaanites, Hivites, and Jebusites, and I will destroy them.

24"You must not bow down to their gods or worship them. You must not live the way those people live. You must destroy their idols, breaking into pieces the stone pillars they use in worship. 25If you worship the LORD your God, I will bless your bread and your water. I will take away sickness from you. 26None of your women will have her baby die before it is born, and all women will have children. I will allow you to live long lives.

27"I will make your enemies afraid of me. I will confuse any people you fight against, and I will make all your enemies run away from you. 28I will send terror ahead of you that will force the Hivites, Canaanites, and Hittites out of your way. 29But I will not force all those people out in only one year. If I did, the land would become a desert and the wild animals would become too many for you. 30Instead, I will force those people out slowly, until there are enough of you to take over the land.

31"I will give you the land from the Red Sea to the Mediterranean Sea, and from the desert to the Euphrates River. I will give you power over the people who now live in the land, and you will force them out ahead of you. 32You must not make an agreement with those people or with their gods. 33You must not let them live in your land, or they will make you sin against me. If you worship their gods, you will be caught in a trap."

God and Israel Make Their Agreement

24 The LORD told Moses, "You, Aaron, Nadab, Abihu, and seventy of the older leaders of Israel must come up to me and worship me from a distance. 2Then Moses alone must come near me; the others must not come near. The rest of the people must not come up the mountain with Moses."

3Moses told the people all the LORD's words and laws for living. Then all of the people answered out loud together, "We will do all the things the LORD has said." 4So Moses wrote down all the

23:12 Sabbath: Leviticus 26:2
23:19 Community: Exodus 32
23:19 *Holy Tent.* Literally, "house of the LORD your God." See Exodus 25:9.
23:23 See note at 3:8.
23:26 Sickness, Disease, Healing: Deuteronomy 7:12–15
23:28 See note at 3:8.

words of the LORD. And he got up early the next morning and built an altar near the bottom of the mountain. He set up twelve stones, one stone for each of the twelve tribes of Israel. 5Then Moses sent young Israelite men to offer whole burnt offerings and to sacrifice young bulls as fellowship offerings to the LORD. 6Moses put half of the blood of these animals in bowls, and he sprinkled the other half of the blood on the altar. 7Then he took the Book of the Agreement and read it so the people could hear him. And they said, "We will do everything that the LORD has said; we will obey."

8Then Moses took the blood from the bowls and sprinkled it on the people, saying, "This is the blood that begins the Agreement, the Agreement which the LORD has made with you about all these words."

9Moses, Aaron, Nadab, Abihu, and seventy of the older leaders of Israel went up the mountain 10and saw the God of Israel. Under his feet was a surface that looked as if it were paved with blue sapphire stones, and it was as clear as the sky! 11These leaders of the Israelites saw God, but God did not destroy them. Then they ate and drank together.

God Promises Moses the Stone Tablets

12The LORD said to Moses, "Come up the mountain to me. Wait there, and I will give you two stone tablets. On these are the teachings and the commands I have written to instruct the people."

13So Moses and his helper Joshua set out, and Moses went up to Sinai, the mountain of God. 14Moses said to the older leaders, "Wait here for us until we come back to you. Aaron and Hur are with you, and anyone who has a disagreement with others can take it to them."

Moses Meets with God

15When Moses went up on the mountain, the cloud covered it. 16The glory of the LORD came down on Mount Sinai, and the cloud covered it for six days. On the seventh day the LORD called to Moses from inside the cloud. 17To the Israelites the glory of the LORD looked like a fire burning on top of the mountain. 18Then Moses went into the cloud and went higher up the mountain. He was on the mountain for forty days and forty nights.

Gifts for the Lord

25 The LORD said to Moses, 2"Tell the Israelites to bring me gifts. Receive for me the gifts each person wants to give. 3These are the gifts that you should receive from them: gold, silver, bronze; 4blue, purple, and red thread; fine linen, goat hair, 5sheepskins that are dyed red; fine leather; acacia wood; 6olive oil to burn in the lamps; spices for sweet-smelling incense, and the special olive oil poured on a person's head to make him a priest; 7onyx stones, and other jewels to be put on the holy vest and the chest covering.

8"The people must build a holy place for me so that I can live among them. 9Build this Holy Tent and everything in it by the plan I will show you.

The Ark of the Agreement

10"Use acacia wood and build an Ark forty-five inches long, twenty-seven inches wide, and twenty-seven inches high. 11Cover the Ark inside and out with pure gold, and put a gold strip all around it. 12Make four gold rings for the Ark and attach them to its four feet, two rings on each side. 13Then make poles from acacia wood and cover them with gold. 14Put the poles through the rings on the sides of the Ark, and use these poles to carry it. 15These poles must always stay in the rings of the Ark. Do not take them out. 16Then put in the Ark the Agreement which I will make with you.

17"Then make a lid of pure gold for the Ark; this is the mercy seat. Make it forty-five inches long and twenty-seven inches wide. 18Then hammer gold to make two creatures with wings, and put one on each end of the lid. 19Attach one creature on one end of the lid and the other creature on the other end. Make them to be one piece with the lid at the ends. 20The creatures' wings should be spread upward, covering the lid, and the creatures are to face each other across the lid. 21Put this lid on top of the Ark, and put in the Ark the Agreement which I will make with you. 22I will meet with you there, above the lid between the two winged creatures on the Ark of the Agreement. There I will give you all my commands for the Israelites.

The Table

23"Make a table out of acacia wood, thirty-six

24:7 *Agreement.* The agreement is a legal contract like a treaty between nations. Here God enters into a treaty with his people—Israel. In other versions of the Bible, agreement is often translated by the word "covenant."

24:8 Reconciliation: Exodus30:10

24:11 Table Fellowship/Lord's Supper: Leviticus 23:40

24:17 Glory: Exodus 40:34–35

25:5 *acacia wood.* A very expensive and precious wood.

25:17 *mercy seat.* The Ark was the throne of God and the mercy seat was the top of the Ark. It was where God would sit in his Holy Tent. Since the place is holy, it is made of pure gold.

25:18 *creatures.* These creatures, known as "cherubim," are powerful angelic creatures who serve to protect God's holiness.

inches long, eighteen inches wide, and twenty-seven inches high. [24]Cover it with pure gold, and put a gold strip around it. [25]Make a frame three inches high that stands up all around the edge, and put a gold strip around it. [26]Then make four gold rings. Attach them to the four corners of the table where the four legs are. [27]Put the rings close to the frame around the top of the table, because they will hold the poles for carrying it. [28]Make the poles out of acacia wood, cover them with gold, and carry the table with these poles. [29]Make the plates and bowls for the table, as well as the jars and cups, out of pure gold. They will be used for pouring out the drink offerings. [30]On this table put the bread that shows you are in my presence so that it is always there in front of me.

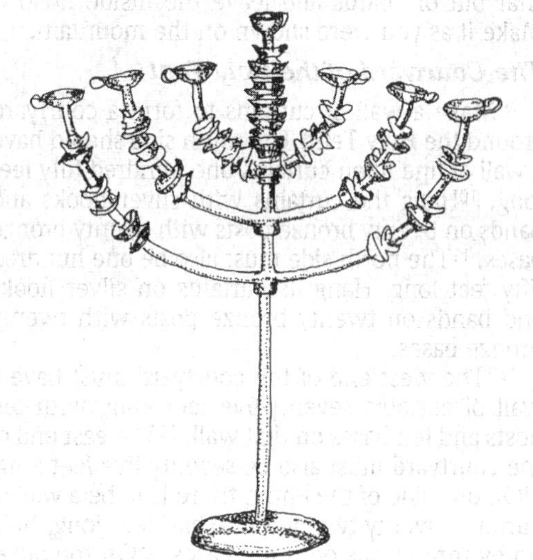

A model of the seven-branched lampstand first made for the Holy Tent (See 25:31–40)

The Lampstand

[31]"Hammer pure gold to make a lampstand. Its base, stand, flower-like cups, buds, and petals must all be joined together in one piece. [32]The lampstand must have six branches going out from its sides—three on one side and three on the other. [33]Each branch must have three cups shaped like almond flowers on it. Each cup must have a bud and a petal. Each of the six branches going out from the lampstand must be the same. [34]And there must be four more cups made like almond flowers on the lampstand itself. These cups must also have buds and petals. [35]Put a bud under each pair of branches that goes out from the lampstand. Each of the six branches going out from the lampstand must be the same. [36]The branches, buds, and lampstand must be made of one piece, hammered out of pure gold.

[37]"Then make seven small oil lamps and put them on the lampstand so that they give light to the area in front of it. [38]The wick trimmers and trays must be made of pure gold. [39]Use seventy-five pounds of pure gold to make the lampstand and everything with it. [40]Be very careful to make them by the plan I showed you on the mountain.

The Holy Tent

26 "Make for the Holy Tent ten curtains of fine linen and blue, purple, and red thread. Have a skilled craftsman sew designs of creatures with wings on the pieces of cloth. [2]Make each curtain the same size—forty-two feet long and six feet wide. [3]Sew five curtains together for one set, and sew the other curtains together for the second set. [4]Make loops of blue cloth on the edge of the end curtain of one set, and do the same for the end curtain of the other set. [5]Make fifty loops on the end curtain of the first set and fifty loops on the end curtain of the second set. These loops must be opposite each other. [6]And make fifty gold hooks to join the two sets of curtains so that the Holy Tent is one piece.

[7]"Then make another tent that will cover the Holy Tent, using eleven curtains made from goat hair. [8]All these curtains must be the same size—forty-five feet long and six feet wide. [9]Sew five of the curtains together into one set. Then sew the other six curtains together into the second set. Fold the sixth curtain double over the front of the Tent. [10]Make fifty loops down the edge of the end curtain of one set, and do the same for the end curtain of the other set. [11]Then make fifty bronze hooks and put them in the loops to join the tent together so that the covering is one piece. [12]Let the extra half piece of cloth hang over the back of the Holy Tent. [13]There will be eighteen inches hanging over the sides of the Holy Tent, to protect it. [14]Make a covering for the Holy Tent from sheepskins colored red, and over that make a covering from fine leather.

[15]"Use acacia wood to make upright frames for the Holy Tent. [16]Each frame must be fifteen feet long and twenty-seven inches wide, [17]with two pegs side by side. Every frame must be made the

25:31 *lampstand.* The lampstand, known as the "menorah," had the form of a tree, which represents the presence of the living God (see note to 4:2).

26:4 *blue cloth.* This is the innermost of the four coverings of the Holy Tent. As the innermost, it is the one seen by someone inside the Tent. It gives the interior a sky-like feeling. It represents heaven. The Holy Tent is heaven on earth, the place where God dwells.

same way. 18Make twenty frames for the south side of the Holy Tent. 19Each frame must have two silver bases to go under it, a peg fitting into each base. You must make forty silver bases for the frames. 20Make twenty more frames for the north side of the Holy Tent 21and forty silver bases for them—two bases for each frame. 22You must make six frames for the rear or west end of the Holy Tent 23and two frames for each corner at the rear. 24The two frames are to be doubled at the bottom and joined at the top with a metal ring. Both corner frames must be made this way. 25So there will be a total of eight frames at the rear of the Tent, and there will be sixteen silver bases—two bases under each frame.

26“Make crossbars of acacia wood to connect the upright frames of the Holy Tent. Make five crossbars to hold the frames together on one side 27and five to hold the frames together on the other side. Also make five crossbars to hold the frames together on the west end, at the rear. 28The middle crossbar is to be set halfway up the frames, and it is to run along the entire length of each side and rear. 29Make gold rings on the sides of the frames to hold the crossbars, and cover the frames and the crossbars with gold. 30Set up the Holy Tent by the plan shown to you on the mountain.

31“Make a curtain of fine linen and blue, purple, and red thread, and have a skilled craftsman sew designs of creatures with wings on it. 32Hang the curtain by gold hooks on four posts of acacia wood that are covered with gold, and set them in four silver bases. 33Hang the curtain from the hooks in the roof, and put the Ark of the Agreement containing the two stone tablets behind it. This curtain will separate the Holy Place from the Most Holy Place. 34Put the lid on the Ark of the Agreement in the Most Holy Place.

35“Outside the curtain, put the table on the north side of the Holy Tent. Put the lampstand on the south side of the Holy Tent across from the table.

The Entrance of the Holy Tent

36“Then, for the entrance of the Tent, make a curtain with fine linen and blue, purple, and red thread. Someone who can sew well is to sew designs on it. 37Make five posts of acacia wood covered with gold. Make gold hooks for them on which to hang the curtain, and make five bronze bases for them.

The Altar for Burnt Offerings

27 “Make an altar of acacia wood, four and one-half feet high. It should be square—seven and one-half feet long and seven and one-half feet wide. 2Make each of the four corners of the altar stick out like a horn, in such a way that the corners with their horns are all one piece. Then cover the whole altar with bronze.

3“Use bronze to make all the tools and dishes that will be used on the altar: the pots to remove the ashes, the shovels, the bowls for sprinkling blood, the meat forks, and the pans for carrying the burning wood.

4“Make a large bronze screen to hold the burning wood, and put a bronze ring at each of the four corners of it. 5Put the screen inside the altar, under its rim, halfway up from the bottom.

6“Make poles of acacia wood for the altar, and cover them with bronze. 7Put the poles through the rings on both sides of the altar to carry it. 8Make the altar out of boards and leave the inside hollow. Make it as you were shown on the mountain.

The Courtyard of the Holy Tent

9“Make a wall of curtains to form a courtyard around the Holy Tent. The south side should have a wall of fine linen curtains one hundred fifty feet long. 10Hang the curtains with silver hooks and bands on twenty bronze posts with twenty bronze bases. 11The north side must also be one hundred fifty feet long. Hang its curtains on silver hooks and bands on twenty bronze posts with twenty bronze bases.

12“The west end of the courtyard must have a wall of curtains seventy-five feet long, with ten posts and ten bases on that wall. 13The east end of the courtyard must also be seventy-five feet long. 14On one side of the entry, there is to be a wall of curtains twenty-two and one-half feet long, held up by three posts on three bases. 15On the other side of the entry, there is also to be a wall of curtains twenty-two and one-half feet long, held up by three posts on three bases.

16“The entry to the courtyard is to be a curtain thirty feet wide, made of fine linen with blue, purple, and red thread. Someone who can sew well is to sew designs on it. It is to be held up by four posts on four bases. 17All the posts around the courtyard must have silver bands and hooks and bronze bases. 18The courtyard must be one hundred fifty feet long and seventy-five feet wide, with a wall of curtains around it seven and one-half feet high, made of fine linen. The bases in which the posts are set must be bronze. 19All the things used in the Holy Tent and all the tent pegs for the Holy Tent and the wall around the courtyard must be made of bronze.

Oil for the Lamp

20“Command the people of Israel to bring you

26:37 Holiness: Exodus 29

Noah

Genesis 6:9

What does the story of Noah and the flood show us about how God saves his people? How is the agreement between God and Noah related to other agreements God made with his people?

The story of Noah and the flood (Genesis 6–9) is well known to children and adults alike. It is the fourth story of the Bible (after creation, Adam and Eve's disobedience, and Cain's murder of Abel).

The setting of the story is the growing number of people on the earth and the marriage of women to the "sons of God" (6:1–2). The identity of these sons of God is not clear (they seem to be related to the "Nephilim," a race of giants, in verse 4), but whoever they were, their actions were worthy of God's punishment: the life expectancy of humans would be limited to 120 years (verse 3). Apparently, the wickedness and evil of humanity became so widespread (verse 5) that God actually regretted having created them (verse 6). He decided that he would "destroy every animal and everything that crawls on the earth and the birds of the air" (verse 7). Noah, however, was to escape this punishment, because he "pleased the Lord" (verse 8).

The Lord spoke to Noah and told him what he was about to do. Noah was to build a boat, which was to provide a means for him and his family to escape the coming flood that the Lord would use to destroy all life on earth. The Lord made an "agreement" with Noah (verse 18) that he and his wife, his sons, and their wives would enter safely into the boat and ride out the storm.

The flood began (7:17) and it was not until more than a year later (see 7:11 and 8:14) that the waters had receded enough for Noah and the others to set foot on dry ground.

Noah, perhaps somewhat surprisingly, is mentioned only a few times throughout the Bible. Where he is mentioned, he serves as a model for righteous conduct. That Noah's behavior was pleasing to God is made explicit in Genesis 6:8–9: Noah "pleased the Lord;" he was "a good man, the most innocent man of his time, and he walked with God." Noah's morality is seen as a standard of conduct in Ezekiel 14:14 and 20: even the goodness of Noah, Daniel, or Job could not save Jerusalem from their coming destruction. In Hebrews 11:7, Noah is said to have shown his faithful obedience to God by building a boat to save him and his family.

Elsewhere in the New Testament, God's deliverance of Noah and his family through water is seen as similar to baptism. Peter writes that the water of the flood "is like baptism that now saves you—not the washing of dirt from the body, but the promise made to God from a good conscience" (1 Peter 3:21).

But there is even more to this similarity between salvation in Noah and the Christian's salvation in Christ. First, we see throughout the Bible that God always delivers a "remnant" of his people, even though they all deserve his punishment. This is a sign of God's free grace and mercy in the midst of his judgment. God's salvation of a "remnant" is seen most clearly perhaps in his deliverance of the Israelites from captivity in Babylon. Although the nation is guilty of serving other gods, and hence deserves God's terrible punishment (exile to a foreign land), God reserves a portion of his people whom he, by his grace, will bring back to the land and build up once again into a people devoted to him. (See, for example, Jeremiah 23:1–8.)

God's plan for saving a remnant comes to its fullest expression in the New Testament. Although humanity as a whole is fully deserving of God's eternal punishment (Romans 3:9–31), God does not act according to what we deserve. Rather, as Paul says, "There are a few people that God has chosen by his grace" (Romans 11:5). Just as in the time of Elijah, where God kept for himself a remnant of faithful Israelites who had not turned to worshipping Baal (Romans 11:2–4; 1 Kings 19:9–18), God now preserves for himself the church. This is not an "exclusive club" that calls for boasting from its members; it is not our doing, but God's: "And if he chose them by grace, it is not for the things they have done" (Romans 11:6).

Another similarity between God's deliverance of Noah and salvation in Christ is the "agreement" God makes with his people. On Noah's side we see this in Genesis 6:18 and 9:8–17. God committed himself to saving Noah, and after he saved him, he committed himself never to destroy the earth again by water. The rainbow was a sign of this commitment, or "agreement."

God also made an agreement with Abraham (Genesis 15 and 17), the Israelites at Sinai (Exodus 19–24), and David and his descendants (2 Samuel 7:5–16). Each instance is one where God committed himself to be with his people no matter what. In Christ, God made a "new agreement" with his people (Luke 22:20; see also Jeremiah 31:31–34). Christ's death and resurrection is the surest sign that he will be faithful to us always. It is God's final statement that he is with us and will never abandon us, both in this life and the next (Romans 5:6–11).

Noah: For additional scriptures on this topic go to Ezekiel 14:4.

Noah's Ark

Genesis 6:14

What is the purpose of the ark? What do other biblical passages have to say about it? How does the ark help us understand salvation?

According to Genesis 6:1–8, there came a point when the wickedness of humanity became so pronounced that God even regretted having created the world, a world he himself called "very good" in Genesis 1:31. What apparently brought on God's extreme displeasure is described in Genesis 6:1–4. This passage is very difficult to understand (and uncovering its exact meaning should not cause undue concern), but the culprit seems to be the "sons of God" who marry "daughters of human beings" and whose offspring become "the mighty warriors of long ago." The point, however, is that the nature of this was so bad that God's "heart was filled with pain," enough pain to wipe out everything he had made.

As the well-known story goes, God decides to destroy the earth by means of a flood. He gives Noah, a good and innocent man who "walked with God" (verse 9), ample warning and tells him to build an ark. The ark was to be a huge boat (actually a large box), 450 feet long (1 1/2 times the length of a football field), 75 feet wide (1/6 its length) and 45 feet high (1/10 its length), and came fully equipped with three floors, stalls, a window, and doors. The ark was to be a safe haven for God's righteous people while his anger was being poured out (literally!) on sinners. The lesson to be learned from the ark and the flood story itself is that God saves those who live their lives worthy of God's favor (Genesis 6:9).

But the significance of the ark is by no means limited to the flood story. An "ark" is mentioned again in another famous story where water once again becomes the tool of God's judgment: the Exodus. When Pharaoh decrees to drown all the Israelite baby boys in the waters of the Nile (Exodus 1:22), Moses' mother, fearing for her baby's life, put him in a *basket* (Exodus 2:3). The Hebrew word here is the same as for "ark" in Genesis 6:14; the word occurs nowhere else other than the flood story and Exodus 2. Moses is a Noah-like figure. As Noah was saved in an ark from watery judgment, so was Moses—the difference being that the water in Noah's day was God's doing while the watery fate of the Israelite boys was Pharaoh's doing.

Moses' Noah-like deliverance from water sets the stage for the Israelites' deliverance through the Red Sea in Exodus 13–15. It is only because Moses was put in an "ark" in chapter 2 that he was able to lead the Israelites out of Egypt and through the sea. And just as it was in Noah's day, the watery judgment is now God's doing; the sinners are destroyed, and those on whom God's favor rests are brought safely through the water. In a manner of speaking, not only Moses, but all the Israelites, experience a Noah-like deliverance: Moses is saved from water directly by an "ark," and the Israelites are saved from water by virtue of their association with Moses. We see something like this already in the flood story, for although only Noah is specifically called good, his entire family is permitted to enter the ark because of their association with him.

The significance of the ark extends even beyond the Old Testament into the New. In the same way that Noah *and his family* were brought through the flood, and Moses *and the Israelites* were brought through the sea, so does Jesus *bring his church* through the "waters" of sin and death. In this sense, the ark holds an important lesson for understanding salvation in Christ. The direct connection between Jesus and the flood story is made in at least two New Testament passages.

In Matthew 24:37–38, Jesus is talking to his followers about the events surrounding the last days and his Second Coming. When the topic turns specifically to the time of Jesus' return, Jesus compares his coming to the days of Noah. The people living in that time will be like Noah's neighbors: going their own merry way without a care in the world. Then, just as with the flood, God's judgment will come upon those people swiftly and unexpectedly. Jesus' warning to his followers is to be like Noah, always ready and vigilant (verses 42–44). In other words, Jesus' Second Coming and the final judgment will be another Noah-like event: God's people will be taken out of danger while the rest face destruction.

First Peter 3:19–22 has a slightly different way of bringing together Noah and salvation in Christ. Although the specifics of this passage are difficult to sort out, the basic idea is that the water of the flood was a kind of "baptism" (verse 21). Peter highlights the *saving* aspect of the water: Noah and his family "were saved by water" (verse 20). In this sense, Christian baptism by water represents the telling mark of salvation. In other words, the baptized Christian is "in the boat of salvation" so to speak, rather than out if it, through the power of the risen Lord (verse 21).

Noah's Ark: For additional scriptures on this topic go to 1 Peter 3:20

pure olive oil, made from pressed olives, to keep
the lamps on the lampstand burning. 21Aaron
and his sons must keep the lamps burning
before the LORD from evening till morning. This
will be in the Meeting Tent, outside the curtain
which is in front of the Ark. The Israelites and
their descendants must obey this rule from now
on.

Clothes for the Priests

28 "Tell your brother Aaron to come to you,
along with his sons Nadab, Abihu, Eleazar,
and Ithamar. Separate them from the other
Israelites to serve me as priests. 2Make holy clothes
for your brother Aaron to give him honor and
beauty. 3Tell all the skilled craftsmen to whom I
have given wisdom to make special clothes for
Aaron—clothes to show that he belongs to me so
that he may serve me as a priest.⚭ 4These are the
clothes they must make: a chest covering, a holy
vest, an outer robe, a woven inner robe, a turban,
and a cloth belt. The craftsmen must make these
holy clothes for your brother Aaron and his sons.
Then they may serve me as priests. 5The craftsmen
must use gold and blue, purple and red thread, and
fine linen.

The Holy Vest

6"Use gold and blue, purple and red thread, and
fine linen to make the holy vest; skilled craftsmen
are to make it. 7At each top corner of this holy vest
there will be a pair of shoulder straps tied together
over each shoulder.

8"The craftsmen will very carefully weave a belt
on the holy vest that is made with the same materials—gold and blue, purple and red thread, and
fine linen.

9"Take two onyx stones and write the names of
the twelve sons of Israel on them, 10six on one
stone and six on the other. Write the names in
order, from the oldest son to the youngest.
11Carve the names of the sons of Israel on these
stones in the same way a person carves words
and designs on a seal. Put gold around the stones
to hold them on the holy vest. 12Then put the two
stones on the two straps of the holy vest as
reminders of the twelve sons of Israel. Aaron is to
wear their names on his shoulders in the presence of the LORD as reminders of the sons of
Israel. 13Make two gold pieces to hold the stones
14and two chains of pure gold, twisted together
like a rope. Attach the chains to the two gold
pieces that hold the stones.

Holy clothes of the high priest, as described in chapter 28

The Chest Covering

15"Make a chest covering to help in making decisions. The craftsmen should make it as they made
the holy vest, using gold and blue, purple and red
thread, and fine linen. 16The chest covering must
be square—nine inches long and nine inches
wide—and folded double to make a pocket. 17Put
four rows of beautiful gems on the chest covering:
The first row must have a ruby, a topaz, and a yellow quartz; 18the second must have turquoise, a
sapphire, and an emerald; 19the third must have a
jacinth, an agate, and an amethyst; 20the fourth
must have a chrysolite, an onyx, and a jasper. Put
gold around these jewels to attach them to the
chest covering. 21There must be twelve jewels on
the chest covering—one jewel for each of the
names of the sons of Israel. Carve the name of one
of the twelve tribes on each of the stones as you
would carve a seal.⚭

22"Make chains of pure gold, twisted together

⚭**28:3 Wisdom:** 2 Chronicles 1:10

⚭**28:21 Stone:** Deuteronomy 5:22

like rope, for the chest covering. [23]Make two gold rings and put them on the two upper corners of the chest covering. [24]Attach the two gold chains to the two rings at the upper corners of the chest covering. [25]Attach the other ends of the two chains to the two gold pieces on the shoulder straps in the front of the holy vest.

[26]"Make two gold rings and put them at the two lower corners of the chest covering, on the inside edge next to the holy vest. [27]Make two more gold rings and attach them to the bottom of the shoulder straps in the front of the holy vest. Put them close to the seam above the woven belt of the holy vest. [28]Join the rings of the chest covering to the rings of the holy vest with blue ribbon, connecting it to the woven belt so the chest covering will not swing out from the holy vest.

[29]"When Aaron enters the Holy Place, he will wear the names of the sons of Israel over his heart, on the chest covering that helps in making decisions. This will be a continual reminder before the LORD. [30]And put the Urim and Thummim inside the chest covering so that they will be on Aaron's heart when he goes before the LORD. They will help in making decisions for the Israelites. So Aaron will always carry them with him when he is before the LORD.

[31]"Make the outer robe to be worn under the holy vest, using only blue cloth. [32]Make a hole in the center for Aaron's head, with a woven collar around the hole so it will not tear. [33]Make balls like pomegranates of blue, purple, and red thread, and hang them around the bottom of the outer robe with gold bells between them. [34]All around the bottom of the outer robe there should be a gold bell and a pomegranate ball, a gold bell and a pomegranate ball. [35]Aaron must wear this robe when he serves as priest. The ringing of the bells will be heard when he enters and leaves the Holy Place before the LORD so that Aaron will not die.

[36]"Make a strip of pure gold and carve these words on it as you would carve a seal: 'Holy to the LORD.' [37]Use blue ribbon to tie it to the turban; put it on the front of the turban. [38]Aaron must wear this on his forehead. In this way, he will be blamed if anything is wrong with the gifts of the Israelites. Aaron must always wear this on his head so the LORD will accept the gifts of the people.

[39]"Make the woven inner robe of fine linen, and make the turban of fine linen also. Make the cloth belt with designs sewn on it. [40]Also make woven inner robes, cloth belts, and headbands for Aaron's sons, to give them honor and beauty. [41]Put these clothes on your brother Aaron and his sons, and pour olive oil on their heads to appoint them as priests. Make them belong to me so they may serve me as priests.

[42]"Make for them linen underclothes to cover them from the waist to the upper parts of the legs. [43]Aaron and his sons must wear these underclothes when they enter the Meeting Tent and anytime they come near the altar to serve as priests in the Holy Place. If they do not wear these clothes, they will be guilty of wrong, and they will die. This will be a law that will last from now on for Aaron and all his descendants.

Appointing the Priests

29 "This is what you must do to appoint Aaron and his sons to serve me as priests. Take one young bull and two male sheep that have nothing wrong with them. [2]Use fine wheat flour without yeast to make bread, cakes mixed with olive oil, and wafers brushed with olive oil. [3]Put these in one basket, and bring them along with the bull and two male sheep. [4]Bring Aaron and his sons to the entrance of the Meeting Tent and wash them with water. [5]Take the clothes and dress Aaron in the inner robe and the outer robe of the holy vest. Then put on him the holy vest and the chest covering, and tie the holy vest on him with its skillfully woven belt. [6]Put the turban on his head, and put the holy crown on the turban. [7]Take the special olive oil and pour it on his head to make him a priest.

[8]"Then bring his sons and put the inner robes on them. [9]Put the headbands on their heads, and tie cloth belts around their waists. Aaron and his descendants will be priests in Israel, according to a rule that will continue from now on. This is how you will appoint Aaron and his sons as priests.

[10]"Bring the bull to the front of the Meeting Tent, and Aaron and his sons must put their hands on the bull's head. [11]Then kill the bull before the LORD at the entrance to the Meeting Tent. [12]Use your finger to put some of the bull's blood on the corners of the altar, and then pour the blood that is left at the bottom of the altar. [13]Take all the fat that covers the inner organs, as well as the best part of the liver, both kidneys, and the fat around them, and burn them on the altar. [14]Take the bull's meat, skin, and intestines, and burn them outside the camp. This is an offering to take away sin.

[15]"Take one of the male sheep, and have Aaron and his sons put their hands on its head. [16]Kill it, and take its blood and sprinkle it on all four sides

29:9 Priesthood: Leviticus 8

of the altar. 17Then cut it into pieces and wash its inner organs and its legs, putting them with its head and its other pieces. 18Burn the whole sheep on the altar; it is a burnt offering made by fire to the LORD. Its smell is pleasing to the LORD.

19"Take the other male sheep, and have Aaron and his sons put their hands on its head. 20Kill it and take some of its blood. Put the blood on the bottom of the right ears of Aaron and his sons and on the thumbs of their right hands and on the big toes of their right feet. Then sprinkle the rest of the blood against all four sides of the altar. 21Take some of the blood from the altar, and mix it with the special oil used in appointing priests. Sprinkle this on Aaron and his clothes and on his sons and their clothes. This will show that Aaron and his sons and their clothes are given to my service.

22"Then take the fat from the male sheep, the fat tail, and the fat that covers the inner organs. In addition, take the best part of the liver, both kidneys, and the fat around them, and the right thigh. (This is the male sheep to be used in appointing priests.)

23"Then take the basket of bread that you made without yeast, which you put before the LORD. From it take a loaf of bread, a cake made with olive oil, and a wafer. 24Put all of these in the hands of Aaron and his sons, and tell them to present them as an offering to the LORD. 25Then take them from their hands and burn them on the altar with the whole burnt offering. This is an offering made by fire to the LORD; its smell is pleasing to the LORD. 26Then take the breast of the male sheep used to appoint Aaron as priest, and present it before the LORD as an offering. This part of the animal will be your share. 27Set aside the breast and the thigh of the sheep that were used to appoint Aaron and his sons as priests. These parts belong to them. 28They are to be the regular share which the Israelites will always give to Aaron and his sons. It is the gift the Israelites must give to the LORD from their fellowship offerings.

29"The holy clothes made for Aaron will belong to his descendants so that they can wear these clothes when they are appointed as priests. 30Aaron's son, who will become high priest after Aaron, will come to the Meeting Tent to serve in the Holy Place. He is to wear these clothes for seven days.

31"Take the male sheep used to appoint priests and boil its meat in a place that is holy. 32Then at the entrance of the Meeting Tent, Aaron and his sons must eat the meat of the sheep and the bread that is in the basket. 33They should eat these offerings that were used to remove their sins and to make them holy when they were made priests. But no one else is to eat them, because they are holy things. 34If any of the meat from that sheep or any of the bread is left the next morning, it must be burned. It must not be eaten, because it is holy.

35"Do all these things that I commanded you to do to Aaron and his sons, and spend seven days appointing them. 36Each day you are to offer a bull to remove the sins of Aaron and his sons so they will be given for service to the LORD. Make the altar ready for service to the LORD, and pour oil on it to make it holy. 37Spend seven days making the altar ready for service to God and making it holy. Then the altar will become very holy, and anything that touches it must be holy.

The Daily Sacrifices

38"Every day from now on, offer on the altar two lambs that are one year old. 39Offer one lamb in the morning and the other in the evening before dark. 40In the morning, when you offer the first lamb, offer also two quarts of fine flour mixed with one quart of oil from pressed olives. Pour out a quart of wine as a drink offering. 41Offer the second lamb in the evening with the same grain offering and drink offering as you did in the morning. This is an offering made by fire to the LORD, and its smell is pleasing to him.

42"You must burn these things as an offering to the LORD every day, from now on, at the entrance of the Meeting Tent before the LORD. When you make the offering, I, the LORD, will meet you there and speak to you. 43I will meet with the people of Israel there, and that place will be holy because of my glory.

44"So I will make the Meeting Tent and the altar holy; I will also make Aaron and his sons holy so they may serve me as priests. 45I will live with the people of Israel and be their God. 46And they will know that I am the LORD their God who led them out of Egypt so that I could live with them. I am the LORD their God.

The Altar for Burning Incense

30 "Make an altar out of acacia wood for burning incense. 2Make it square—eighteen inches long and eighteen inches wide—and make it thirty-six inches high. The corners that stick out like horns must be one piece with the altar. 3Cover its top, its sides, and its corners with pure gold, and put a gold strip all around the altar. 4Make two gold rings beneath the gold strip on

29:46 **Holiness:** Leviticus 20:7

29:46 **Mediator:** Exodus 3

opposite sides of the altar, and slide poles through them to carry the altar. 5Make the poles from acacia wood and cover them with gold. 6Put the altar of incense in front of the curtain that is near the Ark of the Agreement, in front of the lid that covers that Ark. There I will meet with you.

7"Aaron must burn sweet-smelling incense on the altar every morning when he comes to take care of the oil lamps. 8He must burn incense again in the evening when he lights the lamps, so incense will burn before the LORD every day from now on. 9Do not use this altar for offering any other incense, or burnt offering, or any kind of grain offering, or drink offering. 10Once a year Aaron must make the altar ready for service to God by putting blood on its corners—the blood of the animal offered to remove sins. He is to do this once a year from now on. This altar belongs completely to the LORD's service."

The Tax for the Meeting Tent

11The LORD said to Moses, 12"When you count the people of Israel, every person must buy back his life from the LORD so that no terrible things will happen to the people when you number them. 13Every person who is counted must pay one-fifth of an ounce of silver. (This is set by using one-half of the Holy Place measure, which weighs two-fifths of an ounce.) This amount is a gift to the LORD. 14Every person who is counted and is twenty years old or older must give this amount to the LORD. 15A rich person must not give more than one-fifth of an ounce, and a poor person must not give less. You are paying this to the LORD to buy back your lives. 16Gather from the people of Israel this money paid to buy back their lives, and spend it on things for the service in the Meeting Tent. This payment will remind the LORD that the Israelites' lives have been bought back."

The Bronze Bowl

17The LORD said to Moses, 18"Make a bronze bowl, on a bronze stand, for washing. Put the bowl and stand between the Meeting Tent and the altar, and put water in the bowl. 19Aaron and his sons must wash their hands and feet with the water from this bowl. 20Each time they enter the Meeting Tent they must wash with water so they will not die. Whenever they approach the altar to serve as priests and offer a sacrifice to the LORD by fire, 21they must wash their hands and their feet so they will not die. This is a rule which Aaron and his descendants are to keep from now on."

Oil for Appointing

22Then the LORD said to Moses, 23"Take the finest spices: twelve pounds of liquid myrrh, half that amount (that is, six pounds) of sweet-smelling cinnamon, six pounds of sweet-smelling cane, 24and twelve pounds of cassia. Weigh all these by the Holy Place measure. Also take four quarts of olive oil, 25and mix all these things like a perfume to make a holy olive oil. This special oil must be put on people and things to make them ready for service to God. 26Put this oil on the Meeting Tent and the Ark of the Agreement, 27on the table and all its dishes, on the lampstand and all its tools, and on the incense altar. 28Also, put the oil on the altar for burnt offerings and on all its tools, as well as on the bowl and the stand under the bowl. 29You will prepare all these things for service to God, and they will be very holy. Anything that touches these things must be holy.

30"Put the oil on Aaron and his sons to give them for service to me, that they may serve me as priests. 31Tell the Israelites, 'This is to be my holy olive oil from now on. It is to be put on people and things to make them ready for service to God. 32Do not pour it on the bodies of ordinary people, and do not make perfume the same way you make this oil. It is holy, and you must treat it as holy. 33If anyone makes perfume like it or puts it on someone who is not a priest, that person must be cut off from his people.'"

Incense

34Then the LORD said to Moses, "Take these sweet-smelling spices: resin, onycha, galbanum, and pure frankincense. Be sure that you have equal amounts of each. 35Make incense as a person who makes perfume would do. Add salt to it to keep it pure and holy. 36Beat some of the incense into a fine powder, and put it in front of the Ark of the Agreement in the Meeting Tent, where I will meet with you. You must use this incense powder only for its very special purpose. 37Do not make incense for yourselves the same way you make this incense. Treat it as holy to the LORD. 38Whoever makes incense like this to use as perfume must be cut off from his people."

Bezalel and Oholiab Help

31 Then the LORD said to Moses, 2"See, I have chosen Bezalel son of Uri from the tribe of Judah. (Uri was the son of Hur.) 3I have filled Bezalel with the Spirit of God and have given him the skill, ability, and knowledge to do all kinds of

30:10 Reconciliation: Leviticus 4:13–16

stood and worshiped, each person at the entrance of his own tent.

11The LORD spoke to Moses face to face as a man speaks with his friend. Then Moses would return to the camp, but Moses' young helper, Joshua son of Nun, did not leave the Tent.

12Moses said to the LORD, "You have told me to lead these people, but you did not say whom you would send with me. You have said to me, 'I know you very well, and I am pleased with you.' 13If I have truly pleased you, show me your plans so that I may know you and continue to please you. Remember that this nation is your people."

14The LORD answered, "I myself will go with you, and I will give you victory."

15Then Moses said to him, "If you yourself don't go with us, then don't send us away from this place. 16If you don't go with us, no one will know that you are pleased with me and with your people. These people and I will be no different from any other people on earth."

17Then the LORD said to Moses, "I will do what you ask, because I know you very well, and I am pleased with you."

Moses Sees God's Glory

18Then Moses said, "Now, please show me your glory."

19The LORD answered, "I will cause all my goodness to pass in front of you, and I will announce my name, the LORD, so you can hear it. I will show kindness to anyone to whom I want to show kindness, and I will show mercy to anyone to whom I want to show mercy. 20But you cannot see my face, because no one can see me and live.

21"There is a place near me where you may stand on a rock. 22When my glory passes that place, I will put you in a large crack in the rock and cover you with my hand until I have passed by. 23Then I will take away my hand, and you will see my back. But my face must not be seen."⚭

Moses Gets New Stone Tablets

34 The LORD said to Moses, "Cut two more stone tablets like the first two, and I will write the same words on them that were on the first two stones which you broke. 2Be ready tomorrow morning, and then come up on Mount Sinai. Stand before me there on the top of the mountain. 3No one may come with you or even be seen any place on the mountain. Not even the flocks or herds may eat grass near that mountain."

4So Moses cut two stone tablets like the first ones. Then early the next morning he went up Mount Sinai, just as the LORD had commanded him, carrying the two stone tablets with him. 5Then the LORD came down in the cloud and stood there with Moses, and the LORD called out his name: the LORD.

6The LORD passed in front of Moses and said, "I am the LORD. The LORD is a God who shows mercy, who is kind, who doesn't become angry quickly, who has great love and faithfulness 7and is kind to thousands of people. The LORD forgives people for evil, for sin, and for turning against him, but he does not forget to punish guilty people. He will punish not only the guilty people, but also their children, their grandchildren, their great-grandchildren, and their great-great-grandchildren."

8Then Moses quickly bowed to the ground and worshiped. 9He said, "Lord, if you are pleased with me, please go with us. I know that these are stubborn people, but forgive our evil and our sin. Take us as your own people."

10Then the LORD said, "I am making this agreement with you. I will do miracles in front of all your people—things that have never before been done for any other nation on earth—and the people with you will see my work. I, the LORD, will do wonderful things for you. 11Obey the things I command you today, and I will force out the Amorites, Canaanites, Hittites, Perizzites, Hivites, and Jebusites ahead of you. 12Be careful that you don't make an agreement with the people who live in the land where you are going, because it will bring you trouble. 13Destroy their altars, break their stone pillars, and cut down their Asherah idols. 14Don't worship any other god, because I, the LORD, the Jealous One, am a jealous God.⚭

15"Be careful that you don't make an agreement with the people who live in that land. When they worship their gods, they will invite you to join them. Then you will eat their sacrifices. 16If you choose some of their daughters as wives for your sons and those daughters worship gods, they will lead your sons to do the same thing.⚭

⚭**33:23 Apostasy:** Numbers 14

34:11 See note at 3:8.

34:13 *Asherah idols.* Asherah was a very popular goddess worshipped by those who lived in Palestine before the Israelites did.

34:14 We think of jealousy as a bad and destructive emotion, and indeed it often is (1 Samuel 18:9). But two relationship are exclusive; they tolerate no rivals. These include the marriage relationship and the bond between God and his people. When these are threatened then jealousy is appropriate because a person can have only one spouse and only one God.

⚭**34:14 Trinity:** Deuteronomy 6:4–6

⚭**34:16 Nehemiah:** Deuteronomy 7:3–4

⚭**34:16 Racism:** Leviticus 19:33–34

17“Do not make gods of melted metal.

18“Celebrate the Feast of Unleavened Bread. For seven days you must eat bread made without yeast as I commanded you. Do this during the month I have chosen, the month of Abib, because in that month you came out of Egypt.

19“The firstborn of every mother belongs to me, including every firstborn male animal that is born in your flocks and herds. 20You may buy back a donkey by paying for it with a lamb, but if you don't want to buy back a donkey, you must break its neck. You must buy back all your firstborn sons.

“No one is to come before me without a gift.

21“You must work for six days, but on the seventh day you must rest—even during the planting season and the harvest season.

22“Celebrate the Feast of Weeks when you gather the first grain of the wheat harvest. And celebrate the Feast of Shelters in the fall.

23“Three times each year all your males must come before the Lord GOD, the God of Israel. 24I will force out nations ahead of you and expand the borders of your land. You will go before the LORD your God three times each year, and at that time no one will try to take your land from you.

25“Do not offer the blood of a sacrifice to me with anything containing yeast, and do not leave any of the sacrifice of the Feast of Passover until the next morning.

26“Bring the best first crops that you harvest from your ground to the Tent of the LORD your God.

“You must not cook a young goat in its mother's milk.”

27Then the LORD said to Moses, “Write down these words, because with these words I have made an agreement with you and Israel.”

28Moses stayed there with the LORD forty days and forty nights, and during that time he did not eat food or drink water. And Moses wrote the words of the Agreement—the Ten Commandments—on the stone tablets.

The Face of Moses Shines

29Then Moses came down from Mount Sinai, carrying the two stone tablets of the Agreement in his hands. But he did not know that his face was shining because he had talked with the LORD. 30When Aaron and all the people of Israel saw that Moses' face was shining, they were afraid to go near him. 31But Moses called to them, so Aaron and all the leaders of the people returned to Moses, and he talked with them. 32After that, all the people of Israel came near him, and he gave them all the commands that the LORD had given him on Mount Sinai.

33When Moses finished speaking to the people, he put a covering over his face. 34Anytime Moses went before the LORD to speak with him, Moses took off the covering until he came out. Then Moses would come out and tell the Israelites what the LORD had commanded. 35They would see that Moses' face was shining. So he would cover his face again until the next time he went in to speak with the LORD.

Rules About the Sabbath

35 Moses gathered all the Israelite community together and said to them, “These are the things the LORD has commanded you to do. 2You are to work for six days, but the seventh day will be a holy day, a Sabbath of rest to honor the LORD. Anyone who works on that day must be put to death. 3On the Sabbath day you must not light a fire in any of your houses.”

4Moses said to all the Israelites, “This is what the LORD has commanded: 5From what you have, take an offering for the LORD. Let everyone who is willing bring this offering to the LORD: gold, silver, bronze, 6blue, purple and red thread, and fine linen, goat hair 7and male sheepskins that are colored red. They may also bring fine leather, acacia wood, 8olive oil for the lamps, spices for the special olive oil used for appointing priests and for the sweet-smelling incense, 9onyx stones, and other jewels to be put on the holy vest and chest covering of the priests.

10“Let all the skilled workers come and make everything the LORD commanded: 11the Holy Tent, its outer tent and its covering, the hooks, frames, crossbars, posts, and bases; 12the Ark of the Agreement, its poles, lid, and the curtain in front of it; 13the table, and its poles, all the things that go with the table, and the bread that shows we are in God's presence; 14the lampstand for the light and all the things that go with it, the lamps, and olive oil for the light; 15the altar of incense and its poles, the special oil and the sweet-smelling incense, the curtain for the entrance of the Meeting Tent; 16the altar of burnt offering and its bronze screen, its poles and all its tools, the bronze bowl and its base; 17the curtains around the courtyard, their posts and bases, and the curtain at the entry to the courtyard; 18the pegs of the Holy Tent and of the courtyard and their ropes; 19the special

34:18 *the month of Abib.* This month was the first of the year for Israel. It comes around the time of our March and April.

34:26 *“You must not cook a young goat in its mother's milk.”* This law probably forbids a Canaanite religious ritual.

34:35 Mountain: Numbers 20:23–39

35:2 Capital Punishment: Leviticus 20:2–16

House/Home

Genesis 7:21

What, according to the Bible, is the role of the house or household? How central is it to the fulfilling of God's basic purposes?

The earliest references to *house/home* are to the extended family rather than a building (Genesis 7:1; 12:1), or a group of people in the camp following an itinerant figure (Genesis 17:12–27). It is through the families and descendants of key figures in the Bible—especially Abraham and David—that God's basic promises to all people will be realized (Genesis 12:1–3; 17:1–8; 2 Samuel 7:13–16; 1 Chronicles 17:10–14). However, it can also refer to a place in which to stay (Genesis 24:31; 33:17). When it refers to a physical building, it means any kind of human residence, not necessarily a free-standing house. A residence could even be part of a city wall (Joshua 2:15).

These places could be owned and sold (Leviticus 14:35; 25:29), and as a protection against a forced sale the seller had a right to buy back a house within a year. Investing time and energy into building programs does not bring contentment (Ecclesiastes 2:4): too much laziness, on the other hand, results in a house falling into disrepair (Proverbs 10:18). One of the most serious sins an Israelite could commit was to covet their neighbor's house (Deuteronomy 5:21), and one of the most serious losses an Israelite could suffer was the unjust loss of their own house (Job 20:19). Those who simply accumulate houses or build fancy ones at the expense of others will face a frightful punishment (Isaiah 5:8; Amos 5:11; Micah 2:2).

On the other hand, when the people of God are in exile they should not act as if they are transients but build houses and have families. They should do this as part of their commitment to the city in which God has placed them (Jeremiah 29:5, 28). Though the turning over of their original houses to aliens and strangers is a sign of God's judgment (Lamentations 5:2; Ezekiel 7:24), the day will come when they will return to their homeland and again buy houses and fields there (Jeremiah 32:15). While the idea of each person having their own home had a long history in Israel (1 Samuel 10:25), there was one group or order, the Rechabites, who were called to continue living in tents instead of building houses for themselves or others (Jeremiah 35:8–9).

The word for house can also refer to an outside location in which God is experienced as especially present: such a place is "surely the house of God" (Genesis 28:17). A shrine dedicated to God could also be described loosely as "the house of the LORD" (1 Samuel 1:7), as could the Tabernacle that went with the Israelites wherever they traveled (1 Chronicles 6:48). God says to David: "I have not lived in a house. I have been moving around all this time with a tent as my home" (2 Samuel 7:6). Though he does not allow David to build him a house, that is, a temple, God promises the king that his son Solomon will do so (2 Samuel 7:13; 8:27; 1 Chronicles 17:14). A deep longing of the pious Israelite was to frequent this special place throughout their whole lives (Psalm 23:6; 27:4). Even the birds of the air find a rightful resting place there (Psalm 84:3).

In the New Testament, references to house/home are of many different kinds. Jesus' teachings provide many examples:

1. As in the Old Testament (Psalm 127:1), Jesus uses the building of houses as an illustration of right and wrong attitudes. He does this especially with regard to properly grounding one's life on God (Matthew 7:24–27). Heaven is also described by him as a large house with many guest rooms (John 14:2), or as a banquet in a wealthy home (Luke 14:23).

2. Jesus conducted much of his ministry to the people in their homes as he ate, drank, and conversed with them (Matthew 9:10, 28; 13:36; Luke 7:36ff.). Those who believed him and his disciples were encouraged to do the same, and should shake the dust off their feet outside any place they were not accepted (Mark 5:19; Luke 10:5–11).

3. Although he occasionally taught the crowds in the temple or in the open, Jesus instructed his disciples primarily in homes (Mark 3:20; 7:17; 9:28, 33; 10:10). Although he also called the Temple a "house of prayer" (Mark 11:17), from this time the ordinary house became the main meeting place for believers.

4. This is fitting because Jesus describes his followers as a family (Mark 3:31–34). Even though his disciples may have left houses and households to accompany him, within this new community they will receive both back multiplied (Mark 10:28–30).

Many of these themes are picked up elsewhere in the New Testament (compare Hebrews 3:3–6; 2 John 10). This is especially true in Acts and in Paul.

1. Heaven is again described as a house that is being built for us by God now, which unlike our existing bodies is permanent and free of faults. When we arrive there, for us this will really be home (2 Corinthians 5:1–10).

2. The gospel was shared and received frequently in people's homes, and there whole households believed the message (Acts 5:42; 11:14; 16:31–34; 18:8; 1 Corinthians 16:15). Apostles also spread the good news through other homes into which they were invited (Acts 13:7; 28:7), or in houses which they rented for themselves over a longer period of time (Acts 28:30–31). Further instruction also took place in homes (Acts 20:20), and there were warnings against false teachers who sought to gain entrance into people's homes and undermine whole households (2 Timothy 3:6; Titus 1:11).

3. Although in early days of the church believers gathered around the Temple to hear the apostles (Acts 2:46), from the outset they met regularly in homes to worship with one another (Acts 2:46; 8:3; 16:40; 20:7–12) and for specific prayer (Acts 4:31; 12:12). This practice was continued under Paul, whose converts met regularly as house churches (Romans 16:5; 1 Corinthians 16:19; Colossians 4:15; Philemon 2) and also in larger gatherings as the whole church (Romans 16:23), though still in a home.

4. The church is described as a family (Galatians 6:10; Ephesians 2:19; 1 Timothy 3:15) or as the objects in a house (2 Timothy 2:20–21). According to Acts, as there was need believers sold their surplus houses and lands so that they could distribute the proceeds among the poorer members (Acts 4:34). According to Paul, all Christians should privately set aside money so that it can be shared with the needy (1 Corinthians 16:2).

Two final issues should be mentioned, one to do with leaderhip in the church, the other to do with baptism of children. With respect to leadership, emphasis is laid on the importance of designating key people in the church only if they have already demonstrated their ability to look after their own households well (1 Timothy 3:4–5, 12). They should also treat others in the church as they would senior and junior, male and female, members of their own family (1 Timothy 5:1–2).

With respect to baptism, the reference to whole households receiving the message and being baptized has often been understood to include small children. However, this issue cannot be decided on the grounds of language alone. "Household" or "all the household" (or such translations as "family", "descendants") can be used of adults alone (Genesis 7:1; 39:5; 45:7) or has "children" added to it to distinguish between the two (Genesis 18:19; 36:6; 50:7; 1 Samuel 1:21). The New Testament also refers to all-adult households (Acts 10:33–34; 1 Corinthians 16:15ff.), and has the same distinction between household or families and children (1 Timothy 3:12).

House/Home: For additional scriptures on this topic go to Leviticus 14:35.

clothes that the priest will wear in the Holy Place.
These are the holy clothes for Aaron the priest and
his sons to wear when they serve as priests."
20Then all the people of Israel went away from
Moses. 21Everyone who wanted to give came and
brought a gift to the LORD for making the Meeting
Tent, all the things in the Tent, and the special
clothes. 22All the men and women who wanted to
give brought gold jewelry of all kinds—pins, earrings, rings, and bracelets. They all presented
their gold to the LORD. 23Everyone who had blue,
purple, and red thread, and fine linen, and anyone
who had goat hair or male sheepskins colored red
or fine leather brought them to the LORD.
24Everyone who could give silver or bronze
brought that as a gift to the LORD, and everyone
who had acacia wood to be used in the work
brought it. 25Every skilled woman used her hands
to make the blue, purple, and red thread, and fine
linen, and they brought what they had made. 26All
the women who were skilled and wanted to help
made thread of the goat hair. 27The leaders brought
onyx stones and other jewels to put on the holy
vest and chest covering for the priest. 28They also
brought spices and olive oil for the sweet-smelling
incense, the special oil, and the oil to burn in the
lamps. 29All the men and women of Israel who
wanted to help brought gifts to the LORD for all the
work the LORD had commanded Moses and the
people to do.
30Then Moses said to the Israelites, "Look, the
LORD has chosen Bezalel son of Uri the son of Hur,
from the tribe of Judah. 31The LORD has filled
Bezalel with the Spirit of God and has given him the
skill, ability, and knowledge to do all kinds of work.
32He is able to design pieces to be made of gold, silver, and bronze, 33to cut stones and jewels and put
them in metal, to carve wood, and to do all kinds
of work. 34Also, the LORD has given Bezalel and
Oholiab, the son of Ahisamach from the tribe of
Dan, the ability to teach others. 35The LORD has
given them the skill to do all kinds of work. They
are able to cut designs in metal and stone. They
can plan and sew designs in the fine linen with
the blue, purple, and red thread. And they
36 are also able to weave things. 1So Bezalel,
Oholiab, and every skilled person will do
the work the Lord has commanded, because he
gave them the wisdom and understanding to do all
the skilled work needed to build the Holy Tent."
2Then Moses called Bezalel, Oholiab, and all
the other skilled people to whom the LORD had
given skills, and they came because they wanted
to help with the work. 3They received from Moses
everything the people of Israel had brought as gifts
to build the Holy Tent. The people continued to
bring gifts each morning because they wanted to.
4So all the skilled workers left the work they were
doing on the Holy Tent, 5and they said to Moses,
"The people are bringing more than we need to do
the work the LORD commanded."
6Then Moses sent this command throughout
the camp: "No man or woman should make anything else as a gift for the Holy Tent." So the people
were kept from giving more, 7because what they
had was already more than enough to do all the
work.

The Holy Tent

8Then the skilled workers made the Holy Tent.
They made the ten curtains of blue, purple, and
red cloth, and they sewed designs of creatures with
wings on the curtains. 9Each curtain was the same
size—forty-two feet long and six feet wide. 10Five
of the curtains were fastened together to make
one set, and the other five were fastened together
to make another set. 11Then they made loops of
blue cloth along the edge of the end curtain on the
first set of five, and they did the same thing with
the other set of five. 12There were fifty loops on
one curtain and fifty loops on the other curtain,
with the loops opposite each other. 13They made
fifty gold hooks to join the two curtains together so
that the Holy Tent was joined together as one piece.
14Then the workers made another tent of eleven
curtains made of goat hair, to put over the Holy
Tent. 15All eleven curtains were the same size—
forty-five feet long and six feet wide. 16The workers
sewed five curtains together into one set and six
together into another set. 17They made fifty loops
along the edge of the outside curtain of one set and
fifty loops along the edge of the outside curtain of
the other set. 18Then they made fifty bronze rings
to join the two sets of cloth together and make
the tent one piece. 19They made two more coverings for the outer tent—one made of male sheepskins colored red and the other made of fine
leather.
20Then they made upright frames of acacia
wood for the Holy Tent. 21Each frame was fifteen
feet tall and twenty-seven inches wide, 22and there
were two pegs side by side on each one. Every
frame of the Holy Tent was made this same way.
23They made twenty frames for the south side of
the Tent, 24and they made forty silver bases that
went under the twenty frames. There were two
bases for every frame—one for each peg of each
frame. 25They also made twenty frames for the
north side of the Holy Tent 26and forty silver
bases—two to go under each frame. 27They made

six frames for the rear or west end of the Holy Tent 28and two frames for the corners at the rear of the Holy Tent. 29These two frames were doubled at the bottom and joined at the top with a metal ring. They did this for each of these corners. 30So there were eight frames and sixteen silver bases—two bases under each frame.

31Then they made crossbars of acacia wood to connect the upright frames of the Holy Tent. Five crossbars held the frames together on one side of the Tent, 32and five held the frames together on the other side. Also, five crossbars held the frames together on the west end, at the rear of the Tent. 33They made the middle crossbar run along the entire length of each side and rear of the Tent. It was set halfway up the frames. 34They made gold rings on the sides of the frames to hold the crossbars, and they covered the frames and the crossbars with gold.

35Then they made the curtain of blue, purple, and red thread, and fine linen. A skilled craftsman sewed designs of creatures with wings on it. 36They made four posts of acacia wood for it and covered them with gold. Then they made gold hooks for the posts, as well as four silver bases in which to set the posts. 37For the entrance to the Tent, they made a curtain of blue, purple, and red thread, and fine linen. A person who sewed well sewed designs on it. 38Then they made five posts and hooks for it. They covered the tops of the posts and their bands with gold, and they made five bronze bases for the posts.

The Ark of the Agreement

37 Bezalel made the Ark of acacia wood; it was forty-five inches long, twenty-seven inches wide, and twenty-seven inches high. 2He covered it, both inside and out, with pure gold, and he put a gold strip around it. 3He made four gold rings for it and attached them to its four feet, with two rings on each side. 4Then he made poles of acacia wood and covered them with gold. 5He put the poles through the rings on each side of the Ark to carry it. 6Then he made a lid of pure gold that was forty-five inches long and twenty-seven inches wide. 7Then Bezalel hammered gold to make two creatures with wings and attached them to each end of the lid. 8He made one creature on one end of the lid and the other creature on the other end. He attached them to the lid so that it would be one piece. 9The creatures' wings were spread upward, covering the lid, and the creatures faced each other across the lid.⚭

The Table

10Then he made the table of acacia wood; it was thirty-six inches long, eighteen inches wide, and twenty-seven inches high. 11He covered it with pure gold and put a gold strip around it. 12He made a frame three inches high that stood up all around the edge, and he put a gold strip around it. 13Then he made four gold rings for the table and attached them to the four corners of the table where the four legs were. 14The rings were put close to the frame around the top of the table, because they held the poles for carrying it. 15The poles for carrying the table were made of acacia wood and were covered with gold. 16He made of pure gold all the things that were used on the table: the plates, bowls, cups, and jars used for pouring the drink offerings.

The Lampstand

17Then he made the lampstand of pure gold, hammering out its base and stand. Its flower-like cups, buds, and petals were joined together in one piece with the base and stand. 18Six branches went out from the sides of the lampstand—three on one side and three on the other. 19Each branch had three cups shaped like almond flowers, and each cup had a bud and a petal. Each of the six branches going out from the lampstand was the same. 20There were four more cups shaped like almond flowers on the lampstand itself, each with its buds and petals. 21Three pairs of branches went out from the lampstand. A bud was under the place where each pair was attached to the lampstand. Each of the six branches going out from the lampstand was the same. 22The buds, branches, and lampstand were all one piece of pure, hammered gold. 23He made seven pure gold lamps for this lampstand, and he made pure gold wick trimmers and trays. 24He used about seventy-five pounds of pure gold to make the lampstand and all the things that go with it.

The Altar for Burning Incense

25Then he made the altar of incense out of acacia wood. It was square—eighteen inches long and eighteen inches wide—and it was thirty-six inches high. Each corner that stuck out like a horn was joined into one piece with the altar. 26He covered the top and all the sides and the corners with pure gold, and he put gold trim around the altar. 27He made two gold rings and put them below the trim on opposite sides of the altar; these rings held the poles for carrying it. 28He made the poles of acacia wood and covered them with gold.

⚭**37:9 Ark of the Agreement:** Numbers 10:33–36

29Then he made the holy olive oil for appointing the priests and the pure, sweet-smelling incense. He made them like a person who mixes perfumes.

The Altar for Burnt Offerings

38 Then he built the altar for burnt offerings out of acacia wood. The altar was square—seven and one-half feet long and seven and one-half feet wide—and it was four and one-half feet high. 2He made each corner stick out like a horn so that the horns and the altar were joined together in one piece. Then he covered the altar with bronze. 3He made all the tools of bronze to use on the altar: the pots, shovels, bowls for sprinkling blood, meat forks, and pans for carrying the fire. 4He made a large bronze screen to hold the burning wood for the altar and put it inside the altar, under its rim, halfway up from the bottom. 5He made bronze rings to hold the poles for carrying the altar, and he put them at the four corners of the screen. 6Then he made poles of acacia wood and covered them with bronze. 7He put the poles through the rings on both sides of the altar, to carry it. He made the altar of boards and left the inside hollow.

The Bronze Bowl

8He made the bronze bowl for washing, and he built it on a bronze stand. He used the bronze from mirrors that belonged to the women who served at the entrance to the Meeting Tent.

The Courtyard of the Holy Tent

9Then he made a wall of curtains to form a courtyard around the Holy Tent. On the south side the curtains were one hundred fifty feet long and were made of fine linen. 10The curtains hung on silver hooks and bands, placed on twenty bronze posts with twenty bronze bases. 11On the north side the wall of curtains was also one hundred fifty feet long, and it hung on silver hooks and bands on twenty posts with twenty bronze bases.

12On the west side of the courtyard, the wall of curtains was seventy-five feet long. It was held up by silver hooks and bands on ten posts with ten bases. 13The east side was also seventy-five feet long. 14On one side of the entry there was a wall of curtains twenty-two and one-half feet long, held up by three posts and three bases. 15On the other side of the entry there was also a wall of curtains twenty-two and one-half feet long, held up by three posts and three bases. 16All the curtains around the courtyard were made of fine linen. 17The bases for the posts were made of bronze. The hooks and the bands on the posts were made of silver, and the tops of the posts were covered with silver also. All the posts in the courtyard had silver bands.

18The curtain for the entry of the courtyard was made of blue, purple, and red thread, and fine linen, sewn by a person who could sew well. The curtain was thirty feet long and seven and one-half feet high, the same height as the curtains around the courtyard. 19It was held up by four posts and four bronze bases. The hooks and bands on the posts were made of silver, and the tops on the posts were covered with silver. 20All the tent pegs for the Holy Tent and for the curtains around the courtyard were made of bronze.

21This is a list of the materials used to make the Holy Tent, where the Agreement was kept. Moses ordered the Levites to make this list, and Ithamar son of Aaron was in charge of keeping it. 22Bezalel son of Uri, the son of Hur of the tribe of Judah, made everything the LORD commanded Moses. 23Oholiab son of Ahisamach of the tribe of Dan helped him. He could cut designs into metal and stone; he was a designer and also skilled at sewing the blue, purple, and red thread, and fine linen.

24The total amount of gold used to build the Holy Tent was presented to the LORD. It weighed over 2,000 pounds, as set by the Holy Place measure.

25The silver was given by the members of the community who were counted. It weighed 7,550 pounds, as set by the Holy Place measure. 26All the men twenty years old or older were counted. There were 603,550 men, and each man had to pay one-fifth of an ounce of silver, as set by the Holy Place measure. 27Of this silver, 7,500 pounds were used to make the one hundred bases for the Holy Tent and for the curtain—75 pounds of silver in each base. 28They used 50 pounds of silver to make the hooks for the posts and to cover the tops of the posts and to make the bands on them.

29The bronze which was presented to the LORD weighed about 5,000 pounds. 30They used the bronze to make the bases at the entrance of the Meeting Tent, to make the altar and the bronze screen, and to make all the tools for the altar. 31This bronze was also used to make bases for the wall of curtains around the courtyard and bases for curtains at the entry to the courtyard, as well as to make the tent pegs for the Holy Tent and the curtains that surrounded the courtyard.

Clothes for the Priests

39 They used blue, purple, and red thread to make woven clothes for the priests to wear when they served in the Holy Place. They

made the holy clothes for Aaron as the LORD had commanded Moses.

2They made the holy vest of gold, and blue, purple, and red thread, and fine linen. 3They hammered the gold into sheets and then cut it into long, thin strips. They worked the gold into the blue, purple, and red thread, and fine linen. This was done by skilled craftsmen. 4They made the shoulder straps for the holy vest, which were attached to the top corners of the vest and tied together over each shoulder. 5The skillfully woven belt was made in the same way; it was joined to the holy vest as one piece. It was made of gold, and blue, purple, and red thread, and fine linen, the way the LORD commanded Moses.

6They put gold around the onyx stones and then wrote the names of the sons of Israel on these gems, as a person carves words and designs on a seal. 7Then they attached the gems on the shoulder straps of the holy vest, as reminders of the twelve sons of Israel. This was done just as the LORD had commanded Moses.

8The skilled craftsmen made the chest covering like the holy vest; it was made of gold, and blue, purple, and red thread, and fine linen. 9The chest covering was square—nine inches long and nine inches wide—and it was folded double to make a pocket. 10Then they put four rows of beautiful jewels on it: In the first row there was a ruby, a topaz, and a yellow quartz; 11in the second there was a turquoise, a sapphire, and an emerald; 12in the third there was a jacinth, an agate, and an amethyst; 13in the fourth there was a chrysolite, an onyx, and a jasper. Gold was put around these jewels to attach them to the chest covering, 14and the names of the sons of Israel were carved on these twelve jewels as a person carves a seal. Each jewel had the name of one of the twelve tribes of Israel.

15They made chains of pure gold, twisted together like a rope, for the chest covering. 16The workers made two gold pieces and two gold rings. They put the two gold rings on the two upper corners of the chest covering. 17Then they put two gold chains in the two rings at the ends of the chest covering, 18and they fastened the other two ends of the chains to the two gold pieces. They attached these gold pieces to the two shoulder straps in the front of the holy vest. 19They made two gold rings and put them at the lower corners of the chest covering on the inside edge next to the holy vest. 20They made two more gold rings on the bottom of the shoulder straps in front of the holy vest, near the seam, just above the woven belt of the holy vest. 21They used a blue ribbon and tied the rings of the chest covering to the rings of the holy vest, connecting it to the woven belt. In this way the chest covering would not swing out from the holy vest. They did all these things the way the LORD commanded.

22Then they made the outer robe to be worn under the holy vest. It was woven only of blue cloth. 23They made a hole in the center of the outer robe, with a woven collar sewn around it so it would not tear. 24Then they made balls like pomegranates of blue, purple, and red thread, and fine linen and hung them around the bottom of the outer robe. 25They also made bells of pure gold and hung these around the bottom of the outer robe between the balls. 26So around the bottom of the outer robe there was a bell and a pomegranate ball, a bell and a pomegranate ball. The priest wore this outer robe when he served as priest, just as the LORD had commanded Moses.

27They wove inner robes of fine linen for Aaron and his sons, 28and they made turbans, headbands, and underclothes of fine linen. 29Then they made the cloth belt of fine linen, and blue, purple, and red thread, and designs were sewn onto it, just as the LORD had commanded Moses.

30They made a strip of pure gold, which is the holy crown, and carved these words in the gold, as one might carve on a seal: "Holy to the LORD." 31Then they tied this flat piece to the turban with a blue ribbon, as the LORD had commanded Moses.

32So all the work on the Meeting Tent was finished. The Israelites did everything just as the LORD had commanded Moses. 33Then they brought the Holy Tent to Moses: the Tent and all its furniture, hooks, frames, crossbars, posts, and bases; 34the covering made of male sheepskins colored red, the covering made of fine leather, and the curtain that covered the entrance to the Most Holy Place; 35the Ark of the Agreement, its poles and lid; 36the table, all its containers, and the bread that showed they were in God's presence; 37the pure gold lampstand with its lamps in a row, all its tools, and the olive oil for the light; 38the gold altar, the special olive oil used for appointing priests, the sweet-smelling incense, and the curtain that covered the entrance to the Tent; 39the bronze altar and its screen, its poles and all its tools, the bowl and its stand; 40the curtains for the courtyard with their posts and bases, the curtain that covered the entry to the courtyard, the cords, pegs, and all the things in the Meeting Tent. 41They brought the clothes for the priests to wear when they served in the Holy Tent—the holy clothes for Aaron the priest and the clothes for his sons, which they wore when they served as priests.

42The Israelites had done all this work just as

the LORD had commanded Moses. 43Moses looked
closely at all the work and saw they had done it just
as the LORD had commanded. So Moses blessed
them.

Setting Up the Holy Tent

40 Then the LORD said to Moses: 2"On the first
day of the first month, set up the Holy
Tent, which is the Meeting Tent. 3Put the Ark of
the Agreement in it and hang the curtain in front
of the Ark. 4Bring in the table and arrange everything on the table that should be there. Then
bring in the lampstand and set up its lamps. 5Put
the gold altar for burning incense in front of the
Ark of the Agreement, and put the curtain at the
entrance to the Holy Tent.
6"Put the altar of burnt offerings in front of the
entrance of the Holy Tent, the Meeting Tent. 7Put
the bowl between the Meeting Tent and the altar,
and put water in it. 8Set up the courtyard around
the Holy Tent, and put the curtain at the entry to
the courtyard.
9"Use the special olive oil and pour it on the
Holy Tent and everything in it, in order to give
the Tent and all that is in it for service to the LORD.
They will be holy. 10Pour the special oil on the
altar for burnt offerings and on all its tools. Give
the altar for service to God, and it will be very
holy. 11Then pour the special olive oil on the bowl
and the base under it so that they will be given for
service to God.
12"Bring Aaron and his sons to the entrance of
the Meeting Tent, and wash them with water.
13Then put the holy clothes on Aaron. Pour the
special oil on him, and give him for service to
God so that he may serve me as a priest. 14Bring
Aaron's sons and put the inner robes on them.
15Pour the special oil on them in the same way
that you appointed their father as priest so that
they may also serve me as priests. Pouring oil on
them will make them a family of priests, they and
their descendants from now on." 16Moses did
everything that the LORD commanded him.
17So the Holy Tent was set up on the first day of
the first month during the second year after they
left Egypt. 18When Moses set up the Holy Tent,
he put the bases in place, and he put the frames
on the bases. Next he put the crossbars through
the rings of the frames and set up the posts.
19After that, Moses spread the cloth over the Holy
Tent and put the covering over it, just as the LORD
commanded.
20Moses put the stone tablets that had the
Agreement written on them into the Ark. He put
the poles through the rings of the Ark and put the
lid on it. 21Next he brought the Ark into the Tent
and hung the curtain to cover the Ark, just as the
LORD commanded him.
22Moses put the table in the Meeting Tent on
the north side of the Holy Tent in front of the
curtain. 23Then he put the bread on the table
before the LORD, just as the LORD commanded
him. 24Moses put the lampstand in the Meeting
Tent on the south side of the Holy Tent across
from the table. 25Then he put the lamps on the
lampstand before the LORD, just as the LORD commanded him.
26Moses put the gold altar for burning incense
in the Meeting Tent in front of the curtain. 27Then
he burned sweet-smelling incense on it, just as the
LORD commanded him. 28Then he hung the curtain at the entrance to the Holy Tent.
29He put the altar for burnt offerings at the
entrance to the Holy Tent, the Meeting Tent, and

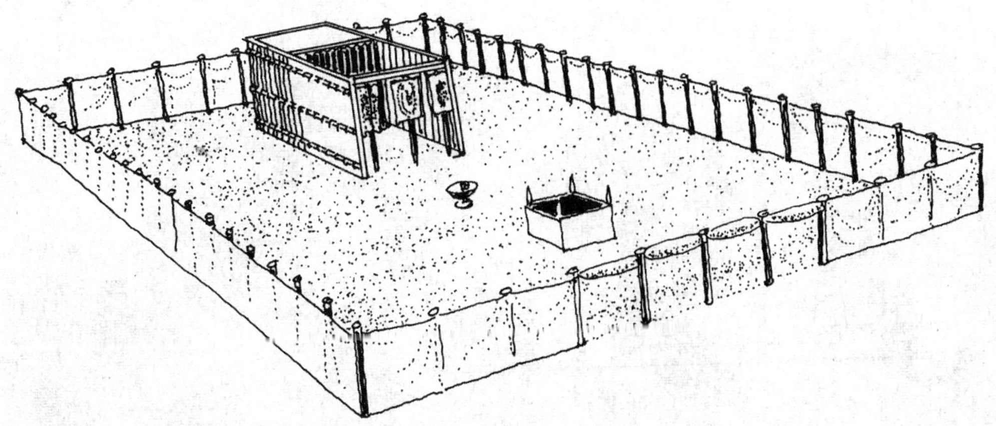

The Holy Tent, as described in chapter 26

offered a whole burnt offering and grain offerings on it, just as the LORD commanded him. 30Moses put the bowl between the Meeting Tent and the altar for burnt offerings, and he put water in it for washing. 31Moses, Aaron, and Aaron's sons used this water to wash their hands and feet. 32They washed themselves every time they entered the Meeting Tent and every time they went near the altar for burnt offerings, just as the LORD commanded Moses.

33Then Moses set up the courtyard around the Holy Tent and the altar, and he put up the curtain at the entry to the courtyard. So Moses finished the work.

The Cloud over the Holy Tent

34Then the cloud covered the Meeting Tent, and the glory of the LORD filled the Holy Tent. 35Moses could not enter the Meeting Tent, because the cloud had settled on it, and the glory of the LORD filled the Holy Tent.

36When the cloud rose from the Holy Tent, the Israelites would begin to travel, 37but as long as the cloud stayed on the Holy Tent, they did not travel. They stayed in that place until the cloud rose. 38So the cloud of the LORD was over the Holy Tent during the day, and there was a fire in the cloud at night. So all the Israelites could see the cloud while they traveled.

40:34 *the cloud.* God chose to represent his presence in the Holy Tent by means of a cloud. The cloud is associated with the heavens above.

40:35 Glory: Deuteronomy 5:24

40:38 Presence of God: Psalm 84

INTRODUCTION TO THE BOOK OF

LEVITICUS

Rules for Worship and Living

WHO WROTE THIS BOOK?

As one of the first five books of the Bible, called the Pentateuch, Leviticus is ascribed to Moses, the leader of God's people, Israel.

TO WHOM WAS THIS BOOK WRITTEN?

The Book of Leviticus was written for the people of Israel. Its name relates to the people of Levi, who were in charge of worship in the Holy Tent of God.

WHERE WAS IT WRITTEN?

This book was probably written in the desert area where Moses lead the people of Israel.

WHEN WAS IT WRITTEN?

Like the other books in the Pentateuch, Leviticus was probably written between 1446 and 1406 B.C., during the forty years when Israel was wandering in the desert. More specifically, this book may have been written during the year that Israel camped at Mount Sinai and Moses received the laws from God.

WHAT IS THE BOOK ABOUT?

Leviticus is, in effect, God's book of laws and rules for living and for worshiping him. The primary theme for the book is the holiness of God, man's need for that holiness, and God's plan to atone for man's unholiness.

WHY WAS THIS BOOK WRITTEN?

God gave his laws and rules through Moses to his people—the people he loved. The guidelines he gave, if followed by the people, would bring the people of Israel great blessings and happiness. Ignoring his rules would, however, bring the people troubles and sorrow. God's ways are right and good, and following them was the path to the Promised Land—the path to holiness.

SO WHAT DOES THIS BOOK MEAN TO US?

While specific laws and rules for worship in the Holy Tent are, perhaps, not still applicable to us today, God's call to holiness in the Book of Leviticus rings down through the ages as fresh and vital as the day it was given. Following God's guidelines for living and worship will still bring his people great blessings and happiness. Ignoring them will bring us trouble and eternal sorrow.

SUMMARY:

The name of the book, Leviticus, highlights its contents. The name means "concerning the Levites," and although the tribe of Levi is not emphasized throughout the book, the priestly subject matter shows the title to be appropriate.

Many Christians pass over Leviticus as not applying to the present day because we no longer have priests or sacrifices. But a close look at the book will show that it makes a rich contribution to our understanding of God and how he saves us from our sins.

The Book of Exodus ends with a description of the building of the Meeting Tent, the place where God is worshiped during the desert wanderings. So Leviticus, which is the third part of the five-part Torah, continues the discussion of the forms of worship used during this period of history.

Leviticus begins with a description of the five main kinds of sacrifices: burnt offerings, grain offerings, fellowship offerings, sin offerings, and penalty offerings. The various sacrifices have three main purposes. (1) They are a gift to God. (2) They provide the opportunity for fellowship among worshipers. (3) Perhaps most importantly, they were a way that the sinful people of Israel could seek God's forgiveness by offering a substitute to take the penalty for their sin.

The priesthood itself is a second major topic of concern in Leviticus. Much of the book is instruction to priests or to laypeople as they related to priests. Leviticus also includes the story of the beginning of the formal priesthood (chapters 8 and 9). The priests are set apart from other people because they minister in the presence of God. In Old Testament times, sinful people cannot simply walk into the presence of a holy God.

Leviticus also contains many laws intended to keep sinful, unrepentant human beings away from God's holy presence. There are laws about what foods to eat, about diseases, about bodily discharges, sexual relations, Sabbath observance, and much more. These laws not only describe those who should be kept away from God's presence, but also how to get right with God again.

These three major topics of sacrifice, priesthood, and law may be seen in the structure of the book:

I. Sacrificial Laws (1:1–7:38)
II. Stories about Priests (8:1–10:20)
III. Laws to Preserve God's Holiness (11:1–27:34)

For the Christian, the Book of Hebrews shows how the Book of Leviticus is relevant for us today. It presents Jesus Christ as the perfect High Priest who offers himself as the perfect sacrifice. As it says in Hebrews 9:26: "But Christ came only once and for all time at just the right time to take away all sin by sacrificing himself."

I. Sacrificial Laws (1:1–7:38)

Sacrifice is the first topic treated in the Book of Leviticus. Christians often stop reading at the beginning of the book, since the ancient sacrificial system is no longer in use. Of course, we no longer sacrifice animals to the Lord, but this is because Jesus Christ has offered himself once and for all as the sacrifice (Hebrews 9:26). Here, Leviticus gives us the background for understanding the sacrifice of Jesus on the cross.

II. Stories about Priests (8:1–10:20)

The next three chapters of Leviticus tell about the beginning of the priesthood. First, Aaron and his sons are set apart from the rest of the people of Israel as priests. Then, the account of the death of Nadab and Abihu is given. Nadab and Abihu are sons of Aaron, but they did not worship God in the way that God desired. In this way the Book of Leviticus shows the limits of the priesthood.

III. Laws to Preserve God's Holiness (11:1–27:34)

The Book of Leviticus contains many laws on a variety of subjects, including sexuality, religious observance, proper foods to eat, and certain types of diseases. Since God was actually present with Israel, the purity of the camp had to be maintained. These laws guided Israel and the guardians of God's holiness, the priests, about how to keep the camp pure.

LEVITICUS

The Burnt Offering

The LORD called to Moses and spoke to him from the Meeting Tent, saying, 2“Tell the people of Israel: ‘When you bring an offering to the LORD, bring as your offering an animal from the herd or flock.

3“‘If the offering is a whole burnt offering from the herd, it must be a male that has nothing wrong with it. The person must take the animal to the entrance of the Meeting Tent so that the LORD will accept the offering. 4He must put his hand on the animal’s head, and the LORD will accept it to remove the person’s sin so he will belong to God. 5He must kill the young bull before the LORD, and Aaron’s sons, the priests, must bring its blood and sprinkle it on all sides of the altar at the entrance to the Meeting Tent. 6After that he will skin the animal and cut it into pieces. 7The priests, when they have put wood and fire on the altar, 8are to lay the head, the fat, and other pieces on the wood that is on the fire of the altar. 9The animal’s inner organs and legs must be washed with water. Then the priest must burn all the animal’s parts on the altar. It is a whole burnt offering, an offering made by fire, and its smell is pleasing to the LORD.

10“‘If the burnt offering is a sheep or a goat from the flock, it must be a male that has nothing wrong with it. 11The person must kill the animal on the north side of the altar before the LORD, and Aaron’s sons, the priests, must sprinkle its blood on all sides of the altar. 12The person must cut the animal into pieces, and the priest must lay them, with the head and fat, on the wood that is on the fire of the altar. 13The person must wash the animal’s inner organs and legs with water, and then the priest must burn all its parts on the altar. It is a whole burnt offering, an offering made by fire, and its smell is pleasing to the LORD.

14“‘If the whole burnt offering for the LORD is a bird, it must be a dove or a young pigeon. 15The priest will bring it to the altar and pull off its head, which he will burn on the altar; the bird’s blood must be drained out on the side of the altar. 16The priest must remove the bird’s crop and its contents and throw them on the east side of the altar, where the ashes are. 17Then he must tear the bird open by its wings without dividing it into two parts. He must burn the bird on the altar, on the wood which is on the fire. It is a whole burnt offering, an offering made by fire, and its smell is pleasing to the LORD.

The Grain Offering

2 “‘When anyone offers a grain offering to the LORD, it must be made from fine flour. The person must pour oil on it, put incense on it, 2and then take it to Aaron’s sons, the priests. The priest must take a handful of the fine flour and oil and all the incense, and burn it on the altar as a memorial portion. It is an offering made by fire, and its smell is pleasing to the LORD. 3The rest of the grain offering will belong to Aaron and the priests; it is a most holy part of the offerings made by fire to the LORD.

4“‘If you bring a grain offering that was baked in the oven, it must be made from fine flour. It may be loaves made without yeast and mixed with oil, or it may be wafers made without yeast that have oil poured over them. 5If your grain offering is cooked on a griddle, it must be made, without yeast, of fine flour mixed with oil. 6Crumble it and pour oil over it; it is a grain offering. 7If your grain offering is cooked in a pan, it must be made from fine flour and oil. 8Bring the grain offering made of these things to the LORD. Give it to the priest, and he will take it to the altar. 9He will take out the memorial portion from the grain offering and burn it on the altar, as an offering made by fire. Its smell is pleasing to the LORD. 10The rest of the grain offering belongs to Aaron and the priests. It is a most holy part of the offerings made to the LORD by fire.

11“‘Every grain offering you bring to the LORD must be made without yeast, because you must not burn any yeast or honey in an offering made by fire to the LORD. 12You may bring yeast and honey to the LORD as an offering from the first harvest, but they must not be burned on the altar

1:3 *burnt offering.* The burnt offering was an offering which highlighted the forgiveness of sin. The animal was completely burned on the altar as a substitute for the sinner who actually deserved to die for his own sin.

1:5 The blood of the offering is to be sprinkled against the altar. The altar symbolizes God’s presence with his people. The blood of the sacrifice is not magical, but symbolizes the death of the animal. The animal stands in the place of the person who offers it. The dead animal stands in his place, because he deserves to die for his sins. The New Testament tells us that these bloody animal sacrifices are a shadow of the sacrifice of Christ. It is the shed blood of Jesus which has true power to cover our sins.

1:16 *crop.* A small bag inside a bird’s throat. When a bird eats, its food goes into this part first. There, the food is made soft before it goes into the stomach.

2:1 *grain offering.* The grain offering gets its name from its main ingredient, fine flour. Two other parts of this offering were oil and incense. A small part of the flour was combined with the oil and incense, and they were burned as a gift for the Lord. The rest of the flour was given to the priests as a gift. This sacrifice is primarily a gift to God.

as a pleasing smell. 13You must also put salt on all your grain offerings. Salt stands for your agreement with God that will last forever; do not leave it out of your grain offering. You must add salt to all your offerings.

14"'If you bring a grain offering from the first harvest to the LORD, bring crushed heads of new grain roasted in the fire. 15Put oil and incense on it; it is a grain offering. 16The priest will burn the memorial portion of the crushed grain and oil, with the incense on it. It is an offering by fire to the LORD.

The Fellowship Offering

3 "'If a person's fellowship offering to the LORD is from the herd, it may be a male or female, but it must have nothing wrong with it. 2The person must put his hand on the animal's head and kill it at the entrance to the Meeting Tent. Then Aaron's sons, the priests, must sprinkle the blood on all sides of the altar. 3From the fellowship offering he must make a sacrifice by fire to the LORD. He must offer the fat of the animal's inner organs (both the fat that is in them and that covers them), 4both kidneys with the fat that is on them near the lower back muscle, and the best part of the liver, which he will remove with the kidneys. 5Then the priests will burn these parts on the altar, on the whole burnt offering that is on the wood of the fire. It is an offering made by fire, and its smell is pleasing to the LORD.

6"'If a person's fellowship offering to the LORD is a lamb or a goat, it may be a male or female, but it must have nothing wrong with it. 7If he offers a lamb, he must bring it before the LORD 8and put his hand on its head. Then he must kill the animal in front of the Meeting Tent, and the priests must sprinkle its blood on all sides of the altar. 9From the fellowship offering the person must make a sacrifice by fire to the LORD. He must bring the fat, the whole fat tail cut off close to the backbone, the fat of the inner organs (both the fat that is in them and that covers them), 10both kidneys with the fat that is on them, near the lower back muscle, and the best part of the liver, which he will remove with the kidneys. 11Then the priest will burn these parts on the altar as food; it will be an offering made by fire to the LORD.

12"'If a person's offering is a goat, he must offer it before the LORD 13and put his hand on its head. Then he must kill it in front of the Meeting Tent, and the priests must sprinkle its blood on all sides of the altar. 14From this offering the person must make a sacrifice by fire to the LORD. He must offer all the fat of the goat's inner organs (both the fat that is in them and that covers them), 15both kidneys with the fat that is on them near the lower back muscle, and the best part of the liver, which he will remove with the kidneys. 16The priest will burn these parts on the altar as food. It is an offering made by fire, and its smell is pleasing to the LORD. All the fat belongs to the LORD.

17"'This law will continue for people from now on, wherever you live: You must not eat any fat or blood.'"

The Sin Offering

4 The LORD said to Moses, 2"Tell the people of Israel this: 'When a person sins by accident and does some things the LORD has commanded not to be done, that person must do these things:

3"'If the appointed priest sins so that he brings guilt on the people, then he must offer a young bull to the LORD, one that has nothing wrong with it, as a sin offering for the sin he has done. 4He will bring the bull to the entrance of the Meeting Tent in front of the LORD, put his hand on its head, and kill it before the LORD. 5Then the appointed priest must bring some of the bull's blood into the Meeting Tent. 6The priest is to dip his finger into the blood and sprinkle it seven times before the LORD in front of the curtain of the Most Holy Place. 7The priest must also put some of the blood on the corners of the altar of incense that stands before the LORD in the Meeting Tent. The rest of the blood he must pour out at the bottom of the altar of burnt offering, which is at the entrance of the Meeting Tent. 8He must remove all the fat from the bull of the sin offering—the fat on and around the inner organs, 9both kidneys with the fat that is on them near the lower back muscle, and the best part of the liver which he will remove with the kidneys. 10(He must do this in the same way the fat is removed from the bull of the fellowship offering.) Then the priest must burn the animal parts on the altar of burnt offering. 11But the priest must carry off the skin of the bull and all its meat, along with the rest of the bull—its head, legs, intestines, and other inner organs. 12He must take it outside the camp to the special clean place where the ashes are poured out. He must burn it on a wood fire on the pile of ashes.

13"'If the whole nation of Israel sins accidentally without knowing it and does something the LORD

3:1 *Fellowship offering.* This sacrifice is mainly for fellowship between both the worshiper and God and also among the worshipers.

4:3 *sin offering.* This sacrifice is connected with the forgiveness of sin.

Capital Punishment

Genesis 9:6

Why do so many laws in the Old Testament require the death penalty? What about capital punishment today?

A person could argue that capital punishment was established at the very beginning when God told Adam, "You must not eat the fruit from the tree which gives the knowledge of good and evil. If you ever eat fruit from that tree, you will die" (Genesis 2:17)! God established this penalty to impress upon Adam the seriousness of disobedience. Soon after Adam disobeyed, Adam's firstborn son, Cain, killed his brother Abel. Violence increased in the world to such an extent that God executed capital punishment for everyone except Noah and his family. The Bible contains other examples of God executing capital punishment directly. Genesis 18:16–19:19 records God's destruction of Sodom and Gomorrah. Genesis 38:7, 10 describes how God killed Er and Onan for their evil ways.

Does Genesis 9:4–7 indicate that the death penalty for murder has a special justification?

Immediately after the flood God gave instructions about capital punishment. From that time forward man would serve as God's instrument in protecting life by punishing those who took the life of another: "I will demand blood for life. I will demand the life of any animal that kills a person, and I will demand the life of anyone who takes another person's life. 'Whoever kills a human being will be killed by a human being, because God made humans in his own image'" (Genesis 9:5–6).

The Old Testament required capital punishment for a multitude of crimes. Genesis 9:6 is the first place that God actually establishes the law that man will execute capital punishment on man. Exodus 21:15–17; 22:18–19; and 35:2 require death as punishment for striking one's parents, kidnapping, sacrificing to false gods, and profaning the Sabbath. Leviticus 20:2–16; 21:9; and 24:11–23 require death for adultery, incest, bestiality, sodomy, fornication, blasphemy, and offering a human sacrifice. Numbers 15:32–36 and 35:29–34 require death for murder and desecration of the Sabbath. Numbers 35:31 also states that the death penalty may never be remitted when it applies. Deuteronomy 13:1–10; 17:6–12; 21:18–21; and 22:21–25 require death for crimes such as rape and false teaching.

God is too holy to look upon evil. It is God's intent to put an end to evil as quickly and completely as possible. He does this in the interest of preserving life. Exodus 20:1–6 explains that God required severe punishment for evil because he had rescued Israel from bondage to the Egyptians. Israelites were not to do evil as the Egyptians did, from whom God had saved them. Rather, Israel was to be holy, as God their rescuer was holy.

Several explanations for the number of crimes requiring the death penalty are found in Deuteronomy. In Deuteronomy 21:21 God tells Israel that by means of capital punishment they are to put away the evil person from their midst. He also says that all Israel will hear of this and fear. Thus God wants to stop the activity of the evildoer, and he wants to prevent others from doing anything similar. Deuteronomy 20:16–18 explains that God required the Israelites to put certain foreign people to death so that the Israelites would not learn any of their abominable practices. In certain cases, like those mentioned in Deuteronomy 7:10 and 25:17–19, God decrees death for members of nations because of particular wrongs they had done against God or his people. Numbers 35:33 says that God has instituted the death penalty in the interest of keeping the land pure.

It is important to recognize the origin and purpose of capital punishment. It is of equal importance to know the restrictions that God has placed on the enforcement of this law. Numbers 35:30 warns that no one is to be put to death on the testimony of one witness. Numbers 35:19, 24 notes that the actual execution of a person for murder is restricted to the "avenger of blood," that is, the victim's next of kin who bears that responsibility. Romans 13:1–7, in a similar way, restricts the enforcement of the death penalty to civil authorities. Numbers 35:9–15 tells us that a distinction was made in case of an accident. Cities of refuge were required to be provided for a person who killed someone else accidentally.

Most of all, it is important to know that capital punishment is not to be motivated by an attitude of revenge on the part of individuals. In Matthew 5:38–42 Jesus notes that the Jews had heard it said, "An eye for an eye, and a tooth for a tooth." Jesus responds to this misuse of Scripture by commanding people to turn the other cheek. The saying that people were using to justify their revenge was based on Exodus 21:22–25. This passage did require life for life, eye for eye, and tooth for tooth. However, the decision to execute such judgment was restricted to the judges.

Capital Punishment: For additional scriptures on this topic go to Exodus 21:15–17.

AGREEMENT

GENESIS 9:9

In what way can our relationship with God be called an agreement? How are the different agreements in the Bible related? What is the new agreement?

The Bible explains that God desires a relationship with his human creatures. That relationship is described in a number of different ways, but perhaps the most common picture the Bible draws of the divine-human relationship is that of an agreement. *Agreement* is the NCV choice for translating a Hebrew and Greek word that is sometimes translated "covenant" or "testament."

No English word is perfect for translating the original word that lies behind the word *agreement. Covenant* is an obscure English word that communicates little to many readers of the Bible. On the other hand, while *agreement* is understandable, it is also slightly incomplete in meaning.

The problem is that it is not as if God and his human creatures are sitting down on equal terms and negotiating a relationship on which they agree. No, this agreement is more like the relationship between two nations, one led by the ruler of a superpower and the other a weak and dependent king of a small nation. In other words, God, the Great King, enters into an agreement with his servant people, and it is God who begins the relationship and who sets the terms for the relationship, not his human creatures.

We can see God's primary role in the biblical agreement by looking at the first clear use of the term to describe the relationship between God and humanity in the account of Noah. After the flood waters recede, God says to Noah, "Now I am making my agreement with you and your people who will live after you" (Genesis 9:9). God is the one who initiates the relationship and establishes the terms by which it continues. In this case he agrees not to judge the world by means of a flood again. He also makes certain demands of Noah, including the command to "to have many children, to grow in number on the earth, and to become many" (Genesis 9:7). God also presents a sign of his commitment to continue in this relationship with Noah and those who are descended from him (all humanity) by placing a rainbow in the sky. Every time a rainbow appears we are to remember that God has entered into an agreement with us through Noah.

We should also notice that before God came to Noah to make an agreement with him, Noah sacrificed to the Lord. This is something that happens whenever a divine-human agreement is made. After all, God is holy and humans are sinful, and sacrifice is a way of acknowledging sin before entering into God's presence (see Sacrifice).

There are at least three other agreements in the Old Testament. One does not replace the other, but they all build on each other. The next agreement is God's agreement with Abraham. Once again, he made certain promises to Abraham (Genesis 12:1–3) and also placed demands upon him (to leave Ur and go to Canaan). The promises to Abraham include the promise that he will give birth to a mighty nation. This promise, of course, implies that he will have children and eventually come to own the land of Canaan. Much of the following Scripture has as its focus the granting of these promises. God also promises Abraham that he will bring a blessing upon all the nations of the world.

The third agreement in the Old Testament is between Moses and God (Exodus 19–24). God has saved Israel from Egyptian slavery. He then directs Moses to bring them to Mount Sinai so he can establish them as a nation. The Ten Commandments and the many laws associated with the Ten Commandments are the demands that God places upon his Old Testament covenant people.

The last agreement in the Old Testament is between David and God (2 Samuel 7). Here God promises David a dynasty; his descendants will follow him on the throne of Israel. In turn, God calls on David and his offspring to follow his laws and be faithful to him.

Many other passages describe a renewal, or reconfirmation, of the agreement. Moses led the people of Israel in a reconfirmation of the agreement before they went into the Promised Land (Deuteronomy); Joshua had the people renew the agreement before his death (Joshua 24), and so on. Furthermore, the prophet's main job was to remind God's people that they should obey God's agreement, and when they didn't he warned them that they would face an angry God.

Jesus Christ is the final fulfillment and climax of the agreements. He established the new agreement (Luke 22:20). He is the descendent of David who is on the throne forever (Romans 1:3). He is the seed of Abraham and the fulfillment of the promise of land. He is the one who fulfills the Law of Moses (Matthew 5:17–20).

Agreement: For additional scriptures on this topic go to Exodus 2:24.

has commanded not to be done, they are guilty. 14When they learn about the sin they have done, they must offer a young bull as a sin offering and bring it before the Meeting Tent. 15The older leaders of the group of people must put their hands on the bull's head before the LORD, and it must be killed before the LORD. 16Then the appointed priest must bring some of the bull's blood into the Meeting Tent. 17Dipping his finger in the blood, he must sprinkle it seven times before the LORD in front of the curtain. 18Then he must put some of the blood on the corners of the altar that is before the LORD in the Meeting Tent. The priest must pour out the rest of the blood at the bottom of the altar of burnt offering, which is at the entrance to the Meeting Tent. 19He must remove all the fat from the animal and burn it on the altar; 20he will do the same thing with this bull that he did with the first bull of the sin offering. In this way the priest removes the sins of the people so they will belong to the LORD and be forgiven. 21Then the priest must carry the bull outside the camp and burn it, just as he did with the first bull. This is the sin offering for the whole community.

22"'If a ruler sins by accident and does something the LORD his God has commanded must not be done, he is guilty. 23When he learns about his sin, he must bring a male goat that has nothing wrong with it as his offering. 24The ruler must put his hand on the goat's head and kill it in the place where they kill the whole burnt offering before the LORD; it is a sin offering. 25The priest must take some of the blood of the sin offering on his finger and put it on the corners of the altar of burnt offering. He must pour out the rest of the blood at the bottom of the altar of burnt offering. 26He must burn all the goat's fat on the altar in the same way he burns the fat of the fellowship offerings. In this way the priest removes the ruler's sin so he belongs to the LORD, and the LORD will forgive him.

27"'If any person in the community sins by accident and does something which the LORD has commanded must not be done, he is guilty. 28When the person learns about his sin, he must bring a female goat that has nothing wrong with it as an offering for his sin. 29He must put his hand on the animal's head and kill it at the place of the whole burnt offering. 30Then the priest must take some of the goat's blood on his finger and put it on the corners of the altar of burnt offering. He must pour out the rest of the goat's blood at the bottom of the altar. 31Then the priest must remove all the goat's fat in the same way the fat is removed from the fellowship offerings. He must burn it on the altar as a smell pleasing to the LORD. In this way the priest will remove that person's sin so he will belong to the LORD, and the LORD will forgive him.

32"'If this person brings a lamb as his offering for sin, he must bring a female that has nothing wrong with it. 33He must put his hand on the animal's head and kill it as a sin offering in the place where the whole burnt offering is killed. 34The priest must take some of the blood from the sin offering on his finger and put it on the corners of the altar of burnt offering. He must pour out the rest of the lamb's blood at the bottom of the altar. 35Then the priest must remove all the lamb's fat in the same way that the lamb's fat is removed from the fellowship offerings. He must burn the pieces on the altar on top of the offerings made by fire for the LORD. In this way the priest will remove that person's sins so he will belong to the LORD, and the LORD will forgive him.

Special Types of Accidental Sins

5 "'If a person is ordered to tell in court what he has seen or what he knows and he does not tell the court, he is guilty of sin.

2"'Or someone might touch something unclean, such as the dead body of an unclean wild animal or an unclean farm animal or an unclean crawling animal. Even if he does not know that he touched it, he will still be unclean and guilty of sin.

3"'Someone might touch human uncleanness—anything that makes someone unclean—and not know it. But when he learns about it, he will be guilty.

4"'Or someone might make a promise before the LORD without thinking. It might be a promise to do something bad or something good; it might be about anything. Even if he forgets about it, when he remembers, he will be guilty.

5"'When anyone is guilty of any of these things, he must tell how he sinned. 6He must bring an offering to the LORD as a penalty for sin; it must be a female lamb or goat from the flock. The priest will perform the acts to remove that person's sin so he will belong to the LORD.

7"'But if the person cannot afford a lamb, he must bring two doves or two young pigeons to the LORD as the penalty for his sin. One bird must be for a sin offering, and the other must be for a whole burnt offering. 8He must bring them to the priest, who will first offer the one for the sin offering. He will pull the bird's head from its neck, but

4:16 Reconciliation: Leviticus 5:9

4:35 Sin: 1 Kings 8:46–51

he will not pull it completely off. 9He must sprinkle the blood from the sin offering on the side of the altar, and then he must pour the rest of the blood at the bottom of the altar; it is a sin offering. 10Then the priest must offer the second bird as a whole burnt offering, as the law says. In this way the priest will remove the person's sin so he will belong to the LORD, and the LORD will forgive him.

11"'If the person cannot afford two doves or two pigeons, he must bring about two quarts of fine flour as an offering for sin. He must not put oil or incense on the flour, because it is a sin offering. 12He must bring the flour to the priest. The priest will take a handful of the flour as a memorial offering and burn it on the altar on top of the offerings made by fire to the LORD; it is a sin offering. 13In this way the priest will remove the person's sins so he will belong to the LORD, and the LORD will forgive him. What is left of the sin offering belongs to the priest, like the grain offering.'"

The Penalty Offering

14The LORD said to Moses, 15"If a person accidentally sins and does something against the holy things of the LORD, he must bring from the flock a male sheep that has nothing wrong with it. This will be his penalty offering to the LORD. Its value in silver must be correct as set by the Holy Place measure. It is a penalty offering. 16That person must pay for the sin he did against the holy thing, adding one-fifth to its value. Then he must give it all to the priest. In this way the priest will remove the person's sin so he will belong to the LORD, by using the male sheep as the penalty offering. And the LORD will forgive the person.

17"If a person sins and does something the LORD has commanded not to be done, even if he does not know it, he is still guilty. He is responsible for his sin. 18He must bring the priest a male sheep from the flock, one that has nothing wrong with it and that is worth the correct amount. It will be a penalty offering. Though the person sinned without knowing it, with this offering the priest will remove the sin so the person will belong to the LORD, and the LORD will forgive him. 19The person is guilty of doing wrong, so he must give the penalty offering to the LORD."

6

The LORD said to Moses, 2"A person might sin against the LORD by doing one of these sins: He might lie about what happened to something he was taking care of for someone else, or he might lie about a promise he made. He might steal something or cheat someone. 3He might find something that had been lost and then lie about it. He might make a promise before the LORD about something and not mean it, or he might do some other sin. 4If he does any of these things, he is guilty of sin. He must bring back whatever he stole or whatever he took by cheating. He must bring back the thing he took care of for someone else. He must bring back what he found and lied about 5or what he made a false promise about. He must pay the full price plus an extra one-fifth of the value of what he took. He must give the money to the true owner on the day he brings his penalty offering. 6He must bring his penalty to the priest—a male sheep from the flock, one that does not have anything wrong with it and that is worth the correct amount. It will be a penalty offering to the LORD. 7Then the priest will perform the acts to remove that person's sin so he will belong to the LORD, and the LORD will forgive him for the sins that made him guilty."

The Whole Burnt Offering

8The LORD said to Moses, 9"Give this command to Aaron and the priests: 'These are the teachings about the whole burnt offering: The burnt offering must stay on the altar all night until morning, and the altar's fire must be kept burning. 10The priest must put on his linen robe and linen underclothes next to his body. Then he will remove the ashes from the burnt offering on the altar and put them beside the altar. 11Then he must take off those clothes and put on others and carry the ashes outside the camp to a special clean place. 12But the fire must be kept burning on the altar; it must not be allowed to go out. The priest must put more firewood on the altar every morning, place the whole burnt offering on the fire, and burn the fat of the fellowship offerings. 13The fire must be kept burning on the altar all the time; it must not go out.

The Grain Offering

14"'These are the teachings about the grain offering: The priests must bring it to the LORD in front of the altar. 15The priest must take a handful of fine flour, with the oil and all of the incense on it, and burn the grain offering on the altar as a memorial offering to the LORD. Its smell is pleasing to him. 16Aaron and the priests may eat what is left, but it must be eaten without yeast in a holy place. They

---

5:9 Reconciliation: Isaiah 53:5

5:15 *penalty offering.* This sacrifice, like the sin offering, is connected with the forgiveness of sin. But the penalty offering is particularly important when the sin is committed against the "holy things of the Lord."

6:9 Sacrifice: Leviticus 7:11

must eat it in the courtyard of the Meeting Tent. 17It must not be cooked with yeast. I have given it as their share of the offerings made to me by fire; it is most holy, like the sin offering and the penalty offering. 18Any male descendant of Aaron may eat it as his share of the offerings made to the LORD by fire, and this will continue from now on. Whatever touches these offerings shall become holy.'"

19The LORD said to Moses, 20"This is the offering Aaron and the priests must bring to the LORD on the day they appoint Aaron as high priest: They must bring two quarts of fine flour for a continual grain offering, half of it in the morning and half in the evening. 21The fine flour must be mixed with oil and cooked on a griddle. Bring it when it is well mixed. Present the grain offering that is broken into pieces, and it will be a smell that is pleasing to the LORD. 22One of the priests appointed to take Aaron's place as high priest must make the grain offering. It is a rule forever that the grain offering must be completely burned to the LORD. 23Every grain offering made by a priest must be completely burned; it must not be eaten."

The Sin Offering

24The LORD said to Moses, 25"Tell Aaron and the priests: 'These are the teachings about the sin offering: The sin offering must be killed in front of the LORD in the same place the whole burnt offering is killed; it is most holy. 26The priest who offers the sin offering must eat it in a holy place, in the courtyard of the Meeting Tent. 27Whatever touches the meat of the sin offering must be holy, and if the blood is sprinkled on any clothes, you must wash them in a holy place. 28The clay pot the meat is cooked in must be broken, or if a bronze pot is used, it must be scrubbed and rinsed with water. 29Any male in a priest's family may eat the offering; it is most holy. 30But if the blood of the sin offering is taken into the Meeting Tent and used to remove sin in the Holy Place, that sin offering must be burned with fire. It must not be eaten.

The Penalty Offering

7 "'These are the teachings about the penalty offering, which is most holy: 2The penalty offering must be killed where the whole burnt offering is killed. Then the priest must sprinkle its blood on all sides of the altar. 3He must offer all the fat from the penalty offering—the fat tail, the fat that covers the inner organs, 4both kidneys with the fat that is on them near the lower back muscle, and the best part of the liver, which is to be removed with the kidneys. 5The priest must burn all these things on the altar as an offering made by fire to the LORD. It is a penalty offering. 6Any male in a priest's family may eat it. It is most holy, so it must be eaten in a holy place.

7"'The penalty offering is like the sin offering in that the teachings are the same for both. The priest who offers the sacrifice to remove sins will get the meat for food. 8The priest who offers the burnt offering may also have the skin from it. 9Every grain offering that is baked in an oven, cooked on a griddle, or baked in a dish belongs to the priest who offers it. 10Every grain offering, either dry or mixed with oil, belongs to the priests, and all priests will share alike.

The Fellowship Offering

11"'These are the teachings about the fellowship offering a person may offer to the LORD:⚭ 12If he brings the fellowship offering to show his thanks, he should also bring loaves of bread made without yeast that are mixed with oil, wafers made without yeast that have oil poured over them, and loaves of fine flour that are mixed with oil. 13He must also offer loaves of bread made with yeast along with his fellowship offering, which he gives to show thanks. 14One of each kind of offering will be for the LORD; it will be given to the priest who sprinkles the blood of the fellowship offering. 15When the fellowship offering is given to thank the LORD, the meat from it must be eaten the same day it is offered; none of it must be left until morning.

16"'If a person brings a fellowship offering just to give a gift to God or because of a special promise to him, the sacrifice should be eaten the same day he offers it. If there is any left, it may be eaten the next day. 17If any meat from this sacrifice is left on the third day, it must be burned up. 18Any meat of the fellowship offering eaten on the third day will not be accepted, nor will the sacrifice count for the person who offered it. It will become unclean, and anyone who eats the meat will be guilty of sin.

19"'People must not eat meat that touches anything unclean; they must burn this meat with fire. Anyone who is clean may eat other meat. 20But if anyone is unclean and eats the meat from the fellowship offering that belongs to the LORD, he must be cut off from his people.

21"'If anyone touches something unclean—uncleanness that comes from people, from an

---

⚭**7:11 Sacrifice:** Leviticus 23:13

7:12 There were a number of different types of sacrifices during the Old Testament period, and they had a variety of purposes. They were to provide a substitute death for our sins, to provide food for fellowship meals, and to offer thanks to God. A thankful heart toward God is what separates a person who loves God from one who does not.

animal, or from some hated thing—touching it
will make him unclean. If he then eats meat from
the fellowship offering that belongs to the LORD,
he must be cut off from his people.'"
22The LORD said to Moses, 23"Tell the people of
Israel: 'You must not eat any of the fat from cattle,
sheep, or goats. 24If an animal is found dead or
torn by wild animals, you may use its fat for other
things, but you must not eat it. 25If someone eats
fat from an animal offering made by fire to the
LORD, he must be cut off from his people. 26No
matter where you live, you must not eat blood
from any bird or animal. 27Anyone who eats blood
must be cut off from his people.'"

The Priests' Share

28The LORD said to Moses, 29"Tell the people of
Israel: 'If someone brings a fellowship offering to
the LORD, he must give part of it as his sacrifice to
the LORD. 30He must carry that part of the gift in
his own hands as an offering made by fire to the
LORD. He must bring the fat and the breast of the
animal to the priest, to be presented to the LORD
as the priests' share. 31Then the priest must burn
the fat on the altar, but the breast of the animal
will belong to Aaron and the priests. 32You must
also give the right thigh from the fellowship offering
to the priest as a gift; 33it will belong to the priest
who offers the blood and fat of the fellowship offering. 34I have taken the breast and the thigh from
the fellowship offerings of the Israelites, and I
have given these parts to Aaron and the priests as
their share for all time from the Israelites.'"
35This is the portion that belongs to Aaron and
his sons from the offerings made by fire to the
LORD. They were given this share on the day they
were presented to the LORD as priests. 36On the
day the LORD appointed the priests, he commanded
Israel to give this share to them, and it is to be
given to the priests as their share from now on.
37These are the teachings about the whole
burnt offering, the grain offering, the sin offering,
the penalty offering, the offering for the appointment of priests, and the fellowship offering. 38The
LORD gave these teachings to Moses on Mount Sinai
on the day he commanded the Israelites to bring
their offerings to the LORD in the Sinai Desert.

Aaron and His Sons Appointed

8 The LORD said to Moses, 2"Bring Aaron and
his sons and their clothes, the special olive oil
used in appointing people and things to the service
of the LORD, the bull of the sin offering and the
two male sheep, and the basket of bread made
without yeast. 3Then gather the people together
at the entrance to the Meeting Tent." 4Moses did
as the LORD commanded him, and the people met
together at the entrance to the Meeting Tent.
5Then Moses spoke to the people and said,
"This is what the LORD has commanded to be
done." 6Bringing Aaron and his sons forward,
Moses washed them with water. 7He put the inner
robe on Aaron and tied the cloth belt around him.
Then Moses put the outer robe on him and
placed the holy vest on him. He tied the skillfully
woven belt around him so that the holy vest was
tied to Aaron. 8Then Moses put the chest covering on him and put the Urim and the Thummim
in the chest covering. 9He also put the turban on
Aaron's head. He put the strip of gold, the holy
crown, on the front of the turban, as the LORD
commanded him to do.
10Then Moses put the special oil on the Holy
Tent and everything in it, making them holy for
the LORD. 11He sprinkled some oil on the altar
seven times, sprinkling the altar and all its tools
and the large bowl and its base. In this way he
made them holy for the LORD. 12He poured some
of the special oil on Aaron's head to make Aaron
holy for the LORD. 13Then Moses brought Aaron's
sons forward. He put the inner robes on them,
tied cloth belts around them, and put headbands
on them, as the LORD had commanded him.
14Then Moses brought the bull for the sin offering, and Aaron and his sons put their hands on its
head. 15Moses killed the bull, took the blood, and
with his finger put some of it on all the corners of
the altar, to make it pure. Then he poured out the
rest of the blood at the bottom of the altar. In this
way he made it holy and ready for service to God.
16Moses took all the fat from the inner organs of
the bull, the best part of the liver, and both kidneys
with the fat that is on them, and he burned them
on the altar. 17But he took the bull's skin, its meat,
and its intestines and burned them in a fire outside the camp, as the LORD had commanded him.
18Next Moses brought the male sheep of the
burnt offering, and Aaron and his sons put their
hands on its head. 19Then Moses killed it and sprinkled the blood on all sides of the altar. 20He cut the
male sheep into pieces and burned the head, the
pieces, and the fat. 21He washed the inner organs
and legs with water and burned the whole sheep
on the altar as a burnt offering made by fire to the

8:10 *the special oil.* The priests are anointed with the same special oil as the Holy Tent. In this way, they are both set apart. The priests become a part of the Holy Tent itself.

LORD; its smell was pleasing to the LORD. Moses did these things as the LORD had commanded him.

[22]Then Moses brought the other male sheep, the one used in appointing Aaron and his sons as priests, and Aaron and his sons put their hands on its head. [23]Then Moses killed the sheep and put some of its blood on the bottom of Aaron's right ear, some on the thumb of Aaron's right hand, and some on the big toe of his right foot. [24]Then Moses brought Aaron's sons close to the altar. He put some of the blood on the bottom of their right ears, some on the thumbs of their right hands, and some on the big toes of their right feet. Then he sprinkled blood on all sides of the altar. [25]He took the fat, the fat tail, all the fat on the inner organs, the best part of the liver, both kidneys with their fat, and the right thigh. [26]From the basket of bread made without yeast that is put before the LORD each day, Moses took a loaf of bread, a loaf made with oil, and a wafer. He put these pieces of bread on the fat and right thigh of the male sheep. [27]All these things he put in the hands of Aaron and his sons and presented them as an offering before the LORD. [28]Then Moses took them from their hands and burned them on the altar on top of the burnt offering. So this was the offering for appointing Aaron and his sons as priests. It was an offering made by fire to the LORD, and its smell was pleasing to him. [29]Moses also took the breast and presented it as an offering before the LORD. It was Moses' share of the male sheep used in appointing the priests, as the LORD had commanded him.

[30]Moses took some of the special oil and some of the blood which was on the altar, and he sprinkled them on Aaron and Aaron's clothes and on Aaron's sons and their clothes. In this way Moses made Aaron, his clothes, his sons, and their clothes holy for the LORD.

[31]Then Moses said to Aaron and his sons, "I gave you a command, saying, 'Aaron and his sons will eat these things.' So take the meat and basket of bread from the offering for appointing priests. Boil the meat at the door of the Meeting Tent, and eat it there with the bread. [32]If any of the meat or bread is left, burn it. [33]The time of appointing will last seven days; you must not go outside the entrance of the Meeting Tent until that time is up. Stay there until the time of your appointing is finished. [34]The LORD commanded the things that were done today to remove your sins so you will belong to him. [35]You must stay at the entrance of the Meeting Tent day and night for seven days. If you don't obey the LORD's commands, you will die. The LORD has given me these commands."

[36]So Aaron and his sons did everything the LORD had commanded through Moses.

Aaron and His Sons Offer Sacrifices

9 On the eighth day after the time of appointing, Moses called for Aaron and his sons and for the older leaders of Israel. [2]He said to Aaron, "Take a bull calf and a male sheep that have nothing wrong with them, and offer them to the LORD. The calf will be a sin offering, and the male sheep will be a whole burnt offering. [3]Tell the people of Israel, 'Take a male goat for a sin offering and a calf and a lamb for a whole burnt offering; each must be one year old, and it must have nothing wrong with it. [4]Also take a bull and a male sheep for fellowship offerings, along with a grain offering mixed with oil. Offer all these things to the LORD, because the LORD will appear to you today.'"

[5]So all the people came to the front of the Meeting Tent, bringing the things Moses had commanded them to bring, and they stood before the LORD. [6]Moses said, "You have done what the LORD commanded, so you will see the LORD's glory."

[7]Then Moses told Aaron, "Go to the altar and offer sin offerings and whole burnt offerings. Do this to remove your sins and the people's sins so you will belong to God. Offer the sacrifices for the people and perform the acts to remove their sins for them so they will belong to the LORD, as the LORD has commanded."

[8]So Aaron went to the altar and killed the bull calf as a sin offering for himself. [9]Then his sons brought the blood to him, and he dipped his finger in the blood and put it on the corners of the altar. He poured out the rest of the blood at the bottom of the altar. [10]Aaron took the fat, the kidneys, and the best part of the liver from the sin offering and burned them on the altar, in the way the LORD had commanded Moses. [11]The meat and skin he burned outside the camp.

[12]Then Aaron killed the animal for the whole burnt offering. His sons brought the blood to him, and he sprinkled it on all sides of the altar. [13]As they gave him the pieces and head of the burnt offering, Aaron burned them on the altar. [14]He also washed the inner organs and the legs of the burnt offering and burned them on top of the burnt offering on the altar.

[15]Then Aaron brought the offering that was for the people. He took the goat of the people's sin offering and killed it and offered it for the sin

8:36 Priesthood: Numbers 25:13

offering, just as he had done the first sin offering. [16]Then Aaron brought the whole burnt offering and offered it in the way that the LORD had commanded. [17]He also brought the grain offering to the altar. He took a handful of the grain and burned it on the altar, in addition to the morning's burnt offering.

[18]Aaron also killed the bull and the male sheep as the fellowship offerings for the people. His sons brought him the blood, and he sprinkled it on all sides of the altar. [19]Aaron's sons also brought to Aaron the fat of the bull and the male sheep—the fat tail, the fat covering the inner organs, the kidneys, and the best part of the liver. [20]Aaron's sons put them on the breasts of the bull and the sheep. Then Aaron burned these fat parts on the altar. [21]He presented the breasts and the right thigh before the LORD as the priests' share of the offering, as Moses had commanded.

[22]Then Aaron lifted his hands toward the people and blessed them. When he had finished offering the sin offering, the burnt offering, and the fellowship offering, he stepped down from the altar.

[23]Moses and Aaron went into the Meeting Tent. Then they came out and blessed the people, and the LORD's glory came to all the people. [24]Fire came out from the LORD and burned up the burnt offering and fat on the altar. When the people saw this, they shouted with joy and bowed facedown on the ground.

God Destroys Nadab and Abihu

10 Aaron's sons Nadab and Abihu took their pans for burning incense, put fire in them, and added incense; but they did not use the special fire Moses had commanded them to use in the presence of the LORD. [2]So fire came down from the LORD and destroyed Nadab and Abihu, and they died in front of the LORD. [3]Then Moses said to Aaron, "This is what the LORD was speaking about when he said,

'I must be respected as holy
  by those who come near me;
before all the people
  I must be given honor.'"

So Aaron did not say anything about the death of his sons.

[4]Aaron's uncle Uzziel had two sons named Mishael and Elzaphan. Moses said to them, "Come here and pick up your cousins' bodies. Carry them outside the camp away from the front of the Holy Place." [5]So Mishael and Elzaphan obeyed Moses and carried the bodies of Nadab and Abihu, still clothed in the special priest's inner robes, outside the camp.

[6]Then Moses said to Aaron and his other sons, Eleazar and Ithamar, "Don't show sadness by tearing your clothes or leaving your hair uncombed. If you do, you will die, and the LORD will be angry with all the people. All the people of Israel, your relatives, may cry loudly about the LORD burning Nadab and Abihu, [7]but you must not even leave the Meeting Tent. If you go out of the entrance, you will die, because the LORD has appointed you to his service." So Aaron, Eleazar, and Ithamar obeyed Moses.

[8]Then the LORD said to Aaron, [9]"You and your sons must not drink wine or beer when you go into the Meeting Tent. If you do, you will die. This law will continue from now on.⚭ [10]You must keep what is holy separate from what is not holy; you must keep what is clean separate from what is unclean. [11]You must teach the people all the laws that the LORD gave to them through Moses."

[12]Moses said to Aaron and his remaining sons, Eleazar and Ithamar, "Eat the part of the grain offering that is left from the sacrifices offered by fire to the LORD, but do not add yeast to it. Eat it near the altar because it is most holy. [13]You must eat it in a holy place, because this part of the offerings made by fire to the LORD belongs to you and your sons. I have been commanded to tell you this.

[14]"Also, you and your sons and daughters may eat the breast and thigh of the fellowship offering that was presented to the LORD. You must eat them in a clean place; they are your share of the fellowship offerings given by the Israelites. [15]The people must bring the fat from their animals that was part of the offering made by fire, and they must present it to the LORD along with the thigh and the breast of the fellowship offering. They will be the regular share of the offerings for you and your children, as the LORD has commanded."

[16]Moses looked for the goat of the sin offering, but it had already been burned up. So he became very angry with Eleazar and Ithamar, Aaron's remaining sons. He said, [17]"Why didn't you eat that goat in a holy place? It is most holy, and the LORD gave it to you to take away the guilt of the people, to remove their sins so they will belong to the LORD. [18]You didn't bring the goat's blood inside the Holy Place. You were supposed to eat the goat in a holy place, as I commanded!"

[19]But Aaron said to Moses, "Today they brought their sin offering and burnt offering before the

9:23 *the LORD's glory.* God is holy and powerful. Human beings cannot stand in his presence without harm. God, though, will often reveal himself through his glory, which often takes the form of smoke and fire. This is a veiled glimpse of his presence.

⚭**10:9 Alcohol:** Numbers 6:1–3

LORD, but these terrible things have still happened
to me! Do you think the LORD would be any happier
if I ate the sin offering today?" 20When Moses
heard this, he was satisfied.

Rules About What May Be Eaten

11 The LORD said to Moses and Aaron, 2"Tell
the Israelites this: 'These are the land animals
you may eat: 3You may eat any animal that has split
hoofs completely divided and that chews the cud.
4"'Some animals only chew the cud or only have
split hoofs, and you must not eat them. The camel
chews the cud but does not have a split hoof; it is
unclean for you. 5The rock badger chews the cud
but does not have a split hoof; it is unclean for you.
6The rabbit chews the cud but does not have a split
hoof; it is unclean for you. 7Now the pig has a split
hoof that is completely divided, but it does not
chew the cud; it is unclean for you. 8You must not
eat the meat from these animals or even touch
their dead bodies; they are unclean for you.
9"'Of the animals that live in the sea or in a
river, if the animal has fins and scales, you may
eat it. 10But whatever lives in the sea or in a river
and does not have fins and scales—including the
things that fill the water and all other things that
live in it—you should hate. 11You must not eat
any meat from them or even touch their dead
bodies, because you should hate them. 12You
must hate any animal in the water that does not
have fins and scales.
13"'Also, these are the birds you are to hate.
They are hateful and should not be eaten. You
must not eat eagles, vultures, black vultures,
14kites, any kind of falcon, 15any kind of raven,
16horned owls, screech owls, sea gulls, any kind
of hawk, 17little owls, cormorants, great owls,
18white owls, desert owls, ospreys, 19storks, any
kind of heron, hoopoes, or bats.
20"'Don't eat insects that have wings and walk
on all four feet; they also are to be hated.
21"'But you may eat certain insects that have
wings and walk on four feet. You may eat those that
have legs with joints above their feet so they can
jump. 22These are the insects you may eat: all kinds
of locusts, winged locusts, crickets, and grasshoppers. 23But all other insects that have wings and
walk on four feet you are to hate. 24Those insects
will make you unclean, and anyone who touches
the dead body of one of these insects will become
unclean until evening. 25Anyone who picks up one
of these dead insects must wash his clothes and be
unclean until evening.
26"'Some animals have split hoofs, but the hoofs
are not completely divided; others do not chew
the cud. They are unclean for you, and anyone
who touches the dead body of one of these animals
will become unclean. 27Of all the animals that
walk on four feet, the animals that walk on their
paws are unclean for you. Anyone who touches
the dead body of one of these animals will
become unclean until evening. 28Anyone who
picks up their dead bodies must wash his clothes
and be unclean until evening; these animals are
unclean for you.
29"'These crawling animals are unclean for you:
moles, rats, all kinds of great lizards, 30geckos,
crocodiles, lizards, sand reptiles, and chameleons.
31These crawling animals are unclean for you;
anyone who touches their dead bodies will be
unclean until evening.
32"'If an unclean animal dies and falls on something, that item will also become unclean. This
includes anything made from wood, cloth, leather,
or rough cloth, regardless of its use. Whatever the
animal falls on must be washed with water and
be unclean until evening; then it will become clean
again. 33If the dead, unclean animal falls into a clay
bowl, anything in the bowl will become unclean,
and you must break the bowl. 34If water from the
unclean clay bowl gets on any food, that food will
become unclean. 35If any dead, unclean animal
falls on something, it becomes unclean. If it is a
clay oven or a clay baking pan, it must be broken
into pieces. These things will be unclean; they
are unclean for you.

A great owl

36"'A spring or well that collects water will stay
clean, but anyone who touches the dead body of
any unclean animal will become unclean. 37If a
dead, unclean animal falls on a seed to be planted,
that seed is still clean. 38But if you put water on
some seeds and a dead, unclean animal falls on
them, they are unclean for you.

39“‘Also, if an animal which you use for food dies, anyone who touches its body will be unclean until evening. 40Anyone who eats meat from this animal’s dead body must wash his clothes and be unclean until evening. Anyone who picks up the animal’s dead body must wash his clothes and be unclean until evening.

41“‘Every animal that crawls on the ground is to be hated; it must not be eaten. 42You must not eat any of the animals that crawl on the ground, including those that crawl on their stomachs, that walk on all four feet, or on many feet. They are to be hated. 43Do not make yourself unclean by these animals; you must not become unclean by them. 44I am the LORD your God. Keep yourselves holy for me because I am holy. Don’t make yourselves unclean with any of these crawling animals. 45I am the LORD who brought you out of Egypt to be your God; you must be holy because I am holy.

46“‘These are the teachings about all of the cattle, birds, and other animals on earth, as well as the animals in the sea and those that crawl on the ground. 47These teachings help people know the difference between unclean animals and clean animals; they help people know which animals may be eaten and which ones must not be eaten.’”

Rules for New Mothers

12 The LORD said to Moses, 2“Tell the people of Israel this: ‘If a woman gives birth to a son, she will become unclean for seven days, as she is unclean during her monthly period. 3On the eighth day the boy must be circumcised. 4Then it will be thirty-three days before she becomes clean from her loss of blood. She must not touch anything that is holy or enter the Holy Tent until her time of cleansing is finished. 5But if she gives birth to a daughter, the mother will be unclean for two weeks, as she is unclean during her monthly period. It will be sixty-six days before she becomes clean from her loss of blood.

6“‘After she has a son or daughter and her days of cleansing are over, the new mother must bring certain sacrifices to the Meeting Tent. She must give the priest at the entrance a year-old lamb for a burnt offering and a dove or young pigeon for a sin offering. 7He will offer them before the LORD to make her clean so she will belong to the LORD again; then she will be clean from her loss of blood. These are the teachings for a woman who gives birth to a boy or girl.

8“‘If she cannot afford a lamb, she is to bring two doves or two young pigeons, one for a burnt offering and one for a sin offering. In this way the priest will make her clean so she will belong to the LORD again, and she will be clean.’”

Rules About Skin Diseases

13 The LORD said to Moses and Aaron, 2“Someone might have on his skin a swelling or a rash or a bright spot. If the sore looks like a harmful skin disease, the person must be brought to Aaron the priest or to one of Aaron’s sons, the priests. 3The priest must look at the sore on the person’s skin. If the hair in the sore has become white, and the sore seems deeper than the person’s skin, it is a harmful skin disease. When he has finished looking at the person, the priest must announce that the person is unclean.

4“If there is a white spot on a person’s skin, but the spot does not seem deeper than the skin, and if the hair from the spot has not turned white, the priest must separate that person from other people for seven days. 5On the seventh day the priest must look at the person again. If he sees that the sore has not changed and it has not spread on the skin, the priest must keep the person separated for seven more days. 6On the seventh day the priest must look at the person again. If the sore has faded and has not spread on the skin, the priest must announce that the person is clean. The sore is only a rash. The person must wash his clothes, and he will become clean again.

7“But if the rash spreads again after the priest has announced him clean, the person must come again to the priest. 8The priest must look at him, and if the rash has spread on the skin, the priest must announce that the person is unclean; it is a harmful skin disease.

9“If a person has a harmful skin disease, he must be brought to the priest, 10and the priest must look at him. If there is a white swelling in the skin, and the hair has become white, and the skin looks raw in the swelling, 11it is a harmful skin disease. It is one he has had for a long time. The priest must announce that the person is unclean. He will not need to separate that person from other people, because everyone already knows that the person is unclean.

12“If the skin disease spreads all over a person’s body, covering his skin from his head to his feet, as far as the priest can see, the priest must look at the person’s whole body. 13If the priest sees that the disease covers the whole body and has turned all of the person’s skin white, he must announce that the person is clean.

11:47 Animals: Psalm 8:4–8

12:3 Circumcision: Joshua 5

IDOLATRY

GENESIS 11:4

What is an idol? What happens to those who worship idols?
Is there an image of God today that humans are to worship?

The Bible has much to say about idols and idolatry. We all have some notion of what an idol is—a type of statue. So we may ask, "If I don't own any idols, what does all of this talk of idols and idolatry have to do with me?" However, is it possible that the idols that the Bible talks about point to something beyond the mere statue? Could it be that this "something" affects the lives of all people, including people who are living today? Just what is an idol then?

To better understand idols and idolatry, it is helpful to understand what people in Old Testament times thought about them. Did those people really believe that an idol was a god? In a sense, yes. Idols were physical objects, or a kind of statue. But ancient people believed these statues also stood for real gods. When the people of Thessalonica became Christians they "stopped worshiping idols and began serving the living and true God" (1 Thessalonians 1:9). The idols that they now rejected had earlier stood for real gods in their lives.

If early peoples believed idols were real gods, what were these gods and where did they come from? In old times, the gods were nothing more than humankind's way of explaining their everyday world. We need to remember that this was before the day of scientific discoveries, which explain how the world that we see works. This is why the names of the gods as well as their activities reflected life as they knew it. People today try to explain most everything by science. By way of contrast, people of ancient times tried to explain the world around them by making gods out of different things in nature, such as the sea, the river, the sun, the moon, and the stars. This, then, was their way of explaining their world.

Another important idea in ancient times was how life was made—plant, animal, and human. This idea was closely connected to idol worship. In those days, farming was the major industry, and all human life depended upon it. In turn, farming depended upon rain to grow crops. If the rain did not come, then the crops would not grow, and famine threatened human life (see Genesis 41:27, 36, 50, 56; 42:5; 1 Kings 17:1–16). Since human life depended upon the weather, people began to make idols in the images of weather gods as well as goddesses connected with human reproduction.

So what did the worship of these idols accomplish? The worship of idols was closely connected with magic. Early humans tried to deal with the world of the gods by using magic (1 Samuel 28:7–20; Isaiah 8:19). They believed they could get answers to special problems and that these answers were the secrets of the gods. It was also their way of trying to control the world in which they lived. All of the sacrifices and worship were done to get something in return.

An idol, whether it is a physical object, a statue, or simply an idea, is anything that takes first place in a person's life instead of the true and living God (Deuteronomy 5:7–9; see also Colossians 1:18). The Bible makes much mention of idols. But it is not so much the object itself that the Bible speaks against. Rather, it is the condition of the hearts of the people who worship them. The worship of idols, then, is a spiritual attitude that does not give God his proper place in a person's life.

Is there a connection between worship, sacrifices, and idolatry? Yes, from the very beginning it is clear that humans were accountable to God and that they were to give him their worship. In Genesis 4:3–4, both Cain and Abel presented themselves to God along with their sacrifices. God accepted Abel's sacrifice, but rejected Cain's. The story indicates that the approval or rejection of the sacrifices was not necessarily due to the kind of sacrifice, although Abel did offer a blood sacrifice. Rather, it depended upon the spiritual attitude of the worshiper. Cain's sacrifice was rejected because his heart was not right with God.

This attitude eventually affected all humankind. It is seen in the judgment of the earth with the flood (Genesis 6–8) and in the confusion of languages at the tower of Babel (Genesis 11:1–9). In the story of Babel, the tower contained idols, and the idol of the most powerful god was at the very top. The tower itself served as a symbol of human pride. Humans believed they could come together and reach God with their own human efforts. In many ways we do this in our own lives when we try do something our own way without prayerfully asking for God's approval or direction in our decision. In his judgment upon the people at Babel, God showed his mercy (see "Mercy"). He sometimes has to do something special in order to get our attention and keep us from making choices that would harm us.

In spite of God's judgment, humans again began to build towers just like the one at Babel. It was from such a situation that God called Abram (Genesis 12:1–3). Joshua 24:15 suggests that Abram, the father of Israel, had worshiped false gods in a far country before God saved him and called him to serve the true God.

During its whole history, Israel had a problem with idolatry. Even from its very beginning, God gave Israel a set of special rules (see "Law," "Teachings of Moses," "Ten Commandments"). The first two of the Ten Commandments forbade people from giving any god first place before the true and living God. These rules also do not allow anyone to make idols or to worship any other god except the Lord himself (Exodus 20:3–5; Deuteronomy 5:7–9).

However, as soon as God gave these rules, Israel began to break them. While Moses was still on Mount Sinai, the Israelites threw a wild party and built an idol. The idol was a golden calf, one of the gods of Egypt. When Moses came down, he found them worshiping this idol. Because they had broken his rules, God had to discipline and correct his people.

What does God think of idolatry? God hates idolatry (1 Peter 4:3). He thinks it is foolish (Isaiah 40:18–20). In Isaiah 40, God makes fun of idols by picturing skillful workmen making expensive chains to tie idols to trees so that they will not fall over on their faces (see also 1 Samuel 5:3–4). If an idol is so helpless that it cannot even stand up by itself, then it is foolish to worship it. How could such a helpless object have any special powers to help humans? Idolatry simply does not make any sense (Acts 17:29).

So how did all of this idolatry affect God's people, Israel? The sad part of Israel's idolatry was that they made God look bad to their neighbors who were lost and in need of salvation. God's main purpose for Israel was that she would show the world how good God was. By seeing how good and great God is, they too would want to know and worship him (Isaiah 60:1–3) and to experience his salvation (Isaiah 56:1–7). This is also the purpose of the church today. God desires that Christians show the world how wonderful their Savior Jesus Christ is. In that way, they too might desire a special relationship with him.

Is there an image of God that God himself accepts? If so, how does this affect me? The only image of God that God approves is that which God himself has made. From the dust of the earth God placed his own image within the first man, Adam. However, due to Adam's sin of disobedience, that image has become tarnished. Since then, man's sinfulness causes him to dishonor God's image in him by his sinful acts (Romans 1:18–32). All idolatry, then, is degrading, defiling (1 Corinthians 6:15–18), and enslaving to humans (Galatians 4:8–9). It makes human beings less than what God would like them to be.

Today, the only true and pure image of God is Jesus Christ (Hebrews 1:3). All other images of God are fakes. With the birth of Jesus, God himself became a person with human flesh. The difference between Jesus Christ and the rest of humankind is that Jesus is God in human flesh. He therefore has no sin. If we want to see what God is really like, a good way is to look at Jesus' life as described in the first four books of the New Testament.

Is there an image of God today that humans are to worship? The rules in the Old Testament said that people are not allowed to make idols or worship images. But there is an image of God today that the Bible commands us to worship. Jesus Christ, as the exact image and likeness of God, deserves all the worship and praise of humankind. This is the same worship that is due only to God. Because of Jesus' sacrifice on the cross, God his Father has "raised him to the highest place" and "made his name greater than every other name" (Philippians 2:8–9). As a result of this, someday every living being will worship Jesus Christ— "every knee will bow to the name of Jesus . . . and confess that Jesus Christ is Lord" (Philippians 2:10–11).

What is idolatry today? How can I keep it out of my life? Idolatry today is the same as it has always been. It is putting something first in our lives besides God. The biggest idol in all of our hearts is the one named "self." The main motto of our day is "me first." People living today, as in ancient times, could be called the "me first" generation. In light of this tendency, Jesus gave a very important teaching for living in his kingdom. Those who give themselves first place in this life will be given last place in his kingdom. Likewise, those who give themselves the lowest place by placing others first will be given first place (Matthew 23:11–12).

Idolatry: For additional scriptures on this topic go to Joshua 24:1–5.

14“But when the person has an open sore, he is unclean. 15When the priest sees the open sore, he must announce that the person is unclean. The open sore is not clean; it is a harmful skin disease. 16If the open sore becomes white again, the person must come to the priest. 17The priest must look at him, and if the sores have become white, the priest must announce that the person with the sores is clean. Then he will be clean.

18“Someone may have a boil on his skin that is healed. 19If in the place where the boil was, there is a white swelling or a bright red spot, this place on the skin must be shown to the priest. 20And the priest must look at it. If the spot seems deeper than the skin and the hair on it has become white, the priest must announce that the person is unclean. The spot is a harmful skin disease that has broken out from inside the boil. 21But if the priest looks at the spot and there are no white hairs in it and the spot is not deeper than the skin and it has faded, the priest must separate the person from other people for seven days. 22If the spot spreads on the skin, the priest must announce that the person is unclean; it is a disease that will spread. 23But if the bright spot does not spread or change, it is only the scar from the old boil. Then the priest must announce that the person is clean.

24“When a person gets a burn on his skin, if the open sore becomes white or red, 25the priest must look at it. If the white spot seems deeper than the skin and the hair at that spot has become white, it is a harmful skin disease. The disease has broken out in the burn, and the priest must announce that the person is unclean. It is a harmful skin disease. 26But if the priest looks at the spot and there is no white hair in the bright spot, and the spot is no deeper than the skin and has faded, the priest must separate the person from other people for seven days. 27On the seventh day the priest must look at him again. If the spot has spread on the skin, the priest must announce that the person is unclean. It is a harmful skin disease. 28But if the bright spot has not spread on the skin but has faded, it is the swelling from the burn. The priest must announce that the person is clean, because the spot is only a scar from the burn.

29“When a man or a woman gets a sore on the scalp or on the chin, 30a priest must look at the sore. If it seems deeper than the skin and the hair around it is thin and yellow, the priest must announce that the person is unclean. It is an itch, a harmful skin disease of the head or chin. 31But if the priest looks at it and it does not seem deeper than the skin and there is no black hair in it, the priest must separate the person from other people for seven days. 32On the seventh day the priest must look at the sore. If it has not spread, and there are no yellow hairs growing in it, and the sore does not seem deeper than the skin, 33the person must shave himself, but he must not shave the sore place. The priest must separate that person from other people for seven more days. 34On the seventh day the priest must look at the sore. If it has not spread on the skin and it does not seem deeper than the skin, the priest must announce that the person is clean. So the person must wash his clothes and become clean. 35But if the sore spreads on the skin after the person has become clean, 36the priest must look at him again. If the sore has spread on the skin, the priest doesn’t need to look for the yellowish hair; the person is unclean. 37But if the priest thinks the sore has stopped spreading, and black hair is growing in it, the sore has healed. The person is clean, and the priest must announce that he is clean.

38“When a man or a woman has white spots on the skin, 39a priest must look at them. If the spots on the skin are dull white, the disease is only a harmless rash. That person is clean.

40“When anyone loses hair from his head and is bald, he is clean. 41If he loses hair from the front of his head and has a bald forehead, he is clean. 42But if there is a red-white sore on his bald head or forehead, it is a skin disease breaking out in those places. 43A priest must look at that person. If the swelling of the sore on his bald head or forehead is red-white, like a skin disease that spreads, 44that person has a skin disease. He is unclean. The priest must announce that the person is unclean because of the sore on his head.

45“If a person has a skin disease that spreads, he must warn other people by shouting, ‘Unclean, unclean!’ His clothes must be torn at the seams, he must let his hair stay uncombed, and he must cover his mouth. 46That person will be unclean the whole time he has the disease; he is unclean. He must live alone outside the camp.

Rules About Mildew

47“Clothing might have mildew on it. It might be clothing made of linen or wool 48(either woven or knitted), or of leather, or something made from leather. 49If the mildew in the clothing, leather, or woven or knitted material is green or red, it is a spreading mildew. It must be shown to the priest. 50The priest must look at the mildew, and he must put that piece of clothing in a separate place for seven days. 51On the seventh day he must look at the mildew again. If the mildew has spread on the cloth (either woven or knitted) or the leather, no matter what the leather was used for, it is a mildew that destroys; it is unclean. 52The priest must burn the clothing. It does not matter if it is woven or knitted, wool or linen, or made of leather, because the mildew is spreading. It must be burned.

53"If the priest sees that the mildew has not spread in the cloth (either knitted or woven) or leather, 54he must order the people to wash that piece of leather or cloth. Then he must separate the clothing for seven more days. 55After the piece with the mildew has been washed, the priest must look at it again. If the mildew still looks the same, the piece is unclean, even if the mildew has not spread. You must burn it in fire; it does not matter if the mildew is on one side or the other.

56"But when the priest looks at that piece of leather or cloth, the mildew might have faded after the piece has been washed. Then the priest must tear the mildew out of the piece of leather or cloth (either woven or knitted). 57But if the mildew comes back to that piece of leather or cloth (either woven or knitted), the mildew is spreading. And whatever has the mildew must be burned with fire. 58When the cloth (either woven or knitted) or the leather is washed and the mildew is gone, it must be washed again; then it will be clean.

59"These are the teachings about mildew on pieces of cloth (either woven or knitted) or leather, to decide if they are clean or unclean."

Rules for Cleansing from Skin Diseases

14 The LORD said to Moses, 2"These are the teachings for the time at which people who had a harmful skin disease are made clean.

"The person shall be brought to the priest, 3and the priest must go outside the camp and look at the one who had the skin disease. If the skin disease is healed, 4the priest will command that two living, clean birds, a piece of cedar wood, a piece of red string, and a hyssop plant be brought for cleansing the person with the skin disease.

5"The priest must order one bird to be killed in a clay bowl containing fresh water. 6Then he will take the living bird, the piece of cedar wood, the red string, and the hyssop; all these he will dip into the blood of the bird that was killed over the fresh water. 7The priest will sprinkle the blood seven times on the person being cleansed from the skin disease. He must announce that the person is clean and then go to an open field and let the living bird go free.

8"The person to be cleansed must wash his clothes, shave off all his hair, and bathe in water. Then he will be clean and may go into the camp, though he must stay outside his tent for the first seven days. 9On the seventh day he must shave off all his hair—the hair from his head, his beard, his eyebrows, and the rest of his hair. He must wash his clothes and bathe his body in water, and he will be clean.

10"On the eighth day the person who had the skin disease must take two male lambs that have nothing wrong with them and a year-old female lamb that has nothing wrong with it. He must also take six quarts of fine flour mixed with oil for a grain offering and two-thirds of a pint of olive oil. 11The priest who is to announce that the person is clean must bring him and his sacrifices before the LORD at the entrance of the Meeting Tent. 12The priest will take one of the male lambs and offer it with the olive oil as a penalty offering; he will present them before the LORD as an offering. 13Then he will kill the male lamb in the holy place, where the sin offering and the whole burnt offering are killed. The penalty offering is like the sin offering—it belongs to the priest and it is most holy.

14"The priest will take some of the blood of the penalty offering and put it on the bottom of the right ear of the person to be made clean. He will also put some of it on the thumb of the person's right hand and on the big toe of the person's right foot. 15Then the priest will take some of the oil and pour it into his own left hand. 16He will dip a finger of his right hand into the oil that is in his left hand, and with his finger he will sprinkle some of the oil seven times before the LORD. 17The priest will put some oil from his hand on the bottom of the right ear of the person to be made clean, some on the thumb of the person's right hand, and some on the big toe of the person's right foot. The oil will go on these places on top of the blood for the penalty offering. 18He will put the rest of the oil that is in his left hand on the head of the person to be made clean. In this way the priest will make that person clean so he can belong to the LORD again.

19"Next the priest will offer the sin offering to make that person clean so he can belong to the LORD again. After this the priest will kill the animal for the whole burnt offering, 20and he will offer the burnt offering and grain offering on the altar. In this way he will make that person clean so he can belong to the LORD again.

21"But if the person is poor and unable to afford these offerings, he must take one male lamb for a penalty offering. It will be presented to the LORD to make him clean so he can belong to the LORD again. The person must also take two quarts of fine flour mixed with oil for a grain offering. He must also take two-thirds of a pint of olive oil 22and two doves or two young pigeons, which he can afford. One bird is for a sin offering and the other for a whole burnt offering. 23On the eighth day the person will bring them for his cleansing to the priest at the entrance of the Meeting Tent, before the LORD. 24The priest will take the lamb for the penalty offering and the oil, and he will present them as an offering before the LORD. 25Then he will kill the lamb of the penalty offering, take some of its blood, and put it on the bottom of the right ear of the person to be made clean. The priest will put some of this blood on the thumb of the person's right hand and some on the big toe of the person's right foot. 26He will also pour some of the oil into his own left hand. 27Then with a finger of his right hand, he will sprinkle some of the oil from his left hand seven times before the LORD. 28The priest will take some of the oil from his hand and put it on the bottom of the right ear of the person to be made clean. He will also put some of it on the thumb of the person's right hand and some on the big toe of the person's right foot. The oil will go on these places on top of the blood from the penalty offering. 29The priest must put the rest of the oil that is in his hand on the head of the person to be made clean, to make him clean so he can belong to the LORD again. 30Then the priest will offer one of the doves or young pigeons, which the person can afford. 31He must offer one of the birds for a sin offering and the other for a whole burnt offering, along with the grain offering. In this way the priest will make the person clean so he can belong to the LORD again; he will become clean.

32"These are the teachings for making a person clean after he has had a skin disease, if he cannot afford the regular sacrifices for becoming clean."

Rules for Cleaning Mildew

33The LORD also said to Moses and Aaron, 34"I am giving the land of Canaan to your people. When they enter that land, if I cause mildew to grow in someone's house in that land, 35the owner of that house must come and tell the priest. He should say, 'I have seen something like mildew in my house.' 36Then the priest must order the people to empty the house before he goes in to look at the mildew. This is so he will not have to say that everything in the house is unclean. After this, the priest will go in to look at it. 37He will look at the mildew, and if the mildew on the walls of the house is green or red and goes into the wall's surface, 38he must go out and close up the house for seven days. 39On the seventh day the priest must come back and check the house. If the mildew has spread on the walls of the house, 40the priest must order the people to tear out the stones with the mildew on them. They should throw them away, at a certain unclean place outside the city. 41Then the priest must have all the inside of the house scraped. The people must throw away the plaster they scraped off the walls, at a certain unclean place outside the city. 42Then the owner must put new stones in the walls, and he must cover the walls with new clay plaster.

43"Suppose a person has taken away the old stones and plaster and put in new stones and plaster. If mildew again appears in his house, 44the priest must come back and check the house again. If the mildew has spread in the house, it is a mildew that destroys things; the house is unclean. 45Then the owner must tear down the house, remove all its stones, plaster, and wood, and take them to the unclean place outside the city. 46Anyone who goes into that house while it is closed up will be unclean until evening. 47Anyone who eats in that house or lies down there must wash his clothes.

48"Suppose after new stones and plaster have been put in a house, the priest checks it again and the mildew has not spread. Then the priest will announce that the house is clean, because the mildew is gone.

49"Then, to make the house clean, the priest must take two birds, a piece of cedar wood, a piece of red string, and a hyssop plant. 50He will kill one bird in a clay bowl containing fresh water. 51Then he will take the bird that is still alive, the cedar wood, the hyssop, and the red string, and he will dip them into the blood of the bird that was killed over the fresh water. The priest will sprinkle the blood on the house seven times. 52He will use the bird's blood, the fresh water, the live bird, the cedar wood, the hyssop, and the red string to make the house clean. 53He will then go to an open field outside the city and let the living bird go free. This is how the priest makes the house clean and ready for service to the LORD."

54These are the teachings about any kind of skin disease, 55mildew on pieces of cloth or in a house, 56swellings, rashes, or bright spots on the skin; 57they help people decide when things are unclean and when they are clean. These are the teachings about all these kinds of diseases.

14:35 House/Home: Deuteronomy 5:21

Rules About a Person's Body

15 The LORD also said to Moses and Aaron,
2"Say to the people of Israel: 'When a fluid
comes from a person's body, the fluid is unclean.
3It doesn't matter if the fluid flows freely or if it is
blocked from flowing; the fluid will make him
unclean. This is the way the fluid makes him
unclean:
4"'If the person who discharges the body fluid
lies on a bed, that bed becomes unclean, and everything he sits on becomes unclean. 5Anyone who
touches his bed must wash his clothes and bathe in
water, and the person will be unclean until
evening. 6Whoever sits on something that the person who discharges the fluid sat on must wash his
clothes and bathe in water; he will be unclean until
evening. 7Anyone who touches the person who discharges the body fluid must wash his clothes and
bathe in water; he will be unclean until evening.
8"'If the person who discharges the body fluid
spits on someone who is clean, that person must
wash his clothes and bathe in water; he will be
unclean until evening. 9Everything on which the
person who is unclean sits when riding will
become unclean. 10Anyone who touches something that was under him will be unclean until
evening. And anyone who carries these things
must wash his clothes and bathe in water; he will
be unclean until evening.
11"'If the person who discharges a body fluid has
not washed his hands in water and touches another
person, that person must wash his clothes and
bathe in water; he will be unclean until evening.
12"'If a person who discharges a body fluid
touches a clay bowl, that bowl must be broken. If
he touches a wooden bowl, that bowl must be
washed in water.
13"'When a person who discharges a body fluid
is made clean, he must count seven days for himself for his cleansing. He must wash his clothes
and bathe his body in fresh water, and he will be
clean. 14On the eighth day he must take two
doves or two young pigeons before the LORD at the
entrance of the Meeting Tent. He will give the two
birds to the priest. 15The priest will offer the birds,
one for a sin offering and the other for a burnt
offering. And the priest will make that person
clean so he can belong to the LORD again.
16"'If semen goes out from a man, he must bathe
in water; he will be unclean until evening. 17If the
fluid gets on any clothing or leather, it must be
washed with water; it will be unclean until evening.
18"'If a man has sexual relations with a woman
and semen comes out, both people must bathe in
water; they will be unclean until evening.

Rules About a Woman's Body

19"'When a woman has her monthly period,
she is unclean for seven days; anyone who
touches her will be unclean until evening.
20Anything she lies on during this time will be
unclean, and everything she sits on during this
time will be unclean. 21Anyone who touches her
bed must wash his clothes and bathe in water;
that person will be unclean until evening.
22Anyone who touches something she has sat on
must wash his clothes and bathe in water; that
person will be unclean until evening. 23It does
not matter if the person touched the woman's
bed or something she sat on; he will be unclean
until evening.
24"'If a man has sexual relations with a woman
and her monthly period touches him, he will be
unclean for seven days; every bed he lies on will
be unclean.
25"'If a woman has a loss of blood for many days
and it is not during her regular monthly period, or
if she continues to have a loss of blood after her
regular period, she will be unclean, as she is during her monthly period. She will be unclean for as
long as she continues to bleed. 26Any bed she lies
on during all the time of her bleeding will be like
her bed during her regular monthly period.
Everything she sits on will be unclean, as during
her regular monthly period.
27"'Whoever touches those things will be
unclean and must wash his clothes and bathe in
water; he will be unclean until evening. 28When
the woman becomes clean from her bleeding, she
must wait seven days, and after this she will be
clean. 29Then on the eighth day she must take
two doves or two young pigeons and bring them
to the priest at the entrance of the Meeting Tent.
30The priest must offer one bird for a sin offering
and the other for a whole burnt offering. In this
way the priest will make her clean so she can
belong to the LORD again.
31"'So you must warn the people of Israel to
stay separated from things that make them unclean. If you don't warn the people, they might
make my Holy Tent unclean, and then they
would have to die!'"
32These are the teachings for the person who
discharges a body fluid and for the man who
becomes unclean from semen coming out of his

15:16 *semen.* A man's body fluid by which he can make a woman pregnant.

15:32 *semen.* See note at 15:16.

body. 33These are the teachings for the woman who becomes unclean from her monthly period, for a man or woman who has a discharge, and for a man who becomes unclean by having sexual relations with a woman who is unclean.

The Day of Cleansing

16 Now two of Aaron's sons had died while offering incense to the LORD, and after that time the LORD spoke to Moses. 2The LORD said to him, "Tell your brother Aaron that there are times when he cannot go behind the curtain into the Most Holy Place where the Ark is. If he goes in when I appear in a cloud over the lid on the Ark, he will die.

3"This is how Aaron may enter the Most Holy Place: Before he enters, he must offer a bull for a sin offering and a male sheep for a whole burnt offering. 4He must put on the holy linen inner robe, with the linen underclothes next to his body. His belt will be the cloth belt, and he will wear the linen turban. These are holy clothes, so he must bathe his body in water before he puts them on.

5"Aaron must take from the people of Israel two male goats for a sin offering and one male sheep for a burnt offering. 6Then he will offer the bull for the sin offering for himself to remove sins from him and his family so they will belong to the LORD.

7"Next Aaron will take the two goats and bring them before the LORD at the entrance to the Meeting Tent. 8He will throw lots for the two goats—one will be for the LORD and the other for the goat that removes sin. 9Then Aaron will take the goat that was chosen for the LORD by throwing the lot, and he will offer it as a sin offering. 10The other goat, which was chosen by lot to remove the sin, must be brought alive before the LORD. The priest will use it to perform the acts that remove Israel's sin so they will belong to the LORD. Then this goat will be sent out into the desert as a goat that removes sin.

11"Then Aaron will offer the bull as a sin offering for himself, to remove the sins from him and his family so they will belong to the LORD; he will kill the bull for the sin offering for himself. 12Then he must take a pan full of burning coals from the altar before the LORD and two handfuls of sweet incense that has been ground into powder. He must bring it into the room behind the curtain. 13He must put the incense on the fire before the LORD so that the cloud of incense will cover the lid on the Ark. Then when Aaron comes in, he will not die. 14Also, he must take some of the blood from the bull and sprinkle it with his finger on the front of the lid; with his finger he will sprinkle the blood seven times in front of the lid.

15"Then Aaron must kill the goat of the sin offering for the people and bring its blood into the room behind the curtain. He must do with the goat's blood as he did with the bull's blood, sprinkling it on the lid and in front of the lid. 16Because the people of Israel have been unclean, Aaron will perform the acts to make the Most Holy Place ready for service to the LORD. Then it will be clean from the sins and crimes of the Israelites. He must also do this for the Meeting Tent, because it stays in the middle of unclean people. 17When Aaron makes the Most Holy Place ready for service to the LORD, no one is allowed in the Meeting Tent until he comes out. So Aaron will perform the acts to remove sins from himself, his family, and all the people of Israel, so they will belong to the LORD. 18Afterward he will go out to the altar that is before the LORD and will make it ready for service to the LORD. Aaron will take some of the bull's blood and some of the goat's blood and put it on the corners of the altar on all sides. 19Then, with his finger, he will sprinkle some of the blood on the altar seven times to make the altar holy for the LORD and clean from all the sins of the Israelites.

20"When Aaron has finished making the Most Holy Place, the Meeting Tent, and the altar ready for service to the LORD, he will offer the living goat. 21He will put both his hands on the head of the living goat, and he will confess over it all the sins and crimes of Israel. In this way Aaron will put the people's sins on the goat's head. Then he will send the goat away into the desert, and a man who has been appointed will lead the goat away. 22So the goat will carry on itself all the people's sins to a lonely place in the desert. The man who leads the goat will let it loose there.

23"Then Aaron will enter the Meeting Tent and take off the linen clothes he had put on before he went into the Most Holy Place; he must leave these clothes there. 24He will bathe his body in water in a holy place and put on his regular clothes. Then he will come out and offer the whole burnt offering for himself and for the people, to remove sins from himself and the people so they will belong to the LORD. 25Then he will burn the fat of the sin offering on the altar.

26"The person who led the goat, the goat to remove sins, into the desert must wash his clothes and bathe his body in water. After that, he may come back into the camp.

27"The bull and the goat for the sin offerings, whose blood was brought into the Most Holy Place to make it ready for service to the LORD, must be taken outside the camp; the animals' skins, bodies, and intestines will be burned in the fire. 28Then the one who burns them must wash his clothes and bathe his body in water. After that, he may come back into the camp.

29"This law will always continue for you: On the tenth day of the seventh month, you must not eat and you must not do any work. The travelers or foreigners living with you must not work either. 30It is on this day that the priests will make you clean so you will belong to the LORD again. All your sins will be removed. 31This is a very important day of rest for you, and you must not eat. This law will continue forever.

32"The priest appointed to take his father's place, on whom the oil was poured, will perform the acts for making things ready for service to the LORD. He must put on the holy linen clothes 33and make the Most Holy Place, the Meeting Tent, and the altar ready for service to the LORD. He must also remove the sins of the priests and all the people of Israel so they will belong to the LORD. 34That law for removing the sins of the Israelites so they will belong to the LORD will continue forever. You will do these things once a year."

So they did the things the LORD had commanded Moses.

Offering Sacrifices

17 The LORD said to Moses, 2"Speak to Aaron, his sons, and all the people of Israel. Tell them: 'This is what the LORD has commanded. 3If an Israelite kills an ox, a lamb, or a goat either inside the camp or outside it, 4when he should have brought the animal to the entrance of the Meeting Tent as a gift to the LORD in front of the LORD's Holy Tent, he is guilty of killing. He has killed, and he must be cut off from the people. 5This rule is so people will bring their sacrifices, which they have been sacrificing in the open fields, to the LORD. They must bring those animals to the LORD at the entrance of the Meeting Tent; they must bring them to the priest and offer them as fellowship offerings. 6Then the priest will sprinkle the blood from those animals on the LORD's altar near the entrance of the Meeting Tent. And he will burn the fat from those animals on the altar, as a smell pleasing to the LORD. 7They must not offer any more sacrifices to their goat idols, which they have chased like prostitutes. These rules will continue for people from now on.'

8"Tell the people this: 'If any citizen of Israel or foreigner living with you offers a burnt offering or sacrifice, 9that person must take his sacrifice to the entrance of the Meeting Tent to offer it to the LORD. If he does not do this, he must be cut off from the people.

10"'I will be against any citizen of Israel or foreigner living with you who eats blood. I will cut off that person from the people. 11This is because the life of the body is in the blood, and I have given you rules for pouring that blood on the altar to remove your sins so you will belong to the LORD. It is the blood that removes the sins, because it is life. 12So I tell the people of Israel this: "None of you may eat blood, and no foreigner living among you may eat blood."

13"'If any citizen of Israel or foreigner living among you catches a wild animal or bird that can be eaten, that person must pour the blood on the ground and cover it with dirt. 14If blood is still in the meat, the animal's life is still in it. So I give this command to the people of Israel: "Don't eat meat that still has blood in it, because the animal's life is in its blood. Anyone who eats blood must be cut off."

15"'If a person, either a citizen or a foreigner, eats an animal that died by itself or was killed by another animal, he must wash his clothes and bathe in water. He will be unclean until evening; then he will be clean. 16If he does not wash his clothes and bathe his body, he will be guilty of sin.'"

Rules About Sexual Relations

18 The LORD said to Moses, 2"Tell the people of Israel: 'I am the LORD your God. 3In the past you lived in Egypt, but you must not do what was done in that country. And you must not do as they do in the land of Canaan, where I am bringing you. Do not follow their customs. 4You must obey my rules and follow them. I am the LORD your God. 5Obey my laws and rules; a person who obeys them will live because of them. I am the LORD.

6"'You must never have sexual relations with your close relatives. I am the LORD.

7"'You must not shame your father by having sexual relations with your mother. She is your mother; do not have sexual relations with her. 8You must not have sexual relations with your father's wife; that would shame your father.

9"'You must not have sexual relations with your sister, either the daughter of your father or your mother. It doesn't matter if she was born in your house or somewhere else.

10"'You must not have sexual relations with

16:29 Fasting: 2 Chronicles 20:3

16:34 Clean & Unclean: Numbers 8:5–26

Abraham

Genesis 12

Who was Abraham? Why is Abraham considered a "patriarch" of the Jewish faith? How is Abraham an encouragement to our faith?

Abraham is the first of the patriarchs of the Israelites. All God's chosen people of Israel are his descendants. God chose him to leave Ur, a Mesopotamian city, to travel to Canaan, known today as Palestine, and become the first of a people specially chosen by God to be his people.

The agreement between Abraham and God spells out the relationship. This agreement was stated for the first time in Genesis 12:1–3:

The LORD said to Abram, "Leave your country, your relatives, and your father's family, and go to the land I will show you.

I will make you a great nation,
  and I will bless you.
I will make you famous,
  and you will be a blessing to others.
I will bless those who bless you,
  and I will place a curse on those who harm you.
And all the people on earth
  will be blessed through you."

The story of Abraham is found in Genesis 12:1–25:18 and follows Abraham's reaction to these great promises. It is a story of the ups and downs of faith as it encounters threats and obstacles.

Abraham obeys God and makes the long and difficult journey to Canaan. Obstacles threaten Abraham's faith the moment he enters the new land. After his arrival, the land is rocked by a famine. Abraham feels he has to go to Egypt to survive the famine (Genesis 12:10–20). He reacts in fear as he goes to Egypt, telling Sarah to lie about her relationship with him. He fears the king of Egypt much more than he trusts God.

In the next story, though, Abraham reacts with faith as an obstacle arises. In this case, the problem is a good one. He and his nephew Lot have both prospered, and now they need to separate (Genesis 13). Abraham does not grasp at the promises here but allows Lot to chose the part of the land that he desires. Lot, of course, chooses the best part of the land, the prime real estate around the thriving towns of Sodom and Gomorrah (but see Genesis 18).

Abraham experiences the same high and low points of faith as he confronts the threat to the promise of descendants. On at least two occasions he takes matters into his own hands and tries to manufacture a descendant. The first instance is in Genesis 15 when he names Eliezer of Damascus, his top household servant, his heir. In Genesis 16 he follows another ancient practice and takes a concubine, Hagar, who gives birth to Ishmael.

In both cases, God appears to Abraham reaffirming his intention to give him and Sarah a real son. The fulfillment to the promise takes place in Genesis 21 when Isaac their son is born when they are in their extreme old age. This just underlines the fact that this child is a gift from God.

But the story of the struggle of faith in the promises does not end yet for Abraham. In Genesis 22 God gives Abraham a heart-rending command to take his new son and sacrifice him in the land of Moriah. By this time, though, Abraham has a deep and abiding trust in God and his love for him. So, without a word, he takes his son to the sacrifice. God, in his goodness, stops the sacrifice at the last minute and supplies an animal substitute in Isaac's place (Genesis 22:12–14).

Abraham becomes an example for us in our own struggle with faith. With the Book of Hebrews in the New Testament we can use Abraham as a model of a struggling faith that at the end comes to a firm confidence in God's goodness and power (Hebrews 11:8–19). Paul also uses Abraham as an example of how we are made right with God. He points out that Abraham did not have a relationship with God because he did all the right things, but because he put his trust in God. He quotes Genesis 15:6 in Romans 4:3: "Abraham believed God, and God accepted Abraham's faith, and that faith made him right with God."

Abraham: For additional scriptures on this topic go to Genesis 11:26–25:18.

CAREER/CAREERISM

GENESIS 12

How do you determine your career in a way that is sensitive to God's purpose and values? What is "careerism"? How does "seeking first the kingdom of God" relate to "careerism" today?

In Genesis 12:1 the Lord called Abram to "go" to a new land and then promised him great blessing. In verse 4 we read that Abram went "as the LORD had told him." This brief account of a call, a promise, and the subsequent action of obedience is replayed in different settings throughout the Bible.

In Exodus 3:10 God called Moses saying, "So now I am sending you to the king of Egypt. Go! Bring my people, the Israelites, out of Egypt!" Moses went and through the power of God set the captives free. In the book of Ruth, Naomi ordered Ruth to return to her own people and to her old gods, but Ruth refused and cried out, "Where you go, I will go. . . . Your people will be my people, and your God will be my God" (Ruth 1:16). Because of her devotion to her mother-in-law and to the God of Israel, Ruth became King David's great-grandmother and thus part of the very lineage of Jesus himself. Then in the New Testament, Jesus gathered all of his followers together and "chose twelve men and called them apostles" (Mark 3:14).

Just as God the Father called Abraham, Moses, Ruth, the apostles, and all of the great people of the Bible, so too does he call all people today. Without question, the *first* and *primary* call upon each of our lives is to acknowledge Jesus Christ as our personal Lord and Savior and to live in obedience to him. This means that we are called to follow him in our daily lives: in our family, career, church, and community life.

But there is a secondary call for each of us as well, and that is the call to a *specific form of service to humanity*. Traditionally, the church has named this "vocation," or "calling." Each person in Christ is called to fulfill a small part of the divine plan for history. Following Jesus, therefore, must translate itself into actual work for the Lord. Like Jesus, we too are called to "continue doing the work of the [Lord]" (John 9:4).

Many wrongly think that doing the work of the Lord mainly means full-time Christian ministry. While the ministry is important, it is very wrong to limit Christian vocation to being a full-time preacher, missionary, or church worker. Our careers are called to be in Christ, that is, in alignment with his reign. If we understand our lifetime work to be both a response of obedience to the calling of God upon our lives and an avenue of serving humanity, then our careers can be the very avenue of service God has chosen for us. This means that auto mechanics, research scientists, or homemakers who follow Jesus in their everyday lives and who view their careers as a means of living for him are every bit as much "in the ministry" as any pastor. In the kingdom of God there is no hierarchy of Christian service; there is only fidelity or lack of fidelity to the call to serve.

Determining a career, therefore, hinges on several important factors. First is the primary issue of seeking the will of God for your life. Implied in the personal acknowledgment of Jesus as Lord is the concerted effort to structure one's entire life—including career—around his purpose and will. When choosing a career such questions as, "How is he calling me to invest my life?" and "What are the particular gifts and graces he has given me to serve humanity and praise his name?" become most important. The patient seeking of clear guidance through prayer and Scripture study as well as the advice of godly people is critical in choosing a career wisely.

One of the ways to know whether or not you are in alignment with the will of God in regard to your career is to understand the temptation of careerism. Careerism is approaching any job with the dominant thought of, "What's in it for me?" It is the plague of living a self-centered existence that looks upon others as a means of exploitation for the sake of self-advancement. Clients, for instance, become objects to help a person get ahead in life.

If someone's primary motivation for entering any career is financial gain, or making a name for themselves, they likely have fallen prey to the temptation of careerism. Jesus said, "The thing you should want most is God's kingdom and doing what God wants. Then all these other things you need will be given to you" (Matthew 6:33). The Good News is that Jesus forgives all who truly repent of their sins (1 John 1:9) and can transform even a selfish career into one of true obedience to him and service to others. Jesus can also lead beyond present careers that are completely out of his will for our lives by opening new and surprising doors of service.

Career/Careerism: For additional scriptures on this topic go to Mark 3:14.

your son's daughter or your daughter's daughter;
that would bring shame on you.
11"'If your father and his wife have a daughter,
she is your sister. You must not have sexual relations with her.
12"'You must not have sexual relations with
your father's sister; she is your father's close relative. 13You must not have sexual relations with
your mother's sister; she is your mother's close
relative. 14You must not have sexual relations
with the wife of your father's brother, because
this would shame him. She is your aunt.
15"'You must not have sexual relations with
your daughter-in-law; she is your son's wife. Do
not have sexual relations with her.
16"'You must not have sexual relations with your
brother's wife. That would shame your brother.
17"'You must not have sexual relations with
both a woman and her daughter. And do not have
sexual relations with this woman's granddaughter,
either the daughter of her son or her daughter;
they are her close relatives. It is evil to do this.
18"'While your wife is still living, you must not
take her sister as another wife. Do not have sexual relations with her.
19"'You must not go near a woman to have sexual relations with her during her monthly period,
when she is unclean.
20"'You must not have sexual relations with
your neighbor's wife and make yourself unclean
with her.
21"'You must not give any of your children to
be sacrificed to Molech, because this would show
that you do not respect your God. I am the LORD.
22"'You must not have sexual relations with a
man as you would a woman. That is a hateful sin.⚭
23"'You must not have sexual relations with an
animal and make yourself unclean with it. Also a
woman must not have sexual relations with an
animal; it is not natural.
24"'Don't make yourself unclean by any of
these wrong things. I am forcing nations out of
their countries because they did these sins, and I
am giving their land to you. 25The land has become
unclean, and I punished it for its sins, so the land
is throwing out those people who live there.
26"'You must obey my laws and rules, and you
must not do any of these hateful sins. These rules
are for the citizens of Israel and for the people who
live with you. 27The people who lived in the land
before you did all these hateful things and made the
land unclean. 28If you do these things, you will also
make the land unclean, and it will throw you out as
it threw out the nations before you. 29Anyone who
does these hateful sins must be cut off from the
people. 30Keep my command not to do these hateful sins that were done by the people who lived in
the land before you. Don't make yourself unclean
by doing them. I am the LORD your God.'"⚭

Other Laws

19 The LORD said to Moses, 2"Tell all the people
of Israel: 'I am the LORD your God. You
must be holy because I am holy.
3"'You must respect your mother and father,
and you must keep my Sabbaths. I am the LORD
your God.
4"'Do not worship idols or make statues or gods
for yourselves. I am the LORD your God.
5"'When you sacrifice a fellowship offering to
the LORD, offer it in such a way that will be
accepted. 6You may eat it the same day you offer
it or on the next day. But if any is left on the third
day, you must burn it up. 7If any of it is eaten on
the third day, it is unclean, and it will not be
accepted. 8Anyone who eats it then will be guilty
of sin, because he did not respect the holy things
that belong to the LORD. He must be cut off from
the people.
9"'When you harvest your crops on your land,
do not harvest all the way to the corners of your
fields. If grain falls onto the ground, don't gather
it up. 10Don't pick all the grapes in your vineyards, and don't pick up the grapes that fall to the
ground. You must leave those things for poor
people and for people traveling through your
country. I am the LORD your God.⚭
11"'You must not steal. You must not cheat
people, and you must not lie to each other. 12You
must not make a false promise by my name, or
you will show that you don't respect your God. I
am the LORD.
13"'You must not cheat your neighbor or rob
him. You must not keep a hired worker's salary
all night until morning. 14You must not curse a
deaf person or put something in front of a blind
person to make him fall. But you must respect
your God. I am the LORD.⚭

⚭**18:22 Homosexuality:** Leviticus 20:13

18:22 Homosexuality is specifically prohibited by the Law of Moses. This perversion is called a "hateful sin" and is an act that calls for the death penalty (Leviticus 20:13). Though homosexuals may claim that their behavior is genetically rooted, the Law regards those who commit homosexual acts as accountable for their sins (implying they have a choice in the matter): "They have brought it on themselves."

⚭**18:30 Sexuality:** Leviticus 20

⚭**18:30 Divorce:** Leviticus 20

⚭**19:10 Ruth:** Deuteronomy 24:19

⚭**19:14 Physical Handicap:** Leviticus 21:18–20

15"'Be fair in your judging. You must not show
special favor to poor people or great people, but
be fair when you judge your neighbor. 16You
must not spread false stories against other people,
and you must not do anything that would put
your neighbor's life in danger. I am the LORD.

17"'You must not hate your fellow citizen in
your heart. If your neighbor does something
wrong, tell him about it, or you will be partly to
blame. 18Forget about the wrong things people do
to you, and do not try to get even. Love your
neighbor as you love yourself. I am the LORD.

19"'Obey my laws. You must not mate two different kinds of cattle or sow your field with two
different kinds of seed. You must not wear clothing made from two different kinds of material
mixed together.

20"'If a man has sexual relations with a slave
girl of another man, but this slave girl has not
been bought or given her freedom, there must be
punishment. But they are not to be put to death,
because the woman was not free. 21The man
must bring a male sheep as his penalty offering to
the LORD at the entrance to the Meeting Tent.
22The priest will offer the sheep as a penalty offering before the LORD for the man's sin, to remove
the sins of the man so he will belong to the LORD.
Then he will be forgiven for his sin.

23"'In the future, when you enter your country,
you will plant many kinds of trees for food. After
planting a tree, wait three years before using its
fruit. 24In the fourth year the fruit from the tree
will be the LORD's, a holy offering of praise to
him. 25Then in the fifth year, you may eat the
fruit from the tree. The tree will then produce
more fruit for you. I am the LORD your God.

26"'You must not eat anything with the blood
in it.

"'You must not try to tell the future by signs or
black magic.

27"'You must not cut the hair on the sides of
your heads or cut the edges of your beard. 28You
must not cut your body to show sadness for someone who died or put tattoo marks on yourselves.
I am the LORD.

29"'Do not dishonor your daughter by making
her become a prostitute. If you do this, the country will be filled with all kinds of sin.

30"'Obey the laws about Sabbaths, and respect
my Most Holy Place. I am the LORD.

31"'Do not go to mediums or fortune-tellers for
advice, or you will become unclean. I am the
LORD your God.

32"'Show respect to old people; stand up in
their presence. Show respect also to your God. I
am the LORD.

33"'Do not mistreat foreigners living in your
country, 34but treat them just as you treat your own
citizens. Love foreigners as you love yourselves,
because you were foreigners one time in Egypt. I
am the LORD your God.

35"'Do not cheat when you measure the length
or weight or amount of something. 36Your
weights and balances should weigh correctly,
with your weighing baskets the right size and
your jars holding the right amount of liquid. I am
the LORD your God. I brought you out of the land
of Egypt.

37"'Remember all my laws and rules, and obey
them. I am the LORD.'"

Warnings About Various Sins

20 The LORD said to Moses, 2"You must
also tell the people of Israel these things:
'If a person in your country gives one of his children to Molech, that person must be killed. It
doesn't matter if he is a citizen or a foreigner living in Israel; you must throw stones at him and
kill him. 3I will be against him and cut him off
from his people, because he gave his children to
Molech. He showed that he did not respect my
holy name, and he made my Holy Place unclean.
4The people of the community might ignore that
person and not kill the one who gave his children
to Molech. 5But I will be against him and his family, and I will cut him off from his people. I will do
this to anyone who follows him in being unfaithful to me by worshiping Molech.

6"'I will be against anyone who goes to mediums and fortune-tellers for advice, because that
person is being unfaithful to me. So I will cut him
off from his people.

19:18 This command became the famous "second greatest commandment" in the New Testament (Matthew 19:19; 22:39; Mark 12:31, 33; Romans 13:9; Galatians 5:14). It calls us to love and care for our neighbor as much as we love and care for ourselves. The New Testament, especially the parable of the Good Samaritan, clarifies who our neighbor is. A neighbor is "anyone with whom we come in contact, who has a need, and whom we can help."

19:18 Neighbor: Deuteronomy 19:4–6
19:26 Magic: Leviticus 19:31
19:26 Astrology: Deuteronomy 17:3
19:31 Magic: Leviticus 20:6

19:32 Today our society celebrates youth over age. The Bible, though, honors the old. Through experience they have acquired wisdom that they pass down to the young. As a result, the young owe older people respect and honor.

19:32 Growing Old: Deuteronomy 21:15–17
19:34 Racism: Deuteronomy 7:3–4
20:6 Magic: Leviticus 20:27

7"'Be my holy people. Be holy because I am the LORD your God. 8Remember and obey my laws. I am the LORD, and I have made you holy.

9"'Anyone who curses his father or mother must be put to death. He has cursed his father or mother, so he has brought his own death on himself.

Punishments for Sexual Sins

10"'If a man has sexual relations with his neighbor's wife, both the man and the woman are guilty of adultery and must be put to death. 11If a man has sexual relations with his father's wife, he has shamed his father, and both the man and his father's wife must be put to death. They have brought it on themselves.

12"'If a man has sexual relations with his daughter-in-law, both of them must be put to death. What they have done is not natural. They have brought their own deaths on themselves.

13"'If a man has sexual relations with another man as a man does with a woman, these two men have done a hateful sin. They must be put to death. They have brought it on themselves.

14"'If a man has sexual relations with both a woman and her mother, this is evil. The people must burn that man and the two women in fire so that your people will not be evil.

15"'If a man has sexual relations with an animal, he must be put to death. You must also kill the animal. 16If a woman approaches an animal and has sexual relations with it, you must kill the woman and the animal. They must be put to death. They have brought it on themselves.

17"'It is shameful for a brother to marry his sister, the daughter of either his father or his mother, and to have sexual relations with her. In front of everyone they must both be cut off from their people. The man has shamed his sister, and he is guilty of sin.

18"'If a man has sexual relations with a woman during her monthly period, both the woman and the man must be cut off from their people. They sinned because they showed the source of her blood.

19"'Do not have sexual relations with your mother's sister or your father's sister, because that would shame a close relative. Both of you are guilty of this sin.

20"'If a man has sexual relations with his uncle's wife, he has shamed his uncle. That man and his uncle's wife will die without children; they are guilty of sin.

21"'It is unclean for a man to marry his brother's wife. That man has shamed his brother, and they will have no children.

22"'Remember all my laws and rules, and obey them. I am leading you to your own land, and if you obey my laws and rules, that land will not throw you out. 23I am forcing out ahead of you the people who live there. Because they did all these sins, I have hated them. Do not live the way those people lived.

24"'I have told you that you will get their land, which I will give to you as your very own; it is a fertile land. I am the LORD your God, and I have set you apart from other people and made you my own. 25So you must treat clean animals and birds differently from unclean animals and birds. Do not make yourselves unclean by any of these unclean birds or animals or things that crawl on the ground, which I have made unclean for you. 26So you must be holy to me because I, the LORD, am holy, and I have set you apart from other people to be my own.

27"'A man or woman who is a medium or a fortune-teller must be put to death. You must stone them to death; they have brought it on themselves.'"

How Priests Must Behave

21 The LORD said to Moses, "Tell these things to Aaron's sons, the priests: 'A priest must not make himself unclean by touching a dead person. 2But if the dead person was one of his close relatives, he may touch him. The priest may make himself unclean if the dead person is his mother or father, son or daughter, brother or 3unmarried sister who is close to him because she has no husband. The priest may make himself unclean for her if she dies. 4But a priest must not make himself unclean if the dead person was only related to him by marriage.

5"'Priests must not shave their heads, or shave off the edges of their beards, or cut their bodies. 6They must be holy to their God and show respect for God's name, because they present the offerings made by fire to the LORD, which is the food of their God. So they must be holy.

7"'A priest must not marry an unclean prostitute or a divorced woman, because he is holy to his God. 8Treat him as holy, because he offers up the food of your God. Think of him as holy; I am the LORD who makes you holy, and I am holy.

20:7 Holiness: Isaiah 6:3
20:10 Adultery: Deuteronomy 5:18
20:13 Homosexuality: 1 Corinthians 6:9–10
20:16 Capital Punishment: Leviticus 21:9
20:27 Magic: Isaiah 47:9–15
20:27 Spirituality/Spiritual Dryness: Matthew 5:1–7:29
20:27 Sexuality: Numbers 5
20:27 Divorce: Deuteronomy 22:13–30
21:7 Celibacy: Leviticus 21:13–14

9“‘If a priest’s daughter makes herself unclean by becoming a prostitute, she shames her father. She must be burned with fire.

10“‘The high priest, who was chosen from among his brothers, had the special olive oil poured on his head. He was also appointed to wear the priestly clothes. So he must not show his sadness by letting his hair go uncombed or tearing his clothes. 11He must not go into a house where there is a dead body. He must not make himself unclean, even if it is for his own father or mother. 12The high priest must not go out of the Holy Place, because if he does and becomes unclean, he will make God’s Holy Place unclean. The special oil used in appointing priests was poured on his head to separate him from the rest of the people. I am the LORD.

13“‘The high priest must marry a woman who is a virgin. 14He must not marry a widow, a divorced woman, or a prostitute. He must marry a virgin from his own people 15so the people will respect his children as his own. I am the LORD. I have set the high priest apart for his special job.’”

16The LORD said to Moses, 17“Tell Aaron: ‘If any of your descendants have something wrong with them, they must never come near to offer the special food of their God. 18Anyone who has something wrong with him must not come near: blind men, crippled men, men with damaged faces, deformed men, 19men with a crippled foot or hand, 20hunchbacks, dwarfs, men who have something wrong with their eyes, men who have an itching disease or a skin disease, or men who have damaged sex glands.

21“‘If one of Aaron’s descendants has something wrong with him, he cannot come near to make the offerings made by fire to the LORD. He has something wrong with him; he cannot offer the food of his God. 22He may eat the most holy food and also the holy food. 23But he may not go through the curtain into the Most Holy Place, and he may not go near the altar, because he has something wrong with him. He must not make my Holy Place unfit. I am the LORD who makes these places holy.’”

24So Moses told these things to Aaron, Aaron’s sons, and all the people of Israel.

22 The LORD said to Moses, 2“Tell Aaron and his sons: ‘The people of Israel will give offerings to me. These offerings are holy, and they are mine, so you must respect them to show that you respect my holy name. I am the LORD.’ 3Say to them: ‘If any one of your descendants from now on is unclean and comes near the offerings that the Israelites made holy for me, that person must be cut off from appearing before me. I am the LORD.

4“‘If one of Aaron’s descendants has a harmful skin disease, or if he discharges a body fluid, he cannot eat the holy offerings until he becomes clean. He could also become unclean from touching a dead body, from his own semen, 5from touching any unclean crawling animal, or from touching an unclean person (no matter what made the person unclean). 6Anyone who touches those things will become unclean until evening. That person must not eat the holy offerings unless he washes with water. 7He will be clean only after the sun goes down. Then he may eat the holy offerings; the offerings are his food.

8“‘If a priest finds an animal that died by itself or that was killed by some other animal, he must not eat it. If he does, he will become unclean. I am the LORD.

9“‘If the priests keep all the rules I have given, they will not become guilty; if they are careful, they will not die. I am the LORD who has made them holy. 10Only people in a priest’s family may eat the holy offering. A visitor staying with the priest or a hired worker must not eat it. 11But if the priest buys a slave with his own money, that slave may eat the holy offerings; slaves who were born in his house may also eat his food. 12If a priest’s daughter marries a person who is not a priest, she must not eat any of the holy offerings. 13But if the priest’s daughter becomes widowed or divorced, with no children to support her, and if she goes back to her father’s house where she lived as a child, she may eat some of her father’s food. But only people from a priest’s family may eat this food.

14“‘If someone eats some of the holy offering by mistake, that person must pay back the priest for that holy food, adding another one-fifth of the price of that food.

15“‘When the Israelites give their holy offerings to the LORD, the priest must not treat these holy things as though they were not holy. 16The priests must not allow those who are not priests to eat the holy offerings. If they do, they cause the ones who eat the holy offerings to become guilty, and they will have to pay for it. I am the LORD, who makes them holy.’”

17The LORD said to Moses, 18“Tell Aaron and his sons and all the people of Israel: ‘A citizen of Israel or a foreigner living in Israel might want to bring a whole burnt offering, either for some special promise he has made or for a special gift he wants

21:9 Capital Punishment: Leviticus 24:11–23
21:14 Celibacy: Jeremiah 16:2
21:20 Physical Handicap: Matthew 9:32

22:4 *semen.* A man’s body fluid by which he can make a woman pregnant.

to give to the LORD. 19If he does, he must bring a
male animal that has nothing wrong with it—a bull,
a sheep, or a goat—so it might be accepted for him.
20He must not bring an animal that has something
wrong with it, or it will not be accepted for him.
21"'If someone brings a fellowship offering to
the LORD, either as payment for a special promise
the person has made or as a special gift the person
wants to give the LORD, it might be from the herd
or from the flock. But it must be healthy, with
nothing wrong with it, so that it will be accepted.
22You must not offer to the LORD any animal that
is blind, that has broken bones or is crippled, that
has running sores or any sort of skin disease. You
must not offer any animals like these on the altar
as an offering by fire to the LORD.
23"'If an ox or lamb is smaller than normal or is
not perfectly formed, you may give it as a special
gift to the LORD; it will be accepted. But it will not
be accepted as payment for a special promise you
have made.
24"'If an animal has bruised, crushed, torn, or
cut sex glands, you must not offer it to the LORD.
You must not do this in your own land, 25and you
must not take such animals from foreigners as sacrifices to the LORD. Because the animals have been
hurt in some way and have something wrong with
them, they will not be accepted for you.'"
26The LORD said to Moses, 27"When an ox, a
sheep, or a goat is born, it must stay seven days
with its mother. But from the eighth day on, this
animal will be accepted as a sacrifice by fire to the
LORD. 28But you must not kill the animal and its
mother on the same day, either an ox or a sheep.
29"If you want to offer some special offering of
thanks to the LORD, you must do it in a way that
pleases him. 30You must eat the whole animal
that same day and not leave any of the meat for
the next morning. I am the LORD.
31"Remember my commands and obey them; I
am the LORD. 32Show respect for my holy name.
You Israelites must remember that I am holy; I
am the LORD, who has made you holy. 33I brought
you out of Egypt to be your God. I am the LORD."

Special Holidays

23 The LORD said to Moses, 2"Tell the people
of Israel: 'You will announce the LORD's
appointed feasts as holy meetings. These are my
special feasts.

The Sabbath

3"'There are six days for you to work, but the
seventh day will be a special day of rest. It is a day
for a holy meeting; you must not do any work. It
is a Sabbath to the LORD in all your homes.

The Passover and Unleavened Bread

4"'These are the LORD's appointed feasts, the holy
meetings, which you will announce at the times set
for them. 5The LORD's Passover is on the fourteenth
day of the first month, beginning at twilight. 6The
Feast of Unleavened Bread begins on the fifteenth
day of the same month. You will eat bread made
without yeast for seven days. 7On the first day of
this feast you will have a holy meeting, and you
must not do any work. 8For seven days you will
bring an offering made by fire to the LORD. There
will be a holy meeting on the seventh day, and on
that day you must not do any regular work.'"

The First of the Harvest

9The LORD said to Moses, 10"Tell the people of
Israel: 'You will enter the land I will give you and
gather its harvest. At that time you must bring the
first bundle of grain from your harvest to the
priest. 11The priest will present the bundle before
the LORD, and it will be accepted for you; he will
present the bundle on the day after the Sabbath.
12"'On the day when you present the bundle of
grain, offer a male lamb, one year old, that has
nothing wrong with it, as a burnt offering to the
LORD. 13You must also offer a grain offering—four
quarts of fine flour mixed with olive oil as an
offering made by fire to the LORD; its smell will be
pleasing to him. You must also offer a quart of
wine as a drink offering. 14Until the day you
bring your offering to your God, do not eat any
new grain, roasted grain, or bread made from
new grain. This law will always continue for people from now on, wherever you live.

The Feast of Weeks

15"'Count seven full weeks from the morning
after the Sabbath. (This is the Sabbath that you
bring the bundle of grain to present as an offering.) 16On the fiftieth day, the first day after the
seventh week, you will bring a new grain offering
to the LORD. 17On that day bring two loaves of
bread from your homes to be presented as an
offering. Use yeast and four quarts of flour to
make those loaves of bread; they will be your gift
to the LORD from the first wheat of your harvest.
18"'Offer with the bread one young bull, two
male sheep, and seven male lambs that are one
year old and have nothing wrong with them.

22:29 Thanks: 1 Chronicles 25:3

23:13 Sacrifice: Numbers 28:7

Offer them with their grain offerings and drink
offerings, as a burnt offering to the LORD. They
will be an offering made by fire, and the smell
will be pleasing to the LORD. 19You must also offer
one male goat for a sin offering and two male,
one-year-old lambs as a fellowship offering.
20"'The priest will present the two lambs as an
offering before the LORD, along with the bread
from the first wheat of the harvest. They are holy
to the LORD, and they will belong to the priest.
21On that same day you will call a holy meeting;
you must not do any work that day. This law will
continue for you from now on, wherever you live.
22"'When you harvest your crops on your land,
do not harvest all the way to the corners of your
field. If grain falls onto the ground, don't gather it
up. Leave it for poor people and foreigners in
your country. I am the LORD your God.'"

The Feast of Trumpets

23Again the LORD said to Moses, 24"Tell the people of Israel: 'On the first day of the seventh
month you must have a special day of rest, a holy
meeting, when you blow the trumpet for a special
time of remembering. 25Do not do any work, and
bring an offering made by fire to the LORD.'"

The Day of Cleansing

26The LORD said to Moses, 27"The Day of Cleansing will be on the tenth day of the seventh month.
There will be a holy meeting, and you will give up
eating and bring an offering made by fire to the
LORD. 28Do not do any work on that day, because it
is the Day of Cleansing. On that day the priests will
go before the LORD and perform the acts to make
you clean so you will belong to the LORD.
29"Anyone who refuses to give up food on this
day must be cut off from the people. 30If anyone
works on this day, I will destroy that person from
among the people. 31You must not do any work at
all; this law will continue for people from now on
wherever you live. 32It will be a special day of rest
for you, and you must not eat. You will start this
special day of rest on the evening after the ninth
day of the month, and it will continue from that
evening until the next evening."

The Feast of Shelters

33Again the LORD said to Moses, 34"Tell the people of Israel: 'On the fifteenth day of the seventh
month is the Feast of Shelters. This feast to the
LORD will continue for seven days. 35There will be
a holy meeting on the first day; do not do any
work. 36You will bring an offering made by fire to
the LORD each day for seven days. On the eighth
day you will have another holy meeting, and you
will bring an offering made by fire to the LORD.
This will be a holy meeting; do not do any work.
37("'These are the LORD's special feasts, when
there will be holy meetings and when you bring
offerings made by fire to the LORD. You will bring
whole burnt offerings, grain offerings, sacrifices,
and drink offerings—each at the right time. 38These
offerings are in addition to those for the LORD's
Sabbath days, in addition to offerings you give as
payment for special promises, and in addition to
special offerings you want to give to the LORD.)
39"'So on the fifteenth day of the seventh
month, after you have gathered in the crops of
the land, celebrate the LORD's festival for seven
days. You must rest on the first day and the eighth
day. 40On the first day you will take good fruit
from the fruit trees, as well as branches from
palm trees, poplars, and other leafy trees. You
will celebrate before the LORD your God for seven
days. 41Celebrate this festival to the LORD for
seven days each year. This law will continue from
now on; you will celebrate it in the seventh
month. 42Live in shelters for seven days. All the
people born in Israel must live in shelters 43so
that all your descendants will know I made Israel
live in shelters during the time I brought them
out of Egypt. I am the LORD your God.'"
44So Moses told the people of Israel about all of
the LORD's appointed feast days.

The Lampstand and the Holy Bread

24 The LORD said to Moses, 2"Command the
people of Israel to bring you pure oil from
crushed olives. That oil is for the lamps so that
these lamps may never go out. 3Aaron will keep
the lamps burning in the Meeting Tent from
evening until morning before the LORD; this is in
front of the curtain of the Ark of the Agreement.
This law will continue from now on. 4Aaron must
always keep the lamps burning on the lampstands
of pure gold before the LORD.
5"Take fine flour and bake twelve loaves of
bread with it, using four quarts of flour for each
loaf. 6Put them in two rows on the golden table
before the LORD, six loaves in each row. 7Put pure
incense on each row as the memorial portion to
take the place of the bread. It is an offering made
by fire to the LORD. 8Every Sabbath day Aaron will
put the bread in order before the LORD, as an agreement with the people of Israel that will continue

23:40 **Table Fellowship/Lord's Supper:** Deuteronomy 12:11

23:44 **Feasts/Festivals:** Numbers 28:16

forever. 9That bread will belong to Aaron and his sons. They will eat it in a holy place, because it is a most holy part of the offerings made by fire to the LORD. That bread is their share forever."

The Man Who Cursed God

10Now there was a son of an Israelite woman and an Egyptian father who was walking among the Israelites. A fight broke out in the camp between him and an Israelite. 11The son of the Israelite woman began cursing and speaking against the LORD, so the people took him to Moses. (The mother's name was Shelomith, the daughter of Dibri from the family of Dan.) 12The people held him as a prisoner while they waited for the LORD's command to be made clear to them.

13Then the LORD said to Moses, 14"Take the one who spoke against me outside the camp. Then all the people who heard him must put their hands on his head, and all the people must throw stones at him and kill him. 15Tell the people of Israel this: 'If anyone curses his God, he is guilty of sin. 16Anyone who speaks against the LORD must be put to death; all the people must kill him by throwing stones at him. Foreigners must be punished just like the people born in Israel; if they speak against the LORD, they must be put to death.

17"'Whoever kills another person must be put to death. 18Whoever kills an animal that belongs to another person must give that person another animal to take its place. 19And whoever causes an injury to a neighbor must receive the same kind of injury in return: 20Broken bone for broken bone, eye for eye, tooth for tooth. Anyone who injures another person must be injured in the same way in return. 21Whoever kills another person's animal must give that person another animal to take its place. But whoever kills another person must be put to death.

22"'The law will be the same for the foreigner as for those from your own country. I am the LORD your God.'"

23Then Moses spoke to the people of Israel, and they took the person who had cursed outside the camp and killed him by throwing stones at him. So the people of Israel did as the LORD had commanded Moses.

The Time of Rest for the Land

25 The LORD said to Moses at Mount Sinai, 2"Tell the people of Israel this: 'When you enter the land I will give you, let it have a special time of rest, to honor the LORD. 3You may plant seed in your field for six years, and you may trim your vineyards for six years and bring in their fruits. 4But during the seventh year, you must let the land rest. This will be a special time to honor the LORD. You must not plant seed in your field or trim your vineyards. 5You must not cut the crops that grow by themselves after harvest, or gather the grapes from your vines that are not trimmed. The land will have a year of rest.

6"'You may eat whatever the land produces during that year of rest. It will be food for your men and women servants, for your hired workers, and for the foreigners living in your country. 7It will also be food for your cattle and the wild animals of your land. Whatever the land produces may be eaten.

The Year of Jubilee

8"'Count off seven groups of seven years, or forty-nine years. During that time there will be seven years of rest for the land. 9On the Day of Cleansing, you must blow the horn of a male sheep; this will be on the tenth day of the seventh month. You must blow the horn through the whole country. 10Make the fiftieth year a special year, and announce freedom for all the people living in your country. This time will be called Jubilee. You will each go back to your own property, each to your own family and family group. 11The fiftieth year will be a special time for you to celebrate. Don't plant seeds, or harvest the crops that grow by themselves, or gather grapes from the vines that are not trimmed. 12That year is Jubilee; it will be a holy time for you. You may eat only the crops that come from the field. 13In the year of Jubilee you each must go back to your own property.

14"'If you sell your land to your neighbor, or if you buy land from your neighbor, don't cheat each other. 15If you want to buy your neighbor's land, count the number of years since the last Jubilee, and use that number to decide the right price. If your neighbor sells the land to you, count

---

24:16 The context of this passage shows that blasphemy is open defiance of and disrespect towards the Lord. In the Old Testament, such an act was worthy of death by stoning, both for native-born Israelites and foreigners.

24:22 Foreigner (Alien): Deuteronomy 10:19

24:23 Capital Punishment: Numbers 15:32–36

25:1–22 Not only was the seventh day (the Sabbath) and the seventh month special (Leviticus 23:3, 23–43), the seventh year was "a special time of rest, to honor the Lord" (Leviticus 25:2). The people were not to plant crops so that the land could rest. The fiftieth year, called the year of Jubilee, was also a special year of celebration with no planting of crops. Freedom was announced so that all who had had to sell their property could go back to it (Leviticus 25:11–13).

25:10 *Jubilee.* This word comes from the Hebrew word for a horn of a male sheep.

the number of years left for harvesting crops, and
use that number to decide the right price. 16If there
are many years, the price will be high. But if there
are only a few years, lower the price, because
your neighbor is really selling only a few crops to
you. 17You must not cheat each other, but you
must respect your God. I am the LORD your God.
18"'Remember my laws and rules, and obey
them so that you will live safely in the land. 19The
land will give good crops to you, and you will eat
as much as you want and live safely in the land.
20"'But you might ask, "If we don't plant seeds or
gather crops, what will we eat the seventh year?" 21I
will send you such a great blessing during the sixth
year that the land will produce enough crops for
three years. 22When you plant in the eighth year,
you will still be eating from the old crop; you will eat
the old crop until the harvest of the ninth year.

Property Laws

23"'The land really belongs to me, so you can't
sell it for all time. You are only foreigners and
travelers living for a while on my land. 24People
might sell their land, but it must always be possible for the family to get its land back. 25If a person
in your country becomes very poor and sells some
land, then close relatives must come and buy it
back. 26If there is not a close relative to buy the
land back, but if the person makes enough money
to be able to buy it back, 27the years must be
counted since the land was sold. That number
must be used to decide how much the first owner
should pay back the one who bought it. Then the
land will belong to the first owner again. 28But if
there is not enough money to buy it back, the one
who bought it will keep it until the year of
Jubilee. During that celebration, the land will go
back to the first owner's family.
29"'If someone sells a home in a walled city, for
a full year after it is sold, the person has the right
to buy it back. 30But if the owner does not buy
back the house before a full year is over, it will
belong to the one who bought it and to his future
sons. The house will not go back to the first
owner at Jubilee. 31But houses in small towns
without walls are like open country; they can be
bought back, and they must be returned to their
first owner at Jubilee.
32"'The Levites may always buy back their
houses in the cities that belong to them. 33If someone buys a house from a Levite, that house in the
Levites' city will again belong to the Levites in the
Jubilee. This is because houses in Levite cities
belong to the people of Levi; the Israelites gave
these cities to them. 34Also the fields and pastures
around the Levites' cities cannot be sold, because
those fields belong to the Levites forever.

Rules for Slave Owners

35"'If anyone from your country becomes too
poor to support himself, help him to live among
you as you would a stranger or foreigner. 36Do not
charge him any interest on money you loan to
him, but respect your God; let the poor live
among you. 37Don't lend him money for interest,
and don't try to make a profit from the food he
buys. 38I am the LORD your God, who brought you
out of the land of Egypt to give the land of Canaan
to you and to become your God.
39"'If anyone from your country becomes very
poor and sells himself as a slave to you, you must
not make him work like a slave. 40He will be like
a hired worker and a visitor with you until the
year of Jubilee. 41Then he may leave you, take his
children, and go back to his family and the land of
his ancestors. 42This is because the Israelites are
my servants, and I brought them out of slavery in
Egypt. They must not become slaves again.
43You must not rule this person cruelly, but you
must respect your God.
44"'Your men and women slaves must come from
other nations around you; from them you may buy
slaves. 45Also you may buy as slaves children from
the families of foreigners living in your land. These
child slaves will belong to you, 46and you may even
pass them on to your children after you die; you can
make them slaves forever. But you must not rule
cruelly over your own people, the Israelites.
47"'Suppose a foreigner or visitor among you
becomes rich. If someone in your country becomes
so poor that he has to sell himself as a slave to the
foreigner living among you or to a member of the
foreigner's family, 48the poor person has the right
to be bought back and become free. One of his
relatives may buy him back: 49His uncle, his
uncle's son, or any one of his close relatives may
buy him back. Or, if he gets enough money, he
may pay the money to free himself.
50"'He and the one who bought him must
count the time from when he sold himself up to

25:28 Land/Inheritance: Numbers 36:5–7

25:35–38 The ground of this commandment, as with many others, is that the Lord brought Israel out of Egypt (this is even the ground of the Ten Commandments in Exodus 20:2). God's grace to them, when they were oppressed slaves, was to serve as a model in their treatment of unfortunate people in their country (see also Leviticus 19:33–34). In this way they showed respect for God (compare Leviticus 22:31–33). We can show our respect for God and our appreciation of our salvation in Christ by being gracious and charitable to others.

25:42 Servant of the Lord: Leviticus 25:55

LAND/INHERITANCE

GENESIS 12

Why was the land so central in God's promise to Abraham and, then, to the life of Israel in the Old Testament? What happened to the central role of the land following the exile? What role does the theme of land/inheritance have in the New Testament?

In Genesis 12:1–3, God called Abraham to leave his home country for the land he had promised. Hundreds of years later, when the nation of Israel had finally taken possession of Canaan, God allotted the land to each tribe and family as their inheritance (Joshua 13:6–8). The land, however, belonged wholly to God. No family could ever sell their land; it was meant to provide lasting sustenance and security for them and their descendants (Leviticus 25:23; see also Numbers 36:5–9). The Israelites could only sell the use of their land for a period of time, and, even then, every fifty years the land would revert to the original family during the year of Jubilee (Leviticus 25:23–28). God also intended that the land of Israel would bless all the people, even the poor and the powerless: farmers were not allowed to harvest their fields completely, thus allowing the widows, orphans, and foreigners in the land to have what was left over (Deuteronomy 24:19–22).

Yet the promise to Abraham was about more than just land for the people of Israel. The promise in Genesis 12:1–3 was threefold: Abraham would be given a land; he would be the father of a great nation; and in him "all the people of the earth will be blessed." All three elements of this promise were to work together to achieve a single purpose: to bring all the nations of the earth back into fellowship with God. God would make Israel a prosperous and mighty nation, enjoying great abundance, and in response to God Israel would act holy, as God is holy, *in the land* in the sight of her neighbor nations. These other nations would realize that Israel's greatness was due to her God, and to the keeping of his law (Deuteronomy 4:5–8). Israel's life in the land would be a light for all nations, calling them to the one true God (Isaiah 42:6; 49:6).

But Israel was never able to live faithfully before God in the land, and instead worshiped false gods and oppressed the poor in the land. In judgment God took away their land and sent the people into exile (see Nehemiah 9 for a summary of this). In the absence of a faithful Israel in the land, a new means of witnessing to the other nations was necessary. The books of Jeremiah and Ezekiel, written just before and during the exile, speak to this: "The Lord has made something new happen in the land" (Jeremiah 31:22). God would enact a new agreement with his people, one in which his teachings would be written on their hearts (Jeremiah 31:31–34), and God's Spirit within them would enable them to live a holy life (Ezekiel 36:26–27).

The idea of physical land disappears in the promise/inheritance language of the New Testament. Although land is missing, the two other elements of the promise to Abraham are carried forward into the New Testament. Relative to the promise, however, the descendants of Abraham are now no longer the physical nation of Israel, but rather "the true children of Abraham are those who have faith" (Galatians 3:7; see also Romans 4:16–17). The idea that God's people are called to bring the good news to all the world becomes the explicit focal point of the New Testament, the very heart of Jesus' ministry and the work of the church (Matthew 28:18–20; Mark 1:14–15). Christ died on the cross "so that God's blessing promised to Abraham might come through Jesus Christ to those who are not Jews" (Galatians 3:14).

The lack of focus on land is paralleled by other changes as well. In contrast with the year of Jubilee and widows gleaning in the fields, the members of the New Testament church gave freely, even *selling their fields* to care for the needy (Acts 4:34–37). Jesus speaks only of the most basic of needs—food, water, clothing—not the abundant Old Testament blessings experienced in the land. Instead, Jesus encourages his disciples to trust in God daily for supplying these essentials, and to seek instead the kingdom of God (Matthew 6:24–33; Luke 12:22–31). The full blessing of the faithful takes on a future orientation. Amid suffering, disciples are called upon to "be full of joy, because you have a reward waiting for you in heaven" (Matthew 5:12; Luke 6:23).

Christians in the New Testament look forward to an inheritance not of land but of eternal life (Matthew 19:29). The new agreement promises "blessings that will last forever" (Hebrews 9:15), and the Holy Spirit becomes in this life the down payment of this inheritance (Ephesians 1:13–14; see also Romans 8:23; 2 Corinthians 1:22). It is by this same Spirit that Christians can be a true and effective witness of God's glory (Galatians 5:22–25; see also Acts 1:8). This life by the power of the Holy Spirit is the light to a dark world, enabling the church, as the spiritual children of Abraham, to bless all nations (Galatians 3:8).

Land/Inheritance: For additional scriptures on this topic go to Leviticus 25:23–28.

CURSE

GENESIS 12:3

How effective is a curse? What is the relationship between cursing and blessing? What does it mean to be under God's curse and how can we escape it?

The Bible takes cursing much more seriously than we do. We may think of a curse as a word or phrase spoken in frustration, anger or hatred which expresses our attitude toward someone, but in the Bible, a curse invokes God's anger and judgment against its object.

Because curses depend upon God's power to make them effective, curses can bring no harm upon those who are innocent, and they fly around like birds that never land (Proverbs 26:2).

But for the guilty, God's curse will land with sudden and total destruction (Zechariah 5:1–4). Even a curse spoken in God's name may bring God's judgment suddenly and decisively upon the guilty. After the prophet Elisha cursed boys who mocked his baldness, two bears immediately tore them apart (2 Kings 2:24). Jesus cursed an unfruitful fig tree, which withered within a day (Mark 11:12–14, 20–21).

In our culture, words are usually considered powerless to bring physical harm, as illustrated in the familiar children's rhyme, "Sticks and stones may break my bones but words will never hurt me." But in the world of the Old Testament, people considered words themselves to have the power to bring destruction, and a curse was a potent weapon against an enemy.

God's promise to Abraham was extended to Abraham's descendants and identified them as a people in a special relationship with God. When Abraham's son, Isaac, was approaching death, he repeated the Abrahamic blessing to his son Jacob, from whom the people of Israel traced their descent: "may everyone who curses you be cursed, and may everyone who blesses you be blessed" (Genesis 27:29). The elaborate deception which Jacob planned to secure his father's blessing (Genesis 27) demonstrates the great importance attached to a father's blessing. Blessing and cursing dedicate all available resources either toward or against the object of the action and leave no room for halfhearted commitment. After Isaac blessed Jacob, he had nothing left with which to bless Esau, who was entitled to the blessing by birth (Genesis 27:37).

Blessing and cursing are opposite ways of experiencing God's presence. God pledged himself to be with Abraham and the nation of his descendants (Genesis 17:7–8), and God's presence with them required their obedience. In the covenant God established with Israel, the nation of Abraham's descendants, God prescribed both blessings and curses (Deuteronomy 11:26–29; 30:19). For those living in obedience to God's commands, his presence would bring blessing (Deuteronomy 28:1–14), but for those living in disobedience, God's presence would bring curses (Deuteronomy 27:15–26; 28:15–68). Because Israel as an entire nation disobeyed the commands God gave in his covenant with them God brought the curses of the covenant upon them (Daniel 9:11).

The blessings and curses that were set before Israel parallel the blessings and curses that were set before Adam and Eve in the Garden of Eden (Genesis 2:9, 16–17). Rather than choosing the tree that gives life, Adam and Eve ate from the tree that gives the knowledge of good and evil in direct disobedience to God's command. Their sin brought God's curse upon the serpent who had tempted them (Genesis 3:14) and upon all human efforts to cultivate the earth given to them (Genesis 3:17).

Everyone who lives in disobedience to God's law is under his curse (Galatians 3:10), but for those who put their trust in Jesus, he has taken the curse upon himself. In dying on a cross, Jesus endured the death of one cursed by God. "Anyone whose body is displayed on a tree is cursed by God" (Deuteronomy 21:23). By exchanging places with those under the curse, Jesus took the curse upon himself so that those who believe might receive the blessings promised to Abraham (Galatians 3:9, 13–14). Just as Abraham was blessed because he believed God (Galatians 3:6), only faith in Jesus Christ can bring freedom from God's curse to those who live in disobedience to God's commands (Galatians).

God's curse will be removed from the creation after his final judgment of the earth. In the heavenly city which God will establish, any threat of curse will be replaced by the tree that brings only the blessing of life (Revelation 22:2), the same tree that Adam and Eve chose against in the Garden of Eden. Because God himself will be present, nothing under the curse of his judgment will remain in the city (Revelation 22:3). God's presence with his people will be the greatest blessing of the heavenly city (Revelation 21:3) and the final fulfillment of his promise to Abraham that he would be God to Abraham and to those who are his children by faith (Genesis 17:7–8; Galatians 3:7).

Curse: For additional scriptures on this topic go to Genesis 3:14.

the next year of Jubilee. Use that number to decide the price, because the person really only hired himself out for a certain number of years. 51If there are still many years before the year of Jubilee, the person must pay back a large part of the price. 52If there are only a few years left until Jubilee, the person must pay a small part of the first price. 53But he will live like a hired person with the foreigner every year; don't let the foreigner rule cruelly over him.

54"'Even if no one buys him back, at the year of Jubilee, he and his children will become free. 55This is because the people of Israel are servants to me. They are my servants, whom I brought out of Egypt. I am the LORD your God.

Rewards for Obeying God

26 "'Don't make idols for yourselves or set up statues or memorials. Don't put stone statues in your land to bow down to, because I am the LORD your God.

2"'Remember my Sabbaths, and respect my Holy Place. I am the LORD.

3"'If you remember my laws and commands and obey them, 4I will give you rains at the right season; the land will produce crops, and the trees of the field will produce their fruit. 5Your threshing will continue until the grape harvest, and your grape harvest will continue until it is time to plant. Then you will have plenty to eat and live safely in your land. 6I will give peace to your country; you will lie down in peace, and no one will make you afraid. I will keep harmful animals out of your country, and armies will not pass through it.

7"'You will chase your enemies and defeat them, killing them with your sword. 8Five of you will chase a hundred men; a hundred of you will chase ten thousand men. You will defeat your enemies and kill them with your sword.

9"'Then I will show kindness to you and let you have many children; I will keep my agreement with you. 10You will have enough crops to last for more than a year. When you harvest the new crops, you will have to throw out the old ones to make room for them. 11Also I will place my Holy Tent among you, and I will not turn away from you. 12I will walk with you and be your God, and you will be my people. 13I am the LORD your God, who brought you out of Egypt, where you were slaves. I broke the heavy weights that were on your shoulders and let you walk proudly again.

Punishment for Not Obeying God

14"'But if you do not obey me and keep all my commands, 15and if you turn away from my rules and hate my laws, refusing to obey all my commands, you have broken our agreement. 16As a result, I will do this to you: I will cause terrible things to happen to you. I will cause you to have disease and fever that will destroy your eyes and slowly kill you. You will not have success when you plant your seed, and your enemy will eat your crops. 17I will be against you, and your enemies will defeat you. These people who hate you will rule over you, and you will run away even when no one is chasing you.

18"'If after all this you still do not obey me, I will punish you seven times more for your sins. 19I will break your great pride, and I will make the sky like iron and the earth like bronze. 20You will work hard, but it will not help. Your land will not grow any crops, and your trees will not give their fruit.

21"'If you still turn against me and refuse to obey me, I will beat you seven times harder. The more you sin, the more you will be punished. 22I will send wild animals to attack you, and they will take your children away from you and destroy your cattle. They will make you so few in number the roads will be empty.

23"'If you don't learn your lesson after all these things, and if you still turn against me, 24I will also turn against you. I will punish you seven more times for your sins. 25You broke my agreement, and I will punish you. I will bring armies against you, and if you go into your cities for safety, I will cause diseases to spread among you so that your enemy will defeat you. 26There will be very little bread to eat; ten women will be able to cook all your bread in one oven. They will measure each piece of bread, and you will eat, but you will still be hungry.

27"'If you still refuse to listen to me and still turn against me, 28I will show my great anger; I will punish you seven more times for your sins. 29You will eat the bodies of your sons and daughters. 30I will destroy your places where gods are worshiped and cut down your incense altars. I will pile your dead bodies on the lifeless forms of your idols. I will hate you. 31I will destroy your

25:55 Servant of the Lord: Numbers 14:24
25:55 Materialism/Possessions: Deuteronomy 15
25:55 Slavery: Isaiah 61:1–2
26:2 Sabbath: Leviticus 26:34–35
26:6 Peace: Psalm 4:8
26:13 Commitment: 1 Samuel 18:1–4
26:19 *sky . . . bronze.* This means the sky will give no rain and the earth will produce no crops.
26:20 Famine: Deuteronomy 28:15–24

cities and make your holy places empty, and I will not smell the pleasing smell of your offerings. 32I will make the land empty so that your enemies who come to live in it will be shocked at it. 33I will scatter you among the nations, and I will pull out my sword and destroy you. Your land will become empty, your cities a waste. 34When you are taken to your enemy's country, your land will finally get its rest. It will enjoy its time of rest all the time it lies empty. 35During the time the land is empty, it will have the rest you should have given it while you lived in it.

36"'Those of you who are left alive will lose their courage in the land of their enemies. They will be frightened by the sound of a leaf being blown by the wind. They will run as if someone were chasing them with a sword, and they will fall even when no one is chasing them. 37They will fall over each other, as if someone were chasing them with a sword, even though no one is chasing them. You will not be strong enough to stand up against your enemies. 38You will die among other nations and disappear in your enemies' countries. 39So those who are left alive will rot away in their enemies' countries because of their sins. They will also rot away because of their ancestors' sins.

There Is Always Hope

40"'But maybe the people will confess their sins and the sins of their ancestors; maybe they will admit they turned against me and sinned against me, 41which made me turn against them and send them into the land of their enemies. If these disobedient people are sorry for what they did and accept punishment for their sin, 42I will remember my agreement with Jacob, my agreement with Isaac, and my agreement with Abraham, and I will remember the land. 43The land will be left empty by its people, and it will enjoy its time of rest as it lies bare without them. Then those who are left alive will accept the punishment for their sins. They will learn that they were punished because they hated my laws and refused to obey my rules. 44But even though this is true, I will not turn away from them when they are in the land of their enemies. I will not hate them so much that I completely destroy them and break my agreement with them, because I am the LORD their God. 45For their good I will remember the agreement with their ancestors, whom I brought out of the land of Egypt so I could become their God; the other nations saw these things. I am the LORD.'"

46These are the laws, rules, and teachings the LORD made between himself and the Israelites through Moses at Mount Sinai.

Promises Are Important

27 The LORD said to Moses, 2"Speak to the people of Israel and tell them: 'If someone makes a special promise to give a person as a servant to the LORD by paying a price that is the same value as that person, 3the price for a man twenty to sixty years old is about one and one-fourth pounds of silver. (You must use the measure as set by the Holy Place.) 4The price for a woman twenty to sixty years old is about twelve ounces of silver. 5The price for a man five to twenty years old is about eight ounces of silver; for a woman it is about four ounces of silver. 6The price for a baby boy one month to five years old is about two ounces of silver; for a baby girl the price is about one and one-half ounces of silver. 7The price for a man sixty years old or older is about six ounces of silver; for a woman it is about four ounces of silver.

8"'If anyone is too poor to pay the price, bring him to the priest, and the priest will set the price. The priest will decide how much money the person making the vow can afford to pay.

Gifts to the Lord

9"'Some animals may be used as sacrifices to the LORD. If someone promises to bring one of these to the LORD, it will become holy. 10That person must not try to put another animal in its place or exchange it, a good animal for a bad one, or a bad animal for a good one. If this happens, both animals will become holy.

11"'Unclean animals cannot be offered as sacrifices to the LORD, and if someone brings one of them to the LORD, that animal must be brought to the priest. 12The priest will decide a price for the animal, according to whether it is good or bad; as the priest decides, that is the price for the animal. 13If the person wants to buy back the animal, an additional one-fifth must be added to the price.

Value of a House

14"'If a person gives a house as holy to the LORD, the priest must decide its value, according to whether the house is good or bad; as the priest decides, that is the price for the house. 15But if the person who gives the house wants to buy it back, an additional one-fifth must be added to the price. Then the house will belong to that person again.

26:35 Sabbath: Nehemiah 13:15–22

Value of Land

16“‘If a person gives some family property to the LORD, the value of the fields will depend on how much seed is needed to plant them. It will cost about one and one-fourth pounds of silver for each six bushels of barley seed needed. 17If the person gives a field at the year of Jubilee, its value will stay at what the priest has decided. 18But if the person gives the field after the Jubilee, the priest must decide the exact price by counting the number of years to the next year of Jubilee. Then he will subtract that number from its value. 19If the person who gave the field wants to buy it back, one-fifth must be added to that price, and the field will belong to the first owner again.

20“‘If the person does not buy back the field, or if it is sold to someone else, the first person cannot ever buy it back. 21When the land is released at the year of Jubilee, it will become holy to the LORD, like land specially given to him. It will become the property of the priests.

22“‘If someone gives to the LORD a field he has bought, which is not a part of his family land, 23the priest must count the years to the next Jubilee. He must decide the price for the land, and the price must be paid on that day. Then that land will be holy to the LORD. 24At the year of Jubilee, the land will go back to its first owner, to the family who sold the land.

25“‘You must use the measure as set by the Holy Place in paying these prices; it weighs two-fifths of an ounce.

Value of Animals

26“‘If an animal is the first one born to its parent, it already belongs to the LORD, so people may not give it again. If it is a cow or a sheep, it is the LORD’s. 27If the animal is unclean, the person must buy it back for the price set by the priest, and the person must add one-fifth to that price. If it is not bought back, the priest must sell it for the price he had decided.

28“‘There is a special kind of gift that people set apart to give to the LORD; it may be a person, animal, or field from the family property. That gift cannot be bought back or sold. Every special kind of gift is most holy to the LORD.

29“‘If anyone is given for the purpose of being destroyed, he cannot be bought back; he must be put to death.

30“‘One-tenth of all crops belongs to the LORD, including the crops from fields and the fruit from trees. That one-tenth is holy to the LORD. 31If a person wants to get back that tenth, one-fifth must be added to its price.

32“‘The priest will take every tenth animal from a person’s herd or flock, and it will be holy to the LORD. 33The owner should not pick out the good animals from the bad or exchange one animal for another. If that happens, both animals will become holy; they cannot be bought back.’”

34These are the commands the LORD gave to Moses at Mount Sinai for the people of Israel.

Notes:

INTRODUCTION TO THE BOOK OF NUMBERS

Wandering in the Desert

WHO WROTE THIS BOOK?

Numbers, along with the other five books of the Torah or Pentateuch, are traditionally attributed to Moses.

TO WHOM WAS THIS BOOK WRITTEN?

This book was written to and for the people of Israel.

WHERE WAS IT WRITTEN?

Like the other four books of the Pentateuch (the first five books of the Bible), Numbers was probably composed by Moses in the desert area where the people of Israel wandered, or perhaps in the Moabite region as they prepared to enter the Promised Land.

WHEN WAS IT WRITTEN?

This book, written near the end of the forty-year desert wanderings, would bear a date between 1446 and 1406 B.C.

WHAT IS THE BOOK ABOUT?

The Book of Numbers tells the story of Israel's journey from Mount Sinai to Moab, the country that bordered Canaan—the Promised Land. The tale continues with Israel's refusal to trust God's leading and power when they would not conquer their enemies in Canaan and claim the land promised to them by God. As a result, God sent them in to the desert to wander aimlessly for forty long years.

WHY WAS THIS BOOK WRITTEN?

With God in the lead, Israel marches from Mount Sinai to Kadesh to Moab as his conquering army to establish God's kingdom prominently in the world. The book shows us that as long as they were faithful and followed God's lead they were, indeed, victorious. But when they rebelled and retreated from him, they found themselves lost and wandering in the desert, a result of his anger.

SO WHAT DOES THIS BOOK MEAN TO US?

Christians today are appointed to be God's conquering army to continue spreading his kingdom in the world. As long as we are faithful to God and follow his lead, "we have full victory through God who showed his love for us" (Romans 8:37). We are conquerors; we are his ambassadors. But when we rebel against him and retreat from his leading we find ourselves lost in the desert of sin and sorrow. Even then, God does not abandon us or fail to meet our needs as he brings circumstances into our lives that will lead us to change our hearts and lives back to him.

SUMMARY:

With a title like Numbers, most Christians expect to find a boring book with lists of people. There *are* such lists in the book, but there are also many interesting stories and important laws.

Numbers serves an important role as the fourth part of the five-part Torah (Pentateuch). It tells the story of the change that took place: from the old generation that left Egypt at the time of the Exodus and sinned in the desert, to the new generation that stands on the edge of the Promised Land. The book presents the reader with a vision of new beginnings and hope.

Numbers, like the other parts of the Torah, was written by Moses and may be divided into three parts:

I. Organizing at Sinai Israel for the March (1:1–9:14)
II. The Journey through the Desert—Its Progress and Failures (9:15–25:18)
III. On the Edge of Settlement (26:1–36:13)

The message of the Book of Numbers is one of hope and promise. The first part of the book describes judgments which came upon the people who left Egypt because of their continued rebellion against God. Still God continued to treat them as his special people. At the end of the book, a second generation stands before the Lord and has the promise of a new future as they approach the Promised Land.

I. Organizing Israel at Sinai for the March (1:1–9:14)

The first part of Numbers describes how Israel, under Moses' leadership, prepared to leave the Sinai region and head toward the Promised Land. They now had the Ten Commandments and God's blessing to proceed, thanks to Moses' prayer after they sinned by worshiping the gold calf.

The first chapter counts the fighting men in Israel and concludes that there are 603,550 men. The next chapter informs the tribes where they are to camp whenever they temporarily stop their march. The Meeting Tent, which represented God's presence, is to be in the middle of the camp, and all the tribes are to be around it, just like the camp of an army. The point of these chapters and the preparations is to show that Israel is God's army marching to battle in the Promised Land. Little do they know at this time that it will be a forty-year march.

II. The Journey through the Desert—Its Progress and Failures (9:15–25:18)

The people of Israel set out from the area around Mount Sinai and begin their march toward the Promised Land. During the day they follow a cloud and at night a pillar of fire. These, along with the Ark of the Agreement, represent God's presence with his people.

In spite of God's presence, they still complained about the hardships of the march. God provides for them in wonderful ways, but they still grumble.

While in the desert, the people of Israel send out spies to explore the Promised Land. They return with reports of a fertile land and warlike inhabitants. The people grow fearful, showing their lack of trust in God. For their lack of faith, God condemns them to wander in the desert for forty years until that generation dies off.

But even this event does not satisfy all the people of Israel. Korah and Dathan, Abiram and On lead a rebellion against Moses and Aaron, but God judges them.

Finally, even Moses disobeys God in his anger, and he is punished by not being permitted to lead the people into the Promised Land.

As they get closer to the Promised Land, they run into resistance from the various kings of the land surrounding Palestine, but God gives them the power to defeat their enemies, even when their enemies are assisted by a powerful prophet named Balaam.

III. On the Edge of Settlement (26:1–36:13)

The last section of Numbers begins with a second census of all Israel (see Numbers 1 for the first census). None of these people who are now ready to go into the Promised Land were in the first census except Moses, Joshua, and Caleb. The rest of this section narrates laws and the final preparations of Israel before they attack Palestine.

NUMBERS

The People of Israel Are Counted

The LORD spoke to Moses in the Meeting Tent
in the Desert of Sinai. This was on the first
day of the second month in the second year
after the Israelites left Egypt. He said to Moses:
2"You and Aaron must count all the people of
Israel by families and family groups, listing the
name of each man. 3You and Aaron must count
every man twenty years old or older who will
serve in the army of Israel, and list them by their
divisions. 4One man from each tribe, the leader of
his family, will help you. 5These are the names of
the men who will help you:
from the tribe of Reuben—Elizur son of
Shedeur;
6from the tribe of Simeon—Shelumiel
son of Zurishaddai;
7from the tribe of Judah—Nahshon son
of Amminadab;
8from the tribe of Issachar—Nethanel
son of Zuar;
9from the tribe of Zebulun—Eliab son
of Helon;
10from the tribe of Ephraim son of
Joseph—Elishama son of Ammihud;
from the tribe of Manasseh son of
Joseph—Gamaliel son of Pedahzur;
11from the tribe of Benjamin—Abidan
son of Gideoni;
12from the tribe of Dan—Ahiezer son of
Ammishaddai;
13from the tribe of Asher—Pagiel son of
Ocran;
14from the tribe of Gad—Eliasaph son of
Deuel;
15from the tribe of Naphtali—Ahira son
of Enan."
16These were the men chosen from the people
to be leaders of their tribes, the heads of Israel's
family groups.
17Moses and Aaron took these men who had
been picked 18and called all the people of Israel
together on the first day of the second month.
Then the people were listed by their families and
family groups, and all the men who were twenty
years old or older were listed by name. 19Moses did
exactly what the LORD had commanded and listed
the people while they were in the Desert of Sinai.
20The tribe of Reuben, the first son born to Israel,
was counted; all the men twenty years old or
older who were able to serve in the army were
listed by name with their families and family
groups. 21The tribe of Reuben totaled 46,500 men.
22The tribe of Simeon was counted; all the men
twenty years old or older who were able to serve in
the army were listed by name with their families
and family groups. 23The tribe of Simeon totaled
59,300 men.
24The tribe of Gad was counted; all the men
twenty years old or older who were able to serve
in the army were listed by name with their families and family groups. 25The tribe of Gad totaled
45,650 men.
26The tribe of Judah was counted; all the men
twenty years old or older who were able to serve in
the army were listed by name with their families
and family groups. 27The tribe of Judah totaled
74,600 men.
28The tribe of Issachar was counted; all the men
twenty years old or older who were able to serve
in the army were listed by name with their families
and family groups. 29The tribe of Issachar totaled
54,400 men.
30The tribe of Zebulun was counted; all the men
twenty years old or older who were able to serve in
the army were listed by name with their families
and family groups. 31The tribe of Zebulun totaled
57,400 men.
32The tribe of Ephraim, a son of Joseph, was
counted; all the men twenty years old or older who
were able to serve in the army were listed by name
with their families and family groups. 33The tribe
of Ephraim totaled 40,500 men.
34The tribe of Manasseh, also a son of Joseph,
was counted; all the men twenty years old or older
who were able to serve in the army were listed by
name with their families and family groups. 35The
tribe of Manasseh totaled 32,200 men.
36The tribe of Benjamin was counted; all the
men twenty years old or older who were able to
serve in the army were listed by name with their
families and family groups. 37The tribe of Benjamin
totaled 35,400 men.
38The tribe of Dan was counted; all the men
twenty years old or older who were able to serve in
the army were listed by name with their families
and family groups. 39The tribe of Dan totaled
62,700 men.
40The tribe of Asher was counted; all the men
twenty years old or older who were able to serve
in the army were listed by name with their families and family groups. 41The tribe of Asher totaled
41,500 men.
42The tribe of Naphtali was counted; all the men
twenty years old or older who were able to serve

in the army were listed by name with their families and family groups. [43]The tribe of Naphtali totaled 53,400 men.

[44]Moses, Aaron, and the twelve leaders of Israel, one from each of the families, counted these men. [45]Every man of Israel twenty years old or older who was able to serve in the army was counted and listed with his family. [46]The total number of men was 603,550.

[47]The families from the tribe of Levi were not listed with the others, because [48]the LORD had told Moses: [49]"Do not count the tribe of Levi or include them with the other Israelites. [50]Instead put the Levites in charge of the Holy Tent of the Agreement and everything that is with it. They must carry the Holy Tent and everything in it, and they must take care of it and make their camp around it. [51]Any time the Holy Tent is moved, the Levites must take it down, and any time it is set up, the Levites must do it. Anyone else who goes near the Holy Tent will be put to death. [52]The Israelites will make their camps in separate divisions, each family near its flag. [53]But the Levites must make their camp around the Holy Tent of the Agreement so that I will not be angry with the Israelites. The Levites will take care of the Holy Tent of the Agreement."

[54]So the Israelites did everything just as the LORD commanded Moses.

The Camp Arrangement

2 The LORD said to Moses and Aaron: [2]"The Israelites should make their camps around the Meeting Tent, but they should not camp too close to it. They should camp under their family flag and banners."

[3]The camp of Judah will be on the east side, where the sun rises, and they will camp by divisions there under their flag. The leader of the people of Judah is Nahshon son of Amminadab. [4]There are 74,600 men in his division.

[5]Next to them the tribe of Issachar will camp. The leader of the people of Issachar is Nethanel son of Zuar. [6]There are 54,400 men in his division.

[7]Next is the tribe of Zebulun. The leader of the people of Zebulun is Eliab son of Helon. [8]There are 57,400 men in his division.

[9]There are a total of 186,400 men in the camps of Judah and its neighbors, in all their divisions. They will be the first to march out of camp.

[10]The divisions of the camp of Reuben will be on the south side, where they will camp under their flag. The leader of the people of Reuben is Elizur son of Shedeur. [11]There are 46,500 men in his division.

[12]Next to them the tribe of Simeon will camp. The leader of the people of Simeon is Shelumiel son of Zurishaddai. [13]There are 59,300 men in his division.

[14]Next is the tribe of Gad. The leader of the people of Gad is Eliasaph son of Deuel. [15]There are 45,650 men in his division.

[16]There are a total of 151,450 men in the camps of Reuben and its neighbors, in all their divisions. They will be the second group to march out of camp.

[17]When the Levites march out with the Meeting Tent, they will be in the middle of the other camps. The tribes will march out in the same order as they camp, each in its place under its flag.

[18]The divisions of the camp of Ephraim will be on the west side, where they will camp under their flag. The leader of the people of Ephraim is Elishama son of Ammihud. [19]There are 40,500 men in his division.

[20]Next to them the tribe of Manasseh will camp. The leader of the people of Manasseh is Gamaliel son of Pedahzur. [21]There are 32,200 men in his division.

[22]Next is the tribe of Benjamin. The leader of the people of Benjamin is Abidan son of Gideoni. [23]There are 35,400 men in his division.

[24]There are a total of 108,100 men in the camps of Ephraim and its neighbors, in all their divisions. They will be the third group to march out of camp.

[25]The divisions of the camp of Dan will be on the north side, where they will camp under their flag. The leader of the people of Dan is Ahiezer son of Ammishaddai. [26]There are 62,700 men in his division.

[27]Next to them the tribe of Asher will camp. The leader of the people of Asher is Pagiel son of Ocran. [28]There are 41,500 men in his division.

[29]Next is the tribe of Naphtali. The leader of the people of Naphtali is Ahira son of Enan. [30]There are 53,400 men in his division.

[31]There are 157,600 men in the camps of Dan and its neighbors. They will be the last to march out of camp, and they will travel under their own flag.

[32]These are the Israelites who were counted by families. The total number of Israelites in the camps, counted by divisions, is 603,550. [33]Moses obeyed the LORD and did not count the Levites among the other people of Israel.

[34]So the Israelites obeyed everything the LORD commanded Moses. They camped under their flags and marched out by families and family groups.

1:45 *who was able to serve in the army.* The census counts potential soldiers because they were marching toward war with the present inhabitants of the Promised Land.

2:27 Music: Joshua 6

DREAMS

GENESIS 15:9–21

Why were dreams important in the Bible?
Does God still speak to his people through dreams today?

Throughout the Bible God commonly reveals himself and his will through dreams. In Genesis 15:9–21, God seals his agreement with Abram (or Abraham), in a dream. Up to this point, God has spoken directly to people (Genesis 3:9; 12:1), but now he speaks to Abram while he is in a deep sleep. As it happens in many of the dreams mentioned in the Bible, a vision appears in Abram's dream. He sees a smoking firepot and a blazing torch pass between the sacrificed animals. Thus Abram not only has God's words of promise to rely upon in the future; he also has a dream from God that grants a vivid picture or image of that promise. God speaks to Abram through both word and image.

In a few Bible passages we can clearly distinguish between a vision and a dream, but in many instances there is little that separates them. In most cases, God reveals himself in a dream when the person is asleep (Laban in Genesis 31:24), or he reveals his message in a vision when the person is in a trance or in a wakeful state of mind (John in Revelation 1:10). In either case, God's revelation of his will is the most consistent theme. Job 33:14 tells us that "God does speak—sometimes one way and sometimes another—even though people may not understand it." And 1 Samuel 28:6 says that God speaks primarily in three ways: he speaks directly to and through the prophets; he manifests his will through the Urim; and he speaks indirectly through the medium of dreams.

Whenever we consider dreams in the Bible, we need to understand that God spoke through them to reveal his will for the future, to encourage his people, and to communicate new truths.

In Genesis 37:5–10, Joseph dreams that he will be the leader of his family one day. In one dream his brothers' bundles of wheat bow down to him, and in a second dream the earth, moon, and stars bow down to him. These dreams about the future become a reality in Genesis 42 when Joseph is made ruler over Egypt.

In Judges 7:13, God encourages Gideon with a dream before he goes into battle with the Midianites. Gideon, while spying on the enemy, overhears two men talk of a dream. In this dream, a barley loaf, symbolizing Gideon, flattened the tent of Midian. After Gideon hears the dream, he worships God and goes boldly into battle.

God also uses dreams or visions to announce the birth of Christ (Matthew 1:20–24), to inaugurate the church age (Acts 10), and to envision the future revelation of Christ (Revelation 1:10). Each of these different dreams teach us that God speaks to his people, and that he is with them in numerous ways.

In the book of Daniel, God uses many dreams to speak to King Nebuchadnezzar (Daniel 2, 4). Daniel makes it clear to the king that he could not interpret dreams without the help of God. God is the one who gives the dream and God is the one who interprets the dream. He alone knows the hearts of people and what will occur in the future.

Clearly, God speaks through dreams in the Bible. Yet does that mean he speaks to us through dreams today as well? We must be careful that our theology does not limit God by saying he cannot use dreams in the present or that he will not use dreams in the future to give new insights. On the other hand, we must submit every dream to the authority of Scripture. God will not give any insight contrary to what he has revealed already.

Ecclesiastes wisely reminds us that dreams can merely be a result of being preoccupied with everyday matters: "Bad dreams come from too much worrying" (5:3). Furthermore, Jeremiah warns the people of his day that dreams can be nothing more than self-deluded imagination: "They [the false prophets] prophesy from their own wishful thinking" (23:26). These false prophets invent their own message and pretend that it is God's message (23:31).

The strongest warning about dreams occurs in Deuteronomy 13:1–5. Even in the early days of Israel, God's people are concerned with discerning between true and false prophecy. Moses warns that false prophets will come and use dreams to turn the people away from God. But dreams, even when they are accompanied by signs and miracles, are not to be readily accepted. Instead, they are to be put to a twofold test: dreams are false dreams (1) if they draw a person's heart away from the one true God or (2) if they deny any truth about God as revealed in Scripture. "Serve only the Lord your God. Respect him, keep his commands, and obey him" (13:4).

Dreams: For additional scriptures on this topic go to Genesis 20:3–7.

CIRCUMCISION

GENESIS 17:10

What is circumcision? What did it represent in the Old Testament? Should we perform circumcisions today?

Circumcision was a fairly common custom practiced in the ancient world of the Bible. It is the surgical practice of cutting off the foreskin of the male sex organ. (The foreskin is a fold of skin that covers the end of the sex organ.)

Today doctors routinely circumcise infants because the size of the foreskin opening is often too small, making cleansing difficult and leading to irritation and inflammation. In biblical times, however, circumcision was not always practice and when practiced it was performed at different ages and for different reasons.

Bible scholars have discerned basically three reasons why ancient peoples may have practiced circumcision. The first reason may have been for the purpose of cleanliness and hygiene. The second reason is not as clear and has to do with the notion of sacrifice. The idea was that with the shedding of blood and the cutting off of the foreskin a kind of "part for the whole" sacrifice was envisioned. The third reason is probably the most significant and most common reason why circumcision was performed. It represented a ritual of initiation. Initiation means to admit someone into some new membership or status usually by some official ceremony, often implying the abandoning of a former membership or status.

What does circumcision mean in the Bible? In the Bible, our first and most important reference to circumcision is in Genesis 17. Here circumcision is given by God to Abraham and his descendants as a sign of the agreement (or covenant) he is making with them: "Your bodies will be marked to show that you are part of my agreement that lasts forever" (Genesis 17:13). This agreement or covenant began in Genesis 12 and was repeated and elaborated upon in Genesis 15 and 17. God had promised to Abraham numerous descendants, the land of Canaan, and that from him would come a great nation. Thus, the circumcision of Abraham in Genesis 17 represents an initiation rite in the formation of a new people, a new nation to be brought about by God himself through Abraham.

By adopting circumcision, Abraham was accepting the agreement both on his part and for his descendants after him. In fact, anyone who rejected the circumcision would be cut off from the agreement and the people just as the flesh of the foreskin is cut off in circumcision: "Any male who is not circumcised will be cut off from his people, because he has broken my agreement" (Genesis 17:14). Abraham and his descendants would no longer identify with their Mesopotamian roots but through circumcision would become members of a new community, later to become ancient Israel. What distinguished Abraham's circumcision from the circumcision of other nations around him was the timing of it, being performed not at puberty but at birth on a child who was only eight days old. The command to circumcise was also to include Abraham's slaves (Genesis 17:12,13) and not just his own blood relatives. Thus, Genesis 17 began the custom of Israelite circumcision, which became their distinguishing mark as a people for centuries to come.

Sometimes the Bible uses the word circumcise in a figurative sense to mean "dedicating one's self to God" or "being open to God's instruction." For example, Jeremiah 4:4 states, "Give yourselves [literally, 'circumcise yourselves'] to the service of the LORD, and decide to obey him" [literally, 'remove the foreskin of your hearts']. Jeremiah 6:10 says, "the people of Israel have closed ears [literally "uncircumcised ears"], so they cannot hear my warnings. They don't like the word of the LORD; they don't want to listen to it!"

In the New Testament, it is clear that circumcision was no longer required of believers (See Galatians 5:6; 6:15; Acts 15). Instead, there was a new shift towards a spiritual and inner significance of circumcision, namely that done by the Holy Spirit upon the heart (Romans 2:29; Philippians 3:3).

Many Christians today believe that we have an equivalent form of Old Testament circumcision in the New Testament practice of baptism. In that baptism is also an initiation rite into membership in the people of God, the church, there is a parallel. Colossians 2:11–12 brings the two practices together. Here we see the idea that Christian baptism is the New Testament equivalent of circumcision in the Old Testament. Just as circumcision initiated a person into membership in the Old Testament people of God, Israel, baptism initiates a person into membership in the New Testament people of God, the church.

Circumcision: For additional scriptures on this topic go to Exodus 12:43–49.

Aaron's Family, the Priests

3 This is the family history of Aaron and Moses at the time the LORD talked to Moses on Mount Sinai.

2Aaron had four sons: Nadab, the oldest, Abihu, Eleazar, and Ithamar. 3These were the names of Aaron's sons, who were appointed to serve as priests. 4But Nadab and Abihu died in the presence of the LORD when they offered the wrong kind of fire before the LORD in the Desert of Sinai. They had no sons. So Eleazar and Ithamar served as priests during the lifetime of their father Aaron.

5The LORD said to Moses, 6"Bring the tribe of Levi and present them to Aaron the priest to help him. 7They will help him and all the Israelites at the Meeting Tent, doing the work in the Holy Tent. 8The Levites must take care of everything in the Meeting Tent and serve the people of Israel by doing the work in the Holy Tent. 9Give the Levites to Aaron and his sons; of all the Israelites, the Levites are given completely to him. 10Appoint Aaron and his sons to serve as priests, but anyone else who comes near the holy things must be put to death."

11The LORD also said to Moses, 12"I am choosing the Levites from all the Israelites to take the place of all the firstborn children of Israel. The Levites will be mine, 13because the firstborn are mine. When you were in Egypt, I killed all the firstborn children of the Egyptians and took all the firstborn of Israel to be mine, both animals and children. They are mine. I am the LORD."

14The LORD again said to Moses in the Desert of Sinai, 15"Count the Levites by families and family groups. Count every male one month old or older." 16So Moses obeyed the LORD and counted them all.

17Levi had three sons, whose names were Gershon, Kohath, and Merari.

18The Gershonite family groups were Libni and Shimei.

19The Kohathite family groups were Amram, Izhar, Hebron, and Uzziel.

20The Merarite family groups were Mahli and Mushi.

These were the family groups of the Levites.

21The family groups of Libni and Shimei belonged to Gershon; they were the Gershonite family groups. 22The number that was counted was 7,500 males one month old or older. 23The Gershonite family groups camped on the west side, behind the Holy Tent. 24The leader of the families of Gershon was Eliasaph son of Lael. 25In the Meeting Tent the Gershonites were in charge of the Holy Tent, its covering, the curtain at the

A model of Levites offering sacrifices in front of the Holy Tent

entrance to the Meeting Tent, 26the curtains in the courtyard, the curtain at the entry to the courtyard around the Holy Tent and the altar, the ropes, and all the work connected with these items.

27The family groups of Amram, Izhar, Hebron, and Uzziel belonged to Kohath; they were the Kohathite family groups. 28They had 8,600 males one month old or older, and they were responsible for taking care of the Holy Place. 29The Kohathite family groups camped south of the Holy Tent. 30The leader of the Kohathite families was Elizaphan son of Uzziel. 31They were responsible for the Ark, the table, the lampstand, the altars, the tools of the Holy Place which they were to use, the curtain, and all the work connected with these items. 32The main leader of the Levites was Eleazar son of Aaron, the priest, who was in charge of all those responsible for the Holy Place.

33The family groups of Mahli and Mushi belonged to Merari; they were the Merarite family groups. 34The number that was counted was 6,200 males one month old or older. 35The leader of the Merari families was Zuriel son of Abihail, and they were to camp north of the Holy Tent. 36The Merarites were responsible for the frames of the Holy Tent, the braces, the posts, the bases, and all the work connected with these items. 37They were also responsible for the posts in the courtyard around the Holy Tent and their bases, tent pegs, and ropes.

38Moses, Aaron, and his sons camped east of the Holy Tent, toward the sunrise, in front of the Meeting Tent. They were responsible for the Holy Place for the Israelites. Anyone else who came near the Holy Place was to be put to death.

39Moses and Aaron counted the Levite men by their families, as the LORD commanded, and there were 22,000 males one month old or older.

Levites Take the Place of the Firstborn Sons

40The LORD said to Moses, "Count all the firstborn sons in Israel one month old or older, and list
their names. 41Take the Levites for me instead of
the firstborn sons of Israel; take the animals of the
Levites instead of the firstborn animals from the
rest of Israel. I am the LORD."
42So Moses did what the LORD commanded and
counted all the firstborn sons of the Israelites.
43When he listed all the firstborn sons one month
old or older, there were 22,273 names.
44The LORD also said to Moses, 45"Take the
Levites instead of all the firstborn sons of the Israelites, and take the animals of the Levites instead
of the animals of the other people. The Levites are
mine. I am the LORD. 46Since there are 273 more
firstborn sons than Levites, 47collect two ounces of
silver for each of the 273 sons. Use the measure
as set by the Holy Place, which is two-fifths of an
ounce. 48Give the silver to Aaron and his sons as
the payment for the 273 Israelites."
49So Moses collected the money for the people
the Levites could not replace. 50From the firstborn
of the Israelites, he collected thirty-five pounds of
silver, using the measure set by the Holy Place.
51Moses obeyed the command of the LORD and
gave the silver to Aaron and his sons.⚭

The Jobs of the Kohath Family

4 The LORD said to Moses and Aaron, 2"Count
the Kohathites among the Levites by family
groups and families. 3Count the men from thirty
to fifty years old, all who come to serve in the
Meeting Tent.
4"The Kohathites are responsible for the most
holy things in the Meeting Tent. 5When the Israelites are ready to move, Aaron and his sons must
go into the Holy Tent, take down the curtain, and
cover the Ark of the Agreement with it. 6Over this
they must put a covering made from fine leather,
then spread the solid blue cloth over that, and put
the poles in place.
7"Then they must spread a blue cloth over the
table for the bread that shows a person is in God's
presence. They must put the plates, pans, bowls,
and the jars for drink offerings on the table; they
must leave the bread that is always there on the
table. 8Then they must put a red cloth over all of
these things, cover everything with fine leather,
and put the poles in place.
9"With a blue cloth they must cover the lampstand, its lamps, its wick trimmers, its trays, and
all the jars for the oil used in the lamps. 10Then
they must wrap everything in fine leather and put
all these things on a frame for carrying them.
11"They must spread a blue cloth over the gold
altar, cover it with fine leather, and put the poles
in place.
12"They must gather all the things used for
serving in the Holy Place and wrap them in a
blue cloth. Then they must cover that with fine
leather and put these things on a frame for carrying them.
13"They must clean the ashes off the bronze
altar and spread a purple cloth over it. 14They
must gather all the things used for serving at the
altar—the pans for carrying the fire, the meat
forks, the shovels, and the bowls—and put them
on the bronze altar. Then they must spread a
covering of fine leather over it and put the poles
in place.
15"When the Israelites are ready to move, and
when Aaron and his sons have covered the holy
furniture and all the holy things, the Kohathites
may go in and carry them away. In this way they
won't touch the holy things and die. It is the
Kohathites' job to carry the things that are in the
Meeting Tent.
16"Eleazar son of Aaron, the priest, will be
responsible for the Holy Tent and for everything in
it, for all the holy things it has: the oil for the lamp,
the sweet-smelling incense, the continual grain
offering, and the oil used to appoint priests and
things to the LORD's service."
17The LORD said to Moses and Aaron, 18"Don't
let the Kohathites be cut off from the Levites. 19Do
this for the Kohathites so that they may go near the
Most Holy Place and not die: Aaron and his sons
must go in and show each Kohathite what to do
and what to carry. 20The Kohathites must not enter
and look at the holy things, even for a second, or
they will die."

The Jobs of the Gershon Family

21The LORD said to Moses, 22"Count the Gershonites by families and family groups. 23Count the men
from thirty to fifty years old, all who have a job to
do in the Meeting Tent.
24"This is what the Gershonite family groups
must do and what they must carry. 25They must
carry the curtains of the Holy Tent, the Meeting
Tent, its covering, and its outer covering made
from fine leather. They must also carry the curtains
for the entrance to the Meeting Tent, 26the curtains of the courtyard that go around the Holy
Tent and the altar, the curtain for the entry to the

⚭**3:51 Mediator:** Exodus 29

courtyard, the ropes, and all the things used with the curtains. They must do everything connected with these things. 27Aaron and his sons are in charge of what the Gershonites do or carry; you tell them what they are responsible for carrying. 28This is the work of the Gershonite family group at the Meeting Tent. Ithamar son of Aaron, the priest, will direct their work.

The Jobs of the Merari Family

29"Count the Merarite families and family groups. 30Count the men from thirty to fifty years old, all who work at the Meeting Tent. 31It is their job to carry the following as they serve in the Meeting Tent: the frames of the Holy Tent, the crossbars, the posts, and bases, 32in addition to the posts that go around the courtyard, their bases, tent pegs, ropes, and everything that is used with the poles around the courtyard. Tell each man exactly what to carry. 33This is the work the Merarite family group will do for the Meeting Tent. Ithamar son of Aaron, the priest, will direct their work."

The Levite Families

34Moses, Aaron, and the leaders of Israel counted the Kohathites by families and family groups, 35the men from thirty to fifty years old who were to work at the Meeting Tent. 36There were 2,750 men in the family groups. 37This was the total of the Kohath family groups who worked at the Meeting Tent, whom Moses and Aaron counted as the LORD had commanded Moses.

38Also, the Gershonites were counted by families and family groups, 39the men from thirty to fifty years old who were given work at the Meeting Tent. 40The families and family groups had 2,630 men. 41This was the total of the Gershon family groups who worked at the Meeting Tent, whom Moses and Aaron counted as the LORD had commanded.

42Also, the men in the families and family groups of the Merari family were counted, 43the men from thirty to fifty years old who were to work at the Meeting Tent. 44The family groups had 3,200 men. 45This was the total of the Merari family groups, whom Moses and Aaron counted as the LORD had commanded Moses.

46So Moses, Aaron, and the leaders of Israel counted all the Levites by families and family groups. 47They counted the men from thirty to fifty years old who were given work at the Meeting Tent and who carried the Tent. 48The total number of these men was 8,580. 49Each man was counted as the LORD had commanded Moses; each man was given his work and told what to carry as the LORD had commanded Moses.

Rules About Cleanliness

5 The LORD said to Moses, 2"Command the Israelites to send away from camp anyone with a harmful skin disease. Send away anyone who gives off body fluid or who has become unclean by touching a dead body. 3Send both men and women outside the camp so that they won't spread the disease there, where I am living among you." 4So Israel obeyed the LORD's command and sent those people outside the camp. They did just as the LORD had told Moses.

Paying for Doing Wrong

5The LORD said to Moses, 6"Tell the Israelites: 'When a man or woman does something wrong to another person, that is really sinning against the LORD. That person is guilty 7and must admit the wrong that has been done. The person must fully pay for the wrong that has been done, adding one-fifth to it, and giving it to the person who was wronged. 8But if that person is dead and does not have any close relatives to receive the payment, the one who did wrong owes the LORD and must pay the priest. In addition, the priest must sacrifice a male sheep to remove the wrong so that the person will belong to the LORD. 9When an Israelite brings a holy gift, it should be given to the priest. 10No one has to give these holy gifts, but if someone does give them, they belong to the priest.'"

Suspicious Husbands

11Then the LORD said to Moses, 12"Tell the Israelites: 'A man's wife might be unfaithful to him 13and have sexual relations with another man. Her sin might be kept hidden from her husband so that he does not know about the wrong she did. Perhaps no one saw it, and she wasn't caught. 14But if her husband has feelings of jealousy and suspects she has sinned—whether she has or not— 15he should take her to the priest. The husband must also take an offering for her of two quarts of barley flour. He must not pour oil or incense on it, because this is a grain offering for jealousy, an offering of remembrance. It is to find out if she is guilty.

4:49 Births: Joshua 13–19
4:49 Numbers: Deuteronomy 6:4
5:5–8 Although confession is important when a person does wrong, some wrongs should also include payment. If people steal or cheat, they should not only return what was taken but must also add one-fifth to the value of what was taken. (Leviticus 6:1–5). Such a "paying back" policy is very helpful in making sure the matter is resolved fairly.
5:14 Jealousy: Psalm 78:58

On the eighth day Gamaliel son of Pedahzur brought his gifts. He was the leader of the tribe of Manasseh.

On the ninth day Abidan son of Gideoni brought his gifts. He was the leader of the tribe of Benjamin.

On the tenth day Ahiezer son of Ammishaddai brought his gifts. He was the leader of the tribe of Dan.

On the eleventh day Pagiel son of Ocran brought his gifts. He was the leader of the tribe of Asher.

On the twelfth day Ahira son of Enan brought his gifts. He was the leader of the tribe of Naphtali.

84So these were the gifts from the Israelite leaders when oil was poured on the altar and it was given for service to the LORD: twelve silver plates, twelve silver bowls, and twelve gold dishes. 85Each silver plate weighed about three and one-fourth pounds, and each bowl weighed about one and three-fourths pounds. All the silver plates and silver bowls together weighed about sixty pounds according to a weight set by the Holy Place measure. 86The twelve gold dishes filled with incense weighed four ounces each, according to the weight set by the Holy Place measure. Together the gold dishes weighed about three pounds. 87The total number of animals for the burnt offering was twelve bulls, twelve male sheep, and twelve male lambs a year old. There was also a grain offering, and there were twelve male goats for a sin offering. 88The total number of animals for the fellowship offering was twenty-four bulls, sixty male sheep, sixty male goats, and sixty male lambs a year old. All these offerings were for giving the altar to the service of the LORD after the oil had been poured on it.

89When Moses went into the Meeting Tent to speak with the LORD, he heard the LORD speaking to him. The voice was coming from between the two gold creatures with wings that were above the lid of the Ark of the Agreement. In this way the LORD spoke with him.

The Lampstand

8 The LORD said to Moses, 2"Speak to Aaron and tell him, 'Put the seven lamps where they can light the area in front of the lampstand.'"

3Aaron did this, putting the lamps so they lighted the area in front of the lampstand; he obeyed the command the LORD gave Moses. 4The lampstand was made from hammered gold, from its base to the flowers. It was made exactly the way the LORD had showed Moses.

The Levites Are Given to God

5The LORD said to Moses, 6"Take the Levites away from the other Israelites and make them clean. 7This is what you should do to make them clean: Sprinkle the cleansing water on them, and have them shave their bodies and wash their clothes so they will be clean. 8They must take a young bull and the grain offering of flour mixed with oil that goes with it. Then take a second young bull for a sin offering. 9Bring the Levites to the front of the Meeting Tent, and gather all the Israelites around. 10When you bring the Levites before the LORD, the Israelites should put their hands on them. 11Aaron will present the Levites before the LORD as an offering presented from the Israelites. Then the Levites will be ready to do the work of the LORD.

12"The Levites will put their hands on the bulls' heads—one bull will be a sin offering to the LORD, and the other will be a burnt offering, to remove the sins of the Levites so they will belong to the LORD. 13Make the Levites stand in front of Aaron and his sons and present the Levites as an offering to the LORD. 14In this way you must set apart the Levites from the other Israelites; the Levites will be mine.

15"Make the Levites pure, and present them as an offering so that they may come to work at the Meeting Tent. 16They will be given completely to me from the Israelites; I have taken them for myself instead of the firstborn of every Israelite woman. 17All the firstborn in Israel—people or animals—are mine. When I killed all the firstborn in Egypt, I set the firstborn in Israel aside for myself. 18But I have taken the Levites instead of all the firstborn in Israel. 19From all the Israelites I have given the Levites to Aaron and his sons so that they may serve the Israelites at the Meeting Tent. They will help remove the Israelites' sins so they will belong to the LORD and so that no disaster will strike the Israelites when they approach the Holy Place."

20So Moses, Aaron, and all the Israelites obeyed and did with the Levites what the LORD commanded Moses. 21The Levites made themselves clean and washed their clothes. Then Aaron presented them as an offering to the LORD. He also removed their sins so they would be pure. 22After that, the Levites came to the Meeting Tent to work, and Aaron and his sons told them what to do. They did with the Levites what the LORD commanded Moses.

23The LORD said to Moses, 24"This command is for the Levites. Everyone twenty-five years old or older must come to the Meeting Tent, because

8:10 *put . . . them.* This showed that the people had a part in giving the Levites their special work.

they all have jobs to do there. 25At the age of fifty, they must retire from their jobs and not work again. 26They may help their fellow Levites with their work at the Meeting Tent, but they must not do the work themselves. This is the way you are to give the Levites their jobs."

The Passover Is Celebrated

9 The LORD spoke to Moses in the Desert of Sinai in the first month of the second year after the Israelites left Egypt. He said, 2"Tell the Israelites to celebrate the Passover at the appointed time. 3That appointed time is the fourteenth day of this month at twilight; they must obey all the rules about it."

4So Moses told the Israelites to celebrate the Passover, 5and they did; it was in the Desert of Sinai at twilight on the fourteenth day of the first month. The Israelites did everything just as the LORD commanded Moses.

6But some of the people could not celebrate the Passover on that day because they were unclean from touching a dead body. So they went to Moses and Aaron that day and 7said to Moses, "We are unclean because of touching a dead body. But why should we be kept from offering gifts to the LORD at this appointed time? Why can't we join the other Israelites?"

8Moses said to them, "Wait, and I will find out what the LORD says about you."

9Then the LORD said to Moses, 10"Tell the Israelites this: 'If you or your descendants become unclean because of a dead body, or if you are away on a trip during the Passover, you must still celebrate the LORD's Passover. 11But celebrate it at twilight on the fourteenth day of the second month. Eat the lamb with bitter herbs and bread made without yeast. 12Don't leave any of it until the next morning or break any of its bones. When you celebrate the Passover, follow all the rules. 13Anyone who is clean and is not away on a trip but does not eat the Passover must be cut off from the people. That person did not give an offering to the LORD at the appointed time and must be punished for the sin.

14"'Foreigners among you may celebrate the LORD's Passover, but they must follow all the rules. You must have the same rules for foreigners as you have for yourselves.'"

The Cloud Above the Tent

15On the day the Holy Tent, the Tent of the Agreement, was set up, a cloud covered it. From dusk until dawn the cloud above the Tent looked like fire. 16The cloud stayed above the Tent, and at night it looked like fire. 17When the cloud moved from its place over the Tent, the Israelites moved, and wherever the cloud stopped, the Israelites camped. 18So the Israelites moved at the LORD's command, and they camped at his command. While the cloud stayed over the Tent, they remained camped. 19Sometimes the cloud stayed over the Tent for a long time, but the Israelites obeyed the LORD and did not move. 20Sometimes the cloud was over it only a few days. At the LORD's command the people camped, and at his command they moved. 21Sometimes the cloud stayed only from dusk until dawn; when the cloud lifted the next morning, the people moved. When the cloud lifted, day or night, the people moved. 22The cloud might stay over the Tent for two days, a month, or a year. As long as it stayed, the people camped, but when it lifted, they moved. 23At the LORD's command the people camped, and at his command they moved. They obeyed the LORD's order that he commanded through Moses.

The Silver Trumpets

10 The LORD said to Moses, 2"Make two trumpets of hammered silver, and use them to call the people together and to march out of camp. 3When both trumpets are blown, the people should gather before you at the entrance to the Meeting Tent. 4If you blow only one trumpet, the leaders, the heads of the family groups of Israel, should meet before you. 5When you loudly blow the trumpets, the tribes camping on the east should move. 6When you loudly blow them again, the tribes camping on the south should move; the loud sound will tell them to move. 7When you want to gather the people, blow the trumpets, but don't blow them as loudly.

8"Aaron's sons, the priests, should blow the trumpets. This is a law for you and your descendants from now on. 9When you are fighting an enemy who attacks you in your own land, blow the trumpets loudly. The LORD your God will take notice of you and will save you from your enemies. 10Also blow your trumpets at happy times and during your feasts and at New Moon festivals. Blow them over your burnt offerings and fellowship offerings, because they will help you remember your God. I am the LORD your God."

The Israelites Move Camp

11The cloud lifted from the Tent of the Agreement on the twentieth day of the second month of the second year. 12So the Israelites moved from

8:26 Clean & Unclean: Psalm 51:2

the Desert of Sinai and continued until the cloud stopped in the Desert of Paran. 13This was their first time to move, and they did it as the LORD had commanded Moses.

14The divisions from the camp of Judah moved first under their flag. Nahshon son of Amminadab was the commander. 15Nethanel son of Zuar was over the division of the tribe of Issachar. 16Eliab son of Helon was over the division of the tribe of Zebulun. 17Then the Holy Tent was taken down, and the Gershonites and Merarites, who carried it, moved next.

18Then came the divisions from the camp of Reuben under their flag, and Elizur son of Shedeur was the commander. 19Shelumiel son of Zurishaddai was over the division of the tribe of Simeon. 20Eliasaph son of Deuel was over the division of the tribe of Gad. 21Then came the Kohathites, who carried the holy things; the Holy Tent was to be set up before they arrived.

22Next came the divisions from the camp of Ephraim under their flag, and Elishama son of Ammihud was the commander. 23Gamaliel son of Pedahzur was over the division of the tribe of Manasseh, 24and Abidan son of Gideoni was over the division of the tribe of Benjamin.

25The last ones were the rear guard for all the tribes. These were the divisions from the camp of Dan under their flag, and Ahiezer son of Ammishaddai was the commander. 26Pagiel son of Ocran was over the division of the tribe of Asher; 27Ahira son of Enan was over the division of the tribe of Naphtali. 28This was the order the Israelite divisions marched in when they moved.

29Hobab was the son of Reuel the Midianite, who was Moses' father-in-law. Moses said to Hobab, "We are moving to the land the LORD promised to give us. Come with us and we will be good to you, because the LORD has promised good things to Israel."

30But Hobab answered, "No, I will not go. I will go back to my own land where I was born."

31But Moses said, "Please don't leave us. You know where we can camp in the desert, and you can be our guide. 32Come with us. We will share with you all the good things the LORD gives us." 33So they left the mountain of the LORD and traveled for three days. The Ark of the LORD's Agreement went in front of the people for those three days, as they looked for a place to camp. 34The LORD's cloud was over them during the day when they left their camp.

35When the Ark left the camp, Moses said,
"Rise up, LORD!
Scatter your enemies:
make those who hate you run from you."
36And when the Ark was set down, Moses said,
"Return, LORD,
to the thousands of people of Israel."

Fire from the Lord

11 Now the people complained to the LORD about their troubles, and when he heard them, he became angry. Then fire from the LORD burned among the people at the edge of the camp. 2The people cried out to Moses, and when he prayed to the LORD, the fire stopped burning. 3So that place was called Taberah, because the LORD's fire had burned among them.

Seventy Older Leaders Help Moses

4Some troublemakers among them wanted better food, and soon all the Israelites began complaining. They said, "We want meat! 5We remember the fish we ate for free in Egypt. We also had cucumbers, melons, leeks, onions, and garlic. 6But now we have lost our appetite; we never see anything but this manna!"

7The manna was like small white seeds. 8The people would go to gather it, and then grind it in handmills, or crush it between stones. After they cooked it in a pot or made cakes with it, it tasted like bread baked with olive oil. 9When the dew fell on the camp each night, so did the manna.

10Moses heard every family crying as they stood in the entrances of their tents. Then the LORD became very angry, and Moses got upset. 11He asked the LORD, "Why have you brought me, your servant, this trouble? What have I done wrong that you made me responsible for all these people? 12I am not the father of all these people, and I didn't give birth to them. So why do you make me carry them to the land you promised to our ancestors? Must I carry them in my arms as a nurse carries a baby? 13Where can I get meat for all these people? They keep crying to me, 'We want meat!' 14I can't take care of all these people alone. It is too much for me. 15If you are going to continue doing this to me, then kill me now. If you care about me, put me to death, and then I won't have any more troubles."

16The LORD said to Moses, "Bring me seventy of Israel's older leaders, men that you know are leaders

10:29 *Reuel the Midianite.* Also called Jethro.
10:36 Ark of the Agreement: Numbers 14:44
11:3 *Taberah.* This name means "burning."
11:6 *manna.* Manna is a Hebrew word which means "What is it?" It is described in Numbers 11:7 but is like nothing we know today. Many people try to associate it with a natural phenomenon in the desert, but it is more likely that the manna was a miraculous gift from God.

SARAH

GENESIS 17:15,16

How does the story of Sarah point forward to the gospel? How is Sarah a model for Christian women?

The story of Sarah should be set in the context of God's promise to make Abraham into a great nation (Genesis 12:2), to give him a vast number of descendants (Genesis 13:16; 15:5; 16:10; 17:20) and to cause kings to come from him (Genesis 17:6). Sarah herself receives a similar set of promises. She would be "the mother of many nations," and "kings of nations" would come from her as well (Genesis 17:16). When God made these promises he also changed her name (from Sarai) thus indicating a new beginning in her relationship with him (Genesis 17:15).

The first step in the fulfillment of these promises was the birth of a son. The problem was that Sarah was unable to have children (Genesis 11:30, 16:1). Recognizing that it was impossible to have a child herself, Sarah suggested to Abraham that he have sexual relations with her slave girl, Hagar (Genesis 16:2). This was a common practice in the ancient world. By this means the barren wife could provide her husband with a son through the slave and so keep the family line from dying out (Genesis 16:2).

But Sarah and Abraham had to learn that God could do the impossible. The promise of descendants would not come through human strategies. It would be accomplished by a miracle. This point is made clear in Genesis 17. After the incident with Hagar, God explained to Abraham that the promised son must be born through Sarah. God repeated the promise that Abraham would be the father of many nations (Genesis 17:4) and to remove any doubt about Sarah's role in this, he promised that "Sarah your wife will have a son" (Genesis 17:19). By the time God made this promise, Sarah was not only still barren but, at ninety, well past the age of childbearing (Genesis 17:17; 18:11,12). For Sarah to bear a child, God had to bring life to her dead womb. So the birth of Isaac (Genesis 21:1–3) was an act of salvation, a partial reversal of the curse of death that haunts humanity since the Fall.

Certainly the New Testament writers understood the birth of Isaac as the rejuvenation of Sarah's dead womb. In Romans 4 Paul discusses Abraham's faith in God's promise to make him the father of many nations (Romans 4:18). Specifically, Abraham believed that he would be a father even though Sarah "could not have children" (literally, "Sarah's womb was *dead*") (Romans 4:19). In believing that God could do this, Abraham trusted in "the God who gives life to the dead and who creates something out of nothing" (Romans 4:17). The same interpretation of Sarah's experience undergirds Hebrews 11:11, 12.

Therefore, the New Testament writers understand the reversal of Sarah's barrenness as a demonstration of God's resurrection power and as a foreshadowing of the much greater transformation of death into life that occurred when God raised Jesus from the dead (Romans 4:25).

In Galatians 4, Sarah is used to illustrate a different point. Here Paul picks up on the contrast between Hagar's role as a slave and Sarah's status as a free woman. Hagar is like the agreement that God made with Israel at Mount Sinai when he gave them the law. The Jews — those under the law — are regarded as the children of Hagar because they, like her, are slaves. In the case of the Jews, they are slaves to the law (Galatians 4:24, 25). Christians, on the other hand, are regarded as children of the free woman Sarah because they are free from the law. In addition, Paul compares Christians to Isaac, the child of the promise through Sarah (Galatians 4:28). Like Isaac they are heirs to all the promises God gave to Abraham (Galatians 4:30, 31; see also 3:14).

The Bible, therefore, presents Sarah as the mother of a great nation: the people of God. Her descendants were first the Israelites and then Christians, who through Christ are the spiritual descendants of Abraham and Sarah (Galatians 4:21–28). Furthermore, she is mother of many kings. This is fulfilled first in David and his descendants, but most completely fulfilled in David's greatest descendant, Jesus Christ, who rules at God's right hand (Acts 2:32, 33).

There is only one clear instance where the New Testament presents Sarah as a model for Christian behavior. First Peter 3 argues that a woman's beauty comes from within her — "a gentle and quiet spirit" — and not from outward appearances (1 Peter 3:1–4). Specifically, the writer focuses on a woman's willingness to yield to her husband and offers Sarah as an illustration of this virtue. This is a particularly striking choice since Genesis emphasizes Sarah's physical beauty (Genesis 12:11, 14). Nonetheless, Peter praises Sarah's obedience to her husband, which he deduces from the fact that she referred to Abraham as "master" (1 Peter 3:6, citing Genesis 18:12, where the word translated "husband" can also mean "master").

Sarah: For additional scriptures on this topic go to Genesis 11:30.

Obedience

Genesis 22

What should we obey? Can we obey? Will we obey? What does obedience gain?

The Bible draws our attention not only to the reality of God, but also to the way he demands and deserves to be the central reference point of our lives. When Adam and Eve ate from "the tree which gives the knowledge of good and evil" (Genesis 2:17; 3:6), they took it upon themselves to define right and wrong, a right the Bible reserves for God alone (Genesis 3:5, 22).

Obedience to God, on the other hand, is guiding and submitting our conduct to God's standards, rather than our own. We study the nature of obedience in the hope that it will help us avoid the failures and repeat the victories of people of God in the past.

Abraham's binding of his son Isaac in Genesis 22 serves as a good model of obedience for several reasons. First, Abraham occupies a prominent place in the Bible's story of salvation, functioning as something of a prototype for all believers in God (see Galatians 3:6–9; John 8:39–40). Second, the story illustrates the intimate connection between trust and obedience, between "faith" and "works." Finally, the New Testament (Hebrews 11:17–19; James 2:21–24) presents this story as an example to Christians.

What, then, is the nature of obedience? First, human obedience must always be to the revealed will of God. We can obey only what we've understood to be God's communication to us.

God made his intentions known to Abraham with a command in Genesis 22:2: "Take your only son, Isaac, the son you love, and go to the land of Moriah. Kill him there and offer him as a whole burnt offering. . . ." Abraham, unaware that this command was a "test" (verse 1), might have legitimately questioned its rationality and uprightness: why sacrifice the very child he received through God's promise (Genesis 21:1–7)? But in the end, these possible questions, which stood outside the realm of his own understanding, did not deter him from obeying (22:9–10). Abraham is commended because he humbly submitted to what he held to be the word of God.

The rest of the Bible also makes it clear that obedience is recognizing God's revealed word and yielding our minds and wills to it. For the people of Israel, obedience meant following the Book of the Agreement (Exodus 24:7; 2 Kings 23:2–3), God's law (Ezra 7:26; Psalm 119:106), and God's prophets (Jeremiah 26:13; 2 Chronicles 20:20). For Christians, it means obeying the truth of the Good News (2 Corinthians 9:13; 2 Thessalonians 1:8), the commands of Jesus Christ (Matthew 7:24; John 14:15, 23), the teaching of his apostles (Matthew 28:20; 1 Thessalonians 3:8), and the voice of his Holy Spirit (Acts 13:2–3; Galatians 5:16). It is, in fact, walking in the Spirit (Romans 8:4) and being filled with the Spirit (Ephesians 5:18).

Second, human obedience is possible only in the context of a faith-relationship with God. We can obey only when we savingly know and trust the one we are obeying.

The test of Abraham's obedience at Moriah was really a test of his "faith" (Genesis 22:1). After he obeyed, the angel of the Lord said, "Now I can see that you trust God" (vv. 8, 12). The Book of Hebrews shows how Abraham's faith made his obedience possible: Abraham was ready to offer Isaac because he believed that God could raise the dead (11:19). If this trust in God were absent, it is not difficult to imagine Abraham failing to obey. But as it turned out, "Abraham's faith and the things he did worked together" (James 2:22).

The rest of the Bible confirms that faith in God must be firmly in place before true obedience can come about. Obedience is not the means of securing God's favor; it is the grateful response to his favor, which is seen and received by believing in him (Romans 1:5; Acts 6:7).

Prior to having the desire and power to obey, which are granted only by God (Ezekiel 11:19–20; Philippians 2:13), the Christian must first trust Jesus Christ and possess his empowering Holy Spirit (John 14:15–17; 15:5; Acts 5:31–32; Romans 15:18–19; 1 Peter 1:2; 1 John 3:23–24).

Third, human obedience is honored and blessed by God. We understand the meaning of our obedience better when we know what it means to God.

God responds to Abraham's obedience at Moriah by reaffirming his promises: "I will surely bless you. . . . Through your descendants all the nations on the earth will be blessed, because you obeyed me" (Genesis 22:17–18). These words express God's delight in obedience, his desire to reward obedience, and his plan to use these rewards to bring humankind closer to him.

Obedience: For additional scriptures on this topic go to Genesis 2:16–17.

among the people. Bring them to the Meeting Tent,
and have them stand there with you. 17I will come
down and speak with you there. I will take some of
the Spirit that is in you, and I will give it to them.
They will help you care for the people so that you
will not have to care for them alone.

18"Tell the people this: 'Make yourselves holy
for tomorrow, and you will eat meat. You cried to
the LORD, "We want meat! We were better off in
Egypt!" So now the LORD will give you meat to eat.
19You will eat it not for just one, two, five, ten, or
even twenty days, 20but you will eat that meat for
a whole month. You will eat it until it comes out
your nose, and you will grow to hate it. This is
because you have rejected the LORD, who is with
you. You have cried to him, saying, "Why did we
ever leave Egypt?"' "

21Moses said, "LORD, here are six hundred thousand people standing around me, and you say, 'I
will give them enough meat to eat for a month!'
22If we killed all the flocks and herds, that would
not be enough. If we caught all the fish in the sea,
that would not be enough."

23But the LORD said to Moses, "Do you think I'm
weak? Now you will see if I can do what I say."

24So Moses went out to the people and told them
what the LORD had said. He gathered seventy of the
older leaders together and had them stand around
the Tent. 25Then the LORD came down in the cloud
and spoke to Moses. The LORD took some of the
Spirit Moses had, and he gave it to the seventy
leaders. With the Spirit in them, they prophesied,
but just that one time.

26Two men named Eldad and Medad were also
listed as leaders, but they did not go to the Tent.
They stayed in the camp, but the Spirit was also
given to them, and they prophesied in the camp.
27A young man ran to Moses and said, "Eldad and
Medad are prophesying in the camp."

28Joshua son of Nun said, "Moses, my master,
stop them!" (Ever since he was a young boy,
Joshua had been Moses' assistant.)

29But Moses answered, "Are you jealous for me?
I wish all the LORD's people could prophesy. I wish
the LORD would give his Spirit to all of them!"
30Then Moses and the leaders of Israel went back
to the camp.

The Lord Sends Quail

31The LORD sent a strong wind from the sea, and
it blew quail into the area all around the camp. The
quail were about three feet deep on the ground,
and there were quail a day's walk in any direction.
32The people went out and gathered quail all that
day, that night, and the next day. Everyone gathered at least sixty bushels, and they spread them
around the camp. 33But the LORD became very
angry, and he gave the people a terrible sickness
that came while the meat was still in their mouths.
34So the people named that place Kibroth Hattaavah, because there they buried those who wanted
other food.

35From Kibroth Hattaavah the people went to
stay at Hazeroth.

Miriam and Aaron Speak Against Moses

12 Miriam and Aaron began to talk against
Moses because of his Cushite wife (he had
married a Cushite). 2They said, "Is Moses the only
one the LORD speaks through? Doesn't he also
speak through us?" And the LORD heard this.

3(Now Moses was very humble. He was the least
proud person on earth.)

4So the LORD suddenly spoke to Moses, Aaron,
and Miriam and said, "All three of you come to the
Meeting Tent." So they went. 5The LORD came
down in a pillar of cloud and stood at the entrance to
the Tent. He called to Aaron and Miriam, and they
both came near. 6He said, "Listen to my words:

When a prophet is among you,
I, the LORD, will show myself to him in
visions;
I will speak to him in dreams.
7But this is not true with my servant Moses.
I trust him to lead all my people.
8I speak face to face with him—
clearly, not with hidden meanings.
He has even seen the form of the LORD.
You should be afraid
to speak against my servant Moses."

9The LORD was very angry with them, and he left.
10When the cloud lifted from the Tent and Aaron
turned toward Miriam, she was as white as snow;
she had a skin disease. 11Aaron said to Moses,
"Please, my master, forgive us for our foolish sin.
12Don't let her be like a baby who is born dead.
(Sometimes a baby is born with half of its flesh
eaten away.)"

13So Moses cried out to the LORD, "God, please
heal her!"

14The LORD answered Moses, "If her father had
spit in her face, she would have been shamed for
seven days, so put her outside the camp for seven
days. After that, she may come back." 15So Miriam
was put outside of the camp for seven days, and

11:34 *Kibroth Hattaavah.* This name in Hebrew means "graves of wanting."

12:2 Spiritual Gifts: Judges 3:10

12:6 Dreams: 1 Kings 3:5–15

12:8 Prophetic Symbolism: Numbers 24:2–4

the people did not move on until she came back. 16After that, the people left Hazeroth and camped in the Desert of Paran.

The Spies Explore Canaan

13 The LORD said to Moses, 2"Send men to explore the land of Canaan, which I will give to the Israelites. Send one leader from each tribe."

3So Moses obeyed the LORD's command and sent the Israelite leaders out from the Desert of Paran. 4These are their names: from the tribe of Reuben, Shammua son of Zaccur; 5from the tribe of Simeon, Shaphat son of Hori; 6from the tribe of Judah, Caleb son of Jephunneh; 7from the tribe of Issachar, Igal son of Joseph; 8from the tribe of Ephraim, Hoshea son of Nun; 9from the tribe of Benjamin, Palti son of Raphu; 10from the tribe of Zebulun, Gaddiel son of Sodi; 11from the tribe of Manasseh (a tribe of Joseph), Gaddi son of Susi; 12from the tribe of Dan, Ammiel son of Gemalli; 13from the tribe of Asher, Sethur son of Michael; 14from the tribe of Naphtali, Nahbi son of Vophsi; 15from the tribe of Gad, Geuel son of Maki.

16These are the names of the men Moses sent to explore the land. (Moses gave Hoshea son of Nun the new name Joshua.)

17Moses sent them to explore Canaan and said, "Go through southern Canaan and then into the mountains. 18See what the land looks like. Are the people who live there strong or weak? Are there a few or many? 19What kind of land do they live in? Is it good or bad? What about the towns they live in—are they open like camps, or do they have walls? 20What about the soil? Is it fertile or poor? Are there trees there? Try to bring back some of the fruit from that land." (It was the season for the first grapes.)

21So they went up and explored the land, from the Desert of Zin all the way to Rehob by Lebo Hamath. 22They went through the southern area to Hebron, where Ahiman, Sheshai, and Talmai, the descendants of Anak lived. (The city of Hebron had been built seven years before Zoan in Egypt.) 23In the Valley of Eshcol, they cut off a branch of a grapevine that had one bunch of grapes on it and carried that branch on a pole between two of them. They also got some pomegranates and figs. 24That place was called the Valley of Eshcol, because the Israelites cut off the bunch of grapes there. 25After forty days of exploring the land, the men returned to the camp.

26They came back to Moses and Aaron and all the Israelites at Kadesh, in the Desert of Paran. The men reported to them and showed everybody the fruit from the land. 27They told Moses, "We went to the land where you sent us, and it is a fertile land! Here is some of its fruit. 28But the people who live there are strong. Their cities are walled and very large. We even saw some Anakites there. 29The Amalekites live in the southern area; the Hittites, Jebusites, and Amorites live in the mountains; and the Canaanites live near the sea and along the Jordan River."

30Then Caleb told the people near Moses to be quiet, and he said, "We should certainly go up and take the land for ourselves. We can certainly do it."

31But the men who had gone with him said, "We can't attack those people; they are stronger than we are." 32And those men gave the Israelites a bad report about the land they explored, saying, "The land that we explored is too large to conquer. All the people we saw are very tall. 33We saw the Nephilim people there. (The Anakites come from the Nephilim people.) We felt like grasshoppers, and we looked like grasshoppers to them."

The People Complain Again

14 That night all the people in the camp began crying loudly. 2All the Israelites complained against Moses and Aaron, and all the people said to them, "We wish we had died in Egypt or in this desert. 3Why is the LORD bringing us to this land to be killed with swords? Our wives and children will be taken away. We would be better off going back to Egypt." 4They said to each other, "Let's choose a leader and go back to Egypt."

5Then Moses and Aaron bowed facedown in front of all the Israelites gathered there. 6Joshua son of Nun and Caleb son of Jephunneh, who had explored the land, tore their clothes. 7They said to all of the Israelites, "The land we explored is very good. 8If the LORD is pleased with us, he will lead us into that land and give us that fertile land. 9Don't turn against the LORD! Don't be afraid of the people in that land! We will chew them up. They have no protection, but the LORD is with us. So don't be afraid of them."

10Then all the people talked about killing them with stones. But the glory of the LORD appeared at the Meeting Tent to all the Israelites. 11The LORD said to Moses, "How long will these people ignore me? How long will they not believe me in spite of the miracles I have done among them? 12I will

---

13:24 *Eshcol.* This name in Hebrew means "bunch."

13:28 *Anakites.* Anakites are a physically large, warlike tribe of whom the people of Israel are especially afraid.

13:33 *Nephilim.* We first hear about the Nephilim in Genesis 6:4, but they are only mentioned three times in the Bible. However, they are an unusually large and warlike people.

14:6 Joshua: Deuteronomy 1:38

give them a terrible sickness and get rid of them.
But I will make you into a great nation that will be
stronger than they are."
13Then Moses said to the LORD, "The Egyptians
will hear about it! You brought these people from
there by your great power, 14and the Egyptians
will tell this to those who live in this land. They
have already heard about you, LORD. They know
that you are with your people and that you were
seen face to face. They know that your cloud stays
over your people and that you lead your people
with that cloud during the day and with fire at
night. 15If you put these people to death all at once,
the nations who have heard about your power
will say, 16'The LORD was not able to bring them
into the land he promised them. So he killed them
in the desert.'
17"So show your strength now, Lord. Do what
you said: 18'The LORD doesn't become angry quickly,
but he has great love. He forgives sin and law
breaking. But the LORD never forgets to punish
guilty people. When parents sin, he will also punish their children, their grandchildren, their
great-grandchildren, and their great-great-grandchildren.' 19By your great love, forgive these people's sin, just as you have forgiven them from the
time they left Egypt until now."
20The LORD answered, "I have forgiven them as
you asked. 21But, as surely as I live and as surely as
my glory fills the whole earth, I make this promise:
22All these men saw my glory and the miracles I
did in Egypt and in the desert, but they disobeyed
me and tested me ten times. 23So not one of them
will see the land I promised to their ancestors. No
one who rejected me will see that land. 24But my
servant Caleb thinks differently and follows me
completely. So I will bring him into the land he
has already seen, and his children will own that
land. 25Since the Amalekites and the Canaanites
are living in the valleys, leave tomorrow and follow the desert road toward the Red Sea."

The Lord Punishes the People

26The LORD said to Moses and Aaron, 27"How
long will these evil people complain about me? I
have heard the grumbling and complaining of
these Israelites. 28So tell them, 'This is what the
LORD says. I heard what you said, and as surely as
I live, I will do those very things to you: 29You will
die in this desert. Every one of you who is twenty
years old or older and who was counted with the
people—all of you who complained against me—
will die. 30Not one of you will enter the land where
I promised you would live; only Caleb son of Jephunneh and Joshua son of Nun will go in. 31You said
that your children would be taken away, but I will
bring them into the land to enjoy what you
refused. 32As for you, you will die in this desert.
33Your children will be shepherds here for forty
years. Because you were not loyal, they will suffer
until you lie dead in the desert. 34For forty years
you will suffer for your sins—a year for each of the
forty days you explored the land. You will know
me as your enemy.' 35I, the LORD, have spoken,
and I will certainly do these things to all these evil
people who have come together against me. So
they will all die here in this desert."
36The men Moses had sent to explore the land
had returned and spread complaints among all the
people. They had given a bad report about the
land. 37The men who gave a very bad report died;
the LORD killed them with a terrible sickness.
38Only two of the men who explored the land did
not die—Joshua son of Nun and Caleb son of
Jephunneh.
39When Moses told these things to all the Israelites, they were very sad. 40Early the next morning
they started to go toward the top of the mountains,
saying, "We have sinned. We will go where the
LORD told us."
41But Moses said, "Why are you disobeying the
LORD's command? You will not win! 42Don't go,
because the LORD is not with you and you will be
beaten by your enemies. 43You will run into the
Amalekites and Canaanites, who will kill you with
swords. You have turned away from the LORD, so
the LORD will not be with you."
44But they were proud. They went toward the
top of the mountains, but Moses and the Ark of
the Agreement with the LORD did not leave the
camp. 45The Amalekites and the Canaanites
who lived in those mountains came down and
attacked the Israelites and beat them back all the
way to Hormah.

Rules About Sacrifices

15 The LORD said to Moses, 2"Speak to the Israelites and say to them, 'When you enter the
land that I am giving you as a home, 3give the
LORD offerings made by fire. These may be from
your herds or flocks, as a smell pleasing to the
LORD. These may be burnt offerings or sacrifices
for special promises, or as gifts to him, or as festival offerings. 4The one who brings the offering

14:24 Servant of the Lord: Deuteronomy 32:36
14:38 Perseverance: Hosea 12:6
14:44 Ark of the Agreement: Numbers 17:10
14:45 Apostasy: Numbers 16

shall also give the LORD a grain offering. It should be two quarts of fine flour mixed with one quart of olive oil. 5Each time you offer a lamb as a burnt offering or sacrifice, also prepare a quart of wine as a drink offering.

6"'If you are giving a male sheep, also prepare a grain offering of four quarts of fine flour mixed with one and one-fourth quarts of olive oil. 7Also prepare one and one-fourth quarts of wine as a drink offering. Its smell will be pleasing to the LORD.

8"'If you prepare a young bull as a burnt offering or sacrifice, whether it is for a special promise or a fellowship offering to the LORD, 9bring a grain offering with the bull. It should be six quarts of fine flour mixed with two quarts of olive oil. 10Also bring two quarts of wine as a drink offering. This offering is made by fire, and its smell will be pleasing to the LORD. 11Prepare each bull or male sheep, lamb or young goat this way. 12Do this for every one of the animals you bring.

13"'All citizens must do these things in this way, and the smell of their offerings by fire will be pleasing to the LORD. 14From now on if foreigners who live among you want to make offerings by fire so the smell will be pleasing to the LORD, they must offer them the same way you do. 15The law is the same for you and for foreigners, and it will be from now on; you and the foreigners are alike before the LORD. 16The teachings and rules are the same for you and for the foreigners among you.'"

17The LORD said to Moses, 18"Tell the Israelites: 'You are going to another land, where I am taking you. 19When you eat the food there, offer part of it to the LORD. 20Offer a loaf of bread from the first of your grain, which will be your offering from the threshing floor. 21From now on offer to the LORD the first part of your grain.

22"'Now what if you forget to obey any of these commands the LORD gave Moses? 23These are the LORD's commands given to you through Moses, which began the day the LORD gave them to you and will continue from now on. 24If the people forget to obey one of these commands, all the people must offer a young bull as a burnt offering, a smell pleasing to the LORD. By law you must also give the grain offering and the drink offering with it, and you must bring a male goat as a sin offering.

25"'The priest will remove that sin for all the Israelites so they will belong to the LORD. They are forgiven, because they didn't know they were sinning. For the wrong they did they brought offerings to the LORD, an offering by fire and a sin offering. 26So all of the people of Israel and the foreigners living among them will be forgiven. No one meant to do wrong.

27"'If just one person sins without meaning to, a year-old female goat must be brought for a sin offering. 28The priest will remove the sin of the person who sinned accidentally. He will remove it before the LORD, and the person will be forgiven. 29The same teaching is for everyone who sins accidentally—for those born Israelites and for foreigners living among you.

30"'But anyone who sins on purpose is against the LORD and must be cut off from the people, whether it is someone born among you or a foreigner.⚭ 31That person has turned against the LORD's word and has not obeyed his commands. Such a person must surely be cut off from the others. He is guilty.'"

A Man Worked on the Sabbath

32When the Israelites were still in the desert, they found a man gathering wood on the Sabbath day. 33Those who found him gathering wood brought him to Moses and Aaron and all the people. 34They held the man under guard, because they did not know what to do with him. 35Then the LORD said to Moses, "The man must surely die. All the people must kill him by throwing stones at him outside the camp." 36So all the people took him outside the camp and stoned him to death, as the LORD commanded Moses.⚭

The Tassels

37The LORD said to Moses, 38"Speak to the Israelites and tell them this: 'Tie several pieces of thread together and attach them to the corners of your clothes. Put a blue thread in each one of these tassels. Wear them from now on. 39You will have these tassels to look at to remind you of all the LORD's commands. Then you will obey them and not be disloyal by following what your bodies and eyes want. 40Then you will remember to obey all my commands, and you will be God's holy people. 41I am the LORD your God, who brought you out of Egypt to be your God. I am the LORD your God.'"

Korah, Dathan, Abiram, and On

16 Korah, Dathan, Abiram, and On turned against Moses. (Korah was the son of Izhar, the son of Kohath, the son of Levi; Dathan and Abiram were brothers, the sons of Eliab; and On was the son of Peleth; Dathan, Abiram, and On were from the tribe of Reuben.) 2These men gathered two hundred fifty other Israelite men, well-known leaders chosen by the community, and

⚭**15:30 Blasphemy:** 2 Kings 19:6

⚭**15:36 Capital Punishment:** Numbers 35:9–31

challenged Moses. 3They came as a group to speak to Moses and Aaron and said, "You have gone too far. All the people are holy, every one of them, and the LORD is among them. So why do you put yourselves above all the people of the LORD?"

4When Moses heard this, he bowed facedown. 5Then he said to Korah and all his followers: "Tomorrow morning the LORD will show who belongs to him. He will bring the one who is holy near to him; he will bring to himself the person he chooses. 6So Korah, you and all your followers do this: Get some pans for burning incense. 7Tomorrow put fire and incense in them and take them before the LORD. He will choose the man who is holy. You Levites have gone too far."

8Moses also said to Korah, "Listen, you Levites. 9The God of Israel has separated you from the rest of the Israelites. He brought you near to himself to do the work in the LORD's Holy Tent and to stand before all the Israelites and serve them. Isn't that enough? 10He has brought you and all your fellow Levites near to himself, yet now you want to be priests. 11You and your followers have joined together against the LORD. Your complaint is not against Aaron."

12Then Moses called Dathan and Abiram, the sons of Eliab, but they said, "We will not come! 13You have brought us out of a fertile land to this desert to kill us, and now you want to order us around. 14You haven't brought us into a fertile land; you haven't given us any land with fields and vineyards. Will you put out the eyes of these men? No! We will not come!"

15Then Moses became very angry and said to the LORD, "Don't accept their gifts. I have not taken anything from them, not even a donkey, and I have not done wrong to any of them."

16Then Moses said to Korah, "You and all your followers must stand before the LORD tomorrow. And Aaron will stand there with you and them. 17Each of you must take your pan and put incense in it; present these two hundred fifty pans before the LORD. You and Aaron must also present your pans." 18So each man got his pan and put burning incense in it and stood with Moses and Aaron at the entrance to the Meeting Tent. 19Korah gathered all his followers who were against Moses and Aaron, and they stood at the entrance to the Meeting Tent. Then the glory of the LORD appeared to everyone.

20The LORD said to Moses and Aaron, 21"Move away from these men so I can destroy them quickly."

22But Moses and Aaron bowed facedown and cried out, "God, you are the God over the spirits of all people. Please don't be angry with this whole group. Only one man has really sinned."

23Then the LORD said to Moses, 24"Tell everyone to move away from the tents of Korah, Dathan, and Abiram."

25Moses stood and went to Dathan and Abiram; the older leaders of Israel followed him. 26Moses warned the people, "Move away from the tents of these evil men! Don't touch anything of theirs, or you will be destroyed because of their sins." 27So they moved away from the tents of Korah, Dathan, and Abiram. Dathan and Abiram were standing outside their tents with their wives, children, and little babies.

28Then Moses said, "Now you will know that the LORD has sent me to do all these things; it was not my idea. 29If these men die a normal death—the way men usually die—then the LORD did not really send me. 30But if the LORD does something new, you will know they have insulted the LORD. The ground will open and swallow them. They will be buried alive and will go to the place of the dead, and everything that belongs to them will go with them."

31When Moses finished saying these things, the ground under the men split open. 32The earth opened and swallowed them and all their families. All Korah's men and everything they owned went down. 33They were buried alive, going to the place of the dead, and everything they owned went with them. Then the earth covered them. They died and were gone from the community. 34The people of Israel around them heard their screams and ran away, saying, "The earth will swallow us, too!"

35Then a fire came down from the LORD and destroyed the two hundred fifty men who had presented the incense.

36The LORD said to Moses, 37"Tell Eleazar son of Aaron, the priest, to take all the incense pans out of the fire. Have him scatter the coals a long distance away. But the incense pans are still holy. 38Take the pans of these men who sinned and lost their lives, and hammer them into flat sheets that will be used to cover the altar. They are holy, because they were presented to the LORD, and they will be a sign to the Israelites."

39So Eleazar the priest gathered all the bronze pans that had been brought by the men who were burned up. He had the pans hammered into flat sheets to put on the altar, 40as the LORD had commanded him through Moses. These

16:14 Rebellion: Numbers 20:1–13

sheets were to remind the Israelites that only descendants of Aaron should burn incense before the LORD. Anyone else would die like Korah and his followers.

Aaron Saves the People

41The next day all the Israelites complained against Moses and Aaron and said, "You have killed the LORD's people."

42When the people gathered to complain against Moses and Aaron, they turned toward the Meeting Tent, and the cloud covered it. The glory of the LORD appeared. 43Then Moses and Aaron went in front of the Meeting Tent.

44The LORD said to Moses, 45"Move away from these people so I can destroy them quickly." So Moses and Aaron bowed facedown.

46Then Moses said to Aaron, "Get your pan, and put fire from the altar and incense in it. Hurry to the people and remove their sin. The LORD is angry with them; the sickness has already started." 47So Aaron did as Moses said. He ran to the middle of the people, where the sickness had already started among them. So Aaron offered the incense to remove their sin. 48He stood between the dead and the living, and the sickness stopped there. 49But 14,700 people died from that sickness, in addition to those who died because of Korah. 50Then Aaron went back to Moses at the entrance to the Meeting Tent. The terrible sickness had been stopped.

Aaron's Walking Stick Buds

17 The LORD said to Moses, 2"Speak to the people of Israel and get twelve walking sticks from them—one from the leader of each tribe. Write the name of each man on his stick, and 3on the stick from Levi, write Aaron's name. There must be one stick for the head of each tribe. 4Put them in the Meeting Tent in front of the Ark of the Agreement, where I meet with you. 5I will choose one man whose walking stick will begin to grow leaves; in this way I will stop the Israelites from always complaining against you."

6So Moses spoke to the Israelites. Each of the twelve leaders gave him a walking stick—one from each tribe—and Aaron's walking stick was among them. 7Moses put them before the LORD in the Tent of the Agreement.

8The next day, when Moses entered the Tent, he saw that Aaron's stick (which stood for the family of Levi) had grown leaves. It had even budded, blossomed, and produced almonds. 9So Moses brought out to the Israelites all the walking sticks from the LORD's presence. They all looked, and each man took back his stick.

10Then the LORD said to Moses, "Put Aaron's walking stick back in front of the Ark of the Agreement. It will remind these people who are always turning against me to stop their complaining against me so they won't die." 11So Moses obeyed what the LORD commanded him.

12The people of Israel said to Moses, "We are going to die! We are destroyed. We are all destroyed! 13Anyone who even comes near the Holy Tent of the LORD will die. Will we all die?"

The Work of the Priests and Levites

18 The LORD said to Aaron, "You, your sons, and your family are now responsible for any wrongs done against the Holy Place; you and your sons are responsible for any wrongs done against the priests. 2Bring with you your fellow Levites from your tribe, and they will help you and your sons serve in the Tent of the Agreement. 3They are under your control, to do all the work that needs to be done in the Tent. But they must not go near the things in the Holy Place or near the altar. If they do, both you and they will die. 4They will join you in taking care of the Meeting Tent. They must do the work at the Tent, and no one else may come near you.

5"You must take care of the Holy Place and the altar so that I won't become angry with the Israelites again. 6I myself chose your fellow Levites from among the Israelites as a gift given for you to the LORD, to work at the Meeting Tent. 7But only you and your sons may serve as priests. Only you may serve at the altar or go behind the curtain. I am giving you this gift of serving as a priest, and anyone else who comes near the Holy Place will be put to death."

8Then the LORD said to Aaron, "I myself make you responsible for the offerings given to me. All the holy offerings that the Israelites give to me, I give to you and your sons as your share, your continual portion. 9Your share of the holy offerings is that part which is not burned. When the people bring me gifts as most holy offerings, whether they are grain or sin or penalty offerings, they will be set apart for you and your sons. 10You must eat the offering in a most holy place. Any male may eat it, but you must respect it as holy.

11"I also give you the offerings the Israelites present to me. I give these to you and your sons and

16:50 Apostasy: Philippians 3:18

17:2 *walking sticks.* These wooden sticks each represent a tribe. The stick which buds indicates which tribe God has chosen to be set aside to serve him. The living stick represents God's presence.

17:10 Ark of the Agreement: Deuteronomy 10:1–5

daughters as your continual share. Anyone in your family who is clean may eat it.

12"And I give you all the best olive oil and all the best new wine and grain. This is what the Israelites give to me, the LORD, from the first crops they harvest. 13When they bring to the LORD all the first things they harvest, they will be yours. Anyone in your family who is clean may eat these things.

14"Everything in Israel that is given to the LORD is yours. 15The first one born to any family, whether people or animals, will be offered to the LORD. And that will be yours. But you must make a payment for every firstborn child and every firstborn animal that is unclean. 16When they are one month old, you must make a payment for them of two ounces of silver, as set by the Holy Place measure.

17"But you must not make a payment for the firstborn ox or sheep or goat. Those animals are holy. Sprinkle their blood on the altar and burn their fat as an offering made by fire. The smell is pleasing to the LORD. 18But the meat will be yours, just as the breast that is presented and the right thigh will be yours. 19Anything the Israelites present as holy gifts I, the LORD, give to you, your sons and daughters as your continual portion. This is a lasting agreement of salt before the LORD for you and your children forever."

20The LORD also said to Aaron, "You will not inherit any of the land, and you will not own any land among the other people. I will be yours. Out of all the Israelites, only you will inherit me.

21"When the people of Israel give me a tenth of what they make, I will give that tenth to the Levites. This is their payment for the work they do serving at the Meeting Tent. 22But the other Israelites must never go near the Meeting Tent, or they will die for their sin. 23Only the Levites should work in the Meeting Tent and be responsible for any sins against it. This is a rule from now on. The Levites will not inherit any land among the other Israelites, 24but when the Israelites give a tenth of everything they make to me, I will give that tenth to the Levites as a reward. That is why I said about the Levites: 'They will not inherit any land among the Israelites.'"

25The LORD said to Moses, 26"Speak to the Levites and tell them: 'You will receive a tenth of everything the Israelites make, which I will give to you. But you must give a tenth of that back to the LORD. 27I will accept your offering just as much as I accept the offerings from others, who give new grain or new wine. 28In this way you will present an offering to the LORD as the other Israelites do. When you receive a tenth from the Israelites, you will give a tenth of that to Aaron, the priest, as the LORD's share. 29Choose the best and holiest part from what you are given as the portion you must give to the LORD.'

30"Say to the Levites: 'When you present the best, it will be accepted as much as the grain and wine from the other people. 31You and your families may eat all that is left anywhere, because it is your pay for your work in the Meeting Tent. 32And if you always give the best part to the LORD, you will never be guilty. If you do not sin against the holy offerings of the Israelites, you will not die.'"

The Offering for Cleansing

19 The LORD said to Moses and Aaron, 2"These are the teachings that the LORD commanded. Tell the Israelites to get a young red cow that does not have anything wrong with it and that has never been worked. 3Give the cow to Eleazar the priest; he will take it outside the camp and kill it. 4Then Eleazar the priest must put some of its blood on his finger and sprinkle it seven times toward the front of the Meeting Tent. 5The whole cow must be burned while he watches; the skin, the meat, the blood, and the intestines must all be burned. 6Then the priest must take a cedar stick, a hyssop branch, and a red string and throw them onto the burning cow. 7After the priest has washed himself and his clothes with water, he may come back into the camp, but he will be unclean until evening. 8The man who burns the cow must wash himself and his clothes in water; he will be unclean until evening.

9"Then someone who is clean will collect the ashes from the cow and put them in a clean place outside the camp. The Israelites will keep these ashes to use in the cleansing water, in a special ceremony to cleanse away sin. 10The man who collected the cow's ashes must wash his clothes and be unclean until evening. This is a lasting rule for the Israelites and for the foreigners among them.

11"Those who touch a dead person's body will be unclean for seven days. 12They must wash themselves with the cleansing water on the third day and on the seventh day, then they will be

18:19 *agreement of salt.* The meaning is not clear, but Leviticus 2:13 says, "Salt stands for your agreement with God that will last forever." Salt survives fire intact, and so it represents the fact that the Agreement lasts through time. See Thematic Article entitled "Agreement."

18:19 Salt: Judges 9:45

19 The ashes of the red cow were to be used in the cleansing water. This water was sprinkled on those who had become unclean by contact with a dead person, a human bone, or a grave to make them clean again. This outward cleansing pointed toward the deeper spiritual cleansing that would be accomplished for sinners by the blood of Christ (see Hebrews 9:13–14).

clean. But if they do not wash themselves on the third day and the seventh day, they cannot be clean. [13]If those who touch a dead person's body stay unclean and go to the LORD's Holy Tent, it becomes unclean; they must be cut off from Israel. If the cleansing water is not sprinkled on them, they are unclean and will stay unclean.

[14]"This is the teaching about someone who dies in a tent: Anyone in the tent or anyone who enters it will be unclean for seven days. [15]And every open jar or pot without a cover becomes unclean. [16]If anyone is outside and touches someone who was killed by a sword or who died a natural death, or if anyone touches a human bone or a grave, that person will be unclean for seven days.

[17]"So you must use the ashes from the burnt offering to make that person clean again. Pour fresh water over the ashes into a jar. [18]A clean person must take a hyssop branch and dip it into the water, and then he must sprinkle it over the tent and all its objects. He must also sprinkle the people who were there, as well as anyone who touched a bone, or the body of someone who was killed, or a dead person, or a grave. [19]The person who is clean must sprinkle this water on the unclean people on the third day and on the seventh day. On the seventh day they will become clean. They must wash their clothes and take a bath, and they will be clean that evening. [20]If any who are unclean do not become clean, they must be cut off from the community. Since they were not sprinkled with the cleansing water, they stay unclean, and they could make the LORD's Holy Tent unclean. [21]This is a lasting rule. Those who sprinkle the cleansing water must also wash their clothes, and anyone who touches the water will be unclean until evening. [22]Anything an unclean person touches becomes unclean, and whoever touches it will be unclean until evening."

Moses Disobeys God

20 In the first month all the people of Israel arrived at the Desert of Zin, and they stayed at Kadesh. There Miriam died and was buried. [2]There was no water for the people, so they came together against Moses and Aaron. [3]They argued with Moses and said, "We should have died in front of the LORD as our brothers did. [4]Why did you bring the LORD's people into this desert? Are we and our animals to die here? [5]Why did you bring us from Egypt to this terrible place? It has no grain, figs, grapevines, or pomegranates, and there's no water to drink!"

[6]So Moses and Aaron left the people and went to the entrance of the Meeting Tent. There they bowed facedown, and the glory of the LORD appeared to them. [7]The LORD said to Moses, [8]"Take your walking stick, and you and your brother Aaron should gather the people. Speak to that rock in front of them so that its water will flow from it. When you bring the water out from that rock, give it to the people and their animals."

[9]So Moses took the stick from in front of the LORD, as he had said. [10]Moses and Aaron gathered the people in front of the rock, and Moses said, "Now listen to me, you who turn against God! Do you want us to bring water out of this rock?" [11]Then Moses lifted his hand and hit the rock twice with his stick. Water began pouring out, and the people and their animals drank it.

[12]But the LORD said to Moses and Aaron, "Because you did not believe me, and because you did not honor me as holy before the people, you will not lead them into the land I will give them."

[13]These are the waters of Meribah, where the Israelites argued with the LORD and where he showed them he was holy.

Edom Will Not Let Israel Pass

[14]From Kadesh, Moses sent messengers to the king of Edom. He said, "Your brothers, the Israelites, say to you: You know about all the troubles we have had, [15]how our ancestors went down into Egypt and we lived there for many years. The people of Egypt were cruel to us and our ancestors, [16]but when we cried out to the LORD, he heard us and sent us an angel to bring us out of Egypt.

"Now we are here at Kadesh, a town on the edge of your land. [17]Please let us pass through your country. We will not touch any fields of grain or vineyards, and will not drink water from the wells. We will travel only along the king's road, not turning right or left until we have passed through your country."

[18]But the king of Edom answered: "You may not pass through here. If you try, I will come and meet you with swords."

[19]The Israelites answered: "We will go along the main road, and if we or our animals drink any of your water, we will pay for it. We only want to walk through. That's all."

20:3–5 Here the Israelites complain to Moses and Aaron about their difficult life in the desert. The psalms show us that it is appropriate to be honest with God about what is bothering us, but here the Israelites are complaining with an attitude that God cannot help them. They are simply mad at God and his servants Moses and Aaron. They should have come to God with their problems but have an open attitude that God can change their present difficult situation.

20:13 *Meribah.* This name in Hebrew means "argument."

20:13 Rebellion: Numbers 20:24

Blessing

Genesis 27:31–34

What does it mean for a parent to give his or her child a blessing? What are the consequences of a child not receiving parental blessing? What are the various aspects of giving/receiving a blessing?

All of us long to be accepted by others. While we may say out loud, "I don't care what other people think about me," on the inside we all yearn for intimacy and affection. This yearning is especially true in our relationships with our parents. Gaining or missing out on parental approval, or blessing, has a tremendous effect on us, even if it has been years since we have had any regular contact with them. In fact, what happens in our relationships with our parents can greatly affect all our present and future relationships, including our relationships with God.

For almost all children who miss out on their parents' blessing, at some level this lack of acceptance sets off a lifelong search. This search for the blessing is not just a modern-day phenomenon. It is actually centuries old. In fact, we can find a clear picture in the Old Testament of a person who missed out on his family's blessing. This person was a confused and angry man named Esau.

What was this blessing that Esau had waited for over the years? For sons or daughters in biblical times, receiving their father's blessing was a momentous event. This blessing gave these children a tremendous sense of being highly valued by their parents and even pictured a special future for them. At a specific time they would hear words of love and acceptance from their parents.

The story of Jacob's stealing the blessing that was to go to Esau is a familiar one.

With the help of his mother, Rebekah, Jacob deceived his father, Isaac, and tricked him into giving him the blessing reserved for the firstborn. In blessing Jacob, Isaac touched him and spoke a blessing to him aloud. He expressed his high regard for Jacob and told of a future that made Jacob the master over his brothers and the beneficiary of the promise to Abraham to rule the land in which they lived. He even helped Jacob achieve his blessing by sending him to the house of his uncle, Laban, to find a wife (Genesis 27: 22–29; 28:1–4).

When Esau returned from hunting and discovered that Jacob had stolen his blessing, he cried out bitterly: "Bless me—me, too, my father" (Genesis 27:34)! But it was too late. For a father in biblical times, once a blessing was spoken, it could not be taken back. In response to his pitiful cries, Esau did receive a blessing of sorts from his father (Genesis 27:39–40), but not the one he longed for.

Some aspects of this blessing were unique to that time; however, the *relationship elements* of this blessing are still true today. In Old Testament times, this blessing was primarily reserved for one special occasion. Parents today can decide to build these elements of blessing into their children's lives daily.

By examining the case of Jacob and Esau, we can see both the pattern of biblical blessing and the pain that results from the failure to receive parental blessing. If you are a parent, learning about the family blessing can help you provide your child or children with a protective tool. The best defense against a child's longing for imaginary acceptance is to provide him or her with true acceptance. By providing a child with true acceptance and affirmation at home, you can greatly reduce the likelihood that he or she will seek acceptance in the arms of a cult member or with someone in an immoral relationship. True acceptance radiates from the concept of the blessing.

There were four elements in Isaac's blessing of Jacob that form a definition of parental blessing. A family blessing begins with *meaningful touching.* It continues with a *spoken message of high value,* a message that pictures a *special future* for the individual being blessed, and one that is based on an *active commitment* to see the blessing come to pass.

While Old Testament blessings were based on a spiritual covenant with one nation and contained prophetic elements, the concept of blessing children continued on into the New Testament. We read in Mark 10:13–16 that Jesus took children up into his arms, put his hands on them, and blessed them. Because of what Jesus did for all people in dying for them, now every family and each family member can experience a blessing through God's Son.

While people may grow up without receiving the love and acceptance from parents that they long for, it is still possible for the devastating effects of not receiving a blessing to be reversed. For the Christian, healing begins with a knowledge that he or she is accepted by God because of his beloved Son (Ephesians 1:3–6). It is then extended from one believer to another as each fulfills Christ's commandment to love one another.

Blessing: For additional scriptures on this topic go to Deuteronomy 33:1–29.

OATH/VOW

GENESIS 28:20–22

What is the difference between a vow and an oath? Can we still make vows like Jacob's? Does Jesus forbid Christians to make any oath?

A vow is a promise to worship God in some particular way. An oath is a promise backed by a "conditional curse" upon oneself: "May God punish me terribly if I eat bread or anything else before the sun sets" (2 Samuel 3:35)! They are both special promises, but a vow is between a person and God, while an oath is between two people with God invited to enforce it.

In the Old Testament a vow was a voluntary promise to worship God, usually by offering a sacrifice above and beyond any regular obligation. For example, knowing that he was entirely dependent upon God for the outcome of his situation, Jacob prayed to God for help, and promised to worship him if he succeeded (Genesis 28:20–22). In another case, when the sailors realized that it was Jonah's God that had caused the great storm and the calm that followed, they promised to worship him (Jonah 1:16). It is permissible never to make a vow, but if one is made it must be kept (Leviticus 5:4; Deuteronomy 23:21–3; Ecclesiastes 5:1–7). Such is the obligation two people undertake when they exchange vows during the marriage ceremony.

The Nazirite vow (Numbers 6) involves dedication to the service of God with certain specific restrictions: (1) consume nothing made from grapes, (2) never cut one's hair, (3) have no contact with the dead. It was generally entered into voluntarily and for a certain period of time (Paul, in Acts 18:18), but in special cases people were dedicated from before birth by their parents, and remained under the vow for life (Samson, in Judges 13:4–5; Samuel, in 1 Samuel 1:11).

With regard to any vow: (1) it is necessary to know and respect God before our worship is acceptable to him (Hosea 6:6; Isaiah 19:21), and (2) we cannot use the system to force God to bless our plans (Jeremiah 11:13–15).

On the cross Jesus made and kept the vow to end all vows. (The italicized words are related to the Hebrew *Shalom,* completeness, often meaning completing or paying a vow.) The words of Psalm 22 call to mind Christ on the cross, and verse 25 says, "LORD, I praise you in the great meeting of your people; these worshipers will see me *do* what I promised." God accepted this ultimate self-sacrifice: "The LORD made his life a penalty offering, but he will still see his descendants and live a long life. He will *complete* the things the LORD wants him to do" (Isaiah 53:10). This was for our sake, in effect to pay all our vows: "The punishment, which *made us well,* was given to him, and we are healed because of his wounds" (Isaiah 53:5).

With regard to oaths, Christians can take oaths, but very cautiously. The Bible says we can take an oath in God's name (Deuteronomy 6:13; Joshua 23:7; Psalm 24:4; 63:11). Swearing "As surely as the LORD lives" is sanctioned in Jeremiah 4:2 and 12:16. God swears in his own name (Genesis 22:16; Hebrews 6:13). Jesus submitted to an oath (Matthew 26:63), and Paul calls God as his witness (Romans 1:9; 2 Corinthians 1:23; Galatians 1:20). Thus we are not afraid to swear in court with our hand on the Bible, first because we are simply acknowledging that God witnesses our promise to tell the truth (Exodus 22:11; 1 Kings 8:31–32), and second because we intend to tell the truth anyway: such an oath only emphasizes the obligation we already have as a Christian to tell the truth before God.

An oath is asking God to harm or kill you if you don't keep your word (2 Samuel 3:35). It is important to understand the seriousness of swearing in God's name. Like a hasty vow, a hasty oath can have dire consequences (Judges 21; Joshua 9; 2 Samuel 21:1–14). Swearing falsely in God's name shows lack of respect for God (Leviticus 19:12) and violates the third and ninth commandments (Exodus 20:7, 16).

In Jesus' day some people did not take oaths seriously. The Pharisees had set up a sort of sliding scale of truthfulness based on the relative value of the religious icon that was invoked (Matthew 23:16–22); this way they could take advantage of those who didn't know their system. They also tried to avoid swearing by God directly, thinking that they would not be as guilty when they did not keep their oath. That is why in Matthew 5:33–36 Jesus refutes their argument by saying that we should not swear by heaven, earth, Jerusalem, or the hair on our head; since God is sovereign, these things are under his control, not ours, and to swear by them is to swear by him. In order to avoid the deviousness of the Pharisees, in verse 37 Jesus says we should just tell the plain truth (see also James 5:12).

Oath/Vow: For additional scriptures on this topic go to Numbers 6.

[20]But he answered: "You may not pass through here."

Then the Edomites went out to meet the Israelites with a large and powerful army. [21]The Edomites refused to let them pass through their country, so the Israelites turned back.

Aaron Dies

[22]All the Israelites moved from Kadesh to Mount Hor, [23]near the border of Edom. There the LORD said to Moses and Aaron, [24]"Aaron will die. He will not enter the land that I'm giving to the Israelites, because you both acted against my command at the waters of Meribah. [25]Take Aaron and his son Eleazar up on Mount Hor, [26]and take off Aaron's special clothes and put them on his son Eleazar. Aaron will die there; he will join his ancestors."

[27]Moses obeyed the LORD's command. They climbed up Mount Hor, and all the people saw them go. [28]Moses took off Aaron's clothes and put them on Aaron's son Eleazar. Then Aaron died there on top of the mountain. Moses and Eleazar came back down the mountain, [29]and when all the people learned that Aaron was dead, everyone in Israel cried for him for thirty days.

War with the Canaanites

21 The Canaanite king of Arad lived in the southern area. When he heard that the Israelites were coming on the road to Atharim, he attacked them and captured some of them. [2]Then the Israelites made this promise to the LORD: "If you will help us defeat these people, we will completely destroy their cities." [3]The LORD listened to the Israelites, and he let them defeat the Canaanites. The Israelites completely destroyed the Canaanites and their cities, so the place was named Hormah.

The Bronze Snake

[4]The Israelites left Mount Hor and went on the road toward the Red Sea, in order to go around the country of Edom. But the people became impatient on the way [5]and grumbled at God and Moses. They said, "Why did you bring us out of Egypt to die in this desert? There is no bread and no water, and we hate this terrible food!"

[6]So the LORD sent them poisonous snakes; they bit the people, and many of the Israelites died. [7]The people came to Moses and said, "We sinned when we grumbled at you and the LORD. Pray that the LORD will take away these snakes." So Moses prayed for the people.

[8]The LORD said to Moses, "Make a bronze snake, and put it on a pole. When anyone who is bitten looks at it, that person will live." [9]So Moses made a bronze snake and put it on a pole. Then when a snake bit anyone, that person looked at the bronze snake and lived.

The Journey to Moab

[10]The Israelites went and camped at Oboth. [11]They went from Oboth to Iye Abarim, in the desert east of Moab. [12]From there they went and camped in the Zered Valley. [13]From there they went and camped across the Arnon, in the desert just inside the Amorite country. The Arnon is the border between the Moabites and the Amorites. [14]That is why the Book of the Wars of the LORD says:

"... and Waheb in Suphah, and the ravines,
the Arnon, [15]and the slopes of the ravines
that lead to the settlement of Ar.
These places are at the border of Moab."

[16]The Israelites went from there to Beer; a well is there where the Lord said to Moses, "Gather the people and I will give them water."

[17]Then the Israelites sang this song:

"Pour out water, well!
Sing about it.
[18]Princes dug this well.
Important men made it.
With their scepters and poles, they dug it."

The people went from the desert to Mattanah. [19]From Mattanah they went to Nahaliel and on to Bamoth. [20]From Bamoth they went to the valley of Moab where the top of Mount Pisgah looks over the desert.

Israel Kills Sihon and Og

[21]The Israelites sent messengers to Sihon, king of the Amorites, saying, [22]"Let us pass through your country. We will not go through any fields of grain or vineyards, or drink water from the wells. We will travel only along the king's road until we have passed through your country."

[23]But King Sihon would not let the Israelites pass through his country. He gathered his whole army together, and they marched out to meet Israel in the desert. At Jahaz they fought the Israelites. [24]Israel killed the king and captured his land from the Arnon River to the Jabbok River. They took the land as far as the Ammonite border, which was strongly defended. [25]Israel captured all the Amorite cities and lived in them, taking Heshbon and all

20:24 Rebellion: Deuteronomy 31:27
20:29 Mountain: Numbers 27:12–14

21:3 *Hormah.* This name in Hebrew means "completely destroyed."
21:6 Mediator: Numbers 3

the towns around it. 26 Heshbon was the city where
Sihon, the Amorite king, lived. In the past he had
fought with the king of Moab and had taken all the
land as far as the Arnon.

27 That is why the poets say:
"Come to Heshbon
  and rebuild it;
  rebuild Sihon's city.
28 A fire began in Heshbon;
  flames came from Sihon's city.
It destroyed Ar in Moab,
  and it burned the Arnon highlands.
29 How terrible for you, Moab!
  The people of Chemosh are ruined.
His sons ran away
  and his daughters were captured
  by Sihon, king of the Amorites.
30 But we defeated those Amorites.
  We ruined their towns from Heshbon to
    Dibon,
  and we destroyed them as far as Nophah,
    near Medeba."

31 So Israel lived in the land of the Amorites.

32 After Moses sent spies to the town of Jazer,
they captured the towns around it, forcing out the
Amorites who lived there.

33 Then the Israelites went up the road toward
Bashan. Og king of Bashan and his whole army
marched out to meet the Israelites, and they
fought at Edrei.

34 The Lord said to Moses, "Don't be afraid of
him. I will hand him, his whole army, and his
land over to you. Do to him what you did to
Sihon, the Amorite king who lived in Heshbon."

35 So the Israelites killed Og and his sons and all
his army; no one was left alive. And they took his
land.

Balak Sends for Balaam

22 Then the people of Israel went to the plains
of Moab, and they camped near the Jordan
River across from Jericho.

2 Balak son of Zippor saw everything the Israelites had done to the Amorites. 3 And Moab was
scared of so many Israelites; truly, Moab was terrified by them.

4 The Moabites said to the older leaders of Midian, "These people will take everything around us
like an ox eating grass."

Balak son of Zippor was the king of Moab at this
time. 5 He sent messengers to Balaam son of Beor
at Pethor, near the Euphrates River in his native
land. Balak said, "A nation has come out of Egypt
that covers the land. They have camped next to
me, 6 and they are too powerful for me. So come
and put a curse on them. Maybe then I can defeat
them and make them leave the area. I know that
if you bless someone, the blessings happen, and if
you put a curse on someone, it happens."

7 The older leaders of Moab and Midian went
with payment in their hands. When they found
Balaam, they told him what Balak had said.

8 Balaam said to them, "Stay here for the night,
and I will tell you what the Lord tells me." So the
Moabite leaders stayed with him.

9 God came to Balaam and asked, "Who are these
men with you?"

10 Balaam said to God, "The king of Moab, Balak
son of Zippor, sent them to me with this message:
11 'A nation has come out of Egypt that covers the
land. So come and put a curse on them, and maybe
I can fight them and force them out of my land.'"

12 But God said to Balaam, "Do not go with them.
Don't put a curse on those people, because I have
blessed them."

13 The next morning Balaam awoke and said to
Balak's leaders, "Go back to your own country; the
Lord has refused to let me go with you."

14 So the Moabite leaders went back to Balak and
said, "Balaam refused to come with us."

15 So Balak sent other leaders—this time there
were more of them, and they were more important. 16 They went to Balaam and said, "Balak son of
Zippor says this: Please don't let anything stop you
from coming to me. 17 I will pay you very well, and
I will do what you say. Come and put a curse on
these people for me."

18 But Balaam answered Balak's servants, "King
Balak could give me his palace full of silver and
gold, but I cannot disobey the Lord my God in anything, great or small. 19 You stay here tonight as the
other men did, and I will find out what more the
Lord tells me."

20 That night God came to Balaam and said,
"These men have come to ask you to go with them.
Go, but only do what I tell you."

Balaam's Donkey Speaks

21 Balaam got up the next morning and put a saddle on his donkey. Then he went with the Moabite
leaders. 22 But God became angry because Balaam
went, so the angel of the Lord stood in the road to
stop Balaam. Balaam was riding his donkey, and he
had two servants with him. 23 When the donkey
saw the angel of the Lord standing in the road with
a sword in his hand, the donkey left the road and

22:7 *Balaam.* Balaam is a foreign prophet whom Balak hires in order to curse the people of Israel. It is interesting that recent archaeological research has found mention of Balaam in ancient Near Eastern inscriptions.

went into the field. Balaam hit the donkey to force
her back on the road.
24Later, the angel of the Lord stood on a narrow
path between two vineyards, with walls on both
sides. 25Again the donkey saw the angel of the
Lord, and she walked close to one wall, crushing
Balaam's foot against it. So he hit her again.
26The angel of the Lord went ahead again and
stood at a narrow place, too narrow to turn left or
right. 27When the donkey saw the angel of the
Lord, she lay down under Balaam. This made him
so angry that he hit her with his stick. 28Then the
Lord made the donkey talk, and she said to
Balaam, "What have I done to make you hit me
three times?"
29Balaam answered the donkey, "You have made
me look foolish! I wish I had a sword in my hand!
I would kill you right now!"
30But the donkey said to Balaam, "I am your very
own donkey, which you have ridden for years. Have
I ever done this to you before?"
"No," Balaam said.
31Then the Lord let Balaam see the angel of the
Lord, who was standing in the road with his
sword drawn. Then Balaam bowed facedown on
the ground.
32The angel of the Lord asked Balaam, "Why
have you hit your donkey three times? I have stood
here to stop you, because what you are doing is
wrong. 33The donkey saw me and turned away
from me three times. If she had not turned away,
I would have killed you by now, but I would have
let her live."
34Then Balaam said to the angel of the Lord, "I
have sinned; I did not know you were standing in
the road to stop me. If I am wrong, I will go back."
35The angel of the Lord said to Balaam, "Go with
these men, but say only what I tell you." So Balaam
went with Balak's leaders.
36When Balak heard that Balaam was coming,
he went out to meet him at Ar in Moab, which
was beside the Arnon, at the edge of his country.
37Balak said to Balaam, "I had asked you before to
come quickly. Why didn't you come to me? I am
able to reward you well."
38But Balaam answered, "I have come to you
now, but I can't say just anything. I can only say
what God tells me to say."
39Then Balaam went with Balak to Kiriath
Huzoth. 40Balak offered cattle and sheep as a sacrifice and gave some meat to Balaam and the leaders with him.
41The next morning Balak took Balaam to Bamoth Baal; from there he could see the edge of the
Israelite camp.

Balaam's First Message

23 Balaam said to Balak, "Build me seven altars
here, and prepare seven bulls and seven
male sheep for me." 2Balak did what Balaam asked,
and they offered a bull and a male sheep on each of
the altars.
3Then Balaam said to Balak, "Stay here beside
your burnt offering and I will go. If the Lord comes
to me, I will tell you whatever he shows me." Then
Balaam went to a higher place.
4God came to Balaam there, and Balaam said to
him, "I have prepared seven altars, and I have
offered a bull and a male sheep on each altar."
5The Lord told Balaam what he should say. Then
the Lord said, "Go back to Balak and give him this
message."
6So Balaam went back to Balak. Balak and all the
leaders of Moab were still standing beside his burnt
offering 7when Balaam gave them this message:
"Balak brought me here from Aram;
the king of Moab brought me from the eastern
mountains.
Balak said, 'Come, put a curse on the people of
Jacob for me.
Come, call down evil on the people of Israel.'
8But God has not cursed them,
so I cannot curse them.
The LORD has not called down evil on them,
so I cannot call down evil on them.
9I see them from the top of the mountains;
I see them from the hills.
I see a people who live alone,
who think they are different from other
nations.
10No one can number the many people of Jacob,
and no one can count a fourth of Israel.
Let me die like good men,
and let me end up like them!"
11Balak said to Balaam, "What have you done to
me? I brought you here to curse my enemies, but
you have only blessed them!"
12But Balaam answered, "I must say what the
Lord tells me to say."

Balaam's Second Message

13Then Balak said to him, "Come with me to
another place, where you can also see the people.
But you can only see part of them, not all of them.
Curse them for me from there." 14So Balak took
Balaam to the field of Zophim, on top of Mount
Pisgah. There Balak built seven altars and offered
a bull and a male sheep on each altar.
15So Balaam said to Balak, "Stay here by your
burnt offering, and I will meet with God over
there."

16 So the Lord came to Balaam and told him what
to say. Then he said, "Go back to Balak and say
such and such."
17 So Balaam went to Balak, where he and the
leaders of Moab were standing beside his burnt
offering. Balak asked him, "What did the Lord
say?"
18 Then Balaam gave this message:
"Stand up, Balak, and listen.
Hear me, son of Zippor.
19 God is not a human being, and he will not lie.
He is not a human, and he does not change
his mind.
What he says he will do, he does.
What he promises, he makes come true.
20 He told me to bless them,
so I cannot change the blessing.
21 He has found no wrong in the people of Jacob;
he saw no fault in Israel.
The LORD their God is with them,
and they praise their King.
22 God brought them out of Egypt;
they are as strong as a wild ox.
23 No tricks will work on the people of Jacob,
and no magic will work against Israel.
People now say about them,
'Look what God has done for Israel!'
24 The people rise up like a lioness;
they get up like a lion.
Lions don't rest until they have eaten,
until they have drunk their enemies' blood."
25 Then Balak said to Balaam, "You haven't
cursed these people, so at least, don't bless them!"
26 Balaam answered Balak, "I told you before
that I can only do what the Lord tells me."

Balaam's Third Message

27 Then Balak said to Balaam, "Come, I will take
you to another place. Maybe God will be pleased
to let you curse them from there." 28 So Balak took
Balaam to the top of Peor, the mountain that looks
over the desert.
29 Balaam told Balak, "Build me seven altars here
and prepare for me seven bulls and seven male
sheep." 30 Balak did what Balaam asked, and he
offered a bull and a male sheep on each altar.

24 Balaam saw that the Lord wanted to bless
Israel, so he did not try to use any magic
but looked toward the desert. 2 When Balaam saw
the Israelites camped in their tribes, the Spirit of
God took control of him, 3 and he gave this message:
"This is the message of Balaam son of Beor,
the message of a man who sees clearly;
4 this is the message of a man who hears the
words of God.
I see a vision from the Almighty,
and my eyes are open as I fall before him.
5 Your tents are beautiful, people of Jacob!
So are your homes, Israel!
6 Your tents spread out like valleys,
like gardens beside a river.
They are like spices planted by the LORD,
like cedar trees growing by the water.
7 Israel's water buckets will always be full,
and their crops will have plenty of water.
Their king will be greater than Agag;
their kingdom will be very great.
8 God brought them out of Egypt;
they are as strong as a wild ox.
They will defeat their enemies
and break their enemies' bones;
they will shoot them with arrows.
9 Like a lion, they lie waiting to attack;
like a lioness, no one would be brave enough
to wake them.
Anyone who blesses you will be blessed,
and anyone who curses you will be cursed."
10 Then Balak was angry with Balaam, and he
pounded his fist. He said to Balaam, "I called you
here to curse my enemies, but you have continued to bless them three times. 11 Now go home! I
said I would pay you well, but the Lord has made
you lose your reward."
12 Balaam said to Balak, "When you sent messengers to me, I told them, 13 'Balak could give me
his palace filled with silver and gold, but I still
cannot go against the Lord's commands. I could
not do anything, good or bad, on my own, but I
must say what the Lord says.' 14 Now I am going
back to my own people, but I will tell you what
these people will do to your people in the future."

Balaam's Final Message

15 Then Balaam gave this message:
"This is the message of Balaam son of Beor,
the message of a man who sees clearly;
16 this is the message of a man who hears the
words of God.
I know well the Most High God.
I see a vision from the Almighty,
and my eyes are open as I fall before him.
17 I see someone who will come some day,
someone who will come, but not soon.
A star will come from Jacob;
a ruler will rise from Israel.
He will crush the heads of the Moabites
and smash the skulls of the sons of Sheth.
18 Edom will be conquered;

24:4 Prophetic Symbolism: Psalm 78:1–3

his enemy Edom will be conquered,
but Israel will grow wealthy.
19A ruler will come from the descendants of Jacob
and will destroy those left in the city."

20Then Balaam saw Amalek and gave this message:

"Amalek was the most important nation,
but Amalek will be destroyed at last."

21Then Balaam saw the Kenites and gave this message:

"Your home is safe,
like a nest on a cliff.
22But you Kenites will be burned up;
Assyria will keep you captive."

23Then Balaam gave this message:

"No one can live when God does this.
24 Ships will sail from the shores of Cyprus
and defeat Assyria and Eber,
but they will also be destroyed."

25Then Balaam got up and returned home, and Balak also went on his way.

Israel Worships Baal at Peor

25 While the people of Israel were still camped at Acacia, the men began sinning sexually with Moabite women. 2The women invited them to their sacrifices to their gods, and the Israelites ate food there and worshiped these gods. 3So the Israelites began to worship Baal of Peor, and the LORD was very angry with them.

4The LORD said to Moses, "Get all the leaders of the people and kill them in open daylight in the presence of the LORD. Then the LORD will not be angry with the people of Israel."

5So Moses said to Israel's judges, "Each of you must put to death your people who have become worshipers of Baal of Peor."

6Moses and the Israelites were gathered at the entrance to the Meeting Tent, crying there. Then an Israelite man brought a Midianite woman to his brothers in plain sight of Moses and all the people. 7Phinehas son of Eleazar, the son of Aaron, the priest, saw this, so he left the meeting and got his spear. 8He followed the Israelite into his tent and drove his spear through both the Israelite man and the Midianite woman. Then the terrible sickness among the Israelites stopped.

9This sickness had killed twenty-four thousand people.

10The LORD said to Moses, 11"Phinehas son of Eleazar, the son of Aaron, the priest, has saved the Israelites from my anger. He hates sin as much as I do. Since he tried to save my honor among them, I will not kill them. 12So tell Phinehas that I am making my peace agreement with him. 13He and his descendants will always be priests, because he had great concern for the honor of his God. He removed the sins of the Israelites so they would belong to God."

14The Israelite man who was killed with the Midianite woman was named Zimri son of Salu. He was the leader of a family in the tribe of Simeon. 15And the name of the Midianite woman who was put to death was Cozbi daughter of Zur, who was the chief of a Midianite family.

16The LORD said to Moses, 17"The Midianites are your enemies, and you should kill them. 18They have already made you their enemies, because they tricked you at Peor and because of their sister Cozbi, the daughter of a Midianite leader. She was the woman who was killed when the sickness came because the people sinned at Peor."

The People Are Counted

26 After the great sickness, the LORD said to Moses and Eleazar son of Aaron, the priest, 2"Count all the people of Israel by families. Count all the men who are twenty years old or older who will serve in the army of Israel." 3Moses and Eleazar the priest spoke to the people on the plains of Moab near the Jordan River, across from Jericho. They said, 4"Count the men twenty years old or older, as the LORD commanded Moses."

Here are the Israelites who came out of Egypt:

5The tribe of Reuben, the first son born to Israel, was counted. From Hanoch came the Hanochite family group; from Pallu came the Palluite family group; 6from Hezron came the Hezronite family group; from Carmi came the Carmite family group. 7These were the family groups of Reuben, and the total number of men was 43,730.

8The son of Pallu was Eliab, 9and Eliab's sons were Nemuel, Dathan, and Abiram. Dathan and Abiram were the leaders who turned against Moses and Aaron and followed Korah when he turned against the LORD. 10The earth opened up and swallowed them and Korah; they died at the same time the fire burned up the 250 men. This was a warning, 11but the children of Korah did not die.

12These were the family groups in the tribe of Simeon: From Nemuel came the Nemuelite family group; from Jamin came the Jaminite family group; from Jakin came the Jakinite family group; 13from Zerah came the Zerahite family group; from Shaul came the Shaulite family group. 14These were the

25:13 Priesthood: Psalm 110:4

family groups of Simeon, and the total number of men was 22,200.

15These were the family groups in the tribe of Gad: From Zephon came the Zephonite family group; from Haggi came the Haggite family group; from Shuni came the Shunite family group; 16from Ozni came the Oznite family group; from Eri came the Erite family group; 17from Arodi came the Arodite family group; from Areli came the Arelite family group. 18These were the family groups of Gad, and the total number of men was 40,500.

19Two of Judah's sons, Er and Onan, died in Canaan.

20These were the family groups in the tribe of Judah: From Shelah came the Shelanite family group; from Perez came the Perezite family group; from Zerah came the Zerahite family group. 21These were the family groups from Perez: From Hezron came the Hezronite family group; from Hamul came the Hamulite family group. 22These were the family groups of Judah, and the total number of men was 76,500.

23These were the family groups in the tribe of Issachar: From Tola came the Tolaite family group; from Puah came the Puite family group; 24from Jashub came the Jashubite family group; from Shimron came the Shimronite family group. 25These were the family groups of Issachar, and the total number of men was 64,300.

26These were the family groups in the tribe of Zebulun: From Sered came the Seredite family group; from Elon came the Elonite family group; from Jahleel came the Jahleelite family group. 27These were the family groups of Zebulun, and the total number of men was 60,500.

28These were the family groups of Joseph through Manasseh and Ephraim.

29These were the family groups of Manasseh: From Makir came the Makirite family group (Makir was the father of Gilead); from Gilead came the Gileadite family group. 30These were the family groups that came from Gilead: From Iezer came the Iezerite family group; from Helek came the Helekite family group; 31from Asriel came the Asrielite family group; from Shechem came the Shechemite family group; 32from Shemida came the Shemidaite family group; from Hepher came the Hepherite family group. 33(Zelophehad son of Hepher had no sons; he had only daughters, and their names were Mahlah, Noah, Hoglah, Milcah, and Tirzah.) 34These were the family groups of Manasseh, and the total number of men was 52,700.

35These were the family groups in the tribe of Ephraim: From Shuthelah came the Shuthelahite family group; from Beker came the Bekerite family group; from Tahan came the Tahanite family group. 36This was the family group from Shuthelah: From Eran came the Eranite family group. 37These were the family groups of Ephraim, and the total number of men was 32,500. These are the family groups that came from Joseph.

38These were the family groups in the tribe of Benjamin: From Bela came the Belaite family group; from Ashbel came the Ashbelite family group; from Ahiram came the Ahiramite family group; 39from Shupham came the Shuphamite family group; from Hupham came the Huphamite family group. 40These were the family groups from Bela through Ard and Naaman: From Ard came the Ardite family group; from Naaman came the Naamite family group. 41These were the family groups of Benjamin, and the total number of men was 45,600.

42This was the family group in the tribe of Dan: From Shuham came the Shuhamite family group. That was the family of Dan, 43and the total number of men in the Shuhamite family group of Dan was 64,400.

44These were the family groups in the tribe of Asher: From Imnah came the Imnite family group; from Ishvi came the Ishvite family group; from Beriah came the Beriite family group. 45These were the family groups that came from Beriah: From Heber came the Heberite family group; from Malkiel came the Malkielite family group. 46(Asher also had a daughter named Serah.) 47These were the family groups of Asher, and the total number of men was 53,400.

48These were the family groups in the tribe of Naphtali: From Jahzeel came the Jahzeelite family group; from Guni came the Gunite family group; 49from Jezer came the Jezerite family group; from Shillem came the Shillemite family group. 50These were the family groups of Naphtali, and the total number of men was 45,400.

51So the total number of the men of Israel was 601,730.

52The LORD said to Moses, 53"Divide the land among these people by the number of names. 54A large tribe will get more land, and a small tribe will get less land; the am ount of land each tribe gets will depend on the number of its people. 55Divide the land by drawing lots, and the land each tribe gets will be named for that tribe. 56Divide the land between large and small groups by drawing lots."

57The tribe of Levi was also counted. These were the family groups of Levi: From Gershon came the Gershonite family group; from Kohath came the Kohathite family group; from Merari came the Merarite family group. 58These also were Levite family

groups: the Libnite family group, the Hebronite
family group, the Mahlite family group, the
Mushite family group, and the Korahite family
group. (Kohath was the ancestor of Amram,
59whose wife was named Jochebed. She was from
the tribe of Levi and she was born in Egypt. She
and Amram had two sons, Aaron and Moses, and
their sister Miriam. 60Aaron was the father of Nadab, Abihu, Eleazar, and Ithamar. 61But Nadab and
Abihu died because they made an offering before
the LORD with the wrong kind of fire.)

62The total number of male Levites one month
old or older was 23,000. But these men were not
counted with the other Israelites, because they
were not given any of the land among the other
Israelites.

63Moses and Eleazar the priest counted all these
people. They counted the Israelites on the plains of
Moab across the Jordan River from Jericho. 64Moses
and Aaron the priest had counted the Israelites in
the Desert of Sinai, but no one Moses counted on
the plains of Moab was in the first counting.
65The LORD had told the Israelites they would all
die in the desert, and the only two left were
Caleb son of Jephunneh and Joshua son of Nun.

Zelophehad's Daughters

27 Then the daughters of Zelophehad came
near. Zelophehad was the son of Hepher,
the son of Gilead, the son of Makir, the son of
Manasseh. Zelophehad's daughters belonged to
the family groups of Manasseh son of Joseph. The
daughters' names were Mahlah, Noah, Hoglah,
Milcah, and Tirzah. 2They went to the entrance of
the Meeting Tent and stood before Moses, Eleazar
the priest, the leaders, and all the people. They
said, 3"Our father died in the desert. He was not
one of Korah's followers who came together
against the LORD, but he died because of his own
sin, and he had no sons. 4Our father's name will
die out because he had no sons. Give us property
among our father's relatives."

5So Moses brought their case to the LORD, 6and
the LORD said to him, 7"The daughters of Zelophehad are right; they should certainly get what their
father owned. Give them property among their
father's relatives.

8"Tell the Israelites, 'If a man dies and has no
son, then everything he owned should go to his
daughter. 9If he has no daughter, then everything
he owned should go to his brothers. 10If he has no
brothers, then everything he owned should go to
his father's brothers. 11And if his father had no
brothers, then everything he owned should go to
the nearest relative in his family group. This should
be a rule among the people of Israel, as the LORD
has given this command to Moses.'"

Joshua Is the New Leader

12Then the LORD said to Moses, "Climb this
mountain in the Abarim Mountains, and look at
the land I have given to the Israelites. 13After you
have seen it, you will die and join your ancestors
as your brother Aaron did, 14because you both
acted against my command in the Desert of Zin.
You did not honor me as holy before the people at
the waters of Meribah." (This was at Meribah in
Kadesh in the Desert of Zin.)

15Moses said to the LORD, 16"The LORD is the
God of the spirits of all people. May he choose a
leader for these people, 17who will go in and out
before them. He must lead them out like sheep
and bring them in; the LORD's people must not be
like sheep without a shepherd."

18So the LORD said to Moses, "Take Joshua son
of Nun, because my Spirit is in him. Put your hand
on him, 19and have him stand before Eleazar the
priest and all the people. Then give him his orders
as they watch. 20Let him share your honor so that
all the Israelites will obey him. 21He must stand
before Eleazar the priest, and Eleazar will get
advice from the LORD by using the Urim. At his
command all the Israelites will go out, and at his
command they will all come in."

22Moses did what the LORD told him. He took
Joshua and had him stand before Eleazar the priest
and all the people, 23and he put his hands on him
and gave him orders, just as the LORD had told
him.

Daily Offerings

28 The LORD said to Moses, 2"Give this command to the Israelites. Tell them: 'Bring
me food offerings made by fire, for a smell that is
pleasing to me, and be sure to bring them at the
right time.' 3Say to them, 'These are the offerings
you must bring to the LORD: two male lambs, a
year old, as a burnt offering each day. They must
have nothing wrong with them. 4Offer one lamb
in the morning and the other lamb at twilight.
5Also bring a grain offering of two quarts of fine
flour, mixed with one quart of oil from pressed

26:65 Genealogy: 1 Chronicles 1–9

27:14 Mountain: Deuteronomy 27:9–28:68

27:17 Leadership: Deuteronomy 1:15

27:21 *Urim.* The Urim is usually mentioned along with the Thummim. They are Hebrew words which mean "Light" and "Truth" respectively. They were some sort of lot by which the priest could determine God's will for a certain situation.

olives. 6This is the daily burnt offering which began at Mount Sinai; its smell is pleasing to the LORD. 7Offer one quart of wine with each lamb as a drink offering; pour it out to the LORD at the Holy Place. 8Offer the second lamb at twilight. As in the morning, also give a grain offering and a drink offering. This offering is made by fire, and its smell is pleasing to the LORD.

Sabbath Offerings

9"'On the Sabbath day you must give two male lambs, a year old, that have nothing wrong with them. Also give a drink offering and a grain offering; the grain offering must be four quarts of fine flour mixed with olive oil. 10This is the burnt offering for every Sabbath, in addition to the daily burnt offering and drink offering.

Monthly Offerings

11"'On the first day of each month bring a burnt offering to the LORD. This will be two young bulls, one male sheep, and seven male lambs a year old, and they must have nothing wrong with them. 12Give a grain offering with each bull of six quarts of fine flour mixed with olive oil. Also give a grain offering with the male sheep. It must be four quarts of fine flour mixed with olive oil. 13And give a grain offering with each lamb of two quarts of fine flour mixed with olive oil. This is a burnt offering, and its smell is pleasing to the LORD. 14The drink offering with each bull will be two quarts of wine, with the male sheep it will be one and one-third quarts, and with each lamb it will be one quart of wine. This is the burnt offering that must be offered each month of the year. 15Besides the daily burnt offerings and drink offerings, bring a sin offering of one goat to the LORD.

The Passover

16"'The LORD's Passover will be on the fourteenth day of the first month. 17The Feast of Unleavened Bread begins on the fifteenth day of that month. For seven days, you may eat only bread made without yeast. 18Have a holy meeting on the first day of the festival, and don't work that day. 19Bring to the LORD an offering made by fire, a burnt offering of two young bulls, one male sheep, and seven male lambs a year old. They must have nothing wrong with them. 20With each bull give a grain offering of six quarts of fine flour mixed with olive oil. With the male sheep it must be four quarts of fine flour mixed with oil. 21With each of the seven lambs, it must be two quarts of fine flour mixed with oil. 22Bring one goat as a sin offering, to remove your sins so you will belong to God. 23Bring these offerings in addition to the burnt offerings you give every morning. 24So bring food for the offering made by fire each day for seven days, for a smell that is pleasing to the LORD. Do it in addition to the daily burnt offering and its drink offering. 25On the seventh day have a holy meeting, and don't work that day.

The Feast of Weeks

26"'On the day of firstfruits when you bring new grain to the LORD during the Feast of Weeks, have a holy meeting. Don't work that day. 27Bring this burnt offering to the LORD: two young bulls, one male sheep, and seven male lambs a year old. This smell is pleasing to the LORD. 28Also, with each bull give a grain offering of six quarts of fine flour mixed with oil. With the male sheep, it must be four quarts of flour, 29and with each of the seven lambs offer two quarts of flour. 30Offer one male goat to remove your sins so you will belong to God. 31Bring these offerings and their drink offerings in addition to the daily burnt offering and its grain offering. The animals must have nothing wrong with them.

The Feast of Trumpets

29 "'Have a holy meeting on the first day of the seventh month, and don't work on that day. That is the day you blow the trumpets. 2Bring these burnt offerings as a smell pleasing to the LORD: one young bull, one male sheep, and seven male lambs a year old. They must have nothing wrong with them. 3With the bull give a grain offering of six quarts of fine flour mixed with oil. With the male sheep offer four quarts, 4and with each of the seven lambs offer two quarts. 5Offer one male goat for a sin offering to remove your sins so you will belong to God. 6These offerings are in addition to the monthly and daily burnt offerings. Their grain offerings and drink offerings must be done as you have been told. These offerings are made by fire to the LORD, and their smell is pleasing to him.

The Day of Cleansing

7"'Have a holy meeting on the tenth day of the seventh month. On that day do not eat and do not work. 8Bring these burnt offerings as a smell pleasing to the LORD: one young bull, one male sheep, and seven male lambs a year old. They must have nothing wrong with them. 9With the bull give a grain offering of six quarts of fine flour mixed with oil. With the male sheep it must be four

28:7 Sacrifice: Isaiah 43:23

28:16 Feasts/Festivals: Deuteronomy 16:1–17

HATE

GENESIS 37:4

Is hate ever legitimate? Does God hate?

Generally speaking, a person who hates has intense feelings of strong dislike or animosity toward someone or something. In the Bible hate can be understood in a number of different ways, and it is important to know the differences. First, an individual may have such deep-seated hostility toward another person that it results in that person's murder. We only need to turn a few pages into Genesis to find the very first instance of this, where Cain's hatred for his brother Abel resulted in murder (Genesis 4:8; 1 John 3:11–15). Second, there is a hate that despises someone so much that they are rejected or spurned, but without the malicious intent to kill. Jephthah was the object of this kind of hatred at the hands of his half-brothers because he was an illegitimate son and was thus rejected (Judges 11:7). Third, the concept of hate is used vividly to describe a vehement dislike toward someone which is reflected in an attitude of indifference or disregard toward them. Samson was thought to have had this type of attitude toward his Philistine wife (Judges 14:16; 15:2; 2 Samuel 13:15). The kinds of hate thus far described are characteristic of the old life before one's coming to Christ (Galatians 5:20; Titus 3:3; 1 John 2:9, 11; 3:15).

Finally, "hate" can be understood in a comparative sense, meaning to love something or someone less than something or someone else. For example, Jesus requires that his true disciples are those who "hate their lives in this world" in order that they might "keep true life forever" (John 12:25). By this is meant that the disciple loves his earthly life less than the life to come (Luke 14:26; see Romans 9:13 and note).

Since this last instance of "hate" is of a positive nature, this leads us to explore the instances where "hate" can be legitimate for the child of God. Because believers sustain a relationship to God that is based upon holiness, loyalty, and reverence, among many other qualities, they will come to love the things that God loves, and to hate the things that God hates. The psalmist writes, "People who love the LORD hate evil" (Psalm 97:10). The writer of Proverbs adds, "If you respect the LORD, you will also hate evil" (Proverbs 8:13). The prophet Jehu rebuked King Jehoshaphat for loving those who hate the Lord (2 Chronicles 19:2). In the New Testament, James tells us that "loving the world is the same as hating God" (James 4:4; 1 John 2:15). Paul commmands us to "hate what is evil," and hold on to what is good (Romans 12:9). As a result, the people of God will also hate various evil deeds, including pride, evil ways, and lies (Proverbs 8:13).

There are passages, however, especially in the Old Testament, where the righteous are said to hate, not just evil deeds, but also evil-doers. The psalmist writes with such great intensity of emotion that all he feels toward the enemies of God is hate (Psalm 139:21–22). Such passages as this one should be understood not as contradicting Jesus' command to love one's enemies (Matthew 5:43–44), but as seen in the light of the psalmist's fierce loyalty and jealousy for God's honor. There is a kind of holy hatred which is not malicious, retaliatory, or personal, nor is it based upon a fleeting emotion, but is a settled condition of the mind and will that stands opposed to anyone who defies God and his ways. It is a hatred which expresses itself not in wishing harm to God's enemies, but in seeking their repentance through deeds of kindness.

Although the Bible teaches us that God is love (1 John 4:8), the Bible also teaches us that God is holy (Isaiah 6:3), which means that he is supremely great (Psalm 145:3), awe-inspiring (Psalm 89:7), perfect (Psalm 50:2), and pure in all that he is and does (Isaiah 5:16). God "cannot stand to see those who do wrong" (Habakkuk 1:13). Therefore, God hates all that offends his holy character and turns people's hearts away from the worship he alone deserves.

God displays a holy hatred for such disgusting practices and attitudes as these of the nations that surround Israel (Leviticus 18) which, sadly, were sometimes borrowed by God's own people, including child sacrifice (Deuteronomy 12:31; 2 Kings 16:3) and the worship of idols (Deuteronomy 16:21–22; 27:15; Jeremiah 44:4). Among the many other things God hates (see especially Proverbs 6:16–19 and note there) include flawed sacrifices (Deuteronomy 17:1), stealing (Isaiah 61:8), dishonesty (Proverbs 11:1), divorce (Malachi 2:16), injustice (Proverbs 17:15), "the sacrifice that the wicked offer" (Proverbs 15:8), and empty worship (Isaiah 1:14). In the New Testament, we read that Jesus hates the lawless deeds of the Nicolaitans (Revelation 2:6). Furthermore, God hates not only these practices, but also those who do them (Leviticus 20:23; Psalm 5:5), therefore they will be punished (Deuteronomy 5:9; Psalm 81:15). Yet God takes no pleasure in the death of the wicked, but longs that they repent and live (Ezekiel 18:23, 32).

Hate: For additional scriptures on this topic go to Exodus 20:5.

FAMINE

GENESIS 41:30–31

What are some examples of famine in the Bible?
What was God's role in famine, and how did he use it?

The possibility of famine was one of the most common and feared troubles of the world of the Bible. What was famine, what were its causes, and did God have anything to do with it?

The subject of famine in the Bible stretches from Genesis to Revelation. Famine is the extreme shortage of food in a society or community, giving rise to great hunger and even starvation among its people. It can come about by any number of causes both human and natural, but it was apparently a fact of life in the ancient world. Probably the most notable examples in the Bible are the famine in Egypt during Joseph's time (Genesis 41), the famine prophesied by Elijah during King Ahab's reign (1 Kings 17), and the prophesy of Agabus in Acts 11:27–28. There are, however, many other references to famine in the Bible.

Famines could last any length of time including three to up to seven years. Joseph's famine lasted seven years and so did that of Elisha and the Shunammite woman (2 Kings 8:1). A three-year famine is mentioned in David's time (2 Samuel 21:1), and Jesus refers to Elijah's famine as being three-and-a-half years long (Luke 4:25). According to the Jewish historian Josephus, a great famine lasted in Palestine from 44 to 48 C.E. Famines could be local as—for example, those limited to the Palestine area in the days of Ruth and Abraham (Ruth 1:1; Genesis 12:10)—or even limited to a particular region as in the days of Elisha (2 Kings 4:38). In these situations, the people often moved temporarily to other places where food was available. Ruth's mother-in-law moved to Moab, Abraham to Egypt, and Elisha's Shunammite woman to the land of the Philistines (2 Kings 8:2). Sometimes the shortage of food was widespread and universal as in the case of Joseph in Egypt (Genesis 41:54) and Agabus's prophecy (Acts 11:28).

Famine was something greatly feared in the Bible. We find many descriptions of famine: "The babies are so thirsty their tongues stick to the roofs of their mouths. Children beg for bread but no one gives them any" (Lamentations 4:4). Sometimes the famine was so severe animals had to be killed (1 Kings 18:5), and in the worst situations cannibalism took place (for example, during the military sieges of Ben-Hadad, 2 Kings 6:27–29; and Nebuchadnezzar, Lamentations 2:20; 4:10). Famine was one of the three great terrors in the Bible; nothing was worse than "war, hunger and terrible disease" (Jeremiah 14:12; 2 Samuel 24:13; Revelation 6:8).

When famine came, what was God's role in it? It is clear in the Old Testament that God often used this calamity as discipline upon his sinning people. "But if you do not obey me and keep all my commands . . . I will make the sky like iron and the earth like bronze. . . . Your land will not grow any crops, and your trees will not give their fruit" (Leviticus 26:14–20; Deuteronomy 28:15–24). God's chastisement was not meant to destroy his people but to bring them to repentance and to obedience to his ways (Leviticus 26:40–42; 1 Kings 8:35–40; Amos 4:6; Haggai 1:10). Not all famines, however, were because God was chastising his people. The famines of Joseph in Genesis and Agabus in Acts were upon all people and were part of God's ordering of natural events to bring about his divine purposes. In the case of Joseph, God was working his purposes by using the coming famine as the occasion to elevate Joseph to power in Egypt and reunite him with his family. In Acts 11, Agabus's prophecy provided the opportunity and advance notice for the fellow believers of Antioch to help the mother church in Jerusalem. In 2 Samuel 21, there had been famine for three years, yet David did not know why God had sent it. He prayed and learned that God had sent the famine because of a specific wrong committed by King Saul against the Gibeonites. Once the wrong had been addressed, "God answered the prayers for the land" (2 Samuel 21: 14). In the psalms and wisdom literature, we learn that God preserves the righteous and those who trust in him in times of famine (Psalms 33:18–19; 37:19; Proverbs 10:3; Job 5:20).

In the New Testament, the only major references to famine other than the one prophesied by Agabus in Acts 11 are in the passages concerning Jesus' Second Coming (Matthew 24:7; Mark 13:8; Luke 21:11). Famine will be part of the many troubles that come upon the world just prior to the Lord's return. In these references, however, famine does not appear to function as discipline but as pure judgment upon the unbelieving (Revelation 6:8; 18:8).

Famine: For additional scriptures on this topic go to Genesis 12:10.

quarts, 10and with each of the seven lambs it must be two quarts. 11Offer one male goat as a sin offering. This will be in addition to the sin offering which removes your sins, the daily burnt offering with its grain offering, and the drink offerings.

The Feast of Shelters

12"'Have a holy meeting on the fifteenth day of the seventh month, and do not work on that day. Celebrate a festival to the LORD for seven days. 13Bring these burnt offerings, made by fire, as a smell pleasing to the LORD: thirteen young bulls, two male sheep, and fourteen male lambs a year old. They must have nothing wrong with them. 14With each of the thirteen bulls offer a grain offering of six quarts of fine flour mixed with oil. With each of the two male sheep it must be four quarts, 15and with each of the fourteen lambs it must be two quarts. 16Offer one male goat as a sin offering in addition to the daily burnt offering with its grain and drink offerings.

17"'On the second day of this festival give an offering of twelve bulls, two male sheep, and fourteen male lambs a year old. They must have nothing wrong with them. 18Bring the grain and drink offerings for the bulls, sheep, and lambs, according to the number required. 19Offer one male goat as a sin offering, in addition to the daily burnt offering with its grain and drink offerings.

20"'On the third day offer eleven bulls, two male sheep, and fourteen male lambs a year old. They must have nothing wrong with them. 21Bring the grain and drink offerings for the bulls, sheep, and lambs, according to the number required. 22Offer one male goat as a sin offering, in addition to the daily burnt offering with its grain and drink offerings.

23"'On the fourth day offer ten bulls, two male sheep, and fourteen male lambs a year old. They must have nothing wrong with them. 24Bring the grain and drink offerings for the bulls, sheep, and lambs, according to the number required. 25Offer one male goat as a sin offering, in addition to the daily burnt offering with its grain and drink offerings.

26"'On the fifth day offer nine bulls, two male sheep, and fourteen male lambs a year old. They must have nothing wrong with them. 27Bring the grain and drink offerings for the bulls, sheep, and lambs, according to the number required. 28Offer one male goat as a sin offering, in addition to the daily burnt offering with its grain and drink offerings.

29"'On the sixth day offer eight bulls, two male sheep, and fourteen male lambs a year old. They must have nothing wrong with them. 30Bring the grain and drink offerings for the bulls, sheep, and lambs, according to the number required. 31Offer one male goat as a sin offering, in addition to the daily burnt offering with its grain and drink offerings.

32"'On the seventh day offer seven bulls, two male sheep, and fourteen male lambs a year old. They must have nothing wrong with them. 33Bring the grain and drink offerings for the bulls, sheep, and lambs, according to the number required. 34Offer one male goat as a sin offering, in addition to the daily burnt offering with its grain and drink offerings.

35"'On the eighth day have a closing meeting, and do not work on that day. 36Bring an offering made by fire, a burnt offering, as a smell pleasing to the LORD. Offer one bull, one male sheep, and seven male lambs a year old. They must have nothing wrong with them. 37Bring the grain and drink offerings for the bull, the male sheep, and the lambs, according to the number required. 38Offer one male goat as a sin offering, in addition to the daily burnt offering with its grain and drink offerings.

39"'At your festivals you should bring these to the LORD: your burnt offerings, grain offerings, drink offerings and fellowship offerings. These are in addition to other promised offerings and special gifts you want to give to the LORD.'"

40Moses told the Israelites everything the LORD had commanded him.

Rules About Special Promises

30 Moses spoke with the leaders of the Israelite tribes. He told them these commands from the LORD.

2"If a man makes a promise to the LORD or says he will do something special, he must keep his promise. He must do what he said. 3If a young woman still living at home makes a promise to the LORD or pledges to do something special, 4and if her father hears about the promise or pledge and says nothing, she must do what she promised. She must keep her pledge. 5But if her father hears about the promise or pledge and does not allow it, then the promise or pledge does not have to be kept. Her father would not allow it, so the LORD will free her from her promise.

6"If a woman makes a pledge or a careless promise and then gets married, 7and if her husband hears about it and says nothing, she must keep her

29:40 Celebration: Deuteronomy 16:1-17

promise or the pledge she made. [8]But if her husband hears about it and does not allow it, he cancels her pledge or the careless promise she made. The LORD will free her from keeping it.

[9]"If a widow or divorced woman makes a promise, she must do whatever she promised.

[10]"If a woman makes a promise or pledge while she is married, [11]and if her husband hears about it but says nothing and does not stop her, she must keep her promise or pledge. [12]But if her husband hears about it and cancels it, she does not have to do what she said. Her husband has canceled it, so the LORD will free her from it. [13]A woman's husband may make her keep or cancel any promise or pledge she has made. [14]If he says nothing to her about it for several days, she must keep her promises. If he hears about them and says nothing, she must keep her promises. [15]But if he cancels them long after he heard about them, he is responsible if she breaks her promise."

[16]These are commands that the LORD gave to Moses for husbands and wives, and for fathers with daughters living at home.

Israel Attacks the Midianites

31 The LORD spoke to Moses and said, [2]"Pay back the Midianites for what they did to the Israelites; after that you will die."

[3]So Moses said to the people, "Get some men ready for war. The LORD will use them to pay back the Midianites. [4]Send to war a thousand men from each of the tribes of Israel." [5]So twelve thousand men got ready for war, a thousand men from each tribe. [6]Moses sent those men to war; Phinehas son of Eleazar the priest was with them. He took with him the holy things and the trumpets for giving the alarm. [7]They fought the Midianites as the LORD had commanded Moses, and they killed every Midianite man. [8]Among those they killed were Evi, Rekem, Zur, Hur, and Reba, who were the five kings of Midian. They also killed Balaam son of Beor with a sword.

[9]The Israelites captured the Midianite women and children, and they took all their flocks, herds, and goods. [10]They burned all the Midianite towns where they had settled and all their camps, [11]but they took all the people and animals and goods. [12]Then they brought the captives, the animals, and the goods back to Moses and Eleazar the priest and all the Israelites. Their camp was on the plains of Moab near the Jordan River, across from Jericho.

[13]Moses, Eleazar the priest, and all the leaders of the people went outside the camp to meet them. [14]Moses was angry with the army officers, the commanders over a thousand men, and those over a hundred men, who returned from war.

[15]He asked them, "Why did you let the women live? [16]They were the ones who followed Balaam's advice and turned the Israelites from the LORD at Peor. Then a terrible sickness struck the LORD's people. [17]Kill all the Midianite boys, and kill all the Midianite women who have had sexual relations. [18]But save for yourselves the girls who have not had sexual relations with a man.

[19]"All you men who killed anyone or touched a dead body must stay outside the camp for seven days. On the third and seventh days you and your captives must make yourselves clean. [20]You must clean all your clothes and anything made of leather, goat hair, or wood."

[21]Then Eleazar the priest said to the soldiers who had gone to war, "These are the teachings that the LORD gave to Moses: [22]Put any gold, silver, bronze, iron, tin, or lead— [23]anything that will not burn—into the fire, and then it will be clean. But also purify those things with the cleansing water. Then they will be clean. If something cannot stand the fire, wash it with the water. [24]On the seventh day wash your clothes, and you will be clean. After that you may come into the camp."

Dividing the Goods

[25]The LORD said to Moses, [26]"You, Eleazar the priest, and the leaders of the family groups should take a count of the goods, the men, and the animals that were taken. [27]Then divide those possessions between the soldiers who went to war and the rest of the people. [28]From the soldiers who went to war, take a tax for the LORD of one item out of every five hundred. This includes people, cattle, donkeys, or sheep. [29]Take it from the soldiers' half, and give it to Eleazar the priest as the LORD's share. [30]And from the people's half, take one item out of every fifty. This includes people, cattle, donkeys, sheep, or other animals. Give that to the Levites, who take care of the LORD's Holy Tent." [31]So Moses and Eleazar did as the LORD commanded Moses.

[32]There remained from what the soldiers had taken 675,000 sheep, [33]72,000 cattle, [34]61,000 donkeys, [35]and 32,000 women who had not had sexual relations with a man. [36]The soldiers who went to war got 337,000 sheep, [37]and they gave 675 of them to the LORD. [38]They got 36,000 cattle,

31:17 *Kill all* . . . . God used the people of Israel to execute his judgment against the people of Canaan for all their wicked acts. The laws of holy war are found in Deuteronomy 7 and 20.

and they gave 72 of them to the LORD. 39They got 30,500 donkeys, and they gave 61 of them to the LORD. 40They got 16,000 people, and they gave 32 of them to the LORD. 41Moses gave the LORD's share to Eleazar the priest, as the LORD had commanded him.

42Moses separated the people's half from the soldiers' half. 43The people got 337,500 sheep, 4436,000 cattle, 4530,500 donkeys, 46and 16,000 people. 47From the people's half Moses took one item out of every fifty for the LORD. This included the animals and the people. Then he gave them to the Levites, who took care of the LORD's Holy Tent. This was what the LORD had commanded Moses.

48Then the officers of the army, the commanders of a thousand men and commanders of a hundred men, came to Moses. 49They told Moses, "We, your servants, have counted our soldiers under our command, and not one of them is missing. 50So we have brought the LORD a gift of the gold things that each of us found: arm bands, bracelets, signet rings, earrings, and necklaces. These are to remove our sins so we will belong to the LORD."

51So Moses and Eleazar the priest took the gold from them, which had been made into all kinds of objects. 52The commanders of a thousand men and the commanders of a hundred men gave the LORD the gold, and all of it together weighed about 420 pounds; 53each soldier had taken something for himself. 54Moses and Eleazar the priest took the gold from the commanders of a thousand men and the commanders of a hundred men. Then they put it in the Meeting Tent as a memorial before the LORD for the people of Israel.

The Tribes East of the Jordan

32 The people of Reuben and Gad had large flocks and herds. When they saw that the lands of Jazer and Gilead were good for the animals, 2they came to Moses, Eleazar the priest, and the leaders of the people. 3-4They said, "We, your servants, have flocks and herds. The LORD has captured for the Israelites a land that is good for animals—the land around Ataroth, Dibon, Jazer, Nimrah, Heshbon, Elealeh, Sebam, Nebo, and Beon. 5If it pleases you, we would like this land to be given to us. Don't make us cross the Jordan River."

6Moses told the people of Gad and Reuben, "Shall your brothers go to war while you stay behind? 7You will discourage the Israelites from going over to the land the LORD has given them. 8Your ancestors did the same thing. I sent them from Kadesh Barnea to look at the land. 9They went as far as the Valley of Eshcol, and when they saw the land, they discouraged the Israelites from going into the land the LORD had given them. 10The LORD became very angry that day and made this promise: 11'None of the people who came from Egypt and who are twenty years old or older will see the land that I promised to Abraham, Isaac, and Jacob. These people have not followed me completely. 12Only Caleb son of Jephunneh the Kenizzite and Joshua son of Nun followed the LORD completely.'

13"The LORD was angry with Israel, so he made them wander in the desert for forty years. Finally all the people who had sinned against the LORD died, 14and now you are acting just like your ancestors! You sinful people are making the LORD even more angry with Israel. 15If you quit following him, it will add to their stay in the desert, and you will destroy all these people."

16Then the Reubenites and Gadites came up to Moses and said, "We will build pens for our animals and cities for our children here. 17Then our children will be in strong, walled cities, safe from the people who live in this land. Then we will prepare for war. We will help the other Israelites get their land, 18and we will not return home until every Israelite has received his land. 19We won't take any of the land west of the Jordan River; our part of the land is east of the Jordan."

20So Moses told them, "You must do these things. You must go before the LORD into battle 21and cross the Jordan River armed, until the LORD forces out the enemy. 22After the LORD helps us take the land, you may return home. You will have done your duty to the LORD and Israel, and you may have this land as your own.

23"But if you don't do these things, you will be sinning against the LORD; know for sure that you will be punished for your sin. 24Build cities for your children and pens for your animals, but then you must do what you promised."

25The Gadites and Reubenites said to Moses, "We are your servants, and we will do what you, our master, command. 26Our children, wives, and all our cattle will stay in the cities of Gilead, 27but we, your servants, will prepare for battle. We will go over and fight for the LORD, as you, our master, have said."

28So Moses gave orders about them to Eleazar the priest, to Joshua son of Nun, and to the leaders of the tribes of Israel. 29Moses said to them, "If the Gadites and Reubenites prepare for battle and cross the Jordan River with you, to go before the LORD and help you take the land, give them the land of Gilead for their own. 30But if they do not go

over armed, they will not receive it; their land will
be in Canaan with you."
31 The Gadites and Reubenites answered, "We
are your servants, and we will do as the LORD said.
32 We will cross over into Canaan and go before
the LORD ready for battle. But our land will be east
of the Jordan River."
33 So Moses gave that land to the tribes of Gad,
Reuben, and East Manasseh. (Manasseh was
Joseph's son.) That land had been the kingdom of
Sihon, king of the Amorites, and the kingdom of
Og, king of Bashan, as well as all the cities and the
land around them.
34 The Gadites rebuilt the cities of Dibon, Ataroth, Aroer, 35 Atroth Shophan, Jazer, Jogbehah,
36 Beth Nimrah, and Beth Haran. These were
strong, walled cities. And they built sheep pens.
37 The Reubenites rebuilt Heshbon, Elealeh, Kiriathaim, 38 Nebo, Baal Meon, and Sibmah. They
renamed Nebo and Baal Meon when they rebuilt
them.
39 The descendants of Makir son of Manasseh
went and captured Gilead and forced out the
Amorites who were there. 40 So Moses gave Gilead to the family of Makir son of Manasseh, and
they settled there. 41 Jair son of Manasseh went
out and captured the small towns there, and he
called them the Towns of Jair. 42 Nobah went and
captured Kenath and the small towns around it;
then he named it Nobah after himself.

Israel's Journey from Egypt

33 These are the places the Israelites went as
Moses and Aaron led them out of Egypt in
divisions. 2 At the LORD's command Moses recorded
the places they went, and these are the places they
went.
3 On the fifteenth day of the first month, the day
after the Passover, the Israelites left Rameses and
marched out boldly in front of all the Egyptians.
4 The Egyptians were burying their firstborn sons,
whom the LORD had killed; the LORD showed that
the gods of Egypt were false.
5 The Israelites left Rameses and camped at
Succoth.
6 They left Succoth and camped at Etham, at the
edge of the desert.
7 They left Etham and went back to Pi Hahiroth,
to the east of Baal Zephon, and camped near Migdol.
8 They left Pi Hahiroth and walked through the
sea into the desert. After going three days through
the Desert of Etham, they camped at Marah.
9 They left Marah and went to Elim; there were
twelve springs of water and seventy palm trees
where they camped.
10 They left Elim and camped near the Red Sea.
11 They left the Red Sea and camped in the Desert
of Sin.
12 They left the Desert of Sin and camped at
Dophkah.
13 They left Dophkah and camped at Alush.
14 They left Alush and camped at Rephidim, where
the people had no water to drink.
15 They left Rephidim and camped in the Desert
of Sinai.
16 They left the Desert of Sinai and camped at
Kibroth Hattaavah.
17 They left Kibroth Hattaavah and camped at
Hazeroth.
18 They left Hazeroth and camped at Rithmah.
19 They left Rithmah and camped at Rimmon
Perez.
20 They left Rimmon Perez and camped at Libnah.
21 They left Libnah and camped at Rissah.
22 They left Rissah and camped at Kehelathah.
23 They left Kehelathah and camped at Mount
Shepher.
24 They left Mount Shepher and camped at
Haradah.
25 They left Haradah and camped at Makheloth.
26 They left Makheloth and camped at Tahath.
27 They left Tahath and camped at Terah.
28 They left Terah and camped at Mithcah.
29 They left Mithcah and camped at Hashmonah.
30 They left Hashmonah and camped at Moseroth.
31 They left Moseroth and camped at Bene Jaakan.
32 They left Bene Jaakan and camped at Hor
Haggidgad.
33 They left Hor Haggidgad and camped at
Jotbathah.
34 They left Jotbathah and camped at Abronah.
35 They left Abronah and camped at Ezion Geber.
36 They left Ezion Geber and camped at Kadesh
in the Desert of Zin.
37 They left Kadesh and camped at Mount Hor,
on the border of Edom. 38 Aaron the priest obeyed
the LORD and went up Mount Hor. There he died
on the first day of the fifth month in the fortieth
year after the Israelites left Egypt. 39 Aaron was
123 years old when he died on Mount Hor.
40 The Canaanite king of Arad, who lived in the
southern area of Canaan, heard that the Israelites
were coming.
41 The people left Mount Hor and camped at
Zalmonah.
42 They left Zalmonah and camped at Punon.
43 They left Punon and camped at Oboth.
44 They left Oboth and camped at Iye Abarim,
on the border of Moab.
45 They left Iye Abarim and camped at Dibon Gad.
46 They left Dibon Gad and camped at Almon
Diblathaim.

47They left Almon Diblathaim and camped in the mountains of Abarim, near Nebo.

48They left the mountains of Abarim and camped on the plains of Moab near the Jordan River across from Jericho. 49They camped along the Jordan on the plains of Moab, and their camp went from Beth Jeshimoth to Abel Acacia.

50On the plains of Moab by the Jordan River across from Jericho, the LORD spoke to Moses. He said, 51"Speak to the Israelites and tell them, 'When you cross the Jordan River and go into Canaan, 52force out all the people who live there. Destroy all of their carved statues and metal idols. Wreck all of their places of worship. 53Take over the land and settle there, because I have given this land to you to own. 54Throw lots to divide up the land by family groups, giving larger portions to larger family groups and smaller portions to smaller family groups. The land will be given as the lots decide; each tribe will get its own land.

55"'But if you don't force those people out of the land, they will bring you trouble. They will be like sharp hooks in your eyes and thorns in your sides. They will bring trouble to the land where you live. 56Then I will punish you as I had planned to punish them.'"

The Borders of Canaan

34 The LORD said to Moses, 2"Give this command to the people of Israel: 'You will soon enter Canaan and it will be yours. These shall be the borders: 3On the south you will get part of the Desert of Zin near the border of Edom. On the east side your southern border will start at the south end of the Dead Sea, 4cross south of Scorpion Pass, and go through the Desert of Zin and south of Kadesh Barnea. Then it will go to Hazar Addar and over to Azmon. 5From Azmon it will go to the brook of Egypt, and it will end at the Mediterranean Sea.

6"'Your western border will be the Mediterranean Sea.

7"'Your northern border will begin at the Mediterranean Sea and go to Mount Hor. 8From Mount Hor it will go to Lebo Hamath, and on to Zedad. 9Then the border will go to Ziphron, and it will end at Hazar Enan. This will be your northern border.

10"'Your eastern border will begin at Hazar Enan and go to Shepham. 11From Shepham the border will go east of Ain to Riblah and along the hills east of Lake Galilee. 12Then the border will go down along the Jordan River and end at the Dead Sea.

"'These are the borders around your country.'"

13So Moses gave this command to the Israelites: "This is the land you will receive. Throw lots to divide it among the nine and one-half tribes, because the LORD commanded that it should be theirs. 14The tribes of Reuben, Gad, and East Manasseh have already received their land. 15These two and one-half tribes received land east of the Jordan River, across from Jericho."

16Then the LORD said to Moses, 17"These are the men who will divide the land: Eleazar the priest and Joshua son of Nun. 18Also take one leader from each tribe to help divide the land. 19These are the names of the leaders: from the tribe of Judah, Caleb son of Jephunneh; 20from the tribe of Simeon, Shemuel son of Ammihud; 21from the tribe of Benjamin, Elidad son of Kislon; 22from the tribe of Dan, Bukki son of Jogli; 23from the tribe of Manasseh son of Joseph, Hanniel son of Ephod; 24from the tribe of Ephraim son of Joseph, Kemuel son of Shiphtan; 25from the tribe of Zebulun, Elizaphan son of Parnach; 26from the tribe of Issachar, Paltiel son of Azzan; 27from the tribe of Asher, Ahihud son of Shelomi; 28from the tribe of Naphtali, Pedahel son of Ammihud."

29The LORD commanded these men to divide the land of Canaan among the Israelites.

The Levites' Towns

35 The LORD spoke to Moses on the plains of Moab across from Jericho by the Jordan River. He said, 2"Command the Israelites to give the Levites cities to live in from the land they receive. Also give the Levites the pastureland around these cities. 3Then the Levites will have cities where they may live and pastureland for their cattle, flocks, and other animals. 4The pastureland you give the Levites will extend fifteen hundred feet from the city wall. 5Also measure three thousand feet in each direction outside the city wall—three thousand feet east of the city, three thousand feet south of the city, three thousand feet west of the city, and three thousand feet north of the city, with the city in the center. This will be pastureland for the Levites' cities.

Cities of Safety

6"Six of the cities you give the Levites will be cities of safety. A person who accidentally kills someone may run to one of those cities for safety. You must also give forty-two other cities to the Levites; 7give the Levites a total of forty-eight cities and their pastures. 8The larger tribes of Israel must give more cities, and the smaller tribes must give fewer cities. Each tribe must give some of its cities to the Levites, but the number of cities they give will depend on the size of their land."

9Then the LORD said to Moses, 10"Tell the Israelites these things: 'When you cross the Jordan River and go into Canaan, 11you must choose cities to be cities of safety, so that a person who accidentally kills someone may run to them for safety. 12There the person will be safe from the dead person's relative who has the duty of punishing the killer. He will not die before he receives a fair trial in court. 13The six cities you give will be cities of safety. 14Give three cities east of the Jordan River and three cities in Canaan as cities of safety. 15These six cities will be places of safety for citizens of Israel, as well as for foreigners and other people living with you. Any of these people who accidentally kills someone may run to one of these cities.

16"'Anyone who uses an iron weapon to kill someone is a murderer. He must be put to death. 17Anyone who takes a rock and kills a person with it is a murderer. He must be put to death. 18Anyone who picks up a piece of wood and kills someone with it is a murderer. He must be put to death. 19A relative of the dead person must put the murderer to death; when they meet, the relative must kill the murderer. 20A person might shove someone or throw something at someone and cause death. 21Or a person might hit someone with his hand and cause death. If it were done from hate, the person is a murderer and must be put to death. A relative of the dead person must kill the murderer when they meet.

22"'But a person might suddenly shove someone, and not from hatred. Or a person might accidentally throw something and hit someone. 23Or a person might drop a rock on someone he couldn't see and kill that person. There was no plan to hurt anyone and no hatred for the one who was killed. 24If that happens, the community must judge between the relative of the dead person and the killer, according to these rules. 25They must protect the killer from the dead person's relative, sending the killer back to the original city of safety, to stay there until the high priest dies (the high priest had the holy oil poured on him).

26"'Such a person must never go outside the limits of the city of safety. 27If a relative of the dead person finds the killer outside the city, the relative may kill that person and not be guilty of murder. 28The killer must stay in the city of safety until the high priest dies. After the high priest dies, the killer may go home.

29"'These laws are for you from now on, wherever you live.

30"'If anyone kills a person, the murderer may be put to death only if there are witnesses. No one may be put to death with only one witness.

31"'Don't take money to spare the life of a murderer who should be put to death. A murderer must be put to death.

32"'If someone has run to a city of safety, don't take money to let the person go back home before the high priest dies.

33"'Don't let murder spoil your land. The only way to remove the sin of killing an innocent person is for the murderer to be put to death. 34I am the LORD, and I live among the Israelites. I live in that land with you, so do not spoil it with murder.'"

Land for Zelophehad's Daughters

36 The leaders of Gilead's family group went to talk to Moses and the leaders of the families of Israel. (Gilead was the son of Makir, the son of Manasseh, the son of Joseph.) 2They said, "The LORD commanded you, our master, to give the land to the Israelites by throwing lots, and the LORD commanded you to give the land of Zelophehad, our brother, to his daughters. 3But if his daughters marry men from other tribes of Israel, then that land will leave our family, and the people of the other tribes will get that land. So we will lose some of our land. 4When the time of Jubilee comes for the Israelites, their land will go to the tribes of the people they marry; their land will be taken away from us, the land we received from our fathers."

5Then Moses gave the Israelites this command from the LORD: "These men from the tribe of Joseph are right. 6This is the LORD's command to Zelophehad's daughters: You may marry anyone you wish, as long as the person is from your own tribe. 7In this way the Israelites' land will not pass from tribe to tribe, and each Israelite will keep the land in the tribe that belonged to his ancestors. 8A woman who inherits her father's land may marry, but she must marry someone from her own tribe. In this way every Israelite will keep the land that belonged to his ancestors. 9The land must not pass from tribe to tribe, and each Israelite tribe will keep the land it received from its ancestors."

10Zelophehad's daughters obeyed the LORD's command to Moses.

11So Zelophehad's daughters—Mahlah, Tirzah, Hoglah, Milcah, and Noah—married their cousins, their father's relatives. 12Their husbands were from the tribe of Manasseh son of Joseph, so their land stayed in their father's family group and tribe.

13These were the laws and commands that the LORD gave to the Israelites through Moses on the plains of Moab by the Jordan River, across from Jericho.

35:31 Murder: Deuteronomy 5:17

35:31 Capital Punishment: Deuteronomy 13:1–10

35:33–34 In this text, God adds another consideration to the Law's requirement that murderers be executed: shedding innocent blood pollutes the land given by God to his people. God is the giver of life, and he lives in the land with his people. So then, the taking of life by a murderer "spoils" the land where God dwells.

35:34 City: Isaiah 62

36:7 Land/Inheritance: Deuteronomy 24:19–22

JOSEPH

GENESIS 50:20

Who was Joseph? How does his life illustrate God's care for us? How does Joseph's life anticipate Jesus Christ?

The account of Joseph's life is found in Genesis 37, 39–50. The story takes us from Joseph's childhood to his death and recounts how and why the people of God wound up in Egypt.

When we first hear of Joseph, he was a young man with eleven brothers. He was the youngest and the son of his father Jacob's favorite wife, and so he was favored by his father over the other young men. This caused his brothers to be jealous of him, as demonstrated at the time he received Jacob's gift of a "special robe with long sleeves" (Genesis 37:3).

God gave Joseph an awareness of his future crucial role in the family by dreams, but he did not endear himself to his brothers in the way that he shared this information with the family (Genesis 37:5–11). Joseph, in a phrase, was something of a spoiled child, and his brothers responded with jealousy and anger.

These emotions exploded into action one fateful day when Joseph was sent out to check on his brothers, who were taking care of the flocks away from home. The brothers at first thought to kill him, but then decided to throw him into a pit. While Reuben intended to later rescue him, another brother, Judah, sold him into slavery to a group of Midianite traders on their way to Egypt.

From this point on, Joseph's life was out of his control. From a human perspective it seemed like he was at the mercy of his various masters, but, as we soon see, God was the one who was in control.

At first, Joseph was sold to an Egyptian named Potiphar, the captain of the palace guard. Because God was with Joseph, the affairs of Potiphar's house prospered well. However, a problem arose when Potiphar's wife desired to sleep with her husband's attractive slave. Joseph, though, realized that such an act would not only betray his human master but also his divine one (Genesis 39:9). In her anger Potiphar's wife framed Joseph and made it look like he tried to assault her.

The result was that Joseph was thrown into jail. Once again, though, it was God who was in control. Joseph's presence in the jail meant that God was also present, and the jail prospered. Joseph also showed his ability to interpret dreams when he told two of the king's chief officers what their dreams meant.

Joseph's ability to interpret dreams played a major role in the next stage of his life. The king's two officers were eventually released from prison and, just as Joseph had said, one was restored to his old position and the other was hanged.

Thus, when the Egyptian king had a striking dream that needed interpretation, the remaining official finally remembered Joseph. The king called Joseph to him, and Joseph successfully interpreted the dream and allowed the king to prepare for a lengthy famine. For his efforts, Joseph was made a ruler in Egypt (Genesis 41:41–45). When the famine hit years later, Egypt was the only nation that was prepared. Back in Canaan, Jacob, who believed his son to be dead, and his brothers, who thought he was a lowly slave, were hit hard by the famine. The brothers, with the exception of Benjamin, went to Egypt where they encountered Joseph.

Joseph knew his brothers, but they did not recognize him. Thus, Joseph could test their characters by presenting them with obstacles and dangers in which they had to decide whether they would look out for themselves or for others. The final test concerned Benjamin, and when Judah showed himself willing to offer himself in place of Benjamin (Genesis 44:32–34), Joseph revealed himself to his brothers and insisted that the whole family move to Egypt where they weathered the famine and prospered.

When his father died and his brothers once again feared for their lives, expecting Joseph to take his revenge against them finally, Joseph told them what had really gone on in his life: "You meant to hurt me, but God turned your evil into good to save the lives of many people, which is being done" (Genesis 50:20).

This important biblical principle that God overrules evil for good stands behind many of God's actions in biblical history, but it reaches its climax at the cross. Peter echoed Joseph's words here when he reflected on what happened at the cross of Christ: "Jesus was given to you, and with the help of those who don't know the law, you put him to death by nailing him to a cross. But this was God's plan which he had made long ago; he knew all this would happen. God raised Jesus from the dead and set him free from the pain of death, because death could not hold him" (Acts 2:23–24).

Joseph: For additional scriptures on this topic go to Genesis 37.

Adoption

EXODUS 2

What does the Bible teach about orphans and adoption?
Can this help us understand our adoption into God's family?

Nothing touches our hearts more than the sight of an orphan. Without parents to protect and nurture them, orphans are incredibly vulnerable to great suffering and harm. They are at the mercy of others who have power over them to either help or hurt.

God recognizes the great danger that orphans face, and he gives the fate of orphans the highest priority in the law that he gave his people Israel through Moses. He warns, them, especially the king, to take care of the orphans in their midst (Exodus 22:22; Deuteronomy 10:18; 24:17–22; 27:19). Orphans (along with widows, aliens, and the poor) are to receive unique attention, including protection and provisions. They are to receive part of a special tithe, and they are to be included in festivals. Those priorities—and the prophets—remind rulers that orphans are to receive attentive care or God will bring harsh judgment (Isaiah 1:17, 23; Jeremiah 22:2–3; Ezekiel 22:6–7). It is in God's character to give a unique love and attentiveness to those cut off from a society's protection and economic provision (Deuteronomy 10:18; Psalm 10:18; 146:9). God expects rulers and believers to conform to that priority. In the Old Testament, one of the king's highest duties was to care for and protect the orphan.

The story of Esther illustrates one Israelite's care for a family member who was orphaned in her youth. Esther's parents had died in her youth. Her cousin Mordecai took it upon himself to care for her (Esther 2:7). Of course, the purpose of the story of Esther in the Bible is to show how these two people were used by God in order to save the Jewish people from extermination during a particularly dangerous period of their history.

In another Bible story we learn how another adoption also leads to the salvation of God's people. Moses' mother decided that by making her baby an orphan she was giving him the best opportunity she could. She knew Moses had bad prospects if she kept him. Moses' sister, participating in this risky plot, helped ensure that he would be found. Further, when Pharaoh's daughter retrieved Moses from the river, Moses' sister suggested a strategy that temporarily reunited mother and baby. Later, Pharaoh's daughter adopted the baby Moses (Exodus 2:10). Thus Moses, instead of dying at the hands of Pharaoh's command, lived in his household, where God used him to rescue his people from slavery.

Moses eventually rejected his adopted status and reclaimed his original family and people (Hebrews 11:24). But, as is not uncommon, God used an evil situation for good. Moses, as an adopted bicultural person, was being prepared for a unique leadership role.

So we see from the Old Testament that God's concern for the helpless orphans leads him to insist that his people care for those without parents. This mandate continues in the New Testament (James 1:27).

In large and small ways, the church can keep children from becoming orphans. Christians can work to reduce or stop wars, famines, or disease. On personal and political levels, churches can help make it possible for men and women to keep their babies by providing resources, including a welcoming church "family," employment opportunities, basic provisions, and education. The church can help make adoptions easier by underwriting service agencies and providing support for adopting parents and adopted children.

The apostle Paul uses the idea of adoption to teach readers about our relationship with God. This is what is meant by "The Spirit . . . makes us children of God" (Romans 8:15). We were spiritual orphans, and God chose us. Paul uses this term in describing Israel (Romans 9:4; Galatians 4:5) and in describing the church (Ephesians 1:5), with a special word to the non-Jewish believers (Galatians 3:29; 4:7; Ephesians 3:6). Like any adopted children, our receptivity to our new father and his family makes a profound difference in the relationship. Just as the Spirit made us God's children, we are to follow that Spirit (Romans 8:14). Our lives are to reflect in our attitudes, actions, and words the character of the one who intervened in our marginalized status and made us his own sons and daughters. And because our full inheritance is still to come, Paul later instructs us to be hopeful as we wait for that completion of our adoptive status (Romans 8:23).

An orphan makes no choice about being orphaned or about being adopted, whether his parents die or decide not to raise their child. Without parents, orphans are powerless and in danger. So, according to the New Testament, it is with all of us. We are without full identity; we are without spiritual protection; we are without a home, until we receive the Father who adopts us and nurtures us in his holy family.

Adoption: For additional scriptures on this topic go to Exodus 22:22.

INTRODUCTION TO THE BOOK OF

DEUTERONOMY

Moses' Last Message to Israel

WHO WROTE THIS BOOK?

As with the other four books in the Pentateuch (or Torah), which is the name given to the first five books of the Bible, Deuteronomy is ascribed to Moses. However, the preamble and the account of the death of Moses were added by someone else unknown to us, perhaps Joshua.

TO WHOM WAS THIS BOOK WRITTEN?

Moses is writing to Israel, God's people.

WHERE WAS IT WRITTEN?

It is probable that Deuteronomy was written in Moab, east of the Jordan River (1:5).

WHEN WAS IT WRITTEN?

The Book of Deuteronomy, like the rest of the Pentateuch, was likely written about 1406 B.C., near the end of Israel's desert wanderings.

WHAT IS THE BOOK ABOUT?

Deuteronomy contains Moses' farewell speeches to God's people, including his review of the Law, as he handed over leadership of the nation of Israel to Joshua, who would lead them into the Promised Land.

WHY WAS THE BOOK WRITTEN?

Deuteronomy is a great spiritual message that reminds its readers of God's love for his people, Israel. It also tells of Israel's love for him. With the death of their earthly leader, Moses, Israel is called to a complete commitment to their God, both in their worship and their obedience to him. They are reminded that following God's teachings will bring them into the Promised Land.

SO WHAT DOES THIS BOOK MEAN TO US?

God still loves us as his people. And we must continue to love him with all our hearts. With the death of Christ, our leader, we are also called to a complete commitment to God in our worship and obedience. If we, like Israel, continue to follow God's teachings, because we are members of his family, we will also be ushered into the eternal land of promise—our heavenly home.

SUMMARY:

The Book of Deuteronomy contains Moses' final speeches to the people of Israel. He is about to die, and they are going to enter the Promised Land under the leadership of Joshua. His speech reminds them of all they have been through together in the desert. He also reminds them how often they did not trust God and warns them that they need to obey him in the future, if they want God to bless them.

Many of the stories and laws Moses tells the people at this historic time are repeats of what we have read earlier in Exodus, Leviticus, and Numbers. This explains why the book is called Deuteronomy, which means "repetition of the law." But the laws and events are not repeated exactly the same way. They are usually given a new slant, making them relevant for the new situation in the Promised Land, where the people will be living without Moses as their leader.

By recounting what happened in the past and the laws the people of Israel needed to obey, Moses is leading the people in a renewal of their agreement with God (see "agreement" in the Dictionary/Concordance). As a matter of fact, the whole Book of Deuteronomy has the structure of an agreement.

I. Introduction of the Parties Making an Agreement (1:1–5)
II. History of the Relationship (1:6–3:29)
III. Laws Which Govern the Relationship (4:1–26:19)
IV. Curses and Blessings (27:1–30:20)
V. Witnesses to the Agreement (31:1–34:12)

Moses, the one who speaks in this book, is the author of the Book of Deuteronomy. This book brings to a completion the five-part Torah (Pentateuch), or Law of Moses.

I. Introduction of the Parties Making an Agreement (1:1–5)

The first few verses give the setting for the book. Moses is on the plains of Moab just outside the Promised Land. He speaks to the gathered people and reminds them of the agreement they have with God.

II. History of the Relationship (1:6–3:29)

As is common in agreements from the ancient world, Moses begins by reminding the people of Israel of the relationship they have had with God. He focuses on the time since they left Mount Sinai up to the time they arrived on the plains of Moab. This period was a time when Israel rebelled against God, but God continued to love them.

III. Laws Which Govern the Relationship (4:1–26:19)

The longest section of Deuteronomy contains laws. Many are given a second time, though often with some slight changes. The highlight of the law in Deuteronomy is the Ten Commandments (Deuteronomy 5:1–22; see Exodus 20:1–17). And many of the other laws are applications of the Ten Commandments to more specific cases. Some of the most notable laws in the book include the command for a single place of worship (chapter 12), prohibitions for false prophecy (13:1–11; 18:14–21), and guidelines for the godly king (17:14–21).

IV. Curses and Blessings (27:1–30:20)

Moses' sermon comes to an end. He brings it to a climax by naming the blessings that will come to Israel if they obey God's teachings and the curses that will afflict them if they don't. He then calls on Israel to obey God, and by doing that, they choose life rather than death.

V. Witnesses to the Agreement (31:1–34:12)

Now that Moses' speech is over, we hear about the end of his ministry. Joshua is appointed to replace him as leader of Israel. Moses sings a final song, blesses the people, then goes up Mount Nebo and dies.

DEUTERONOMY

Moses Talks to the Israelites

This is the message Moses gave to all the people of Israel in the desert east of the Jordan River. They were in the desert area near Suph, between Paran and the towns of Tophel, Laban, Hazeroth, and Dizahab.

2(The trip from Mount Sinai to Kadesh Barnea on the Mount Seir road takes eleven days.) 3Forty years after the Israelites had left Egypt, on the first day of the eleventh month, Moses told the people of Israel everything the LORD had commanded him to tell them. 4This was after the LORD had defeated Sihon and Og. Sihon was king of the Amorite people and lived in Heshbon. Og was king of Bashan and lived in Ashteroth and Edrei.

5Now the Israelites were east of the Jordan River in the land of Moab, and there Moses began to explain what God had commanded. He said:

6The LORD our God spoke to us at Mount Sinai and said, "You have stayed long enough at this mountain. 7Get ready, and go to the mountain country of the Amorites, and to all the places around there—the Jordan Valley, the mountains, the western hills, the southern area, the seacoast, the land of Canaan, and Lebanon. Go as far as the great river, the Euphrates. 8See, I have given you this land, so go in and take it for yourselves. The LORD promised it to your ancestors—Abraham, Isaac, and Jacob and their descendants."

Moses Appoints Leaders

9At that time I said, "I am not able to take care of you by myself. 10The LORD your God has made you grow in number so that there are as many of you as there are stars in the sky. 11I pray that the LORD, the God of your ancestors, will give you a thousand times more people and do all the wonderful things he promised. 12But I cannot take care of your problems, your troubles, and your arguments by myself. 13So choose some men from each tribe—wise men who have understanding and experience—and I will make them leaders over you."

14And you said, "That's a good thing to do."

15So I took the wise and experienced leaders of your tribes, and I made them your leaders. I appointed commanders over a thousand people, over a hundred people, over fifty people, and over ten people and made them officers over your tribes. 16Then I told your leaders, "Listen to the arguments between your people. Judge fairly between two Israelites or between an Israelite and a foreigner. 17When you judge, be fair to everyone; don't act as if one person is more important than another, and don't be afraid of anyone, because your decision comes from God. Bring the hard cases to me, and I will judge them." 18At that time I told you everything you must do.

Spies Enter the Land

19Then, as the LORD our God commanded us, we left Mount Sinai and went toward the mountain country of the Amorite people. We went through that large and terrible desert you saw, and then we came to Kadesh Barnea. 20I said to you, "You have now come to the mountain country of the Amorites, to the land the LORD our God will give us. 21Look, here it is! Go up and take it. The LORD, the God of your ancestors, told you to do this, so don't be afraid and don't worry."

22Then all of you came to me and said, "Let's send men before us to spy out the land. They can come back and tell us about the way we should go and the cities we will find."

23I thought that was a good idea, so I chose twelve of your men, one for each tribe. 24They left and went up to the mountains, and when they came to the Valley of Eshcol they explored it. 25They took some of the fruit from that land and brought it down to us, saying, "It is a good land that the LORD our God is giving us."

Israel Refuses to Enter

26But you refused to go. You would not obey the command of the LORD your God, 27but grumbled in your tents, saying, "The LORD hates us. He brought us out of Egypt just to give us to the Amorites, who will destroy us. 28Where can we go now? The spies we sent have made us afraid, because they said, 'The people there are stronger and taller than we are. The cities are big, with walls up to the sky. And we saw the Anakites there!' "

1:5 Law: Psalm 1:2

1:10 *stars in the sky.* The picture which God draws indicates that Israel's population has burst at the seams. This saying goes back to Genesis 15:5 when God promised Abram that his offspring would be too many to count, like the stars in the sky.

1:15 Leadership: 1 Kings 14:7–8

1:17 Fear: Joshua 8:1

1:17 Citizen: Deuteronomy 17:15

29Then I said to you, "Don't be frightened; don't be afraid of those people. 30The LORD your God will go ahead of you and fight for you as he did in Egypt; you saw him do it. 31And in the desert you saw how the LORD your God carried you, like one carries a child. And he has brought you safely all the way to this place."

32But you still did not trust the LORD your God, even though 33he had always gone before you to find places for you to camp. In a fire at night and in a cloud during the day, he showed you which way to go.

34When the LORD heard what you said, he was angry and made an oath, saying, 35"I promised a good land to your ancestors, but none of you evil people will see it. 36Only Caleb son of Jephunneh will see it. I will give him and his descendants the land he walked on, because he followed the LORD completely."

37Because of you, the LORD was also angry with me and said, "You won't enter the land either, 38but your assistant, Joshua son of Nun, will enter it. Encourage him, because he will lead Israel to take the land for their own.

39"Your little children that you said would be captured, who do not know right from wrong at this time, will go into the land. I will give the land to them, and they will take it for their own. 40But you must turn around and follow the desert road toward the Red Sea."

41Then you said to me, "We have sinned against the LORD, but now we will go up and fight, as the LORD our God commanded us." Then all of you put on weapons, thinking it would be easy to go into the mountains.

42But the LORD said to me, "Tell the people, 'You must not go up there and fight. I will not be with you, and your enemies will defeat you.' "

43So I told you, but you would not listen. You would not obey the LORD's command. You were proud, so you went on up into the mountains, 44and the Amorites who lived in those mountains came out and fought you. They chased you like bees and defeated you from Edom to Hormah. 45So you came back and cried before the LORD, but the LORD did not listen to you; he refused to pay attention to you. 46So you stayed in Kadesh a long time.

Israel Wanders in the Desert

2 Then we turned around, and we traveled on the desert road toward the Red Sea, as the LORD had told me to do. We traveled through the mountains of Edom for many days.

2Then the LORD said to me, 3"You have traveled through these mountains long enough. Turn north 4and give the people this command: 'You will soon go through the land that belongs to your relatives, the descendants of Esau who live in Edom. They will be afraid of you, but be very careful. 5Do not go to war against them. I will not give you any of their land—not even a foot of it, because I have given the mountains of Edom to Esau as his own. 6You must pay them in silver for any food you eat or water you drink.' "

7The LORD your God has blessed everything you have done; he has protected you while you traveled through this great desert. The LORD your God has been with you for the past forty years, and you have had everything you needed.

8So we passed by our relatives, the descendants of Esau who lived in Edom. We turned off the Jordan Valley road that comes from the towns of Elath and Ezion Geber and traveled along the desert road to Moab.

The Land of Ar

9Then the LORD said to me, "Don't bother the people of Moab. Don't go to war against them, because I will not give you any of their land as your own; I have given Ar to the descendants of Lot as their own." 10(The Emites, who lived in Ar before, were strong people, and there were many of them. They were very tall, like the Anakites. 11The Emites were thought to be Rephaites, like the Anakites, but the Moabite people called them Emites. 12The Horites also lived in Edom before, but the descendants of Esau forced them out and destroyed them, taking their place as Israel did in the land the LORD gave them as their own.)

13And the LORD said to me, "Now get up and cross the Zered Valley." So we crossed the valley. 14It had been thirty-eight years from the time we left Kadesh Barnea until we crossed the Zered Valley. By then, all the fighting men from that time had died, as the LORD had promised would happen. 15The LORD continued to work against them to remove them from the camp until they were all dead.

16When the last of those fighting men had died, 17the LORD said to me, 18"Today you will pass by Ar, on the border of Moab. 19When you come near the people of Ammon, don't bother them or go to war against them, because I will not give you any of their land as your own. I have given it to the descendants of Lot for their own."

20(That land was also thought to be a land of the Rephaites, because those people used to live there,

1:31 Road/Way: 2 Samuel 22:31

1:38 Joshua: Deuteronomy 31:14

but the Ammonites called them Zamzummites.
21They were strong people, and there were many
of them; they were very tall, like the Anakites.
The LORD destroyed the Zamzummites, and the
Ammonites forced them out of the land and took
their place. 22The LORD did the same thing for the
descendants of Esau, who lived in Edom, when
he destroyed the Horites. The Edomites forced
them out of the land and took their place, and
they live there to this day. 23The Cretan people
came from Crete and destroyed the Avvites, who
lived in towns all the way to Gaza; the Cretans
destroyed them and took their place.)

Fighting the Amorites

24The LORD said, "Get up and cross the Arnon
Ravine. See, I am giving you the power to defeat
Sihon the Amorite, king of Heshbon, and I am
giving you his land. So fight against him and
begin taking his land. 25Today I will begin to
make all the people in the world afraid of you.
When they hear reports about you, they will
shake with fear, and they will be terrified of you."

26I sent messengers from the desert of Kedemoth to Sihon king of Heshbon. They offered him
peace, saying, 27"If you let us pass through your
country, we will stay on the road and not turn
right or left. 28We will pay you in silver for any food
we eat or water we drink. We only want to walk
through your country. 29The descendants of Esau
in Edom let us go through their land, and so did
the Moabites in Ar. We want to cross the Jordan
River into the land the LORD our God has given
us." 30But Sihon king of Heshbon would not let us
pass, because the LORD your God had made him
stubborn. The LORD wanted you to defeat Sihon,
and now this has happened.

31The LORD said to me, "See, I have begun to give
Sihon and his country to you. Begin taking the land
as your own."

32Then Sihon and all his army came out and
fought us at Jahaz, 33but the LORD our God gave
Sihon to us. We defeated him, his sons, and all
his army. 34We captured all his cities at that time
and completely destroyed them, as well as the
men, women, and children. We left no one alive.
35But we kept the cattle and valuable things from
the cities for ourselves. 36We defeated Aroer on
the edge of the Arnon Ravine, and we defeated
the town in the ravine, and even as far as Gilead.
No town was too strong for us; the LORD our God
gave us all of them. 37But you did not go near the
land of the Ammonites, on the shores of the
Jabbok River, or the towns in the mountains, as
the LORD our God had commanded.

The Battle at Bashan

3 When we turned and went up the road toward
Bashan, Og king of Bashan and all his army
came out to fight us at Edrei. 2The LORD said to
me, "Don't be afraid of Og, because I will hand
him, his whole army, and his land over to you. Do
to him what you did to Sihon king of the
Amorites, who ruled in Heshbon."

3So the LORD our God gave us Og king of Bashan
and all his army; we defeated them and left no
one alive. 4Then we captured all of Og's cities, all
sixty of them, and took the whole area of Argob,
Og's kingdom in Bashan. 5All these were strong
cities, with high walls and gates with bars. And
there were also many small towns with no walls.
6We completely destroyed them, just like the
cities of Sihon king of Heshbon. We killed all the
men, women, and children, 7but we kept all the
cattle and valuable things from the cities for ourselves.

8So at that time we took the land east of the
Jordan River, from the Arnon Ravine to Mount
Hermon, from these two Amorite kings. 9(Hermon is called Sirion by the Sidonian people, but
The Amorites call it Senir.) 10We captured all the
cities on the high plain and all of Gilead, and we
took all of Bashan as far as Salecah and Edrei, towns
in Og's kingdom of Bashan. 11(Only Og king of
Bashan was left of the few Rephaites. His bed was
made of iron, and it was more than thirteen feet
long and six feet wide! It is still in the Ammonite
city of Rabbah.)

The Land Is Divided

12At that time we took this land to be our own.
I gave the people of Reuben and Gad the land from
Aroer by the Arnon Ravine, as well as half of the
mountain country of Gilead and the cities in it.
13To the people of East Manasseh I gave the rest
of Gilead and all of Bashan, the kingdom of Og.
(The area of Argob in Bashan was called the land
of the Rephaites. 14Jair, a descendant of Manasseh,
took the whole area of Argob, all the way to the
border of the Geshurites and Maacathites. So that
land was named for Jair, and even today Bashan is
called the Towns of Jair.) 15I gave Gilead to Makir.
16I gave the Reubenites and the Gadites the land
that begins at Gilead and goes from the Arnon
Ravine (the middle of the Arnon is the border) to
the Jabbok River, which is the Ammonite border.
17The border on the west was the Jordan River in
the Jordan Valley, and it goes from Lake Galilee to
the Dead Sea west of Mount Pisgah.

18At that time I gave you this command: "The

LORD your God has given you this land as your own. Now your fighting men must take their weapons, and you must lead the other Israelites across the river. 19Your wives, your young children, and your cattle may stay here. I know you have many cattle, and they may stay here in the cities I have given you, 20until the LORD also gives your Israelite relatives a place to rest. They will receive the land the LORD your God has given them on the other side of the Jordan River. After that, you may each return to the land I have given you."

21Then I gave this command to Joshua: "You have seen for yourself all that the LORD your God has done to these two kings. The LORD will do the same thing to all the kingdoms where you are going. 22Don't be afraid of them, because the LORD your God will fight for you."

Moses Cannot Enter the Land

23Then I begged the LORD: 24"Lord GOD, you have begun to show me, your servant, how great you are. You have great strength, and no other god in heaven or on earth can do the powerful things you do. There is no other god like you. 25Please let me cross the Jordan River so that I may see the good land by the Jordan. I want to see the beautiful mountains and Lebanon."

26But the LORD was angry with me because of you, and he would not listen to me. The LORD said to me, "That's enough. Don't talk to me anymore about it. 27Climb to the top of Mount Pisgah and look west, north, south, and east. You can look at the land, but you will not cross the Jordan River. 28Appoint Joshua and help him be brave and strong. He will lead the people across the river and give them the land that they are to inherit, but you can only look at it." 29So we stayed in the valley opposite Beth Peor.

Moses Tells Israel to Obey

4 Now, Israel, listen to the laws and commands I will teach you. Obey them so that you will live and so that you will go over and take the land the LORD, the God of your ancestors, is giving to you. 2Don't add to these commands, and don't leave anything out, but obey the commands of the LORD your God that I give you.

3You have seen for yourselves what the LORD did at Baal Peor, how the LORD your God destroyed everyone among you who followed Baal in Peor. 4But all of you who continued following the LORD your God are still alive today.

5Look, I have taught you the laws and rules the LORD my God commanded me. Now you can obey the laws in the land you are entering, in the land you will take. 6Obey these laws carefully, in order to show the other nations that you have wisdom and understanding. When they hear about these laws, they will say, "This great nation of Israel is wise and understanding." 7No other nation is as great as we are. Their gods do not come near them, but the LORD our God comes near when we pray to him. 8And no other nation has such good teachings and commands as those I am giving to you today.

9But be careful! Watch out and don't forget the things you have seen. Don't forget them as long as you live, but teach them to your children and grandchildren. 10Remember the day you stood before the LORD your God at Mount Sinai. He said to me, "Bring the people together so I can tell them what I have to say. Then they will respect me as long as they live in the land, and they will teach these things to their children." 11When you came and stood at the bottom of the mountain, it blazed with fire that reached to the sky, and black clouds made it very dark. 12The LORD spoke to you from the fire. You heard the sound of words, but you did not see him; there was only a voice. 13The LORD told you about his Agreement, the Ten Commandments. He told you to obey them, and he wrote them on two stone tablets. 14Then the LORD commanded me to teach you the laws and rules that you must obey in the land you will take when you cross the Jordan River.

Laws About Idols

15Since the LORD spoke to you from the fire at Mount Sinai, but you did not see him, watch yourselves carefully! 16Don't sin by making idols of any kind, and don't make statues—of men or women, 17of animals on earth or birds that fly in the air, 18of anything that crawls on the ground, or of fish in the water below. 19When you look up at the sky, you see the sun, moon, and stars, and everything in the sky. But don't bow down and worship them, because the LORD your God has made these things for all people everywhere. 20But the LORD brought you out of Egypt, which tested you like a furnace for melting iron, and he made you his very own people, as you are now.

4:5–8 Israel's life of obedience to God while in the land would show the other nations around them that their God was the one true God. They would fulfill the promise God made to Abram that he and his descendants would be a blessing to all the people of the world (see Genesis 12:1–3).

4:9 Instruction: Deuteronomy 11:19
4:10 Church: Matthew 18:17-20
4:10 Community: Deuteronomy 6:3–9
4:13 Agreement: Joshua 24:25

21The LORD was angry with me because of you, and he swore that I would not cross the Jordan River to go into the good land the LORD your God is giving you as your own. 22I will die here in this land and not cross the Jordan, but you will soon go across and take that good land. 23Be careful. Don't forget the Agreement of the LORD your God that he made with you, and don't make any idols for yourselves, as the LORD your God has commanded you not to do. 24The LORD your God is a jealous God, like a fire that burns things up.

25Even after you have lived in the land a long time and have had children and grandchildren, don't do evil things. Don't make any kind of idol, and don't do what the LORD your God says is evil, because that will make him angry. 26If you do, I ask heaven and earth to speak against you this day that you will quickly be removed from this land that you are crossing the Jordan River to take. You will not live there long after that, but you will be completely destroyed. 27The LORD will scatter you among the other nations. Only a few of you will be left alive, and those few will be in other nations where the LORD will send you. 28There you will worship gods made by people, gods made of wood and stone, that cannot see, hear, eat, or smell. 29But even there you can look for the LORD your God, and you will find him if you look for him with your whole being. 30It will be hard when all these things happen to you. But after that you will come back to the LORD your God and obey him, 31because the LORD your God is a merciful God. He will not leave you or destroy you. He will not forget the Agreement with your ancestors, which he swore to them.

The Lord Is Great

32Nothing like this has ever happened before! Look at the past, long before you were even born. Go all the way back to when God made humans on the earth, and look from one end of heaven to the other. Nothing like this has ever been heard of! 33No other people have ever heard God speak from a fire and have still lived. But you have. 34No other god has ever taken for himself one nation out of another. But the LORD your God did this for you in Egypt, right before your own eyes. He did it with tests, signs, miracles, war, and great sights, by his great power and strength.

35He showed you things so you would know that the LORD is God, and there is no other God besides him. 36He spoke to you from heaven to teach you. He showed you his great fire on earth, and you heard him speak from the fire. 37Because the LORD loved your ancestors, he chose you, their descendants, and he brought you out of Egypt himself by his great strength. 38He forced nations out of their land ahead of you, nations that were bigger and stronger than you were. The LORD did this so he could bring you into their land and give it to you as your own, and this land is yours today.

39Know and believe today that the LORD is God. He is God in heaven above and on the earth below. There is no other god! 40Obey his laws and commands that I am giving you today so that things will go well for you and your children. Then you will live a long time in the land that the LORD your God is giving to you forever.

Cities of Safety

41Moses chose three cities east of the Jordan River, 42where a person who accidentally killed someone could go. If the person was not killed because of hatred, the murderer's life could be saved by running to one of these cities. 43These were the cities: Bezer in the desert high plain was for the Reubenites; Ramoth in Gilead was for the Gadites; and Golan in Bashan was for the Manassites.

The Laws Moses Gave

44These are the teachings Moses gave to the people of Israel. 45They are the rules, commands, and laws he gave them when they came out of Egypt. 46They were in the valley near Beth Peor, east of the Jordan River, in the land of Sihon. Sihon king of the Amorites ruled in Heshbon and was defeated by Moses and the Israelites as they came out of Egypt. 47The Israelites took his land and the land of Og king of Bashan, the two Amorite kings east of the Jordan River. 48This land went from Aroer, on the edge of the Arnon Ravine, to Mount Hermon. 49It included all the Jordan Valley east of the Jordan River, and it went as far as the Dead Sea below Mount Pisgah.

The Ten Commandments

5 Moses called all the people of Israel together and said: Listen, Israel, to the commands and laws I am giving you today. Learn them and obey them carefully. 2The LORD our God made an Agreement with us at Mount Sinai. 3He did not make this Agreement with our ancestors, but he made it with us, with all of us who are alive here today. 4The LORD spoke to you face to face from the fire on the mountain. 5(At that time I stood between you and the LORD in order to tell you what the LORD said; you were afraid of the fire, so you would not go up on the mountain.) The LORD said:

6“I am the LORD your God; I brought you out of the land of Egypt where you were slaves.

7“You must not have any other gods except me.

8“You must not make for yourselves any idols or anything to worship that looks like something in the sky above or on the earth below or in the water below the land. 9You must not worship or serve any idol, because I, the LORD your God, am a jealous God. If people sin against me and hate me, I will punish their children, even their grandchildren and great-grandchildren. 10But I will be very kind for a thousand lifetimes to those who love me and obey my commands.

11“You must not use the name of the LORD your God thoughtlessly, because the LORD will punish anyone who uses his name in this way.

12“Keep the Sabbath as a holy day, as the LORD your God has commanded you. 13You may work and get everything done during six days each week, 14but the seventh day is a day of rest to honor the LORD your God. On that day no one may do any work: not you, your son or daughter, your male or female slaves, your ox, your donkey, or any of your animals, or the foreigners living in your cities. That way your servants may rest as you do. 15Remember that you were slaves in Egypt and that the LORD your God brought you out of there by his great power and strength. So the LORD your God has commanded you to rest on the Sabbath day.

16“Honor your father and your mother as the LORD your God has commanded you. Then you will live a long time, and things will go well for you in the land that the LORD your God is going to give you.

17“You must not murder anyone.

18“You must not be guilty of adultery.

19“You must not steal.

20“You must not tell lies about your neighbor.

21“You must not want to take your neighbor's wife. You must not want to take your neighbor's house or land, his male or female slaves, his ox or his donkey, or anything that belongs to your neighbor.”

22The LORD spoke these commands to all of you on the mountain in a loud voice out of the fire, the cloud, and the deep darkness; he did not say anything else. Then he wrote them on two stone tablets, and he gave them to me.

23When you heard the voice from the darkness, as the mountain was blazing with fire, all your older leaders and leaders of your tribes came to me. 24And you said, “The LORD our God has shown us his glory and majesty, and we have heard his voice from the fire. Today we have seen that a person can live even if God speaks to him. 25But now, we will die! This great fire will burn us up, and we will die if we hear the LORD our God speak anymore. 26No human being has ever heard the living God speaking from a fire and still lived, but we have. 27Moses, you go near and listen to everything the LORD our God says. Then you tell us what the LORD our God tells you, and we will listen and obey.”

28The LORD heard what you said to me, and he said to me, “I have heard what the people said to you. Everything they said was good. 29I wish their hearts would always respect me and that they would always obey my commands so that things would go well for them and their children forever!

30“Go and tell the people to return to their tents, 31but you stay here with me so that I may give you all the commands, rules, and laws that you must teach the people to obey in the land I am giving them as their own.”

32So be careful to do what the LORD your God has commanded you, and follow the commands exactly. 33Live the way the LORD your God has commanded you so that you may live and have what is good and have a long life in the land you will take.

The Command to Love God

6 These are the commands, rules, and laws that the LORD your God told me to teach you to obey in the land you are crossing the Jordan River to take. 2You, your children, and your grandchildren must respect the LORD your God as long as

5:6 Freedom: Deuteronomy 7:6–8

5:7–9 God demands first place in the lives of his people. He is the only one who can save people and provide for their needs. To give worship to anything else brings God's displeasure and judgment.

5:9 *a jealous God.* Jealousy is often seen as a negative, harmful emotion (see “jealousy” in the Dictionary/Concordance). But with God it is a virtue because his jealousy guards his people against entering into a destructive relationship with a false god.

5:12–15 Deuteronomy gives a second telling of the Ten Commandments. There are changes from the first telling found in Exodus 20, nowhere shown more than in this the fourth commandment. In Exodus the Sabbath observance was grounded in the Creation; here it is based on Israel's salvation from Egypt. Just as God gave Israel rest from their bondage in Egypt, so the Sabbath provides rest from the work of the week.

5:16 Parenting: Deuteronomy 6:2

5:17 Murder: 2 Samuel 3:26–34

5:18 Adultery: Jeremiah 3:8

5:21 House/Home: 2 Samuel 7:13–16

5:21 Greed: Proverbs 15:27

5:22 Stone: Deuteronomy 27:6

5:24 Glory: Psalm 3:3

you live. Obey all his rules and commands I give
you so that you will live a long time. 3Listen,
Israel, and carefully obey these laws. Then all will
go well for you, and you will become a great nation
in a fertile land, just as the LORD, the God of your
ancestors, has promised you.
4Listen, people of Israel! The LORD our God is the
only LORD. 5Love the LORD your God with all your
heart, all your soul, and all your strength. 6Always
remember these commands I give you today.
7Teach them to your children, and talk about
them when you sit at home and walk along the
road, when you lie down and when you get up.
8Write them down and tie them to your hands as
a sign. Tie them on your forehead to remind you,
9and write them on your doors and gates.
10The LORD your God will bring you into the
land he promised to your ancestors, to Abraham,
Isaac, and Jacob, and he will give it to you. The
land has large, growing cities you did not build,
11houses full of good things you did not buy, wells
you did not dig, and vineyards and olive trees you
did not plant. You will eat as much as you want.
12But be careful! Do not forget the LORD, who
brought you out of the land of Egypt where you
were slaves.
13Respect the LORD your God. You must worship
him and make your promises only in his name.
14Do not worship other gods as the people around
you do, 15because the LORD your God is a jealous
God. He is present with you, and if you worship
other gods, he will become angry with you and
destroy you from the earth. 16Do not test the LORD
your God as you did at Massah. 17Be sure to obey
the commands of the LORD your God and the rules
and laws he has given you. 18Do what the LORD says
is good and right so that things will go well for
you. Then you may go in and take the good land
the LORD promised to your ancestors. 19He will force
all your enemies out as you go in, as the LORD has
said.
20In the future when your children ask you,
"What is the meaning of the laws, commands, and
rules the LORD our God gave us?" 21tell them, "We
were slaves to the king of Egypt, but the LORD
brought us out of Egypt by his great power. 22The
LORD showed us great and terrible signs and miracles, which he did to Egypt, the king, and his
whole family. 23The LORD brought us out of Egypt
to lead us here and to give us the land he promised
our ancestors. 24The LORD ordered us to obey all
these commands and to respect the LORD our God
so that we will always do well and stay alive, as
we are today. 25The right thing for us to do is this:
Obey all these rules in the presence of the LORD
our God, as he has commanded."

You Are God's People

7 The LORD your God will bring you into the land
that you are entering and that you will have
as your own. As you go in, he will force out these
nations: the Hittites, Girgashites, Amorites, Canaanites, Perizzites, Hivites, and Jebusites—seven
nations that are stronger than you. 2The LORD
your God will hand these nations over to you, and
when you defeat them, you must destroy them
completely. Do not make a peace treaty with them
or show them any mercy. 3Do not marry any of
them, or let your daughters marry their sons, or
let your sons marry their daughters. 4If you do,
those people will turn your children away from
me, to begin serving other gods. Then the LORD will
be very angry with you, and he will quickly destroy
you. 5This is what you must do to those people:
Tear down their altars, smash their holy stone pillars, cut down their Asherah idols, and burn their
idols in the fire. 6You are holy people who belong
to the LORD your God. He has chosen you from all
the people on earth to be his very own.
7The LORD did not care for you and choose you
because there were many of you—you are the
smallest nation of all. 8But the LORD chose you
because he loved you, and he kept his promise to
your ancestors. So he brought you out of Egypt by
his great power and freed you from the land of
slavery, from the power of the king of Egypt. 9So
know that the LORD your God is God, the faithful
God. He will keep his agreement of love for a

6:2 Parenting: Proverbs 13:24

6:4 Numbers: 2 Kings 19:32

6:5 Since the God of Israel is the only LORD, he is to be loved with one's whole being, including: one's heart (mind, emotions, and will); one's soul (that part of human existence that is eternal); and one's strength (that is, the material body). This, for Jesus, is the greatest commandment of them all (Matthew 22:37).

6:5 Will of God: 1 Kings 19:12

6:6 Trinity: Judges 6:11–24

6:9 Community: Deuteronomy 10:12–22

6:15 *a jealous God.* See 5:9.

7 War is conflict among nations which leads to fighting. God tells Israel to destroy all the people when they enter the land of Canaan because of their wickedness and the problem of their influencing the Israelites to do wrong. God also promises Israel that if she disobeys, God will bring nations against her in judgment (Deuteronomy 28:48–57). Although it was proper for God's people to fight as a way of furthering the purposes of God in the Old Testament, God's people now use different methods (John 18:36; 2 Corinthians 5:18–21; Ephesians 6).

7:4 Nehemiah: 2 Kings 25:10

7:4 Racism: Joshua 23:12–13

7:6 Gentiles (Non-Jews): Isaiah 42:6

7:8 Love: Proverbs 10:12

7:8 Freedom: Isaiah 61:1–4

thousand lifetimes for people who love him and
obey his commands. 10But he will pay back those
people who hate him. He will destroy them, and he
will not be slow to pay back those who hate him.
11So be careful to obey the commands, rules, and
laws I give you today.

12If you pay attention to these laws and obey
them carefully, the LORD your God will keep his
agreement and show his love to you, as he promised
your ancestors. 13He will love and bless you. He
will make the number of your people grow; he will
bless you with children. He will bless your fields
with good crops and will give you grain, new wine,
and oil. He will bless your herds with calves and
your flocks with lambs in the land he promised your
ancestors he would give you. 14You will be blessed
more than any other people. Every husband and
wife will have children, and all your cattle will
have calves. 15The LORD will take away all disease
from you; you will not have the terrible diseases
that were in Egypt, but he will give them to all the
people who hate you. 16You must destroy all
the people the LORD your God hands over to you.
Do not feel sorry for them, and do not worship
their gods, or they will trap you.

17You might say to yourselves, "Because these
nations are stronger than we are, we can't force
them out." 18But don't be afraid of them. Remember
what the LORD your God did to all of Egypt and its
king. 19You saw for yourselves the troubles, signs,
and miracles he did, how the LORD's great power
and strength brought you out of Egypt. The LORD
your God will do the same thing to all the nations
you now fear. 20The LORD your God will also send
terror among them so that even those who are
alive and hiding from you will die. 21Don't be
afraid of them, because the LORD your God is with
you; he is a great God and people are afraid of him.
22When the LORD your God forces those nations
out of the land, he will do it little by little ahead of
you. You won't be able to destroy them all at once;
otherwise, the wild animals will grow too many in
number. 23But the LORD your God will hand those
nations over to you, confusing them until they are
destroyed. 24The LORD will help you defeat their
kings, and the world will forget who they were. No
one will be able to stop you; you will destroy them
all. 25Burn up their idols in the fire. Do not wish for
the silver and gold they have, and don't take it for
yourselves, or you will be trapped by it. The LORD
your God hates it. 26Do not bring one of those hateful things into your house, or you will be completely
destroyed along with it. Hate and reject those
things; they must be completely destroyed.

Remember the Lord

8 Carefully obey every command I give you today.
Then you will live and grow in number, and
you will enter and take the land the LORD promised
your ancestors. 2Remember how the LORD your
God has led you in the desert for these forty years,
taking away your pride and testing you, because
he wanted to know what was in your heart. He
wanted to know if you would obey his commands.
3He took away your pride when he let you get
hungry, and then he fed you with manna, which
neither you nor your ancestors had ever seen. This
was to teach you that a person does not live by eating only bread, but by everything the LORD says.
4During these forty years, your clothes did not
wear out, and your feet did not swell. 5Know in
your heart that the LORD your God corrects you as
a parent corrects a child.

6Obey the commands of the LORD your God, living as he has commanded you and respecting him.
7The LORD your God is bringing you into a good
land, a land with rivers and pools of water, with
springs that flow in the valleys and hills, 8a land
that has wheat and barley, vines, fig trees, pomegranates, olive oil, and honey. 9It is a land where
you will have plenty of food, where you will have
everything you need, where the rocks are iron,
and where you can dig copper out of the hills.

10When you have all you want to eat, then praise
the LORD your God for giving you a good land. 11Be
careful not to forget the LORD your God so that you
fail to obey his commands, laws, and rules that I
am giving to you today. 12When you eat all you
want and build nice houses and live in them,
13when your herds and flocks grow large and your
silver and gold increase, when you have more of
everything, 14then your heart will become proud.
You will forget the LORD your God, who brought
you out of the land of Egypt, where you were
slaves. 15He led you through the large and terrible
desert that was dry and had no water, and that
had poisonous snakes and stinging insects. He
gave you water from a solid rock 16and manna to eat

7:11 Election (Chosen): Jeremiah 31:31-34

7:12 Good Works: Daniel 9:18

7:15 Sickness, Disease, Healing: Psalm 6

8:1–5 The wilderness (desert) is a most dangerous and inhospitable land. Here, the Israelites are tested and the true nature of their hearts becomes known: they are unbelieving, complaining, and rebellious. The Lord, meanwhile, as a parent, feeds them, preserves them, and corrects them. During this care and trial, Israel and her Lord get to know each other. He is mighty, powerful, and loving; they are proud, stubborn, and disobedient.

8:16 *manna.* See Numbers 11:6.

MOSES

EXODUS 2:10

Who is Moses and what did he do?
How is Jesus like Moses and why is this important for understanding the Christian life?

Moses stands out as one of the most prominent and important figures in the Old Testament. His greatness and importance lie in two areas. First, it was through his leadership that God brought the Israelites out of generations of slavery in Egypt to become the Israelite nation. Second, it was through Moses that God gave Israel their most treasured gift, the law.

Moses was born at an unsettling time in Israel's history. The Israelites had moved from the land of Canaan to Egypt several hundred years earlier under Joseph (Genesis 47:27; 50:14; Exodus 1:1–5). There they apparently lived in peace and safety. But after the death of Joseph and his generation, "a new king began to rule Egypt, who did not know who Joseph was" (Exodus 1:8). This new Pharaoh grew concerned about the ever-growing Israelite population and sought to stem the tide before their great numbers should pose a serious military threat. First, he tried enslaving them, but that only caused them to thrive all the more (1:12–13). Then, he instructed two Hebrew nurses to kill the newborn males, but they feared God rather than Pharaoh and refused to carry out his scheme (1:15–21). Finally, in a last-ditch attempt, Pharaoh commanded that all newborn males be thrown into the Nile (1:22). We are told that at least one child escaped: Moses. He was put into a basket by his mother and set on the water. He was found downstream by Pharaoh's daughter, of all people, who raised him as her own.

In preparation for his great task, God himself appeared to Moses in a burning bush (Exodus 3). It was here that God told Moses that he had shown him to be his servant to deliver the Israelites out of Egyptian bondage and bring them safely into their new land, the land of Canaan. It was through Moses that God inflicted the ten plagues upon Egypt (Exodus 7–11), which in the end finally convinced the hard-hearted Pharaoh to release the Israelites. Yet despite the disasters that had befallen his people, Pharaoh changed his mind one last time (14:5) and chased the Israelites into the desert. It was here that, trapped between the onrushing Egyptian army and the sea, God opened the sea and allowed the Israelites to pass through safely to the other side. After they crossed the sea, the Israelites began their period of wilderness wandering. Forty years later they finally entered the land of Canaan.

Along the way to the promised land, the Israelites stopped at Mount Sinai (Exodus 19), the very mountain where God had earlier revealed himself to Moses (Exodus 3). It was here that God gave the Israelites, through Moses, the law. This law included not only the Ten Commandments (20:1–17), but other laws concerning the day-to-day lives of the Israelites with one another (chapters 21–23), all of which is called the Book of the Agreement (24:7). Moses alone was permitted to be in God's presence on the mountain and receive the law. In this respect, he played the role of the mediator between God and his people, the Israelites.

Jesus is often described in the New Testament in a way that reminds us of Moses. As well as Jesus being the "second Adam," he is also the "second Moses." This is brought out both plainly and subtly in the New Testament. As the "new Moses," Jesus is the ultimate fulfillment of the prophet like Moses promised in Deuteronomy 18:15: "The LORD your God will give you a prophet like me."

Perhaps the most straightforward passage that describes Jesus in Moses-like terms is Hebrews 3:1–4:13. The writer of Hebrews compares the church to the Israelites wandering in the desert between Egypt and the promised land. Like the ancient Israelites of old, the church exists between its "Egypt" (bondage to sin) and its "promised land" (heaven). Jesus is the church's Moses who is faithfully bringing his people through this period of wilderness wandering. Hebrews 3:1–6 especially compares Jesus and Moses. However great Moses was, Jesus is greater still: "Jesus has more honor than Moses" (verse 3).

There are other passages that should also be understood in this light. One example is the sermon Jesus gave from a "hill" in Matthew 5–7. Like Moses receiving the law on a mountain, Jesus give his followers instructions on how they should live. Throughout this sermon, Jesus seems to be contrasting his "new law" with Moses' "old law" (see also John 1:17).

Jesus is our new Moses. The church has been delivered from its bondage to sin and awaits its entrance to the promised land. Until that time, Jesus faithfully guides his people through the trials and difficulties of everyday life.

Moses: For additional scriptures on this topic go to Matthew 2:10.

Growing Old

Exodus 4

How are older people viewed in the Old and New Testaments? Is there a biblical example for the modern fear of growing old? How is growing older understood—say, in the case of Moses?

Throughout the Old and New Testaments, older people are celebrated as leaders, prophets, judges, and people of God (Deuteronomy 33:1; Judges 2; 1 Kings 19; Luke 2:25–26, 36–37). Though there are many stories about young children who were chosen or set apart in a special way, their impact on society often did not take place until they were well along in years (Exodus 2:1–10; 1 Samuel 16). This is due, in part, to the cultural understanding that wisdom was gained through a long life. "Those who have lived many years should teach wisdom" (Job 32:7).

Wisdom was a necessary factor in establishing one's honor in biblical social systems (Proverbs 4:7–8). Even Jesus himself had to be described as wise before his earthly ministry could truly begin (Luke 2:52). We might want to think of wisdom in terms of wealth of experience. The length of a person's years would quite naturally go hand in hand with the wealth of that same person's experience. Thus, as illustrated by the Job passage above, wisdom is most easily gained through the passage of time. Therefore, it was the older and not the younger people who had the status and respect necessary to influence society.

The Bible itself insists that the younger generation gives honor and respect to those older than they are. Children are especially commanded to honor their parents. The fifth of the Ten Commandments begins, "Honor your father and your mother" (Exodus 20:12), and Paul repeats this in the book of Ephesians (6:1). Also, during the Old Testament period, the elders were important local leaders of the people of God. The New Testament, also, called its local leaders "elders," those who were mature in the faith. Instead of being fearful of growing old, then, in biblical times one might fear much more a youth spent unwisely. "So be very careful how you live. Do not live like those who are not wise, but live wisely" (Ephesians 5:5).

Ironically, Jesus said the children should not be kept from him (Matthew 19:14) in order to question his culture's disregard for youth in favor of those who had grown older. Therefore, although our modern-day understanding of growing old does not equate with theirs, our issues are the same. While we honor youth and productivity to the disregard of older people, they honored old age and wisdom to the disregard of their youth.

Consider Moses. God chose Moses to lead his people out of Israel. Moses was an oldest son, and an older man (Exodus 2:11–25). Yet despite his age and thus his acquired status, Moses was a humble man (Exodus 4; Numbers 12:3). Though in his society his status as an older person gave him the credibility to lead the people, his humility forced him to rely on God's power and not his own. The people may have allowed him to lead because he had the kind of wisdom and status that could only come from many years of living, but God chose him for other reasons as well.

As Moses grew older, in contrast to losing his influence or ability, he became even more honorable in the eyes of the people. He continued to lead the people through the wilderness and teach them the ways of God (Exodus, Leviticus, Numbers, Deuteronomy). It is God, and not the people, who decided when Moses would pass on the responsibility of leadership. And this, surprisingly, did not happen until his death. Growing older did not mean that Moses would have less to give. On the contrary, as seen in Deuteronomy 32–34, the people relied on and respected him more.

In Deuteronomy 32–34 Moses told the people of Israel their story of redemption from bondage through song. In the retelling, he reminded them of their past mistakes. He specifically told them to learn from their fathers and "older leaders," who would indeed know about past failures (Deuteronomy 32:7). By doing that, Moses reminded the community that the older people have stories to share from the past that would help younger people make wise decisions in the future. Moses, in turn, shared his wisdom with Joshua, to whom he gave over leadership of the people (Deuteronomy 34:9).

Most of the great things that Moses accomplished occurred while he was a very old man (Deuteronomy 34:7). We should celebrate this fact in our communities today by asking retirees and senior citizens to share their wealth of experience and be leaders among us. We must remember that it is God, and not those with status, who decides the length of our usefulness on earth.⚭

⚭**Growing Old:** For additional scriptures on this topic go to Exodus 11.

in the desert. Manna was something your ancestors
had never seen. He did this to take away your pride
and to test you, so things would go well for you in
the end. [17]You might say to yourself, "I am rich
because of my own power and strength," [18]but
remember the LORD your God! It is he who gives you
the power to become rich, keeping the agreement
he promised to your ancestors, as it is today.
[19]If you ever forget the LORD your God and follow other gods and worship them and bow down to
them, I warn you today that you will be destroyed.
[20]Just as the LORD destroyed the other nations for
you, you can be destroyed if you do not obey the
LORD your God.

The Lord Will Be with Israel

9 Listen, Israel. You will soon cross the Jordan
River to go in and force out nations that are
bigger and stronger than you. They have large cities
with walls up to the sky. [2]The people there are
Anakites, who are strong and tall. You know about
them, and you have heard it said: "No one can stop
the Anakites." [3]But today remember that the LORD
your God goes in before you to destroy them like a
fire that burns things up. He will defeat them ahead
of you, and you will force them out and destroy
them quickly, just as the LORD has said.
[4]After the LORD your God has forced those
nations out ahead of you, don't say to yourself, "The
LORD brought me here to take this land because I
am so good." No! It is because these nations are
evil that the LORD will force them out ahead of you.
[5]You are going in to take the land, not because you
are good and honest, but because these nations
are evil. That is why the LORD your God will force
them out ahead of you, to keep his promise to your
ancestors, to Abraham, Isaac, and Jacob. [6]The LORD
your God is giving you this good land to take as
your own. But know this: It is not because you
are good; you are a stubborn people.

Remember the Lord's Anger

[7]Remember this and do not forget it: You made
the LORD your God angry in the desert. You would
not obey the LORD from the day you left Egypt
until you arrived here. [8]At Mount Sinai you made
the LORD angry—angry enough to destroy you.
[9]When I went up on the mountain to receive the
stone tablets, the tablets with the Agreement the
LORD had made with you, I stayed on the mountain
for forty days and forty nights; I did not eat bread
or drink water. [10]The LORD gave me two stone
tablets, which God had written on with his own
finger. On them were all the commands that the
LORD gave to you on the mountain out of the fire,
on the day you were gathered there.
[11]When the forty days and forty nights were
over, the LORD gave me the two stone tablets, the
tablets with the Agreement on them. [12]Then the
LORD told me, "Get up and go down quickly from
here, because the people you brought out from
Egypt are ruining themselves. They have quickly
turned away from what I commanded and have
made an idol for themselves."
[13]The LORD said to me, "I have watched these
people, and they are very stubborn! [14]Get away so
that I may destroy them and make the whole world
forget who they are. Then I will make another
nation from you that will be bigger and stronger
than they are."
[15]So I turned and came down the mountain that
was burning with fire, and the two stone tablets
with the Agreement were in my hands. [16]When I
looked, I saw you had sinned against the LORD
your God and had made an idol in the shape of a
calf. You had quickly turned away from what the
LORD had told you to do. [17]So I took the two stone
tablets and threw them down, breaking them
into pieces right in front of you.
[18]Then I again bowed facedown on the ground
before the LORD for forty days and forty nights; I
did not eat bread or drink water. You had sinned
by doing what the LORD said was evil, and you
made him angry. [19]I was afraid of the LORD's anger
and rage, because he was angry enough with you
to destroy you, but the LORD listened to me again.
[20]And the LORD was angry enough with Aaron to
destroy him, but then I prayed for Aaron, too. [21]I
took that sinful calf idol you had made and burned
it in the fire. I crushed it into a powder like dust
and threw the dust into a stream that flowed down
the mountain.
[22]You also made the LORD angry at Taberah,
Massah, and Kibroth Hattaavah.
[23]Then the LORD sent you away from Kadesh
Barnea and said, "Go up and take the land I have
given you." But you rejected the command of the
LORD your God. You did not trust him or obey
him. [24]You have refused to obey the LORD as long
as I have known you.
[25]The LORD had said he would destroy you, so I
threw myself down in front of him for those forty

8:18 Memory: Nehemiah 4:14

9:2 *Anakites.* See Numbers 13:28.

9:23–29 Moses here reviews the rebellion at Kadesh along with other rebellions against God's authority while Israel was journeying in the wilderness (vv. 7–22). His purpose is to remind the people before they enter the Promised Land of the Lord's great anger toward rebelliousness and his swiftness to purge rebels from his holy people.

days and forty nights. 26I prayed to the LORD and said, "Lord GOD, do not destroy your people, your own people, whom you freed and brought out of Egypt by your great power and strength. 27Remember your servants Abraham, Isaac, and Jacob. Don't look at how stubborn these people are, and don't look at their sin and evil. 28Otherwise, Egypt will say, 'It was because the LORD was not able to take his people into the land he promised them, and it was because he hated them that he took them into the desert to kill them.' 29But they are your people, LORD, your own people, whom you brought out of Egypt with your great power and strength."

New Stone Tablets

10 At that time the LORD said to me, "Cut two stone tablets like the first ones and come up to me on the mountain. Also make a wooden Ark. 2I will write on the tablets the same words that were on the first tablets, which you broke, and you will put the new tablets in the Ark."

3So I made the Ark out of acacia wood, and I cut out two stone tablets like the first ones. Then I went up on the mountain with the two tablets in my hands. 4The LORD wrote the same things on these tablets he had written before—the Ten Commandments that he had told you on the mountain from the fire, on the day you were gathered there. And the LORD gave them to me. 5Then I turned and came down the mountain; I put the tablets in the Ark I had made, as the LORD had commanded, and they are still there.

6(The people of Israel went from the wells of the Jaakanites to Moserah. Aaron died there and was buried; his son Eleazar became priest in his place. 7From Moserah they went to Gudgodah, and from Gudgodah they went to Jotbathah, a place with streams of water. 8At that time the LORD chose the tribe of Levi to carry the Ark of the Agreement with the LORD. They were to serve the LORD and to bless the people in his name, which they still do today. 9That is why the Levites did not receive any land of their own; instead, they received the LORD himself as their gift, as the LORD your God told them.)

10I stayed on the mountain forty days and forty nights just like the first time, and the LORD listened to me this time also. He did not want to destroy you. 11The LORD said to me, "Go and lead the people so that they will go in and take the land I promised their ancestors."

What the Lord Wants You To Do

12Now, Israel, this is what the LORD your God wants you to do: Respect the LORD your God, and do what he has told you to do. Love him. Serve the LORD your God with your whole being, 13and obey the LORD's commands and laws that I am giving you today for your own good.

14The LORD owns the world and everything in it—the heavens, even the highest heavens, are his. 15But the LORD cared for and loved your ancestors, and he chose you, their descendants, over all the other nations, just as it is today. 16Give yourselves completely to serving him, and do not be stubborn any longer. 17The LORD your God is God of all gods and Lord of all lords. He is the great God, who is strong and wonderful. He does not take sides, and he will not be talked into doing evil. 18He helps orphans and widows, and he loves foreigners and gives them food and clothes. 19You also must love foreigners, because you were foreigners in Egypt. 20Respect the LORD your God and serve him. Be loyal to him and make your promises in his name. 21He is the one you should praise; he is your God, who has done great and wonderful things for you, which you have seen with your own eyes. 22There were only seventy of your ancestors when they went down to Egypt, and now the LORD your God has made you as many as the stars in the sky.

Great Things Israel Saw

11 Love the LORD your God and always obey his orders, rules, laws, and commands. 2Remember today it was not your children who saw and felt the correction of the LORD your God. They did not see his majesty, his power, his strength, 3or his signs and the things he did in Egypt to the king and his whole country. 4They did not see what he did to the Egyptian army, its horses and chariots, when he drowned them in the Red Sea as they were chasing you. The LORD ruined them forever. 5They did not see what he did for you in the desert until you arrived here. 6They did not see what he did to Dathan and Abiram, the sons of Eliab the Reubenite, when the ground opened up and swallowed them, their families, their tents, and everyone who stood

10:3 *acacia wood.* See Exodus 25:5.

10:5 Ark of the Agreement: Joshua 3–4

10:17–19 The basis for Israelite hospitality toward foreigners is God's hospitable treatment toward them when they themselves were slaves and homeless wanderers. Hospitality toward foreigners is to arise not from fear but from the tender heart, from feelings evoked by the people's memory of what it was like to be foreigners themselves.

10:18 Adoption: Deuteronomy 24:17–21

10:19 Foreigner (Alien): Psalm 39:12

10:19 Hospitality: Deuteronomy 24:17–22

10:22 Community: Deuteronomy 15:7–8

with them in Israel. 7It was you who saw all these great things the LORD has done.

8So obey all the commands I am giving you today so that you will be strong and can go in and take the land you are going to take as your own. 9Then you will live a long time in the land that the LORD promised to give to your ancestors and their descendants, a fertile land. 10The land you are going to take is not like Egypt, where you were. There you had to plant your seed and water it, like a vegetable garden, by using your feet. 11But the land that you will soon cross the Jordan River to take is a land of hills and valleys, a land that drinks rain from heaven. 12It is a land the LORD your God cares for. His eyes are on it continually, and he watches it from the beginning of the year to the end.∞

13If you carefully obey the commands I am giving you today and love the LORD your God and serve him with your whole being, 14then he will send rain on your land at the right time, in the fall and spring, and you will be able to gather your grain, new wine, and oil. 15He will put grass in the fields for your cattle, and you will have plenty to eat.

16Be careful, or you will be fooled and will turn away to serve and worship other gods. 17If you do, the LORD will become angry with you and will shut the heavens so it will not rain. Then the land will not grow crops, and you will soon die in the good land the LORD is giving you. 18Remember my words with your whole being. Write them down and tie them to your hands as a sign; tie them on your foreheads to remind you. 19Teach them well to your children, talking about them when you sit at home and walk along the road, when you lie down and when you get up.∞ 20Write them on your doors and gates 21so that both you and your children will live a long time in the land the LORD promised your ancestors, as long as the skies are above the earth.

22If you are careful to obey every command I am giving you to follow, and love the LORD your God, and do what he has told you to do, and are loyal to him, 23then the LORD will force all those nations out of the land ahead of you, and you will take the land from nations that are bigger and stronger than you. 24Everywhere you step will be yours. Your land will go from the desert to Lebanon and from the Euphrates River to the Mediterranean Sea. 25No one will be able to stop you. The LORD your God will do what he promised and will make the people afraid everywhere you go.

26See, today I am letting you choose a blessing or a curse. 27You will be blessed if you obey the commands of the LORD your God that I am giving you today. 28But you will be cursed if you disobey the commands of the LORD your God. So do not disobey the commands I am giving you today, and do not worship other gods you do not know. 29When the LORD your God brings you into the land you will take as your own, you are to announce the blessings from Mount Gerizim and the curses from Mount Ebal. 30(These mountains are on the other side of the Jordan River, to the west, toward the sunset. They are near the great trees of Moreh in the land of the Canaanites who live in the Jordan Valley opposite Gilgal.) 31You will soon cross the Jordan River to enter and take the land the LORD your God is giving you. When you take it over and live there, 32be careful to obey all the commands and laws I am giving you today.

The Place for Worship

12 These are the commands and laws you must carefully obey in the land the LORD, the God of your ancestors, is giving you. Obey them as long as you live in the land. 2When you inherit the lands of these nations, you must completely destroy all the places where they serve their gods, on high mountains and hills and under every green tree. 3Tear down their altars, smash their holy stone pillars, and burn their Asherah idols in the fire. Cut down their idols and destroy their names from those places.

4Don't worship the LORD your God that way, 5but look for the place the LORD your God will choose—a place among your tribes where he is to be worshiped. Go there, 6and bring to that place your burnt offerings and sacrifices; bring a tenth of what you gain and your special gifts; bring what you have promised and the special gifts you want to give the LORD, and bring the first animals born to your herds and flocks.

7There you will be together with the LORD your God. There you and your families will eat, and you will enjoy all the good things for which you have worked, because the LORD your God has blessed you.

8Do not worship the way we have been doing today, each person doing what he thinks is right. 9You have not yet come to a resting place, to the land the LORD your God will give you as your own. 10But soon you will cross the Jordan River to live

∞**11:12 Garden of Eden:** Song of Solomon 4:12–15
∞**11:19 Instruction:** Psalm 51:13
12:5 *a place.* Deuteronomy 12 commands that a single place be chosen for worshiping God. This commandment goes into effect when they inherit the lands of the nations (verse 2). This describes the time when David rids the Promised Land of all God's enemies and then the Temple is built by Solomon. Mount Zion, the location of the Temple, is the place referred to in this law.

in the land the LORD your God is giving you as your own, where he will give you rest from all your enemies and you will live in safety. 11Then the LORD your God will choose a place where he is to be worshiped. To that place you must bring everything I tell you: your burnt offerings and sacrifices, your offerings of a tenth of what you gain, your special gifts, and all your best things you promised to the LORD. 12There rejoice before the LORD your God. Everyone should rejoice: you, your sons and daughters, your male and female servants, and the Levites from your towns who have no land of their own. 13Be careful that you don't sacrifice your burnt offerings just anywhere you please. 14Offer them only in the place the LORD will choose. He will choose a place in one of your tribes, and there you must do everything I am commanding you.

15But you may kill your animals in any of your towns and eat as much of the meat as you want, as if it were a deer or a gazelle; this is the blessing the LORD your God is giving you. Anyone, clean or unclean, may eat this meat, 16but do not eat the blood. Pour it out on the ground like water. 17Do not eat in your own towns what belongs to the LORD: one-tenth of your grain, new wine, or oil; the first animals born to your herds or flocks; whatever you have promised to give; the special gifts you want to give to the LORD, or any other gifts. 18Eat these things when you are together with the LORD your God, in the place the LORD your God chooses to be worshiped. Everyone must do this: you, your sons and daughters, your male and female servants, and the Levites from your towns. Rejoice in the LORD your God's presence about the things you have worked for. 19Be careful not to forget the Levites as long as you live in the land.

20When the LORD your God enlarges your country as he has promised, and you want some meat so you say, "I want some meat," you may eat as much meat as you want. 21If the LORD your God chooses a place where he is to be worshiped that is too far away from you, you may kill animals from your herds and flocks, which the LORD has given to you. I have commanded that you may do this. You may eat as much of them as you want in your own towns, 22as you would eat gazelle or deer meat. Both clean and unclean people may eat this meat, 23but be sure you don't eat the blood, because the life is in the blood. Don't eat the life with the meat. 24Don't eat the blood, but pour it out on the ground like water. 25If you don't eat it, things will go well for you and your children, because you will be doing what the LORD says is right.

26Take your holy things and the things you have promised to give, and go to the place the LORD will choose. 27Present your burnt offerings on the altar of the LORD your God, both the meat and the blood. The blood of your sacrifices should be poured beside the altar of the LORD your God, but you may eat the meat. 28Be careful to obey all the rules I am giving you so that things will always go well for you and your children, and you will be doing what the LORD your God says is good and right.

29You will enter the land and take it away from the nations that the LORD your God will destroy ahead of you. When you force them out and live in their land, 30they will be destroyed for you, but be careful not to be trapped by asking about their gods. Don't say, "How do these nations worship? I will do the same." 31Don't worship the LORD your God that way, because the LORD hates the evil ways they worship their gods. They even burn their sons and daughters as sacrifices to their gods!

32Be sure to do everything I have commanded you. Do not add anything to it, and do not take anything away from it.

False Prophets

13 Prophets or those who tell the future with dreams might come to you and say they will show you a miracle or a sign. 2The miracle or sign might even happen, and then they might say, "Let's serve other gods" (gods you have not known) "and let's worship them." 3But you must not listen to those prophets or dreamers. The LORD your God is testing you, to find out if you love him with your whole being. 4Serve only the LORD your God. Respect him, keep his commands, and obey him. Serve him and be loyal to him. 5The prophets or dreamers must be killed, because they said you should turn against the LORD your God, who brought you out of Egypt and saved you from the land where you were slaves. They tried to turn you

12:11 Table Fellowship/Lord's Supper: Deuteronomy 12:17–18

12:18 Table Fellowship/Lord's Supper: Deuteronomy 16

13:1–5 Anyone can join God's community and claim that God has revealed some new truth through a dream. This passage is a strong warning to the community of faith to properly discern the wrong use of dreams. Dreams—even when accompanied by "miracles" or "signs"—must be submitted to what has already been established to be true about God. God would never reveal anything that is contrary to his character or his commands (see Jeremiah 23:25–32). In fact, we should be especially wise in this matter of dreams because verse 3 tells us God may be testing our discernment and obedience. God also issues a severe warning to false prophets who use dreams to deceive: "The prophets or dreamers must be killed," (13:5).

from doing what the LORD your God commanded you to do. You must get rid of the evil among you.

[6]Someone might try to lead you to serve other gods—it might be your brother, your son or daughter, the wife you love, or a close friend. The person might say, "Let's go and worship other gods." (These are gods that neither you nor your ancestors have known, [7]gods of the people who live around you, either nearby or far away, from one end of the land to the other.) [8]Do not give in to such people. Do not listen or feel sorry for them, and do not let them go free or protect them. [9]You must put them to death. You must be the first one to start to kill them, and then everyone else must join in. [10]You must throw stones at them until they die, because they tried to turn you away from the LORD your God, who brought you out of the land of Egypt, where you were slaves. [11]Then everyone in Israel will hear about this and be afraid, and no one among you will ever do such an evil thing again.

Cities to Destroy

[12]The LORD your God is giving you cities in which to live, and you might hear something about one of them. Someone might say [13]that evil people have moved in among you. And they might lead the people of that city away from God, saying, "Let's go and worship other gods." (These are gods you have not known.) [14]Then you must ask about it, looking into the matter and checking carefully whether it is true. If it is proved that a hateful thing has happened among you, [15]you must kill with a sword everyone who lives in that city. Destroy the city completely and kill everyone in it, as well as the animals, with a sword. [16]Gather up everything those people owned, and put it in the middle of the city square. Then completely burn the city and everything they owned as a burnt offering to the LORD your God. That city should never be rebuilt; let it be ruined forever. [17]Don't keep for yourselves any of the things found in that city, so the LORD will not be angry anymore. He will give you mercy and feel sorry for you, and he will make your nation grow larger, as he promised to your ancestors. [18]You will have obeyed the LORD your God by keeping all his commands that I am giving to you today, and you will be doing what the LORD says is right.

God's Special People

14 You are the children of the LORD your God. When someone dies, do not cut yourselves or shave your heads to show your sadness. [2]You are holy people, who belong to the LORD your God. He has chosen you from all the people on earth to be his very own.

[3]Do not eat anything the LORD hates. [4]These are the animals you may eat: oxen, sheep, goats, [5]deer, gazelle, roe deer, wild goats, ibex, antelope, and mountain sheep. [6]You may eat any animal that has a split hoof and chews the cud, [7]but you may not eat camels, rabbits, or rock badgers. These animals chew the cud, but they do not have split hoofs, so they are unclean for you. [8]Pigs are also unclean for you; they have split hoofs, but they do not chew the cud. Do not eat their meat or touch their dead bodies.

[9]There are many things that live in the water. You may eat anything that has fins and scales, [10]but do not eat anything that does not have fins and scales. It is unclean for you.

[11]You may eat any clean bird. [12]But do not eat these birds: eagles, vultures, black vultures, [13]red kites, falcons, any kind of kite, [14]any kind of raven, [15]horned owls, screech owls, sea gulls, any kind of hawk, [16]little owls, great owls, white owls, [17]desert owls, ospreys, cormorants, [18]storks, any kind of heron, the hoopoes, or bats.

[19]All insects with wings are unclean for you; do not eat them. [20]Other things with wings are clean, and you may eat them.

[21]Do not eat anything you find that is already dead. You may give it to a foreigner living in your town, and he may eat it, or you may sell it to a foreigner. But you are holy people, who belong to the LORD your God.

Do not cook a baby goat in its mother's milk.

Giving One-Tenth

[22]Be sure to save one-tenth of all your crops each year. [23]Take it to the place the LORD your God will choose where he is to be worshiped. There, where you will be together with the LORD, eat the tenth of your grain, new wine, and oil, and eat the animals born first to your herds and flocks. Do this so that you will learn to respect the LORD your God always. [24]But if the place the LORD will choose to be worshiped is too far away and he has blessed you so much you cannot carry a tenth, [25]exchange your one-tenth for silver. Then take the silver with you to the place the LORD your God shall choose. [26]Use the silver to buy anything you wish—cattle, sheep, wine, beer, or anything you wish. Then you and your family will eat and celebrate there before the LORD your God. [27]Do not

13:10 Capital Punishment: Deuteronomy 17:6–12
13:11 Prophet & Prophecy: Isaiah 41:21–24
13:18 Cults: Deuteronomy 18

forget the Levites in your town, because they have no land of their own among you.

28 At the end of every third year, everyone should bring one-tenth of that year's crop and store it in your towns. 29 This is for the Levites so they may eat and be full. (They have no land of their own among you.) It is also for strangers, orphans, and widows who live in your towns so that all of them may eat and be full. Then the LORD your God will bless you and all the work you do.

The Special Seventh Year

15 At the end of every seven years, you must tell those who owe you anything that they do not have to pay you back. 2 This is how you must do it: Everyone who has loaned money must cancel the loan and not make a neighbor or relative pay it back. This is the LORD's time for canceling what people owe. 3 You may make a foreigner pay what is owed to you, but you must not collect what another Israelite owes you. 4 But there should be no poor people among you, because the LORD your God will richly bless you in the land he is giving you as your own. 5 He will bless you if you obey the LORD your God completely, but you must be careful to obey all the commands I am giving you today. 6 The LORD your God will bless you as he promised, and you will lend to other nations, but you will not need to borrow from them. You will rule over many nations, but none will rule over you.

7 If there are poor among you, in one of the towns of the land the LORD your God is giving you, do not be selfish or greedy toward them. 8 But give freely to them, and freely lend them whatever they need. 9 Beware of evil thoughts. Don't think, "The seventh year is near, the year to cancel what people owe." You might be mean to the needy and not give them anything. Then they will complain to the LORD about you, and he will find you guilty of sin. 10 Give freely to the poor person, and do not wish that you didn't have to give. The LORD your God will bless your work and everything you touch. 11 There will always be poor people in the land, so I command you to give freely to your neighbors and to the poor and needy in your land.

Letting Slaves Go Free

12 If one of your own people sells himself to you as a slave, whether it is a Hebrew man or woman, that person will serve you for six years. But in the seventh year you must let the slave go free. 13 When you let slaves go, don't send them away without anything. 14 Give them some of your flock, your grain, and your wine, giving to them as the LORD has given to you. 15 Remember that you were slaves in Egypt, and the LORD your God saved you. That is why I am commanding this to you today.

16 But if your slave says to you, "I don't want to leave you," because he loves you and your family and has a good life with you, 17 stick an awl through his ear into the door; he will be your slave for life. Also do this to a female slave.

18 Do not think of it as a hard thing when you let your slaves go free. After all, they served you six years and did twice the work of a hired person. The LORD your God will bless you in everything you do.

Rules About Firstborn Animals

19 Save all the first male animals born to your herds and flocks. They are for the LORD your God. Do not work the first calf born to your oxen, and do not cut off the wool from the first lamb born to your sheep. 20 Each year you and your family are to eat these animals in the presence of the LORD your God, in the place he will choose to be worshiped. 21 If an animal is crippled or blind or has something else wrong, do not sacrifice it to the LORD your God. 22 But you may eat that animal in your own town. Both clean and unclean people may eat it, as they would eat a gazelle or a deer. 23 But don't eat its blood; pour it out on the ground like water.

The Passover

16 Celebrate the Passover of the LORD your God during the month of Abib, because it was during Abib that he brought you out of Egypt at night. 2 As the sacrifice for the Passover to the LORD your God, offer an animal from your flock or herd at the place the LORD will choose to be worshiped. 3 Do not eat it with bread made with yeast. But for seven days eat bread made without yeast, the bread of suffering, because you left Egypt in a hurry. So all your life you will remember the time you left Egypt. 4 There must be no yeast anywhere

---

15:1 *seven.* Not all numbers in the Bible are symbolic, but sometimes they are used for more than their literal meaning (see "numbers" in the Dictionary/Concordance). Seven is one of the more frequently used symbolic numbers. Based on the fact that God created the world in six days and rested on the seventh, the number seven often stands for completion or wholeness.

15:4 Poverty: 1 Samuel 2:8

15:8 Community: Amos 2:6–16

15:8 Debt/Loan: Deuteronomy 23:19–20

15:17 *awl.* A tool like a big needle with a handle at one end.

15:23 Materialism/Possessions: Psalm 49

15:23 Money: Deuteronomy 24:10–22

16:1 Feasts/Festivals: Matthew 26:17

16:1 Table Fellowship/Lord's Supper: Deuteronomy 16:15

in your land for seven days. Offer the sacrifice on the evening of the first day, and eat all the meat before morning; do not leave it overnight.

5Do not offer the Passover sacrifice in just any town the LORD your God gives you, 6but offer it in the place he will choose to be worshiped. Offer it in the evening as the sun goes down, which is when you left Egypt. 7Roast the meat and eat it at the place the LORD your God will choose. The next morning go back to your tents. 8Eat bread made without yeast for six days. On the seventh day have a special meeting for the LORD your God, and do not work that day.

The Feast of Weeks

9Count seven weeks from the time you begin to harvest the grain, 10and then celebrate the Feast of Weeks for the LORD your God. Bring an offering as a special gift to him, giving to him just as he has blessed you. 11Rejoice before the LORD your God at the place he will choose to be worshiped. Everybody should rejoice: you, your sons and daughters, your male and female servants, the Levites in your town, the strangers, orphans, and widows living among you. 12Remember that you were slaves in Egypt, and carefully obey all these laws.

The Feast of Shelters

13Celebrate the Feast of Shelters for seven days, after you have gathered your harvest from the threshing floor and winepress. 14Everybody should rejoice at your Feast: you, your sons and daughters, your male and female servants, the Levites, strangers, orphans, and widows who live in your towns. 15Celebrate the Feast to the LORD your God for seven days at the place he will choose, because the LORD your God will bless all your harvest and all the work you do, and you will be completely happy.

16All your men must come before the LORD three times a year to the place he will choose. They must come at these times: the Feast of Unleavened Bread, the Feast of Weeks, and the Feast of Shelters. No man should come before the LORD without a gift. 17Each of you must bring a gift that will show how much the LORD your God has blessed you.

Judges for the People

18Appoint judges and officers for your tribes in every town the LORD your God is giving you; they must judge the people fairly. 19Do not judge unfairly or take sides. Do not let people pay you to make wrong decisions, because that kind of payment makes wise people seem blind, and it changes the words of good people. 20Always do what is right so that you will live and always have the land the LORD your God is giving you.

God Hates Idols

21Do not set up a wooden Asherah idol next to the altar you build for the LORD your God, 22and do not set up holy stone pillars. The LORD your God hates them.

17 If an ox or sheep has something wrong with it, do not offer it as a sacrifice to the LORD your God. He would hate that.

2A man or woman in one of the towns the LORD gave you might be found doing something evil and breaking the Agreement. 3That person may have served other gods and bowed down to them or to the sun or moon or stars of the sky, which I have commanded should not be done. 4If someone has told you about it, you must look into the matter carefully. If it is true that such a hateful thing has happened in Israel, 5take the man or woman who has done the evil thing to the city gates and throw stones at that person until he dies. 6There must be two or three witnesses that it is true before the person is put to death; if there is only one witness, the person should not be put to death. 7The witnesses must be the first to throw stones at the person, and then everyone else will follow. You must get rid of the evil among you.

Courts of Law

8Some cases that come before you, such as murder, quarreling, or attack, may be too difficult to judge. Take these cases to the place the LORD your God will choose. 9Go to the priests who are Levites and to the judge who is on duty at that time. Ask them about the case, and they will decide. 10You must follow the decision they give you at the place the LORD your God will choose. Be careful to do everything they tell you. 11Follow the teachings they give you, and do whatever they decide, exactly as they tell you. 12The person who does not show respect for the judge or priest who is there serving the LORD your God must be put to death. You must get rid of that evil from Israel. 13Then everyone will hear about this and will be afraid, and they will not show disrespect anymore.

Choosing a King

14When you enter the land the LORD your God is giving you, taking it as your own and living in it, you will say, "Let's appoint a king over us like the nations all around us." 15Be sure to appoint over

16:15 Table Fellowship/Lord's Supper: Isaiah 25:6–7
16:17 Celebration: Matthew 26:26–30
17:3 Astrology: 2 Kings 17:16
17:12 Capital Punishment: Deuteronomy 21:18–21

you the king the LORD your God chooses. He must
be one of your own people. Do not appoint as your
king a foreigner who is not a fellow Israelite.
[16]The king must not have too many horses for
himself, and he must not send people to Egypt to
get more horses, because the LORD has told you,
"Don't return that way again." [17]The king must not
have many wives, or his heart will be led away from
God. He must not have too much silver and gold.

[18]When he becomes king, he should write a
copy of the teachings on a scroll for himself, a copy
taken from the priests and Levites. [19]He should
keep it with him all the time and read from it every
day of his life. Then he will learn to respect the
LORD his God, and he will obey all the teachings and
commands. [20]He should not think he is better than
his fellow Israelites, and he must not stop obeying the law in any way so that he and his descendants may rule the kingdom for a long time.

Shares for Priests and Levites

18 The priests are from the tribe of Levi, and
that tribe will not receive a share of the land
with the Israelites. They will eat the offerings made
to the LORD by fire, which is their share. [2]They
will not inherit any of the land like their brothers,
but they will inherit the LORD himself, as he has
promised them.

[3]When you offer a bull or sheep as a sacrifice,
you must share with the priests, giving them the
shoulder, the cheeks, and the inner organs. [4]Give
them the first of your grain, new wine, and oil, as
well as the first wool you cut from your sheep.
[5]The LORD your God has chosen the priests and
their descendants out of all your tribes to stand and
serve the LORD always.

[6]If a Levite moves from one of your towns anywhere in Israel where he lives and comes to the
place the LORD will choose, because he wants to
serve the LORD there, [7]he may serve the LORD his
God. He will be like his fellow Levites who serve
there before the LORD. [8]They all will have an equal
share of the food. That is separate from what he has
received from the sale of family possessions.

Do Not Follow Other Nations

[9]When you enter the land the LORD your God is
giving you, don't learn to do the hateful things the
other nations do. [10]Don't let anyone among you
offer a son or daughter as a sacrifice in the fire.
Don't let anyone use magic or witchcraft, or try to
explain the meaning of signs. [11]Don't let anyone
try to control others with magic, and don't let them
be mediums or try to talk with the spirits of dead
people. [12]The LORD hates anyone who does these
things. Because the other nations do these things,
the LORD your God will force them out of the land
ahead of you. [13]But you must be innocent in the
presence of the LORD your God.

The Lord's Special Prophet

[14]The nations you will force out listen to people
who use magic and witchcraft, but the LORD your
God will not let you do those things. [15]The LORD
your God will give you a prophet like me, who is
one of your own people. Listen to him. [16]This is
what you asked the LORD your God to do when
you were gathered at Mount Sinai. You said,
"Don't make us listen to the voice of the LORD our
God again, and don't make us look at this terrible
fire anymore, or we will die."

[17]So the LORD said to me, "What they have said
is good. [18]So I will give them a prophet like you,
who is one of their own people. I will tell him what
to say, and he will tell them everything I command. [19]This prophet will speak for me; anyone
who does not listen when he speaks will answer
to me. [20]But if a prophet says something I did not
tell him to say as though he were speaking for
me, or if a prophet speaks in the name of other
gods, that prophet must be killed."

[21]You might be thinking, "How can we know if a
message is not from the LORD?" [22]If what a prophet
says in the name of the LORD does not happen, it is
not the LORD's message. That prophet was speaking
his own ideas. Don't be afraid of him.

Cities of Safety

19 When the LORD your God gives you land
that belongs to the other nations, nations that
he will destroy, you will force them out and live

17:15 Citizen: Ezra 6:10

18:14–21 God used prophets to communicate to his people. They brought them warnings and messages of comfort. They revealed the future, but only as it related to their present situation.

Moses was a prophet, and this passage tells the Israelites that more prophets will follow him. Since the danger of false prophets was always present, the Lord gave the people tests to see if a prophet was from him or not. In Deuteronomy 13:1–11 God described a false prophet as one who would lead them to worship a different god. In Deuteronomy 18:14–21, the false prophet was one whose prophecy did not come true. Israel was to reject false prophets and follow the true prophet. Deuteronomy 18 anticipates a steady succession of prophets, but also looked forward to one prophet who would fulfill all prophecy (Acts 3:22–23).

18:15 Moses was the great deliverer whom God used to bring the Israelites out of Egypt. But Moses' days were limited and he, like all men, would have to die. So a prophet like Moses was promised to the Israelites to take his place. This promise is partially fulfilled by the Old Testament prophets whom God raised up throughout Israel's history, but it is ultimately fulfilled by Jesus, who is like Moses, but who "has more honor than Moses" (Hebrews 3:3).

18:22 Anti-Christ (Enemy of Christ): Jeremiah 28:9

18:22 Cults: 2 Corinthians 11:4

18:22 Obedience: Deuteronomy 28:1–14

Names of God

Exodus 6:2, 3

What function do the different names of God play in the Bible in terms of revealing his character?

Names were very important to the Hebrews because they believed a person's name revealed the person's character. If you knew someone's name you had an idea of his or her personality because the name was a window to the soul. Jacob's life of deceit was prophesied when he was given his name—the name Jacob literally meant "deceiver" (Genesis 27:34–36). Rachel, while dying in childbirth, named her son Ben-oni, "son of my sorrow." Jacob, though, changed their child's name to Ben-jamin, which meant "son of my right hand" (Genesis 35:18).

Exodus 6:2 is one of the most important passages in the Bible because God discloses himself with a new name—*Yahweh* (translated Lord) is God's personal name for Israel only. Before this time, he revealed himself with names like "God Almighty" (*El Shaddai*) or God (*El, Elohim*). These Old Testament names were used by both Israel and the nations surrounding them. But *Yahweh* was the personal name that spoke of the intimate, redemptive relationship God had with his chosen people.

God promises Moses that he will deliver his people from the oppressive Egyptians through his "great power." As a guarantee that he will keep his promise, God offers the name *Yahweh,* which literally means "I am that I am" or "I cause to be what will be." Jehovah—a name that says God is intimately connected to his people—he will certainly act on their behalf.

Throughout the Scriptures God is called and known by many names. He is called God (*El, Elohim* in the Old Testament, *Theos* in the New Testament). This name highlights the transcendence and absolute otherness of God. *El* is the creator and ruler of the universe. (Genesis 1:1; 17:1; 28:3; Joshua 3:10; 2 Samuel 22:31). *Theos* (God) is the New Testament name equivalent to *El* and *Elohim* and was the generic name for God used by the Greeks. Like *El* this name emphasizes God's transcendence (1 Corinthians 8:4; Ephesians 1:3; 1 Thessalonians 1:1; Revelation 16:9).

God is called Lord (*Adonai* in the OT, *Kurios* in the NT). When it is used to denote God, like *Yahweh*, the name Lord stresses the relational aspect of God. But *Adonai* also speaks of his authority and loftiness (Genesis 15:2; Exodus 4:10; Joshua 3:11).

God is called Savior (*Yasha* in the OT, Jesus in the NT). This is God's redemptive name. Salvation in the Bible included deliverance from dangers and enemies, but it also involved rescue from human guilt and eternal punishment. Jesus is the name of the son of God in the New Testament. The name Jesus reflects the Old Testament concept of God as personal deliverer from the chaos of the world and the evil of Satan (Matthew 1:21; John 1:29). Jesus is also called the Christ, which fulfills the OT prophecy of the Messiah (John 1:41) the Anointed One.

God is the Most High (*Elyon*). The name suggests a God who is majestic and exalted above all other gods (Genesis 14:18–20; Numbers 24:16; Psalm 97:9).

God is called Almighty (*El Shaddai*). This was God's covenant name and used primarily by the patriarchs. It most likely means the "God of the mountains." This name reflects the covenant agreement between God and the leader of the family or clan. *El Shaddai* was the God who nourished, guided, and protected the family (Genesis 49:25; Exodus 6:2–3). Later in the Bible the name occurs most frequently in the book of Job (31 times).

There were special names of God. He was called *El Olam*, "Eternal God" (Genesis 21:33); *El Roi*, "The God who sees" (Genesis 16:13); *El Berith*, "God of the covenant" (Judges 9:46); Lord All-Powerful (1 Samuel 17:45); The Beginning and the End (Isaiah 48:12); God, who has been alive forever (Daniel 7:9); The Alpha and Omega (Revelation 1:8, 17).

Like any person, God is known by his names. Because believers know the name of God, we know his identity and character, and thus we trust in his name (Genesis 12:8; Philippians 2:9, 10). God's people can also take great comfort and hope in his name. God's names are descriptive and predictive: they describe his nature, and they predict his faithfulness. His name tells us that he will act on the behalf of those who trust in his name.

Names of God: For additional scriptures on this topic go to Exodus 3:13–14.

FEASTS/FESTIVALS

EXODUS 12

What significance did feasts have in the life of Israel; in the life of the early church?
In what way do we see the faith of Israel and of the church embodied in these celebrations?
What is the role of similar celebrations in the life of the church today?

The feasts and festivals of the Old Testament provided a religious pattern to the year of the ancient Israelite. The festivals combined the practical events of life, such as harvest and planting, with the history of Israel and the great saving events of God. In the New Testament these feasts and events are seen as anticipations of the work of God in Christ and are taken up into the Christian worship cycle.

The Jewish calendar was dominated by the three main feasts of the year: Passover (which took place in the month of Nissan, which is modern March or April); Weeks (or the Feast of Harvest, which occurred in the month of Sivan, or later May and early June); and Tabernacles (or the Feast of Booths, which took place just after the Jewish New Year, Rosh Ha-Shanah, in the month of Tishri, which is our late September/early October). Each of these feasts has connections with the agricultural calendar of the early Israelites, and further connections with important events in the history of Israel.

The Feast of Passover celebrates first and foremost the victory of God that allowed Israel to escape their slavery in Egypt. The feast commemorates the night when the angel of the Lord "passed over" the houses of Israel and took every firstborn from the Egyptians. The details of the feast are covered in several locations in the Pentateuch (Exodus 12:1–27; 23:15; Leviticus 23:4–8; Numbers 28:16–25; Deuteronomy 16:1–8). The highlight of the seven-day festival is the meal where the Passover is celebrated and the story of Israel's redemption retold. The family gathers together to eat the Passover lamb and the unleavened bread—reminders how the blood of the lamb kept the angel of death away from the Israelite households on the night of the Passover, and how the Israelites ate the unleavened bread when they made their departure from Egypt. The Exodus is the defining event of Israel's relationship with God.

In the New Testament we find many motifs and ideas from the Exodus event and Passover, in particular, reapplied and interpreted in light of Christ. Paul can call Jesus, "Christ our Paschal (or Passover) lamb" seeing in the sacrifice of Christ a similar deliverance and salvation as that first offered in the Passover (1 Corinthians 5:7). The Christian meal, The Eucharist or the Lord's Supper, takes in many of the themes and motifs of the Passover supper. The supper Jesus offered to his disciples was a "new agreement" (Luke 22:20) in his blood and body just as the old Passover remembered the blood and sacrifice of the Passover lamb (Matthew 26:26–29; Mark 14:22–25; Luke 22:14–23). The bread and the wine of the passover meal are now for Christians interpreted as symbols of the redemption offered through Christ's atoning death.

The Feast of Weeks (Exodus 23:16; 34:22; Leviticus 23:15–22; Numbers 28:26–31; Deuteronomy 16:9–12) celebrates the wheat harvest. In later times this festival also became known as "Pentecost" because it is celebrated fifty days after the first sabbath beginning Passover. This one-day festival was the most clearly agricultural of all the festivals. The Feast of Weeks, or Pentecost, celebrated the harvest, and also served as the time when the offering of first fruits were brought to the Temple. The feast included a meal for the poor, so that the people were given a opportunity in the Feast of Weeks to share the bounty of the harvest both with God and with their needy neighbors.

In Acts 2:1 on the Day of Pentecost the disciples were filled with the Spirit. The great missionary harvest of the church began with Peter's sermon on Pentecost. In the modern Christian church "Pentecost" has become a celebration of the work and person of the Holy Spirit.

The last major feast of Israel was the Feast of Tabernacles (Exodus 23:16; 34:22; Leviticus 23:33–36, 39–43; Numbers 29:12–32; Deuteronomy 16:13–16). This feast celebrated the grape harvest in the fall and commemorated the wanderings of the Israelites in the wilderness.

Two other significant feasts were added to commemorate Israelite victories after the Exodus period. Purim was established as a two-day feast on the fourteenth and fifteenth of Adar (February/March) to celebrate the deliverance of Israel from the plots of Haman during the reign of the Persian King Xerxes (Esther 9:18–28). The Festival of Lights or "Hanukkah" celebrates the re-establishment of the Temple and temple worship during the Maccabean struggle (1 Maccabees 4:36–59; 2 Maccabees 10:6–8). Hanukkah, or the Feast of Dedication as it is called in John 10:22, is celebrated in the month of Tebeth (or December).

Feasts/Festivals: For additional scriptures on this topic go to Leviticus 23:1.

in their cities and houses. 2Then choose three cities in the middle of the land the LORD your God is giving you as your own. 3Build roads to these cities, and divide the land the LORD is giving you into three parts so that someone who kills another person may run to these cities.

4This is the rule for someone who kills another person and runs to one of these cities in order to save his life. But the person must have killed a neighbor without meaning to, not out of hatred. 5For example, suppose someone goes into the forest with a neighbor to cut wood and swings an ax to cut down a tree. If the ax head flies off the handle, hitting and killing the neighbor, the one who killed him may run to one of these cities to save his life. 6Otherwise, the dead person's relative who has the duty of punishing a murderer might be angry and chase him. If the city is far away, the relative might catch and kill the person, even though he should not be killed because there was no intent to kill his neighbor. 7This is why I command you to choose these three cities.

8-9Carefully obey all these laws I'm giving you today. Love the LORD your God, and always do what he wants you to do. Then the LORD your God will enlarge your land as he promised your ancestors, giving you the whole land he promised to them. After that, choose three more cities of safety 10so that innocent people will not be killed in your land, the land that the LORD your God is giving you as your own. By doing this you will not be guilty of allowing the death of innocent people.

11But if a person hates his neighbor and, after hiding and waiting, attacks and kills him and then runs to one of these cities for safety, 12the older leaders of his own city should send for the murderer. They should bring the person back from the city of safety and hand him over to the relative who has the duty of punishing the murderer. 13Show no mercy. You must remove from Israel the guilt of murdering innocent people so that things will go well for you.

14Do not move the stone that marks the border of your neighbor's land, which people long ago set in place. It marks what you inherit in the land the LORD your God is giving you as your own.

Rules About Witnesses

15One witness is not enough to accuse a person of a crime or sin. A case must be proved by two or three witnesses.

16If a witness lies and accuses a person of a crime, 17the two people who are arguing must stand in the presence of the LORD before the priests and judges who are on duty. 18The judges must check the matter carefully. The witness who is a liar, lying about a fellow Israelite, 19must be punished. He must be punished in the same way the other person would have been punished. You must get rid of the evil among you. 20The rest of the people will hear about this and be afraid, and no one among you will ever do such an evil thing again. 21Show no mercy. A life must be paid for a life, an eye for an eye, a tooth for a tooth, a hand for a hand, a foot for a foot.

Laws for War

20 When you go to war against your enemies and you see horses and chariots and an army that is bigger than yours, don't be afraid of them. The LORD your God, who brought you out of Egypt, will be with you. 2The priest must come and speak to the army before you go into battle. 3He will say, "Listen, Israel! Today you are going into battle against your enemies. Don't lose your courage or be afraid. Don't panic or be frightened, 4because the LORD your God goes with you, to fight for you against your enemies and to save you."

5The officers should say to the army, "Has anyone built a new house but not given it to God? He may go home, because he might die in battle and someone else would get to give his house to God. 6Has anyone planted a vineyard and not begun to enjoy it? He may go home, because he might die in battle and someone else would enjoy his vineyard. 7Is any man engaged to a woman and not yet married to her? He may go home, because he might die in battle and someone else would marry her." 8Then the officers should also say, "Is anyone here afraid? Has anyone lost his courage? He may go home so that he will not cause others to lose their courage, too." 9When the officers finish speaking to the army, they should appoint commanders to lead it.

10When you march up to attack a city, first make them an offer of peace. 11If they accept your offer and open their gates to you, all the people of that city will become your slaves and work for you. 12But if they do not make peace with you and fight you in battle, you should surround that city. 13The LORD your God will give it to you. Then kill all the men with your swords, 14and you may take everything else in the city for yourselves. Take the women, children, and animals, and you may use these things the LORD your God gives you from your enemies. 15Do this to all the cities that are far away, that do not belong to the nations nearby.

19:6 Neighbor: Deuteronomy 27:24

19:15 Crime: Deuteronomy 21:1–22:25

20:2 *the priest.* The priest played an important role in the wars of Israel. Since God led the army, the priests were needed to lead the troops in worship. War was holy in Israel.

20:7 Marriage: Psalm 45

[16]But leave nothing alive in the cities of the land the LORD your God is giving you. [17]Completely destroy these people: the Hittites, Amorites, Canaanites, Perizzites, Hivites, and Jebusites, as the LORD your God has commanded. [18]Otherwise, they will teach you what they do for their gods, and if you do these hateful things, you will sin against the LORD your God.

[19]If you surround and attack a city for a long time, trying to capture it, do not destroy its trees with an ax. You can eat the fruit from the trees, but do not cut them down. These trees are not the enemy, so don't make war against them. [20]But you may cut down trees that you know are not fruit trees and use them to build devices to attack the city walls, until the city is captured.

A Person Found Murdered

21 Suppose someone is found murdered, lying in a field in the land the LORD your God is giving you as your own, and no one knows who killed the person. [2]Your older leaders and judges should go to where the body was found, and they should measure how far it is to the nearby cities. [3]The older leaders of the city nearest the body must take a young cow that has never worked or worn a yoke, [4]and they must lead her down to a valley that has never been plowed or planted, with a stream flowing through it. There they must break the young cow's neck. [5]The priests, the sons of Levi, should come forward, because they have been chosen by the LORD your God to serve him and to give blessings in the LORD's name. They are the ones who decide cases of quarreling and attacks. [6]Then all the older leaders of the city nearest the murdered person should wash their hands over the young cow whose neck was broken in the valley. [7]They should declare: "We did not kill this person, and we did not see it happen. [8]LORD, remove this sin from your people Israel, whom you have saved. Don't blame your people, the Israelites, for the murder of this innocent person." And so the murder will be paid for. [9]Then you will have removed from yourselves the guilt of murdering an innocent person, because you will be doing what the LORD says is right.

Captive Women as Wives

[10]When you go to war against your enemies, the LORD will help you defeat them so that you will take them captive. [11]If you see a beautiful woman among the captives and are attracted to her, you may take her as your wife. [12]Bring her into your home, where she must shave her head and cut her nails [13]and change the clothes she was wearing when you captured her. After she has lived in your house and cried for her parents for a month, you may marry her. You will be her husband, and she will be your wife. [14]But if you are not pleased with her, you must let her go anywhere she wants. You must not sell her for money or make her a slave, because you have taken away her honor.

The Oldest Son

[15]A man might have two wives, one he loves and one he doesn't. Both wives might have sons by him. If the older son belongs to the wife he does not love, [16]when that man wills his property to his sons he must not give the son of the wife he loves what belongs to the older son, the son of the wife he does not love. [17]He must agree to give the older son two shares of everything he owns, even though the older son is from the wife he does not love. That son was the first to prove his father could have children, so he has the rights that belong to the older son.

Sons Who Refuse to Obey

[18]If someone has a son who is stubborn, who turns against his father and mother and doesn't obey them or listen when they correct him, [19]his parents must take him to the older leaders at the city gate. [20]They will say to the leaders, "Our son is stubborn and turns against us. He will not obey us. He eats too much, and he is always drunk." [21]Then all the men in his town must throw stones at him until he dies. Get rid of the evil among you, because then all the people of Israel will hear about this and be afraid.

Other Laws

[22]If someone is guilty of a sin worthy of death, he must be put to death and his body displayed on a tree. [23]But don't leave his body hanging on the tree overnight; be sure to bury him that same day, because anyone whose body is displayed on a tree is cursed by God. You must not ruin the land the LORD your God is giving you as your own.

21:17 Growing Old: 1 Samuel 2:30–35

21:21 Capital Punishment: Deuteronomy 22:21–25

21:22–23 A number of sins were capital offenses according to the Old Testament law. This law describes what is done with the body of such a criminal after his death; it is to be publicly displayed on a tree. But, the passage is careful to warn, that the body must not stay displayed through the night. To hang on a tree was considered a curse and a danger to the land. The cross of Christ was considered a tree, and Paul understood that the crucifixion made Christ a curse (Galatians 3:13). He became a curse in our place in order to free us from the curse of sin.

21:23 Curse: Deuteronomy 30:19

21:23 The Crucifixion of Jesus (The Way of the Cross): Matthew 10:38–39

22 If you see your fellow Israelite's ox or sheep wandering away, don't ignore it. Take it back to its owner. 2If the owner does not live close to you, or if you do not know who the owner is, take the animal home with you. Keep it until the owner comes looking for it; then give it back. 3Do the same thing if you find a donkey or coat or anything someone lost. Don't just ignore it.

4If you see your fellow Israelite's donkey or ox fallen on the road, don't ignore it. Help the owner get it up.

5A woman must not wear men's clothes, and a man must not wear women's clothes. The LORD your God hates anyone who does that.

6If you find a bird's nest by the road, either in a tree or on the ground, and the mother bird is sitting on the young birds or eggs, do not take the mother bird with the young birds. 7You may take the young birds, but you must let the mother bird go free. Then things will go well for you, and you will live a long time.

8When you build a new house, build a low wall around the edge of the roof so you will not be guilty if someone falls off the roof.

9Don't plant two different kinds of seeds in your vineyard. Otherwise, both crops will be ruined.

10Don't plow with an ox and a donkey tied together.

11Don't wear clothes made of wool and linen woven together.

12Tie several pieces of thread together; then put these tassels on the four corners of your coat.

Marriage Laws

13If a man marries a girl and has sexual relations with her but then decides he does not like her, 14he might talk badly about her and give her a bad name. He might say, "I married this woman, but when I had sexual relations with her, I did not find that she was a virgin." 15Then the girl's parents must bring proof that she was a virgin to the older leaders at the city gate. 16The girl's father will say to the leaders, "I gave my daughter to this man to be his wife, but now he does not want her. 17This man has told lies about my daughter. He has said, 'I did not find your daughter to be a virgin,' but here is the proof that my daughter was a virgin." Then her parents are to show the sheet to the city leaders, 18and the leaders must take the man and punish him. 19They must make him pay about two and one-half pounds of silver to the girl's father, because the man has given an Israelite virgin a bad name. The girl will continue to be the man's wife, and he may not divorce her as long as he lives.

20But if the things the husband said about his wife are true, and there is no proof that she was a virgin, 21the girl must be brought to the door of her father's house. Then the men of the town must put her to death by throwing stones at her. She has done a disgraceful thing in Israel by having sexual relations before she was married. You must get rid of the evil among you.

22If a man is found having sexual relations with another man's wife, both the woman and the man who had sexual relations with her must die. Get rid of this evil from Israel.

23If a man meets a virgin in a city and has sexual relations with her, but she is engaged to another man, 24you must take both of them to the city gate and put them to death by throwing stones at them. Kill the girl, because she was in a city and did not scream for help. And kill the man for having sexual relations with another man's wife. You must get rid of the evil among you.

25But if a man meets an engaged girl out in the country and forces her to have sexual relations with him, only the man who had sexual relations with her must be put to death. 26Don't do anything to the girl, because she has not done a sin worthy of death. This is like the person who attacks and murders a neighbor; 27the man found the engaged girl in the country and she screamed, but no one was there to save her.

28If a man meets a virgin who is not engaged to be married and forces her to have sexual relations with him and people find out about it, 29the man must pay the girl's father about one and one-fourth pounds of silver. He must also marry the girl, because he has dishonored her, and he may never divorce her for as long as he lives.

30A man must not marry his father's wife; he must not dishonor his father in this way.

The Lord's People

23 No man who has had part of his sex organ cut off may come into the meeting to worship the LORD.

2No one born to parents who were forbidden by law to marry may come into the meeting to worship the LORD. The descendants for ten generations may not come in either.

22:8 *roof.* In Bible times houses were built with flat roofs. The roof was used for drying things such as flax and fruit. And it was used as an extra room, as a place for worship, and as a place to sleep in the summer.

22:22 Sexuality: Song of Solomon
22:25 Capital Punishment: 1 Kings 2:25
22:25 Crime: Deuteronomy 25:2
22:30 Divorce: Deuteronomy 24:1–5

3No Ammonite or Moabite may come into the
meeting to worship the LORD, and none of their
descendants for ten generations may come in. 4This
is because the Ammonites and Moabites did not
give you bread and water when you came out of
Egypt. And they hired Balaam son of Beor, from
Pethor in Northwest Mesopotamia, to put a curse
on you. 5But the LORD your God would not listen to Balaam. He turned the curse into a blessing
for you, because the LORD your God loves you.
6Don't wish for their peace or success as long as
you live.

7Don't hate Edomites; they are your close relatives. Don't hate Egyptians, because you were foreigners in their country. 8The great-grandchildren
of these two peoples may come into the meeting
to worship the LORD.

Keeping the Camp Clean

9When you are camped in time of war, keep
away from unclean things. 10If a man becomes
unclean during the night, he must go outside the
camp and not come back. 11But when evening
comes, he must wash himself, and at sunset he
may come back into the camp.

12Choose a place outside the camp where people may go to relieve themselves. 13Carry a tent
peg with you, and when you relieve yourself, dig
a hole and cover up your dung. 14The LORD your
God moves around through your camp to protect
you and to defeat your enemies for you, so the
camp must be holy. He must not see anything
unclean among you so that he will not leave you.

Other Laws

15If an escaped slave comes to you, do not hand
over the slave to his master. 16Let the slave live
with you anywhere he likes, in any town he
chooses. Do not mistreat him.

17No Israelite man or woman must ever become a temple prostitute. 18Do not bring a male
or female prostitute's pay to the Temple of the
LORD your God to pay what you have promised to
the LORD, because the LORD your God hates prostitution.

19If you loan your fellow Israelites money or
food or anything else, don't make them pay back
more than you loaned them. 20You may charge
foreigners, but not fellow Israelites. Then the
LORD your God will bless everything you do in the
land you are entering to take as your own.

21If you make a promise to give something to the
LORD your God, do not be slow to pay it, because
the LORD your God demands it from you. Do not be
guilty of sin. 22But if you do not make the promise,
you will not be guilty. 23You must do whatever
you say you will do, because you chose to make
the promise to the LORD your God.

24If you go into your neighbor's vineyard, you
may eat as many grapes as you wish, but do not
put any grapes into your basket. 25If you go into
your neighbor's grainfield, you may pick grain
with your hands, but you must not cut down your
neighbor's grain with your sickle.

24 A man might marry a woman but later
decide she doesn't please him because he
has found something bad about her. He writes
out divorce papers for her, gives them to her, and
sends her away from his house. 2After she leaves
his house, she goes and marries another man,
3but her second husband does not like her either.
So he writes out divorce papers for her, gives
them to her, and sends her away from his house.
Or the second husband might die. 4In either case,
her first husband who divorced her must not marry
her again, because she has become unclean. The
LORD would hate this. Don't bring this sin into the
land the LORD your God is giving you as your own.

5A man who has just married must not be sent to
war or be given any other duty. He should be free to
stay home for a year to make his new wife happy.

6If someone owes you something, do not take
his two stones for grinding grain—not even the
upper one—in place of what he owes, because
this is how the person makes a living.

7If someone kidnaps a fellow Israelite, either to
make him a slave or sell him, the kidnapper must
be killed. You must get rid of the evil among you.

8Be careful when someone has a skin disease.
Do exactly what the priests, the Levites, teach you,
being careful to do what I have commanded them.
9Remember what the LORD your God did to Miriam
on your way out of Egypt.

10When you make a loan to your neighbors, don't
go into their homes to get something in place of
it. 11Stay outside and let them go in and get what
they promised you. 12If a poor person gives you a

23:4 Ruth: Nehemiah 13:1–2
23:20 Debt/Loan: Amos 2:6–8
23:23 Oath/Vow: Psalm 66:13–15

24:1–4 This law is somewhat complicated. The actual reason the law was written is not given until verse 4. The phrase "something bad about her," which is the reason for the divorce, brought about an argument over what "something bad" meant. The first three verses merely set the stage for the law — they are not commands or laws. This law is a recognition that divorce happened then, as it does now. It instructs people how to live after divorce. The person who puts away his wife must not marry her again if she, in the meantime, was married to another (verse 4). Perhaps human nature took this law to be a commandment allowing divorce.

24:5 Divorce: Deuteronomy 25:5–10

coat to show he will pay the loan back, don't keep it overnight. [13]Give the coat back at sunset, because your neighbor needs that coat to sleep in, and he will be grateful to you. And the LORD your God will see that you have done a good thing.

[14]Don't cheat hired servants who are poor and needy, whether they are fellow Israelites or foreigners living in one of your towns. [15]Pay them each day before sunset, because they are poor and need the money. Otherwise,they may complain to the LORD about you, and you will be guilty of sin.

[16]Parents must not be put to death if their children do wrong, and children must not be put to death if their parents do wrong. Each person must die for his own sin.

[17]Do not be unfair to a foreigner or an orphan. Don't take a widow's coat to make sure she pays you back. [18]Remember that you were slaves in Egypt, and the LORD your God saved you from there. That is why I am commanding you to do this.

[19]When you are gathering your harvest in the field and leave behind a bundle of grain, don't go back and get it. Leave it there for foreigners, orphans, and widows so that the LORD your God can bless everything you do. [20]When you beat your olive trees to knock the olives off, don't beat the trees a second time. Leave what is left for foreigners, orphans, and widows. [21]When you harvest the grapes in your vineyard, don't pick the vines a second time. Leave what is left for foreigners, orphans, and widows. [22]Remember that you were slaves in Egypt; that is why I am commanding you to do this.

25

If two people have an argument and go to court, the judges will decide the case. They will declare one person right and the other guilty. [2]If the guilty person has to be punished with a beating, the judge will make that person lie down and be beaten in front of him. The number of lashes should match the crime. [3]But don't hit a person more than forty times, because more than that would disgrace him before others.

[4]When an ox is working in the grain, do not cover its mouth to keep it from eating.

[5]If two brothers are living together, and one of them dies without having a son, his widow must not marry someone outside her husband's family. Her husband's brother must marry her, which is his duty to her as a brother-in-law. [6]The first son she has counts as the son of the dead brother so that his name will not be forgotten in Israel.

[7]But if a man does not want to marry his brother's widow, she should go to the older leaders at the town gate. She should say, "My brother-in-law will not carry on his brother's name in Israel. He refuses to do his duty for me."

[8]Then the older leaders of the town must call for the man and talk to him. But if he is stubborn and says, "I don't want to marry her," [9]the woman must go up to him in front of the leaders. She must take off one of his sandals and spit in his face and say, "This is for the man who won't continue his brother's family!" [10]Then that man's family shall be known in Israel as the Family of the Unsandaled.

[11]If two men are fighting and one man's wife comes to save her husband from his attacker, grabbing the attacker by his sex organs, [12]you must cut off her hand. Show her no mercy.

[13]Don't carry two sets of weights with you, one heavy and one light. [14]Don't have two different sets of measures in your house, one large and one small. [15]You must have true and honest weights and measures so that you will live a long time in the land the LORD your God is giving you. [16]The LORD your God hates anyone who is dishonest and uses dishonest measures.

[17]Remember what the Amalekites did to you when you came out of Egypt. [18]When you were tired and worn out, they met you on the road and attacked all those lagging behind. They were not afraid of God. [19]When the LORD your God gives you rest from all the enemies around you in the land he is giving you as your own, you shall destroy any memory of the Amalekites on the earth. Do not forget!

24:17 Abortion and Crisis Pregnancy: Job 31:15

24:17–22 The people's memory of how hard slavery and homelessness were for them, and of the love and blessing God gave them through his care and provision, is foundational to the Law's provisions for the weakest and most powerless in their own society—foreigners, orphans, and widows.

24:19 Ruth: See article on page 389.

24:19–22 The land of Canaan (Promised Land) was "a fertile land," a land of abundant life. It would be a denial of this truth if a person had to go without food in the land God had given to Israel. Laws like these were supposed to ensure that even the poorest people—the widows and orphans—could enjoy some of the blessings of living in the Promised Land.

24:21 Adoption: Deuteronomy 27:19

24:22 Hospitality: Judges 19:14–23

24:22 Land/Inheritance: Joshua 13:6–8

24:22 Widow, The: Psalm 94:6

24:22 Money: Nehemiah 5:1–3

25:2 Crime: Psalm 58:2

25:2 Crime is deserving of punishment, but the severity of a punishment should match the crime. Even a criminal should be treated as a human being who bears the image of God.

25:5–10 This law formalizes an ancient custom that was meant to ensure the continuation of a man's name even after he had died. For specific examples of this custom, see Genesis 38 and Ruth 3–4.

25:10 Divorce: Malachi 2:13–16

The First Harvest

26 When you go into the land the LORD your God is giving you as your own, to take it over and live in it, 2you must take some of the first harvest of crops that grow from the land the LORD your God is giving you. Put the food in a basket and go to the place where the LORD your God will choose to be worshiped. 3Say to the priest on duty at that time, "Today I declare before the LORD your God that I have come into the land the LORD promised our ancestors that he would give us." 4The priest will take your basket and set it down in front of the altar of the LORD your God. 5Then you shall announce before the LORD your God: "My father was a wandering Aramean. He went down to Egypt with only a few people, but they became a great, powerful, and large nation there. 6But the Egyptians were cruel to us, making us suffer and work very hard. 7So we prayed to the LORD, the God of our ancestors, and he heard us. When he saw our trouble, hard work, and suffering, 8the LORD brought us out of Egypt with his great power and strength, using great terrors, signs, and miracles. 9Then he brought us to this place and gave us this fertile land. 10Now I bring part of the first harvest from this land that you, LORD, have given me." Place the basket before the LORD your God and bow down before him. 11Then you and the Levites and foreigners among you should rejoice, because the LORD your God has given good things to you and your family.

12Bring a tenth of all your harvest the third year (the year to give a tenth of your harvest). Give it to the Levites, foreigners, orphans, and widows so that they may eat in your towns and be full. 13Then say to the LORD your God, "I have taken out of my house the part of my harvest that belongs to God, and I have given it to the Levites, foreigners, orphans, and widows. I have done everything you commanded me; I have not broken your commands, and I have not forgotten any of them. 14I have not eaten any of the holy part while I was in sorrow. I have not removed any of it while I was unclean, and I have not offered it for dead people. I have obeyed you, the LORD my God, and have done everything you commanded me. 15So look down from heaven, your holy home. Bless your people Israel and bless the land you have given us, which you promised to our ancestors— a fertile land."

Obey the Lord's Commands

16Today the LORD your God commands you to obey all these rules and laws; be careful to obey them with your whole being. 17Today you have said that the LORD is your God, and you have promised to do what he wants you to do—to keep his rules, commands, and laws. You have said you will obey him. 18And today the LORD has said that you are his very own people, as he has promised you. But you must obey his commands. 19He will make you greater than all the other nations he made. He will give you praise, fame, and honor, and you will be a holy people to the LORD your God, as he has said.

The Law Written on Stones

27 Then Moses, along with the older leaders of Israel, commanded the people, saying, "Keep all the commands I have given you today. 2Soon you will cross the Jordan River to go into the land the LORD your God is giving you. On that day set up some large stones and cover them with plaster. 3When you cross over, write all the words of these teachings on them. Then you may enter the land the LORD your God is giving you, a fertile land, just as the LORD, the God of your ancestors, promised. 4After you have crossed the Jordan River, set up these stones on Mount Ebal, as I command you today, and cover them with plaster. 5Build an altar of stones there to the LORD your God, but don't use any iron tool to cut the stones; 6build the altar of the LORD your God with stones from the field. Offer burnt offerings on it to the LORD your God, 7and offer fellowship offerings there, and eat them and rejoice before the LORD your God. 8Then write clearly all the words of these teachings on the stones."

Curses of the Law

9Then Moses and the Levites who were priests spoke to all Israel and said, "Be quiet, Israel. Listen! Today you have become the people of the LORD your God. 10Obey the LORD your God, and keep his commands and laws that I give you today."

11That day Moses also gave the people this command:

12When you cross the Jordan River, these tribes must stand on Mount Gerizim to bless the people: Simeon, Levi, Judah, Issachar, Joseph and Benjamin. 13And these tribes must stand on Mount

26:12–13 Scripture suggests an undesignated portion of the tithe was to be used to care for those without money. It has been argued by Christians in modern Western societies that we are taxed heavily for programs geared to benefit the poor. Thus a large part of the tithing obligation has been covered by involuntary contributions to the state. This is the sort of half-truth that often confuses our thinking about the tithe. This way of thinking is a sort of legalism in reverse. It also works against the attitude of gratitude (thankfulness) that the tithe is meant to represent.

27:6 Stone: Joshua 8:31

Ebal to announce the curses: Reuben, Gad, Asher,
Zebulun, Dan, and Naphtali.
14The Levites will say to all the people of Israel
in a loud voice:
15"Anyone will be cursed who makes an idol or
statue and secretly sets it up, because the LORD
hates the idols people make."
Then all the people will say, "Amen!"
16"Anyone will be cursed who dishonors his
father or mother."
Then all the people will say, "Amen!"
17"Anyone will be cursed who moves the stone
that marks a neighbor's border."
Then all the people will say, "Amen!"
18"Anyone will be cursed who sends a blind
person down the wrong road."
Then all the people will say, "Amen!"
19"Anyone will be cursed who is unfair to foreigners, orphans, or widows."
Then all the people will say, "Amen!"
20"A man will be cursed who has sexual relations with his father's wife, because it is a dishonor to his father."
Then all the people will say, "Amen!"
21"Anyone will be cursed who has sexual relations with an animal."
Then all the people will say, "Amen!"
22"A man will be cursed who has sexual relations with his sister, whether she is his father's
daughter or his mother's daughter."
Then all the people will say, "Amen!"
23"A man will be cursed who has sexual relations with his mother-in-law."
Then all the people will say, "Amen!"
24"Anyone will be cursed who kills a neighbor
secretly."
Then all the people will say, "Amen!"
25"Anyone will be cursed who takes money to
murder an innocent person."
Then all the people will say, "Amen!"
26"Anyone will be cursed who does not agree
with the words of these teachings and does not
obey them."
Then all the people will say, "Amen!"

Blessings for Obeying

28 You must completely obey the LORD your
God, and you must carefully follow all his
commands I am giving you today. Then the LORD
your God will make you greater than any other
nation on earth. 2Obey the LORD your God so that
all these blessings will come and stay with you:
3You will be blessed in the city and blessed in
the country.
4Your children will be blessed, as well as your
crops; your herds will be blessed with calves
and your flocks with lambs.
5Your basket and your kitchen will be blessed.
6You will be blessed when you come in and
when you go out.
7The LORD will help you defeat the enemies
that come to fight you. They will attack you from
one direction, but they will run from you in seven
directions.
8The LORD your God will bless you with full
barns, and he will bless everything you do. He will
bless the land he is giving you.
9The LORD will make you his holy people, as he
promised. But you must obey his commands and
do what he wants you to do. 10Then everyone on
earth will see that you are the LORD's people, and
they will be afraid of you. 11The LORD will make you
rich: You will have many children, your animals
will have many young, and your land will give
good crops. It is the land that the LORD promised
your ancestors he would give to you.
12The LORD will open up his heavenly storehouse
so that the skies send rain on your land at the
right time, and he will bless everything you do.
You will lend to other nations, but you will not
need to borrow from them. 13The LORD will make
you like the head and not like the tail; you will be
on top and not on bottom. But you must obey the
commands of the LORD your God that I am giving
you today, being careful to keep them. 14Do not disobey anything I command you today. Do exactly
as I command, and do not follow other gods or
serve them.

Curses for Disobeying

15But if you do not obey the LORD your God and
carefully follow all his commands and laws I am
giving you today, all these curses will come upon
you and stay:
16You will be cursed in the city and cursed in the
country.
17Your basket and your kitchen will be cursed.
18Your children will be cursed, as well as your
crops; the calves of your herds and the lambs of your
flocks will be cursed.
19You will be cursed when you go in and when
you go out.
20The LORD will send you curses, confusion, and
punishment in everything you do. You will be

27:19 Adoption: Psalm 10:14–18
27:24 Neighbor: 1 Kings 8:31
28:14 Obedience: 1 Kings 2:1–4

destroyed and suddenly ruined because you did
wrong when you left him. 21The LORD will give you
terrible diseases and destroy you from the land you
are going to take. 22The LORD will punish you with
disease, fever, swelling, heat, lack of rain, plant
diseases, and mildew until you die. 23The sky
above will be like bronze, and the ground below
will be like iron. 24The LORD will turn the rain into
dust and sand, which will fall from the skies until
you are destroyed.

25The LORD will help your enemies defeat you.
You will attack them from one direction, but you
will run from them in seven directions. And you
will become a thing of horror among all the kingdoms on earth. 26Your dead bodies will be food for
all the birds and wild animals, and there will be no
one to scare them away. 27The LORD will punish
you with boils like those the Egyptians had. You
will have bad growths, sores, and itches that can't
be cured. 28The LORD will give you madness, blindness, and a confused mind. 29You will have to feel
around in the daylight like a blind person. You will
fail in everything you do. People will hurt you and
steal from you every day, and no one will save you.

30You will be engaged to a woman, but another
man will force her to have sexual relations with him.
You will build a house, but you will not live in it. You
will plant a vineyard, but you will not get its grapes.
31Your ox will be killed before your eyes, but you
will not eat any of it. Your donkey will be taken
away from you, and it will not be brought back.
Your sheep will be given to your enemies, and no
one will save you. 32Your sons and daughters will
be given to another nation, and you will grow tired
looking for them every day, but there will be
nothing you can do. 33People you don't know will
eat the crops your land and hard work have produced. You will be mistreated and abused all your
life. 34The things you see will cause you to go mad.
35The LORD will give you sore boils on your knees
and legs that cannot be cured, and they will go from
the soles of your feet to the tops of your heads.

36The LORD will send you and your king away to
a nation neither you nor your ancestors know,
where you will serve other gods made of wood
and stone. 37You will become a hated thing to the
nations where the LORD sends you; they will laugh
at you and make fun of you.

38You will plant much seed in your field, but your
harvest will be small, because locusts will eat the
crop. 39You will plant vineyards and work hard in
them, but you will not pick the grapes or drink the
wine, because the worms will eat them. 40You will
have olive trees in all your land, but you will not get
any olive oil, because the olives will drop off the
trees. 41You will have sons and daughters, but you
will not be able to keep them, because they will
be taken captive. 42Locusts will destroy all your
trees and crops.

43The foreigners who live among you will get
stronger and stronger, and you will get weaker
and weaker. 44Foreigners will lend money to you,
but you will not be able to lend to them. They will
be like the head, and you will be like the tail.

45All these curses will come upon you. They will
chase you and catch you and destroy you, because
you did not obey the LORD your God and keep the
commands and laws he gave you. 46The curses will
be signs and miracles to you and your descendants
forever. 47You had plenty of everything, but you did
not serve the LORD your God with joy and a pure
heart, 48so you will serve the enemies the LORD
sends against you. You will be hungry, thirsty,
naked, and poor, and the LORD will put a load on
you until he has destroyed you.

The Curse of an Enemy Nation

49The LORD will bring a nation against you from
far away, from the end of the world, and it will
swoop down like an eagle. You won't understand
their language, 50and they will look mean. They
will not respect old people or feel sorry for the
young. 51They will eat the calves from your herds
and the harvest of your field, and you will be
destroyed. They will not leave you any grain, new
wine or oil, or any calves from your herds or lambs
from your flocks. You will be ruined. 52That nation
will surround and attack all your cities. You trust
in your high, strong walls, but they will fall down.
That nation will surround all your cities everywhere in the land the LORD your God is giving you.

53Your enemy will surround you. Those people
will make you starve so that you will eat your own
babies, the bodies of the sons and daughters the
LORD your God gave you. 54Even the most gentle
and kind man among you will become cruel to his
brother, his wife whom he loves, and his children
who are still alive. 55He will not even give them any
of the flesh of his children he is eating, because it
will be all he has left. Your enemy will surround
you and make you starve in all your cities. 56The
most gentle and kind woman among you, so gentle
and kind she would hardly even walk on the ground,
will be cruel to her husband whom she loves and
to her son and daughter. 57She will give birth to a

28:23 *sky . . . bronze.* This means the sky will give no rain and the earth will produce no crops.

28:24 Famine: Ruth 1:1
28:49 Tongues: Daniel 7:13–14

Exodus/New Exodus

Exodus 12:31–51

What is the Exodus and how did it come about? Why do the later prophets use exodus language to describe later divine rescues? How does the Exodus look forward to Jesus Christ?

The word *exodus* comes from a Greek term which means "departure." It is related to our English word "exit." It comes to refer especially to Israel's departure from Egypt under the leadership of Moses. The Exodus is, without a doubt, the most important act of salvation in the entire Old Testament. The Hebrew people were slaves in Egypt. They had no power, and their masters were the most powerful nation at the time. Their freedom could not come through human means. Only God could save them.

God chose to save them by using Moses as his spokesperson. God had rescued Moses from death, the fate that Pharaoh had commanded for all the Hebrew baby boys. But more than that, God had worked events so that Moses was raised in the very household of Pharaoh.

When he was older, Moses left Egypt and sought refuge in the desert. While there, God confronted him in the form of a burning bush and called him to return to Egypt to lead his people out of slavery.

At first it appeared as if Moses would have no success. Pharaoh resisted all attempts to free the Hebrew slaves, even after Moses showed the power of God through the plagues he sent against that land. It was not until the tenth and final plague, the death of the firstborn, that Pharaoh allowed the Israelites to leave. Even then, Pharaoh had a change of heart and decided to hunt down the Hebrews when their backs were against the Red Sea.

It is the Red Sea crossing that most characterizes the Exodus. The Hebrews had no human hope. They faced an impassable sea, and the Egyptian army was bearing down on them. They had no weapons, but they did have prayer. As Moses raised his walking stick in prayer, God used the wind to split the sea, permitting the Israelites to walk through on dry ground. When the Egyptians tried to follow, God caused the sea to close, killing that army. The only appropriate response was a song of praise to God:

The LORD is a warrior;
  the LORD is his name.
The chariots and soldiers of the king of Egypt
  he has thrown into the sea. (Exodus 15:3–4)

Since the Exodus was such a dramatic display of God's saving power, it has been remembered throughout the centuries that followed. Prophets who lived hundreds of years after Moses saw in the Exodus a pattern for the kind of rescues God would accomplish for Israel in the future. Isaiah, Jeremiah, Ezekiel, Hosea, and others saw the coming judgment, when Babylon would destroy and exile Judah, as a second Egyptian bondage, so their return from that bondage, the restoration to the land, was a second exodus experience.

Isaiah's prophecy regarding this return, however, makes us look beyond the immediate fulfillment in the return to the land of Palestine. Isaiah 40:3 is quoted in Mark 1:1–3 to refer to John the Baptist preparing the way for the coming Messiah. He is one who brings salvation, a new Exodus, and his earthly ministry is patterned after the Exodus event.

Jesus began his ministry by being baptized in the desert (Matthew 3:13–17). He then continued in the desert for forty days and forty nights where he was tempted by the devil (Matthew 4:1–11). These forty days and nights reflected the forty years Israel spent in the desert, and so it is not surprising that Jesus was tempted with the same things as Israel, but Jesus did not cave in to the temptations, but rather quoted the Book of Deuteronomy, the sermon of Moses in the desert, three times.

After he came out of the desert, Jesus then went to the mountain where he preached a sermon on the law (Matthew 5–7). This reflects the giving of the Ten Commandments on Mount Sinai in the desert. Many other events in Jesus' life also reflect the Exodus and desert wanderings, but note especially that Jesus was crucified on or near the time of the Passover; indeed he was the Passover lamb (1 Corinthians 5:7), the Passover being the festival of the Exodus. Jesus is the fulfillment of the Exodus.

But there is more to be said. The author of the Book of Hebrews tells Christians that they are wanderers in the desert waiting for entry into the promised land, heaven (Hebrews 3:7–4:13).

So the original exodus at the time of Moses becomes the prime example of salvation in the Old Testament. Later Old Testament authors use it to describe the new work of salvation in their own day. Finally Jesus reveals himself as the fulfillment of the Exodus, an Exodus that Christians today wait to fully experience.

Exodus/New Exodus: For additional scriptures on this topic go to Exodus 15.

Holy War & Divine Warrior

Exodus 15

Why is there so much war in the Bible? How was war waged?
How is spiritual warfare related to the actual warfare of the Old Testament?

The Bible is full of the sights, sounds, and smells of warfare. This statement is especially true of the Old Testament, but close reading of the New Testament shows that warfare is a major theme there as well. Study of the Bible reveals that there is a theology of warfare that runs from Genesis to Revelation. Not every passage containing descriptions of battle or military language fits in here, but the Bible does present a coherent and developing conception of what Bible scholars have called Holy War. Holy war is holy because God is present with Israel's army. He tells the Israelites against whom to go to war (Joshua 5:13–15; 1 Samuel 23:1–6), and they must spiritually prepare themselves through circumcision (Joshua 5:1–12) and the offering of pre-war sacrifices (1 Samuel 13). Since God is in their midst, the warriors must remain in a ritually "clean" state (like Uriah in 2 Samuel 11:10–11) and the war camp itself must remain pure (Deuteronomy 23:9–14). When the Israelites march off to battle, they sing hymns of praise just as if they were in the Temple (2 Chronicles 20:20–23).

The Israelites win the war only because God delivers their enemies into their hand. For this reason, the number of troops and the quality of their weaponry is unimportant. Indeed, as the story of Gideon demonstrates (Judges 7), God requires fewer rather than more troops. In this way, the Israelites know that the victory is God's and not theirs, so they have no basis on which to boast in themselves.

After the victory, the Israelites should acknowledge the Lord through praise (Exodus 15; Judges 5) and offer him all the plunder. The plunder includes material goods that are given to the treasury of the sanctuary and not used for personal gain and also prisoners of war who are normally executed.

This is the picture of holy war in the Old Testament. At the center stands God, the divine warrior.

As we read from Genesis to Revelation, though, we can discern different stages of God's battle as it relates to his plan of redemption. The stage we just described is the typical one during the early Old Testament period: God battles his flesh and blood enemies. However, even during this early period and certainly coming to culmination later in Israel's history, we see that God turns against Israel itself. Israel was used as God's tool of judgment against the unbelieving nations of its day, but when Israel itself turned its back on God, he promised to judge them as well (Deuteronomy 28:49–52) using Babylonia to take his people into exile.

However, this is not the end of the story in the Old Testament. As the last prophets speak in the context of restoration to the land, they look forward to the day when God will intervene as a warrior to deliver them from their foreign oppressors (Daniel 7; Zechariah 14). It is on this note of expectation that the Old Testament closes.

The Good News of Mark opens with John the Baptist preaching in the wilderness. His message focuses on a coming deliverer who will bring judgment on the unbeliever. He baptizes Jesus and then is jailed.

While in jail, John hears disturbing reports about Jesus. He is not destroying the enemies of God; he is healing them, exorcising demons, and preaching the gospel of peace. Jesus has come to direct the war not against the flesh and blood enemies of God's people, but against Satan himself. This warfare was carried on through exorcism and ultimately by his crucifixion.

Paul understands Jesus' crucifixion and resurrection in this way. This is how Jesus defeated Satan, by dying and not by killing. He triumphed over the "spiritual rulers and powers" by defeating them on the cross (Colossians 2:15).

As a result, Ephesians 6:10–20 describes the Christian as engaged in warfare against the powers, but wearing the "full armor of God." In the New Testament epistles, the Christian struggle against the evil of this present world, evangelism, and sanctification are all pictured as part of our present holy war.

The last phase of holy war is presented in the apocalyptic literature of the New Testament, the scriptures that describe the end times. Here Christ will appear at the head of the heavenly army and finish the victory that he won on the cross (Revelation 19:11–21).⚭

⚭**Holy War & Divine Warrior:** For additional scriptures on this topic go to Genesis 3:15.

baby, but she will plan to eat the baby and what comes after the birth itself. She will eat them secretly while the enemy surrounds the city. Those people will make you starve in all your cities.

[58]Be careful to obey everything in these teachings that are written in this book. You must respect the glorious and wonderful name of the LORD your God, [59]or the LORD will give terrible diseases to you and your descendants. You will have long and serious diseases, and long and miserable sicknesses. [60]He will give you all the diseases of Egypt that you dread, and the diseases will stay with you. [61]The LORD will also give you every disease and sickness not written in this Book of the Teachings, until you are destroyed. [62]You people may have outnumbered the stars, but only a few of you will be left, because you did not obey the LORD your God. [63]Just as the LORD was once happy with you and gave you good things and made you grow in number, so then the LORD will be happy to ruin and destroy you, and you will be removed from the land you are entering to take as your own.

[64]Then the LORD will scatter you among the nations—from one end of the earth to the other. There you will serve other gods of wood and stone, gods that neither you nor your ancestors have known. [65]You will have no rest among those nations and no place that is yours. The LORD will make your mind worried, your sight weak, and your soul sad. [66]You will live with danger and be afraid night and day. You will not be sure that you will live. [67]In the morning you will say, "I wish it were evening," and in the evening you will say, "I wish it were morning." Terror will be in your heart, and the things you have seen will scare you. [68]The LORD will send you back to Egypt in ships, even though I, Moses, said you would never go back to Egypt. And there you will try to sell yourselves as slaves to your enemies, but no one will buy you.

The Agreement in Moab

29 The LORD commanded Moses to make an agreement with the Israelites in Moab in addition to the agreement he had made with them at Mount Sinai. These are the words of that agreement.

[2]Moses called all the Israelites together and said to them:

You have seen everything the LORD did before your own eyes to the king of Egypt and to the king's leaders and to the whole country. [3]With your own eyes you saw the great troubles, signs, and miracles. [4]But to this day the LORD has not given you a mind that understands; you don't really understand what you see with your eyes or hear with your ears. [5]I led you through the desert for forty years, and during that time neither your clothes nor sandals wore out. [6]You ate no bread and drank no wine or beer. This was so you would understand that I am the LORD your God.

[7]When you came to this place, Sihon king of Heshbon and Og king of Bashan came out to fight us, but we defeated them. [8]We captured their land and gave it to the tribes of Reuben, Gad, and East Manasseh to be their own.

[9]You must carefully obey everything in this agreement so that you will succeed in everything you do. [10]Today you are all standing here before the LORD your God—your leaders and important men, your older leaders, officers, and all the other men of Israel, [11]your wives and children and the foreigners who live among you, who chop your wood and carry your water. [12]You are all here to enter into an agreement and a promise with the LORD your God, an agreement the LORD your God is making with you today. [13]This will make you today his own people. He will be your God, as he told you and as he promised your ancestors Abraham, Isaac, and Jacob. [14]But I am not just making this agreement and its promises with you [15]who are standing here before the LORD your God today, but also with those who are not here today.

[16]You know how we lived in Egypt and how we passed through the countries when we came here. [17]You saw their hateful idols made of wood, stone, silver, and gold. [18]Make sure no man, woman, family group, or tribe among you leaves the LORD our God to go and serve the gods of those nations. They would be to you like a plant that grows bitter, poisonous fruit.

[19]These are the kind of people who hear these curses but bless themselves, thinking, "We will be safe even though we continue doing what we want to do." Those people may destroy all of your land, both wet and dry. [20]The LORD will not forgive them. His anger will be like a burning fire against those people, and all the curses written in this book will come on them. The LORD will destroy any memory of them on the earth. [21]He will separate them from all the tribes of Israel for punishment. All the curses of the Agreement that are written in this Book of the Teachings will happen to them.

[22]Your children who will come after you, as well

28:68 Mountain: Psalm 68

28:68 Promise: Joshua 21:43–45

as foreigners from faraway lands, will see the disasters that come to this land and the diseases the LORD will send on it. They will say, 23"The land is nothing but burning cinders and salt. Nothing is planted, nothing grows, and nothing blooms. It is like Sodom and Gomorrah, and Admah and Zeboiim, which the LORD destroyed because he was very angry." 24All the other nations will ask, "Why has the LORD done this to the land? Why is he so angry?"

25And the answer will be, "It is because the people broke the Agreement of the LORD, the God of their ancestors, which he made with them when he brought them out of Egypt. 26They went and served other gods and bowed down to gods they did not even know. The LORD did not allow that, 27so he became very angry at the land and brought all the curses on it that are written in this book. 28Since the LORD became angry and furious with them, he took them out of their land and put them in another land where they are today."

29There are some things the LORD our God has kept secret, but there are some things he has let us know. These things belong to us and our children forever so that we will do everything in these teachings.

The Israelites Will Return

30 When all these blessings and curses I have described happen to you, and the LORD your God has sent you away to other nations, think about these things. 2Then you and your children will return to the LORD your God, and you will obey him with your whole being in everything I am commanding you today. 3Then the LORD your God will give you back your freedom. He will feel sorry for you, and he will bring you back again from the nations where he scattered you. 4He may send you to the ends of the earth, but he will gather you and bring you back from there, 5back to the land that belonged to your ancestors. It will be yours. He will give you success, and there will be more of you than there were of your ancestors. 6The LORD your God will prepare you and your descendants to love him with your whole being so that you will live. 7The LORD your God will put all these curses on your enemies, who hate you and are cruel to you. 8And you will again obey the LORD, keeping all his commands that I give you today. 9The LORD your God will make you successful in everything you do. You will have many children, your cattle will have many calves, and your fields will produce good crops, because the LORD will again be happy with you, just as he was with your ancestors. 10But you must obey the LORD your God by keeping all his commands and rules that are written in this Book of the Teachings. You must return to the LORD your God with your whole being.

Choose Life or Death

11This command I give you today is not too hard for you; it is not beyond what you can do. 12It is not up in heaven. You do not have to ask, "Who will go up to heaven and get it for us so we can obey it and keep it?" 13It is not on the other side of the sea. You do not have to ask, "Who will go across the sea and get it? Who will tell it to us so we can keep it?" 14No, the word is very near you. It is in your mouth and in your heart so you may obey it.

15Look, today I offer you life and success, death and destruction. 16I command you today to love the LORD your God, to do what he wants you to do, and to keep his commands, his rules, and his laws. Then you will live and grow in number, and the LORD your God will bless you in the land you are entering to take as your own.

17But if you turn away from the LORD and do not obey him, if you are led to bow and serve other gods, 18I tell you today that you will surely be destroyed. And you will not live long in the land you are crossing the Jordan River to enter and take as your own.

19Today I ask heaven and earth to be witnesses. I am offering you life or death, blessings or curses. Now, choose life! Then you and your children may live. 20To choose life is to love the LORD your God, obey him, and stay close to him. He is your life, and he will let you live many years in the land, the land he promised to give your ancestors Abraham, Isaac, and Jacob.

Joshua Takes Moses' Place

31 Then Moses went and spoke these words to all the Israelites: 2"I am now one hundred twenty years old, and I cannot lead you anymore. The LORD told me I would not cross the Jordan River; 3the LORD your God will lead you across himself. He will destroy those nations for you, and you will take over their land. Joshua will also lead you across, as the LORD has said. 4The LORD will do to those nations what he did to Sihon and Og, the kings of the Amorites, when he destroyed them and their land. 5The LORD will give those nations to you; do to them everything I told you. 6Be strong and brave. Don't be afraid of them and don't be frightened, because the LORD your God will go with you. He will not leave you or forget you."

30:17 Death: Job 14:1-2

30:19 Curse: Job 2:9

7Then Moses called Joshua and said to him in front of the people, "Be strong and brave, because you will lead these people into the land the LORD promised to give their ancestors, and help them take it as their own. 8The LORD himself will go before you. He will be with you; he will not leave you or forget you. Don't be afraid and don't worry."

Moses Writes the Teachings

9So Moses wrote down these teachings and gave them to the priests and all the older leaders of Israel. (The priests are the sons of Levi, who carry the Ark of the Agreement with the LORD.) 10-11Then Moses commanded them: "Read these teachings for all Israel to hear at the end of every seven years, which is the year to cancel what people owe. Do it during the Feast of Shelters, when all the Israelites will come to appear before the LORD your God and stand at the place he will choose. 12Gather all the people: the men, women, children, and foreigners living in your towns so that they can listen and learn to respect the LORD your God and carefully obey everything in this law. 13Since their children do not know this law, they must hear it. They must learn to respect the LORD your God for as long as they live in the land you are crossing the Jordan River to take for your own."

The Lord Calls Moses and Joshua

14The LORD said to Moses, "Soon you will die. Get Joshua and come to the Meeting Tent so that I may command him." So Moses and Joshua went to the Meeting Tent.

15The LORD appeared at the Meeting Tent in a cloud; the cloud stood over the entrance of the Tent. 16And the LORD said to Moses, "You will soon die. Then these people will not be loyal to me but will worship the foreign gods of the land they are entering. They will leave me, breaking the Agreement I made with them. 17Then I will become very angry at them, and I will leave them. I will turn away from them, and they will be destroyed. Many terrible things will happen to them. Then they will say, 'It is because God is not with us that these terrible things are happening.' 18I will surely turn away from them then, because they have done wrong and have turned to other gods.

19"Now write down this song and teach it to the Israelites. Then have them sing it, because it will be my witness against them. 20When I bring them into the land I promised to their ancestors, a fertile land, they will eat as much as they want and get fat. Then they will turn to other gods and serve them. They will reject me and break my Agreement. 21Then when many troubles and terrible things happen to them, this song will testify against them, because the song will not be forgotten by their descendants. I know what they plan to do, even before I take them into the land I promised them." 22So Moses wrote down the song that day, and he taught it to the Israelites.

23Then the LORD gave this command to Joshua son of Nun: "Be strong and brave, because you will lead the people of Israel to the land I promised them, and I will be with you."

24After Moses finished writing all the words of the teachings in a book, 25he gave a command to the Levites, who carried the Ark of the Agreement with the LORD. 26He said, "Take this Book of the Teachings and put it beside the Ark of the Agreement with the LORD your God. It must stay there as a witness against you. 27I know how stubborn and disobedient you are. You have disobeyed the LORD while I am alive and with you, and you will disobey even more after I die! 28Gather all the older leaders of your tribes and all your officers to me so that I may say these things for them to hear, and so that I may ask heaven and earth to testify against them. 29I know that after I die you will become completely evil. You will turn away from the commands I have given you. Terrible things will happen to you in the future when you do what the LORD says is evil, and you will make him angry with the idols you have made."

Moses' Song

30And Moses spoke this whole song for all the people of Israel to hear:

32 Hear, heavens, and I will speak.
Listen, earth, to what I say.
2My teaching will drop like rain;
my words will fall like dew.
They will be like showers on the grass;
they will pour down like rain on young plants.
3I will announce the name of the LORD.
Praise God because he is great!
4He is like a rock; what he does is perfect,
and he is always fair.
He is a faithful God who does no wrong,
who is right and fair.

31:14 Joshua: Joshua 1–24

31:27 Rebellion: 1 Samuel 12:14–15

32:4 Justice is measured by God himself. By his actions and commands, he sets the standards of fairness and unfairness. Although human standards of justice may change with time and circumstances, God's justice is as unchangeable as a rock.

32:4 Justice: 2 Chronicles 19:7

[5]They have done evil against him.
To their shame they are no longer
his children;
they are an evil and lying people.
[6]This is not the way to repay the LORD,
you foolish and unwise people.
He is your Father and Maker,
who made you and formed you.

[7]Remember the old days.
Think of the years already passed.
Ask your father and he will tell you;
ask your older leaders and they will
inform you.
[8]God Most High gave the nations their lands,
dividing up the human race.
He set up borders for the people
and even numbered the Israelites.
[9]The LORD took his people as his share,
the people of Jacob as his very own.

[10]He found them in a desert,
a windy, empty land.
He surrounded them and brought them up,
guarding them as those he loved
very much.
[11]He was like an eagle building its nest
that flutters over its young.
It spreads its wings to catch them
and carries them on its feathers.
[12]The LORD alone led them,
and there was no foreign god helping him.

[13]The LORD brought them to the heights of
the land
and fed them the fruit of the fields.
He gave them honey from the rocks,
bringing oil from the solid rock.
[14]There were milk curds from the cows and
milk from the flock;
there were fat sheep and goats.
There were sheep and goats from Bashan
and the best of the wheat.
You drank the juice of grapes.

[15]Israel grew fat and kicked;
they were fat and full and firm.
They left the God who made them
and rejected the Rock who saved them.
[16]They made God jealous with foreign gods
and angry with hateful idols.
[17]They made sacrifices to demons, not God,
to gods they had never known,
new gods from nearby,
gods your ancestors did not fear.
[18]You left God who is the Rock, your Father,
and you forgot the God who gave you birth.

[19]The LORD saw this and rejected them;
his sons and daughters had made
him angry.
[20]He said, "I will turn away from them
and see what will happen to them.
They are evil people,
unfaithful children.
[21]They used things that are not gods to make
me jealous
and worthless idols to make me angry.
So I will use those who are not a nation to
make them jealous;
I will use a nation that does not understand
to make them angry.
[22]My anger has started a fire
that burns down to the place of the dead.
It will burn up the ground and its crops,
and it will set fire to the base of the
mountains.

[23]"I will pile troubles upon them
and shoot my arrows at them.
[24]They will be starved and sick,
destroyed by terrible diseases.
I will send them vicious animals
and gliding, poisonous snakes.
[25]In the streets the sword will kill;
in their homes there will be terror.
Young men and women will die,
and so will babies and gray-haired men.
[26]I will scatter them as I said,
and no one will remember them.
[27]But I didn't want their enemy to brag;
their enemy might misunderstand
and say, 'We have won!
The LORD has done none of this.'"

[28]Israel has no sense;
they do not understand.
[29]I wish they were wise and understood this;
I wish they could see what will happen
to them.
[30]One person cannot chase a thousand people,
and two people cannot fight ten thousand

32:10 The wilderness (desert) is the birthplace of Israel as a people, a holy nation belonging to God. In the Desert of Sinai the Lord offers them a new life, an agreement with him—a relationship that gives them their identity, purpose, religion, and laws.

32:16 *jealous.* See 5:9.
32:17 *demons.* This verse teaches that evil spiritual forces—demons—often stood behind the false gods of the nations.
32:21 *jealous.* See 5:9.

unless their Rock has sold them,
unless the LORD has given them up.
31The rock of these people is not like our Rock;
our enemies agree to that.
32Their vine comes from Sodom,
and their fields are like Gomorrah.
Their grapes are full of poison;
their bunches of grapes are bitter.
33Their wine is like snake poison,
like the deadly poison of cobras.

34"I have been saving this,
and I have it locked in my storehouses.
35I will punish those who do wrong; I will
repay them.
Soon their foot will slip,
because their day of trouble is near,
and their punishment will come quickly."

36The LORD will defend his people
and have mercy on his servants.
He will see that their strength is gone,
that nobody is left, slaves or free.⚭
37Then he will say, "Where are their gods?
Where is the rock they trusted?
38Who ate the fat from their sacrifices,
and who drank the wine of their drink
offerings?
Let those gods come to help you!
Let them protect you!

39"Now you will see that I am the
one God!
There is no god but me.
I send life and death;
I can hurt, and I can heal.
No one can escape from me.
40I raise my hand toward heaven and make
this promise:
As surely as I live forever,⚭
41I will sharpen my flashing sword,
and I will take it in my hand to judge.
I will punish my enemies
and pay back those who hate me.
42My arrows will be covered with their blood;
my sword will eat their flesh.
The blood will flow from those who are killed
and the captives.
The heads of the enemy leaders will be
cut off."

43Be happy, nations, with his people,
because he will repay you for the blood of
his servants.
He will punish his enemies,
and he will remove the sin of his land
and people.⚭

44Moses came with Joshua son of Nun, and
they spoke all the words of this song for the people to hear. 45When Moses finished speaking
these words to all Israel, 46he said to them: "Pay
careful attention to all the words I have said to
you today, and command your children to obey
carefully everything in these teachings. 47These
should not be unimportant words for you, but
rather they mean life for you! By these words you
will live a long time in the land you are crossing
the Jordan River to take as your own."

Moses Goes Up to Mount Nebo

48The LORD spoke to Moses again that same day
and said, 49"Go up the Abarim Mountains, to
Mount Nebo in the country of Moab, across from
Jericho. Look at the land of Canaan that I am giving to the Israelites as their own. 50On that mountain that you climb, you will die and join your
ancestors, just as your brother Aaron died on
Mount Hor and joined his ancestors. 51You both
sinned against me at the waters of Meribah Kadesh
in the Desert of Zin, and you did not honor me as
holy there among the Israelites. 52So now you will
only look at the land from far away. You will not
enter the land I am giving the people of Israel."

Moses Blesses the People

33 Moses, the man of God, gave this blessing to
the Israelites before he died. 2He said:

"The LORD came from Mount Sinai
and rose like the sun from Edom;
he showed his greatness from
Mount Paran.
He came with thousands of angels
from the southern mountains.
3The LORD surely loves his people
and takes care of all those who belong
to him.
They bow down at his feet,
and they are taught by him.
4Moses gave us the teachings
that belong to the people of Jacob.
5The LORD became king of Israel
when the leaders of the people gathered,
when the tribes of Israel came together.

⚭**32:36 Servant of the Lord:** Deuteronomy 32:43
⚭**32:40 The People of God :** Isaiah 62:1–5
⚭**32:43 Servant of the Lord:** Joshua 1:7

6“Let the people of Reuben live and not die,
but let the people be few.”

7Moses said this about the people of Judah:
“LORD, listen to Judah’s prayer;
bring them back to their people.
They defend themselves with their hands.
Help them fight their enemies!”

8Moses said this about the people of Levi:
“LORD, your Thummim and Urim belong
to Levi, whom you love.
LORD, you tested him at Massah
and argued with him at the waters of
Meribah.
9He said about his father and mother,
‘I don’t care about them.’
He did not treat his brothers as favorites
or give special favors to his children,
but he protected your word
and guarded your agreement.
10He teaches your laws to the people of Jacob
and your teachings to the people of Israel.
He burns incense before you
and makes whole burnt offerings on
your altar.
11LORD, make them strong;
be pleased with the work they do.
Defeat those who attack them,
and don’t let their enemies rise up again.”

12Moses said this about the people of
Benjamin:
“The LORD’s loved ones will lie down in safety,
because he protects them all day long.
The ones he loves rest with him.”

13Moses said this about the people of Joseph:
“May the LORD bless their land with wonderful
dew from heaven,
with water from the springs below,
14with the best fruits that the sun brings,
and with the best fruits that the moon
brings.
15Let the old mountains give the finest crops,
and let the everlasting hills give the best
fruits.
16Let the full earth give the best fruits,
and let the LORD who lived in the burning
bush be pleased.
May these blessings rest on the head of Joseph,
on the forehead of the one who was blessed
among his brothers.
17Joseph has the majesty of a firstborn bull;
he is as strong as a wild ox.
He will stab other nations,
even those nations far away.
These are the ten thousands of Ephraim,
and these are the thousands of Manasseh.”

18Moses said this about the people of Zebulun:
“Be happy when you go out, Zebulun,
and be happy in your tents, Issachar.
19They will call the people to the mountain,
and there they will offer the right sacrifices.
They will do well from all that is in the sea,
and they will do well from the treasures
hidden in the sand on the shore.”

20Moses said this about the people of Gad:
“Praise God who gives Gad more land!
Gad lives there like a lion,
who tears off arms and heads.
21They chose the best land for themselves.
They received a large share, like that given
to an officer.
When the leaders of the people gathered,
the people of Gad did what the LORD said
was right,
and they judged Israel fairly.”

22Moses said this about the people of Dan:
“Dan is like a lion’s cub,
who jumps out of Bashan.”

23Moses said this about the people of Naphtali:
“Naphtali enjoys special kindnesses,
and they are full of the LORD’s blessings.
Take as your own the west and south.”

24Moses said this about the people of Asher:
“Asher is the most blessed of the sons;
let him be his brothers’ favorite.
Let him bathe his feet in olive oil.
25Your gates will have locks of iron and bronze,
and you will be strong as long as you live.
26“There is no one like the God of Israel,
who rides through the skies to help you,
who rides on the clouds in his majesty.
27The everlasting God is your place of safety,
and his arms will hold you up forever.
He will force your enemy out ahead of you,
saying, ‘Destroy the enemy!’
28The people of Israel will lie down in safety.
Jacob’s spring is theirs alone.

33:26 *rides on the clouds.* God was often seen as riding a cloud, especially into battle. The cloud may represent his chariot.

Theirs is a land full of grain and new wine,
where the skies drop their dew.
29Israel, you are blessed!
No one else is like you,
because you are a people saved by
the LORD.
He is your shield and helper,
your glorious sword.
Your enemies will be afraid of you,
and you will walk all over their
holy places."

Moses Dies

34 Then Moses climbed Mount Nebo from the
plains of Moab to the top of Mount Pisgah,
across from Jericho. From there the LORD showed
him all the land from Gilead to Dan, 2all of
Naphtali and the lands of Ephraim and Manasseh,
all the land of Judah as far as the Mediterranean
Sea, 3as well as the southern desert and the whole
Valley of Jericho up to Zoar. (Jericho is called the
city of palm trees.) 4Then the LORD said to Moses,
"This is the land I promised to Abraham, Isaac,
and Jacob when I said to them, 'I will give this land
to your descendants.' I have let you look at it, Moses,
but you will not cross over there."

5Then Moses, the servant of the LORD, died there
in Moab, as the LORD had said. 6He buried Moses
in Moab in the valley opposite Beth Peor, but even
today no one knows where his grave is. 7Moses
was one hundred twenty years old when he died.
His eyes were not weak, and he was still strong.
8The Israelites cried for Moses for thirty days,
staying in the plains of Moab until the time of sadness was over.

9Joshua son of Nun was then filled with wisdom, because Moses had put his hands on him.
So the Israelites listened to Joshua, and they did
what the LORD had commanded Moses.

10There has never been another prophet in
Israel like Moses. The Lord knew Moses face to
face 11and sent him to do signs and miracles in
Egypt—to the king, to all his officers, and to the
whole land of Egypt. 12Moses had great power,
and he did great and wonderful things for all the
Israelites to see.

33:29 Happiness: Job 5:17
33:29 Blessing: Joshua 14:13–14
34:4 Abraham: Joshua 24:2

Notes:

INTRODUCTION TO THE BOOK OF

JOSHUA

Israel Conquers the Promised Land

WHO WROTE THIS BOOK?

Unfortunately, it cannot be concluded who the actual author of the Book of Joshua was. However, it is most likely that Joshua himself wrote the book, which is claimed by earliest Jewish traditions, except for the final passage about Joshua's own funeral. That section is ascribed to Eleazar, son of Aaron.

TO WHOM WAS THIS BOOK WRITTEN?

Joshua, the leader of the people of Israel, was writing to his own people.

WHERE WAS IT WRITTEN?

If, indeed, Joshua was the author of the book, it was likely composed in Canaan, the Promised Land, during Israel's conquest of the land.

WHEN WAS IT WRITTEN?

Since this book records the invasion and conquest of Canaan by Israel, which immediately followed the death of Moses and the end of Israel's forty-year desert wanderings, it is possible to set the date of its writing about the year 1406 B.C. and following.

WHAT IS THE BOOK ABOUT?

The Book of Joshua takes up where Deuteronomy left off. It records the historical events surrounding Israel's victorious march into the Promised Land, led by God himself. Israel progressed around the east side of the Dead Sea, and the only country to give them any substantial resistance was Edom. Joshua led them into Canaan, conducted successful conquests, and gave land to each of the tribes. They were home at last and in possession of the land that God had promised their father, Abraham, so many years earlier.

WHY WAS THIS BOOK WRITTEN?

Joshua, which means "the LORD saves" or "the LORD gives victory," tells the story of God's leading his people victoriously into the Promised Land and, thus, fulfilling the promise he had made so many years before. The writer of Joshua recorded this great event, providing them with a written and constant reminder that God is faithful; he always keeps his promises. And as long as God's people are faithful to him, they will ultimately be victorious.

SO WHAT DOES THIS BOOK MEAN TO US?

In the Greek language of the New Testament, the name "Joshua" becomes "Jesus." And, like Joshua, Jesus shows us today that "the LORD saves" and "the LORD gives victory." God has never stopped leading his people to the land he has promised us. And as long as we, as Christians, are faithful to him, we will be eternally victorious as he defeats our enemy, the devil, and leads us safely into heaven—the land he has promised us.

SUMMARY:

The Book of Deuteronomy ends on the plains of Moab with Moses climbing Mount Nebo to die. Joshua picks up the story and tells of the people of Israel at long last crossing into Canaan, the Promised Land.

We first learn about the great wars that Israel fights against the people of Canaan. These are no ordinary wars. They are wars with God at the head of the army, using even nature to help Israel win. At first, Israel defeats Jericho; then, after a setback, they conquer Ai; and finally, Gibeon surrenders to them. In this first move into the land, Palestine is split in half.

The kings of southern Canaan gather together to fight Joshua and the people of Israel. God defeats the armies of Canaan, even causing the sun to stand still so Israel's victory can be completed.

After the south is subdued, the kings of northern Canaan band together to try to stop Joshua. But once again, God gives Israel the victory.

As we quickly learn, the people of Canaan still live in the land, but Israel now has effective control over all of Palestine, and only after a few years of fighting.

The second half of the Book of Joshua describes how the now-conquered land is divided up and given to the various tribes of Israel. The list of towns, cities, and villages, which seem endless and boring to modern readers, were a song of praise to the ancient people of Israel, who were witnesses to the fulfillment of God's promise to Abraham that one day the land of Palestine would be their own.

The book ends on a dramatic note as Joshua, now old and near death, leads Israel in a reaffirmation of their agreement with the Lord (Joshua 24).

The Book of Joshua may be divided as follows:

I. Preparations and Crossing (1:1–5:12)
II. The Conquest of Palestine (5:13–12:24)
III. The Division of the Land (13:1–22:34)
IV. Joshua's Last Words (12:1–24:33)

A Christian reads Joshua for more than history. We learn that God can do wonderful things in the life of his people. We see that he fights for his people against their enemies. In our time, according to the New Testament, he leads us in battle with spiritual weapons, which are more powerful than swords and spears, against Satan himself (Ephesians 6:10–20).

I. Preparations and Crossing (1:1–5:12)

God makes sure to encourage Joshua by saying that he is still with Joshua, just as he was with Moses. He tells Joshua to remain faithful. With that, the action begins. Joshua first sends spies into Jericho. When they return, the people of Israel cross the Jordan River. God reminds this new generation that he is still the God of power when he splits the waters of the Jordan River so they can walk across on dry ground. When the people cross, they spiritually prepare themselves with circumcision and by observing the Passover.

II. The Conquest of Palestine (5:13–12:24)

Joshua leads Israel to victory against Canaan. Though some land remains to be conquered when he is done, the promises of Abraham are being fulfilled in these wars. God leads the army, and he is the one who gives them victory.

III. The Division of the Land (13:1–22:34)

Joshua has now grown old. Though there were still Canaanites left in the land, it was now time to divide up the land among the people of Israel. The naming of many cities, towns, and villages strike us today as tedious, but it is a way of making the fulfillment of the ancient promise of a homeland concrete to the people of Israel.

IV. Joshua's Last Words (23:1–24:33)

The Book of Joshua ends with the last words of Joshua and the report of a ceremony in which Joshua leads Israel as they recommit themselves to the Lord.

JOSHUA

God's Command to Joshua

After Moses, the servant of the LORD, died,
the LORD spoke to Joshua son of Nun,
Moses' assistant. 2The LORD said, "My
servant Moses is dead. Now you and all these
people go across the Jordan River into the land
I am giving to the Israelites. 3I promised Moses I
would give you this land, so I will give you every
place you go in the land. 4All the land from the
desert in the south to Lebanon in the north will
be yours. All the land from the great river, the
Euphrates, in the east, to the Mediterranean Sea in
the west will be yours, too, including the land of
the Hittites. 5No one will be able to defeat you all
your life. Just as I was with Moses, so I will be with
you. I will not leave you or forget you.

6"Joshua, be strong and brave! You must lead
these people so they can take the land that I
promised their fathers I would give them. 7Be
strong and brave. Be sure to obey all the teachings my servant Moses gave you. If you follow
them exactly, you will be successful in everything you do. 8Always remember what is written in the Book of the Teachings. Study it day
and night to be sure to obey everything that is
written there. If you do this, you will be wise and
successful in everything. 9Remember that I
commanded you to be strong and brave. Don't
be afraid, because the LORD your God will be
with you everywhere you go."

Joshua's Orders to the People

10Then Joshua gave orders to the officers of the
people: 11"Go through the camp and tell the people, 'Get your supplies ready. Three days from
now you will cross the Jordan River and take the
land the LORD your God is giving you.'"

12Then Joshua said to the people of Reuben, Gad,
and East Manasseh, 13"Remember what Moses,
the servant of the LORD, told you. He said the LORD
your God would give you rest and would give you
this land. 14Now the LORD has given you this land
east of the Jordan River. Your wives, children, and
animals may stay here, but your fighting men must
dress for war and cross the Jordan River ahead of
your brothers to help them. 15The LORD has given
you a place to rest and will do the same for your
brothers. But you must help them until they take
the land the LORD their God is giving them. Then
you may return to your own land east of the Jordan
River, the land that Moses, the servant of the LORD,
gave you."

16Then the people answered Joshua, "Anything
you command us to do, we will do. Any place you
send us, we will go. 17Just as we fully obeyed
Moses, we will obey you. We ask only that the
LORD your God be with you just as he was with
Moses. 18Whoever refuses to obey your commands
or turns against you will be put to death. Just be
strong and brave!"

Spies Sent to Jericho

2 Joshua son of Nun secretly sent out two spies
from Acacia and said to them, "Go and look
at the land, particularly at the city of Jericho."

So the men went to Jericho and stayed at the
house of a prostitute named Rahab.

2Someone told the king of Jericho, "Some
men from Israel have come here tonight to spy
out the land."

3So the king of Jericho sent this message to
Rahab: "Bring out the men who came to you and
entered your house. They have come to spy out
our whole land."

4But the woman had hidden the two men. She
said, "They did come here, but I didn't know where
they came from. 5In the evening, when it was time
to close the city gate, they left. I don't know where
they went, but if you go quickly, maybe you can
catch them." 6(The woman had taken the men up
to the roof and had hidden them there under stalks
of flax that she had spread out.) 7So the king's men
went out looking for the spies on the road that leads

1:7 Servant of the Lord: Joshua 5:14

1:7 Success is rooted in obedience to the will of God. The successful person is the one who seeks God's will more than anything else and delights in doing that will more than anything else.

1:8 Meditation: Psalm 1:2–3

1:8 *the Book of the Teachings.* The Book refers to Moses' writings, the Pentateuch (or Torah), which are the first five books of the Bible.

1:9 Moses was dead. Joshua was now the leader and given the command to enter Canaan and possess it. These were dangerous times, but Joshua is told not to be afraid. Why? In this passage God reminds Joshua that he is not alone, rather he is with him. God is more powerful than all the enemies of his people and will bring them the victory.

2:1–14 This passage raises ethical problems, in that it records that Rahab lied to the citizens of Jericho regarding the whereabouts of the spies, and yet she was commended in Hebrews 11:31 and James 2:25 for her deeds. Note, however, that she was commended, not for her dishonesty, but for her protection of the spies. God's approval of a person does not necessarily include his uncritical approval of each act of that person.

2:6 *roof.* In Bible times houses were built with flat roofs. The roof was used for drying things such as flax and fruit. It was also used as an extra room, as a place for worship, and as a cool place to sleep in the summer.

Flax flowers ripen into seeds used to produce linseed oil.

to the crossings of the Jordan River. The city gate
was closed just after the king's men left the city.
8Before the spies went to sleep for the night,
Rahab went up to the roof. 9She said to them, "I
know the LORD has given this land to your people.
You frighten us very much. Everyone living in
this land is terribly afraid of you 10because we
have heard how the LORD dried up the Red Sea
when you came out of Egypt. We have heard how
you destroyed Sihon and Og, two Amorite kings
who lived east of the Jordan. 11When we heard
this, we were very frightened. Now our men are
afraid to fight you because the LORD your God
rules the heavens above and the earth below!
12So now, promise me before the LORD that you
will show kindness to my family just as I showed
kindness to you. Give me some proof that you
will do this. 13Allow my father, mother, brothers,
sisters, and all of their families to live. Save us
from death."
14The men agreed and said, "It will be our lives
for your lives if you don't tell anyone what we are
doing. When the LORD gives us the land, we will
be kind and true to you."
15The house Rahab lived in was built on the
city wall, so she used a rope to let the men down
through a window. 16She said to them, "Go into
the hills so the king's men will not find you. Hide
there for three days. After the king's men return,
you may go on your way."
17The men said to her, "You must do as we say.
If not, we cannot be responsible for keeping this
oath you have made us swear. 18When we return
to this land, you must tie this red rope in the
window through which you let us down. Bring
your father, mother, brothers, and all your family
into your house. 19If anyone leaves your house
and is killed, it is his own fault. We cannot be
responsible for him. If anyone in your house is
hurt, we will be responsible. 20But if you tell anyone about this, we will be free from the oath you
made us swear."
21Rahab answered, "I agree to this." So she
sent them away, and they left. Then she tied the
red rope in the window.
22The men left and went into the hills where
they stayed for three days. The king's men looked
for them all along the road, but after three days,
they returned to the city without finding them.
23Then the two men started back. They left the
hills and crossed the river and came to Joshua son
of Nun and told him everything that had happened to them. 24They said, "The LORD surely has
given us all of the land. All the people in that land
are terribly afraid of us."

Crossing the Jordan

3 Early the next morning Joshua and all the
Israelites left Acacia. They traveled to the
Jordan River and camped there before crossing it.
2After three days the officers went through the
camp 3and gave orders to the people: "When you
see the priests and Levites carrying the Ark of the
Agreement with the LORD your God, leave where
you are and follow it. 4That way you will know
which way to go since you have never been here
before. But do not follow too closely. Stay about a
thousand yards behind the Ark."
5Then Joshua told the people, "Make yourselves holy, because tomorrow the LORD will do
amazing things among you."
6Joshua said to the priests, "Take the Ark of
the Agreement and go ahead of the people." So the
priests lifted the Ark and carried it ahead of the
people.
7Then the LORD said to Joshua, "Today I will
begin to make you great in the opinion of all the
Israelites so the people will know I am with you
just as I was with Moses. 8Tell the priests who
carry the Ark of the Agreement to go to the edge
of the Jordan River and stand in the water."
9Then Joshua said to the Israelites, "Come here
and listen to the words of the LORD your God.
10Here is proof that the living God is with you and

2:8 *to the roof.* It was not uncommon for people to sleep on their cool, flat roofs in ancient times.

2:21 Deborah: Judges 1:14–15
2:24 Mission: 2 Kings 5

Sickness, Disease, Healing

Exodus 15:26

What is the biblical perspective on sickness and health? What causes sickness? Can God heal sickness, and does he always heal sickness?

The Bible is not concerned only with abstract, spiritual concepts. It is not out of touch with reality. Rather, the Word of God is thoroughly practical. Nowhere is this seen more clearly than in the Bible's treatment of the subjects of sickness, disease, and health.

Generally speaking, sickness is viewed as negative, while healing is viewed as positive. In and of themselves, sickness and disease are bad while health and healing are good. Long, vibrant life is viewed as a gift from God (Psalm 91:16), while premature death, especially as a result of debilitating sickness, is considered tragic (1 Samuel 2:31–33). Disease cuts life short and often drastically affects the quality of life.

Today, we often separate physical, emotional, and spiritual health, associating doctors with the body, psychologists with the mind, and ministers with the spirit. The biblical mentality was much more holistic: God was the giver of health, be it physical, emotional, or spiritual. He might use human physicians or natural means (2 Kings 20:1–7; 1 Timothy 5:23), but he alone was the ultimate source of life, health, and fertility, whatever the need might be.

If the land was desolate, God could restore it (2 Chronicles 7:14); if the womb was barren, God could make it fertile (Genesis 20:17–18); if the body was sick, God could cure it (Numbers 12:10–13); if the water was unwholesome, God could make it fresh (2 Kings 2:21–22). In all these verses, the same Hebrew word is used: it is God who "heals" —he restores and makes whole, whatever the condition.

Because God is a God of life, and since his laws are good, it stands to reason that living in harmony with him would lead to health and protection (Psalm 91; Proverbs 3:7–8; 4:20–22), while ignoring him and his Word would lead to death (Proverbs 8:36). Why then could godly people become sick? It is true that sin is the *ultimate* cause of sickness and death, even though not all sickness in the Bible was viewed as the result of specific, individual sin (John 9:1–3). In other words, because of the fall of the human race, disease and death have become our common lot. But not all sickness is "spiritually" rooted.

Many times sickness is simply viewed as a natural process. All of us get old, the body wears out, and even the most righteous people on earth may ultimately die of illness (2 Kings 13:14). At other times, minor sickness or injury is just the result of living in this world. Not every bump, bruise, headache, or pain is of spiritual significance! Yet there are times when sudden, serious, or acute illness is a divine messenger saying, "Something is wrong! You have strayed from the path of life! Turn back before it's too late!" (See Job 33:19–30.)

Was there any hope that one day God would rid the earth of the terrible curse of sickness and disease? Yes. The prophets declared that a day would come when great miracles of healing would become commonplace (Isaiah 35:3–6), and eventually both sickness and sin would be no more (Isaiah 33:24).

This new day *began* when Jesus came into the world. His ministry was not only characterized by teaching and preaching, but by healing as well (Matthew 4:23–25). He opened blind eyes, made cripples whole, unstopped deaf ears, and even raised the dead (Matthew 15:30–31; Luke 7:11–17). These healings were a sign of his deity, and proof that he was the Messiah (Luke 7:21–23; John 10:37–38). But they also reflected the loving heart of God the Father (John 14:9–11), moved with compassion for a dying race (Matthew 14:14). The Lord was troubled by human suffering, and he did something about it (Mark 1:40–42).

We see then that the miracles of Jesus indicated that God's kingdom of life and love had broken into this present age. For this reason, healings and miracles continued to take place, at first through the followers of Jesus in the book of Acts, and right up to this day. Prayer for the sick was also a trademark of the church, with the assurance that "the prayer that is said in faith will make the sick person well" (James 5:14–16; see also John 14:12–14).

Of course, there is still sickness and death in this age, and it is not realistic to expect universal, perfect health for all Christians. Yet there is no question that the revelation of God as Healer is still relevant, and that through Jesus, he has made healing accessible to us through dependence on him.

Sickness, Disease, Healing: For additional scriptures on this topic go to Exodus 23:25–26.

SABBATH

EXODUS 20:8–11

What is the connection between Sabbath and rest? Why is there a Sabbath? Do we observe the Sabbath today? When is the final and complete Sabbath?

The idea of Sabbath, or rest, appears early in Bible history. At the end of the sixth day of creation, when God had finished his work and declared that it was very good, he rested. Genesis 2:2–3 tell's us, "By the seventh day God finished the work he had been doing, so he rested from all his work. God blessed the seventh day and made it a holy day, because on that day he rested." When Moses gave the commandments on Mount Sinai, he referred back to God's rest after creation, "The reason is that in six days the Lord made everything. . . . On the seventh day he rested. So the LORD blessed the Sabbath day and made it holy" (Exodus 20:11). The importance of keeping the Sabbath is supported by a reminder and warning in the Book of Leviticus (Leviticus 26:2, 27–35). Again, God commanded the people to keep his Sabbaths.

There were several reasons for keeping the Sabbath, that is, resting on the seventh day. The first reason is based on God's rest after his work of creation. If it is good for the Creator to rest, it makes sense that his creation would benefit from rest also. Exodus 23:10–11 reminds us that even the land needs to rest. This is what farmers practice when they rotate their crops in a seven-year cycle. Exodus 23 goes on to tell us that the purpose for this rest is that land, animals, servants, masters, and all people might be refreshed. Exodus 31:13–17 and Ezekiel 20:12 tell us that God also gave the Sabbath as a sign between himself and his people. By keeping the Sabbath, people would remember that God had made his people holy, just as he had sanctified the seventh day.

The keeping of the Sabbath was even more important after God brought the children of Israel out of slavery in Egypt. The Egyptians forced the people of God to work without rest. God rescued his people from that bondage. God wanted the people to keep the Sabbath so they would never forget how he had set them free from their forced labor (Deuteronomy 5:12–15).

The serious nature of keeping the Sabbath may be seen from a few examples. Exodus 16 describes how God gave the people manna to eat while they were in the desert. If the people collected more manna than they were supposed to for one day, what was left over would rot. However, on the sixth day God instructed them to collect twice as much manna, yet it would last through the Sabbath without spoiling. Both Isaiah (Isaiah 56:2–7) and Amos (Amos 8:5) tried to teach people the importance of remembering the Sabbath faithfully. The people refused and were eventually taken into captivity, just as God had warned in Leviticus 26. After God brought his people back from exile, teachers like Nehemiah were very serious about keeping the Sabbath properly (Nehemiah 13:15–22).

Now we can see that the Sabbath rest was founded on God's rest after creation and on the rest he gave his people after he brought them out of slavery in Egypt. We also know how important and serious the Sabbath law was in the Old Testament. But does it still apply today? If it does apply, what is a person allowed to do on that day? Jesus confirmed the importance of rest. Jesus often went away from the crowds with his disciples so they could rest (Mark 6:31). However, the New Testament records how Jesus consistently taught and healed on the Sabbath (Matthew 12:1–3; Mark 6:2; Luke 4:16). The apostles also taught on the Sabbath (Acts 13:14–52). When religious leaders criticized Jesus for this, he gave two important answers. First, Jesus reminded them that the Sabbath was made for people, not people for the Sabbath. Second, Jesus told them it was lawful to do good on the Sabbath. Paul wrote in Colossians 2:16 that Christians should let no one judge them with regard to the Sabbath, which is a shadow of things to come. Therefore, a Christian is free in regard to keeping the Sabbath in a particular way or on a certain day of the week. However, we do well to remember that God gave the Sabbath so that we might benefit (by remembering and resting), and so others might benefit (by our teaching and doing good).

The Bible also teaches that there is a final fulfillment of a Sabbath rest. Hebrews 4 reminds us that there is a rest for the people of God and encourages us to be diligent to enter that rest. This rest is enjoyed by Christians to some degree in this life, but will not be enjoyed completely until the next. Revelation 6:11 records that the saints were told to rest until the rest of their brothers and sisters came to heaven. In Revelation 14:12–13 John says that the saints are those who keep the commandments of God and the faith of Jesus. He goes on to say that the dead who die in the Lord are blessed because they rest from their labors.

Sabbath: For additional scriptures on this topic go to Genesis 2:2–3.

that he will force out the Canaanites, Hittites, Hivites, Perizzites, Girgashites, Amorites, and Jebusites. 11The Ark of the Agreement with the Lord of the whole world will go ahead of you into the Jordan River. 12Now choose twelve men from among you, one from each of the twelve tribes of Israel. 13The priests will carry the Ark of the LORD, the Master of the whole world, into the Jordan ahead of you. When they step into the water, it will stop. The river will stop flowing and will stand up in a heap."

14So the people left the place where they had camped, and they followed the priests who carried the Ark of the Agreement across the Jordan River. 15During harvest the Jordan overflows its banks. When the priests carrying the Ark came to the edge of the river and stepped into the water, 16the water upstream stopped flowing. It stood up in a heap a great distance away at Adam, a town near Zarethan. The water flowing down to the Sea of Arabah (the Dead Sea) was completely cut off. So the people crossed the river near Jericho. 17The priests carried the Ark of the Agreement with the LORD to the middle of the river and stood there on dry ground. They waited there while all the people of Israel walked across the Jordan River on dry land.

Rocks to Remind the People

4 After all the people had finished crossing the Jordan, the LORD said to Joshua, 2"Choose twelve men from among the people, one from each tribe. 3Tell them to get twelve rocks from the middle of the river, from where the priests stood. Carry the rocks and put them down where you stay tonight."

4So Joshua chose one man from each tribe. Then he called the twelve men together 5and said to them, "Go out into the river where the Ark of the LORD your God is. Each of you bring back one rock, one for each tribe of Israel, and carry it on your shoulder. 6They will be a sign among you. In the future your children will ask you, 'What do these rocks mean?' 7Tell them the water stopped flowing in the Jordan when the Ark of the Agreement with the LORD crossed the river. These rocks will always remind the Israelites of this."

8So the Israelites obeyed Joshua and carried twelve rocks from the middle of the Jordan River, one rock for each of the twelve tribes of Israel, just as the LORD had commanded Joshua. They carried the rocks with them and put them down where they made their camp. 9Joshua also put twelve rocks in the middle of the Jordan River where the priests had stood while carrying the Ark of the Agreement. These rocks are still there today.

10The priests carrying the Ark continued standing in the middle of the river until everything was done that the LORD had commanded Joshua to tell the people, just as Moses had told Joshua. The people hurried across the river. 11After they finished crossing the river, the priests carried the Ark of the LORD to the other side as the people watched. 12The men from the tribes of Reuben, Gad, and East Manasseh obeyed what Moses had told them. They were dressed for war, and they crossed the river ahead of the other people. 13About forty thousand soldiers prepared for war passed before the LORD as they marched across the river, going toward the plains of Jericho.

14That day the LORD made Joshua great in the opinion of all the Israelites. They respected Joshua all his life, just as they had respected Moses.

15Then the LORD said to Joshua, 16"Command the priests to bring the Ark of the Agreement out of the river."

17So Joshua commanded the priests, "Come up out of the Jordan."

18Then the priests carried the Ark of the Agreement with the LORD out of the river. As soon as their feet touched dry land, the water began flowing again. The river again overflowed its banks, just as it had before they crossed.

19The people crossed the Jordan on the tenth day of the first month and camped at Gilgal, east of Jericho. 20They carried with them the twelve rocks taken from the Jordan, and Joshua set them up at Gilgal. 21Then he spoke to the Israelites: "In the future your children will ask you, 'What do these rocks mean?' 22Tell them, 'Israel crossed the Jordan River on dry land. 23The LORD your God caused the water to stop flowing until you finished crossing it, just as the LORD did to the Red Sea. He stopped the water until we crossed it. 24The LORD did this so all people would know he has great power and so you would always respect the LORD your God.'"

5 All the kings of the Amorites west of the Jordan and the Canaanite kings living by the Mediterranean Sea heard that the LORD dried up

4:7 After forty years of wandering in the desert, the Israelites were finally entering the Promised Land. This was a momentous occasion as God stopped the waters of the Jordan so the Israelites could have a second "Red Sea" experience. In response they set up a mound of twelve stones so they could look back and remember the occasion of God's miracle. Their remembrance of God would help them in the troubled days ahead. They would be reminded that God is a powerful God who saves.

4:24 Ark of the Agreement: Joshua 6

the Jordan River until the Israelites had crossed it.
After that they were scared and too afraid to face
the Israelites.

The Israelites Are Circumcised

2At that time the LORD said to Joshua, "Make
knives from flint stones and circumcise the
Israelites." 3So Joshua made knives from flint stones
and circumcised the Israelites at Gibeath Haaraloth.
4This is why Joshua circumcised the men: After
the Israelites left Egypt, all the men old enough to
serve in the army died in the desert on the way
out of Egypt. 5The men who had come out of
Egypt had been circumcised, but none of those
who were born in the desert on the trip from
Egypt had been circumcised. 6The Israelites had
moved about in the desert for forty years. During
that time all the fighting men who had left Egypt
had died because they had not obeyed the LORD.
So the LORD swore they would not see the land he
had promised their ancestors to give them, a fertile land. 7Their sons took their places. But none
of the sons born on the trip from Egypt had been
circumcised, so Joshua circumcised them. 8After
all the Israelites had been circumcised, they
stayed in camp until they were healed.
9Then the LORD said to Joshua, "As slaves in
Egypt you were ashamed, but today I have
removed that shame." So Joshua named that
place Gilgal, which it is still named today.
10The people of Israel were camped at Gilgal on
the plains of Jericho. It was there, on the evening
of the fourteenth day of the month, they celebrated
the Passover Feast. 11The day after the Passover, the
people ate food grown on that land: bread made
without yeast and roasted grain. 12The day they ate
this food, the manna stopped coming. The Israelites
no longer got the manna from heaven. They ate the
food grown in the land of Canaan that year.
13Joshua was near Jericho when he looked up
and saw a man standing in front of him with a
sword in his hand. Joshua went to him and asked,
"Are you a friend or an enemy?"
14The man answered, "I am neither. I have
come as the commander of the LORD's army."
Then Joshua bowed facedown on the ground
and asked, "Does my master have a command for
me, his servant?"
15The commander of the LORD's army answered,
"Take off your sandals, because the place where
you are standing is holy." So Joshua did.

The Fall of Jericho

6 The people of Jericho were afraid because the
Israelites were near. They closed the city
gates and guarded them. No one went into the
city, and no one came out.
2Then the LORD said to Joshua, "Look, I have
given you Jericho, its king, and all its fighting
men. 3March around the city with your army once
a day for six days. 4Have seven priests carry trumpets made from horns of male sheep and have
them march in front of the Ark. On the seventh
day march around the city seven times and have
the priests blow the trumpets as they march.
5They will make one long blast on the trumpets.
When you hear that sound, have all the people
give a loud shout. Then the walls of the city will
fall so the people can go straight into the city."
6So Joshua son of Nun called the priests
together and said to them, "Carry the Ark of the
Agreement. Tell seven priests to carry trumpets
and march in front of it." 7Then Joshua ordered
the people, "Now go! March around the city. The
soldiers with weapons should march in front of
the Ark of the Agreement with the LORD."
8When Joshua finished speaking to the people,
the seven priests began marching before the
LORD. They carried the seven trumpets and blew
them as they marched. The priests carrying the
Ark of the Agreement with the LORD followed
them. 9Soldiers with weapons marched in front of
the priests, and armed men walked behind the
Ark. The priests were blowing their trumpets.
10But Joshua had told the people not to give a war
cry. He said, "Don't shout. Don't say a word until
the day I tell you. Then shout." 11So Joshua had
the Ark of the LORD carried around the city one
time. Then they went back to camp for the night.
12Early the next morning Joshua got up, and the
priests carried the Ark of the LORD again. 13The
seven priests carried the seven trumpets and
marched in front of the Ark of the LORD, blowing
their trumpets. Soldiers with weapons marched in
front of them, and other soldiers walked behind the
Ark of the LORD. All this time the priests were blowing their trumpets. 14So on the second day they
marched around the city one time and then went
back to camp. They did this every day for six days.
15On the seventh day they got up at dawn and
marched around the city, just as they had on the
days before. But on that day they marched around

5:14 Servant of the Lord: 1 Samuel 1:11
5:15 Circumcision: Jeremiah 9:25–26
5:15 Holy War & Divine Warrior: Joshua 10:14

6:4 *Ark.* The Ark is described in Exodus 25:10–22, and it represented God's presence on earth. It often went with Israel's army into battle.

the city seven times. 16The seventh time around the priests blew their trumpets. Then Joshua gave the command: "Now, shout! The LORD has given you this city! 17The city and everything in it are to be destroyed as an offering to the LORD. Only Rahab the prostitute and everyone in her house should remain alive. They must not be killed, because Rahab hid the two spies we sent out. 18Don't take any of the things that are to be destroyed as an offering to the LORD. If you take them and bring them into our camp, you yourselves will be destroyed, and you will bring trouble to all of Israel. 19All the silver and gold and things made from bronze and iron belong to the LORD and must be saved for him."

20When the priests blew the trumpets, the people shouted. At the sound of the trumpets and the people's shout, the walls fell, and everyone ran straight into the city. So the Israelites defeated that city. 21They completely destroyed with the sword every living thing in the city—men and women, young and old, cattle, sheep, and donkeys.

22Joshua said to the two men who had spied out the land, "Go into the prostitute's house. Bring her out and bring out those who are with her, because of the promise you made to her." 23So the two men went into the house and brought out Rahab, her father, mother, brothers, and all those with her. They put all of her family in a safe place outside the camp of Israel.

24Then Israel burned the whole city and everything in it, but they did not burn the things made from silver, gold, bronze, and iron. These were saved for the LORD. 25Joshua saved Rahab the prostitute, her family, and all who were with her, because Rahab had helped the men he had sent to spy out Jericho. Rahab still lives among the Israelites today.

26Then Joshua made this oath:

"Anyone who tries to rebuild this city
of Jericho
will be cursed by the LORD.
The one who lays the foundation of this city
will lose his oldest son,
and the one who sets up the gates
will lose his youngest son."

27So the LORD was with Joshua, and Joshua became famous through all the land.

The Sin of Achan

7 But the Israelites did not obey the LORD. There was a man from the tribe of Judah named Achan. (He was the son of Carmi and grandson of Zabdi, who was the son of Zerah.) Because Achan kept some of the things that were to be given to the LORD, the LORD became very angry at the Israelites.

2Joshua sent some men from Jericho to Ai, which was near Beth Aven, east of Bethel. He told them, "Go to Ai and spy out the area." So the men went to spy on Ai.

3Later they came back to Joshua and said, "There are only a few people in Ai, so we will not need all our people to defeat them. Send only two or three thousand men to fight. There is no need to send all of our people." 4So about three thousand men went up to Ai, but the people of Ai beat them badly. 5The people of Ai killed about thirty-six Israelites and then chased the rest from the city gate all the way down to the canyon, killing them as they went down the hill. When the Israelites saw this, they lost their courage.

6Then Joshua tore his clothes in sorrow. He bowed facedown on the ground before the Ark of the LORD and stayed there until evening. The leaders of Israel did the same thing. They also threw dirt on their heads to show their sorrow. 7Then Joshua said, "Lord GOD, you brought our people across the Jordan River. Why did you bring us this far and then let the Amorites destroy us? We would have been happy to stay on the other side of the Jordan. 8Lord, there is nothing I can say now. Israel has been beaten by the enemy. 9The Canaanites and all the other people in this country will hear about this and will surround and kill us all! Then what will you do for your own great name?"

10The LORD said to Joshua, "Stand up! Why are you down on your face? 11The Israelites have sinned; they have broken the agreement I commanded them to obey. They took some of the things I commanded them to destroy. They have stolen and lied and have taken those things for themselves. 12That is why the Israelites cannot face their enemies. They turn away from the fight and run, because I have commanded that they be destroyed. I will not help you anymore unless you destroy everything as I commanded you.

13"Now go! Make the people holy. Tell them, 'Set yourselves apart to the LORD for tomorrow. The LORD, the God of Israel, says some of you are keeping things he commanded you to destroy. You will never defeat your enemies until you throw away those things.

14"'Tomorrow morning you must be present with your tribes. The LORD will choose one tribe

6:17 Rahab: Joshua 6:22–23
6:23 Rahab: Joshua 6:25
6:25 Rahab: Ruth 1:16
6:27 Ark of the Agreement: 1 Samuel 3:3
6:27 Music: 1 Samuel 16:14–23
7:12 God's Anger: Daniel 8:19

to stand alone before him. Then the LORD will choose one family group from that tribe to stand before him. Then the LORD will choose one family from that family group to stand before him, person by person. 15The one who is keeping what should have been destroyed will himself be destroyed by fire. Everything he owns will be destroyed with him. He has broken the agreement with the LORD and has done a disgraceful thing among the people of Israel!'"

16Early the next morning Joshua led all of Israel to present themselves in their tribes, and the LORD chose the tribe of Judah. 17So the family groups of Judah presented themselves, and the LORD then chose the family group of Zerah. When all the families of Zerah presented themselves, the family of Zabdi was chosen. 18And Joshua told all the men in that family to present themselves. The LORD chose Achan son of Carmi. (Carmi was the son of Zabdi, who was the son of Zerah.)

19Then Joshua said to Achan, "My son, tell the truth. Confess to the LORD, the God of Israel. Tell me what you did, and don't try to hide anything from me."

20Achan answered, "It is true! I have sinned against the LORD, the God of Israel. This is what I did: 21Among the things I saw was a beautiful coat from Babylonia and about five pounds of silver and more than one and one-fourth pounds of gold. I wanted these things very much for myself, so I took them. You will find them buried in the ground under my tent, with the silver underneath."

22So Joshua sent men who ran to the tent and found the things hidden there, with the silver. 23The men brought them out of the tent, took them to Joshua and all the Israelites, and spread them out on the ground before the LORD. 24Then Joshua and all the people led Achan son of Zerah to the Valley of Trouble. They also took the silver, the coat, the gold, Achan's sons, daughters, cattle, donkeys, sheep, tent, and everything he owned. 25Joshua said, "I don't know why you caused so much trouble for us, but now the LORD will bring trouble to you." Then all the people threw stones at Achan and his family until they died. Then the people burned them. 26They piled rocks over Achan's body, and they are still there today. That is why it is called the Valley of Trouble. After this the LORD was no longer angry.

Ai Is Destroyed

8 Then the LORD said to Joshua, "Don't be afraid or give up. Lead all your fighting men to Ai. I will help you defeat the king of Ai, his people, his city, and his land. 2You will do to Ai and its king what you did to Jericho and its king. Only this time you may take all the wealth and keep it for yourselves. Now tell some of your soldiers to set up an ambush behind the city."

3So Joshua led his whole army toward Ai. Then he chose thirty thousand of his best fighting men and sent them out at night. 4Joshua gave them these orders: "Listen carefully. You must set up an ambush behind the city. Don't go far from it, but continue to watch and be ready. 5I and the men who are with me will march toward the city, and the men in the city will come out to fight us, just as they did before. Then we will turn and run away from them. 6They will chase us away from the city, thinking we are running away from them as we did before. When we run away, 7come out from your ambush and take the city. The LORD your God will give you the power to win. 8After you take the city, burn it. See to it! You have your orders."

9Then Joshua sent them to wait in ambush between Bethel and Ai, to the west of Ai. But Joshua stayed the night with his people.

10Early the next morning Joshua gathered his men together. He and the older leaders of Israel led them up to Ai. 11All of the soldiers who were with Joshua marched up to Ai and stopped in front of the city and made camp north of it. There was a valley between them and the city. 12Then Joshua chose about five thousand men and set them in ambush in the area west of the city between Bethel and Ai. 13So the people took their positions; the main camp was north of the city, and the other men were hiding to the west. That night Joshua went down into the valley.

14Now when the king of Ai saw the army of Israel, he and his people got up early the next morning and hurried out to fight them. They went out to a place east of the city, but the king did not know soldiers were waiting in ambush behind the city. 15Joshua and all the men of Israel let the army of Ai push them back. Then they ran toward the desert. 16The men in Ai were called to chase Joshua and his men, so they left the city and went after them. 17All the men of Ai and Bethel chased the army of Israel. The city was left open; not a man stayed to protect it.

18Then the LORD said to Joshua, "Hold your spear toward Ai, because I will give you that city." So Joshua held his spear toward the city of Ai. 19When the Israelites who were in ambush saw this, they quickly came out of their hiding

8:1 Fear: Psalm 55:4–8

place and hurried toward the city. They entered the city, took control of it, and quickly set it on fire.

20 When the men of Ai looked back, they saw smoke rising from their city. At the same time the Israelites stopped running and turned against the men of Ai, who could not escape in any direction. 21 When Joshua and all his men saw that the army had taken control of the city and saw the smoke rising from it, they stopped running and turned to fight the men of Ai. 22 The men who were in ambush also came out of the city to help with the fight. So the men of Ai were caught between the armies of Israel. None of the enemy escaped. The Israelites fought until not one of the men of Ai was left alive, except 23 the king of Ai, and they brought him to Joshua.

A Review of the Fighting

24 During the fighting the army of Israel chased the men of Ai into the fields and desert and killed all of them. Then they went back to Ai and killed everyone there. 25 All the people of Ai died that day, twelve thousand men and women. 26 Joshua had held his spear toward Ai, as a sign to destroy the city, and did not draw it back until all the people of Ai were destroyed. 27 The people of Israel kept for themselves the animals and the other things the people of Ai had owned, as the LORD had commanded Joshua to do.

28 Then Joshua burned the city of Ai and made it a pile of ruins. And it is still like that today. 29 Joshua hanged the king of Ai on a tree and left him there until evening. At sunset Joshua told his men to take the king's body down from the tree and to throw it down at the city gate. Then they covered it with a pile of rocks, which is still there today.

30 Joshua built an altar for the LORD, the God of Israel, on Mount Ebal, as 31 Moses, the LORD's servant, had commanded. Joshua built the altar as it was explained in the Book of the Teachings of Moses. It was made from uncut stones; no tool was ever used on them. On that altar the Israelites offered burnt offerings to the LORD and fellowship offerings.∞ 32 There Joshua wrote the teachings of Moses on stones for all the people of Israel to see. 33 The older leaders, officers, judges, and all the Israelites were there; Israelites and non-Israelites were all standing around the Ark of the Agreement with the LORD in front of the priests, the Levites who had carried the Ark. Half of the people stood in front of Mount Ebal, and half stood in front of Mount Gerizim. This was the way the LORD's servant Moses had earlier commanded the people to be blessed.

34 Then Joshua read all the words of the teachings, the blessings and the curses, exactly as they were written in the Book of the Teachings. 35 All the Israelites were gathered together—men, women, and children—along with the non-Israelites who lived among them. Joshua read every command that Moses had given.

The Gibeonite Trickery

9 All the kings west of the Jordan River heard about these things: the kings of the Hittites, Amorites, Canaanites, Perizzites, Hivites, and Jebusites. They lived in the mountains and on the western hills and along the whole Mediterranean Sea coast. 2 So all these kings gathered to fight Joshua and the Israelites.

3 When the people of Gibeon heard how Joshua had defeated Jericho and Ai, 4 they decided to trick the Israelites. They gathered old sacks and old leather wine bags that were cracked and mended, and they put them on the backs of their donkeys. 5 They put old sandals on their feet and wore old clothes, and they took some dry, moldy bread. 6 Then they went to Joshua in the camp near Gilgal.

The men said to Joshua and the Israelites, "We have traveled from a faraway country. Make a peace agreement with us."

7 The Israelites said to these Hivites, "Maybe you live near us. How can we make a peace agreement with you?"

8 The Hivites said to Joshua, "We are your servants."

But Joshua asked, "Who are you? Where do you come from?"

9 The men answered, "We are your servants who have come from a far country, because we heard of the fame of the LORD your God. We heard about what he has done and everything he did in Egypt. 10 We heard that he defeated the two kings of the Amorites from the east side of the Jordan River—Sihon king of Heshbon and Og king of Bashan who ruled in Ashtaroth. 11 So our older leaders and our people said to us, 'Take food for your journey and go and meet the Israelites. Tell them, "We are your servants. Make a peace agreement with us."'

∞**8:31 Stone:** Joshua 24:26–27

9 Israel got themselves into trouble by making an oath without first asking the LORD what to do (verse 14). They had to keep their word, though they did force the Gibeonites into servitude (verse 23). Later King Saul went back on the oath, and it brought a curse on Israel until David made up for it (2 Samuel 21:1–14).

9:3 *to trick the Israelites.* In Deuteronomy 20:16–18 God commanded Israel to destroy the Canaanites completely, but they could spare people who lived outside of Palestine. That is why the Gibeonites thought up this trick.

12“Look at our bread. On the day we left home
to come to you it was warm and fresh, but now it
is dry and moldy. 13Look at our leather wine bags.
They were new and filled with wine, but now
they are cracked and old. Our clothes and sandals
are worn out from the long journey.”
14The men of Israel tasted the bread, but they
did not ask the LORD what to do. 15So Joshua
agreed to make peace with the Gibeonites and to
let them live. And the leaders of the Israelites
swore an oath to keep the agreement.
16Three days after they had made the agreement, the Israelites learned that the Gibeonites
lived nearby. 17So the Israelites went to where
they lived and on the third day came to their
cities: Gibeon, Kephirah, Beeroth, and Kiriath
Jearim. 18But the Israelites did not attack those
cities, because they had made a promise to them
before the LORD, the God of Israel.
All the Israelites grumbled against the leaders.
19But the leaders answered, “We have given our
promise before the LORD, the God of Israel, so we
cannot attack them now. 20This is what we must
do. We must let them live. Otherwise, God’s
anger will be against us for breaking the oath we
swore to them. 21So let them live, but they will
cut wood and carry water for our people.” So the
leaders kept their promise to them.
22Joshua called for the Gibeonites and asked,
“Why did you lie to us? Your land was near our
camp, but you told us you were from a far country. 23Now, you will be placed under a curse to be
our slaves. You will have to cut wood and carry
water for the house of my God.”
24The Gibeonites answered Joshua, “We lied to
you because we were afraid you would kill us. We
heard that the LORD your God commanded his
servant Moses to give you all of this land and to
kill all the people who lived in it. That is why we
did this. 25Now you can decide what to do with
us, whatever you think is right.”
26So Joshua saved their lives by not allowing
the Israelites to kill them, 27but he made the
Gibeonites slaves. They cut wood and carried
water for the Israelites, and they did it for the altar
of the LORD—wherever he chose it to be. They are
still doing this today.

The Sun Stands Still

10 At this time Adoni-Zedek king of Jerusalem
heard that Joshua had defeated Ai and
completely destroyed it, as he had also done to
Jericho and its king. The king also learned that
the Gibeonites had made a peace agreement with
Israel and that they lived nearby.∞ 2Adoni-Zedek
and his people were very afraid because of this.
Gibeon was not a little town like Ai; it was a large
city, as big as a city that had a king, and all its men
were good fighters. 3So Adoni-Zedek king of Jerusalem sent a message to Hoham king of Hebron,
Piram king of Jarmuth, Japhia king of Lachish, and
Debir king of Eglon. He begged them, 4“Come with
me and help me attack Gibeon, which has made
a peace agreement with Joshua and the Israelites.”
5Then these five Amorite kings—the kings of
Jerusalem, Hebron, Jarmuth, Lachish, and Eglon—
gathered their armies, went to Gibeon, surrounded
it, and attacked it.
6The Gibeonites sent this message to Joshua in
his camp at Gilgal: “Don’t let us, your servants,
be destroyed. Come quickly and help us! Save us!
All the Amorite kings from the mountains have
joined their armies and are fighting against us.”
7So Joshua marched out of Gilgal with his whole
army, including his best fighting men. 8The LORD
said to Joshua, “Don’t be afraid of those armies,
because I will hand them over to you. None of
them will be able to stand against you.”
9Joshua and his army marched all night from
Gilgal for a surprise attack. 10The LORD confused
those armies when Israel attacked, so Israel defeated them in a great victory at Gibeon. They
chased them along the road going up to Beth
Horon and killed men all the way to Azekah and
Makkedah. 11As they chased the enemy down the
Beth Horon Pass to Azekah, the LORD threw large
hailstones on them from the sky and killed them.
More people were killed by the hailstones than
by the Israelites’ swords.
12On the day that the LORD gave up the Amorites to the Israelites, Joshua stood before all the
people of Israel and said to the LORD:
“Sun, stand still over Gibeon.
Moon, stand still over the Valley of Aijalon.”
13So the sun stood still,
and the moon stopped
until the people defeated their enemies.
These words are written in the Book of Jashar.
The sun stopped in the middle of the sky and
waited to go down for a full day. 14That has never
happened at any time before that day or since.
That was the day the LORD listened to a human
being. Truly the LORD was fighting for Israel!∞

∞**10:1 Jerusalem:** Joshua 15:63

10:13 *the sun stood still.* While many have tried to explain the stopping of the sun as a result of a natural occurrence, the best understanding is that it is a miracle where God overruled laws of nature.

∞**10:14 Holy War & Divine Warrior:** Judges 7:14

ADULTERY

EXODUS 20:14

What is the biblical teaching on adultery? What does biblical teaching have to tell us about promiscuity today? Does the Bible's definition of adultery say anything of our spiritual lives?

Adultery is sexual unfaithfulness toward your spouse, and a topic that comes up again and again in the Bible. It is unanimously condemned, not only in the Ninth Commandment (see also Deuteronomy 5:18), but also in such passages as Leviticus 20:10 and 1 Corinthians 6:9–10.

Perhaps the most well-known story of adultery in the Bible is David's sin with Bathsheba in 2 Samuel 11. It was in the spring, when kings normally go out at war, that David stayed behind in Jerusalem. He went up to the roof of his house and saw Bathsheba, wife of Uriah, one of his soldiers. She became pregnant by David, and in an effort to conceal his sin, David tried to get Uriah to sleep with Bathsheba. When he nobly refused (thinking of his faithful comrades in battle), David assigned Uriah to the front line of battle with the intent that he be killed in action, which is precisely what happened. God punished David by the death of their child shortly after its birth (2 Samuel 12:13–23) and by the deadly political intrigue surrounding his sons Amnon and Absolom (2 Samuel 13–18). David later came to realize what he had done, and his deep sorrow and regret are recounted in Psalm 51.

The other prominent example in the Bible is Joseph's temptation by Potiphar's wife in Genesis 39. There, Joseph finds himself alone with the wife of Potiphar, the captain of Pharaoh's palace guard. But the outcome is quite different than with David: Joseph resists the strong temptation of the adulteress and does not give in. He recognizes that such an act would not only betray the trust of Potiphar, who had come to trust Joseph completely (Genesis 39:6), but would be a "sin against God" (Genesis 39:9). David finally learned the same lesson, as we see in Psalm 51:4: "You are the only one I have sinned against."

Two valuable lessons may be learned from these two stories. First, adultery, in addition to the harm done to the parties involved, is ultimately a sin against God himself. To put it another way, there is a spiritual dimension to adultery that permits no excuses such as "it's all right as long as no one finds out." The wrong done against God cannot be swept under the rug. This holds not only for adultery, but for any sin: God is always the "third party" involved.

The second lesson is that adultery in the Bible, like today, is truly a temptation, even for such pillars of faith as Joseph and David. Although only David gave in, it is clear that the temptation to sin was a struggle for both of them. The difference lies in how each of them handled that temptation. In these two stories, the Bible gives both a how-to and a how-not-to of resisting adultery.

Adultery, therefore, is not a uniquely modern problem. Despite the "glamorous" and enticing images that invade our daily lives, seemingly wherever we turn, it should be remembered that adultery has *always* been a matter of concern for God's people. And the response of God's people should always be the same: No. The fact that the Bible mentions adultery as often as it does, in addition to the fact that it is one of the Ten Commandments, shows how concerned God is that we remain faithful to our spouses.

Also, no doubt the primary reason why adultery continues to be an issue (and even endorsed in today's world) is that the spiritual dimension has been lost. If there is no fear of God and no shame in sinning against him, there is no adultery to speak of, only "extra-marital relationships."

The spiritual dimension of adultery also has another level of meaning in the Bible, one that gets at the very heart of the Christian life. The Bible not only describes our unfaithfulness to our spouses as adultery, but our unfaithfulness to God himself. The most extended example of this is Hosea 1–3. There, Hosea's marriage to the adulterous Gomer is presented as a graphic picture of God's continued faithfulness to his unfaithful people. A similar parable is also found in Jeremiah 3:6–10.

As the Israelites are God's bride in the Old Testament, so is the church in the New Testament. In Revelation 19:7; 21:2, 9, the church is called the bride of the Lamb (Christ), and is to be kept pure and holy for her husband. Christians are to be truly faithful, not only to our earthly spouse, but to our heavenly spouse as well. Intimacy with any other husband is considered adultery and not without terrible consequences.

The Good News, however, also includes forgiveness for those who have done wrong yet are truly sorry for what they have done. We see this not only in Psalm 51 and Hosea 3, but in the well-known story of the adulterous woman whom Jesus saves from being stoned (John 8:1–11).

Adultery: For additional scriptures on this topic go to Genesis 2:24.

ABORTION

EXODUS 21:22

Does the Bible have anything to say directly about abortion?
How can the Bible be properly used to help Christians think about abortion?

Abortion has been the subject of heated debate, particularly since the early seventies. And although the response of the Christian church has been virtuously unanimous against this practice, many believers are often at a loss to give biblical grounds for their position.

Perhaps the main reason for this is the fact that there is no passage in the Bible that definitively comments on abortion. There is no commandment against (or for!) the practice. There is no description of an abortion, nor is there an allusion to abortion. Although the practice of abortion was not unknown in the ancient world in general, it apparently was not an issue for the biblical writers.

Some would respond by saying that the sixth commandment, "You must not murder anyone" (Exodus 20:13), covers abortion, since a fetus is a person who is killed in the act. But that is precisely the question: Does the Bible recognize the fetus as a living being? So while abortion is not specifically addressed in the Bible, there are certain Old Testament passages that speak indirectly to the issue.

Perhaps the most often cited passage is Exodus 21:22. There is, however, considerable ambiguity with this verse, which certainly explains why it can be cited by both pro-life and pro-choice advocates. For one thing, what does it mean for the baby to "come out"? The Hebrew is quite unclear and could refer to premature delivery (miscarriage) or full-term delivery. Also, whose "harm" is being referred to, the mother's or the child's? If the child's, it is still worth pointing out that Exodus 21:22 speaks of the accidental death of a child against its mother's wishes. How does this relate to the "woman's right to choose" in today's debate? It is difficult to know exactly what this verse means, or its exact relevance to the abortion debate.

However, there are other passages that refer to the womb and the child in the womb. The two most often cited passages in the Old Testament are Jeremiah 1:5 and Psalm 139:13–16. The first refers to Jeremiah's call to be a prophet. It declares that God had Jeremiah "set apart" even before he was born, more specifically, before God formed him in the womb. Such a notion would seem to have at least some bearing on the status of the fetus, since Jeremiah was in God's mind, so to speak, before his birth. Yet the relevance of this passage should not be pressed too far, since it states explicitly that Jeremiah was known by God *before* he was even in the womb. In other words, the status of the fetus in the womb seems to be beside the point. Furthermore, the general context of Jeremiah 1 is the appointment of Jeremiah as a "prophet to the nations" and not a comment on personhood of the fetus. Too much should not be expected from this passage. Nevertheless, one should neither ignore the clear implication that, from God's point of view, his concern for his people does not begin merely at birth.

Perhaps more pertinent is Psalm 139:13–16. Here the writer refers specifically to the wonder of God "creating" and "forming" him in the womb. Again, the context is not the status of the fetus as a person, but at the very least this passage refers to God's planning of the believer's *entire life* (verse 16), a life that apparently began in the womb, and not at birth or the third trimester. Verse 15 is especially important as it describes, in a manner of speaking, fetal development. Yet neither should this passage be pushed too far. Although the writer praises God for the "amazing and wonderful way" he was made, this does not necessarily imply that the fetus is considered a person, which is at the heart of the abortion controversy. Although the wonderful act of God in the womb most likely implies the personhood of the fetus, it is not certain.

Job 10:10–11, like Psalm 139, speaks of the formation of "skin and flesh . . . bones and muscles" inside the mother. The context here is Job's complaint against God. Job reminds God of how he created him in the womb. Why, Job seems to ask, would God want to harm him now? (See also 10:3, 18.)

A strong implication to be drawn from at least Job 10 and Psalm 139 is that God's involvement in our lives does not begin at birth. Rather, God is seen to be "active" in the womb; he "forms," "makes," "puts together," "dresses," "sews" the body in the womb. In fact, and this is where Jeremiah 1:4, 5 becomes relevant, God's care for his people begins even *before* the womb. In this sense, the development of the fetus may be seen as one stage along the way in the realization of God's design. It should be kept in mind that the Bible does not address abortion directly. Nevertheless, the Bible teaches that the unborn child is firmly in God's mind, for he made it.

Abortion: For additional scriptures on this topic go to Jeremiah 20:14–18.

15After this, Joshua and his army went back to
the camp at Gilgal.
16During the fight the five kings ran away and
hid in a cave near Makkedah, 17but someone found
them hiding in the cave at Makkedah and told
Joshua. 18So he said, "Cover the opening of the
cave with large rocks. Put some men there to guard
it, 19but don't stay there yourselves. Continue
chasing the enemy and attacking them from
behind. Don't let them get to their cities, because
the LORD your God will hand them over to you."
20So Joshua and the Israelites killed the enemy,
but a few were able to get back to their strong,
walled cities. 21After the fighting, Joshua's men
came back safely to him at Makkedah. No one was
brave enough to say a word against the Israelites.
22Joshua said, "Move the rocks that are covering the opening of the cave and bring those five
kings out to me." 23So Joshua's men brought the
five kings out of the cave—the kings of Jerusalem,
Hebron, Jarmuth, Lachish, and Eglon. 24When
they brought the five kings out to Joshua, he
called for all his men. He said to the commanders
of his army, "Come here! Put your feet on the
necks of these kings." So they came close and put
their feet on their necks.
25Joshua said to his men, "Be strong and brave!
Don't be afraid, because I will show you what the
LORD will do to the enemies you will fight in the
future." 26Then Joshua killed the five kings and
hung their bodies on five trees, where he left them
until evening.
27At sunset Joshua told his men to take the bodies down from the trees. Then they threw them
into the same cave where they had been hiding
and covered the opening of the cave with large
rocks, which are still there today.
28That day Joshua defeated Makkedah. He killed
the king and completely destroyed all the people
in that city as an offering to the LORD; no one was
left alive. He did the same thing to the king of
Makkedah that he had done to the king of Jericho.

Defeating Southern Cities

29Joshua and all the Israelites traveled from
Makkedah to Libnah and attacked it. 30The LORD
handed over the city and its king. They killed
every person in the city; no one was left alive.
And they did the same thing to that king that they
had done to the king of Jericho.
31Then Joshua and all the Israelites left Libnah
and went to Lachish, which they surrounded and
attacked. 32The LORD handed over Lachish on the
second day. The Israelites killed everyone in that
city just as they had done to Libnah. 33During this
same time Horam king of Gezer came to help
Lachish, but Joshua also defeated him and his
army; no one was left alive.
34Then Joshua and all the Israelites went from
Lachish to Eglon. They surrounded Eglon,
attacked it, and 35captured it the same day. They
killed all its people and completely destroyed
everything in it as an offering to the LORD, just as
they had done to Lachish.
36Then Joshua and the Israelites went from
Eglon to Hebron and attacked it, 37capturing it
and all the little towns near it. The Israelites killed
everyone in Hebron; no one was left alive there.
Just as they had done to Eglon, they completely
destroyed the city and all its people as an offering to
the LORD.
38Then Joshua and the Israelites went back to
Debir and attacked it. 39They captured that city, its
king, and all the little towns near it, completely
destroying everyone in Debir as an offering to the
LORD; no one was left alive there. Israel did to
Debir and its king just as they had done to Libnah
and its king, just as they had done to Hebron.
40So Joshua defeated all the kings of the cities of
these areas: the mountains, southern Canaan, the
western hills, and the slopes. The LORD, the God
of Israel, had told Joshua to completely destroy all
the people as an offering to the LORD, so he left no
one alive in those places. 41Joshua captured all
the cities from Kadesh Barnea to Gaza, and from
Goshen to Gibeon. 42He captured all these cities
and their kings on one trip, because the LORD, the
God of Israel, was fighting for Israel.
43Then Joshua and all the Israelites returned to
their camp at Gilgal.

Defeating Northern Kings

11 When Jabin king of Hazor heard about all
that had happened, he sent messages to
Jobab king of Madon, to the king of Shimron, and to
the king of Acshaph. 2He sent messages to the kings
in the northern mountains and also to the kings in
the Jordan Valley south of Lake Galilee and in the
western hills. He sent a message to the king of
Naphoth Dor in the west 3and to the kings of the
Canaanites in the east and in the west. He sent
messages to the Amorites, Hittites, Perizzites, and
Jebusites in the mountains. Jabin also sent one to
the Hivites, who lived below Mount Hermon in
the area of Mizpah. 4So the armies of all these
kings came together with their horses and chariots.

10:24 *put their feet on their necks.* We know from ancient Near Eastern art and literature that this is a symbolic gesture of defeat.

There were as many soldiers as grains of sand on the seashore.

[5]All of these kings met together at the waters of Merom, joined their armies together into one camp, and made plans to fight against the Israelites.

[6]Then the LORD said to Joshua, "Don't be afraid of them, because at this time tomorrow I will give them to you. You will cripple their horses and burn all their chariots."

[7]So Joshua and his whole army surprised the enemy by attacking them at the waters of Merom. [8]The LORD handed them over to Israel. They chased them to Greater Sidon, Misrephoth Maim, and the Valley of Mizpah in the east. Israel fought until none of the enemy was left alive. [9]Joshua did what the LORD said to do; he crippled their horses and burned their chariots.

[10]Then Joshua went back and captured the city of Hazor and killed its king. (Hazor had been the leader of all the kingdoms that fought against Israel.) [11]Israel killed everyone in Hazor, completely destroying them; no one was left alive. Then they burned Hazor itself.

[12]Joshua captured all of these cities, killed all of their kings, and completely destroyed everything in these cities. He did this just as Moses, the servant of the LORD, had commanded. [13]But the Israelites did not burn any cities that were built on their mounds, except Hazor; only that city was burned by Joshua. [14]The people of Israel kept for themselves everything they found in the cities, including all the animals. But they killed all the people there; they left no one alive. [15]Long ago the LORD had commanded his servant Moses to do this, and then Moses had commanded Joshua to do it. Joshua did everything the LORD had commanded Moses.

[16]So Joshua defeated all the people in the land. He had control of the mountains and the area of southern Canaan, all the areas of Goshen, the western hills, and the Jordan Valley. He controlled the mountains of Israel and all the hills near them. [17]Joshua controlled all the land from Mount Halak near Edom to Baal Gad in the Valley of Lebanon, below Mount Hermon. Joshua also captured all the kings in the land and killed them. [18]He fought against them for many years. [19]The people of only one city in all the land had made a peace agreement with Israel—the Hivites living in Gibeon. All the other cities were defeated in war. [20]The LORD made those people stubborn so they would fight against Israel and he could completely destroy them without mercy. This is what the LORD had commanded Moses to do.⚭

[21]Now Joshua fought the Anakites who lived in the mountains of Hebron, Debir, Anab, Judah, and Israel, and he completely destroyed them and their towns. [22]There were no Anakites left living in the land of the Israelites and only a few were left in Gaza, Gath, and Ashdod. [23]Joshua took control of all the land of Israel as the LORD had told Moses to do long ago. He gave the land to Israel, because he had promised it to them. Then Joshua divided the land among the tribes of Israel, and there was peace in the land.

Kings Defeated by Israel

12 The Israelites took control of the land east of the Jordan River from the Arnon Ravine to Mount Hermon and all the land along the eastern side of the Jordan Valley. These lands belonged to the kings whom the Israelites defeated.

[2]Sihon king of the Amorites lived in the city of Heshbon and ruled the land from Aroer at the Arnon Ravine to the Jabbok River. His land started in the middle of the ravine, which was their border with the Ammonites. Sihon ruled over half the land of Gilead [3]and over the eastern side of the Jordan Valley from Lake Galilee to the Dead Sea. And he ruled from Beth Jeshimoth south to the slopes of Pisgah.

[4]Og king of Bashan was one of the last of the Rephaites. He ruled the land in Ashtaroth and Edrei. [5]He ruled over Mount Hermon, Salecah, and all the area of Bashan up to where the people of Geshur and Maacah lived. Og also ruled half the land of Gilead up to the border of Sihon king of Heshbon.

[6]The LORD's servant Moses and the Israelites defeated all these kings, and Moses gave that land to the tribes of Reuben and Gad and to East Manasseh as their own.

[7]Joshua and the Israelites also defeated kings in the land west of the Jordan River. He gave the people the land and divided it among the twelve tribes to be their own. It was between Baal Gad in the Valley of Lebanon and Mount Halak near Edom. [8]This included the mountains, the western hills, the Jordan Valley, the slopes, the desert, and southern Canaan. This was the land where the Hittites, Amorites, Canaanites, Perizzites, Hivites, and Jebusites had lived. The Israelites defeated the king of each of the following cities: [9]Jericho, Ai (near Bethel), [10]Jerusalem, Hebron, [11]Jarmuth, Lachish, [12]Eglon, Gezer, [13]Debir, Geder, [14]Hormah, Arad, [15]Libnah, Adullam, [16]Makkedah, Bethel, [17]Tappuah, Hepher, [18]Aphek, Lasharon, [19]Madon, Hazor,

---

⚭**11:20 Stubbornness:** Judges 2:19

11:21 *Anakites.* See Numbers 13:28.

20 Shimron Meron, Acshaph, 21 Taanach, Megiddo, 22 Kedesh, Jokneam in Carmel, 23 Dor (in Naphoth Dor), Goyim in Gilgal, and 24 Tirzah.

The total number of kings was thirty-one.

Land Still to Be Taken

13 When Joshua was very old, the LORD said to him, "Joshua, you have grown old, but there is still much land for you to take. 2 This is what is left: the regions of Geshur and of the Philistines; 3 the area from the Shihor River at the border of Egypt to Ekron in the north, which belongs to the Canaanites; the five Philistine leaders at Gaza, Ashdod, Ashkelon, Gath, and Ekron; the Avvites, 4 who live south of the Canaanite land; 5 the Gebalites, and the area of Lebanon east of Baal Gad below Mount Hermon to Lebo Hamath.

6 "The Sidonians are living in the hill country from Lebanon to Misrephoth Maim, but I will force all of them out ahead of the Israelites. Be sure to remember this land when you divide the land among the Israelites, as I told you.

7 "Now divide the land among the nine tribes and West Manasseh."

Dividing the Land

8 East Manasseh and the tribes of Reuben and Gad had received their land. The LORD's servant Moses had given them the land east of the Jordan River. 9 Their land started at Aroer at the Arnon Ravine and continued to the town in the middle of the ravine, and it included the whole plain from Medeba to Dibon. 10 All the towns ruled by Sihon king of the Amorites, who ruled in the city of Heshbon, were in that land. The land continued to the area where the Ammonites lived. 11 Gilead was also there, as well as the area where the people of Geshur and Maacah lived, and all of Mount Hermon and Bashan as far as Salecah. 12 All the kingdom of Og king of Bashan was in the land. Og was one of the last of the Rephaites, and in the past he ruled in Ashtaroth and Edrei. Moses had defeated them and had taken their land. 13 Because the Israelites did not force out the people of Geshur and Maacah, they still live among the Israelites today.

14 The tribe of Levi was the only one that did not get any land. Instead, they were given all the burned sacrifices made to the LORD, the God of Israel, as he had promised them.

15 Moses had given each family group from the tribe of Reuben some land: 16 Theirs was the land from Aroer near the Arnon Ravine to the town of Medeba, including the whole plain and the town in the middle of the ravine; 17 Heshbon and all the towns on the plain: Dibon, Bamoth Baal, and Beth Baal Meon, 18 Jahaz, Kedemoth, Mephaath, 19 Kiriathaim, Sibmah, Zereth Shahar on the hill in the valley, 20 Beth Peor, the hills of Pisgah, and Beth Jeshimoth. 21 So that land included all the towns on the plain and all the area that Sihon king of the Amorites had ruled from the town of Heshbon. Moses had defeated him along with the leaders of the Midianites, including Evi, Rekem, Zur, Hur, and Reba. All these leaders fought together with Sihon and lived in that country. 22 The Israelites killed many people during the fighting, including Balaam of Beor, who tried to use magic to tell the future. 23 The land given to Reuben stopped at the shore of the Jordan River. So the land given to the family groups of Reuben included all these towns and their villages that were listed.

24 This is the land Moses gave to the tribe of Gad, to all its family groups: 25 the land of Jazer and all the towns of Gilead; half the land of the Ammonites that went as far as Aroer near Rabbah; 26 the area from Heshbon to Ramath Mizpah and Betonim; the area from Mahanaim to the land of Debir; 27 in the valley, Beth Haram, Beth Nimrah, Succoth, and Zaphon, the other land Sihon king of Heshbon had ruled east of the Jordan River and continuing to the end of Lake Galilee. 28 All this land went to the family groups of Gad, including all these towns and their villages.

29 This is the land Moses had given to East Manasseh. Half of all the family groups in the tribe of Manasseh were given this land: 30 The land started at Mahanaim and included all of Bashan and the land ruled by Og king of Bashan; all the towns of Jair in Bashan, sixty cities in all; 31 half of Gilead, Ashtaroth, and Edrei, the cities where Og king of Bashan had ruled. All this went to the family of Makir son of Manasseh, and half of all his sons were given this land.

32 Moses had given this land to these tribes on the plains of Moab across the Jordan River east of Jericho. 33 But Moses had given no land to the tribe of Levi because the LORD, the God of Israel, promised that he himself would be the gift for the Levites.

14 Eleazar the priest, Joshua son of Nun, and the leaders of all the tribes of Israel decided what land to give to the people in the land of Canaan. 2 The LORD had commanded Moses long

13:8 Land/Inheritance: Nehemiah 9:36–37

13:14 *Levi . . . did not get any land.* See Genesis 34 and 49:5–7.

ago how he wanted the people to choose their land. The people of the nine-and-a-half tribes threw lots to decide which land they would receive. [3]Moses had already given the two-and-a-half tribes their land east of the Jordan River. But the tribe of Levi was not given any land like the others. [4]The sons of Joseph had divided into two tribes—Manasseh and Ephraim. The tribe of Levi was not given any land. It was given only some towns in which to live and pastures for its animals. [5]The LORD had told Moses how to give the land to the tribes of Israel, and the Israelites divided the land.

Caleb's Land

[6]One day some men from the tribe of Judah went to Joshua at Gilgal. Among them was Caleb son of Jephunneh the Kenizzite. He said to Joshua, "You remember what the LORD said at Kadesh Barnea when he was speaking to the prophet Moses about you and me. [7]Moses, the LORD's servant, sent me to look at the land where we were going. I was forty years old then. When I came back, I told Moses what I thought about the land. [8]The other men who went with me frightened the people, but I fully believed the LORD would allow us to take the land. [9]So that day Moses promised me, 'The land where you went will become your land, and your children will own it forever. I will give you that land because you fully believed in the LORD, my God.'

[10]"Now then, the LORD has kept his promise. He has kept me alive for forty-five years from the time he said this to Moses during the time we all wandered in the desert. Now here I am, eighty-five years old. [11]I am still as strong today as I was the day Moses sent me out, and I am just as ready to fight now as I was then. [12]So give me the mountain country the LORD promised me that day long ago. Back then you heard that the Anakite people lived there and the cities were large and well protected. But now with the LORD helping me, I will force them out, just as the LORD said."

[13]Joshua blessed Caleb son of Jephunneh and gave him the city of Hebron as his own. [14]Hebron still belongs to the family of Caleb son of Jephunneh the Kenizzite because he had faith and obeyed the LORD, the God of Israel.∞ [15](In the past it was called Kiriath Arba, named for Arba, the greatest man among the Anakites.)

After this there was peace in the land.

Land for Judah

15 The land that was given to the tribe of Judah was divided among all the family groups. It went all the way to the Desert of Zin in the far south, at the border of Edom.

[2]The southern border of Judah's land started at the south end of the Dead Sea [3]and went south of Scorpion Pass to Zin. From there it passed to the south of Kadesh Barnea and continued past Hezron to Addar. From Addar it turned and went to Karka. [4]It continued to Azmon, the brook of Egypt, and then to the Mediterranean Sea. This was the southern border.

[5]The eastern border was the shore of the Dead Sea, as far as the mouth of the Jordan River.

The northern border started at the bay of the sea at the mouth of the Jordan River. [6]Then it went to Beth Hoglah and continued north of Beth Arabah to the stone of Bohan son of Reuben. [7]Then the northern border went through the Valley of Achor to Debir where it turned toward the north and went to Gilgal. Gilgal is across from the road that goes through Adummim Pass, on the south side of the ravine. The border continued to the waters of En Shemesh and stopped at En Rogel. [8]Then it went through the Valley of Ben Hinnom, next to the southern side of the Jebusite city (which is called Jerusalem). There the border went to the top of the hill on the west side of Hinnom Valley, at the northern end of the Valley of Giants. [9]From there it went to the spring of the waters of Nephtoah and then it went to the cities near Mount Ephron. There it turned and went toward Baalah, which is called Kiriath Jearim. [10]At Baalah the border turned west and went toward Mount Seir. It continued along the north side of Mount Jearim (also called Kesalon) and came to Beth Shemesh. From there it went past Timnah [11]to the hill north of Ekron. Then it turned toward Shikkeron and went past Mount Baalah and continued on to Jabneel, ending at the sea.

[12]The Mediterranean Sea was the western border. Inside these borders lived the family groups of Judah.

[13]The LORD had commanded Joshua to give Caleb son of Jephunneh part of the land in Judah, so he gave Caleb the town of Kiriath Arba, also called Hebron. (Arba was the father of Anak.) [14]Caleb forced out the three Anakite families living in Hebron: Sheshai, Ahiman, and Talmai, the descendants of Anak. [15]Then he left there and went to fight against the people living in Debir. (In the past Debir had been called Kiriath Sepher.) [16]Caleb said, "I will give Acsah, my daughter, as a wife to the man who attacks and

∞**14:14 Blessing:** 2 Kings 2:9

15:14 *Anakite.* See Numbers 13:28.

captures the city of Kiriath Sepher." [17]Othniel son of Kenaz, Caleb's brother, captured the city, so Caleb gave his daughter Acsah to Othniel to be his wife. [18]When Acsah came to Othniel, she told him to ask her father for a field.

So Acsah went to her father. When she got down from her donkey, Caleb asked her, "What do you want?"

[19]Acsah answered, "Do me a special favor. Since you have given me land in southern Canaan, also give me springs of water." So Caleb gave her the upper and lower springs.

[20]The tribe of Judah got the land God had promised them. Each family group got part of the land.

[21]The tribe of Judah got all these towns in the southern part of Canaan near the border of Edom: Kabzeel, Eder, Jagur, [22]Kinah, Dimonah, Adadah, [23]Kedesh, Hazor, Ithnan, [24]Ziph, Telem, Bealoth, [25]Hazor Hadattah, Kerioth Hezron (also called Hazor), [26]Amam, Shema, Moladah, [27]Hazar Gaddah, Heshmon, Beth Pelet, [28]Hazar Shual, Beersheba, Biziothiah, [29]Baalah, Iim, Ezem, [30]Eltolad, Kesil, Hormah, [31]Ziklag, Madmannah, Sansannah, [32]Lebaoth, Shilhim, Ain, and Rimmon. There were twenty-nine towns and their villages.

[33]The tribe of Judah got these towns in the western hills: Eshtaol, Zorah, Ashnah, [34]Zanoah, En Gannim, Tappuah, Enam, [35]Jarmuth, Adullam, Socoh, Azekah, [36]Shaaraim, Adithaim, and Gederah (also called Gederothaim). There were fourteen towns and their villages.

[37]Judah was also given these towns in the western hills: Zenan, Hadashah, Migdal Gad, [38]Dilean, Mizpah, Joktheel, [39]Lachish, Bozkath, Eglon, [40]Cabbon, Lahmas, Kitlish, [41]Gederoth, Beth Dagon, Naamah, and Makkedah. There were sixteen towns and their villages.

[42]Judah was also given these towns in the western hills: Libnah, Ether, Ashan, [43]Iphtah, Ashnah, Nezib, [44]Keilah, Aczib, and Mareshah. There were nine towns and their villages.

[45]The tribe of Judah was also given these towns: Ekron and all the small towns and villages near it; [46]the area west of Ekron and all the villages and small towns near Ashdod; [47]Ashdod and the small towns and villages around it; the villages and small towns around Gaza as far as the brook of Egypt and along the coast of the Mediterranean Sea.

[48]The tribe of Judah was also given these towns in the mountains: Shamir, Jattir, Socoh, [49]Dannah, Kiriath Sannah (also called Debir), [50]Anab, Eshtemoh, Anim, [51]Goshen, Holon, and Giloh. There were eleven towns and their villages.

[52]They were also given these towns in the mountains: Arab, Dumah, Eshan, [53]Janim, Beth Tappuah, Aphekah, [54]Humtah, Kiriath Arba (also called Hebron), and Zior. There were nine towns and their villages.

[55]Judah was also given these towns in the mountains: Maon, Carmel, Ziph, Juttah, [56]Jezreel, Jokdeam, Zanoah, [57]Kain, Gibeah, and Timnah. There were ten towns and their villages.

[58]They were also given these towns in the mountains: Halhul, Beth Zur, Gedor, [59]Maarath, Beth Anoth, and Eltekon. There were six towns and their villages.

[60]The people of Judah were also given the two towns of Rabbah and Kiriath Baal (also called Kiriath Jearim) and their villages.

[61]Judah was given these towns in the desert: Beth Arabah, Middin, Secacah, [62]Nibshan, the City of Salt, and En Gedi. There were six towns and all their villages.

[63]The army of Judah was not able to force out the Jebusites living in Jerusalem, so the Jebusites still live among the people of Judah to this day.⚭

Land for Ephraim and Manasseh

16 This is the land the tribe of Joseph received. It started at the Jordan River near Jericho and continued to the waters of Jericho, just east of the city. The border went up from Jericho to the mountains of Bethel. [2]Then it continued from Bethel (also called Luz) to the Arkite border at Ataroth. [3]From there it went west to the border of the Japhletites and continued to the area of the Lower Beth Horon. Then it went to Gezer and ended at the sea.

[4]So Manasseh and Ephraim, sons of Joseph, received their land.

[5]This is the land that was given to the family groups of Ephraim: Their border started at Ataroth Addar in the east, went to Upper Beth Horon, [6]and then to the sea. From Micmethath it turned eastward toward Taanath Shiloh and continued eastward to Janoah. [7]Then it went down from Janoah to Ataroth and to Naarah. It continued until it touched Jericho and stopped at the Jordan River. [8]The border went from Tappuah west to Kanah Ravine and ended at the sea. This is all the land that was given to each family group in the tribe of the Ephraimites. [9]Many of the towns were actually within Manasseh's borders, but the people of Ephraim got those towns and their villages. [10]The Ephraimites could not force the Canaanites to leave Gezer, so the Canaanites

⚭**15:63 Jerusalem:** 1 Samuel 24

still live among the Ephraimites today, but they became slaves of the Ephraimites.

17 Then land was given to the tribe of Manasseh, Joseph's first son. Manasseh's first son was Makir, the father of Gilead. Makir was a great soldier, so the lands of Gilead and Bashan were given to his family. 2Land was also given to the other family groups of Manasseh—Abiezer, Helek, Asriel, Shechem, Hepher, and Shemida. These were all the other sons of Manasseh son of Joseph.

3Zelophehad was the son of Hepher, who was the son of Gilead, who was the son of Makir, who was the son of Manasseh. Zelophehad had no sons, but he had five daughters, named Mahlah, Noah, Hoglah, Milcah, and Tirzah. 4They went to Eleazar the priest and to Joshua son of Nun and all the leaders. They said, "The LORD told Moses to give us land like the men received." So Eleazar obeyed the LORD and gave the daughters some land, just like the brothers of their father. 5So the tribe of Manasseh had ten sections of land west of the Jordan River and two more sections, Gilead and Bashan, on the east side of the Jordan River. 6The daughters of Manasseh received land just as the sons did. Gilead was given to the rest of the families of Manasseh.

7The lands of Manasseh were in the area between Asher and Micmethath, near Shechem. The border went south to the En Tappuah area, 8which belonged to Manasseh, except for the town of Tappuah. It was along the border of Manasseh's land and belonged to the sons of Ephraim. 9The border of Manasseh continued south to Kanah Ravine. The cities in this area of Manasseh belonged to Ephraim. Manasseh's border was on the north side of the ravine and went to the sea. 10The land to the south belonged to Ephraim, and the land to the north belonged to Manasseh. The Mediterranean Sea was the western border. The border touched Asher's land on the north and Issachar's land on the east.

11In the areas of Issachar and Asher, the people of Manasseh owned these towns: Beth Shan and its small towns; Ibleam and its small towns; the people who lived in Dor and its small towns; the people in Naphoth Dor and its small towns; the people who lived in Taanach and its small towns; the people in Megiddo and its small towns. 12Manasseh was not able to defeat those cities, so the Canaanites continued to live there. 13When the Israelites grew strong, they forced the Canaanites to work for them, although they did not force them to leave the land.

14The people from the tribes of Joseph said to Joshua, "You gave us only one area of land, but we are many people. Why did you give us only one part of all the land the LORD gave his people?"

15And Joshua answered them, "If you have too many people, go up to the forest and make a place for yourselves to live there in the land of the Perizzites and the Rephaites. The mountain country of Ephraim is too small for you."

16The people of Joseph said, "It is true. The mountain country of Ephraim is not enough for us, but the land where the Canaanites live is dangerous. They are skilled fighters. They have powerful weapons in Beth Shan and all the small towns in that area, and they are also in the Valley of Jezreel."

17Then Joshua said to the people of Joseph—to Ephraim and Manasseh, "There are many of you, and you have great power. You should be given more than one share of land. 18You also will have the mountain country. It is a forest, but you can cut down the trees and make it a good place to live. You will own all of it because you will force the Canaanites to leave the land even though they have powerful weapons and are strong."

The Rest of the Land Divided

18 All of the Israelites gathered together at Shiloh where they set up the Meeting Tent. The land was now under their control. 2But there were still seven tribes of Israel that had not yet received their land.

3So Joshua said to the Israelites: "Why do you wait so long to take your land? The LORD, the God of your ancestors, has given this land to you. 4Choose three men from each tribe, and I will send them out to study the land. They will describe in writing the land their tribe wants as its share, and then they will come back to me. 5They will divide the land into seven parts. The people of Judah will keep their land in the south, and the people of Joseph will keep their land in the north. 6You should describe the seven parts of land in writing and bring what you have written to me. Then I will throw lots in the presence of the LORD our God. 7But the Levites do not get any part of these lands, because they are priests, and their work is to serve the LORD. Gad, Reuben, and East Manasseh have received the land promised to them, which is east of the Jordan River. Moses, the servant of the LORD, gave it to them."

8So the men who were chosen to map the land started out. Joshua told them, "Go and study the land and describe it in writing. Then come back to me, and I will throw lots in the presence of the LORD here in Shiloh." 9So the men left and went into the land. They described in a scroll each

Ark of the Agreement

Exodus 25:10

What was the Ark of the Agreement? How was the Ark used? What did it represent?

The Ark of the Agreement was the most important furnishing of the Holy Tent (the Tabernacle). It was Israel's movable sanctuary in the wilderness, and had a long history in the growth of the nation.

The Ark of the Agreement was a portable wooden chest specially made to be a sacred and central piece of furniture among the other furnishings in the Holy Tent. It consisted also of a special cover or lid called the "mercy seat" (Exodus 25:17–22) made of gold with two winged creatures (angels/cherubim) on both ends facing each other with their wings arching over the center of the cover. Moses was commanded to place in the Ark the two stone tablets upon which were written the Ten Commandments (Deuteronomy 10:1–5). In Exodus 25:21, the stone tablets are referred to as the "Agreement which I will make with you." Later on, a pot of manna and Aaron's walking stick were also included (see Exodus 16:33–34; Numbers 17:10; Hebrews 9:4–5).

The Ark is referred to in the Bible in many different ways. There are over twenty different designations. It is called the Ark of the Agreement, Ark of the testimony, the Ark of the Agreement of the Lord, and sometimes simply the Ark. It must not be confused with Noah's Ark, however. It is called the Ark of the Agreement because of its primary contents, the Ten Commandments, which in summary form represent the agreement between God and his people (see Exodus 24).

During Moses' time, God met with and instructed him before the Ark (Exodus 25:22). During the wilderness journey, the Ark guided the Israelites from place to place (Numbers 10:33–36; 14:44). In Joshua's day, the Ark was an important sign of God's power as it was used in the miraculous crossing of the Jordan River and the fall of the city of Jericho (Joshua 3–7). In Samuel's time, the Ark had a precarious existence, first residing in Shiloh from where it was taken into battle by the Israelites against the Philistines (1 Samuel 4). Israel was defeated, the Ark captured and taken into Philistine territory where it was moved from one town to another because of its ill effects on the local people (1 Samuel 5). Finally, the Philistines returned the Ark to Israel where it ended up in the house of Abinadab (1 Samuel 6). In 2 Samuel 6, David brought the Ark from Abinadab's house to a tent in Jerusalem, and in 1 Kings 8 we learn that Solomon installed the Ark in the permanent sanctuary of the Temple. Very little is known of what happened to the Ark after that. It was probably destroyed or stolen during the invasion of Nebuchadnezzar in 586 B.C. (2 Kings 25:8–21), but its disappearance remains a mystery.

Throughout the Old Testament, the Ark represented many things. It was a channel of revelation as God spoke with Moses before the Ark and as young Samuel heard the voice of the Lord (1 Samuel 3). It guided the people of Israel in the wilderness. The Ark was often seen as an instrument of God's protection and guarantor of success in military battle (Numbers 10:35–36; Joshua 6; 1 Samuel 4:3). It is sometimes referred to as if to emphasize the Lord's might and strength. It is called "the Ark of the Agreement with the LORD All-Powerful" (1 Samuel 4:4) and the "Ark that shows your strength" (Psalm 132:8). Something of its otherworldly power and sacredness is seen when seventy men of Beth Shemesh were struck down for looking into it (1 Samuel 6:19) and when Uzzah died for touching it (2 Samuel 6:6–7).

In spite of the many representations of the significance of the Ark, they may all be combined under the one idea of God's presence. The Ark represents God's special presence in the midst of his people. Because God is present in the Ark, the Ark has power to reveal, to guide, to give victory in battle. It cannot be manipulated, however, as the people of Israel discovered in 1 Samuel 4, and it can afflict the enemy terribly (1 Samuel 5). To speak of God's glory and strength is another way of referring to God's presence. In the Psalms, God's presence and the Ark are intimately associated in the context of a gathered worshipping community (Psalm 78:60–61; 132:8).

In the New Testament, the ultimate expression of God's Presence is none other than Jesus Christ, the one who "lived among us" and of whom John says, "we saw his glory—the glory that belongs to the only Son of the Father" (John 1:14). Indeed, Jeremiah 3:16 speaks of the day when the Ark would no longer be important but that Jerusalem would be the "Throne of the Lord." Hebrews 9–10 speaks of the Ark and Holy Tent furnishings as merely shadows of the reality which would come, namely Christ.

Ark of the Agreement: For additional scriptures on this topic go to Exodus 37:1–9.

IMAGES OF GOD

EXODUS 33:18–23

Can human beings understand or relate to a God who is far, far above them? How do the images of God used in Scripture help bridge the chasm between people and God Almighty?

We humans are earth-bound, flesh-and-blood, flawed creatures, while God is a spirit, perfect, unlimited by space or time. In 1 Timothy 6:15–16, Paul reminds us that there is no way our minds can grasp this divine being. God "is the blessed and only Ruler, the King of all kings and the Lord of all lords. He is the only one who never dies. He lives in light so bright no one can go near it. No one has ever seen God, or can see him."

Yet in spite of the chasm that separates God and people, the good news of the Bible is that God wants to give himself to us. This apparent paradox—that God is beyond our knowing, yet makes himself known—is captured in the strange account in Exodus 33:18–23 when Moses begs God, "Please show me your glory." God allows Moses to glimpse his goodness from the back, but he shields Moses from seeing his full glory because "no one can see me and live." In this story God clearly wants to fulfill Moses' desire to see him, but he must make a way for Moses to view him indirectly; an indirect view is all Moses is capable of taking in.

What was true for Moses is true for all humans—we cannot literally see God or comprehend his full, glorious perfection. But God has made a way for us to see him indirectly; he has inspired the Bible's writers to present God in concrete, down-to-earth word pictures.

Most often the images for God in Scripture are human images. Not only is God portrayed with a human body (eyes, ears, nostrils, mouth, arms, hands, feet), but also with human emotions (love, delight, patience, anger, jealousy, disappointment). Furthermore, God is frequently portrayed in human roles—husband, parent, king, warrior, judge, doctor, teacher, shepherd, farmer, potter, party host, to name a few.

God is also pictured frequently in non-human images. Sometimes he is pictured in terms of man-made implements or structures—he is like a cup, a shield, a dwelling, a walled city. But more often the Bible uses images for God drawn from the world of nature. God is embodied in earthquake, storm, and fire. He is pictured as the sun, as a wild animal or bird, as a rock.

Sometimes a passage will present God in terms of a single image—he is a shepherd in Psalm 23, a father in the parable of the prodigal son in Luke 15:11–32. But quite often several images, perhaps wildly different images, are used for God in a single passage. Why do we find such a variety of images for God in Scripture? In part because no one image could do him justice. Each image by itself suggests certain truths about God, but also misrepresents him. The image of a shepherd embodies God's tender care, but not his exalted status. The image of a lion suggests God's majesty and might, but carries no hint of his compassion, creativity, or power to communicate with us. The image of a rock shows God's strength and dependability, but in no way suggests his active involvement in human affairs. Thus we can assume that God inspired the Bible's writers to use many different images in order to give us a fuller, truer picture of himself while preventing us from adopting the false ideas that single images might suggest.

Perhaps God had a further reason for using such a variety of images for himself. Readers come to the Bible with different personalities and backgrounds, different needs and desires. Particular images may move certain people yet leave others untouched. In Hosea 5:11–6:3, the prophet warned idol worshippers that God would come to punish them like a moth, like rot, and like a ferocious lion. Then he promised the people that if they returned to God, he would be to them like a healing physician, like dawn breaking, and like spring rain that waters the ground. Surely God intended this variety of images to touch all kinds of people—housewives and soldiers and farmers, vain people and fearful people and hurt people—and cause them to repent.

As we read the various images for God in Scripture, there may be some value in reminding ourselves that we, like Moses, are only seeing God in part, not in his full glory. But that should not prevent us from taking biblical pictures for God very seriously and meditating on them with great care. When God is described as a shepherd in Isaiah 40:11, we should feel the comfort of his arms tight around us and rest gratefully in the fact that he keeps us safe. When God is described as a righteous judge in Romans 2:2–8, we should hear the wrath in his voice and visualize his disappointment, and then tremble to realize how much he is hurt by our rebelliousness. Only as we enter imaginatively into the full power of the images will they touch us as God intends they should, allowing him to become more real to us, allowing us to draw closer to him.

Images of God: For additional scriptures on this topic go to Exodus 15:3–8.

town in the seven parts of the land. Then they came back to Joshua, who was still at the camp at Shiloh. [10]There Joshua threw lots in the presence of the LORD to choose the lands that should be given to each tribe.

Land for Benjamin

[11]The first part of the land was given to the tribe of Benjamin. Each family group received some land between the land of Judah and the land of Joseph. This is the land chosen for Benjamin: [12]The northern border started at the Jordan River and went along the northern edge of Jericho, and then it went west into the mountains. That boundary continued until it was just east of Beth Aven. [13]From there it went south to Luz (also called Bethel) and then down to Ataroth Addar, which is on the hill south of Lower Beth Horon.

[14]At the hill to the south of Beth Horon, the border turned and went south near the western side of the hill. It went to Kiriath Baal (also called Kiriath Jearim), a town where people of Judah lived. This was the western border.

[15]The southern border started near Kiriath Jearim and went west to the waters of Nephtoah. [16]Then it went down to the bottom of the hill, which was near the Valley of Ben Hinnom, on the north side of the Valley of Rephaim. The border continued down the Hinnom Valley just south of the Jebusite city to En Rogel. [17]There it turned north and went to En Shemesh. It continued to Geliloth near the Adummim Pass. Then it went down to the great Stone of Bohan son of Reuben. [18]The border continued to the northern part of Beth Arabah and went down into the Jordan Valley. [19]From there it went to the northern part of Beth Hoglah and ended at the north shore of the Dead Sea, where the Jordan River flows into the sea. This was the southern border.

[20]The Jordan River was the border on the eastern side. So this was the land given to the family groups of Benjamin with the borders on all sides.

[21]The family groups of Benjamin received these cities: Jericho, Beth Hoglah, Emek Keziz, [22]Beth Arabah, Zemaraim, Bethel, [23]Avvim, Parah, Ophrah, [24]Kephar Ammoni, Ophni, and Geba. There were twelve towns and all their villages.

[25]The tribe of Benjamin also received Gibeon, Ramah, Beeroth, [26]Mizpah, Kephirah, Mozah, [27]Rekem, Irpeel, Taralah, [28]Zelah, Haeleph, the Jebusite city (Jerusalem), Gibeah, and Kiriath. There were fourteen towns and their villages. All these areas are the lands the family groups of Benjamin were given.

Land for Simeon

19 The second part of the land was given to the tribe of Simeon. Each family group received some of the land inside the area of Judah. [2]They received Beersheba (also called Sheba), Moladah, [3]Hazar Shual, Balah, Ezem, [4]Eltolad, Bethul, Hormah, [5]Ziklag, Beth Marcaboth, Hazar Susah, [6]Beth Lebaoth, and Sharuhen. There were thirteen towns and their villages.

[7]They received the towns of Ain, Rimmon, Ether, and Ashan, four towns and their villages. [8]They also received all the very small areas with people living in them as far as Baalath Beer (this is the same as Ramah in southern Canaan). So these were the lands given to the family groups in the tribe of Simeon. [9]The land of the Simeonites was taken from part of the land of Judah. Since Judah had much more land than they needed, the Simeonites received part of their land.

Land for Zebulun

[10]The third part of the land was given to the tribe of Zebulun. Each family group of Zebulun received some of the land. The border of Zebulun went as far as Sarid. [11]Then it went west to Maralah and came near Dabbesheth and then near Jokneam. [12]Then it turned to the east. It went from Sarid to the area of Kisloth Tabor and on to Daberath and to Japhia. [13]It continued eastward to Gath Hepher and Eth Kazin, ending at Rimmon. There the border turned and went toward Neah. [14]At Neah it turned again and went to the north to Hannathon and continued to the Valley of Iphtah El. [15]Inside this border were the cities of Kattath, Nahalal, Shimron, Idalah, and Bethlehem. There were twelve towns and their villages.

[16]So these are the towns and the villages that were given to the family groups of Zebulun.

Land for Issachar

[17]The fourth part of the land was given to the tribe of Issachar. Each family group of Issachar received some of the land. [18]Their land included Jezreel, Kesulloth, Shunem, [19]Hapharaim, Shion, Anaharath, [20]Rabbith, Kishion, Ebez, [21]Remeth, En Gannim, En Haddah, and Beth Pazzez.

18:28 Benjamin inherited the city of Jerusalem (Judges 1:21). This might be surprising to some readers who have usually associated the tribe of Judah with Jerusalem. Saul, a Benjaminite, never conquered the Jebusites or their city Jerusalem. When David, of the tribe of Judah, conquered Jerusalem, the city began to be associated with Judah (2 Samuel 5). Earlier the tribe of Judah had fought Jerusalem and burned it, but they did not destroy the inhabitants (Judges 1:8).

[22]The border of their land touched the area called Tabor, Shahazumah, and Beth Shemesh and stopped at the Jordan River. There were sixteen towns and their villages.

[23]These cities and towns were part of the land that was given to the family groups of Issachar.

Land for Asher

[24]The fifth part of the land was given to the tribe of Asher. Each family group of Asher received some of the land. [25]Their land included Helkath, Hali, Beten, Acshaph, [26]Allammelech, Amad, and Mishal.

The western border touched Mount Carmel and Shihor Libnath. [27]Then it turned east and went to Beth Dagon, touching Zebulun and the Valley of Iphtah El. Then it went north of Beth Emek and Neiel and passed north to Cabul. [28]From there it went to Abdon, Rehob, Hammon, and Kanah and continued to Greater Sidon. [29]Then the border went back south toward Ramah and continued to the strong, walled city of Tyre. There it turned and went toward Hosah, ending at the sea. This was in the area of Aczib, [30]Ummah, Aphek, and Rehob. There were twenty-two towns and their villages.

[31]These cities and their villages were part of the land that was given to the family groups of Asher.

Land for Naphtali

[32]The sixth part of the land was given to the tribe of Naphtali. Each family group of Naphtali received some of the land. [33]The border of their land started at the large tree in Zaanannim, which is near Heleph. Then it went through Adami Nekeb and Jabneel, as far as Lakkum, and ended at the Jordan River. [34]Then it went to the west through Aznoth Tabor and stopped at Hukkok. It went to the area of Zebulun on the south, Asher on the west, and Judah, at the Jordan River, on the east. [35]The strong, walled cities inside these borders were called Ziddim, Zer, Hammath, Rakkath, Kinnereth, [36]Adamah, Ramah, Hazor, [37]Kedesh, Edrei, En Hazor, [38]Iron, Migdal El, Horem, Beth Anath, and Beth Shemesh. There were nineteen towns and all their villages.

[39]The towns and the villages around them were in the land that was given to the family groups of Naphtali.

Land for Dan

[40]The seventh part of the land was given to the tribe of Dan. Each family group of Dan received some of the land. [41]Their land included Zorah, Eshtaol, Ir Shemesh, [42]Shaalabbin, Aijalon, Ithlah, [43]Elon, Timnah, Ekron, [44]Eltekeh, Gibbethon, Baalath, [45]Jehud, Bene Berak, Gath Rimmon, [46]Me Jarkon, Rakkon, and the area near Joppa.

[47](But the Danites had trouble taking their land. They went and fought against Leshem, defeated it, and killed the people who lived there. So the Danites moved into the town of Leshem and changed its name to Dan, because he was the father of their tribe.) [48]All of these towns and villages were given to the family groups of Dan.

Land for Joshua

[49]After the leaders finished dividing the land and giving it to the different tribes, the Israelites gave Joshua son of Nun his land also. [50]They gave Joshua the town he asked for, Timnath Serah in the mountains of Ephraim, just as the LORD commanded. He built up the town and lived there.

[51]So these lands were given to the different tribes of Israel. Eleazar the priest, Joshua son of Nun, and the leaders of each tribe divided up the land by lots at Shiloh. They met in the presence of the LORD at the entrance to the Meeting Tent. Now they were finished dividing the land.∞

Cities of Safety

20 Then the LORD said to Joshua: [2]"Tell the Israelites to choose the special cities of safety, as I had Moses command you to do. [3]If a person kills someone accidentally and without meaning to kill him, that person may go to a city of safety to hide. There the killer will be safe from the relative who has the duty of punishing a murderer.

[4]"When the killer runs to one of those cities, he must stop at the entrance gate, stand there, and tell the leaders of the people what happened. Then that person will be allowed to enter the city and will be given a place to live among them. [5]But if the one who is chasing him follows him to that city, the leaders of the city must not hand over the killer. It was an accident. He did not hate him beforehand or kill him on purpose. [6]The killer must stay in the city until a court comes to a decision and until the high priest dies. Then he may go back home to the town from which he ran away."

[7]So the Israelites chose these cities to be cities of safety: Kedesh in Galilee in the mountains of Naphtali; Shechem in the mountains of Ephraim; Kiriath Arba (also called Hebron) in the mountains of Judah; [8]Bezer on the east side of the Jordan River near Jericho in the desert in the land of Reuben; Ramoth in Gilead in the land of Gad; and Golan in Bashan in the land of Manasseh.

∞**19:51 Births:** 2 Samuel 7:12–16

[9]Any Israelite or anyone living among them who killed someone accidentally was to be allowed to run to one of these cities of safety. There he would not be killed, before he was judged, by the relative who had the duty of punishing a murderer.

Towns for the Levites

21 The heads of the Levite families went to talk to Eleazar the priest, to Joshua son of Nun, and to the heads of the families of all the tribes of Israel. [2]At Shiloh in the land of Canaan, the heads of the Levite families said to them, "The LORD commanded Moses that you give us towns where we may live and pastures for our animals." [3]So the Israelites obeyed this command of the LORD and gave the Levite people these towns and pastures for their own land: [4]The Kohath family groups were part of the tribe of Levi. Some of the Levites in the Kohath family groups were from the family of Aaron the priest. To these Levites were given thirteen towns in the areas of Judah, Simeon, and Benjamin. [5]The other family groups of Kohath were given ten towns in the areas of Ephraim, Dan, and West Manasseh.

[6]The people from the Gershon family groups were given thirteen towns in the land of Issachar, Asher, Naphtali, and the East Manasseh in Bashan.

[7]The family groups of Merari were given twelve towns in the areas of Reuben, Gad, and Zebulun.

[8]So the Israelites gave the Levites these towns and the pastures around them, just as the LORD had commanded Moses.

[9]These are the names of the towns that came from the lands of Judah and Simeon. [10]The first choice of towns was given to the Kohath family groups of the Levites. [11]They gave them Kiriath Arba, also called Hebron, and all its pastures in the mountains of Judah. (Arba was the father of Anak.) [12]But the fields and the villages around Kiriath Arba had been given to Caleb son of Jephunneh.

[13]So they gave the city of Hebron to the descendants of Aaron (Hebron was a city of safety). They also gave them the towns of Libnah, [14]Jattir, Eshtemoa, [15]Holon, Debir, [16]Ain, Juttah, and Beth Shemesh, and all the pastures around them. Nine towns were given from these two tribes.

[17]They also gave the people of Aaron these cities that belonged to the tribe of Benjamin: Gibeon, Geba, [18]Anathoth, and Almon. They gave them these four towns and the pastures around them.

[19]So these thirteen towns with their pastures were given to the priests, who were from the family of Aaron.

[20]The other Kohathite family groups of the Levites were given these towns from the tribe of Ephraim: [21]Shechem in the mountains of Ephraim (which was a city of safety), Gezer, [22]Kibzaim, and Beth Horon. There were four towns and their pastures.

[23]The tribe of Dan gave them Eltekeh, Gibbethon, [24]Aijalon, and Gath Rimmon. There were four towns and their pastures.

[25]West Manasseh gave them Taanach and Gath Rimmon and the pastures around these two towns.

[26]So these ten towns and the pastures around them were given to the rest of the Kohathite family groups.

[27]The Gershonite family groups of the Levite tribe were given these towns: East Manasseh gave them Golan in Bashan, which was a city of safety, and Be Eshtarah, and the pastures around these two towns.

[28]The tribe of Issachar gave them Kishion, Daberath, [29]Jarmuth, and En Gannim, and the pastures around these four towns.

[30]The tribe of Asher gave them Mishal, Abdon, [31]Helkath, and Rehob, and the pastures around these four towns.

[32]The tribe of Naphtali gave them Kedesh in Galilee (a city of safety), Hammoth Dor, and Kartan, and the pastures around these three towns.

[33]So the Gershonite family groups received thirteen towns and the pastures around them.

[34]The Merarite family groups (the rest of the Levites) were given these towns: The tribe of Zebulun gave them Jokneam, Kartah, [35]Dimnah, and Nahalal, and the pastures around these four towns.

[36]The tribe of Reuben gave them Bezer, Jahaz, [37]Kedemoth, and Mephaath, along with the pastures around these four towns.

[38]The tribe of Gad gave them Ramoth in Gilead (a city of safety), Mahanaim, [39]Heshbon, and Jazer, and the pastures around these four towns.

[40]So the total number of towns given to the Merarite family groups was twelve.

[41]A total of forty-eight towns with their pastures in the land of Israel were given to the Levites. [42]Each town had pastures around it.

[43]So the LORD gave the people all the land he had promised their ancestors. The people took the land and lived there. [44]The LORD gave them peace on all sides, as he had promised their ancestors. None of their enemies defeated them; the LORD handed all their enemies over to them. [45]He kept every promise he had made to the Israelites; each one came true.⚭

⚭**21:45 Promise:** Psalm 89:30–37

Three Tribes Go Home

22 Then Joshua called a meeting of all the people from the tribes of Reuben, Gad, and East Manasseh. 2He said to them, "You have done everything Moses, the LORD's servant, told you to do. You have also obeyed all my commands. 3For a long time you have supported the other Israelites. You have been careful to obey the commands the LORD your God gave you. 4The LORD your God promised to give the Israelites peace, and he has kept his promise. Now you may go back to your homes, to the land that Moses, the LORD's servant, gave you, on the east side of the Jordan River. 5But be careful to obey the teachings and laws Moses, the LORD's servant, gave you: to love the LORD your God and obey his commands, to continue to follow him and serve him the very best you can."

6Then Joshua said good-bye to them, and they left and went away to their homes. 7Moses had given the land of Bashan to East Manasseh. Joshua gave land on the west side of the Jordan River to West Manasseh. And he sent them to their homes and he blessed them. 8He said, "Go back to your homes and your riches. You have many animals, silver, gold, bronze, and iron, and many beautiful clothes. Also, you have taken many things from your enemies that you should divide among yourselves."

9So the people from the tribes of Reuben, Gad, and East Manasseh left the other Israelites at Shiloh in Canaan and went back to Gilead. It was their own land, given to them by Moses as the LORD had commanded.

10The people of Reuben, Gad, and East Manasseh went to Geliloth, near the Jordan River in the land of Canaan. There they built a beautiful altar. 11The other Israelites still at Shiloh heard about the altar these three tribes built at the border of Canaan at Geliloth, near the Jordan River on Israel's side. 12All the Israelites became very angry at these three tribes, so they met together and decided to fight them.

13The Israelites sent Phinehas son of Eleazar the priest to Gilead to talk to the people of Reuben, Gad, and East Manasseh. 14They also sent one leader from each of the ten tribes at Shiloh. Each of them was a leader of his family group of Israelites.

15These leaders went to Gilead to talk to the people of Reuben, Gad, and East Manasseh. They said: 16"All the Israelites ask you: 'Why did you turn against the God of Israel by building an altar for yourselves? You know that this is against God's law. 17Remember what happened at Peor? We still suffer today because of that sin, for which God made many Israelites very sick. 18And now are you turning against the LORD and refusing to follow him?

"'If you don't stop what you're doing today, the LORD will be angry with everyone in Israel tomorrow. 19If your land is unclean, come over into our land where the LORD's Tent is. Share it with us. But don't turn against the LORD and us by building another altar for the LORD our God. 20Remember how Achan son of Zerah refused to obey the command about what must be completely destroyed. That one man broke God's law, but all the Israelites were punished. Achan died because of his sin, but others also died.'"

21The people from Reuben, Gad, and East Manasseh answered, 22"The LORD is God of gods! The LORD is God of gods! God knows, and we want you to know also. If we have done something wrong, you may kill us. 23If we broke God's law, we ask the LORD himself to punish us. We did not build this altar to offer burnt offerings or grain and fellowship offerings.

24"We did not build it for that reason. We feared that some day your people would not accept us as part of your nation. Then they might say, 'You cannot worship the LORD, the God of Israel. 25The LORD made the Jordan River a border between us and you people of Reuben and Gad. You cannot worship the LORD.' So we feared that your children might make our children stop worshiping the LORD.

26"That is why we decided to build this altar. But it is not for burnt offerings and sacrifices. 27This altar is proof to you and us and to all our children who will come after us that we worship the LORD with our whole burnt offerings, grain, and fellowship offerings. This was so your children would not say to our children, 'You are not the LORD's.'

28"In the future if your children say that, our children can say, 'See the altar made by our ancestors. It is exactly like the LORD's altar, but we do not use it for sacrifices. It shows that we are part of Israel.'

29"Truly, we don't want to be against the LORD or to stop following him by building an altar for burnt offerings, grain offerings, or sacrifices. We know the only true altar to the LORD our God is in front of the Holy Tent."

30When Phinehas the priest and the ten leaders heard the people of Reuben, Gad, and East Manasseh, they were pleased. 31So Phinehas, son of Eleazar the priest, said, "Now we know the

LORD is with us and that you didn't turn against him. Now the Israelites will not be punished by the LORD."

32Then Phinehas and the leaders left the people of Reuben and Gad in Gilead and went back to Canaan where they told the Israelites what had happened. 33They were pleased and thanked God. So they decided not to fight the people of Reuben and Gad and destroy those lands.

34And the people of Reuben and Gad named the altar Proof That We Believe the LORD Is God.

The Last Words of Joshua

23 The LORD gave Israel peace from their enemies around them. Many years passed, and Joshua grew very old. 2He called a meeting of all the older leaders, heads of families, judges, and officers of Israel. He said, "I am now very old. 3You have seen what the LORD has done to our enemies to help us. The LORD your God fought for you. 4Remember that your people have been given their land between the Jordan River and the Mediterranean Sea in the west, the land I promised to give you. 5The LORD your God will force out the people living there. The LORD will push them out ahead of you. And you will own the land, as he has promised you.

6"Be strong. You must be careful to obey everything commanded in the Book of the Teachings of Moses. Do exactly as it says. 7Don't become friends with the people living among us who are not Israelites. Don't say the names of their gods or make anyone swear by them. Don't serve or worship them. 8You must continue to follow the LORD your God, as you have done in the past.

9"The LORD has forced many great and powerful nations to leave ahead of you. No nation has been able to defeat you. 10With his help, one Israelite could defeat a thousand, because the LORD your God fights for you, as he promised to do. 11So you must be careful to love the LORD your God.

12"If you turn away from the way of the LORD and become friends with these people who are not part of Israel and marry them, 13the LORD your God will not help you defeat your enemies. They will be like traps for you, like whips on your back and thorns in your eyes, and none of you will be left in this good land the LORD your God has given you.

14"It's almost time for me to die. You know and fully believe that the LORD has done great things for you. You know that he has not failed to keep any of his promises. 15Every good promise that the LORD your God made has come true, and in the same way, his other promises will come true. He promised that evil will come to you and that he will destroy you from this good land that he gave you. 16This will happen if you don't keep your agreement with the LORD your God. If you go and serve other gods and worship them, the LORD will become very angry with you. Then none of you will be left in this good land he has given you."

24 Joshua gathered all the tribes of Israel together at Shechem. He called the older leaders, heads of families, judges, and officers of Israel to stand before God.

2Then Joshua said to all the people, "Here's what the LORD, the God of Israel, says to you: 'A long time ago your ancestors lived on the other side of the Euphrates River. Terah, the father of Abraham and Nahor, worshiped other gods. 3But I, the LORD, took your ancestor Abraham from the other side of the river and led him through the land of Canaan. And I gave him many children, including his son Isaac. 4I gave Isaac two sons named Jacob and Esau. I gave the land around the mountains of Edom to Esau, but Jacob and his sons went down to Egypt. 5Then I sent Moses and Aaron to Egypt, where I brought many disasters on the Egyptians. Afterwards I brought you out. 6When I brought your ancestors out of Egypt, they came to the Red Sea, and the Egyptians chased them with chariots and men on horses. 7So the people called out to the LORD. And I brought darkness between you and the Egyptians and made the sea to cover them. You yourselves saw what I did to the army of Egypt. After that, you lived in the desert for a long time.

8"'Then I brought you to the land of the Amorites, east of the Jordan River. They fought against you, but I handed them over to you. I destroyed them before you, and you took control of that land. 9But the king of Moab, Balak son of Zippor, prepared to fight against the Israelites. The king sent for Balaam son of Beor to curse you, 10but I refused to listen to Balaam. So he asked for good things to happen to you! I saved you and brought you out of his power.

11"'Then you crossed the Jordan River and came to Jericho, where the people of Jericho fought against you. Also, the Amorites, Perizzites, Canaanites, Hittites, Girgashites, Hivites, and

23:13 Racism: Isaiah 42:6
24:2 Abraham: Isaiah 29:22
24:5 Idolatry: 1 Kings 12:26–33

Jebusites fought against you. But I handed them over to you. [12]I sent terror ahead of you to force out two Amorite kings. You took the land without using swords and bows. [13]I gave you that land where you did not have to work. I gave you cities that you did not have to build. And now you live in that land and in those cities, and you eat from vineyards and olive trees that you did not plant.'"

[14]Then Joshua said to the people, "Now respect the LORD and serve him fully and sincerely. Throw away the gods that your ancestors worshiped on the other side of the Euphrates River and in Egypt. Serve the LORD. [15]But if you don't want to serve the LORD, you must choose for yourselves today whom you will serve. You may serve the gods that your ancestors worshiped when they lived on the other side of the Euphrates River, or you may serve the gods of the Amorites who lived in this land. As for me and my family, we will serve the LORD."

[16]Then the people answered, "We will never stop following the LORD to serve other gods! [17]It was the LORD our God who brought our ancestors out of Egypt. We were slaves in that land, but the LORD did great things for us there. He brought us out and protected us while we traveled through other lands. [18]Then he forced out all the people living in these lands, even the Amorites. So we will serve the LORD, because he is our God."

[19]Then Joshua said, "You are not able to serve the LORD, because he is a holy God and a jealous God. If you turn against him and sin, he will not forgive you. [20]If you leave the LORD and serve other gods, he will send you great trouble. The LORD may have been good to you, but if you turn against him, he will destroy you."

[21]But the people said to Joshua, "No! We will serve the LORD."

[22]Then Joshua said, "You are your own witnesses that you have chosen to serve the LORD."

The people said, "Yes, we are."

[23]Then Joshua said, "Now throw away the gods that you have. Love the LORD, the God of Israel, with all your heart."

[24]Then the people said to Joshua, "We will serve the LORD our God, and we will obey him."

[25]On that day at Shechem Joshua made an agreement for the people. He made rules and laws for them to follow. [26]Joshua wrote these things in the Book of the Teachings of God. Then he took a large stone and set it up under the oak tree near the LORD's Holy Tent.

[27]Joshua said to all the people, "See this stone! It will remind you of what we did today. It was here the LORD spoke to us today. It will remind you of what happened so you will not turn against your God."

Joshua Dies

[28]Then Joshua sent the people back to their land.

[29]After that, Joshua son of Nun died at the age of one hundred ten. [30]They buried him in his own land at Timnath Serah, in the mountains of Ephraim, north of Mount Gaash.

[31]The Israelites served the LORD during the lifetime of Joshua and during the lifetimes of the older leaders who lived after Joshua who had seen what the LORD had done for Israel.

Joseph Comes Home

[32]When the Israelites left Egypt, they carried the bones of Joseph with them. They buried them at Shechem, in the land Jacob had bought for a hundred pieces of silver from the sons of Hamor (Hamor was the father of Shechem). This land now belonged to Joseph's children.

[33]And Eleazar son of Aaron died and was buried at Gibeah in the mountains of Ephraim, which had been given to Eleazar's son Phinehas.

24:15 Even for the people of Israel, the children of those who had received the agreement at Mount Sinai and witnessed the miracles of the Exodus, there was a choice to be made. Joshua put the issue bluntly: either serve the God of Israel, or worship the other gods. God always gives human beings the freedom to choose whether to serve him or not. Making that choice, or reaffirming a previous choice, can be a turning experience away from sin and toward the Lord. This turning is conversion.

24:15 Near the end of Joshua's life, he assembled the tribes of Israel together, recounted their history, and reminded them of the Lord's faithfulness in bringing them into the land and defeating their enemies. With all this as background, Joshua challenged the leaders and people to make a commitment to serving the Lord and him only, a decision he had already made for his family.

24:25 Agreement: 1 Kings 19:10

24:27 Stone: 1 Samuel 7:12

24:33 Joshua: Judges 1:1

INTRODUCTION TO THE BOOK OF JUDGES

Great Leaders Rescue Israel

WHO WROTE THIS BOOK?

According to Jewish tradition, the Book of Judges was written by Samuel. However, that fact cannot be totally verified. It has been suggested that Nathan and Gad, both prophets of God, may have helped put the accounts together.

TO WHOM WAS THIS BOOK WRITTEN?

Judges was written for and about the people of Israel, God's special nation.

WHERE WAS IT WRITTEN?

This portion of Israel's history was likely written in Canaan, the Promised Land, since that's where the judges ruled the people of Israel.

WHEN WAS IT WRITTEN?

Judges was probably written in the tenth or eleventh century B.C., sometime just before or after David had been established as king.

WHAT IS THE BOOK ABOUT?

The Book of Judges describes the history of the people of Israel from the time of Joshua's death until the time of the kings of Israel. During this time Israel often turns away from God. They are then oppressed by foreign nations. But when they get into trouble, as a result of their unfaithfulness to God, they cry out for God to deliver them from the enemies that overwhelm them. "Then the LORD chose leaders called judges, who saved the Israelites . . ." (2:16).

WHY WAS THIS BOOK WRITTEN?

The writer of Judges constantly reminds the readers that God is their Lord and ruler (8:23), and that he is their king, which they often forget in favor of earthly kings and gods of their society. Their forgetfulness is recorded in 17:6: "At that time Israel did not have a king, so everyone did what seemed right." The result of Israel's repeated unfaithfulness to God creates an erratic history of ups and downs for them. When they remember God as their Lord and king, they are up; when they forget him, they are down. The truth is, whether they are up or down, God is still the Lord.

SO WHAT DOES THIS BOOK MEAN TO US?

The echo of the words of Judges tells us today that God is still the Lord of our lives. He is the king of all earthly kings; he is the true ruler of the world. When we, as Christians, remember to pay homage to God as our Lord and king, we reap his blessings in our lives. When we forget to acknowledge him, our lives suffer. The truth remains: whether we recognize him or not, God is the Lord of life. For life to be blessed here on earth, we must be humble servants of the One who can add blessings to life.

SUMMARY:

The Book of Judges covers the period of time between the death of Joshua and the rise of the kings in Israel. The title of the book highlights the main characters of this period of history, who are called judges. The name judges can be misleading. The people are not called judges because they preside in a courtroom. Rather, they were military or tribal leaders who appeared from time to time in different areas of Israel to deliver God's people from their enemies.

The largest part of the Book of Judges follows the exploits of these leaders, and their stories have a similar pattern. The account begins with the notice that the people of God have rebelled against God. Because they have sinned, God allows a foreign enemy to come in and rule over them. As a result of their suffering, the people turn back to God and ask his forgiveness and help. God then sends a judge to deliver them. Most of the story develops around how God uses the judge to deliver Israel. Once they are freed from their oppression they enjoy a period of peace, but it is not too long before they rebel against the Lord again, and the cycle begins all over.

Still, Judges is more than the same story over and over again. Actually, as time wears on, the moral situation among God's people gets worse, and the judges are less and less respectable people. Deborah, Othniel, and Ehud, whose stories are given first, have admirable qualities, but the final two judges, Jephthah and Samson, are shady characters, whom God nonetheless uses to work his deliverance.

The book ends with two stories that depart from the cycle described above. They are both stories about an individual Levite whose sins are heightened to national catastrophes. These two stories highlight the message of the Book of Judges: the spiritual state of the people of God is low. The repeated statement at the end of the book—"In those days Israel did not have a king. Everyone did what seemed right" (e.g. Judges 21:25)—indicates that the book was written in part to support the new institution of kingship as a solution to the problems of the period of judges.

The Book of Judges can be outlined briefly as follows:

I. The Conquest Continues (1:1–2:5)
II. The Judges (2:6–16:31)
III. Sinful Levites and Troubled Israel (17:1–21:25)

The office of judge was used by God to save Israel from foreign oppression. However, as we have seen, the judge was an imperfect deliverer, full of faults, and rescuing Israel for only brief periods of time. The kingship was a better, more stable human institution. However, the imperfections of both judge and king caused the people of God to yearn for someone whose salvation was sure and long lasting. The answer came in the form of Jesus Christ, the perfect deliverer, the King of kings.

I. The Conquest Continues (1:1–2:5)

The Book of Judges begins with stories from the continuing war with the Canaanites who lived in Palestine even after the death of Joshua. Even when they had opportunity, the people of Israel did not always force the Canaanites to leave the Promised Land as God wanted them to. As a result, God would let the Canaanites stay in the land as a constant temptation to Israel.

II. The Judges (2:6–16:31)

The centerpiece of the Book of Judges is the collection of stories of the war leaders who rise up and deliver Israel from foreign enemies who have taken over their land or part of it. (For a fuller description of the pattern behind these stories, see the summary above.) These leaders include Othniel, Ehud, Shamgar, Deborah, Gideon, Jephthah, and Samson. Other individuals are also called judges, but they do not have war stories associated with them. The latter judges include Tola, Jair, Ibzan, Elon, and Abdon (Judges 10:1–5; 12:8–15).

III. Sinful Levites and Troubled Israel (17:1–21:25)

The Book of Judges ends with two stories that show again just how sinful the period of the judges really is. We don't know exactly when these events took place, but they did occur before kings ruled Israel. Both stories start out with a family tragedy that quickly becomes a national calamity. Both stories also have Levites, the tribe especially devoted to the Lord's service, at the center.

JUDGES

Judah Fights the Canaanites

After Joshua died, the Israelites asked the LORD, "Who will be first to go and fight for us against the Canaanites?"

2The LORD said to them, "The tribe of Judah will go. I have handed the land over to them."

3The men of Judah said to the men of Simeon, their relatives, "Come and help us fight the Canaanites for our land. If you do, we will go and help you fight for your land." So the men of Simeon went with them.

4When Judah attacked, the LORD handed over the Canaanites and the Perizzites to them, and they defeated ten thousand men at the city of Bezek. 5There they found Adoni-Bezek, the ruler of the city, and fought him. The men of Judah defeated the Canaanites and the Perizzites, 6but Adoni-Bezek ran away. The men of Judah chased him, and when they caught him, they cut off his thumbs and big toes.

7Adoni-Bezek said, "Seventy kings whose thumbs and big toes had been cut off used to eat scraps that fell from my table. Now God has paid me back for what I did to them." The men of Judah took Adoni-Bezek to Jerusalem, and he died there.

8Then the men of Judah fought against Jerusalem and captured it. They attacked with their swords and burned the city.

9Later, they went down to fight the Canaanites who lived in the mountains, in the dry country to the south, and in the western hills. 10The men of Judah went to fight against the Canaanites in the city of Hebron (which used to be called Kiriath Arba). And they defeated Sheshai, Ahiman, and Talmai.

Caleb and His Daughter

11Then they left there and went to fight against the people living in Debir. (In the past Debir had been called Kiriath Sepher.) 12Before attacking the city, Caleb said, "I will give Acsah, my daughter, as a wife to the man who attacks and captures the city of Kiriath Sepher." 13Othniel son of Kenaz, Caleb's younger brother, captured the city, so Caleb gave his daughter Acsah to Othniel to be his wife.

14When Acsah came to Othniel, she told him to ask her father for a field. When she got down from her donkey, Caleb asked her, "What do you want?"

15Acsah answered him, "Do me a special favor. Since you have given me land in southern Canaan, also give me springs of water." So Caleb gave her the upper and lower springs.

Fights with the Canaanites

16The Kenite people, who were from the family of Moses' father-in-law, left Jericho, the city of palm trees. They went with the men of Judah to the Desert of Judah to live with them there in southern Judah near the city of Arad.

17The men of Judah and the men of Simeon, their relatives, defeated the Canaanites who lived in Zephath. They completely destroyed the city, so they called it Hormah. 18The men of Judah captured Gaza, Ashkelon, Ekron, and the lands around them.

19The LORD was with the men of Judah. They took the land in the mountains, but they could not force out the people living on the plain, because they had iron chariots. 20As Moses had promised, Hebron was given to Caleb, and Caleb forced out the three sons of Anak. 21But the people of Benjamin could not make the Jebusite people leave Jerusalem. Since that time the Jebusites have lived with the Benjaminites in Jerusalem.

22The men of Joseph went to fight against the city of Bethel, and the LORD was with them. 23They sent some spies to Bethel (which used to be called Luz). 24The spies saw a man coming out of the city and said to him, "Show us a way into the city, and we will be kind to you." 25So the man showed them the way into the city. The men of Joseph attacked with swords the people in Bethel, but they let the man and his family go free. 26He went to the land where the Hittites lived and built a city. He named it Luz, which it is called even today.

27There were Canaanites living in the cities of Beth Shan, Taanach, Dor, Ibleam, Megiddo, and the small towns around them. The people of Manasseh did not force those people out of their towns, because the Canaanites were determined to stay there. 28Later, the Israelites grew strong and forced the Canaanites to work as slaves, but they did not make all the Canaanites leave their land. 29The people of Ephraim did not force out all of the

1:1 Joshua: Nehemiah 8:17

1:6 *cut off his thumbs and big toes.* This practice made sure that prisoners of war would not be able to use weapons and fight again.

1:16 *the city of palm trees.* Jericho was a tropical oasis in the middle of a barren desert.

1:17 *Hormah.* Hormah sounds like the Hebrew word meaning "to destroy completely."

1:20 *Anak.* See Numbers 13:28.

Canaanites living in Gezer. So the Canaanites continued to live in Gezer with the people of Ephraim.
30The people of Zebulun did not force out the
Canaanites living in the cities of Kitron and
Nahalol. They stayed and lived with the people of
Zebulun, but Zebulun made them work as slaves.
31The people of Asher did not force the Canaanites from the cities of Acco, Sidon, Ahlab,
Aczib, Helbah, Aphek, and Rehob. 32Since the
people of Asher did not force them out, the
Canaanites continued to live with them. 33The
people of Naphtali did not force out the people of
the cities of Beth Shemesh and Beth Anath. So
they continued to live with the Canaanites in
those cities, and the Canaanites worked as slaves.
34The Amorites forced the Danites back into the
mountains and would not let them come down to
live in the plain. 35The Amorites were determined
to stay in Mount Heres, Aijalon, and Shaalbim. But
when the Israelites grew stronger, they made the
Amorites work as slaves. 36The land of the Amorites
was from Scorpion Pass to Sela and beyond.

The Angel of the Lord at Bokim

2 The angel of the LORD went up from Gilgal to
Bokim and said, "I brought you up from Egypt
and led you to the land I promised to give your
ancestors. I said, 'I will never break my agreement
with you. 2But you must not make an agreement
with the people who live in this land. You must
destroy their altars.' But you did not obey me.
How could you do this? 3Now I tell you, 'I will not
force out the people in this land. They will be your
enemies, and their gods will be a trap for you.'"
4After the angel gave Israel this message from the
LORD, they cried loudly. 5So they named the place
Bokim. There they offered sacrifices to the LORD.

Joshua Dies

6Then Joshua sent the people back to their land.
7The people served the LORD during the lifetime of
Joshua and during the lifetimes of the older leaders who lived after Joshua and who had seen what
great things the LORD had done for Israel. 8Joshua
son of Nun, the servant of the LORD, died at the
age of one hundred ten. 9They buried him in his
own land at Timnath Serah in the mountains of
Ephraim, north of Mount Gaash.

The People Disobey

10After those people had died, their children
grew up and did not know the LORD or what he
had done for Israel. 11So they did what the LORD
said was wrong, and they worshiped the Baal idols.
12They quit following the LORD, the God of their
ancestors who had brought them out of Egypt.
They began to worship the gods of the people
who lived around them, and that made the LORD
angry. 13The Israelites quit following the LORD and
worshiped Baal and Ashtoreth. 14The LORD was
angry with the people of Israel, so he handed
them over to robbers who took their possessions.
He let their enemies who lived around them
defeat them; they could not protect themselves.
15When the Israelites went out to fight, they
always lost, because the LORD was not with them.
The LORD had sworn to them this would happen.
So the Israelites suffered very much.

God Chooses Judges

16Then the LORD chose leaders called judges,
who saved the Israelites from the robbers. 17But
the Israelites did not listen to their judges. They
were not faithful to God but worshiped other
gods instead. Their ancestors had obeyed the
LORD's commands, but they quickly turned away
and did not obey. 18When their enemies hurt
them, the Israelites cried for help. So the LORD
felt sorry for them and sent judges to save them
from their enemies. The LORD was with those
judges all their lives. 19But when the judges died,
the Israelites again sinned and worshiped other
gods. They became worse than their ancestors.
The Israelites were very stubborn and refused to
change their evil ways.
20So the LORD became angry with the Israelites.
He said, "These people have broken the agreement I made with their ancestors. They have not
listened to me. 21I will no longer defeat the
nations who were left when Joshua died. 22I will
use them to test Israel, to see if Israel will keep the
LORD's commands as their ancestors did." 23In
the past the LORD had permitted those nations to
stay in the land. He did not quickly force them
out or help Joshua's army defeat them.

3 These are the nations the LORD did not force
to leave. He wanted to test the Israelites who
had not fought in the wars of Canaan. 2(The only
reason the LORD left those nations in the land was
to teach the descendants of the Israelites who had
not fought in those wars how to fight.) 3These are
the nations: the five rulers of the Philistines, all
the Canaanites, the people of Sidon, and the
Hivites who lived in the Lebanon mountains from
Mount Baal Hermon to Lebo Hamath. 4Those
nations were in the land to test the Israelites—to

2:5 *Bokim.* This name means "crying."
2:16 *judges.* They were not judges in courts of law, but leaders of the people in times of emergency.
2:19 Stubbornness: 2 Kings 17:13–18

GLORY

EXODUS 33:18

What is glory? Where is glory found? Who has glory?
What makes God glorious? Can we share in God's glory?

In the Old Testament, no one was permitted to look directly at God (Exodus 19:21–22). Such an experience would have overwhelmed a sinful human being and caused their death. God appeared to his people in indirect ways, ways that revealed his glory to them. This glory gave his people a taste of what God was all about, while protecting them from the danger of meeting with God directly.

What is the glory of the Lord? It seems to be such an abstract concept. How can we make it concrete in a way that will lead us to a greater appreciation of the believers during the biblical period?

God's glory reflects his uniqueness and refers to his importance. The countries of the ancient Near East believed in thousands of gods, but the God of the Bible is like none other. Indeed, he is distinctive in every aspect of his being, and so, in a sense, God's glory is God himself.

Since God himself is so great and our human minds so incapable of grasping him completely, the glory of the Lord is indicated by symbols. In the first place, the glory of the Lord often took the form of a cloud (or smoke) and fire. When Moses went up Mount Sinai to receive the Ten Commandments, the top of the mountain was covered by a cloud and it "looked like a fire burning on top of the mountain" (Exodus 24:15–18). The fire indicated God's purity, and the cloud hid his dangerous presence from those who were looking on.

The cloud, which symbolized God's glory, also filled the innermost and most holy part of the Temple. This cloud represented God's presence with his people.

But still, the idea of God's glory is elusive. As we have seen, part of the reason for this is because its purpose is to reveal, but also to conceal God from view. This is especially true in the Old Testament. When Jesus Christ came, we recieved a clearer vision of what the glory of the Lord is: "The Word became a human and lived among us. We saw his glory—the glory that belongs to the only Son of the Father—and he was full of grace and truth" (John 1:14).

This verse teaches that Jesus is God's glory. When he is present, it means that God is present. Jesus has the power, the authority, the distinction, and the importance of God. As we come to know Jesus, we come to know God himself. As the glory of God he deserves our respect, our honor, our esteem, and our worship. Revelation 5:12 gives us a window into the heavenly worship of Jesus Christ, the type of worship that he so richly deserves here on earth: "The Lamb who was killed is worthy to receive power, wealth, wisdom, and strength, honor, glory, and praise!"

The Book of Revelation makes it clear that Jesus' glory is a glory that fills all the earth, but the fact that God's glory fills the entire earth is not a truth restricted to the New Testament. When Isaiah (6:3) received his call to the prophetic ministry, he was transported to heaven where he saw angelic creatures who cried out, "Holy, holy, holy is the LORD All-Powerful. His glory fills the whole earth."

Glory, thus, belongs to God, and to his son Jesus Christ. The Bible also teaches that God gives his human creatures glory. We reflect his glory. After all, we are made in his image.

The Fall into sin tarnished the reflection of divine glory, but it is still there. Furthermore, Jesus prayed in his priestly prayer just before his death that God enhance his people's glory. "I have given these people the glory that you gave me so that they can be one, just as you and I are one." (John 17:22) The glory that Jesus gives to his people results in their unity, and their unity is a sign to the world that God sent Jesus into the world (John 17:21).

Contemporary Christians should realize that we are glorious creatures created by God. This realization should lead to greater respect for ourselves and for other people. This understanding of human beings must be balanced with the fact that we are also sinners.

The most important thing that the Bible teaches about glory is that God is the source of it. He is glory itself, and because of that, it is God who deserves all our praise and worship.⚭

⚭**Glory:** For additional scriptures on this topic go to Exodus 24:16–17.

ANGER

EXODUS 34:6

What is anger? Why do we get angry?
Is anger always a negative emotion? Why does God get angry?

Anger is a response to an assault. Someone attacks us, and one of our options is to lash back. The emotion of anger can run from a minor irritation to an intense rage or fury. As human beings and as Christians we struggle with any anger that we feel. The effects which our anger has on other people can be quite damaging, and the guilty feelings which we often feel after we cool down also give us pause. We often respond by labeling all anger as wrong or bad. But as we turn to the Bible we are surprised to see that God does not always condemn anger, and as a matter of fact, God himself frequently is described as angry toward humanity.

We must distinguish a destructive anger from a righteous anger. That some anger is wrong is clear from the Bible's warnings to avoid it:

Wait and trust the LORD.
  Don't be upset when others get rich
  or when someone else's plans succeed.
Don't get angry.
  Don't be upset; it only leads to trouble. (Psalm 37:7–8)

Anger here is a response to a perceived injustice. A good person deserves something, but godless people get it instead. The psalmist tells the angry person to be patient because in the long run people who follow God will come out on top.

God wants us to adopt a selfless, gentle approach to those who assault us. As Jesus instructed in the Sermon on the Mount, "If someone slaps you on the right cheek, turn to him the other cheek also. If someone wants to sue you in court and take your shirt, let him have your coat also. If someone forces you to go with him one mile, go with him two miles" (Matthew 5:39–41). And James along the same line says, "Do not become angry easily, because anger will not help you live the right kind of life God wants" (James 1:19b-20).

Indeed, selfish, unthinking anger which is often an automatic response when our desires are not met are ultimately directed at God, and we become rebels like those described at the beginning of Psalm 2:

Why are the nations so angry?
  Why are the people making useless plans?
The kings of the earth prepare to fight,
  and their leaders made plans together
against the LORD
  and against his appointed one.

And, of course, we can see the wisdom of God's advice, especially after we have let anger take over our minds and make us act in ways that we come to regret afterwards.

However, the Bible does not teach that all anger is wrong. We should not become angry easily, but there are times when anger is the only appropriate response. The Bible recognizes that it is possible to be right in our anger. There is anger without sin. "When you are angry, do not sin, and be sure to stop being angry before the end of the day" (Ephesians 4:26; see also Psalm 4:4).

While we are angry, we should be careful not to adopt the world's methods of dealing with anger, lashing out with violence and hate ourselves. We should rather remember that our weapons are the more powerful spiritual weapons of prayer, faith, and love (see Ephesians 6:10–20).

What is most wonderful, though, is that the focus of God's rage against sin has not been directed against us, but against himself. This is the heart of the death of Christ. God often speaks of the judgment which is due against sinners as the "cup of anger" (Psalm 75:8). But ultimately it is Jesus Christ who drinks this cup (Matthew 26:39) and feels the force of God's anger in the place of those who put their trust in him.

Anger: For additional scriptures on this topic go to Psalm 2:1.

see if they would obey the commands the LORD
had given to their ancestors by Moses.
[5]The people of Israel lived with the Canaanites,
Hittites, Amorites, Perizzites, Hivites, and
Jebusites. [6]The Israelites began to marry the
daughters of those people, and they allowed their
daughters to marry the sons of those people.
Israel also served their gods.

Othniel, the First Judge

[7]The Israelites did what the LORD said was
wrong. They forgot about the LORD their God and
served the idols of Baal and Asherah. [8]So the LORD
was angry with Israel and allowed Cushan-
Rishathaim king of Northwest Mesopotamia to
rule over the Israelites for eight years. [9]When
Israel cried to the LORD, the LORD sent someone to
save them. Othniel son of Kenaz, Caleb's younger
brother, saved the Israelites. [10]The Spirit of the
LORD entered Othniel, and he became Israel's
judge. When he went to war, the LORD handed
over to him Cushan-Rishathaim king of Northwest
Mesopotamia. [11]So the land was at peace for
forty years. Then Othniel son of Kenaz died.

Ehud, the Judge

[12]Again the people of Israel did what the LORD said
was wrong. So the LORD gave Eglon king of Moab
power to defeat Israel because of the evil Israel did.
[13]Eglon got the Ammonites and the Amalekites to
join him. Then he attacked Israel and took Jericho,
the city of palm trees. [14]So the people of Israel were
ruled by Eglon king of Moab for eighteen years.
[15]When the people cried to the LORD, he sent
someone to save them. He was Ehud, son of Gera
from the people of Benjamin, who was left-
handed. Israel sent Ehud to give Eglon king of
Moab the payment he demanded. [16]Ehud made
himself a sword with two edges, about eighteen
inches long, and he tied it to his right hip under
his clothes. [17]Ehud gave Eglon king of Moab the
payment he demanded. Now Eglon was a very fat
man. [18]After he had given Eglon the payment,
Ehud sent away the people who had carried it.
[19]When he passed the statues near Gilgal, he
turned around and said to Eglon, "I have a secret
message for you, King Eglon."
The king said, "Be quiet!" Then he sent all of
his servants out of the room. [20]Ehud went to King
Eglon, as he was sitting alone in the room above
his summer palace.
Ehud said, "I have a message from God for
you." As the king stood up from his chair, [21]Ehud
reached with his left hand and took out the sword
that was tied to his right hip. Then he stabbed the
sword deep into the king's belly! [22]Even the handle sank in, and the blade came out his back. The
king's fat covered the whole sword, so Ehud left
the sword in Eglon. [23]Then he went out of the
room and closed and locked the doors behind him.
[24]When the servants returned just after Ehud
left, they found the doors to the room locked. So
they thought the king was relieving himself.
[25]They waited for a long time. Finally they became worried because he still had not opened the
doors. So they got the key and unlocked them and
saw their king lying dead on the floor!
[26]While the servants were waiting, Ehud had
escaped. He passed by the statues and went to
Seirah. [27]When he reached the mountains of
Ephraim he blew the trumpet. The people of Israel
heard it and went down from the hills with Ehud
leading them.
[28]He said to them, "Follow me! The LORD has
helped you to defeat your enemies, the Moabites." So Israel followed Ehud and captured the
crossings of the Jordan River. They did not allow
the Moabites to cross the Jordan River. [29]Israel
killed about ten thousand strong and able men
from Moab; not one escaped. [30]So that day Moab
was forced to be under the rule of Israel, and
there was peace in the land for eighty years.

Shamgar, the Judge

[31]After Ehud, Shamgar son of Anath saved
Israel. Shamgar killed six hundred Philistines
with a sharp stick used to guide oxen.

Deborah, the Woman Judge

4 After Ehud died, the Israelites again did what
the LORD said was wrong. [2]So he let Jabin, a
king of Canaan who ruled in the city of Hazor,
defeat Israel. Sisera, who lived in Harosheth
Haggoyim, was the commander of Jabin's army.
[3]Because he had nine hundred iron chariots and
was very cruel to the people of Israel for twenty
years, they cried to the LORD for help.
[4]A prophetess named Deborah, the wife of
Lappidoth, was judge of Israel at that time.
[5]Deborah would sit under the Palm Tree of Deborah, which was between the cities of Ramah
and Bethel, in the mountains of Ephraim. And

3:10 Spiritual Gifts: 2 Samuel 23:2

3:15 *left-handed.* In the ancient world, left-handedness was considered strange and abnormal. Here it may also be seen as a secret weapon of sorts (compare Judges 20:16). No one would expect him to conceal the weapon on the right side and grasp it with his left hand.

4:3 *iron chariots.* The Philistines had a monopoly on iron weapons in Palestine at this time.

the people of Israel would come to her to settle their arguments.

[6]Deborah sent a message to Barak son of Abinoam. Barak lived in the city of Kedesh, which is in the area of Naphtali. Deborah said to Barak, "The LORD, the God of Israel, commands you: 'Go and gather ten thousand men of Naphtali and Zebulun and lead them to Mount Tabor. [7]I will make Sisera, the commander of Jabin's army, and his chariots, and his army meet you at the Kishon River. I will hand Sisera over to you.'"

[8]Then Barak said to Deborah, "I will go if you will go with me, but if you won't go with me, I won't go."

[9]"Of course I will go with you," Deborah answered, "but you will not get credit for the victory. The LORD will let a woman defeat Sisera." So Deborah went with Barak to Kedesh. [10]At Kedesh, Barak called the people of Zebulun and Naphtali together. From them, he gathered ten thousand men to follow him, and Deborah went with him also.

[11]Now Heber the Kenite had left the other Kenites, the descendants of Hobab, Moses' brother-in-law. Heber had put up his tent by the great tree in Zaanannim, near Kedesh.

[12]When Sisera was told that Barak son of Abinoam had gone to Mount Tabor, [13]Sisera gathered his nine hundred iron chariots and all the men with him, from Harosheth Haggoyim to the Kishon River.

[14]Then Deborah said to Barak, "Get up! Today is the day the LORD will hand over Sisera. The LORD has already cleared the way for you." So Barak led ten thousand men down Mount Tabor. [15]As Barak approached, the LORD confused Sisera and his army and chariots. The LORD defeated them with the sword, but Sisera left his chariot and ran away on foot. [16]Barak and his men chased Sisera's chariots and army to Harosheth Haggoyim. With their swords they killed all of Sisera's men; not one of them was left alive.

[17]But Sisera himself ran away to the tent where Jael lived. She was the wife of Heber, one of the Kenite family groups. Heber's family was at peace with Jabin king of Hazor. [18]Jael went out to meet Sisera and said to him, "Come into my tent, master! Come in. Don't be afraid." So Sisera went into Jael's tent, and she covered him with a rug.

[19]Sisera said to Jael, "I am thirsty. Please give me some water to drink." So she opened a leather bag of milk and gave him a drink. Then she covered him up.

[20]He said to her, "Go stand at the entrance to the tent. If anyone comes and asks you, 'Is anyone here?' say, 'No.'"

[21]But Jael, the wife of Heber, took a tent peg and a hammer and quietly went to Sisera. Since he was very tired, he was in a deep sleep. She hammered the tent peg through the side of Sisera's head and into the ground. And so Sisera died.

[22]At that very moment Barak came by Jael's tent, chasing Sisera. Jael went out to meet him and said, "Come. I will show you the man you are looking for." So Barak entered her tent, and there Sisera lay dead, with the tent peg in his head.

[23]On that day God defeated Jabin king of Canaan in the sight of Israel.

[24]Israel became stronger and stronger against Jabin king of Canaan until finally they destroyed him.

The Song of Deborah

5 On that day Deborah and Barak son of Abinoam sang this song:

[2]"The leaders led Israel.
The people volunteered to go to battle.
Praise the LORD!
[3]Listen, kings.
Pay attention, rulers!
I myself will sing to the LORD.
I will make music to the LORD, the God of Israel.

[4]"LORD, when you came from Edom,
when you marched from the land of Edom,
the earth shook,
the skies rained,
and the clouds dropped water.
[5]The mountains shook before the LORD, the
God of Mount Sinai,
before the LORD, the God of Israel!

4:5 Deborah: Ruth 3:5–15

4:17 We cannot understand Jael apart from her close tie to Deborah. Both Deborah and Jael are women who lure the Lord's enemies to destruction. Jael, in a bold stroke of heroism, goes out to meet Sisera and invites him to the supposed safety of her tent. She uses hospitality and cunning to lure and then finally bring down her enemy. When Jael drives the tent peg through Sisera's temple, she fulfills Deborah's prophecy, "The Lord will let a woman defeat Sisera" (4:9).

5:1 Deborah's song is similar to the song of Moses in Deuteronomy 32. Moses sings his song before Israel enters the Promised Land; Deborah sings her song long after Israel has possessed the land. Both songs celebrate God as the warrior who delivers Israel in times of obedience and punishes them in times of disobedience. God knew before Israel entered the Promised Land that his people would worship pagan gods. Moses' song was a future warning for the Israelites to remember and worship the Lord only. His song details the punishment that would come upon Israel if they disobeyed: "I will use a nation that does not understand to make them angry" (Deuteronomy 32:21). Deborah's song recalls God's punishment of Israel at the hands of Canaan. Indeed, God's awful punishment had come upon Israel; their worship of false gods had caused God to place Israel under the slavery of the Canaanites. Yet more importantly, Deborah's song celebrates the destruction of the Canaanites, and God's deliverance of Israel.

6"In the days of Shamgar son of Anath,
in the days of Jael, the main roads were empty.
Travelers went on the back roads.
7There were no warriors in Israel
until I, Deborah, arose,
until I arose to be a mother to Israel.
8At that time they chose to follow new gods.
Because of this, enemies fought us at
our city gates.
No one could find a shield or a spear
among the forty thousand people of Israel.
9My heart is with the commanders of Israel.
They volunteered freely from among
the people.
Praise the LORD!

10"You who ride on white donkeys
and sit on saddle blankets,
and you who walk along the road, listen!
11Listen to the sound of the singers
at the watering holes.
There they tell about the victories of the LORD,
the victories of the LORD's warriors in Israel.
Then the LORD's people went down to
the city gates.

12"Wake up, wake up, Deborah!
Wake up, wake up, sing a song!
Get up, Barak!
Go capture your enemies, son of Abinoam!

13"Then those who were left came down to the
important leaders.
The LORD's people came down to me with
strong men.
14They came from Ephraim in the mountains
of Amalek.
Benjamin was among the people who
followed you.
From the family group of Makir, the commanders
came down.
And from Zebulun came those who lead.
15The princes of Issachar were with Deborah.
The people of Issachar were loyal to Barak
and followed him into the valley.
The Reubenites thought hard
about what they would do.
16Why did you stay by the sheepfold?
Was it to hear the music played for
your sheep?
The Reubenites thought hard
about what they would do.
17The people of Gilead stayed east of the
Jordan River.
People of Dan, why did you stay by the ships?
The people of Asher stayed at the seashore,
at their safe harbors.
18But the people of Zebulun risked their lives,
as did the people of Naphtali on the
battlefield.

19"The kings came, and they fought.
At that time the kings of Canaan fought
at Taanach, by the waters of Megiddo.
But they took away no silver or possessions
of Israel.
20The stars fought from heaven;
from their paths, they fought Sisera.
21The Kishon River swept Sisera's men away,
that old river, the Kishon River.
March on, my soul, with strength!
22Then the horses' hoofs beat the ground.
Galloping, galloping go Sisera's mighty horses.
23'May the town of Meroz be cursed,' said the
angel of the LORD.
'Bitterly curse its people,
because they did not come to help the LORD.
They did not fight the strong enemy.'

24"May Jael, the wife of Heber the Kenite,
be blessed above all women who live
in tents.
25Sisera asked for water,
but Jael gave him milk.
In a bowl fit for a ruler,
she brought him cream.
26Jael reached out and took the tent peg.
Her right hand reached for the workman's
hammer.
She hit Sisera! She smashed his head!
She crushed and pierced the side of his head!
27At Jael's feet he sank.
He fell, and he lay there.
At her feet he sank. He fell.
Where Sisera sank, there he fell, dead!

28"Sisera's mother looked out through
the window.
She looked through the curtains and cried out,
'Why is Sisera's chariot so late in coming?
Why are sounds of his chariots' horses
delayed?'
29The wisest of her servant ladies answer her,
and Sisera's mother says to herself,
30'Surely they are robbing the people they
defeated!
Surely they are dividing those things among
themselves!
Each soldier is given a girl or two.
Maybe Sisera is taking pieces of dyed cloth.

Maybe they are even taking
pieces of dyed, embroidered cloth for the
necks of the victors!'

31"Let all your enemies die this way, LORD!
But let all the people who love you
be as strong as the rising sun!"

Then there was peace in the land for forty years.

The Midianites Attack Israel

6 Again the Israelites did what the LORD said
was wrong. So for seven years the LORD handed
them over to Midian. 2Because the Midianites were
very powerful and were cruel to Israel, the Israelites made hiding places in the mountains, in caves,
and in safe places. 3Whenever the Israelites planted
crops, the Midianites, Amalekites, and other peoples from the east would come and attack them.
4They camped in the land and destroyed the crops
that the Israelites had planted as far away as Gaza.
They left nothing for Israel to eat, and no sheep, cattle, or donkeys. 5The Midianites came with their
tents and their animals like swarms of locusts to
ruin the land. There were so many people and
camels they could not be counted. 6Israel became
very poor because of the Midianites, so they cried
out to the LORD.

7When the Israelites cried out to the LORD
against the Midianites, 8the LORD sent a prophet
to them. He said, "This is what the LORD, the God
of Israel, says: I brought you out of Egypt, the land
of slavery. 9I saved you from the Egyptians and
from all those who were against you. I forced the
Canaanites out of their land and gave it to you.
10Then I said to you, 'I am the LORD your God.
Live in the land of the Amorites, but do not worship their gods.' But you did not obey me."

The Angel of the Lord Visits Gideon

11The angel of the LORD came and sat down
under the oak tree at Ophrah that belonged to
Joash, one of the Abiezrite people. Gideon, Joash's
son, was separating some wheat from the chaff in a
winepress to keep the wheat from the Midianites.
12The angel of the LORD appeared to Gideon and
said, "The LORD is with you, mighty warrior!"

13Then Gideon said, "Sir, if the LORD is with us,
why are we having so much trouble? Where are
the miracles our ancestors told us he did when the
LORD brought them out of Egypt? But now he has
left us and has handed us over to the Midianites."

14The LORD turned to Gideon and said, "Go with
your strength and save Israel from the Midianites.
I am the one who is sending you."

15But Gideon answered, "Lord, how can I save
Israel? My family group is the weakest in Manasseh,
and I am the least important member of my family."

16The LORD answered him, "I will be with you.
It will seem as if the Midianites you are fighting
are only one man."

17Then Gideon said to the LORD, "If you are
pleased with me, give me proof that it is really
you talking with me. 18Please wait here until I
come back to you. Let me bring my offering and
set it in front of you."

And the LORD said, "I will wait until you return."

19So Gideon went in and cooked a young goat,
and with twenty quarts of flour, made bread without yeast. Then he put the meat into a basket and
the broth into a pot. He brought them out and
gave them to the angel under the oak tree.

20The angel of God said to Gideon, "Put the
meat and the bread without yeast on that rock
over there. Then pour the broth on them." And
Gideon did as he was told. 21The angel of the
LORD touched the meat and the bread with the
end of the stick that was in his hand. Then fire
jumped up from the rock and completely burned
up the meat and the bread! And the angel of the
LORD disappeared! 22Then Gideon understood he
had been talking to the angel of the LORD. So
Gideon cried out, "Lord GOD! I have seen the
angel of the LORD face to face!"

23But the LORD said to Gideon, "Calm down!
Don't be afraid! You will not die!"

24So Gideon built an altar there to worship the
LORD and named it The LORD Is Peace. It still
stands at Ophrah, where the Abiezrites live.

Gideon Tears Down the Altar of Baal

25That same night the LORD said to Gideon,
"Take the bull that belongs to your father and a
second bull seven years old. Pull down your
father's altar to Baal, and cut down the Asherah
idol beside it. 26Then build an altar to the LORD
your God with its stones in the right order on this
high ground. Kill and burn a second bull on this
altar, using the wood from the Asherah idol."

27So Gideon got ten of his servants and did what
the LORD had told him to do. But Gideon was
afraid that his family and the men of the city might
see him, so he did it at night, not in the daytime.

28When the men of the city got up the next
morning, they saw that the altar for Baal had been
destroyed and that the Asherah idol beside it had
been cut down! They also saw the altar Gideon had
built and the second bull that had been sacrificed
on it. 29The men of the city asked each other, "Who
did this?"

6:16 Angels/Guardian Angels: Daniel 7:13–14

6:24 Trinity: Isaiah 45:21–22

After they asked many questions, someone told them, "Gideon son of Joash did this."

30So they said to Joash, "Bring your son out. He has pulled down the altar of Baal and cut down the Asherah idol beside it. He must die!"

31But Joash said to the angry crowd around him, "Are you going to take Baal's side? Are you going to defend him? Anyone who takes Baal's side will be killed by morning! If Baal is a god, let him fight for himself. It's his altar that has been pulled down." 32So on that day Gideon got the name Jerub-Baal, which means "let Baal fight against him," because Gideon pulled down Baal's altar.

Gideon Defeats Midian

33All the Midianites, the Amalekites, and other peoples from the east joined together and came across the Jordan River and camped in the Valley of Jezreel. 34But the Spirit of the LORD entered Gideon, and he blew a trumpet to call the Abiezrites to follow him. 35He sent messengers to all of Manasseh, calling them to follow him. He also sent messengers to the people of Asher, Zebulun, and Naphtali. So they also went up to meet Gideon and his men.

36Then Gideon said to God, "You said you would help me save Israel. 37I will put some wool on the threshing floor. If there is dew only on the wool but all of the ground is dry, then I will know that you will use me to save Israel, as you said." 38And that is just what happened. When Gideon got up early the next morning and squeezed the wool, he got a full bowl of water from it.

39Then Gideon said to God, "Don't be angry with me if I ask just one more thing. Please let me make one more test. Let only the wool be dry while the ground around it gets wet with dew." 40That night God did that very thing. Just the wool was dry, but the ground around it was wet with dew.

7 Early in the morning Jerub-Baal (also called Gideon) and all his men set up their camp at the spring of Harod. The Midianites were camped north of them in the valley at the bottom of the hill called Moreh. 2Then the LORD said to Gideon, "You have too many men to defeat the Midianites. I don't want the Israelites to brag that they saved themselves. 3So now, announce to the people, 'Anyone who is afraid may leave Mount Gilead and go back home.'" So twenty-two thousand men returned home, but ten thousand remained.

4Then the LORD said to Gideon, "There are still too many men. Take the men down to the water, and I will test them for you there. If I say, 'This man will go with you,' he will go. But if I say, 'That one will not go with you,' he will not go."

5So Gideon led the men down to the water. There the LORD said to him, "Separate them into those who drink water by lapping it up like a dog and those who bend down to drink." 6There were three hundred men who used their hands to bring water to their mouths, lapping it as a dog does. All the rest got down on their knees to drink.

7Then the LORD said to Gideon, "Using the three hundred men who lapped the water, I will save you and hand Midian over to you. Let all the others go home." 8So Gideon sent the rest of Israel to their homes. But he kept three hundred men and took the jars and the trumpets of those who left.

Now the camp of Midian was in the valley below Gideon. 9That night the LORD said to Gideon, "Get up. Go down and attack the camp of the Midianites, because I will give them to you. 10But if you are afraid to go down, take your servant Purah with you. 11When you come to the camp of Midian, you will hear what they are saying. Then you will not be afraid to attack the camp."

Gideon Is Encouraged

So Gideon and his servant Purah went down to the edge of the enemy camp. 12The Midianites, the Amalekites, and all the peoples from the east were camped in that valley. There were so many of them they seemed like locusts. Their camels could not be counted because they were as many as the grains of sand on the seashore!

13When Gideon came to the enemy camp, he heard a man telling his friend about a dream. He was saying, "I dreamed that a loaf of barley bread rolled into the camp of Midian. It hit the tent so hard that the tent turned over and fell flat!"

14The man's friend said, "Your dream is about the sword of Gideon son of Joash, a man of Israel. God will hand Midian and the whole army over to him!"⚭

15When Gideon heard about the dream and what it meant, he worshiped God. Then Gideon went back to the camp of Israel and called out to them, "Get up! The LORD has handed the army of Midian over to you!" 16Gideon divided the three hundred men into three groups. He gave each man a trumpet and an empty jar with a burning torch inside.

17Gideon told the men, "Watch me and do what I do. When I get to the edge of the camp, do what I do. 18Surround the enemy camp. When I and everyone with me blow our trumpets, you blow your trumpets, too. Then shout, 'For the LORD and for Gideon!'"

7:5 *lapping it up like a dog.* While some try to find a reason why God chose the "dog lappers" to fight, it seems a test designed simply to cut down the number of warriors for the battle.

⚭**7:14 Holy War & Divine Warrior:** 1 Samuel 17:45–47

Midian Is Defeated

19 So Gideon and the one hundred men with him came to the edge of the enemy camp just after they had changed guards. It was during the middle watch of the night. Then Gideon and his men blew their trumpets and smashed their jars. 20 All three groups of Gideon's men blew their trumpets and smashed their jars. They held the torches in their left hands and the trumpets in their right hands. Then they shouted, "A sword for the LORD and for Gideon!" 21 Each of Gideon's men stayed in his place around the camp, but the Midianites began shouting and running to escape.

22 When Gideon's three hundred men blew their trumpets, the LORD made all the Midianites fight each other with their swords! The enemy army ran away to the city of Beth Shittah toward Zererah. They ran as far as the border of Abel Meholah, near the city of Tabbath. 23 Then men of Israel from Naphtali, Asher, and all of Manasseh were called out to chase the Midianites. 24 Gideon sent messengers through all the mountains of Ephraim, saying, "Come down and attack the Midianites. Take control of the Jordan River as far as Beth Barah before the Midianites can get to it."

So they called out all the men of Ephraim, who took control of the Jordan River as far as Beth Barah. 25 The men of Ephraim captured two princes of Midian named Oreb and Zeeb. They killed Oreb at the rock of Oreb and Zeeb at the winepress of Zeeb, and they continued chasing the Midianites. They brought the heads of Oreb and Zeeb to Gideon, who was east of the Jordan River.

8 The men of Ephraim asked Gideon, "Why did you treat us this way? Why didn't you call us when you went to fight against Midian?" They argued angrily with Gideon.

2 But he answered them, "I have not done as well as you! The small part you did was better than all that my people of Abiezer did. 3 God let you capture Oreb and Zeeb, the princes of Midian. How can I compare what I did with what you did?" When the men of Ephraim heard Gideon's answer, they were not as angry anymore.

Gideon Captures Two Kings

4 When Gideon and his three hundred men came to the Jordan River, they were tired, but they chased the enemy across to the other side. 5 Gideon said to the men of Succoth, "Please give my soldiers some bread because they are very tired. I am chasing Zebah and Zalmunna, the kings of Midian."

6 But the leaders of Succoth said, "Why should we give your soldiers bread? You haven't caught Zebah and Zalmunna yet."

7 Then Gideon said, "The LORD will surrender Zebah and Zalmunna to me. After that, I will whip your skin with thorns and briers from the desert."

8 Gideon left Succoth and went to the city of Peniel and asked them for food. But the people of Peniel gave him the same answer as the people of Succoth. 9 So Gideon said to the men of Peniel, "After I win the victory, I will return and pull down this tower."

10 Zebah and Zalmunna and their army were in the city of Karkor. About fifteen thousand men were left of the armies of the peoples of the east. Already one hundred twenty thousand soldiers had been killed. 11 Gideon went up the road of those who live in tents east of Nobah and Jogbehah, and he attacked the enemy army when they did not expect it. 12 Zebah and Zalmunna, the kings of Midian, ran away, but Gideon chased and captured them and frightened away their army.

13 Then Gideon son of Joash returned from the battle by the Pass of Heres. 14 Gideon captured a young man from Succoth and asked him some questions. So the young man wrote down for Gideon the names of seventy-seven officers and older leaders of Succoth.

Gideon Punishes Succoth

15 When Gideon came to Succoth, he said to the people of that city, "Here are Zebah and Zalmunna. You made fun of me by saying, 'Why should we give bread to your tired men? You have not caught Zebah and Zalmunna yet.'" 16 So Gideon took the older leaders of the city and punished them with thorns and briers from the desert. 17 He also pulled down the tower of Peniel and killed the people in that city.

18 Gideon asked Zebah and Zalmunna, "What were the men like that you killed on Mount Tabor?"

They answered, "They were like you. Each one of them looked like a prince."

19 Gideon said, "Those were my brothers, my mother's sons. As surely as the LORD lives, I would not kill you if you had spared them." 20 Then Gideon said to Jether, his oldest son, "Kill them." But Jether was only a boy and was afraid, so he did not take out his sword.

21 Then Zebah and Zalmunna said to Gideon, "Come on. Kill us yourself. As the saying goes, 'It takes a man to do a man's job.'" So Gideon got up and killed Zebah and Zalmunna and took the decorations off their camels' necks.

SALT

LEVITICUS 2:13 OR NUMBERS 18:19

What does salt symbolize in the Bible? Why was salt offered with every sacrifice? Why does Jesus call his followers "the salt of the earth"?

Like clean drinking water and efficient sanitation systems, salt is a very important ingredient of life that most people today take for granted. In Bible times, even though salt was available and affordable to everyone, it was more valuable and appreciated than it is to people today. The harvesting and transport of salt was often taxed by the governments of that day. Salt was harvested from pits or low-lying areas where the heat of the sun had evaporated the collected water, a process called salinization. The coastal areas of the Mediterranean Sea and the areas surrounding the Dead Sea were locations for the harvesting of salt. By means of a pick or tool, the salt could be broken into small pieces, which could then be loaded onto camels to be taken to marketplaces in surrounding cities or distant lands. The properties of salt lead to its association with several themes in the Bible, some peculiar to readers today. Salt is beneficial to people because it can be used to preserve and season food (Job 6:6; Matthew 5:13). However, too much salt may cause death to people and animals and makes the ground and water unfit to support life. This is why "salt" has both positive and negative connotations in the Bible.

The Dead Sea and the surrounding region were apparently once fertile and populated. Genesis 14 records an ancient battle among nine kings who ruled cities in what is now the Salt or Dead Sea. Of these cities, the most recognizable to Bible readers today are Sodom and Gomorrah. Abraham's nephew Lot chose to live in these cities because they had much water and good grazing lands for his sheep (Genesis 13:8–13). Due to the sins of the citizens of these cities, God destroyed them with fire. Lot and his family escaped, but his wife became a pillar of salt when she disobeyed God's command not to look back at the cities after they left them (Genesis 19:24–26). Her punishment is fitting because the places occupied by these cities now lie underneath a sea of salt water. In warfare, armies punished their enemies by making their enemies' lands unusable. After Abimelech destroyed the city of Shechem, he sowed the land of the city with salt (Judges 9:45).

Salt can also be symbol of blessing and favor in the Bible. The first few chapters of Leviticus concern the proper offerings that are to be made to God and the proper way to make those offerings. The passage here states, "Salt stands for your agreement with God that will last forever . . ." and commands, "You must add salt to all your offerings" (Leviticus 2:13). The use of salt as a food preservative is probably the basis for its symbolism in the sacrifice as a sign that the agreement between God and Israel is to last forever. This phrase "agreement of salt" also occurs in Numbers 18:19, though there it refers to the agreement between the LORD and Aaron and his family (the priests). Salt implies that the parties must remain loyal to the agreement (2 Chronicles 13:5–7).

Second Kings 2:20–21 speaks of a time when the prophet Elisha "healed" a spring near Jericho, which was unable to grow crops due to bad water. Elisha throws salt in the spring and God heals the water. The salt symbolizes God's blessing. In Ezekiel 16:4, a very interesting use of salt is mentioned. God compares Jerusalem's beginnings to an unwanted infant. An unwanted infant was not washed with water, rubbed with salt, or wrapped in cloths. Apparently the practice of the people was to rub their newborn children with salt to bless and protect them.

From these positive and negative aspects of salt, come the spiritual meaning of salt that Jesus uses in his teaching. When Jesus calls his followers "the salt of the earth," he reminds them that they are God's blessing and have a responsibility to bless and make peace with the people and world around them by remaining loyal to God. He also warns the people that "if the salt loses its salty taste, you cannot make it salty again. It is good for nothing except to be thrown out and walked on" (Matthew 5:13). This means that if the people do not remain loyal to God and to each other, they lose God's blessing and can no longer be a blessing. When he warns then that such salt is only good for being thrown out and walked on, he probably means that it is no longer useful to bless or enhance anything, but only to curse the ground. Nothing could grow there, but at least people could walk on the useless soil.

Salt: For additional scriptures on this topic go to Genesis 19:26.

SACRIFICE

LEVITICUS 4:29

What is a sacrifice? What are the different types of sacrifices? What was their purpose? Why is Jesus' death called a sacrifice? Do we offer sacrifices today?

Sacrifice has the idea of giving something valuable to God. In Bible times, most people were farmers. Therefore, food items were given as things of value for sacrifice — grain, olive oil, wine, and animals. Some offerings were burned, others were eaten, still others were poured out as drink offerings (Genesis 28:18; 35:14; Leviticus 23:13; Numbers 15:5; 28:7;Philippians 2:17). Whatever people gave to God, it was always to be from the best that they had(Leviticus 22:19; Deuteronomy 26:2). However, God's people often tried to give him their leftovers which made God very unhappy with them (Malachi 1:8; Isaiah 1:11–15). Because of how good God is, we should always give him our very best.

How long have people been offering sacrifices? The offering of sacrifices seems to be as old as humankind itself. God killed animals to clothe Adam and Eve after they had sinned (Genesis3:21). The deaths of the animals point to the serious nature of sin. Also, Cain and Abel's sacrifices (Genesis 4:3–4) indicate that the offering of sacrifices was common at that time. Why are there different kinds of sacrifices and what are they? During the time of Moses, God's people something special about their friendship with God. There are basically three different groups of sacrifices: gift/present offerings, fellowship/friendship offerings (see"Fellowship"), and sin/guilt offerings (see "Sin," "Guilt"). The first group, gift/present offerings, involves giving special presents to God. In everything that a person offered to God, he or she had to realize that every good thing comes from God (Deuteronomy 26:1–10; 1 Chronicles 29:10–19; see James 1:17). The burnt (or whole) offering was a special kind of present because all of the sacrifice was burned up and given over to God. It more than any other pictured the most generous giving (Leviticus 1:1–17; 6:8–13). There was also a special gift or free-will offering. In this offering, a person showed special loyalty or devotion to God by giving him gifts above what the rules required (Exodus 35:27–29; Deuteronomy 12:17, 16:10; 23:23; 2 Chronicles 31:14; 35:8). These sacrifices teach us that God wants his people to give generously and completely of themselves in serving him. This kind of service might include the giving of our time and special abilities he has given us, as well as the giving of our money in supporting his work. The second group—fellowship offerings—concerns friendship between people and friendship with God. In this offering, the people making the offerings along with the priest share the sacrifice as a meal in God's presence (1 Samuel 1:4–5, see also verse 9). There were basically two kinds of friendship offerings: peace offerings and thank offerings. The peace offering pictured friendship between God's people and friendship with God. Christians take part in a special friendship meal today, the Lord's Supper (see note: 1 Corinthians 11:23). In the thank offering, the person making the sacrifice gave thanks to God for special blessings received (2 Chronicles 33:16; Psalms 50:14; 107:22; 116:17). The third group of sacrifices, sin/guilt offerings, is concerned with being made right with God when a person has done something wrong. Sin hurts a person's friendship with God. In Bible times, when a person did something wrong, he brought a bloody sacrifice (Leviticus 4:29). This was a teaching picture of how bad sin is. The only thing that can make things right and make God happy again is for the person to admit to God how bad his or her sin is (Proverbs 28:13; 1 John 1:9). The guilt offering was given when a person did something wrong to someone else (Leviticus 4:1–5). This offering teaches that the person who did the wrong must make things right with the person who was wronged.

Why don't we have sacrifices today? The sacrifices in the Old Testament were not enough to bring complete salvation. Thankfully, a time came when God expressed his love to us in a very special way. He offered a way for us to be made right with him by sacrificing his special only Son (John 3:16). This sacrifice is the only one which makes God completely happy. Jesus' sacrifice on the cross is a once-and-for-all-time offering for sin (Hebrews 9:12). No more sin offerings are needed.

Are there sacrifices that the Christian can offer today? The New Testament uses the language of sacrifices to describe what God wants from the Christian. Instead of animal sacrifices, the Christian is to give spiritual service to God (Ephesians 5:2; Philippians 4:18; 1 Peter 2:5). He wants a sacrifice from us in the form of living service (see note, Romans 12:1).

Sacrifice: For additional scriptures on this topic go to Genesis 3:21.

Gideon Makes an Idol

22The people of Israel said to Gideon, "You
saved us from the Midianites. Now, we want you
and your son and your grandson to rule over us."
23But Gideon told them, "The LORD will be your
ruler. I will not rule over you, nor will my son rule
over you." 24He said, "I want you to do this one
thing for me. I want each of you to give me a gold
earring from the things you took in the fighting."
(The Ishmaelites wore gold earrings.)
25They said, "We will gladly give you what you
want." So they spread out a coat, and everyone
threw down an earring from what he had taken.
26The gold earrings weighed about forty-three
pounds. This did not count the decorations, necklaces, and purple robes worn by the kings of
Midian, nor the chains from the camels' necks.
27Gideon used the gold to make a holy vest, which
he put in his hometown of Ophrah. But all the
Israelites were unfaithful to God and worshiped it,
so it became a trap for Gideon and his family.

The Death of Gideon

28So Midian was under the rule of Israel; they
did not cause trouble anymore. And the land had
peace for forty years, as long as Gideon was alive.
29Gideon son of Joash went to his home to live.
30He had seventy sons of his own, because he had
many wives. 31He had a slave woman who lived
in Shechem, and he had a son by her, whom he
named Abimelech. 32So Gideon son of Joash died
at a good old age. He was buried in the tomb of
Joash, his father, in Ophrah, where the Abiezrites
live.
33As soon as Gideon died, the people of Israel
were again unfaithful to God and followed the
Baals. They made Baal-Berith their god. 34The
Israelites did not remember the LORD their God,
who had saved them from all their enemies living
all around them. 35And they were not kind to the
family of Jerub-Baal, also called Gideon, for all the
good he had done for Israel.

Abimelech Becomes King

9 Abimelech son of Gideon went to his uncles
in the city of Shechem. He said to his uncles
and all of his mother's family group, 2"Ask the
leaders of Shechem, 'Is it better for the seventy
sons of Gideon to rule over you or for one man to
rule?' Remember, I am your relative."
3Abimelech's uncles spoke to all the leaders of
Shechem about this. And they decided to follow
Abimelech, because they said, "He is our relative."
4So the leaders of Shechem gave Abimelech about
one and three-quarter pounds of silver from the
temple of the god Baal-Berith. Abimelech used
the silver to hire some worthless, reckless men,
who followed him wherever he went. 5He went to
Ophrah, the hometown of his father, and murdered
his seventy brothers, the sons of Gideon. He killed
them all on one stone. But Gideon's youngest son,
Jotham, hid from Abimelech and escaped. 6Then
all of the leaders of Shechem and Beth Millo gathered beside the great tree standing in Shechem.
There they made Abimelech their king.

Jotham's Story

7When Jotham heard this, he went and stood
on the top of Mount Gerizim. He shouted to the
people: "Listen to me, you leaders of Shechem, so
that God will listen to you! 8One day the trees
decided to appoint a king to rule over them. They
said to the olive tree, 'You be king over us!'
9"But the olive tree said, 'Men and gods are
honored by my oil. Should I stop making it and go
and sway over the other trees?'
10"Then the trees said to the fig tree, 'Come
and be king over us!'
11"But the fig tree answered, 'Should I stop
making my sweet and good fruit and go and sway
over the other trees?'
12"Then the trees said to the vine, 'Come and
be king over us!'
13"But the vine answered, 'My new wine makes
men and gods happy. Should I stop making it and
go and sway over the trees?'
14"Then all the trees said to the thornbush,
'Come and be king over us.'
15"But the thornbush said to the trees, 'If you
really want to appoint me king over you, come
and find shelter in my shade! But if not, let fire
come out of the thornbush and burn up the cedars
of Lebanon!'
16"Now, were you completely honest and sincere
when you made Abimelech king? Have you been
fair to Gideon and his family? Have you treated
Gideon as you should? 17Remember, my father
fought for you and risked his life to save you from
the power of the Midianites. 18But now you have
turned against my father's family and have killed
his seventy sons on one stone. You have made
Abimelech, the son of my father's slave girl, king
over the leaders of Shechem just because he is
your relative! 19So then, if you have been honest
and sincere to Gideon and his family today, be

8:24 *Gideon.* Also called Jerub-Baal.
8:24 *Ishmaelites.* Another name for the Midianites.
See Genesis 37:25–28.

9:15 Proverb: 1 Kings 4:29–34

happy with Abimelech as your king. And may he be happy with you! 20But if not, may fire come out of Abimelech and completely burn you leaders of Shechem and Beth Millo! Also may fire come out of the leaders of Shechem and Beth Millo and burn up Abimelech!"

21Then Jotham ran away and escaped to the city of Beer. He lived there because he was afraid of his brother Abimelech.

Abimelech Fights Against Shechem

22Abimelech ruled Israel for three years. 23Then God sent an evil spirit to make trouble between Abimelech and the leaders of Shechem so that the leaders of Shechem turned against him. 24Abimelech had killed Gideon's seventy sons, his own brothers, and the leaders of Shechem had helped him. So God sent the evil spirit to punish them. 25The leaders of Shechem were against Abimelech then. They put men on the hilltops in ambush who robbed everyone going by. And Abimelech was told.

26A man named Gaal son of Ebed and his brothers moved into Shechem, and the leaders of Shechem trusted him. 27They went out to the vineyards to pick grapes, and they squeezed the grapes. Then they had a feast in the temple of their god, where they ate and drank and cursed Abimelech. 28Gaal son of Ebed said, "We are the men of Shechem. Who is Abimelech that we should serve him? Isn't he one of Gideon's sons, and isn't Zebul his officer? We should serve the men of Hamor, Shechem's father. Why should we serve Abimelech? 29If you made me commander of these people, I would get rid of Abimelech. I would say to him, 'Get your army ready and come out to battle.'"

30Now when Zebul, the ruler of Shechem, heard what Gaal son of Ebed said, he was very angry. 31He sent secret messengers to Abimelech, saying, "Gaal son of Ebed and Gaal's brothers have come to Shechem, and they are turning the city against you! 32You and your men should get up during the night and hide in the fields outside the city. 33As soon as the sun comes up in the morning, attack the city. When Gaal and his men come out to fight you, do what you can to them."

34So Abimelech and all his soldiers got up during the night and hid near Shechem in four groups. 35Gaal son of Ebed went out and was standing at the entrance to the city gate. As he was standing there, Abimelech and his soldiers came out of their hiding places.

36When Gaal saw the soldiers, he said to Zebul, "Look! There are people coming down from the mountains!"

But Zebul said, "You are seeing the shadows of the mountains. The shadows just look like people."

37But again Gaal said, "Look, there are people coming down from the center of the land, and there is a group coming from the fortune-tellers' tree!"

38Zebul said to Gaal, "Where is your bragging now? You said, 'Who is Abimelech that we should serve him?' You made fun of these men. Now go out and fight them."

39So Gaal led the men of Shechem out to fight Abimelech. 40Abimelech and his men chased them, and many of Gaal's men were killed before they could get back to the city gate. 41While Abimelech stayed at Arumah, Zebul forced Gaal and his brothers to leave Shechem.

42The next day the people of Shechem went out to the fields. When Abimelech was told about it, 43he separated his men into three groups and hid them in the fields. When he saw the people coming out of the city, he jumped up and attacked them. 44Abimelech and his group ran to the entrance gate to the city. The other two groups ran out to the people in the fields and struck them down. 45Abimelech and his men fought the city of Shechem all day until they captured it and killed its people. Then he tore it down and threw salt over the ruins.

The Tower of Shechem Burns

46When the leaders who were in the Tower of Shechem heard what had happened to Shechem, they gathered in the safest room of the temple of El Berith. 47Abimelech heard that all the leaders of the Tower of Shechem had gathered there. 48So he and all his men went up Mount Zalmon, near Shechem. Abimelech took an ax and cut some branches and put them on his shoulders. He said to all those with him, "Hurry! Do what I have done!" 49So all those men cut branches and followed Abimelech and piled them against the safest room of the temple. Then they set them on fire and burned the people inside. So all the people who were at the Tower of Shechem also died—about a thousand men and women.

Abimelech's Death

50Then Abimelech went to the city of Thebez. He surrounded the city, attacked it, and captured it. 51But inside the city was a strong tower, so all the men, women, and leaders of that city ran to the

9:24 *Gideon* See note at 8:22.
9:45 *salt.* The salt would keep crops from growing there.

9:45 Salt: 2 Kings 2:20

tower. When they got inside, they locked the door
behind them. Then they climbed up to the roof of
the tower. 52Abimelech came to the tower to attack
it. He approached the door of the tower to set it
on fire, 53but as he came near, a woman dropped
a grinding stone on his head, crushing his skull.
54He quickly called to the officer who carried
his armor and said, "Take out your sword and kill
me. I don't want people to say, 'A woman killed
Abimelech.'" So the officer stabbed Abimelech,
and he died. 55When the people of Israel saw
Abimelech was dead, they all returned home.
56In that way God punished Abimelech for all
the evil he had done to his father by killing his
seventy brothers. 57God also punished the men of
Shechem for the evil they had done. So the curse
spoken by Jotham, the youngest son of Gideon,
came true.

Tola, the Judge

10 After Abimelech died, another judge came
to save Israel. He was Tola son of Puah, the
son of Dodo. Tola was from the people of Issachar
and lived in the city of Shamir in the mountains of
Ephraim. 2Tola was a judge for Israel for twenty-
three years. Then he died and was buried in
Shamir.

Jair, the Judge

3After Tola died, Jair from the region of Gilead
became judge. He was a judge for Israel for twenty-
two years. 4Jair had thirty sons, who rode thirty
donkeys. These thirty sons controlled thirty towns
in Gilead, which are called the Towns of Jair to this
day. 5Jair died and was buried in the city of Kamon.

The Ammonites Trouble Israel

6Again the Israelites did what the LORD said
was wrong. They worshiped Baal and Ashtoreth,
the gods of Aram, Sidon, Moab, and Ammon, and
the gods of the Philistines. The Israelites left the
LORD and stopped serving him. 7So the LORD was
angry with them and handed them over to the
Philistines and the Ammonites. 8In the same year
those people destroyed the Israelites who lived
east of the Jordan River in the region of Gilead,
where the Amorites lived. So the Israelites suffered
for eighteen years. 9The Ammonites then crossed
the Jordan River to fight the people of Judah,
Benjamin, and Ephraim, causing much trouble to
the people of Israel. 10So the Israelites cried out to
the LORD, "We have sinned against you. We left our
God and worshiped the Baal idols."

11The LORD answered the Israelites, "When the
Egyptians, Amorites, Ammonites, Philistines,
12Sidonians, Amalekites, and Maonites were
cruel to you, you cried out to me, and I saved you.
13But now you have left me again and have worshiped other gods. So I refuse to save you again.
14You have chosen those gods. So go call to them for
help. Let them save you when you are in trouble."
15But the people of Israel said to the LORD, "We
have sinned. Do to us whatever you want, but
please save us today!" 16Then the Israelites threw
away the foreign gods among them, and they
worshiped the LORD again. So he felt sorry for
them when he saw their suffering.
17The Ammonites gathered for war and
camped in Gilead. The Israelites gathered and
camped at Mizpah. 18The leaders of the people of
Gilead said, "Who will lead us to attack the
Ammonites? He will become the head of all those
who live in Gilead."

Jephthah Is Chosen as Leader

11 Jephthah was a strong soldier from Gilead.
His father was named Gilead, and his mother
was a prostitute. 2Gilead's wife had several sons.
When they grew up, they forced Jephthah to leave
his home, saying to him, "You will not get any of
our father's property, because you are the son of
another woman." 3So Jephthah ran away from his
brothers and lived in the land of Tob. There some
worthless men began to follow him.
4After a time the Ammonites fought against
Israel. 5When the Ammonites made war against
Israel, the older leaders of Gilead went to Jephthah to bring him back from Tob. 6They said to
him, "Come and lead our army so we can fight
the Ammonites."
7But Jephthah said to them, "Didn't you hate me?
You forced me to leave my father's house. Why are
you coming to me now that you are in trouble?"
8The older leaders of Gilead said to Jephthah,
"It is because of those troubles that we come to
you now. Please come with us and fight against
the Ammonites. You will be the ruler over everyone who lives in Gilead."
9Then Jephthah answered, "If you take me
back to Gilead to fight the Ammonites and the
LORD helps me win, I will be your ruler."
10The older leaders of Gilead said to him, "The
LORD is listening to everything we are saying. We
promise to do all that you tell us to do." 11So
Jephthah went with the older leaders of Gilead,

9:57 *Gideon.* Also called Jerub-Baal.

10:4 *donkeys.* During some periods of Israel's history, the donkey was a status symbol.

and the people made him their leader and commander of their army. Jephthah repeated all of his
words in front of the LORD at Mizpah.

Jephthah Sends Messengers to the Ammonite King

12Jephthah sent messengers to the king of the
Ammonites, asking, "What have you got against
Israel? Why have you come to attack our land?"
13The king of the Ammonites answered the
messengers of Jephthah, "We are fighting Israel
because you took our land when you came up
from Egypt. You took our land from the Arnon
River to the Jabbok River to the Jordan River.
Now give our land back to us peacefully."
14Jephthah sent the messengers to the Ammonite
king again. 15They said:
"This is what Jephthah says: Israel did not take
the land of the people of Moab or Ammon.
16When the Israelites came out of Egypt, they
went into the desert to the Red Sea and then to
Kadesh. 17Israel sent messengers to the king of
Edom, saying, 'Let the people of Israel go across
your land.' But the king of Edom refused. We sent
the same message to the king of Moab, but he
also refused. So the Israelites stayed at Kadesh.
18"Then the Israelites went into the desert
around the borders of the lands of Edom and
Moab. Israel went east of the land of Moab and
camped on the other side of the Arnon River, the
border of Moab. They did not cross it to go into
the land of Moab.
19"Then Israel sent messengers to Sihon king
of the Amorites, king of the city of Heshbon, asking, 'Let the people of Israel pass through your land
to go to our land.' 20But Sihon did not trust the
Israelites to cross his land. So he gathered all of his
people and camped at Jahaz and fought with Israel.
21"But the LORD, the God of Israel, handed
Sihon and his army over to Israel. All the land of
the Amorites became the property of Israel. 22So
Israel took all the land of the Amorites from the
Arnon River to the Jabbok River, from the desert
to the Jordan River.
23"It was the LORD, the God of Israel, who
forced out the Amorites ahead of the people of
Israel. So do you think you can make them leave?
24Take the land that your god Chemosh has given
you. We will live in the land the LORD our God
has given us!
25"Are you any better than Balak son of Zippor,
king of Moab? Did he ever quarrel or fight with
the people of Israel? 26For three hundred years
the Israelites have lived in Heshbon and Aroer
and the towns around them and in all the cities
along the Arnon River. Why have you not taken
these cities back in all that time? 27I have not
sinned against you, but you are sinning against
me by making war on me. May the LORD, the
Judge, decide whether the Israelites or the
Ammonites are right."
28But the king of the Ammonites ignored this
message from Jephthah.

Jephthah's Promise

29Then the Spirit of the LORD entered Jephthah.
Jephthah passed through Gilead and Manasseh
and the city of Mizpah in Gilead to the land of the
Ammonites. 30Jephthah made a promise to the
LORD, saying, "If you will hand over the Ammonites to me, 31I will give you as a burnt offering the
first thing that comes out of my house to meet me
when I return from the victory. It will be the
LORD's."
32Then Jephthah went over to fight the
Ammonites, and the LORD handed them over to
him. 33In a great defeat Jephthah struck them
down from the city of Aroer to the area of
Minnith, and twenty cities as far as the city of
Abel Keramim. So the Ammonites were defeated
by the Israelites.
34When Jephthah returned to his home in
Mizpah, his daughter was the first one to come
out to meet him, playing a tambourine and dancing. She was his only child; he had no other sons
or daughters. 35When Jephthah saw his daughter, he tore his clothes to show his sorrow. He
said, "My daughter! You have made me so sad
because I made a promise to the LORD, and I cannot break it!"
36Then his daughter said, "Father, you made
a promise to the LORD. So do to me just what
you promised, because the LORD helped you
defeat your enemies, the Ammonites." 37She
also said, "But let me do one thing. Let me be
alone for two months to go to the mountains.
Since I will never marry, let me and my friends
go and cry together."
38Jephthah said, "Go." So he sent her away
for two months. She and her friends stayed in

11:29–40 In making his vow Jephthah made two errors: (1) he did not need to make any vow—the LORD was already with him (verse 29), and (2) he did not think carefully about the possible outcome of his vow. Jephthah's vow turned out to be tragic, as he was forced to sacrifice his only daughter. God does not condone human sacrifice (Leviticus 18:21; Deuteronomy 12:31). Many of the examples in the Book of Judges are meant to be avoided, not emulated.

11:31 *burnt offering.* While some interpreters try to downplay the reference, it does appear that Jephthah committed himself to provide such a burnt offering and actually sacrificed his daughter in this way.

the mountains and cried for her because she would never marry. [39]After two months she returned to her father, and Jephthah did to her what he had promised. Jephthah's daughter never had a husband.

From this came a custom in Israel that [40]every year the young women of Israel would go out for four days to remember the daughter of Jephthah from Gilead.

Jephthah and Ephraim

12 The men of Ephraim called all their soldiers together and crossed the river to the town of Zaphon. They said to Jephthah, "Why didn't you call us to help you fight the Ammonites? We will burn your house down with you in it."

[2]Jephthah answered them, "My people and I fought a great battle against the Ammonites. I called you, but you didn't come to help me. [3]When I saw that you would not help me, I risked my own life and went against the Ammonites. The LORD handed them over to me. So why have you come to fight against me today?"

[4]Then Jephthah called the men of Gilead together and fought the men of Ephraim. The men of Gilead struck them down because the Ephraimites had said, "You men of Gilead are nothing but deserters from Ephraim—living between Ephraim and Manasseh." [5]The men of Gilead captured the crossings of the Jordan River that led to the country of Ephraim. A person from Ephraim trying to escape would say, "Let me cross the river." Then the men of Gilead would ask him, "Are you from Ephraim?" If he replied no, [6]they would say to him, "Say the word 'Shibboleth.'" The men of Ephraim could not say that word correctly. So if the person from Ephraim said, "Sibboleth," the men of Gilead would kill him at the crossing. So forty-two thousand people from Ephraim were killed at that time.

[7]Jephthah was a judge for Israel for six years. Then Jephthah, the man from Gilead, died and was buried in a town in Gilead.

Ibzan, the Judge

[8]After Jephthah died, Ibzan from Bethlehem was a judge for Israel. [9]He had thirty sons and thirty daughters. He let his daughters marry men who were not in his family group, and he brought thirty women who were not in his tribe to be wives for his sons. Ibzan judged

Relief of a Philistine

Israel for seven years. [10]Then he died and was buried in Bethlehem.

Elon, the Judge

[11]After Ibzan died, Elon from the tribe of Zebulun was a judge for Israel. He judged Israel for ten years. [12]Then Elon, the man of Zebulun, died and was buried in the city of Aijalon in the land of Zebulun.

Abdon, the Judge

[13]After Elon died, Abdon son of Hillel from the city of Pirathon was a judge for Israel. [14]He had forty sons and thirty grandsons, who rode on seventy donkeys. He judged Israel for eight years. [15]Then Abdon son of Hillel died and was buried in Pirathon in the land of Ephraim, in the mountains where the Amalekites lived.

The Birth of Samson

13 Again the people of Israel did what the LORD said was wrong. So he handed them over to the Philistines for forty years.

[2]There was a man named Manoah from the tribe of Dan, who lived in the city of Zorah. He had a wife, but she could not have children. [3]The angel of the LORD appeared to Manoah's wife and said, "You have not been able to have children, but you will become pregnant and give birth to a son. [4]Be careful not to drink wine or beer or eat anything that is unclean, [5]because you will become

12:6 *Shibboleth.* Jephthah used what was obviously a difference in speech between tribes to identify those who were from Ephraim. It would be similar to the difference between the dialects of a northerner and a southerner in the same country.

12:14 *donkeys.* See 10:4.

13:5 *Nazirite.* The Nazirite vow is described in Numbers 6:1–21. A Nazirite was one who was dedicated to the Lord in a special way.

pregnant and have a son. You must never cut his
hair, because he will be a Nazirite, given to God
from birth. He will begin to save Israel from the
power of the Philistines."
6Then Manoah's wife went to him and told him
what had happened. She said, "A man from God
came to me. He looked like an angel from God;
his appearance was frightening. I didn't ask him
where he was from, and he didn't tell me his
name. 7But he said to me, 'You will become pregnant and will have a son. Don't drink wine or
beer or eat anything that is unclean, because the
boy will be a Nazirite to God from his birth until
the day of his death.'"
8Then Manoah prayed to the LORD: "Lord, I beg
you to let the man of God come to us again. Let
him teach us what we should do for the boy who
will be born to us."
9God heard Manoah's prayer, and the angel of
God came to Manoah's wife again while she was
sitting in the field. But her husband Manoah
was not with her. 10So she ran to tell him, "He
is here! The man who appeared to me the other
day is here!"
11Manoah got up and followed his wife. When
he came to the man, he said, "Are you the man
who spoke to my wife?"
The man said, "I am."
12So Manoah asked, "When what you say happens, what kind of life should the boy live? What
should he do?"
13The angel of the LORD said, "Your wife must be
careful to do everything I told her to do. 14She must
not eat anything that grows on a grapevine, or drink
any wine or beer, or eat anything that is unclean.
She must do everything I have commanded her."
15Manoah said to the angel of the LORD, "We
would like you to stay awhile so we can cook a
young goat for you."
16The angel of the LORD answered, "Even if I
stay awhile, I would not eat your food. But if you
want to prepare something, offer a burnt offering
to the LORD." (Manoah did not understand that
the man was really the angel of the LORD.)
17Then Manoah asked the angel of the LORD,
"What is your name? Then we will honor you
when what you have said really happens."
18The angel of the LORD said, "Why do you ask
my name? It is too amazing for you to understand."
19So Manoah sacrificed a young goat on a rock
and offered some grain as a gift to the LORD. Then
an amazing thing happened as Manoah and his
wife watched. 20The flames went up to the sky
from the altar. As the fire burned, the angel of the
LORD went up to heaven in the flame. When
Manoah and his wife saw that, they bowed facedown on the ground. 21The angel of the LORD did
not appear to them again. Then Manoah understood that the man was really the angel of the
LORD. 22Manoah said, "We have seen God, so we
will surely die."
23But his wife said to him, "If the LORD wanted
to kill us, he would not have accepted our burnt
offering or grain offering. He would not have
shown us all these things or told us all this."
24So the woman gave birth to a boy and named
him Samson. He grew, and the LORD blessed him.
25The Spirit of the LORD began to work in Samson
while he was in the city of Mahaneh Dan,
between the cities of Zorah and Eshtaol.

Samson's First Marriage

14 Samson went down to the city of Timnah
where he saw a Philistine woman. 2When
he returned home, he said to his father and
mother, "I saw a Philistine woman in Timnah. I
want you to get her for me so I can marry her."
3His father and mother answered, "Surely
there is a woman from Israel you can marry. Do
you have to marry a woman from the Philistines,
who are not circumcised?"
But Samson said, "Get that woman for me! She
is the one I want!" 4(Samson's parents did not
know that the LORD wanted this to happen
because he was looking for a way to challenge the
Philistines, who were ruling over Israel at this
time.) 5Samson went down with his father and
mother to Timnah, as far as the vineyard near
there. Suddenly, a young lion came roaring
toward Samson! 6The Spirit of the LORD entered
Samson with great power, and he tore the lion
apart with his bare hands. For him it was as easy
as tearing apart a young goat. But Samson did not
tell his father or mother what he had done. 7Then
he went down to the city and talked to the
Philistine woman, and he liked her.
8Several days later Samson went back to marry
her. On his way he went over to look at the body
of the dead lion and found a swarm of bees and
honey in it. 9Samson got some of the honey with
his hands and walked along eating it. When he
came to his parents, he gave some to them. They
ate it, too, but Samson did not tell them he had
taken the honey from the body of the dead lion.

They were like lay priests, so it was a way for a non-Levite to draw close to God in service.

13:22 Angels: 2 Chronicles 18:18
13:25 Infertility (Childlessness/Barrenness): 1 Samuel 1:1–20

10Samson's father went down to see the Philistine woman. And Samson gave a feast, as was the custom for the bridegroom. 11When the people saw him, they sent thirty friends to be with him.

Samson's Riddle

12Samson said to them, "Let me tell you a riddle. Try to find the answer during the seven days of the feast. If you can, I will give you thirty linen shirts and thirty changes of clothes. 13But if you can't, you must give me thirty linen shirts and thirty changes of clothes."

So they said, "Tell us your riddle so we can hear it."

14Samson said,

"Out of the eater comes something to eat.
Out of the strong comes something sweet."

After three days, they had not found the answer.

15On the fourth day they said to Samson's wife, "Did you invite us here to make us poor? Trick your husband into telling us the answer to the riddle. If you don't, we will burn you and everyone in your father's house."

16So Samson's wife went to him, crying, and said, "You hate me! You don't really love me! You told my people a riddle, but you won't tell me the answer."

Samson said, "I haven't even told my father or mother. Why should I tell you?"

17Samson's wife cried for the rest of the seven days of the feast. So he finally gave her the answer on the seventh day, because she kept bothering him. Then she told her people the answer to the riddle.

18Before sunset on the seventh day of the feast, the Philistine men had the answer. They came to Samson and said,

"What is sweeter than honey?
What is stronger than a lion?"

Then Samson said to them,

"If you had not plowed with my young cow,
you would not have solved my riddle!"

19Then the Spirit of the LORD entered Samson and gave him great power. Samson went down to the city of Ashkelon and killed thirty of its men and took all that they had and gave the clothes to the men who had answered his riddle. Then he went to his father's house very angry. 20And Samson's wife was given to his best man.

Samson Troubles the Philistines

15 At the time of the wheat harvest, Samson went to visit his wife, taking a young goat with him. He said, "I'm going to my wife's room," but her father would not let him go in.

2He said to Samson, "I thought you really hated your wife, so I gave her to your best man. Her younger sister is more beautiful. Take her instead."

3But Samson said to them, "This time no one will blame me for hurting you Philistines!" 4So Samson went out and caught three hundred foxes. He took two foxes at a time, tied their tails together, and then tied a torch to the tails of each pair of foxes. 5After he lit the torches, he let the foxes loose in the grainfields of the Philistines so that he burned up their standing grain, the piles of grain, their vineyards, and their olive trees.

6The Philistines asked, "Who did this?"

Someone told them, "Samson, the son-in-law of the man from Timnah, did because his father-in-law gave his wife to his best man."

So the Philistines burned Samson's wife and her father to death. 7Then Samson said to the Philistines, "Since you did this, I won't stop until I pay you back!" 8Samson attacked the Philistines and killed many of them. Then he went down and stayed in a cave in the rock of Etam.

9The Philistines went up and camped in the land of Judah, near a place named Lehi. 10The men of Judah asked them, "Why have you come here to fight us?"

They answered, "We have come to make Samson our prisoner, to pay him back for what he did to our people."

11Then three thousand men of Judah went to the cave in the rock of Etam and said to Samson, "What have you done to us? Don't you know that the Philistines rule over us?"

Samson answered, "I only paid them back for what they did to me."

12Then they said to him, "We have come to tie you up and to hand you over to the Philistines."

Samson said to them, "Promise me you will not hurt me yourselves."

13The men from Judah said, "We agree. We will just tie you up and give you to the Philistines. We will not kill you." So they tied Samson with two new ropes and led him up from the cave in the rock. 14When Samson came to the place named Lehi, the Philistines came to meet him, shouting for joy. Then the Spirit of the LORD entered Samson and gave him great power. The ropes on him weakened like burned strings and fell off his hands! 15Samson found the jawbone of a dead donkey, took it, and killed a thousand men with it!

16Then Samson said,

"With a donkey's jawbone
I made donkeys out of them.

14:15 *fourth.* The Hebrew word is "seventh." Some old translations say "fourth," which fits the order of events better.

With a donkey's jawbone
I killed a thousand men!"
17 When he finished speaking, he threw away the
jawbone. So that place was named Ramath Lehi.
18 Samson was very thirsty, so he cried out to the
LORD, "You gave me, your servant, this great victory. Do I have to die of thirst now? Do I have to be
captured by people who are not circumcised?"
19 Then God opened up a hole in the ground at
Lehi, and water came out. When Samson drank,
he felt better; he felt strong again. So he named
that spring Caller's Spring, which is still in Lehi.
20 Samson judged Israel for twenty years in the
days of the Philistines.

Samson Goes to the City of Gaza

16 One day Samson went to Gaza and saw a
prostitute there. He went in to spend the
night with her. 2 When the people of Gaza heard,
"Samson has come here!" they surrounded the
place and waited for him near the city gate all
night. They whispered to each other, "When
dawn comes, we will kill Samson!"
3 But Samson only stayed with the prostitute
until midnight. Then he got up and took hold of
the doors and the two posts of the city gate and
tore them loose, along with the bar. He put them
on his shoulders and carried them to the top of
the hill that faces the city of Hebron.

Samson and Delilah

4 After this, Samson fell in love with a woman
named Delilah, who lived in the Valley of Sorek.
5 The Philistine rulers went to Delilah and said,
"Find out what makes Samson so strong. Trick him
into telling you how we can overpower him and
capture him and tie him up. If you do this, each one
of us will give you twenty-eight pounds of silver."
6 So Delilah said to Samson, "Tell me why you
are so strong. How can someone tie you up and
capture you?"
7 Samson answered, "Someone would have to
tie me up with seven new bowstrings that have
not been dried. Then I would be as weak as any
other man."
8 The Philistine rulers brought Delilah seven new
bowstrings that had not been dried, and she tied
Samson with them. 9 Some men were hiding in
another room. Delilah said to him, "Samson, the
Philistines are here!" But Samson broke the bowstrings like pieces of burned string. So the Philistines
did not find out the secret of Samson's strength.
10 Then Delilah said to Samson, "You made a fool
of me. You lied to me. Now tell me how someone
can tie you up."
11 Samson said, "They would have to tie me
with new ropes that have not been used before.
Then I would become as weak as any other man."
12 So Delilah took new ropes and tied Samson.
Some men were hiding in another room. She called
out to him, "Samson, the Philistines are here!" But
he broke the ropes as easily as if they were threads.
13 Then Delilah said to Samson, "Again you
have made a fool of me. You lied to me. Tell me
how someone can tie you up."
He said, "Using the loom, weave the seven
braids of my hair into the cloth, and tighten it with
a pin. Then I will be as weak as any other man."
While Samson slept, Delilah wove the seven
braids of his hair into the cloth. 14 Then she fastened it with a pin.
Again she said to him, "Samson, the Philistines
are here!" Samson woke up and pulled out the
pin and the loom with the cloth.
15 Then Delilah said to him, "How can you say,
'I love you,' when you don't even trust me? This
is the third time you have made a fool of me. You
haven't told me the secret of your great strength."
16 She kept bothering Samson about his secret day
after day until he felt he was going to die!
17 So he told her everything. He said, "I have
never had my hair cut, because I have been set
apart to God as a Nazirite since I was born. If
someone shaved my head, I would lose my
strength and be as weak as any other man."
18 When Delilah saw that he had told her everything sincerely, she sent a message to the
Philistine rulers. She said, "Come back one more
time, because he has told me everything." So the
Philistine rulers came back to Delilah and
brought the silver with them. 19 Delilah got
Samson to sleep, lying in her lap. Then she called
in a man to shave off the seven braids of Samson's
hair. In this way she began to make him weak,
and his strength left him.
20 Then she said, "Samson, the Philistines are
here!"
He woke up and thought, "I'll leave as I did
before and shake myself free." But he did not know
that the LORD had left him.

15:17 *Ramath Lehi.* This name means Jawbone Hill.

15:18 Complaint/Lament/Protest: Job 3

16:7 *bowstrings.* The Hebrew word makes it clear that this string was made out of the gut of animals. It should be remembered that a Nazirite was not allowed to touch any dead animal. Samson is already playing loose with his Nazirite vow.

16:13 *loom.* A machine for making cloth from thread.

16:17 *hair cut.* A Nazirite (Numbers 6:1–21) was not permitted to cut his hair.

Clean & Unclean

Leviticus 11

How are these words used in the Old Testament?
How does the coming of Christ affect the Christian understanding of what is clean and what is unclean?

Clean and unclean are terms that describe those things that are pleasing and acceptable to God on the one hand, or displeasing and unacceptable to him on the other. These classifications can be applied to animals, objects, practices, or people.

The distinction between clean and unclean animals first occurs in the Old Testament at the time of the Flood (Genesis 7:2–3, 8). This distinction continues and is described in detail in the laws about food that God later gave to the Israelites (Leviticus 11). These laws establishing a difference between clean and unclean animals point to the difference God was establishing between Israel and the other nations who did not worship him (Leviticus 20:25–26).

The difference between the categories of clean and unclean also points toward the difference between the ultimate cleanness, or holiness, of God and the uncleanness of sin and its effects.

When sin entered the world because of Adam and Eve's disobedience to God's command (Genesis 3), the perfect order of creation was disrupted and all sorts of harmful consequences followed. In the Old Testament, these harmful consequences of sin are classified as unclean, and include bleeding associated with childbirth and menstruation (Leviticus 12), infectious skin diseases (Leviticus 13:1–46), mildew (Leviticus 13:47–59), bodily discharges (Leviticus 15), and a dead person or animal (Leviticus 11:24, 39; Numbers 19:11). Anyone or anything that came into contact with these things was also considered unclean. Therefore, a person could become unclean without actually having committed any sinful act.

Those who found themselves in such an unclean state were not allowed to participate in the ceremonies of the sanctuary, but had to remain separated from the rest of the community. Usually, however, they could take steps to make themselves clean again. These involved a time of separation from the community, washing with water, and offering certain sacrifices.

Besides the uncleanness produced by the effects of sin in the world, there is also the uncleanness that arises from sin itself. Sin causes a separation between the individual and God. Sacrifices were prescribed to restore the broken fellowship and provide for the removal of the guilt of sin. Chief among these were those performed on the annual Day of Cleansing (Leviticus 16). On this day animals were sacrificed and their blood was sprinkled on and in front of the lid of the Ark. The sins of the people were confessed over a scapegoat that was then led out into the wilderness, symbolizing the removal of the sins of the people from their midst. These action cleansed the people so that they would again be acceptable and pleasing to the Lord (Leviticus 16:30). But all of these sacrifices of the Old Testament had no lasting effect and had to be performed repeatedly.

The measures taken in the Old Testament to remove the guilt of sin find their ultimate expression in the work of Christ. Sin has caused an uncleanness in all of us which makes us displeasing and unacceptable to God (Romans 3:9–18). As a result, we are separated from God and the community of his people. In the Old Testament, washing with water and the performance of sacrifices were necessary to become clean again. In the New Testament those temporary actions find a perfect and final realization in the sacrifice of Christ, who "used the word to make the church clean by washing it with water" (Ephesians 5:26). There is no longer any need to make repeated sacrifices for the removal of the guilt of sin because the perfect sacrifice of Christ is more than sufficient to take away the sins of the world once for all (Hebrews 10:1–18). Therefore, those who trust in Christ as the perfect sacrifice for their uncleanness can now draw near to God with confidence, knowing that they have been cleansed (Hebrews 10:22).

Clean & Unclean: For additional scriptures on this topic go to Leviticus 12–16.

CELEBRATION

LEVITICUS 23

What is celebrated in the Bible?
What do we celebrate today?

We have many different types of celebration today. We celebrate religious holidays like Christmas and Easter, and other non-religious events like birthdays. What does the Bible say about celebrations, and does it have anything to say about our own practice today?

Celebrations with special religious significance were established at set times for the nation of Israel. Leviticus 23:1 calls them "the Lord's appointed feasts." These included the weekly Sabbath, the Passover or the Feast of Unleavened Bread, the Feast of the Harvest, the Feast of Weeks, the Feast of Trumpets, the Day of Cleansing, and the Feast of Shelters. All these feasts, except the Feast of the Harvest, had a day of no work and a holy meeting. They also included offerings to the Lord. At three of these feasts (Unleavened Bread, Weeks, and Shelters) all males had to come to worship the Lord at the Holy Tent (later, at the Temple in Jerusalem; Exodus 23:17).

The feasts were celebrated with rest, offerings to the Lord, and food in remembrance of the Exodus from Egypt and God's continued goodness to the people in providing for them.

Besides having set times of celebration, the people could bring a fellowship offering any time to the Lord to show their thanks, to give God a gift, or because of a special promise made to God. In these offerings the people were given some meat back from the animal offered so that they could have a meal with family and friends (Leviticus 7:11–18).

Sometimes celebrations occurred when something major had been accomplished, such as the crossing of the Red Sea and the destruction of the Egyptian army (Exodus 15), the bringing of the Ark of the Lord to Jerusalem (2 Samuel 6:12–23), the completion of the Temple (1 Kings 8:62–63), and the rebuilding of the wall of Jerusalem (Nehemiah 12:27–47). Most of these celebrations included singing, music, and dancing.

People also celebrated important events, such as birthdays (Genesis 40:20; Mark 6:21) and weddings (Judges 14:10). Jesus attended a wedding feast where he performed his first miracle by providing more wine for the festivities (John 2:1–11).

The feasts continued to be observed by Jewish people in the New Testament. Jesus used many of them to teach about himself. Indeed, we can see that Jesus fulfilled the feasts, so we don't observe them anymore.

For instance, on the last day of the Feast of Shelters, Jesus promised thirsty people could have rivers of water flowing from them if they believe in him (John 7:37–38). At the Feast of Weeks (called Pentecost) in Acts 2, God poured out his Spirit to equip the church for spreading the gospel. But perhaps most dramatically, the Passover was celebrated by Jesus and became the Lord's Supper (Matthew 26:26–30; 1 Corinthians 11:23–26). Indeed, Jesus is our Passover lamb (1 Corinthians 5:7), having been sacrificed once and for all for our sins.

We don't celebrate these Old Testament festivals any more because Jesus has fulfilled them. They were shadows that were looking forward to New Testament realities. Indeed, Paul makes it very clear that no one is obligated to celebrate these old special days, including the Sabbath, in the way they did during the Old Testament period (Colossians 2:16).

But the church does celebrate the death and resurrection of Christ by participating in the Lord's Supper. At this time, we not only remember Jesus with the bread and wine, we also look forward to the time when Jesus will come again. His return is also described as a great celebration. At that time, there will be a great wedding meal as God's people celebrate with great joy their union with Jesus and their deliverance from all enemies (Matthew 26:29; Revelation 19:6–11).

Until then, everyday is a celebration. We have no special religious requirement to celebrate events like Christmas, Easter, or birthdays, but neither are they prohibited. Our lives will be characterized by joy thanks to God's great work of salvation in the world and our lives. It is, therefore, not surprising that we will have times of joyous celebrations in our lives.

Celebration: For additional scriptures on this topic go to Exodus 12.

21Then the Philistines captured Samson and tore out his eyes. They took him down to Gaza, where they put bronze chains on him and made him grind grain in the prison. 22But his hair began to grow again.

Samson Dies

23The Philistine rulers gathered to celebrate and to offer a great sacrifice to their god Dagon. They said, "Our god has handed Samson our enemy over to us." 24When the people saw him, they praised their god, saying,

"This man destroyed our country.
He killed many of us!
But our god handed over
our enemy to us."

25While the people were enjoying the celebration, they said, "Bring Samson out to perform for us." So they brought Samson from the prison, and he performed for them. They made him stand between the pillars. 26Samson said to the servant holding his hand, "Let me feel the pillars that hold up the temple so I can lean against them." 27Now the temple was full of men and women. All the Philistine rulers were there, and about three thousand men and women were on the roof watching Samson perform. 28Then Samson prayed to the LORD, "Lord GOD, remember me. God, please give me strength one more time so I can pay these Philistines back for putting out my two eyes!" 29Then Samson turned to the two center pillars that supported the whole temple. He braced himself between the two pillars, with his right hand on one and his left hand on the other. 30Samson said, "Let me die with these Philistines!" Then he pushed as hard as he could, causing the temple to fall on the rulers and all the people in it. So Samson killed more of the Philistines when he died than when he was alive.

31Samson's brothers and his whole family went down to get his body. They brought him back and buried him in the tomb of Manoah, his father, between the cities of Zorah and Eshtaol. Samson was a judge for the people of Israel for twenty years.

Micah's Idols

17 There was a man named Micah who lived in the mountains of Ephraim. 2He said to his mother, "I heard you speak a curse about the twenty-eight pounds of silver that were taken from you. I have the silver with me; I took it."

His mother said, "The LORD bless you, my son!"

3Micah gave the twenty-eight pounds of silver to his mother. Then she said, "I will give this silver to the LORD. I will have my son make an idol and a statue. So I will give the silver back to you."

4When he gave the silver back to his mother, she took about five pounds and gave it to a silversmith. With it he made an idol and a statue, which stood in Micah's house. 5Micah had a special holy place, and he made a holy vest and some household idols. Then Micah chose one of his sons to be his priest. 6At that time Israel did not have a king, so everyone did what seemed right.

7There was a young man who was a Levite from the city of Bethlehem in Judah who was from the people of Judah. 8He left Bethlehem to look for another place to live, and on his way he came to Micah's house in the mountains of Ephraim. 9Micah asked him, "Where are you from?"

He answered, "I'm a Levite from Bethlehem in Judah. I'm looking for a place to live."

10Micah said to him, "Live with me and be my father and my priest. I will give you four ounces of silver each year and clothes and food." So the Levite went in. 11He agreed to live with Micah and became like one of Micah's own sons. 12Micah made him a priest, and he lived in Micah's house. 13Then Micah said, "Now I know the LORD will be good to me, because I have a Levite as my priest."

Dan's Family Captures Laish

18 At that time Israel did not have a king. And at that time the tribe of Dan was still looking for a land where they could live, a land of their own. The Danites had not yet been given their own land among the tribes of Israel. 2So, from their family groups, they chose five soldiers from the cities of Zorah and Eshtaol to spy out and explore the land. They were told, "Go, explore the land."

They came to the mountains of Ephraim, to Micah's house, where they spent the night. 3When they came near Micah's house, they recognized the voice of the young Levite. So they stopped there and asked him, "Who brought you here? What are you doing here? Why are you here?"

4He told them what Micah had done for him, saying "He hired me. I am his priest."

5They said to him, "Please ask God if our journey will be successful."

16:27 *roof.* In Bible times houses were built with flat roofs. The roof was used for drying things such as flax and fruit. And it was used as an extra room, as a place for worship, and as a cool place to sleep in the summer.

16:31 Samson: See article on page 380.

16:31 Martyrdom: Psalm 44:22

18:3 *Levite.* The Levites were the only ones God had appointed as priests.

6The priest said to them, "Go in peace. The
LORD is pleased with your journey."
7So the five men left. When they came to the
city of Laish, they saw that the people there lived
in safety, like the people of Sidon. They thought
they were safe and had plenty of everything.
They lived a long way from the Sidonians and had
no dealings with anyone else.
8When the five men returned to Zorah and
Eshtaol, their relatives asked them, "What did
you find?"
9They answered, "We have seen the land, and
it is very good. We should attack them. Aren't
you going to do something? Don't wait! Let's go
and take that land! 10When you go, you will see
there is plenty of land—plenty of everything! The
people are not expecting an attack. Surely God
has handed that land over to us!"
11So six hundred Danites left Zorah and Eshtaol
ready for war. 12On their way they set up camp
near the city of Kiriath Jearim in Judah. That is
why the place west of Kiriath Jearim is named
Mahaneh Dan to this day. 13From there they traveled on to the mountains of Ephraim. Then they
came to Micah's house.
14The five men who had explored the land
around Laish said to their relatives, "Do you
know in one of these houses there are a holy vest,
household gods, an idol, and a statue? You know
what to do." 15So they stopped at the Levite's
house, which was also Micah's house, and greeted
the Levite. 16The six hundred Danites stood at
the entrance gate, wearing their weapons of war.
17The five spies went into the house and took the
idol, the holy vest, the household idols, and the
statue. The priest and the six hundred men
armed for war stood by the entrance gate.
18When the spies went into Micah's house and
took the image, the holy vest, the household
idols, and the statue, the priest asked them,
"What are you doing?"
19They answered, "Be quiet! Don't say a word.
Come with us and be our father and priest. Is it
better for you to be a priest for one man's house
or for a tribe and family group in Israel?" 20This
made the priest happy. So he took the holy vest,
the household idols, and the idol and went with
the Danites. 21They left Micah's house, putting
their little children, their animals, and everything
they owned in front of them.
22When they had gone a little way from Micah's
house, the men who lived near Micah were called
out and caught up with them. 23The men with
Micah shouted at the Danites, who turned around
and said to Micah, "What's the matter with you?
Why have you been called out to fight?"
24Micah answered, "You took my gods that I
made and my priest. What do I have left? How
can you ask me, 'What's the matter?'"
25The Danites answered, "You should not argue
with us. Some of our angry men might attack you,
killing you and your family." 26Then the Danites
went on their way. Micah knew they were too
strong for him, so he turned and went back home.
27Then the Danites took what Micah had made
and his priest and went on to Laish. They
attacked those peaceful people and killed them
with their swords and then burned the city.
28There was no one to save the people of Laish.
They lived too far from Sidon, and they had no
dealings with anyone else. Laish was in a valley
near Beth Rehob.
The people of Dan rebuilt the city and lived
there. 29They changed the name of Laish to Dan,
naming it for their ancestor Dan, one of the sons
of Israel.
30The people of Dan set up the idols in the city
of Dan. Jonathan son of Gershom, Moses' son,
and his sons served as priests for the tribe of Dan
until the land was captured. 31The people of Dan
set up the idols Micah had made as long as the
Holy Tent of God was in Shiloh.

A Levite and His Servant

19 At that time Israel did not have a king.
There was a Levite who lived in the faraway mountains of Ephraim. He had taken a slave
woman from the city of Bethlehem in the land of
Judah to live with him, 2but she was unfaithful to
him. She left him and went back to her father's
house in Bethlehem in Judah and stayed there for
four months. 3Then her husband went to ask her
to come back to him, taking with him his servant
and two donkeys. When the Levite came to her
father's house, she invited him to come in, and
her father was happy to see him. 4The father-in-
law, the young woman's father, asked him to
stay. So he stayed for three days and ate, drank,
and slept there.
5On the fourth day they got up early in the
morning. The Levite was getting ready to leave,
but the woman's father said to his son-in-law,
"Refresh yourself by eating something. Then go."
6So the two men sat down to eat and drink
together. After that, the father said to him, "Please
stay tonight. Relax and enjoy yourself." 7When the

18:12 *Mahaneh Dan.* This name means "the camp of Dan."

man got up to go, his father-in-law asked him to
stay. So he stayed again that night. 8On the fifth
day the man got up early in the morning to leave.
The woman's father said, "Refresh yourself. Wait
until this afternoon." So the two men ate together.
9When the Levite, his slave woman, and his
servant got up to leave, the father-in-law, the
young woman's father, said, "It's almost night.
The day is almost gone. Spend the night here and
enjoy yourself. Tomorrow morning you can get up
early and go home." 10But the Levite did not want
to stay another night. So he took his two saddled
donkeys and his slave woman and traveled toward
the city of Jebus (also called Jerusalem).
11As the day was almost over, they came near
Jebus. So the servant said to his master, "Let's
stop at this city of the Jebusites, and spend the
night here."
12But his master said, "No. We won't go inside
a foreign city. Those people are not Israelites. We
will go on to the city of Gibeah." 13He said,
"Come on. Let's try to make it to Gibeah or
Ramah so we can spend the night in one of those
cities." 14So they went on. The sun went down as
they came near Gibeah, which belongs to the
tribe of Benjamin. 15They stopped there to spend
the night. They came to the public square of the
city and sat down, but no one invited them home
to spend the night.
16Finally, in the evening an old man came in
from his work in the fields. His home was in the
mountains of Ephraim, but now he was living in
Gibeah. (The people of Gibeah were from the
tribe of Benjamin.) 17He saw the traveler in the
public square and asked, "Where are you going?
Where did you come from?"
18The Levite answered, "We are traveling from
Bethlehem in Judah to my home in the mountains of Ephraim. I have been to Bethlehem in
Judah, but now I am going to the Holy Tent of the
LORD. No one has invited me to stay in his house.
19We already have straw and food for our donkeys
and bread and wine for me, the young woman,
and my servant. We don't need anything."
20The old man said, "You are welcome to stay
at my house. Let me give you anything you need,
but don't spend the night in the public square."
21So the old man took the Levite into his house,
and he fed their donkeys. They washed their feet
and had something to eat and drink.
22While they were enjoying themselves, some
wicked men of the city surrounded the house and
beat on the door. They shouted to the old man
who owned the house, "Bring out the man who
came to your house. We want to have sexual relations with him."
23The owner of the house went outside and
said to them, "No, my friends. Don't be so evil.
This man is a guest in my house. Don't do this
terrible thing! 24Look, here are my daughter,
who has never had sexual relations before, and
the man's slave woman. I will bring them out to
you now. Do anything you want with them, but
don't do such a terrible thing to this man."
25But the men would not listen to him. So the
Levite took his slave woman and sent her outside
to them. They forced her to have sexual relations
with them, and they abused her all night long.
Then, at dawn, they let her go. 26She came back
to the house where her master was staying and
fell down at the door and lay there until daylight.
27In the morning when the Levite got up, he
opened the door of the house and went outside to
go on his way. But his slave woman was lying at
the doorway of the house, with her hands on the
doorsill. 28The Levite said to her, "Get up; let's
go." But she did not answer. So he put her on his
donkey and went home.
29When the Levite got home, he took a knife
and cut his slave woman into twelve parts, limb
by limb. Then he sent a part to each area of Israel.
30Everyone who saw this said, "Nothing like this
has ever happened before, not since the people of
Israel came out of Egypt. Think about it. Tell us
what to do."

The War Between Israel and Benjamin

20 So all the Israelites from Dan to Beersheba,
including the land of Gilead, joined together
before the LORD in the city of Mizpah. 2The leaders
of all the tribes of Israel took their places in the
meeting of the people of God. There were
400,000 soldiers with swords. 3(The people of
Benjamin heard that the Israelites had gone up to
Mizpah.) Then the Israelites said to the Levite,
"Tell us how this evil thing happened."

19:14–23 Several features of Old Testament hospitality practices are displayed here. (1) Strangers wait in the public square for an invitation. (2) A local asks them questions to discern their intentions and destination, screening them. (3) A local offers to provide food, water, protection, and shelter for the travelers and their animals. (4) Protection, in this case, breaks down and violence results, bringing shame and judgment on the entire community (Judges 19:30–21:2).

19:23 Hospitality: Psalm 107:1–9

19:29 *cut his slave woman into twelve parts.* This act shows that the Levite did not really care about the woman, but rather his own pride. There are stories from the ancient Near East where an animal was divided and sent to tribal leaders as a call to war.

20:1 *Dan . . . Beersheba.* Dan was the city farthest north in Israel. Beersheba was the city farthest south. So this means all the people of Israel.

4So the husband of the murdered woman answered, "My slave woman and I came to Gibeah in Benjamin to spend the night. 5During the night the men of Gibeah came after me. They surrounded the house and wanted to kill me. They forced my slave woman to have sexual relations and she died. 6I took her and cut her into parts and sent one part to each area of Israel because the people of Benjamin did this wicked and terrible thing in Israel. 7Now, all you Israelites, speak up. What is your decision?"

8Then all the people stood up at the same time, saying, "None of us will go home. Not one of us will go back to his house! 9Now this is what we will do to Gibeah. We will throw lots. 10That way we will choose ten men from every hundred men from all the tribes of Israel, and we will choose a hundred men from every thousand, and a thousand men from every ten thousand. These will find supplies for the army. Then the army will go to the city of Gibeah of Benjamin to repay them for the terrible thing they have done in Israel." 11So all the men of Israel were united and gathered against the city.

12The tribes of Israel sent men throughout the tribe of Benjamin demanding, "What is this evil thing some of your men have done? 13Hand over the wicked men in Gibeah so that we can put them to death. We must remove this evil from Israel."

But the Benjaminites would not listen to their fellow Israelites. 14The Benjaminites left their own cities and met at Gibeah to fight the Israelites. 15In only one day the Benjaminites got 26,000 soldiers together who were trained with swords. They also had 700 chosen men from Gibeah. 16Seven hundred of these trained soldiers were left-handed, each of whom could sling a stone at a hair and not miss!

17The Israelites, except for the Benjaminites, gathered 400,000 soldiers with swords.

18The Israelites went up to the city of Bethel and asked God, "Which tribe shall be first to attack the Benjaminites?"

The LORD answered, "Judah shall go first."

19The next morning the Israelites got up and made a camp near Gibeah. 20The men of Israel went out to fight the Benjaminites and took their battle position at Gibeah. 21Then the Benjaminites came out of Gibeah and killed 22,000 Israelites during the battle that day. 22-23The Israelites went before the LORD and cried until evening. They asked the LORD, "Shall we go to fight our relatives, the Benjaminites, again?"

The LORD answered, "Go up and fight them." The men of Israel encouraged each other. So they took the same battle positions they had taken the first day.

24The Israelites came to fight the Benjaminites the second day. 25The Benjaminites came out of Gibeah to attack the Israelites. This time, the Benjaminites killed 18,000 Israelites, all of whom carried swords.

26Then the Israelites went up to Bethel. There they sat down and cried to the LORD and went without food all day until evening. They also brought burnt offerings and fellowship offerings to the LORD. 27The Israelites asked the LORD a question. (In those days the Ark of the Agreement with God was there at Bethel. 28A priest named Phinehas son of Eleazar, the son of Aaron, served before the Ark of the Agreement.) They asked, "Shall we go to fight our relatives, the Benjaminites, again, or shall we stop fighting?"

The LORD answered, "Go, because tomorrow I will hand them over to you."

29Then the Israelites set up ambushes all around Gibeah. 30They went to fight against the Benjaminites at Gibeah on the third day, getting into position for battle as they had done before. 31When the Benjaminites came out to fight them, the Israelites backed up and led the Benjaminites away from the city. The Benjaminites began to kill some of the Israelites as they had done before. About thirty Israelites were killed—some in the fields and some on the roads leading to Bethel and to Gibeah.

32The Benjaminites said, "We are winning as before!"

But the Israelites said, "Let's run. Let's trick them into going farther away from their city and onto the roads."

33All the Israelites moved from their places and got into battle positions at a place named Baal Tamar. Then the Israelites ran out from their hiding places west of Gibeah. 34Ten thousand of the best trained soldiers from all of Israel attacked Gibeah. The battle was very hard. The Benjaminites did not know disaster was about to come to them. 35The LORD used the Israelites to defeat the Benjaminites. On that day the Israelites killed 25,100 Benjaminites, all armed with swords. 36Then the Benjaminites saw that they were defeated.

The Israelites had moved back because they were depending on the surprise attack they had set up near Gibeah. 37The men in hiding rushed

20:16 *left-handed.* See 3:15.

into Gibeah, spread out, and killed everyone in the city with their swords. 38Now the Israelites had set up a signal with the men in hiding. The men in the surprise attack were to send up a cloud of smoke from the city. 39Then the army of Israel turned around in the battle.

The Benjaminites had killed about thirty Israelites. They were saying, "We are winning, as in the first battle!" 40But then a cloud of smoke began to rise from the city. The Benjaminites turned around and saw that the whole city was going up in smoke. 41Then the Israelites turned and began to fight. The Benjaminites were terrified because they knew that disaster was coming to them. 42So the Benjaminites ran away from the Israelites toward the desert, but they could not escape the battle. And the Israelites who came out of the cities killed them. 43They surrounded the Benjaminites and chased them and caught them in the area east of Gibeah. 44So 18,000 brave Benjaminite fighters were killed. 45The Benjaminites ran toward the desert to the rock of Rimmon, but the Israelites killed 5,000 Benjaminites along the roads. They chased them as far as Gidom and killed 2,000 more Benjaminites there.

46On that day 25,000 Benjaminites were killed, all of whom had fought bravely with swords. 47But 600 Benjaminites ran to the rock of Rimmon in the desert, where they stayed for four months. 48Then the Israelites went back to the land of Benjamin and killed the people in every city and also the animals and everything they could find. And they burned every city they found.

Wives for the Men of Benjamin

21 At Mizpah the men of Israel had sworn, "Not one of us will let his daughter marry a man from the tribe of Benjamin."

2The people went to the city of Bethel and sat before God until evening, crying loudly. 3They said, "LORD, God of Israel, why has this terrible thing happened to us so that one tribe of Israel is missing today?"

4Early the next day the people built an altar and put burnt offerings and fellowship offerings to God on it.

5Then the Israelites asked, "Did any tribe of Israel not come here to meet with us in the presence of the LORD?" They asked this question because they had sworn that anyone who did not meet with them at Mizpah would be killed.

6The Israelites felt sorry for their relatives, the Benjaminites. They said, "Today one tribe has been cut off from Israel. 7We swore before the LORD that we would not allow our daughters to marry a Benjaminite. How can we make sure that the remaining men of Benjamin will have wives?" 8Then they asked, "Which one of the tribes of Israel did not come here to Mizpah?" They found that no one from the city of Jabesh Gilead had come. 9The people of Israel counted everyone, but there was no one from Jabesh Gilead.

10So the whole group of Israelites sent twelve thousand soldiers to Jabesh Gilead to kill the people with their swords, even the women and children.

11"This is what you must do: Kill every man in Jabesh Gilead and every married woman." 12The soldiers found four hundred young unmarried women in Jabesh Gilead, so they brought them to the camp at Shiloh in Canaan.

13Then the whole group of Israelites sent a message to the men of Benjamin, who were at the rock of Rimmon, offering to make peace with them. 14So the men of Benjamin came back at that time. The Israelites gave them the women from Jabesh Gilead who had not been killed, but there were not enough women.

15The people of Israel felt sorry for the Benjaminites because the LORD had separated the tribes of Israel. 16The older leaders of the Israelites said, "The women of Benjamin have been killed. Where can we get wives for the men of Benjamin who are still alive? 17These men must have children to continue their families so a tribe in Israel will not die out. 18But we cannot allow our daughters to marry them, because we swore, 'Anyone who gives a wife to a man of Benjamin is cursed.' 19We have an idea! There is a yearly festival of the LORD at Shiloh, which is north of the city of Bethel, east of the road that goes from Bethel to Shechem, and south of the city of Lebonah."

20So the older leaders told the men of Benjamin, "Go and hide in the vineyards. 21Watch for the young women from Shiloh to come out to join the dancing. Then run out from the vineyards and take one of the young Shiloh women and return to the land of Benjamin. 22If their fathers or brothers come to us and complain, we will say: 'Be kind to the men of Benjamin. We did not get wives for Benjamin during the war, and you did not give the women to the men from Benjamin. So you are not guilty.'"

23So that is what the Benjaminites did. While the young women were dancing, each man caught one of them, took her away, and married her. Then they went back to the land God had given them and rebuilt their cities and lived there.

24Then the Israelites went home to their own tribes and family groups, to their own land that God had given them.

25In those days Israel did not have a king. Everyone did what seemed right.

Notes:

INTRODUCTION TO THE BOOK OF

RUTH

The Story of a Girl from Moab

WHO WROTE THIS BOOK?

The author of Ruth is not known. Even though Jewish tradition suggests that Samuel is the author, his writing of the book cannot be confirmed.

TO WHOM WAS THIS BOOK WRITTEN?

The Book of Ruth was written as a part of Israel's history and, therefore, for them.

WHERE WAS IT WRITTEN?

Since this book is set in the land of Judah, it is probable that its writing also took place there. Naomi was, in fact, from Bethlehem of Judah, and 1:6 says that Naomi and her daughters-in-law prepared to "go home" from there (Moab).

WHEN WAS IT WRITTEN?

The opening verse of Ruth sets the date of the story as "in the days when the judges ruled." Therefore, we can conclude that it took place between 1380 and 1050 B.C. The days of the judges were well known as wild and dangerous times. Though the events of the book are set in the time of the judges, the earliest the book could have been written is the time of David who is mentioned at the end (4:17–22).

WHAT IS THE BOOK ABOUT?

Ruth is a story of love and loyalty. It begins with the touching tale of young Ruth's devotion to her widowed mother-in-law, Naomi. Then the story blossoms into the Bible's most elegant human love story between Ruth and Boaz—two people of integrity and fine character in the midst of cultural chaos and confusion. The story shows Naomi's destitution turned into comfort and happiness through the love and loyalty of Ruth and Boaz.

WHY WAS THIS BOOK WRITTEN?

The story of Ruth is an important link in the history of the people of Israel, since Jesus later comes to earth through Ruth's direct lineage. The Book of Ruth describes the kind of selfless love that God desires from his people. Ruth's constant devotion and care for Naomi, as well as Boaz's generosity and kindness, are reenactments of God's love for his people. Ruth shows how those traits are rewarded with great blessings from God.

SO WHAT DOES THIS BOOK MEAN TO US?

God still desires selfless love, devotion, generosity, and kindness from his people. When we, as Christians, exhibit those traits, people around us actually see God himself in action through us. We are, in fact, the spirit of God with skin on in this world. And just as God blessed Naomi, Ruth, and Boaz for their faithfulness to his laws, he will bless us today when we show the world his love and kindness.

SUMMARY:

The Book of Ruth is named after one of its main characters, a Moabite woman, who marries a man from Israel. After her husband's death, she journeys back to Israel with her mother-in-law, Naomi.

All the action of the book takes place during the period of the judges, but unlike most of the people in the book, the main characters of Ruth are people of strength and moral character.

The purpose of the book is twofold, but the two purposes are related. In the first place, the Book of Ruth tells us something about where David came from. He was a descendant of Ruth and Boaz. The book also teaches us that God works wonders in his quiet guidance of human affairs. He works through ordinary people like Ruth and Boaz to provide extraordinary help to his people. In this case the help comes in the person of the great king David. David the king was the eventual fruit of this, from a human perspective, *coincidental* meeting of Ruth and Boaz. God's hand guides the events of this story as directly as it did in the story of the Exodus from Egypt. The Book of Ruth not only amazes us with an insider's look at how God brought David to Israel in such an extraordinary way, but assures us that God works in our ordinary lives as well.

Matthew 1:5 reminds the reader that Ruth was the grandmother of David, but then continues by showing that the line of descent leads to Jesus. Only a handful of women are included in this genealogy: Tamar, Rahab, Ruth, and Mary. All of them had aspersions cast on them: prostitute, foreigner, unwed mother. But God used each of them to further the line that led to the Messiah.

RUTH

Long ago when the judges ruled Israel,
there was a shortage of food in the land.∞
2So a man named Elimelech left the town
of Bethlehem in Judah to live in the country of
Moab with his wife and his two sons. His wife was
named Naomi, and his two sons were named
Mahlon and Kilion. They were Ephrathahites from
Bethlehem in Judah. When they came to Moab,
they settled there.
3Then Naomi's husband, Elimelech, died, and
she was left with her two sons. 4These sons married women from Moab. One was named Orpah,
and the other was named Ruth. Naomi and her
sons had lived in Moab about ten years 5when
Mahlon and Kilion also died. So Naomi was left
alone without her husband or her two sons.
6While Naomi was in Moab, she heard that the
LORD had come to help his people and had given
them food again. So she and her daughters-in-law
got ready to leave Moab and return home. 7Naomi
and her daughters-in-law left the place where
they had lived and started back to the land of
Judah. 8But Naomi said to her two daughters-in-
law, "Go back home, each of you to your own
mother's house. May the LORD be as kind to you as
you have been to me and my sons who are now
dead. 9May the LORD give you another happy home
and a new husband."
When Naomi kissed the women good-bye, they
began to cry out loud. 10They said to her, "No, we
want to go with you to your people."
11But Naomi said, "My daughters, return to
your own homes. Why do you want to go with
me? I cannot give birth to more sons to give you
new husbands; 12go back, my daughters, to your
own homes. I am too old to have another husband.
Even if I told myself, 'I still have hope' and had
another husband tonight, and even if I had more
sons, 13should you wait until they were grown into
men? Should you live for so many years without
husbands? Don't do that, my daughters. My life is
much too sad for you to share, because the LORD
has been against me!"
14The women cried together out loud again.
Then Orpah kissed her mother-in-law Naomi
good-bye, but Ruth held on to her tightly.
15Naomi said to Ruth, "Look, your sister-in-law
is going back to her own people and her own gods.
Go back with her."

Ruth Stays with Naomi

16But Ruth said, "Don't beg me to leave you or to
stop following you. Where you go, I will go. Where
you live, I will live. Your people will be my people,
and your God will be my God.∞ 17And where you
die, I will die, and there I will be buried. I ask the
LORD to punish me terribly if I do not keep this
promise: Not even death will separate us."
18When Naomi saw that Ruth had firmly made
up her mind to go with her, she stopped arguing
with her. 19So Naomi and Ruth went on until
they came to the town of Bethlehem. When they
entered Bethlehem, all the people became very
excited. The women of the town said, "Is this
really Naomi?"
20Naomi answered the people, "Don't call me
Naomi. Call me Mara, because the Almighty has
made my life very sad. 21When I left, I had all I
wanted, but now, the LORD has brought me home
with nothing. Why should you call me Naomi
when the LORD has spoken against me and the
Almighty has given me so much trouble?"
22So Naomi and her daughter-in-law Ruth, the
Moabite, returned from Moab and arrived at
Bethlehem at the beginning of the barley harvest.∞

Ruth Meets Boaz

2 Now Naomi had a rich relative named Boaz,
from Elimelech's family.
2One day Ruth, the Moabite, said to Naomi, "I
am going to the fields. Maybe someone will be
kind enough to let me gather the grain he leaves
behind."
Naomi said, "Go, my daughter."
3So Ruth went to the fields and gathered the
grain that the workers cutting the grain had left
behind. It just so happened that the field belonged
to Boaz, from Elimelech's family.
4Soon Boaz came from Bethlehem and greeted
his workers, "The LORD be with you!"

1:1 *judges.* They were not judges in courts of law, but leaders of the people in times of emergency.

∞**1:1 Famine:** 2 Samuel 21:1–14

1:11 *I cannot give birth to more sons to give you new husbands.* While this may be a reference to the practice of a person marrying a deceased brother's wife (Genesis 38; Deuteronomy 25:5–10; Matthew 22:23–33), it is unlikely since this practice assumes a brother of near equal age and the same father. Naomi is simply telling her daughters-in-law that she cannot help them find marriage partners.

∞**1:16 Rahab:** Isaiah 2:2–5

1:20 *Naomi.* This name means "happy" or "pleasant."

1:20 *Mara.* This name means "bitter" or "sad."

∞**1:22 Self-Control:** Jeremiah 17:8

2:2 *to let me gather the grain he leaves behind.* The law of Moses allows the poor to pick grain that remains after the harvest is taken (Leviticus 19:9–10; 23:22; Deuteronomy 24:19–22).

And the workers answered, "May the LORD bless you!"

5Then Boaz asked his servant in charge of the workers, "Whose girl is that?"

6The servant answered, "She is the young Moabite woman who came back with Naomi from the country of Moab. 7She said, 'Please let me follow the workers cutting grain and gather what they leave behind.' She came and has remained here, from morning until just now. She has stopped only a few moments to rest in the shelter."

8Then Boaz said to Ruth, "Listen, my daughter. Don't go to gather grain for yourself in another field. Don't even leave this field at all, but continue following closely behind my women workers. 9Watch to see into which fields they go to cut grain and follow them. I have warned the young men not to bother you. When you are thirsty, you may go and drink from the water jugs that the young men have filled."

10Then Ruth bowed low with her face to the ground and said to him, "I am not an Israelite. Why have you been so kind to notice me?"

11Boaz answered her, "I know about all the help you have given your mother-in-law after your husband died. You left your father and mother and your own country to come to a nation where you did not know anyone. 12May the LORD reward you for all you have done. May your wages be paid in full by the LORD, the God of Israel, under whose wings you have come for shelter."

13Then Ruth said, "I hope I can continue to please you, sir. You have said kind and encouraging words to me, your servant, though I am not one of your servants."

14At mealtime Boaz told Ruth, "Come here. Eat some of our bread and dip it in our sauce."

So Ruth sat down beside the workers. Boaz handed her some roasted grain, and she ate until she was full; she even had some food left over. 15When Ruth rose and went back to work, Boaz commanded his workers, "Let her gather even around the piles of cut grain. Don't tell her to go away. 16In fact, drop some full heads of grain for her from what you have in your hands, and let her gather them. Don't tell her to stop."

17So Ruth gathered grain in the field until evening. Then she separated the grain from the chaff, and there was about one-half bushel of barley. 18Ruth carried the grain into town, and her mother-in-law saw how much she had gathered. Ruth also took out the food that was left over from lunch and gave it to Naomi.

19Naomi asked her, "Where did you gather all this grain today? Where did you work? Blessed be whoever noticed you!"

Ruth told her mother-in-law whose field she had worked in. She said, "The man I worked with today is named Boaz."

20Naomi told her daughter-in-law, "The LORD bless him! He continues to be kind to us—both the living and the dead!" Then Naomi told Ruth, "Boaz is one of our close relatives, one who should take care of us."

21Then Ruth, the Moabite, said, "Boaz also told me, 'Keep close to my workers until they have finished my whole harvest.'"

22But Naomi said to her daughter-in-law Ruth, "It is better for you to continue working with his women workers. If you work in another field, someone might hurt you." 23So Ruth continued working closely with the workers of Boaz, gathering grain until the barley harvest and the wheat harvest were finished. And she continued to live with Naomi, her mother-in-law.

Naomi's Plan

3 Then Naomi, Ruth's mother-in-law, said to her, "My daughter, I must find a suitable home for you, one that will be good for you. 2Now Boaz, whose young women you worked with, is our close relative. Tonight he will be working at the threshing floor. 3Wash yourself, put on perfume, change your clothes, and go down to the threshing floor. But don't let him know you're there until he has finished his dinner. 4Watch him so you will know where he lies down to sleep. When he lies down, go and lift the cover off his feet and lie down. He will tell you what you should do."

5Then Ruth answered, "I will do everything you say."

6So Ruth went down to the threshing floor and did all her mother-in-law told her to do. 7After his evening meal, Boaz felt good and went to sleep lying beside the pile of grain. Ruth went to him quietly and lifted the cover from his feet and lay down.

8About midnight Boaz was startled and rolled over. There was a woman lying near his feet! 9Boaz asked, "Who are you?"

2:20 *one who should take care of us.* The Hebrew phrase behind this translation indicates a formal role in that society known as the "kinsman-redeemer." Close relatives had responsibilities to help a person if a catastrophe struck. This included death and the leaving behind of wife and mother.

2:23 Crossing Cultural Boundaries: Esther 4:13–14

3:2 *close relatives.* In Bible times the closest relative could marry a widow without children so she could have children. He would care for this family, but they and their property would not belong to him. They would belong to the dead husband.

3:4 *lift . . . feet.* This showed Ruth was asking him to be her husband.

HOLINESS

LEVITICUS 11:44–45

What does it mean to be holy? How is God Holy? How can we be holy?

Holiness is an idea that is found very often throughout the Bible. It involves a complete separation from anything that is sinful or impure and a commitment to serve God and bring him honor. God himself is the only one who is perfectly good and separate from sin (1 John 1:5). He alone is so pure that his eyes cannot even look at evil (Habakkuk 1:13). He, too, is the only one whose actions always bring him honor. Therefore, God is the only one who is perfectly holy (1 Samuel 2:2). Jesus called God the Father holy (John 17:11). Even the evil spirits acknowledged that God the Son is holy (Mark 1:24). The very name of the Holy Spirit indicates his holiness. All through the Bible, people acknowledge and praise the holiness of God. In a vision, the prophet Isaiah even saw heavenly beings praising God on his throne as "holy, holy, holy" (Isaiah 6:1–3). Because God is so holy, everything that is associated with him is holy, too. His heavenly dwelling is holy (Deuteronomy 26:15). His name is holy (Matthew 6:9) and must not be misused (Exodus 20:7). His throne (Psalm 47:8), his power (Isaiah 52:10), his word (the *Holy* Scriptures), and all of his ways (Psalm 77:13) are holy. In short, everything about God is entirely free from sin and brings him honor.

God's complete separation from sin requires that those who would draw near to him must also be holy. His ministering angels, who continually praise him and do his bidding, are without sin and called holy (Mark 8:38). For human beings to be able to be friends with God they must also be holy, but they can't do this by themselves. Human beings already bear the guilt of the first sin. In addition, the corruption of our human nature that was produced when sin came into the world has made us unable to please God. God himself must take action to cleanse us from our sin and make us able to serve him in a way that brings him honor.

In the Old Testament, God set apart the nation of Israel to be those people who would receive his special attention and favor. In order for the Israelites to be able to have this special relationship with God, it was necessary for him to make them holy. He did this by providing for the removal of their sins and by giving them guidelines for living their lives in ways that honored him (Leviticus 20:7–8; 22:31–32). Animal sacrifices were the means that God provided for removing their sins. These sacrifices themselves were considered holy because they brought honor to God by reminding people that he was without sin and that those who would be friends with him must also be without sin. The sacrifices were offered to God on behalf of the people by priests, who had been set apart for this task by means of special procedures that ensured they were free from all impurity and sin before they entered into God's holy presence (Exodus 29; Leviticus 8). The sacrifices that the priests offered to God for the people made them clean from the guilt of sin so that they were able to draw near to God in fellowship. To be holy, however, they still had to honor God in the way they led their lives. God commanded the Israelites to live holy lives so that they could continue to enjoy friendship with him (Leviticus 11:44–45; 20:7–8). He gave them the law so that they would know how to honor him with their lives. Because the law comes from God, it, too, is considered holy (Romans 7:12). By obeying the law, the Israelites would bring honor to God (Deuteronomy 28:9–10; Romans 2:23).

God had cleansed the Israelites from their sin by means of sacrifices and had given them guidelines for how to conduct their lives in a way that would bring him honor. In this way, God had made them holy or sanctified them. He could not have fellowship with them and be present among them. From the time God delivered the Israelites from Egypt until the time of King Solomon, the physical place where his presence was located in their midst was the Meeting Tent. After King Solomon built the Temple, God's presence with the Israelites was located there. Everything about this place was holy, and the inner and most special room in it that was particularly identified with the presence of the most holy God was called the Most Holy Place. This room was so holy that the Israelite high priest could only enter it once a year, and then only with an offering of blood for is own and the people's sins (Leviticus 16:29–34; Hebrews 9:7, 25).

The New Testament talks abut holiness in the same way as the Old Testament. Just as the Israelites were commanded to be holy, so God commands believers today to be holy (1 Peter 1:15–16). Holiness for the Israelites involved sacrifices for the forgiveness of their sins and living according to God's laws so that he would be honored. Holiness for believers in the church today involves the same things, but today sacrifice for sin and living to honor God are possible because of Jesus Christ.

Everything that God had previously required to make his people holy in the Old Testament is provided in a more complete way by Jesus Christ. The sacrifices of the Old Testament times were really inadequate to make the people holy. They had to be performed again and again and never removed the people's sin Hebrews 10:1–4). The animal sacrifices pointed toward a future time when God would provide the perfect sacrifice for sin, Jesus Christ, who sacrificed himself only once and for all time "so that the church could be pure and without fault, with no evil or sin or any other wrong" (Ephesians 5:27). He was the perfect sacrifice for our sin because he had no sin of his own. By trusting in his self-sacrifice on our behalf, we have become right with God (2 Corinthians 5:21). Through Christ our sins are forgiven and we are made holy (1 Corinthians 1:30), so that we now have free access to enter the Most Holy Place of God's presence at any time without fear (Hebrews 10:19–22).

Holiness, however, also involves serving God and bringing him honor. Jesus brought the Father honor by living in perfect obedience to him. Though Jesus was tempted in every way that we are, he committed no sin (Hebrews 4:15). Christ's continual right behavior in the service of God is attributed to all those who trust in him, so that God sees us as being perfectly obedient as well. God can always regard us as holy because we are united with Christ by faith. Our relationship with God is now just as secure as the relationship between God the Father and God the Son. Therefore, nothing will ever be able to separate us from the love of God that we have through faith in Jesus Christ (Romans 8:31–39). But because we are now identified with Christ, we should notice that our lives are beginning to become more like his in his holiness. Christ's self-sacrifice on our behalf actually enables this to happen. In the past, we were controlled by our own sinful selves and were slaves to sin so that we could not live the type of lives that brought honor to God. But "our old life died with Christ on the cross so that our sinful selves would have no power over us and we would not be slaves to sin" (Romans 6:6). Through faith in Jesus Christ we are now free to serve God instead of sin (Hebrews 9:14–15). In addition, God has sent his Holy Spirit to give us new life and strengthen us in our efforts to honor God with our behavior (Galatians 5:16–26). When we live by following the Spirit, we can be the kind of people that God wants us to be—those who bring honor to him (Romans 8:1–17).

In the Old testament, the presence of the holy God with his people was associated with the holy Meeting Tent or Temple. Because God has made his people holy through the perfect sacrifice of Christ, he can now dwell within and among them. In fact, Peter describes believers as living stones that are being built up into God's new temple (1 Peter 2:5). In the old Temple, special actions were taken by the priests to ensure that they were cleansed from sin and able to offer the sacrifices. In the new spiritual temple formed by the community of those who trust in Jesus Christ, believers themselves are described as holy priests (1 Peter 2:5, 9) who are cleansed by his sacrifice. The sacrifices that we offer are the words and activities of our lives that bring honor to God (Romans 12:1; Hebrews 13:15–16). We try to be holy in all that we do because the one who has called us to have friendship with him is holy (1 Peter 1:15).

We know, however, that we do not always live holy lives, lives that please God and bring honor to him. Sometimes God even has to discipline his children when they go astray so that they might return quickly to the holy lifestyle that gives him honor and that he has commanded (Hebrews 12:10–11). In our individual experiences we struggle daily against temptation and sin. When we do sin, we need to confess our sin right away, relying on the sacrifice of Jesus Christ that was made on our behalf, so that we can be made clean again (1 John 1:9). In our daily efforts to become more holy in the way we live, we can take encouragement from God's promises that one day he will remove all sin from the world so that everything will be holy (Zechariah 14:20–21). Then we will be able to enjoy perfect fellowship with God without anything impure or unholy interfering (Revelation 21:1–22:6). Until then, believers are urged to be filled with the Spirit (Ephesians 5:18) and to make every effort to bring honor to God by living holy lives (2 Corinthians 7:1). We can succeed in this effort by relying on the power of the Holy Spirit, by prayer (Ephesians 6:18), by the encouragement of other Christians (1 Thessalonians 5:11; Hebrews 10:24–25), and by an increasing understanding of God's word (John 17:17).⚭

⚭**Holiness:** For additional scriptures on this topic go to Exodus 26.

She said, "I am Ruth, your servant girl. Spread
your cover over me, because you are a relative who
is supposed to take care of me."
10Then Boaz said, "The LORD bless you, my
daughter. This act of kindness is greater than the
kindness you showed to Naomi in the beginning.
You didn't look for a young man to marry, either
rich or poor. 11Now, my daughter, don't be afraid.
I will do everything you ask, because all the people in our town know you are a good woman. 12It
is true that I am a relative who is to take care of
you, but you have a closer relative than I. 13Stay
here tonight, and in the morning we will see if he
will take care of you. If he decides to take care of
you, that is fine. But if he refuses, I will take care
of you myself, as surely as the LORD lives. So stay
here until morning."
14So Ruth stayed near his feet until morning but
got up while it was still too dark to recognize anyone. Boaz thought, "People in town must not
know that the woman came here to the threshing
floor." 15So Boaz said to Ruth, "Bring me your
shawl and hold it open."

So Ruth held her shawl open, and Boaz poured
six portions of barley into it. Boaz then put it on
her head and went back to the city.
16When Ruth went back to her mother-in-law,
Naomi asked, "How did you do, my daughter?"

Ruth told Naomi everything that Boaz did for
her. 17She said, "Boaz gave me these six portions
of barley, saying, 'You must not go home without
a gift for your mother-in-law.'"
18Naomi answered, "Ruth, my daughter, wait
here until you see what happens. Boaz will not
rest until he has finished doing what he should do
today."

Boaz Marries Ruth

4 Boaz went to the city gate and sat there until
the close relative he had mentioned passed
by. Boaz called to him, "Come here, friend, and
sit down." So the man came over and sat down.
2Boaz gathered ten of the older leaders of the city
and told them, "Sit down here!" So they sat
down.
3Then Boaz said to the close relative, "Naomi,
who has come back from the country of Moab,
wants to sell the piece of land that belonged to
our relative Elimelech. 4So I decided to tell you
about it: If you want to buy back the land, then
buy it in front of the people who are sitting here
and in front of the older leaders of my people. But
if you don't want to buy it, tell me, because you
are the only one who can buy it, and I am next
after you."

The close relative answered, "I will buy back
the land."
5Then Boaz explained, "When you buy the
land from Naomi, you must also marry Ruth, the
Moabite, the dead man's wife. That way, the land
will stay in the dead man's name."
6The close relative answered, "I can't buy back
the land. If I did, I might harm what I can pass on
to my own sons. I cannot buy the land back, so
buy it yourself."
7Long ago in Israel when people traded or
bought back something, one person took off his
sandal and gave it to the other person. This was
the proof of ownership in Israel.
8So the close relative said to Boaz, "Buy the land
yourself," and he took off his sandal.
9Then Boaz said to the older leaders and to all
the people, "You are witnesses today. I am buying
from Naomi everything that belonged to Elimelech
and Kilion and Mahlon. 10I am also taking Ruth,
the Moabite who was the wife of Mahlon, as my
wife. I am doing this so her dead husband's property will stay in his name and his name will not
be separated from his family and his hometown.
You are witnesses today."
11So all the people and older leaders who were
at the city gate said, "We are witnesses. May the
LORD make this woman, who is coming into your
home, like Rachel and Leah, who had many children and built up the people of Israel. May you
become powerful in the district of Ephrathah and
famous in Bethlehem. 12As Tamar gave birth to
Judah's son Perez, may the LORD give you many
children through Ruth. May your family be great
like his."
13So Boaz took Ruth home as his wife and had
sexual relations with her. The LORD let her become
pregnant, and she gave birth to a son. 14The
women told Naomi, "Praise the LORD who gave
you this grandson. May he become famous in
Israel. 15He will give you new life and will take care
of you in your old age because of your daughter-in-
law who loves you. She is better for you than seven
sons, because she has given birth to your grandson."
16Naomi took the boy, held him in her arms,
and cared for him. 17The neighbors gave the boy
his name, saying, "This boy was born for Naomi."
They named him Obed. Obed was the father of

3:9 *Spread your cover over me.* By this, Ruth was asking Boaz to marry her.

3:15 Deborah: 1 Samuel 18:20–21

4:12 *Perez.* One of Boaz's ancestors.

Jesse, and Jesse was the father of David.

18This is the family history of Perez, the father
of Hezron. 19Hezron was the father of Ram, who
was the father of Amminadab. 20Amminadab was
the father of Nahshon, who was the father of
Salmon. 21Salmon was the father of Boaz, who was
the father of Obed. 22Obed was the father of
Jesse, and Jesse was the father of David.

4:18–22 The family history of Perez at the end of Ruth connects David to the tribe of Judah (Perez was the son of Judah, Genesis 38:29). It also seems to provide justification for David being king even though there was a Moabitess in his family background (see the prohibition against Moabites in Deuteronomy 23:3–6).

4:22 Self-Control: Jeremiah 17:8

INTRODUCTION TO THE BOOK OF

1 SAMUEL

Samuel and King Saul

WHO WROTE THIS BOOK?

The author of 1 Samuel is uncertain, since the book itself does not name its writer. Some people have suggested that, perhaps, the author was Zabud, who was the personal adviser to King Solomon and the son of Nathan the prophet. However, that cannot be verified.

TO WHOM WAS THIS BOOK WRITTEN?

The Book of 1 Samuel was intended for readers in Israel, the people of God.

WHERE WAS IT WRITTEN?

Since Israel was living in Canaan, the Promised Land, during the period of the judges and the kings, it is probable that 1 Samuel was written there, too.

WHEN WAS IT WRITTEN?

Based on several passages in the Book of 1 Samuel, the author evidently lived and wrote shortly after King Solomon's death, which was in 930 B.C., and when the kingdom of Israel divided (see comments about "Israel and Judah" in 11:8; 17:52; 18:16).

WHAT IS THIS BOOK ABOUT?

This book records the birth and ministry of Samuel the prophet, as well as the beginning of the rule of kings in Israel (the "monarchy"). The first two kings—Saul and David—were anointed by Samuel, this book's namesake. Before the actual anointing is described, however, 1 Samuel rehearses historical and theological events that brought about the establishment of the kingship.

WHY WAS THIS BOOK WRITTEN?

The Book of 1 Samuel vividly depicts God as the King of kings. While he charged Samuel to anoint Saul as king over Israel, God made it clear that he would continue to be the real king over Israel. Saul soon forgot that his kingship was dependent on his submission to the Great King of heaven. As a result, God began preparing David to take his place. Through the writings of the author of 1 Samuel, Israel was reminded to give homage to God who had constantly cared for them and protected them.

SO WHAT DOES THIS BOOK MEAN TO US?

God still appoints kings and rulers in the world today (see Romans 13:1), and yet he remains the King of those kings and Ruler of all rulers (1 Timothy 6:15). We are reminded, through the words of 1 Samuel, to continually pay homage to the Great King of heaven and to give him all the praise and glory for his constant care and protection.

SUMMARY:

1 and 2 Samuel were originally one book. Beginning with Samuel, the last judge, it tells the story of the rise of kingship in Israel. The book was split into two parts at least by the time of the ancient Greek translation of the Old Testament known as the Septuagint.

1 and 2 Samuel are named after the person whom God used to introduce the kingship in Israel. Samuel worried that the kingship could use its influence to lead people away from the Lord, but it was God's will that Israel be ruled by a king at this time, so he anointed first Saul and then David as kings of Israel.

1 Samuel has the following outline:

I. Samuel, the Last Judge of Israel (1:1–7:17)
II. Samuel and Saul: From Judge to King (8:1–12:25)
III. Saul, Rejected King (13:1–15:35)
IV. Saul and David: Love Turns to Hate (16:1–30:31)
V. The End of Saul (31:1–13)

Kingship is the major theme of the Book of 1 Samuel. The king was the "anointed one." The Hebrew term *messiah* means "anointed one," and the idea of a Messiah as a king like David flows out of the Book of Samuel.

I. Samuel, the Last Judge of Israel (1:1–7:17)

The Book of Samuel opens with Eli as judge in Shiloh. But things are not well. He is not competent, and his sons are evil. God decides to remove him from being priest and judge and raise up someone who will obey him. This person is Samuel. He is a gift to his mother, Hannah, from God because she had been barren up to this point. Hannah knows that he is a special gift from God and sets him apart for service as a Nazirite (Numbers 6:1–21). The first seven chapters tell us about the youth of Samuel, the downfall of Eli's household, and the early victories under Samuel.

II. Samuel and Saul: From Judge to King (8:1–12:25)

The people approach Samuel and ask for a king. Up to this point God was the only king of Israel; so the request was an insult to God himself. But God felt that it was the right time for Israel to have a king rather than a judge to lead them. Saul is chosen by God, and then Samuel leads Israel in a renewal of their agreement (see "agreement" in the Dictionary/Concordance) with God to remind them that, though they now have a human king, their real leader is still God.

III. Saul, Rejected King (13:1–15:35)

The kingship gets off to a bad start with Saul. God uses him to win great victories over many of Israel's enemies, especially the feared Philistines. But Saul is not careful to obey God's law. As a result, Samuel tells him that God is going to remove the kingship from his family.

IV. Saul and David: Love Turns to Hate (16:1–30:31)

The focus of attention switches from Saul to David. Samuel anoints David as the next king of Israel. Saul grows jealous of David and wants him killed, but God allows David to escape to the deserted areas of Israel, where he lives until the death of Saul.

V. The End of Saul (31:1–13)

The last chapter of 1 Samuel gives the account of the death of Saul. A new era was about to begin in Israel.

1 Samuel

Samuel's Birth

There was a man named Elkanah son of Jeroham from Ramathaim in the mountains of Ephraim. Elkanah was from the family of Zuph. (Jeroham was Elihu's son. Elihu was Tohu's son, and Tohu was the son of Zuph from the family group of Ephraim.) [2]Elkanah had two wives named Hannah and Peninnah. Peninnah had children, but Hannah had none.

[3]Every year Elkanah left his town of Ramah and went up to Shiloh to worship the LORD All-Powerful and to offer sacrifices to him. Shiloh was where Hophni and Phinehas, the sons of Eli, served as priests of the LORD. [4]When Elkanah offered sacrifices, he always gave a share of the meat to his wife Peninnah and to her sons and daughters. [5]But Elkanah always gave a special share of the meat to Hannah, because he loved Hannah and because the LORD had kept her from having children. [6]Peninnah would tease Hannah and upset her, because the LORD had made her unable to have children. [7]This happened every year when they went up to the house of the LORD at Shiloh. Peninnah would upset Hannah until Hannah would cry and not eat anything. [8]Her husband Elkanah would say to her, "Hannah, why are you crying and why won't you eat? Why are you sad? Don't I mean more to you than ten sons?"

[9]Once, after they had eaten their meal in Shiloh, Hannah got up. Now Eli the priest was sitting on a chair near the entrance to the LORD's house. [10]Hannah was so sad that she cried and prayed to the LORD. [11]She made a promise, saying, "LORD All-Powerful, see how sad I am. Remember me and don't forget me. If you will give me a son, I will give him back to you all his life, and no one will ever cut his hair with a razor."

[12]While Hannah kept praying, Eli watched her mouth. [13]She was praying in her heart so her lips moved, but her voice was not heard. Eli thought she was drunk [14]and said to her, "Stop getting drunk! Throw away your wine!"

[15]Hannah answered, "No, sir, I have not drunk any wine or beer. I am a deeply troubled woman, and I was telling the LORD about all my problems. [16]Don't think I am an evil woman. I have been praying because I have many troubles and am very sad."

[17]Eli answered, "Go! I wish you well. May the God of Israel give you what you asked of him."

[18]Hannah said, "May I always please you." When she left and ate something, she was not sad anymore.

[19]Early the next morning Elkanah's family got up and worshiped the LORD. Then they went back home to Ramah. Elkanah had sexual relations with his wife Hannah, and the LORD remembered her. [20]So Hannah became pregnant, and in time she gave birth to a son. She named him Samuel, saying, "His name is Samuel because I asked the LORD for him."

Hannah Gives Samuel to God

[21]Every year Elkanah went with his whole family to Shiloh to offer sacrifices and to keep the promise he had made to God. [22]But one time Hannah did not go with him. She told him, "When the boy is old enough to eat solid food, I will take him to Shiloh. Then I will give him to the LORD, and he will always live there."

[23]Elkanah, Hannah's husband, said to her, "Do what you think is best. You may stay home until the boy is old enough to eat. May the LORD do what you have said." So Hannah stayed at home to nurse her son until he was old enough to eat.

[24]When Samuel was old enough to eat, Hannah took him to the house of the LORD at Shiloh, along with a three-year-old bull, one-half bushel of flour, and a leather bag filled with wine. [25]After they had killed the bull for the sacrifice, Hannah brought Samuel to Eli. [26]She said to Eli, "As surely as you live, sir, I am the same woman who stood near you praying to the LORD. [27]I prayed for this child, and the LORD answered my prayer and gave him to me. [28]Now I give him back to the LORD. He will belong to the LORD all his life." And he worshiped the LORD there.

1:9–11 Hannah's desperation over her infertility drove her to make a promise to the Lord. If he gave her a son, she would give him back to the Lord. While some might consider this bargaining with God, in Hannah's case it showed both the depth of her desire for a child and her devotion to the Lord. All of us are loaned our children only for a while, and we must yield the control over their future to the Lord.

1:11 *cut . . . razor.* People who made special promises not to cut their hair or to drink wine or beer were called Nazirites. These people gave a specific time in their lives, or sometimes their entire lives, to the Lord. See Numbers 6:1-5.

1:11 Servant of the Lord: 2 Samuel 7

1:20 *Samuel.* This name sounds like the Hebrew word for "God heard."

1:20 *I asked the LORD for him.* Samuel's name sounds like it has the Hebrew verb "to ask" in it.

1:20 Samuel: 1 Samuel 2:11–3:21

1:20 Infertility (Childlessness/Barrenness): Psalm 128

Hannah Gives Thanks

2 Hannah prayed:
"The LORD has filled my heart with joy;
I feel very strong in the LORD.
I can laugh at my enemies;
I am glad because you have helped me!

2"There is no one holy like the LORD.
There is no God but you;
there is no Rock like our God.

3"Don't continue bragging,
don't speak proud words.
The LORD is a God who knows everything,
and he judges what people do.

4"The bows of warriors break,
but weak people become strong.
5Those who once had plenty of food now must
work for food,
but people who were hungry are
hungry no more.
The woman who could not have children
now has seven,
but the woman who had many children
now is sad.

6"The LORD sends death,
and he brings to life.
He sends people to the grave,
and he raises them to life again.
7The LORD makes some people poor,
and others he makes rich.
He makes some people humble,
and others he makes great.
8The LORD raises the poor up from the dust,
and he lifts the needy from the ashes.
He lets the poor sit with princes
and receive a throne of honor.

"The foundations of the earth
belong to the LORD,
and the LORD set the world upon them.
9He protects those who are loyal to him,
but evil people will be silenced
in darkness.
Power is not the key to success.
10The LORD destroys his enemies;
he will thunder in heaven against them.
The LORD will judge all the earth.
He will give power to his king
and make his appointed king strong."

Eli's Evil Sons

11Then Elkanah went home to Ramah, but the
boy continued to serve the LORD under Eli the
priest.
12Now Eli's sons were evil men; they did not
care about the LORD. 13This is what the priests
would normally do to the people: Every time someone brought a sacrifice, the meat would be cooked
in a pot. The priest's servant would then come carrying a fork that had three prongs. 14He would
plunge the fork into the pot or the kettle. Whatever
the fork brought out of the pot belonged to the
priest. But this is how they treated all the Israelites
who came to Shiloh to offer sacrifices. 15Even
before the fat was burned, the priest's servant
would come to the person offering sacrifices and
say, "Give the priest some meat to roast. He won't
accept boiled meat from you, only raw meat."
16If the one who offered the sacrifice said, "Let
the fat be burned up first as usual, and then take
anything you want," the priest's servant would
answer, "No, give me the meat now. If you don't,
I'll take it by force."
17The LORD saw that the sin of the servants was
very great because they did not show respect for
the offerings made to the LORD.

Samuel Grows Up

18But Samuel obeyed the LORD. As a boy he
wore a linen holy vest. 19Every year Samuel's
mother made a little coat for him and took it to
him when she went with her husband to Shiloh
for the sacrifice. 20When Eli blessed Elkanah and
his wife, he would say, "May the LORD repay you
with children through Hannah to take the place
of the boy Hannah prayed for and gave back to the
LORD." Then Elkanah and Hannah would go home.
21The LORD was kind to Hannah, so she became
the mother of three sons and two daughters. And
the boy Samuel grew up serving the LORD.
22Now Eli was very old. He heard about everything his sons were doing to all the Israelites and
how his sons had sexual relations with the women
who served at the entrance to the Meeting Tent.
23Eli said to his sons, "Why do you do these evil
things that the people tell me about? 24No, my sons.
The LORD's people are spreading a bad report about
you. 25If you sin against someone, God can help you.
But if you sin against the LORD himself, no one can
help you!" But Eli's sons would not listen to him,
because the LORD had decided to put them to death.
26The boy Samuel grew physically. He pleased
the LORD and the people.

2:8 Poverty: Psalm 22:26

VISION

NUMBERS 12:6–8

What is the relationship between prophetic vision and vision in terms of a hoped-for future? How might vision for a church or person best be defined today?

Throughout the Bible there are prophets and saintly people who share visions of a hoped-for future. From the beginning, God has allowed his character and word to us to be revealed through visions he gives to his people. Through visions, the Lord reveals what he wants known about his desires or what he wants to do, and shows it to an appointed person elected for this purpose.

What is vision? Basically, it is an act of prophetic seeing, an imaginative intellectual or spiritual perception of things. The visionary person in this sense addresses the real-life circumstances and issues of his day. Ultimately, this is a message to the church that warns, educates, challenges, or foresees the future. The focus is on the creation of a new reality.

Biblical visions are concerned both with immediate and specific situations such as God's speaking to Abraham (Genesis 15:1–21) and Moses (Numbers 12:6–8), injustices such as Peter's being put in jail (Acts 12:7), and future events of the kingdom of God, as in the prophetic writings of Ezekiel, Daniel, Isaiah, and John in the Book of Revelation. It is recorded how some visions came to people in the day (Daniel 10:4–9; Acts 9:3–4; 10:3, 9–10), while others came at night (Genesis 46:2; Job 33:15; Acts 18:9).

One of the Hebrew words often translated as vision comes from a root word related to the beholding of a vision while in a trancelike state, which is in fact how many of the visions are recorded as having come to pass (Isaiah 1:1), especially among the prophets. In this sense it points to a special awareness of God shared by devoted and committed people (Daniel 2:19; Acts 9:10; 16:9–10). Another word also used means vision as revelation, such as when God addresses Moses, Aaron, and Miriam with the words, "When a prophet is among you, I, the LORD, will show myself to him in visions; I will speak to him in dreams" (Numbers 12:6; see also 1 Samuel 3:15). As we see in the lives of the Old Testament prophets, it is often compounded by a deep dissatisfaction with things as they are because of a vision of how things could be. "The vision that Ezekiel sees is for a time many years from now. He is prophesying about times far away" (Ezekiel 12:27). It begins with indignation over the way things are, and it grows into looking for something from the future that will make a difference in the present.

Old Testament history is filled with examples of just this kind of vision. Moses was very upset by the cruel oppression of his fellow Israelites in Egypt. But he remembered God's covenant with Abraham, Isaac, and Jacob and was sustained throughout his long life by the vision of the Promised Land. The Scriptures suggest that God trusted Moses so much to lead his people that he spoke "face to face to him—clearly, not with hidden meanings" (Numbers 12:7–8). While Nehemiah was a captive in Persia, he heard that the wall of the Holy City was in ruins, and its inhabitants in great distress. The news overwhelmed him, until God put into his heart a vision of what he could and should do. "Come, let's rebuild the wall of Jerusalem, so we won't be full of shame any longer. . . . Then they answered, 'Let's start rebuilding'" (Nehemiah 2:17–18).

Moving on to New Testament times, we see this theme of vision especially in the public ministry of Jesus. He was very dissatisfied with the way things were because he knew how they could be. He was angry over disease and death, and the spiritual hunger of a people who wanted to know God. But while he was angry, he also felt compassion. This is a powerful combination, and at the very center of true vision.

At the center of Paul's defense of himself and his ministry before King Agrippa was his retelling of his vision of the Lord at his conversion on the Damascus Road. He told how God said to "tell people the things . . . that I will show you. . . . I am sending you to them to open their eyes so that they may turn away from darkness to the light, away from the power of Satan and to God" (Acts 26:15–20). The person to whom God has given the vision has a responsibility to obey it (Acts 26:19). Finally, this shared vision is always and basically about repentance and turning to God.

The early Christians were the subject of much of Rome's hatred, as well as the victims of much Jewish animosity. But Jesus had told them he had given them the power to "go and make followers of all people in the world" and armed them with the promise "I will be with you always, even until the end of this age" (Matthew 28:18–20). Indeed, it was this vision that gave them the courage and freedom to take the Gospel to a world that often didn't want to hear it.

These then are the biblical examples for the Christian community today as we try to understand God's vision for God's people.

True vision has as much to do with the ability to see what is present as it does with an ability to imagine the future. While such an ability might seem rather ordinary, real vision helps make God's direction for the present clearer. Examples of this are Moses and his circumstances while leading the people of Israel to the Promised Land, and before him, Abraham (see Genesis 12:1–3). The Lord did not talk to Moses "with hidden meanings." He was clear about the vision he gave him (Numbers 12:8).

Vision is not only about the grand events of history such as the leading of a people or the building of a church. It also concerns itself with the opening of an individual's eyes "so that they may turn away from darkness to the light, away from the power of Satan and to God. Then their sins can be forgiven" (Acts 26:18).⚭

⚭**Vision:** For additional scriptures on this topic go to Genesis 15:1.

27 A man of God came to Eli and said, "This is
what the LORD says: 'I clearly showed myself to the
family of your ancestor Aaron when they were
slaves to the king of Egypt. 28 I chose them from all
the tribes of Israel to be my priests. I wanted them
to go up to my altar, to burn incense, and to wear
the holy vest. I also let the family of your ancestor
have part of all the offerings sacrificed by the
Israelites. 29 So why don't you respect the sacrifices
and gifts? You honor your sons more than me. You
grow fat on the best parts of the meat the Israelites
bring to me.'
30 "So the LORD, the God of Israel, says: 'I
promised that your family and your ancestor's family would serve me always.' But now the LORD says:
'This must stop! I will honor those who honor me,
but I will dishonor those who ignore me. 31 The
time is coming when I will destroy the descendants of both you and your ancestors. No man will
grow old in your family. 32 You will see trouble in
my house. No matter what good things happen to
Israel, there will never be an old man in your family. 33 I will not totally cut off your family from my
altar. But your eyes will cry and your heart be sad,
because all your descendants will die.
34 " 'I will give you a sign. Both your sons, Hophni
and Phinehas, will die on the same day. 35 I will
choose a loyal priest for myself who will listen to
me and do what I want. I will make his family continue, and he will always serve before my appointed
king. 36 Then everyone left in your family will
come and bow down before him. They will beg
for a little money or a little food and say, "Please
give me a job as priest so I can have food to eat." ' "

God Calls Samuel

3 The boy Samuel served the LORD under Eli.
In those days the LORD did not speak directly
to people very often; there were very few visions.
2 Eli's eyes were so weak he was almost blind.
One night he was lying in bed. 3 Samuel was also
in bed in the LORD's house, where the Ark of the
Agreement was. God's lamp was still burning.
4 Then the LORD called Samuel, and Samuel
answered, "I am here!" 5 He ran to Eli and said,
"I am here. You called me."
But Eli said, "I didn't call you. Go back to bed."
So Samuel went back to bed.
6 The LORD called again, "Samuel!"
Samuel again went to Eli and said, "I am here.
You called me."
Again Eli said, "I didn't call you. Go back to bed."
7 Samuel did not yet know the LORD, and the
LORD had not spoken directly to him yet.
8 The LORD called Samuel for the third time.
Samuel got up and went to Eli and said, "I am here.
You called me."
Then Eli realized the LORD was calling the boy.
9 So he told Samuel, "Go to bed. If he calls you again,
say, 'Speak, LORD. I am your servant and I am listening.' " So Samuel went and lay down in bed.
10 The LORD came and stood there and called as
he had before, "Samuel, Samuel!"
Samuel said, "Speak, LORD. I am your servant
and I am listening."
11 The LORD said to Samuel, "Watch, I am going
to do something in Israel that will shock those who
hear about it. 12 At that time I will do to Eli and his
family everything I promised, from beginning to
end. 13 I told Eli I would punish his family always,
because he knew his sons were evil. They acted
without honor, but he did not stop them. 14 So I
swore to Eli's family, 'Your guilt will never be
removed by sacrifice or offering.' "
15 Samuel lay down until morning. Then he
opened the doors of the house of the LORD. He was
afraid to tell Eli about the vision, 16 but Eli called to
him, "Samuel, my son!"
Samuel answered, "I am here."
17 Eli asked, "What did the LORD say to you?
Don't hide it from me. May God punish you terribly if you hide from me anything he said to you."
18 So Samuel told Eli everything and did not hide
anything from him. Then Eli said, "He is the LORD.
Let him do what he thinks is best."
19 The LORD was with Samuel as he grew up; he
did not let any of Samuel's messages fail to come
true. 20 Then all Israel, from Dan to Beersheba,
knew Samuel was a true prophet of the LORD. 21 And
the LORD continued to show himself at Shiloh, and
he showed himself to Samuel through his word.
4 So, news about Samuel spread through all of
Israel.

The Philistines Capture the Ark of the Agreement

At that time the Israelites went out to fight the
Philistines. The Israelites camped at Ebenezer
and the Philistines at Aphek. 2 The Philistines went
to meet the Israelites in battle. And as the battle
spread, they defeated the Israelites, killing about
four thousand soldiers on the battlefield.

2:35 Growing Old: 1 Corinthians 13:11
3:3 Ark of the Agreement: 1 Samuel 4–6
3:4 Communication: Isaiah 6

3:20 *Dan to Beersheba.* Dan was the city farthest north in Israel, and Beersheba was the city farthest south. So this means all the people of Israel.
3:21 Samuel: 1 Samuel 7:2–11

3When some Israelite soldiers went back to their
camp, the older leaders of Israel asked, "Why did
the LORD let the Philistines defeat us? Let's bring
the Ark of the Agreement with the LORD here
from Shiloh and take it with us into battle. Then
God will save us from our enemies."
4So the people sent men to Shiloh. They brought
back the Ark of the Agreement with the LORD All-
Powerful, who sits between the gold creatures
with wings. Eli's two sons, Hophni and Phinehas,
were there with the Ark.
5When the Ark of the Agreement with the
LORD came into the camp, all the Israelites gave a
great shout of joy that made the ground shake.
6When the Philistines heard Israel's shout, they
asked, "What's all this shouting in the Hebrew
camp?"
Then the Philistines found out that the Ark of
the LORD had come into the Hebrew camp. 7They
were afraid and said, "A god has come into the
Hebrew camp! We're in trouble! This has never
happened before! 8How terrible it will be for us!
Who can save us from these powerful gods? They
are the ones who struck the Egyptians with all
kinds of disasters in the desert. 9Be brave,
Philistines! Fight like men! In the past they were
our slaves. So fight like men, or we will become
their slaves."
10So the Philistines fought hard and defeated the
Israelites, and every Israelite soldier ran away to his
own home. It was a great defeat for Israel, because
thirty thousand Israelite soldiers were killed. 11The
Ark of God was taken by the Philistines, and Eli's
two sons, Hophni and Phinehas, died.
12That same day a man from the tribe of
Benjamin ran from the battle. He tore his clothes
and put dust on his head to show his great sadness.
13When he arrived in Shiloh, Eli was by the side of
the road. He was sitting there in a chair, watching,
because he was worried about the Ark of God.
When the Benjaminite entered Shiloh, he told
the bad news. Then all the people in town cried
loudly. 14Eli heard the crying and asked, "What's all
this noise?"
The Benjaminite ran to Eli and told him what
had happened. 15Eli was now ninety-eight years
old, and he was blind. 16The Benjaminite told him,
"I have come from the battle. I ran all the way here
today."
Eli asked, "What happened, my son?"
17The Benjaminite answered, "Israel ran away
from the Philistines, and the Israelite army has lost
many soldiers. Your two sons are both dead, and
the Philistines have taken the Ark of God."
18When he mentioned the Ark of God, Eli fell
backward off his chair. He fell beside the gate,
broke his neck, and died, because he was old and
fat. He had led Israel for forty years.

The Glory Is Gone

19Eli's daughter-in-law, the wife of Phinehas,
was pregnant and was about to give birth. When
she heard the news that the Ark of God had been
taken and that Eli, her father-in-law, and Phinehas,
her husband, were both dead, she began to give
birth to her child. The child was born, but the
mother had much trouble in giving birth. 20As
she was dying, the women who helped her said,
"Don't worry! You've given birth to a son!" But
she did not answer or pay attention. 21She named
the baby Ichabod, saying, "Israel's glory is gone."
She said this because the Ark of God had been
taken and her father-in-law and husband were
dead. 22She said, "Israel's glory is gone, because the
Ark of God has been taken away."

Trouble for the Philistines

5 After the Philistines had captured the Ark of
God, they took it from Ebenezer to Ashdod.
2They carried it into Dagon's temple and put it
next to Dagon. 3When the people of Ashdod rose
early the next morning, they found that Dagon had
fallen on his face on the ground before the Ark of
the LORD. So they put Dagon back in his place.
4The next morning when they rose, they again
found Dagon fallen on the ground before the Ark
of the LORD. His head and hands had broken off
and were lying in the doorway. Only his body was
still in one piece. 5So, even today, Dagon's priests
and others who enter his temple at Ashdod refuse
to step on the doorsill.
6The LORD was hard on the people of Ashdod
and their neighbors. He caused them to suffer and
gave them growths on their skin. 7When the
people of Ashdod saw what was happening, they
said, "The Ark of the God of Israel can't stay with
us. God is punishing us and Dagon our god." 8The
people of Ashdod called all five Philistine kings

4:3 *take it with us into battle.* The Ark represented God's presence with his people. Since it was moveable, it was taken into battle with the army. Here, however, Eli's sons treat the Ark like a magical box.

4:4 The expression "whose throne is between the gold creatures with wings" (2 Samuel 6:2; 2 Kings 19:15; Psalm 80:1) emphasizes Israel's understanding that the Ark was the 'throneseat' of God's invisible presence.

4:7 *A god has come into the Hebrew camp!* The Philistines believed in many false gods, including the false gods of other nations.

4:21 *Ichabod.* This name means "no glory."

5:4 *His head and hands had broken off.* Like a defeated enemy. In the ancient Near Eastern world the practice of cutting off heads and hands of slain enemies was known. Counting these could give an accurate body count.

together and asked them, "What should we do
with the Ark of the God of Israel?"

The rulers answered, "Move the Ark of the
God of Israel to Gath." So the Philistines moved it
to Gath.

9But after they moved it to Gath, there was a
great panic. The LORD was hard on that city also,
and he gave both old and young people in Gath
growths on their skin. 10Then the Philistines sent
the Ark of God to Ekron.

But when it came into Ekron, the people of
Ekron yelled, "Why are you bringing the Ark of the
God of Israel to our city? Do you want to kill us
and our people?" 11So they called all the kings of
the Philistines together and said, "Send the Ark
of the God of Israel back to its place before it kills
us and our people!" All the people in the city
were struck with terror because God was so hard
on them there. 12The people who did not die
were troubled with growths on their skin. So the
people of Ekron cried loudly to heaven.

The Ark of God Is Sent Home

6 The Philistines kept the Ark of God in their
land seven months. 2Then they called for their
priests and magicians and said, "What should we
do with the Ark of the LORD? Tell us how to send
it back home!"

3The priests and magicians answered, "If you
send back the Ark of the God of Israel, don't send
it back empty. You must give a penalty offering. If
you are then healed, you will know that it was
because of the Ark that you had such trouble."

4The Philistines asked, "What kind of penalty
offering should we send to Israel's God?"

They answered, "Make five gold models of the
growths on your skin and five gold models of rats.
The number of models must match the number
of Philistine kings, because the same sickness has
come on you and your kings. 5Make models of the
growths and the rats that are ruining the country,
and give honor to Israel's God. Then maybe he
will stop being so hard on you, your gods, and your
land. 6Don't be stubborn like the king of Egypt and
the Egyptians. After God punished them terribly,
they let the Israelites leave Egypt.

7"You must build a new cart and get two cows
that have just had calves. These must be cows that
have never had yokes on their necks. Hitch the
cows to the cart, and take the calves home, away
from their mothers. 8Put the Ark of the LORD on
the cart and the gold models for the penalty offering
in a box beside the Ark. Then send the cart straight
on its way. 9Watch the cart. If it goes toward Beth
Shemesh in Israel's own land, the LORD has given
us this great sickness. But if it doesn't, we will
know that Israel's God has not punished us. Our
sickness just happened by chance."

10The Philistines did what the priests and
magicians said. They took two cows that had just
had calves and hitched them to the cart, but they
kept their calves at home. 11They put the Ark of
the LORD and the box with the gold rats and models of growths on the cart. 12Then the cows went
straight toward Beth Shemesh. They stayed on the
road, mooing all the way, and did not turn right or
left. The Philistine kings followed the cows as far
as the border of Beth Shemesh.

13Now the people of Beth Shemesh were harvesting their wheat in the valley. When they
looked up and saw the Ark of the LORD, they were
very happy. 14The cart came to the field belonging
to Joshua of Beth Shemesh and stopped near a
large rock. The people of Beth Shemesh chopped
up the wood of the cart. Then they sacrificed the
cows as burnt offerings to the LORD. 15The Levites
took down the Ark of the LORD and the box that
had the gold models, and they put both on the
large rock. That day the people of Beth Shemesh
offered whole burnt offerings and made sacrifices
to the LORD. 16After the five Philistine kings saw
this, they went back to Ekron the same day.

17The Philistines had sent these gold models of
the growths as penalty offerings to the LORD. They
sent one model for each Philistine town: Ashdod,
Gaza, Ashkelon, Gath, and Ekron. 18And the
Philistines also sent gold models of rats. The number of rats matched the number of towns belonging to the Philistine kings, including both strong,
walled cities and country villages. The large rock
on which they put the Ark of the LORD is still there
in the field of Joshua of Beth Shemesh.

19But some of the men of Beth Shemesh looked
into the Ark of the LORD. So God killed seventy of
them. The people of Beth Shemesh cried because
the LORD had struck them down. 20They said,
"Who can stand before the LORD, this holy God?
Whom will he strike next?"

21Then they sent messengers to the people of
Kiriath Jearim, saying, "The Philistines have
brought back the Ark of the LORD. Come down
and take it to your city."⚭

7 The men of Kiriath Jearim came and took the
Ark of the LORD to Abinadab's house on a hill.

6:4 *models.* In the ancient world there was a form of magic by which the magician made a model of an object that was feared for the purpose of getting rid of it. Here the skin growths and the rats represented the disease and the means of spreading it.

⚭**6:21 Ark of the Agreement:** 2 Samuel 6

There they made Abinadab's son Eleazar holy for the LORD so he could guard the Ark of the LORD.

The Lord Saves the Israelites

2The Ark stayed at Kiriath Jearim a long time—twenty years in all. And the people of Israel began to follow the LORD again. 3Samuel spoke to the whole group of Israel, saying, "If you're turning back to the LORD with all your hearts, you must remove your foreign gods and your idols of Ashtoreth. You must give yourselves fully to the LORD and serve only him. Then he will save you from the Philistines."

4So the Israelites put away their idols of Baal and Ashtoreth, and they served only the LORD.

5Samuel said, "All Israel must meet at Mizpah, and I will pray to the LORD for you." 6So the Israelites met together at Mizpah. They drew water from the ground and poured it out before the LORD and did not eat that day. They confessed, "We have sinned against the LORD." And Samuel served as judge of Israel at Mizpah.

7The Philistines heard the Israelites were meeting at Mizpah, so the Philistine kings came up to attack them. When the Israelites heard they were coming, they were afraid. 8They said to Samuel, "Don't stop praying to the LORD our God for us! Ask him to save us from the Philistines!" 9Then Samuel took a baby lamb and offered it to the LORD as a whole burnt offering. He called to the LORD for Israel's sake, and the LORD answered him.

10While Samuel was burning the offering, the Philistines came near to attack Israel. But the LORD thundered against them with loud thunder. They were so frightened they became confused. So the Israelites defeated the Philistines in battle. 11The men of Israel ran out of Mizpah and chased the Philistines almost to Beth Car, killing the Philistines along the way.⚭

Peace Comes to Israel

12After this happened Samuel took a stone and set it up between Mizpah and Shen. He named the stone Ebenezer, saying, "The LORD has helped us to this point."⚭ 13So the Philistines were defeated and did not enter the Israelites' land again.

The LORD was against the Philistines all Samuel's life. 14Earlier the Philistines had taken towns from the Israelites, but the Israelites won them back, from Ekron to Gath. They also took back from the Philistines the lands near these towns. There was peace also between Israel and the Amorites.

15Samuel continued as judge of Israel all his life. 16Every year he went from Bethel to Gilgal to Mizpah and judged the Israelites in all these towns. 17But Samuel always went back to Ramah, where his home was. There he judged Israel and built an altar to the LORD.

Israel Asks for a King

8 When Samuel was old, he made his sons judges for Israel. 2His first son was named Joel, and his second son was named Abijah. Joel and Abijah were judges in Beersheba. 3But Samuel's sons did not live as he did. They tried to get money dishonestly, and they accepted money secretly to make wrong judgments.

4So all the older leaders came together and met Samuel at Ramah. 5They said to him, "You're old, and your sons don't live as you do. Give us a king to rule over us like all the other nations."

6When the older leaders said that, Samuel was not pleased. He prayed to the LORD, 7and the LORD told Samuel, "Listen to whatever the people say to you. They have not rejected you. They have rejected me from being their king. 8They are doing as they have always done. When I took them out of Egypt, they left me and served other gods. They are doing the same to you. 9Now listen to the people, but warn them what the king who rules over them will do."

10So Samuel told those who had asked him for a king what the LORD had said. 11Samuel said, "If you have a king ruling over you, this is what he will do: He will take your sons and make them serve with his chariots and his horses, and they will run in front of the king's chariot. 12The king will make some of your sons commanders over thousands or over fifties. He will make some of your other sons plow his ground and reap his harvest. He will take others to make weapons of war and equipment for his chariots. 13He will take your daughters to make perfume and cook and bake for him. 14He will take your best fields, vineyards, and olive groves and give them to his servants. 15He will take one-tenth of your grain and grapes and give it to his officers and servants. 16He will take your male and female servants, your best cattle, and your donkeys and use them all for his own work. 17He will take one-tenth of your flocks, and you yourselves will become his slaves. 18When that time comes, you will cry out because of the king you chose. But the LORD will not answer you then."

19But the people would not listen to Samuel.

⚭**7:11 Samuel:** 1 Samuel 15:1–16:13
7:12 *Ebenezer.* This name means "stone of help."

⚭**7:12 Stone:** Psalm 118:22

They said, "No! We want a king to rule over us.
20Then we will be the same as all the other
nations. Our king will judge for us and go with us
and fight our battles."
21After Samuel heard all that the people said,
he repeated their words to the LORD. 22The LORD
answered, "You must listen to them. Give them a
king."
Then Samuel told the people of Israel, "Go
back to your towns."

Saul Looks for His Father's Donkeys

9 Kish, son of Abiel from the tribe of Benjamin,
was an important man. (Abiel was the son of
Zeror, who was the son of Becorath, who was the
son of Aphiah of Benjamin.) 2Kish had a son named
Saul, who was a fine young man. There was no
Israelite better than he. Saul stood a head taller
than any other man in Israel.
3Now the donkeys of Saul's father, Kish, were
lost. So Kish said to Saul, his son, "Take one of
the servants, and go and look for the donkeys."
4Saul went through the mountains of Ephraim
and the land of Shalisha, but he and the servant
could not find the donkeys. They went into the
land of Shaalim, but the donkeys were not there.
They went through the land of Benjamin, but
they still did not find them. 5When they arrived
in the area of Zuph, Saul said to his servant, "Let's
go back or my father will stop thinking about the
donkeys and will start worrying about us."
6But the servant answered, "A man of God is in
this town. People respect him because everything
he says comes true. Let's go into the town now.
Maybe he can tell us something about the journey
we have taken."
7Saul said to his servant, "If we go into the town,
what can we give him? The food in our bags is
gone. We have no gift to give him. Do we have
anything?"
8Again the servant answered Saul. "Look, I have
one-tenth of an ounce of silver. Give it to the man
of God. Then he will tell us about our journey."
9(In the past, if someone in Israel wanted to ask
something from God, he would say, "Let's go to
the seer." We call the person a prophet today, but
in the past he was called a seer.)
10Saul said to his servant, "That's a good idea.
Come, let's go." So they went toward the town
where the man of God was.
11As Saul and the servant were going up the hill
to the town, they met some young women coming
out to get water. Saul and the servant asked them,
"Is the seer here?"
12The young women answered, "Yes, he's here.
He's ahead of you. Hurry now. He has just come
to our town today, because the people will offer a
sacrifice at the place of worship. 13As soon as you
enter the town, you will find him before he goes
up to the place of worship to eat. The people will
not begin eating until the seer comes, because he
must bless the sacrifice. After that, the guests will
eat. Go now, and you should find him."

Saul Meets Samuel

14Saul and the servant went up to the town. Just
as they entered it, they saw Samuel coming toward
them on his way up to the place of worship.
15The day before Saul came, the LORD had told
Samuel: 16"About this time tomorrow I will send
you a man from the land of Benjamin. Appoint
him to lead my people Israel. He will save my people from the Philistines. I have seen the suffering
of my people, and I have listened to their cry."
17When Samuel first saw Saul, the LORD said to
Samuel, "This is the man I told you about. He will
organize my people."
18Saul approached Samuel at the gate and said,
"Please tell me where the seer's house is."
19Samuel answered, "I am the seer. Go with me
to the place of worship. Today you and your servant are to eat with me. Tomorrow morning I will
answer all your questions and send you home.
20Don't worry about the donkeys you lost three
days ago, because they have been found. Soon all
the wealth of Israel will belong to you and your
family."
21Saul answered, "But I am from the tribe of
Benjamin, the smallest tribe in Israel. And my
family group is the smallest in the tribe of Benjamin. Why are you saying such things?"
22Then Samuel took Saul and his servant into a
large room and gave them a choice place at the
table. About thirty guests were there. 23Samuel
said to the cook, "Bring the meat I gave you, the
portion I told you to set aside."
24So the cook took the thigh and put it on the
table in front of Saul. Samuel said, "This is the
meat saved for you. Eat it, because it was set aside
for you for this special time. As I said, 'I had invited
the people.'" So Saul ate with Samuel that day.
25After they finished eating, they came down
from the place of worship and went to the town.
Then Samuel talked with Saul on the roof of his

9:25 *roof.* In Bible times houses were built with flat roofs. The roof was used for drying things such as flax and fruit. And it was used as an extra room, as a place for worship, and as a cool place to sleep in the summer. See Deuteronomy 22:8.

house. 26At dawn they got up, and Samuel called to Saul on the roof. He said, "Get up, and I will send you on your way." So Saul got up and went out of the house with Samuel. 27As Saul, his servant, and Samuel were getting near the edge of the city, Samuel said to Saul, "Tell the servant to go on ahead of us, but you stay, because I have a message from God for you."

Samuel Appoints Saul

10 Samuel took a jar of olive oil and poured it on Saul's head. He kissed Saul and said, "The LORD has appointed you to lead his people. 2After you leave me today, you will meet two men near Rachel's tomb on the border of Benjamin at Zelzah. They will say to you, 'The donkeys you were looking for have been found. But now your father has stopped thinking about his donkeys and is worrying about you. He is asking, "What will I do about my son?"'

3"Then you will go on until you reach the big tree at Tabor. Three men on their way to worship God at Bethel will meet you there. One man will be carrying three goats. Another will be carrying three loaves of bread. And the third will have a leather bag full of wine. 4They will greet you and offer you two loaves of bread, which you must accept. 5Then you will go to Gibeah of God, where a Philistine camp is. When you approach this town, a group of prophets will come down from the place of worship. They will be playing harps, tambourines, flutes, and lyres, and they will be prophesying. 6Then the Spirit of the LORD will rush upon you with power. You will prophesy with these prophets, and you will be changed into a different man. 7After these signs happen, do whatever you find to do, because God will help you.

8"Go ahead of me to Gilgal. I will come down to you to offer whole burnt offerings and fellowship offerings. But you must wait seven days. Then I will come and tell you what to do."

Saul Made King

9When Saul turned to leave Samuel, God changed Saul's heart. All these signs came true that day. 10When Saul and his servant arrived at Gibeah, Saul met a group of prophets. The Spirit of God rushed upon him, and he prophesied with the prophets. 11When people who had known Saul before saw him prophesying with the prophets, they asked each other, "What has happened to Kish's son? Is even Saul one of the prophets?"

12A man who lived there said, "Who is the father of these prophets?" So this became a famous saying: "Is even Saul one of the prophets?" 13When Saul finished prophesying, he entered the place of worship.

14Saul's uncle asked him and his servant, "Where have you been?"

Saul said, "We were looking for the donkeys. When we couldn't find them, we went to talk to Samuel."

15Saul's uncle asked, "Please tell me. What did Samuel say to you?"

16Saul answered, "He told us the donkeys had already been found." But Saul did not tell his uncle what Samuel had said about his becoming king.

17Samuel called all the people of Israel to meet with the LORD at Mizpah. 18He said, "This is what the LORD, the God of Israel, says: 'I led Israel out of Egypt. I saved you from Egypt's control and from other kingdoms that were troubling you.' 19But now you have rejected your God. He saves you from all your troubles and problems, but you said, 'No! We want a king to rule over us.' Now come, stand before the LORD in your tribes and family groups."

20When Samuel gathered all the tribes of Israel, the tribe of Benjamin was picked. 21Samuel had them pass by in family groups, and Matri's family was picked. Then he had each man of Matri's family pass by, and Saul son of Kish was picked. But when they looked for Saul, they could not find him. 22They asked the LORD, "Has Saul come here yet?"

The LORD said, "Yes. He's hiding behind the baggage."

23So they ran and brought him out. When Saul stood among the people, he was a head taller than anyone else. 24Then Samuel said to the people, "See the man the LORD has chosen. There is no one like him among all the people."

Then the people shouted, "Long live the king!"

25Samuel explained the rights and duties of the king and then wrote them in a book and put it before the LORD. Then he told the people to go to their homes.

26Saul also went to his home in Gibeah. God touched the hearts of certain brave men who went along with him. 27But some troublemakers said, "How can this man save us?" They disapproved of Saul and refused to bring gifts to him. But Saul kept quiet.

10:1 *took a jar of olive oil and poured it.* This ritual is called "anointing" and represented the Spirit of God coming on a person in order to equip him for a special task.

Nahash Troubles Jabesh Gilead

11 About a month later Nahash the Ammonite and his army surrounded the city of Jabesh in Gilead. All the people of Jabesh said to Nahash, "Make a treaty with us, and we will serve you."

2But he answered, "I will make a treaty with you only if I'm allowed to poke out the right eye of each of you. Then all Israel will be ashamed!"

3The older leaders of Jabesh said to Nahash, "Give us seven days to send messengers through all Israel. If no one comes to help us, we will give ourselves up to you."

4When the messengers came to Gibeah where Saul lived and told the people the news, they cried loudly. 5Saul was coming home from plowing the fields with his oxen when he heard the people crying. He asked, "What's wrong with the people that they are crying?" Then they told Saul what the messengers from Jabesh had said. 6When Saul heard their words, God's Spirit rushed upon him with power, and he became very angry. 7So he took a pair of oxen and cut them into pieces. Then he gave the pieces of the oxen to messengers and ordered them to carry them through all the land of Israel.

The messengers said, "This is what will happen to the oxen of anyone who does not follow Saul and Samuel." So the people became very afraid of the LORD. They all came together as if they were one person. 8Saul gathered the people together at Bezek. There were three hundred thousand men from Israel and thirty thousand men from Judah.

9They said to the messengers who had come, "Tell the people at Jabesh Gilead this: 'Before the day warms up tomorrow, you will be saved.'" So the messengers went and reported this to the people at Jabesh, and they were very happy. 10The people said to Nahash the Ammonite, "Tomorrow we will come out to meet you. Then you can do anything you want to us."

11The next morning Saul divided his soldiers into three groups. At dawn they entered the Ammonite camp and defeated them before the heat of the day. The Ammonites who escaped were scattered; no two of them were still together.

12Then the people said to Samuel, "Who didn't want Saul as king? Bring them here and we will kill them!"

13But Saul said, "No! No one will be put to death today. Today the LORD has saved Israel!"

14Then Samuel said to the people, "Come, let's go to Gilgal. There we will again promise to obey the king." 15So all the people went to Gilgal, and there, before the LORD, the people made Saul king. They offered fellowship offerings to the LORD, and Saul and all the Israelites had a great celebration.

Samuel's Farewell Speech

12 Samuel said to all Israel, "I have done every thing you wanted me to do and have put a king over you. 2Now you have a king to lead you. I am old and gray, and my sons are here with you. I have been your leader since I was young. 3Here I am. If I have done anything wrong, you must testify against me before the LORD and his appointed king. Did I steal anyone's ox or donkey? Did I hurt or cheat anyone? Did I ever secretly accept money to pretend not to see something wrong? If I did any of these things, I will make it right."

4The Israelites answered, "You have not cheated us, or hurt us, or taken anything unfairly from anyone."

5Samuel said to them, "The LORD is a witness to what you have said. His appointed king is also a witness today that you did not find anything wrong in me."

"He is our witness," they said.

6Then Samuel said to the people, "It is the LORD who chose Moses and Aaron and brought your ancestors out of Egypt. 7Now, stand there, and I will remind you of all the good things the LORD did for you and your ancestors.

8"After Jacob entered Egypt, his descendants cried to the LORD for help. So the LORD sent Moses and Aaron, who took your ancestors out of Egypt and brought them to live in this place.

9"But they forgot the LORD their God. So he handed them over as slaves to Sisera, the commander of the army of Hazor, and as slaves to the Philistines and the king of Moab. They all fought against your ancestors. 10Then your ancestors cried to the LORD and said, 'We have sinned. We have left the LORD and served the Baals and the Ashtoreths. But now save us from our enemies, and we will serve you.' 11So the LORD sent Gideon, Barak, Jephthah, and Samuel. He saved you from your enemies around you, and you lived in safety. 12But when you saw Nahash king of the Ammonites coming against you, you said, 'No! We want a king to rule over us!'—even though

11:7 See Judges 19:29. Saul's act is a call to war and a threat to anyone within Israel who would not join him.

12:11 *Gideon.* Also called Jerub-Baal.

the LORD your God was your king. 13Now here is the king you chose, the one you asked for. The LORD has put him over you. 14You must honor the LORD and serve him. You must obey his word and not turn against his commands. Both you and the king ruling over you must follow the LORD your God. If you do, it will be well with you. 15But if you don't obey the LORD, and if you turn against his commands, he will be against you. He will do to you what he did to your ancestors.

16"Now stand still and see the great thing the LORD will do before your eyes. 17It is now the time of the wheat harvest. I will pray for the LORD to send thunder and rain. Then you will know what an evil thing you did against the LORD when you asked for a king."

18Then Samuel prayed to the LORD, and that same day the LORD sent thunder and rain. So the people were very afraid of the LORD and Samuel. 19They said to Samuel, "Pray to the LORD your God for us, your servants! Don't let us die! We've added to all our sins the evil of asking for a king."

20Samuel answered, "Don't be afraid. It's true that you did wrong, but don't turn away from the LORD. Serve the LORD with all your heart. 21Idols are of no use, so don't worship them. They can't help you or save you. They are useless! 22For his own sake, the LORD won't leave his people. Instead, he was pleased to make you his own people. 23I will surely not stop praying for you, because that would be sinning against the LORD. I will teach you what is good and right. 24You must honor the LORD and truly serve him with all your heart. Remember the wonderful things he did for you! 25But if you are stubborn and do evil, he will sweep you and your king away."

13 Saul was thirty years old when he became king, and he was king over Israel forty-two years. 2Saul chose three thousand men from Israel. Two thousand men stayed with him at Micmash in the mountains of Bethel, and one thousand men stayed with Jonathan at Gibeah in Benjamin. Saul sent the other men in the army back home.

3Jonathan attacked the Philistine camp in Geba, and the other Philistines heard about it. Saul said, "Let the Hebrews hear what happened." So he told the men to blow trumpets through all the land of Israel. 4All the Israelites heard the news. The men said, "Saul has defeated the Philistine camp. Now the Philistines will really hate us!" Then the Israelites were called to join Saul at Gilgal.

5The Philistines gathered to fight Israel with three thousand chariots and six thousand men to ride in them. Their soldiers were as many as the grains of sand on the seashore. The Philistines went and camped at Micmash, which is east of Beth Aven. 6When the Israelites saw that they were in trouble, they went to hide in caves and bushes, among the rocks, and in pits and wells. 7Some Hebrews even went across the Jordan River to the land of Gad and Gilead.

But Saul stayed at Gilgal, and all the men in his army were shaking with fear. 8Saul waited seven days, because Samuel had said he would meet him then. But Samuel did not come to Gilgal, and the soldiers began to leave.

9So Saul said, "Bring me the whole burnt offering and the fellowship offerings." Then Saul offered the whole burnt offering. 10Just as he finished, Samuel arrived, and Saul went to greet him.

11Samuel asked, "What have you done?"

Saul answered, "I saw the soldiers leaving me, and you were not here when you said you would be. The Philistines were gathering at Micmash. 12Then I thought, 'The Philistines will come against me at Gilgal, and I haven't asked for the LORD's approval.' So I forced myself to offer the whole burnt offering."

13Samuel said, "You acted foolishly! You haven't obeyed the command of the LORD your God. If you had obeyed him, the LORD would have made your kingdom continue in Israel always, 14but now your kingdom will not continue. The LORD has looked for the kind of man he wants. He has appointed him to rule his people, because you haven't obeyed his command."

15Then Samuel left Gilgal and went to Gibeah in Benjamin. Saul counted the men who were still with him, and there were about six hundred.

Hard Times for Israel

16Saul and his son Jonathan and the soldiers with him stayed in Gibeah in the land of Benjamin. The Philistines made their camp at Micmash. 17Three groups went out from the Philistine camp to make raids. One group went on the Ophrah road in the land of Shual. 18The second group

12:15 Rebellion: Nehemiah 9:26–31
12:17 *time . . . harvest.* This was a dry time in the summer when no rains fell.
13:1 *Saul . . . years.* This is how the verse is worded in some early Greek copies. The Hebrew is not clear here.
13:5 *three thousand.* Some Greek copies say three thousand. The Hebrew copies say thirty thousand.
13:11 *What have you done?* Only priests were allowed to offer sacrifices to the Lord.

Rebellion

Numbers 14

What makes a person a rebel in the Bible? What does God do with rebels?

The Bible speaks just as passionately about unbelief as it does about belief. There are many terms for rejecting God, but the one which perhaps carries the most notoriety is "rebellion" (or, "turning away"). Whenever God speaks like a betrayed parent or a wounded lover, it is in response to human rebellion (Ezekiel 16:1–34; Hosea 11:1–4).

What is rebellion against God? In one sense, it refers to something specific: to particular moments in the Bible's recorded history when God's people ungratefully rejected his love and contemptuously defied his authority. Human sinfulness is specifically labeled as "rebellion" in four main periods: (1) when Israel wandered in the wilderness (Numbers 14:9), (2) when Israel was taken captive (Ezekiel 2:3), (3) the time of Jesus (Hebrews 12:3; John 1:11), and (4) the last days before Jesus' return (2 Thessalonians 2:2–3). Each time is marked with people who "shake their fists at God and try to get their own way against the Almighty" (Job 15:25).

In another sense, however, rebellion against God refers to something more general: all human beings as sinners are in rebellion. Paul writes in Romans 8:7: "When people's thinking is controlled by the sinful self, they are against God, because they refuse to obey God's law." Apart from Christ, the general direction of people's lives makes them "God's enemies" (Romans 5:10). The study of rebellion is important because it sheds light upon ourselves.

What, then, characterizes rebellion against God? First, there is a total rejection of God's call to trust in him. To rebel is to renounce the authority's believability. The people at Kadesh angrily spurned the Lord's goodness and interpreted it as evil: "We wish we had died in Egypt or in this desert. Why is the LORD bringing us to this land to be killed with swords?" (Numbers 14:2–3). They were so set against God that they were blind to his grace and power (v. 11).

Other rebellious behavior in the Bible reflects its opposing and distrustful nature. God explained to Moses and Aaron that their rebellion in striking the rock to provide water at Meribah (Numbers 20:1–13), instead of following his command, was "because you did not believe me" (v. 12). The same can be said about the Pharisees' hateful response to Jesus, which is attributed to the fact that they did not believe in him (John 8:23–24, 39–47). They similarly interpreted Jesus' goodness as evil (Matthew 12:22–24).

A second characteristic of rebellion is willful and deliberate disobedience to the instruction God gives. To rebel is to defy openly the authority's commands. "Those who fight against the light do not know God's ways or stay in his paths" (Job 24:13). The people at Kadesh angrily chose not to follow God's course, but to chart their own (Numbers 14:3: "We would be better off going back to Egypt"). Despite the foolishness of their disobedience, illustrated by their defeat at the end of the chapter (vv. 42–45), they persisted in desiring to do things their own way. Their rebellion was seen in their idolatry (Ezekiel 20:8) and disregard for the law (Daniel 9:5). God's exasperation is captured in Psalm 50:16–17: "Why do you talk about my laws? Why do you mention my agreement? You hate my teachings and turn your back on what I say."

A third characteristic of rebellion is the prideful refusal to acknowledge the authority God claims. To rebel is to deny the preeminence of another in order to bolster oneself. The people at Kadesh were proud (Numbers 14:44). They wished to replace God's appointed leaders with ones who would do their bidding: "Let's choose a leader and go back to Egypt," (v. 4); "Then all the people talked about killing [Moses and Aaron] with stone," (v. 10). The arrogance one shows in attempting to eliminate God so that one might become one's own authority is pictured well by Isaiah 45:9: "How terrible it will be for those who argue with the God who made them. . . . The clay does not ask the potter, 'What are you doing?'"

What then is to become of the rebellious? The Bible makes it clear that they cannot share in the promise of eternal rest (Hebrews 3:15–19). God's sifting out the rebellious from the faithful at Kadesh (Numbers 14:29–30) is indicative of his more general plan for only a faithful remnant to receive his eternal blessings (Ezekiel 20:38). The rebellious are promised only eternal punishment (Revelation 20:10, 15).

Rebellion: For additional scriptures on this topic go to Exodus 14:10–12.

LYING/DISHONESTY

NUMBERS 23:19

Is all lying wrong? What happens to liars? What is the truth?

The importance of truthfulness and honesty (as opposed to lying and dishonesty) can be seen in the emphasis the Bible places upon the ultimate source of truth, which, simply stated, is God and his teachings. Truth is an inseparable part of the very character of God, namely, his integrity, trustworthiness, and faithfulness. He is, for example, called the "God of truth" (Psalm 31:5), who "cannot lie" (Titus 1:2; Hebrews 6:18). The Bible relates this quality of truthfulness to all three persons of the Trinity. In Jesus' Upper Room prayer he addressed the Father as "the only true God" (John 17:3). Jesus himself is described as "full of grace and truth" (John 1:14, 17; 14:6), and the Holy Spirit as the "Spirit of truth" (John 14:17; 15:26; 16:13). Not only God's person but also his teaching is truth (John 17:17; Psalm 33:4; 119:142, 151, 160).

Truth is not only a moral quality, but we can also speak of it as that which is revealed for what it really is—open, uncovered, and authentic, opposed to what is false or phony. God reveals himself to us this way, as the One True God (vs. the false gods of idolatry, Jeremiah 13:25; 16:19). Finally, truth can be understood in terms of statements which are accurate, correct, or right. God's words are true, and we can respond to them with faith. The Good News is described in many places as the "truth of the Good News" (Galatians 2:5, 14; 5:7; 1 Timothy 2:4). The entire body of Christian teaching is also sometimes described as the "true teaching" (2 Timothy 2:15).

In contrast, the source and basis of lying is in Satan, who is called "the father of lies" (John 8:44), standing in fundamental opposition to the truth of God. Among his sinister purposes is to deceive people and cause them through unbelief to question God's integrity (Genesis 3:4-6), for not to believe God is to make God out to be a liar (1 John 5:10). Lying is also rooted in the minds and hearts of sinful humanity (Jeremiah 17:9) "who tells lies as soon as they are born" (Psalm 58:3), "hide the truth" (Romans 1:18), and "trade the truth of God for a lie" (Romans 1:25). Lying can become such a habit that it is ingrained in one's very lifestyle (Jeremiah 9:5; 23:14) to the point that one's conscience can be destroyed or rendered insensitive (1 Timothy 4:2). Those who lie will themselves be the recipients of lies (compare Genesis 27:35 with Genesis 29:25). The fruit of lying and dishonesty is the breakdown of society (Isaiah 59:14–15). Those who reject the Good News are at the same time believing the lie, living under its dominance, and becoming liars themselves (1 John 2:22). The ultimate destiny of liars is judgment (2 Thessalonians 2:10–11) in the lake of fire (Revelation 21:8; 21:27; 22:15).

As we have seen, truthfulness is fundamental to God's very person. As such, he fiercely opposes lying and dishonesty, for it offends his holy character in which resides absolutely no darkness (1 John 1:5). Lying is listed among the sins that he especially hates (Deuteronomy 25:16; see Proverbs 6:16–19 where two of the seven sins are related to lying). Lying is part of the old life before salvation in Christ (Colossians 3:9) and violates the clear command of God (Exodus 20:26; Leviticus 19:11–12). Believers are to follow the way of truth (Psalm 86:11; 2 John 4), hate lying (Proverbs 13:5), and reject the company of liars (Psalm 101:7). Because they are members of the same body (Ephesians 4:25), God's people are to refrain from lying and be "completely truthful" (Psalm 51:6). The very serious nature of lying can be seen in one dramatic incident in the life of the early church (Acts 5:1–11).

Although some may feel that lying or "fudging on the truth" is acceptable (or even encouraged) under certain circumstances as perhaps the most loving thing or best thing to do, the Bible in its entirety uniformly condemns all forms of lying. For one thing, "love is not happy with evil but . . . with the truth" (1 Corinthians 13:6). For another, we are not to "do evil so that good will come" (Romans 3:8). In other words the Bible is concerned with the way we do things, not just the rightness or wrongness of the things themselves. The Romans passage is of special significance since Paul uses lying to illustrate this very point (Romans 3:7).

It is true that some of God's choicest servants were guilty of lying at some point in their lives (Genesis 20:2; 1 Samuel 21:2; Matthew 26:72), but we must remember that the Bible does not approve everything it reports. In addition, God does not and cannot lie, but he is still able to use the lies of others to accomplish his purposes.

Lying/Dishonesty: For additional scriptures on this topic go to 1 Samuel 15:29.

went on the Beth Horon road. The third group went on the border road that overlooks the Valley of Zeboim toward the desert.

[19]The whole land of Israel had no blacksmith because the Philistines had said, "The Hebrews might make swords and spears." [20]So all the Israelites had to go down to the Philistines to have their plows, hoes, axes, and sickles sharpened. [21]The Philistine blacksmiths charged about one-fourth of an ounce of silver for sharpening plows and hoes. And they charged one-eighth of an ounce of silver for sharpening picks, axes, and the sticks used to guide oxen.

[22]So when the battle came, the soldiers with Saul and Jonathan had no swords or spears. Only Saul and his son Jonathan had them.

Israel Defeats the Philistines

[23]A group from the Philistine army had gone out to the pass at Micmash.

14 One day Jonathan, Saul's son, said to the officer who carried his armor, "Come, let's go over to the Philistine camp on the other side." But Jonathan did not tell his father.

[2]Saul was sitting under a pomegranate tree at the threshing floor near Gibeah. He had about six hundred men with him. [3]One man was Ahijah who was wearing the holy vest. (Ahijah was a son of Ichabod's brother Ahitub. Ichabod was the son of Phinehas, the son of Eli, the LORD's priest in Shiloh.) No one knew Jonathan had left.

[4]There was a steep slope on each side of the pass that Jonathan planned to go through to reach the Philistine camp. The cliff on one side was named Bozez, and the cliff on the other side was named Seneh. [5]One cliff faced north toward Micmash. The other faced south toward Geba.

[6]Jonathan said to his officer who carried his armor, "Come. Let's go to the camp of those men who are not circumcised. Maybe the LORD will help us. The LORD can give us victory if we have many people, or just a few."

[7]The officer who carried Jonathan's armor said to him, "Do whatever you think is best. Go ahead. I'm with you."

[8]Jonathan said, "Then come. We will cross over to the Philistines and let them see us. [9]If they say to us, 'Stay there until we come to you,' we will stay where we are. We won't go up to them. [10]But if they say, 'Come up to us,' we will climb up, and the LORD will let us defeat them. This will be the sign for us."

[11]When both Jonathan and his officer let the Philistines see them, the Philistines said, "Look! The Hebrews are crawling out of the holes they were hiding in!" [12]The Philistines in the camp shouted to Jonathan and his officer, "Come up to us. We'll teach you a lesson!"

Jonathan said to his officer, "Climb up behind me, because the LORD has given the Philistines to Israel!" [13]So Jonathan climbed up, using his hands and feet, and his officer climbed just behind him. Jonathan struck down the Philistines as he went, and his officer killed them as he followed behind him. [14]In that first fight Jonathan and his officer killed about twenty Philistines over a half acre of ground.

[15]All the Philistine soldiers panicked—those in the camp and those in the raiding party. The ground itself shook! God had caused the panic.

[16]Saul's guards were at Gibeah in the land of Benjamin when they saw the Philistine soldiers running in every direction. [17]Saul said to his army, "Check to see who has left our camp." When they checked, they learned that Jonathan and his officer were gone.

[18]So Saul said to Ahijah the priest, "Bring the Ark of God." (At that time it was with the Israelites.) [19]While Saul was talking to the priest, the confusion in the Philistine camp was growing. Then Saul said to Ahijah, "Put your hand down!"

[20]Then Saul gathered his army and entered the battle. They found the Philistines confused, striking each other with their swords! [21]Earlier, there were Hebrews who had served the Philistines and had stayed in their camp, but now they joined the Israelites with Saul and Jonathan. [22]When all the Israelites hidden in the mountains of Ephraim heard that the Philistine soldiers were running away, they also joined the battle and chased the Philistines. [23]So the LORD saved the Israelites that day, and the battle moved on past Beth Aven.

Saul Makes Another Mistake

[24]The men of Israel were miserable that day because Saul had made an oath for all of them. He had said, "No one should eat food before evening and before I finish defeating my enemies. If he does, he will be cursed!" So no Israelite soldier ate food.

[25]Now the army went into the woods, where there was some honey on the ground. [26]They came upon some honey, but no one took any because they were afraid of the oath. [27]Jonathan had not heard the oath Saul had put on the army, so he

13:19 *no blacksmith.* During this time period the Philistines had a monopoly on the manufacture of iron, thus putting the people of Israel at a distinct disadvantage.

dipped the end of his stick into the honey and lifted some out and ate it. Then he felt better. 28Then one of the soldiers told Jonathan, "Your father made an oath for all the soldiers. He said any man who eats today will be cursed! That's why they are so weak."

29Jonathan said, "My father has made trouble for the land! See how much better I feel after just tasting a little of this honey! 30It would have been much better for the men to eat the food they took from their enemies today. We could have killed many more Philistines!"

31That day the Israelites defeated the Philistines from Micmash to Aijalon. After that, they were very tired. 32They had taken sheep, cattle, and calves from the Philistines. Now they were so hungry they killed the animals on the ground and ate them, without draining the blood from them! 33Someone said to Saul, "Look! The men are sinning against the LORD. They're eating meat without draining the blood from it!"

Saul said, "You have sinned! Roll a large stone over here now!" 34Then he said, "Go to the men and tell them that each person must bring his ox and sheep to me and kill it here and eat it. Don't sin against the LORD by eating meat without draining the blood from it."

That night everyone brought his animals and killed them there. 35Then Saul built an altar to the LORD. It was the first altar he had built to the LORD.

36Saul said, "Let's go after the Philistines tonight and rob them. We won't let any of them live!"

The men answered, "Do whatever you think is best."

But the priest said, "Let's ask God."

37So Saul asked God, "Should I chase the Philistines? Will you let us defeat them?" But God did not answer Saul at that time. 38Then Saul said to all the leaders of his army, "Come here. Let's find out what sin has been done today. 39As surely as the LORD lives who has saved Israel, even if my son Jonathan did the sin, he must die." But no one in the army spoke.

40Then Saul said to all the Israelites, "You stand on this side. I and my son Jonathan will stand on the other side."

The men answered, "Do whatever you think is best."

41Then Saul prayed to the LORD, the God of Israel, "Give me the right answer."

And Saul and Jonathan were picked; the other men went free. 42Saul said, "Now let us discover if it is I or Jonathan my son who is guilty." And Jonathan was picked.

43Saul said to Jonathan, "Tell me what you have done."

So Jonathan told Saul, "I only tasted a little honey from the end of my stick. And must I die now?"

44Saul said, "Jonathan, if you don't die, may God punish me terribly."

45But the soldiers said to Saul, "Must Jonathan die? Never! He is responsible for saving Israel today! As surely as the LORD lives, not even a hair of his head will fall to the ground! Today Jonathan fought against the Philistines with God's help!" So the army saved Jonathan, and he did not die.

46Then Saul stopped chasing the Philistines, and they went back to their own land.

Saul Fights Israel's Enemies

47When Saul became king over Israel, he fought against Israel's enemies all around. He fought Moab, the Ammonites, Edom, the king of Zobah, and the Philistines. Everywhere Saul went he defeated Israel's enemies. 48He fought bravely and defeated the Amalekites. He saved the Israelites from their enemies who had robbed them.

49Saul's sons were Jonathan, Ishvi, and Malki-Shua. His older daughter was named Merab, and his younger daughter was named Michal. 50Saul's wife was Ahinoam daughter of Ahimaaz. The commander of his army was Abner son of Ner, Saul's uncle. 51Saul's father Kish and Abner's father Ner were sons of Abiel.

52All Saul's life he fought hard against the Philistines. When he saw strong or brave men, he took them into his army.

Saul Rejected as King

15 Samuel said to Saul, "The LORD sent me to appoint you king over Israel. Now listen to his message. 2This is what the LORD All-Powerful says: 'When the Israelites came out of Egypt, the Amalekites tried to stop them from going to Canaan. So I will punish them. 3Now go, attack the Amalekites and destroy everything they own as an offering to the LORD. Don't let anything live. Put to death men and women, children and small babies, cattle and sheep, camels and donkeys.' "

4So Saul called the army together at Telaim. There were two hundred thousand foot soldiers and ten thousand men from Judah. 5Then Saul went to the city of Amalek and set up an ambush in the ravine. 6He said to the Kenites, "Go away.

14:33 *without draining the blood from it.* According to Genesis 9:4, people were not allowed to eat the meat of animals with the blood still in it.

Leave the Amalekites so that I won't destroy you
with them, because you showed kindness to the
Israelites when they came out of Egypt." So the
Kenites moved away from the Amalekites.
7Then Saul defeated the Amalekites. He fought
them all the way from Havilah to Shur, at the border of Egypt. 8He took King Agag of the
Amalekites alive, but he killed all of Agag's army
with the sword. 9Saul and the army let Agag live,
along with the best sheep, fat cattle, and lambs.
They let every good animal live, because they did
not want to destroy them. But when they found an
animal that was weak or useless, they killed it.
10Then the LORD spoke his word to Samuel: 11"I
am sorry I made Saul king, because he has stopped
following me and has not obeyed my commands."
Samuel was upset, and he cried out to the LORD
all night long.
12Early the next morning Samuel got up and
went to meet Saul. But the people told Samuel,
"Saul has gone to Carmel, where he has put up a
monument in his own honor. Now he has gone
down to Gilgal."
13When Samuel came to Saul, Saul said, "May
the LORD bless you! I have obeyed the LORD's
commands."
14But Samuel said, "Then why do I hear cattle
mooing and sheep bleating?"
15Saul answered, "The soldiers took them from
the Amalekites. They saved the best sheep and
cattle to offer as sacrifices to the LORD your God,
but we destroyed all the other animals."
16Samuel said to Saul, "Stop! Let me tell you
what the LORD said to me last night."
Saul answered, "Tell me."
17Samuel said, "Once you didn't think much of
yourself, but now you have become the leader of
the tribes of Israel. The LORD appointed you to be
king over Israel. 18And he sent you on a mission.
He said, 'Go and destroy those evil people, the
Amalekites. Make war on them until all of them
are dead.' 19Why didn't you obey the LORD? Why
did you take the best things? Why did you do what
the LORD said was wrong?"
20Saul said, "But I did obey the LORD. I did what
the LORD told me to do. I destroyed all the
Amalekites, and I brought back Agag their king.
21The soldiers took the best sheep and cattle to
sacrifice to the LORD your God at Gilgal."
22But Samuel answered,

"What pleases the LORD more:
burnt offerings and sacrifices
or obedience to his voice?
It is better to obey than to sacrifice.
It is better to listen to God than to offer the
fat of sheep.
23Disobedience is as bad as the sin of sorcery.
Pride is as bad as the sin of worshiping idols.
You have rejected the LORD's command.
Now he rejects you as king."

24Then Saul said to Samuel, "I have sinned. I
didn't obey the LORD's commands and your words.
I was afraid of the people, and I did what they
said. 25Now, I beg you, forgive my sin. Come back
with me so I may worship the LORD."
26But Samuel said to Saul, "I won't go back with
you. You rejected the LORD's command, and now
he rejects you as king of Israel."
27As Samuel turned to leave, Saul caught his
robe, and it tore. 28Samuel said to him, "The LORD
has torn the kingdom of Israel from you today and
has given it to one of your neighbors who is better than you. 29The LORD is the Eternal One of
Israel. He does not lie or change his mind. He is
not a human being, so he does not change his
mind."
30Saul answered, "I have sinned. But please
honor me in front of the older leaders of my people
and in front of the Israelites. Come back with me
so that I can worship the LORD your God." 31So
Samuel went back with Saul, and Saul worshiped
the LORD.
32Then Samuel said, "Bring me King Agag of
the Amalekites."
Agag came to Samuel in chains, but Agag
thought, "Surely the threat of death has passed."
33Samuel said to him, "Your sword made other
mothers lose their children. Now your mother will
have no children." And Samuel cut Agag to pieces
before the LORD at Gilgal.
34Then Samuel left and went to Ramah, but Saul
went up to his home in Gibeah. 35And Samuel

15:8 King Agag ruled the Amalekites, the first nation that tried to destroy the newly formed nation of ancient Israel many years earlier (Exodus 17:8–15). Because of this, God promised to completely destroy the Amalekites. God commanded Saul, Israel's first king, to carry out this promise. In the Book of Esther, Haman, the enemy of the Jews of Persia, is called an Agagite to show that he is under the same promise of destruction.

15:9 King Saul had a wrong attitude when he offered his sacrifice because he kept the best parts for himself. God desires the best from his people, which is complete obedience. Partial obedience comes from sinful thinking.

15:11 *not obeyed my commands.* Here Saul specifically disobeyed the command to execute all the inhabitants of a defeated city and turn the plunder over to the LORD (Deuteronomy 20).

15:22 Samuel's words of rebuke to Saul, after Saul disobediently spared the Amalekite animals for the purpose of sacrifice (1 Samuel 15:3, 9), show that obedience is more than mere formal compliance with written codes; it is also having a humble and faithful disposition of submission. This inward aspect of obedience was missing also in the Pharisees of Jesus' day (Matthew 6:2, 5, 16; 12:7).

15:29 Lying/Dishonesty: Psalm 96:13

never saw Saul again the rest of his life, but he was sad for Saul. And the LORD was very sorry he had made Saul king of Israel.

Samuel Goes to Bethlehem

16 The LORD said to Samuel, "How long will you continue to feel sorry for Saul? I have rejected him as king of Israel. Fill your container with olive oil and go. I am sending you to Jesse who lives in Bethlehem, because I have chosen one of his sons to be king."

2But Samuel said, "If I go, Saul will hear the news and will try to kill me."

The LORD said, "Take a young calf with you. Say, 'I have come to offer a sacrifice to the LORD.'
3Invite Jesse to the sacrifice. Then I will tell you what to do. You must appoint the one I show you."

4Samuel did what the LORD told him to do. When he arrived at Bethlehem, the older leaders of Bethlehem shook with fear. They met him and asked, "Are you coming in peace?"

5Samuel answered, "Yes, I come in peace. I have come to make a sacrifice to the LORD. Set yourselves apart to the LORD and come to the sacrifice with me." Then he set Jesse and his sons apart to the LORD, and he invited them to come to the sacrifice.

6When they arrived, Samuel saw Eliab, and he thought, "Surely the LORD has appointed this person standing here before him."

7But the LORD said to Samuel, "Don't look at how handsome Eliab is or how tall he is, because I have not chosen him. God does not see the same way people see. People look at the outside of a person, but the LORD looks at the heart."

8Then Jesse called Abinadab and told him to pass by Samuel. But Samuel said, "The LORD has not chosen this man either." 9Then Jesse had Shammah
pass by. But Samuel said, "No, the LORD has not
chosen this one." 10Jesse had seven of his sons pass
by Samuel. But Samuel said to him, "The LORD has not chosen any of these."

11Then he asked Jesse, "Are these all the sons you have?"

Jesse answered, "I still have the youngest son. He is out taking care of the sheep."

Samuel said, "Send for him. We will not sit down to eat until he arrives."

12So Jesse sent and had his youngest son brought in. He was a fine boy, tanned, and handsome.

The LORD said to Samuel, "Go, appoint him, because he is the one."

13So Samuel took the container of olive oil and poured it on Jesse's youngest son to appoint him in front of his brothers. From that day on, the LORD's Spirit worked in David. Samuel then went back to Ramah.⊂⊃

David Serves Saul

14But the LORD's Spirit had left Saul, and an evil spirit from the LORD troubled him.

15Saul's servants said to him, "See, an evil spirit
from God is troubling you. 16Give us the command
to look for someone who can play the harp. When the evil spirit from God troubles you, he will play, and you will feel better."

17So Saul said to his servants, "Find someone who can play well and bring him to me."

18One of the servants said, "I have seen a son of Jesse of Bethlehem play the harp. He is brave and courageous. He is a good speaker and handsome, and the LORD is with him."

19Then Saul sent messengers to Jesse, saying, "Send me your son David, who is with the sheep."
20So Jesse loaded a donkey with bread, a leather bag full of wine, and a young goat, and he sent them with his son David to Saul.

21When David came to Saul, he began to serve him. Saul liked David and made him the officer
who carried his armor. 22Saul sent a message to
Jesse, saying, "Let David stay and serve me because I like him."

23When the evil spirit from God troubled Saul, David would take his harp and play. Then the evil spirit would leave him, and Saul would feel better.⊂⊃

David and Goliath

17 The Philistines gathered their armies for war. They met at Socoh in Judah and camped at Ephes Dammim between Socoh and Azekah.
2Saul and the Israelites gathered in the Valley of Elah and camped there and took their positions to
fight the Philistines. 3The Philistines controlled
one hill while the Israelites controlled another. The valley was between them.

4The Philistines had a champion fighter from Gath named Goliath. He was about nine feet, four inches tall. He came out of the Philistine camp
5with a bronze helmet on his head and a coat of bronze armor that weighed about one hundred
twenty-five pounds. 6He wore bronze protectors

⊂⊃**16:13 Samuel:** 1 Samuel 25:1

16:13 *took the container of olive oil.* See 1 Samuel 10:1.

⊂⊃**16:23 Loneliness:** 1 Samuel 28:1–20

⊂⊃**16:23 Music:** 2 Samuel 1:17–27

⊂⊃**16:23 Demon:** Job 1:6–12

17:4 *a champion fighter.* In the ancient Near East, two armies could settle their differences by picking champions who would represent their sides. The champion who won the fight also won the battle for their army.

on his legs, and he had a bronze spear on his back.
7The wooden part of his larger spear was like a
weaver's rod, and its blade weighed about fifteen
pounds. The officer who carried his shield walked
in front of him.
8Goliath stood and shouted to the Israelite soldiers, "Why have you taken positions for battle? I
am a Philistine, and you are Saul's servants! Choose
a man and send him to fight me. 9If he can fight and
kill me, we will be your servants. But if I can kill
him, you will be our servants." 10Then he said,
"Today I stand and dare the army of Israel! Send
one of your men to fight me!" 11When Saul and the
Israelites heard the Philistine's words, they were
very scared.
12Now David was the son of Jesse, an Ephrathite
from Bethlehem in Judah. Jesse had eight sons. In
Saul's time Jesse was an old man. 13His three oldest sons followed Saul to the war. The first son
was Eliab, the second was Abinadab, and the third
was Shammah. 14David was the youngest. Jesse's
three oldest sons followed Saul, 15but David went
back and forth from Saul to Bethlehem, where he
took care of his father's sheep.
16For forty days the Philistine came out every
morning and evening and stood before the Israelite
army.
17Jesse said to his son David, "Take this half
bushel of cooked grain and ten loaves of bread to
your brothers in the camp. 18Also take ten pieces
of cheese to the commander and to your brothers.
See how your brothers are and bring back some
proof to show me that they are all right. 19Your
brothers are with Saul and the army in the Valley
of Elah, fighting against the Philistines."
20Early in the morning David left the sheep
with another shepherd. He took the food and left
as Jesse had told him. When David arrived at the
camp, the army was going out to their battle positions, shouting their war cry. 21The Israelites and
Philistines were lining up their men to face each
other in battle.
22David left the food with the man who kept
the supplies and ran to the battle line to talk to his
brothers. 23While he was talking with them,
Goliath, the Philistine champion from Gath, came
out. He shouted things against Israel as usual, and
David heard him. 24When the Israelites saw
Goliath, they were very much afraid and ran away.
25They said, "Look at this man! He keeps coming out to challenge Israel. The king will give much
money to whoever kills him. He will also let whoever kills him marry his daughter. And his father's
family will not have to pay taxes in Israel."
26David asked the men who stood near him,

A shepherd and his sling

"What will be done to reward the man who kills
this Philistine and takes away the shame from
Israel? Who does this uncircumcised Philistine
think he is? Does he think he can speak against the
armies of the living God?"
27The Israelites told David what would be done
for the man who would kill Goliath.
28When David's oldest brother Eliab heard
David talking with the soldiers, he was angry
with David. He asked David, "Why did you come
here? Who's taking care of those few sheep of
yours in the desert? I know you are proud and
wicked at heart. You came down here just to
watch the battle."
29David asked, "Now what have I done wrong?
Can't I even talk?" 30When he turned to other
people and asked the same questions, they gave
him the same answer as before. 31Yet what David
said was told to Saul, and he sent for David.
32David said to Saul, "Don't let anyone be discouraged. I, your servant, will go and fight this
Philistine!"
33Saul answered, "You can't go out against this
Philistine and fight him. You're only a boy. Goliath
has been a warrior since he was a young man."
34But David said to Saul, "I, your servant, have
been keeping my father's sheep. When a lion or
bear came and took a sheep from the flock, 35I
would chase it. I would attack it and save the sheep
from its mouth. When it attacked me, I caught it by
its fur and hit it and killed it. 36I, your servant,
have killed both a lion and a bear! This uncircumcised Philistine will be like them, because he has
spoken against the armies of the living God. 37The
LORD who saved me from a lion and a bear will save
me from this Philistine."
Saul said to David, "Go, and may the LORD be
with you." 38Saul put his own clothes on David.

He put a bronze helmet on his head and dressed him in armor. 39David put on Saul's sword and tried to walk around, but he was not used to all the armor Saul had put on him.

He said to Saul, "I can't go in this, because I'm not used to it." Then David took it all off. 40He took his stick in his hand and chose five smooth stones from a stream. He put them in his shepherd's bag and grabbed his sling. Then he went to meet the Philistine.

41At the same time, the Philistine was coming closer to David. The man who held his shield walked in front of him. 42When Goliath looked at David and saw that he was only a boy, tanned and handsome, he looked down on David with disgust. 43He said, "Do you think I am a dog, that you come at me with a stick?" He used his gods' names to curse David. 44He said to David, "Come here. I'll feed your body to the birds of the air and the wild animals!"

45But David said to him, "You come to me using a sword and two spears. But I come to you in the name of the LORD All-Powerful, the God of the armies of Israel! You have spoken against him. 46Today the LORD will hand you over to me, and I'll kill you and cut off your head. Today I'll feed the bodies of the Philistine soldiers to the birds of the air and the wild animals. Then all the world will know there is a God in Israel! 47Everyone gathered here will know the LORD does not need swords or spears to save people. The battle belongs to him, and he will hand you over to us."

48As Goliath came near to attack him, David ran quickly to meet him. 49He took a stone from his bag, put it into his sling, and slung it. The stone hit the Philistine and went deep into his forehead, and Goliath fell facedown on the ground.

50So David defeated the Philistine with only a sling and a stone. He hit him and killed him. He did not even have a sword in his hand. 51Then David ran and stood beside him. He took Goliath's sword out of its holder and killed him by cutting off his head.

When the Philistines saw that their champion was dead, they turned and ran. 52The men of Israel and Judah shouted and chased the Philistines all the way to the entrance of the city of Gath and to the gates of Ekron.

The Philistines' bodies lay on the Shaaraim road as far as Gath and Ekron. 53The Israelites returned after chasing the Philistines and robbed their camp. 54David took Goliath's head to Jerusalem and put Goliath's weapons in his own tent.

55When Saul saw David go out to meet Goliath, Saul asked Abner, commander of the army, "Abner, who is that young man's father?"

Abner answered, "As surely as you live, my king, I don't know."

56The king said, "Find out whose son he is."

57When David came back from killing Goliath, Abner brought him to Saul. David was still holding Goliath's head.

58Saul asked him, "Young man, who is your father?"

David answered, "I am the son of your servant Jesse of Bethlehem."

Saul Fears David

18 When David finished talking with Saul, Jonathan felt very close to David. He loved David as much as he loved himself. 2Saul kept David with him from that day on and did not let him go home to his father's house. 3Jonathan made an agreement with David, because he loved David as much as himself. 4He took off his coat and gave it to David, along with his armor, including his sword, bow, and belt.

5Saul sent David to fight in different battles, and David was very successful. Then Saul put David over the soldiers, which pleased Saul's officers and all the other people.

6After David had killed the Philistine, he and the men returned home. Women came out from all the towns of Israel to meet King Saul. They sang songs of joy, danced, and played tambourines and stringed instruments. 7As they played, they sang,

"Saul has killed thousands of his enemies,
but David has killed tens of thousands."

8The women's song upset Saul, and he became very angry. He thought, "The women say David has killed tens of thousands, but they say I have killed only thousands. The only thing left for him to have is the kingdom!" 9So Saul watched David

---

17:46 *to the birds of the air and the wild animals.* People of the ancient Near East feared not having a proper burial.

17:47 Holy War & Divine Warrior: 2 Samuel 5:24

18:4 *He took off his coat . . . along with his armor, including his sword, bow, and belt.* This ritual not only shows the close friendship between David and Jonathan but also indicated that Jonathan, who was the heir to the throne, knew that David would be the next king of Israel.

18:4 Commitment: Ephesians 2:12–13

18:4 Friend: 1 Samuel 19:1–7

closely from then on, because he was jealous.

10The next day an evil spirit from God rushed upon Saul, and he prophesied in his house. David was playing the harp as he usually did, but Saul had a spear in his hand. 11He threw the spear, thinking, "I'll pin David to the wall." But David escaped from him twice.

12The LORD was with David but had left Saul. So Saul was afraid of David. 13He sent David away and made him commander of a thousand soldiers. So David led them in battle. 14He had great success in everything he did because the LORD was with him. 15When Saul saw that David was very successful, he feared David even more. 16But all the people of Israel and Judah loved David because he led them well in battle.

Saul's Daughter Marries David

17Saul said to David, "Here is my older daughter Merab. I will let you marry her. All I ask is that you remain brave and fight the LORD's battles." Saul thought, "I won't have to kill David. The Philistines will do that."

18But David answered Saul, saying, "Who am I? My family is not important enough for me to become the king's son-in-law." 19So, when the time came for Saul's daughter Merab to marry David, Saul gave her instead to Adriel of Meholah.

20Now Saul's other daughter, Michal, loved David. When they told Saul, he was pleased. 21He thought, "I will let her marry David. Then she will be a trap for him, and the Philistines will defeat him." So Saul said to David a second time, "You may become my son-in-law."

22And Saul ordered his servants to talk with David in private and say, "Look, the king likes you. His servants love you. You should be his son-in-law."

23Saul's servants said these words to David, but David answered, "Do you think it is easy to become the king's son-in-law? I am poor and unimportant."

24When Saul's servants told him what David had said, 25Saul said, "Tell David, 'The king doesn't want money for the bride. All he wants is a hundred Philistine foreskins to get even with his enemies.'" Saul planned to let the Philistines kill David.

26When Saul's servants told this to David, he was pleased to become the king's son-in-law. 27So he and his men went out and killed two hundred Philistines. David brought all their foreskins to Saul so he could be the king's son-in-law. Then Saul gave him his daughter Michal for his wife. 28Saul saw that the LORD was with David and that his daughter Michal loved David. 29So he grew even more afraid of David, and he was David's enemy all his life.

30The Philistine commanders continued to go out to fight the Israelites, but every time, David was more skillful than Saul's officers. So he became famous.

Saul Tries to Kill David

19 Saul told his son Jonathan and all his servants to kill David, but Jonathan liked David very much. 2So he warned David, "My father Saul is looking for a chance to kill you. Watch out in the morning. Hide in a secret place. 3I will go out and stand with my father in the field where you are hiding, and I'll talk to him about you. Then I'll let you know what I find out."

4When Jonathan talked to Saul his father, he said good things about David. Jonathan said, "The king should do no wrong to your servant David since he has done nothing wrong to you. What he has done has helped you greatly. 5David risked his life when he killed Goliath the Philistine, and the LORD won a great victory for all Israel. You saw it and were happy. Why would you do wrong against David? He's innocent. There's no reason to kill him!"

6Saul listened to Jonathan and then made this promise: "As surely as the LORD lives, David won't be put to death."

7So Jonathan called to David and told him everything that had been said. He brought David to Saul, and David was with Saul as before.

8When war broke out again, David went out to fight the Philistines. He defeated them, and they ran away from him.

9But once again an evil spirit from the LORD rushed upon Saul as he was sitting in his house with his spear in his hand. David was playing the harp. 10Saul tried to pin David to the wall with his spear, but David jumped out of the way. So Saul's spear went into the wall, and David ran away that night.

11Saul sent messengers to David's house to watch it and to kill him in the morning. But

18:9 Jealousy can be an incredibly destructive emotion. It can destroy relationships like David and Saul's. It can be a fruit of sin and at odds with spirituality (Galatians 5:20 and 1 Corinthians 5:20). However, in certain circumstances jealousy is a godly response to the threat of a marriage relationship (Song of Songs 8:6) or the relationship between God and his people (Exodus 34:14).

18:14 Success: 2 Kings 18:5–7

18:21 Deborah: 1 Kings 2:13–25

19:7 Friend: 1 Sam 20:1–42

Michal, David's wife, warned him, saying,
"Tonight you must run for your life. If you don't,
you will be dead in the morning." 12So she let
David down out of a window, and he ran away and
escaped. 13Then Michal took an idol, laid it on the
bed, covered it with clothes, and put goats' hair at
its head.
14Saul sent messengers to take David prisoner,
but Michal said, "He is sick."
15Saul sent them back to see David, saying,
"Bring him to me on his bed so I can kill him."
16When the messengers entered David's house,
they found just an idol on the bed with goats' hair
on its head.
17Saul said to Michal, "Why did you trick me this
way? You let my enemy go so he could run away!"
Michal answered Saul, "David told me if I did
not help him escape, he would kill me."
18After David had escaped from Saul, he went
to Samuel at Ramah and told him everything Saul
had done to him. Then David and Samuel went to
Naioth and stayed there. 19Saul heard that David
was in Naioth at Ramah. 20So he sent messengers
to capture him. But they met a group of prophets
prophesying, with Samuel standing there leading
them. So the Spirit of God entered Saul's men,
and they also prophesied.
21When Saul heard the news, he sent more
messengers, but they also prophesied. Then he
sent messengers a third time, but they also prophesied. 22Finally, Saul himself went to Ramah, to
the well at Secu. He asked, "Where are Samuel and
David?"
The people answered, "In Naioth at Ramah."
23When Saul went to Naioth at Ramah, the Spirit
of God also rushed upon him. And he walked on,
prophesying until he came to Naioth at Ramah.
24He took off his robes and prophesied in front of
Samuel. He lay that way all day and all night. That
is why people ask, "Is even Saul one of the
prophets?"

Jonathan Helps David

20 Then David ran away from Naioth in
Ramah. He went to Jonathan and asked,
"What have I done? What is my crime? How did
I sin against your father? Why is he trying to kill
me?"
2Jonathan answered, "No! You won't die! See,
my father doesn't do anything great or small without first telling me. Why would he keep this from
me? It's not true!"
3But David took an oath, saying, "Your father
knows very well that you like me. He says to
himself, 'Jonathan must not know about it, or he
will tell David.' As surely as the LORD lives and as
you live, I am only a step away from death!"
4Jonathan said to David, "I'll do anything you
want me to do."
5So David said, "Look, tomorrow is the New
Moon festival. I am supposed to eat with the king,
but let me hide in the field until the third evening.
6If your father notices I am gone, tell him, 'David
begged me to let him go to his hometown of
Bethlehem. Every year at this time his family group
offers a sacrifice.' 7If your father says, 'Fine,' I am
safe. But if he becomes angry, you will know that
he wants to hurt me. 8Jonathan, be loyal to me,
your servant. You have made an agreement with
me before the LORD. If I am guilty, you may kill me
yourself! Why hand me over to your father?"
9Jonathan answered, "No, never! If I learn that
my father plans to hurt you, I will warn you!"
10David asked, "Who will let me know if your
father answers you unkindly?"
11Then Jonathan said, "Come, let's go out into
the field." So the two of them went out into the
field.
12Jonathan said to David, "I promise this before
the LORD, the God of Israel: At this same time the
day after tomorrow, I will find out how my father
feels. If he feels good toward you, I will send word
to you and let you know. 13But if my father plans
to hurt you, I will let you know and send you
away safely. May the LORD punish me terribly if I
don't do this. And may the LORD be with you as
he has been with my father. 14But show me the
kindness of the LORD as long as I live so that I may
not die. 15You must never stop showing your kindness to my family, even when the LORD has
destroyed all your enemies from the earth."
16So Jonathan made an agreement with David.
He said, "May the LORD hold David's enemies
responsible." 17And Jonathan asked David to
repeat his promise of love for him, because he
loved David as much as he loved himself.
18Jonathan said to David, "Tomorrow is the New
Moon festival. Your seat will be empty, so my father
will miss you. 19On the third day go to the place
where you hid when this trouble began. Wait by
the rock Ezel. 20On the third day I will shoot three
arrows to the side of the rock as if I am shooting at
a target. 21Then I will send a boy to find the arrows.
If I say to him, 'The arrows are near you; bring
them here,' you may come out of hiding. You are
safe. As the LORD lives, there is no danger. 22But if
I say to the boy, 'Look, the arrows are beyond you,'
you must go, because the LORD is sending you
away. 23Remember what we talked about. The
LORD is a witness between you and me forever."

INSTRUCTION

DEUTERONOMY 6:4–9

What does the Bible say about instruction and teaching? Who does the instructing? What is the content of the instruction?

The idea of instruction is an important one in the Bible. Throughout the Bible, the Lord shows that he is concerned that his people are properly grounded in the faith. They must be taught the ways of the Lord, what is right and wrong, how to live a life that conforms to God's will.

Children are common objects of instruction in the Bible. In the Old Testament, it was important for the Israelites to pass on the traditions of what God had done for his people. In particular, the Exodus was the key event that brought the nation of Israel into existence. But since only one generation actually experienced God's mighty acts, future generations needed to hear about what God had done. For example, Exodus 10:2 says: "I also did this so you could tell your children and your grandchildren how I was hard on the Egyptians. Tell them about the miracles I did among them so that all of you will know that I am the LORD." Other passages that have a similar idea are Exodus 12:26; 13:8, 14; Deuteronomy 4:9; 6:4–9, 20; 11:19.

Children are also instructed not only in the knowledge of God's mighty acts, but also in what it means to live godly lives. This is a popular idea in the book of Proverbs and is summarized in Proverbs 22:6: "Train children how to live right, and when they are old, they will not change." The importance of teaching children is also seen in the refrain found in several places in Proverbs, that children should listen to their father's teaching (for example 1:8; 4:1; 8:33). In Psalm 34:11, children are called to come and listen in order to learn how to worship the Lord. Ephesians 6:4 firmly grounds this idea in New Testament teaching: "Fathers, do not make your children angry, but raise them with the training and teaching of the Lord."

Adults also need instruction. As much as children need to be taught the ways of the Lord, adults need continually to be reminded of what it means to live in a relationship with God. Instruction in the faith is a common theme in both the Old and New Testaments. And this pertains not to those outside of the faith who are being instructed to enter, but to those on the inside who are entering into an ever deeper relationship with the Lord. Once again, Proverbs provides a host of relevant passages. One example is 23:12: "Remember what you are taught, and listen carefully to words of knowledge" (see also Proverbs 13:13; 16:20; 19:20; 21:11). In Psalm 51:13, David promises the Lord that he will learn from his experiences and teach the Lord's ways to those who do wrong. In Exodus 18:20, Moses' father-in-law advises Moses to choose elders to help him to teach the Israelites "the right way to live and what they should do." As with children, adults are also reminded of God's mighty acts of the past (Psalms 77; 78; 105; 106).

Such adult instruction in the New Testament concerns instruction in the Gospel. Paul in particular was in the habit of telling his readers to listen to his instruction and to instruct each other properly in the faith (for example Romans 15:14; 1 Corinthians 14:6, 26, 31; Galatians 6:6; 1 Timothy 1:18; 3:14–15; 2 Timothy 4:6).

Instruction not only occurs from one person to another. God is also an instructor—*the* instructor. The Book of Psalms occasionally refers to God as an instructor of the faithful (25:9; 32:8; 119:33; 143:10; see also Micah 4:2; Exodus 33:13; 1 Kings 8:36). We also see that one reason for the Lord's instructing his people is so that they can instruct one another (Deuteronomy 6:1; Isaiah 50:4).

Jesus is also *the* instructor in the New Testament. Much of his earthly life was about teaching his disciples and other followers about the Kingdom of God, how they may enter and how they ought to act within it. One need only think of the many parables and the Sermon on the Mount (Matthew 5–7). Jesus taught his disciples to pray (Luke 11:1). He refers to himself as "Teacher" in John 13:12–14.

As the master teacher, Jesus taught his followers, who in turn became teachers themselves. This "changing of the guard" begins in Matthew 28:20: what Jesus taught the disciples, they are now to go and teach others. As we instruct one another, we are acting like Jesus (see Deuteronomy 6:1 and Isaiah 50:4 above) It is a small wonder, then, that since teaching is such a high calling, with it goes much responsibility (James 3:1; 2 Timothy 2:2–4). Teaching is an official job in the church assigned by God for his people (1 Corinthians 12:28; Ephesians 4:11).

Instruction: For additional scriptures on this topic go to Exodus 12:26.

Gentiles (Non-Jews)

Deuteronomy 7

What is a Gentile? Why were Gentiles excluded from the people of God in the Old Testament? Why were they included in the people of God in the New Testament?

Racism ignites more passions, incites more wars, and instigates more oppression than almost any other prejudice. Although people may be divided by economies, religions, and geography, some of the most powerful forces which separate people are racial and ethnic.

One of the main dividing lines running throughout much of the Bible is the division between the Jewish nation of Israel and all other nations and races. Although the Bible uses several words such as nations, tribes, tongues, peoples, Greeks, and uncircumcised, all of these mean non-Jewish people who are often called Gentiles. The sometimes bitter opposition between Jewish people and Gentiles still persisting today extends back into the earliest books of the Bible and created a major conflict in the early church.

Much of the bloodshed in the Old Testament occurred during Israel's conquest of the land of Canaan when they were authorized by God to destroy all the Gentiles living in the land which had been promised to them (Deuteronomy 2–3; 7:1–3; Joshua 6; 8; 10–12). The people of Israel, composed of a race first called Hebrews and later Jewish people, identified themselves as the descendants of Abraham, Isaac, and Jacob and the unique heirs to the promises which God gave to Abraham (Genesis 12:2–3; 15:18–19; 17:3–8). Although Israelites rooted their identity in Abraham, they celebrated their deliverance from Egypt as the proof that they were set apart from all the other nations as God's chosen people (Exodus 19:3–6; Deuteronomy 7:7–8).

In the Old Testament, the Gentiles usually worshipped idols and false gods (Deuteronomy 7:3–6), and their widespread idolatry demonstrated their rejection of God as the only God deserving their worship (Romans 1:23). Their idolatry brought them under God's curse (Exodus 20:4; Deuteronomy 27:15) and committed them to destruction at the hands of God's servant nation Israel (see essay on "Divine Warrior").

Israel was commanded by God to destroy the Gentiles living in Canaan so that the land would be purified of any idolatry which might corrupt the kingdom of priests which God was to establish there (Exodus 19:3–6; Deuteronomy 7:3–6). God desired Israel to be a nation free of idolatrous corruption which would serve as an example of the holy kingdom of priests gathered from every nation who will serve God alone for eternity (Revelation 5:9–10). As an example to the other nations, Israel was to be a beacon of light attracting the Gentiles to worship God in his Temple in Jerusalem (Isaiah 42:6; 49:6; 60).

Israel often rejected its responsibility to be a light to the Gentiles, as illustrated by the story of the prophet Jonah. Jonah was so narrow-minded in his loyalty to his own nation that he disobeyed God's explicit command to go to the city of Nineveh in order to warn them of God's impending judgment. Even after he went to the Ninevites and persuaded them to repent, Jonah was disappointed that God had shown them mercy (Jonah 3:10–4:3). In contrast to Jonah's racial prejudice, God expressed his deep concern for a great city of Gentiles (Jonah 4:11).

God's choice of Abraham was never intended to restrict God's blessings to a single race of people. Even in God's promise to Abraham that God would make him a great nation, God intended that all the nations of the earth would be blessed through him (Genesis 12:2–3). Jesus Christ's death and resurrection opened the way for both Jewish people and Gentiles to inherit the blessing which God promised to Abraham (Galatians 3:6–14). Like Abraham, it is only through faith that Jewish people and Gentiles can be considered righteous before God (Romans 3:29–30; 4:9–12). In Christ, God makes no distinction between Jewish people and Gentiles (Galatians 3:28).

Even in the New Testament church, Jewish believers doubted that Christ died for Jewish people and Gentiles alike. Like Jonah, Peter thought that God's mercy was restricted to the Jewish people, but his experience while visiting the Gentile Cornelius showed the early church that God had poured out his Spirit on both Jewish people and Gentiles (Acts 10–11:18).

Christ's commission to his disciples that they should be his witnesses in every part of the world (Acts 1:8) reverses the narrow focus of the Old Testament on the nation of Israel and directs the church to bring the Good News to all the races and nations. Isaiah's vision of the Gentile nations worshipping God in his city will finally be fulfilled in God's heavenly city when all the nations will walk by its light (Revelation 21:24).

Gentiles (Non-Jews): For additional scriptures on this topic go to Genesis 12:3.

24So David hid in the field. When the New Moon festival came, the king sat down to eat. 25He sat where he always sat, near the wall. Jonathan sat across from him, and Abner sat next to Saul, but David's place was empty. 26That day Saul said nothing. He thought, "Maybe something has happened to David so that he is unclean." 27But the next day was the second day of the month, and David's place was still empty. So Saul said to Jonathan, "Why hasn't the son of Jesse come to the feast yesterday or today?"

28Jonathan answered, "David begged me to let him go to Bethlehem. 29He said, 'Let me go, because our family has a sacrifice in the town, and my brother has ordered me to be there. Now if I am your friend, please let me go to see my brothers.' That is why he has not come to the king's table."

30Then Saul became very angry with Jonathan. He said, "You son of a wicked, worthless woman! I know you are on the side of David son of Jesse! You bring shame on yourself and on your mother who gave birth to you. 31As long as Jesse's son lives, you will never be king or have a kingdom. Now send for David and bring him to me. He must die!"

32Jonathan asked his father, "Why should David be killed? What wrong has he done?" 33Then Saul threw his spear at Jonathan, trying to kill him. So Jonathan knew that his father really wanted to kill David. 34Jonathan was very angry and left the table. That second day of the month he refused to eat. He was ashamed of his father and upset over David.

35The next morning Jonathan went out to the field to meet David as they had agreed. He had a young boy with him. 36Jonathan said to the boy, "Run and find the arrows I shoot." When he ran, Jonathan shot an arrow beyond him. 37The boy ran to the place where Jonathan's arrow fell, but Jonathan called, "The arrow is beyond you!" 38Then he shouted, "Hurry! Go quickly! Don't stop!" The boy picked up the arrow and brought it back to his master. 39(The boy knew nothing about what this meant; only Jonathan and David knew.) 40Then Jonathan gave his weapons to the boy and told him, "Go back to town."

41When the boy left, David came out from the south side of the rock. He bowed facedown on the ground before Jonathan three times. Then David and Jonathan kissed each other and cried together, but David cried the most.

42Jonathan said to David, "Go in peace. We have promised by the LORD that we will be friends. We said, 'The LORD will be a witness between you and me, and between our descendants always.'" Then David left, and Jonathan went back to town.∞

David Goes to See Ahimelech

21 David went to Nob to see Ahimelech the priest. Ahimelech shook with fear when he saw David, and he asked, "Why are you alone? Why is no one with you?"

2David answered him, "The king gave me a special order. He told me, 'No one must know what I am sending you to do or what I told you to do.' I told my men where to meet me. 3Now, what food do you have with you? Give me five loaves of bread or anything you find."

4The priest said to David, "I don't have any plain bread here, but I do have some holy bread. You may eat it if your men have kept themselves from women."

5David answered, "No women have been near us for days. My men always keep themselves holy, even when we do ordinary work. And this is especially true when the work is holy."

6So the priest gave David the holy bread from the presence of God because there was no other. Each day the holy bread was replaced with hot bread.

7One of Saul's servants happened to be there that day. He had been held there before the LORD. He was Doeg the Edomite, the chief of Saul's shepherds.

8David asked Ahimelech, "Do you have a spear or sword here? The king's business was very important, so I left without my sword or any other weapon."

9The priest answered, "The sword of Goliath the Philistine, the one you killed in the Valley of Elah, is here. It is wrapped in a cloth behind the holy vest. If you want it, you may take it. There's no other sword here but that one."

David said, "There is no other sword like it. Give it to me."

David Goes to Gath

10That day David ran away from Saul and went to Achish king of Gath. 11But the servants of Achish said to him, "This is David, the king of the Israelites. He's the man they dance and sing about, saying:

∞**20:42 Friend:** Proverbs 17:17
21:4 *holy bread.* This was the bread that showed the people were in the presence of God. Normally only the priests ate this bread.

'Saul has killed thousands of his enemies,
but David has killed tens of thousands.' "

12David paid attention to these words and was very much afraid of Achish king of Gath. 13So he pretended to be crazy in front of Achish and his servants. While he was with them, he acted like a madman and clawed on the doors of the gate and let spit run down his beard.

14Achish said to his servants, "Look at the man! He's crazy! Why do you bring him to me? 15I have enough madmen. I don't need you to bring him here to act like this in front of me! Don't let him in my house!"

David at Adullam and Mizpah

22 David left Gath and escaped to the cave of Adullam. When his brothers and other relatives heard that he was there, they went to see him. 2Everyone who was in trouble, or who owed money, or who was unsatisfied gathered around David, and he became their leader. About four hundred men were with him.

3From there David went to Mizpah in Moab and spoke to the king of Moab. He said, "Please let my father and mother come and stay with you until I learn what God is going to do for me." 4So he left them with the king of Moab, and they stayed with him as long as David was hiding in the stronghold.

5But the prophet Gad said to David, "Don't stay in the stronghold. Go to the land of Judah." So David left and went to the forest of Hereth.

Saul Destroys Ahimelech's Family

6Saul heard that David and his men had been seen. Saul was sitting under the tamarisk tree on the hill at Gibeah, and all his officers were standing around him. He had a spear in his hand. 7Saul said to them, "Listen, men of Benjamin! Do you think the son of Jesse will give all of you fields and vineyards? Will David make you commanders over thousands of men or hundreds of men? 8You have all made plans against me! No one tells me when my son makes an agreement with the son of Jesse! No one cares about me! No one tells me when my son has encouraged my servant to ambush me this very day!"

9Doeg the Edomite, who was standing there with Saul's officers, said, "I saw the son of Jesse. He came to see Ahimelech son of Ahitub at Nob. 10Ahimelech prayed to the LORD for David and gave him food and gave him the sword of Goliath the Philistine."

11Then the king sent for the priest Ahimelech son of Ahitub and for all of Ahimelech's relatives who were priests at Nob. And they all came to the king. 12Saul said to Ahimelech, "Listen now, son of Ahitub."

Ahimelech answered, "Yes, master."

13Saul said, "Why are you and Jesse's son against me? You gave him bread and a sword! You prayed to God for him. David has turned against me and is waiting to attack me even now!"

14Ahimelech answered, "You have no other servant who is as loyal as David, your own son-in-law and captain of your bodyguards. Everyone in your house respects him. 15That was not the first time I prayed to God for David. Don't blame me or any of my relatives. I, your servant, know nothing about what is going on."

16But the king said, "Ahimelech, you and all your relatives must die!" 17Then he told the guards at his side, "Go and kill the priests of the LORD, because they are on David's side. They knew he was running away, but they didn't tell me."

But the king's officers refused to kill the priests of the LORD.

18Then the king ordered Doeg, "Go and kill the priests." So Doeg the Edomite went and killed the priests. That day he killed eighty-five men who wore the linen holy vest. 19He also killed the people of Nob, the city of the priests. With the sword he killed men, women, children, babies, cattle, donkeys, and sheep.

20But Abiathar, a son of Ahimelech, who was the son of Ahitub, escaped. He ran away and joined David. 21He told David that Saul had killed the LORD's priests. 22Then David told him, "Doeg the Edomite was there at Nob that day. I knew he would surely tell Saul. So I am responsible for the death of all your father's family. 23Stay with me. Don't be afraid. The man who wants to kill you also wants to kill me. You will be safe with me."

David Saves the People of Keilah

23 Someone told David, "Look, the Philistines are fighting against Keilah and stealing grain from the threshing floors."

2David asked the LORD, "Should I go and fight these Philistines?"

The LORD answered him, "Go. Attack them, and save Keilah."

3But David's men said to him, "We're afraid here in Judah. We will be more afraid if we go to Keilah where the Philistine army is."

4David again asked the LORD, and the LORD answered, "Go down to Keilah. I will help you defeat the Philistines." 5So David and his men went to Keilah and fought the Philistines and took their cattle. David killed many Philistines and saved the people of Keilah. [6](Now Abiathar son of Ahimelech had brought the holy vest with him when he came to David at Keilah.)

Saul Chases David

[7]Someone told Saul that David was now at Keilah. Saul said, "God has handed David over to me! He has trapped himself, because he has entered a town with gates and bars." [8]Saul called all his army together for battle, and they prepared to go down to Keilah to attack David and his men.

[9]David learned Saul was making evil plans against him. So he said to Abiathar the priest, "Bring the holy vest." [10]David prayed, "LORD, God of Israel, I have heard that Saul plans to come to Keilah to destroy the town because of me. [11]Will the leaders of Keilah hand me over to Saul? Will Saul come down to Keilah, as I heard? LORD, God of Israel, tell me, your servant!"

The LORD answered, "Saul will come down."

[12]Again David asked, "Will the leaders of Keilah hand me and my men over to Saul?"

The LORD answered, "They will."

[13]So David and his six hundred men left Keilah and kept moving from place to place. When Saul found out that David had escaped from Keilah, he did not go there.

[14]David stayed in the desert hideouts and in the hills of the Desert of Ziph. Every day Saul looked for David, but the LORD did not surrender David to him.

[15]While David was at Horesh in the Desert of Ziph, he learned that Saul was coming to kill him. [16]But Saul's son Jonathan went to David at Horesh and strengthened his faith in God. [17]Jonathan told him, "Don't be afraid, because my father won't touch you. You will be king of Israel, and I will be second to you. Even my father Saul knows this." [18]The two of them made an agreement before the LORD. Then Jonathan went home, but David stayed at Horesh.

[19]The people from Ziph went to Saul at Gibeah and told him, "David is hiding in our land. He's at the hideouts of Horesh, on the hill of Hakilah, south of Jeshimon. [20]Now, our king, come down anytime you want. It's our duty to hand David over to you."

[21]Saul answered, "The LORD bless you for helping me. [22]Go and learn more about him. Find out where he is staying and who has seen him there. I have heard that he is clever. [23]Find all the hiding places he uses, and come back and tell me everything. Then I'll go with you. If David is in the area, I will track him down among all the families in Judah."

[24]So they went back to Ziph ahead of Saul. Now David and his men were in the Desert of Maon in the desert area south of Jeshimon. [25]Saul and his men went to look for David, but David heard about it and went down to a rock and stayed in the Desert of Maon. When Saul heard that, he followed David into the Desert of Maon.

[26]Saul was going along one side of the mountain, and David and his men were on the other side. They were hurrying to get away from Saul, because Saul and his men were closing in on them. [27]But a messenger came to Saul, saying, "Come quickly! The Philistines are attacking our land!" [28]So Saul stopped chasing David and went to challenge the Philistines. That is why people call this place Rock of Parting. [29]David also left the Desert of Maon and stayed in the hideouts of En Gedi.

David Shames Saul

24 After Saul returned from chasing the Philistines, he was told, "David is in the Desert of En Gedi." [2]So he took three thousand chosen men from all Israel and began looking for David and his men near the Rocks of the Wild Goats.

[3]Saul came to the sheep pens beside the road. A cave was there, and he went in to relieve himself. Now David and his men were hiding far back in the cave. [4]The men said to David, "Today is the day the LORD spoke of when he said, 'I will give your enemy over to you. Do anything you want with him.' "

Then David crept up to Saul and quietly cut off a corner of Saul's robe. [5]Later David felt guilty because he had cut off a corner of Saul's robe.⚭ [6]He said to his men, "May the LORD keep me from doing such a thing to my master! Saul is the LORD's appointed king. I should not do anything against him, because he is the LORD's appointed king!" [7]David used these words to stop his men; he did not let them attack Saul. Then Saul left the cave and went his way.

[8]When David came out of the cave, he shouted to Saul, "My master and king!" Saul looked back, and David bowed facedown on the ground. [9]He said to Saul, "Why do you listen when people say, 'David wants to harm you'? [10]You have seen

23:24 *Maon.* Some early Greek copies say "Maon." The Hebrew copies say "Paran."

⚭**24:5 Conscience:** 2 Samuel 24:10

something with your own eyes today. The LORD put you in my power in the cave. They said I should kill you, but I was merciful. I said, 'I won't harm my master, because he is the LORD's appointed king.' 11My father, look at this piece of your robe in my hand! I cut off the corner of your robe, but I didn't kill you. Now understand and know I am not planning any evil against you. I did nothing wrong to you, but you are hunting me to kill me. 12May the LORD judge between us, and may he punish you for the wrong you have done to me! But I am not against you. 13There is an old saying: 'Evil things come from evil people.' But I am not against you. 14Whom is the king of Israel coming out against? Whom are you chasing? It's as if you are chasing a dead dog or a flea. 15May the LORD be our judge and decide between you and me. May he support me and show that I am right. May he save me from you!"

16When David finished saying these words, Saul asked, "Is that your voice, David my son?" And he cried loudly. 17He said, "You are a better man than I am. You have been good to me, but I have done wrong to you. 18You told me what good things you did. The LORD handed me over to you, but you did not kill me. 19If a person finds his enemy, he doesn't just send him on his way, does he? May the LORD reward you because you were good to me today. 20I know you will surely be king, and you will rule the kingdom of Israel. 21Now swear to me by the LORD that you will not kill my descendants and that you won't wipe out my name from my father's family."

22So David made the promise to Saul. Then Saul went back home, and David and his men went up to their hideout.∞

Nabal Insults David

25 Now Samuel died, and all the Israelites met and had a time of sadness for him. Then they buried him at his home in Ramah.

David moved to the Desert of Maon.∞ 2A man in Maon who had land at Carmel was very rich. He had three thousand sheep and a thousand goats. He was cutting the wool off his sheep at Carmel. 3His name was Nabal, and he was a descendant of Caleb. His wife was named Abigail. She was wise and beautiful, but Nabal was cruel and mean.

4While David was in the desert, he heard that Nabal was cutting the wool from his sheep. 5So he sent ten young men and told them, "Go to Nabal at Carmel, and greet him for me. 6Say to Nabal, 'May you and your family and all who belong to you have good health! 7I have heard that you are cutting the wool from your sheep. When your shepherds were with us, we did not harm them. All the time your shepherds were at Carmel, we stole nothing from them. 8Ask your servants, and they will tell you. We come at a happy time, so be kind to my young men. Please give anything you can find for them and for your son David.' "

9When David's men arrived, they gave the message to Nabal, but Nabal insulted them. 10He answered them, "Who is David? Who is this son of Jesse? Many slaves are running away from their masters today! 11I have bread and water, and I have meat that I killed for my servants who cut the wool. But I won't give it to men I don't know."

12David's men went back and told him all Nabal had said. 13Then David said to them, "Put on your swords!" So they put on their swords, and David put on his also. About four hundred men went with David, but two hundred men stayed with the supplies.

14One of Nabal's servants said to Abigail, Nabal's wife, "David sent messengers from the desert to greet our master, but Nabal insulted them. 15These men were very good to us. They did not harm us. They stole nothing from us during all the time we were out in the field with them. 16Night and day they protected us. They were like a wall around us while we were with them caring for the sheep. 17Now think about it, and decide what you can do. Terrible trouble is coming to our master and all his family. Nabal is such a wicked man that no one can even talk to him."

18Abigail hurried. She took two hundred loaves of bread, two leather bags full of wine, five cooked sheep, a bushel of cooked grain, a hundred cakes of raisins, and two hundred cakes of pressed figs and put all these on donkeys. 19Then she told her servants, "Go on. I'll follow you." But she did not tell her husband.

20Abigail rode her donkey and came down toward the mountain hideout. There she met David and his men coming down toward her.

21David had just said, "It's been useless! I watched over Nabal's property in the desert. I made sure none of his sheep was missing. I did good to him, but he has paid me back with evil. 22May God punish my enemies even more. I will not leave one of Nabal's men alive until morning."

23When Abigail saw David, she quickly got off her donkey and bowed facedown on the ground

∞**24:22 Jerusalem:** 2 Kings 19:31
25:1 *Maon.* Some early Greek copies say "Maon." The Hebrew copies say "Paran."
∞**25:1 Samuel:** Luke 24:19

before him. 24She fell at David's feet and said, "My
master, let the blame be on me! Please let me talk
to you. Listen to what I say. 25My master, don't pay
attention to this worthless man Nabal. He is like
his name. His name means 'fool,' and he is truly
a fool. But I, your servant, didn't see the men you
sent. 26The LORD has kept you from killing and punishing anyone. As surely as the LORD lives and as
surely as you live, may your enemies become like
Nabal! 27I have brought a gift to you for the men
who follow you. 28Please forgive my wrong. The
LORD will certainly let your family have many
kings, because you fight his battles. As long as you
live, may you do nothing bad. 29Someone might
chase you to kill you, but the LORD your God will
keep you alive. He will throw away your enemies'
lives as he would throw a stone from a sling. 30The
LORD will keep all his promises of good things for
you. He will make you leader over Israel. 31Then
you won't feel guilty or troubled because you
killed innocent people and punished them. Please
remember me when the LORD brings you success."

32David answered Abigail, "Praise the LORD,
the God of Israel, who sent you to meet me.
33May you be blessed for your wisdom. You have
kept me from killing or punishing people today.
34As surely as the LORD, the God of Israel, lives, he
has kept me from hurting you. If you hadn't come
quickly to meet me, not one of Nabal's men would
have lived until morning."

35Then David accepted Abigail's gifts. He told
her, "Go home in peace. I have heard your words,
and I will do what you have asked."

Nabal's Death

36When Abigail went back to Nabal, he was in
the house, eating like a king. He was very drunk
and in a good mood. So she told him nothing until
the next morning. 37In the morning when he was
not drunk, his wife told him everything. His heart
stopped, and he became like stone. 38About ten
days later the LORD struck Nabal and he died.

39When David heard that Nabal was dead, he
said, "Praise the LORD! Nabal insulted me, but the
LORD has supported me! He has kept me from doing
wrong. The LORD has punished Nabal for his wrong."

Then David sent a message to Abigail, asking her
to be his wife. 40His servants went to Carmel and
said to Abigail, "David sent us to take you so you
can become his wife."

41Abigail bowed facedown on the ground and
said, "I am your servant. I'm ready to serve you
and to wash the feet of my master's servants."
42Abigail quickly got on a donkey and went with
David's messengers, with her five maids following her. And she became David's wife.

43David also had married Ahinoam of Jezreel. So
they were both David's wives. 44Saul's daughter
Michal was also David's wife, but Saul had given
her to Paltiel son of Laish, who was from Gallim.

David Shames Saul Again

26 The people of Ziph went to Saul at Gibeah
and said to him, "David is hiding on the hill
of Hakilah opposite Jeshimon."

2So Saul went down to the Desert of Ziph with
three thousand chosen men of Israel to look for
David there. 3Saul made his camp beside the road
on the hill of Hakilah opposite Jeshimon, but David
stayed in the desert. When he heard Saul had followed him, 4he sent out spies and learned for certain that Saul had come to Hakilah.

5Then David went to the place where Saul had
camped. He saw where Saul and Abner son of
Ner, the commander of Saul's army, were sleeping. Saul was sleeping in the middle of the camp
with all the army around him.

6David asked Ahimelech the Hittite and Abishai
son of Zeruiah, Joab's brother, "Who will go down
into Saul's camp with me?"

Abishai answered, "I'll go with you."

7So that night David and Abishai went into
Saul's camp. Saul was asleep in the middle of the
camp with his spear stuck in the ground near his
head. Abner and the army were sleeping around
Saul. 8Abishai said to David, "Today God has
handed your enemy over to you. Let me pin Saul
to the ground with my spear. I'll only have to do it
once. I won't need to hit him twice."

9But David said to Abishai, "Don't kill Saul! No
one can harm the LORD's appointed king and still
be innocent! 10As surely as the LORD lives, the
LORD himself will punish Saul. Maybe Saul will
die naturally, or maybe he will go into battle and
be killed. 11But may the LORD keep me from harming his appointed king! Take the spear and water
jug that are near Saul's head. Then let's go."

12So David took the spear and water jug that
were near Saul's head, and they left. No one saw
them or knew about it or woke up, because the
LORD had put them sound asleep.

13David crossed over to the other side of the
hill and stood on top of the mountain far from
Saul's camp. They were a long way away from each
other. 14David shouted to the army and to Abner
son of Ner, "Won't you answer me, Abner?"

Abner answered, "Who is calling for the king?
Who are you?"

25:44 Folly/Foolishness: Psalm 14:1

15David said, "You're the greatest man in Israel. Isn't that true? Why didn't you guard your master the king? Someone came into your camp to kill your master the king! 16You have not done well. As surely as the LORD lives, you and your men should die. You haven't guarded your master, the LORD's appointed king. Look! Where are the king's spear and water jug that were near his head?"

17Saul knew David's voice. He said, "Is that your voice, David my son?"

David answered, "Yes, it is, my master and king." 18David also said, "Why are you chasing me, my master? What wrong have I done? What evil am I guilty of? 19My master and king, listen to me. If the LORD made you angry with me, let him accept an offering. But if people did it, may the LORD curse them! They have made me leave the land the LORD gave me. They have told me, 'Go and serve other gods.' 20Now don't let me die far away from the LORD's presence. The king of Israel has come out looking for a flea! You're just hunting a bird in the mountains!"

21Then Saul said, "I have sinned. Come back, David my son. Today you respected my life, so I will not try to hurt you. I have been very stupid and foolish."

22David answered, "Here is your spear. Let one of your young men come here and get it. 23The LORD rewards us for the things we do right and for our loyalty to him. The LORD handed you over to me today, but I wouldn't harm the LORD's appointed king. 24As I respected your life today, may the LORD also respect my life and save me from all trouble."

25Then Saul said to David, "You are blessed, my son David. You will do great things and succeed."

So David went on his way, and Saul went back home.

David Lives with the Philistines

27 But David thought to himself, "Saul will catch me someday. The best thing I can do is escape to the land of the Philistines. Then he will give up looking for me in Israel, and I can get away from him."

2So David and his six hundred men left Israel and went to Achish son of Maoch, king of Gath. 3David, his men, and their families made their home in Gath with Achish. David had his two wives with him—Ahinoam of Jezreel and Abigail of Carmel, the widow of Nabal. 4When Saul heard that David had run away to Gath, he stopped looking for him.

5Then David said to Achish, "If you are pleased with me, give me a place in one of the country towns where I can live. I don't need to live in the royal city with you."

6That day Achish gave David the town of Ziklag, and Ziklag has belonged to the kings of Judah ever since. 7David lived in the Philistine land a year and four months.

8David and his men raided the people of Geshur, Girzi, and Amalek. (These people had lived for a long time in the land that reached to Shur and Egypt.) 9When David fought them, he killed all the men and women and took their sheep, cattle, donkeys, camels, and clothes. Then he returned to Achish.

10Achish would ask David, "Where did you go raiding today?" And David would tell him that he had gone to the southern part of Judah, or Jerahmeel, or to the land of the Kenites. 11David never brought a man or woman alive to Gath. He thought, "If we bring people alive, they may tell Achish, 'This is what David really did.'" David did this all the time he lived in the Philistine land. 12So Achish trusted David and said to himself, "David's own people, the Israelites, now hate him very much. He will serve me forever."

Saul and the Witch of Endor

28 Later, the Philistines gathered their armies to fight against Israel. Achish said to David, "You understand that you and your men must join my army."

2David answered, "You will see for yourself what I, your servant, can do!"

Achish said, "Fine, I'll make you my permanent bodyguard."

3Now Samuel was dead, and all the Israelites had shown their sadness for him. They had buried Samuel in his hometown of Ramah.

And Saul had forced out the mediums and fortune-tellers from the land.

4The Philistines came together and made camp at Shunem. Saul gathered all the Israelites and made camp at Gilboa. 5When he saw the Philistine army, he was afraid, and his heart pounded with fear. 6He prayed to the LORD, but the LORD did not answer him through dreams, Urim, or prophets.

28 Rejected by the people, and challenged for the kingship by David, Saul knew in his heart that the root of his despair was to be found in his own disobedience to the word of God brought to him through the prophet Samuel. Feeling deserted by God, Saul consults a witch who would bring up the spirit of the dead Samuel. Samuel's spirit confirms that Saul's tragic position is the result of his previous unwillingness to obey the instructions God gave him. The use of magic and occult powers to change things is condemned throughout Scripture, and Saul is left in no doubt that God's mind certainly cannot be changed by such means.

7Then Saul said to his servants, "Find me a woman
who is a medium so I may go and ask her what will
happen."
His servants answered, "There is a medium in
Endor."
8Then Saul put on other clothes to disguise himself, and at night he and two of his men went to
see the woman. Saul said to her, "Talk to a spirit
for me. Bring up the person I name."
9But the woman said to him, "Surely you know
what Saul has done. He has forced the mediums
and fortune-tellers from the land. You are trying to
trap me and get me killed."
10Saul made a promise to the woman in the
name of the LORD. He said, "As surely as the LORD
lives, you won't be punished for this."
11The woman asked, "Whom do you want me to
bring up?"
He answered, "Bring up Samuel."
12When the woman saw Samuel, she screamed.
She said, "Why have you tricked me? You are
Saul!"
13The king said to the woman, "Don't be afraid!
What do you see?"
The woman said, "I see a spirit coming up out
of the ground."
14Saul asked, "What does he look like?"
The woman answered, "An old man wearing a
coat is coming up."
Then Saul knew it was Samuel, and he bowed
facedown on the ground.
15Samuel asked Saul, "Why have you disturbed
me by bringing me up?"
Saul said, "I am greatly troubled. The Philistines
are fighting against me, and God has left me. He
won't answer me anymore, either by prophets or
in dreams. That's why I called for you. Tell me
what to do."
16Samuel said, "The LORD has left you and has
become your enemy. So why do you call on me?
17He has done what he said he would do—the
things he said through me. He has torn the kingdom out of your hands and given it to one of your
neighbors, David. 18You did not obey the LORD; you
did not show the Amalekites how angry he was
with them. That's why he has done this to you
today. 19The LORD will hand over both Israel and
you to the Philistines. Tomorrow you and your
sons will be with me. The LORD will hand over the
army of Israel to the Philistines."
20Saul quickly fell flat on the ground and was
afraid of what Samuel had said. He was also very
weak because he had eaten nothing all that day
and night.
21Then the woman came to Saul and saw that he
was really frightened. She said, "Look, I, your servant, have obeyed you. I have risked my life and
done what you told me to do. 22Now please listen
to me. Let me give you some food so you may eat
and have enough strength to go on your way."
23But Saul refused, saying, "I won't eat."
His servants joined the woman in asking him to
eat, and he listened to them. So he got up from the
ground and sat on the bed.
24At the house the woman had a fat calf, which
she quickly killed. She took some flour and mixed
dough with her hands. Then she baked some
bread without yeast. 25She put the food before
them, and they ate. That same night they got up
and left.

David Goes Back to Ziklag

29 The Philistines gathered all their soldiers
at Aphek. Israel camped by the spring at
Jezreel. 2The Philistine kings were marching with
their groups of a hundred and a thousand men.
David and his men were marching behind Achish.
3The Philistine commanders asked, "What are
these Hebrews doing here?"
Achish told them, "This is David. He served Saul
king of Israel, but he has been with me for over a
year now. I have found nothing wrong in David
since the time he left Saul."
4But the Philistine commanders were angry
with Achish and said, "Send David back to the city
you gave him. He cannot go with us into battle. If
he does, we'll have an enemy in our own camp.
He could please his king by killing our own men.
5David is the one the Israelites dance and sing
about, saying:

'Saul has killed thousands of his enemies,
but David has killed tens of thousands.'"

6So Achish called David and said to him, "As
surely as the LORD lives, you are loyal. I would be
pleased to have you serve in my army. Since the
day you came to me, I have found no wrong in you.
But the other kings don't trust you. 7Go back in
peace. Don't do anything to displease the Philistine
kings."
8David asked, "What wrong have I done? What
evil have you found in me from the day I came to
you until now? Why can't I go fight your enemies,
my lord and king?"

28:6 *Urim.* The Urim, along with the Thummim, belonged to the priests and was used by them to determine God's will.

28:20 Loneliness: Psalm 13

9Achish answered, "I know you are as good as
an angel from God. But the Philistine commanders
have said, 'David must not go with us into battle.'
10Early in the morning you and your master's servants should leave. Get up as soon as it is light
and go."
11So David and his men got up early in the
morning and went back to the country of the
Philistines. And the Philistines went up to Jezreel.

David's War with the Amalekites

30 On the third day, when David and his men
arrived at Ziklag, he found that the
Amalekites had raided southern Judah and Ziklag,
attacking Ziklag and burning it. 2They captured
the women and everyone, young and old, but they
had not killed anyone. They had only taken them
away.
3When David and his men came to Ziklag, they
found the town had been burned and their wives,
sons, and daughters had been taken as prisoners.
4Then David and his army cried loudly until they
were too weak to cry anymore. 5David's two wives
had also been taken—Ahinoam of Jezreel and
Abigail the widow of Nabal from Carmel. 6The men
in the army were threatening to kill David with
stones, which greatly upset David. Each man was
sad and angry because his sons and daughters had
been captured, but David found strength in the
LORD his God. 7David said to Abiathar the priest,
"Bring me the holy vest."
8Then David asked the LORD, "Should I chase the
people who took our families? Will I catch them?"
The LORD answered, "Chase them. You will
catch them, and you will succeed in saving your
families."
9David and the six hundred men with him came
to the Besor Ravine, where some of the men
stayed. 10David and four hundred men kept up the
chase. The other two hundred men stayed behind
because they were too tired to cross the ravine.
11They found an Egyptian in a field and brought
him to David. They gave the Egyptian some water
to drink and some food to eat. 12And they gave him
a piece of a fig cake and two clusters of raisins.
Then he felt better, because he had not eaten any
food or drunk any water for three days and nights.
13David asked him, "Who is your master?
Where do you come from?"
He answered, "I'm an Egyptian, the slave of an
Amalekite. Three days ago my master left me,
because I was sick. 14We had raided the southern
area of the Kerethites, the land of Judah, and the
southern area of Caleb. We burned Ziklag, as well.
15David asked him, "Can you lead me to the
people who took our families?"
He answered, "Yes, if you promise me before
God that you won't kill me or give me back to my
master. Then I will take you to them."
16So the Egyptian led David to the Amalekites.
They were lying around on the ground, eating and
drinking and celebrating with the things they had
taken from the land of the Philistines and from
Judah. 17David fought them from sunset until the
evening of the next day. None of them escaped,
except four hundred young men who rode off on
their camels. 18David got his two wives back and
everything the Amalekites had taken. 19Nothing
was missing. David brought back everyone, young
and old, sons and daughters. He recovered the
valuable things and everything the Amalekites
had taken. 20David took all the sheep and cattle, and
his men made these animals go in front, saying,
"They are David's prize."
21Then David came to the two hundred men
who had been too tired to follow him, who had
stayed at the Besor Ravine. They came out to meet
David and the people with him. When he came
near, David greeted the men at the ravine.
22But the evil men and troublemakers among
those who followed David said, "Since these two
hundred men didn't go with us, we shouldn't give
them any of the things we recovered. Just let each
man take his wife and children and go."
23David answered, "No, my brothers. Don't do
that after what the LORD has given us. He has protected us and given us the enemy who attacked
us. 24Who will listen to what you say? The share
will be the same for the one who stayed with the
supplies as for the one who went into battle. All
will share alike." 25David made this an order and
rule for Israel, which continues even today.
26When David arrived in Ziklag, he sent some
of the things he had taken from the Amalekites to
his friends, the leaders of Judah. He said, "Here is
a present for you from the things we took from
the LORD's enemies."
27David also sent some things to the leaders in
Bethel, Ramoth in the southern part of Judah, Jattir,
28Aroer, Siphmoth, Eshtemoa, 29Racal, the cities of
the Jerahmeelites and the Kenites, 30Hormah, Bor
Ashan, Athach, 31Hebron, and to the people in all
the other places where he and his men had been.

The Death of Saul

31 The Philistines fought against Israel, and the
Israelites ran away from them. Many
Israelites were killed on Mount Gilboa. 2The
Philistines fought hard against Saul and his sons,
killing his sons Jonathan, Abinadab, and Malki-

Shua. [3]The fighting was heavy around Saul. The
archers shot him, and he was badly wounded. [4]He
said to the officer who carried his armor, "Pull out
your sword and kill me. Then those uncircumcised
men won't make fun of me and kill me." But Saul's
officer refused, because he was afraid. So Saul
took his own sword and threw himself on it.
[5]When the officer saw that Saul was dead, he
threw himself on his own sword, and he died
with Saul. [6]So Saul, his three sons, and the officer
who carried his armor died together that day.

[7]When the Israelites who lived across the Jezreel
Valley and those who lived across the Jordan River
saw how the Israelite army had run away, and that
Saul and his sons were dead, they left their cities
and ran away. Then the Philistines came and lived
there.

[8]The next day when the Philistines came to
take all the valuable things from the dead soldiers, they found Saul and his three sons dead on
Mount Gilboa. [9]They cut off Saul's head and took
off his armor. Then they sent messengers through
all the land of the Philistines to tell the news in
the temple of their idols and to their people.
[10]They put Saul's armor in the temple of the
Ashtoreths and hung his body on the wall of Beth
Shan.

[11]When the people living in Jabesh Gilead heard
what the Philistines had done to Saul, [12]the brave
men of Jabesh marched all night and came to Beth
Shan. They removed the bodies of Saul and his sons
from the wall of Beth Shan and brought them to
Jabesh. There they burned the bodies. [13]They took
their bones and buried them under the tamarisk
tree in Jabesh. Then the people of Jabesh gave up
eating for seven days.

Notes:

INTRODUCTION TO THE BOOK OF 2 SAMUEL

David, the Greatest King

WHO WROTE THIS BOOK?

The author of 2 Samuel is uncertain, since the book itself does not name its writer. Some people have suggested that, perhaps, the author was Zabud, who was the personal adviser to King Solomon and son of Nathan the prophet. However, that cannot be verified.

TO WHOM WAS THIS BOOK WRITTEN?

The Book of 2 Samuel was intended for readers in Israel, the people of God.

WHERE WAS IT WRITTEN?

Since Israel was living in Canaan, the Promised Land, during the period of the judges and the kings, it is probable that 2 Samuel was written there, too.

WHEN WAS IT WRITTEN?

Based on several passages in the Book of Samuel, the author evidently lived and wrote shortly after King Solomon's death, which was in 930 B.C., and when the kingdom of Israel divided (see comments about "Israel and Judah" in 1 Samuel 11:8; 17:52; 18:16).

WHAT IS IT ABOUT?

The Book of 2 Samuel records the historical events surrounding the kingship of David, who is portrayed as a great king in the eyes of God, even though he was far from perfect. Under David's leadership Israel recaptured Jerusalem and brought the Ark of the Agreement home. David also led them in conquering their enemies from Egypt to the Euphrates (see chapter 8). In chapters 10–20 we are shown David's imperfections, including his sin with Bathsheba (chapters 11–12) and his lack of discipline with his sons (see 13:21; 14:1,33). At last we hear David's glorious words of praise to God (22:31–51) for his care and deliverance.

WHY WAS THIS BOOK WRITTEN?

David is called "the kind of man he (the LORD) wants" (1 Samuel 13:14), even though he sinned greatly. The key to David's close relationship with God was David's willingness to repent of his grievous sins and always turn back to God for forgiveness. God knew David's weaknesses, but he also knew David's repentant heart. And that's the kind of heart that pleases him. This book reminds Israel to keep their hearts tuned to God.

SO WHAT DOES THIS BOOK MEAN TO US?

If we want to be the kind of people God wants, we must be constant in our repentance. God knows our weaknesses, too. As Psalm 103:14 says, "He knows how we were made; he remembers that we are dust." And yet, he is more concerned about the state of our hearts and our repentant spirits. If we continually turn back to God, he will continually forgive us.

SUMMARY:

The Book of 2 Samuel continues the account of the early kingship that was begun in 1 Samuel, since 1 and 2 Samuel were originally one book giving the account of the rise of Israel's kingship.

Three parts make up 2 Samuel. The first part of the book tells us about the rise of David and his great accomplishments. The second part begins with the report of David's sin with Bathsheba and then continues with all the family and political troubles that resulted from that sin. The third part of 2 Samuel gives some additional information about David's kingship.

I. The Rise of David (1:1–10:19)
II. David's Failures (11:1–20:26)
III. More Stories about David (21:1–24:25)

I. The Rise of David (1:1–10:19)

The first part of 2 Samuel recounts the rise of David to the kingship. This happened in two stages. After the death of Saul, the southern tribe of Judah immediately recognized David as king, but in the north, Ish-bosheth, the son of Saul, was made king. After seven and a half years, Ish-bosheth was assassinated and David became king of the north, too. David then captured Jerusalem, made it his capital, and brought the Ark to it. God then entered into an agreement with David, assuring him that his sons would follow him on the throne. Everything was looking up for David.

II. David's Failures (11:1–20:26)

God had blessed David, but now he was going to stumble in a way that would affect the rest of his life. He took another man's wife, Bathsheba. From this episode in his life, his family life began to unravel in ways that led to political trouble.

III. More Stories about David (21:1–24:25)

The Book of 2 Samuel ends with additional stories about David. They are not in chronological order, but are stories and speeches of David during his life.

2 SAMUEL

David Learns About Saul's Death

Now Saul was dead. After David had
defeated the Amalekites, he returned to
Ziklag and stayed there two days. 2On
the third day a young man from Saul's camp came
to Ziklag. To show his sadness, his clothes were
torn and he had dirt on his head. He came and
bowed facedown on the ground before David.
3David asked him, "Where did you come from?"
The man answered, "I escaped from the Israelite
camp."
4David asked him, "What happened? Please tell
me!"
The man answered, "The people have run
away from the battle, and many of them have
fallen and are dead. Saul and his son Jonathan are
dead also."
5David asked him, "How do you know Saul and
his son Jonathan are dead?"
6The young man answered, "I happened to be
on Mount Gilboa. There I saw Saul leaning on his
spear. The Philistine chariots and the men riding
in them were coming closer to Saul. 7When he
looked back and saw me, he called to me. I
answered him, 'Here I am!'
8"Then Saul asked me, 'Who are you?'
"I told him, 'I am an Amalekite.'
9"Then Saul said to me, 'Please come here and
kill me. I am badly hurt and am almost dead
already.'
10"So I went over and killed him. He had been
hurt so badly I knew he couldn't live. Then I took
the crown from his head and the bracelet from
his arm, and I have brought them here to you, my
master."
11Then David tore his clothes to show his sorrow, and all the men with him did also. 12They
were very sad and cried and did not eat until
evening. They cried for Saul and his son Jonathan
and for all the people of the LORD and for all the
Israelites who had died in the battle.

David Orders the Amalekite Killed

13David asked the young man who brought the
report, "Where are you from?"
The young man answered, "I am the son of a
foreigner, an Amalekite."
14David asked him, "Why were you not afraid
to kill the LORD's appointed king?"
15Then David called one of his men and told
him, "Go! Kill the Amalekite!" So the Israelite
killed him. 16David had said to the Amalekite, "You
are responsible for your own death. You confessed
by saying, 'I have killed the LORD's appointed
king.'"

David's Song About Saul and Jonathan

17David sang a funeral song about Saul and his
son Jonathan, 18and he ordered that the people of
Judah be taught this song. It is called "The Bow,"
and it is written in the Book of Jashar:

19"Israel, your leaders have been killed
on the hills.
How the mighty have fallen in battle!
20Don't tell it in Gath.
Don't announce it in the streets of Ashkelon.
If you do, the Philistine women will
be happy.
The daughters of the Philistines will rejoice.

21"May there be no dew or rain on the
mountains of Gilboa,
and may their fields produce no grain,
because there the mighty warrior's shield
was dishonored.
Saul's shield will no longer be rubbed
with oil.
22Jonathan's bow did not fail
to kill many soldiers.
Saul's sword did not fail
to wound many strong men.

23"We loved Saul and Jonathan
and enjoyed them while they lived.
They are together even in death.
They were faster than eagles.
They were stronger than lions.

24"You daughters of Israel, cry for Saul.
Saul clothed you with red dresses
and put gold decorations on them.

25"How the mighty have fallen in battle!
Jonathan is dead on Gilboa's hills.
26I cry for you, my brother Jonathan.
I enjoyed your friendship so much.
Your love to me was wonderful,
better than the love of women.

27"How the mighty have fallen!
The weapons of war are gone."

1:27 Music: 1 Kings 1:39–40

David Is Made King of Judah

2 Later, David prayed to the LORD, saying, "Should I go up to any of the cities of Judah?"

The LORD said to David, "Go."

David asked, "Where should I go?"

The LORD answered, "To Hebron."

2So David went up to Hebron with his two wives: Ahinoam from Jezreel and Abigail, the widow of Nabal from Carmel. 3David also brought his men and their families, and they all made their homes in the cities of Hebron. 4Then the men of Judah came to Hebron and appointed David king over Judah.

They told David that the men of Jabesh Gilead had buried Saul. 5So David sent messengers to the men of Jabesh Gilead and said to them, "The LORD bless you. You have shown loyalty to your master Saul by burying him. 6May the LORD now be loyal and true to you. I will also treat you well because you have done this. 7Now be strong and brave. Saul your master is dead, and the people of Judah have appointed me their king."

War Between Judah and Israel

8Abner son of Ner was the commander of Saul's army. Abner took Saul's son Ish-Bosheth to Mahanaim 9and made him king of Gilead, Ashuri, Jezreel, Ephraim, Benjamin, and all Israel. 10Saul's son Ish-Bosheth was forty years old when he became king over Israel, and he ruled two years. But the people of Judah followed David. 11David was king in Hebron for seven years and six months.

12Abner son of Ner and the servants of Ish-Bosheth son of Saul left Mahanaim and went to Gibeon. 13Joab son of Zeruiah and David's men also went there and met Abner and Ish-Bosheth's men at the pool of Gibeon. Abner's group sat on one side of the pool; Joab's group sat on the other.

14Abner said to Joab, "Let the young men have a contest here."

Joab said, "Yes, let them have a contest."

15Then the men got up and were counted—twelve from the people of Benjamin for Ish-Bosheth son of Saul, and twelve from David's men. 16Each man grabbed the one opposite him by the head and stabbed him in the side with a knife. So the men fell down together. For that reason, that place in Gibeon is called the Field of Knives. 17That day there was a terrible battle, and David's men defeated Abner and the Israelites.

Abner Kills Asahel

18Zeruiah's three sons, Joab, Abishai, and Asahel, were there. Now Asahel was a fast runner, as fast as a deer in the field. 19Asahel chased Abner, going straight toward him. 20Abner looked back and asked, "Is that you, Asahel?"

Asahel said, "Yes, it is."

21Then Abner said to Asahel, "Turn to your right or left and catch one of the young men and take his armor." But Asahel refused to stop chasing him.

22Abner again said to Asahel, "Stop chasing me! If you don't stop, I'll have to kill you! Then I won't be able to face your brother Joab again!"

23But Asahel refused to stop chasing Abner. So using the back end of his spear, Abner stabbed Asahel in the stomach, and the spear came out of his back. Asahel died right there, and everyone stopped when they came to the place where Asahel's body lay.

24But Joab and Abishai continued chasing Abner. As the sun was going down, they arrived at the hill of Ammah, near Giah on the way to the desert near Gibeon. 25The men of Benjamin came to Abner, and all stood together at the top of the hill.

26Abner shouted to Joab, "Must the sword kill forever? Surely you must know this will only end in sadness! Tell the people to stop chasing their own brothers!"

27Then Joab said, "As surely as God lives, if you had not said anything, the people would have chased their brothers until morning." 28Then Joab blew a trumpet, and his people stopped chasing the Israelites. They did not fight them anymore.

29Abner and his men marched all night through the Jordan Valley. They crossed the Jordan River, and after marching all day, arrived at Mahanaim.

30After he had stopped chasing Abner, Joab came back and gathered the people together. Asahel and nineteen of David's men were missing. 31But David's men had killed three hundred sixty Benjaminites who had followed Abner. 32David's men took Asahel and buried him in the tomb of his father at Bethlehem. Then Joab and his men marched all night. The sun came up as they reached Hebron.

3 There was a long war between the people who supported Saul's family and those who supported David's family. The supporters of David's family became stronger and stronger, but

2:4 *king over Judah.* The south made decisions separately from the north on these matters. Later in history, after Solomon, the north and the south would permanently separate from one another.

2:28 The trumpet was actually a ram's horn. It was hollowed out and holes were drilled in it so that when blown into, it would produce sounds. It could be blown very loudly and make different types of sounds or notes. This made it an important instrument to help the captain communicate to his army during battle.

Election (Chosen)

Deuteronomy 7:6–11

How did Israel experience being chosen by God? What does "election" ("chosen" NCV) mean from the standpoint of God's action and the related responsibility of "the elect"? How does the New Testament understand election?

Election is a hard term for people in democratic societies to accept. When "all are created equal," it is difficult to think that God would choose some people instead of others. The Bible does not primarily concern itself with the rightness of election from a human perspective, but takes the view that God has the right to elect and begins there. This perspective emphasizes not which group of human beings is chosen, but the purposes for which God chooses, or elects, a certain people. Those elected are to reflect God's character and are thus to do God's work in the world for the benefit of all creation.

It is important first to understand the various uses of "election" or "chosen" in the Old Testament. Election means primarily three things. It can be used (1) of human choice (I Samuel 2:30), (2) of God's choice of Jerusalem (1 Kings 14:21), and most importantly, (3) of God's choice of a people. (Only rarely does the Old Testament speak of God's choosing individuals.) In Deuteronomy 7:6–11, God chooses Israel out of love. God called them out of all the nations of the earth. "You are holy people, who belong to the Lord your God. He has chosen you from all the people on earth to be his very own" (Deuteronomy 14:2). God chose Israel to reflect God's character and thus to be God's representative on earth, and for this reason, Israel is called God's "firstborn son" in Exodus 4:22.

There are two sides to election, divine initiative and human response. Sometimes divine faithfulness is underlined, as in Psalm 89:1–4, where the agreement with David is said to "continue forever." Because *God*, whose love is "loyal" or "steadfast," has made this agreement through David, it will stand. On the other hand, the Bible also teaches that human response is crucial. Amos 3:1–15 and 9:7–10 emphasize the importance of the chosen to respond in an ethical life, and in fact, declares that election actually means that God has a particular claim over Israel because of Israel's election.

The New Testament retains the Old Testament's emphasis on choice as a human act, as in Mary's choice to listen to Jesus in Luke 10:42 and Paul's choice between life and death in Philippians 1:22. (In contrast to the Old Testament, it does not speak of God's choosing Jerusalem.) The main focus falls upon God's election of a people, as in Ephesians 1:3–10.

In the end, the choice of the elect is completely God's decision and initiative (Romans 9:11–12). And yet, the New Testament emphasizes, like the Old Testament, that election demands moral response (2 Peter 1:10). Ultimately, the New Testament affirms that Jesus is God's chosen One (Hebrews 1:2) and we are called to respond to Jesus: "Come to the Lord Jesus, the stone that lives. The people of the world did not want this stone, but he was the stone God chose, and he was precious" (1 Peter 2:4).

In God's election, there is an emphasis on the undeserved favor or divine "grace" (Ephesians 2:8–10). Human beings can never earn this favor. Only Christ can. God is the One who takes initiative in offering salvation. Pride as a response to election is unacceptable since election implies *God's* choice and has nothing to do with human merit. The Bible is not a story of human beings' search for God. It is quite opposite. In the Bible, God searches for men and women.

Can some resist their election and then lose their salvation? This is a perplexing question that has advocates for both sides. On the one hand, certain passages emphasize the need for human response (Hebrews 6:4–6; 10:26–31) and others give assurance of divine initiative through Christ (John 10:28–29). The former passages sound as if election can be forfeited, the latter, as if this is impossible. Christians who emphasize human response say that salvation can be lost if people turn away from faith, while those who emphasize God's decision say if salvation seems to be "lost," it is only because these people were never chosen in the first place. (Some commentators on Scripture, citing passages such as Romans 5:18–19, Colossians 1:20, and 1 Timothy 4:10, sidestep the issue by saying that God in Christ has elected *all* people.) What is sure, is that those who have received Christ may be said to be both chosen by God and to have chosen God. Election should give believers assurance that God's love and favor does not rest in our actions, but in God's faithfulness. It should also give believers the confidence that God's commitment to his own is permanent and irrevocable.

Election (Chosen): For additional scriptures on this topic go to Genesis 12:1–3.

MOUNTAIN

DEUTERONOMY 11

Why are mountains mentioned so often in biblical narrative?
Are there places that serve the same function for us today?

The numerous biblical references to mountains should not surprise the reader, since mountains constitute the chief topographical feature of Palestine; thus they have deep meaning in the history of the region. Therefore, when the biblical writers mention mountains, it is not only to communicate location data; many times these references are also channels to convey theological ideas. This is a common occurrence in both Old and New Testaments.

Mount Ebal and Mount Gerizim, for example, were more than geographical landmarks for the people of Israel. They represented the blessings of obeying God's law—Mount Gerizim—and the curses that resulted from disobeying his commands. When the Israelites looked at these two mountains, the most prominent in central Palestine, they were to remember that the whole future of the nation depended on their choice between obedience or disobedience, blessing or curse; this should move them to obey the Lord (Deuteronomy 27:9–28:68).

Mount Sinai, the mountain of God, is in Israel's early history a mediating place between heaven and earth. There the Lord appears to Moses and recruits him to bring the Israelites out of Egypt. The proof of God's presence and authority behind Moses in this mission will be the arrival of the people at Sinai to worship the Lord (Exodus 3:1–12). At this site, with the people camping in front of the mountain, Israel becomes God's people. Moses summons their elders and sets before them God's purpose for Israel to be his own possession if they keep his agreement. They, in turn, commit themselves to his words. The mountain, in and of itself, does not bring the presence of God to the people. This is evident when at its very foot they build a calf and worship it as their god (Exodus 32:1–6).

Once Moses and the people have settled in the land, Mount Zion, the mountain on which the Temple stands, and Jerusalem by extension, becomes the holy mountain of the Lord. The Lord's presence in the Temple turns Mount Zion into his holy mountain; a mediating place between the divine and the human realms.

Just as mountains are places of judgment and blessing, they are also associated with Israel's pagan worship (Isaiah 57:7; 65:7; Ezekiel 6:13) and are related to the Lord's judgment upon Israel. Mountains are called as witnesses, in God's case, against Israel for their sins (Micah 6:1–2). They are addressed in representation of the people when the prophet is ordered to prophesy against them (Ezekiel 6:1–7); the mountain on which the Temple stands will fall prey into their enemies' hands and become a neglected place (Micah 3:12). The anger of God against the nations and the force of his judgment are also announced by the prophets in relation to mountains: their blood will flow down the mountains, kings will be thrown in disgrace from the mountain of God, and the flesh of their dead will fill the mountains and be scattered upon them (Isaiah 34:1–3; Ezekiel 28:14–16).

On the other hand, the high mountain of Israel also represents a healing place after God's judgment. There he will gather his people back from exile. To this mountain they will come to worship and serve him (Isaiah 27:13; Ezekiel 20:40). The nations will gather on the Lord's holy mountain, in his house of prayer, to join him, love him, serve him, learn his law, and obey him (Isaiah 56:6–8; Micah 4:1–4). Jesus affirms this universal scope of God's purpose.

In the four books of Good News (Matthew, Mark, Luke, and John), mountains are places where utter loyalty to the Lord and exclusivity of service to him are affirmed (Matthew 4:8–10); where the community of the kingdom takes form (Matthew 5–7; Mark 3:13–19); where appearances of God (theophanies) that define the identity and mission of Jesus takes place (Matthew 17:1–13; Luke 9:28–36); sites of prayer where Jesus identifies himself with God's purposes (Matthew 14:23; Luke 6:12; John 6:15); and platforms from where judgment is declared (Mark 13:3–37).

Today, geographical places do not serve as channels for theological meaning. However, one could argue that the church is the one place that serves for us the same function mountains served in the biblical story. Here, people from all nations come to join him, love him, serve him, hear him, and go out to serve him. His presence, his word, his judgments, and his mercy are announced from this place, calling people to decide for or against him. Yet the church cannot contain, restrain, or assure his presence.

Mountain: For additional scriptures on this topic go to Exodus 19.

the supporters of Saul's family became weaker
and weaker.

David's Sons

2Sons were born to David at Hebron. The first
was Amnon, whose mother was Ahinoam from
Jezreel. 3The second son was Kileab, whose mother
was Abigail, the widow of Nabal from Carmel.
The third son was Absalom, whose mother was
Maacah daughter of Talmai, the king of Geshur.
4The fourth son was Adonijah, whose mother
was Haggith. The fifth son was Shephatiah,
whose mother was Abital. 5The sixth son was
Ithream, whose mother was Eglah, David's wife.
These sons were born to David at Hebron.

Abner Joins David

6During the war between the supporters of
Saul's family and the supporters of David's family,
Abner made himself a main leader among the
supporters of Saul.
7Saul once had a slave woman named Rizpah,
who was the daughter of Aiah. Ish-Bosheth said
to Abner, "Why did you have sexual relations
with my father's slave woman?"
8Abner was very angry because of what Ish-
Bosheth said, and he replied, "I have been loyal
to Saul and his family and friends! I didn't hand
you over to David. I am not a traitor working for
Judah! But now you are saying I did something
wrong with this woman! 9May God help me if I
don't join David! I will make sure that what the
LORD promised does happen! 10I will take the
kingdom from the family of Saul and make
David king of Israel and Judah, from Dan to
Beersheba!"
11Ish-Bosheth couldn't say anything to Abner,
because he was afraid of him.
12Then Abner sent messengers to ask David,
"Who is going to rule the land? Make an agreement with me, and I will help you unite all Israel."
13David answered, "Good! I will make an agreement with you, but I ask you one thing. I will not
meet with you unless you bring Saul's daughter
Michal to me." 14Then David sent messengers to
Saul's son Ish-Bosheth, saying, "Give me my wife
Michal. She was promised to me, and I killed a
hundred Philistines to get her."
15So Ish-Bosheth sent men to take Michal from
her husband Paltiel son of Laish. 16Michal's husband went with her, crying as he followed her to
Bahurim. But Abner said to Paltiel, "Go back
home." So he went home.
17Abner sent this message to the older leaders
of Israel: "You have been wanting to make David
your king. 18Now do it! The LORD said of David,
'Through my servant David, I will save my people
Israel from the Philistines and all their enemies.'"
19Abner also said these things to the people of
Benjamin. He then went to Hebron to tell David
what the Benjaminites and Israel wanted to do.
20Abner came with twenty men to David at
Hebron. There David prepared a feast for them.
21Abner said to David, "My master and king, I
will go and bring all the Israelites to you. Then
they will make an agreement with you so you will
rule over all Israel as you wanted." So David let
Abner go, and he left in peace.

Abner's Death

22Just then Joab and David's men came from a
battle, bringing many valuable things they had
taken from the enemy. David had let Abner leave
in peace, so he was not with David at Hebron.
23When Joab and all his army arrived at Hebron,
the army said to Joab, "Abner son of Ner came to
King David, and David let him leave in peace."
24Joab came to the king and said, "What have
you done? Abner came to you. Why did you let
him go? Now he's gone. 25You know Abner son of
Ner! He came to trick you! He came to learn
about everything you are doing!"
26After Joab left David, he sent messengers
after Abner, and they brought him back from the
well of Sirah. But David did not know this.
27When Abner arrived at Hebron, Joab took him
aside into the gateway. He acted as though he
wanted to talk with Abner in private, but Joab
stabbed him in the stomach, and Abner died.
Abner had killed Joab's brother Asahel, so Joab
killed Abner to pay him back.
28Later when David heard the news, he said,
"My kingdom and I are innocent forever of the
death of Abner son of Ner. The LORD knows this.
29Joab and his family are responsible for this. May
his family always have someone with sores or
with a skin disease. May they always have someone who must lean on a crutch. May some of his
family be killed in war. May they always have
someone without food to eat."
30(Joab and his brother Abishai killed Abner,
because he had killed their brother Asahel in the
battle at Gibeon.)
31Then David said to Joab and to all the people
with Joab, "Tear your clothes and put on rough
cloth to show how sad you are. Cry for Abner."

3:10 *Dan to Beersheba.* Dan was the city farthest north in Israel, and Beersheba was the city farthest south. So this means all the people of Israel.

King David himself followed the body of Abner.
32They buried Abner in Hebron, and David and
all the people cried at Abner's grave.
33King David sang this funeral song for Abner.

"Did Abner die like a fool?
34 His hands were not tied.
His feet were not in chains.
He fell at the hands of evil men."

Then all the people cried again for Abner.
35They came to encourage David to eat while it
was still day. But he made a promise, saying,
"May God punish me terribly if I eat bread or anything else before the sun sets!"
36All the people saw what happened, and they
agreed with what the king was doing, just as they
agreed with everything he did. 37That day all the
people of Judah and Israel understood that David
did not order the killing of Abner son of Ner.
38David said to his officers, "You know that a
great man died today in Israel. 39Even though I
am the appointed king, I feel empty. These sons
of Zeruiah are too much for me. May the LORD
give them the punishment they should have."

Ish-Bosheth's Death

4 When Ish-Bosheth son of Saul heard that
Abner had died at Hebron, he was shocked
and all Israel became frightened. 2Two men who
were captains in Saul's army came to Ish-
Bosheth. One was named Baanah, and the other
was named Recab. They were the sons of Rimmon
of Beeroth, who was a Benjaminite. (The town
Beeroth belonged to the tribe of Benjamin. 3The
people of Beeroth ran away to Gittaim, and they
still live there as foreigners today.)
4(Saul's son Jonathan had a son named Mephibosheth, who was crippled in both feet. He was
five years old when the news came from Jezreel
that Saul and Jonathan were dead. Mephibosheth's nurse had picked him up and run away.
But as she hurried to leave, she dropped him, and
now he was lame.)
5Recab and Baanah, sons of Rimmon from
Beeroth, went to Ish-Bosheth's house in the afternoon while he was taking a nap. 6-7They went
into the middle of the house as if to get some
wheat. Ish-Bosheth was lying on his bed in his
bedroom. Then Recab and Baanah stabbed him in
the stomach, killed him, cut off his head, and took
it with them. They escaped and traveled all night
through the Jordan Valley. 8When they arrived at
Hebron, they gave his head to David and said to
the king, "Here is the head of Ish-Bosheth son of
Saul, your enemy. He tried to kill you! Today the
LORD has paid back Saul and his family for what
they did to you!"
9David answered Recab and his brother Baanah,
the sons of Rimmon of Beeroth, "As surely as the
LORD lives, he has saved me from all trouble!
10Once a man thought he was bringing me good
news. When he told me, 'Saul is dead!' I seized
him and killed him at Ziklag. That was the reward
I gave him for his news! 11So even more I must put
you evil men to death because you have killed an
innocent man on his own bed in his own house!"
12So David commanded his men to kill Recab
and Baanah. They cut off the hands and feet of
Recab and Baanah and hung them over the pool
of Hebron. Then they took Ish-Bosheth's head
and buried it in Abner's tomb at Hebron.

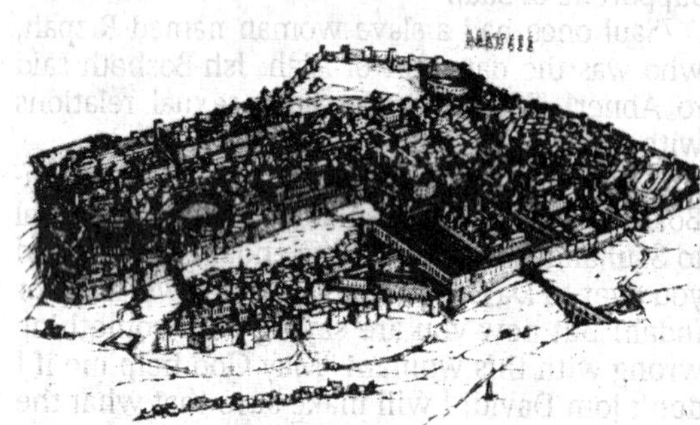

Jerusalem in Jesus' day. The Temple is in the foreground. Herod's palace is on the far side of the city.

David Is Made King of Israel

5 Then all the tribes of Israel came to David at
Hebron and said to him, "Look, we are your
own family. 2Even when Saul was king, you were
the one who led Israel in battle. The LORD said to
you, 'You will be a shepherd for my people Israel.
You will be their leader.'"
3So all the older leaders of Israel came to King
David at Hebron, and he made an agreement
with them in Hebron in the presence of the LORD.
Then they poured oil on David to make him king
over Israel.
4David was thirty years old when he became
king, and he ruled forty years. 5He was king over
Judah in Hebron for seven years and six months,
and he was king over all Israel and Judah in
Jerusalem for thirty-three years.

3:34 Murder: Psalm 94:6
4:4 *run away.* A conquering army would often completely kill off the defeated king's children.

6When the king and his men went to Jerusalem
to attack the Jebusites who lived there, the
Jebusites said to David, "You can't get inside our
city. Even the blind and the crippled can stop
you." They thought David could not enter their
city. 7But David did take the city of Jerusalem with
its strong walls, and it became the City of David.
8That day David said to his men, "To defeat the
Jebusites you must go through the water tunnel.
Then you can reach those 'crippled' and 'blind'
enemies. This is why people say, 'The blind and
the crippled may not enter the palace.'"
9So David lived in the strong, walled city and
called it the City of David. David built more buildings around it, beginning where the land was
filled in. He also built more buildings inside the
city. 10He became stronger and stronger, because
the LORD God All-Powerful was with him.
11Hiram king of the city of Tyre sent messengers to David, along with cedar logs, carpenters,
and stonecutters. They built a palace for David.
12Then David knew that the LORD really had made
him king of Israel and that the LORD had made his
kingdom great because the LORD loved his people
Israel.
13After he came from Hebron, David took for
himself more slave women and wives in Jerusalem.
More sons and daughters were born to David.
14These are the names of the sons born to David
in Jerusalem: Shammua, Shobab, Nathan, Solomon,
15Ibhar, Elishua, Nepheg, Japhia, 16Elishama,
Eliada, and Eliphelet.

David Defeats the Philistines

17When the Philistines heard that David had
been made king over Israel, all the Philistines
went to look for him. But when David heard the
news, he went down to the stronghold. 18The
Philistines came and camped in the Valley of
Rephaim. 19David asked the LORD, "Should I attack
the Philistines? Will you hand them over to me?"
The LORD said to David, "Go! I will certainly
hand them over to you."
20So David went to Baal Perazim and defeated
the Philistines there. David said, "Like a flood of
water, the LORD has broken through my enemies
in front of me." So David named the place Baal
Perazim. 21The Philistines left their idols behind
at Baal Perazim, so David and his men carried
them away.
22Once again the Philistines came and camped
at the Valley of Rephaim. 23When David prayed to
the LORD, he answered, "Don't attack the Philistines from the front. Instead, go around and
attack them in front of the balsam trees. 24When
you hear the sound of marching in the tops of the
balsam trees, act quickly. I, the LORD, will have
gone ahead of you to defeat the Philistine
army." 25So David did what the LORD commanded. He defeated the Philistines and chased
them all the way from Gibeon to Gezer.

The Ark Is Brought to Jerusalem

6 David again gathered all the chosen men of
Israel—thirty thousand of them. 2Then he
and all his people went to Baalah in Judah to
bring back the Ark of God. The Ark is called by
the Name, the name of the LORD All-Powerful,
whose throne is between the gold creatures with
wings. 3They put the Ark of God on a new cart
and brought it out of Abinadab's house on the hill.
Uzzah and Ahio, sons of Abinadab, led the new
cart 4which had the Ark of God on it. Ahio was
walking in front of it. 5David and all the Israelites
were celebrating in the presence of the LORD. They
were playing wooden instruments: lyres, harps,
tambourines, rattles, and cymbals.
6When David's men came to the threshing floor
of Nacon, the oxen stumbled. So Uzzah reached
out to steady the Ark of God. 7The LORD was angry
with Uzzah and killed him because of what he did.
So Uzzah died there beside the Ark of God. 8David
was angry because the LORD had killed Uzzah.
Now that place is called the Punishment of Uzzah.
9David was afraid of the LORD that day, and he
said, "How can the Ark of the LORD come to me
now?" 10So David would not move the Ark of the
LORD to be with him in Jerusalem. Instead, he
took it to the house of Obed-Edom, a man from
Gath. 11The Ark of the LORD stayed in Obed-
Edom's house for three months, and the LORD
blessed Obed-Edom and all his family.
12The people told David, "The LORD has blessed
the family of Obed-Edom and all that belongs to
him, because the Ark of God is there." So David
went and brought it up from Obed-Edom's house
to Jerusalem with joy. 13When the men carrying
the Ark of the LORD had walked six steps, David
sacrificed a bull and a fat calf. 14Then David danced
with all his might before the LORD. He had on a
holy linen vest. 15David and all the Israelites
shouted with joy and blew the trumpets as they
brought the Ark of the LORD to the city.
16As the Ark of the LORD came into the city,
Saul's daughter Michal looked out the window.

5:20 *Baal Perazim.* This name means "the Lord breaks through."
5:24 Holy War & Divine Warrior: 2 Chronicles 20:20–23
6:2 *Baalah in Judah.* Another name for Kiriath Jearim.

When she saw David jumping and dancing in the presence of the LORD, she hated him.

17David put up a tent for the Ark of the LORD, and then the Israelites put it in its place inside the tent. David offered whole burnt offerings and fellowship offerings before the LORD. 18When David finished offering the whole burnt offerings and the fellowship offerings, he blessed the people in the name of the LORD All-Powerful. 19David gave a loaf of bread, a cake of dates, and a cake of raisins to every Israelite, both men and women. Then all the people went home.

20David went back to bless the people in his home, but Saul's daughter Michal came out to meet him. She said, "With what honor the king of Israel acted today! You took off your clothes in front of the servant girls of your officers like one who takes off his clothes without shame!"

21Then David said to Michal, "I did it in the presence of the LORD. The LORD chose me, not your father or anyone from Saul's family. The LORD appointed me to be over Israel. So I will celebrate in the presence of the LORD. 22Maybe I will lose even more honor, and maybe I will be brought down in my own opinion, but the girls you talk about will honor me!"

23And Saul's daughter Michal had no children to the day she died.∞

David Wants to Build a Temple

7 King David was living in his palace, and the LORD had given him peace from all his enemies around him. 2Then David said to Nathan the prophet, "Look, I am living in a palace made of cedar wood, but the Ark of God is in a tent!"

3Nathan said to the king, "Go and do what you really want to do, because the LORD is with you."

4But that night the LORD spoke his word to Nathan, 5"Go and tell my servant David, 'This is what the LORD says: Will you build a house for me to live in? 6From the time I brought the Israelites out of Egypt until now I have not lived in a house. I have been moving around all this time with a tent as my home. 7As I have moved with the Israelites, I have never said to the tribes, whom I commanded to take care of my people Israel, "Why haven't you built me a house of cedar?"'

8"You must tell my servant David, 'This is what the LORD All-Powerful says: I took you from the pasture and from tending the sheep and made you leader of my people Israel. 9I have been with you everywhere you have gone and have defeated your enemies for you. I will make you as famous as any of the great people on the earth. 10Also I will choose a place for my people Israel, and I will plant them so they can live in their own homes. They will not be bothered anymore. Wicked people will no longer bother them as they have in the past 11when I chose judges for my people Israel. But I will give you peace from all your enemies. I also tell you that I will make your descendants kings of Israel after you.

12"'When you die and join your ancestors, I will make one of your sons the next king, and I will set up his kingdom. 13He will build a house for me, and I will let his kingdom rule always. 14I will be his father, and he will be my son. When he sins, I will use other people to punish him. They will be my whips.∞ 15I took away my love from Saul, whom I removed before you, but I will never stop loving your son. 16But your family and your kingdom will continue always before me. Your throne will last forever.'"∞

17Nathan told David everything God had said in this vision.

David Prays to God

18Then King David went in and sat in front of the LORD. David said, "Lord GOD, who am I? What is my family? Why did you bring me to this point? 19But even this is not enough for you, Lord GOD. You have also made promises about my future family. This is not normal, Lord GOD.

20"What more can I say to you, Lord GOD, since you know me, your servant, so well! 21You have done this great thing because you said you would and because you wanted to, and you have let me know about it. 22This is why you are great, Lord GOD! There is no one like you. There is no God except you. We have heard all this ourselves! 23There is no nation like your people Israel. They are the only people on earth that God chose to be his own. You made your name well known. You did great and wonderful miracles for them. You went ahead of them and forced other nations and their gods out of the land. You freed your people from slavery in Egypt. 24You made the people of Israel your very own people forever, and, LORD, you are their God.

25"Now, LORD God, keep the promise forever that you made about my family and me, your servant.

∞**6:23 Ark of the Agreement:** 1 Kings 8:1–21
7:6 *a tent as my home.* The Holy Tent was, indeed, a tent-like structure.
∞**7:14 Jesus:** Psalm 2:7
7:16 The word *agreement* is not used here, but later passages look back on this episode as the time God entered into an agreement with David (Psalm 89:3). God would raise up a line of kings from David. David responded to this agreement with great joy and gratitude.
∞**7:16 Births:** 1 Chronicles 1–9
∞**7:16 House/Home:** Psalm 127:1–2

Do what you have said. 26Then you will be honored always, and people will say, 'The LORD All-
Powerful is God over Israel!' And the family of
your servant David will continue before you.
27"LORD All-Powerful, the God of Israel, you
have said to me, 'I will make your family great.'
So I, your servant, am brave enough to pray to
you. 28Lord GOD, you are God, and your words
are true. And you have promised these good
things to me, your servant. 29Please, bless my
family. Let it continue before you always. Lord
GOD, you have said so. With your blessing let my
family always be blessed."

David Wins Many Wars

8 Later, David defeated the Philistines, conquered them, and took the city of Metheg
Ammah.
2He also defeated the people of Moab. He made
them lie on the ground, and then he used a rope to
measure them. Those who were measured within
two rope lengths were killed, but those who were
within the next rope length were allowed to live.
So the people of Moab became servants of David
and gave him the payment he demanded.
3David also defeated Hadadezer son of Rehob,
king of Zobah, as he went to take control again at
the Euphrates River. 4David captured one thousand chariots, seven thousand men who rode in
chariots, and twenty thousand foot soldiers. He
crippled all but a hundred of the chariot horses.
5Arameans from Damascus came to help
Hadadezer king of Zobah, but David killed
twenty-two thousand of them. 6Then David put
groups of soldiers in Damascus in Aram. The
Arameans became David's servants and gave him
the payment he demanded. The LORD gave David
victory everywhere he went.
7David took the shields of gold that had belonged to Hadadezer's officers and brought them
to Jerusalem. 8David also took many things made
of bronze from Tebah and Berothai, which had
been cities under Hadadezer's control.
9Toi king of Hamath heard that David had
defeated all the army of Hadadezer. 10So Toi sent
his son Joram to greet and congratulate King
David for defeating Hadadezer. (Hadadezer had
been at war with Toi.) Joram brought items made
of silver, gold, and bronze. 11King David gave
them to the LORD, along with the silver and gold
he had taken from the other nations he had
defeated. 12These nations were Edom, Moab,
Ammon, Philistia, and Amalek. David also gave
the LORD what he had taken from Hadadezer son
of Rehob, king of Zobah.
13David was famous after he returned from
defeating eighteen thousand Arameans in the
Valley of Salt. 14He put groups of soldiers all over
Edom, and all the Edomites became his servants.
The LORD gave David victory everywhere he went.
15David was king over all Israel, and he did what
was fair and right for all his people. 16Joab son of
Zeruiah was commander over the army. Jehoshaphat son of Ahilud was the recorder. 17Zadok son
of Ahitub and Abiathar son of Ahimelech were
priests. Seraiah was the royal secretary. 18Benaiah
son of Jehoiada was over the Kerethites and
Pelethites. And David's sons were priests.

David Helps Saul's Family

9 David asked, "Is anyone still left in Saul's
family? I want to show kindness to that person
for Jonathan's sake!"
2Now there was a servant named Ziba from
Saul's family. So David's servants called Ziba to
him. King David said to him, "Are you Ziba?"
He answered, "Yes, I am your servant."
3The king asked, "Is anyone left in Saul's family?
I want to show God's kindness to that person."
Ziba answered the king, "Jonathan has a son
still living who is crippled in both feet."
4The king asked Ziba, "Where is this son?"
Ziba answered, "He is at the house of Makir
son of Ammiel in Lo Debar."
5Then King David had servants bring Jonathan's
son from the house of Makir son of Ammiel in Lo
Debar. 6Mephibosheth, Jonathan's son, came
before David and bowed facedown on the floor.
David said, "Mephibosheth!"
Mephibosheth said, "I am your servant."
7David said to him, "Don't be afraid. I will be
kind to you for your father Jonathan's sake. I will
give you back all the land of your grandfather
Saul, and you will always eat at my table."
8Mephibosheth bowed to David again and said,
"You are being very kind to me, your servant!
And I am no better than a dead dog!"
9Then King David called Saul's servant Ziba.
David said to him, "I have given your master's
grandson everything that belonged to Saul and his
family. 10You, your sons, and your servants will
farm the land and harvest the crops. Then your family will have food to eat. But Mephibosheth, your
master's grandson, will always eat at my table."

7:29 Servant of the Lord: 1 Kings 8:26
8:18 *Kerethites and Pelethites.* These were probably special units of the army that were responsible for the king's safety, a kind of palace guard.

(Now Ziba had fifteen sons and twenty servants.) 11 Ziba said to King David, "I, your servant, will do everything my master, the king, commands me."

So Mephibosheth ate at David's table as if he were one of the king's sons. 12 Mephibosheth had a young son named Mica. Everyone in Ziba's family became Mephibosheth's servants. 13 Mephibosheth lived in Jerusalem, because he always ate at the king's table. And he was crippled in both feet.

War with the Ammonites and Arameans

10 When Nahash king of the Ammonites died, his son Hanun became king after him. 2 David said, "Nahash was loyal to me, so I will be loyal to his son Hanun." So David sent his messengers to comfort Hanun about his father's death.

David's officers went to the land of the Ammonites. 3 But the Ammonite leaders said to Hanun, their master, "Do you think David wants to honor your father by sending men to comfort you? No! David sent them to study the city and spy it out and capture it!" 4 So Hanun arrested David's officers. To shame them he shaved off half their beards and cut off their clothes at the hips. Then he sent them away.

5 When the people told David, he sent messengers to meet his officers because they were very ashamed. King David said, "Stay in Jericho until your beards have grown back. Then come home."

6 The Ammonites knew that they had insulted David. So they hired twenty thousand Aramean foot soldiers from Beth Rehob and Zobah. They also hired the king of Maacah with a thousand men and twelve thousand men from Tob.

7 When David heard about this, he sent Joab with the whole army. 8 The Ammonites came out and prepared for battle at the city gate. The Arameans from Zobah and Rehob and the men from Tob and Maacah were out in the field by themselves.

9 Joab saw that there were enemies both in front of him and behind him. So he chose some of the best soldiers of Israel and sent them out to fight the Arameans. 10 Joab put the rest of the army under the command of Abishai, his brother. Then he sent them out to fight the Ammonites. 11 Joab said to Abishai, "If the Arameans are too strong for me, you must help me. Or, if the Ammonites are too strong for you, I will help you. 12 Be strong. We must fight bravely for our people and the cities of our God. The LORD will do what he thinks is right."

13 Then Joab and the army with him went to attack the Arameans, and the Arameans ran away. 14 When the Ammonites saw that the Arameans were running away, they also ran away from Abishai and went back to their city. So Joab returned from the battle with the Ammonites and came to Jerusalem.

15 When the Arameans saw that Israel had defeated them, they came together into one big army. 16 Hadadezer sent messengers to bring the Arameans from east of the Euphrates River, and they went to Helam. Their leader was Shobach, the commander of Hadadezer's army.

17 When David heard about this, he gathered all the Israelites together. They crossed over the Jordan River and went to Helam. There the Arameans prepared for battle and attacked him. 18 But the Arameans ran away from the Israelites. David killed seven hundred Aramean chariot drivers and forty thousand Aramean horsemen. He also killed Shobach, the commander of the Aramean army.

19 When the kings who served Hadadezer saw that the Israelites had defeated them, they made peace with the Israelites and served them. And the Arameans were afraid to help the Ammonites again.

David Sins with Bathsheba

11 In the spring, when the kings normally went out to war, David sent out Joab, his servants, and all the Israelites. They destroyed the Ammonites and attacked the city of Rabbah. But David stayed in Jerusalem. 2 One evening David got up from his bed and walked around on the roof of his palace. While he was on the roof, he saw a woman bathing. She was very beautiful. 3 So David sent his servants to find out who she was. A servant answered, "That woman is Bathsheba daughter of Eliam. She is the wife of Uriah the Hittite." 4 So David sent messengers to bring Bathsheba to him. When she came to him, he had sexual relations with her. (Now Bathsheba had purified herself from her monthly period.) Then she went back to her house. 5 But Bathsheba became pregnant and sent word to David, saying, "I am pregnant."

10:5 *your beards.* All mature men in Israel had beards. Only eunuchs were bare-chinned in the ancient Near East, thus the embarrassment associated with this shaving.

11:1 Military campaigns were an annual event in ancient times in this part of the world. Spring was the time to begin. This note introduces David, who is not on the battlefield but getting into trouble at home. The implied message is that David should have been with the army, and the sin with Bathsheba might have been avoided.

11:1 *when the kings normally went out to war.* Kings of the ancient Near East launched their annual military campaigns in the spring when the weather allowed it. The passage implies that David should have been on the battlefield with Joab rather than staying in Jerusalem and getting into trouble.

11:2 *roof.* In Bible times houses were built with flat roofs. The roof was used for drying things such as flax and fruit, as an extra room, as a place for worship, and as a cool place to sleep in the summer.

11:2 *on the roof.* See Deuteronomy 22:8. The roof of a house in ancient Israel was a living space. Houses in David's Jerusalem were built into a slope on a hillside.

TITHE

DEUTERONOMY 14:22–23

What is a tithe? Is tithing an Old Testament practice no longer in effect in the New Testament?

A tithe is one-tenth of the produce of a person's land over a season or one-tenth of a person's annual income. The practice of tithing has a long and varied history. The cultural practice of "tenthing" was established before the first Biblical record of the practice. The early records of the tithe indicate that they were offered to the gods out of gratitude (thankfulness) for life's blessing or the hope of getting a blessing. We see an example of this sort of tithing in the earliest Biblical examples. Abram gave a tithe, a tenth, of the spoils of battle to Melchizedek, the king of Salem and the priest of "God Most High" (Genesis 14:20). Jacob promised to practice the giving of one-tenth out of gratitude to God for the blessing of his heritage, land, protection, food, and clothing (Genesis 28:22). The attitude of giving out of gratitude is necessary to understand the tithe.

The concept of Lordship is a second theme central to the tithe. The important question to Jews and Christians alike is who or what will be first in their lives. The Old Testament developed complex and sometimes confusing rules for the tithe, but it also reminds us of the purpose of the tithe. That purpose is "that you will learn to respect the LORD your God always" (Deuteronomy 14:23). The teachings of Jesus reinforce this point. His statement, "Your heart will be where your treasure is," deals directly to the Lordship question (Matthew 6:21).

Making tithing a law is developed in the Old Testament books of Leviticus, Numbers, and Deuteronomy. It was first a way of celebrating the goodness and blessings of God. Second, it proved again the Lordship of the God Most High. Third, it provided a means of support for the priestly ministry of the Levites. Forth, it maintained the place of worship. Fifth, it was a way of providing care for the poor.

By the end of the Old Testament, not giving the tithe was regarded as robbing the LORD All-Powerful and as a means of securing future blessing (Malachi 3:6–12). Malachi charged the people to be obedient and promised that God would provide for them out of abundance.

The ancient practice of tithing was changed by Israel in the first five books of the Old Testament. Then it was ruined by trivial changes that made laws besides those in the Bible. Jewish commentaries on the Law added layer upon layer of complexity. This turned a beautiful and relatively simple practice into a legalistic burden. These additions are found in the Mishnah and Talmud.

By New Testament times tithing was an expected practice of the people of Jesus' day. Jesus liked the tithing of the Pharisees by saying, "These things you should do" (Matthew 23:23 and Luke 11:42). But he warned them that they needed to do more. The attitude of thankfulness, the focus on Lordship, and concern for the poor were missing from their legalistic practice.

Is tithing an Old Testament practice no longer in effect for New Testament Christians? There are very few verses in Scripture that deal with this. Jesus' teaching for the tithe, however qualified, has been cited. It seems that Jesus wanted us to better understand giving. He opposed the legalism associated with giving which was taught by the Pharisees and religious leaders of his day. He liked the gratitude that accompanies the giving of Zacchaeus (Luke 19:8–9); the widow's few cents that provided for worship (Mark 12:41–44); and gifts that support the poor. He taught that what people do with their money and possessions should be ordered by God's priorities in order to settle the question of Lordship (Matthew 6).

The apostle Paul does not use the term tithe. He instructs new Christians: "Now I will write about the collection of money. . . . On the first day of every week, each one of you should put aside money as you have been blessed." His teaching of giving "as you have been blessed" stops just short of using the word tithe (1 Corinthians 16:1–2).

Christians live by God's grace as revealed in Jesus Christ and not by the burdensome laws of the Pharisees and religious leaders of Jesus' day. Now freed from that law by the sacrifice of Christ, we should not think of doing less than the law previously required. We should express our gratitude to God in our giving, discipline ourselves to show respect for the Lord by giving a tithe, provide for the ministry, and take care of the poor. The practice of tithing seems as proper to the task of the church today as it did in the days of the kings of Israel and Judah.

Tithe: For additional scriptures on this topic go to Genesis 14:20.

MAGIC

DEUTERONOMY 18

What is magic?

For most people, "magic" means a stage show with conjuring tricks and illusions. But it can also have a more sinister ring to it: all over the Western world today there is a renewed interest in the occult, coupled with the rise of so-called neopaganism.

The anthropologist James G. Frazer (1854–1941) related magic to people's need to control the natural environment. Faced with the impossibility of doing this, he suggested that they concluded nature itself was controlled by other powerful forces (gods), and developed religion to control the gods. With science and technology, everything seemed to work by "laws of nature," and so both magic and religion were done away with once people saw they themselves had the power to control it.

Magic Powers

Magic consists of actions designed to produce certain consequences by the operation of mystical or spiritual powers. To do that, magicians use special rituals, secret words (magic spells) and objects. Clients pay for these services to ensure their own lives run smoothly.

Magic was widespread in the world of the Bible, and involved in every aspect of life: agriculture, rites of passage, burial customs, and so on—anything in which success seemed to depend on influences from some other mystical or spiritual world.

Many magicians' handbooks survived from New Testament times. They show how widespread magical practices could be. Spells were used for weather forecasting, healings, exorcisms, and even ancient science. Magic could also mean getting in touch with the spirits of the dead. On occasion, it involved sacrifice, either of animals or people, or both. Mithraism was a secret society with a special attraction for Roman soldiers, and it was founded on the practice of magic.

The church has always had an uneasy relationship with all this. Some sections of the Gnostic movement of the second and third centuries became in effect a kind of Christian magic. Eight hundred years later, the Cathars took a similar position, while in more recent times some of the founding fathers of the modern U.S.A. came under the influence of the same type of thinking. To this day, the back of a dollar bill still carries magical symbols whose origins go back to the amulets and curse tablets of the ancient world.

The Bible's Teaching on Magic

The Bible has no time for all this (Exodus 22:18; Leviticus 19:26, 31; 20:6, 27; Deuteronomy 18:9–22). That did not stop people experimenting with magic, and judging from the amount of time the prophets spent warning people against it, it must have been a serious social and religious problem (Isaiah 47:9–15; Jeremiah 27:9; Ezekiel 13:17–19; Micah 5:11–12; Nahum 3:4; Malachi 3:5). Even members of the royal families of Israel and Judah sometimes got involved (2 Kings 9:22; 2 Chronicles 33:6), and they too were condemned for ignoring God's law in this way. The New Testament takes the same approach (Galatians 5:19–20; Acts 8:9–24; 13:6–12; 19:13–19).

The Bible's understanding of God is quite different from the world's view of magic.

1. The Bible never endows nature with divinity. There is no such thing as objects or activities that contain spiritual or psychic power by themselves. The physical environment is good, and is to be preserved and valued, but God is the one who is to be worshiped, for all that there is depends on God for its nurture and continued life.

2. God is not an unpredictable "force" to be appeased and humored by magical performances, but a personal being made known especially through the life, death, and resurrection of Jesus. Knowing God is about believing Jesus, not manipulating alien spiritual forces.

3. Magic depends on some people's having secret knowledge which the majority do not possess. The Bible teaches that anyone can have direct access to God, and so there is nothing left for the magician to do. Indeed, by getting involved in magic, people can find themselves lining up not on God's side, but on the devil's.

4. The Bible condemns efforts to manipulate the details of our own life and to exploit other people for our own benefit. It affirms that God is in sole control of this world, and can be trusted to do what is right.

Magic: For additional scriptures on this topic go to Exodus 22:18.

6So David sent a message to Joab: "Send Uriah
the Hittite to me." And Joab sent Uriah to David.
7When Uriah came to him, David asked him how
Joab was, how the soldiers were, and how the
war was going. 8Then David said to Uriah, "Go
home and rest."
So Uriah left the palace, and the king sent a gift
to him. 9But Uriah did not go home. Instead, he
slept outside the door of the palace as all the
king's officers did.
10The officers told David, "Uriah did not go
home."
Then David said to Uriah, "You came from a
long trip. Why didn't you go home?"
11Uriah said to him, "The Ark and the soldiers
of Israel and Judah are staying in tents. My master
Joab and his officers are camping out in the fields.
It isn't right for me to go home to eat and drink
and have sexual relations with my wife!"
12David said to Uriah, "Stay here today. Tomorrow I'll send you back to the battle." So Uriah
stayed in Jerusalem that day and the next. 13Then
David called Uriah to come to see him, so Uriah
ate and drank with David. David made Uriah
drunk, but he still did not go home. That evening
Uriah again slept with the king's officers.
14The next morning David wrote a letter to
Joab and sent it by Uriah. 15In the letter David
wrote, "Put Uriah on the front lines where the
fighting is worst and leave him there alone. Let
him be killed in battle."
16Joab watched the city and saw where its
strongest defenders were and put Uriah there.
17When the men of the city came out to fight
against Joab, some of David's men were killed.
And Uriah the Hittite was one of them.
18Then Joab sent David a complete account of the
war. 19Joab told the messenger, "Tell King David
what happened in the war. 20After you finish, the
king may be angry and ask, 'Why did you go so near
the city to fight? Didn't you know they would
shoot arrows from the city wall? 21Do you remember who killed Abimelech son of Jerub-Besheth?
It was a woman on the city wall. She threw a
large stone for grinding grain on Abimelech and
killed him there in Thebez. Why did you go so
near the wall?' If King David asks that, tell him,
'Your servant Uriah the Hittite also died.'"
22The messenger left and went to David and
told him everything Joab had told him to say.
23The messenger told David, "The men of Ammon
were winning. They came out and attacked us in
the field, but we fought them back to the city
gate. 24The archers on the city wall shot at your
servants, and some of your men were killed. Your
servant Uriah the Hittite also died."
25David said to the messenger, "Say this to
Joab: 'Don't be upset about this. The sword kills
everyone the same. Make a stronger attack against
the city and capture it.' Encourage Joab with
these words."
26When Bathsheba heard that her husband was
dead, she cried for him. 27After she finished her
time of sadness, David sent servants to bring her
to his house. She became David's wife and gave
birth to his son, but the LORD did not like what
David had done.

David's Son Dies

12 The LORD sent Nathan to David. When he
came to David, he said, "There were two
men in a city. One was rich, but the other was poor.
2The rich man had many sheep and cattle. 3But the
poor man had nothing except one little female
lamb he had bought. The poor man fed the lamb,
and it grew up with him and his children. It
shared his food and drank from his cup and slept
in his arms. The lamb was like a daughter to him.
4"Then a traveler stopped to visit the rich man.
The rich man wanted to feed the traveler, but he
didn't want to take one of his own sheep or cattle. Instead, he took the lamb from the poor man
and cooked it for his visitor."
5David became very angry at the rich man. He
said to Nathan, "As surely as the LORD lives, the
man who did this should die! 6He must pay for the
lamb four times for doing such a thing. He had no
mercy!"
7Then Nathan said to David, "You are the man!
This is what the LORD, the God of Israel, says: 'I
appointed you king of Israel and saved you from
Saul. 8I gave you his kingdom and his wives. And
I made you king of Israel and Judah. And if that
had not been enough, I would have given you
even more. 9So why did you ignore the LORD's
command? Why did you do what he says is
wrong? You killed Uriah the Hittite with the
sword of the Ammonites and took his wife to be
your wife! 10Now there will always be people in
your family who will die by a sword, because you
did not respect me; you took the wife of Uriah the
Hittite for yourself!'
11"This is what the LORD says: 'I am bringing
trouble to you from your own family. While you

11:11 *It isn't right for me to . . . have sexual relations with my wife.* See Leviticus 15:16–18 for the laws that explain Uriah's statement. The emission of semen, even in marital intercourse, made someone unclean for a day. That meant Uriah could not go on holy ground, like the battlefield where the Ark of the Agreement accompanied the army.

11:21 *Jerub-Besheth.* Another name for Gideon.

watch, I will take your wives from you and give them to someone who is very close to you. He will have sexual relations with your wives, and everyone will know it. 12You had sexual relations with Bathsheba in secret, but I will do this so all the people of Israel can see it.'"

13Then David said to Nathan, "I have sinned against the LORD."

Nathan answered, "The LORD has taken away your sin. You will not die. 14But what you did caused the LORD's enemies to lose all respect for him. For this reason the son who was born to you will die."

15Then Nathan went home. And the LORD caused the son of David and Bathsheba, Uriah's widow, to be very sick. 16David prayed to God for the baby. David refused to eat or drink. He went into his house and stayed there, lying on the ground all night. 17The older leaders of David's family came to him and tried to pull him up from the ground, but he refused to get up or to eat food with them.

18On the seventh day the baby died. David's servants were afraid to tell him that the baby was dead. They said, "Look, we tried to talk to David while the baby was alive, but he refused to listen to us. If we tell him the baby is dead, he may do something awful."

19When David saw his servants whispering, he knew that the baby was dead. So he asked them, "Is the baby dead?"

They answered, "Yes, he is dead."

20Then David got up from the floor, washed himself, put lotions on, and changed his clothes. Then he went into the LORD's house to worship. After that, he went home and asked for something to eat. His servants gave him some food, and he ate.

21David's servants said to him, "Why are you doing this? When the baby was still alive, you refused to eat and you cried. Now that the baby is dead, you get up and eat food."

22David said, "While the baby was still alive, I refused to eat, and I cried. I thought, 'Who knows? Maybe the LORD will feel sorry for me and let the baby live.' 23But now that the baby is dead, why should I go without food? I can't bring him back to life. Some day I will go to him, but he cannot come back to me."

24Then David comforted Bathsheba his wife. He slept with her and had sexual relations with her. She became pregnant again and had another son, whom David named Solomon. The LORD loved Solomon. 25The LORD sent word through Nathan the prophet to name the baby Jedidiah, because the LORD loved the child.

David Captures Rabbah

26Joab fought against Rabbah, a royal city of the Ammonites, and he was about to capture it. 27Joab sent messengers to David and said, "I have fought against Rabbah and have captured its water supply. 28Now bring the other soldiers together and attack this city. Capture it before I capture it myself and it is called by my name!"

29So David gathered all the army and went to Rabbah and fought against it and captured it. 30David took the crown off their king's head and had it placed on his own head. That gold crown weighed about seventy-five pounds, and it had valuable gems in it. And David took many valuable things from the city. 31He also brought out the people of the city and forced them to work with saws, iron picks, and axes. He also made them build with bricks. David did this to all the Ammonite cities. Then David and all his army returned to Jerusalem.

Amnon and Tamar

13 David had a son named Absalom and a son named Amnon. Absalom had a beautiful sister named Tamar, and Amnon loved her. 2Tamar was a virgin. Amnon made himself sick just thinking about her, because he could not find any chance to be alone with her.

3Amnon had a friend named Jonadab son of Shimeah, David's brother. Jonadab was a very clever man. 4He asked Amnon, "Son of the king, why do you look so sad day after day? Tell me what's wrong!"

Amnon told him, "I love Tamar, the sister of my half-brother Absalom."

5Jonadab said to Amnon, "Go to bed and act as if you are sick. Then your father will come to see you. Tell him, 'Please let my sister Tamar come in and give me food to eat. Let her make the food in front of me so I can watch and eat it from her hand.'"

6So Amnon went to bed and acted sick. When King David came in to see him, Amnon said to him, "Please let my sister Tamar come in. Let her make two of her special cakes for me while I watch. Then I will eat them from her hands."

7David sent for Tamar in the palace, saying, "Go to your brother Amnon's house and make some food for him." 8So Tamar went to her brother Amnon's house, and he was in bed. Tamar took some dough and pressed it together with her hands. She made some special cakes while Amnon watched. Then she baked them. 9Next she took the pan and served him, but he refused to eat.

12:25 *Jedidiah.* This name means "loved by the LORD."

He said to his servants, "All of you, leave me alone!" So they all left him alone. 10Amnon said to Tamar, "Bring the food into the bedroom so I may eat from your hand."

Tamar took the cakes she had made and brought them to her brother Amnon in the bedroom. 11She went to him so he could eat from her hands, but Amnon grabbed her. He said, "Sister, come and have sexual relations with me."

12Tamar said to him, "No, brother! Don't force me! This should never be done in Israel! Don't do this shameful thing! 13I could never get rid of my shame! And you will be like the shameful fools in Israel! Please talk with the king, and he will let you marry me."

14But Amnon refused to listen to her. He was stronger than she was, so he forced her to have sexual relations with him. 15After that, Amnon hated Tamar. He hated her more than he had loved her before. Amnon said to her, "Get up and leave!"

16Tamar said to him, "No! Sending me away would be worse than what you've already done!"

But he refused to listen to her. 17He called his young servant back in and said, "Get this woman out of here and away from me! Lock the door after her." 18So his servant led her out of the room and bolted the door after her.

Tamar was wearing a special robe with long sleeves, because the king's virgin daughters wore this kind of robe. 19To show how upset she was, Tamar put ashes on her head and tore her special robe and put her hand on her head. Then she went away, crying loudly.

20Absalom, Tamar's brother, said to her, "Has Amnon, your brother, forced you to have sexual relations with him? For now, sister, be quiet. He is your half-brother. Don't let this upset you so much!" So Tamar lived in her brother Absalom's house and was sad and lonely.

21When King David heard the news, he was very angry. 22Absalom did not say a word, good or bad, to Amnon. But he hated Amnon for disgracing his sister Tamar.

Absalom's Revenge

23Two years later Absalom had some men come to Baal Hazor, near Ephraim, to cut the wool from his sheep. Absalom invited all the king's sons to come also. 24Absalom went to the king and said, "I have men coming to cut the wool. Please come with your officers and join me."

25King David said to Absalom, "No, my son. We won't all go, because it would be too much trouble for you." Although Absalom begged David, he would not go, but he did give his blessing.

26Absalom said, "If you don't want to come, then please let my brother Amnon come with us."

King David asked, "Why should he go with you?"

27Absalom kept begging David until he let Amnon and all the king's sons go with Absalom.

28Then Absalom instructed his servants, "Watch Amnon. When he is drunk, I will tell you, 'Kill Amnon.' Right then, kill him! Don't be afraid, because I have commanded you! Be strong and brave!" 29So Absalom's young men killed Amnon as Absalom commanded, but all of David's other sons got on their mules and escaped.

30While the king's sons were on their way, the news came to David, "Absalom has killed all of the king's sons! Not one of them is left alive!" 31King David tore his clothes and lay on the ground to show his sadness. All his servants standing nearby tore their clothes also.

32Jonadab son of Shimeah, David's brother, said to David, "Don't think all the young men, your sons, are killed. No, only Amnon is dead! Absalom has planned this ever since Amnon forced his sister Tamar to have sexual relations with him. 33My master and king, don't think that all of the king's sons are dead. Only Amnon is dead!"

34In the meantime Absalom had run away.

A guard standing on the city wall saw many people coming from the other side of the hill. 35So Jonadab said to King David, "Look, I was right! The king's sons are coming!"

36As soon as Jonadab had said this, the king's sons arrived, crying loudly. David and all his servants began crying also. 37David cried for his son every day.

But Absalom ran away to Talmai son of Ammihud, the king of Geshur. 38After Absalom ran away to Geshur, he stayed there for three years. 39When King David got over Amnon's death, he missed Absalom greatly.

Joab Sends a Wise Woman to David

14 Joab son of Zeruiah knew that King David missed Absalom very much. 2So Joab sent messengers to Tekoa to bring a wise woman from there. He said to her, "Pretend to be very sad. Put on funeral clothes and don't put lotion on yourself. Act like a woman who has been crying many days for someone who died. 3Then go to the king and say these words." Then Joab told her what to say.

4So the woman from Tekoa spoke to the king. She bowed facedown on the ground to show respect and said, "My king, help me!"

13:37 *Talmai.* He was Absalom's grandfather.

5King David asked her, "What is the matter?"

The woman said, "I am a widow; my husband is dead. 6I had two sons. They were out in the field fighting, and no one was there to stop them. So one son killed the other son. 7Now all the family group is against me. They said to me, 'Bring the son who killed his brother so we may kill him for killing his brother. That way we will also get rid of the one who would receive what belonged to his father.' My son is like the last spark of a fire. He is all I have left. If they kill him, my husband's name and property will be gone from the earth."

8Then the king said to the woman, "Go home. I will take care of this for you."

9The woman of Tekoa said to him, "Let the blame be on me and my father's family. My master and king, you and your throne are innocent."

10King David said, "Bring me anyone who says anything bad to you. Then he won't bother you again."

11The woman said, "Please promise in the name of the LORD your God. Then my relative who has the duty of punishing a murderer won't add to the destruction by killing my son."

David said, "As surely as the LORD lives, no one will hurt your son. Not one hair from his head will fall to the ground."

12The woman said, "Let me say something to you, my master and king."

The king said, "Speak."

13Then the woman said, "Why have you decided this way against the people of God? When you judge this way, you show that you are guilty for not bringing back your son who was forced to leave home. 14We will all die some day. We're like water spilled on the ground; no one can gather it back. But God doesn't take away life. Instead, he plans ways that those who have been sent away will not have to stay away from him! 15My master and king, I came to say this to you because the people have made me afraid! I thought, 'Let me talk to the king. Maybe he will do what I ask. 16Maybe he will listen. Perhaps he will save me from those who want to keep both me and my son from getting what God gave us.'

17"Now I say, 'May the words of my master the king give me rest. Like an angel of God, you know what is good and what is bad. May the LORD your God be with you!'"

18Then King David said, "Do not hide the truth. Answer me one question."

The woman said, "My master the king, please ask your question."

19The king said, "Did Joab tell you to say all these things?"

The woman answered, "As you live, my master the king, no one could avoid that question. You are right. Your servant Joab did tell me to say these things. 20Joab did it so you would see things differently. My master, you are wise like an angel of God who knows everything that happens on earth."⚭

Absalom Returns to Jerusalem

21The king said to Joab, "Look, I will do what I promised. Bring back the young man Absalom."

22Joab bowed facedown on the ground and blessed the king. Then he said, "Today I know you are pleased with me, because you have done what I asked."

23Then Joab got up and went to Geshur and brought Absalom back to Jerusalem. 24But King David said, "Absalom must go to his own house. He may not come to see me." So Absalom went to his own house and did not go to see the king.

25Absalom was greatly praised for his handsome appearance. No man in Israel was as handsome as he. No blemish was on him from his head to his foot. 26At the end of every year, Absalom would cut his hair, because it became too heavy. When he weighed it, it would weigh about five pounds by the royal measure.

27Absalom had three sons and one daughter. His daughter's name was also Tamar, and she was a beautiful woman.

28Absalom lived in Jerusalem for two full years without seeing King David. 29Then Absalom sent for Joab so he could send him to the king, but Joab would not come. Absalom sent a message a second time, but Joab still refused to come. 30Then Absalom said to his servants, "Look, Joab's field is next to mine, and he has barley growing there. Go burn it." So Absalom's servants set fire to Joab's field.

31Then Joab went to Absalom's house and said to him, "Why did your servants burn my field?"

32Absalom said to Joab, "I sent a message to you, asking you to come here. I wanted to send you to the king to ask him why he brought me home from Geshur. It would have been better for me to stay there! Now let me see the king. If I have sinned, he can put me to death!"

33So Joab went to the king and told him Absalom's words. Then the king called for Absalom. Absalom came and bowed facedown on the ground before the king, and the king kissed him.

⚭**14:20 Parables:** 1 Kings 20:35–40

Absalom Plans to Take David's Kingdom

15 After this, Absalom got a chariot and
horses for himself and fifty men to run
before him. 2Absalom would get up early and stand
near the city gate. Anyone who had a problem for
the king to settle would come here. When someone came, Absalom would call out and say,
"What city are you from?"
The person would answer, "I'm from one of
the tribes of Israel."
3Then Absalom would say, "Look, your claims
are right, but the king has no one to listen to
you." 4Absalom would also say, "I wish someone
would make me judge in this land! Then people
with problems could come to me, and I could
help them get justice."
5People would come near Absalom to bow to
him. When they did, Absalom would reach out
his hand and take hold of them and kiss them.
6Absalom did that to all the Israelites who came
to King David for decisions. In this way, Absalom
stole the hearts of all Israel.
7After four years Absalom said to King David,
"Please let me go to Hebron. I want to carry out
my promise that I made to the LORD 8while I was
living in Geshur in Aram. I said, 'If the LORD
takes me back to Jerusalem, I will worship him
in Hebron.'"
9The king said, "Go in peace."
So Absalom went to Hebron. 10But he sent
secret messengers through all the tribes of
Israel. They told the people, "When you hear
the trumpets, say this: 'Absalom is the king at
Hebron!'"
11Absalom had invited two hundred men to go
with him. So they went from Jerusalem with him,
but they didn't know what he was planning.
12While Absalom was offering sacrifices, he sent
for Ahithophel, one of the people who advised
David, to come from his hometown of Giloh. So
Absalom's plans were working very well. More
and more people began to support him.
13A messenger came to David, saying, "The
Israelites are giving their loyalty to Absalom."
14Then David said to all his officers who were
with him in Jerusalem, "We must leave quickly!
If we don't, we won't be able to get away from
Absalom. We must hurry before he catches us
and destroys us and kills the people of Jerusalem."
15The king's officers said to him, "We will do
anything you say."
16The king set out with everyone in his house,
but he left ten slave women to take care of the
palace. 17The king left with all his people following him, and they stopped at a house far
away. 18All the king's servants passed by him—
the Kerethites and Pelethites, all those from
Gath, and the six hundred men who had followed him.
19The king said to Ittai, a man from Gath, "Why
are you also going with us? Turn back and stay
with King Absalom because you are a foreigner.
This is not your homeland. 20You joined me only
a short time ago. Should I make you wander with
us when I don't even know where I'm going?
Turn back and take your brothers with you. May
kindness and loyalty be shown to you."
21But Ittai said to the king, "As surely as the
LORD lives and as you live, I will stay with you,
whether it means life or death."
22David said to Ittai, "Go, march on." So Ittai
from Gath and all his people with their children
marched on. 23All the people cried loudly as
everyone passed by. King David crossed the
Kidron Valley, and then all the people went on to
the desert. 24Zadok and all the Levites with him
carried the Ark of the Agreement with God. They
set it down, and Abiathar offered sacrifices until
all the people had left the city.
25The king said to Zadok, "Take the Ark of God
back into the city. If the LORD is pleased with me,
he will bring me back and will let me see both it
and Jerusalem again. 26But if the LORD says he is
not pleased with me, I am ready. He can do what
he wants with me."
27The king also said to Zadok the priest, "Aren't
you a seer? Go back to the city in peace and take
your son Ahimaaz and Abiathar's son Jonathan
with you. 28I will wait near the crossings into the
desert until I hear from you." 29So Zadok and
Abiathar took the Ark of God back to Jerusalem
and stayed there.
30David went up the Mount of Olives, crying as
he went. He covered his head and went barefoot.
All the people with David covered their heads
also and cried as they went. 31Someone told
David, "Ahithophel is one of the people with
Absalom who made secret plans against you."
So David prayed, "LORD, please make Ahithophel's advice foolish."
32When David reached the top of the mountain
where people used to worship God, Hushai the
Arkite came to meet him. Hushai's coat was torn,

15:2 *city gate.* People came here to conduct business. Public meetings and court cases were also held here.
15:18 *Kerethites and Pelethites.* These were probably special units of the army that were responsible for the king's safety, a kind of palace guard.

and there was dirt on his head to show how sad he was. 33David said to Hushai, "If you go with me, you will be just one more person for me to take care of. 34But if you return to the city, you can make Ahithophel's advice useless. Tell Absalom, 'I am your servant, my king. In the past I served your father, but now I will serve you.' 35The priests Zadok and Abiathar will be with you. Tell them everything you hear in the royal palace. 36Zadok's son Ahimaaz and Abiathar's son Jonathan are with them. Send them to tell me everything you hear." 37So David's friend Hushai entered Jerusalem just as Absalom arrived.

Ziba Meets David

16 When David had passed a short way over the top of the Mount of Olives, Ziba, Mephibosheth's servant, met him. Ziba had a row of donkeys loaded with two hundred loaves of bread, one hundred cakes of raisins, one hundred cakes of figs, and leather bags full of wine. 2The king asked Ziba, "What are these things for?"

Ziba answered, "The donkeys are for your family to ride. The bread and cakes of figs are for the servants to eat. And the wine is for anyone to drink who might become weak in the desert."

3The king asked, "Where is Mephibosheth?"

Ziba answered him, "Mephibosheth is staying in Jerusalem because he thinks, 'Today the Israelites will give my father's kingdom back to me!'"

4Then the king said to Ziba, "All right. Everything that belonged to Mephibosheth, I now give to you!"

Ziba said, "I bow to you. I hope I will always be able to please you."

Shimei Curses David

5As King David came to Bahurim, a man came out and cursed him. He was from Saul's family group, and his name was Shimei son of Gera. 6He threw stones at David and his officers, but the people and soldiers gathered all around David. 7Shimei cursed David, saying, "Get out, get out, you murderer, you troublemaker. 8The LORD is punishing you for the people in Saul's family you killed! You took Saul's place as king, but now the LORD has given the kingdom to your son Absalom! Now you are ruined because you are a murderer!"

9Abishai son of Zeruiah said to the king, "Why should this dead dog curse you, the king? Let me go over and cut off his head!"

10But the king answered, "This does not concern you, sons of Zeruiah! If he is cursing me because the LORD told him to, who can question him?"

11David also said to Abishai and all his officers, "My own son is trying to kill me! This man is a Benjaminite and has more right to kill me! Leave him alone, and let him curse me because the LORD told him to do this. 12Maybe the LORD will see my misery and repay me with something good for Shimei's curses today!"

13So David and his men went on down the road, but Shimei followed on the nearby hillside. He kept cursing David and throwing stones and dirt at him. 14When the king and all his people arrived at the Jordan, they were very tired, so they rested there.

15Meanwhile, Absalom, Ahithophel, and all the Israelites arrived at Jerusalem. 16David's friend Hushai the Arkite came to Absalom and said to him, "Long live the king! Long live the king!"

17Absalom asked, "Why are you not loyal to your friend David? Why didn't you leave Jerusalem with your friend?"

18Hushai said, "I belong to the one chosen by the LORD and by these people and everyone in Israel. I will stay with you. 19In the past I served your father. So whom should I serve now? David's son! I will serve you as I served him."

Ahithophel's Advice

20Absalom said to Ahithophel, "Tell us what we should do."

21Ahithophel said, "Your father left behind some of his slave women to take care of the palace. Have sexual relations with them. Then all Israel will hear that your father is your enemy, and all your people will be encouraged to give you more support." 22So they put up a tent for Absalom on the roof of the palace where everyone in Israel could see it. And Absalom had sexual relations with his father's slave women.

23At that time people thought Ahithophel's advice was as reliable as God's own word. Both David and Absalom thought it was that reliable.

17 Ahithophel said to Absalom, "Let me choose twelve thousand men and chase David tonight. 2I'll catch him while he is tired and weak, and I'll frighten him so all his people will run away. But I'll kill only King David. 3Then I'll bring everyone back to you. If the man you are looking for is dead, everyone else will return safely." 4This plan seemed good to Absalom and to all the leaders of Israel.

5But Absalom said, "Now call Hushai the Arkite, so I can hear what he says." 6When Hushai came to Absalom, Absalom said to him, "This is

16:22 *roof.* In Bible times houses were built with flat roofs. The roof was used for drying things such as flax and fruit. And it was used as an extra room, as a place for worship, and as a cool place to sleep in the summer.

the plan Ahithophel gave. Should we follow it? If
not, tell us."
7Hushai said to Absalom, "Ahithophel's advice
is not good this time." 8Hushai added, "You know
your father and his men are strong. They are as
angry as a bear that is robbed of its cubs. Your
father is a skilled fighter. He won't stay all night
with the army. 9He is probably already hiding in a
cave or some other place. If the first attack fails,
people will hear the news and think, 'Absalom's
followers are losing!' 10Then even the men who
are as brave as lions will be frightened, because
all the Israelites know your father is a fighter.
They know his men are brave!
11"This is what I suggest: Gather all the Israelites from Dan to Beersheba. There will be as
many people as grains of sand by the sea. Then
you yourself must go into the battle. 12We will go
to David wherever he is hiding. We will fall on
him as dew falls on the ground. We will kill him
and all of his men so that no one will be left alive.
13If David escapes into a city, all the Israelites will
bring ropes to that city and pull it into the valley.
Not a stone will be left!"
14Absalom and all the Israelites said, "The
advice of Hushai the Arkite is better than that of
Ahithophel." (The LORD had planned to destroy
the good advice of Ahithophel so the LORD could
bring disaster on Absalom.)
15Hushai told Zadok and Abiathar, the priests,
what Ahithophel had suggested to Absalom and
the older leaders of Israel. He also reported to
them what he himself had suggested. Hushai
said, 16"Quickly! Send a message to David. Tell
him not to stay tonight at the crossings into the
desert but to cross over the Jordan River at once.
If he crosses the river, he and all his people won't
be destroyed."
17Jonathan and Ahimaaz were waiting at En
Rogel. They did not want to be seen going into
the city, so a servant girl would go out to them
and give them messages. Then Jonathan and
Ahimaaz would go and tell King David.
18But a boy saw Jonathan and Ahimaaz and told
Absalom. So Jonathan and Ahimaaz left quickly
and went to a man's house in Bahurim. He had a
well in his courtyard, and they climbed down into
it. 19The man's wife spread a sheet over the opening of the well and covered it with grain. No one
could tell that anyone was hiding there.
20Absalom's servants came to the woman at the
house and asked, "Where are Ahimaaz and
Jonathan?"
She said to them, "They have already crossed
the brook."
Absalom's servants then went to look for Jonathan and Ahimaaz, but they could not find them.
So they went back to Jerusalem.
21After Absalom's servants left, Jonathan and
Ahimaaz climbed out of the well and went to tell
King David. They said, "Hurry, cross over the river!
Ahithophel has said these things against you!"
22So David and all his people crossed the Jordan
River. By dawn, everyone had crossed the Jordan.
23When Ahithophel saw that the Israelites did
not accept his advice, he saddled his donkey and
went to his hometown. He left orders for his family and property, and then he hanged himself. He
died and was buried in his father's tomb.

War Between David and Absalom

24David arrived at Mahanaim. And Absalom
and all his Israelites crossed over the Jordan
River. 25Absalom had made Amasa captain of the
army instead of Joab. Amasa was the son of a man
named Jether the Ishmaelite. Amasa's mother
was Abigail daughter of Nahash and sister of
Zeruiah, Joab's mother. 26Absalom and the
Israelites camped in the land of Gilead.
27Shobi, Makir, and Barzillai were at Mahanaim
when David arrived. Shobi son of Nahash was
from the Ammonite town of Rabbah. Makir son of
Ammiel was from Lo Debar, and Barzillai was
from Rogelim in Gilead. 28They brought beds,
bowls, clay pots, wheat, barley, flour, roasted grain,
beans, small peas, 29honey, milk curds, sheep,
and cheese made from cows' milk for David and
his people. They said, "The people are hungry
and tired and thirsty in the desert."

18 David counted his men and placed over
them commanders of thousands and commanders of hundreds. 2He sent the troops out in
three groups. Joab commanded one-third of the
men. Joab's brother Abishai son of Zeruiah commanded another third. And Ittai from Gath commanded the last third. King David said to them, "I
will also go with you."
3But the men said, "You must not go with us! If
we run away in the battle, Absalom's men won't
care. Even if half of us are killed, Absalom's men
won't care. But you're worth ten thousand of us!
You can help us most by staying in the city."
4The king said to his people, "I will do what you
think is best." So the king stood at the side of the
gate as the army went out in groups of a hundred
and a thousand.

17:11 *Dan to Beersheba.* Dan was the city farthest north in Israel, and Beersheba was the city farthest south. So this means all the people of Israel.

5The king commanded Joab, Abishai, and Ittai,
"Be gentle with young Absalom for my sake."
Everyone heard the king's orders to the commanders about Absalom.
6David's army went out into the field against
Absalom's Israelites, and they fought in the forest
of Ephraim. 7There David's army defeated the
Israelites. Many died that day—twenty thousand
men. 8The battle spread through all the country,
but that day more men died in the forest than in
the fighting.

Absalom Dies

9Then Absalom happened to meet David's
troops. As Absalom was riding his mule, it went
under the thick branches of a large oak tree.
Absalom's head got caught in the tree, and his
mule ran out from under him. So Absalom was
left hanging above the ground.
10When one of the men saw it happen, he told
Joab, "I saw Absalom hanging in an oak tree!"
11Joab said to him, "You saw him? Why didn't
you kill him and let him fall to the ground? I would
have given you a belt and four ounces of silver!"
12The man answered, "I wouldn't touch the
king's son even if you gave me twenty-five pounds
of silver. We heard the king command you, Abishai,
and Ittai, 'Be careful not to hurt young Absalom.'
13If I had killed him, the king would have found
out, and you would not have protected me!"
14Joab said, "I won't waste time here with you!"
Absalom was still alive in the oak tree, so Joab took
three spears and stabbed him in the heart. 15Ten
young men who carried Joab's armor also gathered
around Absalom and struck him and killed him.
16Then Joab blew the trumpet, so the troops
stopped chasing the Israelites. 17Then Joab's men
took Absalom's body and threw it into a large pit
in the forest and filled the pit with many stones.
All the Israelites ran away to their homes.
18When Absalom was alive, he had set up a pillar for himself in the King's Valley. He said, "I
have no son to keep my name alive." So he
named the pillar after himself, and it is called
Absalom's Monument even today.
19Ahimaaz son of Zadok said to Joab, "Let me
run and take the news to King David. I'll tell him
the LORD has saved him from his enemies."
20Joab answered Ahimaaz, "No, you are not the
one to take the news today. You may do it another
time, but do not take it today, because the king's
son is dead."
21Then Joab said to a man from Cush, "Go, tell
the king what you have seen." The Cushite
bowed to Joab and ran to tell David.
22But Ahimaaz son of Zadok begged Joab again,
"No matter what happens, please let me go along
with the Cushite!"
Joab said, "Son, why do you want to carry the
news? You won't get any reward."
23Ahimaaz answered, "No matter what happens,
I will run."
So Joab said to Ahimaaz, "Run!" Then Ahimaaz
ran by way of the Jordan Valley and passed the
Cushite.
24David was sitting between the inner and
outer gates of the city. The watchman went up to
the roof of the gate by the walls, and as he looked
up, he saw a man running alone. 25He shouted
the news to the king.
The king said, "If he is alone, he is bringing
good news!"
The man came nearer and nearer to the city.
26Then the watchman saw another man running,
and he called to the gatekeeper, "Look! Another
man is running alone!"
The king said, "He is also bringing good news!"
27The watchman said, "I think the first man
runs like Ahimaaz son of Zadok."
The king said, "Ahimaaz is a good man. He
must be bringing good news!"
28Then Ahimaaz called a greeting to the king.
He bowed facedown on the ground before the
king and said, "Praise the LORD your God! The
LORD has defeated those who were against you,
my king."
29The king asked, "Is young Absalom all right?"
Ahimaaz answered, "When Joab sent me, I saw
some great excitement, but I don't know what it
was."
30The king said, "Step over here and wait." So
Ahimaaz stepped aside and stood there.
31Then the Cushite arrived. He said, "Master
and king, hear the good news! Today the LORD
has punished those who were against you!"
32The king asked the Cushite, "Is young Absalom all right?"
The Cushite answered, "May your enemies and
all who come to hurt you be like that young man!"
33Then the king was very upset, and he went to
the room over the city gate and cried. As he
went, he cried out, "My son Absalom, my son
Absalom! I wish I had died and not you. Absalom,
my son, my son!"

Joab Scolds David

19 People told Joab, "Look, the king is sad and
crying because of Absalom." 2David's army
had won the battle that day. But it became a very sad
day for all the people, because they heard that the

king was very sad for his son. 3The people came into the city quietly that day. They were like an army that had been defeated in battle and had run away. 4The king covered his face and cried loudly, "My son Absalom! Absalom, my son, my son!"

5Joab went into the king's house and said, "Today you have shamed all your men. They saved your life and the lives of your sons, daughters, wives, and slave women. 6You have shamed them because you love those who hate you, and you hate those who love you. Today you have made it clear that your commanders and men mean nothing to you. What if Absalom had lived and all of us were dead? I can see you would be pleased. 7Now go out and encourage your servants. I swear by the LORD that if you don't go out, no man will be left with you by tonight! That will be worse than all the troubles you have had from your youth until today."

8So the king went to the city gate. When the news spread that the king was at the gate, everyone came to see him.

David Goes Back to Jerusalem

All the Israelites who had followed Absalom had run away to their homes. 9People in all the tribes of Israel began to argue, saying, "The king saved us from the Philistines and our other enemies, but he left the country because of Absalom. 10We appointed Absalom to rule us, but now he has died in battle. We should make David the king again."

11King David sent a message to Zadok and Abiathar, the priests, that said, "Speak to the older leaders of Judah. Say, 'Even in my house I have heard what all the Israelites are saying. So why are you the last tribe to bring the king back to his palace? 12You are my brothers, my own family. Why are you the last tribe to bring back the king?' 13And say to Amasa, 'You are part of my own family. May God punish me terribly if I don't make you commander of the army in Joab's place!'"

14David touched the hearts of all the people of Judah at once. They sent a message to the king that said, "Return with all your men." 15Then the king returned as far as the Jordan River. The men of Judah came to Gilgal to meet him and to bring him across the Jordan.

16Shimei son of Gera, a Benjaminite who lived in Bahurim, hurried down with the men of Judah to meet King David. 17With Shimei came a thousand Benjaminites. Ziba, the servant from Saul's family, also came, bringing his fifteen sons and twenty servants with him. They all hurried to the Jordan River to meet the king. 18The people went across the Jordan to help bring the king's family back to Judah and to do whatever the king wanted. As the king was crossing the river, Shimei son of Gera came to him and bowed face-down on the ground in front of the king. 19He said to the king, "My master, don't hold me guilty. Don't remember the wrong I did when you left Jerusalem! Don't hold it against me. 20I know I have sinned. That is why I am the first person from Joseph's family to come down and meet you today, my master and king!"

21But Abishai son of Zeruiah said, "Shimei should die because he cursed you, the LORD's appointed king!"

22David said, "This does not concern you, sons of Zeruiah! Today you're against me! No one will be put to death in Israel today. Today I know I am king over Israel!" 23Then the king promised Shimei, "You won't die."

24Mephibosheth, Saul's grandson, also went down to meet King David. Mephibosheth had not cared for his feet, cut his beard, or washed his clothes from the time the king had left Jerusalem until he returned safely. 25When Mephibosheth came from Jerusalem to meet the king, the king asked him, "Mephibosheth, why didn't you go with me?"

26He answered, "My master, my servant Ziba tricked me! I said to Ziba, 'I am crippled, so saddle a donkey. Then I will ride it so I can go with the king.' 27But he lied about me to you. You, my master and king, are like an angel from God. Do what you think is good. 28You could have killed all my grandfather's family. Instead, you put me with those people who eat at your own table. So I don't have a right to ask anything more from the king!"

29The king said to him, "Don't say anything more. I have decided that you and Ziba will divide the land."

30Mephibosheth said to the king, "Let Ziba take all the land now that my master the king has arrived safely home."

31Barzillai of Gilead came down from Rogelim to cross the Jordan River with the king. 32Barzillai was a very old man, eighty years old. He had taken care of the king when David was staying at Mahanaim, because Barzillai was a very rich man. 33David said to Barzillai, "Cross the river with me. Come with me to Jerusalem, and I will take care of you."

19:8 *city gate.* People came here to conduct business. Public meetings and court cases were also held here.

34But Barzillai answered the king, "Do you
know how old I am? Do you think I can go with
you to Jerusalem? 35I am eighty years old! I am too
old to taste what I eat or drink. I am too old to hear
the voices of men and women singers. Why should
you be bothered with me? 36I am not worthy of a
reward from you, but I will cross the Jordan River
with you. 37Then let me go back so I may die in my
own city near the grave of my father and mother.
But here is Kimham, your servant. Let him go with
you, my master and king. Do with him whatever
you want."

38The king answered, "Kimham will go with
me. I will do for him anything you wish, and I will
do anything for you that you wish." 39The king
kissed Barzillai and blessed him. Then Barzillai
returned home, and the king and all the people
crossed the Jordan.

40When the king crossed over to Gilgal, Kimham went with him. All the troops of Judah and
half the troops of Israel led David across the river.

41Soon all the Israelites came to the king and said
to him, "Why did our relatives, the people of Judah,
steal you away? Why did they bring you and your
family across the Jordan River with your men?"

42All the people of Judah answered the Israelites, "We did this because the king is our close
relative. Why are you angry about it? We have not
eaten food at the king's expense or taken anything for ourselves!"

43The Israelites answered the people of Judah,
"We have ten tribes in the kingdom, so we have
more right to David than you do! But you ignored
us! We were the first ones to talk about bringing
our king back!"

But the people of Judah spoke even more
unkindly than the people of Israel.

Sheba Leads Israel Away from David

20 It happened that a troublemaker named
Sheba son of Bicri from the tribe of Benjamin was there. He blew the trumpet and said:

"We have no share in David!
We have no part in the son of Jesse!
People of Israel, let's go home!"

2So all the Israelites left David and followed
Sheba son of Bicri. But the people of Judah stayed
with their king all the way from the Jordan River
to Jerusalem.

3David came back to his palace in Jerusalem.
He had left ten of his slave women there to take
care of the palace. Now he put them in a locked
house. He gave them food, but he did not have
sexual relations with them. So they lived like widows until they died.

4The king said to Amasa, "Tell the men of
Judah to meet with me in three days, and you
must also be here." 5So Amasa went to call the
men of Judah together, but he took more time
than the king had said.

6David said to Abishai, "Sheba son of Bicri is
more dangerous to us than Absalom was. Take
my men and chase him before he finds walled
cities and escapes from us." 7So Joab's men, the
Kerethites and the Pelethites, and all the soldiers
went with Abishai. They went out from Jerusalem to chase Sheba son of Bicri.

8When Joab and the army came to the great
rock at Gibeon, Amasa came out to meet them.
Joab was wearing his uniform, and at his waist he
wore a belt that held his sword in its case. As Joab
stepped forward, his sword fell out of its case.
9Joab asked Amasa, "Brother, is everything all
right with you?" Then with his right hand he took
Amasa by the beard to kiss him. 10Amasa was not
watching the sword in Joab's hand. So Joab
pushed the sword into Amasa's stomach, causing
Amasa's insides to spill onto the ground. Joab did
not have to stab Amasa again; he was already
dead. Then Joab and his brother Abishai continued to chase Sheba son of Bicri.

11One of Joab's young men stood by Amasa's
body and said, "Everyone who is for Joab and
David should follow Joab!" 12Amasa lay in the
middle of the road, covered with his own blood.
When the young man saw that everyone was
stopping to look at the body, he dragged it from
the road, laid it in a field, and put a cloth over it.
13After Amasa's body was taken off the road, all
the men followed Joab to chase Sheba son of Bicri.

14Sheba went through all the tribes of Israel to
Abel Beth Maacah. All the Berites also came
together and followed him. 15So Joab and his men
came to Abel Beth Maacah and surrounded it.
They piled dirt up against the city wall, and they
began hacking at the walls to bring them down.

16But a wise woman shouted out from the city,
"Listen! Listen! Tell Joab to come here. I want to
talk to him!"

17So Joab came near her. She asked him, "Are
you Joab?"

He answered, "Yes, I am."

Then she said, "Listen to what I say."

Joab said, "I'm listening."

18Then the woman said, "In the past people
would say, 'Ask for advice at Abel,' and the problem

20:7 *Kerethites and Pelethites.* These were probably special units of the army that were responsible for the king's safety, a kind of palace guard.

would be solved. 19I am one of the peaceful, loyal people of Israel. You are trying to destroy an important city of Israel. Why must you destroy what belongs to the LORD?"

20Joab answered, "I would prefer not to destroy or ruin anything! 21That is not what I want. But there is a man here from the mountains of Ephraim, who is named Sheba son of Bicri. He has turned against King David. If you bring him to me, I will leave the city alone."

The woman said to Joab, "His head will be thrown over the wall to you."

22Then the woman spoke very wisely to all the people of the city. They cut off the head of Sheba son of Bicri and threw it over the wall to Joab. So he blew the trumpet, and the army left the city. Every man returned home, and Joab went back to the king in Jerusalem.

23Joab was commander of all the army of Israel. Benaiah son of Jehoiada led the Kerethites and Pelethites. 24Adoniram was in charge of the men who were forced to do hard work. Jehoshaphat son of Ahilud was the recorder. 25Sheba was the royal secretary. Zadok and Abiathar were the priests, 26and Ira the Jairite was David's priest.

The Gibeonites Punish Saul's Family

21 During the time David was king, there was a shortage of food that lasted for three years. So David prayed to the LORD.

The LORD answered, "Saul and his family of murderers are the reason for this shortage, because he killed the Gibeonites." 2(Now the Gibeonites were not Israelites; they were a group of Amorites who were left alive. The Israelites had promised not to hurt the Gibeonites, but Saul had tried to kill them, because he was eager to help the people of Israel and Judah.)

King David called the Gibeonites together and spoke to them. 3He asked, "What can I do for you? How can I make up for the harm done so you can bless the LORD's people?"

4The Gibeonites said to David, "We cannot demand silver or gold from Saul or his family. And we don't have the right to kill anyone in Israel."

Then David asked, "What do you want me to do for you?"

5The Gibeonites said, "Saul made plans against us and tried to destroy all our people who are left in the land of Israel. 6So bring seven of his sons to us. Then we will kill them and hang them on stakes in the presence of the LORD at Gibeah, the hometown of Saul, the LORD's chosen king."

The king said, "I will give them to you." 7But the king protected Mephibosheth, the son of Jonathan, the son of Saul, because of the promise he had made to Jonathan in the LORD's name. 8The king did take Armoni and Mephibosheth, sons of Rizpah and Saul. (Rizpah was the daughter of Aiah.) And the king took the five sons of Saul's daughter Merab. (Adriel son of Barzillai the Meholathite was the father of Merab's five sons.) 9David gave these seven sons to the Gibeonites. Then the Gibeonites killed them and hung them on stakes on a hill in the presence of the LORD. All seven sons died together. They were put to death during the first days of the harvest season at the beginning of barley harvest.

10Aiah's daughter Rizpah took the rough cloth that was worn to show sadness and put it on a rock for herself. She stayed there from the beginning of the harvest until the rain fell on her sons' bodies. During the day she did not let the birds of the sky touch her sons' bodies, and during the night she did not let the wild animals touch them.

11People told David what Aiah's daughter Rizpah, Saul's slave woman, was doing. 12Then David took the bones of Saul and Jonathan from the men of Jabesh Gilead. (The Philistines had hung the bodies of Saul and Jonathan in the public square of Beth Shan after they had killed Saul at Gilboa. Later the men of Jabesh Gilead had secretly taken them from there.) 13David brought the bones of Saul and his son Jonathan from Gilead. Then the people gathered the bodies of Saul's seven sons who were hanged on stakes. 14The people buried the bones of Saul and his son Jonathan at Zela in Benjamin in the tomb of Saul's father Kish. The people did everything the king commanded.

Then God answered the prayers for the land.∞

Wars with the Philistines

15Again there was war between the Philistines and Israel. David and his men went out to fight the Philistines, but David became tired. 16Ishbi-Benob, one of the sons of Rapha, had a bronze spearhead weighing about seven and one-half pounds and a new sword. He planned to kill David, 17but Abishai son of Zeruiah killed the Philistine and saved David's life.

Then David's men made a promise to him, saying, "Never again will you go out with us to battle. If you were killed, Israel would lose its greatest leader."

18Later, at Gob, there was another battle with the Philistines. Sibbecai the Hushathite killed Saph, another one of the sons of Rapha.

21:8 *Mephibosheth.* This is not Jonathan's son but another man with the same name.

∞**21:14 Famine:** 2 Samuel 24:13

[19]Later, there was another battle at Gob with
the Philistines. Elhanan son of Jaare-Oregim from
Bethlehem killed Goliath from Gath. His spear
was as large as a weaver's rod.
[20]At Gath another battle took place. A huge
man was there; he had six fingers on each hand
and six toes on each foot—twenty-four fingers
and toes in all. This man also was one of the sons
of Rapha. [21]When he challenged Israel, Jonathan
son of Shimeah, David's brother, killed him.
[22]These four sons of Rapha from Gath were
killed by David and his men.

David's Song of Praise

22 David sang this song to the LORD when
the LORD saved him from Saul and all his
other enemies. [2]He said:

"The LORD is my rock, my protection,
my Savior.
[3]My God is my rock.
I can run to him for safety.
He is my shield and my saving strength,
my defender and my place of safety.
The LORD saves me from those who
want to harm me.∞
[4]I will call to the LORD, who is worthy of praise,
and I will be saved from my enemies.

[5]"The waves of death came around me;
the deadly rivers overwhelmed me.
[6]The ropes of death wrapped around me.
The traps of death were before me.
[7]In my trouble I called to the LORD;
I cried out to my God.
From his temple he heard my voice;
my call for help reached his ears.

[8]"The earth trembled and shook.
The foundations of heaven began to shake.
They trembled because the LORD was angry.
[9]Smoke came out of his nose,
and burning fire came out of his mouth.
Burning coals went before him.
[10]He tore open the sky and came down
with dark clouds under his feet.
[11]He rode a creature with wings and flew.
He raced on the wings of the wind.
[12]He made darkness his shelter,
surrounded by fog and clouds.
[13]Out of the brightness of his presence
came flashes of lightning.
[14]The LORD thundered from heaven;
the Most High raised his voice.
[15]He shot his arrows and scattered his enemies.
His bolts of lightning confused them with fear.
[16]The LORD spoke strongly.
The wind blew from his nose.
Then the valleys of the sea appeared,
and the foundations of the earth were seen.

[17]"The LORD reached down from above
and took me;
he pulled me from the deep water.
[18]He saved me from my powerful enemies,
from those who hated me, because they
were too strong for me.
[19]They attacked me at my time of trouble,
but the LORD supported me.
[20]He took me to a safe place.
Because he delights in me, he saved me.

[21]"The LORD spared me because I did
what was right.
Because I have not done evil,
he has rewarded me.
[22]I have followed the ways of the LORD;
I have not done evil by turning from my God.
[23]I remember all his laws
and have not broken his rules.
[24]I am innocent before him;
I have kept myself from doing evil.
[25]The LORD rewarded me because I did
what was right,
because I did what the LORD said was right.

[26]"LORD, you are loyal to those who are loyal,
and you are good to those who are good.
[27]You are pure to those who are pure,
but you are against those who are evil.
[28]You save the humble,
but you bring down those who are proud.
[29]LORD, you give light to my lamp.
The LORD brightens the darkness around me.
[30]With your help I can attack an army.
With God's help I can jump over a wall.

21:19 *Goliath.* In 1 Chronicles 20:5 he is called Lahmi, brother of Goliath.

∞**22:3 Weapons:** Psalm 3:3

22:7–20 This poetic passage (written by David, and essentially identical to Psalm 18:6–19) shows how a variety of images can give us a fuller, deeper understanding of God's nature. The images in verses 7 and 17–20 portray God as David's personal friend who listens to him and reaches down to rescue him. Such images remind us that God is close to and cares for those who put their faith in him. But verses 8–16 combine images of an angry warrior with images that suggest God is an earthquake, volcano, or storm. This combination of military and nature imagery reminds us that in spite of God's loving nature and his desire to save, he also has a frightening, overpowering capacity for destruction that he may exercise when people defy his purposes.

22:9 *smoke . . . burning fire.* God often appeared to his people in the form of smoke and fire. This represented his glory.

Rahab

Joshua 2

Is Rahab an example of an Old Testament convert? Why does Rahab help the spies? Is it right that Rahab lied? What can her conversion teach us?

Did Rahab have a true "conversion experience" or did she just "get religion" in a crisis situation? The Book of Joshua portrays her as having a living faith. In her conversation with the spies, Rahab said that she has known about the Lord because of his mighty deeds (Joshua 2:9–10). Not only did Rahab have factual information about the Lord, but the facts had made an impression on her heart. When she said, "the LORD your God rules the heavens above and the earth below" (verse 11), she acknowledged the Lord as the one true God. She believed that he was all-powerful and that he kept his word. Her statement, "I *know* the LORD has given this land to your people" (Joshua 2:9, emphasis mine), indicates that she believed the Lord's promise to give the land to Israel was as good as accomplished. Because of her faith in Israel's God, Rahab made a covenant (see "agreement") with the spies, and she did not turn over the two men to Jericho's leaders.

After Rahab's family was safely brought out of Jericho, they were put in a place outside the Israelite camp (Joshua 6:23). (They could not be taken into the Israelite camp because non-Israelite people were ritually unclean.) If her trust in the Lord had not been genuine, Rahab could have gone off on her own at this point. Instead she officially joined herself with the people of Israel. Joshua 6:25 relates that Rahab did not remain outside the camp, but that she was still living among the Israelites when the Book of Joshua was written. Matthew 1:5 fills in an important detail in her life by relating that Rahab married an Israelite man, Salmon, and was in the family tree of Jesus.

The New Testament praises Rahab's faith on two occasions. The author of Hebrews includes her in the roll call of faithful people. He says, "it was by faith that Rahab, the prostitute, welcomed the spies and was not killed with those who disobeyed God" (Hebrews 11:31). James uses Rahab as an example of someone who shows her faith by what she does. According to James, Rahab's faith was genuine because she acted on her belief by hiding the spies (James 2:25).

Was it right for Rahab to lie in order to protect the spies? This is a very difficult question, and biblical writers do not evaluate whether her action was right or wrong. Clearly, Rahab's actions were motivated by faith in the God of Israel. But the Bible also teaches that lying is sinful (Exodus 20:16). An incident recorded in Acts 4 and 5 sheds light on her situation. The apostles Peter and John were commanded by the Jewish leaders to stop teaching in the name of Jesus (Acts 4:18), but they continued preaching the good news about Jesus. When Jewish leaders demanded to know why the apostles had not stopped teaching about Jesus, Peter and the others answered, "We must obey God, not human authority!" (Acts 5:29). There are times when believers are to follow the kingdom of God rather than obey their government. Decisions to disobey civil authority should not be made lightly, but with careful thought. Rahab disobeyed her city leaders because she believed that the kingdom of Israel's God, the true God, must go forward.

God's plan of salvation includes the whole world because everyone in the world is a sinner in need of a savior. "God loved the world so much that he gave his one and only Son so that whoever believes in him may not be lost, but have eternal life" (John 3:16). Rahab, the prostitute, is a great example of God's love for the lost. Rahab was not at the top of society in Jericho; she was at the bottom. God did not shun her because of her sinful life, but accepted her because of her faith. He loved her even though she was not from his chosen people, the Israelites. Rahab's story is a reminder that Christians have no reason to judge someone harshly because they have a different color skin or because they have a different culture or because they come from a questionable background. Jesus died for the whole world, including people with whom we are not comfortable.

Christians are God's hands and feet in the continuing work of bringing this message of salvation to the nations. Matthew records that one of the last things Jesus told his disciples was that they were to go and make disciples of all the peoples on the earth and teach them everything Jesus had commanded them (Matthew 28:18–20).

Rahab: For additional scriptures on this topic go to Joshua 6:17.

Jordan River

Joshua 3

Where is the river Jordan? What is its importance as a boundary for Israel? What is its symbolic value in view of the book of Joshua? Why did John the Baptist choose this location for his ministry? What associations did Jesus have with John? Is there a difference between John's baptism and Christian baptism?

This river, which runs from Mount Hermon to the Dead Sea and forms part of the eastern border of Israel, is usually divided into the upper Jordan (from Hermon to the Sea of Galilee) and the lower Jordan (from the sea of Galilee south). It is possible that the meaning of the Hebrew word *yarden* is "perennial river." This describes the river quite well, for it becomes little more than a creek in places during the dry, summer months, but every winter it turns into a river of considerable size and force. In biblical times, the Jordan was never of the size or significance of the Nile or other large rivers in the area such as the Euphrates. The Jordan's significance was perhaps symbolic as a source of water.

Since the time of the events recorded in Joshua (if not before, see Genesis 13:10), the Jordan has been seen as a boundary marker of the Promised Land, and the crossing of it a type of passage, the entering into the Holy Land, the place where God lives. It is interesting that already in the Scriptures the crossing of the Jordan can be used in symbolic ways, for instance to describe the passage from life to death or, better said, from this world into heaven (Hebrews 3:17–19). It has also been suggested that the phrase "land of Jordan" (Psalm 42) refers to the passage into the underworld or land of the dead (called Sheol in the Old Testament).

When the Israelites were taken into exile, first the representatives of the northern tribes by the Assyrians about 722 B.C. and then the southern tribes about 595 B.C., crossing the Jordan in reverse became a symbol of slavery, just as re-entering the land was associated with recrossing the Jordan. Of course, the primary events that were referred to over and over again that had to do with a pilgrimage up to the Jordan were the Exodus-Sinai wanderings (see Exodus, Numbers, Deuteronomy), and thus the crossing of the Jordan was associated not just with the taking of a promised land, but also with deliverance from slavery in Egypt.

These last overtones come into play in the history of Jesus in Matthew's gospel where Jesus, like Israel, was called up out of Egypt (2:15) and then baptized in the Jordan as he entered into the ministry phase of his life in the Promised Land (Matthew 3). Jesus was to be seen as the one who brings the new exodus from bondage, the new deliverance. Only this time it was not mainly from external oppressors but from the internal ones (sin, disease, demons). Conversion is a passing over into a new state of being and is appropriately symbolized by baptism, especially symbolic if done in the Jordan.

It is not by accident that John the Baptist's prophetic ministry focused on the region of the Jordan. His message makes clear (Matthew 3; Luke 3) that in his view Israel was still in bondage, in a sort of spiritual exile, even though many Jews resided in the land. They needed repentance, forgiveness from sin, and a new devotion to be God's people in preparation for the coming judgment of God. Perhaps the most striking thing about John's ministry is that he believed forgiveness could be offered quite apart from the sacrificial system in the Temple in Jerusalem. God was the God of the Exodus and the wilderness wandering and could not be confined to a particular place or holy zone. Thus God would meet the chosen people again at the river Jordan and usher them into a new state of being. Baptism in the Jordan symbolized cleansing, and John's message was that Israel had fallen into spiritual exile and needed this cleansing.

Some have suggested that John had been part of the Qumran community that lived at the Dead Sea, but if so, his approach to preparing for the coming of God was very different. Rather than withdrawing from corrupt Israel and involving himself in endless daily ritual cleansings with the Qumran dwellers, John chose to go out to the Jordan and call Israel to repentance, which would be symbolized by a decisive one-time baptismal experience.⚭

⚭**Jordan River:** For additional scriptures on this topic go to 2 Kings 5:8–14.

31“The ways of God are without fault;
the LORD’s words are pure.
He is a shield to those who trust him.
32Who is God? Only the LORD.
Who is the Rock? Only our God.
33God is my protection.
He makes my way free from fault.
34He makes me like a deer that does not
stumble;
he helps me stand on the steep mountains.
35He trains my hands for battle
so my arms can bend a bronze bow.
36You protect me with your saving shield.
You have stooped to make me great.
37You give me a better way to live,
so I live as you want me to.
38I chased my enemies and destroyed them.
I did not quit till they were destroyed.
39I destroyed and crushed them
so they couldn’t rise up again.
They fell beneath my feet.
40You gave me strength in battle.
You made my enemies bow before me.
41You made my enemies turn back,
and I destroyed those who hated me.
42They called for help,
but no one came to save them.
They called to the LORD,
but he did not answer them.
43I beat my enemies into pieces,
like dust on the ground.
I poured them out and walked on them
like mud in the streets.

44“You saved me when my people attacked me.
You kept me as the leader of nations.
People I never knew serve me.
45Foreigners obey me.
As soon as they hear me, they obey me.
46They all become afraid
and tremble in their hiding places.

47“The LORD lives!
May my Rock be praised!
Praise God, the Rock, who saves me!
48God gives me victory over my enemies
and brings people under my rule.
49He frees me from my enemies.

“You set me over those who hate me.
You saved me from cruel men.
50So I will praise you, LORD, among the nations.
I will sing praises to your name.
51The LORD gives great victories to his king.
He is loyal to his appointed king,
to David and his descendants forever.”

David’s Last Words

23 These are the last words of David.

This is the message of David son of Jesse.
The man made great by the Most High
God speaks.
He is the appointed king of the God of Jacob;
he is the sweet singer of Israel:

2“The LORD’s Spirit spoke through me,
and his word was on my tongue.
3The God of Israel spoke;
the Rock of Israel said to me:
‘Whoever rules fairly over people,
who rules with respect for God,
4is like the morning light at dawn,
like a morning without clouds.
He is like sunshine after a rain
that makes the grass sprout from the ground.’

5“This is how God has cared for my family.
God made a lasting agreement with me,
right and sure in every way.
He will accomplish my salvation
and satisfy all my desires.

6“But all evil people will be thrown away
like thorns
that cannot be held in a hand.
7No one can touch them
except with a tool of iron or wood.
They will be thrown in the fire and burned
where they lie.”

David’s Army

8These are the names of David’s warriors:
Josheb-Basshebeth, the Tahkemonite, was head
of the Three. He killed eight hundred men at one
time.
9Next was Eleazar son of Dodai the Ahohite.
Eleazar was one of the three soldiers who were
with David when they challenged the Philistines.
The Philistines were gathered for battle, and the
Israelites drew back. 10But Eleazar stayed where
he was and fought the Philistines until he was so
tired his hand stuck to his sword. The LORD gave
a great victory for the Israelites that day. The troops

22:31 Road/Way: Psalm 1:1
23:2 Spiritual Gifts: Acts 10:46

23:8 *Three.* These were David’s most powerful soldiers. See 1 Chronicles 11:11.

came back after Eleazar had won the battle, but
only to take weapons and armor from the enemy.
11Next there was Shammah son of Agee the
Hararite. The Philistines came together to fight in
a vegetable field. Israel's troops ran away from
the Philistines, 12but Shammah stood in the middle of the field and fought for it and killed the
Philistines. And the LORD gave a great victory.
13Once, three of the Thirty, David's chief soldiers, came down to him at the cave of Adullam
during harvest. The Philistine army had camped
in the Valley of Rephaim. 14At that time David
was in the stronghold, and some of the Philistines
were in Bethlehem.
15David had a strong desire for some water. He
said, "Oh, I wish someone would get me water
from the well near the city gate of Bethlehem!"
16So the three warriors broke through the
Philistine army and took water from the well near
the city gate of Bethlehem. Then they brought it
to David, but he refused to drink it. He poured it
out before the LORD, 17saying, "May the LORD
keep me from drinking this water! It would be
like drinking the blood of the men who risked
their lives!" So David refused to drink it. These
were the brave things that the three warriors did.
18Abishai, brother of Joab son of Zeruiah, was
captain of the Three. Abishai fought three hundred soldiers with his spear and killed them. He
became as famous as the Three 19and was more
honored than the Three. He became their commander even though he was not one of them.
20Benaiah son of Jehoiada was a brave fighter
from Kabzeel who did mighty things. He killed
two of the best warriors from Moab. He also went
down into a pit and killed a lion on a snowy day.
21Benaiah killed a large Egyptian who had a spear
in his hand. Benaiah had a club, but he grabbed
the spear from the Egyptian's hand and killed him
with his own spear. 22These were the things
Benaiah son of Jehoiada did. He was as famous as
the Three. 23He received more honor than the
Thirty, but he did not become a member of the
Three. David made him leader of his bodyguards.

The Thirty Chief Soldiers

24The following men were among the Thirty:

Asahel brother of Joab;
Elhanan son of Dodo from Bethlehem;
25Shammah the Harodite;
Elika the Harodite;
26Helez the Paltite;
Ira son of Ikkesh from Tekoa;
27Abiezer the Anathothite;
Mebunnai the Hushathite;
28Zalmon the Ahohite;
Maharai the Netophathite;
29Heled son of Baanah the Netophathite;
Ithai son of Ribai from Gibeah in Benjamin;
30Benaiah the Pirathonite;
Hiddai from the ravines of Gaash;
31Abi-Albon the Arbathite;
Azmaveth the Barhumite;
32Eliahba the Shaalbonite;
the sons of Jashen;
Jonathan 33son of Shammah the Hararite;
Ahiam son of Sharar the Hararite;
34Eliphelet son of Ahasbai the Maacathite;
Eliam son of Ahithophel the Gilonite;
35Hezro the Carmelite;
Paarai the Arbite;
36Igal son of Nathan of Zobah;
the son of Hagri;
37Zelek the Ammonite;
Naharai the Beerothite, who carried the armor of Joab son of Zeruiah;
38Ira the Ithrite;
Gareb the Ithrite,
39and Uriah the Hittite.

There were thirty-seven in all.

David Counts His Army

24 The LORD was angry with Israel again,
and he caused David to turn against the
Israelites. He said, "Go, count the people of Israel
and Judah."
2So King David said to Joab, the commander of
the army, "Go through all the tribes of Israel, from
Dan to Beersheba, and count the people. Then I
will know how many there are."
3But Joab said to the king, "May the LORD your
God give you a hundred times more people, and
may my master the king live to see this happen.
Why do you want to do this?"
4But the king commanded Joab and the commanders of the army, so they left the king to
count the Israelites.
5After crossing the Jordan River, they camped
near Aroer on the south side of the city in the
ravine. They went through Gad and on to Jazer.
6Then they went to Gilead and the land of Tahtim
Hodshi and to Dan Jaan and around to Sidon.
7They went to the strong, walled city of Tyre and

24:2 *Dan to Beersheba.* Dan was the city farthest north in Israel, and Beersheba was the city farthest south. So this means all the people of Israel.

to all the cities of the Hivites and Canaanites.
Finally, they went to southern Judah, to Beersheba.
8After nine months and twenty days, they had
gone through all the land. Then they came back
to Jerusalem.
9Joab gave the list of the people to the king.
There were eight hundred thousand men in Israel who could use the sword and five hundred
thousand men in Judah.
10David felt ashamed after he had counted the
people. He said to the LORD, "I have sinned greatly
by what I have done. LORD, I beg you to forgive me,
your servant, because I have been very foolish."
11When David got up in the morning, the LORD
spoke his word to Gad, who was a prophet and
David's seer. 12The LORD told Gad, "Go and tell
David, 'This is what the LORD says: I offer you
three choices. Choose one of them and I will do it
to you.'"
13So Gad went to David and said to him,
"Should three years of hunger come to you and
your land? Or should your enemies chase you for
three months? Or should there be three days of
disease in your land? Think about it. Then decide
which of these things I should tell the LORD who
sent me."
14David said to Gad, "I am in great trouble. Let
the LORD punish us, because the LORD is very
merciful. Don't let my punishment come from
human beings!"
15So the LORD sent a terrible disease on Israel. It
began in the morning and continued until the
chosen time to stop. From Dan to Beersheba seventy thousand people died. 16When the angel
raised his arm toward Jerusalem to destroy it, the
LORD felt very sorry about the terrible things that
had happened. He said to the angel who was
destroying the people, "That is enough! Put down
your arm!" The angel of the LORD was then by the
threshing floor of Araunah the Jebusite.
17When David saw the angel that killed the
people, he said to the LORD, "I am the one who
sinned and did wrong. These people only followed me like sheep. They did nothing wrong.
Please punish me and my family."
18That day Gad came to David and said, "Go and
build an altar to the LORD on the threshing floor of
Araunah the Jebusite." 19So David did what Gad
told him to do, just as the LORD commanded.
20Araunah looked and saw the king and his servants coming to him. So he went out and bowed
facedown on the ground before the king. 21He
said, "Why has my master the king come to me?"
David answered, "To buy the threshing floor
from you so I can build an altar to the LORD. Then
the terrible disease will stop."
22Araunah said to David, "My master and king,
you may take anything you want for a sacrifice.
Here are some oxen for the whole burnt offering
and the threshing boards and the yokes for the
wood. 23My king, I give everything to you."
Araunah also said to the king, "May the LORD
your God be pleased with you."
24But the king answered Araunah, "No, I will
pay you for the land. I won't offer to the LORD my
God burnt offerings that cost me nothing."
So David bought the threshing floor and the
oxen for one and one-fourth pounds of silver.
25He built an altar to the LORD there and offered
whole burnt offerings and fellowship offerings.
Then the LORD answered his prayer for the country,
and the disease in Israel stopped.

24:10 Conscience: Mark 3:5

24:13 Famine: 1 Kings 8:37

Notes:

INTRODUCTION TO THE BOOK OF

1 KINGS

The Kingdom Is Divided

WHO WROTE THIS BOOK?

Although Jewish tradition holds that Jeremiah was the author of 1 Kings, that fact is inconclusive. Whoever the author/compiler was, he was obviously well acquainted with the Book of Deuteronomy. He also depended on other resources to develop 1 Kings, such as "the book of the history of Solomon" (see 11:41), "the book of the history of the kings of Israel" (14:19), and "the book of the history of the kings of Judah" (14:29) and, possibly, others, such as the records of the prophets.

TO WHOM WAS THIS BOOK WRITTEN?

The author of 1 Kings, while fully aware of the separation of Judah and Israel, is recording these events for the benefit of the whole nation of Israel—all of the people with whom God had made his agreement.

WHERE WAS IT WRITTEN?

The exact location of the author during the writing of 1 Kings is not known. However, it is likely that its writing took place somewhere within the boundaries of Israel.

WHEN WAS IT WRITTEN?

The most likely date for the writing of 1 Kings is between 562 and 538 B.C., although these dates are debatable.

WHAT IS THE BOOK ABOUT?

1 Kings is a continuation of the history of the kings of Israel begun in 1 and 2 Samuel. David's son, Solomon the wise ruler (see chapter 3), has become king after his father. And the first eleven chapters of the book describe his reign, including the building of the magnificent Temple of God in Jerusalem (chapters 5–8). The remainder of the book deals with the kingdom's being divided and the reigns of various kings in each part of the kingdom.

WHY WAS THIS BOOK WRITTEN?

Like the books of 1 and 2 Samuel, 1 Kings presents God as the supreme King and Ruler. It emphasizes that Israel's well-being depended on her kings' faithfulness to the agreement Israel had made with God. The author's intent is to help Israel understand that their exile is due to their rebellion against God and his agreement. However, he continues to remind them that their sincere repentance and return to following the agreement with God offers hope in light of God's promise to David.

SO WHAT DOES THIS BOOK MEAN TO US?

We, too, have an agreement with God, which was sealed by Jesus Christ on the cross. Our well-being, as Christians, is dependent on our faithfulness to that agreement, the New Testament, and its teachings. Like the people of Israel, we have a great promise from God—a promise of eternal life, as described in Revelation 2:10: "Be faithful, even if you have to die, and I will give you the crown of life."

SUMMARY:

The two books of Kings were originally a unified work. As they now exist, 1 Kings covers the history of Israel from the rise of Solomon through the division of the kingdom into two parts during the reign of his son Rehoboam, continuing all the way to the death of Ahab and the coronation of his son Ahaziah.

The books of 1 and 2 Kings, like 1 and 2 Samuel, look at Israel's history in the light of the laws of Deuteronomy. It was written during the exile and wrestles with the question of how the people of God could be defeated by the Babylonians. The answer that Kings implies is that they were punished because they broke the laws of Deuteronomy, for example the law that God be worshiped at one central location (Deuteronomy 12).

First Kings has the following outline:

I. The Rise and Decline of Solomon (1:1–11:43)
II. The Division of the Kingdom (12:1–14:31)
III. From Abijah of Judah to the Rise of Ahaziah of Israel (15:1–22:53)

I. The Rise and Decline of Solomon (1:1–11:43)

Family and political intrigue continued in David's old age. When one of his sons, Adonijah, tried to set himself up as king, David made Solomon, another son, his co-regent. When David died, Solomon became the king. At first Solomon was totally committed to the Lord. He sought God's wisdom and built the Temple. Later in his life, apparently under the influence of his foreign wives, he turned against the Lord—an act that led to the division of the kingdom.

II. The Division of the Kingdom (12:1–14:31)

After Solomon's death, his son Rehoboam expected to become the king of a united Israel like his father. But because of the sin of Rehoboam's father, God planned to divide the nation. So when Rehoboam expected to be crowned the king of the north and south, the northern tribes rejected him and, instead, put Jeroboam on the throne. It was at this time that Jeroboam built places where the people of Israel could worship a calf idol. This sin affected the northern kingdom for the rest of its history.

III. From Abijah of Judah to the Rise of Ahaziah of Israel (15:1–22:53)

The last chapters of 1 Kings give the story of the early days of the divided kingdom. While some kings do seek to obey God, most of them lead the people to false worship. The story of Elijah begins at the end of 1 Kings.

1 KINGS

Adonijah Tries to Become King

At this time King David was very old, and although his servants covered him with blankets, he could not keep warm. 2They said to him, "We will look for a young woman to care for you. She will lie close to you and keep you warm." 3After searching everywhere in Israel for a beautiful young woman, they found a girl named Abishag from Shunam and brought her to the king. 4The girl was very beautiful, and she cared for the king and served him. But the king did not have sexual relations with her.

5Adonijah was the son of King David and Haggith, and he was very proud. "I will be the king," he said. So he got chariots and horses for himself and fifty men for his personal bodyguard. 6Now David had never interfered with Adonijah by questioning what he did. Born next after Absalom, Adonijah was a very handsome man.

7Adonijah spoke with Joab son of Zeruiah and Abiathar the priest, and they agreed to help him. 8But Zadok the priest, Benaiah son of Jehoiada, Nathan the prophet, Shimei, Rei, and King David's special guard did not join Adonijah.

9Then Adonijah killed some sheep, cows, and fat calves for sacrifices at the Stone of Zoheleth near the spring of Rogel. He invited all his brothers, the other sons of King David, to come, as well as all the men of Judah. 10But Adonijah did not invite Nathan the prophet, Benaiah, his father's special guard, or his brother Solomon.

11When Nathan heard about this, he went to Bathsheba, Solomon's mother. "Have you heard that Adonijah, Haggith's son, has made himself king?" Nathan asked. "Our real king, David, does not know it. 12I strongly advise you to save yourself and your sons. 13Go to King David and tell him, 'My master and king, you promised that my son Solomon would be king and would rule on your throne after you. Why then has Adonijah become king?' 14While you are still talking to the king, I will come in and tell him that what you have said about Adonijah is true."

15So Bathsheba went in to see the aged king in his bedroom, where Abishag, the girl from Shunam, was caring for him. 16Bathsheba bowed and knelt before the king. He asked, "What do you want?"

17She answered, "My master, you made a promise to me in the name of the LORD your God. You said, 'Your son Solomon will become king after me, and he will rule on my throne.' 18But now, unknown to you, Adonijah has become king. 19He has killed many cows, fat calves, and sheep for sacrifices. And he has invited all your sons, as well as Abiathar the priest and Joab the commander of the army, but he did not invite Solomon, who serves you. 20My master and king, all the Israelites are watching you, waiting for you to decide who will be king after you. 21As soon as you die, Solomon and I will be treated as criminals."

22While Bathsheba was still talking with the king, Nathan the prophet arrived. 23The servants told the king, "Nathan the prophet is here." So Nathan went to the king and bowed facedown on the ground before him.

24Nathan said, "My master and king, have you said that Adonijah will be the king after you and that he will rule on your throne? 25Today he has sacrificed many cows, fat calves, and sheep, and he has invited all your other sons, the commanders of the army, and Abiathar the priest. Right now they are eating and drinking with him. They are saying, 'Long live King Adonijah!' 26But he did not invite me, your own servant, or Zadok the priest, or Benaiah son of Jehoiada, or your son Solomon. 27Did you do this? Since we are your servants, why didn't you tell us who should be king after you?"

David Makes Solomon King

28Then the king said, "Tell Bathsheba to come in!" So she came in and stood before the king.

29Then the king made this promise, "The LORD has saved me from all trouble. As surely as he lives, 30I will do today what I have promised you in the name of the LORD, the God of Israel. I promised that your son Solomon would be king after me and rule on my throne in my place."

31Then Bathsheba bowed facedown on the ground and knelt before the king and said, "Long live my master King David!"

32Then King David said, "Tell Zadok the priest, Nathan the prophet, and Benaiah son of Jehoiada to come in." When they came before the king, 33he said to them, "Take my servants with you and put my son Solomon on my own mule. Take him down to the spring called Gihon. 34There Zadok the priest and Nathan the prophet should pour olive oil on him and make him king over Israel. Blow the trumpet and shout, 'Long live King Solomon!' 35Then come back up here with him. He will sit on my throne and rule in my place, because he is the one I have chosen to be the ruler over Israel and Judah."

1:33 *mule.* See Judges 10:4 for the fact that mules/donkeys were animals of prestige during some periods in the ancient Near Eastern world.

36Benaiah son of Jehoiada answered the king,
"Amen! This is what the LORD, the God of my
master, has declared! 37The LORD has always
helped you, our king. May he also help Solomon
and make King Solomon's throne an even greater
throne than yours."
38So Zadok the priest, Nathan the prophet, and
Benaiah son of Jehoiada left with the Kerethites
and Pelethites. They put Solomon on King
David's mule and took him to the spring called
Gihon. 39Zadok the priest took the container of
olive oil from the Holy Tent and poured the oil on
Solomon's head to show he was the king. Then
they blew the trumpet, and all the people
shouted, "Long live King Solomon!" 40All the people followed Solomon into the city. Playing flutes
and shouting for joy, they made so much noise
the ground shook.
41At this time Adonijah and all the guests with
him were finishing their meal. When he heard the
sound from the trumpet, Joab asked, "What does
all that noise from the city mean?"
42While Joab was speaking, Jonathan son of Abiathar the priest arrived. Adonijah said, "Come in!
You are an important man, so you must be bringing good news."
43But Jonathan answered, "No! Our master
King David has made Solomon the new king.
44King David sent Zadok the priest, Nathan the
prophet, Benaiah son of Jehoiada, and all the
king's bodyguards with him, and they have put
Solomon on the king's own mule. 45Then Zadok
the priest and Nathan the prophet poured olive
oil on Solomon at Gihon to make him king. After
that they went into the city, shouting with joy.
Now the whole city is excited, and that is the
noise you hear. 46Solomon has now become the
king. 47All the king's officers have come to tell
King David that he has done a good thing. They
are saying, 'May your God make Solomon even
more famous than you and an even greater king
than you.'" Jonathan continued, "And King David
bowed down on his bed to worship God, 48say-
ing, 'Bless the LORD, the God of Israel. Today he
has made one of my sons the king and allowed
me to see it.'"
49Then all of Adonijah's guests were afraid, and
they left quickly and scattered. 50Adonijah was
also afraid of Solomon, so he went and took hold
of the corners of the altar. 51Then someone told
Solomon, "Adonijah is afraid of you, so he is at
the altar, holding on to its corners. He says, 'Tell
King Solomon to promise me today that he will
not kill me.'"
52So Solomon answered, "Adonijah must show
that he is a man of honor. If he does that, I
promise he will not lose even a single hair from
his head. But if he does anything wrong, he will
die." 53Then King Solomon sent some men to get
Adonijah. When he was brought from the altar,
he came before King Solomon and bowed down.
Solomon told him, "Go home."

The Death of David

2 Since it was almost time for David to die, he
gave his son Solomon his last commands.
2David said, "My time to die is near. Be a good and
strong leader. 3Obey the LORD your God. Follow
him by obeying his demands, his commands, his
laws, and his rules that are written in the teachings
of Moses. If you do these things, you will be successful in all you do and wherever you go. 4And if
you obey the LORD, he will keep the promise he
made to me. He said: 'If your descendants live as
I tell them and have complete faith in me, a man
from your family will always be king over the people of Israel.'
5"Also, you remember what Joab son of Zeruiah
did to me. He killed the two commanders of Israel's
armies: Abner son of Ner and Amasa son of Jether.
He did this as if he and they were at war, although
it was a time of peace. He put their blood on the
belt around his waist and on his sandals on his feet.
6Punish him in the way you think is wisest, but do
not let him die peacefully of old age.
7"Be kind to the children of Barzillai of Gilead,
and allow them to eat at your table. They welcomed
me when I ran away from your brother Absalom.
8"And remember, Shimei son of Gera, the
Benjaminite, is here with you. He cursed me the
day I went to Mahanaim. But when he came down
to meet me at the Jordan River, I promised him
before the LORD, 'Shimei, I will not kill you.' 9But
you should not leave him unpunished. You are a
wise man, and you will know what to do to him,
but you must be sure he is killed."
10Then David died and was buried with his
ancestors in Jerusalem. 11He had ruled over Israel
forty years—seven years in Hebron and thirty-three
years in Jerusalem.

1:38 *Kerethites and Pelethites.* These were probably special units of the army that were responsible for the king's safety, a kind of palace guard.

1:39 *poured the oil.* See 1 Samuel 10:1.

1:40 Music: 2 Chronicles 5:11–14

1:50 *corners of the altar.* If a person were innocent of a crime, he could run into the Holy Place where the altar was. If he held on to the corners of the altar, which looked like horns, he would be safe.

2:4 Obedience: Nehemiah 1:4-9

DEBORAH

JUDGES 4–5

Deborah was the only woman who judged Israel in the time of the judges. Was this a sign that Israel was weak? Is Deborah then a warning or an example for women in today's society?

Deborah judged in a time when "there were no warriors in Israel" (Judges 5:7). She was a poet, warrior, prophetess, and judge who delivered the Israelites from slavery with heroic courage and passionate faith. But Christians have not been comfortable with this powerful, influential woman. Some biblical scholars have argued that Deborah was a judge only as a concession to the weakness of the male judges or the perilous times of the judges. Yet the Bible never relegates Deborah to "second best" as a choice to judge Israel. Nowhere does the Book of Judges hint that Deborah was anything less than God's appointed leader for the day.

The story of Deborah is unique among Bible stories in that the women are the major players, and the men are passive characters who are influenced by the women. For example, Barak was the general of Deborah's army but was a reluctant hero who demanded that Deborah go with him into battle. Deborah's faith was contrasted with Barak's fear, and as a result, Deborah spoke a significant prophecy to Barak: "But you [Barak] will not get credit for the victory. The LORD will let a woman defeat Sisera" (4:9).

This prophecy found its fulfillment in another important woman closely allied with Deborah. Jael was the woman who defeated the Canaanites by killing their general. Jael invited the retreating Sisera into her tent and drove a tent peg through his temple while he slept. Barak routed the Canaanite army, but Sisera died not at Barak's hands, but at the hands of Jael, a woman. Both Deborah and Jael were successful warriors against God's enemies, while Barak was a hesitant hero who could not defeat God's enemies without their help.

Furthermore, Deborah's and Jael's actions in battle were identified with the actions of the Lord. Deborah and Jael were the "helpers" who fulfilled God's prophecy: "I [the LORD] will make Sisera, the commander of Jabin's army, and his chariots, and his army, meet you at the Kishon River. and I will hand Sisera over to you" (Judges 4:7). In a dramatic comparison, Deborah and Jael demonstrated the aspect of God that lures people to salvation or destruction.

Deborah, however, was not the only woman who influenced the destiny of the Israelites. A comparison with other women in the Bible will shed more light on Deborah's importance.

In Genesis 38, the patriarch Judah failed to fulfill his obligation to his daughter-in-law Tamar. After the death of his first two sons, Judah promised his third son to Tamar. But instead, Judah held on to his third son and broke his promise to her. Yet Judah's actions did not deter Tamar from doing what was right. Even though Judah was passive with his promise, Tamar took matters into her own hands and guaranteed Judah's lineage, which included David and Christ.

Ruth was another woman who dramatically changed the history of Israel. Though she was a Moabite woman, she boldly asked Boaz to marry her and become her kinsman-redeemer (Ruth 3:6–9). Ruth's boldness brought redemption to Naomi's family. More importantly, Ruth and Boaz had a son who was King David's grandfather (Ruth 4:17).

Esther was a woman who, like Deborah, delivered Israel from destruction by a foreign nation (Esther 5:7–8). Esther was the wife of King Xerxes when Israel was in exile in the Persian Empire. During this time, the wicked Haman conspired to destroy the Jews, but his plan was discovered and told to Esther. She bravely approached the king, and in an elaborate plan, she exposed Haman saving the Jews from destruction (Esther 7).

Deborah was one of many women in the Bible who fulfilled God's plans through ingenuity and faith. After Deborah, all the judges who came upon the scene were men, but each was a reluctant or dubious hero.

But there is one shining example in Judges. In a book where powerless women were sacrificed, raped, dismembered, and bartered by their own families and nation, Deborah stands out as a stark contrast. Like Tamar, Ruth, and Esther, Deborah was a woman in the midst of a male-dominated society who influenced the history of Israel and hence the Christian church. She is an example to men and women of all generations of what one woman can accomplish through her wisdom and bravery.

Deborah: For additional scriptures on this topic go to Genesis 38:13–26.

SAMSON

JUDGES 13

Who is Samson? Does Samson ever do anything to please God? How does God use him? In what sense is Samson a "hero of faith" (Hebrews 11:32)?

The period of the judges of Israel was a time of great spiritual decline in Israel. After Joshua defeated the Canaanites, he led Israel in a rededication to the Lord (Joshua 24). Even so, soon after his death, the people began to wander not only from the Lord, but also from each other.

The real cause of their political troubles, though, was spiritual. As the beginning of the Book of Judges points out (2:10–3:5), God allowed Israel's enemies to control them when they turned their back on him and started worshiping foreign gods. At this point, the people realized how weak and powerless they were without the Lord, and they turned to him for help. In response, God raised up deliverers who are called "judges".

The story of Samson is found in Judges 13–16 and begins before his birth. An unnamed woman, the wife of Manoah, is barren. God gives her the good news that she will give birth to a special son, so she needs to prepare for the event. The fact that God must intervene in the birth by allowing Manoah's wife to conceive and give birth shows that the child is a gift from God, and that Israel's deliverance is ultimately God's doing.

The child is to be specially dedicated to the Lord as a Nazirite (see Numbers 6:1–21). A Nazirite is someone who lives an especially holy life. Only a male Levite could be a priest, but a man or a woman from any other tribe could serve as a Nazirite. Samson's special dedication plays a very important role in the account of his life.

Imagine his mother and father's excitement at the birth of this long-desired child, and then their confusion and frustration at his actions as a young man. Samson acts like a spoiled brat, the ultimate rebellious teenager. The only difference is that his incredibly strong will is matched by his physical strength. What is so amazing is that God uses this selfish man to accomplish the good purpose that he intends for him.

The first story we hear of Samson as a young man illustrates this point. Samson does not lead an army to liberate the Israelites from the Philistines; he would rather marry one of their pretty young women (Judges 14). He demands that his parents arrange a wedding. After trying to talk him out of it, they give in. Neither they nor Samson have any idea that God is going to use this wedding to inflict heavy damages on the enemy!

On the trip to the Philistine town where the girl lives, Samson is attacked by a lion. He rips the lion apart. Later when he passes that way again, he notices that some bees have built a nest in the dead carcass of the lion. He reaches inside to scoop some honey out. This act later becomes the basis of a riddle that Samson poses to thirty men who are attending his wedding feast.

How does God use this whole fiasco to help Israel against the Philistines? The thirty friends force Samson's young wife to give them the answer to the riddle, so he loses the bet and has to pay up with thirty changes of clothes. He is so angry that he goes down to Philistia, kills thirty Philistines, and takes their clothes.

Time and again God overrules Samson's selfish impulses and uses them to inflict damage against Israel's enemies, the Philistines. This comes to a climax at the end of his life.

Samson later marries a second Philistine girl named Delilah. She badgers him to tell her his source of his strength. He keeps trying to put her off, but finally gives in and tells her that his strength comes from his long hair. One part of the vow a Nazirite makes is never to cut his hair (Numbers 6:5). Samson's hair is not magical, but it is a sign that he has a special relationship with God. So when Delilah cuts it off, Samson loses his strength, because God has abandoned him for his betrayal.

But once again God uses Samson. Samson is captured, blinded, and put on display in the city of Gaza. All the Philistine rulers are there. Again, Samson prays to God selfishly. He asks for God to return his strength one more time, so he could get revenge for the loss of his eyes (Judges 16:28). He is able to push apart two pillars, causing the whole temple to collapse on the leading citizens of Philistia.

As the New Testament reminds us (Hebrews 11:32) Samson was, in spite of his deep failings, a man of faith. He knew that God's Spirit gave him the power that he had (Judges 13:24; 14:6, 19; 15:14). Though he was motivated by his selfishness, he did pray to God for the strength he needed at the end. The story of Samson teaches us that God is not limited by those he wants to use. He can overrule the evil and incompetence of his servants.

Samson: For additional scriptures on this topic go to Judges 13:1–16:31.

Solomon Takes Control as King

12Solomon became king after David, his father,
and he was in firm control of his kingdom.
13At this time Adonijah son of Haggith went to
Bathsheba, Solomon's mother. "Do you come in
peace?" Bathsheba asked.
"Yes. This is a peaceful visit," Adonijah answered.
14"I have something to say to you."
"You may speak," she said.
15"You remember that at one time the kingdom
was mine," Adonijah said. "All the people of Israel
recognized me as their king, but things have
changed. Now my brother is the king, because the
LORD chose him. 16Now I have one thing to ask you;
please do not refuse me."
Bathsheba answered, "What do you want?"
17"I know King Solomon will do anything you
ask him," Adonijah continued. "Please ask him to
give me Abishag the Shunammite to be my wife."
18"Very well," she answered. "I will speak to the
king for you."
19So Bathsheba went to King Solomon to speak
to him for Adonijah. When Solomon saw her, he
stood up to meet her, then bowed down, and sat
on the throne. He told some servants to bring
another throne for his mother. Then she sat down
at his right side.
20Bathsheba said, "I have one small thing to ask
you. Please do not refuse me."
"Ask, mother," the king answered. "I will not
refuse you."
21So she said, "Allow Abishag the Shunammite
to marry your brother Adonijah."
22King Solomon answered his mother, "Why do
you ask me to give him Abishag? Why don't you
also ask for him to become the king since he is my
older brother? Abiathar the priest and Joab son of
Zeruiah would support him!"
23Then King Solomon swore by the name of the
LORD, saying, "May God punish me terribly if this
doesn't cost Adonijah his life! 24By the LORD who
has given me the throne that belonged to my father
David and who has kept his promise and given
the kingdom to me and my people, Adonijah will
die today!" 25Then King Solomon gave orders to
Benaiah son of Jehoiada, and he went and killed
Adonijah.
26King Solomon said to Abiathar the priest, "I
should kill you too, but I will allow you to go back
to your fields in Anathoth. I will not kill you at this
time, because you helped carry the Ark of the Lord
GOD while marching with my father David. And I
know you shared in all the hard times with him."
27Then Solomon removed Abiathar from being the
LORD's priest. This happened as the LORD had said
it would, when he was speaking in Shiloh about
the priest Eli and his descendants.
28When Joab heard about what had happened,
he was afraid. He had supported Adonijah but not
Absalom. So Joab ran to the Tent of the LORD and
took hold of the corners of the altar. 29Someone
told King Solomon that Joab had run to the Tent of
the LORD and was beside the altar. Then Solomon
ordered Benaiah to go and kill him.
30Benaiah went into the Tent of the LORD and
said to Joab, "The king says, 'Come out!'"
But Joab answered, "No, I will die here."
So Benaiah went back to the king and told him
what Joab had said. 31Then the king ordered
Benaiah, "Do as he says! Kill him there and bury
him. Then my family and I will be free of the guilt
of Joab, who has killed innocent people. 32Without
my father knowing it, he killed two men who were
much better than he was—Abner son of Ner, the
commander of Israel's army, and Amasa son of
Jether, the commander of Judah's army. So the LORD
will pay him back for those deaths. 33Joab and his
family will be forever guilty for their deaths, but
there will be peace from the LORD for David, his
descendants, his family, and his throne forever."
34So Benaiah son of Jehoiada killed Joab, and he
was buried near his home in the desert. 35The king
then made Benaiah son of Jehoiada commander of
the army in Joab's place. He also made Zadok the
new high priest in Abiathar's place.
36Next the king sent for Shimei. Solomon said to
him, "Build a house for yourself in Jerusalem and
live there. Don't leave the city. 37The very day you
leave and cross the Kidron Valley, someone will kill
you, and it will be your own fault."
38So Shimei answered the king, "I agree with
what you say. I will do what you say, my master and
king." So Shimei lived in Jerusalem for a long time.
39But three years later two of Shimei's slaves ran
away to Achish king of Gath, who was the son of
Maacah. Shimei heard that his slaves were in Gath,
40so he put his saddle on his donkey and went to
Achish at Gath to find them. Then he brought
them back from Gath.
41Someone told Solomon that Shimei had gone
from Jerusalem to Gath and had returned. 42So

2:17 *Abishag the Shunammite.* To marry the wife or concubine of the previous king was to make a power play on the throne.

2:25 Capital Punishment: Zechariah 5:3–4

2:25 Deborah: Esther 5:1–8

2:28 *corners of the altar.* If a person were innocent of a crime, he could run into the Holy Place where the altar was. If he held on to the corners of the altar, which looked like horns, he would be safe.

Solomon sent for Shimei and said, "I made you
promise in the name of the LORD not to leave Jerusalem. I warned you if you went out anywhere you
would die, and you agreed to what I said. 43Why
did you break your promise to the LORD and disobey my command?" 44The king also said, "You
know the many wrong things you did to my father
David, so now the LORD will punish you for those
wrongs. 45But the LORD will bless me and make
the rule of David safe before the LORD forever."
46Then the king ordered Benaiah to kill Shimei,
and he did. Now Solomon was in full control of his
kingdom.

Solomon Asks for Wisdom

3 Solomon made an agreement with the king of
Egypt by marrying his daughter and bringing
her to Jerusalem. At this time Solomon was still
building his palace and the Temple of the LORD, as
well as a wall around Jerusalem. 2The Temple for
the worship of the LORD had not yet been finished,
so people were still sacrificing at altars in many
places of worship. 3Solomon showed he loved the
LORD by following the commands his father David
had given him, except many other places of worship were still used to offer sacrifices and to burn
incense.
4King Solomon went to Gibeon to offer a sacrifice, because it was the most important place of
worship. He offered a thousand burnt offerings
on that altar. 5While he was at Gibeon, the LORD
appeared to him in a dream during the night. God
said, "Ask for whatever you want me to give you."
6Solomon answered, "You were very kind to
your servant, my father David. He obeyed you, and
he was honest and lived right. You showed great
kindness to him when you allowed his son to be
king after him. 7LORD my God, now you have made
me, your servant, king in my father's place. But I
am like a little child; I don't know how to do what
must be done. 8I, your servant, am here among
your chosen people, and there are too many of
them to count. 9I ask that you give me an obedient
heart so I can rule the people in the right way and
will know the difference between right and wrong.
Otherwise, it is impossible to rule this great people
of yours."
10The Lord was pleased that Solomon had asked
this. 11So God said to him, "You did not ask for a
long life, or riches for yourself, or the death of your
enemies. Since you asked for wisdom to make the
right decisions, 12I will do what you asked. I will
give you wisdom and understanding that is greater
than anyone has had in the past or will have in the
future. 13I will also give you what you did not ask
for: riches and honor. During your life no other
king will be as great as you. 14If you follow me and
obey my laws and commands, as your father
David did, I will also give you a long life."
15After Solomon woke up from the dream, he
went to Jerusalem. He stood before the Ark of the
Agreement with the Lord, where he made burnt
offerings and fellowship offerings. After that, he
gave a feast for all his leaders and officers.⚭

Solomon Makes a Wise Decision

16One day two women who were prostitutes
came to Solomon. As they stood before him, 17one
of the women said, "My master, this woman and I
live in the same house. I gave birth to a baby while
she was there with me. 18Three days later this
woman also gave birth to a baby. No one else was
in the house with us; it was just the two of us.
19One night this woman rolled over on her baby,
and he died. 20So she took my son from my bed
during the night while I was asleep, and she carried him to her bed. Then she put the dead baby in
my bed. 21The next morning when I got up to feed
my baby, I saw that he was dead! When I looked at
him more closely, I realized he was not my son."
22"No!" the other woman cried. "The living baby
is my son, and the dead baby is yours!"
But the first woman said, "No! The dead baby
is yours, and the living one is mine!" So the two
women argued before the king.
23Then King Solomon said, "One of you says, 'My
son is alive and your son is dead.' Then the other
one says, 'No! Your son is dead and my son is
alive.'"
24The king sent his servants to get a sword. When
they brought it to him, 25he said, "Cut the living
baby into two pieces, and give each woman half."
26The real mother of the living child was full of
love for her son. So she said to the king, "Please,
my master, don't kill him! Give the baby to her!"
But the other woman said, "Neither of us will
have him. Cut him into two pieces!"
27Then King Solomon said, "Don't kill him. Give
the baby to the first woman, because she is the real
mother."
28When the people of Israel heard about King
Solomon's decision, they respected him very much.
They saw he had wisdom from God to make the
right decisions.

3:1 *made an agreement.* Treaties between nations in ancient times were often sealed by a marriage between the two ruling families.

⚭**3:15 Dreams:** Job 33:15

Solomon's Officers

4 King Solomon ruled over all Israel. [2]These are the names of his leading officers:
Azariah son of Zadok was the priest;
[3]Elihoreph and Ahijah, sons of Shisha, recorded what happened in the courts;
Jehoshaphat son of Ahilud recorded the history of the people;
[4]Benaiah son of Jehoiada was commander of the army;
Zadok and Abiathar were priests;
[5]Azariah son of Nathan was in charge of the district governors;
Zabud son of Nathan was a priest and adviser to the king;
[6]Ahishar was responsible for everything in the palace;
Adoniram son of Abda was in charge of the labor force.

A cedar of Lebanon, used to construct the Temple

[7]Solomon placed twelve governors over the districts of Israel, who gathered food from their districts for the king and his family. Each governor was responsible for bringing food to the king one month of each year. [8]These are the names of the twelve governors:
Ben-Hur was governor of the mountain country of Ephraim.
[9]Ben-Deker was governor of Makaz, Shaalbim, Beth Shemesh, and Elon Bethhanan.
[10]Ben-Hesed was governor of Arubboth, Socoh, and all the land of Hepher.
[11]Ben Abinadab was governor of Naphoth Dor. (He was married to Taphath, Solomon's daughter.)
[12]Baana son of Ahilud was governor of Taanach, Megiddo, and all of Beth Shan next to Zarethan. This was below Jezreel from Beth Shan to Abel Meholah across from Jokmeam.
[13]Ben-Geber was governor of Ramoth in Gilead. (He was governor of all the towns of Jair in Gilead. Jair was the son of Manasseh. Ben-Geber was also over the district of Argob in Bashan, which had sixty large, walled cities with bronze bars on their gates.)
[14]Ahinadab son of Iddo was governor of Mahanaim.
[15]Ahimaaz was governor of Naphtali. (He was married to Basemath, Solomon's daughter.)
[16]Baana son of Hushai was governor of Asher and Aloth.
[17]Jehoshaphat son of Paruah was governor of Issachar.
[18]Shimei son of Ela was governor of Benjamin.
[19]Geber son of Uri was governor of Gilead. Gilead had been the country of Sihon king of the Amorites and Og king of Bashan. But Geber was the only governor over this district.

Solomon's Kingdom

[20]There were as many people in Judah and
Israel as grains of sand on the seashore. The people ate, drank, and were happy. [21]Solomon ruled
over all the kingdoms from the Euphrates River to
the land of the Philistines, as far as the border of
Egypt. These countries brought Solomon the payments he demanded, and they were under his
control all his life.
[22]Solomon needed much food each day to feed
himself and all the people who ate at his table: one
hundred ninety-five bushels of fine flour, three hundred ninety bushels of grain, [23]ten cows that were
fed on good grain, twenty cows that were raised in
the fields, one hundred sheep, three kinds of deer,
and fattened birds.
[24]Solomon controlled all the countries west of
the Euphrates River—the land from Tiphsah to
Gaza. And he had peace on all sides of his kingdom. [25]During Solomon's life Judah and Israel,
from Dan to Beersheba, also lived in peace; all of
his people were able to sit under their own fig
trees and grapevines.
[26]Solomon had four thousand stalls for his chariot horses and twelve thousand horses. [27]Each
month one of the district governors gave King
Solomon all the food he needed—enough for
every person who ate at the king's table. The governors made sure he had everything he needed.
[28]They also brought enough barley and straw for
Solomon's chariot and work horses; each person
brought this grain to the right place.

4:25 *Dan to Beersheba.* Dan was the city farthest north in Israel, and Beersheba was the city farthest south. So this means all the people of Israel.

Solomon's Wisdom

29God gave Solomon great wisdom so he could
understand many things. His wisdom was as hard
to measure as the grains of sand on the seashore.
30His wisdom was greater than any wisdom of the
East, or any wisdom in Egypt. 31He was wiser
than anyone on earth. He was even wiser than
Ethan the Ezrahite, as well as Heman, Calcol, and
Darda—the three sons of Mahol. King Solomon
became famous in all the surrounding countries.
32During his life he spoke three thousand wise sayings and also wrote one thousand five songs. 33He
taught about many kinds of plants—everything
from the great cedar trees of Lebanon to the weeds
that grow out of the walls. He also taught about
animals, birds, crawling things, and fish. 34People
from all nations came to listen to King Solomon's
wisdom. The kings of all nations sent them to him,
because they had heard of Solomon's wisdom.⚭

Builders' tools found in Egypt dating back to about 2000 B.C.—wooden mallet, bronze chisels, and plumb-bob

Preparing to Build the Temple

5 Hiram, the king of Tyre, had always been
David's friend. When Hiram heard that Solomon had been made king in David's place, he sent
his messengers to Solomon. 2Solomon sent this
message back to King Hiram: 3"You remember
my father David had to fight many wars with the
countries around him, so he was never able to build
a temple for worshiping the LORD his God. David
was waiting until the LORD allowed him to defeat all
his enemies. 4But now the LORD my God has given
me peace on all sides of my country. I have no enemies now, and no danger threatens my people.
5"The LORD promised my father David, 'I will
make your son king after you, and he will build a
temple for worshiping me.' Now, I plan to build
that temple for worshiping the LORD my God. 6So
send your men to cut down cedar trees for me
from Lebanon. My servants will work with yours,
and I will pay them whatever wages you decide.
We don't have anyone who can cut down trees as
well as the people of Sidon."
7When Hiram heard what Solomon asked, he
was very happy. He said, "Praise the LORD today!
He has given David a wise son to rule over this
great nation!" 8Then Hiram sent back this message to Solomon: "I received the message you sent,
and I will give you all the cedar and pine trees you
want. 9My servants will bring them down from
Lebanon to the sea. There I will tie them together
and float them along the shore to the place you
choose. Then I will separate the logs there, and
you can take them away. In return it is my wish
that you give food to all those who live with me."
10So Hiram gave Solomon as much cedar and pine
as he wanted. 11And Solomon gave Hiram about
one hundred twenty-five thousand bushels of
wheat each year to feed the people who lived
with him. Solomon also gave him about one hundred fifteen thousand gallons of pure olive oil
every year.
12The LORD gave Solomon wisdom as he had
promised. And there was peace between Hiram
and Solomon; these two kings made a treaty
between themselves.
13King Solomon forced thirty thousand men of
Israel to help in this work. 14He sent a group of ten
thousand men each month to Lebanon. Each
group worked in Lebanon one month, then went
home for two months. A man named Adoniram
was in charge. 15Solomon forced eighty thousand
men to work in the hill country, cutting stone, and
he had seventy thousand men to carry the stones.
16There were also thirty-three hundred men who
directed the workers. 17King Solomon commanded
them to cut large blocks of fine stone to be used
for the foundation of the Temple. 18Solomon's and
Hiram's builders and the men from Byblos carved
the stones and prepared the stones and the logs for
building the Temple.

Solomon Builds the Temple

6 Solomon began to build the Temple four hundred eighty years after the people of Israel had
left Egypt. This was during the fourth year of King
Solomon's rule over Israel. It was the second
month, the month of Ziv.

⚭**4:34 Proverb:** Job 28:28

2The Temple was ninety feet long, thirty feet wide, and forty-five feet high. 3The porch in front of the main room of the Temple was fifteen feet deep and thirty feet wide. This room ran along the front of the Temple itself. Its width was equal to that of the Temple. 4The Temple also had windows that opened and closed. 5Solomon also built some side rooms against the walls of the main room and the inner room of the Temple. He built rooms all around. 6The rooms on the bottom floor were seven and one-half feet wide. Those on the middle floor were nine feet wide, and the rooms above them were ten and one-half feet wide. The Temple wall that formed the side of each room was thinner than the wall in the room below. These rooms were pushed against the Temple wall, but they did not have their main beams built into this wall.

7The stones were prepared at the same place where they were cut from the ground. Since these stones were the only ones used to build the Temple, there was no noise of hammers, axes, or any other iron tools at the Temple.

8The entrance to the lower rooms beside the Temple was on the south side. From there, stairs went up to the second-floor rooms. And from there, stairs went on to the third-floor rooms. 9Solomon put a roof made from beams and cedar boards on the Temple. So he finished building the Temple 10as well as the bottom floor that was beside the Temple. This bottom floor was seven and one-half feet high and was attached to the Temple by cedar beams.

11The LORD said to Solomon: 12"If you obey all my laws and commands, I will do for you what I promised your father David. 13I will live among the Israelites in this Temple, and I will never leave my people Israel."

14So Solomon finished building the Temple. 15The inside walls were covered from floor to ceiling with cedar boards. The floor was made from pine boards. 16A room thirty feet long was built in the back part of the Temple. This room, called the Most Holy Place, was separated from the rest of the Temple by cedar boards which reached from floor to ceiling. 17The main room, the one in front of the Most Holy Place, was sixty feet long. 18Everything inside the Temple was covered with cedar, which was carved with pictures of flowers and plants. A person could not see the stones of the wall, only the cedar.

19Solomon prepared the inner room at the back of the Temple to keep the Ark of the Agreement with the LORD. 20This inner room was thirty feet long, thirty feet wide, and thirty feet high. He covered this room with pure gold, and he also covered the altar of cedar. 21He covered the inside of the Temple with pure gold, placing gold chains across the front of the inner room, which was also covered with gold. 22So all the inside of the Temple, as well as the altar of the Most Holy Place, was covered with gold.

23Solomon made two creatures from olive wood and placed them in the Most Holy Place. Each creature was fifteen feet tall 24and had two wings. Each wing was seven and one-half feet long, so it was fifteen feet from the end of one wing to the end of the other. 25The creatures were the same size and shape; 26each was fifteen feet tall. 27These creatures were put beside each other in the Most Holy Place with their wings spread out. One creature's wing touched one wall, and the other creature's wing touched the other wall with their wings touching each other in the middle of the room. 28These two creatures were covered with gold.

29All the walls around the Temple were carved with pictures of creatures with wings, as well as palm trees and flowers. This was true for both the main room and the inner room. 30The floors of both rooms were covered with gold.

31Doors made from olive wood were placed at the entrance to the Most Holy Place. These doors had five-sided frames. 32Creatures with wings, as well as palm trees and flowers, were also carved on the two olive wood doors that were covered with gold. The creatures and the palm trees on the doors were covered with gold as well. 33At the entrance to the main room there was a square door frame made of olive wood. 34Two doors were made from pine. Each door had two parts so the doors folded. 35The doors were covered with pictures of creatures with wings, as well as palm trees and flowers. All of the carvings were covered with gold, which was evenly spread over them.

36The inner courtyard was enclosed by walls, which were made of three rows of cut stones and one row of cedar boards.

37Work began on the Temple in Ziv, the second month, during the fourth year Solomon was king over Israel. 38The Temple was finished during the eleventh year he was king, in the eighth month, the month of Bul. It was built exactly as it was planned. Solomon had spent seven years building it.

Solomon's Palace

7 King Solomon also built a palace for himself; it took him thirteen years to finish it. 2Built of cedars from the Forest of Lebanon, it was one hundred fifty feet long, seventy-five feet wide, and forty-five feet high. It had four rows of cedar columns which supported the cedar beams. 3There were forty-five beams on the roof, with fifteen

beams in each row, and the ceiling was covered with cedar above the beams. 4Windows were placed in three rows facing each other. 5All the doors were square, and the three doors at each end faced each other.

6Solomon also built the porch that had pillars. This porch was seventy-five feet long and forty-five feet wide. Along the front of the porch was a roof supported by pillars.

7Solomon also built a throne room where he judged people, called the Hall of Justice. This room was covered with cedar from the floor to the ceiling. 8The palace where Solomon lived was built like the Hall of Justice, and it was behind this hall. Solomon also built the same kind of palace for his wife, who was the daughter of the king of Egypt.

9All these buildings were made with blocks of fine stone. First they were carefully cut. Then they were trimmed with a saw in the front and back. These fine stones went from the foundations of the buildings to the top of the walls. Even the courtyard was made with blocks of stone. 10The foundations were made with large blocks of fine stone, some as long as fifteen feet. Others were twelve feet long. 11On top of these foundation stones were other blocks of fine stone and cedar beams. 12The palace courtyard, the courtyard inside the Temple, and the porch of the Temple were surrounded by walls. All of these walls had three rows of stone blocks and one row of cedar beams.

The Temple Is Completed Inside

13King Solomon sent to Tyre and had Huram brought to him. 14Huram's mother was a widow from the tribe of Naphtali. His father was from Tyre and had been skilled in making things from bronze. Huram was also very skilled and experienced in bronze work. So he came to King Solomon and did all the bronze work.

15He made two bronze pillars, each one twenty-seven feet tall and eighteen feet around. 16He also made two bronze capitals that were seven and one-half feet tall, and he put them on top of the pillars. 17Then he made a net of seven chains for each capital, which covered the capitals on top of the two pillars. 18He made two rows of bronze pomegranates to go on the nets. These covered the capitals at the top of the pillars. 19The capitals on top of the pillars in the porch were shaped like lilies, and they were six feet tall. 20The capitals were on top of both pillars, above the bowl-shaped section and next to the nets. At that place there were two hundred pomegranates in rows all around the capitals. 21Huram put these two bronze pillars at the porch of the Temple. He named the south pillar He Establishes and the north pillar In Him Is Strength. 22The capitals on top of the pillars were shaped like lilies. So the work on the pillars was finished.

23Then Huram made from bronze a large round bowl, which was called the Sea. It was forty-five feet around, fifteen feet across, and seven and one-half feet deep. 24Around the outer edge of the bowl was a rim. Under this rim were two rows of bronze plants which surrounded the bowl. There were ten plants every eighteen inches, and these plants were made in one piece with the bowl. 25The bowl rested on the backs of twelve bronze bulls that faced outward from the center of the bowl. Three bulls faced north, three faced west, three faced south, and three faced east. 26The sides of the bowl were four inches thick, and it held about eleven thousand gallons. The rim of the bowl was like the rim of a cup or like a lily blossom.

27Then Huram made ten bronze stands, each one six feet long, six feet wide, and four and one-half feet high. 28The stands were made from square sides, which were put on frames. 29On the sides were bronze lions, bulls, and creatures with wings. On the frames above and below the lions and bulls were designs of flowers hammered into the bronze. 30Each stand had four bronze wheels with bronze axles. At the corners there were bronze supports for a large bowl, and the supports had designs of flowers. 31There was a frame on top of the bowls, eighteen inches high above the bowls. The opening of the bowl was round, twenty-seven inches deep. Designs were carved into the bronze on the frame, which was square, not round. 32The four wheels, placed under the frame, were twenty-seven inches high. The axles between the wheels were made as one piece with the stand. 33The wheels were like a chariot's wheels. Everything on the wheels—the axles, rims, spokes, and hubs—were made of bronze.

34The four supports were on the four corners of each stand. They were made as one piece with the stand. 35A strip of bronze around the top of each stand was nine inches deep. It was also made as one piece with the stand. 36The sides of the stand and the frames were covered with carvings of creatures with wings, as well as lions, palm trees, and flowers. 37This is the way Huram made the ten stands. The bronze for each stand was melted

7:15 *two bronze pillars.* The pillars represent the stability of the Temple and the stability of the presence of Israel in the Promised Land.

7:23 *the Sea.* Besides serving as a place for ceremonial bathing, the Sea before the Temple represented the subduing of the forces of chaos by God.

and poured into a mold, so all the stands were the same size and shape.

[38]Huram also made ten bronze bowls, one bowl for each of the ten stands. Each bowl was six feet across and could hold about two hundred thirty gallons. [39]Huram put five stands on the south side of the Temple and five on the north side. He put the large bowl in the southeast corner of the Temple. [40]Huram also made bowls, shovels, and small bowls.

So Huram finished all his work for King Solomon on the Temple of the LORD:

[41]two pillars;
two large bowls for the capitals on top of the pillars;
two nets to cover the two large bowls for the capitals on top of the pillars;
[42]four hundred pomegranates for the two nets (there were two rows of pomegranates for each net covering the bowls for the capitals on top of the pillars);
[43]ten stands with a bowl on each stand;
[44]the large bowl with twelve bulls under it;
[45]the pots, shovels, small bowls, and all the utensils for the Temple of the LORD.

Huram made everything King Solomon wanted from polished bronze. [46]The king had these things poured into clay molds that were made in the plain of the Jordan River between Succoth and Zarethan. [47]Solomon never weighed the bronze used to make these things, because there was too much to weigh. So the total weight of all the bronze was never known.

[48]Solomon also made all the items for the Temple of the LORD:

the golden altar;
the golden table which held the bread that shows God's people are in his presence;
[49]the lampstands of pure gold (five on the right side and five on the left side in front of the Most Holy Place);
the flowers, lamps, and tongs of gold;
[50]the pure gold bowls, wick trimmers, small bowls, pans, and dishes used to carry coals;
the gold hinges for the doors of the Most Holy Place and the main room of the Temple.

[51]Finally the work King Solomon did for the Temple of the LORD was finished. Solomon brought in everything his father David had set apart for the Temple—silver, gold, and other articles. He put everything in the treasuries of the Temple of the LORD.

The Ark Is Brought into the Temple

8 King Solomon called for the older leaders of Israel, the heads of the tribes, and the leaders of the families to come to him in Jerusalem. He wanted them to bring the Ark of the Agreement with the LORD from the older part of the city. [2]So all the Israelites came together with King Solomon during the festival in the month of Ethanim, the seventh month.

[3]When all the older leaders of Israel arrived, the priests lifted up the Ark. [4]They carried the Ark of the LORD, the Meeting Tent, and the holy utensils; the priests and the Levites brought them up. [5]King Solomon and all the Israelites gathered before the Ark and sacrificed so many sheep and cattle no one could count them all. [6]Then the priests put the Ark of the Agreement with the LORD in its place inside the Most Holy Place in the Temple, under the wings of the golden creatures. [7]The wings of these creatures were spread out over the place for the Ark, covering it and its carrying poles. [8]The carrying poles were so long that anyone standing in the Holy Place in front of the Most Holy Place could see the ends of the poles, but no one could see them from outside the Holy Place. The poles are still there today. [9]The only things inside the Ark were two stone tablets that Moses had put in the Ark at Mount Sinai. That was where the LORD made his agreement with the Israelites after they came out of Egypt.

[10]When the priests left the Holy Place, a cloud filled the Temple of the LORD. [11]The priests could not continue their work, because the Temple was filled with the glory of the LORD.

Solomon Speaks to the People

[12]Then Solomon said, "The LORD said he would live in a dark cloud. [13]LORD, I have truly built a wonderful Temple for you—a place for you to live forever."

[14]While all the Israelites were standing there, King Solomon turned to them and blessed them.

[15]Then he said, "Praise the LORD, the God of Israel. He has done what he promised to my father David. The LORD said, [16]'Since the time I brought my people Israel out of Egypt, I have not chosen a

8:9 *stone tablets.* They were the two tablets on which God wrote the Ten Commandments.

city in any tribe of Israel where a temple will be built for me. But I have chosen David to lead my people Israel.’

17“My father David wanted to build a temple for the LORD, the God of Israel. 18But the LORD said to my father David, ‘It was good that you wanted to build a temple for me. 19But you are not the one to build it. Your son, who comes from your own body, is the one who will build my temple.’

20“Now the LORD has kept his promise. I am the king now in place of David my father. Now I rule Israel as the LORD promised, and I have built the Temple for the LORD, the God of Israel. 21I have made a place there for the Ark, in which is the Agreement the LORD made with our ancestors when he brought them out of Egypt.”

Solomon’s Prayer

22Then Solomon stood facing the LORD’s altar, and all the Israelites were standing behind him. He spread out his hands toward the sky 23and said:

“LORD, God of Israel, there is no god like you in heaven above or on earth below. You keep your agreement of love with your servants who truly follow you. 24You have kept the promise you made to your servant David, my father. You spoke it with your own mouth and finished it with your hands today. 25Now LORD, God of Israel, keep the promise you made to your servant David, my father. You said, ‘If your sons are careful to obey me as you have obeyed me, there will always be someone from your family ruling Israel.’ 26Now, God of Israel, please continue to keep that promise you made to your servant David, my father.

27“But, God, can you really live here on the earth? The sky and the highest place in heaven cannot contain you. Surely this house which I have built cannot contain you. 28But please listen to my prayer and my request, because I am your servant. LORD my God, hear this prayer your servant prays to you today. 29Night and day please watch over this Temple where you have said, ‘I will be worshiped there.’ Hear the prayer I pray facing this Temple. 30Hear my prayers and the prayers of your people Israel when we pray facing this place. Hear from your home in heaven, and when you hear, forgive us.

31“If someone wrongs another person, he will be brought to the altar in this Temple. If he swears an oath that he is not guilty, 32then hear in heaven. Judge the case, punish the guilty, but declare that the innocent person is not guilty.

33“When your people, the Israelites, sin against you, their enemies will defeat them. But if they come back to you and praise you and pray to you in this Temple, 34then hear them in heaven. Forgive the sins of your people Israel, and bring them back to the land you gave to their ancestors.

35“When they sin against you, you will stop the rain from falling on their land. Then they will pray, facing this place and praising you; they will stop sinning when you make them suffer. 36When this happens, please hear their prayer in heaven, and forgive the sins of your servants, the Israelites. Teach them to do what is right. Then please send rain to this land you have given particularly to them.

37“At times the land will become so dry that no food will grow, or a great sickness will spread among the people. Sometimes all the crops will be destroyed by locusts or grasshoppers. Your people will be attacked in their cities by their enemy or will become sick. 38When any of these things happen, the people will become truly sorry. If your people spread their hands in prayer toward this Temple, 39then hear their prayers from your home in heaven. Forgive and treat each person as he should be treated because you know what is in a person’s heart. Only you know what is in everyone’s heart. 40Then your people will respect you as long as they live in this land you gave to our ancestors.

41-42“People who are not Israelites, foreigners from other lands, will hear about your greatness and power. They will come from far away to pray at this Temple. 43Then hear from your home in heaven, and do whatever they ask you. Then people everywhere will know you and respect you, just as your people in Israel do. Then everyone will know I built this Temple as a place to worship you.

44“When your people go out to fight their enemies along some road on which you send them, your people will pray to you, facing the city which you have chosen and the Temple I have built for you. 45Then hear in heaven their prayers, and do what is right.

46“Everyone sins, so your people will also sin against you. You will become angry with them and hand them over to their enemies. Their enemies will capture them and take them away to their

---

8:21 Ark of the Agreement: Jeremiah 3:16–17

8:26 Servant of the Lord: 1 Kings 8:29

8:29 Servant of the Lord: Job 1:8

8:31 Neighbor: Proverbs 3:27–29

8:31–32 An oath was used in cases where it was not humanly possible to determine the truth of a statement (Exodus 22:1–13; Numbers 5:11–31). This brought an end to argument (Hebrews 6:16). Of course, it is not valid if the person swearing the oath does not take it seriously.

8:35 Repentance: Isaiah 1:16–17

8:37 Famine: 2 Kings 6:24–25

RUTH

RUTH 1

What is the story about Ruth, a woman and a Gentile, doing in the Old Testament?

From an ancient Israelite perspective, Ruth seems poor material for a heroine. She is a Moabitess, a citizen of a nation condemned for its unkindness to Israel (Deuteronomy 23:3–4; Nehemiah 13:1–2). Furthermore, she was a woman and lived in poverty. As a widow and a foreigner living away from the protection and support of her own family and people, she was among the most powerless and victimized members of Israelite society.

But Ruth did more than passively receive Boaz's kindness. She was a heroine in her own right, equal in standing to her Israelite rescuer. She was the ideal Gentile, the appropriate counterpart to the virtuous Boaz.

The Book of Ruth makes this point by using identical expressions to describe the qualities of both Boaz and Ruth. Boaz was Naomi's "rich relative" (Ruth 2:1), but the same Hebrew word is used when Boaz tells Ruth that she is "a good woman" (Ruth 3:11). The point is that they share the same noble character. The other virtue Boaz and Ruth share is "kindness" (Ruth 2:20; 3:10). This refers to their commitment to the welfare of the family of Elimelech.

"Kindness" is also a quality of God himself (Ruth 1:8) so it is not surprising that the story focuses on the virtue of keeping agreements in its portrayal of Ruth.

In ancient Israel, when a woman married, she transferred her allegiance from her father's family to her husband's family (Psalm 45:10–11; Judges 1:13–15; 1 Samuel 19:11–14). When Ruth married Mahlon, she was expected to devote herself to the welfare of his family. But after Elimelech and his sons died, Naomi released Ruth and Orpah from this duty. They were free to return to their families and resume their lives as Moabites (Ruth 1:8, 11–12). In contrast to Orpah, Ruth refused to leave. Her commitment to the welfare of the family went beyond what social custom expected. She turned her back on her own family and homeland and continued to seek the welfare of her husband's family. First, she accepted the responsibility of providing food for Naomi (Ruth 2:2, 18). Second, when Ruth boldly asked that Boaz marry her (3:9), she was seeking to revive the family line of Elimelech and Mahlon. Ruth based her appeal to Boaz on the fact that he was a "close relative"—a protector—of Naomi and the family of Elimelech. By custom, the first son from the marriage of Ruth and Boaz was also regarded as the heir of Mahlon (Ruth 4:10, 13–15; Deuteronomy 25:5–10; Genesis 38). By marrying Boaz, Ruth showed the depth of her commitment to her dead husband and his family long after she had been released from any obligations to them. In so doing, she went far beyond what would be expected of an Israelite (Ruth 4:3–6), let alone a Gentile.

Ruth was also an ideal Gentile because of her commitment to Israel's God. She is contrasted with Orpah who returned to her family. But that also meant returning to the gods of Moab (Ruth 1:15). Ruth, on the other hand, remained committed to Naomi, to the family of her dead husband, and more importantly, to the God of that family (Ruth 1:16–17). When Ruth says, "Your God will be my God" (1:16), these are the words of an ideal Gentile who rejected her gods and turned to follow the God of Israel. At this point, Ruth may also be contrasted with other Moabite wives of the Old Testament. Among Solomon's many wives were Moabites (1 Kings 11:1). Unlike Ruth, they continued to worship the gods of their homeland and so led Solomon away from following the Lord (1 Kings 11:3–4, 7). Later, in Ezra and Nehemiah, marriage between the men of Judah and Moabite women seriously threatened the spiritual purity of the nation (Ezra 9:1–2; Nehemiah 13:23–27). Ruth was different from these women. Her commitment to an Israelite family and to the God of Israel showed her to be a worthy successor to Leah and Rachel, the mothers of Israel (Ruth 4:11), and a noble ancestor of one of the greatest Israelites, King David (Ruth 4:22). Placed between these heroes of Israel, Ruth the Moabitess is portrayed as a "true Israelite." The story of Ruth's inclusion into the people of Israel expresses the Old Testament's conviction that the kingdom of God was meant to be much larger than national Israel. Matthew's gospel shares this viewpoint. In the Great Commission (Matthew 28:18–20) Jesus commands his Israelite disciples to take the Good News of salvation to "all people in the world." For Matthew, Ruth is a prototype of those Gentiles who would follow Christ. This is why she joins three other Gentiles—Tamar, Rahab, and Uriah—in the list of Jesus' ancestors (Matthew 1:3–6). She is an Old Testament example of the ideal Gentile who is included in the people of God.

Ruth: For additional scriptures on this topic go to Genesis 38:6–11.

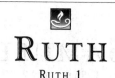

SAMUEL

1 SAMUEL 12

How did Samuel lead Israel? How does his leadership point to the leadership of Jesus Christ?

When God called Samuel (1 Samuel 3), Israel was in a leadership crisis. There was no prophet who could guide the people in their relationship with the Lord (1 Samuel 3:1). The priesthood had become corrupt (1 Samuel 2:12, 17), and the nation was hard-pressed by their enemies and had no one to lead them. God raised up Samuel to meet these three needs. Samuel led Israel as a prophet, priest, and judge. His leadership in Israel is unique because he is the only individual in the Old Testament who held all three offices.

As a priest, Samuel offered sacrifices (1 Samuel 7:9–10; 9:12) and obeyed the Lord, unlike the priests Phinehas and Hophni (1 Samuel 2:17–3:1). He also offered up prayers to God on behalf of the Israelites (1 Samuel 7:7–8; 12:23). Both prayers and sacrifices were a priest's means of interceding on behalf of the people in the presence of God.

Samuel fulfilled the role of prophet by bringing God's messages to the people. Samuel was "a true prophet of the LORD" because God "did not let any of Samuel's messages fail to come true" (1 Samuel 3:19, 20; see also Deuteronomy 18:21–22). Not only did prophets foretell future events, but they delivered messages from God concerning situations in the present. For example, Samuel brought God's command to Saul regarding the fate of the Amalekites and their possessions (1 Samuel 15:1–3) and later expressed God's displeasure with Saul's disobedience (1 Samuel 15:16–18). After Saul became king, Samuel's major role was that of prophet.

Before kings ruled in Israel, God periodically raised up leaders called "judges" who led the nation during turbulent times (1 Samuel 12:9–11; Judges 2). These leaders did have judicial functions, but they also led the nation militarily and spiritually. According to 1 Samuel 7:15, Samuel judged Israel "all his life." One of his recorded activities as judge was gathering Israelites to Mizpah and leading them in repentance and renewal (1 Samuel 7:5–6). Samuel's actions were instrumental in Israel's defeat of the Philistines at Mizpah (1 Samuel 7:8–13).

A basic principle of interpreting and understanding the Bible is that events, things, or people in the Old Testament are often similar to events, things, and people in the New Testament. The substance of the New Testament can be found in the Old Testament, and the meaning of the Old Testament is revealed and explained in the New Testament. Images or pictures of Christ in the Old Testament can seem fuzzy and shadowy, but Jesus, the Light of the World, brings them into focus (see Hebrews 10:1). Images of Christ in the Old Testament are not understandable without the New Testament. The three roles of leadership filled by Samuel—prophet, priest, and judge/king)—all point to the work and ministry of Jesus Christ.

Deuteronomy 18:16–19 defines a prophet as someone who speaks God's very own words to people. As a prophet, Jesus speaks God's word and his will. One mark of Jesus' ministry which distinguished him from other teachers is that "he taught like a person who had authority." Because Jesus is one with the Father (John 10:30), he hears and says exactly what the Father commands (John 14:10). Jesus continues his role as a prophet in the lives of believers today through his word in the Bible.

Priests intercede before God with sacrifices and prayers on behalf of a community. In the Old Testament, God graciously accepted the life of the sacrificial animal instead of taking the life of the person offering the sacrifice as punishment for sin. Jesus was both the priest who offered the sacrifice, and he himself was the sacrifice to take away the sins of his people. Jesus' life was the perfect sacrifice because it did away with the need for any more animal sacrifices (Hebrews 9:26b).

The office of judge was limited to a very specific time in Israel's history, but its major functions of providing direction and leadership for God's people are part of kingship. As the Son of God, King Jesus has been given "all power in heaven and on earth" (Matthew 28:18). But Jesus has a kingdom which is not an earthly kingdom (John 18:36–37). Colossians 1:13 says, "God has freed us from the power of darkness, and he brought us into the kingdom of his dear Son." Jesus rules his kingdom by ruling in the hearts of his people through the Holy Spirit. One day, Jesus will return to earth as a kingly warrior and subdue all those who oppose him (Revelation 19:11–16).⚭

⚭**Samuel:** For additional scriptures on this topic go to 1 Samuel 1:1–20.

countries far or near. 47Your people will be sorry for their sins when they are held as prisoners in another country. They will be sorry and pray to you in the land where they are held as prisoners, saying, 'We have sinned. We have done wrong and acted wickedly.' 48They will truly turn back to you in the land of their enemies. They will pray to you, facing this land you gave their ancestors, this city you have chosen, and the Temple I have built for you. 49Then hear their prayers from your home in heaven, and do what is right. 50Forgive your people of all their sins and for turning against you. Make those who have captured them show them mercy. 51Remember, they are your special people. You brought them out of Egypt, as if you were pulling them out of a blazing furnace.

52"Give your attention to my prayers and the prayers of your people Israel. Listen to them anytime they ask you for help. 53You chose them from all the nations on earth to be your very own people. This is what you promised through Moses your servant when you brought our ancestors out of Egypt, Lord GOD."

54Solomon prayed this prayer to the LORD, kneeling in front of the altar with his arms raised toward heaven. When he finished praying, he got up. 55Then, in a loud voice, he stood and blessed all the people of Israel, saying: 56"Praise the LORD! He promised he would give rest to his people Israel, and he has given us rest. The LORD has kept all the good promises he gave through his servant Moses. 57May the LORD our God be with us as he was with our ancestors. May he never leave us, 58and may he turn us to himself so we will follow him. Let us obey all the laws and commands he gave our ancestors. 59May the LORD our God remember this prayer day and night and do what is right for his servant and his people Israel day by day. 60Then all the people of the world will know the LORD is the only true God. 61You must fully obey the LORD our God and follow all his laws and commands. Continue to obey in the future as you do now."

Sacrifices Are Offered

62Then King Solomon and all Israel with him offered sacrifices to the LORD. 63Solomon killed twenty-two thousand cattle and one hundred twenty thousand sheep as fellowship offerings. So the king and all the people gave the Temple to the LORD.

64On that day King Solomon made holy the middle part of the courtyard which is in front of the Temple of the LORD. There he offered whole burnt offerings, grain offerings, and the fat of the fellowship offerings. He offered them in the courtyard, because the bronze altar before the LORD was too small to hold all the burnt offerings, the grain offerings, and the fat of the fellowship offerings.

65Solomon and all the Israelites celebrated the other festival that came at that time. People came from as far away as Lebo Hamath and the brook of Egypt. A great many people celebrated before the LORD for seven days, then seven more days, for a total of fourteen days. 66On the following day Solomon sent the people home. They blessed the king as they went, happy because of all the good things the LORD had done for his servant David and his people Israel.

The Lord Appears to Solomon Again

9 Solomon finished building the Temple of the LORD and his royal palace and everything he wanted to build. 2Then the LORD appeared to him again just as he had done before, in Gibeon. 3The LORD said to him: "I have heard your prayer and what you have asked me to do. You built this Temple, and I have made it a holy place. I will be worshiped there forever and will watch over it and protect it always.

4"But you must serve me as your father David did; he was fair and sincere. You must obey all I have commanded and keep my laws and rules. 5If you do, I will make your kingdom strong. This is the promise I made to your father David—that someone from his family would always rule Israel.

6"But you and your children must follow me and obey the laws and commands I have given you. You must not serve or worship other gods. 7If you do, I will force Israel to leave the land I have given them, and I will leave this Temple that I have made holy. All the nations will make fun of Israel and speak evil about them. 8If the Temple is destroyed, everyone who passes by will be shocked. They will make fun of you and ask, 'Why did the LORD do this terrible thing to this land and this Temple?' 9People will answer, 'This happened because they left the LORD their God. This was the God who brought their ancestors out of Egypt, but they decided to follow other gods. They worshiped and served those gods, so the LORD brought all this disaster on them.'"

Solomon's Other Achievements

10By the end of twenty years, King Solomon had built two buildings—the Temple of the LORD and the royal palace. 11At that time King Solomon gave

8:51 Sin: Psalms 51

9:5 Integrity: Job 2:3

twenty towns in Galilee to Hiram king of Tyre,
because Hiram had helped with the buildings.
Hiram had given Solomon all the cedar, pine, and
gold he wanted. 12So Hiram traveled from Tyre to
see the towns Solomon had given him, but when
he saw them, he was not pleased. 13He asked,
"What good are these towns you have given me,
my brother?" So he named them the Land of
Cabul, and they are still called that today. 14Hiram
had sent Solomon about nine thousand pounds of
gold.

15This is the account of the forced labor Solomon
used to build the Temple and the palace. He had
them fill in the land and build the wall around
Jerusalem. He also had them rebuild the cities of
Hazor, Megiddo, and Gezer. 16(In the past the king
of Egypt had attacked and captured Gezer. After
burning it, he killed the Canaanites who lived
there. Then he gave it as a wedding present to his
daughter, who married Solomon. 17So Solomon
rebuilt it.) He also built the cities of Lower Beth
Horon 18and Baalath, as well as Tadmor, which is
in the desert. 19King Solomon also built cities for
storing grain and supplies and cities for his chariots and horses. He built whatever he wanted in
Jerusalem, Lebanon, and everywhere he ruled.

20There were other people in the land who were
not Israelites—Amorites, Hittites, Perizzites,
Hivites, and Jebusites. 21They were descendants
of people that the Israelites had not destroyed.
Solomon forced them to work for him as slaves,
as is still true today. 22But Solomon did not make
slaves of the Israelites. They were his soldiers,
government leaders, officers, captains, chariot
commanders, and drivers.

23These were his most important officers over
the work. There were five hundred fifty supervisors over the people who did the work on Solomon's projects.

24The daughter of the king of Egypt moved from
the old part of Jerusalem to the palace that Solomon had built for her. Then Solomon filled in the
surrounding land.

25Three times each year Solomon offered whole
burnt offerings and fellowship offerings on the altar
he had built for the LORD. He also burned incense
before the LORD. So he finished the work on the
Temple.

26King Solomon also built ships at Ezion Geber,
a town near Elath on the shore of the Red Sea, in
the land of Edom. 27Hiram had skilled sailors, so
he sent them to serve in these ships with Solomon's men. 28The ships sailed to Ophir and brought
back about thirty-two thousand pounds of gold to
King Solomon.

The Queen of Sheba Visits Solomon

10 When the queen of Sheba heard about Solomon, she came to test him with hard questions. 2She traveled to Jerusalem with a large group
of servants and camels carrying spices, jewels, and
much gold. When she came to Solomon, she talked
with him about all she had in mind, 3and Solomon
answered all her questions. Nothing was too hard
for him to explain to her. 4The queen of Sheba
learned that Solomon was very wise. She saw the
palace he had built, 5the food on his table, his many
officers, the palace servants, and their good clothes.
She saw the servants who served him at feasts and
the whole burnt offerings he made in the Temple
of the LORD. All these things amazed her.

6So she said to King Solomon, "What I heard in
my own country about your achievements and wisdom is true. 7I could not believe it then, but now I
have come and seen it with my own eyes. I was not
told even half of it! Your wisdom and wealth are
much greater than I had heard. 8Your men and officers are very lucky, because in always serving you,
they are able to hear your wisdom. 9Praise the LORD
your God, who was pleased to make you king of
Israel. The LORD has constant love for Israel, so he
made you king to keep justice and to rule fairly."

10Then she gave the king about nine thousand
pounds of gold and many spices and jewels. No one
since that time has brought more spices than the
queen of Sheba gave to King Solomon.

11(Hiram's ships brought gold from Ophir, as well
as much juniper wood and jewels. 12Solomon used
the juniper wood to build supports for the Temple
of the LORD and the palace, and to make harps and
lyres for the musicians. Such fine juniper wood has
not been brought in or been seen since that time.)

13King Solomon gave the queen of Sheba everything she wanted and asked for, in addition to what
he had already given her of his wealth. Then she
and her servants returned to her own country.⚭

Solomon's Wealth

14Every year King Solomon received about fifty
thousand pounds of gold. 15Besides that, he also
received gold from the traders and merchants, as
well as from the kings of Arabia and governors of
the land.

16King Solomon made two hundred large shields
of hammered gold, each of which contained about
seven and one-half pounds of gold. 17He also made

9:13 *Cabul.* This name sounds like the Hebrew word for "worthless."

⚭**10:13 Reputation:** Proverbs 12:2

three hundred smaller shields of hammered gold, each of which contained about four pounds of gold. The king put them in the Palace of the Forest of Lebanon.

18The king built a large throne of ivory and covered it with fine gold. 19The throne had six steps on it, and its back was round at the top. There were armrests on both sides of the chair, and each armrest had a lion beside it. 20Twelve lions stood on the six steps, one lion at each end of each step. Nothing like this had ever been made for any other kingdom. 21All of Solomon's drinking cups, as well as the dishes in the Palace of the Forest of Lebanon, were made of pure gold. Nothing was made from silver, because silver was not valuable in Solomon's time.

22King Solomon also had many trading ships at sea, along with Hiram's ships. Every three years the ships returned, bringing back gold, silver, ivory, apes, and baboons.

23So Solomon had more riches and wisdom than all the other kings on earth. 24People everywhere wanted to see King Solomon and listen to the wisdom God had given him. 25Every year those who came brought gifts of silver and gold, clothes, weapons, spices, horses, and mules.

26Solomon had fourteen hundred chariots and twelve thousand horses. He kept some in special cities for the chariots, and others he kept with him in Jerusalem. 27In Jerusalem Solomon made silver as common as stones and cedar trees as common as the fig trees on the western hills. 28He imported horses from Egypt and Kue. His traders bought them in Kue. 29A chariot from Egypt cost about fifteen pounds of silver, and a horse cost nearly four pounds of silver. Solomon's traders also sold horses and chariots to all the kings of the Hittites and the Arameans.

Solomon's Many Wives

11 King Solomon loved many women who were not from Israel. He loved the daughter of the king of Egypt, as well as women of the Moabites, Ammonites, Edomites, Sidonians, and Hittites. 2The LORD had told the Israelites, "You must not marry people of other nations. If you do, they will cause you to follow their gods." But Solomon fell in love with these women. 3He had seven hundred wives who were from royal families and three hundred slave women who gave birth to his children. His wives caused him to turn away from God. 4As Solomon grew old, his wives caused him to follow other gods. He did not follow the LORD completely as his father David had done. 5Solomon worshiped Ashtoreth, the goddess of the people of Sidon, and Molech, the hated god of the Ammonites. 6So Solomon did what the LORD said was wrong and did not follow the LORD completely as his father David had done.

7On a hill east of Jerusalem, Solomon built two places for worship. One was a place to worship Chemosh, the hated god of the Moabites, and the other was a place to worship Molech, the hated god of the Ammonites. 8Solomon did the same thing for all his foreign wives so they could burn incense and offer sacrifices to their gods.

9The LORD had appeared to Solomon twice, but the king turned away from following the LORD, the God of Israel. The LORD was angry with Solomon, 10because he had commanded Solomon not to follow other gods. But Solomon did not obey the LORD's command. 11So the LORD said to Solomon, "Because you have chosen to break your agreement with me and have not obeyed my commands, I will tear your kingdom away from you and give it to one of your officers. 12But I will not take it away while you are alive because of my love for your father David. I will tear it away from your son when he becomes king. 13I will not tear away all the kingdom from him, but I will leave him one tribe to rule. I will do this because of David, my servant, and because of Jerusalem, the city I have chosen."

Solomon's Enemies

14The LORD caused Hadad the Edomite, a member of the family of the king of Edom, to become Solomon's enemy. 15Earlier, David had defeated Edom. When Joab, the commander of David's army, went into Edom to bury the dead, he killed all the males. 16Joab and all the Israelites stayed in Edom for six months and killed every male in Edom. 17At that time Hadad was only a young boy, so he ran away to Egypt with some of his father's officers. 18They left Midian and went to Paran, where they were joined by other men. Then they all went to Egypt to see the king, who gave Hadad a house, some food, and some land.

19The king liked Hadad so much he gave Hadad a wife—the sister of Tahpenes, the king's wife. 20They had a son named Genubath. Queen Tahpenes brought him up in the royal palace with the king's own children.

11:1 Solomon: 1 Kings 11:40

11:1–8 Rather than depend on God for his needs, King Solomon married many foreign wives. Such practices served as insurance policies for peace with neighboring nations. This was a problem because Solomon's wives brought their false gods with them. God wanted Solomon to display to the nations the good news of his saving power. Instead, Solomon brought the worship of false gods into Israel in a very big way. Sadly, idolatry led God's people away from him.

21While he was in Egypt, Hadad heard that David had died and that Joab, the commander of the army, was dead also. So Hadad said to the king, "Let me go; I will return to my own country."

22"Why do you want to go back to your own country?" the king asked. "What haven't I given you here?"

"Nothing," Hadad answered, "but please, let me go."

23God also caused another man to be Solomon's enemy—Rezon son of Eliada. Rezon had run away from his master, Hadadezer king of Zobah. 24After David defeated the army of Zobah, Rezon gathered some men and became the leader of a small army. They went to Damascus and settled there, and Rezon became king of Damascus. 25Rezon ruled Aram, and he hated Israel. So he was an enemy of Israel all the time Solomon was alive. Both Rezon and Hadad made trouble for Israel.

26Jeroboam son of Nebat was one of Solomon's officers. He was an Ephraimite from the town of Zeredah, and he was the son of a widow named Zeruah. Jeroboam turned against the king.

27This is the story of how Jeroboam turned against the king. Solomon was filling in the land and repairing the wall of Jerusalem, the city of David, his father. 28Jeroboam was a capable man, and Solomon saw that this young man was a good worker. So Solomon put him over all the workers from the tribes of Ephraim and Manasseh.

29One day as Jeroboam was leaving Jerusalem, Ahijah, the prophet from Shiloh, who was wearing a new coat, met him on the road. The two men were alone out in the country. 30Ahijah took his new coat and tore it into twelve pieces. 31Then he said to Jeroboam, "Take ten pieces of this coat for yourself. The LORD, the God of Israel, says: 'I will tear the kingdom away from Solomon and give you ten tribes. 32But I will allow him to control one tribe. I will do this for the sake of my servant David and for Jerusalem, the city I have chosen from all the tribes of Israel. 33I will do this because Solomon has stopped following me and has worshiped the Sidonian god Ashtoreth, the Moabite god Chemosh, and the Ammonite god Molech. Solomon has not obeyed me by doing what I said is right and obeying my laws and commands, as his father David did.

34"'But I will not take all the kingdom away from Solomon. I will let him rule all his life because of my servant David, whom I chose, who obeyed all my commands and laws. 35But I will take the kingdom away from his son, and I will allow you to rule over the ten tribes. 36I will allow Solomon's son to continue to rule over one tribe so that there will always be a descendant of David, my servant, in Jerusalem, the city where I chose to be worshiped. 37But I will make you rule over everything you want. You will rule over all of Israel, 38and I will always be with you if you do what I say is right. You must obey all my commands. If you obey my laws and commands as David did, I will be with you. I will make your family a lasting family of kings, as I did for David, and give Israel to you. 39I will punish David's children because of this, but I will not punish them forever.'"

Solomon's Death

40Solomon tried to kill Jeroboam, but he ran away to Egypt, to Shishak king of Egypt, where he stayed until Solomon died.∞

41Everything else King Solomon did, and the wisdom he showed, is written in the book of the history of Solomon. 42Solomon ruled in Jerusalem over all Israel for forty years. 43Then he died and was buried in Jerusalem, the city of David, his father. And his son Rehoboam became king in his place.

Israel Turns Against Rehoboam

12 Rehoboam went to Shechem, where all the Israelites had gone to make him king. 2Jeroboam son of Nebat was still in Egypt, where he had gone to escape from Solomon. When Jeroboam heard about Rehoboam being made king, he was living in Egypt. 3After the people sent for him, he and the people went to Rehoboam and said to him, 4"Your father forced us to work very hard. Now, make it easier for us, and don't make us work as hard as he did. Then we will serve you."

5Rehoboam answered, "Go away for three days, and then come back to me." So the people left.

6King Rehoboam asked the older leaders who had advised Solomon during his lifetime, "How do you think I should answer these people?"

7They said, "You should be like a servant to them today. If you serve them and give them a kind answer, they will serve you always."

8But Rehoboam rejected this advice. Instead, he asked the young men who had grown up with him and who served as his advisers. 9Rehoboam asked them, "What is your advice? How should we answer these people who said, 'Don't make us work as hard as your father did'?"

10The young men who had grown up with him answered, "Those people said to you, 'Your father

∞**11:40 Solomon:** 1 Chronicles 29:28

forced us to work very hard. Now make our work
easier.' You should tell them, 'My little finger is
bigger than my father's legs. 11He forced you to
work hard, but I will make you work even harder.
My father beat you with whips, but I will beat you
with whips that have sharp points.'"
12Rehoboam had told the people, "Come back
to me in three days." So after three days Jeroboam
and all the people returned to Rehoboam. 13King
Rehoboam spoke cruel words to them, because he
had rejected the advice the older leaders had given
him. 14He followed the advice of the young men
and said to the people, "My father forced you to
work hard, but I will make you work even harder.
My father beat you with whips, but I will beat you
with whips that have sharp points." 15So the king
did not listen to the people. The LORD caused this
to happen to keep the promise he had made to
Jeroboam son of Nebat through Ahijah, a prophet
from Shiloh.
16When all the Israelites saw that the new king
refused to listen to them, they said to the king,
"We have no share in David!
We have no part in the son of Jesse!
People of Israel, let's go to our own homes!
Let David's son rule his own people!"
So the Israelites went home. 17But Rehoboam still
ruled over the Israelites who lived in the towns of
Judah.
18Adoniram was in charge of the forced labor.
When Rehoboam sent him to the people of Israel,
they threw stones at him until he died. But King
Rehoboam ran to his chariot and escaped to
Jerusalem. 19Since then, Israel has been against
the family of David.
20When all the Israelites heard that Jeroboam
had returned, they called him to a meeting and
made him king over all Israel. Only the tribe of
Judah continued to follow the family of David.
21When Rehoboam arrived in Jerusalem, he
gathered one hundred eighty thousand of the best
soldiers from the tribes of Judah and Benjamin. As
son of Solomon, Rehoboam wanted to fight the
people of Israel to take back his kingdom.
22But God spoke his word to Shemaiah, a man of
God, saying, 23"Speak to Solomon's son Rehoboam,
the king of Judah, and to all the people of Judah and
Benjamin and the rest of the people. Say to them,
24'The LORD says you must not go to war against
your brothers, the Israelites. Every one of you
should go home, because I made all these things
happen.'" So they obeyed the LORD's command
and went home as the LORD had commanded.
25Then Jeroboam made Shechem in the mountains of Ephraim a very strong city, and he lived
there. He also went to the city of Peniel and made
it stronger.

Jeroboam Builds Golden Calves

26Jeroboam said to himself, "The kingdom will
probably go back to David's family. 27If the people
continue going to the Temple of the LORD in
Jerusalem to offer sacrifices, they will want to be
ruled again by Rehoboam. Then they will kill me
and follow Rehoboam king of Judah."
28King Jeroboam asked for advice. Then he made
two golden calves. "It is too long a journey for you
to go to Jerusalem to worship," he said to the people. "Israel, here are your gods who brought you
out of Egypt." 29Jeroboam put one golden calf in
the city of Bethel and the other in the city of Dan.
30This became a very great sin, because the people
traveled as far as Dan to worship the calf there.
31Jeroboam built temples on the places of worship. He also chose priests from all the people, not
just from the tribe of Levi. 32And he started a new
festival on the fifteenth day of the eighth month,
just like the festival in Judah. During that time the
king offered sacrifices on the altar, along with sacrifices to the calves in Bethel he had made. He
also chose priests in Bethel to serve at the places
of worship he had made. 33So Jeroboam chose his
own time for a festival for the Israelites—the fifteenth day of the eighth month. During that time
he offered sacrifices on the altar he had built in
Bethel. He set up a festival for the Israelites and
offered sacrifices on the altar.

The Man of God Speaks Against Bethel

13 The LORD commanded a man of God from
Judah to go to Bethel. When he arrived, Jeroboam was standing by the altar to offer a sacrifice.
2The LORD had commanded the man of God to
speak against the altar. The man said, "Altar, altar,
the LORD says to you: 'David's family will have a
son named Josiah. The priests for the places of
worship now make their sacrifices on you, but
Josiah will sacrifice those priests on you. Human
bones will be burned on you.'" 3That same day the
man of God gave proof that these things would
happen. "This is the LORD's sign that this will happen," he said. "This altar will break apart, and the
ashes on it will fall to the ground."
4When King Jeroboam heard what the man of
God said about the altar in Bethel, the king raised
his hand from the altar and pointed at the man.

12:33 Idolatry: Isaiah 40:18–20
12:33 Samaria: 1 Kings 16:21–24

"Take him!" he said. But when the king said this, his arm was paralyzed, and he could not move it. 5The altar also broke into pieces, and its ashes fell to the ground. This was the sign the LORD had told the man of God to give.

6Then the king said to the man of God, "Please pray to the LORD your God for me, and ask him to heal my arm."

So the man of God prayed to the LORD, and the king's arm was healed, becoming as it was before.

7Then the king said to the man of God, "Please come home and eat with me, and I will give you a gift."

8But the man of God answered the king, "Even if you gave me half of your kingdom, I would not go with you. I will not eat or drink anything in this place. 9The LORD commanded me not to eat or drink anything nor to return on the same road by which I came." 10So he took a different road and did not return on the same road by which he had come to Bethel.

11Now an old prophet was living in Bethel. His sons came and told him what the man of God had done there that day. They also told their father what he had said to King Jeroboam. 12The father asked, "Which road did he use when he left?" So his sons showed him the road the man of God from Judah had taken. 13Then the prophet told his sons to put a saddle on his donkey. So they saddled the donkey, and he left.

14He went after the man of God and found him sitting under an oak tree. The prophet asked, "Are you the man of God who came from Judah?"

The man answered, "Yes, I am."

15The prophet said, "Please come home and eat with me."

16"I can't go home with you," the man of God answered. "I can't eat or drink with you in this place. 17The LORD said to me, 'Don't eat or drink anything there or return on the same road by which you came.'"

18Then the old prophet said, "But I also am a prophet like you." Then he told a lie. He said, "An angel from the LORD came to me and told me to bring you to my home. He said you should eat and drink with me." 19So the man of God went to the old prophet's house, and he ate and drank with him there.

20While they were sitting at the table, the LORD spoke his word to the old prophet. 21The old prophet cried out to the man of God from Judah, "The LORD said you did not obey him! He said you did not do what the LORD your God commanded you. 22The LORD commanded you not to eat or drink anything in this place, but you came back and ate and drank. So your body will not be buried in your family grave."

23After the man of God finished eating and drinking, the prophet put a saddle on his donkey for him, and the man left. 24As he was traveling home, a lion attacked and killed him. His body lay on the road, with the donkey and the lion standing nearby. 25Some men who were traveling on that road saw the body and the lion standing nearby. So they went to the city where the old prophet lived and told what they had seen.

26The old prophet who had brought back the man of God heard what had happened. "It is the man of God who did not obey the LORD's command," he said. "So the LORD sent a lion to kill him, just as he said he would."

27Then the prophet said to his sons, "Put a saddle on my donkey," which they did. 28The old prophet went out and found the body lying on the road, with the donkey and the lion still standing nearby. The lion had not eaten the body or hurt the donkey. 29The prophet put the body on his donkey and carried it back to the city to have a time of sadness for him and to bury him. 30The prophet buried the body in his own family grave, and they were sad for the man of God and said, "Oh, my brother."

31After the prophet buried the body, he said to his sons, "When I die, bury me in this same grave. Put my bones next to his. 32Through him the LORD spoke against the altar at Bethel and against the places of worship in the towns of Samaria. What the LORD spoke through him will certainly come true."

33After this incident King Jeroboam did not stop doing evil. He continued to choose priests for the places of worship from among all the people. Anyone who wanted to be a priest for the places of worship was allowed to be one. 34In this way the family of Jeroboam sinned, and this sin caused its ruin and destruction from the earth.

Jeroboam's Son Dies

14 At that time Jeroboam's son Abijah became very sick. 2So Jeroboam said to his wife, "Go to Shiloh to see the prophet Ahijah. He is the one who said I would become king of Israel. But dress yourself so people won't know you are my wife. 3Take the prophet ten loaves of bread, some cakes, and a jar of honey. Then ask him what will happen to our son, and he will tell you." 4So the king's wife did as he said and went to Ahijah's home in Shiloh.

Now Ahijah was very old and blind. 5The LORD said to him, "Jeroboam's son is sick, and Jeroboam's wife is coming to ask you about him. When she arrives, she will pretend to be someone else." Then the LORD told Ahijah what to say.

[6]When Ahijah heard her walking to the door, he said, "Come in, wife of Jeroboam. Why are you pretending to be someone else? I have bad news for you. [7]Go back and tell Jeroboam that this is what the LORD, the God of Israel, says: 'Jeroboam, I chose you from among all the people and made you the leader of my people Israel. [8]I tore the kingdom away from David's family, and I gave it to you. But you are not like my servant David, who always obeyed my commands and followed me with all his heart. He did only what I said was right.⚭ [9]But you have done more evil than anyone who ruled before you. You have quit following me and have made other gods and idols of metal. This has made me very angry, [10]so I will soon bring disaster to your family. I will kill all the men in your family, both slaves and free men. I will destroy your family as completely as fire burns up manure. [11]Anyone from your family who dies in the city will be eaten by dogs, and those who die in the fields will be eaten by the birds. The LORD has spoken.'"

[12]Then Ahijah said to Jeroboam's wife, "Go home now. As soon as you enter your city, your son will die, [13]and all Israel will be sad for him and bury him. He is the only one of Jeroboam's family who will be buried, because he is the only one in the king's family who pleased the LORD, the God of Israel.

[14]"The LORD will put a new king over Israel, who will destroy Jeroboam's family, and this will happen soon. [15]Then the LORD will punish Israel, which will be like grass moving in the water. The LORD will pull up Israel from this good land, the land he gave their ancestors. He will scatter Israel beyond the Euphrates River, because he is angry with the people. They made the LORD angry when they set up idols to worship Asherah. [16]Jeroboam sinned, and then he made the people of Israel sin. So the LORD will let the people of Israel be defeated."

[17]Then Jeroboam's wife left and returned to Tirzah. As soon as she entered her home, the boy died. [18]After they buried him, all Israel had a time of sadness for him, just as the LORD had said through his servant, the prophet Ahijah.

[19]Everything else Jeroboam did is written in the book of the history of the kings of Israel. He fought wars and continued to rule the people, [20]serving as king for twenty-two years. Then he died, and his son Nadab became king in his place.

The Death of Rehoboam

[21]Solomon's son Rehoboam was forty-one years old when he became king of Judah. His mother was Naamah from Ammon. Rehoboam ruled in Jerusalem for seventeen years. (The LORD had chosen that city from all the land of Israel as the place where he would be worshiped.)

[22]The people of Judah did what the LORD said was wrong. Their sins made the LORD very angry, even more angry than he had been at their ancestors. [23]The people built stone pillars and places to worship gods and Asherah idols on every high hill and under every green tree. [24]There were even male prostitutes in the land. They acted like the people who had lived in the land before the Israelites. They had done many evil things, and God had taken the land away from them.

[25]During the fifth year Rehoboam was king, Shishak king of Egypt attacked Jerusalem. [26]He took the treasures from the Temple of the LORD and the king's palace. He took everything, even the gold shields Solomon had made. [27]So King Rehoboam made bronze shields to put in their place and gave them to the commanders of the guards for the palace gates. [28]Whenever the king went to the Temple of the LORD, the guards carried the shields. Later, they would put them back in the guardroom.

[29]Everything else King Rehoboam did is written in the book of the history of the kings of Judah. [30]There was war between Rehoboam and Jeroboam the whole time. [31]Rehoboam, son of Naamah from Ammon, died and was buried with his ancestors in Jerusalem, and his son Abijah became king in his place.

Abijah King of Judah

15 Abijah became king of Judah during the eighteenth year Jeroboam son of Nebat was king of Israel. [2]Abijah ruled in Jerusalem for three years. His mother was Maacah daughter of Abishalom. [3]He did all the same sins his father before him had done. Abijah was not faithful to the LORD his God as David, his great-grandfather, had been. [4]Because the LORD loved David, the LORD gave him a kingdom in Jerusalem and allowed him to have a son to be king after him. The LORD also kept Jerusalem safe. [5]David always did what the LORD said was right and obeyed his commands all his life, except the one time when David sinned against Uriah the Hittite.

⚭**14:8 Leadership:** 1 Kings 16:2

14:19 *the book of the history of the kings of Israel.* Kings often refers to another history book that kept an account of the great events of the northern kingdom (there was also one for the kings of Judah). This book has never been discovered and is not inspired.

14:29 *the book of the history of the kings of Judah.* See 14:19.

6There was war between Abijah and Jeroboam during Abijah's lifetime. 7Everything else Abijah did is written in the book of the history of the kings of Judah. During the time Abijah ruled, there was war between Abijah and Jeroboam. 8Abijah died and was buried in Jerusalem, and his son Asa became king in his place.

Asa King of Judah

9During the twentieth year Jeroboam was king of Israel, Asa became king of Judah. 10His grandmother's name was Maacah, the daughter of Abishalom. Asa ruled in Jerusalem for forty-one years.

11Asa did what the LORD said was right, as his ancestor David had done. 12He forced the male prostitutes at the worship places to leave the country. He also took away the idols that his ancestors had made. 13His grandmother Maacah had made a terrible Asherah idol, so Asa removed her from being queen mother. He cut down that idol and burned it in the Kidron Valley. 14The places of worship to gods were not removed. Even so, Asa was faithful to the LORD all his life. 15Asa brought into the Temple of the LORD the gifts he and his father had given: gold, silver, and utensils.

16There was war between Asa and Baasha king of Israel all the time they were kings. 17Baasha attacked Judah, and he made the town of Ramah strong so he could keep people from leaving or entering Judah, Asa's country.

18Asa took the rest of the silver and gold from the treasuries of the Temple of the LORD and his own palace and gave it to his officers. Then he sent them to Ben-Hadad son of Tabrimmon, who was the son of Hezion. Ben-Hadad was the king of Aram and ruled in the city of Damascus. Asa said, 19"Let there be a treaty between you and me as there was between my father and your father. I am sending you a gift of silver and gold. Break your treaty with Baasha king of Israel so he will leave my land."

20Ben-Hadad agreed with King Asa, so he sent the commanders of his armies to attack the towns of Israel. They defeated the towns of Ijon, Dan, and Abel Beth Maacah, as well as all Galilee and the area of Naphtali. 21When Baasha heard about these attacks, he stopped building up Ramah and returned to Tirzah. 22Then King Asa gave an order to all the people of Judah; everyone had to help. They carried away all the stones and wood Baasha had been using in Ramah, and they used them to build up Geba and Mizpah in the land of Benjamin.

23Everything else Asa did—his victories and the cities he built—is written in the book of the history of the kings of Judah. When he became old, he got a disease in his feet. 24After Asa died, he was buried with his ancestors in Jerusalem, the city of David, his ancestor. Then Jehoshaphat, Asa's son, became king in his place.

Nadab King of Israel

25Nadab son of Jeroboam became king of Israel during the second year Asa was king of Judah. Nadab was king of Israel for two years, 26and he did what the LORD said was wrong. Jeroboam had led the people of Israel to sin, and Nadab sinned in the same way as his father Jeroboam.

27Baasha son of Ahijah, from the tribe of Issachar, made plans to kill Nadab. Nadab and all Israel were attacking the Philistine town of Gibbethon, so Baasha killed Nadab there. 28This happened during Asa's third year as king of Judah, and Baasha became the next king of Israel.

Baasha King of Israel

29As soon as Baasha became king, he killed all of Jeroboam's family, leaving no one in Jeroboam's family alive. He destroyed them all as the LORD had said would happen through his servant Ahijah from Shiloh. 30King Jeroboam had sinned very much and had led the people of Israel to sin, so he made the LORD, the God of Israel, very angry.

31Everything else Nadab did is written in the book of the history of the kings of Israel. 32There was war between Asa king of Judah and Baasha king of Israel all the time they ruled.

33Baasha son of Ahijah became king of Israel during Asa's third year as king of Judah. Baasha ruled in Tirzah for twenty-four years, 34and he did what the LORD said was wrong. Jeroboam had led the people of Israel to sin, and Baasha sinned in the same way as Jeroboam.

16 Jehu son of Hanani spoke the word of the LORD against King Baasha. 2The LORD said, "You were nothing, but I took you and made you a leader over my people Israel. But you have followed the ways of Jeroboam and have led my people Israel to sin. Their sins have made me angry, 3so, Baasha, I will soon destroy you and your family. I will do to you what I did to the family of Jeroboam son of Nebat. 4Anyone from your family who dies in the city will be eaten by dogs,

15:7 *the book of the history of the kings of Judah.* See 14:19.
15:23 *the book of the history of the kings of Judah.* See 14:19.
15:31 *the book of the history of the kings of Israel.* See 14:19.
16:2 Leadership: 1 Chronicles 13:1

16:4 *will be eaten by dogs . . . will be eaten by birds.* In the ancient Near East in general, and in the Old Testament in particular, it was considered a curse not to receive a regular burial.

CHILDREN

1 SAMUEL 16

What role did children play in biblical times?
What does it mean to inherit the kingdom of God "as children"?

In spite of the magnitude of his extended family and his great wealth, Abraham still felt the loss of having no children. Similarly, Zechariah and Elizabeth, though they were righteous before God, suffered on account of their childlessness (Luke 1). In the Old Testament, the bearing and rearing of children was not only regarded as the greatest of God's gifts, but was seen as one of the primary ways for God's people to maintain their relationship to him. "Have many children and grow in number," God had instructed the first parents (Genesis 1:28). Baby boys were to be circumcised (Genesis 17), and ancient Jews adopted the custom of blessing all children (see Numbers 6:24–26). They were gifts from God, and they were the guarantee of the ongoing covenant between God and the people of Israel.

It is surprising, then, that children had virtually no respect in ancient Israel. In spite of their importance to the agreement God had made with his people, children were not highly regarded in everyday social interaction. This may be due in part to the short life expectancy of children in the ancient world. In addition, according to tradition the most important position in the ancient village was held by the older people.

This is not to say that God lacked interest in children, however. Even if the structures of local communities provided little esteem for children, God could and often did choose to work with and through children. Though he was only a boy, David was God's choice to be the king of Israel. Samuel himself was called to serve God when Samuel was a little boy (1 Samuel 3). Jeremiah is called to be a prophet even though he is only a boy (Jeremiah 1:4–10). In the New Testament, a girl named Rhoda is the only one who recognizes that God has rescued Peter from prison (Acts 12:6–17); she has a hard time convincing the adults that what she had seen was true! The psalm says to the Lord, "You have taught children and babies to sing praises to you" (Psalm 8:2).

By the time of Jesus, the lot of children in larger society had not improved. Jesus and his early followers lived in a time when people were very concerned with questions about who was the greatest. In this society it was easy to say who was the least important: children. Their fathers had almost absolute control over their lives, from the time children were born until the death of their fathers. Children were important only as much as they contributed to the family livelihood through their work in the field. Otherwise, they should neither be seen nor heard.

This is what makes Jesus' interest in children so surprising. Although his followers were acting in the normal way in refusing to allow children to come near Jesus, he welcomed children into his presence and blessed them (see Mark 10:13–16). He restores to life the twelve-year-old daughter of Jairus (Mark 5:35–43) and casts a demon out of a young boy (Mark 9:14–29).

Even more surprising is the way Jesus uses children as examples of what it means to follow him. For example, in the Gospel of Mark, Jesus took a small child and had him stand among his disciples. "Taking the child in his arms, he said, 'Whoever accepts a child like this in my name accepts me'" (Mark 9:33–37). What would it mean "to accept" or "to receive" a little child? In the world of Jesus, this would mean to treat children as special guests, as though they were the most important members of the community. In order to do this, Jesus' followers would have to stop thinking of themselves as so important.

This is also the message of Jesus when he says that people must receive the kingdom of God "as if you were a little child" (Mark 10:15). He is not trying to say that followers of Jesus should have childlike faith or innocence. After all, children in the world of Jesus were not known for their faith or innocence; they were hardly known at all, since they were regarded as unimportant. When Jesus instructs people to act as though they were little children, then, he is asking them to quit thinking so highly of themselves. He is asking them to stop thinking of themselves as more important than others. Like the children of the world of Jesus, followers of Jesus need to content themselves with having little or no power to make people act like they want them to act.

The practices of God in the Old Testament and the message about children in Jesus' ministry remain as fresh today as when they were first recorded.⚭

⚭**Children:** For additional scriptures on this topic go to Genesis 1:28.

DAVID

1 SAMUEL 16

How did David come to be King of Israel? Why was David not allowed by God to build the Temple? Even though David sinned grievously, he was called "the kind of man (God) wants" (1 Samuel 13:14). Why?

David is one of the most exciting figures of the Old Testament. Not only is he pivotal in the history of Israel, but we feel like we get to know him in his strengths and weaknesses.

Two major events were recorded about David's youth, both anticipating his impact on the history of Israel and the Bible. First (1 Samuel 16:14–22), David was hired to be a harp player in Saul's court. The troubled king was soothed by the young man's playing. This episode set the stage for the adult David who contributed so many songs (psalms) to the Bible.

Next, 1 Samuel 17 recounts the encounter between David and the Philistine mercenary Goliath. Though Goliath was huge, trained and well-armored, David, a simple shepherd boy armed only with a slingshot, killed him and won the victory for Israel. This story anticipated the adult David who would become Israel's warrior-king.

Though David never tried to take the kingship form Saul or hurry the end of his kingship, Saul became extremely jealous of this young man. Though he allowed him to marry into the family (1 Samuel 18:17–31) and though Saul's son, Jonathan, was his close friend, "Saul watched David closely because he was jealous" (1 Samuel 18:9).

Even when David had the opportunity to kill Saul and take the throne, he refused to do so (1 Samuel 24 and 26). In the spirit of Psalm 131, he did not grasp at the promises but demonstrated a calmness of spirit that waited for God to give him the kingship.

That time came when Saul and Jonathan were killed in battle with the Philistines (1 Samuel 31). One would think that David would rejoice that the man who was chasing him so unjustly had died, but David responded with great sadness to the death of Saul, his enemy, and Jonathan, his closest friend (2 Samuel 1:17–27).

Now that he was king, David brought the Ark of God to Jerusalem with the intention of building the Temple and making the city the religious capital as well. However, God felt that the time was not quite right for the building of the Temple, so David's role was to prepare for its building (1 Chronicles 22:2–29:30).

Around this time, the single greatest event of David's kingship occurred. God rejected David's wish to build the Temple, but he nonetheless blessed David with the promise of a dynasty. Indeed, he said to David that "your throne will last forever" (2 Samuel 7:16).

David was overwhelmed with thankfulness (2 Samuel 7:18–29), but he soon sinned. At a time he should have been out fighting the Lord's battles, he was at home with time on his hands. He saw a beautiful woman, Bathsheba, whom he desired even though she was married. She became pregnant by him, and to cover over his sin, he had Uriah, her husband, killed on the battlefield. He was confronted by Nathan the prophet and repented (see Psalm 51), but the consequences of his act reached down to the end of his reign.

David's life ended in the middle of family feuds. However, in the final analysis, he remained the standard by which all subsequent kings were judged. Few of his descendants even came close to his level of devotion and obedience to God.

What then happened to the promise of an eternal kingship of David? God's fulfillment of this promise far exceeded human ability to imagine it. David's greater son, Jesus, was born in Bethlehem. He was proclaimed king not just of the Jewish people, but of the whole world. David, the king, was a pale reflection of Jesus, our divine king, who came here to establish a kingdom among us.

David: For additional scriptures on this topic go to 1 Chronicles 10–2 Chronicles 29:30.

and anyone from your family who dies in the fields will be eaten by birds."

5Everything else Baasha did and all his victories are written down in the book of the history of the kings of Israel. 6So Baasha died and was buried in Tirzah, and his son Elah became king in his place.

7The LORD spoke his word against Baasha and his family through the prophet Jehu son of Hanani. Baasha had done many things the LORD said were wrong, which made the LORD very angry. He did the same evil deeds that Jeroboam's family had done before him. The LORD also spoke against Baasha because he killed all of Jeroboam's family.

Elah King of Israel

8Elah son of Baasha became king of Israel during Asa's twenty-sixth year as king of Judah, and Elah ruled in Tirzah for two years.

9Zimri, one of Elah's officers, commanded half of Elah's chariots. Zimri made plans against Elah while the king was in Tirzah, getting drunk at Arza's home. (Arza was in charge of the palace at Tirzah.) 10Zimri went into Arza's house and killed Elah during Asa's twenty-seventh year as king of Judah. Then Zimri became king of Israel in Elah's place.

Zimri King of Israel

11As soon as Zimri became king, he killed all of Baasha's family, not allowing any of Baasha's family or friends to live. 12So Zimri destroyed all of Baasha's family just as the LORD had said it would happen through the prophet Jehu. 13Baasha and his son Elah sinned and led the people of Israel to sin, and they made the LORD, the God of Israel, angry because of their worthless idols.

14Everything else Elah did is written in the book of the history of the kings of Israel.

15So during Asa's twenty-seventh year as king of Judah, Zimri became king of Israel and ruled in Tirzah seven days.

The army of Israel was camped near Gibbethon, a Philistine town. 16The men in the camp heard that Zimri had made secret plans against King Elah and had killed him. So that day in the camp they made Omri, the commander of the army, king over Israel. 17So Omri and all the Israelite army left Gibbethon and attacked Tirzah. 18When Zimri saw that the city had been captured, he went into the palace and set it on fire, burning the palace and himself with it. 19So Zimri died because he had sinned by doing what the LORD said was wrong. Jeroboam had led the people of Israel to sin, and Zimri sinned in the same way as Jeroboam.

20Everything else Zimri did and the story of how he turned against King Elah are written down in the book of the history of the kings of Israel.

Omri King of Israel

21The people of Israel were divided into two groups. Half of the people wanted Tibni son of Ginath to be king, while the other half wanted Omri. 22Omri's followers were stronger than the followers of Tibni son of Ginath, so Tibni died, and Omri became king.

23Omri became king of Israel during the thirty-first year Asa was king of Judah. Omri ruled Israel for twelve years, six of those years in the city of Tirzah. 24He bought the hill of Samaria from Shemer for about one hundred fifty pounds of silver. Omri built a city on that hill and called it Samaria after the name of its earlier owner, Shemer.

25But Omri did what the LORD said was wrong; he did more evil than all the kings who came before him. 26Jeroboam son of Nebat had led the people of Israel to sin, and Omri sinned in the same way as Jeroboam. The Israelites made the LORD, the God of Israel, very angry because they worshiped worthless idols.

27Everything else Omri did and all his successes are written in the book of the history of the kings of Israel. 28So Omri died and was buried in Samaria, and his son Ahab became king in his place.

Ahab King of Israel

29Ahab son of Omri became king of Israel during Asa's thirty-eighth year as king of Judah, and Ahab ruled Israel in the city of Samaria for twenty-two years. 30More than any king before him, Ahab son of Omri did many things the LORD said were wrong. 31He sinned in the same ways as Jeroboam son of Nebat, but he did even worse things. He married Jezebel daughter of Ethbaal, the king of Sidon. Then Ahab began to serve Baal and worship him. 32He built a temple in Samaria for worshiping Baal and put an altar there for Baal. 33Ahab also made an idol for worshiping Asherah. He did more things to make the LORD, the God of Israel, angry than all the other kings before him.

16:5 *the book of the history of the kings of Israel.* See 14:19.

16:14 *the book of the history of the kings of Israel.* See 14:19.

16:20 *the book of the history of the kings of Israel.* See 14:19.

16:23 *Omri.* Though he is only briefly mentioned in the Bible, other ancient Near Eastern texts refer to Omri as a particularly powerful king of Israel.

16:24 Samaria: Isaiah 10:10–11

16:27 *the book of the history of the kings of Israel.* See 14:19.

16:31 Jezebel: 1 Kings 18:4–21

Baal: the people of Canaan's false god of weather and fertility

[34]During the time of Ahab, Hiel from Bethel rebuilt the city of Jericho. It cost Hiel the life of Abiram, his oldest son, to begin work on the city, and it cost the life of Segub, his youngest son, to build the city gates. This happened just as the LORD, speaking through Joshua son of Nun, said it would happen.

Elijah Stops the Rain

17 Now Elijah the Tishbite was a prophet from the settlers in Gilead. "I serve the LORD, the God of Israel," Elijah said to Ahab. "As surely as the LORD lives, no rain or dew will fall during the next few years unless I command it."

[2]Then the LORD spoke his word to Elijah: [3]"Leave this place and go east and hide near Kerith Ravine east of the Jordan River. [4]You may drink from the stream, and I have commanded ravens to bring you food there." [5]So Elijah did what the LORD said; he went to Kerith Ravine, east of the Jordan, and lived there. [6]The birds brought Elijah bread and meat every morning and evening, and he drank water from the stream.

[7]After a while the stream dried up because there was no rain. [8]Then the LORD spoke his word to Elijah, [9]"Go to Zarephath in Sidon and live there. I have commanded a widow there to take care of you."

[10]So Elijah went to Zarephath. When he reached the town gate, he saw a widow gathering wood for a fire. Elijah asked her, "Would you bring me a little water in a cup so I may have a drink?" [11]As she was going to get his water, Elijah said, "Please bring me a piece of bread, too."

[12]The woman answered, "As surely as the LORD your God lives, I have no bread. I have only a handful of flour in a jar and only a little olive oil in a jug. I came here to gather some wood so I could go home and cook our last meal. My son and I will eat it and then die from hunger."

[13]"Don't worry," Elijah said to her. "Go home and cook your food as you have said. But first make a small loaf of bread from the flour you have, and bring it to me. Then cook something for yourself and your son. [14]The LORD, the God of Israel, says, 'That jar of flour will never be empty, and the jug will always have oil in it, until the day the LORD sends rain to the land.'"

[15]So the woman went home and did what Elijah told her to do. And the woman and her son and Elijah had enough food every day. [16]The jar of flour and the jug of oil were never empty, just as the LORD, through Elijah, had promised.

Elijah Brings a Boy Back to Life

[17]Some time later the son of the woman who owned the house became sick. He grew worse and worse and finally stopped breathing. [18]The woman said to Elijah, "Man of God, what have you done to me? Did you come here to remind me of my sin and to kill my son?"

[19]Elijah said to her, "Give me your son." Elijah took the boy from her, carried him upstairs, and laid him on the bed in the room where he was staying. [20]Then he prayed to the LORD: "LORD my

16:34 *the LORD . . . happen.* When Joshua destroyed Jericho, he said whoever rebuilt the city would lose his oldest and youngest sons. See Joshua 6:26.

16:34 *Joshua, son of Nun, said it would happen.* See Joshua 6:26.

17:1 Here famine by drought was not only God's discipline and chastisement upon his sinning people as was so often the case in the Old Testament (Leviticus 26:14–20; Deuteronomy 28:15–24; 2 Samuel 21, 24; Ezekiel 4:16), it was also part of God's means of authenticating Elijah's ministry as a true prophet and of demonstrating that the God of Israel, and not the foreign god, Baal, was truly "lord of the rains" (Leviticus 26:3–4; Hosea 2:5, 8).

17:1 *no rain or dew will fall.* God stopped the rain and dew because the people worshiped Baal, the god of rain and dew. In this way God was showing the people who really controlled the rain and dew.

God, this widow is letting me stay in her house.
Why have you done this terrible thing to her and
caused her son to die?" 21Then Elijah lay on top of
the boy three times. He prayed to the LORD, "LORD
my God, let this boy live again!"
22The LORD answered Elijah's prayer; the boy
began breathing again and was alive. 23Elijah carried the boy downstairs and gave him to his
mother and said, "See! Your son is alive!"
24"Now I know you really are a man from God,"
the woman said to Elijah. "I know that the LORD
truly speaks through you!"

Elijah Kills the Prophets of Baal

18 During the third year without rain, the LORD
spoke his word to Elijah: "Go and meet King
Ahab, and I will soon send rain." 2So Elijah went to
meet Ahab.
By this time there was no food in Samaria.
3King Ahab sent for Obadiah, who was in charge
of the king's palace. (Obadiah was a true follower of
the LORD. 4When Jezebel was killing all the LORD's
prophets, Obadiah hid a hundred of them in two
caves, fifty in one cave and fifty in another. He
also brought them food and water.) 5Ahab said to
Obadiah, "Let's check every spring and valley in
the land. Maybe we can find enough grass to keep
our horses and mules alive and not have to kill
our animals." 6So each one chose a part of the
country to search; Ahab went in one direction
and Obadiah in another.
7While Obadiah was on his way, Elijah met him.
Obadiah recognized Elijah, so he bowed down to the
ground and said, "Elijah? Is it really you, master?"
8"Yes," Elijah answered. "Go tell your master
that I am here."
9Then Obadiah said, "What wrong have I done
for you to hand me over to Ahab like this? He will
put me to death. 10As surely as the LORD your God
lives, the king has sent people to every country to
search for you. If the ruler said you were not there,
Ahab forced the ruler to swear you could not be
found in his country. 11Now you want me to go to
my master and tell him, 'Elijah is here'? 12The
Spirit of the LORD may carry you to some other
place after I leave. If I go tell King Ahab you are
here, and he comes and doesn't find you, he will
kill me! I have followed the LORD since I was a boy.
13Haven't you been told what I did? When Jezebel
was killing the LORD's prophets, I hid a hundred
of them, fifty in one cave and fifty in another. I
brought them food and water. 14Now you want

Raven: a large, black, flesh-eating bird

me to go and tell my master you are here? He will
kill me!"
15Elijah answered, "As surely as the LORD All-
Powerful lives, whom I serve, I will be seen by
Ahab today."
16So Obadiah went to Ahab and told him where
Elijah was. Then Ahab went to meet Elijah.
17When he saw Elijah, he asked, "Is it you—
the biggest troublemaker in Israel?"
18Elijah answered, "I have not made trouble in
Israel. You and your father's family have made all
this trouble by not obeying the LORD's commands.
You have gone after the Baals. 19Now tell all Israel
to meet me at Mount Carmel. Also bring the four
hundred fifty prophets of Baal and the four hundred
prophets of Asherah, who eat at Jezebel's table."
20So Ahab called all the Israelites and those
prophets to Mount Carmel. 21Elijah approached
the people and said, "How long will you not decide
between two choices? If the LORD is the true God,
follow him, but if Baal is the true God, follow him!"
But the people said nothing.
22Elijah said, "I am the only prophet of the LORD
here, but there are four hundred fifty prophets of
Baal. 23Bring two bulls. Let the prophets of Baal
choose one bull and kill it and cut it into pieces.
Then let them put the meat on the wood, but they
are not to set fire to it. I will prepare the other
bull, putting the meat on the wood but not setting
fire to it. 24You prophets of Baal, pray to your god,
and I will pray to the LORD. The god who answers
by setting fire to his wood is the true God."
All the people agreed that this was a good idea.
25Then Elijah said to the prophets of Baal,
"There are many of you, so you go first. Choose a
bull and prepare it. Pray to your god, but don't start
the fire."

17:23 Intercession: Daniel 9:3–19

18:2–40 In this worship encounter that preserved the worship of the Lord in Israel, Mount Carmel follows the tradition of mountain sites in the history of the Israelites. The people are called to gather at a mountain site to decide if they are going to acknowledge, worship, and serve the Lord, or if they are going to reject him. On the mountain, the Lord reveals himself as the true God, and the relationship between God and his people is reaffirmed.

18:21 Jezebel: 1 Kings 21

18:24 *by setting fire.* That is, which god would send his lightning down from heaven. Baal was the god of the rain, which included lightning. So God was taking Baal on in the area of his specialty.

26So they took the bull that was given to them and prepared it. They prayed to Baal from morning until noon, shouting "Baal, answer us!" But there was no sound, and no one answered. They danced around the altar they had built.

27At noon Elijah began to make fun of them. "Pray louder!" he said. "If Baal really is a god, maybe he is thinking, or busy, or traveling! Maybe he is sleeping so you will have to wake him!" 28The prophets prayed louder, cutting themselves with swords and spears until their blood flowed, which was the way they worshiped. 29The afternoon passed, and the prophets continued to act like this until it was time for the evening sacrifice. But no voice was heard; Baal did not answer, and no one paid attention.

30Then Elijah said to all the people, "Now come to me." So they gathered around him, and Elijah rebuilt the altar of the LORD, which had been torn down. 31He took twelve stones, one stone for each of the twelve tribes, the number of Jacob's sons. (The LORD changed Jacob's name to Israel.) 32Elijah used these stones to rebuild the altar in honor of the LORD. Then he dug a ditch around the altar that was big enough to hold about thirteen quarts of seed. 33Elijah put the wood on the altar, cut the bull into pieces, and laid the pieces on the wood. 34Then he said, "Fill four jars with water, and pour it on the meat and on the wood." Then Elijah said, "Do it again," and they did it again. Then he said, "Do it a third time," and they did it the third time. 35So the water ran off the altar and filled the ditch.

36At the time for the evening sacrifice, the prophet Elijah went near the altar. "LORD, you are the God of Abraham, Isaac, and Israel," he prayed. "Prove that you are the God of Israel and that I am your servant. Show these people that you commanded me to do all these things. 37LORD, answer my prayer so these people will know that you, LORD, are God and that you will change their minds."

38Then fire from the LORD came down and burned the sacrifice, the wood, the stones, and the ground around the altar. It also dried up the water in the ditch. 39When all the people saw this, they fell down to the ground, crying, "The LORD is God! The LORD is God!"

40Then Elijah said, "Capture the prophets of Baal! Don't let any of them run away!" The people captured all the prophets. Then Elijah led them down to the Kishon Valley, where he killed them.⚭

The Rain Comes Again

41Then Elijah said to Ahab, "Now, go, eat, and drink, because a heavy rain is coming." 42So King Ahab went to eat and drink. At the same time Elijah climbed to the top of Mount Carmel, where he bent down to the ground with his head between his knees.

43Then Elijah said to his servant, "Go and look toward the sea."

The servant went and looked. "I see nothing," he said.

Elijah told him to go and look again. This happened seven times. 44The seventh time, the servant said, "I see a small cloud, the size of a human fist, coming from the sea."

Elijah told the servant, "Go to Ahab and tell him to get his chariot ready and go home now. Otherwise, the rain will stop him."

45After a short time the sky was covered with dark clouds. The wind began to blow, and soon a heavy rain began to fall. Ahab got in his chariot and started back to Jezreel. 46The LORD gave his power to Elijah, who tightened his clothes around him and ran ahead of King Ahab all the way to Jezreel.

Elijah Runs Away

19 King Ahab told Jezebel everything Elijah had done and how Elijah had killed all the prophets with a sword. 2So Jezebel sent a messenger to Elijah, saying, "May the gods punish me terribly if by this time tomorrow I don't kill you just as you killed those prophets."

3When Elijah heard this, he was afraid and ran for his life, taking his servant with him. When they came to Beersheba in Judah, Elijah left his servant there. 4Then Elijah walked for a whole day into the desert. He sat down under a bush and asked to die. "I have had enough, LORD," he prayed. "Let me die. I am no better than my ancestors." 5Then he lay down under the tree and slept.

Suddenly an angel came to him and touched him. "Get up and eat," the angel said. 6Elijah saw near his head a loaf baked over coals and a jar of water, so he ate and drank. Then he went back to sleep.

7Later the LORD's angel came to him a second time. The angel touched him and said, "Get up and eat. If you don't, the journey will be too hard for you." 8So Elijah got up and ate and drank. The food made him strong enough to walk for forty days and nights to Mount Sinai, the mountain of God. 9There Elijah went into a cave and stayed all night.

18:28 *cutting themselves.* This mourning ritual is verified in the ancient Canaanite texts from Ugarit.

⚭**18:40 Evangelism:** 2 Kings 5.1–15

Then the LORD spoke his word to him: "Elijah! Why are you here?"

10He answered, "LORD God All-Powerful, I have always served you as well as I could. But the people of Israel have broken their agreement with you, destroyed your altars, and killed your prophets with swords. I am the only prophet left, and now they are trying to kill me, too."

11The LORD said to Elijah, "Go, stand in front of me on the mountain, and I will pass by you." Then a very strong wind blew until it caused the mountains to fall apart and large rocks to break in front of the LORD. But the LORD was not in the wind. After the wind, there was an earthquake, but the LORD was not in the earthquake. 12After the earthquake, there was a fire, but the LORD was not in the fire. After the fire, there was a quiet, gentle sound. 13When Elijah heard it, he covered his face with his coat and went out and stood at the entrance to the cave.

Then a voice said to him, "Elijah! Why are you here?"

14He answered, "LORD God All-Powerful, I have always served you as well as I could. But the people of Israel have broken their agreement with you, destroyed your altars, and killed your prophets with swords. I am the only prophet left, and now they are trying to kill me, too."

15The LORD said to him, "Go back on the road that leads to the desert around Damascus. Enter that city, and pour olive oil on Hazael to make him king over Aram. 16Then pour oil on Jehu son of Nimshi to make him king over Israel. Next, pour oil on Elisha son of Shaphat from Abel Meholah to make him a prophet in your place. 17Jehu will kill anyone who escapes from Hazael's sword, and Elisha will kill anyone who escapes from Jehu's sword. 18I have seven thousand people left in Israel who have never bowed down before Baal and whose mouths have never kissed his idol."

Elisha Becomes a Prophet

19So Elijah left that place and found Elisha son of Shaphat plowing a field with a team of oxen. He owned twelve teams of oxen and was plowing with the twelfth team. Elijah came up to Elisha, took off his coat, and put it on Elisha. 20Then Elisha left his oxen and ran to follow Elijah. "Let me kiss my father and my mother good-bye," Elisha said. "Then I will go with you."

Elijah answered, "Go back. It does not matter to me."

21So Elisha went back and took his pair of oxen and killed them. He used their wooden yoke for a fire. Then he cooked the meat and gave it to the people. After they ate it, Elisha left and followed Elijah and became his helper.

Ben-Hadad and Ahab Go to War

20 Ben-Hadad king of Aram gathered together all his army. There were thirty-two kings with their horses and chariots who went with him and surrounded Samaria and attacked it. 2The king sent messengers into the city to Ahab king of Israel.

This was his message: "Ben-Hadad says, 3'Your silver and gold belong to me, as well as the best of your wives and children.'"

4Ahab king of Israel answered, "My master and king, I agree to what you say. I and everything I have belong to you."

5Then the messengers came to Ahab again. They said, "Ben-Hadad says, 'I told you before that you must give me your silver and gold, your wives and your children. 6About this time tomorrow I will send my men, who will search everywhere in your palace and in the homes of your officers. Whatever they want they will take and carry off.'"

7Then Ahab called a meeting of all the older leaders of his country. He said, "Ben-Hadad is looking for trouble. First he said I had to give him my wives, my children, my silver, and my gold, and I have not refused him."

8The older leaders and all the people said, "Don't listen to him or agree to this."

9So Ahab said to Ben-Hadad's messengers, "Tell my master the king: 'I will do what you said at first, but I cannot allow this second command.'" And King Ben-Hadad's men carried the message back to him.

10Then Ben-Hadad sent another message to Ahab: "May the gods punish me terribly if I don't completely destroy Samaria. There won't be enough left for each of my men to get a handful of dust!"

11Ahab answered, "Tell Ben-Hadad, 'The man who puts on his armor should not brag. It's the man who lives to take it off who has the right to brag.'"

12Ben-Hadad was drinking in his tent with the other rulers when the message came from Ahab. Ben-Hadad commanded his men to prepare to attack the city, and they moved into place for battle.

13At the same time a prophet came to Ahab king of Israel. The prophet said, "Ahab, the LORD says to you, 'Do you see that big army? I will hand it over

19:9 Depression: Nehemiah 2:1–3
19:10 Agreement: Ezra 10:3
19:12 Will of God: Proverbs 3:5–7

19:16 *pour oil on.* See 1 Samuel 10:1

19:21 Wilderness (Desert): Psalm 95

to you today so you will know I am the LORD.'"

14 Ahab asked, "Who will you use to defeat them?"

The prophet answered, "The LORD says, 'The young officers of the district governors will defeat them.'"

Then the king asked, "Who will command the main army?"

The prophet answered, "You will."

15 So Ahab gathered the young officers of the district governors, two hundred thirty-two of them. Then he called together the army of Israel, about seven thousand people in all.

16 They marched out at noon, while Ben-Hadad and the thirty-two rulers helping him were getting drunk in their tents. 17 The young officers of the district governors attacked first. Ben-Hadad sent out scouts who told him that soldiers were coming from Samaria. 18 Ben-Hadad said, "They may be coming to fight, or they may be coming to ask for peace. In either case capture them alive."

19 The young officers of the district governors led the attack, followed by the army of Israel. 20 Each officer of Israel killed the man who came against him. The men from Aram ran away as Israel chased them, but Ben-Hadad king of Aram escaped on a horse with some of his horsemen. 21 Ahab king of Israel led the army and destroyed the Arameans' horses and chariots. King Ahab thoroughly defeated the Aramean army.

22 Then the prophet went to Ahab king of Israel and said, "The king of Aram will attack you again next spring. So go home now and strengthen your army and see what you need to do."

23 Meanwhile the officers of Ben-Hadad king of Aram said to him, "The gods of Israel are mountain gods. Since we fought in a mountain area, Israel won. Let's fight them on the flat land, and then we will win. 24 This is what you should do. Don't allow the thirty-two rulers to command the armies, but put other commanders in their places. 25 Gather an army like the one that was destroyed and as many horses and chariots as before. We will fight the Israelites on flat land, and then we will win." Ben-Hadad agreed with their advice and did what they said.

26 The next spring Ben-Hadad gathered the army of Aram and went up to Aphek to fight against Israel.

27 The Israelites also had prepared for war. They marched out to meet the Arameans and camped opposite them. The Israelites looked like two small flocks of goats, but the Arameans covered the area.

28 A man of God came to the king of Israel with this message: "The LORD says, 'The people of Aram say that I, the LORD, am a god of the mountains, not a god of the valleys. So I will allow you to defeat this huge army, and then you will know I am the LORD.'"

29 The armies were camped across from each other for seven days. On the seventh day the battle began. The Israelites killed one hundred thousand Aramean soldiers in one day. 30 The rest of them ran away to the city of Aphek, where a city wall fell on twenty-seven thousand of them. Ben-Hadad also ran away to the city and hid in a room.

31 His officers said to him, "We have heard that the kings of Israel are trustworthy. Let's dress in rough cloth to show our sadness, and wear ropes on our heads. Then we will go to the king of Israel, and perhaps he will let you live."

32 So they dressed in rough cloth and wore ropes on their heads and went to the king of Israel. They said, "Your servant Ben-Hadad says, 'Please let me live.'"

Ahab answered, "Is he still alive? He is my brother."

33 Ben-Hadad's men had wanted a sign from Ahab. So when Ahab called Ben-Hadad his brother, they quickly said, "Yes! Ben-Hadad is your brother."

Ahab said, "Bring him to me." When Ben-Hadad came, Ahab asked him to join him in the chariot.

34 Ben-Hadad said to him, "Ahab, I will give you back the cities my father took from your father. And you may put shops in Damascus, as my father did in Samaria."

Ahab said, "If you agree to this, I will allow you to go free." So the two kings made a peace agreement. Then Ahab let Ben-Hadad go free.

A Prophet Speaks Against Ahab

35 One prophet from one of the groups of prophets told another, "Hit me!" He said this because the LORD had commanded it, but the other man refused. 36 The prophet said, "You did not obey the LORD's command, so a lion will kill you as soon as you leave me." When the man left, a lion found him and killed him.

37 The prophet went to another man and said, "Hit me, please!" So the man hit him and hurt him. 38 The prophet wrapped his face in a cloth so no one could tell who he was. Then he went and waited by the road for the king. 39 As Ahab king of Israel passed by, the prophet called out to him. "I went to fight in the battle," the prophet said. "One

20:23 *mountain gods.* The Arameans apparently had little precise knowledge of Israel's religion. They just heard that God's house, the Temple, was on Mount Zion.

of our men brought an enemy soldier to me. Our man said, ‘Guard this man. If he runs away, you will have to give your life in his place. Or, you will have to pay a fine of seventy-five pounds of silver.’ 40But I was busy doing other things, so the man ran away.”

The king of Israel answered, “You have already said what the punishment is. You must do what the man said.”

41Then the prophet quickly took the cloth from his face. When the king of Israel saw him, he knew he was one of the prophets. 42The prophet said to the king, “This is what the LORD says: ‘You freed the man I said should die, so your life will be taken instead of his. The lives of your people will also be taken instead of the lives of his people.’”

43Then King Ahab went back to his palace in Samaria, angry and upset.

Ahab Takes Naboth's Vineyard

21 After these things had happened, this is what followed. A man named Naboth owned a vineyard in Jezreel, near the palace of Ahab king of Israel. 2One day Ahab said to Naboth, “Give me your vineyard. It is near my palace, and I want to make it into a vegetable garden. I will give you a better vineyard in its place, or, if you prefer, I will pay you what it is worth.”

3Naboth answered, “May the LORD keep me from ever giving my land to you. It belongs to my family.”

4Ahab went home angry and upset, because he did not like what Naboth from Jezreel had said. (Naboth had said, “I will not give you my family's land.”) Ahab lay down on his bed, turned his face to the wall, and refused to eat.

5His wife, Jezebel, came in and asked him, “Why are you so upset that you refuse to eat?”

6Ahab answered, “I talked to Naboth, the man from Jezreel. I said, ‘Sell me your vineyard, or, if you prefer, I will give you another vineyard for it.’ But Naboth refused.”

7Jezebel answered, “Is this how you rule as king over Israel? Get up, eat something, and cheer up. I will get Naboth's vineyard for you.”

8So Jezebel wrote some letters, signed Ahab's name to them, and used his own seal to seal them. Then she sent them to the older leaders and important men who lived in Naboth's town. 9The letter she wrote said: “Declare a day during which the people are to give up eating. Call the people together, and give Naboth a place of honor among them. 10Seat two troublemakers across from him, and have them say they heard Naboth speak against God and the king. Then take Naboth out of the city and kill him with stones.”

11The older leaders and important men of Jezreel obeyed Jezebel's command, just as she wrote in the letters. 12They declared a special day on which the people were to give up eating. And they put Naboth in a place of honor before the people. 13Two troublemakers sat across from Naboth and said in front of everybody that they had heard him speak against God and the king. So the people carried Naboth out of the city and killed him with stones. 14Then the leaders sent a message to Jezebel, saying, “Naboth has been killed.”

15When Jezebel heard that Naboth had been killed, she told Ahab, “Naboth of Jezreel is dead. Now you may go and take for yourself the vineyard he would not sell to you.” 16When Ahab heard that Naboth of Jezreel was dead, he got up and went to the vineyard to take it for his own.

17At this time the LORD spoke his word to the prophet Elijah the Tishbite. The LORD said, 18“Go to Ahab king of Israel in Samaria. He is at Naboth's vineyard, where he has gone to take it as his own. 19Tell Ahab that I, the LORD, say to him, ‘You have murdered Naboth and taken his land. So I tell you this: In the same place the dogs licked up Naboth's blood, they will also lick up your blood!’”

20When Ahab saw Elijah, he said, “So you have found me, my enemy!”

Elijah answered, “Yes, I have found you. You have always chosen to do what the LORD says is wrong. 21So the LORD says to you, ‘I will soon destroy you. I will kill you and every male in your family, both slave and free. 22Your family will be like the family of King Jeroboam son of Nebat and like the family of King Baasha son of Ahijah. I will destroy you, because you have made me angry and have led the people of Israel to sin.’

23“And the LORD also says, ‘Dogs will eat the body of Jezebel in the city of Jezreel.’

24“Anyone in your family who dies in the city will be eaten by dogs, and anyone who dies in the fields will be eaten by birds.”

25There was no one like Ahab who had chosen so often to do what the LORD said was wrong, because his wife Jezebel influenced him to do evil. 26Ahab sinned terribly by worshiping idols, just as the Amorite people did. And the LORD had taken away their land and given it to the people of Israel.

27After Elijah finished speaking, Ahab tore his clothes. He put on rough cloth, refused to eat, and even slept in the rough cloth to show how sad and upset he was.

20:40 Parables: Isaiah 5:1–7

[28]The LORD spoke his word to Elijah the Tishbite:
[29]"I see that Ahab is now sorry for what he has
done. So I will not cause the trouble to come to him
during his life, but I will wait until his son is king.
Then I will bring this trouble to Ahab's family."

The Death of Ahab

22 For three years there was peace between
Israel and Aram. [2]During the third year
Jehoshaphat king of Judah went to visit Ahab king
of Israel.
[3]At that time Ahab asked his officers, "Do you
remember that the king of Aram took Ramoth in
Gilead from us? Why have we done nothing to get
it back?" [4]So Ahab asked King Jehoshaphat, "Will
you go with me to fight at Ramoth in Gilead?"
"I will go with you," Jehoshaphat answered.
"My soldiers are yours, and my horses are yours."
[5]Jehoshaphat also said to Ahab, "But first we
should ask if this is the LORD's will."
[6]Ahab called about four hundred prophets together and asked them, "Should I go to war against
Ramoth in Gilead or not?"
They answered, "Go, because the Lord will hand
them over to you."
[7]But Jehoshaphat asked, "Isn't there a prophet of
the LORD here? Let's ask him what we should do."
[8]Then King Ahab said to Jehoshaphat, "There is
one other prophet. We could ask the LORD through
him, but I hate him. He never prophesies anything
good about me, but something bad. He is Micaiah
son of Imlah."
Jehoshaphat said, "King Ahab, you shouldn't say
that!"
[9]So Ahab king of Israel told one of his officers to
bring Micaiah to him at once.
[10]Ahab king of Israel and Jehoshaphat king of
Judah had on their royal robes and were sitting on
their thrones at the threshing floor, near the
entrance to the gate of Samaria. All the prophets
were standing before them, speaking their messages. [11]Zedekiah son of Kenaanah had made some
iron horns. He said to Ahab, "This is what the LORD
says, 'You will use these horns to fight the Arameans until they are destroyed.'"
[12]All the other prophets said the same thing.
"Attack Ramoth in Gilead and win, because the
LORD will hand the Arameans over to you."
[13]The messenger who had gone to get Micaiah
said to him, "All the other prophets are saying King
Ahab will succeed. You should agree with them
and give the king a good answer."
[14]But Micaiah answered, "As surely as the LORD
lives, I can tell him only what the LORD tells me."
[15]When Micaiah came to Ahab, the king asked
him, "Micaiah, should we attack Ramoth in Gilead
or not?"
Micaiah answered, "Attack and win! The LORD
will hand them over to you."
[16]But Ahab said to Micaiah, "How many times
do I have to tell you to speak only the truth to me
in the name of the LORD?"
[17]So Micaiah answered, "I saw the army of Israel
scattered over the hills like sheep without a shepherd. The LORD said, 'They have no leaders. They
should go home and not fight.'"
[18]Then Ahab king of Israel said to Jehoshaphat,
"I told you! He never prophesies anything good
about me, but only bad."
[19]But Micaiah said, "Hear the message from the
LORD: I saw the LORD sitting on his throne with his
heavenly army standing near him on his right and
on his left. [20]The LORD said, 'Who will trick Ahab
into attacking Ramoth in Gilead where he will be
killed?'
"Some said one thing; some said another. [21]Then
one spirit came and stood before the LORD and said,
'I will trick him.'
[22]"The LORD asked, 'How will you do it?'
"The spirit answered, 'I will go to Ahab's prophets and make them tell lies.'
"So the LORD said, 'You will succeed in tricking
him. Go and do it.'"
[23]Micaiah said, "Ahab, the LORD has made your
prophets lie to you, and the LORD has decided that
disaster should come to you."
[24]Then Zedekiah son of Kenaanah went up to
Micaiah and slapped him in the face. Zedekiah said,
"Has the LORD's spirit left me to speak through you?"
[25]Micaiah answered, "You will find out on the
day you go to hide in an inside room."
[26]Then Ahab king of Israel ordered, "Take
Micaiah and send him to Amon, the governor of the
city, and to Joash, the king's son. [27]Tell them I said
to put this man in prison and give him only bread
and water until I return safely from the battle."
[28]Micaiah said, "Ahab, if you come back safely
from battle, the LORD has not spoken through me.
Remember my words, all you people!"

21:29 Jezebel: Revelations 17

22:19–23 This passage seems at first to suggest that God is the author of lying, which the Bible elsewhere indicates is contrary to his character (Numbers 23:19; Titus 1:2). The passage indicates however, that it was not God, but a "spirit," which is probably Satan or one of his demons that influenced the false prophets. It should also be pointed out that Micaiah's vision was revealed to Ahab so that Ahab was aware of it, yet he ignored the warning anyway. This passage vividly illustrates 2 Thessalonians 2:9–12 and is descriptive of Ahab, who made a deliberate choice to do what was wrong (1 Kings 21:20, 25) and thus subjected himself to the power of delusion. He loved lies and hated the truth (Psalm 52:3).

A Matter of the Heart

I Samuel 16:7

What matters most to God—true beliefs, right actions, proper worship, the beauty of appearance, or purity of heart? What does the Bible mean by "heart"? How can hearts be changed?

There are many things which are important in religion: what one believes (doctrines, beliefs, theology); what one does (actions, conduct, works, morals, ethics); how one feels (sincere, good, bad, indifferent); how one worships (ritual, liturgy, tradition,); public appearance, etc. Scripturally, what is essential to true religion is simply the condition of one's heart. Is it open or closed, contrite or stubborn, soft like a pillow or hard like a stone? "The sacrifice God wants is a broken spirit. God, you will you not reject a heart that is broken and sorry for sin" (Psalm 51:17).

What does the Bible mean by "heart"? There are three Hebrew words and equivalent Greek terms for "heart" which appear over 850 times in the Old and New Testaments. Rarely do they refer to the physical organ that pumps blood (perhaps only in 1 Samuel 25:37 and 2 Kings 9:24 in reference to paralysis or death when the heart stops). Generally, it is meant as a metaphor for the spiritual organ of the core self. In biblical psychology, the heart is the innermost spring of personal life; the source of all thoughts and plans, attitudes and desires, motives and choices; the deep seat of the 1) intellect, 2) emotions, and 3) will.

1) *The Seat of Intellect:* The heart is the center of cognitive and imaginative processes, in both Hebrew and Greek conception. In many traditional translations of the Bible, heart is used to refer to the mind (1 Chronicles 29:9), knowledge (Ecclesiastes 8:16), understanding (Job 12:3), discernment (1 Kings 3:9), and memory (Proverbs 3:3). Knowing God involves the spiritual, non-material mind, which is in the heart.

2) *The Seat of Emotions:* The heart can be happy (Proverbs 27:11; Acts 14:17) or sad (Nehemiah 2:2), troubled (John 12:27) or at peace (Colossians 3:15). It can be courageous (2 Samuel 17:10), fearful (Isaiah 35:11), discouraged (Numbers 32:7), envious (Proverbs 23:17), generous (2 Chronicles 29:31), proud (Deuteronomy 8:14), or pure (Matthew 5:8). It can be moved by compassion (Luke 7:13) or hardened by hatred (Leviticus 19:17). The heart can burn with spiritual vitality (Luke 24:32) or grow cold with indifference (Revelation 2:4, 5). "The mouth speaks the things that are in the heart" (Matthew 12:34).

3) *The Seat of the Will:* A person's character is determined by the condition of his or her heart. The heart can be "stubborn" (2 Chronicles 36:13) or "steady" (Psalm 108:1), "desperately wicked" (Jeremiah 17:9) or "broken and contrite" (Psalm 51), depending on its fundamental response to God. The heart is the center where decisions, obedience, intentionality, and devotion are formed. It is where conversion and communion take place. What God wants is what John Wesley called the "perfection of the will"—human hearts transformed and made responsive to grace, overflowing with love for God, neighbor, and oneself. Hearts that have hardened to human need and grown cold to divine love can soften, warm, change, and be renewed (and sometimes even replaced), through the gracious gift of God (See Ezekiel 36:24–28).

"We believe with our hearts, and so we are made right with God" (Romans 10:10). However, the condition of a person's heart is known only to God. To be human is to make judgments based on external criteria: what one believes, how one behaves, and the way one appears. But God sees beneath the surface to the heart of the matter. For example, when the LORD was seeking someone after his own heart to be king of Israel, he sent Samuel to the house of Jesse. After examining all the externally qualified candidates, who the Lord rejected, the prophet found a young shepherd boy, David. "God does not see the same way people see. People look at the outside of a person, but the Lord looks at the heart" (1 Samuel 16:7).

Scripture sometimes uses the term "heart" in a deeper sense, to refer not only to a person's inner thoughts, emotions, and volition, but to a sacred sphere within the core self which is immortal (1 Peter 3:4). Augustine called it a God-shaped vacuum, and said "our hearts are restless till they find there rest in Thee." The heart, in this sense, is that deeper spiritual point of contact with the Divine, roughly equivalent to spirit—as in Psalm 51:10). In this more mystical understanding, the heart is that which speaks directly with God (Psalm 27:8), and is subject to divine revelation, influence, and activity (Romans 2:15, Acts 15:9).

In mysterious ways, God can harden hearts (Exodus 4:21) or change them into responsive vessels of his will (Ezra 6:22). God can put fear into human hearts (Jeremiah 32:40) or inspire them for his purposes (Nehemiah 2:12). The Devil has similar access to the human heart: he persuaded Judas to turn against Jesus (John 13:2); and possessed Ananias to lie to the Spirit and to the Church (Acts 5:3).

A Matter of the Heart: For additional scriptures on this topic go to Jeremiah 17:9.

JERUSALEM

2 SAMUEL 5:5

Why was Jerusalem such an important place?

Jerusalem is one of the oldest cities in the world. It played an important role in the history of Israel and her neighbors because it was situated between three continents (Europe, Asia and Africa) and between two main trade routes ("the way of the sea" in the plains to the west of Jerusalem and "the king's highway" across the Jordan River to the east). Set upon steep slopes, the city was well protected from invading forces (Psalm 125:2 states, "As the mountains surround Jerusalem, the LORD surrounds his people now and forever"). The addition of walls to the city made it very hard for an enemy force to subdue it. The name of this ancient city may mean "possession of peace" or "city of peace." Jerusalem was also called "Zion," the name of one of the mountains on which it was built (2 Kings 19:31). Melchizedek (whose name means "king of righteousness"), the king of Salem, brought out bread and wine to Abraham after Abraham defeated five kings in battle (Genesis 14:18). Salem is probably another, older name for Jerusalem. The first mention of "Jerusalem" is found in Joshua 10:1. The inhabitants of Jerusalem, called Jebusites (Joshua 15:63), feared the invading Israelites and the peace treaty that they made with the Gibeonites (Judges 9). The king of Jerusalem, Adoni-Zedek, asked four other kings to fight against Gibeon because they made peace with Israel. Joshua and Israel honored the treaty they made with Gibeon, defeated the armies, and killed the five kings, but did not take their cities at that time.

The tribes of Benjamin and Judah are both associated with Jerusalem. Sometimes Jerusalem is said to be of the tribe of Judah and at other times to be of the tribe of Benjamin. Joshua 18:28 and Judges 1:21 clearly state that Jerusalem was an inheritance of the tribe of Benjamin. However, Judah was the first to battle the city and destroy the buildings (Judges 1:8).

The tribe of Benjamin was never able to subdue the inhabitants of Jerusalem, the Jebusites. The Israelites and Jebusites lived beside each other until the time of David. When David became the king of Judah and Israel, his first act was to battle the Jebusites for Jerusalem (2 Samuel 5:5). The city, set on three high ridges, was very defensible. The Jebusites were certain that David could not defeat them. They even taunted David and the army of Israel. David defeated the Jebusites and made Jerusalem his capital. Second Samuel 5:7 tells us that Jerusalem became the "City of David." Since David was a member of the tribe of Judah, Jerusalem from this time forward is usually associated with Judah rather than Benjamin (but note 2 Chronicles 34:32; Ezra 1:5; 10:9; Jeremiah 6:1; 32:44; 33:13). The close proximity of Benjamin, Jerusalem, and Judah helped David to unite the northern tribes with the southern tribes. David's choice of Jerusalem as his capital, within Benjamin's inheritance, was a more neutral and acceptable site for him to reign than any site in Judah. Jerusalem remained the capital of the southern kingdom, Judah, until it was destroyed by the Babylonian King Nebuchadnezzar in 586 B.C.

The main reason Jerusalem is important in the Bible, however, is because it is there that the LORD chose to dwell and be worshiped by his chosen people, Israel. Second Chronicles 6:6 states, "But now I have chosen Jerusalem as the place I am to be worshiped." God had previously shown that Jerusalem was his holy city by allowing David to take the Ark of the Agreement into Jerusalem (2 Samuel 6:12). The threshing floor of a Jebusite named Araunah (2 Chronicles 3:1; 2 Samuel 24) became the location for the Temple in which God would live. David bought the threshing floor from Araunah and built an altar there to save the Israelites from a plague his sin had brought on them (2 Samuel 24). God lived on Mount Zion (another name for Jerusalem, Psalm 74:2); it was his home (Psalm 76:2). For the Israelites, this meant that God loved them out of all the other people on earth, since he chose to live with them. The presence of God in Jerusalem was a sign of his love and the agreement he had made with Abraham and David. After the nation of Israel sinned and was defeated by the Assyrians, the people of Judah became too confident in Jerusalem. They began to boast that because the Lord had chosen Jerusalem, it could never be defeated (Jeremiah 7:3,10). They worshiped Baal and other gods and forgot that it was God's presence, not the city or Temple, that protected Jerusalem. Because of their sin, God became angry with Jerusalem and let the Babylonians destroy it (Jeremiah 27; 39). The Temple was sacked and emptied, and 4,600 people were taken captive (Jeremiah 52:30). However, the Lord promised that after Jerusalem was destroyed, he would again build it up. He also promised that he would make a new agreement with his people that would last forever (Jeremiah 31).

Jerusalem: For additional scriptures on this topic go to Genesis 14:18.

29So Ahab king of Israel and Jehoshaphat king of Judah went to Ramoth in Gilead. 30King Ahab said to Jehoshaphat, "I will go into battle, but I will wear other clothes so no one will recognize me. But you wear your royal clothes." So Ahab wore other clothes and went into battle.

31The king of Aram had ordered his thirty-two chariot commanders, "Don't fight with anyone—important or unimportant—except the king of Israel." 32When these commanders saw Jehoshaphat, they thought he was certainly the king of Israel, so they turned to attack him. But Jehoshaphat began shouting. 33When they saw he was not King Ahab, they stopped chasing him.

34By chance, a soldier shot an arrow, but he hit Ahab king of Israel between the pieces of his armor. King Ahab said to his chariot driver, "Turn around and get me out of the battle, because I am hurt!" 35The battle continued all day. King Ahab was held up in his chariot and faced the Arameans. His blood flowed down to the bottom of the chariot. That evening he died. 36Near sunset a cry went out through the army of Israel: "Each man go back to his own city and land."

37In that way King Ahab died. His body was carried to Samaria and buried there. 38The men cleaned Ahab's chariot at a pool in Samaria where prostitutes bathed, and the dogs licked his blood from the chariot. These things happened as the LORD had said they would.

39Everything else Ahab did is written in the book of the history of the kings of Israel. It tells about the palace Ahab built and decorated with ivory and the cities he built. 40So Ahab died, and his son Ahaziah became king in his place.

Jehoshaphat King of Judah

41Jehoshaphat son of Asa became king of Judah during Ahab's fourth year as king of Israel. 42Jehoshaphat was thirty-five years old when he became king, and he ruled in Jerusalem for twenty-five years. His mother's name was Azubah daughter of Shilhi. 43Jehoshaphat was good, like his father Asa, and he did what the LORD said was right. But Jehoshaphat did not destroy the places where gods were worshiped, so the people continued offering sacrifices and burning incense there. 44Jehoshaphat was at peace with the king of Israel. 45Jehoshaphat fought many wars, and these wars and his successes are written in the book of the history of the kings of Judah. 46There were male prostitutes still in the places of worship from the days of his father, Asa. So Jehoshaphat forced them to leave.

47During this time the land of Edom had no king; it was ruled by a governor.

48King Jehoshaphat built trading ships to sail to Ophir for gold. But the ships were wrecked at Ezion Geber, so they never set sail. 49Ahaziah son of Ahab went to help Jehoshaphat, offering to give Jehoshaphat some men to sail with his men, but Jehoshaphat refused.

50Jehoshaphat died and was buried with his ancestors in Jerusalem, the city of David, his ancestor. Then his son Jehoram became king in his place.

Ahaziah King of Israel

51Ahaziah son of Ahab became king of Israel in Samaria during Jehoshaphat's seventeenth year as king over Judah. Ahaziah ruled Israel for two years, 52and he did what the LORD said was wrong. He did the same evil his father Ahab, his mother Jezebel, and Jeroboam son of Nebat had done. All these rulers led the people of Israel into more sin. 53Ahaziah worshiped and served the god Baal, and this made the LORD, the God of Israel, very angry. In these ways Ahaziah did what his father had done.

Notes:

INTRODUCTION TO THE BOOK OF

2 KINGS

Two Kingdoms Are Destroyed

SEE THE INTRODUCTION TO 1 KINGS.

SUMMARY:

The Book of 2 Kings continues the account given in 1 Kings. In the original Hebrew, 1 and 2 Kings were a single, unified work. Thus, the introduction to 1 Kings also covers the main features of 2 Kings.

Second Kings opens with the reign of Ahaziah, introduced at the end of 1 Kings. The story of Elijah and Elisha, which spans the reigns of six northern kings, continues from 1 Kings into 2 Kings. The book concludes with the fall of Jerusalem and a brief account of episodes from the exile.

The outline of 2 Kings is as follows:

I. From Ahaziah's Rule to the Fall of the Northern Kingdom (1:1–17:41)
II. From Hezekiah to the Fall of Judah and the Exile (18:1–25:30)

I. From Ahaziah's Rule to the Fall of the Northern Kingdom (1:1–17:41)

First Kings and 2 Kings were originally a single composition. The break between the two contains no special significance, occurring in the middle of the report of the reign of King Ahaziah.

The first seventeen chapters of 2 Kings covers the period of time when the northern and southern kingdoms both exist. The biblical account shifts back and forth from one kingdom to another. In this way they cover the reigns of overlapping kings. At the end of this section of Kings, the northern kingdom is carried off into captivity.

II. From Hezekiah to the Fall of Judah and the Exile (18:1–25:30)

After the fall of the ten northern tribes, only the south, Judah, remains. While a number of kings try to follow the Lord the best that they can (Hezekiah and Josiah most notably), most of the kings continue the evil practices that brought them into conflict with God.

Finally, God uses the Babylonians as his tool of judgment, and the people of Israel are sent into exile for their sins of idolatry and pride. At the very end of the story, we learn that the Babylonian king, Evil-Merodach, releases Jehoiachin, the exiled king of Judah, from prison, showing that God has not completely abandoned his people in their exile.

2 KINGS

Elijah and King Ahaziah

1 After Ahab died, Moab broke away from
Israel's rule. 2Ahaziah fell down through
the wooden bars in his upstairs room in
Samaria and was badly hurt. He sent messengers
and told them, "Go, ask Baal-Zebub, god of Ekron,
if I will recover from my injuries."
3But the LORD's angel said to Elijah the Tishbite, "Go up and meet the messengers sent by the
king of Samaria. Ask them, 'Why are you going to
ask questions of Baal-Zebub, god of Ekron? Is it
because you think there is no God in Israel?'
4This is what the LORD says: 'You will never get
up from the bed you are lying on; you will die.'"
Then Elijah left.
5When the messengers returned to Ahaziah, he
asked them, "Why have you returned?"
6They said, "A man came to meet us. He said,
'Go back to the king who sent you and tell him
what the LORD says: "Why do you send messengers to ask questions of Baal-Zebub, god of Ekron?
Is it because you think there is no God in Israel?
You will never get up from the bed you are lying
on; you will die."' "
7Ahaziah asked them, "What did the man look
like who met you and told you this?"
8They answered, "He was a hairy man and
wore a leather belt around his waist."
Ahaziah said, "It was Elijah the Tishbite."
9Then he sent a captain with his fifty men to
Elijah. The captain went to Elijah, who was sitting on top of the hill, and said to him, "Man of
God, the king says, 'Come down!'"
10Elijah answered the captain, "If I am a man of
God, let fire come down from heaven and burn
up you and your fifty men." Then fire came down
from heaven and burned up the captain and his
fifty men.
11Ahaziah sent another captain and fifty men to
Elijah. The captain said to him, "Man of God, this
is what the king says: 'Come down quickly!'"
12Elijah answered, "If I am a man of God, let
fire come down from heaven and burn up you and
your fifty men!" Then fire came down from heaven
and burned up the captain and his fifty men.
13Ahaziah then sent a third captain with his
fifty men. The third captain came and fell down
on his knees before Elijah and begged, "Man of
God, please respect my life and the lives of your
fifty servants. 14See, fire came down from heaven
and burned up the first two captains of fifty with
all their men. But now, respect my life."
15The LORD's angel said to Elijah, "Go down
with him and don't be afraid of him." So Elijah
got up and went down with him to see the king.
16Elijah told Ahaziah, "This is what the LORD
says: 'You have sent messengers to ask questions
of Baal-Zebub, god of Ekron. Is it because you
think there is no God in Israel to ask? Because of
this, you will never get up from your bed; you will
die.'" 17So Ahaziah died, just as the LORD,
through Elijah, had said he would.
Joram became king in Ahaziah's place during
the second year Jehoram son of Jehoshaphat was
king of Judah. Joram ruled because Ahaziah had
no son to take his place. 18The other things
Ahaziah did are written in the book of the history
of the kings of Israel.

Elijah Is Taken to Heaven

2 It was almost time for the LORD to take Elijah
by a whirlwind up into heaven. While Elijah
and Elisha were leaving Gilgal, 2Elijah said to Elisha,
"Please stay here. The LORD has told me to go to
Bethel."
But Elisha said, "As the LORD lives, and as you
live, I won't leave you." So they went down to
Bethel. 3The groups of prophets at Bethel came
out to Elisha and said to him, "Do you know the
LORD will take your master away from you today?"
Elisha said, "Yes, I know, but don't talk about it."
4Elijah said to him, "Stay here, Elisha, because
the LORD has sent me to Jericho."
But Elisha said, "As the LORD lives, and as you
live, I won't leave you."
So they went to Jericho. 5The groups of prophets at Jericho came to Elisha and said, "Do you
know that the LORD will take your master away
from you today?"
Elisha answered, "Yes, I know, but don't talk
about it."
6Elijah said to Elisha, "Stay here. The LORD has
sent me to the Jordan River."
Elisha answered, "As the LORD lives, and as you
live, I won't leave you."
So the two of them went on. 7Fifty men of the
groups of prophets came and stood far from
where Elijah and Elisha were by the Jordan.
8Elijah took off his coat, rolled it up, and hit the

1:1 In the ancient Near East it was common for conquered lands to try to assert their independence at the time of the death of a powerful king.
1:3 Baal-Zebub was the local manifestation of the Canaanite god Baal. Literally, the name means "Lord of the flies," but this may be a derisive nickname given to the god who was probably known by his worshipers as Baal-Zebul, "the Lord Prince."

water. The water divided to the right and to the left,
and Elijah and Elisha crossed over on dry ground.
9After they had crossed over, Elijah said to
Elisha, "What can I do for you before I am taken
from you?"
Elisha said, "Leave me a double share of your
spirit."
10Elijah said, "You have asked a hard thing. But
if you see me when I am taken from you, it will
be yours. If you don't, it won't happen."
11As they were walking and talking, a chariot
and horses of fire appeared and separated Elijah
from Elisha. Then Elijah went up to heaven in a
whirlwind. 12Elisha saw it and shouted, "My
father! My father! The chariots of Israel and their
horsemen!" And Elisha did not see him anymore.
Then Elisha grabbed his own clothes and tore
them to show how sad he was.
13He picked up Elijah's coat that had fallen from
him. Then he returned and stood on the bank of
the Jordan. 14Elisha hit the water with Elijah's
coat and said, "Where is the LORD, the God of
Elijah?" When he hit the water, it divided to the
right and to the left, and Elisha crossed over.
15The groups of prophets at Jericho were
watching and said, "Elisha now has the spirit
Elijah had." And they came to meet him, bowing
down to the ground before him. 16They said to
him, "There are fifty strong men with us. Please
let them go and look for your master. Maybe the
Spirit of the LORD has taken Elijah up and set him
down on some mountain or in some valley."
But Elisha answered, "No, don't send them."
17When the groups of prophets had begged
Elisha until he couldn't refuse them anymore, he
said, "Send them." So they sent fifty men who
looked for three days, but they could not find
him. 18Then they came back to Elisha at Jericho
where he was staying. He said to them, "I told
you not to go, didn't I?"

Elisha Makes the Water Pure

19The people of the city said to Elisha, "Look,
master, this city is a nice place to live as you can
see. But the water is so bad the land cannot grow
crops."
20Elisha said, "Bring me a new bowl and put
salt in it." So they brought it to him.
21Then he went out to the spring and threw the
salt in it. He said, "This is what the LORD says: 'I
have healed this water. From now on it won't
cause death, and it won't keep the land from
growing crops.'" 22So the water has been healed
to this day just as Elisha had said.

Boys Make Fun of Elisha

23From there Elisha went up to Bethel. On the
way some boys came out of the city and made fun
of him. They said to him, "Go up too, you baldhead! Go up too, you baldhead!" 24Elisha turned
around, looked at them, and put a curse on them
in the name of the LORD. Then two mother bears
came out of the woods and tore forty-two of the
boys to pieces. 25Elisha went to Mount Carmel
and from there he returned to Samaria.

War Between Israel and Moab

3 Joram son of Ahab became king over Israel at
Samaria in Jehoshaphat's eighteenth year as
king of Judah. And Joram ruled twelve years. 2He
did what the LORD said was wrong, but he was
not like his father and mother; he removed the
stone pillars his father had made for Baal. 3But he
continued to sin like Jeroboam son of Nebat who
had led Israel to sin. Joram did not stop doing
these same sins.
4Mesha king of Moab raised sheep. He paid the
king of Israel one hundred thousand lambs and
the wool of one hundred thousand sheep. 5But
when Ahab died, the king of Moab turned against
the king of Israel. 6So King Joram went out from
Samaria and gathered Israel's army. 7He also sent
messengers to Jehoshaphat king of Judah. "The
king of Moab has turned against me," he said.
"Will you go with me to fight Moab?"
Jehoshaphat replied, "I will go with you. My
soldiers and my horses are yours."
8Jehoshaphat asked, "Which way should we
attack?"
Joram answered, "Through the Desert of Edom."
9So the king of Israel went with the king of Judah
and the king of Edom. After they had marched
seven days, there was no more water for the army
or for their animals that were with them. 10The
king of Israel said, "This is terrible! The LORD has
called us three kings together to hand us over to
the Moabites!"
11But Jehoshaphat asked, "Is there a prophet of
the LORD here? We can ask the LORD through him."
An officer of the king of Israel answered, "Elisha
son of Shaphat is here. He was Elijah's servant."
12Jehoshaphat said, "He speaks the LORD's
truth." So the king of Israel and Jehoshaphat and
the king of Edom went down to see Elisha.

2:9 *Leave . . . spirit.* By law, the first son in a family would inherit a double share of his father's possessions. Elisha is asking to inherit a share of his master's power as his follower. He is not asking for twice as much power as Elijah had.

2:9 Blessing: Psalm 128

2:20 Salt: Job 6:6

13Elisha said to the king of Israel, "I have nothing to do with you. Go to the prophets of your father and to the prophets of your mother!"

The king of Israel said to Elisha, "No, the LORD has called us three kings together to hand us over to the Moabites."

14Elisha said, "As surely as the LORD All-Powerful lives, whom I serve, I tell you the truth. I wouldn't even look at you or notice you if Jehoshaphat king of Judah were not here. I respect him. 15Now bring me someone who plays the harp."

While the harp was being played, the LORD gave Elisha power. 16Then Elisha said, "The LORD says to dig holes in the valley. 17The LORD says you won't see wind or rain, but the valley will be filled with water. Then you, your cattle, and your other animals can drink. 18This is easy for the LORD to do; he will also hand Moab over to you. 19You will destroy every strong, walled city and every important town. You will cut down every good tree and stop up all springs. You will ruin every good field with rocks."

20The next morning, about the time the sacrifice was offered, water came from the direction of Edom and filled the valley.

21All the Moabites heard that the kings had come up to fight against them. So they gathered everyone old enough to put on armor and waited at the border. 22But when the Moabites got up early in the morning, the sun was shining on the water. They saw the water across from them, and it looked as red as blood. 23Then they said, "This is blood! The kings must have fought and killed each other! Come, Moabites, let's take the valuables from the dead bodies!"

24When the Moabites came to the camp of Israel, the Israelites came out and fought them until they ran away. Then the Israelites went on into the land, killing the Moabites. 25They tore down the cities and threw rocks all over every good field. They stopped up all the springs and cut down all the good trees. Kir Hareseth was the only city with its stones still in place, but the men with slingshots surrounded it and conquered it, too.

26When the king of Moab saw that the battle was too much for him, he took seven hundred men with swords to try to break through to the king of Edom. But they could not break through. 27Then the king of Moab took his oldest son, who would have been king after him, and offered him as a burnt offering on the wall. So there was great anger against the Israelites, who left and went back to their own land.

A Widow Asks Elisha for Help

4 The wife of a man from the groups of prophets said to Elisha, "Your servant, my husband, is dead. You know he honored the LORD. But now the man he owes money to is coming to take my two boys as his slaves!"

2Elisha answered, "How can I help you? Tell me, what do you have in your house?"

The woman said, "I don't have anything there except a pot of oil."

3Then Elisha said, "Go and get empty jars from all your neighbors. Don't ask for just a few. 4Then go into your house and shut the door behind you and your sons. Pour oil into all the jars, and set the full ones aside."

5So she left Elisha and shut the door behind her and her sons. As they brought the jars to her, she poured out the oil. 6When the jars were all full, she said to her son, "Bring me another jar."

But he said, "There are no more jars." Then the oil stopped flowing.

7She went and told Elisha. And the prophet said to her, "Go, sell the oil and pay what you owe. You and your sons can live on what is left."

The Shunammite Woman

8One day Elisha went to Shunem, where an important woman lived. She begged Elisha to stay and eat. So every time Elisha passed by, he stopped there to eat. 9The woman said to her husband, "I know that this is a holy man of God who passes by our house all the time. 10Let's make a small room on the roof and put a bed in the room for him. We can put a table, a chair, and a lampstand there. Then when he comes by, he can stay there."

11One day Elisha came to the woman's house. After he went to his room and rested, 12he said to his servant Gehazi, "Call the Shunammite woman."

When the servant had called her, she stood in front of him. 13Elisha had told his servant, "Now say to her, 'You have gone to all this trouble for us. What can I do for you? Do you want me to

3:27 Child sacrifice on the battlefield was a rare but verifiable practice in the ancient Near East. Israel may have withdrawn out of simple disgust.

4:8–10 Hospitality was, and is, very important in the Middle East. The story of the Shunammite woman who had a room constructed on the roof of her house where the prophet Elisha could stay whenever he was in the area is especially touching. By opening her home to the prophet, the woman was greatly blessed by God. Today, when families show similar hospitality to missionaries, they are also blessed.

4:10 *roof.* In Bible times houses were built with flat roofs. The roof was used for drying things such as flax and fruit, as an extra room, as a place for worship, and as a cool place to sleep in the summer.

speak to the king or the commander of the army
for you?'"

She answered, "I live among my own people."
14Elisha said to Gehazi, "But what can we do
for her?"

He answered, "She has no son, and her husband is old."

15Then Elisha said to Gehazi, "Call her." When
he called her, she stood in the doorway. 16Then
Elisha said, "About this time next year, you will
hold a son in your arms."

The woman said, "No, master, man of God,
don't lie to me, your servant!"

17But the woman became pregnant and gave
birth to a son at that time the next year, just as
Elisha had told her.

18The boy grew up and one day went out to his
father, who was with the grain harvesters. 19The
boy said to his father, "My head! My head!"

The father said to his servant, "Take him to his
mother!" 20The servant took him to his mother,
and he lay on his mother's lap until noon. Then
he died. 21So she took him up and laid him on
Elisha's bed. Then she shut the door and left.

22She called to her husband, "Send me one of
the servants and one of the donkeys. Then I can
go quickly to the man of God and return."

23The husband said, "Why do you want to go to
him today? It isn't the New Moon or the Sabbath
day."

She said, "It will be all right."

24Then she saddled the donkey and said to her
servant, "Lead on. Don't slow down for me
unless I tell you." 25So she went to Elisha, the
man of God, at Mount Carmel.

When he saw her coming from far away, he said
to his servant Gehazi, "Look, there's the Shunammite woman! 26Run to meet her and ask, 'Are you all
right? Is your husband all right? Is the boy all right?'"

She answered, "Everything is all right."

27Then she came to Elisha at the hill and
grabbed his feet. Gehazi came near to pull her
away, but Elisha said to him, "Leave her alone.
She's very upset, and the LORD has not told me
about it. He has hidden it from me."

28She said, "Master, did I ask you for a son?
Didn't I tell you not to lie to me?"

29Then Elisha said to Gehazi, "Get ready. Take
my walking stick in your hand and go quickly. If
you meet anyone, don't say hello. If anyone
greets you, don't respond. Lay my walking stick
on the boy's face."

30The boy's mother said, "As surely as the LORD
lives and as you live, I won't leave you!" So Elisha
got up and followed her.

31Gehazi went on ahead and laid the walking
stick on the boy's face, but the boy did not talk or
move. Then Gehazi went back to meet Elisha.
"The boy has not awakened," he said.

32When Elisha came into the house, the boy
was lying dead on his bed. 33Elisha entered the
room and shut the door, so only he and the boy
were in the room. Then he prayed to the LORD.
34He went to the bed and lay on the boy, putting his
mouth on the boy's mouth, his eyes on the boy's
eyes, and his hands on the boy's hands. He
stretched himself out on top of the boy. Soon the
boy's skin became warm. 35Elisha turned away and
walked around the room. Then he went back and
put himself on the boy again. The boy sneezed
seven times and opened his eyes.

36Elisha called Gehazi and said, "Call the Shunammite!" So he did. When she came, Elisha
said, "Pick up your son." 37She came in and fell at
Elisha's feet, bowing facedown to the floor. Then
she picked up her son and went out.

Elisha and the Stew

38When Elisha returned to Gilgal, there was a
shortage of food in the land. While the groups of
prophets were sitting in front of him, he said to
his servant, "Put the large pot on the fire, and boil
some stew for these men."

39One of them went out into the field to gather
plants. Finding a wild vine, he picked fruit from
the vine and filled his robe with it. Then he came
and cut up the fruit into the pot. But they didn't
know what kind of fruit it was. 40They poured out
the stew for the others to eat. When they began
to eat it, they shouted, "Man of God, there's death
in the pot!" And they could not eat it.

41Elisha told them to bring some flour. He
threw it into the pot and said, "Pour it out for the
people to eat." Then there was nothing harmful
in the pot.

Elisha Feeds the People

42A man from Baal Shalishah came to Elisha,
bringing him twenty loaves of barley bread from
the first harvest. He also brought fresh grain in
his sack. Elisha said, "Give it to the people to
eat."

43Elisha's servant asked, "How can I feed a
hundred people with so little?"

"Give the bread to the people to eat," Elisha
said. "This is what the LORD says: 'They will eat
and will have food left over.'" 44After he gave it to
them, the people ate and had food left over, as the
LORD had said.

Naaman Is Healed

5 Naaman was commander of the army of the king of Aram. He was honored by his master, and he had much respect because the LORD used him to give victory to Aram. He was a mighty and brave man, but he had a skin disease.

2The Arameans had gone out to raid the Israelites and had taken a little girl as a captive. This little girl served Naaman's wife. 3She said to her mistress, "I wish my master would meet the prophet who lives in Samaria. He would cure him of his disease."

4Naaman went to the king and told him what the girl from Israel had said. 5The king of Aram said, "Go ahead, and I will send a letter to the king of Israel." So Naaman left and took with him about seven hundred fifty pounds of silver, as well as one hundred fifty pounds of gold and ten changes of clothes. 6He brought the letter to the king of Israel, which read, "I am sending my servant Naaman to you so you can heal him of his skin disease."

7When the king of Israel read the letter, he tore his clothes to show how upset he was. He said, "I'm not God! I can't kill and make alive again! Why does this man send someone with a skin disease for me to heal? You can see that the king of Aram is trying to start trouble with me."

8When Elisha, the man of God, heard that the king of Israel had torn his clothes, he sent the king this message: "Why have you torn your clothes? Let Naaman come to me. Then he will know there is a prophet in Israel." 9So Naaman went with his horses and chariots to Elisha's house and stood outside the door.

10Elisha sent Naaman a messenger who said, "Go and wash in the Jordan River seven times. Then your skin will be healed, and you will be clean."

11Naaman became angry and left. He said, "I thought Elisha would surely come out and stand before me and call on the name of the LORD his God. I thought he would wave his hand over the place and heal the disease. 12The Abana and the Pharpar, the rivers of Damascus, are better than all the waters of Israel. Why can't I wash in them and become clean?" So Naaman went away very angry.

13Naaman's servants came near and said to him, "My father, if the prophet had told you to do some great thing, wouldn't you have done it? Doesn't it make more sense just to do it? After all, he only told you, 'Wash, and you will be clean.'" 14So Naaman went down and dipped in the Jordan seven times, just as Elisha had said. Then his skin became new again, like the skin of a child. And he was clean.

15Naaman and all his group returned to Elisha. He stood before Elisha and said, "Look, I now know there is no God in all the earth except in Israel. Now please accept a gift from me."

16But Elisha said, "As surely as the LORD lives whom I serve, I won't accept anything." Naaman urged him to take the gift, but he refused.

17Then Naaman said, "If you won't take the gift, then please give me some soil—as much as two of my mules can carry. From now on I'll not offer any burnt offering or sacrifice to any other gods but the LORD. 18But let the LORD pardon me for this: When my master goes into the temple of Rimmon to worship, he leans on my arm. Then I must bow in that temple. May the LORD pardon me when I do that."

19Elisha said to him, "Go in peace."

Naaman left Elisha and went a short way. 20Gehazi, the servant of Elisha the man of God, thought, "My master has not accepted what Naaman the Aramean brought. As surely as the LORD lives, I'll run after him and get something from him." 21So Gehazi went after Naaman.

When Naaman saw someone running after him, he got off the chariot to meet Gehazi. He asked, "Is everything all right?"

22Gehazi said, "Everything is all right. My master has sent me. He said, 'Two young men from the groups of prophets in the mountains of Ephraim just came to me. Please give them seventy-five pounds of silver and two changes of clothes.'"

23Naaman said, "Please take one hundred fifty pounds," and he urged Gehazi to take it. He tied one hundred fifty pounds of silver in two bags with two changes of clothes. Then he gave them to two of his servants to carry for Gehazi. 24When they came to the hill, Gehazi took these things from Naaman's servants and put them in the house. Then he let Naaman's servants go, and they left.

25When he came in and stood before his master, Elisha said to him, "Where have you been, Gehazi?"

"I didn't go anywhere," he answered.

26But Elisha said to him, "My spirit was with

5:8–14 The incident of the healing of the Syrian general, Naaman, by having him bathe seven times in the Jordan River reveals the power of God. It also reveals the contempt with which other nations viewed this river, which is full and swift in winter but slow and shallow in summer. Naaman's derogatory comparison of the Jordan River with the rivers of Damascus says it all (verse 12).

5:14 Jordan River: Psalm 42

5:15 Evangelism: Nehemiah 6:15–16

5:18 *temple of Rimmon.* The place where the Aramean people worshiped the god Rimmon.

SOLOMON

1 KINGS 1

Who was Solomon? How did Solomon become wise?
Why did Solomon turn against the Lord?

Solomon was the third (after Saul and David) and last king of a united Israel, when both the northern and southern kingdoms were one. He was the son of David and Bathsheba (2 Samuel 12:24–25). He was not the oldest son of David, but his father nonetheless chose him to follow him on the throne of Israel. When David was very old, another son, Adonijah, tried to put himself on the throne of Israel. He had some very powerful allies, but when Bathsheba and Nathan the prophet reminded David of his earlier promise, the king declared that Solomon was his successor (1 Kings 1). Apparently, Solomon ruled with David during the last days of that great king's life.

After David died, Solomon became the sole ruler of Israel. During the early years of his rule, Solomon showed that he was a godly king, earnest in his desire to serve the Lord. First Kings 3:1–15 describes his trip to Gibeon, which was the most important place of worship before the Temple was built. In his love for the Lord, Solomon offered a thousand burnt offerings (1 Kings 3:4). In response, God gave Solomon the most incredible opportunity. He said to him, "Ask for whatever you want me to give you" (1 Kings 3:5).

Solomon could have asked for anything. But he looked into his heart and knew what he needed. He asked for wisdom from God, whom he knew was the source of all real wisdom. Solomon understood that the kingship would demand great things from him, and so he requested God's wisdom.

God was pleased with Solomon's request. It was, after all, motivated by Solomon's concerns for others rather than for himself. He told Solomon that he would not only become the wisest person alive, but he would also become rich and famous. Indeed, as we read through the account of Solomon's rule (1 Kings 2–11), we see how God made Solomon rich through his wisdom.

Solomon's wisdom became proverbial. In 1 Kings 3:16–28 we read an account of a court case involving two women. He insightfully solved a dispute over a child, a case made difficult because no witnesses were present to speak on behalf of either woman. With the understanding of motherhood, Solomon ordered the child cut in two so that each woman could have half. Solomon knew that the true mother would rather give up the child than see him die. As a result of this ruling, Israel marveled: "They saw he had wisdom from God to make the right decisions" (1 Kings 3:28).

Solomon's reputation, however, extended far beyond the borders of Israel. His widespread fame is evidenced in the story of the queen of Sheba (1 Kings 10:1–13). Sheba was a wealthy country because of its trade in spices and precious metals. While the exact location of Sheba is disputed, the best guess places it at approximately the same area as modern Yemen. This identification means that the queen traveled about 1,400 miles to meet Solomon in Jerusalem. The queen was amazed by Solomon's wisdom and his wealth. Solomon's wisdom caused this Gentile queen to praise God: "Praise the LORD your God, who was pleased to make you king of Israel" (1 Kings 10:9).

Solomon's wisdom was practical. It was not abstract knowledge, but it taught people how to live. Solomon did not write the whole Book of Proverbs, but he was responsible for most of that book (Proverbs 1:1). In that book, he taught that "knowledge begins with respect for the LORD, but fools hate wisdom and self-control" (Proverbs 1:7) and gave much practical advice about how one should behave in everyday life. Solomon's name is also associated with two other books of wisdom in the Old Testament: Ecclesiastes (see 1:12) and the Song of Solomon (1:1).

One of the first items on Solomon's kingly agenda was the building of the Temple (1 Kings 6:1–8:66). David, his father, had desired to build the Temple (2 Samuel 7), but God had told him that the time was not yet right. Instead, his son, Solomon, was the one who would build the Temple (2 Samuel 7:13). The Temple, in contrast to the Meeting Tent or Tabernacle, symbolized God's permanent dwelling and Israel's final settlement of the land. David was the one to finish the settlement, and so it was left to Solomon—whose very name means "Peace"—to build this place of worship.

One of the great ironic tragedies of the Bible is Solomon's fall into sin. Here is one who earnestly sought God with all his heart and received God's abundant blessing, but, nonetheless, by the time of his death, "the king turned away from following the LORD" (1 Kings 11:9). He was worshiping false gods at strange altars.

Solomon: For additional scriptures on this topic go to 1 Kings 11:1.

Elijah and Elisha

1 Kings 17:1

Who are Elijah and Elisha, and what role do they play in the history of Israel? How do they combat false religion? How does their prophetic ministry look forward to Jesus Christ?

Elijah and Elisha were prophets sent by the Lord to counter the growing unbelief and idolatry of the northern kingdom of Israel during the eighth century B.C. Their story takes up a large portion of the Book of Kings (1 Kings 17:1–2 Kings 13:21). The parallel history in Chronicles, however, only briefly mentions Elijah (2 Chronicles 21:12) due to its focus on the southern kingdom of Judah.

Elijah appeared on the scene before Elisha. Ahab was king, and he had just married a woman named Jezebel, the daughter of the king of the Sidonians and a worshiper of Baal. Baal was the main god of the Canaanites and throughout the whole period of the Old Testament. Jezebel wanted to promote the worship of Baal in Israel. Baal was the god of rain, dew, and fertility, and these were valued highly in the rather dry land of Israel. The evidence indicates that many Israelites turned away from the Lord to worship Baal during Ahab's kingship.

As a result, God sent Elijah to confront Ahab and lead the people back to true worship. When Elijah first appeared, he spoke boldly to Ahab and proclaimed, "As surely as the LORD lives, no rain or dew will fall during the next few years unless I command it" (1 Kings 17:1). It was as if God said to Israel, "Since you are seeking fertility from a false god like Baal, I will keep it from you." God was going to show Ahab and Israel who really controlled the fertility of the land and the blessings of life.

This initial confrontation led to the famous contest on Mount Carmel (1 Kings 18). Here Elijah met four hundred and fifty prophets of Baal. The object of the contest was to see whose god could light the fire on the altar. From a human point of view, Elijah had the definite disadvantage. Besides the numerical advantage, the prophets of Baal went first. Also remember that Baal was the god of rain which included lightning. But, since Baal was a figment of the people's imagination, the prophets of Baal were unsuccessful. Then it was the turn of Elijah's God.

In order to emphasize the divine origin of the fire, Elijah began by making the odds even worse by pouring water on the wood (1 Kings 18:34–35). He then prayed, and God answered the prayer by sending fire down from the sky which consumed the sacrifice. This contest showed the people that Baal was nothing, and God controlled the powers of nature. Elijah prayed again, and the rains which had been withheld since 1 Kings 17:1 came down (1 Kings 18:41–46).

While this contest had a huge impact on the people, the problem of false worship continued. The prophet also attracted the special hatred of Jezebel. This reaction sent Elijah into a depression, and he ran away to the wilderness, where God bolstered his confidence by appearing to him and telling him that a remnant of the faithful remained in Israel. "I have seven thousand people left in Israel who have never bowed down before Baal and whose mouths have never kissed his idol" (1 Kings 19:18). God also blessed Elijah by sending him an apprentice, an energetic young man named Elisha. Together, they continued their divinely given work to counter the forces of evil in God's kingdom.

Eventually, the time came for Elijah to be with God. As a sign of his grace, Elijah did not die. Rather, he was taken up to heaven in a chariot of fire (2 Kings 2:1–18). Further, Elisha was appointed Elijah's successor to lead the fight against Baal worship in Israel.

The account of Elisha's solo ministry is filled with amazing accounts of miracles. To the modern reader, some of the stories seem strange and out of place. For instance, in one place one of Elisha's apprentices lost an axhead in a body of water (2 Kings 6:1–7). This represented a huge loss since iron was rare and expensive, and the ax was borrowed. But when Elisha came and caused the axhead to float, it did more than save them lots of money. It also showed God's power over the waters. This has special significance because Baal worship claimed that Baal was in charge of the waters. When this is realized, it becomes obvious why so many of the miracles concern water.

While Elijah and Elisha are not mentioned frequently outside of the Book of Kings, it is indeed noteworthy that the Old Testament ends with the promise that Elijah is coming again (Malachi 4:5–6).

Elijah and Elisha: For additional scriptures on this topic go to 1 Kings 17:1–2 Kings 13:21.

you. I knew when the man turned from his chariot to meet you. This isn't a time to take money, clothes, olives, grapes, sheep, oxen, male servants, or female servants. 27So Naaman's skin disease will come on you and your children forever." When Gehazi left Elisha, he had the disease and was as white as snow.

An Axhead Floats

6 The groups of prophets said to Elisha, "The place where we meet with you is too small for us. 2Let's go to the Jordan River. There everyone can get a log, and let's build a place there to live."

Elisha said, "Go."

3One of them said, "Please go with us."

Elisha answered, "I will go," 4so he went with them. When they arrived at the Jordan, they cut down some trees. 5As one man was cutting down a tree, the head of his ax fell into the water. He yelled, "Oh, my master! I borrowed that ax!"

6Elisha asked, "Where did it fall?" The man showed him the place. Then Elisha cut down a stick and threw it into the water, and it made the iron head float. 7Elisha said, "Pick up the axhead." Then the man reached out and took it.

Elisha and the Blinded Arameans

8The king of Aram was at war with Israel. He had a council meeting with his officers and said, "I will set up my camp in this place."

9Elisha, the man of God, sent a message to the king of Israel, saying, "Be careful! Don't pass that place, because the Arameans are going down there!"

10The king of Israel checked the place about which Elisha had warned him. Elisha warned him several times, so the king protected himself there.

11The king of Aram was angry about this. He called his officers together and demanded, "Tell me who of us is working for the king of Israel."

12One of the officers said, "None, my master and king. It's Elisha, the prophet from Israel. He can tell you what you speak in your bedroom."

13The king said, "Go and find him so I can send men and catch him."

The servants came back and reported, "He is in Dothan."

14Then the king sent horses, chariots, and many troops to Dothan. They arrived at night and surrounded the city.

15Elisha's servant got up early, and when he went out, he saw an army with horses and chariots all around the city. The servant said to Elisha, "Oh, my master, what can we do?"

16Elisha said, "Don't be afraid. The army that fights for us is larger than the one against us."

17Then Elisha prayed, "LORD, open my servant's eyes, and let him see."

The LORD opened the eyes of the young man, and he saw that the mountain was full of horses and chariots of fire all around Elisha.

18As the enemy came down toward Elisha, he prayed to the LORD, "Make these people blind." So he made the Aramean army blind, as Elisha had asked.

19Elisha said to them, "This is not the right road or the right city. Follow me and I'll take you to the man you are looking for." Then Elisha led them to Samaria.

20After they entered Samaria, Elisha said, "LORD, open these men's eyes so they can see." So the LORD opened their eyes, and the Aramean army saw that they were inside the city of Samaria!

21When the king of Israel saw the Aramean army, he said to Elisha, "My father, should I kill them? Should I kill them?"

22Elisha answered, "Don't kill them. You wouldn't kill people whom you captured with your sword and bow. Give them food and water, and let them eat and drink and then go home to their master." 23So he prepared a great feast for the Aramean army. After they ate and drank, the king sent them away, and they went home to their master. The soldiers of Aram did not come anymore into the land of Israel.

A Shortage of Food

24Later, Ben-Hadad king of Aram gathered his whole army and surrounded and attacked Samaria. 25There was a shortage of food in Samaria. It was so bad that a donkey's head sold for about two pounds of silver, and half of a pint of dove's dung sold for about two ounces of silver.

26As the king of Israel was passing by on the wall, a woman yelled out to him, "Help me, my master and king!"

27The king said, "If the LORD doesn't help you, how can I? Can I get help from the threshing floor or from the winepress?" 28Then the king said to her, "What is your trouble?"

She answered, "This woman said to me, 'Give up your son so we can eat him today. Then we will eat

5:27 Mission: Matthew 10:1–15

6:5 An ax, with an iron head, was an incredibly expensive tool in the ancient world. The miracle of its recovery shows the power of God, through the prophet, to control the waters, which throughout this section have symbolic overtones. On the basis of ancient Near Eastern texts, the Bible often uses the waters to stand for the forces of chaos that stand in conflict against God.

6:25 Famine: 2 Kings 8:1

my son tomorrow.' 29So we boiled my son and ate him. Then the next day I said to her, 'Give up your son so we can eat him.' But she had hidden him."

30When the king heard the woman's words, he tore his clothes in grief. As he walked along the wall, the people looked and saw he had on rough cloth under his clothes to show his sadness. 31He said, "May God punish me terribly if the head of Elisha son of Shaphat isn't cut off from his body today!"

32The king sent a messenger to Elisha, who was sitting in his house with the older leaders. But before the messenger arrived, Elisha said to them, "See, this murderer is sending men to cut off my head. When the messenger arrives, shut the door and hold it; don't let him in. The sound of his master's feet is behind him."

33Elisha was still talking with the leaders when the messenger arrived. The king said, "This trouble has come from the LORD. Why should I wait for the LORD any longer?"

7 Elisha said, "Listen to the LORD's word. This is what the LORD says: 'About this time tomorrow seven quarts of fine flour will be sold for two-fifths of an ounce of silver, and thirteen quarts of barley will be sold for two-fifths of an ounce of silver. This will happen at the gate of Samaria.'"

2Then the officer who was close to the king answered Elisha, "Even if the LORD opened windows in the sky, that couldn't happen."

Elisha said, "You will see it with your eyes, but you will not eat any of it."

3There were four men with a skin disease at the entrance to the city gate. They said to each other, "Why do we sit here until we die? 4There is no food in the city. So if we go into the city, we will die there. If we stay here, we will die. So let's go to the Aramean camp. If they let us live, we will live. If they kill us, we die."

5So they got up at twilight and went to the Aramean camp, but when they arrived, no one was there. 6The Lord had caused the Aramean army to hear the sound of chariots, horses, and a large army. They had said to each other, "The king of Israel has hired the Hittite and Egyptian kings to attack us!" 7So they got up and ran away in the twilight, leaving their tents, horses, and donkeys. They left the camp standing and ran for their lives.

8When the men with the skin disease came to the edge of the camp, they went into one of the tents and ate and drank. They carried silver, gold, and clothes out of the camp and hid them. Then they came back and entered another tent. They carried things from this tent and hid them, also.

9Then they said to each other, "We're doing wrong. Today we have good news, but we are silent. If we wait until the sun comes up, we'll be discovered. Let's go right now and tell the people in the king's palace."

10So they went and called to the gatekeepers of the city. They said, "We went to the Aramean camp, but no one is there; we didn't hear anyone. The horses and donkeys were still tied up, and the tents were still standing." 11Then the gatekeepers shouted out and told the people in the palace.

12The king got up in the night and said to his officers, "I'll tell you what the Arameans are doing to us. They know we are starving. They have gone out of the camp to hide in the field. They're saying, 'When the Israelites come out of the city, we'll capture them alive. Then we'll enter the city.'"

13One of his officers answered, "Let some men take five of the horses that are still left in the city. These men are like all the Israelites who are left; they are also about to die. Let's send them to see what has happened."

14So the men took two chariots with horses. The king sent them after the Aramean army, saying, "Go and see what has happened." 15The men followed the Aramean army as far as the Jordan River. The road was full of clothes and equipment that the Arameans had thrown away as they had hurriedly left. So the messengers returned and told the king. 16Then the people went out and took valuables from the Aramean camp. So seven quarts of fine flour were sold for two-fifths of an ounce of silver, and thirteen quarts of barley were sold for two-fifths of an ounce of silver, just as the LORD had said.

17The king chose the officer who was close to him to guard the gate, but the people trampled the officer to death. This happened just as Elisha had told the king when the king came to his house. 18He had said, "Thirteen quarts of barley and seven quarts of fine flour will each sell for two-fifths of an ounce of silver about this time tomorrow at the gate of Samaria."

19But the officer had answered, "Even if the LORD opened windows in the sky, that couldn't happen." And Elisha had told him, "You will see it with your eyes, but you won't eat any of it." 20It happened to the officer just that way. The people trampled him in the gateway, and he died.

The Shunammite Regains Her Land

8 Elisha spoke to the woman whose son he had brought back to life. He said, "Get up and go with your family. Stay any place you can, because the LORD has called for a time without food that

will last seven years." 2So the woman got up and did as the man of God had said. She left with her family, and they stayed in the land of the Philistines for seven years. 3After seven years she returned from the land of the Philistines and went to beg the king for her house and land. 4The king was talking with Gehazi, the servant of the man of God. The king had said, "Please tell me all the great things Elisha has done." 5Gehazi was telling the king how Elisha had brought a dead boy back to life. Just then the woman whose son Elisha had brought back to life came and begged the king for her house and land.

Gehazi said, "My master and king, this is the woman, and this is the son Elisha brought back to life."

6The king asked the woman, and she told him about it. Then the king chose an officer to help her. "Give the woman everything that is hers," the king said. "Give her all the money made from her land from the day she left until now."

Ben-Hadad Is Killed

7Then Elisha went to Damascus, where Ben-Hadad king of Aram was sick. Someone told him, "The man of God has arrived."

8The king said to Hazael, "Take a gift in your hand and go meet him. Ask the LORD through him if I will recover from my sickness."

9So Hazael went to meet Elisha, taking with him a gift of forty camels loaded with every good thing in Damascus. He came and stood before Elisha and said, "Your son Ben-Hadad king of Aram sent me to you. He asks if he will recover from his sickness."

10Elisha said to Hazael, "Go and tell Ben-Hadad, 'You will surely recover,' but the LORD has told me he will really die." 11Hazael stared at Elisha until he felt ashamed. Then Elisha cried.

12Hazael asked, "Why are you crying, master?"

Elisha answered, "Because I know what evil you will do to the Israelites. You will burn their strong, walled cities with fire and kill their young men with swords. You will throw their babies to the ground and split open their pregnant women."

13Hazael said, "Am I a dog? How could I do such things?"

Elisha answered, "The LORD has shown me that you will be king over Aram."

14Then Hazael left Elisha and came to his master. Ben-Hadad said to him, "What did Elisha say to you?"

Hazael answered, "He told me that you will surely recover." 15But the next day Hazael took a blanket and dipped it in water. Then he put it over Ben-Hadad's face, and he died. So Hazael became king in Ben-Hadad's place.

Jehoram King of Judah

16While Jehoshaphat was king in Judah, Jehoram son of Jehoshaphat became king of Judah. This was during the fifth year Joram son of Ahab was king of Israel. 17Jehoram was thirty-two years old when he began to rule, and he ruled eight years in Jerusalem. 18He followed the ways of the kings of Israel, just as the family of Ahab had done, because he married Ahab's daughter. Jehoram did what the LORD said was wrong. 19But the LORD would not destroy Judah because of his servant David. The LORD had promised that one of David's descendants would always rule.

20In Jehoram's time Edom broke away from Judah's rule and chose their own king. 21So Jehoram and all his chariots went to Zair. The Edomites surrounded him and his chariot commanders. Jehoram got up and attacked the Edomites at night, but his army ran away to their tents. 22From then until now the country of Edom has fought against the rule of Judah. At the same time Libnah also broke away from Judah's rule.

23The other acts of Jehoram and all the things he did are written in the book of the history of the kings of Judah. 24Jehoram died and was buried with his ancestors in Jerusalem, and Jehoram's son Ahaziah ruled in his place.

25Ahaziah son of Jehoram became king of Judah during the twelfth year Joram son of Ahab was king of Israel. 26Ahaziah was twenty-two years old when he became king, and he ruled one year in Jerusalem. His mother's name was Athaliah, a granddaughter of Omri king of Israel. 27Ahaziah followed the ways of Ahab's family. He did what the LORD said was wrong, as Ahab's family had done, because he was a son-in-law to Ahab.

28Ahaziah went with Joram son of Ahab to Ramoth in Gilead, where they fought against Hazael king of Aram. The Arameans wounded Joram. 29So King Joram returned to Jezreel to heal from the wound he had received from the Arameans at Ramoth when he fought Hazael king of Aram. Ahaziah son of Jehoram king of Judah went down to visit Joram son of Ahab at Jezreel, because he had been wounded.

8:1 Famine: 2 Kings 25:3

8:23 *the book of the history of the kings of Judah.* Book 2 of Kings often refers to another history book that kept an account of the great events of the southern kingdom (there was also one for the kings of Israel). This book has never been discovered and is not inspired.

Jehu Is Chosen King

9 At the same time, Elisha the prophet called a man from the groups of prophets. Elisha said, "Get ready, and take this small bottle of olive oil in your hand. Go to Ramoth in Gilead. 2When you arrive, find Jehu son of Jehoshaphat, the son of Nimshi. Go in and make Jehu get up from among his brothers, and take him to an inner room. 3Then take the bottle and pour the oil on Jehu's head and say, 'This is what the LORD says: I have appointed you king over Israel.' Then open the door and run away. Don't wait!"

4So the young man, the prophet, went to Ramoth in Gilead. 5When he arrived, he saw the officers of the army sitting together. He said, "Commander, I have a message for you."

Jehu asked, "For which one of us?"

The young man said, "For you, commander."

6Jehu got up and went into the house. Then the young prophet poured the olive oil on Jehu's head and said to him, "This is what the LORD, the God of Israel says: 'I have appointed you king over the LORD's people Israel. 7You must destroy the family of Ahab your master. I will punish Jezebel for the deaths of my servants the prophets and for all the LORD's servants who were murdered. 8All of Ahab's family must die. I will not let any male child in Ahab's family live in Israel, whether slave or free. 9I will make Ahab's family like the family of Jeroboam son of Nebat and like the family of Baasha son of Ahijah. 10The dogs will eat Jezebel at Jezreel, and no one will bury her.'"

Then the young prophet opened the door and ran away.

11When Jehu went back to his master's officers, one of them said to Jehu, "Is everything all right? Why did this crazy man come to you?"

Jehu answered, "You know the man and how he talks."

12They answered, "That's not true. Tell us."

Jehu said, "He said to me, 'This is what the LORD says: I have appointed you to be king over Israel.'"

13Then the officers hurried, and each man took off his own coat and put it on the stairs for Jehu. They blew the trumpet and shouted, "Jehu is king!"

Joram and Ahaziah Are Killed

14So Jehu son of Jehoshaphat, the son of Nimshi, made plans against Joram. Now Joram and all Israel had been defending Ramoth in Gilead from Hazael king of Aram. 15But King Joram had to return to Jezreel to heal from the injuries the Arameans had given him when he fought against Hazael king of Aram.

Jehu said, "If you agree with this, don't let anyone leave the city. They might tell the news in Jezreel." 16Then he got into his chariot and set out for Jezreel, where Joram was resting. Ahaziah king of Judah had gone down to see him.

17The lookout was standing on the watchtower in Jezreel when he saw Jehu's troops coming. He said, "I see some soldiers!"

Joram said, "Take a horseman and send him to meet them. Tell him to ask, 'Is all in order?'"

18The horseman rode out to meet Jehu, and he said, "This is what the king says: 'Is all in order?'"

Jehu said, "Why bother yourself with order? Come along behind me."

The lookout reported, "The messenger reached them, but he is not coming back."

19Then Joram sent out a second horseman. This rider came to Jehu's group and said, "This is what the king says: 'Is all in order?'"

Jehu answered, "Why bother yourself with order? Come along behind me."

20The lookout reported, "The second man reached them, but he is not coming back. The man in the chariot is driving like Jehu son of Nimshi. He drives as if he were crazy!"

21Joram said, "Get my chariot ready." Then the servant got Joram's chariot ready. Joram king of Israel and Ahaziah king of Judah went out, each in his own chariot, to meet Jehu at the property of Naboth the Jezreelite.

22When Joram saw Jehu, he said, "Is all in order, Jehu?"

Jehu answered, "There will never be any order as long as your mother Jezebel worships idols and uses witchcraft."

23Joram turned the horses to run away and yelled to Ahaziah, "It's a trick, Ahaziah!"

24Then Jehu drew his bow and shot Joram between his shoulders. The arrow went through Joram's heart, and he fell down in his chariot.

25Jehu ordered Bidkar, his chariot officer, "Pick up Joram's body, and throw it into the field of Naboth the Jezreelite. Remember when you and I rode together with Joram's father Ahab. The LORD made this prophecy against him: 26'Yesterday I saw the blood of Naboth and his sons, says the LORD, so I will punish Ahab in his field, says the LORD.' Take Joram's body and throw it into the field, as the LORD has said."

9:3 *pour the oil.* This ritual of anointing is a method of commissioning Jehu for his task and may represent his receiving the power of the Holy Spirit for the job God has given him.

10He gave the commanders the spears and shields that had belonged to King David and that were kept in the Temple of the LORD.

Joash Becomes King

11Then each guard took his place with his weapons in his hand. There were guards from the south side of the Temple to the north side. They stood by the altar and the Temple and around the king. 12Jehoiada brought out the king's son and put the crown on him and gave him a copy of the agreement. They appointed him king and poured olive oil on him. Then they clapped their hands and said, "Long live the king!"

13When Athaliah heard the noise of the guards and the people, she went to them at the Temple of the LORD. 14She looked, and there was the king, standing by the pillar, as the custom was. The officers and trumpeters were standing beside him, and all the people of the land were very happy and were blowing trumpets. Then Athaliah tore her clothes and screamed, "Traitors! Traitors!"

15Jehoiada the priest gave orders to the commanders of a hundred men, who led the army. He said, "Surround her with soldiers and kill with a sword anyone who follows her." He commanded this because he had said, "Don't put Athaliah to death in the Temple of the LORD." 16So they caught her when she came to the horses' entrance near the palace. There she was put to death.

17Then Jehoiada made an agreement between the LORD and the king and the people that they would be the LORD's special people. He also made an agreement between the king and the people. 18All the people of the land went to the temple of Baal and tore it down, smashing the altars and idols. They also killed Mattan, the priest of Baal, in front of the altars.

Then Jehoiada the priest placed guards at the Temple of the LORD. 19He took with him the commanders of a hundred men and the Carites, the royal bodyguards, as well as the guards and all the people of the land. Together they took the king out of the Temple of the LORD and went into the palace through the gate of the guards. Then the king sat on the royal throne. 20So all the people of the land were very happy, and Jerusalem had peace, because Athaliah had been put to death with the sword at the palace.

21Joash was seven years old when he became king.

12 Joash became king of Judah in Jehu's seventh year as king of Israel, and he ruled for forty years in Jerusalem. His mother's name was Zibiah, and she was from Beersheba. 2Joash did what the LORD said was right as long as Jehoiada the priest taught him. 3But the places where gods were worshiped were not removed; the people still made sacrifices and burned incense there.

Joash Repairs the Temple

4Joash said to the priests, "Take all the money brought as offerings to the Temple of the LORD. This includes the money each person owes in taxes and the money each person promises or brings freely to the LORD. 5Each priest will take the money from the people he serves. Then the priests must repair any damage they find in the Temple."

6But by the twenty-third year Joash was king, the priests still had not repaired the Temple. 7So King Joash called for Jehoiada the priest and the other priests and said to them, "Why aren't you repairing the damage of the Temple? Don't take any more money from the people you serve, but hand over the money for the repair of the Temple." 8The priests agreed not to take any more money from the people and not to repair the Temple themselves.

9Jehoiada the priest took a box and made a hole in the top of it. Then he put it by the altar, on the right side as the people came into the Temple of the LORD. The priests guarding the doorway put all the money brought to the Temple of the LORD into the box.

10Each time the priests saw that the box was full of money, the king's royal secretary and the high priest came. They counted the money that had been brought to the Temple of the LORD, and they put it into bags. 11Next they weighed the money and gave it to the people in charge of the work on the Temple. With it they paid the carpenters and the builders who worked on the Temple of the LORD, 12as well as the bricklayers and stonecutters. They also used the money to buy timber and cut stone to repair the damage of the Temple of the LORD. It paid for everything.

13The money brought into the Temple of the LORD was not used to make silver cups, wick trimmers, bowls, trumpets, or gold or silver vessels. 14They paid the money to the workers, who used it to repair the Temple of the LORD. 15They did not demand to know how the money was spent, because the workers were honest. 16The money from the penalty offerings and sin offerings was not brought into the Temple of the LORD, because it belonged to the priests.

Joash Saves Jerusalem

17About this time Hazael king of Aram attacked Gath and captured it. Then he went to attack

Jerusalem. 18Joash king of Judah took all the holy things given by his ancestors, the kings of Judah—Jehoshaphat, Jehoram, and Ahaziah. He also took his own holy things as well as the gold that was found in the treasuries of the Temple of the LORD and the gold from the palace. Joash sent all this treasure to Hazael king of Aram, who turned away from Jerusalem.

19Everything else Joash did is written in the book of the history of the kings of Judah. 20His officers made plans against him and killed him at Beth Millo on the road down to Silla. 21The officers who killed him were Jozabad son of Shimeath and Jehozabad son of Shomer. Joash was buried with his ancestors in Jerusalem, and Amaziah, his son, became king in his place.

Jehoahaz King of Israel

13 Jehoahaz son of Jehu became king over Israel in Samaria during the twenty-third year Joash son of Ahaziah was king of Judah. Jehoahaz ruled seventeen years, 2and he did what the LORD said was wrong. Jehoahaz did the same sins Jeroboam son of Nebat had done. Jeroboam had led Israel to sin, and Jehoahaz did not stop doing these same sins. 3So the LORD was angry with Israel and handed them over to Hazael king of Aram and his son Ben-Hadad for a long time.

4Then Jehoahaz begged the LORD, and the LORD listened to him. The LORD had seen the troubles of Israel; he saw how terribly the king of Aram was treating them. 5He gave Israel a man to save them, and they escaped from the Arameans. The Israelites then lived in their own homes as they had before, 6but they still did not stop doing the same sins that the family of Jeroboam had done. He had led Israel to sin, and they continued doing those sins. The Asherah idol also was left standing in Samaria.

7Nothing was left of Jehoahaz's army except fifty horsemen, ten chariots, and ten thousand foot soldiers. The king of Aram had destroyed them and made them like chaff.

8Everything else Jehoahaz did and all his victories are written in the book of the history of the kings of Israel. 9Jehoahaz died and was buried in Samaria, and his son Jehoash became king in his place.

Jehoash King of Israel

10Jehoash son of Jehoahaz became king of Israel in Samaria during Joash's thirty-seventh year as king of Judah. Jehoash ruled sixteen years, 11and he did what the LORD said was wrong. He did not stop doing the same sins Jeroboam son of Nebat had done. Jeroboam had led Israel to sin, and Jehoash continued to do the same thing. 12Everything else he did and all his victories, including his war against Amaziah king of Judah, are written in the book of the history of the kings of Israel. 13Jehoash died, and Jeroboam took his place on the throne. Jehoash was buried in Samaria with the kings of Israel.

The Death of Elisha

14At this time Elisha became sick. Before he died, Jehoash king of Israel went to Elisha and cried for him. Jehoash said, "My father, my father! The chariots of Israel and their horsemen!"

15Elisha said to Jehoash, "Take a bow and arrows." So he took a bow and arrows. 16Then Elisha said to him, "Put your hand on the bow." So Jehoash put his hand on the bow. Then Elisha put his hands on the king's hands. 17Elisha said, "Open the east window." So Jehoash opened the window. Then Elisha said, "Shoot," and Jehoash shot. Elisha said, "The LORD's arrow of victory over Aram! You will defeat the Arameans at Aphek until you destroy them."

18Elisha said, "Take the arrows." So Jehoash took them. Then Elisha said to him, "Strike the ground." So Jehoash struck the ground three times and stopped. 19The man of God was angry with him. "You should have struck five or six times!" Elisha said. "Then you would have struck Aram until you had completely destroyed it. But now you will defeat it only three times."

20Then Elisha died and was buried.

At that time groups of Moabites would rob the land in the springtime. 21Once as some Israelites were burying a man, suddenly they saw a group of Moabites coming. The Israelites threw the dead man into Elisha's grave. When the man touched Elisha's bones, the man came back to life and stood on his feet.

War with Aram

22During all the days Jehoahaz was king, Hazael king of Aram troubled Israel. 23But the LORD was kind to the Israelites; he had mercy on them and helped them because of his agreement with Abraham, Isaac, and Jacob. To this day he has never wanted to destroy them or reject them.

24When Hazael king of Aram died, his son Ben-Hadad became king in his place. 25During a war

12:19 *the book of the history of the kings of Judah.* See 8:23.
13:12 *the book of the history of the kings of Israel.* See 8:23.

13:21 Elijah and Elisha: 2 Chronicles 21:12

SAMARIA

2 KINGS 17

What is the nature of the relationship between the Jewish people and the Samaritans? What is the source of the hostility from these two groups of people? What can we learn from the Samaritans?

The hostile relationship between Jewish people and Samaritans is reminiscent of the bloody battles still fought today in Northern Ireland. The Samaritans and Jews come from a similar faith background, but disagreements led them on a hostile path of hatred.

One of their chief disagreements with most Jews is the Samaritans' acceptance of only the Pentateuch, the first five books of the Bible, as authoritative Scripture. A second, equally important difference that arose after the exile was over the issue of the place of worship. Jewish people believed that they should approach God on Mount Zion in Jerusalem, while Samaritans worshiped God at Mount Gerezim near the city of Shechem.

The Books of Kings reveal a smidgeon of what went on between these closely related enemies. Until the death of King Solomon Israel was a united kingdom (1 Kings 12). But at the end of his life, he began to follow the gods of his many wives. As a consequence, God tore the tribes of Israel apart, leaving only the tribe of Judah to be ruled by the house of David. This tribe lived in the area surrounding the Temple in Jerusalem—the house of the Lord. The other tribes were ruled by a succession of kings, none of which came from the house of David (1 Kings 12:19). The place of government in that northern kingdom was built on a hill called Samaria (1 Kings 16:21–24). At some later point, the people of the northern kingdom of Israel worshiped in Samaria, while the people of the southern kingdom of Judah worshiped in Jerusalem, another city on a hill. Israel would not leave Judah alone, though, and continually advanced on that city in an attempt to capture the southern kingdom for its own (2 Chronicles 25:20–24; 28:8). Thus, the rivalry grew.

The kings of Samaria did evil in the eyes of the Lord by worshiping other gods of the surrounding nations (1 Kings 16:25, 30, 52). After two hundred years of disobedience to the Lord, Israel was conquered by the Assyrians, and all of God's people were dispersed to other nations. People from five nations were then sent to resettle the land that God had set apart for his people (2 Kings 17:24–33). These people intermarried with Jewish people left in the land and became the ancestors of the Samaritans that we read about in the New Testament. A large part of the anti-Samaritan feeling on the part of Jewish people in the books of Ezra and Nehemiah as well as the New Testament has to do with the mixed heritage of the Samaritans.

Thus, the prophets used Samaria as an example of the kind of punishment that would be dealt out to Judah if they continued in their worship of other gods (Isaiah 10:10–11; Ezekiel 23; Hosea 8:5–6). God, through the prophets, promised to redeem Samaria back to the agreement God had made with them. He promised to make it an everlasting covenant that they might know that he is the Lord (Ezekiel 16:53–63).

The effect of this everlasting covenant is not realized, however, until Jesus begins his ministry. Throughout his travels with his disciples, Jesus slowly begins to teach them and others that God's love extends beyond the borders of Jerusalem even to their hated enemies—the Samaritans.

In John 4, Jesus' disciples are surprised to find him speaking with a Samaritan woman (John 4:27). Indeed, the woman herself was shocked that Jesus would ask to use her drinking utensil, considering the poor relationship between the two peoples. Yet Jesus, by breaking down the social barriers, reveals to this woman his desire that all people know to worship the Lord in spirit and in truth (John 4:22–24) and not restrict their worship to a place, whether Jerusalem or Mount Gerezim in Samaria. As the disciples witness his interaction, they are exposed to the far-reaching boundaries of God's kingdom.

Luke does not mention Jesus' primary interaction with Samaritans, but the parable of the good Samaritan (Luke 10:30–35) is just as shocking. By surprising his audience with such a generous account of one of their most hated enemies, Jesus teaches that he does not judge people by their heritage, but rather by who they are as people. "Love your neighbor as you love yourself" (Luke 10:27) is easy as long as you do not hate your neighbor. It was important that he open this window of reconciliation in the minds of his followers so that they would carry out his mission, even to the dreaded Samaritans (Acts 1:8).

The disciples pick up in Acts where Jesus left off in Luke and go to the city of Samaria to preach about the risen Lord (Acts 8). There, the Good News is received with joy, and at last God's promise of an everlasting kingdom is fulfilled in Samaria. But even more, this everlasting kingdom is inclusive of all who will believe in God's love through Jesus, regardless of heritage, race, or religion (Acts 15:3).

Samaria: For additional scriptures on this topic go to 1 Kings 12.

MUSIC

1 CHRONICLES 16

The Old Testament is filled with music and psalms. Why does the New Testament not have any? What role did music play in worship?

Music in the Bible is a topic about which, unfortunately, few precise answers can be given. The importance of music is emphasized in Genesis 4:21. There music is listed as one of three main occupations or classes of the earliest society, along with cattle-raising and tool-making. Most often, music was used to express joy (Luke 15:25), grief (2 Samuel 1:17–27) or to worship God. In Saul's case, it was used to relieve depression (1 Samuel 16:23). Music may have accompanied the prophets' poems (Isaiah 5:1). The use of music to worship God was very important in both the Old and New Testaments. The most famous pieces of music in the Bible are in the Book of Psalms.

A psalm was a song written to be sung in the temple worship of the Old Testament. The heading of the psalms may give instructions and information about that psalm. These instructions may tell the reader how the psalm was to be sung and played, the tune or melody of the music, the instruments to be used in the song's performance, the author's name, and the purpose of the psalm. However, exactly what the instructions meant is unknown because no one knows the precise meaning for many of the words used. A psalm could be a song about praise, in which it would celebrate God and all the good things he did (Psalm 68). A psalm could be a song about doubt, or death, or feared (Psalm 22). The writer of such a song might be in danger or trouble or have sinned against God and needed to change his heart and life (Psalm 51). Many psalms are prayers and combine confessions of fear or sins and trust in God, who protects and forgives his people. The tune used for the song, its melody, reflected the lyrics or words that were to be sung. The song of praise was usually a loud, lively song to which people could sing, jump, shout, or otherwise express themselves (2 Samuel 6:5, 15–16), while the tune sung by a sad person helped others share his pain (Matthew 11:16).

The Bible mentions three main types of musical instruments. There were musical instruments that were beaten or struck to produce sounds (drums, cymbals, tambourines). There were instruments that had strings, which could be plucked or strummed to produce sound (lyres, harps). There were instruments that could be blown into to produce sound (flutes, trumpets).

The trumpet was a very important musical instrument, not anything like modern trumpets. It was a long, curved ram's horn, hollowed out and drilled so that it could produce sounds more like a noisemaker than a musical instrument. It was blown at feasts, at the enthronement of a king, as a warning alert, and during battles. The trumpet could be blown to sound the attack charge (Judges 7:20–21; Job 39:24–25), as well as the retreat (2 Samuel 20:1, 22). The trumpet was heard at Mount Sinai to announce the presence of God on the mountain (Exodus 19:19). The trumpet's blast came to symbolize God's judgment against a nation. It signaled doom for those who were his enemies and peace for his allies (Joel 2:1; 1 Corinthians 15:52; Revelation 8:6–9:13). For Christians, the trumpet announces the Second Coming of Jesus and the judgment at the end of time (1 Thessalonians 4:16).

Music was also used in daily life for entertainment. The prophet Amos condemned the wealthy Israelites of his time because they abused the poor, but feasted and made music to make themselves happy (Amos 6:5). He told them that their "palace songs will become funeral songs." (Amos 8:3). "I will explain my riddle on the harp" (Psalm 49:4) may reflect an ancient practice of telling stories, riddles, and singing to the music of a harp for entertainment. There were poets and singers and musicians who formed groups and played in the temples and in the courts of the kings (1 Kings 10:12; 1 Chronicles 15:24–25; 2 Chronicles 9:11).

In the New Testament little mention is made of how the church used music in worship, but music was important for the first Christians. The apostle Paul tells the Christians to "Speak to each other with psalms, hymns, and spiritual songs, singing and making music in your hearts to the Lord" (Ephesians 5:19; see also Colossians 3:16). Philippians 2:6–11 and 1 Timothy 3:16 may be examples of worship songs used in the first churches. For the most part, the churches' first worship was much like that of the synagogues, in which music was simply the singing of psalms and scripture songs. In Revelation, the temple is again the place of worship. The worshipers there sing and play songs just as in the earthly Temple in Jerusalem (Revelation 5:8–10, 19).

⚭**Music:** For additional scriptures on this topic go to Genesis 4:21.

Hazael had taken some cities from Jehoahaz,
Jehoash's father. Now Jehoash took back those
cities from Hazael's son Ben-Hadad. He defeated
Ben-Hadad three times and took back the cities of
Israel.

Amaziah King of Judah

14 Amaziah son of Joash became king of Judah
during the second year Jehoash son of
Jehoahaz was king of Israel. 2Amaziah was twenty-
five years old when he became king, and he ruled
twenty-nine years in Jerusalem. His mother was
named Jehoaddin, and she was from Jerusalem.
3Amaziah did what the LORD said was right. He
did everything his father Joash had done, but he
did not do as his ancestor David had done. 4The
places where gods were worshiped were not
removed, so the people still sacrificed and burned
incense there.

5As soon as Amaziah took control of the kingdom, he executed the officers who had murdered
his father the king. 6But he did not put to death
the children of the murderers because of the rule
written in the Book of the Teachings of Moses.
The LORD had commanded: "Parents must not be
put to death when their children do wrong, and
children must not be put to death when their parents do wrong. Each must die for his own sins."

7In battle Amaziah killed ten thousand Edomites in the Valley of Salt. He also took the city of
Sela. He called it Joktheel, as it is still called today.
8Amaziah sent messengers to Jehoash son of
Jehoahaz, the son of Jehu, king of Israel. They
said, "Come, let's meet face to face."

9Then Jehoash king of Israel answered Amaziah king of Judah, "A thornbush in Lebanon sent
a message to a cedar tree in Lebanon. It said, 'Let
your daughter marry my son.' But then a wild animal from Lebanon came by, walking on and
crushing the thornbush. 10You have defeated
Edom, but you have become proud. Stay at home
and brag. Don't ask for trouble, or you and Judah
will be defeated."

11But Amaziah would not listen, so Jehoash king
of Israel went to attack. He and Amaziah king of
Judah faced each other in battle at Beth Shemesh
in Judah. 12Israel defeated Judah, and every man
of Judah ran away to his home. 13At Beth
Shemesh Jehoash king of Israel captured Amaziah
king of Judah. (Amaziah was the son of Joash,
who was the son of Ahaziah.) Jehoash went up to
Jerusalem and broke down the wall of Jerusalem

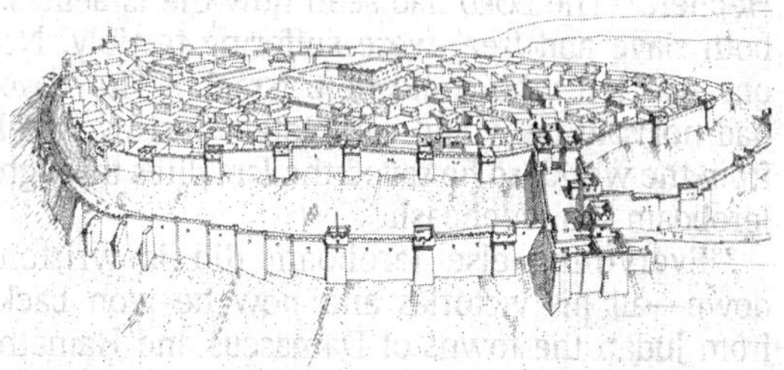

The town of Lachish built by Rehoboam, tenth century B.C. The large building in the center is the palace of Israel.

from the Gate of Ephraim to the Corner Gate,
which was about six hundred feet. 14He took all
the gold and silver and all the utensils in the
Temple of the LORD, and he took the treasuries of
the palace and some hostages. Then he returned
to Samaria.

15The other acts of Jehoash and his victories,
including his war against Amaziah king of Judah,
are written in the book of the history of the kings
of Israel. 16Jehoash died and was buried in Samaria
with the kings of Israel, and his son Jeroboam
became king in his place.

17Amaziah son of Joash, the king of Judah, lived
fifteen years after the death of Jehoash son of
Jehoahaz, the king of Israel. 18The other things
Amaziah did are written in the book of the history
of the kings of Judah. 19The people in Jerusalem
made plans against him. So he ran away to the
town of Lachish, but they sent men after him to
Lachish and killed him. 20They brought his body
back on horses, and he was buried with his
ancestors in Jerusalem, in the city of David.

21Then all the people of Judah made Uzziah
king in place of his father Amaziah. Uzziah was
sixteen years old. 22He rebuilt the town of Elath
and made it part of Judah again after Amaziah died.

Jeroboam King of Israel

23Jeroboam son of Jehoash became king of
Israel in Samaria during the fifteenth year Amaziah was king of Judah. (Amaziah was the son of
Joash.) Jeroboam ruled forty-one years, 24and he
did what the LORD said was wrong. Jeroboam son
of Nebat had led Israel to sin, and Jeroboam son of
Jehoash did not stop doing the same sins.
25Jeroboam won back Israel's border from Lebo
Hamath to the Dead Sea. This happened as the
LORD, the God of Israel, had said through his servant Jonah son of Amittai, the prophet from Gath

14:6 *"Parents . . . sins."* See Deuteronomy 24:16.
14:15 *the book of the history of the kings of Israel.* See 8:23.
14:21 *Uzziah.* Also called Azariah.

Hepher. 26The LORD had seen how the Israelites, both slave and free, were suffering terribly. No one was left who could help Israel. 27The LORD had not said he would completely destroy Israel from the world, so he saved the Israelites through Jeroboam son of Jehoash.

28Everything else Jeroboam did is written down—all his victories and how he won back from Judah the towns of Damascus and Hamath for Israel. All this is written in the book of the history of the kings of Israel. 29Jeroboam died and was buried with his ancestors, the kings of Israel. Jeroboam's son Zechariah became king in his place.

Uzziah King of Judah

15 Uzziah son of Amaziah became king of Judah during Jeroboam's twenty-seventh year as king of Israel. 2Uzziah was sixteen years old when he became king, and he ruled fifty-two years in Jerusalem. His mother was named Jecoliah, and she was from Jerusalem. 3He did what the LORD said was right, just as his father Amaziah had done. 4But the places where gods were worshiped were not removed, so the people still made sacrifices and burned incense there.

5The LORD struck Uzziah with a skin disease, which he had until the day he died. So he had to live in a separate house. Jotham, the king's son, was in charge of the palace, and he governed the people of the land.

6All the other things Uzziah did are written in the book of the history of the kings of Judah. 7Uzziah died and was buried near his ancestors in Jerusalem, and his son Jotham became king in his place.

Zechariah King of Israel

8Zechariah son of Jeroboam was king over Israel in Samaria. He ruled for six months during Uzziah's thirty-eighth year as king of Judah. 9Zechariah did what the LORD said was wrong, just as his ancestors had done. Jeroboam son of Nebat had led the people of Israel to sin, and Zechariah did not stop doing the same sins.

10Shallum son of Jabesh made plans against Zechariah and killed him in front of the people. Then Shallum became king in his place. 11The other acts of Zechariah are written in the book of the history of the kings of Israel. 12The LORD had told Jehu: "Your sons down to your great-great-grandchildren will be kings of Israel," and the LORD's word came true.

Shallum King of Israel

13Shallum son of Jabesh became king during Uzziah's thirty-ninth year as king of Judah. Shallum ruled for a month in Samaria. 14Then Menahem son of Gadi came up from Tirzah to Samaria and attacked Shallum son of Jabesh in Samaria. He killed him and became king in Shallum's place.

15The other acts of Shallum and his secret plans are written in the book of the history of the kings of Israel.

Menahem King of Israel

16Menahem started out from Tirzah and attacked Tiphsah, destroying the city and the area nearby. This was because the people had refused to open the city gate for him. He defeated them and ripped open all their pregnant women.

17Menahem son of Gadi became king over Israel during Uzziah's thirty-ninth year as king of Judah. Menahem ruled ten years in Samaria, 18and he did what the LORD said was wrong. Jeroboam son of Nebat had led Israel to sin, and all the time Menahem was king, he did not stop doing the same sins.

19Pul king of Assyria came to attack the land. Menahem gave him about seventy-four thousand pounds of silver so Pul would support him and make his hold on the kingdom stronger. 20Menahem taxed Israel to pay about one and one-fourth pounds of silver to each soldier of the king of Assyria. So the king left and did not stay in the land.

21Everything else Menahem did is written in the book of the history of the kings of Israel. 22Then Menahem died, and his son Pekahiah became king in his place.

Pekahiah King of Israel

23Pekahiah son of Menahem became king over Israel in Samaria during Uzziah's fiftieth year as king of Judah. Pekahiah ruled two years, 24and he did what the LORD said was wrong. Jeroboam son of Nebat had led Israel to sin, and Pekahiah did not stop doing the same sins.

25Pekah son of Remaliah was one of Pekahiah's captains, and he made plans against Pekahiah. He took fifty men of Gilead with him and killed Pekahiah, as well as Argob and Arieh, in the palace at Samaria. Then Pekah became king in Pekahiah's place.

15:1, 8, 23 *Uzziah.* Also called Azariah.

15:5 *skin disease.* Traditionally understood to be leprosy, but now taken more generally because the translation "leprosy" is known to be a mistake.

15:6 *the book of the history of the kings of Judah.* See 8:23.

15:19 *Pul.* Another name for the Assyrian king, Tiglath-pileser III.

[26]Everything else Pekahiah did is written in the book of the history of the kings of Israel.

Pekah King of Israel

[27]Pekah son of Remaliah became king over Israel in Samaria during Uzziah's fifty-second year as king of Judah. Pekah ruled twenty years, [28]and he did what the LORD said was wrong. Jeroboam son of Nebat had led Israel to sin, and Pekah did not stop doing the same sins.

[29]Tiglath-Pileser was king of Assyria. He attacked while Pekah was king of Israel, capturing the cities of Ijon, Abel Beth Maacah, Janoah, Kedesh, and Hazor. He also captured Gilead and Galilee and all the land of Naphtali and carried the people away to Assyria. [30]Then Hoshea son of Elah made plans against Pekah son of Remaliah and attacked and killed him. Then Hoshea became king in Pekah's place during the twentieth year Jotham son of Uzziah was king.

[31]Everything else Pekah did is written in the book of the history of the kings of Israel.

Jotham King of Judah

[32]Jotham son of Uzziah became king of Judah during the second year Pekah son of Remaliah was king of Israel. [33]Jotham was twenty-five years old when he became king, and he ruled sixteen years in Jerusalem. His mother's name was Jerusha daughter of Zadok. [34]Jotham did what the LORD said was right, just as his father Uzziah had done. [35]But the places where gods were worshiped were not removed, and the people still made sacrifices and burned incense there. Jotham rebuilt the Upper Gate of the Temple of the LORD.

[36]The other things Jotham did while he was king are written in the book of the history of the kings of Judah. [37]At that time the LORD began to send Rezin king of Aram and Pekah son of Remaliah against Judah. [38]Jotham died and was buried with his ancestors in Jerusalem, the city of David, his ancestor. Then Jotham's son Ahaz became king in his place.

Ahaz King of Judah

16 Ahaz was the son of Jotham king of Judah. Ahaz became king of Judah in the seventeenth year Pekah son of Remaliah was king of Israel. [2]Ahaz was twenty years old when he became king, and he ruled sixteen years in Jerusalem. Unlike his ancestor David, he did not do what the LORD his God said was right. [3]Ahaz did the same things the kings of Israel had done. He even made his son pass through fire. He did the same hateful sins as the nations had done whom the LORD had forced out of the land ahead of the Israelites. [4]Ahaz offered sacrifices and burned incense at the places where gods were worshiped, on the hills, and under every green tree.

[5]Rezin king of Aram and Pekah son of Remaliah, the king of Israel, came up to attack Jerusalem. They surrounded Ahaz but could not defeat him. [6]At that time Rezin king of Aram took back the city of Elath for Aram, and he forced out all the people of Judah. Then Edomites moved into Elath, and they still live there today.

[7]Ahaz sent messengers to Tiglath-Pileser king of Assyria, saying, "I am your servant and your friend. Come and save me from the king of Aram and the king of Israel, who are attacking me." [8]Ahaz took the silver and gold that was in the Temple of the LORD and in the treasuries of the palace, and he sent these as a gift to the king of Assyria. [9]So the king of Assyria listened to Ahaz. He attacked Damascus and captured it and sent all its people away to Kir. And he killed Rezin.

[10]Then King Ahaz went to Damascus to meet Tiglath-Pileser king of Assyria. Ahaz saw an altar at Damascus, and he sent plans and a pattern of this altar to Uriah the priest. [11]So Uriah the priest built an altar, just like the plans King Ahaz had sent him from Damascus. Uriah finished the altar before King Ahaz came back from Damascus. [12]When the king arrived from Damascus, he saw the altar and went near and offered sacrifices on it. [13]He burned his burnt offerings and grain offerings and poured out his drink offering. He also sprinkled the blood of his fellowship offerings on the altar.

[14]Ahaz moved the bronze altar that was before the LORD at the front of the Temple. It was between Ahaz's altar and the Temple of the LORD, but he put it on the north side of his altar. [15]King Ahaz commanded Uriah the priest, "On the large altar burn the morning burnt offering, the evening grain offering, the king's burnt offering and grain offering, and the whole burnt offering, the grain offering, and the drink offering for all the people of the land. Sprinkle on the altar all the blood of the burnt offering and of the sacrifice. But I will use the bronze altar to ask questions of God." [16]So Uriah the priest did everything as King Ahaz commanded him.

[17]Then King Ahaz took off the side panels from the bases and removed the washing bowls from

15:27 *Uzziah* Also called Azariah.
15:29 *Tiglath-Pileser* Also called Pul.
15:36 *in the book of the history of the kings of Judah.* See 8:23.

the top of the bases. He also took the large bowl, which was called the Sea, off the bronze bulls that held it up, and he put it on a stone base. 18Ahaz took away the platform for the royal throne, which had been built at the Temple of the LORD. He also took away the outside entrance for the king. He did these things because of the king of Assyria.

19The other things Ahaz did as king are written in the book of the history of the kings of Judah. 20Ahaz died and was buried with his ancestors in Jerusalem, and Ahaz's son Hezekiah became king in his place.

Hoshea, Last King of Israel

17 Hoshea son of Elah became king over Israel during Ahaz's twelfth year as king of Judah. Hoshea ruled in Samaria nine years. 2He did what the LORD said was wrong, but he was not as bad as the kings of Israel who had ruled before him.

3Shalmaneser king of Assyria came to attack Hoshea. Hoshea had been Shalmaneser's servant and had made the payments to Shalmaneser that he had demanded. 4But the king of Assyria found out that Hoshea had made plans against him by sending messengers to So, the king of Egypt. Hoshea had also stopped giving Shalmaneser the payments, which he had paid every year in the past. For that, the king put Hoshea in prison. 5Then the king of Assyria came and attacked all the land of Israel. He surrounded Samaria and attacked it for three years. 6He defeated Samaria in the ninth year Hoshea was king, and he took the Israelites away to Assyria. He settled them in Halah, in Gozan on the Habor River, and in the cities of the Medes.

Israelites Punished for Sin

7All these things happened because the Israelites had sinned against the LORD their God. He had brought them out of Egypt and had rescued them from the power of the king of Egypt, but the Israelites had honored other gods. 8They lived like the nations the LORD had forced out of the land ahead of them. They lived as their evil kings had shown them, 9secretly sinning against the LORD their God. They built places to worship gods in all their cities, from the watchtower to the strong, walled city. 10They put up stone pillars to gods and Asherah idols on every high hill and under every green tree. 11The Israelites burned incense everywhere gods were worshiped, just as the nations who lived there before them had done, whom the LORD had forced out of the land. The Israelites did wicked things that made the LORD angry. 12They served idols when the LORD had said, "You must not do this." 13The LORD used every prophet and seer to warn Israel and Judah. He said, "Stop your evil ways and obey my commands and laws. Follow all the teachings that I commanded your ancestors, the teachings that I gave you through my servants the prophets."

14But the people would not listen. They were stubborn, just as their ancestors had been who did not believe in the LORD their God. 15They rejected the LORD's laws and the agreement he had made with their ancestors. And they refused to listen to his warnings. They worshiped useless idols and became useless themselves. They did what the nations around them did, which the LORD had warned them not to do.

16The people rejected all the commands of the LORD their God. They molded statues of two calves, and they made an Asherah idol. They worshiped all the stars of the sky and served Baal.⚭ 17They made their sons and daughters pass through fire and tried to find out the future by magic and witchcraft. They always chose to do what the LORD said was wrong, which made him angry. 18Because he was very angry with the people of Israel, he removed them from his presence. Only the tribe of Judah was left.⚭

Judah Is Also Guilty

19But even Judah did not obey the commands of the LORD their God. They did what the Israelites had done, 20so the LORD rejected all the people of Israel. He punished them and let others destroy them; he threw them out of his presence. 21When the LORD separated them from the family of David, the Israelites made Jeroboam son of Nebat their king. Jeroboam led the Israelites away from the LORD and led them to sin greatly. 22So they continued to do all the sins Jeroboam did. They did not stop doing these sins 23until the LORD removed the Israelites from his presence, just as he had said through all his servants the prophets. So the Israelites were taken out of their land to Assyria, and they have been there to this day.

16:19 *in the book of the history of the kings of Judah.* See 8:23.

17:5–23 The northern kingdom of Israel was removed from their land to Assyria because they worshiped the idols of the nations around them. God had been patient with Israel by giving them every chance to change their hearts and lives. However, he finally kept his promise to punish his people for not turning from their sin of idolatry.

⚭**17:16 Astrology:** 2 Kings 21:3–5

⚭**17:18 Stubbornness:** Proverbs 1:22–32

Relief of an Assyrian hunter from the palace of King Sargon II at Khorsabad, eighth century B.C.

The Beginning of the Samaritan People

24 The king of Assyria brought people from Babylon, Cuthah, Avva, Hamath, and Sepharvaim and put them in the cities of Samaria to replace the Israelites. These people took over Samaria and lived in the cities. 25 At first they did not worship the LORD, so he sent lions among them which killed some of them. 26 The king of Assyria was told, "You sent foreigners into the cities of Samaria who do not know the law of the god of the land. This is why he has sent lions among them. The lions are killing them because they don't know what the god wants."

27 Then the king of Assyria commanded, "Send back one of the priests you took away. Let him live there and teach the people what the god wants." 28 So one of the priests who had been carried away from Samaria returned to live in Bethel. And he taught the people how to honor the LORD.

29 But each nation made gods of its own and put them in the cities where they lived and in the temples where gods were worshiped. These temples had been built by the Samaritans. 30 The people from Babylon made Succoth Benoth their god. The people from Cuthah worshiped Nergal. The people of Hamath worshiped Ashima. 31 The Avvites worshiped Nibhaz and Tartak. The Sepharvites burned their children in the fire, sacrificing them to Adrammelech and Anammelech, the gods of Sepharvaim. 32 They also honored the LORD, but they chose priests for the places where gods were worshiped. The priests were chosen from among themselves, and they made sacrifices for the people. 33 The people honored the LORD but also served their own gods, just as the nations did from which they had been brought. 34 Even today they do as they did in the past. They do not worship the LORD nor obey his rules and commands. They do not obey the teachings or the commands of the LORD, which he gave to the children of Jacob, whom he had named Israel. 35 The LORD had made an agreement with them and had commanded them, "Do not honor other gods. Do not bow down to them or worship them or offer sacrifices to them. 36 Worship the LORD who brought you up out of the land of Egypt with great power and strength. Bow down to him and offer sacrifices to him. 37 Always obey the rules, orders, teachings, and commands he wrote for you. Do not honor other gods. 38 Do not forget the agreement I made with you, and do not honor other gods. 39 Instead worship the LORD your God, who will save you from all your enemies."

40 But the Israelites did not listen. They kept on doing the same things they had done before. 41 So these nations honored the LORD but also worshiped their idols, and their children and grandchildren still do as their ancestors did.

Hezekiah King of Judah

18 Hezekiah son of Ahaz king of Judah became king during the third year Hoshea son of Elah was king of Israel. 2 Hezekiah was twenty-five years old when he became king, and he ruled twenty-nine years in Jerusalem. His mother's name was Abijah daughter of Zechariah. 3 Hezekiah did what the LORD said was right, just as his ancestor David had done. 4 He removed the places where gods were worshiped. He smashed the stone pillars and cut down the Asherah idols. Also the Israelites had been burning incense to Nehushtan, the bronze snake Moses had made. But Hezekiah broke it into pieces.

5 Hezekiah trusted in the LORD, the God of Israel. There was no one like him among all the kings of Judah, either before him or after him. 6 Hezekiah was loyal to the LORD and did not stop following him; he obeyed the commands the LORD had given Moses. 7 And the LORD was with Hezekiah, so he had success in everything he did. He turned against the king of Assyria and stopped serving him.

18:7 Success: 1 Chronicles 22:13

8Hezekiah defeated the Philistines all the way to
Gaza and its borders, including the watchtowers
and the strong, walled cities.

The Assyrians Capture Samaria

9Shalmaneser king of Assyria surrounded Samaria and attacked it in the fourth year Hezekiah
was king. This was the seventh year Hoshea son
of Elah was king of Israel. 10After three years the
Assyrians captured Samaria. This was in the sixth
year Hezekiah was king, which was Hoshea's ninth
year as king of Israel. 11The king of Assyria took the
Israelites away to Assyria and settled them in
Halah, in Gozan on the Habor River, and in the
cities of the Medes. 12This happened because
they did not obey the LORD their God. They broke
his agreement and did not obey all that Moses,
the LORD's servant, had commanded. They would
not listen to the commands or do them.

Assyria Attacks Judah

13During Hezekiah's fourteenth year as king,
Sennacherib king of Assyria attacked all the
strong, walled cities of Judah and captured them.
14Then Hezekiah king of Judah sent a message to
the king of Assyria at Lachish. He said, "I have
done wrong. Leave me alone, and I will pay anything you ask." So the king of Assyria made
Hezekiah pay about twenty-two thousand pounds
of silver and two thousand pounds of gold.
15Hezekiah gave him all the silver that was in the
Temple of the LORD and in the palace treasuries.
16Hezekiah stripped all the gold that covered the
doors and doorposts of the Temple of the LORD.
Hezekiah had put gold on these doors himself,
but he gave it all to the king of Assyria.

17The king of Assyria sent out his supreme
commander, his chief officer, and his field commander. They went with a large army from
Lachish to King Hezekiah in Jerusalem. When
they came near the waterway from the upper
pool on the road where people do their laundry,
they stopped. 18They called for the king, so the
king sent Eliakim, Shebna, and Joah out to meet
them. Eliakim son of Hilkiah was the palace manager, Shebna was the royal secretary, and Joah
son of Asaph was the recorder.

19The field commander said to them, "Tell
Hezekiah this:

"'The great king, the king of Assyria, says:
What can you trust in now? 20You say you have
battle plans and power for war, but your words
mean nothing. Whom are you trusting for help so
that you turn against me? 21Look, you are depending on Egypt to help you, but Egypt is like a splintered walking stick. If you lean on it for help, it
will stab your hand and hurt you. The king of
Egypt will hurt all those who depend on him.
22You might say, "We are depending on the LORD
our God," but Hezekiah destroyed the LORD's
altars and the places of worship. Hezekiah told
Judah and Jerusalem, "You must worship only at
this one altar in Jerusalem."

23"'Now make an agreement with my master,
the king of Assyria: I will give you two thousand
horses if you can find enough men to ride them.
24You cannot defeat one of my master's least
important officers, so why do you depend on
Egypt to give you chariots and horsemen? 25I have
not come to attack and destroy this place without
an order from the LORD. The LORD himself told me
to come to this country and destroy it.'"

26Then Eliakim son of Hilkiah, Shebna, and
Joah said to the field commander, "Please speak
to us in the Aramaic language. We understand it.
Don't speak to us in Hebrew, because the people
on the city wall can hear you."

27"No," the commander said, "my master did
not send me to tell these things only to you and
your king. He sent me to speak also to those people sitting on the wall who will have to eat their
own dung and drink their own urine like you."

28Then the commander stood and shouted loudly
in the Hebrew language, "Listen to what the great
king, the king of Assyria, says! 29The king says
you should not let Hezekiah fool you, because he
can't save you from my power. 30Don't let
Hezekiah talk you into trusting the LORD by saying, 'The LORD will surely save us. This city won't
be handed over to the king of Assyria.'

31"Don't listen to Hezekiah. The king of Assyria
says, 'Make peace with me, and come out of the
city to me. Then everyone will be free to eat the
fruit from his own grapevine and fig tree and to
drink water from his own well. 32After that I will
come and take you to a land like your own—a
land with grain and new wine, bread and vineyards, olives, and honey. Choose to live and not
to die!'

"Don't listen to Hezekiah. He is fooling you
when he says, 'The LORD will save us.' 33Has a
god of any other nation saved his people from the
power of the king of Assyria? 34Where are the
gods of Hamath and Arpad? Where are the gods
of Sepharvaim, Hena, and Ivvah? They did not

18:22 Here the Assyrians clearly misunderstand that Hezekiah was destroying illegitimate altars in favor of the one central altar in Jerusalem.

save Samaria from my power. [35]Not one of all the
gods of these countries has saved his people from
me. Neither can the LORD save Jerusalem from my
power."
[36]The people were silent. They didn't answer
the commander at all, because King Hezekiah had
ordered, "Don't answer him."
[37]Then Eliakim, Shebna, and Joah tore their
clothes to show how upset they were. (Eliakim son
of Hilkiah was the palace manager, Shebna was the
royal secretary, and Joah son of Asaph was the
recorder.) The three men went to Hezekiah and told
him what the field commander had said.

Jerusalem Will Be Saved

19 When King Hezekiah heard the message,
he tore his clothes and put on rough cloth
to show how sad he was. Then he went into the
Temple of the LORD. [2]Hezekiah sent Eliakim, the
palace manager, and Shebna, the royal secretary,
and the older priests to Isaiah. They were all
wearing rough cloth when they came to Isaiah
the prophet, the son of Amoz. [3]They told Isaiah,
"This is what Hezekiah says: Today is a day of sorrow and punishment and disgrace, as when a child
should be born, but the mother is not strong
enough to give birth to it. [4]The king of Assyria
sent his field commander to make fun of the living
God. Maybe the LORD your God will hear what
the commander said and will punish him for it.
So pray for the few of us who are left alive."⚭
[5]When Hezekiah's officers came to Isaiah, [6]he
said to them, "Tell your master this: The LORD
says, 'Don't be afraid of what you have heard.
Don't be frightened by the words the servants of
the king of Assyria have spoken against me.⚭
[7]Listen! I am going to put a spirit in the king of
Assyria. He will hear a report that will make him
return to his own country, and I will cause him to
die by the sword there.'"
[8]The field commander heard that the king of
Assyria had left Lachish. When he went back, he
found the king fighting against the city of Libnah.
[9]The king received a report that Tirhakah, the
Cushite king of Egypt, was coming to attack him.
When the king of Assyria heard this, he sent messengers to Hezekiah, saying, [10]"Tell Hezekiah
king of Judah: Don't be fooled by the god you
trust. Don't believe him when he says Jerusalem
will not be handed over to the king of Assyria.
[11]You have heard what the kings of Assyria have
done. They have completely defeated every country, so do not think you will be saved. [12]Did the
gods of those people save them? My ancestors
destroyed them, defeating the cities of Gozan,
Haran, and Rezeph, and the people of Eden living
in Tel Assar. [13]Where are the kings of Hamath
and Arpad? Where are the kings of Sepharvaim,
Hena, and Ivvah?"

Hezekiah Prays to the Lord

[14]When Hezekiah received the letter from the
messengers and read it, he went up to the
Temple of the LORD. He spread the letter out
before the LORD [15]and prayed to the LORD:
"LORD, God of Israel, whose throne is between
the gold creatures with wings, only you are God
of all the kingdoms of the earth. You made the
heavens and the earth. [16]Hear, LORD, and listen.
Open your eyes, LORD, and see. Listen to the
words Sennacherib has said to insult the living
God. [17]It is true, LORD, that the kings of Assyria
have destroyed these countries and their lands.
[18]They have thrown the gods of these nations
into the fire, but they were only wood and rock
statues that people made. So the kings have
destroyed them. [19]Now, LORD our God, save us
from the king's power so that all the kingdoms
of the earth will know that you, LORD, are the
only God."

God Answers Hezekiah

[20]Then Isaiah son of Amoz sent a message to
Hezekiah that said, "This is what the LORD, the
God of Israel, says: I have heard your prayer to me
about Sennacherib king of Assyria. [21]This is what
the LORD has said against Sennacherib:

'The people of Jerusalem
  hate you and make fun of you.
The people of Jerusalem
  laugh at you as you run away.
[22]You have insulted me and spoken against me;
  you have raised your voice against me.
You have a proud look on your face,
  which is against me, the Holy One of Israel.
[23]You have sent your messengers to insult
    the Lord.
  You have said, "With my many chariots
I have gone to the tops of the mountains,
  to the highest mountains of Lebanon.
I have cut down its tallest cedars
  and its best pine trees.
I have gone to its farthest places
  and to its best forests.
[24]I have dug wells in foreign countries
  and drunk water there.

⚭**19:4 The Remnant:** 2 Kings 19:30–31

⚭**19:6 Blasphemy:** Nehemiah 9:18

By the soles of my feet,
I have dried up all the rivers of Egypt."

25"'King of Assyria, surely you have heard.
Long ago I, the LORD, planned these things.
Long ago I designed them,
and now I have made them happen.
I allowed you to turn those strong, walled
cities
into piles of rocks.
26The people in those cities were weak;
they were frightened and put to shame.
They were like grass in the field,
like tender, young grass,
like grass on the housetop
that is burned by the wind before it can grow.

27"'I know when you rest,
when you come and go,
and how you rage against me.
28Because you rage against me,
and because I have heard your proud words,
I will put my hook in your nose
and my bit in your mouth.
Then I will force you to leave my country
the same way you came.'

29"Then the LORD said, 'Hezekiah, I will give you
this sign:
This year you will eat the grain that grows wild,
and the second year you will eat what grows
wild from that.
But in the third year, plant grain and harvest it.
Plant vineyards and eat their fruit.
30Some of the people in the family of Judah
will escape.
Like plants that take root,
they will grow strong and have
many children.
31A few people will come out of Jerusalem alive;
a few from Mount Zion will live.
The strong love of the LORD All-Powerful
will make this happen.'

32"So this is what the LORD says about the king
of Assyria:
'He will not enter this city
or even shoot an arrow here.
He will not fight against it with shields
or build a ramp to attack the city walls.
33He will return to his country the same way
he came,
and he will not enter this city,'
says the LORD.
34'I will defend and save this city
for my sake and for the sake of David,
my servant.'"

35That night the angel of the LORD went out and
killed one hundred eighty-five thousand men in
the Assyrian camp. When the people got up early
the next morning, they saw all the dead bodies.
36So Sennacherib king of Assyria left and went
back to Nineveh and stayed there.
37One day as Sennacherib was worshiping in the
temple of his god Nisroch, his sons Adrammelech
and Sharezer killed him with a sword. Then they
escaped to the land of Ararat. So Sennacherib's son
Esarhaddon became king of Assyria.

Hezekiah's Illness

20 At that time Hezekiah became so sick he
almost died. The prophet Isaiah son of
Amoz went to see him and told him, "This is what
the LORD says: Make arrangements because you
are not going to live, but die."
2Hezekiah turned toward the wall and prayed to
the LORD, 3"LORD, please remember that I have
always obeyed you. I have given myself completely
to you and have done what you said was right."
Then Hezekiah cried loudly.
4Before Isaiah had left the middle courtyard, the
LORD spoke his word to Isaiah: 5"Go back and tell
Hezekiah, the leader of my people: 'This is what
the LORD, the God of your ancestor David, says: I
have heard your prayer and seen your tears, so I
will heal you. Three days from now you will go up
to the Temple of the LORD. 6I will add fifteen years
to your life. I will save you and this city from the
king of Assyria; I will protect the city for my sake
and for the sake of my servant David.'"
7Then Isaiah said, "Make a paste from figs." So
they made it and put it on Hezekiah's boil, and he
got well.
8Hezekiah had asked Isaiah, "What will be the
sign that the LORD will heal me and that I will go
up to the Temple of the LORD on the third day?"
9Isaiah said, "The LORD will do what he says.
This is the sign from the LORD to show you: Do
you want the shadow to go forward ten steps or
back ten steps?"
10Hezekiah answered, "It's easy for the shadow
to go forward ten steps. Instead, let it go back ten
steps."

19:28 *hook in your nose.* Referring to the treatment of prisoners of war. They would be led by a leash attached to the nose through the streets of the victor's hometown.

19:31 Jerusalem: 2 Chronicles 3:1
19:31 The Remnant: 2 Chronicles 34:21
19:32 Numbers: 1 Chronicles 12:23–37

NEHEMIAH

NEHEMIAH 1

How is a story about rebuilding city walls and racially mixed marriages relevant for modern Christians?

The people of Israel were proud of Jerusalem. They praised its beauty (Psalms 48:2; 50:2; Ezekiel 16:14) and admired its majestic walls (Psalm 48:12–13). But because of Israel's long history of idolatry, God let the Babylonian king Nebuchadnezzar destroy Jerusalem in 587–586 B.C. The Temple was burned to the ground, the city walls were broken down, and the inhabitants led into exile (2 Kings 25:1–21; 2 Chronicles 36:17–20; Jeremiah 52:4–27). Pride turned to shame as the city lay empty and ruined (Lamentations 1:1, 4; 2:1, 8–9; 5:18). Nations that had once admired Jerusalem's majesty made fun of its misfortune (Lamentations 1:7; 2:15–16).

Through the years of exile, Israel anticipated the time when their punishment would be reversed, and Jerusalem would be rebuilt (Isaiah 44:28; 45:13; 58:12; Jeremiah 30:18; 31:38; Ezekiel 36:10, 33) and inhabited once again (Isaiah 44:26; 49:17–20; Jeremiah 33:10, 11).

The books of Ezra and Nehemiah tell the story of that reversal. In 538 B.C. the Persian king Cyrus allowed the Jewish exiles to return to Judah and rebuild the Temple (2 Chronicles 36:22–23; Ezra 1:1–4). The Book of Ezra describes how this was accomplished.

The rebuilding of the Temple, however, was not a full reversal of God's judgment on Israel. Jerusalem and its walls remained in ruins (Nehemiah 1:3; 2:3, 17). The people who had returned from exile were living in the towns of Judah, but Jerusalem itself was uninhabited (Nehemiah 7:4; 11:1). The desolation and emptiness of the city was a lingering reminder of God's judgment (Leviticus 26:31; Deuteronomy 28:52) and the incompleteness of the nation's salvation. Also, Jerusalem's condition continued to bring shame on the people; it was an invitation to their enemies to make fun of their misfortune. This problem of shame is uppermost in Nehemiah's mind. Certainly, the broken walls created a problem of national security. Without a walled city to retreat to, the residents of Judah were defenseless against their enemies (Nehemiah 4:7–23). But, the greater problem was the national disgrace of a ruined city (Nehemiah 1:3; 2:17).

Nehemiah's task was to restore Jerusalem to its former glory and so remove this shame. He achieved success in two ways. The first is seen in the change in the attitude of the surrounding nations. As the people attempted to rebuild the wall, their enemies stood around making fun of their efforts (Nehemiah 4:1–3). This increased the disgrace of the Jewish people, so Nehemiah prayed that God would turn the insults of the enemies back on their own heads (Nehemiah 4:4). This prayer was answered when the walls were completed. The enemies were now disgraced (Nehemiah 6:16). This is the first way Nehemiah achieved his goal: the enemies' shame replaced Israel's shame. The second change is seen in the joyful celebration that followed the completion of the wall (Nehemiah 12:27, 43). Israel's shame had turned to joy.

In addition to rebuilding the walls of Jerusalem, Nehemiah faced a second challenge: the spiritual rebuilding of the community. In this task he was less successful. He first had to stop the economic oppression of the poor by the rich (Nehemiah 5:1–5). Again, his motivation was to prevent disgrace from falling on the nation (Nehemiah 5:9). Later he joined Ezra in calling the people to obedience to the Teachings of Moses (Nehemiah 8:9, 10). At first, it seemed that both efforts were successful (Nehemiah 5:12; 9:1–10:39). But, the people's repentance was only superficial and temporary. When Nehemiah returned to Jerusalem after spending time in Persia (Nehemiah 13:6, 7), he discovered that the people were committing the same sins they had earlier repented of: not caring for the temple (Nehemiah 10:37; 13:10, 11), breaking the Sabbath (Nehemiah 10:31; 13:15–17), and, most serious of all, marrying foreigners (Nehemiah 10:30; 13:23, 24). The same sinfulness that had earlier sent Israel into captivity was still a problem for the group that returned from captivity (Nehemiah 13:18, 26, 27). The city had been rebuilt, but the people's hearts needed to be transformed (Jeremiah 31:33; Ezekiel 11:19; 36:26).

The New Testament is also concerned about mixed marriages. Clearly, there is no problem with interracial marriages. Because Christians are "one in Christ" racial barriers are broken down (Galatians 3:28). The type of mixed marriages that are not permitted are those between Christians and non-Christians (2 Corinthians 6:14). If Nehemiah is any guide, the danger is that the non-Christian will lead the Christian away from worship of God in the same way that the idol-worshiping Gentiles led their Israelite husbands and wives into sin (Nehemiah 13:23–27).

Nehemiah: For additional scriptures on this topic go to Exodus 34:16.

Esther

ESTHER 4:14

Who was Esther? Since the Book of Esther does not mention God, why is it included as an inspired Bible book? Why is the Book of Esther important?

Esther was a Jewish woman who lived in Persia (modern Iran) about 480 B.C. She was an orphan who was raised by Mordecai, a relative who worked in the service of the Persian king, Xerxes (486—465 B.C.). Through providential circumstances Esther won the favor of Xerxes, who married her and crowned her queen.

Esther's story is quite different from those of other biblical women. Unlike other famous women of the Old Testament—for instance, Sarah, Rachel, Ruth, and Hannah—Esther did not bear a son who became great in Israel's history. It is not known if Esther ever became a mother. The memory of Esther is preserved in the Bible because she played an important role in the political intrigue of the Persian court. Because of her action in court politics, Esther was highly esteemed and had great influence over the Jews of Persia.

The title of the book, "Esther," indicates that she is its main character. Mordecai also played a prominent role in the events commemorated by the Jewish holiday of Purim. Esther and Mordecai foiled the plot of Haman, their political enemy, who intended to kill all the Jewish people living in the Persian Empire. Esther wrote to the Jewish people with full authority, establishing a holiday called Purim to celebrate this deliverance. Esther's decree was written down in the official records (9:29, 32). The holiday Esther and Mordecai established many centuries ago is still celebrated by the Jews today. No other woman in biblical history has had such direct and far-reaching influence on the religious practices of her people.

The holiday is called *Purim* because that is a Hebrew word for "dice" or "lots." In ancient biblical times, dice were thrown to get answers from the gods. Haman consulted his gods about the best time to attack the Jews by having the Pur—that is, the lot—thrown before him (3:7). The roll of the die was to determine the day on which the Jews would be killed. When that day finally arrived, Haman himself was dead and Mordecai, a Jew, had been promoted to Haman's place.

Although the Book of Esther is the only book in the Bible that does not mention God, the story it tells is linked to the previous history of the Jewish people in two ways. First, the story of Esther is found in the Hebrew Bible, which shows that it was recognized as an important part of their religious history. Secondly, Haman, who plotted to kill all the Jews in Persia, is called an Agagite (3:1, 8:5). Agag was the king of the Amalekites during the reign of Israel's first king, Saul (1 Samuel 15:8). The Amalekites were the first nation to try to destroy ancient Israel immediately after they left Egypt in the Exodus. Because of this, God promised he would completely destroy them (Exodus 17:8–16). Many years later God commanded Israel's King Saul to carry out his promise by completely destroying the Amalekites and everything that belonged to them. Instead of being obedient, Saul spared King Agag and the best of the booty because he thought God would be pleased to receive it as a sacrifice. The prophet Samuel rebuked Saul, saying that in God's eyes, obedience is better than sacrifice. By calling Haman an Agagite, the Book of Esther shows him to be an enemy of the Jews who is under God's promise of destruction. When Haman and those who are on his side are killed, the Jewish people understood that God was still protecting them from destruction just as he protected their ancient ancestors.

Esther and Mordecai became great because of their roles in saving the Jewish people from destruction, but they do not seem to be ideal Jews compared to other Old Testament heroes. Daniel and his friends refused to violate the Jewish dietary laws by eating the food of the pagan king of Babylon. Esther not only ate the court food, she also did not protest when taken to have intimate relations with the pagan king to whom she was not married. Mordecai forbade Esther to reveal her identity as a Jew, putting her in a compromising position. Because Mordecai didn't get along with Haman, the entire Jewish people were threatened with death. The Bible does not tell us why Esther and Mordecai acted as they did or what God thought about their behavior. It is an encouragement to us that though Esther and Mordecai were not perfect people, God still worked out his perfect plan through their imperfect decisions and actions. This is an example of what theologians call "divine providence,"—that is, how God invisibly controls everything for his good purposes.

The story of Esther and Mordecai shows that God keeps his promises, both to bless and to destroy, even many centuries after he makes them.

Esther: For additional scriptures on this topic go to Psalm 16:5.

11Then Isaiah the prophet called to the LORD, and the LORD brought the shadow ten steps back up the stairway of Ahaz that it had gone down.

Messengers from Babylon

12At that time Merodach-Baladan son of Baladan was king of Babylon. He sent letters and a gift to Hezekiah, because he had heard that Hezekiah was sick. 13Hezekiah listened to the messengers, so he showed them what was in his storehouses: the silver, gold, spices, expensive perfumes, his swords and shields, and all his wealth. He showed them everything in his palace and his kingdom.

14Then Isaiah the prophet went to King Hezekiah and asked him, "What did these men say? Where did they come from?"

Hezekiah said, "They came from a faraway country—from Babylon."

15So Isaiah asked him, "What did they see in your palace?"

Hezekiah said, "They saw everything in my palace. I showed them all my wealth."

16Then Isaiah said to Hezekiah, "Listen to the words of the LORD: 17'In the future everything in your palace and everything your ancestors have stored up until this day will be taken away to Babylon. Nothing will be left,' says the LORD. 18'Some of your own children, those who will be born to you, will be taken away. And they will become servants in the palace of the king of Babylon.'"

19Hezekiah told Isaiah, "These words from the LORD are good." He said this because he thought, "There will be peace and security in my lifetime."

20Everything else Hezekiah did—all his victories, his work on the pool, his work on the tunnel to bring water into the city—is written in the book of the history of the kings of Judah. 21Then Hezekiah died, and his son Manasseh became king in his place.

Manasseh King of Judah

21 Manasseh was twelve years old when he became king, and he was king fifty-five years in Jerusalem. His mother's name was Hephzibah. 2He did what the LORD said was wrong. He did the hateful things the other nations had done—the nations that the LORD had forced out of the land ahead of the Israelites. 3Manasseh's father, Hezekiah, had destroyed the places where gods were worshiped, but Manasseh rebuilt them. He built altars for Baal, and he made an Asherah idol as Ahab king of Israel had done. Manasseh also worshiped all the stars of the sky and served them. 4The LORD had said about the Temple, "I will be worshiped in Jerusalem," but Manasseh built altars in the Temple of the LORD. 5He built altars to worship the stars in the two courtyards of the Temple of the LORD.⚭ 6He made his own son pass through fire. He practiced magic and told the future by explaining signs and dreams, and he got advice from mediums and fortune-tellers. He did many things the LORD said were wrong, which made the LORD angry.

7Manasseh carved an Asherah idol and put it in the Temple. The LORD had said to David and his son Solomon about the Temple, "I will be worshiped forever in this Temple and in Jerusalem, which I have chosen from all the tribes of Israel. 8I will never again make the Israelites wander out of the land I gave their ancestors. But they must obey everything I have commanded them and all the teachings my servant Moses gave them." 9But the people did not listen. Manasseh led them to do more evil than the nations the LORD had destroyed ahead of the Israelites.

10The LORD said through his servants the prophets, 11"Manasseh king of Judah has done these hateful things. He has done more evil than the Amorites before him. He also has led Judah to sin with his idols. 12So this is what the LORD, the God of Israel, says: 'I will bring so much trouble on Jerusalem and Judah that anyone who hears about it will be shocked. 13I will stretch the measuring line of Samaria over Jerusalem, and the plumb line used against Ahab's family will be used on Jerusalem. I will wipe out Jerusalem as a person wipes a dish and turns it upside down. 14I will throw away the rest of my people who are left. I will give them to their enemies, and they will be robbed by all their enemies, 15because my people did what I said was wrong. They have made me angry from the day their ancestors left Egypt until now.'"

16Manasseh also killed many innocent people, filling Jerusalem from one end to the other with their blood. This was besides the sin he led Judah to do; he led Judah to do what the LORD said was wrong.

17The other things Manasseh did as king, even the sin he did, are written in the book of the history of the kings of Judah. 18Manasseh died and was buried in the garden of his own palace, the garden of Uzza. Then Manasseh's son Amon became king in his place.

Amon King of Judah

19Amon was twenty-two years old when he

⚭**21:5 Astrology:** 2 Kings 23:4–5

became king, and he was king for two years in Jerusalem. His mother's name was Meshullemeth
daughter of Haruz, who was from Jotbah. 20Amon
did what the LORD said was wrong, as his father
Manasseh had done. 21He lived in the same way
his father had lived: he worshiped the idols his
father had worshiped, and he bowed down
before them. 22Amon rejected the LORD, the God
of his ancestors, and did not follow the ways of
the LORD.
23Amon's officers made plans against him and
killed him in his palace. 24Then the people of the
land killed all those who had made plans to kill
King Amon, and they made his son Josiah king in
his place.
25Everything else Amon did is written in the
book of the history of the kings of Judah. 26He was
buried in his grave in the garden of Uzza, and his
son Josiah became king in his place.

Josiah King of Judah

22 Josiah was eight years old when he became
king, and he ruled thirty-one years in Jerusalem. His mother's name was Jedidah daughter of
Adaiah, who was from Bozkath. 2Josiah did what
the LORD said was right. He lived as his ancestor
David had lived, and he did not stop doing what
was right.
3In Josiah's eighteenth year as king, he sent
Shaphan to the Temple of the LORD. Shaphan son
of Azaliah, the son of Meshullam, was the royal
secretary. Josiah said, 4"Go up to Hilkiah the high
priest, and have him empty out the money the
gatekeepers have gathered from the people. This
is the money they have brought into the Temple
of the LORD. 5Have him give the money to the
supervisors of the work on the Temple of the
LORD. They must pay the workers who repair the
Temple of the LORD— 6the carpenters, builders,
and bricklayers. Also use the money to buy timber and cut stone to repair the Temple. 7They do
not need to report how they use the money given
to them, because they are working honestly."

The Book of the Teachings Is Found

8Hilkiah the high priest said to Shaphan the
royal secretary, "I've found the Book of the
Teachings in the Temple of the LORD." He gave it
to Shaphan, who read it.
9Then Shaphan the royal secretary went to the
king and reported to Josiah, "Your officers have
paid out the money that was in the Temple of the
LORD. They have given it to the workers and
supervisors at the Temple." 10Then Shaphan the
royal secretary told the king, "Hilkiah the priest
has given me a book." And Shaphan read from
the book to the king.
11When the king heard the words of the Book
of the Teachings, he tore his clothes to show how
upset he was. 12He gave orders to Hilkiah the
priest, Ahikam son of Shaphan, Acbor son of
Micaiah, Shaphan the royal secretary, and Asaiah
the king's servant. These were the orders: 13"Go
and ask the LORD about the words in the book
that was found. Ask for me, for all the people, and
for all Judah. The LORD's anger is burning against
us, because our ancestors did not obey the words
of this book; they did not do all the things written
for us to do."
14So Hilkiah the priest, Ahikam, Acbor, Shaphan, and Asaiah went to talk to Huldah the
prophetess. She was the wife of Shallum son of
Tikvah, the son of Harhas, who took care of the
king's clothes. Huldah lived in Jerusalem, in the
new area of the city.
15She said to them, "This is what the LORD, the
God of Israel, says: Tell the man who sent you to
me, 16'This is what the LORD says: I will bring
trouble to this place and to the people living here,
as it is written in the book which the king of
Judah has read. 17The people of Judah have left
me and have burned incense to other gods. They
have made me angry by all that they have done.
My anger burns against this place like a fire, and
it will not be put out.' 18Tell the king of Judah,
who sent you to ask the LORD, 'This is what the
LORD, the God of Israel, says about the words you
heard: 19When you heard my words against this
place and its people, you became sorry for what
you had done and humbled yourself before me. I
said they would be cursed and would be
destroyed. You tore your clothes to show how
upset you were, and you cried in my presence.
This is why I have heard you, says the LORD. 20So
I will let you die, and you will be buried in peace.
You won't see all the trouble I will bring to this
place.'"
So they took her message back to the king.

The People Hear the Agreement

23 Then the king gathered all the older leaders
of Judah and Jerusalem together. 2He went
up to the Temple of the LORD, and all the people
from Judah and Jerusalem went with him. The
priests, prophets, and all the people—from the
least important to the most important—went with

21:17 *in the book of the history of the kings of Judah.* See 8:23.

21:25 *in the book of the history of the kings of Judah.* See 8:23.

him. He read to them all the words of the Book of the Agreement that was found in the Temple of the LORD. 3The king stood by the pillar and made an agreement in the presence of the LORD to follow the LORD and obey his commands, rules, and laws with his whole being, and to obey the words of the agreement written in this book. Then all the people promised to obey the agreement.

Josiah Destroys the Places for Idol Worship

4The king commanded Hilkiah the high priest and the priests of the next rank and the gatekeepers to bring out of the Temple of the LORD everything made for Baal, Asherah, and all the stars of the sky. Then Josiah burned them outside Jerusalem in the open country of the Kidron Valley and carried their ashes to Bethel. 5The kings of Judah had chosen priests for these gods. These priests burned incense in the places where gods were worshiped in the cities of Judah and the towns around Jerusalem. They burned incense to Baal, the sun, the moon, the planets, and all the stars of the sky. But Josiah took those priests away.⚭ 6He removed the Asherah idol from the Temple of the LORD and took it outside Jerusalem to the Kidron Valley, where he burned it and beat it into dust. Then he threw the dust on the graves of the common people. 7He also tore down the houses of the male prostitutes who were in the Temple of the LORD, where the women did weaving for Asherah.

8King Josiah brought all the false priests from the cities of Judah. He ruined the places where gods were worshiped, where the priests had burned incense, from Geba to Beersheba. He destroyed the places of worship at the entrance to the Gate of Joshua, the ruler of the city, on the left side of the city gate. 9The priests at the places where gods were worshiped were not allowed to serve at the LORD's altar in Jerusalem. But they could eat bread made without yeast with their brothers.

10Josiah ruined Topheth, in the Valley of Ben Hinnom, so no one could sacrifice his son or daughter to Molech. 11Judah's kings had placed horses at the front door of the Temple of the LORD in the courtyard near the room of Nathan-Melech, an officer. These horses were for the worship of the sun. So Josiah removed them and burned the chariots that were for sun worship also.

12The kings of Judah had built altars on the roof of the upstairs room of Ahaz. Josiah broke down these altars and the altars Manasseh had made in the two courtyards of the Temple of the LORD. Josiah smashed them to pieces and threw their dust into the Kidron Valley. 13King Josiah ruined the places where gods were worshiped east of Jerusalem, south of the Mount of Olives. Solomon king of Israel had built these places. One was for Ashtoreth, the hated goddess of the Sidonians. One was for Chemosh, the hated god of Moab. And one was for Molech, the hated god of the Ammonites. 14Josiah smashed to pieces the stone pillars they worshiped, and he cut down the Asherah idols. Then he covered the places with human bones.

15Josiah also broke down the altar at Bethel—the place of worship made by Jeroboam son of Nebat, who had led Israel to sin. Josiah burned that place, broke the stones of the altar into pieces, then beat them into dust. He also burned the Asherah idol. 16When he turned around, he saw the graves on the mountain. He had the bones taken from the graves, and he burned them on the altar to ruin it. This happened as the LORD had said it would through the man of God.

17Josiah asked, "What is that monument I see?"

The people of the city answered, "It's the grave of the man of God who came from Judah. This prophet announced the things you have done against the altar of Bethel."

18Josiah said, "Leave the grave alone. No one may move this man's bones." So they left his bones and the bones of the prophet who had come from Samaria.

19The kings of Israel had built temples for worshiping gods in the cities of Samaria, which had caused the LORD to be angry. Josiah removed all those temples and did the same things as he had done at Bethel. 20He killed all the priests of those places of worship; he killed them on the altars and burned human bones on the altars. Then he went back to Jerusalem.

Josiah Celebrates the Passover

21The king commanded all the people, "Celebrate the Passover to the LORD your God as it is written in this Book of the Agreement." 22The Passover had not been celebrated like this since the judges led Israel. Nor had one like it happened while there were kings of Israel and kings of Judah. 23This Passover was celebrated to the LORD in Jerusalem in the eighteenth year of King Josiah's rule.

24Josiah destroyed the mediums, fortune-tellers, house gods, and idols. He also destroyed all the

⚭**23:5 Astrology:** 2 Chronicles 33:3

23:12 *roof.* In Bible times houses were built with flat roofs. The roof was used for drying things such as flax and fruit, as an extra room, as a place for worship, and as a cool place to sleep in the summer.

23:13 *Mount of Olives.* Literally, "The Mountain of Ruin."

23:17 A fulfillment of the prophecy found in 1 Kings 13:1–2.

hated gods seen in the land of Judah and
Jerusalem. This was to obey the words of the
teachings written in the book Hilkiah the priest
had found in the Temple of the LORD.
25There was no king like Josiah before or after
him. He obeyed the LORD with all his heart, soul,
and strength, following all the Teachings of Moses.
26Even so, the LORD did not stop his strong and
terrible anger. His anger burned against Judah
because of all Manasseh had done to make him
angry. 27The LORD said, "I will send Judah out of
my sight, as I have sent Israel away. I will reject
Jerusalem, which I chose. And I will take away
the Temple about which I said, 'I will be worshiped there.'"
28Everything else Josiah did is written in the
book of the history of the kings of Judah.
29While Josiah was king, Neco king of Egypt
went to help the king of Assyria at the Euphrates
River. King Josiah marched out to fight against
Neco, but at Megiddo, Neco faced him and killed
him. 30Josiah's servants carried his body in a chariot from Megiddo to Jerusalem and buried him in
his own grave. Then the people of Judah chose
Josiah's son Jehoahaz and poured olive oil on him
to make him king in his father's place.

Jehoahaz King of Judah

31Jehoahaz was twenty-three years old when
he became king, and he was king in Jerusalem for
three months. His mother's name was Hamutal,
who was the daughter of Jeremiah from Libnah.
32Jehoahaz did what the LORD said was wrong,
just as his ancestors had done.
33King Neco took Jehoahaz prisoner at Riblah
in the land of Hamath so that Jehoahaz could not
rule in Jerusalem. Neco made the people of Judah
pay about seventy-five hundred pounds of silver
and about seventy-five pounds of gold.
34King Neco made Josiah's son Eliakim the king
in place of Josiah his father. Then Neco changed
Eliakim's name to Jehoiakim. But Neco took
Jehoahaz to Egypt, where he died. 35Jehoiakim
gave King Neco the silver and gold he demanded.
Jehoiakim taxed the land and took silver and gold
from the people of the land to give to King Neco.
Each person had to pay his share.

Jehoiakim King of Judah

36Jehoiakim was twenty-five years old when he
became king, and he was king in Jerusalem for
eleven years. His mother's name was Zebidah
daughter of Pedaiah, who was from Rumah.
37Jehoiakim did what the LORD said was wrong,
just as his ancestors had done.

24 While Jehoiakim was king, Nebuchadnezzar king of Babylon attacked the land of
Judah. So Jehoiakim became Nebuchadnezzar's
servant for three years. Then he turned against
Nebuchadnezzar and broke away from his rule.
2The LORD sent raiding parties from Babylon,
Aram, Moab, and Ammon against Jehoiakim to
destroy Judah. This happened as the LORD had
said it would through his servants the prophets.
3The LORD commanded this to happen to the
people of Judah, to remove them from his presence, because of all the sins of Manasseh. 4He
had killed many innocent people and had filled
Jerusalem with their blood. And the LORD would
not forgive these sins.
5The other things that happened while Jehoiakim
was king and all he did are written in the book of
the history of the kings of Judah. 6Jehoiakim died,
and his son Jehoiachin became king in his place.
7The king of Egypt did not leave his land again,
because the king of Babylon had captured all that
belonged to the king of Egypt, from the brook of
Egypt to the Euphrates River.

Jehoiachin King of Judah

8Jehoiachin was eighteen years old when he
became king, and he was king three months in
Jerusalem. His mother's name was Nehushta
daughter of Elnathan from Jerusalem. 9Jehoiachin
did what the LORD said was wrong, just as his
father had done.
10At that time the officers of Nebuchadnezzar
king of Babylon came up to Jerusalem. When they
reached the city, they attacked it. 11Nebuchad-
nezzar himself came to the city while his officers
were attacking it. 12Jehoiachin king of Judah surrendered to the king of Babylon, along with
Jehoiachin's mother, servants, older leaders, and
officers. So Nebuchadnezzar made Jehoiachin a
prisoner in the eighth year he was king of
Babylon. 13Nebuchadnezzar took all the treasures
from the Temple of the LORD and from the palace.
He cut up all the gold objects Solomon king of
Israel had made for the Temple of the LORD. This
happened as the LORD had said it would.
14Nebuchadnezzar took away all the people of
Jerusalem, including all the leaders, all the
wealthy people, and all the craftsmen and metal
workers. There were ten thousand prisoners in
all. Only the poorest people in the land were left.
15Nebuchadnezzar carried away Jehoiachin to

23:28 *in the book of the history of the kings of Judah.* See 8:23.

24:5 *in the book of the history of the kings of Judah.* See 8:23.

Babylon, as well as the king's mother and his wives, the officers, and the leading men of the land. They were taken captive from Jerusalem to Babylon. 16The king of Babylon also took all seven thousand soldiers, who were strong and able to fight in war, and about a thousand craftsmen and metal workers. Nebuchadnezzar took them as prisoners to Babylon. 17Then he made Mattaniah, Jehoiachin's uncle, king in Jehoiachin's place. He also changed Mattaniah's name to Zedekiah.

Zedekiah King of Judah

18Zedekiah was twenty-one years old when he became king, and he was king in Jerusalem for eleven years. His mother's name was Hamutal daughter of Jeremiah from Libnah. 19Zedekiah did what the LORD said was wrong, just as Jehoiakim had done. 20All this happened in Jerusalem and Judah because the LORD was angry with them. Finally, he threw them out of his presence.

The Fall of Jerusalem

Zedekiah turned against the king of Babylon.

25 Nebuchadnezzar king of Babylon marched against Jerusalem with his whole army during Zedekiah's ninth year as king, on the tenth day of the tenth month. He made a camp around the city and piled dirt against the city walls to attack it. 2The city was under attack until Zedekiah's eleventh year as king. 3By the ninth day of the fourth month, the hunger was terrible in the city. There was no food for the people to eat. 4Then the city was broken into, and the whole army ran away at night through the gate between the two walls by the king's garden. While the Babylonians were still surrounding the city, Zedekiah and his men ran away toward the Jordan Valley. 5But the Babylonian army chased King Zedekiah and caught up with him in the plains of Jericho. All of his army was scattered from him, 6so they captured Zedekiah and took him to the king of Babylon at Riblah. There he passed sentence on Zedekiah. 7They killed Zedekiah's sons as he watched. Then they put out his eyes and put bronze chains on him and took him to Babylon.

8Nebuzaradan was the commander of the king's special guards. This officer of the king of Babylon came to Jerusalem on the seventh day of the fifth month, in Nebuchadnezzar's nineteenth year as king of Babylon. 9Nebuzaradan set fire to the Temple of the LORD and the palace and all the houses of Jerusalem. Every important building was burned.

10The whole Babylonian army, led by the commander of the king's special guards, broke down the walls around Jerusalem. 11Nebuzaradan, the commander of the guards, captured the people left in Jerusalem, those who had surrendered to the king of Babylon, and the rest of the people. 12But the commander left behind some of the poorest people of the land to take care of the vineyards and fields.

13The Babylonians broke up the bronze pillars, the bronze stands, and the large bronze bowl, which was called the Sea, in the Temple of the LORD. Then they carried the bronze to Babylon. 14They also took the pots, shovels, wick trimmers, dishes, and all the bronze objects used to serve in the Temple. 15The commander of the king's special guards took away the pans for carrying hot coals, the bowls, and everything made of pure gold or silver. 16There were two pillars and the large bronze bowl and the movable stands which Solomon had made for the Temple of the LORD. There was so much bronze that it could not be weighed. 17Each pillar was about twenty-seven feet high. The bronze capital on top of the pillar was about four and one-half feet high. It was decorated with a net design and bronze pomegranates all around it. The other pillar also had a net design and was like the first pillar.

Judah Is Taken Prisoner

18The commander of the guards took some prisoners—Seraiah the chief priest, Zephaniah the priest next in rank, and the three doorkeepers. 19Of the people who were still in the city, he took the officer in charge of the fighting men, as well as five people who advised the king. He took the royal secretary who selected people for the army and sixty other men who were in the city. 20Nebuzaradan, the commander, took all these people and brought them to the king of Babylon at Riblah. 21There at Riblah, in the land of Hamath, the king had them killed. So the people of Judah were led away from their country as captives.

Gedaliah Becomes Governor

22Nebuchadnezzar king of Babylon left some people in the land of Judah. He appointed Gedaliah son of Ahikam, the son of Shaphan, as governor.

24:18 *Jeremiah.* This is not the prophet Jeremiah, but a different man with the same name.

25:1 *piled dirt against the city walls.* This was a common practice in siege warfare. The attacking army would construct a ramp of dirt against the wall of the city in order to allow the army to climb it and overrun the walls.

25:3 Famine: Jeremiah 14:3–5

25:10 Nehemiah: 2 Chronicles 36:19

23The army captains and their men heard that
the king of Babylon had made Gedaliah governor,
so they came to Gedaliah at Mizpah. They were
Ishmael son of Nethaniah, Johanan son of Kareah,
Seraiah son of Tanhumeth the Netophathite,
Jaazaniah son of the Maacathite, and their men.
24Then Gedaliah promised these army captains
and their men, "Don't be afraid of the Babylonian
officers. Live in the land and serve the king of
Babylon, and everything will go well for you."
25In the seventh month Ishmael son of Nethaniah, son of Elishama from the king's family, came
with ten men and killed Gedaliah. They also killed
the men of Judah and Babylon who were with
Gedaliah at Mizpah. 26Then all the people, from the
least important to the most important, along with
the army leaders, ran away to Egypt, because they
were afraid of the Babylonians.

Jehoiachin Is Set Free

27Jehoiachin king of Judah was held in Babylon
for thirty-seven years. In the thirty-seventh year
Evil-Merodach became king of Babylon, and he let
Jehoiachin out of prison on the twenty-seventh
day of the twelfth month. 28Evil-Merodach spoke
kindly to Jehoiachin and gave him a seat of honor
above the seats of the other kings who were with
him in Babylon. 29So Jehoiachin put away his
prison clothes. For the rest of his life, he ate at the
king's table. 30Every day, for as long as Jehoiachin
lived, the king gave him an allowance.

25:29 *the king's table.* Not that he ate with the king, but that the king provided him a regular allowance, thus showing him some favor.

INTRODUCTION TO THE BOOK OF

1 CHRONICLES

Israel's History from Adam to David

WHO WROTE THIS BOOK?

It is traditionally believed that Ezra, the prophet, wrote the Chronicles, but this fact cannot be completely confirmed.

TO WHOM WAS THIS BOOK WRITTEN?

Like its companion book, the Book of Kings, Chronicles is a part of the history of Israel and, thus, written for and about them. However, unlike Kings, which is written for Israel in captivity, Chronicles is written for Israel following the exile and during her restoration days.

WHERE WAS IT WRITTEN?

The location of the author during his writing is not specifically known; however, it is possible that Jerusalem might be the site, since the rebuilding of the Temple is a central idea of the book.

WHEN WAS IT WRITTEN?

Latest opinion among biblical scholars places the writing of Chronicles in the latter half of the fifth century B.C., probably between 539 and 400 B.C., which would correspond with the life of Ezra and the period of restoration.

WHAT IS THIS BOOK ABOUT?

The Book of Chronicles overviews the entire history of the people of Israel from the time of Adam down through their captivity. These historical events are recited with a focus on Israel's restored status. It assures them of God's continuing interest in his people, the ongoing force of the agreement he made with them at Mount Sinai, his faithfulness to the promises he made to Abraham and David, and a renewal of their relationship to him. The book ends with the death of David and the anointing of Solomon as King of the United Kingdom.

WHY WAS THIS BOOK WRITTEN?

The author of Chronicles obviously wanted to reinforce Israel's hope of a coming Savior (Messiah), who had been promised to them as a "son of David." It is his intention to reaffirm God's promise as sure and dependable. He also highlights the need for their continued obedience to the law and the prophets. The point is, God is always faithful, and Israel must be faithful, too.

SO WHAT DOES THIS BOOK MEAN TO US?

God's promise to Israel was that Christ was coming to deliver them from their persecutors and restore them to glory as God's favored people. God's promise to us, as Christians, is that Christ is coming again to deliver us from our persecutor, Satan, and take us to the glory that is awaiting us in heaven as God's favored people. The message both to Israel and to us is, "Be faithful! He's coming."

SUMMARY:

Chronicles is a book that Christians often skip or skim. We often feel that we have already read the history of the period from David to the exile in Samuel and Kings. Why bother to do it twice? First Chronicles begins with an imposing genealogy that most modern readers find monotonous.

But to pass over Chronicles is to miss a special treat. Like the multiple gospels in the New Testament, the presence of two accounts of Israel's history is not boring but exciting in that they give us two important and true perspectives on the same period of time.

Samuel and Kings were written during the exile where the burning question in the minds of the original readers concerned how God could have let them be defeated by their enemies and thrown out of the Promised Land. Chronicles was written in the period after the exile, during the restoration when the faithful few returned to the Land. They had questions too, and they turned to their history for answers. They were asking about their relationship with the past, and they were looking for positive role models for their life in Judah. What Chronicles gives them is not only a pattern from the past for living in the present, but also increases the expectation that something even better would come in the future.

First and Second Chronicles were originally one writing in the Hebrew Bible. It was divided into two books by the translators of the Old Testament into the Greek language (called the Septuagint).

The book of 1 Chronicles has the following outline:

I. The Genealogies (1:1–9:44)
II. The Story of David (10:1–29:30)

I. The Genealogies (1:1–9:44)

The genealogies connect the Israel of the time of the restoration with the people of the past. The people of God who have returned from the Babylonian captivity are interested in how they relate to the past, and the genealogies take them all the way back to Adam.

II. The Story of David (10:1–29:30)

The rest of the Book of 1 Chronicles focuses on David. It is interesting to note the difference of emphasis between the account of Kings and Chronicles concerning the early period of Israel's kingship. Chronicles tells us little about Saul compared to Kings. It devotes most of its attention to David, but even here it is selective. Most of the stories that throw a bad light on David are not given. This emphasis is in keeping with the purpose of wanting to give a positive history of the past as a model for how to behave now that they have returned to the land of Palestine. Much emphasis is placed on David's and Solomon's activities in building the Temple, since at the time Chronicles was written the Temple was being rebuilt.

1 CHRONICLES

From Adam to Abraham

Adam was the father of Seth. Seth was the
father of Enosh. Enosh was the father of
Kenan. 2Kenan was the father of Mahalalel. Mahalalel was the father of Jared. Jared was
the father of Enoch. 3Enoch was the father of
Methuselah. Methuselah was the father of
Lamech, and Lamech was the father of Noah.
4The sons of Noah were Shem, Ham, and
Japheth.
5Japheth's sons were Gomer, Magog, Madai,
Javan, Tubal, Meshech, and Tiras.
6Gomer's sons were Ashkenaz, Riphath, and
Togarmah.
7Javan's sons were Elishah, Tarshish, Kittim,
and Rodanim.
8Ham's sons were Cush, Mizraim, Put, and
Canaan.
9Cush's sons were Seba, Havilah, Sabta, Raamah, and Sabteca.
Raamah's sons were Sheba and Dedan.
10Cush was the father of Nimrod, who grew up
to become a mighty warrior on the earth.
11Mizraim was the father of the Ludites, Anamites, Lehabites, and Naphtuhites,
12Pathrusites, Casluhites, and Caphtorites. (The
Philistines came from the Casluhites.)
13Canaan's first child was Sidon. He was also
the father of the Hittites, 14Jebusites, Amorites,
Girgashites, 15Hivites, Arkites, Sinites, 16Arvadites,
Zemarites, and Hamathites.
17Shem's sons were Elam, Asshur, Arphaxad,
Lud, and Aram.
Aram's sons were Uz, Hul, Gether, and Meshech.
18Arphaxad was the father of Shelah, who was
the father of Eber.
19Eber had two sons. One son was named
Peleg, because the people on the earth were
divided into different languages during his life.
Peleg's brother was named Joktan.
20Joktan was the father of Almodad, Sheleph,
Hazarmaveth, Jerah, 21Hadoram, Uzal, Diklah,
22Obal, Abimael, Sheba, 23Ophir, Havilah, and
Jobab. All these were Joktan's sons. 24The family
line included Shem, Arphaxad, Shelah, 25Eber,
Peleg, Reu, 26Serug, Nahor, Terah, 27and Abram,
who was called Abraham.

Abraham's Family

28Abraham's sons were Isaac and Ishmael.
29These were the sons of Isaac and Ishmael.
Ishmael's first son was Nebaioth. His other sons
were Kedar, Adbeel, Mibsam, 30Mishma, Dumah, Massa, Hadad, Tema, 31Jetur, Naphish, and
Kedemah. These were Ishmael's sons. 32Keturah,
Abraham's slave woman, gave birth to Zimran,
Jokshan, Medan, Midian, Ishbak, and Shuah.
Jokshan's sons were Sheba and Dedan.
33Midian's sons were Ephah, Epher, Hanoch,
Abida, and Eldaah. All these were descendants of
Keturah.
34Abraham was the father of Isaac, and Isaac's
sons were Esau and Israel.
35Esau's sons were Eliphaz, Reuel, Jeush, Jalam, and Korah.
36Eliphaz's sons were Teman, Omar, Zepho,
Gatam, Kenaz, Timna, and Amalek.
37Reuel's sons were Nahath, Zerah, Shammah,
and Mizzah.

The Edomites from Seir

38Seir's sons were Lotan, Shobal, Zibeon, Anah,
Dishon, Ezer, and Dishan.
39Lotan's sons were Hori and Homam, and his
sister was Timna.
40Shobal's sons were Alvan, Manahath, Ebal,
Shepho, and Onam.
Zibeon's sons were Aiah and Anah.
41Anah's son was Dishon.
Dishon's sons were Hemdan, Eshban, Ithran,
and Keran.
42Ezer's sons were Bilhan, Zaavan, and Akan.
Dishan's sons were Uz and Aran.

The Kings of Edom

43These kings ruled in Edom before there were
kings in Israel. Bela son of Beor was king of Edom,
and his city was named Dinhabah.
44When Bela died, Jobab son of Zerah became
king. He was from Bozrah.
45When Jobab died, Husham became king. He
was from the land of the Temanites.
46When Husham died, Hadad son of Bedad
became king, and his city was named Avith.
Hadad defeated Midian in the country of Moab.
47When Hadad died, Samlah became king. He
was from Masrekah.
48When Samlah died, Shaul became king. He
was from Rehoboth by the river.
49When Shaul died, Baal-Hanan son of Acbor
became king.

1:7 *Kittim.* His descendants were the people of Cyprus.
1:8 *Mizraim.* This is another name for Egypt.
1:19 *Peleg.* This name sounds like the Hebrew word for "divided."

[50]When Baal-Hanan died, Hadad became king, and his city was named Pau. Hadad's wife was named Mehetabel, and she was the daughter of Matred, who was the daughter of Me-Zahab. [51]Then Hadad died.

The leaders of the family groups of Edom were Timna, Alvah, Jetheth, [52]Oholibamah, Elah, Pinon, [53]Kenaz, Teman, Mibzar, [54]Magdiel, and Iram. These were the leaders of Edom.

Israel's Family

2 The sons of Israel were Reuben, Simeon, Levi, Judah, Issachar, Zebulun, [2]Dan, Joseph, Benjamin, Naphtali, Gad, and Asher.

Judah's Family

[3]Judah's sons were Er, Onan, and Shelah. A Canaanite woman, the daughter of Shua, was their mother. Judah's first son, Er, did what the LORD said was wicked, so the LORD put him to death. [4]Judah's daughter-in-law Tamar gave birth to Perez and Zerah. Judah was the father, so Judah had five sons.

[5]Perez's sons were Hezron and Hamul.

[6]Zerah had five sons: Zimri, Ethan, Heman, Calcol, and Darda.

[7]Carmi's son was Achan, who caused trouble for Israel because he took things that had been given to the LORD to be destroyed.

[8]Ethan's son was Azariah.

[9]Hezron's sons were Jerahmeel, Ram, and Caleb.

[10]Ram was Amminadab's father, and Amminadab was Nahshon's father. Nahshon was the leader of the people of Judah. [11]Nahshon was the father of Salmon, who was the father of Boaz. [12]Boaz was the father of Obed, and Obed was the father of Jesse.

[13]Jesse's first son was Eliab. His second son was Abinadab, his third was Shimea, [14]his fourth was Nethanel, his fifth was Raddai, [15]his sixth was Ozem, and his seventh son was David. [16]Their sisters were Zeruiah and Abigail. Zeruiah's three sons were Abishai, Joab, and Asahel. [17]Abigail was the mother of Amasa, and his father was Jether, an Ishmaelite.

Caleb's Family

[18]Caleb son of Hezron had children by his wife Azubah and by Jerioth. Caleb and Azubah's sons were Jesher, Shobab, and Ardon. [19]When Azubah died, Caleb married Ephrath. They had a son named Hur, [20]who was the father of Uri, who was the father of Bezalel.

[21]Later, when Hezron was sixty years old, he married the daughter of Makir, Gilead's father. Hezron had sexual relations with Makir's daughter, and she had a son named Segub. [22]Segub was the father of Jair. Jair controlled twenty-three cities in the country of Gilead. [23](But Geshur and Aram captured the Towns of Jair, as well as Kenath and the small towns around it—sixty towns in all.) All these were descendants of Makir, the father of Gilead.

[24]After Hezron died in Caleb Ephrathah, his wife Abijah had his son, named Ashhur. Ashhur became the father of Tekoa.

Jerahmeel's Family

[25]Hezron's first son was Jerahmeel. Jerahmeel's sons were Ram, Bunah, Oren, Ozem, and Ahijah. Ram was Jerahmeel's first son. [26]Jerahmeel had another wife, named Atarah. She was the mother of Onam.

[27]Jerahmeel's first son, Ram, had sons. They were Maaz, Jamin, and Eker.

[28]Onam's sons were Shammai and Jada.

Shammai's sons were Nadab and Abishur.

[29]Abishur's wife was named Abihail, and their sons were Ahban and Molid.

[30]Nadab's sons were Seled and Appaim. Seled died without having children.

[31]Appaim's son was Ishi, who became the father of Sheshan.

Sheshan was the father of Ahlai.

[32]Jada was Shammai's brother, and Jada's sons were Jether and Jonathan. Jether died without having children.

[33]Jonathan's sons were Peleth and Zaza.

These were Jerahmeel's descendants.

[34]Sheshan did not have any sons, only daughters. He had a servant from Egypt named Jarha. [35]Sheshan let his daughter marry his servant Jarha, and she had a son named Attai.

[36]Attai was the father of Nathan. Nathan was the father of Zabad. [37]Zabad was the father of Ephlal. Ephlal was the father of Obed. [38]Obed was the father of Jehu. Jehu was the father of Azariah. [39]Azariah was the father of Helez. Helez was the father of Eleasah. [40]Eleasah was the father of Sismai. Sismai was the father of Shallum. [41]Shallum was the father of Jekamiah, and Jekamiah was the father of Elishama.

Caleb's Family

[42]Caleb was Jerahmeel's brother. Caleb's first son was Mesha. Mesha was the father of Ziph, and his son Mareshah was the father of Hebron.

[43]Hebron's sons were Korah, Tappuah, Rekem, and Shema. [44]Shema was the father of Raham, who was the father of Jorkeam. Rekem was the

2:1 *Israel.* Another name for Jacob.

2:7 Achan's story is found in Joshua 7. His crime against the Lord led to the defeat of Israel in its battle against Ai.

JOB

JOB 1

What is the story of Job? Is he an innocent sufferer? What do we learn from his suffering?

Job's story is found in the book that bears his name. We learn a little bit about Job's life in the introduction to the book (Job 1). He lived in the land of Uz, which was probably located east of Palestine in what is today the country of Jordan. The significance of this location is that it indicates that Job was not an Israelite. For this reason, most students of the Bible date Job to the time before Abraham when God entered into a special relationship with a particular people.

Job's lifestyle was similar to Abraham's. He had a large family and his wealth was composed of large herds and flocks as well as a large number of servants (Job 1:2–3). Right from the start we learn that Job was "an honest and innocent man" (1:1). According to a common belief in ancient times, such a godly person would obviously be blessed with health, wealth, and success. But that was not the case with Job. God allowed him to be hit by tragedy after tragedy. Job's servants, his animals, and even his children were killed in one disaster after another. After these horrible events, Job himself was struck with a debilitating, painful, and humiliating disease.

These events raise certain questions about life, suffering, and God. While the focus is on one person, the Book of Job intends to take this concrete case and address these issues that are so crucial to us all. The question that is raised right from the very start is, How can an all-powerful and all-loving God allow his faithful and innocent children suffer?

Of course, readers have more information than the characters of the story, since the first chapter of Job has informed us that Job is innocent. Neither Job nor his three friends know this, and so they begin a lengthy debate over the cause of Job's suffering.

While there may be subtle differences between Eliphaz, Bildad, and Zophar, they all agree in their basic position that Job is suffering because he is a sinner and needs to repent (Job 4:7–11; 11:13–20). They don't know any specific sin in his life, but they believe that all suffering is caused by sin. So, if Job is suffering, then he is sinning. No other option is possible.

On the other hand, Job knows his own heart, and he knows that his suffering is out of proportion to his sinfulness. He denies that his loss and pain are the results of sin. God is basically unfair and "destroys both the innocent and the guilty" (9:22, see verses 21–24). In turn, Eliphaz, Bildad, and Zophar bombard Job with their arguments, probing him to admit his sin, and calling him a liar when he does not. Job defends himself and comes close to calling God unfair. He demands that God reveal himself and set the record straight.

The three friends, on the one hand (see 11:12; 15:1–3), and Job, on the other (12:1–3; 13:12), set themselves up as wise men, each with their perspective. They think they have an insight into the workings of the world, based on their underlying philosophy. As they present their own views, they attack the integrity and competence of the other. After three cycles of discussion between Job and his friends (Job 4–31) their debate reaches an end, but no final resolution. Job hints at the truth (Job 28, the poem on God's wisdom), but then continues his lament about his suffering (Job 29–31).

At this point, a new character bursts onto the scene. Elihu is a brash young man who has hesitated to speak up to this point because of his age. Frustrated that his elders were unable to bring Job to recognition of his failings, Elihu now tries. He attempts to bring new arguments, but just repeats the old formulas that have not proved persuasive. His long speech (Job 32–37) is ignored by all, including God at the end.

All throughout his speech, Job had been calling on God to come and speak to him. If he was expecting an apology or even an explanation, he was sadly mistaken. God comes, but he comes with power and accusations against Job: "Who is this that makes my purpose unclear by saying things that are not true?" (Job 38:2).

God then gives Job a speech about where wisdom comes from. The three friends have been saying they are wise; Job in his turn has made the same claim. God speaks out of the whirlwind and says, in effect, "I am the one who is all-wise!"

When Job hears God, he respectfully submits to his Maker (Job 40:3–5; 42:1–6). God never directly answers Job's question about the cause of his suffering. God's answer is, "I am wise. Submit yourself to me!" Job does and teaches all who suffer that we should trust our heavenly Father, even when life seems irrational.

After Job's repentance, God restores his health and wealth and even raises up a new family for him.

Note: All Scripture references on Job are included in this article.

SATAN/SATANISM

JOB 1

What does the term Satan mean? Why is he so seldom mentioned in the Old Testament? Does the Bible tell us where Satan came from or what type of being he is?

The English term "Satan" is a transliteration of the Hebrew word *satan,* which means "adversary." It was not originally a proper name or a technical term, but came to be used in that way in early Judaism and then in early Christianity. In other words, except perhaps for Job, we do not find it as a proper name in the Old Testament.

The word first appears in some of the later material in the Old Testament, such as Job 1:6–2:7; 1 Chronicles 21:1; Zechariah 3:1–2; and occurs as another name for "the devil" in the New Testament (see Mark 3:23, 26; Luke 10:18).

As the Hebrew word *satan* (adversary), it refers to a being that tests, persecutes, tempts, misleads, accuses believers, and, hence, is their nemesis or adversary. The term comes from the arena of the court and makes us think of images of a prosecuting attorney or perhaps a legal adversary.

As with many other doctrines (for example, the Trinity), God slowly revealed the details concerning his supernatural enemy to his people. God's people probably did not have a full understanding and belief in such a being until later in the Old Testament period. Even so, it is hard to doubt that God's people, like other ancient Near Eastern peoples, believed in supernatural evil of a personal nature as well as supernatural good.

And when we turn to Genesis 3, we find a character, who, though not identified explicitly at that time as Satan, fits that bill. Genesis 3 gives the account of humankind's fall into sin. The one who tempts the woman, then tempts the man to rebel against God is the snake. It is hard to doubt the author believed that the powers of darkness were using this creature to purposely mislead Adam and Eve. The element of speech, plus purposeful evil intent, points to a larger supernatural being manipulating the situation.

Thus, we are not surprised to see that the New Testament makes the connection between the snake and Satan explicit (Romans 16:20; Revelation 12:9). It is Satan himself who tempts human beings into rebellion against God. In the context of the curse God places on him (Genesis 3:15), we learn that a lasting conflict will take place between him and the "seed of the woman." The rest of Scripture tells the story of that battle; the battle between the kingdom of God and the kingdom of evil.

In Job 1–2 we find a being who is part of the heavenly court, whose primary domain seems to be the earth which he roams. In these chapters it is made clear that the major function of Satan is to put people, in particular God's servants, to the test. It is also made clear that he does nothing without the permission of God. In the Old Testament Satan is not specifically associated with an otherworldly place called hell, in part because God was just beginning to reveal more about the afterlife and hell as opposed to heaven at the end of the Old Testament period.

Satan is not seen as a mere personification in this material. While it is too much to see Satan as in open conflict with God in Job 1–2, since he is still part of the heavenly court, nevertheless his malicious intent distinguishes him from God and God's character. God allows Job to be tested so that his good character may be demonstrated or even proved, while Satan's desire is to so try Job that he will renounce his God. As the scenes in Job 1–2 and in Zechariah 3:1–2 make clear, the major function of Satan in the Old Testament is to be the accuser (before God) of believers. While such things seem to be occasionally hinted at in the Old Testament, it is only in the New Testament that we find a full-blown development of the understanding of Satan, demons, hell, and supernatural conflict.

As we turn to the New Testament, we see Jesus' ministry is set against the backdrop of a personal devil that tempts him at crucial junctures of his life (compare Matthew 4:1–11 to Luke 4:13), and again and again he confronts demons (sometimes called unclean spirits), who are viewed as underlings of Satan (see Mark 1:23–26; 3:22–30; 5:1–20). Satan in Mark 3 is viewed as the strong man, whose captives Jesus came to set free. Luke 10:17–18 indicates that there is a connection between exorcisms on earth and the fall of Satan. In short, Jesus and his followers' appearance on the stage of human history means the beginning of the end for the devil and his work. In particular, Paul and other New Testament writers came to see Christ's death on the cross as the decisive victory against the powers of darkness which makes their eventual doom certain (see Colossians 1:21–23).

Satan/Satanism: For additional scriptures on this topic go to Zechariah 3:1–2.

father of Shammai. 45Shammai was the father of Maon, and Maon was the father of Beth Zur.

46Caleb's slave woman was named Ephah, and she was the mother of Haran, Moza, and Gazez. Haran was the father of Gazez.

47Jahdai's sons were Regem, Jotham, Geshan, Pelet, Ephah, and Shaaph.

48Caleb had another slave woman named Maacah. She was the mother of Sheber, Tirhanah, 49Shaaph, and Sheva. Shaaph was the father of Madmannah. Sheva was the father of Macbenah and Gibea. Caleb's daughter was Acsah.

50-51These were Caleb's descendants: Caleb's son Hur was the first son of his mother Ephrathah. Hur's sons were Shobal, Salma, and Hareph. Shobal was the father of Kiriath Jearim. Salma was the father of Bethlehem. And Hareph was the father of Beth Gader.

52Shobal was the father of Kiriath Jearim. Shobal's descendants were Haroeh, half the Manahathites, 53and the family groups of Kiriath Jearim: the Ithrites, Puthites, Shumathites, and Mishraites. The Zorathites and the Eshtaolites came from the Mishraite people.

54Salma's descendants were Bethlehem, the Netophathites, Atroth Beth Joab, half the Manahathites, and the Zorites. 55His descendants included the families who lived at Jabez, who wrote and copied important papers. They were called the Tirathites, Shimeathites, and Sucathites and were from the Kenite family group who came from Hammath. He was the father of the people living in Recab.

David's Family

3 These are David's sons who were born in Hebron. The first was Amnon, whose mother was Ahinoam from Jezreel. The second son was Daniel, whose mother was Abigail from Carmel. 2The third son was Absalom, whose mother was Maacah daughter of Talmai, the king of Geshur. The fourth son was Adonijah, whose mother was Haggith. 3The fifth son was Shephatiah, whose mother was Abital. The sixth son was Ithream, whose mother was Eglah. 4These six sons of David were born to him in Hebron, where David ruled for seven and one-half years.

David ruled in Jerusalem thirty-three years. 5These were his children who were born in Jerusalem: Shammua, Shobab, Nathan, and Solomon—the four children of David and Bathsheba, Ammiel's daughter. 6-8David's other nine children were Ibhar, Elishua, Eliphelet, Nogah, Nepheg, Japhia, Elishama, Eliada, and Eliphelet. 9These were all of David's sons, except for those born to his slave women. David also had a daughter named Tamar.

The Kings of Judah

10Solomon's son was Rehoboam. Rehoboam's son was Abijah. Abijah's son was Asa. Asa's son was Jehoshaphat. 11Jehoshaphat's son was Jehoram. Jehoram's son was Ahaziah. Ahaziah's son was Joash. 12Joash's son was Amaziah. Amaziah's son was Azariah. Azariah's son was Jotham. 13Jotham's son was Ahaz. Ahaz's son was Hezekiah. Hezekiah's son was Manasseh. 14Manasseh's son was Amon, and Amon's son was Josiah.

15These were Josiah's sons: His first son was Johanan, his second was Jehoiakim, his third was Zedekiah, and his fourth was Shallum.

16Jehoiakim was followed by Jehoiachin, and he was followed by Zedekiah.

David's Descendants After the Babylonian Captivity

17Jehoiachin was taken as a prisoner. His sons were Shealtiel, 18Malkiram, Pedaiah, Shenazzar, Jekamiah, Hoshama, and Nedabiah.

19Pedaiah's sons were Zerubbabel and Shimei.

Zerubbabel's sons were Meshullam and Hananiah, and their sister was Shelomith. 20Zerubbabel also had five other sons: Hashubah, Ohel, Berekiah, Hasadiah, and Jushab-Hesed.

21Hananiah's descendants were Pelatiah and Jeshaiah, and the sons of Rephaiah, Arnan, Obadiah, and Shecaniah.

22Shecaniah's son was Shemaiah. Shemaiah's sons were Hattush, Igal, Bariah, Neariah, and Shaphat. There were six in all.

23Neariah had three sons: Elioenai, Hizkiah, and Azrikam.

24Elioenai had seven sons: Hodaviah, Eliashib, Pelaiah, Akkub, Johanan, Delaiah, and Anani.

Other Family Groups of Judah

4 Judah's descendants were Perez, Hezron, Carmi, Hur, and Shobal.

2Reaiah was Shobal's son. Reaiah was the father of Jahath, and Jahath was the father of Ahumai and Lahad. They were the family groups of the Zorathite people.

3-4Hur was the oldest son of Caleb and his wife Ephrathah. Hur was the leader of Bethlehem. His three sons were Etam, Penuel, and Ezer. Etam's sons were Jezreel, Ishma, and Idbash. They had a sister named Hazzelelponi. Penuel was the father of Gedor, and Ezer was the father of Hushah.

5Tekoa's father was Ashhur. Ashhur had two wives named Helah and Naarah.

6The sons of Ashhur and Naarah were Ahuzzam, Hepher, Temeni, and Haahashtari. These were the descendants of Naarah.

7Helah's sons were Zereth, Zohar, Ethnan,
8and Koz. Koz was the father of Anub, Haz-
zobebah, and the Aharhel family group. Aharhel
was the son of Harum.

9There was a man named Jabez, who was respected more than his brothers. His mother
named him Jabez because she said, "I was in
much pain when I gave birth to him." 10Jabez
prayed to the God of Israel, "Please do good things
for me and give me more land. Stay with me, and
don't let anyone hurt me. Then I won't have any
pain." And God did what Jabez had asked.

11Kelub, Shuhah's brother, was the father of
Mehir. Mehir was the father of Eshton. 12Eshton
was the father of Beth Rapha, Paseah, and Tehinnah.
Tehinnah was the father of the people from the
town of Nahash. These people were from Recah.

13The sons of Kenaz were Othniel and Seraiah.
Othniel's sons were Hathath and Meonothai.
14Meonothai was the father of Ophrah.

Seraiah was the father of Joab. Joab was the ancestor of the people from Craftsmen's Valley, named
that because the people living there were craftsmen.

15Caleb was Jephunneh's son. Caleb's sons
were Iru, Elah, and Naam. Elah's son was Kenaz.

16Jehallelel's sons were Ziph, Ziphah, Tiria, and
Asarel.

17-18Ezrah's sons were Jether, Mered, Epher,
and Jalon. Mered married Bithiah, the daughter
of the king of Egypt. The children of Mered and
Bithiah were Miriam, Shammai, and Ishbah.
Ishbah was the father of Eshtemoa. Mered also
had a wife from Judah, who gave birth to Jered,
Heber, and Jekuthiel. Jered became the father of
Gedor. Heber became the father of Soco. And
Jekuthiel became the father of Zanoah.

19Hodiah's wife was Naham's sister. The sons
of Hodiah's wife were Eshtemoa and the father of
Keilah. Keilah was from the Garmite people, and
Eshtemoa was from the Maacathite people.

20Shimon's sons were Amnon, Rinnah, Ben-
Hanan, and Tilon.

Ishi's sons were Zoheth and Ben-Zoheth.

21-22Shelah was Judah's son. Shelah's sons were
Er, Laadah, Jokim, the men from Cozeba, Joash,
and Saraph. Er was the father of Lecah. Laadah
was the father of Mareshah and the family groups
of linen workers at Beth Ashbea. Joash and
Saraph ruled in Moab and Jashubi Lehem. The
writings about this family are very old. 23These
sons of Shelah were potters. They lived in Netaim
and Gederah and worked for the king.

Simeon's Children

24Simeon's sons were Nemuel, Jamin, Jarib,
Zerah, and Shaul. 25Shaul's son was Shallum. Shallum's son was Mibsam. Mibsam's son was Mishma.

26Mishma's son was Hammuel. Hammuel's son
was Zaccur. Zaccur's son was Shimei. 27Shimei
had sixteen sons and six daughters, but his brothers did not have many children, so there were not
as many people in their family group as there
were in Judah.

28Shimei's children lived in Beersheba, Moladah,
Hazar Shual, 29Bilhah, Ezem, Tolad, 30Bethuel,
Hormah, Ziklag, 31Beth Marcaboth, Hazar Susim,
Beth Biri, and Shaaraim. They lived in these cities
until David became king. 32The five villages near
these cities were Etam, Ain, Rimmon, Token, and
Ashan. 33There were also other villages as far
away as Baalath. This is where they lived. And
they wrote the history of their family.

34-38The men in this list were leaders of their
family groups: Meshobab, Jamlech, Joshah son of
Amaziah, Joel, Jehu son of Joshibiah (Joshibiah
was the son of Seraiah, who was the son of Asiel),
Elioenai, Jaakobah, Jeshohaiah, Asaiah, Adiel,
Jesimiel, Benaiah, and Ziza. (Ziza was the son of
Shiphi, who was the son of Allon. Allon was the
son of Jedaiah, who was the son of Shimri. And
Shimri was the son of Shemaiah.)

These families grew very large. 39They went
outside the city of Gedor to the east side of the
valley to look for pasture for their flocks. 40They
found good pastures with plenty of grass, and the
land was open country and peaceful and quiet.
Ham's descendants had lived there in the past.

41These men who were listed came to Gedor
while Hezekiah was king of Judah. They fought
against the Hamites, destroying their tents, and
also against the Meunites who lived there, and
completely destroyed them. So there are no
Meunites there even today. Then these men began
to live there, because there was pasture for their
flocks. 42Ishi's sons, Pelatiah, Neariah, Rephaiah,
and Uzziel, led five hundred of the Simeonites and
attacked the people living in the mountains of
Edom. 43They killed the few Amalekites who were
still alive. From that time until now these
Simeonites have lived in Edom.

Reuben's Children

5 Reuben was Israel's first son. Reuben should
have received the special privileges of the

4:9 *Jabez.* This name in Hebrew sounds like the word for "pain."

5:1 The story of Reuben's offense against his father is found in Genesis 35:22 and 49:3–4.

oldest son, but he had sexual relations with his father's slave woman. So those special privileges were given to Joseph's sons. (Joseph was a son of Israel.) In the family history Reuben's name is not listed as the first son. 2Judah became stronger than his brothers, and a leader came from his family. But Joseph's family received the privileges that belonged to the oldest son. 3Reuben was Israel's first son. Reuben's sons were Hanoch, Pallu, Hezron, and Carmi.

4These were the children of Joel: Shemaiah was Joel's son. Gog was Shemaiah's son. Shimei was Gog's son. 5Micah was Shimei's son. Reaiah was Micah's son. Baal was Reaiah's son. 6Beerah was Baal's son. Beerah was a leader of the tribe of Reuben. Tiglath-Pileser king of Assyria captured him and took him away.

7Joel's brothers and all his family groups are listed just as they are written in their family histories: Jeiel was the first, then Zechariah, 8and Bela. (Bela was the son of Azaz. Azaz was the son of Shema, and Shema was the son of Joel.) They lived in the area of Aroer all the way to Nebo and Baal Meon. 9Bela's people lived to the east—as far as the edge of the desert, which is beside the Euphrates River—because they had too many cattle for the land of Gilead.

10When Saul was king, Bela's people fought a war against the Hagrite people and defeated them. Then Bela's people lived in the tents that had belonged to the Hagrites in all the area east of Gilead.

Gad's Children

11The people from the tribe of Gad lived near the Reubenites. The Gadites lived in the area of Bashan all the way to Salecah. 12Joel was the main leader, Shapham was second, and then Janai and Shaphat were leaders in Bashan.

13The seven relatives in their families were Michael, Meshullam, Sheba, Jorai, Jacan, Zia, and Eber. 14They were the descendants of Abihail. Abihail was Huri's son. Huri was Jaroah's son. Jaroah was Gilead's son. Gilead was Michael's son. Michael was Jeshishai's son. Jeshishai was Jahdo's son, and Jahdo was the son of Buz. 15Ahi was Abdiel's son, and Abdiel was Guni's son. Ahi was the leader of their family.

16The Gadites lived in Gilead, Bashan and the small towns around it, and on all the pasturelands in the Plain of Sharon all the way to the borders.

17All these names were written in the family history of Gad during the time Jotham was king of Judah and Jeroboam was king of Israel.

Soldiers Skilled in War

18There were forty-four thousand seven hundred sixty soldiers from the tribes of Reuben and Gad and East Manasseh who carried shields and swords and bows. They were skilled in war. 19They started a war against the Hagrites and the people of Jetur, Naphish, and Nodab. 20The men from the tribes of Manasseh, Reuben, and Gad prayed to God during the war, asking him to help them. So he helped them because they trusted him. He handed over to them the Hagrites and all those who were with them. 21They took the animals that belonged to the Hagrites: fifty thousand camels, two hundred fifty thousand sheep, and two thousand donkeys. They also captured one hundred thousand people. 22Many Hagrites were killed because God helped the people of Reuben, Gad, and Manasseh. Then they lived there until Babylon captured them and took them away.

East Manasseh

23There were many people in East Manasseh, and they lived in the area of Bashan all the way to Baal Hermon, Senir, and Mount Hermon.

24These were the family leaders: Epher, Ishi, Eliel, Azriel, Jeremiah, Hodaviah, and Jahdiel. They were all strong, brave, and famous men, and leaders in their families. 25But they sinned against the God that their ancestors had worshiped. They began worshiping the gods of the people in that land, and those were the people God was destroying. 26So the God of Israel made Pul king of Assyria want to go to war. (Pul was also called Tiglath-Pileser.) He captured the people of Reuben, Gad, and East Manasseh, and he took them away to Halah, Habor, Hara, and near the Gozan River. They have lived there from that time until this day.

Levi's Children

6 Levi's sons were Gershon, Kohath, and Merari. 2Kohath's sons were Amram, Izhar, Hebron, and Uzziel.

3Amram's children were Aaron, Moses, and Miriam.

Aaron's sons were Nadab, Abihu, Eleazar, and Ithamar. 4Eleazar was the father of Phinehas. Phinehas was the father of Abishua. 5Abishua was the father of Bukki. Bukki was the father of Uzzi. 6Uzzi was the father of Zerahiah. Zerahiah was the father of Meraioth. 7Meraioth was the father of Amariah. Amariah was the father of Ahitub. 8Ahitub was the father of Zadok. Zadok was the father of Ahimaaz. 9Ahimaaz was the father of

Azariah. Azariah was the father of Johanan.
10Johanan was the father of Azariah. (Azariah was
a priest in the Temple Solomon built in Jerusalem.)
11Azariah was the father of Amariah. Amariah
was the father of Ahitub. 12Ahitub was the father
of Zadok. Zadok was the father of Shallum.
13Shallum was the father of Hilkiah. Hilkiah was
the father of Azariah. 14Azariah was the father of
Seraiah, and Seraiah was the father of Jehozadak.

15Jehozadak was forced to leave his home
when the LORD sent Judah and Jerusalem into
captivity under the control of Nebuchadnezzar.

16Levi's sons were Gershon, Kohath, and Merari.

17The names of Gershon's sons were Libni and
Shimei.

18Kohath's sons were Amram, Izhar, Hebron,
and Uzziel.

19Merari's sons were Mahli and Mushi.

This is a list of the family groups of Levi, listed
by the name of the father of each group.

20Gershon's son was Libni. Libni's son was
Jehath. Jehath's son was Zimmah. 21Zimmah's
son was Joah. Joah's son was Iddo. Iddo's son was
Zerah. And Zerah's son was Jeatherai.

22Kohath's son was Amminadab. Amminadab's
son was Korah. Korah's son was Assir. 23Assir's son
was Elkanah. Elkanah's son was Ebiasaph. Ebiasaph's son was Assir. 24Assir's son was Tahath.
Tahath's son was Uriel. Uriel's son was Uzziah,
and Uzziah's son was Shaul.

25Elkanah's sons were Amasai and Ahimoth.
26Ahimoth's son was Elkanah. Elkanah's son was
Zo-phai. Zophai's son was Nahath. 27Nahath's son
was Eliab. Eliab's son was Jeroham. Jeroham's
son was Elkanah, and Elkanah's son was Samuel.

28Samuel's sons were Joel, the first son, and
Abijah, the second son.

29Merari's son was Mahli. Mahli's son was Libni.
Libni's son was Shimei. Shimei's son was Uzzah.
30Uzzah's son was Shimea. Shimea's son was
Haggiah, and Haggiah's son was Asaiah.

The Temple Musicians

31David chose some people to be in charge of
the music in the house of the LORD. They began
their work after the Ark of the Agreement was
put there. 32They served by making music at the
Holy Tent (also called the Meeting Tent), and
they served until Solomon built the Temple of the
LORD in Jerusalem. They followed the rules for
their work.

33These are the musicians and their sons:

From Kohath's family there was Heman the
singer. Heman was Joel's son. Joel was Samuel's
son. 34Samuel was Elkanah's son. Elkanah was
Jeroham's son. Jeroham was Eliel's son. Eliel was
Toah's son. 35Toah was Zuph's son. Zuph was
Elkanah's son. Elkanah was Mahath's son. Mahath
was Amasai's son. 36Amasai was Elkanah's son.
Elkanah was Joel's son. Joel was Azariah's son.
Azariah was Zephaniah's son. 37Zephaniah was
Tahath's son. Tahath was Assir's son. Assir was
Ebiasaph's son. Ebiasaph was Korah's son. 38Korah
was Izhar's son. Izhar was Kohath's son. Kohath
was Levi's son. Levi was Israel's son.

39There was Heman's helper Asaph, whose
group stood by Heman's right side. Asaph was
Berekiah's son. Berekiah was Shimea's son.
40Shimea was Michael's son. Michael was Baaseiah's son. Baaseiah was Malkijah's son. 41Mal-
kijah was Ethni's son. Ethni was Zerah's son.
Zerah was Adaiah's son. 42Adaiah was Ethan's
son. Ethan was Zimmah's son. Zimmah was
Shimei's son. 43Shimei was Jahath's son. Jahath
was Gershon's son, and Gershon was Levi's son.

44Merari's family were the helpers of Heman
and Asaph, and they stood by Heman's left side. In
this group was Ethan son of Kishi. Kishi was
Abdi's son. Abdi was Malluch's son. 45Malluch was
Hashabiah's son. Hashabiah was Amaziah's son.
Amaziah was Hilkiah's son. 46Hilkiah was Amzi's
son. Amzi was Bani's son. Bani was Shemer's son.
47Shemer was Mahli's son. Mahli was Mushi's
son. Mushi was Merari's son, and Merari was
Levi's son.

48The other Levites served by doing their own
special work in the Holy Tent, the house of God.
49Aaron and his descendants offered the sacrifices
on the altar of burnt offering and burned the
incense on the altar of incense. They offered the
sacrifices that removed the Israelites' sins so they
could belong to God. They did all the work in the
Most Holy Place and followed all the laws that
Moses, God's servant, had commanded.

50These were Aaron's sons: Eleazar was Aaron's
son. Phinehas was Eleazar's son. Abishua was
Phinehas' son. 51Bukki was Abishua's son. Uzzi
was Bukki's son. Zerahiah was Uzzi's son.
52Meraioth was Zerahiah's son. Amariah was Meraioth's son. Ahitub was Amariah's son. 53Zadok
was Ahitub's son, and Ahimaaz was Zadok's son.

Land for the Levites

54These are the places where Aaron's descendants lived. His descendants from the Kohath
family group received the first share of the land.

55They were given the city of Hebron in Judah
and the pastures around it, 56but the fields farther from the city and the villages near Hebron
were given to Caleb son of Jephunneh.

57So the descendants of Aaron were given Hebron, one of the cities of safety. They also received the towns and pastures of Libnah, Jattir,
Eshtemoa, 58Hilen, Debir, 59Ashan, Juttah, and
Beth Shemesh. 60They also received these towns
and pastures from the tribe of Benjamin: Gibeon,
Geba, Alemeth, and Anathoth.

The Kohath family groups received a total of thirteen towns.

61The rest of the Kohath family group was giv-
en ten towns from the family groups of West Manasseh. The towns were chosen by throwing lots.

62The Gershon family group received thirteen
towns from the tribes of Issachar, Asher, Naphtali, and the part of Manasseh living in Bashan.

63The Merari family group received twelve
towns from the tribes of Reuben, Gad, and Zebulun. Those towns were chosen by throwing lots.

64So the Israelites gave these towns and their
pastures to the Levites. 65The towns from the
tribes of Judah, Simeon, and Benjamin, which
were named, were chosen by throwing lots.

66Some of the Kohath family groups received
towns and pastures from the tribe of Ephraim.
67They received Shechem, one of the cities of
safety, with its pastures in the mountains of Ephraim. They also received the towns and pastures of
Gezer, 68Jokmeam, Beth Horon, 69Aijalon, and
Gath Rimmon.

70The rest of the people in the Kohath family
group received the towns of Aner and Bileam and
their pastures from West Manasseh.

71From East Manasseh, the Gershon family received the towns and pastures of Golan in Bashan
and Ashtaroth.

72-73From the tribe of Issachar, the Gershon family received the towns and pastures of Kedesh,
Daberath, Ramoth, and Anem.

74-75From the tribe of Asher, the Gershon family received the towns and pastures of Mashal,
Abdon, Hukok, and Rehob.

76From the tribe of Naphtali, the Gershon family received the towns and pastures of Kedesh in
Galilee, Hammon, and Kiriathaim.

77The rest of the Levites, the people from the
Merari family, received from the tribe of Zebulun
the towns and pastures of Jokneam, Kartah,
Rimmono, and Tabor.

78-79From the tribe of Reuben, the Merari family received the towns and pastures of Bezer in
the desert, Jahzah, Kedemoth, and Mephaath.
(The tribe of Reuben lived east of the Jordan
River, across from Jericho.)

80-81From the tribe of Gad, the Merari family
received the towns and pastures of Ramoth in
Gilead, Mahanaim, Heshbon, and Jazer.

Issachar's Children

7 Issachar had four sons: Tola, Puah, Jashub,
and Shimron.

2Tola's sons were Uzzi, Rephaiah, Jeriel, Jahmai,
Ibsam, and Samuel, and they were leaders of
their families. In the family history of Tola's
descendants, twenty-two thousand six hundred
men were listed as fighting men during the time
David was king.

3Uzzi's son was Izrahiah.

Izrahiah's sons were Michael, Obadiah, Joel,
and Isshiah. All five of them were leaders. 4Their
family history shows they had thirty-six thousand
men ready to serve in the army, because they had
many wives and children.

5The records of the family groups of Issachar show
there were eighty-seven thousand fighting men.

Benjamin's Children

6Benjamin had three sons: Bela, Beker, and
Jediael.

7Bela had five sons: Ezbon, Uzzi, Uzziel,
Jerimoth, and Iri, and they were leaders of their
families. Their family history shows they had
twenty-two thousand thirty-four fighting men.

8Beker's sons were Zemirah, Joash, Eliezer,
Elioenai, Omri, Jeremoth, Abijah, Anathoth, and
Alemeth. They all were Beker's sons. 9Their family history listed the family leaders and twenty
thousand two hundred fighting men.

10Jediael's son was Bilhan.

Bilhan's sons were Jeush, Benjamin, Ehud,
Kenaanah, Zethan, Tarshish, and Ahishahar. 11All
these sons of Jediael were leaders of their families. They had seventeen thousand two hundred
fighting men ready to serve in the army.

12The Shuppites and Huppites were descendants of Ir, and the Hushites were descendants of
Aher.

Naphtali's Children

13Naphtali's sons were Jahziel, Guni, Jezer, and
Shillem. They were Bilhah's grandsons.

Manasseh's Children

14These are Manasseh's descendants. Manasseh
had an Aramean slave woman, who was the
mother of Asriel and Makir. Makir was Gilead's
father. 15Makir took a wife from the Huppites and

6:57 *cities of safety.* A person who had accidentally killed someone could go to one of the six cities of safety to receive protection and a fair trial.

Shuppites. His sister was named Maacah. His second son was named Zelophehad, and he had only daughters. 16Makir's wife Maacah had a son whom she named Peresh. Peresh's brother was named Sheresh. Sheresh's sons were Ulam and Rakem.

17Ulam's son was Bedan.

These were the sons of Gilead, who was the son of Makir. Makir was Manasseh's son. 18Makir's sister Hammoleketh gave birth to Ishhod, Abiezer, and Mahlah.

19The sons of Shemida were Ahian, Shechem, Likhi, and Aniam.

Ephraim's Children

20These are the names of Ephraim's descendants. Ephraim's son was Shuthelah. Shuthelah's son was Bered. Bered's son was Tahath. Tahath's son was Eleadah. Eleadah's son was Tahath. 21Tahath's son was Zabad. Zabad's son was Shuthelah.

Ezer and Elead went to Gath to steal cows and sheep and were killed by some men who grew up in that city. 22Their father Ephraim cried for them many days, and his family came to comfort him. 23Then he had sexual relations with his wife again. She became pregnant and gave birth to a son whom Ephraim named Beriah because of the trouble that had happened to his family. 24Ephraim's daughter was Sheerah. She built Lower Beth Horon, Upper Beth Horon, and Uzzen Sheerah.

25Rephah was Ephraim's son. Resheph was Rephah's son. Telah was Resheph's son. Tahan was Telah's son. 26Ladan was Tahan's son. Ammihud was Ladan's son. Elishama was Ammihud's son. 27Nun was Elishama's son, and Joshua was the son of Nun.

28Ephraim's descendants lived in these lands and towns: Bethel and the villages near it, Naaran on the east, Gezer and the villages near it on the west, and Shechem and the villages near it. These villages went all the way to Ayyah and its villages. 29Along the borders of Manasseh's land were the towns of Beth Shan, Taanach, Megiddo, and Dor, and the villages near them. The descendants of Joseph son of Israel lived in these towns.

Asher's Children

30Asher's sons were Imnah, Ishvah, Ishvi, and Beriah. Their sister was Serah.

31Beriah's sons were Heber and Malkiel. Malkiel was Birzaith's father.

32Heber was the father of Japhlet, Shomer, Hotham, and their sister Shua.

33Japhlet's sons were Pasach, Bimhal, and Ashvath. They were Japhlet's children.

34Japhlet's brother was Shomer. Shomer's sons were Rohgah, Hubbah, and Aram.

35Shomer's brother was Hotham. Hotham's sons were Zophah, Imna, Shelesh, and Amal.

36Zophah's sons were Suah, Harnepher, Shual, Beri, Imrah, 37Bezer, Hod, Shamma, Shilshah, Ithran, and Beera.

38Jether's sons were Jephunneh, Pispah, and Ara.

39Ulla's sons were Arah, Hanniel, and Rizia.

40All these men were descendants of Asher and leaders of their families. They were powerful warriors and outstanding leaders. Their family history lists that they had twenty-six thousand soldiers ready to serve in the army.

The Family History of King Saul

8 Benjamin was the father of Bela, his first son. Ashbel was his second son, Aharah was his third, 2Nohah was his fourth, and Rapha was his fifth son.

3Bela's sons were Addar, Gera, Abihud, 4Abishua, Naaman, Ahoah, 5Gera, Shephuphan, and Huram.

6These were the descendants of Ehud and leaders of their families in Geba. They were forced to move to Manahath. 7Ehud's descendants were Naaman, Ahijah, and Gera. Gera forced them to leave. He was the father of Uzza and Ahihud.

8-11Shaharaim and his wife Hushim had sons named Abitub and Elpaal. In Moab, Shaharaim divorced his wives Hushim and Baara. Shaharaim and his wife Hodesh had these sons: Jobab, Zibia, Mesha, Malcam, Jeuz, Sakia, and Mirmah. They were leaders of their families.

12-13Elpaal's sons were Eber, Misham, Shemed, Beriah, and Shema. Shemed built the towns of Ono and Lod and the villages around them. Beriah and Shema were leaders of the families living in Aijalon, and they forced out the people who lived in Gath.

14Beriah's sons were Ahio, Shashak, Jeremoth, 15Zebadiah, Arad, Eder, 16Michael, Ishpah, and Joha.

17Elpaal's sons were Zebadiah, Meshullam, Hizki, Heber, 18Ishmerai, Izliah, and Jobab.

19Shimei's sons were Jakim, Zicri, Zabdi, 20Elienai, Zillethai, Eliel, 21Adaiah, Beraiah, and Shimrath.

22Shashak's sons were Ishpan, Eber, Eliel, 23Abdon, Zicri, Hanan, 24Hananiah, Elam, Anthothijah, 25Iphdeiah, and Penuel.

26Jeroham's sons were Shamsherai, Shehariah, Athaliah, 27Jaareshiah, Elijah, and Zicri.

7:23 *Beriah.* This name sounds like the Hebrew word for "trouble."

JUSTICE

JOB 1 OR 40:8

What defines justice? Should God's justice be feared?
If God is just, then why do the innocent suffer? How is justice achieved?

At one time or another, nearly everyone has uttered the complaint, "It's just not fair!" Although people may disagree over defining what's fair and what's not, this common complaint shows that human beings all share a sense that there is a difference between fair and unfair, right and wrong, justice and injustice. In order for this difference to be more than a matter of personal opinion, justice must be weighed according to a universal and absolute standard.

The Bible tells us that the universal and absolute standard of justice is God himself. He is the absolute standard of justice because justice comes from his nature. God defines justice for us by his actions and commands (Deuteronomy 10:17; 32:4; Psalm 19:7–9; Daniel 9:14; Romans 2:2; Revelation 15:3). Though lawyers, judges, and juries seek after justice, only God can deliver it perfectly since he is its source. Where corruption may be found in human courts, only true justice will be found with God (2 Chronicles 19:7; Psalm 9:7–8; Proverbs 29:26; Ecclesiastes 3:16; 5:8; Isaiah 59:14–15).

Because God is just, he must punish those who go against his commandments. If God did not punish sin, he would violate his own nature. When Adam and Eve disobeyed God's command, his justice required that they be punished. From that day forward, Adam and all his descendants were placed under a sentence of death (Genesis 2:17). Although all of Adam's descendants are deserving of death, Christ's sacrificial death on the cross satisfied God's justice on behalf of those believing in him and freed them from the sentence of death (Romans 5:16–17).

We often think of justice only as fairness in judgment, but the Bible closely links justice with the idea of righteousness. Although God's justice demands that he punish the guilty (Exodus 34:7), his justice and righteousness are also revealed in his fair treatment of sinners who have trusted in Christ's sacrifice for forgiveness (Romans 3:26; 1 John 1:9). One of the turning points in the history of the Christian church occurred when Martin Luther, the sixteenth-century German theologian, realized that God's justice includes the righteous activity by which he makes sinners right with himself through the gift of faith in Christ (Romans 1:17; 3:21–26). While God's justice should be feared by those who have rejected Christ and continued to live against his commands, it should be warmly accepted by those who have received salvation in Christ.

Since the Bible tells us God is just, the widespread suffering and oppression in the world has led many people to question why God permits such injustice. The Bible recounts the doubts of even godly people as they wondered about God's justice. Jeremiah had confidence in God's justice, but he did not understand the prosperity of the wicked (Jeremiah 12:1). Although Job was an honest and innocent man (Job 1:1), he faced such horrible suffering that he cursed the day of his birth (Job 3:1). As Job struggled to understand the reason for his suffering, he questioned God's justice (Job 40:8). After God reminded Job of God's power, glory, and mastery of creation, Job humbly realized that he was in no position to accuse God (Job 42:1–6). The Bible does not offer a simple explanation of injustice, but it clearly states that God is not responsible for it.

Injustice does not come from God's hand, but from our own. Since the beginning of the world, people have turned away from the knowledge God has revealed in order to hide the evil of their own deeds (Romans 1:18–20). As creatures made in the image of God (Genesis 1:26–27), human beings were created just and had the capacity to act rightly in perfect obedience to God's command (Genesis 2:16–17). When Adam and Eve rejected God's righteous command in order to gain a knowledge of good and evil apart from God, human beings lost the ability to act justly and judge rightly. Because human beings willingly chose to do evil, God allowed them to live out the consequences of their choice in violence, deceit, and injustice (Romans 1:28–32). Suffering comes because of the sin of Adam and Eve.

God will not allow injustice to continue indefinitely. His justice will be openly demonstrated on the last day when he will judge everything, even what is done in secret (Ecclesiastes 12:14; Romans 2:5–16; 1 Corinthians 4:5). On that day, he will reward and punish each person according to his or her deeds (Matthew 16:27; 2 Corinthians 5:10; Revelation 22:12). For those who have been made just through faith in Christ, that day will not bring punishment but forgiveness as Christ confesses them before the father (Matthew 10:32).

Justice: For additional scriptures on this topic go to Deuteronomy 32:4.

DEATH

JOB 1:13–22; 2:11–13

What did death mean to the people of the Old Testament? When God sent his Son Jesus to earth, did this change the meaning of death for those who put their faith in him?

In different times and places, people have viewed death differently. Some people have exalted death as a glorious opportunity for human heroism. Other people have accepted death as a natural, inevitable part of life. Many contemporary Americans seem determined to ignore death, letting relatives die out of sight in hospitals, practicing few if any rituals of mourning.

Death in the Old Testament is neither ignored, nor accepted, nor glorified. Generally, people see death as tragic and act out this viewpoint through dramatic, emotional mourning customs like the ones described in these passages from Job. Such rituals not only honor those who have died and comfort their survivors, they also acknowledge the power and terror of death itself (See 2 Samuel 1:1–2, 11–12, 17 and Ezekiel 27:27–32 for further descriptions of mourning customs practiced by people in the Bible.)

From the beginning of the Old Testament, death is portrayed as a dreaded intruder. When God created Adam and Eve, his perfect plan was for them to live forever in fellowship with him. But he warned them that if they disobeyed him, they would die. When they disobeyed, their proud rebellion disrupted their fellowship with God and let death into their world (Genesis 2:15–3:24). Since their fall, all humans have contended with the triple curse of sin, death, and separation from God.

Throughout the Old Testament, the threat of death and its horrors is used to encourage God's people to remain faithful to him. Often God is seen bringing sudden or violent death to punish sinners (Jeremiah 9:13–24). Yet there is also the recognition that all people, even those faithful to God, will die (Isaiah 40:6–8). Awareness of their own mortality is a powerful incentive for God's people to fear God, obey him, and enjoy his blessings while they still can.

In spite of the threat of death hanging over everyone's head in the Old Testament, the underlying conviction of the writers was that God would far rather show love and mercy than bring death (Psalm 103). Sometimes these writers did glimpse the possibility that their fellowship with God could continue after death (Psalm 73:23–28). In the New Testament, these Old Testament glimpses of everlasting life with God became a bright reality when God sent his Son Jesus to offer all people eternal life. Because Jesus died to pay for our sins, he freed us from the power sin and death have over us. Jesus first demonstrated his ability to defeat death by raising Jarius' daughter, the widow's son, and Lazarus from the dead.

Death and sin are still closely connected in the New Testament. Paul explains in Romans 6:23, "When people sin, they earn what sin pays—death." Elsewhere, people who reject God's gift of eternal life and thus remain in the grip of sin are pictured as already being spiritually dead (Ephesians 2:1). But those who put their faith in Jesus and the forgiveness he offers no longer need to fear death as God's punishment for sin. Jesus assures them, "Whoever hears what I say and believes in the One who sent me has eternal life. That person will not be judged guilty but has already left death and entered life" (John 5:24).

In light of his triumphant work on the cross, such death takes on a meaning very different from the Old Testament view. Death is no longer seen as final, but only temporary. Paul assured the Thessalonians that when the Lord comes again, "those who have died believing in Christ will rise first" (1 Thessalonians 4:15–16). Furthermore, for Christians death is no longer assumed to bring separation from God, but rather is seen as the gateway to closer communion with him. Thus, Paul can say in Philippians 1:21–23, "Dying would be profit for me. . . . I want to leave this life and be with Christ, which is much better."

In the New Testament, death becomes a powerful positive metaphor for how we gain salvation. As Jesus had to literally die to save us, we must figuratively "die to our old selves" (that is, surrender our sinful determination to run our own lives) before we can experience the life God wants to give us. Paul explains in Romans 6:2–4, "We died to our old sinful lives, so how can we continue living with sin? . . . When we were baptized, we were buried with Christ and shared his death. So, just as Christ was raised from the dead by the wonderful power of the Father, we also can live a new life."

Yet in spite of the positive perspectives on death which we gain from the New Testament, death remains a powerful threat for those who refuse to accept the salvation Christ offers (John 8:23–24). And even for believers, death still brings with it pain and sadness. Only when Jesus returns to establish the new heaven and new earth will sin and death be destroyed.

Death: For additional scriptures on this topic go to Deuteronomy 30:15–17.

28The family histories show that all these men
were leaders of their families and lived in
Jerusalem.
29Jeiel lived in the town of Gibeon, where he
was the leader. His wife was named Maacah.
30Jeiel's first son was Abdon. His other sons were
Zur, Kish, Baal, Ner, Nadab, 31Gedor, Ahio,
Zeker, 32and Mikloth. Mikloth was the father of
Shimeah. These sons also lived near their relatives in Jerusalem.
33Ner was the father of Kish. Kish was the father
of Saul, and Saul was the father of Jonathan,
Malki-Shua, Abinadab, and Esh-Baal.
34Jonathan's son was Merib-Baal, who was the
father of Micah.
35Micah's sons were Pithon, Melech, Tarea, and
Ahaz. 36Ahaz was the father of Jehoaddah. Jehoaddah was the father of Alemeth, Azmaveth, and
Zimri. Zimri was the father of Moza. 37Moza was the
father of Binea. Raphah was Binea's son. Eleasah
was Raphah's son, and Azel was Eleasah's son.
38Azel had six sons: Azrikam, Bokeru, Ishmael,
Sheariah, Obadiah, and Hanan. All these were
Azel's sons.
39Azel's brother was Eshek. Eshek's first son
was Ulam, his second was Jeush, and Eliphelet
was his third. 40Ulam's sons were mighty warriors and good archers. They had many sons and
grandsons—one hundred fifty of them in all.
All these men were Benjamin's descendants.

9 The names of all the people of Israel were
listed in their family histories, and those family
histories were put in the book of the kings of Israel.

The People in Jerusalem

The people of Judah were captured and forced
to go to Babylon, because they were not faithful
to God. 2The first people to come back and live in
their own lands and towns were some Israelites,
priests, Levites, and Temple servants.
3People from the tribes of Judah, Benjamin,
Ephraim, and Manasseh lived in Jerusalem. This
is a list of those people.
4There was Uthai son of Ammihud. (Ammihud
was Omri's son. Omri was Imri's son. Imri was
Bani's son. Bani was a descendant of Perez, and
Perez was Judah's son.)
5Of the Shilonite people there were Asaiah and
his sons. Asaiah was the oldest son in his family.
6Of the Zerahite people there were Jeuel and
other relatives of Zerah. There were six hundred
ninety of them in all.
7From the tribe of Benjamin there was Sallu
son of Meshullam. (Meshullam was Hodaviah's
son, and Hodaviah was Hassenuah's son.) 8There
was also Ibneiah son of Jeroham and Elah son of
Uzzi. (Uzzi was Micri's son.) And there was
Meshullam son of Shephatiah. (Shephatiah was
Reuel's son, and Reuel was Ibnijah's son.) 9The
family history of Benjamin lists nine hundred
fifty-six people living in Jerusalem, and all these
were leaders of their families.
10Of the priests there were Jedaiah, Jehoiarib,
Jakin, and 11Azariah son of Hilkiah. (Hilkiah was
Meshullam's son. Meshullam was Zadok's son.
Zadok was Meraioth's son. Meraioth was
Ahitub's son. Ahitub was the officer responsible
for the Temple of God.) 12Also there was Adaiah
son of Jeroham. (Jeroham was Pashhur's son, and
Pashhur was Malkijah's son.) And there was Maasai
son of Adiel. (Adiel was Jahzerah's son. Jahzerah
was Meshullam's son. Meshullam was Meshillemith's son, and Meshillemith was Immer's son.)
13There were one thousand seven hundred sixty
priests. They were leaders of their families, and
they were responsible for serving in the Temple
of God.
14Of the Levites there was Shemaiah son of
Hasshub. (Hasshub was Azrikam's son, and Azrikam was Hashabiah's son. Hashabiah was from
the family of Merari.) 15There were also Bak-
bakkar, Heresh, Galal, and Mattaniah son of
Mica. (Mica was Zicri's son, and Zicri was
Asaph's son.) 16There was also Obadiah son of
Shemaiah. (Shemaiah was Galal's son, and Galal
was Jeduthun's son.) And there was Berekiah son
of Asa. (Asa was the son of Elkanah, who lived in
the villages of the Netophathites.)
17Of the gatekeepers there were Shallum, Akkub, Talmon, Ahiman, and their relatives. Shallum was their leader. 18These gatekeepers from
the tribe of Levi still stand next to the King's Gate
on the east side of the city. 19Shallum was Kore's
son. Kore was Ebiasaph's son, and Ebiasaph was
Korah's son. Shallum and his relatives from the
family of Korah were gatekeepers and were
responsible for guarding the gates of the Temple.
Their ancestors had also been responsible for
guarding the entrance to the Temple of the LORD.
20In the past Phinehas, Eleazar's son, was in
charge of the gatekeepers, and the LORD was with
Phinehas. 21Zechariah son of Meshelemiah was
the gatekeeper at the entrance to the Temple.
22In all, two hundred twelve men were chosen
to guard the gates, and their names were written
in their family histories in their villages. David and
Samuel the seer chose these men because they
were dependable. 23The gatekeepers and their
descendants had to guard the gates of the Temple of

the LORD. (The Temple took the place of the Holy
Tent.) 24There were gatekeepers on all four sides
of the Temple: east, west, north, and south. 25The
gatekeepers' relatives who lived in the villages
had to come and help them at times. Each time
they came they helped the gatekeepers for seven
days. 26Because they were dependable, four gatekeepers were made the leaders of all the gatekeepers. They were Levites, and they were responsible
for the rooms and treasures in the Temple of God.
27They stayed up all night guarding the Temple of
God, and they opened it every morning.

28Some of the gatekeepers were responsible for
the utensils used in the Temple services. They
counted these utensils when people took them
out and when they brought them back. 29Other
gatekeepers were chosen to take care of the furniture and utensils in the Holy Place. They also
took care of the flour, wine, oil, incense, and spices,
30but some of the priests took care of mixing the
spices. 31There was a Levite named Mattithiah
who was dependable and had the job of baking
the bread used for the offerings. He was the first
son of Shallum, who was from the family of Korah.
32Some of the gatekeepers from the Kohath family
had the job of preparing the special bread that was
put on the table every Sabbath day.

33Some of the Levites were musicians in the
Temple. The leaders of these families stayed in
the rooms of the Temple. Since they were on
duty day and night, they did not do other work in
the Temple.

34These are the leaders of the Levite families.
Their names were listed in their family histories,
and they lived in Jerusalem.

The Family History of King Saul

35Jeiel lived in the town of Gibeon, where he was
the leader. His wife was named Maacah. 36Jeiel's
first son was Abdon. His other sons were Zur, Kish,
Baal, Ner, Nadab, 37Gedor, Ahio, Zechariah, and
Mikloth. 38Mikloth was Shimeam's father. Jeiel's
family lived near their relatives in Jerusalem.

39Ner was Kish's father. Kish was Saul's father.
Saul was the father of Jonathan, Malki-Shua,
Abinadab, and Esh-Baal.

40Jonathan's son was Merib-Baal, who was the
father of Micah.

41Micah's sons were Pithon, Melech, Tahrea,
and Ahaz. 42Ahaz was Jadah's father. Jadah was
the father of Alemeth, Azmaveth, and Zimri. Zimri
was Moza's father. 43Moza was Binea's father.
Rephaiah was Binea's son. Eleasah was Rephaiah's
son, and Azel was Eleasah's son.

44Azel had six sons: Azrikam, Bokeru, Ishmael,
Sheariah, Obadiah, and Hanan. They were Azel's
sons.

The Death of King Saul

10 The Philistines fought against Israel, and
the Israelites ran away from them. Many
Israelites were killed on Mount Gilboa. 2The Philistines fought hard against Saul and his sons, killing
his sons Jonathan, Abinadab, and Malki-Shua. 3The
fighting was heavy around Saul, and the archers
shot him with their arrows and wounded him.

4Then Saul said to the officer who carried his
armor, "Pull out your sword and stab me. If you
don't, these Philistines who are not circumcised
will come and hurt me." But Saul's officer refused,
because he was afraid. So Saul took his own sword
and threw himself on it. 5When the officer saw
that Saul was dead, he threw himself on his own
sword and died. 6So Saul and three of his sons died;
all his family died together.

7When the Israelites living in the valley saw that
their army had run away and that Saul and his sons
were dead, they left their towns and ran away.
Then the Philistines came and settled in them.

8The next day when the Philistines came to strip
the dead soldiers, they found Saul and his sons dead
on Mount Gilboa. 9The Philistines stripped Saul's
body and took his head and his armor. Then they
sent messengers through all their country to tell the
news to their idols and to their people. 10The
Philistines put Saul's armor in the temple of their
idols and hung his head in the temple of Dagon.

11All the people in Jabesh Gilead heard what the
Philistines had done to Saul. 12So the brave men of
Jabesh went and got the bodies of Saul and his
sons and brought them to Jabesh. They buried
their bones under the large tree in Jabesh. Then
the people of Jabesh gave up eating for seven days.

13Saul died because he was not faithful to the
LORD and did not obey the LORD. He even went to
a medium and asked her for advice 14instead of
asking the LORD. This is why the LORD put Saul to
death and gave the kingdom to Jesse's son David.

David Becomes King

11 Then the people of Israel came to David at
the town of Hebron and said, "Look, we are

9:44 Births: 1 Chronicles 23–24

9:44 Genealogy: See article on page 672.

10:11 *Jabesh Gilead.* The people of Jabesh Gilead had a special relationship with Saul since the time he saved their city from destruction and humiliation, during his early years as king (1 Samuel 11).

11:1 *Hebron.* David was a southerner, a Judean, so it is not surprising that the core of his support came from the powerful southern city of Hebron.

your own family. 2Even when Saul was king, you
were the one who led Israel in battle. The LORD
your God said to you, 'You will be the shepherd
for my people Israel. You will be their leader.'"
3So all the older leaders of Israel came to King
David at Hebron. He made an agreement with
them in Hebron in the presence of the LORD.
Then they poured oil on David to make him king
over Israel. The LORD had promised through
Samuel that this would happen.

David Captures Jerusalem

4David and all the Israelites went to the city of
Jerusalem. At that time Jerusalem was called Jebus,
and the people living there were named Jebusites.
5They said to David, "You can't get inside our
city." But David did take the city of Jerusalem with
its strong walls, and it became the City of David.
6David had said, "The person who leads the attack
against the Jebusites will become the commander
over all my army." Joab son of Zeruiah led the attack,
so he became the commander of the army.
7Then David made his home in the strong,
walled city, which is why it was named the City
of David. 8David rebuilt the city, beginning where
the land was filled in and going to the wall that
was around the city. Joab repaired the other parts
of the city. 9David became stronger and stronger,
and the LORD All-Powerful was with him.

David's Mighty Warriors

10This is a list of the leaders over David's warriors
who helped make David's kingdom strong. All the
people of Israel also supported David's kingdom.
These heroes and all the people of Israel made
David king, just as the LORD had promised.
11This is a list of David's warriors:
Jashobeam was from the Hacmonite people. He
was the head of the Three, David's most powerful
soldiers. He used his spear to fight three hundred
men at one time, and he killed them all.
12Next was Eleazar, one of the Three. Eleazar
was Dodai's son from the Ahohite people. 13Eleazar
was with David at Pas Dammim when the
Philistines came there to fight. There was a field of
barley at that place. The Israelites ran away from
the Philistines, 14but they stopped in the middle
of that field and fought for it and killed the
Philistines. The LORD gave them a great victory.
15Once, three of the Thirty, David's chief soldiers, came down to him at the rock by the cave
near Adullam. At the same time the Philistine
army had camped in the Valley of Rephaim.
16At that time David was in a stronghold, and
some of the Philistines were in Bethlehem.
17David had a strong desire for some water. He
said, "Oh, I wish someone would get me water
from the well near the city gate of Bethlehem!"
18So the Three broke through the Philistine army
and took water from the well near the city gate in
Bethlehem. Then they brought it to David, but he
refused to drink it. He poured it out before the
LORD, 19saying, "May God keep me from drinking
this water! It would be like drinking the blood of
the men who risked their lives to bring it to me!"
So David refused to drink it.
These were the brave things that the three
warriors did.
20Abishai brother of Joab was the captain of the
Three. Abishai fought three hundred soldiers
with his spear and killed them. He became as
famous as the Three 21and was more honored
than the Three. He became their commander
even though he was not one of them.
22Benaiah son of Jehoiada was a brave fighter
from Kabzeel who did mighty things. He killed
two of the best warriors from Moab. He also went
down into a pit and killed a lion on a snowy day.
23Benaiah killed an Egyptian who was about seven
and one-half feet tall and had a spear as large as a
weaver's rod. Benaiah had a club, but he grabbed
the spear from the Egyptian's hand and killed him
with his own spear. 24These were the things
Benaiah son of Jehoiada did. He was as famous as
the Three. 25He received more honor than the
Thirty, but he did not become a member of the
Three. David made him leader of his bodyguards.

The Thirty Chief Soldiers

26These were also mighty warriors:
Asahel brother of Joab; Elhanan son
of Dodo from Bethlehem;
27Shammoth the Harorite; Helez the
Pelonite;
28Ira son of Ikkesh from Tekoa; Abiezer
the Anathothite;
29Sibbecai the Hushathite; Ilai the
Ahohite;
30Maharai the Netophathite; Heled son
of Baanah the Netophathite;
31Ithai son of Ribai from Gibeah in
Benjamin; Benaiah the Pirathonite;
32Hurai from the ravines of Gaash;
Abiel the Arbathite;
33Azmaveth the Baharumite; Eliahba
the Shaalbonite;

11:11 *Three.* Or maybe "Thirty." These were David's most powerful soldiers. See 2 Samuel 23:8.

34the sons of Hashem the Gizonite;
Jonathan son of Shagee
the Hararite;
35Ahiam son of Sacar the Hararite;
Eliphal son of Ur;
36Hepher the Mekerathite; Ahijah
the Pelonite;
37Hezro the Carmelite; Naarai son
of Ezbai;
38Joel brother of Nathan; Mibhar son
of Hagri;
39Zelek the Ammonite; Naharai the
Berothite, the officer who carried
the armor for Joab son of Zeruiah;
40Ira the Ithrite;
Gareb the Ithrite;
41Uriah the Hittite;
Zabad son of Ahlai;
42Adina son of Shiza the Reubenite,
who was the leader of the
Reubenites, and his thirty soldiers;
43Hanan son of Maacah;
Joshaphat the Mithnite;
44Uzzia the Ashterathite;
Shama and Jeiel sons of Hotham the
Aroerite;
45Jediael son of Shimri;
Joha, Jediael's brother, the Tizite;
46Eliel the Mahavite;
Jeribai and Joshaviah, Elnaam's sons;
Ithmah the Moabite;
47Eliel, Obed, and Jaasiel the Mezobaites.

Warriors Join David

12 These were the men who came to David
at Ziklag when David was hiding from
Saul son of Kish. They were among the warriors
who helped David in battle. 2They came with
bows for weapons and could use either their
right or left hands to shoot arrows or to sling
rocks. They were Saul's relatives from the tribe
of Benjamin. 3Ahiezer was their leader, and
there was Joash. (Ahiezer and Joash were sons of
Shemaah, who was from the town of Gibeah.)
There were also Jeziel and Pelet, the sons of
Azmaveth. There were Beracah and Jehu from the
town of Anathoth. 4And there was Ishmaiah from
the town of Gibeon; he was one of the Thirty. In
fact, he was the leader of the Thirty. There were
Jeremiah, Jahaziel, Johanan, and Jozabad from
Gederah. 5There were Eluzai, Jerimoth, Bealiah,
and Shemariah. There was Shephatiah from
Haruph. 6There were Elkanah, Isshiah, Azarel,
Joezer, and Jashobeam from the family group of
Korah. 7And there were Joelah and Zebadiah, the
sons of Jeroham, from the town of Gedor.
8Part of the people of Gad joined David at his
stronghold in the desert. They were brave warriors
trained for war and skilled with shields and spears.
They were as fierce as lions and as fast as gazelles
over the hills.
9Ezer was the leader of Gad's army, and Obadiah
was second in command. Eliab was third, 10Mish-
mannah was fourth, Jeremiah was fifth, 11Attai was
sixth, Eliel was seventh, 12Johanan was eighth,
Elzabad was ninth, 13Jeremiah was tenth, and
Macbannai was eleventh in command.
14They were the commanders of the army
from Gad. The least of these leaders was in
charge of a hundred soldiers, and the greatest
was in charge of a thousand. 15They crossed the
Jordan River and chased away the people living in
the valleys, to the east and to the west. This happened in the first month of the year when the
Jordan floods the valley.
16Other people from the tribes of Benjamin and
Judah also came to David at his stronghold.
17David went out to meet them and said to them,
"If you have come peacefully to help me, I welcome you. Join me. But if you have come to turn
me over to my enemies, even though I have done
nothing wrong, the God of our fathers will see
this and punish you."
18Then the Spirit entered Amasai, the leader of
the Thirty, and he said:
"We belong to you, David.
We are with you, son of Jesse.
Success, success to you.
Success to those who help you,
because your God helps you."
So David welcomed these men and made them
leaders of his army.
19Some of the men from Manasseh also joined
David when he went with the Philistines to fight
Saul. But David and his men did not really help
the Philistines. After talking about it, the
Philistine leaders decided to send David away.
They said, "If David goes back to his master Saul,
we will be killed." 20These are the men from
Manasseh who joined David when he went to
Ziklag: Adnah, Jozabad, Jediael, Michael, Jozabad,
Elihu, and Zillethai. Each of them was a leader of
a thousand men from Manasseh. 21All these men
of Manasseh were brave soldiers, and they
helped David fight against groups of men who
went around the country robbing people. These
soldiers became commanders in David's army.
22Every day more men joined David, and his army
became large, like the army of God.

Others Join David at Hebron

23 These are the numbers of the soldiers ready
for battle who joined David at Hebron. They came
to help turn the kingdom of Saul over to David,
just as the LORD had said.
24 There were sixty-eight hundred men with
their weapons from Judah. They carried shields
and spears.
25 There were seventy-one hundred men from
Simeon. They were warriors ready for war.
26 There were forty-six hundred men from Levi.
27 Jehoiada, a leader from Aaron's family, was in
that group. There were thirty-seven hundred with
him. 28 Zadok was also in that group. He was a
strong young warrior, and with him came twenty-
two leaders from his family.
29 There were three thousand men from Benjamin, who were Saul's relatives. Most of them had
remained loyal to Saul's family until then.
30 There were twenty thousand eight hundred
men from Ephraim. They were brave warriors
and were famous men in their own family groups.
31 There were eighteen thousand men from
West Manasseh. Each one was especially chosen
to make David king.
32 There were two hundred leaders from Issachar. They knew what Israel should do, and they
knew the right time to do it. Their relatives were
with them and under their command.
33 There were fifty thousand men from Zebulun.
They were trained soldiers and knew how to use
every kind of weapon of war. They followed David
completely.
34 There were one thousand officers from
Naphtali. They had thirty-seven thousand soldiers
with them who carried shields and spears.
35 There were twenty-eight thousand six hundred men from Dan, who were ready for war.
36 There were forty thousand trained soldiers
from Asher, who were ready for war.
37 There were one hundred twenty thousand
soldiers from the east side of the Jordan River
from the people of Reuben, Gad, and East Manasseh. They had every kind of weapon.
38 All these fighting men were ready to go to war.
They came to Hebron fully agreed to make David
king of all Israel. All the other Israelites also agreed
to make David king. 39 They spent three days there
with David, eating and drinking, because their relatives had prepared food for them. 40 Also, their
neighbors came from as far away as Issachar,
Zebulun, and Naphtali, bringing food on donkeys,
camels, mules, and oxen. They brought much
flour, fig cakes, raisins, wine, oil, cows, and sheep,
because the people of Israel were very happy.

Bringing Back the Ark

13 David talked with all the officers of his
army, the commanders of a hundred men
and the commanders of a thousand men. 2 Then
David called the people of Israel together and said,
"If you think it is a good idea, and if it is what the
LORD our God wants, let's send a message. Let's
tell our fellow Israelites in all the areas of Israel
and the priests and Levites living with them in
their towns and pastures to come and join us.
3 Let's bring the Ark of our God back to us. We did
not use it to ask God for help while Saul was
king." 4 All the people agreed with David, because
they all thought it was the right thing to do.
5 So David gathered all the Israelites, from the
Shihor River in Egypt to Lebo Hamath, to bring
the Ark of God back from the town of Kiriath
Jearim. 6 David and all the Israelites with him
went to Baalah of Judah, which is Kiriath Jearim,
to get the Ark of God the LORD. God's throne is
between the golden, winged creatures on the
Ark, and the Ark is called by his name.
7 The people carried the Ark of God from
Abinadab's house on a new cart, and Uzzah and
Ahio guided it. 8 David and all the Israelites were
celebrating in the presence of God. With all their
strength they were singing and playing lyres,
harps, tambourines, cymbals, and trumpets.
9 When David's men came to the threshing floor of
Kidon, the oxen stumbled, and Uzzah reached out
his hand to steady the Ark. 10 The LORD was angry
with Uzzah and killed him, because he had touched
the Ark. So Uzzah died there in the presence of God.
11 David was angry because the LORD had punished Uzzah in his anger. Now that place is called
The Punishment of Uzzah.
12 David was afraid of God that day and asked,
"How can I bring the Ark of God home to me?" 13 So
David did not take the Ark with him to Jerusalem.
Instead, he took it to the house of Obed-Edom
who was from Gath. 14 The Ark of God stayed with
Obed-Edom's family in his house for three months,
and the LORD blessed Obed-Edom's family and
everything he owned.

David's Kingdom Grows

14 Hiram king of the city of Tyre sent messengers to David. He also sent cedar logs,

12:37 Numbers: Ezekiel 1:5

13:1 Leadership: 1 Chronicles 28:4

13:3 *Ark.* The Ark of God was the most powerful representation of God's presence with his people. Moving the Ark back to Jerusalem makes it the religious center of Israel.

bricklayers, and carpenters to build a palace for
David. 2Then David knew that the LORD really
had made him king of Israel and that he had made
his kingdom great. The LORD did this because he
loved his people Israel.
3David married more women in Jerusalem and
had more sons and daughters. 4These are the
names of David's children born in Jerusalem:
Shammua, Shobab, Nathan, Solomon, 5Ibhar,
Elishua, Elpelet, 6Nogah, Nepheg, Japhia, 7Elish-
ama, Beeliada, and Eliphelet.

David Defeats the Philistines

8When the Philistines heard that David had
been made king of all Israel, they went to look for
him. But David heard about it and went out to
fight them. 9The Philistines had attacked and
robbed the people in the Valley of Rephaim.
10David asked God, "Should I go and attack the
Philistines? Will you hand them over to me?"
The LORD answered him, "Go, I will hand them
over to you."
11So David and his men went up to the town of
Baal Perazim and defeated the Philistines. David
said, "Like a flood of water, God has broken through
my enemies by using me." So that place was named
Baal Perazim. 12The Philistines had left their idols
there, so David ordered his men to burn them.
13Soon the Philistines attacked the people in
the valley again. 14David prayed to God again, and
God answered him, saying, "Don't attack the
Philistines from the front. Instead, go around
them and attack them in front of the balsam trees.
15When you hear the sound of marching in the
tops of the balsam trees, then attack. I, God, will
have gone out before you to defeat the Philistine
army." 16David did as God commanded, and he
and his men defeated the Philistine army all the
way from Gibeon to Gezer.
17So David became famous in all the countries,
and the LORD made all nations afraid of him.

The Ark Is Brought to Jerusalem

15 David built houses for himself in Jerusalem. Then he prepared a place for the
Ark of God, and he set up a tent for it. 2David
said, "Only the Levites may carry the Ark of God.
The LORD chose them to carry the Ark of the LORD
and to serve him forever."
3David called all the people of Israel to come to
Jerusalem. He wanted to bring the Ark of the
LORD to the place he had made for it. 4David called
together the descendants of Aaron and the Levites.
5There were one hundred twenty people from
Kohath's family group, with Uriel as their leader.
6There were two hundred twenty people from
Merari's family group, with Asaiah as their leader.
7There were one hundred thirty people from
Gershon's family group, with Joel as their leader.
8There were two hundred people from Elizaphan's
family group, with Shemaiah as their leader.
9There were eighty people from Hebron's family
group, with Eliel as their leader. 10And there were
one hundred twelve people from Uzziel's family
group, with Amminadab as their leader.
11Then David asked the priests Zadok and
Abiathar and these Levites to come to him: Uriel,
Asaiah, Joel, Shemaiah, Eliel, and Amminadab.
12David said to them, "You are the leaders of the
families of Levi. You and the other Levites must
give yourselves for service to the LORD. Bring up
the Ark of the LORD, the God of Israel, to the place
I have made for it. 13The last time we did not ask
the LORD how to carry it. You Levites didn't carry
it, so the LORD our God punished us."
14Then the priests and Levites prepared themselves for service to the LORD so they could carry
the Ark of the LORD, the God of Israel. 15The
Levites used special poles to carry the Ark of God
on their shoulders, as Moses had commanded,
just as the LORD had said they should.
16David told the leaders of the Levites to
appoint their brothers as singers to play their
lyres, harps, and cymbals and to sing happy songs.

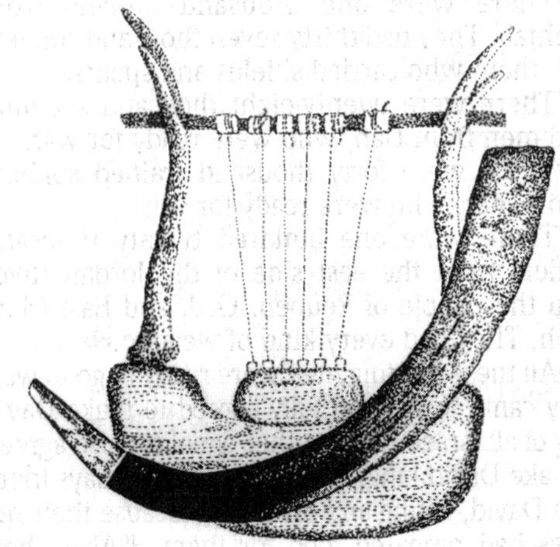

The horn and lyre were common musical instruments of Israel.

14:8 Up to this point the Philistines may have thought David to be sympathetic toward their interests in Palestine. After all, he had earlier been on their side (1 Samuel 27), but now he was growing too strong and dangerous. God used this to help David win a great victory over this old enemy of Israel.

14:11 *Baal Perazim.* This name means "the Lord breaks through."

17So the Levites appointed Heman and his rela-
tives Asaph and Ethan. Heman was Joel's son.
Asaph was Berekiah's son. And Ethan, from the
Merari family group, was Kushaiah's son. 18There
was also a second group of Levites: Zechariah,
Jaaziel, Shemiramoth, Jehiel, Unni, Eliab, Benaiah,
Maaseiah, Mattithiah, Eliphelehu, Mikneiah, Obed-
Edom, and Jeiel. They were the Levite guards.
19The singers Heman, Asaph, and Ethan played
bronze cymbals. 20Zechariah, Jaaziel, Shemiramoth,
Jehiel, Unni, Eliab, Maaseiah, and Benaiah played
the lyres. 21Mattithiah, Eliphelehu, Mikneiah,
Obed-Edom, Jeiel, and Azaziah played the harps.
22The Levite leader Kenaniah was in charge of the
singing, because he was very good at it.
23Berekiah and Elkanah were two of the guards
for the Ark of the Agreement. 24The priests
Shebaniah, Joshaphat, Nethanel, Amasai, Zechariah, Benaiah, and Eliezer had the job of blowing
trumpets in front of the Ark of God. Obed-Edom
and Jehiah were also guards for the Ark.
25David, the leaders of Israel, and the commanders of a thousand soldiers went to get the Ark of
the Agreement with the LORD. They all went to
bring the Ark from Obed-Edom's house with great
joy. 26Because God helped the Levites who carried
the Ark of the Agreement with the LORD, they
sacrificed seven bulls and seven male sheep. 27All
the Levites who carried the Ark, and Kenaniah, the
man in charge of the singing, and all the singers
wore robes of fine linen. David also wore a robe of
fine linen and a holy vest of fine linen. 28So all the
people of Israel brought up the Ark of the Agreement with the LORD. They shouted, blew horns and
trumpets, and played cymbals, lyres, and harps.
29As the Ark of the Agreement with the LORD
entered Jerusalem, Saul's daughter Michal
watched from a window. When she saw King
David dancing and celebrating, she hated him.

16 They brought the Ark of God and put it
inside the tent that David had set up for it.
Then they offered burnt offerings and fellowship
offerings to God. 2When David had finished giving the burnt offerings and fellowship offerings,
he blessed the people in the name of the LORD.
3He gave a loaf of bread, some dates, and raisins
to every Israelite man and woman.
4Then David appointed some of the Levites to
serve before the Ark of the LORD. They had the job of
leading the worship and giving thanks and praising
the LORD, the God of Israel. 5Asaph, who played the
cymbals, was the leader. Zechariah was second to
him. The other Levites were Jaaziel, Shemiramoth,
Jehiel, Mattithiah, Eliab, Benaiah, Obed-Edom, and
Jeiel. They played the lyres and harps. 6Benaiah and
Jahaziel were priests who blew the trumpets regularly before the Ark of the Agreement with God.
7That day David first gave Asaph and his relatives
the job of singing praises to the LORD.

David's Song of Thanks

8Give thanks to the LORD and pray to him.
Tell the nations what he has done.
9Sing to him; sing praises to him.
Tell about all his miracles.
10Be glad that you are his;
let those who seek the LORD be happy.
11Depend on the LORD and his strength;
always go to him for help.
12Remember the miracles he has done,
his wonders, and his decisions.
13You are the descendants of his servant, Israel;
you are the children of Jacob, his chosen
people.

14He is the LORD our God.
His laws are for all the world.
15He will keep his agreement forever;
he will keep his promises always.
16He will keep the agreement he made with
Abraham
and the promise he made to Isaac.
17He made it a law for the people of Jacob;
he made it an agreement with Israel to
last forever.
18He said, "I will give the land of Canaan to you,
to belong to you."

19Then God's people were few in number,
and they were strangers in the land.
20They went from one nation to another,
from one kingdom to another.
21But he did not let anyone hurt them;
he warned kings not to harm them.
22He said, "Don't touch my chosen people,
and don't harm my prophets."

23Sing to the LORD, all the earth.
Every day tell how he saves us.
24Tell the nations about his glory;
tell all peoples the miracles he does.
25The LORD is great; he should be praised.
He should be respected more than all the gods.
26All the gods of the nations are only idols,
but the LORD made the skies.
27He has glory and majesty;
he has power and joy in his Temple.

28Praise the LORD, all nations on earth.
Praise the LORD's glory and power;

29 praise the glory of the LORD's name.
Bring an offering and come to him.
Worship the LORD because he is holy.
30 Tremble before him, everyone on earth.
The earth is set, and it cannot be moved.
31 Let the skies rejoice and the earth be glad.
Let people everywhere say, "The LORD is king!"
32 Let the sea and everything in it shout;
let the fields and everything in them rejoice.
33 Then the trees of the forest will sing
for joy before the LORD.
They will sing because he is coming
to judge the world.

34 Thank the LORD because he is good.
His love continues forever.
35 Say to him, "Save us, God our Savior,
and bring us back and save us from
other nations.
Then we will thank you
and will gladly praise you."
36 Praise the LORD, the God of Israel.
He always was and always will be.

All the people said "Amen" and praised the LORD.
37 Then David left Asaph and the other Levites
there in front of the Ark of the Agreement with
the LORD. They were to serve there every day.
38 David also left Obed-Edom and sixty-eight other
Levites to serve with them. Hosah and Obed-
Edom son of Jeduthun were guards.
39 David left Zadok the priest and the other
priests who served with him in front of the Tent of
the LORD at the place of worship in Gibeon. 40 Every
morning and evening they offered burnt offerings
on the altar of burnt offerings, following the rules
written in the Teachings of the LORD, which he had
given Israel. 41 With them were Heman and Jeduthun and other Levites. They were chosen by
name to sing praises to the LORD because his love
continues forever. 42 Heman and Jeduthun also
had the job of playing the trumpets and cymbals
and other musical instruments when songs were
sung to God. Jeduthun's sons guarded the gates.
43 Then all the people left. Each person went
home, and David also went home to bless the
people in his home.

God's Promise to David

17 When David moved into his palace, he said
to Nathan the prophet, "Look, I am living
in a palace made of cedar, but the Ark of the
Agreement with the LORD sits in a tent."
2 Nathan said to David, "Do what you want to
do, because God is with you."
3 But that night God spoke his word to Nathan,
saying, 4 "Go and tell David my servant, 'This is
what the LORD says: You are not the person to
build a house for me to live in. 5 From the time I
brought Israel out of Egypt until now I have not
lived in a house. I have moved from one tent site
to another and from one place to another. 6 As I
have moved with the Israelites to different places,
I have never said to the leaders, whom I commanded to take care of my people, "Why haven't
you built me a house of cedar?"'
7 "Now, tell my servant David: 'This is what the
LORD All-Powerful says: I took you from the pasture
and from tending the sheep and made you king of
my people Israel. 8 I have been with you everywhere you have gone. I have defeated your enemies for you. I will make you as famous as any of the
great people on the earth. 9 I will choose a place for
my people Israel, and I will plant them so they can
live in their own homes. They will not be bothered
anymore. Wicked people will no longer hurt them
as they have in the past 10 when I chose judges for
my people Israel. I will defeat all your enemies.
"'I tell you that the LORD will make your
descendants kings of Israel after you. 11 When you
die and join your ancestors, I will make one of your
sons the new king, and I will set up his kingdom.
12 He will build a house for me, and I will let his
kingdom rule always. 13 I will be his father, and he
will be my son. I took away my love from Saul, who
ruled before you, but I will never stop loving your
son. 14 I will put him in charge of my house and
kingdom forever. His family will rule forever.'"
15 Nathan told David everything God had said in
this vision.

David Prays to God

16 Then King David went in and sat in front of the
LORD. David said, "LORD God, who am I? What is my
family? Why did you bring me to this point? 17 But
that was not enough for you, God. You have also
made promises about my future family. LORD God,
you have treated me like a very important person.
18 "What more can I say to you for honoring me,
your servant? You know me so well. 19 LORD, you
have done this wonderful thing for my sake and
because you wanted to. You have made known all
these great things.
20 "There is no one like you, LORD. There is no
God except you. We have heard all this ourselves!

17:10–15 Here the Lord enters into an agreement (see "agreement" in the Dictionary/Concordance) with David, building on those with Noah, Abraham, and Moses. He promises David that his offspring will rule Israel. This agreement is ultimately fulfilled when Jesus, a descendent of David (Romans 1:3), is proclaimed King forever.

17:14 Kingdom of God: Matthew 13:24

INTEGRITY

JOB 2:1–10

What do we mean by integrity? What are the various ingredients that make up the person of integrity?

Integrity is an all-encompassing concept most often having to do with the matter of personal character or relationships. It is by no accident that the word *integral* is a derivative of the word integrity, because at its very core the word has to do with the condition of something or someone being undivided, and thereby suggests a simplicity and completeness. The concern for personal integration and completeness is as much a concern in our day as it was for the authors of the various books of the Bible.

Throughout both the Old and the New Testaments, the question of integrity is most often related to the character of persons in relation to God and to their community. Perhaps this concept is most poignantly presented in the story of Job. Despite the challenges and unimaginable trials he faces which include the murder of his family (Job 1:13–15, 18–20), the killing of his herds and servants, and thereby loss of all means of support for he and his family (Job 1:16–17), and being afflicted with painful sores from the top of his head to the soles of his feet (Job 2:17), he is able to remain an "honest and innocent man; he honored God and stayed away from evil" (Job 1:1). Despite his wife's inability to not appreciate his commitment to innocence (Job 2:9), Job "did not sin in what he said," thereby retaining his faith and integrity (Job 2:10).

Integrity is made up of several ingredients, the first of which is honesty. One cannot have any integrity before God or with other persons if there is a lack of honesty. "Good people will be guided by honesty; dishonesty will destroy those who are not trustworthy" (Proverbs 11:3). Truthfulness is at the core of integrity. In the New Testament there is a fundamental distaste about appearing as honest when, in fact, one is not truthful. In confronting the Pharisees, Jesus talks about how when people see them they think they look good, "but on the inside you are full of hypocrisy and evil" (Matthew 23:28). Even some of the Jewish leaders who were against Jesus' ministry nevertheless acknowledged his integrity. "You are an honest man. You are not afraid of what other people think about you, because you pay no attention to who they are" (Mark 12:13–14). Jesus condemned the false and ambiguous piety of the Pharisees and in the same way requires from each of us a whole and integrated commitment to God. Therefore honesty, as an ingredient of integrity, means the relationship we say we have with God is sincere and straightforward, suggesting the absence of dishonesty or duplicity. Only in this way is God truly honored, and are we truly leading lives marked by integrity. It means the good people we represent ourselves to be are the good people we truly are. Such simple honesty brings freedom that can be achieved no other way (see Proverbs 11:6).

That brings us to another suggested ingredient of integrity, which is wholeness. This implies also a certain commitment to innocence. We have a commitment as integrated people to be "careful to live an innocent life" and to not look at anything wicked and therefore not relevant to a pure and holy relationship with God (Psalm 101:2–3). The gift back to us with this commitment to integrity is a confidence and hope in our knowledge that "honest people will never be destroyed" (Job 4:6–7). In our commitment to innocence and integrity, we have the assurance of God being with us forever (see Psalm 41:12). Simple integrity makes our choices and therefore our lives simpler (see Proverbs 11:5).

To be this whole and undivided person committed to sincerely serving Jesus Christ, we must stay away from evil and pursue the things of God with all our heart. No one can serve two masters (Matthew 6:24), and the thing we should want most is God's kingdom and doing what God wants (see Matthew 6:33). Throughout the Bible there is a concern for uncorrupted character. In the Psalms and the Proverbs these themes especially emerge. In one of the epistles of Peter we are told that we must "rid [ourselves] of all evil, all lying, hypocrisy, jealousy, and evil speech. As newborn babies want milk, you should want the pure and simple teaching" (1 Peter 2:2). The Lord said to Solomon that "you must serve me as your father David did; he was fair and sincere" (1 Kings 9:4–5). This mark of integrity is undergirded by obedience to all that God has commanded, keeping all his rules and laws. We are reminded in the Gospel of Matthew that we must be as "innocent as doves" and therefore immune to falsehood (Matthew 10:16).

People of integrity can be trusted to be faithful—faithful to their word, to God, and to their community. It means keeping our promises to God and to others. It means doing what we do and meaning it, representing ourselves as godly and actually being holy! "Say only yes if you mean yes, and no if you mean no" (Matthew 5:37). Integrity is ultimately about the quality of our relationship to God and to each other.

Integrity: For additional scriptures on this topic go to 1 Kings 9:4–5.

ROAD/WAY

PSALM 1

How does the Bible use the image of a road? How is life like a journey?

Life is a journey. We travel a road from birth to death. The Bible describes life as a journey down a road where we encounter many obstacles and points of decision. Which road should we take, and where are we going anyway?

In one sense, the human journey began in Genesis 3 when Adam and Eve were thrown out of the Garden of Eden because of their sin. They and their descendants, including us today, became wanderers (Genesis 4:12), seeking a way back to the rest, safety, and joy of the Garden.

The story of the Bible may be described as the journey of humanity along the road of life as it seeks the way back to the Garden. That road is a long and painful one. Because of human sin, God set up angelic guards to prevent anyone "from getting to the tree of life" (Genesis 3:24).

God in his grace gives tokens of the final destination to his people. For instance, he promised Abraham that his offspring would find rest in the Promised Land. Abraham himself had to wander in the land as a stranger, waiting for God's timing to give it to his children. When the time came for the Israelites to enter the Promised Land, they were in Egypt and had to travel to Palestine in order to claim the land. This period of time is commonly known as the wilderness wanderings and is described in the Bible as a road along which God led his people to their new home. According to Exodus 13:21, "The LORD showed them the way; during the day he went ahead of them in a pillar of cloud, and during the night he was in a pillar of fire to give them light." Further, Deuteronomy 1:31 remembers that "in the desert you saw how the LORD your God carried you, like one carries a child. And he has brought you safely all the way to this place."

There were threats and obstacles along the way. The first major obstacle was the Red Sea which blocked their road as the Egyptian army came to kill them all. God however provided a way of escape.

Some of the obstacles were a result of the disobedience of the Israelites themselves. They chose to go down the wrong way. For instance, while Moses was on the mount getting the Ten Commandments, the people began to worship a golden calf (Exodus 32). This act almost led to God's abandoning his people in the wilderness (Exodus 33:3), but Moses prayed and God continued with them along their journey.

The wilderness wanderings ended successfully when the Israelites entered the Promised Land and God gave them victory under the leadership of Joshua, but they nonetheless remained pilgrims on the road of life. The Promised Land was just a taste of the final rest, which no one enters before the end of time.

The Bible describes our life as a decision concerning which of two roads we will travel. On the one hand, there is the road that God has placed before us. It is called the way of the Lord, the way of righteousness, or the way of obedience (Genesis 18:19; 2 Samuel 22:31; Psalms 1:1; 18:30; 37:5).

On the other hand, there is the way of folly and disobedience. The first road leads to God and life and ultimate joy. The second road leads to death. Many choose the second road because it seems so right, so easy, so pleasurable. As the New Testament states it, "Enter through the narrow gate. The gate is wide and the road is wide that leads to hell, and many people enter through that gate. But the gate is small and the road is narrow that leads to true life. Only a few people find that road" (Matthew 7:13–14).

The Book of Proverbs uses the image of the road or way more than any other book of the Bible. The reader of the book is assumed to be a young man who is walking down the path of life. As he does so, he will be ambushed and enticed to turn off that road and go down the road of quick, sensual pleasure. His teachers warn him of these dangers. They tell him to stick to the proper path, the path of righteousness and wisdom (4:11; 10:29; 12:28), and they warn him to avoid the way of folly (4:14, 19; 13:15).

The road image comes to a climax in Proverbs 9. The young man encounters two female figures on the side of the road. They call to him and invite him into their homes at the top of the hill. The one woman is Wisdom. She wants him to join her and become wise in order to live. The other woman is Folly. She sounds just as pleasant, but Proverbs 9:18 warns the reader that "her guests end up deep in the grave." In the New Testament we learn that Jesus Christ is Wisdom (Matthew 11:18–19; Colossians 2:3). He invites us to join him on the road of life. He is not only the guide on the road; he is the road itself. "I am the way, and the truth, and the life. The only way to the Father is through me" (John 14:6).

Road/Way: For additional scriptures on this topic go to Genesis 4:12.

21There is no nation like your people Israel. They are the only people on earth that God chose to be his own. You made your name well known by the great and wonderful things you did for them. You went ahead of them and forced other nations out of the land. You freed your people from slavery in Egypt. 22You made the people of Israel your very own people forever, and, LORD, you are their God.

23"LORD, keep the promise forever that you made about my family and me, your servant. Do what you have said. 24Then you will be honored always, and people will say, 'The LORD All-Powerful, the God over Israel, is Israel's God!' And the family of your servant David will continue before you.

25"My God, you have told me that you would make my family great. So I, your servant, am brave enough to pray to you. 26LORD, you are God, and you have promised these good things to me, your servant. 27You have chosen to bless my family. Let it continue before you always. LORD, you have blessed my family, so it will always be blessed."

David Defeats Nations

18 Later, David defeated the Philistines, conquered them, and took the city of Gath and the small towns around it.

2He also defeated the people of Moab. So the people of Moab became servants of David and gave him the payment he demanded.

3David also defeated Hadadezer king of Zobah all the way to the town of Hamath as he tried to spread his kingdom to the Euphrates River. 4David captured one thousand of his chariots, seven thousand men who rode in chariots, and twenty thousand foot soldiers. He crippled all but a hundred of the chariot horses.

5Arameans from Damascus came to help Hadadezer king of Zobah, but David killed twenty-two thousand of them. 6Then David put groups of soldiers in Damascus in Aram. The Arameans became David's servants and gave him the payments he demanded. So the LORD gave David victory everywhere he went.

7David took the shields of gold that had belonged to Hadadezer's officers and brought them to Jerusalem. 8David also took many things made of bronze from Tebah and Cun, which had been cities under Hadadezer's control. Later, Solomon used this bronze to make things for the Temple: the large bronze bowl, which was called the Sea, the pillars, and other bronze utensils.

9Toi king of Hamath heard that David had defeated all the army of Hadadezer king of Zobah. 10So Toi sent his son Hadoram to greet and congratulate King David for defeating Hadadezer. (Hadadezer had been at war with Toi.) Hadoram brought items made of gold, silver, and bronze. 11King David gave them to the LORD, along with the silver and gold he had taken from these nations: Edom, Moab, the Ammonites, the Philistines, and Amalek.

12Abishai son of Zeruiah killed eighteen thousand Edomites in the Valley of Salt. 13David put groups of soldiers in Edom, and all the Edomites became his servants. The LORD gave David victory everywhere he went.

David's Important Officers

14David was king over all of Israel, and he did what was fair and right for all his people. 15Joab son of Zeruiah was commander over the army. Jehoshaphat son of Ahilud was the recorder. 16Zadok son of Ahitub and Abiathar son of Ahimelech were priests. Shavsha was the royal secretary. 17Benaiah son of Jehoiada was over the Kerethites and Pelethites. And David's sons were important officers who served at his side.

War with the Ammonites and Arameans

19 When Nahash king of the Ammonites died, his son became king after him. 2David said, "Nahash was loyal to me, so I will be loyal to his son Hanun." So David sent messengers to comfort Hanun about his father's death.

David's officers went to the land of the Ammonites to comfort Hanun. 3But the Ammonite leaders said to Hanun, "Do you think David wants to honor your father by sending men to comfort you? No! David sent them to study the land and capture it and spy it out." 4So Hanun arrested David's officers. To shame them he shaved their beards and cut off their clothes at the hips. Then he sent them away.

5When the people told David what had happened to his officers, he sent messengers to meet them, because they were very ashamed. King David said, "Stay in Jericho until your beards have grown back. Then come home."

6The Ammonites knew that they had insulted David. So Hanun and the Ammonites sent about seventy-four thousand pounds of silver to hire chariots and chariot drivers from Northwest Mesopotamia, Aram Maacah, and Zobah. 7The

---

18:17 *Kerethites and Pelethites.* These were probably special units of the army that were responsible for the king's safety, a kind of palace guard.

19:4 *shaved their beards.* According to the art and literature of the ancient Near East, a beard was worn by all adult males and was likely a sign of maturity. Even if these men shaved the remaining half of their beards off, they would still feel public shame.

Ammonites hired thirty-two thousand chariots
and the king of Maacah and his army. So they
came and set up camp near the town of Medeba.
The Ammonites themselves came out of their
towns and got ready for battle.
8When David heard about this, he sent Joab with
the whole army. 9The Ammonites came out and prepared for battle at the city gate. The kings who had
come to help were out in the field by themselves.
10Joab saw that there were enemies both in front
of him and behind him. So he chose some of the
best soldiers of Israel and sent them out to fight the
Arameans. 11Joab put the rest of the army under
the command of Abishai, his brother. Then they
went out to fight the Ammonites. 12Joab said to
Abishai, "If the Arameans are too strong for me,
you must help me. Or, if the Ammonites are too
strong for you, I will help you. 13Be strong. We
must fight bravely for our people and the cities of
our God. The LORD will do what he thinks is right."
14Then Joab and the army with him went to
attack the Arameans, and the Arameans ran
away. 15When the Ammonites saw that the Arameans were running away, they also ran away
from Joab's brother Abishai and went back to
their city. So Joab went back to Jerusalem.
16When the Arameans saw that Israel had
defeated them, they sent messengers to bring
other Arameans from east of the Euphrates River.
Their leader was Shophach, the commander of
Hadadezer's army.
17When David heard about this, he gathered all
the Israelites, and they crossed over the Jordan
River. He prepared them for battle, facing the
Arameans. The Arameans fought with him, 18but
they ran away from the Israelites. David killed
seven thousand Aramean chariot drivers and forty
thousand Aramean foot soldiers. He also killed
Shophach, the commander of the Aramean army.
19When those who served Hadadezer saw that
the Israelites had defeated them, they made
peace with David and served him. So the Arameans refused to help the Ammonites again.

Joab Destroys the Ammonites

20 In the spring, the time of year when kings
normally went out to battle, Joab led out
the army of Israel. But David stayed in Jerusalem.
The army of Israel destroyed the land of Ammon
and went to the city of Rabbah and attacked it.
2David took the crown off the head of their king,
and had it placed on his own head. That gold crown
weighed about seventy-five pounds, and it had
valuable gems in it. And David took many valuable things from the city. 3He also brought out the
people of the city and forced them to work with
saws, iron picks, and axes. David did this to all
the Ammonite cities. Then David and all his army
returned to Jerusalem.

Philistine Giants Are Killed

4Later, at Gezer, war broke out with the Philistines. Sibbecai the Hushathite killed Sippai, who
was one of the descendants of the Rephaites. So
those Philistines were defeated.
5Later, there was another battle with the Philistines. Elhanan son of Jair killed Lahmi, the brother
of Goliath, who was from the town of Gath. His
spear was as large as a weaver's rod.
6At Gath another battle took place. A huge man
was there; he had six fingers on each hand and six
toes on each foot—twenty-four fingers and toes in
all. This man also was one of the sons of Rapha.
7When he spoke against Israel, Jonathan son of
Shimea, David's brother, killed him.
8These descendants of Rapha from Gath were
killed by David and his men.

David Counts the Israelites

21 Satan was against Israel, and he caused
David to count the people of Israel. 2So
David said to Joab and the commanders of the
troops, "Go and count all the Israelites from Beersheba to Dan. Then tell me so I will know how
many there are."
3But Joab said, "May the LORD give the nation a
hundred times more people. My master the king,
all the Israelites are your servants. Why do you
want to do this, my master? You will make Israel
guilty of sin."
4But the king commanded Joab, so Joab left and
went through all Israel. Then he returned to Jerusalem. 5Joab gave the list of the people to David.
There were one million one hundred thousand
men in all of Israel who could use the sword, and
there were four hundred seventy thousand men
in Judah who could use the sword. 6But Joab did
not count the tribes of Levi and Benjamin,
because he didn't like King David's order. 7David
had done something God had said was wrong, so
God punished Israel.

20:2 *their king.* Or, "Milcom," the god of the Ammonite people.

21:1 Satan is rarely mentioned in the Old Testament, and this is one of his earliest appearances. It is interesting to compare this passage with 2 Samuel 24:1, which is another telling of the same story, because in that verse it is the Lord who is said to be "against Israel." What can we learn by comparing these two passages? The key thing we learn is that Satan can only act with the permission of God. He cannot act independently, as we also see in the first part of the Book of Job. This truth gives comfort to Christians because we know that Satan cannot tear us away from the love of God against God's will.

21:2 *Beersheba to Dan.* Beersheba was the city farthest south in Israel. Dan was the city farthest north. So this means all the people of Israel.

8Then David said to God, "I have sinned greatly
by what I have done! Now, I beg you to forgive me,
your servant, because I have been very foolish."
9The LORD said to Gad, who was David's seer,
10"Go and tell David, 'This is what the LORD says:
I offer you three choices. Choose one of them and I
will do it.'"
11So Gad went to David and said to him, "This
is what the LORD says: 'Choose for yourself
12three years of hunger. Or choose three months
of running from your enemies as they chase you
with their swords. Or choose three days of punishment from the LORD, in which a terrible disease will spread through the country. The angel
of the LORD will go through Israel destroying the
people.' Now, David, decide which of these
things I should tell the LORD who sent me."
13David said to Gad, "I am in great trouble. Let
the LORD punish me, because the LORD is very merciful. Don't let my punishment come from human
beings."
14So the LORD sent a terrible disease on Israel,
and seventy thousand people died. 15God sent an
angel to destroy Jerusalem, but when the angel
started to destroy it, the LORD saw it and felt very
sorry about the terrible things that had happened.
So he said to the angel who was destroying, "That
is enough! Put down your arm!" The angel of the
LORD was then standing at the threshing floor of
Araunah the Jebusite.
16David looked up and saw the angel of the LORD
in the sky, holding his sword drawn and pointed at
Jerusalem. Then David and the older leaders bowed
facedown on the ground. They were wearing
rough cloth to show their grief. 17David said to
God, "I am the one who sinned and did wrong. I
gave the order for the people to be counted. These
people only followed me like sheep. They did
nothing wrong. LORD my God, please punish me
and my family, but stop the terrible disease that is
killing your people."
18Then the angel of the LORD told Gad to tell
David that he should build an altar to the LORD on
the threshing floor of Araunah the Jebusite. 19So
David did what Gad told him to do, in the name
of the LORD.
20Araunah was separating the wheat from the
straw. When he turned around, he saw the angel.
Araunah's four sons who were with him hid.
21David came to Araunah, and when Araunah
saw him, he left the threshing floor and bowed
facedown on the ground before David.
22David said to him, "Sell me your threshing floor
so I can build an altar to the LORD here. Then the terrible disease will stop. Sell it to me for the full price."
23Araunah said to David, "Take this threshing
floor. My master the king, do anything you want.
Look, I will also give you oxen for the whole
burnt offerings, the threshing boards for the
wood, and wheat for the grain offering. I give
everything to you."
24But King David answered Araunah, "No, I will
pay the full price for the land. I won't take anything that is yours and give it to the LORD. I won't
offer a burnt offering that costs me nothing."
25So David paid Araunah about fifteen pounds
of gold for the place. 26David built an altar to the
LORD there and offered whole burnt offerings and
fellowship offerings. David prayed to the LORD,
and he answered him by sending down fire from
heaven on the altar of burnt offering. 27Then the
LORD commanded the angel to put his sword back
into its holder.
28When David saw that the Lord had answered
him on the threshing floor of Araunah, he offered
sacrifices there. 29The Holy Tent that Moses
made while the Israelites were in the desert and
the altar of burnt offerings were in Gibeon at the
place of worship. 30But David could not go to the
Holy Tent to speak with God, because he was
afraid of the angel of the Lord and his sword.
22 David said, "The Temple of the LORD God
and the altar for Israel's burnt offerings
will be built here."

David Makes Plans for the Temple

2So David ordered all foreigners living in Israel
to gather together. From that group David chose
stonecutters to cut stones to be used in building
the Temple of God. 3David supplied a large amount
of iron to be used for making nails and hinges for
the gate doors. He also supplied more bronze than
could be weighed, 4and he supplied more cedar
logs than could be counted. Much of the cedar
had been brought to David by the people from
Sidon and Tyre.
5David said, "We should build a great Temple for
the LORD, which will be famous everywhere for its
greatness and beauty. But my son Solomon is young.
He hasn't yet learned what he needs to know, so
I will prepare for the building of it." So David got
many of the materials ready before he died.
6Then David called for his son Solomon and told
him to build the Temple for the LORD, the God of

22:1 This verse explains why the author decided to include this story of David's sin. Usually the Book of Chronicles, with its interest in holding up role models for the late Israelite community, avoided stories that cast a negative light on David. But the story of the census is evidently included here because it explains how the land was purchased for the Temple.

Israel. 7David said to him, "My son, I wanted to build a temple for worshiping the LORD my God. 8But the LORD spoke his word to me, 'David, you have killed many people. You have fought many wars. You cannot build a temple for worship to me, because you have killed many people.⚭ 9But, you will have a son, a man of peace and rest. I will give him rest from all his enemies around him. His name will be Solomon, and I will give Israel peace and quiet while he is king. 10Solomon will build a temple for worship to me. He will be my son, and I will be his father. I will make his kingdom strong; someone from his family will rule Israel forever.'"

11David said, "Now, my son, may the LORD be with you. May you build a temple for the LORD your God, as he said you would. 12He will make you the king of Israel. May the LORD give you wisdom and understanding so you will be able to obey the teachings of the LORD your God. 13Be careful to obey the rules and laws the LORD gave Moses for Israel. If you obey them, you will have success. Be strong and brave. Don't be afraid or discouraged.⚭

14"Solomon, I have worked hard getting many of the materials for building the Temple of the LORD. I have supplied about seven and one-half million pounds of gold, about seventy-five million pounds of silver, so much bronze and iron it cannot be weighed, and wood and stone. You may add to them. 15You have many workmen—stonecutters, bricklayers, carpenters, and people skilled in every kind of work. 16They are skilled in working with gold, silver, bronze, and iron. You have more craftsmen than can be counted. Now begin the work, and may the LORD be with you."

17Then David ordered all the leaders of Israel to help his son Solomon. 18David said to them, "The LORD your God is with you. He has given you rest from our enemies. He has handed over to me the people living around us. The LORD and his people are in control of this land. 19Now give yourselves completely to obeying the LORD your God. Build the holy place of the LORD God; build the Temple for worship to the LORD. Then bring the Ark of the Agreement with the LORD and the holy items that belong to God into the Temple."

The Levites

23 After David had lived long and was old, he made his son Solomon the new king of Israel. 2David gathered all the leaders of Israel, along with the priests and Levites. 3He counted the Levites who were thirty years old and older. In all, there were thirty-eight thousand Levites. 4David said, "Of these, twenty-four thousand Levites will direct the work of the Temple of the LORD, six thousand Levites will be officers and judges, 5four thousand Levites will be gatekeepers, and four thousand Levites will praise the LORD with musical instruments I made for giving praise."

6David separated the Levites into three groups that were led by Levi's three sons: Gershon, Kohath, and Merari.

The People of Gershon

7From the people of Gershon, there were Ladan and Shimei.

8Ladan had three sons. His first son was Jehiel, and his other sons were Zetham and Joel.

9Shimei's sons were Shelomoth, Haziel, and Haran. These three sons were leaders of Ladan's families. 10Shimei had four sons: Jahath, Ziza, Jeush, and Beriah. 11Jahath was the first son, and Ziza was the second son. But Jeush and Beriah did not have many children, so they were counted as if they were one family.

The People of Kohath

12Kohath had four sons: Amram, Izhar, Hebron, and Uzziel.

13Amram's sons were Aaron and Moses. Aaron and his descendants were chosen to be special forever. They were chosen to prepare the holy things for the LORD's service, to offer sacrifices before the LORD, and to serve him as priests. They were to give blessings in his name forever.

14Moses was the man of God, and his sons were counted as part of the tribe of Levi. 15Moses' sons were Gershom and Eliezer. 16Gershom's first son was Shubael. 17Eliezer's first son was Rehabiah. Eliezer had no other sons, but Rehabiah had many sons.

18Izhar's first son was Shelomith.

19Hebron's first son was Jeriah, his second was Amariah, his third was Jahaziel, and his fourth was Jekameam.

20Uzziel's first son was Micah and his second was Isshiah.

The People of Merari

21Merari's sons were Mahli and Mushi. Mahli's sons were Eleazar and Kish. 22Eleazar died without sons; he had only daughters. Eleazar's daughters married their cousins, the sons of Kish. 23Mushi's three sons were Mahli, Eder, and Jerimoth.

⚭**22:8 Ambition:** Psalm 69:9

22:9 *Solomon.* This name sounds like the Hebrew word for "peace."

⚭**22:13 Success:** Proverbs 16:3

The Levites' Work

24These were Levi's descendants listed by their families. They were the leaders of families. Each person who was twenty years old or older was listed. They served in the LORD's Temple.

25David had said, "The LORD, the God of Israel, has given rest to his people. He has come to live in Jerusalem forever. 26So the Levites don't need to carry the Holy Tent or any of the things used in its services anymore." 27David's last instructions were to count the Levites who were twenty years old and older.

28The Levites had the job of helping Aaron's descendants in the service of the Temple of the LORD. They cared for the Temple courtyard and side rooms, and they made all the holy things pure. Their job was to serve in the Temple of God. 29They were responsible for putting the holy bread on the table, for the flour in the grain offerings, for the bread made without yeast, for the baking and mixing, and for the measuring. 30The Levites also stood every morning and gave thanks and praise to the LORD. They also did this every evening. 31The Levites offered all the burnt offerings to the LORD on the special days of rest, at the New Moon festivals, and at all appointed feasts. They served before the LORD every day. They were to follow the rules for how many Levites should serve each time. 32So the Levites took care of the Meeting Tent and the Holy Place. And they helped their relatives, Aaron's descendants, with the services at the Temple of the LORD.

The Groups of the Priests

24 These were the groups of Aaron's sons: Aaron's sons were Nadab, Abihu, Eleazar, and Ithamar. 2But Nadab and Abihu died before their father did, and they had no sons. So Eleazar and Ithamar served as the priests. 3David, with the help of Zadok, a descendant of Eleazar, and Ahimelech, a descendant of Ithamar, separated their family groups into two different groups. Each group had certain duties. 4There were more leaders from Eleazar's family than from Ithamar's—sixteen leaders from Eleazar's family and eight leaders from Ithamar's family. 5Men were chosen from Eleazar's and Ithamar's families by throwing lots. Some men from each family were chosen to be in charge of the Holy Place, and some were chosen to serve as priests.

6Shemaiah son of Nethanel, from the tribe of Levi, was the secretary. He recorded the names of those descendants in front of King David, the officers, Zadok the priest, Ahimelech son of Abiathar, and the leaders of the families of the priests and Levites. The work was divided by lots among the families of Eleazar and Ithamar. The following men with their groups were chosen.

7The first one chosen was Jehoiarib. The second was Jedaiah. 8The third was Harim. The fourth was Seorim. 9The fifth was Malkijah. The sixth was Mijamin. 10The seventh was Hakkoz. The eighth was Abijah. 11The ninth was Jeshua. The tenth was Shecaniah. 12The eleventh was Eliashib. The twelfth was Jakim. 13The thirteenth was Huppah. The fourteenth was Jeshebeab. 14The fifteenth was Bilgah. The sixteenth was Immer. 15The seventeenth was Hezir. The eighteenth was Happizzez. 16The nineteenth was Pethahiah. The twentieth was Jehezkel. 17The twenty-first was Jakin. The twenty-second was Gamul. 18The twenty-third was Delaiah. The twenty-fourth was Maaziah.

19These were the groups chosen to serve in the Temple of the LORD. They obeyed the rules given them by Aaron, just as the LORD, the God of Israel, had commanded him.

The Other Levites

20These are the names of the rest of Levi's descendants:

Shubael was a descendant of Amram, and Jehdeiah was a descendant of Shubael.

21Isshiah was the first son of Rehabiah.

22From the Izhar family group, there was Shelomoth, and Jahath was a descendant of Shelomoth.

23Hebron's first son was Jeriah, Amariah was his second, Jahaziel was his third, and Jekameam was his fourth.

24Uzziel's son was Micah. Micah's son was Shamir. 25Micah's brother was Isshiah, and Isshiah's son was Zechariah.

26Merari's descendants were Mahli and Mushi. Merari's son was Jaaziah. 27Jaaziah son of Merari had sons named Shoham, Zaccur, and Ibri. 28Mahli's son was Eleazar, but Eleazar did not have any sons.

29Kish's son was Jerahmeel.

30Mushi's sons were Mahli, Eder, and Jerimoth.

These are the Levites, listed by their families. 31They were chosen for special jobs by throwing lots in front of King David, Zadok, Ahimelech, the leaders of the families of the priests, and the Levites. They did this just as their relatives, the priests, Aaron's descendants, had done. The families of the oldest brother and the youngest brother were treated the same.

24:31 Births: Ezra 2

The Music Groups

25 David and the commanders of the army chose some of the sons of Asaph, Heman, and Jeduthun to preach and play harps, lyres, and cymbals. Here is a list of the men who served in this way:

2Asaph's sons who served were Zaccur, Joseph, Nethaniah, and Asarelah. King David chose Asaph to preach, and Asaph directed his sons.

3Jeduthun's sons who served were Gedaliah, Zeri, Jeshaiah, Shimei, Hashabiah, and Mattithiah. There were six of them, and Jeduthun directed them. He preached and used a harp to give thanks and praise to the LORD.

4Heman's sons who served were Bukkiah, Mattaniah, Uzziel, Shubael, Jerimoth, Hananiah, Hanani, Eliathah, Giddalti, Romamti-Ezer, Joshbekashah, Mallothi, Hothir, and Mahazioth. 5All these were sons of Heman, David's seer. God promised to make Heman strong, so Heman had many sons. God gave him fourteen sons and three daughters. 6Heman directed all his sons in making music for the Temple of the LORD with cymbals, lyres, and harps; that was their way of serving in the Temple of God. King David was in charge of Asaph, Jeduthun, and Heman. 7These men and their relatives were trained and skilled in making music for the LORD. There were two hundred eighty-eight of them. 8Everyone threw lots to choose the time his family was to serve at the Temple. The young and the old, the teacher and the student, had to throw lots.

9First, the lot fell to Joseph, from the family of Asaph.

Second, twelve men were chosen from Gedaliah, his sons and relatives.

10Third, twelve men were chosen from Zaccur, his sons and relatives.

11Fourth, twelve men were chosen from Izri, his sons and relatives.

12Fifth, twelve men were chosen from Nethaniah, his sons and relatives.

13Sixth, twelve men were chosen from Bukkiah, his sons and relatives.

14Seventh, twelve men were chosen from Jesarelah, his sons and relatives.

15Eighth, twelve men were chosen from Jeshaiah, his sons and relatives.

16Ninth, twelve men were chosen from Mattaniah, his sons and relatives.

17Tenth, twelve men were chosen from Shimei, his sons and relatives.

18Eleventh, twelve men were chosen from Azarel, his sons and relatives.

19Twelfth, twelve men were chosen from Hashabiah, his sons and relatives.

20Thirteenth, twelve men were chosen from Shubael, his sons and relatives.

21Fourteenth, twelve men were chosen from Mattithiah, his sons and relatives.

22Fifteenth, twelve men were chosen from Jerimoth, his sons and relatives.

23Sixteenth, twelve men were chosen from Hananiah, his sons and relatives.

24Seventeenth, twelve men were chosen from Joshbekashah, his sons and relatives.

25Eighteenth, twelve men were chosen from Hanani, his sons and relatives.

26Nineteenth, twelve men were chosen from Mallothi, his sons and relatives.

27Twentieth, twelve men were chosen from Eliathah, his sons and relatives.

28Twenty-first, twelve men were chosen from Hothir, his sons and relatives.

29Twenty-second, twelve men were chosen from Giddalti, his sons and relatives.

30Twenty-third, twelve men were chosen from Mahazioth, his sons and relatives.

31Twenty-fourth, twelve men were chosen from Romamti-Ezer, his sons and relatives.

The Gatekeepers

26 These are the groups of the gatekeepers. From the family of Korah, there was Meshelemiah son of Kore, who was from Asaph's family. 2Meshelemiah had sons. Zechariah was his first son, Jediael was second, Zebadiah was third, Jathniel was fourth, 3Elam was fifth, Jehohanan was sixth, and Eliehoenai was seventh.

4Obed-Edom had sons. Shemaiah was his first son, Jehozabad was second, Joah was third, Sacar was fourth, Nethanel was fifth, 5Ammiel was sixth, Issachar was seventh, and Peullethai was eighth. God blessed Obed-Edom with children.

6Obed-Edom's son Shemaiah also had sons. They were leaders in their father's family because they were capable men. 7Shemaiah's sons were Othni, Rephael, Obed, Elzabad, Elihu, and Semakiah. Elihu, and Semakiah were skilled workers. 8All these were Obed-Edom's descendants. They and their sons and relatives were capable men and strong workers. Obed-Edom had sixty-two descendants in all.

9Meshelemiah had sons and relatives who were skilled workers. In all, there were eighteen.

10From the Merari family, Hosah had sons.

25:3 Thanks: 2 Chronicles 29:31

Shimri was chosen to be in charge. Although he
was not the oldest son, his father chose him to be
in charge. 11Hilkiah was his second son, Tabaliah
was third, and Zechariah was fourth. In all, Hosah
had thirteen sons and relatives.
12These were the leaders of the groups of gatekeepers, and they served in the Temple of the
LORD. Their relatives also worked in the Temple.
13By throwing lots, each family chose a gate to
guard. Young and old threw lots.
14Meshelemiah was chosen by lot to guard the
East Gate. Then lots were thrown for Meshelemiah's son Zechariah. He was a wise counselor
and was chosen for the North Gate. 15Obed-Edom
was chosen for the South Gate, and Obed-Edom's
sons were chosen to guard the storehouse.
16Shuppim and Hosah were chosen for the West
Gate and the Shalleketh Gate on the upper road.
Guards stood side by side with guards. 17Six
Levites stood guard every day at the East Gate;
four Levites stood guard every day at the North
Gate; four Levites stood guard every day at the
South Gate; and two Levites at a time guarded the
storehouse. 18There were two guards at the western court and four guards on the road to the court.
19These were the groups of the gatekeepers from
the families of Korah and Merari.

Other Leaders

20Other Levites were responsible for guarding
the treasuries of the Temple of God and for the
places where the holy items were kept.
21Ladan was Gershon's son and the ancestor of
several family groups. Jehiel was a leader of one
of the family groups. 22His sons were Zetham and
Joel his brother, and they were responsible for
the treasuries of the Temple of the LORD.
23Other leaders were chosen from the family
groups of Amram, Izhar, Hebron, and Uzziel.
24Shubael, the descendant of Gershom, who was
Moses' son, was the leader responsible for the
treasuries. 25These were Shubael's relatives from
Eliezer: Eliezer's son Rehabiah, Rehabiah's son
Jeshaiah, Jeshaiah's son Joram, Joram's son Zicri,
and Zicri's son Shelomith. 26Shelomith and his
relatives were responsible for everything that had
been collected for the Temple by King David, by
the heads of families, by the commanders of a
thousand men and of a hundred men, and by
other army commanders. 27They also gave some
of the things they had taken in wars to be used in
repairing the Temple of the LORD. 28Shelomith and
his relatives took care of all the holy items. Some
had been given by Samuel the seer, Saul son of
Kish, Abner son of Ner, and Joab son of Zeruiah.
29Kenaniah was from the Izhar family. He and
his sons worked outside the Temple as officers
and judges in different places in Israel.
30Hashabiah was from the Hebron family. He
and his relatives were responsible for the LORD's
work and the king's business in Israel west of the
Jordan River. There were seventeen hundred
skilled men in Hashabiah's group. 31The history
of the Hebron family shows that Jeriah was their
leader. In David's fortieth year as king, the
records were searched, and some capable men of
the Hebron family were found living at Jazer in
Gilead. 32Jeriah had twenty-seven hundred relatives who were skilled men and leaders of families. King David gave them the responsibility of
directing the tribes of Reuben, Gad, and East
Manasseh in God's work and the king's business.

Army Divisions

27 This is the list of the Israelites who served
the king in the army. Each division was on
duty one month each year. There were leaders of
families, commanders of a hundred men, commanders of a thousand men, and other officers.
Each division had twenty-four thousand men.
2Jashobeam son of Zabdiel was in charge of the
first division for the first month. There were
twenty-four thousand men in his division.
3Jashobeam, one of the descendants of Perez, was
leader of all the army officers for the first month.
4Dodai, from the Ahohites, was in charge of the
division for the second month. Mikloth was a
leader in the division. There were twenty-four
thousand men in Dodai's division.
5The third commander, for the third month,
was Benaiah son of Jehoiada the priest. There were
twenty-four thousand men in his division. 6He
was the Benaiah who was one of the Thirty soldiers. Benaiah was a brave warrior who led those
men. Benaiah's son Ammizabad was in charge of
Benaiah's division.
7The fourth commander, for the fourth month,
was Asahel, the brother of Joab. Later, Asahel's son
Zebadiah took his place as commander. There
were twenty-four thousand men in his division.
8The fifth commander, for the fifth month, was
Shamhuth, from Izrah's family. There were twenty-
four thousand men in his division.
9The sixth commander, for the sixth month, was
Ira son of Ikkesh from the town of Tekoa. There
were twenty-four thousand men in his division.

27:6 *Thirty.* These were David's most powerful soldiers. See 2 Samuel 23:24.

10The seventh commander, for the seventh month, was Helez. He was from the Pelonites and a descendant of Ephraim. There were twenty-four thousand men in his division.

11The eighth commander, for the eighth month, was Sibbecai. He was from Hushah and was from Zerah's family. There were twenty-four thousand men in his division.

12The ninth commander, for the ninth month, was Abiezer. He was from Anathoth in Benjamin. There were twenty-four thousand men in his division.

13The tenth commander, for the tenth month, was Maharai. He was from Netophah and was from Zerah's family. There were twenty-four thousand men in his division.

14The eleventh commander, for the eleventh month, was Benaiah. He was from Pirathon in Ephraim. There were twenty-four thousand men in his division.

15The twelfth commander, for the twelfth month, was Heldai. He was from Netophah and was from Othniel's family. There were twenty-four thousand men in his division.

Leaders of the Tribes

16These were the leaders of the tribes of Israel. Eliezer son of Zicri was over the tribe of Reuben. Shephatiah son of Maacah was over the tribe of Simeon. 17Hashabiah son of Kemuel was over the tribe of Levi. Zadok was over the people of Aaron. 18Elihu, one of David's brothers, was over the tribe of Judah. Omri son of Michael was over the tribe of Issachar. 19Ishmaiah son of Obadiah was over the tribe of Zebulun. Jerimoth son of Azriel was over the tribe of Naphtali. 20Hoshea son of Azaziah was over the tribe of Ephraim. Joel son of Pedaiah was over West Manasseh. 21Iddo son of Zechariah was over East Manasseh. Jaasiel son of Abner was over the tribe of Benjamin. 22Azarel son of Jeroham was over the tribe of Dan.

These were the leaders of the tribes of Israel.

23The LORD had promised to make the Israelites as many as the stars in the sky. So David only counted the men who were twenty years old and older. 24Joab son of Zeruiah began to count the people, but he did not finish. God became angry with Israel for counting the people, so the number of the people was not put in the history book about King David's rule.

The King's Directors

25Azmaveth son of Adiel was in charge of the royal storehouses.

Jonathan son of Uzziah was in charge of the storehouses in the country, towns, villages, and towers.

26Ezri son of Kelub was in charge of the field workers who farmed the land.

27Shimei, from the town of Ramah, was in charge of the vineyards.

Zabdi, from Shapham, was in charge of storing the wine that came from the vineyards.

28Baal-Hanan, from Geder, was in charge of the olive trees and sycamore trees in the western hills.

Joash was in charge of storing the olive oil.

29Shitrai, from Sharon, was in charge of the herds that fed in the Plain of Sharon.

Shaphat son of Adlai was in charge of the herds in the valleys.

30Obil, an Ishmaelite, was in charge of the camels.

Jehdeiah, from Meronoth, was in charge of the donkeys.

31Jaziz, from the Hagrites, was in charge of the flocks.

All these men were the officers who took care of King David's property.

32Jonathan was David's uncle, and he advised David. Jonathan was a wise man and a teacher of the law. Jehiel son of Hacmoni took care of the king's sons. 33Ahithophel advised the king. Hushai, from the Arkite people, was the king's friend. 34Jehoiada and Abiathar later took Ahithophel's place in advising the king. Jehoiada was Benaiah's son. Joab was the commander of the king's army.

David's Plans for the Temple

28 David commanded all the leaders of Israel to come to Jerusalem. There were the leaders of the tribes, commanders of the divisions serving the king, commanders of a thousand men and of a hundred men, leaders who took care of the property and animals that belonged to the king and his sons, men over the palace, the powerful men, and all the brave warriors.

2King David stood up and said, "Listen to me, my relatives and my people. I wanted to build a place to keep the Ark of the Agreement with the LORD. I wanted it to be God's footstool. So I made plans to build a temple. 3But God said to me, 'You must not build a temple for worshiping me, because you are a soldier and have killed many people.'

4"But the LORD, the God of Israel, chose me from my whole family to be king of Israel forever. He chose the tribe of Judah to lead, and from the people of Judah, he chose my father's family. From that family God was pleased to make me king of Israel. 5The LORD has given me many sons, and

28:4 Leadership: Psalm 23

SUCCESS

PSALM 1:3

How do God's people define and measure success? How can we put a proper idea of success into our lives? What does Jesus teach us about being successful?

Success is a word that has been greatly misused. Too often it has been used to mean power, wealth, status, self-fulfillment, and happiness. Christians have also stumbled into worldly ideas of success through non-biblical teachings like, to become a Christian means to become rich. It is extremely important for us to return to a correct idea of success. We need to study it, but carefully.

The Bible teaches that both the righteous and the wicked may succeed. The success of the righteous is described in our location text, Psalm 1. We see it elsewhere in such passages as Genesis 39:23, Deuteronomy 29:9, 1 Chronicles 22:13, and Nehemiah 2:20. In the New Testament we can infer that Simon and Andrew had a successful fishing business when Jesus found them (Matthew 4:18), and the apostle Paul was able to support himself successfully through tent-making (Acts 18:3). Over the centuries, Christians have been successful in a variety of ways and in all walks of life.

But the Bible also shows the success of the wicked in such passages as Job 12:6, Psalm 73:3, and Jeremiah 5:28. The writer of Ecclesiastes describes the false success of labor and achievement when it is rooted in jealousy (4:4). In the New Testament we meet prosperous people like Herod (Matthew 2:3–19), Ananias and Sapphira (Acts 5:1–11), and Alexander (2 Timothy 4:14–15), but we would hardly want to pattern our lives after any of them. By linking success to evil people as well as righteous people, we cannot say that successful people are godly or that being godly means getting rich.

What then is success? The Bible answers this question in a number of ways, but underlying them all is the dominant motif of *character.* Successful people are successful because of who they are, not because of what they do. Joshua is the chosen successor to Moses because God's Spirit is in him (Numbers 27:18). He will succeed only to the extent that he obeys the Lord (Joshua 1:7). Later on in Judah's history, Uzziah is one of the best kings to ever rule. It is said of him, "as long as Uzziah obeyed the LORD, God gave him success" (2 Chronicles 26:5). The writer of Proverbs underscores the secret of success by writing, "Knowledge begins with respect for the LORD, but fools hate wisdom and self-control" (1:7). Success is rooted in character.

The Hebrew word *blessed* that begins the psalm is translated by the NCV as "happy." The successful person experiences and then expresses "the blessed (happy) life." In this psalm the characteristics of the successful person include not listening to the wicked or making their places one's hangout. Successful people do not do what evil people do. They love the Lord's teachings and take them into their lives day and night. As a result, they show a strength comparable to trees firmly rooted by riverbeds, producing one good thing after another.

Once again, we see the idea that success flows from character. When the psalmist writes, "everything they do will succeed," that success is based more upon the quality of their lives than the skillfulness of their activities. For this reason, we are on the right track to define success with such words as "holiness," "godliness," and "obedience." In terms of success, the Bible is much more interested in showing us where it comes from than in describing all of its results.

Jesus amplifies this theme in the Beatitudes, as he describes various aspects of the "blessed (happy) life" (Matthew 5:1–10). We can be considered successful when we know we have great spiritual needs, when we are willing to grieve over our losses, when we live humble lives, when we want to do what is right more than anything else, when we show mercy to others, when we are pure in our thinking, when we work to bring peace to life, and when we are treated badly for doing good. In fact, it is not inaccurate to say that the rest of the Sermon on the Mount is Christ's views on success. If we would live the "blessed life," we would be considered successful whether we have much or little, whether we live famous or ordinary lives.

But what about conduct—what we do and the way we do it? The Bible is filled with verse after verse describing the lifestyles of the truly successful. Our two primary passages in Psalm 1 and Matthew 5 give hundreds of concrete examples. Ask the psalmist how many different ways there are to "produce fruit," or ask Jesus how many different ways there are to "work to bring peace." Behind every principle of character there are many specific applications in conduct. Once we make this connection, almost every passage in the Bible opens up as a "manual of success" either in terms of character or conduct, promise or forbidding, allowance or warning.

If we wish to include the Bible's definition of success into our lives, we can do so by studying the lives of successful biblical people: Moses and David, Ruth and Esther—people who lived successfully in the Old Testament. In the New Testament we can study people like Simon Peter and Paul. Exploring their lives confirms all the things we have talked about up to now, but it does one other important thing. It shows us that "success" is not the same as perfection. Each of these people, while truly successful, made mistakes. Some of them committed heartbreaking sin. The saints are not successful because they are perfect; they are successful because they are rooted in God—ready to repent when they fail God, ready to obey when they follow him.

Finally, of course, we take our cues for success from Christ. As we become more familiar with his life, we more clearly see what success is all about. To be sure, Christ is not "successful" if we apply many of today's measurements used by the world. But when we see success for what it really is, we see in him the life of deepest success. It would be impossible to fully describe all the elements of success in Christ, so let's take a different approach. Let's see how he is the example of success in relation to the words which we used to begin this essay: power, wealth, status, self-fulfillment, and happiness.

Jesus certainly had power! Even a quick reading of the Gospels shows Christ's power in relation to the natural and supernatural. But what we see is not one who "throws power around" either for show or the mere demonstration of it. Instead, we see Jesus using his power constructively and compassionately. He uses his power to take a stand against evil and to promote the physical, emotional, and spiritual well-being of people. Jesus changes power from its tempting and destructive display and shows us how to use power.

What about wealth? At first glance, it may seem that Jesus has very little to teach us about success in relation to that. It is true that he himself did not have a lot of wealth, but neither did he avoid fellowship with rich people or automatically condemn anyone for being wealthy. Instead, he taught two very important lessons. First, he taught that "life is not measured by how much one owns" (Luke 12:15). He consistently steers us away from measuring our success by how much more we have than others. Rather, he tells us to measure our wealth in terms of those things which we store away in heaven, where "they cannot be destroyed by moths or rust and where thieves cannot break in and steal them" (Matthew 6:20).

His second teaching encouraged those with wealth to consider how they might use it for the good of others. In the parable of the rich man who built bigger barns (Luke 12:13–21), he condemned selfishness and the temptation to use one's wealth to provide false security. By this parable, he is telling us to be grateful for any material riches which might come our way, but at the same time to be seeking for ways to share what we have with others. Jesus understood that wealth is never "equally distributed" on the earth; that the task of stewardship is given to those who are blessed with a lot of this world's goods. By viewing wealth in this way, we do not have to keep prosperity and success separate.

Turning to status, we find puzzlement. On one occasion, Jesus draws back from someone even calling him "good" (Mark 10:18). But at another time, he frankly says, "You call me 'Teacher' and 'Lord,' and you are right, because that is what I am" (John 13:13). What are we to make of this? How are we to understand Jesus' relationship to status? The answer comes from the context in John 13. He is willing to be called "teacher" and "Lord" in relation to servanthood. He had just washed the feet of his disciples. In effect, Christ was saying, "If you are willing to let me *teach* you about service, then I am your Teacher. If you are willing to let me show you how to be *lord* of ordinary tasks, then I am your Lord." Or to say it another way, Jesus rejected ideas of status which artificially elevated him above others. He redefined status in terms of humble acts of kindness which edify others. In this way he keeps status and success in their proper relationship.

Self-fulfillment likewise finds its transformation in Christ. It is not to be seen as "doing your own thing" or "getting your own way." Instead, it is finding your highest joy in doing the will of God (John 4:34). By comparing this with food, Jesus is telling us that there is a nourishment of the self which is incomparable when God's will is the source. Once again we find a puzzle: we discover that, "those who want to save their lives will give up true life, and those who give up their lives for me will have true life" (Matthew 16:25). Self-fulfillment and success can be partners when doing God's will is at the center of our lives.

Needless to say, happiness is the greatest outcome of this kind of living. Jesus demonstrates that this kind of happiness is not the result of self-seeking, but rather the product of self-giving. Through his example the simplest, yet most profound definition of success emerges: knowing and doing the will of God.

A present-day writer has said that the successful person is the one who ends up with the most "toys." The Bible disagrees, and in place of such a weak idea of success, it teaches us that the truly successful person is the one who ends up with the most "joys"—joys rooted in character, experienced in the blessed life, and expressed in countless acts of service. On these terms, we need never avoid success.

Success: For additional scriptures on this topic go to Genesis 39:23.

from those sons he has chosen Solomon to be the new king of Israel. Israel is the LORD's kingdom. 6The LORD said to me, 'Your son Solomon will build my Temple and its courtyards. I have chosen Solomon to be my son, and I will be his father. 7He is obeying my laws and commands now. If he continues to obey them, I will make his kingdom strong forever.'"

8David said, "Now, in front of all Israel, the assembly of the LORD, and in the hearing of God, I tell you these things: Be careful to obey all the commands of the LORD your God. Then you will keep this good land and pass it on to your descendants forever.

9"And you, my son Solomon, accept the God of your father. Serve him completely and willingly, because the LORD knows what is in everyone's mind. He understands everything you think. If you go to him for help, you will get an answer. But if you turn away from him, he will leave you forever. 10Solomon, you must understand this. The LORD has chosen you to build the Temple as his holy place. Be strong and finish the job."

11Then David gave his son Solomon the plans for building the Temple and the courtyard around the Temple. They included its buildings, its storerooms, its upper rooms, its inside rooms, and the place where the people's sins were removed. 12David gave him plans for everything he had in mind: the courtyards around the LORD's Temple and all the rooms around it, the Temple treasuries, and the treasuries of the holy items used in the Temple. 13David gave Solomon directions for the groups of the priests and Levites. David told him about all the work of serving in the Temple of the LORD and about the items to be used in the Temple service 14that were made of gold or silver. David told Solomon how much gold or silver should be used to make each thing. 15David told him how much gold to use for each gold lampstand and its lamps and how much silver to use for each silver lampstand and its lamps. The different lampstands were to be used where needed. 16David told how much gold should be used for each table that held the holy bread and how much silver should be used for the silver tables. 17He told how much pure gold should be used to make the forks, bowls, and pitchers and how much gold should be used to make each gold dish. He told how much silver should be used to make each silver dish 18and how much pure gold should be used for the altar of incense. He also gave Solomon the plans for the chariot of the golden creatures that spread their wings over the Ark of the Agreement with the LORD.

19David said, "All these plans were written with the LORD guiding me. He helped me understand everything in the plans."

20David also said to his son Solomon, "Be strong and brave, and do the work. Don't be afraid or discouraged, because the LORD God, my God, is with you. He will not fail you or leave you until all the work for the Temple of the LORD is finished. 21The groups of the priests and Levites are ready for all the work on the Temple of God. Every skilled worker is ready to help you with all the work. The leaders and all the people will obey every command you give."

Gifts for Building the Temple

29 King David said to all the Israelites who were gathered, "God chose my son Solomon, who is young and hasn't yet learned what he needs to know, but the work is important. This palace is not for people; it is for the LORD God. 2I have done my best to prepare for building the Temple of God. I have given gold for the things made of gold and silver for the things made of silver. I have given bronze for the things made of bronze and iron for the things made of iron. I have given wood for the things made of wood and onyx for the settings. I have given turquoise gems of many different colors, valuable stones, and white marble. I have given much of all these things. 3I have already given this for the Temple, but now I am also giving my own treasures of gold and silver, because I really want the Temple of my God to be built. 4I have given about two hundred twenty thousand pounds of pure gold from Ophir and about five hundred twenty thousand pounds of pure silver. They will be used to cover the walls of the buildings 5and for all the gold and silver work. Skilled men may use the gold and silver to make things for the Temple. Now, who is ready to give himself to the service of the LORD today?"

6The family leaders and the leaders of the tribes of Israel, the commanders of a thousand men and of a hundred men, and the leaders responsible for the king's work gave their valuable things. 7They donated about three hundred eighty thousand pounds of gold, about seven hundred fifty thousand pounds of silver, about one million three hundred fifty thousand pounds of bronze, and about seven million five hundred thousand pounds of iron to the Temple of God. 8People who had valuable gems gave them to the treasury of the Temple of the LORD, and Jehiel, from the Gershon family, took care of the valuable gems. 9The leaders gave willingly and completely to the LORD. The people rejoiced to see their leaders give so gladly, and King David was also very happy.

David's Prayer

10David praised the LORD in front of all the people who were gathered. He said:
"We praise you, LORD,
God of our father Israel.
We praise you forever and ever.
11LORD, you are great and powerful.
You have glory, victory, and honor.
Everything in heaven and on earth
belongs to you.
The kingdom belongs to you, LORD;
you are the ruler over everything.
12Riches and honor come from you.
You rule everything.
You have the power and strength
to make anyone great and strong.
13Now, our God, we thank you
and praise your glorious name.

14"These things did not really come from me
and my people.
Everything comes from you;
we have given you back what you gave us.
15We are like foreigners and strangers,
as our ancestors were.
Our time on earth is like a shadow.
There is no hope.
16LORD our God, we have gathered all this
to build your Temple for worship to you.
But everything has come from you;
everything belongs to you.
17I know, my God, that you test people's hearts.
You are happy when people do what is right.
I was happy to give all these things,
and I gave with an honest heart.
Your people gathered here are happy to
give to you,
and I rejoice to see their giving.
18LORD, you are the God of our ancestors,
the God of Abraham, Isaac, and Jacob.
Make your people want to serve you always,
and make them want to obey you.
19Give my son Solomon a desire to serve you.
Help him always obey your commands,
laws, and rules.
Help him build the Temple
for which I have prepared."

20Then David said to all the people who were gathered, "Praise the LORD your God." So they all praised the LORD, the God of their ancestors, and they bowed to the ground to give honor to the LORD and the king.

Solomon Becomes King

21The next day the people sacrificed to the LORD. They offered burnt offerings to him of a thousand bulls, a thousand male sheep, and a thousand male lambs. They also brought drink offerings. Many sacrifices were made for all the people of Israel.
22That day the people ate and drank with much joy, and the LORD was with them.

And they made David's son Solomon king for the second time. They poured olive oil on Solomon to appoint him king in the presence of the LORD. And they poured oil on Zadok to appoint him as priest. 23Then Solomon sat on the LORD's throne as king and took his father David's place. Solomon was very successful, and all the people of Israel obeyed him. 24All the leaders and soldiers and King David's sons accepted Solomon as king and promised to obey him. 25The LORD made Solomon great before all the Israelites and gave Solomon much honor. No king of Israel before Solomon had such honor.

David's Death

26David son of Jesse was king over all Israel.
27He had ruled over Israel forty years—seven years in Hebron and thirty-three years in Jerusalem. 28David died when he was old. He had lived a good, long life and had received many riches and honors. His son Solomon became king after him.

29Everything David did as king, from beginning to end, is recorded in the records of Samuel the seer, the records of Nathan the prophet, and the records of Gad the seer. 30Those writings tell what David did as king of Israel. They tell about his power and what happened to him and to Israel and to all the kingdoms around them.

29:14 Stewardship: Psalm 8:6
29:22 Perhaps taking into account the fact that Solomon had been made co-king with his father David earlier (see 23:1).
29:28 Solomon: 2 Chronicles 6:12

INTRODUCTION TO THE BOOK OF
2 CHRONICLES

Israel's History from Solomon to the Captivity

SUMMARY:

The outline of 2 Chronicles is as follows:

I. The Story of Solomon (1:1–9:31)
II. The Kings of Judah (10:1–36:23)

Chronicles is composed of two parts, 1 and 2 Chronicles, in our English Bibles, but originally the two parts were one book. For that reason, the introduction to 1 Chronicles should be read as an introduction to 2 Chronicles.

I. The Story of Solomon (1:1–9:31)

The Book of 2 Chronicles continues the narrative of 1 Kings. The first nine chapters focus on Solomon, the third and last king of a united Israel. In keeping with the major themes of the Book of Chronicles there is a focus on the Temple of Solomon. After all, at the time of the composition of Chronicles, they were building the second Temple, and hearing about the construction of the now-destroyed first Temple would have been an encouragement to them. Also in keeping with the emphasis in Chronicles is the fact that Solomon is presented in positive terms. The stories of his sin emphasized in Kings are here excluded.

II. The Kings of Judah (10:1–36:23)

These chapters give the story of the period known as the divided kingdom. After Solomon's death, the ten northern tribes, known after that as Israel, split off from the two southern tribes, called Judah. This division resulted from Solomon's sins, and the relationship between the northern and southern tribes was usually tense.

The Book of Kings also covers this period of time, but with a difference. Since Kings was written during the period of the exile, the burning question was, "Why were we defeated?" So throughout the book the sins of the kings of Israel and Judah are told.

In Chronicles, written during the period of the restoration, the burning question was, "What is our connection with the past?" Since only Judah is left, the accounts of the divided kingdom only concern the southern part of the kingdom. The north is just mentioned as it comes into contact with the south. Also, the subject matter of the narratives about the individual southern kings is more positive than their parallels in the Book of Kings.

2 Chronicles

Solomon Asks for Wisdom

1 Solomon, David's son, became a powerful king, because the LORD his God was with him and made him very great.

2Solomon spoke to all the people of Israel—the commanders of a hundred men and of a thousand men, the judges, every leader in all Israel, and the leaders of the families. 3Then Solomon and all the people with him went to the place of worship at the town of Gibeon. God's Meeting Tent, which Moses the LORD's servant had made in the desert, was there. 4David had brought the Ark of God from Kiriath Jearim to Jerusalem, where he had made a place for it and had set up a tent for it. 5The bronze altar that Bezalel son of Uri, who was the son of Hur, had made was in Gibeon in front of the Holy Tent. So Solomon and the people worshiped there. 6Solomon went up to the bronze altar in the presence of the LORD at the Meeting Tent and offered a thousand burnt offerings on it.

7That night God appeared to Solomon and said to him, "Ask for whatever you want me to give you."

8Solomon answered, "You have been very kind to my father David, and you have made me king in his place. 9Now, LORD God, may your promise to my father David come true. You have made me king of a people who are as many as the dust of the earth. 10Now give me wisdom and knowledge so I can lead these people in the right way, because no one can rule them without your help."

11God said to Solomon, "You have not asked for wealth or riches or honor, or for the death of your enemies, or for a long life. But since you have asked for wisdom and knowledge to lead my people, over whom I have made you king, 12I will give you wisdom and knowledge. I will also give you more wealth, riches, and honor than any king who has lived before you or any who will live after you."

13Then Solomon left the place of worship, the Meeting Tent, at Gibeon and went back to Jerusalem. There King Solomon ruled over Israel.

Solomon's Wealth

14Solomon had fourteen hundred chariots and twelve thousand horses. He kept some in special cities for the chariots, and others he kept with him in Jerusalem. 15In Jerusalem Solomon made silver and gold as plentiful as stones and cedar trees as plentiful as the fig trees on the western hills. 16He imported horses from Egypt and Kue; his traders bought them in Kue. 17They imported chariots from Egypt for about fifteen pounds of silver apiece, and horses cost nearly four pounds of silver apiece. Then they sold the horses and chariots to all the kings of the Hittites and the Arameans.

Solomon Prepares for the Temple

2 Solomon decided to build a temple as a place to worship the LORD and also a palace for himself. 2He chose seventy thousand men to carry loads, eighty thousand men to cut stone in the hill country, and thirty-six hundred men to direct the workers.

3Solomon sent this message to Hiram king of the city of Tyre: "Help me as you helped my father David by sending him cedar logs so he could build himself a palace to live in. 4I will build a temple for worshiping the LORD my God, and I will give this temple to him. There we will burn sweet-smelling spices in his presence. We will continually set out the holy bread in God's presence. And we will burn sacrifices every morning and evening, on Sabbath days and New Moons, and on the other feast days commanded by the LORD our God. This is a rule for Israel to obey forever.

5"The temple I build will be great, because our God is greater than all gods. 6But no one can really build a house for our God. Not even the highest of heavens can hold him. How then can I build a temple for him except as a place to burn sacrifices to him?

7"Now send me a man skilled in working with gold, silver, bronze, and iron, and with purple, red, and blue thread. He must also know how to make engravings. He will work with my skilled craftsmen in Judah and Jerusalem, whom my father David chose.

8"Also send me cedar, pine, and juniper logs from Lebanon. I know your servants are experienced at cutting down the trees in Lebanon, and my servants will help them. 9Send me a lot of wood, because the temple I am going to build will be large and wonderful. 10I will give your servants who cut the wood one hundred twenty-five thousand bushels of wheat, one hundred twenty-five thousand bushels of barley, one hundred fifteen thousand gallons of wine, and one hundred fifteen thousand gallons of oil."

11Then Hiram king of Tyre answered Solomon with this letter: "Solomon, because the LORD loves his people, he chose you to be their king." 12Hiram

1:10 Wisdom: Job 28

also said: "Praise the LORD, the God of Israel, who
made heaven and earth! He has given King David
a wise son, one with wisdom and understanding,
who will build a temple for the LORD and a palace
for himself.
13"I will send you a skilled and wise man
named Huram-Abi. 14His mother was from the
people of Dan, and his father was from Tyre.
Huram-Abi is skilled in working with gold, silver,
bronze, iron, stone, and wood, and with purple,
blue, and red thread, and expensive linen. He is
skilled in making engravings and can make any
design you show him. He will help your craftsmen
and the craftsmen of your father David.
15"Now send my servants the wheat, barley, oil,
and wine you promised. 16We will cut as much
wood from Lebanon as you need and will bring it
on rafts by sea to Joppa. Then you may carry it to
Jerusalem."
17Solomon counted all the foreigners living in
Israel. (This was after the time his father David had
counted the people.) There were one hundred
fifty-three thousand six hundred foreigners in the
country. 18Solomon chose seventy thousand of
them to carry loads, eighty thousand of them to
cut stone in the mountains, and thirty-six hundred
of them to direct the workers and to keep the
people working.

Solomon Builds the Temple

3 Then Solomon began to build the Temple of the
LORD in Jerusalem on Mount Moriah. This was
where the LORD had appeared to David, Solomon's
father. Solomon built the Temple on the place
David had prepared on the threshing floor of
Araunah the Jebusite.⚭ 2Solomon began building in
the second month of the fourth year he ruled Israel.
3Solomon used these measurements for building the Temple of God. It was ninety feet long and
thirty feet wide, using the old measurement. 4The
porch in front of the main room of the Temple was
thirty feet long and thirty feet high.
He covered the inside of the porch with pure
gold. 5He put panels of pine on the walls of the
main room and covered them with pure gold. Then
he put designs of palm trees and chains in the
gold. 6He decorated the Temple with gems and
gold from Parvaim. 7He put gold on the Temple's
ceiling beams, doorposts, walls, and doors, and he
carved creatures with wings on the walls.
8Then he made the Most Holy Place. It was thirty
feet long and thirty feet wide, as wide as the
Temple. He covered its walls with about forty-six
thousand pounds of pure gold. 9The gold nails
weighed over a pound. He also covered the upper
rooms with gold.
10He made two creatures with wings for the
Most Holy Place and covered them with gold.
11The wings of the gold creatures were thirty feet
across. One wing of one creature was seven and
one-half feet long and touched the Temple wall.
The creature's other wing was also seven and one-
half feet long, and it touched a wing of the second
creature. 12One wing of the second creature
touched the other side of the room and was also
seven and one-half feet long. The second creature's
other wing touched the first creature's wing, and it
was also seven and one-half feet long. 13Together,
the creatures' wings were thirty feet across. The
creatures stood on their feet, facing the main room.
14He made the curtain of blue, purple, and red
thread, and expensive linen, and he put designs of
creatures with wings in it.
15He made two pillars to stand in front of the
Temple. They were about fifty-two feet tall, and the
capital of each pillar was over seven feet tall. 16He
made a net of chains and put them on the tops of
the pillars. He made a hundred pomegranates and
put them on the chains. 17Then he put the pillars
up in front of the Temple. One pillar stood on the
south side, the other on the north. He named the
south pillar He Establishes and the north pillar In
Him Is Strength.

Things for the Temple

4 He made a bronze altar thirty feet long thirty
feet wide, and fifteen feet tall. 2Then he made
from bronze a large round bowl, which was called
the Sea. It was forty-five feet around, fifteen feet
across, and seven and one-half feet deep. 3There
were carvings of bulls under the rim of the bowl—
ten bulls every eighteen inches. They were in two
rows and were made in one piece with the bowl.
4The bowl rested on the backs of twelve bronze
bulls that faced outward from the center of the
bowl. Three bulls faced north, three faced west,

⚭**3:1 Jerusalem:** Psalm 125:2

3:6 *Parvaim.* There was much gold there. It may have been in the country of Ophir.

3:10 *creatures with wings.* These creatures with wings are known as cherubim. Solomon made artistic representations of cherubim, who are powerful angelic beings.

3:15 *two pillars.* The Temple has many points of similarity with the Holy Tent, but the two pillars are new. Their names and their shape show that they symbolize the fact that Israel is now firmly settled in the land of Palestine.

4:2 *The Sea* is a huge bowl of water. It probably was used for ritual washings by priests and other worshipers. But its name, Sea, has further significance. The Sea in the Bible and ancient Near East often stands for the forces of chaos that are in conflict with God, the Creator. The presence of the Sea in front of the Temple shows that these forces of chaos are under God's control.

three faced south, and three faced east. 5The sides of the bowl were four inches thick, and it held about seventeen thousand five hundred gallons. The rim of the bowl was like the rim of a cup or like a lily blossom.

6He made ten smaller bowls and put five on the south side and five on the north. They were for washing the animals for the burnt offerings, but the large bowl was for the priests to wash in.

7He made ten lampstands of gold, following the plans. He put them in the Temple, five on the south side and five on the north.

8He made ten tables and put them in the Temple, five on the south side and five on the north. And he used gold to make a hundred other bowls.

9He also made the priests' courtyard and the large courtyard. He made the doors that opened to the courtyard and covered them with bronze. 10Then he put the large bowl in the southeast corner of the Temple.

11Huram also made bowls, shovels, and small bowls. So he finished his work for King Solomon on the Temple of God:

12two pillars;
two large bowls for the capitals on top of the pillars;
two nets to cover the two large bowls for the capitals on top of the pillars;
13four hundred pomegranates for the two nets (there were two rows of pomegranates for each net covering the bowls for the capitals on top of the pillars);
14the stands with a bowl on each stand;
15the large bowl with twelve bulls under it;
16the pots, shovels, forks, and all the things to go with them.

All the things that Huram-Abi made for King Solomon for the Temple of the LORD were made of polished bronze. 17The king had these things poured into clay molds that were made in the plain of the Jordan River between Succoth and Zarethan. 18Solomon had so many things made that the total weight of all the bronze was never known.

19Solomon also made all the things for God's Temple: the golden altar; tables which held the bread that shows God's people are in his presence; 20the lampstands and their lamps of pure gold, to burn in front of the Most Holy Place as planned; 21the flowers, lamps, and tongs of pure gold; 22the pure gold wick trimmers, small bowls, pans, and dishes used to carry coals, the gold doors for the Temple, and the inside doors of the Most Holy Place and of the main room.

5 Finally all the work Solomon did for the Temple of the LORD was finished. He brought in everything his father David had set apart for the Temple—all the silver and gold and other articles. And he put everything in the treasuries of God's Temple.

The Ark Is Brought into the Temple

2Solomon called for the older leaders of Israel, the heads of the tribes, and the leaders of the families to come to him in Jerusalem. He wanted them to bring the Ark of the Agreement with the LORD from the older part of the city. 3So all the Israelites came together with the king during the festival in the seventh month.

4When all the older leaders of Israel arrived, the Levites lifted up the Ark. 5They carried the Ark of the Agreement, the Meeting Tent, and the holy utensils in it; the priests and the Levites brought them up. 6King Solomon and all the Israelites gathered before the Ark of the Agreement and sacrificed so many sheep and bulls no one could count them.

7Then the priests put the Ark of the Agreement with the LORD in its place inside the Most Holy Place in the Temple, under the wings of the golden creatures. 8The wings of these creatures were spread out over the place for the Ark, covering it and its carrying poles. 9The carrying poles were so long that anyone standing in the Holy Place in front of the Most Holy Place could see the ends of the poles. But no one could see them from outside the Holy Place. The poles are still there today. 10The only things inside the Ark were two stone tablets that Moses had put in the Ark at Mount Sinai. That was where the LORD made his agreement with the Israelites after they came out of Egypt.

11Then all the priests left the Holy Place. (All the priests from each group had made themselves ready to serve the LORD.) 12All the Levite musicians—Asaph, Heman, Jeduthun, and all their sons and relatives—stood on the east side of the altar. They were dressed in white linen and played cymbals, harps, and lyres. With them were one hundred twenty priests who blew trumpets. 13Those who blew the trumpets and those who sang together sounded like one person as they praised

5:2 *The Ark of the Agreement.* A wooden box that symbolized God's presence with his people. When the Ark was placed in the Temple, it symbolized God's presence in the Temple.

5:10 *stone tablets.* They were the two stone tablets on which God wrote the Ten Commandments.

and thanked the LORD. They sang as others played their trumpets, cymbals, and other instruments. They praised the LORD with this song:

"He is good;
his love continues forever."

Then the Temple of the LORD was filled with a cloud. 14The priests could not continue their work because of the cloud, because the LORD's glory filled the Temple of God.⚭

Solomon Speaks to the People

6 Then Solomon said, "The LORD said he would live in the dark cloud. 2LORD, I have built a wonderful Temple for you—a place for you to live forever."

3While all the Israelites were standing there, King Solomon turned to them and blessed them. 4Then he said, "Praise the LORD, the God of Israel. He has done what he promised to my father David. The LORD said, 5'Since the time I brought my people out of Egypt, I have not chosen a city in any tribe of Israel where a temple will be built for me. I did not choose a man to lead my people Israel. 6But now I have chosen Jerusalem as the place I am to be worshiped, and I have chosen David to lead my people Israel.'

7"My father David wanted to build a temple for the LORD, the God of Israel. 8But the LORD said to my father David, 'It was good that you wanted to build a temple for me. 9But you are not the one to build it. Your son, who comes from your own body, is the one who will build my temple.'

10"Now the LORD has kept his promise. I am the king now in place of David my father. Now I rule Israel as the LORD promised, and I have built the Temple for the LORD, the God of Israel. 11There I have put the Ark, in which is the Agreement the LORD made with the Israelites."

Solomon's Prayer

12Then Solomon stood facing the LORD's altar, and all the Israelites were standing behind him. He spread out his hands.⚭ 13He had made a bronze platform seven and one-half feet long, seven and one-half feet wide, and seven and one-half feet high, and he had placed it in the middle of the outer courtyard. Solomon stood on the platform. Then he kneeled in front of all the people of Israel gathered there, and he spread out his hands toward the sky. 14He said, "LORD, God of Israel, there is no god like you in heaven or on earth. You keep your agreement of love with your servants who truly follow you. 15You have kept the promise you made to your servant David, my father. You spoke it with your own mouth and finished it with your hands today.

16"Now, LORD, God of Israel, keep the promise you made to your servant David, my father. You said, 'If your sons are careful to obey my teachings as you have obeyed, there will always be someone from your family ruling Israel.' 17Now, LORD, God of Israel, please continue to keep that promise you made to your servant.

18"But, God, can you really live here on the earth with people? The sky and the highest place in heaven cannot contain you. Surely this house which I have built cannot contain you. 19But please listen to my prayer and my request, because I am your servant. LORD my God, hear this prayer your servant prays to you. 20Day and night please watch over this Temple where you have said you would be worshiped. Hear the prayer I pray facing this Temple. 21Hear my prayers and the prayers of your people Israel when we pray facing this place. Hear from your home in heaven, and when you hear, forgive us.

22"If someone wrongs another person, he will be brought to the altar in this Temple. If he swears an oath that he is not guilty, 23then hear in heaven. Judge the case, punish the guilty, but declare that the innocent person is not guilty.

24"When your people, the Israelites, sin against you, their enemies will defeat them. But if they come back to you and praise you and pray to you in this Temple, 25then listen from heaven. Forgive the sin of your people Israel, and bring them back to the land you gave to them and their ancestors.

26"When they sin against you, you will stop the rain from falling on their land. Then they will pray, facing this place and praising you; they will stop sinning when you make them suffer. 27When this happens, hear their prayer in heaven, and forgive the sins of your servants, the Israelites. Teach them to do what is right. Then please send rain to this land you have given particularly to them.

28"At times the land will get so dry that no food will grow, or a great sickness will spread among the people. Sometimes the crops will be destroyed by locusts or grasshoppers. Your people will be attacked in their cities by their enemies, or will become sick. 29When any of these things happens, the people will become truly sorry. If your people spread their hands in prayer toward this Temple, 30then hear their prayers from your home in heaven. Forgive and treat each person as he should be treated because you know what is in a person's

⚭**5:14 Music:** Daniel 3:5

⚭**6:12 Solomon:** 2 Chronicles 9:3

heart. Only you know what is in people's hearts.
31Then the people will respect and obey you as
long as they live in this land you gave our ancestors.

32"People who are not Israelites, foreigners from
other lands, will hear about your greatness and
power. They will come from far away to pray at this
Temple. 33Then hear from your home in heaven,
and do whatever they ask you. Then people everywhere will know you and respect you, just as your
people Israel do. Then everyone will know that I
built this Temple as a place to worship you.

34"When your people go out to fight their enemies along some road on which you send them,
your people will pray to you, facing this city
which you have chosen and the Temple I have built
for you. 35Then hear in heaven their prayers, and
do what is right.

36"Everyone sins, so your people will also sin
against you. You will become angry with them and
will hand them over to their enemies. Their enemies will capture them and take them away to a
country far or near. 37Your people will be sorry for
their sins when they are held as prisoners in another
country. They will be sorry and pray to you in the
land where they are held as prisoners, saying, 'We
have sinned. We have done wrong and acted
wickedly.' 38They will truly turn back to you in the
land where they are captives. They will pray, facing this land you gave their ancestors, this city you
have chosen, and the Temple I have built for you.
39Then hear their prayers from your home in
heaven and do what is right. Forgive your people
who have sinned against you.

40"Now, my God, look at us. Listen to the
prayers we pray in this place.

41Now, rise, LORD God, and come to your resting
place.
Come with the Ark of the Agreement that
shows your strength.
Let your priests receive your salvation, LORD
God,
and may your holy people be happy because
of your goodness.
42LORD God, do not reject your appointed one.
Remember your love for your servant David."

The Temple Is Given to the Lord

7 When Solomon finished praying, fire came
down from the sky and burned up the burnt
offering and the sacrifices. The LORD's glory filled
the Temple. 2The priests could not enter the
Temple of the LORD, because the LORD's glory filled
it. 3When all the people of Israel saw the fire
come down from heaven and the LORD's glory on
the Temple, they bowed down on the pavement
with their faces to the ground. They worshiped
and thanked the LORD, saying,

"He is good;
his love continues forever."

4Then King Solomon and all the people offered
sacrifices to the LORD. 5King Solomon offered a
sacrifice of twenty-two thousand cattle and one
hundred twenty thousand sheep. So the king and
all the people gave the Temple to God. 6The priests
stood ready to do their work. The Levites also
stood with the instruments of the LORD's music
that King David had made for praising the LORD.
The priests and Levites were saying, "His love continues forever." The priests, who stood across from
the Levites, blew their trumpets, and all the
Israelites were standing.

7Solomon made holy the middle part of the courtyard, which is in front of the Temple of the LORD.
There he offered whole burnt offerings and the fat
of the fellowship offerings. He offered them in the
courtyard, because the bronze altar he had made
could not hold the burnt offerings, grain offerings, and fat.

8Solomon and all the Israelites celebrated the
festival for seven days. There were many people,
and they came from as far away as Lebo Hamath
and the brook of Egypt. 9For seven days they celebrated giving the altar for the worship of God. Then
they celebrated the festival for seven days. On the
eighth day they had a meeting. 10On the twenty-
third day of the seventh month Solomon sent the
people home, full of joy. They were happy because
the LORD had been so good to David, Solomon,
and his people Israel.

The Lord Appears to Solomon

11Solomon finished the Temple of the LORD and
his royal palace. He had success in doing everything he planned in the Temple of the LORD and his
own palace. 12Then the LORD appeared to Solomon
at night and said to him, "I have heard your
prayer and have chosen this place for myself to be
a Temple for sacrifices.

13"I may stop the sky from sending rain. I may
command the locusts to destroy the land. I may send
sicknesses to my people. 14Then if my people,
who are called by my name, are sorry for what
they have done, if they pray and obey me and stop
their evil ways, I will hear them from heaven. I will
forgive their sin, and I will heal their land.⚭ 15Now

⚭**7:14 Healing:** Psalm 38

I will see them, and I will listen to the prayers
prayed in this place. [16]I have chosen this Temple
and made it holy. So I will be worshiped there forever. Yes, I will always watch over it and love it.
[17]"But you must serve me as your father David
did. You must obey all I have commanded and
keep my laws and rules. [18]If you do, I will make
your kingdom strong. This is the agreement I made
with your father David, saying, 'Someone from
your family will always rule in Israel.'
[19]"But you must follow me and obey the laws and
commands I have given you. You must not serve or
worship other gods. [20]If you do, I will take the
Israelites out of my land, the land I have given
them, and I will leave this Temple that I have made
holy. All the nations will make fun of it and speak
evil about it. [21]This Temple is honored now, but
then, everyone who passes by will be shocked.
They will ask, 'Why did the LORD do this terrible
thing to this land and this Temple?' [22]People will
answer, 'This happened because they left the LORD,
the God of their ancestors, the God who brought
them out of Egypt. They decided to follow other
gods and worshiped and served them, so he
brought all this disaster on them.'"

Solomon's Other Achievements

8 By the end of twenty years, Solomon had built
the Temple of the LORD and the royal palace.
[2]Solomon rebuilt the towns that Hiram had given
him, and Solomon sent Israelites to live in them.
[3]Then he went to Hamath Zobah and captured it.
[4]Solomon also built the town of Tadmor in the
desert, and he built all the towns in Hamath as
towns for storing grain and supplies. [5]He rebuilt
the towns of Upper Beth Horon and Lower Beth
Horon, protecting them with strong walls, gates,
and bars in the gates. [6]He also rebuilt the town of
Baalath. And he built all the other towns for storage and all the cities for his chariots and horses.
He built all he wanted in Jerusalem, Lebanon, and
everywhere he ruled.
[7]There were other people in the land who were
not Israelites—the Hittites, Amorites, Perizzites,
Hivites, and Jebusites. [8]They were descendants of
the people that the Israelites had not destroyed.
Solomon forced them to be slave workers, as is still
true today. [9]But Solomon did not make slaves of the
Israelites. They were his soldiers, chief captains,
commanders of his chariots, and his chariot drivers. [10]These were his most important officers.
There were two hundred fifty of them to direct
the people.
[11]Solomon brought the daughter of the king of
Egypt from the older part of Jerusalem to the palace
he had built for her. Solomon said, "My wife must
not live in King David's palace, because the places
where the Ark of the Agreement has been are
holy."
[12]Then Solomon offered burnt offerings to the
LORD on the altar he had built for the LORD in front
of the Temple porch. [13]He offered sacrifices every
day as Moses had commanded. They were offered
on the Sabbath days, New Moons, and the three
yearly feasts—the Feast of Unleavened Bread, the
Feast of Weeks, and the Feast of Shelters. [14]Solo-
mon followed his father David's instructions and
chose the groups of priests for their service and
the Levites to lead the praise and to help the
priests do their daily work. And he chose the
gatekeepers by their groups to serve at each gate,
as David, the man of God, had commanded. [15]They
obeyed all of Solomon's commands to the priests
and Levites, as well as his commands about the
treasuries.
[16]All Solomon's work was done as he had said
from the day the foundation of the Temple of the
LORD was begun, until it was finished. So the
Temple was finished.
[17]Then Solomon went to the towns of Ezion
Geber and Elath near the Red Sea in the land of
Edom. [18]Hiram sent ships to Solomon that were
commanded by his own men, who were skilled
sailors. Hiram's men went with Solomon's men to
Ophir and brought back about thirty-four thousand pounds of gold to King Solomon.

The Queen of Sheba Visits

9 When the queen of Sheba heard about Solomon's fame, she came to Jerusalem to test him
with hard questions. She had a large group of servants with her and camels carrying spices, jewels,
and much gold. When she came to Solomon, she
talked with him about all she had in mind, [2]and
Solomon answered all her questions. Nothing was
too hard for him to explain to her. [3]The queen of
Sheba saw that Solomon was very wise. She saw
the palace he had built, ⚭ [4]the food on his table,
his many officers, the palace servants and their
good clothes, the servants who served Solomon his
wine and their good clothes. She saw the whole
burnt offerings he made in the Temple of the LORD.
All these things amazed her.
[5]So she said to King Solomon, "What I heard in
my own country about your achievements and wisdom is true. [6]I did not believe it then, but now I

⚭ **9:3 Solomon:** Proverbs 1:1

have come and seen it with my own eyes. I was
not told even half of your great wisdom! You are
much greater than I had heard. 7Your men and
officers are very lucky, because in always serving
you, they are able to hear your wisdom. 8Praise
the LORD your God who was pleased to make you
king. He has put you on his throne to rule for the
LORD your God, because your God loves the people
of Israel and supports them forever. He has made
you king over them to keep justice and to rule
fairly."

9Then she gave the king about nine thousand
pounds of gold and many spices and jewels. No
one had ever given such spices as the queen of
Sheba gave to King Solomon.

10Hiram's men and Solomon's men brought gold
from Ophir, juniper wood, and jewels. 11King
Solomon used the juniper wood to build steps for
the Temple of the LORD and the palace and to make
lyres and harps for the musicians. No one in Judah
had ever seen such beautiful things as these.

12King Solomon gave the queen of Sheba everything she wanted and asked for, even more than
she had brought to him. Then she and her servants
returned to her own country.

Solomon's Wealth

13Every year King Solomon received about fifty
thousand pounds of gold. 14Besides that, he also
received gold from traders and merchants. All the
kings of Arabia and the governors of the land also
brought gold and silver.

15King Solomon made two hundred large shields
of hammered gold, each of which contained about
seven and one-half pounds of hammered gold. 16He
also made three hundred smaller shields of hammered gold, each of which contained about four
pounds of gold. The king put them in the Palace
of the Forest of Lebanon.

17The king built a large throne of ivory and covered it with pure gold. 18The throne had six steps
on it and a gold footstool. There were armrests on
both sides of the chair, and each armrest had a lion
beside it. 19Twelve lions stood on the six steps,
one lion at each end of each step. Nothing like this
had ever been made for any other kingdom. 20All
of Solomon's drinking cups, as well as the dishes
in the Palace of the Forest of Lebanon, were made
of pure gold. In Solomon's time people did not
think silver was valuable.

21King Solomon had many ships that he sent out
to trade, with Hiram's men as the crews. Every
three years the ships returned, bringing back gold,
silver, ivory, apes, and baboons.

22King Solomon had more riches and wisdom
than all the other kings on earth. 23All the kings
of the earth wanted to see Solomon and listen to
the wisdom God had given him. 24Year after year
everyone who came brought gifts of silver and
gold, clothes, weapons, spices, horses, and mules.

25Solomon had four thousand stalls for horses
and chariots, and he had twelve thousand horses.
He kept some in special cities for the chariots, and
others he kept with him in Jerusalem. 26Solomon
ruled over all the kingdoms from the Euphrates
River to the land of the Philistines, as far as the border of Egypt. 27In Jerusalem the king made silver as
common as stones and cedar trees as plentiful as
the fig trees on the western hills. 28Solomon
imported horses from Egypt and all other countries.

Solomon's Death

29Everything else Solomon did, from the beginning to the end, is written in the records of Nathan
the prophet, and in the prophecy of Ahijah the
Shilonite, and in the visions of Iddo the seer, who
wrote about Jeroboam, Nebat's son. 30Solomon
ruled in Jerusalem over all Israel for forty years.
31Then Solomon died and was buried in Jerusalem,
the city of David, his father. And Solomon's son
Rehoboam became king in his place.

Israel Turns Against Rehoboam

10 Rehoboam went to Shechem, where all the
Israelites had gone to make him king.
2Jeroboam son of Nebat was in Egypt, where he
had gone to escape from King Solomon. When
Jeroboam heard about Rehoboam being made
king, he returned from Egypt. 3After the people
sent for him, he and the people went to Rehoboam
and said to him, 4"Your father forced us to work
very hard. Now, make it easier for us, and don't
make us work as he did. Then we will serve you."

5Rehoboam answered, "Come back to me in
three days." So the people left.

6King Rehoboam asked the older leaders who
had advised Solomon during his lifetime, "How do
you think I should answer these people?"

7They answered, "Be kind to these people. If you
please them and give them a kind answer, they
will serve you always."

8But Rehoboam rejected this advice. Instead,
he asked the young men who had grown up with
him and who served as his advisers. 9Rehoboam
asked them, "What is your advice? How should we
answer these people who said, 'Don't make us
work as hard as your father did'?"

10The young men who had grown up with him
answered, "The people said to you, 'Your father
forced us to work very hard. Now make our work

Judah won, because they depended on the LORD, the God of their ancestors.

19Abijah's army chased Jeroboam's army and captured from him the towns of Bethel, Jeshanah, and Ephron, and the small villages near them. 20Jeroboam never became strong again while Abijah was alive. The LORD struck Jeroboam, and he died.

21But Abijah became strong. He married fourteen women and was the father of twenty-two sons and sixteen daughters. 22Everything else Abijah did—what he said and what he did—is recorded in the writings of the prophet Iddo.

14 Abijah died and was buried in Jerusalem. His son Asa became king in his place, and there was peace in the country for ten years during Asa's time.

Asa King of Judah

2Asa did what the LORD his God said was good and right. 3He removed the foreign altars and the places where gods were worshiped. He smashed the stone pillars that honored other gods, and he tore down the Asherah idols. 4Asa commanded the people of Judah to follow the LORD, the God of their ancestors, and to obey his teachings and commandments. 5He also removed the places where gods were worshiped and the incense altars from every town in Judah. So the kingdom had peace while Asa was king. 6Asa built strong, walled cities in Judah during the time of peace. He had no war in these years, because the LORD gave him peace.

7Asa said to the people of Judah, "Let's build up these towns and put walls around them. Let's make towers, gates, and bars in the gates. This country is ours, because we have obeyed the LORD our God. We have followed him, and he has given us peace all around." So they built and had success.

8Asa had an army of three hundred thousand men from Judah and two hundred eighty thousand men from Benjamin. The men from Judah carried large shields and spears. The men from Benjamin carried small shields and bows and arrows. All of them were brave fighting men.

9Then Zerah from Cush came out to fight them with an enormous army and three hundred chariots. They came as far as the town of Mareshah. 10So Asa went out to fight Zerah and prepared for battle in the Valley of Zephathah at Mareshah.

11Asa called out to the LORD his God, saying, "LORD, only you can help weak people against the strong. Help us, LORD our God, because we depend on you. We fight against this enormous army in your name. LORD, you are our God. Don't let anyone win against you."

12So the LORD defeated the Cushites when Asa's army from Judah attacked them, and the Cushites ran away. 13Asa's army chased them as far as the town of Gerar. So many Cushites were killed that the army could not fight again; they were crushed by the LORD and his army. Asa and his army carried many valuable things away from the enemy. 14They destroyed all the towns near Gerar, because the people living in these towns were afraid of the LORD. Since these towns had many valuable things, Asa's army took them away. 15Asa's army also attacked the camps where the shepherds lived and took many sheep and camels. Then they returned to Jerusalem.

Asa's Changes

15 The Spirit of God entered Azariah son of Oded. 2Azariah went to meet Asa and said, "Listen to me, Asa and all you people of Judah and Benjamin. The LORD is with you when you are with him. If you obey him, you will find him, but if you leave him, he will leave you. 3For a long time Israel was without the true God and without a priest to teach them and without the teachings. 4But when they were in trouble, they turned to the LORD, the God of Israel. They looked for him and found him. 5In those days no one could travel safely. There was much trouble in all the nations. 6One nation would destroy another nation, and one city would destroy another city, because God troubled them with all kinds of distress. 7But you should be strong. Don't give up, because you will get a reward for your good work."

8Asa felt brave when he heard these words and the message from Azariah son of Oded the prophet. So he removed the hateful idols from all of Judah and Benjamin and from the towns he had captured in the hills of Ephraim. He repaired the LORD's altar that was in front of the porch of the Temple of the LORD.

9Then Asa gathered all the people from Judah and Benjamin and from the tribes of Ephraim, Manasseh, and Simeon who were living in Judah. Many people came to Asa even from Israel, because they saw that the LORD, Asa's God, was with him.

10Asa and these people gathered in Jerusalem in the third month of the fifteenth year of Asa's rule. 11At that time they sacrificed to the LORD seven hundred bulls and seven thousand sheep and goats from the valuable things Asa's army had taken from their enemies. 12Then they made an agreement to obey the LORD, the God of their ancestors, with their whole being. 13Anyone who refused to obey the LORD, the God of Israel, was to be killed. It did not matter if that person was important or unimportant, a man or woman. 14Then Asa and the people made a promise before the LORD, shouting with a loud voice and blowing trumpets and sheep's horns. 15All the people of Judah were happy about the promise, because they had promised with all their heart. They looked for God and found him. So the LORD gave them peace in all the country.

16King Asa also removed Maacah, his grandmother, from being queen mother, because she had made a terrible Asherah idol. Asa cut down that idol, smashed it into pieces, and burned it in the Kidron Valley. 17But the places of worship to gods were not removed from Judah. Even so, Asa was faithful all his life.

18Asa brought into the Temple of God the gifts he and his father had given: silver, gold, and utensils.

19There was no more war until the thirty-fifth year of Asa's rule.

Asa's Last Years

16 In the thirty-sixth year of Asa's rule, Baasha king of Israel attacked Judah. He made the town of Ramah strong so he could keep people from leaving or entering Judah, Asa's country.

2Asa took silver and gold from the treasuries of the Temple of the LORD and out of his own palace. Then he sent it with messengers to Ben-Hadad king of Aram, who lived in Damascus. Asa said, 3"Let there be a treaty between you and me as there was between my father and your father. I am sending you silver and gold. Break your treaty with Baasha king of Israel so he will leave my land."

4Ben-Hadad agreed with King Asa and sent the commanders of his armies to attack the towns of Israel. They defeated the towns of Ijon, Dan, and Abel Beth Maacah, and all the towns in Naphtali where treasures were stored. 5When Baasha heard about this, he stopped building up Ramah and left his work. 6Then King Asa brought all the people of Judah to Ramah, and they carried away the rocks and wood that Baasha had used. And they used them to build up Geba and Mizpah.

7At that time Hanani the seer came to Asa king of Judah and said to him, "You depended on the king of Aram to help you and not on the LORD your God. So the king of Aram's army escaped from you. 8The Cushites and Libyans had a large and powerful army and many chariots and horsemen. But you depended on the LORD to help you, so he handed them over to you. 9The LORD searches all the earth for people who have given themselves completely to him. He wants to make them strong. Asa, you did a foolish thing, so from now on you will have wars."

10Asa was angry with Hanani the seer because of what he had said; he was so angry that he put Hanani in prison. And Asa was cruel to some of the people at the same time.

11Everything Asa did as king, from the beginning to the end, is written in the book of the kings of Judah and Israel. 12In the thirty-ninth year of his rule, Asa got a disease in his feet. Though his disease was very bad, he did not ask for help from the LORD, but only from the doctors. 13Then Asa died in the forty-first year of his rule. 14The people buried Asa in the tomb he had made for himself in Jerusalem. They laid him on a bed filled with spices and different kinds of mixed perfumes, and they made a large fire to honor him.

Jehoshaphat King of Judah

17 Jehoshaphat, Asa's son, became king of Judah in his place. Jehoshaphat made Judah strong so they could fight against Israel. 2He put troops in all the strong, walled cities of Judah, in the land of Judah, and in the towns of Ephraim that his father Asa had captured.

3The LORD was with Jehoshaphat, because he lived as his ancestor David had lived when he first became king. Jehoshaphat did not ask for help from the Baal idols, 4but from the God of his father. He obeyed God's commands and did not live as the people of Israel lived. 5The LORD made Jehoshaphat a strong king over Judah. All the people of Judah brought gifts to Jehoshaphat, so he had much wealth and honor. 6He wanted very much to obey the LORD. He also removed the places for worshiping gods and the Asherah idols from Judah.

7During the third year of his rule, Jehoshaphat sent his officers to teach in the towns of Judah. These officers were Ben-Hail, Obadiah, Zechariah, Nethanel, and Micaiah. 8Jehoshaphat sent with them these Levites: Shemaiah, Nethaniah, Zebadiah, Asahel, Shemiramoth, Jehonathan, Adonijah, Tobijah, and Tob-Adonijah. He also sent

16:11 *the book of the kings of Judah and Israel.* This book was in existence at the time of the writing of Chronicles, but it has never been discovered and is not inspired.

16:12–13 Many people think that King Asa sinned by going to the doctors, thus explaining why he died of his disease. Actually, there is much more to the story. For most of his life, he was known as a man who depended on the Lord, even when the odds were completely against him (see 2 Chronicles 14–15). But toward the end of his life, during a terrible crisis, he sought the help of a foreign king instead of crying out to God, Israel's true King (2 Chronicles 16:1–9). After that, he became very sick, but even in his sickness he did not ask the Lord for help, but instead turned to doctors (meaning magical or idol-worshiping "physicians"). And so he died.

the priests Elishama and Jehoram. 9These leaders, Levites, and priests taught the people in Judah. They took the Book of the Teachings of the LORD and went through all the towns of Judah and taught the people.

10The nations near Judah were afraid of the LORD, so they did not start a war against Jehoshaphat. 11Some of the Philistines brought gifts and silver to Jehoshaphat as he demanded. Some Arabs brought him flocks: seventy-seven hundred sheep and seventy-seven hundred goats.

12Jehoshaphat grew more and more powerful. He built strong, walled cities and towns for storing supplies in Judah. 13He kept many supplies in the towns of Judah, and he kept trained soldiers in Jerusalem. 14These soldiers were listed by families. From the families of Judah, these were the commanders of groups of a thousand men: Adnah was the commander of three hundred thousand soldiers; 15Jehohanan was the commander of two hundred eighty thousand soldiers; 16Amasiah was the commander of two hundred thousand soldiers. Amasiah son of Zicri had volunteered to serve the LORD.

17These were the commanders from the families of Benjamin: Eliada, a brave soldier, had two hundred thousand soldiers who used bows and shields. 18And Jehozabad had one hundred eighty thousand men armed for war.

19All these soldiers served King Jehoshaphat. The king also put other men in the strong, walled cities through all of Judah.

Micaiah Warns King Ahab

18 Jehoshaphat had much wealth and honor, and he made an agreement with King Ahab through marriage. 2A few years later Jehoshaphat went to visit Ahab in Samaria. Ahab sacrificed many sheep and cattle as a great feast to honor Jehoshaphat and the people with him. He encouraged Jehoshaphat to attack Ramoth in Gilead. 3Ahab king of Israel asked Jehoshaphat king of Judah, "Will you go with me to attack Ramoth in Gilead?"

Jehoshaphat answered, "I will go with you, and my soldiers are yours. We will join you in the battle." 4Jehoshaphat also said to Ahab, "But first we should ask if this is the LORD's will."

5So King Ahab called four hundred prophets together and asked them, "Should we go to war against Ramoth in Gilead or not?"

They answered, "Go, because God will hand them over to you."

6But Jehoshaphat asked, "Isn't there a prophet of the LORD here? Let's ask him what we should do."

7Then King Ahab said to Jehoshaphat, "There is one other prophet. We could ask the LORD through him, but I hate him. He never prophesies anything good about me, but always something bad. He is Micaiah son of Imlah."

Jehoshaphat said, "King Ahab, you shouldn't say that!"

8So Ahab king of Israel told one of his officers to bring Micaiah to him at once.

9Ahab king of Israel and Jehoshaphat king of Judah had on their royal robes and were sitting on their thrones at the threshing floor, near the entrance to the gate of Samaria. All the prophets were standing before them speaking their messages. 10Zedekiah son of Kenaanah had made some iron horns. He said to Ahab, "This is what the LORD says: 'You will use these horns to fight the Arameans until they are destroyed.'"

11All the other prophets said the same thing, "Attack Ramoth in Gilead and win, because the LORD will hand the Arameans over to you."

12The messenger who had gone to get Micaiah said to him, "All the other prophets are saying King Ahab will win. You should agree with them and give the king a good answer."

13But Micaiah answered, "As surely as the LORD lives, I can tell him only what my God says."

14When Micaiah came to Ahab, the king asked him, "Micaiah, should we attack Ramoth in Gilead or not?"

Micaiah answered, "Attack and win! They will be handed over to you."

15But Ahab said to Micaiah, "How many times do I have to tell you to speak only the truth to me in the name of the LORD?"

16So Micaiah answered, "I saw the army of Israel scattered over the hills like sheep without a shepherd. The LORD said, 'They have no leaders. They should go home and not fight.'"

17Then Ahab king of Israel said to Jehoshaphat, "I told you! He never prophesies anything good about me, but only bad."

18But Micaiah said, "Hear the message from the LORD: I saw the LORD sitting on his throne with his heavenly army standing on his right and on his left. 19The LORD said, 'Who will trick King Ahab

17:9 *the Book of the Teachings of the LORD.* This is a reference to the first five books of the Old Testament.

18:1 *agreement . . . through marriage.* Jehoshaphat's son Jehoram married Athaliah, Ahab's daughter. See 2 Chronicles 21:6.

18:14 Because of the reaction of Ahab and the whole context, it is clear that Micaiah spoke with a sarcastic tone in this verse.

18:18 Angels: Job 38:7

of Israel into attacking Ramoth in Gilead where
he will be killed?'

"Some said one thing; some said another.
20Then one spirit came and stood before the LORD
and said, 'I will trick him.'

"The LORD asked, 'How will you do it?'

21"The spirit answered, 'I will go to Ahab's
prophets and make them tell lies.'

"So the LORD said, 'You will succeed in tricking
him. Go and do it.'"

22Micaiah said, "Ahab, the LORD has made your
prophets lie to you, and the LORD has decided that
disaster should come to you."

23Then Zedekiah son of Kenaanah went up to
Micaiah and slapped him in the face. Zedekiah
said, "Has the LORD's Spirit left me to speak
through you?"

24Micaiah answered, "You will find out on the
day you go to hide in an inside room."

25Then Ahab king of Israel ordered, "Take
Micaiah and send him to Amon, the governor of
the city, and to Joash, the king's son. 26Tell them
I said to put this man in prison and give him only
bread and water until I return safely from the
battle."

27Micaiah said, "Ahab, if you come back safely
from the battle, the LORD has not spoken through
me. Remember my words, all you people!"

Ahab Is Killed

28So Ahab king of Israel and Jehoshaphat king of
Judah went to Ramoth in Gilead. 29King Ahab said
to Jehoshaphat, "I will go into battle, but I will wear
other clothes so no one will recognize me. But
you wear your royal clothes." So Ahab wore other
clothes, and they went into battle.

30The king of Aram ordered his chariot commanders, "Don't fight with anyone—important or
unimportant—except the king of Israel." 31When
these commanders saw Jehoshaphat, they thought
he was the king of Israel, so they turned to attack
him. But Jehoshaphat began shouting, and the LORD
helped him. God made the chariot commanders
turn away from Jehoshaphat. 32When they saw he
was not King Ahab, they stopped chasing him.

33By chance, a soldier shot an arrow which hit
Ahab king of Israel between the pieces of his
armor. King Ahab said to his chariot driver, "Turn
around and get me out of the battle, because I am
hurt!" 34The battle continued all day. King Ahab
held himself up in his chariot and faced the
Arameans until evening. Then he died at sunset.

19 Jehoshaphat king of Judah came back safely
to his palace in Jerusalem. 2Jehu son of
Hanani, a seer, went out to meet him and said to
the king, "Why did you help evil people? Why do
you love those who hate the LORD? That is the reason the LORD is angry with you. 3But there is some
good in you. You took the Asherah idols out of this
country, and you have tried to obey God."

Jehoshaphat Chooses Judges

4Jehoshaphat lived in Jerusalem. He went out
again to be with the people, from Beersheba to the
mountains of Ephraim, and he turned them back to
the LORD, the God of their ancestors. 5Jehoshaphat
appointed judges in all the land, in each of the
strong, walled cities of Judah. 6Jehoshaphat said to
them, "Watch what you do, because you are not
judging for people but for the LORD. He will be with
you when you make a decision. 7Now let each of
you fear the LORD. Watch what you do, because the
LORD our God wants people to be fair. He wants all
people to be treated the same, and he doesn't want
decisions influenced by money."

8And in Jerusalem Jehoshaphat appointed some
of the Levites, priests, and leaders of Israelite families to be judges. They were to decide cases about
the law of the LORD and settle problems between
the people who lived in Jerusalem. 9Jehoshaphat
commanded them, "You must always serve the
LORD completely, and you must fear him. 10Your
people living in the cities will bring you cases
about killing, about the teachings, commands,
rules, or some other law. In all these cases you
must warn the people not to sin against the LORD.
If you don't, he will be angry with you and your
people. But if you warn them, you won't be guilty.

11"Amariah, the leading priest, will be over you
in all cases about the LORD. Zebadiah son of
Ishmael, a leader in the tribe of Judah, will be over
you in all cases about the king. Also, the Levites
will serve as officers for you. Have courage. May
the LORD be with those who do what is right."

Jehoshaphat Faces War

20 Later the Moabites, Ammonites, and some
Meunites came to start a war with Jehoshaphat. 2Messengers came and told Jehoshaphat,
"A large army is coming against you from Edom,
from the other side of the Dead Sea. They are
already in Hazazon Tamar!" (Hazazon Tamar is
also called En Gedi.) 3Jehoshaphat was afraid, so he
decided to ask the LORD what to do. He announced

18:33 *by chance.* From a human point of view. The archer shot at random, but the implicit message is that God directed the shot.

19:7 Justice: Job 40:8

WATER

PSALM 46

Water appears in Scripture in many forms ranging from dew to flood, from desert wells to ocean waves. What truths can we learn from the water images in the Bible?

As Psalm 46 demonstrates, water images can carry different meanings. Verses 2–3 describe violent seas resulting from an earthquake. Verses 4–5 picture a gently flowing river providing life-giving water to the people in a city surrounded by enemy troops. In the space of four verses, water represents danger and comfort, destruction and help, terror and joy.

We can see this "split personality" of water all through the Bible. Water can either be a friend that sustains life, quenches thirst, and helps plants grow, or an enemy that threatens death and destruction. The people of the Bible who lived in desert lands had a great appreciation for "friendly" forms of water. Dew, rain, snow, streams, rivers, pools, springs, and wells are usually pictured positively in Scripture. On the other hand, biblical writings not only view storms and floods as the enemy, but also associate lakes and seas with danger. They sometimes envision evil forces and monsters residing in deep waters. The writers of the Bible would have been surprised at the way we view rivers, lakes, and oceans as vacation playgrounds.

The biblical viewpoint on water differs from our modern viewpoint in another, more important way. With our scientific mind-set, we tend to assume that all forms of water are simply natural. But in the Bible, water is seen to have supernatural significance. God not only created water in the beginning, he continually controls its actions and effects to further his own purposes. Thus, when rain falls and streams flow, this is evidence that God takes care of his world like a devoted gardener.

Biblical writers also believed that God used water, or the lack of water, to punish people who tried to block his purposes. He told Noah, "Because people have made the earth full of violence, . . . I will bring a flood of water on the earth to destroy all living things that live under the sky" (Genesis 6:13, 17). Later God used water to defeat the Egyptians who had made his people slaves: "The chariots and soldiers of the king of Egypt he has thrown into the sea. . . . They sank like lead in the raging water" (Exodus 15:4, 10). Still later, when God's people failed to rebuild the Temple in Jerusalem, God proclaimed, "Because of what you have done, the sky holds back its rain and the ground holds back its crops" (Haggai 1:10).

In the New Testament, one sign that Jesus is indeed God is that he has the same power over water that God used throughout the Old Testament. However, Jesus never used water to punish sinners. Instead, he walked on the waves to bring comfort to his disciples and calmed the storm to build their faith.

Since water plays such a crucial role in the world and for humans, it is not surprising that it is often used to mean other things in Scripture. Some forms stand for trouble and evil. Military conquest is compared to a flood in Isaiah 8:7–8. Divine judgment affects sinners like poisoned water in Jeremiah 8:14. False teachings are like waves that can push immature Christians one way, then another in Ephesians 4:14. Satan's opposition to the coming of Christ is symbolized by water poured from a serpent's mouth in Revelation 12:15.

Friendly forms of water are used in the Bible to represent all kinds of good gifts God gives us—his Word, the Holy Spirit, life, strength, joy, peace, renewal, fruitfulness, healing, salvation. Isaiah 55:10–11 compares God's words to rain and snow that water the ground and bring growth and nourishment. Jeremiah 17:7–8 says that "the person who trusts in the LORD will be . . . strong, like a tree planted near water that sends its roots by a stream." The "living water" Jesus offers the Samaritan woman in John 4:7–14 symbolizes the eternal life and fulfillment that can be found only in him. In Titus 3:4–6, the Holy Spirit is pictured as water which is poured out on believers to cleanse them and give them new life.

Because water can stand for so many of the blessings God gives, it is often used to show us the perfect kingdom God will establish at the end of time. In Revelation 22:1–2 John sees "the river of the water of life" flowing through the new Jerusalem. "It was shining like crystal and was flowing from the throne of God and of the Lamb down the middle of the street of the city. The tree of life was on each side of the river. . . . The leaves of the tree are for the healing of all the nations."

From Genesis, when "God's Spirit was moving over the water," to Revelation, which promises "the water of life as a free gift," we see water playing a powerful role, emphasizing God's personal involvement in his world. Sometimes water images are frightening, reminding us of God's determination to judge sin and wipe out evil. But often water shows us God's deep desire to give his human creatures abundant life and everlasting joy.

Water: For additional scriptures on this topic go to Genesis 6–7.

Praise

Psalm 66

What are psalms of praise? How do we worship God?
How do the Psalms speak about living in a fallen world?

The Book of Psalms is a collection of songs Israelite people used when they worshipped God. Many psalms are songs of praise which declare God's greatness, power, and excellence. But psalms are more than praise songs. They show a wide range of emotions—gladness, joy, hope, sadness, grief, and despair. The Psalms are very personal conversations with God in which the writers' deepest longings and beliefs are expressed. By looking at Psalm 66 and other passages we learn who is to praise God, how to praise God, and where and when to praise God.

Psalm 66:1 is clear that "everything on earth" is to praise God. This "everything" includes God's chosen people (Psalm 148:14 and 135:19), the nations and rulers of this earth (Psalm 67:34), angels (Psalm 148:2 and 103:20), and all of creation (Psalm 148 and Psalm 69:34).

God can be praised anytime, anywhere, but Scripture does mention some specific times and places. God should be praised in public settings. For Old Testament Israel, this meant praising God in the Temple. For Christians, it means praising God in church meetings. God is also praised in private and in the evening. Psalm 63:6–7 says, "I remember you while I'm lying in bed; I think about you through the night. You are my help. Because of your protection, I sing." Psalm 35:28 encourages men and women to praise God every day.

It would be impossible to give a complete list of the kinds of things for which we praise God, but Psalm 66 offers several examples. First, the writer praises God for his character. In verse 2–3 he mentions God's glory and power. Verse 7 proclaims, "He rules forever with his power" (Psalm 66:7). In other words, God sits on the throne of the universe and controls its destiny. A second reason to praise God is "what God has done, the amazing things he has done for people" (Psalm 66:5). In verse 6 the writer mentions two events from Israel's history: when God turned the Red Sea into dry land (Exodus 14) and when the Israelites crossed the Jordan River on foot (Joshua 3). In verses 8–12 the writer moves from past acts of God to his current deeds. The people had gone through a time of testing when they feared defeat by their enemies. But God protected their lives, kept them from defeat, and brought them to a place filled with good things. Praise is also offered to God for listening to the prayers of his people in Psalm 66:20.

God is a good and all-powerful God, but suffering, sin, and death continue to exist and affect God's people. This concern appears briefly in Psalm 66:8–12. The people went through a time of testing and sank into despair, but God brought Israel through the fire and flood to a place filled with good things. God saves and delivers them from their suffering. The Book of Psalms addresses our everyday life by showing the tension which exists between good and evil in the lives of believers.

The writer does not say whether or not the suffering was a result of the nation's sin, and it would be impossible to figure out the specific reason why the predicament occurred. But the event illustrates the fact that believers come into contact with pain and suffering regularly. Psalms which focus on asking God for relief from troubles reflect the problem of suffering and evil. "Lord, why are you so far away? Why do you hide when there is trouble? Proudly the wicked chase down those who suffer. Let them be caught in their own traps" (Psalm 10:1–2). (See also: Psalms 13:1–3, 69:1–4, 73:1–12.)

But the Psalms also speak of God's love and protection. "The Lord defends those who suffer; he defends them in times of trouble. Those who know the LORD trust him, because he will not leave those who come to him" (Psalm 9:9–10). (See also: Psalms 28:6–9, 34:4–5, 36:5–7.) These Psalms affirm God's love and protection toward those who seek him. The writers speak of God's deliverance from suffering and persecution, but they do not speak of God keeping us from all pain and trials.

The tension of a good and all-powerful God ruling a world in which evil exists is resolved at the second coming of Christ, when evil, suffering, oppression, and death are ended (Revelation 21:1–4). The consummation of God's kingdom is celebrated through songs recorded in the book of Revelation. These songs are the psalms of the New Testament. "The power to rule the world now belongs to our Lord and to his Christ, and he will rule forever and ever" (Revelation 11:15). "We give thanks to you, Lord God Almighty, who is and who was, because you have used your great power and have begun to rule (v. 16)!" Give thanks to God for delivering you from daily troubles and praise him for the ultimate victory he has won in Jesus Christ!⚭

⚭ **Praise:** For additional sriptures on this topic go to Psalm 18.

that no one in Judah should eat during this special time of prayer to God. 4The people of Judah came together to ask the LORD for help; they came from every town in Judah.

5The people of Judah and Jerusalem met in front of the new courtyard in the Temple of the LORD. Then Jehoshaphat stood up, 6and he said, "LORD, God of our ancestors, you are the God in heaven. You rule over all the kingdoms of the nations. You have power and strength, so no one can stand against you. 7Our God, you forced out the people who lived in this land as your people Israel moved in. And you gave this land forever to the descendants of your friend Abraham. 8They lived in this land and built a Temple for you. They said, 9'If trouble comes upon us, or war, punishment, sickness, or hunger, we will stand before you and before this Temple where you have chosen to be worshiped. We will cry out to you when we are in trouble. Then you will hear and save us.'

10"But now here are men from Ammon, Moab, and Edom. You wouldn't let the Israelites enter their lands when the Israelites came from Egypt. So the Israelites turned away and did not destroy them. 11But see how they repay us for not destroying them! They have come to force us out of your land, which you gave us as our own. 12Our God, punish those people. We have no power against this large army that is attacking us. We don't know what to do, so we look to you for help."

13All the men of Judah stood before the LORD with their babies, wives, and children. 14Then the Spirit of the LORD entered Jahaziel. (Jahaziel was Zechariah's son. Zechariah was Benaiah's son. Benaiah was Jeiel's son, and Jeiel was Mattaniah's son.) Jahaziel, a Levite and a descendant of Asaph, stood up in the meeting. 15He said, "Listen to me, King Jehoshaphat and all you people living in Judah and Jerusalem. The LORD says this to you: 'Don't be afraid or discouraged because of this large army. The battle is not your battle, it is God's. 16Tomorrow go down there and fight those people. They will come up through the Pass of Ziz. You will find them at the end of the ravine that leads to the Desert of Jeruel. 17You won't need to fight in this battle. Just stand strong in your places, and you will see the LORD save you. Judah and Jerusalem, don't be afraid or discouraged, because the LORD is with you. So go out against those people tomorrow.'"

18Jehoshaphat bowed facedown on the ground. All the people of Judah and Jerusalem bowed down before the LORD and worshiped him. 19Then some Levites from the Kohathite and Korahite people stood up and praised the LORD, the God of Israel, with very loud voices.

20Jehoshaphat's army went out into the Desert of Tekoa early in the morning. As they were starting out, Jehoshaphat stood and said, "Listen to me, people of Judah and Jerusalem. Have faith in the LORD your God, and you will stand strong. Have faith in his prophets, and you will succeed." 21Jehoshaphat listened to the people's advice. Then he chose men to be singers to the LORD, to praise him because he is holy and wonderful. As they marched in front of the army, they said,

"Thank the LORD,
because his love continues forever."

22As they began to sing and praise God, the LORD set ambushes for the people of Ammon, Moab, and Edom who had come to attack Judah. And they were defeated. 23The Ammonites and Moabites attacked the Edomites, destroying them completely. After they had killed the Edomites, they killed each other.

24When the men from Judah came to a place where they could see the desert, they looked at the enemy's large army. But they only saw dead bodies lying on the ground; no one had escaped. 25When Jehoshaphat and his army came to take their valuables, they found many supplies, much clothing, and other valuable things. There was more than they could carry away; there was so much it took three days to gather it all. 26On the fourth day Jehoshaphat and his army met in the Valley of Beracah and praised the LORD. That is why that place has been called the Valley of Beracah to this day.

27Then Jehoshaphat led all the men from Judah and Jerusalem back to Jerusalem. The LORD had made them happy because their enemies were defeated. 28They entered Jerusalem with harps, lyres, and trumpets and went to the Temple of the LORD.

29When all the kingdoms of the lands around them heard how the LORD had fought Israel's enemies, they feared God. 30So Jehoshaphat's kingdom was not at war. His God gave him peace from all the countries around him.

Jehoshaphat's Rule Ends

31Jehoshaphat ruled over the country of Judah. He was thirty-five years old when he became king, and he ruled in Jerusalem for twenty-five years. His mother's name was Azubah daughter of

20:3 Fasting: Ezra 8:21–23
20:23 Holy War & Divine Warrior: Psalm 24:8

20:26 *Beracah.* This name means "blessing" or "praise."

Shilhi. 32Jehoshaphat was good like his father Asa, and he did what the LORD said was right. 33But the places where gods were worshiped were not removed, and the people did not really want to follow the God of their ancestors.

34The other things Jehoshaphat did as king, from the beginning to the end, are written in the records of Jehu son of Hanani, which are in the book of the kings of Israel.

35Later, Jehoshaphat king of Judah made a treaty with Ahaziah king of Israel, which was a wrong thing to do. 36Jehoshaphat agreed with Ahaziah to build trading ships, which they built in the town of Ezion Geber. 37Then Eliezer son of Dodavahu from the town of Mareshah spoke against Jehoshaphat. He said, "Jehoshaphat, because you joined with Ahaziah, the LORD will destroy what you have made." The ships were wrecked so they could not sail out to trade.

21 Jehoshaphat died and was buried with his ancestors in Jerusalem, the city of David. Then his son Jehoram became king in his place. 2Jehoram's brothers were Azariah, Jehiel, Zechariah, Azariahu, Michael, and Shephatiah. They were the sons of Jehoshaphat king of Judah. 3Jehoshaphat gave his sons many gifts of silver, gold, and valuable things, and he gave them strong, walled cities in Judah. But Jehoshaphat gave the kingdom to Jehoram, because he was the first son.

Jehoram King of Judah

4When Jehoram took control of his father's kingdom, he killed all his brothers with a sword and also killed some of the leaders of Judah. 5He was thirty-two years old when he began to rule, and he ruled eight years in Jerusalem. 6He followed in the ways of the kings of Israel, just as the family of Ahab had done, because he married Ahab's daughter. Jehoram did what the LORD said was wrong. 7But the LORD would not destroy David's family because of the agreement he had made with David. He had promised that one of David's descendants would always rule.

8In Jehoram's time, Edom broke away from Judah's rule and chose their own king. 9So Jehoram went to Edom with all his commanders and chariots. The Edomites surrounded him and his chariot commanders, but Jehoram got up and attacked the Edomites at night. 10From then until now the country of Edom has fought against the rule of Judah. At the same time the people of Libnah also broke away from Jehoram because Jehoram left the LORD, the God of his ancestors.

11Jehoram also built places to worship gods on the hills in Judah. He led the people of Jerusalem to sin, and he led the people of Judah away from the LORD. 12Then Jehoram received this letter from Elijah the prophet:

> This is what the LORD, the God of your ancestor David, says, "Jehoram, you have not lived as your father Jehoshaphat lived and as Asa king of Judah lived.∞ 13But you have lived as the kings of Israel lived, leading the people of Judah and Jerusalem to sin against God, as Ahab and his family did. You have killed your brothers, and they were better than you. 14So now the LORD is about to punish your people, your children, wives, and everything you own. 15You will have a terrible disease in your intestines that will become worse every day. Finally it will cause your intestines to come out."

16The LORD caused the Philistines and the Arabs who lived near the Cushites to be angry with Jehoram. 17So the Philistines and Arabs attacked Judah and carried away all the wealth of Jehoram's palace, as well as his sons and wives. Only Jehoram's youngest son, Ahaziah, was left.

18After these things happened, the LORD gave Jehoram a disease in his intestines that could not be cured. 19After he was sick for two years, Jehoram's intestines came out because of the disease, and he died in terrible pain. The people did not make a fire to honor Jehoram as they had done for his ancestors.

20Jehoram was thirty-two years old when he became king, and he ruled eight years in Jerusalem. No one was sad when he died. He was buried in Jerusalem, but not in the graves for the kings.

Ahaziah King of Judah

22 The people of Jerusalem chose Ahaziah, Jehoram's youngest son, to be king in his place. The robbers who had come with the Arabs to attack Jehoram's camp had killed all of Jehoram's older sons. So Ahaziah began to rule Judah. 2Ahaziah was twenty-two years old when he became king, and he ruled one year in Jerusalem. His mother's name was Athaliah, a granddaughter of Omri. 3Ahaziah followed the ways of Ahab's family, because his mother encouraged him to do wrong. 4Ahaziah did what the LORD said was wrong, as Ahab's family had done. They gave advice to Ahaziah after his father died, and

∞**21:12 Elijah and Elisha:** Malachi 4:5–6

their bad advice led to his death. 5Following their advice, Ahaziah went with Joram son of Ahab to Ramoth in Gilead, where they fought against Hazael king of Aram. The Arameans wounded Joram. 6So Joram returned to Jezreel to heal from the wounds he received at Ramoth when he fought Hazael king of Aram.

Ahaziah son of Jehoram and king of Judah went down to visit Joram son of Ahab at Jezreel because he had been wounded.

7God caused Ahaziah's death when he went to visit Joram. Ahaziah arrived and went out with Joram to meet Jehu son of Nimshi, whom the LORD had appointed to destroy Ahab's family. 8While Jehu was punishing Ahab's family, he found the leaders of Judah and the sons of Ahaziah's relatives who served Ahaziah, and Jehu killed them all. 9Then Jehu looked for Ahaziah. Jehu's men caught him hiding in Samaria, so they brought him to Jehu. Then they killed and buried him. They said, "Ahaziah is a descendant of Jehoshaphat, and Jehoshaphat obeyed the LORD with all his heart." No one in Ahaziah's family had the power to take control of the kingdom of Judah.

Athaliah and Joash

10When Ahaziah's mother, Athaliah, saw that her son was dead, she killed all the royal family in Judah. 11But Jehosheba, King Jehoram's daughter, took Joash, Ahaziah's son. She stole him from among the other sons of the king who were going to be murdered and put him and his nurse in a bedroom. So Jehosheba, who was King Jehoram's daughter and Ahaziah's sister and the wife of Jehoiada the priest, hid Joash so Athaliah could not kill him. 12He hid with them in the Temple of God for six years. During that time Athaliah ruled the land.

23 In the seventh year Jehoiada decided to do something. He made an agreement with the commanders of the groups of a hundred men: Azariah son of Jeroham, Ishmael son of Jehohanan, Azariah son of Obed, Maaseiah son of Adaiah, and Elishaphat son of Zicri. 2They went around in Judah and gathered the Levites from all the towns, and they gathered the leaders of the families of Judah. Then they went to Jerusalem. 3All the people together made an agreement with the king in the Temple of God.

Jehoiada said to them, "The king's son will rule, as the LORD promised about David's descendants. 4Now this is what you must do: You priests and Levites go on duty on the Sabbath. A third of you will guard the doors. 5A third of you will be at the king's palace, and a third of you will be at the Foundation Gate. All the other people will stay in the courtyards of the Temple of the LORD. 6Don't let anyone come into the Temple of the LORD except the priests and Levites who serve. They may come because they have been made ready to serve the LORD, but all the others must do the job the LORD has given them. 7The Levites must stay near the king, each man with his weapon in his hand. If anyone tries to enter the Temple, kill him. Stay close to the king when he goes in and when he goes out."

Joash Becomes King

8The Levites and all the people of Judah obeyed everything Jehoiada the priest had commanded. He did not excuse anyone from the groups of the priests. So each commander took his men who came on duty on the Sabbath with those who went off duty on the Sabbath. 9Jehoiada gave the commanders of a hundred men the spears and the large and small shields that had belonged to King David and that were kept in the Temple of God. 10Then Jehoiada told the men where to stand, each man with his weapon in his hand. There were guards from the south side of the Temple to the north side. They stood by the altar and the Temple and around the king.

11Jehoiada and his sons brought out the king's son and put the crown on him and gave him a copy of the agreement. Then they appointed him king and poured olive oil on him and shouted, "Long live the king!"

12When Athaliah heard the noise of the people running and praising the king, she went to them at the Temple of the LORD. 13She looked, and there was the king standing by his pillar at the entrance. The officers and the trumpeters were standing beside him, and all the people of the land were happy and blowing trumpets. The singers were playing musical instruments and leading praises. Then Athaliah tore her clothes and screamed, "Traitors! Traitors!"

14Jehoiada the priest sent out the commanders of a hundred men, who led the army. He said, "Surround her with soldiers and take her out of the Temple area. Kill with a sword anyone who follows her." He had said, "Don't put Athaliah to death in the Temple of the LORD." 15So they caught her when she came to the entrance of the Horse Gate near the palace. There they put her to death.

16Then Jehoiada made an agreement with the people and the king that they would be the LORD's special people. 17All the people went to the temple of Baal and tore it down, smashing the altars and idols. They killed Mattan, the priest of Baal, in front of the altars.

18Then Jehoiada chose the priests, who were Levites, to be responsible for the Temple of the LORD. David had given them duties in the Temple of the LORD. They were to offer the burnt offerings to the LORD as the Teachings of Moses commanded, and they were to offer them with much joy and singing as David had commanded. 19Jehoiada put guards at the gates of the Temple of the LORD so that anyone who was unclean in any way could not enter.

20Jehoiada took with him the commanders of a hundred men, the important men, the rulers of the people, and all the people of the land to take the king out of the Temple of the LORD. They went through the Upper Gate into the palace, and then they seated the king on the throne. 21So all the people of the land were very happy, and Jerusalem had peace, because Athaliah had been put to death with the sword.

Joash Repairs the Temple

24 Joash was seven years old when he became king, and he ruled forty years in Jerusalem. His mother's name was Zibiah, and she was from Beersheba. 2Joash did what the LORD said was right as long as Jehoiada the priest was alive. 3Jehoiada chose two wives for Joash, and Joash had sons and daughters.

4Later, Joash decided to repair the Temple of the LORD. 5He called the priests and the Levites together and said to them, "Go to the towns of Judah and gather the money all the Israelites have to pay every year. Use it to repair the Temple of your God. Do this now." But the Levites did not hurry.

6So King Joash called for Jehoiada the leading priest and said to him, "Why haven't you made the Levites bring in from Judah and Jerusalem the tax money that Moses, the LORD's servant, and the people of Israel used for the Holy Tent?"

7In the past the sons of wicked Athaliah had broken into the Temple of God and used its holy things for worshiping the Baal idols.

8King Joash commanded that a box for contributions be made. They put it outside, at the gate of the Temple of the LORD. 9Then the Levites made an announcement in Judah and Jerusalem, telling people to bring to the LORD the tax money Moses, the servant of God, had made the Israelites give while they were in the desert. 10All the officers and people were happy to bring their money, and they put it in the box until the box was full. 11When the Levites would take the box to the king's officers, they would see that it was full of money. Then the king's royal secretary and the leading priest's officer would come and take out the money and return the box to its place. They did this often and gathered much money. 12King Joash and Jehoiada gave the money to the people who worked on the Temple of the LORD. And they hired stoneworkers and carpenters to repair the Temple of the LORD. They also hired people to work with iron and bronze to repair the Temple.

13The people worked hard, and the work to repair the Temple went well. They rebuilt the Temple of God to be as it was before, but even stronger. 14When the workers finished, they brought the money that was left to King Joash and Jehoiada. They used that money to make utensils for the Temple of the LORD, utensils for the service in the Temple and for the burnt offerings, and bowls and other utensils from gold and silver. Burnt offerings were given every day in the Temple of the LORD while Jehoiada was alive.

15Jehoiada grew old and lived many years. Then he died when he was one hundred thirty years old. 16Jehoiada was buried in Jerusalem with the kings, because he had done much good in Judah for God and his Temple.

Joash Does Evil

17After Jehoiada died, the officers of Judah came and bowed down to King Joash, and he listened to them. 18The king and these leaders stopped worshiping in the Temple of the LORD, the God of their ancestors. Instead, they began to worship the Asherah idols and other idols. Because they did wrong, God was angry with the people of Judah and Jerusalem. 19Even though the LORD sent prophets to the people to turn them back to him and even though the prophets warned them, they refused to listen.

20Then the Spirit of God entered Zechariah son of Jehoiada the priest. Zechariah stood before the people and said, "This is what God says: 'Why do you disobey the LORD's commands? You will not be successful. Because you have left the LORD, he has also left you.'"

21But the king and his officers made plans against Zechariah. At the king's command they threw stones at him in the courtyard of the Temple of the LORD until he died. 22King Joash did not remember Jehoiada's kindness to him, so Joash killed Zechariah, Jehoiada's son. Before Zechariah died, he said, "May the LORD see what you are doing and punish you."

23At the end of the year, the Aramean army came against Joash. They attacked Judah and Jerusalem, killed all the leaders of the people, and sent all the valuable things to their king in Damascus. 24The Aramean army came with only a small group of men, but the LORD handed over to them a very large army from Judah, because the people of Judah had left the LORD, the God of their ancestors. So Joash was punished. 25When the Arameans left, Joash was badly wounded. His own officers made plans against him because he had killed Zechariah son of Jehoiada the priest. So they killed Joash in his own bed. He died and was buried in Jerusalem but not in the graves of the kings.

26The officers who made plans against Joash were Jozabad and Jehozabad. Jozabad was the son of Shimeath, a woman from Ammon. And Jehozabad was the son of Shimrith, a woman from Moab. 27The story of Joash's sons, the great prophecies against him, and how he repaired the Temple of God are written in the book of the kings. Joash's son Amaziah became king in his place.

Amaziah King of Judah

25 Amaziah was twenty-five years old when he became king, and he ruled for twenty-nine years in Jerusalem. His mother's name was Jehoaddin, and she was from Jerusalem. 2Amaziah did what the LORD said was right, but he did not really want to obey him. 3As soon as Amaziah took strong control of the kingdom, he executed the officers who had murdered his father the king. 4But Amaziah did not put to death their children. He obeyed what was written in the Book of Moses, where the LORD commanded, "Parents must not be put to death when their children do wrong, and children must not be put to death when their parents do wrong. Each must die for his own sins."

5Amaziah gathered the people of Judah together. He grouped all the people of Judah and Benjamin by families, and he put commanders over groups of a thousand and over groups of a hundred. He counted the men who were twenty years old and older. In all there were three hundred thousand soldiers ready to fight and skilled with spears and shields. 6Amaziah also hired one hundred thousand soldiers from Israel for about seventy-five hundred pounds of silver. 7But a man of God came to Amaziah and said, "My king, don't let the army of Israel go with you. The LORD is not with Israel or the people from the tribe of Ephraim. 8You can make yourself strong for war, but God will defeat you. He has the power to help you or to defeat you."

9Amaziah said to the man of God, "But what about the seventy-five hundred pounds of silver I paid to the Israelite army?"

The man of God answered, "The LORD can give you much more than that."

10So Amaziah sent the Israelite army back home to Ephraim. They were very angry with the people of Judah and went home angry.

11Then Amaziah became very brave and led his army to the Valley of Salt in the country of Edom. There Amaziah's army killed ten thousand Edomites. 12The army of Judah also captured ten thousand and took them to the top of a cliff and threw them off so that they split open.

13At the same time the Israelite troops that Amaziah had not let fight in the war were robbing towns in Judah. From Samaria to Beth Horon they killed three thousand people and took many valuable things.

14When Amaziah came home after defeating the Edomites, he brought back the idols they worshiped and started to worship them himself. He bowed down to them and offered sacrifices to them. 15The LORD was very angry with Amaziah, so he sent a prophet to him who said, "Why have you asked their gods for help? They could not even save their own people from you!"

16As the prophet spoke, Amaziah said to him, "We never gave you the job of advising the king. Stop, or you will be killed."

The prophet stopped speaking except to say, "I know that God has decided to destroy you because you have done this. You did not listen to my advice."

17Amaziah king of Judah talked with those who advised him. Then he sent a message to Jehoash son of Jehoahaz, who was the son of Jehu king of Israel. Amaziah said to Jehoash, "Come, let's meet face to face."

18Then Jehoash king of Israel answered Amaziah king of Judah, "A thornbush in Lebanon sent a message to a cedar tree in Lebanon. It said, 'Let your daughter marry my son.' But then a wild animal from Lebanon came by, walking on and crushing the thornbush. 19You say to yourself that you have defeated Edom, but you have become proud, and you brag. But you stay at home! Don't ask for trouble, or you and Judah will be defeated."

20But Amaziah would not listen. God caused this to happen so that Jehoash would defeat Judah, because Judah asked for help from the gods of Edom. 21So Jehoash king of Israel went to attack. He and Amaziah king of Judah faced each other in battle at Beth Shemesh in Judah. 22Israel defeated Judah, and every man of Judah ran away to his

25:4 *"Parents . . . sins."* See Deuteronomy 24:16.

home. 23At Beth Shemesh Jehoash king of Israel captured Amaziah king of Judah. (Amaziah was the son of Joash, who was the son of Ahaziah.) Then Jehoash brought him to Jerusalem. Jehoash broke down the wall of Jerusalem, from the Gate of Ephraim to the Corner Gate, about six hundred feet. 24He took all the gold and silver and all the utensils from the Temple of God that Obed-Edom had taken care of. He also took the treasures from the palace and some hostages. Then he returned to Samaria.

25Amaziah son of Joash, the king of Judah, lived fifteen years after the death of Jehoash son of Jehoahaz, the king of Israel. 26The other things Amaziah did as king, from the beginning to the end, are written in the book of the kings of Judah and Israel. 27When Amaziah stopped obeying the LORD, the people in Jerusalem made plans against him. So he ran away to the town of Lachish, but they sent men after him to Lachish and killed him. 28They brought his body back on horses, and he was buried with his ancestors in Jerusalem, the city of David.

Uzziah King of Judah

26 Then all the people of Judah made Uzziah king in place of his father Amaziah. Uzziah was sixteen years old. 2He rebuilt the town of Elath and made it part of Judah again after Amaziah died.

3Uzziah was sixteen years old when he became king, and he ruled fifty-two years in Jerusalem. His mother's name was Jecoliah, and she was from Jerusalem. 4He did what the LORD said was right, just as his father Amaziah had done. 5Uzziah obeyed God while Zechariah was alive, because he taught Uzziah how to respect and obey God. And as long as Uzziah obeyed the LORD, God gave him success.

6Uzziah fought a war against the Philistines. He tore down the walls around their towns of Gath, Jabneh, and Ashdod and built new towns near Ashdod and in other places among the Philistines. 7God helped Uzziah fight the Philistines, the Arabs living in Gur Baal, and the Meunites. 8Also, the Ammonites made the payments Uzziah demanded. He was very powerful, so his name became famous all the way to the border of Egypt.

9Uzziah built towers in Jerusalem at the Corner Gate, the Valley Gate, and where the wall turned, and he made them strong. 10He also built towers in the desert and dug many wells, because he had many cattle on the western hills and in the plains. He had people who worked his fields and vineyards in the hills and in the fertile lands, because he loved the land.

11Uzziah had an army of trained soldiers. They were counted and put in groups by Jeiel the royal secretary and Maaseiah the officer. Hananiah, one of the king's commanders, was their leader. 12There were twenty-six hundred leaders over the soldiers. 13They were in charge of an army of three hundred seven thousand five hundred men who fought with great power to help the king against the enemy. 14Uzziah gave his army shields, spears, helmets, armor, bows, and stones for their slings. 15In Jerusalem Uzziah made devices that were invented by clever men. These devices on the towers and corners of the city walls were used to shoot arrows and large rocks. So Uzziah became famous in faraway places, because he had much help until he became powerful.

16But when Uzziah became powerful, his pride led to his ruin. He was unfaithful to the LORD his God; he went into the Temple of the LORD to burn incense on the altar for incense. 17Azariah and eighty other brave priests who served the LORD followed Uzziah into the Temple. 18They told him he was wrong and said to him, "You don't have the right to burn incense to the LORD. Only the priests, Aaron's descendants, should burn the incense, because they have been made holy. Leave this holy place. You have been unfaithful, and the LORD God will not honor you for this."

19Uzziah was standing beside the altar for incense in the Temple of the LORD, and in his hand was a pan for burning incense. He was very angry with the priests. As he was standing in front of the priests, a skin disease broke out on his forehead. 20Azariah, the leading priest, and all the other priests looked at him and saw the skin disease on his forehead. So they hurried him out of the Temple. Uzziah also rushed out, because the LORD was punishing him. 21So King Uzziah had the skin disease until the day he died. He had to live in a separate house and could not enter the Temple of the LORD. His son Jotham was in charge of the palace, and he governed the people of the land.

22The other things Uzziah did as king, from beginning to end, were written down by the prophet Isaiah son of Amoz. 23Uzziah died and was buried near his ancestors in a graveyard that belonged to the kings. This was because people

25:26 *the book of the kings of Judah and Israel.* See 16:11.
26:1 *Uzziah.* Also called Azariah.
26:19 *skin disease.* Traditionally understood to be leprosy, but taken more generally because this traditional translation is now known to be a mistake.

said, "He had a skin disease." And his son Jotham became king in his place.

Jotham King of Judah

27 Jotham was twenty-five years old when he became king, and he ruled sixteen years in Jerusalem. His mother's name was Jerusha daughter of Zadok. [2]Jotham did what the LORD said was right, just as his father Uzziah had done. But Jotham did not enter the Temple of the LORD to burn incense as his father had. But the people continued doing wrong. [3]Jotham rebuilt the Upper Gate of the Temple of the LORD, and he added greatly to the wall at Ophel. [4]He also built towns in the hill country of Judah, as well as walled cities and towers in the forests.

[5]Jotham also fought the king of the Ammonites and defeated them. So each year for three years they gave Jotham about seventy-five hundred pounds of silver, about sixty-two thousand bushels of wheat, and about sixty-two thousand bushels of barley. [6]Jotham became powerful, because he always obeyed the LORD his God.

[7]The other things Jotham did while he was king and all his wars are written in the book of the kings of Israel and Judah. [8]Jotham was twenty-five years old when he became king, and he ruled sixteen years in Jerusalem. [9]Jotham died and was buried in Jerusalem, the city of David. Then Jotham's son Ahaz became king in his place.

Ahaz King of Judah

28 Ahaz was twenty years old when he became king, and he ruled sixteen years in Jerusalem. Unlike his ancestor David, he did not do what the LORD said was right. [2]Ahaz did the same things the kings of Israel had done. He made metal idols to worship Baal. [3]He burned incense in the Valley of Ben Hinnom and made his children pass through the fire. He did the same hateful sins as the nations had done whom the LORD had forced out of the land ahead of the Israelites. [4]Ahaz offered sacrifices and burned incense at the places where gods were worshiped, and on the hills, and under every green tree.

[5]So the LORD his God handed over Ahaz to the king of Aram. The Arameans defeated Ahaz and took many people of Judah as prisoners to Damascus.

He also handed over Ahaz to Pekah king of Israel, and Pekah's army killed many soldiers of Ahaz. [6]The army of Pekah son of Remaliah killed one hundred twenty thousand brave soldiers from Judah in one day. Pekah defeated them because they had left the LORD, the God of their ancestors. [7]Zicri, a warrior from Ephraim, killed King Ahaz's son Maaseiah. He also killed Azrikam, the officer in charge of the palace, and Elkanah, who was second in command to the king. [8]The Israelite army captured two hundred thousand of their own relatives. They took women, sons and daughters, and many valuable things from Judah and carried them back to Samaria. [9]But a prophet of the LORD named Oded was there. He met the Israelite army when it returned to Samaria and said to them, "The LORD, the God of your ancestors, handed Judah over to you, because he was angry with those people. But God has seen the cruel way you killed them. [10]Now you plan to make the people of Judah and Jerusalem your slaves, but you also have sinned against the LORD your God. [11]Now listen to me. Send back your brothers and sisters whom you captured, because the LORD is very angry with you."

[12]Then some of the leaders in Ephraim—Azariah son of Jehohanan, Berekiah son of Meshillemoth, Jehizkiah son of Shallum, and Amasa son of Hadlai—met the Israelite soldiers coming home from war. [13]They warned the soldiers, "Don't bring the prisoners from Judah here. If you do, we will be guilty of sin against the LORD, and that will make our sin and guilt even worse. Our guilt is already so great that he is angry with Israel."

[14]So the soldiers left the prisoners and valuable things in front of the officers and people there. [15]The leaders who were named took the prisoners and gave those who were naked the clothes that the Israelite army had taken. They gave the prisoners clothes, sandals, food, drink, and medicine. They put the weak prisoners on donkeys and took them back to their families in Jericho, the city of palm trees. Then they returned home to Samaria.

[16-17]At that time the Edomites came again and attacked Judah and carried away prisoners. So King Ahaz sent to the king of Assyria for help. [18]The Philistines also robbed the towns in the western hills and in southern Judah. They captured the towns of Beth Shemesh, Aijalon, Gederoth, Soco, Timnah, and Gimzo, and the villages around them. Then the Philistines lived in those towns. [19]The LORD brought trouble on Judah because Ahaz their king led the people of Judah to sin, and he was unfaithful to the LORD. [20]Tiglath-Pileser king of Assyria came to Ahaz, but he gave Ahaz trouble instead of help. [21]Ahaz took some valuable things from the Temple of the LORD, from the palace, and

27:7 *the book of the kings of Israel and Judah.* See 16:11.

from the princes, and he gave them to the king of Assyria, but it did not help.

[22]During Ahaz's troubles he was even more unfaithful to the LORD. [23]He offered sacrifices to the gods of the people of Damascus, who had defeated him. He thought, "The gods of the kings of Aram helped them. If I offer sacrifices to them, they will help me also." But this brought ruin to Ahaz and all Israel.

[24]Ahaz gathered the things from the Temple of God and broke them into pieces. Then he closed the doors of the Temple of the LORD. He made altars and put them on every street corner in Jerusalem. [25]In every town in Judah, Ahaz made places for burning sacrifices to worship other gods. So he made the LORD, the God of his ancestors, very angry.

[26]The other things Ahaz did as king, from beginning to end, are written in the book of the kings of Judah and Israel. [27]Ahaz died and was buried in the city of Jerusalem, but not in the graves of the kings of Israel. Ahaz's son Hezekiah became king in his place.

Hezekiah Purifies the Temple

29 Hezekiah was twenty-five years old when he became king, and he ruled twenty-nine years in Jerusalem. His mother's name was Abijah daughter of Zechariah. [2]Hezekiah did what the LORD said was right, just as his ancestor David had done.

[3]Hezekiah opened the doors of the Temple of the LORD and repaired them in the first month of the first year he was king. [4]Hezekiah brought in the priests and Levites and gathered them in the courtyard on the east side of the Temple. [5]Hezekiah said, "Listen to me, Levites. Make yourselves ready for the LORD's service, and make holy the Temple of the LORD, the God of your ancestors. Remove from the Temple everything that makes it impure. [6]Our ancestors were unfaithful to God and did what the LORD said was wrong. They left the LORD and stopped worshiping at the Temple where he lives. They rejected him. [7]They shut the doors of the porch of the Temple, and they let the fire go out in the lamps. They stopped burning incense and offering burnt offerings in the holy place to the God of Israel. [8]So the LORD became very angry with the people of Judah and Jerusalem, and he punished them. Other people are frightened and shocked by what he did to them. So they insult the people of Judah. You know these things are true. [9]That is why our ancestors were killed in battle and our sons, daughters, and wives were taken captive. [10]Now I, Hezekiah, have decided to make an agreement with the LORD, the God of Israel, so he will not be angry with us anymore. [11]My sons, don't waste any more time. The LORD chose you to stand before him, to serve him, to be his servants, and to burn incense to him."

[12]These are the Levites who started to work. From the Kohathite family there were Mahath son of Amasai and Joel son of Azariah. From the Merarite family there were Kish son of Abdi and Azariah son of Jehallelel. From the Gershonite family there were Joah son of Zimmah and Eden son of Joah. [13]From Elizaphan's family there were Shimri and Jeiel. From Asaph's family there were Zechariah and Mattaniah. [14]From Heman's family there were Jehiel and Shimei. From Jeduthun's family there were Shemaiah and Uzziel.

[15]These Levites gathered their brothers together and made themselves holy for service in the Temple. Then they went into the Temple of the LORD to purify it. They obeyed the king's command that had come from the LORD. [16]When the priests went into the Temple of the LORD to purify it, they took out all the unclean things they found in the Temple of the LORD and put them in the Temple courtyard. Then the Levites took these things out to the Kidron Valley. [17]Beginning on the first day of the first month, they made the Temple holy for the LORD's service. On the eighth day of the month, they came to the porch of the Temple, and for eight more days they made the Temple of the LORD holy. So they finished on the sixteenth day of the first month.

[18]Then they went to King Hezekiah and said, "We have purified the entire Temple of the LORD, the altar for burnt offerings and its utensils, and the table for the holy bread and all its utensils. [19]When Ahaz was king, he was unfaithful to God and removed some things from the Temple. But we have put them back and made them holy for the LORD. They are now in front of the LORD's altar."

[20]Early the next morning King Hezekiah gathered the leaders of the city and went up to the Temple of the LORD. [21]They brought seven bulls, seven male sheep, seven lambs, and seven male goats. These animals were an offering to remove the sin of the people and the kingdom of Judah and to make the Temple ready for service to God. King Hezekiah commanded the priests, the descendants of Aaron, to offer these animals on the LORD's altar. [22]So the priests killed the bulls and sprinkled

28:26 *the book of the kings of Judah and Israel.* See 16:11.

CRIME

EXODUS 21:12

What is crime in the Bible? How is crime related to the law of God?
Can we derive our understanding of crime from the Bible?
What is the Bible's solution to the problem of crime?

The Bible does not use any single word alone to refer to crime, but it speaks of "sin," "evil," "wickedness," and "charge," as well as "crime" as violations of an established law, whether it is a civil, criminal, or religious law. In modern usage, crime refers to any violation of the criminal code established by the regional authorities. But the Bible does not distinguish criminal law from civil and religious law. Why? Because all law established for the nation of Israel was set up by the same authority—God himself. The Books of Exodus, Leviticus, and Deuteronomy list many of the laws, crimes, and penalties which God defined and established for the nation after he had entered into agreement with Israel.

The Old Testament closely connects civil, criminal, and religious laws because all of them were given in the context of the agreement God made with Israel at Mount Sinai through Moses. In that agreement, God promised to protect the people of Israel from all threats, as long as they remained obedient to the laws he established. Therefore, any crime committed against a person of Israel was also a crime committed against the God who had promised to protect Israel.

In establishing the agreement with Moses at Sinai, God treated Israel as a unified nation so that the actions of individual people of Israel would have consequences for the entire nation. For example, although Achan alone kept plunder from the fallen city of Jericho, God said, "The Israelites have sinned . . ." (Joshua 7:11). Achan's religious crime against God brought a penalty upon the entire nation and made Achan guilty of a crime against his fellow Israelites. Achan's sin shows that in Israel it was impossible to distinguish violations of religious commands from civil laws, since both were offenses against God and had direct consequences for the welfare of the nation.

In the world of the New Testament, legal authority rested in the hands of the Roman government, although the Romans delegated a degree of legal authority to native officials who were empowered to enforce both local and Roman law. Although the Roman government later enforced conformity to certain religious laws such as the worship of the Roman Emperor during the period of the New Testament, Roman authorities such as Pilate (Matthew 27:24) and Gallio (Acts 18:14–16) were reluctant to judge religious crimes.

The New Testament was directed to readers living under the authority of a corrupt, tyrannical, pagan government. The apostle Paul recognized that God himself is the source of the authority given to the governing officials to establish laws and to prosecute and punish offenders (Romans 13:1–7). Paul instructed his Christian readers to submit to the civil government.

As the Bible's terms for crime show, crime is one of the many ways by which sin comes to expression. Although crime and sinful behavior may be curtailed by the strict enforcement of laws, laws themselves more often incite the sinful desires which result in sinful, criminal behavior (Romans 7:5).

The penalties for many crimes described in the Old Testament seem harsh when compared to those imposed by modern civil authorities. Some of the crimes for which death was prescribed as punishment are murder (Exodus 21:12), kidnapping (Exodus 21:16), rape (Deuteronomy 22:25), adultery (Deuteronomy 22:22), relations with animals (Exodus 22:19), idolatry (Exodus 22:20), evil magic (Exodus 22:18), speaking against the Lord (Leviticus 24:13–16), Sabbath-breaking (Exodus 31:14), and juvenile delinquency (Deuteronomy 21:18–21). When the crime was directed against an individual, the responsibility for carrying out the death sentence on the offender often rested on the victim's family.

The penalty for crimes involving the damage or loss of property usually required that the offender make restitution to the victim in an amount equal to or greater than the loss, depending on whether the loss resulted from negligence or intentional actions (Exodus 21:28–22:15).

Although many biblical characters experienced imprisonment, such as Joseph, Samson, Jeremiah, John the Baptist, Peter, and Paul, the Bible nowhere prescribes physical imprisonment as a means of criminal punishment or rehabilitation. The only imprisonment the Bible prescribes follows the final judgment of the wicked (Isaiah 24:22), and this imprisonment intends only punishment with no possibility of rehabilitation.

Crime: For additional scriptures on this topic go to Exodus 21:1–22:31.

MEMORY

PSALM 77

What role does memory play in faith?
How can memory strengthen trust in God?
What does God want us to remember?

Memory plays a crucial role in the Bible. It has an important role to play in faith. Memory is the ability to recall people, events, and ideas from the past. But it is really more than just the power to recall something to mind. It is more than thought; it includes the imagination. It is more than an act of the mind; it involves action. And it has significance beyond the past; it affects the present and can give us hope for the future.

God shows his goodness and power to his people through great acts that he performs in the past, in history. And indeed, the list of God's great accomplishments—"his miracles" or "mighty deeds"—is very long. He is the One who made the whole universe and gave human beings life. He is the One who made barren women have children and provided food for his people in the desert. He is the One who defeated great armies who wanted to kill all the Israelites, and he did this many, many times. But perhaps the most remembered of all God's great acts in the past was the time that he brought his people out of slavery in Egypt and brought them to the promised land. And the most dramatic moment of that great rescue was the crossing of the Red Sea (Exodus 14; 15).

After the plague that killed all the Egyptian firstborn, the king of Egypt finally let the Hebrews leave. After their departure, however, he changed his mind, grew angry, and chased after them with his army of chariots. The king caught up with the Hebrews when they had their backs against the Red Sea, which was impossible to cross. It looked like it was all over for the people of God. But at this moment, God used the winds to cause the sea to divide into two parts, leaving dry ground for the Hebrews to cross. The Egyptians tried to pursue them, but when they got into the sea, God stopped the winds and the Egyptians were all destroyed.

God rescued his people from impossible odds during this escape from Egypt. It stuck to the memory of the whole nation, and it became a memory that gave God's people hope in later years. Psalm 77 is a good example of this remembrance and its resulting hope.

> I cry out to God;
> I call to God, and he will hear me.
> I look for the Lord on the day of trouble.
> All night long I reach out my hands,
> but I cannot be comforted (v. 1–2).

The psalm continues in its expression of doubt and trouble until verse 11. At that point, the psalmist begins to remember God's great acts in the past—specifically, the crossing of the Red Sea:

> You made a way through the sea
> and paths through the deep waters,
> but your footprints were not seen.
> You led your people like a flock
> by using Moses and Aaron (v. 9–20).

By the time this psalm was composed, the Exodus was ancient history. The psalmist puts himself back in the time of the deliverance from Egypt. He knows that his own present troubles aren't even worth comparing to the danger that Moses faced from Egypt. He also knows the outcome: Israel was saved and Egypt destroyed. This memory gives him hope for his own future. If God could deliver his people from such danger, he can certainly help him handle his problems. Thus, memory becomes a shield against depression and fear.

The Christian has an even greater shield than the Old Testament believer. After all, the Exodus was a temporary rescue from danger and merely anticipated the greater salvation given by Jesus Christ. In the words of Paul, we are called to "Remember Jesus Christ, who was raised from the dead, who is from the family of David" (2 Timothy 2:8). If Jesus can save us from our sins by his dying on the cross and his resurrection, what do we really have to be afraid of? Indeed, the Lord's Supper is a sacrament whose main purpose is to cause us to remember Jesus' death as a mighty act of deliverance and calls us to order our life in light of it (1 Corinthians 11:23–26).⚭

⚭**Memory:** For additional scriptures on this topic go to Genesis 9:15.

their blood on the altar. They killed the sheep and
sprinkled their blood on the altar. Then they killed
the lambs and sprinkled their blood on the altar.
23Then the priests brought the male goats for the
sin offering before the king and the people there.
After the king and the people put their hands on
the goats, 24the priests killed them. With the goats'
blood they made an offering on the altar to remove
the sins of the Israelites so they would belong to
God. The king had said that the burnt offering
and sin offering should be made for all Israel.
25King Hezekiah put the Levites in the Temple
of the LORD with cymbals, harps, and lyres, as
David, Gad, and Nathan had commanded. (Gad
was the king's seer, and Nathan was a prophet.)
This command came from the LORD through his
prophets. 26So the Levites stood ready with David's
instruments of music, and the priests stood ready
with their trumpets.
27Then Hezekiah gave the order to sacrifice the
burnt offering on the altar. When the burnt offering began, the singing to the LORD also began. The
trumpets were blown, and the musical instruments of David king of Israel were played. 28All the
people worshiped, the singers sang, and the trumpeters blew their trumpets until the burnt offering
was finished.
29When the sacrifices were completed, King
Hezekiah and everyone with him bowed down
and worshiped. 30King Hezekiah and his officers
ordered the Levites to praise the LORD, using the
words David and Asaph the seer had used. So
they praised God with joy and bowed down and
worshiped.
31Then Hezekiah said, "Now that you people of
Judah have given yourselves to the LORD, come
near to the Temple of the LORD. Bring sacrifices
and offerings, to show thanks to him." So the people brought sacrifices and thank offerings, and
anyone who was willing also brought burnt offerings. 32For burnt offerings they brought a total
of seventy bulls, one hundred male sheep, and
two hundred lambs; all these animals were sacrificed as burnt offerings to the LORD. 33The holy
offerings totaled six hundred bulls and three
thousand sheep and goats. 34There were not
enough priests to skin all the animals for the
burnt offerings. So their relatives the Levites
helped them until the work was finished and other
priests could be made holy. The Levites had been
more careful to make themselves holy for the
LORD's service than the priests. 35There were

The Kidron Valley lies just east of Jerusalem.

many burnt offerings along with the fat of fellowship offerings and drink offerings. So the service
in the Temple of the LORD began again. 36And
Hezekiah and the people were very happy that
God had made it happen so quickly for his people.

The Passover Celebration

30 King Hezekiah sent messages to all the people of Israel and Judah, and he wrote letters
to the people of Ephraim and Manasseh. Hezekiah
invited all these people to come to the Temple of
the LORD in Jerusalem to celebrate the Passover for
the LORD, the God of Israel. 2King Hezekiah, his
officers, and all the people in Jerusalem agreed to
celebrate the Passover in the second month. 3They
could not celebrate it at the normal time, because
not enough priests had made themselves ready to
serve the LORD, and the people had not yet gathered
in Jerusalem. 4This plan satisfied King Hezekiah
and all the people. 5So they made an announcement everywhere in Israel, from Beersheba to
Dan, telling the people to come to Jerusalem to
celebrate the Passover for the LORD, the God of
Israel. For a long time most of the people had not
celebrated the Passover as the law commanded. 6At
the king's command, the messengers took letters
from him and his officers all through Israel and
Judah. This is what the letters said:

People of Israel, return to the LORD, the
God of Abraham, Isaac, and Israel. Then God
will return to you who are still alive, who have
escaped from the kings of Assyria. 7Don't be
like your ancestors or your relatives. They
turned against the LORD, the God of their
ancestors, so he caused other people to be
disgusted with them. You know this is true.
8Don't be stubborn as your ancestors were,
but obey the LORD willingly. Come to the

29:30 David: Psalm 78:70

29:31 Thanks: Psalm 30

30:5 *Beersheba to Dan.* Dan was the city farthest north in Israel, and Beersheba was the city farthest south. So this means all the people of Israel.

Temple, which he has made holy forever. Serve the LORD your God so he will not be angry with you. 9Come back to the LORD. Then the people who captured your relatives and children will be kind to them and will let them return to this land. The LORD your God is kind and merciful. He will not turn away from you if you return to him.

10The messengers went to every town in Ephraim and Manasseh, and all the way to Zebulun, but the people laughed at them and made fun of them. 11But some men from Asher, Manasseh, and Zebulun were sorry for what they had done and went to Jerusalem. 12And God united all the people of Judah in obeying King Hezekiah and his officers, because their command had come from the LORD.

13In the second month a large crowd came together in Jerusalem to celebrate the Feast of Unleavened Bread. 14The people removed the altars and incense altars to gods in Jerusalem and threw them into the Kidron Valley.

15They killed the Passover lamb on the fourteenth day of the second month. The priests and the Levites were ashamed, so they made themselves holy and brought burnt offerings into the Temple of the LORD. 16They took their regular places in the Temple as the Teachings of Moses, the man of God, commanded. The Levites gave the blood of the sacrifices to the priests, who sprinkled it on the altar. 17Since many people in the crowd had not made themselves holy, the Levites killed the Passover lambs for everyone who was not clean. The Levites made each lamb holy for the LORD. 18-19Although many people from Ephraim, Manasseh, Issachar, and Zebulun had not purified themselves for the feast, they ate the Passover even though it was against the law. So Hezekiah prayed for them, saying, "LORD, you are good. You are the LORD, the God of our ancestors. Please forgive all those who try to obey you even if they did not make themselves clean as the rules of the Temple command." 20The LORD listened to Hezekiah's prayer, and he healed the people. 21The Israelites in Jerusalem celebrated the Feast of Unleavened Bread for seven days with great joy to the LORD. The Levites and priests praised the LORD every day with loud music. 22Hezekiah encouraged all the Levites who showed they understood well how to do their service for the LORD. The people ate the feast for seven days, offered fellowship offerings, and praised the LORD, the God of their ancestors.

23Then all the people agreed to stay seven more days, so they celebrated with joy for seven more days. 24Hezekiah king of Judah gave one thousand bulls and seven thousand sheep to the people. The officers gave one thousand bulls and ten thousand sheep to the people. Many priests made themselves holy. 25All the people of Judah, the priests, the Levites, those who came from Israel, the foreigners from Israel, and the foreigners living in Judah were very happy. 26There was much joy in Jerusalem, because there had not been a celebration like this since the time of Solomon son of David and king of Israel. 27The priests and Levites stood up and blessed the people, and God heard them because their prayer reached heaven, his holy home.

The Collection for the Priests

31 When the Passover celebration was finished, all the Israelites in Jerusalem went out to the towns of Judah. There they smashed the stone pillars used to worship gods. They cut down the Asherah idols and destroyed the altars and places for worshiping gods in all of Judah, Benjamin, Ephraim, and Manasseh. After they had destroyed all of them, the Israelites returned to their own towns and homes.

2King Hezekiah appointed groups of priests and Levites for their special duties. They were to offer burnt offerings and fellowship offerings, to worship, and to give thanks and praise at the gates of the LORD's house. 3Hezekiah gave some of his own animals for the burnt offerings, which were given every morning and evening, on Sabbath days, during New Moons, and at other feasts commanded in the LORD's Teachings.

4Hezekiah commanded the people living in Jerusalem to give the priests and Levites the portion that belonged to them. Then the priests and Levites could give all their time to the LORD's Teachings. 5As soon as the king's command went out to the Israelites, they gave freely of the first portion of their grain, new wine, oil, honey, and everything they grew in their fields. They brought a large amount, one-tenth of everything. 6The people of Israel and Judah who lived in Judah also brought one-tenth of their cattle and sheep and one-tenth of the holy things that were given to the LORD their God, and they put all of them in piles. 7The people began the piles in the third month and finished in the seventh month. 8When Hezekiah and his officers came and saw the piles, they praised the LORD and his people, the people of Israel. 9Hezekiah asked the priests and Levites about the piles. 10Azariah, the leading priest from Zadok's family, answered Hezekiah, "Since the people began to bring their offerings to the Temple of the LORD, we have had plenty to eat and plenty left over, because the LORD has blessed his people. So we have all this left over."

11Then Hezekiah commanded the priests to prepare the storerooms in the Temple of the LORD. So this was done. 12Then the priests brought in the offerings and the things given to the LORD and one-tenth of everything the people had given. Conaniah the Levite was in charge of these things, and his brother Shimei was second to him. 13Conaniah and his brother Shimei were over these supervisors: Jehiel, Azaziah, Nahath, Asahel, Jerimoth, Jozabad, Eliel, Ismakiah, Mahath, and Benaiah. King Hezekiah and Azariah the officer in charge of the Temple of God had chosen them.

14Kore son of Imnah the Levite was in charge of the special gifts the people wanted to give to God. He was responsible for giving out the contributions made to the LORD and the holy gifts. Kore was the guard at the East Gate. 15Eden, Miniamin, Jeshua, Shemaiah, Amariah, and Shecaniah helped Kore in the towns where the priests lived. They gave from what was collected to the other groups of priests, both young and old.

16From what was collected, these men also gave to the males three years old and older who had their names in the Levite family histories. They were to enter the Temple of the LORD for their daily service, each group having its own responsibilities. 17The priests were given their part of the collection, by families, as listed in the family histories. The Levites twenty years old and older were given their part of the collection, based on their responsibilities and their groups. 18The Levites' babies, wives, sons, and daughters also got part of the collection. This was done for all the Levites who were listed in the family histories, because they always kept themselves ready to serve the LORD.

19Some of Aaron's descendants, the priests, lived on the farmlands near the towns or in the towns. Men were chosen by name to give part of the collection to these priests. All the males and those named in the family histories of the Levites received part of the collection.

20This is what King Hezekiah did in Judah. He did what was good and right and obedient before the LORD his God. 21Hezekiah tried to obey God in his service of the Temple of God, and he tried to obey God's teachings and commands. He gave himself fully to his work for God. So he had success.

Assyria Attacks Judah

32 After Hezekiah did all these things to serve the LORD, Sennacherib king of Assyria came and attacked Judah. He and his army surrounded and attacked the strong, walled cities, hoping to take them for himself. 2Hezekiah knew that Sennacherib had come to Jerusalem to attack it. 3So Hezekiah and his officers and army commanders decided to cut off the water from the springs outside the city. So the officers and commanders helped Hezekiah. 4Many people came and cut off all the springs and the stream that flowed through the land. They said, "The king of Assyria will not find much water when he comes here." 5Then Hezekiah made Jerusalem stronger. He rebuilt all the broken parts of the wall and put towers on it. He also built another wall outside the first one and strengthened the area that was filled in on the east side of the old part of Jerusalem. He also made many weapons and shields.

6Hezekiah put army commanders over the people and met with them at the open place near the city gate. Hezekiah encouraged them, saying, 7"Be strong and brave. Don't be afraid or worried because of the king of Assyria or his large army. There is a greater power with us than with him. 8He only has men, but we have the LORD our God to help us and to fight our battles." The people were encouraged by the words of Hezekiah king of Judah.

9After this King Sennacherib of Assyria and all his army surrounded and attacked Lachish. Then he sent his officers to Jerusalem with this message for King Hezekiah of Judah and all the people of Judah in Jerusalem:

> 10Sennacherib king of Assyria says this: "You have nothing to trust in to help you. It is no use for you to stay in Jerusalem under attack. 11Hezekiah says to you, 'The LORD our God will save us from the king of Assyria,' but he is fooling you. If you stay in Jerusalem, you will die from hunger and thirst. 12Hezekiah himself removed your LORD's places of worship and altars. He told you people of Judah and Jerusalem that you must worship and burn incense on only one altar.
>
> 13"You know what my ancestors and I have done to all the people in other nations. The gods of those nations could not save their people from my power. 14My ancestors destroyed those nations; none of their gods could save

32:3 *cut off the water.* Hezekiah attempts to hide or divert the water supplies that are outside the city walls to keep them from the Assyrians.

them from me. So your god cannot save you from my power. 15Do not let Hezekiah fool you or trick you, and do not believe him. No god of any nation or kingdom has been able to save his people from me or my ancestors. Your god is even less able to save you from me."

16Sennacherib's officers said worse things against the LORD God and his servant Hezekiah. 17King Sennacherib also wrote letters insulting the LORD, the God of Israel. They spoke against him, saying, "The gods of the other nations could not save their people from me. In the same way Hezekiah's god won't be able to save his people from me." 18Then the king's officers shouted in Hebrew, calling out to the people of Jerusalem who were on the city wall. The officers wanted to scare the people away so they could capture Jerusalem. 19They spoke about the God of Jerusalem as though he were like the gods the people of the world worshiped, which are made by human hands.

20King Hezekiah and the prophet Isaiah son of Amoz prayed to heaven about this. 21Then the LORD sent an angel who killed all the soldiers, leaders, and officers in the camp of the king of Assyria. So the king went back to his own country in disgrace. When he went into the temple of his god, some of his own sons killed him with a sword.

22So the LORD saved Hezekiah and the people in Jerusalem from Sennacherib king of Assyria and from all other people. He took care of them on every side. 23Many people brought gifts for the LORD to Jerusalem, and they also brought valuable gifts to King Hezekiah of Judah. From then on all the nations respected Hezekiah.

Hezekiah Dies

24At that time Hezekiah became so sick he almost died. When he prayed to the LORD, the LORD spoke to him and gave him a sign. 25But Hezekiah did not thank God for his kindness, because he was so proud. So the LORD was angry with him and the people of Judah and Jerusalem. 26But later Hezekiah and the people of Jerusalem were sorry and stopped being proud, so the LORD did not punish them while Hezekiah was alive.

27Hezekiah had many riches and much honor. He made treasuries for his silver, gold, gems, spices, shields, and other valuable things. 28He built storage buildings for grain, new wine, and oil and stalls for all the cattle and pens for the sheep. 29He also built many towns. He had many flocks and herds, because God had given Hezekiah much wealth.

30It was Hezekiah who cut off the upper pool of the Gihon spring and made those waters flow straight down to the west side of the older part of Jerusalem. And Hezekiah was successful in everything he did. 31But one time the leaders of Babylon sent messengers to Hezekiah, asking him about a strange sign that had happened in the land. When they came, God left Hezekiah alone to test him so he could know everything that was in Hezekiah's heart.

32Hezekiah's love for God and the other things he did as king are written in the vision of the prophet Isaiah son of Amoz. This is in the book of the kings of Judah and Israel. 33Hezekiah died and was buried on a hill, where the graves of David's ancestors are. All the people of Judah and Jerusalem honored Hezekiah when he died, and his son Manasseh became king in his place.

Manasseh King of Judah

33 Manasseh was twelve years old when he became king, and he was king for fifty-five years in Jerusalem. 2He did what the LORD said was wrong. He did the hateful things the nations had done—the nations that the LORD had forced out of the land ahead of the Israelites. 3Manasseh's father, Hezekiah, had torn down the places where gods were worshiped, but Manasseh rebuilt them. He also built altars for the Baal gods, and he made Asherah idols and worshiped all the stars of the sky and served them. 4The LORD had said about the Temple, "I will be worshiped in Jerusalem forever," but Manasseh built altars in the Temple of the LORD. 5He built altars to worship the stars in the two courtyards of the Temple of the LORD. 6He made his children pass through fire in the Valley of Ben Hinnom. He practiced magic and witchcraft and told the future by explaining signs and dreams. He got advice from mediums and fortune-tellers. He did many things the LORD said were wrong, which made the LORD angry.

7Manasseh carved an idol and put it in the Temple of God. God had said to David and his son Solomon about the Temple, "I will be worshiped forever in this Temple and in Jerusalem, which I have chosen from all the tribes of Israel. 8I will never again make the Israelites leave the land I

32:24, 31 *sign.* See Isaiah 38:1–8. It tells the story about the sign and how the Lord gave Hezekiah fifteen more years to live.

32:31 *God . . . heart.* See 2 Kings 20:12–19.

32:32 *the book of the kings of Judah and Israel.* See 16:11.

33:5 Astrology: Isaiah 47:13–14

33:6 Magic: Galatians 5:20

gave to their ancestors. But they must obey everything I have commanded them in all the teachings, rules, and commands I gave them through Moses."
[9]But Manasseh led the people of Judah and Jerusalem to do wrong. They did more evil than the nations the LORD had destroyed ahead of the Israelites.
[10]The LORD spoke to Manasseh and his people, but they did not listen. [11]So the LORD brought the king of Assyria's army commanders to attack Judah. They captured Manasseh, put hooks in him, placed bronze chains on his hands, and took him to Babylon. [12]As Manasseh suffered, he begged the LORD his God for help and humbled himself before the God of his ancestors. [13]When Manasseh prayed, the LORD heard him and had pity on him. So the LORD let him return to Jerusalem and to his kingdom. Then Manasseh knew that the LORD is the true God.
[14]After that happened, Manasseh rebuilt the outer wall of Jerusalem and made it higher. It was in the valley on the west side of the Gihon spring and went to the entrance of the Fish Gate and around the hill of Ophel. Then he put commanders in all the strong, walled cities in Judah.
[15]Manasseh removed the idols of other nations, including the idol in the Temple of the LORD. He removed all the altars he had built on the Temple hill and in Jerusalem and threw them out of the city. [16]Then he set up the LORD's altar and sacrificed on it fellowship offerings and offerings to show thanks to God. Manasseh commanded all the people of Judah to serve the LORD, the God of Israel. [17]The people continued to offer sacrifices at the places of worship, but their sacrifices were only to the LORD their God. [18]The other things Manasseh did as king, his prayer to his God, and what the seers said to him in the name of the LORD, the God of Israel—all are recorded in the book of the history of the kings of Israel. [19]Manasseh's prayer and God's pity for him, his sins, his unfaithfulness, the places he built for worshiping gods and the Asherah idols before he humbled himself—all are written in the book of the seers. [20]Manasseh died and was buried in his palace. Then Manasseh's son Amon became king in his place.

Amon King of Judah

[21]Amon was twenty-two years old when he became king, and he was king for two years in Jerusalem. [22]He did what the LORD said was wrong, as his father Manasseh had done. Amon worshiped and offered sacrifices to all the carved idols Manasseh had made. [23]Amon did not humble himself before the LORD as his father Manasseh had done. Instead, Amon sinned even more.
[24]King Amon's officers made plans against him and killed him in his palace. [25]Then the people of the land killed all those who had made plans to kill King Amon, and they made his son Josiah king in his place.

Josiah King of Judah

34 Josiah was eight years old when he became king, and he ruled thirty-one years in Jerusalem. [2]He did what the LORD said was right. He lived as his ancestor David had lived, and he did not stop doing what was right.
[3]In his eighth year as king while he was still young, Josiah began to obey the God of his ancestor David. In his twelfth year as king, Josiah began to remove from Judah and Jerusalem the gods, the places for worshiping gods, the Asherah idols, and the wooden and metal idols. [4]The people tore down the altars for the Baal gods as Josiah directed. Then Josiah cut down the incense altars that were above them. He broke up the Asherah idols and the wooden and metal idols and beat them into powder. Then he sprinkled the powder on the graves of the people who had offered sacrifices to these gods. [5]He burned the bones of their priests on their own altars. So Josiah removed idol worship from Judah and Jerusalem, [6]and from the towns in the areas of Manasseh, Ephraim, and Simeon all the way to Naphtali, and in the ruins near these towns. [7]Josiah broke down the altars and Asherah idols and beat the idols into powder. He cut down all the incense altars in all of Israel. Then he went back to Jerusalem.
[8]In Josiah's eighteenth year as king, he made Judah and the Temple pure again. He sent Shaphan son of Azaliah, Maaseiah the city leader, and Joah son of Joahaz the recorder to repair the Temple of the LORD, the God of Josiah. [9]These men went to Hilkiah the high priest and gave him the money the Levite gatekeepers had gathered from the people of Manasseh, Ephraim, and all the Israelites who were left alive, and also from all the people of Judah, Benjamin, and Jerusalem. This is the money they had brought into the Temple of God. [10]Then the Levites gave it to the supervisors of the work on the Temple of the LORD, and they paid the workers who rebuilt and repaired the Temple. [11]They gave money to carpenters and builders to buy cut stone and wood. The wood was used to rebuild the buildings and to make beams for them, because the

33:11 *put hooks in him.* From ancient Near Eastern art we learn that these hooks were put through his nose and attached to a chain. Thus, he was treated like a captured animal.

kings of Judah had let the buildings fall into ruin. 12The men did their work well. Their supervisors were Jahath and Obadiah, who were Levites from the family of Merari, and Zechariah and Meshullam, who were from the family of Kohath. These Levites were all skilled musicians. 13They were also in charge of the workers who carried loads and all the other workers. Some Levites worked as secretaries, officers, and gatekeepers.

The Book of the Teachings Is Found

14The Levites brought out the money that was in the Temple of the LORD. As they were doing this, Hilkiah the priest found the Book of the LORD's Teachings that had been given through Moses. 15Hilkiah said to Shaphan the royal secretary, "I've found the Book of the Teachings in the Temple of the LORD!" Then he gave it to Shaphan.

16Shaphan took the book to the king and reported to Josiah, "Your officers are doing everything you told them to do. 17They have paid out the money that was in the Temple of the LORD and have given it to the supervisors and the workers." 18Then Shaphan the royal secretary told the king, "Hilkiah the priest has given me a book." And Shaphan read from the book to the king.

19When the king heard the words of the Teachings, he tore his clothes to show how upset he was. 20He gave orders to Hilkiah, Ahikam son of Shaphan, Acbor son of Micaiah, Shaphan the royal secretary, and Asaiah, the king's servant. These were the orders: 21"Go and ask the LORD about the words in the book that was found. Ask for me and for the people who are left alive in Israel and Judah. The LORD is very angry with us, because our ancestors did not obey the LORD's word; they did not do everything this book says to do."

22So Hilkiah and those the king sent with him went to talk to Huldah the prophetess. She was the wife of Shallum son of Tikvah, the son of Harhas, who took care of the king's clothes. Huldah lived in Jerusalem, in the new area of the city.

23She said to them, "This is what the LORD, the God of Israel, says: Tell the man who sent you to me, 24'This is what the LORD says: I will bring trouble to this place and to the people living here. I will bring all the curses that are written in the book that was read to the king of Judah. 25The people of Judah have left me and have burned incense to other gods. They have made me angry by all the evil things they have made. So I will punish them in my anger, which will not be put out.' 26Tell the king of Judah, who sent you to ask the LORD, 'This is what the LORD, the God of Israel, says about the words you heard: 27When you heard my words against this place and its people, you became sorry for what you had done and you humbled yourself before me. You tore your clothes to show how upset you were, and you cried in my presence. This is why I have heard you, says the LORD. 28So I will let you die and be buried in peace. You won't see all the trouble I will bring to this place and the people living here.'"

So they took her message back to the king.

29Then the king gathered all the older leaders of Judah and Jerusalem together. 30He went up to the Temple of the LORD, and all the people from Judah and from Jerusalem went with him. The priests, the Levites, and all the people—from the most important to the least important—went with him. He read to them all the words in the Book of the Agreement that was found in the Temple of the LORD. 31The king stood by his pillar and made an agreement in the presence of the LORD to follow the LORD and obey his commands, rules, and laws with his whole being and to obey the words of the agreement written in this book. 32Then Josiah made all the people in Jerusalem and Benjamin promise to accept the agreement. So the people of Jerusalem obeyed the agreement of God, the God of their ancestors.

33And Josiah threw out the hateful idols from all the land that belonged to the Israelites. He led everyone in Israel to serve the LORD their God. While Josiah lived, the people obeyed the LORD, the God of their ancestors.

Josiah Celebrates the Passover

35 King Josiah celebrated the Passover to the LORD in Jerusalem. The Passover lamb was killed on the fourteenth day of the first month. 2Josiah chose the priests to do their duties, and he encouraged them as they served in the Temple of the LORD. 3The Levites taught the Israelites and were made holy for service to the LORD. Josiah said to them, "Put the Holy Ark in the Temple that David's son Solomon, the king of Israel, built. Do not carry it from place to place on your shoulders anymore. Now serve the LORD your God and his people Israel. 4Prepare yourselves by your family groups for service, and do the jobs that King David and his son Solomon gave you to do.

5"Stand in the holy place with a group of the Levites for each family group of the people. 6Kill the

34:15 *the Book of the Teachings that had been given through Moses.* This reference indicates that either the whole or a part of the first five books of the Bible had been lost and now rediscovered. Due to Josiah's reaction, it is usually thought that the discovered portion was the whole or a part of the Book of Deuteronomy.

34:21 The Remnant: Ezra 9:8

Passover lambs, and make yourselves holy to the
LORD. Prepare the lambs for your relatives, the
people of Israel, as the LORD through Moses commanded us to do."
7Josiah gave the Israelites thirty thousand sheep
and goats to kill for the Passover sacrifices, and he
gave them three thousand cattle. They were all
his own animals.
8Josiah's officers also gave willingly to the people,
the priests, and the Levites. Hilkiah, Zechariah, and
Jehiel, the officers in charge of the Temple, gave
the priests twenty-six hundred lambs and goats
and three hundred cattle for Passover sacrifices.
9Conaniah, his brothers Shemaiah and Nethanel,
and Hashabiah, Jeiel, and Jozabad gave the Levites
five thousand sheep and goats and five hundred
cattle for Passover sacrifices. These men were leaders of the Levites.
10When everything was ready for the Passover
service, the priests and Levites went to their places,
as the king had commanded. 11The Passover
lambs were killed. Then the Levites skinned the
animals and gave the blood to the priests, who
sprinkled it on the altar. 12Then they gave the
animals for the burnt offerings to the different
family groups so the burnt offerings could be
offered to the LORD as was written in the book of
Moses. They also did this with the cattle. 13The
Levites roasted the Passover sacrifices over the
fire as they were commanded, and they boiled
the holy offerings in pots, kettles, and pans.
Then they quickly gave the meat to the people.
14After this was finished, the Levites prepared
meat for themselves and for the priests, the
descendants of Aaron. The priests worked until
night, offering the burnt offerings and burning the
fat of the sacrifices.
15The Levite singers from Asaph's family stood in
the places chosen for them by King David, Asaph,
Heman, and Jeduthun, the king's seer. The gatekeepers at each gate did not have to leave their
places, because their fellow Levites had prepared
everything for them for the Passover.
16So everything was done that day for the worship of the LORD, as King Josiah commanded. The
Passover was celebrated, and the burnt offerings
were offered on the LORD's altar. 17The Israelites
who were there celebrated the Passover and the
Feast of Unleavened Bread for seven days. 18The
Passover had not been celebrated like this in
Israel since the prophet Samuel was alive. None
of the kings of Israel had ever celebrated a
Passover like it was celebrated by King Josiah, the
priests, the Levites, the people of Judah and Israel
who were there, and the people of Jerusalem.
19This Passover was celebrated in the eighteenth
year Josiah was king.

The Death of Josiah

20After Josiah did all this for the Temple, Neco
king of Egypt led an army to attack Carchemish, a
town on the Euphrates River. And Josiah marched
out to fight against Neco. 21But Neco sent messengers to Josiah, saying, "King Josiah, there should
not be war between us. I did not come to fight you,
but my enemies. God told me to hurry, and he is
on my side. So don't fight God, or he will destroy
you."
22But Josiah did not go away. He wore different
clothes so no one would know who he was.
Refusing to listen to what Neco said at God's command, Josiah went to fight on the plain of
Megiddo. 23In the battle King Josiah was shot by
archers. He told his servants, "Take me away
because I am badly wounded." 24So they took
him out of his chariot and put him in another
chariot and carried him to Jerusalem. There he
died and was buried in the graves where his ancestors were buried. All the people of Judah and
Jerusalem were very sad because he was dead.
25Jeremiah wrote some sad songs about Josiah.
Even to this day all the men and women singers
remember and honor Josiah with these songs. It
became a custom in Israel to sing these songs that
are written in the collection of sad songs.
26-27The other things Josiah did as king, from
beginning to end, are written in the book of the
kings of Israel and Judah. It tells how he loved
what was written in the LORD's teachings.

Jehoahaz King of Judah

36 The people of Judah chose Josiah's son
Jehoahaz and made him king in Jerusalem
in his father's place.
2Jehoahaz was twenty-three years old when he
became king, and he was king in Jerusalem for
three months. 3Then King Neco of Egypt removed
Jehoahaz from being king in Jerusalem. Neco made
the people of Judah pay about seventy-five hundred
pounds of silver and about seventy-five pounds of
gold. 4The king of Egypt made Jehoahaz's brother
Eliakim the king of Judah and Jerusalem and
changed his name to Jehoiakim. But Neco took his
brother Jehoahaz to Egypt.

Jehoiakim King of Judah

5Jehoiakim was twenty-five years old when he
became king, and he was king in Jerusalem for
eleven years. He did what the LORD his God said
was wrong. 6King Nebuchadnezzar of Babylon
attacked Judah, captured Jehoiakim, put bronze

chains on him, and took him to Babylon.
[7]Nebuchadnezzar removed some of the things
from the Temple of the LORD, took them to
Babylon, and put them in his own palace.
[8]The other things Jehoiakim did as king, the
hateful things he did, and everything he was guilty
of doing, are written in the book of the kings of
Israel and Judah. And Jehoiakim's son Jehoiachin
became king in his place.

Jehoiachin King of Judah

[9]Jehoiachin was eighteen years old when he
became king of Judah, and he was king in Jerusalem
for three months and ten days. He did what the
LORD said was wrong. [10]In the spring King
Nebuchadnezzar sent for Jehoiachin and brought
him and some valuable treasures from the Temple
of the LORD to Babylon. Then Nebuchadnezzar
made Jehoiachin's uncle Zedekiah the king of Judah
and Jerusalem.

Zedekiah King of Judah

[11]Zedekiah was twenty-one years old when he
became king of Judah, and he was king in
Jerusalem for eleven years. [12]Zedekiah did what
the LORD his God said was wrong. The prophet
Jeremiah spoke messages from the LORD, but
Zedekiah did not obey. [13]Zedekiah turned against
King Nebuchadnezzar, who had forced him to
swear in God's name to be loyal to him. But
Zedekiah became stubborn and refused to obey the
LORD, the God of Israel. [14]Also, all the leaders of the
priests and the people of Judah became more
wicked, following the evil example of the other
nations. The LORD had made the Temple in
Jerusalem holy, but the leaders made it unholy.

The Fall of Jerusalem

[15]The LORD, the God of their ancestors, sent
prophets again and again to warn his people,
because he had pity on them and on his Temple.
[16]But they made fun of God's prophets and hated
God's messages. They refused to listen to the
prophets until, finally, the LORD became so angry
with his people that he could not be stopped. [17]So
God brought the king of Babylon to attack them.
The king killed the young men even when they
were in the Temple. He had no mercy on the young
men or women, the old men or those who were
sick. God handed all of them over to Nebuchadnezzar. [18]Nebuchadnezzar carried away to Babylon all
the things from the Temple of God, both large
and small, and all the treasures from the Temple
of the LORD and from the king and his officers.
[19]Nebuchadnezzar and his army set fire to God's
Temple and broke down Jerusalem's wall and
burned all the palaces. They took or destroyed
every valuable thing in Jerusalem.
[20]Nebuchadnezzar took captive to Babylon the
people who were left alive, and he forced them to
be slaves for him and his descendants. They
remained there as slaves until the Persian kingdom
defeated Babylon. [21]And so what the LORD had
told Israel through the prophet Jeremiah happened: The country was an empty wasteland for
seventy years to make up for the years of Sabbath
rest that the people had not kept.
[22]In the first year Cyrus was king of Persia, the
LORD had Cyrus send an announcement to his
whole kingdom. This happened so the LORD's message spoken by Jeremiah would come true. He
wrote:

[23]This is what Cyrus king of Persia says:
The LORD, the God of heaven, has given me
all the kingdoms of the earth, and he has
appointed me to build a Temple for him at
Jerusalem in Judah. Now may the LORD your
God be with all of you who are his people.
You are free to go to Jerusalem.

36:19 Nehemiah: Ezra 9:2

36:21 *Sabbath rest.* The Law said that every seventh year the land was not to be farmed. See Leviticus 25:1–7.

Angels

Psalm 103:20

What place do angels have in God's creation? What do they do? Who is the angel of the Lord?

Although the Bible does not specifically talk about when the angels were created, Colossians 1:16 mentions that all powers in heaven and earth, seen and unseen, were created by Christ. The angels were present when God created the earth, for they "shouted with joy" in response to God's creating activity (Job 38:7).

The angels have a unique place in the world. According to Psalm 8:5 angels are on a higher level than humans. They are heavenly creatures who surround the throne of God (Daniel 7:10). They worship and praise God (Psalm 148:2). Although angels are heavenly creatures, they can appear as normal humans to other humans. In Genesis 18 three angels appear to Abraham as men. Hebrews 13:2 states that in reaching out to strangers some have entertained angels without knowing it. However, there are times when angels appear very different than humans. They exhibit knowledge that is beyond humans (in Daniel 8:17 an angel explains a vision to Daniel). They have great strength (in Matthew 28:2 an angel rolls the heavy stone away from the tomb). And sometimes when they appear there are other manifestations, such as a bright light (Matthew 28:3; Acts 12:7). Angels are also different from humans in that they do not marry (Luke 20:35–36).

The angels also have a unique function in the world. The Hebrew and Greek word for *angel* also means "messenger." Angels are messengers of God who are sent out to accomplish the purposes of God. They are servants who do what God wants (Psalm 103:20). They delivered important messages from God at key points in the salvation story (Numbers 20:16; Luke 1:36; Acts 10:3). They took part in the giving of the law (Acts 7:53). Angels are also sent to assist God's people in a number of ways. They offer guidance (Genesis 24:7; Acts 8:26). They minister to the needs of God's servants (Elijah in 1 Kings 19:5; Jesus in Luke 22:43; Paul in Acts 27:23). They give protection, such as when an angel shut the mouths of the lions (Daniel 6:22). A warning to those who think that little children are not important is supported by the fact that "they have angels in heaven who are always with my Father in heaven" (Matthew 18:10).

Angels are part of the army of God who fight for God's people in behalf of God (2 Chronicles 18:18). They are mighty warriors who obey God's voice (Psalm 103:20). An angel destroyed the Assyrian army, sending the Assyrians back to their own country in disgrace (2 Chronicles 32:21). Psalm 78:49 speaks of God's anger against the sin of Israel and that he sent "his destroying angels" among them. In this role, angels become messengers of God's judgment. They play a major role in the Book of Revelation and will accompany Jesus when he returns to earth (2 Thessalonians 1:7). They will be sent out to gather people for judgment (Matthew 13:41).

Angels are also involved in spiritual warfare. Some angels rebelled against God and are actively trying to hinder the purposes of God (Daniel 10:12–14; Revelation 12:7). The leader of these angels is called Satan (Luke 10:18), or the devil (Matthew 25:41). Jesus has authority over all the angels, authorities, and powers (1 Peter 3:22) so that one day they will all be defeated and experience God's judgment (Matthew 25:41).

There are only two angels named in the Bible: Gabriel and Michael. Gabriel delivered a message to Mary (Luke 1:26). Michael is called the archangel and is the leader of the army of angels (Revelation 12:7).

An interesting figure in the Old Testament is the angel of the Lord. It becomes evident that this angel is not just an angel but is the Lord. He appeared to Samson's parents to tell them about the birth of Samson. When they offered a sacrifice to God, the angel went up to heaven in the flame. They became afraid because they understood that they had seen God (Judges 13:22). The angel of the Lord appeared to Moses in the burning bush, but it is God who called to Moses from the bush. There is a clear identification of the angel of the Lord with God (Exodus 3:2–4). A strong connection can also be made between the angel of the Lord and Jesus. The angel of the Lord is identified with God in Exodus 3. God tells Moses that his name is "I am who I am" (verse 14). Jesus identifies himself as "I am" in John 8:58. Not only does Jesus claim to be God, but it is likely that many appearances of the angel of the Lord are appearances of Jesus before he became a human.

God's people can take great comfort in knowing that angels are God's messengers. They help believers in a number of ways (Hebrews 1:14), including guidance and protection.

Angels: For additional scriptures on this topic go to Judges 13:18–22.

ALCOHOL

PSALM 104

Does the Bible prohibit the use of alcohol? Does it provide guidelines?

The use and abuse of alcohol was a serious matter in Old Testament and early New Testament times, just as it is today. The Old Testament provides examples like Noah. Soon after the flood Noah planted a vineyard, made wine, and became drunk (Genesis 9:20–21). Many kings and armies in Old Testament times were defeated while under the influence of too much wine (1 Kings 16:9; 20:16). In the New Testament, Jesus told the parable of the unfaithful servant who drank too much and beat the other servants because he thought the master was not coming soon (Matthew 24:48–49). Jesus also said in plain words that people will be drinking too much wine and becoming drunk instead of being prepared for His return on judgment day (Luke 21:34). The Book of Revelation uses the image of drunkenness with wine often to describe those who will be condemned (Revelation 17:2). Do all these examples mean that alcohol is bad and drinking is wrong?

The Bible does not forbid drinking alcohol. While Noah did not set a good example, the Bible does not comment on his overindulgence. It was his son Ham who was cursed for tricking his father who had fallen asleep uncovered in his tent. Psalm 104:15 tells us that God has given us bread and wine which "makes happy hearts." Isaiah described the time when Christ would come as a feast of the best wines, prepared by God. Wine seems to be connected with the idea of feasting and celebration. A clear example of this is found on the occasion when Jesus changed many gallons of water into wine at the wedding in Cana (John 2:1–12) and the finest of wine at that.

Some people suggest that wine may mean grape juice in the Bible. However, the words describing wine show that it is alcoholic. In John 2, we learn that the poorer wine was served last because no one could tell how the wine tasted after they had drunk the best. This practice would make no sense if nonalcoholic grape juice were being served. At Pentecost the apostles were accused of being drunk on "new wine" because of the way they were acting. Acting in strange ways is considered a result of intoxication from alcohol. A group of people in the church of Corinth were admonished by Paul for being careless in drinking and becoming drunk with the wine which was to be used for communion.

Although wine is a gift from God, we must be very careful concerning its use. There are also commands in the Bible against the use of wine by certain people at certain times and against the misuse of alcohol by all people. Nazarites were not allowed to drink any alcohol during the time of their separation (Numbers 6:1–4). Since Samson and John the Baptist were to be Nazarites all their life, they were never to drink. Priests were told in Leviticus never to drink when they served in the Meeting Tent, or Tabernacle. In a similar way, pastors of the New Testament are not allowed to be drunkards. Public servants are spoken to in Proverbs 31:4, which says that wine is not for kings because it will get in the way of clear thinking and good judgment.

All people are warned not to misuse alcohol. That is, they are not to drink so much that they become drunk. Proverbs 23:29 describes the woe, sorrow, contentions, and other problems of a person who spends too much time drinking. Belshazzar, king of Babylon, drank too much wine at a party and brought immediate condemnation on himself from God because of his foolish actions. Christians in general are warned that no drunkard has any part in the kingdom of heaven (Romans 14:21; 1 Corinthians 6:10; Galatians 5:21; Ephesians 5:18). Therefore, many Christians choose to abstain from alcohol as the wiser course in our culture.

Just as alcohol can be used for good reasons or misused for bad, so the term "cup" can describe something positive or negative in the Bible. The suffering and death of Jesus is called the cup which he must drink. James and John were reminded by Jesus that sharing in his glory meant drinking from this cup. In the garden of Gethsemane, Jesus prayed to be delivered from drinking this cup, yet only if it was God's will (Matthew 24:42). It was indeed God's will that Jesus taste death for all, that all might be saved.

First Corinthians 10:14–17 calls the cup of wine used in the Lord's Supper the "cup of blessing." It is a cup of blessing because it passes along to those who receive it the saving work accomplished by the shedding of Jesus' blood.

Finally, in Revelation 17, all those who are condemned by God are said to have drunk and become drunk from the cup of the prostitute. On judgment day these people will drink from the wine of God's wrath, which is the torment of eternal punishment in hell.⚭

⚭ **Alcohol:** For additional scriptures on this topic go to Genesis 9:21–24.

INTRODUCTION TO THE BOOK OF

EZRA

The Return from Captivity

WHO WROTE THIS BOOK?

It is traditionally believed that Ezra the prophet wrote the Book of Ezra, but this fact cannot be completely confirmed. Whoever the author, the form and language patterns of the Book of Ezra are highly similar to the Books of Chronicles. In fact, the final verses of Chronicles and the opening verses of Ezra are almost identical, thus lending credence to the books' having the same author.

TO WHOM WAS THIS BOOK WRITTEN?

The Book of Ezra was written for and about the people of Israel.

WHERE WAS IT WRITTEN?

In the fifth month of the seventh year of King Artaxerxes I, Ezra came to Jerusalem (458 B.C.), according to Jewish tradition (see 7:8). From that verifiable fact we may deduce that the Book of Ezra was written in and around Jerusalem.

WHEN WAS IT WRITTEN?

This book was probably written sometime in the fifth century B.C., perhaps about 440 B.C.

WHAT IS THE BOOK ABOUT?

Ezra continues the story of Israel that was begun in the Books of Chronicles. It tells the tale that Israel's remaining people returned to Judah, just as God had said they would do, and overcame opposition to rebuild the Temple at Jerusalem. It also tells of how Ezra purified the nation of intermarriage in obedience to the Law of Moses.

WHY WAS THIS BOOK WRITTEN?

Ezra shows the restoration of holiness among the people of God. When the faithful few people of Israel return to Jerusalem, God returns with them. Together, God and the people rebuild the Temple. At the end of the story, we find God's people celebrating the dedication of the Temple and renewing their own dedication to holiness.

SO WHAT DOES THIS BOOK MEAN TO US?

The rewards for holiness have not changed among God's people. When we, as Christians, remain faithful to God's teachings until the end, God will remain with us (see Revelation 2:10). At the end of our story as God's people in the present age, we will find ourselves—a holy people—living in the holy city (heaven) with our holy God. This is the fulfillment of his divine promises to us through Jesus—the new David. Meanwhile we must renew our dedication to living holy lives before God and the world, just as the returned exiles did under Ezra.

SUMMARY:

While our Bible treats Ezra and Nehemiah as two separate books, they were originally one book, sharing many similar themes and continuing the same story. Indeed, Ezra continues the story that began in Chronicles. Second Chronicles 36:22–23 is actually repeated at the beginning of the Book of Ezra.

Ezra-Nehemiah is the story of Israel's return to the land of Judah after their exile in Babylonia. God now honors his word to his people that the faithful few people of Israel will return to the Promised Land. The Book of Ezra begins with the decree of the Persian king, Cyrus, that the people of Israel who want to may return to Judah. This decree may be dated to 539 B.C., and the story continues to the time of Ezra. The traditional date for Ezra's return to Judah in 458 B.C.

The Book of Ezra is named after the main character of the second part of the book. He writes in the first person about his return to Jerusalem. He describes his mission to instruct the people in the law of God and to support the rebuilding of the Temple and the city.

While we can date Ezra's mission with some confidence, this does not allow us to date the book.

Ezra's own first person story (chapters 7–10) was written by him, but then it was included in the larger story of the book, which includes the Book of Nehemiah.

The message of Ezra-Nehemiah is an important window to late Old Testament thought. It shows a transition from the importance of charismatic individuals to the importance of community. Ezra and Nehemiah are leaders, but the great acts of rebuilding are accomplished by the whole community of God. Second, we see the concept of holiness expand. The task of building the house of God does not stop with the Temple alone (6:15), but it continues and includes the city and the walls, all of which are consecrated (recognized as holy) in the grand opening ceremonies at the end (Nehemiah 8–13).

There is also a strong emphasis in the book on the distinctiveness of the people of God. They are to obey God's law and keep separate from the people on the outside. For instance, the prohibition on intermarriage is a major topic in the book. In other words, there is the building of both a physical wall and a spiritual wall in Jerusalem. At the end of the book, we have a holy people dwelling in a holy city.

The Book of Ezra has the following outline:

I. From the Decree of Cyrus to the Construction of the Temple (1:1–6:22)
II. Ezra's Mission (Ezra 7:1–10:44)

I. From the Decree of Cyrus to the Construction of the Temple (1:1—6:22)

The opening chapters of the Book of Ezra narrate events that took place between the decree that allowed the people of God to return to Judah and the rebuilding of the Temple (539–515 B.C.). Only a few people of Israel chose to return to the land, and they did so under the leadership of Zerubbabel, a descendant of David, and Sheshbazzar. The main purpose of the return was to rebuild the Temple. They encountered opposition from those who were already living in the land, but God allowed the Temple to be finally finished.

II. Ezra's Mission (7:1—10:44)

Time has passed since the end of chapter 6. Ezra's return to Jerusalem is usually dated to 458 B.C. Ezra's purpose is to rebuild Jerusalem both physically and spiritually. He is a priest, and he wants to teach the people God's law. When he returns, he finds the people of God in a sorry spiritual state, especially because many of them had married non-Jewish women. He calls on them to repent, and the people confess their sin.

EZRA

Cyrus Helps the Captives Return

In the first year Cyrus was king of Persia, the
LORD caused Cyrus to send an announcement to his whole kingdom and to put it in
writing. This happened so the LORD's message
spoken by Jeremiah would come true. He wrote:

2This is what Cyrus king of Persia says:
The Lord, the God of heaven, has given all
the kingdoms of the earth to me, and he has
appointed me to build a Temple for him at
Jerusalem in Judah. 3May God be with all of
you who are his people. You are free to go to
Jerusalem in Judah and build the Temple of
the Lord, the God of Israel, who is in Jerusalem. 4Those who stay behind, wherever
they live, should support those who want to
go. Give them silver and gold, supplies and
cattle, and special gifts for the Temple of God
in Jerusalem.

5Then the family leaders of Judah and Benjamin
and the priests and Levites got ready to go to Jerusalem—everyone God had caused to want to go
to Jerusalem to build the Temple of the LORD. 6All
their neighbors helped them, giving them things
made of silver and gold, along with supplies, cattle,
valuable gifts, and special gifts for the Temple. 7Also,
King Cyrus brought out the bowls and pans that
belonged in the Temple of the LORD, which Nebuchadnezzar had taken from Jerusalem and put in
the temple of his own god. 8Cyrus king of Persia
had Mithredath the treasurer bring them and count
them out for Sheshbazzar, the prince of Judah.
9He listed thirty gold dishes, one thousand silver dishes, twenty-nine pans, 10thirty gold bowls,
four hundred ten matching silver bowls, and one
thousand other pieces.
11There was a total of fifty-four hundred pieces
of gold and silver. Sheshbazzar brought all these
things along when the captives went from Babylon
to Jerusalem.

The Captives Who Returned

2 These are the people of the area who returned
from captivity, whom Nebuchadnezzar king of
Babylon had taken away to Babylon. They returned
to Jerusalem and Judah, each going back to his own
town. 2These people returned with Zerubbabel,
Jeshua, Nehemiah, Seraiah, Reelaiah, Mordecai,
Bilshan, Mispar, Bigvai, Rehum, and Baanah.
These are the people from Israel: 3the descendants of Parosh—2,172; 4the descendants of
Shephatiah—372; 5the descendants of Arah—
775; 6the descendants of Pahath-Moab (through
the family of Jeshua and Joab)—2,812; 7the descendants of Elam—1,254; 8the descendants of
Zattu—945; 9the descendants of Zaccai—760;
10the descendants of Bani—642; 11the descendants of Bebai—623; 12the descendants of Azgad—1,222; 13the descendants of Adonikam—
666; 14the descendants of Bigvai—2,056; 15the
descendants of Adin—454; 16the descendants of
Ater (through the family of Hezekiah)—98; 17the
descendants of Bezai—323; 18the descendants of
Jorah—112; 19the descendants of Hashum—223;
20the descendants of Gibbar—95.
21These are the people from the towns: of
Bethlehem—123; 22of Netophah—56; 23of Anathoth—128; 24of Azmaveth—42; 25of Kiriath
Jearim, Kephirah, and Beeroth—743; 26of Ramah
and Geba—621; 27of Micmash—122; 28of Bethel
and Ai—223; 29of Nebo—52; 30of Magbish—
156; 31of the other town of Elam—1,254; 32of
Harim—320; 33of Lod, Hadid and Ono—725;
34of Jericho—345; 35of Senaah—3,630.
36These are the priests: the descendants of
Jedaiah (through the family of Jeshua)—973;
37the descendants of Immer—1,052; 38the descendants of Pashhur—1,247; 39the descendants
of Harim—1,017.
40These are the Levites: the descendants of
Jeshua and Kadmiel (through the family of Hodaviah)—74.
41These are the singers: the descendants of
Asaph—128.
42These are the gatekeepers of the Temple: the
descendants of Shallum, Ater, Talmon, Akkub,
Hatita, and Shobai—139.
43These are the Temple servants: the descendants
of Ziha, Hasupha, Tabbaoth, 44Keros, Siaha, Padon,
45Lebanah, Hagabah, Akkub, 46Hagab, Shalmai,
Hanan, 47Giddel, Gahar, Reaiah, 48Rezin, Nekoda,
Gazzam, 49Uzza, Paseah, Besai, 50Asnah, Meunim,
Nephussim, 51Bakbuk, Hakupha, Harhur, 52Bazluth,
Mehida, Harsha, 53Barkos, Sisera, Temah, 54Neziah,
and Hatipha.
55These are the descendants of the servants of
Solomon: the descendants of Sotai, Hassophereth,

1:2 *The LORD, the God of heaven.* Cyrus here uses the language of the Jewish people themselves to refer to their God. As a believer in a vast number of gods, Cyrus would have acknowledged the existence of *Yahweh,* but his language here does not mean he became a convert to Judaism.

Peruda, 56Jaala, Darkon, Giddel, 57Shephatiah,
Hattil, Pokereth-Hazzebaim, and Ami.
58The Temple servants and the descendants of
the servants of Solomon numbered 392.
59Some people came to Jerusalem from the
towns of Tel Melah, Tel Harsha, Kerub, Addon,
and Immer, but they could not prove that their
ancestors came from Israel. 60They were the descendants of Delaiah, Tobiah, and Nekoda—652.
61Also these priests: the descendants of Hobaiah, Hakkoz, and Barzillai, who had married a
daughter of Barzillai from Gilead and was called
by her family name.
62These people searched for their family records
but could not find them. So they could not be
priests, because they were thought to be unclean.
63The governor ordered them not to eat any of
the food offered to God until a priest had settled
this matter by using the Urim and Thummim.
64The total number of those who returned was
42,360. 65This is not counting their 7,337 male and
female servants and the 200 male and female
singers they had with them. 66They had 736 horses,
245 mules, 67435 camels, and 6,720 donkeys.
68When they arrived at the Temple of the LORD
in Jerusalem, some of the leaders of families gave
offerings to rebuild the Temple of God on the
same site as before. 69They gave as much as they
could to the treasury to rebuild the Temple—
about 1,100 pounds of gold, about 6,000 pounds
of silver, and 100 pieces of clothing for the priests.
70All the Israelites settled in their hometowns.
The priests, Levites, singers, gatekeepers, and
Temple servants, along with some of the other
people, settled in their own towns as well.

Rebuilding the Altar

3 In the seventh month, after the Israelites
were settled in their hometowns, they met
together in Jerusalem. 2Then Jeshua son of
Jozadak and his fellow priests joined Zerubbabel
son of Shealtiel and began to build the altar of the
God of Israel where they could offer burnt offerings, just as it is written in the Teachings of
Moses, the man of God. 3Even though they were
afraid of the people living around them, they built
the altar where it had been before. And they
offered burnt offerings on it to the LORD morning
and evening. 4Then, to obey what was written,
they celebrated the Feast of Shelters. They offered
the right number of sacrifices for each day of the
festival. 5After the Feast of Shelters, they had regular sacrifices every day, as well as sacrifices for
the New Moon and all the festivals commanded
by the LORD. Also there were special offerings
brought as gifts to the LORD. 6On the first day of the
seventh month they began to bring burnt offerings
to the LORD, but the foundation of the LORD's Temple
had not yet been laid.

Rebuilding the Temple

7Then they gave money to the bricklayers and
carpenters. They also gave food, wine, and oil to
the cities of Sidon and Tyre so they would float
cedar logs from Lebanon to the seacoast town of
Joppa. Cyrus king of Persia had given permission
for this.
8In the second month of the second year after
their arrival at the Temple of God in Jerusalem,
Zerubbabel son of Shealtiel, Jeshua son of
Jozadak, their fellow priests and Levites, and all
who had returned from captivity to Jerusalem
began to work. They chose Levites twenty years
old and older to be in charge of the building of the
Temple of the LORD. 9These men were in charge
of the work of building the Temple of God: Jeshua
and his sons and brothers; Kadmiel and his sons
who were the descendants of Hodaviah; and the
sons of Henadad and their sons and brothers.
They were all Levites.
10The builders finished laying the foundation of
the Temple of the LORD. Then the priests, dressed
in their robes, stood with their trumpets, and the
Levites, the sons of Asaph, stood with their cymbals. They all took their places and praised the LORD
just as David king of Israel had said to do. 11With
praise and thanksgiving, they sang to the LORD:
"He is good;
his love for Israel continues forever."
And then all the people shouted loudly, "Praise
the LORD! The foundation of his Temple has been
laid." 12But many of the older priests, Levites, and
family leaders who had seen the first Temple cried
when they saw the foundation of this Temple.
Most of the other people were shouting with joy.
13The people made so much noise it could be
heard far away, and no one could tell the difference
between the joyful shouting and the sad crying.

Enemies of the Rebuilding

4 When the enemies of the people of Judah
and Benjamin heard that the returned captives were building a Temple for the LORD, the
God of Israel, 2they came to Zerubbabel and the
leaders of the families. The enemies said, "Let us

2:70 Births: Nehemiah 7
3:12 Some of the older leaders wept because this new Temple did not compare to the outward glory of the old one.

help you build, because we are like you and want
to worship your God. We have been offering sacrifices to him since the time of Esarhaddon king
of Assyria, who brought us here."
3But Zerubbabel, Jeshua, and the leaders of
Israel answered, "You will not help us build a
Temple to our God. We will build it ourselves for
the LORD, the God of Israel, as King Cyrus, the
king of Persia, commanded us to do."
4Then the people around them tried to discourage the people of Judah by making them afraid to
build. 5Their enemies hired others to delay the
building plans during the time Cyrus was king of
Persia. And it continued to the time Darius was
king of Persia.

More Problems for the Builders

6When Xerxes first became king, those enemies
wrote a letter against the people of Judah and
Jerusalem.
7When Artaxerxes became king of Persia,
Bishlam, Mithredath, Tabeel, and those with
them wrote a letter to Artaxerxes. It was written
in the Aramaic language and translated.
8Rehum the governor and Shimshai the governor's secretary wrote a letter against Jerusalem to
Artaxerxes the king. It said:

9This letter is from Rehum the governor,
Shimshai the secretary, and their fellow
workers—the judges and important officers
over the men who came from Tripolis,
Persia, Erech, and Babylon, the Elamite people of Susa, 10and those whom the great and
honorable Ashurbanipal forced out of their
countries and settled in the city of Samaria
and in other places of the Trans-Euphrates.

11(This is a copy of the letter they sent to
Artaxerxes.)

To King Artaxerxes.
From your servants who live in Trans-
Euphrates.

12King Artaxerxes, you should know that
the Jewish people who came to us from you
have gone to Jerusalem to rebuild that evil city
that refuses to obey. They are fixing the walls
and repairing the foundations of the buildings.
13Now, King Artaxerxes, you should know
that if Jerusalem is built and its walls are
fixed, Jerusalem will not pay taxes of any
kind. Then the amount of money your government collects will be less. 14Since we
must be loyal to the government, we don't
want to see the king dishonored. So we are
writing to let the king know. 15We suggest
you search the records of the kings who
ruled before you. You will find out that the
city of Jerusalem refuses to obey and makes
trouble for kings and areas controlled by
Persia. Since long ago it has been a place
where disobedience has started. That is why
it was destroyed. 16We want you to know,
King Artaxerxes, that if this city is rebuilt
and its walls fixed, you will be left with nothing in Trans-Euphrates.

17King Artaxerxes sent this answer:

To Rehum the governor and Shimshai the
secretary, to all their fellow workers living in
Samaria, and to those in other places in
Trans-Euphrates.

Greetings.
18The letter you sent to us has been translated and read to me. 19I ordered the
records to be searched, and it was done. We
found that Jerusalem has a history of disobedience to kings and has been a place of
problems and trouble. 20Jerusalem has had
powerful kings who have ruled over the
whole area of Trans-Euphrates, and taxes of
all kinds have been paid to them. 21Now,
give an order for those men to stop work.
The city of Jerusalem will not be rebuilt
until I say so. 22Make sure you do this,
because if they continue, it will hurt the
government.

23A copy of the letter that King Artaxerxes sent
was read to Rehum and Shimshai the secretary
and the others. Then they quickly went to the
Jewish people in Jerusalem and forced them to
stop building.
24So the work on the Temple of God in
Jerusalem stopped until the second year Darius
was king of Persia.

4:13 Walls provided a city with a defense against an enemy army. To build walls could be interpreted as a preparation for war.

4:17 When Ezra came back to the land, he set about to rebuild the decimated community of God's people. His task was to build the Temple. He found opposition from the north. These people lived in Samaria, and this conflict was an instance of a long-standing conflict between Jewish people and Samaritans that stands behind the parable of the good Samaritan, and the conversation between Jesus and the woman at the well in John 4.

KINGS AND PROPHETS OF JUDAH

KINGS	DATE	PROPHETS
Rehoboam	930-913 B.C.	
Abijah	913-910 B.C.	
Asa[g]	911-870 B.C.	
Jehoshaphat[g]	872-848 B.C.	
Jehoram	853-841 B.C.	
Ahaziah	841 B.C.	
Athaliah	841-835 B.C.	
Joash[g]	835-796 B.C.	*Joel*
Amaziah[g]	796-767 B.C.	
Azariah (Uzziah)[g]	792-740 B.C.	*Isaiah*
Jotham[g]	750-732 B.C.	*Isaiah*
		Micah
Ahaz	750-715 B.C.	*Micah*
		Isaiah
Hezekiah[g]	715-686 B.C.	*Isaiah*
		Micah
Manasseh	697-642 B.C.	
Amon	642-640 B.C.	
Josiah[g]	640-609 B.C.	*Huldah*
		Nahum
		Habakkuk
		Jeremiah
Jehoahaz[g]	609 B.C.	*Zephaniah*
		Jeremiah
Jehoiakim[g]	609-598 B.C.	*Jeremiah*
Jehoiachin[g]	598-597 B.C.	*Jeremiah*
Zedekiah[g]	597-586 B.C.	*Jeremiah*

Note: Sometimes kings ruled at the same time as their fathers or sons.
A [g] indicates good kings.

Kings and Prophets of Israel

KINGS	DATE	PROPHETS
Jeroboam I	930-909 B.C.	*Unnamed man of God*
		Ahijah
Nadab	909-908 B.C.	
Baasha	908-886 B.C.	*Jehu son of Hanani*
Elah	886-885 B.C.	
Zimri	885 B.C.	
Tibni	885-880 B.C.	
Omri	880-874 B.C.	
Ahab	874-853 B.C.	*Elijah*
		Elisha
		An unnamed prophet
		Micaiah
		Obadiah (?)
Ahaziah	853-852 B.C.	
Joram	852-841 B.C.	*Elisha*
Jehu	841-814 B.C.	*Elisha*
Jehoahaz	814-798 B.C.	
Jehoash	798-782 B.C.	*Elisha*
Jeroboam II	793-753 B.C.	*Jonah*
		Amos
		Hosea
Zechariah	753 B.C.	
Shallum	752 B.C.	
Menahem	752-742 B.C.	*Hosea*
Pekah	752-732 B.C.	
Pekahiah	742-740 B.C.	
Hoshea	732-723 B.C.	

Tattenai's Letter to Darius

5 The prophets Haggai and Zechariah, a descendant of Iddo, prophesied to the Jewish people
in Judah and Jerusalem in the name of the God of
Israel, who was over them. 2Then Zerubbabel son
of Shealtiel and Jeshua son of Jozadak started
working again to rebuild the Temple of God in
Jerusalem. And the prophets of God were there,
helping them.
3At that time Tattenai, the governor of Trans-
Euphrates, and Shethar-Bozenai, and their fellow
workers went to the Jewish people and asked,
"Who gave you permission to rebuild this Temple
and fix these walls?" 4They also asked, "What are
the names of the men working on this building?"
5But their God was watching over the older leaders of the Jewish people. The builders were not
stopped until a report could go to King Darius and
his written answer could be received.
6This is a copy of the letter that was sent to
King Darius by Tattenai, the governor of Trans-
Euphrates, Shethar-Bozenai, and the other important officers of Trans-Euphrates. 7This is what
was said in the report they sent to him:

To King Darius.

Greetings. May you have peace.
8King Darius, you should know that we
went to the district of Judah where the
Temple of the great God is. The people are
building that Temple with large stones, and
they are putting timbers in the walls. They are
working very hard and are building very fast.
9We asked their older leaders, "Who gave
you permission to rebuild this Temple and
these walls?" 10We also asked for their names,
and we wrote down the names of their leaders
so you would know who they are.
11This is the answer they gave to us: "We
are the servants of the God of heaven and
earth. We are rebuilding the Temple that a
great king of Israel built and finished many
years ago. 12But our ancestors made the God
of heaven angry, so he handed them over to
Nebuchadnezzar king of Babylon, who
destroyed this Temple and took the people to
Babylon as captives.
13"Later, in the first year Cyrus was king of
Babylon, he gave a special order for this
Temple to be rebuilt. 14Cyrus brought out
from the temple in Babylon the gold and silver bowls and pans that came from the
Temple of God. Nebuchadnezzar had taken
them from the Temple in Jerusalem and had
put them in the temple in Babylon.
"Then King Cyrus gave them to Sheshbazzar, his appointed governor. 15Cyrus said to
him, 'Take these gold and silver bowls and
pans, and put them back in the Temple in
Jerusalem and rebuild the Temple of God
where it was.' 16So Sheshbazzar came and
laid the foundations of the Temple of God in
Jerusalem. From that day until now the work
has been going on, but it is not yet finished."
17Now, if the king wishes, let a search be
made in the royal records of Babylon. See if
King Cyrus gave an order to rebuild this
Temple in Jerusalem. Then let the king write
us and tell us what he has decided.

The Order of Darius

6 So King Darius gave an order to search the
records kept in the treasury in Babylon. 2A
scroll was found in Ecbatana, the capital city of
Media. This is what was written on it:

Note:

3King Cyrus gave an order about the Temple
of God in Jerusalem in the first year he was
king. This was the order:
"Let the Temple be rebuilt as a place to
present sacrifices. Let its foundations be laid;
it should be ninety feet high and ninety feet
wide. 4It must have three layers of large
stones and then one layer of timbers. The
costs should be paid from the king's treasury.
5The gold and silver utensils from the
Temple of God should be put back in their
places. Nebuchadnezzar took them from the
Temple in Jerusalem and brought them to
Babylon, but they are to be put back in the
Temple of God in Jerusalem."
6Now then, Tattenai, governor of Trans-
Euphrates, Shethar-Bozenai, and all the officers of that area, stay away from there. 7Do
not bother the work on that Temple of God.
Let the governor of the Jewish people and
the older Jewish leaders rebuild this Temple
where it was before.
8Also, I order you to do this for those older
leaders of the Jewish people who are building this Temple: The cost of the building is to
be fully paid from the royal treasury, from
taxes collected from Trans-Euphrates. Do
this so the work will not stop. 9Give those
people anything they need—young bulls,
male sheep, or lambs for burnt offerings to

the God of heaven, or wheat, salt, wine, or olive oil. Give the priests in Jerusalem anything they ask for every day without fail. 10Then they may offer sacrifices pleasing to the God of heaven, and they may pray for the life of the king and his sons.

11Also, I give this order: If anyone changes this order, a wood beam is to be pulled from his house and driven through his body. Because of his crime, make his house a pile of ruins. 12God has chosen Jerusalem as the place he is to be worshiped. May he punish any king or person who tries to change this order and destroy this Temple.

I, Darius, have given this order. Let it be obeyed quickly and carefully.

Completion of the Temple

13So, Tattenai, the governor of Trans-Euphrates, Shethar-Bozenai, and their fellow workers carried out King Darius' order quickly and carefully. 14The older Jewish leaders continued to build and were successful because of the preaching of Haggai the prophet and Zechariah, a descendant of Iddo. They finished building the Temple as the God of Israel had commanded and as kings Cyrus, Darius, and Artaxerxes of Persia had ordered. 15The Temple was finished on the third day of the month of Adar in the sixth year Darius was king.

16Then the people of Israel celebrated and gave the Temple to God to honor him. Everybody was happy: the priests, the Levites, and the rest of the Jewish people who had returned from captivity. 17They gave the Temple to God by offering a hundred bulls, two hundred male sheep, and four hundred lambs as sacrifices. And as an offering to forgive the sins of all Israel, they offered twelve male goats, one goat for each tribe in Israel. 18Then they put the priests and the Levites into their separate groups. Each group had a certain time to serve God in the Temple at Jerusalem as it is written in the Book of Moses.

The Passover Is Celebrated

19The Jewish people who returned from captivity celebrated the Passover on the fourteenth day of the first month. 20The priests and Levites had made themselves clean. Then the Levites killed the Passover lambs for all the people who had returned from captivity, for their relatives the priests, and for themselves. 21So all the people of Israel who returned from captivity ate the Passover lamb. So did the people who had given up the unclean ways of their non-Jewish neighbors in order to worship the LORD, the God of Israel. 22For seven days they celebrated the Feast of Unleavened Bread in a very joyful way. The LORD had made them happy by changing the mind of the king of Assyria so that he helped them in the work on the Temple of the God of Israel.

Ezra Comes to Jerusalem

7 After these things during the rule of Artaxerxes king of Persia, Ezra came up from Babylon. Ezra was the son of Seraiah, the son of Azariah, the son of Hilkiah, 2the son of Shallum, the son of Zadok, the son of Ahitub, 3the son of Amariah, the son of Azariah, the son of Meraioth, 4the son of Zerahiah, the son of Uzzi, the son of Bukki, 5the son of Abishua, the son of Phinehas, the son of Eleazar, the son of Aaron the high priest. 6This Ezra came to Jerusalem from Babylon. He was a teacher and knew well the Teachings of Moses that had been given by the LORD, the God of Israel. Ezra received everything he asked for from the king, because the LORD his God was helping him. 7In the seventh year of King Artaxerxes more Israelites came to Jerusalem. Among them were priests, Levites, singers, gatekeepers, and Temple servants.

8Ezra arrived in Jerusalem in the fifth month of Artaxerxes' seventh year as king. 9Ezra had left Babylon on the first day of the first month, and he arrived in Jerusalem on the first day of the fifth month, because God was helping him. 10Ezra had worked hard to know and obey the Teachings of the LORD and to teach his rules and commands to the Israelites.

Artaxerxes' Letter to Ezra

11King Artaxerxes had given a letter to Ezra, a priest and teacher who taught about the commands and laws the LORD gave Israel. This is a copy of the letter:

> 12From Artaxerxes, king of kings, to Ezra the priest, a teacher of the Law of the God of heaven.
>
> Greetings.
>
> 13Now I give this order: Any Israelite in my kingdom who wishes may go with you to Jerusalem, including priests and Levites. 14Ezra, you are sent by the king and the seven people who

6:10 Citizen: Ecclesiastes 8:2–4

7:1 *After these things.* There is a time period of about sixty years between chapters six and seven.

advise him to ask how Judah and Jerusalem
are obeying the Law of your God, which you
are carrying with you. 15Also take with you
the silver and gold that the king and those
who advise him have given freely to the God
of Israel, whose Temple is in Jerusalem.
16Also take the silver and gold you receive
from the area of Babylon. Take the offerings
the Israelites and their priests have given as
gifts for the Temple of your God in
Jerusalem. 17With this money buy bulls, male
sheep, and lambs, and the grain offerings and
drink offerings that go with those sacrifices.
Then sacrifice them on the altar in the
Temple of your God in Jerusalem.
18You and your fellow Jews may spend the
silver and gold left over as you want and as
God wishes. 19Take to the God of Jerusalem
all the utensils for worship in the Temple of
your God, 20which we have given you. Use
the royal treasury to pay for anything else
you need for the Temple of your God.
21Now I, King Artaxerxes, give this order
to all the men in charge of the treasury of
Trans-Euphrates: Give Ezra, a priest and a
teacher of the Law of the God of heaven,
whatever he asks for. 22Give him up to seventy-
five hundred pounds of silver, six hundred
bushels of wheat, six hundred gallons of wine,
and six hundred gallons of olive oil. And give
him as much salt as he wants. 23Carefully
give him whatever the God of heaven wants
for the Temple of the God of heaven. We do
not want God to be angry with the king and
his sons. 24Remember, you must not make
these people pay taxes of any kind: priests,
Levites, singers, gatekeepers, Temple servants,
and other workers in this Temple of God.
25And you, Ezra, use the wisdom you have
from your God to choose judges and lawmak-
ers to rule the Jewish people of Trans-
Euphrates. They know the laws of your God,
and you may teach anyone who does not
know them. 26Whoever does not obey the
law of your God or of the king must be punished. He will be killed, or sent away, or have
his property taken away, or be put in jail.

27Praise the LORD, the God of our ancestors. He
caused the king to want to honor the Temple of
the LORD in Jerusalem. 28The LORD has shown me,
Ezra, his love in the presence of the king, those
who advise the king, and the royal officers. Because
the LORD my God was helping me, I had courage,
and I gathered the leaders of Israel to return with
me.

Leaders Who Returned with Ezra

8 These are the leaders of the family groups
and those who were listed with them who
came back with me from Babylon during the rule
of King Artaxerxes.
2From the descendants of Phinehas: Gershom.
From the descendants of Ithamar: Daniel.
From the descendants of David: Hattush 3of the
descendants of Shecaniah.
From the descendants of Parosh: Zechariah,
with one hundred fifty men.
4From the descendants of Pahath-Moab: Eliehoenai son of Zerahiah, with two hundred men.
5From the descendants of Zattu: Shecaniah son
of Jahaziel, with three hundred men.
6From the descendants of Adin: Ebed son of
Jonathan, with fifty men.
7From the descendants of Elam: Jeshaiah son of
Athaliah, with seventy men.
8From the descendants of Shephatiah: Zebadiah son of Michael, with eighty men.
9From the descendants of Joab: Obadiah son of
Jehiel, with two hundred eighteen men.
10From the descendants of Bani: Shelomith son
of Josiphiah, with one hundred sixty men.
11From the descendants of Bebai: Zechariah
son of Bebai, with twenty-eight men.
12From the descendants of Azgad: Johanan son
of Hakkatan, with one hundred ten men.
13From the descendants of Adonikam, these
were the last ones: Eliphelet, Jeuel, and Shemaiah, with sixty men.
14From the descendants of Bigvai: Uthai and
Zaccur, with seventy men.

The Return to Jerusalem

15I called all those people together at the canal
that flows toward Ahava, where we camped for
three days. I checked all the people and the priests,
but I did not find any Levites. 16So I called these
leaders: Eliezer, Ariel, Shemaiah, Elnathan, Jarib,
Elnathan, Nathan, Zechariah, and Meshullam.
And I called Joiarib and Elnathan, who were
teachers. 17I sent these men to Iddo, the leader at
Casiphia, and told them what to say to Iddo and
his relatives, who are the Temple servants in
Casiphia. I sent them to bring servants to us for
the Temple of our God. 18Our God was helping us,

8:15 *Ahava.* A location and the name of a canal (see 8:21) in the vicinity of Babylon.

MEDITATION

PSALM 119

What are Christians doing when they are meditating?
How is meditation different from prayer?
What are the objects of the Christian's meditation?
How can meditation benefit the believer today?

To meditate is to focus one's thoughts on something, or to reflect or ponder something. The Bible speaks about meditation with words like "remember," "think about," and "consider." For example, in Psalm 63:6, the psalmist says, "I remember you while I'm lying in bed; I think about you through the night." To "think about," to meditate, is to allow one's mind to return again and again to thoughts of God. Whereas meditation refers to bringing one's mind to thoughts about God, prayer is most often used for talking to God. For example, in Phillipians 4:6, the apostle Paul encourages the believer to "pray and ask God for everything you need." It is easy to see how "thinking about" God and "praying to" God often happen together as our minds are focused on One who is always with us. Still, meditation can be distinguished from prayer in that the focus in meditation is the repeated bringing of thoughts about God to our minds.

Meditation often joins thinking, feeling, and imagination in a time of being with God or thinking about God. A good example of this is found in Psalm 77. The psalmist says, "When I remember God, I become upset; when I think, I become afraid" (verse 3). The thought of God stirs up the emotions of this person. He says, "I think and I ask myself: Will the Lord reject us forever'"(vv. 6–7)? He is sad, because he had been taught that God was a mighty God, but he does not experience God's power in his own life. The psalmist then decides to remember the mighty deeds of God which he had heard about. He says, "I think about all the things you did and consider your deeds" (verse 12). He imagines the story of Moses and Aaron crossing the Red Sea, and the power of God separating the waters. "Lightning lit up the world. The earth trembled and shook," he writes. "You made a way through the sea and paths through the deep waters" (vv. 18–19). His prayerful imagination of the mighty acts of God renews his confidence that God's "ways are holy. No God is as great as our God" (verse 13).

When we meditate as Christians, we think about different things related to our faith. We think about his words, his works, his ways, and about God himself. The Book of Psalms speaks often about meditating on the words of God. Psalm 1:2 states that those whom God loves most, "love the Lord's teachings, and they think about those teachings day and night." Psalm 119 presents this theme repeatedly. "I think about your orders and study your ways," he says (verse 15). "I, your servant, will think about your demands." "How I love your teachings! I think about them all day long" (vv. 23, 97). "I stay awake all night," he says, "so I can think about your promises" (verse 148). But we not only meditate on God's words, we also meditate on his works, either the majesty of his creation, or his mighty deeds of the past. We have seen in Psalm 77 how God's past deeds can be the object of meditation. The writer of Psalm 143:5 states, "I remember what happened long ago; I consider everything you have done. I think about all you have made." We also can find ourselves meditating on the ways of God. Paul urged the Phillippians to "think about the things that are good and worthy of praise. Think about the things that are true and honorable and right and pure and beautiful and respected" (Phillippians 4:8). Finally, we meditate on God himself. He becomes the object of our thought and the One present in our thought. The author of Hebrews encourages us to "think about Jesus' example" (Hebrews 12:3). Psalm 107:43 states, "Whoever is wise will remember these things and will think about the love of the Lord."

To spend time focusing our mind, our imagination, and our emotions on the things of the Lord is an enriching experience for the believer. Psalm 119:99 states, "I am wiser than all my teachers, because I think about your rules." Those who think about the Lord's teachings day and night are called "strong, like a tree planted by a river. . . . Everything they do will succeed" (Psalm 1:3). "Think only about the things in heaven," Paul encourages. "Christ is our life, and when he comes again, you will share in his glory" (Colossians 3:2, 4).

As God is present in our times with him, prayer and meditation blend, for God is not only the One about whom we think, but also the One to whom we pray and with whom we are present. To spend time bringing our mind to God is a special experience for the believer, one which helps us to find success on earth and prepares us to share his glory in heaven.

Meditation: For additional scriptures on this topic go to Joshua 1:8.

Abortion and Crisis Pregnancy

Psalm 139

What themes in the Bible help us form a biblical viewpoint on abortion? Do we have examples of "crisis pregnancies" in the Bible? How does God respond to them? How are we to respond to them?

Few issues are as controversial and confusing as abortion. Many Christians turn to the Bible for moral guidance on this problem. They are often surprised to find that there is no single passage of Scripture that directly addresses abortion. This does not mean, however, that the Bible is silent on the issue. Rather, there are a number of themes that, when understood together, help us to form a biblical view of abortion. These themes include: the values of unborn human life; God's care for women in crisis pregnancies; and God's call for Christians to care for these women and their children.

Unborn human life is valuable because God is the creator of life. In Psalm 139, David declares the wonder and intimacy of God's creative act. He affirms that God is at work forming human life within the womb. Other Old Testament writers understood God to be active in the conception and development of prenatal life, (Job 31:15; Isaiah 44:2). David also speaks of the intimate relationship between God and the unborn. "You saw my bones being formed as I took shape in my mother's body" (Psalm 139:15). David is claiming here that God knew him completely before he was born.

God places value upon unborn human life by designing a special purpose for each individual life. Several biblical figures claim that God's plan for their lives was given to them while still in their mother's womb. The Old Testament prophet Isaiah said that God had both named him and called him to God's service before his birth (Isaiah 49:1). The apostle Paul testifies that "God had special plans for me and set me apart for his work even before I was born" (Galatians 1:15). And Jeremiah recounts God's proclamation to him that he was chosen by God even before his conception (Jeremiah 1:5). Creating, "seeing," calling, and naming are all acts of God showing that his presence is with the unborn. In these ways we see that God values prenatal life. When we seek the Bible's view of abortion, we must begin with this notion of the God-given value of unborn human life.

The story of Hagar and Ishmael in the Book of Genesis tells us how God also values and cares for women in crisis pregnancies. Hagar's barren mistress Sarai told her husband to conceive a child with Hagar so that she could "have [her] own family through her" (Genesis 16:2). When Hagar became pregnant, Sarai mistreated her. Rejected and abused, Hagar fled to the desert. There an angel of the Lord greeted her with the promise that God would bless her with "so many descendants they cannot be counted" (Genesis 16:10). In God's provision for Hagar, he also affirms the value of the life growing within her womb. God's chosen name for her unborn is Ishmael, "because the Lord has heard your cries" (Genesis 16:11).

What does it mean that God "hears" Hagar's cries? God knows Hagar and her circumstances, and he is moved to give tangible care to this woman and her unborn child. This is reflected in Hagar's name for the Lord, "God who sees me" (Genesis 16:13). This language is reminiscent of Psalm 139 which speaks of God's "seeing" unborn life in the womb. God sees and hears the needs of both mother and unborn child. Unlike God, we often elevate the life of one over the other. A biblical view would call us to weigh each life as valuable before God, and to be responsive as God is to the needs of women in crisis pregnancies and their unborn children.

This theme of caring for the outcast and needy is present throughout the Bible. In Matthew, Jesus teaches that we are to feed, clothe, and comfort "the least of" God's people (Matthew 25:40). The New Testament church of Acts concerned themselves with feeding the widows of their group (Acts 6:1–7). James claims that pure and faultless religion is "caring for orphans or widows who need help" (James 1:27). The Old Testament, too, attests to this call to care for the orphan (Deuteronomy 24:17; Job 31:17). How do these passages help us to form a biblical view of abortion? Simply put, our care for women facing crisis pregnancies and the unborn is an expression of the kind of neighbor love that is exemplified in these texts. Such a response gives witness to the value of every human life—born and unborn, mother and child.

Abortion and Crisis Pregnancy: For additional scriptures on this topic go to Job 31:15.

so Iddo's relatives gave us Sherebiah, a wise man from the descendants of Mahli son of Levi, who was the son of Israel. And they brought Sherebiah's sons and brothers, for a total of eighteen men. 19And they brought to us Hashabiah and Jeshaiah from the descendants of Merari, and his brothers and nephews. In all there were twenty men. 20They also brought two hundred twenty of the Temple servants, a group David and the officers had set up to help the Levites. All of those men were listed by name.

21There by the Ahava Canal, I announced we would all give up eating and humble ourselves before our God. We would ask God for a safe trip for ourselves, our children, and all our possessions. 22I was ashamed to ask the king for soldiers and horsemen to protect us from enemies on the road. We had said to the king, "Our God helps everyone who obeys him, but he is very angry with all who reject him." 23So we gave up eating and prayed to our God about our trip, and he answered our prayers.

24Then I chose twelve of the priests who were leaders, Sherebiah, Hashabiah, and ten of their relatives. 25I weighed the offering of silver and gold and the utensils given for the Temple of our God, and I gave them to the twelve priests I had chosen. The king, the people who advised him, his officers, and all the Israelites there with us had given these things for the Temple. 26I weighed out and gave them about fifty thousand pounds of silver, about seventy-five hundred pounds of silver objects, and about seventy-five hundred pounds of gold. 27I gave them twenty gold bowls that weighed about nineteen pounds and two fine pieces of polished bronze that were as valuable as gold.

28Then I said to the priests, "You and these utensils belong to the LORD for his service. The silver and gold are gifts to the LORD, the God of your ancestors. 29Guard these things carefully. In Jerusalem, weigh them in front of the leading priests, Levites, and the leaders of the family groups of Israel in the rooms of the Temple of the LORD." 30So the priests and Levites accepted the silver, the gold, and the utensils that had been weighed to take them to the Temple of our God in Jerusalem.

31On the twelfth day of the first month we left the Ahava Canal and started toward Jerusalem. Our God helped us and protected us from enemies and robbers along the way. 32Finally we arrived in Jerusalem where we rested three days.

33On the fourth day we weighed out the silver, the gold, and the utensils in the Temple of our God. We handed them to the priest Meremoth son of Uriah. Eleazar son of Phinehas was with him, as were the Levites Jozabad son of Jeshua and Noadiah son of Binnui. 34We checked everything by number and by weight, and the total weight was written down.

35Then the captives who returned made burnt offerings to the God of Israel. They sacrificed twelve bulls for all Israel, ninety-six male sheep, and seventy-seven lambs. For a sin offering there were twelve male goats. All this was a burnt offering to the LORD. 36They took King Artaxerxes' orders to the royal officers and to the governors of Trans-Euphrates. Then these men gave help to the people and the Temple of God.

Ezra's Prayer

9 After these things had been done, the leaders came to me and said, "Ezra, the Israelites, including the priests and Levites, have not kept themselves separate from the people around us. Those neighbors do evil things, as the Canaanites, Hittites, Perizzites, Jebusites, Ammonites, Moabites, Egyptians, and Amorites did. 2The Israelite men and their sons have married these women. They have mixed the people who belong to God with the people around them. The leaders and officers of Israel have led the rest of the Israelites to do this unfaithful thing."

3When I heard this, I angrily tore my robe and coat, pulled hair from my head and beard, and sat down in shock. 4Everyone who trembled in fear at the word of the God of Israel gathered around me because of the unfaithfulness of the captives who had returned. I sat there in shock until the evening sacrifice.

5At the evening sacrifice I got up from where I had shown my shame. My robe and coat were torn, and I fell on my knees with my hands spread out to the LORD my God. 6I prayed,

"My God, I am too ashamed and embarrassed to lift up my face to you, my God, because our sins are so many. They are higher than our heads. Our guilt even reaches up to the sky. 7From the days of our ancestors until now, our guilt has been great. Because of our sins, we, our kings, and our priests have been punished by the sword and captivity. Foreign kings have taken away our things and shamed us, even as it is today.

8"But now, for a short time, the LORD our God has been kind to us. He has let some of us come back from captivity and has let us live in safety in

8:23 Fasting: Nehemiah 1:4–11

9:2 Nehemiah: Ezra 9:10–12

his holy place. And so our God gives us hope and
a little relief from our slavery.⚭ 9Even though we
are slaves, our God has not left us. He caused the
kings of Persia to be kind to us and has given us
new life. We can rebuild the Temple and repair
its ruins. And he has given us a wall to protect us
in Judah and Jerusalem.

10"But now, our God, what can we say after
you have done all this? We have disobeyed your
commands 11that you gave through your servants
the prophets. You said, 'The land you are entering to own is ruined; the people living there have
spoiled it by the evil they do. Their evil filled the
land with uncleanness from one end to the other.
12So do not let your daughters marry their sons,
and do not let their daughters marry your sons.
Do not wish for their peace or success. Then you
will be strong and eat the good things of the land.
Then you can leave this land to your descendants
forever.'⚭

13"What has happened to us is our own fault.
We have done evil things, and our guilt is great.
But you, our God, have punished us less than we
deserve; you have left a few of us alive. 14We
should not again break your commands by allowing marriages with these wicked people. If we
did, you would get angry enough to destroy us,
and none of us would be left alive. 15LORD, God of
Israel, by your goodness a few of us are left alive
today. We admit that we are guilty and none of us
should be allowed to stand before you."⚭

The People Confess Sin

10 As Ezra was praying and confessing and
crying and throwing himself down in front
of the Temple, a large group of Israelite men,
women, and children gathered around him who
were also crying loudly. 2Then Shecaniah son of
Jehiel the Elamite said to Ezra, "We have been
unfaithful to our God by marrying women from
the peoples around us. But even so, there is still
hope for Israel. 3Now let us make an agreement
before our God. We will send away all these
women and their children as you and those who
respect the commands of our God advise. Let it
be done to obey God's Teachings.⚭ 4Get up,
Ezra. You are in charge, and we will support you.
Have courage and do it."

5So Ezra got up and made the priests, Levites,
and all the people of Israel promise to do what was
suggested; and they promised. 6Then Ezra left the
Temple and went to the room of Jehohanan son
of Eliashib. While Ezra was there, he did not eat
or drink, because he was still sad about the
unfaithfulness of the captives who had returned.

7They sent an order in Judah and Jerusalem for
all the captives who had returned to meet
together in Jerusalem. 8Whoever did not come to
Jerusalem within three days would lose his property and would no longer be a member of the
community of the returned captives. That was
the decision of the officers and older leaders.

9So within three days all the people of Judah
and Benjamin gathered in Jerusalem. It was the
twentieth day of the ninth month. All the people
were sitting in the open place in front of the
Temple and were upset because of the meeting
and because it was raining. 10Ezra the priest stood
up and said to them, "You have been unfaithful
and have married non-Jewish women. You have
made Israel more guilty. 11Now, confess it to the
LORD, the God of your ancestors. Do his will and
separate yourselves from the people living around
you and from your non-Jewish wives."

12Then the whole group answered Ezra with a
loud voice, "Ezra, you're right! We must do what
you say. 13But there are many people here, and
it's the rainy season. We can't stand outside, and
this problem can't be solved in a day or two,
because we have sinned badly. 14Let our officers
make a decision for the whole group. Then let
everyone in our towns who has married a non-
Jewish woman meet with the older leaders and
judges of each town at a planned time, until the
hot anger of our God turns away from us." 15Only
Jonathan son of Asahel, Jahzeiah son of Tikvah,
Meshullam, and Shabbethai the Levite were
against the plan.

16So the returned captives did what was suggested. Ezra the priest chose men who were
leaders of the family groups and named one
from each family division. On the first day of the
tenth month they sat down to study each case.
17By the first day of the first month, they had finished with all the men who had married non-
Jewish women.

⚭**9:8 The Remnant:** Ezra 9:13–15
⚭**9:12 Nehemiah:** Nehemiah 10:30
⚭**9:15 The Remnant:** Isaiah 10:20–22
⚭**10:3 Agreement:** Psalm 89

10:10–19 When the Jewish captives of Babylonia returned to Jerusalem, Ezra reminds them that they are not to marry the people who live there who are not Jewish (verse 10; see Deuteronomy 7:1–4). The problem is that some of the people were already involved in such marriages. The people who have married non-Jewish persons are told to separate themselves from them. The leaders of each family division studied each case (verse 16). The people promised to divorce their wives, and offer a penalty offering (verse 19). The Bible does not mention whether or not they carried through with their promise.

Those Guilty of Marrying Non-Jewish Women

18These are the descendants of the priests who had married foreign women:

From the descendants of Jeshua son of Jozadak and Jeshua's brothers: Maaseiah, Eliezer, Jarib, and Gedaliah. 19(They all promised to divorce their wives, and each one brought a male sheep from the flock as a penalty offering.)

20From the descendants of Immer: Hanani and Zebadiah.

21From the descendants of Harim: Maaseiah, Elijah, Shemaiah, Jehiel, and Uzziah.

22From the descendants of Pashhur: Elioenai, Maaseiah, Ishmael, Nethanel, Jozabad, and Elasah.

23Among the Levites: Jozabad, Shimei, Kelaiah (also called Kelita), Pethahiah, Judah, and Eliezer.

24Among the singers: Eliashib.

Among the gatekeepers: Shallum, Telem, and Uri.

25And among the other Israelites, these married non-Jewish women:

From the descendants of Parosh: Ramiah, Izziah, Malkijah, Mijamin, Eleazar, Malkijah, and Benaiah.

26From the descendants of Elam: Mattaniah, Zechariah, Jehiel, Abdi, Jeremoth, and Elijah.

27From the descendants of Zattu: Elioenai, Eliashib, Mattaniah, Jeremoth, Zabad, and Aziza.

28From the descendants of Bebai: Jehohanan, Hananiah, Zabbai, and Athlai.

29From the descendants of Bani: Meshullam, Malluch, Adaiah, Jashub, Sheal, and Jeremoth.

30From the descendants of Pahath-Moab: Adna, Kelal, Benaiah, Maaseiah, Mattaniah, Bezalel, Binnui, and Manasseh.

31From the descendants of Harim: Eliezer, Ishijah, Malkijah, Shemaiah, Shimeon, 32Benjamin, Malluch, and Shemariah.

33From the descendants of Hashum: Mattenai, Mattattah, Zabad, Eliphelet, Jeremai, Manasseh, and Shimei.

34From the descendants of Bani: Maadai, Amram, Uel, 35Benaiah, Bedeiah, Keluhi, 36Vaniah, Meremoth, Eliashib, 37Mattaniah, Mattenai, and Jaasu.

38From the descendants of Binnui: Shimei, 39Shelemiah, Nathan, Adaiah, 40Macnadebai, Shashai, Sharai, 41Azarel, Shelemiah, Shemariah, 42Shallum, Amariah, and Joseph.

43From the descendants of Nebo: Jeiel, Mattithiah, Zabad, Zebina, Jaddai, Joel, and Benaiah.

44All these men had married non-Jewish women, and some of them had children by these wives.

Notes:

INTRODUCTION TO THE BOOK OF

NEHEMIAH

Rebuilding the Walls of Jerusalem

Nehemiah continues the account begun in the Book of Ezra. Indeed, Nehemiah and Ezra originally were one unified work. The introduction to the Book of Ezra, therefore, should be read also as an introduction to the Book of Nehemiah. The Nehemiah memoirs can be dated about 430 B.C.

SUMMARY:

The Book of Nehemiah begins with the first-person account of Nehemiah himself. Nehemiah was one who served wine to the king of Persia, who at this time was Artaxerxes. The book covers the period of time from Ezra's commission to return to Judah to help restore the city up to the time that not only the Temple, but also the city and its walls, are built and given to the Lord. So, we can date the opening of this book to 445 B.C.

Nehemiah's main task was to rebuild the wall and the city. Though he faced great opposition, he turned to God, and with God's strength he accomplished this important work.

For a summary of the theological message of Nehemiah, please see the introduction to Ezra.

The Book of Nehemiah has the following outline:

I. Nehemiah Leads the People in Rebuilding the Walls of Jerusalem (1:1–7:73)
II. Ezra Leads the People in Reaffirming their Relationship with God (7:74–10:39)
III. Celebration and Continuing Trouble (11:1–13:31)

I. Nehemiah Leads the People in Rebuilding the Walls of Jerusalem (1:1–7:73)

Nehemiah, a servant of the Persian king, hears a sad report about the condition of Jerusalem. His unhappiness catches the attention of the king, who determines to send him back to his homeland. Once there, Nehemiah takes over the leadership of the city, and he puts his efforts into rallying the people to rebuild the destroyed walls. Though there is external opposition, they accomplish this task in record time.

II. Ezra Leads the People in Reaffirming their Relationship with God (7:74–10:39)

Ezra reads the law of Moses to the people, and they confess their sin and renew their relationship with God.

III. Celebration and Continuing Trouble (11:1–13:31)

Now the Temple, the city, and the walls are all restored. They are dedicated to the Lord. However, even after this, problems remain, and the Book of Nehemiah continues with a list of problems that still beset the people. By ending with the problems still facing the people, the book makes us aware that more is to come.

NEHEMIAH

Nehemiah's Prayer

These are the words of Nehemiah son of
Hacaliah.
In the month of Kislev in the twentieth
year, I, Nehemiah, was in the capital city of Susa.
2One of my brothers named Hanani came with
some other men from Judah. I asked them about
Jerusalem and the Jewish people who lived
through the captivity.
3They answered me, "Those who are left from
the captivity are back in Judah, but they are in
much trouble and are full of shame. The wall
around Jerusalem is broken down, and its gates
have been burned."
4When I heard these things, I sat down and cried
for several days. I was sad and ate nothing. I prayed
to the God of heaven, 5"LORD, God of heaven, you
are the great God who is to be respected. You are
loyal, and you keep your agreement with those who
love you and obey your commands. 6Look and listen
carefully. Hear the prayer that I, your servant, am
praying to you day and night for your servants, the
Israelites. I confess the sins we Israelites have done
against you. My father's family and I have sinned
against you. 7We have been wicked toward you and
have not obeyed the commands, rules, and laws you
gave your servant Moses.
8"Remember what you taught your servant
Moses, saying, 'If you are unfaithful, I will scatter
you among the nations. 9But if you return to me
and obey my commands, I will gather your people
from the far ends of the earth. And I will bring
them from captivity to where I have chosen to be
worshiped.'
10"They are your servants and your people,
whom you have saved with your great strength
and power. 11Lord, listen carefully to the prayer of
your servant and the prayers of your servants who
love to honor you. Give me, your servant, success
today; allow this king to show kindness to me."
I was the one who served wine to the king.

Nehemiah Is Sent to Jerusalem

2 It was the month of Nisan in the twentieth
year Artaxerxes was king. He wanted some
wine, so I took some and gave it to the king. I had
not been sad in his presence before. 2So the king
said, "Why does your face look sad even though
you are not sick? Your heart must be sad."
Then I was very afraid. 3I said to the king, "May
the king live forever! My face is sad because the
city where my ancestors are buried lies in ruins,
and its gates have been destroyed by fire."
4Then the king said to me, "What do you want?"
First I prayed to the God of heaven. 5Then I
answered the king, "If you are willing and if I have
pleased you, send me to the city in Judah where
my ancestors are buried so I can rebuild it."
6The queen was sitting next to the king. He
asked me, "How long will your trip take, and
when will you get back?" It pleased the king to
send me, so I set a time.
7I also said to him, "If you are willing, give me
letters for the governors of Trans-Euphrates. Tell
them to let me pass safely through their lands on
my way to Judah. 8And may I have a letter for
Asaph, the keeper of the king's forest, telling him
to give me timber? I will need it to make boards
for the gates of the palace, which is by the
Temple, and for the city wall, and for the house in
which I will live." So the king gave me the letters,
because God was showing kindness to me. 9Then
I went to the governors of Trans-Euphrates and
gave them the king's letters. The king had also
sent army officers and soldiers on horses with me.
10When Sanballat the Horonite and Tobiah the
Ammonite officer heard about this, they were
upset that someone had come to help the
Israelites.

Nehemiah Inspects Jerusalem

11I went to Jerusalem and stayed there three
days. 12Then at night I started out with a few
men. I had not told anyone what God had caused
me to do for Jerusalem. There were no animals
with me except the one I was riding.
13I went out at night through the Valley Gate. I
rode toward the Dragon Well and the Trash Gate,
inspecting the walls of Jerusalem that had been broken down and the gates that had been destroyed
by fire. 14Then I rode on toward the Fountain Gate
and the King's Pool, but there was not enough
room for the animal I was riding to pass through.
15So I went up the valley at night, inspecting the

1:1 *twentieth year.* This is probably referring to the twentieth year King Artaxerxes I ruled Persia.

1:9 Obedience: Psalm 119

1:11 *the one who served wine to the king.* Nehemiah's profession explains why he was allowed to be in intimate contact with the powerful king of Persia. People in Nehemiah's profession had to be expert in selecting and tasting wines, as well as detecting poisons.

1:11 Fasting: Jonah 3

2:3 Depression: Psalm 88

2:10 *Sanballat . . . and Tobiah.* These are men of some importance and are non-Judeans. Sanballat may well have been the governor of Samaria at this time, as we know he was later in life, according to extra-biblical texts.

wall. Finally, I turned and went back in through
the Valley Gate. 16The guards did not know
where I had gone or what I was doing. I had not
yet said anything to the Jewish people, the
priests, the important men, the officers, or any of
the others who would do the work.

17Then I said to them, "You can see the trouble
we have here. Jerusalem is a pile of ruins, and its
gates have been burned. Come, let's rebuild the
wall of Jerusalem so we won't be full of shame
any longer." 18I also told them how God had been
kind to me and what the king had said to me.

Then they answered, "Let's start rebuilding."
So they began to work hard.

19But when Sanballat the Horonite, Tobiah the
Ammonite officer, and Geshem the Arab heard
about it, they made fun of us and laughed at us.
They said, "What are you doing? Are you turning
against the king?"

20But I answered them, "The God of heaven
will give us success. We, his servants, will start
rebuilding, but you have no share, claim, or
memorial in Jerusalem."

Builders of the Wall

3 Eliashib the high priest and his fellow priests
went to work and rebuilt the Sheep Gate.
They gave it to the Lord's service and set its doors
in place. They worked as far as the Tower of the
Hundred and gave it to the Lord's service. Then
they went on to the Tower of Hananel. 2Next to
them, the men of Jericho built part of the wall,
and Zaccur son of Imri built next to them.

3The sons of Hassenaah rebuilt the Fish Gate,
laying its boards and setting its doors, bolts, and
bars in place. 4Meremoth son of Uriah, the son of
Hakkoz, made repairs next to them. Meshullam
son of Berekiah, the son of Meshezabel, made
repairs next to Meremoth. And Zadok son of
Baana made repairs next to Meshullam. 5The
men from Tekoa made repairs next to them, but
the leading men of Tekoa would not work under
their supervisors.

6Joiada son of Paseah and Meshullam son of
Besodeiah repaired the Old Gate. They laid its
boards and set its doors, bolts, and bars in place.
7Next to them, Melatiah from Gibeon, other men
from Gibeon and Mizpah, and Jadon from
Meronoth made repairs. These places were ruled
by the governor of Trans-Euphrates. 8Next to
them, Uzziel son of Harhaiah, a goldsmith, made
repairs. And next to him, Hananiah, a perfume
maker, made repairs. These men rebuilt Jerusalem
as far as the Broad Wall. 9The next part of the wall
was repaired by Rephaiah son of Hur, the ruler of
half of the district of Jerusalem. 10Next to him,
Jedaiah son of Harumaph made repairs opposite his
own house. And next to him, Hattush son of Hashabneiah made repairs. 11Malkijah son of Harim and
Hasshub son of Pahath-Moab repaired another part
of the wall and the Tower of the Ovens. 12Next to
them Shallum son of Hallohesh, the ruler of half of
the district of Jerusalem, and his daughters made
repairs.

13Hanun and the people of Zanoah repaired the
Valley Gate, rebuilding it and setting its doors,
bolts, and bars in place. They also repaired the
five hundred yards of the wall to the Trash Gate.

14Malkijah son of Recab, the ruler of the district
of Beth Hakkerem, repaired the Trash Gate. He
rebuilt that gate and set its doors, bolts, and bars
in place.

15Shallun son of Col-Hozeh, the ruler of the district of Mizpah, repaired the Fountain Gate. He
rebuilt it, put a roof over it, and set its doors,
bolts, and bars in place. He also repaired the wall
of the Pool of Siloam next to the King's Garden all
the way to the steps that went down from the older
part of the city. 16Next to Shallun was Nehemiah
son of Azbuk, the ruler of half of the district of Beth
Zur. He made repairs opposite the tombs of David
and as far as the man-made pool and the House of
the Heroes.

17Next to him, the Levites made repairs, working
under Rehum son of Bani. Next to him, Hashabiah,
the ruler of half of the district of Keilah, for his
district. 18Next to him, Binnui son of Henadad
and his Levites made repairs. Binnui was the
ruler of the other half of the district of Keilah.
19Next to them, Ezer son of Jeshua, the ruler of
Mizpah, repaired another part of the wall. He
worked across from the way up to the armory, as
far as the bend. 20Next to him, Baruch son of
Zabbai worked hard on the wall that went from
the bend to the entrance to the house of Eliashib,
the high priest. 21Next to him, Meremoth son of
Uriah, the son of Hakkoz, repaired the wall that
went from the entrance to Eliashib's house to the
far end of it.

22Next to him worked the priests from the surrounding area. 23Next to them, Benjamin and
Hasshub made repairs in front of their own
house. Next to them, Azariah son of Maaseiah,
the son of Ananiah, made repairs beside his own

2:18 Vision: Proverbs 29:18

3:16 *Nehemiah.* This is a different Nehemiah than the one who wrote this book.

house. 24Next to him, Binnui son of Henadad repaired the wall that went from Azariah's house to the bend and on to the corner. 25Palal son of Uzai worked across from the bend and by the tower on the upper palace, which is near the courtyard of the king's guard. Next to Palal, Pedaiah son of Parosh made repairs. 26The Temple servants who lived on the hill of Ophel made repairs as far as a point opposite the Water Gate. They worked toward the east and the tower that extends from the palace. 27Next to them, the people of Tekoa repaired the wall from the great tower that extends from the palace to the wall of Ophel.

28The priests made repairs above the Horse Gate, each working in front of his own house. 29Next to them, Zadok son of Immer made repairs across from his own house. Next to him, Shemaiah son of Shecaniah, the guard of the East Gate, made repairs. 30Next to him, Hananiah son of Shelemiah, and Hanun, the sixth son of Zalaph, made repairs on another part of the wall. Next to them, Meshullam son of Berekiah made repairs across from where he lived. 31Next to him, Malkijah, one of the goldsmiths, made repairs. He worked as far as the house of the Temple servants and the traders, which is across from the Inspection Gate, and as far as the room above the corner of the wall. 32The goldsmiths and the traders made repairs between the room above the corner of the wall and the Sheep Gate.

Those Against the Rebuilding

4 When Sanballat heard we were rebuilding the wall, he was very angry, even furious. He made fun of the Jewish people. 2He said to his friends and those with power in Samaria, "What are these weak Jews doing? Will they rebuild the wall? Will they offer sacrifices? Can they finish it in one day? Can they bring stones back to life from piles of trash and ashes?"

3Tobiah the Ammonite, who was next to Sanballat, said, "If a fox climbed up on the stone wall they are building, it would break it down."

4I prayed, "Hear us, our God. We are hated. Turn the insults of Sanballat and Tobiah back on their own heads. Let them be captured and stolen like valuables. 5Do not hide their guilt or take away their sins so that you can't see them, because they have insulted the builders."

6So we rebuilt the wall to half its height, because the people were willing to work.

7But Sanballat, Tobiah, the Arabs, the Ammonites, and the people from Ashdod were very angry when they heard that the repairs to Jerusalem's walls were continuing and that the holes in the wall were being closed. 8So they all made plans to come to Jerusalem and fight and stir up trouble. 9But we prayed to our God and appointed guards to watch for them day and night.

10The people of Judah said, "The workers are getting tired. There is so much trash we cannot rebuild the wall."

11And our enemies said, "The Jews won't know or see anything until we come among them and kill them and stop the work."

12Then the Jewish people who lived near our enemies came and told us ten times, "Everywhere you turn, the enemy will attack us." 13So I put people behind the lowest places along the wall—the open places—and I put families together with their swords, spears, and bows. 14Then I looked around and stood up and said to the important men, the leaders, and the rest of the people: "Don't be afraid of them. Remember the Lord, who is great and powerful. Fight for your brothers, your sons and daughters, your wives, and your homes."

15Then our enemies heard that we knew about their plans and that God had ruined their plans. So we all went back to the wall, each to his own work.

16From that day on, half my people worked on the wall. The other half was ready with spears, shields, bows, and armor. The officers stood in back of the people of Judah 17who were building the wall. Those who carried materials did their work with one hand and carried a weapon with the other. 18Each builder wore his sword at his side as he worked. The man who blew the trumpet to warn the people stayed next to me.

A gold adze, dagger, and sheath from about 2000 B.C., found in the Royal Graves at Ur

4:14 Memory: Psalm 74:2

Folly/Foolishness

Proverbs 1:7

What is folly and who is a fool? Is a fool simply someone who does not know much? What is the difference between foolishness and wisdom?

Foolishness is the opposite of wisdom in the Bible. The Book of Proverbs, in particular, contrasts a wise person and a fool.

In the first place, fools are angry, arrogant, and self-centered. Their tempers are quick to flare up (Proverbs 14:17, 29; 29:11). They seem to enjoy quarrels and fights (Proverbs 20:3). They also think a lot of themselves, rarely taking advice from anyone else (Proverbs 12:15; 28:26). They even reject the guidance of their parents as being beneath them (Proverbs 15:5).

Fools also find it impossible to control their emotions and their actions. In Proverbs 12:23 fools and wise people are contrasted on this point: "Wise people keep what they know to themselves, but fools can't keep from showing how foolish they are." They are quick to act on their impulses, not thinking about their actions.

Fools lack control in many areas of their lives, but Proverbs especially focuses on their inabilities to control their tongues. Fools talk too much, and it hurts them (Proverbs 10:14). It is good advice for fools to keep their mouths closed, otherwise, their stupidity shows (Proverbs 17:28). They speak without thinking (Proverbs 18:13). And when they have something good to say, they say it in such a way as to make it ineffective (Proverbs 26:7). Even worse, when fools speak, they lie and gossip (Proverbs 10:18; 11:12; 18:6). This quality is what makes fools such dangerous messengers. "Sending a message by a foolish person is like cutting off your feet or drinking poison" (Proverbs 26:6). As opposed to the wise, they act out of ignorance , not knowledge: "Wise people see where they are going, but fools walk around in the dark" (Ecclesiastes 2:14). The amazing thing is that fools do not want to get better. They avoid and ridicule instruction and discipline. As Proverbs 15:5 puts it, "Fools reject their parents' correction, but anyone who accepts correction is wise." Fools are not just stupid; they are bad people. According to Proverbs 10:23, "A foolish person enjoys doing wrong, but a person with understanding enjoys doing what is wise."

Nabal is a good example of a fool in the Bible (1 Samuel 25). His very name means "fool" in Hebrew. The story is set during the days that David and his men were fleeing from Saul, who wanted to kill David. David had to stay out in the uninhabited parts of Israel, and so at the time of the passage, David was helping the men of Nabal, a rich herdsman. However, when David tried to get supplies for his men, Nabal impulsively refused David and insulted him in the process. His quick tongue landed him in a dangerous situation because David prepared to go to battle against him. If it were not for Abigail, Nabal's wise wife, the situation would have surely escalated into a bloody confrontation.

As we continue to explore foolishness in the Bible we see that it is more than a mental or ethical category; it is rebellion against God. As the beginning of Psalm 14 says, "Fools say to themselves, 'There is no God'" (verse 1). The fool is not denying the existence of God or a god, but what he is saying is that God does not matter. Indeed, everybody has to make a decision in life whether to pursue wisdom or foolishness. Proverbs 9 illustrates this choice by describing two women. One is Wisdom (verses 1–6) and the other is Foolishness (verses 13–18). The reader of Proverbs must make a choice whether to go with one or the other. It is a question whether to pursue the true God or false gods. This is why the Bible is clear that those who remain fools will end up destroying themselves.

The final question is how we are to relate to a fool. Proverbs gives guidance in 26:4 and 5:

Don't give fools a foolish answer,
  or you will be just like them.
But answer fools as they should be answered,
  or they will think they are really wise.

To call someone a fool is no casual comment. It is to attribute to that person not just ignorance, but also wickedness, and ultimately godlessness. That is why Jesus warns that calling someone a fool can put you "in danger of the fire of hell" (Matthew 5:22).

For the Christian the best solution to foolishness is to turn to Christ, who is the one in whom are "all the treasures of wisdom and knowledge" (Colossians 2:3).

Folly/Foolishness: For additional scriptures on this topic go to 1 Samuel 25.

WISDOM

PROVERBS 1:7

What is wisdom? Where do we go to become wise?
How is Jesus related to God's wisdom?

Wisdom is insight into the workings of the world. A wise person knows how to handle the difficult times of life. To be wise means to be in tune with how the world works and to know the proper behavior for each situation.

Of course, the Bible roots wisdom in God. After all, only God, the creator and sustainer of the universe, knows how the world works in all of its different ways. That is why Proverbs, the most obvious of all books of wisdom, begins with the famous statement, "Knowledge [another word for wisdom] begins with respect for the LORD" (Proverbs 1:7). The only true wisdom in this world comes from God.

That is the message of Job for instance. Job and his three friends have an argument about the cause of Job's pain. His children have been killed, his wealth taken away, and his body has painful sores from his head to his feet. His three friends, Eliphaz, Bildad, and Zophar, believe they have the correct answer to the cause of his sickness. They argue that Job suffers because he has sinned. They believe that if Job would listen to them and repent, then he would get better immediately. On the other hand, Job knows they are wrong. He questions God's justice and wisdom. The point of the Book of Job, however, is that only God knows (Job 38–42). God is the only one who is completely wise. As the famous poem on wisdom says, "The fear of the Lord is wisdom; to stay away from evil is understanding" (Job 28:28).

The second half of Job 28:28 leads us to another important quality of biblical wisdom. Wisdom is right, and its opposite, foolishness, is wrong. Many proverbs make this contrast:

A wise person will understand what to do,
    but a foolish person is dishonest.
Fools don't care if they sin,
    but honest people work at being right. (Proverbs 14:8, 9)

The Bible leads people in the direction of wisdom and doing right, while avoiding their opposites foolishness and evil. The Book of Proverbs sets up a very sharp contrast between wisdom and foolishness in Proverbs 8 and 9, and these chapters give us an excellent understanding of how wisdom works. They also show the close connection between wisdom and God.

Proverbs 8 gives the speech of Wisdom as though she were a woman. The reader has met her earlier in the book (Proverbs 1:20), but now we have a lengthy and revealing chapter about her. She is standing on the hilltop next to the road, which is the path of life, calling to the young men, who stand for the readers of the book. Wisdom warns them to avoid another woman named Foolishness (see Proverbs 9:1–6 and 9:13–18). Foolishness is trying to get the young men to come to her house, which is also on the hilltop.

Those who follow Wisdom will be good and will have what they need in life. Her advice is better than silver and gold (Proverbs 8:10–11). Still, what Foolishness has to offer seems so good, so right, so profitable, but it is nothing. Those who follow Foolishness are evil and will die (Proverbs 9:18). She is a liar, while Wisdom tells the truth.

Lady Wisdom is the same as God's quality of wisdom. Lady Wisdom stands for God himself. If that is so, what about Foolishness? Foolishness stands for all the false gods and goddesses, the idols, that turned Israel away from the true God. So, the decision whether to follow Wisdom or Folly is a choice to love God or worship an idol, which is Satan himself.

This contrast of Wisdom and Foolishness in Proverbs 8 and 9, is repeated through the rest of the Book of Proverbs. Proverbs 10–31 contain the short, meaningful statements that we tend to call "proverbs." They provide the message of wisdom in the Bible. They are the nitty-gritty advice about how to live life well, in a way that will lead to success. Often this is all that they are taken to be—good advice—but reading them in the light of Proverbs 8–9, we see that they are much more.

According to Colossians 2:3, it is Jesus in whom "all the treasures of wisdom and knowledge are safely kept." In 1 Corinthians 1:30 Paul teaches that it is Christ "who has become for us wisdom from God." We are not to follow or seek out the wisdom of the world, but rather we are to seek Jesus Christ who makes us wise. And once we have found him we find goodness and life.

Wisdom: For additional scriptures on this topic go to Genesis 3:6.

19Then I said to the important men, the leaders, and the rest of the people, "This is a very big job. We are spreading out along the wall so that we are far apart. 20Wherever you hear the sound of the trumpet, assemble there. Our God will fight for us."

21So we continued to work with half the men holding spears from sunrise till the stars came out. 22At that time I also said to the people, "Let every man and his helper stay inside Jerusalem at night. They can be our guards at night and workmen during the day." 23Neither I, my brothers, my workers, nor the guards with me ever took off our clothes. Each person carried his weapon even when he went for water.

Nehemiah Helps Poor People

5 The men and their wives complained loudly against their fellow Jews. 2Some of them were saying, "We have many sons and daughters in our families. To eat and stay alive, we need grain."

3Others were saying, "We are borrowing money against our fields, vineyards, and homes to get grain because there is not much food."

4And still others were saying, "We are borrowing money to pay the king's tax on our fields and vineyards. 5We are just like our fellow Jews, and our sons are like their sons. But we have to sell our sons and daughters as slaves. Some of our daughters have already been sold. But there is nothing we can do, because our fields and vineyards already belong to other people."

6When I heard their complaints about these things, I was very angry. 7After I thought about it, I accused the important people and the leaders, "You are charging your own brothers too much interest." So I called a large meeting to deal with them. 8I said to them, "As much as possible, we have bought freedom for our fellow Jews who had been sold to foreigners. Now you are selling your fellow Jews to us!" The leaders were quiet and had nothing to say.

9Then I said, "What you are doing is not right. Don't you fear God? Don't let our foreign enemies shame us. 10I, my brothers, and my men are also lending money and grain to the people. But stop charging them so much for this. 11Give back their fields, vineyards, olive trees, and houses right now. Also give back the extra amount you charged—the hundredth part of the money, grain, new wine, and oil."

12They said, "We will give it back and not demand anything more from them. We will do as you say."

Then I called for the priests, and I made the important men and leaders take an oath to do what they had said. 13Also I shook out the folds of my robe and said, "In this way may God shake out everyone who does not keep his promise. May God shake him out of his house and out of the things that are his. Let that person be shaken out and emptied!"

Then the whole group said, "Amen," and they praised the LORD. So the people did what they had promised.

14I was appointed governor in the land of Judah in the twentieth year of King Artaxerxes' rule. I was governor of Judah for twelve years, until his thirty-second year. During that time neither my brothers nor I ate the food that was allowed for a governor. 15But the governors before me had placed a heavy load on the people. They took about one pound of silver from each person, along with food and wine. The governors' helpers before me also controlled the people, but I did not do that, because I feared God. 16I worked on the wall, as did all my men who were gathered there. We did not buy any fields.

17Also, I fed one hundred fifty Jewish people and officers at my table, as well as those who came from the nations around us. 18This is what was prepared every day: one ox, six good sheep, and birds. And every ten days there were all kinds of wine. But I never demanded the food that was due a governor, because the people were already working very hard.

19Remember to be kind to me, my God, for all the good I have done for these people.

More Problems for Nehemiah

6 Then Sanballat, Tobiah, Geshem the Arab, and our other enemies heard that I had rebuilt the wall and that there was not one gap in it. But I had not yet set the doors in the gates. 2So Sanballat and Geshem sent me this message: "Come, Nehemiah, let's meet together in Kephirim on the plain of Ono."

But they were planning to harm me. 3So I sent messengers to them with this answer: "I am doing a great work, and I can't come down. I don't want the work to stop while I leave to meet you." 4Sanballat and Geshem sent the same message to me four times, and each time I sent back the same answer.

5The fifth time Sanballat sent his helper to me with the message, and in his hand was an unsealed letter. 6This is what was written:

5:3 Money: Isaiah 3:14

6:6 *rebuilding the wall.* Rebuilding the walls of a city strengthened its

A report is going around to all the nations,
and Geshem says it is true, that you and the
Jewish people are planning to turn against
the king and that you are rebuilding the wall.
They say you are going to be their king 7and
that you have appointed prophets to announce
in Jerusalem: "There is a king of Judah!" The
king will hear about this. So come, let's discuss this together.

8So I sent him back this answer: "Nothing you
are saying is really happening. You are just making it up in your own mind."
9Our enemies were trying to scare us, thinking,
"They will get too weak to work. Then the wall
will not be finished."
But I prayed, "God, make me strong."
10One day I went to the house of Shemaiah son
of Delaiah, the son of Mehetabel. Shemaiah had
to stay at home. He said, "Nehemiah, let's meet
in the Temple of God. Let's go inside the Temple
and close the doors, because men are coming at
night to kill you."
11But I said, "Should a man like me run away?
Should I run for my life into the Temple? I will
not go." 12I knew that God had not sent him but
that Tobiah and Sanballat had paid him to prophesy against me. 13They paid him to frighten me so
I would do this and sin. Then they could give me
a bad name to shame me.
14I prayed, "My God, remember Tobiah and Sanballat and what they have done. Also remember
the prophetess Noadiah and the other prophets
who have been trying to frighten me."

The Wall Is Finished

15The wall of Jerusalem was completed on the
twenty-fifth day of the month of Elul. It took fifty-
two days to rebuild. 16When all our enemies
heard about it and all the nations around us saw
it, they were shamed. They then understood that
the work had been done with the help of our God.
17Also in those days the important men of Judah
sent many letters to Tobiah, and he answered
them. 18Many Jewish people had promised to be
faithful to Tobiah, because he was the son-in-law
of Shecaniah son of Arah. And Tobiah's son
Jehohanan had married the daughter of Meshullam son of Berekiah. 19These important men
kept telling me about the good things Tobiah was
doing, and then they would tell Tobiah what I said
about him. So Tobiah sent letters to frighten me.

7 After the wall had been rebuilt and I had set
the doors in place, the gatekeepers, singers, and
Levites were chosen. 2I put my brother Hanani,
along with Hananiah, the commander of the palace,
in charge of Jerusalem. Hananiah was honest and
feared God more than most people. 3I said to them,
"The gates of Jerusalem should not be opened until
the sun is hot. While the gatekeepers are still on
duty, have them shut and bolt the doors. Appoint
people who live in Jerusalem as guards, and put
some at guard posts and some near their own
houses."

The Captives Who Returned

4The city was large and roomy, but there were
few people in it, and the houses had not yet been
rebuilt. 5Then my God caused me to gather the
important men, the leaders, and the common
people so I could register them by families. I
found the family history of those who had
returned first. This is what I found written there:
6These are the people of the area who returned
from captivity, whom Nebuchadnezzar king of
Babylon had taken away. They returned to Jerusalem and Judah, each going back to his own
town. 7These people returned with Zerubbabel,
Jeshua, Nehemiah, Azariah, Raamiah, Nahamani,
Mordecai, Bilshan, Mispereth, Bigvai, Nehum,
and Baanah.
These are the people from Israel: 8the descendants of Parosh—2,172; 9the descendants of Shephatiah—372; 10the descendants of Arah—652;
11the descendants of Pahath-Moab (through the
family of Jeshua and Joab)—2,818; 12the descendants of Elam—1,254; 13the descendants of
Zattu—845; 14the descendants of Zaccai—760;
15the descendants of Binnui—648; 16the descendants of Bebai—628; 17the descendants of Azgad—
2,322; 18the descendants of Adonikam—667; 19the
descendants of Bigvai—2,067; 20the descendants of
Adin—655; 21the descendants of Ater (through
Hezekiah)—98; 22the descendants of Hashum—
328; 23the descendants of Bezai—324; 24the
descendants of Hariph—112; 25the descendants of
Gibeon—95.
26These are the people from the towns of
Bethlehem and Netophah—188; 27of Anathoth—
128; 28of Beth Azmaveth—42; 29of Kiriath Jearim,
Kephirah, and Beeroth—743; 30of Ramah and
Geba—621; 31of Micmash—122; 32of Bethel and
Ai—123; 33of the other Nebo—52; 34of the other
Elam—1,254; 35of Harim—320; 36of Jericho—345;

defenses and could be seen as an act of aggression against Israel's master, the Persian king.

6:16 Evangelism: Matthew 10:1–15

37of Lod, Hadid, and Ono—721; 38of Senaah—3,930.

39These are the priests: the descendants of Jedaiah (through the family of Jeshua)—973; 40the descendants of Immer—1,052; 41the descendants of Pashhur—1,247; 42the descendants of Harim—1,017.

43These are the Levites: the descendants of Jeshua (through Kadmiel through the family of Hodaviah)—74.

44These are the singers: the descendants of Asaph—148.

45These are the gatekeepers: the descendants of Shallum, Ater, Talmon, Akkub, Hatita, and Shobai—138.

46These are the Temple servants: the descendants of Ziha, Hasupha, Tabbaoth, 47Keros, Sia, Padon, 48Lebana, Hagaba, Shalmai, 49Hanan, Giddel, Gahar, 50Reaiah, Rezin, Nekoda, 51Gazzam, Uzza, Paseah, 52Besai, Meunim, Nephussim, 53Bakbuk, Hakupha, Harhur, 54Bazluth, Mehida, Harsha, 55Barkos, Sisera, Temah, 56Neziah, and Hatipha.

57These are the descendants of the servants of Solomon: the descendants of Sotai, Sophereth, Perida, 58Jaala, Darkon, Giddel, 59Shephatiah, Hattil, Pokereth-Hazzebaim, and Amon.

60The Temple servants and the descendants of the servants of Solomon totaled 392 people.

61Some people came to Jerusalem from the towns of Tel Melah, Tel Harsha, Kerub, Addon, and Immer, but they could not prove that their ancestors came from Israel. Here are their names and their number: 62the descendants of Delaiah, Tobiah, and Nekoda—642.

63And these priests could not prove that their ancestors came from Israel: the descendants of Hobaiah, Hakkoz, and Barzillai. (He had married a daughter of Barzillai from Gilead and was called by her family name.)

64These people searched for their family records, but they could not find them. So they could not be priests, because they were thought to be unclean. 65The governor ordered them not to eat any of the holy food until a priest settled this matter by using the Urim and Thummim.

66The total number of those who returned was 42,360. 67This is not counting their 7,337 male and female servants and the 245 male and female singers with them. 68They had 736 horses, 245 mules, 69435 camels, and 6,720 donkeys.

70Some of the family leaders gave to the work. The governor gave to the treasury about 19 pounds of gold, 50 bowls, and 530 pieces of clothing for the priests. 71Some of the family leaders gave about 375 pounds of gold and about 2,660 pounds of silver to the treasury for the work. 72The total of what the other people gave was about 375 pounds of gold, about 2,250 pounds of silver, and 67 pieces of clothing for the priests. 73So these people all settled in their own towns: the priests, the Levites, the gatekeepers, the singers, the Temple servants, and all the other people of Israel.⚭

Ezra Reads the Teachings

By the seventh month the Israelites were settled in their own towns.

8 All the people of Israel gathered together in the square by the Water Gate. They asked Ezra the teacher to bring out the Book of the Teachings of Moses, which the LORD had given to Israel.

2So on the first day of the seventh month, Ezra the priest brought out the Teachings for the crowd. Men, women, and all who could listen and understand had gathered. 3At the square by the Water Gate Ezra read the Teachings out loud from early morning until noon to the men, women, and everyone who could listen and understand. All the people listened carefully to the Book of the Teachings.

4Ezra the teacher stood on a high wooden platform that had been built just for this time. On his right were Mattithiah, Shema, Anaiah, Uriah, Hilkiah, and Maaseiah. And on his left were Pedaiah, Mishael, Malkijah, Hashum, Hashbaddanah, Zechariah, and Meshullam.

5Ezra opened the book in full view of everyone, because he was above them. As he opened it, all the people stood up. 6Ezra praised the LORD, the great God, and all the people held up their hands and said, "Amen! Amen!" Then they bowed down and worshiped the LORD with their faces to the ground.

7These Levites explained the Teachings to the people as they stood there: Jeshua, Bani, Sherebiah, Jamin, Akkub, Shabbethai, Hodiah, Maaseiah, Kelita, Azariah, Jozabad, Hanan, and Pelaiah. 8They read from the Book of the Teachings of God and explained what it meant so the people understood what was being read.

9Then Nehemiah the governor, Ezra the priest and teacher, and the Levites who were teaching said to all the people, "This is a holy day to the LORD your God. Don't be sad or cry." All the people had been crying as they listened to the words of the Teachings.

⚭**7:73 Births:** Luke 3:23–38

8 While there is evidence of scribes teaching the Law prior to the exile (see Jeremiah 8:8–9), during and after the exile such a role gained increasing prominence. Perhaps the most celebrated figure is Ezra. Although he was of the priestly line, Ezra was most noted for his responsibilities as scribe, which centered on teaching the Law to the people.

[10]Nehemiah said, "Go and enjoy good food and
sweet drinks. Send some to people who have
none, because today is a holy day to the Lord.
Don't be sad, because the joy of the LORD will
make you strong."
[11]The Levites helped calm the people, saying,
"Be quiet, because this is a holy day. Don't be sad."
[12]Then all the people went away to eat and
drink, to send some of their food to others, and to
celebrate with great joy. They finally understood
what they had been taught.
[13]On the second day of the month, the leaders
of all the families, the priests, and the Levites met
with Ezra the teacher. They gathered to study the
words of the Teachings. [14]This is what they found
written in the Teachings: The LORD commanded
through Moses that the people of Israel were to
live in shelters during the feast of the seventh
month. [15]The people were supposed to preach
this message and spread it through all their towns
and in Jerusalem: "Go out into the mountains, and
bring back branches from olive and wild olive trees,
myrtle trees, palms, and shade trees. Make shelters with them, as it is written."
[16]So the people went out and got tree branches.
They built shelters on their roofs, in their courtyards, in the courtyards of the Temple, in the
square by the Water Gate, and in the square next
to the Gate of Ephraim. [17]The whole group that
had come back from captivity built shelters and
lived in them. The Israelites had not done this
since the time of Joshua son of Nun. And they were
very happy.
[18]Ezra read to them every day from the Book of
the Teachings, from the first day to the last. The
people of Israel celebrated the feast for seven
days, and then on the eighth day the people gathered as the law said.

Israel Confesses Sins

9 On the twenty-fourth day of that same
month, the people of Israel gathered. They
did not eat, and they wore rough cloth and put
dust on their heads to show their sadness. [2]Those
people whose ancestors were from Israel had separated themselves from all foreigners. They stood
and confessed their sins and their ancestors' sins.
[3]For a fourth of the day they stood where they
were and read from the Book of the Teachings of
the LORD their God. For another fourth of the day
they confessed their sins and worshiped the LORD
their God. [4]These Levites were standing on the
stairs: Jeshua, Bani, Kadmiel, Shebaniah, Bunni,
Sherebiah, Bani, and Kenani. They called out to the
LORD their God with loud voices. [5]Then these
Levites spoke: Jeshua, Kadmiel, Bani, Hashabneiah,
Sherebiah, Hodiah, Shebaniah, and Pethahiah.
They said, "Stand up and praise the LORD your God,
who lives forever and ever."

The People's Prayer

"Blessed be your wonderful name.
It is more wonderful than all blessing
and praise.
[6]You are the only LORD.
You made the heavens, even the
highest heavens,
with all the stars.
You made the earth and everything on it,
the seas and everything in them;
you give life to everything.
The heavenly army worships you.

[7]"You are the LORD,
the God who chose Abram
and brought him out of Ur in Babylonia
and named him Abraham.
[8]You found him faithful to you,
so you made an agreement with him
to give his descendants the land of the
Canaanites,
Hittites, Amorites,
Perizzites, Jebusites, and Girgashites.
You have kept your promise,
because you do what is right.

[9]"You saw our ancestors suffering in Egypt
and heard them cry out at the Red Sea.
[10]You did signs and miracles against the
king of Egypt,
and against all his officers and all
his people,
because you knew how proud they were.
You became as famous as you are today.
[11]You divided the sea in front of our ancestors;
they walked through on dry ground.
But you threw the people chasing them into
the deep water,
like a stone thrown into mighty waters.
[12]You led our ancestors with a pillar of
cloud by day
and with a pillar of fire at night.

8:16 *roofs.* In Bible times houses were built with flat roofs. The roof was used for drying things such as flax and fruit. And it was used as an extra room, as a place for worship, and as a cool place to sleep in the summer.

8:17 Joshua: Acts 7:45

9:8 *agreement.* This is a reference to the agreement made between Abram and the Lord, which may be found in Genesis 12:1–3; 15; 17. Also see "agreement" in the Dictionary/Concordance.

It lit the way
they were supposed to go.
13You came down to Mount Sinai
and spoke from heaven to our ancestors.
You gave them fair rules and true teachings,
good orders and commands.
14You told them about your holy Sabbath
and gave them commands, orders,
and teachings
through your servant Moses.
15When they were hungry, you gave them bread
from heaven.
When they were thirsty, you brought them
water from the rock.
You told them to enter and take over
the land you had promised to give them.

16"But our ancestors were proud and stubborn
and did not obey your commands.
17They refused to listen;
they forgot the miracles you did for them.
So they became stubborn and turned
against you,
choosing a leader to take them back to slavery.
But you are a forgiving God.
You are kind and full of mercy.
You do not become angry quickly, and you
have great love.
So you did not leave them.
18Our ancestors even made an idol of a calf for
themselves.
They said, 'This is your god, Israel,
who brought you up out of Egypt.'
They spoke against you.

19"You have great mercy,
so you did not leave them in the desert.
The pillar of cloud guided them by day,
and the pillar of fire led them at night,
lighting the way they were to go.
20You gave your good Spirit to teach them.
You gave them manna to eat
and water when they were thirsty.
21You took care of them for forty years
in the desert;
they needed nothing.
Their clothes did not wear out,
and their feet did not swell.

22"You gave them kingdoms and nations;
you gave them more land.
They took over the country of Sihon king
of Heshbon
and the country of Og king of Bashan.
23You made their children as many as the stars
in the sky,
and you brought them into the land
that you told their fathers to enter and take
over.
24So their children went into the land and took
over.
The Canaanites lived there, but you defeated
them for our ancestors.
You handed over to them the Canaanites,
their kings, and the people of the land.
Our ancestors could do what they wanted
with them.
25They captured strong, walled cities and
fertile land.
They took over houses full of good things,
wells that were already dug,
vineyards, olive trees, and many fruit trees.
They ate until they were full and grew fat;
they enjoyed your great goodness.

26"But they were disobedient and turned
against you
and ignored your teachings.
Your prophets warned them to come
back to you,
but they killed those prophets
and spoke against you.
27So you handed them over to their enemies,
and their enemies treated them badly.
But in this time of trouble our ancestors
cried out to you,
and you heard from heaven.
You had great mercy
and gave them saviors who saved them from
the power of their enemies.
28But as soon as they had rest,
they again did what was evil.
So you left them to their enemies
who ruled over them.
When they cried out to you again,
you heard from heaven.
Because of your mercy, you saved them again
and again.
29You warned them to return to your teachings,
but they were proud and did not obey your
commands.
If someone obeys your laws, he will live,
but they sinned against your laws.
They were stubborn, unwilling, and disobedient.
30You were patient with them for many years
and warned them by your Spirit through
the prophets,

9:18 Blasphemy: Isaiah 37:6

but they did not pay attention.
So you handed them over to other countries.
31But because your mercy is great, you did not
kill them all or leave them.
You are a kind and merciful God.

32"And so, our God, you are the great and
mighty and wonderful God.
You keep your agreement of love.
Do not let all our trouble seem unimportant
to you.
This trouble has come to us, to our kings
and our leaders,
to our priests and prophets,
to our ancestors and all your people
from the days of the kings of Assyria until
today.
33You have been fair in everything that has
happened to us;
you have been loyal, but we have been
wicked.
34Our kings, leaders, priests, and ancestors did
not obey your teachings;
they did not pay attention to the commands
and warnings you gave them.
35Even when our ancestors were living in
their kingdom,
enjoying all the good things you had
given them,
enjoying the land that was fertile and
full of room,
they did not stop their evil ways.

36"Look, we are slaves today
in the land you gave our ancestors.
They were to enjoy its fruit and its good things,
but look, we are slaves here.
37The land's great harvest belongs to the kings
you have put over us
because of our sins.
Those kings rule over us and our cattle
as they please,
so we are in much trouble.

The People's Agreement

38"Because of all this, we are making an agreement in writing, and our leaders, Levites, and priests are putting their seals on it."

10 These are the men who sealed the agreement:
Nehemiah the governor, son of Hacaliah.
Zedekiah, 2Seraiah, Azariah, Jeremiah, 3Pashhur,
Amariah, Malkijah, 4Hattush, Shebaniah, Malluch,
5Harim, Meremoth, Obadiah, 6Daniel, Ginnethon,
Baruch, 7Meshullam, Abijah, Mijamin, 8Maaziah,
Bilgai, and Shemaiah. These are the priests.
9These are the Levites who sealed it: Jeshua
son of Azaniah, Binnui of the sons of Henadad,
Kadmiel, 10and their fellow Levites: Shebaniah,
Hodiah, Kelita, Pelaiah, Hanan, 11Mica, Rehob,
Hashabiah, 12Zaccur, Sherebiah, Shebaniah,
13Hodiah, Bani, and Beninu.
14These are the leaders of the people who sealed
the agreement: Parosh, Pahath-Moab, Elam, Zattu,
Bani, 15Bunni, Azgad, Bebai, 16Adonijah, Bigvai,
Adin, 17Ater, Hezekiah, Azzur, 18Hodiah, Hashum,
Bezai, 19Hariph, Anathoth, Nebai, 20Magpiash,
Meshullam, Hezir, 21Meshezabel, Zadok, Jaddua,
22Pelatiah, Hanan, Anaiah, 23Hoshea, Hananiah,
Hasshub, 24Hallohesh, Pilha, Shobek, 25Rehum,
Hashabnah, Maaseiah, 26Ahiah, Hanan, Anan,
27Malluch, Harim, and Baanah.
28The rest of the people took an oath. They were
the priests, Levites, gatekeepers, singers, Temple
servants, all those who separated themselves
from foreigners to keep the Teachings of God,
and also their wives and their sons and daughters
who could understand. 29They joined their fellow
Israelites and their leading men in taking an oath,
which was tied to a curse in case they broke the
oath. They promised to follow the Teachings of
God, which they had been given through Moses
the servant of God, and to obey all the commands, rules, and laws of the LORD our God.
30They said:

We promise not to let our daughters marry
foreigners nor to let our sons marry their
daughters. 31Foreigners may bring goods or
grain to sell on the Sabbath, but we will not
buy on the Sabbath or any holy day. Every
seventh year we will not plant, and that year
we will forget all that people owe us.
32We will be responsible for the commands
to pay for the service of the Temple of our God.
We will give an eighth of an ounce of silver
each year. 33It is for the bread that is set out on
the table; the regular grain offerings and burnt
offerings; the offerings on the Sabbaths, New
Moon festivals, and special feasts; the holy
offerings; the offerings to remove the sins of
the Israelites so they will belong to God; and
for the work of the Temple of our God.

9:31 Rebellion: Psalm 95:8–10
9:37 Land/Inheritance: Nehemiah 13
10:30 Nehemiah: Nehemiah 11:1

34We, the priests, the Levites, and the people, have thrown lots to decide at what time
of year each family must bring wood to the
Temple. The wood is for burning on the altar
of the LORD our God, and we will do this as it
is written in the Teachings.
35We also will bring the first fruits from
our crops and the first fruits of every tree to
the Temple each year.
36We will bring to the Temple our firstborn sons and cattle and the firstborn of our
herds and flocks, as it is written in the
Teachings. We will bring them to the priests
who are serving in the Temple.
37We will bring to the priests at the storerooms of the Temple the first of our ground
meal, our offerings, the fruit from all our
trees, and our new wine and oil. And we will
bring a tenth of our crops to the Levites, who
will collect these things in all the towns
where we work. 38A priest of Aaron's family
must be with the Levites when they receive
the tenth of the people's crops. The Levites
must bring a tenth of all they receive to the
Temple of our God to put in the storerooms
of the treasury. 39The people of Israel and the
Levites are to bring to the storerooms the gifts
of grain, new wine, and oil. That is where the
utensils for the Temple are kept and where
the priests who are serving, the gatekeepers,
and singers stay.
We will not ignore the Temple of our God.

New People Move into Jerusalem

11 The leaders of Israel lived in Jerusalem. But
the rest of the people threw lots to choose
one person out of every ten to come and live in
Jerusalem, the holy city. The other nine could
stay in their own cities.∞ 2The people blessed
those who volunteered to live in Jerusalem.
3These are the area leaders who lived in Jerusalem. (Some people lived on their own land in
the cities of Judah. These included Israelites,
priests, Levites, Temple servants, and descendants
of Solomon's servants. 4Others from the families of
Judah and Benjamin lived in Jerusalem.)
These are the descendants of Judah who moved
into Jerusalem. There was Athaiah son of Uzziah.
(Uzziah was the son of Zechariah, the son of
Amariah. Amariah was the son of Shephatiah, the
son of Mahalalel. Mahalalel was a descendant of
Perez.) 5There was also Masseiah son of Baruch.
(Baruch was the son of Col-Hozeh, the son of
Hazaiah. Hazaiah was the son of Adaiah, the son
of Joiarib. Joiarib was the son of Zechariah, a
descendant of Shelah.) 6All the descendants of
Perez who lived in Jerusalem totaled 468 men.
They were soldiers.
7These are descendants of Benjamin who moved
into Jerusalem. There was Sallu son of Meshullam. (Meshullam was the son of Joed, the son of
Pedaiah. Pedaiah was the son of Kolaiah, the son
of Maaseiah. Maaseiah was the son of Ithiel, the
son of Jeshaiah.) 8Following him were Gabbai and
Sallai, for a total of 928 men. 9Joel son of Zicri was
appointed over them, and Judah son of Hassenuah
was second in charge of the new area of the city.
10These are the priests who moved into Jerusalem. There was Jedaiah son of Joiarib, Jakin,
11and Seraiah son of Hilkiah, the supervisor in the
Temple. (Hilkiah was the son of Meshullam, the son
of Zadok. Zadok was the son of Meraioth, the son of
Ahitub.) 12And there were others with them who
did the work for the Temple. All together there
were 822 men. Also there was Adaiah son of Jeroham. (Jeroham was the son of Pelaliah, the son of
Amzi. Amzi was the son of Zechariah, the son
of Pashhur. Pashhur was the son of Malkijah.)
13And there were family heads with him. All
together there were 242 men. Also there was
Amashsai son of Azarel. (Azarel was the son of
Ahzai, the son of Meshillemoth. Meshillemoth
was the son of Immer.) 14And there were brave
men with Amashsai. All together there were 128
men. Zabdiel son of Haggedolim was appointed
over them.
15These are the Levites who moved into Jerusalem. There was Shemaiah son of Hasshub.
(Hasshub was the son of Azrikam, the son of
Hashabiah. Hashabiah was the son of Bunni.)
16And there were Shabbethai and Jozabad, two of
the leaders of the Levites who were in charge of the
work outside the Temple. 17There was Mattaniah
son of Mica. (Mica was the son of Zabdi, the son
of Asaph.) Mattaniah was the director who led
the people in thanksgiving and prayer. There was
Bakbukiah, who was second in charge over his
fellow Levites. And there was Abda son of Shammua. (Shammua was the son of Galal, the son of
Jeduthun.) 18All together 284 Levites lived in the
holy city of Jerusalem.
19The gatekeepers who moved into Jerusalem
were Akkub, Talmon, and others with them. There
was a total of 172 men who guarded the city gates.
20The other Israelites, priests, and Levites lived
on their own land in all the cities of Judah.
21The Temple servants lived on the hill of Ophel,
and Ziha and Gishpa were in charge of them.

∞ **Nehemiah:** 13:23–27

22Uzzi son of Bani was appointed over the Levites in Jerusalem. (Bani was the son of Hashabiah, the son of Mattaniah. Mattaniah was the son of Mica.) Uzzi was one of Asaph's descendants, who were the singers responsible for the service of the Temple. 23The singers were under the king's orders, which regulated them day by day.

24Pethahiah son of Meshezabel was the king's spokesman. (Meshezabel was a descendant of Zerah, the son of Judah.)

25Some of the people of Judah lived in villages with their surrounding fields. They lived in Kiriath Arba and its surroundings, in Dibon and its surroundings, in Jekabzeel and its surroundings, 26in Jeshua, Moladah, Beth Pelet, 27Hazar Shual, Beersheba and its surroundings, 28in Ziklag and Meconah and its surroundings, 29in En Rimmon, Zorah, Jarmuth, 30Zanoah, Adullam and their villages, in Lachish and the fields around it, and in Azekah and its surroundings. So they settled from Beersheba all the way to the Valley of Hinnom.

31The descendants of the Benjaminites from Geba lived in Micmash, Aija, Bethel and its surroundings, 32in Anathoth, Nob, Ananiah, 33Hazor, Ramah, Gittaim, 34Hadid, Zeboim, Neballat, 35Lod, Ono, and in the Valley of the Craftsmen.

36Some groups of the Levites from Judah settled in the land of Benjamin.

Priests and Levites

12 These are the priests and Levites who returned with Zerubbabel son of Shealtiel and with Jeshua. There were Seraiah, Jeremiah, Ezra, 2Amariah, Malluch, Hattush, 3Shecaniah, Rehum, Meremoth, 4Iddo, Ginnethon, Abijah, 5Mijamin, Moadiah, Bilgah, 6Shemaiah, Joiarib, Jedaiah, 7Sallu, Amok, Hilkiah, and Jedaiah. They were the leaders of the priests and their relatives in the days of Jeshua.

8The Levites were Jeshua, Binnui, Kadmiel, Sherebiah, Judah, and Mattaniah. Mattaniah and his relatives were in charge of the songs of thanksgiving. 9Bakbukiah and Unni, their relatives, stood across from them in the services.

10Jeshua was the father of Joiakim. Joiakim was the father of Eliashib. Eliashib was the father of Joiada. 11Joiada was the father of Jonathan, and Jonathan was the father of Jaddua.

12In the days of Joiakim, these priests were the leaders of the families of priests: Meraiah, from Seraiah's family; Hananiah, from Jeremiah's family; 13Meshullam, from Ezra's family; Jehohanan, from Amariah's family; 14Jonathan, from Malluch's family; Joseph, from Shecaniah's family; 15Adna, from Harim's family; Helkai, from Meremoth's family; 16Zechariah, from Iddo's family; Meshullam, from Ginnethon's family; 17Zicri, from Abijah's family; Piltai, from Miniamin's and Moadiah's families; 18Shammua, from Bilgah's family; Jehonathan, from Shemaiah's family; 19Mattenai, from Joiarib's family; Uzzi, from Jedaiah's family; 20Kallai, from Sallu's family; Eber, from Amok's family; 21Hashabiah, from Hilkiah's family; and Nethanel, from Jedaiah's family.

22The leaders of the families of the Levites and the priests were written down in the days of Eliashib, Joiada, Johanan, and Jaddua, while Darius the Persian was king. 23The family leaders among the Levites were written down in the history book, but only up to the time of Johanan son of Eliashib. 24The leaders of the Levites were Hashabiah, Sherebiah, Jeshua son of Kadmiel, and their relatives. Their relatives stood across from them and gave praise and thanksgiving to God. One group answered the other group, as David, the man of God, had commanded.

25These were the gatekeepers who guarded the storerooms next to the gates: Mattaniah, Bakbukiah, Obadiah, Meshullam, Talmon, and Akkub. 26They served in the days of Joiakim son of Jeshua, the son of Jozadak. They also served in the days of Nehemiah the governor and Ezra the priest and teacher.

The Wall of Jerusalem

27When the wall of Jerusalem was offered as a gift to God, they asked the Levites to come from wherever they lived to Jerusalem to celebrate with joy the gift of the wall. They were to celebrate with songs of thanksgiving and with the music of cymbals, harps, and lyres. 28They also brought together singers from all around Jerusalem, from the Netophathite villages, 29from Beth Gilgal, and from the areas of Geba and Azmaveth. The singers had built villages for themselves around Jerusalem. 30The priests and Levites made themselves pure, and they also made the people, the gates, and the wall of Jerusalem pure.

31I had the leaders of Judah go up on top of the wall, and I appointed two large choruses to give thanks. One chorus went to the right on top of the wall, toward the Trash Gate. 32Behind them went Hoshaiah and half the leaders of Judah. 33Azariah, Ezra, Meshullam, 34Judah, Benjamin, Shemaiah, and Jeremiah also went. 35Some priests with trumpets also went, along with Zechariah son of Jonathan. (Jonathan was the son of Shemaiah, the son of Mattaniah. Mattaniah was the son of

Parenting

PROVERBS 1:8–9:18

What can we learn from the Bible about being good parents? How are parents to teach their children about the Lord?

The wealth of books on parenting in today's bookstores shows the great concern and desire among both Christians and non-Christians to understand how to raise their children. Woven throughout the Scriptures are principles and teachings about parenting as relevant and sufficient today as they were when first written. These principles, along with biblical examples, provide a clear and consistent picture of what godly parenting looks like.

Throughout the Bible the acceptance or rejection of godly parental instruction is treated as a matter of life and death for the children (Exodus 20:12; Deuteronomy 5:16; Ephesians 6:1–3). In the biblical model of parenting, the parents stand under God's authority and serve as his stewards in passing on his truth to their children. The story of Hannah (1 Samuel 1:1) illustrates this dramatically.

Hannah could not have children for many years, until the Lord answered her prayers and gave her a son, Samuel. As a demonstration of her trust in the Lord and her thankfulness for his provision, Hannah entrusted Samuel, when he was "old enough to eat," into the hands of the high priest Eli to assist the priests in their service to the Lord (1 Samuel 1:24). Hannah understood that her son belonged to the Lord from birth.

Generally, it is not good or necessary for today's parents to surrender their children wholesale into someone else's care as an act of commitment to the Lord. It is good for today's parents to recognize that their children belong to God. As such, while their children are young and extremely dependent, parents are responsible to teach them how to trust in God. As children age, the human parents must begin to step out of the way of the Divine Parent. The role of their restrictions, protection, and affections in the child's life must diminish. As the children mature through their teen years to become fully independent and responsible adults, the parental role becomes one of guidance and friendship.

Scripture also portrays parenting as an activity with a goal. That goal is to create and maintain an environment in which God is the center of all thought and activities (Deuteronomy 6:4–25). In other words, God is present (Acts 17:28) and demands to receive glory (1 Corinthians 10:31) in every area of the child's life. Parents must work to put God's truth into every sphere of daily life in order to help their children develop a way of thinking and living that consistently pleases God.

According to the biblical model, this way of life is taught not simply by precept, but also by example (Proverbs 31:27–28; 2 Timothy 1:5). On the other hand, when parents teach the truth but live a lie, their children become confused and angry. An example of the destructive power of hypocrisy can be seen in the life of Gideon, the judge whom God raised up to deliver the Israelites from the Midianites. When an angel visited Gideon to inform him of his chosen role as Israel's deliverer, Gideon remembered what his parents had taught him about God's power and character (Judges 6:13). Clearly, Gideon's parents had partly kept Moses' command to teach their child about God. However, their hypocrisy is uncovered in verse 25 when God commanded Gideon to destroy his father's pagan altars! They taught, but did not believe and obey. Their son struggled with spiritual confusion for the rest of his life. The incident of the fleece reveals the initial weakness of Gideon's faith (Judges 6:33–40). By various means God educated him on how to fight by faith, and Gideon learned well enough to overcome opposition from his countrymen and achieve a great victory (Judges 7:19–8:21). In his moment of triumph Gideon mixed up wisdom and folly. He refused to become king but fashioned a "holy vest" that became an idol to the Israelites (Judges 8:22–27). The parental regulations in Deuteronomy 6:6–9, 12 are preceded by the command to love God completely. Without practicing love for God, a parent dare not hope that even the most effective verbal instruction will produce godly children.

Coupled with this emphasis on teaching by precept and example is the Bible's emphasis on the need for parents to guide their children's hearts. God is chiefly concerned about the development of the person within, where thoughts, motives, and desires dwell. The Bible warns that unless the inner person is transformed from natural rebellion against God to sincere love and worship of God the best parenting will lead to a dead legalism (Proverbs 4:23; 16:2; 21:2). By guiding the heart parents will make it easier for their children to understand and acknowledge their need for Christ.⚭

⚭**Parenting:** For additional scriptures on this topic go to Exodus 20:12.

FEAR

PROVERBS 1:7

What is fear and why are we afraid? Is fear always bad? What does it mean to "fear the LORD"?

When we find ourselves in danger, we often react with fear. Fear is the desire to flee before an attack that we know we cannot win. In this sense, it is the other side of anger which responds to danger by lashing out at it. Fear can run the gamut of intensity from nervousness to horror, but in each case, it is a realization that something or someone threatens us, and we cannot control the situation.

In a sinful world, God's creatures have much that can cause them to be afraid. Because of sin, the world has grown hostile and threatening. Before the Fall, Adam and Eve felt perfectly comfortable in their world. In particular, they felt no threat from God, but immediately after they ate the fruit of the tree of knowledge, they fled from God. When God confronted Adam and asked why he ran away from him, Adam replied, "I heard you walking in the garden, and I was afraid because I was naked, so I hid" (Genesis 3:10).

Sin separated human beings from God, so they no longer enjoyed his protection from the threats of the world. The result was that fear and dread entered the human experience.

Psalms 55:4–8 gives voice to this unpleasant human emotion. David says this:

I am frightened inside;
  the terror of death has attacked me.
I am scared and shaking,
  and terror grips me.
I said, "I wish I had wings like a dove.
  Then I would fly away and rest.
I would wander far away
  and stay in the desert.
I would hurry to my place of escape,
  far away from the wind and storm.

We only get a hint of the immediate threat that causes David's fear (verses 9–11). The Psalms are never specific about the events behind their composition because they were written for others to use, others who came later and had similar, though not identical, problems. But David's ultimate fear, and the fear of every one of God's human creatures, is the terror of death. Death, after all, is the ultimate assault, and one that no human can escape since we will all die.

We can see that there is good reason to be afraid in the world. We might get hurt, abused, victimized, assaulted, even killed. So why does the Bible keep saying, "Don't be afraid" (Genesis 15:1; 21:17; 43:23; Deuteronomy 1:17; Joshua 8:1)?

The Bible encourages us by telling us that there is a fear that melts away all of our little anxieties, including what appears to us to be a monster—the fear of death. God tells us that we should not fear other people, creatures, nature, or anything as long as we fear the Lord. Jesus told his disciples not to fear those who could kill the body, but the One (God) who could throw them into hell (Luke 12:4–5).

Indeed, the fear of the world will either drive us away from God or right into his protective and powerful arms. We should fear only the Lord because we know that he is the only one who can protect us.

Many Bible versions translate the Hebrew term not as "fear," but rather as "respect." We do this because we want to avoid the impression that we fear God in the same way that we would fear an encounter with an ax murderer in an alley. On the other hand, we should not so tame the concept that we forget that God is so great and powerful that, as we reflect on him, our knees should knock, and we should feel like bowing down to him.

The Bible encourages a type of fear that God desires us to have. Psalm 147:11 states,

The LORD is pleased with those who respect him,
  with those who trust his love.

Fearing the Lord puts all our other fears in perspective. After all, with God on our side "no one can defeat us" (Romans 8:31). Thus, with the psalmist we can confidently boast, "I will not be afraid, because the LORD is with me. People can't do anything to me" (Psalm 118:6).

Fear: For additional scriptures on this topic go to Genesis 15:1

INTRODUCTION TO THE BOOK OF ESTHER

Esther Saves Her People

WHO WROTE THIS BOOK?

Although we do not know who the author of the Book of Esther is, it is obvious that the person was of Jewish origin, due to his focus on a Jewish festival and Jewish nationalism.

TO WHOM WAS THIS BOOK WRITTEN?

The author of the Book of Esther was writing to the Jewish people who were saved by God through Esther in this story.

WHERE WAS IT WRITTEN?

From the author's knowledge of Persian customs, and with the setting of the story in the Persian city of Susa, it is likely that the Book of Esther was written somewhere in Persia, the author's probable residence.

WHEN WAS IT WRITTEN?

Esther was probably written sometime between 460 B.C., when the book's events took place, and 331 B.C., before the fall of the Persian empire to Greece.

WHAT IS THE BOOK ABOUT?

At the opening of the Book of Esther, King Xerxes of Persia has dethroned Queen Vashti. He then selects Esther, a young Jewish woman, as his new queen. A story of intrigue and political treason follow, centered around a powerful government leader named Haman and Esther's relative and caregiver, Mordecai. Their confrontation results in Haman's tricking Xerxes into signing a decree to eliminate the Jewish people from Persia. This dastardly deed finally requires Esther to risk her life to save her people from destruction.

WHY WAS THIS BOOK WRITTEN?

The Book of Esther was primarily recorded to establish the celebration of the Feast of Purim for Israel. It is also a written reminder to the people of Israel of their great rescue from annihilation through the courage and faithfulness of a young Jewish woman. The story shows that God protects his people through the directed actions of his faithful servants, such as Esther.

SO WHAT DOES THIS BOOK MEAN TO US?

The political intrigue and evil plots against God's people in the days of Esther are as contemporary today as they were in Persia. As in the days of Esther, Satan attacks God's people through evil-minded men and even laws of the land. But God still uses his faithful people today to protect and rescue his people, even though we may not always recognize it as God's leading. Proposed laws that are detrimental to the church are often defeated, and Satan's plot is foiled. There is no doubt that God is still in control, just as in the days of Esther, and that he raises up leaders to protect his people during times of crisis and to accomplish his purposes in the world.

SUMMARY:

Esther is a strange part of the Bible in that it never once mentions God or any of the great saving events of Israel's previous history. The book's action is set in the period after Israel's return from the exile, but the scene is Persia, not Palestine. God's people find themselves in trouble with the authorities, but seeming *coincidences* abound in an amazing way that not only allows God's people to escape a horrible fate but also sees their enemies suffer the end which they tried to impose on the Jewish people.

Haman, an important leader in Persia, takes an intense dislike to Mordecai, a Jewish man who has also assumed importance in the Persian empire. Haman manipulates events so that the king decrees the total annihilation of the Jewish people.

But while Haman works for the destruction of the Jewish people, an *unknown* force seems to be guiding events for their salvation. Vashti, the queen of the Persian empire, displeases the king, and he searches for a new queen. As a result, Esther, a Jewish girl, and Mordecai's ward, is taken into the king's harem where she can be close to him. Mordecai saves the king from an assassination plot, and his name is written in the royal record books. Thus, when the moment is right, Esther and Mordecai are in a position to stop Haman's plan and bring the destruction he intended for the Jews on himself.

Of course, the narrator is being subtle here. The *unknown force,* who is not named, is known by every faithful reader to be God. God saves Israel through the amazing events in the book.

The facts of the book come from the kingship of Xerxes (486–465 B.C.). The Book of Esther may have been written soon after; certainly the vividness and accuracy of the descriptions of the Persian court support such a date.

The outline of Esther is as follows:

I. Xerxes' Feasts (1:1–2:18)
II. Esther's Feasts (2:19–7:10)
III. The Feasts of Purim (8:1–10:3)

I. Xerxes' Feasts (1:1–2:18)

The Book of Esther opens with a great feast given by the Persian king, Xerxes. At one point he calls for his wife Vashti, so he can exploit her beauty before the crowds. She refuses, and this leads Xerxes to depose her from the throne. He then seeks a replacement, and Esther is chosen. A Jewish girl becomes queen in Persia, though she keeps her ethnic identity a secret from the king.

II. Esther's Feasts (2:19–7:10)

Secret plots abound in the Book of Esther. Mordecai uncovers a plot by two officers to assassinate the king and reports it to the royal court, thus saving the king's life. His name and good deed are entered in the royal record books. Haman plots secretly to kill the Jewish people, which now includes Queen Esther.

When Mordecai discovers Haman's plan, he tells Esther she must tell the king. Knowing the danger of approaching the king unsummoned, Esther at first hesitates, but Mordecai stirs her on. Esther invites the king and Haman to two feasts. At the second feast she breaks the news of Haman's plot to the king whose anger against Haman results in his being hanged on the gallows Haman had constructed to kill Mordecai.

III. The Feasts of Purim (8:1–10:3)

King Xerxes had already issued an unchangeable decree that allowed Haman's people to kill the people of Israel. Xerxes could not change that decree, but he did issue another decree allowing the Jewish people to defend themselves. As a result, they defeated their enemies, and then established a new festival called Purim, which is celebrated to the present day.

ESTHER

Queen Vashti Disobeys the King

This is what happened during the time of
King Xerxes, the king who ruled the one
hundred twenty-seven states from India to
Cush. 2In those days King Xerxes ruled from his
capital city of Susa. 3In the third year of his rule,
he gave a banquet for all his important men and
royal officers. The army leaders from the countries of Persia and Media and the important men
from all Xerxes' empire were there.
4The banquet lasted one hundred eighty days.
All during that time King Xerxes was showing off
the great wealth of his kingdom and his own
great riches and glory. 5When the one hundred
eighty days were over, the king gave another banquet. It was held in the courtyard of the palace
garden for seven days, and it was for everybody in
the palace at Susa, from the greatest to the least.
6The courtyard had fine white curtains and purple drapes that were tied to silver rings on marble
pillars by white and purple cords. And there were
gold and silver couches on a floor set with tiles of
white marble, shells, and gems. 7Wine was
served in gold cups of various kinds. And there
was plenty of the king's wine, because he was
very generous. 8The king commanded that the
guests be permitted to drink as much as they
wished. He told the wine servers to serve each
person what he wanted.
9Queen Vashti also gave a banquet for the
women in the royal palace of King Xerxes.
10On the seventh day of the banquet, King
Xerxes was very happy, because he had been drinking much wine. He gave a command to the seven
eunuchs who served him—Mehuman, Biztha,
Harbona, Bigtha, Abagtha, Zethar, and Carcas. 11He
commanded them to bring him Queen Vashti,
wearing her royal crown. She was to come to show
her beauty to the people and important men,
because she was very beautiful. 12The eunuchs told
Queen Vashti about the king's command, but she
refused to come. Then the king became very angry;
his anger was like a burning fire.
13It was a custom for the king to ask advice from
experts about law and order. So King Xerxes spoke
with the wise men who would know the right
thing to do. 14The wise men the king usually talked
to were Carshena, Shethar, Admatha, Tarshish,
Meres, Marsena, and Memucan, seven of the
important men of Persia and Media. These seven
had special privileges to see the king and had the
highest rank in the kingdom. 15The king asked
them, "What does the law say must be done to
Queen Vashti? She has not obeyed the command
of King Xerxes, which the eunuchs took to her."

A relief of Xerxes I (Ahasuerus) from the treasury at Persepolis, Iran

16Then Memucan said to the king and the other
important men, "Queen Vashti has not done
wrong to the king alone. She has also done wrong
to all the important men and all the people in all
the empire of King Xerxes. 17All the wives of the
important men of Persia and Media will hear
about the queen's actions. Then they will no
longer honor their husbands. They will say, 'King
Xerxes commanded Queen Vashti to be brought
to him, but she refused to come.' 18Today the
wives of the important men of Persia and Media
have heard about the queen's actions. So they
will speak in the same way to their husbands, and
there will be no end to disrespect and anger.

1:1 *one hundred twenty-seven states from India to Cush.* Xerxes' empire is the largest empire known up to this point in time in the ancient Near Eastern world. Cush is south of Egypt and roughly the same as modern Ethiopia.

19“So, our king, if it pleases you, give a royal
order, and let it be written in the laws of Persia and
Media, which cannot be changed. The law should
say Vashti is never again to enter the presence of
King Xerxes. Also let the king give her place as
queen to someone who is better than she is. 20And
let the king’s order be announced everywhere in
his enormous kingdom. Then all the women will
respect their husbands, from the greatest to the
least.”
21The king and his important men were happy
with this advice, so King Xerxes did as Memucan
suggested. 22He sent letters to all the states of the
kingdom in the writing of each state and in the language of each group of people. These letters
announced that each man was to be the ruler of
his own family.

Esther Is Made Queen

2 Later, when King Xerxes was not so angry,
he remembered Vashti and what she had
done and his order about her. 2Then the king’s
personal servants suggested, “Let a search be
made for beautiful young girls for the king. 3Let
the king choose supervisors in every state of his
kingdom to bring every beautiful young girl to the
palace at Susa. They should be taken to the
women’s quarters and put under the care of Hegai,
the king’s eunuch in charge of the women. And
let beauty treatments be given to them. 4Then let
the girl who most pleases the king become queen
in place of Vashti.” The king liked this idea, so he
did as they said.
5Now there was a Jewish man in the palace of
Susa whose name was Mordecai son of Jair. Jair
was the son of Shimei, the son of Kish. Mordecai
was from the tribe of Benjamin, 6which had been
taken captive from Jerusalem by Nebuchadnezzar
king of Babylon. They were part of the group
taken into captivity with Jehoiachin king of Judah.
7Mordecai had a cousin named Hadassah, who
had no father or mother, so Mordecai took care of
her. Hadassah was also called Esther, and she had
a very pretty figure and face. Mordecai had
adopted her as his own daughter when her father
and mother died.
8When the king’s command and order had
been heard, many girls had been brought to the
palace in Susa and put under the care of Hegai.
Esther was also taken to the king’s palace and put
under the care of Hegai, who was in charge of the
women. 9Esther pleased Hegai, and he liked her.
So Hegai quickly began giving Esther her beauty
treatments and special food. He gave her seven
servant girls chosen from the king’s palace. Then
he moved her and her seven servant girls to the
best part of the women’s quarters.
10Esther did not tell anyone about her family or
who her people were, because Mordecai had told
her not to. 11Every day Mordecai walked back and
forth near the courtyard where the king’s women
lived to find out how Esther was and what was
happening to her.
12Before a girl could take her turn with King
Xerxes, she had to complete twelve months of
beauty treatments that were ordered for the
women. For six months she was treated with oil
and myrrh and for six months with perfumes and
cosmetics. 13Then she was ready to go to the
king. Anything she asked for was given to her to
take with her from the women’s quarters to the
king’s palace. 14In the evening she would go to
the king’s palace, and in the morning she would
return to another part of the women’s quarters.
There she would be placed under the care of
Shaashgaz, the king’s eunuch in charge of the slave
women. The girl would not go back to the king
again unless he was pleased with her and asked
for her by name.
15The time came for Esther daughter of Abihail,
Mordecai’s uncle, who had been adopted by
Mordecai, to go to the king. She asked for only
what Hegai suggested she should take. (Hegai
was the king’s eunuch who was in charge of the
women.) Everyone who saw Esther liked her.
16So Esther was taken to King Xerxes in the royal
palace in the tenth month, the month of Tebeth,
during Xerxes’ seventh year as king.
17And the king was pleased with Esther more
than with any of the other girls. He liked her
more than any of the other girls, so he put a royal
crown on her head and made her queen in place
of Vashti. 18Then the king gave a great banquet
for Esther and invited all his important men and
royal officers. He announced a holiday for all the
empire and had the government give away gifts.

Mordecai Discovers an Evil Plan

19Now Mordecai was sitting at the king’s gate
when the girls were gathered the second time.
20Esther still had not told anyone about her family or who her people were, just as Mordecai had
commanded her. She obeyed Mordecai just as
she had done when she was under his care.

2:7 Esther’s adoption, like that of Moses, provided a unique opportunity for God to work. Adoption can create new relationships, new opportunities, new hopes. As cousins, Esther and Mordecai already had some family lineage, but the adoption made it more formal and legally recognized. Thereafter they could work together as God’s special agents to protect the Jews.

21Now Bigthana and Teresh were two of the king's officers who guarded the doorway. While Mordecai was sitting at the king's gate, they became angry and began to make plans to kill King Xerxes. 22But Mordecai found out about their plans and told Queen Esther. Then Esther told the king how Mordecai had discovered the evil plan. 23When the report was investigated, it was found to be true, and the two officers who had planned to kill the king were hanged. All this was written down in the daily court record in the king's presence.

Haman Plans to Destroy the Jewish People

3 After these things happened, King Xerxes honored Haman son of Hammedatha the Agagite. He gave him a new rank that was higher than all the important men. 2All the royal officers at the king's gate would bow down and kneel before Haman, as the king had ordered. But Mordecai would not bow down or show him honor.

3Then the royal officers at the king's gate asked Mordecai, "Why don't you obey the king's command?" 4And they said this to him every day. When he did not listen to them, they told Haman about it. They wanted to see if Haman would accept Mordecai's behavior because Mordecai had told them he was Jewish.

5When Haman saw that Mordecai would not bow down to him or honor him, he became very angry. 6He thought of himself as too important to try to kill only Mordecai. He had been told who the people of Mordecai were, so he looked for a way to destroy all of Mordecai's people, the Jews, in all of Xerxes' kingdom.

7It was in the first month of the twelfth year of King Xerxes' rule—the month of Nisan. Pur (that is, the lot) was thrown before Haman to choose a day and a month. So the twelfth month, the month of Adar, was chosen.

8Then Haman said to King Xerxes, "There is a certain group of people scattered among the other people in all the states of your kingdom. Their customs are different from those of all the other people, and they do not obey the king's laws. It is not right for you to allow them to continue living in your kingdom. 9If it pleases the king, let an order be given to destroy those people. Then I will pay seven hundred fifty thousand pounds of silver to those who do the king's business, and they will put it into the royal treasury."

10So the king took his signet ring off and gave it to Haman son of Hammedatha, the Agagite, the enemy of the Jewish people. 11Then the king said to Haman, "The money and the people are yours. Do with them as you please."

12On the thirteenth day of the first month, the royal secretaries were called, and they wrote out all of Haman's orders. They wrote to the king's governors and to the captains of the soldiers in each state and to the important men of each group of people. The orders were written in the writing of each state and in the language of each people. They were written in the name of King Xerxes and sealed with his signet ring. 13Letters were sent by messengers to all the king's empire ordering them to destroy, kill, and completely wipe out all the Jewish people. That meant young and old, women and little children, too. It was to happen on a single day—the thirteenth day of the twelfth month, which was Adar. And they could take everything the Jewish people owned. 14A copy of the order was given out as a law in every state so all the people would be ready for that day.

15The messengers set out, hurried by the king's command, as soon as the order was given in the palace at Susa. The king and Haman sat down to drink, but the city of Susa was in confusion.

Mordecai Asks Esther to Help

4 When Mordecai heard about all that had been done, he tore his clothes, put on rough cloth and ashes, and went out into the city crying loudly and painfully. 2But Mordecai went only as far as the king's gate, because no one was allowed to enter that gate dressed in rough cloth. 3As the king's order reached every area, there was great sadness and loud crying among the Jewish people. They gave up eating and cried out loud, and many of them lay down on rough cloth and ashes to show how sad they were.

4When Esther's servant girls and eunuchs came to her and told her about Mordecai, she was very upset and afraid. She sent clothes for Mordecai to put on instead of the rough cloth, but he would not wear them. 5Then Esther called for Hathach, one of the king's eunuchs chosen by the king to serve her. Esther ordered him to find out what was bothering Mordecai and why.

6So Hathach went to Mordecai, who was in the city square in front of the king's gate. 7Mordecai told Hathach everything that had happened to

3:1 Haman is a descendant of Agag, the Amalekite king whom Saul fought, while Mordecai is a Benjaminite who is related to Saul's clan (2:5). Amalek had tried to hinder Israel early on, and Moses revealed that God had declared war against them (Exodus 17:16). Saul should have destroyed the Amalekites when he had the chance (1 Samuel 15), but he didn't. Now one of his descendants has a new opportunity.

him, and he told Hathach about the amount of
money Haman had promised to pay into the
king's treasury for the killing of the Jewish people. 8Mordecai also gave him a copy of the order
to kill the Jewish people, which had been given
in Susa. He wanted Hathach to show it to Esther
and to tell her about it. And Mordecai told him to
order Esther to go into the king's presence to beg
for mercy and to plead with him for her people.
9Hathach went back and reported to Esther
everything Mordecai had said. 10Then Esther told
Hathach to tell Mordecai, 11"All the royal officers
and people of the royal states know that no man
or woman may go to the king in the inner courtyard without being called. There is only one law
about this: Anyone who enters must be put to
death unless the king holds out his gold scepter.
Then that person may live. And I have not been
called to go to the king for thirty days."
12Esther's message was given to Mordecai.
13Then Mordecai sent back word to Esther: "Just
because you live in the king's palace, don't think
that out of all the Jewish people you alone will
escape. 14If you keep quiet at this time, someone
else will help and save the Jewish people, but you
and your father's family will all die. And who
knows, you may have been chosen queen for just
such a time as this."
15Then Esther sent this answer to Mordecai:
16"Go and get all the Jewish people in Susa
together. For my sake, give up eating; do not eat
or drink for three days, night and day. I and my
servant girls will also give up eating. Then I will
go to the king, even though it is against the law,
and if I die, I die."
17So Mordecai went away and did everything
Esther had told him to do.

Esther Speaks to the King

5 On the third day Esther put on her royal robes
and stood in the inner courtyard of the king's
palace, facing the king's hall. The king was sitting
on his royal throne in the hall, facing the doorway. 2When the king saw Queen Esther standing
in the courtyard, he was pleased. He held out to
her the gold scepter that was in his hand, so
Esther went forward and touched the end of it.
3The king asked, "What is it, Queen Esther?
What do you want to ask me? I will give you as
much as half of my kingdom."
4Esther answered, "My king, if it pleases you,
come today with Haman to a banquet that I have
prepared for him."
5Then the king said, "Bring Haman quickly so
we may do what Esther asks."
So the king and Haman went to the banquet
Esther had prepared for them. 6As they were
drinking wine, the king said to Esther, "Now,
what are you asking for? I will give it to you. What
is it you want? I will give you as much as half of
my kingdom."
7Esther answered, "This is what I want and
what I ask for. 8My king, if you are pleased with
me and if it pleases you, give me what I ask for
and do what I want. Come with Haman tomorrow to the banquet I will prepare for you. Then I
will answer your question about what I want."

Haman's Plans Against Mordecai

9Haman left the king's palace that day happy
and content. But when he saw Mordecai at the
king's gate and saw that Mordecai did not stand
up or tremble with fear before him, Haman
became very angry with Mordecai. 10But he controlled his anger and went home.
Then Haman called together his friends and his
wife, Zeresh. 11He told them how wealthy he was
and how many sons he had. He also told them all
the ways the king had honored him and how the
king had placed him higher than his important
men and his royal officers. 12He also said, "I'm
the only person Queen Esther invited to come
with the king to the banquet she gave. And
tomorrow also the queen has asked me to be her
guest with the king. 13But all this does not really
make me happy when I see that Jew Mordecai sitting at the king's gate."
14Then Haman's wife, Zeresh, and all his
friends said, "Have a seventy-five foot platform
built, and in the morning ask the king to have
Mordecai hanged on it. Then go to the banquet
with the king and be happy." Haman liked this
suggestion, so he ordered the platform to be built.

Mordecai Is Honored

6 That same night the king could not sleep. So
he gave an order for the daily court record to
be brought in and read to him. 2It was found
recorded that Mordecai had warned the king
about Bigthana and Teresh, two of the king's officers who guarded the doorway and who had
planned to kill the king.
3The king asked, "What honor and reward
have been given to Mordecai for this?"
The king's personal servants answered, "Nothing has been done for Mordecai."

4:14 Crossing Cultural Boundaries: Matthew 8:1–4

5:8 Deborah: John 2:1–5

NUMBERS

PROVERBS 6:16–19

Are there symbolic numbers with theological meanings? Sometimes it seems like people go too far when explaining the meaning of the numbers. How can I know when too much is being made of the meanings of numbers?

Numbers can be among the most interesting study topics of the Bible (for instance the number 666 in Revelation 13:18). Most numbers in the Bible, however, are not deep, theological, hidden clues to the "true" meaning of Scripture (1 Chronicles 12:23–37 are among the most dry). Indeed, numbers can be informative, poetic, or figurative (symbolic). When the people of Israel are counted in the wilderness of Sinai, the numbers are informative. They were written to impart information to the reader (Numbers 1–4). Other times numbers do carry a special significance. This may be due to a meaning associated with the number itself, or the way the number is used in a sentence. For example, consider the above passage, Proverbs 6:16–19. The numbers six and seven do have symbolic meanings in Scripture. Six sometimes represents imperfection, while seven implies perfection or completeness. In this case, six may have a symbolic meaning. Since the writer is listing sins, he may have chosen to begin with six since it often represents that which is incomplete, not whole, or sinful. Seven definitely has poetic or symbolic force. Seven, when used poetically, means completeness or wholeness. This use of seven stresses the complete hate God has for these things, particularly, the seventh. But overshadowing the poetic use of both numbers is the way the entire phrase increases the displeasure of the Lord. Raising the preceding number, in this case six, by one to seven in this verse has far more meaning than the "inherent" symbolism of the numbers.

In the Bible numbers must be examined to see how they contribute to the meaning of the passage. Again, take an example of the number seven. Methuselah, who lived longer than any other man in the Bible, is said to have had a son, Lamech, when he was 187 years old (Genesis 5:25). The number seven here does not have a special import in this verse. On the other hand in Genesis 4:23–24, Lamech says, "I killed a man for wounding me, a young man for hitting me. If Cain's killer is punished seven times, then Lamech's killer will be punished seventy-seven times." In these verses, seven definitely carries the meaning of completeness. The number seventy-seven, multiplies the completeness of the punishment.

Generally, numbers are more likely to be significant and symbolic in such books as Revelation, Daniel, Ezekiel, and Zechariah, though they may be used symbolically anywhere in the Bible. The following are some numbers which are often used symbolically. The number one is an important number because it expresses unity and strength in union (Deuteronomy 6:4; Ephesians 4:1–16). The number three also has the connotation of completeness (Jonah spent three days in the whale and Christ three in the tomb). Sometimes it may simply mean a "few" (2 Kings 19:31). The number four is especially important in the books of Daniel, Ezekiel, and Revelation. The number four is often used to describe power and probably owes its meaning to the four directions, North, South, East, and West. Special attention must be paid to the number seven in the Book of Revelation. There are seven angels, bowls, churches, eyes, heads, hills, lampstands, seals, spirits, stars, thunders, and trumpets. The number twelve and its multiples also play a significant role in Revelation: the twenty-four elders (Revelation 4:4), the twelve tribes of Israel (Revelation 7), the twelve apostles, and the one hundred forty-four thousand marked on the forehead (Revelation 7). Some ancient numbering systems used twelve as their base.

Students of the Bible should also look out for words or phrases that are repeated. Often the number of times they are repeated imports a special meaning to the phrase. The heavenly creature in Isaiah 6:3 calls out, "Holy, holy, holy is the Lord. . . ." The repetition of the word three times means that God is the holiest. There is no one to compare to him. It is a superlative. Revelation 5:12 is a sevenfold blessing for Christ, "The Lamb who is worthy to receive power, wealth, wisdom, and strength, honor, glory, and praise!"

Readers of the Bible sometimes fail to appreciate how they use numbers in symbolic speech today. The number "thirteen" only recently began appearing on elevators and hotel plans. It was left out due to its negative and perceived evil connotations. Reminding oneself of how and how often such speech is used today will probably help in determining the deeper meanings of numbers in the Bible. Generally speaking, if the study or use of the numbers in the Bible becomes more important than the overall meaning of the passages from which they come, it is probably being overdone.

Numbers: For additional scriptures on this topic go to Genesis 4:23–24.

Happiness

Proverbs 16:20

Describe the emotion. What makes us happy? What should make us happy?

God promises happiness to everyone who trusts him. However, it is important to see how God defines happiness by understanding this verse in light of the rest of Scripture. Happiness and its synonyms—joy, blessedness, and peace (*shalom*)—are persistent topics throughout the Bible. Both God and humanity are concerned with happiness in life, both now and in the hereafter.

God is happy and joyous: "The Lord your God is with you; the mighty One will save you. He will rejoice over you. You will rest in his love; he will sing and be joyful about you" (Zephaniah 3:17).

Many people in the Bible are happy over positive events in their lives: Leah rejoiced over the birth of a son (Genesis 30:13), and David celebrated before the LORD (2 Samuel 6:5).

Happiness in the Bible is both an emotion and a state of being. It is a response to life (emotion) and a way of living (state of being). Thus, the Scriptures speak of happiness as an intense emotion (joy) we can experience throughout life. But happiness can be much more. It also includes mental well-being and ultimate satisfaction in life. In both Testaments happiness is equated to success, health, safety, prosperity, and an internal sense of peace and contentment (Esther 9:22; Proverbs 12:20; John 16:19–24; Romans 15:32).

Consequently, it is the Christian who can enjoy happiness in two dimensions of reality—here on earth and, more importantly, in the age to come. "I have seen what is best for people here on earth. They should eat and drink and enjoy their work, because the life God has given them on earth is short" (Ecclesiastes 5:18). The writer of Ecclesiastes teaches a simple but important message: Enjoy life and all its pleasures while living on this earth. Why? Because God has given life as a gift for every person to enjoy.

Unbelievers though can enjoy happiness in this life only. And more significantly, most of the time the wicked derive their temporal happiness from their vices such as gluttony, adultery, wealth, drunkenness, and selfish pleasure. "If people please God, God will give them wisdom, knowledge, and joy. But sinners will get only the work of gathering and storing wealth that they will have to give to the ones who please God" (Ecclesiastes 2:26).

Christians and unbelievers should see happiness in life very differently. Since the unbeliever has no real hope in the future, suffering or adverse circumstances ruins happiness. That is what a Christian should also understand though—happiness never excludes or denies the presence of suffering or sadness. However, many Christians today believe that happiness should not include suffering, or they deny the effects of suffering. For the Christian, happiness is never the ultimate goal of life but a result of living an obedient, compassionate life. Ironically, we can be happy and still have great sadness in life.

As opposed to secular thinking, a Christian worldview enriches the concept of happiness. It is never a denial of suffering or its consequences but an honest appraisal of life and its many difficulties. The Christian's view of happiness will be tempered by how he or she views suffering and misfortune in this life.

Christ lived this kind of happiness while ministering on earth. Hebrews 12:2 says, "But he accepted the shame [of the cross] as if it were nothing because of the joy that God put before him." In fact, according to a biblical definition of happiness, suffering is an opportunity for joy. James, too, speaks of this strange joy: "When you have many kinds of troubles, you should be full of joy" (James 1:2).

In his Sermon on the Mount (Matthew 5), Christ spoke of happiness for the Christian. Happy people are those who recognize their desperate spiritual need (Matthew 5:3). Happy people are sad but God comforts them (5:4). They are humble (5:5), righteous (5:6), full of mercy (5:7), pure (5:8), and peaceful (5:9). And finally, happy, blessed people suffer great injustice (5:10).

Jesus gave this encouragement to those who would receive such treatment "People will insult you and hurt you. But when they do you will be happy" (5:11).

This can be the greatest hope of the Christian—that no matter what tragedy transpires here on earth, one day there will be a perfect and permanent happiness for the one who trusts the Lord. Hence a Christian can enjoy happiness in both the good and bad circumstances of life.

Happiness: For additional scriptures on this topic go to Genesis 30:13.

4The king said, "Who is in the courtyard?" Now Haman had just entered the outer court of the king's palace. He had come to ask the king about hanging Mordecai on the platform he had prepared.

5The king's personal servants said, "Haman is standing in the courtyard."

The king said, "Bring him in."

6So Haman came in. And the king asked him, "What should be done for a man whom the king wants very much to honor?"

And Haman thought to himself, "Whom would the king want to honor more than me?" 7So he answered the king, "This is what you could do for the man you want very much to honor. 8Have the servants bring a royal robe that the king himself has worn. And also bring a horse with a royal crown on its head, a horse that the king himself has ridden. 9Let the robe and the horse be given to one of the king's most important men. Let the servants put the robe on the man the king wants to honor, and let them lead him on the horse through the city streets. As they are leading him, let them announce: 'This is what is done for the man whom the king wants to honor!'"

10The king commanded Haman, "Go quickly. Take the robe and the horse just as you have said, and do all this for Mordecai the Jew who sits at the king's gate. Do not leave out anything you have suggested."

11So Haman took the robe and the horse, and he put the robe on Mordecai. Then he led him on horseback through the city streets, announcing before Mordecai: "This is what is done for the man whom the king wants to honor!"

12Then Mordecai returned to the king's gate, but Haman hurried home with his head covered, because he was embarrassed and ashamed. 13He told his wife, Zeresh, and all his friends everything that had happened to him.

Haman's wife and the men who gave him advice said, "You are starting to lose power to Mordecai. Since he is a Jew, you cannot win against him. You will surely be ruined." 14While they were still talking, the king's eunuchs came to Haman's house and made him hurry to the banquet Esther had prepared.

Haman Is Hanged

7 So the king and Haman went in to eat with Queen Esther. 2As they were drinking wine on the second day, the king asked Esther again, "What are you asking for? I will give it to you. What is it you want? I will give you as much as half of my kingdom."

3Then Queen Esther answered, "My king, if you are pleased with me, and if it pleases you, let me live. This is what I ask. And let my people live, too. This is what I want. 4My people and I have been sold to be destroyed, to be killed and completely wiped out. If we had been sold as male and female slaves, I would have kept quiet, because that would not be enough of a problem to bother the king."

5Then King Xerxes asked Queen Esther, "Who is he, and where is he? Who has done such a thing?"

6Esther said, "Our enemy and foe is this wicked Haman!"

Then Haman was filled with terror before the king and queen. 7The king was very angry, so he got up, left his wine, and went out into the palace garden. But Haman stayed inside to beg Queen Esther to save his life. He could see that the king had already decided to kill him.

8When the king returned from the palace garden to the banquet hall, he saw Haman falling on the couch where Esther was lying. The king said, "Will he even attack the queen while I am in the house?"

As soon as the king said that, servants came in and covered Haman's face. 9Harbona, one of the eunuchs there serving the king, said, "Look, a seventy-five foot platform stands near Haman's house. This is the one Haman had prepared for Mordecai, who gave the warning that saved the king."

The king said, "Hang Haman on it!" 10So they hanged Haman on the platform he had prepared for Mordecai. Then the king was not so angry anymore.

The King Helps the Jewish People

8 That same day King Xerxes gave Queen Esther everything Haman, the enemy of the Jewish people, had left when he died. And Mordecai came in to see the king, because Esther had told the king how he was related to her. 2Then the king took off his signet ring that he had taken back from Haman, and he gave it to Mordecai. Esther put Mordecai in charge of everything Haman left when he died.

3Once again Esther spoke to the king. She fell at the king's feet and cried and begged him to stop the evil plan that Haman the Agagite had planned against the Jews. 4The king held out the gold scepter to Esther. So Esther got up and stood in front of him.

5She said, "My king, if you are pleased with me, and if it pleases you to do this, if you think it is the right thing to do, and if you are happy with me, let an order be written to cancel the letters

Haman wrote. Haman the Agagite sent messages to destroy all the Jewish people in all of your kingdom. 6I could not stand to see that terrible thing happen to my people. I could not stand to see my family killed."

7King Xerxes answered Queen Esther and Mordecai the Jew, "Because Haman was against the Jewish people, I have given his things to Esther, and my soldiers have hanged him. 8Now, in the king's name, write another order to the Jewish people as it seems best to you. Then seal the order with the king's signet ring, because no letter written in the king's name and sealed with his signet ring can be canceled."

9At that time the king's secretaries were called. This was the twenty-third day of the third month, which is Sivan. The secretaries wrote out all of Mordecai's orders to the Jews, to the governors, to the captains of the soldiers in each state, and to the important men of the one hundred twenty-seven states that reached from India to Cush. They wrote in the writing of each state and in the language of each people. They also wrote to the Jewish people in their own writing and language. 10Mordecai wrote orders in the name of King Xerxes and sealed the letters with the king's signet ring. Then he sent the king's orders by messengers on fast horses, horses that were raised just for the king.

11These were the king's orders: The Jewish people in every city have the right to gather together to protect themselves. They may destroy, kill, and completely wipe out the army of any state or people who attack them. And they are to do the same to the women and children of that army. They may also take by force the property of their enemies. 12The one day set for the Jewish people to do this in all the empire of King Xerxes was the thirteenth day of the twelfth month, the month of Adar. 13A copy of the king's order was to be sent out as a law in every state. It was to be made known to the people of every nation living in the kingdom so the Jewish people would be ready on that set day to strike back at their enemies.

14The messengers hurried out, riding on the royal horses, because the king commanded those messengers to hurry. And the order was also given in the palace at Susa.

15Mordecai left the king's presence wearing royal clothes of blue and white and a large gold crown. He also had a purple robe made of the best linen. And the people of Susa shouted for joy. 16It was a time of happiness, joy, gladness, and honor for the Jewish people. 17As the king's order went to every state and city, there was joy and gladness among the Jewish people. In every state and city to which the king's order went, they were having feasts and celebrating. And many people through all the empire became Jews, because they were afraid of the Jewish people.

Victory for the Jewish People

9 The order the king had commanded was to be done on the thirteenth day of the twelfth month, the month of Adar. That was the day the enemies of the Jewish people had hoped to defeat them, but that was changed. So the Jewish people themselves defeated those who hated them. 2The Jews met in their cities in all the empire of King Xerxes in order to attack those who wanted to harm them. No one was strong enough to fight against them, because all the other people living in the empire were afraid of them. 3All the important men of the states, the governors, captains of the soldiers, and the king's officers helped the Jewish people, because they were afraid of Mordecai. 4Mordecai was very important in the king's palace. He was famous in all the empire, because he was becoming a leader of more and more people.

5And, with their swords, the Jewish people defeated all their enemies, killing and destroying them. And they did what they wanted with those people who hated them. 6In the palace at Susa, they killed and destroyed five hundred men. 7They also killed: Parshandatha, Dalphon, Aspatha, 8Poratha, Adalia, Aridatha, 9Parmashta, Arisai, Aridai, and Vaizatha, 10the ten sons of Haman, son of Hammedatha, the enemy of the Jewish people. But the Jewish people did not take their belongings.

11On that day the number killed in the palace at Susa was reported to the king. 12The king said to Queen Esther, "The Jewish people have killed and destroyed five hundred people in the palace at Susa, and they have also killed Haman's ten sons. What have they done in the rest of the king's empire! Now what else are you asking? I will do it! What else do you want? It will be done!"

13Esther answered, "If it pleases the king, give the Jewish people who are in Susa permission to do again tomorrow what the king ordered for today. And let the bodies of Haman's ten sons be hanged on the platform."

14So the king ordered that it be done. A law was given in Susa, and the bodies of the ten sons of Haman were hanged. 15The Jewish people in Susa came together on the fourteenth day of the month of Adar. They killed three hundred people in Susa, but they did not take their belongings.

16At that same time, all the Jewish people in
the king's empire also met to protect themselves
and get rid of their enemies. They killed seventy-
five thousand of those who hated them, but they
did not take their belongings. 17This happened on
the thirteenth day of the month of Adar. On the
fourteenth day they rested and made it a day of
joyful feasting.

The Feast of Purim

18But the Jewish people in Susa met on the thirteenth and fourteenth days of the month of Adar.
Then they rested on the fifteenth day and made it
a day of joyful feasting.

19This is why the Jewish people who live in the
country and small villages celebrate on the fourteenth day of the month of Adar. It is a day of joyful feasting and a day for exchanging gifts.

20Mordecai wrote down everything that had
happened. Then he sent letters to all the Jewish
people in all the empire of King Xerxes, far and
near. 21He told them to celebrate every year on
the fourteenth and fifteenth days of the month of
Adar, 22because that was when the Jewish people
got rid of their enemies. They were also to celebrate it as the month their sadness was turned to
joy and their crying for the dead was turned into
celebration. He told them to celebrate those days
as days of joyful feasting and as a time for giving
food to each other and presents to the poor.

23So the Jewish people agreed to do what
Mordecai had written to them, and they agreed to
hold the celebration every year. 24Haman son of
Hammedatha, the Agagite, was the enemy of all
the Jewish people. He had made an evil plan
against the Jewish people to destroy them, and he
had thrown the Pur (that is, the lot) to choose a
day to ruin and destroy them. 25But when the
king learned of the evil plan, he sent out written
orders that the evil plans Haman had made
against the Jewish people would be used against
him. And those orders said that Haman and his
sons should be hanged on the platform. 26So these
days were called Purim, which comes from the
word "Pur" (the lot). Because of everything written in this letter and what they had seen and
what happened to them, 27the Jewish people set
up this custom. They and their descendants and
all those who join them are always to celebrate
these two days every year. They should do it in the
right way and at the time Mordecai had ordered
them in the letter. 28These two days should be
remembered and celebrated from now on in every
family, in every state, and in every city. These
days of Purim should always be celebrated by the
Jewish people, and their descendants should
always remember to celebrate them, too.

29So Queen Esther daughter of Abihail, along
with Mordecai the Jew, wrote this second letter
about Purim. Using the power they had, they
wrote to prove the first letter was true. 30And
Mordecai sent letters to all the Jewish people in
the one hundred twenty-seven states of the kingdom of Xerxes, writing them a message of peace
and truth. 31He wrote to set up these days of
Purim at the chosen times. Mordecai the Jew and
Queen Esther had sent out the order for the
Jewish people, just as they had set up things for
themselves and their descendants: On these two
days the people should give up eating and cry
loudly. 32Esther's letter set up the rules for Purim,
and they were written down in the records.

The Greatness of Mordecai

10 King Xerxes demanded taxes everywhere,
even from the cities on the seacoast. 2And
all the great things Xerxes did by his power and
strength are written in the record books of the
kings of Media and Persia. Also written in those
record books are all the things done by Mordecai,
whom the king made great. 3Mordecai the Jew was
second in importance to King Xerxes, and he
was the most important man among the Jewish
people. His fellow Jews respected him very much,
because he worked for the good of his people and
spoke up for the safety of all the Jewish people.

9:18–32 The Feast of Purim was established in the fourth century B.C. when a plot to destroy the Jewish people living in Persia failed. Haman had decided by lot (Pur) the day for the destruction of the people, but through some surprising turns of events God delivered the people through Esther's and Mordecai's intervention. Haman himself was destroyed. This deliverance was celebrated by a day of joyful feasting and exchanging of gifts.

Notes:

INTRODUCTION TO SECTION TWO
JOB – SONG OF SOLOMON

THE BOOKS OF POETRY

JOB	PSALMS	PROVERBS	ECCLESIASTES	SONG OF SOLOMON

Much of the Bible is written in poetry. Job, Psalms, Ecclesiastes, Song of Solomon, Proverbs, Isaiah, Micah, and many other books are poetic in large measure. Genesis, Exodus, Matthew, Philippians, and most other Bible books also contain some poetry.

How can we recognize poetry in the Bible? Poetry is easy to identify in the Bible because of all the white space on the page! As opposed to prose, which is written in sentences and paragraphs, poetry is made up of short phrases that are grouped in stanzas. Poetry, in other words, says a lot using as few words as possible. This makes the poetical portions of the Bible especially rich in meaning and also somewhat harder to grasp at first reading. Indeed, poetry invites the reader to slow down and meditate on the meaning of the text. We should savor and ponder, not skim the poems of the Bible.

Why is there so much poetry in the Bible? This question intensifies as we realize that poetry does not communicate very precisely. It uses much imagery and many other figures of speech; poetry is not the language of choice for communicating detailed information. But what poetry lacks in precision of detail it more than makes up in vividness and its ability to speak to the whole person. Poetry not only informs our intellects, it also arouses our emotions, stimulates our imaginations, and directs our wills by telling us how to act. Poetry speaks to the whole person, not just the brain.

Poetry has certain characteristic features, which are important to understand in order to interpret poetry correctly.

In the first place, most biblical poetry contains parallel lines. Psalm 131:1 is a good example:

> LORD, my heart is not proud;
>   I don't look down on others.
> I don't do great things,
>   and I can't do miracles.

We can notice a kind of echoing effect here. The lines are not saying the same thing, but they are related to one another. In each sentence the psalmist, David, denies something. As we study it closely and ask how the sentences are like and unlike each other, we see that David distances himself from pride in three areas. First, he says his heart, which is the core of his personality, is not proud. In the second line he says that his body language, his demeanor, doesn't radiate pride. Then in the next two sentences (in themselves forming an echoing effect) he says his actions are not those of a proud person. The point is that when we study poetry, which is made up of parallelism, we need to reflect on how the lines relate to each other.

Second, poetry is made up of a lot of imagery. Imagery is the bringing together of two things that are essentially different from each other so that we can learn something about one of the things. "The LORD is my shepherd" (Psalm 23:1) brings together God and the shepherd, two people that are very unlike, in order to teach us about God. After all, we know that shepherds care for and guide their sheep. So the Lord must care for and provide for his sheep—namely us! Images also pull at our emotions in ways that flat, plain prose cannot.

God speaks to us in the language of a poet. By doing so, he shows us that he cares for more than just our minds; he cares about our souls.

Lord, you give light to my lamp.
My God brightens the darkness around me.

Psalm 18:28

INTRODUCTION TO THE BOOK OF
JOB
A Good Man Suffers

WHO WROTE THIS BOOK?

Uncertain, but evidently a person from Israel since he often refers to God as *Yahweh* (NCV: "the LORD").

TO WHOM WAS THIS BOOK WRITTEN?

The people of Israel.

WHERE WAS IT WRITTEN?

Probably in or near Uz, the country where Job lived, east of the Jordan River.

WHEN WAS IT WRITTEN?

The date of this writing appears to be from 2000–1000 B.C.

WHAT IS THE BOOK ABOUT?

Human suffering and God's justice.

WHY WAS THIS BOOK WRITTEN?

To encourage God's people to remain faithful to him, even during difficult times, and to trust him even when it is hard to understand his purposes.

SO WHAT DOES THIS BOOK MEAN TO US?

Your faithfulness to God is not always easy, but it is always rewarded by him in the long run.

SUMMARY:

The human experience does not escape suffering, pain, and trouble. For this reason, many people are attracted to the Book of Job where the topic of discussion is the suffering of the main character—Job.

Job's suffering is especially problematic because it can be connected to no sin that he has committed. The narrator informs the reader right at the beginning that Job was "an honest and innocent man; he honored God and stayed away from evil" (Job 1:1). According to a mechanical reading of the blessings and curses of the Book of Deuteronomy (27:9–28:68) and a large number of Proverbs (i.e. 3:1–2; 10:16; 19:15; 21:20), we might expect Job to be healthy, successful, and wealthy.

So the main issue addressed by the Book of Job is how an innocent and godly person can suffer so horribly. He is approached by three friends who advocate the traditional connection between sin and punishment, but he refuses to agree with them, since he knows he does not deserve the pain he is experiencing. Once they are done with him, another young man, Elihu, addresses him, urging him to repent.

None of these human explanations succeed. *Yahweh* (God) finally speaks to Job at the end of the book. Interestingly, he does not tell Job why he is suffering. Instead, he tells Job that his attempts at wisdom are vain. He needs to acknowledge that it is God who is all-wise. Job learns from this speech and repents in dust and ashes. God then more than restores Job's previous prosperity.

The New Testament also addresses the issue of human suffering. Indeed, Jesus Christ is the truly innocent sufferer, being the only one who has not committed any sin. He submitted himself to the suffering of the world in order to free from the pain of the world those people who believe in him. It's not that Christians escape suffering in this life. The New Testament is clear that Christians will suffer this side of heaven. In 2 Corinthians 1:3–11 Paul tells Christians that they share in Christ's suffering and have his comfort available to them.

The action of the Book of Job is set in very early biblical times. Job is from the country of Uz, which is not part of Israel. This may date Job to the time just before God entered into a relationship with Abraham's descendants, choosing them as his special family.

An outline of the Book of Job is as follows:

I. Job's Prosperity Turned to Suffering (1:1–2:13)
II. Job Laments His Pain (3:1–26)
III. The Three Friends Come to "Console" Him (4:1–31:40)
IV. Elihu Takes His Turn Against Job (32:1–37:24)
V. God's Speech and Job's Response (38:1–42:17)

I. Job's Prosperity Turned to Suffering (1:1–2:13)

The book opens with a description of Job, who is honest and innocent. He is also very prosperous with a large family and many possessions. Satan and God enter into a debate about why Job is so devoted to God. As a result God gives permission for Satan to test Job's devotion. Job is unaware of the reasons for his suffering, and so the question naturally arises, "Why is an apparently innocent man like Job suffering?" At the end of this section, his three friends, Eliphaz, Bildad, and Zophar arrive, and they press this question.

II. Job Laments His Pain (3:1–26)

Job responds to his pain and suffering with a lament, a prayer of complaint to God. This prayer stirs the three friends to respond in the next section of the book.

III. The Three Friends Come to "Console" Him (4:1–31:40)

Job's three friends now give him advice. They all have essentially the same message—he must have sinned; otherwise he would not be suffering. They make a offhand connection between one's behavior and reward and punishment. Job responds to each of their speeches. He rejects their interpretation of his situation in no uncertain terms. There are three cycles of speeches. In each cycle Eliphaz, Bildad, and Zophar speak in turn, and Job responds to each of them. When all is said and done, though, they are no closer to the truth than when they began.

IV. Elihu Takes His Turn Against Job (32:1–37:24)

The three older friends are out of arguments; their debate with Job has ended. Now a previously unmentioned young man named Elihu steps up to the plate, unhappy that Job is unconvinced that he is the cause of his suffering. Elihu thinks that he has the answers, but as he speaks he contributes nothing new and his comments are ignored in all that follows.

V. God's Speech and Job's Response (38:1–42:17)

God interrupts the speeches of the human characters of the book and speaks to Job out of the storm. His tone is angry and challenging. Job has set himself up as a wise person who wants to understand why he is suffering. God's answer is to remind Job who is really the wise one of the universe. The implicit message to Job is that the proper response to his suffering is to put his trust and confidence in God. Job does that, and God restores him.

JOB

Job, the Good Man

A man named Job lived in the land of Uz.
He was an honest and innocent man; he
honored God and stayed away from evil.
2Job had seven sons and three daughters. 3He
owned seven thousand sheep, three thousand
camels, five hundred teams of oxen, and five hundred female donkeys. He also had a large number
of servants. He was the greatest man among all
the people of the East.
4Job's sons took turns holding feasts in their
homes and invited their sisters to eat and drink
with them. 5After a feast was over, Job would
send and have them made clean. Early in the
morning Job would offer a burnt offering for each
of them, because he thought, "My children may
have sinned and cursed God in their hearts." Job
did this every time.

Satan Appears Before the LORD

6One day the angels came to show themselves
before the LORD, and Satan was with them. 7The
LORD said to Satan, "Where have you come from?"
Satan answered the LORD, "I have been wandering around the earth, going back and forth in it."
8Then the LORD said to Satan, "Have you noticed
my servant Job? No one else on earth is like him.
He is an honest and innocent man, honoring God
and staying away from evil."
9But Satan answered the LORD, "Job honors God
for a good reason. 10You have put a wall around
him, his family, and everything he owns. You
have blessed the things he has done. His flocks
and herds are so large they almost cover the land.
11But reach out your hand and destroy everything
he has, and he will curse you to your face."
12The LORD said to Satan, "All right, then.
Everything Job has is in your power, but you must
not touch Job himself." Then Satan left the LORD's
presence.
13One day Job's sons and daughters were eating
and drinking wine together at the oldest
brother's house. 14A messenger came to Job and
said, "The oxen were plowing and the donkeys
were eating grass nearby, 15when the Sabeans
attacked and carried them away. They killed the
servants with swords, and I am the only one who
escaped to tell you!"
16The messenger was still speaking when
another messenger arrived and said, "Lightning
from God fell from the sky. It burned up the sheep
and the servants, and I am the only one who
escaped to tell you!"
17The second messenger was still speaking when
another messenger arrived and said, "The Babylonians sent three groups of attackers that swept
down and stole your camels and killed the servants.
I am the only one who escaped to tell you!"
18The third messenger was still speaking when
another messenger arrived and said, "Your sons
and daughters were eating and drinking wine
together at the oldest brother's house. 19Suddenly
a great wind came from the desert, hitting all four
corners of the house at once. The house fell in on
the young people, and they are all dead. I am the
only one who escaped to tell you!"
20When Job heard this, he got up and tore his
robe and shaved his head to show how sad he
was. Then he bowed down to the ground to worship God. 21He said:

"I was naked when I was born,
and I will be naked when I die.
The LORD gave these things to me,
and he has taken them away.
Praise the name of the LORD."

22In all this Job did not sin or blame God.

Satan Appears Before the LORD Again

2 On another day the angels came to show themselves before the LORD, and Satan was with
them again. 2The LORD said to Satan, "Where have
you come from?"
Satan answered the LORD, "I have been wandering around the earth, going back and forth in it."
3Then the LORD said to Satan, "Have you
noticed my servant Job? No one else on earth is
like him. He is an honest and innocent man, honoring God and staying away from evil. You caused
me to ruin him for no good reason, but he continues to be without blame."
4"One skin for another!" Satan answered. "A
man will give all he has to save his own life. 5But
reach out your hand and destroy his flesh and
bones, and he will curse you to your face."
6The LORD said to Satan, "All right, then. Job is
in your power, but you may not take his life."
7So Satan left the LORD's presence. He put painful sores on Job's body, from the top of his head to

1:1 *Uz.* Uz is located to the east of the land of Israel. Most scholars associate Uz with what is later known as Edom.
1:8 Servant of the Lord: Job 42:7–8
1:12 Evil: Job 16:11
1:12 Demon: Isaiah 14:12–15
1:21 Names of God: Ezekiel 20:44
1:22 Family: 1 Corinthians 13:12
2:3 Integrity: Job 31:6

the soles of his feet. 8Job took a piece of broken pottery to scrape himself, and he sat in ashes in misery.
9Job's wife said to him, "Why are you trying to
stay innocent? Curse God and die!"
10Job answered, "You are talking like a foolish
woman. Should we take only good things from
God and not trouble?" In spite of all this Job did
not sin in what he said.

Job's Three Friends Come to Help

11Now Job had three friends: Eliphaz the
Temanite, Bildad the Shuhite, and Zophar the
Naamathite. When these friends heard about
Job's troubles, they agreed to meet and visit him.
They wanted to show their concern and to comfort
him. 12They saw Job from far away, but he looked
so different they almost didn't recognize him. They
began to cry loudly and tore their robes and put
dirt on their heads to show how sad they were.
13Then they sat on the ground with Job seven
days and seven nights. No one said a word to him
because they saw how much he was suffering.

Job Curses His Birth

3 After seven days Job cried out and cursed the
day he had been born, 2saying:

3"Let the day I was born be destroyed,
and the night it was said, 'A boy is born!'
4Let that day turn to darkness.
Don't let God care about it.
Don't let light shine on it.
5Let darkness and gloom have that day.
Let a cloud hide it.
Let thick darkness cover its light.
6Let thick darkness capture that night.
Don't count it among the days of the year
or put it in any of the months.
7Let that night be empty,
with no shout of joy to be heard.
8Let those who curse days curse that day.
Let them prepare to wake up the sea
monster Leviathan.
9Let that day's morning stars never appear;
let it wait for daylight that never comes.
Don't let it see the first light of dawn,
10because it allowed me to be born
and did not hide trouble from my eyes.

11"Why didn't I die as soon as I was born?
Why didn't I die when I came out of the
womb?
12Why did my mother's knees receive me,
and my mother's breasts feed me?
13If they had not been there,
I would be lying dead in peace;
I would be asleep and at rest
14with kings and wise men of the earth
who built places for themselves that are now
ruined.
15I would be asleep with rulers
who filled their houses with gold and silver.
16Why was I not buried like a child born dead,
like a baby who never saw the light of day?
17In the grave the wicked stop making trouble,
and the weary workers are at rest.
18In the grave there is rest for the captives
who no longer hear the shout of the
slave driver.
19People great and small are in the grave,
and the slave is freed from his master.

20"Why is light given to those in misery?
Why is life given to those who are so
unhappy?
21They want to die, but death does not come.
They search for death more than for
hidden treasure.
22They are very happy
when they get to the grave.
23They cannot see where they are going.
God has hidden the road ahead.
24I make sad sounds as I eat;
my groans pour out like water.
25Everything I feared and dreaded
has happened to me.
26I have no peace or quietness.
I have no rest, only trouble."

Eliphaz Speaks

4 Then Eliphaz the Temanite answered:

2"If someone tried to speak with you, would
you be upset?
I cannot keep from speaking.
3Think about the many people you
have taught
and the weak hands you have made strong.
4Your words have comforted those who fell,
and you have strengthened those who
could not stand.
5But now trouble comes to you, and you are
discouraged;
trouble hits you, and you are terrified.

2:9 Curse: Proverbs 26:2
2:11 Comfort: Job 42:11
3:8 *Leviathan.* Leviathan was the sea monster that stood against the force of creation order and represented chaos. Job invokes an ancient curse to arouse Leviathan to wipe out or destroy the day Job was born.
3:26 Complaint/Lament/Protest: Psalm 5

Reputation

PROVERBS 22:1

What is a good reputation? How does one get a good reputation? How does one get a bad reputation?

Possessing a good name is the greatest asset a person can own. This proverb tells us that a good name, a good reputation, is far greater than even great riches. The rest of the Old Testament confirms this proverb for in the days of ancient Israel a person's name and the reputation that accompanied the name was a life-and-death matter. The people of Israel were continually concerned that they did not lose their individual names or that their names were not tarnished by a bad reputation. Since the name of the person represented the essence of his or her personality, losing the name would be tantamount to losing the person. Hence, name was associated with words such as *fame*, *memory*, and *remembering.*

The name was an external expression of an individual's internal nature. In biblical thinking there was an intimate connection between the person's reputation and the name. The name manifested the character and, consequently, a person's name eventually gained a reputation, whether good or bad.

The name Jacob means "deceiver" or "one who supplants by deceit." After Jacob received the birthright by deceiving Isaac, his twin brother Esau offered up this lament: "Jacob is the right name for him. He has tricked me these two times" (Genesis 27:34–36). The conniving Jacob lived out his name and confirmed his reputation. Later on in the Genesis story, Jacob encountered God at Jabbok and was forever changed (Genesis 32:23–33). Jacob's name was changed to Israel to represent a change of character and reputation.

Prior to sending Moses back to Egypt, God reveals a new truth of his character by revealing a new name. "Then God said to Moses, 'I am the LORD. I appeared to Abraham, Isaac, and Jacob by the name God Almighty [*El Shaddai*], but they did not know me by my name, the LORD [*Jehovah*]' " (Exodus 6:2–3). Moses was to return to Egypt with the name and reputation of Jehovah, the God who is present, the God who acts on behalf of Israel.

If reputation is so advantageous in the Bible and in our lives today, then how does one receive a good reputation? Once again, Proverbs cuts to the core of the matter and offers sage advice. "Knowledge [living with wisdom] begins with the respect of the LORD" (Proverbs 1:7). Our faith must precede our actions. Our relationship with God determines whether or not we have a good or bad reputation. A good reputation begins with a good relationship with God, and the result is a life of exemplary actions.

Proverbs 1:7 teaches that wise living begins in faith. The remainder of the Book of Proverbs gives practical, down-to-earth advice on how to live a life that is wise and good and hence a life that has a good reputation. Here are just a few: One who fears the LORD is successful, righteous, just, and fair (1:3). One who has a good reputation is industrious (10:4); honest (10:9); wise (10:32); kind (11:17); open to learning (12:1); capable and competent (12:4); and responsible for other human beings (14:31).

Hebrews 11 speaks of women and men in the past whose reputations encourage Christians in the present—people like Abel, Enoch, Noah, Abraham, Isaac, Jacob, Joseph, Moses, Rahab, and the judges. "All these people are known for their faith." These men and women teach two essential truths about having a good reputation: a good reputation does not mean a perfect life. These verses offer great hope to our everyday lives. These were men and women of faith, but they were not perfect. They had lapses of faith. Some lied. Some feared and faltered. Each one had something in his or her life that had the potential of ruining a good reputation. But over the span of their lives they were people who patiently waited "for the city that has real foundations" (Hebrews 11:10). Secondly, these heroes and heroines of faith remind us that a good reputation takes a lifetime to acquire. A bad reputation can be gained in one single moment of life—an affair, a lie, a failure. But one who fails can gain a good reputation simply by being forgiven. Jacob was a testament to a man who could change his reputation from good to bad, and in spite of all his failures he is remembered as a man of faith.

One's reputation could advance or destroy his or her lot in life. Thus, losing great riches is nothing in comparison to losing a good reputation. Riches are great to have, but a good reputation will evoke God's blessing on our lives both here on earth and in heaven. A good reputation is eminently valuable because it calls people to the God whose name and reputation we bear. Modern Christians will do much for the eternal kingdom by living lives of redemptive actions.

Reputation: For additional scriptures on this topic go to 1 Kings 10:1–13.

Proverb

Ecclesiastes 12:9–12

What is the nature of the proverb in the Bible? What makes proverbs unique, and what is their purpose in Scripture? Are parables proverbs?

All of us are familiar with proverbs: short, wise sayings that are straight to the point, easy to understand and easy to remember. In fact, some of the earliest instruction we received as children came in the form of proverbial sayings. In this way, complex philosophies and principles of life were boiled down to sentences of just three or four words. Who among us hasn't heard, "Haste makes waste," "Waste not, want not," or the more recent, "No pain, no gain"? And how often did we learn the hard way that, "You get what you pay for?"

The world of nature also provided numerous proverbial lessons. Just consider some of the better-known "fowl" proverbs, such as: "Birds of a feather flock together;" "Don't count your chickens before they hatch;" "A bird in the hand is worth two in the bush;" and "Kill two birds with one stone."

It is no surprise, then, that the Bible too is full of proverbs, seeing that proverbial sayings serve as such an effective teaching tool. In addition to the many hundreds of proverbs in the Book of Proverbs, as well as several dozen in Ecclesiastes, proverbial expressions are found throughout the Scriptures, beginning with the most basic form of proverbial speech, the comparison. (The Hebrew word for "proverb" comes from a root meaning "compare.") The simplest example of this is found in Ezekiel 16:44: "The daughter is like her mother."

These vivid comparisons can paint powerful word pictures, forcefully driving home the point, as in Proverbs 11:22, "A beautiful woman without good sense is like a gold ring in a pig's snout"; or, 17:14, "Starting a quarrel is like a leak in a dam, so stop it before a fight breaks out." Other proverbs contrast and compare the final results of two opposite kinds of behavior, such as, "A wise son makes his father happy, but a foolish son makes his mother sad" (Proverbs 10:1); or, "A lazy person will end up poor, but a hard worker will become rich" (Proverbs 10:4).

Many proverbial expressions contain no comparisons at all, but simply consist of a short saying that has become well known. In this category would be the words of King Ahab to King Ben Hadad in 1 Kings 20:11, "The man who puts on his armor should not brag. It's the man who lives to take it off who has the right to brag." (In Hebrew, these two sentences are just four words, typical of proverbial sayings.) Ecclesiastes has many examples of this too, such as, "Whoever loves money will never have enough money; whoever loves wealth will not be satisfied with it" (5:10).

Sayings like these are found throughout the Bible, and they carry a special authority because they ring true. They are easily memorized, they communicate clearly, and they have a certain familiarity because they are so well known.

There are also extended forms of proverbs, longer teachings of wisdom, found especially in Proverbs 1–9 and 31. Of course, the purpose of these sayings is to impart instruction and offer clear, strong, and practical guidelines for living. But the extended proverbial expression is like a fatherly talk on a specific theme, reinforced with examples from real life.

For example, Proverbs 1 deals with the dangers of going along with the sinful crowd. Wisdom herself warns, "Fools will die because they refuse to listen; they will be destroyed because they do not care. But those who listen to me will live in safety and be at peace, without fear or injury" (Proverbs 1:32–33).

In the New Testament, Jesus occasionally used proverbs in his teaching (for example, Luke 4:23a; Matthew 9:13, quoting from Hosea 6:6; Matthew 11:17).

The fact that proverbs and parables are so common in the Bible reminds us that the biblical authors, inspired as they were by the Spirit, were more interested in communicating to their hearers with forceful memorable speech than in impressing them with flowery speech. Although their words are often beautiful and majestic, their overall goal was to hit home and make a lasting impact. Nothing does this better than the proverbial saying.

So, read carefully and listen well, and, as Proverbs 19:20 says, "In the end you will be wise." That is the purpose of the biblical proverb.∞

∞**Proverb:** For additional scriptures on this topic go to Judges 9:7–15.

6You should have confidence because you
respect God;
you should have hope because you
are innocent.

7"Remember that the innocent will not die;
honest people will never be destroyed.
8I have noticed that people who plow evil
and plant trouble, harvest it.
9God's breath destroys them,
and a blast of his anger kills them.
10Lions may roar and growl,
but when the teeth of a strong lion are broken,
11that lion dies of hunger.
The cubs of the mother lion are scattered.

12"A word was brought to me in secret,
and my ears heard a whisper of it.
13It was during a nightmare
when people are in deep sleep.
14I was trembling with fear;
all my bones were shaking.
15A spirit glided past my face,
and the hair on my body stood on end.
16The spirit stopped,
but I could not see what it was.
A shape stood before my eyes,
and I heard a quiet voice.
17It said, 'Can a human be more right than God?
Can a person be pure before his maker?
18God does not trust his angels;
he blames them for mistakes.
19So he puts even more blame on people who
live in clay houses,
whose foundations are made of dust,
who can be crushed like a moth.
20Between dawn and sunset many people are
broken to pieces;
without being noticed, they die and
are gone forever.
21The ropes of their tents are pulled up,
and they die without wisdom.'

5 "Call if you want to, Job, but no one will
answer you.
You can't turn to any of the holy ones.
2Anger kills the fool,
and jealousy slays the stupid.
3I have seen a fool succeed,
but I cursed his home immediately.
4His children are far from safety
and are crushed in court with no defense.
5The hungry eat his harvest,
even taking what grew among the thorns,
and thirsty people want his wealth.
6Hard times do not come up from the ground,
and trouble does not grow from the earth.
7People produce trouble
as surely as sparks fly upward.

8"But if I were you, I would call on God
and bring my problem before him.
9God does wonders that cannot be understood;
he does so many miracles they cannot
be counted.
10He gives rain to the earth
and sends water on the fields.
11He makes the humble person important
and lifts the sad to places of safety.
12He ruins the plans of those who trick others
so they have no success.
13He catches the wise in their own clever traps
and sweeps away the plans of those who
try to trick others.
14Darkness covers them up in the daytime;
even at noon they feel around in the dark.
15God saves the needy from their lies
and from the harm done by powerful people.
16So the poor have hope,
while those who are unfair are silenced.

17"The one whom God corrects is happy,
so do not hate being corrected by
the Almighty.⚭
18God hurts, but he also bandages up;
he injures, but his hands also heal.
19He will save you from six troubles;
even seven troubles will not harm you.
20God will buy you back from death in times
of hunger,
and in battle he will save you from
the sword.
21You will be protected from the tongue that
strikes like a whip,
and you will not be afraid when destruction
comes.
22You will laugh at destruction and hunger,
and you will not fear the wild animals,
23because you will have an agreement with the
stones in the field,
and the wild animals will be at peace with you.
24You will know that your tent is safe,
because you will check the things you own
and find nothing missing.

4:19 *clay houses.* This is probably talking about people's bodies.
⚭**5:17 Happiness:** Psalm 128:1

⚭**5:17 Beatitudes:** Proverbs 3:13

25You will know that you will have many children,
and your descendants will be like the grass
on the earth.
26You will come to the grave with all your
strength,
like bundles of grain gathered at the
right time.

27"We have checked this, and it is true,
so hear it and decide what it means to you."

Job Answers Eliphaz

6 Then Job answered:

2"I wish my suffering could be weighed
and my misery put on scales.
3My sadness would be heavier than the sand of
the seas.
No wonder my words seem careless.
4The arrows of the Almighty are in me;
my spirit drinks in their poison;
God's terrors are gathered against me.
5A wild donkey does not bray when it has grass
to eat,
and an ox is quiet when it has feed.
6Tasteless food is not eaten without salt,
and there is no flavor in the white of an egg.
7I refuse to touch it;
such food makes me sick.

8"How I wish that I might have what I ask for
and that God would give me what I hope for.
9How I wish God would crush me
and reach out his hand to destroy me.
10Then I would have this comfort
and be glad even in this unending pain,
because I would know I did not reject the
words of the Holy One.

11"I do not have the strength to wait.
There is nothing to hope for,
so why should I be patient?
12I do not have the strength of stone;
my flesh is not bronze.
13I have no power to help myself,
because success has been taken
away from me.

14"They say, 'A man's friends should be kind to
him when he is in trouble,
even if he stops fearing the Almighty.'
15But my brothers cannot be counted on.
They are like streams that do not always flow,
streams that sometimes run over.
16They are made dark by melting ice
and rise with melting snow.
17But they stop flowing in the dry season;
they disappear when it is hot.
18Travelers turn away from their paths
and go into the desert and die.
19The groups of travelers from Tema
look for water,
and the traders of Sheba look hopefully.
20They are upset because they had been sure;
when they arrive, they are disappointed.
21You also have been no help.
You see something terrible, and you are afraid.
22I have never said, 'Give me a gift.
Use your wealth to pay my debt.
23Save me from the enemy's power.
Buy me back from the clutches of
cruel people.'

24"Teach me, and I will be quiet.
Show me where I have been wrong.
25Honest words are painful,
but your arguments prove nothing.
26Do you mean to correct what I say?
Will you treat the words of a troubled man as
if they were only wind?
27You would even gamble for orphans
and would trade away your friend.

28"But now please look at me.
I would not lie to your face.
29Change your mind; do not be unfair;
think again, because my innocence is being
questioned.
30What I am saying is not wicked;
I can tell the difference between
right and wrong.

7 "People have a hard task on earth,
and their days are like those of a laborer.
2They are like a slave wishing for the evening
shadows,
like a laborer waiting to be paid.
3But I am given months that are empty,
and nights of misery have been given to me.
4When I lie down, I think, 'How long until
I get up?'
The night is long, and I toss until dawn.

6:6 Salt: Ezekiel 16:4

6:11 Here Job says he is losing his patience. How does this square with James 5:11 where Job is given as an example of patience? The Greek word in James is better translated "perseverance." Patience is more passive than Job's attitude allows. In other words, Job displays a kind of active, occasionally combative, relationship with God, but he sticks with him, not cursing God as his wife suggests.

[5]My body is covered with worms and scabs,
and my skin is broken and full of sores.

[6]"My days go by faster than a weaver's tool,
and they come to an end without hope.
[7]Remember, God, that my life is only a breath.
My eyes will never see happy times again.
[8]Those who see me now will see me no more;
you will look for me, but I will be gone.
[9]As a cloud disappears and is gone,
people go to the grave and never return.
[10]They will never come back to their
houses again,
and their places will not know them anymore.

[11]"So I will not stay quiet;
I will speak out in the suffering of my spirit.
I will complain because I am so unhappy.
[12]I am not the sea or the sea monster.
So why have you set a guard over me?
[13]Sometimes I think my bed will comfort me
or that my couch will stop my complaint.
[14]Then you frighten me with dreams
and terrify me with visions.
[15]My throat prefers to be choked;
my bones welcome death.
[16]I hate my life; I don't want to live forever.
Leave me alone, because my days
have no meaning.

[17]"Why do you make people so important
and give them so much attention?
[18]You examine them every morning
and test them every moment.
[19]Will you never look away from me
or leave me alone even long enough
to swallow?
[20]If I have sinned, what have I done to you,
you watcher of humans?
Why have you made me your target?
Have I become a heavy load for you?
[21]Why don't you pardon my wrongs
and forgive my sins?
I will soon lie down in the dust of death.
Then you will search for me, but I will
be no more."

Bildad Speaks to Job

8 Then Bildad the Shuhite answered:

[2]"How long will you say such things?
Your words are no more than wind.

Papyrus: used for making writing material, boats, baskets, ropes, and sandals

[3]God does not twist justice;
the Almighty does not make wrong
what is right.
[4]Your children sinned against God,
and he punished them for their sins.
[5]But you should ask God for help
and pray to the Almighty for mercy.
[6]If you are good and honest,
he will stand up for you
and bring you back where you belong.
[7]Where you began will seem unimportant,
because your future will be so successful.

[8]"Ask old people;
find out what their ancestors learned,
[9]because we were only born yesterday and
know nothing.
Our days on earth are only a shadow.
[10]Those people will teach you and tell you
and speak about what they know.
[11]Papyrus plants cannot grow where
there is no swamp,
and reeds cannot grow tall without water.
[12]While they are still growing and not yet cut,
they will dry up quicker than grass.
[13]That is what will happen to those who
forget God;
the hope of the wicked will be gone.
[14]What they hope in is easily broken;
what they trust is like a spider's web.

7:12 *the sea or the sea monster.* In ancient thought the sea monster was the symbol of chaos. God subdued and controlled the sea in order to bring about creation.

8:8 *Ask old people.* In the ancient world the wisdom of aged people was valued because they had more experience in the world than the young.

15They lean on the spider's web, but it breaks.
They grab it, but it does not hold up.
16They are like well-watered plants in
the sunshine
that spread their roots all through the garden.
17They wrap their roots around a pile of rocks
and look for a place among the stones.
18But if a plant is torn from its place,
then that place rejects it and says, 'I
never saw you.'
19Now joy has gone away;
other plants grow up from the same dirt.

20"Surely God does not reject the innocent
or give strength to those who do evil.
21God will yet fill your mouth with laughter
and your lips with shouts of joy.
22Your enemies will be covered with shame,
and the tents of the wicked will be gone."

Job Answers Bildad

9 Then Job answered:

2"Yes, I know that this is true,
but how can anyone be right in the
presence of God?
3Someone might want to argue with God,
but no one could answer God,
not one time out of a thousand.
4God's wisdom is deep, and his power is great;
no one can fight him without getting hurt.
5God moves mountains without anyone
knowing it
and turns them over when he is angry.
6He shakes the earth out of its place
and makes its foundations tremble.
7He commands the sun not to shine
and shuts off the light of the stars.
8He alone stretches out the skies
and walks on the waves of the sea.
9It is God who made the Bear, Orion, and
the Pleiades
and the groups of stars in the southern sky.
10He does wonders that cannot be understood;
he does so many miracles they cannot
be counted.
11When he passes me, I cannot see him;
when he goes by me, I do not recognize him.
12If he snatches something away, no one
can stop him
or say to him, 'What are you doing?'
13God will not hold back his anger.
Even the helpers of the monster Rahab lie at
his feet in fear.
14So how can I argue with God,
or even find words to argue with him?
15Even if I were right, I could not answer him;
I could only beg God, my Judge, for mercy.
16If I called to him and he answered,
I still don't believe he would listen to me.
17He would crush me with a storm
and multiply my wounds for no reason.
18He would not let me catch my breath
but would overwhelm me with misery.
19When it comes to strength, God is
stronger than I;
when it comes to justice, no one can
accuse him.
20Even if I were right, my own mouth would
say I was wrong;
if I were innocent, my mouth would say
I was guilty.

21"I am innocent,
but I don't care about myself.
I hate my own life.
22It is all the same. That is why I say,
'God destroys both the innocent and the guilty.'
23If the whip brings sudden death,
God will laugh at the suffering of the innocent.
24When the land falls into the hands of
evil people,
he covers the judges' faces so they can't
see it.
If it is not God who does this, then who is it?

25"My days go by faster than a runner;
they fly away without my seeing any joy.
26They glide past like paper boats.
They attack like eagles swooping down to feed.
27Even though I say, 'I will forget my complaint;
I will change the look on my face and smile,'
28I still dread all my suffering.
I know you will hold me guilty.
29I have already been found guilty,
so why should I struggle for no reason?
30I might wash myself with soap
and scrub my hands with strong soap,
31but you would push me into a dirty pit,
and even my clothes would hate me.

32"God is not a man like me, so I cannot
answer him.
We cannot meet each other in court.

9:9 *Bear . . . Pleiades.* Names of well-known groups of stars.
9:13 *Rahab.* Rahab, like Leviathan (see 3:8), is a sea monster and, as such, symbolizes the forces of chaos that stand against the creator God.

[33]I wish there were someone to make
peace between us,
someone to decide our case.
[34]Maybe he could remove God's punishment
so his terror would no longer frighten me.
[35]Then I could speak without being afraid,
but I am not able to do that.

10 "I hate my life,
so I will complain without holding back;
I will speak because I am so unhappy.
[2]I will say to God: Do not hold me guilty,
but tell me what you have against me.
[3]Does it make you happy to trouble me?
Don't you care about me, the work of
your hands?
Are you happy with the plans of evil people?
[4]Do you have human eyes
that see as we see?
[5]Are your days like the days of humans,
and your years like our years?
[6]You look for the evil I have done
and search for my sin.
[7]You know I am not guilty,
but no one can save me from your power.

[8]"Your hands shaped and made me.
Do you now turn around and destroy me?
[9]Remember that you molded me like a
piece of clay.
Will you now turn me back into dust?
[10]You formed me inside my mother
like cheese formed from milk.
[11]You dressed me with skin and flesh;
you sewed me together with bones
and muscles.⚭
[12]You gave me life and showed me kindness,
and in your care you watched over my life.

[13]"But in your heart you hid other plans.
I know this was in your mind.
[14]If I sinned, you would watch me
and would not let my sin go unpunished.
[15]How terrible it will be for me if I am guilty!
Even if I am right, I cannot lift my head.
I am full of shame
and experience only pain.
[16]If I hold up my head, you hunt me like a lion
and again show your terrible power
against me.
[17]You bring new witnesses against me
and increase your anger against me.
Your armies come against me.

[18]"So why did you allow me to be born?
I wish I had died before anyone saw me.
[19]I wish I had never lived,
but had been carried straight from birth
to the grave.
[20]The few days of my life are almost over.
Leave me alone so I can have a
moment of joy.
[21]Soon I will leave; I will not return
from the land of darkness and gloom,
[22]the land of darkest night,
from the land of gloom and confusion,
where even the light is darkness."

Zophar Speaks to Job

11 Then Zophar the Naamathite answered:

[2]"Should these words go unanswered?
Is this talker in the right?
[3]Your lies do not make people quiet;
people should correct you when you
make fun of God.
[4]You say, 'My teachings are right,
and I am clean in God's sight.'
[5]I wish God would speak
and open his lips against you
[6]and tell you the secrets of wisdom,
because wisdom has two sides.
Know this: God has even forgotten some of
your sin.

[7]"Can you understand the secrets of God?
Can you search the limits of the Almighty?
[8]His limits are higher than the heavens;
you cannot reach them!
They are deeper than the grave;
you cannot understand them!
[9]His limits are longer than the earth
and wider than the sea.

[10]"If God comes along and puts you in prison
or calls you into court, no one can stop him.
[11]God knows who is evil,
and when he sees evil, he takes note of it.
[12]A fool cannot become wise
any more than a wild donkey can be
born tame.

[13]"You must give your whole heart to him
and hold out your hands to him for help.
[14]Put away the sin that is in your hand;
let no evil remain in your tent.

10:10–11 Today, many people think that birth is when human life begins. Before that moment, we are just so much human tissue. But these verses, though poetic, indicate that God tenderly cares for the fetus in the mother's womb.

⚭**10:11 Abortion:** Jeremiah 20:14–18

15Then you can lift up your face without shame,
and you can stand strong without fear.
16You will forget your trouble
and darkness will seem like morning.
17Your life will be as bright as the noonday sun,
and darkness will seem like morning.
18You will feel safe because there is hope;
you will look around and rest in safety.
19You will lie down, and no one will scare you.
Many people will want favors from you.
20But the wicked will not be able to see,
so they will not escape.
Their only hope will be to die."

Job Answers Zophar

12 Then Job answered:

2"You really think you are the only wise people
and that when you die, wisdom will die
with you!
3But my mind is as good as yours;
you are not better than I am.
Everyone knows all these things.
4My friends all laugh at me
when I call on God and expect him to
answer me;
they laugh at me even though I am right
and innocent!
5Those who are comfortable don't care
that others have trouble;
they think it right that those people should
have troubles.
6The tents of robbers are not bothered,
and those who make God angry are safe.
They have their god in their pocket.

7"But ask the animals, and they will teach you,
or ask the birds of the air, and they
will tell you.
8Speak to the earth, and it will teach you,
or let the fish of the sea tell you.
9Every one of these knows
that the hand of the LORD has done this.
10The life of every creature
and the breath of all people are
in God's hand.
11The ear tests words
as the tongue tastes food.
12Older people are wise,
and long life brings understanding.

13"But only God has wisdom and power,
good advice and understanding.
14What he tears down cannot be rebuilt;
anyone he puts in prison cannot be let out.
15If God holds back the waters, there is no rain;
if he lets the waters go, they flood the land.
16He is strong and victorious;
both the one who fools others and the one
who is fooled belong to him.
17God leads the wise away as captives
and turns judges into fools.
18He takes off chains that kings put on
and puts a garment on their bodies.
19He leads priests away naked
and destroys the powerful.
20He makes trusted people be silent
and takes away the wisdom of older leaders.
21He brings disgrace on important people
and takes away the weapons of the strong.
22He uncovers the deep things of darkness
and brings dark shadows into the light.
23He makes nations great and then destroys them;
he makes nations large and then scatters them.
24He takes understanding away from the leaders
of the earth
and makes them wander through a
pathless desert.
25They feel around in darkness with no light;
he makes them stumble like drunks.

13 "Now my eyes have seen all this;
my ears have heard and understood it.
2What you know, I also know.
You are not better than I am.
3But I want to speak to the Almighty
and to argue my case with God.
4But you smear me with lies.
You are worthless doctors, all of you!
5I wish you would just stop talking;
then you would really be wise!
6Listen to my argument,
and hear the pleading of my lips.
7You should not speak evil in the name of God;
you cannot speak God's truth by telling lies.
8You should not unfairly choose his side
against mine;
you should not argue the case for God.
9You will not do well if he examines you;
you cannot fool God as you might fool humans.
10God would surely scold you
if you unfairly took one person's side.
11His bright glory would scare you,
and you would be very much afraid of him.
12Your wise sayings are worth no more
than ashes,
and your arguments are as weak as clay.

13"Be quiet and let me speak.
Let things happen to me as they will.

TIME

ECCLESIASTES 3:1–11

How much does our view and use of time match that found in the biblical writings? What can it teach us so that we approach both from God's point of view rather than a human or simply modern point of view?

Basic to all the Bible says about time is that time is a gift of God. Days and weeks came into being with the Creation (Genesis 1:3–2:3). Seasons also have their source in God (Psalm 74:16), and years marked the main religious festivals (Leviticus 23). Time, then, is made and marked by God. It is not under human control or arrangement.

Those who think otherwise are firmly corrected. This was the mistake of the rich fool in Jesus' parable, who thought that he could determine the length of his life and the order it would take (Luke 12:16–20). It is tempting to say, as the person referred to in the letter of James, that "Today or tomorrow we will go to some city. We will stay there a year, do business, and make money." But we can only see "a short time" ahead. Only God knows the future, and only what God grants us will take place (James 4:13–17). As Proverbs says: "People can make all kinds of plans, but only the LORD's plan will happen (Proverbs 19:21).

According to the Bible, the period of time for normally given by God to human beings is "seventy years, or, if we are strong, eighty years" (Psalm 90:10). This is a reminder that the human lifespan has not changed significantly from biblical times to the present: the increasing number of people who reach old age is mainly due to the lower death rates for children and pregnant women. Even so, the days "pass quickly," are often filled with "hard work and pain," and all too soon "are gone;" if we are wise, we will notice that our lives are "short" and act wisely (Psalm 90:10–12). In other words, we should have a sense of the brevity of life and seek to use it wisely and responsibly.

In the Bible we find two basic ways of looking at everyday time.

1. *Measurable time.* This is divided up into parts of the day, like dawn, morning, midday, dark, and evening. Or, as aboard ships still today, into various 'watches' during the night (three in the Old Testament, four in the New Testament). There was no Hebrew word for *hours*, only a Greek word later. This suggests that marking the day by hours was more a Western than Eastern development. In biblical languages there is nothing that matches our word *minutes.* This means that our sense of very small measurements of time, and of very exact counting of it, was not done in Bible times.

On the whole, biblical references to time are fairly general. In the Gospels, for example, events are generally introduced with such words as "then," "after," "about," "later," "once," "one day," "another day," "a few days," "a short time," "a while," "another time," "after some time." Sometimes, without pinning down the exact time, time references are more specific, such as "immediately," "very early," "the night before," "the same day," "that evening," "at that time," "the next day," "after two days," "the next sabbath." In both Hebrew and Greek there were terms for month and year, and these could be calculated with some accuracy. Mostly this was done by reference to the number of years since a king began to reign (Jeremiah 1:2), or when a king died (Isaiah 6:1). Often the future is described simply as "the age," or "the days," to come (Amos 8:11).

2. *Another approach to time.* Here time is not counted but is noted from the experience or event that takes place within it. In other words, time is defined by *what* happens rather than *when* something happens or *how long* it happens. The best description of this way of viewing and using time comes in the Book of Ecclesiastes, which says, "There is a time for everything, and everything on earth has its special season" (Ecclesiastes 3:1). As the passage goes on to note, this includes birth and death, crying and laughing, being sad and dancing, planting and pulling up plants, collecting and throwing things away, hugging and not hugging, looking for something and giving up, sewing and tearing apart, speaking and being silent, loving and hating, fighting and making peace. As we read this poem in Ecclesiastes, we must be sure to see it as a description of the time, not as what should or must take place.

Other passages indicate that there is a proper time for youth, marriage, and old age. Also for leaving and returning (Micah 7:15), feasting or going hungry (Psalm 37:19), beautifying and having a regular monthly period (Esther 2:12; Leviticus 15:25), working and resting (John 9:4), traveling and staying in one place (Deuteronomy 2:14), worshiping God and healing others (Psalm 122:1–4; Jeremiah 8:15). Part of the time that God gives daily is for sleep. God grants us this out of love. Always getting up too early or staying up too late rejects God's generous arrangement and fails to accomplish God's purposes (Psalm 127:1–2).

According to the Bible, there is a clear cycle for the use of time. Daylight hours are for work, and evening hours for relaxation and sleep (1 Thessalonians 5:6). Six days a week shall be given over to work, the seventh to rest, for animals as well as people (Exodus 20:8–11; 23:12–13). Even during busy periods such as harvest time the sabbath should be oberved (Exodus 34:21). There were also several main feasts throughout the year, some celebrating great actions God had performed on behalf of the people—such as the Passover and the Feast of Trumpets—and others connected with God's providing food at harvest times—such as the Feast of Weeks and of Harvest (Leviticus 23).

Christ's life and work fulfilled the purpose of feasts like the Passover (1 Corinthians 5:7), and Gentile Christians were under no obligation to keep the sabbath or any monthly festival (Romans 14:5–6; Colossians 2:16–17). For Christ is our Passsover, and through him we have already entered into God's rest (Hebrews 4:3). In honor of Christ's resurrection on the first day of the week (John 20:1), the early Christians met on Sundays for fellowship with God and one another (Acts 20:7). They also each set aside money that day to give to those who were in need (1 Corinthians 16:2). But they also met at other times (Acts 2: 42).

Everyone should seek to view and use time responsibly. As Paul wrote: "be very careful how you live. Do not live like those who are not wise, but live wisely. Use every chance you have for doing good, because these are evil times. So do not be foolish but learn what the Lord wants you to do" (Ephesians 5:15–17). This means always using good sense, and making sure that what we do is useful and does not waste time. Believers should encourage one another daily to do this (Hebrews 3:13).

Using "every chance" to do good means living responsibly and giving time to what God wants. This is more important than filling every moment with activities or trying to do everything that comes our way. Giving time to what God wants made it possible for Paul to pass by places in which he could have spent time because he did not sense God's direction (Acts 16:6–9). He also experiences frustrations and delays in fulfilling his plans (Acts 13:49–51; 2 Corinthians 1:23–2:1), but knows that things only happen or come together "if the Lord allows it" (1 Corinthians 16:7). This does not mean that Paul did not do his best and work hard (Acts 20:31). But he had a clear sense of how he should use his time (Romans 15:20), what his main work was (1 Corinthians 3:10), and that he should finish what he had started (Romans 15:23).

Understanding when, where, and how to use time involves knowing the difference between what is really important—things that must be done—and what seems urgent but can be set aside (Luke 10:38–42). It means knowing the opportunity that should not be taken up and the clear call of God that must be obeyed (2 Corinthians 2:12–13). It also allows us to tell the difference between our own human plans and God's purposes (Proverbs 19:21). Wise people plan in such a way that they keep their time more flexible the further it is from the present (1 Corinthians 16:5–9), because no one can know too far ahead what God has in mind.

In general there should be an ongoing awareness that becoming too busy or anxious is to forget the temporary nature of this life (1 Corinthians 7:29–30), and that God will both provide for material needs (Matthew 6:25–34) and accomplish evangelistic results (Isaiah 55:10–11). Believers should also live in the trust that the Lord's coming is nearer than before (Romans 13:12), and will not be long (Revelation 22:20). No one knows exactly when this will be (Mark 13:32), and it might seem like a long time, for to God "one day is as a thousand years, and a thousand years is as one day" (2 Peter 3:8). As in the past, though God's purposes sometimes seem to move slowly, at other times God acts quickly to save, protect, or honor his people.

Finally, the most important thing for us to know is that the whole of our life is in God's hands (Psalm 31:15). God is in control of time; times does not control him. He is not bound by time; he is eternal (1 Timothy 1:17). The fact that God is not bound by time makes clearer such biblical teachings as God's plannings long ago. How else could he choose "us before the world was made" (Ephesians 1:4)? We can't completely understand it; after all, we are creatures of time. Our eternal God knows not only the past and the present, but also the future. That is what gives us confidence in the prophecy of the Bible. That is why we know for certain that he will win the victory in the end. To our eternal God, the future is not a matter of time and chance, as it often seems to us from our point of view "here on earth" (Ecclesiastes 9:11). It is a matter of absolute certainty!∞

∞**Time:** For additional scriptures on this topic go to Exodus 20:8–11.

[14]Why should I put myself in danger
and take my life in my own hands?
[15]Even if God kills me, I have hope in him;
I will still defend my ways to his face.
[16]This is my salvation.
The wicked cannot come before him.
[17]Listen carefully to my words;
let your ears hear what I say.
[18]See, I have prepared my case,
and I know I will be proved right.
[19]No one can accuse me of doing wrong.
If someone can, I will be quiet and die.

[20]"God, please just give me these two things,
and then I will not hide from you:
[21]Take your punishment away from me,
and stop frightening me with your terrors.
[22]Then call me, and I will answer,
or let me speak, and you answer.
[23]How many evil things and sins have I done?
Show me my wrong and my sin.
[24]Don't hide your face from me;
don't think of me as your enemy.
[25]Don't punish a leaf that is blown by the wind;
don't chase after straw.
[26]You write down cruel things against me
and make me suffer for my boyhood sins.
[27]You put my feet in chains
and keep close watch wherever I go.
You even mark the soles of my feet.

[28]"Everyone wears out like something rotten,
like clothing eaten by moths.

14 "All of us born to women
live only a few days and have lots of trouble.
[2]We grow up like flowers and then dry
up and die.
We are like a passing shadow that does
not last.⚭
[3]Lord, do you need to watch me like this?
Must you bring me before you to be judged?
[4]No one can bring something clean from
something dirty.
[5]Our time is limited.
You have given us only so many months
to live
and have set limits we cannot go beyond.
[6]So look away from us and leave us alone
until we put in our time like a laborer.

[7]"If a tree is cut down,
there is hope that it will grow again
and will send out new branches.
[8]Even if its roots grow old in the ground,
and its stump dies in the dirt,
[9]at the smell of water it will bud
and put out new shoots like a plant.
[10]But we die, and our bodies are laid in
the ground;
we take our last breath and are gone.⚭
[11]Water disappears from a lake,
and a river loses its water and dries up.
[12]In the same way, we lie down and do
not rise again;
we will not get up or be awakened
until the heavens disappear.

[13]"I wish you would hide me in the grave;
hide me until your anger is gone.
I wish you would set a time
and then remember me!
[14]If a person dies, will he live again?
All my days are a struggle;
I will wait until my change comes.
[15]You will call, and I will answer you;
you will desire the creature your hands
have made.
[16]Then you will count my steps,
but you will not keep track of my sin.
[17]My wrongs will be closed up in a bag,
and you will cover up my sin.

[18]"A mountain washes away and crumbles;
and a rock can be moved from its place.
[19]Water washes over stones and wears
them down,
and rushing waters wash away the dirt.
In the same way, you destroy my hope.
[20]You defeat a person forever, and he is gone;
you change his appearance and send
him away.
[21]His sons are honored, but he does
not know it;
his sons are disgraced, but he does not see it.
[22]He only feels the pain of his body
and feels sorry for himself."

Eliphaz Answers Job

15 Then Eliphaz the Temanite answered:
[2]"A wise person would not answer with
empty words
or fill his stomach with the hot east wind.
[3]He would not argue with useless words
or make speeches that have no value.
[4]But you even destroy respect for God
and limit the worship of him.

⚭**14:2 Death:** Job 14:7–10

⚭**14:10 Death:** Psalm 49:13–20

5Your sin teaches your mouth what to say;
you use words to trick others.
6It is your own mouth, not mine, that shows
you are wicked;
your own lips testify against you.

7"You are not the first man ever born;
you are not older than the hills.
8You did not listen in on God's secret council.
But you limit wisdom to yourself.
9You don't know any more than we know.
You don't understand any more than we
understand.
10Old people with gray hair are on our side;
they are even older than your father.
11Is the comfort God gives you not enough for you,
even when words are spoken gently to you?
12Has your heart carried you away from God?
Why do your eyes flash with anger?
13Why do you speak out your anger against God?
Why do these words pour out of your mouth?

14"How can anyone be pure?
How can someone born to a woman
be good?
15God places no trust in his holy ones,
and even the heavens are not pure
in his eyes.
16How much less pure is one who is
terrible and rotten
and drinks up evil as if it were water!

17"Listen to me, and I will tell you about it;
I will tell you what I have seen.
18These are things wise men have told;
their fathers told them, and they have
hidden nothing.
19(The land was given to their fathers only,
and no foreigner lived among them.)
20The wicked suffer pain all their lives;
the cruel suffer during all the years saved
up for them.
21Terrible sounds fill their ears,
and when things seem to be going well,
robbers attack them.
22Evil people give up trying to escape from
the darkness;
it has been decided that they will die
by the sword.
23They wander around and will become food
for vultures.
They know darkness will soon come.∞
24Worry and suffering terrify them;
they overwhelm them, like a king ready
to attack,
25because they shake their fists at God
and try to get their own way against
the Almighty.
26They stubbornly charge at God
with thick, strong shields.

27"Although the faces of the wicked are
thick with fat,
and their bellies are fat with flesh,
28they will live in towns that are ruined,
in houses where no one lives,
which are crumbling into ruins.
29The wicked will no longer get rich,
and the riches they have will not last;
the things they own will no longer spread
over the land.
30They will not escape the darkness.
A flame will dry up their branches;
God's breath will carry the wicked away.
31The wicked should not fool themselves by
trusting what is useless.
If they do, they will get nothing in return.
32Their branches will dry up before they
finish growing
and will never turn green.
33They will be like a vine whose grapes are
pulled off before they are ripe,
like an olive tree that loses its blossoms.
34People without God can produce nothing.
Fire will destroy the tents of those who take
money to do evil,
35who plan trouble and give birth to evil,
whose hearts plan ways to trick others."

Job Answers Eliphaz

16 Then Job answered:

2"I have heard many things like these.
You are all painful comforters!
3Will your long-winded speeches never end?
What makes you keep on arguing?
4I also could speak as you do
if you were in my place.
I could make great speeches against you
and shake my head at you.
5But, instead, I would encourage you,
and my words would bring you relief.

6"Even if I speak, my pain is not less,
and if I don't speak, it still does not go away.

15:8 *God's secret council.* Here, and in a number of passages in the Old Testament, there are allusions to a divine council. In this council, God tells his angelic servants how to accomplish his will in the world.

∞**15:23 Darkness:** Isaiah 9:2

7God, you have surely taken away my strength
and destroyed my whole family.
8You have made me thin and weak,
and this shows I have done wrong.
9God attacks me and tears me with anger;
he grinds his teeth at me;
my enemy stares at me with his angry eyes.
10People open their mouths to make fun of me
and hit my cheeks to insult me.
They join together against me.
11God has turned me over to evil people
and has handed me over to the wicked.
12Everything was fine with me,
but God broke me into pieces;
he held me by the neck and crushed me.
He has made me his target;
13 his archers surround me.
He stabs my kidneys without mercy;
he spills my blood on the ground.
14Again and again God attacks me;
he runs at me like a soldier.

15"I have sewed rough cloth over my skin to
show my sadness
and have buried my face in the dust.
16My face is red from crying;
I have dark circles around my eyes.
17Yet my hands have never done
anything cruel,
and my prayer is pure.

18"Earth, please do not cover up my blood.
Don't let my cry ever stop being heard!
19Even now I have one who speaks for
me in heaven;
the one who is on my side is high above.
20The one who speaks for me is my friend.
My eyes pour out tears to God.
21He begs God on behalf of a human
as a person begs for his friend.

22"Only a few years will pass
before I go on the journey of no return.

17 My spirit is broken;
the days of my life are almost gone.
The grave is waiting for me.
2Those who laugh at me surround me;
I watch them insult me.

3"God, make me a promise.
No one will make a pledge for me.
4You have closed their minds to understanding.
Do not let them win over me.
5A person might speak against his friends
for money,
but if he does, the eyes of his children
go blind.

6"God has made my name a curse word;
people spit in my face.
7My sight has grown weak because of my sadness,
and my body is as thin as a shadow.
8Honest people are upset about this;
innocent people are upset with those
who do wrong.

9But those who do right will continue to do right,
and those whose hands are not dirty with sin
will grow stronger.
10"But, all of you, come and try again!
I do not find a wise person among you.
11My days are gone, and my plans have
been destroyed,
along with the desires of my heart.
12These men think night is day;
when it is dark, they say, 'Light is near.'
13If the only home I hope for is the grave,
if I spread out my bed in darkness,
14if I say to the grave, 'You are my father,'
and to the worm, 'You are my mother'
or 'You are my sister,'
15where, then, is my hope?
Who can see any hope for me?
16Will hope go down to the gates of death?
Will we go down together into the dust?"

Bildad Answers Job

18 Then Bildad the Shuhite answered:

2"When will you stop these speeches?
Be sensible, and then we can talk.
3You think of us as cattle,
as if we are stupid.
4You tear yourself to pieces in your anger.
Should the earth be vacant just for you?
Should the rocks move from their places?

5"The lamp of the wicked will be put out,
and the flame in their lamps will stop burning.
6The light in their tents will grow dark,
and the lamps by their sides will go out.
7Their strong steps will grow weak;
they will fall into their own evil traps.
8Their feet will be caught in a net
when they walk into its web.
9A trap will catch them by the heel
and hold them tight.

16:11 Evil: Job 30:26

10A trap for them is hidden on the ground,
right in their path.
11Terrible things startle them from every side
and chase them at every step.
12Hunger takes away their strength,
and disaster is at their side.
13Disease eats away parts of their skin;
death gnaws at their arms and legs.
14They are torn from the safety of their tents
and dragged off to Death, the King of Terrors.
15Their tents are set on fire,
and sulfur is scattered over their homes.
16Their roots dry up below ground,
and their branches die above ground.
17People on earth will not remember them;
their names will be forgotten in the land.
18They will be driven from light into darkness
and chased out of the world.
19They have no children or descendants among
their people,
and no one will be left alive where they
once lived.
20People of the west will be shocked at what has
happened to them,
and people of the east will be very frightened.
21Surely this is what will happen to the wicked;
such is the place of one who does not
know God."

Job Answers Bildad

19 Then Job answered:

2"How long will you hurt me
and crush me with your words?
3You have insulted me ten times now
and attacked me without shame.
4Even if I have sinned,
it is my worry alone.
5If you want to make yourselves look
better than I,
you can blame me for my suffering.
6Then know that God has wronged me
and pulled his net around me.

7"I shout, 'I have been wronged!'
But I get no answer.
I scream for help
but I get no justice.
8God has blocked my way so I cannot pass;
he has covered my paths with darkness.
9He has taken away my honor
and removed the crown from my head.
10He beats me down on every side until
I am gone;
he destroys my hope like a fallen tree.
11His anger burns against me,
and he treats me like an enemy.
12His armies gather;
they prepare to attack me.
They camp around my tent.

13"God has made my brothers my enemies,
and my friends have become strangers.
14My relatives have gone away,
and my friends have forgotten me.
15My guests and my female servants treat
me like a stranger;
they look at me as if I were a foreigner.
16I call for my servant, but he does not answer,
even when I beg him with my own mouth.
17My wife can't stand my breath,
and my own family dislikes me.
18Even the little boys hate me
and talk about me when I leave.
19All my close friends hate me;
even those I love have turned against me.
20I am nothing but skin and bones;
I have escaped by the skin of my teeth.
21Pity me, my friends, pity me,
because the hand of God has hit me.
22Why do you chase me as God does?
Haven't you hurt me enough?

23"How I wish my words were written down,
written on a scroll.
24I wish they were carved with an iron
pen into lead,
or carved into stone forever.
25I know that my Defender lives,
and in the end he will stand upon the earth.
26Even after my skin has been destroyed,
in my flesh I will see God.
27I will see him myself;
I will see him with my very own eyes.
How my heart wants that to happen!⚭

28"If you say, 'We will continue to trouble Job,
because the problem lies with him,'
29you should be afraid of the sword yourselves.
God's anger will bring punishment
by the sword.
Then you will know there is judgment."

Zophar Answers

20 Then Zophar the Naamathite answered:

2"My troubled thoughts cause me to answer,
because I am very upset.

⚭**19:27 Mourning:** Isaiah 61:2–3

3You correct me and I am insulted,
but I understand how to answer you.

4"You know how it has been for a long time,
ever since people were first put on the earth.
5The happiness of evil people is brief,
and the joy of the wicked lasts only
a moment.
6Their pride may be as high as the heavens,
and their heads may touch the clouds,
7but they will be gone forever, like their
own dung.
People who knew them will say,
'Where are they?'
8They will fly away like a dream
and not be found again;
they will be chased away like a vision
in the night.
9Those who saw them will not see them again;
the places where they lived will see them no
more.
10Their children will have to pay back the poor,
and they will have to give up their wealth.
11They had the strength of their youth
in their bones,
but it will lie with them in the dust of death.

12"Evil may taste sweet in their mouths,
and they may hide it under their tongues.
13They cannot stand to let go of it;
they keep it in their mouths.
14But their food will turn sour in their stomachs,
like the poison of a snake inside them.
15They have swallowed riches, but they will
spit them out;
God will make them vomit their riches up.
16They will suck the poison of snakes,
and the snake's fangs will kill them.
17They will not admire the sparkling streams
or the rivers flowing with honey and cream.
18They must give back what they worked for
without eating it;
they will not enjoy the money they made
from their trading,
19because they troubled the poor and left them
with nothing.
They have taken houses they did not build.

20"Evil people never lack an appetite,
and nothing escapes their selfishness.
21But nothing will be left for them to eat;
their riches will not continue.
22When they still have plenty, trouble will catch
up to them,
and great misery will come down on them.
23When the wicked fill their stomachs,
God will send his burning anger against them,
and blows of punishment will fall on
them like rain.
24The wicked may run away from an iron weapon,
but a bronze arrow will stab them.
25They will pull the arrows out of their backs
and pull the points out of their livers.
Terrors will come over them;
26 total darkness waits for their treasure.
A fire not fanned by people will destroy them
and burn up what is left of their tents.
27The heavens will show their guilt,
and the earth will rise up against them.
28A flood will carry their houses away,
swept away on the day of God's anger.
29This is what God plans for evil people;
this is what he has decided they will receive."

Job Answers Zophar

21 Then Job answered:

2"Listen carefully to my words,
and let this be the way you comfort me.
3Be patient while I speak.
After I have finished, you may continue
to make fun of me.

4"My complaint is not just against people;
I have reason to be impatient.
5Look at me and be shocked;
put your hand over your mouth in shock.
6When I think about this, I am terribly afraid
and my body shakes.
7Why do evil people live a long time?
They grow old and become more powerful.
8They see their children around them;
they watch them grow up.
9Their homes are safe and without fear;
God does not punish them.
10Their bulls never fail to mate;
their cows have healthy calves.
11They send out their children like a flock;
their little ones dance about.
12They sing to the music of tambourines and harps,
and the sound of the flute makes them happy.
13Evil people enjoy successful lives
and then go peacefully to the grave.
14They say to God, 'Leave us alone!
We don't want to know your ways.
15Who is the Almighty that we should serve him?
What would we gain by praying to him?'
16The success of the wicked is not their
own doing.
Their way of thinking is different from mine.

17Yet how often are the lamps of evil people
turned off?
How often does trouble come to them?
How often do they suffer God's
angry punishment?
18How often are they like straw in the wind
or like chaff that is blown away by a storm?
19It is said, 'God saves up a person's punishment
for his children.'
But God should punish the wicked themselves
so they will know it.
20Their eyes should see their own destruction,
and they should suffer the anger of
the Almighty.
21They do not care about the families
they leave behind
when their lives have come to an end.

22"No one can teach knowledge to God;
he is the one who judges even the
most important people.
23One person dies while he still has
all his strength,
feeling completely safe and comfortable.
24His body was well fed,
and his bones were strong and healthy.
25But another person dies with an
unhappy heart,
never enjoying any happiness.
26They are buried next to each other,
and worms cover them both.

27"I know very well your thoughts
and your plans to wrong me.
28You ask about me, 'Where is this great
man's house?
Where are the tents where the
wicked live?'
29Have you never asked those who travel?
Have you never listened to their stories?
30On the day of God's anger and punishment,
it is the wicked who are spared.
31Who will accuse them to their faces?
Who will pay them back for the evil they
have done?
32They are carried to their graves,
and someone keeps watch over their tombs.
33The dirt in the valley seems sweet to them.
Everybody follows after them,
and many people go before them.

34"So how can you comfort me with
this nonsense?
Your answers are only lies!"

Eliphaz Answers

22 Then Eliphaz the Temanite answered:

2"Can anyone be of real use to God?
Can even a wise person do him good?
3Does it help the Almighty for you
to be good?
Does he gain anything if you are innocent?
4Does God punish you for respecting him?
Does he bring you into court for this?
5No! It is because your evil is without limits
and your sins have no end.
6You took your brothers' things for a debt
they didn't owe;
you took clothes from people and left
them naked.
7You did not give water to tired people,
and you kept food from the hungry.
8You were a powerful man who owned land;
you were honored and lived in the land.
9But you sent widows away empty-handed,
and you mistreated orphans.
10That is why traps are all around you
and sudden danger frightens you.
11That is why it is so dark you cannot see
and a flood of water covers you.

12"God is in the highest part of heaven.
See how high the highest stars are!
13But you ask, 'What does God know?
Can he judge us through the dark clouds?
14Thick clouds cover him so he cannot see us
as he walks around high up in the sky.'
15Are you going to stay on the old path
where evil people walk?
16They were carried away before their
time was up,
and their foundations were washed away
by a flood.
17They said to God, 'Leave us alone!
The Almighty can do nothing to us.'
18But it was God who filled their houses with
good things.
Their way of thinking is different from mine.

19"Good people can watch and be glad;
the innocent can laugh at them and say,
20'Surely our enemies are destroyed,
and fire burns up their wealth.'

21"Obey God and be at peace with him;
this is the way to happiness.
22Accept teaching from his mouth,
and keep his words in your heart.

23If you return to the Almighty, you will be
blessed again.
So remove evil from your house.
24Throw your gold nuggets into the dust
and your fine gold among the rocks in the
ravines.
25Then the Almighty will be your gold
and the best silver for you.
26You will find pleasure in the Almighty,
and you will look up to him.
27You will pray to him, and he will hear you,
and you will keep your promises to him.
28Anything you decide will be done,
and light will shine on your ways.
29When people are made humble and you say,
'Have courage,'
then the humble will be saved.
30Even a guilty person will escape
and be saved because your hands are clean."

Job Answers

23 Then Job answered:
2"My complaint is still bitter today.
I groan because God's heavy hand is on me.
3I wish I knew where to find God
so I could go to where he lives.
4I would present my case before him
and fill my mouth with arguments.
5I would learn how he would answer me
and would think about what he would say.
6Would he not argue strongly against me?
No, he would really listen to me.
7Then an honest person could present his
case to God,
and I would be saved forever by my judge.

8"If I go to the east, God is not there;
if I go to the west, I do not see him.
9When he is at work in the north, I catch no
sight of him;
when he turns to the south, I cannot see him.
10But God knows the way that I take,
and when he has tested me, I will come
out like gold.
11My feet have closely followed his steps;
I have stayed in his way;
I did not turn aside.
12I have never left the commands he has spoken;
I have treasured his words more than
my own.

13"But he is the only God.
Who can come against him?
He does anything he wants.
14He will do to me what he said he would do,
and he has many plans like this.
15That is why I am frightened of him;
when I think of this, I am afraid of him.
16God has made me afraid;
the Almighty terrifies me.
17But I am not hidden by the darkness,
by the thick darkness that covers my face.

24 "I wish the Almighty would set a time
for judging.
Those who know God do not see such a day.
2Wicked people take other people's land;
they steal flocks and take them to
new pastures.
3They chase away the orphan's donkey
and take the widow's ox when she has
no money.
4They push needy people off the path;
all the poor of the land hide from them.
5The poor become like wild donkeys in the desert
who go about their job of finding food.
The desert gives them food for their children.
6They gather hay and straw in the fields
and pick up leftover grapes from the vineyard
of the wicked.
7They spend the night naked, because they
have no clothes,
nothing to cover themselves in the cold.
8They are soaked from mountain rains
and stay near the large rocks because they
have no shelter.
9The fatherless child is grabbed from its
mother's breast;
they take a poor mother's baby to pay for
what she owes.
10So the poor go around naked without
any clothes;
they carry bundles of grain but still go hungry;
11they crush olives to get oil
and grapes to get wine, but they still go thirsty.
12Dying people groan in the city,
and the injured cry out for help,
but God accuses no one of doing wrong.

13"Those who fight against the light
do not know God's ways
or stay in his paths.
14When the day is over, the murderers get up
to kill the poor and needy.
At night they go about like thieves.
15Those who are guilty of adultery watch
for the night,
thinking, 'No one will see us,'
and they keep their faces covered.

16In the dark, evil people break into houses.
In the daytime they shut themselves up in their own houses,
because they want nothing to do with the light.
17Darkness is like morning to all these evil people
who make friends with the terrors of darkness.

18"They are like foam floating on the water.
Their part of the land is cursed;
no one uses the road that goes by their vineyards.
19As heat and dryness quickly melt the snow,
so the grave quickly takes away the sinners.
20Their mothers forget them,
and worms will eat their bodies.
They will not be remembered,
so wickedness is broken in pieces like a stick.
21These evil people abuse women who cannot have children
and show no kindness to widows.
22But God drags away the strong by his power.
Even though they seem strong, they do not know how long they will live.
23God may let these evil people feel safe,
but he is watching their ways.
24For a little while they are important, and then they die;
they are laid low and buried like everyone else;
they are cut off like the heads of grain.
25If this is not true, who can prove I am wrong?
Who can show that my words are worth nothing?"

Bildad Answers

25 Then Bildad the Shuhite answered:
2"God rules and he must be honored;
he set up order in his high heaven.
3No one can count God's armies.
His light shines on all people.
4So no one can be good in the presence of God,
and no one born to a woman can be pure.
5Even the moon is not bright
and the stars are not pure in his eyes.
6People are much less! They are like insects.
They are only worms!"

Job Answers Bildad

26 Then Job answered:
2"You are no help to the helpless!
You have not aided the weak!
3Your advice lacks wisdom!
You have shown little understanding!
4Who has helped you say these words?
And where did you get these ideas?

5"The spirits of the dead tremble,
those who are beneath and in the waters.
6Death is naked before God;
destruction is uncovered before him.
7God stretches the northern sky out over empty space
and hangs the earth on nothing.
8He wraps up the waters in his thick clouds,
but the clouds do not break under their weight.
9He covers the face of the moon,
spreading his clouds over it.
10He draws the horizon like a circle on the water
at the place where light and darkness meet.
11Heaven's foundations shake
when he thunders at them.
12With his power he quiets the sea;
by his wisdom he destroys Rahab, the sea monster.
13He breathes, and the sky clears.
His hand stabs the fleeing snake.
14And these are only a small part of God's works.
We only hear a small whisper of him.
Who could understand God's thundering power?"

27 And Job continued speaking:
2"As surely as God lives, who has taken away my rights,
the Almighty, who has made me unhappy,
3as long as I am alive
and God's breath of life is in my nose,
4my lips will not speak evil,
and my tongue will not tell a lie.
5I will never agree you are right;
until I die, I will never stop saying I am innocent.
6I will insist that I am right; I will not back down.
My conscience will never bother me.

7"Let my enemies be like evil people,
my foes like those who are wrong.
8What hope do the wicked have when they die,
when God takes their life away?
9God will not listen to their cries
when trouble comes to them.
10They will not find joy in the Almighty,
even though they call out to God all the time.

11"I will teach you about the power of God
and will not hide the ways of the Almighty.

26:12 See 9:13.

EVIL

ECCLESIASTES 6:2

Why did a good God allow for the presence of evil in the world?
What is "evil" and how can we recognize it in day-to-day life?
What resources do we have for dealing with evil?

Evil is a word with broad applications and is therefore difficult to define. In the Bible, *evil* is anything that brings sorrow, distress, or calamity, including moral wrongdoing, where human beings choose to do what hurts other human beings, or any part of creation. Generally, evil works against the life-giving power of God and seeks to thwart God's will. The ultimate evil, therefore, is to reject the one, true, living God and to put anything in God's place.

There was a time, in the late nineteenth and early twentieth century, when optimism in human achievement was so strong that evil's existence was associated with ignorance, and its disappearance with greater knowledge. If humankind only knew more, soon would come the end of all evil in the world. Since then, two world wars—especially with chemical warfare, the Holocaust, and Hiroshima and Nagasaki—combined with growing problems of over-population, racism, ecological destruction, and worldwide disease have cured humankind of that illusion. The Bible throughout clearly presents evil as a reality that clings to us. As Paul declares in Romans 7:21, "So I have learned this rule: When I want to do good, evil is there with me."

In the Old Testament, there is no distinction between moral evil and calamity in the words used for evil. Some basic meanings are sadness (Genesis 44:34), harm ("harmful" in Leviticus 26:6), "serious problems" (Ecclesiastes 6:2), and wickedness (1 Samuel 12:17). The most important definition of evil is a rejection of God's way and law (Deuteronomy 4:25; 1 Kings 11:6; 2 Kings 21:2; see Hebrews 3:12).

The problem with the presence of evil arises from the essential biblical confession that God created the world and called it good. In Genesis 1, God states five times that the creation is "good" (verses 10, 12, 18, 21, 25), and even in verse 31, "very good."

This raises the problem of evil in the world: if God has created the heaven and earth good, then why is evil around in any form? In this sense, every friend who dies of cancer, every soul that ends up rebelling against God, every person killed by an earthquake or flood, is one more argument against the existence of a good, all-powerful God. At times the presence of evil in the creation is so strong that "the world" becomes associated with the realm of evil. In the Gospel of John, for instance, there is a clear indication that God created the world (John 1:10), but that the world is now a place largely in rebellion against its Creator (John 12:31; 15:19). The Bible never describes evil as greater than the good that is in creation: "The Light shines in the darkness, and the darkness has not overpowered it" (John 1:5).

There is no extended discussion in the Bible for why evil exists in the world, but *freedom* plays a significant part in the entrance of evil into the Garden in Genesis 3. In Genesis 2:16–17, God allows the man to eat from any tree, except the tree "which gives the knowledge of good and evil." The meanings of this tree have been hotly debated, but what is most important for an understanding of evil is that here, from the beginning of creation, the human being is given free choice: first of all, an ability to select from many good alternatives, and second, a freedom to disobey. So when the woman and man eat from this tree in Genesis 3:6, there is an abuse of freedom that breaks their relationship with God (Genesis 3:8–10) and leads God to curse them (Genesis 3:16–19). (It should also be noted that after their sin in Genesis 3:21, God makes clothes for them, showing care for them.) Genesis teaches here that evil enters from an abuse of freedom.

The Book of Job has often been a source for reflection on the nature of evil and the existence of a good God. Job 1:6–12 begins by describing Satan (or "the adversary"), who is responsible for the evil that will happen to Job and that God allows (but does not cause). The presence of evil spirits (also described in 1 Samuel 16:14–23 and 1 Kings 22:19–23) does not solve the problem of the origin of evil, but simply adds a complexity that behind all earthly evil, there is cosmic evil. (It should be noted here that the power of evil is never set as an equal to God, for God alone controls the universe.) As Job's trials continue, he raises the biblical question of why the righteous (and especially Job!) suffer (Job 16:11; 30:26). What emerges from the final section of Job (38:1–42:6), however, is not a definitive answer, but that the suffering of the righteous is a mysterious part of creation and that God's presence is more important than answers to the questions evil raises.

The Old Testament responds to the problem of evil in other passages in three ways. (1) God's will is not thwarted by evil, but God can take evil and make it result in good. As Joseph said to his brothers who sold him into slavery, "You meant to hurt me, but God turned your evil into good to save the lives of many people, which is being done" (Genesis 50:20; see also Romans 8:28). (2) God uses evil to test righteous people, as God tested Job. (3) Evil will not win in the long run; it may promise short-term benefits, but cuts off women and men from the greatest good, God (Psalm 37:16–17; 73:15–28; Proverbs 10:29; 11:19; 17:13).

The New Testament understands evil in the same way that the Old Testament does—as both moral wrong and calamity—and, from this definition, adds some new insights into how Christians are to understand evil.

The New Testament affirms that God is not responsible for evil. James says that God is neither tempted by evil nor tempts people to do evil (James 1:13). Though evil exists in the world, it can never overcome good (John 1:5). Jesus instructs his disciples to pray nevertheless that God would deliver them from evil in Matthew 6:13. Christians are to watch out for the heart, where much evil resides (Mark 7:21). Christians are to be careful of their speech (James 3:8) and the love of money, which "causes all kinds of evil" (1 Timothy 6:10). Christians are encouraged never to repay evil for evil (Romans 12:17; 1 Peter 2:16), but are to actively to resist it in their own behavior (Romans 16:19; 1 Corinthians 14:20; 1 Thessalonians 5:22; 3 John 11).

When the problem of evil comes to the New Testament, there is a distinct twist: Jesus, the very Son of God, died at the hands of evil women and men. Thus, God clearly has overcome evil by Jesus' bearing its full consequences (1 Peter 2:18–25). This means that God is not far from the human struggle with evil, and that Jesus, himself God, has taken on evil.

The New Testament declares that the final victory over evil will come when God creates a new heaven and a new earth. Then God "will wipe away every tear from their eyes, and there will no more death, sadness, crying, or pain, because all the old ways are gone" (Revelation 21:4). This affirmation has certainly been used as a rationalization for ignoring evil and oppression on the earth, but it has similarly given hope in the midst of injustice that a day is coming when every evil and injustice will be righted.

Evil is around us every day. This fact raises both philosophical and practical questions.

Reflection on the presence of evil has led to the question, How can a good and all-powerful God create a world that has evil in it? The Bible, however, does not concern itself directly with this philosophical problem. Still there will always be a search to work with the biblical texts and find responses to the problem of evil. The most simple answer is that natural evil is the price paid for regularity in nature (the same log that burns and keeps someone warm cannot suddenly stop burning if it is part of a house), and moral evil is the price paid for human freedom (the same hand that can reach out and console can strike and injure). For God to create a world that is ordered and not simply chaotic, there must be natural law. And for there to be the possibility of good, ethical behavior—and especially where we can love God and other human beings—there has to be freedom. This freedom allows for both good and evil action. Ultimately, it must be admitted that any answers are tentative, do not answer every objection, and are best when they do not attempt to resolve all of the mystery in the kind of world God has created. Christians look to complete answers and, most importantly, to the end of all evil, at the end of history.

The Bible takes evil as a given, and therefore offers a realistic picture of life and calls people to offer practical solutions to evil. In Western societies, and particularly in the United States, there is a general cultural unwillingness to admit that evil is a daily reality, not only in widespread calamities like earthquakes, wars, and personal suffering such as cancer and injury, but also in daily psychological brokenness. The Bible is much more realistic than many contemporary Westerners often are. Consequently, Christians are called to be a healing influence in a world of evil; we can, in fact, be part of God's solution to evil. The Scriptures emphasize that God's coming in Christ takes on and defeats evil through Christ's suffering on the cross and his resurrection. Therefore, we can mirror God's work through acts of compassion and efforts to liberate people from evil. We can also respond through lament and we can gain a foretaste of God's final victory over evil through prayer and worship. Evil raises considerable questions about the nature of God and God's redemptive creation, but also offers concrete opportunities for doing God's work in the world.⚭

⚭**Evil:** For additional scriptures on this topic go to Genesis 1.

12You have all seen this yourselves.
So why are we having all this talk that
means nothing?

13"Here is what God has planned for evil people,
and what the Almighty will give to
cruel people:
14They may have many children, but the sword
will kill them.
Their children who are left will never have
enough to eat.
15Then they will die of disease and be buried,
and the widows will not even cry for them.
16The wicked may heap up silver like piles of dirt
and have so many clothes they are like
piles of clay.
17But good people will wear what evil people
have gathered,
and the innocent will divide up their silver.
18The houses the wicked build are like
a spider's web,
like a hut that a guard builds.
19The wicked are rich when they go to bed,
but they are rich for the last time;
when they open their eyes, everything is gone.
20Fears come over them like a flood,
and a storm snatches them away in the night.
21The east wind will carry them away, and then
they are gone,
because it sweeps them out of their place.
22The wind will hit them without mercy
as they try to run away from its power.
23It will be as if the wind is clapping its hands;
it will whistle at them as they run
from their place.

28 "There are mines where people dig silver
and places where gold is made pure.
2Iron is taken from the ground,
and copper is melted out of rocks.
3Miners bring lights
and search deep into the mines
for ore in thick darkness.
4Miners dig a tunnel far from where people live,
where no one has ever walked;
they work far from people, swinging and
swaying from ropes.
5Food grows on top of the earth,
but below ground things are changed
as if by fire.
6Sapphires are found in rocks,
and gold dust is also found there.
7No hawk knows that path;
the falcon has not seen it.
8Proud animals have not walked there,
and no lions cross over it.
9Miners hit the rocks of flint
and dig away at the bottom of the mountains.
10They cut tunnels through the rock
and see all the treasures there.
11They search for places where rivers begin
and bring things hidden out into the light.

12"But where can wisdom be found,
and where does understanding live?
13People do not understand the value of wisdom;
it cannot be found among those who are alive.
14The deep ocean says, 'It's not in me;'
the sea says, 'It's not in me.'
15Wisdom cannot be bought with gold,
and its cost cannot be weighed in silver.
16Wisdom cannot be bought with fine gold
or with valuable onyx or sapphire gems.
17Gold and crystal are not as valuable as wisdom,
and you cannot buy it with jewels of gold.
18Coral and jasper are not worth talking about,
and the price of wisdom is much greater
than rubies.
19The topaz from Cush cannot compare
to wisdom;
it cannot be bought with the purest gold.

20"So where does wisdom come from,
and where does understanding live?
21It is hidden from the eyes of every living thing,
even from the birds of the air.
22The places of destruction and death say,
'We have heard reports about it.'
23Only God understands the way to wisdom,
and he alone knows where it lives,
24because he looks to the farthest parts
of the earth
and sees everything under the sky.
25When God gave power to the wind
and measured the water,
26when he made rules for the rain
and set a path for a thunderstorm to follow,
27then he looked at wisdom and decided
its worth;
he set wisdom up and tested it.
28Then he said to humans,
'The fear of the Lord is wisdom;
to stay away from evil is understanding.'"

28:18–19 *Cush.* Cush is far away Ethiopia. This reference continues the theme that wisdom is more precious and inaccessible than even the most precious stones and metals.

28:28 Proverb: Psalm 49:4
28:28 Wisdom: Proverbs 4:5–9

Job Continues

29 Job continued to speak:

2"How I wish for the months that have passed
and the days when God watched over me.
3God's lamp shined on my head,
and I walked through darkness by his light.
4I wish for the days when I was strong,
when God's close friendship blessed my house.
5The Almighty was still with me,
and my children were all around me.
6It was as if my path were covered with cream
and the rocks poured out olive oil for me.
7I would go to the city gate
and sit in the public square.
8When the young men saw me, they would
step aside,
and the old men would stand up in respect.
9The leading men stopped speaking
and covered their mouths with their hands.
10The voices of the important men were quiet,
as if their tongues stuck to the roof
of their mouths.
11Anyone who heard me spoke well of me,
and those who saw me praised me,
12because I saved the poor who called out
and the orphan who had no one to help.
13The dying person blessed me,
and I made the widow's heart sing.
14I put on right living as if it were clothing;
I wore fairness like a robe and a turban.
15I was eyes for the blind
and feet for the lame.
16I was like a father to needy people,
and I took the side of strangers who
were in trouble.
17I broke the fangs of evil people
and snatched the captives from their teeth.

18"I thought, 'I will live for as many days as
there are grains of sand,
and I will die in my own house.
19My roots will reach down to the water.
The dew will lie on the branches all night.
20New honors will come to me continually,
and I will always have great strength.'

21"People listened to me carefully
and waited quietly for my advice.
22After I finished speaking, they
spoke no more.
My words fell very gently on their ears.
23They waited for me as they would for rain
and drank in my words like spring rain.
24I smiled at them when they doubted,
and my approval was important to them.
25I chose the way for them and was their leader.
I lived like a king among his army,
like a person who comforts sad people.

30 "But now men who are younger than I
make fun of me.
I would not have even let their fathers
sit with my sheep dogs.
2What use did I have for their strength
since they had lost their strength to work?
3They were thin from hunger
and wandered the dry and ruined
land at night.
4They gathered desert plants among the brush
and ate the root of the broom tree.
5They were forced to live away from people;
people shouted at them as if they were thieves.
6They lived in dried up streambeds,
in caves, and among the rocks.
7They howled like animals among the bushes
and huddled together in the brush.
8They are worthless people without names
and were forced to leave the land.

9"Now they make fun of me with songs;
my name is a joke among them.
10They hate me and stay far away from me,
but they do not mind spitting in my face.
11God has taken away my strength and
made me suffer,
so they attack me with all their anger.
12On my right side they rise up like a mob.
They lay traps for my feet
and prepare to attack me.
13They break up my road
and work to destroy me,
and no one helps me.
14They come at me as if through a hole in the wall,
and they roll in among the ruins.
15Great fears overwhelm me.
They blow my honor away as if by
a great wind,
and my safety disappears like a cloud.

16"Now my life is almost over;
my days are full of suffering.
17At night my bones ache;
gnawing pains never stop.
18In his great power God grabs hold of
my clothing
and chokes me with the collar of my coat.
19He throws me into the mud,
and I become like dirt and ashes.

[20]"I cry out to you, God, but you do not answer;
I stand up, but you just look at me.
[21]You have turned on me without mercy;
with your powerful hand you attacked me.
[22]You snatched me up and threw me into the wind
and tossed me about in the storm.
[23]I know you will bring me down to death,
to the place where all living people must go.

[24]"Surely no one would hurt a ruined man
when he cries for help in his time of trouble.
[25]I cried for those who were in trouble;
I have been very sad for poor people.
[26]But when I hoped for good, only evil
came to me;
when I looked for light, darkness came.
[27]I never stop being upset;
days of suffering are ahead of me.
[28]I have turned black, but not by the sun.
I stand up in public and cry for help.
[29]I have become a brother to wild dogs
and a friend to ostriches.
[30]My skin has become black and peels off,
as my body burns with fever.
[31]My harp is tuned to sing a sad song,
and my flute is tuned to moaning.

31

"But I made an agreement with my eyes
not to look with desire at a girl.
[2]What has God above promised for people?
What has the Almighty planned from on high?
[3]It is ruin for evil people
and disaster for those who do wrong.
[4]God sees my ways
and counts every step I take.

[5]"If I have been dishonest
or lied to others,
[6]then let God weigh me on honest scales.
Then he will know I have done
nothing wrong.
[7]If I have turned away from doing what is right,
or my heart has been led by my eyes
to do wrong,
or my hands have been made unclean,
[8]then let other people eat what I have planted,
and let my crops be plowed up.

[9]"If I have desired another woman
or have waited at my neighbor's door
for his wife,
[10]then let my wife grind another man's grain,
and let other men have sexual relations
with her.
[11]That would be shameful,
a sin to be punished.
[12]It is like a fire that burns and destroys;
all I have done would be plowed up.

[13]"If I have been unfair to my male
and female slaves
when they had a complaint against me,
[14]how could I tell God what I did?
What will I answer when he asks me to
explain what I've done?
[15]God made me in my mother's womb, and he
also made them;
the same God formed both of us in
our mothers' wombs.

[16]"I have never refused the appeals of the poor
or let widows give up hope while looking
for help.
[17]I have not kept my food to myself
but have given it to the orphans.
[18]Since I was young, I have been like a father
to the orphans.
From my birth I guided the widows.
[19]I have not let anyone die for lack of clothes
or let a needy person go without a coat.
[20]That person's heart blessed me,
because I warmed him with the wool
of my sheep.
[21]I have never hurt an orphan
even when I knew I could win in court.
[22]If I have, then let my arm fall off my shoulder
and be broken at the joint.
[23]I fear destruction from God,
and I fear his majesty, so I could not
do such things.

[24]"I have not put my trust in gold
or said to pure gold, 'You are my security.'
[25]I have not celebrated my great wealth
or the riches my hands had gained.
[26]I have not thought about worshiping the sun
in its brightness
nor admired the moon moving in glory
[27]so that my heart was pulled away from God.
My hand has never offered the sun and
moon a kiss of worship.
[28]If I had, these also would have been sins
to be punished,
because I would have been unfaithful to God.

30:26 Evil: Job 42:1–6
30:28 *I have turned black.* He has turned black because of his disease and perhaps because of his excessive worry.
31:6 Integrity: Psalm 26:1
31:10 *grind another man's grain.* The agricultural allusion is a metaphor for sexual intercourse.
31:15 Abortion and Crisis Pregnancy: Isaiah 44:2
31:17 Abortion and Crisis Pregnancy: Psalm 139:13–16

29"I have not been happy when my enemy fell
or laughed when he had trouble.
30I have not let my mouth sin
by cursing my enemy's life.
31The men of my house have always said,
'Everyone has eaten all he wants of Job's
food.'
32No stranger ever had to spend the night in the
street,
because I always let travelers stay in my
home.
33I have not hidden my sin as others do,
secretly keeping my guilt to myself.
34I was not so afraid of the crowd
that I kept quiet and stayed inside
because I feared being hated by other families.

35("How I wish a court would hear my case!
Here I sign my name to show I have
told the truth.
Now let the Almighty answer me;
let the one who accuses me write it down.
36I would wear the writing on my shoulder;
I would put it on like a crown.
37I would explain to God every step I took,
and I would come near to him like a prince.)

38"If my land cries out against me
and its plowed rows are not wet with tears,
39if I have taken the land's harvest without paying
or have broken the spirit of those who
worked the land,
40then let thorns come up instead of wheat,
and let weeds come up instead of barley."

The words of Job are finished.

Elihu Speaks

32 These three men stopped trying to answer
Job, because he was so sure he was right.
2But Elihu son of Barakel the Buzite, from the family of Ram, became very angry with Job, because
Job claimed he was right instead of God. 3Elihu
was also angry with Job's three friends who had no
answer to show that Job was wrong, yet continued
to blame him. 4Elihu had waited before speaking to
Job, because the three friends were older than he
was. 5But when Elihu saw that the three men had
nothing more to say, he became very angry.
6So Elihu son of Barakel the Buzite said this:

"I am young,
and you are old.
That is why I was afraid
to tell you what I know.
7I thought, 'Older people should speak,
and those who have lived many years should
teach wisdom.'
8But it is the spirit in a person,
the breath of the Almighty, that
gives understanding.
9It is not just older people who are wise;
they are not the only ones who understand
what is right.
10So I say, listen to me.
I too will tell you what I know.
11I waited while you three spoke,
and listened to your explanations.
While you looked for words to use,
12 I paid close attention to you.
But not one of you has proved Job wrong;
none of you has answered his arguments.
13Don't say, 'We have found wisdom;
only God will show Job to be wrong,
not people.'
14Job has not spoken his words against me,
so I will not use your arguments to answer Job.

15"These three friends are defeated and have
no more to say;
words have failed them.
16Now they are standing there with no
answers for Job.
Now that they are quiet, must I wait to speak?
17No, I too will speak
and tell what I know.
18I am full of words,
and the spirit in me causes me to speak.
19I am like wine that has been bottled up;
I am ready to burst like a new leather wine bag.
20I must speak so I will feel relief;
I must open my mouth and answer.
21I will be fair to everyone
and not flatter anyone.
22I don't know how to flatter,
and if I did, my Maker would quickly take
me away.

33 "Now, Job, listen to my words.
Pay attention to everything I say.
2I open my mouth
and am ready to speak.
3My words come from an honest heart,
and I am sincere in saying what I know.
4The Spirit of God created me,
and the breath of the Almighty gave me life.

32:4 Age was supposed to give people wisdom. Thus the elder friends were given the respect of speaking first, but now that they have failed, Elihu steps forward to speak.

5Answer me if you can;
get yourself ready and stand before me.
6I am just like you before God;
I too am made out of clay.
7Don't be afraid of me;
I will not be hard on you.

8"But I heard what you have said;
I heard every word.
9You said, 'I am pure and without sin;
I am innocent and free from guilt.
10But God has found fault with me;
he considers me his enemy.
11He locks my feet in chains
and closely watches everywhere I go.'

12"But I tell you, you are not right in saying this,
because God is greater than we are.
13Why do you accuse God
of not answering anyone?
14God does speak—sometimes one way and
sometimes another—
even though people may not understand it.
15He speaks in a dream or a vision of the night
when people are in a deep sleep,
lying on their beds.
16He speaks in their ears
and frightens them with warnings
17to turn them away from doing wrong
and to keep them from being proud.
18God does this to save a person from death,
to keep him from dying.
19A person may be corrected while in bed in
great pain;
he may have continual pain in his very bones.
20He may be in such pain that he even hates food,
even the very best meal.
21His body becomes so thin there is almost
nothing left of it,
and his bones that were hidden now stick out.
22He is near death,
and his life is almost over.

23"But there may be an angel to speak for him,
one out of a thousand, who will tell him
what to do.
24The angel will beg for mercy and say:
'Save him from death.
I have found a way to pay for his life.'
25Then his body is made new like a child's.
It will return to the way it was when
he was young.
26That person will pray to God, and God
will listen to him.
He will see God's face and will shout
with happiness.
And God will set things right for him again.
27Then he will say to others,
'I sinned and twisted what was right,
but I did not receive the punishment I
should have received.
28God bought my life back from death,
and I will continue to enjoy life.'

29"God does all these things to a person
two or even three times
30so he won't die as punishment for his sins
and so he may still enjoy life.

31"Job, pay attention and listen to me;
be quiet, and I will speak.
32If you have anything to say, answer me;
speak up, because I want to prove you right.
33But if you have nothing to say, then listen to me;
be quiet, and I will teach you wisdom."

34 Then Elihu said:

2"Hear my words, you wise men;
listen to me, you who know a lot.
3The ear tests words
as the tongue tastes food.
4Let's decide for ourselves what is right,
and let's learn together what is good.

5"Job says, 'I am not guilty,
and God has refused me a fair trial.
6Instead of getting a fair trial,
I am called a liar.
I have been seriously hurt,
even though I have not sinned.'
7There is no other man like Job;
he takes insults as if he were drinking water.
8He keeps company with those who do evil
and spends time with wicked men,
9because he says, 'It is no use
to try to please God.'

10"So listen to me, you who can understand.
God can never do wrong!
It is impossible for the Almighty to do evil.
11God pays a person back for what he has done
and gives him what his actions deserve.
12Truly God will never do wrong;
the Almighty will never twist what is right.
13No one chose God to rule over the earth
or put him in charge of the whole world.

33:15 Dreams: Jeremiah 23:25–32

33:30 Pride: Job 40:6–14

14If God should decide
to take away life and breath,
15then everyone would die together
and turn back into dust.

16"If you can understand, hear this;
listen to what I have to say.
17Can anyone govern who hates what is right?
How can you blame God who is both fair
and powerful?
18God is the one who says to kings, 'You
are worthless,'
or to important people, 'You are evil.'
19He is not nicer to princes than other people,
nor kinder to rich people than poor people,
because he made them all with his own hands.
20They can die in a moment, in the middle of
the night.
They are struck down, and then they
pass away;
powerful people die without help.

21"God watches where people go;
he sees every step they take.
22There is no dark place or deep shadow
where those who do evil can hide from him.
23He does not set a time
for people to come before him for judging.
24Without asking questions, God breaks
powerful people into pieces
and puts others in their place.
25Because God knows what people do,
he defeats them in the night, and
they are crushed.
26He punishes them for the evil they do
so that everyone else can watch,
27because they stopped following God
and did not care about any of his ways.
28The cry of the poor comes to God;
he hears the cry of the needy.
29But if God keeps quiet, who can blame him?
If he hides his face, who can see him?
God still rules over both nations
and persons alike.
30 He keeps the wicked from ruling
and from trapping others.

31"But suppose someone says to God,
'I am guilty, but I will not sin anymore.
32Teach me what I cannot see.
If I have done wrong, I will not do it again.'
33So, Job, should God reward you as you want
when you refuse to change?
You must decide, not I,
so tell me what you know.

34"Those who understand speak,
and the wise who hear me say,
35'Job speaks without knowing what is true;
his words show he does not understand.'
36I wish Job would be tested completely,
because he answered like an evil man!
37Job now adds to his sin by turning against God.
He claps his hands in protest,
speaking more and more against God."

35 Then Elihu said:

2"Do you think this is fair?
You say, 'God will show that I am right,'
3but you also ask, 'What's the use?
I don't gain anything by not sinning.'

4"I will answer you
and your friends who are with you.
5Look up at the sky
and see the clouds so high above you.
6If you sin, it does nothing to God;
even if your sins are many, they do nothing
to him.
7If you are good, you give nothing to God;
he receives nothing from your hand.
8Your evil ways only hurt a man like yourself,
and the good you do only helps other
human beings.

9"People cry out when they are in trouble;
they beg for relief from powerful people.
10But no one asks, 'Where is God, my Maker,
who gives us songs in the night,
11who makes us smarter than the animals
of the earth
and wiser than the birds of the air?'
12God does not answer evil people when
they cry out,
because the wicked are proud.
13God does not listen to their useless begging;
the Almighty pays no attention to them.
14He will listen to you even less
when you say that you do not see him,
that your case is before him,
that you must wait for him,
15 that his anger never punishes,
and that he doesn't notice evil.
16So Job is only speaking nonsense,
saying many words without knowing
what is true."

Elihu's Speech Continues

36 Elihu continued:

2"Listen to me a little longer, and I will show you
that there is more to be said for God.

[3]What I know comes from far away.
I will show that my Maker is right.
[4]You can be sure that my words are not false;
one who really knows is with you.

[5]"God is powerful, but he does not hate people;
he is powerful and sure of what he wants to do.
[6]He will not keep evil people alive,
but he gives the poor their rights.
[7]He always watches over those who do right;
he sets them on thrones with kings
and they are honored forever.
[8]If people are bound in chains,
or if trouble, like ropes, ties them up,
[9]God tells them what they have done,
that they have sinned in their pride.
[10]God makes them listen to his warning
and commands them to change from
doing evil.
[11]If they obey and serve him,
the rest of their lives will be successful,
and the rest of their years will be happy.
[12]But if they do not listen,
they will die by the sword,
and they will die without knowing why.

[13]"Those who have wicked hearts hold
on to anger.
Even when God punishes them, they do not
cry for help.
[14]They die while they are still young,
and their lives end in disgrace.
[15]But God saves those who suffer through their
suffering;
he gets them to listen through their pain.

[16]"God is gently calling you from the
jaws of trouble
to an open place of freedom
where he has set your table full of the best
food.
[17]But now you are being punished like the wicked;
you are getting justice.
[18]Be careful! Don't be led away from God by
riches;
don't let much money turn you away.
[19]Neither your wealth nor all your great strength
will keep you out of trouble.
[20]Don't wish for the night
when people are taken from their homes.
[21]Be careful not to turn to evil,
which you seem to want more
than suffering.

[22]"God is great and powerful;
no other teacher is like him.
[23]No one has planned his ways for him;
no one can say to God, 'You have done wrong.'
[24]Remember to praise his work,
about which people have sung.
[25]Everybody has seen it;
people look at it from far off.
[26]God is so great, greater than we can understand!
No one knows how old he is.

[27]"He evaporates the drops of water from
the earth
and turns them into rain.
[28]The rain then pours down from the clouds,
and showers fall on people.
[29]No one understands how God spreads
out the clouds
or how he sends thunder from where he lives.
[30]Watch how God scatters his lightning
around him,
lighting up the deepest parts of the sea.
[31]This is the way God governs the nations;
this is how he gives us enough food.
[32]God fills his hands with lightning
and commands it to strike its target.
[33]His thunder announces the coming storm,
and even the cattle know it is near.

37 "At the sound of his thunder, my heart
pounds
as if it will jump out of my chest.
[2]Listen! Listen to the thunder of God's voice
and to the rumbling that comes from
his mouth.
[3]He turns his lightning loose under the whole sky
and sends it to the farthest parts of the earth.
[4]After that you can hear the roar
when he thunders with a great sound.
He does not hold back the flashing
when his voice is heard.
[5]God's voice thunders in wonderful ways;
he does great things we cannot understand.
[6]He says to the snow, 'Fall on the earth,'
and to the shower, 'Be a heavy rain.'⚭
[7]With it, he stops everyone from working
so everyone knows it is the work of God.
[8]The animals take cover from the rain
and stay in their dens.
[9]The storm comes from where it was stored;
the cold comes with the strong winds.
[10]The breath of God makes ice,
and the wide waters become frozen.

⚭**37:6 Environment:** Job 38–41

[11]He fills the clouds with water
and scatters his lightning through them.
[12]At his command they swirl around
over the whole earth,
doing whatever he commands.
[13]He uses the clouds to punish people
or to water his earth and show his love.

[14]"Job, listen to this:
Stop and notice God's miracles.
[15]Do you know how God controls the clouds
and makes his lightning flash?
[16]Do you know how the clouds hang in the sky?
Do you know the miracles of God, who
knows everything?
[17]You suffer in your clothes
when the land is silenced by the hot,
south wind.
[18]You cannot stretch out the sky like God
and make it look as hard as polished bronze.
[19]Tell us what we should say to him;
we cannot get our arguments ready because
we do not have enough understanding.
[20]Should God be told that I want to speak?
Would a person ask to be swallowed up?
[21]No one can look at the sun
when it is bright in the sky
after the wind has blown all the clouds away.
[22]God comes out of the north in golden light,
in overwhelming greatness.
[23]The Almighty is too high for us to reach.
He has great strength;
he is always right and never punishes unfairly.
[24]That is why people honor him;
he does not respect those who say
they are wise."

The LORD Questions Job

38 Then the LORD answered Job from the storm. He said:
[2]"Who is this that makes my purpose unclear
by saying things that are not true?
[3]Be strong like a man!
I will ask you questions,
and you must answer me.
[4]Where were you when I made the earth's
foundation?
Tell me, if you understand.
[5]Who marked off how big it should be?
Surely you know!
Who stretched a ruler across it?
[6]What were the earth's foundations set on,
or who put its cornerstone in place
[7]while the morning stars sang together
and all the angels shouted with joy?

[8]"Who shut the doors to keep the sea in
when it broke through and was born,
[9]when I made the clouds like a coat for the sea
and wrapped it in dark clouds,
[10]when I put limits on the sea
and put its doors and bars in place,
[11]when I said to the sea, 'You may come this far,
but no farther;
this is where your proud waves must stop'?

[12]"Have you ever ordered the morning to begin,
or shown the dawn where its place was
[13]in order to take hold of the earth by its edges
and shake evil people out of it?
[14]At dawn the earth changes like clay being
pressed by a seal;
the hills and valleys stand out like folds
in a coat.
[15]Light is not given to evil people;
their arm is raised to do harm, but it is broken.

[16]"Have you ever gone to where the sea begins
or walked in the valleys under the sea?
[17]Have the gates of death been opened to you?
Have you seen the gates of the deep darkness?
[18]Do you understand how wide the earth is?
Tell me, if you know all these things.

[19]"What is the path to light's home,
and where does darkness live?
[20]Can you take them to their places?
Do you know the way to their homes?
[21]Surely you know, if you were already born
when all this happened!
Have you lived that many years?

[22]"Have you ever gone into the storehouse
of the snow
or seen the storehouses for hail,
[23]which I save for times of trouble,
for days of war and battle?
[24]Where is the place from which light comes?
Where is the place from which the east
winds blow over the earth?
[25]Who cuts a waterway for the heavy rains
and sets a path for the thunderstorm?

37:13 Water: Psalm 104:1–18

38:1 God appears to Job, and he speaks to him through the covering of a storm cloud. God's glory is too overwhelming for people to have any kind of direct contact with his divinity, and so the clouds protect Job. God's appearing with a storm highlights God's anger with Job.

38:7 Angels: Daniel 6:22

38:10 *limits on the sea.* See 3:8. In the ancient Near Eastern world the sea was a symbol of the forces of chaos that God needed to control as he established order in creation.

JEALOUSY

SONG OF SOLOMON 8:6

What is jealousy? Is jealousy ever a good emotion? How can the Bible call God "jealous"?

Jealousy is an angry desire to protect what we have, or wrongly think that we have. We usually think of male-female relationships when we talk about jealousy; after all, it is the stuff of movies and soap operas. But it is also the stuff of real life in all relationships.

A woman can be jealous of her husband if she suspects a threat to their relationship. A child can be jealous of a brother if he thinks his mother favors him. A friend can be jealous of the person he consider to be his best friend, if that person does not call to keep in touch. It is even possible to be jealous of possessions and hoard them for one's own use.

The Bible recognizes jealousy. King Saul illustrated how jealousy affects relationships and distorts how someone views his world (see 1 Samuel 16–19). When Saul and David first met, Saul loved the young shepherd boy. David's music calmed the king's soul, and his bravery in fighting the Philistine giant Goliath rid Israel of a great external threat (chapter 17).

Saul had position; he was the first king of Israel. But as he heard others compare David's abilities to his own, he grew jealous. More frightening than David's greater abilities was the fact that Saul had been disobedient to God, and God's presence had left him.

Saul's jealousy became obsessive. When he heard the popular song being chanted in the streets, "Saul has killed thousands of his enemies, but David has killed tens of thousands," he became incredibly jealous. "So Saul watched David closely from then on, because he was jealous" (1 Samuel 18:7–9).

Saul recognized David's gifts and courage; he knew his own lack and failure. His desire to protect his kingship escalated his feelings toward David from affection, to annoyance, to murderous obsession. He was blinded by jealousy.

The amazing thing about jealousy is that the jealous person often destroys or loses what he was trying to protect, precisely because of his jealousy. This happened with Saul who lost the kingship to David, though David had no intention of stealing it from the king.

The Bible clearly recognizes a dark emotion called jealousy, which is destructive of human relationships. Paul tells us that jealousy is at odds with spirituality (1 Corinthians 3:3) and lists it as one of the fruits of sin (Galatians 5:20).

We must not lose sight, however, that jealousy also has a good side. Some jealousy is not a sin, but rather it is a virtue. In the first place, God is often said to be a jealous God. According to Exodus 34:14, "Don't worship any other god, because I, the LORD, the Jealous One, am a jealous God."

Of whom is God jealous? He is jealous of idols, whose worship seduced Israel. God desires to protect his people when they cozy up to foreign gods. God wants an intimate relationship with us, and cannot stand it when someone or something else gets in the way, especially something as powerful and destructive as idolatry.

Moses calls God jealous in the context of presenting the Israelites with a new set of tablets engraved with the Ten Commandments. The first set had been smashed when Moses came down from Mount Sinai to find the Israelites worshiping a golden calf. God was furious, and in holy jealousy he called on the Levites to kill a number of the traitorous Israelites. This passage is just one example of many where God is described as jealously protecting his people from a relationship with false gods.

Jealousy is legitimate only in one type of human relationship according to the Bible—marriage. Not that all jealousy in marriage is appropriate. Often, it is just suspicious and petty even in a marriage. But if there is a clear threat to a marriage relationship, then jealousy is a divinely instilled emotion which has as its purpose the preservation of the exclusive marriage relationship.

It is not surprising that these are the only two relationships where jealousy is permitted. After all, they are the only ones which are exclusive. We can worship only one God, and we may have only one wife or husband.⚭

⚭**Jealousy:** For additional scriptures on this topic go to Numbers 5:14.

Sexuality

Song of Solomon

Should we enjoy and explore our sexuality as Christians? Is sex always right or always wrong? How does sexual experience help us understand God?

Sexuality is a major part of being a human being. We are sexual beings, created either male or female (Genesis 1:27). We have strong sexual desires, so the Bible has a lot to say about sex.

Most people are aware that the Bible addresses the issue of human sexuality, but until they really study the subject they believe that the Bible's main teaching is to warn against the dangers of sexuality. After all, they reason, the Bible is concerned with spiritual life and sees it as at war with the body. That must mean that the Bible wants us to turn from a strong concern with sexuality and the body to a devotion to God and our spiritual life.

It is true that the Bible warns us that not all sexual behavior is good, but it also proclaims the good news that our sexuality is divinely created and that it is a gift from God for our enjoyment.

The story of our sexuality begins at the time of creation. Adam was created first, but as he named all the other creatures, he felt something missing. There was no "helper that was right for him" (Genesis 2:20). In a word, he was lonely and needed the companionship of an equal.

In his great wisdom, God caused Adam to fall asleep and created Eve, the first woman, from one of Adam's ribs (Genesis 2:20–22). The choice of a rib was intentional. Eve was created from Adam, showing that there was an original unity, which is recreated in marriage and specifically the sex act. Also, the rib is something from Adam's side, not his head nor his feet, illustrating that Eve was an equal partner with Adam. Eve is a distinct, unique creature who is nonetheless similar to Adam in ways that the other creatures were not. In a word, Adam now had an intimate partner in creation. Marriage was an institution created by God so that a man and a woman could come together and express their union in the most intimate way possible. "So a man will leave his father and mother and be united with his wife, and the two will become one body. The man and his wife were both naked, but they were not ashamed" (Genesis 2:24–25).

Unfortunately, the story did not end there. Genesis 3 narrates the fall into sin. Eve took the forbidden fruit of the tree of the knowledge of good and evil and ate it against the clear command of God. Adam, too, took the fruit and ate it. As a result, sin entered the world and humanity was separated from God. They could no longer enjoy the wonderful, intimate relationship they had with the Lord without repentance and sacrifice. A further impact of the fall was a separation between the man and the woman. No longer could they stand naked in the garden and feel no shame. They ran away from each other. God in his mercy gave them clothes (Genesis 3:21).

Sexuality now was beset with problems, as were all other areas of human life. Men and women struggle in their relationships with each other.

Sex often becomes an idol of sorts. People are obsessed with it, as can be seen in the contemporary media. Television and the movies are filled with references to sex outside of marriage and lewd sexual scenes. Advertising uses the lure of sex to sell its products. Passages like 1 Thessalonians 4:3–8 are needed warnings to avoid sexual excesses and a call to live a sexual life pleasing to God.

On the other hand, sexuality is also mistreated when it is ruthlessly repressed, that is, when it is treated as a taboo subject. The church has sometimes fallen into this trap when it considers sexuality as something fleshly and in conflict with the spiritual life.

The Bible recognizes the danger of sinful sexuality in its laws against sexual perversions. That is, it warns against the dangers of misusing sex in ways for which God did not intend it. God created sexuality for enjoyment within a marriage relationship. That is why the Bible forbids sexual intercourse outside of marriage. For that reason, premarital sex (Exodus 22:16), adultery (Numbers 5; Deuteronomy 22:22), incest (Leviticus 18 and 20), homosexuality (Leviticus 18:22), and relations with animals (Leviticus 18:23) are all forbidden by God's law.

Even with all the dangers associated with sex, the Bible invites us to celebrate sexuality within marriage. The book that sounds the loudest call to enjoy sex is the Song of Solomon. This book's primary message is that sex is a wonderful gift from God to be enjoyed for the pure sensual pleasure it provides a husband and a wife.⚭

⚭**Sexuality:** For additional scriptures on this topic go to Genesis 1:27.

[26]Who waters the land where no one lives,
the desert that has no one in it?
[27]Who sends rain to satisfy the empty land
so the grass begins to grow?
[28]Does the rain have a father?
Who is father to the drops of dew?
[29]Who is the mother of the ice?
Who gives birth to the frost from the sky
[30]when the water becomes hard as stone,
and even the surface of the ocean is frozen?

[31]"Can you tie up the stars of the Pleiades
or loosen the ropes of the stars in Orion?
[32]Can you bring out the stars on time
or lead out the stars of the Bear with its cubs?
[33]Do you know the laws of the sky
and understand their rule over the earth?

[34]"Can you shout an order to the clouds
and cover yourself with a flood of water?
[35]Can you send lightning bolts on their way?
Do they come to you and say, 'Here we are'?
[36]Who put wisdom inside the mind
or understanding in the heart?
[37]Who has the wisdom to count the clouds?
Who can pour water from the jars of the sky
[38]when the dust becomes hard
and the clumps of dirt stick together?

[39]"Do you hunt food for the female lion
to satisfy the hunger of the young lions
[40]while they lie in their dens
or hide in the bushes waiting to attack?
[41]Who gives food to the birds
when their young cry out to God
and wander about without food?

39

"Do you know when the mountain goats
give birth?
Do you watch when the deer gives birth to
her fawn?
[2]Do you count the months until they give birth
and know the right time for them
to give birth?
[3]They lie down, their young are born,
and then the pain of giving birth is over.
[4]Their young ones grow big and strong in
the wild country.
Then they leave their homes and do not return.

[5]"Who let the wild donkey go free?
Who untied its ropes?
[6]I am the one who gave the donkey the desert
as its home;
I gave it the desert lands as a place to live.
[7]The wild donkey laughs at the confusion
in the city,
and it does not hear the drivers shout.
[8]It roams the hills looking for pasture,
looking for anything green to eat.

[9]"Will the wild ox agree to serve you
and stay by your feeding box at night?
[10]Can you hold it to the plowed row with
a harness
so it will plow the valleys for you?
[11]Will you depend on the wild ox for its
great strength
and leave your heavy work for it to do?
[12]Can you trust the ox to bring in your grain
and gather it to your threshing floor?

[13]"The wings of the ostrich flap happily,
but they are not like the feathers of the stork.
[14]The ostrich lays its eggs on the ground
and lets them warm in the sand.
[15]It does not stop to think that a foot might step
on them and crush them;
it does not care that some animal might
walk on them.
[16]The ostrich is cruel to its young, as if they
were not even its own.
It does not care that its work is for nothing,
[17]because God did not give the ostrich wisdom;
God did not give it a share of good sense.
[18]But when the ostrich gets up to run, it is so fast
that it laughs at the horse and its rider.

[19]"Job, are you the one who gives the horse
its strength
or puts a flowing mane on its neck?
[20]Do you make the horse jump like a locust?
It scares people with its proud snorting.
[21]It paws wildly, enjoying its strength,
and charges into battle.
[22]It laughs at fear and is afraid of nothing;
it does not run away from the sword.
[23]The bag of arrows rattles against the horse's side,
along with the flashing spears and swords.
[24]With great excitement, the horse races over
the ground;
and it cannot stand still when it hears
the trumpet.
[25]When the trumpet blows, the horse snorts, 'Aha!'
It smells the battle from far away;

38:36 Job and his three friends have been debating the cause of his sufferings. They differ but they all think they have the truth. At the end of the book God appears to Job and challenges his understanding of himself. God tells Job that he is not as wise as he thought. God himself is the only one who knows the answers to the difficult questions of the universe.

it hears the shouts of commanders and the
battle cry.

26"Is it through your wisdom that the hawk flies
and spreads its wings toward the south?
27Are you the one that commands the eagle to fly
and build its nest so high?
28It lives on a high cliff and stays there at night;
the rocky peak is its protected place.
29From there it looks for its food;
its eyes can see it from far away.
30Its young eat blood,
and where there is something dead, the
eagle is there."

40 The LORD said to Job:
2"Will the person who argues with the
Almighty correct him?
Let the person who accuses God answer him."

3Then Job answered the LORD:
4"I am not worthy; I cannot answer you anything,
so I will put my hand over my mouth.
5I spoke one time, but I will not answer again;
I even spoke two times, but I will say
nothing more."

6Then the LORD spoke to Job from the storm:
7"Be strong, like a man!
I will ask you questions,
and you must answer me.
8Would you say that I am unfair?
Would you blame me to make yourself
look right?
9Are you as strong as God?
Can your voice thunder like his?
10If so, then decorate yourself with glory
and beauty;
dress in honor and greatness as if they
were clothing.
11Let your great anger punish;
look at the proud and bring them down.
12Look at the proud and make them humble.
Crush the wicked wherever they are.
13Bury them all in the dirt together;
cover their faces in the grave.
14If you can do that, then I myself will praise you,
because you are strong enough to
save yourself.

15"Look at the behemoth,
which I made just as I made you.
It eats grass like an ox.
16Look at the strength it has in its body;
the muscles of its stomach are powerful.
17Its tail is like a cedar tree;
the muscles of its thighs are woven together.
18Its bones are like tubes of bronze;
its legs are like bars of iron.
19It is one of the first of God's works,
but its Maker can destroy it.
20The hills, where the wild animals play,
provide food for it.
21It lies under the lotus plants,
hidden by the tall grass in the swamp.
22The lotus plants hide it in their shadow;
the poplar trees by the streams surround it.
23If the river floods, it will not be afraid;
it is safe even if the Jordan River rushes
to its mouth.
24Can anyone blind its eyes and capture it?
Can anyone put hooks in its nose?

41 "Can you catch the leviathan on a
fish hook
or tie its tongue down with a rope?
2Can you put a cord through its nose
or a hook in its jaw?
3Will it keep begging you for mercy
and speak to you with gentle words?
4Will it make an agreement with you
and let you take it as your slave for life?
5Can you make a pet of the leviathan as you
would a bird
or put it on a leash for your girls?
6Will traders try to bargain with you for it?
Will they divide it up among
the merchants?
7Can you stick darts all over its skin
or fill its head with fishing spears?
8If you put one hand on it,
you will never forget the battle,
and you will never do it again!
9There is no hope of defeating it;
just seeing it overwhelms people.
10No one is brave enough to make it angry,
so who would be able to stand up against me?
11No one has ever given me anything that I
must pay back,

40:8 Justice: Psalm 9:8
40:14 Pride: Psalm 10:4
40:15 *behemoth.* The behemoth is a huge animal that God made and only he can control. The behemoth has been identified as a hippopotamus or a buffalo. Whatever it is, it is an illustration of God's great power and wisdom.

41:1 *leviathan.* See 3:8. Though many people identify leviathan here with the crocodile, it is most likely a reference to the primordial sea monster. Its description here shows it to be a wonderfully powerful creature whom only God could create and control.

because everything under the sky
belongs to me.

12“I will speak about Leviathan’s arms and legs,
its great strength and well-formed body.
13No one can tear off its outer hide
or poke through its double armor.
14No one can force open its great jaws;
they are filled with frightening teeth.
15It has rows of shields on its back
that are tightly sealed together.
16Each shield is so close to the next one
that no air can go between them.
17They are joined strongly to one another;
they hold on to each other and cannot
be separated.
18When it snorts, flashes of light are thrown out,
and its eyes look like the light at dawn.
19Flames blaze from its mouth;
sparks of fire shoot out.
20Smoke pours out of its nose,
as if coming from a large pot over a hot fire.
21Its breath sets coals on fire,
and flames come out of its mouth.
22There is great strength in its neck.
People are afraid and run away.
23The folds of its skin are tightly joined;
they are set and cannot be moved.
24Its chest is as hard as a rock,
even as hard as a grinding stone.
25The powerful fear its terrible looks
and draw back in fear as it moves.
26The sword that hits it does not hurt it,
nor the arrows, darts, and spears.
27It treats iron as if it were straw
and bronze metal as if it were rotten wood.
28It does not run away from arrows;
stones from slings are like chaff to it.
29Clubs feel like pieces of straw to it,
and it laughs when they shake a spear at it.
30The underside of its body is like broken pieces
of pottery.
It leaves a trail in the mud like a
threshing board.
31It makes the deep sea bubble like a boiling pot;
it stirs up the sea like a pot of oil.
32When it swims, it leaves a shining path in
the water
that makes the sea look as if it had white hair.
33Nothing else on earth is equal to it;
it is a creature without fear.
34It looks down on all those who are too proud;
it is king over all proud creatures.”

Job Answers the Lord

42 Then Job answered the LORD:
2“I know that you can do all things
and that no plan of yours can be ruined.
3You asked, ‘Who is this that made my purpose
unclear by saying things that are not true?’
Surely I spoke of things I did not understand;
I talked of things too wonderful for me to know.
4You said, ‘Listen now, and I will speak.
I will ask you questions,
and you must answer me.’
5My ears had heard of you before,
but now my eyes have seen you.
6So now I hate myself;
I will change my heart and life.
I will sit in the dust and ashes.”

End of the Story

7After the LORD had said these things to Job, he
said to Eliphaz the Temanite, “I am angry with
you and your two friends, because you have not
said what is right about me, as my servant Job
did. 8Now take seven bulls and seven male sheep,
and go to my servant Job, and offer a burnt offering for yourselves. My servant Job will pray for
you, and I will listen to his prayer. Then I will not
punish you for being foolish. You have not said
what is right about me, as my servant Job did.”
9So Eliphaz the Temanite, Bildad the Shuhite, and
Zophar the Naamathite did as the LORD said, and
the LORD listened to Job’s prayer.
10After Job had prayed for his friends, the LORD
gave him success again. The LORD gave Job twice as
much as he had owned before. 11Job’s brothers and
sisters came to his house, along with everyone who
had known him before, and they all ate with him
there. They comforted him and made him feel better
about the trouble the LORD had brought on him, and
each one gave Job a piece of silver and a gold ring.
12The LORD blessed the last part of Job’s life even
more than the first part. Job had fourteen thousand
sheep, six thousand camels, a thousand teams of
oxen, and a thousand female donkeys. 13Job also
had seven sons and three daughters. 14He named
the first daughter Jemimah, the second daughter
Keziah, and the third daughter Keren-Happuch.
15There were no other women in all the land as
beautiful as Job’s daughters. And their father Job
gave them land to own along with their brothers.
16After this, Job lived one hundred forty years.
He lived to see his children, grandchildren, great-
grandchildren, and great-great-grandchildren. 17Then
Job died; he was old and had lived many years.

41:34 Environment: Psalm 23:1
42:6 Evil: Ecclesiastes 9:3
42:8 Servant of the Lord: Psalm 34:22
42:11 Comfort: Psalm 69:20

Notes:

INTRODUCTION TO THE BOOK OF

PSALMS

The Songbook of Israel

WHO WROTE THIS BOOK?

The Psalms are a collection of songs, poems, and prayers written by various people, probably including David, Asaph, the Sons of Korah, Moses, Solomon, and perhaps others.

TO WHOM WAS THIS BOOK WRITTEN?

These songs, poems, and prayers are addressed to God, or are about God, even when the author, the king, or wisdom is the apparent subject.

WHERE WAS IT WRITTEN?

The Psalms were probably written in and around Israel, the homeland of the assumed writers.

WHEN WAS IT WRITTEN?

The writing of Psalms took centuries to complete. It was probably put into its final form around the third century B.C.

WHAT IS THE BOOK ABOUT?

Psalms is a collection of poems and prayers intended to be sung by the people of Israel in praise, thanksgiving, lament, and/or petition to God.

WHY WAS THIS BOOK WRITTEN?

The psalms were written for various reasons. Some are praises of God's mighty works; some are prayers and pleas for his help and deliverance; some are reflections of God's wisdom and faithfulness to his people; some are songs of confidence and victory. The psalms, in fact, mirror the joys and sorrows of God's people.

SO WHAT DOES THIS BOOK MEAN TO US?

Many contemporary hymns and songs used in the church are still based on these beautiful ancient prayers and poems. We, like Israel, can express our heartfelt joys and sorrows through the psalms today. And with the psalms we can praise and worship our God.

SUMMARY:

The Book of Psalms is like no other book in the Bible. It is not a running story, a letter, or a prophecy. It is a collection of poems that are prayers set to music. They constitute the hymnbook of the Old Testament people of God.

The Psalms express Israel's faith in God. They are prayers of a people who have a close, intimate relationship with him. In the context of dialogue with God, the Psalms express every important religious truth taught in the Old Testament.

Jesus expressed his pain and joy by often citing the Psalms (see Luke 24:44, and for an example Matthew 27:46 which cites Psalm 22:1). Indeed, every psalm may be used as a prayer to Jesus, but it is true that certain psalms are more pointed than others in their anticipation of the Messiah (Psalms 2; 16; 22; 69; 110).

The Psalms have no overall structure. Once completed, the book was divided into five separate sections, perhaps imitating the five books of Moses or "the Law."

I. Book 1: Psalms 1–41
II. Book 2: Psalms 42–72
III. Book 3: Psalms 73–89
IV. Book 4: Psalms 90–106
V. Book 5: Psalms 107–150

Each book, however, contains psalms from a variety of time periods and also many different types of hymns. We can identify three major and four minor types of psalms. Descriptions of these types of psalms may be found with the following psalms:

MAJOR

Hymns (Psalm 98)
Laments (Psalm 77)
Thanksgivings (Psalm 30)

MINOR

Psalms of Confidence (Psalm 23)
Psalms of Remembrance (Psalm 78)
Wisdom Psalms (Psalm 1)
Kingship Psalms (Psalm 2)

Psalm 98 (Hymn)

Hymns are psalms of praise to God. They are songs that are sung when the psalmist feels nothing but love and appreciation and awe toward God. Other examples include Psalms 8; 24; 29; 33; 47; 48. While not the most common type of psalm (see lament), hymns occur with increasing frequency toward the end of the book. It is not surprising that the Hebrew name of the book, then, is *Tehillim* — "Praises."

Psalm 77 (Lament)

Laments express the psalmist's disappointments, fears, or anger toward life and, occasionally, toward God. They are characterized by brutal honesty; the psalmist holds back no punches from God. Almost always, as here, the psalmist turns toward God at the end with hope. These are the most frequently occurring type of psalm. Other examples include Psalms 3; 22; 69; 130.

Psalm 30 (Thanksgiving)

These psalms begin like hymns praising the Lord. As a matter of fact, the only difference between thanksgivings and hymns are that the latter refer to an earlier lament or petition that the worshiper prayed to God. God answered the earlier prayer, and now the psalmist thanks God for hearing him. Other examples of thanksgivings include Psalms 18; 66; 107; 118; 138.

Psalm 23 (Confidence)

These psalms are noted by their mood of trust in the Lord. They are usually brief and have a clear image of our relationship with God that imparts a feeling of confidence. Here, of course, that image is the shepherd who guides and protects his sheep. Other examples of this type of psalm include Psalms 121 and 131.

Psalm 78 (Psalms of Remembrance)

Throughout the psalms the composer reminds himself and his readers of the past great acts of God. However, in a handful of psalms the great acts of God make up the main subject of the psalm. The purpose of calling these events to remembrance is to lead the people of Israel to praise God for directing their steps. Other examples include Psalms 105; 106; 136.

Psalm 1 (Wisdom)

Wisdom is the application of God's truth to life. A wise person is one who seeks out and lives by God's will. Proverbs, Ecclesiastes, Job, and Song of Solomon are known as wisdom books in the Bible, but there are a number of psalms which share similar ideas with these books. Psalm 1 is a wisdom psalm since it describes how the godly should live—by avoiding evil and following the teachings of the Lord. Other wisdom psalms include Psalms 37; 49; 119.

Psalm 2 (Kingship)

Kingship is an important topic of the Psalms. God is praised as king of the universe and David, the human king, composed many psalms and others sing about him. Psalm 2 is an example where both the divine and human king are praised. Other kingship psalms include 24 and 93 (divine king) and 20; 21 45 (the human king).

Happy are the people who know how to praise you.
Lord, let them live in the light of your presence.
In your name they rejoice and continually praise your goodness.

Psalm 89:15–16

PSALMS

Book 1

Two Ways to Live

Happy are those who don't listen to
the wicked,
who don't go where sinners go,
who don't do what evil people do.
2 They love the LORD's teachings,
and they think about those teachings
day and night.
3 They are strong, like a tree planted by a river.
The tree produces fruit in season,
and its leaves don't die.
Everything they do will succeed.

4 But wicked people are not like that.
They are like chaff that the wind blows away.
5 So the wicked will not escape
God's punishment.
Sinners will not worship with God's people.
6 This is because the LORD takes care of his people,
but the wicked will be destroyed.

The LORD's Chosen King

2 Why are the nations so angry?
Why are the people making useless plans?
2 The kings of the earth prepare to fight,
and their leaders make plans together
against the LORD
and his appointed one.
3 They say, "Let's break the chains that
hold us back
and throw off the ropes that tie us down."

4 But the one who sits in heaven laughs;
the Lord makes fun of them.
5 Then the LORD warns them
and frightens them with his anger.
6 He says, "I have appointed my own king
to rule in Jerusalem on my holy
mountain, Zion."

7 Now I will tell you what the LORD
has declared:
He said to me, "You are my son.
Today I have become your father.
8 If you ask me, I will give you the nations;
all the people on earth will be yours.
9 You will rule over them with an iron rod.
You will break them into pieces
like pottery."

10 So, kings, be wise;
rulers, learn this lesson.
11 Obey the LORD with great fear.
Be happy, but tremble.
12 Show that you are loyal to his son,
or you will be destroyed by his anger,
because he can quickly become angry.
But happy are those who trust
him for protection.

A Morning Prayer

David sang this when he ran away from his son Absalom.

3 LORD, I have many enemies!
Many people have turned against me.
2 Many are saying about me,
"God won't rescue him." *Selah*

3 But, LORD, you are my shield,
my wonderful God who gives
me courage.
4 I will pray to the LORD,
and he will answer me from his
holy mountain. *Selah*

1:1 Road/Way: Psalm 18:30

1:1 Many people think that happiness can be found in illicit sex, overdrinking, taking drugs, or in some other hedonistic way. The psalmist, though, presents a totally different view. How is happiness found? It is found in avoiding sin and obeying and loving God!

1:1–2 True happiness, according to the psalmist, flows from listening and obeying God's law. The blessed stay away from evil and do what God wants them to do.

1:2 Law: Romans 13:8–10

1:3 Meditation: Psalm 19:14

1:4 *chaff.* Chaff are plants that are dead, have no roots, and are blown about by the wind. The contrast with the river and deep-rooted tree is obvious.

2:1 Anger: Psalm 4:4

2:2 *his appointed one.* The "appointed" one is the one anointed for kingship. The immediate reference is the human king of Israel, but the ultimate reference is to Jesus Christ.

2:7 Jesus: Daniel 7

2:7 Psalm 2 was likely a coronation psalm, sung when a new king took the throne. It showed the special relationship between the king, especially David, and God. Godly kings represented the Lord's rule over his people. That the king was God's special son was a point made in the agreement God made with David (2 Samuel 7). In the New Testament, Jesus Christ shows himself to be the king of God's people when, at his baptism, a voice from heaven says, "This is my Son, whom I love, and I am very pleased with him" (Matthew 3:17).

3 *David sang this when he ran away from his son Absalom.* This is the first title to be found in the Book of Psalms. These titles do not have verse numbers in English translations of the Bible, but they are part of the original Hebrew.

3:2 *Selah.* Selah is simply a Hebrew word that gives directions for the reading or performance of the Psalm. It may mean "interlude" or it may instruct the person who prays to lie down in worship.

3:3 Glory: Psalm 24:9

3:3 Weapons: Hosea 1:7

Encouragement

Isaiah 40:31

How can a person find/give encouragement in the midst of problems?
What resources are available to lift and motivate someone, no matter what the circumstances?
What mindset is required for real success?

"The people who trust the Lord will become strong again" (Isaiah 40:31). The Lord might strengthen you through some person, or an unexpected meeting. It may come through someone God uses to encourage you. I know this is true because there have been times when I needed to be encouraged. And there have been other times when God used me to give encouragement to someone else. "Trust the Lord." Remain in touch with God through prayer. Remind yourself of how important you are to him. After all, he loved you enough to send his Son into the world to be your Savior.

Just because you are a child of God does not mean you will never have problems and never need encouragement. Nobody is free from problems. A problem-free life is an illusion—a mirage in the desert. It is a dangerously deceptive perception, which can mislead, blind, and distract. To pursue a problem-free life is to run after an elusive fantasy; it is a waste of mental and physical energies. Jesus told the truth when he said, "In this world you will have trouble" (John 16:33) But he immediately added a word of encouragement: "But be brave! I have defeated the world."

Encouragement is available to you, if you have problem-solving, mountain-moving faith. There is no substitute for deep abiding faith. If we hold on, we will win out! Unquestionably the profound faith and the beautiful providence of God produce a strong and unquenchable optimistic mental attitude. Tough people have it. And they can weather the worst storm. They can rough out the toughest times. They win! They come out on top. This faith requires activation. It yields hope and encouragement. But four steps are necessary to come out on top.

The first step will be to put your problems into perspective. Sure, you have problems. They may be the worst you've ever faced. But chances are, they are not the worst thing that could possibly have happened. No matter how bad it is, it could always be worse. Be glad it is not.

The second step is to learn to solve and manage problems. And there is not necessarily a solution for every problem; however, every problem can be managed positively. To do so, it is necessary to take charge and control of your problems. I call this "possibility thinking." Possibility thinking. What is it? In essence, it is the management of ideas. Possibility thinking focuses not on the management of time, money, energy, or persons, but on the management of ideas. It is rejecting the negatives, the impossibilities, associated with your problems, and seeing the potential for something good and constructive in every problem. Joseph expressed this very kind of thinking to the brothers who had sold him into slavery: "You meant to hurt me, but God turned your evil into good to save the lives of many people, which is being done" (Genesis 50:20).

The third step is to be open to the positive ideas God will place in your mind, if you have faith and bring your needs to him in prayer. A simple approach is to take out a sheet of paper and list ten possible solutions to your problem. I call it, "Count to ten and win!" Approach this step with a "game attitude." To play this game, which involves setting your imagination free from the fear of failure and thinking bigger than you ever have done before, you must begin by believing that God wants to give you the wisdom you seek, that he has given you latent gifts of creativity. Remember: "If any of you needs wisdom, you should ask God for it. He is generous and enjoys giving to all people, so he will give you wisdom. But when you ask God, you must believe and not doubt" (James 1:5–6).

The fourth step is to take action on the positive ideas God places in your mind. People who win over tough times are people who never stop believing. They have faith in themselves and their Lord and in the ideas that God gives them. These winners, survivors, pray for God's guidance, and when they know what it is they have to do, then they take action. They do something about it.

I say to you: you can do anything you want to do. You can be anything you want to be. You can go anywhere from where you are—if you are willing to believe God, dream big and work hard. With Paul, you can say: "I can to all things through Christ, because he gives me strength" (Philippians 4:13).⚭

⚭**Encouragement:** For additional scriptures on this topic go to Genesis 50:20.

SERVANT OF THE LORD

ISAIAH 52:13

What does it mean to be a servant of the Lord? Who is the servant of the Lord in the Book of Isaiah? How can we be servants of God today?

By definition, if someone is a "master" then he must have a servant. The greater the power, resources, and influence of the master, the more servants he will have. What about God, who is the Master of the universe and the Lord of all? The Bible teaches that the angels are his servants (Psalm 103:19–21), that the forces of nature are his servants (Psalm 104:4), that whole nations are his servants (see below), that foreign kings are his servants (Jeremiah 27:6), and that each individual who comes to know him becomes his servant.

To be a servant of God is a great privilege, but it carries responsibility. In a real sense, servants do not have "a life of their own." Their will is to do the bidding of their master. In fact, the Hebrew and Greek words for "servant" can also mean "slave." Slaves are the property of their masters!

Depending on the type of master we serve, our lives can be wonderful or terrible. Jesus explained that "everyone who lives in sin is a slave to sin" (John 8:34), and Proverbs teaches that the sins of an evil man will tie him up like ropes (Proverbs 5:22). Serving sin means bondage and degradation. Serving sin means that the devil himself is our master: "The devil has been sinning from the beginning, so anyone who continues to sin belongs to the devil" (1 John 3:8). "You belong to your father the devil, and you want to do what he wants" (John 8:44a).

There is nothing good about the devil. He is full of hate and only seeks to bring down and destroy. The sinful pleasures he offers are only temporary. He uses them as bait to entrap wandering souls. In the end, being his servant is misery. But serving God is wonderful! Although he requires our total submission, it is a submission based on love, not terror. Jesus said, "Come to me all of you who are tired and have heavy loads, and I will give you rest" (Matthew 11:28).

When we really come to know him, we delight to do his will: "My God, I want to do what you want. Your teachings are in my heart" (Psalms 40:8). "Loving God means obeying his commands. And God's commands are not too hard for us" (1 John 5:3).

Moses is often called a servant of the Lord in the Old Testament. In fact, God seems to speak of his servant Moses with pride: "I speak face to face to him—clearly, not with hidden meanings. He has even seen the form of the Lord. You should be afraid to speak against my servant Moses. . . . I trust him to lead all my people" (Numbers 12:8, 7b). Being God's servant means having a close relationship with him. That's why Jesus told his disciples that they were not merely servants, but actually friends (John 15:15). We serve him out of deep loyalty, love, and respect.

Israel is also called the servant of the Lord in the Bible, especially in the Book of Isaiah: "The Lord says, 'People of Israel, you are my servants'" (Isaiah 41:8a). But Isaiah sometimes speaks of Israel as a blind and deaf servant, refusing to obey or listen to the voice of God (42:19–20). At other times, he speaks of the servant as perfectly righteous (53:9b), even calling him his "good servant" (53:11b). Is he speaking of two different servants?

Actually, God called the people of Israel as a nation to be his servants, but instead, they went their own way. Yet there was one within Israel, the ideal representative of the nation, who perfectly obeyed and submitted, even to the point of laying down his life. He is Jesus, the Messiah and King of Israel, and he fulfills God's purposes for the nation.

We are called to follow in his footsteps, to be his servants, laying down our lives for the people of this world, so that they too may know the Lord. Paul understood this well, introducing his letters with the words, "From Paul, a servant of Jesus Christ" (Romans 1:1a). For him, this meant that he no longer lived to do his will and fulfill his own goals. Rather, he said, "I still live in my body, but I live by faith in the Son of God who loved me and gave himself for me" (Galatians 2:20b).

As servants of the Lord, we too are called to fully surrender our wills and desires, living the rest of our days in joyful obedience to our heavenly Master: "So you do not belong to yourselves, because you were bought by God for a price. So honor God with your bodies" (1 Corinthians 6:20).⚭

⚭**Servant of the Lord:** For additional scriptures on this topic go to Exodus 14:31.

[5]I can lie down and go to sleep,
and I will wake up again,
because the LORD gives me strength.
[6]Thousands of troops may surround me,
but I am not afraid.

[7]LORD, rise up!
My God, come save me!
You have struck my enemies on the cheek;
you have broken the teeth of the wicked.
[8]The LORD can save his people.
LORD, bless your people. *Selah*

An Evening Prayer

For the director of music. With stringed instruments. A psalm of David.

4 Answer me when I pray to you,
my God who does what is right.
Make things easier for me when I am in trouble.
Have mercy on me and hear my prayer.

[2]People, how long will you turn my honor
into shame?
How long will you love what is false and look
for new lies? *Selah*
[3]You know that the LORD has chosen for himself
those who are loyal to him.
The LORD listens when I pray to him.
[4]When you are angry, do not sin.
Think about these things quietly
as you go to bed. *Selah*
[5]Do what is right as a sacrifice to the LORD
and trust the LORD.

[6]Many people ask,
"Who will give us anything good?"
LORD, be kind to us.
[7]But you have made me very happy,
happier than they are,
even with all their grain and new wine.
[8]I go to bed and sleep in peace,
because, LORD, only you keep me safe.

A Morning Prayer for Protection

For the director of music. For flutes. A psalm of David.

5 LORD, listen to my words.
Understand my sadness.
[2]Listen to my cry for help, my King and my God,
because I pray to you.
[3]LORD, every morning you hear my voice.
Every morning, I tell you what I need,
and I wait for your answer.
[4]You are not a God who is pleased with
the wicked;
you do not live with those who do evil.
[5]Those people who make fun of you cannot
stand before you.
You hate all those who do evil.
[6]You destroy liars;
the LORD hates those who kill and
trick others.

[7]Because of your great love,
I can come into your Temple.
Because I fear and respect you,
I can worship in your holy Temple.
[8]LORD, since I have many enemies,
show me the right thing to do.
Show me clearly how you want me to live.

[9]My enemies' mouths do not tell the truth;
in their hearts they want to destroy others.
Their throats are like open graves;
they use their tongues for telling lies.
[10]God, declare them guilty!
Let them fall into their own traps.
Send them away because their sins are many;
they have turned against you.

[11]But let everyone who trusts you be happy;
let them sing glad songs forever.
Protect those who love you
and who are happy because of you.
[12]LORD, you bless those who do what is right;
you protect them like a soldier's shield.

A Prayer for Mercy in Troubled Times

For the director of music. With stringed instruments. Upon the sheminith. A psalm of David.

6 LORD, don't correct me when you are angry;
don't punish me when you are
very angry.
[2]LORD, have mercy on me because I am weak.
Heal me, LORD, because my bones ache.
[3]I am very upset.
LORD, how long will it be?

[4]LORD, return and save me;
save me because of your kindness.
[5]Dead people don't remember you;
those in the grave don't praise you.

[6]I am tired of crying to you.
Every night my bed is wet with tears;

4:4 Anger: Psalm 37:7–8
4:8 Peace: Psalm 119:165
5:12 Complaint/Lament/Protest: Psalm 7

my bed is soaked from my crying.
7My eyes are weak from so much crying;
they are weak from crying about my enemies.

8Get away from me, all you who do evil,
because the LORD has heard my crying.
9The LORD has heard my cry for help;
the LORD will answer my prayer.
10All my enemies will be ashamed and troubled.
They will turn and suddenly leave in shame.

A Prayer for Fairness

A shiggaion of David which he sang to the Lord about Cush, from the tribe of Benjamin.

7 LORD my God, I trust in you for protection.
Save me and rescue me
from those who are chasing me.
2Otherwise, like a lion they will tear me apart.
They will rip me to pieces, and no one can
save me.

3LORD my God, what have I done?
Have my hands done something wrong?
4Have I done wrong to my friend
or stolen without reason from my enemy?
5If I have, let my enemy chase me and
capture me.
Let him trample me into the dust
and bury me in the ground. *Selah*

6LORD, rise up in your anger;
stand up against my enemies' anger.
Get up and demand fairness.
7Gather the nations around you
and rule them from above.
8LORD, judge the people.
LORD, defend me because I am right,
because I have done no wrong,
God Most High.
9God, you do what is right.
You know our thoughts and feelings.
Stop those wicked actions done by evil people,
and help those who do what is right.

10God protects me like a shield;
he saves those whose hearts are right.
11God judges by what is right,
and God is always ready to punish
the wicked.
12If they do not change their lives,
God will sharpen his sword;
he will string his bow and take aim.
13He has prepared his deadly weapons;
he has made his flaming arrows.

14There are people who think up evil
and plan trouble and tell lies.
15They dig a hole to trap others,
but they will fall into it themselves.
16They will get themselves into trouble;
the violence they cause will hurt
only themselves.

17I praise the LORD because he does what
is right.
I sing praises to the LORD Most High.

The LORD's Greatness

For the director of music. On the gittith. A psalm of David.

8 LORD our Lord,
your name is the most wonderful name
in all the earth!
It brings you praise in heaven above.
2You have taught children and babies
to sing praises to you
because of your enemies.
And so you silence your enemies
and destroy those who try to get even.

3I look at your heavens,
which you made with your fingers.
I see the moon and stars,
which you created.
4But why are people important to you?
Why do you take care of human beings?
5You made them a little lower than
the angels
and crowned them with glory and honor.
6You put them in charge of everything
you made.
You put all things under their control:
7all the sheep, the cattle,
and the wild animals,
8the birds in the sky,

6:10 Sickness, Disease, Healing: Psalm 30
7:17 Complaint/Lament/Protest: Psalm 22
8:4–8 The spiritual life is rooted in the magnificence and magnitude of our creation. We are the ultimate objects of God's marvelous love. Spirituality includes our recognition of who we are and our response to God, seeking grace to be who we are all the days of our lives.
8:5 The Bible has a high view of humanity. We are created in God's image. We have honor and glory. God cares for us and loves us.
8:5 Glory: Psalm 24:9
8:5 Humans and angels are different. Angels are heavenly creatures attending the throne of God (Daniel 7:10) and sent out as messengers for God (Psalms 103:20; Luke 1:35). Humans live on the earth and have charge over God's created world. Both humans and angels should seek to obey and honor God in their God-given areas of service.
8:6 Stewardship: Malachi 3:6–12

the fish in the sea,
and everything that lives under water.⚭

9LORD our Lord,
your name is the most wonderful name in
all the earth!

Thanksgiving for Victory

For the director of music. To the tune of "The Death of the Son." A psalm of David.

9 I will praise you, LORD, with all my heart.
I will tell all the miracles you have done.
2I will be happy because of you;
God Most High, I will sing praises to
your name.

3My enemies turn back;
they are overwhelmed and die
because of you.
4You have heard my complaint;
you sat on your throne and judged by what
was right.
5You spoke strongly against the foreign nations
and destroyed the wicked;
you wiped out their names forever and ever.
6The enemy is gone forever.
You destroyed their cities;
no one even remembers them.

7But the LORD rules forever.
He sits on his throne to judge,
8and he will judge the world in fairness;
he will decide what is fair for the nations.⚭
9The LORD defends those who suffer;
he defends them in times of trouble.
10Those who know the LORD trust him,
because he will not leave those who
come to him.⚭

11Sing praises to the LORD who is king on
Mount Zion.
Tell the nations what he has done.
12He remembers who the murderers are;
he will not forget the cries of those
who suffer.
13LORD, have mercy on me.
See how my enemies hurt me.
Do not let me go through the gates of death.
14Then, at the gates of Jerusalem, I will
praise you;
I will rejoice because you saved me.

15The nations have fallen into the
pit they dug.
Their feet are caught in the nets they laid.
16The LORD has made himself known by his
fair decisions;
the wicked get trapped by
what they do. *Higgaion. Selah*
17Wicked people will go to the grave,
and so will all those who forget God.
18But those who have troubles will not be
forgotten.
The hopes of the poor will never die.

19LORD, rise up and judge the nations.
Don't let people think they are strong.
20Teach them to fear you, LORD.
The nations must learn that they are
only human. *Selah*

A Complaint About Evil People

10 LORD, why are you so far away?
Why do you hide when there is trouble?
2Proudly the wicked chase down those
who suffer.
Let them be caught in their own traps.
3They brag about the things they want.
They bless the greedy but hate the LORD.
4The wicked people are too proud.
They do not look for God;
there is no room for God
in their thoughts.⚭
5They always succeed.
They are far from keeping your laws;
they make fun of their enemies.
6They say to themselves, "Nothing bad will
ever happen to me;
I will never be ruined."
7Their mouths are full of curses, lies,
and threats;
they use their tongues for sin and evil.
8They hide near the villages.
They look for innocent people to kill;
they watch in secret for the helpless.
9They wait in hiding like a lion.
They wait to catch poor people;
they catch the poor in nets.
10The poor are thrown down and crushed;
they are defeated because the others
are stronger.
11The wicked think, "God has forgotten us.
He doesn't see what is happening."

⚭**8:8 Animals:** Psalm 104:10–11
⚭**9:8 Justice:** Proverbs 29:26
⚭**9:10 Stress:** Proverbs 3:5–6
9:11 *Mount Zion.* Mount Zion is the place that God chose in Jerusalem to make his presence known. After David's death the Temple was located there.

⚭**10:4 Pride:** Proverbs 16:18

12LORD, rise up and punish the wicked.
Don't forget those who need help.
13Why do wicked people hate God?
They say to themselves, "God won't
punish us."
14LORD, surely you see these cruel and evil things;
look at them and do something.
People in trouble look to you for help.
You are the one who helps the orphans.
15Break the power of wicked people.
Punish them for the evil they have done.

16The LORD is King forever and ever.
Destroy from your land those nations that do
not worship you.
17LORD, you have heard what the poor people want.
Do what they ask, and listen to them.
18Protect the orphans and put an end to suffering
so they will no longer be afraid of evil people.⚭

Trust in the LORD

For the director of music. Of David.

11 I trust in the LORD for protection.
So why do you say to me,
"Fly like a bird to your mountain.
2Like hunters, the wicked string their bows;
they set their arrows on the bowstrings.
They shoot from dark places
at those who are honest.
3When all that is good falls apart,
what can good people do?"

4The LORD is in his holy temple;
the LORD sits on his throne in heaven.
He sees what people do;
he keeps his eye on them.
5The LORD tests those who do right,
but he hates the wicked and those who love
to hurt others.
6He will send hot coals and burning sulfur on
the wicked.
A whirlwind is what they will get.
7The LORD does what is right, and he
loves justice,
so honest people will see his face.

A Prayer Against Liars

For the director of music. Upon the sheminith. A psalm of David.

12 Save me, LORD, because the good people
are all gone;
no true believers are left on earth.
2Everyone lies to his neighbors;
they say one thing and mean another.

3The LORD will stop those flattering lips
and cut off those bragging tongues.
4They say, "Our tongues will help us win.
We can say what we wish; no one is
our master."

5But the LORD says,
"I will now rise up,
because the poor are being hurt.
Because of the moans of the helpless,
I will give them the help they want."
6The LORD's words are pure,
like silver purified by fire,
like silver purified seven times over.

7LORD, you will keep us safe;
you will always protect us from
such people.
8But the wicked are all around us;
everyone loves what is wrong.⚭

A Prayer for God to Be Near

For the director of music. A psalm of David.

13 How long will you forget me, LORD?
Forever?
How long will you hide from me?
2How long must I worry
and feel sad in my heart all day?
How long will my enemy win over me?

3LORD, look at me.
Answer me, my God;
tell me, or I will die.
4Otherwise my enemy will say, "I have won!"
Those against me will rejoice that I've
been defeated.

5I trust in your love.
My heart is happy because you
saved me.
6I sing to the LORD
because he has taken care of me.⚭

The Unbelieving Fool

For the director of music. Of David.

14 Fools say to themselves,
"There is no God."

⚭**10:18 Doubt:** Psalm 14:1
⚭**10:18 Adoption:** Psalm 68:5
⚭**12:8 Tongue:** Psalm 19:14

⚭**13:6 Loneliness:** Psalm 22
⚭**13:6 Suffering:** Psalm 22
14:1 *"There is no God."* The fool does not deny the *existence* of God,

Fools are evil and do terrible things;
there is no one who does anything good.

[2]The LORD looked down from heaven on all people
to see if anyone understood,
if anyone was looking to God for help.
[3]But all have turned away.
Together, everyone has become evil.
There is no one who does anything good,
not even one.

[4]Don't the wicked understand?
They destroy my people as if they were eating bread.
They do not ask the LORD for help.
[5]But the wicked are filled with terror,
because God is with those who do what is right.
[6]The wicked upset the plans of the poor,
but the LORD will protect them.

[7]I pray that victory will come to Israel from Mount Zion!
May the LORD bring them back.
Then the people of Jacob will rejoice,
and the people of Israel will be glad.

What the LORD Demands

A psalm of David.

15 LORD, who may enter your Holy Tent?
Who may live on your holy mountain?

[2]Only those who are innocent
and who do what is right.
Such people speak the truth from their hearts
[3] and do not tell lies about others.
They do no wrong to their neighbors
and do not gossip.
[4]They do not respect hateful people
but honor those who honor the LORD.
They keep their promises to their neighbors,
even when it hurts.
[5]They do not charge interest on money they lend
and do not take money to hurt innocent people.

Whoever does all these things will never be destroyed.

The LORD Takes Care of His People

A miktam of David.

16 Protect me, God,
because I trust in you.
[2]I said to the LORD, "You are my Lord.
Every good thing I have comes from you."
[3]As for the godly people in the world,
they are the wonderful ones I enjoy.
[4]But those who turn to idols
will have much pain.
I will not offer blood to those idols
or even speak their names.

[5]No, the LORD is all I need.
He takes care of me.
[6]My share in life has been pleasant;
my part has been beautiful.

[7]I praise the LORD because he advises me.
Even at night, I feel his leading.
[8]I keep the LORD before me always.
Because he is close by my side,
I will not be hurt.
[9]So I rejoice and am glad.
Even my body has hope,
[10]because you will not leave me in the grave.
You will not let your holy one rot.
[11]You will teach me how to live a holy life.
Being with you will fill me with joy;
at your right hand I will find pleasure forever.

A Prayer for Protection

A prayer of David.

17 LORD, hear me begging for fairness;
listen to my cry for help.
Pay attention to my prayer,
because I speak the truth.
[2]You will judge that I am right;
your eyes can see what is true.
[3]You have examined my heart;
you have tested me all night.
You questioned me without finding anything wrong;
I have not sinned with my mouth.
[4]I have obeyed your commands,
so I have not done what evil people do.
[5]I have done what you told me;
I have not failed.

---

but rather the *relevance* of God. A fool could be well-educated and smart, but since he denies the relevance of God, he lives in a fantasy world.

14:1 Folly/Foolishness: Proverbs 10:14

14:1 Doubt: Matthew 13:58

14:7 *Mount Zion.* See 9:11.

15:5 See Deuteronomy 23:19, 20. Only foreigners could be charged interest on loans, not the people of Israel.

16:5 Esther: Proverbs 16:33

6I call to you, God,
and you answer me.
Listen to me now,
and hear what I say.
7Your love is wonderful.
By your power you save those who trust you
from their enemies.
8Protect me as you would protect your own eye.
Hide me under the shadow of your wings.
9Keep me from the wicked who attack me,
from my enemies who surround me.
10They are selfish
and brag about themselves.
11They have chased me until they have
surrounded me.
They plan to throw me to the ground.
12They are like lions ready to kill;
like lions, they sit in hiding.

13LORD, rise up, face the enemy, and throw them
down.
Save me from the wicked with your sword.
14LORD, save me by your power
from those whose reward is in this life.
They have plenty of food.
They have many sons
and leave much money to their children.

15Because I have lived right, I will see your face.
When I wake up, I will see your likeness and
be satisfied.

A Song of Victory

For the director of music. By the LORD's servant, David.
David sang this song to the LORD when the LORD had saved him from
Saul and all his other enemies.

18 I love you, LORD. You are my strength.

2The LORD is my rock, my protection,
my Savior.
My God is my rock.
I can run to him for safety.
He is my shield and my saving strength,
my defender.
3I will call to the LORD, who is worthy of praise,
and I will be saved from my enemies.

4The ropes of death came around me;
the deadly rivers overwhelmed me.
5The ropes of death wrapped around me.
The traps of death were before me.
6In my trouble I called to the LORD.
I cried out to my God for help.
From his temple he heard my voice;
my call for help reached his ears.

7The earth trembled and shook.
The foundations of the mountains began
to shake.
They trembled because the LORD was angry.
8Smoke came out of his nose,
and burning fire came out of his mouth.
Burning coals went before him.
9He tore open the sky and came down
with dark clouds under his feet.
10He rode a creature with wings and flew.
He raced on the wings of the wind.
11He made darkness his covering, his shelter
around him,
surrounded by fog and clouds.
12Out of the brightness of his presence
came clouds
with hail and lightning.
13The LORD thundered from heaven;
the Most High raised his voice,
and there was hail and lightning.
14He shot his arrows and scattered
his enemies.
His many bolts of lightning confused them
with fear.
15LORD, you spoke strongly.
The wind blew from your nose.
Then the valleys of the sea appeared,
and the foundations of the earth were seen.

16The LORD reached down from above and
took me;
he pulled me from the deep water.
17He saved me from my powerful enemies,
from those who hated me, because they
were too strong for me.
18They attacked me at my time of trouble,
but the LORD supported me.
19He took me to a safe place.
Because he delights in me, he saved me.

20The LORD spared me because I did
what was right.

18:9 *He tore open the sky.* Here God is seen riding his storm cloud chariot into battle.
18:10 *a creature with wings.* This is a reference to angelic creatures sometimes called cherubim. Cherubim are particularly powerful spiritual creatures.
18:14 *He shot his arrows.* His arrows are a reference to the bolts of lightning that God sends to the earth.
18:16 *the deep water.* The reference to deep water is a reference to the chaotic waters of the sea that are often symbolic of those forces that stand against God, who is the God of creation and order. Someone who is in deep water is being overwhelmed by the troubles of life.

Because I have not done evil, he has
rewarded me.
21 I have followed the ways of the LORD;
I have not done evil by turning away from
my God.
22 I remember all his laws
and have not broken his rules.
23 I am innocent before him;
I have kept myself from doing evil.
24 The LORD rewarded me because I did what
was right,
because I did what the LORD said was right.

25 LORD, you are loyal to those who are loyal,
and you are good to those who are good.
26 You are pure to those who are pure,
but you are against those who are bad.
27 You save the humble,
but you bring down those who are proud.
28 LORD, you give light to my lamp.
My God brightens the darkness around me.
29 With your help I can attack an army.
With God's help I can jump over a wall.

30 The ways of God are without fault.
The LORD's words are pure.
He is a shield to those who trust him.⚭
31 Who is God? Only the LORD.
Who is the Rock? Only our God.
32 God is my protection.
He makes my way free from fault.
33 He makes me like a deer that does not stumble;
he helps me stand on the steep mountains.
34 He trains my hands for battle
so my arms can bend a bronze bow.
35 You protect me with your saving shield.
You support me with your right hand.
You have stooped to make me great.
36 You give me a better way to live,
so I live as you want me to.
37 I chased my enemies and caught them.
I did not quit until they were destroyed.
38 I crushed them so they couldn't rise up again.
They fell beneath my feet.
39 You gave me strength in battle.
You made my enemies bow before me.
40 You made my enemies turn back,
and I destroyed those who hated me.
41 They called for help,
but no one came to save them.
They called to the LORD,
but he did not answer them.
42 I beat my enemies into pieces, like dust
in the wind.
I poured them out like mud in the streets.

43 You saved me when the people attacked me.
You made me the leader of nations.
People I never knew serve me.
44 As soon as they hear me, they obey me.
Foreigners obey me.
45 They all become afraid
and tremble in their hiding places.

46 The LORD lives!
May my Rock be praised.
Praise the God who saves me!
47 God gives me victory over my enemies
and brings people under my rule.
48 He saves me from my enemies.

You set me over those who hate me.
You saved me from cruel men.
49 So I will praise you, LORD, among the nations.
I will sing praises to your name.
50 The LORD gives great victories to his king.
He is loyal to his appointed king,
to David and his descendants forever.⚭

God's Works and Word

For the director of music. A psalm of David.

19 The heavens tell the glory of God,
and the skies announce what his hands
have made.
2 Day after day they tell the story;
night after night they tell it again.
3 They have no speech or words;
they have no voice to be heard.
4 But their message goes out through all the world;
their words go everywhere on earth.
The sky is like a home for the sun.
5 The sun comes out like a bridegroom from
his bedroom.
It rejoices like an athlete eager to run a race.
6 The sun rises at one end of the sky
and follows its path to the other end.
Nothing hides from its heat.

7 The teachings of the LORD are perfect;
they give new strength.
The rules of the LORD can be trusted;
they make plain people wise.
8 The orders of the LORD are right;
they make people happy.

⚭**18:30 Road/Way:** Psalm 37:5
⚭**18:50 Praise:** Psalm 47:1–3

19:5 The sun is like a bridegroom that is strong and vital.

The commands of the LORD are pure;
they light up the way.
9Respect for the LORD is good;
it will last forever.
The judgments of the LORD are true;
they are completely right.
10They are worth more than gold,
even the purest gold.
They are sweeter than honey,
even the finest honey.
11By them your servant is warned.
Keeping them brings great reward.

12People cannot see their own mistakes.
Forgive me for my secret sins.
13Keep me from the sins of pride;
don't let them rule me.
Then I can be pure
and innocent of the greatest of sins.

14I hope my words and thoughts please you.
LORD, you are my Rock, the one who
saves me.

A Prayer for the King

For the director of music. A psalm of David.

20 May the LORD answer you in times of
trouble.
May the God of Jacob protect you.
2May he send you help from his Temple
and support you from Mount Zion.
3May he remember all your offerings
and accept all your sacrifices. *Selah*
4May he give you what you want
and make all your plans succeed,
5and we will shout for joy when you succeed,
and we will raise a flag in the name
of our God.
May the LORD give you all that you ask for.

6Now I know the LORD helps his
appointed king.
He answers him from his holy heaven
and saves him with his strong right hand.
7Some trust in chariots, others in horses,
but we trust the LORD our God.
8They are overwhelmed and defeated,
but we march forward and win.
9LORD, save the king!
Answer us when we call for help.

Thanksgiving for the King

For the director of music. A psalm of David.

21 LORD, the king rejoices because of your
strength;
he is so happy when you save him!
2You gave the king what he wanted
and did not refuse what he asked for. *Selah*
3You put good things before him
and placed a gold crown on his head.
4He asked you for life,
and you gave it to him,
so his years go on and on.
5He has great glory because you gave
him victories;
you gave him honor and praise.
6You always gave him blessings;
you made him glad because you were
with him.
7The king truly trusts the LORD.
Because God Most High always loves him,
he will not be overwhelmed.
8Your hand is against all your enemies;
those who hate you will feel your power.
9When you appear,
you will burn them as in a furnace.
In your anger you will swallow them up,
and fire will burn them up.
10You will destroy their families from the earth;
their children will not live.
11They made evil plans against you,
but their traps won't work.
12You will make them turn their backs
when you aim your arrows at them.
13Be supreme, LORD, in your power.
We sing and praise your greatness.

The Prayer of a Suffering Man

For the director of music. To the tune of "The Doe of Dawn."
A psalm of David.

22 My God, my God, why have you
rejected me?
You seem far from saving me,
far from the words of my groaning.
2My God, I call to you during the day,
but you do not answer.
I call at night;
I am not silent.

3You sit as the Holy One.
The praises of Israel are your throne.

19:14 Meditation: Psalm 63:6
19:14 Tongue: Proverbs 7:21
20:1 This prayer is addressed to the human king. It is a request that God aid the king during difficult times.
20:6 *appointed.* See 2:2.

Decision Making/Plan

Jeremiah 10:23

If God is in control of everything, can we really talk about making decisions? Does the Bible give any guidance in how we make our decisions? Does God "plan"?

Decision making and planning are part of our everyday lives. From the time we wake up to the time we go to bed at night, whether we work outside the home or inside the home, no matter how we spend our days, we are constantly making decisions and planning what we will do next. The decisions can be anything from mundane happenings to significant decisions that may affect the rest of our lives.

A prominent biblical teaching is God's absolute power and control of all he has created (often called God's "sovereignty"). God is the creator of the universe; nothing exists apart from his will. He is in control of the seasons, the wind, the rain (Genesis 8:22; 1 Kings 17:1; 18:1), and the rise and fall of world powers (Isaiah 40:15). We, too, are God's created beings. Since God is in control of all his creation, can we then meaningfully speak of "making decisions"? Doesn't this imply *our,* rather than God's, control over our lives?

There are several passages that speak of God's control over our lives, even to the smallest detail (for example Proverbs 16:9 and 20:24). Two explicit passages are Proverbs 19:21: "People can make all kinds of plans, but only the Lord's plan will happen," and Jeremiah 10:23: "Lord, I know that a person's life doesn't really belong to him. No one can control his own life." Clearly, our lives are not our own.

Yet this is not the whole story. The Bible is full of instances where people make all sorts of decisions. In Genesis 13:11, Lot *chose* to live in the Jordan Valley, leaving Abram the land of Canaan. In Romans 1:13, Paul speaks of his *planning* to visit the Christians in Rome. In fact, much of the Bible is made up of urging God's people to choose right over wrong. We need only think of the kings of Israel who, one after the other, with few exceptions, made the wrong decision by worshiping false gods (throughout 1 and 2 Kings). In fact, the whole rationale for exhorting the people of God to act correctly assumes their ability to choose the wrong path (Deuteronomy 30:19; Joshua 24:15; John 7:17).

It seems, then, that there is some tension in the Bible between these two ideas: God is in complete control of our lives, yet people in the Bible are forever making decisions and are even commanded to make decisions. There is one particular biblical question where this tension comes to a head: God's plan of salvation. Do we make "decisions for Christ" or does God "choose us" to be saved?

Both ideas find scriptural support. On one hand, we read that Christ "chose us before the world was made" (Ephesians 1:4); Jesus says to his disciples, "You did not choose me; I chose you" (John 15:16); Paul tells the Thessalonians, "Brothers and sisters, God loves you, and we know he has chosen you" (1 Thessalonians 1:4). On the other hand, there are some passages that clearly extend a universal call to all people to be saved, such as, 2 Peter 3:9 and 1 Timothy 2:4, and others that emphasize the importance of receiving Christ into our lives (John 1:12; Revelation 3:2a).

The question of how people are saved is a constant topic of discussion among Christians. Yet the proper way of handling this issue, regardless of what side we come down on, is *not* to accept one set of verses and reject another set. How are we saved? Is it by God's decision or ours? The biblical answer seems to be *yes*—to both! Both human decision and God's will are real and active in the process. Perhaps Paul states the mystery best in Philippians 2:12–13: "Keep on working to complete your salvation with fear and trembling [our decision], because God is working in you to help you want to do and be able to do what pleases him [God's will]."

How we make our everyday decisions can be understood in the same way. Does God direct our steps, or are we responsible for making our own thoughtful decisions? Again, the answer to both is *yes.* But how can that be? It is certainly a mystery to us how both can be real, but God understands. Scripture, however, gives us insight into how these two ideas come together. As Christians grow in faith, God works in us to bring our will to conform to his will. As Paul says, "Be changed within by a new way of thinking. Then you will be able to decide what God wants for you" (Romans 12:2). Our way of thinking can actually become like God's way of thinking! This is not a quick process; there is no magic formula. It takes time—perhaps a lifetime of growing in Christ—but the Christian is continually being conformed to God's will.

So we are to make *faithful decisions*, always striving to conform to God's will, yet not paralyzed, for we know that "God is working in you" (Philippians 2:13) and that "in everything God works for the good of those who love him" (Romans 8:28).∞

∞**Decision Making/Plan:** For additional scriptures on this topic go to Proverbs 3:5–6.

CELIBACY

JEREMIAH 16:2

Is there any place in the Bible that requires or suggests voluntary celibacy for spiritual life? Why have some religious denominations insisted upon celibacy for their leaderships?

Genesis 2:18 records God saying, "It is not good for the man to be alone." In Genesis 1:28 God tells Adam and Eve to be fruitful and multiply. This same command is given again to Noah after the Flood (Genesis 9:1). It would appear from God's word that celibacy is not the norm for human beings.

Other references from the Bible tell us that God's word and intent continue to apply. Leviticus 21:7, 13–14 records instructions for Levites who were to serve as priests. While they were restricted as to whom they might marry, it was assumed that they would marry in order to raise up the next generation of priests. Hosea, the prophet, provides an interesting example of how God would use the marriage of his prophet in a special way. God commanded Hosea to marry a prostitute and bear children in order to make his message clear to Israel (Hosea 1:2–3).

In the New Testament we find that Paul approved of people who wanted to be married so that their sexual desires might find proper expression within marriage (1 Corinthians 7:1–8). Paul warns those who are married not to avoid showing their love in sexual ways, unless it is by mutual consent and for a specific period of time. Paul also warns married Christians not to seek any sort of separation from their spouses, as if Christianity required it. On the contrary, Paul urges them to remain as they are, that is, married (1 Corinthians 7:25–26). First Corinthians 7:32–40 gives the impression that some people who were engaged to be married thought it was their duty as Christians to abstain from marriage. Paul commended their willingness to make this sacrifice for the kingdom, but urged them not to feel compelled to do so. He encouraged them to marry if they so desired. Finally, 1 Corinthians 9:5 records Paul's vehement response to some who were saying Paul had no right to a wife. Paul contends that he does have the right to take a believing wife as the examples of Peter, the brothers of Jesus, and the other apostles prove.

Clearly, God's intent is that most people should marry and bear children. Therefore, it is no surprise that the Bible never commands people, in general, to be celibate. Jeremiah, the prophet, is the only example of someone who was commanded to remain single (Jeremiah 16:2). While we cannot be certain, it appears that Daniel and his companions in Babylon also were celibate (Daniel 1:1–21). In New Testament times we have two obvious examples of celibacy in Jesus and the apostle Paul.

If it is God's intent that people marry and bear children, why did some people practice celibacy? Even though Jeremiah is the only example of someone commanded to be celibate, there must be some importance to all of these examples. The key is provided by Paul in 1 Corinthians 7:26–33. Paul says, "The present time is a time of trouble, so I think it is good for you to stay the way you are . . . If you are not married, do not try to find a wife . . . I want you to be free from worry." It is understandable that people who are in danger because of their work might remain single so that the trouble they encounter would not affect families. The suffering of Paul was difficult enough for his friends to witness; how much worse would it have been for a spouse or children? Paul also mentions the distraction of marriage. Spouses are concerned with one another, and rightly so. But single, celibate people are free to devote themselves entirely to the work of God's kingdom, at least that is the proper reason for making a commitment to remain single. Some Christian groups feel so strongly about this that they require their priests to be celibate. The Bible commends those who are celibate for the sake of giving unrestricted service to God. However, the Bible warns against demanding celibacy (1 Timothy 4:1–3).

In Matthew 19:1–12 Jesus responds to questions about marriage and divorce. After listening to Jesus' teaching, his followers asked him if it would be better for a person to stay single. Jesus said it was true, a person would be better off single (remember the reasons Paul gives in 1 Corinthians 7). However, Jesus goes on to say that not everyone can live that way. Only people who are given the ability to remain celibate by God should remain so. Thus Jesus warns against requiring celibacy of people, since everyone is not capable.

In 1 Timothy 4:1–3 Paul responds to the situation that Jesus warned about. Paul wrote that in the latter times people would forbid others to marry. Paul calls this teaching the doctrine of demons and lying hypocrisy. Hebrews 13:4 confirms this by saying, "Marriage should be honored by everyone." Celibacy is a choice, not a command.

Celibacy: For additional scriptures on this topic go to Genesis 2:18.

4 Our ancestors trusted you;
they trusted, and you saved them.
5 They called to you for help
and were rescued.
They trusted you
and were not disappointed.

6 But I am like a worm instead of a man.
People make fun of me and hate me.
7 Those who look at me laugh.
They stick out their tongues and shake
their heads.
8 They say, "Turn to the LORD for help.
Maybe he will save you.
If he likes you,
maybe he will rescue you."

9 You had my mother give birth to me.
You made me trust you
while I was just a baby.
10 I have leaned on you since the day I was born;
you have been my God since my mother
gave me birth.
11 So don't be far away from me.
Now trouble is near,
and there is no one to help.
12 People have surrounded me like angry bulls.
Like the strong bulls of Bashan, they are on
every side.
13 Like hungry, roaring lions
they open their mouths at me.
14 My strength is gone,
like water poured out onto the ground,
and my bones are out of joint.
My heart is like wax;
it has melted inside me.
15 My strength has dried up like a clay pot,
and my tongue sticks to the top of my mouth.
You laid me in the dust of death.
16 Evil people have surrounded me;
like dogs they have trapped me.
They have bitten my arms and legs.
17 I can count all my bones;
people look and stare at me.
18 They divided my clothes among them,
and they threw lots for my clothing.

19 But, LORD, don't be far away.
You are my strength; hurry to help me.
20 Save me from the sword;
save my life from the dogs.
21 Rescue me from the lion's mouth;
save me from the horns of the bulls.

22 Then I will tell my fellow Israelites about you;
I will praise you in the public meeting.
23 Praise the LORD, all you who respect him.
All you descendants of Jacob, honor him;
fear him, all you Israelites.
24 He does not ignore those in trouble.
He doesn't hide from them
but listens when they call out to him.
25 LORD, I praise you in the great meeting of
your people;
these worshipers will see me do what
I promised.
26 Poor people will eat until they are full;
those who look to the LORD will praise him.
May your hearts live forever!
27 People everywhere will remember
and will turn to the LORD.
All the families of the nations
will worship him
28 because the LORD is King,
and he rules the nations.

29 All the powerful people on earth will eat
and worship.
Everyone will bow down to him,
all who will one day die.
30 The people in the future will serve him;
they will always be told about the Lord.
31 They will tell that he does what is right.
People who are not yet born
will hear what God has done.

The LORD the Shepherd

A psalm of David.

23 The LORD is my shepherd;
I have everything I need.
2 He lets me rest in green pastures.
He leads me to calm water.
3 He gives me new strength.
He leads me on paths that are right
for the good of his name.
4 Even if I walk through a very dark valley,
I will not be afraid,
because you are with me.

22:12 *the strong bulls of Bashan.* These bulls (see Amos 4:1) are strong and large.

22:26 Poverty: Proverbs 10:4

22:31 Loneliness: Isaiah 6:1–8

22:31 Complaint/Lament/Protest: Psalm 26

22:31 Suffering: Psalm 42

23:1 Environment: Psalm 48:1–2

23:1 *The LORD is my shepherd.* The shepherd image emphasizes God's protection and guidance of his people. In the ancient Near East, kings were known as the shepherds of their people, so Psalm 23 may also be alluding to God's royalty.

23:4 The presence of the shepherd with his rod and walking stick brings reassurance to the sheep, for these instruments picture the

Your rod and your walking stick
comfort me.

5You prepare a meal for me
in front of my enemies.
You pour oil on my head;
you fill my cup to overflowing.
6Surely your goodness and love
will be with me
all my life,
and I will live in the house of the
LORD forever.

A Welcome for God into the Temple

A psalm of David.

24 The earth belongs to the LORD, and
everything in it—
the world and all its people.
2He built it on the waters
and set it on the rivers.

3Who may go up on the mountain
of the LORD?
Who may stand in his holy Temple?
4Only those with clean hands and
pure hearts,
who have not worshiped idols,
who have not made promises in the name of
a false god.
5They will receive a blessing from the LORD;
the God who saves them will declare
them right.
6They try to follow God;
they look to the God of Jacob for help. *Selah*

7Gates, open all the way.
Open wide, aged doors
so the glorious King will come in.
8Who is this glorious King?
The LORD, strong and mighty.
The LORD, the powerful warrior.
9Gates, open all the way.
Open wide, aged doors
so the glorious King will come in.
10Who is this glorious King?
The LORD All-Powerful—
he is the glorious King. *Selah*

A Prayer for God to Guide

Of David.

25 LORD, I give myself to you;
2 my God, I trust you.
Do not let me be disgraced;
do not let my enemies laugh at me.
3No one who trusts you will be disgraced,
but those who sin without excuse will
be disgraced.

4LORD, tell me your ways.
Show me how to live.
5Guide me in your truth,
and teach me, my God, my Savior.
I trust you all day long.
6LORD, remember your mercy and love
that you have shown since long ago.
7Do not remember the sins
and wrong things I did when I was young.
But remember to love me always
because you are good, LORD.

8The LORD is good and right;
he points sinners to the right way.
9He shows those who are humble how to
do right,
and he teaches them his ways.
10All the LORD's ways are loving and true
for those who follow the demands of
his agreement.
11For the sake of your name, LORD,
forgive my many sins.
12Are there those who respect the LORD?
He will point them to the best way.
13They will enjoy a good life,
and their children will inherit the land.
14The LORD tells his secrets to those who
respect him;
he tells them about his agreement.
15My eyes are always looking to the
LORD for help.
He will keep me from any traps.
16Turn to me and have mercy on me,
because I am lonely and hurting.
17My troubles have grown larger;
free me from my problems.
18Look at my suffering and troubles,
and take away all my sins.

Lord's watchful care over his own people. Both these instruments were essential for the shepherd's trade and served as symbols of his authority. The rod was a weapon of protection, and the walking stick, or staff, a means of guidance and direction.

23:5 *You pour oil on my head.* Guests were refreshed by having their heads anointed with oil. This can mean that God gave him great wealth and blessed him.

23:6 Leadership: Psalm 31:3

23:6 Pleasure: Psalm 119:16

24:1–2 *He built it on waters.* On the third day of creation God caused the dry land to emerge from the waters.

24:8 Holy War & Divine Warrior: Lamentations 2:4–5

24:9 Glory: Isaiah 6:3

[19]Look at how many enemies I have!
See how much they hate me!⚭
[20]Protect me and save me.
I trust you, so do not let me be disgraced.
[21]My hope is in you,
so may goodness and honesty guard me.
[22]God, save Israel from all their troubles!

The Prayer of an Innocent Believer

Of David.

26 LORD, defend me because I have lived an innocent life.
I have trusted the LORD and never doubted.⚭
[2]LORD, try me and test me;
look closely into my heart and mind.
[3]I see your love,
and I live by your truth.
[4]I do not spend time with liars,
nor do I make friends with those who hide their sin.
[5]I hate the company of evil people,
and I won't sit with the wicked.
[6]I wash my hands to show I am innocent,
and I come to your altar, LORD.
[7]I raise my voice in praise
and tell of all the miracles you have done.
[8]LORD, I love the Temple where you live,
where your glory is.
[9]Do not kill me with those sinners
or take my life with those murderers.
[10]Evil is in their hands,
and they do wrong for money.
[11]But I have lived an innocent life,
so save me and have mercy on me.
[12]I stand in a safe place.
LORD, I praise you in the great meeting.⚭

A Song of Trust in God

Of David.

27 The LORD is my light and the one who saves me.
I fear no one.
The LORD protects my life;
I am afraid of no one.
[2]Evil people may try to destroy my body.
My enemies and those who hate me attack me,
but they are overwhelmed and defeated.
[3]If an army surrounds me,
I will not be afraid.
If war breaks out,
I will trust the LORD.

[4]I ask only one thing from the LORD.
This is what I want:
Let me live in the LORD's house
all my life.
Let me see the LORD's beauty
and look with my own eyes at his Temple.
[5]During danger he will keep me safe in his shelter.
He will hide me in his Holy Tent,
or he will keep me safe on a high mountain.
[6]My head is higher than my enemies around me.
I will offer joyful sacrifices in his Holy Tent.
I will sing and praise the LORD.

[7]LORD, hear me when I call;
have mercy and answer me.
[8]My heart said of you, "Go, worship him."
So I come to worship you, LORD.
[9]Do not turn away from me.
Do not turn your servant away in anger;
you have helped me.
Do not push me away or leave me alone,
God, my Savior.
[10]If my father and mother leave me,
the LORD will take me in.⚭
[11]LORD, teach me your ways,
and guide me to do what is right
because I have enemies.
[12]Do not hand me over to my enemies,
because they tell lies about me
and say they will hurt me.

[13]I truly believe
I will live to see the LORD's goodness.
[14]Wait for the LORD's help.
Be strong and brave,
and wait for the LORD's help.

A Prayer in Troubled Times

Of David.

28 LORD, my Rock, I call out to you for help.
Do not be deaf to me.

⚭**25:19 Hate:** Psalm 119:104
⚭**26:1 Integrity:** Psalm 41:12
⚭**26:12 Complaint/Lament/Protest:** Psalm 42–43
27:1 Many times in the Old Testament salvation is described as salvation from danger, from illness, or from enemies. Here we see someone trusting God for protection and thanking him for his goodness. Our response to God's salvation is worship, trust, and obedience.

27:4 *live in the LORD's house.* The LORD's house is the Holy Tent. Of course, there are no living quarters at the Holy Tent, but the psalmist thus expresses his desire to be in God's presence as often as possible.

⚭**27:10 Family:** See article on page 841.

28:1 *my Rock.* The Rock is a cliff, not a pebble or small stone. Thus, this image is one of God as our protector and fortress.

If you are silent,
  I will be like those in the grave.
2 Hear the sound of my prayer,
  when I cry out to you for help.
I raise my hands
  toward your Most Holy Place.
3 Don't drag me away with the wicked,
  with those who do evil.
They say "Peace" to their neighbors,
  but evil is in their hearts.
4 Pay them back for what they have done,
  for their evil deeds.
Pay them back for what they have done;
  give them their reward.
5 They don't understand what the
    LORD has done
  or what he has made.
So he will knock them down
  and not lift them up.

6 Praise the LORD,
  because he heard my prayer for help.
7 The LORD is my strength and shield.
  I trust him, and he helps me.
I am very happy,
  and I praise him with my song.
8 The LORD is powerful;
  he gives victory to his chosen one.
9 Save your people
  and bless those who are your own.
  Be their shepherd and carry them forever.

God in the Thunderstorm

A psalm of David.

29 Praise the LORD, you angels;
  praise the LORD's glory and power.
2 Praise the LORD for the glory of his name;
  worship the LORD because he is holy.

3 The LORD's voice is heard over the sea.
  The glorious God thunders;
  the LORD thunders over the ocean.
4 The LORD's voice is powerful;
  the LORD's voice is majestic.
5 The LORD's voice breaks the trees;
  the LORD breaks the cedars of Lebanon.
6 He makes the land of Lebanon dance like a calf
  and Mount Hermon jump like a baby bull.
7 The LORD's voice makes the lightning flash.
8 The LORD's voice shakes the desert;
  the LORD shakes the Desert of Kadesh.
9 The LORD's voice shakes the oaks
  and strips the leaves off the trees.
In his Temple everyone says, "Glory to God!"

10 The LORD controls the flood.
  The LORD will be King forever.
11 The LORD gives strength to his people;
  the LORD blesses his people with peace.

Thanksgiving for Escaping Death

A psalm of David. A song for giving the Temple to the LORD.

30 I will praise you, LORD,
  because you rescued me.
  You did not let my enemies laugh at me.
2 LORD, my God, I prayed to you,
  and you healed me.
3 You lifted me out of the grave;
  you spared me from going down to the place
    of the dead.

4 Sing praises to the LORD, you who belong to him;
  praise his holy name.
5 His anger lasts only a moment,
  but his kindness lasts for a lifetime.
Crying may last for a night,
  but joy comes in the morning.

6 When I felt safe, I said,
  "I will never fear."
7 LORD, in your kindness you made my
    mountain safe.
  But when you turned away, I was frightened.

8 I called to you, LORD,
  and asked you to have mercy on me.
9 I said, "What good will it do if I die
  or if I go down to the grave?
Dust cannot praise you;
  it cannot speak about your truth.
10 LORD, hear me and have mercy on me.
  LORD, help me."

11 You changed my sorrow into dancing.
  You took away my clothes of sadness,
  and clothed me in happiness.

28:9 *shepherd.* See Psalm 23:1.

29:2 Worship: Psalm 40:3

29:3 The imagery of this psalm may be compared to the imagery devoted to Baal in the people of Canaan's literature. God—not Baal—here is seen to be the one who controls the rains, fertility, and subdues the sea.

30:5 History teaches us that every problem and every experience of suffering has a life span. No problem is permanent. Are you suffering? Do you have problems? They will pass; they will not last. Your problem will not live forever, but you will! Storms always give way to the sun. Winter always thaws into springtime. Your storm will pass. Your winter will thaw. Your crying will end. Your problem will be resolved.

30:7 *made my mountain safe.* Mountains, in contrast to the sea, represent stability. They often symbolize the security that God gives us.

[12]I will sing to you and not be silent.
LORD, my God, I will praise you forever.⚭

A Prayer of Faith in Troubled Times

For the director of music. A psalm of David.

31 LORD, I trust in you;
let me never be disgraced.
Save me because you do what is right.
[2]Listen to me
and save me quickly.
Be my rock of protection,
a strong city to save me.
[3]You are my rock and my protection.
For the good of your name, lead me and
guide me.⚭
[4]Set me free from the trap they set for me,
because you are my protection.
[5]I give you my life.
Save me, LORD, God of truth.

[6]I hate those who worship false gods.
I trust only in the LORD.
[7]I will be glad and rejoice in your love,
because you saw my suffering;
you knew my troubles.
[8]You have not handed me over to my enemies
but have set me in a safe place.

[9]LORD, have mercy, because I am in misery.
My eyes are weak from so much crying,
and my whole being is tired from grief.
[10]My life is ending in sadness,
and my years are spent in crying.
My troubles are using up my strength,
and my bones are getting weaker.
[11]Because of all my troubles, my enemies hate me,
and even my neighbors look down on me.
When my friends see me,
they are afraid and run.
[12]I am like a piece of a broken pot.
I am forgotten as if I were dead.
[13]I have heard many insults.
Terror is all around me.
They make plans against me
and want to kill me.

[14]LORD, I trust you.
I have said, "You are my God."
[15]My life is in your hands.
Save me from my enemies
and from those who are chasing me.
[16]Show your kindness to me, your servant.
Save me because of your love.
[17]LORD, I called to you,
so do not let me be disgraced.
Let the wicked be disgraced
and lie silent in the grave.
[18]With pride and hatred
they speak against those who do right.
So silence their lying lips.

[19]How great is your goodness
that you have stored up for
those who fear you,
that you have given to those who trust you.
You do this for all to see.
[20]You protect them by your presence
from what people plan against them.
You shelter them from evil words.
[21]Praise the LORD.
His love to me was wonderful
when my city was attacked.
[22]In my distress, I said,
"God cannot see me!"
But you heard my prayer
when I cried out to you for help.
[23]Love the LORD, all you who belong to him.
The LORD protects those who truly believe,
but he punishes the proud as much as they
have sinned.
[24]All you who put your hope in the LORD
be strong and brave.

It Is Better to Confess Sin

A maskil of David.

32 Happy is the person
whose sins are forgiven,
whose wrongs are pardoned.⚭
[2]Happy is the person
whom the LORD does not consider guilty
and in whom there is nothing false.

[3]When I kept things to myself,
I felt weak deep inside me.
I moaned all day long.
[4]Day and night you punished me.
My strength was gone as in the
summer heat. *Selah*
[5]Then I confessed my sins to you
and didn't hide my guilt.
I said, "I will confess my sins
to the LORD,"
and you forgave my guilt. *Selah*

⚭**30:12 Sickness, Disease, Healing:** Psalm 38
⚭**30:13 Thanks:** Mark 14:22
⚭**31:3 Leadership:** Psalm 139:24
⚭**32:1 Beatitudes:** Psalm 85:12

6For this reason, all who obey you
should pray to you while they still can.
When troubles rise like a flood,
they will not reach them.
7You are my hiding place.
You protect me from my troubles
and fill me with songs of salvation. *Selah*

8The LORD says, "I will make you wise and
show you where to go.
I will guide you and watch over you.
9So don't be like a horse or donkey,
that doesn't understand.
They must be led with bits and reins,
or they will not come near you."

10Wicked people have many troubles,
but the LORD's love surrounds those who
trust him.
11Good people, rejoice and be happy
in the LORD.
Sing all you whose hearts are right.

Praise God Who Creates and Saves

33 Sing to the LORD, you who do
what is right;
honest people should praise him.
2Praise the LORD on the harp;
make music for him on a ten-stringed lyre.
3Sing a new song to him;
play well and joyfully.

4God's word is true,
and everything he does is right.
5He loves what is right and fair;
the LORD's love fills the earth.

6The sky was made at the LORD's command.
By the breath from his mouth, he made all
the stars.
7He gathered the water of the sea into a heap.
He made the great ocean stay in its place.
8All the earth should worship the LORD;
the whole world should fear him.
9He spoke, and it happened.
He commanded, and it appeared.
10The LORD upsets the plans of nations;
he ruins all their plans.
11But the LORD's plans will stand forever;
his ideas will last from now on.
12Happy is the nation whose God is the LORD,
the people he chose for his very own.
13The LORD looks down from heaven
and sees every person.
14From his throne he watches
all who live on earth.
15He made their hearts
and understands everything they do.
16No king is saved by his great army.
No warrior escapes by his great strength.
17Horses can't bring victory;
they can't save by their strength.
18But the LORD looks after those who fear him,
those who put their hope in his love.
19He saves them from death
and spares their lives in times of hunger.
20So our hope is in the LORD.
He is our help, our shield to protect us.
21We rejoice in him,
because we trust his holy name.
22LORD, show your love to us
as we put our hope in you.

Praise God Who Judges and Saves

David's song from the time he acted crazy so Abimelech would send him away, and David did leave.

34 I will praise the LORD at all times;
his praise is always on my lips.
2My whole being praises the LORD.
The poor will hear and be glad.
3Glorify the LORD with me,
and let us praise his name together.

4I asked the LORD for help, and he answered me.
He saved me from all that I feared.
5Those who go to him for help are happy,
and they are never disgraced.
6This poor man called, and the LORD heard him
and saved him from all his troubles.
7The angel of the LORD camps around those
who fear God,
and he saves them.

8Examine and see how good the LORD is.
Happy is the person who trusts him.
9You who belong to the LORD, fear him!
Those who fear him will have everything
they need.
10Even lions may get weak and hungry,
but those who look to the LORD will have
every good thing.
11Children, come and listen to me.
I will teach you to worship the LORD.
12You must do these things

32:6 *flood.* See 18:16.
33:3 *a new song.* A new song is a song that is almost always associated with a military victory.
34:7 *The angel of the LORD.* God's heavenly army protects his people. See "angel" in the concordance.

to enjoy life and have many happy days.
13You must not say evil things,
and you must not tell lies.
14Stop doing evil and do good.
Look for peace and work for it.

15The LORD sees the good people
and listens to their prayers.
16But the LORD is against those who do evil;
he makes the world forget them.
17The LORD hears good people when they cry out
to him,
and he saves them from all their troubles.
18The LORD is close to the brokenhearted,
and he saves those whose spirits have
been crushed.

19People who do what is right may have
many problems,
but the LORD will solve them all.
20He will protect their very bones;
not one of them will be broken.
21Evil will kill the wicked;
those who hate good people will be
judged guilty.
22But the LORD saves his servants' lives;
no one who trusts him will be judged guilty.⚭

A Prayer for Help

Of David.

35 LORD, battle with those who battle
with me.
Fight against those who fight against me.
2Pick up the shield and armor.
Rise up and help me.
3Lift up your spears, both large and small,
against those who chase me.
Tell me, "I will save you."

4Make those who want to kill me
be ashamed and disgraced.
Make those who plan to harm me
turn back and run away.
5Make them like chaff blown by the wind
as the angel of the LORD forces them away.
6Let their road be dark and slippery
as the angel of the LORD chases them.
7For no reason they spread out their net to
trap me;
for no reason they dug a pit for me.
8So let ruin strike them suddenly.
Let them be caught in their own nets;
let them fall into the pit and die.
9Then I will rejoice in the LORD;
I will be happy when he saves me.
10Even my bones will say,
"LORD, who is like you?
You save the weak from the strong,
the weak and poor from robbers."

11Men without mercy stand up to testify.
They ask me things I do not know.
12They repay me with evil for the good I have done,
and they make me very sad.
13Yet when they were sick, I put on clothes
of sadness
and showed my sorrow by going without food.
But my prayers were not answered.
14 I acted as if they were my friends or brothers.
I bowed in sadness as if I were crying for
my mother.
15But when I was in trouble, they gathered
and laughed;
they gathered to attack before I knew it.
They insulted me without stopping.
16They made fun of me and were cruel to me
and ground their teeth at me in anger.

17Lord, how long will you watch this happen?
Save my life from their attacks;
save me from these people who are
like lions.
18I will praise you in the great meeting.
I will praise you among crowds of people.
19Do not let my enemies laugh at me;
they hate me for no reason.
Do not let them make fun of me;
they have no cause to hate me.
20Their words are not friendly
but are lies about peace-loving people.
21They speak against me
and say, "Aha! We saw what you did!"

22LORD, you have been watching. Do not
keep quiet.
Lord, do not leave me alone.
23Wake up! Come and defend me!
My God and Lord, fight for me!
24LORD my God, defend me with your justice.
Don't let them laugh at me.
25Don't let them think, "Aha! We got what
we wanted!"
Don't let them say, "We destroyed him."
26Let them be ashamed and embarrassed,
because they were happy when I hurt.

34:14 This verse is not about finding inner peace. Believers are to work for the well-being of those around them, so that they and their neighbors can live secure, undisturbed, and satisfying lives.

⚭**34:22 Servant of the Lord:** Psalm 35:27

35:5 *chaff.* See 1:4.

Cover them with shame and disgrace,
because they thought they were
better than I was.
27May my friends sing and shout for joy.
May they always say, "Praise the
greatness of the LORD,⚭
who loves to see his servants do well."
28I will tell of your goodness
and will praise you every day.

Wicked People and a Good God

For the director of music. Of David, the servant of the LORD.

36 Sin speaks to the wicked in their hearts.
They have no fear of God.
2They think too much of themselves
so they don't see their sin and hate it.
3Their words are wicked lies;
they are no longer wise or good.
4At night they make evil plans;
what they do leads to nothing good.
They don't refuse things that are evil.

5LORD, your love reaches to the heavens,
your loyalty to the skies.
6Your goodness is as high as the mountains.
Your justice is as deep as the great ocean.
LORD, you protect both people and animals.
7God, your love is so precious!
You protect people in the shadow of your
wings.
8They eat the rich food in your house,
and you let them drink from your
river of pleasure.
9You are the giver of life.
Your light lets us enjoy life.⚭

10Continue to love those who know you
and to do good to those who are good.
11Don't let proud people attack me
and the wicked force me away.
12Those who do evil have been defeated.
They are overwhelmed;
they cannot do evil any longer.

God Will Reward Fairly

Of David.

37 Don't be upset because of evil people.
Don't be jealous of those who do wrong,
2because like the grass, they will soon dry up.
Like green plants, they will soon die away.
3Trust the LORD and do good.
Live in the land and feed on truth.
4Enjoy serving the LORD,
and he will give you what you want.
5Depend on the LORD;
trust him, and he will take care of you.⚭
6Then your goodness will shine like the sun,
and your fairness like the noonday sun.

7Wait and trust the LORD.
Don't be upset when others get rich
or when someone else's plans succeed.
8Don't get angry.
Don't be upset; it only leads to trouble.⚭
9Evil people will be sent away,
but those who trust the LORD will inherit
the land.
10In a little while the wicked will be no more.
You may look for them, but they will be gone.
11People who are not proud will inherit the land
and will enjoy complete peace.

12The wicked make evil plans against good people.
They grind their teeth at them in anger.
13But the Lord laughs at the wicked,
because he sees that their day is coming.
14The wicked draw their swords
and bend their bows
to kill the poor and helpless,
to kill those who are honest.
15But their swords will stab their own hearts,
and their bows will break.

16It is better to have little and be right
than to have much and be wrong.
17The power of the wicked will be broken,
but the LORD supports those who do right.
18The LORD watches over the lives of
the innocent,
and their reward will last forever.
19They will not be ashamed when trouble comes.
They will be full in times of hunger.⚭
20But the wicked will die.
The LORD's enemies will be like the
flowers of the fields;
they will disappear like smoke.
21The wicked borrow and don't pay back,
but those who do right give freely to others.
22Those whom the LORD blesses will inherit
the land,
but those he curses will be sent away.

⚭**35:27 Servant of the Lord:** Psalm 90:13

36:7 *in the shadow of your wings.* God is often likened to a mother bird who protectively guards her young under her wings.

⚭**36:9 Images of God:** Psalm 144:1–2

⚭**37:5 Road/Way:** Psalm 77:19

⚭**37:8 Anger:** Psalm 75:8

⚭**37:19 Famine:** Romans 8:35

COMPLAINT/LAMENT/PROTEST

LAMENTATIONS 5

Is it appropriate to complain? Can we complain about God? What is the difference between complaint and grumbling? Does God himself complain?

Christians feel it is appropriate to seek an attitude of humble submission to God. After all, God is all-powerful and he is good. Though life's circumstances may seem hard, Christians ought to "trust the Lord."

Such an approach to life has an element of truth to it, but it is not the only biblical teaching on how to approach God in the middle of life's hard realities. Indeed, there is a substantial number of passages that show God's people turning to God in protest. These passages should not be explained away in support of a quiet, passionless attitude toward God.

The Psalms contain a number of prayers that begin with complaints toward the Lord (for instance, Psalms 3, 5, 7, 26, 70). These prayers are characterized by a brutal honesty that expresses disappointment and even anger with God. Psalm 77 is a good example of the psalmist's insistent questioning of God's justice and goodness. The psalmist is troubled by some unspecified problem that causes him to spend the night awake and in confrontation with God. Indeed, the psalmist realizes that his trouble stems from God's inability or unwillingness to help him. Thus, he blames God and even throws accusations in his face (vv. 7–9). God had promised to protect them, but was not following through.

As with all the complaint psalms (and they are the single most commonly occurring type of psalm in the Bible), Psalm 77 turns toward God with trust and praise at the end. The psalmist finds hope in the future as he remembers the past. He finally remembers how God rescued his people in the past when they were in deep distress. Specifically, the psalmist remembers the Exodus when God saved Israel at the Red Sea (vv. 16–20).

Psalm 77 is typical in its main structure to other complaints in the Psalms in that they always (though see a notable exception in Psalm 88) turn to God in a positive way at the end and the complaints cease.

While Psalm 77 is an example of an individual complaint, the Book of Lamentations demonstrates that the whole nation could turn to God with their troubles.

Lamentations was written immediately after Babylon defeated the Israelite kingdom of Judah, destroying Jerusalem and its Temple (586 B.C.). Though it was the Babylonian army with its weapons that did the physical work, the author of Lamentations knew that God was the real actor in this defeat. According to Lamentations 2:5, "The LORD was like an enemy; he swallowed up Israel."

With this in mind, the Book of Lamentations was written to express the people's grief to God. Though the faithful who survived the defeat knew that their sin caused God to judge them, their response also expressed their complaint to him, "Why have you forgotten us for so long? Have you left us forever?" (5:20).

Laments and protests may be found throughout the Bible. Abraham complained to God that he had not yet given him a son as he promised (Genesis 15:2, 3). Samson protested that God gave him nothing to drink after he defeated some Philistines with the jawbone of a donkey (Judges 15:18). Job complained that God had brought him into the world to suffer (Job 3). Jeremiah faulted the Lord for favoring evil people over good ones (Jeremiah 12:1–4) and putting him in difficult spots. The list goes on and on.

Complaints are brought against other people, ourselves, or God himself. All three are illustrated in Psalms 42–43. Psalm 42:3 talks about wicked men who question the psalmist's God. The repeated refrain of the psalms is a complaint directed by the psalmist against himself, "Why am I so sad? Why am I so upset? I should put my hope in God and keep praising him, my Savior and my God" (Psalm 42:5).

These biblical examples show us that it is sometimes appropriate to approach God with complaints. This is true even when we look at the New Testament. Old Testament complaints are the key to the presentation of the Gospel. Jesus and the apostles expressed the depths of the Savior's anguish and pain through the laments, particularly Psalms 22 and 69. For instance, Jesus on the cross expressed his pain and anguish with the words of Psalm 22:1: "My God, my God, why have you rejected me?" (See Mark 15:34.) Jesus shows grief because he suffers. Indeed, he is the ultimate innocent sufferer.

Complaint/Lament/Protest: For additional scriptures on this topic go to Genesis 15:2–3.

Ezekiel

Ezekiel 2:9

Who was Ezekiel? What did his prophetic actions mean?

Ezekiel is an unusual figure among the Old Testament prophets. He often supplemented his preaching with graphic symbolic acts to drive home God's message of judgment and hope. What were the unique circumstances surrounding Ezekiel's ministry that led him to use striking symbolic actions? What was the meaning of these peculiar prophetic actions?

Ezekiel was commissioned in his thirtieth year (Ezekiel 1:1) to prophesy to his fellow exiles in Babylon. The time was one of great anxiety for the exiles. Just a few years earlier (597–596 B.C.) Nebuchadnezzar, the Babylonian king, had besieged Jerusalem, taken King Jehoiachin and many important citizens into exile in Babylon, and set up Jehoiachin's Uncle Zedekiah as king. At that time in Judah, there was a widespread belief that the Lord would protect Jerusalem and the kings descended from David from disaster, no matter how badly God's people had sinned. False prophets were proclaiming the imminent overthrow of the Babylonians by God, and the subsequent return of Jehoiachin to the throne (Jeremiah 23:17; 28:1–17).

Ezekiel, like his older contemporary Jeremiah, was called by God to preach a different message. The ancient Sinai covenant threatened the kings and people of Israel with destruction of the land and exile because of their sins. Nebuchadnezzar was God's instrument to punish his people for idolatry and injustice. The nation had to repent or face disaster! Far from recognizing these events as God's judgment for their sins, the people arrogantly claimed God's favor and believed the optimistic messages of the false prophets.

The people of Israel were in such deep spiritual darkness that extreme measures were needed to bring them out of it. One of those measures was to announce an impending judgment so terrible that God's wrath against the people could no longer be denied (Ezekiel 20:4–44). Another measure was to describe the people's sins and the looming judgment in terms graphic and lurid enough to shock them to their senses (see Ezekiel 16; 23). Finally, there were the symbolic actions: puzzling, scandalizing, and thought-provoking.

The first symbolic act performed by Ezekiel (Ezekiel 2:9–3:3) occurred immediately after his call to be a prophet. God held out a scroll covered with "funeral songs, sad writings, and words about troubles" (verse 10) and commanded him to eat it. The act of eating the scroll symbolized that God gave Ezekiel his words to speak. So then, Ezekiel's words and symbolic actions brought God's message to the people.

God then afflicted Ezekiel with inability to speak (Ezekiel 3:26–27). This inability to speak lasted until Jerusalem's destruction about six years later (Ezekiel 24:25–27; 33:21–22). Since Ezekiel gave several long speeches in chapters 3–30 during this period, his dumbness must have been partial and intermittent. Ezekiel was only able to speak when God opened his mouth. This arrangement further identified the prophet's words with the words of the Lord.

Ezekiel began his public prophetic ministry with a series of symbolic acts which emphasized God's approaching judgment on Jerusalem (Ezekiel 4:1–6:7). Jerusalem's judgment is graphically and repeatedly portrayed to the exiles because Jerusalem was their source of hope. First, Ezekiel was commanded to draw a picture of Jerusalem on a brick and construct a siege model depicting the city under attack. Next, Ezekiel was commanded to set up an iron plate between himself and the map of Jerusalem. The iron plate symbolized the insurmountable barrier that then existed between God and his people. God then commanded Ezekiel to "attack" the map of the city, symbolizing that God himself would attack Jerusalem.

Immediately after this, Ezekiel was commanded to lie on his left side for 390 days, then on his right side for forty days, signifying God's judgment on the northern and southern kingdoms respectively. Since Ezekiel also baked bread during this time (verse 9) he must have lain on his side for only a portion of each day. The limited rations he was allowed to eat represent the scarcity of food during a long siege. He cooked his food over dung to illustrate how the Israelites would be forced to act impurely during the siege (see Deuteronomy 23:12–14). Next, Ezekiel was commanded to shave his head (Ezekiel 5:1–4), signifying grief (Isaiah 15:2; Jeremiah 48:37) and shame (2 Samuel 10:4). Ezekiel was then commanded to divide up his hair and perform symbolic acts with the portions. These acts symbolized various aspects of God's judgment on Jerusalem (5:5–9). The few hairs which Ezekiel was commanded to tie in his clothing (verse 3) signified a remnant of survivors. These few would look back on the disaster and realize that God had truly spoken to them through Ezekiel (5:13).

Ezekiel: For additional scriptures on this topic go to Ezekiel 3:26–27.

23When a person's steps follow the LORD,
God is pleased with his ways.
24If he stumbles, he will not fall,
because the LORD holds his hand.

25I was young, and now I am old,
but I have never seen good people
left helpless
or their children begging for food.
26Good people always lend freely to others,
and their children are a blessing.

27Stop doing evil and do good,
so you will live forever.
28The LORD loves justice
and will not leave those who worship him.
He will always protect them,
but the children of the wicked will die.
29Good people will inherit the land
and will live in it forever.

30A good person speaks with wisdom,
and he says what is fair.
31The teachings of his God are in his heart,
so he does not fail to keep them.
32The wicked watch for good people
so that they may kill them.
33But the LORD will not take away his protection
or let good people be judged guilty.

34Wait for the LORD's help
and follow him.
He will honor you and give you the land,
and you will see the wicked sent away.

35I saw a wicked and cruel man
who looked strong like a healthy tree in
good soil.
36But he died and was gone;
I looked for him, but he couldn't be found.

37Think of the innocent person,
and watch the honest one.
The man who has peace
will have children to live after him.
38But sinners will be destroyed;
in the end the wicked will die.

39The LORD saves good people;
he is their strength in times of trouble.
40The LORD helps them and saves them;
he saves them from the wicked,
because they trust in him for protection.

A Prayer in Time of Sickness

A psalm of David to remember.

38 LORD, don't correct me when you are
angry.
Don't punish me when you are furious.
2Your arrows have wounded me,
and your hand has come down on me.
3My body is sick from your punishment.
Even my bones are not healthy because
of my sin.
4My guilt has overwhelmed me;
like a load it weighs me down.
5My sores stink and become infected
because I was foolish.
6I am bent over and bowed down;
I am sad all day long.
7I am burning with fever,
and my whole body is sore.
8I am weak and faint.
I moan from the pain I feel.

9Lord, you know everything I want;
my cries are not hidden from you.
10My heart pounds, and my strength is gone.
I am losing my sight.
11Because of my wounds, my friends and
neighbors avoid me,
and my relatives stay far away.
12Some people set traps to kill me.
Those who want to hurt me plan trouble;
all day long they think up lies.

13I am like a deaf man; I cannot hear.
Like a mute, I cannot speak.
14I am like a person who does not hear,
who has no answer to give.
15I trust you, LORD.
You will answer, my Lord and God.
16I said, "Don't let them laugh at me
or brag when I am defeated."
17I am about to die,
and I cannot forget my pain.
18I confess my guilt;
I am troubled by my sin.
19My enemies are strong and healthy,
and many hate me for no reason.
20They repay me with evil for the good I did.
They lie about me because I try to do good.

21LORD, don't leave me;
my God, don't go away.
22Quickly come and help me,
my Lord and Savior.

38:22 Healing: Jeremiah 33:6–8

38:22 Sickness, Disease, Healing: Psalm 41:1–3

Life Is Short

For the director of music. For Jeduthun. A psalm of David.

39 I said, "I will be careful how I act
and will not sin by what I say.
I will be careful what I say
around wicked people."
2So I kept very quiet.
I didn't even say anything good,
but I became even more upset.
3I became very angry inside,
and as I thought about it, my anger burned.
So I spoke:
4"LORD, tell me when the end will come
and how long I will live.
Let me know how long I have.
5You have given me only a short life;
my lifetime is like nothing to you.
Everyone's life is only a breath. *Selah*
6People are like shadows moving about.
All their work is for nothing;
they collect things but don't know who will
get them.

7"So, Lord, what hope do I have?
You are my hope.
8Save me from all my sins.
Don't let wicked fools make fun of me.
9I am quiet; I do not open my mouth,
because you are the one who has done this.
10Quit punishing me;
your beating is about to kill me.
11You correct and punish people for their sins;
like a moth, you destroy what they love.
Everyone's life is only a breath. *Selah*

12"LORD, hear my prayer,
and listen to my cry.
Do not ignore my tears.
I am like a visitor with you.
Like my ancestors, I'm only here a short time.⚭
13Leave me alone so I can be happy
before I leave and am no more."

Praise and Prayer for Help

For the director of music. A psalm of David.

40 I waited patiently for the LORD.
He turned to me and heard my cry.
2He lifted me out of the pit of destruction,
out of the sticky mud.
He stood me on a rock

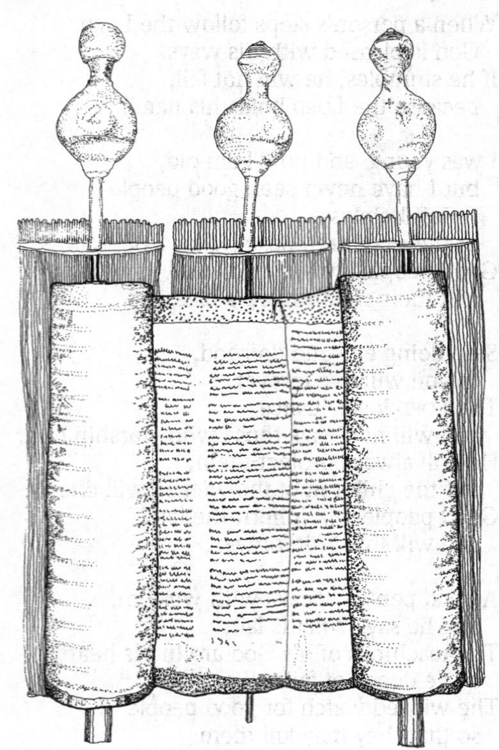

An ancient scroll containing the Pentateuch (Torah)—the first five books of the Old Testament

and made my feet steady.
3He put a new song in my mouth,
a song of praise to our God.
Many people will see this and worship him.
Then they will trust the LORD.⚭

4Happy is the person
who trusts the LORD,
who doesn't turn to those who are proud
or to those who worship false gods.
5LORD my God, you have done many miracles.
Your plans for us are many.
If I tried to tell them all,
there would be too many to count.

6You do not want sacrifices and offerings.
But you have made a hole in my ear
to show that my body and life are yours.
You do not ask for burnt offerings
and sacrifices to take away sins.

⚭**39:12 Foreigner (Alien):** Psalm 146:9

40:2 *sticky mud.* The sticky mud of the pit is contrasted with the firmness of rock. The pit is an allusion to the grave, and God has saved him from that fate.

⚭**40:3 Worship:** Psalm 42:1–2

[7]Then I said, "Look, I have come.
It is written about me in the book.
[8]My God, I want to do what you want.
Your teachings are in my heart."

[9]I will tell about your goodness in the great
meeting of your people.
LORD, you know my lips are not silent.
[10]I do not hide your goodness in my heart;
I speak about your loyalty and salvation.
I do not hide your love and truth
from the people in the great meeting.

[11]LORD, do not hold back your mercy from me;
let your love and truth always protect me.
[12]Troubles have surrounded me;
there are too many to count.
My sins have caught me
so that I cannot see a way to escape.
I have more sins than hairs on my head,
and I have lost my courage.
[13]Please, LORD, save me.
Hurry, LORD, to help me.
[14]People are trying to kill me.
Shame them and disgrace them.
People want to hurt me.
Let them run away in disgrace.
[15]People are making fun of me.
Let them be shamed into silence.
[16]But let those who follow you
be happy and glad.
They love you for saving them.
May they always say, "Praise the LORD!"

[17]Lord, because I am poor and helpless,
please remember me.
You are my helper and savior.
My God, do not wait.

A Prayer in Time of Sickness

For the director of music. A psalm of David.

41 Happy is the person who thinks about
the poor.
When trouble comes, the LORD will
save him.
[2]The LORD will protect him and spare his life
and will bless him in the land.
He will not let his enemies take him.
[3]The LORD will give him strength when he is sick,
and he will make him well again.
[4]I said, "LORD, have mercy on me.
Heal me, because I have sinned against you."
[5]My enemies are saying evil things about me.
They say, "When will he die and
be forgotten?"
[6]Some people come to see me,
but they lie.
They just come to get bad news.
Then they go and gossip.
[7]All my enemies whisper about me
and think the worst about me.
[8]They say, "He has a terrible disease.
He will never get out of bed again."
[9]My best and truest friend, who ate at my table,
has even turned against me.

[10]LORD, have mercy on me.
Give me strength so I can pay them back.
[11]Because my enemies do not defeat me,
I know you are pleased with me.
[12]Because I am innocent, you support me
and will let me be with you forever.

[13]Praise the LORD, the God of Israel.
He has always been,
and he will always be.
Amen and amen.

Book 2

Wishing to Be Near God

For the director of music. A maskil of the sons of Korah.

42 As a deer thirsts for streams of water,
so I thirst for you, God.
[2]I thirst for the living God.
When can I go to meet with him?
[3]Day and night, my tears have been my food.
People are always saying,
"Where is your God?"
[4]When I remember these things,
I speak with a broken heart.
I used to walk with the crowd
and lead them to God's Temple
with songs of praise.

[5]Why am I so sad?
Why am I so upset?
I should put my hope in God
and keep praising him,
my Savior and [6]my God.

40:9 *in the great meeting of your people.* The great meeting is perhaps referring to all the people of Israel, or else specifically, the worshipers at the Temple.

40:14 Honor & Shame: Matthew 18:4

41:3 Sickness, Disease, Healing: Proverbs 4:20–22

41:12 Integrity: Psalm 101:2–3

42:2 Worship: Psalm 51:16–17

42:6 *Mount Hermon and Mount Mizar.* The psalmist is separated

I am very sad.
So I remember you where the Jordan River begins,
near the peaks of Hermon and Mount Mizar.
7Troubles have come again and again,
sounding like waterfalls.
Your waves are crashing all around me.
8The LORD shows his true love every day.
At night I have a song,
and I pray to my living God.
9I say to God, my Rock,
"Why have you forgotten me?
Why am I sad
and troubled by my enemies?"
10My enemies' insults make me feel
as if my bones were broken.
They are always saying,
"Where is your God?"

11Why am I so sad?
Why am I so upset?
I should put my hope in God
and keep praising him,
my Savior and my God.

A Prayer for Protection

43 God, defend me.
Argue my case against those who don't follow you.
Save me from liars and those who do evil.
2God, you are my strength.
Why have you rejected me?
Why am I sad
and troubled by my enemies?
3Send me your light and truth
to guide me.
Let them lead me to your holy mountain,
to where you live.
4Then I will go to the altar of God,
to God who is my joy and happiness.
I will praise you with a harp,
God, my God.

5Why am I so sad?
Why am I so upset?
I should put my hope in God
and keep praising him,
my Savior and my God.

A Prayer for Help

For the director of music. A maskil of the sons of Korah.

44 God, we have heard about you.
Our ancestors told us
what you did in their days,
in days long ago.
2With your power you forced the nations out of the land
and placed our ancestors here.
You destroyed those other nations,
but you made our ancestors grow strong.
3It wasn't their swords that took the land.
It wasn't their power that gave them victory.
But it was your great power and strength.
You were with them because you loved them.

4My God, you are my King.
Your commands led Jacob's people to victory.
5With your help we pushed back our enemies.
In your name we trampled those who came against us.
6I don't trust my bow to help me,
and my sword can't save me.
7You saved us from our foes,
and you made our enemies ashamed.
8We will praise God every day;
we will praise your name forever. *Selah*

9But you have rejected us and shamed us.
You don't march with our armies anymore.
10You let our enemies push us back,
and those who hate us have taken our wealth.
11You gave us away like sheep to be eaten
and have scattered us among the nations.
12You sold your people for nothing
and made no profit on the sale.

13You made us a joke to our neighbors;
those around us laugh and make fun of us.
14You made us a joke to the other nations;
people shake their heads.
15I am always in disgrace,
and I am covered with shame.
16My enemy is getting even
with insults and curses.

17All these things have happened to us,
but we have not forgotten you
or failed to keep our agreement with you.

---

from God's presence at the Temple. He mentions Mount Hermon to the far north of Israel's border, where the Jordan River begins its southerly flow. We do not know the identity of Mount Mizar.

42:11 Jordan River: Matthew 3

42:11 Suffering: Isaiah 52:13–53:12

43:3 *your holy mountain.* This mountain is Mount Zion where the Temple is located.

43:5 Complaint/Lament/Protest: Psalm 69

44:7 Salvation: Psalm 53:6

[18]Our hearts haven't turned away from you,
and we haven't stopped following you.
[19]But you crushed us in this place where
wild dogs live,
and you covered us with deep darkness.

[20]If we had forgotten our God
or lifted our hands in prayer to foreign gods,
[21]God would have known,
because he knows what is in our hearts.
[22]But for you we are in danger of death
all the time.
People think we are worth no more than
sheep to be killed.

[23]Wake up, Lord! Why are you sleeping?
Get up! Don't reject us forever.
[24]Why do you hide from us?
Have you forgotten our pain and troubles?

[25]We have been pushed down into the dirt;
we are flat on the ground.
[26]Get up and help us.
Because of your love, save us.

A Song for the King's Wedding

For the director of music. To the tune of "Lilies." A maskil.
A love song of the sons of Korah.

45 Beautiful words fill my mind.
I am speaking of royal things.
My tongue is like the pen of a skilled writer.

[2]You are more handsome than anyone,
and you are an excellent speaker,
so God has blessed you forever.
[3]Put on your sword, powerful warrior.
Show your glory and majesty.
[4]In your majesty win the victory
for what is true and right.
Your power will do amazing things.
[5]Your sharp arrows will enter
the hearts of the king's enemies.
Nations will be defeated before you.
[6]God, your throne will last forever and ever.
You will rule your kingdom with fairness.
[7]You love right and hate evil,
so God has chosen you from among
your friends;
he has set you apart with much joy.
[8]Your clothes smell like myrrh, aloes, and cassia.
From palaces of ivory
music comes to make you happy.
[9]Kings' daughters are among your
honored women.
Your bride stands at your right side
wearing gold from Ophir.

[10]Listen to me, daughter; look and pay attention.
Forget your people and your father's family.
[11]The king loves your beauty.
Because he is your master, you should
obey him.
[12]People from the city of Tyre have brought a gift.
Wealthy people will want to meet you.

[13]The princess is very beautiful.
Her gown is woven with gold.
[14]In her beautiful clothes she is brought to
the king.
Her bridesmaids follow behind her,
and they are also brought to him.
[15]They come with happiness and joy;
they enter the king's palace.

[16]You will have sons to replace your fathers.
You will make them rulers through all the land.
[17]I will make your name famous from now on,
so people will praise you forever and ever.

God Protects His People

For the director of music. By alamoth. A psalm of the sons of Korah.

46 God is our protection and our strength.
He always helps in times of trouble.
[2]So we will not be afraid even if the earth shakes,
or the mountains fall into the sea,
[3]even if the oceans roar and foam,
or the mountains shake at the
raging sea. *Selah*

[4]There is a river that brings joy to the city of God,
the holy place where God Most High lives.
[5]God is in that city, and so it will not
be shaken.
God will help her at dawn.
[6]Nations tremble and kingdoms shake.
God shouts and the earth crumbles.

[7]The LORD All-Powerful is with us;
the God of Jacob is our defender. *Selah*

44:22 Martyrdom: Isaiah 53
45:17 Marriage: Malachi 2:16
46:2 *mountains fall into the sea.* The oceans and seas represent the forces of chaos and disorder, while mountains are the height of geographical stability. The psalmist can retain his calm even when it looks as if his whole world is caving in.

46:4 *a river that brings joy to the city of God.* Since Jerusalem has no river, this is an attempt to liken Jerusalem, the "city of God," to the Garden of Eden.

[8]Come and see what the LORD has done,
the amazing things he has done on the earth.
[9]He stops wars everywhere on the earth.
He breaks all bows and spears
and burns up the chariots with fire.
[10]God says, "Be quiet and know that I am God.
I will be supreme over all the nations;
I will be supreme in the earth."

[11]The LORD All-Powerful is with us;
the God of Jacob is our defender. *Selah*

God, the King of the World

For the director of music. A psalm of the sons of Korah.

47 Clap your hands, all you people.
Shout to God with joy.
[2]The LORD Most High is wonderful.
He is the great King over all the earth!
[3]He defeated nations for us
and put them under our control.⚭
[4]He chose the land we would inherit.
We are the children of Jacob, whom
he loved. *Selah*

[5]God has risen with a shout of joy;
the LORD has risen as the
trumpets sounded.
[6]Sing praises to God. Sing praises.
Sing praises to our King. Sing praises.
[7]God is King of all the earth,
so sing a song of praise to him.
[8]God is King over the nations.
God sits on his holy throne.
[9]The leaders of the nations meet
with the people of the God of Abraham,
because the leaders of the earth belong to God.
He is supreme.

Jerusalem, the City of God

A psalm of the sons of Korah.

48 The LORD is great; he should be praised
in the city of our God, on his
holy mountain.
[2]It is high and beautiful
and brings joy to the whole world.
Mount Zion is like the high mountains of
the north;
it is the city of the Great King.⚭
[3]God is within its palaces;
he is known as its defender.
[4]Kings joined together
and came to attack the city.
[5]But when they saw it, they were amazed.
They ran away in fear.
[6]Fear took hold of them;
they hurt like a woman having a baby.
[7]You destroyed the large trading ships
with an east wind.

[8]First we heard
and now we have seen
that God will always keep his city safe.
It is the city of the LORD All-Powerful,
the city of our God. *Selah*

[9]God, we come into your Temple
to think about your love.
[10]God, your name is known everywhere;
all over the earth people praise you.
Your right hand is full of goodness.
[11]Mount Zion is happy
and all the towns of Judah rejoice,
because your decisions are fair.

[12]Walk around Jerusalem
and count its towers.
[13]Notice how strong they are.
Look at the palaces.
Then you can tell your children
about them.
[14]This God is our God forever and ever.
He will guide us from now on.

Trusting Money Is Foolish

For the director of music. A psalm of the sons of Korah.

49 Listen to this, all you nations;
listen, all you who live on earth.
[2]Listen, both great and small,
rich and poor together.
[3]What I say is wise,
and my heart speaks with understanding.

⚭**47:3 Praise:** Psalm 65:13

48 Jerusalem was the called the "City of David." This was because the Israelites were unable to conquer it until David fought against it (2 Samuel 5). But in a truer sense, the real king in Jerusalem was God. This psalm praises the God who was king in Jerusalem. He was the one who lived in its palace and fought its battles (48:3).

48 In the Old Testament the beauty and security of Jerusalem (Psalm 50:2; Ezekiel 16:14) was a picture of salvation. That glory was lost when Nebuchadnezzar destroyed the city in 587–586 B.C., although Nehemiah's reconstruction of the city restored it to a measure of its glory after the Babylonian exile (Nehemiah 12:27–43). Both the glorious Jerusalem described in this psalm and the Jerusalem rebuilt by Nehemiah point forward to the New Jerusalem of Revelation 21.

48:1 *on his holy mountain.* The mountain is Mount Zion where the Temple is located. The mountains of Lebanon, where pagans believed the gods of the people of Canaan dwelled, were physically much larger, but Zion is compared to it favorably because of its significance due to the location of the Temple.

⚭**48:2 Environment:** Psalm 52:8

4I will pay attention to a wise saying;
I will explain my riddle on the harp.⚭

5Why should I be afraid of bad days?
Why should I fear when evil men
surround me?
6They trust in their money
and brag about their riches.
7No one can buy back the life of another.
No one can pay God for his own life,
8because the price of a life is high.
No payment is ever enough.
9Do people live forever?
Don't they all face death?

10See, even wise people die.
Fools and stupid people also die
and leave their wealth to others.
11Their graves will always be their homes.
They will live there from now on,
even though they named places after
themselves.
12Even rich people do not live forever;
like the animals, people die.

13This is what will happen to those who trust
in themselves
and to their followers who
believe them. *Selah*
14Like sheep, they must die,
and death will be their shepherd.
Honest people will rule over them in
the morning,
and their bodies will rot in a grave far
from home.
15But God will save my life
and will take me from the grave. *Selah*

16Don't be afraid of rich people
because their houses are more beautiful.
17They don't take anything to the grave;
their wealth won't go down with them.
18Even though they were praised when they
were alive—
and people may praise you when
you succeed—
19they will go to where their ancestors are.
They will never see light again.
20Rich people with no understanding
are just like animals that die.⚭

God Wants True Worship

A psalm of Asaph.

50 The God of gods, the LORD, speaks.
He calls the earth from the rising to the
setting sun.
2God shines from Jerusalem,
whose beauty is perfect.
3Our God comes, and he will not be silent.
A fire burns in front of him,
and a powerful storm surrounds him.
4He calls to the sky above and to the earth
that he might judge his people.
5He says, "Gather around, you who worship
me,
who have made an agreement with me,
using a sacrifice."
6God is the judge,
and even the skies say he is right. *Selah*

7God says, "My people, listen to me;
Israel, I will testify against you.
I am God, your God.
8I do not scold you for your sacrifices.
You always bring me your burnt offerings.
9But I do not need bulls from your stalls
or goats from your pens,
10because every animal of the forest is
already mine.
The cattle on a thousand hills are mine.
11I know every bird on the mountains,
and every living thing in the fields is mine.
12If I were hungry, I would not tell you,
because the earth and everything in it
are mine.
13I don't eat the meat of bulls
or drink the blood of goats.
14Give an offering to show thanks to God.
Give God Most High what you
have promised.
15Call to me in times of trouble.
I will save you, and you will honor me."

16But God says to the wicked,
"Why do you talk about my laws?
Why do you mention my agreement?
17You hate my teachings
and turn your back on what I say.
18When you see a thief, you join him.
You take part in adultery.

⚭**49:4 Proverb:** Proverbs 1:1–6
⚭**49:20 Materialism/Possessions:** Ezekiel 27–28
⚭**49:20 Death:** Ecclesiastes 9:2–6
50:1–7 In this psalm, God is portrayed as a judge speaking in court, but the imagery used shows that his power and righteousness go far beyond the power and righteousness of any human judge. His courtroom takes in the whole earth and sky, and when he enters the courtroom, fire and storm accompany him. When such a judge commands people to listen, surely we should listen.

19You don't stop your mouth from speaking evil,
and your tongue makes up lies.
20You speak against your brother
and lie about your mother's son.
21I have kept quiet while you did these things,
so you thought I was just like you.
But I will scold you
and accuse you to your face.

22"Think about this, you who forget God.
Otherwise, I will tear you apart,
and no one will save you.
23Those people honor me
who bring me offerings to show thanks.
And I, God, will save those who do that."

A Prayer for Forgiveness

For the director of music.
A psalm of David when the prophet Nathan came to David after David's sin with Bathsheba.

51 God, be merciful to me
because you are loving.
Because you are always ready to be merciful,
wipe out all my wrongs.
2Wash away all my guilt
and make me clean again.⚭

3I know about my wrongs,
and I can't forget my sin.
4You are the only one I have sinned against;
I have done what you say is wrong.
You are right when you speak
and fair when you judge.
5I was brought into this world in sin.
In sin my mother gave birth to me.

6You want me to be completely truthful,
so teach me wisdom.
7Take away my sin, and I will be clean.
Wash me, and I will be whiter than snow.
8Make me hear sounds of joy and gladness;
let the bones you crushed be happy again.
9Turn your face from my sins
and wipe out all my guilt.
10Create in me a pure heart, God,
and make my spirit right again.⚭
11Do not send me away from you
or take your Holy Spirit away from me.
12Give me back the joy of your salvation.
Keep me strong by giving me a
willing spirit.
13Then I will teach your ways to those who
do wrong,
and sinners will turn back to you.⚭

14God, save me from the guilt of murder,
God of my salvation,
and I will sing about your goodness.
15Lord, let me speak
so I may praise you.
16You are not pleased by sacrifices, or I would
give them.
You don't want burnt offerings.
17The sacrifice God wants is a broken spirit.
God, you will not reject a heart that
is broken and sorry for sin.⚭

18Do whatever good you wish
for Jerusalem.
Rebuild the walls of Jerusalem.
19Then you will be pleased with right sacrifices
and whole burnt offerings,
and bulls will be offered on your altar.⚭

God Will Punish the Proud

For the director of music. A maskil of David.
When Doeg the Edomite came to Saul and said to him, "David is in Ahimelech's house."

52 Mighty warrior, why do you brag about
the evil you do?
God's love will continue forever.
2You think up evil plans.
Your tongue is like a sharp razor,
making up lies.
3You love wrong more than right
and lies more than truth. *Selah*
4You love words that bite
and tongues that lie.

51 David here wrestles with the guilt of his horrible sin against Bathsheba, with whom he committed adultery, and her husband Uriah, whom he had killed. He turns to God, who alone can "wash away" his guilt (verse 2). He acknowledges that it is God against whom he has ultimately sinned (verse 4). He prays this prayer with the understanding that God "will not reject a heart that is broken and sorry for sin" (verse 17). In this penitential Psalm, David prays for a spirit of true repentance after being confronted by the prophet Nathan for his sins of murder and adultery. It is not enough to simply say he's sorry, nor to offer the traditional sacrifice for sin. What David needs is for God to have mercy and forgive; to "wash away all my guilt and make me clean again" (verse 2). He asks God to do the otherwise impossible: to create in him a "pure heart"—one that is broken by the things that breaks God's heart; one that is remorseful for the sin of hurting people as well as offending God (10–17); one that seeks to be transformed in the inner being. Inward transformation, not the external sacrifice, is what is required in order for the joy of the Lord to return to David.

⚭**51:2 Clean & Unclean:** Psalm 51:7–10

⚭**51:10 Clean & Unclean:** Isaiah 64:6

⚭**51:13 Instruction:** Psalm 119:33

51:17 *you will not reject a heart that is broken and sorry.* David understands that God wants his heart. Sacrifices that are given by a person who loves God are pleasing to him, as verse 19 shows.

⚭**51:17 Worship:** Psalm 63:1–4

⚭**51:19 Sin:** Matthew 5:29–30

Prophetic Symbolism

Ezekiel 4

Why did the prophets use symbolic language and actions to convey their message? Did the prophets sometimes speak with a kind of secret language? How does this language speak to us today?

When we think of the ancient prophets like Elijah, Ezekiel, and John the Baptist, we think of unusual, bearded men who see strange visions and have odd dreams. They seem to be totally caught up with God. In fact, they are sure that they have heard his voice and that he has told them to speak to the people. Sometimes their words seem mystical and hard to understand. But they didn't only *speak* for the Lord. They also *acted* for him. How do we explain their difficult words and unusual deeds?

Let's look first at the symbolic actions of the prophets. The prophet was not just a messenger; the prophet's very life was also a message. God called the whole person, and the life he lived before the people was also a loud sermon. Isaiah said that he and his children were "signs and proofs for the people of Israel from the Lord" (Isaiah 8:18), and he even gave one of his sons, Shear-Jashub, a symbolic name (Isaiah 7:3).

Similarly, the prophet Hosea was commanded by God to marry an unfaithful woman (a prostitute), representing the Lord's relationship to unfaithful Israel (Hosea 1:2–3). Each of the children was then given an expressive name (Hosea 1:4–9). What a message this conveyed to the people! Every time they saw the prophet, his wife, or children they were reminded of God's message. In fact, there must have been lots of talk each time Hosea's wife had a new baby: "What will he name this one?"

Sometimes the prophets were called on to perform very painful tasks. God informed Ezekiel that his dear wife was about to die, and said, "You must not be sad or cry loudly for her or shed any tears. Groan silently; do not cry loudly for the dead" (Ezekiel 24:16b-17a). Why? Ezekiel explained to the people that . . . your sons and daughters that you left behind in Jerusalem will fall dead by the sword. When that happens, you are to act as I have" (Ezekiel 24:21b-22a). Yes, "Ezekiel is to be an example to you" (24:24a).

There are many other symbolic actions that were performed by the prophets, proving that, very often, actions do speak louder than words. Isaiah walked around naked and barefoot as a sign that "old people and young people will be led away naked and barefoot, with their buttocks bare" (Isaiah 20:2–4), and Jeremiah shattered a jar in public symbolizing that God would soon shatter the city of Jerusalem (Jeremiah 19:1–15).

But the prophets spoke mainly with words, not actions. Why then is their language sometimes difficult to understand? One reason is that they were frequently reporting the contents of dreams and visions. These often need to be interpreted if they are to be relevant (see Genesis 40–41 and Daniel 2), so it is important not to read more into them than what the Scripture actually tells us.

Many times, it is only the overall meaning of the dream or vision that is clear. For example, the visions of John in the Book of Revelation have been the subject of all kinds of speculation. What is the exact interpretation of every beast, every creature, every bowl, and every trumpet? In each generation, different opinions have been offered, with all kinds of disagreement and guesswork. This, of course, is to be expected, although we would be wise not to be too dogmatic. But one thing is clear: Revelation points to the ultimate triumph of the power of God over the powers of darkness. In spite of a severe battle and great suffering, the people of the Lord will ultimately rule with him in a perfect kingdom free from sin or strife.

The prophets, especially Ezekiel, also spoke in parables, representing the nations as birds, trees, or different animals. While the specific details are often meaningful, it is the overall thrust of the message that is important, and the prophets were careful to make that clear.

Another reason that the prophets' words do not always read like a history book is because their message is relevant for every age. If they were totally specific in their message all the time, always supplying details of names, places, and events, they would quickly have become dated. But in the wisdom of God, the prophets had a message for their own day, as well as a message for ours, twenty-five hundred years later. Their words are both timely and timeless. And so, when reading the prophetic books, it is always good to ask, What was the relevance of the message to the prophet's own generation? And, how does it speak to me today? Use this method when studying the Book of Amos: His words confronted social injustice and empty religion then, and they confront us today.

If we read the prophets correctly, we will never make these mistakes. We will be challenged and encouraged, but we will leave the mysteries to God (Deuteronomy 29:29).⚭

⚭**Prophetic Symbolism:** For additional scriptures on this topic go to Genesis 49:1–27.

DANIEL

DANIEL 1

How did Daniel, a young man from Israel, come to a prominent place in the leadership of Babylon, his captors? How was Daniel able to interpret the king's dreams? Why did God rescue and protect Daniel on so many occasions?

Daniel is one of the main examples of faith in the Old Testament. Indeed, he may be the most consistent example of deep-seated and unwavering confidence in God found in the Old Testament. His character is all the more remarkable because he lived during a time of tremendous instability and confusion. Again and again, God strengthened his trust in him by saving him from difficult circumstances.

Daniel was a young man when Nebuchadnezzar first imposed his authority over Jerusalem around 605 B.C. At that time the Babylonian king placed his own choice on the throne of Judah and then deported Jehoiachin and other leading citizens of Judah to Babylon. Young men like Daniel and his friends were brought along and then trained in the Babylonian court for service to the king.

One of the purposes for this type of training was to encourage the bright and privileged youths of Judah to adopt pro-Babylonian ways. It was an attempt to gain their lifelong loyalty. Right from the start, though, Daniel and his three friends retained their Israelite distinctiveness. They "decided not to eat the king's food or drink his wine" (Daniel 1:8). In turn, God blessed them for their obedience to him, and so they prospered and grew important in the Babylonian kingdom.

Like Joseph (Genesis 37–50) before him, Daniel gained the attention of the king by means of his ability to interpret dreams. That ability was not learned or cultivated, as Daniel himself indicated when he told Nebuchadnezzar, "No wise man, magician, or fortune-teller can explain to the king the secret he has asked about. But there is a God in heaven who explains secret things . . ." (Daniel 2:27–28).

Indeed, three times Daniel was called upon to interpret dreams or some other symbolic prophecy. First, he interpreted Nebuchadnezzar's dream of a statue composed of four parts: a gold head, a silver chest and arms, a stomach and upper legs of bronze, legs of iron and feet of mixed iron and clay (Daniel 2:31–36). The top was precious and hard, while the bottom was cheap and vulnerable. The whole statue was toppled when a rock hit the feet. God told Daniel that the dream spoke of the progression of human kingdoms starting with Nebuchadnezzar's, the head of gold. But eventually these kingdoms would crumble before the rock that no human hand touched, surely a reference to a divine intervention.

Second, Nebuchadnezzar had a vision of a large tree that housed all the wild animals and birds of the earth (Daniel 4). It was a wonderful tree, but an angel came down and called for its destruction. It also spoke of a man who would become like an animal.

Daniel, under divine inspiration, also interpreted that dream. Nebuchadnezzar was the tree. But God would teach him that his kingdom is not the result of his own power, but rather God's. God would take the kingdom away from this most powerful of human beings and reduce him for a period of time to the level of an animal. These events took place precisely as Daniel explained.

Daniel was also called to interpret a vision when Belshazzar was ruling in Babylon (Daniel 5). During an evening of feasting and drinking, a hand wrote strange words on the wall: *Mene*, *mene*, *teke*, and *parsin*. When Daniel was called in to interpret, he pointed out that these words signaled the end of the Babylonian kingdom, and indeed that very night Darius the Mede took Babylon and Belshazzar was killed.

Daniel was used by God to interpret the dreams and visions of the kings of Israel's oppressors. In these stories, as well as in others (for example, Daniel in the lions' den [Daniel 6]), Daniel provides a model of faithful and successful behavior of an Israelite living in the exile, a period of the scattering of the Jewish people. Indeed, Daniel is an example to Jewish and Christian people throughout the centuries as they live in hostile cultures and societies (see especially Daniel 9).

But Daniel was more than a role model. He was also privileged by God to receive visions that extended farther into the future than any other Old Testament prophet, and perhaps more than any prophet other than John in the Book of Revelation, who quoted Daniel frequently.

Daniel was a model of faithful and successful obedience in the midst of oppression. He was also the recipient of visions of the end that impacted the New Testament, especially the Book of Revelation, in a powerful way.

Daniel: For additional scriptures on this topic go to Daniel 1:6–7.

5But God will ruin you forever.
He will grab you and throw you out of your tent;
he will tear you away from the land of the living. *Selah*
6Those who do right will see this and fear God.
They will laugh at you and say,
7"Look what happened to the man
who did not depend on God
but depended on his money.
He grew strong by his evil plans."

8But I am like an olive tree
growing in God's Temple.
I trust God's love
forever and ever.
9God, I will thank you forever for what you have done.
With those who worship you, I will trust you because you are good.

The Unbelieving Fool

For the director of music. By mahalath. A maskil of David.

53 Fools say to themselves,
"There is no God."
Fools are evil and do terrible things;
none of them does anything good.

2God looked down from heaven on all people
to see if anyone was wise,
if anyone was looking to God for help.
3But all have turned away.
Together, everyone has become evil;
none of them does anything good.
Not a single person.

4Don't the wicked understand?
They destroy my people as if they were eating bread.
They do not ask God for help.
5The wicked are filled with terror
where there had been nothing to fear.
God will scatter the bones of your enemies.
You will defeat them,
because God has rejected them.

6I pray that victory will come to Israel from Mount Zion!
May God bring them back.
Then the people of Jacob will rejoice,
and the people of Israel will be glad.

A Prayer for Help

For the director of music. With stringed instruments. A maskil of David when the Ziphites went to Saul and said, "We think David is hiding among our people."

54 God, save me because of who you are.
By your strength show that I am innocent.
2Hear my prayer, God;
listen to what I say.
3Strangers turn against me,
and cruel men want to kill me.
They do not care about God. *Selah*

4See, God will help me;
the Lord will support me.
5Let my enemies be punished with their own evil.
Destroy them because you are loyal to me.

6I will offer a sacrifice as a special gift to you.
I will thank you, LORD, because you are good.
7You have saved me from all my troubles,
and I have seen my enemies defeated.

A Prayer About a False Friend

For the director of music. With stringed instruments. A maskil of David.

55 God, listen to my prayer
and do not ignore my cry for help.
2Pay attention to me and answer me.
I am troubled and upset
3by what the enemy says
and how the wicked look at me.
They bring troubles down on me,
and in anger they attack me.

4I am frightened inside;
the terror of death has attacked me.
5I am scared and shaking,
and terror grips me.
6I said, "I wish I had wings like a dove.
Then I would fly away and rest.
7I would wander far away
and stay in the desert. *Selah*
8I would hurry to my place of escape,
far away from the wind and storm."
9Lord, destroy and confuse their words,
because I see violence and fighting in the city.
10Day and night they are all around its walls,
and evil and trouble are everywhere inside.

52:8 Environment: Psalm 90:1–2

52:8 *like an olive tree.* Olive trees were plentiful in Israel. They represent fertility and also long life since olive trees live for centuries.

53:6 Salvation: Isaiah 12:2

55:8 Fear: Psalm 118:6

11Destruction is everywhere in the city;
trouble and lying never leave its streets.

12It was not an enemy insulting me.
I could stand that.
It was not someone who hated me.
I could hide from him.
13But it is you, a person like me,
my companion and good friend.
14We had a good friendship
and walked together to God's Temple.

15Let death take away my enemies.
Let them die while they are still young
because evil lives with them.
16But I will call to God for help,
and the LORD will save me.
17Morning, noon, and night I am troubled
and upset,
but he will listen to me.
18Many are against me,
but he keeps me safe in battle.
19God who lives forever
will hear me and punish them. *Selah*
But they will not change;
they do not fear God.

20The one who was my friend attacks
his friends
and breaks his promises.
21His words are slippery like butter,
but war is in his heart.
His words are smoother than oil,
but they cut like knives.

22Give your worries to the LORD,
and he will take care of you.
He will never let good people down.
23But, God, you will bring down
the wicked to the grave.
Murderers and liars will live
only half a lifetime.
But I will trust in you.

Trusting God for Help

For the director of music. To the tune of "The Dove in the Distant Oak." A miktam of David when the Philistines captured him in Gath.

56 God, be merciful to me because people are
chasing me;
the battle has pressed me all day long.
2My enemies have chased me all day;
there are many proud people fighting me.
3When I am afraid,
I will trust you.
4I praise God for his word.
I trust God, so I am not afraid.
What can human beings do to me?

5All day long they twist my words;
all their evil plans are against me.
6They wait. They hide.
They watch my steps,
hoping to kill me.
7God, do not let them escape;
punish the foreign nations in your anger.
8You have recorded my troubles.
You have kept a list of my tears.
Aren't they in your records?

9On the day I call for help, my enemies
will be defeated.
I know that God is on my side.
10I praise God for his word to me;
I praise the LORD for his word.
11I trust in God. I will not be afraid.
What can people do to me?

12God, I must keep my promises to you.
I will give you my offerings to thank you,
13because you have saved me from death.
You have kept me from being defeated.
So I will walk with God
in light among the living.

A Prayer in Troubled Times

For the director of music. To the tune of "Do Not Destroy." A miktam of David when he escaped from Saul in the cave.

57 Be merciful to me, God; be merciful to me
because I come to you for protection.
Let me hide under the shadow of
your wings
until the trouble has passed.

2I cry out to God Most High,
to the God who does everything for me.
3He sends help from heaven and saves me.
He punishes those who chase me. *Selah*
God sends me his love and truth.

4Enemies, like lions, are all around me;
I must lie down among them.
Their teeth are like spears and arrows,
their tongues as sharp as swords.

57:1 *the shadow of your wings.* See 36:7.

57:4 *lions.* Lions, which lived in great numbers in ancient Israel, were known for their ruthlessness and strength.

[5]God is supreme over the skies;
his majesty covers the earth.

[6]They set a trap for me.
I am very worried.
They dug a pit in my path,
but they fell into it themselves. *Selah*

[7]My heart is steady, God; my heart is steady.
I will sing and praise you.
[8]Wake up, my soul.
Wake up, harp and lyre!
I will wake up the dawn.
[9]Lord, I will praise you among the nations;
I will sing songs of praise about you
to all the nations.
[10]Your great love reaches to the skies,
your truth to the clouds.
[11]God, you are supreme above the skies.
Let your glory be over all the earth.

Unfair Judges

For the director of music. To the tune of "Do Not Destroy." A miktam of David.

58 Do you rulers really say what is right?
Do you judge people fairly?
[2]No, in your heart you plan evil;
you think up violent crimes in the land.⚭
[3]From birth, evil people turn away from God;
they wander off and tell lies as soon
as they are born.
[4]They are like poisonous snakes,
like deaf cobras that stop up their ears
[5]so they cannot hear the music of the
snake charmer
no matter how well he plays.

[6]God, break the teeth in their mouths!
Tear out the fangs of those lions, LORD!
[7]Let them disappear like water that
flows away.
Let them be cut short like a broken arrow.
[8]Let them be like snails that melt as they move.
Let them be like a child born dead who
never saw the sun.
[9]His anger will blow them away alive
faster than burning thorns can heat a pot.
[10]Good people will be glad when they see
him get even.
They will wash their feet in the blood
of the wicked.
[11]Then people will say,
"There really are rewards for doing what is
right.
There really is a God who judges the world."

A Prayer for Protection

For the director of music. To the tune of "Do Not Destroy." A miktam of David when Saul sent men to watch David's house to kill him.

59 God, save me from my enemies.
Protect me from those who come
against me.
[2]Save me from those who do evil
and from murderers.

[3]Look, men are waiting to ambush me.
Cruel men attack me,
but I have not sinned or done wrong, LORD.
[4]I have done nothing wrong, but they are ready
to attack me.
Wake up to help me, and look.
[5]You are the LORD God All-Powerful, the
God of Israel.
Arise and punish those people.
Do not give those traitors any mercy. *Selah*

[6]They come back at night.
Like dogs they growl and roam around the city.
[7]Notice what comes from their mouths.
Insults come from their lips,
because they say, "Who's listening?"
[8]But, LORD, you laugh at them;
you make fun of all of them.

[9]God, my strength, I am looking to you,
because God is my defender.
[10]My God loves me, and he goes in
front of me.
He will help me defeat my enemies.
[11]Lord, our protector, do not kill them, or my
people will forget.
With your power scatter them and defeat
them.
[12]They sin by what they say;
they sin with their words.
They curse and tell lies,
so let their pride trap them.
[13]Destroy them in your anger;
destroy them completely!
Then they will know
that God rules over Israel
and to the ends of the earth. *Selah*

57:6 The enemies of the psalmist are here likened to hunters who set out traps for the godly.
⚭**58:2 Crime:** Isaiah 53:12

59:6 *dogs.* Dogs were not loved pets in ancient Israel. They were dangerous pests who could seriously injure a person.

14They come back at night.
Like dogs they growl
and roam around the city.
15They wander about looking for food,
and they howl if they do not find enough.
16But I will sing about your strength.
In the morning I will sing about your love.
You are my defender,
my place of safety in times of trouble.
17God, my strength, I will sing praises to you.
God, my defender, you are the God who
loves me.

A Prayer After a Defeat

For the director of music. To the tune of "Lily of the Agreement." A miktam of David. For teaching. When David fought the Arameans of Northwest Mesopotamia and Zobah, and when Joab returned and defeated twelve thousand Edomites at the Valley of Salt.

60 God, you have rejected us and
scattered us.
You have been angry, but please come back
to us.
2You made the earth shake and crack.
Heal its breaks because it is shaking.
3You have given your people trouble.
You made us unable to walk straight, like
people drunk with wine.
4You have raised a banner to gather those who
fear you.
Now they can stand up against
the enemy. *Selah*

5Answer us and save us by your power
so the people you love will be rescued.

6God has said from his Temple,
"When I win, I will divide Shechem
and measure off the Valley of Succoth.
7Gilead and Manasseh are mine.
Ephraim is like my helmet.
Judah holds my royal scepter.
8Moab is like my washbowl.
I throw my sandals at Edom.
I shout at Philistia."

9Who will bring me to the strong,
walled city?
Who will lead me to Edom?
10God, surely you have rejected us;
you do not go out with our armies.
11Help us fight the enemy.
Human help is useless,
12but we can win with God's help.
He will defeat our enemies.

A Prayer for Protection

For the director of music. With stringed instruments. Of David.

61 God, hear my cry;
listen to my prayer.
2I call to you from the ends of the earth
when I am afraid.
Carry me away to a high mountain.
3You have been my protection,
like a strong tower against my enemies.

4Let me live in your Holy Tent forever.
Let me find safety in the shelter of
your wings. *Selah*

5God, you have heard my promises.
You have given me what belongs to those
who fear you.

6Give the king a long life;
let him live many years.
7Let him rule in the presence of God forever.
Protect him with your love and truth.
8Then I will praise your name forever,
and every day I will keep my promises.

Trust Only in God

For the director of music. For Jeduthun. A psalm of David.

62 I find rest in God;
only he can save me.
2He is my rock and my salvation.
He is my defender;
I will not be defeated.

3How long will you attack someone?
Will all of you kill that person?
Who is like a leaning wall, like a fence ready
to fall?
4They are planning to make that person fall.
They enjoy telling lies.
With their mouths they bless,
but in their hearts they curse. *Selah*

5I find rest in God;
only he gives me hope.

60:7 *Gilead, Manasseh, Ephraim, and Judah.* These four locations are all parts of Israel.
60:8 *Moab, Edom, and Philistia.* Moab, Edom, and Philistia are all traditional enemies of Israel, and the gesture of throwing sandals is one which expresses anger and contempt.
61:4 *shelter of your wings.* See 36:7.
62:3 *a leaning wall.* The images of the leaning wall, or the fence about to fall, are referring to someone who is about to be defeated. The enemy of the psalmist is pushing someone over the edge.

[6]He is my rock and my salvation.
He is my defender;
I will not be defeated.
[7]My honor and salvation come from God.
He is my mighty rock and my protection.

[8]People, trust God all the time.
Tell him all your problems,
because God is our protection. *Selah*

[9]The least of people are only a breath,
and even the greatest are just a lie.
On the scales, they weigh nothing;
together they are only a breath.
[10]Do not trust in force.
Stealing is of no use.
Even if you gain more riches,
don't put your trust in them.

[11]God has said this,
and I have heard it over and over:
God is strong.
[12]The Lord is loving.
You reward people for what they have done.

Wishing to Be Near God

A psalm of David when he was in the desert of Judah.

63 God, you are my God.
I search for you.
I thirst for you
like someone in a dry, empty land
where there is no water.
[2]I have seen you in the Temple
and have seen your strength and glory.
[3]Because your love is better than life,
I will praise you.
[4]I will praise you as long as I live.
I will lift up my hands in prayer to your name.
[5]I will be content as if I had eaten the best foods.
My lips will sing, and my mouth will
praise you.

[6]I remember you while I'm lying in bed;
I think about you through the night.
[7]You are my help.
Because of your protection, I sing.
[8]I stay close to you;
you support me with your right hand.

[9]Some people are trying to kill me,
but they will go down to the grave.
[10]They will be killed with swords
and eaten by wild dogs.
[11]But the king will rejoice in his God.
All who make promises in his name will
praise him,
but the mouths of liars will be shut.

A Prayer Against Enemies

For the director of music. A psalm of David.

64 God, listen to my complaint.
I am afraid of my enemies;
protect my life from them.
[2]Hide me from those who plan wicked things,
from that gang who does evil.
[3]They sharpen their tongues like swords
and shoot bitter words like arrows.
[4]From their hiding places they shoot at
innocent people;
they shoot suddenly and are not afraid.
[5]They encourage each other to do wrong.
They talk about setting traps,
thinking no one will see them.
[6]They plan wicked things and say,
"We have a perfect plan."
The mind of human beings is hard
to understand.

[7]But God will shoot them with arrows;
they will suddenly be struck down.
[8]Their own words will be used against them.
All who see them will shake their heads.
[9]Then everyone will fear God.
They will tell what God has done,
and they will learn from what he has done.
[10]Good people will be happy in the LORD
and will find protection in him.
Let everyone who is honest praise the LORD.

A Hymn of Thanksgiving

For the director of music. A psalm of David. A song.

65 God, you will be praised in Jerusalem.
We will keep our promises to you.
[2]You hear our prayers.
All people will come to you.
[3]Our guilt overwhelms us,
but you forgive our sins.
[4]Happy are the people you choose
and invite to stay in your court.
We are filled with good things in your house,
your holy Temple.

63:4 Worship: Psalm 103:1–5
63:6 Meditation: Psalm 77
65:1 *you will be praised in Jerusalem.* Jerusalem is the location of the Temple where formal worship of God takes place.
65:2 Prayer: Psalm 141:2

5You answer us in amazing ways,
God our Savior.
People everywhere on the earth
and beyond the sea trust you.
6You made the mountains by your strength;
you are dressed in power.
7You stopped the roaring seas,
the roaring waves,
and the uproar of the nations.
8Even those people at the ends of the earth fear
your miracles.
You are praised from where the sun rises to
where it sets.

9You take care of the land and water it;
you make it very fertile.
The rivers of God are full of water.
Grain grows because you make it grow.
10You send rain to the plowed fields;
you fill the rows with water.
You soften the ground with rain,
and then you bless it with crops.
11You give the year a good harvest,
and you load the wagons with many crops.
12The desert is covered with grass
and the hills with happiness.
13The pastures are full of flocks,
and the valleys are covered with grain.
Everything shouts and sings for joy.⚭

Praise God for What He Has Done

For the director of music. A song. A psalm.

66 Everything on earth, shout with
joy to God!
2Sing about his glory!
Make his praise glorious!
3Say to God, "Your works are amazing!
Because your power is great,
your enemies fall before you.
4All the earth worships you
and sings praises to you.
They sing praises to your name." *Selah*

5Come and see what God has done,
the amazing things he has done
for people.
6He turned the sea into dry land.
The people crossed the river on foot.
So let us rejoice because of what he did.⚭
7He rules forever with his power.
He keeps his eye on the nations,
so people should not turn against him. *Selah*

8You people, praise our God;
loudly sing his praise.
9He protects our lives
and does not let us be defeated.
10God, you have tested us;
you have purified us like silver.
11You let us be trapped
and put a heavy load on us.
12You let our enemies walk on our heads.
We went through fire and flood,
but you brought us to a place with good things.

13I will come to your Temple with burnt offerings.
I will give you what I promised,
14 things I promised when I was in trouble.
15I will bring you offerings of fat animals,
and I will offer sheep, bulls,
and goats.⚭ *Selah*

16All of you who fear God, come and listen,
and I will tell you what he has done for me.
17I cried out to him with my mouth
and praised him with my tongue.
18If I had known of any sin in my heart,
the Lord would not have listened to me.
19But God has listened;
he has heard my prayer.
20Praise God,
who did not ignore my prayer
or hold back his love from me.

Everyone Should Praise God

For the director of music. With stringed instruments.
A psalm. A song.

67 God, have mercy on us and bless us
and show us your kindness *Selah*
2so the world will learn your ways,
and all nations will learn that you can save.

3God, the people should praise you;
all people should praise you.
4The nations should be glad and sing
because you judge people fairly.
You guide all the nations on earth. *Selah*
5God, the people should praise you;
all people should praise you.

65:7 *roaring seas* and *roaring waves.* The waters are symbolic of the forces of chaos and disorder that God confronts.
⚭**65:13 Praise:** Psalm 77:13–15
⚭**66:6 Flood:** Psalm 93:3–4
66:6 *sea into dry land* and *crossed the river on foot.* The first line refers to the crossing of the Red Sea (Exodus 14–15) and the second line to the crossing of the Jordan River (Joshua 3).
66:13 The psalmist apparently promised the Lord a sacrifice if he answered a request. The psalm is a thanksgiving for hearing a previously given prayer.
⚭**66:15 Oath/Vow:** Proverbs 20:25

[6]The land has given its crops.
God, our God, blesses us.
[7]God blesses us
so people all over the earth will fear him.

Praise God Who Saved the Nation

For the director of music. A psalm of David. A song.

68 Let God rise up and scatter his enemies;
let those who hate him run away
from him.
[2]Blow them away as smoke
is driven away by the wind.
As wax melts before a fire,
let the wicked be destroyed before God.
[3]But those who do right should be glad
and should rejoice before God;
they should be happy and glad.

[4]Sing to God; sing praises to his name.
Prepare the way for him
who rides through the desert,
whose name is the LORD.
Rejoice before him.
[5]God is in his holy Temple.
He is a father to orphans,
and he defends the widows.⚭
[6]God gives the lonely a home.
He leads prisoners out with joy,
but those who turn against God will live in a
dry land.

[7]God, you led your people out
when you marched through
the desert. *Selah*

[8]The ground shook
and the sky poured down rain
before God, the God of Mount Sinai,
before God, the God of Israel.
[9]God, you sent much rain;
you refreshed your tired land.
[10]Your people settled there.
God, in your goodness
you took care of the poor.

[11]The Lord gave the command,
and a great army told the news:
[12]"Kings and their armies run away.
In camp they divide the wealth taken in war.
[13]Those who stayed by the campfires
will share the riches taken in battle."
[14]The Almighty scattered kings
like snow on Mount Zalmon.

[15]The mountains of Bashan are high;
the mountains of Bashan have many peaks.
[16]Why do you mountains with many peaks
look with envy
on the mountain that God chose for his home?
The LORD will live there forever.
[17]God comes with millions of chariots;
the Lord comes from Mount Sinai to
his holy place.
[18]When you went up to the heights,
you led a parade of captives.
You received gifts from the people,
even from those who turned against you.
And the LORD God will live there.

[19]Praise the Lord, God our Savior,
who helps us every day. *Selah*
[20]Our God is a God who saves us;
the LORD God saves us from death.

[21]God will crush his enemies' heads,
the hairy skulls of those who continue
to sin.
[22]The Lord said, "I will bring the enemy back
from Bashan;
I will bring them back from the depths of
the sea.
[23]Then you can stick your feet in their blood,
and your dogs can lick their share."

[24]God, people have seen your victory march;
God my King marched into the holy place.
[25]The singers are in front and the instruments
are behind.
In the middle are the girls with
the tambourines.
[26]Praise God in the meeting place;
praise the LORD in the gathering of Israel.
[27]There is the smallest tribe, Benjamin,
leading them.
And there are the leaders of Judah with
their group.
There also are the leaders of Zebulun
and of Naphtali.

⚭**68:5 Adoption:** Proverbs 23:9–11

68:5 *father to orphans, and defends the widows.* In the ancient world, widows and orphans were especially vulnerable to social exploitation because the husband/father was missing from the scene. God then has special concern to protect the weak.

68:16 Though many mountains, including those of Bashan, far outshone Zion physically, that hill was by far the most important because the Temple was there.

68:22 *bring the enemy back from Bashan.* The reference to Bashan here is probably a reference to the defeat of Og during the period of the desert wanderings (Deuteronomy 3).

28God, order up your power;
show the mighty power you have used
for us before.
29Kings will bring their wealth to you,
to your Temple in Jerusalem.
30Punish Egypt, the beast in the tall grass
along the river.
Punish the leaders of nations, those bulls
among the cows.
Defeated, they will bring you their silver.
Scatter those nations that love war.
31Messengers will come from Egypt;
the people of Cush will pray to God.

32Kingdoms of the earth, sing to God;
sing praises to the Lord. *Selah*
33Sing to the one who rides through the skies,
which are from long ago.
He speaks with a thundering voice.
34Announce that God is powerful.
He rules over Israel,
and his power is in the skies.
35God, you are wonderful in your Temple.
The God of Israel gives his people strength
and power.

Praise God!

A Cry for Help

For the director of music. To the tune of "Lilies." A psalm of David.

69 God, save me,
because the water has risen
to my neck.
2I'm sinking down into the mud,
and there is nothing to stand on.
I am in deep water,
and the flood covers me.
3I am tired from calling for help;
my throat is sore.
My eyes are tired from waiting
for God to help me.
4There are more people who hate me for no
reason than hairs on my head;
powerful enemies want to destroy me
for no reason.
They make me pay back
what I did not steal.
5God, you know what I have done wrong;
I cannot hide my guilt from you.
6Lord God All-Powerful,
do not let those who hope in you be ashamed
because of me.
God of Israel,
do not let your worshipers be disgraced
because of me.
7For you, I carry this shame,
and my face is covered with disgrace.
8I am like a stranger to my closest relatives
and a foreigner to my mother's children.
9My strong love for your Temple completely
controls me.
When people insult you, it hurts me.
10When I cry and go without food,
they make fun of me.
11When I wear clothes of sadness,
they joke about me.
12They make fun of me in public places,
and the drunkards make up songs about me.

13But I pray to you, Lord, for favor.
God, because of your great love, answer me.
You are truly able to save.
14Pull me from the mud,
and do not let me sink.
Save me from those who hate me
and from the deep water.
15Do not let the flood drown me
or the deep water swallow me
or the grave close its mouth over me.
16Lord, answer me because your love is
so good.
Because of your great kindness, turn to me.
17Do not hide from me, your servant.
I am in trouble. Hurry to help me!
18Come near and save me;
rescue me from my enemies.

19You see my shame and disgrace.
You know all my enemies and what they
have said.
20Insults have broken my heart
and left me weak.
I looked for sympathy, but there was none;
I found no one to comfort me.

68:35 Mountain: Psalm 97:5

69:1 *water has risen to my neck.* The waters represent chaos or disorder. Here they stand for chaos in the psalmist's own life.

69:1–4, 13–18 In Psalm 69 David pictures himself caught in a flood and calls out to God for help, but the deep waters he is experiencing are not literal. They mean something else. The swirling currents that have caught him off balance and threaten to overwhelm him stand for the hatred and derision of his enemies. The mud that is sucking him down stands for his feelings of confusion, loneliness, shame, and despair. However, David keeps his faith in God's power to save him, both from his enemies and from his own turbulent emotions.

69:9 Ambition: John 4:34

69:11 *clothes of sadness.* The clothes of sadness are a reference to sackcloth, a very poor, rough fabric, which was worn during periods of mourning.

69:15 Fasting: Mark 1:9–13

69:20 Comfort: Psalm 77:2

Martyrdom

Daniel 3, 6; Matthew 5:10, 16:24; Acts 7

What does "martyrdom" mean? Who are some Old Testament examples of martyrdom? What does it mean that Christians are also called to be "witnesses" (martyrs) for Christ?

The Greek word which sounds like our English *martyr* originally meant "witness," either in the sense of giving testimony at a trial or confessing personal experience of an event. The English term *martyr* refers to a person who suffers and is put to death for refusing to renounce their faith and beliefs. Witnesses and martyrs are closely related from the time of the Bible, where many gave their lives because of their faithful adherence to God's commands in the face of violent opposition. Shortly after, the New Testament "witnesses" became a shorthand way of referring to those who died for their faithfulness to Christ (see Revelation 2:13).

In the Old Testament there are several examples of martyrs, and others who barely escape martyrdom due to God's last-minute deliverance. These stories model that zeal for the Lord knows no limits. Martyrs demonstrated their confidence in God by their willingness to sacrifice their lives rather than to renounce their faith. Samson is perhaps the earliest example of a martyr (Judges 16), and Daniel the latest. In Daniel 3, Shadrach, Meshach, and Abednego chose to be thrown into a blazing furnace rather than to worship a statue made of gold in violation of the Ten Commandments (Exodus 20:3–5). Though God delivered them and spared them from martyrdom, they are the pattern of faithful obedience and ultimate faithfulness to God. A few chapters later, Daniel himself chose death in the lions' den, though he, too, is graciously delivered before he had to face the consequences of his choice (Daniel 6).

In the 400-year-period between the Old and New Testaments, martyrdom is continually portrayed in the books of Apocrapha (books considered by some scholars to not have been inspired by God and are not included in this or most other Bibles) as the noblest choice one can make in faithfulness to God's commands. The radical faith-commitment of the martyrs is well summarized: "Let us die rather than transgress the commandments of the Lord of lords, the God of our Fathers" (Testament of Moses 9:7 in the Apocrypha). First Maccabees reports the revolt of Jewish rebels against Rome and how they refused to fight on the Sabbath day, even when attacked. They would rather die than violate the command of God to "Remember to keep the Sabbath holy" (Exodus 20:8–11). These brief examples illustrate the extent of Jewish devotion to God, a pattern that is essential background for understanding many of the references to martyrdom and suffering in the New Testament (2 Maccabees 6:1–7:42; 12:39–45 in the Apocrypha).

Jesus taught his followers to brace themselves for the violent opposition sure to come against them because of their faithfulness to him. To encourage them amidst their suffering, he taught that the heavenly reward would justify the cost of earthly faithfulness (Matthew 5:10–11; 10:5–42). John the Baptist is the first example in the New Testament of martyrdom. In his case he was executed for his faithfulness to the command, "It is not lawful for you to be married to your brother's wife" (Mark 6:14–29).

Of course, Jesus himself is the model martyr of the New Testament (Revelation 1:5; 3:14),although it may be more accurate to say that he is the ultimate sacrifice. He predicted his own death at Jerusalem, including his trial, suffering, and execution (Matthew 16:21). All four gospels emphasize that this was not simply the result of cruel fate, but the direct result of his choice to give his life in obedience to his heavenly Father: "No one takes it away from me; I give my own life freely . . . This is what my Father commanded me to do" (John 10:18). An early hymn says that "he humbled himself and was fully obedient to God, even when that caused his death—death on a cross" (Philippians 2:8). As Daniel and John the Baptist prefigured, so Christ became the exemplary martyr, witnessing to his zeal for the Lord through his willingness to die and sacrificing himself for the sins of the world.

This same pattern was embodied by the followers of Jesus. He admonished his followers, "If people want to follow me, they must give up the things they want. They must be willing even to give up their lives to follow me" (Matthew 16:24). Followers and pupils of Jesus are to expect the same treatment as their master and teacher (John 15:18–27).⚭

⚭**Martyrdom:** For additional scriptures on this topic go to Judges 16.

Angels/Guardian Angels

Daniel 9

*Where do angels come from? Do we each have "guardian" angels?
What is the role of angels in God's activity?*

Hundreds of popular books, cover stories in news magazines, and testimonials of close encounters with celestial beings speak to a renewed interest in angels today. In one sense, this is surprising, since many modern people, both in and outside of the church, have been taken captive by the world of science and technology and have left little room in their lives for the mysterious. True, heavenly creatures have made their appearances as the crowning glory of Christmas trees and are trotted out each year in Christmas musicals, but, for most Americans, they have not been free to leave the front covers of Christmas cards, the walls of art museums, or the stories of our childhood.

In ancient Israel, speculation about the spiritual world arose in the midst of difficult times. Following the capture of Jerusalem and the Exile of the people of Israel into Babylon in the late 6th century B.C., and especially in the midst of the challenges of foreign influence and dominion under the Greeks and Romans in the three centuries before the birth of Jesus, many within Israel learned to look beyond present realities for answers to hard questions. The failure of its primary religious institutions, the prominence of evil, the suffering of the righteous—these and related crises led Israel to open its eyes to another world, another time and space inhabited by heavenly creatures.

The Bible tells us that there is a whole world out there that we cannot see. God has not only created the world that is before our eyes, but also spiritual creatures that we cannot see. These spiritual creatures have a variety of names—angels, demons, cherubim, seraphim. Some are good and some are bad. We don't know the details of their origins or their lives. The Bible does not focus on these creatures; they focus on our relationship with God. However, from time to time, the curtains draw back and the Bible gives us a glimpse of these beings we call angels. These spiritual creatures appear on the scene as early as Genesis 3 when God placed armed angels at the entrance to the Garden of Eden so that Adam and Eve could not return to paradise. They appear throughout the Bible through the very last chapters of Revelation where angels give a tour of the new Jerusalem.

What did Jesus and his followers make of such speculation? Very little, actually. Angels are present in the New Testament, of course, but they hardly occupy center stage. They are most active in the narrative of Jesus' birth in Luke 1–2, in accounts of Jesus being tested (for example, Matthew 4:11; Mark 1:13; Luke 22:43–44), in the resurrection narratives (Matthew 28, Mark 16, Luke 24, John 20), and in images of the coming of the Son of Man and final judgment (for example, Mark 13:26; 14:62; see Daniel 7:13–14).

As in the Old Testament, descriptions of the activity of angels in the New Testament are often ways of referring to the active presence of God in human affairs that also protect the transcendence of God. The "angel of the Lord" present at the beginning of the Book of Luke is none other than God's special agent to accomplish his will (see Exodus 3:2; Judges 6:11–16). In Luke he is Gabriel, and he communicates God's purpose, favor, and judgment.

Angels often appear as God's mouthpieces—as interpreters of dreams, as in Daniel 8–10; or as those who confirm the earlier words of Jesus, as in Luke 24:1–9. In Jesus' teaching, angels appear as members of the heavenly entourage (Luke 9:26; 12:8–9), they rejoice when humans turn to embrace God's purpose for themselves (Luke 15:10), and they act on behalf of a beggar so poor that he does not even receive proper burial (Luke 16:22).

Angels can be portrayed in a guardian role—over children (Matthew 18:10) and adults (Acts 5:19–20; 12:6–11, 15), even over churches (Revelation 2–3). In addition to serving as messengers of God (see Matthew 1–2; Luke 1–2; and Acts 10:1–6), angels are said to be active in judgment, both in the present (see Acts 12:20–23) and on the Last Day (see, for example, Matthew 16:27; 1 Thessalonians 4:16; Jude 14–15).

Angels are not, according to the teaching of the Bible, here to soothe, satisfy, and cuddle. Such angels might make us feel good, or at least better. But can they really address the problem of evil in our world? Can they join us as we join God in his redemptive project? Can they help us to look beyond ourselves to grapple with the impressive resources God has in bringing peace with justice? These are the roles given angels, according to Scripture.

Angels/Guardian Angels: For additional scriptures on this topic go to Judges 6:11–16.

21They put poison in my food
and gave me vinegar to drink.

22Let their own feasts cause their ruin;
let their feasts trap them and pay them back.
23Let their eyes be closed so they cannot see
and their backs be forever weak from troubles.
24Pour your anger out on them;
let your anger catch up with them.
25May their place be empty;
leave no one to live in their tents.
26They chase after those you have hurt,
and they talk about the pain of those you
have wounded.
27Charge them with crime after crime,
and do not let them have anything good.
28Wipe their names from the book of life,
and do not list them with those who do what
is right.

29I am sad and hurting.
God, save me and protect me.

30I will praise God in a song
and will honor him by giving thanks.
31That will please the LORD more than offering
him cattle,
more than sacrificing a bull with horns
and hoofs.
32Poor people will see this and be glad.
Be encouraged, you who worship God.
33The LORD listens to those in need
and does not look down on captives.

34Heaven and earth should praise him,
the seas and everything in them.
35God will save Jerusalem
and rebuild the cities of Judah.
Then people will live there and own the land.
36 The descendants of his servants will inherit
that land,
and those who love him will live there.

A Cry for God to Help Quickly

For the director of music. A psalm of David.
To help people remember.

70 God, come quickly and save me.
LORD, hurry to help me.
2Let those who are trying to kill me
be ashamed and disgraced.
Let those who want to hurt me
run away in disgrace.
3Let those who make fun of me
stop because of their shame.
4But let all those who worship you
rejoice and be glad.
Let those who love your salvation
always say, "Praise the greatness of God."
5I am poor and helpless;
God, hurry to me.
You help me and save me.
LORD, do not wait.

An Old Person's Prayer

71 In you, LORD, is my protection.
Never let me be ashamed.
2Because you do what is right, save and
rescue me;
listen to me and save me.
3Be my place of safety
where I can always come.
Give the command to save me,
because you are my rock and my strong,
walled city.
4My God, save me from the power of the wicked
and from the hold of evil and cruel people.
5LORD, you are my hope.
LORD, I have trusted you since I was young.
6I have depended on you since I was born;
you helped me even on the day of my birth.
I will always praise you.

7I am an example to many people,
because you are my strong protection.
8I am always praising you;
all day long I honor you.
9Do not reject me when I am old;
do not leave me when my strength is gone.
10My enemies make plans against me,
and they meet together to kill me.
11They say, "God has left him.
Go after him and take him,
because no one will save him."

12God, don't be far off.
My God, hurry to help me.
13Let those who accuse me
be ashamed and destroyed.

69:22–28 The psalmist has been wrongly treated by his enemies, and here he lets them feel the full force of his anger. He holds back no punches as he asks God to give them what they deserve. The psalms invite us to express our anger to God honestly. Anger is not always wrong. After all, God himself is angry toward those who oppress the helpless and subvert justice.

69:31 Sacrifices of cattle, or the bull, were the most expensive that could be made. Thus the poor are especially thankful that God honors prayer even more than such a sacrifice.

69:36 Complaint/Lament/Protest: Psalm 70

70:5 Complaint/Lament/Protest: Psalm 77

Let those who are trying to hurt me
be covered with shame and disgrace.
14But I will always have hope
and will praise you more and more.
15I will tell how you do what is right.
I will tell about your salvation all
day long,
even though it is more than I can tell.
16I will come and tell about your powerful
works, Lord GOD.
I will remind people that only you do
what is right.

17God, you have taught me since
I was young.
To this day I tell about the miracles you do.
18Even though I am old and gray,
do not leave me, God.
I will tell the children about your power;
I will tell those who live after me about
your might.

19God, your justice reaches to the skies.
You have done great things;
God, there is no one like you.
20You have given me many troubles
and bad times,
but you will give me life again.
When I am almost dead,
you will keep me alive.
21You will make me greater than ever,
and you will comfort me again.

22I will praise you with the harp.
I trust you, my God.
I will sing to you with the lyre,
Holy One of Israel.
23I will shout for joy when I sing praises to you.
You have saved me.
24I will tell about your justice all day long.
And those who want to hurt me
will be ashamed and disgraced.

A Prayer for the King

Of Solomon.

72 God, give the king your good judgment
and the king's son your goodness.
2Help him judge your people fairly
and decide what is right for the poor.
3Let there be peace on the mountains
and goodness on the hills for the people.
4Help him be fair to the poor
and save the needy
and punish those who hurt them.

5May they respect you as long as the sun shines
and as long as the moon glows.
6Let him be like rain on the grass,
like showers that water the earth.
7Let goodness be plentiful while he lives.
Let peace continue as long as there is a moon.

8Let his kingdom go from sea to sea,
and from the Euphrates River to the ends of
the earth.
9Let the people of the desert bow down to him,
and make his enemies lick the dust.
10Let the kings of Tarshish and the faraway lands
bring him gifts.
Let the kings of Sheba and Seba
bring their presents to him.
11Let all kings bow down to him
and all nations serve him.

12He will help the poor when they cry out
and will save the needy when no one else
will help.
13He will be kind to the weak and poor,
and he will save their lives.
14He will save them from cruel people who try
to hurt them,
because their lives are precious to him.

15Long live the king!
Let him receive gold from Sheba.
Let people always pray for him
and bless him all day long.
16Let the fields grow plenty of grain
and the hills be covered with crops.
Let the land be as fertile as Lebanon,
and let the cities grow like the grass in a field.
17Let the king be famous forever;
let him be remembered as long as the
sun shines.
Let the nations be blessed because of him,
and may they all bless him.

18Praise the LORD God, the God of Israel,
who alone does such miracles.
19Praise his glorious name forever.
Let his glory fill the whole world.
Amen and amen.

20This ends the prayers of David son of Jesse.

72:10 *Tarshish.* Tarshish is far away from Israel, thought to be located in what is today known as Spain.

Book 3

Should the Wicked Be Rich?

A psalm of Asaph.

73 God is truly good to Israel,
to those who have pure hearts.
2But I had almost stopped believing;
I had almost lost my faith
3because I was jealous of proud people.
I saw wicked people doing well.

4They are not suffering;
they are healthy and strong.
5They don't have troubles like the rest of us;
they don't have problems like other people.
6They wear pride like a necklace
and put on violence as their clothing.
7They are looking for profits
and do not control their selfish desires.
8They make fun of others and speak evil;
proudly they speak of hurting others.
9They brag to the sky.
They say that they own the earth.
10So their people turn to them
and give them whatever they want.
11They say, "How can God know?
What does God Most High know?"
12These people are wicked,
always at ease, and getting richer.
13So why have I kept my heart pure?
Why have I kept my hands from doing wrong?
14I have suffered all day long;
I have been punished every morning.

15God, if I had decided to talk like this,
I would have let your people down.
16I tried to understand all this,
but it was too hard for me to see
17until I went to the Temple of God.
Then I understood what will happen to them.
18You have put them in danger;
you cause them to be destroyed.
19They are destroyed in a moment;
they are swept away by terrors.
20It will be like waking from a dream.
Lord, when you rise up, they will disappear.

21When my heart was sad
and I was angry,
22I was senseless and stupid.
I acted like an animal toward you.

23But I am always with you;
you have held my hand.
24You guide me with your advice,
and later you will receive me in honor.
25I have no one in heaven but you;
I want nothing on earth besides you.
26My body and my mind may become weak,
but God is my strength.
He is mine forever.

27Those who are far from God will die;
you destroy those who are unfaithful.
28But I am close to God, and that is good.
The Lord GOD is my protection.
I will tell all that you have done.

A Nation in Trouble Prays

A maskil of Asaph.

74 God, why have you rejected us for so long?
Why are you angry with us, the sheep of
your pasture?
2Remember the people you bought
long ago.
You saved us, and we are your very own.
After all, you live on Mount Zion.∞
3Make your way through these old ruins;
the enemy wrecked everything in the
Temple.

4Those who were against you shouted in your
meeting place
and raised their flags there.
5They came with axes raised
as if to cut down a forest of trees.
6They smashed the carved panels
with their axes and hatchets.
7They burned your Temple to the ground;
they have made the place where you
live unclean.
8They thought, "We will completely
crush them!"
They burned every place where God was
worshiped in the land.
9We do not see any signs.
There are no more prophets,
and no one knows how long this will last.
10God, how much longer will the enemy make
fun of you?
Will they insult you forever?
11Why do you hold back your power?
Bring your power out in the open and
destroy them!

74:1 *sheep.* See 23:1.
∞**74:2 Memory:** Psalm 105:5

74:2 *Mount Zion.* Mount Zion was the location of the Temple in Israel, the place where God's presence dwelt.

12God, you have been our king for a long time.
You bring salvation to the earth.⚭
13You split open the sea by your power
and broke the heads of the sea monster.
14You smashed the heads of the
monster Leviathan
and gave him to the desert creatures as food.
15You opened up the springs and streams
and made the flowing rivers run dry.
16Both the day and the night are yours;
you made the sun and the moon.
17You set all the limits on the earth;
you created summer and winter.

18LORD, remember how the enemy insulted you.
Remember how those foolish people made
fun of you.
19Do not give us, your doves, to those
wild animals.
Never forget your poor people.
20Remember the agreement you made with us,
because violence fills every dark corner of
this land.
21Do not let your suffering people be disgraced.
Let the poor and helpless praise you.

22God, arise and defend yourself.
Remember the insults that come from those
foolish people all day long.
23Don't forget what your enemies said;
don't forget their roar as they rise against
you always.

God the Judge

For the director of music. To the tune of "Do Not Destroy."
A psalm of Asaph. A song.

75 God, we thank you;
we thank you because you are near.
We tell about the miracles you do.

2You say, "I set the time for trial,
and I will judge fairly.
3The earth with all its people may shake,
but I am the one who holds
it steady. *Selah*
4I say to those who are proud, 'Don't brag,'
and to the wicked, 'Don't show your power.
5Don't try to use your power against heaven.
Don't be stubborn.'"

6No one from the east or the west
or the desert can judge you.
7God is the judge;
he judges one person as guilty and another
as innocent.
8The LORD holds a cup of anger in his hand;
it is full of wine mixed with spices.
He pours it out even to the last drop,
and the wicked drink it all.⚭

9I will tell about this forever;
I will sing praise to the God of Jacob.
10He will take all power away from the wicked,
but the power of good people will grow.

The God Who Always Wins

For the director of music. With stringed instruments.
A psalm of Asaph. A song.

76 People in Judah know God;
his fame is great in Israel.
2His Tent is in Jerusalem;
his home is on Mount Zion.
3There God broke the flaming arrows,
the shields, the swords, and the
weapons of war. *Selah*

4God, how wonderful you are!
You are more splendid than the hills full
of animals.
5The brave soldiers were stripped
as they lay asleep in death.
Not one warrior
had the strength to stop it.
6God of Jacob, when you spoke strongly,
horses and riders fell dead.
7You are feared;
no one can stand against you when you
are angry.
8From heaven you gave the decision,
and the earth was afraid and silent.

⚭**74:12 Earth:** Psalm 104:5

74:12–15 Many ancient peoples believed deep waters were the dwelling place of monsters and evil spirits. Some pagan myths pictured God creating order out of chaos by conquering a sea monster. The writer of Psalm 74 alludes to such a story, as do other biblical writers (Job 41; Isaiah 27:1; 51:9–10). In the New Testament, deep waters are sometimes associated with demons and evil. For example, in Revelation 13 when Satan calls the beast who is against God to lead the people of the earth astray, John pictures the beast "coming up out of the sea" (verse 1). But the main point the biblical writers make is this: God has control over every form of evil as surely as he controls every form of water.

74:13 *sea.* The sea was often personified and represented the forces of chaos and disorder that God fought against to establish his creation order.

74:14 *Leviathan.* Leviathan is a reference to a sea monster that represents chaos which God fights against to establish order. Leviathan is known from ancient writings from Canaan.

⚭**75:8 Anger:** Psalm 78:49

76:2 *Mount Zion.* Mount Zion was the location of the Temple in Jerusalem.

9God, you stood up to judge
and to save the needy people
of the earth. *Selah*
10People praise you for your anger against evil.
Those who live through your anger are
stopped from doing more evil.⚭

11Make and keep your promises to the LORD
your God.
From all around, gifts should come to the
God we worship.
12God breaks the spirits of great leaders;
the kings on earth fear him.

Remembering God's Help

For the director of music. For Jeduthun. A psalm of Asaph.

77 I cry out to God;
I call to God, and he will hear me.
2I look for the Lord on the day of trouble.
All night long I reach out my hands,
but I cannot be comforted.⚭
3When I remember God, I become upset;
when I think, I become afraid. *Selah*

4You keep my eyes from closing.
I am too upset to say anything.
5I keep thinking about the old days,
the years of long ago.
6At night I remember my songs.
I think and I ask myself:
7"Will the Lord reject us forever?
Will he never be kind to us again?
8Is his love gone forever?
Has he stopped speaking for all time?
9Has God forgotten mercy?
Is he too angry to pity us?" *Selah*
10Then I say "This is what makes me sad:
For years the power of God Most High was
with us."

11I remember what the LORD did;
I remember the miracles you did long ago.
12I think about all the things you did
and consider your deeds.

13God, your ways are holy.
No god is as great as our God.
14You are the God who does miracles;
you have shown people your power.
15By your power you have saved your people,
the descendants of Jacob and
Joseph. *Selah*

16God, the waters saw you;
they saw you and became afraid;
the deep waters shook with fear.
17The clouds poured down their rain.
The sky thundered.
Your lightning flashed back and forth
like arrows.
18Your thunder sounded in the whirlwind.
Lightning lit up the world.
The earth trembled and shook.
19You made a way through the sea
and paths through the deep waters,
but your footprints were not seen.⚭
20You led your people like a flock
by using Moses and Aaron.⚭

God Saved Israel from Egypt

A maskil of Asaph.

78 My people, listen to my teaching;
listen to what I say.
2I will speak using stories;
I will tell secret things from long ago.
3We have heard them and known them
by what our ancestors have told us.⚭
4We will not keep them from our children;
we will tell those who come later
about the praises of the LORD.
We will tell about his power
and the miracles he has done.⚭

5The LORD made an agreement with Jacob
and gave the teachings to Israel,
which he commanded our ancestors
to teach to their children.
6Then their children would know them,
even their children not yet born.
And they would tell their children.
7So they would all trust God
and would not forget what he had done
but would obey his commands.

⚭**76:10 Praise:** Psalm 92
77 This psalm is an excellent example of the type of boldness God invites us to in prayer. The psalmist does not hold anything back. He tells God his deepest needs. He also does not fall short of charging God with being the source of his confusion. At the end, as he remembers God's great acts of deliverance in the past, he turns to God in trust.
⚭**77:2 Comfort:** Psalm 86:17
77:16 *waters.* The waters of the Red Sea are here personified and seen as an enemy of God. Once again the waters are seen as symbolic of the forces of chaos that stand against God. God defeats them as he saves the people of Israel.
⚭**77:19 Road/Way:** Proverbs 4:11
⚭**77:20 Complaint/Lament/Protest:** Psalm 83
⚭**77:20 Meditation:** Psalm 143:5
⚭**77:20 Exodus/New Exodus:** Hosea 2:14–15
⚭**78:3 Prophetic Symbolism:** Jeremiah 1:11–16
⚭**78:4 Praise:** Psalm 92

8They would not be like their ancestors
who were stubborn and disobedient.
Their hearts were not loyal to God,
and they were not true to him.

9The men of Ephraim had bows for weapons,
but they ran away on the day of battle.
10They didn't keep their agreement with God
and refused to live by his teachings.
11They forgot what he had done
and the miracles he had shown them.
12He did miracles while their ancestors watched,
in the fields of Zoan in Egypt.
13He divided the Red Sea and led them through.
He made the water stand up like a wall.
14He led them with a cloud by day
and by the light of a fire by night.
15He split the rocks in the desert
and gave them more than enough water, as if
from the deep ocean.
16He brought streams out of the rock
and caused water to flow down like rivers.

17But the people continued to sin against him;
in the desert they turned against God
Most High.
18They decided to test God
by asking for the food they wanted.
19Then they spoke against God,
saying, "Can God prepare food in the desert?
20When he hit the rock, water poured out
and rivers flowed down.
But can he give us bread also?
Will he provide his people with meat?"
21When the LORD heard them, he was very angry.
His anger was like fire to the people of Jacob;
his anger grew against the people of Israel.
22They had not believed God
and had not trusted him to save them.
23But he gave a command to the clouds above
and opened the doors of heaven.
24He rained manna down on them to eat;
he gave them grain from heaven.
25So they ate the bread of angels.
He sent them all the food they could eat.
26He sent the east wind from heaven
and led the south wind by his power.
27He rained meat on them like dust.
The birds were as many as the sand of the sea.
28He made the birds fall inside the camp,
all around the tents.
29So the people ate and became very full.
God had given them what they wanted.
30While they were still eating,
and while the food was still in their mouths,
31God became angry with them.
He killed some of the healthiest of them;
he struck down the best young men of Israel.

32But they kept on sinning;
they did not believe even with the miracles.
33So he ended their days without meaning
and their years in terror.
34Anytime he killed them, they would look to
him for help;
they would come back to God and follow him.
35They would remember that God was their Rock,
that God Most High had saved them.
36But their words were false,
and their tongues lied to him.
37Their hearts were not really loyal to God;
they did not keep his agreement.
38Still God was merciful.
He forgave their sins
and did not destroy them.
Many times he held back his anger
and did not stir up all his anger.
39He remembered that they were only human,
like a wind that blows and does not
come back.

40They turned against God so often
in the desert
and grieved him there.
41Again and again they tested God
and brought pain to the Holy One of Israel.
42They did not remember his power
or the time he saved them from the enemy.
43They forgot the signs he did in Egypt
and his wonders in the fields of Zoan.
44He turned their rivers to blood
so no one could drink the water.
45He sent flies that bit the people.
He sent frogs that destroyed them.
46He gave their crops to grasshoppers
and what they worked for to locusts.
47He destroyed their vines with hail
and their sycamore trees with sleet.
48He killed their animals with hail
and their cattle with lightning.
49He showed them his hot anger.
He sent his strong anger against them,
his destroying angels.⚭
50He found a way to show his anger.
He did not keep them from dying
but let them die by a terrible disease.

⚭**78:49 Anger:** Psalm 109:9–12

[51]God killed all the firstborn sons in Egypt,
the oldest son of each family of Ham.
[52]But God led his people out like sheep
and he guided them like a flock through
the desert.
[53]He led them to safety so they had nothing
to fear,
but their enemies drowned in the sea.
[54]So God brought them to his holy land,
to the mountain country he took with his
own power.
[55]He forced out the other nations,
and he had his people inherit the land.
He let the tribes of Israel settle there in tents.

[56]But they tested God
and turned against God Most High;
they did not keep his rules.
[57]They turned away and were disloyal just like
their ancestors.
They were like a crooked bow that does not
shoot straight.
[58]They made God angry by building places to
worship gods;
they made him jealous with their idols.⚭
[59]When God heard them, he became very angry
and rejected the people of Israel completely.
[60]He left his dwelling at Shiloh,
the Tent where he lived among the people.
[61]He let the Ark, his power, be captured;
he let the Ark, his glory, be taken by enemies.
[62]He let his people be killed;
he was very angry with his children.
[63]The young men died by fire,
and the young women had no one to marry.
[64]Their priests fell by the sword,
but their widows were not allowed to cry.

[65]Then the Lord got up as if he had been asleep;
he awoke like a man who had been drunk
with wine.
[66]He struck down his enemies
and disgraced them forever.
[67]But God rejected the family of Joseph;
he did not choose the tribe of Ephraim.
[68]Instead, he chose the tribe of Judah
and Mount Zion, which he loves.
[69]And he built his Temple high like
the mountains.
Like the earth, he built it to last forever.
[70]He chose David to be his servant
and took him from the sheep pens.⚭
[71]He brought him from tending the sheep
so he could lead the flock, the people
of Jacob,
his own people, the people of Israel.
[72]And David led them with an innocent heart
and guided them with skillful hands.

The Nation Cries for Jerusalem

A psalm of Asaph.

79 God, nations have come against your
chosen people.
They have ruined your holy Temple.
They have turned Jerusalem into ruins.
[2]They have given the bodies of your servants as
food to the wild birds.
They have given the bodies of those who
worship you to the wild animals.
[3]They have spilled blood like water all
around Jerusalem.
No one was left to bury the dead.
[4]We are a joke to the other nations;
they laugh and make fun of us.

[5]LORD, how long will this last?
Will you be angry forever?
How long will your jealousy burn like a fire?⚭
[6]Be angry with the nations that do not know you
and with the kingdoms that do not honor you.
[7]They have gobbled up the people of Jacob
and destroyed their land.
[8]Don't punish us for our past sins.
Show your mercy to us soon,
because we are helpless!
[9]God our Savior, help us
so people will praise you.
Save us and forgive our sins
so people will honor you.

78:51 *Ham.* The people in Egypt were descendants of Ham, one of Noah's sons. See Genesis 10:6.
78:52 *sheep.* See Psalm 23:1.
⚭**78:58 Jealousy:** Psalm 79:5
78:60 *Shiloh.* Right after the conquest under Joshua, God directed them to set up the Meeting Tent at Shiloh, which is about twenty miles north of Jerusalem, in the tribe of Ephraim (Joshua 18:1).
78:61 Although the word "Ark" is not in the original Hebrew, it is most certainly alluded to by the phrase, "his power" (see Psalm 132:8 where the word "Ark" is present) and the historical context (1 Samuel 4). Although there is only one clear reference to the Ark in the Psalms (132:8), there may be other veiled references in the form of similar expressions (e.g. "your glory," Psalm 26:8; 1 Samuel 4:22; "the one who sits on his throne between the gold creatures with wings," Psalms 80:1; 99:1). This suggests the importance of the Ark and its significance as God's presence in the worship of ancient Israel.
78:65 A provocative image to use of God. The idea is that someone who is asleep from the effects of wine is in a deep sleep and aroused only with difficulty.
78:67 God rejected Shiloh as the place where his Temple would be and chose Jerusalem instead. Also he ultimately rejected Saul's kingship and chose David, who was of the tribe of Judah.
⚭**78:70 David:** Psalm 132:10–18
⚭**79:5 Jealousy:** Proverbs 6:34

10Why should the nations say,
"Where is their God?"
Tell the other nations in our presence
that you punish those who kill your servants.
11Hear the moans of the prisoners.
Use your great power
to save those sentenced to die.

12Repay those around us seven times over
for their insults to you, Lord.
13We are your people, the sheep of your flock.
We will thank you always;
forever and ever we will praise you.

A Prayer to Bring Israel Back

For the director of music. To the tune of "Lilies of the Agreement." A psalm of Asaph.

80 Shepherd of Israel, listen to us.
You lead the people of Joseph like a flock.
You sit on your throne between the gold
creatures with wings.
Show your greatness 2to the people of
Ephraim, Benjamin, and Manasseh.
Use your strength,
and come to save us.

3God, take us back.
Show us your kindness so we can be saved.

4LORD God All-Powerful,
how long will you be angry
at the prayers of your people?
5You have fed your people with tears;
you have made them drink many tears.
6You made those around us fight over us,
and our enemies make fun of us.

7God All-Powerful, take us back.
Show us your kindness so we can be saved.

8You brought us out of Egypt as if we were a vine.
You forced out other nations and planted us in
the land.
9You cleared the ground for us.
Like a vine, we took root and filled the land.
10We covered the mountains with our shade.
We had limbs like the mighty cedar tree.
11Our branches reached the Mediterranean Sea,
and our shoots went to the Euphrates River.
12So why did you pull down our walls?
Now everyone who passes by steals from us.
13Like wild pigs they walk over us;
like wild animals they feed on us.

14God All-Powerful, come back.
Look down from heaven and see.
Take care of us, your vine.
15 You planted this shoot with your own hands
and strengthened this child.
16Now it is cut down and burned with fire;
you destroyed us by your angry looks.
17With your hand,
strengthen the one you have chosen
for yourself.
18Then we will not turn away from you.
Give us life again, and we will call to you
for help.

19LORD God All-Powerful, take us back.
Show us your kindness so we can be saved.

A Song for a Holiday

For the director of music. By the gittith. A psalm of Asaph.

81 Sing for joy to God, our strength;
shout out loud to the God of Jacob.
2Begin the music. Play the tambourines.
Play pleasant music on the harps and lyres.
3Blow the trumpet at the time of the New Moon,
when the moon is full, when our
feast begins.
4This is the law for Israel;
it is the command of the God of Jacob.
5He gave this rule to the people of Joseph
when they went out of the land of Egypt.

I heard a language I did not know, saying:
6"I took the load off their shoulders;
I let them put down their baskets.
7When you were in trouble, you called, and I
saved you.
I answered you with thunder.
I tested you at the waters of Meribah. *Selah*
8My people, listen. I am warning you.
Israel, please listen to me!
9You must not have foreign gods;
you must not worship any false god.
10I, the LORD, am your God,
who brought you out of Egypt.
Open your mouth and I will feed you.

11"But my people did not listen to me;
Israel did not want me.

80:1 *Shepherd.* See Psalm 23:1.
80:11 The geographical area here is similar to the extent of the land promised to Abram (Genesis 15:18–20).
81:3 *time of the New Moon.* For the New Moon celebration, consult 1 Samuel 20:5, 18; 2 Kings 4:23; Isaiah 66:23.

Day of the Lord

Joel 2:31

What is the "day of the Lord?" Is it something that has happened or something that will happen? Is it to be looked forward to or avoided?

The Bible shows us in various places that God's patience does not last forever. Eventually, God will judge and punish those who deserve it. A common phrase used throughout the Bible to express this is "day of the LORD." It refers to a future time, either very soon to come or far off (the "last day"), when God's justice will be satisfied. The phrase is also often found in a shorter form, "on that day." A closely related term is "at that time."

In the Old Testament, the "day of the LORD" is often directed toward Israel's enemies. They were to be punished for the way they treated the Israelites. Two examples are the Israelites' archenemies, the Egyptians (Isaiah 19:16; Jeremiah 46:10; Ezekiel 30:3) and the Babylonians (Isaiah 13:6). The idea here is probably the punishment of those nations sometime in the prophet's near future, rather than some "last future" judgment, although often it is difficult to distinguish between the two. But the main point is still clear: the enemies of God's people will not escape punishment.

Zechariah 14 speaks of the "LORD's day of judging" (verse 1) when he will "go to war" against all of Israel's enemies (verse 3). This is a particularly important passage because it has a certain "last day" feel to it (verse 9 speaks of the Lord becoming the only "king over the whole world"). This is very relevant to the New Testament passages discussed below.

The Old Testament also teaches that the "day of the LORD" was not only against other nations, but against disobedient Israel as well. God is patient and just; he punishes all who deserve it. Amos 5:18 says, "Why do you want *that day* to come? It will bring darkness for you, not light." There were those in Israel who were unrepentant and arrogantly thought that God's coming wrath would only be against "someone else." Even today, some people suppress the conviction of the Gospel and avoid any commitment to God. They say that we can't know for certain now, but "we'll all find out in the end." This is certainly true, but, as Amos wrote, this is not necessarily something to look forward to. The answer will certainly come, but there are those who may not find the answer to be what they expected. Similar to this is Zephaniah 1. The "LORD's day of judging" (verse 14) will "sweep away everything from the earth" (verse 2) and bring an end to "everyone on earth" (verse 18). This includes Judah (verses 4–13).

In the Old Testament, God's wrath against Israel on "that day" often took the form of some natural disaster. One example is the locust plague that destroyed the vegetation in Joel 1 (especially verse 15, "The LORD's day of judging is near"). Another example is Amos 5:18 (and 20) mentioned above. At other times, the punishment was in the form of an oppressive nation (for example, the Assyrians in Isaiah 5:26–30).

There are certain Old Testament passages that seem to present the "day of the LORD" as an event of universal and lasting consequence. Two of these passages have already been mentioned: Zechariah 14 and Zephaniah 1. Another passage is Malachi 4:1–5. Here we read that "there is a day coming" (verse 1), "that great and terrifying day of the LORD's judging" (verse 5). But before that day, the Lord will send "Elijah the prophet" (verse 5). Who was this Elijah? According to the New Testament, it was John the Baptist (Matthew 17:9–13; Mark 9:9–13; Luke 1:17). John was an Elijah-like prophet who warned the people of coming judgment (Luke 3:7–9). And that coming judgment will be executed by the coming Christ of whom John spoke (Luke 3:16–18).

The "day of the LORD" is very much a New Testament idea. It continues the notion of sweeping, universal wrath and judgment found in various Old Testament passages. It refers consistently to the future return of Christ to judge the world. It is also related to similar terms, such as the "coming of Christ" (Philippians *1:10; 2:16*), "the day" (for example, 1 Thessalonians 5:2), and "the day" (Romans 2:16), and "that day" (1 Corinthians 3:13).

God's future judgment in Christ will be terrible, final, and permanent. Yet for those who are in Christ, the "day of the LORD" will bring about the beginning of eternity. Although it will bring the destruction of the "sinful self" (perhaps referring to the body), our "spirit will be saved on the day of the LORD" (1 Corinthians 5:5). As such, the "day of the LORD comes again" is something that we "wait for and look forward to" (2 Peter 3:12).

Day of the Lord: For additional scriptures on this topic go to Joel 1:15.

Astrology

ZEPHANIAH 1

What is astrology? How does it work? What does the Bible say about it?

Astrology today is big business. Millions of people consult their horoscopes every day in the newspaper, while business tycoons sell stocks on the basis of advice from astrologers. Even leading world politicians have been known to make decisions that way.

In Western history, the practice of astrology can be traced through the Renaissance period, back into ancient Greece and Rome, and before that into Egypt and Babylonia. Elsewhere, Chinese and Indian cultures both have long astrological traditions, and the same phenomenon can also be found in some sections of Islam.

Astrology takes many forms. Modern Western astrology is generally based on twelve "signs of the zodiac" (though some identify thirteen). These are identified as twelve constellations, or groups of stars, each corresponding to particular dates within the year, and with names drawn from ancient mythology: Aries (the Ram), Taurus (the Bull), Gemini (the Twins), Cancer (the Crab), Leo (the Lion), Virgo (the Virgin), Libra (the Scales), Scorpio (the Scorpion), Sagittarius (the Archer), Capricorn (the Goat), Aquarius (the Waterbearer), and Pisces (the Fish). These constellations are grouped into four triangles identified with fire, air, earth, and water, while the entire zodiac is divided into (usually) twelve "houses" corresponding to different aspects of human experience: life, wealth, brothers and sisters, parents, sons, health, marriage, death, travels, honors, friends, and enemies.

It is often claimed that astrology has a modern scientific basis, but its foundational assumptions are essentially identical with the flat-earth cosmology of ancient Greece. Pluto and Neptune, for instance, do not feature in astrological calculations, because they were not discovered until after the rules of astrology were first set out. There are many complex and esoteric calculations involved in interpreting the movements of the stars and planets, and these, too, are drawn from ancient (mostly Greek) mythology and science.

Ultimately, all astrology is based on reverence for the stars and the planets, and the belief that they control or determine the course of human life. Even the details of everyday life are somehow preprogrammed through the power of these celestial bodies. Since there is nothing much anyone can do to alter things, astrologers aim to help their clients be aware of what is coming (as determined by astral bodies), in order to help them make the best of their situation. Magic would typically claim to change the way things are or seem to be, whereas astrology starts from the belief that nothing can be fundamentally changed. Consequently, it presents an essentially pessimistic outlook, tempered only by the claim that if people can know what is to come they may be better equipped to handle it. It is not hard to see why astrology has suddenly become very popular in the West, with a loss of confidence in the scientific materialist world view, and the widespread feeling that humankind has somehow lost control of what is going on in the world.

This is all far removed from the teaching of the Bible, where the world and its people are not in the control of impersonal cosmic forces, but in the hands of a loving and generous God who can be known and enjoyed in a personal relationship. The very first chapter of Genesis emphasizes that the stars and planets are to be understood as part of the creation of God. They are certainly among the most striking parts of God's creation, and many passages celebrate their beauty and attractiveness (for example, Genesis 15:5; 1 Corinthians 15:41; 2 Peter 1:19). They can even be used as symbols of the Messiah (Numbers 24:17; Revelation 22:16), while the way they dance around in the sky is an expression of the way the whole universe joins in the praise of God (Job 38:7; Psalm 148:3).

But the stars and planets are not themselves divine. On the contrary, they are part of God's own creation (Genesis 1:16; Nehemiah 9:6; Job 9:7, 9:9, 38:32; Psalms 8:3, 33:6, 136:9, 147:4; Isaiah 40:26, 45:12; Jeremiah 31:35; Amos 5:8). They can occasionally be used by God to impinge on human life, as when the sun and moon stood still at Joshua's command (Joshua 10:12–13), or "the stars fought from heaven" to support Deborah against the Canaanites (Judges 5:20). But they have no independent status, and both the worship of stars and the use of them to try and predict the future is specifically forbidden (Leviticus 19:26; Deuteronomy 17:2, 3).

Astrology: For additional scriptures on this topic go to Leviticus 19:26.

[12]So I let them go their stubborn way
and follow their own advice.
[13]I wish my people would listen to me;
I wish Israel would live my way.
[14]Then I would quickly defeat their enemies
and turn my hand against their foes.
[15]Those who hate the LORD would bow before him.
Their punishment would continue forever.
[16]But I would give you the finest wheat
and fill you with honey from the rocks."

A Cry for Justice

A psalm of Asaph.

82 God is in charge of the great meeting;
he judges among the "gods."
[2]He says, "How long will you defend evil people?
How long will you show greater kindness to
the wicked? *Selah*
[3]Defend the weak and the orphans;
defend the rights of the poor and suffering.
[4]Save the weak and helpless;
free them from the power of the wicked.

[5]"You know nothing. You don't understand.
You walk in the dark,
while the world is falling apart.
[6]I said, 'You are "gods."
You are all sons of God Most High.'
[7]But you will die like any other person;
you will fall like all the leaders."

[8]God, come and judge the earth,
because you own all the nations.

A Prayer Against the Enemies

A song. A psalm of Asaph.

83 God, do not keep quiet;
God, do not be silent or still.
[2]Your enemies are making noises;
those who hate you are getting ready to attack.
[3]They are making secret plans against
your people;
they plot against those you love.
[4]They say, "Come, let's destroy them as
a nation.
Then no one will ever remember the
name 'Israel.'"
[5]They are united in their plan.
These have made an agreement against you:
[6]the families of Edom and the Ishmaelites,
Moab and the Hagrites,
[7]the people of Byblos, Ammon, Amalek,
Philistia, and Tyre.
[8]Even Assyria has joined them
to help Ammon and Moab, the descendants
of Lot. *Selah*

[9]God, do to them what you did to Midian,
what you did to Sisera and Jabin at the
Kishon River.
[10]They died at Endor,
and their bodies rotted on the ground.
[11]Do to their important leaders what you did to
Oreb and Zeeb.
Do to their princes what you did to Zebah
and Zalmunna.
[12]They said, "Let's take for ourselves
the pasturelands that belong to God."
[13]My God, make them like tumbleweed,
like chaff blown away by the wind.
[14]Be like a fire that burns a forest
or like flames that blaze through the hills.
[15]Chase them with your storm,
and frighten them with your wind.
[16]Cover them with shame.
Then people will look for you, LORD.
[17]Make them afraid and ashamed forever.
Disgrace them and destroy them.
[18]Then they will know that you are the LORD,
that only you are God Most High over all
the earth.∞

Wishing to Be in the Temple

For the director of music. On the gittith.
A psalm of the sons of Korah.

84 LORD All-Powerful,
how lovely is your Temple!
[2]I want more than anything
to be in the courtyards of the LORD's Temple.
My whole being wants
to be with the living God.
[3]The sparrows have found a home,
and the swallows have nests.
They raise their young near your altars,
LORD All-Powerful, my King and my God.

82:1 *"gods."* From the following context it seems clear that these "gods" are humans who just think themselves powerful enough to be gods. They are human rulers and judges.

83 In a number of psalms the singer turns to God and honestly complains about the troubles in his life. Here the psalmist speaks for all of Israel as they are threatened with destruction by a number of nations. Through psalms like this one, God encourages our honest prayers that protest our present situations and ask for his help.

∞**83:18 Complaint/Lament/Protest:** Jeremiah 12:1–4

83:18 *God Most High.* God Most High is a rare title for the Lord. Its special significance is that it is often used by the people of Canaan to refer to their god Baal in their own literature. The psalmist is saying that it is only the Lord who is God Most High, not Baal.

4Happy are the people who live at your Temple;
they are always praising you. *Selah*

5Happy are those whose strength comes from you,
who want to travel to Jerusalem.
6As they pass through the Valley of Baca,
they make it like a spring.
The autumn rains fill it with pools of water.
7The people get stronger as they go,
and everyone meets with God in Jerusalem.

8LORD God All-Powerful, hear my prayer;
God of Jacob, listen to me. *Selah*
9God, look at our shield;
be kind to your appointed king.

10One day in the courtyards of your Temple
is better
than a thousand days anywhere else.
I would rather be a doorkeeper in the Temple
of my God
than live in the homes of the wicked.
11The LORD God is like a sun and shield;
the LORD gives us kindness and honor.
He does not hold back anything good
from those whose lives are innocent.
12LORD All-Powerful,
happy are the people who trust you!⚭

A Prayer for the Nation

For the director of music. A psalm of the sons of Korah.

85 LORD, you have been kind to your land;
you brought back the people of Jacob.
2You forgave the guilt of the people
and covered all their sins. *Selah*
3You stopped all your anger;
you turned back from your strong anger.

4God our Savior, bring us back again.
Stop being angry with us.
5Will you be angry with us forever?
Will you stay angry from now on?
6Won't you give us life again?
Your people would rejoice in you.
7LORD, show us your love,
and save us.

8I will listen to God the LORD.
He has ordered peace for those who
worship him.
Don't let them go back to foolishness.
9God will soon save those who respect him,
and his glory will be seen in our land.
10Love and truth belong to God's people;
goodness and peace will be theirs.
11On earth people will be loyal to God,
and God's goodness will shine down
from heaven.
12The LORD will give his goodness,
and the land will give its crops.⚭
13Goodness will go before God
and prepare the way for him.

A Cry for Help

A prayer of David.

86 LORD, listen to me and answer me.
I am poor and helpless.
2Protect me, because I worship you.
My God, save me, your servant who trusts
in you.
3Lord, have mercy on me,
because I have called to you all day.
4Give happiness to me, your servant,
because I give my life to you, Lord.
5Lord, you are kind and forgiving
and have great love for those who
call to you.
6LORD, hear my prayer,
and listen when I ask for mercy.
7I call to you in times of trouble,
because you will answer me.

8Lord, there is no god like you
and no works like yours.
9Lord, all the nations you have made
will come and worship you.
They will honor you.
10You are great and you do miracles.
Only you are God.
11LORD, teach me what you want me to do,
and I will live by your truth.
Teach me to respect you completely.
12Lord, my God, I will praise you with all my heart,
and I will honor your name forever.
13You have great love for me.
You have saved me from death.

14God, proud men are attacking me;
a gang of cruel men is trying to kill me.
They do not respect you.

84:5 *to travel to Jerusalem.* This reference to traveling to Jerusalem is in association with the holy feasts, like Passover, that took place every year in Jerusalem. Faithful people of Israel would have to make the trip to participate.

84:7 *Jerusalem.* Jerusalem was the city where Mount Zion, the mountain of the Temple, was located.

⚭84:12 Presence of God: Psalm 139

⚭85:12 Beatitudes: Psalm 106:3

[15]But Lord, you are a God who shows mercy and
is kind.
You don't become angry quickly.
You have great love and faithfulness.
[16]Turn to me and have mercy.
Give me, your servant, strength.
Save me, the son of your female servant.
[17]Show me a sign of your goodness.
When my enemies look, they
will be ashamed.
You, LORD, have helped me and
comforted me.

God Loves Jerusalem

A song. A psalm of the sons of Korah.

87 The LORD built Jerusalem on the holy
mountain.
2 He loves its gates more than any other
place in Israel.
[3]City of God,
wonderful things are said about you. *Selah*
[4]God says, "I will put Egypt and Babylonia
on the list of nations that know me.
People from Philistia, Tyre, and Cush
will be born there."

[5]They will say about Jerusalem,
"This one and that one were born there.
God Most High will strengthen her."
[6]The LORD will keep a list of the nations.
He will note, "This person was
born there." *Selah*

[7]They will dance and sing,
"All good things come from Jerusalem."

A Sad Complaint

A song. A psalm of the sons of Korah. For the director of music. By the mahalath leannoth. A maskil of Heman the Ezrahite.

88 LORD, you are the God who saves me.
I cry out to you day and night.
[2]Receive my prayer,
and listen to my cry.

[3]My life is full of troubles,
and I am nearly dead.
[4]They think I am on the way to my grave.
I am like a man with no strength.
[5]I have been left as dead,
like a body lying in a grave
whom you don't remember anymore,
cut off from your care.
[6]You have brought me close to death;
I am almost in the dark place of the dead.
[7]You have been very angry with me;
all your waves crush me. *Selah*
[8]You have taken my friends away from me
and have made them hate me.
I am trapped and cannot escape.
9 My eyes are weak from crying.
LORD, I have prayed to you every day;
I have lifted my hands in prayer to you.

[10]Do you show your miracles for the dead?
Do their spirits rise up and
praise you? *Selah*

[11]Will your love be told in the grave?
Will your loyalty be told in the place of death?
[12]Will your miracles be known in the dark grave?
Will your goodness be known in the land
of forgetfulness?

[13]But, LORD, I have called out to you for help;
every morning I pray to you.
[14]LORD, why do you reject me?
Why do you hide from me?
[15]I have been weak and dying since
I was young.
I suffer from your terrors, and I am helpless.
[16]You have been angry with me,
and your terrors have destroyed me.
[17]They surround me daily like a flood;
they are all around me.
[18]You have taken away my loved ones and friends.
Darkness is my only friend.

A Song About God's Loyalty

A maskil of Ethan the Ezrahite.

89 I will always sing about the LORD's love;
I will tell of his loyalty from now on.
[2]I will say, "Your love continues forever;
your loyalty goes on and on like the sky."
[3]You said, "I made an agreement with the man
of my choice;
I made a promise to my servant David.
[4]I told him, 'I will make your family
continue forever.
Your kingdom will go on and on.'" *Selah*

86:17 Comfort: Psalm 119:50–52

87:5 Not that they are literally born in Jerusalem, but they are spiritually born in that city where God's presence dwells.

88:17 *like a flood.* The waters symbolize the forces of chaos, the troubles that plague the psalmist.

88:18 Depression: Proverbs 13:12

5LORD, the heavens praise you for your miracles
and for your loyalty in the meeting of your
holy ones.
6Who in heaven is equal to the LORD?
None of the angels is like the LORD.
7When the holy ones meet, it is God they fear.
He is more frightening than all who surround
him.
8LORD GOD All-Powerful, who is like you?
LORD, you are powerful and completely
trustworthy.
9You rule the mighty sea
and calm the stormy waves.
10You crushed the sea monster Rahab;
by your power you scattered your enemies.

11The skies and the earth belong to you.
You made the world and everything in it.
12You created the north and the south.
Mount Tabor and Mount Hermon sing for joy
at your name.
13Your arm has great power.
Your hand is strong; your right hand is lifted up.
14Your kingdom is built on what is right and fair.
Love and truth are in all you do.

15Happy are the people who know how to
praise you.
LORD, let them live in the light of your presence.
16In your name they rejoice
and continually praise your goodness.
17You are their glorious strength,
and in your kindness you honor our king.
18Our king, our shield, belongs to the LORD,
to the Holy One of Israel.

19Once, in a vision, you spoke
to those who worship you.
You said, "I have given strength to a warrior;
I have raised up a young man from my people.
20I have found my servant David;
I appointed him by pouring holy oil on him.
21I will steady him with my hand
and strengthen him with my arm.
22No enemy will make him give forced payments,
and wicked people will not defeat him.
23I will crush his enemies in front of him;
I will defeat those who hate him.
24My loyalty and love will be with him.
Through me he will be strong.
25I will give him power over the sea
and control over the rivers.
26He will say to me, 'You are my father,
my God, the Rock, my Savior.'
27I will make him my firstborn son,
the greatest king on earth.
28My love will watch over him forever,
and my agreement with him will never end.
29I will make his family continue,
and his kingdom will last as long as the skies.

30"If his descendants reject my teachings
and do not follow my laws,
31if they ignore my demands
and disobey my commands,
32then I will punish their sins with a rod
and their wrongs with a whip.
33But I will not hold back my love from David,
nor will I stop being loyal.
34I will not break my agreement
nor change what I have said.
35I have promised by my holiness,
I will not lie to David.
36His family will go on forever.
His kingdom will last before me like the sun.
37It will continue forever, like the moon,
like a dependable witness in
the sky."⚭ *Selah*

38But now you have refused and rejected your
appointed king.
You have been angry with him.
39You have abandoned the agreement with
your servant
and thrown his crown to the ground.
40You have torn down all his city walls;
you have turned his strong cities into ruins.
41Everyone who passes by steals from him.
His neighbors insult him.
42You have given strength to his enemies
and have made them all happy.
43You have made his sword useless;
you did not help him stand in battle.
44You have kept him from winning
and have thrown his throne to the ground.
45You have cut his life short
and covered him with shame. *Selah*

46LORD, how long will this go on?
Will you ignore us forever?
How long will your anger burn like a fire?
47Remember how short my life is.
Why did you create us? For nothing?
48What person alive will not die?
Who can escape the grave? *Selah*

89:10 *Rahab.* Like Leviathan (see Job 3:8), Rahab is a sea monster and, as such, symbolizes the forces of chaos that stand against the creator God.

⚭**89:37 Promise:** Jeremiah 33:19–26

49Lord, where is your love from times past,
which in your loyalty you promised to David?
50Lord, remember how they insulted your servant;
remember how I have suffered the insults of the nations.
51LORD, remember how your enemies insulted you
and how they insulted your appointed king wherever he went.

52Praise the LORD forever!
Amen and amen.⚭

Book 4

God Is Eternal, and We Are Not

A prayer of Moses, the man of God.

90 Lord, you have been our home
since the beginning.
2Before the mountains were born
and before you created the earth and the world,
you are God.
You have always been, and you will always be.⚭

3You turn people back into dust.
You say, "Go back into dust, human beings."
4To you, a thousand years
is like the passing of a day,
or like a few hours in the night.
5While people sleep, you take their lives.
They are like grass that grows up in the morning.
6In the morning they are fresh and new,
but by evening they dry up and die.

7We are destroyed by your anger;
we are terrified by your hot anger.
8You have put the evil we have done right in front of you;
you clearly see our secret sins.
9All our days pass while you are angry.
Our years end with a moan.
10Our lifetime is seventy years
or, if we are strong, eighty years.
But the years are full of hard work and pain.
They pass quickly, and then we are gone.
11Who knows the full power of your anger?
Your anger is as great as our fear of you should be.
12Teach us how short our lives really are
so that we may be wise.⚭

13LORD, how long before you return
and show kindness to your servants?⚭
14Fill us with your love every morning.
Then we will sing and rejoice all our lives.
15We have seen years of trouble.
Now give us as much joy as you gave us sorrow.
16Show your servants the wonderful things you do;
show your greatness to their children.
17Lord our God, treat us well.
Give us success in what we do;
yes, give us success in what we do.

Safe in the LORD

91 Those who go to God Most High for safety
will be protected by the Almighty.
2I will say to the LORD, "You are my place of safety and protection.
You are my God and I trust you."

3God will save you from hidden traps
and from deadly diseases.
4He will cover you with his feathers,
and under his wings you can hide.
His truth will be your shield and protection.
5You will not fear any danger by night
or an arrow during the day.
6You will not be afraid of diseases that come in the dark
or sickness that strikes at noon.
7At your side one thousand people may die,
or even ten thousand right beside you,
but you will not be hurt.
8You will only watch
and see the wicked punished.

9The LORD is your protection;
you have made God Most High your place of safety.
10Nothing bad will happen to you;
no disaster will come to your home.
11He has put his angels in charge of you
to watch over you wherever you go.

⚭**89:52 Agreement:** Psalm 132:11

90 This psalm paints a terrifying picture of human mortality. Contrasted with the awesome, eternal power of God, people's lives are seen to be as fragile and fleeting as grass. The threat of death is particularly horrible because death is viewed as a punishment from God, an expression of his anger against sin. Yet this psalm shows us that, while the focus on death in Scripture may be bitter medicine, it is actually very good for our spiritual health. When we acknowledge our mortality, we are forced to admit that we do not control our lives, God does. We learn to turn to him and depend on him as our only true home (verse 1), our only true source of success (verse 17).

⚭**90:2 Environment:** Psalm 96:11–12

⚭**90:12 Time:** Psalm 127:1–2

⚭**90:13 Servant of the Lord:** Psalm 113:1

[12]They will catch you in their hands
so that you will not hit your foot on a rock.
[13]You will walk on lions and cobras;
you will step on strong lions and snakes.

[14]The LORD says, "Whoever loves me, I will save.
I will protect those who know me.
[15]They will call to me, and I will answer them.
I will be with them in trouble;
I will rescue them and honor them.
[16]I will give them a long, full life,
and they will see how I can save."

Thanksgiving for God's Goodness

A psalm. A song for the Sabbath day.

92 It is good to praise you, LORD,
to sing praises to God Most High.
[2]It is good to tell of your love in the morning
and of your loyalty at night.
[3]It is good to praise you with the ten-stringed lyre
and with the soft-sounding harp.

[4]LORD, you have made me happy by what you
have done;
I will sing for joy about what your hands
have done.
[5]LORD, you have done such great things!
How deep are your thoughts!
[6]Stupid people don't know these things,
and fools don't understand.
[7]Wicked people grow like the grass.
Evil people seem to do well,
but they will be destroyed forever.
[8]But, LORD, you will be honored forever.

[9]LORD, surely your enemies,
surely your enemies will be destroyed,
and all who do evil will be scattered.
[10]But you have made me as strong as an ox.
You have poured fine oils on me.
[11]When I looked, I saw my enemies;
I heard the cries of those who are against me.

[12]But good people will grow like palm trees;
they will be tall like the cedars of Lebanon.
[13]Like trees planted in the Temple of the LORD,
they will grow strong in the courtyards
of our God.
[14]When they are old, they will still produce fruit;
they will be healthy and fresh.
[15]They will say that the LORD is good.
He is my Rock, and there is no wrong
in him.

The Majesty of the LORD

93 The LORD is king. He is clothed in majesty.
The LORD is clothed in majesty
and armed with strength.
The world is set,
and it cannot be moved.
[2]LORD, your kingdom was set up long ago;
you are everlasting.

[3]LORD, the seas raise,
the seas raise their voice.
The seas raise up their pounding waves.
[4]The sound of the water is loud;
the ocean waves are powerful,
but the LORD above is much greater.

[5]LORD, your laws will stand forever.
Your Temple will be holy forevermore.

God Will Pay Back His Enemies

94 The LORD is a God who punishes.
God, show your greatness and punish!
[2]Rise up, Judge of the earth,
and give the proud what they deserve.
[3]How long will the wicked be happy?
How long, LORD?

[4]They are full of proud words;
those who do evil brag about what they
have done.
[5]LORD, they crush your people
and make your children suffer.
[6]They kill widows and foreigners
and murder orphans.
[7]They say, "The LORD doesn't see;
the God of Jacob doesn't notice."

[8]You stupid ones among the people, pay attention.
You fools, when will you understand?
[9]Can't the creator of ears hear?
Can't the maker of eyes see?
[10]Won't the one who corrects nations punish you?
Doesn't the teacher of people know everything?

92:12 *Palm trees* and *cedars.* Majestic, vital, strong trees.

92:15 Praise: Psalm 95:3

93:4 Flood: Ezekiel 31:15

94:6 Murder: Jeremiah 7:9–10

94:6 Widows, orphans, and foreigners living away from home did not have a family (and especially a male guardian) to protect them from the criminal elements in Israelite society (see also Jeremiah 22:3; Malachi 3:5). The Law of Moses required that all Israelites be responsible for the care and protection of these vulnerable groups (Exodus 22:21–27; Deuteronomy 14:28–29; 24:14–22; 26:12; 27:19). In the same way, Christians are required to protect and care for the poor and weak in the church (Acts 6:1–3; Galatians 2:10; 1 Timothy 5:3–10; James 1:27).

94:6 The Widow: James 1:27

11The LORD knows what people think.
He knows their thoughts are just a puff of wind.

12LORD, those you correct are happy;
you teach them from your law.
13You give them rest from times of trouble
until a pit is dug for the wicked.
14The LORD won't leave his people
nor give up his children.
15Judgment will again be fair,
and all who are honest will follow it.

16Who will help me fight against the wicked?
Who will stand with me against those who do evil?
17If the LORD had not helped me,
I would have died in a minute.
18I said, "I am about to fall,"
but, LORD, your love kept me safe.
19I was very worried,
but you comforted me and made me happy.

20Crooked leaders cannot be your friends.
They use the law to cause suffering.
21They join forces against people who do right
and sentence to death the innocent.
22But the LORD is my defender;
my God is the rock of my protection.
23God will pay them back for their sins
and will destroy them for their evil.
The LORD our God will destroy them.

A Call to Praise and Obedience

95 Come, let's sing for joy to the LORD.
Let's shout praises to the Rock who saves us.
2Let's come to him with thanksgiving.
Let's sing songs to him,
3because the LORD is the great God,
the great King over all gods.
4The deepest places on earth are his,
and the highest mountains belong to him.
5The sea is his because he made it,
and he created the land with his own hands.

6Come, let's worship him and bow down.
Let's kneel before the LORD who made us,
7because he is our God
and we are the people he takes care of
and the sheep that he tends.
Today listen to what he says:
8 "Do not be stubborn, as your ancestors were at Meribah,
as they were that day at Massah in the desert.
9There your ancestors tested me
and tried me even though they saw what I did.
10I was angry with those people for forty years.
I said, 'They are not loyal to me
and have not understood my ways.'
11I was angry and made a promise,
'They will never enter my rest.'"

Praise for the LORD's Glory

96 Sing to the LORD a new song;
sing to the LORD, all the earth.
2Sing to the LORD and praise his name;
every day tell how he saves us.
3Tell the nations of his glory;
tell all peoples the miracles he does,

4because the LORD is great; he should be praised at all times.
He should be honored more than all the gods,
5because all the gods of the nations are only idols,
but the LORD made the heavens.
6The LORD has glory and majesty;
he has power and beauty in his Temple.

7Praise the LORD, all nations on earth;
praise the LORD's glory and power.
8Praise the glory of the LORD's name.
Bring an offering and come into his Temple courtyards.
9Worship the LORD because he is holy.
Tremble before him, everyone on earth.
10Tell the nations, "The LORD is king."
The earth is set, and it cannot be moved.
He will judge the people fairly.
11Let the skies rejoice and the earth be glad;
let the sea and everything in it shout.
12 Let the fields and everything in them rejoice.
Then all the trees of the forest will sing for joy
13 before the LORD, because he is coming.
He is coming to judge the world;
he will judge the world with fairness
and the peoples with truth.

A Hymn About the LORD's Power

97 The LORD is king. Let the earth rejoice;
faraway lands should be glad.
2Thick, dark clouds surround him.
His kingdom is built on what is right and fair.

95:3 Praise: Psalm 108:8–11
95:10 Rebellion: Ezekiel 16:1–34
95:11 Wilderness (Desert): Isaiah 6:11–12
96:1 *a new song.* See Psalm 33:3.
96:12 Environment: Psalm 98:7–9
96:13 Lying/Dishonesty: Proverbs 12:19

3A fire goes before him
and burns up his enemies all around.
4His lightning lights up the world;
when the people see it, they tremble.
5The mountains melt like wax before the LORD,
before the Lord of all the earth.⚭
6The heavens tell about his goodness,
and all the people see his glory.

7Those who worship idols should be ashamed;
they brag about their gods.
All the gods should worship the LORD.
8When Jerusalem hears this, she is glad,
and the towns of Judah rejoice.
They are happy because of your
judgments, LORD.
9You are the LORD Most High over
all the earth;
you are supreme over all gods.

10People who love the LORD hate evil.
The LORD watches over those who
follow him
and frees them from the power of the wicked.
11Light shines on those who do right;
joy belongs to those who are honest.
12Rejoice in the LORD, you who do right.
Praise his holy name.

The LORD of Power and Justice

A psalm.

98 Sing to the LORD a new song,
because he has done miracles.
By his right hand and holy arm
he has won the victory.
2The LORD has made known his power to save;
he has shown the other nations his victory
for his people.
3He has remembered his love
and his loyalty to the people of Israel.
All the ends of the earth have seen
God's power to save.

4Shout with joy to the LORD, all the earth;
burst into songs and make music.
5Make music to the LORD with harps,
with harps and the sound of singing.
6Blow the trumpets and the sheep's horns;
shout for joy to the LORD the King.
7Let the sea and everything in it shout;
let the world and everyone in it sing.
8Let the rivers clap their hands;
let the mountains sing together for joy.
9Let them sing before the LORD,
because he is coming to judge the world.
He will judge the world fairly;
he will judge the peoples with fairness.⚭

The LORD, the Fair and Holy King

99 The LORD is king.
Let the peoples shake with fear.
He sits between the gold creatures
with wings.
Let the earth shake.
2The LORD in Jerusalem is great;
he is supreme over all the peoples.
3Let them praise your name;
it is great, holy and to be feared.

4The King is powerful and loves justice.
LORD, you made things fair;
you have done what is fair and right
for the people of Jacob.
5Praise the LORD our God,
and worship at the Temple, his footstool.
He is holy.

6Moses and Aaron were among his priests,
and Samuel was among his worshipers.
They called to the LORD,
and he answered them.
7He spoke to them from the pillar of cloud.
They kept the rules and laws he
gave them.

8LORD our God, you answered them.
You showed them that you are a
forgiving God,
but you punished them for their wrongs.
9Praise the LORD our God,
and worship at his holy mountain,
because the LORD our God is holy.

A Call to Praise the LORD

A psalm of thanks.

100 Shout to the LORD, all the earth.
2 Serve the LORD with joy;
come before him with singing.

⚭**97:5 Mountain:** Psalm 104
97:5 *mountains.* Mountains, which are symbolic of power and stability, here melt before God, showing his even greater power.
98:1 *a new song.* See 33:3.
⚭**98:9 Environment:** Psalm 104
99:1 *the gold creatures with wings.* These are the angelic creatures who are known for their having outstretched wings over the Ark of the Agreement in the Holy Place of the Holy Tent (Exodus 37:1–9).
99:6 Samuel here is associated with Moses and Aaron, all three being great men of prayer. They effectively talked with God, and he answered their prayers. Samuel associates himself with Moses and Aaron in 1 Samuel 12:6.

THE REMNANT

ZEPHANIAH 3:12–14

What is the meaning of the term "remnant"? Where is the remnant concept found in the Scriptures?

Although the Bible speaks of a time when righteousness will fill the earth and wickedness will be no more, the sad fact is that in every generation, only a few, relatively speaking, are faithful to the Lord. They are the godly minority, those who remain true to the Word and go against the grain of society. They are the remnant, those "who are left alive" when God's judgments sweep away the rebels and sinners. As expressed in Zephaniah 3:12–13: "But I will leave in the city the humble and those who are not proud, and they will trust in the LORD. Those who are left alive in Israel won't do wrong or tell lies; they won't trick people with their words. They will eat and lie down and no one will make them afraid."

From the very beginning of human history, the great mass of people went their own way. In the days of the Flood, only Noah and his family were spared from destruction. Out of the entire population of the world, God could find only one righteous man, along with his wife, their three sons and their wives — a remnant of just eight (Genesis 6:9–18). They alone were preserved in the midst of the divine judgment that literally wiped out their entire generation. Through them the earth was repopulated (Genesis 9:1–2).

Several generations later, there was another worldwide falling away from God, this time a corporate rebellion of pride and self-will. The Bible refers to this as the building of the Tower of Babel (Genesis 11:1–9). Once again the Lord found a man who would listen to his voice. He was Abram (later called Abraham), and he and his descendants formed the remnant through whom God's plan was carried out. As promised to Abram, "And all the people on earth will be blessed through you" (Genesis 12:3b).

Abraham's descendants (through his son Isaac and his grandson Jacob, also called Israel) became known as the twelve tribes of Israel, or the Israelites. Technically speaking, these tribes now formed the remnant, even though their numbers increased into the hundreds and hundreds of thousands. God singled them out, gave them his laws and made his agreement with them. They alone were to be his people, living in separation from the corrupting influences of the surrounding nations. They alone would have direct access to the Lord, and his Temple would be in their midst.

Yet, for the most part, it was only a small percentage *even of the Israelites*, the chosen nation, that remained faithful. Virtually every book of the Bible paints a similar picture: Most people refuse to obey God's commandments, living in ignorance and often rebellion. But there is always that faithful remnant, a light shining in the midst of darkness, confronting the world and its sin and offering it hope if it will turn back. God always has his witnesses in the earth!

When the Son of God came into the world, great crowds were attracted to him by his teaching and miracles. They wanted to go everywhere he went. But when he told them the cost of following him — giving up the things they want and even giving up their own lives (Matthew 16:24–26; Luke 14:25–33) — most of them turned away (John 6:66). The price was too steep, the stakes too high. Once again, there was only a small group that remained true, no matter what the consequences (John 6:67–68).

Jesus was not disappointed. He was determined to reproduce himself in a quality way in the small group of men who would be leaders after his death and resurrection. He knew the principle of the remnant only too well. He chose 12 which soon turned into 120, which quickly became 3000, and then 5000 (Mark 3:14; Acts 1:15; 2:41; 4:4).

The apostle Paul was also intimately acquainted with the biblical pattern of the remnant. Although he was deeply grieved by the fact that the great majority of his own Jewish people were rejecting Jesus as their Messiah and Lord, he pointed out that, now too, "There are a few people God has chosen by his grace" (Romans 11:5).

Ultimately, although the "road is narrow that leads to life," and "Only a few people find that road" (Matthew 7:14), this remnant of true believers will continue to grow until they constitute "a great number of people, so many that no one could count them . . . from every nation, tribe, people, and language of the earth" (Revelation 7:9). In the end, they "will inherit the land and will enjoy complete peace" (Psalm 37:11).

The Remnant: For additional scriptures on this topic go to Genesis 45:7.

GENEALOGY

MATTHEW 1

Why does the Bible have so many genealogies? Why were genealogies important? Why are the two genealogies of Jesus somewhat different?

A genealogy is a record of a family; it tells who descended from whom. Genealogies were very important to people in the Bible, for many reasons. Genealogies told who owned what land, and who inherited certain offices, especially the priesthood and the kingship. Genealogies told people who they were in relation to their families, and who the head of each family was. And for the people of Israel, genealogies were the means of remembering God's faithfulness "from generation to generation."

There are over two dozen genealogies in the Old Testament. The most important ones are found in Genesis 5, 10, 11, 46; Numbers 26; and 1 Chronicles 1–9 (nine whole chapters!). The only genealogies in the New Testament are genealogies of Jesus (Matthew 1 and Luke 3).

Genealogies did not always list every single ancestor. Sometimes generations were skipped, with only the most important ancestors named. For example, although the *New Century Version* translates Matthew 1:12, "Shealtiel was the *grandfather* of Zerubbabel" (because Pedaiah is left out of the list; see 1 Chronicles 3:17–19), the Greek simply reads "Shealtiel fathered Zerubbabel," just as it says "David fathered Solomon" (verse 6). Sometimes people have tried to figure out the date of creation by adding up the ages of people in the genealogies, but since some generations were probably skipped, this is unreliable.

Also, genealogies can be patterned. The genealogy of Jesus in Matthew 1 is divided into three blocks of fourteen generations each. Each block represents the major stages of God's saving his people: "There were fourteen generations from Abraham to David. And there were fourteen generations from David until the people were taken to Babylon. And there were fourteen generations from the time when the people were taken to Babylon until Christ was born" (Matthew 1:17). This shows that the genealogies in the Bible do more than just chart someone's ancestry. They trace how God has worked in that family. God promised that he would bless the descendants of Abraham, through Isaac, and give them the Promised Land. The genealogy of the people soon to enter Palestine after the Exodus showed that God had fulfilled his promise to that family (Numbers 26).

Some societies today still regard genealogies as very important. Many missionaries have told how they have translated parts of the Bible for a people that have never heard it before, and it has little effect, until they translate the genealogies, and then people become Christians. Genealogies say, "This is not just a story; it is history about real people."

Many people have noticed that the genealogy of Jesus in Matthew 1 is different from that in Luke 3. Matthew's genealogy identifies Joseph's father as Jacob (Matthew 1:16) and traces the descent through David's son Solomon (Matthew 1:6). Luke says that Joseph was the son of Heli (Luke 3:23) and traces Jesus' ancestry through David's son, Nathan (Luke 3:31). One possible solution to this problem is that Luke is actually tracing Mary's ancestry instead of Joseph's, and that "son" in Luke 3:23 means "son-in-law." Another solution is to understand either Heli or Jacob as Joseph's stepfather. These are both possible solutions, but there is a further problem in Luke 3:27 where Zerubbabel and Shealtiel are mentioned. These names also occur in Matthew's genealogy, but Shealtiel's father in Luke is Neri, not Jehoiachin as in Matthew, and the genealogies do not coincide again until David. The best solution is that Matthew is tracing the *royal* descent, whereas Luke is tracing the actual physical descent. Matthew's genealogy answers the question, Who would inherit the kingship if Israel had never gone into exile?

This strange divergence in the genealogy actually solves a seemingly unsolvable problem in the Old Testament. In Jeremiah 22:30 God prophesied that "none of his [Jehoiachin's] descendants will be successful; none will sit on the throne of David." But in 2 Samuel 7:16 God had also prophesied to David that "your family and your kingdom will continue always before me. Your throne will last forever." Perhaps Jesus' physical descent through a different line means the curse of Jeremiah 22 did not apply to him or keep him from fulfilling the promise of 2 Samuel 7.

Many people today do not even know who their fathers, grandfathers, or great–grandfathers were. But even though we do not know our physical genealogy, Christians are the *spiritual* descendants of Abraham by faith (Galatians 3:29). Indeed we are the children of God himself (Galatians 3:26; 1 John 3:1), and are the brothers and sisters of Jesus (Hebrews 2:11). Everyone who believes in Jesus has the best genealogy of all.

Genealogy: For additional scriptures on this topic go to Genesis 5.

[3]Know that the LORD is God.
He made us, and we belong to him;
we are his people, the sheep he tends.

[4]Come into his city with songs of thanksgiving
and into his courtyards with songs
of praise.
Thank him and praise his name.
[5]The LORD is good. His love is forever,
and his loyalty goes on and on.

A Promise to Rule Well

A psalm of David.

101 I will sing of your love and fairness;
LORD, I will sing praises to you.
[2]I will be careful to live an innocent life.
When will you come to me?

I will live an innocent life in my house.
[3] I will not look at anything wicked.
I hate those who turn against you;
they will not be found near me.⚭
[4]Let those who want to do wrong stay away
from me;
I will have nothing to do with evil.
[5]If anyone secretly says things against
his neighbor,
I will stop him.
I will not allow people
to be proud and look down on others.

[6]I will look for trustworthy people
so I can live with them in the land.
Only those who live innocent lives
will be my servants.
[7]No one who is dishonest will live in
my house;
no liars will stay around me.
[8]Every morning I will destroy the wicked
in the land.
I will rid the LORD's city of people who do evil.

A Cry for Help

A prayer of a person who is suffering when he is discouraged and tells the LORD his complaints.

102 LORD, listen to my prayer;
let my cry for help come to you.
[2]Do not hide from me
in my time of trouble.
Pay attention to me.
When I cry for help, answer me quickly.
[3]My life is passing away like smoke,
and my bones are burned up with fire.
[4]My heart is like grass
that has been cut and dried.
I forget to eat.
[5]Because of my grief,
my skin hangs on my bones.
[6]I am like a desert owl,
like an owl living among the ruins.
[7]I lie awake.
I am like a lonely bird on a housetop.
[8]All day long enemies insult me;
those who make fun of me use my name as
a curse.
[9]I eat ashes for food,
and my tears fall into my drinks.
[10]Because of your great anger,
you have picked me up and thrown me away.
[11]My days are like a passing shadow;
I am like dried grass.

[12]But, LORD, you rule forever,
and your fame goes on and on.
[13]You will come and have mercy on Jerusalem,
because the time has now come to be
kind to her;
the right time has come.
[14]Your servants love even her stones;
they even care about her dust.
[15]Nations will fear the name of the LORD,
and all the kings on earth will honor you.
[16]The LORD will rebuild Jerusalem;
there his glory will be seen.
[17]He will answer the prayers of the needy;
he will not reject their prayers.

[18]Write these things for the future
so that people who are not yet born will
praise the LORD.
[19]The LORD looked down from his holy
place above;
from heaven he looked down at the earth.
[20]He heard the moans of the prisoners,
and he freed those sentenced to die.
[21]The name of the LORD will be heard in
Jerusalem;
his praise will be heard there.
[22]People will come together,
and kingdoms will serve the LORD.

[23]God has made me tired of living;
he has cut short my life.

100:3 *sheep.* See Psalm 23:1.
⚭**101:3 Integrity:** Proverbs 11:3

102:6 *owl.* He is like an owl, quiet and lonely.

[24]So I said, "My God, do not take me in the
middle of my life.
Your years go on and on.
[25]In the beginning you made the earth,
and your hands made the skies.
[26]They will be destroyed, but you will remain.
They will all wear out like clothes.
And, like clothes, you will change them
and throw them away.
[27]But you never change,
and your life will never end.
[28]Our children will live in your presence,
and their children will remain with you."

Praise to the LORD of Love

Of David.

103 My whole being, praise the LORD;
all my being, praise his holy name.
[2]My whole being, praise the LORD
and do not forget all his kindnesses.
[3]He forgives all my sins
and heals all my diseases.
[4]He saves my life from the grave
and loads me with love and mercy.
[5]He satisfies me with good things
and makes me young again, like the eagle.

[6]The LORD does what is right and fair
for all who are wronged by others.
[7]He showed his ways to Moses
and his deeds to the people of Israel.
[8]The LORD shows mercy and is kind.
He does not become angry quickly, and he
has great love.
[9]He will not always accuse us,
and he will not be angry forever.
[10]He has not punished us as our sins should
be punished;
he has not repaid us for the evil we have done.
[11]As high as the sky is above the earth,
so great is his love for those who respect him.
[12]He has taken our sins away from us
as far as the east is from west.
[13]The LORD has mercy on those who respect him,
as a father has mercy on his children.
[14]He knows how we were made;
he remembers that we are dust.

[15]Human life is like grass;
we grow like a flower in the field.
[16]After the wind blows, the flower is gone,
and there is no sign of where it was.
[17]But the LORD's love for those who respect him
continues forever and ever,
and his goodness continues to their
grandchildren
[18]and to those who keep his agreement
and who remember to obey his orders.

[19]The LORD has set his throne in heaven,
and his kingdom rules over everything.
[20]You who are his angels, praise the LORD.
You are the mighty warriors who do what
he says
and who obey his voice.
[21]You, his armies, praise the LORD;
you are his servants who do what he wants.
[22]Everything the LORD has made
should praise him in all the places he rules.
My whole being, praise the LORD.

Praise to God Who Made the World

104 My whole being, praise the LORD.
LORD my God, you are very great.
You are clothed with glory and majesty;
[2] you wear light like a robe.
You stretch out the skies like a tent.
[3] You build your room above the clouds.
You make the clouds your chariot,
and you ride on the wings of the wind.
[4]You make the winds your messengers,
and flames of fire are your servants.

[5]You built the earth on its foundations
so it can never be moved.
[6]You covered the earth with oceans;
the water was above the mountains.
[7]But at your command, the water rushed away.
When you thundered your orders,
it hurried away.

103:1–5 This psalm was probably written in celebration of a miraculous healing. Forgiveness of sin and healing of sickness go hand in hand, and so the psalmist praises the Lord as the one who is faithful to forgive and heal. Also, the seriously ill person felt as if he already had one foot in the grave, as if death already had a grip on him. So he thanks God for saving him from the grave and for making him feel young again.

103:5 Worship: Matthew 6:9–13

103:12 *as far as the east is from west.* He has removed our sins from us as far as it is humanly possible to imagine.

104:1–2 The first, and perhaps the highest, element of worship is to praise God for all that he is and all his achievements. The primary acts of worship are those which focus on God directly—those in which God is to us not simply "he" but "you." This means that we must not imagine that work for God in the world is a substitute for direct fellowship with him in praise and prayer and devotion, when we talk not merely about God but to him.

104:3 *above the clouds.* God is envisioned as riding a cloud chariot. See Psalm 18:9.

104:4 *flames of fire are your servants.* God's servants have an awesome appearance. These references are aggressive attacks on the religion of Israel's neighbors because they also likened their gods' servants in the same way.

104:5 Earth: Psalm 146:6

The mountains rose; the valleys sank.
The water went to the places you made for it.
You set borders for the seas that
they cannot cross,
so water will never cover the earth again.

You make springs pour into the ravines;
they flow between the mountains.
They water all the wild animals;
the wild donkeys come there to drink.
Wild birds make nests by the water;
they sing among the tree branches.
You water the mountains from above.
The earth is full of the things you made.
You make the grass for cattle
and vegetables for the people.
You make food grow from the earth.
You give us wine that makes happy hearts
and olive oil that makes our faces shine.
You give us bread that gives us strength.
The LORD's trees have plenty of water;
they are the cedars of Lebanon,
which he planted.
7The birds make their nests there;
the stork's home is in the fir trees.
8The high mountains belong to the wild goats.
The rocks are hiding places for the badgers.

9You made the moon to mark the seasons,
and the sun always knows when to set.
0You make it dark, and it becomes night.
Then all the wild animals creep around.
1The lions roar as they attack.
They look to God for food.
2When the sun rises, they leave
and go back to their dens to lie down.
3Then people go to work
and work until evening.

24LORD, you have made many things;
with your wisdom you made them all.
The earth is full of your riches.
25Look at the sea, so big and wide,
with creatures large and small that
cannot be counted.
26Ships travel over the ocean,
and there is the sea monster Leviathan,
which you made to play there.

The Rock Partridge was a typical bird of Bible times.

27All these things depend on you
to give them their food at the right time.
28When you give it to them,
they gather it up.
When you open your hand,
they are filled with good food.
29When you turn away from them,
they become frightened.
When you take away their breath,
they die and turn to dust.
30When you breathe on them,
they are created,
and you make the land new again.

31May the glory of the LORD be forever.
May the LORD enjoy what he has made.
32He just looks at the earth, and it shakes.
He touches the mountains, and they smoke.

33I will sing to the LORD all my life;
I will sing praises to my God as long as I live.
34May my thoughts please him;
I am happy in the LORD.
35Let sinners be destroyed from the earth,
and let the wicked live no longer.

My whole being, praise the LORD.
Praise the LORD.

104:11 Animals: Proverbs 12:10
104:15 God is good to his human creatures, giving them many gifts for their enjoyment. Psalm 104:15 names three luxuries that give pleasure to men and women: wine, olive oil, and bread. The mention of wine, along with olive oil and bread, shows that, if used properly, wine can be a blessing and not a curse.
104:18 Water: Psalm 104:24–26
104:20 Often darkness carries symbolic overtones. It represents ignorance, death, and the unknown. Here, however, it has a literal meaning. The night is dark. The important teaching of this verse, however, is that it is God who created the darkness. It may represent evil or ignorance, but is not evil. Darkness is also a creation of God and serves his purpose for his creation.
104:26 *Leviathan.* See Psalm 74:14.
104:26 Water: Isaiah 12:1–3
104:32 The mountains are symbolic of stability and power, but God's touch causes them to smoke.
104:35 Environment: Psalm 145:9–10
104:35 Mountain: Psalm 114:4–6

God's Love for Israel

105 Give thanks to the LORD and pray to him.
Tell the nations what he has done.
2 Sing to him; sing praises to him.
Tell about all his miracles.
3 Be glad that you are his;
let those who seek the LORD be happy.
4 Depend on the LORD and his strength;
always go to him for help.
5 Remember the miracles he has done;
remember his wonders and his decisions.
6 You are descendants of his servant Abraham,
the children of Jacob, his chosen people.
7 He is the LORD our God.
His laws are for all the world.

8 He will keep his agreement forever;
he will keep his promises always.
9 He will keep the agreement he made
with Abraham
and the promise he made to Isaac.
10 He made it a law for the people of Jacob;
he made it an agreement with Israel to
last forever.
11 The LORD said, "I will give you the land
of Canaan,
and it will belong to you."

12 Then God's people were few in number.
They were strangers in the land.
13 They went from one nation to another,
from one kingdom to another.
14 But the LORD did not let anyone hurt them;
he warned kings not to harm them.
15 He said, "Don't touch my chosen people,
and don't harm my prophets."

16 God ordered a time of hunger in the land,
and he destroyed all the food.
17 Then he sent a man ahead of them—
Joseph, who was sold as a slave.
18 They put chains around his feet
and an iron ring around his neck.
19 Then the time he had spoken of came,
and the LORD's words proved that Joseph
was right.
20 The king of Egypt sent for Joseph and freed him;
the ruler of the people set him free.
21 He made him the master of his house;
Joseph was in charge of his riches.
22 He could order the princes as he wished.
He taught the older men to be wise.
23 Then his father Israel came to Egypt;
Jacob lived in Egypt.
24 The LORD made his people grow in number,
and he made them stronger than their enemies.
25 He caused the Egyptians to hate his people
and to make plans against his servants.
26 Then he sent his servant Moses,
and Aaron, whom he had chosen.
27 They did many signs among the Egyptians
and worked wonders in Egypt.
28 The LORD sent darkness and made
the land dark,
but the Egyptians turned against
what he said.
29 So he changed their water into blood
and made their fish die.
30 Then their country was filled with frogs,
even in the bedrooms of their rulers.
31 The LORD spoke and flies came,
and gnats were everywhere in the country.
32 He made hail fall like rain
and sent lightning through their land.
33 He struck down their grapevines
and fig trees,
and he destroyed every tree in the country.
34 He spoke and grasshoppers came;
the locusts were too many to count.
35 They ate all the plants in the land
and everything the earth produced.
36 The LORD also killed all the firstborn sons
in the land,
the oldest son of each family.

37 Then he brought his people out,
and they carried with them silver and gold.
Not one of his people stumbled.
38 The Egyptians were glad when they left,
because the Egyptians were afraid of them.
39 The LORD covered them with a cloud
and lit up the night with fire.
40 When they asked, he brought them quail
and filled them with bread from heaven.
41 God split the rock, and water flowed out;
it ran like a river through the desert.
42 He remembered his holy promise
to his servant Abraham.

105:5 Memory: Ecclesiastes 12:1

105:16–23 This psalm worships the Lord by remembering how he has dealt with his people through history. One of the high points was how God preserved Jacob and his family through a devastating famine in Palestine. He did this in a most surprising way, through Joseph—sold into slavery, but raised to a position of power and authority in Egypt. Joseph is an example of how God can overrule difficult circumstances and use them for great good.

105:23 *Jacob.* Also called Israel.

105:23 *Egypt.* Literally, "the land of Ham." Also in verse 27. The people in Egypt were descendants of Ham, one of Noah's sons. See Genesis 10:6.

o God brought his people out with joy,
his chosen ones with singing.
le gave them lands of other nations,
so they received what others had worked for.
'his was so they would keep his orders
and obey his teachings.

'raise the LORD!

ael's Failure to Trust God

)6 Praise the LORD!
Thank the LORD because he is good.
His love continues forever.
Jo one can tell all the mighty things
the LORD has done;
no one can speak all his praise.
Iappy are those who do right,
who do what is fair at all times.

.ORD, remember me when you are kind
to your people;
help me when you save them.
.et me see the good things you do for your
chosen people.
Let me be happy along with your happy nation;
let me join your own people in praising you.

Ve have sinned just as our ancestors did.
We have done wrong; we have done evil.
)ur ancestors in Egypt
did not learn from your miracles.
'hey did not remember all your kindnesses,
so they turned against you at the Red Sea.
ut the LORD saved them for his own sake,
to show his great power.
Ie commanded the Red Sea, and it dried up.
He led them through the deep sea
as if it were a desert.
Ie saved them from those who hated them.
He saved them from their enemies,
nd the water covered their foes.
Not one of them escaped.
'hen the people believed what the LORD said,
and they sang praises to him.

ut they quickly forgot what he had done;
they did not wait for his advice.
'hey became greedy for food in the desert,
and they tested God there.
o he gave them what they wanted,
but he also sent a terrible disease among them.

16 The people in the camp were jealous of Moses
and of Aaron, the holy priest of the LORD.
17 Then the ground opened up and
swallowed Dathan
and closed over Abiram's group.
18 A fire burned among their followers,
and flames burned up the wicked.

19 The people made a gold calf at Mount Sinai
and worshiped a metal statue.
20 They exchanged their glorious God
for a statue of a bull that eats grass.
21 They forgot the God who saved them,
who had done great things in Egypt,
22 who had done miracles in Egypt
and amazing things by the Red Sea.
23 So God said he would destroy them.
But Moses, his chosen one, stood before him
and stopped God's anger from
destroying them.

24 Then they refused to go into the beautiful land
of Canaan;
they did not believe what God promised.
25 They grumbled in their tents
and did not obey the LORD.
26 So he swore to them
that they would die in the desert.
27 He said their children would be killed by
other nations
and that they would be scattered among
other countries.

28 They joined in worshiping Baal at Peor
and ate meat that had been sacrificed to
lifeless statues.
29 They made the LORD angry by what they did,
so many people became sick with a
terrible disease.
30 But Phinehas prayed to the LORD,
and the disease stopped.
31 Phinehas did what was right,
and it will be remembered from now on.

32 The people also made the LORD angry
at Meribah,
and Moses was in trouble because of them.
33 The people turned against the Spirit of God,
so Moses spoke without stopping to think.

34 The people did not destroy the other nations
as the LORD had told them to do.

06:3 Beatitudes: Psalm 112:1
:9 God controls the waters of chaos. He uses them for his own
)oses.

106:22 *Egypt.* Literally, "the land of Ham." The people in Egypt were descendants of Ham, one of Noah's sons. See Genesis 10:6.

35 Instead, they mixed with the other nations
and learned their customs.
36 They worshiped other nations' idols
and were trapped by them.
37 They even killed their sons and daughters
as sacrifices to demons.
38 They killed innocent people,
their own sons and daughters,
as sacrifices to the idols of Canaan.
So the land was made unholy by their blood.
39 The people became unholy by their sins;
they were unfaithful to God in what they did.

40 So the LORD became angry with his people
and hated his own children.
41 He handed them over to other nations
and let their enemies rule over them.
42 Their enemies were cruel to them
and kept them under their power.
43 The LORD saved his people many times,
but they continued to turn against him.
So they became even more wicked.

44 But God saw their misery
when he heard their cry.
45 He remembered his agreement with them,
and he felt sorry for them because of his
great love.
46 He caused them to be pitied
by those who held them captive.

47 LORD our God, save us
and bring us back from other nations.
Then we will thank you
and will gladly praise you.

48 Praise the LORD, the God of Israel.
He always was and always will be.
Let all the people say, "Amen!"

Praise the LORD!

Book 5

God Saves from Many Dangers

107 Thank the LORD because he is good.
His love continues forever.
2 That is what those whom the LORD has saved
should say.
He has saved them from the enemy
3 and has gathered them from other lands,
from east and west, north and south.

4 Some people had wandered in the desert lands.
They found no city in which to live.
5 They were hungry and thirsty,
and they were discouraged.
6 In their misery they cried out to the LORD,
and he saved them from their troubles.
7 He led them on a straight road
to a city where they could live.
8 Let them give thanks to the LORD for his love
and for the miracles he does for people.
9 He satisfies the thirsty
and fills up the hungry.∞

10 Some sat in gloom and darkness;
they were prisoners suffering in chains.
11 They had turned against the words of God
and had refused the advice of God Most High.
12 So he broke their pride by hard work.
They stumbled, and no one helped.
13 In their misery they cried out to the LORD,
and he saved them from their troubles.
14 He brought them out of their gloom
and darkness
and broke their chains.
15 Let them give thanks to the LORD for his love
and for the miracles he does for people.
16 He breaks down bronze gates
and cuts apart iron bars.

17 Some fools turned against God
and suffered for the evil they did.
18 They refused to eat anything,
so they almost died.
19 In their misery they cried out to the LORD,
and he saved them from their troubles.
20 God gave the command and healed them,
so they were saved from dying.
21 Let them give thanks to the LORD for his love
and for the miracles he does for people.
22 Let them offer sacrifices to thank him.
With joy they should tell what he has done.

23 Others went out to sea in ships
and did business on the great oceans.
24 They saw what the LORD could do,
the miracles he did in the deep oceans.
25 He spoke, and a storm came up,
which blew up high waves.

106:37 *as sacrifices to demons.* Though the idols they worshiped were false, non-existent gods, evil spiritual realities used them for their own purposes. Sacrificing to false gods, was in actuality, serving demons.

107:1–9 God's people are pictured as desert wanderers—homeless, hungry, and thirsty. God is their gracious host, quenching their thirst and filling them with food.

∞**107:9 Hospitality:** Matthew 9:9–13

he ships were tossed as high as the sky and
fell low to the depths.
The storm was so bad that they lost
their courage.
hey stumbled and fell like people who
were drunk.
They did not know what to do.
ı their misery they cried out to the LORD,
and he saved them from their troubles.
e stilled the storm
and calmed the waves.
hey were happy that it was quiet,
and God guided them to the port they wanted.
et them give thanks to the LORD for his love
and for the miracles he does for people.
et them praise his greatness in the meeting of
the people;
let them praise him in the meeting of the
older leaders.

e changed rivers into a desert
and springs of water into dry ground.
e made fertile land salty,
because the people there did evil.
e changed the desert into pools of water
and dry ground into springs of water.
e had the hungry settle there
so they could build a city in which to live.
hey planted seeds in the fields and vineyards,
and they had a good harvest.
od blessed them, and they grew in number.
Their cattle did not become fewer.

ecause of disaster, troubles, and sadness,
their families grew smaller and weaker.
e showed he was displeased with their leaders
and made them wander in a pathless desert.
ut he lifted the poor out of their suffering
and made their families grow like
flocks of sheep.
ood people see this and are happy,
but the wicked say nothing.

'hoever is wise will remember these things
and will think about the love of the LORD.

'rayer for Victory

A song. A psalm of David.

)8 God, my heart is steady.
I will sing and praise you with
all my being.

2 Wake up, harp and lyre!
I will wake up the dawn.
3 LORD, I will praise you among the nations;
I will sing songs of praise about you to
all the nations.
4 Your great love reaches to the skies,
your truth to the heavens.
5 God, you are supreme above the skies.
Let your glory be over all the earth.

6 Answer us and save us by your power
so the people you love will be rescued.
7 God has said from his Temple,
"When I win, I will divide Shechem
and measure off the Valley of Succoth.
8 Gilead and Manasseh are mine.
Ephraim is like my helmet.
Judah holds my royal scepter.
9 Moab is like my washbowl.
I throw my sandals at Edom.
I shout at Philistia."

10 Who will bring me to the strong, walled city?
Who will lead me to Edom?
11 God, surely you have rejected us;
you do not go out with our armies.
12 Help us fight the enemy.
Human help is useless,
13 but we can win with God's help.
He will defeat our enemies.

A Prayer Against an Enemy

For the director of music. A psalm of David.

109 God, I praise you.
Do not be silent.
2 Wicked people and liars have spoken
against me;
they have told lies about me.
3 They have said hateful things about me
and attack me for no reason.
4 They attacked me, even though I loved them
and prayed for them.
5 I was good to them, but they repay me
with evil.
I loved them, but they hate me in return.

6 They say about me, "Have an evil person work
against him,
and let an accuser stand against him.
7 When he is judged, let him be found guilty,
and let even his prayers show his guilt.

29 *waves.* The seas often represent the forces of chaos, and here shows he is in control. He can bring them to order. Jesus will show that he is God by stilling the sea.

108:8 *Gilead, Manasseh, Ephraim, and Judah.* See Psalm 60:7.
108:9 *Moab, Edom, and Philistia.* See Psalm 60:8.
108:11 Praise: Revelation 11:15–18

8 Let his life be cut short,
and let another man replace him as leader.
9 Let his children become orphans
and his wife a widow.
10 Make his children wander around, begging
for food.
Let them be forced out of the ruins in which
they live.
11 Let the people to whom he owes money take
everything he owns,
and let strangers steal everything he has
worked for.
12 Let no one show him love
or have mercy on his orphaned children.
13 Let all his descendants die
and be forgotten by those who live after him.
14 LORD, remember how wicked his
ancestors were,
and don't let the sins of his mother be
wiped out.
15 LORD, always remember their sins.
Then make people forget about
them completely.

16 "He did not remember to be loving.
He hurt the poor, the needy, and those who
were sad
until they were nearly dead.
17 He loved to put curses on others,
so let those same curses fall on him.
He did not like to bless others,
so do not let good things happen to him.
18 He cursed others as often as he wore clothes.
Cursing others filled his body and his life,
like drinking water and using olive oil.
19 So let curses cover him like clothes
and wrap around him like a belt."
20 May the LORD do these things to those who
accuse me,
to those who speak evil against me.

21 But you, Lord GOD,
be kind to me so others will know you are
good.
Because your love is good, save me.
22 I am poor and helpless
and very sad.
23 I am dying like an evening shadow;
I am shaken off like a locust.
24 My knees are weak from hunger,
and I have grown thin.
25 My enemies insult me;
they look at me and shake their heads.

26 LORD my God, help me;
because you are loving, save me.
27 Then they will know that your power has
done this;
they will know that you have done it, LORD.
28 They may curse me, but you bless me.
They may attack me, but they will
be disgraced.
Then I, your servant, will be glad.
29 Let those who accuse me be disgraced
and covered with shame like a coat.
30 I will thank the LORD very much;
I will praise him in front of many people.
31 He defends the helpless
and saves them from those who accuse them.

The LORD Appoints a King

A psalm of David.

110 The LORD said to my Lord,
"Sit by me at my right side
until I put your enemies under your control."
2 The LORD will enlarge your kingdom
beyond Jerusalem,
and you will rule over your enemies.
3 Your people will join you on your day of battle.
You have been dressed in holiness from birth;
you have the freshness of a child.

4 The LORD has made a promise
and will not change his mind.
He said, "You are a priest forever,
a priest like Melchizedek."

5 The Lord is beside you to help you.
When he becomes angry, he will crush kings.
6 He will judge those nations, filling them with
dead bodies;
he will defeat rulers all over the world.
7 The king will drink from the brook on the way.
Then he will be strengthened.

109:8 Judas: Zechariah 11:12
109:9 Through his death the enemy's wife would become a widow and his children would become orphans, thus losing their normal social support and rendering them vulnerable to poverty and other problems.
109:12 Anger: Psalm 145:8
109:25 *shake their heads.* They shake their heads because they are disgusted.
110:4 Priesthood: Malachi 2:7
110:4 *a priest like Melchizedek.* The regular priesthood was established through Aaron, so this is a special type of priesthood. Since Melchizedek (Genesis 14:18–20) was king as well as priest, this may be the force of the verse. Jesus Christ will later be called a priest like Melchizedek (Hebrews 7).

Jesus

Matthew 1

What does the name Jesus mean? What does calling Jesus "Son of God" tell us about him? What did the term Savior mean when applied to Jesus?

Jesus is the English form of the late Hebrew name form *Yehoshua* (Joshua), which means "*Yahweh* is salvation" or possibly "*Yahweh* has saved." The name itself reminds us that Jesus was a Jew, born of a Jewish mother named Miriam (in English, Mary). As such, Jesus was born into the world of early Judaism with its religious focus on the Torah (the Law), Temple (in Jerusalem), Territory (the Holy Land), and being the chosen and set-apart people of God. He was born into a world, however, where all was not well for God's own, for they were under the rule of people, either directly under Roman rule (in Judea), or under the rule of kings who were clients of Rome (in Galilee).

Since, to our knowledge, Jesus never left the vicinity of Israel, nor interacted with non-Jews to any great extent, he must be understood in his own Jewish historical context. This, in principle, means that we should not be surprised that his ministry was taken up with discussions of matters such as the proper observance of the Sabbath, clean and unclean food and persons, Jewish marriage and divorce customs, how to properly honor parents, prayer and fasting, the proper way to treat terrible sinners, how one should relate to Caesar and his taxes, the coming of God's kingdom and anointed One (Messiah), and related matters. Jesus' own preferred way to refer to himself was as the Son of Man, a phrase taken from Daniel 7, but a term the early church seems not to have used much to speak of Jesus (see Acts 7:56, but the phrase is never found in the New Testament letters). Jesus' Jewishness is also shown by his frequent association with the great prophet, John the Baptist, his baptism by John, and the fact that people were comparing and contrasting Jesus' ministry with that of John (see Mark 2:18–22; 8:28; Luke 3:1–20).

Though Jesus was certainly a Jew and talked in terms early Jews could understand, he was not simply a product of his environment, for he saw it as his ministry to be a reformer of sorts. For example, Jesus did not observe the Old Testament laws of clean and unclean (see Mark 7). He would frequently dine with or touch and heal the unclean, the diseased, and the possessed. As a result, he got a reputation for being a "friend of sinners," which in his day was seen as a bad thing. Then, too, Jesus felt it was right that he help and heal people on the Sabbath, even though most Jews understood that the Law said such activity was work and, thus, forbidden unless the life of the person about to be helped or healed was at risk. In general, Jesus agreed with the Pharisees that there needed to be a renewal of holiness and loyalty to God in the land, but he disagreed with how this should be accomplished.

In thinking of Jesus as the Son of God, one must keep in mind that this phrase is used in Old Testament texts like 2 Samuel 7:14 and Psalm 2:7 to refer to the Davidic king, not a divine being. In other words, its primary meaning in Jewish contexts was to refer to a royal human being, not a divine being.

The New Testament portrays Jesus as God's unique and divine Son. Relevant to the discussion of Jesus as Son of God is the fact that Jesus prayed to God as *Abba*, the Aramaic term of endearment which means "dearest Father" (Mark 14:36). The term itself implies a certain kind of intimate relationship between Jesus and God, suggesting he saw himself as God's special Son. The parable of the vineyard, found in Mark 12:1–12, is also of relevance for it suggests Jesus saw himself as God's last ambassador to his people, indeed as God's only and beloved Son. Equally important is Mark 13:32 which has Jesus admitting in the same breath that he, as the Son of Man, does not know the timing of the Second Coming and also suggesting that as God's Son he had greater knowledge of God and his plans than men or even angels.

The term Savior is not found on Jesus' lips, but it is clear that he saw himself seeking and saving the lost (see Luke 15). It is important to make clear that when Jesus speaks of salvation, he is not just referring to a spiritual change in a person's life, though that is the beginning of it (Luke 7:36–50). As God's salvation breaks into the world, it is a powerful force that changes the structure of human society—the prisoners are set free, the poor hear Good News, and the oppressed are released from oppression (Luke 4:18–19). In short, salvation is viewed as a holistic matter involving the body, human spirit, and human relationships. Jesus comes to minister to the whole person, for salvation means total human change in preparation for the full coming of the Kingdom in which there will be no disease, decay, death, no suffering or sorrow, and in which true *shalom,* true peace, the well-being of both humans and all of creation will be reestablished (see Revelation 21).

Jesus: For additional scriptures on this topic go to 2 Samuel 7:14.

BAPTISM

MATTHEW 3

Why do Christians baptize? Should only believers be baptized?

Christians baptize for two reasons: Jesus' example and his clear instructions. Jesus set an example for us when he allowed John to baptize him in the Jordan River (Matthew 3:13–15). Jesus also gave us clear instructions on this matter when he commanded his followers to baptize new believers (Matthew 28:19–20). The earliest Christians took this example and instruction to heart and made it their practice. When people responded to Peter's convicting message about the crucifixion of Jesus by asking what they should do, Peter answered, "Change your hearts and lives and be baptized, each one of you, in the name of the Lord Jesus Christ for the forgiveness of your sins. And you will receive the gift of the Holy Spirit" (Acts 2:38). Philip demonstrated this same practice when he baptized many people who came to believe in Jesus Christ (Acts 8). Paul was baptized (9:18), and he himself baptized Lydia in Philippi ("she and all the people in her house," Acts 16:15), Crispus, Gaius, and "the family of Stephanas" in Corinth (Acts 18:8; 1 Corinthians 1:14–16).

The key elements in baptisms in the New Testament are (1) that people repent (change their hearts and lives); (2) that they are baptized with water in the name of the Father, Son, and Holy Spirit; (3) that they realize that the Holy Spirit is present in their lives making them children of God by grace through faith in Christ; and (4) that they are added to the fellowship of those who believe in and belong to God through Christ. These elements are probably rooted in early Christian reflection on such Old Testament texts as Ezekiel 36:25–27, where cleansing with water is associated with cleansing of the heart. Similarly, the New Testament teaching that being baptized is being clothed with Christ (for example, Galatians 3:26–27) is rooted in an Old Testament text like Zechariah 3:3–5.

Baptize means to dip or plunge into water. The examples of baptism recorded in the Bible happen in the open air at a river. There is no biblical instruction that a river is the only place a baptism can be done. The later church practiced baptism indoors, with a smaller amount of water. Presumably the Lord is pleased that, regardless of the location of the water used, people fulfill the purpose of baptism by public identification with Christ and incorporation into Christ's family, the church (see 1 Corinthians 1:17). It is not as important where a person is baptized (church building, swimming pool, river), as it is that they *are* baptized. It is important that they are identified with the crucified and risen Jesus Christ (Romans 6:1–14). To be baptized into Christ is to admit and commit to living in the sphere of Christ's control and will as expressed in the community of believers, the Body of Christ, his church (1 Corinthians 12:13).

A long-debated question in the history of the church is how old one should be when baptized. The Bible does not specifically say how old one must be. The biblical examples are adults who consciously acknowledge their wrongdoing, but there are less definitive passages that have been interpreted by some to mean that children and slaves were baptized because of their parents' or masters' repentance and faith. For example, who was included in "all the people in [Lydia's] house" (Acts 16:15) or "the family of Stephanas" (1 Corinthians 1:16)? Children and slaves may have been included, but the text does not say so.

There are two basic lines of tradition in the church. In one tradition, only adults who have repented and believed are baptized. In the other tradition, both believing adults and the infants of believing parents are baptized. Both traditions emphasize the true meaning of baptism as a confession of faith in and identification with the death and resurrection of Christ for the forgiveness of sins. Both traditions view baptism as a commitment that must be lived out in the person's life. Both traditions see baptism as an initiation into Christ's body, the church (1 Corinthians 12:13). However, only the first tradition can actually be supported by biblical example.

There is no doubt that baptism is both right and good. And true followers of Jesus Christ will follow his example and command in this rite as well.⚭

⚭**Baptism:** For additional scriptures on this topic go to Ezekiel 26:25–26.

Praise the LORD's Goodness

111 Praise the LORD!
I will thank the LORD with all my heart
in the meeting of his good people.
2The LORD does great things;
those who enjoy them seek them.
3What he does is glorious and splendid,
and his goodness continues forever.
4His miracles are unforgettable.
The LORD is kind and merciful.
5He gives food to those who fear him.
He remembers his agreement forever.
6He has shown his people his power
when he gave them the lands of other nations.

7Everything he does is good and fair;
all his orders can be trusted.
8They will continue forever.
They were made true and right.
9He sets his people free.
He made his agreement everlasting.
He is holy and wonderful.

10Wisdom begins with respect for the LORD;
those who obey his orders have
good understanding.
He should be praised forever.

Honest People Are Blessed

112 Praise the LORD!
Happy are those who respect the LORD,
who want what he commands.⚭
2Their descendants will be powerful in the land;
the children of honest people will be blessed.
3Their houses will be full of wealth and riches,
and their goodness will continue forever.
4A light shines in the dark for honest people,
for those who are merciful and
kind and good.
5It is good to be merciful and generous.
Those who are fair in their business
6will never be defeated.
Good people will always be remembered.
7They won't be afraid of bad news;
their hearts are steady because they
trust the LORD.
8They are confident and will not be afraid;
they will look down on their enemies.
9They give freely to the poor.
The things they do are right and will
continue forever.
They will be given great honor.

10The wicked will see this and become angry;
they will grind their teeth in anger and then
disappear.
The wishes of the wicked will come
to nothing.

Praise for the LORD's Kindness

113 Praise the LORD!
Praise him, you servants of the LORD;
praise the name of the LORD.⚭
2The LORD's name should be praised
now and forever.
3The LORD's name should be praised
from where the sun rises to where it sets.
4The LORD is supreme over all the nations;
his glory reaches to the skies.

5No one is like the LORD our God,
who rules from heaven,
6who bends down to look
at the skies and the earth.
7The LORD lifts the poor from the dirt
and takes the helpless from the ashes.
8He seats them with princes,
the princes of his people.
9He gives children to the woman who has none
and makes her a happy mother.

Praise the LORD!

God Brought Israel from Egypt

114 When the Israelites went out of Egypt,
the people of Jacob left that
foreign country.
2Then Judah became God's holy place;
Israel became the land he ruled.

3The Red Sea looked and ran away;
the Jordan River turned back.
4The mountains danced like sheep
and the hills like little lambs.
5Sea, why did you run away?
Jordan, why did you turn back?
6Mountains, why did you dance like sheep?
Hills, why did you dance like little lambs?⚭

⚭**112:1 Beatitudes:** Job 5:17
⚭**113:1 Servant of the Lord:** Psalm 119:17

113:3 *from where the sun rises to where is sets.* That is, he should be praised everywhere.
⚭**114:6 Mountain:** Isaiah 2:2–3

7Earth, shake with fear before the Lord,
before the God of Jacob.
8He turned a rock into a pool of water,
a hard rock into a spring of water.

The One True God

115 It does not belong to us, LORD.
The glory belongs to you
because of your love and loyalty.

2Why do the nations ask,
"Where is their God?"
3Our God is in heaven.
He does what he pleases.
4Their idols are made of silver and gold,
the work of human hands.
5They have mouths, but they cannot speak.
They have eyes, but they cannot see.
6They have ears, but they cannot hear.
They have noses, but they cannot smell.
7They have hands, but they cannot feel.
They have feet, but they cannot walk.
No sounds come from their throats.
8People who make idols will be like them,
and so will those who trust them.

9Family of Israel, trust the LORD;
he is your helper and your protection.
10Family of Aaron, trust the LORD;
he is your helper and your protection.
11You who respect the LORD should trust him;
he is your helper and your protection.

12The LORD remembers us and will bless us.
He will bless the family of Israel;
he will bless the family of Aaron.
13The LORD will bless those who respect him,
from the smallest to the greatest.

14May the LORD give you success,
and may he give you and your children success.
15May you be blessed by the LORD,
who made heaven and earth.

16Heaven belongs to the LORD,
but he gave the earth to people.
17Dead people do not praise the LORD;
those in the grave are silent.
18But we will praise the LORD
now and forever.

Praise the LORD!

Thanksgiving for Escaping Death

116 I love the LORD,
because he listens to my prayers
for help.
2He paid attention to me,
so I will call to him for help as long as I live.
3The ropes of death bound me,
and the fear of the grave took hold of me.
I was troubled and sad.
4Then I called out the name of the LORD.
I said, "Please, LORD, save me!"

5The LORD is kind and does what is right;
our God is merciful.
6The LORD watches over the foolish;
when I was helpless, he saved me.
7I said to myself, "Relax,
because the LORD takes care of you."
8LORD, you saved me from death.
You stopped my eyes from crying;
you kept me from being defeated.
9So I will walk with the LORD
in the land of the living.
10I believed, so I said,
"I am completely ruined."
11In my distress I said,
"All people are liars."

12What can I give the LORD
for all the good things he has given
to me?
13I will lift up the cup of salvation,
and I will pray to the LORD.
14I will give the LORD what I promised
in front of all his people.

15The death of one that belongs to the LORD
is precious in his sight.
16LORD, I am your servant;
I am your servant and the son of your
female servant.
You have freed me from my chains.
17I will give you an offering to show thanks
to you,
and I will pray to the LORD.
18I will give the LORD what I promised
in front of all his people,
19in the Temple courtyards
in Jerusalem.

Praise the LORD!

114:8 *a hard rock into a spring of water.* This reference is to the provision of water at Kadesh (Numbers 20:1–13).
116:3 It was as if ropes came out of the ground and began pulling the psalmist into the grave.
116:13 *the cup of salvation.* The psalmist knew there were two cups, figuratively speaking—a cup of God's anger or judgment and a cup of his blessing or salvation.

Hymn of Praise

117 All you nations, praise the LORD.
All you people, praise him
because the LORD loves us very much,
and his truth is everlasting.

Praise the LORD!

Thanksgiving for Victory

118 Thank the LORD because he is good.
His love continues forever.
Let the people of Israel say,
"His love continues forever."
Let the family of Aaron say,
"His love continues forever."
Let those who respect the LORD say,
"His love continues forever."

I was in trouble, so I called to the LORD.
The LORD answered me and set me free.
I will not be afraid, because the LORD is with me.
People can't do anything to me.
The LORD is with me to help me,
so I will see my enemies defeated.
It is better to trust the LORD
than to trust people.
It is better to trust the LORD
than to trust princes.

All the nations surrounded me,
but I defeated them in the name of the LORD.
They surrounded me on every side,
but with the LORD's power I defeated them.
They surrounded me like a swarm of bees,
but they died as quickly as thorns burn.
By the LORD's power, I defeated them.
They chased me until I was almost defeated,
but the LORD helped me.
The LORD gives me strength and a song.
He has saved me.

Shouts of joy and victory
come from the tents of those who do right:
"The LORD has done powerful things."
The power of the LORD has won the victory;
with his power the LORD has done
mighty things.

I will not die, but live,
and I will tell what the LORD has done.
18 The LORD has taught me a hard lesson,
but he did not let me die.

19 Open for me the Temple gates.
Then I will come in and thank the LORD.
20 This is the LORD's gate;
only those who are good may enter through it.
21 LORD, I thank you for answering me.
You have saved me.

22 The stone that the builders rejected
became the cornerstone.
23 The LORD did this,
and it is wonderful to us.
24 This is the day that the LORD has made.
Let us rejoice and be glad today!

25 Please, LORD, save us;
please, LORD, give us success.
26 God bless the one who comes in the name of
the LORD.
We bless all of you from the Temple of
the LORD.
27 The LORD is God,
and he has shown kindness to us.
With branches in your hands, join the feast.
Come to the corners of the altar.

28 You are my God, and I will thank you;
you are my God, and I will praise
your greatness.

29 Thank the LORD because he is good.
His love continues forever.

The Word of God

119 Happy are those who live pure lives,
who follow the LORD's teachings.
2 Happy are those who keep his rules,
who try to obey him with their
whole heart.
3 They don't do what is wrong;
they follow his ways.
4 LORD, you gave your orders
to be obeyed completely.
5 I wish I were more loyal
in obeying your demands.
6 Then I would not be ashamed
when I study your commands.

118:6 Fear: Psalm 147:11
118:22 Stone: Isaiah 8:14
8:22 *The stone that the builders rejected.* The least desirable
came the most important as the rejected stone is placed in the
st obvious place. Jesus used this verse in reference to himself
atthew 21:42; Mark 12:10; Luke 20:17; Acts 4:11; I Peter 2:7).

119:1 Throughout this psalm, the joys of God's Law for God's people are sung. The Law is God's gift to his people to show them how they ought to live. In Matthew 5:17–20, and throughout Matthew 5–7, Jesus teaches us how we ought to understand the Law in light of his coming.

[7]When I learned that your laws are fair,
I praised you with an honest heart.
[8]I will obey your demands,
so please don't ever leave me.

[9]How can a young person live a pure life?
By obeying your word.
[10]With all my heart I try to obey you.
Don't let me break your commands.
[11]I have taken your words to heart
so I would not sin against you.
[12]LORD, you should be praised.
Teach me your demands.
[13]My lips will tell about
all the laws you have spoken.
[14]I enjoy living by your rules
as people enjoy great riches.
[15]I think about your orders
and study your ways.
[16]I enjoy obeying your demands,
and I will not forget your word.⚭

[17]Do good to me, your servant, so I can live,
so I can obey your word.⚭
[18]Open my eyes to see
the miracles in your teachings.
[19]I am a stranger on earth.
Do not hide your commands from me.
[20]I wear myself out with desire
for your laws all the time.
[21]You scold proud people;
those who ignore your commands are cursed.
[22]Don't let me be insulted and hated
because I keep your rules.
[23]Even if princes speak against me,
I, your servant, will think about your demands.
[24]Your rules give me pleasure;
they give me good advice.⚭

[25]I am about to die.
Give me life, as you have promised.
[26]I told you about my life, and you answered me.
Teach me your demands.
[27]Help me understand your orders.
Then I will think about your miracles.
[28]I am sad and tired.
Make me strong again as you have promised.
[29]Don't let me be dishonest;
have mercy on me by helping me obey
your teachings.
[30]I have chosen the way of truth;
I have obeyed your laws.
[31]I hold on to your rules.
LORD, do not let me be disgraced.
[32]I will quickly obey your commands,
because you have made me happy.

[33]LORD, teach me your demands,
and I will keep them until the end.⚭
[34]Help me understand, so I can keep
your teachings,
obeying them with all my heart.
[35]Lead me in the path of your commands,
because that makes me happy.
[36]Make me want to keep your rules
instead of wishing for riches.
[37]Keep me from looking at worthless things.
Let me live by your word.
[38]Keep your promise to me, your servant,
so you will be respected.
[39]Take away the shame I fear,
because your laws are good.
[40]How I want to follow your orders.
Give me life because of your goodness.

[41]LORD, show me your love,
and save me as you have promised.
[42]I have an answer for people who insult me,
because I trust what you say.
[43]Never keep me from speaking your truth,
because I depend on your fair laws.
[44]I will obey your teachings
forever and ever.
[45]So I will live in freedom,
because I want to follow your orders.
[46]I will discuss your rules with kings
and will not be ashamed.
[47]I enjoy obeying your commands,
which I love.
[48]I praise your commands, which I love,
and I think about your demands.

[49]Remember your promise to me, your servant;
it gives me hope.⚭
[50]When I suffer, this comforts me:
Your promise gives me life.
[51]Proud people always make fun of me,
but I do not reject your teachings.

119:15 The psalmist loves to obey God's laws, but he is not content just doing that. He also thinks about God's orders, no doubt seeking to understand the purposes God has in giving them. He turns them over and over in his mind, meditating on the commandments. He contemplates God's ways, his patterns of dealing with his children. In so doing, his joy in following those ways only increases.

⚭**119:16 Pleasure:** Psalm 119:24
⚭**119:17 Servant of the Lord:** Psalm 119:140
⚭**119:24 Pleasure:** Jeremiah 2:13
⚭**119:33 Instruction:** Micah 4:2
⚭**119:49 Hope:** Psalm 119:74

52I remember your laws from long ago,
and they comfort me, LORD.
53I become angry with wicked people
who do not keep your teachings.
54I sing about your demands
wherever I live.
55LORD, I remember you at night,
and I will obey your teachings.
56This is what I do:
I follow your orders.

57LORD, you are my share in life;
I have promised to obey your words.
58I prayed to you with all my heart.
Have mercy on me as you have promised.
59I thought about my life,
and I decided to follow your rules.
60I hurried and did not wait
to obey your commands.
61Wicked people have tied me up,
but I have not forgotten your teachings.
62In the middle of the night, I get up to thank you
because your laws are right.
63I am a friend to everyone who fears you,
to anyone who obeys your orders.
64LORD, your love fills the earth.
Teach me your demands.

65You have done good things for your servant,
as you have promised, LORD.
66Teach me wisdom and knowledge
because I trust your commands.
67Before I suffered, I did wrong,
but now I obey your word.
68You are good, and you do what is good.
Teach me your demands.
69Proud people have made up lies about me,
but I will follow your orders with all my heart.
70Those people have no feelings,
but I love your teachings.
71It was good for me to suffer
so I would learn your demands.
72Your teachings are worth more to me
than thousands of pieces of gold and silver.

73You made me and formed me with your hands.
Give me understanding so I can learn
your commands.
74Let those who respect you rejoice when
they see me,
because I put my hope in your word.
75LORD, I know that your laws are right
and that it was right for you to punish me.
76Comfort me with your love,
as you promised me, your servant.
77Have mercy on me so that I may live.
I love your teachings.
78Make proud people ashamed because they lied
about me.
But I will think about your orders.
79Let those who respect you return to me,
those who know your rules.
80Let me obey your demands perfectly
so I will not be ashamed.

81I am weak from waiting for you to save me,
but I hope in your word.
82My eyes are tired from looking for
your promise.
When will you comfort me?
83Even though I am like a wine bag going up
in smoke,
I do not forget your demands.
84How long will I live?
When will you judge those who are
hurting me?
85Proud people have dug pits to trap me.
They have nothing to do with your teachings.
86All of your commands can be trusted.
Liars are hurting me. Help me!
87They have almost put me in the grave,
but I have not rejected your orders.
88Give me life by your love
so I can obey your rules.

89LORD, your word is everlasting;
it continues forever in heaven.
90Your loyalty will go on and on;
you made the earth, and it still stands.
91All things continue to this day because of
your laws,
because all things serve you.
92If I had not loved your teachings,
I would have died from my sufferings.
93I will never forget your orders,
because you have given me life by them.
94I am yours. Save me.
I want to obey your orders.
95Wicked people are waiting to destroy me,
but I will think about your rules.
96Everything I see has its limits,
but your commands have none.

97How I love your teachings!

119:52 Comfort: Psalm 119:76
119:74 Hope: Psalm 119:81
119:76 Comfort: Isaiah 12:1
119:81 Hope: Psalm 119:114

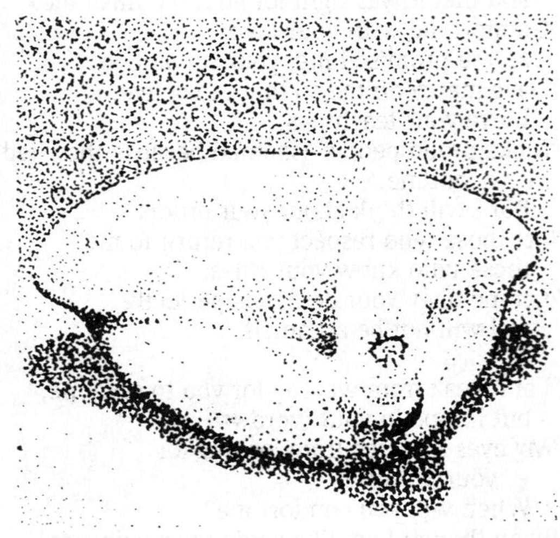

"Your word is like a lamp for my feet and a light for my path" (119:105).

I think about them all day long.
98Your commands make me wiser than
my enemies,
because they are mine forever.
99I am wiser than all my teachers,
because I think about your rules.
100I have more understanding than the older
leaders,
because I follow your orders.
101I have avoided every evil way
so I could obey your word.
102I haven't walked away from your laws,
because you yourself are my teacher.
103Your promises are sweet to me,
sweeter than honey in my mouth!
104Your orders give me understanding,
so I hate lying ways.

105Your word is like a lamp for my feet
and a light for my path.
106I will do what I have promised
and obey your fair laws.
107I have suffered for a long time.
LORD, give me life by your word.
108LORD, accept my willing praise
and teach me your laws.
109My life is always in danger,
but I haven't forgotten your teachings.
110Wicked people have set a trap for me,
but I haven't strayed from your orders.
111I will follow your rules forever,
because they make me happy.
112I will try to do what you demand
forever, until the end.
113I hate disloyal people,
but I love your teachings.
114You are my hiding place and my shield;
I hope in your word.
115Get away from me, you who do evil,
so I can keep my God's commands.
116Support me as you promised so I can live.
Don't let me be embarrassed because of
my hopes.
117Help me, and I will be saved.
I will always respect your demands.
118You reject those who ignore your demands,
because their lies mislead them.
119You throw away the wicked of the world
like trash.
So I will love your rules.
120I shake in fear of you;
I respect your laws.

121I have done what is fair and right.
Don't leave me to those who wrong me.
122Promise that you will help me, your servant.
Don't let proud people wrong me.
123My eyes are tired from looking for
your salvation
and for your good promise.
124Show your love to me, your servant,
and teach me your demands.
125I am your servant. Give me wisdom
so I can understand your rules.
126LORD, it is time for you to do something,
because people have disobeyed your teachings.
127I love your commands
more than the purest gold.
128I respect all your orders,
so I hate lying ways.

129Your rules are wonderful.
That is why I keep them.
130Learning your words gives wisdom
and understanding for the foolish.
131I am nearly out of breath.
I really want to learn your commands.
132Look at me and have mercy on me
as you do for those who love you.
133Guide my steps as you promised;
don't let any sin control me.
134Save me from harmful people
so I can obey your orders.
135Show your kindness to me, your servant.
Teach me your demands.

119:104 Hate: Proverbs 1:22

119:114 Hope: Psalm 119:147

36Tears stream from my eyes,
because people do not obey your teachings.

37LORD, you do what is right,
and your laws are fair.
38The rules you commanded are right
and completely trustworthy.
39I am so upset I am worn out,
because my enemies have forgotten
your words.
40Your promises are proven,
so I, your servant, love them.
41I am unimportant and hated,
but I have not forgotten your orders.
42Your goodness continues forever,
and your teachings are true.
43I have had troubles and misery,
but I love your commands.
44Your rules are always good.
Help me understand so I can live.

45LORD, I call to you with all my heart.
Answer me, and I will keep your demands.
46I call to you.
Save me so I can obey your rules.
47I wake up early in the morning and cry out.
I hope in your word.
48I stay awake all night
so I can think about your promises.
49Listen to me because of your love;
LORD, give me life by your laws.
50Those who love evil are near,
but they are far from your teachings.
51But, LORD, you are also near,
and all your commands are true.
52Long ago I learned from your rules
that you made them to continue forever.

53See my suffering and rescue me,
because I have not forgotten
your teachings.
54Argue my case and save me.
Let me live by your promises.
55Wicked people are far from being saved,
because they do not want
your demands.
56LORD, you are very kind;
give me life by your laws.
57Many enemies are after me,
but I have not rejected your rules.
58I see those traitors, and I hate them,
because they do not obey what you say.

159See how I love your orders.
LORD, give me life by your love.
160Your words are true from the start,
and all your laws will be fair forever.

161Leaders attack me for no reason,
but I fear your law in my heart.
162I am as happy over your promises
as if I had found a great treasure.
163I hate and despise lies,
but I love your teachings.
164Seven times a day I praise you
for your fair laws.
165Those who love your teachings will
find true peace,
and nothing will defeat them.
166I am waiting for you to save me, LORD.
I will obey your commands.
167I obey your rules,
and I love them very much.
168I obey your orders and rules,
because you know everything I do.

169Hear my cry to you, LORD.
Let your word help me understand.
170Listen to my prayer;
save me as you promised.
171Let me speak your praise,
because you have taught me
your demands.
172Let me sing about your promises,
because all your commands are fair.
173Give me your helping hand,
because I have chosen your commands.
174I want you to save me, LORD.
I love your teachings.
175Let me live so I can praise you,
and let your laws help me.
176I have wandered like a lost sheep.
Look for your servant, because I have not
forgotten your commands.

A Prayer of Someone Far from Home

A psalm for going up to worship.

120 When I was in trouble, I called to the LORD,
and he answered me.
2LORD, save me from liars
and from those who plan evil.

3You who plan evil, what will God do to you?
How will he punish you?

119:140 Servant of the Lord: Psalm 123:1–2
119:147 Hope: Matthew 25:1–13
119:165 Peace: Isaiah 9:6
119:176 Obedience: Nehemiah 1:4–9

4He will punish you with the sharp arrows
of a warrior
and with burning coals of wood.

5How terrible it is for me to live in the
land of Meshech,
to live among the people of Kedar.
6I have lived too long
with people who hate peace.
7When I talk peace,
they want war.

The LORD Guards His People

A song for going up to worship.

121 I look up to the hills,
but where does my help come from?
2My help comes from the LORD,
who made heaven and earth.

3He will not let you be defeated.
He who guards you never sleeps.
4He who guards Israel
never rests or sleeps.
5The LORD guards you.
The LORD is the shade that protects
you from the sun.
6The sun cannot hurt you during the day,
and the moon cannot hurt you at night.
7The LORD will protect you from
all dangers;
he will guard your life.
8The LORD will guard you as you
come and go,
both now and forever.

Happy People in Jerusalem

A song for going up to worship. Of David.

122 I was happy when they said to me,
"Let's go to the Temple of the LORD."
2Jerusalem, we are standing
at your gates.

3Jerusalem is built as a city
with the buildings close together.
4The tribes go up there,
the tribes who belong to the LORD.
It is the rule in Israel
to praise the LORD at Jerusalem.
5There the descendants of David
set their thrones to judge the people.

6Pray for peace in Jerusalem:
"May those who love her be safe.
7May there be peace within her walls
and safety within her strong towers."
8To help my relatives and friends,
I say, "Let Jerusalem have peace."
9For the sake of the Temple of the LORD
our God,
I wish good for her.⚭

A Prayer for Mercy

A song for going up to worship.

123 LORD, I look upward to you,
you who live in heaven.
2Slaves depend on their masters,
and a female servant depends on
her mistress.
In the same way, we depend on the LORD
our God;
we wait for him to show us mercy.⚭

3Have mercy on us, LORD. Have mercy on us,
because we have been insulted.
4We have suffered many insults from
lazy people
and much cruelty from the proud.

The LORD Saves His People

A song for going up to worship. Of David.

124 What if the LORD had not been on
our side?
(Let Israel repeat this.)
2What if the LORD had not been on our side
when we were attacked?
3When they were angry with us,
they would have swallowed us alive.
4They would have been like a flood
drowning us;
they would have poured over us like a river.
5 They would have swept us away like a
mighty stream.

6Praise the LORD,
who did not let them chew us up.
7We escaped like a bird
from the hunter's trap.
The trap broke,
and we escaped.
8Our help comes from the LORD,
who made heaven and earth.

120:5 *Meshech and Kedar.* Meshech and Kedar are far away from Israel. Meshech was in Asia Minor (Genesis 10:2; Ezekiel 38:2), and Kedar was in Arabia (Isaiah 21:16).

⚭**122:9 City:** Matthew 5:14

⚭**123:2 Servant of the Lord:** Isaiah 41:8

TEST/TEMPTATION

MATTHEW 4:1

Does God test his people? For what purpose? How does the temptation of Jesus relate to the temptations of Israel in the desert? Are Christians tested today?

The themes of testing and temptation are very important for the Christian. We must look at the difference between these themes in order to avoid confusion. Testing in the Bible can be understood in three ways. First, it is something that is done by God in order to strengthen, develop, or purify our character d usually takes the form of some kind of trouble, hardship, or discipline (Daniel 11:35; Romans 5:3–5; ebrews 12:4–11). Sometimes it is described under the image of refining something, which means to make mething, like gold or silver, pure in a fire (Psalm 66:10; Malachi 3:2–3). God removes impurities from our aracters (Isaiah 48:10) so that we may be holy. A special character quality produced is patience or durance (James 1:3–4). Second, testing is done by God to prove how genuine our faith is, to see what our arts are really like (Deuteronomy 8:2) and to see whether we will obey him (Exodus 16:4) and this, too, ually involves some kind of hardship. The story of Abraham and Isaac in Genesis 22 is a good example of is (Genesis 22:1, 12; Hebrews 11:17–19). This type of testing can also occur under the image of refining mething, for as gold is refined its true nature is seen. This is how our faith is shown to be real (Job 23:10; Peter 1:7). These kinds of testings are done by God for our benefit. A third kind of testing described in the ble is from Satan and is very destructive. This temptation might cause Christians to lose their influence rough some sin. Or it could get them into such a difficult situation that they might give up their faith.

Temptation in the Bible always has a negative meaning, which is, namely, to try to get someone to do mething sinful. It is done by Satan (Mark 1:13), or by our own evil desires (James 1:14), but never by God mes 1:13). However, we must remember that God allows temptations and can use them to strengthen d prove our faith in the ways described above (James 1:12), if we know how to respond to them.

We can learn much about Satan's methods and how to respond to them by studying the temptation of sus in the desert (Matthew 4:1–11) and comparing it to Israel's experience (Deuteronomy 8:2), for there many important similarities. Besides the similar setting (the desert) and numbering (forty), we can serve that Satan's first temptation (Matthew 4:3–4) was to try to get Jesus to act without God's help and isfy his hunger by relying upon himself to provide his needs.

The people of Israel were tested in the same way. The issue was whether they would accept God's provin for their needs or be unhappy with what God fed them. We know the sad answer to that (Numbers :4–6). Fortunately, Jesus responded differently. He quoted Deuteronomy 8:2–3, which in effect says that is more than just the satisfaction of our wants but includes obedience to God's word. Satan's second nptation (Matthew 4:5–7) was to try to get Jesus to jump off the Temple on purpose. Satan even quoted ripture (Psalm 91:11–12) as part of his temptation. The idea was to test God to see if he would protect sus from harm as God had promised. In the same way the people of Israel were protected by God in the sert (Deuteronomy 1:32; 32:10) because of his presence with them. Later in Old Testament history the mple came to symbolize God's protective presence, and Psalm 91 (which was quoted by Satan) was probly written with that in mind. Tragically, God's people questioned whether he was really with them during eir desert experience (Exodus 17:76) and, in doing so, were guilty of testing the Lord (Numbers 14:22; alm 78:41). This means they doubted or questioned his ability to lovingly provide, protect, or care for his n. Jesus rejects Satan's approach by quoting Deuteronomy 6:16. He rightly saw that demanding miracus protection as proof of God's care was wrong. The proper attitude is trust and obedience.

Satan's third temptation (Matthew 4:8–10) had to do with Jesus' ultimate loyalty. Would Jesus remain thful to God and his plan, even if it meant great suffering, or would he take a shortcut, worship Satan and cept his attractive offer of the kingdoms of the world? This, too, relates to Israel's experience in the desert, Moses warns them that once they enter the Promised Land with all of its riches they might forget God d be attracted to other gods (Deuteronomy 6:10–15; 8:10–20). Jesus' answer is seen against this backound. Again, tragically, the people of Israel failed this test (Judges 2:10–15), but Jesus overcomes this nptation by quoting Deuteronomy 6:13, which immediately follows the great love commandment (6:5).

Christians are tested and tempted today in similar ways. Are we willing to trust God to provide for us ilippians 4:19) and protect us (Psalm 91:9), or do we doubt him?

Test/Temptation: For additional scriptures on this topic go to Exodus 15:25.

DARKNESS

MATTHEW 4:12–16

What is the symbolic significance of "darkness" in the Bible?

Darkness appears throughout the Bible as a symbol for ignorance and evil. It is often used in conjunction with night and is contrasted with light and day, which are symbols of God's presence and salvation.

No one can see in the dark. To people unaware of the scientific explanations of the rotation of the earth and its revolutions around the sun, the darkness of night was a mysterious and divine act. The only way to light up a dark room or to light the way in the dark night was with an oil lamp or a fire. But these only provided a small amount of light around the flame. It is hard to imagine the complete darkness people experienced without electric lights inside and street lights outside. Such darkness meant it was impossible to travel or work or to even know what was going on around you. Not knowing made many people feel uncomfortable, even afraid. It was probably for these simple reasons that darkness became a symbol for things people could not understand or feared.

Genesis began with the world in darkness. History began with God's words, "'Let there be light,' and there was light. God saw that the light was good, so he divided the light from the darkness" (Genesis 1:3–4). The idea that light and day are "good" and that darkness and night are "evil" is carried through the Old Testament into the New Testament.

In the Old Testament darkness is primarily a symbol of death and judgment. The Old Testament does not contain much teaching on what happens after death. The after-life was something many feared and did not understand. Job spoke of his death as darkness. In Job 10:21–22 Job lamented, "Soon I will leave; I will not return from the land of darkness and gloom, the land of darkest night, from the land of gloom and confusion, where even the light is darkness" (see also 17:13). The Psalms use the symbol in the same way (88:6, 18; 143:3). Psalm 88:6 says, "You have brought me close to death; I am almost in the dark place of the dead."

Darkness as divine judgment is the most frequent use of the symbol. It was used as a plague against the Egyptians in Exodus 10 (see also Psalm 105:28); as a curse against those who disobey their parents in Proverbs 20:20; and as a symbol of the impending destruction of Babylon in Isaiah 47:5. Darkness is also used by the prophets as a symbol of the destruction of Israel and Judah (Jeremiah 13:16; Joel 2:2; Amos 5:18; Zephaniah 1:15). Finally, it is used by Jesus to describe hell, which is called "darkness" (Matthew 25:30).

In Isaiah, darkness is often a symbol of people who do not know God's laws and God's grace. There are those who are in "darkness" by their own choice, rejecting God's laws and grace (Isaiah 5:20), and those who have never had the chance to see, for whom God provides light and salvation.

Today, to say someone is "in the dark" means that they do not understand or do not know the truth about something. In the New Testament, "darkness" and "night" are used in this way to refer to people who do not understand the Good News Jesus brings. When Nicodemus questioned Jesus, the writer noted that he came at night (John 3:2). Matthew 4:13–16 is a quote from the Old Testament prophet Isaiah stating that the non-Jewish people who did not know God are said to be in darkness. Jesus is the great light Matthew was describing. Jesus has come to bring "light" or to help people understand God's love for them. In John 8:12, Jesus said, "I am the light of the world. The person who follows me will never live in darkness but will have the light that gives life. Jesus also speaks of his followers as the light of the world (Matthew 5:14). Like Jesus, they are to let people know about God's love for them.

Darkness and night are also used to symbolize the behavior of people who do not understand the Good News of Jesus. Paul compared the way people lived their lives before they knew Jesus to the way they should live after they received the Good News of Christ. In Ephesians 5:8–9, Paul wrote, "In the past you were full of darkness, but now you are full of light in the Lord. So live like children who belong to the light." In 2 Corinthians 6:14 he made the same point, "You are not the same as those who do not believe. So do not join yourselves to them. Good and bad do not belong together. Light and darkness cannot share together."

Today, "darkness" and "night" are still used as symbols of that which we fear or do not understand. Though we now have electric lights everywhere on a dark night, people still need the kind of light Christ brings into the world. That is the knowledge of God's grace that turns lack of understanding into confidence and fear into trust.

Darkness: For additional scriptures on this topic go to Job 15:23.

God Protects Those Who Trust Him

A song for going up to worship.

125 Those who trust the LORD are like
Mount Zion,
which sits unmoved forever.
2As the mountains surround Jerusalem,
the LORD surrounds his people
now and forever.⚭

3The wicked will not rule
over those who do right.
If they did, the people who do right
might use their power to do evil.

4LORD, be good to those who are good,
whose hearts are honest.
5But, LORD, when you remove those
who do evil,
also remove those who stop following you.

Let there be peace in Israel.

LORD, Bring Your People Back

A song for going up to worship.

126 When the LORD brought the prisoners
back to Jerusalem,
it seemed as if we were dreaming.
2Then we were filled with laughter,
and we sang happy songs.
Then the other nations said,
"The LORD has done great things
for them."
3The LORD has done great things for us,
and we are very glad.

4LORD, return our prisoners again,
as you bring streams to the desert.
5Those who cry as they plant crops
will sing at harvest time.
6Those who cry
as they carry out the seeds
will return singing
and carrying bundles of grain.

All Good Things Come from God

A song for going up to worship. Of Solomon.

127 If the LORD doesn't build the house,
the builders are working for nothing.
If the LORD doesn't guard the city,
the guards are watching for nothing.
2It is no use for you to get up early
and stay up late,
working for a living.
The LORD gives sleep to those he loves.⚭
3Children are a gift from the LORD;
babies are a reward.
4Children who are born to a young man
are like arrows in the hand of a warrior.
5Happy is the man
who has his bag full of arrows.
They will not be defeated
when they fight their enemies at the city gate.⚭

The Happy Home

A song for going up to worship.

128 Happy are those who respect the LORD
and obey him.⚭
2You will enjoy what you work for,
and you will be blessed with good things.
3Your wife will give you many children,
like a vine that produces much fruit.
Your children will bring you much good,
like olive branches that produce many olives.
4This is how the man who respects the LORD
will be blessed.
5May the LORD bless you from Mount Zion;
may you enjoy the good things of
Jerusalem all your life.
6May you see your grandchildren.

Let there be peace in Israel.⚭

A Prayer Against the Enemies

A song for going up to worship.

129 They have treated me badly all my life.
(Let Israel repeat this.)

⚭**125:2 Jerusalem:** Jeremiah 7:3

125:2 *the mountains surround Jerusalem.* The mountains surround Jerusalem and serve as their first line of defense.

126:1 *brought the prisoners back to Jerusalem.* This may be a reference to the return of the exiles from the Babylonian captivity (see the Book of Ezra) after 539 B.C.

⚭**127:2 House/Home:** Jeremiah 29:5

⚭**127:2 Time:** Proverbs 19:21

127:4–5 The psalmist compares children to a warrior's arrows, because one's children are a source of family strength in trouble. Today's children are tomorrow's church. They must be guided and prepared to continue the spiritual warfare in which the church is engaged until Christ returns.

⚭**127:5 Children:** Psalm 128

⚭**128:1 Happiness:** Psalm 137:8

128:3 *vine.* Olive trees and vines produced olives and grapes, staples of Israel's diet.

128:5 *Zion.* The location of the Temple.

⚭**128:6 Blessing:** Proverbs 10:6

⚭**128:6 Children:** Matthew 18:1–5

⚭**128:6 Infertility (Childlessness/Barrenness):** See article on page 862.

129:1 *They have treated me badly all my life.* Israel was oppressed throughout its history, and so the Israelites speak with one voice here and express their pain.

2They have treated me badly all my life,
but they have not defeated me.
3Like farmers plowing, they plowed over
my back,
making long wounds.
4But the LORD does what is right;
he has set me free from those wicked people.

5Let those who hate Jerusalem
be turned back in shame.
6Let them be like the grass on the roof
that dries up before it has grown.
7There is not enough of it to fill a hand
or to make into a bundle to fill one's arms.
8Let those who pass by them not say,
"May the LORD bless you.
We bless you by the power of the LORD."

A Prayer for Mercy

A song for going up to worship.

130 LORD, I am in great trouble,
so I call out to you.
2Lord, hear my voice;
listen to my prayer for help.
3LORD, if you punished people for all their sins,
no one would be left, Lord.
4But you forgive us,
so you are respected.

5I wait for the LORD to help me,
and I trust his word.
6I wait for the Lord to help me
more than night watchmen wait for the dawn,
more than night watchmen wait for the dawn.

7People of Israel, put your hope in the LORD
because he is loving
and able to save.
8He will save Israel
from all their sins.

Childlike Trust in the LORD

A song for going up to worship. Of David.

131 LORD, my heart is not proud;
I don't look down on others.
I don't do great things,
and I can't do miracles.
2But I am calm and quiet,
like a baby with its mother.
I am at peace, like a baby with its mother.

3People of Israel, put your hope in the LORD
now and forever.

In Praise of the Temple

A song for going up to worship.

132 LORD, remember David
and all his suffering.
2He made an oath to the LORD,
a promise to the Mighty God of Jacob.
3He said, "I will not go home to my house,
or lie down on my bed,
4or close my eyes,
or let myself sleep
5until I find a place for the LORD.
I want to provide a home for the Mighty God
of Jacob."

6We heard about the Ark in Bethlehem.
We found it at Kiriath Jearim.
7Let's go to the LORD's house.
Let's worship at his footstool.
8Rise, LORD, and come to your resting place;
come with the Ark that shows
your strength.
9May your priests do what is right.
May your people sing for joy.

10For the sake of your servant David,
do not reject your appointed king.
11The LORD made a promise to David,
a sure promise that he will not take back.
He promised, "I will make one of
your descendants
rule as king after you.
12If your sons keep my agreement
and the rules that I teach them,
then their sons after them will rule
on your throne forever and ever."∞

13The LORD has chosen Jerusalem;
he wants it for his home.
14He says, "This is my resting place forever.
Here is where I want to stay.
15I will bless her with plenty;
I will fill her poor with food.
16I will cover her priests with salvation,
and those who worship me will really
sing for joy.

17"I will make a king come from the family
of David.

132:7 *at his footstool.* The Ark of the Agreement that was kept in the Holy Place in the Holy Tent was sometimes referred to as God's footstool (1 Chronicles 28:2).

132:12 This reminds God of the promise he made to David in 2 Samuel 7:11–16.

∞**132:12 Agreement:** Isaiah 24:5

I will provide my appointed one descendants
to rule after him.
I will cover his enemies with shame,
but his crown will shine."

he Love of God's People

A song for going up to worship. Of David.

133 It is good and pleasant
when God's people live together in
peace!
It is like perfumed oil poured on the priest's head
and running down his beard.
It ran down Aaron's beard
and on to the collar of his robes.
It is like the dew of Mount Hermon
falling on the hills of Jerusalem.
There the LORD gives his blessing
of life forever.

emple Guards, Praise the LORD

A song for going up to worship.

134 Praise the LORD, all you servants of
the LORD,
you who serve at night in the Temple of
the LORD.
Raise your hands in the Temple
and praise the LORD.

May the LORD bless you from Mount Zion,
he who made heaven and earth.

he LORD Saves, Idols Do Not

135 Praise the LORD!

Praise the name of the LORD;
praise him, you servants of the LORD,
you who stand in the LORD's Temple
and in the Temple courtyards.
Praise the LORD, because he is good;
sing praises to him, because it is pleasant.

The LORD has chosen the people of Jacob
for himself;
he has chosen the people of Israel for his
very own.
5I know that the LORD is great.
Our Lord is greater than all the gods.
6The LORD does what he pleases,
in heaven and on earth,
in the seas and the deep oceans.
7He brings the clouds from the ends of the earth.
He sends the lightning with the rain.
He brings out the wind from his storehouses.

8He destroyed the firstborn sons in Egypt
the firstborn of both people and animals.
9He did many signs and miracles in Egypt
against the king and his servants.
10He defeated many nations
and killed powerful kings:
11Sihon king of the Amorites,
Og king of Bashan,
and all the kings of Canaan.
12Then he gave their land as a gift,
a gift to his people, the Israelites.

13LORD, your name is everlasting;
LORD, you will be remembered forever.
14The LORD defends his people
and has mercy on his servants.

15The idols of other nations are made of silver
and gold,
the work of human hands.
16They have mouths, but they cannot speak.
They have eyes, but they cannot see.
17They have ears, but they cannot hear.
They have no breath in their mouths.
18People who make idols will be like them,
and so will those who trust them.

19Family of Israel, praise the LORD.
Family of Aaron, praise the LORD.
20Family of Levi, praise the LORD.
You who respect the LORD should praise him.
21You people of Jerusalem, praise the LORD on
Mount Zion.
Praise the LORD!

132:18 David: Isaiah 55:3
3 The psalmist expresses wonder at the sight of people living gether in peace. Since the Fall, human beings have been separated m one another, more interested in themselves than in other peo-. As the New Testament teaches, it is only as God reconciles us to nself that we can truly become close to one another.
3:3 *like the dew of Mount Hermon.* The unity between brother aelites is likened to the dew of Mount Hermon—a majestic moun-n on the north border of Israel—falling on the hills of Jerusalem ny miles away.
4:3 *Mount Zion.* Mount Zion was the location of the Temple of the d.

135:1 *you servants of the LORD.* The context indicates that these servants are the priests who serve in the Temple area.
135:5–6 In these verses the psalmist proclaims that the God of Israel is greater than all other gods because he does whatever he pleases. This claim is meaningful because the psalmist knows exactly what God has done in the past and gives him praise for his actions on behalf of Israel in the following verses. Take some time to think about what God has done for his people—including you—and give him praise for his greatness.
135:7 Since many people of Israel were tempted to worship Baal, the god of the storm, this reference to God's ability to control the rains may have had special significance.

God's Love Continues Forever

136 Give thanks to the LORD because he
is good.
His love continues forever.
2Give thanks to the God of gods.
His love continues forever.
3Give thanks to the Lord of lords.
His love continues forever.

4Only he can do great miracles.
His love continues forever.
5With his wisdom he made the skies.
His love continues forever.
6He spread out the earth on the seas.
His love continues forever.
7He made the sun and the moon.
His love continues forever.
8He made the sun to rule the day.
His love continues forever.
9He made the moon and stars to rule the night.
His love continues forever.

10He killed the firstborn sons of the Egyptians.
His love continues forever.
11He brought the people of Israel out of Egypt.
His love continues forever.
12He did it with his great power and strength.
His love continues forever.
13He parted the water of the Red Sea.
His love continues forever.
14He brought the Israelites through the middle
of it.
His love continues forever.
15But the king of Egypt and his army drowned in
the Red Sea.
His love continues forever.

16He led his people through the desert.
His love continues forever.
17He defeated great kings.
His love continues forever.
18He killed powerful kings.
His love continues forever.
19He defeated Sihon king of the Amorites.
His love continues forever.
20He defeated Og king of Bashan.
His love continues forever.
21He gave their land as a gift.
His love continues forever.
22It was a gift to his servants, the Israelites.
His love continues forever.
23He remembered us when we were in trouble.
His love continues forever.
24He freed us from our enemies.
His love continues forever.
25He gives food to every living creature.
His love continues forever.

26Give thanks to the God of heaven.
His love continues forever.

Israelites in Captivity

137 By the rivers in Babylon we sat and cried
when we remembered Jerusalem.
2On the poplar trees nearby
we hung our harps.
3Those who captured us asked us to sing;
our enemies wanted happy songs.
They said, "Sing us a song
about Jerusalem!"

4But we cannot sing songs about the LORD
while we are in this foreign country!
5Jerusalem, if I forget you,
let my right hand lose its skill.
6Let my tongue stick to the roof of my mouth
if I do not remember you,
if I do not think about Jerusalem
as my greatest joy.

7LORD, remember what the Edomites did
on the day Jerusalem fell.
They said, "Tear it down!
Tear it down to its foundations!"

8People of Babylon, you will be destroyed.
The people who pay you back for what you
did to us will be happy.∞
9They will grab your babies
and throw them against the rocks.∞

A Hymn of Thanksgiving

A psalm of David.

138 LORD, I will thank you with all my heart;
I will sing to you before the gods.
2I will bow down facing your holy Temple,
and I will thank you for your love and loyalty.

136:1 Psalm 136 was probably a liturgical poem. The priest would say the first line of each verse, and then the congregation would together give the response, "his love continues forever."

137:1 This psalm was certainly written during the time that Israel was in captivity in Babylon.

137:7 The people of Edom were especially cruel to Israel during the time of their defeat. The prophet Obadiah looks forward to their coming punishment.

∞**137:8 Happiness:** Psalm 144:15

∞**137:9 Babylon:** Isaiah 13:1–14:27

You have made your name and your word
greater than anything.
3On the day I called to you, you answered me.
You made me strong and brave.

4LORD, let all the kings of the earth praise you
when they hear the words you speak.
5They will sing about what the LORD has done,
because the LORD's glory is great.

6Though the LORD is supreme,
he takes care of those who are humble,
but he stays away from the proud.
7LORD, even when I have trouble all around me,
you will keep me alive.
When my enemies are angry,
you will reach down and save me by
your power.
8LORD, you do everything for me.
LORD, your love continues forever.
Do not leave us, whom you made.

God Knows Everything

For the director of music. A psalm of David.

139 LORD, you have examined me
and know all about me.⚭
2You know when I sit down and when I get up.
You know my thoughts before I think them.
3You know where I go and where I lie down.
You know thoroughly everything I do.
4LORD, even before I say a word,
you already know it.
5You are all around me—in front and in back—
and have put your hand on me.
6Your knowledge is amazing to me;
it is more than I can understand.

7Where can I go to get away from your Spirit?
Where can I run from you?
8If I go up to the heavens, you are there.
If I lie down in the grave, you are there.
9If I rise with the sun in the east
and settle in the west beyond the sea,
10even there you would guide me.
With your right hand you would hold me.

11I could say, "The darkness will hide me.
Let the light around me turn into night."
12But even the darkness is not dark to you.
The night is as light as the day;
darkness and light are the same to you.

13You made my whole being;
you formed me in my mother's body.
14I praise you because you made me in an
amazing and wonderful way.
What you have done is wonderful.
I know this very well.
15You saw my bones being formed
as I took shape in my mother's body.
When I was put together there,
16 you saw my body as it was formed.
All the days planned for me
were written in your book
before I was one day old.⚭

17God, your thoughts are precious to me.
They are so many!
18If I could count them,
they would be more than all the grains
of sand.
When I wake up,
I am still with you.

19God, I wish you would kill the wicked!
Get away from me, you murderers!
20They say evil things about you.
Your enemies use your name thoughtlessly.
21LORD, I hate those who hate you;
I hate those who rise up against you.
22I feel only hate for them;
they are my enemies.

23God, examine me and know my heart;
test me and know my nervous thoughts.⚭
24See if there is any bad thing in me.
Lead me on the road to everlasting life.⚭

A Prayer for Protection

For the director of music. A psalm of David.

140 LORD, rescue me from evil people;
protect me from cruel people
2who make evil plans,
who always start fights.
3They make their tongues sharp as a snake's;
their words are like snake poison. *Selah*

139 Psalm 139:13–16 is one of the few biblical passages that speaks of fetal life. As such, it is one of the few passages that has some relevance to the abortion issue. These verses strongly suggest that God spans the believer's *entire life* (v. 16), and this life apparently begins in the womb (v. 13). It should be remembered, however, that Psalm 139 does not address the abortion issue directly. For this reason, it is perhaps wise not to treat this passage as a proof text.

⚭**139:1 Test/Temptation:** Psalm 139:23–24
⚭**139:16 Abortion and Crisis Pregnancy:** See article on page 532.
⚭**139:23 A Matter of the Heart:** Luke 16:15
⚭**139:24 Leadership:** Psalm 143:10
⚭**139:24 Presence of God:** Jeremiah 7:4
⚭**139:24 Test/Temptation:** Jeremiah 17:10

4LORD, guard me from the power of
wicked people;
protect me from cruel people
who plan to trip me up.
5The proud hid a trap for me.
They spread out a net beside the road;
they set traps for me. *Selah*

6I said to the LORD, "You are my God."
LORD, listen to my prayer for help.
7LORD God, my mighty savior,
you protect me in battle.
8LORD, do not give the wicked what
they want.
Don't let their plans succeed,
or they will become proud. *Selah*

9Those around me have
planned trouble.
Now let it come to them.
10Let burning coals fall on them.
Throw them into the fire
or into pits from which they
cannot escape.
11Don't let liars settle in the land.
Let evil quickly hunt down cruel people.

12I know the LORD will get justice for the poor
and will defend the needy in court.
13Good people will praise his name;
honest people will live in his presence.

A Prayer Not to Sin

A psalm of David.

141 LORD, I call to you. Come quickly.
Listen to me when I call to you.
2Let my prayer be like incense placed before you,
and my praise like the evening sacrifice.⚭

3LORD, help me control my tongue;
help me be careful about what I say.
4Take away my desire to do evil
or to join others in doing wrong.
Don't let me eat tasty food
with those who do evil.

5If a good person punished me, that would
be kind.
If he corrected me, that would be like
perfumed oil on my head.
I shouldn't refuse it.
But I pray against those who do evil.

6 Let their leaders be thrown down the cliffs.
Then people will know that I have
spoken correctly:
7"The ground is plowed and broken up.
In the same way, our bones have been
scattered at the grave."

8GOD, I look to you for help.
I trust in you, LORD. Don't let me die.
9Protect me from the traps they set for me
and from the net that evil people have spread.
10Let the wicked fall into their own nets,
but let me pass by safely.

A Prayer for Safety

A maskil of David when he was in the cave. A prayer.

142 I cry out to the LORD;
I pray to the LORD for mercy.
2I pour out my problems to him;
I tell him my troubles.
3When I am afraid,
you, LORD, know the way out.
In the path where I walk,
a trap is hidden for me.
4Look around me and see.
No one cares about me.
I have no place of safety;
no one cares if I live.

5LORD, I cry out to you.
I say, "You are my protection.
You are all I want in this life."
6Listen to my cry,
because I am helpless.
Save me from those who are chasing me,
because they are too strong for me.
7Free me from my prison,
and then I will praise your name.
Then good people will surround me,
because you have taken care of me.

A Prayer Not to Be Killed

A psalm of David.

143 LORD, hear my prayer;
listen to my cry for mercy.
Answer me
because you are loyal and good.
2Don't judge me, your servant,
because no one alive is right before you.
3My enemies are chasing me;
they crushed me to the ground.

⚭**141:2 Prayer:** Isaiah 56:7

141:2 *like incense place before you.* Incense was valuable and it was something that brought pleasure to the Lord (Exodus 30:34–38).

They made me live in darkness
like those long dead.
4I am afraid;
my courage is gone.

5I remember what happened long ago;
I consider everything you have done.
I think about all you have made.
6I lift my hands to you in prayer.
As a dry land needs rain, I thirst
for you. *Selah*

7LORD, answer me quickly,
because I am getting weak.
Don't turn away from me,
or I will be like those who are dead.
8Tell me in the morning about your love,
because I trust you.
Show me what I should do,
because my prayers go up to you.
9LORD, save me from my enemies;
I hide in you.
10Teach me to do what you want,
because you are my God.
Let your good Spirit
lead me on level ground.

11LORD, let me live
so people will praise you.
In your goodness
save me from my troubles.
12In your love defeat my enemies.
Destroy all those who trouble me,
because I am your servant.

A Prayer for Victory

Of David.

144 Praise the LORD, my Rock,
who trains me for war,
who trains me for battle.
2He protects me like a strong, walled city, and
he loves me.
He is my defender and my Savior,
my shield and my protection.
He helps me keep my people under control.

3LORD, why are people important to you?
Why do you even think about human beings?
4People are like a breath;
their lives are like passing shadows.
5LORD, tear open the sky and come down.
Touch the mountains so they will smoke.
6Send the lightning and scatter my enemies.
Shoot your arrows and force them away.
7Reach down from above.
Save me and rescue me out of this sea
of enemies,
from these foreigners.
8They are liars;
they are dishonest.

9God, I will sing a new song to you;
I will play to you on the ten-stringed harp.
10You give victory to kings.
You save your servant David from cruel swords.
11Save me, rescue me from these foreigners.
They are liars; they are dishonest.

12Let our sons in their youth
grow like plants.
Let our daughters be
like the decorated stones in the Temple.
13Let our barns be filled
with crops of all kinds.
Let our sheep in the fields have
thousands and tens of thousands of lambs.
14 Let our cattle be strong.
Let no one break in.
Let there be no war,
no screams in our streets.

15Happy are those who are like this;
happy are the people whose God is the LORD.

Praise to God the King

A psalm of praise. Of David.

145 I praise your greatness, my God the King;
I will praise you forever and ever.
2I will praise you every day;
I will praise you forever and ever.
3The LORD is great and worthy of our praise;
no one can understand how great he is.

4Parents will tell their children what you
have done.
They will retell your mighty acts,
5wonderful majesty, and glory.
And I will think about your miracles.
6They will tell about the amazing things you do,
and I will tell how great you are.

143:5 Meditation: Philippians 4:8
143:10 Leadership: Proverbs 15:21
144:1 *who trains me for war.* Warfare was an act of worship for the people of Israel (Deuteronomy 7, 20). After all, God was with them as their divine warrior (Exodus 15:3).

144:2 Images of God: Isaiah 5:1–7
144:9 *a new song.* See 33:3.
144:12 Women: Matthew 19:3–12
144:15 Happiness: Psalm 146:5

7 They will remember your great goodness
and will sing about your fairness.

8 The LORD is kind and shows mercy.
He does not become angry quickly but
is full of love.
9 The LORD is good to everyone;
he is merciful to all he has made.
10 LORD, everything you have made will
praise you;
those who belong to you will bless you.
11 They will tell about the glory of your kingdom
and will speak about your power.
12 Then everyone will know the mighty
things you do
and the glory and majesty of your kingdom.
13 Your kingdom will go on and on,
and you will rule forever.

The LORD will keep all his promises;
he is loyal to all he has made.
14 The LORD helps those who have been defeated
and takes care of those who are in trouble.
15 All living things look to you for food,
and you give it to them at the right time.
16 You open your hand,
and you satisfy all living things.

17 Everything the LORD does is right.
He is loyal to all he has made.
18 The LORD is close to everyone who prays to him,
to all who truly pray to him.
19 He gives those who respect him what they want.
He listens when they cry, and he saves them.
20 The LORD protects everyone who loves him,
but he will destroy the wicked.

21 I will praise the LORD.
Let everyone praise his holy name forever.

Praise God Who Helps the Weak

146 Praise the LORD!
My whole being, praise the LORD.
2 I will praise the LORD all my life;
I will sing praises to my God as long as I live.

3 Do not put your trust in princes
or other people, who cannot save you.
4 When people die, they are buried.
Then all of their plans come to an end.

5 Happy are those who are helped by the God
of Jacob.
Their hope is in the LORD their God.
6 He made heaven and earth,
the sea and everything in it.
He remains loyal forever.
7 He does what is fair for those who
have been wronged.
He gives food to the hungry.
The LORD sets the prisoners free.
8 The LORD gives sight to the blind.
The LORD lifts up people who are
in trouble.
The LORD loves those who do right.
9 The LORD protects the foreigners.
He defends the orphans and widows,
but he blocks the way of the wicked.

10 The LORD will be King forever.
Jerusalem, your God is everlasting.

Praise the LORD!

Praise God Who Helps His People

147 Praise the LORD!

It is good to sing praises to our God;
it is good and pleasant to praise him.
2 The LORD rebuilds Jerusalem;
he brings back the captured Israelites.
3 He heals the brokenhearted
and bandages their wounds.

4 He counts the stars
and names each one.
5 Our Lord is great and very powerful.
There is no limit to what he knows.
6 The LORD defends the humble,
but he throws the wicked to the ground.

7 Sing praises to the LORD;
praise our God with harps.
8 He fills the sky with clouds
and sends rain to the earth
and makes grass grow on the hills.
9 He gives food to cattle
and to the little birds that call.

10 He does not enjoy the strength of a horse
or the strength of a man.

145:8 Anger: Matthew 26:39
145:10 Environment: Psalm 148
146:5 Happiness: Jeremiah 12:1
146:6 Earth: Isaiah 65:17
146:9 Foreigner (Alien): Ezekiel 47:22

147:2 *the captured Israelites.* This reference to returning captured Israelites is most likely associated with the return of a remnant of Israel after the Babylonian captivity (see the Book of Ezra and Thematic Ariticle, "The Remnant").

BEATITUDES

MATTHEW 5

Do the Beatitudes describe character qualities or blessings from God?

What person would not like to find the secret of happiness? The Beatitudes in Matthew 5 (and the parallel passage in Luke 6) describe the happiness that comes with membership in God's kingdom—and the price of that happiness.

The expression "happy are those" translates into English the Greek word *makarios*, which, in turn translates a similar phrase in the Old Testament (based on the Hebrew word *'aser*). These phrases describe the person who is "happy" or "fortunate" or "blessed." In the Old Testament, happiness comes to people who are faithful in their relationships with God. Those who belong to God are fortunate and blessed (Psalm 33:12). Being chosen by God makes Israel a blessed people (Psalm 65:4). Naturally, those who trust in God find well-being and blessing (Psalms 40:4; 85:10–14).

Blessing and happiness flow to those people who seek God in order to obey the Lord (Psalms 106:3; 112:1; 128:1, 2). Therefore, happiness comes when we avoid those things which would bring us misery by leading us away from God—the sad influence of the wicked (Psalm 1:1–2) and the misleading influence of idols (Psalm 40:4). If obedience leads to happiness, then even God's correction leads to happiness, if we learn to leave disobedience behind (Job 5:17). God not only corrects us, but he also forgives us, renewing our happiness as we renew our relationships with him (Psalm 32:1–2).

The happy person is the wise person, who knows God and seeks to know the ways of God better (Proverbs 3:13; 8:32). Happiness comes with doing the right thing, and with respect and hard work (Proverbs 20:9; 28:14). In short, the righteous person experiences the blessings of God and lives the fortunate life.

Matthew 5:1–12 describes the fortunate person as a member of the community of the kingdom of God. The Beatitudes do not describe different people who are blessed, but different aspects of what it means to belong to God's kingdom and so find happiness. Each of the Beatitudes is a couplet: the first part describing the characteristic of the believer ("those people who know they have great spiritual need are happy"), and the second part the result of that characteristic ("because the kingdom of heaven belongs to them").

Matthew 5 lists seven beatitudes. In some there is a contrast between the characteristics of the person and what they receive. Those with "great spiritual need" receive the kingdom as a result. Those in grief receive comfort. The humble inherit the earth. These Beatitudes stress that God seeks people who come humbly and with a sense of their own sinfulness and need. The Kingdom belongs only to those who know they need it, not to those who think they are self-sufficient. Thus the Beatitudes invite repentance, a turning away from sin and toward God, who gives such good gifts to his people.

Other beatitudes stress a more positive relationship between the character and acts of the person and their relationship with the kingdom of God. The merciful receive mercy (5:7). The pure will see God (5:8). The peacemakers will be accepted as God's children (5:9). Purity, mercy, and peace are attributes of God's own character. As the people of God take on the character of God, they will be fortunate and blessed.

Other beatitudes warn that being a part of God's kingdom will mean opposition and even suffering (5:10–11). In these last beatitudes we see the Christian nature of the Kingdom. Those who are persecuted "because you follow me" (5:11) are promised happiness. The person willing to witness about Christ and trust in him may have to endure the censure and evil opinions of others, but in God's eyes that person is still fortunate.

Luke 6:20–26 recounts only four Beatitudes. These stress a reversal of the condition of those who belong to the kingdom of God. Presently, the faithful are those who are hungry, who weep, who are poor and hated by others for their faith in Jesus (6:20–23). But, in the Kingdom, they will find joy and plenty to make up for their sacrifice.

The Beatitudes set the standards of the Kingdom for happiness and meaning in life—and the way to happiness is quite different from the usual way of the world. Riches, peace, and comfort may be traps that help us ignore God. We are fortunate in the depth of our hunger for God and our sense of need for belonging to God. We are happy if we take on the character of God. We are blessed if we are willing to witness to Christ, even at the cost of embracing rejection and opposition.

Beatitudes: For additional scriptures on this topic go to Psalm 32:1.

LAW

MATTHEW 5:17–20

What is the Old Testament's view of the Law? What is the New Testament's view of the Law? What does keeping the Law have to do with living the Christian life?

It is difficult to overstate the importance of the Law for the Israelites in the Old Testament. It was God's gift to his people. It showed how they should live in order to please God. It was not a burden, but a joy. Speaking of the Law, the writer of Psalm 119 says, "Happy are those who live pure lives, who follow the LORD's teachings" (verse 1); "I will never forget your orders, because you have given me life by them" (verse 93); "Your word is like a lamp for my feet and a light for my path. I will do what I have promised and obey your fair laws" (verses 105–106).

It is perhaps a common misunderstanding of the Law to think that it was imposed upon the Israelites in order for them to become God's people. This is not the case. God chose Israel first among all the nations, beginning with Abram and culminating in the Exodus. God did not say to Abram that he had to obey before he would call him up from Ur (see Genesis 15:6; Romans 4); nor did God tell the Israelites in Egypt that they first had to prove themselves faithful before he would bring them out of slavery. To put it another way, God did not say, "These are the things you have to do if you want to become my people." Rather he said, "I have made you my people, now these are the things I want you to do." The Law was a gift to the Israelites to teach them how they might obey God and fully enjoy his blessings.

When understood in this way, the relevance of the Law for Christians takes on a different spin than is sometimes thought. Jesus tells us in Matthew 5:17–20 how he relates to the Law. Several general principles can be drawn from this passage: (1) Jesus was not "anti-law." He saw himself as fulfilling the Law of Moses and the teaching of the prophets (verse 17). (2) In some sense, even the very details of the Law are of vital importance. In fact, they will remain "until heaven and earth are gone" (verse 18). The Law is not to be taken lightly. (3) There are consequences for those who do not obey or teach others not to obey. These will be "least important in the kingdom of heaven" (verse 19). The "kingdom of heaven" does not refer to where you go after you die. It refers to those who are a part of God's kingdom here and now. It is also clear that he is not speaking here of what to do in order to enter this kingdom, but proper conduct for those *already a part of the kingdom*. As in the Old Testament, law is not a condition for entering God's family, but the rules for those who are in God's family. (4) True obedience to the Law, which is what Jesus sets out to explain in the Sermon on the Mount (chapters 5–7), exceeds that of the so-called experts (Pharisees), who understood law merely in the outward, legalistic sense.

Such a view of the Law, however, seems difficult to square with some of Paul's statements. For example, Romans 3:21: "But God has a way to make people right with him without the law." Or Galatians 3:11: "Now it is clear that no one can be made right with God by the law." But several points should be brought out to help clarify Paul's understanding of the law. First of all, even these statements are not really very different from what Jesus said. Paul says here that the law cannot make you right with God. Elsewhere he says that we are not saved by our own efforts; salvation is a gift (Ephesians 2:9). Likewise, Jesus never says that you are saved by the law. Jesus' high regard for the law is for those who are already in the "kingdom of heaven."

Also, Paul's view of the law is not completely negative. The remainder of Romans 3:21 says that this "way to make people right with him without the law" is precisely what the Old Testament itself intended: "He has now shown us that way *which the law and the prophets told us about*." Like Jesus, Paul claims that the proper understanding of the law is in complete harmony with the intention of the Old Testament.

Finally, Paul's more extreme statements on the law must be understood in the context of his audience. Paul was a theologian, this is true. But he was also a pastor. He was writing to people in particular circumstances with particular needs. In Galatians especially, the vitality of the gospel was threatened by those who wanted to mix law (specifically circumcision) and gospel as a *means for salvation* (see Galatians 5:1–15). It is this that is an improper use of the law, denying both the freedom and grace that is ours in Christ as well as the teachings of the law and the prophets on the Old Testament.

What is the Christian's response to the law? We are saved not by any of our own efforts, but by Christ's supreme effort on the cross. But as Christians, we take God's law to heart, not legalistically, but as a pattern of conduct in God's world. That pattern is perhaps best expressed in the "law of love" (Matthew 5:43–48; 7:12; 22:40), for as we love others, we will be perfect as our Father in heaven is perfect (Matthew 5:48), and we will fulfill the requirements for righteousness contained in the law (Romans 13:8–10).

Law: For additional scriptures on this topic go to Deuteronomy 1:5.

[11]The LORD is pleased with those who respect him,
with those who trust his love.

[12]Jerusalem, praise the LORD;
Jerusalem, praise your God.
[13]He makes your city gates strong
and blesses your children inside.
[14]He brings peace to your country
and fills you with the finest grain.

[15]He gives a command to the earth,
and it quickly obeys him.
[16]He spreads the snow like wool
and scatters the frost like ashes.
[17]He throws down hail like rocks.
No one can stand the cold he sends.
[18]Then he gives a command, and it melts.
He sends the breezes, and the
waters flow.

[19]He gave his word to Jacob,
his laws and demands to Israel.
[20]He didn't do this for any other nation.
They don't know his laws.

Praise the LORD!

The World Should Praise the LORD

148 Praise the LORD!

Praise the LORD from the skies.
Praise him high above the earth.
[2]Praise him, all you angels.
Praise him, all you armies of heaven.
[3]Praise him, sun and moon.
Praise him, all you shining stars.
[4]Praise him, highest heavens
and you waters above the sky.
[5]Let them praise the LORD,
because they were created by
his command.
[6]He put them in place forever and ever;
he made a law that will never change.

[7]Praise the LORD from the earth,
you large sea animals and all the oceans,
[8]lightning and hail, snow and mist,
and stormy winds that obey him,
[9]mountains and all hills,
fruit trees and all cedars,
[10]wild animals and all cattle,
crawling animals and birds,
[11]kings of the earth and all nations,
princes and all rulers of the earth,
[12]young men and women,
old people and children.

[13]Praise the LORD,
because he alone is great.
He is more wonderful than heaven
and earth.
[14]God has given his people a king.
He should be praised by all who belong
to him;
he should be praised by the Israelites, the
people closest to his heart.

Praise the LORD!

Praise the God of Israel

149 Praise the LORD!

Sing a new song to the LORD;
sing his praise in the meeting of
his people.

[2]Let the Israelites be happy because of God,
their Maker.
Let the people of Jerusalem rejoice because
of their King.
[3]They should praise him with dancing.
They should sing praises to him with
tambourines and harps.
[4]The LORD is pleased with his people;
he saves the humble.
[5]Let those who worship him rejoice in
his glory.
Let them sing for joy even in bed!

[6]Let them shout his praise
with their two-edged swords in
their hands.
[7]They will punish the nations
and defeat the people.
[8]They will put those kings in chains
and those important men in iron bands.
[9]They will punish them as God has written.
God is honored by all who worship him.

Praise the LORD!

147:11 Fear: Proverbs 1:7

147:13 *your city gates strong.* The city gates were the most vulnerable part of the wall. God strengthens Jerusalem's gates to make them safe.

148:7 The sea and its creatures often stood for the forces of chaos. Here even the seas and the sea animals praise God, showing that he is indeed LORD of all.

148:14 Environment: Ecclesiastes 3:11

149:1 *a new song.* See 33:3.

Praise the Lord with Music

150 Praise the Lord!

Praise God in his Temple;
praise him in his mighty heaven.
2 Praise him for his strength;
praise him for his greatness.
3 Praise him with trumpet blasts;
praise him with harps and lyres.
4 Praise him with tambourines and dancing;
praise him with stringed instruments
and flutes.
5 Praise him with loud cymbals;
praise him with crashing cymbals.
6 Let everything that breathes praise the Lord.

Praise the Lord!

INTRODUCTION TO THE BOOK OF

PROVERBS

Wise Teachings for God's People

WHO WROTE THIS BOOK?

These wise teachings are probably from a circle of wise men, including Solomon, Agur, Lemuel, and perhaps others.

TO WHOM WAS THIS BOOK WRITTEN?

Proverbs was primarily intended for the young people of Israel, which is shown by frequent use of the phrase "my son."

WHERE WAS IT WRITTEN?

It is likely that Proverbs originated in and around Israel where Solomon lived and reigned as king.

WHEN WAS IT WRITTEN?

Assuming Solomon is, indeed, the author, it was probably written during the tenth century B.C.—the time of Israel's united kingdom—but was later compiled into this collection during Hezekiah's reign in the seventh century B.C.

WHAT IS THE BOOK ABOUT?

Proverbs is a collection of wise sayings and teachings about life and how to live it successfully in God's eyes.

WHY WAS THIS BOOK WRITTEN?

The purpose of Proverbs is summarized well in the opening of verses of Proverbs 1, especially verse 4: "They make the uneducated smarter and give knowledge and sense to the young."

SO WHAT DOES THIS BOOK MEAN TO US?

Since Solomon, the presumed author of Proverbs, was the wisest man who ever lived (see 1 Kings 3:5–13), his words are valuable guides for the way we live our lives before God today.

SUMMARY:

Proverbs attracts much interest today because of its insightful, practical advice concerning daily life. Christians desire wisdom from God, and Proverbs offers it in abundance.

Much of the book's teaching is addressed to young men about to embark on a career in government service. This explains why there is so much advice on avoiding dubious women in the book. The principles of the book, however, apply to women as well, and so our translation takes that into account.

Solomon, who lived in the tenth century B.C., is the source of the wisdom found in the Book of Proverbs (1:1), though the book gives indication that others were also involved in the final version (25:1; 30:1; 31:1).

The book is more than just good advice. God is not mentioned explicitly, but the structure of the book points to the fact that people have a basic choice to make. They can either ally themselves with foolishness, who represents the "wisdom" of worldly gods (Proverbs 9:13–18) or wisdom, who represents God himself (Proverbs 8 and 9:1–6). A wise person is a good person—that is, he is following God—while a fool is a bad person who follows idols.

The Book of Proverbs encourages its readers to seek out and follow wisdom. Wisdom takes on a personal face in the New Testament. According to Paul in 1 Corinthians 1:30, Jesus is the one "who has become for us the wisdom of God." In Colossians 2:3, he exclaims that it is in Jesus that "all the treasures of wisdom and knowledge are safely kept."

The outline of the Book of Proverbs is as follows:

I. Preamble (1:1–7)
II. Wisdom Discourses (1:8–9:18)

III. Solomon's Proverbs, including the Sayings of the Wise (10:1–29:27)
IV. Sayings of Agur and King Lemuel (30:1–31:9)
V. Poem to the Virtuous Woman (31:10–31)

I. Preamble (1:1–7)

Here the author clearly states his purpose. He wants to teach both the wise and the uneducated. The preamble also lays down the foundation of all wisdom: respect for the Lord.

II. Wisdom Discourses (1:8–9:18)

The first nine chapters of the book are made up of long speeches about wisdom, often between parent and child. Throughout the section, the parents encourage their child to follow wisdom and avoid folly. The section comes to a climax when a clear choice must be made between following the woman named Wisdom (9:1–6) or the woman named Foolishness (9:13–18).

III. Solomon's Proverbs, including the Sayings of the Wise (10:1–29:27)

This, the largest section of the Book of Proverbs, is also the part that is most characteristic of it. Throughout these chapters we find the short, pithy sayings that we associate with the book. They give good advice about life. We must remember that these are not law; they are not rules that are always applicable in every situation. It takes a wise person to know when to apply the proverb in real life. We must also keep in mind that these proverbs are to be read in the light of the first nine chapters that have identified the way of wisdom with God and the way of foolishness with idolatry. So these proverbs are more than good advice; they are pointing the way to God. Lastly, keep in mind that these proverbs are a collection that have no obvious structure. Proverbs on the same themes (the tongue, laziness, difficult spouse, how to act with the king) are sprinkled throughout the collection and are not placed in any systematic order.

IV. Sayings of Agur and King Lemuel (30:1–31:9)

The last three sections of the book are brief, and the first two of those are especially difficult. We don't know who Agur or Lemuel were; this is their only mention in the whole Bible. The book concludes with a powerful poem on the characteristics of a godly woman.

V. Poem to the Virtuous Woman (31:10–31)

PROVERBS

The Importance of Proverbs

1 These are the wise words of Solomon son of
David, king of Israel.
2 They teach wisdom and self-control;
they will help you understand wise words.
3 They will teach you how to be wise and
self-controlled
and will teach you to do what is honest and
fair and right.
4 They make the uneducated smarter
and give knowledge and sense to the young.
5 Wise people can also listen and learn;
even smart people can find good advice in
these words.
6 Then anyone can understand wise words
and stories,
the words of the wise and their riddles.

7 Knowledge begins with respect for the LORD,
but fools hate wisdom and self-control.

Warnings Against Evil

8 My child, listen to your father's teaching
and do not forget your mother's advice.
9 Their teaching will be like flowers in your hair
or a necklace around your neck.

10 My child, if sinners try to lead you into sin,
do not follow them.
11 They will say, "Come with us.
Let's ambush and kill someone;
let's attack some innocent people just for fun.
12 Let's swallow them alive, as death does;
let's swallow them whole, as the grave does.
13 We will take all kinds of valuable things
and fill our houses with stolen goods.
14 Come join us,
and we will share with you stolen goods."
15 My child, do not go along with them;
do not do what they do.
16 They are eager to do evil
and are quick to kill.
17 It is useless to spread out a net
right where the birds can see it.
18 But sinners will fall into their own traps;
they will only catch themselves!
19 All greedy people end up this way;
greed kills selfish people.

Wisdom Speaks

20 Wisdom is like a woman shouting in the street;
she raises her voice in the city squares.
21 She cries out in the noisy street
and shouts at the city gates:
22 "You fools, how long will you be foolish?
How long will you make fun of wisdom
and hate knowledge?
23 If only you had listened when I corrected you,
I would have told you what's in my heart;
I would have told you what I am thinking.
24 I called, but you refused to listen;
I held out my hand, but you paid no attention.
25 You did not follow my advice
and did not listen when I corrected you.
26 So I will laugh when you are in trouble.
I will make fun when disaster strikes you,
27 when disaster comes over you like a storm,
when trouble strikes you like a whirlwind,
when pain and trouble overwhelm you.

28 "Then you will call to me,
but I will not answer.
You will look for me,
but you will not find me.
29 It is because you rejected knowledge
and did not choose to respect the LORD.
30 You did not accept my advice,
and you rejected my correction.
31 So you will get what you deserve;
you will get what you planned for others.
32 Fools will die because they refuse to listen;
they will be destroyed because they
do not care.
33 But those who listen to me will live in safety
and be at peace, without fear of injury."

1:1 Solomon: Song of Solomon 1:1
1:6 Proverb: Proverbs 4:20–22
1:7 Fear: Luke 22:44

1:7 In today's society, people seek knowledge in the world of education, and college and graduate degrees are often taken as a sign of learning. From the biblical perspective, that is not totally accurate. True knowledge begins with a recognition of who God is and what he requires. It is based on a deep respect for him and his law.

So also, real wisdom cannot be acquired through book-learning alone. Instead, a wise life is a disciplined life, a life of self-control, a life of restraint. In a similar way, a fool is not an intellectually stupid person, but a morally dense person.

1:8 *My child.* The original Book of Proverbs is addressed to young men, so the Hebrew specifically says "my son." However, the principles that are addressed to the young men are for the most part relevant for all people, and in those places we have translated it "my child."

1:20 *Wisdom.* Throughout the first nine chapters of the book, wisdom is personified as a woman. Of course, the reference is to God's wisdom, which is desirable for the young men to look for and establish a relationship with.

1:22 Hate: Proverbs 1:29
1:29 Hate: Proverbs 10:12
1:32 Stubbornness: Isaiah 30:8–11
1:33 Incarnation: Proverbs 3:13–18

Rewards of Wisdom

2 My child, listen to what I say
and remember what I command you.
2Listen carefully to wisdom;
set your mind on understanding.
3Cry out for wisdom,
and beg for understanding.
4Search for it like silver,
and hunt for it like hidden treasure.
5Then you will understand respect for the LORD,
and you will find that you know God.
6Only the LORD gives wisdom;
he gives knowledge and understanding.
7He stores up wisdom for those who are honest.
Like a shield he protects the innocent.
8He makes sure that justice is done,
and he protects those who are loyal to him.

9Then you will understand what is honest and fair
and what is the good and right thing to do.
10Wisdom will come into your mind,
and knowledge will be pleasing to you.
11Good sense will protect you;
understanding will guard you.
12It will keep you from the wicked,
from those whose words are bad,
13who don't do what is right
but what is evil.
14They enjoy doing wrong
and are happy to do what is crooked and evil.
15What they do is wrong,
and their ways are dishonest.

16It will save you from the unfaithful wife
who tries to lead you into adultery with
pleasing words.
17She leaves the husband she married when she
was young.
She ignores the promise she made before God.
18Her house is on the way to death;
those who took that path are now all dead.
19No one who goes to her comes back
or walks the path of life again.

20But wisdom will help you be good
and do what is right.
21Those who are honest will live in the land,
and those who are innocent will remain in it.
22But the wicked will be removed from the land,
and the unfaithful will be thrown
out of it.

Advice to Children

3 My child, do not forget my teaching,
but keep my commands in mind.
2Then you will live a long time,
and your life will be successful.

3Don't ever forget kindness and truth.
Wear them like a necklace.
Write them on your heart as if on a tablet.
4Then you will be respected
and will please both God and people.

5Trust the LORD with all your heart,
and don't depend on your own understanding.
6Remember the LORD in all you do,
and he will give you success.⚭

7Don't depend on your own wisdom.
Respect the LORD and refuse to do wrong.⚭
8Then your body will be healthy,
and your bones will be strong.

9Honor the LORD with your wealth
and the firstfruits from all your crops.
10Then your barns will be full,
and your wine barrels will overflow
with new wine.

11My child, do not reject the LORD's discipline,
and don't get angry when he corrects you.
12The LORD corrects those he loves,
just as parents correct the child they
delight in.

13Happy is the person who finds wisdom,
the one who gets understanding.⚭
14Wisdom is worth more than silver;
it brings more profit than gold.
15Wisdom is more precious than rubies;
nothing you could want is equal to it.
16With her right hand wisdom offers you
a long life,
and with her left hand she gives you riches
and honor.
17Wisdom will make your life pleasant
and will bring you peace.
18As a tree produces fruit, wisdom gives life to
those who use it,
and everyone who uses it will be happy.⚭

⚭**3:6 Decision Making/Plan:** Proverbs 16:9
⚭**3:6 Stress:** Isaiah 40:29–31
⚭**3:7 Will of God:** Matthew 6:10
⚭**3:13 Beatitudes:** Proverbs 8:32
3:16 Where is honor found? According to the Book of Proverbs, it is found in wisdom, which begins with respect for the Lord (Proverbs 1:7). The Christian knows that Jesus is the source of all true wisdom (Colossians 2:3). To gain honor, according to the Bible, is to associate yourself with Jesus Christ.
⚭**3:18 Incarnation:** Proverbs 8:1

19The LORD made the earth, using his wisdom.
He set the sky in place, using his understanding.
20With his knowledge, he made springs flow into rivers
and the clouds drop rain on the earth.

21My child, hold on to wisdom and good sense.
Don't let them out of your sight.
22They will give you life
and beauty like a necklace around your neck.
23Then you will go your way in safety,
and you will not get hurt.
24When you lie down, you won't be afraid;
when you lie down, you will sleep in peace.
25You won't be afraid of sudden trouble;
you won't fear the ruin that comes to the wicked,
26because the LORD will keep you safe.
He will keep you from being trapped.

27Whenever you are able,
do good to people who need help.
28If you have what your neighbor asks for,
don't say, "Come back later.
I will give it to you tomorrow."
29Don't make plans to hurt your neighbor
who lives nearby and trusts you.
30Don't accuse a person for no good reason;
don't accuse someone who has not harmed you.

31Don't be jealous of those who use violence,
and don't choose to be like them.
32The LORD hates those who do wrong,
but he is a friend to those who are honest.
33The LORD will curse the evil person's house,
but he will bless the home of those who do right.
34The LORD laughs at those who laugh at him,
but he gives grace to those who are not proud.
35Wise people will receive honor,
but fools will be disgraced.

Wisdom Is Important

4 My children, listen to your father's teaching;
pay attention so you will understand.
2What I am telling you is good,
so do not forget what I teach you.
3When I was a young boy in my father's house
and like an only child to my mother,
4my father taught me and said,
"Hold on to my words with all your heart.
Keep my commands and you will live.
5Get wisdom and understanding.
Don't forget or ignore my words.
6Hold on to wisdom, and it will take care of you.
Love it, and it will keep you safe.
7Wisdom is the most important thing;
so get wisdom.
If it costs everything you have, get understanding.
8Treasure wisdom, and it will make you great;
hold on to it, and it will bring you honor.
9It will be like flowers in your hair
and like a beautiful crown on your head."

10My child, listen and accept what I say.
Then you will have a long life.
11I am guiding you in the way of wisdom,
and I am leading you on the right path.
12Nothing will hold you back;
you will not be overwhelmed.
13Always remember what you have been taught,
and don't let go of it.
Keep all that you have learned;
it is the most important thing in life.
14Don't follow the ways of the wicked;
don't do what evil people do.
15Avoid their ways, and don't follow them.
Stay away from them and keep on going,
16because they cannot sleep until they do evil.
They cannot rest until they harm someone.
17They feast on wickedness and cruelty
as if they were eating bread and drinking wine.

18The way of the good person is like the light of dawn,
growing brighter and brighter until full daylight.
19But the wicked walk around in the dark;
they can't even see what makes them stumble.

20My child, pay attention to my words;
listen closely to what I say.
21Don't ever forget my words;
keep them always in mind.
22They are the key to life for those who find them;
they bring health to the whole body.
23Be careful what you think,
because your thoughts run your life.

3:29 Neighbor: Proverbs 14:21
4:9 Wisdom: Proverbs 8
4:11 Road/Way: Proverbs 4:14
4:14 Road/Way: Proverbs 4:19
4:19 Road/Way: Proverbs 9
4:22 Sickness, Disease, Healing: Proverbs 12:18
4:22 Proverb: Proverbs 25:1

24Don't use your mouth to tell lies;
don't ever say things that are not true.
25Keep your eyes focused on what is right,
and look straight ahead to what is good.
26Be careful what you do,
and always do what is right.
27Don't turn off the road of goodness;
keep away from evil paths.

Warning About Adultery

5 My son, pay attention to my wisdom;
listen to my words of understanding.
2Be careful to use good sense,
and watch what you say.
3The words of another man's wife may seem
sweet as honey;
they may be as smooth as olive oil.
4But in the end she will bring you sorrow,
causing you pain like a two-edged sword.
5She is on the way to death;
her steps are headed straight to the grave.
6She gives little thought to life.
She doesn't even know that her ways
are wrong.

7Now, my sons, listen to me,
and don't ignore what I say.
8Stay away from such a woman.
Don't even go near the door of her house,
9or you will give your riches to others,
and the best years of your life will be given
to someone cruel.
10Strangers will enjoy your wealth,
and what you worked so hard for will go to
someone else.
11You will groan at the end of your life
when your health is gone.
12Then you will say, "I hated being told
what to do!
I would not listen to correction!
13I would not listen to my teachers
or pay attention to my instructors.
14I came close to being completely ruined
in front of a whole group of people."

15Be faithful to your own wife,
just as you drink water from your own well.
16Don't pour your water in the streets;
don't give your love to just any woman.
17These things are yours alone
and shouldn't be shared with strangers.
18Be happy with the wife you married when
you were young.
She gives you joy, as your fountain
gives you water.
19She is as lovely and graceful as a deer.
Let her love always make you happy;
let her love always hold you captive.
20My son, don't be held captive by a woman
who takes part in adultery.
Don't hug another man's wife.

21The LORD sees everything you do,
and he watches where you go.
22An evil man will be caught in his wicked ways;
the ropes of his sins will tie him up.
23He will die because he does not control himself,
and he will be held captive by his foolishness.

Dangers of Being Foolish

6 My child, be careful about giving a
guarantee for somebody else's loan,
about promising to pay what someone
else owes.
2You might get trapped by what you say;
you might be caught by your own words.
3My child, if you have done this and are under
your neighbor's control,
here is how to get free.
Don't be proud. Go to your neighbor
and beg to be free from your promise.
4Don't go to sleep
or even rest your eyes,
5but free yourself like a deer running
from a hunter,
like a bird flying away from a trapper.

6Go watch the ants, you lazy person.
Watch what they do and be wise.
7Ants have no commander,
no leader or ruler,
8but they store up food in the summer
and gather their supplies at harvest.
9How long will you lie there, you lazy person?
When will you get up from sleeping?
10You sleep a little; you take a nap.
You fold your hands and lie down to rest.
11So you will be as poor as if you had
been robbed;
you will have as little as if you had
been held up.

12Some people are wicked and no good.
They go around telling lies,
13winking with their eyes, tapping with their feet,
and making signs with their fingers.

6:11 Leisure: Proverbs 10:26

6:13 *winking with their eyes.* A wink was a sign of insincerity in speech or action.

WILL OF GOD

MATTHEW 6:10

Is the will of God clearly spelled out in detail for each believer?
How did people throughout the Old and New Testaments recognize God's will?
What habits might we learn from them in our own attempts to grasp God's will?

When Jesus taught us how to pray by giving the model prayer in Matthew 6, he said in verse 10, "May your kingdom come and what you want be done, here on earth as it is in heaven." He was saying that in heaven the will and desire of God is carried out without the sin getting in the way and without any hesitation on the part of the angels. In heaven the will of God to bless, to love, and to receive worship, praise, and thanksgiving is done completely. Psalm 46:4–5 says clearly,

There is a river that brings joy
 to the city of God,
the holy place where God Most High lives.
God is in that city, and so it will
 not be shaken.

The river stands for the grace of God that flows through heaven, enabling all the heavenly host to faithfully carry out the perfect will of the creator and sustainer of all that is.

Jesus prayed that what his Father wants (his Father's will)—which is perfectly fulfilled in heaven—would also be brought about on earth. His entire life became an example for each person of how to listen for, carry out, and fulfill the will of the heavenly Father.

As Christians we believe that God has placed us on earth for a very short time in order to love him, to spread his kingdom, and to love and serve others. If this is true, then nothing becomes more important for us than to understand and carry out what the Father wants in our lives.

There are parts of God's will that are clear for each person. We call these "revelation" (meaning revealed to us in Scripture), and they must become *top* values for us in our everyday lives. In the Old Testament these values are in the Ten Commandments found in Exodus 20. They were summed up in Deuteronomy 6:4–5, "Listen, people of Israel! The LORD our God is the only LORD. Love the LORD your God with all your heart, all your soul, and all your strength," and in Leviticus 19:18, "Love your neighbor as you love yourself."

Then in the New Testament there are scriptures that clearly teach the will of God for each person. Without question, the single most important part of God's will is that we change our hearts and lives (2 Peter 3:9) and place our faith and trust in Jesus as Lord and Savior. God gives us eternal life through his Son: "Whoever has the Son has life, but whoever does not have the Son of God does not have life" (1 John 5:12).

God wants us to change our hearts and lives and be baptized in the name of Christ (Acts 2:38). He wants us to be filled with the Holy Spirit (Ephesians 5:17), attend all church meetings (Hebrews 10:25), continue praying (Colossians 4:2), to study his Word, the Bible (Colossians 3:16), and take care of all that he has given us (Matthew 25:14–30). This includes giving to God as he has blessed us (1 Corinthians 16:2). Also, all Christians are to be about the lifelong business of growing in grace (2 Peter 3:18). This causes us to want to, "go and make followers of all people in the world" (Matthew 28:18–20).

There are many other Scriptures that clearly tell us what the Lord wants for our lives. They tell us how to live our daily lives. Such Scriptures teach us, for example, to be sexually pure, not to lie, and not to let evil thoughts control us (Colossians 3:5–17). They teach us to be honest in all of our work (Proverbs 16:11), to pray for those in authority (1 Timothy 2:2), to follow the laws of the land as well as the moral laws of God (Romans 13; 1 Corinthians 6:8–10), to marry only another believer (2 Corinthians 6:14). They also teach us to love, help each other, and respect each other at home (Ephesians 5:21–6:4) and to lead lives that give praise to God (Ephesians 1:12). These are all clearly taught as what God wants for every person. How wonderful it is to be able to plainly know the will of the One who created us!

The Bible says, therefore, that there are to values that are for every person and these are the will of God for all. But what does God want or plan for an individual life? For instance, the Bible does not tell us what job to work at or where to live or who to marry. To properly know what God wants in these areas, we must now look at some proven biblical teachings.

First we must understand that God loves us. Each created individual is a loved and cherished one-of-a-kind creation of God. We have all been chosen, not "to suffer his anger but to have salvation through our Lord Jesus Christ," (1 Thessalonians 5:9) and to be his people, "because from the very beginning God had decided this in keeping with his plan. And he is the One who makes everything agree with what he decides and wants" (Ephesians 1:11).

As loved creations we are without question meant to be part of God's overall plan for history. Paul says in Ephesians 2:10 that, "God has made us what we are. In Christ Jesus, God made us to do good works, which God planned in advance for us to live our lives doing." Oh, the wonder of the thought that before the beginning of time, we were in the mind and heart of God as a part of his marvelous plan for history! Before our actual creation, there was a loving plan for each of us. We all have a specific work to do.

But if this specific, individual work is not explained in detail, then how in this world can we know it? How does God tell his specific will to us as individuals?

We must begin by faithfully doing what we already know to be God's will for us. For instance, daily prayer, Bible study, fellowship, and service are the very works which God can use to help us know his specific will for us as individuals. When we hear the words of Christ and obey them, we become like the wise person of Matthew 7:24–25. He built the house of his life upon the rock and it did not fall when the storms of life came. But if we are not obedient to what we already know to be the will of God, then we become like the foolish person Christ spoke of in Matthew 7:26–27 whose house fell because it was built upon the sand and could not withstand the storms of life.

Through a disciplined, ongoing life of trust in Christ, grace allows us to slowly build our "response-ability" factor. This is the ability the Lord gives us first to *hear* his word and then to do what we hear through actions of *obedience*. As we first learn to hear him speak to us in Scripture, then our ability to hear him in other ways begins to grow. We may hear him in the spectacular events of our life such as when Moses heard God speak from the burning bush (Exodus 3), or when he received the Ten Commandments on Mount Sinai (Exodus 19–20). God even speaks to us in the hard times of our lives, assuring us that we will be protected and that he is all that we need (Psalm 16).

But most often God speaks to us in a quiet, gentle sound as he did to Elijah in 1 Kings 19:12 and to Samuel in 1 Samuel 3. This quiet, gentle voice of the Lord may come through reading and studying the Bible (Psalm 119:1–16). It might come while reading a great spiritual classic or listening to a sermon. It might come to us in a time of prayer or even from trusted Christian friends.

However it comes, if it is truly what God wants for our lives it will have certain qualities. First, it will never go against Scripture and will always be supported by it. Second, it will come more than once. It will not just be a one-time thought but will burn in our mind and heart over a necessary period of time. Third, it will be supported by the history of how God has dealt with humanity. Our cherished Christian tradition will show us that, "Yes, indeed, God taught in such a manner to people in the past and he continues to work the same way today." Fourth, if it is a true word of the Lord, it may very well stretch our faith, our trust, and even our reason. It may at first seem to be out of the question in terms of whether it can be done. It will not be silly or foolhardy. Often, basic common sense will protect us from being tricked by Satan. Finally, if it is the true will of the Father, it will give him praise and will be centered around obedience to him. Jesus said in John 5:30, "I don't try to please myself, but I try to please the One who sent me." Jesus says to us, "if you love me, you will obey my commands" (John 14:15).

When we seek with all that we are to follow the will of God for our lives, we can count on some marvelous promises from the Lord. We can depend on living forever with God (see Psalm 23; 1 John 2:17); we can enjoy the new life that he provides now through the Son (Romans 6:4); and we can trust in the promise of his guidance for our lives:

Trust the LORD with all your heart,
and don't depend on your own understanding.
Remember the LORD in all you do,
and he will give you success.
Don't depend on your own wisdom.
Respect the LORD and refuse to do wrong.
(Proverbs 3:5–7)⚭

⚭**Will of God:** For additional scriptures on this topic go to Deuteronomy 6:4–5.

[14]They make evil plans in their hearts
and are always starting arguments.
[15]So trouble will strike them in an instant;
suddenly they will be so hurt no one
can help them.

[16]There are six things the LORD hates.
There are seven things he cannot stand:
17 a proud look,
a lying tongue,
hands that kill innocent people,
18 a mind that thinks up evil plans,
feet that are quick to do evil,
19 a witness who lies,
and someone who starts arguments
among families.

Warning About Adultery

[20]My son, keep your father's commands,
and don't forget your mother's teaching.
[21]Keep their words in mind forever
as though you had them tied around
your neck.
[22]They will guide you when you walk.
They will guard you when you sleep.
They will speak to you when you are awake.
[23]These commands are like a lamp;
this teaching is like a light.
And the correction that comes from them
will help you have life.
[24]They will keep you from sinful women
and from the pleasing words of another
man's unfaithful wife.
[25]Don't desire her because she is beautiful.
Don't let her capture you by the way
she looks at you.
[26]A prostitute will treat you like a loaf of bread,
and a woman who takes part in adultery may
cost you your life.
[27]You cannot carry hot coals against your chest
without burning your clothes,
[28]and you cannot walk on hot coals
without burning your feet.
[29]The same is true if you have sexual relations
with another man's wife.
Anyone who does so will be punished.
[30]People don't hate a thief
when he steals because he is hungry.
[31]But if he is caught, he must pay back seven
times what he stole,
and it may cost him everything he owns.
[32]A man who takes part in adultery has
no sense;
he will destroy himself.
[33]He will be beaten up and disgraced,
and his shame will never go away.
[34]Jealousy makes a husband very angry,
and he will have no pity when he
gets revenge.⚭
[35]He will accept no payment for the wrong;
he will take no amount of money.

The Woman of Adultery

7
My son, remember what I say, and treasure
my commands.
[2]Obey my commands, and you will live.
Guard my teachings as you would your
own eyes.
[3]Remind yourself of them;
write them on your heart as if on a tablet.
[4]Treat wisdom as a sister,
and make understanding your closest friend.
[5]Wisdom and understanding will keep you
away from adultery,
away from the unfaithful wife and her
pleasing words.

[6]Once while I was at the window of my house
I looked out through the shutters
[7]and saw some foolish, young men.
I noticed one of them had no wisdom.
[8]He was walking down the street near
the corner
on the road leading to her house.
[9]It was the twilight of the evening;
the darkness of the night was just beginning.
[10]Then the woman approached him,
dressed like a prostitute
and planning to trick him.

6:16–18 A close look at this passage reveals that God shows his holy hate for a misuse of various parts of the human makeup (see 6:13) that were intended to honor and not offend him: eyes, tongue, hands, mind, and feet. One's attitudes, thoughts, speech, behavior, and relationship to others are of great importance to God.

⚭**6:34 Jealousy:** Proverbs 27:4

7 The Book of Proverbs never uses the name Jezebel, but the adulteress certainly portrays the characteristics we have come to expect from a "Jezebel." Just like the historical Jezebel written of in 1–2 Kings, and the character Jezebel in Revelation, the adulteress of Proverbs 7 is about the work of leading people astray. Like the adulteress in Revelation 2, the Proverbs 7 adulteress finds notoriety in leading men into sexual sin (Proverbs 5, 7). This, however, does not distance her from the historical Jezebel. She caused the death of many people (1 Kings 18:4,40) by encouraging the worship of false gods. Ultimately her family's house fell (1 Kings 21:22) and her relations were killed (1 Kings 22:35, 2 Kings 9:7–10) because of her evil influence (1 Kings 21:25). Similarly, Proverbs warns that "[the adulteress] has ruined many good men, and many have died because of her. Her house is on the road to death, the road that leads down to the grave" (Proverbs 7:26–27). Though one engages in idolatry and the other in adultery—the connection is clear. A "Jezebel" is one who leads God's people from the path of life to death.

11 She was loud and stubborn
and never stayed at home.
12 She was always out in the streets or in
the city squares,
waiting around on the corners of the streets.
13 She grabbed him and kissed him.
Without shame she said to him,
14 "I made my fellowship offering and took some
of the meat home.
Today I have kept my special promises.
15 So I have come out to meet you;
I have been looking for you and
have found you.
16 I have covered my bed
with colored sheets from Egypt.
17 I have made my bed smell sweet
with myrrh, aloes, and cinnamon.
18 Come, let's make love until morning.
Let's enjoy each other's love.
19 My husband is not home;
he has gone on a long trip.
20 He took a lot of money with him
and won't be home for weeks."
21 By her clever words she made him give in;
by her pleasing words she led him
into doing wrong.
22 All at once he followed her,
like an ox led to the butcher,
like a deer caught in a trap
23 and shot through the liver with an arrow.
Like a bird caught in a trap,
he didn't know what he did would
kill him.

24 Now, my sons, listen to me;
pay attention to what I say.
25 Don't let yourself be tricked by such a woman;
don't go where she leads you.
26 She has ruined many good men,
and many have died because of her.
27 Her house is on the road to death,
the road that leads down to the grave.

Listen to Wisdom

8 Wisdom calls to you like someone shouting;
understanding raises her voice.
2 On the hilltops along the road
and at the crossroads, she stands calling.
3 Beside the city gates,
at the entrances into the city, she calls out:
4 "Listen, everyone, I'm calling out to you;
I am shouting to all people.
5 You who are uneducated, be smarter.
You who are foolish, get understanding.
6 Listen, because I have important things to say,
and what I tell you is right.
7 What I say is true,
I refuse to speak evil.
8 Everything I say is honest;
nothing I say is crooked or false.
9 People with good sense know what I say is true;
and those with knowledge know my
words are right.
10 Choose my teachings instead of silver,
and knowledge rather than the finest gold.
11 Wisdom is more precious than rubies.
Nothing you could want is equal to it.

12 "I am wisdom, and I am smart.
I also have knowledge and good sense.
13 If you respect the LORD, you will also hate evil.
I hate pride and bragging,
evil ways and lies.
14 I have good sense and advice,
and I have understanding and power.
15 I help kings to govern
and rulers to make fair laws.
16 Princes use me to lead,
and so do all important people
who judge fairly.
17 I love those who love me,
and those who seek me find me.
18 Riches and honor are mine to give.
So are wealth and lasting success.
19 What I give is better than the finest gold,
better than the purest silver.
20 I do what is right
and follow the path of justice.
21 I give wealth to those who love me,
filling their houses with treasures.

22 "I, wisdom, was with the LORD when
he began his work,
long before he made anything else.
23 I was created in the very beginning,
even before the world began.

7:21 Tongue: Jeremiah 20:10
8:1 Incarnation: Daniel 10:6
8:1 *Wisdom.* See 1:20.
8:13 The Book of Proverbs calls on God's people to "fear" the Lord. To avoid misunderstanding, the *Everyday Bible* translates the word "fear" as "respect." However we must not lose sight of the fact that God is so great and we are so sinful that our knees should knock when we imagine ourselves in such an intimate relationship with such a powerful being. To fear God drives away all the other fears of this world.
8:23 The language of this chapter is highly figurative. God's wisdom is personified as a woman. The antiquity of God's wisdom is figuratively represented by her early birth. This language should not be taken literally.

[24]I was born before there were oceans,
or springs overflowing with water,
[25]before the hills were there,
before the mountains were put in place.
[26]God had not made the earth or fields,
not even the first dust of the earth.
[27]I was there when God put the skies in place,
when he stretched the horizon over
the oceans,
[28]when he made the clouds above
and put the deep underground springs
in place.
[29]I was there when he ordered the sea
not to go beyond the borders he had set.
I was there when he laid the earth's foundation.
[30] I was like a child by his side.
I was delighted every day,
enjoying his presence all the time,
[31]enjoying the whole world,
and delighted with all its people.

[32]"Now, my children, listen to me,
because those who follow my ways are happy.⚭
[33]Listen to my teaching, and you will be wise;
do not ignore it.
[34]Happy are those who listen to me,
watching at my door every day,
waiting at my open doorway.
[35]Those who find me find life,
and the LORD will be pleased with them.
[36]Those who do not find me hurt themselves.
Those who hate me love death."⚭

Being Wise or Foolish

9 Wisdom has built her house;
she has made its seven columns.
[2]She has prepared her food and wine;
she has set her table.
[3]She has sent out her servant girls,
and she calls out from the highest place
in the city.
[4]She says to those who are uneducated,
"Come in here, you foolish people!
[5]Come and eat my food
and drink the wine I have prepared.
[6]Stop your foolish ways, and you will live;
take the road of understanding.⚭

[7]"If you correct someone who makes fun of
wisdom, you will be insulted.
If you correct an evil person, you will get hurt.
[8]Do not correct those who make fun of wisdom,
or they will hate you.
But correct the wise, and they will love you.
[9]Teach the wise, and they will become
even wiser;
teach good people, and they will learn
even more.

[10]"Wisdom begins with respect for the LORD,
and understanding begins with knowing
the Holy One.
[11]If you live wisely, you will live a long time;
wisdom will add years to your life.
[12]The wise person is rewarded by wisdom,
but whoever makes fun of wisdom will
suffer for it."

[13]Foolishness is like a loud woman;
she does not have wisdom or knowledge.
[14]She sits at the door of her house
at the highest place in the city.
[15]She calls out to those who are passing by,
who are going along, minding their
own business.
[16]She says to those who are uneducated,
"Come in here, you foolish people!
[17]Stolen water is sweeter,
and food eaten in secret tastes better."
[18]But these people don't know that everyone
who goes there dies,
that her guests end up deep in the grave.⚭

The Wise Words of Solomon

10 These are the wise words of Solomon:

A wise son makes his father happy,
but a foolish son makes his mother sad.

[2]Riches gotten by doing wrong have no value,
but right living will save you from death.

⚭**8:32 Beatitudes:** Revelation 14:13
⚭**8:36 Wisdom:** Proverbs 9:1–6
9:3 *the highest place in the city.* Wisdom's house is at the highest point of the city. In the ancient Near East the high point was the location of the temple. This is true in Israel as well, since the Temple was built on Mount Zion. The location of Wisdom's house indicates that Wisdom is God himself.
⚭**9:6 Wisdom:** Proverbs 13:14
9:13 *Foolishness.* As Wisdom is the personification of God's wisdom, so Foolishness represents the advice one might get from false gods. Note as well that Foolishness has her house on the high point of the city, the place normally occupied by the Temple. See 9:3.
9:13–18 In this passage Foolishness is likened to a woman who sits at the entrance to her house and invites men in for a meal. She entices them with food and drink, but her real desire is to kill them. In this way Foolishness is contrasted with Wisdom (Proverbs 9:1–6), another woman who invites men into her house. But she wants to educate them. Both women have their houses on a high hill in the city, the location of temples in ancient cities, showing that the poet intends to say that the woman Wisdom is God, and the woman Foolishness is idols, false gods who try to lure the Israelites away.
⚭**9:18 Road/Way:** Proverbs 10:29

3The LORD does not let good people go hungry,
but he keeps evil people from getting what
they want.

4A lazy person will end up poor,
but a hard worker will become rich.

5Those who gather crops on time are wise,
but those who sleep through the harvest
are a disgrace.

6Good people will have rich blessings,
but the wicked will be overwhelmed
by violence.

7Good people will be remembered as a blessing,
but evil people will soon be forgotten.

8The wise do what they are told,
but a talkative fool will be ruined.

9The honest person will live in safety,
but the dishonest will be caught.

10A wink may get you into trouble,
and foolish talk will lead to your ruin.

11The words of a good person give life, like a
fountain of water,
but the words of the wicked contain nothing
but violence.

12Hatred stirs up trouble,
but love forgives all wrongs.

13Smart people speak wisely,
but people without wisdom should
be punished.

14The wise don't tell everything they know,
but the foolish talk too much and
are ruined.

15Having lots of money protects the rich,
but having no money destroys the poor.

16Good people are rewarded with life,
but evil people are paid with punishment.

17Whoever accepts correction is on the way to life,
but whoever ignores correction will lead
others away from life.

18Whoever hides hate is a liar.
Whoever tells lies is a fool.

19If you talk a lot, you are sure to sin;
if you are wise, you will keep quiet.

20The words of a good person are like pure silver,
but an evil person's thoughts are worth
very little.
21Good people's words will help many others,
but fools will die because they don't
have wisdom.

22The LORD's blessing brings wealth,
and no sorrow comes with it.

23A foolish person enjoys doing wrong,
but a person with understanding enjoys
doing what is wise.

24Evil people will get what they fear most,
but good people will get what they
want most.

25A storm will blow the evil person away,
but a good person will always be safe.

26A lazy person affects the one he works for
like vinegar on the teeth or smoke in
the eyes.

27Whoever respects the LORD will have a
long life,
but the life of an evil person will be
cut short.

28A good person can look forward to happiness,
but an evil person can expect nothing.

29The LORD will protect good people
but will ruin those who do evil.

30Good people will always be safe,
but evil people will not remain in the land.

31A good person says wise things,
but a liar's tongue will be stopped.

10:4 Poverty: Proverbs 29:14
10:6 Blessing: Proverbs 28:20
10:10 *wink.* See 6:13.
10:12 Hate: Ecclesiastes 3:8
10:12 Love: Proverbs 17:17
10:14 Folly/Foolishness: Proverbs 10:18
10:18 Folly/Foolishness: Proverbs 10:23
10:23 Folly/Foolishness: Proverbs 11:12
10:26 Leisure: Proverbs 13:4
10:29 Road/Way: Proverbs 12:28

32Good people know the right thing to say,
but evil people only tell lies.

11

The LORD hates dishonest scales, but he is pleased with honest weights.

2Pride leads only to shame;
it is wise to be humble.

3Good people will be guided by honesty;
dishonesty will destroy those who are not trustworthy.

4Riches will not help when it's time to die,
but right living will save you from death.

5The goodness of the innocent makes life easier,
but the wicked will be destroyed by their wickedness.

6Doing right brings freedom to honest people,
but those who are not trustworthy will be caught by their own desires.

7When the wicked die, hope dies with them;
their hope in riches will come to nothing.

8The good person is saved from trouble;
it comes to the wicked instead.

9With words an evil person can destroy a neighbor,
but a good person will escape by being smart.

10When good people succeed, the city is happy.
When evil people die, there are shouts of joy.

11Good people bless and build up their city,
but the wicked can destroy it with their words.

12People without good sense find fault with their neighbors,
but those with understanding keep quiet.

13Gossips can't keep secrets,
but a trustworthy person can.

14Without leadership a nation falls,
but lots of good advice will save it.

15Whoever guarantees to pay somebody else's loan will suffer.
It is safer to avoid such promises.

16A kind woman gets respect,
but cruel men get only wealth.

17Kind people do themselves a favor,
but cruel people bring trouble on themselves.

18An evil person really earns nothing,
but a good person will surely be rewarded.

19Those who are truly good will live,
but those who chase after evil will die.

20The LORD hates those with evil hearts
but is pleased with those who are innocent.

21Evil people will certainly be punished,
but those who do right will be set free.

22A beautiful woman without good sense
is like a gold ring in a pig's snout.

23Those who do right only wish for good,
but the wicked can expect to be defeated by God's anger.

24Some people give much but get back even more.
Others don't give what they should and end up poor.
25Whoever gives to others will get richer;
those who help others will themselves be helped.

26People curse those who keep all the grain,
but they bless the one who is willing to sell it.

27Whoever looks for good will find kindness,
but whoever looks for evil will find trouble.

28Those who trust in riches will be ruined,
but a good person will be healthy like a green leaf.

29Whoever brings trouble to his family
will be left with nothing but the wind.
A fool will be a servant to the wise.

11:3 Integrity: Proverbs 14:32

11:1–23 The Proverbs of Solomon are full of sage advice for living the wise and honest life. In this chapter, there is special focus on honesty, certainly one of the most important ingredients of integrity. "Good people will be guided by honesty; dishonesty will destroy those who are not trustworthy" (11:3).

11:12 Folly/Foolishness: Proverbs 12:15

30A good person gives life to others;
the wise person teaches others how to live.

31Good people will be rewarded on earth,
and the wicked and the sinners will
be punished.

12 Anyone who loves learning accepts
correction,
but a person who hates being corrected
is stupid.

2The LORD is pleased with a good person,
but he will punish anyone who plans evil.

3Doing evil brings no safety at all,
but a good person has safety and security.

4A good wife is like a crown for her husband,
but a disgraceful wife is like a disease
in his bones.

5The plans that good people make are fair,
but the advice of the wicked will trick you.

6The wicked talk about killing people,
but the words of good people will save them.

7Wicked people die and they are no more,
but a good person's family continues.

8The wisdom of the wise wins praise,
but there is no respect for the stupid.

9A person who is not important but has a
servant is better off
than someone who acts important but
has no food.

10Good people take care of their animals,
but even the kindest acts of the wicked
are cruel.

11Those who work their land will have plenty
of food,
but the one who chases empty dreams
is not wise.

12The wicked want what other evil people
have stolen,
but good people want to give what they have
to others.

13Evil people are trapped by their evil talk,
but good people stay out of trouble.

14People will be rewarded for what they say,
and they will also be rewarded for what
they do.

15Fools think they are doing right,
but the wise listen to advice.

16Fools quickly show that they are upset,
but the wise ignore insults.

17An honest witness tells the truth,
but a dishonest witness tells lies.

18Careless words stab like a sword,
but wise words bring healing.

19Truth will continue forever,
but lies are only for a moment.

20Those who plan evil are full of lies,
but those who plan peace are happy.

21No harm comes to a good person,
but an evil person's life is full of trouble.

22The LORD hates those who tell lies
but is pleased with those who keep
their promises.

23Wise people keep what they know to
themselves,
but fools can't keep from showing how
foolish they are.

24Hard workers will become leaders,
but those who are lazy will be slaves.

25Worry is a heavy load,
but a kind word cheers you up.

26Good people take advice from their friends,
but an evil person is easily led to do wrong.

27The lazy catch no food to cook,
but a hard worker will have great wealth.

28Doing what is right is the way to life,
but there is another way that leads to death.

12:2 Reputation: Ecclesiastes 7:1
12:10 Animals: Isaiah 11:6–9
12:16 Folly/Foolishness: Proverbs 12:23
12:18 Sickness, Disease, Healing: Isaiah 30:26
12:19 Lying/Dishonesty: Isaiah 44:20
12:23 Folly/Foolishness: Proverbs 14:15–18
12:28 Road/Way: Matthew 7:13–14

13 Wise children take their parents' advice,
but whoever makes fun of wisdom won't
listen to correction.

2People will be rewarded for what they say,
but those who can't be trusted want
only violence.

3Those who are careful about what they say
protect their lives,
but whoever speaks without thinking
will be ruined.

4The lazy will not get what they want,
but those who work hard will.⚭

5Good people hate what is false,
but the wicked do shameful and
disgraceful things.

6Doing what is right protects the honest person,
but doing evil ruins the sinner.

7Some people pretend to be rich but really
have nothing.
Others pretend to be poor but really
are wealthy.

8The rich may have to pay a ransom for
their lives,
but the poor will face no such danger.

9Good people can look forward to a bright future,
but the future of the wicked is like a flame
going out.

10Pride only leads to arguments,
but those who take advice are wise.

11Money that comes easily disappears quickly,
but money that is gathered little by little
will grow.

12It is sad not to get what you hoped for.
But wishes that come true are like eating
fruit from the tree of life.⚭

13Those who reject what they are taught will
pay for it,
but those who obey what they are told
will be rewarded.

14The teaching of a wise person gives life.
It is like a fountain that can save people
from death.⚭

15People with good understanding will be
well liked,
but the lives of those who are not trustworthy
are hard.

16Every wise person acts with good sense,
but fools show how foolish they are.

17A wicked messenger brings nothing
but trouble,
but a trustworthy one makes everything right.

18A person who refuses correction will end up
poor and disgraced,
but the one who accepts correction will
be honored.

19It is so good when wishes come true,
but fools hate to stop doing evil.

20Spend time with the wise and you will
become wise,
but the friends of fools will suffer.

21Trouble always comes to sinners,
but good people enjoy success.

22Good people leave their wealth to their
grandchildren,
but a sinner's wealth is stored up for
good people.

23A poor person's field might produce plenty
of food,
but others often steal it away.

24If you do not punish your children, you don't
love them,
but if you love your children, you will
correct them.⚭

25Good people have enough to eat,
but the wicked will go hungry.

14 A wise woman strengthens her family,
but a foolish woman destroys hers by
what she does.⚭

⚭**13:4 Leisure:** Proverbs 20:4
⚭**13:12 Depression:** Ecclesiastes 7:3
⚭**13:14 Wisdom:** Proverbs 16:16
13:24 To the writer of Proverbs, failure to correct a child is tantamount to hating him, since such neglect may leave the child vulnerable to dangerous, life-threatening influences.
⚭**13:24 Parenting:** Proverbs 14:1
⚭**14:1 Parenting:** Proverbs 19:18

2People who live good lives respect the LORD,
but those who live evil lives don't.

3Fools will be punished for their proud words,
but the words of the wise will protect them.

4When there are no oxen, no food is in the barn.
But with a strong ox, much grain can
be grown.

5A truthful witness does not lie,
but a false witness tells nothing but lies.

6Those who make fun of wisdom look for it
and do not find it,
but knowledge comes easily to those with
understanding.

7Stay away from fools,
because they can't teach you anything.

8A wise person will understand what to do,
but a foolish person is dishonest.

9Fools don't care if they sin,
but honest people work at being right.

10No one else can know your sadness,
and strangers cannot share your joy.

11The wicked person's house will be destroyed,
but a good person's tent will still
be standing.

12Some people think they are doing right,
but in the end it leads to death.

13Someone who is laughing may be sad inside,
and joy may end in sadness.

14Evil people will be paid back for their
evil ways,
and good people will be rewarded for their
good ones.

15Fools will believe anything,
but the wise think about what they do.

16Wise people are careful and stay out of trouble,
but fools are careless and quick to act.

17Someone with a quick temper does foolish things,
but someone with understanding
remains calm.

18Fools are rewarded with nothing but
more foolishness,
but the wise are rewarded with knowledge.

19Evil people will bow down to those who
are good;
the wicked will bow down at the door of
those who do right.

20The poor are rejected, even by their neighbors,
but the rich have many friends.

21It is a sin to hate your neighbor,
but being kind to the needy brings
happiness.

22Those who make evil plans will be ruined,
but those who plan to do good will be loved
and trusted.

23Those who work hard make a profit,
but those who only talk will be poor.

24Wise people are rewarded with wealth,
but fools only get more foolishness.

25A truthful witness saves lives,
but a false witness is a traitor.

26Those who respect the LORD will have security,
and their children will be protected.

27Respect for the LORD gives life.
It is like a fountain that can save people
from death.

28A king is honored when he has many people
to rule,
but a prince is ruined if he has none.

29Patient people have great understanding,
but people with quick tempers show
their foolishness.

30Peace of mind means a healthy body,
but jealousy will rot your bones.

14:18 Folly/Foolishness: Proverbs 14:29

14:21 Neighbor: Proverbs 27:14

14:29 Folly/Foolishness: Proverbs 15:5

14:30 The Bible has a high view of the human body. It was created by God and is an integral part of all of us. God's Word does not support a strong distinction between the body, which is evil and of this world, and the spirit, which is good and belongs to God. Here the wise teacher offers his advice for good body health. A calm mind leads to a healthy body, while one agitated by the stress of jealousy is prone to disease.

FASTING

MATTHEW 6:16–18

What does the Bible teach about fasting—voluntarily abstaining a while from food? Did Jesus fast? Does he expect it of his followers? What are the spiritual benefits of fasting?

In the Old Testament there are two kinds of fasting, individual and community. Although the practice was common in Israel, it was obligatory only on the Day of Cleansing or Atonement (Leviticus 16:29). Individual fasts were observed in Israel as a sign of affliction (2 Samuel 12:15–23), contrition (Psalm 69:15), or in sympathy for someone who had become ill (Psalm 35:13–14). Moses, David, Elijah, Esther, Daniel, and Anna were among the many leaders who fasted and encouraged others to do so.

Community fasts were called by prophets, priests, and kings as a sign of the people's repentance (Jonah 3) and as part of fervent prayers for deliverance from enemies (Esther 4:16). Fasts were usually accompanied by the wearing of sackcloth and the imposition of ashes as a sign of penance, mourning, and humility (Nehemiah 9:1; Joel 1:8–2:17).

In the New Testament, the practice of individual fasting continues with John the Baptist and Jesus, but apparently not with his disciples until after the resurrection and ascension.

John the Baptist, who fasted from normal food—eating only locusts and wild honey—called people to the desert. "Change your hearts and lives because the kingdom of heaven is near." Those who heeded his call "confessed their sins, and he baptized them in the Jordan River" (Matthew 3:1–6). Some became his disciples. Apparently, it was their custom to fast often to help prepare the way for the Lord (Matthew 9:14).

Before beginning his public ministry, Jesus wanted to be baptized by John, in accordance with God's will (Matthew 3:13–15). Immediately afterward, Jesus was led by the Spirit into the desert for forty days and nights of solitude. He ate nothing, he prayed, he was tempted by Satan, he was with wild animals, and angels took care of him (Matthew 4:1–11; Mark 1:9–13; Luke 4:1–13). There is no other reference to Jesus fasting, although it is reasonable to assume that he and his disciples fasted corporately during the annual Day of Cleansing.

In his Sermon on the Mount, Jesus taught that individual fasting should be done in secret, as an inward act of spiritual devotion rather than as an outward sign of being religious: "When you give up eating, don't put on a sad face like the hypocrites." Instead, fast without letting people know what you are doing, and your Father in heaven will reward you (Matthew 6:16–18).

It is significant that Jesus did not say, "*If* you fast," nor, "You *must* fast," but rather, *"When* you fast . . ." The practice is assumed, but not explicitly commanded. It was Jesus' intention to give instructions concerning the common practice of fasting, rather than issuing a new commandment. His counsel is directed to our motivations and attitudes about fasting. If we call attention to our fast, people will certainly be impressed, and that is our reward. If we fast humbly and in secret, as Jesus taught, our motivation is pure, and our reward inward.

The Pharisees fasted ritualistically twice a week (Luke 18:9–14). Jesus' disciples apparently did not. When asked why not, Jesus replied: "The friends of the bridegroom are not sad while he is with them. But the time will come when the bridegroom will be taken from them, and then they will give up eating" (Matthew 9:14–15). It is important to know what time and season it is, spiritually (and liturgically) speaking. When the bridegroom is in your midst, it is time for feasting. When the bridegroom is absent, it is time for prayer and fasting. There is plenty of time for both in the rhythm and flow of spiritual life.

Clearly, Jesus expects his followers to fast, struggle, and pray (as he did in the desert) at the appropriate time and season. Spiritual battles are recognized, fought, and won in the spiritual desert of prayer and solitude. Certain kinds of demons, Jesus knew, could only be driven out by prayer (and fasting, as some manuscripts add to Mark 9:29).

What is the spiritual benefit of fasting? According to Richard Foster, more than any other discipline, fasting reveals those things that control us. Food or drink, or any other idol or addiction, must ultimately bow to the Lordship of Christ. Fasting purges the soul of that which claims to be but is not God. Fasting can help us experience the grace of God in unique ways. It should not be neglected by believers today.

Fasting: For additional scriptures on this topic go to Leviticus 16:29.

SCRIBES (TEACHERS OF THE LAW)

MATTHEW 7:28–29

Who are the scribes mentioned in the Bible? What role did they play in Israel's history? What function do they have in the Gospels? Why do they oppose Jesus?

Imagine our world without computers, tape recorders, or even typewriters. Imagine what life would be like without easy access to paper, pens, and pencils. How would life be different if we did not have books, or even our own Bible to read?

Such was life in the ancient world. Only a privileged few were trained to read and write. Only a special segment of people regularly worked with writing materials. And even fewer had access to books or Scriptures. Therefore, the skills of writing and reading were highly valued in the ancient world. Throughout the ancient world a class of people arose called "teachers of the law," or "scribes," who were trained with the rudimentary skills of their trade: reading, writing, and transcribing. Because of the importance of that trade, the role of scribes often went far beyond simple secretarial skills to include teaching, interpretation, and regulation of laws found in official documents.

Scribal skills were especially valued by the people of Israel because God had revealed himself and his plan for humanity in written Scriptures. Since they were required to read and copy and interpret the written Scriptures, scribes were given special prominence. Some scribes in ancient Israel were even given political responsibilities as advisers in the royal court (see 2 Samuel 8:16–18; 1 Kings 4:1–6).

Even greater significance was given to scribes after Solomon's Temple was destroyed by the Babylonians. The Temple had been the national symbol of God's presence and covenant, but with its destruction increasing importance was given to the role of the Scriptures in the national life. While we find evidence of scribes teaching the Teachings of Moses, or the Law, prior to the exile (see Jeremiah 8:8–9), we see that during and after the exile such a role gained increasing prominence. Perhaps the most celebrated scribe is Ezra. Although he was of the priestly line, Ezra was most noted for his responsibilities as scribe, which centered on teaching the Law to the people (Nehemiah 8).

Scribes played an increasingly influential role into the era of the second Temple and the New Testament. Although the term scribe (*grammateus*) was once most closely associated with reading and writing and making copies of the Scriptures, it came to signify an expert in relation to the Teachings, and could be translated as "teacher of the law" (Mark 7:5) and used interchangeably with the term "lawyer" or "expert in the law" (*nomikos*; see Luke 11:45–46; Matthew 23:4). The Pharisee Gamaliel was called a "teacher of the Law" (*nomodidaskaloi*; Acts 5:34), an equivalent expression for scribe. The scribes were not only curators of the text of the Old Testament, but also taught the Teachings of Moses (Matthew 7:29; Mark 1:22), held themselves responsible to interpret and preserve the Law (Mark 7:5–8), elaborate doctrine from the Law (Matthew 17:10), and gather around themselves disciples whom they could train to carry on the profession.

In Galilee the scribes may appear as lower-level officials who acted in the synagogue as teachers or interpreters (Mark 1:22), or the scribes may appear in Jerusalem as high-level officials linked with the chief priests and the Sanhedrin (Matthew 2:4). Scribes can join with Pharisees to question Jesus in Galilee (Matthew 15:1) or Jerusalem (Matthew 23:13), or link forces with the chief priests in Jerusalem in their condemnation of Jesus (Matthew 21:15).

Why do we find the scribes so often opposing Jesus? The scribes were officials charged with preserving the law and traditions. But now Jesus claims to speak and act for God. From the very beginning of Jesus' public ministry the people saw that Jesus gave new teaching with authority, which directly contrasted with the scribes (see Matthew 7:28–29; Mark 1:22, 27).

But we must not suppose that all scribes opposed Jesus. Apparently, some among the scribes were able to set aside their professional blinders to see and hear Jesus' ministry and message. On one occasion Luke tells us that some of the scribes complimented Jesus for his interpretation of a theological issue (Luke 20:39). On another occasion Mark tells us that Jesus recognized the sincerity of a scribe who came questioning his understanding of the law: "When Jesus saw that the man answered him wisely, Jesus said to him, 'You are close to the kingdom of God'" (Mark 12:34; see 12:28–33).

Scribes (Teachers of the Law): For additional scriptures on this topic go to Matthew 5:20.

31Whoever mistreats the poor insults their Maker,
but whoever is kind to the needy honors God.

32The wicked are ruined by their own evil,
but those who do right are protected
even in death.⚭

33Wisdom lives in those with understanding,
and even fools recognize it.

34Doing what is right makes a nation great,
but sin will bring disgrace to any people.

35A king is pleased with a wise servant,
but he will become angry with one who
causes him shame.

15 A gentle answer will calm a person's anger,
but an unkind answer will cause
more anger.

2Wise people use knowledge when
they speak,
but fools pour out foolishness.

3The LORD's eyes see everything;
he watches both evil and good people.

4As a tree gives fruit, healing words give life,
but dishonest words crush the spirit.

5Fools reject their parents' correction,
but anyone who accepts correction is wise.⚭

6Much wealth is in the houses of good people,
but evil people get nothing but trouble.

7Wise people use their words to spread
knowledge,
but there is no knowledge in the thoughts
of fools.

8The LORD hates the sacrifice that the
wicked offer,
but he likes the prayers of honest people.

9The LORD hates what evil people do,
but he loves those who do what is right.

10The person who quits doing what is right will
be punished,
and the one who hates to be corrected will die.

11The LORD knows what is happening in the
world of the dead,
so he surely knows the thoughts
of the living.

12Those who make fun of wisdom don't like to
be corrected;
they will not ask the wise for advice.

13Happiness makes a person smile,
but sadness can break a person's spirit.

14People with understanding want more
knowledge,
but fools just want more foolishness.

15Every day is hard for those who suffer,
but a happy heart is like a continual feast.

16It is better to be poor and respect the LORD
than to be wealthy and have much trouble.

17It is better to eat vegetables with those who
love you
than to eat meat with those who hate you.

18People with quick tempers cause trouble,
but those who control their tempers
stop a quarrel.

19A lazy person's life is like a patch of thorns,
but an honest person's life is like a
smooth highway.

20A wise son makes his father happy,
but a foolish son disrespects his mother.

21A person without wisdom enjoys being foolish,
but someone with understanding does
what is right.⚭

22Plans fail without good advice,
but they succeed with the advice of
many others.

⚭**14:32 Integrity:** Malachi 2:6

15:1 The Book of Proverbs is filled with many helpful sayings about both a proper and improper use of the tongue. To get the most out of a study of the tongue, look for examples of the proper use of the tongue and its influence either on the speaker or the listeners. Then do the same for the improper use. Sometimes you will find both the proper and improper use in the same verse. Look at Proverbs 15:1 as an example. See the proper use: "a gentle answer"; and its influence: "will calm a person's anger." Now note improper use: "an unkind answer," and its influence: "will cause more anger." Another good example of this exercise is Proverbs 13:3.

⚭**15:5 Folly/Foolishness:** Proverbs 17:28

⚭**15:21 Leadership:** Isaiah 3:12

[23]People enjoy giving good advice.
Saying the right word at the right time is
so pleasing.

[24]Wise people's lives get better and better.
They avoid whatever would cause their death.

[25]The LORD will tear down the proud
person's house,
but he will protect the widow's property.

[26]The LORD hates evil thoughts
but is pleased with kind words.

[27]Greedy people bring trouble to their families,
but the person who can't be paid to do
wrong will live.

[28]Good people think before they answer,
but the wicked simply pour out evil.

[29]The LORD does not listen to the wicked,
but he hears the prayers of those who do right.

[30]Good news makes you feel better.
Your happiness will show in your eyes.

[31]If you listen to correction to improve your life,
you will live among the wise.

[32]Those who refuse correction hate themselves,
but those who accept correction gain
understanding.

[33]Respect for the LORD will teach you wisdom.
If you want to be honored, you must
be humble.

16

People may make plans in their minds,
but only the LORD can make them come
true.

[2]You may believe you are doing right,
but the LORD will judge your reasons.

[3]Depend on the LORD in whatever you do,
and your plans will succeed.

[4]The LORD makes everything go as he pleases.
He has even prepared a day of disaster for
evil people.

[5]The LORD hates those who are proud.
They will surely be punished.

[6]Love and truth bring forgiveness of sin.
By respecting the LORD you will avoid evil.

[7]When people live so that they please the LORD,
even their enemies will make peace
with them.

[8]It is better to be poor and right
than to be wealthy and dishonest.

[9]People may make plans in their minds,
but the LORD decides what they will do.

[10]The words of a king are like a message from God,
so his decisions should be fair.

[11]The LORD wants honest balances and scales;
all the weights are his work.

[12]Kings hate those who do wrong,
because governments only continue if
they are fair.

[13]Kings like honest people;
they value someone who speaks the truth.

[14]An angry king can put someone to death,
so a wise person will try to make him happy.

[15]A smiling king can give people life;
his kindness is like a spring shower.

[16]It is better to get wisdom than gold,
and to choose understanding rather
than silver!

[17]Good people stay away from evil.
By watching what they do, they protect
their lives.

[18]Pride will destroy a person;
a proud attitude leads to ruin.

[19]It is better to be humble and be with those
who suffer
than to share stolen property with
the proud.

15:25 *the widow's property.* A widow in the ancient Near East was highly vulnerable, having no husband who could provide for her needs. The Lord therefore assures her well-being by backing it up with his power.

15:27 Greed: Mark 7:20–23

16:3 Success: Matthew 5:1–10

16:9 Decision Making/Plan: Proverbs 20:24

16:16 Wisdom: Ecclesiastes 2:12–16

16:18 Pride: Isaiah 2:6–22

20Whoever listens to what is taught will succeed,
and whoever trusts the LORD will be happy.

21The wise are known for their understanding.
Their pleasant words make them better
teachers.

22Understanding is like a fountain which gives
life to those who use it,
but foolishness brings punishment to fools.

23Wise people's minds tell them what to say,
and that helps them be better teachers.

24Pleasant words are like a honeycomb,
making people happy and healthy.

25Some people think they are doing right,
but in the end it leads to death.

26The workers' hunger helps them,
because their desire to eat makes them work.

27Useless people make evil plans,
and their words are like a burning fire.

28A useless person causes trouble,
and a gossip ruins friendships.

29Cruel people trick their neighbors
and lead them to do wrong.

30Someone who winks is planning evil,
and the one who grins is planning
something wrong.

31Gray hair is like a crown of honor;
it is earned by living a good life.

32Patience is better than strength.
Controlling your temper is better than
capturing a city.

33People throw lots to make a decision,
but the answer comes from the LORD.⚭

17 It is better to eat a dry crust of bread in peace
than to have a feast where there
is quarreling.

2A wise servant will rule over the master's
disgraceful child
and will even inherit a share of what the
master leaves his children.

3A hot furnace tests silver and gold,
but the LORD tests hearts.

4Evil people listen to evil words.
Liars pay attention to cruel words.

5Whoever mistreats the poor insults their Maker;
whoever enjoys someone's trouble will
be punished.

6Old people are proud of their grandchildren,
and children are proud of their parents.

7Fools should not be proud,
and rulers should not be liars.

8Some people think they can pay others to do
anything they ask.
They think it will work every time.

9Whoever forgives someone's sin makes a friend,
but gossiping about the sin breaks
up friendships.

10A wise person will learn more from a warning
than a fool will learn from a hundred lashings.

11Disobedient people look only for trouble,
so a cruel messenger will be sent against them.

12It is better to meet a bear robbed of her cubs
than to meet a fool doing foolish things.

13Whoever gives evil in return for good
will always have trouble at home.

14Starting a quarrel is like a leak in a dam,
so stop it before a fight breaks out.

15The LORD hates both of these things:
freeing the guilty and punishing the innocent.

16It won't do a fool any good to try to buy wisdom,
because he doesn't have the ability
to be wise.

17A friend loves you all the time,
and a brother helps in time of trouble.⚭

16:30 *winks.* See 6:13.
16:31 *Gray hair.* Old age was highly prized in ancient Israel and the broader Near East, since those who were old had lived long and learned by experience.

⚭**16:33 Esther:** Proverbs 21:30–31
⚭**17:17 Love:** Jeremiah 31:3
⚭**17:17 Friend:** Proverbs 18:24

18It is not wise to promise
to pay what your neighbor owes.

19Whoever loves to argue loves to sin.
Whoever brags a lot is asking for trouble.

20A person with an evil heart will find no success,
and the person whose words are evil will get
into trouble.

21It is sad to have a foolish child;
there is no joy in being the parent of a fool.

22A happy heart is like good medicine,
but a broken spirit drains your strength.

23When the wicked accept money to do wrong
there can be no justice.

24The person with understanding is always
looking for wisdom,
but the mind of a fool wanders everywhere.

25A foolish son makes his father sad
and causes his mother great sorrow.

26It is not good to punish the innocent
or to beat leaders for being honest.

27The smart person says very little,
and one with understanding stays calm.

"The LORD is like a strong tower; those who do right can run to him for safety" (18:10).

28Even fools seem to be wise if they keep quiet;
if they don't speak, they appear to
understand.⚭

18

Unfriendly people are selfish
and hate all good sense.

2Fools do not want to understand anything.
They only want to tell others what they think.

3Do something evil, and people won't like you.
Do something shameful, and they will make
fun of you.

4Spoken words can be like deep water,
but wisdom is like a flowing stream.

5It is not good to honor the wicked
or to be unfair to the innocent.

6The words of fools start quarrels.
They make people want to beat them.

7The words of fools will ruin them;
their own words will trap them.⚭

8The words of a gossip are like tasty bits of food.
People like to gobble them up.

9A person who doesn't work hard
is just like someone who destroys things.

10The LORD is like a strong tower;
those who do right can run to him for safety.

11Rich people trust their wealth to protect them.
They think it is like the high walls of a city.

12Proud people will be ruined,
but the humble will be honored.

13Anyone who answers without listening
is foolish and confused.⚭

14The will to live can get you through sickness,
but no one can live with a broken spirit.

15The mind of a person with understanding
gets knowledge;
the wise person listens to learn more.

16Taking a gift to an important man
will help get you in to see him.

⚭**17:28 Folly/Foolishness:** Proverbs 18:6–7
⚭**18:7 Folly/Foolishness:** Proverbs 18:13
⚭**18:13 Folly/Foolishness:** Proverbs 26:4–7

17The person who tells one side of a story
seems right,
until someone else comes and asks questions.

18Throwing lots can settle arguments
and keep the two sides from fighting.

19A brother who has been insulted is harder to
win back than a walled city,
and arguments separate people like the
barred gates of a palace.

20People will be rewarded for what they say;
they will be rewarded by how they speak.

21What you say can mean life or death.
Those who speak with care will be rewarded.

22When a man finds a wife, he finds something
good.
It shows that the LORD is pleased with him.

23The poor beg for mercy,
but the rich give rude answers.

24Some friends may ruin you,
but a real friend will be more loyal than
a brother.

19 It is better to be poor and honest
than to be foolish and tell lies.

2Enthusiasm without knowledge is not good.
If you act too quickly, you might
make a mistake.

3People's own foolishness ruins their lives,
but in their minds they blame the LORD.

4Wealthy people are always finding more friends,
but the poor lose all theirs.

5A witness who lies will not go free;
liars will never escape.

6Many people want to please a leader,
and everyone is friends with those
who give gifts.

7Poor people's relatives avoid them;
even their friends stay far away.
They run after them, begging,
but they are gone.

8Those who get wisdom do themselves a favor,
and those who love learning will succeed.

9A witness who lies will not go free,
liars will die.

10A fool should not live in luxury.
A slave should not rule over princes.

11Smart people are patient;
they will be honored if they ignore insults.

12An angry king is like a roaring lion,
but his kindness is like the dew on the grass.

13A foolish son will ruin his father,
and a quarreling wife is like dripping water.

14Houses and wealth are inherited from parents,
but a wise wife is a gift from the LORD.

15Lazy people sleep a lot,
and idle people will go hungry.

16Those who obey the commands protect
themselves,
but those who are careless will die.

17Being kind to the poor is like lending
to the LORD;
he will reward you for what you have done.

18Correct your children while there is still hope;
do not let them destroy themselves.

19People with quick tempers will have to
pay for it.
If you help them out once, you will have to
do it again.

20Listen to advice and accept correction,
and in the end you will be wise.

21People can make all kinds of plans,
but only the LORD's plan will happen.

22People want others to be loyal,
so it is better to be poor than to be a liar.

18:24 Friend: Ecclesiastes 4:9–12
19:18 Parenting: Proverbs 19:27
19:21 People's plans cannot upset God's. Nothing happens by accident, but only by God's plan. This, however, does not mean that Christians are not to plan or make decisions. Decisions are constantly being made, not only in our lives, but were made even more in the lives of biblical figures. One of the great joys of the Good News is that God teaches us throughout our lives to want what he wants. In this way we become more like Christ.
19:21 Time: Ecclesiastes 3:1–14

23Those who respect the LORD will live
and be satisfied, unbothered by trouble.

24Though the lazy person puts his hand in the dish,
he won't lift the food to his mouth.

25Whip those who make fun of wisdom, and
perhaps foolish people will gain
some wisdom.
Correct those with understanding, and they
will gain knowledge.

26A son who robs his father and sends away
his mother
brings shame and disgrace on himself.

27Don't stop listening to correction, my child,
or you will forget what you have
already learned.⚭

28An evil witness makes fun of fairness,
and wicked people love what is evil.

29People who make fun of wisdom will
be punished,
and the backs of foolish people will be beaten.

20 Wine and beer make people loud and
uncontrolled;
it is not wise to get drunk on them.

2An angry king is like a roaring lion.
Making him angry may cost you your life.

3Foolish people are always fighting,
but avoiding quarrels will bring you honor.

4Lazy farmers don't plow when they should;
they expect a harvest, but there is none.⚭

5People's thoughts can be like a deep well,
but someone with understanding can find
the wisdom there.

6Many people claim to be loyal,
but it is hard to find a trustworthy person.

7The good people who live honest lives
will be a blessing to their children.⚭

8When a king sits on his throne to judge,
he knows evil when he sees it.

9No one can say, "I am innocent;
I have never done anything wrong."

10The LORD hates both these things:
dishonest weights and dishonest measures.

11Even children are known by their behavior;
their actions show if they are innocent
and good.⚭

12The LORD has made both these things:
ears to hear and eyes to see.

13If you love to sleep, you will be poor.
If you stay awake, you will have
plenty of food.

14Buyers say, "This is bad. It's no good."
Then they go away and brag about what
they bought.

15There is gold and plenty of rubies,
but only a few people speak with
knowledge.

16Take the coat of someone who promises to pay
a stranger's debts,
and keep it until he pays what the
stranger owes.

17Stolen food may taste sweet at first,
but later it will feel like a mouth full of gravel.

18Get advice if you want your plans to work.
If you go to war, get the advice of others.

19Gossips can't keep secrets,
so avoid people who talk too much.

20Those who curse their father or mother
will be like a light going out in darkness.

21Wealth inherited quickly in the beginning
will do you no good in the end.

22Don't say, "I'll pay you back for the wrong
you did."
Wait for the LORD, and he will make
things right.

23The LORD hates dishonest weights,
and dishonest scales do not please him.

⚭**19:27 Parenting:** Proverbs 20:7
⚭**20:4 Leisure:** Proverbs 21:17
⚭**20:7 Parenting:** Proverbs 20:11
⚭**20:11 Parenting:** Proverbs 22:6

24The LORD decides what a person will do;
no one understands what his life is all about.

25It's dangerous to promise something to God
too quickly.
After you've thought about it, it may
be too late.

26A wise king sorts out the evil people,
and he punishes them as they deserve.

27The LORD looks deep inside people
and searches through their thoughts.

28Loyalty and truth keep a king in power;
he continues to rule if he is loyal.

29Young men glory in their strength,
and old men are honored for their gray hair.

30Hard punishment will get rid of evil,
and whippings can change an evil heart.

21 The LORD can control a king's mind as he
controls a river;
he can direct it as he pleases.

2You may believe you are doing right,
but the LORD judges your reasons.

3Doing what is right and fair
is more important to the LORD
than sacrifices.

4Proud looks, proud thoughts,
and evil actions are sin.

5The plans of hard-working people earn a profit,
but those who act too quickly become poor.

6Wealth that comes from telling lies
vanishes like a mist and leads to death.

7The violence of the wicked will destroy them,
because they refuse to do what is right.

8Guilty people live dishonest lives,
but honest people do right.

9It is better to live in a corner on the roof
than inside the house with a quarreling wife.

10Evil people only want to harm others.
Their neighbors get no mercy from them.

11If you punish those who make fun of wisdom,
a foolish person may gain some wisdom.
But if you teach the wise, they will
get knowledge.

12God, who is always right, watches the house of
the wicked
and brings ruin on every evil person.

13Whoever ignores the poor when they
cry for help
will also cry for help and not be answered.

14A secret gift will calm an angry person;
a present given in secrecy will quiet
great anger.

15When justice is done, good people are happy,
but evil people are ruined.

16Whoever does not use good sense
will end up among the dead.

17Whoever loves pleasure will become poor;
whoever loves wine and perfume will
never be rich.

18Wicked people will suffer instead of good people,
and those who cannot be trusted will suffer
instead of those who do right.

19It is better to live alone in the desert
than with a quarreling and complaining wife.

20Wise people's houses are full of the best foods
and olive oil,
but fools waste everything they have.

21Whoever tries to live right and be loyal
finds life, success, and honor.

22A wise person can defeat a city full of warriors
and tear down the defenses they trust in.

23Those who are careful about what they say
keep themselves out of trouble.

24People who act with stubborn pride
are called "proud," "bragger," and "mocker."

20:24 Decision Making/Plan: See article on page 621.
20:25 Oath/Vow: Ecclesiastes 5:4–7
21:9 *roof.* In Bible times houses were built with flat roofs. The roof was used for drying things such as flax and fruit. And it was used as an extra room, as a place for worship, and as a cool place to sleep in the summer.
21:17 Leisure: Proverbs 21:25

25Lazy people's desire for sleep will kill them,
because they refuse to work.
26All day long they wish for more,
but good people give without holding back.

27The LORD hates sacrifices brought by evil people,
particularly when they offer them for the
wrong reasons.

28A lying witness will be forgotten,
but a truthful witness will speak on.

29Wicked people are stubborn,
but good people think carefully about
what they do.

30There is no wisdom, understanding, or advice
that can succeed against the LORD.

31You can get the horses ready for battle,
but it is the LORD who gives the victory.

22 Being respected is more important than
having great riches.
To be well thought of is better than
silver or gold.

2The rich and the poor are alike
in that the LORD made them all.

3The wise see danger ahead and avoid it,
but fools keep going and get into trouble.

4Respecting the LORD and not being proud
will bring you wealth, honor, and life.
5Evil people's lives are like paths covered with
thorns and traps.
People who guard themselves don't have
such problems.

6Train children how to live right,
and when they are old, they will not change.

7The rich rule over the poor,
and borrowers are servants to lenders.

8Those who plan evil will receive trouble.
Their cruel anger will come to an end.

9Generous people will be blessed,
because they share their food with the poor.

10Get rid of the one who makes fun of wisdom.
Then fighting, quarrels, and insults will stop.

11Whoever loves pure thoughts and kind words
will have even the king as a friend.

12The LORD guards knowledge,
but he destroys false words.

13The lazy person says, "There's a lion outside!
I might get killed out in the street!"

14The words of an unfaithful wife are like
a deep trap.
Those who make the LORD angry will get
caught by them.

15Every child is full of foolishness,
but punishment can get rid of it.

16Whoever gets rich by mistreating the poor,
and gives presents to the wealthy, will
become poor.

Other Wise Sayings

17Listen carefully to what wise people say;
pay attention to what I am teaching you.
18It will be good to keep these things in mind
so that you are ready to repeat them.
19I am teaching them to you now
so that you will put your trust in the LORD.
20I have written thirty sayings for you,
which give knowledge and good advice.
21I am teaching you true and reliable words
so that you can give true answers to
anyone who asks.

22Do not abuse poor people because they
are poor,
and do not take away the rights of the
needy in court.
23The LORD will defend them in court
and will take the life of those who take
away their rights.

24Don't make friends with quick-tempered
people
or spend time with those who have
bad tempers.
25If you do, you will be like them.
Then you will be in real danger.

21:25 Leisure: Proverbs 24:30–34
21:31 Esther: Romans 8:28
22:6 Parenting: Colossians 3:21
22:17 *wise people.* The Book of Proverbs now quotes the wisdom of a group of unnamed "wise people." Scholars have noticed that the following section is close in its surface content to wisdom from ancient Egypt.

MIRACLES

MATTHEW 8

What is a miracle? Do miracles still happen today? Are there different types of miracles? How did Jesus interpret his miracles? Are the miracles recorded in Acts different from Jesus' miracles?

In the four books of Good News (the Gospels: Matthew, Mark, Luke, and John), the term *miracle* is not really used to describe Jesus' remarkable actions to help and heal various people. What we have called *miracles* are called "mighty works" in the Gospels and "signs" and "wonders" in the fourth gospel. In the Gospels, miracles are seen as evidence that God's kingdom, his divine saving activity, has broken into the midst of God's people (Luke 11:20–23). The fourth gospel focuses a good deal more on the person of Jesus, and the "signs" and "wonders" recounted there point beyond themselves to the presence of the King.

To a great extent, the ancients would not have shared our rather clear-cut separation of the supernatural and the natural, since they believed that God or the gods were operative in nature and throughout the ordinary course of human affairs as well as through prodigies and unusual healings and happenings. It is also confusing when various dictionaries define miracles as events that apparently violate the known laws of nature, for what sense can be made of the idea of a God who violates the very laws or principles that he used to set up the universe in the first place? It is better to say that miracles are surprising and unusual events (wonders) that go beyond, but not against, the so-called laws of nature. It is best to avoid the notion that God has basically wound up the universe and let it run on its own except for occasional miraculous incursions, for the Bible sees God involved in all the ordinary as well as the extraordinary affairs of life. God has not withdrawn from creation and left it to its own devices.

Miracles can then be distinguished from God's ordinary day-to-day providential guidance and protection in that miracles involve the using of extraordinary or unusual means to accomplish some end. By definition, miracles are something out of the ordinary and exceptional. While it is, perhaps, true that some of the events depicted in the Bible which have traditionally been seen as miracles can be given a natural explanation (such as the falling of quail in the desert to feed the Israelites, or the healing of a paralytic whose illness may have been psychosomatic in nature), on the whole, the miracles in the Bible cannot be explained away.

A belief in miracles depends in part on a prior belief about what is and is not possible in this world. In particular, belief in miracles depends on a prior belief in God. If one believes there is an all-powerful creator God who made the universe and all that is in it out of nothing, it follows then that all sorts of miracles are possible for such a being. An all-powerful being is free to arrange or rearrange various facets of creation according to a divine will or plan. The "laws" of nature are, after all, just the ways God chooses ordinarily to run his universe.

Whether or not we can believe that a particular event is a miracle will depend in part on the trustworthiness of those who bear witness to the events. It may also depend in part on whether or not we, ourselves, have personally experienced or know someone who has experienced a miracle, and so have a personal understanding of what is involved. Since God is the same God and the universe and humankind have not changed in decisive ways since the beginning of creation, it is no more difficult to believe in miracles happening today than in the past, unless we are persuaded that God does not do those sorts of things anymore. That belief, however, falls on the hard rocks of the thousands of personal testimonies of reliable witnesses to the miraculous in all ages since biblical times. It is well to add that science is not able to absolutely rule out the miraculous, especially because there is no proof that the universe is a closed system that runs purely on the basis of impersonal natural laws.

The miracles of Jesus and those recorded in Acts and elsewhere in the New Testament help us to understand that the message of salvation is holistic in character—it involves real human lives and physical conditions, as well as spiritual renewal. The Good News is regularly associated with physical healing as well as with spiritual transformation or help with a mental or emotional problem.

We are reminded by these stories that we must not preach a half-gospel that offers only spiritual consolation and change, but does not affect human bodies or human social relationships and situations. Jesus says clearly in Luke 4 that he came to help the poor, to set the prisoner free, to heal the sick, as well as to save the soul. This is still the Good News the church should offer today—the story of a Savior who can work all sorts of wonders, physical, mental, spiritual, emotional, and social.

Miracles: For additional scriptures on this topic go to Matthew 9.

HEALING
MATTHEW 8

What does the Bible say about healing? Why do the Gospels spend so much time talking about Jesus healing people? How does the church experience God's healing power in Scripture and today?

The Good News of the Bible is news of healing. From beginning to end we find that God is interested in restoring things to wholeness. This is most clearly shown in the healing ministry of Jesus, a ministry which is shared by the church after his resurrection.

The Old Testament laws sought to protect the people of God from sickness by keeping them from the sources of disease—physical, spiritual, and social. For example, God was careful to keep his people away from animals which might carry disease (Leviticus 11:31–39), as well as from fortune tellers who could also make one "unclean" (Leviticus 19:31). At times God would punish people with sickness for doing things against his will. Yet he was always there to supply healing to those who returned to him (Genesis 20:17; Numbers 21:4–9). The way of Old Testament law is summarized in Exodus 15:26, "If you obey all his commands and keep his rules, I will not bring on you any of the sickness I brought on the Egyptians. I am the LORD who heals."

Sickness, in the Old Testament, was often understood as punishment for sin. David prays, "LORD have mercy on me. Heal me because I have sinned against you" (Psalm 41:4). Likewise, the Lord tells Solomon that God will "forgive their sin" and "heal their land" (2 Chronicles 7:13–14). However, in the Book of Job we learn that sickness is not always due to sin. Even when the causes of suffering are unknown, God can still be trusted, as we see in the ministry of Elisha whom God used to multiply food, heal the sick, and "heal" dirty water (2 Kings 2–7).

The prophets of Israel were painfully aware of how their nation had rejected God. They envisioned a time when the Lord would heal the "sicknesses" of the nation. "Come, let's go back to the LORD," Hosea calls, "He has hurt us but he will heal us. He has wounded us, but he will bandage our wounds" (Hosea 6:1). At times, the hopes of the prophets turned to a Savior, about whom they could say, "And we are healed because of his wounds" (Isaiah 53:5).

The New Testament tells of the fulfillment of God's desire to deliver, to save, and to heal his people. Healing is seen as one part of the Lord's work of setting people free. The Gospels summarize the ministry of Jesus in Matthew 9:35, "Jesus traveled through all the towns and villages, teaching in their synagogues, preaching the Good News about the kingdom, and healing all kinds of diseases and sicknesses." He forgave their sins (Matthew 9:1–8), he cast cruel demons out from them (Matthew 8:28–34); he taught them (Matthew 7:28–29); and he healed them.

In Jesus' healings, we see God in the flesh. Jesus healed "all the sick" (Matthew 8:16). Blindness, fevers, skin diseases, mental problems, and many other hurts were healed by Jesus. Jesus' healings were miraculous "signs and wonders," showing that his message was from God. But the healings *themselves* were part of Jesus' message of hope to the hurting. They flowed from his care for others (Luke 7:11–16), from the faith of those who came to him (Matthew 8:5–13), and from his hatred of the forces which torment human life (Matthew 8:16–17). He used faith, speech, and touch to bring the healing power of God to the sick (Matthew 8:1–3).

Jesus did not reserve the healing ministry for himself, but passed on to his disciples "authority to drive out evil spirits and to heal every kind of disease and sickness" (Matthew 10:1). His followers became apostles of salvation: announcing the Good News of God's kingdom, and demonstrating this Good News by restoring people to wholeness. This ministry greatly increased after Jesus' resurrection and the outpouring of his Spirit. Healing was an important part of the apostles' evangelism. They prayed, "Help us to be brave by showing us your power to heal. Give proofs and make miracles happen by the power of Jesus, your holy servant" (Acts 4:29–30).

The healing ministry passed from the apostles to the churches. Paul speaks to the Galatian church of God still working "miracles among you" (Galatians 3:5). The New Testament letters give two models of healing. Paul presents a model which emphasizes "gifts of healing" (1 Corinthians 12:9, 28). The Holy Spirit gives some believers special abilities to heal others. These are given by God for "the common good" (1 Corinthians 12:7). By using these gifts, the sick are made well and the whole church is encouraged. ⚭

⚭**Healing:** For additional scriptures on this topic go to 2 Chronicles 7:13–14.

[26]Don't promise to pay what someone else owes,
and don't guarantee anyone's loan.
[27]If you cannot pay the loan,
your own bed may be taken right out from
under you.

[28]Don't move an old stone that marks a border,
because those stones were set up by
your ancestors.

[29]Do you see people skilled in their work?
They will work for kings, not for ordinary
people.⚭

23 If you sit down to eat with a ruler,
notice the food that is in front of you.
[2]Control yourself
if you have a big appetite.
[3]Don't be greedy for his fine foods,
because that food might be a trick.

[4]Don't wear yourself out trying to get rich;
be wise enough to control yourself.
[5]Wealth can vanish in the wink of an eye.
It can seem to grow wings
and fly away like an eagle.

[6]Don't eat the food of selfish people;
don't be greedy for their fine foods.
[7]Selfish people are always worrying
about how much the food costs.
They tell you, "Eat and drink,"
but they don't really mean it.
[8]You will throw up the little you have eaten,
and you will have wasted your kind words.

[9]Don't speak to fools;
they will only ignore your wise words.

[10]Don't move an old stone that marks a border,
and don't take fields that belong to orphans.
[11]God, their defender, is strong;
he will take their side against you.⚭

[12]Remember what you are taught,
and listen carefully to words of knowledge.
[13]Don't fail to punish children.
If you spank them, they won't die.
[14]If you spank them,
you will save them from death.

[15]My child, if you are wise,
then I will be happy.
[16]I will be so pleased
if you speak what is right.

[17]Don't envy sinners,
but always respect the LORD.
[18]Then you will have hope for the future,
and your wishes will come true.

[19]Listen, my child, and be wise.
Keep your mind on what is right.
[20]Don't drink too much wine
or eat too much food.
[21]Those who drink and eat too much
become poor.
They sleep too much and end up
wearing rags.

[22]Listen to your father, who gave you life,
and do not forget your mother when she is old.
[23]Learn the truth and never reject it.
Get wisdom, self-control, and understanding.
[24]The father of a good child is very happy;
parents who have wise children are glad
because of them.
[25]Make your father and mother happy;
give your mother a reason to be glad.

[26]My son, pay attention to me,
and watch closely what I do.
[27]A prostitute is as dangerous as a deep pit,
and an unfaithful wife is like a narrow well.
[28]They ambush you like robbers
and cause many men to be unfaithful
to their wives.

[29]Who has trouble? Who has pain?
Who fights? Who complains?
Who has unnecessary bruises?
Who has bloodshot eyes?

22:26–27 Often the books of wisdom offer what is more like practical advice than a command. Certainly we should not guarantee such a large loan that our own home would be lost if the borrower defaults. Better to refrain from co-signing entirely. (Compare Ecclesiastes 5:5. Even though it is permissible to make a promise, it may be better not to promise at all, in order to avoid the consequences of breaking our word.) Perhaps we can also learn that charity is better than lending, as in Jesus' admonishment to be willing to give to the poor without expecting to get paid back.

22:28 *an old stone that marks a border.* In ancient times carved boundary stones marked the extent of one's property.

⚭**22:29 Work:** Proverbs 26:14–15

23:10 *an old stone that marks a border.* See 22:28.

⚭**23:11 Adoption:** Isaiah 1:17

23:26–35 Alcoholism is a serious problem, and Proverbs speaks against it by describing the pitiful effects that drinking too much has on people. While it may taste good, it can create horrible and painful problems. Elsewhere in the Bible, it is clear that alcohol is a gift from God (Psalm 104:15; John 2:1–12), but everyone must be warned about its abuses.

⚭**23:30 Alcohol:** Proverbs 31:4

30It is people who drink too much wine,
who try out all different kinds of strong drinks.
31Don't stare at the wine when it is red,
when it sparkles in the cup,
when it goes down smoothly.
32Later it bites like a snake
with poison in its fangs.
33Your eyes will see strange sights,
and your mind will be confused.
34You will feel dizzy as if you're in a storm on
the ocean,
as if you're on top of a ship's sails.
35You will think, "They hit me, but I'm not hurt.
They beat me up, but I don't remember it.
I wish I could wake up.
Then I would get another drink."

24 Don't envy evil people
or try to be friends with them.
2Their minds are always planning violence,
and they always talk about making trouble.

3It takes wisdom to have a good family,
and it takes understanding to make it strong.
4It takes knowledge to fill a home
with rare and beautiful treasures.

5Wise people have great power,
and those with knowledge have great
strength.
6So you need advice when you go to war.
If you have lots of good advice, you will win.

7Foolish people cannot understand wisdom.
They have nothing to say in a discussion.

8Whoever makes evil plans
will be known as a troublemaker.
9Making foolish plans is sinful,
and making fun of wisdom is hateful.

10If you give up when trouble comes,
it shows that you are weak.

11Save those who are being led to their death;
rescue those who are about to be killed.
12If you say, "We don't know anything about this,"
God, who knows what's in your mind,
will notice.
He is watching you, and he will know.
He will reward each person for what
he has done.

13My child, eat honey because it is good.
Honey from the honeycomb tastes sweet.
14In the same way, wisdom is pleasing to you.
If you find it, you have hope for the future,
and your wishes will come true.

15Don't be wicked and attack a good
family's house;
don't rob the place where they live.
16Even though good people may be bothered
by trouble seven times, they are
never defeated,
but the wicked are overwhelmed
by trouble.

17Don't be happy when your enemy is defeated;
don't be glad when he is overwhelmed.
18The LORD will notice and be displeased.
He may not be angry with them anymore.

19Don't envy evil people,
and don't be jealous of the wicked.
20An evil person has nothing to hope for;
the wicked will die like a flame that is put out.

21My child, respect the LORD and the king.
Don't join those people who refuse
to obey them.
22The LORD and the king will quickly destroy
such people.
Those two can cause great disaster!

More Words of Wisdom

23These are also sayings of the wise:

It is not good to take sides when you
are the judge.
24Don't tell the wicked that they
are innocent;
people will curse you, and nations
will hate you.
25But things will go well if you punish
the guilty,
and you will receive rich blessings.

26An honest answer is as pleasing
as a kiss on the lips.

27First, finish your outside work
and prepare your fields.
After that, you can build your house.

28Don't testify against your neighbor for
no good reason.
Don't say things that are false.
29Don't say, "I'll get even;
I'll do to him what he did to me."

30 I passed by a lazy person's field
and by the vineyard of someone with no sense.
31 Thorns had grown up everywhere.
The ground was covered with weeds,
and the stone walls had fallen down.
32 I thought about what I had seen;
I learned this lesson from what I saw.
33 You sleep a little; you take a nap.
You fold your hands and lie down to rest.
34 Soon you will be as poor as if you had
been robbed;
you will have as little as if you had
been held up.

More Wise Sayings of Solomon

25 These are more wise sayings of Solomon, copied by the men of Hezekiah king of Judah.

2 God is honored for what he keeps secret.
Kings are honored for what they
can discover.

3 No one can measure the height of the skies or
the depth of the earth.
So also no one can understand the mind
of a king.

4 Remove the scum from the silver,
so the silver can be used by the silversmith.
5 Remove wicked people from the king's presence;
then his government will be honest and last
a long time.

6 Don't brag to the king
and act as if you are great.
7 It is better for him to give you a higher position
than to bring you down in front of the prince.

Because of something you have seen,
8 do not quickly take someone to court.
What will you do later
when your neighbor proves you wrong?

9 If you have an argument with your neighbor,
don't tell other people what was said.
10 Whoever hears it might shame you,
and you might not ever be respected again.

11 The right word spoken at the right time
is as beautiful as gold apples in a silver bowl.

12 A wise warning to someone who will listen
is as valuable as gold earrings or fine
gold jewelry.

13 Trustworthy messengers refresh those
who send them,
like the coolness of snow in the summertime.

14 People who brag about gifts they never give
are like clouds and wind that give no rain.

15 With patience you can convince a ruler,
and a gentle word can get through to
the hard-headed.

16 If you find honey, don't eat too much,
or it will make you throw up.
17 Don't go to your neighbor's house too often;
too much of you will make him hate you.

18 When you lie about your neighbors,
it hurts them as much as a club, a sword, or
a sharp arrow.

19 Trusting unfaithful people when you are
in trouble
is like eating with a broken tooth or walking
with a crippled foot.

20 Singing songs to someone who is sad
is like taking away his coat on a cold day
or pouring vinegar on soda.

21 If your enemy is hungry, feed him.
If he is thirsty, give him a drink.
22 Doing this will be like pouring burning coals
on his head,
and the LORD will reward you.

23 As the north wind brings rain,
telling gossip brings angry looks.

24 It is better to live in a corner on the roof
than inside the house with a
quarreling wife.

25 Good news from a faraway place
is like a cool drink when you are tired.

26 A good person who gives in to evil
is like a muddy spring or a dirty well.

24:34 Leisure: Proverbs 26:13–16
25:1 Proverb: Ezekiel 12:22–23
25:1 Apparently wisdom teachers from the time of Hezekiah encouraged the spread of wisdom teaching from the Book of Proverbs at the end of the eighth century B.C.

25:24 *roof.* In Bible times houses were built with flat roofs. The roof was used for drying things such as flax and fruit. And it was used as an extra room, as a place for worship, and as a cool place to sleep in the summer.

27It is not good to eat too much honey,
nor does it bring you honor to brag about
yourself.

28Those who do not control themselves
are like a city whose walls are broken down.

26 It shouldn't snow in summer or rain at
harvest.
Neither should a foolish person ever
be honored.

2Curses will not harm someone who is innocent;
they are like sparrows or swallows that fly
around and never land.

3Whips are for horses, and harnesses are
for donkeys,
so paddles are good for fools.

4Don't give fools a foolish answer,
or you will be just like them.

5But answer fools as they should be answered,
or they will think they are really wise.

6Sending a message by a foolish person
is like cutting off your feet or drinking poison.

7A wise saying spoken by a fool
is as useless as the legs of a crippled person.

8Giving honor to a foolish person
is like tying a stone in a slingshot.

9A wise saying spoken by a fool
is like a thorn stuck in the hand of a drunk.

10Hiring a foolish person or anyone just passing by
is like an archer shooting at just anything.

11A fool who repeats his foolishness
is like a dog that goes back to what it has
thrown up.

12There is more hope for a foolish person
than for those who think they are wise.

13The lazy person says, "There's a lion
in the road!
There's a lion in the streets!"

14Like a door turning back and forth on
its hinges,
the lazy person turns over and over in bed.

15Lazy people may put their hands in the dish,
but they are too tired to lift the food to
their mouths.

16The lazy person thinks he is wiser
than seven people who give
sensible answers.

17Interfering in someone else's quarrel as
you pass by
is like grabbing a dog by the ears.

18Like a madman shooting
deadly, burning arrows
19is the one who tricks a neighbor
and then says, "I was just joking."

20Without wood, a fire will go out,
and without gossip, quarreling will stop.

21Just as charcoal and wood keep a fire going,
a quarrelsome person keeps an
argument going.

22The words of a gossip are like tasty bits of food;
people like to gobble them up.

23Kind words from a wicked mind
are like a shiny coating on a clay pot.

24Those who hate you may try to fool you
with their words,
but in their minds they are planning evil.
25People's words may be kind, but don't
believe them,
because their minds are full of
evil thoughts.
26Lies can hide hate,
but the evil will be plain to everyone.

25:28 This is one of the few Old Testament references to "self-control" and has to do with being unable to rule one's spirit. In contemporary terms, a person without self-control is a person with weak boundaries, someone unable to restrain his or her own impulses and unable to protect him or herself from the intrusions of others. The Bible encourages us to trust in the Lord for strength and guidance in exerting self-control, so that our lives serve him and reflect faith, love, and hope.

26:2 Curse: 1 Corinthians 4:12

26:2 Curses have no magical power to cause harm. Only God has the power to make a curse effective, and he will bring harm only upon the guilty.

26:7 Folly/Foolishness: Proverbs 28:26

26:15 Work: Proverbs 31:10–31

26:16 Leisure: Isaiah 5:11–12

26:23 *a shiny coating on a clay pot.* Some clay pottery in ancient Israel was covered with a shiny glaze.

27Whoever digs a pit for others will fall into it.
Whoever tries to roll a boulder down
on others will be crushed by it.

28Liars hate the people they hurt,
and false praise can ruin others.

27 Don't brag about tomorrow;
you don't know what may happen then.

2Don't praise yourself. Let someone else do it.
Let the praise come from a stranger and not
from your own mouth.

3Stone is heavy, and sand is weighty,
but a complaining fool is worse than either.

4Anger is cruel and destroys like a flood,
but no one can put up with jealousy!

5It is better to correct someone openly
than to have love and not show it.

6The slap of a friend can be trusted to help you,
but the kisses of an enemy are nothing but lies.

7When you are full, not even honey tastes good,
but when you are hungry, even something
bitter tastes sweet.

8A person who leaves his home
is like a bird that leaves its nest.

9The sweet smell of perfume and oils
is pleasant,
and so is good advice from a friend.

10Don't forget your friend or your parent's friend.
Don't always go to your family for help when
trouble comes.
A neighbor close by is better than a
family far away.

11Be wise, my child, and make me happy.
Then I can respond to any insult.

12The wise see danger ahead and avoid it,
but fools keep going and get into trouble.

13Take the coat of someone who promises to pay
a stranger's loan,
and keep it until he pays what the
stranger owes.

14If you loudly greet your neighbor early
in the morning,
he will think of it as a curse.

15A quarreling wife is as bothersome
as a continual dripping on a rainy day.
16Stopping her is like stopping the wind
or trying to grab oil in your hand.

17As iron sharpens iron,
so people can improve each other.

18Whoever tends a fig tree gets to eat its fruit,
and whoever takes care of his master will
receive honor.

19As water reflects your face,
so your mind shows what kind of
person you are.

20People will never stop dying and being
destroyed,
and they will never stop wanting more
than they have.

21A hot furnace tests silver and gold,
and people are tested by the praise
they receive.

22Even if you ground up a foolish person like
grain in a bowl,
you couldn't remove the foolishness.

23Be sure you know how your sheep are doing,
and pay attention to the condition
of your cattle.
24Riches will not go on forever,
nor do governments go on forever.
25Bring in the hay, and let the new
grass appear.
Gather the grass from the hills.
26Make clothes from the lambs' wool,
and sell some goats to buy a field.

27:4 Jealousy: Ecclesiastes 9:6
27:7 Conflict: Proverbs 27:17
27:14 Neighbor: Jeremiah 31:34
27:17 Conflict: Matthew 18:15–17

27:17 How can we sharpen one another as "iron sharpens iron"? We have to rub up against one another on a regular basis—that is, we need to relate to our friends often enough and deeply enough to have an influence on one another. But as people relate and really get involved in one another's lives, friction and heat are inevitable. Some issues are sensitive and confronting them will result in conflict. Sparks may fly. But all of this is part of the process of sharpening one another. To follow this biblical command, we have to be loving enough and courageous enough to challenge one another for the sake of growth and restoration (Matthew 18:15–17).

27There will be plenty of goat's milk
to feed you and your family
and to make your servant girls healthy.

28 Evil people run even though no one is
chasing them,
but good people are as brave as a lion.

2When a country is lawless, it has one ruler
after another;
but when it is led by a man with understanding
and knowledge, it continues strong.

3Rulers who mistreat the poor
are like a hard rain that destroys the crops.

4Those who disobey what they have been
taught praise the wicked,
but those who obey what they have been
taught are against them.

5Evil people do not understand justice,
but those who follow the LORD understand
it completely.

6It is better to be poor and innocent
than to be rich and wicked.

7Children who obey what they have been
taught are smart,
but friends of troublemakers disgrace
their parents.

8Some people get rich by overcharging others,
but their wealth will be given to those who
are kind to the poor.

9If you refuse to obey what you have been taught,
your prayers will not be heard.

10Those who lead good people to do wrong
will be ruined by their own evil,
but the innocent will be rewarded with
good things.

11Rich people may think they are wise,
but the poor with understanding will prove
them wrong.

12When good people triumph, there is
great happiness,
but when the wicked get control,
everybody hides.

13If you hide your sins, you will not succeed.
If you confess and reject them, you will
receive mercy.

14Those who are always respectful will be happy,
but those who are stubborn will get
into trouble.

15A wicked ruler is as dangerous to poor people
as a roaring lion or a charging bear.

16A ruler without wisdom will be cruel,
but the one who refuses to take dishonest
money will rule a long time.

17Don't help those who are guilty of murder;
let them run until they die.

18Innocent people will be kept safe,
but those who are dishonest will suddenly
be ruined.

19Those who work their land will have
plenty of food,
but the ones who chase empty dreams
instead will end up poor.

20A truthful person will have many blessings,
but those eager to get rich will be punished.

21It is not good for a judge to take sides,
but some will sin for only a piece of bread.

22Selfish people are in a hurry to get rich
and do not realize they soon will be poor.

23Those who correct others will later be liked
more than those who give false praise.

24Whoever robs his father or mother
and says, "It's not wrong,"
is just like someone who destroys things.

25A greedy person causes trouble,
but the one who trusts the LORD will succeed.

26Those who trust in themselves are foolish,
but those who live wisely will be kept safe.

27Whoever gives to the poor will have
everything he needs,
but the one who ignores the poor will
receive many curses.

28:20 Blessing: Ezekiel 34:25–31

28:26 Folly/Foolishness: Proverbs 29:11

28When the wicked get control, everybody hides,
but when they die, good people do well.

29 Whoever is stubborn after being
corrected many times
will suddenly be hurt beyond cure.

2When good people do well, everyone is happy,
but when evil people rule, everyone groans.

3Those who love wisdom make their
parents happy,
but friends of prostitutes waste their money.

4If a king is fair, he makes his country strong,
but if he takes gifts dishonestly, he tears his
country down.

5Those who give false praise to their neighbors
are setting a trap for them.

6Evil people are trapped by their own sin,
but good people can sing and be happy.

7Good people care about justice for the poor,
but the wicked are not concerned.

8People who make fun of wisdom cause
trouble in a city,
but wise people calm anger down.

9When a wise person takes a foolish person
to court,
the fool only shouts or laughs, and there is
no peace.

10Murderers hate an honest person
and try to kill those who do right.

11Foolish people lose their tempers,
but wise people control theirs.⚭

12If a ruler pays attention to lies,
all his officers will become wicked.

13The poor person and the cruel person are alike
in that the LORD gave eyes to both
of them.

14If a king judges poor people fairly,
his government will continue forever.⚭

15Correction and punishment make children wise,
but those left alone will disgrace their mother.

16When there are many wicked people, there is
much sin,
but those who do right will see them destroyed.

17Correct your children, and you will be proud;
they will give you satisfaction.

18Where there is no word from God, people
are uncontrolled,
but those who obey what they have been
taught are happy.⚭

19Words alone cannot correct a servant,
because even if he understands, he
won't respond.

20Do you see people who speak too quickly?
There is more hope for a foolish person than
for them.

21If you spoil your servants when they are young,
they will bring you grief later on.

22An angry person causes trouble;
a person with a quick temper sins a lot.

23Pride will ruin people,
but those who are humble will be honored.

24Partners of thieves are their own worst enemies.
If they have to testify in court, they are afraid
to say anything.

25Being afraid of people can get you into trouble,
but if you trust the LORD, you will be safe.

26Many people want to speak to a ruler,
but justice comes only from the LORD.⚭

27Good people hate those who are dishonest,
and the wicked hate those who are honest.

Wise Words from Agur

30 These are the words of Agur son of Jakeh.
This is his message to Ithiel and Ucal:

2"I am the most stupid person there is,
and I have no understanding.

⚭**29:11 Folly/Foolishness:** Ecclesiastes 2:14
⚭**29:14 Poverty:** Ezekiel 16:49
⚭**29:18 Vision:** Isaiah 1:1
⚭**29:26 Justice:** Ecclesiastes 5:8

30:1 *Agur son of Jakeh.* There is some difficulty over whether these are personal names of people who are otherwise unknown or actually Hebrew words that should be translated. The former is most likely.

3I have not learned to be wise,
and I don't know much about God,
the Holy One.
4Who has gone up to heaven and come
back down?
Who can hold the wind in his hand?
Who can gather up the waters in his coat?
Who has set in place the ends of the earth?
What is his name or his son's name?
Tell me, if you know!

5"Every word of God is true.
He guards those who come to him for safety.
6Do not add to his words,
or he will correct you and prove you
are a liar.

7"I ask two things from you, LORD.
Don't refuse me before I die.
8Keep me from lying and being dishonest.
And don't make me either rich or poor;
just give me enough food for each day.
9If I have too much, I might reject you
and say, 'I don't know the LORD.'
If I am poor, I might steal
and disgrace the name of my God.

10"Do not say bad things about servants to their
masters,
or they will curse you, and you will
suffer for it.

11"Some people curse their fathers
and do not bless their mothers.
12Some people think they are pure,
but they are not really free from evil.
13Some people have such a proud look!
They look down on others.
14Some people have teeth like swords;
their jaws seem full of knives.
They want to remove the poor from the earth
and the needy from the land.

15"Greed has two daughters
named 'Give' and 'Give.'
There are three things that are never satisfied,
really four that never say, 'I've had enough!':
16the cemetery, the childless mother,
the land that never gets enough rain,
and fire that never says, 'I've had enough!'

17"If you make fun of your father
and refuse to obey your mother,
the birds of the valley will peck out your eyes,
and the vultures will eat them.

18"There are three things that are too hard for me,
really four I don't understand:
19the way an eagle flies in the sky,
the way a snake slides over a rock,
the way a ship sails on the sea,
and the way a man and a woman fall in love.

20"This is the way of a woman who takes
part in adultery:
She acts as if she had eaten and washed
her face;
she says, 'I haven't done anything wrong.'

21"There are three things that make the
earth tremble,
really four it cannot stand:
22a servant who becomes a king,
a foolish person who has plenty to eat,
23a hated woman who gets married,
and a maid who replaces her mistress.

24"There are four things on earth that are small,
but they are very wise:
25Ants are not very strong,
but they store up food in the summer.
26Rock badgers are not very powerful,
but they can live among the rocks.
27Locusts have no king,
but they all go forward in formation.
28Lizards can be caught in the hand,
but they are found even in kings' palaces.

29"There are three things that strut proudly,
really four that walk as if they were
important:
30a lion, the proudest animal,
which is strong and runs from nothing,
31a rooster, a male goat,
and a king when his army is around him.

32"If you have been foolish and proud,
or if you have planned evil, shut
your mouth.
33Just as stirring milk makes butter,
and twisting noses makes them bleed,
so stirring up anger causes trouble."

Wise Words of King Lemuel

31 These are the words of King Lemuel, the message his mother taught him:

2"My son, I gave birth to you.
You are the son I prayed for.
3Don't waste your strength on women
or your time on those who ruin kings.

BLASPHEMY

MATTHEW 9:3

What does it mean to blaspheme in the Bible? Why was Jesus accused of blasphemy? How does one blaspheme today?

Blasphemy is commonly understood to mean that a human being claims to be God in some sense. This is certainly correct to a certain extent, but biblically speaking the definition of blasphemy is a bit different. It concerns itself basically with an improper manner of relating to the Lord, which can mean several specific things. In the Bible, the penalty for blasphemy is death, specifically stoning (Leviticus 24:16; John 10:31).

Anyone can blaspheme. In the Old Testament, blasphemy is committed not only by Israel's enemies (2 Kings 19:6, 22; see also Isaiah 37:6, 23), but by God's chosen people, the Israelites themselves (Numbers 15:30). Blasphemy is not a sin that is restricted to those who are either outside or inside of God's family.

There are many ways in which blasphemy is committed in the Bible:

(1) Cursing and speaking against God (Leviticus 24:10–23).

(2) Purposefully committing a sin (Numbers 15:30).

(3) Insulting or mocking God (2 Kings 19:6, 22 [Isaiah 37:6, 23] Isaiah 52:5).

(4) Forsaking God (Ezekiel 20:27; perhaps also Acts 26:11 and 1 Timothy 1:20).

(5) Making an idol (Nehemiah 9:18).

(6) Speaking against God by mistreating his messengers (Nehemiah 9:26; Acts 6:11; 1 Timothy 1:13; 2 Peter 2:12).

(7) Speaking against the Holy Spirit by attributing his miracles to Satan (Matthew 12:31; see also Mark 3:29 and Luke 12:10).

(8) Claiming divine authority (Revelation 13:1, 5, 6; 17:3).

A closer look at these examples shows that blasphemy has much to do with speaking or acting "against God." It is showing hatred and disrespect for God's authority by mocking God, disbelieving in him, defying him, discrediting or harming those whom God has sent to act on his behalf, or holding any created thing (including oneself) in God's rightful place.

Blasphemy is more than simply saying "I am God," or something similar. Rather, it is displaying an insubordinate attitude toward the King of the universe. Such insubordination puts the blasphemer in a "contest" against God, so to speak. In so doing, the blasphemer thinks him- or herself as being in a position to compete with God on the same playing field.

Jesus was accused of blasphemy, but falsely so. Jesus said and did things that should, by normal standards, have been considered blasphemous. In this respect, the religious leaders of Jesus' day were consistent with the Old Testament concept when they accused him of blasphemy. Yet, Jesus was unique and did not operate under "normal standards."

How did Jesus blaspheme? First, he is accused of blasphemy because he takes it upon himself to forgive sin (Matthew 9:3; Luke 5:21). In one sense, there is nothing unusual about Jesus, or anyone else, forgiving someone when he or she sins. But what makes Jesus' declaration blasphemous to the "teachers of the law" is that he forgave a man's sins that were not committed against Jesus personally.

People are to forgive others when they themselves are wronged, but only God can forgive someone's sins when they are committed against another person. Why is it that God does this? It is because all sins committed against other people are ultimately sins against God. Hence, when Jesus forgives the paralyzed man for his "sins," he is speaking not of some disrespect that man had shown towards him, but his sins in general. And the teachers of the law were quick (and quite correct!) to point out that God, and God alone, can do this. What the teachers of the law did not understand, however, was that the One whom they were accusing of blasphemy was God himself in the flesh.

Blasphemy is by no means a dead issue today. When God is made fun of, or when his commands are disregarded, that is blasphemy. Anytime one's central focus is anything other than the Lord, that is blasphemy. Blasphemy is not simply an open claim to divinity. It is very subtle and pervasive and is certainly a common occurrence today. Although subtle, blasphemy is the ultimate rebellion against God. But, like all sin, there is forgiveness with God through the God-man, Jesus Christ.

Blasphemy: For additional scriptures on this topic go to Numbers 15:30.

Demon

Matthew 12:22–29

What is a demon and where do demons come from? What is the relation between demonic influence and psychological illness? Can a believer be taken over by a demon?

There was a time when demons were considered to be the remnant of primitive superstition, a superstition that would soon be overcome by the force of reason. This thought obviously made accepting the biblical representation of demons difficult, especially the New Testament's portrayals of Christ's encounters with demons. Certainly, many popular images are superstitious and need to be rethought in light of the Bible's direct and simple portrayal of demons. Demons are understood in the Scripture as an unseen part of the creation that seeks to thwart God's work and over which Christ has power.

In the Old Testament, various evil spirits provoke unexpected behavior: for example, they arouse a desire for vengeance (Judges 9:23), provoke mental confusion (1 Samuel 16:14), and may influence the words of a false prophet (1 Kings 22:22; compare 1 Timothy 4:1).

The existence of a single powerful adversary to God's rule is described in Isaiah 14:12–15 and Ezekiel 28:11–19. This adversary is clarified in the New Testament to be Satan, although this is not as clearly distinguished in the Old Testament. First Chronicles 21:1, Job 1–2, and Zechariah 3:1 speak of "Satan" or "the satan" (meaning "adversary" in Hebrew), but not until the New Testament does this adversary clearly command evil spiritual beings, or demons.

The Bible takes the existence of demons for granted. As such, the origin of demons is never answered. Demons seem to be angels that have turned from serving God now and are with the devil (Matthew 25:41; Revelation 12:7–9), but this does not offer any real clarity about their origin.

The first four books of the New Testament present Jesus as bringing about the fall of Satan and having authority over demons. The fall of Satan is a definite sign that the kingdom of God is at hand. In Luke 10:18, Jesus says, "I saw Satan fall like lightning from heaven." (Compare, for example, John 12:31; 14:30; 16:11 where the term "ruler of this world" is used for Satan.) Satan is also called Beelzebul, which literally means the "ruler of demons" (Matthew 12:24; Mark 3:22). It is important to note that, though Satan is the archenemy of God, he is in no way equal to God in power. In this sense, Satan is the opposite of Michael, the prince of angels (Jude 9; Revelation 12:7). Because Satan is not equal to God, his doom is sure (Revelation 20:9–10).

In the New Testament, certain persons are said "to have demons" (for example, Matthew 8:28–32; 9:32–33; Mark 7:24–30; 9:17–29). This is a better translation than "demon-possessed" since the demon or evil spirit does not continuously take over the person, but only causes erratic and violent behavior. Jesus clearly has power over demons, as in the story of the man from Gerasene (Mark 5:1–19), where the demons recognize Christ, and he casts them out, restoring the man to his community. It can be noted that although some sickness is associated with demons, there are some distinctions made between demon-influenced behavior and illness. For example, Mark 6:13 says, "They forced many demons out and put olive oil on many sick people and healed them."

The apostles, as part of their commissioning, were given power by Christ to overcome demons (Mark 3:14–15). From the New Testament viewpoint, it is unnecessary for Christians to preoccupy themselves with the existence of demons. It is clear, however, that Christians are involved in warfare against spiritual powers, for which Paul lists a variety of weapons in Ephesians 6:12–18, such as prayer, Scripture, etc. Since Christians have the Spirit of Christ in their lives (Romans 8:9–17; 1 Corinthians 12:3), they cannot be overcome by demons, but are only open to Satan's attack (2 Corinthians 12:7).

On the one hand, it would be inconsistent with biblical revelation to discount completely evil spiritual forces at work in the world. This is mainly a problem for the secularized Western cultures who feel they have outgrown their belief in demons. A particular case is psychological disorder, where it is asserted that formerly psychological problems were misdiagnosed as demon-possession. Some, in fact, do not want to draw too fine a distinction between demon-influence and psychological disorder. One can say that anything that is against fullness of life—disease, psychological disorder, and more pure forms of demonic harassment—is against God's will and represents the work of evil forces. Still not every paranoia is directly demonic, and not every form of demon-influence can be explained psychologically. It takes Christians with spiritual discernment and psychological insight to know the difference.

Demon: For additional scriptures on this topic go to 1 Samuel 16:14–23.

4“Kings should not drink wine, Lemuel,
and rulers should not desire beer.
5If they drink, they might forget the law
and keep the needy from getting
their rights.
6Give beer to people who are dying
and wine to those who are sad.
7Let them drink and forget their need
and remember their misery no more.

8“Speak up for those who cannot speak
for themselves;
defend the rights of all those who
have nothing.
9Speak up and judge fairly,
and defend the rights of the poor and needy.”

A woman using her right hand to twist combed wool into yarn, which is then wound onto the shaft of her spindle

The Good Wife

10It is hard to find a good wife,
because she is worth more than rubies.
11Her husband trusts her completely.
With her, he has everything he needs.
12She does him good and not harm
for as long as she lives.
13She looks for wool and flax
and likes to work with her hands.
14She is like a trader’s ship,
bringing food from far away.
15She gets up while it is still dark
and prepares food for her family
and feeds her servant girls.
16She inspects a field and buys it.
With money she earned, she plants
a vineyard.
17She does her work with energy,
and her arms are strong.
18She knows that what she makes is good.
Her lamp burns late into the night.
19She makes thread with her hands
and weaves her own cloth.
20She welcomes the poor
and helps the needy.
21She does not worry about her family
when it snows,
because they all have fine clothes to keep
them warm.
22She makes coverings for herself;
her clothes are made of linen and other
expensive material.
23Her husband is known at the city meetings,
where he makes decisions as one of
the leaders of the land.
24She makes linen clothes and sells them
and provides belts to the merchants.
25She is strong and is respected by the people.
She looks forward to the future with joy.
26She speaks wise words
and teaches others to be kind.
27She watches over her family
and never wastes her time.
28Her children speak well of her.
Her husband also praises her,
29saying, “There are many fine women,
but you are better than all of them.”
30Charm can fool you, and beauty can trick you,
but a woman who respects the LORD
should be praised.
31Give her the reward she has earned;
she should be praised in public for
what she has done.

31:4 Alcohol: Proverbs 31:6–7
31:7 Alcohol: Isaiah 25:6
31:10–31 The description of a “good wife” in this passage is remarkable for its balance. While her main responsibility is to her husband and children, she is also involved in business and works of charity. She completely meets the needs of her husband and enhances his reputation. She works with her hands and prepares meals for her household. She is strong and tireless in her labors. She makes clothing for her family. She has a positive outlook, and she is a teacher of wisdom. Most importantly, she respects the Lord. Such a woman is, indeed, deserving of praise.
31:24 The woman is engaged in an occupation. It was a domestic occupation, but then again so were most male occupations in ancient Israel.
31:31 Work: Ecclesiastes 2:4–11

She does her work with energy,
and her arms are strong.
She knows that what she makes is good.
Her lamp burns late into the night.

PROVERBS 31:17–18

INTRODUCTION TO THE BOOK OF ECCLESIASTES

A Wise Man Believes in God

WHO WROTE THIS BOOK?

Although no author's name appears in the Book of Ecclesiastes, it is highly likely that Solomon wrote it, based on such passages as 1:1, 12, 16 and others.

TO WHOM WAS THIS BOOK WRITTEN?

Like Proverbs, it may have been intended to benefit young people (12:1) or those less wise than the author.

WHERE WAS IT WRITTEN?

If Solomon is the author, it is likely that Ecclesiastes was written in or around his homeland—Israel.

WHEN WAS IT WRITTEN?

It was probably written during Solomon's era—the tenth century B.C.

WHAT IS THE BOOK ABOUT?

Ecclesiastes seem to be the author's personal reflections on life, people, and the world. The theme of Ecclesiastes centers on the author's pursuit of knowledge, pleasure, possessions, and projects. Without God, the author concludes, a person's efforts are useless and life is without meaning.

WHY WAS THIS BOOK WRITTEN?

As verse three of Ecclesiastes 1 questions, "What do people really gain from all the hard work they do here on earth?" The author of Ecclesiastes seemingly stops to take stock of his life and to show the uselessness of life without God so that his young readers will put God first in their lives.

SO WHAT DOES THIS BOOK MEAN TO US?

Like Solomon, we must also take stock of our lives at various times. And like Solomon, if we are honest in our examinations, we will likewise determine that life without God is "useless—a chasing after wind."

SUMMARY:

The Book of Ecclesiastes strikes readers as different than other biblical books. Instead of encouragement and faith, its statements seem to raise doubts and voice skepticism. The most frequent statement in the book is "Everything is useless!" (See Ecclesiastes 1:2 and 12:8 and many other places.)

It is important to recognize the overall structure of the book in order to see its important contribution to the Bible.

I. Introduction to the Teacher's Thought (1:1–11)
II. The Teacher's View of Life and Advice (1:12–12:7)
III. The Wise Person's View of the Teacher and His Final Advice (12:8–14)

The most important thing to keep in mind as we read Ecclesiastes is that the long middle section of the book (1:12–12:7) is the opinion of a person identified as the Teacher. In this section he is the one who tells people that everything is useless and that there is no real difference between good and evil (7:15–18). His view of life is rendered negative by the fact that we all have to die and that is the end of it all (3:18–21 and 12:1–7).

The book's teaching, though, is not the same as the teaching of the Teacher in this section of the book. There is a shift in speaker in 12:8, and in the closing verses we are told that what is important is our relationship with God and how we behave in the light of it.

Whether the person who speaks in 12:8–14 is the aged, repentant Teacher, who is commenting on his younger self who speaks in 1:11–12:7, or whether it is a second unnamed wise person is beside the point. The important thing to keep in mind is that the last verses provide the perspective through which we must understand the dubious teaching of 1:12–12:7. In this way Ecclesiastes is similar to the Book of Job that quotes chapters of the dubious theology of Job and his friends, and then, only at the end, with the speeches of God, do we get the true teaching of the book.

The Teacher informs us that the world is a dangerous and hostile place with no use or meaning. The wise man at the end of the Teacher's speech points us back to God. We must remember that the Teacher is right in that the world apart from God is useless or meaningless (Romans 8:18–21). Jesus Christ came into this useless world and died on the cross in order to free us from its uselessness.

Many people identify the Teacher with Solomon (1:12). Those who do would date the book to the time of this king (tenth century B.C.), but others suggest a later date.

I. Introduction to the Teacher's Thought (1:1–11)

The first few verses prepare the reader for the long speech by the Teacher. Here, as in the final few verses, the Teacher is addressed in the third person, rather than speaking in the first. The mood, sad and skeptical, is set right from the beginning.

II. The Teacher's View of Life and Advice (1:12–12:7)

The Teacher now introduces himself and begins his long and rather negative speech. He looks for meaning in the world but fails. He fears death and the fact that he cannot control time.

III. The Wise Person's View of the Teacher and His Final Advice (12:8–14)

Now that the Teacher has finished his lesson in life, another voice speaks and talks about the Teacher with his son. Though he is complimentary at first, at the end he turns his son to the really important teachings about God: honor and obey him.

ECCLESIASTES

These are the words of the Teacher, a son of David, king in Jerusalem.

2The Teacher says,
"Useless! Useless!
Completely useless!
Everything is useless."

3What do people really gain
from all the hard work they do
here on earth?

Things Never Change

4People live, and people die,
but the earth continues forever.
5The sun rises, the sun sets,
and then it hurries back to where it
rises again.
6The wind blows to the south;
it blows to the north.
It blows from one direction and then another.
Then it turns around and repeats the same
pattern, going nowhere.
7All the rivers flow to the sea,
but the sea never becomes full.
8Everything is boring,
so boring that you don't even want to talk
about it.
Words come again and again to our ears,
but we never hear enough,
nor can we ever really see all we want
to see.
9All things continue the way they have been
since the beginning.
What has happened will happen again;
there is nothing new here on earth.
10Someone might say,
"Look, this is new,"
but really it has always been here.
It was here before we were.
11People don't remember what happened
long ago,
and in the future people will not remember
what happens now.
Even later, other people will not remember
what was done before them.

Does Wisdom Bring Happiness?

12I, the Teacher, was king over Israel in Jerusalem. 13I decided to use my wisdom to learn
about everything that happens on earth. I learned
that God has given us terrible things to face. 14I
looked at everything done on earth and saw that it
is all useless, like chasing the wind.

15If something is crooked,
you can't make it straight.
If something is missing,
you can't say it is there.

16I said to myself, "I have become very wise
and am now wiser than anyone who ruled Jerusalem before me. I know what wisdom and
knowledge really are." 17So I decided to find out
about wisdom and knowledge and also about foolish thinking, but this turned out to be like chasing
the wind.

18With much wisdom comes much
disappointment;
the person who gains more knowledge also
gains more sorrow.

Does "Having Fun" Bring Happiness?

2 I said to myself, "I will try having fun. I will
enjoy myself." But I found that this is also
useless. 2It is foolish to laugh all the time, and
having fun doesn't accomplish anything. 3I
decided to cheer myself up with wine while my
mind was still thinking wisely. I wanted to find a
way to enjoy myself and see what was good for
people to do during their few days of life.

Does Hard Work Bring Happiness?

4Then I did great things: I built houses and
planted vineyards for myself. 5I made gardens and

1:2 *useless.* The word "useless" literally means vapor or bubble. The idea is that nothing has meaning or use in the world.

1:12 The Teacher introduces and describes himself in a way that sounds like Solomon, and perhaps he is Solomon. However, the fact that he does not name himself Solomon, and the fact that there are some differences between the Teacher and Solomon, have led many people to believe that the Teacher is just adopting Solomon to make points about finding meaning in things that Solomon had plenty of, such as women and money.

2:1 The theme of pleasure is viewed from two angles in Ecclesiastes by a person who experienced earthly pleasures at a level and to a degree that are afforded to very few others. From the negative standpoint, he eventually came to realize that, when pleasures are pursued from God independently, they are empty as this passage shows. However, in other places he recommends the enjoyment of life and its God-appointed pleasures as long as they are viewed from a proper perspective, namely the shortness of life and the need to reverence God (5:18–20; 9:7–10; 12:13–14).

2:1–2 Devoting all of our time and effort to satisfying our desires for pleasure is selfish and describes how we were before we trusted in Jesus (Titus 3:3). Now that we have been set free from this slavery to sin, we are free to spend our time doing good things (Romans 6:17–18). Any leisure time that we have can be used for personal rest and recreation in order to refresh us and make us better able to do those things that bring honor to God (Colossians 3:17; Titus 3:8).

parks, and I planted all kinds of fruit trees in them.
6I made pools of water for myself and used them to
water my growing trees. 7I bought male and
female slaves, and slaves were also born in my
house. I had large herds and flocks, more than
anyone in Jerusalem had ever had before. 8I also
gathered silver and gold for myself, treasures
from kings and other areas. I had male and female
singers and all the women a man could ever
want. 9I became very famous, even greater than
anyone who had lived in Jerusalem before me. My
wisdom helped me in all this.

10Anything I saw and wanted, I got for myself;
I did not miss any pleasure I desired.
I was pleased with everything I did,
and this pleasure was the reward for all my hard work.
11But then I looked at what I had done,
and I thought about all the hard work.
Suddenly I realized it was useless, like chasing the wind.
There is nothing to gain from anything we do here on earth.

Maybe Wisdom Is the Answer

12Then I began to think again about being wise,
and also about being foolish and doing crazy things.
But after all, what more can anyone do?
He can't do more than what the other king has already done.
13I saw that being wise is certainly better than being foolish,
just as light is better than darkness.
14Wise people see where they are going,
but fools walk around in the dark.
Yet I saw that
both wise and foolish people end the same way.

15I thought to myself,
"What happens to a fool will happen to me, too,
so what is the reward for being wise?"
I said to myself,
"Being wise is also useless."
16The wise person and the fool
will both die,
and no one will remember either one for long.
In the future, both will be forgotten.

Is There Real Happiness in Life?

17So I hated life. It made me sad to think that
everything here on earth is useless, like chasing
the wind. 18I hated all the things I had worked for
here on earth, because I must leave them to
someone who will live after me. 19Someone else
will control everything for which I worked so
hard here on earth, and I don't know if he will be
wise or foolish. This is also useless. 20So I became
sad about all the hard work I had done here on
earth. 21People can work hard using all their wisdom, knowledge, and skill, but they will die, and
other people will get the things for which they
worked. They did not do the work, but they will
get everything. This is also unfair and useless.
22What do people get for all their work and struggling here on earth? 23All of their lives their work
is full of pain and sorrow, and even at night their
minds don't rest. This is also useless.

24The best that people can do is eat, drink, and
enjoy their work. I saw that even this comes from
God, 25because no one can eat or enjoy life without him. 26If people please God, God will give
them wisdom, knowledge, and joy. But sinners
will get only the work of gathering and storing
wealth that they will have to give to the ones who
please God. So all their work is useless, like chasing
the wind.

There Is a Time for Everything

3 There is a time for everything,
and everything on earth has its special season.
2There is a time to be born
and a time to die.
There is a time to plant
and a time to pull up plants.
3There is a time to kill
and a time to heal.
There is a time to destroy
and a time to build.
4There is a time to cry
and a time to laugh.
There is a time to be sad
and a time to dance.
5There is a time to throw away stones
and a time to gather them.
There is a time to hug
and a time not to hug.
6There is a time to look for something
and a time to stop looking for it.

2:11 Work: Ecclesiastes 4:4–12
2:13 Blindness: Isaiah 42:6–7
2:14 Folly/Foolishness: Colossians 2:3
2:16 Wisdom: Jeremiah 18:18

There is a time to keep things
  and a time to throw things away.
[7]There is a time to tear apart
  and a time to sew together.
There is a time to be silent
  and a time to speak.
[8]There is a time to love
  and a time to hate.
There is a time for war
  and a time for peace.∞

God Controls His World

[9]Do people really gain anything from their
work? [10]I saw the hard work God has given people to do. [11]God has given them a desire to know
the future. He does everything just right and on
time, but people can never completely understand
what he is doing.∞ [12]So I realize that the best
thing for them is to be happy and enjoy themselves as long as they live. [13]God wants all people
to eat and drink and be happy in their work, which
are gifts from God. [14]I know that everything God
does will continue forever. People cannot add anything to what God has done, and they cannot take
anything away from it. God does it this way to make
people respect him.∞

[15]What happens now has happened in
    the past,
  and what will happen in the future has hap-
    pened before.
  God makes the same things happen again
    and again.

Unfairness on Earth

[16]I also saw this here on earth:
Where there should have been justice, there
    was evil;
  where there should have been right, there
    was wrong.
[17]I said to myself,
God has planned a time for every thing and
    every action,
  so he will judge both good people and bad.

[18]I decided that God leaves it the way it is to
test people and to show them they are just like
animals. [19]The same thing happens to animals
and to people; they both have the same breath, so
they both die. People are no better off than the
animals, because everything is useless. [20]Both
end up the same way; both came from dust and
both will go back to dust. [21]Who can be sure that
the human spirit goes up to God and that the
spirit of an animal goes down into the ground?
[22]So I saw that the best thing people can do is to
enjoy their work, because that is all they have. No
one can help another person see what will happen in the future.∞

Is It Better to Be Dead?

4 Again I saw all the people who were mistreated here on earth.
I saw their tears
  and that they had no one to
    comfort them.
Cruel people had all the power,
  and there was no one to comfort those they
    hurt.
[2]I decided that the dead
  are better off than the living.
[3]But those who have never been born
  are better off still;
they have not seen the evil
  that is done here on earth.

Why Work So Hard?

[4]I realized the reason people work hard and try
to succeed: They are jealous of each other. This,
too, is useless, like chasing the wind.

[5]Some say it is foolish to fold your hands and do
    nothing,
  because you will starve to death.
[6]Maybe so, but I say it is better to be content
  with what little you have.
Otherwise, you will always be struggling
    for more,
  and that is like chasing the wind.

∞**3:8 Hate:** Matthew 24:9
∞**3:11 Environment:** Ecclesiastes 3:18–22
∞**3:14 Time:** 1 Corinthians 16:1–9
∞**3:22 Environment:** Isaiah 35:1–2

4:3 The Teacher describes what the world is like "under the sun," that is apart from God and his redeeming grace. Such a world is filled with all kinds of evil. In the section which this verse concludes, the Teacher specifically highlights the way people are mistreated and oppressed by others. Indeed, there is so much evil that it would be better never to have been born!

The Teacher's insights into what the world is like without God makes us look for a solution "above the sun." That answer is Jesus Christ, who subjected himself to the evil of this world, in order to free us from its curse!

4:4 Through the lessons of painful experience, the writer of Ecclesiastes shows the uselessness of frantic work: jealousy. We need to ask ourselves how much of our quest for success is fueled by unhealthy desires to keep up with others, or to surpass them.

4:4–8 The main speaker in the Book of Ecclesiastes talks about what life is like "here on earth" (Ecclesiastes 1:9) apart from a relationship with God. Here he talks about how difficult our work can be. It is fueled out of jealousy and leads to little if any profit. If we try to find our ultimate meaning in our work, we will surely be frustrated. However, as long as our work is second to God, as long as we work for the glory of God and to help other people, our work can have significance and meaning.

7Again I saw something here on earth that was
useless:
8I saw a man who had no family,
no son or brother.
He always worked hard
but was never satisfied with what he had.
He never asked himself, "For whom am I
working so hard?
Why don't I let myself enjoy life?"
This also is very sad and useless.

Friends and Family Give Strength

9Two people are better than one,
because they get more done by working
together.
10If one falls down,
the other can help him up.
But it is bad for the person who is alone
and falls,
because no one is there to help.
11If two lie down together,
they will be warm,
but a person alone will not be warm.
12An enemy might defeat one person,
but two people together can defend
themselves;
a rope that is woven of three strings is
hard to break.

Fame and Power Are Useless

13A poor but wise boy is better than a foolish
but old king who doesn't listen to advice. 14A boy
became king. He had been born poor in the kingdom and had even gone to prison before becoming king. 15I watched all the people who live on
earth follow him and make him their king.
16Many followed him at first, but later, they did
not like him, either. So fame and power are useless, like chasing the wind.

Be Careful About Making Promises

5 Be careful when you go to worship at the
Temple. It is better to listen than to offer foolish sacrifices without even knowing you are doing
wrong.

2Think before you speak,
and be careful about what you say to God.
God is in heaven,
and you are on the earth,
so say only a few words to God.
3The saying is true: Bad dreams come
from too much worrying,
and too many words come from
foolish people.

4If you make a promise to God, don't be slow to
keep it. God is not happy with fools, so give God
what you promised. 5It is better not to promise
anything than to promise something and not do
it. 6Don't let your words cause you to sin, and
don't say to the priest at the Temple, "I didn't mean
what I promised." If you do, God will become angry
with your words and will destroy everything you
have worked for. 7Many useless promises are like
so many dreams; they mean nothing. You should
respect God.

Officers Cheat Each Other

8In some places you will see poor people mistreated. Don't be surprised when they are not
treated fairly or given their rights. One officer is
cheated by a higher officer who in turn is cheated
by even higher officers. 9The wealth of the
country is divided up among them all. Even the
king makes sure he gets his share of the profits.

Wealth Cannot Buy Happiness

10Whoever loves money
will never have enough money;
Whoever loves wealth
will not be satisfied with it.
This is also useless.
11The more wealth people have,
the more friends they have to help
spend it.
So what do people really gain?
They gain nothing except to look
at their riches.
12Those who work hard sleep in peace;
it is not important if they eat little
or much.
But rich people worry about
their wealth
and cannot sleep.

4:12 Work: Ecclesiastes 5:18–6:9
4:12 Friend: John 13:1–17
5:7 Oath/Vow: Matthew 5:33–37
5:8 Because all human beings are corrupt by nature, we should not expect to receive just treatment from human authorities. Although legal systems may claim to uphold justice, they are unable to escape the corruption of those who administer them.

5:8 Justice: Isaiah 1:17
5:10–17 The Teacher looked hard at the world to find ultimate meaning to life. One area that he hoped would make life meaningful was wealth. His conclusion, however, was clear. Wealth did not bring meaning; it often brought trouble. Wealth apart from God is not worth having.

CHURCH

MATTHEW 16:18

Was Jesus working to establish the church? What is the purpose of the church today?

It is hard to talk about present-day followers of Jesus without talking about the church. Throughout the world, people gather in Christ's name to worship, study, serve, and proclaim the message of this first-century Palestinian Jew. Many of these groups are highly organized, own property and buildings, and join together with hundreds of other groups to form large organizations. Was Jesus working to establish this vast entity we know as the institutional church?

Jesus himself used the expression "kingdom" more often than the "church" to describe the object of his mission. He was here to announce the coming of the kingdom of God. His message about the kingdom and his healing attracted large crowds. The Gospels give accounts of Jesus calling people out of these crowds to follow him. Luke 8:1–3 provides a general picture of the ministry of Jesus and the women and men that followed him: "While Jesus was traveling through some cities and small towns, he preached and told about the Good News of God's kingdom. The twelve apostles were with him and also some women who had been healed. . . ."

Jesus gives his followers special teaching about the kingdom and says that they are like his true family (Mark 3:34), like a light on a hill giving light to the whole world (Matthew 5:14) and he calls them his little flock to whom God wants to give the kingdom (Luke 12:32). Jesus sends his followers out to tell about God's kingdom and heal the sick (Luke 9:2). Did he intend these followers to form the foundation of the institutional church?

While Jesus uses many images to describe his relationship with his followers, he uses the word "church" in two instances. The word *church* at the time the New Testament was written refers to a gathering of people for a central purpose, such as an army for battle, citizens for political proceedings or the faithful for religious services. In Matthew 16:18, after Simon has identified Jesus as the Christ, the Son of God, he is renamed by Jesus: "You are Peter. On this rock I will build my church, and the power of death will not be able to defeat it."

Many people think this verse makes it clear that Jesus established the church at this point with Peter as its leader. Others believe this verse indicates that the church is founded on the content of Peter's confession that "Jesus is Christ." In the second instance of the word *church* Jesus explains that a new relationship with God requires a new relationship with each other as well. Matthew 18:15–17 provides an example of how members of this new community should deal with conflict within the church. The conflict should only become public if all private attempts at reconciliation are exhausted.

When we look at Jesus' preaching on the kingdom and his two brief statements about the church, they seem to be related to one another. As we read on in the New Testament, we learn more about the church. It appears that the church is one term, perhaps even the major term, for those who are part of God's kingdom. The church is the visible manifestation of the kingdom of God.

By the time of the Book of Acts, the church has taken on a kind of institutional status. The narrator of the book speaks of the church as an organization that acts in concert (Acts 8:1, 3; 11:22, 26). The church is persecuted together and prays together (Acts 12:5). It has leaders who are called elders (Acts 14:23; 15:22). When Paul leaves Ephesus, he encourages the elders there to "be like shepherds to the church of God" (Acts 20:28). In 1 Timothy and Titus, Paul lays down specific qualifications for those who will serve in leadership positions in the church.

By the time of the early church and at the command of Christ, the church is an institution. But does that mean it is like our church today in the twentieth century? That is hard to answer as a general principle since there are a number of different churches today around the globe with many different characteristics. None of these specific churches can be identified exclusively or totally with the kingdom of God. They contain the faithful and the impostor. No one church follows the teachings of Jesus completely and faithfully. But Jesus and his followers founded the organized church as a visible manifestation of his kingdom.

As such, the most important thing to remember about the church is that it is the church, not of human beings, but of God (1 Timothy 3:5, 15). Jesus Christ is not only its founder, but also its head. He is over the whole church (Ephesians 1:22; 5:23, 24; Colossians 1:18).⚭

⚭**Church:** For additional scriptures on this topic go to Matthew 18:17–20.

Debt/Loan

Matthew 18:21–35

What does the Old Testament say about lending money? What is the basis for the commands? Should Christians lend and borrow money? What did Jesus say about debt?

The Old Testament law allows Israel to lend money to foreigners and charge interest. In fact, it says that having enough money to be able to make loans is evidence of the blessing of God (Deuteronomy 15:6; compare 28:12 and 44; see also Proverbs 22:7). But they are not allowed to charge interest to other Israelites (Deuteronomy 23:19–20). There were also other laws concerning special grace for needy Israelites (Deuteronomy 24:10–15; Exodus 22:25–27). This is because these loans are not commercial loans for expansion of business, but charitable loans to carry a farmer over a difficult year.

With regard, then, to the literal lending and borrowing of money, the Bible clearly teaches that interest should not be charged to those who cannot afford it. Therefore, special grace and charity should be extended to those who are in financial trouble, especially to those in our "family." However, those who bring such trouble upon themselves should not be supported in their sinful practice: "Anyone who refuses to work should not eat" (2 Thessalonians 3:10). This applies even to those who are among the people of God (see the context, 2 Thessalonians 3:6–15).

It is clear that getting into debt is unwise. Like starvation, a plague of locusts, or being forced out of one's homeland, it is not something we should bring upon ourselves on purpose (Proverbs 22:26–27). We should ponder these things when considering institutional debt—in a congregation, a denomination, or a government. Those who are tempted by credit cards should not carry them, (just as we should flee from other temptations (Proverbs 23:31; 1 Thessalonians 5:22). This also means that a Christian lender should not encourage another person to get into credit trouble.

Whether Christian lenders should charge interest to Christian borrowers is a difficult question. The Old Testament law regarding Israel is not reaffirmed in the New Testament but neither is it specifically repealed. Where the Jewish lawyers concern themselves with technicalities and loopholes, Jesus calls for ethics, justice, and mercy. So if there is a mutually beneficial business transaction between those who can afford to lend and those who can afford to borrow, perhaps it is acceptable. On the other hand, if either party is taking advantage of the other, it is clearly sinful (Nehemiah 5:7–11; Amos 2:6–8; 4:1; Mark 12:40). Beyond this point, it is unclear.

The point in the Old Testament was for Israelites to treat other people, especially other Israelites, with the same kind of mercy that God showed to them. Just as God redeemed them from slavery in Egypt, so they should be gracious to those among them who have been forced into slavery for economic reasons (Leviticus 25:35–38). They should freely lend, or even give, to those who are needy (Deuteronomy 15:7–8). Generosity is a universal virtue (Psalms 37:26; 112:5–6; Proverbs 19:17; Ezekiel 18:5–9). Jesus reinforced the practice of charity by saying that we should not just lend with the assurance of being repaid, but give to those who will probably not be able to pay us back. The action is an example of God's kindness. (Luke 6:34–36).

In the New Testament *debt* is most often used figuratively for the theological idea that, since our debt to God because of our sinfulness was infinite, and the price Christ paid on the cross on our behalf was infinite, we should be infinitely grateful. We should not insult God's generosity by trying to repay his gift, yet whenever we take the opportunity to use our resources to promote God's kingdom (Luke 16:9–13), we are only doing what is right: taking what belongs to God and using it for God's purposes. If we realize the enormity of our previous obligation, we gladly pay these relatively small amounts, whether money or time and talent (Romans 15:26–8; 2 Corinthians 8:8–9). We are thankful that we will never be foreclosed on, that is, threatened with spiritual death and forced to pay the full spiritual debt. It has already been paid.

Along with the realization of the size of the debt that Christ paid for our sake comes a readiness to forgive others when they sin against us (Matthew 6:12, 14–15). Our own salvation is dependent upon this because it is a demonstration of our gratitude to God. If we are not grateful, it shows that we do not realize how great a debt has been forgiven for our sake (Luke 7:36–50); that is, we do not realize how sinful we are, and how seriously our sinfulness grieves God. Such an attitude would call into question our entire understanding of salvation, and, therefore, cause doubt whether we are saved at all (Matthew 18:21–35).

Debt/Loan: For additional scriptures on this topic go to Exodus 22:25–27.

[13]I have seen real misery here on earth:
Money saved is a curse to its owners.
[14] They lose it all in a bad deal
and have nothing to give to their children.
[15]People come into this world with nothing,
and when they die they leave with nothing.
In spite of all their hard work,
they leave just as they came.
[16]This, too, is real misery:
They leave just as they came.
So what do they gain from chasing
the wind?
[17]All they get are days full of sadness
and sorrow,
and they end up sick, defeated, and angry.

Enjoy Your Life's Work

[18]I have seen what is best for people here on
earth. They should eat and drink and enjoy their
work, because the life God has given them on
earth is short. [19]God gives some people the ability
to enjoy the wealth and property he gives them,
as well as the ability to accept their state in life
and enjoy their work. [20]They do not worry about
how short life is, because God keeps them busy
with what they love to do.

6 I have seen something else wrong here on
earth that causes serious problems for people.
[2]God gives great wealth, riches, and honor to
some people; they have everything they want. But
God does not let them enjoy such things; a
stranger enjoys them instead. This is useless and
very wrong. [3]A man might have a hundred children and live a long time, but what good is it if he
can't enjoy the good God gives him or have a
proper burial? I say a baby born dead is better off
than he is. [4]A baby born dead is useless. It returns
to darkness without even a name. [5]That baby
never saw the sun and never knew anything, but
it finds more rest than that man. [6]Even if he lives
two thousand years, he doesn't enjoy the good
God gives him. Everyone is going to the same
place.

[7]People work just to feed themselves,
but they never seem to get enough to eat.
[8]In this way a wise person
is no better off than a fool.
Then, too, it does a poor person little good
to know how to get along in life.
[9]It is better to see what you have
than to want more.
Wanting more is useless—
like chasing the wind.

Who Can Understand God's Plan?

[10]Whatever happens was planned long ago.
Everyone knows what people are like.
No one can argue with God,
who is stronger than anyone.
[11]The more you say,
the more useless it is.
What good does it do?

[12]People have only a few useless days of life on
the earth; their short life passes like a shadow. Who
knows what is best for them while they live? Who
can tell them what the future will bring?

Some Benefits of Serious Thinking

7 It is better to have respect than good
perfume.
The day of death is better than the day
of birth.
[2]It is better to go to a funeral
than to a party.
We all must die,
and everyone living should think about this.
[3]Sorrow is better than laughter,
and sadness has a good influence on you.
[4]A wise person thinks about death,
but a fool thinks only about having a good time.
[5]It is better to be criticized by a wise person
than to be praised by a fool.
[6]The laughter of fools
is like the crackling of thorns in
a cooking fire.
Both are useless.

[7]Even wise people are fools
if they let money change their thinking.

[8]It is better to finish something
than to start it.
It is better to be patient
than to be proud.
[9]Don't become angry quickly,
because getting angry is foolish.

[10]Don't ask, "Why was life better in the
'good old days'?"
It is not wise to ask such questions.

6:9 Work: Ecclesiastes 10:18

7:1 Literally, this verse claims that a "good name" or reputation is better than fine perfume. The latter is only superficial, but a good name indicates a person of deep quality.

7:1 Reputation: John 17:6

7:3 Depression: Matthew 19:22

11Wisdom is better when it comes with money.
They both help those who are alive.
12Wisdom is like money:
they both help.
But wisdom is better,
because it can save whoever has it.

13Look at what God has done:
No one can straighten what he has bent.
14When life is good, enjoy it.
But when life is hard, remember:
God gives good times and hard times,
and no one knows what tomorrow
will bring.

It Is Impossible to Be Truly Good

15In my useless life I have seen both of these:
I have seen good people die in spite of
their goodness
and evil people live a long time in spite
of their evil.
16Don't be too right,
and don't be too wise.
Why destroy yourself?
17Don't be too wicked,
and don't be foolish.
Why die before your time?
18It is good to grab the one and not let go of the
other;
those who honor God will hold them both.

19Wisdom makes a person stronger
than ten leaders in a city.

20Surely there is not a good person on earth
who always does good and never sins.

21Don't listen to everything people say,
or you might hear your servant insulting you.
22You know that many times
you have insulted others.

23I used wisdom to test all these things.
I wanted to be wise,
but it was too hard for me.
24I cannot understand why things are as
they are.
It is too hard for anyone to understand.
25I studied and tried very hard to find wisdom,
to find some meaning for everything.
I learned that it is foolish to be evil,
and it is crazy to act like a fool.

26I found that some women are worse
than death
and are as dangerous as traps.
Their love is like a net,
and their arms hold men like chains.
A man who pleases God will be saved
from them,
but a sinner will be caught by them.

27The Teacher says, "This is what I learned:
I added all these things together
to find some meaning for everything.
28While I was searching,
I did not find one man among the thousands I
found.
Nor did I find a woman among all these.
29One thing I have learned:
God made people good,
but they have found all kinds of ways
to be bad."

Obey the King

8 No one is like the wise person
who can understand what things mean.
Wisdom brings happiness;
it makes sad faces happy.

2Obey the king's command, because you made a
promise to God. 3Don't be too quick to leave the
king. Don't support something that is wrong,
because the king does whatever he pleases.
4What the king says is law; no one tells him what
to do.⚭

5Whoever obeys the king's command will
be safe.
A wise person does the right thing at the
right time.
6There is a right time and a right way for everything,
yet people often have many troubles.
7They do not know what the future holds,
and no one can tell them what will happen.
8No one can control the wind
or stop his own death.
No soldier is released in times of war,
and evil does not set free those who do evil.

Justice, Rewards, and Punishment

9I saw all of this as I considered all that is done
here on earth. Sometimes men harm those they
control. 10I saw the funerals of evil people who
used to go in and out of the holy place. They were
honored in the same towns where they had done
evil. This is useless, too.

⚭**8:4 Citizen:** Jeremiah 29:7

[11]When evil people are not punished right
away, it makes others want to do evil, too.
[12]Though a sinner might do a hundred evil things
and might live a long time, I know it will be better for those who honor God. [13]I also know it will
not go well for evil people, because they do not
honor God. Like a shadow, they will not last.
[14]Sometimes something useless happens on earth.
Bad things happen to good people, and good things
happen to bad people. I say that this is also useless.
[15]So I decided it was more important to enjoy life.
The best that people can do here on earth is to
eat, drink, and enjoy life, because these joys will
help them do the hard work God gives them here
on earth.

We Cannot Understand All God Does

[16]I tried to understand all that happens on
earth. I saw how busy people are, working day
and night and hardly ever sleeping. [17]I also saw
all that God has done. Nobody can understand
what God does here on earth. No matter how
hard people try to understand it, they cannot.
Even if wise people say they understand, they
cannot; no one can really understand it.

Is Death Fair?

9 I thought about all this and tried to understand it. I saw that God controls good people
and wise people and what they do, but no one
knows if they will experience love or hate.

[2]Good and bad people end up the same—
those who are right and those
who are wrong,
those who are good and those who are evil,
those who are clean and those
who are unclean,
those who sacrifice and those who do not.
The same things happen to a good person
as happen to a sinner,
to a person who makes promises to God
and to one who does not.

[3]This is something wrong that happens here on
earth: What happens to one happens to all. So
people's minds are full of evil and foolish
thoughts while they live. After that, they join the
dead.∞ [4]But anyone still alive has hope; even a
live dog is better off than a dead lion!

[5]The living know they will die,
but the dead know nothing.
Dead people have no more reward,
and people forget them.
[6]After people are dead,
they can no longer love or hate or envy.
They will never again share
in what happens here on earth.∞

Enjoy Life While You Can

[7]So go eat your food and enjoy it;
drink your wine and be happy,
because that is what God wants you to do.
[8]Put on nice clothes
and make yourself look good.

[9]Enjoy life with the wife you love. Enjoy all the
useless days of this useless life God has given you
here on earth, because it is all you have. So enjoy
the work you do here on earth. [10]Whatever work
you do, do your best, because you are going to the
grave, where there is no working, no planning,
no knowledge, and no wisdom.∞

Time and Chance

[11]I also saw something else here on earth:
The fastest runner does not always win the race,
the strongest soldier does not always
win the battle,
the wisest does not always have food,
the smartest does not always become
wealthy,
and the talented one does not always
receive praise.
Time and chance happen to everyone.
[12]No one knows what will happen next.
Like a fish caught in a net,
or a bird caught in a trap,
people are trapped by evil
when it suddenly falls on them.

Wisdom Does Not Always Win

[13]I also saw something wise here on earth that
impressed me. [14]There was a small town with
only a few people in it. A great king fought against
it and put his armies all around it. [15]Now there was
a poor but wise man in the town who used his
wisdom to save his town. But later on, everyone

∞**9:3 Evil:** Matthew 6:9–13

9:4 *dog.* In the ancient Near Eastern world, dogs were not loved or appreciated but were seen as pests.

∞**9:6 Jealousy:** Acts 5:17

∞**9:6 Death:** Isaiah 38:1–19

∞**9:10 Encouragement:** Matthew 17:20

9:11 The Teacher in the Book of Ecclesiastes is a struggling, doubting wise man. He gives us the viewpoint of someone who looks at life "here on earth," that has no way to know divine revelation. It is not until the last two verses that we get the positive teaching of the book (12:13–14). The believer finds comfort in the fact that it is God who is in control. So even though life seems uncontrolled to us, we know because of what God tells us in his Word that he is in control.

forgot about him. [16]I still think wisdom is better than strength. But those people forgot about the poor man's wisdom and stopped listening to what he said.

[17]The quiet words of a wise person
are better
than the shouts of a foolish ruler.
[18]Wisdom is better than weapons of war,
but one sinner can destroy much good.

10 Dead flies can make even perfume stink.
In the same way, a little foolishness can
spoil wisdom.
[2]The heart of the wise leads to right,
but the heart of a fool leads to wrong.
[3]Even in the way fools walk along the road,
they show they are not wise;
they show everyone how stupid they are.
[4]Don't leave your job
just because your boss is angry with you.
Remaining calm solves great problems.

[5]There is something else wrong that happens
here on earth.
It is the kind of mistake rulers make:
[6]Fools are given important positions
while gifted people are given lower ones;
[7]I have seen servants ride horses
while princes walk like servants on foot.
[8]Anyone who digs a pit might fall into it;
anyone who knocks down a wall might be
bitten by a snake;
[9]anyone who moves boulders might be hurt by
them;
and anyone who cuts logs might be harmed
by them.
[10]A dull ax means
harder work.
Being wise will make it easier.
[11]If a snake bites the tamer before it is tamed,
what good is the tamer?

[12]The words of the wise bring them praise,
but the words of a fool will
destroy them.
[13]A fool begins by saying foolish things
and ends by saying crazy and
wicked things.
[14]A fool talks too much.
No one knows the future,
and no one can tell what will happen
after death.

[15]Work wears fools out;
they don't even know how to get home.

The Value of Work

[16]How terrible it is for a country whose king is a
child
and whose leaders eat all morning.
[17]How lucky a country is whose king comes
from a good family,
whose leaders eat only at mealtime
and for strength, not to get drunk.

[18]If someone is lazy, the roof will begin to fall.
If he doesn't fix it, the house will leak.⚭

[19]A party makes you feel good,
wine makes you feel happy,
and money buys anything.

[20]Don't make fun of the king,
and don't make fun of rich people, even
in your bedroom.
A little bird might carry your words;
a bird might fly and tell what you said.

Boldly Face the Future

11 Invest what you have,
because after a while you will get
a return.
[2]Invest what you have in several different businesses,
because you don't know what disasters
might happen.

[3]If clouds are full of rain,
they will shower on the earth.
A tree can fall to the north or south,
but it will stay where it falls.
[4]Those who wait for perfect weather
will never plant seeds;
those who look at every cloud
will never harvest crops.

[5]You don't know where the wind will blow,
and you don't know how a baby grows
inside the mother.
In the same way, you don't know what
God is doing,
or how he created everything.
[6]Plant early in the morning,
and work until evening,
because you don't know if this or that
will succeed.
They might both do well.

⚭**10:18 Work:** Isaiah 65:21–23

Serve God While You Are Young

7Sunshine is sweet;
it is good to see the light of day.
8People ought to enjoy every day of their lives,
no matter how long they live.
But they should also remember this:
You will be dead a long time.
Everything that happens then is useless.
9Young people, enjoy yourselves while you are young;
be happy while you are young.
Do whatever your heart desires,
whatever you want to do.
But remember that God will judge you
for everything you do.
10Don't worry,
and forget the troubles of your body,
because youth and childhood are useless.

The Problems of Old Age

12 Remember your Creator
while you are young,
before the days of trouble come
and the years when you say,
"I find no pleasure in them."
2When you get old,
the light from the sun, moon, and stars
will grow dark;
the rain clouds will never seem to go away.
3At that time your arms will shake
and your legs will become weak.
Your teeth will fall out so you cannot chew,
and your eyes will not see clearly.
4Your ears will be deaf to the noise in the streets,
and you will barely hear the millstone grinding grain.
You'll wake up when a bird starts singing,
but you will barely hear singing.
5You will fear high places
and will be afraid to go for a walk.
Your hair will become white like the flowers on an almond tree.
You will limp along like a grasshopper
when you walk.
Your appetite will be gone.
Then you will go to your everlasting home,
and people will go to your funeral.

6Soon your life will snap like a silver chain
or break like a golden bowl.
You will be like a broken pitcher
at a spring,
or a broken wheel at a well.
7You will turn back into the dust of the earth again,
but your spirit will return to God who gave it.

8Everything is useless!
The Teacher says that everything is useless.

Conclusion: Honor God

9The Teacher was very wise and taught the people what he knew. He very carefully thought about, studied, and set in order many wise teachings. 10The Teacher looked for just the right words to write what is dependable and true.

11Words from wise people are like sharp sticks used to guide animals. They are like nails that have been driven in firmly. Altogether they are wise teachings that come from one Shepherd. 12So be careful, my son, about other teachings. People are always writing books, and too much study will make you tired.

13Now, everything has been heard,
so I give my final advice:
Honor God and obey his commands,
because this is all people must do.
14God will judge everything,
even what is done in secret,
the good and the evil.

12:1 Memory: Luke 23:42
12:6 *silver chain, golden bowl.* Life is compared to precious, yet easily broken, objects.
12:11 *sharp sticks, nails.* Sticks and nails are sharp and painful to those being directed.

Notes:

INTRODUCTION TO THE BOOK OF

SONG OF SOLOMON

A Love Song

WHO WROTE THIS BOOK?

In the original Hebrew language, this book is titled "Solomon's Song of Songs." Also verse one indicates the writing is by, for, or about Solomon.

TO WHOM WAS THE BOOK WRITTEN?

It seems to be written to the author's lover, whether real or figurative.

WHERE WAS IT WRITTEN?

Specifically this is unknown, but within the general region of Solomon's kingdom.

WHEN WAS IT WRITTEN?

The date of this writing is uncertain. If, indeed, Solomon was the author, then the writing would have been in the tenth century B.C.

WHAT IS THE BOOK ABOUT?

Song of Solomon is a collection of closely related poems on the topic of marital love.

WHY WAS THIS BOOK WRITTEN?

This book shows God's love for people in all its beautiful facets and as a precious gift from him. Also, it indicates that the beauty of marital love is his idea.

SO WHAT DOES THIS BOOK MEAN TO US?

Song of Solomon reminds us of how much God loves us. Our relationship to him is likened to the intimacy and joy of marriage, with all of its intensity and fulfillment.

SUMMARY:

The Song of Solomon is a song of love. First of all, the Song is a book of poems about human, sensual love. They are the songs of a man and woman who care deeply for one another. The lovers remain unnamed, as do the friends who witness their affection.

Secondly, the Song continues the story of human love that began in the Garden of Eden. After they were created, Adam and Eve stood in the garden naked and felt no shame (Genesis 2). Their Fall into sin (Genesis 3) spoiled the bliss of the garden, and now they felt shame and sought the cover of clothes. The Song of Solomon is the story of the return to the garden as the man and the woman are once again naked and feeling no shame.

Thirdly, the Song tells us about God and our relationship with him, but not directly, since God's name never occurs in the book. Throughout the Bible, however, our relationship with God is likened to the marriage relationship. The one reflects on the other. Christians, especially, cannot read the Song of Solomon without thinking of Ephesians 5—the church is the bride of Christ.

Solomon is named in the first verse and also in a few other places in the book. It is a little unclear whether he actually wrote the Song or not. If he did, it was written in the tenth century B.C.

The book is not a story or drama. It is a collection of closely related poems on the same topic, love.

SONG OF SOLOMON

Solomon's Greatest Song.

The Woman Speaks to the Man She Loves

2Kiss me with the kisses of your mouth,
because your love is better than wine.
3The smell of your perfume is pleasant,
and your name is pleasant like expensive perfume.
That's why the young women love you.
4Take me with you; let's run together.
The king takes me into his rooms.

Friends Speak to the Man

We will rejoice and be happy with you;
we praise your love more than wine.
With good reason, the young women love you.

The Woman Speaks

5I'm dark but lovely,
women of Jerusalem,
dark like the tents of Kedar,
like the curtains of Solomon.
6Don't look at how dark I am,
at how dark the sun has made me.
My brothers were angry with me
and made me tend the vineyards,
so I haven't tended my own vineyard!
7Tell me, you whom I love,
where do you feed your sheep?
Where do you let them rest at noon?
Why should I look for you near your friend's sheep,
like a woman who wears a veil?

The Man Speaks to the Woman

8You are the most beautiful of women.
Surely you know to follow the sheep
and feed your young goats
near the shepherds' tents.
9My darling, you are like a mare
among the king's stallions.
10Your cheeks are beautiful with ornaments,
and your neck with jewels.
11We will make for you gold earrings
with silver hooks.

The Woman Speaks

12The smell of my perfume spreads out
to the king on his couch.
13My lover is like a bag of myrrh
that lies all night between my breasts.
14My lover is like a bunch of flowers
from the vineyards at En Gedi.

The Man Speaks

15My darling, you are beautiful!
Oh, you are beautiful,
and your eyes are like doves.

The Woman Answers the Man

16You are so handsome, my lover,
and so pleasant!
Our bed is the grass.
17Cedar trees form our roof;
our ceiling is made of
juniper wood.

The Woman Speaks Again

2 I am a rose in the Plain of Sharon,
a lily in the valleys.

The Man Speaks Again

2Among the young women, my darling
is like a lily among thorns!

The Woman Answers

3Among the young men, my lover
is like an apple tree in the woods!
I enjoy sitting in his shadow;
his fruit is sweet to my taste.
4He brought me to the banquet room,
and his banner over me is love.
5Strengthen me with raisins,
and refresh me with apples,
because I am weak with love.
6My lover's left hand is under my head,
and his right arm holds me tight.

1:1 Solomon: Matthew 1:6–7

1:2–4 The Song of Solomon describes an intimate, sexual relationship between a man and a woman. Though it is never clearly described as such, the assumption is that the man and the woman are married. The Bible would not tolerate such intimacy outside of a marriage. We should read the Song as promoting a closeness within the marriage bond.

1:5 *dark but lovely.* The woman's dark complexion is the result of too much sun exposure as the following verses make clear.

1:7 *veil.* This was the way a prostitute usually dressed.

1:9 *a mare among the king's stallions.* This image reflects the practice of disrupting a chariot attack by sending a mare among the stallions to distract them and send the chariots into disarray.

1:14 *En Gedi.* En Gedi is a beautiful oasis near the Dead Sea.

1:17 Sexuality: 1 Corinthians 7

DIVORCE

MATTHEW 19:1–10

Why and for what grounds is divorce allowed? Is there a difference between the Old and New Testaments' teaching on divorce? Today, many people become Christians after being divorced and remarried. Must that person divorce his or her present spouse in order to obey Jesus?

Instructions and commands about divorce and remarriage are among the most troublesome, agonizing, and perplexing for many Christians. This is due in part to the ongoing association of ex-spouses, the children involved, the emotional and sexual bond which is established between spouses, and in part to the strictness of the words of Christ when he answered the Pharisees: "I tell you that anyone who divorces his wife and marries another woman is guilty of adultery" (Matthew 19:9).

Jesus begins his teaching on divorce with a discussion of marriage. Jesus' teaching may be summarized as follows. Marriage was instituted not by the laws of human beings, but by the decree and creative order of God (Genesis 1:27; 5:2). Further, the marriage of male and female brings about a union of persons—"and the two will become one body" (Genesis 2:24). This union, brought about by God, is not to be affected by the desire, will, or law of a human. The only reason a person may divorce a spouse is if the spouse commits adultery, which means having sexual relations with someone other than one's husband or wife. Divorce by this definition is not the severing of the marriage vows, but the recognition that the vows have been broken. However, just as today's marriages are not ideal, neither were they from earliest times.

In the Book of Genesis, divorce is never mentioned, however, much of the book revolves around the marriage relationship and the problems that surround marriage. As the tribes of Israel formed a nation in the wilderness, laws for marriage relationships and sexual behavior were handed down from God through Moses (Exodus 22:16–17; Leviticus 18; 20; Deuteronomy 22:13–30; 24:1–5; 25:5–10). Because Deuteronomy 24:1–4 mentions "a certificate of divorce" and has commands concerning divorced women, it is often assumed that there is a difference between the Old Testament and New Testament teaching about divorce. Deuteronomy 24:1–4 concerns a man who married a woman and later found out "something bad" about her and wrote divorce papers against her. The argument during Jesus' time was over what the words "something bad" meant. The Pharisees tried to trick Jesus into an argument about these words. Some said that it meant the woman had sexual relations before she was married or that she committed adultery. Others said it was anything that displeased the husband. Since adultery was punishable by death, they reasoned that this law did not apply to adultery since the woman was merely "sent away" (compare Deuteronomy 22:13–22). Jesus said, more or less, "You cannot divorce for just any reason; adultery is the only reason for divorce." The response of Jesus' followers to his teaching shows that they originally believed there were more grounds for divorce than Jesus taught. They responded, "If that [adultery] is the only reason a man can divorce his wife, it is better not to marry" (Matthew 19:10).

God's attitude toward divorce seems to be constant in the Bible. In Malachi 2:13–16, God emphatically says, "I hate divorce." He says this because men were mistreating their first wives, breaking their marriage agreements, and divorcing them (verse 14). God also tells them that he intended married persons to become one in body and spirit so that they would have children who would remain faithful to God.

Throughout the Old Testament the relationship between God and Israel is compared to the relationship between spouses. The only divorce explicitly mentioned in Scripture is God's divorce of Israel (Jeremiah 3:8). God always represents the husband in these comparisons. Whenever God was going to divorce or leave Israel because of its sin, its sin was compared to adultery. "Adultery" in this case means the people were worshiping other gods (Hosea 1; Jeremiah 3). God asked Israel to return , even though they had worshiped other gods and even though he was very angry with them. He threatened to destroy Israel, but hoped that Israel would return to him before he carried out his word.

God does recognize that divorce does occur and people do leave their spouses. He even gives directions for what to do when this happens in Christian marriages. In 1 Corinthians 7:10–24, Paul says that the Lord commands that a husband and wife should not leave or divorce each other. But if they do leave, they are not to marry again. They may only remarry by returning to their original spouse (1 Corinthians 7:10–11). Paul then goes on to say that in his opinion, if a person becomes a Christian and his spouse does not, he or she must not divorce or leave the one who does not believe. But if the spouse who does not believe leaves, the Christian is then free —this may mean free of guilt or free to marry again (7:12–16).

Divorce: For additional scriptures on this topic go to Genesis 1:27.

End Times/Last Days

Matthew 24

Where is the concept of the last days first found in the Bible? What is meant by end times? When are they said in the New Testament to begin? What are some of the events associated with the end times? Does the phrase "end times" really mean the end of the material universe?

The concept of the last days or end times begins to take shape in the writings of the prophets such as Isaiah and Jeremiah, Joel and Amos, and especially in the prophets of the exilic and post-exilic periods such as Ezekiel, Daniel and Zechariah. Closely associated with the idea of the Day of the Lord, the time when God would come to judge the earth, the prophets sought to convey the idea that God would not allow evil and injustice to continue upon the earth forever, especially when God's people were being notably mistreated, sent into exile and the like. Sometimes the concept of last days refers to the time leading up to the Day of the Lord (see Amos 5:18–27). Sometimes in late Jewish literature it seems to refer to a considerable period of time involving a sort of eschatological or golden age that will occur at the end of human history (see Daniel 7), usually called the "millennium."

It would be a mistake, however, to interpret any of this material as referring to the end of the world, if by that we mean the end of the material universe or the space-time continuum. Rather, the vision of the last days or end times has to do with the time immediately preceding and or including the period when God would right all wrongs upon the earth and God's kingdom would reign throughout the world. The prophets were not interested so much in the timing of this final age of human history on earth, as in its character. It would entail the fulfillment of all God's promises of blessing and judgment, the final rectification of all wrongs, and the elimination of evil, both natural and supernatural, including the evils of war, disease, and death (Revelation 21). For the Jew all these promises focused on the restoration of the promised land to them and its renewal to an Edenlike condition (Isaiah 9; 11), along with the renewal of true worship as symbolized by the restoration of the Temple (Ezekiel 40–48).

When Jesus, in Matthew, 24 Mark 13 and elsewhere, refers to the last days or end times he, too, speaks of a period of time that will lead up to the Day of the Lord. This did not prevent Jesus from saying that one could tell if one was in the end times, in the period that leads up to the Day of the Lord. In general, the Gospels suggest that Jesus believed that in his ministry the eschatological age had already broken into human history, which he calls the coming of the kingdom or dominion of God (Luke 11:20). Mark 13 also suggest that Jesus believed that the preliminary eschatological events had already been set in motion, events that would lead up to the destruction of Jerusalem and include the desolation of the Herodian Temple (Mark 13:14) within a generation or forty-year period (Mark 13:30). In fact, all the things Jesus spoke of as being preliminary end-time events occurring before the Day of the Lord did take place in the forty-year period between the end of his life (about A.D. 30) and the destruction of the Temple (A.D. 70). These events include earthquakes, famines, people falsely claiming to be the Messiah, and great tribulation and trial for the residents of Jerusalem as the Roman armies besieged and eventually destroyed most of Jerusalem, including the Temple. What is very striking about Jesus' teaching on these preliminary events is that he warns that those who see these things happening are not to assume the end times or coming of the Son of Man will follow immediately.

All that we are told about the relationship of these preliminary events and the coming of the Son of Man is that the latter will occur some time after those distressing end-time events (Mark 13:24), and that the Second Coming will be accompanied by cosmic signs in the heavens including shooting stars (Mark 13:25).

Thus, we should stress the fact that ever since Christ came and proclaimed the inbreaking of God's kingdom, we have all been living in the end times or eschatological age, with various preliminary events having come and gone. The climax of these times or the very end is yet to come. The counsel of Jesus in Mark 13 is still a valuable one: (1) believers are not to be distressed by preliminary events; (2) since believers do not know the timing when Christ will return they should always be prepared to meet their Maker or, as Mark 13:23 puts it, "be careful"; (3) we are not to be led astray by false prophets and people with messiah complexes, for when Christ returns it will be evident to all, a dramatic and cosmic event; (4) Christians are to live with a sense of eager expectation that in God's timing God will fulfill the divine promises—they are not to live as if this life is the be-all and end-all existence. The best is yet to come when the Son of Man returns.

End Times/Last Days: For additional scriptures on this topic go to Amos 5:18–27.

The Woman Speaks to the Friends

7 Women of Jerusalem, promise me
by the gazelles and the deer
not to awaken
or excite my feelings of love
until it is ready.

The Woman Speaks Again

8 I hear my lover's voice.
Here he comes jumping across the mountains,
skipping over the hills.
9 My lover is like a gazelle or a young deer.
Look, he stands behind our wall
peeking through the windows,
looking through the blinds.
10 My lover spoke and said to me,
"Get up, my darling;
let's go away, my beautiful one.
11 Look, the winter is past;
the rains are over and gone.
12 Blossoms appear through all the land.
The time has come to sing;
the cooing of doves is heard in our land.
13 There are young figs on the fig trees,
and the blossoms on the vines smell sweet.
Get up, my darling;
let's go away, my beautiful one."

The Man Speaks

14 My beloved is like a dove hiding in the cracks
of the rock,
in the secret places of the cliff.
Show me your face,
and let me hear your voice.
Your voice is sweet,
and your face is lovely.
15 Catch the foxes for us—
the little foxes that ruin the vineyards
while they are in blossom.

The Woman Speaks

16 My lover is mine, and I am his.
He feeds among the lilies
17 until the day dawns
and the shadows disappear.
Turn, my lover.
Be like a gazelle or a young deer
on the mountain valleys.

The Woman Dreams

3 At night on my bed,
I looked for the one I love;

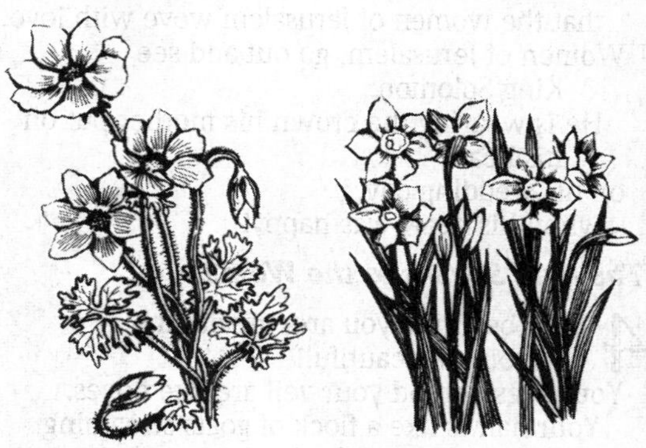

Two flowers that may be called "rose" in the Bible: a mountain tulip (left) and the narcissus (right)

I looked for him, but I could not find him.
2 I got up and went around the city,
in the streets and squares,
looking for the one I love.
I looked for him, but I could not find him.
3 The watchmen found me as they patrolled
the city,
so I asked, "Have you seen the one I love?"
4 As soon as I had left them,
I found the one I love.
I held him and would not let him go
until I brought him to my mother's house,
to the room where I was born.

The Woman Speaks to the Friends

5 Women of Jerusalem, promise me
by the gazelles and the deer
not to awaken
or excite my feelings of love
until it is ready.
6 Who is this coming out of the desert
like a cloud of smoke?
Who is this that smells like myrrh, incense,
and other spices?
7 Look, it's Solomon's couch
with sixty soldiers around it,
the finest soldiers of Israel.
8 These soldiers all carry swords
and have been trained in war.
Every man wears a sword at his side
and is ready for the dangers of the night.
9 King Solomon had a couch made for himself
of wood from Lebanon.
10 He made its posts of silver
and its braces of gold.
The seat was covered with purple cloth

3:7 *couch.* Something like a bed carried by slaves on which the king lay or sat while traveling.

that the women of Jerusalem wove with love.
11Women of Jerusalem, go out and see
King Solomon.
He is wearing the crown his mother put on
his head
on his wedding day,
when his heart was happy!

The Man Speaks to the Woman

4 How beautiful you are, my darling!
Oh, you are beautiful!
Your eyes behind your veil are like doves.
Your hair is like a flock of goats streaming
down Mount Gilead.
2Your teeth are white like newly sheared sheep
just coming from their bath.
Each one has a twin,
and none of them is missing.
3Your lips are like red silk thread,
and your mouth is lovely.
Your cheeks behind your veil
are like slices of a pomegranate.
4Your neck is like David's tower,
built with rows of stones.
A thousand shields hang on its walls;
each shield belongs to a strong soldier.
5Your breasts are like two fawns,
like twins of a gazelle,
feeding among the lilies.
6Until the day dawns
and the shadows disappear,
I will go to that mountain of myrrh
and to that hill of incense.
7My darling, everything about you is beautiful,
and there is nothing at all wrong with you.
8Come with me from Lebanon, my bride.
Come with me from Lebanon,
from the top of Mount Amana,
from the tops of Mount Senir and
Mount Hermon.
Come from the lions' dens
and from the leopards' hills.
9My sister, my bride,
you have thrilled my heart;
you have thrilled my heart
with a glance of your eyes,
with one sparkle from your necklace.
10Your love is so sweet, my sister, my bride.
Your love is better than wine,
and your perfume smells better than
any spice.
11My bride, your lips drip honey;
honey and milk are under your tongue.
Your clothes smell like the cedars of
Lebanon.
12My sister, my bride, you are like a garden
locked up,
like a walled-in spring, a closed-up fountain.
13Your limbs are like an orchard
of pomegranates with all the best fruit,
filled with flowers and nard,
14nard and saffron, calamus, and cinnamon,
with trees of incense, myrrh, and aloes—
all the best spices.
15You are like a garden fountain—
a well of fresh water
flowing down from the mountains of
Lebanon.⚭

The Woman Speaks

16Awake, north wind.
Come, south wind.
Blow on my garden,
and let its sweet smells flow out.
Let my lover enter the garden
and eat its best fruits.

The Man Speaks

5 I have entered my garden, my sister,
my bride.
I have gathered my myrrh with my spice.
I have eaten my honeycomb and my honey.
I have drunk my wine and my milk.

The Friends Speak

Eat, friends, and drink;
yes, drink deeply, lovers.

The Woman Dreams

2I sleep, but my heart is awake.
I hear my lover knocking.
"Open to me, my sister, my darling,
my dove, my perfect one.
My head is wet with dew,
and my hair with the dampness of
the night."
3I have taken off my garment
and don't want to put it on again.
I have washed my feet
and don't want to get them dirty again.
4My lover put his hand through the opening,
and I felt excited inside.
5I got up to open the door for my lover.
Myrrh was dripping from my hands
and flowing from my fingers,

4:4 *Your neck is like David's tower.* This image, like so many of the others, sounds strange to our modern sensibilities. But the comparison of the woman's neck with David's tower evokes majesty and awe.

⚭**4:15 Garden of Eden:** Isaiah 51:3

onto the handles of the lock.
6I opened the door for my lover,
but my lover had left and was gone.
When he spoke, he took my breath away.
I looked for him, but I could not find him;
I called for him, but he did not answer.
7The watchmen found me
as they patrolled the city.
They hit me and hurt me;
the guards on the wall took away my veil.
8Promise me, women of Jerusalem,
if you find my lover,
tell him I am weak with love.

The Friends Answer the Woman

9How is your lover better than other lovers,
most beautiful of women?
How is your lover better than other lovers?
Why do you want us to promise this?

The Woman Answers the Friends

10My lover is healthy and tan,
the best of ten thousand men.
11His head is like the finest gold;
his hair is wavy and black like a raven.
12His eyes are like doves
by springs of water.
They seem to be bathed in cream
and are set like jewels.
13His cheeks are like beds of spices;
they smell like mounds of perfume.
His lips are like lilies
flowing with myrrh.
14His hands are like gold hinges,
filled with jewels.
His body is like shiny ivory
covered with sapphires.
15His legs are like large marble posts,
standing on bases of fine gold.
He is like a cedar of Lebanon,
like the finest of the trees.
16His mouth is sweet to kiss,
and I desire him very much.
Yes, daughters of Jerusalem,
this is my lover
and my friend.

The Friends Speak to the Woman

6 Where has your lover gone,
most beautiful of women?
Which way did your lover turn?
We will look for him with you.

The Woman Answers the Friends

2My lover has gone down to his garden,
to the beds of spices,
to feed in the gardens
and to gather lilies.
3I belong to my lover,
and my lover belongs to me.
He feeds among the lilies.

The Man Speaks to the Woman

4My darling, you are as beautiful as the city
of Tirzah,
as lovely as the city of Jerusalem,
like an army flying flags.
5Turn your eyes from me,
because they excite me too much.
Your hair is like a flock of goats
streaming down Mount Gilead.
6Your teeth are white like sheep
just coming from their bath;
each one has a twin,
and none of them is missing.
7Your cheeks behind your veil
are like slices of a pomegranate.
8There may be sixty queens and eighty
slave women
and so many girls you cannot count them,
9but there is only one like my dove,
my perfect one.
She is her mother's only daughter,
the brightest of the one who gave her birth.
The young women saw her and called
her happy;
the queens and the slave women also
praised her.

The Young Women Praise the Woman

10Who is that young woman
that shines out like the dawn?
She is as pretty as the moon,
as bright as the sun,
as wonderful as an army flying flags.

The Man Speaks

11I went down into the orchard of nut trees
to see the blossoms of the valley,
to look for buds on the vines,
to see if the pomegranate trees had bloomed.
12Before I realized it, my desire for you
made me feel
like a prince in a chariot.

The Friends Call to the Woman

13Come back, come back, woman of Shulam.
Come back, come back,
so we may look at you!

6:13 *woman of Shulam.* This verse identifies the woman as an inhabitant of a village called Shulam, which explains the nickname that many people give her, the "Shulamite."

The Woman Answers the Friends

Why do you want to look at the woman of
Shulam
as you would at the dance of two armies?

The Man Speaks to the Woman

7 Your feet are beautiful in sandals,
you daughter of a prince.
Your round thighs are like jewels
shaped by an artist.
2Your navel is like a round drinking cup
always filled with wine.
Your stomach is like a pile of wheat
surrounded with lilies.
3Your breasts are like two fawns,
like twins of a gazelle.
4Your neck is like an ivory tower.
Your eyes are like the pools in Heshbon
near the gate of Bath Rabbim.
Your nose is like the mountain of Lebanon
that looks down on Damascus.
5Your head is like Mount Carmel,
and your hair is like purple cloth;
the king is captured in its folds.
6You are beautiful and pleasant;
my love, you are full of delights.
7You are tall like a palm tree,
and your breasts are like its bunches of fruit.
8I said, "I will climb up the palm tree
and take hold of its fruit."
Let your breasts be like bunches of grapes,
the smell of your breath like apples,
9 and your mouth like the best wine.

The Woman Speaks to the Man

Let this wine go down sweetly for my lover;
may it flow gently past the lips and teeth.
10I belong to my lover,
and he desires only me.
11Come, my lover,
let's go out into the country
and spend the night in the fields.
12Let's go early to the vineyards
and see if the buds are on the vines.
Let's see if the blossoms have
already opened
and if the pomegranates have bloomed.
There I will give you my love.
13The mandrake flowers give their sweet smell,
and all the best fruits are at our gates.
I have saved them for you, my lover,
the old delights and the new.

8 I wish you were like my brother
who fed at my mother's breasts.
If I found you outside,
I would kiss you,
and no one would look down on me.
2I would lead you and bring you
to my mother's house;
she is the one who taught me.
I would give you a drink of spiced wine
from my pomegranates.

The Woman Speaks to the Friends

3My lover's left hand is under my head,
and his right arm holds me tight.
4Women of Jerusalem,
promise not to awaken
or excite my feelings of love
until it is ready.

The Friends Speak

5Who is this coming out of the desert,
leaning on her lover?

The Man Speaks to the Woman

I woke you under the apple tree
where you were born;
there your mother gave birth to you.
6Put me like a seal on your heart,
like a seal on your arm.
Love is as strong as death;
jealousy is as strong as the grave.
Love bursts into flames
and burns like a hot fire.
7Even much water cannot put out the flame
of love;
floods cannot drown love.
If a man offered everything in his house
for love,
people would totally reject it.

The Woman's Brothers Speak

8We have a little sister,
and her breasts are not yet grown.
What should we do for our sister
on the day she becomes engaged?
9If she is a wall,
we will put silver towers on her.

7:9–13 When Adam and Eve were created, God placed them in a garden where they enjoyed perfect intimacy. However, they did the unthinkable and disobeyed God's command. The result was separation from God and from one another. Adam and Eve no longer could stand in the garden naked and unashamed. The Song of Solomon gives us a picture of restored intimacy. The unnamed lover and beloved are once again in a garden naked and unashamed. Sexual reconciliation has been achieved.

7:13 *mandrake flowers.* Not only was the mandrake sweet smelling, it was also used as an aphrodisiac (Genesis 30:14–16).

If she is a door,
we will protect her with cedar boards.

The Woman Speaks

10I am a wall,
and my breasts are like towers.
So I was to him,
as one who brings happiness.
11Solomon had a vineyard at Baal Hamon.
He rented the vineyards for others to tend,
and everyone who rented had to pay
twenty-five pounds of silver for the fruit.
12But my own vineyard is mine to give.
Solomon, the twenty-five pounds
of silver are for you,
and five pounds are for those who
tend the fruit.

The Man Speaks to the Woman

13You who live in the gardens,
my friends are listening for
your voice;
let me hear it.

The Woman Speaks to the Man

14Hurry, my lover,
be like a gazelle
or a young deer
on the mountains where spices grow.

Notes:

INTRODUCTION TO SECTION THREE
ISAIAH – MALACHI

THE BOOKS OF THE PROPHETS

ISAIAH	EZEKIEL	JOEL	JONAH	HABAKKUK	ZECHARIAH
JEREMIAH	DANIEL	AMOS	MICAH	ZEPHANIAH	MALACHI
LAMENTATIONS	HOSEA	OBADIAH	NAHUM	HAGGAI	

Who are these people called prophets in the Bible? Our minds conjure up images of wild-eyed fanatics, eating locusts and living out in the desert. Indeed, for some of the prophets—Ezekiel and John the Baptist—this description fits well. But for others, we may sense urgency, but not bizarre behavior—Isaiah and Micah, for instance.

The prophets, in the most general sense, are God's spokesmen. They bring God's word to his people. In this sense they are like ambassadors of a great king who deliver the message of their master. This relationship between prophet and God explains why the prophets often speak in God's name and use the first-person "I" as they quote God. They are indeed speaking his words.

Also the prophets are, in a sense, God's lawyers. The people have a formal relationship with God called an agreement (or "covenant"). When the people break the laws of the agreement, God sends the prophets to warn them of the penalties. They urge the people to repent and return to the one, true God.

The prophets also act as the conscience of the human king. Saul had the prophet Samuel, and David had the prophet Nathan to remind them of God's word and ways. Other kings were so sinful that they simply told the prophets to get lost. Even though Ahab didn't want to talk to the prophets, they didn't let him alone when he strayed from following the Lord (1 Kings 20 and 21).

Though the prophets Samuel, Nathan, and Elijah left no personal writings, the inspired records of their ministries help us understand the writings of those who did. For the most part, the writings of the prophets are collections of their sermons. Some, like Nahum, left us just one; others, like Isaiah and Micah, left us whole series of sermons that span years of ministry.

There is an unfortunate tendency among modern readers of the prophets to read them piecemeal, that is to pull out what the prophets said from their broader literary and historical contexts. The prophets are not isolated nuggets of truth; they are unified writings, and the more we understand a prophet's writing as a whole, the better will be our grasp of specific parts. We should always read a prophet's writing in the setting of the whole book.

We also need to know something about the historical setting of the prophecy. Virtually every prophet begins with a superscription (or introduction). This first verse tells us who the author is and at what time he spoke to God's people. The time is usually established by naming the kings who ruled during the prophecy. We can learn about the historical setting by reading the historical books of the Old Testament (in Section One of this book). Then we can fit the prophets into their proper time slots.

Unless we do this we may also commit another common error in our understanding of prophecy. We may think that the prophets are primarily concerned about the future. After all, don't they devote much of the time to telling their readers what is happening in the future? Surprisingly, the answer is no. They do look into the near and distant future, but that is not their main purpose. The prophets are concerned with the present. They are calling the people to turn back from their sins to God. They speak of future judgment and salvation in order to warn and cajole the people of God back into a right relationship with the father.

What can we learn from the prophets? Christians can learn a lot from the prophets. We can learn how God patiently pursued his wayward people. We can learn how God finally punished his people for their stubborn refusal to follow him. But perhaps most importantly, as we see from the use of the prophets' words and examples in the New Testament, we also learn how the prophets revealed the coming of the greatest salvation of all—Jesus Christ.

If you feed those who are hungry
and take care of the needs of
those who are troubled,
then your light will shine in the darkness,
and you will be bright like sunshine at noon.

ISAIAH 58: 10

INTRODUCTION TO THE BOOK OF

ISAIAH

God's Message in Troubled Times

WHO WROTE THIS BOOK?

The author is Isaiah—the greatest of the writing prophets.

TO WHOM WAS THIS BOOK WRITTEN?

Isaiah is writing to Israel and Judah.

WHERE WAS IT WRITTEN?

This great writing was probably done in and around Jerusalem where Isaiah spent most of his life.

WHEN WAS IT WRITTEN?

It is likely that Isaiah wrote this work between 701–681 B.C.

WHAT IS THE BOOK ABOUT?

The prophet Isaiah condemns Ahaz, king of Judah, for his alliance with Assyria in 733 B.C. Isaiah predicts Judah's deliverance from Assyria during Hezekiah's reign and that she will be captured by Babylon. He also prophesies that one day the Redeemer of Israel will come and bear the sins of the people, that the few remaining people of Israel will return from Babylon, and ultimately all nations will experience the "light" of the Redeemer.

WHY WAS THIS BOOK WRITTEN?

Isaiah shows the many dimensions of God's judgment and salvation. His righteousness demands that his erring children be punished, but his love will redeem them once again.

SO WHAT DOES THIS BOOK MEAN TO US?

God is still the "Holy One" (1:4). As his children today, we must still expect his righteousness to require our punishment when we sin against him. By the same token, we are assured of his patient love and eternal redemption.

SUMMARY:

Isaiah's rich teaching can only be hinted at in this brief introduction. He brought a message of coming judgment on Israel and Judah. He told of a coming Assyrian threat that resulted in the destruction of the northern kingdom and danger for the south. But he did not just bring a message of judgment; he also spoke of hope for the remnant that would survive the punishment.

The book is named after its author (1:1). His ministry extended from the time of his calling in the year Uzziah died (740 B.C.—Isaiah 6:1) until the death of Sennacherib (Isaiah 37:38) during the reign of Manasseh (681 B.C.). Many readers have difficulty believing that the whole book was written by Isaiah because of the vivid detail with which he sees the future, even naming a king not yet on the throne (Isaiah 44:28; 45:1, 13). However, God is capable of revealing the future to his prophets, and the New Testament clearly accepted the authorship of Isaiah for the whole book (John 12:38–41; Acts 8:30).

The book rightly attracts a lot of attention because it looks into the near and distant future. Christians note that the book is quoted more often than any other book in the New Testament. John the Baptist is identified as the voice calling in the wilderness anticipated in Isaiah 40:3 (Matthew 3:3). Jesus was associated with Isaiah's "servant of the Lord" (compare Isaiah 53:1 with John 12:38; Acts 8:27–33). The virgin birth was prophesied in Isaiah 7:14, and the list goes on and on.

A general outline of the massive Book of Isaiah is as follows:

I. God Uses Assyria to Judge Israel (Isaiah 1–35)
II. Isaiah and Hezekiah (Isaiah 36–39)
III. Future Deliverance (Isaiah 40–66)

I. God Uses Assyria to Judge Israel (Isaiah 1–35)

Isaiah opens with five chapters of mostly judgment speeches against Israel, but there are also glimmers of hope. This leads to the story of Isaiah's call to the prophetic ministry in chapter 6. In this chapter Isaiah relates a powerful experience of the Lord's presence.

Isaiah then describes his prophetic ministry during the time of the war between Judah on the one hand and Syria and Israel on the other. This draws the attention of Assyria to this region, and Isaiah warns that God will now use Assyria to bring judgment on his people.

This section continues with a lengthy series of judgment speeches against the nations that surround Israel (chapters 13–23). But Israel itself does not escape God's anger. In chapters 24–27, the prophet looks forward to the coming destruction of Jerusalem and the whole world.

II. Isaiah and Hezekiah (Isaiah 36–39)

These chapters narrate the events that took place around 701 B.C. Assyria had already taken the northern kingdom two decades before and had sent the people into exile. Now Sennacherib, the king of Assyria, threatened to take the southern kingdom of Judah. God, though, responded to the prayers of Hezekiah, the king, and Isaiah and allowed Judah to escape. The later visit of Merodach-Baladan of Babylon anticipates the new threat looming on the horizon.

III. Future Deliverance (Isaiah 40–66)

The mood now shifts from mainly negative judgment to promise and hope for the people of God. God will deliver his people from Babylon. Of course, hope for the people of God spells the end of the wicked, so idolaters in particular are told of their coming punishment.

ISAIAH

This is the vision Isaiah son of Amoz saw about what would happen to Judah and Jerusalem. Isaiah saw these things while Uzziah, Jotham, Ahaz, and Hezekiah were kings of Judah.

God's Case Against His Children

2Heaven and earth, listen,
because the LORD is speaking:
"I raised my children and helped them grow up,
but they have turned against me.
3An ox knows its master,
and a donkey knows where its owner feeds it,
but the people of Israel do not know me;
my people do not understand."

4How terrible! Israel is a nation of sin,
a people loaded down with guilt,
a group of children doing evil,
children who are full of evil.
They have left the LORD;
they hate God, the Holy One of Israel,
and have turned away from him as if he were a stranger.

5Why should you continue to be punished?
Why do you continue to turn against him?
Your whole head is hurt,
and your whole heart is sick.
6There is no healthy spot
from the bottom of your foot to the top of your head;
you are covered with wounds, hurts, and open sores
that are not cleaned and covered,
and no medicine takes away the pain.

7Your land is ruined;
your cities have been burned with fire.
While you watch,
your enemies are stealing everything from your land;
it is ruined like a country destroyed by enemies.
8Jerusalem is left alone
like an empty shelter in a vineyard,
like a hut left in a field of melons,
like a city surrounded by enemies.
9The LORD All-Powerful
allowed a few of our people to live.
Otherwise we would have been completely destroyed
like the cities of Sodom and Gomorrah.

10Jerusalem, your rulers are like those of Sodom,
and your people are like those of Gomorrah.
Hear the word of the LORD;
listen to the teaching of our God!
11The LORD says,
"I do not want all these sacrifices.
I have had enough of your burnt sacrifices
of male sheep and fat from fine animals.
I am not pleased
by the blood of bulls, lambs, and goats.
12You come to meet with me,
but who asked you to do
all this running in and out of my Temple's rooms?
13Don't continue bringing me worthless sacrifices!
I hate the incense you burn.
I can't stand your New Moons, Sabbaths, and other feast days;
I can't stand the evil you do in your holy meetings.
14I hate your New Moon feasts
and your other yearly feasts.
They have become a heavy weight on me,
and I am tired of carrying it.
15When you raise your arms to me in prayer,
I will refuse to look at you.
Even if you say many prayers,
I will not listen to you,
because your hands are full of blood.
16Wash yourselves and make yourselves clean.
Stop doing the evil things I see you do.
Stop doing wrong.
17 Learn to do good.
Seek justice.
Punish those who hurt others.
Help the orphans.
Stand up for the rights of widows."

18The LORD says,
"Come, let us talk about these things.
Though your sins are like scarlet,
they can be as white as snow.
Though your sins are deep red,
they can be white like wool.
19If you become willing and obey me,
you will eat good crops from the land.

1:1 Vision: Joel 2:28

1:10 *Sodom and Gomorrah.* Cities that were famous for their great sin (Genesis 19).

1:17 Adoption: Isaiah 1:23

1:17 Justice: Jeremiah 22:3

1:17 Repentance: Jeremiah 3:12–24

20But if you refuse to obey and if you turn
against me,
you will be destroyed by your
enemies' swords."
The LORD himself said these things.

Jerusalem Is Not Loyal to God

21The city of Jerusalem once followed the LORD,
but she is no longer loyal to him.
She used to be filled with fairness;
people there lived the way God wanted.
But now, murderers live there.
22Jerusalem, you have become like the scum left
when silver is purified;
you are like wine mixed with water.
23Your rulers are rebels
and friends of thieves.
They all accept money for doing wrong,
and they are paid to cheat people.
They don't seek justice for the orphans
or listen to the widows' needs.
24So the Lord GOD All-Powerful,
the Mighty One of Israel, says:
"You, my enemies, will not cause me any
more trouble.
I will pay you back for what you did.
25I will turn against you
and clean away all your wrongs as if
with soap;
I will take all the worthless things out
of you.
26I will bring back judges as you had
long ago;
your counselors will be like those you had in
the beginning.
Then you will be called the City That Is Right
with God,
the Loyal City."

27By doing what is fair,
Jerusalem will be free again.
By doing what is right,
her people who come back to the LORD will
have freedom.
28But sinners and those who turn against him
will be destroyed;
those who have left the LORD will die.
29"You will be ashamed,
because you have worshiped gods under
the oak trees.
You will be disgraced,
because you have worshiped idols in
your gardens.
30You will be like an oak whose leaves are dying
or like a garden without water.
31Powerful people will be like small, dry pieces
of wood,
and their works will be like sparks.
They will burn together,
and no one will be able to put out that fire."

The Message About Jerusalem

2 Isaiah son of Amoz saw this message about
Judah and Jerusalem:
2In the last days
the mountain on which the LORD's Temple stands
will become the most important of
all mountains.
It will be raised above the hills,
and people from all nations will come
streaming to it.
3Many nations will come and say,
"Come, let us go up to the mountain of
the LORD,
to the Temple of the God of Jacob.
Then God will teach us his ways,
and we will obey his teachings."
His teachings will go out from Jerusalem;
the message of the LORD will go out
from Jerusalem.
4He will settle arguments among the nations
and will make decisions for many nations.
Then they will make their swords into plows
and their spears into hooks for trimming trees.
Nations will no longer fight other nations,
nor will they train for war anymore.

5Come, family of Jacob,
and let us follow the way of the LORD.

A Terrible Day Is Coming

6LORD, you have left your people,
the family of Jacob,
because they have become filled with wrong
ideas from people in the East.

1:22 *wine mixed with water.* Wine mixed with water was weak and not as good to the taste.
1:23 Adoption: Jeremiah 5:26–29
2:2 Isaiah foresees a time of great blessing for Israel and for the nations during the last days. It is not always entirely clear just when the Old Testament prophets understood this time to come, whether in the near future as a political reality or in the far distant future. But the New Testament explains that the last days began at the first coming of Christ (Acts 2:17–20).
2:2 *the mountain on which the LORD's Temple stands.* Mount Zion was the mountain on which the Temple stood. It was physically a very small hill, but this prophecy envisions a time when its importance will be recognized globally.
2:3 Mountain: Isaiah 25:6–10
2:5 Rahab: Zechariah 8:20–23

They try to tell the future like the Philistines,
and they have completely accepted those
foreign ideas.
7Their land has been filled with silver and gold;
there are a great many treasures there.
Their land has been filled with horses;
there are many chariots there.
8Their land is full of idols.
The people worship these idols they made
with their own hands
and shaped with their own fingers.
9People will not be proud any longer
but will bow low with shame.
God, do not forgive them.

10Go into the caves of the cliffs;
dig holes and hide in the ground
from the anger of the LORD
and from his great power!
11Proud people will be made humble,
and they will bow low with shame.
At that time only the LORD will still be praised.

12The LORD All-Powerful has a certain day planned
when he will punish the proud and those
who brag,
and they will no longer be important.
13He will bring down the tall cedar trees
from Lebanon
and the great oak trees of Bashan,
14all the tall mountains
and the high hills,
15every tall tower
and every high, strong wall,
16all the trading ships
and the beautiful ships.
17At that time proud people will be made humble,
and they will bow low with shame.
At that time only the LORD will be praised,
18 but all the idols will be gone.

19People will run to caves in the rocky cliffs
and will dig holes and hide in the ground
from the anger of the LORD
and his great power,
when he stands to shake the earth.
20At that time people will throw away
their gold and silver idols,
which they made for themselves to worship;
they will throw them away to the bats
and moles.
21Then the people will hide in caves
and cracks in the rocks
from the anger of the LORD
and his great power,
when he stands to shake the earth.

22You should stop trusting in people to save you,
because people are only human;
they aren't able to help you.

God Will Punish Judah and Jerusalem

3 Understand this:
The Lord GOD All-Powerful
will take away everything Judah and Jerusalem
need—
all the food and water,
2the heroes and great soldiers,
the judges and prophets,
people who do magic and older leaders,
3the military leaders and government leaders,
the counselors, the skilled craftsmen, and
those who try to tell the future.
4The LORD says, "I will cause young boys to be
your leaders,
and foolish children will rule over you.
5People will be against each other; everyone
will be against his neighbor.
Young people will not respect older people,
and common people will not respect
important people."
6At that time a man will grab one of his brothers
from his own family and say,
"You have a coat, so you will be our leader.
These ruins will be under your control."
7But that brother will stand up and say,
"I cannot help you,
because I do not have food or clothes in
my house.
You will not make me your leader."
8This will happen because Jerusalem
has stumbled,
and Judah has fallen.
The things they say and do are against
the LORD;
they turn against him.
9The look on their faces shows they are guilty;
like the people of Sodom, they are proud of
their sin.
They don't care who sees it.
How terrible it will be for them,
because they have brought much trouble on
themselves.

2:10 The areas around Jerusalem were filled with cliffs that had a great number of caves.

2:12 Day of the Lord: Isaiah 13:6
2:22 Pride: Jeremiah 17:5–8

[10]Tell those who do what is right that things will go well for them,
because they will receive a reward for what they do.
[11]But how terrible it will be for the wicked!
They will be punished for all the wrong they have done.
[12]Children treat my people cruelly,
and women rule over them.
My people, your guides lead you in the wrong way
and turn you away from what is right.

[13]The LORD takes his place in court
and stands to judge the people.
[14]The LORD presents his case
against the older leaders and other leaders of his people:
"You have burned the vineyard.
Your houses are full of what you took from the poor.
[15]What gives you the right to crush my people
and grind the faces of the poor into the dirt?"
The Lord GOD All-Powerful says this.

A Warning to Women of Jerusalem

[16]The LORD says,
"The women of Jerusalem are proud.
They walk around with their heads held high,
and they flirt with their eyes.
They take quick, short steps,
making noise with their ankle bracelets."
[17]So the Lord will put sores on the heads of those women in Jerusalem,
and he will make them lose their hair.

[18]At that time the Lord will take away everything that makes them proud: their beautiful ankle bracelets, their headbands, their necklaces shaped like the moon, [19]their earrings, bracelets, and veils, [20]their scarves, ankle chains, the cloth belts worn around their waists, their bottles of perfume, and charms, [21]their signet rings, nose rings, [22]their fine robes, capes, shawls, and purses, [23]their mirrors, linen dresses, turbans, and long shawls.

[24]Instead of wearing sweet-smelling perfume,
they will stink.
Instead of fine cloth belts, they will wear the ropes of captives.
Instead of having their hair fixed in fancy ways, they will be bald.
Instead of fine clothes, they will wear clothes of sadness.
Instead of being beautiful, they will wear the brand of a captive.
[25]At that time your men will be killed with swords,
and your heroes will die in war.
[26]There will be crying and sadness near the city gates.
Jerusalem will be like a woman who has lost everything and sits on the ground.

4 At that time seven women
will grab one man
and say, "We will eat our own bread
and make our own clothes,
but please marry us!
Please, take away our shame."

The Branch of the Lord

[2]At that time the LORD's branch will be very
beautiful and great. The people still living in
Israel will be proud of what the land grows.
[3]Those who are still living in Jerusalem will be
called holy; their names are recorded among the
living in Jerusalem. [4]The Lord will wash away the
filth from the women of Jerusalem. He will wash
the bloodstains out of Jerusalem and clean the
city with the spirit of fairness and the spirit of
fire. [5]Then the LORD will cover Mount Zion and
the people who meet there with a cloud of smoke
during the day and with a bright, flaming fire at
night. There will be a covering over every person.
[6]This covering will protect the people from the
heat of the sun and will provide a safe place to
hide from the storm and rain.

Israel, the Lord's Vineyard

5 Now I will sing for my friend a song about his vineyard.
My friend had a vineyard
on a hill with very rich soil.
[2]He dug and cleared the field of stones
and planted the best grapevines there.
He built a tower in the middle of it
and cut out a winepress as well.
He hoped good grapes would grow there,
but only bad ones grew.

3:12 Leadership: Isaiah 40:11
3:14 Money: Isaiah 61:1–2
4:2 *the LORD's branch.* The branch of the Lord ultimately points to Jesus Christ (John 15:1–8).

5:1 *vineyard.* The vineyard is Israel, and God is the person who tends it. This parable should be compared to the one found in Matthew 21:33–44.

BLOOD

MATTHEW 26

What is the importance of blood for the system of sacrifices in Israel? Why did Jesus describe the cup of wine at the Last Supper as "my blood"? What meaning might this have for us today who live in a culture where sacrifice is not practiced?

When Jesus raised his cup of wine at the Last Supper and said, "This is my blood which is the new agreement that God makes with his people" (Matthew 26:28), he is using a very powerful symbol for his Jewish followers gathered to share the Passover with him.

Blood held great significance in the religious life of the people of Israel. It represented deliverance, forgiveness, and God's agreement with the people. The Passover Feast celebrates God's deliverance of the Israelites from slavery in Egypt. God's final punishment of Egypt was the death of all its firstborn male children. The Lord instructed the Israelites to kill an unblemished lamb and put the blood of the lamb on the door frames of their homes. When the angel of the Lord came for the Egyptian children, the homes of God's people, marked with the blood of an unblemished lamb, were passed over and their children were spared (Exodus 11:1–9; 12:21–30). It was as a result of this final punishment that the king of Egypt allowed the Israelites to go free.

The comparison between the blood of the unblemished lamb that spared the Israelite children from death, and the wine symbolizing the blood of the sinless One, Jesus, sparing his followers from eternal death, is present in the Last Supper. When Jesus said, "This blood is poured out for many to forgive their sins" (Matthew 26:28), the allusion to the sacrificial system would have been obvious to the Jewish congregation. Both individuals and the nation of Israel as a whole were required to make sacrifices for breaking the laws of God. These sacrifices involved the shedding of the blood of animals as an offering to God for the forgiveness of their sins (Leviticus 4). Moses instructs Aaron and his sons to make a sacrifice and mix the blood with a special oil to remove their sins when they are appointed priests. (Exodus 29:29, 33). In Leviticus 10:17–18, Moses is upset with them for not performing the sin offering of the people properly, saying, "It is most holy, and the Lord gave it to you to take away the guilt of the people, to remove their sins so they will belong to the Lord. You didn't bring the goat's blood inside the Holy Place . . . as I commanded." When explaining to the people the Lord's command not to eat blood in Leviticus 17:11, Moses says, "This is because the life of the body is in the blood, and I have given you rules for pouring that blood on the altar to remove your sins so you will belong to the Lord."

When Jesus said, "This is my blood which is the new agreement that God makes with his people" (Matthew 26:28), he is using the symbol in a powerful way that would not be lost on the people who identified themselves by the agreement that God made with them through their ancestors. In Exodus 24, after Moses has presented the Law to the people and they pledged themselves to follow God's Law, Moses made a sacrifice. He put half the blood on the altar of the Lord and sprinkled the other half on the people, saying, "This is the blood that begins the Agreement, the Agreement which the Lord has made with you . . ." (Exodus 24:8). Just as the Lord made an agreement with the people of Israel and sealed it with the blood of an animal, Jesus said that God has made a new agreement not just with Israel but with the "many," all people, and it would be sealed with Christ's blood. This would be an agreement once and for all (see Hebrews 9).

It is difficult for Jesus' symbolic statement about the cup of wine as his blood to have the same impact on us today as it did for his original followers. In our culture, blood does not have anything like the meaning it had for them. We do not have a sacrificial system, and blood for us brings up images of pain and violence, though we can still understand its significance. Perhaps the words of Jesus at the Last Supper can have power today when we consider the shedding of blood is always painful, whether it is through violence inflicted by others or ourselves or in healing, as with a surgeon's knife. Though Jesus' blood was shed through the violence of his executioners, it was for us like the healing act of a surgeon. Christ's blood was shed in a procedure that removes our sins and brings about our full recovery. When we take the cup in communion, we can remember that when our very life blood had become poisoned through sin, Christ became a spiritual transfusion for us.

We deserve to die for our sins, but Jesus took our place, shedding his blood that we might live. It is the miraculous act of love by God who raised Jesus from the dead that overcomes spiritual death for all, and that permits us to plead the blood of Jesus when we confess our sins.

Blood: For additional scriptures on this topic go to Romans 5:9.

JUDAS

MATTHEW 26

Who was Judas Iscariot? How could he have betrayed our Lord? How and why did he die?

The name of Judas Iscariot is one that even today carries with it the stigma of betrayal and deception. Even in his introduction to us in scripture he is referred to negatively: ". . . and Judas Iscariot, who later turned against Jesus" (Mark 3:19). It is probable that this infamy did not come to him until after the betrayal of Jesus. He seemed to hold a place of honor and respect as a member of the twelve. He was trusted enough that he was given control of the money box (John 12:6).

This job of treasurer may have been a contributing factor in Judas's fall. He seems to have had a problem with money. John tells us in John 12:6 that Judas "often stole from it." It appears further that the other disciples were unaware of this weakness until after the fact. When Jesus sent him on his way to finish his work of betrayal, the disciples thought he was just running an errand for Jesus (John 13:29). During supper, when Jesus pointed out that he was going to be betrayed, Judas was not suspected by the other disciples. On the contrary, they began to question whether or not they themselves were the ones who would do such a thing (Matthew 26:25).

Judas is mentioned by name only in the list of chosen disciples until the final chapter in the life of Christ begins to be played out. It is then that we begin to see more of the dark character of Judas. What he did was seen by the disciples as an act so evil that it could have only been done through collusion with the forces of darkness (Luke 22:3). The betrayal was premeditated (Luke 22:4), mercenary (Matthew 26:14), and designed to be performed in such a way as to not incite the populace against the Jewish leaders and teachers of the law (Luke 22:6). One of the things that made it particularly repulsive to the disciples was that the betrayal was initiated through the kiss of a friend (Mark 14:45).

There have been some commentators who have tried to clean up the story of Judas by at least giving him a high and noble motive. Some say that he was just trying to force Jesus' hand and cause him to become more aggressive in establishing his kingdom. Scripture does not appear to support such a claim. The motivation that seems to have been driving him was simple greed. "Then one of the twelve apostles, Judas Iscariot, went to talk to the leading priests. He said, 'What will you pay me for giving Jesus to you?' And they gave him thirty silver coins. After that, Judas watched for the best time to turn Jesus in" (Matthew 26:14). This seems to be in line with the character of a thief. It is true, there could also have been anger over a continuing misunderstanding over the kind of kingdom Jesus was bringing. Other disciples seemed to share in this confusion, even after the resurrection prior to Pentecost (Acts 1:6). But to attribute this as a motive to Judas is pure speculation.

Jesus' assessment of Judas was more to the point. He said, "The Son of Man will die, just as the Scriptures say. But how terrible it will be for the person who hands the Son of Man over to be killed. It would be better for him if he had never been born." He also spoke of Judas as being a "devil" (John 6:71). Jesus knew what was in the heart of Judas and that what was there would eventually determine his behavior.

Once Judas realized what the consequences of his betrayal would be for Jesus, he was overcome with guilt and sadness. At that point he could have repented, as Peter had done after he denied Christ three times (Luke 22:61). Instead, he threw the money at the feet of those who had used him to get to Jesus and took his own life (Matthew 27:5). Peter, in his address to those gathered in the upper room, said that in doing this, Judas "turned away and went where he belongs" (Acts 1:25). This appears to be a reference to probable judgment. James tells of the destructive nature of temptation and sin when he says, "People are tempted when their own evil desire leads them away and traps them. This desire leads to sin, and then . . . death" (James 1:14,15).

One of the first items on the agenda in the upper room after the resurrection of Christ was to find a replacement for Judas. The primary requirement was that he be one who had witnessed the life of Jesus from his baptism to his ascension (Acts 1:22). They drew lots and Matthias was chosen (Acts 1:26). It is interesting to note that this is the only place this disciple is ever mentioned in Scripture. One wonders whether Peter and the other apostles might have run ahead of the Lord here.

Judas: For additional scriptures on this topic go to Psalm 109:8.

3My friend says, "You people living
in Jerusalem,
and you people of Judah,
judge between me and my vineyard.
4What more could I have done for my vineyard
than I have already done?
Although I expected good grapes to grow,
why were there only bad ones?
5Now I will tell you
what I will do to my vineyard:
I will remove the hedge,
and it will be burned.
I will break down the stone wall,
and it will be walked on.
6I will ruin my field.
It will not be trimmed or hoed,
and weeds and thorns will grow there.
I will command the clouds
not to rain on it."

7The vineyard belonging to the LORD
All-Powerful
is the nation of Israel;
the garden that he loves
is the people of Judah.
He looked for justice, but there was
only killing.
He hoped for right living, but there were
only cries of pain.⚭

8How terrible it will be for you who add more
houses to your houses
and more fields to your fields
until there is no room left for other people.
Then you are left alone in the land.

9The LORD All-Powerful said this to me:
"The fine houses will be destroyed;
the large and beautiful houses will be
left empty.
10At that time a ten-acre vineyard will make only
six gallons of wine,
and ten bushels of seed will grow only half a
bushel of grain."

11How terrible it will be for people who rise
early in the morning
to look for strong drink,
who stay awake late at night,
becoming drunk with wine.
12At their parties they have lyres, harps,
tambourines, flutes, and wine.
They don't see what the LORD has done
or notice the work of his hands.⚭
13So my people will be captured and taken away,
because they don't really know me.
All the great people will die of hunger,
and the common people will die of thirst.
14So the place of the dead wants more and
more people,
and it opens wide its mouth.
Jerusalem's important people and common
people will go down into it,
with their happy and noisy ones.
15So the common people and the great people
will be brought down;
those who are proud will be humbled.
16The LORD All-Powerful will receive glory by
judging fairly;
the holy God will show himself holy by doing
what is right.
17Then the sheep will go anywhere they want,
and lambs will feed on the land that rich
people once owned.

18How terrible it will be for those people!
They pull their guilt and sins behind them
as people pull wagons with ropes.
19They say, "Let God hurry;
let him do his work soon
so we may see it.
Let the plan of the Holy One of Israel
happen soon
so that we will know what it is."

20How terrible it will be for people who call
good things bad
and bad things good,
who think darkness is light
and light is darkness,
who think sour is sweet
and sweet is sour.

21How terrible it will be for people who think
they are wise
and believe they are clever.

22How terrible it will be for people who are
famous for drinking wine
and are champions at mixing drinks.
23They take money to set the guilty free
and don't allow good people to be
judged fairly.
24They will be destroyed

⚭**5:7 Images of God:** Isaiah 64:8
⚭**5:7 Parables:** Ezekiel 17:2–10
⚭**5:12 Leisure:** 2 Timothy 3:4

just as fire burns straw or dry grass.
They will be destroyed
like a plant whose roots rot
and whose flower dies and blows away
like dust.
They have refused to obey the teachings of the
LORD All-Powerful
and have hated the message from the Holy
God of Israel.
25So the LORD has become very angry with
his people,
and he has raised his hand to punish them.
Even the mountains are frightened.
Dead bodies lie in the streets like garbage.

But the LORD is still angry;
his hand is still raised to strike down
the people.

26He raises a banner for the nations far away.
He whistles to call those people from the
ends of the earth.
Look! The enemy comes quickly!
27Not one of them becomes tired or falls down.
Not one of them gets sleepy and falls asleep.
Their weapons are close at hand,
and their sandal straps are not broken.
28Their arrows are sharp,
and all of their bows are ready to shoot.
The horses' hoofs are hard as rocks,
and their chariot wheels move like a whirlwind.
29Their shout is like the roar of a lion;
it is loud like a young lion.
They growl as they grab their captives.
There is no one to stop them from taking
their captives away.
30On that day they will roar
like the waves of the sea.
And when people look at the land,
they will see only darkness and pain;
all light will become dark in this thick cloud.

Isaiah Becomes a Prophet

6 In the year that King Uzziah died, I saw the
Lord sitting on a very high throne. His long
robe filled the Temple. 2Heavenly creatures of fire
stood above him. Each creature had six wings: It
used two wings to cover its face, two wings to
cover its feet, and two wings for flying. 3Each creature was calling to the others:
"Holy, holy, holy is the LORD All-Powerful.
His glory fills the whole earth."
4Their calling caused the frame around the door
to shake, as the Temple filled with smoke.
5I said, "Oh, no! I will be destroyed. I am not
pure, and I live among people who are not pure,
but I have seen the King, the LORD All-Powerful."
6One of the heavenly creatures used a pair of
tongs to take a hot coal from the altar. Then he flew
to me with the hot coal in his hand. 7The creature
touched my mouth with the hot coal and said,
"Look, your guilt is taken away, because this hot
coal has touched your lips. Your sin is taken away."
8Then I heard the Lord's voice, saying, "Whom
can I send? Who will go for us?"
So I said, "Here I am. Send me!"
9Then the Lord said, "Go and tell this to the
people:
'You will listen and listen, but you will
not understand.
You will look and look, but you will not learn.'

5:26–30 The prophets often painted terrible pictures of the final destruction of the world: The stars would fall from their places, the sun would not give its light, and all the powers of nature would be shaken (Isaiah 24; 34; 2 Peter 3:10). In a similar way, when they spoke of immediate destruction coming upon sinful nations, they also used graphic, seemingly exaggerated, figures of speech. This is because they were not giving literal descriptions but prophetic visions and images. The predicted events would come to pass in a way that was devastating and awesome, although not always exactly as described.

6:1–7 Isaiah's vision of the glory of God is significant for more than one reason. It gives us a glimpse of heaven itself, with God on his throne and heavenly creatures of fire flying and declaring the holiness of God. But it also shows us the effect of a glimpse of God's glory on a human being who sees his own sinfulness by awful contrast, and who, nevertheless, experiences the grace and cleansing God offers.

6:2 *Heavenly creatures.* These heavenly creatures are sometimes called "seraphim," who are among the most mighty of God's creatures.

6:3 Glory: Ezekiel 1:28

6:3 Holiness: Zechariah 14:20–21

6:5–8 Isaiah is brought into the heavenly council chamber, into God's presence, and reacts with shame and guilt. He is aware of his sin and failing his God. God has told us all to "be holy because I am holy" (Leviticus 19:2), and Isaiah recognizes that he has fallen short (Romans 3:23). As Paul goes on to tell us, we have one recourse for our sin and guilt—Jesus Christ whom God sent to provide a way "to forgive sin through faith" (Romans 3:25). Our guilt should drive us to Christ.

6:8 It is interesting that the God of all creation expresses a desire for one to speak on his behalf. The role of a "go-between" was used often in the Old Testament. God called forth persons to mediate with the people, expressing and interpreting God's word and work to them. The role of mediator is a central theme in our understanding of atonement. The gap between God and his human creatures is bridged and mended by a mediating presence.

Prophets, serving God as mediators, spoke of God to the people, pointed to God's activity in the world, and interpreted God's presence. God's "call" was for one to speak out his word, demonstrate his presence, and proclaim his intent. In this way, a prophet revealed God's word to the people.

In the New Testament, Jesus is God's perfect mediator (Hebrews 1:1–3). Christ's followers are also called to go on God's behalf to reveal, to interpret, and to teach (Matthew 28:18–20). Much like God's words heard by Isaiah, Jesus sends us forth into the world. Dare we respond like Isaiah: "Here I am; send me"?

6:8 Loneliness: Jeremiah 1:4–10

[10]Make the minds of these people dumb.
Shut their ears. Cover their eyes.
Otherwise, they might really understand
what they see with their eyes
and hear with their ears.
They might really understand in their minds
and come back to me and be healed."

[11]Then I asked, "Lord, how long should I do this?"
He answered,
"Until the cities are destroyed
and the people are gone,
until there are no people left in the houses,
until the land is destroyed and left empty.
[12]The LORD will send the people far away,
and the land will be left empty.⚭
[13]One-tenth of the people will be left in the land,
but it will be destroyed again.
These people will be like an oak tree
whose stump is left when the tree is
chopped down.
The people who remain will be like a stump
that will sprout again."⚭

Trouble with Aram

7 Now Ahaz was the son of Jotham, who was
the son of Uzziah. When Ahaz was king of
Judah, Rezin king of Aram and Pekah son of Remaliah, the king of Israel, went up to Jerusalem to fight
against it. But they were not able to defeat the city.
[2]Ahaz king of Judah received a message saying, "The armies of Aram and Israel have joined
together."

When Ahaz heard this, he and the people were frightened. They shook with fear like trees of the forest blown by the wind.

[3]Then the LORD told Isaiah, "You and your son
Shear-Jashub should go and meet Ahaz at the
place where the water flows into the upper pool,
on the road where people do their laundry. [4]Tell
Ahaz, 'Be careful. Be calm and don't worry. Don't
let those two men, Rezin and Pekah son of
Remaliah, scare you. Don't be afraid of their anger
or Aram's anger, because they are like two barely
burning sticks that are ready to go out. [5]They have
made plans against you, saying, [6]"Let's fight against
Judah and tear it apart. We will divide the land for
ourselves and make the son of Tabeel the new king
of Judah." [7]But I, the Lord GOD, say,

"'Their plan will not succeed;
it will not happen,
[8]because Aram is led by the city of Damascus,
and Damascus is led by its weak king, Rezin.
Within sixty-five years Israel will no longer be
a nation.
[9]Israel is led by the city of Samaria,
and Samaria is led by its weak king, the son
of Remaliah.
If your faith is not strong,
you will not have strength enough to last.'"

Immanuel—God Is with Us

[10]Then the LORD spoke to Ahaz again, saying,
[11]"Ask for a sign from the LORD your God to prove
to yourself that these things are true. It may be a
sign from as deep as the place of the dead or as
high as the heavens."
[12]But Ahaz said, "I will not ask for a sign or test
the LORD."
[13]Then Isaiah said, "Ahaz, descendant of David,
listen carefully! Isn't it bad enough that you wear
out the patience of people? Do you also have to
wear out the patience of my God? [14]The Lord himself will give you a sign: The virgin will be pregnant. She will have a son, and she will name him
Immanuel. [15]He will be eating milk curds and
honey when he learns to reject what is evil and to
choose what is good. [16]You are afraid of the kings
of Israel and Aram now. But before the child learns
to choose good and reject evil, the lands of Israel
and Aram will be empty. [17]The LORD will bring troubled times to you, your people, and to the people of
your father's family. They will be worse than anything that has happened since Israel separated from
Judah. The LORD will bring the king of Assyria to
fight against you.
[18]"At that time the LORD will whistle for the
Egyptians, and they will come like flies from Egypt's
faraway streams. He will call for the Assyrians, and
they will come like bees. [19]These enemies will
camp in the deep ravines and in the cliffs, by the
thornbushes and watering holes. [20]The Lord will
hire Assyria and use it like a razor to punish Judah.
It will be as if the Lord is shaving the hair from
Judah's head and legs and removing Judah's beard.
[21]"At that time a person will be able to keep
only one young cow and two sheep alive. [22]There

⚭**6:12 Wilderness (Desert):** Isaiah 35
⚭**6:13 Communication:** Hosea 1:2
7:1 This story is set in the context of the war between Israel and Syria on the one hand and Judah on the other. This conflict draws Assyria, the superpower of the day, into the area.
7:2 *Israel.* Literally, "Ephraim." Isaiah often uses "Ephraim" to mean all of Israel.
7:3 *Shear-Jashub.* This name means "a part of the people will come back."
7:14 *virgin.* The Hebrew word means "a young woman." Often this meant a girl who was not married and had not yet had sexual relations with anyone.
7:14 *Immanuel.* This name means "God is with us."

will be only enough milk for that person to eat
milk curds. All who remain in the land will go
back to eating just milk curds and honey. 23In
this land there are now vineyards that have a
thousand grapevines, which are worth about
twenty-five pounds of silver. But these fields
will become full of weeds and thorns. 24The land
will become wild and useful only as a hunting
ground. 25People once worked and grew food on
these hills, but at that time people will not go
there, because the land will be filled with weeds
and thorns. Only sheep and cattle will go to those
places."

Assyria Will Come Soon

8 The LORD told me, "Take a large scroll and
write on it with an ordinary pen: 'Maher-
Shalal-Hash-Baz.' 2I will gather some men to be
reliable witnesses: Uriah the priest and Zechariah
son of Jeberekiah."

3Then I went to the prophetess, and she became
pregnant and had a son. The LORD told me, "Name
the boy Maher-Shalal-Hash-Baz, 4because the king
of Assyria will take away all the wealth and possessions of Damascus and Samaria before the boy
learns to say 'my father' or 'my mother.'"

5Again the LORD spoke to me, saying,

6"These people refuse to accept
the slow-moving waters of the pool of Shiloah
and are terrified of Rezin
and Pekah son of Remaliah.
7So I, the Lord, will bring
the king of Assyria and all his power
against them,
like a powerful flood of water from the
Euphrates River.
The Assyrians will be like water rising over the
banks of the river,
flowing over the land.
8That water will flow into Judah and pass
through it,
rising to Judah's throat.
Immanuel, this army will spread its wings like
a bird
until it covers your whole country."

9Be broken, all you nations,
and be smashed to pieces.
Listen, all you faraway countries.
Prepare for battle and be smashed to pieces!
Prepare for battle and be smashed
to pieces!
10Make your plans for the fight,
but they will be defeated.
Give orders to your armies,
but they will be useless,
because God is with us.

Warnings to Isaiah

11The LORD spoke to me with his great power and
warned me not to follow the lead of the rest of the
people. He said,

12"People are saying that others make plans
against them,
but you should not believe them.
Don't be afraid of what they fear;
do not dread those things.
13But remember that the LORD All-Powerful
is holy.
He is the one you should fear;
he is the one you should dread.
14Then he will be a place of safety for you.
But for the two families of Israel,
he will be like a stone that causes people
to stumble,
like a rock that makes them fall.
He will be like a trap for the people of Jerusalem,
and he will catch them in his trap.⚭
15Many people will fall over this rock.
They will fall and be broken;
they will be trapped and caught."

16Make an agreement.
Seal up the teaching while my followers
are watching.
17I will wait for the LORD to help us,
the LORD who is ashamed of the family
of Israel.
I will wait for him.

18I am here, and with me are the children the
LORD has given me. We are signs and proofs for the
people of Israel from the LORD All-Powerful, who
lives on Mount Zion.

19Some people say, "Ask the mediums and
fortune-tellers, who whisper and mutter, what to
do." But I tell you that people should ask their God
for help. Why should people who are still alive ask
something from the dead? 20You should follow the
teachings and the agreement with the LORD. The
mediums and fortune-tellers do not speak the word
of the LORD, so their words are worth nothing.

21People will wander through the land troubled
and hungry. When they become hungry, they will

8:3 *Maher-Shalal-Hash-Baz.* This name means "there will soon be looting and stealing."

⚭**8:14 Stone:** Isaiah 28:16

8:18 *Mount Zion.* Mount Zion is the location of the Temple of God.

become angry and will look up and curse their king
and their God. 22They will look around them at
their land and see only trouble, darkness, and awful
gloom. And they will be forced into the darkness.

A New Day Is Coming

9 But suddenly there will be no more gloom for
the land that suffered. In the past God made
the lands of Zebulun and Naphtali hang their heads
in shame, but in the future those lands will be made
great. They will stretch from the road along the
Mediterranean Sea to the land beyond the Jordan
River and north to Galilee, the land of people who
are not Israelites.

2Before those people lived in darkness,
but now they have seen a great light.
They lived in a dark land,
but a light has shined on them.⚭
3God, you have caused the nation to grow
and made the people happy.
And they have shown their happiness to you,
like the joy during harvest time,
like the joy of people
taking what they have won in war.
4Like the time you defeated Midian,
you have taken away their heavy load
and the heavy pole from their backs
and the rod the enemy used to
punish them.
5Every boot that marched in battle
and every uniform stained with blood
has been thrown into the fire.
6A child has been born to us;
God has given a son to us.
He will be responsible for leading
the people.
His name will be Wonderful Counselor,
Powerful God,
Father Who Lives Forever, Prince of Peace.⚭
7Power and peace will be in his kingdom
and will continue to grow forever.
He will rule as king on David's throne
and over David's kingdom.
He will make it strong
by ruling with justice and goodness
from now on and forever.
The LORD All-Powerful will do this
because of his strong love for
his people.

God Will Punish Israel

8The Lord sent a message against the people
of Jacob;
it says that God will judge Israel.
9Then everyone in Israel, even the leaders
in Samaria,
will know that God has sent it.
Those people are proud and brag by saying,
10"These bricks have fallen,
but we will build again with cut stones.
These small trees have been chopped down,
but we will put great cedars there."
11But the LORD has brought the enemies of Rezin
against them;
he has stirred up their enemies against them.
12The Arameans came from the east
and the Philistines from the west,
and they ate up Israel with their armies.

But the LORD was still angry;
his hand was still raised to punish the people.

13But the people did not return to the one who
had struck them;
they did not follow the LORD All-Powerful.
14So the LORD cut off Israel's head and tail,
taking away both the branch and stalk in
one day.
15The older leaders and important men were
the head,
and the prophets who speak lies were the tail.
16Those who led the people led them in the
wrong direction,
and those who followed them were destroyed.
17So the Lord is not happy with the young people,
nor will he show mercy to the orphans
and widows.
All the people are separated from God and are
very evil;
they all speak lies.

But the LORD is still angry;
his hand is still raised to strike down the people.

18Evil is like a small fire.
First, it burns weeds and thorns.
Next, it burns the larger bushes in the forest,
and they all go up in a column of smoke.
19The LORD All-Powerful is angry,
so the land will be burned.

⚭**9:2 Darkness:** Matthew 6:23

⚭**9:6 Peace:** Isaiah 54:13

9:6 In this prophecy concerning the coming Messiah, several names are ascribed to him that are descriptive of the ways God relates to his people. As Wonderful Counselor, God responds to our deepest needs; as Powerful God, he rules over this world and guides the course of our lives; as Father Who Lives Forever, he is eternal in his perspective; and as Prince of Peace, he offers to reconcile us to himself and take away our sins.

The people are like fuel for the fire;
no one will try to save his brother or sister.
20People will grab something on the right,
but they will still be hungry.
They will eat something on the left,
but they will not be filled.
Then they will each turn and eat their
own children.
21The people of Manasseh will fight against the
people of Ephraim,
and Ephraim will fight against Manasseh.
Then both of them will turn against Judah.

But the LORD is still angry;
his hand is still raised to strike down
the people.

10 How terrible it will be for those who make
unfair laws,
and those who write laws that make life hard
for people.
2They are not fair to the poor,
and they rob my people of their rights.
They allow people to steal from widows
and to take from orphans what really belongs
to them.
3How will you explain the things you have done?
What will you do when your destruction
comes from far away?
Where will you run for help?
Where will you hide your riches then?
4You will have to bow down among the captives
or fall down among the dead bodies.
But the LORD is still angry;
his hand is still raised to strike down
the people.

God Will Punish Assyria

5God says, "How terrible it will be for the king
of Assyria.
I use him like a rod to show my anger;
in anger I use Assyria like a club.
6I send it to fight against a nation that is separated
from God.
I am angry with those people,
so I command Assyria to fight against them,
to take their wealth from them,
to trample them down like dirt in the streets.
7But Assyria's king doesn't understand that I am
using him;
he doesn't know he is a tool for me.
He only wants to destroy other people
and to defeat many nations.
8The king of Assyria says to himself,
'All of my commanders are like kings.
9The city Calno is like the city Carchemish.
The city Hamath is like the city Arpad.
The city Samaria is like the city Damascus.
10I defeated those kingdoms that worship idols,
and those idols were more than the idols of
Jerusalem and Samaria.
11As I defeated Samaria and her idols,
I will also defeat Jerusalem and her idols.' " ⚭

12When the Lord finishes doing what he planned
to Mount Zion and Jerusalem, he will punish
Assyria. The king of Assyria is very proud, and his
pride has made him do these evil things, so God
will punish him. 13The king of Assyria says this:
"By my own power I have done these things;
by my wisdom I have defeated many nations.
I have taken their wealth,
and, like a mighty one, I have taken
their people.
14I have taken the riches of all these people,
like a person reaching into a bird's nest.
I have taken these nations,
like a person taking eggs.
Not one raised a hand
or opened its mouth to stop me."

15An ax is not better than the person who
swings it.
A saw is not better than the one who uses it.
A stick cannot control the person who picks
it up.
A club cannot pick up the person!
16So the Lord GOD All-Powerful
will send a terrible disease upon
Assyria's soldiers.
The strength of Assyria will be burned up
like a fire burning until everything is gone.
17God, the Light of Israel, will be like a fire;
the Holy One will be like a flame.
He will be like a fire
that suddenly burns the weeds and thorns.
18The fire burns away the great trees and
rich farmlands,
destroying everything.
It will be like a sick person who wastes away.
19The trees left standing will be so few
that even a child could count them.

20At that time some people will be left
alive in Israel
from the family of Jacob.

⚭ **10:11 Samaria:** Ezekiel 23

Pontius Pilate

Matthew 27:1–26

What was Pilate's role in the trial and death of Jesus?

Pontius Pilate is best known to readers of the Bible as the governor of the Roman province of Judea (A.D. 26–36/37) who sentenced Jesus to death on a cross. According to one of the early creeds of the church, Jesus was "crucified under Pontius Pilate." How this happened is described in parallel accounts by each of the New Testament Gospels. A Roman historian, Tacitus, has also reported the execution of Christ under Pilate.

As governor of Judea, Pilate would have been responsible for all aspects of its administration. He would have commanded the Roman troops assigned to this region; he would have been responsible for certain aspects of the finances of the region, including collecting taxes and forwarding them to Rome; and he would have been the head of the legal system in Judea. From Jewish sources outside of the New Testament we gain important insight into Pilate as a ruler. Especially in the earlier part of his career, he was widely known as greedy, brutal, and unbending. He demonstrated little regard for Jewish customs. For example, he seized money from the Jerusalem Temple treasury in order to construct a water system and introduced images of the Roman emperor, portraying him as a god, in the City of Jerusalem. His insensitivity on matters like these, together with the cruelty that characterized his rule more generally, led finally to his being dismissed as governor of Judea. This took place at the end of the year 36 or the beginning of 37, only a few years following Jesus' crucifixion in either A.D. 30 or 33.

This background is important for two reasons. First, it reminds us of the tensions that would seem quite natural in a land that many Jewish people believed belonged to God yet was ruled by Rome. In their records of the trial of Jesus, the Gospels are aware of this mixture of religious and political commitments. On the one hand, we learn that the Jewish council found Jesus guilty of speaking against God and judged him as one who was worthy of death (Matthew 26:59–65; Mark 14:55–64; John 19:7). On the other hand, the Gospels all testify that Jesus was executed as a pretender who claimed to be the king of the Jewish people. This is the content of the inscription on the cross, which summarizes the charges brought against Jesus: "This is Jesus: the King of the Jews" (Matthew 27:37; Mark 15:26; Luke 23:38; and John 19:19–22). Like so many aspects of the story of Jesus' trial, this detail must be understood at more than one level; Jesus' followers realize that the charge brought against Jesus, that he was king of the Jewish people, the Christ, was correct even though others would have seen it as a falsehood.

Luke also reports how Jesus was accused of "telling things that mislead our people. He says that we should not pay taxes to Caesar, and he calls himself the Christ, a king" (Luke 23:2). With this language, Jesus' opponents attempt to discredit him as a false prophet who turns God's people away from the ways of the Lord (Deuteronomy 13; see Matthew 27:63); it also shows how Jesus could be judged as a political threat. In addition, according to John 11:47–53, Jesus' popularity is recognized as a threat to relations between Rome and Jerusalem. This same problem comes to the surface in John 19:12, 15, where the rule of Caesar is contrasted with that of Jesus. Against this background, it becomes easier to understand why Pilate would have gotten involved in deciding Jesus' fate. It also becomes more clear why Pilate's final decision was to have Jesus executed. Pilate's primary concern was to protect Roman interests and, thus, to maintain the peace. If Jesus was presented to him as one who threatened the peace (and this is exactly how Jesus was presented to Pilate by the leaders of the Jewish people), then Jesus must be killed.

Second, what we learn about Pilate from sources outside of the Bible reveals that he had a long history of working with the Jewish leaders in Jerusalem. Indeed, as far as we know, Pilate held the position of governor of Judea longer than anyone else. Apparently, though, it was only with the passing of time that he found ways to keep the peace, and this meant working to stay in good graces with the emperor in Rome. It also meant keeping the leaders of the Jewish people in Jerusalem content enough to keep them from complaining to Rome about his behavior as a ruler. This is certainly a significant part of the portrait of Pontius Pilate found in the Gospels. The most obvious example of this problem arises in John 19:12, where Pilate is threatened with these words, "If you let [Jesus] go, you are no friend of Caesar." Throughout the gospel accounts of the trial of Jesus, however, Pilate appears as someone who is interested primarily not in justice but in conforming to the wishes of the leadership of the Jewish people concerning Jesus.

Pontius Pilate: For additional scriptures on this topic go to Matthew 27:1–2.

THE CRUCIFIXION OF JESUS (THE WAY OF THE CROSS)

MATTHEW 27:32–55

What does the way of the cross mean for contemporary discipleship?
What was the meaning of the crucifixion of Jesus in the first-century Roman world?

The modern-day believer views the crucifixion of Jesus through the victorious resurrection. We have, therefore, lost touch with the scandal of the cross. The fact that Jesus died on a cross had tremendous significance for this followers, for they believed him to be the Messiah, the one to redeem Israel (Luke 24:19–21). Our modern understanding of the crucifixion of Jesus is heightened if we can understand the significance and scandal of the cross of Jesus to the first-century believer.

Crucifixion was a method of capital punishment used by the Roman Empire in the first century. Crucifixion was reserved for people who were guilty of sedition against Rome. It was done in public areas and therefore was not only physically odious and agonizing, but also humiliating. Crucifixion was meant as a vivid public deterrent to crimes against Rome.

From the Gospel accounts, we learn that the victim of crucifixion was first flogged or beaten (Matthew 27:26–31; Mark 15:15–20), and had to carry the cross (John 19:17) to the public place of execution (Matthew 27:38–44, 55–56; Mark 15:27–32, 40–41; Luke 23:27–37, 48–49; John 19:20, 25–27). The condemned was then stripped of his clothing (Matthew 27:35; Mark 15:24; John 19:23) and was crucified.

Death by crucifixion was agonizing. The victim was nailed to the cross or tree through the hands, or wrists and feet, which resulted in very little loss of blood. Because of the nonfatal initial injuries to the condemned, death came slowly by exposure, shock, and asphyxiation caused by exhaustion, with the weakened victim unable to pull himself up in order to breathe.

To see their Messiah put to death in such a manner had to be horrifying for the followers of Jesus. But death by crucifixion had additional frightening and confusing significance to the Jewish followers of Jesus. In Deuteronomy 21:22–23, if someone died by hanging on a cross or tree, they were considered "cursed by God." How could the man they believed to be the Messiah, die on a cross, cursed by God? How scandalous this must have been for the followers of Jesus. This is why Paul wrote in 1 Corinthians, "But we preach a crucified Christ. This is a big problem to the Jews, and it is foolishness to those who are not Jews" (1 Corinthians 1:23). How were the first-century believers, even after the resurrection, to make sense of the cross of Jesus, who was cursed by God?

The New Testament writers had to wrestle and interpret the confusing and scandalous sacrifice of Jesus on the cross. This is a task all followers of Jesus must undertake to better understand discipleship as the way of the cross. The crucifixion of Jesus must first be understood as his taking the penalty, or curse, that each of us deserves for breaking God's law (Galatians 3:13). Christ took our sins and stood as our substitute on the cross. As Paul states it in Galatians 2:20, "I was put to death on the cross with Christ, and I do not live anymore—it is Christ who lives in me."

The writer of Hebrews interpreted the cross of Jesus as atonement as understood through the Old Testament law of sacrifice of animals for the forgiveness of sins (Hebrews 9:18–22). The writer described how in the Old Testament an agreement with God was sealed by mixing the blood of calves with water (9:19), and how an annual blood sacrifice for atonement was required (9:25). Drawing from these very familiar practices, a comparison is made with the once-for-all atoning work of Christ (9:23–24).

The crucifixion of Jesus must also be understood in the context of the life of Jesus. How he died was the result of how he lived, for he lived a life which placed him in direct opposition to the religious leaders of the Jewish people, and ultimately to the Roman Empire.

The gospel writers saw that throughout Jesus' ministry he called people to live a life of service. The life of discipleship which is described in the Gospels is very different from the comfortable standards of lifestyle in the world (Luke 6:20–26). The discipleship lifestyle which Jesus invites believers to follow is consistent with the life he led, which was the way of the cross. In Matthew 10:38–39, Jesus tells his followers, "Whoever is not willing to carry the cross and follow me is not worthy of me. Those who try to hold on to their lives will give up true life."⚭

⚭ **The Crucifixion of Jesus (The Way of the Cross):** For additional scriptures on this topic go to Deuteronomy 21:22–23.

They will not continue to depend
on the person who defeated them.
They will learn truly to depend on the LORD,
the Holy One of Israel.
21Those who are left alive in Jacob's family
will again follow the powerful God.
22Israel, your people are many,
like the grains of sand by the sea.
But only a few of them will be left alive to
return to the LORD.
God has announced that he will
destroy the land
completely and fairly.
23The Lord GOD All-Powerful will certainly
destroy this land,
as he has announced.

24This is what the Lord GOD All-Powerful says:
"My people living in Jerusalem,
don't be afraid of the Assyrians,
who beat you with a rod
and raise a stick against you, as Egypt did.
25After a short time my anger against you will stop,
and then I will turn my anger to
destroying them."

26Then the LORD All-Powerful will beat the
Assyrians with a whip
as he defeated Midian at the rock of Oreb.
He will raise his stick over the waters
as he did in Egypt.
27Then the troubles that Assyria puts on you
will be removed,
and the load they make you carry
will be taken away.

Assyria Invades Israel

28The army of Assyria will enter near Aiath.
Its soldiers will walk through Migron.
They will store their food in Micmash.
29The army will go over the pass.
The soldiers will sleep at Geba.
The people of Ramah will be afraid,
and the people at Gibeah of Saul will run away.
30Cry out, Bath Gallim!
Laishah, listen!
Poor Anathoth!
31The people of Madmenah are running away;
the people of Gebim are hiding.
32This day the army will stop at Nob.
They will shake their fist at Mount Zion,
at the hill of Jerusalem.

33Watch! The Lord GOD All-Powerful
with his great power will chop them down
like a great tree.
Those who are great will be cut down;
those who are important will fall to
the ground.
34He will cut them down
as a forest is cut down with an ax.
And the great trees of Lebanon
will fall by the power of the Mighty One.

The King of Peace Is Coming

11 A new branch will grow
from a stump of a tree;
so a new king will come
from the family of Jesse.
2The Spirit of the LORD will rest upon that king.
The Spirit will give him wisdom and understanding, guidance and power.
The Spirit will teach him to know and
respect the LORD.
3This king will be glad to obey the LORD.
He will not judge by the way things look
or decide by what he hears.
4But he will judge the poor honestly;
he will be fair in his decisions for the poor
people of the land.
At his command evil people will be punished,
and by his words the wicked will be put
to death.
5Goodness and fairness will give him strength,
like a belt around his waist.

6Then wolves will live in peace with lambs,
and leopards will lie down to rest with goats.
Calves, lions, and young bulls will eat together,
and a little child will lead them.
7Cows and bears will eat together in peace.
Their young will lie down to rest together.
Lions will eat hay as oxen do.
8A baby will be able to play near a cobra's hole,
and a child will be able to put his hand into
the nest of a poisonous snake.
9They will not hurt or destroy each other
on all my holy mountain,
because the earth will be full of the knowledge
of the LORD,
as the sea is full of water.

10At that time the new king from the family of
Jesse will stand as a banner for all peoples. The
nations will come together around him, and the
place where he lives will be filled with glory. 11At

10:22 The Remnant: Isaiah 28:5
11:1 *Jesse.* King David's father.
11:1 *branch.* See 4:2
11:9 Animals: Isaiah 65:25

that time the Lord will again reach out and take his
people who are left alive in Assyria, North Egypt,
South Egypt, Cush, Elam, Babylonia, Hamath, and
all the islands of the sea.

12 God will raise a banner as a sign for all nations,
and he will gather the people of Israel who
were forced from their country.
He will gather the scattered people of Judah
from all parts of the earth.
13 At that time Israel will not be jealous anymore,
and Judah will have no more enemies.
Israel will not be jealous of Judah,
and Judah will not hate Israel.
14 But Israel and Judah will attack the Philistines
on the west.
Together they will take the riches from the
people of the east.
They will conquer Edom and Moab,
and the people of Ammon will be under
their control.
15 The LORD will dry up
the Red Sea of Egypt.
He will wave his arm over the
Euphrates River
and dry it up with a scorching wind.
He will divide it into seven small rivers
so that people can walk across them with
their sandals on.
16 So God's people who are left alive
will have a way to leave Assyria,
just like the time the Israelites
came out of Egypt.

A Song of Praise to God

12 At that time you will say:
"I praise you, LORD!
You were angry with me,
but you are not angry with me now!
You have comforted me.
2 God is the one who saves me;
I will trust him and not be afraid.
The LORD, the LORD gives me strength and
makes me sing.
He has saved me."
3 You will receive your salvation with joy
as you would draw water from a well.

4 At that time you will say,
"Praise the LORD and worship him.
Tell everyone what he has done
and how great he is.
5 Sing praise to the LORD, because he has done
great things.
Let all the world know what he has done.
6 Shout and sing for joy, you people of Jerusalem,
because the Holy One of Israel does great
things before your eyes."

God's Message to Babylon

13 God showed Isaiah son of Amoz this message
about Babylon:
2 Raise a flag on the bare mountain.
Call out to the men.
Raise your hand to signal them
to enter through the gates for important people.
3 I myself have commanded those people
whom I have separated as mine.
I have called those warriors to carry out
my anger.
They rejoice and are glad to do my will.

4 Listen to the loud noise in the mountains,
the sound of many people.
Listen to the noise among the kingdoms,
the sound of nations gathering together.
The LORD All-Powerful is calling
his army together for battle.
5 This army is coming from a faraway land,
from the edge of the horizon.
In anger the LORD is using this army like
a weapon
to destroy the whole country.

6 Cry, because the LORD's day of judging is near;
the Almighty is sending destruction.
7 People will be weak with fear,
and their courage will melt away.
8 Everyone will be afraid.
Pain and hurt will grab them;
they will hurt like a woman giving birth to
a baby.
They will look at each other in fear,
with their faces red like fire.

God's Judgment Against Babylon

9 Look, the LORD's day of judging is coming—
a terrible day, a day of God's anger.
He will destroy the land
and the sinners who live in it.
10 The stars will not show their light;
the skies will be dark.
The sun will grow dark as it rises,
and the moon will not give its light.

11:12 The Remnant: Isaiah 28:5
12:1 Comfort: Isaiah 57:18
12:2 Salvation: Luke 18:35–43
12:3 Water: Isaiah 41:17–20
13:6 Day of the Lord: Isaiah 34:2–8

[11]The LORD says, "I will punish the world for its evil
and wicked people for their sins.
I will cause proud people to lose their pride,
and I will destroy the pride of those who are cruel to others.
[12]People will be harder to find than pure gold;
there will be fewer people than there is fine gold in Ophir.
[13]I will make the sky shake,
and the earth will be moved from its place
by the anger of the LORD All-Powerful
at the time of his burning anger.

[14]"Then the people from Babylon will run away like hunted deer
or like sheep who have no shepherd.
Everyone will turn back to his own people;
each will run back to his own land.
[15]Everyone who is captured will be killed;
everyone who is caught will be killed with a sword.
[16]Their little children will be beaten to death in front of them.
Their houses will be robbed
and their wives raped.

[17]"Look, I will cause the armies of Media to attack Babylon.
They do not care about silver
or delight in gold.
[18]Their soldiers will shoot the young men with arrows;
they will show no mercy on children,
nor will they feel sorry for little ones.
[19]Babylon is the most beautiful of all kingdoms,
and the Babylonians are very proud of it.
But God will destroy it
like Sodom and Gomorrah.
[20]No one will ever live there
or settle there again.
No Arab will put a tent there;
no shepherd will bring sheep there.
[21]Only desert animals will live there,
and their houses will be full of wild dogs.
Owls will live there,
and wild goats will leap about in the houses.
[22]Wolves will howl within the strong walls,
and wild dogs will bark in the beautiful buildings.
The end of Babylon is near;
its time is almost over."

Israel Will Return Home

14 The LORD will show mercy to the people of
Jacob, and he will again choose the people
of Israel. He will settle them in their own land. Then
non-Israelite people will join the Israelites and will
become a part of the family of Jacob. [2]Nations will
take the Israelites back to their land. Then those
men and women from the other nations will
become slaves to Israel in the LORD's land. In the
past the Israelites were their slaves, but now the
Israelites will defeat those nations and rule over
them.

The King of Babylon Will Fall

[3]The LORD will take away the Israelites' hard
work and will comfort them. They will no longer
have to work hard as slaves. [4]On that day Israel
will sing this song about the king of Babylon:
The cruel king who ruled us is finished;
his angry rule is finished!
[5]The LORD has broken the scepter of evil rulers
and taken away their power.
[6]The king of Babylon struck people in anger
again and again.
He ruled nations in anger
and continued to hurt them.
[7]But now, the whole world rests and is quiet.
Now the people begin to sing.
[8]Even the pine trees are happy,
and the cedar trees of Lebanon rejoice.
They say, "The king has fallen,
so no one will ever cut us down again."

[9]The place of the dead is excited
to meet you when you come.
It wakes the spirits of the dead,
the leaders of the world.
It makes kings of all nations
stand up from their thrones to greet you.
[10]All these leaders will make fun of you
and will say,
"Now you are weak, as we are.
Now you are just like us."
[11]Your pride has been sent down to the place of the dead.
The music from your harps goes with it.
Flies are spread out like your bed beneath you,
and worms cover your body like a blanket.
[12]King of Babylon, morning star, you have fallen from heaven,

13:17 *armies of Media.* The people of Media were people from the Zagros mountain area. They actually helped Babylon overcome the Assyrians in 612 B.C. They were taken over by the Persians, who then took Babylon in 539 B.C.

13:19 *Sodom and Gomorrah.* The destruction of Sodom and Gomorrah for their horrific sin is described in Genesis 19.

13:20 At this time the Arab people were living like nomads in tents.

even though you were as bright as the rising
sun!
In the past all the nations on earth bowed
down before you,
but now you have been cut down.
13You told yourself,
"I will go up to heaven.
I will put my throne
above God's stars.
I will sit on the mountain of the gods,
on the slopes of the sacred mountain.
14I will go up above the tops of the clouds.
I will be like God Most High."
15But you were brought down to the grave,
to the deep places where the dead are.

16Those who see you stare at you.
They think about what has happened to you
and say, "Is this the same man who caused
great fear on earth,
who shook the kingdoms,
17who turned the world into a desert,
who destroyed its cities,
who captured people in war
and would not let them go home?"

18Every king of the earth has been buried
with honor,
each in his own grave.
19But you are thrown out of your grave,
like an unwanted branch.
You are covered by bodies
that died in battle,
by bodies to be buried in a rocky pit.
You are like a dead body other soldiers
walk on.
20 You will not be buried with those bodies,
because you ruined your own country
and killed your own people.
The children of evil people
will never be mentioned again.

21Prepare to kill his children,
because their father is guilty.
They will never again take control of the earth;
they will never again fill the world with
their cities.

22The LORD All-Powerful says this:
"I will fight against those people;
I will destroy Babylon and its people,
its children and their descendants," says
the LORD.
23"I will make Babylon fit only for owls
and for swamps.
I will sweep Babylon as with a broom
of destruction,"
says the LORD All-Powerful.

God Will Punish Assyria

24The LORD All-Powerful has made this promise:
"These things will happen exactly as I planned
them;
they will happen exactly as I set them up.
25I will destroy the king of Assyria in
my country;
I will trample him on my mountains.
He placed a heavy load on my people,
but that weight will be removed.

26"This is what I plan to do for all the earth.
And this is the hand that I have raised over
all nations."

27When the LORD All-Powerful makes a plan,
no one can stop it.
When the LORD raises his hand to punish people,
no one can stop it.

God's Message to Philistia

28This message was given in the year that King
Ahaz died:
29Country of Philistia, don't be happy
that the king who struck you is now dead.
He is like a snake that will give birth to
another dangerous snake.
The new king will be like a quick, dangerous
snake to bite you.
30Even the poorest of my people will be able to
eat safely,
and people in need will be able to lie down
in safety.
But I will kill your family with hunger,
and all your people who are left will die.

31People near the city gates, cry out!
Philistines, be frightened,
because a cloud of dust comes from
the north.
It is an army, full of men ready to fight.
32What shall we tell the messengers
from Philistia?
Say that the LORD has made
Jerusalem strong
and that his poor people will go there
for safety.

14:15 Demon: Ezekiel 28:11–19

14:27 Babylon: Isaiah 21:1–16

God's Message to Moab

15 This is a message about Moab:
In one night armies took the wealth from
Ar in Moab,
and it was destroyed.
In one night armies took the wealth from Kir
in Moab,
and it was destroyed.
2The people of Dibon go to the places of worship
to cry.
The people of Moab cry for the cities of Nebo
and Medeba.
Every head and beard has been shaved to show
how sad Moab is.
3In the streets they wear rough cloth to show
their sadness.
On the roofs and in the public squares,
they are crying loudly.
4People in the cities Heshbon and Elealeh cry
out loud.
You can hear their voices far away in the city
Jahaz.
Even the soldiers are frightened;
they are shaking with fear.

5My heart cries with sorrow for Moab.
Its people run away to Zoar for safety;
they run to Eglath Shelishiyah.
People are going up the mountain road to Luhith,
crying as they go.
People are going on the road to Horonaim,
crying over their destruction.
6But the water of Nimrim has dried up.
The grass has dried up,
and all the plants are dead;
nothing green is left.
7So the people gather up what they have saved
and carry it across the Ravine of the Poplars.
8Crying is heard everywhere in Moab.
Their crying is heard as far away as the
city Eglaim;
it is heard as far away as Beer Elim.
9The water of the city Dibon is full of blood,
and I, the LORD, will bring even more troubles
to Dibon.
A few people living in Moab have escaped
the enemy,
but I will send lions to kill them.

16 Send the king of the land
the payment he demands.
Send a lamb from Sela through the desert
to the mountain of Jerusalem.
2The women of Moab
try to cross the river Arnon
like little birds
that have fallen from their nest.

3They say: "Help us.
Tell us what to do.
Protect us from our enemies
as shade protects us from the noon sun.
Hide us, because we are running for safety!
Don't give us to our enemies.
4Let those of us who were forced out of Moab
live in your land.
Hide us from our enemies."

The robbing of Moab will stop.
The enemy will be defeated;
those who hurt others will disappear from
the land.
5Then a new loyal king will come;
this faithful king will be from the family
of David.
He will judge fairly
and do what is right.

6We have heard that the people of Moab
are proud
and very conceited.
They are very proud and angry,
but their bragging means nothing.
7So the people of Moab will cry;
they will all be sad.
They will moan and groan
for the raisin cakes they had in Kir Hareseth.
8But the fields of Heshbon and the vines of
Sibmah cannot grow grapes;
foreign rulers have destroyed the grapevines.
The grapevines once spread as far as the city of
Jazer and into the desert;
they had spread as far as the sea.
9I cry with the people of Jazer
for the grapevines of Sibmah.
I will cry with the people of Heshbon
and Elealeh.
There will be no shouts of joy,
because there will be no harvest or ripe fruit.
10There will be no joy and happiness in
the orchards
and no songs or shouts of joy in the vineyards.
No one makes wine in the winepresses,
because I have put an end to shouts of joy.

15:3 *roofs.* In Bible times houses were built with flat roofs. The roof was used for drying things such as flax and fruit. And it was used as an extra room, as a place for worship, and as a cool place to sleep in the summer.

[11]My heart cries for Moab like a harp playing a
funeral song;
I am very sad for Kir Hareseth.
[12]The people of Moab will go to their places of
worship
and will try to pray.
But when they go to their temple to pray,
they will not be able.

[13]Earlier the LORD said these things about Moab.
[14]Now the LORD says, "In three years all those
people and what they take pride in will be hated.
(This is three years as a hired helper would count
time.) There will be a few people left, but they will
be weak."

God's Message to Aram

17 This is a message about Damascus:
"The city of Damascus will be destroyed;
only ruins will remain.
[2]People will leave the cities of Aroer.
Flocks will wander freely in those
empty towns,
and there will be no one to bother them.
[3]The strong, walled cities of Israel will
be destroyed.
The government in Damascus will end.
Those left alive of Aram will be
like the glory of Israel," says the LORD
All-Powerful.

[4]"At that time Israel's wealth will all be gone.
Israel will be like someone who has lost
much weight from sickness.
[5]That time will be like the grain harvest in the
Valley of Rephaim.
The workers cut the wheat.
Then they cut the heads of grain from the plants
and collect the grain.
[6]That time will also be like the olive harvest,
when a few olives are left.
Two or three olives are left in the top branches.
Four or five olives are left on full branches,"
says the LORD, the God of Israel.

[7]At that time people will look to God, their
Maker;
their eyes will see the Holy One of Israel.
[8]They will not trust the altars they have made,
nor will they trust what their hands
have made,
not even the Asherah idols and altars.

[9]In that day all their strong cities will be empty.
They will be like the cities the Hivites and the
Amorites left when the Israelites came to take the
land. Everything will be ruined.

[10]You have forgotten the God who saves you;
you have not remembered that God is your
place of safety.
You plant the finest grapevines
and grapevines from faraway places.
[11]You plant your grapevines one day and try to
make them grow,
and the next day you make them blossom.
But at harvest time everything will be dead;
a sickness will kill all the plants.

[12]Listen to the many people!
Their crying is like the noise from the sea.
Listen to the nations!
Their crying is like the crashing of great waves.
[13]The people roar like the waves,
but when God speaks harshly to them, they
will run away.
They will be like chaff on the hills being blown
by the wind,
or like tumbleweeds blown away by a storm.
[14]At night the people will be very frightened.
Before morning, no one will be left.
So our enemies will come to our land,
but they will become nothing.

God's Message to Cush

18 How terrible it will be for the land beyond
the rivers of Cush.
It is filled with the sound of wings.
[2]That land sends messengers across the sea;
they go on the water in boats made of reeds.

Go, quick messengers,
to a people who are tall and smooth-skinned,
who are feared everywhere.
They are a powerful nation that defeats other
nations.
Their land is divided by rivers.

[3]All you people of the world, look!
Everyone who lives in the world, look!
You will see a banner raised on a mountain.
You will hear a trumpet sound.
[4]The LORD said to me,
"I will quietly watch from where I live,
like heat in the sunshine,

17:13 *chaff.* Chaff is a dry, rootless vegetation that is blown around by the wind. It symbolizes people without purpose or meaning and apart from God.

18:1 *Cush.* Cush is the region of southern Egypt and beyond, including what we call today the Sudan.

EVANGELISM

MATTHEW 28:16–20

What is evangelism? What different perspectives are brought to bear on this question between the Testaments and even between various New Testament books? Can one locate different models for engaging in evangelism in the Bible?

The word *evangelism* comes from a Greek word which means "good news." Those who spread this Good News through their words and actions are evangelists, messengers of good news. Although the word *evangelism* often conjures up pictures of preachers on television or passionate proselytizing on street corners, the Bible provides various models of evangelism.

Compared to the New Testament, the Old Testament has relatively few stories about people specifically sent out as messengers of God's Good News to people who do not know him. But God consistently makes his name and reputation known to non-Jewish people (1 Kings 18:1–40; 2 Kings 5:1–15; Nehemiah 6:15–16). God's purpose for the people of the world is evidenced in his promise to Abram: "All the people on earth will be blessed through you" (Genesis 12:3). According to Isaiah, the message from God to the world includes preaching Good News to the poor, comforting the broken hearted, freeing captives, and declaring the year of God's favor (Isaiah 61:1–2).

Jonah is an Old Testament evangelist, of sorts. He spent three days and three nights inside a big fish because of his refusal to obey God and preach to the great city of Nineveh. The reluctant messenger finally made his way to Nineveh and preached that God was about to destroy the city because of its evil. The people of Nineveh believed his words and repented, and thus, the city and its inhabitants were spared. Despite Jonah's direct disobedience, God's purpose was accomplished.

In the New Testament, the Good News of Jesus Christ is spread through both words and actions. Jesus preached and taught in towns and villages, and many were drawn to follow him because his teaching was with unique authority (Mark 1:27). Jesus also spread the Good News through his actions, both in demonstrations of power in miraculous healings (Matthew 8:1–4) and in his associations with all kinds of people. The despised tax collector Zacchaeus came to faith through Jesus' coming to his house (Luke 19:1–10).

Often Jesus does not directly answer challenges to his authenticity or power. Instead he invited those who wanted to know him to interact and associate with him. He invited two of his earliest followers to "come and see" what he is about. Another follower of Jesus, Philip, is questioned by a skeptic, Nathanael. When questioned about Jesus' authenticity, Philip responded as Jesus did. Rather than arguing, Philip simply invited Nathanael to "come and see" (John 1:35–51).

Early in his ministry, Jesus promised that those who follow him would become people who would follow him would become people who draw others toward God. In Mark 1:16–18 Jesus saw Simon and Andrew and said, "Come follow me, and I will make you fish for people." In Matthew 5:13–16 Jesus called his followers the "light of the world" and "salt of the earth." The follower of Jesus is to not only talk about the Good News, but is to embody it in his or her life and actions.

Evangelism, spreading the Good News about Jesus, is not relegated to a select few or to particular personality types. In Mark 5:1–20 Jesus heals a man tortured by a host of demons. This man, who had spent many demon-possessed years wandering through burial caves and cutting himself with rocks, was sent back to his community with the following command from Jesus: "Go home to your family and tell them how much the Lord has done for you and how he has had mercy on you" (verse 19).

The Samaritan woman in John 4 was another likely evangelist. She had a bad reputation, but her message about Jesus influenced many to hear him for themselves. After hearing him they told the woman, "First we believed in Jesus because of your speech, but now we believe because we heard him ourselves. We know that this man really is the Savior of the world" (John 4:42). The New Testament is filled with people who experienced the Good News and drew others to Jesus, not through complex techniques or arguments, but simply by describing to others what they themselves have experienced as they believed the Good News of Jesus' death, burial, and resurrection (1 Corinthians 15:3–4).

After his resurrection, Jesus promised his followers that they will spread his message throughout the entire world. "All power in heaven and on earth is given to me. So go and make followers of all people in the world" (Matthew 28: 18–19).

Evangelism: For additional scriptures on this topic go to 1 Kings 18:1–40.

MISSION

MATTHEW 28:16–20

According to Scripture, what do we mean by mission? What are its foundations? Its end? In what ways do biblical models suggest ways in which our groups might be involved in mission today?

The mission of God's people is a central part of what God is doing in the world. The Bible tells us that God created human beings and that they enjoyed a harmonious relationship with him. However, human beings rebelled against their Maker, creating a huge gulf between them. Though the earth then became a bad place, God set about to remake the world into a new heaven and a new earth through his activity of forgiveness, guidance, and judgment at the end of the age. The center of God's grand plan is the death and resurrection of Jesus Christ. To share in God's grand plan of salvation, we must confess our sinfulness and turn to Jesus Christ for our salvation. The core of mission is to share this crucial message with everyone.

Since the time of Abraham, God has chosen men and women to be part of that saving process by sharing his plan with others. The descendants of Israel were God's chosen people, given the blessings of many descendants, a rich land, and the Law. God's special relationship with Israel was to be the way in which God's truth and love would be shared with everyone. During this time, Israel was to be a city on a hill. Their devotion and prosperity were to be so appealing that many other people would come to them to meet God. Occasionally, this would happen (think of Rahab [Joshua 2] and Naaman [2 Kings 5] and the people of Nineveh in the Book of Jonah), but on the whole, Israel was disobedient and failed at their task. Their failure makes us yearn for something better.

When Christ came, the angels announced that this was Good News not to just to Israel, but to all humankind (Luke 2:14). Christ started his ministry by announcing the kingdom of God first to the Jewish people. Gradually, the offer of salvation was made to Samaritans, a Roman centurion, and other outsiders. Still, Christianity was primarily a Jewish mission.

In the Great Commission which comes in Matthew 28:16–20, the risen Christ tells the disciples that they were to "make followers of all people in the world." Put simply, the mission of all Christians is to make followers of everyone who will accept God's offer of salvation. This includes a large number of activities, all geared to preparing people to receive his offer.

For example, persons may be prepared to know and trust the love of God through receiving food or money or education or friendship or some other valuable gift. James 2:15–16 says we must feed and clothe persons in addition to wishing them well. Mission must also include being a witness to God's great plan of salvation, accomplished through the work of Christ. After all, as Paul says, "Before people can ask the Lord for help, they must believe in him; and before they can believe in him, they must hear about him; and for them to hear about the Lord, someone must tell them; and before someone can go and tell them, that person must be sent" (Romans 10:14–15). When we are witnesses for Christ, we talk about the God whom we have met in the Bible and experienced in our own lives. We tell them particularly about the death, burial, and resurrection of Jesus. First Peter 3:15 says that we should always be ready "to answer everyone who asks you to explain about the hope you have." Many times the story of a sincere layperson is more convincing than the most learned and scholarly sermon any pastor could preach.

When mission is understood as making followers, it also includes helping them grow in the faith. When we first give our lives to Christ, that is not the end of the process. It is only an important step in the journey of a lifetime. The Bible talks about baby Christians and mature Christians, and we should always be pressing on toward maturity. Through education and many other means, we grow in our faith, in our hope, and in our love. Being sent out in mission is one of the ways in which we grow ourselves. Sometimes Christians engaged in mission receive as big a blessing as the people they actually serve in Christ's name.

The foundation of mission is God's love for the whole world. Because of that, God sends us out so that everyone is cared for. Christ sent out the seventy (Luke 10:1). In Acts 1:8, Christ told the disciples they were to be witnesses for him "in every part of the world." God's plan is clear. Since those who do not accept him will be judged for their sins, he intends to offer salvation to every human being. That means we are called to be in mission in every place possible. It does not matter what race, nation, economic status, or previous religion the person has. Everyone is loved by God, and because of that universal love we should be in mission to the whole world.

Mission: For additional scriptures on this topic go to Genesis 12:1–3.

like the dew in the heat of harvest time."
5The time will come, after the flowers have
bloomed and before the harvest,
when new grapes will be budding and growing.
The enemy will cut the plants with knives;
he will cut down the vines and take
them away.
6They will be left for the birds of the mountains
and for the wild animals.
Birds will feed on them all summer,
and wild animals will eat them
that winter."

7At that time a gift will be brought to the LORD
All-Powerful
from the people who are tall and
smooth-skinned,
who are feared everywhere.
They are a powerful nation that defeats
other nations.
Their land is divided by rivers.
These gifts will be brought to the place of the
LORD All-Powerful,
to Mount Zion.

God's Message to Egypt

19 This is a message about Egypt:
Look, the LORD is coming on a fast cloud
to enter Egypt.
The idols of Egypt will tremble before him,
and Egypt's courage will melt away.

2The LORD says, "I will cause the Egyptians to
fight against themselves.
People will fight with their relatives;
neighbors will fight neighbors;
cities will fight cities;
kingdoms will fight kingdoms.
3The Egyptians will be afraid,
and I will ruin their plans.
They will ask advice from their idols and spirits
of the dead,
from their mediums and fortune-tellers."
4The Lord GOD All-Powerful says,
"I will hand Egypt over to a hard master,
and a powerful king will rule over them."

5The sea will become dry,
and the water will disappear from the
Nile River.
6The canals will stink;
the streams of Egypt will decrease and dry up.
All the water plants will rot;
7 all the plants along the banks of the Nile
will die.
Even the planted fields by the Nile
will dry up, blow away, and disappear.
8The fishermen, all those who catch fish from
the Nile,
will groan and cry;
those who fish in the Nile will be sad.
9All the people who make cloth from flax will
be sad,
and those who weave linen will lose hope.
10Those who weave cloth will be broken.
All those who work for money will be sad.

11The officers of the city of Zoan are fools;
the wise men who advise the king of Egypt
give wrong advice.
How can you say to him, 'I am wise'?
How can you say, 'I am from the old family of
the kings'?
12Egypt, where are your wise men?
Let them show you
what the LORD All-Powerful has planned
for Egypt.
13The officers of Zoan have been fooled;
the leaders of Memphis have believed
false things.
So the leaders of Egypt
lead that nation the wrong way.
14The LORD has made the leaders confused.
They have led Egypt to wander in the
wrong ways,
like drunk people stumbling in their
own vomit.
15There is nothing Egypt can do;
no one there can help.

16In that day the Egyptians will be like women.
They will be afraid of the LORD All-Powerful,
because he will raise his hand to strike them down.
17The land of Judah will bring fear to Egypt. Anyone
there who hears the name Judah will be afraid,
because the LORD All-Powerful has planned terrible
things for them. 18At that time five cities in Egypt
will speak Hebrew, the language of Canaan, and
they will promise to be loyal to the LORD All-
Powerful. One of these cities will be named the
City of Destruction. 19At that time there will be
an altar for the LORD in the middle of Egypt and a
monument to the LORD at the border of Egypt.
20This will be a sign and a witness to the LORD All-
Powerful in the land of Egypt. When the people
cry to the LORD for help, he will send someone to

19:1 *on a fast cloud.* God is often seen riding a cloud into judgment. It is his war chariot.

save and defend them. He will rescue them from
those who hurt them.
21So the LORD will show himself to the Egyptians,
and then they will know he is the LORD. They will
worship God and offer many sacrifices. They
will make promises to the LORD and will keep them.
22The LORD will punish the Egyptians, but then he
will heal them. They will come back to the LORD,
and he will listen to their prayers and heal them.
23At that time there will be a highway from Egypt
to Assyria, and the Assyrians will go to Egypt, and
the Egyptians will go to Assyria. The Egyptians and
Assyrians will worship God together. 24At that time
Israel, Assyria, and Egypt will join together, which
will be a blessing for the earth. 25The LORD All-
Powerful will bless them, saying, "Egypt, you are
my people. Assyria, I made you. Israel, I own you.
You are all blessed!"

Assyria Will Defeat Egypt and Cush

20 Sargon king of Assyria sent a military commander to Ashdod to attack that city. So
the commander attacked and captured it. 2Then
the LORD spoke through Isaiah son of Amoz, saying, "Take the rough cloth off your body, and take
your sandals off your feet." So Isaiah obeyed and
walked around naked and barefoot.
3Then the LORD said, "Isaiah my servant has
walked around naked and barefoot for three years
as a sign against Egypt and Cush. 4The king of
Assyria will carry away prisoners from Egypt and
Cush. Old people and young people will be led
away naked and barefoot, with their buttocks bare.
So the Egyptians will be shamed. 5People who
looked to Cush for help will be afraid, and those
who were amazed by Egypt's glory will be shamed.
6People who live near the sea will say, 'Look at
those countries. We trusted them to help us. We
ran to them so they would save us from the king of
Assyria. So how will we be able to escape?'"

God's Message to Babylon

21 This is a message about the Desert by the
Sea:
Disaster is coming from the desert
like wind blowing in the south.
It is coming from a terrible country.
2I have seen a terrible vision.
I see traitors turning against you
and people taking your wealth.

Elam, attack the people!
Media, surround the city and attack it!
I will bring an end to the pain the city causes.
3I saw those terrible things, and now I am
in pain;
my pains are like the pains of giving birth.
What I hear makes me very afraid;
what I see causes me to shake with fear.
4I am worried,
and I am shaking with fear.
My pleasant evening
has become a night of fear.

5They set the table;
they spread the rugs;
they eat and drink.
Leaders, stand up.
Prepare the shields for battle!

6The Lord said to me,
"Go, place a lookout for the city
and have him report what he sees.
7If he sees chariots and teams of horses,
donkeys, or camels,
he should pay very close attention."

8Then the lookout called out,
"My master, each day I stand in the
watchtower watching;
every night I have been on guard.
9Look, I see a man coming in a chariot
with a team of horses."
The man gives back the answer,
"Babylon has fallen. It has fallen!
All the statues of her gods
lie broken on the ground."
10My people are crushed like grain on the
threshing floor.
My people, I tell you what I have heard
from the LORD All-Powerful,
from the God of Israel.

God's Message to Edom

11This is a message about Dumah:
Someone calls to me from Edom,
"Watchman, how much of the night is left?
Watchman, how much longer will it be night?"
12The watchman answers,
"Morning is coming, but then night will
come again.
If you have something to ask,
then come back and ask."

God's Message to Arabia

13This is a message about Arabia:

21:1. *Desert by the Sea.* Probably Babylon.

21:11 *Dumah.* Another name for Edom.

A group of traders from Dedan
spent the night near some trees in Arabia.
14 They gave water to thirsty travelers;
the people of Tema gave food
to those who were escaping.
15They were running from swords,
from swords ready to kill,
from bows ready to shoot,
from a hard battle.

16This is what the Lord said to me: "In one year
all the glory of the country of Kedar will be gone.
(This is a year as a hired helper counts time.)⚭
17At that time only a few of the archers, the soldiers
of Kedar, will be left alive." The LORD, the God of
Israel, has spoken.

God's Message to Jerusalem

22 This is a message about the Valley of Vision:
What is wrong with you people?
Why are you on your roofs?
2This city was a very busy city,
full of noise and wild parties.
Now your people have been killed,
but not with swords,
nor did they die in battle.
3All your leaders ran away together,
but they have been captured without using
a bow.
All you who were captured
tried to run away before the enemy came.
4So I say, "Don't look at me.
Let me cry loudly.
Don't hurry to comfort me
about the destruction of Jerusalem."
5The Lord GOD All-Powerful has chosen a
special day
of riots and confusion.
People will trample each other in the Valley
of Vision.
The city walls will be knocked down,
and the people will cry out to
the mountain.
6The soldiers from Elam will gather
their arrows
and their chariots and men on horses.
Kir will prepare their shields.
7Your nicest valleys will be filled with chariots.
Horsemen will be ordered to guard the gates
of the city.
8 The walls protecting Judah will fall.
At that time the people of Jerusalem
depended on
the weapons kept at the Palace of the Forest.
9You saw that the walls of Jerusalem
had many cracks that needed repairing.
You stored up water in the lower pool.
10You counted the houses of Jerusalem,
and you tore down houses to repair the walls
with their stones.
11You made a pool between the two walls
to save water from the old pool,
but you did not trust the God who made
these things;
you did not respect the One who planned
them long ago.

12The Lord GOD All-Powerful told the people
to cry and be sad,
to shave their heads and wear rough cloth.
13But look, the people are happy
and are having wild parties.
They kill the cattle and the sheep;
they eat the food and drink the wine.
They say, "Let us eat and drink,
because tomorrow we will die."

14The LORD All-Powerful said to me: "You people
will die before this guilt is forgiven." The Lord GOD
All-Powerful said this.

God's Message to Shebna

15This is what the Lord GOD All-Powerful says:
"Go to this servant Shebna,
the manager of the palace.
16Say to him, 'What are you doing here?
Who said you could cut out a tomb for your
self here?
Why are you preparing your tomb in a
high place?
Why are you carving out a tomb from the rock?
17Look, mighty one! The LORD will throw
you away.
He will take firm hold of you
18and roll you tightly into a ball
and throw you into another country.
There you will die,
and there your fine chariots will remain.
You are a disgrace to your master's house.
19I will force you out of your important job,
and you will be thrown down from your
important place.'

⚭**21:16 Babylon:** Daniel 4:30
22:1 *Valley of Vision.* This probably means a valley near Jerusalem.
22:1 *roofs.* In Bible times houses were built with flat roofs. The roof was used for drying things such as flax and fruit. And it was used as an extra room, as a place for worship, and as a cool place to sleep in the summer.

[20]"At that time I will call for my servant Eliakim
son of Hilkiah. [21]I will take your robe and put it on
him and give him your belt. I will hand over to him
the important job you have, and he will be like a
father to the people of Jerusalem and the family of
Judah. [22]I will put the key to the house of David
around his neck. If he opens a door, no one will be
able to close it; if he closes a door, no one will
be able to open it. [23]He will be like an honored chair
in his father's house. I will make him strong like a
peg that is hammered into a strong board. [24]All the
honored and important things of his family will
depend on him; all the adults and little children will
depend on him. They will be like bowls and jars
hanging on him.

[25]"At that time," says the LORD All-Powerful, "the
peg hammered into the strong board will weaken.
It will break and fall, and everything hanging on it
will be destroyed." The LORD says this.

The harbor at present-day Sidon

God's Message to Lebanon

23 This is a message about Tyre:
You trading ships, cry!
The houses and harbor of Tyre are destroyed.
This news came to the ships
from the land of Cyprus.
[2]Be silent, you who live on the island of Tyre;
you merchants of Sidon, be silent.
Sailors have made you rich.
[3]They traveled the sea to bring grain
from Egypt;
the sailors of Tyre brought grain from the
Nile Valley
and sold it to other nations.

[4]Sidon, be ashamed.
Strong city of the sea, be ashamed, because
the sea says:
"I have not felt the pain of giving birth;
I have not reared young men or women."
[5]Egypt will hear the news about Tyre,
and it will make Egypt hurt with sorrow.

[6]You ships should return to Tarshish.
You people living near the sea should be sad.
[7]Look at your once happy city!
Look at your old, old city!
People from that city have traveled
far away to live.
[8]Who planned Tyre's destruction?
Tyre made others rich.
Its merchants were treated like princes,
and its traders were greatly respected.
[9]It was the LORD All-Powerful who planned this.
He decided to make these proud
people unimportant;
he decided to disgrace those who were
greatly respected.
[10]Go through your land, people of Tarshish,
like the Nile goes through Egypt.
There is no harbor for you now!
[11]The LORD has stretched his hand
over the sea
and made its kingdoms tremble.
He commands that Canaan's
strong, walled cities be destroyed.
[12]He said, "Sidon, you will not rejoice any longer,
because you are destroyed.
Even if you cross the sea to Cyprus,
you will not find a place to rest."
[13]Look at the land of the Babylonians;
it is not a country now.
Assyria has made it a place for wild animals.
Assyria built towers to attack it;
the soldiers took all the treasures from its cities,
and they turned it into ruins.
[14]So be sad, you trading ships,
because your strong city is destroyed.

[15]At that time people will forget about Tyre for
seventy years, which is the length of a king's life.
After seventy years, Tyre will be like the prostitute in this song:

[16]"Oh woman, you are forgotten.
Take your harp and walk through the city.
Play your harp well. Sing your song often.
Then people will remember you."

[17]After seventy years the LORD will deal with
Tyre, and it will again have trade. It will be like a
prostitute for all the nations of the earth. [18]The profits will be saved for the LORD. Tyre will not keep the
money she earns but will give them to the people
who serve the LORD, so they will have plenty of
food and nice clothes.

The Lord Will Punish the World

24 Look! The LORD will destroy the earth and
leave it empty;
he will ruin the surface of the land and scatter
its people.
2At that time the same thing will happen
to everyone:
to common people and priests,
to slaves and masters,
to women slaves and their women masters,
to buyers and sellers,
to those who borrow and those who lend,
to bankers and those who owe the bank.
3The earth will be completely empty.
The wealth will all be taken,
because the LORD has commanded it.
4The earth will dry up and die;
the world will grow weak and die;
the great leaders in this land will
become weak.
5The people of the earth have ruined it,
because they do not follow God's teachings
or obey God's laws
or keep their agreement with God that was
to last forever.
6So a curse will destroy the earth.
The people of the world are guilty,
so they will be burned up;
only a few will be left.
7The new wine will be bad, and the grapevines
will die.
People who were happy will be sad.
8The happy music of the tambourines will end.
The happy sounds of wild parties will stop.
The joyful music from the harps will end.
9People will no longer sing while they drink
their wine.
The beer will taste bitter to those who drink it.
10The ruined city will be empty,
and people will hide behind closed doors.
11People in the streets will ask for wine,
but joy will have turned to sadness;
all the happiness will have left.
12The city will be left in ruins,
and its gates will be smashed to pieces.
13This is what will happen all over the earth
and to all the nations.
The earth will be like an olive tree after
the harvest
or like the few grapes left on a vine
after harvest.
14The people shout for joy.
From the west they praise the greatness of
the LORD.
15People in the east, praise the LORD.
People in the islands of the sea,
praise the name of the LORD, the God of Israel.
16We hear songs from every part of the earth
praising God, the Righteous One.

But I said, "I am dying! I am dying!
How terrible it will be for me!
Traitors turn against people;
with their dishonesty, they turn
against people."
17There are terrors, holes, and traps
for the people of the earth.
18Anyone who tries to escape from the sound
of terror
will fall into a hole.
Anyone who climbs out of the hole
will be caught in a trap.
The clouds in the sky will pour out rain,
and the foundations of the earth
will shake.
19The earth will be broken up;
the earth will split open;
the earth will shake violently.
20The earth will stumble around like someone
who is drunk;
it will shake like a hut in a storm.
Its sin is like a heavy weight on its back;
it will fall and never rise again.

21At that time the LORD will punish
the powers in the sky above
and the rulers on earth below.
22They will be gathered together
like prisoners thrown into a dungeon;
they will be shut up in prison.
After much time they will be punished.
23The moon will be embarrassed,
and the sun will be ashamed,
because the LORD All-Powerful will
rule as king
on Mount Zion in Jerusalem.
Jerusalem's leaders will see his greatness.

A Song of Praise to God

25 LORD, you are my God.
I honor you and praise you,
because you have done amazing things.

24:5 Agreement: Hosea 6:7
24:10 *The ruined city.* The unnamed city may be a reference to Jerusalem, but the context also indicates that it could mean the "world city" and point to the judgment of the entire earth.

24:13 The Remnant: Jeremiah 31:7

24:23 *Mount Zion.* Mount Zion was the location of the Temple, which represented God's presence with his people.

You have always done what you said you
would do;
you have done what you planned long ago.
2 You have made the city a pile of rocks
and have destroyed her walls.
The city our enemies built with strong walls
is gone;
it will never be built again.
3 People from powerful nations will honor you;
cruel people from strong cities will fear you.
4 You protect the poor;
you protect the helpless when they are
in danger.
You are like a shelter from storms,
like shade that protects them from the heat.
The cruel people attack
like a rainstorm beating against the wall,
5 like the heat in the desert.
But you, God, stop their violent attack.
As a cloud cools a hot day,
you silence the songs of those who have
no mercy.

God's Banquet for His Servants

6 The LORD All-Powerful will prepare a feast
on this mountain for all people.
It will be a feast with all the best food and wine,
the finest meat and wine.
7 On this mountain God will destroy
the veil that covers all nations,
the veil that stretches over all peoples;
8 he will destroy death forever.
The Lord GOD will wipe away every tear from
every face.
He will take away the shame of his people
from the earth.
The LORD has spoken.

9 At that time people will say,
"Our God is doing this!
We have waited for him, and he has come to
save us.
This is the LORD. We waited for him,
so we will rejoice and be happy when he
saves us."
10 The LORD will protect Jerusalem,
but he will crush our enemy Moab
like straw that is trampled down in
the manure.
11 They will spread their arms in it
like a person who is swimming.
But God will bring down their pride,
and all the clever things they have made will
mean nothing.
12 Moab's high walls protect them,
but God will destroy these walls.
He will throw them down to the ground,
even to the dust.

A Song of Praise to God

26 At that time people will sing this song
in Judah:
We have a strong city.
God protects us with its strong walls
and defenses.
2 Open the gates,
and the good people will enter,
those who follow God.
3 You, LORD, give true peace
to those who depend on you,
because they trust you.
4 So, trust the LORD always,
because he is our Rock forever.
5 He will destroy the proud city,
and he will punish the people living there.
He will bring that high city down to
the ground
and throw it down into the dust.
6 Then those who were hurt by the city will
walk on its ruins;
those who were made poor by the city will
trample it under their feet.

7 The path of life is level for those who are right
with God;
LORD, you make the way of life smooth for
those people.
8 But, LORD, we are waiting
for your way of justice.
Our souls want to remember
you and your name.
9 My soul wants to be with you at night,
and my spirit wants to be with you at the
dawn of every day.
When your way of justice comes to the land,
people of the world will learn the right way
of living.
10 Evil people will not learn to do good
even if you show them kindness.
They will continue doing evil, even if they live
in a good world;
they never see the LORD's greatness.
11 LORD, you are ready to punish those people,

25:6 Alcohol: Daniel 5:1–6
25:7 Table Fellowship/Lord's Supper: Matthew 9:10–11
25:7 Mountain: Isaiah 40:9–11
25:8 Heaven: Isaiah 35
26:1 *a strong city.* The strong city may be a reference to redeemed Jerusalem or a way of referring to the community of the faithful.

TRINITY

MATTHEW 28:18–20

Does the Bible teach the Trinity? Why do Christians believe in the Trinity, and what does it mean for everyday life?

For many Christian believers, the doctrine of the Trinity either seems far removed from everyday life or is hard to find in the direct teachings of Scripture. In fact, the Trinity was developed as a teaching of the church in relation to the Christian life (specifically how to be saved) and is based on specific biblical approvals.

The Trinity is based on two teachings of the Bible: First of all, there is only one God, confessed in Deuteronomy 6:4, "Listen, people of Israel! The LORD our God is the only LORD," and stated most directly in the later chapters of Isaiah; for example, "I am God. There is no other God" (Isaiah 45:22). This one God is, therefore, the only being worthy of our worship: "Don't worship any other god, because I, the LORD, the Jealous One, am a jealous God" (Exodus 34:14). Second, the Father, the Son, and the Holy Spirit are all said to be divine, or to be God. This leads to a simple definition of the Trinity: God exists in three persons, but is one in being. This three-in-oneness is reflected in Matthew 28:19, where the disciples are commanded to baptize in "the name" (in the singular, representing God's oneness or unity) "of the Father and the Son and the Holy Spirit" (the three persons of the Godhead).

The teaching of the Trinity should be differentiated from seeing God as a simple *unity* (for example, that God merely comes to earth in different modes or ways) or *tritheism* (that there are three gods). The Trinity is a more complex doctrine than these two ideas and is therefore harder to uphold. The first error and tendency (of a strict unity) has been a more frequent problem in the history of theology. Analogies from common experience may help in understanding the Trinity, but all lead to some misunderstanding. For example, an analogy used early in church history was that of ice, water, and fire (for Father, Son, and Holy Spirit, respectively), but this analogy may mislead a person into thinking of God in different modes.

Some attempts have been made to find the Trinity in the Old Testament, either in God's self-reference as a plurality (the "*our* image" of Genesis 1:26) or in early appearances of angels, sometimes called appearances of Christ (Genesis 16:7, 13; Judges 6:11; 22–23). These texts do not *directly* teach, however, that God is Trinity, but they do offer indirect support for the doctrine of the Trinity.

The need for an understanding of God as three-in-one begins with the New Testament understanding of Jesus Christ. John 1:1 describes Christ as "the Word" (which also could be translated "speech" or "reason" or "pattern") and says, "In the beginning there was the Word. The Word was with God [so there is some distinction], and the Word was God [so is also divine]." John 1:14 declares that this Word "became a human and lived among us," and then, in verse 17, that the name of the Word is "Jesus Christ." In this chapter is contained the basis for the Trinity from the New Testament: Christ is the Word, who is both distinct from God the Father, and yet is God. Accordingly, Jesus' special relation with God (Matthew 11:27; John 10:30) and his divinity (John 20:28; Colossians 2:9) can be found in other parts of Scripture.

The early church was not primarily concerned with a number puzzle (how three could be one and one three), but with whether Christ could truly *save* human beings. Human beings cannot rescue themselves from the state of brokenness and sin, and thus need divine help. Jesus has to be God in order to have power to release women and men from their sin. Thus, Paul and Silas tell their jailer, "Believe in the Lord Jesus and you will be saved" (Acts 16:31). This human need for a divine Savior finds its answer in Christ.

The importance and divinity of the Spirit receives less biblical treatment than in the case of the Son, or Jesus. The Bible takes up the nature of the Spirit (as in the case of Jesus) from a practical, and not an abstract, perspective. The Spirit is distinct from Jesus and the Father, since all three are manifested together at the baptism of Jesus (Matthew 3:16–17), and yet the work of the Spirit and the work of Jesus are bound together (John 14:25–26; 15:26–27; Acts 16:6–7; Galatians 4:6).

Finally, the everyday significance of the Trinity for believers today is that God is a being of love who exists eternally in the three persons of the Godhead. This God has really interacted in the created order in Jesus Christ and through the ongoing presence of the Spirit. Christians are invited to participate in this love not only individually, but especially as a community, the church. The promise of the Trinity is that God is not far off, but holds all creation near in love. The call for all people is to enter willingly into this perfect Love.

Trinity: For additional scriptures on this topic go to Genesis 16:7–14.

Gospel/Good News

Mark 1

What is the Gospel?
What form(s) might the Gospel take in contemporary interaction with people?

"That's what he said, but I wouldn't take it as gospel." "The Book of John is the fourth Gospel." "I've always liked Gospel music." These contemporary usages of the word *gospel* do not tell us much about the biblical concept of *gospel* (or Good News). In the ancient world, "good news" was used to describe an announcement of victory and the reward that went to the messenger who brought it; later, it came to apply to other joyful messages. It is not surprising, then, that the biblical writers appropriated this term for the message of the greatest victory and ultimate joy.

The biblical idea of Good News is rooted in the fact that God is the King of everything, and that he will exercise his Kingship to make things right in this fallen creation. Here is the Good News:

• The Lord God is King, and he is coming to free the oppressed (Isaiah 40:3, 9; 52:7–10; 61:1–2)!

• In the coming of Jesus, the kingdom of God is at hand (Mark 1:14–15).

• God is saving us through the work of Christ, who died for our sins according to the Scriptures, was buried, and raised to life on the third day according to the Scriptures (1 Corinthians 15:1–4).

• This salvation is demonstrated in the here-and-now as God releases the captives, heals the sick, comforts the wounded, and liberates the oppressed (Isaiah 61:1–9; Luke 4:18–19). It will be consummated in a time when God remakes heaven and earth, and vanquishes death, pain, and sorrow (Revelation 21:1–4).

• Because of this, even the call to change our hearts and lives is Good News because it prepares the way for the King to come (Isaiah 40:3–4; Mark 1:15; Luke 3:7–18).

When Jesus began his public ministry, he came preaching the Good News: the kingdom of God is near (1:14–15)! This preaching is more than the verbal proclamation of a message—it's show-and-tell! Jesus not only *tells* Good News, he *performs* Good News by demonstrating the saving rule of God in the here-and-now. His Good News speaks to every human need; it refuses to be compartmentalized as merely "spiritual." He sets free those who are oppressed by evil spirits (1:21–28; 5:1–20). He heals the sick (1:29–34). He forgives sins (2:1–12). He relates to outsiders: a leper (1:40–45), a tax collector (2:13–14), a group of sinners (2:15–17), an unclean woman (5:25–34), a non-Jew (7:24–30)—all thought to be outside of God's grace—and personally offers healing and membership in his family (3:31–35). He calms a storm (4:35–41). He raises the dead (5:35–43). He challenges the values, vision, and authority of political and religious leaders (2:18–28; 3:1–6). Jesus' Good News meets every human need: physical, spiritual, emotional, social. And that is just in the first few chapters of Mark!

After Jesus' death and resurrection, there is a shift in the usage of "Good News." Jesus, the proclaimer of the Good News, becomes the center of the Good News message, which is called the "Good News about Jesus Christ, the Son of God" (Mark 1:1; see also Romans 1:9), the "Good News of Christ" (2 Corinthians 2:12), and the "Good News about the glory of Christ" (2 Corinthians 4:4). This Good News about Jesus asserts that in his coming, his life, his death, and his resurrection, Jesus has won the victory over sin, death, and evil, and has fulfilled the promise to Abraham to bless all the nations (Colossians 1:13–22; Galatians 3:8; see also Genesis 12:1–3). The root is still the same: God is the King who has come to exercise his Kingship to set free all of creation from bondage. But now, the plant has flowered, and we can see *how* God has won the decisive battle: through Jesus' coming and redemptive work.

How can we faithfully live out the Good News today, especially in interaction with others? First things first—we need to change our hearts and lives and to acknowledge that Jesus is the King (Mark 1:15). That does not mean we will be perfect, but we need to acknowledge that he is the One with the right to have the final say in our lives—otherwise, how can we call him "Lord" (Luke 6:46)? There is no Good News apart from submitting to Jesus as King; the Good News is to be obeyed (John 3:36; Romans 1:5; 16:26; 1 Peter 4:17). But when we yield ourselves to him, our lives are transformed. We are not only forgiven by God and adopted into his family (Colossians 1:13–14; John 1:12), we also become agents of the Good News—channels through which he demonstrates his rule and makes things right (John 20:21).

We become agents of the Good News when we serve as God's representatives in the world, which means that we must share God's love with people in a way that demonstrates the rule of God in the here-and-now in meeting human needs.

Gospel/Good News: For additional scriptures on this topic go to Isaiah 40:1–11.

but they do not see that.
Show them your strong love for your people.
Then those who are evil will be ashamed.
Burn them in the fire
you have prepared for your enemies.
12LORD, all our success is because of what you have done,
so give us peace.
13LORD, our God, other masters besides you have ruled us,
but we honor only you.
14Those masters are now dead;
their ghosts will not rise from death.
You punished and destroyed them
and erased any memory of them.
15LORD, you multiplied the number of your people;
you multiplied them and brought honor to yourself.
You made the borders of the land wide.
16LORD, people remember you when they are in trouble;
they say quiet prayers to you when you punish them.
17LORD, when we are with you,
we are like a woman giving birth to a baby;
she cries and has pain from the birth.
18In the same way, we had pain.
We gave birth, but only to wind.
We don't bring salvation to the land
or make new people for the world.
19Your people have died, but they will live again;
their bodies will rise from death.
You who lie in the ground,
wake up and be happy!
The dew covering you is like the dew of a new day;
the ground will give birth to the dead.

Judgment: Reward or Punishment

20My people, go into your rooms
and shut your doors behind you.
Hide in your rooms for a short time
until God's anger is finished.
21The LORD will leave his place
to punish the people of the world for their sins.
The earth will show the blood of the people who have been killed;
it will not cover the dead any longer.

27 At that time the LORD will punish
Leviathan, the gliding snake.
He will punish Leviathan, the coiled snake,
with his great and hard and powerful sword.
He will kill the monster in the sea.

2At that time
people will sing about the pleasant vineyard.
3"I, the LORD, will care for that vineyard;
I will water it at the right time.
No one will hurt it,
because I will guard it day and night.
4I am not angry.
If anyone builds a wall of thornbushes in war,
I will march to it and burn it.
5But if anyone comes to me for safety
and wants to make peace with me,
he should come and make peace with me."
6In the days to come, the people of Jacob will be like a plant with good roots;
Israel will grow like a plant beginning to bloom.
Then the world will be filled with their children.

The Lord Will Send Israel Away

7The LORD has not hurt his people as he hurt their enemies;
his people have not been killed like those who tried to kill them.
8He will settle his argument with Israel by sending it far away.
Like a hot desert wind, he will drive it away.
9This is how Israel's guilt will be forgiven;
this is how its sins will be taken away:
Israel will crush the rocks of the altar to dust,
and no statues or altars will be left standing for the Asherah idols.
10At that time the strong, walled city will be empty
like a desert.
Calves will eat grass there.
They will lie down there
and eat leaves from the branches.
11The limbs will become dry and break off,
so women will use them for firewood.
The people refuse to understand,
so God will not comfort them;
their Maker will not be kind to them.

12At that time the LORD will begin gathering his
people one by one from the Euphrates River to the
brook of Egypt. He will separate them from others
as grain is separated from chaff. 13Many of my people
are now lost in Assyria. Some have run away to
Egypt. But at that time a great trumpet will be
blown, and all those people will come and worship
the LORD on that holy mountain in Jerusalem.

27:1 *Leviathan.* Leviathan was a sea monster. The sea and its monsters represented the forces of chaos that raged against God.

Warnings to Israel

28 How terrible it will be for Samaria, the
pride of Israel's drunken people!
That beautiful crown of flowers is just a
dying plant
set on a hill above a rich valley where
drunkards live.
2Look, the Lord has someone who is strong
and powerful.
Like a storm of hail and strong wind,
like a sudden flood of water pouring over
the country,
he will throw Samaria down to the ground.
3That city, the pride of Israel's drunken people,
will be trampled underfoot.
4That beautiful crown of flowers is just a
dying plant
set on a hill above a rich valley.
That city will be like the first fig of summer.
Anyone who sees it
quickly picks it and eats it.

5At that time the LORD All-Powerful
will be like a beautiful crown,
like a wonderful crown of flowers
for his people who are left alive.⚭
6Then he will give wisdom to the judges who
must decide cases
and strength to those who battle at the
city gate.
7But now those leaders are drunk with wine;
they stumble from drinking too much beer.
The priests and prophets are drunk with beer
and are filled with wine.
They stumble from too much beer.
The prophets are drunk when they see
their visions;
the judges stumble when they make
their decisions.
8Every table is covered with vomit,
so there is not a clean place anywhere.

9The LORD is trying to teach the people a lesson;
he is trying to make them understand
his teachings.
But the people are like babies too old for
breast milk,
like those who no longer nurse at their
mother's breast.
10So they make fun of the LORD's prophet and say:
"A command here, a command there.
A rule here, a rule there.
A little lesson here, a little lesson there."
11So the LORD will use strange words and
foreign languages
to speak to these people.
12God said to them,
"Here is a place of rest;
let the tired people come and rest.
This is the place of peace."
But the people would not listen.
13So the words of the LORD will be,
"A command here, a command there.
A rule here, a rule there.
A little lesson here, a little lesson there."
They will fall back and be defeated;
they will be trapped and captured.

14So listen to the LORD's message, you
who brag,
you leaders in Jerusalem.
15You say, "We have made an agreement
with death;
we have a contract with death.
When terrible punishment passes by,
it won't hurt us.
Our lies will keep us safe,
and our tricks will hide us."

16Because of these things, this is what the Lord
GOD says:
"I will put a stone in the ground in Jerusalem,
a tested stone.
Everything will be built on this important and
precious rock.
Anyone who trusts in it will never
be disappointed.⚭
17I will use justice as a measuring line
and goodness as the standard.
The lies you hide behind will be destroyed as if
by hail.
They will be washed away as if in a flood.
18Your agreement with death will be erased;
your contract with death will not help you.
When terrible punishment comes,
you will be crushed by it.
19Whenever punishment comes, it will take
you away.
It will come morning after morning;
it will defeat you by day and by night.
Those who understand this punishment will
be terrified."
20You will be like the person who tried to sleep
on a bed that was too short
and with a blanket that was too narrow
to wrap around himself.

⚭**28:5 The Remnant:** Isaiah 37:32

⚭**28:16 Stone:** Isaiah 54:11–12

21The LORD will fight as he did at Mount Perazim.
He will be angry as he was in the
Valley of Gibeon.
He will do his work, his strange work.
He will finish his job, his strange job.
22Now, you must not make fun of these things,
or the ropes around you will become tighter.
The Lord GOD All-Powerful has told me
how the whole earth will be destroyed.

The Lord Punishes Fairly

23Listen closely to what I tell you;
listen carefully to what I say.
24A farmer does not plow his field all the time;
he does not go on working the soil.
25He makes the ground flat and smooth.
Then he plants the dill and scatters the cumin.
He plants the wheat in rows,
the barley in its special place,
and other wheat as a border around the field.
26His God teaches him
and shows him the right way.
27A farmer doesn't use heavy boards to crush dill;
he doesn't use a wagon wheel to crush cumin.
He uses a small stick to break open the dill,
and with a stick he opens the cumin.
28The grain is ground to make bread.
People do not ruin it by crushing
it forever.
The farmer separates the wheat from the chaff
with his cart,
but he does not let his horses grind it.
29This lesson also comes from the LORD
All-Powerful,
who gives wonderful advice, who is very wise.

Warnings to Jerusalem

29 How terrible it will be for you, Jerusalem,
the city where David camped.
Your festivals have continued
year after year.
2I will attack Jerusalem,
and that city will be filled with sadness
and crying.
It will be like an altar to me.
3I will put armies all around you, Jerusalem;
I will surround you with towers
and with devices to attack you.
4You will be pulled down and will speak from
the ground;
I will hear your voice rising from
the ground.
It will sound like the voice of a ghost;
your words will come like a whisper from
the dirt.

5Your many enemies will become like fine dust;
the many cruel people will be like chaff that
is blown away.
Everything will happen very quickly.
6 The LORD All-Powerful will come
with thunder, earthquakes, and great noises,
with storms, strong winds, and a fire
that destroys.
7Then all the nations that fight against Jerusalem
will be like a dream;
all the nations that attack her
will be like a vision in the night.
8They will be like a hungry man who dreams
he is eating,
but when he awakens, he is still hungry.
They will be like a thirsty man who dreams he
is drinking,
but when he awakens, he is still weak
and thirsty.
It will be the same way with all the nations
who fight against Mount Zion.

9Be surprised and amazed.
Blind yourselves so that you cannot see.
Become drunk, but not from wine.
Trip and fall, but not from beer.
10The LORD has made you go into a deep sleep.
He has closed your eyes. (The prophets are
your eyes.)
He has covered your heads. (The seers are
your heads.)

11This vision is like the words of a book that is
closed and sealed. You may give the book to someone who can read and tell that person to read it.
But he will say, "I can't read the book, because it
is sealed." 12Or you may give the book to someone
who cannot read and tell him to read it. But he
will say, "I don't know how to read."

13The Lord says:
"These people say they love me;
they show honor to me with words,
but their hearts are far from me.
The honor they show me
is nothing but human rules.
14So I will continue to amaze these people
by doing more and more miracles.
Their wise men will lose their wisdom;

28:21 *Mount Perazim and the Valley of Gibeon.* At Mount Perazim the Lord defeated the Philistines (2 Samuel 5:19,20), and at Gibeon he defeated the southern coalition of the city-states of Canaan (Joshua 10:10).

their wise men will not be able
to understand."

Warnings About Other Nations

15How terrible it will be for those who try
to hide things from the LORD
and who do their work in darkness.
They think no one will see them or know
what they do.
16You are confused.
You think the clay is equal to the potter.
You think that an object can tell the one who
made it,
"You didn't make me."
This is like a pot telling its maker,
"You don't know anything."

A Better Time Is Coming

17In a very short time, Lebanon will become
rich farmland,
and the rich farmland will seem
like a forest.
18At that time the deaf will hear the words in
a book.
Instead of having darkness and gloom, the
blind will see.
19The LORD will make the poor people happy;
they will rejoice in the Holy One of Israel.
20Then the people without mercy will come to
an end;
those who do not respect God
will disappear.
Those who enjoy doing evil will be gone:
21those who lie about others in court,
those who trap people in court,
those who lie and take justice from innocent
people in court.

22This is what the LORD who set Abraham free
says to the family of Jacob:
"Now the people of Jacob will
not be ashamed
or disgraced any longer.
23When they see all their children,
the children I made with my hands,
they will say my name is holy.
They will agree that the Holy One of Jacob
is holy,
and they will respect the God of Israel.
24People who do wrong will now understand.
Those who complain will accept
being taught."

Warnings to the Stubborn Nation

30 The LORD said,
"How terrible it will be for these
stubborn children.
They make plans, but they don't ask me to
help them.
They make agreements with other nations,
without asking my Spirit.
They are adding more and more sins
to themselves.
2They go down to Egypt for help
without asking me about it first.
They hope they will be saved by the king
of Egypt;
they want Egypt to protect them.
3But hiding in Egypt will bring you only shame;
Egypt's protection will only disappoint you.
4Your officers have gone to Zoan,
and your messengers have gone to Hanes,
5but they will be put to shame,
because Egypt is useless to them.
It will give no help and will be of no use;
it will cause them only shame
and embarrassment."

God's Message to Judah

6This is a message about the animals in southern Judah:
Southern Judah is a dangerous place
full of lions and lionesses,
poisonous snakes and darting snakes.
The messengers travel through there with
their wealth on the backs of donkeys
and their treasure on the backs of camels.
They carry them to a nation that cannot
help them,
7 to Egypt whose help is useless.
So I call that country Rahab the Do-Nothing.

8Now write this on a sign for the people,
write this on a scroll,
so that for the days to come
this will be a witness forever.
9These people are like children who lie and
refuse to obey;
they refuse to listen to the LORD's teachings.
10They tell the seers,
"Don't see any more visions!"
They say to the prophets,
"Don't tell us the truth!
Say things that will make us feel good;
see only good things for us.

29:22 Abraham: Micah 7:20

30:7 *Rahab.* Egypt is identified with Rahab the sea-monster, who represents the forces of chaos.

[11]Stop blocking our path.
Get out of our way.
Stop telling us
about God, the Holy One of Israel."

[12]So this is what the Holy One of Israel says:
"You people have refused to accept this message
and have depended on cruelty and lies to
help you.
[13]You are guilty of these things.
So you will be like a high wall with cracks in it
that falls suddenly and breaks
into small pieces.
[14]You will be like a clay jar that breaks,
smashed into many pieces.
Those pieces will be too small
to take coals from the fire
or to get water from a well."

[15]This is what the Lord GOD, the Holy One of
Israel, says:
"If you come back to me and trust me,
you will be saved.
If you will be calm and trust me, you will
be strong."
But you don't want to do that.
[16]You say, "No, we need horses to
run away on."
So you will run away on horses.
You say, "We will ride away on fast horses."
So those who chase you will be fast.
[17]One enemy will make threats,
and a thousand of your men will run away.
Five enemies will make threats,
and all of you will run from them.
You will be left alone like a flagpole
on a hilltop,
like a banner on a hill.
[18]The LORD wants to show his mercy to you.
He wants to rise and comfort you.
The LORD is a fair God,
and everyone who waits for his help will
be happy.

The Lord Will Help His People

[19]You people who live on Mount Zion in Jerusalem will not cry anymore. The LORD will hear
your crying, and he will comfort you. When he
hears you, he will help you. [20]The Lord has given
you sorrow and hurt like the bread and water you
ate every day. He is your teacher; he will not continue to hide from you, but you will see your
teacher with your own eyes. [21]If you go the wrong
way—to the right or to the left—you will hear a
voice behind you saying, "This is the right way.
You should go this way." [22]You have statues covered with silver and gold, but you will ruin them
for further use. You will throw them away like
filthy rags and say, "Go away!"
[23]At that time the LORD will send rain for the
seeds you plant in the ground, and the ground will
grow food for you. The harvest will be rich and
great, and you will have plenty of food in the fields
for your animals. [24]Your oxen and donkeys that
work the soil will have all the food they need. You
will have to use shovels and pitchforks to spread
all their food. [25]Every mountain and hill will have
streams filled with water. These things will happen after many people are killed and the towers
are pulled down. [26]At that time the light from the
moon will be bright like the sun, and the light from
the sun will be seven times brighter than now, like
the light of seven days. These things will happen
when the LORD bandages his broken people and
heals the hurts he gave them.

[27]Look! The LORD comes from far away.
His anger is like a fire with thick clouds
of smoke.
His mouth is filled with anger,
and his tongue is like a burning fire.
[28]His breath is like a rushing river,
which rises to the throat.
He will judge the nations as if he is sifting
them through the strainer of destruction.
He will place in their mouths a bit that will
lead them the wrong way.
[29]You will sing happy songs
as on the nights you begin a festival.
You will be happy like people listening to flutes
as they come to the mountain of the LORD,
to the Rock of Israel.
[30]The LORD will cause all people to hear his
great voice
and to see his powerful arm come down
with anger,
like a great fire that burns everything,
like a great storm with much rain and hail.
[31]Assyria will be afraid when it hears the voice
of the LORD,
because he will strike Assyria with a rod.
[32]When the LORD punishes Assyria with a rod,
he will beat them to the music of
tambourines and harps;
he will fight against them with his mighty
weapons.

30:11 Stubbornness: Ezekiel 3:4–11

30:26 Sickness, Disease, Healing: Jeremiah 33:6

[33]Topheth has been made ready for a long time;
it is ready for the king.
It was made deep and wide
with much wood and fire.
And the LORD's breath will come
like a stream of burning sulfur and set it
on fire.

Warnings About Relying on Egypt

31 How terrible it will be for those people who
go down to Egypt for help.
They think horses will save them.
They think their many chariots
and strong horsemen will save them.
But they don't trust God, the Holy One of Israel,
or ask the LORD for help.
[2]But he is wise and can bring them disaster.
He does not change his warnings.
He will rise up and fight against the evil people
and against those who try to help evil people.
[3]The Egyptians are only people and are not God.
Their horses are only animals and are
not spirit.
The LORD will stretch out his arm,
and the one who helps will stumble,
and the people who wanted help will fall.
All of them will be destroyed together.

[4]The LORD says this to me:
"When a lion or a lion's cub kills an animal
to eat,
it stands over the dead animal and roars.
A band of shepherds
may be assembled against it,
but the lion will not be afraid of their yelling
or upset by their noise.
So the LORD All-Powerful will come down
to fight on Mount Zion and on its hill.
[5]The LORD All-Powerful will defend Jerusalem
like birds flying over their nests.
He will defend and save it;
he will 'pass over' and save Jerusalem."

[6]You children of Israel, come back to the God
you fought against. [7]The time is coming when each
of you will stop worshiping idols of gold and silver,
which you sinned by making.

[8]"Assyria will be defeated by a sword, but not
the sword of a person;
Assyria will be destroyed, but not by a
person's sword.
Assyria will run away from the sword of God,
but its young men will be caught and
made slaves.
[9]They will panic, and their protection will
be destroyed.
Their commanders will be terrified when
they see God's battle flag,"
says the LORD,
whose fire is in Jerusalem
and whose furnace is in Jerusalem.

A Good Kingdom Is Coming

32 A king will rule in a way that brings justice,
and leaders will make fair decisions.
[2]Then each ruler will be like a shelter from
the wind,
like a safe place in a storm,
like streams of water in a dry land,
like a cool shadow from a large rock in a
hot land.

[3]People will look to the king for help,
and they will truly listen to what he says.
[4]People who are now worried will be able
to understand.
Those who cannot speak clearly now will
then be able to speak clearly and quickly.
[5]Fools will not be called great,
and people will not respect the wicked.
[6]A fool says foolish things,
and in his mind he plans evil.
A fool does things that are wicked,
and he says wrong things about the LORD.
A fool does not feed the hungry
or let thirsty people drink water.
[7]The wicked person uses evil like a tool.
He plans ways to take everything from
the poor.
He destroys the poor with lies,
even when the poor person is in the right.
[8]But a good leader plans to do good,
and those good things make him a good leader.

Hard Times Are Coming

[9]You women who are calm now,
stand up and listen to me.
You women who feel safe now,
hear what I say.
[10]You women feel safe now,
but after one year you will be afraid.
There will be no grape harvest
and no summer fruit to gather.

30:33 *Topheth.* Gehenna; the Valley of Hinnom. Topheth was a pit near Jerusalem where garbage was thrown, and child sacrifices took place during a period of unbelief.

Women, you are calm now, but you should
shake with fear.
Women, you feel safe now, but you
should tremble.
Take off your nice clothes
and put rough cloth around your waist to
show your sadness.
12Beat your breasts in grief, because the fields
that were pleasant are now empty.
Cry, because the vines that once had fruit
now have no more grapes.
13Cry for the land of my people,
in which only thorns and weeds now grow.
Cry for the city that once was happy
and for all the houses that once were filled
with joy.
14The palace will be empty;
people will leave the noisy city.
Strong cities and towers will be empty.
Wild donkeys will love to live there, and
sheep will go there to eat.

Things Will Get Better

15This will continue until God pours his Spirit
from above upon us.
Then the desert will be like a fertile field
and the fertile field like a forest.
16Justice will be found even in the desert,
and fairness will be found in the fertile fields.
17That fairness will bring peace,
and it will bring calm and safety forever.
18My people will live in peaceful places
and in safe homes
and in calm places of rest.
19Hail will destroy the forest,
and the city will be completely destroyed.
20But you will be happy as you plant seeds near
every stream
and as you let your cattle and donkeys
wander freely.

Warnings to Assyria and Promises to God's People

33 How terrible it will be for you who
destroy others
but have not been destroyed yet.
How terrible it will be for you, traitor,
whom no one has turned against yet.
When you stop destroying,
others will destroy you.
When you stop turning against others,
they will turn against you.

2LORD, be kind to us.
We have waited for your help.
Give us strength every morning.
Save us when we are in trouble.
3Your powerful voice makes people run away
in fear;
your greatness causes the nations to run away.
4Like locusts, your enemies will take away the
things you stole in war.
Like locusts rushing about, they will take
your wealth.
5The LORD is very great, and he lives in a
high place.
He fills Jerusalem with fairness and justice.
6He will be your safety.
He is full of salvation, wisdom, and knowledge.
Respect for the LORD is the greatest treasure.

7See, brave men are crying out in the streets;
those who tried to bring peace are
crying loudly.
8There is no one on the roads,
no one walking in the paths.
People have broken the agreements they made.
They refuse to believe the proof from
witnesses.
No one respects other people.
9The land is sick and dying;
Lebanon is ashamed and dying.
The Plain of Sharon is dry like the desert,
and the trees of Bashan and Carmel are dying.

10The LORD says, "Now, I will stand up
and show my greatness.
Now, I will become important to the people.
11You people do useless things
that are like hay and straw.
A destructive wind will burn you like fire.
12People will be burned until their bones
become like lime;
they will burn quickly like
dry thornbushes."

13You people in faraway lands, hear what I
have done.
You people who are near me, learn about
my power.
14The sinners in Jerusalem are afraid;
those who are separated from God shake
with fear.
They say, "Can any of us live through this fire
that destroys?

33:4 *locusts.* Locusts sweep through an area and consume everything that is edible.
33:9 *Lebanon, Sharon, Bashan, and Carmel.* These places are all very fertile locations. If they are not lush, then the rest of Israel is in bad shape.

Who can live near this fire that burns
on and on?"
15A person who does what is right
and speaks what is right,
who refuses to take money unfairly,
who refuses to take money to hurt others,
who does not listen to plans of murder,
who refuses to think about evil—
16this is the kind of person who will be safe.
He will be protected as he would be in a
high, walled city.
He will always have bread,
and he will not run out of water.
17Your eyes will see the king in his beauty.
You will see the land that stretches far away.
18You will think about the terror of the past:
"Where is that officer?
Where is the one who collected the taxes?
Where is the officer in charge of our
defense towers?"
19No longer will you see those proud people
from other countries,
whose strange language you
couldn't understand.

God Will Protect Jerusalem

20Look at Jerusalem, the city of our festivals.
Look at Jerusalem, that beautiful place of rest.
It is like a tent that will never be moved;
the pegs that hold her in place will never be
pulled up,
and her ropes will never be broken.
21There the LORD will be our Mighty One.
That land is a place with streams and
wide rivers,
but there will be no enemy boats on
those rivers;
no powerful ship will sail on them.
22This is because the LORD is our judge.
The LORD makes our laws.
The LORD is our king.
He will save us.
23You sailors from other lands, hear:
The ropes on your boats hang loose.
The mast is not held firm.
The sails are not spread open.
Then your great wealth will be divided.
There will be so much wealth that even the
crippled people will carry off a share.
24No one living in Jerusalem will say,
"I am sick."
The people who live there will have their
sins forgiven.

God Will Punish His Enemies

34 All you nations, come near and listen.
Pay attention, you peoples!
The earth and all the people in it should listen,
the world and everything in it.
2The LORD is angry with all the nations;
he is angry with their armies.
He will destroy them and kill them all.
3Their bodies will be thrown outside.
The stink will rise from the bodies,
and the blood will flow down the mountains.
4The sun, moon, and stars will dissolve,
and the sky will be rolled up like a scroll.
The stars will fall
like dead leaves from a vine
or dried-up figs from a fig tree.
5The LORD's sword in the sky is covered
with blood.
It will cut through Edom
and destroy those people as an offering to
the LORD.
6The LORD's sword will be covered with blood;
it will be covered with fat,
with the blood from lambs and goats,
with the fat from the kidneys of sheep.
This is because the LORD decided there will be
a sacrifice in Bozrah
and much killing in Edom.
7The oxen will be killed,
and the cattle and the strong bulls.
The land will be filled with their blood,
and the dirt will be covered with their fat.

8The LORD has chosen a time for punishment.
He has chosen a year when people must pay
for the wrongs they did to Jerusalem.
9Edom's rivers will be like hot tar.
Its dirt will be like burning sulfur.
Its land will be like burning tar.
10The fires will burn night and day;
the smoke will rise from Edom forever.
Year after year that land will be empty;
no one will ever travel through that land again.
11Birds and small animals will own that land,
and owls and ravens will live there.
God will make it an empty wasteland;
it will have nothing left in it.
12The important people will have no one left to
rule them;
the leaders will all be gone.
13Thorns will take over the strong towers,
and wild bushes will grow in the walled cities.

33:20 Israel is the land of festivals. The people of Israel were to go to Jerusalem to celebrate the great annual religious festivals.

34:8 Day of the Lord: Jeremiah 30:5

Kingdom of God

Mark 1

Why is the kingdom of God so central to Jesus' message? What might people have understood by this expression? What are the implications of Jesus' message of the kingdom for discipleship today?

The centrality of the kingdom of God in Jesus' message and ministry is clear throughout the Gospels. Perhaps Jesus' whole ministry can best be summarized by his own words at the beginning of the Gospel of Mark, "The right time has come. The kingdom of God is near. Change your hearts and lives and believe the Good News!" (1:15).

But what would the image "kingdom of God" have meant to Jesus' audience? Though the exact phrase "kingdom of God" is absent, in the Old Testament we meet a people yearning to have God's promises fulfilled in them—the promises of an everlasting kingdom (1 Chronicles 17:14). The God of Israel had always been Israel's only Lord over their kingdom. This was the basis of their faith—what set them apart as a people. However, tired of being deprived of what other nations had, they asked for a king. Acknowledging their rejection of him as their king, God granted their wish (1 Samuel 8:4–9). The subsequent rulers over Israel led to the nation's demise, and ultimately they were taken captive into Babylon. The everlasting kingdom promised to them seemed nothing more than a dream.

Daniel gave a picture of the new future kingdom of Israel. "The God of heaven will set up another kingdom that will never be destroyed or given to another group of people. This kingdom will crush all the other kingdoms and bring them to an end, but it will continue forever" (Daniel 2:44). And thus began the images of this "new" kingdom of God. Isaiah, Ezekiel, Hosea, and Amos also proclaimed the hope of such a kingdom—a future time when God would restore Israel, and his kingdom would rule forever.

But what is the essence of the kingdom of God? The kingdom would certainly include God's everlasting reign, but the above-mentioned prophets spoke of more. Perhaps what was expected in the future kingdom would best be understood in light of what was missing in the lives of the people. Even before captivity, the Israelites were torn by civil and foreign wars. So then God was expected to bring peace to the people and to their land (Ezekiel 37:26–28) as well as freedom from foreign oppression. In addition, the people of Israel were not living justly toward one another (see Leviticus 25:8–18; Exodus 22:22–23; Deuteronomy 24:19–22; Amos 5:7; 11–12). Thus, God says through the prophet Amos, "Let justice flow like a river, and let goodness flow like a stream that never stops" (5:24).

Jesus in his many parables beginning, "The kingdom is like . . ." (see Matthew 13:24, 31, 33), builds on the expectations of the kingdom as defined by the prophets of the Old Testament. Again under foreign rule, this time by the Romans, the people of Israel were still waiting for the coming of God's kingdom. They were hoping for the peace, justice, and freedom from oppression they had come to anticipate in God's future reign. Jesus was the fulfillment of that promise (Matthew 3:2–3; Luke 4:21).

Today we, as followers of Christ, must consider Jesus' message of the kingdom as Son of Man and as risen Lord. Is the kingdom fulfilled now, or are we to wait for some future time when Jesus comes again? The question is crucial, for our answer will determine our understanding of discipleship. In Luke 4:21 Jesus says, "While you heard these words just now, they were coming true!" Similarly, in Mark 1:15, Jesus calls us to change our hearts and minds in light of the fact that the time has come. Later, when teaching about prayer, Jesus says to pray for things to be done on earth as they are done in heaven (Matthew 6:10). Finally, in response to a question about the time of the kingdom, Jesus answers, "God's kingdom is within you" (Luke 17:21). However, Jesus also anticipates the *future* coming of God's kingdom. Mark 13 tells of the future destruction of the world before God's ultimate reign. In Luke 13:30 Jesus says, "Those who have the lowest place in life now . . . will have the highest place in the future [at the table in the kingdom of God (verse 29)]." So which is it? Is the kingdom here, or is the kingdom still to come?

In light of the teaching of Jesus throughout the Gospels, we must conclude that the kingdom of God began when Jesus began his ministry. Just like the seed in Mark 4:26–29, the kingdom of God began to grow when God entered his creation at the incarnation. That seed has been planted in the hearts and minds of all believers. The seed grows as the work of heaven is done here on earth. The seed will be experienced in its fullness when Jesus comes again. At that time "*every* knee will bow . . . and *every* one will confess that Jesus Christ is Lord" (Philippians 2:10) and then, we will finally and completely experience God's everlasting kingdom.

Kingdom of God: For additional scriptures on this topic go to 1 Chronicles 17:14.

Wilderness (Desert)

Mark 1:2

What is the importance of the wilderness (desert) for Israel, then for John and Jesus? Do Christians continue to have "wilderness experiences"? How does the Bible address the idea of Christians being tested in this way?

In Israel's early history, the wilderness (desert) is the place of divine provision and testing. Here, the Lord delivers them from Pharaoh's army and other enemies, leads them day and night, quenches their thirst with water from a rock, feeds them with manna, and preserves their clothing and their health (Exodus 14–17). However, the wilderness is not only a symbol of divine direction and protection. The prophets made clear that Israel's spiritual condition would be reflected in the state of their land. If they rejected God's care and his commands, he would turn their cities and fruitful land into empty desert (Jeremiah 22:6; 51:43; Joel 2:1–3). On the other hand, when the Lord delivers his people from the exile and brings them home, he will make a way for them in a wilderness; a wilderness where waters flow, where the danger of wild beasts ceases, and vegetation is renewed (Isaiah 41:17–19; 43:18–21). The transformation of the desert reflects the renewal of Israel's relationship with her Lord and the outpouring of his Spirit upon them (Isaiah 44:3; 63:10–14).

For Israel, the way of the wilderness (desert) is the way from slavery and captivity to the freedom of serving the Lord; the way from lost national identity to recognizing themselves as God's people. It is the way from lostness and wanderings to being found by their Lord; the way from rebellion and rejection to renewal; the way from being spiritually cut off to spiritual sonship. It is the place of new beginnings.

Gospel uses of *wilderness* should be read against this background, keeping in mind that in the Gospels wilderness does not refer only to desert landscapes; the same word is used to speak of lonely or isolated places. The four gospel writers describe the person and ministry of John the Baptist in terms of the wilderness: he is called out of the wilderness or desert (Luke 3:2), and he preaches and baptizes in the wilderness (Matthew 3:1–6; Mark 1:4). So, all four writers identify him as the fulfillment of Isaiah 40:3: "This is the voice of one who calls: 'Prepare in the desert the way for the Lord. Make a straight road in the dry lands for our God." He is the forerunner of the expected Messiah. The one who brings the kingdom that comes in the person of Jesus.

In the wilderness Jesus reenacts and redefines some of the Exodus events. Once baptized by John, Jesus goes to the wilderness. During forty days that remind us of Israel's wanderings in the desert (Numbers 14:33; 32:13), Jesus faces confrontation with the devil. Tempted by him, Jesus triumphs in the test Israel failed in the wilderness. Quoting from the Book of Deuteronomy, he declares his final dependence on God and his Word, his loyalty to God only, and his refusal to test God. The sonship relationship with God is made stronger by his obedience, rejecting Satan's understanding of that relationship (Matthew 4:1–11; Luke 4:1–13). As Israel came to God in the wilderness, so people came there to Jesus (Mark 1:45). In the wilderness he fed them miraculously (Matthew 14:13–21; Mark 8:1–10; Luke 9:10–17), revealing himself not only as the Lord who feeds his people, but as the true bread from heaven (Mark 8:14–21; John 6:25–59). Jesus retreats from the multitudes and goes to a lonely place to pray and to refocus his ministry in terms of the mission the Father entrusted to him (Mark 1:35; Luke 4:42; 5:16).

Christians continue to experience temptations and tests of the wilderness. God promises provision and renewal to withstand. The Bible warns believers that temptations and tests will come (Luke 17:1; James 1:2–4; 12–15). At the same time, it encourages Christians to pray for deliverance from temptation (Matthew 6:13; Mark 14:38; Luke 22:40, 46), and assures us that God will provide a way to escape from it. Because Christ experienced temptation, he understands and helps (1 Corinthians 10:13; Hebrews 2:18; 4:16). Believers are called to learn from Israel's experience in the wilderness and to encourage each other to stay firm in the faith. Otherwise, Christians may show the stubbornness, unbelief, rebelliousness, and blindness to God's ways that the Israelites showed (Hebrews 3:7—4:13). Wilderness experiences are bittersweet for the Christian; while bringing sadness, they promise joy: "These troubles come to prove that your faith is pure. This purity of faith is worth more than gold, which can be proved to be pure by fire but will ruin. But the purity of your faith will bring you praise and glory and honor when Jesus Christ is shown to you" (1 Peter 1:7).

Wilderness (Desert): For additional scriptures on this topic go to Genesis 16:6–14.

It will be a home for wild dogs
and a place for owls to live.
14Desert animals will live with the hyenas,
and wild goats will call to their friends.
Night animals will live there
and find a place of rest.
15Owls will nest there and lay eggs.
When they hatch open, the owls will gather
their young under their wings.
Hawks will gather
with their own kind.

16Look at the LORD's scroll and read what is
written there:
None of these will be missing;
none will be without its mate.
God has given the command,
so his Spirit will gather them together.
17God has divided the land among them,
and he has given them each their portion.
So they will own that land forever
and will live there year after year.

God Will Comfort His People

35 The desert and dry land will become happy;
the desert will be glad and will produce
flowers.
Like a flower, 2it will have many blooms.
It will show its happiness, as if it were
shouting with joy.
It will be beautiful like the forest of Lebanon,
as beautiful as the hill of Carmel and the
Plain of Sharon.
Everyone will see the glory of the LORD
and the splendor of our God.
3Make the weak hands strong
and the weak knees steady.
4Say to people who are frightened,
"Be strong. Don't be afraid.
Look, your God will come,
and he will punish your enemies.
He will make them pay for the wrongs they did,
but he will save you."
5Then the blind people will see again,
and the deaf will hear.
6Crippled people will jump like deer,
and those who can't talk now will
shout with joy.
Water will flow in the desert,
and streams will flow in the dry land.
7The burning desert will have pools of water,
and the dry ground will have springs.
Where wild dogs once lived,
grass and water plants will grow.
8A road will be there;
this highway will be called "The Road to
Being Holy."
Evil people will not be allowed to walk on
that road;
only good people will walk on it.
No fools will go on it.
9No lions will be there,
nor will dangerous animals be on that road.
They will not be found there.
That road will be for the people God saves;
10 the people the LORD has freed will
return there.
They will enter Jerusalem with joy,
and their happiness will last forever.
Their gladness and joy will fill them completely,
and sorrow and sadness will go far away.

The Assyrians Invade Judah

36 During Hezekiah's fourteenth year as king,
Sennacherib king of Assyria attacked all the
strong, walled cities of Judah and captured them.
2The king of Assyria sent out his field commander
with a large army from Lachish to King Hezekiah
in Jerusalem. When the commander came near the
waterway from the upper pool on the road where
people do their laundry, he stopped. 3Eliakim,
Shebna, and Joah went out to meet him. Eliakim
son of Hilkiah was the palace manager, Shebna was
the royal secretary, and Joah son of Asaph was the
recorder.
4The field commander said to them, "Tell
Hezekiah this:
" 'The great king, the king of Assyria, says: What
can you trust in now? 5You say you have battle
plans and power for war, but your words mean
nothing. Whom are you trusting for help so that
you turn against me? 6Look, you are depending
on Egypt to help you, but Egypt is like a splintered
walking stick. If you lean on it for help, it will stab
your hand and hurt you. The king of Egypt will hurt
all those who depend on him. 7You might say, "We

35 To encourage the people of Judah who were being threatened by the military might of Assyria, Isaiah painted this beautiful picture of a future time of blessing God would bring. Notice how water plays an important part in this picture. Springs and streams flowing in the dry land bring new life and healing; the desert produces plants and flowers; frightened people are strengthened; handicapped people become well and whole; sorrow and sadness are banished. Other examples of pictures of future blessedness that use water can be found in Isaiah 30:19–26; 32:15–20; 44:1–5; Ezekiel 47:1–12; Revelation 22:1–2.

35:2 Environment: Isaiah 55:12

35:10 Wilderness (Desert): Isaiah 43:18–21

35:10 Heaven: Isaiah 65:17–25

36:1 *Sennacherib.* Sennacherib was the king of Assyria from 705 to 681 B.C.

are depending on the LORD our God," but Hezekiah
destroyed the LORD's altars and the places of worship. Hezekiah told Judah and Jerusalem, "You
must worship only at this one altar."

[8]" 'Now make an agreement with my master,
the king of Assyria: I will give you two thousand
horses if you can find enough men to ride them.
[9]You cannot defeat one of my master's least important officers, so why do you depend on Egypt to
give you chariots and horsemen? [10]I have not come
to attack and destroy this country without an order
from the LORD. The LORD himself told me to come
to this country and destroy it.' "

[11]Then Eliakim, Shebna, and Joah said to the
field commander, "Please speak to us in the Aramaic language. We understand it. Don't speak to
us in Hebrew, because the people on the city wall
can hear you."

[12]But the commander said, "My master did not
send me to tell these things only to you and your
king. He sent me to speak also to those people sitting on the wall who will have to eat their own
dung and drink their own urine like you."

[13]Then the commander stood and shouted loudly
in the Hebrew language, "Listen to what the great
king, the king of Assyria says, [14]The king says you
should not let Hezekiah fool you, because he can't
save you. [15]Don't let Hezekiah talk you into trusting the LORD by saying, 'The LORD will surely save
us. This city won't be handed over to the king of
Assyria.'

[16]"Don't listen to Hezekiah. The king of Assyria
says, 'Make peace with me, and come out of the
city to me. Then everyone will be free to eat the
fruit from his own grapevine and fig tree and to
drink water from his own well. [17]After that I will
come and take you to a land like your own—a land
with grain and new wine, bread and vineyards.'

[18]"Don't let Hezekiah fool you, saying, 'The LORD
will save us.' Has a god of any other nation saved his
people from the power of the king of Assyria?
[19]Where are the gods of Hamath and Arpad? Where
are the gods of Sepharvaim? They did not save
Samaria from my power. [20]Not one of all the gods
of these countries has saved his people from me.
Neither can the LORD save Jerusalem from my
power."

[21]The people were silent. They didn't answer the
commander at all, because King Hezekiah had
ordered, "Don't answer him."

[22]Then Eliakim, Shebna, and Joah tore their
clothes to show how upset they were. (Eliakim son
of Hilkiah was the palace manager, Shebna was
the royal secretary, and Joah son of Asaph was the
recorder.) The three men went to Hezekiah and
told him what the field commander had said.

Hezekiah Asks God to Help

37 When King Hezekiah heard the message,
he tore his clothes and put on rough cloth
to show how sad he was. Then he went into the
Temple of the LORD. [2]Hezekiah sent Eliakim, the
palace manager, and Shebna, the royal secretary,
and the older priests to Isaiah. They were all wearing rough cloth when they came to Isaiah the
prophet, the son of Amoz. [3]They told Isaiah, "This
is what Hezekiah says: Today is a day of sorrow and
punishment and disgrace, as when a child should
be born, but the mother is not strong enough to
give birth to it. [4]The king of Assyria sent his field
commander to make fun of the living God. Maybe
the LORD your God will hear what the commander
said and will punish him for it. So pray for the few
of us who are left alive."

[5]When Hezekiah's officers came to Isaiah, [6]he
said to them, "Tell your master this: The LORD says,
'Don't be afraid of what you have heard. Don't be
frightened by the words the servants of the king
of Assyria have spoken against me.⚭ [7]Listen! I am
going to put a spirit in the king of Assyria. He will
hear a report that will make him return to his own
country, and I will cause him to die by the sword
there.' "

[8]The field commander heard that the king of
Assyria had left Lachish. When he went back, he
found the king fighting against the city of Libnah.

[9]The king received a report that Tirhakah, the
Cushite king of Egypt, was coming to attack him.
When the king of Assyria heard this, he sent messengers to Hezekiah, saying, [10]"Tell Hezekiah king
of Judah: Don't be fooled by the god you trust.
Don't believe him when he says Jerusalem will not
be handed over to the king of Assyria. [11]You have
heard what the kings of Assyria have done. They
have completely defeated every country, so do not
think you will be saved. [12]Did the gods of those
people save them? My ancestors destroyed them,
defeating the cities of Gozan, Haran, and Rezeph,
and the people of Eden living in Tel Assar. [13]Where
are the kings of Hamath and Arpad? Where are
the kings of Sepharvaim, Hena, and Ivvah?"

Hezekiah Prays to the Lord

[14]When Hezekiah received the letter from the
messengers and read it, he went up to the
Temple of the LORD. He spread the letter out

36:11 *Aramaic and Hebrew.* At this time Hebrew was the language of the people, and Aramaic was the language of international diplomacy.

⚭**37:6 Blasphemy:** Ezekiel 20:27

before the LORD [15]and prayed to the LORD: [16]"LORD
All-Powerful, you are the God of Israel, whose
throne is between the gold creatures with wings,
only you are God of all the kingdoms of the earth.
You made the heavens and the earth. [17]Hear, LORD,
and listen. Open your eyes, LORD, and see. Listen
to all the words Sennacherib has said to insult the
living God.

[18]"It is true, LORD, that the kings of Assyria have
destroyed all these countries and their lands.
[19]They have thrown the gods of these nations into
the fire, but they were only wood and rock statues
that people made. So the kings have destroyed
them. [20]Now, LORD our God, save us from the
king's power so that all the kingdoms of the earth
will know that you, LORD, are the only God."

The Lord Answers Hezekiah

[21]Then Isaiah son of Amoz sent a message to
Hezekiah that said, "This is what the LORD, the
God of Israel, says: 'You prayed to me about
Sennacherib king of Assyria. [22]So this is what the
LORD has said against Sennacherib:

The people of Jerusalem
hate you and make fun of you;
the people of Jerusalem
laugh at you as you run away.
[23]You have insulted me and spoken against me;
you have raised your voice against me.
You have a proud look on your face,
which is against me, the Holy One of Israel!
[24]You have sent your messengers to
insult the Lord.
You have said, "With my many chariots
I have gone to the tops of the mountains,
to the highest mountains of Lebanon.
I have cut down its tallest cedars
and its best pine trees.
I have gone to its greatest heights
and its best forests.
[25]I have dug wells in foreign countries
and drunk water there.
By the soles of my feet,
I have dried up all the rivers of Egypt."

[26]" 'King of Assyria, surely you have heard.
Long ago I, the LORD, planned these things.
Long ago I designed them,
and now I have made them happen.
I allowed you to turn those strong, walled cities
into piles of rocks.
[27]The people in those cities were weak;
they were frightened and put to shame.
They were like grass in the field,
like tender, young grass,
like grass on the housetop
that is burned by the wind before it can grow.
[28]" 'I know when you rest,
when you come and go,
and how you rage against me.
[29]Because you rage against me,
and because I have heard your proud words,
I will put my hook in your nose
and my bit in your mouth.
Then I will force you to leave my country
the same way you came.'

[30]"Then the LORD said, 'Hezekiah, I will give
you this sign:
This year you will eat the grain that grows wild,
and the second year you will eat what grows
wild from that.
But in the third year, plant grain and harvest it.
Plant vineyards and eat their fruit.
[31]Some of the people in the family of Judah
will escape.
Like plants that take root,
they will grow strong and
have many children.
[32]A few people will come out of Jerusalem alive;
a few from Mount Zion will live.
The strong love of the LORD All-Powerful
will make this happen.'⚭

[33]"So this is what the LORD says about the king
of Assyria:
'He will not enter this city
or even shoot an arrow here.
He will not fight against it with shields
or build a ramp to attack the city walls.
[34]He will return to his country the same
way he came,
and he will not enter this city,'
says the LORD.
[35]'I will defend and save this city
for my sake and for David, my servant.' "

[36]Then the angel of the LORD went out and killed
one hundred eighty-five thousand men in the
Assyrian camp. When the people got up early the
next morning, they saw all the dead bodies. [37]So

37:16 *between the gold creatures with wings.* In the Most Holy Place and above the Ark of the Agreement, two powerful heavenly creatures were holding out their wings. These angelic creatures are called "cherubim."

37:29 *my hook in your nose.* Prisoners of war were treated like animals and led through the city by a rope through a hook in the nose.

⚭**37:32 The Remnant:** Jeremiah 23:3

Sennacherib king of Assyria left and went back to
Nineveh and stayed there.
38One day as Sennacherib was worshiping in
the temple of his god Nisroch, his sons Adrammelech and Sharezer killed him with a sword.
Then they escaped to the land of Ararat. So Sennacherib's son Esarhaddon became king of Assyria.

Hezekiah's Illness

38 At that time Hezekiah became very sick; he
was almost dead. The prophet Isaiah son of
Amoz went to see him and told him, "This is what
the LORD says: Make arrangements, because you are
not going to live, but die."
2Hezekiah turned toward the wall and prayed
to the LORD, 3"LORD, please remember that I have
always obeyed you. I have given myself completely
to you and have done what you said was right."
Then Hezekiah cried loudly.
4Then the LORD spoke his word to Isaiah: 5"Go
to Hezekiah and tell him: 'This is what the LORD,
the God of your ancestor David, says: I have
heard your prayer and seen your tears. So I will
add fifteen years to your life. 6I will save you and
this city from the king of Assyria; I will defend
this city.
7" 'The LORD will do what he says. This is the
sign from the LORD to show you: 8The sun has made
a shadow go down the stairway of Ahaz, but I will
make it go back ten steps.' " So the shadow made
by the sun went back up the ten steps it had gone
down.
9After Hezekiah king of Judah got well, he wrote
this song:

10I said, "I am in the middle of my life.
  Do I have to go through the gates of death?
  Will I have the rest of my life taken
    away from me?"
11I said, "I will not see the LORD
  in the land of the living again.
 I will not again see the people
  who live on the earth.
12Like a shepherd's tent,
  my home has been pulled down and
    taken from me.
 I am finished
  like the cloth a weaver rolls up and cuts
    from the loom.
  In one day you brought me to this end.
13All night I cried loudly.
  Like a lion, he crushed all my bones.
  In one day you brought me to this end.
14I cried like a bird
  and moaned like a dove.
 My eyes became tired as I looked to the heavens.
  Lord, I have troubles. Please help me."
15What can I say?
  The Lord told me what would happen and
    then made it happen.
 I have had these troubles in my soul,
  so now I will be humble all my life.
16Lord, because of you, people live.
  Because of you, my spirit also lives;
 you made me well and let me live.
17It was for my own good
  that I had such troubles.
 Because you love me very much,
  you did not let me die
 but threw my sins
  far away.
18People in the place of the dead
    cannot praise you;
  those who have died cannot
    sing praises to you;
 those who die don't trust you
  to help them.
19The people who are alive are the ones
    who praise you.
  They praise you as I praise you today.
 A father should tell his children
  that you provide help.
20The LORD saved me,
  so we will play songs on stringed instruments
 in the Temple of the LORD
  all the days of our lives.

21Then Isaiah said, "Make a paste from figs and
put it on Hezekiah's boil. Then he will get well."
22Hezekiah then asked Isaiah, "What will be the
sign? What will show that I will go up to the Temple
of the LORD?"

Messengers from Babylon

39 At that time Merodach-Baladan son of
Baladan was king of Babylon. He sent letters and a gift to Hezekiah, because he had heard
that Hezekiah had been sick and was now well.
2Hezekiah was pleased and showed the messengers what was in his storehouses: the silver, gold,
spices, expensive perfumes, his swords and shields,
and all his wealth. He showed them everything in
his palace and in his kingdom.
3Then Isaiah the prophet went to King Hezekiah

38:12 *loom.* A machine for making cloth from thread.
38:19 Death: Ezekiel 18:20–24
39:1 *Merodach-Baladan.* Merodach-Baladan was the rebel king of Babylon. At this time Babylon was ruled by Assyria, but Merodach-Baladan was trying to throw off Babylon's masters.

and asked him, "What did these men say? Where
did they come from?"
Hezekiah said, "They came from a faraway
country—from Babylon."
4So Isaiah asked him, "What did they see in your
palace?"
Hezekiah said, "They saw everything in my
palace. I showed them all my wealth."
5Then Isaiah said to Hezekiah: "Listen to the
words of the LORD All-Powerful: 6'In the future
everything in your palace and everything your
ancestors have stored up until this day will be
taken away to Babylon. Nothing will be left,' says
the LORD. 7Some of your own children, those who
will be born to you, will be taken away, and they
will become servants in the palace of the king of
Babylon."
8Hezekiah told Isaiah, "These words from the
LORD are good." He said this because he thought,
"There will be peace and security in my lifetime."

Israel's Punishment Will End

40 Your God says,
"Comfort, comfort my people.
2Speak kindly to the people of Jerusalem
and tell them
that their time of service is finished,
that they have paid for their sins,
that the LORD has punished Jerusalem
twice for every sin they did."

3This is the voice of one who calls out:
"Prepare in the desert
the way for the LORD.
Make a straight road in the dry lands
for our God.
4Every valley should be raised up,
and every mountain and hill
should be made flat.
The rough ground should be made level,
and the rugged ground should be made smooth.
5Then the glory of the LORD will be shown,
and all people together will see it.
The LORD himself said these things."

6A voice says, "Cry out!"
Then I said, "What shall I cry out?"

"Say all people are like the grass,
and all their glory is like the
flowers of the field.
7The grass dies and the flowers fall
when the breath of the LORD blows on them.
Surely the people are like grass.
8The grass dies and the flowers fall,
but the word of our God will live forever."
9Jerusalem, you have good news to tell.
Go up on a high mountain.
Jerusalem, you have good news to tell.
Shout out loud the good news.
Shout it out and don't be afraid.
Say to the towns of Judah,
"Here is your God."
10Look, the Lord GOD is coming with power
to rule all the people.
Look, he will bring reward for his people;
he will have their payment with him.
11He takes care of his people like a shepherd.
He gathers them like lambs in his arms
and carries them close to him.
He gently leads the mothers of the lambs.

God Is Supreme

12Who has measured the oceans in the palm of
his hand?

40:1 Chapters 40–66 are sometimes known as the "Book of Comfort" because the theme of comfort occurs quite frequently in them. In this section Isaiah is writing to the people of Israel to offer them in prophetic fashion the Lord's comfort after they have suffered from the affliction of the exile, a horrible experience for the people of that time which came upon them as a result of their sin (see how the writer of Lamentations felt about it in Lamentations 1:2,9, 16, 17, 21). In this section the Lord continually reminds his people that it is he who brings them comfort (Isaiah 49:13; 51:3, 12; 52:9; 54:11; 61:2). In one notable place the Lord is strikingly compared to a mother who comforts her child (Isaiah 66:13).

40:3 Through Isaiah, God consistently warned that a judgment was coming on the disobedient people of God. Now, in the latter part of the book, God would give a glimpse of the restoration that would follow the judgment. God would judge, purify, and then restore. He would take them out to the desert, then return them to the Promised Land. This verse speaks of the voice that would announce the beginning of that restoration. We know from the beginning of the Book of Mark (1:3) that John the Baptist was the voice of this forerunner. From the desert, he announced the coming of a savior who would lead his people back into the Promised Land of salvation.

40:3–5 Hundreds of years after the Exodus under Moses, Isaiah looks into the future and sees a second exodus. Much of Isaiah's message warns of a coming judgment when the people will be removed from their land because of their sin and will be distributed among the nations. He also gives them hope, however, as in this passage where he describes their return in language reminiscent of the entry into the Promised Land from Egypt.

40:11 Leadership: Isaiah 48:17

40:11 *shepherd.* God is like a shepherd who protects and guides his people.

40:11 Gospel/Good News: Isaiah 52:7

40:11 Mountain: Isaiah 57:7

40:12–26 This beautiful passage proclaims that God is far above anyone or anything in this world, but the writer uses these worldly images to help us grasp this truth. He challenges us to think about humans in various roles, then to recognize how superior God is to humans, no matter what their status or skill. Thus God is portrayed as a craftsman, but one who has fashioned the entire universe (verses 12–15). He is portrayed as a king, but one with the power to put earthly kings in place and then blow them away like chaff (verses 22–24). And he is presented as an army general, but one who has all the stars of heaven at his command (verse 26).

Eagle (left) and vultures (right)—birds of prey, which Israel was forbidden to eat

Who has used his hand to measure the sky?
Who has used a bowl to measure
all the dust of the earth
and scales to weigh the mountains and hills?
13Who has known the mind of the LORD
or been able to give him advice?
14Whom did he ask for help?
Who taught him the right way?
Who taught him knowledge
and showed him the way to understanding?

15The nations are like one small drop in a bucket;
they are no more than the dust on
his measuring scales.
To him the islands are no more than fine
dust on his scales.
16All the trees in Lebanon are not enough
for the altar fires,
and all the animals in Lebanon are not
enough for burnt offerings.
17Compared to the LORD all the nations are
worth nothing;
to him they are less than nothing.

18Can you compare God to anything?
Can you compare him to an image of anything?
19An idol is formed by a craftsman,
and a goldsmith covers it with gold
and makes silver chains for it.
20A poor person cannot buy those
expensive statues,
so he finds a tree that will not rot.
Then he finds a skilled craftsman
to make it into an idol that will not fall over.⚭

21Surely you know. Surely you have heard.
Surely from the beginning someone told you.
Surely you understand how the
earth was created.
22God sits on his throne above the
circle of the earth,
and compared to him, people are
like grasshoppers.
He stretches out the skies like a piece of cloth
and spreads them out like a
tent to sit under.
23He makes rulers unimportant
and the judges of this world worth nothing.
24They are like plants that are placed in the ground,
like seeds that are planted.
As soon as they begin to grow strong,
he blows on them and they die,
and the wind blows them away like chaff.

25God, the Holy One, says, "Can you compare
me to anyone?
Is anyone equal to me?"
26Look up to the skies.
Who created all these stars?
He leads out the army of heaven one by one
and calls all the stars by name.
Because he is strong and powerful,
not one of them is missing.

27People of Jacob, why do you complain?
People of Israel, why do you say,
"The LORD does not see what happens to me;
he does not care if I am treated fairly"?
28Surely you know.
Surely you have heard.
The LORD is the God who lives forever,
who created all the world.
He does not become tired or need to rest.
No one can understand how
great his wisdom is.
29He gives strength to those who are tired
and more power to those who are weak.
30Even children become tired and need to rest,
and young people trip and fall.
31But the people who trust the LORD
will become strong again.
They will rise up as an eagle in the sky;
they will run and not need rest;
they will walk and not become tired.⚭

The Lord Will Help Israel

41 The LORD says, "Faraway countries,
listen to me.
Let the nations become strong.
Come to me and speak;
we will meet together to decide who is right.

⚭**40:20 Idolatry:** Acts 17:29
40:24 *chaff.* See 17:13.

⚭**40:31 Stress:** Isaiah 41:10

[2]"Who caused the one to come from the east?
Who gives him victories everywhere he goes?
The one who brought him gives nations
over to him
and defeats kings.
He uses his sword, and kings become like dust.
He uses his bow, and they are blown
away like chaff.
[3]He chases them and is never hurt,
going places he has never been before.
[4]Who caused this to happen?
Who has controlled history since
the beginning?
I, the LORD, am the one. I was here
at the beginning,
and I will be here when all things are finished."

[5]All you faraway places, look and be afraid;
all you places far away on the earth,
shake with fear.
Come close and listen to me.
[6] The workers help each other
and say to each other, "Be strong!"
[7]The craftsman encourages the goldsmith,
and the workman who smooths the metal
with a hammer encourages the one who
shapes the metal.
He says, "This metal work is good."
He nails the statue to a base
so it can't fall over.

Only the Lord Can Save Us

[8]The LORD says, "People of Israel,
you are my servants.
People of Jacob, I chose you.
You are from the family of my
friend Abraham.
[9]I took you from places far away on the earth
and called you from a faraway country.
I said, 'You are my servants.'
I have chosen you and have
not turned against you.
[10]So don't worry, because I am with you.
Don't be afraid, because I am your God.
I will make you strong and will help you;
I will support you with my
right hand that saves you.
[11]"All those people who are angry with you
will be ashamed and disgraced.
Those who are against you
will disappear and be lost.
[12]You will look for your enemies,
but you will not find them.
Those who fought against you
will vanish completely.
[13]I am the LORD your God,
who holds your right hand,
and I tell you, 'Don't be afraid.
I will help you.'
[14]You few people of Israel who are left,
do not be afraid even though
you are weak as a worm.
I myself will help you," says the LORD.
"The one who saves you is
the Holy One of Israel.
[15]Look, I have made you like a
new threshing board
with many sharp teeth.
So you will walk on mountains and crush them;
you will make the hills like chaff.
[16]You will throw them into the air, and the wind
will carry them away;
a windstorm will scatter them.
Then you will be happy in the LORD;
you will be proud of the Holy One of Israel.

[17]"The poor and needy people look for water,
but they can't find any.
Their tongues are dry with thirst.
But I, the LORD, will answer their prayers;
I, the God of Israel, will not leave them to die.
[18]I will make rivers flow on the dry hills
and springs flow through the valleys.
I will change the desert into a lake of water
and the dry land into fountains of water.
[19]I will make trees grow in the desert—
cedars, acacia, myrtle, and olive trees.
I will put pine, fir, and cypress trees
growing together in the desert.
[20]People will see these things and understand;
they will think carefully about
these things and learn
that the LORD's power did this,
that the Holy One of Israel made
these things."

The Lord Challenges False Gods

[21]The LORD says, "Present your case."
The King of Jacob says, "Tell me
your arguments.
[22]Bring in your idols to tell us
what is going to happen.
Have them tell us what happened
in the beginning.

41:8 Servant of the Lord: Isaiah 42:1
41:10 Stress: Matthew 28:20b
41:20 Water: Jeremiah 2:11–13

Then we will think about these things,
and we will know how they will turn out.
Or tell us what will happen in the future.
23 Tell us what is coming next
so we will believe that you are gods.
Do something, whether it is good or bad,
and make us afraid.
24You gods are less than nothing;
you can't do anything.
Those who worship you should be hated.⚭

25"I have brought someone to
come out of the north.
I have called by name a man from the east,
and he knows me.
He walks on kings as if they were mud,
just as a potter walks on the clay.
26Who told us about this before it happened?
Who told us ahead of time so we could say,
'He was right'?
None of you told us anything;
none of you told us before it happened;
no one heard you tell about it.
27I, the LORD, was the first one to tell Jerusalem
that the people were coming home.
I sent a messenger to Jerusalem with the
good news.
28I look at the idols, but there is
not one that can answer.
None of them can give advice;
none of them can answer my questions.
29Look, all these idols are false.
They cannot do anything;
they are worth nothing.

The Lord's Special Servant

42 "Here is my servant, the one I support.
He is the one I chose, and
I am pleased with him.
I have put my Spirit upon him,
and he will bring justice to all nations.⚭
2He will not cry out or yell
or speak loudly in the streets.
3He will not break a crushed blade of grass
or put out even a weak flame.
He will truly bring justice;
4 he will not lose hope or give up
until he brings justice to the world.
And people far away will trust his teachings."
5God, the LORD, said these things.
He created the skies and stretched them out.
He spread out the earth and everything on it.
He gives life to all people on earth,
to everyone who walks on the earth.
6The LORD says, "I, the LORD, called
you to do right,
and I will hold your hand
and protect you.
You will be the sign of my agreement
with the people,
a light to shine for all people.⚭
7You will help the blind to see.
You will free those who are in prison,
and you will lead those who live in darkness
out of their prison.⚭

8"I am the LORD. That is my name.
I will not give my glory to another;
I will not let idols take the praise
that should be mine.
9The things I said would happen
have happened,
and now I tell you about new things.
Before those things happen,
I tell you about them."

A Song of Praise to the Lord

10Sing a new song to the LORD;
sing his praise everywhere on the earth.
Praise him, you people who sail on the seas
and you animals who live in them.
Praise him, you people living
in faraway places.
11The deserts and their cities
should praise him.
The settlements of Kedar should praise him.
The people living in Sela should sing for joy;
they should shout from the mountaintops.
12They should give glory to the LORD.
People in faraway lands should praise him.
13The LORD will march out like a strong soldier;
he will be excited like a man ready
to fight a war.
He will shout out the battle cry
and defeat his enemies.

⚭**41:24 Prophet & Prophecy:** Jeremiah 18:18
41:25 *someone . . . north.* This probably means Cyrus, a king of Persia.
⚭**42:1 Servant of the Lord:** Isaiah 42:19
⚭**42:6 Gentiles (Non-Jews):** Isaiah 49:6
⚭**42:6 Racism:** Isaiah 54:2–3
42:6–7 It was God's intent from the very start that Israel would be a light to draw all people to God. In this way, all the people of the earth would be blessed through Abram and his descendants (Genesis 12:1-3; see also Isaiah 49:6).
⚭**42:7 Blindness:** Isaiah 42:16–19
42:10 *a new song.* A new song is a victory shout. When God wins a victory, he makes everything new.

Disciple/Discipleship/ Mentoring

(Follow/Follower)

Mark 1:16–20; Matthew 28:18–20

What is a disciple? What differences are found between the different kinds of disciples mentioned in the Gospels? What is Jesus' form of discipleship? How is this related to the idea of mentoring today?

In the ancient world the term *disciple* was used generally to designate a *follower* who was committed to a recognized leader or teacher. When Jesus entered the scene of history in the first century, several other groups of individuals were called disciples. These disciples were similar to, yet quite different from Jesus' disciples.

The Jews who questioned the parents of the man born blind (John 9:13–41) attempted to scorn the blind man by saying that, although he was a follower of Jesus, they were "followers of Moses" (John 9:28). These disciples can be called *devoted traditionalists*. They focused on their privilege to have been born Jews who had a special relationship with God through Moses (see John 9:29). Any true Jew would have been a follower of Moses in this sense, regardless of any secondary commitments to other groups in Israel because God had specially chosen the Jews as his people to be witnesses to the world. But we see in this passage that these Jews were so focused on their privileged position that they missed Jesus.

The followers or disciples of the Pharisees (Matthew 22:15–16; Mark 2:18) were followers of the Pharisaic party, possibly belonging to one of the academic institutions. The Pharisees centered their activities on study and strict application of the Old Testament, developing a complex system of oral interpretations of the Law. These disciples were supremely dedicated people, but are often seen as *academic religionists*, forerunners of the later rabbinical school tradition. The Pharisees had a tendency to do the right things according to their laws without their hearts being rightly motivated (Matthew 15:7–9). Jesus' denunciations of certain Pharisees are among the most scathing in Scripture (for example, Matthew 5:20; 23:1–39). Recognizing the evil intentions of the disciples of the Pharisees who had been sent to trap him, Jesus called them hypocrites (Matthew 22:15–18).

The disciples of John the Baptist (Mark 2:18; John 1:35) were courageous men and women who had left the status quo of institutional Judaism to follow the prophet. They were *members of a movement.* They were attached more to the movement of God through the prophet than to ritualistic practices or traditions. These disciples were a complex group. From them came the first followers of Jesus (John 1:35–51). Some of John's disciples remained in contact with Jesus during his ministry in Galilee (Matthew 14:12). Yet on at least one occasion, they joined forces with the disciples of the Pharisees to question the practices of Jesus and his disciples (Mark 2:18–22). Apparently some of John the Baptist's disciples were so committed to John that they missed the true significance of Jesus' identity and missed becoming his disciples. They were more committed to the movement than to God's revelation through Jesus.

In John 6:60–66 we find what may be the most tragic disciples of all. During the beginning stages of Jesus' ministry, a large, radical group of disciples attached themselves to him. Some, apparently thinking that he was merely a revolutionary prophet, left Jesus when he disappointed their expectations. These disciples were *dedicated revolutionists*. They seemed to be looking for a leader to overthrow the Romans and restore the rule to Israel. Many of them left their homes and jobs to follow Jesus; some were even ready to die for their cause. This attitude is radical on the surface, but when we look deeper, we see people who wanted Jesus to conform to their way of thinking. They were willing to be disciples, but on their terms.

What then was different about Jesus' disciples? Who were they? What were they like? How were they different from these other disciples? Jesus' disciples were those who heard his invitation to begin a new kind of life, accepted his call to the new life, and became obedient to it. The center of this new life was Jesus himself because his disciples gained new life through him (John 10:7–10); they followed him (Mark 1:16–20); they were to hear and obey his teachings (Matthew 5:1–2 ff.); and they were to go into all of the world offering forgiveness of sins to all people who would also become Jesus' followers (Matthew 28:19–20; Luke 24:47).

Discipleship

When Jesus called men and women to follow him, he offered them a personal relationship with him, not simply an alternative lifestyle or a different religious practice or a new social organization. While some of the sectarians within Judaism created man-made separations between the "righteous" and the "unrighteous" by their regulations and traditions, Jesus broke through those barriers by calling to himself those who, in the eyes of sectarians, did not seem to enjoy the necessary qualifications for fellowship with him (Matthew 9:9–13; Mark 2:13–17). Discipleship means the beginning of a new life in intimate fellowship with a living Master and Savior.

Jesus' gracious call to discipleship is accompanied by an intense demand to count the cost of discipleship (see Luke 9:57–62; 14:25–33). Jesus recognized that various securities in this life can be a substitute for allegiance to him. The demand to count the cost of discipleship means exchanging the securities of this world for salvation and security in him. The call to be a disciple in Jesus' lifetime meant to count the cost of full allegiance to him. For some this meant sacrificing riches (Matthew 19:16–26); for others it meant sacrificing attachment to family (Matthew 8:18–22; Luke 14:25–27); for still others it meant abandoning nationalistic feelings of superiority (Luke 10:25–37).

Jesus declares that to be a disciple is to become like the Master (Matthew 10:24–25; Luke 6:40). Becoming like Jesus includes going out with the same message, ministry, and compassion (Matthew 10:5–15), practicing the same religious and social traditions (Matthew 12:1–8; Mark 2:18–22), belonging to the same family of obedience (Matthew 12:46–49), exercising the same servanthood (Matthew 20:26–28; Mark 10:42–45; John 13:12–17), and experiencing the same suffering (Matthew 10:16–25; Mark 10:38–39), doing all as he did. The true disciple is to know Jesus so well, is to follow him so closely, that he or she will become like him (see Luke 6:40; Romans 8:28–29).

John's Gospel carries three challenges that offer the means by which a disciple grows to become like Jesus. First, true discipleship means abiding in Jesus' words as the truth for every area of life (see John 8:31–32). Abiding in Jesus' words means to know and to live according to what Jesus says about life. Instead of listening to the world's values, disciples must listen to what Jesus says. This begins with salvation (see Peter's example in John 6:66–69), but involves every other area of life as well (Matthew 28:19–20). Second, true discipleship means loving one another as Jesus loved his disciples (John 13:34–35). Love is a distinguishing mark of all disciples of Jesus, made possible because of regeneration—where a change has been made in the heart of the believer by God's love—and an endless supply of love from God, who is love (cf. 1 John 4:12–21). Third, Jesus said that the true disciple will bear fruit: the fruit of the Spirit (Galatians 5:22–26), new converts (John 4:3–38; 15:16), righteousness, and good works (Philippians 1:11; Colossians 1:10).

No matter how advanced Jesus' disciples would become, they would always be his disciples. In other master-disciple relationships in Judaism the goal of discipleship was one day to become the master. But followers of Jesus are not simply involved in an educational or vocational form of discipleship. Followers of Jesus have entered into a relationship with the Son of God, which means that Jesus is always Master and Lord (Matthew 23:8–12).

MENTORING

While they vary somewhat, the books of Matthew, Mark, Luke, and John tell us about core of twelve disciples who were called by Jesus into a special relationship with him. Jesus chose the twelve from among the larger number of disciples and named them as *apostles* (Matthew 10:2–4; Luke 6:13, 17): Simon Peter, Andrew, James, John, Philip, Bartholomew, Thomas, Matthew, James the son of Alphaeus, Thaddaeus, Simon the Zealot, and Judas Iscariot. The circumstances of the lives of these twelve were quite different from other disciples, because they were called to follow Jesus around, join him in the missionary outreach to Israel, and be trained for their special roles in the future church.

This leadership role requires special training. Today we call that specialized training "mentoring." As disciples the twelve had a discipleship relationship with Jesus. As apostles they had a *mentoring* relationship with Jesus in which he modeled the kind of ministry they were to have as leaders in the church to come. Mentoring speaks of a relationship in which a more mature person provides personalized help for a specific goal, usually a ministry or professional goal. We might see this today as a more experienced, mature pastor mentors a younger pastor, or where a graduate student has a mentor in a doctoral program. In contrast to this more specialized training, discipleship is the more comprehensive term to describe how disciples of Jesus Christ become like Jesus.

Disciple/Discipleship/Mentoring (Follow/Follower): For additional scriptures on this topic go to Matthew 4:15–22.

14The LORD says, "For a long time
I have said nothing;
I have been quiet and held myself back.
But now I will cry out
and strain like a woman giving birth to a child.
15I will destroy the hills and mountains
and dry up all their plants.
I will make the rivers become dry land
and dry up the pools of water.
16Then I will lead the blind along
a way they never knew;
I will guide them along
paths they have not known.
I will make the darkness become light for them,
and the rough ground smooth.
These are the things I will do;
I will not leave my people.
17But those who trust in idols,
who say to their statues,
'You are our gods'
will be rejected in disgrace.

Israel Refused to Listen to the Lord

18"You who are deaf, hear me.
You who are blind, look and see.
19No one is more blind than my servant Israel
or more deaf than the messenger I send.
No one is more blind than the person I own
or more blind than the servant of the LORD.
20Israel, you have seen much,
but you have not obeyed.
You hear, but you refuse to listen."
21The LORD made his teachings wonderful,
because he is good.
22These people have been defeated and robbed.
They are trapped in pits
or locked up in prison.
Like robbers, enemies have taken them away,
and there is no one to save them.
Enemies carried them off,
and no one said, "Bring them back."

23Will any of you listen to this?
Will you listen carefully in the future?
24Who let the people of Jacob be carried off?
Who let robbers take Israel away?
The LORD allowed this to happen,
because we sinned against him.
We did not live the way he wanted us to live
and did not obey his teaching.
25So he became very angry with us
and brought terrible wars against us.
It was as if the people of Israel had fire all
around them,
but they didn't know what was happening.
It was as if they were burning,
but they didn't pay any attention.

God Is Always with His People

43 Now this is what the LORD says.
He created you, people of Jacob;
he formed you, people of Israel.
He says, "Don't be afraid,
because I have saved you.
I have called you by name, and you are mine.
2When you pass through the waters,
I will be with you.
When you cross rivers, you will not drown.
When you walk through fire,
you will not be burned,
nor will the flames hurt you.
3This is because I, the LORD, am your God,
the Holy One of Israel, your Savior.
I gave Egypt to pay for you,
and I gave Cush and Seba to make you mine.
4Because you are precious to me,
because I give you honor and love you,
I will give other people in your place;
I will give other nations to save your life.
5Don't be afraid, because I am with you.
I will bring your children from the east
and gather you from the west.
6I will tell the north: Give my people to me.
I will tell the south:
Don't keep my people in prison.
Bring my sons from far away
and my daughters from faraway places.
7Bring to me all the people who are mine,
whom I made for my glory,
whom I formed and made."

Judah Is God's Witness

8Bring out the people who have eyes but don't see
and those who have ears but don't hear.
9All the nations gather together,
and all the people come together.
Which of their gods said this would happen?
Which of their gods can tell what happened
in the beginning?
Let them bring their witnesses to prove they
were right.

42:19 Servant of the Lord: Isaiah 44:21
42:19 Blindness: Isaiah 59:10–11
43:8 Isaiah here uses sight and blindness as a metaphor for the quality of one's relationship with God. Those who have physical sight and can see the world around them, but cannot see the world from God's perspective, are blind to the things of God. Therefore, they act in irrational ways by following the advice of gods who don't even exist.

Then others will say, "It is true."
10The LORD says, "You are my witnesses
and the servant I chose.
I chose you so you would know and believe me,
so you would understand that
I am the true God.
There was no God before me,
and there will be no God after me.
11I myself am the LORD;
I am the only Savior.
12I myself have spoken to you, saved you,
and told you these things.
It was not some foreign god among you.
You are my witnesses, and I am God,"
says the LORD.
13 "I have always been God.
No one can save people from my power;
when I do something, no one can change it."

14This is what the LORD, who saves you,
the Holy One of Israel, says:
"I will send armies to Babylon for you,
and I will knock down all its locked gates.
The Babylonians will shout their cries of sorrow.
15I am the LORD, your Holy One,
the Creator of Israel, your King."

God Will Save His People Again

16This is what the LORD says.
He is the one who made a road
through the sea
and a path through rough waters.
17He is the one who defeated the
chariots and horses
and the mighty armies.
They fell together and will never rise again.
They were destroyed as a flame is put out.
18The LORD says, "Forget what happened before,
and do not think about the past.
19Look at the new thing I am going to do.
It is already happening. Don't you see it?
I will make a road in the desert
and rivers in the dry land.
20Even the wild animals will be thankful to me—
the wild dogs and owls.
They will honor me when
I put water in the desert
and rivers in the dry land
to give water to my people, the ones I chose.
21 The people I made
will sing songs to praise me.⚭

22"People of Jacob, you have not called to me;
people of Israel, you have become tired of me.
23You have not brought me your sacrifices of sheep
nor honored me with your sacrifices.
I did not weigh you down with sacrifices to offer
or make you tired with incense to burn.⚭
24So you did not buy incense for me;
you did not freely bring me
fat from your sacrifices.
Instead you have weighed me
down with your many sins;
you have made me tired of your many wrongs.

25"I, I am the One who forgives all your sins,
for my sake;
I will not remember your sins.
26But you should remind me.
Let's meet and decide what is right.
Tell what you have done and
show you are right.
27Your first father sinned,
and your leaders have turned against me.
28So I will make your holy rulers unholy.
I will bring destruction on the people of Jacob,
and I will let Israel be insulted."

The Lord Is the Only God

44 The LORD says, "People of Jacob, you are
my servants. Listen to me!
People of Israel, I chose you."
2This is what the LORD says, who made you,
who formed you in your mother's body,
who will help you:
"People of Jacob, my servants, don't be afraid.
Israel, I chose you.⚭
3I will pour out water for the thirsty land
and make streams flow on dry land.
I will pour out my Spirit into your children
and my blessing on your descendants.⚭
4Your children will grow like a tree in the grass,
like poplar trees growing
beside streams of water.
5One person will say, 'I belong to the LORD,'
and another will use the name Jacob.
Another will sign his name 'I am the LORD's,'
and another will use the name Israel."

43:14–21 As with Noah and the Exodus, God's deliverance of his people is described in "creation-like" language. Throughout the Old and New Testaments, salvation is described as a new creation. This comes to a climax in the New Testament, where Jesus is the "second Adam," and the new heaven and new earth are revealed (Revelation 21).

⚭**43:21 Wilderness (Desert):** Isaiah 63:10–14

⚭**43:23 Sacrifice:** Malachi 1:8

⚭**44:2 Abortion and Crisis Pregnancy:** Isaiah 49:1

⚭**44:3 Spiritual Gifts:** Ezekiel 36:26–28

6The LORD, the king of Israel,
is the LORD All-Powerful, who saves Israel.
This is what he says: "I am the beginning
and the end.
I am the only God.
7Who is a god like me?
That god should come and prove it.
Let him tell and explain all that has happened
since I set up my ancient people.
He should also tell what will happen
in the future.
8Don't be afraid! Don't worry!
I have always told you what will happen.
You are my witnesses.
There is no other God but me.
I know of no other Rock; I am the only One."

Idols Are Useless

9Some people make idols,
but they are worth nothing.
People treasure them, but they are useless.
Those people are witnesses for the statues, but
those people cannot see.
They know nothing, so they will be ashamed.
10Who made these gods?
Who made these useless idols?
11The workmen who made them will be ashamed,
because they are only human.
If they all would come together,
they would all be ashamed and afraid.

12One workman uses tools to heat iron,
and he works over hot coals.
With his hammer he beats the metal and
makes a statue,
using his powerful arms.
But when he becomes hungry,
he loses his power.
If he does not drink water, he becomes tired.

13Another workman uses a line and a compass
to draw on the wood.
Then he uses his chisels to cut a statue
and his calipers to measure the statue.
In this way, the workman makes the wood
look exactly like a person,
and this statue of a person sits in the house.
14He cuts down cedars
or cypress or oak trees.
Those trees grew by their own
power in the forest.
Or he plants a pine tree, and the
rain makes it grow.
15Then he burns the tree.
He uses some of the wood for a fire to keep
himself warm.
He also starts a fire to bake his bread.
But he uses part of the wood to make a god,
and then he worships it!
He makes the idol and bows down to it!
16The man burns half of the wood in the fire.
He uses the fire to cook his meat,
and he eats the meat until he is full.
He also burns the wood to keep himself warm.
He says,
"Good! Now I am warm. I can see because of
the fire's light."
17But he makes a statue from the wood that is
left and calls it his god.
He bows down to it and worships it.
He prays to it and says,
"You are my god. Save me!"
18Those people don't know what they are doing.
They don't understand!
It is as if their eyes are
covered so they can't see.
Their minds don't understand.
19They have not thought about these things;
they don't understand.
They have never thought to themselves,
"I burned half of the wood in the fire
and used the hot coals to bake my bread.
I cooked and ate my meat.
And I used the wood that was
left to make this hateful thing.
I am worshiping a block of wood!"
20He doesn't know what he is doing;
his confused mind leads him the wrong way.
He cannot save himself
or say, "This statue I am
holding is a false god."∞

The Lord Is the True God

21"People of Jacob, remember these things!
People of Israel, remember you
are my servants.∞
I made you, and you are my servants.
So Israel, I will not forget you.
22I have swept away your sins like a big cloud;
I have removed your sins like a cloud that
disappears into the air.
Come back to me because I saved you."

44:8 *God is a Rock.* This does not refer to a small pebble, but a cliff from which his people get protection and help.
44:10 *useless idols.* The idols of the nations were man-made objects that were worshiped. Here Isaiah makes fun of the fact that the same man manufactures and then bows down to idols made of wood.

∞**44:20 Lying/Dishonesty:** Ezekiel 13:6–9
∞**44:21 Servant of the Lord:** Isaiah 53:11–12

23Skies, sing for joy because
the LORD did great things!
Earth, shout for joy, even in your deepest parts!
Sing, you mountains, with thanks to God.
Sing, too, you trees in the forest!
The LORD saved the people of Jacob!
He showed his glory when he saved Israel.
24This is what the LORD says, who saved you,
who formed you in your mother's body:
"I, the LORD, made everything,
stretching out the skies by myself
and spreading out the earth all alone.
25I show that the lying prophets' signs are false;
I make fools of those who do magic.
I confuse even wise men;
they think they know much, but I make
them look foolish.
26I make the messages of my servants come true;
I make the advice of my messengers come true.
I say to Jerusalem,
'People will live in you again!'
I say to the towns of Judah,
'You will be built again!'
I say to Jerusalem's ruins,
'I will repair you.'
27I tell the deep waters, 'Become dry!
I will make your streams become dry!'
28I say of Cyrus, 'He is my shepherd
and will do all that I want him to do.
He will say to Jerusalem,
"You will be built again!"
He will tell the Temple, "Your foundations
will be rebuilt."' "

God Chooses Cyrus to Free Israel

45 This is what the LORD says to Cyrus, his
appointed king:
"I hold your right hand
and will help you defeat nations
and take away other kings' power.
I will open doors for you
so city gates will not stop you.
2I will go before you
and make the mountains flat.
I will break down the bronze gates of the cities
and cut through their iron bars.
3I will give you the wealth that is stored away
and the hidden riches
so you will know I am the LORD,
the God of Israel, who calls you by name.
4I do these things for my servants, the people
of Jacob,
and for my chosen people, the Israelites.
Cyrus, I call you by name,
and I give you a title of honor even though
you don't know me.
5I am the LORD. There is no other God;
I am the only God.
I will make you strong,
even though you don't know me,
6so that everyone will know
there is no other God.
From the east to the west they will know
I alone am the LORD.
7I made the light and the darkness.
I bring peace, and I cause troubles.
I, the LORD, do all these things.

8"Sky above, make victory fall like rain;
clouds, pour down victory.
Let the earth receive it,
and let salvation grow,
and let victory grow with it.
I, the LORD, have created it.

9"How terrible it will be for those who argue
with the God who made them.
They are like a piece of broken pottery
among many pieces.
The clay does not ask the potter,
'What are you doing?'
The thing that is made doesn't say to its maker,
'You have no hands.'
10How terrible it will be for the child who says
to his father,
'Why are you giving me life?'
How terrible it will be for the child who says
to his mother,
'Why are you giving birth to me?' "

11This is what the LORD,
the Holy One of Israel, and its Maker, says:
"You ask me about what will happen.
You question me about my children.
You give me orders about what I have made.
12I made the earth
and all the people living on it.
With my own hands I stretched out the skies,
and I commanded all the armies in the sky.
13I will bring Cyrus to do good things,
and I will make his work easy.
He will rebuild my city
and set my people free
without any payment or reward.
The LORD All-Powerful says this."

44:28 *Cyrus.* Cyrus was the future king of Persia, who would take over Babylon in 539 B.C. and then allow the surviving people of Israel to return to their land. Such a specific prophecy is quite amazing.

14The LORD says,
"The goods made in Egypt and Cush
and the tall people of Seba
will come to you
and will become yours.
The Sabeans will walk behind you,
coming along in chains.
They will bow down before you
and pray to you, saying,
'God is with you,
and there is no other God.'"

15God and Savior of Israel,
you are a God that people cannot see.
16All the people who make idols will
be put to great shame;
they will go off together in disgrace.
17But Israel will be saved by the LORD,
and that salvation will continue forever.
Never again will Israel be put to shame.

18The LORD created the heavens.
He is the God who formed the earth and
made it.
He did not want it to be empty,
but he wanted life on the earth.
This is what the LORD says:
"I am the LORD. There is no other God.
19I did not speak in secret
or hide my words in some dark place.
I did not tell the family of Jacob
to look for me in empty places.
I am the LORD, and I speak the truth;
I say what is right.

20"You people who have escaped from other
nations,
gather together and come before me;
come near together.
People who carry idols of wood don't know
what they are doing.
They pray to a god who cannot save them.
21Tell these people to come to me.
Let them talk about these things together.
Who told you long ago that this would happen?
Who told about it long ago?
I, the LORD, said these things.
There is no other God besides me.
I am the only good God. I am the Savior.
There is no other God.

22"All people everywhere,
follow me and be saved.
I am God. There is no other God.
23I will make a promise by my own power,
and my promise is true;
what I say will not be changed.
I promise that everyone will bow before me
and will promise to follow me.
24People will say about me, 'Goodness and power
come only from the LORD.'"
Everyone who has been angry with him
will come to him and be ashamed.
25But with the LORD's help, the people of Israel
will be found to be good,
and they will praise him.

False Gods Are Useless

46 Bel and Nebo bow down.
Their idols are carried by animals.
The statues are only heavy
loads that must be carried;
they only make people tired.
2These gods will all bow down.
They cannot save themselves
but will all be carried away like prisoners.

3"Family of Jacob, listen to me!
All you people from Israel
who are still alive, listen!
I have carried you since you were born;
I have taken care of you from your birth.
4Even when you are old, I will be the same.
Even when your hair has turned gray,
I will take care of you.
I made you and will take care of you.
I will carry you and save you.

5"Can you compare me to anyone?
No one is equal to me or like me.
6Some people are rich with gold
and weigh their silver on the scales.
They hire a goldsmith, and he
makes it into a god.
Then they bow down and worship it.
7They put it on their shoulders and carry it.
They set it in its place, and there it stands;
it cannot move from its place.
People may yell at it, but it cannot answer.
It cannot save them from their troubles.

8"Remember this, and do not forget it!
Think about these things, you who turn
against God.

45:22 Trinity: Matthew 3:16–17

46:1 *Bel and Nebo.* Bel and Nebo are Hebrew names for the Babylonian gods Marduk and Nabu.

9Remember what happened long ago.
Remember that I am God, and there is no other God.
I am God, and there is no one like me.
10From the beginning I told you what would happen in the end.
A long time ago I told you things that have not yet happened.
When I plan something, it happens.
What I want to do, I will do.
11I am calling a man from the east to carry out my plan;
he will come like a hawk from a country far away.
I will make what I have said come true;
I will do what I have planned.
12Listen to me, you stubborn people,
who are far from what is right.
13I will soon do the things that are right.
I will bring salvation soon.
I will save Jerusalem
and bring glory to Israel."

God Will Destroy Babylon

47 The LORD says, "City of Babylon,
go down and sit in the dirt.
People of Babylon, sit on the ground.
You are no longer the ruler.
You will no longer be called
tender or beautiful.
2 You must use large stones
to grind grain into flour.
Remove your veil and your nice skirts.
Uncover your legs and cross the rivers.
3People will see your nakedness;
they will see your shame.
I will punish you;
I will punish every one of you."

4Our Savior is named the LORD All-Powerful;
he is the Holy One of Israel.

5"Babylon, sit in darkness and say nothing.
You will no longer be called
the queen of kingdoms.
6I was angry with my people,
so I rejected those who belonged to me.
I gave them to you,
but you showed them no mercy.
You even made the old people
work very hard.
7You said, 'I will live forever
as the queen.'
But you did not think about these things
or consider what would happen.

8"Now, listen, you lover of pleasure.
You think you are safe.
You tell yourself,
'I am the only important person.
I will never be a widow
or lose my children.'
9Two things will happen to you suddenly,
in a single day.
You will lose your children and your husband.
These things will truly happen to you,
in spite of all your magic,
in spite of your powerful tricks.
10You do evil things, but you feel safe
and say, 'No one sees what I do.'
Your wisdom and knowledge
have fooled you.
You say to yourself,
'I am God, and no one is equal to me.'
11But troubles will come to you,
and you will not know how to stop them.
Disaster will fall on you,
and you will not be able to keep it away.
You will be destroyed quickly;
you will not even see it coming.

12"Keep on using your tricks
and doing all your magic
that you have used since you were young.
Maybe they will help you;
maybe you will be able to scare someone.
13You are tired of the advice you have received.
So let those who study the sky—
those who tell the future by looking at the stars and the new moons—
let them save you from what is about to happen to you.
14But they are like straw;
fire will quickly burn them up.
They cannot save themselves
from the power of the fire.
They are not like coals that give warmth
nor like a fire that you may sit beside.
15You have worked with these people,
and they have been with you
since you were young,
but they will not be able to help you.
Everyone will go his own way,
and there will be no one left to save you."

47:2 *Remove your veil.* Here the city of Babylon is likened to a whore who is shamed by exposure.
47:13 *by looking at the stars.* This is a reference to astrology. The ancient Near East was filled with astrologers and astrological texts.

47:14 Astrology: Jeremiah 8:2
47:15 Magic: Jeremiah 27:9

God Controls the Future

48 The LORD says, "Family of Jacob,
listen to me.
You are called Israel,
and you come from the family of Judah.
You swear by the LORD's name
and praise the God of Israel,
but you are not honest or sincere.
2You call yourselves people of the holy city,
and you depend on the God of Israel,
who is named the LORD All-Powerful.
3Long ago I told you what would happen.
I said these things and made them known;
suddenly I acted, and these things happened.
4I knew you were stubborn;
your neck was like an iron muscle,
and your head was like bronze.
5So a long time ago I told you about these things;
I told you about them before they happened
so you couldn't say, 'My idols did this,
and my wooden and metal statues made
these things happen.'

6"You heard and saw everything that happened,
so you should tell this news to others.
Now I will tell you about new things,
hidden things that you don't know yet.
7These things are happening now, not long ago;
you have not heard about them before today.
So you cannot say, 'We already
knew about that.'
8But you have not heard me; you have not
understood.
Even long ago you did not listen to me.
I knew you would surely turn against me;
you have fought against
me since you were born.
9But for my own sake I will be patient.
People will praise me for not becoming angry
and destroying you.
10I have made you pure, but not by fire, as silver
is made pure.
I have purified you by giving you troubles.
11I do this for myself, for my own sake.
I will not let people speak evil against me,
and I will not let some god take my glory.

Israel Will Be Free

12"People of Jacob, listen to me.
People of Israel, I have
called you to be my people.
I am God;
I am the beginning and the end.
13I made the earth with my own hands.
With my right hand I spread out the skies.
When I call them,
they come together before me."

14All of you, come together and listen.
None of the gods said these
things would happen.
The LORD has chosen someone
to attack the Babylonians;
he will carry out his wishes against Babylon.

15"I have spoken; I have called him.
I have brought him, and I
will make him successful.
16Come to me and listen to this.
From the beginning I have spoken openly.
From the time it began, I was there."

Now, the Lord GOD
has sent me with his Spirit.

17This is what the LORD, who saves you,
the Holy One of Israel, says:
"I am the LORD your God,
who teaches you to do what is good,
who leads you in the way you should go.⚭
18If you had obeyed me,
you would have had peace
like a full-flowing river.
Good things would have flowed to you like
the waves of the sea.
19You would have had many children,
as many as the grains of sand.
They would never have died out
nor been destroyed."

20My people, leave Babylon!
Run from the Babylonians!
Tell this news with shouts of joy
to the people;
spread it everywhere on earth.
Say, "The LORD has saved his servants,
the people of Jacob."
21They did not become thirsty when he led
them through the deserts.
He made water flow from a rock for them.
He split the rock,
and water flowed out.

22"There is no peace for evil people,"
says the LORD.

48:15 *him.* This probably refers to Cyrus king of Persia.

⚭**48:17 Leadership:** Isaiah 49:10

God Calls His Special Servant

49 All of you people in faraway places, listen to me.
Listen, all you nations far away.
Before I was born, the LORD
called me to serve him.
The LORD named me while I
was still in my mother's body.
2He made my tongue like a sharp sword.
He hid me in the shadow of his hand.
He made me like a sharp arrow.
He hid me in the holder for his arrows.
3He told me, "Israel, you are my servant.
I will show my glory through you."
4But I said, "I have worked hard for nothing;
I have used all my power,
but I did nothing useful.
But the LORD will decide what
my work is worth;
God will decide my reward."
5The LORD made me in the body of my mother
to be his servant,
to lead the people of Jacob back to him
so that Israel might be gathered to him.
The LORD will honor me,
and I will get my strength from my God.
6Now he told me,
"You are an important servant to me
to bring back the tribes of Jacob,
to bring back the people of
Israel who are left alive.
But, more importantly, I will make
you a light for all nations
to show people all over the world
the way to be saved."

7The LORD who saves you
is the Holy One of Israel.
He speaks to the one who is
hated by the people,
to the servant of rulers.
This is what he says: "Kings will see you and
stand to honor you;
great leaders will bow down before you,
because the LORD can be trusted.
He is the Holy One of Israel,
who has chosen you."

The Day of Salvation

8This is what the LORD says:
"At the right time I will hear your prayers.
On the day of salvation I will help you.
I will protect you,
and you will be the sign of my agreement
with the people.
You will bring back the people to the land
and give the land that is now ruined
back to its owners.
9You will tell the prisoners,
'Come out of your prison.'
You will tell those in darkness,
'Come into the light.'
The people will eat beside the roads,
and they will find food even on bare hills.
10They will not be hungry or thirsty.
Neither the hot sun nor the desert
wind will hurt them.
The God who comforts them will lead them
and guide them by springs of water.
11I will make my mountains into roads,
and the roads will be raised up.
12Look, people are coming to me from far away,
from the north and from the west,
from Aswan in southern Egypt."

13Heavens and earth, be happy.
Mountains, shout with joy,
because the LORD comforts his people
and will have pity on those who suffer.

Jerusalem and Her Children

14But Jerusalem said, "The LORD has left me;
the Lord has forgotten me."

15The LORD answers, "Can a woman
forget the baby she nurses?
Can she feel no kindness for the child to
which she gave birth?
Even if she could forget her children,
I will not forget you.
16See, I have written your name on my hand.
Jerusalem, I always think about your walls.
17Your children will soon return to you,
and the people who defeated you and
destroyed you will leave.
18Look up and look around you.
All your children are gathering
to return to you."
The LORD says, "As surely as I live,
your children will be like jewels
that a bride wears proudly.

49:1 Abortion and Crisis Pregnancy: Galatians 1:15

49:6 God raised up his servant so that all people, both Israel and the nations of the earth, might receive his salvation. God never intended to exclude the non-Jewish people from his plan of salvation. Although Israel failed as a light to the nations, Jesus brought salvation to Jewish and non-Jewish people alike (Luke 2:32; Acts 1:8; 22:2; Romans 1:16).

49:6 Gentiles (Non-Jews): Matthew 12:21

49:10 Leadership: Jeremiah 23:32

CROSSING CULTURAL BOUNDARIES

MARK 2:14–17

What are some concrete examples of crossing cultures with the Good News of salvation in the Bible? What can we learn from those examples for faithful discipleship today?

The Bible describes a world where cultural divisions abound. Boundaries were drawn between ethnic groups, rich and poor, men and women, adults and children, healthy and sick, righteous and sinners. An individual who found him or herself on the unfavored side of such boundaries had little hope for change: the poor could not climb a ladder to success, the chronically ill usually did not get better, and the social outcasts stayed on the fringes of everyday life.

Because of the rigidity of these boundaries, it was a notable exception when an individual or individuals chose to cross them. In the Book of Ruth, the Moabite woman Ruth is commended for her willingness to leave her own culture and cross into her mother-in-law's, even after the death of her husband (Ruth 2:11–12). In doing so, she went far above and beyond what was expected of her as a dutiful daughter-in-law.

In the New Testament, Jesus consistently angered and confounded his opponents by crossing existing cultural boundaries. From a Jewish perspective, a key concept in the creation and maintenance of such boundaries was the belief that a firm line needed to be drawn between holy and unholy and between clean and unclean. These boundaries applied to things such as places and food, but they also applied to people. People such as prostitutes, sinners, and tax collectors should not be associated with, at least by "decent people."

When Jesus would go to the house of a tax collector and eat with them, he was extending a most intimate gesture of association and friendship (Mark 2:14–17). He crossed the cultural boundaries that existed to bring the Good News to those most on the outside of respectable society.

Jesus also crossed the boundary between well and sick (Matthew 8:1–4, Mark 5:25–34; Luke 9:37–43). He took the time to speak with and teach women (Luke 10:38–42, John 4:1–26). He crossed ethnic lines and applauded non-Jews as models of faithful behavior (Luke 10:25–37; Matthew 8:5–13). Everywhere he went, Jesus demonstrated that the Good News could not be contained by cultural boundaries.

This was not because Jesus did not acknowledge the existence or importance of such boundaries. Nor did he deny the existence of sin. What is striking about Jesus and the Good News is that as he crosses cultural boundaries, he brings holiness, forgiveness, and cleansing. Instead of being contaminated, he brings new life and hope to those around him.

As Jesus crosses cultural boundaries to draw in a diverse group of people, a new boundary is drawn: it is drawn between those who respond to Jesus' message and those who reject it. When people come to him and tell him that his family is waiting to see him, Jesus comments that those who hear and do the will of God are his family (Mark 3:31–35). He reinterprets the traditional boundaries of "family" to include those who respond to his message. A notable feature about the Good News is that it is always reaching out, crossing boundaries and drawing others in. As Jesus reached across cultural boundaries in his earthly ministry, the members of the early church also crossed boundaries with the message about Jesus.

In the Book of Acts the church in Jerusalem has to deal with the reality that the Good News has gone to non-Jews, on God's divine initiative (Acts 11:1–18). Philip preaches to an Ethiopian he meets on the road, again through divine intervention (Acts 8:26–40). It is clear that God's agenda is that the Good News be spread across cultural and geographic boundaries, from Jerusalem, Judea, Samaria, to every part of the world (Acts 1:8).

Paul understood the expansive and inclusive nature of the Good News. In his letter to the Galatians, Paul criticizes Peter for refusing to eat with non-Jews when his Jewish friends were around. Both Jew and non-Jew, Paul asserts, are made right with God through faith in Jesus Christ. Therefore, it is wrong to reassert the cultural divide between Jew and non-Jew (Galatians 2:11–16).

James also warns his readers about the dangers of treating people according to the cultural boundaries drawn by society, particularly between rich and poor. To treat someone who is wealthy with more honor and respect than someone who is poor is to judge that the wealthy person is more important than the poor person (James 2:1–4).

Crossing Cultural Boundaries: For additional scriptures on this topic go to Genesis 11:1–9.

Ambition

Mark 9:33–37

Can we distinguish between healthy and distorted ambition? What key biblical characters reveal ambition in positive ways? What key biblical characters reveal ambition in negative ways?

In the disciples' era certain questions were often asked. Who is the best? or Who is the wealthiest? or Who is the most important? occupied much of their attention. On the way to Capernaum the disciples began arguing among themselves over who was the greatest in their ranks. Possibly Peter, James, and John were feeling privileged since they had seen the Transfiguration of Jesus. Perhaps others were boasting about how they had performed more miracles than any of the rest. Whatever the source of their conflict, the disciples were about the unhealthy business of ranking themselves. They had allowed the world to infect their spirits with divisive thoughts of competitiveness.

Jesus sat them down around him and told them they had it all wrong. The true way of greatness was this: "Whoever wants to be the most important must be last of all and servant of all" (Mark 9:35). Then to illustrate his point, Jesus stood a little child before them and proclaimed, "Whoever accepts a child like this in my name accepts me. And whoever accepts me accepts the One who sent me" (Mark 9:37).

By calling the disciples to servanthood, and by placing a child before them, Jesus reversed the values of the world as well as those of his disciples. The disciples were demonstrating harmful ambition, the kind that is completely selfish. Such distorted ambition places the self at the center of the creation and then demands that every person, event, and thing revolve around it, including God!

Jesus was coming squarely against an infantile, self-centered world-view that was driven by excessive ambition. The truly great ones, he affirmed, will not see their role as that of getting ahead of others. Instead, they will follow my example and will serve others. The ones who will genuinely be exalted in the kingdom of God will be those who understand their calling as facilitating the love of Christ in others, not in stampeding over others for the sake of self-glory.

Paul was clear in this area as well. He wrote: "When you do things, do not let selfishness or pride be your guide. Instead, be humble and give more honor to others than to yourselves. Do not be interested only in your own life, but be interested in the lives of others" (Philippians 2:3–4). Selfish ambition always results in strife within the church: "arguing, jealousy, anger, selfish fighting, evil talk, gossip, pride, and confusion" (2 Corinthians 12:20). Paul warns us that careless ambition leads to people refusing "to follow truth and, instead, [following] evil" (Romans 2:8).

Christ is always our key example for harmonious living. Paul said Jesus "gave up his place with God and made himself nothing. . . . And when he was living as a man, he humbled himself and was fully obedient to God, even when that caused his death—death on a cross" (Philippians 2:7–8). Jesus descended from a place of magnificent glory to empty himself out in service for us. His sole ambition was to do the will of the Father: "My food is to do what the One who sent me wants me to do and to finish his work" (John 4:34).

In the Old Testament, David had the God-given ambition to build a temple for the Lord. Because of sin in his life, however, he was not allowed to begin the actual construction (1 Chronicles 22:7–8). Nevertheless, he was able to follow his dream by making the necessary preparations for the construction of the temple, which in turn allowed his son Solomon to complete the project.

In the New Testament, Peter demonstrated holy ambition through his obedience to the vision God gave him concerning preaching the gospel to non-Jewish people as well as to the Jews (Acts 10:28–29). Afterward, Paul traveled through much of the northern Mediterranean world preaching the Good News across the Roman empire. His ambition was to spread the knowledge of Christ everywhere, "like a sweet-smelling perfume" (2 Corinthians 2:14).

True ambition is always God-given, God-empowered, and God-directed. It is never focused on self-gain, but on self-sacrifice. Healthy ambition is always fixed upon the Lord and upon service to others. Paul instructed Titus to be one who was "always wanting to do good deeds" (Titus 2:14).

Proper ambition, therefore, is rooted first and last in the Lord. It is the God-given desire to fulfill our purpose in life and to accomplish those things which the Lord has assigned us. It is an attitude of absolute dependence upon God in all things, and a stance which is quick to give God the praise for all successes in life.

Ambition: For additional scriptures on this topic go to 1 Chronicles 22:7–8.

19"You were destroyed and defeated,
and your land was made useless.
But now you will have more people than the
land can hold,
and those people who destroyed
you will be far away.
20Children were born to you while you were sad,
but they will say to you,
'This place is too small for us.
Give us a bigger place to live.'
21Then you will say to yourself,
'Who gave me all these children?
I was sad and lonely,
defeated and separated from my people.
So who reared these children?
I was left all alone.
Where did all these children come from?' "

22This is what the Lord GOD says:
"See, I will lift my hand to signal the nations;
I will raise my banner for all the people to see.
Then they will bring your sons
back to you in their arms,
and they will carry your daughters
on their shoulders.
23Kings will teach your children,
and daughters of kings will take care of them.
They will bow down before you
and kiss the dirt at your feet.
Then you will know I am the LORD.
Anyone who trusts in me will
not be disappointed."

24Can the wealth a soldier wins in war be taken
away from him?
Can a prisoner be freed
from a powerful soldier?
25This is what the LORD says:
"The prisoners will be taken
from the strong soldiers.
What the soldiers have taken will be saved.
I will fight your enemies,
and I will save your children.
26I will force those who trouble you
to eat their own flesh.
Their own blood will be the wine
that makes them drunk.
Then everyone will know
I, the LORD, am the One who saves you;
I am the Powerful One of Jacob who saves you."

Israel Was Punished for Its Sin

50 This is what the LORD says:
"People of Israel, you say I divorced your
mother.
Then where is the paper that proves it?
Or do you think I sold you
to pay a debt?
Because of the evil things you did, I sold you.
Because of the times she turned against me,
your mother was sent away.
2I came home and found no one there;
I called, but no one answered.
Do you think I am not able to save you?
Do I not have the power to save you?
Look, I need only to shout and
the sea becomes dry.
I change rivers into a desert,
and their fish rot because there is no water;
they die of thirst.
3I can make the skies dark;
I can make them black like clothes of sadness."

God's Servant Obeys

4The Lord GOD gave me the ability to teach
so that I know what to say to make
the weak strong.
Every morning he wakes me.
He teaches me to listen like a student.
5The Lord GOD helps me learn,
and I have not turned against him
nor stopped following him.
6I offered my back to those who beat me.
I offered my cheeks to those
who pulled my beard.
I won't hide my face from them
when they make fun of me and spit at me.
7The Lord GOD helps me,
so I will not be ashamed.
I will be determined,
and I know I will not be disgraced.
8He shows that I am innocent,
and he is close to me.
So who can accuse me?
If there is someone, let us go to court together.
If someone wants to prove I have done wrong,
he should come and tell me.
9Look! It is the Lord GOD who helps me.
So who can prove me guilty?
Look! All those who try will become useless
like old clothes;
moths will eat them.

10Who among you fears the LORD
and obeys his servant?
That person may walk in the dark
and have no light.
Then let him trust in the LORD
and depend on his God.

11But instead, some of you want to light your
own fires
and make your own light.
So, go, walk in the light of your fires,
and trust your own light to guide you.
But this is what you will receive from me:
You will lie down in a place of pain.

Jerusalem Will Be Saved

51 The LORD says, "Listen to me,
those of you who try to live right and
follow the LORD.
Look at the rock from which you were cut;
look at the stone quarry from which you
were dug.
2Look at Abraham, your ancestor,
and Sarah, who gave birth to your ancestors.
Abraham had no children when I called him,
but I blessed him and gave
him many descendants.
3So the LORD will comfort Jerusalem;
he will show mercy to those
who live in her ruins.
He will change her deserts
into a garden like Eden;
he will make her empty lands
like the garden of the LORD.
People there will be very happy;
they will give thanks and sing songs.⚭

4"My people, listen to me;
my nation, pay attention to me.
I will give the people my teachings,
and my decisions will be
like a light to all people.
5I will soon show that I do what is right.
I will soon save you.
I will use my power and judge all nations.
All the faraway places are waiting for me;
they wait for my power to help them.
6Look up to the heavens.
Look around you at the earth below.
The skies will disappear like clouds of smoke.
The earth will become useless like old clothes,
and its people will die like flies.
But my salvation will continue forever,
and my goodness will never end.

7"You people who know what is right should
listen to me;
you people who follow my teachings should
hear what I say.
Don't be afraid of the evil things people say,
and don't be upset by their insults.
8Moths will eat those people
as if they were clothes,
and worms will eat them as if they were wool.
But my goodness will continue forever,
and my salvation will continue from now on."

9Wake up, wake up, and use your strength,
powerful LORD.
Wake up as you did in the old times,
as you did a long time ago.
With your own power, you cut Rahab into pieces
and killed that sea monster.
10You dried up the sea
and the waters of the deep ocean.
You made the deepest parts of the sea into a road
for your people to cross over and be saved.
11The people the LORD has freed will return
and enter Jerusalem with joy.
Their happiness will last forever.
They will have joy and gladness,
and all sadness and sorrow
will be gone far away.

12The LORD says, "I am the one who comforts you.
So why should you be afraid of people,
who die?
Why should you fear people
who die like the grass?
13Have you forgotten the LORD who made you,
who stretched out the skies
and made the earth?
Why are you always afraid
of those angry people who trouble you
and who want to destroy?
But where are those angry people now?
14 People in prison will soon be set free;
they will not die in prison,
and they will have enough food.
15I am the LORD your God,
who stirs the sea and makes the waves roar.
My name is the LORD All-Powerful.
16I will give you the words I want you to say.
I will cover you with my
hands and protect you.
I made the heavens and the earth,
and I say to Jerusalem, 'You are my people.'"

51:3 The wasteland is transformed into a garden like Eden. Throughout the Bible, Eden is symbolic of peace, prosperity, and happiness. God's punishment of Israel is compared to the harshness of the desert, but his mercy will redeem the barren lands and transform them into a lush garden that will nourish his chosen people once again.

⚭**51:3 Garden of Eden:** Ezekiel 28:13

51:9 *Rahab.* Rahab was well known in the ancient Near East as a sea monster. The sea and its monsters represented chaos against which the God of creation and order fought. Rahab often stood for Egypt.

God Punished Israel

17Awake! Awake!
Get up, Jerusalem.
The LORD was very angry with you;
your punishment was like wine in a cup.
The LORD made you drink that wine;
you drank the whole cup until you stumbled.
18Jerusalem had many people,
but there was not one to lead her.
Of all the people who grew up there,
no one was there to guide her.
19Troubles came to you two by two,
but no one will feel sorry for you.
There was ruin and disaster,
great hunger and fighting.
No one can comfort you.
20Your people have become weak.
They fall down and lie on every street corner,
like animals caught in a net.
They have felt the full anger of the LORD
and have heard God's angry shout.

21So listen to me, poor Jerusalem,
you who are drunk but not from wine.
22Your God will defend his people.
This is what the LORD your God says:
"The punishment I gave you
is like a cup of wine.
You drank it and could not walk straight.
But I am taking that cup of my anger
away from you,
and you will never be punished
by my anger again.
23I will now give that cup of punishment to
those who gave you pain,
who told you,
'Bow down so we can walk over you.'
They made your back like
dirt for them to walk on;
you were like a street for them to travel on."

Jerusalem Will Be Saved

52 Wake up, wake up, Jerusalem! Become strong!
Be beautiful again,
holy city of Jerusalem.
The people who do not worship God and who
are not pure
will not enter you again.
2Jerusalem, you once were a prisoner.
Now shake off the dust and stand up.
Jerusalem, you once were a prisoner.
Now free yourself from the
chains around your neck.
3This is what the LORD says:
"You were not sold for a price,
so you will be saved without cost."
4This is what the Lord GOD says:
"First my people went down to Egypt to live.
Later Assyria made them slaves.

5"Now see what has happened," says the LORD.
"Another nation has taken
away my people for nothing.
This nation who rules them makes
fun of me," says the LORD.
"All day long they speak against me.
6This has happened so my people
will know who I am,
and so, on that future day, they will know
that I am the one speaking to them.
It will really be me."

7How beautiful is the person
who comes over the mountains
to bring good news,
who announces peace
and brings good news,
who announces salvation
and says to Jerusalem,
"Your God is King."
8Listen! Your guards are shouting.
They are all shouting for joy!
They all will see with their own eyes
when the LORD returns to Jerusalem.
9Jerusalem, your buildings are destroyed now,
but shout and rejoice together,
because the LORD has comforted his people.
He has saved Jerusalem.
10The LORD will show his holy power
to all the nations.
Then everyone on earth
will see the salvation of our God.

11You people, leave, leave; get out of Babylon!
Touch nothing that is unclean.
You men who carry the LORD's
things used in worship,
leave there and make yourselves pure.
12You will not be forced to leave Babylon quickly;
you will not be forced to run away,
because the LORD will go before you,
and the God of Israel will guard you from
behind.

51:23 Hell: Isaiah 66:24
52:1 Nehemiah: Revelation 21:2
52:7 Gospel/Good News: Isaiah 61:1–9

52:7 After a battle, a messenger from the army would be dispatched back home to tell whether the war was won or lost. In this case, the battle was won, and the message was a good one.

The Lord's Suffering Servant

13The LORD says, "See, my servant will act wisely.
People will greatly honor and respect him.
14Many people were shocked when they saw him.
His appearance was so changed he did not
look like a man;
his form was changed so much they could
barely tell he was human.
15But now he will surprise many nations.
Kings will be amazed and shut their mouths.
They will see things they had
not been told about him,
and they will understand things
they had not heard."

53 Who would have believed what we heard?
Who saw the LORD's power in this?
2He grew up like a small plant before the LORD,
like a root growing in a dry land.
He had no special beauty or form to make us
notice him;
there was nothing in his appearance to make
us desire him.
3He was hated and rejected by people.
He had much pain and suffering.
People would not even look at him.
He was hated, and we didn't even notice him.

4But he took our suffering on him
and felt our pain for us.
We saw his suffering
and thought God was punishing him.
5But he was wounded for the wrong we did;
he was crushed for the evil we did.
The punishment, which made us well,
was given to him,
and we are healed because of his wounds.
6We all have wandered away like sheep;
each of us has gone his own way.
But the LORD has put on him the punishment
for all the evil we have done.

7He was beaten down and punished,
but he didn't say a word.
He was like a lamb being led to be killed.
He was quiet, as a sheep is quiet while its
wool is being cut;
he never opened his mouth.
8Men took him away roughly and unfairly.
He died without children to continue
his family.
He was put to death;
he was punished for the sins of my people.
9He was buried with wicked men,
and he died with the rich.
He had done nothing wrong,
and he had never lied.

10But it was the LORD who decided
to crush him and make him suffer.
The LORD made his life a penalty offering,
but he will still see his descendants
and live a long life.
He will complete the things the LORD
wants him to do.
11"After his soul suffers many things,
he will see life and be satisfied.
My good servant will make many
people right with God;
he will carry away their sins.
12For this reason I will make him a great man
among people,
and he will share in all things with those
who are strong.
He willingly gave his life
and was treated like a criminal.
But he carried away the sins of many people
and asked forgiveness for
those who sinned."

People Will Return to Jerusalem

54 The LORD says, "Sing, Jerusalem.
You are like a woman who never gave
birth to children.
Start singing and shout for joy.
You never felt the pain of giving birth,
but you will have more children
than the woman who has a husband.
2Make your tent bigger;
stretch it out and make it wider.
Do not hold back.
Make the ropes longer
and its stakes stronger,
3because you will spread out to the right
and to the left.
Your children will take over other nations,
and they will again live in cities that
once were destroyed.

4"Don't be afraid, because you
will not be ashamed.

53:5 Reconciliation: John 3:16
53:12 Crime: Amos 5:12
53:12 Martyrdom: Daniel 3:1–30
53:12 Suffering: Lamentations
53:12 Servant of the Lord: Isaiah 54:17
54:3 Racism: Matthew 11:20–24
54:4–8 Here God addresses the people of Jerusalem who have

Don't be embarrassed,
because you will not be disgraced.
You will forget the shame you felt earlier;
you will not remember the shame you felt
when you lost your husband.
5The God who made you is like your husband.
His name is the LORD All-Powerful.
The Holy One of Israel is the one who saves you.
He is called the God of all the earth.
6You were like a woman whose husband left her,
and you were very sad.
You were like a wife who married young
and then her husband left her.
But the LORD called you to be his,"
says your God.
7God says, "I left you for a short time,
but with great kindness I will
bring you back again.
8I became very angry
and hid from you for a time,
but I will show you mercy with
kindness forever,"
says the LORD who saves you.
9The LORD says, "This day is like the
time of Noah to me.
I promised then that I would never
flood the world again.
In the same way, I promise I will
not be angry with you
or punish you again.
10The mountains may disappear,
and the hills may come to an end,
but my love will never disappear;
my promise of peace will not come to an end,"
says the LORD who shows mercy to you.

11"You poor city. Storms have hurt you,
and you have not been comforted.
But I will rebuild you with turquoise stones,
and I will build your foundations
with sapphires.
12I will use rubies to build your walls
and shining jewels for the gates
and precious jewels for all your outer walls.⚭
13All your children will be taught by the LORD,
and they will have much peace.⚭
14I will build you using fairness.
You will be safe from those who would hurt you,
so you will have nothing to fear.
Nothing will come to make you afraid.
15I will not send anyone to attack you,
and you will defeat those who do attack you.

16"See, I made the blacksmith.
He fans the fire to make it hotter,
and he makes the kind of tool he wants.
In the same way I have made
the destroyer to destroy.
17 So no weapon that is used against
you will defeat you.
You will show that those who
speak against you are wrong.
These are the good things my servants receive.
Their victory comes from me," says the LORD.⚭

God Gives What Is Good

55 The LORD says, "All you who are thirsty,
come and drink.
Those of you who do not have money,
come, buy and eat!
Come buy wine and milk
without money and without cost.
2Why spend your money on something
that is not real food?
Why work for something that
doesn't really satisfy you?
Listen closely to me, and you will
eat what is good;
your soul will enjoy the rich food that satisfies.
3Come to me and listen;
listen to me so you may live.
I will make an agreement with you
that will last forever.
I will give you the blessings
I promised to David.⚭
4I made David a witness of my
power for all nations,
a ruler and commander of many nations.
5You will call for nations that you don't yet know.
And these nations that do not know you will
run to you
because of the LORD your God,
because of the Holy One of Israel
who honors you."

6So you should look for the LORD before
it is too late;

suffered terrible shame as exiles in Babylon. They deserved to be defeated and taken captive, for they had turned against God. But now God calls himself their husband and expresses his desire to restore them to the place of honor as his wife. Notice how gracious God is in these verses. He acknowledges that he became angry with his people and deserted them, but he does not rub in the truth that they defied and deserted him first. So eager is he to renew a close, loving relationship with them that he pictures himself as a tender, encouraging husband in order to woo them back.

⚭**54:12 Stone:** Matthew 21:42–44
⚭**54:13 Peace:** Ezekiel 34:25
⚭**54:17 Servant of the Lord:** Jeremiah 25:4
⚭**55:3 David:** Jeremiah 33:17
55:3 *the blessings I promised to David.* A reference to the promises to David given in 2 Samuel 7.

you should call to him while he is near.
7The wicked should stop doing wrong,
and they should stop their evil thoughts.
They should return to the LORD so he may
have mercy on them.
They should come to our God, because he
will freely forgive them.

8The LORD says, "My thoughts are
not like your thoughts.
Your ways are not like my ways.
9Just as the heavens are higher than the earth,
so are my ways higher than your ways
and my thoughts higher than your thoughts.
10Rain and snow fall from the sky
and don't return without watering the ground.
They cause the plants to sprout and grow,
making seeds for the farmer
and bread for the people.
11The same thing is true of the words I speak.
They will not return to me empty.
They make the things happen that
I want to happen,
and they succeed in doing what
I send them to do.

12"So you will go out with joy
and be led out in peace.
The mountains and hills will
burst into song before you,
and all the trees in the fields
will clap their hands.
13Large cypress trees will grow where
thornbushes were.
Myrtle trees will grow where weeds were.
These things will be a reminder
of the LORD's promise,
and this reminder will never be destroyed."

All Nations Will Obey the Lord

56 This is what the LORD says:
"Give justice to all people,
and do what is right,
because my salvation will come to you soon.
Soon everyone will know
that I do what is right.
2The person who obeys the
law about the Sabbath
will be blessed,
and the person who does no evil
will be blessed."
3Foreigners who have joined the
LORD should not say,
"The LORD will not accept me with his people."
The eunuch should not say,
"Because I cannot have children, the LORD
will not accept me."
4This is what the LORD says:
"The eunuchs should obey the
law about the Sabbath
and do what I want
and keep my agreement.
5If they do, I will make their names remembered
within my Temple and its walls.
It will be better for them than children.
I will give them a name that will last forever,
that will never be forgotten.
6Foreigners will join the LORD
to worship him and love him,
to serve him,
to obey the law about the Sabbath,
and to keep my agreement.
7I will bring these people to my holy mountain
and give them joy in my house of prayer.
The offerings and sacrifices
they place on my altar will please me,
because my Temple will be called
a house for prayer for people
from all nations."
8The Lord GOD says—
he who gathers the Israelites that were
forced to leave their country:
"I will bring together other people
to join those who are already gathered."

Israel's Leaders Are Evil

9All you animals of the field,
all you animals of the forest, come to eat.
10The leaders who are to guard
the people are blind;
they don't know what they are doing.
All of them are like quiet dogs
that don't know how to bark.
They lie down and dream
and love to sleep.
11They are like hungry dogs
that are never satisfied.
They are like shepherds
who don't know what they are doing.
They all have gone their own way;
all they want to do is satisfy themselves.
12They say, "Come, let's drink some wine;

55:12 Environment: 1 Timothy 4:4
56:7 Prayer: Matthew 6:5–15
56:7 Sabbath: Amos 8:5

let's drink all the beer we want.
And tomorrow we will do this again,
or, maybe we will have an even better time."

Israel Does Not Follow God

57 Those who are right with God may die,
but no one pays attention.
Good people are taken away,
but no one understands.
Those who do right are being
taken away from evil
2 and are given peace.
Those who live as God wants
find rest in death.

3"Come here, you magicians!
Come here, you sons of prostitutes and those
who take part in adultery!
4Of whom are you making fun?
Whom are you insulting?
At whom do you stick out your tongue?
You turn against God,
and you are liars.
5You have sexual relations under every green tree
to worship your gods.
You kill children in the ravines
and sacrifice them in the rocky places.
6You take the smooth rocks from the ravines
as your portion.
You pour drink offerings on them to worship
them,
and you give grain offerings to them.
Do you think this makes me want to show
you mercy?
7You make your bed on every hill and mountain,
and there you offer sacrifices.∞
8You have hidden your idols
behind your doors and doorposts.
You have left me, and you
have uncovered yourself.
You have pulled back the covers
and climbed into bed.
You have made an agreement with those
whose beds you love,
and you have looked at their nakedness.
9You use your oils and perfumes
to look nice for Molech.
You have sent your messengers
to faraway lands;
you even tried to send them to the place of
the dead.
10You were tired from doing these things,
but you never gave up.
You found new strength,
so you did not quit.

11"Whom were you so afraid of
that you lied to me?
You have not remembered me
or even thought about me.
I have been quiet for a long time.
Is that why you are not afraid of me?
12I will tell about your 'goodness' and what you do,
and those things will do you no good.
13When you cry out for help,
let the gods you have gathered help you.
The wind will blow them all away;
just a puff of wind will take them away.
But the person who depends on me will
receive the land
and own my holy mountain."

The Lord Will Save His People

14Someone will say, "Build a road! Build a road!
Prepare the way!
Make the way clear for my people."
15And this is the reason: God lives
forever and is holy.
He is high and lifted up.
He says, "I live in a high and holy place,
but I also live with people who
are sad and humble.
I give new life to those who are humble
and to those whose hearts are broken.
16I will not accuse forever,
nor will I always be angry,
because then human life would grow weak.
Human beings, whom I created, would die.
17I was angry because they were dishonest in
order to make money.
I punished them and turned away from them
in anger,
but they continued to do evil.
18I have seen what they have done, but I will
heal them.
I will guide them and comfort them and
those who felt sad for them.
They will all praise me.∞
19I will give peace, real peace, to those far and near,
and I will heal them," says the LORD.
20But evil people are like the angry sea,
which cannot rest,

57:5 *You kill children in the ravines.* The people of Israel were tempted to worship false gods like the Ammonite god, Molech, who demanded child sacrifices.
∞**57:7 Mountain:** Isaiah 65:7
57:9 *Molech.* Molech was the god of the Ammonite people.
∞**57:18 Comfort:** Philippians 2:1
57:20 *the angry sea.* The sea often represents the forces of chaos which God fights against.

whose waves toss up waste and mud.
21"There is no peace for evil people,"
says my God.

How to Honor God

58 The LORD says, "Shout out loud. Don't hold back.
Shout out loud like a trumpet.
Tell my people what they have done
against their God;
tell the family of Jacob about their sins.
2They still come every day looking for me
and want to learn my ways.
They act just like a nation that does what is right,
that obeys the commands of its God.
They ask me to judge them fairly.
They want God to be near them.
3They say, 'To honor you we had special days
when we gave up eating,
but you didn't see.
We humbled ourselves to honor you,
but you didn't notice.'"
But the LORD says, "You do what pleases
yourselves on these special days,
and you are unfair to your workers.
4On these special days when you do not eat,
you argue and fight
and hit each other with your fists.
You cannot do these things as you do now
and believe your prayers are heard in heaven.
5This kind of special day is not what I want.
This is not the way I want people to be sorry
for what they have done.
I don't want people just to bow their heads
like a plant
and wear rough cloth and lie in ashes to
show their sadness.
This is what you do on your special days when
you do not eat,
but do you think this is what
the LORD wants?

6"I will tell you the kind of special day I want:
Free the people you have put in prison unfairly
and undo their chains.
Free those to whom you are unfair
and stop their hard labor.
7Share your food with the hungry
and bring poor, homeless people
into your own homes.
When you see someone who has no clothes,
give him yours,
and don't refuse to help your own relatives.
8Then your light will shine like the dawn,
and your wounds will quickly heal.
Your God will walk before you,
and the glory of the LORD will protect you
from behind.
9Then you will call out, and the LORD will answer.
You will cry out, and he will say, 'Here I am.'

"If you stop making trouble for others,
if you stop using cruel words and pointing
your finger at others,
10if you feed those who are hungry
and take care of the needs
of those who are troubled,
then your light will shine in the darkness,
and you will be bright like sunshine at noon.
11The LORD will always lead you.
He will satisfy your needs in dry lands
and give strength to your bones.
You will be like a garden that has much water,
like a spring that never runs dry.
12Your people will rebuild the old
cities that are now in ruins;
you will rebuild their foundations.
You will be known for repairing
the broken places
and for rebuilding the roads and houses.

13"You must obey God's law about the Sabbath
and not do what pleases yourselves
on that holy day.
You should call the Sabbath a joyful day
and honor it as the LORD's holy day.
You should honor it by not doing
whatever you please
nor saying whatever you please on that day.
14Then you will find joy in the LORD,
and I will carry you to the high
places above the earth.
I will let you eat the crops of the
land your ancestor Jacob had."
The LORD has said these things.

The Evil That People Do

59 Surely the LORD's power is enough to save you.
He can hear you when you ask him for help.
2It is your evil that has separated
you from your God.
Your sins cause him to turn away from you,
so he does not hear you.
3With your hands you have killed others,
and with your fingers you have done wrong.

58:3–5 Fasting: Psalm 69:1–15

FAMILY

MARK 3:31–35

Does the Bible as a whole have a commitment to a particular notion of family? How do we deal with those passages where Jesus seems to pit faithful discipleship against commitment to one's family? What is the significance of the use of family images and language in descriptions of local communities of God's people?

As children sitting in church with our families, many of us heard for the first time the text of Mark 3:31–35 in which Jesus, told that his family was looking for him, said, "Who are my mother and my brothers?" Then he looked at the crowd gathered around him and said, "Here are my mother and my brothers! My true brother and sister and mother are those who do what God wants." For many of us those words were disturbing. Church taught us the value of family and many other lessons about love, respect, loyalty, and authority within families, yet Jesus seemed to be speaking as a disrespectful son and a disloyal brother. This text and others like it push us to examine the significance of family in the Bible.

The Bible records God's relationship with the beings in his creation to whom he relates as a father to his children. From the first chapter of Genesis it is evident that the Lord God created humankind, and humankind alone, in his image. The image-bearer that God created was fundamentally social—"He created them male and female" (Genesis 1:27)—and familial. The initial human creation was in the form of a family, and after that every child has been born to a mother and a father.

Given the importance of the family, God's role in its creation, and God's desire to communicate with people, it is not surprising that families and family metaphors abound from the beginning to the end of the Bible. Most significantly for Christians, Jesus' birth (Matthew 1:2; Luke 1:2) and death stories (Jesus' commissioning John to care for his mother Mary, John 19:26–27) concern family. And just as creation involves the family, so the apocalyptic vision of the new earth is familial, for of his people God says, "I will be their God, and they will be my children" (Revelation 21:7) and all will celebrate the "marriage" of Jesus, the Lamb, with his people of the holy city (Revelation 21:9–10).

Not only was the creation of humankind familial, but family terms are used to describe God himself whose trinity is composed of the Father, Son, and Holy Spirit. It seems clear that family relationships are inseparable from the nature of God, and, therefore, from the nature of those made in his image. The relationships within the trinity of God are a mystery to us, but we know that they are characterized by love (1 John 4:8), commitment, and communication (John 1:1), and the Father's unquestioned authority (Luke 12:49: Acts 2:17). As Christians striving to follow Jesus, we understand we are to love, commit to, communicate with, and obey God. We are wrong when we fail to do so, and much of our confusion about biblical texts on the family disappears when our focus is placed on a right relationship with God our Father.

What is true about human beings is true about human families: They are characterized by the goodness of God's image in them as well as by sin. The first created family struggled to obey God and failed. They betrayed each other, and Cain killed his brother. From that time forward, the family has been the seat of the strongest emotions and life experiences, a context for scarring, healing, loving, hating, grieving, and rejoicing. Had our original ancestors loved, obeyed, and stayed in conversation with God, their tragedies would have been avoided. They suffered the consequences of their actions as children of God, nevertheless, their Father continued to care for them, making Adam and Eve clothing for their new situation (Genesis 3:20) and placing a protective mark on Cain so that no one would kill him (Genesis 4:15). In the face of his children's betrayal, God continues to love, communicate, and require loving obedience.

With the centrality of family in the Bible, in God, and in our lives, it is difficult to understand Jesus seemingly rejecting his family by saying, "Who are my mother and my brothers" (Mark 3:33)? It seems harsh for Jesus to respond this way when his relatives are trying to protect him from crushing crowds saying, "He was out of his mind" and "Beelzebul is living inside him! He uses power from the ruler of demons to force demons out of people" (Mark 3:21–22). Jesus' family feared their beloved son and brother would be denounced if not destroyed. The reader of this passage knows the concern of his family is justified and wonders why Jesus does not have a gentler response to them.

This passage cuts to the core of many questions about the family and faith. We do not question Jesus' love for his human family, for other passages show it (see Luke 2:41–51; John 2:1–12; John 19:26–27). Also, Jesus exhorts us to love and honor our parents, and has no patience with excuses for not doing so. Questioned by the Pharisees and scribes about honoring tradition, Jesus said, "You have stopped following the commands of God, and you follow only human teaching" (Mark 7:8). He used the example of people claiming that they could not support their parents because their material resources are pledged (or deeded) to the Temple treasury, and declared this as one of many ways people used tradition for "rejecting what God said" (Mark 7:13).

Jesus emphatically warns his listeners then and now against the fabrications of humankind. Tradition, valuable as it may be, is a human creation and stands in contrast to the word of God which is independent of our making. With respect to the family, we are to honor family because we are commanded to do so by God. We are not to place family before God, but, rather, God before family. The sacredness of family derives from God and is violated if family is turned into a freestanding idol.

Jesus drives this point home by what he does and says in Mark 3:33–35. He makes the point that as good and beloved as his human family is, his relationship with God is supreme. In a related passage, Jesus tells his disciples: "Those who love their father or mother more than they love me are not worthy to be my followers. Those who love their son or daughter more than they love me are not worthy to be my followers. Whoever is not willing to carry the cross and follow me is not worthy of me" (Matthew 10:37–39). This is the negative expression of the passage in Mark; it is the "you must not have any other gods except me" (Deuteronomy 5:7) of the New Testament. The biblical mandate for families is that each person in the family be committed to God. From that commitment will flow many blessings to persons and families, the chief of which is inclusion in the family of God.

The tension we experience when we read Mark 3:33–35 and Matthew 10:37–39 has the unfortunate effect of overshadowing the joyful and undeserved family relationship we are granted by Jesus. He freely invites us to be his family and takes us into his heart and life just as he did his mother and earthly father. This is not a privilege we must earn. Jesus does not ask that we be perfect. He asks that we love him first and follow him. He tells us that the members of his family include the hungry, the stranger, the naked, the sick, and the imprisoned (Matthew 25:35–40). It is not a religious or social elite family, and space in the family is not limited. What characterizes the family of God is love, commitment, and communication, and obedience to the Father.

Many instances of biblical conflict between God and his people have to do with idolatry. Other gods, tradition, social order, citizenship, church, friendship, personal development, and family are likely candidates for idolatrous privileging over God and his commandments. In the Old Testament there were occasions when God tested the faith of his people to see whether or not he was first in their hearts. God instructed Abraham to sacrifice his son, Isaac. When Abraham proceeded to obey, the angel of the Lord stopped him and said "I can see that you trust God, and you have not kept your son, your only son, from me" (Genesis 22:12). When God boasted to Satan that Job reverenced him completely, Satan replied that the love was meaningless because it had not been tested. Job, then, is stripped of his human loves, including his children, to see if his love for God is strongest (Job 1). In the gospel story, Jesus loves his family, his friends, and his life, but let go of them all out of love for the Father.

It is a form of idolatry to give human family life—or church community—such eminence that our understanding of God derives from projections of human relationships. To do so is to reverse the proper order of interpretation. Humankind was formed by God in his image, not the reverse. So we seek to know God in order to know how to live, in families and in communities with fellow Christians. It is tempting to take what we know of our families, especially our earthly fathers, and believe that that us knowledge gives knowledge of God. That is truly seeing a "dim reflection" (1 Corinthians 13:12). It is not completely false, for we are created in God's image, but it is distorted.

There is freedom in the biblical message about family, the greatest part of which is our membership by faith in the family of God. We are children of God and related through him to people of faith around the world and throughout history. Another freedom lies in the dethroning of human constructions of ideal families.

Many today are born into families that do not meet our society's or church's ideals. They—we—can seize the good news that these circumstances do not penalize us in the family of God and do not sentence us to replaying our childhood families when we form adult families. For it is God and his relationships with his children that must inspire our own family lives. God blesses families, and parenthood is granted sanctity, authority, and gravity by God's fatherhood. However, the believer who has no parents or spouse or children is neither an orphan nor an outsider, for, as the psalmist says, "If my father and mother leave me, the LORD will take me in" (Psalm 27:10). All who love God are welcomed into the family to which Jesus is referring when he points and says, "Here are my mother and my brothers!" (Mark 3:34).

Family: For additional scriptures on this topic go to Genesis 1:27.

With your lips you have lied,
and with your tongue you say evil things.
4People take each other to court unfairly,
and no one tells the truth in arguing his case.
They accuse each other falsely and tell lies.
They cause trouble and create more evil.
5They hatch evil like eggs from poisonous snakes.
If you eat one of those eggs, you will die,
and if you break one open,
a poisonous snake comes out.
People tell lies as they would spin a spider's web.
6 The webs they make cannot be
used for clothes;
you can't cover yourself with those webs.
The things they do are evil,
and they use their hands to hurt others.
7They eagerly run to do evil,
and they are always ready to
kill innocent people.
They think evil thoughts.
Everywhere they go they
cause ruin and destruction.
8They don't know how to live in peace,
and there is no fairness in their lives.
They are dishonest.
Anyone who lives as they
live will never have peace.

Israel's Sin Brings Trouble

9Fairness has gone far away;
goodness is nowhere to be found.
We wait for the light, but there is
only darkness now.
We hope for a bright light, but all
we have is darkness.
10We are like the blind feeling our
way along a wall.
We feel our way as if we had no eyes.
In the brightness of day we trip
as if it were night.
We are like dead men among the strong.
11All of us growl like the bears.
We call out sadly like the doves.
We look for justice, but there isn't any.
We want to be saved,
but salvation is far away.⚭

12We have done many wrong
things against our God;
our sins show we are wrong.
We know we have turned against God;
we know the evil things we have done:
13sinning and rejecting the LORD,
turning away from our God,
planning to hurt others and to disobey God,
planning and speaking lies.
14So we have driven away justice,
and we have kept away from what is right.
Truth is not spoken in the streets;
what is honest is not allowed to enter the city.
15Truth cannot be found anywhere,
and people who refuse to do evil are attacked.

The LORD looked and could not find any justice,
and he was displeased.
16He could not find anyone to help the people,
and he was surprised that there
was no one to help.
So he used his own power to save the people;
his own goodness gave him strength.
17He covered himself with goodness like armor.
He put the helmet of salvation on his head.
He put on the clothes of punishment
and wrapped himself in
the coat of his strong love.
18The LORD will pay back his
enemies for what they have done.
He will show his anger to
those who were against him;
he will punish the people in
faraway places as they deserve.
19Then people from the west will fear the LORD,
and people from the east will fear his glory.
The LORD will come quickly
like a fast-flowing river,
driven by the breath of the LORD.

20"Then a Savior will come to Jerusalem
and to the people of Jacob who have turned
from sin,"
says the LORD.
21The LORD says, "This is my agreement with
these people: My Spirit and my words that I give
you will never leave you or your children or your
grandchildren, now and forever."

Jerusalem Will Be Great

60 "Jerusalem, get up and shine, because
your light has come,
and the glory of the LORD shines on you.
2Darkness now covers the earth;
deep darkness covers her people.
But the LORD shines on you,
and people see his glory around you.
3Nations will come to your light;
kings will come to the brightness
of your sunrise.

⚭**59:11 Blindness:** Matthew 11:4–14

4"Look around you.
People are gathering and coming to you.
Your sons are coming from far away,
and your daughters are coming with them.
5When you see them, you will
shine with happiness;
you will be excited and full of joy,
because the wealth of the nations across the
seas will be given to you;
the riches of the nations will come to you.
6Herds of camels will cover your land,
young camels from Midian and Ephah.
People will come from Sheba
bringing gold and incense,
and they will sing praises to the LORD.
7All the sheep from Kedar will be given to you;
the sheep from Nebaioth will be
brought to you.
They will be pleasing sacrifices on my altar,
and I will make my beautiful
Temple more beautiful.

8"The people are returning to you like clouds,
like doves flying to their nests.
9People in faraway lands are waiting for me.
The great trading ships will come first,
bringing your children from faraway lands,
and with them silver and gold.
This will honor the LORD your God,
the Holy One of Israel,
who does wonderful things for you.

10"Jerusalem, foreigners will rebuild your walls,
and their kings will serve you.
When I was angry, I hurt you,
but now I want to be kind to
you and comfort you.
11Your gates will always be open;
they will not be closed day or night
so the nations can bring their wealth to you,
and their kings will be led to you.
12The nation or kingdom that doesn't
serve you will be destroyed;
it will be completely ruined.

13"The great trees of Lebanon will be given to you:
its pine, fir, and cypress trees together.
You will use them to make my Temple beautiful,
and I will give much honor to this place
where I rest my feet.
14The people who have hurt you
will bow down to you;
those who hated you will bow
down at your feet.
They will call you The City of the LORD,
Jerusalem, city of the Holy One of Israel.

15"You have been hated and left empty
with no one passing through.
But I will make you great from now on;
you will be a place of happiness
forever and ever.
16You will be given what you need from
the nations,
like a child drinking milk from its mother.
Then you will know that it is I, the LORD,
who saves you.
You will know that the Powerful One of
Jacob protects you.
17I will bring you gold in place of bronze,
silver in place of iron,
bronze in place of wood,
iron in place of rocks.
I will change your punishment into peace,
and you will be ruled by what is right.
18There will be no more violence in your country;
it will not be ruined or destroyed.
You will name your walls Salvation
and your gates Praise.
19The sun will no longer be your
light during the day
nor will the brightness from
the moon be your light,
because the LORD will be your light forever,
and your God will be your glory.
20Your sun will never set again,
and your moon will never be dark,
because the LORD will be your light forever,
and your time of sadness will end.
21All of your people will do what is right.
They will receive the earth forever.
They are the plant I have planted,
the work of my own hands
to show my greatness.
22The smallest family will grow to a thousand.
The least important of you will become a
powerful nation.
I am the LORD,
and when it is time, I will make these things
happen quickly."

The Lord's Message of Freedom

61 The Lord GOD has put his Spirit in me,
because the LORD has appointed me to tell
the good news to the poor.
He has sent me to comfort those whose
hearts are broken,

61 This passage, quoted by Jesus during his first sermon in Nazareth, contains not only the mission agenda of the Messiah, but the urban ministry mandate of all God's people. The Lord God has "put the Spirit" on Jesus and his followers to "tell the good news to the poor . . .

to tell the captives they are free,
and to tell the prisoners they are released.
2He has sent me to announce the time when
the LORD will show his kindness
and the time when our God will
punish evil people.
He has sent me to comfort all
those who are sad⚭
3 and to help the sorrowing people of Jerusalem.
I will give them a crown to replace their ashes,
and the oil of gladness to replace their sorrow,
and clothes of praise to replace their
spirit of sadness.
Then they will be called Trees of Goodness,
trees planted by the LORD to show
his greatness.⚭

4They will rebuild the old ruins
and restore the places destroyed long ago.
They will repair the ruined cities
that were destroyed for so long.⚭

5My people, foreigners will come to
tend your sheep.
People from other countries will tend your
fields and vineyards.
6You will be called priests of the LORD;
you will be named the servants of our God.
You will have riches from all the
nations on earth,
and you will take pride in them.
7Instead of being ashamed, my people will
receive twice as much wealth.
Instead of being disgraced, they will be
happy because of what they receive.
They will receive a double share of the land,
so their happiness will continue forever.
8"I, the LORD, love justice.
I hate stealing and everything that is wrong.
I will be fair and give my people what they
should have,
and I will make an agreement with them that
will continue forever.
9Everyone in all nations will know the children
of my people,
and their children will be
known among the nations.
Anyone who sees them will know
that they are people the LORD has blessed."⚭

10The LORD makes me very happy;
all that I am rejoices in my God.
He has covered me with clothes of salvation
and wrapped me with a coat of goodness,
like a bridegroom dressed for his wedding,
like a bride dressed in jewels.
11The earth causes plants to grow,
and a garden causes the seeds
planted in it to grow.
In the same way the Lord GOD will make
goodness and praise
come from all the nations.

New Jerusalem

62 Because I love Jerusalem, I will continue
to speak for her;
for Jerusalem's sake I will not stop speaking
until her goodness shines like a bright light,
until her salvation burns bright like a flame.
2Jerusalem, the nations will see your goodness,
and all kings will see your glory.
Then you will have a new name,
which the LORD himself will give you.
3You will be like a beautiful crown in the
LORD's hand,
like a king's crown in your God's hand.
4You will never again be called the People
that God Left,
nor your land the Land
that God Destroyed.
You will be called the People God Loves,
and your land will be called the Bride of God,
because the LORD loves you.
And your land will belong to him as a bride
belongs to her husband.
5As a young man marries a woman,
so your children will marry your land.
As a man rejoices over his new wife,
so your God will rejoice over you.⚭

6Jerusalem, I have put guards on the
walls to watch.
They must not be silent day or night.
You people who remind the LORD of your
needs in prayer
should never be quiet.
7You should not stop praying to him until he
builds up Jerusalem
and makes it a city all people will praise.

comfort those whose hearts are broken, to tell the captives they are free." God's people are to show kindness and compassion to the suffering and to "repair the ruined cities." If they do this, they will be called "priests of the Lord," and will fulfill the work the Messiah began.

⚭**61:2 Money:** Amos 8:4

⚭**61:2 Slavery:** Luke 4:18–19
⚭**61:3 Mourning:** Matthew 5:4
⚭**61:4 Freedom:** Luke 4:14–21
⚭**61:9 Gospel/Good News:** Matthew 4:23
⚭**62:5 The People of God:** Romans 8:14–16

[8]The LORD has made a promise,
and by his power he will keep his promise.
He said, "I will never again give your grain
as food to your enemies.
I will not let your enemies drink the new wine
that you have worked to make.
[9]The person who gathers food will eat it,
and he will praise the LORD.
The person who gathers the grapes
will drink the wine
in the courts of my Temple."
[10]Go through, go through the gates!
Make the way ready for the people.
Build up, build up the road!
Move all the stones off the road.
Raise the banner as a sign for the people.

[11]The LORD is speaking
to all the faraway lands:
"Tell the people of Jerusalem,
'Look, your Savior is coming.
He is bringing your reward to you;
he is bringing his payment with him.' "
[12]His people will be called the Holy People,
the Saved People of the LORD,
and Jerusalem will be called the City God Wants,
the City God Has Not Rejected.

The Lord Judges His People

63 Who is this coming from Edom,
from the city of Bozrah, dressed in red?
Who is this dressed in fine clothes
and marching forward with his great power?

He says, "I, the LORD, speak what is right.
I have the power to save you."

[2]Someone asks, "Why are your clothes bright red
as if you had walked on the
grapes to make wine?"

[3]The LORD answers, "I have walked in the
winepress alone,
and no one among the nations helped me.
I was angry and walked on the nations
and crushed them because of my anger.
Blood splashed on my clothes,
and I stained all my clothing.
[4]I chose a time to punish people,
and the time has come for me to save.
[5]I looked around, but I saw no one to help me.
I was surprised that no one supported me.
So I used my own power to save my people;
my own anger supported me.
[6]While I was angry, I walked on the nations.
In my anger I punished them
and poured their blood on the ground."

The Lord's Kindness to His People

[7]I will tell about the LORD's kindness
and praise him for everything he has done.
I will praise the LORD for the many good things
he has given us
and for his goodness to the people of Israel.
He has shown great mercy to us
and has been very kind to us.
[8]He said, "These are my people;
my children will not lie to me."
So he saved them.
[9]When they suffered, he suffered also.
He sent his own angel to save them.
Because of his love and kindness, he saved them.
Since long ago he has picked them up and
carried them.
[10]But they turned against him
and made his Holy Spirit very sad.
So he became their enemy,
and he fought against them.

[11]But then his people remembered what
happened long ago,
in the days of Moses and the
Israelites with him.
Where is the LORD who brought the people
through the sea,
with the leaders of his people?
Where is the one
who put his Holy Spirit among them,
[12]who led Moses by the right hand
with his wonderful power,
who divided the water before them
to make his name famous forever,
[13]who led the people through the deep waters?
Like a horse walking through a desert,
the people did not stumble.
[14]Like cattle that go down to the valley,
the Spirit of the LORD gave the
people a place to rest.
LORD, that is the way you led your people,
and by this you won for
yourself wonderful fame.

A Prayer for Help

[15]LORD, look down from the heavens and see;
look at us from your wonderful and holy
home in heaven.

62:12 City: Psalm 122

63:14 Wilderness (Desert): Jeremiah 50:35–40

Where is your strong love and power?
Why are you keeping your love and
mercy from us?
16You are our father.
Abraham doesn't know we are his children,
and Israel doesn't recognize us.
LORD, you are our father.
You are called "the one who has
always saved us."
17LORD, why are you making us wander
from your ways?
Why do you make us stubborn so that we
don't honor you?
For our sake come back to us,
your servants, who belong to you.
18Your people had your Temple for a while,
but now our enemies have walked on your
holy place and crushed it.
19We have become like people you
never ruled over,
like those who have never worn your name.

64 Tear open the skies and come down to
earth
so that the mountains will tremble before you.
2Like a fire that burns twigs,
like a fire that makes water boil,
let your enemies know who you are.
Then all nations will shake with fear when
they see you.
3You have done amazing things
we did not expect.
You came down, and the mountains
trembled before you.
4From long ago no one has ever
heard of a God like you.
No one has ever seen a God besides you,
who helps the people who trust you.
5You help those who enjoy doing good,
who remember how you want them to live.
But you were angry because we sinned.
For a long time we disobeyed,
so how can we be saved?
6All of us are dirty with sin.
All the right things we have done are like
filthy pieces of cloth.
All of us are like dead leaves,
and our sins, like the wind,
have carried us away.⚭
7No one worships you
or even asks you to help us.
That is because you have turned away from us
and have let our sins destroy us.
8But LORD, you are our father.
We are like clay, and you are the potter;
your hands made us all.⚭
9LORD, don't continue to be angry with us;
don't remember our sins forever.
Please, look at us,
because we are your people.
10Your holy cities are empty like the desert.
Jerusalem is like a desert;
it is destroyed.
11Our ancestors worshiped you
in our holy and wonderful Temple,
but now it has been burned with fire,
and all our precious things have been destroyed.
12When you see these things, will you hold
yourself back from helping us, LORD?
Will you be silent and punish us beyond
what we can stand?

All People Will Learn About God

65 The LORD says, "I made myself known to
people who were not looking for me.
I was found by those who were
not asking me for help.
I said, 'Here I am. Here I am,'
to a nation that was not praying to me.
2All day long I stood ready to accept
people who turned against me,
but the way they continue to live is not good;
they do anything they want to do.
3Right in front of me
they continue to do things
that make me angry.
They offer sacrifices to their gods
in their gardens,
and they burn incense on altars of brick.
4They sit among the graves
and spend their nights waiting to get messages
from the dead.
They eat the meat of pigs,
and their pots are full of soup made from
meat that is wrong to eat.
5But they tell others, 'Stay away, and don't
come near me.
I am too holy for you.'
These people are like smoke in my nose.
Like a fire that burns all the time, they
continue to make me angry.

6"Look, it is written here before me.
I will not be quiet; instead, I will
repay you in full.

⚭**64:6 Clean & Unclean:** Ezekiel 22:26
⚭**64:8 Images of God:** Lamentations 3:1

65:4 *They sit among the graves.* These people worship the dead and expect the departed ghosts to help them in their daily living.

I will punish you for what you have done.
7I will punish you for your sins and
your ancestors' sins,"
says the LORD.
"They burned incense to gods on the mountains
and shamed me on those hills.
So I will punish them as they should be punished
for what they did."

8This is what the LORD says:
"When there is juice left in the grapes,
people do not destroy them,
because they know there is good left in them.
So I will do the same thing to my servants—
I will not completely destroy them.
9I will leave some of the children of Jacob,
and some of the people of Judah will receive
my mountain.
I will choose the people who will live there;
my servants will live there.
10Then the Plain of Sharon will be a field for flocks,
and the Valley of Achor will be a place for
herds to rest.
They will be for the people who want
to follow me.

11"But as for you who left the LORD,
who forgot about my holy mountain,
who worship the god Luck,
who hold religious feasts for the god Fate,
12I decide your fate, and I will punish
you with my sword.
You will all be killed,
because I called you, but you refused to answer.
I spoke to you, but you wouldn't listen.
You did the things I said were evil
and chose to do things that displease me."

13So this is what the Lord GOD says:
"My servants will eat,
but you evil people will be hungry.
My servants will drink,
but you evil people will be thirsty.
My servants will be happy,
but you evil people will be shamed.
14My servants will shout for joy
because of the goodness of their hearts,
but you evil people will cry,
because you will be sad.
You will cry loudly, because your spirits will
be broken.
15Your names will be like curses to my servants,
and the Lord GOD will put you to death.
But he will call his servants by another name.
16People in the land who ask for blessings
will ask for them from the faithful God.
And people in the land who make a promise
will promise in the name of the faithful God,
because the troubles of the past will be forgotten.
I will make those troubles go away.

A New Time Is Coming

17"Look, I will make new heavens and a new earth,
and people will not remember the past
or think about those things.
18My people will be happy forever
because of the things I will make.
I will make a Jerusalem that is full of joy,
and I will make her people a delight.
19Then I will rejoice over Jerusalem
and be delighted with my people.
There will never again be heard in that city
the sounds of crying and sadness.
20There will never be a baby from that city
who lives only a few days.
And there will never be an older person
who doesn't have a long life.
A person who lives a hundred years
will be called young,
and a person who dies before he is a hundred
will be thought of as a sinner.
21In that city those who build
houses will live there.
Those who plant vineyards will get to eat
their grapes.
22No more will one person build a house and
someone else live there.
One person will not plant a garden and
someone else eat its fruit.
My people will live a long time,
as trees live long.
My chosen people will live there
and enjoy the things they make.
23They will never again work for nothing.
They will never again give birth to children
who die young.
All my people will be blessed by the LORD;
they and their children will be blessed.

65:7 Mountain: Ezekiel 34:1–16

65:17 Earth: John 17:4

65:17–25 This passage contains a prophetic vision of the New Jerusalem whose fulfillment is recorded in Revelation 21. Injustice, slavery, hunger, and exploitation will be no more. Spiritually, all God's people will be blessed. This is God's promise for a final restoration of all creation. Among the blessings are eternal joy (v. 18), superlong life (vv. 20, 22), abundance (v. 21), security (v. 22), and peace (v.25). This promised new creation will come after the return of Jesus Christ (Revelation 21:1–4).

65:23 Work: Matthew 20:1–16

24I will provide for their needs before they ask,
and I will help them while they are still asking for help.
25Wolves and lambs will eat together in peace.
Lions will eat hay like oxen,
and a snake on the ground will not hurt anyone.
They will not hurt or destroy each other
on all my holy mountain,"
says the LORD.

The Lord Will Judge All Nations

66 This is what the LORD says:
"Heaven is my throne,
and the earth is my footstool.
So do you think you can build a house for me?
Do I need a place to rest?
2My hand made all things.
All things are here because I made them,"
says the LORD.

"These are the people I am pleased with:
those who are not proud or stubborn
and who fear my word.
3But those people who kill bulls as a sacrifice to me
are like those who kill people.
Those who kill sheep as a sacrifice
are like those who break the necks of dogs.
Those who give me grain offerings
are like those who offer me the blood of pigs.
Those who burn incense
are like those who worship idols.
These people choose their own ways, not mine,
and they love the terrible things they do.
4So I will choose their punishments,
and I will punish them with what they fear most.
This is because I called to them,
but they did not listen.
I spoke to them, but they did not hear me.
They did things I said were evil;
they chose to do things I did not like."

5You people who obey the words of the LORD,
listen to what he says:
"Your brothers hated you
and turned against you
because you followed me.
Your brothers said, 'Let the LORD be honored
so we may see you rejoice,'
but they will be punished.
6Listen to the loud noise coming from the city;
hear the noise from the Temple.
It is the LORD punishing his enemies,
giving them the punishment they should have.

7"A woman does not give
birth before she feels the pain;
she does not give birth
to a son before the pain starts.
8No one has ever heard of that happening;
no one has ever seen that happen.
In the same way no one ever saw a country
begin in one day;
no one has ever heard of a new
nation beginning in one moment.
But Jerusalem will give birth to her children
just as soon as she feels the birth pains.
9In the same way I will not cause pain
without allowing something new to be born,"
says the LORD.
"If I cause you the pain,
I will not stop you from giving birth to your
new nation," says your God.
10"Jerusalem, rejoice.
All you people who love Jerusalem, be happy.
Those of you who felt sad for Jerusalem
should now feel happy with her.
11You will take comfort from her
and be satisfied,
as a child is nursed by its mother.
You will receive her good things
and enjoy her wealth."

12This is what the LORD says:

"I will give her peace that will
flow to her like a river.
The wealth of the nations will come to her
like a river overflowing its banks.
Like babies you will be nursed
and held in my arms
and bounced on my knees.
13I will comfort you
as a mother comforts her child.
You will be comforted in Jerusalem."

14When you see these things, you will be happy,
and you will grow like the grass.
The LORD's servants will see his power,
but his enemies will see his anger.
15Look, the LORD is coming with fire
and his armies with clouds of dust.
He will punish those people with his anger;
he will punish them with flames of fire.

65:25 Heaven: Isaiah 66:22–23
65:25 Animals: Jonah 4:11

66:3 *dogs . . . pigs.* God did not want his people to offer dogs and pigs as sacrifices because they were unclean animals.

[16]The LORD will judge the people with fire,
and he will destroy many
people with his sword;
he will kill many people.

[17]"These people make themselves holy and
pure to go to worship their gods in their gardens.
Following each other into their special gardens,
they eat the meat of pigs and rats and other hateful things. But they will all be destroyed together,"
says the LORD.
[18]"I know they have evil thoughts and do evil
things, so I am coming to punish them. I will
gather all nations and all people, and they will
come together and see my glory.
[19]"I will put a mark on some of the people, and
I will send some of these saved people to the
nations: to Tarshish, Libya, Lud (the land of
archers), Tubal, Greece, and all the faraway lands.
These people have never heard about what I have
done nor seen my glory. So the saved people will
tell the nations about my glory. [20]And they will
bring all your fellow Israelites from all nations to
my holy mountain in Jerusalem. Your fellow
Israelites will come on horses, donkeys, and
camels and in chariots and wagons. They will be
like the grain offerings that the people bring in
clean containers to the Temple," says the LORD.
[21]"And I will choose even some of these people to
be priests and Levites," says the LORD.
[22]"I will make new heavens and the new earth,
which will last forever," says the LORD. "In the
same way, your names and your children will
always be with me. [23]All people will come to worship me every Sabbath and every New Moon,"
says the LORD. [24]"They will go out and see the
dead bodies of the people who sinned against me.
The worms that eat them will never die, and the
fires that burn them will never stop, and everyone will hate to see those bodies."

66:17 *they eat the meat of pigs and rats.* Pigs and rats were considered unclean animals, and the good people of Israel were not to eat them.

66:23 Heaven: Romans 8:18–25
66:24 Hell: Jeremiah 25:15–29

Antichrist (Enemy of Christ)

Mark 13

What does the Bible say about the Antichrist, or enemy of Christ? Should Christians today be concerned about the coming of the Antichrist?

Many Christians today and in every generation since the coming of Christ have concerned themselves with the identity of the Antichrist, or enemy of Christ. This is due in part to the specific warning of Jesus that "false Christs and false prophets . . . will try to fool even the people God has chosen" (Mark 13:22).

This concern is far older than the first century, however. From its earliest days, Israel was interested in distinguishing God's genuine messengers from those who only pretended to represent God. For example, in Deuteronomy 18:21–22, the question is raised, How can we know if a message is not from the Lord? Moses replies that the truth of a prophetic word depends on whether it happens. Passages in the New Testament, too, emphasize the need to distinguish God's message from its counterfeits. First John 4:1–3 warns that false prophets have gone out into the world. These people are false teachers who deny the Father and the Son (1 John 2:22) and refuse to accept that Jesus really came to earth as a human (1 John 4:2; 2 John 7). Such people speak by "the spirit of the enemy of Christ" (1 John 4:3).

The word *Antichrist* itself is rare in the New Testament and absent in the Old Testament. Other words are used for this figure, however. Jesus speaks of "false Christs" as persons who will appear in the period before the end of time. Unlike Jesus, such persons will use their powers to show-off, to prove that they are sent by God. But their real aim is to lead people away from God. The Antichrist is like these "false Christs," except he may even require that people worship him as though he were a god.

Paul does not use the term *Antichrist,* but in 2 Thessalonians 2:3–4 he mentions the "Man of Evil." This person will claim to be God while opposing everything that God stands for. He is the very embodiment of evil. Revelation 13 clearly describes the "beast coming out of the sea" as the Antichrist. It does this not by using the term *Antichrist,* but through portraying the beast as Satan's counterpart to the authentic Christ, Jesus. The beast of the sea in Revelation 13 is Satan's agent to make war against God's people. This description is given in such detail to emphasize the depth of its evil. As one who tries to seize our worship, our loyalty, our obedience, the beast is a counterfeit Christ.

The term *Antichrist* (or "enemy of Christ") appears only in 1 and 2 John. There, John not only prophesies the coming of the Antichrist (2 John 7), he goes on to say that antichrists *have already arrived and are now at work among God's people* (1 John 2:18–20). They are false teachers, people who refuse to accept that Jesus is the authentic Christ. They do not understand who God is, so their relations with others do not exhibit God's love and their actions are immoral. They even separate themselves from God's people. For John, the presence of these enemies of Christ signifies that "the last days" are already present.

As a result, it is clear that concerns about the Antichrist can never be relegated simply to discussions about the end of time. Instead, these passages demonstrate the constant challenge for the people of God to be on the alert.

The enemies of Christ, those who oppose the purposes of God, are not to be expected simply at some future time, just before the end. They are already at work. What is more, they present themselves in subtle ways, beckoning to Christians with showy signs of power. They seem to be from God. They proclaim a message that we want to hear—peace, pleasure, prosperity. But in doing so, they work to entrap us in thoughts and lifestyles that actually work against God's purpose.

The biblical testimony regarding the Antichrist is thus a call to test whether messages and messengers are actually from God. This will be known not only by the consistency of their message with the voice of God in Scripture, but also by the degree to which their lives reflect Christ's selfless character. There is also good news, however: The power of the Antichrist is not absolute, but will be overcome by Christ (see 2 Thessalonians 2:3; 1 John 4:4; Revelation 19:20).

Antichrist (Enemy of Christ): For additional scriptures on this topic go to Deuteronomy 18:21–22.

John the Baptist

Luke 1

Who was John the Baptist? What was his role in the life of Jesus? How did he fulfill Old Testament prophecy?

The voice that opened Jesus' ministry in the New Testament is that of John the Baptist. His preaching was similar to the last prophets of the Old Testament period, proclaiming judgment on the enemies of God. God was about to "burn the chaff with a fire that cannot be put out" (Luke 3:17).

When Jesus came out to be baptized, John recognized him as the One who is "greater than I am" (Luke 3:16). He baptized him, and, then, Jesus became the focus of the gospel story. The next time we see John, he is in prison, worried that perhaps he baptized the wrong person.

Why did John doubt Jesus? While he was in prison, John heard disturbing reports about his ministry. The man whom he said was going to "burn the chaff" was healing the sick, exorcising demons, and preaching the Good News. Where was the judgment, the destruction of the enemies of God?

John was a typical prophet who saw truly into the future, but often saw the future as an undifferentiated unity. Jesus did come as a warrior against the enemy of God, but in his first coming, he focused on defeating Satan and the spiritual enemies. This he accomplished on the cross. When Jesus comes again, according to the teaching of places like Matthew 24 and Revelation, he will bring a fiery judgment.

John the Baptist appears on the scene before Jesus. He was a most unusual character—some would say eccentric. This was seen in his appearance, his lifestyle, and in his ministry style. He wore the rustic clothes of a prophet (Matthew 3:4). His ministry was done in the primitive setting of the desert (Matthew 3:1). He preached a fiery message that would cause the hearers to be, at the least, uncomfortable (Matthew 3:7–10).

Yet, even with these idiosyncrasies, John is a towering figure in the Bible. He stands as a pivotal personality. Closing out the era of the Old Testament prophets and pointing to the reign of the long awaited Messiah (Matthew 3:3, 11). Jesus declared that John was "greater than any other person ever born." But in the same breath he declared, "Even the least important person in the kingdom of heaven is greater than John" (Matthew 11:11).

The story of his birth (Luke 1) is filled with supernatural occurrences. His birth was announced by an angel. It was a miraculous birth, in that his mother was apparently past the normal age of bearing children. This paralleled the Old Testament story of Sarah and Abraham (Genesis 17:17). One important aspect of his birth was that, according to the angel, he would be filled with the Holy Spirit from birth (Luke 1:16). This was no ordinary child. God had big plans for him. His role was twofold. He was both prophet and forerunner. As prophet, he represented the closing chapter of the Old Agreement. As forerunner, he was the bridge to the fulfillment of that agreement through the introduction of the New Agreement in the person of Jesus Christ.

Matthew declares, "This is a voice of one who calls out in the desert: 'Prepare the way for the Lord. Make the road straight for him" (Matthew 3:3). This quote from Isaiah 40:3 points to John as fulfilling Old Testament prophecy, an allusion to the expected return of Elijah prior to the coming of the Messiah (Malachi 4:5–6).

The two roles of prophet and forerunner really complement one another. As prophet, he called the people to a radical commitment to God and his commands. His was a challenge to turn around and walk a new way (Matthew 3:2). He expected that people who claimed to be the people of God would live as though it were true (Matthew 3:7–12). When people were willing to make that commitment, they were invited to publicly proclaim it through confession and baptism (Matthew 3:6).

As forerunner, he showed that this change in the hearts of people who recognized their need for God was precisely what was needed to "prepare the way for the Lord." People are not likely to seek a savior if they do not perceive they are in need of salvation. It is only when we know we are sinners that it is Good News for us that Jesus is "the Lamb of God, who takes away the sin of the world!" (John 1:29).

John's baptism was a central aspect of his ministry. Baptism was not a new rite for John's audience, but the meaning behind it was new. There were others who practiced baptism in that day, among them the Qumran sect, represented by the Dead Sea Scrolls. John is thought to have been a member of that group. But John's baptism was different in that it was offered to whoever would confess and repent.

John the Baptist: For additional scriptures on this topic go to Malachi 4:5–6.

INTRODUCTION TO THE BOOK OF

JEREMIAH

A Warning About Captivity

WHO WROTE THIS BOOK?

The Book of Jeremiah is named for its author, the prophet of God.

TO WHOM WAS THIS BOOK WRITTEN?

Jeremiah prophesied and wrote to the people of Judah.

WHERE WAS IT WRITTEN?

The prophesy was probably written in and around Judah where Jeremiah lived and ministered.

WHEN WAS IT WRITTEN?

Jeremiah's ministry, which included the writing of this book, covered the years 626–586 B.C., from the reign of Josiah until the fall of Jerusalem to the Babylonians.

WHAT IS THE BOOK ABOUT?

Sometimes called "the weeping prophet," Jeremiah wept and prophesied about Judah's idolatry. He warned the people of Judah of God's inevitable judgment against them and advised them to submit to their Babylonian oppressors.

WHY WAS THIS BOOK WRITTEN?

It was Jeremiah's sad but God-ordained task to proclaim Judah's coming destruction and announce the end of an era for them. God would not conclude his work there, however. After the judgment would follow restoration because of his great mercy.

SO WHAT DOES THIS BOOK MEAN TO US?

Like the people of Judah, we are subject to the righteous judgment of God when we sin against him. And like Judah, we also have the promise of his great love and mercy that allows us access to eternal hope and joy through our repentance and his faithful forgiveness. Unlike Judah, we are the beneficiaries of the new agreement and God's grace, prophesied by Jeremiah (31:31) and established by the Lord Jesus Christ.

SUMMARY:

After we read the Book of Jeremiah, we feel as if we not only know the message of the prophet, but we know the prophet himself. Jeremiah, more than the other prophets, shares the struggles of his ministry with the reader, and so we grow close to him as a person.

Jeremiah began his ministry at the end of the seventh century B.C. during the reign of Josiah. He was from the town of Anathoth, which was a couple of miles north of Jerusalem, and he was from a priestly family. His ministry lasted into the exilie (which began in 586 B.C.). We do not know how long Jeremiah lived, but we do know that after the destruction of Jerusalem he was taken to Egypt, the probable place of his death.

This time period was chaotic and uncertain. Assyria was on the downswing when Jeremiah began ministering, and soon Babylon was the superpower of the ancient Near Eastern world. Because of their sins, God was using the people of Babylon to bring judgment on Israel. God called Jeremiah to be his spokesperson to warn them that their demise was in sight.

Jeremiah brought a message of judgment against the people of Israel who had broken their agreement with God. God was about to punish them for their sins. The people thought they were secure even though they were sinners, because the Temple, the symbol of God's presence, was in their midst. Jeremiah told them that God was not going to spare them. As with all the pre-exilic prophets, Jeremiah's message was primarily, but not exclusively, negative. Jeremiah did see hope for the future, particularly in the "good branch in David's family" (23:5). With his prophetic vision Jeremiah saw a future return of a remnant of the people of God and also a future savior who would form a "new agreement" with his people (Jeremiah 31:31). As we might expect, the New Testament points to Jesus Christ as the person who fulfilled Jeremiah's expectations.

The structure of the book is as follows:

I. Judgment against Judah and Jerusalem (1–25)
II. Jeremiah's Life (26–29)
III. Book of Comfort (30–33)
IV. Jeremiah's Life (34–45)
V. Judgment against Foreign Nations (46–51)

I. Judgment against Judah and Jerusalem (1–25)

The first part of the Book of Jeremiah focuses on the judgment coming upon the people of God in Judah. Assyria has already exiled the northern kingdom, and Jeremiah says the same fate is in store for the south, but this time from the Babylonians. Indeed, Jeremiah advises people to surrender to the Babylonians rather than try to resist. False prophets were giving a different message. They said that Jerusalem would stand up before the Babylonian threat, and they hindered and opposed Jeremiah's message. Jeremiah thus turns to God to complain about his treatment by the people. Occasionally, Jeremiah gives hints that God will restore those who survive.

II. Jeremiah's Life (26–29)

Jeremiah recounts how he takes God's message of judgment and repentance to the people. He describes the resistance he gets from false prophets and other religious leaders.

III. Book of Comfort (30–33)

After a message of almost exclusively negative judgment, Jeremiah now turns to the future with hope. God is not going to abandon his people completely. He will turn to them and establish a new relationship with them after they have been purified.

IV. Jeremiah's Life (34–45)

These chapters describe Jeremiah's life in the closing years of the southern kingdom of Judah. Jeremiah is faithfully proclaiming God's message that Babylon will take Judah, but he is perceived as a supporter of the enemy and is imprisoned. When Jerusalem is taken, he is treated well by the Babylonians and allowed to stay in Judah.

V. Judgment against Foreign Nations (46–51)

The Book of Jeremiah ends with a long section which recounts the judgment that is coming upon the godless nations surrounding Israel. The list includes Egypt, Philistia, Moab, Ammon, Edom, Damascus, Kedar, Hazor, and Elam, but the longest judgment speech is against Babylon.

JEREMIAH

These are the words of Jeremiah son of
Hilkiah. He belonged to the family of
priests who lived in the town of Anathoth
in the land of Benjamin. 2The LORD spoke his
word to Jeremiah during the thirteenth year that
Josiah son of Amon was king of Judah. 3The LORD
also spoke to Jeremiah while Jehoiakim son of Josiah was king of Judah and during the eleven years
that Zedekiah son of Josiah was king of Judah. In
the fifth month of his last year, the people of
Jerusalem were taken away as captives.

The Lord Calls Jeremiah

4The LORD spoke his word to me, saying:
5"Before I made you in your mother's womb,
I chose you.
Before you were born, I set you apart for
a special work.
I appointed you as a prophet to
the nations."

6Then I said, "But Lord GOD, I don't know how
to speak. I am only a boy."
7But the LORD said to me, "Don't say, 'I am only
a boy.' You must go everywhere I send you, and
you must say everything I tell you to say. 8Don't
be afraid of anyone, because I am with you to protect you," says the LORD.
9Then the LORD reached out his hand and
touched my mouth. He said to me, "See, I am
putting my words in your mouth. 10Today I have
put you in charge of nations and kingdoms. You
will pull up and tear down, destroy and overthrow, build up and plant."

Jeremiah Sees Two Visions

11The LORD spoke his word to me, saying: "Jeremiah, what do you see?"
I answered, "I see a stick of almond wood."
12The LORD said to me, "You have seen correctly, because I am watching to make sure my
words come true."
13The LORD spoke his word to me again: "What
do you see?"
I answered, "I see a pot of boiling water, tipping
over from the north."
14The LORD said to me, "Disaster will come from
the north and strike all the people who live in this
country. 15In a short time I will call all of the people in the northern kingdoms," said the LORD.
"Those kings will come and set up
their thrones
near the entrance of the gates of Jerusalem.
They will attack all the city walls
around Jerusalem
and all the cities in Judah.
16And I will announce my judgments against
my people
because of their evil in turning away from me.
They offered sacrifices to other gods
and worshiped idols they had made with
their own hands.

17"Jeremiah, get ready. Stand up and tell them
everything I command you to say. Don't be afraid
of the people, or I will give you good reason to be
afraid of them. 18Today I am going to make you a
strong city, an iron pillar, a bronze wall. You will
be able to stand against everyone in the land:
Judah's kings, officers, priests, and the people of
the land. 19They will fight against you, but they
will not defeat you, because I am with you to protect you!" says the LORD.

Israel Turns from God

2 The LORD spoke his word to me, saying: 2"Go
and speak to the people of Jerusalem, saying:
This is what the LORD says:
'I remember how faithful you were to me
when you were a young nation.
You loved me like a young bride.
You followed me through the desert,
a land that had never been planted.
3The people of Israel were holy to the LORD,
like the first fruits from his harvest.
Those who tried to hurt Israel were
judged guilty.
Disasters struck them,'" says the LORD.

1 The fact that, before Jeremiah's birth, God sets him apart to be a prophet is perhaps indirectly relevant to the abortion debate. The point of the passage, however, is that God set Jeremiah apart even *before* he was in his mother's womb. In other words, God's plan for Jeremiah was there long before he was even conceived. This relates to the abortion debate in that God does not begin thinking of us merely at birth, but long before.

1:5 This passage records God's declaration to Jeremiah that he has designed Jeremiah's life since before his birth. This design places value and personhood on Jeremiah while still in his mother's womb. Unborn life is valuable because God forms individual life within the womb, and he instills purpose in that life.

1:5 Abortion and Crisis Pregnancy: Genesis 16

1:10 Loneliness: Matthew 14:23

1:13 *a pot of boiling water.* The pot of boiling water from the north is a symbol which stands for the Babylonians who, though geographically lived due east of Israel, attacked via the road from the north.

1:16 Prophetic Symbolism: Jeremiah 18:1–12

[4]Hear the word of the LORD, family of Jacob,
all you family groups of Israel.
[5]This is what the LORD says:
"I was fair to your ancestors,
so why did they turn away from me?
Your ancestors worshiped useless idols
and became useless themselves.
[6]Your ancestors didn't say,
'Where is the LORD who brought us
out of Egypt?
He led us through the desert,
through a dry and rocky land,
through a dark and dangerous land.
He led us where no one travels or lives.'
[7]I brought you into a fertile land
so you could eat its fruit and produce.
But you came and made my land unclean;
you made it a hateful place.
[8]The priests didn't ask,
'Where is the LORD?'
The people who know the teachings
didn't know me.
The leaders turned against me.
The prophets prophesied in the name of Baal
and worshiped useless idols.

[9]"So now I will again tell what I have against
you," says the LORD.
"And I will tell what I have against
your grandchildren.
[10]Go across the sea to the island of
Cyprus and see.
Send someone to the land of Kedar
to look closely.
See if there has ever been anything like this.
[11]Has a nation ever exchanged its gods?
(Of course, its gods are not really gods at all.)
But my people have exchanged their
glorious God
for idols worth nothing.
[12]Skies, be shocked at the things that
have happened
and shake with great fear!" says the LORD.
[13]"My people have done two evils:
They have turned away from me,
the spring of living water.
And they have dug their own wells,
which are broken wells that cannot
hold water.⚭
[14]Have the people of Israel become slaves?
Have they become like someone who was
born a slave?
Why were they taken captive?
[15]Enemies have roared like lions at Israel;
they have growled at Israel.
They have destroyed the land of Israel.
The cities of Israel lie in ruins,
and all the people have left.
[16]The men from the cities of Memphis
and Tahpanhes
have disgraced you by shaving the
top of your head.
[17]Haven't you brought this on yourselves
by turning away from the LORD your God
when he was leading you in the right way?
[18]It did not help to go to Egypt
and drink from the Shihor River.
It did not help to go to Assyria
and drink from the Euphrates River.
[19]Your evil will bring punishment to you,
and the wrong you have done will teach
you a lesson.
Think about it and understand
that it is a terrible evil to turn away from
the LORD your God.
It is wrong not to fear me,"
says the Lord GOD All-Powerful.

[20]"Long ago you refused to obey me as an ox
breaks its yoke.
You broke the ropes I used to hold you
and said, 'I will not serve you!'
In fact, on every high hill
and under every green tree
you lay down as a prostitute.
[21]But I planted you as a special vine,
as a very good seed.
How then did you turn
into a wild vine that grows bad fruit?
[22]Although you wash yourself with cleanser
and use much soap,
I can still see the stain of your guilt,"
says the Lord GOD.
[23]"How can you say to me, 'I am not guilty.
I have not worshiped the Baal idols'?
Look at the things you did in the valley.
Think about what you have done.

2:7 God sends Israel into exile for defiling the land. Defiling the land today could include pollution and other sinful acts that degrade our environment, as well as our selfishness in other areas of life. One thing is sure, sin in all forms affects the natural world as much as it affects other human beings.

⚭**2:13 Pleasure:** Ezekiel 16:37

⚭**2:13 Water:** Jeremiah 14:1–6

2:20 *on every high hill, under every green tree.* Under green trees and on hills were the locations of pagan altars dedicated to false gods.

You are like a she-camel in mating season
that runs from place to place.
24You are like a wild donkey that lives
in the desert
and sniffs the wind at mating time.
At that time who can hold her back?
Any male who chases her will easily
catch her;
at mating time, it is easy to find her.
25Don't run until your feet are bare
or until your throat is dry.
But you say, 'It's no use!
I love those other gods,
and I must chase them!'

26"A thief is ashamed when someone catches
him stealing.
In the same way, the family of
Israel is ashamed—
they, their kings, their officers,
their priests, and their prophets.
27They say to things of wood, 'You are my father,'
and to idols of stone, 'You gave birth to me.'
Those people won't look at me;
they have turned their backs to me.
But when they get into trouble, they say,
'Come and save us!'
28Where are the idols you made for yourselves?
Let them come and save you
when you are in trouble!
People of Judah, you have as many idols
as you have towns!

29"Why do you complain to me?
All of you have turned against me," says the
LORD.
30"I punished your people, but it did not help.
They didn't come back when they
were punished.
With your swords you killed your prophets
like a hungry lion.

31"People of Judah, pay attention to the word of
the LORD:
Have I been like a desert to the people of Israel
or like a dark and dangerous land?
Why do my people say, 'We are free to wander.
We won't come to you anymore'?
32A young woman does not forget her jewelry,
and a bride does not forget the decorations
for her dress.
But my people have forgotten me
for more days than can be counted.
33You really know how to chase after love.
Even the worst women can learn evil
ways from you.
34Even on your clothes you have the blood
of poor and innocent people,
but they weren't thieves you caught
breaking in.
You do all these things,
35 but you say, 'I am innocent.
God is not angry with me.'
But I will judge you guilty of lying,
because you say, 'I have not sinned.'
36It is so easy for you to change your mind.
Even Egypt will let you down,
as Assyria let you down.
37You will eventually leave that place
with your hands on your head, like captives.
You trusted those countries,
but you will not be helped by them,
because the LORD has rejected them.

Judah Is Unfaithful

3 "If a man divorces his wife
and she leaves him and marries
another man,
should her first husband come back
to her again?
If he went back to her, wouldn't the land
become completely unclean?
But you have acted like a prostitute
with many lovers,
and now you want to come back to me?"
says the LORD.
2"Look up to the bare hilltops, Judah.
Is there any place where you have not
been a prostitute?
You have sat by the road waiting for lovers,
like an Arab in the desert.
You made the land unclean,
because you did evil and were like
a prostitute.
3So the rain has not come,
and there have not been any spring rains.
But your face still looks like the face of
a prostitute.
You refuse even to be ashamed of
what you did.

3:1–25 Divorce is a serious matter. It means that marriage vows are broken, that a unity has been split. God compares his agreement with Israel to a marriage agreement. He says that he divorced Israel because of her adultery (3:8). When God says that Israel and Judah committed adultery against him, he means that they worshiped false gods or idols (3:9). Even though Israel and Judah have hurt him, God still wants them to come back to him (3:12–25). He is still willing to forgive them.

4Now you are calling to me,
'My father, you have been my friend since I was young.
5Will you always be angry at me?
Will your anger last forever?'
Judah, you said this,
but you did as much evil as you could!"

Judah and Israel Are like Sisters

6When King Josiah was ruling Judah, the Lord said to me, "Did you see what unfaithful Israel did? She was like a prostitute with her idols on every hill and under every green tree. 7I said to myself, 'Israel will come back to me after she does this evil,' but she didn't come back. And Israel's wicked sister Judah saw what she did. 8Judah saw that I divorced unfaithful Israel because of her adultery, but that didn't make Israel's wicked sister Judah afraid. She also went out and acted like a prostitute! 9And she didn't care that she was acting like a prostitute. So she made her country unclean and was guilty of adultery, because she worshiped idols made of stone and wood. 10Israel's wicked sister didn't even come back to me with her whole heart, but only pretended," says the Lord.

11The LORD said to me, "Unfaithful Israel had a better excuse than wicked Judah. 12Go and speak this message toward the north:
'Come back, unfaithful people of Israel,'
says the LORD.
'I will stop being angry at you,
because I am full of mercy,' says the LORD.
'I will not be angry with you forever.
13All you have to do is admit your sin—
that you turned against the LORD your God
and worshiped gods under every green tree
and didn't obey me,'" says the LORD.

14"Come back to me, you unfaithful children," says the LORD, "because I am your master. I will take one person from every city and two from every family group, and I will bring you to Jerusalem. 15Then I will give you new rulers who will be faithful to me, who will lead you with knowledge and understanding. 16In those days there will be many of you in the land," says the LORD. "At that time people will no longer say, 'I remember the Ark of the Agreement.' They won't think about it anymore or remember it or miss it or make another one. 17At that time people will call Jerusalem The Throne of the LORD, and all nations will come together in Jerusalem to show respect to the LORD. They will not follow their stubborn, evil hearts anymore. 18In those days the family of Judah will join the family of Israel. They will come together from a land in the north to the land I gave their ancestors.

19"I, the LORD, said,
'How happy I would be to treat you as my own children
and give you a pleasant land,
a land more beautiful than that of any other nation.'
I thought you would call me 'My Father'
and not turn away from me.
20But like a woman who is unfaithful to her husband,
family of Israel, you have been unfaithful to me," says the LORD.

21You can hear crying on the bare hilltops.
It is the people of Israel crying and praying for mercy.
They have become very evil
and have forgotten the LORD their God.
22"Come back to me, you unfaithful children,
and I will forgive you for being unfaithful."

"Yes, we will come to you,
because you are the LORD our God.
23It was foolish to worship idols on the hills
and on the mountains.
Surely the salvation of Israel
comes from the LORD our God.
24Since our youth, shameful gods have eaten up in sacrifice
everything our ancestors worked for—
their flocks and herds,
their sons and daughters.
25Let us lie down in our shame,
and let our disgrace cover us like a blanket.
We have sinned against the LORD our God,
both we and our ancestors.
From our youth until now,
we have not obeyed the LORD our God."

4 "If you will return, Israel,
then return to me," says the LORD.
"If you will throw away your idols that I hate,
then don't wander away from me.
2If you say when you make a promise,
'As surely as the LORD lives,'
and you can say it in a truthful, honest, and right way,
then the nations will be blessed by him,
and they will praise him for what he has done."

3:8 Adultery: Matthew 5:28
3:14 Conversion: Luke 15:17
3:17 Ark of the Agreement: Hebrews 9:3–5
3:24 Repentance: Amos 4:6–13\

[3]This is what the LORD says to the people of Judah and to Jerusalem:
"Plow your unplowed fields,
and don't plant seeds among thorns.
[4]Give yourselves to the service of the LORD,
and decide to obey him,
people of Judah and people of Jerusalem.
If you don't, my anger will spread among you
like a fire,
and no one will be able to put it out,
because of the evil you have done.

Trouble from the North

[5]"Announce this message in Judah and say
it in Jerusalem:
'Blow the trumpet throughout the country!'
Shout out loud and say,
'Come together!
Let's all escape to the strong, walled cities!'
[6]Raise the signal flag toward Jerusalem!
Run for your lives, and don't wait,
because I am bringing disaster from the north
There will be terrible destruction."

[7]A lion has come out of his den;
a destroyer of nations has begun to march.
He has left his home
to destroy your land.
Your towns will be destroyed
with no one left to live in them.
[8]So put on rough cloth,
show how sad you are, and cry loudly.
The terrible anger of the LORD
has not turned away from us.

[9]"When this happens," says the LORD,
"the king and officers will lose their courage.
The priests will be terribly afraid,
and the prophets will be shocked!"

[10]Then I said, "Lord GOD, you have tricked the
people of Judah and Jerusalem. You said, 'You
will have peace,' but now the sword is pointing at
our throats!"
[11]At that time this message will be given to Judah
and Jerusalem: "A hot wind blows from the bare
hilltops of the desert toward the LORD's people. It is
not a gentle wind to separate grain from chaff. [12]I
feel a stronger wind than that. Now even I will
announce judgments against the people of Judah."

[13]Look! The enemy rises up like a cloud,
and his chariots come like a tornado.
His horses are faster than eagles.
How terrible it will be for us! We are ruined!
[14]People of Jerusalem, clean the evil from your
hearts so that you can be saved.
Don't continue making evil plans.
[15]A voice from Dan makes an announcement
and brings bad news from the mountains
of Ephraim.
[16]"Report this to the nations.
Spread this news in Jerusalem:
'Invaders are coming from a faraway country,
shouting words of war against the cities of
Judah.
[17]The enemy has surrounded Jerusalem as men
guard a field,
because Judah turned against me,'"
says the LORD.
[18]"The way you have lived and acted
has brought this trouble to you.
This is your punishment.
How terrible it is!
The pain stabs your heart!"

Jeremiah's Cry

[19]Oh, how I hurt! How I hurt!
I am bent over in pain.
Oh, the torture in my heart!
My heart is pounding inside me.
I cannot keep quiet,
because I have heard the sound of the trumpet.
I have heard the shouts of war.
[20]Disaster follows disaster;
the whole country has been destroyed.
My tents are destroyed in only a moment.
My curtains are torn down quickly.
[21]How long must I look at the war flag?
How long must I listen to the war trumpet?

[22]The LORD says, "My people are foolish.
They do not know me.
They are stupid children;
they don't understand.
They are skillful at doing evil,
but they don't know how to do good."

Disaster Is Coming

[23]I looked at the earth,
and it was empty and had no shape.
I looked at the sky,
and its light was gone.
[24]I looked at the mountains,
and they were shaking.
All the hills were trembling.

4:11 *chaff.* Chaff is dry, rootless vegetation that can be blown about by the wind.

25I looked, and there were no people.
Every bird in the sky had flown away.
26I looked, and the good, rich land had
become a desert.
All its towns had been destroyed
by the LORD and his great anger.

27This is what the LORD says:
"All the land will be ruined,
but I will not completely destroy it.
28So the people in the land will cry loudly,
and the sky will grow dark,
because I have spoken and will not
change my mind.
I have made a decision, and I will not
change it."

29At the sound of the horsemen and the archers,
all the people in the towns run away.
They hide in the thick bushes
and climb up into the rocks.
All of the cities of Judah are empty;
no one lives in them.
30Judah, you destroyed nation, what
are you doing?
Why do you put on your finest dress
and decorate yourself with gold jewelry?
Why do you put color around your eyes?
You make yourself beautiful, but it is
all useless.
Your lovers hate you;
they want to kill you.

31I hear a cry like a woman having a baby,
distress like a woman having her first child.
It is the sound of Jerusalem gasping
for breath.
She lifts her hands in prayer and says,
"Oh! I am about to faint
before my murderers!"

No One Is Right

5 The LORD says, "Walk up and down the
streets of Jerusalem.
Look around and discover these things.
Search the public squares of the city.
If you can find one person who does
honest things,
who searches for the truth,
I will forgive this city.
2Although the people say, 'As surely as the
LORD lives!'
they don't really mean it."
3LORD, don't you look for truth in people?
You struck the people of Judah,
but they didn't feel any pain.
You crushed them,
but they refused to learn what is right.
They became more stubborn than a rock;
they refused to turn back to God.
4But I thought,
"These are only the poor, foolish people.
They have not learned the way of the LORD
and what their God wants them to do.
5So I will go to the leaders of Judah
and talk to them.
Surely they understand the way of the LORD
and know what God wants them to do."
But even the leaders had all joined together to
break away from the LORD;
they had broken their ties with him.
6So a lion from the forest will attack them.
A wolf from the desert will kill them.
A leopard is waiting for them near their towns.
It will tear to pieces anyone who comes
out of the city,
because the people of Judah have sinned greatly.
They have wandered away from the
LORD many times.

7The LORD said, "Tell me why I should forgive
you.
Your children have left me
and have made promises to idols that
are not gods at all.
I gave your children everything they needed,
but they still were like an unfaithful
wife to me.
They spent much time in houses of prostitutes.
8They are like well-fed horses filled
with sexual desire;
each one wants another man's wife.
9Shouldn't I punish the people of Judah for
doing these things?" says the LORD.
"Shouldn't I give a nation such as this the
punishment it deserves?

10"Go along and cut down Judah's vineyards,
but do not completely destroy them.
Cut off all her people as if they were branches,
because they do not belong to the LORD.
11The families of Israel and Judah
have been completely unfaithful to me,"
says the LORD.

12Those people have lied about the LORD
and said, "He will not do anything to us!
Nothing bad will happen to us!

MARY (MOTHER OF JESUS)

LUKE 1

Why does Mary call herself a servant of the Lord? What does Mary's situation teach us today about God's work in the world?

Ironically, the most well-known woman in the Bible—Mary, the mother of Jesus—has only a few small passages devoted to her story. Furthermore, these passages tell us very little about Mary herself. This being the case then, we are forced to focus on God's work in her life and not on Mary herself. Perhaps this is just what God had intended.

Consider the comparison made between Mary and her relations in Luke 1. In the opening scene a portrait is painted of two saintly people—Zechariah and Elizabeth. Both husband *and* wife come from the priestly line of Aaron. Not only did they hold honor due to their family name, but they also acted honorably in keeping God's law (1:6). Despite all of this, however, they were shamed because they were old and had not yet borne any children (verse 25). As the scene shifts, we are taken from Jerusalem and God's holy Temple to the town of Nazareth, a place of no good reputation (John 1:46). We are told that the angel Gabriel went to a virgin whose name was Mary. In essence, Luke gives us nothing of Mary's status. We are not told of her family line. We are not even told of her worthy character or other actions that might *achieve* her the honor that is bestowed on her. With Zechariah and Elizabeth, he shows us the world's expectations—a story that would make his audience sigh with relief to see justice done for these righteous ones. With Mary, Luke dramatically changes the scene and begins to unravel the ways of the "Powerful One [who] has done great things for me" (Luke 1:49).

In Luke 1:30, we are told that God has shown Mary his grace. This little phrase helps to unravel the mystery of God's choosing an unknown, unnamed, poor woman to bring forth his kingdom. Why did God do this? Elizabeth, a virtuous woman from a strong family line, was waiting to have a child. God could have given *her* the Messiah. *She* had all the right credentials! In verses 47 and 49 Mary says, "my heart rejoices in God my Savior, because he has shown his concern for his humble servant girl. . . . The Powerful One has done great things for me." God chose Mary precisely so that his grace in her life would be recognized! If he had chosen Elizabeth, then she would have received the praise for being an honorable woman. Elizabeth appeared *worthy* of God's favor; Mary did not. Or so was the thinking of the day. God wanted to "scatter the people who . . . think great things about themselves" and raise up the humble (1:51–52). In essence, God was about the business of turning upside down the present-day views of who was worthy of his grace and who was not.

In verse 38, a very interesting thing happens. Mary refers to herself as "servant of the Lord." What does she mean by this? Soon after she refers to herself in this manner, in verse 54, she also calls the people of Israel God's servant. In fact, in the first two chapters of Luke alone there are four references to God's servant. In addition to Mary and Israel, King David and Simeon are also referred to as servants of the Lord (1:69; 2:29). In the Old Testament there are others who are referred to as servants of God. They include Moses (2 Chronicles 1:3; Malachi 4:4), Jacob (Isaiah 48:20), Daniel (Daniel 6:20), and even the king of Babylon (Jeremiah 25:9; 27:6). And Luke 12:43 says that a *blessed* servant is one who does God's work. Though Mary puts herself on the level of many great people, we cannot ignore the frequency with which this phrase appears in the Old Testament. Based on the evidence, a servant of God seems, then, to be simply someone who is willing to be obedient to God's work in their lives (whether or not they recognize it, as in the case of the king of Babylon).

At the beginning of Mary's song in 1:48, she repeats that she is God's servant and in the end (1:54) she refers to the people of Israel as God's servant. In between Mary reflects on how God has worked in her life to lift her from humility (1:48a) to fame (1:48b). She then broadens this work of God in her life to include all of Israel. Just as God has done great things for his humble servant, Mary, so shall he lift up his servant, Israel. Mary's song, written in the present-past tense, implies that God has *already* accomplished this. For instance, God chose to bring about his kingdom through a poor girl whose social prestige was nonexistent.

To say that Mary was an extremely virtuous woman, highly favored and *therefore* chosen by God does nothing to unravel the grace of God at work not only in her life, but in the lives of all people (Luke 1:30, 54). Mary was blessed and was a servant of the Lord not because of who she was or what she did, but because God worked in her to bring forth his promise to Israel and, therefore, to all people.

Mary (Mother of Jesus): All scripture references are contained within this article.

INFERTILITY (CHILDLESSNESS/BARRENNESS)

LUKE 1:7

What significance is attached to fertility and childbearing? What about those who are incapable of having children?

Luke presents Zechariah and Elizabeth in an impossible situation. Because they are blameless before the Lord, we might assume that they would share fully in the blessings that come from God. Chief among those blessings is the gift of children, but it is precisely this gift that they have not received. As a result, they (and especially Elizabeth) lived in shame (see Luke 1:25, 28).

The idea that God controls the womb is deeply rooted in the Old Testament (see Psalm 113:9). As a result, the birth of children was regarded as a sign of blessing and a source of esteem in one's larger family and community. On the other hand, the failure to have children was regarded as a curse, a sign of divine punishment. According to Deuteronomy 28:15, 18, failure to follow God's commandments would lead to the cursing of the womb. Blame for the failure to have children typically fell to the woman, so she suffered ridicule from others in the community and, at times, even from her husband (see Genesis 29:32, 34). Rachel, faced with the embarrassment of childlessness, says, "Give me children, or I'll die!" (Genesis 30:1).

The story of Zechariah and Elizabeth has an interesting twist to it. In fact, it is told in such a way as to recall important stories of God's power in the history of Israel. Long before Zechariah and Elizabeth struggled with their inability to have children, Abraham and Sarah suffered because of the lack of children. Like Zechariah and Elizabeth, they had been unable to have children, and, like Zechariah and Elizabeth, they were now too old. Nevertheless, God promised a son to Abraham and Sarah, and she eventually gave birth to Isaac (Genesis 18:1–16; 21:1–7). The birth of a son was a fulfillment of God's promise. It was a miracle, and it was a sign of God's care for Abraham and Sarah. Other Old Testament stories come to mind, too, including the story of Elkanah and Hannah. Hannah cried out in prayer to God for a son, "the Lord remembered her," she became pregnant, and she had a son (1 Samuel 1:1–20).

The way Luke records his story of Elizabeth and Zechariah reminds us of God's miraculous intervention in the past. It also raises our expectations that God might act in a similar way in their case too. Even as we share in their tragedy and pain, we wonder if God will bless them with a child. God hears their prayers and a son, John, is born to them (Luke 1:5–25, 57–66).

Not every story of infertility has such a happy ending. Recent studies estimate that between 10 and 16 percent of all married couples are faced with infertility. Is this a consequence of divine judgment? As we have seen, Deuteronomy 28 notes that failure to observe God's commandments would lead to infertility, and it has always been easy to reverse this logic. Is it not the case, then, that infertility is the consequence of God's curse, itself the result of disobedience? Hardly. To say that disobedience might lead to infertility is not the same thing as saying that infertility is the result of disobedience. Today there is a range of known factors contributing to the incidence of infertility, including the older ages at which people marry or at which they hope to have children. We should also observe that, whereas in biblical times infertility was assumed to result from a problem with the woman, today we know that infertility can result from physical difficulties that originate in the man or in the woman; in some cases, there is a combined problem.

Failure to "fit in" with societal norms of childbearing and childrearing can lead couples to drastic measures. In ways that remind us of biblical stories, many people today experience childlessness as shame and loneliness. Moreover, just as Hannah made a deal with God if only he would give her a son (1 Samuel 1:11) and just as Sarah attempted to achieve God's promise of a son through another woman, so some couples today bargain with God or attempt through reproductive technologies or surrogate mothers to produce a child. Marriage relationships can thus be placed under enormous emotional, social, and financial pressures.

For the people of God, issues of childlessness are ultimately issues of faith to be worked out in conversation with God and God's people. Those of us who struggle with infertility are thus enabled to share our pain and mourn the loss of a child one could never have within a supportive context. Within this same context, we are enabled to grapple with our feelings of isolation and abandonment, to examine the available options, and to explore God's wider purposes beyond the immediacy of our own difficult circumstances.

Infertility (Childlessness/Barrenness): For additional scriptures on this topic go to Genesis 18:1–16.

We will never see war or hunger!
13The prophets are like an empty wind;
the word of God is not in them.
Let the bad things they say happen to them."

14So this is what the LORD God All-Powerful
says:
"The people said I would not punish them.
So, the words I give you will be like fire,
and these people will be like wood that
it burns up.
15Listen, family of Israel," says the LORD,
"I will soon bring a nation from far away to
attack you.
It is an old nation that has lasted a long time.
The people there speak a language you
do not know;
you cannot understand what they say.
16Their arrows bring death.
All their people are strong warriors.
17They will eat your crops and your food.
They will eat your sons and daughters.
They will eat your flocks and herds.
They will eat your grapes and figs.
They will destroy with their swords
the strong, walled cities you trust.

18"Yet even then," says the LORD, "I will not
destroy you completely. 19When the people of
Judah ask, 'Why has the LORD our God done all
these terrible things to us?' then give them this
answer: 'You have left the LORD and served foreign idols in your own land. So now you will serve
foreigners in a land that does not belong to you.'

20"Announce this message to the family of Jacob,
and tell it to the nation of Judah:
21Hear this message, you foolish people who
have no sense.
They have eyes, but they don't really see.
They have ears, but they don't really listen.
22Surely you are afraid of me," says the LORD.
"You should shake with fear in
my presence.
I am the one who made the beaches to be a
border for the sea,
a border the water can never go past.
The waves may pound the beach, but they
can't win over it.
They may roar, but they cannot go beyond it.
23But the people of Judah are stubborn and have
turned against me.
They have turned aside and gone
away from me.
24They do not say to themselves,
'We should fear the LORD our God,
who gives us autumn and spring rains in
their seasons,
who makes sure we have the harvest at
the right time.'
25But your evil has kept away both rain
and harvest.
Your sins have kept you from enjoying
good things.
26There are wicked men among my people.
Like those who make nets for catching birds,
they set their traps to catch people.
27Like cages full of birds,
their houses are full of lies.
They have become rich and powerful.
28 They have grown big and fat.
There is no end to the evil things they do.
They won't plead the case of the orphan
or help the poor be judged fairly.
29Shouldn't I punish the people of Judah for
doing these things?" says the LORD.
"Shouldn't I give a nation such as this the
punishment it deserves?⚭

30"A terrible and shocking thing
has happened in the land of Judah:
31The prophets speak lies,
and the priests take power into their own
hands,
and my people love it this way.
But what will you do when the end comes?

Jerusalem Is Surrounded

6 "Run for your lives, people of Benjamin!
Run away from Jerusalem!
Blow the war trumpet in the town of Tekoa!
Raise the warning flag over the town
of Beth Hakkerem!
Disaster is coming from the north;
terrible destruction is coming to you.
2Jerusalem, I will destroy you,
you who are fragile and gentle.
3Shepherds with their flocks will come
against Jerusalem.
They will set up their tents all around her,
each shepherd taking care of his
own section."
4They say, "Get ready to fight against Jerusalem!
Get up! We will attack at noon!

⚭**5:29 Adoption:** Jeremiah 22:2–3
6:3 *shepherds.* The shepherd was an image of a leader in the ancient Near East. Here, they are the leaders of the armies that come against Jerusalem to destroy her. Their flocks are their troops.

But it is already getting late;
the evening shadows are growing long.
5So get up! We will attack at night.
We will destroy the strong towers
of Jerusalem!"

6This is what the LORD All-Powerful says:
"Cut down the trees around Jerusalem,
and build an attack ramp to the top of its walls.
This city must be punished.
Inside it is nothing but slavery.
7Jerusalem pours out her evil
as a well pours out its water.
The sounds of violence and destruction are
heard within her.
I can see the sickness and hurts of Jerusalem.
8Listen to this warning, Jerusalem,
or I will turn my back on you
and make your land an empty desert
where no one can live."
9This is what the LORD All-Powerful says:
"Gather the few people of Israel who
are left alive,
as you would gather the last grapes
on a grapevine.
Check each vine again,
like someone who gathers grapes."

10To whom can I speak? Whom can I warn?
Who will listen to me?
The people of Israel have closed ears,
so they cannot hear my warnings.
They don't like the word of the LORD;
they don't want to listen to it!
11But I am full of the anger of the LORD,
and I am tired of holding it in.

"Pour out my anger on the children
who play in the street
and on the young men gathered together.
A husband and his wife will both be caught in
his anger,
as will the very old.
12Their houses will be turned over to others,
along with their fields and wives,
because I will raise my hand
and punish the people of Judah,"
says the LORD.
13"Everyone, from the least important to the
greatest,
is greedy for money.
Even the prophets and priests
all tell lies.
14They tried to heal my people's serious injuries
as if they were small wounds.
They said, 'It's all right, it's all right.'
But really, it is not all right.
15They should be ashamed of the terrible
way they act,
but they are not ashamed at all.
They don't even know how to blush
about their sins.
So they will fall, along with everyone else.
They will be thrown to the ground when I
punish them," says the LORD.

16This is what the LORD says:
"Stand where the roads cross and look.
Ask where the old way is,
where the good way is, and walk on it.
If you do, you will find rest for yourselves.
But they have said, 'We will not walk on
the good way.'
17I set watchmen over you
and told you, 'Listen for the sound of the
war trumpet!'
But they said, 'We will not listen.'
18So listen, all you nations,
and pay attention, you witnesses.
Watch what I will do to the people of Judah.
19Hear this, people of the earth:
I am going to bring disaster to the
people of Judah
because of the evil they plan.
They have not listened to my messages
and have rejected my teachings.
20Why do you bring me offerings of incense from
the land of Sheba?
Why do you bring me sweet-smelling cane
from a faraway land?
Your burnt offerings will not be accepted;
your sacrifices do not please me."

21So this is what the LORD says:
"I will put problems in front of Judah.
Fathers and sons will stumble over
them together.
Neighbors and friends will die."

22This is what the LORD says:
"Look, an army is coming
from the land of the north;
a great nation is coming
from the far sides of the earth.
23The soldiers carry bows and spears.
They are cruel and show no mercy.
They sound like the roaring ocean
when they ride their horses.
That army is coming lined up for battle,
ready to attack you, Jerusalem."

[24]We have heard the news about that army
and are helpless from fear.
We are gripped by our pain,
like a woman having a baby.
[25]Don't go out into the fields
or walk down the roads,
because the enemy has swords.
There is terror on every side.
[26]My people, put on rough cloth
and roll in the ashes to show how
sad you are.
Cry loudly for those who are dead,
as if your only son were dead,
because the destroyer
will soon come against us.
[27]"Jeremiah, I have made you like a worker
who tests metal,
and my people are like the ore.
You must observe their ways
and test them.
[28]All my people have turned against me
and are stubborn.
They go around telling lies about others.
They are like bronze and iron
that became covered with rust.
They all act dishonestly.
[29]The fire is fanned to make it hotter,
but the lead does not melt.
The pure metal does not come out;
the evil is not removed from my people.
[30]My people will be called rejected silver,
because the LORD has rejected them."

Jeremiah's Temple Message

7 This is the word that the LORD spoke to Jeremiah: [2]"Stand at the gate of the Temple and
preach this message there:

"'Hear the word of the LORD, all you people of
the nation of Judah! All you who come through
these gates to worship the LORD, listen to this
message! [3]This is what the LORD All-Powerful, the
God of Israel, says: Change your lives and do what
is right! Then I will let you live in this place.⚭
[4]Don't trust the lies of people who say, "This is the
Temple of the LORD. This is the Temple of the LORD.
This is the Temple of the LORD!"⚭ [5]You must
change your lives and do what is right. Be fair to
each other. [6]You must not be hard on strangers,
orphans, and widows. Don't kill innocent people
in this place! Don't follow other gods, or they will
ruin your lives. [7]If you do these things, I will let
you live in this land that I gave to your ancestors
to keep forever.

[8]"'But look, you are trusting lies, which is useless. [9]Will you steal and murder and be guilty of
adultery? Will you falsely accuse other people?
Will you burn incense to the god Baal and follow
other gods you have not known? [10]If you do that,
do you think you can come before me and stand
in this place where I have chosen to be worshiped? Do you think you can say, "We are safe!"
when you do all these hateful things?⚭ [11]This
place where I have chosen to be worshiped is
nothing more to you than a hideout for robbers. I
have been watching you, says the LORD.

[12]"'You people of Judah, go now to the town of
Shiloh, where I first made a place to be worshiped. See what I did to it because of the evil
things the people of Israel had done. [13]You people
of Judah have done all these evil things too, says
the LORD. I spoke to you again and again, but you
did not listen to me. I called you, but you did not
answer. [14]So I will destroy the place where I have
chosen to be worshiped in Jerusalem. You trust in
that place, which I gave to you and your ancestors, but I will destroy it just as I destroyed Shiloh.
[15]I will push you away from me just as I pushed
away your relatives, the people of Israel!'

[16]"As for you, Jeremiah, don't pray for these
people. Don't cry out for them or ask anything for
them or beg me to help them, because I will not
listen to you. [17]Don't you see what they are doing
in the towns of Judah and in the streets of
Jerusalem? [18]The children gather wood, and the
fathers use the wood to make a fire. The women
make the dough for cakes of bread, and they offer
them to the Queen Goddess. They pour out drink
offerings to other gods to make me angry. [19]But I
am not the one the people of Judah are really hurting, says the LORD. They are only hurting themselves and bringing shame upon themselves.

[20]"'So this is what the Lord GOD says: I will
pour out my anger on this place, on people and
animals, on the trees in the field and the crops in
the ground. My anger will be like a hot fire that
no one can put out.

6:29 *pure metal.* The verse describes a failed attempt to extract pure silver from lead. The image means that those who rebelled against God are not removed from the rest of Israel, so they remain evil.

⚭**7:3 Jerusalem:** Jeremiah 7:10

⚭**7:4 Presence of God:** Haggai 2

7:4 *This is the Temple of the LORD.* The people put their hope in the presence of the Temple, which symbolizes God's presence. However, they do not realize that God is not bound by the Temple.

⚭**7:10 Jerusalem:** Jeremiah 31:38

⚭**7:10 Murder:** Matthew 5:21–22

7:18 *Queen Goddess.* The Queen Goddess was the leading deity of the people of Canaan at that time, Astarte, who was known as Ishtar in Mesopotamia.

Obedience Is More than Sacrifice

21“ ‘This is what the LORD All-Powerful, the God
of Israel, says: Offer burnt offerings along with your
other sacrifices, and eat the meat yourselves!
22When I brought your ancestors out of Egypt, I
did not speak to them and give them commands
only about burnt offerings and sacrifices. 23I also
gave them this command: Obey me, and I will be
your God and you will be my people. Do all that I
command so that good things will happen to you.
24But your ancestors did not listen or pay attention to me. They were stubborn and did whatever
their evil hearts wanted. They went backward,
not forward. 25Since the day your ancestors left
Egypt, I have sent my servants, the prophets,
again and again to you. 26But your ancestors did
not listen or pay attention to me. They were very
stubborn and did more evil than their ancestors.’
27“Jeremiah, you will tell all these things to the
people of Judah, but they will not listen to you.
You will call to them, but they will not answer
you. 28So say to them, ‘This is the nation that has
not obeyed the LORD its God. These people do
nothing when I correct them. They do not tell the
truth; it has disappeared from their lips.

The Valley of Killing

29“ ‘Cut off your hair and throw it away. Go up
to the bare hilltop and cry out, because the LORD
has rejected these people. He has turned his back
on them, and in his anger will punish them.
30The people of Judah have done what I said was
evil, says the LORD. They have set up their hateful
idols in the place where I have chosen to be worshiped and have made it unclean. 31The people of
Judah have built places of worship at Topheth in
the Valley of Ben Hinnom. There they burned
their own sons and daughters as sacrifices, something I never commanded. It never even entered
my mind. 32So, I warn you. The days are coming,
says the LORD, when people will not call this place
Topheth or the Valley of Ben Hinnom anymore.
They will call it the Valley of Killing. They will
bury the dead in Topheth until there is no room
to bury anyone else. 33Then the bodies of the
dead will become food for the birds of the sky and
for the wild animals. There will be no one left
alive to chase them away. 34I will end the happy
sounds of the bride and bridegroom. There will
be no happy sounds in the cities of Judah or in the
streets of Jerusalem, because the land will
become an empty desert!

8 “ ‘The LORD says: At that time they will
remove from their tombs the bones of
Judah’s kings and officers, priests and prophets,
and the people of Jerusalem. 2The bones will be
spread on the ground under the sun, moon, and
stars that the people loved and served and went
after and searched for and worshiped. No one
will gather up the bones and bury them. So they
will be like dung thrown on the ground.⚭ 3I will
force the people of Judah to leave their homes
and their land. Those of this evil family who
are not dead will wish they were, says the LORD
All-Powerful.’

Sin and Punishment

4“Say to the people of Judah: ‘This is what
the LORD says:

When people fall down, don’t they get up again?
  And when someone goes the wrong way,
    doesn’t he turn back?
5Why, then, have the people of Jerusalem
    gone the wrong way
  and not turned back?
They believe their own lies
  and refuse to turn around and come back.
6I have listened to them very carefully,
  but they do not say what is right.
They do not feel sorry about their wicked ways,
  saying, “What have I done?”
Each person goes his own way,
  like a horse charging into a battle.
7Even the birds in the sky
  know the right times to do things.
The storks, doves, swifts, and thrushes
  know when it is time to migrate.
But my people don’t know
  what the LORD wants them to do.

8“ ‘You keep saying, “We are wise,
  because we have the teachings of the LORD.”
But actually, those who explain the Scriptures
  have written lies with their pens.
9These wise men refused to listen to the
    word of the LORD,
  so they are not really wise at all.
They will be ashamed.
  They will be shocked and trapped.
10So I will give their wives to other men
  and their fields to new owners.
Everyone, from the least important
    to the greatest,
  is greedy for money.

7:31 *Topheth.* Topheth, located in the Valley of Ben Hinnom, was a garbage dump where children were sacrificed to pagan gods.
⚭**8:2 Astrology:** Jeremiah 10:2

8:2 *No one will gather up the bones.* It was considered a curse during biblical times if one’s body was not given a decent burial.

Even the prophets and priests
all tell lies.
11They tried to heal my people's serious injuries
as if they were small wounds.
They said, "It's all right, it's all right."
But really, it is not all right.
12They should be ashamed of the terrible way
they act,
but they are not ashamed at all.
They don't even know how to blush about
their sins.
So they will fall, along with everyone else.
They will be thrown to the ground when I
punish them, says the LORD.
13" 'I will take away their crops, says the LORD.
There will be no grapes on the vine
and no figs on the fig tree.
Even the leaves will dry up and die.
I will take away what I gave them.' "

14"Why are we just sitting here?
Let's get together!
We have sinned against the LORD,
so he has given us poisoned water to drink.
Come, let's run to the strong, walled cities.
The LORD our God has decided that
we must die,
so let's die there.
15We hoped to have peace,
but nothing good has come.
We hoped for a time when he would heal us,
but only terror has come.
16From the land of Dan,
the snorting of the enemy's horses
is heard.
The ground shakes from the neighing
of their large horses.
They have come and destroyed
the land and everything in it,
the city and all who live there."

17"Look! I am sending poisonous snakes to
attack you.
These snakes cannot be charmed,
and they will bite you," says the LORD.

Jeremiah's Sadness

18God, you are my comfort when I am very sad
and when I am afraid.
19Listen to the sound of my people.
They cry from a faraway land:
"Isn't the LORD still in Jerusalem?
Isn't Jerusalem's king still there?"
But God says, "Why did the people make me
angry by worshiping idols,
useless foreign idols?"

20And the people say, "Harvest time is over;
summer has ended,
and we have not been saved."

21Because my people are crushed, I am crushed.
I cry loudly and am afraid for them.
22Isn't there balm in the land of Gilead?
Isn't there a doctor there?
So why aren't the hurts of my people healed?
9 I wish my head were like a spring of water
and my eyes like a fountain of tears!
Then I could cry day and night
for my people who have been killed.
2I wish I had a place in the desert—
a house where travelers spend the night—
so I could leave my people.
I could go away from them,
because they are all unfaithful to God;
they are all turning against him.

Judah's Failures

3"They use their tongues like a bow,
shooting lies from their mouths like arrows.
Lies, not truth,
have grown strong in the land.
They go from one evil thing to another.
They do not know who I am," says the LORD.
4"Watch out for your friends,
and don't trust your own relatives,
because every relative is a cheater,
and every friend tells lies about you.
5Everyone lies to his friend,
and no one speaks the truth.
The people of Judah have taught their
tongues to lie.
They have become tired from sinning.
6Jeremiah, you live in the middle of lies.
With their lies the people refuse to know me,"
says the LORD.

7So this is what the LORD All-Powerful says:
"I will test the people of Judah as a person
tests metal in a fire.
I have no other choice,
because my people have sinned.
8Their tongues are like sharp arrows.
Their mouths speak lies.
Everyone speaks nicely to his neighbor,
but he is secretly planning to attack him.

8:22 *balm in the land of Gilead.* The balm of Gilead is a reference to some kind of resin used in the healing process.

[9]Shouldn't I punish the people for doing this?"
says the LORD.
"Shouldn't I give a nation like this the
punishment it deserves?"

[10]I, Jeremiah, will cry loudly for the mountains
and sing a funeral song for the empty fields.
They are empty, and no one passes through.
The mooing of cattle cannot be heard.
The birds have flown away,
and the animals are gone.

[11]"I, the LORD, will make the city of Jerusalem
a heap of ruins,
a home for wild dogs.
I will destroy the cities of Judah
so no one can live there."

[12]What person is wise enough to understand
these things? Is there someone who has been
taught by the LORD who can explain them? Why
was the land ruined? Why has it been made like
an empty desert where no one goes?
[13]The LORD answered, "It is because Judah quit
following my teachings that I gave them. They
have not obeyed me or done what I told them to
do. [14]Instead, they were stubborn and followed
the Baals, as their ancestors taught them to do.
[15]So this is what the LORD All-Powerful, the God
of Israel, says: "I will soon make the people of
Judah eat bitter food and drink poisoned water.
[16]I will scatter them through other nations that
they and their ancestors never knew about. I will
chase the people of Judah with the sword until
they are all killed."
[17]This is what the LORD All-Powerful says:
"Now, think about these things!
Call for the women who cry at
funerals to come.
Send for those women who are good
at that job.
[18]Let them come quickly
and cry loudly for us.
Then our eyes will fill with tears,
and streams of water will flow from
our eyelids.
[19]The sound of loud crying is heard from
Jerusalem:
'We are truly ruined!
We are truly ashamed!
We must leave our land,
because our houses are in ruins.' "

[20]Now, women of Judah, listen to the word of
the LORD;
open your ears to hear the words of his
mouth.
Teach your daughters how to cry loudly.
Teach one another a funeral song.
[21]Death has climbed in through our windows
and has entered our strong cities.
Death has taken away our children who play
in the streets
and the young men who meet in the
city squares.

[22]Say, "This is what the LORD says:
'The dead bodies of people will lie
in the open field like dung.
They will lie like grain a farmer has cut,
but there will be no one to gather them.' "
[23]This is what the LORD says:
"The wise must not brag about their wisdom.
The strong must not brag about their strength.
The rich must not brag about their money.
[24]But if someone wants to brag, let him brag
that he understands and knows me.
Let him brag that I am the LORD,
and that I am kind and fair,
and that I do things that are right on earth.
This kind of bragging pleases me,"
says the LORD.⚭

[25]The LORD says, "The time is coming when I
will punish all those who are circumcised only in
the flesh: [26]the people of Egypt, Judah, Edom,
Ammon, Moab, and the desert people who cut
their hair short. The men in all those countries
are not circumcised. And the whole family of
Israel does not give itself to serving me."⚭

The Lord and the Idols

10 Family of Israel, listen to what the LORD
says to you. [2]This is what he says:
"Don't live like the people from other nations,
and don't be afraid of special signs in the sky,
even though the other nations are afraid
of them.⚭
[3]The customs of other people are worth nothing.
Their idols are just wood cut from the forest,
shaped by a worker with his chisel.
[4]They decorate their idols with silver and gold.

9:22 *no one together.* See 8:2.
⚭**9:24 Pride:** Ezekiel 24:21
⚭**9:26 Circumcision:** Ezekiel 44:7–9

⚭**10:2 Astrology:** Jeremiah 19:13
10:2 *special signs in the sky.* The other nations practiced astrology, so signs in the sky that indicated disaster could send them into a panic.

With hammers and nails they fasten
them down
so they won't fall over.
[5]Their idols are like scarecrows in melon fields;
they cannot talk.
Since they cannot walk,
they must be carried.
Do not be afraid of those idols,
because they can't hurt you,
and they can't help you either."

[6]LORD, there is no one like you.
You are great,
and your name is great and powerful.
[7]Everyone should respect you, King of
the nations;
you deserve respect.
Of all the wise people among the nations
and in all the kingdoms,
none of them is as wise as you.
[8]Those wise people are stupid and foolish.
Their teachings come from worthless
wooden idols.
[9]Hammered silver is brought from Tarshish
and gold from Uphaz,
so the idols are made by craftsmen
and goldsmiths.
They put blue and purple clothes on the idols.
All these things are made by skilled workers.
[10]But the LORD is the only true God.
He is the only living God, the King forever.
The earth shakes when he is angry,
and the nations cannot stand up to his anger.

[11]"Tell them this message: 'These gods did not make heaven and earth; they will be destroyed and disappear from heaven and earth.' "

[12]God made the earth by his power.
He used his wisdom to build the world
and his understanding to stretch out the skies.
[13]When he thunders, the waters in the skies roar.
He makes clouds rise in the sky all
over the earth.
He sends lightning with the rain
and brings out the wind from his storehouses.

[14]People are so stupid and know so little.
Goldsmiths are made ashamed by their idols,
because those statues are only false gods.
They have no breath in them.
[15]They are worth nothing; people make
fun of them.
When they are judged, they will
be destroyed.
[16]But God, who is Jacob's Portion, is not
like the idols.
He made everything,
and he chose Israel to be his special people.
The LORD All-Powerful is his name.

Destruction Is Coming

[17]Get everything you own and prepare to leave,
you people who are trapped by your enemies.
[18]This is what the LORD says:
"At this time I will throw out the people who
live in this land.
I will bring trouble to them
so that they may be captured."

[19]How terrible it will be for me because
of my injury.
My wound cannot be healed.
Yet I told myself,
"This is my sickness; I must suffer through it."
[20]My tent is ruined,
and all its ropes are broken.
My children have gone away and left me.
No one is left to put up my tent again
or to set up a shelter for me.
[21]The shepherds are stupid
and don't ask the LORD for advice.
So they do not have success,
and all their flocks are scattered and lost.
[22]Listen! The news is coming.
A loud noise comes from the north
to make the towns of Judah an empty desert
and a home for wild dogs!

Jeremiah's Prayer

[23]LORD, I know that a person's life doesn't really
belong to him.
No one can control his own life.
[24]LORD, correct me, but be fair.
Don't punish me in your anger,
or you will destroy me.
[25]Pour out your anger on other nations
that do not know you
and do not pray to you.
Those nations have destroyed Jacob's family.
They have eaten him up completely
and destroyed his homeland.

The Agreement Is Broken

11 These are the words that the LORD spoke to
Jeremiah: [2]"Listen to the words of this agreement and tell them to the people of Judah and those
living in Jerusalem. [3]Tell them this is what the
LORD, the God of Israel, says: 'Cursed is the person
who does not obey the words of this agreement

4 that I made with your ancestors when I brought
them out of Egypt. Egypt was like a furnace for
melting iron!' I told them, 'Obey me and do
everything I command you. Then you will be my
people, and I will be your God. 5 Then I will keep
the promise I made to your ancestors to give
them a fertile land.' And you are living in that
country today."

I answered, "Amen, LORD."

6 The LORD said to me, "Announce this message
in the towns of Judah and in the streets of
Jerusalem: 'Listen to the words of this agreement
and obey them. 7 I warned your ancestors to obey
me when I brought them out of Egypt. I have
warned them again and again to this very day:
"Obey me!" 8 But your ancestors did not listen to
me. They were stubborn and did what their own
evil hearts wanted. So I made all the curses of this
agreement come upon them. I commanded them
to obey the agreement, but they did not.'"

9 Then the LORD said to me, "I know the people
of Judah and those living in Jerusalem have made
secret plans. 10 They have gone back to the same
sins their ancestors did. Their ancestors refused
to listen to my message and followed and worshiped other gods instead. The families of Israel
and Judah have broken the agreement I made
with their ancestors. 11 So this is what the LORD
says: 'I will soon bring a disaster on the people of
Judah which they will not be able to escape. They
will cry to me for help, but I will not listen to
them. 12 The people living in the towns of Judah
and the city of Jerusalem will pray to their idols to
whom they burn incense. But those idols will not
be able to help when disaster comes. 13 Look,
people of Judah, you have as many idols as there
are towns in Judah. You have built as many altars
to burn incense to that shameful god Baal as there
are streets in Jerusalem.'

14 "As for you, Jeremiah, don't pray for these
people or cry out for them or ask anything for
them. I will not listen when they call to me in the
time of their trouble.

15 "What is my beloved Judah doing in my Temple
when she makes many evil plans?
Do you think animal sacrifices will stop your
punishment?
When you do your evil, then you are happy."
16 The LORD called you "a leafy olive tree,
with beautiful fruit and shape."
But with the roar of a strong storm
he will set that tree on fire,
and its branches will be burned up.

17 The LORD All-Powerful, who planted you, has
announced that disaster will come to you. This is
because the families of Israel and Judah have
done evil and have made him angry by burning
incense to Baal.

Evil Plans Against Jeremiah

18 The LORD showed me that men were making
plans against me. Because he showed me what
they were doing, I knew they were against me.
19 Before this, I was like a gentle lamb waiting to
be butchered. I did not know they had made
plans against me, saying:
"Let us destroy the tree and its fruit.
Let's kill him so people will forget him."
20 But, LORD All-Powerful, you are a fair judge.
You know how to test peoples' hearts
and minds.
I have told you what I have against them.
So let me see you give them the punishment
they deserve.

21 So the LORD speaks about the men from Anathoth who plan to kill Jeremiah and say, "Don't
prophesy in the name of the LORD, or we will kill
you!" 22 So this is what the LORD All-Powerful
says: "I will soon punish the men from Anathoth.
Their young men will die in war. Their sons and
daughters will die from hunger. 23 No one from
the city of Anathoth will be left alive, because I
will cause a disaster to happen to them that year."

Jeremiah's First Complaint

12 LORD, when I bring my case to you,
you are always right.
But I want to ask you about the justice
you give.
Why are evil people successful?
Why do dishonest people have such
easy lives?
2 You have put the evil people here
like plants with strong roots.
They grow and produce fruit.
With their mouths they speak well of you,
but their hearts are really far away from you.
3 But you know my heart, LORD.
You see me and test my thoughts about you.

11:13–15 God does not honor their worship, because they are not really true to him. They are only trying to force God to protect them from trouble by making vows and sacrifices. But we cannot exploit the system of worship that God established as an automatic formula to avoid trouble or to bring prosperity. God knows our thoughts and feelings; he cannot be tricked or forced into doing our will.

12:1 Happiness: Lamentations 5:15

REPENTANCE

LUKE 3:10–14

What does it mean to repent? Who needs to repent and why?

Usually translated in the NCV as "changing our hearts and lives," *repentance* is a key word for the Christian faith. Underlying the notion of repentance are fundamental affirmations about human beings and about God. Especially important is the idea that we have all gone our own ways, not giving ourselves fully to following God. Because of this, we are in need of "changing our hearts and lives" in order to embrace fully God's purpose for our lives. Even Israel, whose faith in God can be assumed, is often called to turn from their evil ways back to God. People who are reared outside the community of God's people are called to repent too; for them, repentance includes coming to trust in God for the first time. Through repentance we turn away from our old ways of life in order to enter into a new relationship with God. In turning to God, we also embrace new ways of living with each other and the world.

The message of repentance, then, is basically good news. It reminds us that sin is not the last word and that judgment for our sin is not inescapable. In the eyes of God, the bad things we have done can be corrected, through changing our hearts and lives. Of course, this might involve paying back the wrongs we have committed (Luke 19:1–10).

Throughout the Bible, the notion of repentance is developed in relationship to the idea of life as a journey. In this way, repentance can be thought of in terms of trading one's life path, one's way of life, for another. In Luke 3:3–6, John's "baptism of changed hearts and lives" is related to the need to make the way of God smooth and straight. Similarly, in the Old Testament, Israel is called to follow the way of the Lord rather than to go the way sinners go (Psalm 1:1). This helps us to realize that repentance is related both to actions and to attitudes. It is more than how we feel or what we say or do. Repentance has to do with a complete change of life. In repentance, our lives become defined by God's goodness toward us and toward others.

John's message makes clear, though, that if our hearts are set on God, our actions will show it. It is not enough to say that we are God's children or that we believe in God. (The Letter of James emphasizes this point too.) John goes on to speak, therefore, of doing "things that show you really have changed your hearts and lives" and of producing "good fruit." When the people ask what this means, John tells them, for example, about the need to share clothing and food with those in need. In this way, John sounds very much like an Old Testament prophet calling the people back to God: "Stop doing wrong. Learn to do good. Seek justice. Punish those who hurt others. Help the orphans. Stand up for the rights of widows" (Isaiah 1:16–17).

The major difference between repentance in John's message and in the message of the Old Testament prophets is John's sense of urgency. Often in the Old Testament, the call to repentance is given in order to remind Israel of what God had called them to be. He delivered them from slavery in Egypt in order to be a different kind of people, a people whose life together would conform to his own will. This perspective is not lost in the New Testament, but there is a new sense of urgency. Salvation and judgment is just around the corner, and the only acceptable response is repentance. Now is the opportunity for response!

Elsewhere in the New Testament, repentance is more and more related to faith. In fact, the word "repentance" is not used very often in the letters of Paul. In Paul's writings and other places in the New Testament, these two words, repentance and faith, are two sides of one coin. "Faith" can include repentance, and "repentance" can thus be used to signify the whole response of people to the Good News of Jesus.

However, just as Israel could be called back to God, so the New Testament shows that Christians can live in need of repentance. Just because they have entered into a new relationship with God does not mean that they cannot or will not turn back to their own way of living, apart from God. God desires that all should repent and so escape the coming judgment (2 Peter 3:8–13). But he also desires that Christians turn from their sin, change their minds, and live lives that produce good fruit: "So be eager to do right," the Lord says, "and change your hearts and lives" (Revelation 3:19).

Repentance can be used to describe the actions people should take toward other people, too. When people have acted in a way that hurts someone else, they are to repent. If they do, they are to be forgiven (Luke 17:3–4).

Repentance: For additional scriptures on this topic go to 1 Kings 8:35.

POVERTY

LUKE 4

What does it mean to be "poor" in the Bible? When Jesus announced that his mission was to bring Good News to the poor, what did he mean? How does the church work to embody this mission today?

When we read the word *poor* in Scripture, we tend to think only of those who have little or no money. This is certainly not without good cause. Throughout Scripture, the poor are contrasted with the rich (Ruth 3:10; Job 34:19; Mark 12:41–42). However, when we too stringently equate poverty with lack of money, we miss out on a wealth of possibilities in relating to this large group throughout Scripture.

In Luke 4:18b, Jesus sets out his mission to the poor. Here the poor appear to include those who need to be released from prison, illness, and oppression. Likewise, in Matthew 11:4–5 and Luke 7:21–23, Jesus recounts those things that have been done for the blind, the lame, the leprous, and even the dead. This is summarized in one final statement: "and the Good News is preached to the poor." In a different context, but with the same effect, Jesus "preaches" to his disciples concerning the poor. Alongside the poor, he includes the hungry, those who weep, the despised, the excluded, and the rejected. They all inherit a specific part of what all the poor who repent will inherit—the kingdom of God (Luke 6:20b–22; Matthew 5:3–11). And when they acknowledge their spiritual poverty, God can lift them up to his kingdom (Revelation 3:17–18).

If this were not enough, then we must be curious about the fact that although Jesus claims to preach Good News to the poor, he, indeed, never goes to the economically poor. Only in Mark are we told of "a poor [person]" (12:42). And here, the fact that she is a widow holds far more social repercussions than the fact that she is economically poor. In a sense, she is poor three times over. We must also be careful to note that she is used as an example of generosity. The Good News is not preached to her.

Throughout the Gospels Jesus is seen with women, children, demoniac, blind people, lame people, and other types of unclean people. In essence, he is drawn to the socially poor. These people lack the human and material supports that often buffer a person against the hard realities of life. They are often more aware of their spiritual needs. Their social poverty may lead to awareness of their spiritual need. It is the latter to whom God promises the kingdom of heaven (Matthew 5:3).

The point is, though, that lack of wealth is only part of what it means to be "poor." For although one would have to have wealth to be in the upper levels of society, one may also have wealth and be without honor (and thus, "poor" in the eyes of society)—for example, women, tax collectors, and Gentiles (Luke 8:2–3; 9:2–4; Matthew 15:21–28).

Perhaps the story of Zacchaeus, the wealthy chief toll collector, illustrates Jesus' mission to "the poor" most explicitly (Luke 19). Not all toll collectors are rich, but because of their position all are despised, and therefore, of low-status. Zacchaeus's status is an important detail in the story. If Jesus came to preach "Good News" to the poor, why is he concerned with Zacchaeus? Zacchaeus is a wealthy man. There are several clues in this story that give away Zacchaeus's "poor" status in society. If status were a result of riches alone, then the crowd would have parted for a man of status equal to Zacchaeus's wealth. Zacchaeus would have been able to see Jesus without climbing a tree. Similarly, Luke tells us that all the people muttered about Jesus' asking for hospitality from a sinner. The people wonder why Jesus would risk his own social status by eating in the home of a low-status person. The final clue is in Jesus' closing statement: "The Son of Man came to find lost people and save them" (Luke 19:10). He refers to Zacchaeus as among the lost. So from all this we must assume that Zacchaeus is low in status, and therefore socially poor.

The Book of Acts and Paul's letters illustrate the ways in which the church carried out Jesus' mission to the poor. They continued to heal those who were crippled and blind (Acts 5:12; 9:36–41). In doing this, they gave more than money could accomplish (Acts 3:6–9). What's more, just like Jesus in Matthew 15:21–28, they opened their circle of fellowship to include those outside of the Jewish faith (Acts 6) and ultimately they actively pursued the inclusion of the Gentiles into the community of believers (Acts 15:7). In addition, Paul spent the majority of his writings working out the practicality of Galatians 3:28, "In Christ, there is no difference between Jew and Greek, slave and free person, male and female." In Paul's time, Jews, free persons, and males held all the social status, which left the others in a condition of social poverty. Paul's message was one that included everyone. In Christ, one's status does not matter.

Poverty: For additional scriptures on this topic go to Deuteronomy 15:4.

Drag the evil people away like sheep
to be butchered.
Set them aside for the day of killing.
4How much longer will the land stay dried up
and the grass in every field be dead?
The animals and birds in the land have died,
because the people are evil.
Yes, they are even saying,
"God does not see what happens to us."

The Lord's Answer to Jeremiah

5"If you get tired while racing
against people,
how can you race against horses?
If you stumble in a country that is safe,
what will you do in the thick thornbushes
along the Jordan River?
6Even your own brothers and members of
your own family
are making plans against you.
They are crying out against you.
Don't trust them,
even when they say nice things to you!

7"I have left Israel;
I have left my people.
I have given the people I love
over to their enemies.
8My people have become to me
like a lion in the forest.
They roar at me,
so I hate them.
9My people have become to me
like a speckled bird attacked on all
sides by hawks.
Go, gather the wild animals.
Bring them to get something to eat.
10Many shepherds have ruined my vineyards
and trampled the plants in my field.
They have turned my beautiful field
into an empty desert.
11They have turned my field into a desert
that is wilted and dead.
The whole country is an empty desert,
because no one who lives there cares.
12Many soldiers have marched over those
barren hills.
The LORD is using the armies to
punish that land
from one end to the other.
No one is safe.
13The people have planted wheat,
but they have harvested only thorns.
They have worked hard until they
were very tired,
but they have nothing for all their work.
They are ashamed of their poor harvest,
because the LORD's terrible anger
has caused this."

14This is what the LORD said to me: "Here is
what I will do to all my wicked neighbors who
take the land I gave my people Israel. I will pull
them up and throw them out of their land. And I
will pull up the people of Judah from among
them. 15But after I pull them up, I will feel sorry
for them again. I will bring each person back to
his own property and to his own land. 16I want
them to learn their lessons well. In the past they
taught my people to swear by Baal's name. But if
they will now learn to swear by my name, saying
'As surely as the LORD lives . . .' I will allow them
to rebuild among my people. 17But if a nation will
not listen to my message, I will pull it up completely and destroy it," says the LORD.

Jeremiah's Linen Belt

13 This is what the LORD said to me: "Go and
buy a linen belt and put it around your
waist. Don't let the belt get wet."
2So I bought a linen belt, just as the LORD told
me, and put it around my waist. 3Then the LORD
spoke his word to me a second time: 4"Take the
belt you bought and are wearing, and go to
Perath. Hide the belt there in a crack in the
rocks." 5So I went to Perath and hid the belt
there, just as the LORD told me.
6Many days later the LORD said to me, "Now go
to Perath and get the belt I told you to hide
there." 7So I went to Perath and dug up the belt
and took it from where I had hidden it. But now
it was ruined; it was good for nothing.
8Then the LORD spoke his word to me. 9This is
what the LORD said: "In the same way I will ruin
the pride of the people of Judah and the great
pride of Jerusalem. 10These evil people refuse to
listen to my warnings. They stubbornly do only
what they want to do, and they follow other gods
to serve and worship them. So they will become
like this linen belt—good for nothing. 11As a belt
is wrapped tightly around a person's waist, I
wrapped the families of Israel and Judah around
me," says the LORD. "I did that so they would be
my people and bring fame, praise, and honor to
me. But my people would not listen.

12:4 Complaint/Lament/Protest: Lamentations 1:1–27

Warnings About Leather Wine Bags

12"Say to them: 'This is what the LORD, the God
of Israel, says: All leather bags for holding wine
should be filled with wine.' People will say to
you: 'Of course, we know all wine bags should be
filled with wine.' 13Then you will say to them,
'This is what the LORD says: I will make everyone
in this land like a drunken person—the kings who
sit on David's throne, the priests and the prophets,
and all the people who live in Jerusalem. 14I will
make them smash against one another, fathers
and sons alike, says the LORD. I will not feel sorry
or have pity on them or show mercy that would
stop me from destroying them.' "

Threat of Slavery

15Listen and pay attention.
Don't be too proud,
because the LORD has spoken to you.
16Give glory to the LORD your God
before he brings darkness
and before you slip and fall
on the dark hills.
You hope for light,
but he will turn it into thick darkness;
he will change it into deep gloom.
17If you don't listen to him,
I will cry secretly
because of your pride.
I will cry painfully,
and my eyes will overflow with tears,
because the LORD's people will be captured.

18Tell this to the king and the queen mother:
"Come down from your thrones,
because your beautiful crowns
have fallen from your heads."
19The cities of southern Judah are locked up,
and no one can open them.
All Judah will be taken as captives to
a foreign land;
they will be carried away completely.

20Jerusalem, look up and see
the people coming from the north.
Where is the flock God gave you to care for,
the flock you bragged about?
21What will you say when they appoint
as your heads
those you had thought were your friends?
Won't you have much pain and trouble,
like a woman giving birth to a baby?
22You might ask yourself,
"Why has this happened to me?"
It happened because of your many sins.
Because of your sins, your skirt was torn off
and your body has been treated badly.
23Can a person from Cush change the color
of his skin?
Can a leopard change his spots?
In the same way, Jerusalem, you cannot
change and do good,
because you are accustomed to doing evil.

24"I will scatter you like chaff that is blown away
by the desert wind.
25This is what will happen to you;
this is your part in my plans," says the LORD.
"Because you forgot me
and trusted in false gods,
26I will pull your skirts up over your face
so everyone will see your shame.
27I have seen the terrible things you
have done:
your acts of adultery and your snorting,
your prostitution,
your hateful acts
on the hills and in the fields.
How terrible it will be for you, Jerusalem.
How long will you continue being unclean?"

A Time Without Rain

14 These are the words that the LORD spoke to
Jeremiah about the time when there was
no rain:
2"The nation of Judah cries as if someone
has died,
and her cities are very sad.
They are distressed over the land.
A cry goes up to God from Jerusalem.
3The important men send their servants
to get water.
They go to the wells,
but they find no water.
So they return with empty jars.
They are ashamed and embarrassed
and cover their heads in shame.
4The ground is dry and cracked open,
because no rain falls on the land.
The farmers are upset and sad,
so they cover their heads in shame.
5Even the mother deer in the field
leaves her newborn fawn to die,
because there is no grass.∞

13:23 *Cush.* The region of Cush is associated with the area south of Egypt, what is today known as Sudan.
13:24 *chaff.* See 4:11.
13:26 *pull your skirts up over your face.* Public exposure was a common punishment for prostitutes in the ancient Near East.
∞**14:5 Famine:** Ezekiel 4:16–17

6 Wild donkeys stand on the bare hills
and sniff the wind like wild dogs.
But their eyes go blind,
because there is no food."∞

7 We know that we suffer because of our sins.
LORD, do something to help us for the good of
your name.
We have left you many times;
we have sinned against you.
8 God, the Hope of Israel,
you have saved Israel in times of trouble.
Why are you like a stranger in the land,
or like a traveler who only stays one night?
9 Why are you like someone who has been
attacked by surprise,
like a warrior who is not able to
save anyone?
But you are among us, LORD,
and we are called by your name
so don't leave us without help!

10 This is what the LORD says about the people
of Judah:
"They really love to wander from me;
they don't stop themselves from leaving me.
So now the LORD will not accept them.
He will now remember the evil they do
and will punish them for their sins."

11 Then the LORD said, "Don't pray for good
things to happen to the people of Judah. 12 Even if
they give up eating, I will not listen to their
prayers. Even if they offer burnt offerings and
grain offerings to me, I will not accept them.
Instead, I will destroy the people of Judah with
war, hunger, and terrible diseases."
13 But I said, "Oh, Lord GOD, the prophets keep
telling the people, 'You will not suffer from an
enemy's sword or from hunger. I, the LORD, will
give you peace in this land.' "
14 Then the LORD said to me, "Those prophets
are prophesying lies in my name. I did not send
them or appoint them or speak to them. They
have been prophesying false visions, idolatries,
worthless magic, and their own wishful thinking.
15 So this is what I say about the prophets who are
prophesying in my name. I did not send them.
They say, 'No enemy will attack this country with
swords. There will never be hunger in this land.'
So those prophets will die from hunger and from
an enemy's sword. 16 And the people to whom the
prophets speak will be thrown into the streets of
Jerusalem. There they will die from hunger and
from an enemy's sword. And no one will be there
to bury them, or their wives, or their sons, or
their daughters. I will punish them.
17 "Jeremiah, speak this message to the people
of Judah:
'Let my eyes be filled with tears
night and day, without stopping.
My people have received a terrible blow;
they have been hurt badly.
18 If I go into the country,
I see people killed by swords.
If I go into the city,
I see much sickness, because the people
have no food.
Both the priests and the prophets
have been taken to a foreign land.' "

19 LORD, have you completely rejected the nation
of Judah?
Do you hate Jerusalem?
Why have you hurt us so badly
that we cannot be made well again?
We hoped for peace,
but nothing good has come.
We looked for a time of healing,
but only terror came.
20 LORD, we admit that we are wicked
and that our ancestors did evil things.
We have sinned against you.
21 For your sake, do not hate us.
Do not take away the honor from your
glorious throne.
Remember your agreement with us,
and do not break it.
22 Do foreign idols have the power to bring rain?
Does the sky itself have the power to send
down showers?
No, it is you, LORD our God.
You are our only hope,
because you are the one who made
all these things.

15 Then the LORD said to me: "I would not
feel sorry for the people of Judah even if
Moses and Samuel prayed for them. Send them
away from me! Tell them to go! 2 When they ask
you, 'Where will we go?' tell them: 'This is what
the LORD says:
Those who are meant to die
will die.

∞**14:6 Water:** Ezekiel 27:1–4
14:12 *give up eating.* The practice of giving up eating for religious purposes, known as fasting, is in view here.

15:1 *Moses and Samuel.* Moses and Samuel were two great, early leaders of Israel, both known for their ability to intercede with prayer on behalf of the people.

Those who are meant to die in war
will die in war.
Those who are meant to die from hunger
will die from hunger.
Those who are meant to be taken captive
will be taken captive.'

3"I will send four kinds of destroyers against
them," says the LORD. "I will send war to kill,
dogs to drag the bodies away, and the birds of the
air and wild animals to eat and destroy the bodies. 4I will make the people of Judah hated by
everyone on earth because of what Manasseh did
in Jerusalem. (Manasseh son of Hezekiah was
king of the nation of Judah.)

5"Who will feel sorry for you, Jerusalem?
Who will be sad and cry for you?
Who will go out of his way to ask
how you are?
6Jerusalem, you have left me," says the LORD.
"You keep going farther and farther away,
so I have taken hold of you and destroyed you.
I was tired of holding back my anger.
7I have separated the people of Judah
with my pitchfork
and scattered them at the city gates of the land.
My people haven't changed their ways.
So I have destroyed them
and taken away their children.
8There are more widows than grains of sand
in the sea.
I brought a destroyer at noontime
against the mothers of the young men of Judah.
I suddenly brought pain and fear
on the people of Judah.
9When the enemy attacked, a woman with
seven sons felt faint because they
would all die.
She became weak and unable to breathe.
Her bright day became dark from sadness.
She felt shame and disgrace.
And everyone else left alive in Judah
I will hand over to the enemies, too!" says
the LORD.

Jeremiah's Second Complaint

10Mother, I am sorry that you gave birth to me
since I must accuse and criticize
the whole land.
I have not loaned or borrowed anything,
but everyone curses me.

11The LORD said,
"I have saved you for a good reason.
I have made your enemies beg you
in times of disaster and trouble.
12No one can smash a piece of iron or bronze
that comes from the north.
13Your wealth and treasures
I will give to others free of charge,
because the people of Judah have sinned
throughout the country.
14I will make you slaves to your enemies
in a land you have never known.
My anger is like a hot fire,
and it will burn against you."

15LORD, you understand.
Remember me and take care of me.
Punish for me those who are hurting me.
Don't destroy me while you remain
patient with them.
Think about the shame I suffer for you.
16Your words came to me, and I listened
carefully to them.
Your words made me very happy,
because I am called by your name,
LORD God All-Powerful.
17I never sat with the crowd
as they laughed and had fun.
I sat by myself, because you were there,
and you filled me with anger at the evil
around me.
18I don't understand why my pain has no end.
I don't understand why my injury is not
cured or healed.
Will you be like a brook that goes dry?
Will you be like a spring that stops flowing?

19So this is what the LORD says:
"If you change your heart and return to me, I
will take you back.
Then you may serve me.
And if you speak things that have worth,
not useless words,
then you may speak for me.
Let the people of Judah turn to you,
but you must not change and be like them.
20I will make you as strong as a wall to
this people,
as strong as a wall of bronze.
They will fight against you,
but they will not defeat you,
because I am with you.

15:3 *destroy the bodies.* See 8:2.
15:4 *Manasseh.* Manasseh sinned greatly against the LORD (2 Kings 21). Even when good king Josiah assumed the throne soon after him, his goodness could not remove the curse that Manasseh's evil had brought on the land (2 Kings 23:26).

I will rescue you and save you,"
says the LORD.
21 "I will save you from these wicked people
and rescue you from these cruel people."

The Day of Disaster

16 Then the LORD spoke his word to me:
2 "You must not get married or have sons
or daughters in this place."⚭
3 The LORD says this about the sons and daughters born in this land and their mothers and
fathers: 4 "They will die of terrible diseases, and
no one will cry for them or bury them. Their bodies will lie on the ground like dung. They will die
in war, or they will starve to death. Their bodies
will be food for the birds of the sky and for the
wild animals."
5 So this is what the LORD says: "Jeremiah, do
not go into a house where there is a funeral meal.
Do not go there to cry for the dead or to show
your sorrow for them, because I have taken back
my blessing, my love, and my pity from these people," says the LORD. 6 "Important people and common people will die in the land of Judah. No one
will bury them or cry for them or cut himself or
shave his head to show sorrow for them. 7 No one
will bring food to comfort those who are crying
for the dead. No one will offer a drink to comfort
someone whose mother or father has died.
8 "Do not go into a house where the people are
having a feast to sit down to eat and drink,
9 because this is what the LORD All-Powerful, the
God of Israel, says: I will soon stop the sounds of
joy and gladness and the happy sounds of brides
and bridegrooms in this place. This will happen
during your lifetime.
10 "When you tell the people of Judah these
things, they will ask you, 'Why has the LORD said
these terrible things to us? What have we done
wrong? What sin have we done against the LORD
our God?'
11 "Then say to them: 'This is because your
ancestors quit following me,' says the LORD. 'And
they followed other gods and served and worshiped them. Your ancestors left me and quit
obeying my teaching. 12 But you have done even
more evil than your ancestors. You are very stubborn and do only what you want to do; you have
not obeyed me. 13 So I will throw you out of this
country and send you into a land that you and
your ancestors never knew. There you can serve
other gods day and night, because I will not help
you or show you any favors.'
14 "People say, 'As surely as the LORD lives, who
brought the people of Israel out of Egypt . . .' But
the time is coming," says the LORD, "when people
will not say this anymore. 15 They will say instead,
'As surely as the LORD lives, who brought the Israelites from the northern land and from all the countries where he had sent them . . .' And I will bring
them back to the land I gave to their ancestors.
16 "I will soon send for many fishermen to come
to this land," says the LORD. "And they will catch
the people of Judah. After that, I will send for
many hunters to come to this land. And they will
hunt the people of Judah on every mountain and
hill and in the cracks of the rocks. 17 I see everything they do. They cannot hide from me the
things they do; their sin is not hidden from my
eyes. 18 I will pay back the people of Judah twice
for every one of their sins, because they have made
my land unclean. They have filled my country with
their hateful idols."

19 LORD, you are my strength and my protection,
my safe place in times of trouble.
The nations will come to you from all
over the world
and say, "Our ancestors had only false gods,
useless idols that didn't help them.
20 Can people make gods for themselves?
They will not really be gods!"
21 The LORD says, "So I will teach those who
make idols.
This time I will teach them
about my power and my strength.
Then they will know
that my name is the LORD.

Judah's Guilty Heart

17 "The sin of the people of Judah is written
with an iron tool.
Their sins were cut with a hard point into
the stone that is their hearts.
Their sins were cut into the corners
of their altars.

⚭**16:2 Celibacy:** Hosea 1:2

16:3–7 Here God is terribly angry with his people because they have rebelled against him and turned to other gods (verses 11–12). Through his prophet Jeremiah, he is trying to jolt them into turning away from their sin and putting their faith in him. So he threatens them not only with terrible death but with a fate worse than death—the humiliation of not being mourned or buried. These verses show us some of the mourning rituals that would have been expected in Judah at that time—a funeral meal, burial of the body, loud crying, cutting oneself or shaving one's head, and bringing food and drink to comfort the family. Other mourning customs in that culture included tearing their garments, beating their breasts, fasting, putting dust or ashes on their heads, sitting or rolling in dirt or ashes, wearing garments made of rough cloth, hiring professional mourners who wailed and played instruments, and composing funeral songs.

16:4 *bodies . . . ground.* See 8:2.

2Even their children remember
their altars to idols and their Asherah idols
beside the green trees
and on the high hills.
3My mountain in the open country
and your wealth and treasures
I will give away to other people.
I will give away the places of worship
in your country,
because you sinned by worshiping there.
4You will lose the land I gave you,
and it is your own fault.
I will let your enemies take you as their slaves
to a land you have never known.
This is because you have made my anger
burn like a hot fire,
and it will burn forever."

Trusting in Humans or God

5This is what the LORD says:
"A curse is placed on those who trust
other people,
who depend on humans for strength,
who have stopped trusting the LORD.
6They are like a bush in a desert
that grows in a land where no one lives,
a hot and dry land with bad soil.
They don't know about the good things
God can give.

7"But the person who trusts in the LORD
will be blessed.
The LORD will show him that he
can be trusted.
8He will be strong, like a tree planted near water
that sends its roots by a stream.
It is not afraid when the days are hot;
its leaves are always green.
It does not worry in a year when no rain comes;
it always produces fruit.
9"More than anything else, a person's
mind is evil
and cannot be healed.
No one truly understands it.
10But I, the LORD, look into a person's heart
and test the mind.
So I can decide what each one deserves;
I can give each one the right payment for
what he does."

11Like a bird hatching an egg it did not lay,
so are the people who get rich by cheating.
When their lives are half finished, they will
lose their riches.
At the end of their lives, it will be clear
they were fools.

12From the beginning, our Temple has
been honored
as a glorious throne for God.
13LORD, hope of Israel,
those who leave you will be shamed.
People who quit following the LORD will be
like a name written in the dust,
because they have left the LORD, the spring of
living water.

Jeremiah's Third Complaint

14LORD, heal me, and I will truly be healed.
Save me, and I will truly be saved.
You are the one I praise.
15The people of Judah keep asking me,
"Where is the word from the LORD?
Let's see that message come true!"

16LORD, I didn't run away from being the shepherd you wanted.
I didn't want the terrible day to come.
You know everything I have said;
you see all that is happening.
17Don't be a terror to me.
I run to you for safety in times of trouble.
18Make those who are hurting me be ashamed,
but don't bring shame to me.
Let them be terrified,
but keep me from terror.
Bring the day of disaster on my enemies.
Destroy them, and destroy them again.

Keeping the Sabbath Holy

19This is what the LORD said to me: "Go and
stand at the People's Gate of Jerusalem, where
the kings of Judah go in and out. And then go to
all the other gates of Jerusalem. 20Say to them there:
'Hear the word of the LORD, kings of Judah, all you
people of Judah, and all who live in Jerusalem,
who come through these gates into the city. 21This
is what the LORD says: Be careful not to carry a
load on the Sabbath day or bring it through the
gates of Jerusalem. 22Don't take a load out of your
houses on the Sabbath or do any work on that day.
But keep the Sabbath as a holy day, as I commanded your ancestors. 23But your ancestors did
not listen or pay attention to me. They were very
stubborn and did not listen. I punished them, but
it didn't do any good. 24But you must be careful to

17:8 Self-Control: Matthew 4:18–22
17:8 Pride: Jeremiah 9:23–24
17:9 A Matter of the Heart: Matthew 22:37
17:10 Test/Temptation: Jeremiah 20:12

obey me, says the LORD. You must not bring a load
through the gates of Jerusalem on the Sabbath,
but you must keep the Sabbath as a holy day and
not do any work on that day.
25“ ‘If you obey this command, kings who sit
on David’s throne will come through the gates of
Jerusalem with their officers. They will come riding
in chariots and on horses, along with the people of
Judah and Jerusalem. And the city of Jerusalem will
have people living in it forever. 26People will come
to Jerusalem from the villages around it, from the
towns of Judah, from the land of Benjamin, from
the western hills, from the mountains, and
from southern Judah. They will all bring to the
Temple of the LORD burnt offerings, sacrifices,
grain offerings, incense, and offerings to show
thanks to God. 27But you must obey me and keep
the Sabbath day as a holy day. You must not carry
any loads into Jerusalem on the Sabbath. If you
don’t obey me, I will start a fire at the gates of
Jerusalem, and it will burn until it burns even the
strong towers. And it will not be put out.’ ”

The Potter and the Clay

18 This is the word the LORD spoke to
Jeremiah: 2“Go down to the potter’s
house, and I will give you my message there.” 3So
I went down to the potter’s house and saw him
working at the potter’s wheel. 4He was using his
hands to make a pot from clay, but something
went wrong with it. So he used that clay to make
another pot the way he wanted it to be.
5Then the LORD spoke his word to me: 6“Family
of Israel, can’t I do the same thing with you?”
says the LORD. “You are in my hands like the clay
in the potter’s hands. 7There may come a time
when I will speak about a nation or a kingdom
that I will pull up by its roots or that I will pull
down to destroy it. 8But if the people of that
nation stop doing the evil they have done, I will
change my mind and not carry out my plans to
bring disaster to them. 9There may come another
time when I will speak about a nation that I will
build up and plant. 10But if I see it doing evil by
not obeying me, I will change my mind and not
carry out my plans to do good for them.
11“So, say this to the people of Judah and those
who live in Jerusalem: ‘This is what the LORD
says: I am preparing disaster for you and making
plans against you. So stop doing evil. Change your
ways and do what is right.’ 12But the people of
Judah will answer, ‘It won’t do any good to try!
We will continue to do what we want. Each of us
will do what his stubborn, evil heart wants!’ ”

Examples of the pottery made by the people of Israel

13So this is what the LORD says:
“Ask the people in other nations this question:
‘Have you ever heard anything like this?’
The people of Israel have done a horrible thing.
14The snow on the mountains of Lebanon
never melts from the rocks.
Its cool, flowing streams
do not dry up.
15But my people have forgotten me.
They burn incense to worthless idols
and have stumbled in what they do
and in the old ways of their ancestors.
They walk along back roads
and on poor highways.
16So Judah’s country will become an empty desert.
People will not stop making fun of it.
They will shake their heads as they pass by;
they will be shocked at how the country
was destroyed.
17Like a strong east wind,
I will scatter them before their enemies.
At that awful time they will not see me coming
to help them;
they will see me leaving.”

Jeremiah’s Fourth Complaint

18Then the people said, “Come, let’s make
plans against Jeremiah. Surely the teaching of the
law by the priest will not be lost. We will still
have the advice from the wise men and the words
of the prophets. So let’s ruin him by telling lies
about him. We won’t pay attention to anything
he says.”

18:12 Prophetic Symbolism: Jeremiah 24:1–10
18:18 Wisdom: Matthew 11:19
18:18 Prophet & Prophecy: 1 Corinthians 12:1–11

19 LORD, listen to me.
Listen to what my accusers are saying!
20 Good should not be paid back with evil,
but they have dug a pit in order to kill me.
Remember that I stood before you
and asked you to do good things for
these people
and to turn your anger away from them.
21 So now, let their children starve,
and let their enemies kill them with swords.
Let their wives lose their children and husbands.
Let the men from Judah be put to death
and the young men be killed with swords
in battle.
22 Let them cry out in their houses
when you bring an enemy against
them suddenly.
Let all this happen, because my enemies
have dug
a pit to capture me and have hidden traps
for my feet.
23 LORD, you know
about all their plans to kill me.
Don't forgive their crimes
or erase their sins from your mind.
Make them fall from their places;
punish them while you are angry.

Judah Is like a Broken Jar

19 This is what the LORD said to me: "Go and
buy a clay jar from a potter. 2 Take some of
the older leaders of the people and the priests,
and go out to the Valley of Ben Hinnom, near the
front of the Potsherd Gate. There speak the
words I tell you. 3 Say, 'Kings of Judah and people
of Jerusalem, listen to this message from the LORD.
This is what the LORD All-Powerful, the God of
Israel, says: I will soon bring a disaster on this
place that will amaze and frighten everyone who
hears about it. 4 The people of Judah have quit following me. They have made this a place for foreign
gods. They have burned sacrifices to other gods
that neither they, nor their ancestors, nor the kings
of Judah had ever known before. They filled this
place with the blood of innocent people. 5 They
have built places on hilltops to worship Baal, where
they burn their children in the fire to Baal. That is
something I did not command or speak about; it
never even entered my mind. 6 Now people call
this place the Valley of Ben Hinnom or Topheth,
but the days are coming, says the LORD, when
people will call it the Valley of Killing.
7 " 'At this place I will ruin the plans of the people of Judah and Jerusalem. The enemy will chase
them, and I will have them killed with swords. I
will make their dead bodies food for the birds and
wild animals. 8 I will completely destroy this city.
People will make fun of it and shake their heads
when they pass by. They will be shocked when
they see how the city was destroyed. 9 An enemy
army will surround the city and will not let anyone go out to get food. I will make the people so
hungry that they will eat the bodies of their own
sons and daughters, and then they will begin to
eat each other.'
10 "While the people with you are watching,
break that jar. 11 Then say this: 'The LORD All-
Powerful says: I will break this nation and this
city just as someone breaks a clay jar that cannot
be put back together again. The dead people will
be buried here in Topheth, because there is no
other place for them. 12 This is what I will do to
these people and to this place, says the LORD. I
will make this city like Topheth. 13 The houses in
Jerusalem and the king's palaces will become as
unclean as this place, Topheth, because the people worshiped gods on the roofs of their houses.
They worshiped the stars and burned incense to
honor them and gave drink offerings to gods.' "
14 When Jeremiah left Topheth where the LORD
had sent him to prophesy, he went to the LORD's
Temple, stood in the courtyard, and said to all the
people: 15 "This is what the LORD All-Powerful, the
God of Israel, says: 'I will soon bring disaster to
Jerusalem and the villages around it, as I said I
would. This will happen because the people are very
stubborn and do not listen at all to what I say.' "

Pashhur Will Be Captured

20 Pashhur son of Immer was a priest and
the highest officer in the Temple of the
LORD. When he heard Jeremiah prophesying in
the Temple courtyard, 2 he had Jeremiah the
prophet beaten. And he locked Jeremiah's hands
and feet between large blocks of wood at the
Upper Gate of Benjamin of the LORD's Temple.
3 The next day when Pashhur took Jeremiah out of
the blocks of wood, Jeremiah said to him, "The
LORD's name for you is not Pashhur. Now his
name for you is Terror on Every Side. 4 This is
what the LORD says: 'I will soon make you a terror
to yourself and to all your friends. You will watch
enemies killing your friends with swords. And I
will give all the people of Judah to the king of

19:6 *Topheth.* See 7:31.
19:13 *roofs.* In Bible times houses were built with flat roofs. The roof was used for drying things such as flax and fruit. And it was used as an extra room, as a place for worship, and as a cool place to sleep in the summer.
19:13 Astrology: Amos 5:26

FORGIVENESS

LUKE 6:27–37

What is forgiveness and why does it occupy so central a place in the offer of redemption and the life of God's people? What are the spiritual and social dimensions of forgiving? Can we forgive too fast or too much?

Forgiveness is an enormously important biblical concept, particularly in the New Testament. It is central to Jesus' ministry: Jesus warmly forgives those who are obviously wrong (Luke 7:36–50), confronts those who cling to their own righteousness (Luke 7:41–47), and teaches radical forgiveness of one another (Luke 6:27–37; Matthew 18:21). God's forgiveness in the Old Testament is less apparent, sometimes indicated in the mercy that God chooses to sustain the human race instead of destroying it but Old Testament forgiveness also often involves ritual acts of repentance or punishment for an offense (Leviticus 4:1–26).

Forgiveness addresses human guilt, but what is guilt? We know that human beings from Creation on have disregarded, or resisted God's priorities. Adam and Eve demonstrate this tendency by seeking to "learn about good and evil and . . . be like God" (Genesis 3:3–5). But is obedience to arbitrary rules required of a tyrannical God, or is there something we can understand for life today? Indeed, the Law God gave to Moses attempted to teach quality living in community and includes justice for the poor. The prophet Micah summarizes God's expectation: "He has told you what he wants from you: to do what is right to other people, love being kind to others, and live humbly, obeying your God" (Micah 6:8). If the Bible describes God's priorities as those which sustain a just and compassionate society, then people departing from these priorities introduce elements of injustice and oppression. Cain, for example, playing out an all-too-familiar sibling rivalry, murders his brother Abel (Genesis 4:1–12). Jacob tricks his blind father to steal a blessing (Genesis 27:1–38). Leah is married off to a man who wants to marry her sister (Genesis 29:21–35). Joseph, Jacob's favored child, lords it over his brothers who retaliate by selling him into slavery (Genesis 37:2b-36). Moses guides the Israelites to freedom, and they complain bitterly about their hard life in the desert (Exodus 16:1–3). Rebellion against God introduces oppression and cruelty. Community and family are torn apart.

When such a wrong has been committed, relationship has been broken, and the damage is not repairable by the one who committed the wrong. These are chilling thoughts. The Bible calls such actions *sin*, a difficult word for a contemporary audience. One theologian suggested that sin is a state of being before it is an action. It is a state of being alienated from ourselves, from others, and from God.

Guilt falls between people, but it also occurs within ourselves when we fail to meet a goal, reach an ideal for ourselves, or hurt someone we didn't intend to hurt. We cannot mend it, and our failure weighs us down. We may ignore it, act cheerful, and put a brave face on things, but the damage done within ourselves remains with us affecting our lives. And guilt occurs in our relationship with God. Perhaps we fail to retain a prayer time, or we do not serve in a way we feel is right. Perhaps in our struggle with faith, we experience doubts and wonder if God condemns us for them. Once we are alienated from God, we do not know how to get back. We may feel afraid of God and then resentful. Only when forgiveness breaks in and frees us can we begin to reverse our self-perpetuating cycles of alienation, fear, and aggression. Without forgiveness we are chained to our past. Paul describes our dilemma, "I do not understand the things I do. I do not do what I want to do, and I do the things I hate" (Romans 7:15), Then he rejoices, "I thank God for saving me through Jesus Christ our Lord" (Romans 7: 25)!

For Jesus, forgiveness is central and occurs repeatedly in both stories and actions. His manner of forgiveness reclaims people from their alienation, returning them to community with others, to God, and to themselves. Jesus' style of forgiveness is unusual. He moves eagerly to offer forgiveness even before he is asked. He does not require that people express being truly sorry. Rather, he assumes that all human beings are weighed down with a need for God's forgiveness. His forgiveness is tender and personal, more resembling acceptance or unconditional positive valuing. Jesus' lavish forgiveness seems to precede repentance. The offering of forgiveness makes a psychological space safe enough for sufferers to acknowledge and face the horrifying prospect of their sins. Repentance then connects them with the healing forgiveness that awaits them, liberating them and offering a new beginning.

Jesus' frequent use of the word *evil* to describe human beings indicates a matter-of-fact recognition that sin is an ordinary part of the human experience. Individuals can either acknowledge it and be reunited with God through forgiveness, or they can deny it and cling to an illusion of their own righteousness. Many people in the Bible and in life today adhere to strict codes of behavior, thereby maintaining a sense of control over their own righteousness and judging those who do not also conform. But denial of sin makes biblical characters as well as modern citizens dangerous. This is the violent underbelly of forgiveness. Jesus knows this and regularly confronts the self-righteous with their need for God's forgiveness. As long as they, or we, cling to our own righteousness, we will be unable to enter into a trusting relationship with God, and like those who sought Jesus' death, we will want to destroy the One who forgives abundantly. In addition, we who are unable to face the frightening reality of our own sins and receive God's tender forgiveness, will be unlikely to forgive those who sin against us.

The theme of forgiveness is prominent in Jesus' ministry. We find the word, for example, used in healing stories. In Matthew 9:1–8, some people bring to Jesus a paralyzed young man. Jesus greets the youth warmly, not with healing, but with forgiveness: "Be encouraged, young man. Your sins are forgiven" (verse 2). Jesus offers forgiveness before inviting him to walk, apparently understanding sin as the root of his paralysis.

In another story (Luke 19:1–10), Jesus cheerfully invites himself to the home of Zacchaeus, a rich tax collector. In the context of first-century hospitality, Jesus is enacting forgiveness. In first-century society, tax collectors were conspirators with Rome, the foreign government which ruled the Jewish homeland. Rich tax collectors were suspected of charging extra taxes to pad their own pockets. They were routinely excluded from society. Receiving hospitality and eating with another person implied intimacy, equality, and acceptance. Zacchaeus would never have presumed to initiate such a scenario, but Jesus, ever eager to forgive sins and include the outcast, enacts forgiveness. And Zacchaeus acts forgiven: "I will give half my possessions to the poor. And if I have cheated anyone, I will pay back four times more" (verse 8). Jesus celebrates Zacchaeus' return to the human family: "Salvation has come to this house today, because this man also belongs to the family of Abraham. The Son of Man came to find lost people and save them" (verse 9–10).

In a third story (John 8:3–11), teachers of the law and the Pharisees bring to Jesus a woman "caught in adultery." Jesus' abundant gracious forgiveness as well as his assumption of universal sinfulness are both apparent here. These men have brought a woman so sinful that no one appears for her defense. Although her crime involved a partner, the partner does not appear. One might suppose that she has been involved in such behavior before. Jesus indicates no interest in discussing her guilt, but rather raises the subject of her accusers' sins. In the end, no one judges her guilty, but Jesus, ever tailoring his forgiveness to the individual, gives her a tool so she will be able to resist further overtures from men—"don't sin anymore" (verse 11).

Jesus repeatedly assumes that all of us bear a terrible need for God's forgiveness. This message consumes much space in Matthew, Mark, Luke, and John. Those who recognize their sin, Jesus tenderly and personally forgives. Those who deny their sin and condemn others, Jesus routinely confronts. We also are called to search our hearts, to bring our broken relationships, our harsh words, and our indifference to suffering to our Lord for healing and forgiveness. And because we know and acknowledge our own sinfulness, we are called as well to graciously and abundantly forgive those who sin against us.

Jesus' teachings on our forgiveness of others are brief compared to his teachings on our need for God's forgiveness, and these teachings are radical. In Matthew 5, Jesus instructs his followers not to fight back. For example, Roman soldiers quartered in a city could legally force citizens to carry their packs one mile. With this practice in mind, Jesus asserts, "If someone forces you to go with him one mile, go with him two miles" (Matthew 5:41). When Peter brings the word *forgiveness* itself into the discussion, asking how often he must forgive his brother, Jesus asserts: "I tell you, you must forgive him more than seven times. You must forgive him even if he does wrong to you seventy-seven times" (Matthew 18:21–22). This number symbolically represents forever.

Contemporary psychology has taught us that denial is dangerous to ourselves and to our families. To deny a family member's outbursts of rage compounds the problem. This caution against denial is consistent with Jesus' teachings. While we may recognize within ourselves our own need for forgiveness and understand the burden of guilt carried by the one who hurt us, forgiving another may be a lengthy process. Following Jesus' method of forgiveness, we do not deny the actions of those who sin against us any more than we deny our own sinfulness. The harsh word hurts; the thoughtless, greedy, or bullying act still stings, the alcoholism is still self-centered, and we do not ignore that. We will need to acknowledge the hurt, and the grief associated with it. As we work these through, we will gradually notice our own complicity in the wrong committed against us. By then, we will know that we have followed Jesus' admonition to forgive as God has forgiven us (Matthew 6:12).⚭

⚭**Forgiveness:** For additional scriptures on this topic go to Matthew 9:1–8.

Babylon, who will take them away as captives to
Babylon and then will kill them with swords. [5]I
will give all the wealth of this city to its enemies—
its goods, its valuables, and the treasures of the
kings of Judah. The enemies will carry all those
valuables off to Babylon. [6]And Pashhur, you and
everyone in your house will be taken captive. You
will be forced to go to Babylon, where you will die
and be buried, you and your friends to whom you
have prophesied lies.'"

Jeremiah's Fifth Complaint

[7]LORD, you tricked me, and I was fooled.
You are stronger than I am, so you won.
I have become a joke;
everyone makes fun of me all day long.
[8]Every time I speak, I shout.
I am always shouting about violence and destruction.
I tell the people about the message I received from the LORD,
but this only brings me insults.
The people make fun of me all day long.
[9]Sometimes I say to myself,
"I will forget about the LORD.
I will not speak anymore in his name."
But then his message becomes like a burning fire inside me,
deep within my bones.
I get tired of trying to hold it inside of me,
and finally, I cannot hold it in.
[10]I hear many people whispering about me:
"Terror on every side!
Tell on him! Let's tell the rulers about him."
My friends are all just waiting for me to make some mistake.
They are saying,
"Maybe we can trick him
so we can defeat him
and pay him back."

[11]But the LORD is with me like a strong warrior,
so those who are chasing me will trip and fall;
they will not defeat me.
They will be ashamed because they have failed,
and their shame will never be forgotten.

[12]LORD All-Powerful, you test good people;
you look deeply into the heart and mind of a person.
I have told you my arguments against these people,
so let me see you give them the punishment they deserve.

[13]Sing to the LORD!
Praise the LORD!
He saves the life of the poor
from the power of the wicked.

Jeremiah's Sixth Complaint

[14]Let there be a curse on the day I was born;
let there be no blessing on the day when my mother gave birth to me.
[15]Let there be a curse on the man
who brought my father the news:
"You have a son!"
This made my father very glad.
[16]Let that man be like the towns
the LORD destroyed without pity.
Let him hear loud crying in the morning
and battle cries at noon,
[17]because he did not kill me before I was born.
Then my mother would have been my grave;
she would have stayed pregnant forever.
[18]Why did I have to come out of my mother's body?
All I have known is trouble and sorrow,
and my life will end in shame.

God Rejects King Zedekiah's Request

21 This is the word that the LORD spoke to
Jeremiah. It came when Zedekiah king of
Judah sent Pashhur son of Malkijah and the priest
Zephaniah son of Maaseiah to Jeremiah. [2]They
said, "Ask the LORD for us what will happen,
because Nebuchadnezzar king of Babylon is
attacking us. Maybe the LORD will do miracles for
us as he did in the past so Nebuchadnezzar will
stop attacking us and leave."

[3]But Jeremiah answered them, "Tell King
Zedekiah this: [4]'Here is what the LORD, the God of
Israel, says: You have weapons of war in your
hands to defend yourselves against the king of
Babylon and the Babylonians, who are all around
the city wall. But I will make those weapons useless. Soon I will bring them into the center of this
city. [5]In my anger, my very great anger, I myself
will fight against you with my great power and
strength. [6]I will kill everything living in
Jerusalem—both people and animals. They will
die from terrible diseases. [7]Then, says the LORD,

20:10 Tongue: Romans 1:29–30
20:12 Test/Temptation: Matthew 26:41
20:18 Abortion: See article on page 252.

I'll hand over Zedekiah king of Judah, his officers,
and the people in Jerusalem who do not die from
the terrible diseases or battle or hunger, to
Nebuchadnezzar king of Babylon. I will let those
win who want to kill the people of Judah, so the
people of Judah and Jerusalem will be killed in
war. Nebuchadnezzar will not show any mercy or
pity or feel sorry for them!'
8"Also tell this to the people of Jerusalem: 'This
is what the LORD says: I will let you choose to live
or die. 9Anyone who stays in Jerusalem will die in
war or from hunger or from a terrible disease. But
anyone who goes out of Jerusalem and surrenders
to the Babylonians who are attacking you will
live. Anyone who leaves the city will save his life
as if it were a prize won in war. 10I have decided
to make trouble for this city and not to help it,
says the LORD. I will give it to the king of Babylon,
and he will burn it with fire.'
11"Say to Judah's royal family: 'Hear the word
of the LORD. 12Family of David, this is what the
LORD says:

You must judge people fairly every morning.
Save the person who has been robbed
from the power of his attacker.
If you don't, I will become very angry.
My anger will be like a fire that no one
can put out,
because you have done evil things.

13" 'Jerusalem, I am against you,
you who live on top of the mountain
over this valley, says the LORD.
You say, "No one can attack us
or come into our strong city."
14But I will give you the punishment you
deserve, says the LORD.
I will start a fire in your forests
that will burn up everything around you!' "

Judgment Against Evil Kings

22 This is what the LORD says: "Go down to
the palace of the king of Judah and prophesy this message there:2'Hear the word of the
LORD, king of Judah, who rules from David's
throne. You and your officers, and your people
who come through these gates, listen! 3This is
what the LORD says: Do what is fair and right.
Save the one who has been robbed from the
power of his attacker. Don't mistreat or hurt the
foreigners, orphans, or widows. Don't kill innocent people here. 4If you carefully obey these
commands, kings who sit on David's throne will
come through the gates of this palace with their
officers and people, riding in chariots and on
horses. 5But if you don't obey these commands,
says the LORD, I swear by my own name that this
king's palace will become a ruin.' "
6This is what the LORD says about the palace
where the king of Judah lives:

"You are tall like the forests of Gilead,
like the mountaintops of Lebanon.
But I will truly make you into a desert,
into towns where no one lives.
7I will send men to destroy the palace,
each with his weapons.
They will cut up your strong, beautiful
cedar beams
and throw them into the fire.

8"People from many nations will pass by this
city and ask each other, 'Why has the LORD done
such a terrible thing to Jerusalem, this great
city?' 9And the answer will be: 'Because the people of Judah quit following the agreement with
the LORD their God. They worshiped and served
other gods.' "

Judgment Against Jehoahaz

10Don't cry for the dead king or be
sad about him.
But cry painfully for the king who is being
taken away,
because he will never return
or see his homeland again.

11This is what the LORD says about Jehoahaz son
of Josiah who became king of Judah after his father
died and who has left this place: "He will never
return. 12He will die where he has been taken
captive, and he will not see this land again."

Judgment Against Jehoiakim

13"How terrible it will be for one who builds
his palace by doing evil,
who cheats people so he can build its
upper rooms.
He makes his own people work for nothing
and does not pay them.
14He says, 'I will build a great palace for myself
with large upper rooms.'
So he builds it with large windows
and uses cedar wood for the walls,
which he paints red.

22:3 Adoption: Ezekiel 22:6–7
22:3 Justice: Amos 5:24
22:3 *the foreigners, orphans, or widows.* Foreigners, orphans, and widows were especially vulnerable to exploitation in ancient biblical society, so God is especially concerned about protecting them with his power.

15"Does having a lot of cedar in your house
make you a great king?
Your father was satisfied to have food and drink.
He did what was right and fair,
so everything went well for him.
16He helped those who were poor and needy,
so everything went well for him.
That is what it means to know God,"
says the LORD.
17"But you only look for and think about
what you can get dishonestly.
You are even willing to kill innocent
people to get it.
You feel free to hurt people and to
steal from them."
18So this is what the LORD says to Jehoiakim son of
Josiah king of Judah:
"The people of Judah will not cry when
Jehoiakim dies,
saying: 'Oh, my brother,' or 'Oh, my sister.'
They will not cry for him, saying:
'Oh, master,' or 'Oh, my king.'
19They will bury him like a donkey,
dragging his body away
and throwing it outside the gates
of Jerusalem.

20"Judah, go up to Lebanon and cry out.
Let your voice be heard in Bashan.
Cry out from Abarim,
because all your friends are destroyed!
21Judah, when you were successful, I warned you,
but you said, 'I won't listen.'
You have acted like this since you were young;
you have not obeyed me.
22Like a storm, my punishment will blow all
your shepherds away
and send your friends into captivity.
Then you will really be ashamed and disgraced
because of all the wicked things you did.
23King, you live in your palace,
cozy in your rooms of cedar.
But when your punishment comes, how you
will groan
like a woman giving birth to a baby!

Judgment upon Jehoiachin

24"As surely as I live," says the LORD, "Jehoiachin
son of Jehoiakim king of Judah, even if you were a
signet ring on my right hand, I would still pull you
off. 25I will hand you over to Nebuchadnezzar king
of Babylon and to the Babylonians—those people
you fear because they want to kill you. 26I will
throw you and your mother into another country.
Neither of you was born there, but both of you
will die there. 27They will want to come back, but
they will never be able to return."

28Jehoiachin is like a broken pot someone
threw away;
he is like something no one wants.
Why will Jehoiachin and his children be
thrown out
and sent into a foreign land?
29Land, land, land of Judah,
hear the word of the LORD!
30This is what the LORD says:
"Write this down in the record about Jehoiachin:
He is a man without children,
a man who will not be successful
in his lifetime.
And none of his descendants will be successful;
none will sit on the throne of David
or rule in Judah."

The Evil Leaders of Judah

23 "How terrible it will be for the leaders of
Judah, who are scattering and destroying
my people," says the LORD.
2They are responsible for the people, so the LORD,
the God of Israel, says to them: "You have scattered my people and forced them away and not
taken care of them. So I will punish you for the
evil things you have done," says the LORD. 3"I sent
my people to other countries, but I will gather
those who are left alive and bring them back to
their own country. Then they will have many children and grow in number. 4I will place new leaders over my people, who will take care of them.
And my people will not be afraid or terrified again,
and none of them will be lost," says the LORD.

The Good Branch Will Come

5"The days are coming," says the LORD,
"when I will raise up a good branch in
David's family.
He will be a king who will rule in a wise way;
he will do what is fair and right in the land.
6In his time Judah will be saved,
and Israel will live in safety.
This will be his name:
The LORD Does What Is Right.

22:24 *a signet ring.* A signet ring was a seal stamp that served as one's personal signature as it was pressed into clay, the paper of Jeremiah's time. It was thus a symbol of a close personal relationship.
23:3 Remnant: Jeremiah 31:7
23:5 Jeremiah prophesied that judgment was coming on the people of God because they had departed from following their Lord. But God allowed Jeremiah to see beyond the Exile. He also saw a future return, a restoration of the people of God. This restoration would include a new king from David's line. In the New Testament, this prophecy came to be fulfilled in Jesus Christ, the greater son of David (Matthew 22:41–46).

7“So the days are coming,” says the LORD, “when
people will not say again: ‘As surely as the LORD
lives, who brought Israel out of Egypt . . .’ 8But
people will say something new: ‘As surely as the
LORD lives, who brought the descendants of Israel
from the land of the north and from all the countries where he had sent them away. . .’ Then the
people of Israel will live in their own land.”

False Prophets Will Be Punished

9A message to the prophets:
My heart is broken.
All my bones shake.
I’m like someone who is drunk,
like someone who has been overcome
with wine.
This is because of the LORD
and his holy words.
10The land of Judah is full of people who
are guilty of adultery.
Because of this, the LORD cursed the land.
It has become a very sad place,
and the pastures have dried up.
The people are evil
and use their power in the wrong way.

11“Both the prophets and the priests live as if
there were no God.
I have found them doing evil things even in
my own Temple,” says the LORD.
12“So they will be in danger.
They will be forced into darkness
where they will be defeated.
I will bring disaster on them
in the year I punish them,” says the LORD.

13“I saw the prophets of Samaria
do something wrong.
Those prophets prophesied by Baal
and led my people Israel away.
14And I have seen the prophets of Jerusalem
do terrible things.
They are guilty of adultery
and live by lies.
They encourage evil people to keep
on doing evil,
so the people don’t stop sinning.
All of those people are like the city of Sodom.
The people of Jerusalem are like the city of
Gomorrah to me!”

15So this is what the LORD All-Powerful says
about the prophets:
“I will make those prophets eat bitter food
and drink poisoned water,
because the prophets of Jerusalem
spread wickedness
through the whole country.”

16This is what the LORD All-Powerful says:
“Don’t pay attention to what those prophets
are saying to you.
They are trying to fool you.
They talk about visions their own
minds made up,
not about visions from me.
17They say to those who hate me:
‘The LORD says: You will have peace.’
They say to all those who are stubborn and
do as they please:
‘Nothing bad will happen to you.’
18But none of these prophets has stood in the
meeting of angels
to see or hear the message of the LORD.
None of them has paid close attention
to his message.
19Look, the punishment from the LORD
will come like a storm.
His anger will be like a hurricane.
It will come swirling down on the heads of
those wicked people.
20The LORD’s anger will not stop
until he finishes what he plans to do.
When that day is over,
you will understand this clearly.
21I did not send those prophets,
but they ran to tell their message.
I did not speak to them,
but they prophesied anyway.
22But if they had stood in the meeting of angels,
they would have told my message
to my people.
They would have turned the people from
their evil ways
and from doing evil.

23“I am a God who is near,” says the LORD.
“I am also a God who is far away.”
24“No one can hide
where I cannot see him,” says the LORD.
“I fill all of heaven and earth,” says the LORD.

25“I have heard the prophets who prophesy lies
in my name. They say, ‘I have had a dream! I have
had a dream!’ 26How long will this continue in the
minds of these lying prophets? They prophesy
from their own wishful thinking. 27They are trying to make the people of Judah forget me by
telling each other these dreams. In the same way,
their ancestors forgot me and worshiped Baal. 28Is

straw the same thing as wheat?" says the LORD. "If a prophet wants to tell about his dreams, let him! But let the person who hears my message speak it truthfully! [29]Isn't my message like a fire?" says the LORD. "Isn't it like a hammer that smashes a rock?

[30]"So I am against the false prophets," says the LORD. "They keep stealing words from each other and say they are from me. [31]I am against the false prophets," says the LORD. "They use their own words and pretend it is a message from me. [32]I am against the prophets who prophesy false dreams," says the LORD. "They mislead my people with their lies and false teachings! I did not send them or command them to do anything for me. They can't help the people of Judah at all," says the LORD.⚭

The Sad Message from the Lord

[33]"Suppose the people of Judah, a prophet, or a priest asks you: 'Jeremiah, what is the message from the LORD?' You will answer them and say, 'You are a heavy load to the LORD, and I will throw you down, says the LORD.' [34]A prophet or a priest or one of the people might say, 'This is a message from the LORD.' That person has lied, so I will punish him and his whole family. [35]This is what you will say to each other: 'What did the LORD answer?' or 'What did the LORD say?' [36]But you will never again say, 'The message of the LORD,' because the only message you speak is your own words. You have changed the words of our God, the living God, the LORD All-Powerful. [37]This is how you should speak to the prophets: 'What answer did the LORD give you?' or 'What did the LORD say?' [38]But don't say, 'The message from the LORD.' If you use these words, this is what the LORD says: Because you called it a 'message from the LORD,' though I told you not to use those words, [39]I will pick you up and throw you away from me, along with Jerusalem, which I gave to your ancestors and to you. [40]And I will make a disgrace of you forever; your shame will never be forgotten."

The Good and Bad Figs

24 Nebuchadnezzar king of Babylon captured Jehoiachin son of Jehoiakim and king of Judah, his officers, and all the craftsmen and metalworkers of Judah. He took them away from Jerusalem and brought them to Babylon. It was then that the LORD showed me two baskets of figs arranged in front of the Temple of the LORD. [2]One of the baskets had very good figs in it, like figs that ripen early in the season. But the other basket had figs too rotten to eat.

[3]The LORD said to me, "What do you see, Jeremiah?"

I answered, "I see figs. The good figs are very good, but the rotten figs are too rotten to eat."

[4]Then the LORD spoke his word to me: [5]"This is what the LORD, the God of Israel, says: 'I sent the people of Judah out of their country to live in the country of Babylon. I think of those people as good, like these good figs. [6]I will look after them and bring them back to the land of Judah. I will not tear them down, but I will build them up. I will not pull them up, but I will plant them so they can grow. [7]I will make them want to know me, that I am the LORD. They will be my people, and I will be their God, because they will return to me with their whole hearts.

[8]" 'But the bad figs are too rotten to eat.' So this is what the LORD says: 'Zedekiah king of Judah, his officers, and all the people from Jerusalem who are left alive, even those who live in Egypt, will be like those rotten figs. [9]I will make those people hated as an evil people by all the kingdoms of the earth. People will make fun of them and tell jokes about them and point fingers at them and curse them everywhere I scatter them. [10]I will send war, hunger, and disease against them. I will attack them until they have all been killed. Then they will no longer be in the land I gave to them and their ancestors.' "⚭

A Summary of Jeremiah's Preaching

25 This is the message that came to Jeremiah concerning all the people of Judah. It came in the fourth year that Jehoiakim son of Josiah was king of Judah and the first year Nebuchadnezzar was king of Babylon. [2]This is the message Jeremiah the prophet spoke to all the people of Judah and Jerusalem:

[3]The LORD has spoken his word to me again and again for these past twenty-three years. I have been a prophet since the thirteenth year of Josiah son of Amon king of Judah. I have spoken messages from the LORD to you from that time until today, but you have not listened.

[4]The LORD has sent all his servants the prophets to you over and over again, but you have not listened or paid any attention to them.⚭ [5]Those prophets have said, "Stop your evil ways. Stop doing what is wrong so you can stay in the land that the LORD gave to you and your ancestors to live in forever. [6]Don't follow other gods to serve them or to worship them. Don't make me, the LORD, angry by worshiping idols that are the work of your own hands, or I will punish you."

⚭**23:32 Leadership:** Micah 3:5
⚭**23:32 Dreams:** Daniel 2:1–47
⚭**24:10 Prophetic Symbolism:** Jeremiah 27:1–7
⚭**25:4 Servant of the Lord:** Malachi 1:6

7“But you people of Judah did not listen to me,”
says the LORD. “You made me angry by worshiping idols that were the work of your own hands,
so I punished you.”
8So this is what the LORD All-Powerful says:
“Since you have not listened to my messages, 9I
will send for all the peoples of the north,” says
the LORD, “along with my servant Nebuchadnezzar king of Babylon. I will bring them all
against Judah, those who live there, and all the
nations around you, too. I will completely destroy
all those countries and leave them in ruins forever. People will be shocked when they see how
badly I have destroyed those countries. 10I will
bring an end to the sounds of joy and happiness,
the sounds of brides and bridegrooms, and the
sound of people grinding meal. And I will take
away the light of the lamp. 11That whole area will
be an empty desert, and these nations will be
slaves of the king of Babylon for seventy years.
12“But when the seventy years have passed, I
will punish the king of Babylon and his entire
nation for their evil,” says the LORD. “I will make
that land a desert forever. 13I will make happen
all the terrible things I said about Babylonia—
everything Jeremiah prophesied about all those
foreign nations, the warnings written in this
book. 14Even the Babylonians will have to serve
many nations and many great kings. I will give
them the punishment they deserve for all their
own hands have done.”

Judgment on the Nations

15The LORD, the God of Israel, said this to me:
“My anger is like the wine in a cup. Take it from
my hand and make all the nations, to whom I am
sending you, drink all of my anger from this cup.
16They will drink my anger and stumble about
and act like madmen because of the war I am
going to send among them.”
17So I took the cup from the LORD's hand and
went to those nations and made them drink from
it. 18I served this wine to the people of Jerusalem
and the towns of Judah, and the kings and officers
of Judah, so they would become a ruin. Then people would be shocked and would insult them and
speak evil of them. And so it has been to this day.
19I also made these people drink of the LORD's
anger: the king of Egypt, his servants, his officers,
all his people, 20and all the foreigners there; all
the kings of the land of Uz; all the kings of the
Philistines (the kings of the cities of Ashkelon,
Gaza, Ekron, and the people left at Ashdod); 21the
people of Edom, Moab, and Ammon; 22all the kings
of Tyre and Sidon; all the kings of the coastal countries to the west; 23the people of Dedan and Tema
and Buz; all who cut their hair short; 24all the
kings of Arabia; and the kings of the people who
live in the desert; 25all the kings of Zimri, Elam,
and Media;26and all the kings of the north, near
and far, one after the other. I made all the kingdoms on earth drink from the cup of the LORD's
anger, but the king of Babylon will drink from this
cup after all the others.
27“Then say to them, ‘This is what the LORD
All-Powerful, the God of Israel, says: Drink this
cup of my anger. Get drunk from it and vomit.
Fall down and don't get up because of the war I
am sending among you!’
28“If they refuse to take the cup from your hand
and drink, say to them, ‘The LORD All-Powerful
says this: You must drink from this cup. 29Look! I
am already bringing disaster on Jerusalem, the
city that is called by my name. Do you think you
will not be punished? You will be punished! I am
sending war on all the people of the earth, says
the LORD All-Powerful.’
30“You, Jeremiah, will prophesy against them
with all these words. Say to them:

‘The LORD will roar from heaven
and will shout from his Holy Temple.
He will roar loudly against his land.
He will shout like people who walk on grapes
to make wine;
he will shout against all who live on the earth.
31The noise will spread all over the earth,
because the LORD will accuse all the nations.
He will judge and tell what is wrong
with all people,
and he will kill the evil people with a
sword,’ ” says the LORD.

32This is what the LORD All-Powerful says:
“Disasters will soon spread
from nation to nation.
They will come like a powerful storm
from the faraway places on earth.”

33At that time those killed by the LORD will reach
from one end of the earth to the other. No one
will cry for them or gather up their bodies and
bury them. They will be left lying on the ground
like dung.

34Cry, you leaders! Cry out loud!
Roll around in the dust, leaders of
the people!

25:29 Hell: Nahum 1:6

It is now time for you to be killed.
You will fall and be scattered,
like pieces of a broken jar.
35 There will be no place for the leaders to hide;
they will not escape.
36 I hear the sound of the leaders shouting.
I hear the leaders of the people crying loudly,
because the LORD is destroying their land.
37 Those peaceful pastures will be like an empty
desert,
because the LORD is very angry.
38 Like a lion, he has left his den.
Their land has been destroyed
because of the terrible war he brought,
because of his fierce anger.

Jeremiah's Lesson at the Temple

26 This message came from the LORD soon
after Jehoiakim son of Josiah became king
of Judah. 2 This is what the LORD said: "Jeremiah,
stand in the courtyard of the Temple of the LORD.
Give this message to all the people of the towns of
Judah who are coming to worship at the Temple
of the LORD. Tell them everything I tell you to say;
don't leave out a word. 3 Maybe they will listen
and stop their evil ways. If they will, I will change
my mind about bringing on them the disaster that
I am planning because of the evil they have done.
4 Say to them: 'This is what the LORD says: You
must obey me and follow my teachings that I gave
you. 5 You must listen to what my servants the
prophets say to you. I have sent them to you again
and again, but you did not listen. 6 If you don't
obey me, I will destroy my Temple in Jerusalem
as I destroyed my Holy Tent at Shiloh. When I do,
people all over the world will curse Jerusalem.'"
7 The priests, the prophets, and all the people
heard Jeremiah speaking these words in the
Temple of the LORD. 8 When Jeremiah finished
speaking everything the LORD had commanded
him to say, the priests, prophets, and all the people grabbed Jeremiah. They said, "You must die!
9 How dare you prophesy in the name of the LORD
that this Temple will be destroyed like the one at
Shiloh! How dare you say that Jerusalem will
become a desert without anyone to live in it!"
And all the people crowded around Jeremiah in
the Temple of the LORD.
10 Now when the officers of Judah heard about
what was happening, they came out of the king's
palace and went up to the Temple of the LORD
and took their places at the entrance of the New
Gate. 11 Then the priests and prophets said to the
officers and all the other people, "Jeremiah
should be killed. He prophesied against Jerusalem, and you heard him yourselves."
12 Then Jeremiah spoke these words to all the
officers of Judah and all the other people: "The
LORD sent me to say everything you have heard
about this Temple and this city. 13 Now change
your lives and start doing good and obey the LORD
your God. Then he will change his mind and not
bring on you the disaster he has told you about.
14 As for me, I am in your power. Do to me what
you think is good and right. 15 But be sure of one
thing. If you kill me, you will be guilty of killing
an innocent person. You will make this city and
everyone who lives in it guilty, too! The LORD
truly sent me to you to give you this message."
16 Then the officers and all the people said to
the priests and the prophets, "Jeremiah must not
be killed. What he told us comes from the LORD
our God."
17 Then some of the older leaders of Judah stood
up and said to all the people, 18 "Micah, from the
city of Moresheth, was a prophet during the time
Hezekiah was king of Judah. Micah said to all the
people of Judah, 'This is what the LORD All-
Powerful says:

Jerusalem will be plowed like a field.
It will become a pile of rocks,
and the hill where the Temple stands will be
covered with bushes.'

19 "Hezekiah king of Judah and the people of
Judah did not kill Micah. You know that Hezekiah
feared the LORD and tried to please the LORD. So the
LORD changed his mind and did not bring on Judah
the disaster he had promised. If we hurt Jeremiah,
we will bring a terrible disaster on ourselves!"
20 (Now there was another man who prophesied in the name of the LORD. His name was Uriah
son of Shemaiah from the city of Kiriath Jearim.
He preached the same things against Jerusalem
and the land of Judah that Jeremiah did. 21 When
King Jehoiakim, all his army officers, and all the
leaders of Judah heard Uriah preach, King
Jehoiakim wanted to kill Uriah. But Uriah heard
about it and was afraid. So he escaped to Egypt.
22 Then King Jehoiakim sent Elnathan son of
Acbor and some other men to Egypt, 23 and they
brought Uriah back from Egypt. Then they took
him to King Jehoiakim, who had Uriah killed with
a sword. His body was thrown into the burial
place where poor people are buried.)
24 Ahikam son of Shaphan supported Jeremiah.
So Ahikam did not hand Jeremiah over to be
killed by the people.

26:15 Jeremiah here reflects Deuteronomy 19:10–13 which says that a whole community is guilty if an innocent person is killed.

Nebuchadnezzar Is Made Ruler

27 The LORD spoke his word to Jeremiah soon after Zedekiah son of Josiah was made king of Judah. 2This is what the LORD said to me: "Make a yoke out of straps and poles, and put it on the back of your neck. 3Then send messages to the kings of Edom, Moab, Ammon, Tyre, and Sidon by their messengers who have come to Jerusalem to see Zedekiah king of Judah. 4Tell them to give this message to their masters: 'The LORD All-Powerful, the God of Israel, says: "Tell your masters: 5I made the earth, its people, and all its animals with my great power and strength. I can give the earth to anyone I want. 6Now I have given all these lands to Nebuchadnezzar king of Babylon, my servant. I will make even the wild animals obey him. 7All nations will serve Nebuchadnezzar and his son and grandson. Then the time will come for Babylon to be defeated, and many nations and great kings will make Babylon their servant.∞

8" ' "But if some nations or kingdoms refuse to serve Nebuchadnezzar king of Babylon and refuse to be under his control, I will punish them with war, hunger, and terrible diseases, says the LORD. I will use Nebuchadnezzar to destroy them. 9So don't listen to your false prophets, those who use magic to tell the future, those who explain dreams, the mediums, or magicians. They all tell you, 'You will not be slaves to the king of Babylon.'∞ 10They are telling you lies that will cause you to be taken far from your homeland. I will force you to leave your homes, and you will die in another land. 11But the nations who put themselves under the control of the king of Babylon and serve him I will let stay in their own country, says the LORD. The people from those nations will live in their own land and farm it." ' "

12I gave the same message to Zedekiah king of Judah. I said, "Put yourself under the control of the king of Babylon and serve him, and you will live. 13Why should you and your people die from war, hunger, or disease, as the LORD said would happen to those who do not serve the king of Babylon? 14But the false prophets are saying, 'You will never be slaves to the king of Babylon.' Don't listen to them because they are prophesying lies to you! 15'I did not send them,' says the LORD. 'They are prophesying lies and saying the message is from me. So I will send you away, Judah. And you and those prophets who prophesy to you will die.' "

16Then I, Jeremiah, said to the priests and all the people, "This is what the LORD says: Those false prophets are saying, 'The Babylonians will soon return what they took from the Temple of the LORD.' Don't listen to them! They are prophesying lies to you. 17Don't listen to those prophets. But serve the king of Babylon, and you will live. There is no reason for you to cause Jerusalem to become a ruin. 18If they are prophets and have the message from the LORD, let them pray to the LORD All-Powerful. Let them ask that the items which are still in the Temple of the LORD and in the king's palace and in Jerusalem not be taken away to Babylon.

19"This is what the LORD All-Powerful says about those items left in Jerusalem: the pillars, the large bronze bowl, which is called the Sea, the stands that can be moved, and other things. 20Nebuchadnezzar king of Babylon did not take these away when he took as captives Jehoiachin son of Jehoiakim king of Judah and all the other important people from Judah and Jerusalem to Babylon. 21This is what the LORD All-Powerful, the God of Israel, says about the items left in the Temple of the LORD and in the king's palace and in Jerusalem:22'All of them will also be taken to Babylon. And they will stay there until the day I go to get them,' says the LORD. 'Then I will bring them back and return them to this place.' "

The False Prophet Hananiah

28 It was in that same year, in the fifth month of Zedekiah's fourth year as king of Judah, soon after he began to rule. The prophet Hananiah son of Azzur, from the town of Gibeon, spoke to me in the Temple of the LORD in front of the priests and all the people. He said: 2"The LORD All-Powerful, the God of Israel, says: 'I have broken the yoke the king of Babylon has put on Judah. 3Before two years are over, I will bring back everything that Nebuchadnezzar king of Babylon took to Babylon from the LORD's Temple. 4I will also bring back Jehoiachin son of Jehoiakim king of Judah and all the other captives from Judah who went to Babylon,' says the LORD. 'So I will break the yoke the king of Babylon put on Judah.' "

5Then the prophet Jeremiah spoke to the prophet Hananiah in front of the priests and all the people who were standing in the Temple of the LORD. 6He said, "Amen! Let the LORD really do that! May the LORD make the message you prophesy come true. May he bring back here everything from the LORD's Temple and all the people who were taken as captives to Babylon.

∞**27:7 Prophetic Symbolism:** Jeremiah 32:1–15

∞**27:9 Magic:** Ezekiel 13:17–19

PARABLES

LUKE 8:10

*Why did Jesus teach in parables?
How should we read them today?*

Speaking of parables in one particularly memorable summary, Mark writes, "Jesus used many stories like these to teach the crowd God's message—as much as they could understand. But when he and his followers were alone, Jesus explained everything to them" (Mark 4:33).

Jesus was not the earliest teacher to use parables. In the Old Testament, Nathan uses a parable about a poor man and his sheep to trap David in his sin (2 Samuel 14:5–20) and Isaiah tells the parable of the vineyard in order to talk about Israel's relationship with God. Many Jewish teachers before and after Jesus filled their teaching with stories that remind us of Jesus' parables. However, no one seems to have been as creative or as consistent in their use of parables as Jesus was. The word *parable* is itself used fifty times in the Books of Matthew, Mark, and Luke. They record as many as sixty-five parables of Jesus, ranging from relatively brief comparisons (like the parable of the leaven in Matthew 13:31–32) to full-blown stories (like the parable of the good Samaritan in Luke 10:25–37).

Why did Jesus teach in parables? Sometimes it was to make his message especially plain to his hearers. Jesus' parables tend to draw on daily life in the villages of Palestine. His basic message is, "Learn from the world what God is like!" Some parables ask the listener simply to learn from the world—such as in Luke 11:5–13. This parable of Jesus does not require that we identify characters within the parable—the homeowner, the friend at midnight, etc.—with anyone outside the parable (God, for example). Instead, Jesus depends on his audience to know that, in the normal setting of village life, a friend will always provide assistance; in the same way, he says, we can depend on God to provide help to those who ask of him. Other parables seem to invite a correspondence between characters in the story and, say, God or Jesus. The Jewish leaders understood that the parable about some farmers who killed the son of the vineyard owner was really about their rejection of God's messengers, including his son (Mark 12:1–12). Similarly, it is easy to see how the father in the parable of the son who left home could be understood to represent the gracious God (Luke 15:11–32).

This does not mean, though, that Jesus taught in parables simply in order to make things plain to his audience. Often his parables have a surprising quality, an unexpected twist in the story. Something does not seem quite right. Even though the mustard seed is very small, just as Jesus says, it does not really produce "the largest of all garden plants" (Mark 4:32). By making this comparison, Jesus is not making a mistake that any gardener would recognize; rather, he is inviting his audience to think with him about the nature of the kingdom of God. If they are looking for the obvious or only working with their usual expectations, they may miss seeing what God is doing in the world.

More often than not, then, parables are not meant to be understood easily on a first reading or first hearing. They invite reflection. In fact, like David, whose sinful plot was unveiled in a parable (2 Samuel 14:5–20), we may not like what we hear. Parables are not usually spoken in order to make us feel good, but to call us into question. They push us to think more deeply about the message of the Good News. They pull the rug out from under the categories with which we normally think. Indeed, it appears that Jesus spoke in parables sometimes because otherwise his message would be too sharp, too difficult. Parables allow Jesus' message to unfold slowly, to challenge us over and over again at deeper and deeper levels.

Jesus' parables are usually focused on the nature of God's kingdom. This is not surprising since the center of his message overall was the kingdom (see Mark 1:15)—that is, the coming of God into the world to bring peace and justice. The problem Jesus faced is that the kingdom he proclaimed was not identical with what his audience expected. Even though he announced the presence of the kingdom in his ministry, much of life still seemed the same. Hence, the question, How could the kingdom have come? Where is peace and justice? Jesus had to explain in new terms the nature of God's rule. Like a mustard seed, the kingdom's beginnings are small. The kingdom is present and growing all around us, even in the midst of evil. Can we see it? Jesus could also speak about the future coming of the kingdom, when evil would be overcome completely and God's peace would be evident to all.

Parables: For additional scriptures on this topic go to 2 Samuel 14:5–20.

LEISURE

LUKE 8:14

What does the Bible say about leisure?
Does the Bible provide any guidelines about how to spend leisure time?

The word *leisure* means time that is free from work or other duties. Because we as Christians should always be giving ourselves fully to the work of the Lord (1 Corinthians 15:58), there is a sense in which we never really have time that is free from wanting to carry out this task. Jesus wants us to be participating in the work of bringing people to God (Matthew 9:35–38). This is a full-time job at which Christians will labor until Christ returns.

We usually use the word *leisure*, however, to mean "the time that we have left over after working the particular jobs at which we earn a living." Modern technology has developed a multitude of labor-saving devices to make our lives easier. As a result, people today probably have more leisure time than at any other time in history. In addition to providing more leisure time, the modern world holds out countless ways to fill that time. In light of these developments, Christians need to seek guidance from the Bible as to how we should deal with this increasing amount of leisure time that is available to us.

The Bible speaks of Sabbath rest (Exodus 20:8–11; Deuteronomy 5:12–15) as rest from our physical labor. Today, however, we usually have much more leisure time than we need simply to rest. How should we occupy this time? While the Bible does not directly address the issue of leisure time, it does provide us with general guidelines to follow.

One principle that we must be careful to observe is that our leisure time should not be the result of refusing to carry out our responsibilities. Paul urges all Christians to do their work diligently (2 Thessalonians 3:6–15). Those who refuse to work are called lazy (Proverbs 6:6–11). Those lazy people who have leisure time because they refuse to work bring hardship to their employers (Proverbs 10:26) and harm to themselves. Laziness results in material poverty (Proverbs 20:4; 24:30–34) and is often characterized by thinking too highly of oneself (Proverbs 26:16). It can even result in physical harm (Proverbs 21:25). We therefore need to make sure that any leisure time we have is not taking time away from important tasks.

When all of our work is done, and we believe that we have legitimate leisure time, how should that time be spent? Again, the Bible gives us another general guideline that we can follow. That is, we should not devote our free time to the exclusive pursuit of pleasure or self-gratification. The author of Ecclesiastes had the time and resources to pursue any pleasure he desired. He tried this for a while, but could only conclude that "It is foolish to laugh all the time, and having fun doesn't accomplish anything" (Ecclesiastes 2:2). As Christians, we should let the teaching of Christ richly live in us (Colossians 3:16) and control our behavior (see Luke 6:46–49). But if we make pleasure the main goal of our spare time, then the teaching of Christ gets "choked out." Jesus said that this can prevent us from growing and producing fruit in our lives (Luke 8:14; see also Isaiah 5:11–12). This slavery to pleasure was part of our old lives apart from Christ (2 Timothy 3:4; Titus 3:3). Now that we have been set free from such selfishness, we can serve God with thankfulness (Romans 6:17–18). We need to make sure that we don't allow the satisfaction of sinful desires to be the main objective of our leisure time. Rather, like everything we do, we must spend our leisure time in a way that brings glory to God (Colossians 3:17).

One way we can do this is to use our leisure time to prepare ourselves to bring the Good News to the world. As we have already seen, this involves physical rest (Mark 6:31). We may also use our leisure time to provide ourselves with spiritual refreshment. We can accomplish this by spending time reading and studying the Bible (Psalm 119:165; 2 Timothy 3:15–17). We also find spiritual refreshment in the time we spend in prayer to God (Philippians 4:6–7). Another way we can wisely use our leisure time is to refresh ourselves mentally and physically with various types of recreation. Paul acknowledges that physical training is helpful in some ways (1 Timothy 4:8). In all of these activities, it is important to remember why we are doing them—to prepare ourselves to better serve God in his kingdom and not simply to satisfy our desires for personal pleasure.

In addition to seeking our own refreshment with our leisure time, we must also be alert for every opportunity that we have for doing good (Galatians 6:10; Ephesians 5:15–20; Colossians 4:5), because our good deeds bring praise to God (Matthew 5:16).

Leisure: For additional scriptures on this topic go to Proverbs 6:6–11.

7“But listen to what I am going to say to you and
all the people. 8There were prophets long before
we became prophets, Hananiah. They prophesied
that war, hunger, and terrible diseases would
come to many countries and great kingdoms. 9But
if a prophet prophesies that we will have peace
and that message comes true, he can be recognized as one truly sent by the LORD.”⚭
10Then the prophet Hananiah took the yoke off
Jeremiah’s neck and broke it. 11Hananiah said in
front of all the people, “This is what the LORD says:
‘In the same way I will break the yoke of
Nebuchadnezzar king of Babylon. He put that yoke
on all the nations of the world, but I will break it
before two years are over.’ ” After Hananiah had
said that, Jeremiah left the Temple.
12The LORD spoke his word to Jeremiah after
the prophet Hananiah had broken the yoke off of
the prophet Jeremiah’s neck. 13The LORD said,
“Go and tell Hananiah, ‘This is what the LORD
says: You have broken a wooden yoke, but I will
make a yoke of iron in its place! 14The LORD All-
Powerful, the God of Israel, says: I will put a yoke
of iron on the necks of all these nations to make
them serve Nebuchadnezzar king of Babylon, and
they will be slaves to him. I will even give Nebuchadnezzar control over the wild animals.’ ”
15Then the prophet Jeremiah said to the
prophet Hananiah, “Listen, Hananiah! The LORD
did not send you, and you have made the people
of Judah trust in lies. 16So this is what the LORD
says: ‘Soon I will remove you from the earth. You
will die this year, because you taught the people
to turn against the LORD.’ ”
17Hananiah died in the seventh month of that
same year.

A Letter to the Captives in Babylon

29 This is the letter that Jeremiah the prophet
sent from Jerusalem to the older leaders
who were among the captives, the priests, and
the prophets. He sent it to all the other people
Nebuchadnezzar had taken as captives from
Jerusalem to Babylon. 2(This letter was sent after
all these people were taken away: Jehoiachin the
king and the queen mother; the officers and leaders of Judah and Jerusalem; and the craftsmen
and metalworkers from Jerusalem.) 3Zedekiah
king of Judah sent Elasah son of Shaphan and
Gemariah son of Hilkiah to Babylon to Nebuchadnezzar king of Babylon. So Jeremiah gave them
this letter to carry to Babylon:
4This is what the LORD All-Powerful, the God of
Israel, says to all those people I sent away from
Jerusalem as captives to Babylon: 5“Build houses
and settle in the land. Plant gardens and eat the
food they grow.⚭ 6Get married and have sons
and daughters. Find wives for your sons, and let
your daughters be married so they also may have
sons and daughters. Have many children in
Babylon; don’t become fewer in number. 7Also
do good things for the city where I sent you as
captives. Pray to the LORD for the city where you
are living, because if good things happen in the
city, good things will happen to you also.”⚭ 8The
LORD All-Powerful, the God of Israel, says: “Don’t
let the prophets among you and the people who
do magic fool you. Don’t listen to their dreams.
9They are prophesying lies to you, saying that
their message is from me. But I did not send
them,” says the LORD.
10This is what the LORD says: “Babylon will be
powerful for seventy years. After that time I will
come to you, and I will keep my promise to bring
you back to Jerusalem. 11I say this because I know
what I am planning for you,” says the LORD. “I
have good plans for you, not plans to hurt you. I
will give you hope and a good future. 12Then you
will call my name. You will come to me and pray
to me, and I will listen to you. 13You will search
for me. And when you search for me with all your
heart, you will find me! 14I will let you find me,”
says the LORD. “And I will bring you back from
your captivity. I forced you to leave this place, but
I will gather you from all the nations, from the
places I have sent you as captives,” says the LORD.
“And I will bring you back to this place.”
15You might say, “The LORD has given us
prophets here in Babylon.”
16But the LORD says this about the king who is
sitting on David’s throne now and all the other
people still in Jerusalem, your relatives who did
not go as captives to Babylon with you. 17The
LORD All-Powerful says: “I will soon send war,

⚭**28:9 Antichrist (Enemy of Christ):** 1 Corinthians 12:1–3

29:4–7 “Do good things for the city” can be more literally translated: “Seek the *shalom* of the city . . . for in its *shalom* you will find your *shalom*.” The Hebrew word *shalom* is usually translated “peace” or “welfare.” It is better left untranslated, for its meaning is too rich to be expressed in English in a single word. Its meaning includes just peace, human wholeness, and social, as well as, spiritual welfare. If God’s people seek justice and peace, healing and wholeness, social and spiritual welfare of the city to which God has called and sent them, they will find their own personal *shalom*.

⚭**29:5 House/Home:** Mark 10:28–30

⚭**29:7 Citizen:** Ezekiel 34:1–2

29:11 Every blessing should contain a note of hope for those who worship and obey the Lord. God promises to bless his rebellious people in the future once they have turned back to him in repentance. In fact, he declares that future blessings are part of his plans for his people. It is important to realize that God wants to give a blessing just as much as we want to receive one.

hunger, and terrible diseases against those still in
Jerusalem. I will make them like bad figs that are
too rotten to eat. 18I will chase them with war,
hunger, and terrible diseases. I will make them
hated by all the kingdoms of the earth. People
will curse them and be shocked and will use them
as a shameful example wherever I make them go.
19This is because they have not listened to my
message," says the LORD. "I sent my message to
them again and again through my servants, the
prophets, but they did not listen," says the LORD.
20You captives, whom I forced to leave Jerusalem and go to Babylon, listen to the message
from the LORD. 21The LORD All-Powerful, the God
of Israel, says this about Ahab son of Kolaiah and
Zedekiah son of Maaseiah: "These two men have
been prophesying lies to you, saying that their
message is from me. But soon I will hand over
those two prophets to Nebuchadnezzar king of
Babylon, and he will kill them in front of you.
22Because of them, all the captives from Judah in
Babylon will use this curse: 'May the LORD treat
you like Zedekiah and Ahab, whom the king of
Babylon burned in the fire.' 23They have done
evil things among the people of Israel. They are
guilty of adultery with their neighbors' wives.
They have also spoken lies and said those lies
were a message from me. I did not tell them to do
that. I know what they have done; I am a witness
to it," says the LORD.
24Also give a message to Shemaiah from the
Nehelamite family. 25The LORD All-Powerful, the
God of Israel, says: "Shemaiah, you sent letters in
your name to all the people in Jerusalem, to the
priest Zephaniah son of Maaseiah, and to all the
priests. 26You said to Zephaniah, 'The LORD has
made you priest in place of Jehoiada. You are to be
in charge of the Temple of the LORD. You should
arrest any madman who acts like a prophet. Lock
his hands and feet between wooden blocks, and
put iron rings around his neck. 27Now Jeremiah
from Anathoth is acting like a prophet. So why
haven't you arrested him? 28Jeremiah has sent this
message to us in Babylon: You will be there for a
long time, so build houses and settle down. Plant
gardens and eat what they grow.' "
29Zephaniah the priest read the letter to Jeremiah
the prophet. 30Then the LORD spoke his word to
Jeremiah: 31"Send this message to all the captives in
Babylon: 'This is what the LORD says about
Shemaiah the Nehelamite: Shemaiah has prophesied to you, but I did not send him. He has made
you believe a lie. 32So the LORD says, I will soon punish Shemaiah the Nehelamite and his family. He
will not see the good things I will do for my people,
says the LORD. None of his family will be left alive
among the people, because he has taught the people to turn against me.' "

Promises of Hope

30 These are the words that the LORD spoke
to Jeremiah. 2The LORD, the God of Israel,
said: "Jeremiah, write in a book all the words I
have spoken to you. 3The days will come when
I will bring Israel and Judah back from captivity,"
says the LORD. "I will return them to the land I
gave their ancestors, and they will own it!" says
the LORD.
4The LORD spoke this message about the people
of Israel and Judah: 5This is what the LORD said:

"We hear people crying from fear.
They are afraid; there is no peace.
6Ask this question, and consider it:
A man cannot have a baby.
So why do I see every strong man
holding his stomach in pain like a woman
having a baby?
Why is everyone's face turning white like a
dead man's face?
7This will be a terrible day!
There will never be another time like this.
This is a time of great trouble for the people
of Jacob,
but they will be saved from it."

8The LORD All-Powerful says, "At that time
I will break the yoke from their necks
and tear off the ropes that hold them.
Foreign people will never again make my
people slaves.
9They will serve the LORD their God
and David their king,
whom I will send to them.

10"So people of Jacob, my servants,
don't be afraid.
Israel, don't be frightened," says
the LORD.
"I will soon save you from that faraway place
where you are captives.
I will save your family from that land.
The people of Jacob will be safe and have
peace again;
there will be no enemy to frighten them.
11I am with you and will save you,"
says the LORD.

30:5 Day of the Lord: Jeremiah 46:10

"I will completely destroy all those nations
where I scattered you,
but I will not completely destroy you.
I will punish you fairly,
but I will still punish you."

12This is what the LORD said:
"You people have a wound that cannot be cured;
your injury will not heal.
13There is no one to argue your case
and no cure for your sores.
So you will not be healed.
14All those nations who were your friends have
forgotten you.
They don't care about you.
I have hurt you as an enemy would.
I punished you very hard,
because your guilt was so great
and your sins were so many.
15Why are you crying out about your injury?
There is no cure for your pain.
I did these things to you because of
your great guilt,
because of your many sins.
16But all those nations that destroyed you will
now be destroyed.
All your enemies will become captives in
other lands.
Those who stole from you will have their own
things stolen.
Those who took things from you in war will
have their own things taken.
17I will bring back your health
and heal your injuries," says the LORD,
"because other people forced you away.
They said about you, 'No one cares
about Jerusalem!' "
18This is what the LORD said:
"I will soon make the tents of Jacob's people
as they used to be,
and I will have pity on Israel's houses.
The city will be rebuilt on its hill of ruins,
and the king's palace will stand in
its proper place.
19People in those places will sing songs of praise.
There will be the sound of laughter.
I will give them many children
so their number will not be small.
I will bring honor to them
so no one will look down on them.
20Their descendants will be as they were
in the old days.
I will set them up as a strong
people before me,
and I will punish the nations who
have hurt them.
21One of their own people will lead them;
their ruler will come from among them.
He will come near to me when I invite him.
Who would dare to come to me uninvited?"
says the LORD.
22"So you will be my people,
and I will be your God."

23Look! It is a storm from the LORD!
He is angry and has gone out to punish
the people.
Punishment will come like a storm
crashing down on the evil people.
24The LORD will stay angry
until he finishes punishing the people.
He will stay angry
until he finishes the punishment he planned.
When that day comes,
you will understand this.

The New Israel

31 The LORD says, "At that time I will be God
of all Israel's family groups, and they will
be my people."
2This is what the LORD says:

"The people who were not killed by the
enemy's sword
found help in the desert.
I came to give rest to Israel."

3And from far away the LORD appeared to his
people and said,
"I love you people
with a love that will last forever.
That is why I have continued
showing you kindness.
4People of Israel, I will build you up again,
and you will be rebuilt.
You will pick up your tambourines again
and dance with those who are joyful.
5You will plant vineyards again
on the hills around Samaria.
The farmers will plant them
and enjoy their fruit.
6There will be a time when watchmen in the
mountains of Ephraim shout this message:
'Come, let's go up to Jerusalem to worship
the LORD our God!' "

7This is what the LORD says:
"Be happy and sing for the people of Jacob.
Shout for Israel, the greatest of the nations.

31:3 Love: Matthew 5:44

Sing your praises and shout this:
'LORD, save your people,
those who are left alive from the nation
of Israel!'

8Look, I will soon bring Israel from the country
in the north,
and I will gather them from the faraway
places on earth.
Some of the people are blind and crippled.
Some of the women are pregnant, and some
are ready to give birth.
A great many people will come back.
9They will be crying as they come,
but they will pray as I bring them back.
I will lead those people by
streams of water
on an even road where they will
not stumble.
I am Israel's father,
and Israel is my firstborn son.

10"Nations, listen to the message from the LORD.
Tell this message in the faraway lands
by the sea:
'The one who scattered the people of Israel
will bring them back,
and he will watch over his people
like a shepherd.'
11The LORD will pay for the people of Jacob
and will buy them back from people stronger
than they were.
12The people of Israel will come to the high
points of Jerusalem
and shout for joy.
Their faces will shine with happiness about all
the good things from the LORD:
the grain, new wine, oil, young sheep,
and young cows.
They will be like a garden that has
plenty of water,
and they will not be troubled anymore.
13Then young women of Israel will be
happy and dance,
the young men and old men also.
I will change their sadness into happiness;
I will give them comfort and joy
instead of sadness.
14The priests will have more than
enough sacrifices,
and my people will be filled with the good
things I give them!" says the LORD.

15This is what the LORD says:
"A voice was heard in Ramah
of painful crying and deep sadness:
Rachel crying for her children.
She refused to be comforted,
because her children are dead!"

16But this is what the LORD says:
"Stop crying;
don't let your eyes fill with tears.
You will be rewarded for your work!" says the
LORD.
"The people will return from their enemy's
land.
17So there is hope for you in the future," says
the LORD.
"Your children will return to their own land.

18"I have heard Israel moaning:
'LORD, you punished me, and I have learned
my lesson.
I was like a calf that had never been trained.
Take me back so that I may come back.
You truly are the LORD my God.
19LORD, after I wandered away from you,
I changed my heart and life.
After I understood,
I beat my breast with sorrow.
I was ashamed and disgraced,
because I suffered for the foolish things I did
when I was young.'

20"You know that Israel is my dear son,
The child I love.
Yes, I often speak against Israel,
but I still remember him.
I love him very much,
and I want to comfort him," says the LORD.

21"People of Israel, fix the road signs.
Put up signs to show you the way home.
Watch the road.
Pay attention to the road on which you travel.
People of Israel, come home,
come back to your towns.
22You are an unfaithful daughter.
How long will you wander before
you come home?
The LORD has made something new
happen in the land:
A woman will go seeking a man."

31:7 The Remnant: Jeremiah 42:2
31:8 Jeremiah says that the restoration of the people of God will come from the north. That is, they will return from Babylon after the Exile.
31:9 *my firstborn son.* The firstborn son during the period of the Old Testament had the rights of inheritance and was typically the favored son.
31:22 Land/Inheritance: Jeremiah 31:31–34

23The LORD All-Powerful, the God of Israel, says:
"I will again do good things for the people of
Judah. At that time the people in the land of Judah
and its towns will again use these words: 'May the
LORD bless you, home of what is good, holy mountain.' 24People in all the towns of Judah will live
together in peace. Farmers and those who move
around with their flocks will live together in
peace. 25I will give rest and strength to those who
are weak and tired."
26After hearing that, I, Jeremiah, woke up and
looked around. My sleep had been very pleasant.
27The LORD says, "The time is coming when I
will help the families of Israel and Judah and their
children and animals to grow. 28In the past I
watched over Israel and Judah, to pull them up
and tear them down, to destroy them and bring
them disaster. But now I will watch over them to
build them up and make them strong," says the
LORD.

29"At that time people will no longer say:
'The parents have eaten sour grapes,
and that caused the children to grind their
teeth from the sour taste.'
30Instead, each person will die for his own sin;
the person who eats sour grapes will grind his
own teeth.

The New Agreement

31"Look, the time is coming," says the LORD,
"when I will make a new agreement
with the people of Israel
and the people of Judah.
32It will not be like the agreement
I made with their ancestors
when I took them by the hand
to bring them out of Egypt.
I was a husband to them,
but they broke that agreement," says the LORD.
33"This is the agreement I will make
with the people of Israel at that time,"
says the LORD:
"I will put my teachings in their minds
and write them on their hearts.
I will be their God,
and they will be my people.
34People will no longer have to teach their
neighbors and relatives
to know the LORD,
because all people will know me,
from the least to the most important," says
the LORD.
"I will forgive them for the wicked
things they did,
and I will not remember their sins anymore."

The Lord Will Never Leave Israel

35The LORD makes the sun shine in the day
and the moon and stars to shine at night.
He stirs up the sea so that its waves crash
on the shore.
The LORD All-Powerful is his name.
This is what the LORD says:
36"Only if these laws should ever fail,"
says the LORD,
"will Israel's descendants ever stop
being a nation before me."

37This is what the LORD says:
"Only if people can measure the sky above
and learn the secrets of the earth below,
will I reject all the descendants of Israel
because of what they have done,"
says the LORD.

The New Jerusalem

38The LORD says, "The time is coming when
Jerusalem will be rebuilt for me—everything
from the Tower of Hananel to the Corner Gate.
39The measuring line will stretch from the Corner
Gate straight to the hill of Gareb. Then it will turn
to the place named Goah. 40The whole valley
where dead bodies and ashes are thrown, and all
the terraces out to the Kidron Valley on the east as
far as the corner of the Horse Gate—all that area
will be holy to the LORD. The city of Jerusalem will
never again be torn down or destroyed."

Jeremiah Buys a Field

32 This is the word the LORD spoke to
Jeremiah in the tenth year Zedekiah was
king of Judah, which was the eighteenth year of
Nebuchadnezzar. 2At that time the army of the
king of Babylon was surrounding Jerusalem.
Jeremiah the prophet was under arrest in the
courtyard of the guard, which was at the palace of
the king of Judah.
3Zedekiah king of Judah had put Jeremiah in
prison there. Zedekiah had asked, "Why have you

31:23 *holy mountain.* The holy mountain of the land of Judah is Mount Zion, the location of God's Temple.
31:31 Agreement: See article on page 122.
31:31 *a new agreement.* The old agreements made with Noah (Genesis 9), Abraham (Genesis 12), Moses (Exodus 19–20), and David (2 Samuel 7) will be replaced by something even better (see Matthew 26:26–29).

31:34 Neighbor: Matthew 19:19
31:34 Land/Inheritance: Ezekiel 36:26–27
31:34 Election (Chosen): Amos 3:1–15
31:38 Jerusalem: Matthew 23:37

prophesied the things you have?" (Jeremiah had said, "This is what the LORD says: 'I will soon hand the city of Jerusalem over to the king of Babylon, and he will capture it. 4Zedekiah king of Judah will not escape from the Babylonian army, but he will surely be handed over to the king of Babylon. And he will speak to the king of Babylon face to face and see him with his own eyes. 5The king will take Zedekiah to Babylon, where he will stay until I have punished him,' says the LORD. 'If you fight against the Babylonians, you will not succeed.' ")

6While Jeremiah was in prison, he said, "The LORD spoke this word to me: 7Your cousin Hanamel, son of your uncle Shallum, will come to you soon. Hanamel will say to you, 'Jeremiah, you are my nearest relative, so buy my field near the town of Anathoth. It is your right and your duty to buy that field.'

8"Then it happened just as the LORD had said. My cousin Hanamel came to me in the courtyard of the guard and said to me, 'Buy for yourself my field near Anathoth in the land of Benjamin. It is your right and duty to buy it and own it.' So I knew this was a message from the LORD.

9"I bought the field at Anathoth from my cousin Hanamel, weighing out seven ounces of silver for him. 10I signed the record and sealed it and had some people witness it. I also weighed out the silver on the scales. 11Then I took both copies of the record of ownership—the one that was sealed that had the demands and limits of ownership, and the one that was not sealed. 12And I gave them to Baruch son of Neriah, the son of Mahseiah. My cousin Hanamel, the other witnesses who signed the record of ownership, and many Jews sitting in the courtyard of the guard saw me give the record of ownership to Baruch.

13"With all the people watching, I told Baruch, 14'This is what the LORD All-Powerful, the God of Israel, says: Take both copies of the record of ownership—the sealed copy and the copy that was not sealed—and put them in a clay jar so they will last a long time. 15This is what the LORD All-Powerful, the God of Israel, says: In the future my people will once again buy houses and fields for grain and vineyards in the land of Israel.'

16"After I gave the record of ownership to Baruch son of Neriah, I prayed to the LORD, 17Oh, Lord GOD, you made the skies and the earth with your very great power. There is nothing too hard for you to do. 18You show love and kindness to thousands of people, but you also bring punishment to children for their parents' sins. Great and powerful God, your name is the LORD All-Powerful. 19You plan and do great things. You see everything that people do, and you reward people for the way they live and for what they do. 20You did miracles and wonderful things in the land of Egypt. You have continued doing them in Israel and among the other nations even until today. So you have become well known. 21You brought your people, the Israelites, out of Egypt using signs and miracles and your great power and strength. You brought great terror on everyone. 22You gave them this land that you promised to their ancestors long ago, a fertile land. 23They came into this land and took it for their own, but they did not obey you or follow your teachings. They did not do everything you commanded. So you made all these terrible things happen to them.

24"Look! The enemy has surrounded the city and has built roads to the top of the walls to capture it. Because of war, hunger, and terrible diseases, the city will be handed over to the Babylonians who are attacking it. You said this would happen, and now you see it is happening. 25But now, Lord GOD, you tell me, 'Buy the field with silver and call in witnesses.' You tell me this while the Babylonian army is ready to capture the city."

26Then the LORD spoke this word to Jeremiah: 27"I am the LORD, the God of every person on the earth. Nothing is impossible for me. 28So this is what the LORD says: I will soon hand over the city of Jerusalem to the Babylonian army and to Nebuchadnezzar king of Babylon, who will capture it. 29The Babylonian army is already attacking the city of Jerusalem. They will soon enter it and start a fire to burn down the city and its houses. The people of Jerusalem offered sacrifices to Baal on the roofs of those same houses and poured out drink offerings to other idols to make me angry. 30From their youth, the people of Israel and Judah have done only the things I said were wrong. They have made me angry by worshiping idols made with their own hands," says the LORD. 31"From the day Jerusalem was built until now, this city has made me angry, so angry that I must remove it from my sight. 32I will destroy it, because of all the evil the people of Israel and Judah have done. The people, their kings and officers, their priests and prophets, all the people of Judah, and the people of Jerusalem have made me

32:7 *my nearest relative.* God distributed the land to families. He also instituted laws to insure that the land stayed with the original family. The law alluded to here is Leviticus 25:25–32.

32:15 Prophetic Symbolism: Ezekiel 1

32:29 *roofs.* In Bible times houses were built with flat roofs. The roof was used for drying things such as flax and fruit. And it was used as an extra room, as a place for worship, and as a cool place to sleep in the summer.

angry. 33They turned their backs to me, not their faces. I tried to teach them again and again, but they wouldn't listen or learn. 34They put their hateful idols in the place where I have chosen to be worshiped, so they made it unclean. 35In the Valley of Ben Hinnom they built places to worship Baal so they could burn their sons and daughters as sacrifices to Molech. But I never commanded them to do such a hateful thing. It never entered my mind that they would do such a thing and cause Judah to sin.

36"You are saying, 'Because of war, hunger, and terrible diseases, the city will be handed over to the king of Babylon.' But the LORD, the God of Israel, says about Jerusalem: 37I forced the people of Israel and Judah to leave their land, because I was furious and very angry with them. But soon I will gather them from all the lands where I forced them to go, and I will bring them back to this place, where they may live in safety. 38The people of Israel and Judah will be my people, and I will be their God. 39I will make them truly want to be one people with one goal. They will truly want to worship me all their lives, for their own good and for the good of their children after them.

40"I will make an agreement with them that will last forever. I will never turn away from them; I will always do good to them. I will make them want to respect me so they will never turn away from me. 41I will enjoy doing good to them. And with my whole being I will surely plant them in this land and make them grow."

42This is what the LORD says: "I have brought this great disaster to the people of Israel and Judah. In the same way I will bring the good things that I promise to do for them. 43You are saying, 'This land is an empty desert, without people or animals. It has been handed over to the Babylonians.' But in the future, people will again buy fields in this land. 44They will use their money to buy fields. They will sign and seal their agreements and call in witnesses. They will again buy fields in the land of Benjamin, in the area around Jerusalem, in the towns of Judah and in the mountains, in the western hills, and in southern Judah. I will make everything as good for them as it once was," says the LORD.

The Promise of the Lord

33 While Jeremiah was still locked up in the courtyard of the guards, the LORD spoke his word to him a second time: 2"These are the words of the LORD, who made the earth, shaped it, and gave it order, whose name is the LORD: 3'Judah, pray to me, and I will answer you. I will tell you important secrets you have never heard before.' 4This is what the LORD, the God of Israel, says about the houses in Jerusalem and the royal palaces of Judah that have been torn down to be used in defense of the attack by the Babylonian army: 5'Some people will come to fight against the Babylonians. They will fill these houses with the bodies of people I killed in my hot anger. I have turned away from this city because of all the evil its people have done.

6"'But then I will bring health and healing to the people there. I will heal them and let them enjoy great peace and safety. 7I will bring Judah and Israel back from captivity and make them strong countries as in the past. 8They sinned against me, but I will wash away that sin. They did evil and turned away from me, but I will forgive them. 9Then "Jerusalem" will be to me a name that brings joy! And people from all nations of the earth will praise it when they hear about the good things I am doing there. They will be surprised and shocked at all the good things and the peace I will bring to Jerusalem.'

10"You are saying, 'Our country is an empty desert, without people or animals.' But this is what the LORD says: It is now quiet in the streets of Jerusalem and in the towns of Judah, without people or animals, but it will be noisy there soon! 11There will be sounds of joy and gladness and the happy sounds of brides and bridegrooms. There will be the sounds of people bringing to the Temple of the LORD their offerings of thanks to the LORD. They will say,

'Praise the LORD All-Powerful,
because the LORD is good!
His love continues forever!'

They will say this because I will again do good things for Judah, as I did in the beginning," says the LORD.

12This is what the LORD All-Powerful says: "This place is empty now, without people or animals. But there will be shepherds in all the towns of Judah and pastures where they let their flocks rest. 13Shepherds will again count their sheep as the sheep walk in front of them. They will count them in the mountains and in the western hills, in southern Judah and the land of Benjamin, and around Jerusalem and the other towns of Judah!" says the LORD.

32:35 *Valley of Ben Hinnom.* See 7:31.
32:41 Obedience: Matthew 7:24–25
33:6 Sickness, Disease, Healing: Matthew 8:16–17
33:8 Healing: Mark 8:2–3

The Good Branch

14The LORD says, "The time is coming when I
will do the good thing I promised to the people of
Israel and Judah.
15In those days and at that time,
I will make a good branch sprout from
David's family.
He will do what is fair and right in the land.
16At that time Judah will be saved,
and the people of Jerusalem will live in safety.
The branch will be named:
The LORD Does What Is Right."
17This is what the LORD says: "Someone from
David's family will always sit on the throne of the
family of Israel. 18And there will always be
priests from the family of Levi. They will always
stand before me to offer burnt offerings and grain
offerings and sacrifices to me."
19The LORD spoke his word to Jeremiah, saying:
20"This is what the LORD says: I have an agreement
with day and night that they will always come at
the right times. If you could change that agreement, 21only then could you change my agreement
with David and Levi. Only then would my servant
David not have a descendant ruling as king on
David's throne. And only then would the family of
Levi not be priests serving me in the Temple. 22But
I will give many descendants to my servant David
and to the family group of Levi who serve me in
the Temple. They will be as many as the stars in
the sky that no one can count. They will be as
many as the grains of sand on the seashore that no
one can measure."
23The LORD spoke his word to Jeremiah, say-
ing:24"Jeremiah, have you heard what the people
are saying? They say: 'The LORD turned away
from the two families of Israel and Judah that he
chose.' Now they don't think of my people as a
nation anymore!"
25This is what the LORD says: "If I had not made
my agreement with day and night, and if I had not
made the laws for the sky and earth, 26only then
would I turn away from Jacob's descendants. And
only then would I not let the descendants of David
my servant rule over the descendants of Abraham,
Isaac, and Jacob. But I will be kind to them and
cause good things to happen to them again."

A Warning to Zedekiah

34 The LORD spoke his word to Jeremiah
when Nebuchadnezzar king of Babylon
was fighting against Jerusalem and all the towns
around it. Nebuchadnezzar had with him all his
army and the armies of all the kingdoms and peoples he ruled. 2This is what the LORD, the God of
Israel, said: "Jeremiah, go to Zedekiah king of
Judah and tell him: 'This is what the LORD says: I
will soon hand the city of Jerusalem over to the
king of Babylon, and he will burn it down! 3You
will not escape from the king of Babylon; you will
surely be captured and handed over to him. You
will see the king of Babylon with your own eyes,
and he will talk to you face to face. And you will
go to Babylon. 4But, Zedekiah king of Judah, listen
to the promise of the LORD. This is what the LORD
says about you: You will not be killed with a
sword. 5You will die in a peaceful way. As people
made funeral fires to honor your ancestors, the
kings who ruled before you, so people will make
a funeral fire to honor you. They will cry for you
and sadly say, "Ah, master!" I myself make this
promise to you, says the LORD.' "
6So Jeremiah the prophet gave this message to
Zedekiah in Jerusalem. 7This was while the army
of the king of Babylon was fighting against Jerusalem and the cities of Judah that had not yet been
taken—Lachish and Azekah. These were the only
strong, walled cities left in the land of Judah.

Slaves Are Mistreated

8The LORD spoke his word to Jeremiah. This
was after King Zedekiah had made an agreement
with all the people in Jerusalem to free all the
Hebrew slaves. 9Everyone was supposed to free
his Hebrew slaves, both male and female. No one
was to keep a fellow Jew as a slave. 10All the officers and all the people accepted this agreement;
they agreed to free their male and female slaves
and no longer keep them as slaves. So all the
slaves were set free. 11But after that, the people
who had slaves changed their minds. So they took
back the people they had set free and made them
slaves again.
12Then the LORD spoke his word to Jeremiah:
13"This is what the LORD, the God of Israel, says: I
brought your ancestors out of Egypt where they
were slaves and made an agreement with them. 14I
said to your ancestors: 'At the end of every seven
years, each one of you must set his Hebrew slaves
free. If a fellow Hebrew has sold himself to you,
you must let him go free after he has served you for
six years.' But your ancestors did not listen or pay
attention to me. 15A short time ago you changed
your hearts and did what I say is right. Each of you
gave freedom to his fellow Hebrews who were
slaves. And you even made an agreement before

33:17 David: Ezekiel 34:23

33:26 Promise: Acts 3:25–26

Neighbor

Luke 10:25–37

Who is our neighbor? How are we to treat a neighbor?

The word *neighbor* occurs over two hundred times in the Bible and is found in the second-greatest commandment, "Love your neighbor as you love yourself" (Matthew 19:19). But what exactly is a neighbor, and how are we to treat a neighbor?

The concept of neighbor is one of the most important concepts in the Old Testament. It is found twice in the Ten Commandments (Exodus 20:16, 17; Deuteronomy 5:20, 21). Simply put, a neighbor is "any member of the community." It has been variously translated "fellow," "fellow-citizen," "brother," or simply "another person." Whereas in English, the word *neighbor* means "one who lives nearby," in the Bible, the term is broader and includes any person belonging to the same social and/or religious community regardless of physical distance.

Naturally, one's neighbor is often the one who does indeed live nearby, and the Bible recognizes this. In Proverbs 3:29, the neighbor is one "who lives nearby and trusts you." "A neighbor close by is better than a family far away" (Proverbs 27:10). The command not to move a neighbor's boundary stone (Deuteronomy 19:14) can only be applicable to people who live next to each other. Many other references, however, are quite general in nature, and it is hard to believe that they would apply only to those who live nearby: "You must not tell lies about your neighbor" (Exodus 20:16). "You must not cheat your neighbor or rob him" (Leviticus 19:13). "If someone wrongs another person [neighbor] . . ." (1 Kings 8:31). Furthermore, the ancient Israelites had a deep sense of their own identity as a community having been specially formed by God and distinguished from other nations by the law of Moses (Genesis 15:14; 19:9–14; Deuteronomy 4:5–8; 7:7). An important reference in this regard is the statement of Moses, who upon seeing two Hebrews fighting each other, spoke up to one of them saying, "Why are you hitting one of your own people?" which is a translation of the original word *neighbor* (Exodus 2:13). Finally, the original language of the Old Testament, Hebrew, has other words which also mean neighbor but which emphasize more the idea of physical proximity (Exodus 32:27; Jeremiah 6:21).

It is in the concept of community that the prohibitions of the Ten Commandments and other laws of the Old Testament take on their force. We are not to tell lies about our neighbor (Exodus 20:16), covet or desire our neighbor's relations or possessions (Exodus 20:17), cheat or rob our neighbor (Leviticus 19:13), plot harm against our neighbor (Proverbs 3:29), or kill our neighbor (Deuteronomy 27:24) precisely because they are our neighbor; that is, a member of our own community and in particular a community established and regulated by God. Wrong committed against anyone is evil, but wrong committed against a member of one's own community is an even greater evil.

A neighbor can be someone who cross-examines you at court (Proverbs 18:17), someone who asks to borrow something (Proverbs 3:28), an acquaintance who is safekeeping another's belongings (Exodus 22:7–14), a fellow woodcutter who is killed accidentally (Deuteronomy 19:4–6), or a person to whom you have loaned money (Deuteronomy 24:10).

In the New Testament, most of the references to "neighbor" are repetitions of the second-greatest commandment found in Leviticus 19:18 (Matthew 19:19; 22:39; Mark 12:31, 33; Romans 13:9; Galatians 5:14; James 2:8). One Greek dictionary defines the word as belonging to a set of words meaning "a person who lives close beside others and who thus by implication is a part of a so-called 'in-group,' that is, the group with which an individual identifies both ethnically and culturally." In this connection, the expert on the Law who asked Jesus in the parable of the good Samaritan, "Who is my neighbor?" understood the word as referring only to "fellow-members of the covenant," that is, the Jewish community. The question then became "to which circle of human relationships are we to demonstrate the command to love as oneself?" Are we to demonstrate love to everyone (which is practically impossible) or show love only to those within our own social and religious circle? Jesus expanded the concept of "neighbor" by including anyone regardless of ethnic or religious heritage with whom we come in contact and can help. In fact, he changed the focus of discussion to what it means to be a neighbor, to involve ourselves in the lives of others.

In addition to the second-greatest commandment, the New Testament specifically says that we should do no harm to our neighbor (Romans 13:10), we should please our neighbor for his or her good (Romans 15:2), we should speak truthfully to our neighbor (Ephesians 4:25), and we should not judge our neighbor (James 4:12).

Neighbor: For additional scriptures on this topic go to Exodus 22:7–14.

PRAYER

LUKE 11:1

Why are believers urged to pray? What are the basic forms of prayer? Does prayer change God's mind? What are some good models for prayer in Scripture?

Prayer is the essence of Christian experience. Christianity is fundamentally a relationship between God and people. Relationships are established, maintained, and enriched by good communication. Prayer is the communication between ourselves and God. We are urged to pray because by doing so, we are engaged in the primary activity which keeps faith vital and strong.

The expression of prayer takes various forms. Adoration affords us the opportunity to praise God. Confession opens the way to forgiveness and restoration. Thanksgiving enables us to express gratitude for specific acts of God in our lives. Intercession invites us to pray for others. Petition gives us permission to pray for ourselves. Each of these types of prayer may be expressed audibly or silently, privately or corporately. Prayer occurs in public worship and even more frequently in private devotion. Most often, it happens as we move through our daily routines. The ordinary circumstances of our lives can be filled with prayer. We can be in a prayerful relation with God all day long. In these ways we fulfill Paul's exhortation to "pray continually" in 1 Thessalonians 5:17. Prayer increasingly becomes a disposition of our mind and heart as we relate all of our life to God's will and direction.

We do not go far in our praying before we confront the question, Does prayer make any difference? Sometimes we pray and we don't seem to get an answer. Does that mean that God does not hear our prayers? Jesus tells us in no uncertain terms that God hears us when we speak to him. He not only hears us but he answers our prayers. In Luke 11:5–13, Jesus says, "Ask, and God will give to you." God indeed does not always give us what we ask for, but perhaps what we ask for isn't good for us. Jesus tells us that he won't give us things that will harm us. He compares our requests to God with a child's request to his parents. He goes on by saying, "If your children ask for an egg, would you give them a scorpion?" The implied answer is no. Parents don't give their children things that will harm them, and neither will God.

The Bible teaches two things that appear contradictory to us from our limited human perspective. The first is that God is in control and knows what he is doing, even from before the beginning of time. And the second is that our prayers influence his actions. A striking example is when Abraham appeals to God for the city of Sodom. In Genesis 18:17–33, God responds to Abraham's intercession by reducing the number of righteous people required to spare Sodom and Gomorrah from fifty to ten! The entire passage resonates with the passionate requests of a sincere man and the compassionate response of a holy God. Abraham is not timid, and God is not put off by his prayer.

Psalm 5:1–3, Jeremiah 12:1–13, John 17, and Acts 12:6–17 show us that genuine, honest conversation takes place in prayer. God truly hears and responds. Prayer is influential. We may not always know how precisely that is so, but are told enough to know that prayer is real two-way talk between ourselves and God.

The most compelling case for the value and power of prayer is Christ himself. Jesus prayed. He prayed often and about many things. Prayer was the "lifeline" between himself and the heavenly Father. From prayer he received inspiration, guidance, and strength. His teaching and example served to encourage others to pray. From Christ, we learn that the most important proof of prayer's value is *not* whether or not it "works," but whether or not it keeps us in touch with God, whose grace can sustain us though both good and bad times. If we limit prayer to "getting answers," we will lose sight of its grandeur, and we will make it more akin to magic than true communion with the living God.

Paul demonstrates this as powerfully as anyone in the Bible. In 2 Corinthians 12:7–9, he prayed three times that his "painful physical problem" would be taken away. But the problem remained. In response to his request God replied, "My grace is enough for you." There's no indication that Paul thought any less of God or prayer because of his experience. Through his example we learn that prayer is much more about receiving grace than it is about getting positive answers.

As the importance of prayer grows in our lives, we will see why the disciples asked Jesus to teach them to pray. Jesus responded with the specific model of the Lord's Prayer here in Luke (11:1–14) and again in Matthew 6 (6:5–15). Through an economy of words we are shown the basic elements of prayer. We can take each phrase in the Lord's Prayer and expand it into a wide range of expressions.

Prayer: For additional scriptures on this topic go to Genesis 4:26.

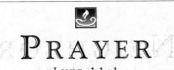

me in the place where I have chosen to be worshiped. 16But now you have changed your minds. You have shown you do not honor me. Each of you has taken back the male and female slaves you had set free, and you have forced them to become your slaves again.

17"So this is what the LORD says: You have not obeyed me. You have not given freedom to your fellow Hebrews, neither relatives nor friends. But now I will give freedom, says the LORD, to war, to terrible diseases, and to hunger. I will make you hated by all the kingdoms of the earth. 18I will hand over the men who broke my agreement, who have not kept the promises they made before me. They cut a calf into two pieces before me and walked between the pieces. 19These people made the agreement before me by walking between the pieces of the calf: the leaders of Judah and Jerusalem, the officers of the court, the priests, and all the people of the land. 20So I will hand them over to their enemies and to everyone who wants to kill them. Their bodies will become food for the birds of the air and for the wild animals of the earth. 21I will hand Zedekiah king of Judah and his officers over to their enemies, and to everyone who wants to kill them, and to the army of the king of Babylon, even though they have left Jerusalem. 22I will give the order, says the LORD, to bring the Babylonian army back to Jerusalem. It will fight against Jerusalem, capture it, set it on fire, and burn it down. I will destroy the towns in Judah so that they become ruins where no one lives!"

The Recabite Family Obeys God

35 When Jehoiakim son of Josiah was king of Judah, the LORD spoke his word to Jeremiah, saying:2 "Go to the family of Recab. Invite them to come to one of the side rooms of the Temple of the LORD, and offer them wine to drink."

3So I went to get Jaazaniah son of Jeremiah, the son of Habazziniah. And I gathered all of Jaazaniah's brothers and sons and the whole family of the Recabites together. 4Then I brought them into the Temple of the LORD. We went into the room of the sons of Hanan son of Igdaliah, who was a man of God. The room was next to the one where the officers stay and above the room of Maaseiah son of Shallum, the doorkeeper in the Temple. 5Then I put some bowls full of wine and some cups before the men of the Recabite family. And I said to them, "Drink some wine."

6But the Recabite men answered, "We never drink wine. Our ancestor Jonadab son of Recab gave us this command: 'You and your descendants must never drink wine. 7Also you must never build houses, plant seeds, or plant vineyards, or do any of those things. You must live only in tents. Then you will live a long time in the land where you are wanderers.' 8So we Recabites have obeyed everything Jonadab our ancestor commanded us. Neither we nor our wives, sons, or daughters ever drink wine. 9We never build houses in which to live, or own fields or vineyards, or plant crops. 10We have lived in tents and have obeyed everything our ancestor Jonadab commanded us. 11But when Nebuchadnezzar king of Babylon attacked Judah, we said to each other, 'Come, we must enter Jerusalem so we can escape the Babylonian army and the Aramean army.' So we have stayed in Jerusalem."

12Then the LORD spoke his word to Jeremiah: 13"This is what the LORD All-Powerful, the God of Israel, says: Jeremiah, go and tell the men of Judah and the people of Jerusalem: 'You should learn a lesson and obey my message,' says the LORD. 14'Jonadab son of Recab ordered his descendants not to drink wine, and that command has been obeyed. Until today they have obeyed their ancestor's command; they do not drink wine. But I, the LORD, have given you messages again and again, but you did not obey me. 15I sent all my servants the prophets to you again and again, saying, "Each of you must stop doing evil. You must change and be good. Do not follow other gods to serve them. If you obey me, you will live in the land I have given to you and your ancestors." But you have not listened to me or paid attention to my message. 16The descendants of Jonadab son of Recab obeyed the commands their ancestor gave them, but the people of Judah have not obeyed me.'

17"So the LORD God All-Powerful, the God of Israel, says: 'I will soon bring every disaster I said would come to Judah and to everyone living in Jerusalem. I spoke to those people, but they refused to listen. I called out to them, but they did not answer me.' "

18Then Jeremiah said to the Recabites, "This is what the LORD All-Powerful, the God of Israel, says: 'You have obeyed the commands of your ancestor Jonadab and have followed all of his teachings; you have done everything he commanded.' 19So this is what the LORD All-Powerful, the God of Israel, says: 'There will always be a descendant of Jonadab son of Recab to serve me.' "

34:18 *They . . . pieces.* This showed that the men were willing to be killed, like this animal, if they did not keep their agreement.

35:3 *Jeremiah.* Not the prophet Jeremiah, but a different man with the same name..

35:6 *Recabite men.* We know little about the Recabites except what is said here and in 2 Kings 10:15–23. Their vows sound similar to those taken by Nazirites (Numbers 6:1–21), but not exactly. The emphasis in this passage is on their faithfulness to their vows.

Jehoiakim Burns Jeremiah's Scroll

36 The LORD spoke this word to Jeremiah during the fourth year that Jehoiakim son of Josiah was king of Judah: 2"Get a scroll. Write on it all the words I have spoken to you about Israel and Judah and all the nations. Write everything from when I first spoke to you, when Josiah was king, until now. 3Maybe the family of Judah will hear what disasters I am planning to bring on them and will stop doing wicked things. Then I would forgive them for the sins and the evil things they have done."

4So Jeremiah called for Baruch son of Neriah. Jeremiah spoke the messages the LORD had given him, and Baruch wrote those messages on the scroll. 5Then Jeremiah commanded Baruch, "I cannot go to the Temple of the LORD. I must stay here. 6So I want you to go to the Temple of the LORD on a day when the people are giving up eating. Read from the scroll to all the people of Judah who come into Jerusalem from their towns. Read the messages from the LORD, which are the words you wrote on the scroll as I spoke them to you. 7Perhaps they will ask the LORD to help them. Perhaps each one will stop doing wicked things, because the LORD has announced that he is very angry with them." 8So Baruch son of Neriah did everything Jeremiah the prophet told him to do. In the LORD's Temple he read aloud the scroll that had the LORD's messages written on it.

9In the ninth month of the fifth year that Jehoiakim son of Josiah was king, a special time to give up eating was announced. All the people of Jerusalem and everyone who had come into Jerusalem from the towns of Judah were supposed to give up eating to honor the LORD. 10At that time Baruch read to all the people there the scroll containing Jeremiah's words. He read the scroll in the Temple of the LORD in the room of Gemariah son of Shaphan, a royal secretary. That room was in the upper courtyard at the entrance of the New Gate of the Temple.

11Micaiah son of Gemariah, the son of Shaphan, heard all the messages from the LORD that were on the scroll. 12Micaiah went down to the royal secretary's room in the king's palace where all of the officers were sitting: Elishama the royal secretary; Delaiah son of Shemaiah; Elnathan son of Acbor; Gemariah son of Shaphan; Zedekiah son of Hananiah; and all the other officers. 13Micaiah told those officers everything he had heard Baruch read to the people from the scroll.

14Then the officers sent a man named Jehudi son of Nethaniah to Baruch. (Nethaniah was the son of Shelemiah, who was the son of Cushi.) Jehudi said to Baruch, "Bring the scroll that you read to the people and come with me."

So Baruch son of Neriah took the scroll and went with Jehudi to the officers. 15Then the officers said to Baruch, "Please sit down and read the scroll to us."

So Baruch read the scroll to them. 16When the officers heard all the words, they became afraid and looked at each other. They said to Baruch, "We must certainly tell the king about these words." 17Then the officers asked Baruch, "Tell us, please, where did you get all these words you wrote on the scroll? Did you write down what Jeremiah said to you?"

18"Yes," Baruch answered. "Jeremiah spoke them all to me, and I wrote them down with ink on this scroll."

19Then the officers said to Baruch, "You and Jeremiah must go and hide, and don't tell anyone where you are."

20The officers put the scroll in the room of Elishama the royal secretary. Then they went to the king in the courtyard and told him all about the scroll. 21So King Jehoiakim sent Jehudi to get the scroll. Jehudi brought the scroll from the room of Elishama the royal secretary and read it to the king and to all the officers who stood around the king. 22It was the ninth month of the year, so King Jehoiakim was sitting in the winter apartment. There was a fire burning in a small firepot in front of him. 23After Jehudi had read three or four columns, the king cut those columns off of the scroll with a penknife and threw them into the firepot. Finally, the whole scroll was burned in the fire. 24King Jehoiakim and his servants heard everything that was said, but they were not frightened! They did not tear their clothes to show their sorrow. 25Elnathan, Delaiah, and Gemariah even tried to talk King Jehoiakim out of burning the scroll, but he would not listen to them. 26Instead, the king ordered Jerahmeel son of the king, Seraiah son of Azriel, and Shelemiah son of Abdeel to arrest Baruch the secretary and Jeremiah the prophet. But the LORD had hidden them.

27So King Jehoiakim burned the scroll where Baruch had written all the words Jeremiah had spoken to him. Then the LORD spoke his word to Jeremiah: 28"Get another scroll. Write all the words on it that were on the first scroll that Jehoiakim

36:9 Fasting: Isaiah 58:1–9

king of Judah burned up. 29Also say this to Jehoiakim king of Judah: 'This is what the LORD says:
You burned up that scroll and said, "Why, Jeremiah, did you write on it 'the king of Babylon will
surely come and destroy this land and the people
and animals in it'?" 30So this is what the LORD
says about Jehoiakim king of Judah: Jehoiakim's
descendants will not sit on David's throne. When
Jehoiakim dies, his body will be thrown out on
the ground. It will be left out in the heat of the
day and in the cold frost of the night. 31I will punish Jehoiakim and his children and his servants,
because they have done evil things. I will bring
disasters upon them and upon all the people in
Jerusalem and Judah—everything I promised but
which they refused to hear.' "
32So Jeremiah took another scroll and gave it to
Baruch son of Neriah, his secretary. As Jeremiah
spoke, Baruch wrote on the scroll the same words
that were on the scroll Jehoiakim king of Judah
had burned in the fire. And many similar words
were added to the second scroll.

Jeremiah in Prison

37 Nebuchadnezzar king of Babylon had
appointed Zedekiah son of Josiah to be
king of Judah. Zedekiah took the place of Jehoiachin son of Jehoiakim. 2But Zedekiah, his servants, and the people of Judah did not listen to the
words the LORD had spoken through Jeremiah the
prophet.
3Now King Zedekiah sent Jehucal son of Shelemiah and the priest Zephaniah son of Maaseiah
with a message to Jeremiah the prophet. This was
the message: "Jeremiah, please pray to the LORD
our God for us."
4At that time Jeremiah had not yet been put
into prison. So he was free to go anywhere he
wanted. 5The army of the king of Egypt had
marched from Egypt toward Judah. Now the
Babylonian army had surrounded the city of Jerusalem. When they heard about the Egyptian army
marching toward them, the Babylonian army left
Jerusalem.
6The LORD spoke his word to Jeremiah the
prophet:7"This is what the LORD, the God of
Israel, says: Jehucal and Zephaniah, I know
Zedekiah king of Judah sent you to seek my help.
Tell this to King Zedekiah: 'The army of the king
of Egypt came here to help you, but they will go
back to Egypt. 8After that, the Babylonian army
will return and attack Jerusalem and capture it
and burn it down.'
9"This is what the LORD says: People of Jerusalem, do not fool yourselves. Don't say, 'The
Babylonian army will surely leave us alone.' They
will not! 10Even if you defeated all of the Babylonian army that is attacking you and there were only
a few injured men left in their tents, they would
come from their tents and burn down Jerusalem!"
11So the Babylonian army left Jerusalem to fight
the army of the king of Egypt. 12Now Jeremiah
tried to travel from Jerusalem to the land of Benjamin to get his share of the property that
belonged to his family. 13When Jeremiah got to
the Benjamin Gate of Jerusalem, the captain in
charge of the guards arrested him. The captain's
name was Irijah son of Shelemiah son of
Hananiah. Irijah said, "You are leaving us to join
the Babylonians!"
14But Jeremiah said to Irijah, "That's not true! I
am not leaving to join the Babylonians." Irijah
refused to listen to Jeremiah, so he arrested
Jeremiah and took him to the officers of
Jerusalem. 15Those rulers were very angry with
Jeremiah and beat him. Then they put him in jail
in the house of Jonathan the royal secretary,
which had been made into a prison. 16So those
people put Jeremiah into a cell in a dungeon, and
Jeremiah was there for a long time.
17Then King Zedekiah sent for Jeremiah and had
him brought to the palace. Zedekiah asked him in
private, "Is there any message from the LORD?"
Jeremiah answered, "Yes, there is. Zedekiah,
you will be handed over to the king of Babylon."
18Then Jeremiah said to King Zedekiah, "What
crime have I done against you or your officers or
the people of Jerusalem? Why have you thrown
me into prison? 19Where are your prophets that
prophesied this message to you: 'The king of
Babylon will not attack you or this land of Judah?'
20But now, my master, king of Judah, please listen
to me, and please do what I ask of you. Do not
send me back to the house of Jonathan the royal
secretary, or I will die there!"
21So King Zedekiah gave orders for Jeremiah to be
put under guard in the courtyard of the guard and to
be given bread each day from the street of the bak-
ers until there was no more bread in the city. So he
stayed under guard in the courtyard of the guard.

Jeremiah Is Thrown into a Well

38 Shephatiah son of Mattan, Gedaliah son
of Pashhur, Jehucal son of Shelemiah, and
Pashhur son of Malkijah heard what Jeremiah was
telling all the people. He said:2 "This is what the

36:30 *body . . . ground.* See 8:2.

LORD says: 'Everyone who stays in Jerusalem will
die from war, or hunger, or terrible diseases. But
everyone who surrenders to the Babylonian army
will live; they will escape with their lives and
live.' 3And this is what the LORD says: 'This city of
Jerusalem will surely be handed over to the army
of the king of Babylon. He will capture this city!' "
4Then the officers said to the king, "Jeremiah
must be put to death! He is discouraging the soldiers who are still in the city, and all the people,
by what he is saying to them. He does not want
good to happen to us; he wants to ruin us."
5King Zedekiah said to them, "Jeremiah is in
your control. I cannot do anything to stop you."
6So the officers took Jeremiah and put him into
the well of Malkijah, the king's son, which was in
the courtyard of the guards. The officers used ropes
to lower Jeremiah into the well, which did not have
any water in it, only mud. And Jeremiah sank
down into the mud.
7But Ebed-Melech, a Cushite and a servant in
the palace, heard that the officers had put
Jeremiah into the well. As King Zedekiah was sitting at the Benjamin Gate, 8Ebed-Melech left the
palace and went to the king. Ebed-Melech said to
him, 9"My master and king, these rulers have
acted in an evil way. They have treated Jeremiah
the prophet badly. They have thrown him into a
well and left him there to die! When there is no
more bread in the city, he will starve to death."
10Then King Zedekiah commanded Ebed-Melech
the Cushite, "Take thirty men from the palace and
lift Jeremiah the prophet out of the well before he
dies."
11So Ebed-Melech took the men with him and
went to a room under the storeroom in the palace.
He took some old rags and worn-out clothes from
that room. Then he let those rags down with some
ropes to Jeremiah in the well. 12Ebed-Melech the
Cushite said to Jeremiah, "Put these old rags and
worn-out clothes under your arms to be pads for
the ropes." So Jeremiah did as Ebed-Melech said.
13The men pulled Jeremiah up with the ropes and
lifted him out of the well. And Jeremiah stayed
under guard in the courtyard of the guard.

Zedekiah Questions Jeremiah

14Then King Zedekiah sent someone to get
Jeremiah the prophet and bring him to the third
entrance to the Temple of the LORD. The king said
to Jeremiah, "I am going to ask you something.
Do not hide anything from me, but tell me everything honestly."
15Jeremiah said to Zedekiah, "If I give you an
answer, you will surely kill me. And even if I give
you advice, you will not listen to me."
16But King Zedekiah made a secret promise to
Jeremiah, "As surely as the LORD lives who has
given us breath and life, I will not kill you. And I
promise not to hand you over to the officers who
want to kill you."
17Then Jeremiah said to Zedekiah, "This is
what the LORD God All-Powerful, the God of
Israel, says: 'If you surrender to the officers of the
king of Babylon, your life will be saved. Jerusalem
will not be burned down, and you and your family will live. 18But if you refuse to surrender to the
officers of the king of Babylon, Jerusalem will be
handed over to the Babylonian army, and they
will burn it down. And you yourself will not
escape from them.' "
19Then King Zedekiah said to Jeremiah, "I'm
afraid of some Jews who have already gone over to
the side of the Babylonian army. If the
Babylonians hand me over to them, they will treat
me badly."
20But Jeremiah answered, "The Babylonians
will not hand you over to the Jews. Obey the LORD
by doing what I tell you. Then things will go well
for you, and your life will be saved. 21But if you
refuse to surrender to the Babylonians, the LORD
has shown me what will happen. 22All the women
left in the palace of the king of Judah will be
brought out and taken to the important officers of
the king of Babylon. Your women will make fun of
you with this song:

'Your good friends misled you
and were stronger than you.
While your feet were stuck in the mud,
they left you.'

23"All your wives and children will be brought
out and given to the Babylonian army. You yourself will not even escape from them. You will be
taken prisoner by the king of Babylon, and Jerusalem will be burned down."
24Then Zedekiah said to Jeremiah, "Do not tell
anyone that I have been talking to you, or you will
die. 25If the officers find out I talked to you, they will
come to you and say, 'Tell us what you said to King
Zedekiah and what he said to you. Don't keep any
secrets from us. If you don't tell us everything, we
will kill you.' 26If they ask you, tell them, 'I was begging the king not to send me back to Jonathan's
house to die.' "
27All the officers did come to question Jeremiah.
So he told them everything the king had ordered

38:7 *Cushite.* See 13:23.

him to say. Then the officers said no more to Jeremiah, because no one had heard what Jeremiah and the king had discussed.

28So Jeremiah stayed under guard in the courtyard of the guard until the day Jerusalem was captured.

The Fall of Jerusalem

39 This is how Jerusalem was captured: Nebuchadnezzar king of Babylon marched against Jerusalem with his whole army and surrounded the city to attack it. This was during the tenth month of the ninth year Zedekiah was king of Judah. 2This lasted until the ninth day of the fourth month in Zedekiah's eleventh year. Then the city wall was broken through. 3And all these officers of the king of Babylon came into Jerusalem and sat down at the Middle Gate: Nergal-Sharezer of the district of Samgar; Nebo-Sarsekim, a chief officer; Nergal-Sharezer, an important leader; and all the other important officers.

4When Zedekiah king of Judah and all his soldiers saw them, they ran away. They left Jerusalem at night and went out from the king's garden. They went through the gate that was between the two walls and then headed toward the Jordan Valley. 5But the Babylonian army chased them and caught up with Zedekiah in the plains of Jericho. They captured him and took him to Nebuchadnezzar king of Babylon, who was at the town of Riblah in the land of Hamath. There Nebuchadnezzar passed his sentence on Zedekiah. 6At Riblah the king of Babylon killed Zedekiah's sons and all the important officers of Judah as Zedekiah watched. 7Then he put out Zedekiah's eyes. He put bronze chains on Zedekiah and took him to Babylon.

8The Babylonians set fire to the palace and to the houses of the people, and they broke down the walls around Jerusalem. 9Nebuzaradan, commander of the king's special guards, took the people left in Jerusalem, those captives who had surrendered to him earlier, and the rest of the people of Jerusalem, and he took them all away to Babylon. 10But Nebuzaradan, commander of the guard, left some of the poorest people of Judah behind. They owned nothing, but that day he gave them vineyards and fields.

11Nebuchadnezzar king of Babylon had given these orders about Jeremiah through Nebuzaradan, commander of the guard: 12"Find Jeremiah and take care of him. Do not hurt him, but do for him whatever he asks you." 13So Nebuchadnezzar sent these men for Jeremiah: Nebuzaradan, commander of the guards; Nebushazban, a chief officer; Nergal-Sharezer, an important leader; and all the other officers of the king of Babylon. 14They had Jeremiah taken out of the courtyard of the guard. Then they turned him over to Gedaliah son of Ahikam son of Shaphan, who had orders to take Jeremiah back home. So they took him home, and he stayed among the people left in Judah.

15While Jeremiah was guarded in the courtyard, the LORD spoke his word to him: 16"Jeremiah, go and tell Ebed-Melech the Cushite this message: 'This is what the LORD All-Powerful, the God of Israel, says: Very soon I will make my words about Jerusalem come true through disaster, not through good times. You will see everything come true with your own eyes. 17But I will save you on that day, Ebed-Melech, says the LORD. You will not be handed over to the people you fear. 18I will surely save you, Ebed-Melech. You will not die from a sword, but you will escape and live. This will happen because you have trusted in me, says the LORD.'"

Jeremiah Is Set Free

40 The LORD spoke his word to Jeremiah after Nebuzaradan, commander of the guards, had set Jeremiah free at the city of Ramah. He had found Jeremiah in Ramah bound in chains with all the captives from Jerusalem and Judah who were being taken away to Babylon. 2When commander Nebuzaradan found Jeremiah, Nebuzaradan said to him, "The LORD your God announced this disaster would come to this place. 3And now the LORD has done everything he said he would do. This disaster happened because the people of Judah sinned against the LORD and did not obey him. 4But today I am freeing you from the chains on your wrists. If you want to, come with me to Babylon, and I will take good care of you. But if you don't want to come, then don't. Look, the whole country is open to you. Go wherever you wish." 5Before Jeremiah turned to leave, Nebuzaradan said, "Or go back to Gedaliah son of Ahikam, the son of Shaphan. The king of Babylon has chosen him to be governor over the towns of Judah. Go and live with Gedaliah among the people, or go anywhere you want."

Then Nebuzaradan gave Jeremiah some food and a present and let him go. 6So Jeremiah went to Gedaliah son of Ahikam at Mizpah and stayed with him there. He lived among the people who were left behind in Judah.

39:12 The Babylonian's positive attitude toward Jeremiah may be explained by the fact that Jeremiah's prophetic message encouraged Judah to surrender to him. Of course, Jeremiah was following God's lead here. He was not trying to win Babylonian favor.

The Short Rule of Gedaliah

7Some officers and their men from the army of
Judah were still out in the open country. They
heard that the king of Babylon had put Gedaliah
son of Ahikam in charge of the people who were
left in the land: the men, women, and children
who were the poorest. They were the ones who
were not taken to Babylon as captives. 8So these
soldiers came to Gedaliah at Mizpah: Ishmael son
of Nethaniah, Johanan and Jonathan sons of
Kareah, Seraiah son of Tanhumeth, the sons of
Ephai the Netophathite, Jaazaniah son of the
Maacathite, and their men.

9Gedaliah son of Ahikam, the son of Shaphan,
made a promise to them, saying, "Do not be
afraid to serve the Babylonians. Stay in the land
and serve the king of Babylon. Then everything
will go well for you. 10I myself will live in Mizpah
and will speak for you before the Babylonians
who come to us here. Harvest the wine, the summer fruit, and the oil, and put what you harvest in
your storage jars. Live in the towns you control."

11The Jews in Moab, Ammon, Edom, and
other countries also heard that the king of Babylon had left a few Jews alive in the land. And
they heard the king of Babylon had chosen
Gedaliah as governor over them. (Gedaliah was
the son of Ahikam, the son of Shaphan.) 12When
the people of Judah heard this news, they came
back to Judah from all the countries where they
had been scattered. They came to Gedaliah at
Mizpah and gathered a large harvest of wine and
summer fruit.

13Johanan son of Kareah and all the army officers
of Judah still in the open country came to Gedaliah
at Mizpah. 14They said to him, "Don't you know that
Baalis king of the Ammonite people wants you dead?
He has sent Ishmael son of Nethaniah to kill you."
But Gedaliah son of Ahikam did not believe them.

15Then Johanan son of Kareah spoke to Gedaliah in private at Mizpah. He said, "Let me go
and kill Ishmael son of Nethaniah. No one will
know anything about it. We should not let
Ishmael kill you. Then all the Jews gathered
around you would be scattered to different countries again, and the few people of Judah who are
left alive would be lost."

16But Gedaliah son of Ahikam said to Johanan
son of Kareah, "Do not kill Ishmael! The things
you are saying about Ishmael are not true."

41 In the seventh month Ishmael son of
Nethaniah and ten of his men came to
Gedaliah son of Ahikam at Mizpah. (Nethaniah
was the son of Elishama.) Now Ishmael was a
member of the king's family and had been one
of the officers of the king of Judah. While they
were eating a meal with Gedaliah at Mizpah,
2Ishmael and his ten men got up and killed
Gedaliah son of Ahikam, the son of Shaphan,
with a sword. (Gedaliah was the man the king
of Babylon had chosen as governor over Judah.)
3Ishmael also killed all the Jews and the Babylonian soldiers who were there with Gedaliah
at Mizpah.

4The day after Gedaliah was murdered, before
anyone knew about it, 5eighty men came to
Mizpah bringing grain offerings and incense to the
Temple of the LORD. Those men from Shechem,
Shiloh, and Samaria had shaved off their beards,
torn their clothes, and cut themselves. 6Ishmael
son of Nethaniah went out from Mizpah to meet
them, crying as he walked. When he met them,
he said, "Come with me to meet Gedaliah son of
Ahikam." 7So they went into Mizpah. Then
Ishmael son of Nethaniah and his men killed seventy of them and threw the bodies into a deep
well. 8But the ten men who were left alive said to
Ishmael, "Don't kill us! We have wheat and barley
and oil and honey that we have hidden in a field."
So Ishmael let them live and did not kill them with
the others. 9Now the well where he had thrown
all the bodies had been made by King Asa as a part
of his defenses against Baasha king of Israel. But
Ishmael son of Nethaniah put dead bodies in it
until it was full.

10Ishmael captured all the other people in
Mizpah: the king's daughters and all the other
people who were left there. They were the ones
whom Nebuzaradan commander of the guard had
chosen Gedaliah son of Ahikam to take care of. So
Ishmael son of Nethaniah captured those people,
and he started to cross over to the country of the
Ammonites.

11Johanan son of Kareah and all his army officers with him heard about all the evil things
Ishmael son of Nethaniah had done. 12So they
took their men and went to fight Ishmael son of
Nethaniah and caught him near the big pool of
water at Gibeon. 13When the captives Ishmael
had taken saw Johanan and the army officers,
they were glad. 14So all the people Ishmael had
taken captive from Mizpah turned around and
ran to Johanan son of Kareah. 15But Ishmael son
of Nethaniah and eight of his men escaped from
Johanan and ran away to the Ammonites.

41:5 *shaved . . . themselves.* The men did this to show they were sad about the Temple in Jerusalem being destroyed.

16So Johanan son of Kareah and all his army
officers saved the captives that Ishmael son of
Nethaniah had taken from Mizpah after he murdered Gedaliah son of Ahikam. Among those left
alive were soldiers, women, children, and palace
officers. And Johanan brought them back from
the town of Gibeon.

The Escape to Egypt

17-18Johanan and the other army officers were
afraid of the Babylonians. Since the king of
Babylon had chosen Gedaliah son of Ahikam to be
governor of Judah but Ishmael son of Nethaniah
had murdered him, Johanan was afraid that the
Babylonians would be angry. So they decided to
run away to Egypt. On the way they stayed at
Geruth Kimham, near the town of Bethlehem.

42 While there, Johanan son of Kareah and
Jezaniah son of Hoshaiah went to Jeremiah the prophet. All the army officers and all the
people, from the least important to the greatest,
went along, too. 2They said to him, "Jeremiah,
please listen to what we ask. Pray to the LORD
your God for all the people left alive from the family of Judah. At one time there were many of us,
but you can see that there are few of us now.⚭ 3So
pray that the LORD your God will tell us where we
should go and what we should do."

4Then Jeremiah the prophet answered, "I
understand what you want me to do. I will pray to
the LORD your God as you have asked. I will tell
you everything he says and not hide anything
from you."

5Then the people said to Jeremiah, "May the
LORD be a true and loyal witness against us if we
don't do everything the LORD your God sends you
to tell us. 6It does not matter if we like the message or not. We will obey the LORD our God, to
whom we are sending you. We will obey what he
says so good things will happen to us."

7Ten days later the LORD spoke his word to Jeremiah. 8Then Jeremiah called for Johanan son of
Kareah, the army officers with him, and all the
other people, from the least important to the greatest. 9Jeremiah said to them, "You sent me to ask
the LORD for what you wanted. This is what the
God of Israel says:10'If you will stay in Judah, I will
build you up and not tear you down. I will plant
you and not pull you up, because I am sad about
the disaster I brought on you. 11Now you fear the
king of Babylon, but don't be afraid of him. Don't
be afraid of him,' says the LORD, 'because I am with
you. I will save you and rescue you from his power.
12I will be kind to you, and he will also treat you
with mercy and let you stay in your land.'

13"But if you say, 'We will not stay in Judah,'
you will disobey the LORD your God. 14Or you
might say, 'No, we will go and live in Egypt. There
we will not see war, or hear the trumpets of war,
or be hungry.' 15If you say that, listen to the message of the LORD, you who are left alive from Judah.
This is what the LORD All-Powerful, the God of
Israel, says: 'If you make up your mind to go and
live in Egypt, these things will happen:16You are
afraid of war, but it will find you in the land of
Egypt. And you are worried about hunger, but it
will follow you into Egypt, and you will die there.
17Everyone who goes to live in Egypt will die in
war or from hunger or terrible disease. No one
who goes to Egypt will live; no one will escape
the terrible things I will bring to them.'

18"This is what the LORD All-Powerful, the God of
Israel, says: 'I showed my anger against the people
of Jerusalem. In the same way I will show my anger
against you when you go to Egypt. Other nations
will speak evil of you. People will be shocked by
what will happen to you. You will become a curse
word, and people will insult you. And you will
never see Judah again.'

19"You who are left alive in Judah, the LORD has
told you, 'Don't go to Egypt.' Be sure you understand this; I warn you today 20that you are making
a mistake that will cause your deaths. You sent
me to the LORD your God, saying, 'Pray to the
LORD our God for us. Tell us everything the LORD
our God says, and we will do it.' 21So today I have
told you, but you have not obeyed the LORD your
God in all that he sent me to tell you. 22So now be
sure you understand this: You want to go to live
in Egypt, but you will die there by war, hunger,
or terrible diseases."

43 So Jeremiah finished telling the people
the message from the LORD their God; he
told them everything the LORD their God had sent
him to tell them.

2Azariah son of Hoshaiah, Johanan son of
Kareah, and some other men were too proud.
They said to Jeremiah, "You are lying! The LORD
our God did not send you to say, 'You must not go
to Egypt to live there.' 3Baruch son of Neriah is
causing you to be against us. He wants you to
hand us over to the Babylonians so they can kill
us or capture us and take us to Babylon."

42:1–6 Here is a representative example of prophetic intercession. In response to the plea of the people, Jeremiah promises to pray and to tell everything he hears from God. Elsewhere, the prophets cry out on behalf of the people, even when Israel or Judah does not ask for it, but rather persists in sin and rebellion.

⚭**42:2 The Remnant:** Amos 5:15

4So Johanan, the army officers, and all the people disobeyed the LORD's command to stay in Judah. 5But Johanan son of Kareah and the army officers led away those who were left alive from Judah. They were the people who had run away from the Babylonians to other countries but then had come back to live in Judah. 6They led away the men, women, and children, and the king's daughters. Nebuzaradan commander of the guard had put Gedaliah son of Ahikam son of Shaphan in charge of those people. Johanan also took Jeremiah the prophet and Baruch son of Neriah. 7These people did not listen to the LORD. So they all went to Egypt to the city of Tahpanhes.

8In Tahpanhes the LORD spoke his word to Jeremiah: 9"Take some large stones. Bury them in the clay in the brick pavement in front of the king of Egypt's palace in Tahpanhes. Do this while the Jews are watching you. 10Then say to them, 'This is what the LORD All-Powerful, the God of Israel, says: I will soon send for my servant, Nebuchadnezzar king of Babylon. I will set his throne over these stones I have buried, and he will spread his covering for shade above them. 11He will come here and attack Egypt. He will bring death to those who are supposed to die. He will make prisoners of those who are to be taken captive, and he will bring war to those who are to be killed with a sword. 12Nebuchadnezzar will set fire to the temples of the gods of Egypt and burn them. And he will take the idols away as captives. As a shepherd wraps himself in his clothes, so Nebuchadnezzar will wrap Egypt around him. Then he will safely leave Egypt. 13He will destroy the stone pillars in the temple of the sun god in Egypt, and he will burn down the temples of the gods of Egypt.' "

Disaster in Egypt

44 Jeremiah received a message from the LORD for all the Jews living in Egypt—in the cities of Migdol, Tahpanhes, Memphis, and in southern Egypt. This was the message: 2"The LORD All-Powerful, the God of Israel, says: You saw all the terrible things I brought on Jerusalem and the towns of Judah, which are ruins today with no one living in them. 3It is because the people who lived there did evil. They made me angry by burning incense and worshiping other gods that neither they nor you nor your ancestors ever knew. 4I sent all my servants, the prophets, to you again and again. By them I said to you, 'Don't do this terrible thing that I hate.' 5But they did not listen or pay attention. They did not stop doing evil things and burning incense to other gods. 6So I showed my great anger against them. I poured out my anger in the towns of Judah and the streets of Jerusalem so they are only ruins and piles of stones today.

7"Now the LORD All-Powerful, the God of Israel, says: Why are you doing such great harm to yourselves? You are cutting off the men and women, children and babies from the family of Judah, leaving yourselves without anyone from the family of Judah. 8Why do you want to make me angry by making idols? Why do you burn incense to the gods of Egypt, where you have come to live? You will destroy yourselves. Other nations will speak evil of you and make fun of you. 9Have you forgotten about the evil things your ancestors did? And have you forgotten the evil the kings and queens of Judah did? Have you forgotten about the evil you and your wives did? These things were done in the country of Judah and in the streets of Jerusalem. 10Even to this day the people of Judah are still too proud. They have not learned to respect me or to follow my teachings. They have not obeyed the laws I gave you and your ancestors.

11"So this is what the LORD All-Powerful, the God of Israel, says: I am determined to bring disasters on you. I will destroy the whole family of Judah. 12The few who were left alive from Judah were determined to go to Egypt and settle there, but they will all die in Egypt. They will be killed in war or die from hunger. From the least important to the greatest, they will be killed in war or die from hunger. Other nations will speak evil about them. People will be shocked by what has happened to them. They will become a curse word, and people will insult them. 13I will punish those people who have gone to live in Egypt, just as I punished Jerusalem, using swords, hunger, and terrible diseases. 14Of the people of Judah who were left alive and have gone to live in Egypt, none will escape my punishment. They want to return to Judah and live there, but none of them will live to return to Judah, except a few people who will escape."

15A large group of the people of Judah who lived in southern Egypt were meeting together. Among them were many women of Judah who were burning incense to other gods, and their husbands knew it. All these people said to Jeremiah, 16"We will not listen to the message from the LORD that you spoke to us. 17We promised to make sacrifices to the Queen Goddess, and we will certainly do everything we promised. We will burn incense and pour out drink offerings to worship her, just as we, our ancestors, kings, and officers did in the past. All of us did these things in the towns of

GREED

LUKE 12:15

What is wrong with wanting money? What happens to the greedy?

Greed is one of the most often-talked-about evils in the Bible. What exactly is greed, why is it so wrong, and what happens to those who are greedy?

Greed is excessive desire to possess more than what one truly needs or more than what others may have. It is clear in the Bible that greed is something that is inside a person, it is an inner attitude. Jesus included greed when he said, "All these evil things come from inside and make people unclean" (Mark 7:23). Criticizing the Pharisees of his day, he remarked, "Inside you are full of greed and evil" (Luke 11:39). Since greed is an inner desire and feeling, no one is free from its temptation. It is not only the rich but the poor who can be greedy (see the parable of the unforgiving servant in Matthew 18:21–35). All of us have at one time or another taken more than we should have. Greed, however, is not only taking but keeping (see the parable of the rich fool, Luke 12:13–21). Often greed is the wanting of money in particular (so translated in 1 Peter 5:2) and not simply of possessions in general.

So what is wrong with wanting money? It is not the wanting of money or possessions which is wrong; it is the *excessive* wanting of these things which is wrong. The Bible acknowledges that humankind has genuine needs (Matthew 6:32; Proverbs 10:15), but these must be kept in balance in a life lived before God. "A person does not live by eating only bread, but by everything God says" (Matthew 4:4). The term "excess," however, is a relative term. What may be excess in one culture or situation may be genuine need in another. How does one know if one is "greedy?"

One way is to ask whether our actions do injury, harm, or wrong to other persons. Do we "try to get rich by cheating others" (1 Timothy 3:8). Have we withheld wages from workers which are due them (James 5:4)? Do we cause unnecessary trouble around us (Proverbs 15:27) or bring trouble upon our families (Proverbs 28:25) because of greed? Unfortunately, some of the most greedy are found among those who profess to be religious, false prophets, and the Pharisees: "Those false teachers only want your money" (2 Peter 2:3). Taking advantage of weak people, false prophets lead others astray, even teaching them to be greedy (2 Peter 2:14). They are compared to the prophet Balaam in the Old Testament who "loved being paid for doing wrong" (2 Peter 2:15). Indeed, the greedy can be said to be those persons who will accept pay for doing wrong (Proverbs 15:27).

Although the Bible is concerned with the impact of greed upon human-to-human relationships, it is the impact upon the divine-and-human relationship which is of greatest concern. Greed and unhealthy desire interfere with our relationship to God, and this is the greatest evil. Greed is, in fact, idolatry (Colossians 3:5). Jesus said, "You cannot serve both God and worldly riches" (Matthew 6:24). "It is easier for a camel to go through the eye of a needle than for a rich person to enter the kingdom of God" (Luke 18:25). As human beings, we will always want more (Proverbs 28:25); the issue is whether money and possessions are more important to us than God. There is nothing wrong with having possessions as long as they do not possess us.

It is our attitude toward money and possessions which marks us as either a believer or a worldly person. Jesus said it is those who do not know God who keep running after these things (Matthew 6:32–33). The opposite of the greedy person is the one who trusts in God (Proverbs 28:25). Like David, our prayer should be, "Everything in heaven and on earth belongs to you. . . . Riches and honor come from you" (1 Chronicles 29:11–12). Like Paul, believers need to learn the secret of contentment: "I have learned the secret of being happy at any time in everything that happens, when I have enough to eat and when I go hungry, when I have more than I need and when I do not have enough" (Philippians 4:12). This does not mean that we should not work and work hard for a living (2 Thessalonians 3:10; Proverbs 14:23; 31:17). It means that we should seek first God's kingdom and what he wants us to do (Matthew 6:32–33). "Honor the LORD with your wealth" (Proverbs 3:9). It is not "money" which is the root of all evil, but the "love" of money (1 Timothy 6:10).

What happens to the greedy? The Bible is clear that the greedy will have no part or inheritance in the kingdom of God (1 Corinthians 6:9–10, Ephesians 5:5).

The Bible exhorts Christians to "Keep your lives free from the love of money, and be satisfied with what you have" (Hebrews 13:5). When it comes to the subject of believers and money, John Wesley, an eighteenth-century revivalist preacher, probably said it best: "Earn as much as you can, save as much as you can, give as much as you can!"

Greed: For additional scriptures on this topic go to Deuteronomy 5:21.

Physical Handicap

LUKE 14

How are persons with physical handicaps looked upon in the Scriptures? What is the Good News for such persons?

For persons living with physical handicaps at the time the Bible was written, the difficulties resulting from their physical limitations were not their greatest problem. It was the way they were treated by the rest of society that caused them the most suffering.

People believed that blindness, deafness, paralysis, various skin diseases, misformed limbs, and other physical handicaps were the result of sin or the presence of an evil spirit. Many of the physical conditions considered "abnormal" made a person "unclean" in the eyes of their communities. An unclean person was not accepted and was not allowed to participate fully in social and spiritual life.

While it was forbidden to purposefully harm a person with a physical handicap (Leviticus 19:14), laws in the Old Testament required that handicapped people be excluded from the community. In Leviticus 21:16–23, Moses commands that if any descendants of Aaron "have something wrong with them," they must be excluded from participation in the rituals for fear they might contaminate the holy places. Leviticus 21:18–20 gives an extensive list of conditions for which they might be excluded: "Anyone who has something wrong with him must not come near: blind men, crippled men, men with damaged faces, deformed men, men with a crippled foot or hand, hunchbacks, dwarfs, men who have something wrong with their eyes, men who have an itching disease or a skin disease, or men who have damaged sex glands." The physically handicapped were also not allowed to enter the palace in Jerusalem (2 Samuel 5:8). If a person had a skin disease and was declared unclean by a priest, they, "must live alone outside the camp" (Leviticus 13:46). No one was allowed to go near them, and they had to shout, "unclean, unclean," to warn people to stay away (Leviticus 13:45). There were also laws that said that God would punish people who disobeyed him by afflicting them with physical handicaps and diseases (Deuteronomy 28:27–29).

These laws were used to exclude people from the community. Jesus defined his mission as one of including the people society had excluded and making clean those people the community considered unclean (Luke 4:18–19). Jesus separated a person's physical handicap from their sinfulness. In John 9, when Jesus and his followers meet a blind man, they ask Jesus if the man is blind because of his sin or his parents' sin. Jesus says, "It is not this man's sin or his parents' sin that made him be blind. This man was born blind so that God's power could be shown in him." In Luke 5:17–26, a paralyzed man is brought before Jesus to be healed. Jesus forgives his sin first and then heals the man's paralysis.

The Gospels make it clear that Jesus did not see a physical handicap as a reason for a person to be separated from the community. In Luke 14, Jesus is eating at the house of a Pharisee on the Sabbath. It was very important to the Pharisees to obey closely the Old Testament laws, especially the laws dealing with what is "clean" and "unclean," and the Sabbath laws. Most of the conflicts Jesus had with the Pharisees were over these laws. In this story, the Pharisees allowed a handicapped man to come into the house where they were eating to see if Jesus would heal him. Jesus had healed other people on the Sabbath who were physically handicapped (Luke 4:31; 6:1–51; Matthew 12:9–14; Mark 3:1–6; Luke 3:10), and the Pharisees thought that this was disobeying the fourth commandment. Jesus healed the man, explaining that it is better to do good on the Sabbath than evil.

In verses 7–11 of Luke 14, the dinner guests are trying to sit in the best seats. Jesus uses this situation to explain that God does not think the same things are important that they do, that acting like you are better than someone else makes you look silly. Everyone is the same in the eyes of God. Giving someone else the more important place, on the other hand, will be seen as an humble act. Jesus applies this idea to the way people treat the physically handicapped. In Luke 14:12–14, he points out that inviting only your friends to a meal at your house is not an act of kindness. It is to the host's benefit because then his friends owe him a favor. It is better to invite people who cannot do you any favors. Jesus says, "Instead, when you give a feast, invite the poor, the crippled, the lame, and the blind. Then you will be blessed, because they have nothing and cannot pay you back. But you will be repaid when the good people rise from the dead." Jesus tells them to invite the people they consider "unclean," to include the people the community has excluded. This, he says, is what God's kingdom is like.

Physical Handicap: For additional scriptures on this topic go to Exodus 15:26–26.

Judah and in the streets of Jerusalem. At that time
we had plenty of food and were successful, and
nothing bad happened to us. 18But since we
stopped making sacrifices to the Queen Goddess
and stopped pouring out drink offerings to her, we
have had great problems. Our people have also
been killed in war and by hunger."

19The women said, "Our husbands knew what
we were doing. We had their permission to burn
incense to the Queen Goddess and to pour out
drink offerings to her. Our husbands knew we
were making cakes that looked like her and were
pouring out drink offerings to her."

20Then Jeremiah spoke to all the people—men
and women—who answered him. 21He said to
them, "The LORD remembered that you and your
ancestors, kings and officers, and the people of
the land burned incense in the towns of Judah
and in the streets of Jerusalem. He remembered
and thought about it. 22Then he could not be
patient with you any longer. He hated the terrible
things you did. So he made your country an
empty desert, where no one lives. Other people
curse that country. And so it is today. 23All this
happened because you burned incense to other
gods. You sinned against the LORD. You did not
obey him or follow his teachings or the laws he
gave you. You did not keep your part of the agreement with him. So this disaster has happened to
you. It is there for you to see."

24Then Jeremiah said to all those men and
women, "People of Judah who are now in Egypt,
hear the word of the LORD: 25The LORD All-
Powerful, the God of Israel, says: You and your
wives did what you said you would do. You said,
'We will certainly keep the promises we made. We
promised to make sacrifices to the Queen Goddess
and to pour out drink offerings to her.' So, go
ahead. Do the things you promised, and keep your
promises. 26But hear the word of the LORD. Listen,
all you Jews living in Egypt. The LORD says, 'I have
sworn by my great name: The people of Judah now
living in Egypt will never again use my name to
make promises. They will never again say in Egypt,
"As surely as the Lord GOD lives. . ." 27I am watching over them, not to take care of them, but to hurt
them. The Jews who live in Egypt will die from
swords or hunger until they are all destroyed. 28A
few will escape being killed by the sword and will
come back to Judah from Egypt. Then, of the people of Judah who came to live in Egypt, those who
are left alive will know if my word or their word
came true. 29I will give you a sign that I will punish
you here in Egypt,' says the LORD. 'When you see it
happen, you will know that my promises to hurt
you will really happen.' 30This is what the LORD
says: 'Hophra king of Egypt has enemies who want
to kill him. Soon I will hand him over to his enemies just as I handed Zedekiah king of Judah over
to Nebuchadnezzar king of Babylon, who wanted
to kill him.' "

A Message to Baruch

45 It was the fourth year that Jehoiakim son
of Josiah was king of Judah. Jeremiah the
prophet told these things to Baruch son of Neriah,
and Baruch wrote them on a scroll: 2"This is what
the LORD, the God of Israel, says to you, Baruch:
3You have said, 'How terrible it is for me! The LORD
has given me sorrow along with my pain. I am
tired because of my suffering and cannot rest.' "

4The LORD said, "Say this to Baruch: 'This is
what the LORD says: I will soon tear down what I
have built, and I will pull up what I have planted
everywhere in Judah. 5Baruch, you are looking
for great things for yourself. Don't look for them,
because I will bring disaster on all the people,
says the LORD. You will have to go many places,
but I will let you escape alive wherever you go.' "

Messages to the Nations

46 The LORD spoke this word to Jeremiah the
prophet about the nations:

2This message is to Egypt. It is about the army
of Neco king of Egypt, which was defeated at the
city of Carchemish on the Euphrates River by
Nebuchadnezzar king of Babylon. This was in the
fourth year that Jehoiakim son of Josiah was king
of Judah. This is the LORD's message to Egypt:

3"Prepare your shields, large and small,
  and march out for battle!
4Harness the horses
  and get on them!
Go to your places for battle
  and put on your helmets!
Polish your spears.
  Put on your armor!
5What do I see?
  That army is terrified,
and the soldiers are running away.
  Their warriors are defeated.
They run away quickly
  without looking back.
  There is terror on every side!"
    says the LORD.

46:2 *Neco king of Egypt.* Neco, king of Egypt, had an army in Syria that threatened to push back the Babylonian army's advances in the area. In 605 B.C. Nebuchadnezzar, then the crown prince, arrived with an army and completely defeated the Egyptians.

[6]"The fast runners cannot run away;
the strong soldiers cannot escape.
They stumble and fall
in the north, by the Euphrates River.
[7]Who is this, rising up like the Nile River,
like strong, fast rivers?
[8]Egypt rises up like the Nile River,
like strong, fast rivers.
Egypt says, 'I will rise up and cover the earth.
I will destroy cities and the people in them!'
[9]Horsemen, charge into battle!
Chariot drivers, drive hard!
March on, brave soldiers—
soldiers from the countries of Cush and Put
who carry shields,
soldiers from Lydia who use bows.

[10]"But that day belongs to the Lord GOD
All-Powerful.
At that time he will give those people the
punishment they deserve.
The sword will kill until it is finished,
until it satisfies its thirst for their blood.
The Lord GOD All-Powerful will offer a sacrifice
in the land of the north, by the
Euphrates River.

[11]"Go up to Gilead and get some balm,
people of Egypt!
You have prepared many medicines,
but they will not work;
you will not be healed.
[12]The nations have heard of your shame,
and your cries fill all the earth.
One warrior has run into another;
both of them have fallen down together!"

[13]This is the message the LORD spoke to Jeremiah
the prophet about Nebuchadnezzar king of
Babylon's coming to attack Egypt:
[14]"Announce this message in Egypt, and
preach it in Migdol.
Preach it also in the cities of Memphis
and Tahpanhes:
'Get ready for war,
because the battle is all around you.'
[15]Egypt, why were your warriors killed?
They could not stand because the LORD
pushed them down.
[16]They stumbled again and again
and fell over each other.
They said, 'Get up. Let's go back
to our own people and our homeland.
We must get away from our enemy's sword!'
[17]In their homelands those soldiers called out,
'The king of Egypt is only a lot of noise.
He missed his chance for glory!' "
[18]The King's name is the LORD All-Powerful.
He says, "As surely as I live,
a powerful leader will come.
He will be like Mount Tabor among
the mountains,
like Mount Carmel by the sea.
[19]People of Egypt, pack your things
to be taken away as captives,
because Memphis will be destroyed.
It will be a ruin, and no one will live there.

[20]"Egypt is like a beautiful young cow,
but a horsefly is coming
from the north to attack her.
[21]The hired soldiers in Egypt's army
are like fat calves,
because even they all turn and
run away together;
they do not stand strong against the attack.
Their time of destruction is coming;
they will soon be punished.
[22]Egypt is like a hissing snake that
is trying to escape.
The enemy comes closer and closer.
They come against Egypt with axes
like men who cut down trees.
[23]They will chop down Egypt's army
as if it were a great forest," says the LORD.
"There are more enemy soldiers than locusts;
there are too many to count.
[24]The people of Egypt will be ashamed.
They will be handed over to the
enemy from the north."

[25]The LORD All-Powerful, the God of Israel,
says: "Very soon I will punish Amon, the god of
the city of Thebes. And I will punish Egypt, her
kings, her gods, and the people who depend on
the king. [26]I will hand those people over to their
enemies, who want to kill them. I will give them
to Nebuchadnezzar king of Babylon and his officers. But in the future, Egypt will live in peace as
it once did," says the LORD.

A Message to Israel

[27]"People of Jacob, my servants, don't be afraid;
don't be frightened, Israel.
I will surely save you from those faraway places
and your children from the lands where they
are captives.

46:10 Day of the Lord: Ezekiel 7:19

The people of Jacob will have peace
and safety again,
and no one will make them afraid.
28People of Jacob, my servants, do not be afraid,
because I am with you," says the LORD.
"I will completely destroy the many
different nations
where I scattered you.
But I will not completely destroy you.
I will punish you fairly,
but I will not let you escape your punishment."

A Message to the Philistines

47 Before the king of Egypt attacked the city
of Gaza, the LORD spoke his word to Jeremiah the prophet. This message is to the Philistine people.
2This is what the LORD says:
"See, the enemy is gathering in the north like
rising waters.
They will become like an overflowing stream
and will cover the whole country like a flood,
even the towns and the people living in them.
Everyone living in that country
will cry for help;
the people will cry painfully.
3They will hear the sound of the running horses
and the noisy chariots
and the rumbling chariot wheels.
Parents will not help their children to safety,
because they will be too weak to help.
4The time has come
to destroy all the Philistines.
It is time to destroy all who are left alive
who could help the cities of Tyre and Sidon.
The LORD will soon destroy the Philistines,
those left alive from the island of Crete.
5The people from the city of Gaza will be sad
and shave their heads.
The people from the city of Ashkelon will
be made silent.
Those left alive from the valley,
how long will you cut yourselves?

6"You cry, 'Sword of the LORD,
how long will you keep fighting?
Return to your holder.
Stop and be still.'
7But how can his sword rest
when the LORD has given it a command?
He has ordered it
to attack Ashkelon and the seacoast."

A Message to Moab

48 This message is to the country of Moab.
This is what the LORD All-Powerful, the
God of Israel, says:

"How terrible it will be for the city of Nebo,
because it will be ruined.
The town of Kiriathaim will be disgraced
and captured;
the strong city will be disgraced and shattered.
2Moab will not be praised again.
Men in the town of Heshbon plan
Moab's defeat.
They say, 'Come, let us put an end
to that nation!'
Town of Madmen, you will also be silenced.
The sword will chase you.
3Listen to the cries from the town of Horonaim,
cries of much confusion and destruction.
4Moab will be broken up.
Her little children will cry for help.
5Moab's people go up the path to the town of
Luhith,
crying loudly as they go.
On the road down to Horonaim,
cries of pain and suffering can be heard.
6Run! Run for your lives!
Go like a bush being blown through the desert.
7You trust in the things you do and in your wealth,
so you also will be captured.
The god Chemosh will go into captivity
and his priests and officers with him.
8The destroyer will come against every town;
not one town will escape.
The valley will be ruined,
and the high plain will be destroyed,
as the LORD has said.
9Give wings to Moab,
because she will surely leave her land.
Moab's towns will become empty,
with no one to live in them.

10A curse will be on anyone who doesn't do
what the LORD says,
and a curse will be on anyone who holds
back his sword from killing.

47:2 *like a flood.* The waters of the chaotic sea were about to overwhelm Philistia. The reference is to Babylonia, which was about to overwhelm the region of Philistia.

47:5 *sad and . . . yourselves.* The people did these things to show their sadness.

48:2 *Madmen.* This name sounds like the Hebrew word for "be silenced."

48:7 *Chemosh.* Chemosh was the god of the Moabites. He was represented by a statue. When the Moabites were defeated, the statue would have been captured and taken back to the victor's temple.

[11]"The people of Moab have never
known trouble.
They are like wine left to settle;
they have never been poured from
one jar to another.
They have not been taken into captivity.
So they taste as they did before,
and their smell has not changed.
[12]A time is coming," says the LORD,
"When I will send people to pour you from
your jars.
They will empty Moab's jars
and smash her jugs.
[13]The people of Israel trusted that god in
the town of Bethel,
and they were ashamed when
there was no help.
In the same way Moab will be ashamed of
their god Chemosh.

[14]"You cannot say, 'We are warriors!
We are brave men in battle!'
[15]The destroyer of Moab and her
towns has arrived.
Her best young men will be killed!"
says the King,
whose name is the LORD All-Powerful.
[16]"The end of Moab is near,
and she will soon be destroyed.
[17]All you who live around Moab,
all you who know her, cry for her.
Say, 'The ruler's power is broken;
Moab's power and glory are gone.'

[18]"You people living in the town of Dibon,
come down from your place of honor
and sit on the dry ground,
because the destroyer of Moab has
come against you.
And he has destroyed your strong,
walled cities.
[19]You people living in the town of Aroer,
stand next to the road and watch.
See the man running away and
the woman escaping.
Ask them, 'What happened?'
[20]Moab is filled with shame, because she is
ruined.
Cry, Moab, cry out!
Announce at the Arnon River
that Moab is destroyed.
[21]People on the high plain have been punished.
Judgment has come to these towns:
Holon, Jahzah, and Mephaath;
[22] Dibon, Nebo, and Beth Diblathaim;
[23]Kiriathaim, Beth Gamul, and Beth Meon;
[24]Kerioth and Bozrah.
Judgment has come to all the towns of Moab,
far and near.
[25]Moab's strength has been cut off,
and its arm broken!" says the LORD.

[26]"The people of Moab thought they were
greater than the LORD,
so punish them until they act as if
they are drunk.
Moab will fall and roll around in its own vomit,
and people will even make fun of it.
[27]Moab, you made fun of Israel.
Israel was caught in the middle of a
gang of thieves.
When you spoke about Israel,
you shook your head and acted as if you were
better than it.
[28]People in Moab, leave your towns empty
and go live among the rocks.
Be like a dove that makes its nest
at the entrance of a cave.

[29]"We have heard that the people of
Moab are proud,
very proud.
They are proud, very proud,
and in their hearts they think they
are important."
[30]The LORD says,
"I know Moab's great pride, but it is useless.
Moab's bragging accomplishes nothing.
[31]So I cry sadly for Moab,
for everyone in Moab.
I moan for the people from the town
of Kir Hareseth.
[32]I cry with the people of the town of Jazer
for you, the grapevines of the town of Sibmah.
In the past your vines spread all the
way to the sea,
as far as the sea of Jazer.
But the destroyer has taken over
your fruit and grapes.
[33]Joy and happiness are gone
from the large, rich fields of Moab.
I have stopped the flow of wine from
the winepresses.
No one walks on the grapes with shouts of joy.
There are shouts,
but not shouts of joy.

[34]"Their crying can be heard from
Moabite towns,
from Heshbon to Elealeh and Jahaz.

It can be heard from Zoar as far away as
Horonaim and Eglath Shelishiyah.
Even the waters of Nimrim are dried up.
35I will stop Moab
from making burnt offerings at the places
of worship
and from burning incense to their gods,"
says the LORD.

36"My heart cries sadly for Moab like a flute
playing a funeral song.
It cries like a flute for the people
from Kir Hareseth.
The money they made has all
been taken away.
37Every head has been shaved
and every beard cut off.
Everyone's hands are cut,
and everyone wears rough cloth
around his waist.
38People are crying on every roof in Moab
and in every public square.
There is nothing but sadness,
because I have broken Moab
like a jar no one wants," says the LORD.
39"Moab is shattered! The people are crying!
Moab turns away in shame!
People all around her make fun of her.
The things that happened fill them
with great fear."

40This is what the LORD says:
"Look! Someone is coming, like an
eagle diving down from the sky
and spreading its wings over Moab.
41The towns of Moab will be captured,
and the strong, walled cities will be defeated.
At that time Moab's warriors will
be frightened,
like a woman who is having a baby.
42The nation of Moab will be destroyed,
because they thought they were greater than
the LORD.
43Fear, deep pits, and traps wait for you,
people of Moab," says the LORD.
44"People will run from fear,
but they will fall into the pits.
Anyone who climbs out of the pits
will be caught in the traps.
I will bring the year of punishment to Moab,"
says the LORD.

45"People have run from the powerful enemy
and have gone to Heshbon for safety.
But fire started in Heshbon;
a blaze has spread from the hometown of
Sihon king of Moab.
It burned up the leaders of Moab
and destroyed those proud people.
46How terrible it is for you, Moab!
The people who worship Chemosh have
been destroyed.
Your sons have been taken captive,
and your daughters have been taken away.
47"But in days to come,
I will make good things happen again to
Moab," says the LORD.

This ends the judgment on Moab.

A Message to Ammon

49 This message is to the Ammonite people.
This is what the LORD says:

"Do you think that Israel has no children?
Do you think there is no one to take the land
when the parents die?
If that were true, why did Molech
take Gad's land
and why did Molech's people settle
in Gad's towns?"
2The LORD says,
"The time will come when I will make Rabbah,
the capital city of the Ammonites, hear the
battle cry.
It will become a hill covered with ruins,
and the towns around it will be burned.
Those people forced Israel out of that land,
but now Israel will force them out!"
says the LORD.
3"People in the town of Heshbon, cry sadly
because the town of Ai is destroyed!
Those who live in Rabbah, cry out!
Put on your rough cloth to show your sadness,
and cry loudly.
Run here and there for safety inside the walls,
because Molech will be taken captive
and his priests and officers with him.
4You brag about your valleys
and about the fruit in your valleys.
You are like an unfaithful child
who believes his treasures will save him.
You think, 'Who would attack me?'

48:37 *Every head . . . waist.* The people did these things to show their sadness for those who had died. These are all mourning rites, and some of them are forbidden by the law of Israel (Leviticus 19:28; 21:5; Deuteronomy 14:1).

48:38 *roof.* In Bible times houses were built with flat roofs. The roof was used for drying things such as flax and fruit. And it was used as an extra room, as a place for worship, and as a cool place to sleep in the summer.

[5]I will soon bring terror on you
from everyone around you,"
says the Lord GOD All-Powerful.
"You will all be forced to run away,
and no one will be able to gather you.

[6]"But the time will come
when I will make good things happen to the
Ammonites again,"
says the LORD.

A Message to Edom

[7]This message is to Edom. This is what the
LORD All-Powerful says:
"Is there no more wisdom in the
town of Teman?
Can the wise men of Edom no longer
give good advice?
Have they lost their wisdom?
[8]You people living in the town of Dedan,
run away and hide in deep caves,
because I will bring disaster on the
people of Esau.
It is time for me to punish them.
[9]If workers came and picked the grapes from
your vines,
they would leave a few grapes behind.
If robbers came at night,
they would steal only enough for themselves.
[10]But I will strip Edom bare.
I will find all their hiding places,
so they will not be able to hide from me.
The children, relatives, and neighbors will die,
and Edom will be no more.
[11]Leave the orphans, and I will take care of them.
Your widows also can trust in me."

[12]This is what the LORD says: "Some people did
not deserve to be punished, but they had to drink
from the cup of suffering anyway. People of
Edom, you deserve to be punished, so you will
not escape punishment. You must certainly drink
from the cup of suffering." [13]The LORD says, "I
swear by my own name that the city of Bozrah
will become a pile of ruins! People will be
shocked by what happened there. They will
insult that city and speak evil of it. And all the
towns around it will become ruins forever."

[14]I have heard a message from the LORD.
A messenger has been sent among
the nations, saying,
"Gather your armies to attack it!
Get ready for battle!"

[15]"Soon I will make you the smallest of nations,
and you will be greatly hated by everyone.
[16]Edom, you frightened other nations,
but your pride has fooled you.
You live in the hollow places of the cliff
and control the high places of the hills.
Even if you build your home as high as
an eagle's nest,
I will bring you down from there,"
says the LORD.
[17]"Edom will be destroyed.
People who pass by will be shocked to see
the destroyed cities,
and they will be amazed at all her injuries.
[18]Edom will be destroyed like the cities of
Sodom and Gomorrah
and the towns around them," says the LORD.
"No one will live there!
No one will stay in Edom."

[19]"Like a lion coming up from the thick bushes
near the Jordan River
to attack a strong pen for sheep,
I will suddenly chase Edom from its land.
Who is the one I have chosen to do this?
There is no one like me,
no one who can take me to court.
None of their leaders can stand
up against me."

[20]So listen to what the LORD has planned
to do against Edom.
Listen to what he has decided to do to the
people in the town of Teman.
He will surely drag away the young
ones of Edom.
Their hometowns will surely be shocked at
what happens to them.
[21]At the sound of Edom's fall, the earth will shake.
Their cry will be heard all the way
to the Red Sea.
[22]The LORD is like an eagle swooping down
and spreading its wings over the
city of Bozrah.
At that time Edom's soldiers will
become very frightened,
like a woman having a baby.

A Message to Damascus

[23]This message is to the city of Damascus:
"The towns of Hamath and Arpad are
put to shame,
because they have heard bad news.

49:7 *Edom, Teman.* These areas, though not in Israel, were famous for their wisdom.

They are discouraged.
They are troubled like the tossing sea.
24The city of Damascus has become weak.
The people want to run away;
they are ready to panic.
The people feel pain and suffering,
like a woman giving birth to a baby.
25Damascus was a city of my joy.
Why have the people not left that
famous city yet?
26Surely the young men will die in
the city squares,
and all her soldiers will be killed at that
time," says the LORD All-Powerful.
27"I will set fire to the walls of Damascus,
and it will completely burn the strong cities
of King Ben-Hadad."

A Message to Kedar and Hazor

28This message is to the tribe of Kedar and the
kingdoms of Hazor, which Nebuchadnezzar king
of Babylon defeated. This is what the LORD says:
"Go and attack the people of Kedar,
and destroy the people of the East.
29Their tents and flocks will be taken away.
Their belongings will be carried off—
their tents, all their goods, and their camels.
Men will shout to them,
'Terror on every side!'

30"Run away quickly!
People in Hazor, find a good place to hide!"
says the LORD.
"Nebuchadnezzar king of Babylon has made
plans against you
and wants to defeat you.

31"Get up! Attack the nation that is comfortable,
that is sure no one will defeat it,"
says the LORD.
"It does not have gates or fences to protect it.
Its people live alone.
32The enemy will steal their camels
and their large herds of cattle as war prizes.
I will scatter the people who cut their hair
short to every part of the earth,
and I will bring disaster on them from everywhere," says the LORD.
33"The city of Hazor will become a home
for wild dogs;
it will be an empty desert forever.
No one will live there,
and no one will stay in it."

A Message to Elam

34Soon after Zedekiah became king of Judah,
the LORD spoke this word to Jeremiah the prophet. This message is to the nation of Elam.
35This is what the LORD All-Powerful says:
"I will soon break Elam's bow,
its greatest strength.
36I will bring the four winds against Elam
from the four corners of the skies.
I will scatter its people everywhere the four
winds blow;
its captives will go to every nation.
37I will terrify Elam in front of their enemies,
who want to destroy them.
I will bring disaster to Elam
and show them how angry I am!" says the LORD.
"I will send a sword to chase Elam
until I have killed them all.
38I will set up my throne in Elam to show
that I am king,
and I will destroy its king and its officers!"
says the LORD.

39"But I will make good things happen
to Elam again
in the future," says the LORD.

A Message to Babylon

50 This is the message the LORD spoke to
Babylon and the Babylonian people through
Jeremiah the prophet.

2"Announce this to the nations.
Lift up a banner and tell them.
Speak the whole message and say:
'Babylon will be captured.
The god Bel will be put to shame,
and the god Marduk will be afraid.
Babylon's gods will be put to shame,
and her idols will be afraid!'
3A nation from the north will attack Babylon
and make it like an empty desert.
No one will live there;
both people and animals will run away."
4The LORD says, "At that time
the people of Israel and Judah will
come together.
They will cry and look for the LORD their God.

49:32 *people who cut their hair short.* This refers to the style of haircut common among the Arabic tribes who are the recipients of this judgment.

50:1 The Babylonians were among Israel's greatest enemies and were a major power in the Old Testament world. They were responsible for taking the Israelites into exile from 597–539 B.C. In so doing, they were the Lord's instrument for punishing the Israelites, who had strayed from their obedience to God. In chapters 50 and 51, Jeremiah delivers a message concerning the ultimate fate of Babylon: this nation will be destroyed, never to rise again. Elsewhere in the Bible, the Babylonians represent the forces of evil pitted against God. They meet their final doom in the Book of Revelation.

[5]Those people will ask how to go to Jerusalem
and will start in that direction.
They will come and join themselves to the LORD.
They will make an agreement with him
that will last forever,
an agreement that will never be forgotten.

[6]"My people have been like lost sheep.
Their leaders have led them in
the wrong way
and made them wander around in
the mountains and hills.
They forgot where their resting place was.
[7]Whoever saw my people hurt them.
And those enemies said, 'We did
nothing wrong.
Those people sinned against the LORD, their
true resting place,
the God their fathers trusted.'

[8]"Run away from Babylon,
and leave the land of the Babylonians.
Be like the goats that lead the flock.
[9]I will soon bring against Babylon
many great nations from the north.
They will take their places for war against it,
and it will be captured by people
from the north.
Their arrows are like trained soldiers
who do not return from war
with empty hands.
[10]The enemy will take all the wealth from
the Babylonians.
Those enemy soldiers will get all they want,"
says the LORD.

[11]"Babylon, you are excited and happy,
because you took my land.
You dance around like a young cow
in the grain.
Your laughter is like the neighing
of male horses.
[12]Your mother will be very ashamed;
the woman who gave birth to you will
be disgraced.
Soon Babylonia will be the least important
of all the nations.
She will be an empty, dry desert.
[13]Because of the LORD's anger,
no one will live there.
She will be completely empty.
Everyone who passes by Babylon will
be shocked.
They will shake their heads when they see
all her injuries.

[14]"Take your positions for war against Babylon,
all you soldiers with bows.
Shoot your arrows at Babylon! Do not save
any of them,
because Babylon has sinned against the LORD.
[15]Soldiers around Babylon, shout the war cry!
Babylon has surrendered, her towers
have fallen,
and her walls have been torn down.
The LORD is giving her people the punishment
they deserve.
You nations should give her what
she deserves;
do to her what she has done to others.
[16]Don't let the people from Babylon
plant their crops
or gather the harvest.
The soldiers treated their captives cruelly.
Now, let everyone go back home.
Let everyone run to his own country.

[17]"The people of Israel are like a flock of
sheep that are scattered
from being chased by lions.
The first lion to eat them up
was the king of Assyria.
The last lion to crush their bones
was Nebuchadnezzar king of Babylon."

[18]So this is what the LORD All-Powerful, the
God of Israel, says:
"I will punish the king of Babylon and his
country
as I punished the king of Assyria.
[19]But I will bring the people of Israel back to
their own pasture.
They will eat on Mount Carmel and in Bashan.
They will eat and be full
on the hills of Ephraim and Gilead."
[20]The LORD says,
"At that time people will try to
find Israel's guilt,
but there will be no guilt.
People will try to find Judah's sins,
but no sins will be found,
because I will leave a few people alive
from Israel and Judah,
and I will forgive their sins.

[21]"Attack the land of Merathaim.
Attack the people who live in Pekod.
Chase them, kill them, and completely
destroy them.
Do everything I commanded you!"
says the LORD.

Hospitality

LUKE 14:12–14

What is hospitality? On what is it based? How is it practiced in Scripture? What might biblical-style hospitality look like in our own setting?

Two kinds of hospitality are practiced in the Bible—hospitality among "insiders" like friends and family, and hospitality towards "outsiders" like strangers, travelers, and people of different religions or ethnic backgrounds. Both kinds of hospitality mark and sustain social structures and community boundaries. Insider hospitality demonstrates and cements kinship, friendship, and belonging, maintaining boundaries from within. Hospitality toward outsiders allows for limited contact that protects both the stranger and the host, guarding the outside boundary of a household, settlement, or community.

Hospitality among kin and friends was one of the joys of life in biblical times. Friends' closeness might be demonstrated and cemented by sharing everyday family meals and special occasions like wedding feasts and Passover celebrations. Trust and harmony were exhibited and enjoyed through such exchanges of hospitality among friends and family.

Travel in the ancient Mediterranean world could be dangerous. Since inns were few and far between, travelers had to rely on locals for access to water, food, shelter, and safety from attack. Locals faced possible physical and social threats from strangers; anyone from outside the kinship group or local social network could upset the social balance of the community and had to be handled carefully. A set of hospitality practices developed to deal with these tensions and dangers. The same basic customs were followed by most of the peoples of the ancient near east.

The Israelites understood their roles as hosts and guests in the light of their unique history. Their hospitality was to go beyond the basic customs, especially in the sense that it was to arise from something other than fear of the stranger or desire to maintain status and honor. Israelite hospitality arises from the heart of a people whose identity, safety, and home rest in the God who came to them when they were strangers and made them welcome (Deuteronomy 10:17–19; 24: 17–19; 26: 5–9; Exodus 22:21). The Law reads, "You must not mistreat a foreigner. You know how it feels to be a foreigner, because you were foreigners in Egypt" (Exodus 23:9). Proper treatment of the stranger is an act in response to God's hospitality. At least ideally, God's people could afford to risk inviting new people in, since they could rely on God to protect.

The code was a process in four phases (initial invitation, screening, provision, and departure) enacted by people taking certain roles (stranger-guest, host, servant). It was important to know what one's role entailed—both its rights and responsibilities—in each of the four phases so that the process would go smoothly. If all went well, the strangers would become friends or allies, and depart well-fed and rested, not as disgruntled enemies.

1) Initial Invitation. Foreigners were eyed with suspicion, but for a settlement or community to fail to offer them shelter, water, and food was dishonorable and even dangerous. In the earliest times, when the people were nomads themselves, approaching strangers might be intercepted and greeted before being invited into the encampment (Genesis 18:2). In villages and towns it was customary for travelers to wait at the well or gate (Genesis 1:1–2; 24:23–25, 31–33; Acts 16:13–15). Before nightfall locals would invite the strangers to stay and dine in a household; to fail to do so was a shameful breach of etiquette on the part of the community (Judges 19:15, 18; and see v. 20, where the custom is properly carried out).

2) Screening. The strangers' intentions, status, and character had to be assessed (Joshua 2:2–3; 2 John 9–11). A traveling rabbi might be invited to speak (Acts 13:15). Sometimes travelers carried letters of recommendation to ease them through this phase (Romans 16:3–16; 1 Corinthians 16:10–11). Sometimes after strangers had spoken or acted in some particular manner they were asked to leave (see Mark 5:17, where this happens to Jesus).

3) Provision and Protection for Guests. In this phase a host welcomes the strangers into the household as guests, offering food, water, and shelter for the travelers and their animals (Genesis 24:23–25; 26:30). The host was usually a male head of household, but might be a woman of means (1 Kings 17:10; Luke 8:2–3; 10:38; Acts 16:13–15). To show the strangers' acceptance as guests, the host (or his servant) washes their feet (Genesis 18:4; 19:2; Luke 7:36–50). The host household provides the best meal possible. Prepared and served by women and household servants, the meal might be lavish and could include entertainment—dancing and music, and Torah reading and discussion. A (male) guest would also be honored by an invitation to speak, an anointing with oil, and a seat near the host at the table. Another key responsibility of the host is to protect guests from harm (Genesis 23:7–9; Joshua 2:1–6; 2 Kings 6:22–23).

4) Departure. It seems to have been a general custom that guests could expect no more than two nights' lodging in any one household. For guests to prolong their stay would be rude and dishonorable, while a host who extends the invitation is unusually generous and kind and signals acceptance into a deeper relationship (Judges 19:1–9). In this phase the aim is to send the guests off well-fed and supplied, well-rested, and with everyone's honor intact (Genesis 26:26–31; Romans 15:24).

Hospitality in the Bible is first of all demonstrated and practiced by God, who hosts a needy humanity (Psalm 107:1–9). The psalmist sees the cosmos as God's place, his house, in which all living creatures are cared for; humanity is especially welcomed and invited to enjoy God's unending hospitality: "You give us wine that makes happy hearts and olive oil that makes our faces shine. You give us bread that gives us strength" (Psalm 104:15).

God hosts his people throughout Israel's history. In the desert *Yahweh* provides water, food, and protection (Exodus 15:24–25, 27; 16) while he screens them prior to their full welcome into the Promised Land (Numbers 14:21–24; Hebrews 3:18–19). Canaan belongs to God: "The land really belongs to me . . . You are only foreigners and travelers living for a while on my land" (Leviticus 25:23; Deuteronomy 26:9). The people's disobedience causes their expulsion from the Promised Land as they are sent into exile in Babylon. The prophet Isaiah announces God's forgiveness in the form of an invitation for his thirsty and hungry people to return to God for refreshment and protection (Isaiah 55:1).

In the Good News accounts, welcoming Jesus, the stranger-guest-messenger from God, is a sign of welcoming God's message of Good News, and of abiding in God's kingdom. It is this kind of receiving and welcoming that is indicated when John writes, "He came to the world that was his own, but his own people did not accept him. But to all who did accept him and believe in him he gave the right to become children of God" (John 1:11–12). Those who reject Jesus or are inhospitable toward him demonstrate their rejection of God's messenger and of the grace and authority he embodies (e.g. Herod the Great, Matthew 2:1–19; Pharisees, Matthew 22:15–16). The Gospels include several stories in which Jesus is a guest (e.g. Matthew 9:10; 26:7; Mark 1:29–31). He follows the hospitality code (by not insulting his hosts, for example), but he also offers revisions of the code and lessons on a new etiquette (Luke 7:36–50). Jesus can openly flout custom by inviting himself to someone's house, and by accepting and giving hospitality to "sinners," who were customarily deemed unworthy of association with good people (Luke 19:1–10). In the Apocalypse, Jesus appears as an unusually bold stranger at the door of those who have been claiming to know him but need to change their hearts and lives: "Here I am! I stand at the door and knock. If you hear my voice and open the door, I will come in and eat with you, and you will eat with me" (Revelation 3:20).

Jesus' invitation, "Come to me, all you who are tired and have heavy loads, and I will give you rest" (Matthew 11:28) is a host's welcome and offer of shelter, lodging, and protection. Jesus hosts and serves thousands at a time in Galilee, providing food in a desert, just as *Yahweh* did through Moses (Luke 9:10–17; John 6:5–13). He shows his willingness to take a servant's position in God's household when he washes his followers' feet, and he says they must be willing to do this kind of serving too (John 13:17). Jesus does this for his closest friends, but he indicates that he expects his friends to actively welcome strangers, which they once were. They are to do as he has done, going out and seeking strangers to invite in, rather than passively waiting for them to arrive. Thus he erases the insider/outsider hospitality distinctions: "When you give a lunch or a dinner, don't invite only your friends, your family, your other relatives, and your rich neighbors . . . Instead, . . . invite the poor, the crippled, the lame, and the blind" (Luke 14:12–13).

Hospitality among the early Christians was central to their life together. They met in houses, not church buildings, and often shared meals—both the *agape*/love feast (Jude 12; 2 Peter 2:13) and Lord's Supper meals (1 Corinthians 10:14–22). Since they were a mixed group, comprised of former Jews and non-Jews, slaves and owners, men and women, simply to eat or lodge together in the same household violated customary boundaries. The challenge of creating and learning hospitality practices among people who once considered each other strangers and outsiders was a source of tension in the church that the apostles had to address (e.g., 1 Corinthians 10 and 11). The writer of 1 Peter urges: "Open your homes to each other, without complaining" (4:9).

Hospitality also made early missionary travels (hence, the explosive expansion of the church) possible (see Acts 10:6, 23; 28:7; 2 Timothy 1:16). The writer of 3 John says: "My dear friend, it is good that you help the brothers and sisters, even those you do not know. They told the church about your love. Please help them to continue their trip in a way worthy of God" (verses 5–6).⚭

⚭**Hospitality:** For additional scriptures on this topic go to Genesis 19:1–16.

22"The noise of battle can be heard all
over the country;
it is the noise of much destruction.
23Babylon was the hammer of the whole earth,
but how broken and shattered that
hammer is now.
It is truly the most ruined
of all the nations.
24Babylon, I set a trap for you,
and you were caught before you knew it.
You fought against the LORD,
so you were found and taken prisoner.
25The LORD has opened up his storeroom
and brought out the weapons of his anger,
because the Lord GOD All-Powerful
has work to do
in the land of the Babylonians.
26Come against Babylon from far away.
Break open her storehouses of grain.
Pile up her dead bodies like heaps of grain.
Completely destroy Babylon
and do not leave anyone alive.
27Kill all the young men in Babylon;
let them be killed like animals.
How terrible it will be for them, because the
time has come for their defeat;
it is time for them to be punished.
28Listen to the people running to escape the
country of Babylon!
They are telling Jerusalem
how the LORD our God is punishing
Babylon as it deserves
for destroying his Temple.

29"Call for the archers
to come against Babylon.
Tell them to surround the city,
and let no one escape.
Pay her back for what she has done;
do to her what she has done to other nations.
Babylon acted with pride against the LORD,
the Holy One of Israel.
30So her young men will be killed in her streets.
All her soldiers will die on that day,"
says the LORD.
31"Babylon, you are too proud, and I
am against you,"
says the Lord GOD All-Powerful.
"The time has come
for you to be punished.
32Proud Babylon will stumble and fall,
and no one will help her get up.
I will start a fire in her towns,
and it will burn up everything around her."

33This is what the LORD All-Powerful says:
"The people of Israel
and Judah are slaves.
The enemy took them as prisoners
and won't let them go.
34But God is strong and will buy them back.
His name is the LORD All-Powerful.
He will surely defend them with power
so he can give rest to their land.
But he will not give rest to those
living in Babylon."

35The LORD says,
"Let a sword kill the people living in Babylon
and her officers and wise men!
36Let a sword kill her false prophets,
and they will become fools.
Let a sword kill her warriors,
and they will be full of terror.
37Let a sword kill her horses and chariots
and all the soldiers hired from
other countries!
Then they will be like frightened women.
Let a sword attack her treasures,
so they will be taken away.
38Let a sword attack her waters
so they will be dried up.
She is a land of idols,
and the people go crazy with fear over them.

39"Desert animals and hyenas will live there,
and owls will live there,
but no people will ever live there again.
She will never be filled with people again.
40God completely destroyed the cities of
Sodom and Gomorrah
and the towns around them," says the LORD.
"In the same way no people will
live in Babylon,
and no human being will stay there.⚭

41"Look! An army is coming from the north.
A powerful nation and many kings
are coming together from all around the
world.
42Their armies have bows and spears.
The soldiers are cruel and have no mercy.
As the soldiers come riding on their horses,
the sound is loud like the roaring sea.
They stand in their places, ready for battle.
They are ready to attack you, city of Babylon.
43The king of Babylon heard about those armies,
and he became helpless with fear.

⚭**50:40 Wilderness (Desert):** Hosea 9:10

Distress has gripped him.
His pain is like that of a woman giving birth to a baby.

44"Like a lion coming up from the thick bushes near the Jordan River
to attack a strong pen for sheep,
I will suddenly chase the people of Babylon from their land.
Who is the one I have chosen to do this?
There is no one like me,
no one who can take me to court.
None of their leaders can stand up against me."

45So listen to what the LORD has planned to do against Babylon.
Listen to what he has decided to do to the people in the city of Babylon.
He will surely drag away the young ones of Babylon.
Their hometowns will surely be shocked at what happens to them.
46At the sound of Babylon's capture,
the earth will shake.
People in all nations will hear Babylon's cry of distress.

51 This is what the LORD says:

"I will soon cause a destroying wind to blow against Babylon and the Babylonian people.
2I will send foreign people to destroy Babylon like a wind that blows chaff away.
They will destroy the land.
Armies will surround the city
when the day of disaster comes upon her.
3Don't let the Babylonian soldiers prepare their bows to shoot.
Don't even let them put on their armor.
Don't feel sorry for the young men of Babylon,
but completely destroy her army.
4They will be killed in the land of the Babylonians
and will die in her streets.
5The Lord GOD All-Powerful
did not leave Israel and Judah,
even though they were completely guilty
in the presence of the Holy One of Israel.
6"Run away from Babylon
and save your lives!
Don't stay and be killed because of Babylon's sins.
It is time for the LORD to punish Babylon;
he will give Babylon the punishment she deserves.
7Babylon was like a gold cup in the LORD's hand
that made the whole earth drunk.
The nations drank Babylon's wine,
so they went crazy.
8Babylon has suddenly fallen and been broken.
Cry for her!
Get balm for her pain,
and maybe she can be healed.

9"Foreigners in Babylon say, 'We tried to heal Babylon,
but she cannot be healed.
So let us leave her and each go to his own country.
Babylon's punishment is as high as the sky;
it reaches to the clouds.'

10"The people of Judah say, 'The LORD has shown us to be right.
Come, let us tell in Jerusalem
what the LORD our God has done.'

11"Sharpen the arrows!
Pick up your shields!
The LORD has stirred up the kings of the Medes,
because he wants to destroy Babylon.
The LORD will punish them as they deserve
for destroying his Temple.
12Lift up a banner against the walls of Babylon!
Bring more guards.
Put the watchmen in their places,
and get ready for a secret attack!
The LORD will certainly do what he has planned
and what he said he would do against the people of Babylon.
13People of Babylon, you live near much water
and are rich with many treasures,
but your end as a nation has come.
It is time to stop you from robbing other nations.
14The LORD All-Powerful has promised in his own name:
'Babylon, I will surely fill you with so many enemy soldiers they will be like a swarm of locusts.
They will stand over you and shout their victory.'

15"The LORD made the earth by his power.
He used his wisdom to build the world
and his understanding to stretch out the skies.

51:8 *balm.* See 8:22.

51:14 *like a swarm of locusts.* Locusts were known for their ability to devastate a land completely.

16When he thunders, the waters in the skies roar.
He makes clouds rise in the sky all
over the earth.
He sends lightning with the rain
and brings out the wind from his storehouses.

17"People are so stupid and know so little.
Goldsmiths are made ashamed by their idols,
because those statues are only false gods.
They have no breath in them.
18They are worth nothing; people make
fun of them.
When they are judged, they will
be destroyed.
19But God, who is Jacob's Portion, is not
like the idols.
He made everything,
and he chose Israel to be his special people.
The LORD All-Powerful is his name.

20"You are my war club,
my battle weapon.
I use you to smash nations.
I use you to destroy kingdoms.
21I use you to smash horses and riders.
I use you to smash chariots and drivers.
22I use you to smash men and women.
I use you to smash old people and
young people.
I use you to smash young men
and young women.
23I use you to smash shepherds and flocks.
I use you to smash farmers and oxen.
I use you to smash governors and officers.

24"But I will pay back Babylon and all the Babylonians for all the evil things they did to Jerusalem
in your sight," says the LORD.

25The LORD says,
"Babylon, you are a destroying mountain,
and I am against you.
You have destroyed the whole land.
I will put my hand out against you.
I will roll you off the cliffs,
and I will make you a burned-out mountain.
26People will not find any rocks in Babylon big
enough for cornerstones.
People will not take any rocks from Babylon
to use for the foundation of a building,
because your city will be just a pile of ruins
forever," says the LORD.

27"Lift up a banner in the land!
Blow the trumpet among the nations!
Get the nations ready for battle against
Babylon.
Call these kingdoms of Ararat, Minni, and
Ashkenaz to fight against her.
Choose a commander to lead the
army against Babylon.
Send so many horses that they are like
a swarm of locusts.
28Get the nations ready for battle
against Babylon—
the kings of the Medes,
their governors and all their officers,
and all the countries they rule.
29The land shakes and moves in pain,
because the LORD will do what he has
planned to Babylon.
He will make Babylon an empty desert,
where no one will live.
30Babylon's warriors have stopped fighting.
They stay in their protected cities.
Their strength is gone,
and they have become like
frightened women.
Babylon's houses are burning.
The bars of her gates are broken.
31One messenger follows another;
messenger follows messenger.
They announce to the king of Babylon
that his whole city has been captured.
32The river crossings have been captured,
and the swamplands are burning.
All of Babylon's soldiers are terribly afraid."
33This is what the LORD All-Powerful, the God
of Israel, says:
"The city of Babylon is like a threshing floor,
where people crush the grain at harvest time.
The time to harvest Babylon is coming soon."

34"Nebuchadnezzar king of Babylon has defeated
and destroyed us.
In the past he took our people away,
and we became like an empty jar.
He was like a giant snake that swallowed us.
He filled his stomach with our best things.
Then he spit us out.
35Babylon did terrible things to hurt us.
Now let those things happen to Babylon,"
say the people of Jerusalem.
"The people of Babylon killed our people.
Now let them be punished for what
they did," says Jerusalem.

36So this is what the LORD says:
"I will soon defend you, Judah,
and make sure that Babylon is punished.

I will dry up Babylon's sea
and make her springs become dry.
37Babylon will become a pile of ruins,
a home for wild dogs.
People will be shocked by what
happened there.
No one will live there anymore.
38Babylon's people roar like young lions;
they growl like baby lions.
39While they are stirred up,
I will give a feast for them
and make them drunk.
They will shout and laugh.
And they will sleep forever and never
wake up!" says the LORD.
40"I will take the people of Babylon to be killed.
They will be like lambs,
like sheep and goats waiting to be killed.

41"How Babylon has been defeated!
The pride of the whole earth has
been taken captive.
People from other nations are shocked at what
happened to Babylon,
and the things they see make them afraid.
42The sea has risen over Babylon;
its roaring waves cover her.
43Babylon's towns are ruined and empty.
It has become a dry, desert land,
a land where no one lives.
People do not even travel through Babylon.
44I will punish the god Bel in Babylon.
I will make him spit out what
he has swallowed.
Nations will no longer come to Babylon;
even the wall around the city will fall.

45"Come out of Babylon, my people!
Run for your lives!
Run from the LORD's great anger.
46Don't lose courage;
rumors will spread through the land, but
don't be afraid.
One rumor comes this year, and another
comes the next year.
There will be rumors of terrible fighting
in the country,
of rulers fighting against rulers.
47The time will surely come
when I will punish the idols of Babylon,
and the whole land will be disgraced.
There will be many dead people
lying all around.
48Then heaven and earth and all that is in them
will shout for joy about Babylon.
They will shout because the army comes
from the north
to destroy Babylon," says the LORD.

49"Babylon must fall, because she killed
people from Israel.
She killed people from everywhere on earth.
50You who have escaped being killed with swords,
leave Babylon! Don't wait!
Remember the LORD in the faraway land
and think about Jerusalem."

51"We people of Judah are disgraced,
because we have been insulted.
We have been shamed,
because strangers have gone into
the holy places of the LORD's Temple!"

52So the LORD says, "The time is coming soon
when I will punish the idols of Babylon.
Wounded people will cry with pain
all over that land.
53Even if Babylon grows until she
touches the sky,
and even if she makes her highest
cities strong,
I will send people to destroy her,"
says the LORD.
54"Sounds of people crying are heard in Babylon.
Sounds of people destroying things
are heard in the land of the Babylonians.
55The LORD is destroying Babylon
and making the loud sounds of the city
become silent.
Enemies come roaring in like ocean waves.
The roar of their voices is heard all around.
56The army has come to destroy Babylon.
Her soldiers have been captured,
and their bows are broken,
because the LORD is a God who punishes
people for the evil they do.
He gives them the full punishment
they deserve.
57I will make Babylon's rulers and
wise men drunk,
and her governors, officers, and soldiers, too.
Then they will sleep forever and never
wake up," says the King,
whose name is the LORD All-Powerful.

58This is what the LORD All-Powerful says:
"Babylon's thick wall will be completely
pulled down
and her high gates burned.
The people will work hard, but it won't help;
their work will only become fuel
for the flames!"

A Message to Babylon

59This is the message that Jeremiah the prophet gave to the officer Seraiah son of Neriah, who was the son of Mahseiah. Seraiah went to Babylon with Zedekiah king of Judah in the fourth year Zedekiah was king of Judah. His duty was to arrange the king's food and housing on the trip. 60Jeremiah had written on a scroll all the terrible things that would happen to Babylon, all these words about Babylon. 61Jeremiah said to Seraiah, "As soon as you come to Babylon, be sure to read this message so all the people can hear you. 62Then say, 'LORD, you have said that you will destroy this place so that no people or animals will live in it. It will be an empty ruin forever.' 63After you finish reading this scroll, tie a stone to it and throw it into the Euphrates River. 64Then say, 'In the same way Babylon will sink and will not rise again because of the terrible things I will make happen here. Her people will fall.' "

The words of Jeremiah end here.

The Fall of Jerusalem

52 Zedekiah was twenty-one years old when he became king, and he was king in Jerusalem for eleven years. His mother's name was Hamutal daughter of Jeremiah, and she was from Libnah. 2Zedekiah did what the LORD said was wrong, just as Jehoiakim had done. 3All this happened in Jerusalem and Judah because the LORD was angry with them. Finally, he threw them out of his presence.

Zedekiah turned against the king of Babylon. 4Then Nebuchadnezzar king of Babylon marched against Jerusalem with his whole army. They made a camp around the city and built devices all around the city walls to attack it. This happened on Zedekiah's ninth year, tenth month, and tenth day as king. 5And the city was under attack until Zedekiah's eleventh year as king.

6By the ninth day of the fourth month, the hunger was terrible in the city; there was no food for the people to eat. 7Then the city wall was broken through, and the whole army of Judah ran away at night. They left the city through the gate between the two walls by the king's garden. Even though the Babylonians were surrounding the city, Zedekiah and his men headed toward the Jordan Valley.

8But the Babylonian army chased King Zedekiah and caught him in the plains of Jericho. All of his army was scattered from him. 9So the Babylonians captured Zedekiah and took him to the king of Babylon at the town of Riblah in the land of Hamath. There he passed sentence on Zedekiah. 10At Riblah the king of Babylon killed Zedekiah's sons as he watched. The king also killed all the officers of Judah. 11Then he put out Zedekiah's eyes, and put bronze chains on him, and took him to Babylon. And the king kept Zedekiah in prison there until the day he died.

12Nebuzaradan, commander of the king's special guards and servant of the king of Babylon, came to Jerusalem on the tenth day of the fifth month. This was in Nebuchadnezzar's nineteenth year as king of Babylon. 13Nebuzaradan set fire to the Temple of the LORD, the palace, and all the houses of Jerusalem; every important building was burned. 14The whole Babylonian army, led by the commander of the king's special guards, broke down all the walls around Jerusalem. 15Nebuzaradan, the commander of the king's special guards, took captive some of the poorest people, those who were left in Jerusalem, those who had surrendered to the king of Babylon, and the skilled craftsmen who were left in Jerusalem. 16But Nebuzaradan left behind some of the poorest people of the land to take care of the vineyards and fields.

17The Babylonians broke into pieces the bronze pillars, the bronze stands, and the large bronze bowl, called the Sea, which were in the Temple of the LORD. Then they carried all the bronze pieces to Babylon. 18They also took the pots, shovels, wick trimmers, bowls, dishes, and all the bronze objects used to serve in the Temple. 19The commander of the king's special guards took away bowls, pans for carrying hot coals, large bowls, pots, lampstands, pans, and bowls used for drink offerings. He took everything that was made of pure gold or silver.

20There was so much bronze that it could not be weighed: two pillars, the large bronze bowl called the Sea with the twelve bronze bulls under it, and the movable stands, which King Solomon had made for the Temple of the LORD.

21Each of the pillars was about twenty-seven feet high, eighteen feet around, and hollow inside. The wall of each pillar was three inches thick. 22The bronze capital on top of the one pillar was about seven and one-half feet high. It was decorated with a net design and bronze pomegranates all around it. The other pillar also had pomegranates and was like the first pillar. 23There were ninety-six pomegranates on the sides of the pillars. There was a total of a hundred pomegranates above the net design.

52:1 *Jeremiah.* This is not the prophet Jeremiah but a different man with the same name.

24The commander of the king's special guards
took as prisoners Seraiah the chief priest, Zephaniah the priest next in rank, and the three doorkeepers. 25He also took from the city the officer in
charge of the soldiers, seven people who advised
the king, the royal secretary who selected people
for the army, and sixty other men from Judah
who were in the city when it fell. 26Nebuzaradan,
the commander, took these people and brought
them to the king of Babylon at the town of Riblah.
27There at Riblah, in the land of Hamath, the king
had them killed.

So the people of Judah were led away from
their country as captives. 28This is the number of
the people Nebuchadnezzar took away as captives:
in the seventh year, 3,023 Jews;29in Nebuchadnezzar's eighteenth year, 832 people from Jerusalem;30in Nebuchadnezzar's twenty-third year,
Nebuzaradan, commander of the king's special
guards, took 745 Jews as captives.

In all 4,600 people were taken captive.

Jehoiachin Is Set Free

31Jehoiachin king of Judah was in prison in
Babylon for thirty-seven years. The year Evil-
Merodach became king of Babylon he let Jehoiachin king of Judah out of prison. He set Jehoiachin
free on the twenty-fifth day of the twelfth month.
32Evil-Merodach spoke kindly to Jehoiachin and
gave him a seat of honor above the seats of the
other kings who were with him in Babylon. 33So
Jehoiachin put away his prison clothes, and for
the rest of his life, he ate at the king's table. 34Every
day the king of Babylon gave Jehoiachin an
allowance. This lasted as long as he lived, until
the day Jehoiachin died.

INTRODUCTION TO THE BOOK OF LAMENTATIONS

Sad Songs About Jerusalem

WHO WROTE THIS BOOK?

The author of Lamentations is uncertain. According to Jewish and Christian traditions, it was written by Jeremiah, who was present at the destruction of Jerusalem and, thus could describe it so vividly.

TO WHOM WAS THIS BOOK WRITTEN?

Lamentations was written for the people of Judah, the citizens of the destroyed Jerusalem.

WHERE WAS IT WRITTEN?

The setting of the book is obviously Jerusalem.

WHEN WAS IT WRITTEN?

Lamentations was probably written between 586 and 516 B.C.

WHAT IS THE BOOK ABOUT?

The Book of Lamentations is a collection of five carefully constructed laments, or sad songs. Four of the songs have 22 verses—the number of letters in the Hebrew alphabet. The third lament has 66 verses—22 times 3.

WHY WAS THIS BOOK WRITTEN?

While Babylon carried out the task, Lamentations reveals that God himself is bringing destruction to his city and Temple as divine punishment for Judah's disloyalty and sin. The book, however, goes on to show God's goodness and mercy. Finally, the laments that began out of rebellion end in repentance and forgiveness.

SO WHAT DOES THIS BOOK MEAN TO US?

The message of Lamentations is clear, both to Judah and to us. God is just. His righteousness can allow no less. And yet, his justice is coupled with his great compassion, mercy, and love for us, which are given to us "new every morning" (3:22–23) when we repent of our rebellion and sin.

SUMMARY:

Lamentations was written in response to the horrible destruction of the city of Jerusalem in 587 B.C. The Babylonian army completely overwhelmed the city and destroyed it, including the Temple, which was the symbol of its relationship with God (see the account in 2 Kings 25:1–21).

Though it was the Babylonians who physically did the destruction, the author of Lamentations knew well that they were just the tool of God's anger. In reality it was God himself who destroyed the city; so it is to God that the author turns to express his pain and to plead for healing.

Though some think that Jeremiah wrote the book, Lamentations nowhere names an author. We are fairly certain, however, that it was written near the time of the destruction of the city of Jerusalem.

The structure of the Book of Lamentations is as follows:

I. Jerusalem Destroyed and Miserable (Lamentations 1)
II. God in His Anger Destroyed the City (Lamentations 2)
III. The Suffering and Hope of the People of God (Lamentations 3)
IV. Sin and Judgment (Lamentations 4)
V. Final Plea for Help (Lamentations 5)

I. Jerusalem Destroyed and Miserable (Lamentations 1)

II. God in His Anger Destroyed the City (Lamentations 2)

God is described as an enemy who wages war and destroys the city of Jerusalem. God is the one who is behind the activity of the Babylonian army.

III. The Suffering and Hope of the People of God (Lamentations 3)

Jerusalem's suffering is here represented as the suffering of a single individual. In the middle of the whole book stands an eloquent expression of future hope in the midst of suffering and pain.

IV. Sin and Judgment (Lamentations 4)

The horrible suffering of the people is described. All the people—rich, poor, priest, prophet, and ruler—sinned against the Lord.

V. Final Plea for Help (Lamentations 5)

The author of this prayer now turns to God and asks for him to stop being angry with them and return and restore them.

LAMENTATIONS

Jerusalem Cries over Her Loss

Jerusalem once was full of people,
but now the city is empty.
Jerusalem once was a great city among the
nations, but now she is like a widow.
She was like a queen of all the other cities,
but now she is a slave.

2 She cries loudly at night,
and tears are on her cheeks.
There is no one to comfort her;
all who loved her are gone.
All her friends have turned against her
and are now her enemies.

3 Judah has gone into captivity
where she suffers and works hard.
She lives among other nations,
but she has found no rest.
Those who chased her caught her
when she was in trouble.

4 The roads to Jerusalem are sad,
because no one comes for the feasts.
No one passes through her gates.
Her priests groan,
her young women are suffering,
and Jerusalem suffers terribly.

5 Her foes are now her masters.
Her enemies enjoy the wealth they
have taken.
The LORD is punishing her
for her many sins.
Her children have gone away
as captives of the enemy.

6 The beauty of Jerusalem
has gone away.
Her rulers are like deer
that cannot find food.
They are weak
and run from the hunters.

7 Jerusalem is suffering and homeless.
She remembers all the good things
from the past.
But her people were defeated by the enemy,
and there was no one to help her.
When her enemies saw her,
they laughed to see her ruined.

8 Jerusalem sinned terribly,
so she has become unclean.
Those who honored her now hate her,
because they have seen her nakedness.
She groans
and turns away.

9 She made herself dirty by her sins
and did not think about what would happen
to her.
Her defeat was surprising,
and no one could comfort her.
She says, "LORD, see how I suffer,
because the enemy has won."

10 The enemy reached out and took
all her precious things.
She even saw foreigners
enter her Temple.
The LORD had commanded foreigners
never to enter the meeting place
of his people.

11 All of Jerusalem's people groan,
looking for bread.
They are trading their precious things for food
so they can stay alive.
The city says, "Look, LORD, and see.
I am hated."

12 Jerusalem says, "You who pass by on the road
don't seem to care.
Come, look at me and see:
Is there any pain like mine?
Is there any pain like that he has caused me?
The LORD has punished me
on the day of his great anger.

13 "He sent fire from above
that went down into my bones.

1 Lamentations expresses grief and shame over the destruction of Jerusalem in 587–586 B.C. The writer is particularly distressed by the arrogant attitude of the surrounding nations who now make fun of Jerusalem's misfortune (Lamentations 1:7; 2:15–16). This scornful attitude continues even after Judah returns from exile (Nehemiah 1:3; 2:17) and is brought to an end only when Nehemiah rebuilds the city and its walls (Nehemiah 6:15, 16; 12:43).

1:1 Jerusalem went from prosperity and joy to devastation and sadness when the Babylonians destroyed and plundered the city, exiling the people, in 587 B.C.

1:1 *she.* In this poem the city of Jerusalem is described as a woman.

1:5 Jerusalem's foes are the Babylonians who were the rising superpower of the day. Babylon was located in Mesopotamia with a center in what is today Iraq.

He stretched out a net for my feet
and turned me back.
He made me so sad and lonely
that I am weak all day.

14"He has noticed my sins;
they are tied together by his hands;
they hang around my neck.
He has turned my strength into weakness.
The Lord has handed me over
to those who are stronger than I.

15"The Lord has rejected
all my mighty men inside my walls.
He brought an army against me
to destroy my young men.
As if in a winepress, the Lord has crushed
the capital city of Judah.

16"I cry about these things;
my eyes overflow with tears.
There is no one near to comfort me,
no one who can give me strength again.
My children are left sad and lonely,
because the enemy has won."

17Jerusalem reaches out her hands,
but there is no one to comfort her.
The LORD commanded the people of Jacob
to be surrounded by their enemies.
Jerusalem is now unclean
like those around her.

18Jerusalem says, "The LORD is right,
but I refused to obey him.
Listen, all you people,
and look at my pain.
My young women and men
have gone into captivity.

19"I called out to my friends,
but they turned against me.
My priests and my older leaders
have died in the city
while looking for food
to stay alive.

20"Look at me, LORD. I am upset
and greatly troubled.
My heart is troubled,
because I have been so stubborn.
Out in the streets, the sword kills;
inside the houses, death destroys.

21"People have heard my groaning,
and there is no one to comfort me.
All my enemies have heard of my trouble,
and they are happy you have done this to me.
Now bring that day you have announced
so that my enemies will be like me.

22"Look at all their evil.
Do to them what you have done to me
because of all my sins.
I groan over and over again,
and I am afraid."

The Lord Destroyed Jerusalem

2 Look how the Lord in his anger
has brought Jerusalem to shame.
He has thrown down the greatness of Israel
from the sky to the earth;
he did not remember the Temple, his footstool,
on the day of his anger.

2The Lord swallowed up without mercy
all the houses of the people of Jacob;
in his anger he pulled down
the strong places of Judah.
He threw her kingdom and its rulers
down to the ground in dishonor.

3In his anger he has removed
all the strength of Israel;
he took away his power from Israel
when the enemy came.
He burned against the people of Jacob like
a flaming fire
that burns up everything around it.

4Like an enemy, he prepared to shoot his bow,
and his hand was against us.
Like an enemy, he killed
all the good-looking people;
he poured out his anger like fire
on the tents of Jerusalem.

5The Lord was like an enemy;
he swallowed up Israel.
He swallowed up all her palaces
and destroyed all her strongholds.
He has caused more moaning and groaning
for Judah.

1:22 Complaint/Lament/Protest: Mark 15:34
1:22 Suffering: Habakkuk 3:17–19
2:1 *his footstool.* The Temple was sometimes imagined to be the place where God rested his feet on earth as he sat on his heavenly throne.

2:4 Israel often spoke of God as the warrior who fought against their enemies. Because of their sins, however, God here fights against his own people.
2:5 Holy War & Divine Warrior: Daniel 7:13

MONEY

LUKE 16:13

Does the Bible talk about money? Is money evil?
How might money best be employed in God's work?

Developments in our systems of exchange and payment in the last century have raised an enormous range of questions about the relationship between wealth and faithfulness to God. Checks and credit cards have become increasingly widespread forms of money, making it easier for a small number of people to accumulate great wealth, and for everyone to purchase goods and services and to get into serious debt. In our world today, it is impossible to be a Christian and not struggle with questions related to money.

Questions related to money were also important among God's people in the Old and New Testaments, even though the word *money* itself is not usually found in the Bible. In fact, after the problem of worshiping idols, the questions most discussed in the Bible have to do with money.

For most of the time covered by the Bible, "money" as we understand it today was not important as a method of payment or exchange. Even in the time of Jesus, in the villages of the countryside, items were "purchased" not so much with money as through the exchange of goods and services (barter). For most of the nation of Israel in the Old Testament and for peasant farmers in the world of Jesus, the idea of "saving" money over a long period was alien. For them, the primary means of exchange was agricultural produce. Each year, the yield from the farm would be divided into three portions: (1) to save enough seed to start next year's crop; (2) to provide for the current needs of the household and livestock, either through direct consumption or by exchanging one's produce for the produce of another family; and (3) to support the authorities of the Temple and state. A farmer might have to borrow money to buy seed for the next year, but payment was more often than not made with a portion of the harvest itself. Often, agricultural goods had to be exchanged for metal money, coins, in order to make the payment of taxes to the state and Temple more manageable.

On the other hand, especially in the cities of the ancient world, and on the major trading routes, money was exchanged. The wealthy loaned money, laborers were paid with coins, the Temple in Jerusalem or the places of worship in other cities were supported with metal coins. In the larger world of Jesus, these coins were produced by the state; for some, these coins were symbols of the ultimate authority of the state and proof that all wealth actually belonged to the emperor.

For this reason, when we read the word "money," or other words like it in biblical texts, we need to remember that these writers were not thinking simply of coins. Instead, "money" refers to wealth, and especially to the potential of wealth to control our lives. This is why Jesus says, "You cannot serve both God and worldly riches [that is, money]" (Luke 16:13).

This is not because Jesus thought money was bad, but he knew how easily we could be drawn away from God by the attraction of money (see Mark 4:18–19). He also knew that money asks for the whole of our lives, just as God does. We cannot give the whole of our lives to both God and money.

What does it mean to serve money? This refers to a way of life described and condemned throughout the Bible. The rule of money is experienced by Israel during their years of slavery in Egypt. In Egypt, they were treated as merchandise to be used by the leaders of Egypt. As a result, when God delivered Israel from Egypt, he provided laws that were to keep the people of Israel from treating each other as property. For example, Israel was not to have another Israelite as a slave; if someone did sell himself to another as a slave, his service was to be temporary (Deuteronomy 15:12–15). Nor were Israelites to lend money and expect interest from each other (Deuteronomy 23:19–22).

The command, "You must not steal" (Exodus 20:15), was to have been central to Israel's practices with money. Today, we often hear in this text a commandment against stealing the private property of others. We must remember, though, that, for Israel, property belongs, ultimately, to God, and that property is given to God's people in order that they might care for it in the name of God (see Genesis 2:8–15; 12:7). Therefore, the command against stealing has less to do with taking what belongs to someone else and more to do with hoarding for oneself what is needed by others. This does not mean that theft as we know it is acceptable, but it does suggest how much more widely stealing must now be understood.

The rule of money is realized, in large part, in the selfishness of those who take for themselves what is needed by others. Indeed, farmers were not even to harvest their crops completely, but were to leave part of the harvest in the field for those who needed it (Leviticus 19:9–10; 23:22). Along the same lines, Jesus told the story of a man who stored up great wealth for himself rather than caring for the needs of his community or giving to the poor; this man was condemned by God as a fool (Luke 12:16–21).

Of course, it is one thing to legislate against the rule of money, but quite another thing to overturn its power. Many Old Testament prophets spoke out against the people of God and their neighboring countries because of their activities with money. The rich dominated the poor, placing them in debt and gaining ownership of their money and land (see Amos 2:6–7; 5:11–12; 8:4–6). Prophets often developed as two sides of the same problem, the two sins of Israel: (1) they worshiped other Gods, and (2) they oppressed other people. In their view, care for the poor, the alien, the orphan, and the widow went hand in glove with faithfulness to God. On the other hand, those whose god was money showed little or no concern for the less fortunate of society.

Similarly, in the Gospels and the Acts of the Apostles, money and possessions are a symbol for how people relate to others and to God. The rich are often recognized by their inattention to the poor (see Luke 16:19–31), but the poor are blessed (Matthew 5:3; Luke 6:20). The early believers formed communities in which there were no needy, where the needs of its members were cared for by those in the church who had possessions to share (Acts 2:44–47; 4:32–37).

In the same way, Paul instructs churches to share their wealth with those churches, sometimes far away, who were in great need (see 1 Corinthians 16:1–4; 2 Corinthians 8–9). What is of special interest about Paul's instructions is that he asks churches largely made up of Gentile Christians to support churches largely made up of Jewish Christians. This demonstrates, first, the importance of money as a symbol of sharing, and, therefore, the fundamental unity of all, whether Jew or Gentile, in Christ (see also Acts 11:27–30).

For this reason, one of the primary ways of understanding the biblical message on money focuses on the understanding of money as a symbol of human relations. Money itself is not evil (1 Timothy 6:10), but can be put to either good purposes or bad. The question is, Who is in charge? Is money controlling us, or are we controlling money? "No servant can serve two masters. . . . You cannot serve both God and worldly riches" (Luke 16:13).

One helpful way of thinking about money is to remember that we use money differently in different settings. We can give money to others, particularly those closest to us, without any strings attached. In this case, the exchange of money symbolizes our close relationships. We can also give money to others with strings attached—for example, in exchange for food at the grocery store. In this case, the exchange of money is set within a business transaction, usually with people with whom we have little or no ongoing relationship. We can also steal money from someone else. In this case, the exchange of money signifies the presence of no relationship at all, or the violent breaking of any relationship we might have had.

Hence, Jesus asked the wealthy man to give his money to the poor (Mark 10:17–22) and Zacchaeus declared that he gave half of his possessions to the poor (Luke 19:8). Giving to the poor was, in Jesus' day, a gift that came with no strings attached. In these cases, then, following Jesus had to do with relating to the poor with help as one would relate to a close friend or member of one's family. Indeed, at one point Jesus counseled his followers to use money to make friends in just this way (Luke 16:9). Similarly, those with wealth in the early Christian community described in Acts gave to those with needs in the community (Acts 2:44–47; 4:32–37). That is, they treated others within the church as though they were family.

At the same time, Jesus can criticize some religious leaders for being more concerned about their own positions in society and their own needs than about the poor around them. Even though they pray and enjoy the respect of others in public, far from assisting the poor they cheat them and steal their homes (see, for example, Luke 20:45–47). They separate themselves from any possible relationship with the poor; they live to serve the rule of money (see Luke 16:14).

It is not too much to say that, for Jesus, the only healthy use of money is to care for the poor. This view is very much in line with Old Testament thinking, for there, too, those in greatest need—the widow, the orphan, and the outsider—need special care. Most Jews in the first century believed that giving money to help those in need was more important than all of the other commandments of God. This was especially important in the world of the New Testament, since the government did not usually provide any help. In the New Testament, James actually says that "caring for orphans or widows who need help" is an expression of the sort of "religion that God accepts as pure and without fault" (James 1:27).⚭

⚭ **Money:** For additional scriptures on this topic go to Deuteronomy 15.

6He cut down his Temple like a garden;
he destroyed the meeting place.
The LORD has made Jerusalem forget
the set feasts and Sabbath days.
He has rejected the king and the priest
in his great anger.

7The Lord has rejected his altar
and abandoned his Temple.
He has handed over to the enemy
the walls of Jerusalem's palaces.
Their uproar in the LORD's Temple
was like that of a feast day.

8The LORD planned to destroy
the wall around Jerusalem.
He measured the wall
and did not stop himself from
destroying it.
He made the walls and defenses sad;
together they have fallen.

9Jerusalem's gates have fallen to the ground;
he destroyed and smashed the bars of the
gates.
Her king and her princes are among the
nations.
The teaching of the LORD has stopped,
and the prophets do not have
visions from the LORD.

10The older leaders of Jerusalem
sit on the ground in silence.
They throw dust on their heads
and put on rough cloth to show
their sadness.
The young women of Jerusalem
bow their heads to the ground in sorrow.

11My eyes have no more tears,
and I am sick to my stomach.
I feel empty inside,
because my people have been destroyed.
Children and babies are fainting
in the streets of the city.

12They ask their mothers,
"Where is the grain and wine?"
They faint like wounded soldiers
in the streets of the city
and die in their mothers' arms.

13What can I say about you, Jerusalem?
What can I compare you to?
What can I say you are like?
How can I comfort you, Jerusalem?
Your ruin is as deep as the sea.
No one can heal you.

14Your prophets saw visions,
but they were false and worth nothing.
They did not point out your sins
to keep you from being captured.
They preached what was false
and led you wrongly.

15All who pass by on the road
clap their hands at you;
they make fun of Jerusalem
and shake their heads.
They ask, "Is this the city that people called
the most beautiful city,
the happiest place on earth?"

16All your enemies open their mouths
to speak against you.
They make fun and grind their teeth in anger.
They say, "We have swallowed you up.
This is the day we were waiting for!
We have finally seen it happen."

17The LORD has done what he planned;
he has kept his word
that he commanded long ago.
He has destroyed without mercy,
and he has let your enemies laugh at you.
He has strengthened your enemies.

18The people cry out to the Lord.
Wall of Jerusalem,
let your tears flow
like a river day and night.
Do not stop
or let your eyes rest.

19Get up, cry out in the night,
even as the night begins.
Pour out your heart like water
in prayer to the Lord.
Lift up your hands in prayer to him
for the life of your children
who are fainting with hunger
on every street corner.

2:7 *abandoned his Temple.* The people of Judah felt confident that they would not be destroyed because God was permanently in the city since he was living in the Temple (Jeremiah 7). This faith was self-centered and arrogant; they felt it didn't matter if they sinned. After all, God can leave his Temple; he is not imprisoned there (see Ezekiel 9–11).

2:15 *"Is this the city . . ."* These words are similar to those found in Psalm 48.

20Jerusalem says: "Look, LORD, and see
to whom you have done this.
Women eat their own babies,
the children they have cared for.
Priests and prophets are killed
in the Temple of the Lord.

21"People young and old
lie outside on the ground.
My young women and young men
have been killed by the sword.
You killed them on the day of your anger;
you killed them without mercy.

22"You invited terrors to come against me on
every side,
as if you were inviting them to a feast.
No one escaped or remained alive
on the day of the LORD's anger.
My enemy has killed
those I cared for and brought up."

The Meaning of Suffering

3 I am a man who has seen the suffering
that comes from the rod of the LORD's anger.⚭
2He led me
into darkness, not light.
3He turned his hand against me
again and again, all day long.

4He wore out my flesh and skin
and broke my bones.
5He surrounded me with sadness
and attacked me with grief.
6He made me sit in the dark,
like those who have been dead a long time.

7He shut me in so I could not get out;
he put heavy chains on me.
8I cry out and beg for help,
but he ignores my prayer.
9He blocked my way with a stone wall
and led me in the wrong direction.

10He is like a bear ready to attack me,
like a lion in hiding.
11He led me the wrong way and let me stray
and left me without help.
12He prepared to shoot his bow
and made me the target for his arrows.⚭

13He shot me in the kidneys
with the arrows from his bag.
14I was a joke to all my people,
who make fun of me with songs all day long.
15The LORD filled me with misery;
he made me drunk with suffering.

16He broke my teeth with gravel
and trampled me into the dirt.
17I have no more peace.
I have forgotten what happiness is.
18I said, "My strength is gone,
and I have no hope in the LORD."

19LORD, remember my suffering and
my misery,
my sorrow and trouble.
20Please remember me
and think about me.
21But I have hope
when I think of this:

22The LORD's love never ends;
his mercies never stop.
23They are new every morning;
LORD, your loyalty is great.
24I say to myself, "The LORD is mine,
so I hope in him."

25The LORD is good to those who hope in him,
to those who seek him.
26It is good to wait quietly
for the LORD to save.
27It is good for someone to work hard
while he is young.

28He should sit alone and be quiet;
the LORD has given him hard work to do.
29He should bow down to the ground;
maybe there is still hope.
30He should let anyone slap his cheek;
he should be filled with shame.

31The Lord will not reject
his people forever.
32Although he brings sorrow,
he also has mercy and great love.
33He does not like to punish people
or make them sad.

34He sees if any prisoner of the earth
is crushed under his feet;
35he sees if someone is treated unfairly
before the Most High God;

⚭**3:1 Images of God:** Lamentations 3:10–12

3:1 The nameless sufferer stands for the combined people of Judah and Jerusalem.

⚭**3:12 Images of God:** Ezekiel 22:17–22

3:21 The hope of restoration expressed here is found in the middle of the book as a whole.

36the Lord sees
if someone is cheated in his case in court.

37Nobody can speak and have it happen
unless the Lord commands it.
38Both bad and good things
come by the command of the Most High God.
39No one should complain
when he is punished for his sins.

40Let us examine and see what we have done
and then return to the LORD.
41Let us lift up our hands and pray from our hearts
to God in heaven:
42"We have sinned and turned against you,
and you have not forgiven us.

43"You wrapped yourself in anger and chased us;
you killed us without mercy.
44You wrapped yourself in a cloud,
and no prayer could get through.
45You made us like scum and trash
among the other nations.

46"All of our enemies
open their mouths and speak against us.
47We have been frightened and fearful,
ruined and destroyed."
48Streams of tears flow from my eyes,
because my people are destroyed.

49My tears flow continually,
without stopping,
50until the LORD looks down
and sees from heaven.
51I am sad when I see
what has happened to all the women
of my city.

52Those who are my enemies for no reason
hunted me like a bird.
53They tried to kill me in a pit;
they threw stones at me.
54Water came up over my head,
and I said, "I am going to die."
55I called out to you, LORD,
from the bottom of the pit.
56You heard me calling, "Do not close your ears
and ignore my gasps and shouts."
57You came near when I called to you;
you said, "Don't be afraid."

58Lord, you have taken my case
and given me back my life.
59LORD, you have seen how I have been wronged.
Now judge my case for me.
60You have seen how my enemies took
revenge on me
and made evil plans against me.

61LORD, you have heard their insults
and all their evil plans against me.
62The words and thoughts of my enemies
are against me all the time.
63Look! In everything they do
they make fun of me with songs.

64Pay them back, LORD,
for what they have done.
65Make them stubborn,
and put your curse on them.
66Chase them in anger, LORD,
and destroy them from under your heavens.

The Attack on Jerusalem

4 See how the gold has lost its shine,
how the pure gold has dulled!
The stones of the Temple are scattered
at every street corner.

2The precious people of Jerusalem
were more valuable than gold,
but now they are thought of as clay jars
made by the hands of a potter.

3Even wild dogs give their milk
to feed their young,
but my people are cruel
like ostriches in the desert.

4The babies are so thirsty
their tongues stick to the roofs of their mouths.
Children beg for bread,
but no one gives them any.

5Those who once ate fine foods
are now starving in the streets.
People who grew up wearing nice clothes
now pick through trash piles.

6My people have been punished
more than Sodom was.
Sodom was destroyed suddenly,
and no hands reached out to help her.

7Our princes were purer than snow,
and whiter than milk.

4:1 *The stones of the Temple are scattered.* The Babylonians pulled down the Temple when they captured the city.

Their bodies were redder than rubies;
they looked like sapphires.

8But now they are blacker than coal,
and no one recognizes them in the streets.
Their skin hangs on their bones;
it is as dry as wood.

9Those who were killed in the war
were better off
than those killed by hunger.
They starve in pain and die,
because there is no food from the field.

Colossal statues of Pharaoh Ramses II at the entrance to the rock-cut temple of Abu-Simbel, Egypt

10With their own hands kind women
cook their own children.
They became food
when my people were destroyed.

11The LORD turned loose all of his anger;
he poured out his strong anger.
He set fire to Jerusalem,
burning it down to the foundations.

12Kings of the earth and people of the world
could not believe
that enemies and foes
could enter the gates of Jerusalem.

13It happened because her prophets sinned
and her priests did evil.
They killed in the city
those who did what was right.

14They wandered in the streets
as if they were blind.
They were dirty with blood,
so no one would touch their clothes.

15"Go away! You are unclean," people
shouted at them.
"Get away! Get away! Don't touch us!"
So they ran away and wandered.
Even the other nations said, "Don't stay here."

16The LORD himself scattered them
and did not look after them anymore.
No one respects the priests
or honors the older leaders.

17Also, our eyes grew tired,
looking for help that never came.
We kept watch from our towers
for a nation to save us.

18Our enemies hunted us,
so we could not even walk in the streets.
Our end is near. Our time is up.
Our end has come.

19Those who chased us
were faster than eagles in the sky.
They ran us into the mountains
and ambushed us in the desert.

20The LORD's appointed king, who was
our very breath,
was caught in their traps.
We had said about him, "We will be
protected by him
among the nations."

21Be happy and glad, people of Edom,
you who live in the land of Uz.
The cup of God's anger will come to you;
then you will get drunk and go naked.

22Your punishment is complete, Jerusalem.
He will not send you into captivity again.
But the LORD will punish the sins of Edom;
he will uncover your evil.

A Prayer to the Lord

5 Remember, LORD, what happened to us.
Look and see our disgrace.
2Our land has been turned over to strangers;
our houses have been given to foreigners.
3We are like orphans with no father;
our mothers are like widows.

4We have to buy the water we drink;
we must pay for the firewood.
5Those who chase after us want to catch
us by the neck.
We are tired and find no rest.
6We made an agreement with Egypt
and with Assyria to get enough food.
7Our ancestors sinned against you, but
they are gone;
now we suffer because of their sins.
8Slaves have become our rulers,
and no one can save us from them.
9We risk our lives to get our food;
we face death in the desert.
10Our skin is hot like an oven;
we burn with starvation.
11The enemy abused the women of Jerusalem
and the girls in the cities of Judah.
12Princes were hung by the hands;
they did not respect our older leaders.
13The young men ground grain at the mill,
and boys stumbled under loads of wood.
14The older leaders no longer sit at the city gates;
the young men no longer sing.
15We have no more joy in our hearts;
our dancing has turned to sadness.
16The crown has fallen from our head.
How terrible it is because we sinned.
17Because of this we are afraid,
and now our eyes are dim.
18Mount Zion is empty,
and wild dogs wander around it.

19But you rule forever, LORD.
You will be King from now on.
20Why have you forgotten us for so long?
Have you left us forever?
21Bring us back to you, LORD, and we will return.
Make our days as they were before,
22or have you completely rejected us?
Are you so angry with us?

5:14 This passage describes the sadness of the Jews as being so great that there was no dancing or singing at city gatherings. Music was of such daily importance that when it could not be heard, it was due to a terrible event, like a death or the loss of a battle.

5:15 Happiness: Matthew 5:3

Notes:

INTRODUCTION TO THE BOOK OF EZEKIEL

God's Message to the Captives

WHO WROTE THIS BOOK?

The Book of Ezekiel is named for its author— the prophet of God.

TO WHOM WAS THIS BOOK WRITTEN?

Ezekiel wrote and prophesied to the people of Judah who had been exiled from Jerusalem to Babylon in 597 B.C. (2 Kings 24:14).

WHERE WAS IT WRITTEN?

These writings were done in Babylon during the exile.

WHEN WAS IT WRITTEN?

Ezekiel's ministry, including this writing, covered the twenty-two years from his call by God in 593 B.C. to 571 B.C. when he received his last message (29:17).

WHAT IS THE BOOK ABOUT?

The Book of Ezekiel contains prophecies and messages of both horror and hope. Chapters 1—24 continually remind Judah of the horrible coming fall of their beloved Jerusalem. Chapters 25—32 are pronouncements of doom on the surrounding nations. In the last chapters of the book, after Jerusalem had, indeed, been destroyed, Ezekiel's words brought comfort and hope to Judah—hope for revival and restoration.

WHY WAS THIS BOOK WRITTEN?

The powerful writing of Ezekiel reveals and reemphasizes God's purpose of saving his people through the history of the world. The world and universe are in his divine control and, therefore, safe and secure. It shows that we as individuals are held responsible for our own actions, according to Ezekiel (18:4, 20).

SO WHAT DOES THIS BOOK MEAN TO US?

With God in control of history, his people have always been protected and loved. God also controls the future and, so, with his ongoing participation in world events assured, Christians can live in peace and confidence, rather than following the worldly call of stress and fear. At the same time, we know we will be held accountable for our actions at the time of the Judgment.

SUMMARY:

Ezekiel was born into a priestly family. He would have begun his priestly ministry at the Temple when he was thirty years old, but was unable to do so since he had been taken into captivity along with many other Judaeans in the year 597 B.C. Instead, when he turned thirty (592 B.C.), God called him as a prophet. His priestly roots, however, explain the source of much of the imagery that he uses throughout the book.

Ezekiel's prophetic ministry took place in Babylonia through the chaotic times that finally saw the complete destruction of Jerusalem in 587 B.C. He carefully dates many of his oracles, and so we know that he ministered at least until Jehoiachin's twenty-seventh year (571 B.C.).

Like Isaiah and Jeremiah, Ezekiel's prophecy contains three major parts: judgment against the people of God, the pronouncement of doom on the surrounding nations, and a message of hope for the remnant of his people. The outline of Ezekiel is as follows:

I. Judgment against Judah and Jerusalem (Ezekiel 1–24)
II. Pronouncement of Doom against the Surrounding Nations (Ezekiel 25–32)
III. Message of Hope for the Remnant (Ezekiel 33–48)

The Book of Ezekiel made a big impact on the writers of the New Testament. At least sixty-five quotes or allusions of the book may be found there, most of them in the Book of Revelation.

I. Judgment against Judah and Jerusalem (Ezekiel 1–24)

The book opens with an account of Ezekiel's call to the prophetic ministry (1–3). He sees an incredible vision of God's holiness. The chapters that follow barrage Judah with judgment speeches and prophetic actions that inform them that Jerusalem is about to be destroyed. The section ends with the death of Ezekiel's wife, symbolizing the destruction of Jerusalem.

II. Pronouncement of Doom against the Surrounding Nations (Ezekiel 25–32)

Ezekiel, speaking as God's representative, now turns from Judah and Jerusalem to the surrounding nations. He brings charges and announces punishment against Ammon, Moab, Edom, Philistia, Tyre, and Egypt. The last two are by far the longest.

III. Message of Hope for the Remnant (Ezekiel 33–48)

While the third and concluding section does contain further threats against Jerusalem and the surrounding nation of Edom, it looks beyond the devastation to restoration. Whether it is the dry bones coming to life or the vision of a new temple, the people of God are here given hope for the future.

EZEKIEL

Ezekiel's Vision of Living Creatures

It was the thirtieth year, on the fifth day of the fourth month of our captivity. I was by the Kebar River among the people who had been carried away as captives. The sky opened, and I saw visions of God.

2It was the fifth day of the month of the fifth year that King Jehoiachin had been a prisoner. 3The LORD spoke his word to Ezekiel son of Buzi in the land of the Babylonians by the Kebar River. There he felt the power of the LORD.

4When I looked, I saw a stormy wind coming from the north. There was a great cloud with a bright light around it and fire flashing out of it. Something that looked like glowing metal was in the center of the fire. 5Inside the cloud was what looked like four living creatures, who were shaped like humans, 6but each of them had four faces and four wings. 7Their legs were straight. Their feet were like a calf's hoofs and sparkled like polished bronze. 8The living creatures had human hands under their wings on their four sides. All four of them had faces and wings, 9and their wings touched each other. The living creatures did not turn when they moved, but each went straight ahead.

10Their faces looked like this: Each living creature had a human face and the face of a lion on the right side and the face of an ox on the left side. And each one also had the face of an eagle. 11That was what their faces looked like. Their wings were spread out above. Each had two wings that touched one of the other living creatures and two wings that covered its body. 12Each went straight ahead. Wherever the spirit would go, the living creatures would also go, without turning. 13The living creatures looked like burning coals of fire or like torches. Fire went back and forth among the living creatures. It was bright, and lightning flashed from it. 14The living creatures ran back and forth like bolts of lightning.

15Now as I looked at the living creatures, I saw a wheel on the ground by each of the living creatures with its four faces. 16The wheels and the way they were made were like this: They looked like sparkling chrysolite. All four of them looked the same, like one wheel crossways inside another wheel. 17When they moved, they went in any one of the four directions, without turning as they went. 18The rims of the wheels were high and frightening and were full of eyes all around.

19When the living creatures moved, the wheels moved beside them. When the living creatures were lifted up from the ground, the wheels also were lifted up. 20Wherever the spirit would go, the living creatures would go. And the wheels were lifted up beside them, because the spirit of the living creatures was in the wheels. 21When the living creatures moved, the wheels moved. When the living creatures stopped, the wheels stopped. And when the living creatures were lifted from the ground, the wheels were lifted beside them, because the spirit of the living creatures was in the wheels.

22Now, over the heads of the living creatures was something like a dome that sparkled like ice and was frightening. 23And under the dome the wings of the living creatures were stretched out straight toward one another. Each living creature also had two wings covering its body. 24I heard the sound of their wings, like the roaring sound of the sea, as they moved. It was like the voice of God Almighty, a roaring sound like a noisy army. When the living creatures stopped, they lowered their wings.

25A voice came from above the dome over the heads of the living creatures. When the living creatures stopped, they lowered their wings. 26Now above the dome there was something that looked like a throne. It looked like a sapphire gem. And on the throne was a shape like a human. 27Then I noticed that from the waist up the shape looked like glowing metal with fire inside. From the waist down it looked like fire, and a bright light was all around. 28The surrounding glow looked like the rainbow in the clouds on a rainy day. It seemed to look like the glory of the LORD. So when I saw it, I bowed facedown on the ground and heard a voice speaking.

The Lord Speaks to Ezekiel

2 He said to me, "Human, stand up on your feet so I may speak with you." 2While he spoke to me, the Spirit entered me and put me on my feet. Then I heard the LORD speaking to me.

1:1 *The thirtieth year . . . .* The date according to our reckoning is July 31, 593 B.C.

1:4 God's appearance to Ezekiel takes the form of smoke (cloud) and fire. God often chose this form when he revealed himself to his people (see Exodus 19:16 at Mount Sinai).

1:5 Numbers: Daniel 7–12

1:5 *four living creatures.* These living creatures are similar to the angels ("cherubim") described later in the Book of Ezekiel (see chapter 9). They are God's powerful and supernatural attendants. In this context they seem to be the driving force of God's cloud chariot.

1:28 Glory: John 1:14

1:28 Prophetic Symbolism: Ezekiel 5

3 He said, "Human, I am sending you to the people of Israel. That nation has turned against me and broken away from me. They and their ancestors have sinned against me until this very day. 4 I am sending you to people who are stubborn and who do not obey. You will say to them, 'This is what the Lord GOD says.' 5 They may listen, or they may not, since they are a people who have turned against me. But they will know that a prophet has been among them. 6 You, human, don't be afraid of the people or their words. Even though they may be like thorny branches and stickers all around you, and though you may feel like you live with poisonous insects, don't be afraid. Don't be afraid of their words or their looks, because they are a people who turn against me. 7 But speak my words to them. They may listen, or they may not, because they turn against me. 8 But you, human, listen to what I say to you. Don't turn against me as those people do. Open your mouth and eat what I am giving you."

9 Then I looked and saw a hand stretched out to me, and a scroll was in it. 10 He opened the scroll in front of me. Funeral songs, sad writings, and words about troubles were written on the front and back.

3 Then the LORD said to me, "Human, eat what you find; eat this scroll. Then go and speak to the people of Israel." 2 So I opened my mouth, and he gave me the scroll to eat.

3 He said to me, "Human, eat this scroll which I am giving you, and fill your stomach with it." Then I ate it, and it was as sweet as honey in my mouth.

4 Then he said to me, "Human, go to the people of Israel, and speak my words to them. 5 You are not being sent to people whose speech you can't understand, whose language is difficult. You are being sent to Israel. 6 You are not being sent to many nations whose speech you can't understand, whose language is difficult, whose words you cannot understand. If I had sent you to them, they would have listened to you. 7 But the people of Israel will not be willing to listen to you, because they are not willing to listen to me. Yes, all the people of Israel are stubborn and will not obey. 8 See, I now make you as stubborn and as hard as they are. 9 I am making you as hard as a diamond, harder than stone. Don't be afraid of them or be frightened by them, though they are a people who turn against me."

10 Also, he said to me, "Human, believe all the words I will speak to you, and listen carefully to them. 11 Then go to the captives, your own people, and say to them, 'The Lord GOD says this.' Tell them this whether they listen or not."

12 Then the Spirit lifted me up, and I heard a loud rumbling sound behind me, saying, "Praise the glory of the LORD in heaven." 13 I heard the wings of the living creatures touching each other and the sound of the wheels by them. It was a loud rumbling sound. 14 So the Spirit lifted me up and took me away. I was unhappy and angry, and I felt the great power of the LORD. 15 I came to the captives from Judah, who lived by the Kebar River at Tel Abib. I sat there seven days where these people lived, feeling shocked.

Israel's Warning

16 After seven days the LORD spoke his word to me again. He said, 17 "Human, I now make you a watchman for Israel. Any time you hear a word from my mouth, warn them for me. 18 When I say to the wicked, 'You will surely die,' you must warn them so they may live. If you don't speak out to warn the wicked to stop their evil ways, they will die in their sin. But I will hold you responsible for their death. 19 If you warn the wicked and they do not turn from their wickedness or their evil ways, they will die because of their sin. But you will have saved your life.

20 "Again, those who do right may turn away from doing good and do evil. If I make something bad happen to them, they will die. Because you have not warned them, they will die because of their sin, and the good they did will not be remembered. But I will hold you responsible for their deaths. 21 But if you have warned those good people not to sin, and they do not sin, they will surely live, because they believed the warning. And you will have saved your life."

22 Then I felt the power of the LORD there. He said to me, "Get up and go out to the plain. There I will speak to you." 23 So I got up and went out to the plain. I saw the glory of the LORD standing there, like the glory I saw by the Kebar River, and I bowed facedown on the ground.

24 Then the Spirit entered me and made me stand on my feet. He spoke to me and said, "Go, shut yourself up in your house. 25 As for you, human, the people will tie you up with ropes so that you will not be able to go out among them. 26 Also, I will make your tongue stick to the roof of your mouth so you will be silent. You will not be able to argue with the people, even though they turn against me. 27 But when I speak to you, I will open your mouth, and you will say to them, 'The

---

3:3 *eat this scroll.* The eating of the scroll indicates the prophet taking the very message of God and making it part of him. Ezekiel then is commanded to speak these words to the people.

3:11 Stubbornness: Matthew 11:20–24

Honor & Shame

Luke 18

How are concerns for honor and shame presented in Scripture? How can people like ourselves, who live in societies not driven by these "pivotal values" relate to concepts that come from such societies? What relevance do these concerns have for us?

The Bible upholds a sense of honor and shame that begins with spiritual realities. Jesus tells a parable with the point that we should serve God in such a way that he is able to honor us with the statement, "You did well. You are a good and loyal servant" (Matthew 25:21). On the other hand, we are to avoid a lifestyle of sin which disgraces the name of Christ (Hebrews 6:6). We are to bring honor to Christ's name through our worship and lifestyle. In addition, we are to be concerned about the honor of others, and even ourselves, because we are all made in God's image and reflect his glory.

We see evidence throughout Scripture of the concern for upholding honor and avoiding shame. This emphasis on one's status was the social scale used to maintain order in that culture. But a close look at our own culture proves that we are not so far removed from honor and shame issues today.

From ancient Israel to the first century when Jesus ministered, God's people concern themselves with avoiding shame and gaining honor. As early as Genesis 4 we are given the story of Cain and Abel. Cain, shamed because God accepted his brother Abel's gift but not his, attempts to regain his honor by getting rid of his rival. This act results in further shame as he is cast outside of his family's protection to "wander around on the earth" (Genesis 4:12). Cain says this is a punishment he cannot bear. Shame, then, is worse even than death. In Psalm 40:14, the writer cries out to God to act against his enemies, "People are trying to kill me. Shame them and disgrace them." And Hebrews 6:6 relates that the tragedy of Jesus' death on the cross was that he was shamed in front of others.

Unlike our culture where status in society is achieved through economic or career success, in biblical societies honor was given to a person based on birthright, not on one's achievements. For example, a healthy, older, free, Jewish man, perhaps even born into the priestly line of Aaron (see Philippians 3:4–6), would have far more honor than a crippled, child, slave, Gentile, girl (see Genesis 21:8–14; Deuteronomy 21:10–14). The emphasis on honor in relation to social status, then, created quite a problem for those not born into an honorable position.

Perhaps this is why we so often hear from Jesus the words, "Whoever wants to be the most important must be last of all and servant of all" (Matthew 18:4; Mark 9:35; 10:43; Luke 22:6). Jesus was committed to breaking down a system that elevated some while oppressing others. In Luke 9:46–48, Jesus responded to an argument between his followers. Though to modern day Christians their argument may seem ridiculous, it was rather pertinent to their social setting. They were expecting Jesus to take over the world soon ,and they would need to know who would be his "right-hand man," so to speak. They, therefore, argued over their seats of status in relation to Jesus so that they could act accordingly when the time came. In an attempt to flatten the system they were working under, Jesus invited a child to him as an example of greatness—a dependent, non-contributing, lowly, no-status, no-worth child.

The realization of this aspect of Jesus' ministry is key to determining how we, as followers of Jesus, should be aware of and respond to honor/shame issues today. As suggested before, first-century Palestine's issue with honor is not much different from twentieth-century America's career/salary issue. In both cases, they allow the people to define social groupings based on the theology of "God's blessing." In biblical times, those with honor were considered blessed, just as those who are successful and prosperous are considered blessed today. By undercutting status issues in his day, Jesus broke the measuring stick used to define those with God's blessing and those without it. The very people who were considered the most outside of God's blessing, the shamed, became those who had access to it all along. Similarly today, without money there would be nothing by which we could measure who has God's favor and who does not. As Americans, especially, we believe that God's blessing is equated with prosperity. God blessed America, after all. We do not believe that we have social groupings that give some persons access, while denying it to others. "If they work hard, they will make it, too" we say, all the while forgetting that our social status, education, health, and gender may have opened doors for us that, though we never acknowledged it, gave us access to opportunities denied to others.

Honor & Shame: For additional scriptures on this topic go to Psalm 40:14.

Materialism/Possessions

Luke 18:18–30

What is "materialism"? What are appropriate uses of possessions?
How many possessions are appropriate?

Materialism refers to an approach to life that places great importance on material possessions. Although biblical authors do not use the word materialism, they do warn against acquiring many possessions, and encourage selling belongings in order to help others. Possessions, like money, are seen as a controlling power that competes with God. The high number of biblical passages that discuss wealth and riches call for our attention, especially since most who read this have many belongings and are wealthy compared to most people in the world.

Much of the biblical discussion of possessions relates to helping the poor. In both Old and New Testaments, people are called to share freely with those in need (Deuteronomy 15:7–11; Luke 11:41; Acts 2:43–47; 2 Corinthians 8:13–15; 1 John 3:17). The Bible, however, does not simply discuss shared riches as a way to alleviate poverty, it also presents the drive to accumulate more possessions as sinful if it causes others to suffer. James condemns those rich who become prosperous and have a life of pleasure by not giving fair wages to their workers (James 5:1–6). Amos condemns those who step on others, taking from the poor in order to fatten their own lifestyle (Amos 2:6–8; 4:1; 5:11). The Jubilee year laws, though not legislating strict equality, show God's concern not to allow some people to become significantly more wealthy than others: every fifty years, the land reverted again to its original owners (Leviticus 25:8–34). Other laws called for all debts to be forgiven every seven years (Deuteronomy 15:1–11). Both sets of laws collide with what our society would consider fair and appropriate rules regulating ownership and the use of money. For God, people are of primary significance—money and possessions are secondary.

The Bible calls the rich to give to the poor not only out of concern for the poor, but also out of concern for the wealthy. As in the case of the rich man in this passage, the wealthy person's need to give may be greater than the poor person's need to receive. The Bible, unlike our society, considers the love of riches a problem. The drive to obtain more belongings can ruin and destroy people (1 Timothy 6:9). The Bible also exposes the lies of materialism. "Life is not measured by how much one owns" (Luke 12:15). The security wealth promises is an illusion, and riches do not satisfy, but this enslaving power will tell us that we will be better off with a little more (Psalm 49; Ecclesiastes 5:10–17; Luke 12:13–34; Revelation 3:17).

Perhaps the most common response to biblical teaching on wealth is to say that the quantity of our wealth is not the issue, but our attitude toward it. This is basically true. For instance, someone who owns very little can still be quite materialistic, and the Bible does not contain a universal call to poverty. Yet too often we say this to escape facing the truth that the quantity of our possession does have significance. It is hard for the rich to enter the kingdom of God (Luke 18:24). Whereas poor people may turn to God because they have little alternative, it is hard for others not to place some security in savings, property, and insurance policies.

What are appropriate uses of possessions? The Bible points to an open-handed ownership that displays a willingness to share or give to others. The Bible does not, however, offer rules on what is an appropriate amount of possessions. Jesus calls one rich man to sell all, but he does not scold Zacchaeus for only giving away half of his possessions (Luke 19:1–9). Just as attempting to achieve the good life through buying more than one needs can consume many people, we could also easily be consumed by attempting to achieve approval from God and status with other Christians by cutting back to a prescribed lifestyle and aiding the poor. Both approaches are based on a materialistic lie that possessions are of central importance. God does not prescribe rules about possessions; rather, God offers us freedom from enslavement to materialism. Any effort at proper use of belongings that is not based in this freedom is only another form of enslavement.

The Bible's strong words against materialism are based on God's love for us. The statement that we cannot serve both God and worldly riches, and the call to sell all, are strong, demanding words, but God has not set up a challenge simply to see if we can achieve it. We should read these as words of rescue from a loving Savior. What would have happened if the rich young ruler had said to Jesus, "I can't; I am trapped by these things. Please help me"? Perhaps the best thing we can do is recognize it is impossible to free ourselves from materialism, and ask God to allow us to experience his love and the reality of his kingdom in such a way that the lies of materialism are no longer compelling.

Materialism/Possessions: For additional scriptures on this topic go to Leviticus 25:8–55.

Lord GOD says this.' Those who will listen, let
them listen. Those who refuse, let them refuse,
because they are a people who turn against me.

The Map of Jerusalem

4 "Now, human, get yourself a brick, put it in
front of you, and draw a map of Jerusalem on
it. 2Then surround it with an army. Build battle
works against the city and a dirt road to the top of
the city walls. Set up camps around it, and put
heavy logs in place to break down the walls. 3Then
get yourself an iron plate and set it up like an iron
wall between you and the city. Turn your face
toward the city as if to attack it and then attack.
This is a sign to Israel.

4"Then lie down on your left side, and take the
guilt of Israel on yourself. Their guilt will be on you
for the number of days you lie on your left side. 5I
have given you the same number of days as the
years of the people's sin. So you will have the
guilt of Israel's sin on you for three hundred
ninety days.

6"After you have finished these three hundred
ninety days, lie down a second time, on your
right side. You will then have the guilt of Judah
on you. I will give it to you for forty days, a day for
each year of their sin. 7Then you will look toward
Jerusalem, which is being attacked. With your
arm bare, you will prophesy against Jerusalem. 8I
will put ropes on you so you cannot turn from one
side to the other until you have finished the days
of your attack on Jerusalem.

9"Take wheat, barley, beans, small peas, and
millet seeds, and put them in one bowl, and make
them into bread for yourself. You will eat it the
three hundred ninety days you lie on your side.
10You will eat eight ounces of food every day at set
times. 11You will drink about two-thirds of a quart
of water every day at set times. 12Eat your food as
you would eat a barley cake, baking it over human
dung where the people can see." 13Then the LORD
said, "In the same way Israel will eat unclean food
among the nations where I force them to go."

14But I said, "No, Lord GOD! I have never been
made unclean. From the time I was young until
now I've never eaten anything that died by itself
or was torn by animals. Unclean meat has never
entered my mouth."

15"Very well," he said. "Then I will give you
cow's dung instead of human dung to use for your
fire to bake your bread."

16He also said to me, "Human, I am going to cut
off the supply of bread to Jerusalem. They will eat
the bread that is measured out to them, and they
will worry as they eat. They will drink water that
is measured out to them, and they will be in shock
as they drink it. 17This is because bread and water
will be hard to find. The people will be shocked at
the sight of each other, and they will become
weak because of their sin.

Ezekiel Cuts His Hair

5 "Now, human, take a sharp sword, and use it
like a barber's razor to shave your head and
beard. Then take scales and weigh and divide the
hair. 2Burn one-third with fire in the middle of the
city when the days of the attack on Jerusalem are
over. Then take one-third and cut it up with the
knife all around the city. And scatter one-third to
the wind. This is how I will chase them with a
sword. 3Also take a few of these hairs and tie them
in the folds of your clothes. 4Take a few more and
throw them into the fire and burn them up. From
there a fire will spread to all the people of Israel.

5"This is what the Lord GOD says: This is Jerusalem. I have put her at the center of the nations
with countries all around her. 6But she has refused
to obey my laws and has been more evil than the
nations. She has refused to obey my rules, even
more than nations around her. The people of
Jerusalem have rejected my laws and have not
lived by my rules.

7"So this is what the Lord GOD says: You have
caused more trouble than the nations around you.
You have not followed my rules or obeyed my laws.
You have not even obeyed the laws of the nations
around you.

8"So this is what the Lord GOD says: I myself am
against you, and I will punish you as the nations
watch. 9I will do things among you that I have not
done before and that I will never do anything like
again, because you do the things I hate. 10So parents among you will eat their children, and children will eat their parents. I will punish you and
will scatter to the winds all who are left alive. 11So
the Lord GOD says: You have made my Temple
unclean with all your evil idols and the hateful

3:27 Ezekiel: Ezekiel 4:1–17
4:17 Famine: Ezekiel 34:29
4:17 Ezekiel: Ezekiel 12:17–20

5:2 Verse 12 explains that each third of Ezekiel's hair represented a third of the people of Jerusalem. One third would die inside the city by famine and disease, another third would die at the hands of the Babylonian army, and the rest would be scattered over the countryside trying to escape. Verses 13–17 are probably a further explanation of Ezekiel's symbolic actions with the two smaller groups of hair in verses 3–4.The few hairs tucked in Ezekiel's clothing represented a small remnant of survivors. The hairs thrown into the fire were those survivors who would later die of famine in the land of Judah.

things you do. Because of this, as surely as I live, I will cut you off. I will have no pity, and I will show no mercy. [12]A third of you will die by disease or be destroyed by hunger inside your walls. A third will fall dead by the sword outside your walls. And a third I will scatter in every direction as I chase them with a sword. [13]Then my anger will come to an end. I will use it up against them, and then I will be satisfied. Then they will know that I, the LORD, have spoken. After I have carried out my anger against them, they will know how strongly I felt.

[14]"I will make you a ruin and a shame among the nations around you, to be seen by all who pass by. [15]Then the nations around you will shame you and make fun of you. You will be a warning and a terror to them. This will happen when I punish you in my great anger. I, the LORD, have spoken. [16]I will send a time of hunger to destroy you, and then I will make your hunger get even worse, and I will cut off your supply of food. [17]I will send a time of hunger and wild animals against you, and they will kill your children. Disease and death will sweep through your people, and I will bring the sword against you to kill you. I, the LORD, have spoken."

Prophecies Against the Mountains

6 Again the LORD spoke his word to me, saying: [2]"Human, look toward the mountains of Israel, and prophesy against them. [3]Say, 'Mountains of Israel, listen to the word of the Lord GOD. The Lord GOD says this to the mountains, the hills, the ravines, and the valleys: I will bring a sword against you, and I will destroy your places of idol worship. [4]Your altars will be destroyed and your incense altars broken down. Your people will be killed in front of your idols. [5]I will lay the dead bodies of the Israelites in front of their idols, and I will scatter your bones around your altars. [6]In all the places you live, cities will become empty. The places of idol worship will be ruined; your altars will become lonely ruins. Your idols will be broken and brought to an end. Your incense altars will be cut down, and the things you made will be wiped out. [7]Your people will be killed and fall among you. Then you will know that I am the LORD.

[8]" 'But I will leave some people alive; some will not be killed by the nations when you are scattered among the foreign lands. [9]Then those who have escaped will remember me, as they live among the nations where they have been taken as captives. They will remember how I was hurt because they were unfaithful to me and turned away from me and desired to worship their idols. They will hate themselves because of the evil things they did that I hate. [10]Then they will know that I am the LORD. I did not bring this terrible thing on them for no reason.

[11]" 'This is what the Lord GOD says: Clap your hands, stamp your feet, and groan because of all the hateful, evil things the people of Israel have done. They will die by war, hunger, and disease. [12]The person who is far away will die by disease. The one who is nearby will die in war. The person who is still alive and has escaped these will die from hunger. So I will carry out my anger on them. [13]Their people will lie dead among their idols around the altars, on every high hill, on all the mountain tops, and under every green tree and leafy oak—all the places where they offered sweet-smelling incense to their idols. Then you will know that I am the LORD. [14]I will use my power against them to make the land empty and wasted from the desert to Diblah, wherever they live. Then they will know that I am the LORD.' "

Ezekiel Tells of the End

7 Again the LORD spoke his word to me, saying: [2]"Human, the Lord GOD says this to the land of Israel: An end! The end has come on the four corners of the land. [3]Now the end has come for you, and I will send my anger against you. I will judge you for the way you have lived, and I will make you pay for all your actions that I hate. [4]I will have no pity on you; I will not hold back punishment from you. Instead, I will make you pay for the way you have lived and for your actions that I hate. Then you will know that I am the LORD.

[5]"This is what the Lord GOD says: Disaster on top of disaster is coming. [6]The end has come! The end has come! It has stirred itself up against you! Look! It has come! [7]Disaster has come for you who live in the land! The time has come; the day of confusion is near. There will be no happy shouting on the mountains. [8]Soon I will pour out my anger against you; I will carry out my anger against you. I will judge you for the way you have lived and will make you pay for everything you have done that I hate. [9]I will show no pity, and I will not hold back punishment. I will pay you back for the way you have lived and the things you have done that I hate. Then you will know that I am the LORD who punishes.

[10]"Look, the day is here. It has come. Disaster has come, violence has grown, and there is more

5:17 Prophetic Symbolism: Ezekiel 12:1–20

6:13 *every high hill.* Hills and mountains were thought to be the dwelling of the gods among Near Eastern people. Altars were located near trees, since they were symbolic of life and fertility.

pride than ever. [11]Violence has grown into a weapon for punishing wickedness. None of the people will be left—none of that crowd, none of their wealth, and nothing of value. [12]The time has come; the day has arrived. Don't let the buyer be happy or the seller be sad, because my burning anger is against the whole crowd. [13]Sellers will not return to the land they have sold as long as they live, because the vision against all that crowd will not be changed. Because of their sins, they will not save their lives. [14]They have blown the trumpet, and everything is ready. But no one is going to the battle, because my anger is against all that crowd.

[15]"The sword is outside, and disease and hunger are inside. Whoever is in the field will die by the sword. Hunger and disease will destroy those in the city. [16]Those who are left alive and who escape will be on the mountains, moaning like doves of the valleys about their own sin. [17]All hands will hang weakly with fear, and all knees will become weak as water. [18]They will put on rough cloth to show how sad they are. They will tremble all over with fear. Their faces will show their shame, and all their heads will be shaved. [19]The people will throw their silver into the streets, and their gold will be like trash. Their silver and gold will not save them from the LORD's anger. It will not satisfy their hunger or fill their stomachs, because it caused them to fall into sin. [20]They were proud of their beautiful jewelry and used it to make their idols and their evil statues, which I hate. So I will turn their wealth into trash. [21]I will give it to foreigners as loot from war and to the most evil people in the world as treasure, and they will dishonor it. [22]I will also turn away from the people of Israel, and they will dishonor my treasured place. Then robbers will enter and dishonor it.

[23]"Make chains for captives, because the land is full of bloody crimes and the city is full of violence. [24]So I will bring the worst of the nations to take over the people's houses. I will also end the pride of the strong, and their holy places will be dishonored. [25]When the people are suffering greatly, they will look for peace, but there will be none. [26]Disaster will come on top of disaster, and rumor will be added to rumor. Then they will try to get a vision from a prophet; the teachings of God from the priest and the advice from the older leaders will be lost. [27]The king will cry greatly, the prince will give up hope, and the hands of the people who own land will shake with fear. I will punish them for the way they have lived. The way they have judged others is the way I will judge them. Then they will know that I am the LORD."

Ezekiel's Vision of Jerusalem

8 It was the sixth year, on the fifth day of the sixth month of our captivity. I was sitting in my house with the older leaders of Judah in front of me. There I felt the power of the Lord GOD. [2]I looked and saw something that looked like a human. From the waist down it looked like fire, and from the waist up it looked like bright glowing metal. [3]It stretched out the shape of a hand and caught me by the hair on my head. The Spirit lifted me up between the earth and the sky. He took me in visions of God to Jerusalem, to the entrance to the north gate of the inner courtyard of the Temple. In the courtyard was the idol that caused God to be jealous. [4]I saw the glory of the God of Israel there, as I had seen on the plain.

[5]Then he said to me, "Human, now look toward the north." So I looked up toward the north, and in the entrance north of the gate of the altar was the idol that caused God to be jealous.

[6]He said to me, "Human, do you see what they are doing? Do you see how many hateful things the people of Israel are doing here that drive me far away from my Temple? But you will see things more hateful than these."

[7]Then he brought me to the entry of the courtyard. When I looked, I saw a hole in the wall. [8]He said to me, "Human, dig through the wall." So I dug through the wall and saw an entrance.

[9]Then he said to me, "Go in and see the hateful, evil things they are doing here." [10]So I entered and looked, and I saw every kind of crawling thing and hateful beast and all the idols of the people of Israel, carved on the wall all around. [11]Standing in front of these carvings and idols were seventy of the older leaders of Israel and Jaazaniah son of Shaphan. Each man had his pan for burning incense in his hand, and a sweet-smelling cloud of incense was rising.

[12]Then he said to me, "Human, have you seen what the older leaders of Israel are doing in the dark? Have you seen each man in the room of his own idol? They say, 'The LORD doesn't see us. The LORD has left the land.' " [13]He also said to me, "You will see even more hateful things that they are doing."

[14]Then he brought me to the entrance of the north gate of the Temple of the LORD, where I saw

7:19 Day of the Lord: Ezekiel 30:3

8:2 *something that looked like a human.* God sent an angel to guide Ezekiel through the remarkable revelations that he describes to the reader.

8:10 These people of Israel were worshiping creatures rather than the Creator, and specifically, they were worshiping unclean animals like those described in Leviticus 11.

8:14 *Tammuz.* Tammuz was a god in Babylon. Every year people

women sitting and crying for Tammuz. 15He said to me, "Do you see, human? You will see things even more hateful than these."

16Then he brought me into the inner courtyard of the Temple. There I saw about twenty-five men at the entrance to the Temple of the LORD, between the porch and the altar. With their backs turned to the Temple of the LORD, they faced east and were worshiping the sun in the east.

17He said to me, "Do you see, human? Is it unimportant that the people of Judah are doing the hateful things they have done here? They have filled the land with violence and made me continually angry. Look, they are insulting me every way they can. 18So I will act in anger. I will have no pity, nor will I show mercy. Even if they shout in my ears, I won't listen to them."

Vision of the Angels

9 Then he shouted with a loud voice in my ears, "You who are chosen to punish this city, come near with your weapon in your hand." 2Then six men came from the direction of the upper gate, which faces north, each with his powerful weapon in his hand. Among them was a man dressed in linen with a writing case at his side. The men went in and stood by the bronze altar.

3Then the glory of the God of Israel went up from above the creatures with wings, where it had been, to the place in the Temple where the door opened. He called to the man dressed in linen who had the writing case at his side. 4He said to the man, "Go through Jerusalem and put a mark on the foreheads of the people who groan and cry about all the hateful things being done among them."

5As I listened, he said to the other men, "Go through the city behind the man dressed in linen and kill. Don't pity anyone, and don't show mercy. 6Kill and destroy old men, young men and women, little children, and older women, but don't touch any who have the mark on them. Start at my Temple." So they started with the older leaders who were in front of the Temple.

7Then he said to the men, "Make the Temple unclean, and fill the courtyards with those who have been killed. Go out!" So the men went out and killed the people in the city. 8While the men were killing the people, I was left alone. I bowed facedown on the ground and I cried out, "Oh, Lord GOD! Will you destroy everyone left alive in Israel when you turn loose your anger on Jerusalem?"

9Then he said to me, "The sin of the people of Israel and Judah is very great. The land is filled with people who murder, and the city is full of people who are not fair. The people say, 'The LORD has left the land, and the LORD does not see.' 10But I will have no pity, nor will I show mercy. I will bring their evil back on their heads."

11Then the man dressed in linen with the writing case at his side reported, "I have done just as you commanded me."

The Coals of Fire

10 Then I looked and saw in the dome above the heads of the living creatures something like a sapphire gem which looked like a throne. 2The LORD said to the man dressed in linen, "Go in between the wheels under the living creatures, fill your hands with coals of fire from between the living creatures, and scatter the coals over the city."

As I watched, the man with linen clothes went in. 3Now the living creatures were standing on the south side of the Temple when the man went in. And a cloud filled the inner courtyard. 4Then the glory of the LORD went up from the living creatures and stood over the door of the Temple. The Temple was filled with the cloud, and the courtyard was full of the brightness from the glory of the LORD. 5The sound of the wings of the living creatures was heard all the way to the outer courtyard. It was like the voice of God Almighty when he speaks.

6When the LORD commanded the man dressed in linen, "Take fire from between the wheels, from between the living creatures," the man went in and stood by a wheel. 7One living creature put out his hand to the fire that was among them, took some of the fire, and put it in the hands of the man dressed in linen. Then the man took the fire and went out.

The Wheels and the Creatures

8Something that looked like a human hand could be seen under the wings of the living creatures. 9I saw the four wheels by the living creatures, one wheel by each living creature. The wheels looked like shining chrysolite. 10All four wheels looked alike: Each looked like a wheel crossways inside another wheel. 11When the wheels moved, they went in any of the directions that the four living creatures faced. The wheels did not turn about, and the living creatures did not turn their bodies

---

thought this god died when the plants died. After they cried for him, they believed he came back to life, and the plants lived again.

9:3 *the creatures with wings.* These cherubim (creatures with wings), who propel God's chariot and are the creatures of chapter 1, are supernatural, angelic beings.

as they went. 12All their bodies, their backs, their
hands, their wings, and the wheels were full of
eyes all over. Each of the four living creatures had
a wheel. 13I heard the wheels being called "whirl-
ing wheels." 14Each living creature had four faces.
The first face was the face of a creature with wings.
The second face was a human face, the third was
the face of a lion, and the fourth was the face of
an eagle.

15Then the living creatures flew up. They were
the same living creatures I had seen by the Kebar
River. 16When the living creatures moved, the
wheels moved beside them. When the living creatures lifted their wings to fly up from the ground,
the wheels did not leave their place beside them.
17When the living creatures stopped, the wheels
stopped. When the creatures went up, the wheels
went up also, because the spirit of the living creatures was in the wheels.

18Then the glory of the LORD left the door of the
Temple and stood over the living creatures. 19As I
watched, the living creatures spread their wings
and flew up from the ground, with the wheels
beside them. They stood where the east gate of
the Temple of the LORD opened, and the glory of
the God of Israel was over them.

20These were the living creatures I had seen
under the God of Israel by the Kebar River. I
knew they were called cherubim. 21Each one
had four faces and four wings, and under their
wings were things that looked like human hands.
22Their faces looked the same as the ones I had
seen by the Kebar River. They each went straight
ahead.

Prophecies Against Evil Leaders

11 The Spirit lifted me up and brought me to
the front gate of the Temple of the LORD,
which faces east. I saw twenty-five men where
the gate opens, among them Jaazaniah son of
Azzur and Pelatiah son of Benaiah, who were
leaders of the people. 2Then the LORD said to me,
"Human, these are the men who plan evil and
give wicked advice in this city of Jerusalem.
3They say, 'It is almost time for us to build
houses. This city is like a cooking pot, and we are
like the best meat.' 4So prophesy against them,
prophesy, human."

5Then the Spirit of the LORD entered me and
told me to say: "This is what the LORD says: You
have said these things, people of Israel, and I
know what you are thinking. 6You have killed
many people in this city, filling its streets with
their bodies.

7"So this is what the Lord GOD says: Those
people you have killed and left in the middle of
the city are like the best meat, and this city is like
the cooking pot. But I will force you out of the
city. 8You have feared the sword, but I will bring
a sword against you, says the Lord GOD. 9I will
force you out of the city and hand you over to
strangers and punish you. 10You will die by the
sword. I will punish you at the border of Israel so
you will know that I am the LORD. 11This city will
not be your cooking pot, and you will not be the
best meat in the middle of it. I will punish you at
the border of Israel. 12Then you will know that I
am the LORD. You did not live by my rules or obey
my laws. Instead, you did the same things as the
nations around you."

13As I prophesied, Pelatiah son of Benaiah died.
Then I bowed facedown on the ground and shouted
with a loud voice, "Oh no, Lord GOD! Will you
completely destroy the Israelites who are left
alive?"

Promise to Those Remaining

14The LORD spoke his word to me, saying,
15"Human, the people still in Jerusalem have spoken about your own relatives and all the people of
Israel who are captives with you, saying, 'They
are far from the LORD. This land has been given to
us as our property.'

16"So say, 'This is what the Lord GOD says: I
sent the people far away among the nations and
scattered them among the countries. But for a little while I have become a Temple to them in the
countries where they have gone.'

17"So say: 'This is what the Lord GOD says: I will
gather you from the nations and bring you together
from the countries where you have been scattered.
Then I will give you back the land of Israel.'

18"When they come to this land, they will
remove all the evil idols and all the hateful images. 19I will give them a desire to respect me
completely, and I will put inside them a new way
of thinking. I will take out the stubborn heart of
stone from their bodies, and I will give them an
obedient heart of flesh. 20Then they will live by
my rules and obey my laws and keep them. They
will be my people, and I will be their God. 21But
those who want to serve their evil statues and
hateful idols, I will pay back for their evil ways,
says the Lord GOD."

11:19–20 God's promise to exiled Israel of a future restoration recognizes that the human heart is disobedient (Ezekiel 2:4–5) and must be changed by God before it can even desire to obey. God's promise to transform people inwardly was given as early as the time of Moses (Deuteronomy 30:6) and now takes place through the renewing work of the Holy Spirit (Ezekiel 36:26–27; John 3:5–6).

Ezekiel's Vision Ends

22Then the living creatures lifted their wings
with the wheels beside them, and the glory of the
God of Israel was above them. 23The glory of the
LORD went up from inside Jerusalem and stopped
on the mountain on the east side of the city. 24The
Spirit lifted me up and brought me to the captives
who had been taken from Judah to Babylonia. This
happened in a vision given by the Spirit of God,
and then the vision I had seen ended. 25And I told
the captives from Judah all the things the LORD had
shown me.

Ezekiel Moves Out

12 Again the LORD spoke his word to me, saying: 2 "Human, you are living among a people who refuse to obey. They have eyes to see, but
they do not see, and they have ears to hear, but
they do not hear, because they are a people who
refuse to obey.

3"So, human, pack your things as if you will be
taken away captive, and walk away like a captive
in the daytime with the people watching. Move
from your place to another with the people watching. Maybe they will understand, even though
they are a people who refuse to obey. 4During the
day when the people are watching, bring out the
things you would pack as captive. At evening, with
the people watching, leave your place like those
who are taken away as captives from their country.
5Dig a hole through the wall while they watch, and
bring your things out through it. 6Lift them onto
your shoulders with the people watching, and
carry them out in the dark. Cover your face so you
cannot see the ground, because I have made you a
sign to the people of Israel."

7I did these things as I was commanded. In the
daytime I brought what I had packed as if I were
being taken away captive. Then in the evening I
dug through the wall with my hands. I brought
my things out in the dark and carried them on my
shoulders as the people watched.

8Then in the morning the LORD spoke his word
to me, saying:9"Human, didn't Israel, who refuses
to obey, ask you, 'What are you doing?'

10"Say to them, 'This is what the Lord GOD says:
This message is about the king in Jerusalem and
all the people of Israel who live there.' 11Say, 'I am
a sign to you.'

"The same things I have done will be done to
the people in Jerusalem. They will be taken away
from their country as captives. 12The king among
them will put his things on his shoulder in the dark
and will leave. The people will dig a hole through
the wall to bring him out. He will cover his face so
he cannot see the ground. 13But I will spread my
net over him, and he will be caught in my trap.
Then I will bring him to Babylon in the land of
the Babylonians. He will not see that land, but he
will die there. 14All who are around the king—his
helpers and all his army—I will scatter in every
direction, and I will chase them with a sword.

15"They will know that I am the LORD when I
scatter them among the nations and spread them
among the countries. 16But I will save a few of
them from the sword and from hunger and disease. Then they can tell about their hateful actions
among the nations where they go. Then they will
know that I am the LORD."

The Lesson of Ezekiel's Shaking

17The LORD spoke his word to me, saying: 18"Human, tremble as you eat your food, and shake with
fear as you drink your water. 19Then say to the people of the land: 'This is what the Lord GOD says
about the people who live in Jerusalem in the land
of Israel: They will eat their food with fear and
drink their water in shock, because their land will
be stripped bare because of the violence of the
people who live in it. 20The cities where people
live will become ruins, and the land will become
empty. Then you will know that I am the LORD.' "

The Visions Will Come True

21The LORD spoke his word to me, saying: 22"Human, what is this saying you have in the land of
Israel: 'The days go by and every vision comes to
nothing'? 23So say to them, 'This is what the Lord
GOD says: I will make them stop saying this, and
nobody in Israel will use this saying anymore.' But
tell them, 'The time is near when every vision will
come true. 24There will be no more false visions
or pleasing prophecies inside the nation of Israel,
25but I, the LORD, will speak. What I say will be
done, and it will not be delayed. You refuse to
obey, but in your time I will say the word and do
it, says the Lord GOD.' "

26The LORD spoke his word to me, saying:
27"Human, the people of Israel are saying, 'The

12:3–7 Ezekiel performed two related symbolic actions. During the day, he took a bundle of belongings from his house and carried them away while all his neighbors were watching. It is assumed that he then returned home. In the evening, he dug a hole in the wall of his house, carried out his belongings, lifted them on his shoulders, and walked away with his face covered. The first action symbolized the departure of the captives from Jerusalem (verse 11). The second action symbolized the desperate escape of King Zedekiah (verse 12; 2 Kings 25:4–7).

12:20 Ezekiel: Ezekiel 24:15–18

12:20 Prophetic Symbolism: Ezekiel 16

12:23 Proverb: Ezekiel 18:2–3

Conversion

Luke 19:2

What does the Bible say about conversion?
Are people raised in families of faith (in Israel and in the church) "converted"?
Does conversion happen only one way? What are concrete signs of conversion?

Conversion is the turning point in the process of salvation. Sin is when we turn away from God and disobey God's commands. God continually seeks for us to turn away from sin and toward him. Such a turning is conversion. In the Old Testament, God sent prophets to tell Israel they should come back to him (Jeremiah 3:14) and should choose him above all other gods (Joshua 24:14–15). In the New Testament, conversion refers specifically to becoming a believer in Christ. Persons who encountered Jesus were changed and learned what a new life in Christ could mean. For Zacchaeus, it meant acceptance when he had been rejected by the people; it meant concern for the poor, and restoring what he had stolen.

Conversion thus is a change in identity, becoming a part of God's new creation (2 Corinthians 5:17). Ephesians 2:12 says we were outside of Israel, and we did not have hope. When someone turns to God, they become again part of God's people and share in the new life that God gives those who belong to him. The deepest question conversion answers is, To whom do you belong? Modern atheists answer, "I belong only to myself. I am committed only to me." Conversion leads people to know the love of God in Christ Jesus.

Conversion happens at some point to every believer. Even those who are raised in families of faith make a decision for themselves about serving God. As a nation, Israel was God's chosen people, and still Joshua told them bluntly, "You must choose for yourselves today whom you will serve" (Joshua 24:15). Despite good upbringing, some individuals stray. They must decide whether to come home, as did the younger son in Jesus' parable who "realized what he was doing" and decided to go home, even if that meant filling a servant's role (Luke 15:17). Others have never known the message of salvation through Christ, and conversion means understanding and accepting it for the first time. In raising children in a Christian family, we hope that the decision to commit one's life to Christ naturally grows out of the education, family prayers, worship, and church activities the young person has experienced. But this developing faith does not take the place of a decision to accept for oneself both the joys and the responsibilities of turning toward God.

Conversion experiences happen in many different ways. The crucial element is that we turn away from sin and toward the Lord. Depending on where a person stands when making the decision, turning takes many different forms. For a gang member involved in criminal activities, conversion means a new set of beliefs, new attitudes, a new group of friends, a new schedule of activities each week. For a teenager raised in church, conversion looks more like a natural outgrowth of the things they have been doing all their lives. When Jesus told Nicodemus that "unless one is born again, he cannot be in God's kingdom" (John 3:3), he was referring to this kind of change that makes one a new person, not a specific kind of experience that everyone must have in the same way. John 3:8 specifically notes that being born again happens by the power of the Spirit, which "blows where it wants to." We know its effects—God is changing people's hearts—but we also know that God acts in many different ways.

We also know the effects of genuine conversion, with only a few exceptions. The new Christian starts to love God in every way possible (Matthew 22:37–38). We begin to put God first in our life, accepting his authority over all that we do. Among other things, loving God means worshiping him in a church, and participating as a member of that body of believers. The New Testament does not have a single example of a believer who was not later connected to a local church. Conversion is seen in love toward others and ourself. It means withdrawing from sinful actions as much as possible, and progressing toward a heart that is completely motivated by love. Someone who turns away from sin is not immediately perfect. In fact, 1 John 2:12 refers to them as children, meaning young Christians. As we grow, sin will have less and less control over our lives. But in conversion, a genuinely new start is made and some fruit of God's love is clearly seen immediately. Zacchaeus's conversion illustrates these principles. He was an isolated individual, condemned by others because he collected taxes for the Romans and cheated the people. Jesus' invitation to eat with him broke down those barriers and showed Zacchaeus the love God had for him. Zacchaeus responded by giving money to the poor and paying back all those he had cheated four times over. He was a new creation.

Conversion: For additional scriptures on this topic go to Jeremiah 3:14.

Mount of Olives

Luke 22:39–46

Why is the Mount of Olives so prominent in the story of Christ? Why is it sometimes called "Gethsemane"? What crucial events happened on the Mount of Olives?

Though they differ in the way they describe the location, all four accounts of the Good News record Jesus crossing over from Jerusalem to the Mount of Olives. During his final stay in Jerusalem, Jesus often went to the Mount of Olives (Gethsemane) in order to pray, rest, and enjoy fellowship with his followers. This was the site of his public betrayal by Judas and his arrest. Before he was arrested, however, it was where Jesus spent the late evening in prayer. According to Acts 1:9–12, Jesus was lifted up into heaven from the Mount of Olives.

Instead of "Mount of Olives," the Books of Matthew and Mark refer to "Gethsemane," which means "oil press." This, along with the reference to a garden in John 18:1, suggests that Gethsemane was an olive tree orchard with an olive press used to squeeze the oil from the olives. It was here, in Gethsemane, on the side of the Mount of Olives, that Jesus often went with his closest followers.

What happened on the night before Jesus' death on the Mount of Olives is crucial to our understanding of Jesus' ministry. In one of the few prayers of Jesus of which we have any record, we hear Jesus seeking to determine God's plan, and to embrace it for himself. In the Books of Matthew and Mark, Jesus prays three times, asking that the cup be removed from him. To speak of the "cup" in this way is to bring to mind God's judgment on the people on account of their wickedness (see Psalm 75:8; Isaiah 51:17). Jesus is thinking of the coming events in the same way: They are so terrible that to experience them is like drinking a cup of something bitter. In spite of the terrible things that were about to happen, though, Jesus is first and foremost committed to God's will. Just as he had taught his followers to pray, "May your kingdom come and what you want be done" (Matthew 6:10), he now prays, "Do what you want, not what I want" (Matthew 26:39).

Also emphasizing Jesus' obedience to God is the way he speaks of God. In Mark 14:36 he says, "Abba, Father!" This is a title for God that highlights the very close relationship they share. In the ancient world, to be a son meant, in part, to be obedient to one's father, and this is precisely what the writers emphasize here. Even in the face of suffering, Jesus affirms his basic commitment to obeying his Father. The Book of John tells this story in a different way, but the same stress on Jesus' obedience is found there, too (John 12:27–29).

Jesus is not the only person in focus in the stories about this night on the Mount of Olives (or Gethsemane). Also of importance are his followers. In fact, Jesus warns his followers several times to watch and pray so that they might have the strength to resist temptation. His warning suggests, first, that he regards his own struggle in prayer as a time to resist the temptation to turn away from the will of God. Second, though, Jesus knows that his followers will face the same temptation. They should face their time of testing in the same way he faces his—in prayer. This, of course, is precisely what the followers do not do—at least, not yet. Throughout the Good News stories, the followers struggle to understand who Jesus is and what it means to follow God's plan. Here, at the end of Jesus' ministry on earth, they show by their sleeping that they have not yet grasped fully the importance of Jesus or of these events.

The parallel between the followers and Jesus is even more stark in the Book of Luke. The story of Jesus' prayer on the Mount of Olives starts and finishes with his instructions to the followers that they should pray. As he prays, they should pray; as he rises, they should rise. That is, they are to act as he does, for he is the perfect example of the way to stand faithfully at the time of testing. Readers of this story will see immediately that they are to follow the example of Jesus, not of the followers.

Jesus' habit of going to the Mount of Olives with his followers is seen not only in the night of his betrayal. Acts 1 also tells the story of his being taken up into heaven from the Mount of Olives. On the Mount of Olives just before his arrest, Jesus declares his ultimate loyalty to God in prayer; then, on the Mount of Olives God lifts Jesus up, affirming him in his obedience. According to Zechariah 14:4, the Mount of Olives was to be the site of important events in God's plan, and this is certainly the case. In fact, not only is it here that Jesus' ascension is located, it is also here that his return is promised.⚭

⚭**Mount of Olives:** For additional scriptures on this topic go to Matthew 14:32–46.

vision that Ezekiel sees is for a time many years
from now. He is prophesying about times far
away.’
28“So say to them: ‘The Lord GOD says this: None
of my words will be delayed anymore. What I have
said will be done, says the Lord GOD.’ ”

Ezekiel Speaks Against False Prophets

13 The LORD spoke his word to me, saying:
2“Human, prophesy against the prophets of
Israel. Say to those who make up their own
prophecies: ‘Listen to the word of the LORD. 3This
is what the Lord GOD says: How terrible it will be
for the foolish prophets who follow their own
ideas and have not seen a vision from me! 4People
of Israel, your prophets have been like wild dogs
hunting to kill and eat among ruins. 5Israel is like
a house in ruins, but you have not gone up into
the broken places or repaired the wall. So how can
Israel hold back the enemy in the battle on the
LORD’s day of judging? 6Your prophets see false
visions and prophesy lies. They say, “This is the
message of the LORD,” when the LORD has not sent
them. But they still hope their words will come
true. 7You said, “This is the message of the LORD,”
but that is a false vision. Your prophecies are lies,
because I have not spoken.
8“ ‘So this is what the Lord GOD says: Because
you prophets spoke things that are false and saw
visions that do not come true, I am against you,
says the Lord GOD. 9I will punish the prophets who
see false visions and prophesy lies. They will have
no place among my people. Their names will not
be written on the list of the people of Israel, and
they will not enter the land of Israel. Then you will
know that I am the Lord GOD.
10“ ‘It is because they lead my people the wrong
way by saying, “Peace!” when there is no peace.
When the people build a weak wall, the prophets
cover it with whitewash to make it look strong.
11So tell those who cover a weak wall with whitewash that it will fall down. Rain will pour down,
hailstones will fall, and a stormy wind will break
the wall down. 12When the wall has fallen, people
will ask you, “Where is the whitewash you used
on the wall?”
13“ ‘So this is what the Lord GOD says: I will
break the wall with a stormy wind. In my anger
rain will pour down, and hailstones will destroy
the wall. 14I will tear down the wall on which you
put whitewash. I will level it to the ground so that
people will see the wall’s foundation. And when
the wall falls, you will be destroyed under it. Then
you will know that I am the LORD. 15So I will carry
out my anger on the wall and against those who
covered it with whitewash. Then I will tell you,
“The wall is gone, and those who covered it with
whitewash are gone. 16The prophets of Israel who
prophesy to Jerusalem and who see visions of peace
for the city, when there is no peace, will be gone,
says the Lord GOD.” ’

False Women Prophets

17“Now, human, look toward the women among
your people who make up their own prophecies.
Prophesy against them. 18Say, ‘This is what the
Lord GOD says: How terrible it will be for women
who sew magic charms on their wrists and make
veils of every length to trap people! You ruin the
lives of my people but try to save your own lives.
19For handfuls of barley and pieces of bread, you
have dishonored me among my people. By lying
to my people, who listen to lies, you have killed
people who should not die, and you have kept
alive those who should not live.
20“ ‘So this is what the Lord GOD says: I am
against your magic charms, by which you trap
people as if they were birds. I will tear those
charms off your arms, and I will free those people
you have trapped like birds. 21I will also tear off
your veils and save my people from your hands.
They will no longer be trapped by your power.
Then you will know that I am the LORD. 22By your
lies you have caused those who did right to be
sad, when I did not make them sad. And you have
encouraged the wicked not to stop being wicked,
which would have saved their lives. 23So you will
not see false visions or prophesy anymore, and I
will save my people from your power so you will
know that I am the LORD.’ ”

Stop Worshiping Idols

14 Some of the older leaders of Israel came to
me and sat down in front of me. 2Then the
LORD spoke his word to me, saying: 3“Human, these
men want to worship idols. They put up evil things
that cause people to sin. Should I allow them to ask
me for help? 4So speak to them and tell them, ‘This
is what the Lord GOD says: When any of the people
of Israel want to worship idols and put up evil
things that cause people to sin and then come to the
prophet, I, the LORD, will answer them myself for
worshiping idols. 5Then I will win back my people
Israel, who have left me because of all their idols.’
6“So say to the people of Israel, ‘This is what the
Lord GOD says: Change your hearts and lives, and

12:27 Vision: Joel 2:28

13:9 Lying/Dishonesty: Ephesians 4:15

13:18 These women are using magic to manipulate the circumstances of their clients. They break the Law of God, and for cheap pay as well.

13:19 Magic: Micah 5:11–12

stop worshiping idols. Stop doing all the things I hate. 7Any of the Israelites or foreigners in Israel can separate themselves from me by wanting to worship idols or by putting up the things that cause people to sin. Then if they come to the prophet to ask me questions, I, the LORD, will answer them myself. 8I will reject them. I will make them a sign and an example, and I will separate them from my people. Then you will know that I am the LORD.

9" 'But if the prophet is tricked into giving a prophecy, it is because I, the LORD, have tricked that prophet to speak. Then I will use my power against him and destroy him from among my people Israel. 10The prophet will be as guilty as the one who asks him for help; both will be responsible for their guilt. 11Then the nation of Israel will not leave me anymore or make themselves unclean anymore with all their sins. They will be my people, and I will be their God, says the Lord GOD.' "

Jerusalem Will Not Be Spared

12The LORD spoke his word to me, saying: 13"Human, if the people of a country sin against me by not being loyal, I will use my power against them. I will cut off their supply of food and send a time of hunger, destroying both people and animals. 14Even if three great men like Noah, Daniel, and Job were in that country, their goodness could save only themselves, says the Lord GOD.

15"Or I might send wild animals into that land, leaving the land empty and without children. Then no one would pass through it because of the animals. 16As surely as I live, says the Lord GOD, even if Noah, Daniel, and Job were in the land, they could not save their own sons or daughters. They could save only themselves, but that country would become empty.

17"Or I might bring a war against that country. I might say, 'Let a war be fought in that land,' in this way destroying its people and its animals. 18As surely as I live, says the Lord GOD, even if those three men were in the land, they could not save their sons or daughters. They could save only themselves.

19"Or I might cause a disease to spread in that country. I might pour out my anger against it, destroying and killing people and animals. 20As surely as I live, says the Lord GOD, even if Noah, Daniel, and Job were in the land, they could not save their son or daughter. They could save only themselves because they did what was right.

21"This is what the Lord GOD says: My plans for Jerusalem are much worse! I will send my four terrible punishments against it—war, hunger, wild animals, and disease—to destroy its people and animals. 22But some people will escape; some sons and daughters will be led out. They will come out to you, and you will see what happens to people who live as they did. Then you will be comforted after the disasters I have brought against Jerusalem, after all the things I have brought against it. 23You will be comforted when you see what happens to them for living as they did, because you will know there was a good reason for what I did to Jerusalem, says the Lord GOD."

Story of the Vine

15 The LORD spoke his word to me, saying: 2"Human, is the wood of the vine better than the wood of any tree in the forest? 3Can wood be taken from the vine to make anything? Can you use it to make a peg on which to hang something? 4If the vine is thrown into the fire for fuel, and the fire burns up both ends and starts to burn the middle, is it useful for anything? 5When the vine was whole, it couldn't be made into anything. When the fire has burned it completely, it certainly cannot be made into anything."

6So this is what the Lord GOD says: "Out of all the trees in the forest, I have given the wood of the vine as fuel for fire. In the same way I have given up the people who live in Jerusalem 7and will turn against them. Although they came through one fire, fire will still destroy them. When I turn against them, you will know that I am the LORD. 8So I will make the land empty, because the people have not been loyal, says the Lord GOD."

The Lord's Kindness to Jerusalem

16 The LORD spoke his word to me, saying: 2"Human, tell Jerusalem about her hateful actions. 3Say, 'This is what the Lord GOD says to Jerusalem: Your beginnings and your ancestors were in the land of the Canaanites. Your father was an Amorite, and your mother was a Hittite. 4On

14:14 Noah: Ezekiel 14:20

14:14 *Noah, Daniel, and Job.* Ezekiel warned of the destruction that was coming on the people of God because of their sins. God here tells Ezekiel that there is no chance of escape. These three are chosen not because they were perfect, but because they pursued God in spite of circumstances which appeared to indicate that he did not care. They are examples of godly, blameless people who could not save their own people or families by their godliness. Ezekiel says that even if they were present at that time, Judah's fate would still be judgment.

14:14, 20 Daniel, probably a younger contemporary of Ezekiel, is used here by the prophet as an example of a person who pleased God. But Daniel, even with Noah and Job (two ancient worthies) could only save themselves from judgment, not Ezekiel's wicked contemporaries.

14:20 Noah: Hebrews 11:7

16:2 *her hateful actions.* Jerusalem was not originally built by the people of Israel, but by pagans (Genesis 10:15,16; Joshua 10:5; 2 Samuel 5:6). Israel itself has pagan ancestors (Deuteronomy 26:5; Joshua 24:14).

the day you were born, your cord was not cut.
You were not washed with water to clean you. You
were not rubbed with salt or wrapped in cloths.
[5]No one felt sorry enough for you to do any of these
things for you. No, you were thrown out into the
open field, because you were hated on the day you
were born.

[6]" 'When I passed by and saw you kicking about
in your blood, I said to you, "Live!" [7]I made you
grow like a plant in the field. You grew up and
became tall and became like a beautiful jewel. Your
breasts formed, and your hair grew, but you were
naked and without clothes.

[8]" 'Later when I passed by you and looked at
you, I saw that you were old enough for love. So I
spread my robe over you and covered your nakedness. I also made a promise to you and entered into
an agreement with you so that you became mine,
says the Lord GOD.

[9]" 'Then I bathed you with water, washed all the
blood off of you, and put oil on you. [10]I put beautiful clothes made with needlework on you and put
sandals of fine leather on your feet. I wrapped you
in fine linen and covered you with silk. [11]I put jewelry on you: bracelets on your arms, a necklace
around your neck, [12]a ring in your nose, earrings in
your ears, and a beautiful crown on your head. [13]So
you wore gold and silver. Your clothes were made
of fine linen, silk, and beautiful needlework. You
ate fine flour, honey, and olive oil. You were very
beautiful and became a queen. [14]Then you became
famous among the nations, because you were so
beautiful. Your beauty was perfect, because of the
glory I gave you, says the Lord GOD.

Jerusalem Becomes a Prostitute

[15]" 'But you trusted in your beauty. You became
a prostitute, because you were so famous. You had
sexual relations with anyone who passed by. [16]You
took some of your clothes and made your places of
worship colorful. There you carried on your prostitution. These things should not happen; they should
never occur. [17]You also took your beautiful jewelry,
made from my gold and silver I had given you, and
you made for yourselves male idols so you could be
a prostitute with them. [18]Then you took your
clothes with beautiful needlework and covered the
idols. You gave my oil and incense as an offering to
them. [19]Also, you took the bread I gave you, the
fine flour, oil, and honey I gave you to eat, and you
offered them before the gods as a pleasing smell.
This is what happened, says the Lord GOD.

[20]" 'But your sexual sins were not enough for
you. You also took your sons and daughters who
were my children, and you sacrificed them to the
idols as food. [21]You killed my children and offered
them up in fire to the idols. [22]While you did all your
hateful acts and sexual sins, you did not remember
when you were young, when you were naked and
had no clothes and were left in your blood.

[23]" 'How terrible! How terrible it will be for you,
says the Lord GOD. After you did all these evil
things, [24]you built yourself a place to worship gods.
You made for yourself a place of worship in every
city square. [25]You built a place of worship at the
beginning of every street. You made your beauty
hateful, offering your body for sex to anyone who
passed by, so your sexual sins became worse and
worse. [26]You also had sexual relations with the
Egyptians, who were your neighbors and partners
in sexual sin. Your sexual sins became even worse,
and they caused me to be angry. [27]So then, I used
my power against you and took away some of your
land. I let you be defeated by those who hate
you, the Philistine women, who were ashamed of
your evil ways. [28]Also, you had sexual relations
with the Assyrians, because you could not be satisfied. Even though you had sexual relations with
them, you still were not satisfied. [29]You did many
more sexual sins in Babylonia, the land of traders,
but even this did not satisfy you.

[30]" 'Truly your will is weak, says the Lord GOD.
You do all the things a stubborn prostitute does.
[31]You built your place to worship gods at the
beginning of every street, and you made places of
worship in every city square. But you were not like
a prostitute when you refused to accept payment.

[32]" 'You are a wife who is guilty of adultery. You
desire strangers instead of your husband. [33]Men
pay prostitutes, but you pay all your lovers to come
to you. And they come from all around for sexual
relations. [34]So you are different from other prostitutes. No man asks you to be a prostitute, and you
pay money instead of having money paid to you.
Yes, you are different.

The Prostitute Is Judged

[35]" 'So, prostitute, hear the word of the LORD.
[36]This is what the Lord GOD says: You showed your
nakedness to other countries. You uncovered your
body in your sexual sins with them as your lovers
and with all your hateful idols. You killed your children and offered their blood to your idols. [37]So I
will gather all your lovers with whom you found

16:4 *cord.* The umbilical cord that gives the unborn baby food and air from its mother.

16:4 Salt: Matthew 5:13
16:34 Rebellion: Ezekiel 20:38

pleasure. Yes, I will gather all those you loved and those you hated. I will gather them against you from all around, and I will strip you naked in front of them so they can see your nakedness. 38I will punish you as women guilty of adultery or as murderers are punished. I will put you to death because I am angry and jealous. 39I will also hand you over to your lovers. They will tear down your places of worship and destroy other places where you worship gods. They will tear off your clothes and take away your jewelry, leaving you naked and bare. 40They will bring a crowd against you to throw stones at you and to cut you into pieces with their swords. 41They will burn down your houses and will punish you in front of many women. I will put an end to your sexual sins, and you will no longer pay your lovers. 42Then I will rest from my anger against you, and I will stop being jealous. I will be quiet and not angry anymore.

43" 'Because you didn't remember when you were young, but have made me angry in all these ways, I will repay you for what you have done, says the Lord GOD. Didn't you add sexual sins to all your other acts which I hate?

44" 'Everyone who uses wise sayings will say this about you: "The daughter is like her mother." 45You are like your mother, who hated her husband and children. You are also like your sisters, who hated their husbands and children. Your mother was a Hittite, and your father was an Amorite. 46Your older sister is Samaria, who lived north of you with her daughters; your younger sister is Sodom, who lived south of you with her daughters. 47You not only followed their ways and did the hateful things they did, but you were soon worse than they were in all your ways. 48As surely as I live, says the Lord GOD, this is true. Your sister Sodom and her daughters never did what you and your daughters have done.

49" 'This was the sin of your sister Sodom: She and her daughters were proud and had plenty of food and lived in great comfort, but she did not help the poor and needy. 50So Sodom and her daughters were proud and did things I hate in front of me. So I got rid of them when I saw what they did. 51Also, Samaria did not do half the sins you do; you have done more hateful things than they did. So you make your sisters look good because of all the hateful things you have done. 52You will suffer disgrace, because you have provided an excuse for your sisters. They are better than you are. Your sins were even more terrible than theirs. Feel ashamed and suffer disgrace, because you made your sisters look good.

53" 'But I will give back to Sodom and her daughters the good things they once had. I will give back to Samaria and her daughters the good things they once had. And with them I will also give back the good things you once had 54so you may suffer disgrace and feel ashamed for all the things you have done. You even gave comfort to your sisters in their sins. 55Your sisters, Sodom with her daughters and Samaria with her daughters, will return to what they were before. You and your daughters will also return to what you were before. 56You humiliated your sister Sodom when you were proud, 57before your evil was uncovered. And now the Edomite women and their neighbors humiliate you. Even the Philistine women humiliate you. Those around you hate you. 58This is your punishment for your terrible sins and for actions that I hate, says the LORD.

God Keeps His Promises

59" 'This is what the Lord GOD says: I will do to you what you have done. You hated and broke the agreement you promised to keep. 60But I will remember my agreement I made with you when you were young, and I will make an agreement that will continue forever with you. 61Then you will remember what you have done and feel ashamed when you receive your sisters—both your older and your younger sisters. I will give them to you like daughters, but not because they share in my agreement with you. 62I will set up my agreement with you, and you will know that I am the LORD. 63You will remember what you did and feel ashamed. You will not open your mouth again because of your shame, when I forgive you for all the things you have done, says the Lord GOD.' "

The Eagle and the Vine

17 The LORD spoke his word to me, saying: 2"Human, give a riddle and tell a story to the people of Israel. 3Say, 'This is what the Lord GOD says: A giant eagle with big wings and long feathers of many different colors came to Lebanon and took hold of the top of a cedar tree. 4He pulled off the top branch and brought it to a land of traders, where he planted it in a city of traders.

5" 'The eagle took some seed from the land and planted it in a good field near plenty of water. He planted it to grow like a willow tree. 6It sprouted and became a low vine that spread over the ground. The branches turned toward the

16:37 Pleasure: Luke 12:19–21
16:49 Poverty: Matthew 11:4–5
16:63 Prophetic Symbolism: Ezekiel 17

eagle, but the roots were under the eagle. So the seed became a vine, and its branches grew, sending out leaves.

7"'But there was another giant eagle with big wings and many feathers. The vine then bent its roots toward this eagle. It sent out its branches from the area where it was planted toward the eagle so he could water it. 8It had been planted in a good field by plenty of water so it could grow branches and give fruit. It could have become a fine vine.'

9"Say to them, 'This is what the Lord GOD says: The vine will not continue to grow. The first eagle will pull up the vine's roots and strip off its fruit. Then the vine and all its new leaves will dry up and die. It will not take a strong arm or many people to pull the vine up by its roots. 10Even if it is planted again, it will not continue to grow. It will completely dry up and die when the east wind hits it in the area where it grew.'"

Zedekiah Against Nebuchadnezzar

11Then the LORD spoke his word to me, saying: 12"Say now to the people who refuse to obey: 'Do you know what these things mean?' Say: 'The king of Babylon came to Jerusalem and took the king and important men of Jerusalem and brought them to Babylon. 13Then he took a member of the family of the king of Judah and made an agreement with him, forcing him to take an oath. The king also took away the leaders of Judah 14to make the kingdom weak so it would not be strong again. Then the kingdom of Judah could continue only by keeping its agreement with the king of Babylon. 15But the king of Judah turned against the king of Babylon by sending his messengers to Egypt and asking them for horses and many soldiers. Will the king of Judah succeed? Will the one who does such things escape? He cannot break the agreement and escape.

16"'As surely as I live, says the Lord GOD, he will die in Babylon, in the land of the king who made him king of Judah. The king of Judah hated his promise to the king of Babylon and broke his agreement with him. 17The king of Egypt with his mighty army and many people will not help the king of Judah in the war. The Babylonians will build devices to attack the cities and to kill many people. 18The king of Judah showed that he hated the promise by breaking the agreement. He promised to support Babylon, but he did all these things. So he will not escape.

19"'So this is what the Lord GOD says: As surely as I live, this is true: I will pay back the king of Judah for hating my promise and breaking my agreement. 20I will spread my net over him, and he will be caught in my trap. Then I will bring him to Babylon, where I will punish him for the unfaithful acts he did against me. 21All the best of his soldiers who escape will die by the sword, and those who live will be scattered to every wind. Then you will know that I, the LORD, have spoken.

22"'This is what the Lord GOD says: I myself will also take a young branch from the top of a cedar tree, and I will plant it. I will cut off a small twig from the top of the tree's young branches, and I will plant it on a very high mountain. 23I will plant it on the high mountain of Israel. Then it will grow branches and give fruit and become a great cedar tree. Birds of every kind will build nests in it and live in the shelter of the tree's branches. 24Then all the trees in the countryside will know that I am the LORD. I bring down the high tree and make the low tree tall. I dry up the green tree and make the dry tree grow. I am the LORD. I have spoken, and I will do it.'"

God Is Fair

18 The LORD spoke his word to me, saying: 2"What do you mean by using this saying about the land of Israel:

'The parents have eaten sour grapes,
and that caused the children to grind their teeth from the sour taste'?

3"As surely as I live, says the Lord GOD, this is true: You will not use this saying in Israel anymore. 4Every living thing belongs to me. The life of the parent is mine, and the life of the child is mine. The person who sins is the one who will die.

5"Suppose a person is good and does what is fair and right. 6He does not eat at the mountain places of worship. He does not look to the idols of Israel for help. He does not have sexual relations with his neighbor's wife or with a woman during her time of monthly bleeding. 7He does not mistreat

17:10 Parables: Ezekiel 19:10–14

17:11–19 The prophet Ezekiel speaks about how the king of Judah had made an agreement with the king of Babylon. But because the king of Judah hated his promise to the Babylonian king, he broke his agreement with him. "The king of Judah showed that he hated the promise by breaking the agreement . . . So he will not escape" (verse 18). Because the king of Judah hated God's promise of protection, he broke his agreement (verse 19).

17:12 This verse and the ones that follow it describe the time of Zedekiah, the last king of the southern kingdom.

17:24 Prophetic Symbolism: Ezekiel 23:1–48

18:2 There was a common belief in Israel at this time that a father's sin would have bad consequences for his children. Ezekiel here explains that people are responsible for their own sins.

18:3 Proverb: Matthew 13:1–52

anyone but returns what was given as a promise
for a loan. He does not rob other people. He gives
bread to the hungry and clothes to those who have
none. 8He does not lend money to get too much
interest or profit. He keeps his hand from doing
wrong. He judges fairly between one person and
another. 9He lives by my rules and obeys my laws
faithfully. Whoever does these things is good and
will surely live, says the Lord GOD.
10"But suppose this person has a wild son who
murders people and who does any of these other
things. 11(But the father himself has not done any
of these things.) This son eats at the mountain
places of worship. He has sexual relations with his
neighbor's wife. 12He mistreats the poor and
needy. He steals and refuses to return what was
promised for a loan. He looks to idols for help. He
does things which I hate. 13He lends money for too
much interest and profit. Will this son live? No, he
will not live! He has done all these hateful things,
so he will surely be put to death. He will be responsible for his own death.
14"Now suppose this son has a son who has
seen all his father's sins, but after seeing them
does not do those things. 15He does not eat at the
mountain places of worship. He does not look to
the idols of Israel for help. He does not have sexual relations with his neighbor's wife. 16He does
not mistreat anyone or keep something promised
for a loan or steal. He gives bread to the hungry
and clothes to those who have none. 17He keeps
his hand from doing wrong. He does not take too
much interest or profit when he lends money. He
obeys my laws and lives by my rules. He will not
die for his father's sin; he will surely live. 18But
his father took other people's money unfairly and
robbed his brother and did what was wrong
among his people. So he will die for his own sin.
19"But you ask, 'Why is the son not punished for
the father's sin?' The son has done what is fair and
right. He obeys all my rules, so he will surely live.
20The person who sins is the one who will die. A
child will not be punished for a parent's sin, and a
parent will not be punished for a child's sin. Those
who do right will enjoy the results of their own
goodness; evil people will suffer the results of their
own evil.
21"But suppose the wicked stop doing all the
sins they have done and obey all my rules and do
what is fair and right. Then they will surely live;
they will not die. 22Their sins will be forgotten.
Because they have done what is right, they will
live. 23I do not really want the wicked to die, says
the Lord GOD. I want them to stop their bad ways
and live.
24"But suppose good people stop doing good
and do wrong and do the same hateful things the
wicked do. Will they live? All their good acts will
be forgotten, because they became unfaithful.
They have sinned, so they will die because of
their sins.
25"But you say, 'What the Lord does isn't fair.'
Listen, people of Israel. I am fair. It is what you do
that is not fair! 26When good people stop doing
good and do wrong, they will die because of it.
They will die, because they did wrong. 27When
the wicked stop being wicked and do what is fair
and right, they will save their lives. 28Because they
thought about it and stopped doing all the sins
they had done, they will surely live; they will not
die. 29But the people of Israel still say, 'What the
Lord does isn't fair.' People of Israel, I am fair. It is
what you do that is not fair.
30"So I will judge you, people of Israel; I will
judge each of you by what you do, says the Lord
GOD. Change your hearts and stop all your sinning
so sin will not bring your ruin. 31Get rid of all the
sins you have done, and get for yourselves a new
heart and a new way of thinking. Why do you want
to die, people of Israel? 32I do not want anyone to
die, says the Lord GOD, so change your hearts and
lives so you may live.

A Sad Song for Israel

19 "Sing a funeral song for the leaders of Israel.
2Say:

'Your mother was like a female lion.
She lay down among the young lions.
She had many cubs.
3When she brought up one of her cubs,
he became a strong lion.
He learned to tear the animals he hunted,
and he ate people.
4The nations heard about him.
He was trapped in their pit,
and they brought him with hooks
to the land of Egypt.

5" 'The mother lion waited and saw
that there was no hope for her cub.
So she took another one of her cubs
and made him a strong lion.
6This cub roamed among the lions.
He was now a strong lion.
He learned to tear the animals he hunted,
and he ate people.

18:24 Death: Matthew 9:18–26

Son/Child of God

John 1:1–18

Why do the early Christians call Jesus "Son of God"? Does this mean he is divine? Who are the children of God?

One of the most popular titles for Jesus in the New Testament is "Son of God." It can be used in a variety of ways by different writers, though there are also many commonalities between these different usages. This is due to the background of the phrase "son of God" in the Old Testament and to general uses of the term "son" in the world of Jesus.

The best way to trace the background of the title of Jesus is first to think of how it is used in the Old Testament. In ancient Israel, the expression "son of God" was used in at least three different ways. First, angels or heavenly beings could be called "sons of God" (for example, Genesis 6:2, 4). These creatures participated in a kind of heavenly council over which God reigned. Second, the people of Israel are sometimes called sons of God, or the nation itself is referred to as a son of God (see Hosea 11:1). This signified their special relationship to God as well as their assignment to allow their lives together to reflect the nature of God and to represent God's ways to the wider world. Finally, the son of God was a title given the king, who represented God's kingship to the people (Psalm 2:7; 89:26–27). These last two are of special importance. They show that human beings who have a special relationship with God and special responsibilities from God might be called God's sons (or God's children).

Also of importance is the everyday use of the term "son" in the world of Jesus. First and foremost, a son was marked by the obedience he showed his father. In the Roman world, where the father had absolute control over his son's life, the fundamental expectation of a son was that he would do whatever his father asked. In Proverbs 4:4 a father says to his son, "Keep my commands and you will live."

Second, sons were expected to learn from their fathers. This was so important in the Roman world that an instructor might even be addressed as "father." Proverbs 4:1 speaks about this: "My children, listen to your father's teaching." Finally, a son might serve as the agent or ambassador of his father. To speak to the son sent on behalf of his father was regarded as the same thing as speaking to the father.

What might it mean, then, to say that Jesus is the Son of God? One can draw out the implications easily. First, as Son of God, Jesus demonstrated absolute obedience to God. This is evident early on in Jesus' life. At his baptism he is called "my Son" by God, then he is immediately tested to see whether he will remain faithful to God (see Matthew 3:13–4:11). Unlike Israel, also tested in the wilderness (Deuteronomy 6–8), he remains faithful to his Father. On the Mount of Olives (see Luke 22:39–46), he submits to the will of his Father even though this will lead to his horrible death on the cross.

Second, the relationship between God and Jesus is one in which Jesus continually seeks to learn God's will and to reveal God's ways to others (see Luke 10:21–24). We see in the Gospels that he often retreats from the crowds in order to pray; he then returns from prayer with a focused sense of why he was sent by God (see, for example, Mark 1:35–39). Third, Jesus is regularly portrayed as having been sent by God as God's agent (see Mark 12:1–12; Galatians 4:4). Throughout the Gospel of John, Jesus is presented as the representative of God, as one who reveals who God is and what God is like (see, for example, John 1:1–18; 14:1–11).

John 1:1–18 shows us that Jesus is the Son of God and as such he reveals God to us. Indeed, this passage teaches that Jesus is the eternal Son of the Father. He was "with God in the beginning" (John 1:2). In this he was totally unique. He bears glory that "belongs to the only Son of the Father" (John 1:14).

But this passage also teaches us that we become the children of God through faith in this Son of God. In him, we "saw his glory." Paul teaches that those who are led by the Spirit are "the true children of God" and address God as "Father" (Romans 8:14–17). This means that Jesus invites people into a new relationship with God. Christians have become like Israel; they share a special relationship with God and they have a special responsibility as his children. They are members of God's family. This means, in part, that they are now to be obedient to God, to learn from him, and to represent to others the character of God. To be called "children of God" also means that Christians are unable to think of themselves as any better or more important than others. There are no bosses within the people of God, no people in charge of anyone else, nobody held in higher esteem than the others, for all are simply children of God.

Son/Child of God: For additional scriptures on this topic go to Matthew 3:13–4:11.

INCARNATION

JOHN 1:14

What do we mean by "incarnation"? Where is it taught and what is its significance in the Bible? What is the relationship between incarnation and ethics?

The word *incarnation* comes specifically from John 1:14: "The Word became a human and lived among us." John is saying that the divine "Word" became the man, Jesus. The incarnation emphasizes the fact that Jesus really was a man. Paul witnesses to the fact that Jesus "gave up his place with God and made himself nothing. He was born to be a man and became like a servant" (Philippians 2:7). In this way, Jesus could identify with us, and we could identify with him (Hebrews 2:5–18).

In addition, in different ways and forms, all the New Testament writers express the idea that Jesus was more than just a man and in some way shared the nature of God. Jesus is not semidivine, or part god and part human, but both fully human and fully God.

It is important to note that this idea arose among Christians who first identified themselves as Jewish. Judaism made a strict separation between God and humanity. There was only one God and that God allowed no rivals (Exodus 20:3–4; Isaiah 44:6; 45:5–6; 46:9). Nevertheless, Christian writers found in the Old Testament suggestions of figures that bridged the gap between God and humanity. The figure of Wisdom in Proverbs 1:20–33; 3:13–18; 8:1–9:22 works alongside God in creation as a skilled artisan. Angels appear that the prophets mistake for God and that bear some of the characteristics of God's glory or name (Daniel 10:6; Ezekiel 1:22–24). Neither Wisdom nor the angels are understood as "gods" in the Old Testament, but both provide a starting point for understanding Christ in the New Testament by providing examples of beings or figures that express part of the character and action of God.

In the New Testament, we find these figures and concepts applied to Christ. John 1:1–18 describes Jesus as "the Word"—a figure related to the concept of Wisdom. The "Word" (or *Logos* in Greek) was the expression of the Divine Ideal in Greek philosophy. John sees Jesus as the human embodiment of the will and being of God (John 4:14; 6:35; 7:37). The Book of John takes this concept further through "reciprocal" formulas that connect the Father to the Son. The works of Jesus reveal the works of the Father (5:36; 10:37; 14:11). The words which the Son says come only from the Father (8:28; 14:10; 17:6–8). To believe in Jesus is to believe in the Father (14:1). To see Jesus is to see the Father (14:9). To be "in" Jesus is to be "in" the Father (10:38; 14:11; 17:20–23). In the end, Jesus claims that he and the Father are one (10:30; 17:11, 22). Those who believe in Jesus belong to God and are accepted by God (John 1:12; 6:40; 12:44–45; 17:3; see also Matthew 11:25–27; Luke 10:21–22). In John these formulas connect the Father and Son in a relationship of absolute continuity.

Paul uses the concept, "the image of God," in much the same way. Christ can be called "exactly like God" because he as God's image expresses in human form the will and the character of God (2 Corinthians 4:4; Colossians 1:15). Using slightly different language, in Philippians 2:6–8 Paul suggests that Christ, though "like God in everything," has come and become a man. The idea is essentially that Christ obediently expresses the nature of God and has come in human form to make God known to us.

And that is the point of the incarnation. Jesus is fully God and fully man; thus his death is able to save us. If he were just a man, his death might be an example of self-sacrifice, but it would have nothing to do with us. If he were just God, we would not be able to identify with him. But since he is God and man, his death and resurrection can save us from sin, guilt, and death.

The worship of the early church in the New Testament addresses Jesus as God. Jesus is the object of prayer, and Jesus receives glory and praise from New Testament writers as God would (Romans 9:5; 2 Peter 3:18; Revelation 1:5b-6). These and other passages underline the fact that the worship of the risen Jesus Christ was fundamental to the worship of the early church.

The incarnation in the end undergirds both the trustworthiness of Jesus' work and words. We can trust Christ as God and his words as God's words because God has come in Christ for us. Jesus becomes the guide for Christian living (see Philippians 2:1–5; John 13:12–20) because Jesus the Son embodies the living will of God.

Incarnation: For additional scriptures on this topic go to Proverbs 1:20–33.

7He tore down their strong places
  and destroyed their cities.
The land and everything in it
  were terrified by the sound of his roar.
8Then the nations came against him
  from areas all around,
and they spread their net over him.
  He was trapped in their pit.
9Then they put him into a cage with chains
  and brought him to the king of Babylon.
They put him into prison
  so his roar could not be heard again
  on the mountains of Israel.

10" 'Your mother was like a vine in your vineyard,
  planted beside the water.
The vine had many branches and gave
    much fruit,
  because there was plenty of water.
11The vine had strong branches,
  good enough for a king's scepter.
The vine became tall
  among the thick branches.
And it was seen, because it was tall
  with many branches.
12But it was pulled up by its roots in anger
  and thrown down to the ground.
The east wind dried it up.
  Its fruit was torn off.
Its strong branches were broken off
  and burned up.
13Now the vine is planted in the desert,
  in a dry and thirsty land.
14Fire spread from the vine's main branch,
  destroying its fruit.
There is not a strong branch left on it
  that could become a scepter for a king.'

This is a funeral song; it is to be used as a funeral song."

Israel Has Refused God

20 It was the seventh year of our captivity, in
the fifth month, on the tenth day of the
month. Some of the older leaders of Israel came to
ask about the LORD and sat down in front of me.
2The LORD spoke his word to me, saying: 3"Human, speak to the older leaders of Israel and say
to them: 'This is what the Lord GOD says: Did you
come to ask me questions? As surely as I live, I will
not let you ask me questions.'
4"Will you judge them? Will you judge them,
human? Let them know the hateful things their
ancestors did. 5Say to them: 'This is what the Lord
GOD says: When I chose Israel, I made a promise
to the descendants of Jacob. I made myself known
to them in Egypt, and I promised them, "I am the
LORD your God." 6At that time I promised them I
would bring them out of Egypt into a land I had
found for them, a fertile land, the best land in the
world. 7I said to them, "Each one of you must
throw away the hateful idols you have seen and
liked. Don't make yourselves unclean with the
idols of Egypt. I am the LORD your God."
8" 'But they turned against me and refused to
listen to me. They did not throw away the hateful
idols which they saw and liked; they did not give
up the idols of Egypt. Then I decided to pour out
my anger against them while they were still in
Egypt. 9But I acted for the sake of my name so it
would not be dishonored in full view of the nations
where the Israelites lived. I made myself known to
the Israelites with a promise to bring them out of
Egypt while the nations were watching. 10So I took
them out of Egypt and brought them into the
desert. 11I gave them my rules and told them
about my laws, by which people will live if they
obey them. 12I also gave them my Sabbaths to be a
sign between us so they would know that I am the
LORD who made them holy.
13" 'But in the desert Israel turned against me.
They did not follow my rules, and they rejected my
laws, by which people will live if they obey them.
They dishonored my Sabbaths. Then I decided to
pour out my anger against them and destroy them
in the desert. 14But I acted for the sake of my
name so it would not be dishonored in full view
of the nations who watched as I had brought the
Israelites out of Egypt. 15And in the desert I swore
to the Israelites that I would not bring them into
the land I had given them. It is a fertile land, the
best land in the world. 16This was because they
rejected my laws and did not follow my rules.
They dishonored my Sabbaths and wanted to worship their idols. 17But I had pity on them. I did not
destroy them or put an end to them in the desert.
18I said to their children in the desert, "Don't live
by the rules of your parents, or obey their laws.
Don't make yourselves unclean with their idols. 19I
am the LORD your God. Live by my rules, obey my
laws, and follow them. 20Keep my Sabbaths holy,
and they will be a sign between me and you. Then
you will know that I am the LORD your God."
21" 'But the children turned against me. They
did not live by my rules, nor were they careful to
obey my laws, by which people will live if they

19:14 Parables: Matthew 7:24–27

obey them. They dishonored my Sabbaths. So I
decided to pour out my anger against them in the
desert. 22But I held back my anger. I acted for the
sake of my name so it would not be dishonored in
full view of the nations who watched as I brought
the Israelites out. 23And in the desert I swore to the
Israelites that I would scatter them among the
nations and spread them among the countries,
24because they had not obeyed my laws. They had
rejected my rules and dishonored my Sabbaths
and worshiped the idols of their parents. 25I also
allowed them to follow rules that were not good
and laws by which they could not live. 26I let the
Israelites make themselves unclean by the gifts
they brought to their gods when they sacrificed
their first children in the fire. I wanted to terrify
them so they would know that I am the LORD.'
27"So, human, speak to the people of Israel. Say
to them, 'This is what the Lord GOD says: Your
ancestors spoke against me by being unfaithful to
me in another way. 28When I had brought them
into the land I promised to give them, they saw
every high hill and every leafy tree. There they
offered their sacrifices to gods. They brought offerings that made me angry and burned their incense
and poured out their drink offerings. 29Then I said
to them: What is this high place where you go to
worship?' " (It is still called High Place today.)
30"So say to the people of Israel: 'This is what
the Lord GOD says: Are you going to make yourselves unclean as your ancestors did? Are you
going to be unfaithful and desire their hateful
idols? 31When you offer your children as gifts and
sacrifice them in the fire, you are making yourselves unclean with all your idols even today. So,
people of Israel, should I let you ask me questions?
As surely as I live, says the Lord GOD, I will not
accept questions from you.
32" 'What you want will not come true. You say,
"We want to be like the other nations, like the
people in other lands. We want to worship idols
made of wood and stone." 33As surely as I live,
says the Lord GOD, I will use my great power and
strength and anger to rule over you. 34I will bring
you out from the foreign nations. With my great
power and strength and anger I will gather you
from the lands where you are scattered. 35I will
bring you among the nations as I brought your
ancestors into the desert with Moses. There I will
judge you face to face. 36I will judge you the same
way I judged your ancestors in the desert of the
land of Egypt, says the Lord GOD. 37I will count
you like sheep and will bring you into line with
my agreement. 38I will get rid of those who refuse
to obey me and who turn against me. I will bring
them out of the land where they are now living,
but they will never enter the land of Israel. Then
you will know that I am the LORD.
39" 'This is what the Lord GOD says: People of
Israel, go serve your idols for now. But later you
will listen to me; you will not continue to dishonor
my holy name with your gifts and gods. 40On my
holy mountain, the high mountain of Israel, all
Israel will serve me in the land, says the Lord GOD.
There I will accept you. There I will expect your
offerings, the first harvest of your offerings, and all
your holy gifts. 41I will accept you like the pleasing
smell of sacrifices when I bring you out from the
foreign nations and gather you from the lands
where you are scattered. Then through you I will
show how holy I am so the nations will see.
42When I bring you into the land of Israel, the land
I promised your ancestors, you will know that I
am the LORD. 43There you will remember everything you did that made you unclean, and then you
will hate yourselves for all the evil things you have
done. 44I will deal with you for the sake of my
name, not because of your evil ways or unclean
actions. Then you will know I am the LORD, people
of Israel, says the Lord GOD.' "

Babylon, the Lord's Sword

45Now the LORD spoke his word to me, saying:
46"Human, look toward the south. Prophesy
against the south and against the forest of the
southern area. 47Say to that forest: 'Hear the word
of the LORD. This is what the Lord GOD says: I am
ready to start a fire in you that will destroy all your
green trees and all your dry trees. The flames that
burn will not be put out. Every face from south to
north will feel their heat. 48Then all the people
will see that I, the LORD, have started the fire. It
will not be put out.' "
49Then I said, "Ah, Lord GOD! The people are
saying about me, 'He is only telling stories.' "
21 Then the LORD spoke his word to me, saying:
2"Human, look toward Jerusalem and speak
against the holy place. Prophesy against the land
of Israel. 3Say to Israel: 'This is what the LORD says:
I am against you. I will pull my sword out of its
holder, and I will cut off from you both the wicked
and those who do right. 4Because I am going to cut
off the wicked and those who do right, my sword
will come out from its holder and attack all people
from south to north. 5Then all people will know

20:27 Blasphemy: Matthew 26:65
20:38 Rebellion: Matthew 12:22–32
20:44 Names of God: Micah 4:5

that I, the LORD, have pulled my sword out from
its holder. My sword will not go back in again.’
6“So, human, groan with breaking heart and
great sadness. Groan in front of the people. 7When
they ask you, ‘Why are you groaning?’ you will say,
‘Because of what I have heard is going to happen.
When it happens, every heart will melt with fear,
and all hands will become weak. Everyone will be
afraid; all knees will become weak as water. Look,
it is coming, and it will happen, says the Lord
GOD.’”
8The LORD spoke his word to me, saying:
9“Human, prophesy and say, ‘This is what the
Lord says:

A sword, a sword,
made sharp and polished.
10It is made sharp for the killing.
It is polished to flash like lightning.

“ ‘You are not happy about this horrible punishment by the sword. But my son Judah, you did
not change when you were only beaten with a rod.

11The sword should be polished.
It is meant to be held in the hand.
It is made sharp and polished,
ready for the hand of a killer.
12Shout and yell, human,
because the sword is meant for my people,
for all the rulers of Israel.
They will be killed by the sword,
along with my people.
So beat your chest in sadness.

13“ ‘The test will come. And Judah, who is hated
by the armies of Babylon, will not last, says the
Lord GOD.’

14“So, human, prophesy
and clap your hands.
Let the sword strike
two or three times.
It is a sword meant for killing,
a sword meant for much killing.
This sword surrounds the people to be killed.
15Their hearts will melt with fear,
and many people will die.
I have placed the killing sword
at all their city gates.
Oh! The sword is made to flash like lightning.
It is held, ready for killing.
16Sword, cut on the right side;
then cut on the left side.
Cut anywhere your blade is turned.
17I will also clap my hands
and use up my anger.
I, the LORD, have spoken.”

Jerusalem to Be Destroyed

18The LORD spoke his word to me, saying:
19“Human, mark two roads that the king of Babylon and his sword can follow. Both of these roads
will start from the same country. And make signs
where the road divides and one way goes toward
the city. 20Mark one sign to show the road he can
take with his sword to Rabbah in the land of the
Ammonites. Mark the other sign to show the road
to Judah and Jerusalem, which is protected with
strong walls. 21The king of Babylon has come to
where the road divides, and he is using magic. He
throws lots with arrows and asks questions of his
family idols. He looks at the liver of a sacrificed
animal to learn where he should go. 22The lot in
his right hand tells him to go to Jerusalem. It tells
him to use logs to break down the city gates, to
shout the battle cry and give the order to kill, and
to build a dirt road to the top of the walls and
devices to attack the walls. 23The people of
Jerusalem have made agreements with other
nations to help them fight Babylon. So they will
think this prediction is wrong, but it is really proof
of their sin, and they will be captured.
24“So this is what the Lord GOD says: ‘You have
shown how sinful you are by turning against the
LORD. Your sins are seen in all the things you do.
Because of this proof against you, you will be taken
captive by the enemy.
25“ ‘You unclean and evil leader of Israel, you
will be killed! The time of your final punishment
has come. 26This is what the Lord GOD says: Take
off the royal turban, and remove the crown. Things
will change. Those who are important now will be
made unimportant, and those who are unimportant now will be made important. 27A ruin! A ruin!
I will make it a ruin! This place will not be rebuilt
until the one comes who has a right to be king.
Then I will give him that right.’

The Punishment of Ammon

28“And you, human, prophesy and say: ‘This is
what the Lord GOD says about the people of
Ammon and their insults:

A sword, a sword
is pulled out of its holder.
It is polished to kill and destroy,
to flash like lightning!
29Prophets see false visions about you
and prophesy lies about you.
The sword will be put on the necks
of these unclean and evil people.
Their day of judging has come;
the time of final punishment has come.
30Put the sword back in its holder.
I will judge you

in the place where you were created,
  in the land where you were born.
31I will pour out my anger against you
  and blast you with the fire of my anger.
I will hand you over to cruel men,
  experts in destruction.
32You will be like fuel for the fire;
  you will die in the land.
You will not be remembered,
  because I, the LORD, have spoken.' "

The Sins of Jerusalem

22 The LORD spoke his word to me, saying:
2"And you, human, will you judge? Will
you judge the city of murderers? Then tell her
about all her hateful acts. 3You are to say: 'This is
what the Lord GOD says: You are a city that kills
those who come to live there. You make yourself
unclean by making idols. 4You have become guilty
of murder and have become unclean by your idols
which you have made. So you have brought your
time of punishment near; you have come to the
end of your years. That is why I have made you a
shame to the nations and why all lands laugh at
you. 5Those near and those far away laugh at you
with your bad name, you city full of confusion.
6" 'Jerusalem, see how each ruler of Israel in
you has been trying to kill people. 7The people in
you hate their fathers and mothers. They mistreat
the foreigners in you and wrong the orphans and
widows in you. 8You hate my holy things and dishonor my Sabbaths. 9The men in you tell lies to
cause the death of others. The people in you eat
food offered to idols at the mountain places of worship, and they take part in sexual sins. 10The men
in you have sexual relations with their fathers'
wives and with women who are unclean, during
their time of monthly bleeding. 11One man in you
does a hateful act with his neighbor's wife, while
another has shamefully made his daughter-in-law
unclean sexually. And another forces his half sister
to have sexual relations with him. 12The people
in you take money to kill others. You take unfair
interest and profits and make profits by mistreating
your neighbor. And you have forgotten me, says
the Lord GOD.
13" 'So, Jerusalem, I will shake my fist at you for
stealing money and for murdering people. 14Will
you still be brave and strong when I punish you? I,
the LORD, have spoken, and I will act. 15I will scatter
you among the nations and spread you through the
countries. That is how I will get rid of your
uncleanness. 16But you, yourself, will be dishonored in the sight of the nations. Then you will
know that I am the LORD.' "

Israel Is Worthless

17The LORD spoke his word to me, saying:
18"Human, the people of Israel have become useless like scum to me. They are like the copper,
tin, iron, and lead left in the furnace when silver
is purified. 19So this is what the Lord GOD says:
'Because you have become useless like scum, I
am going to put you together inside Jerusalem.
20People put silver, copper, iron, lead, and tin
together inside a furnace to melt them down in a
blazing fire. In the same way I will gather you in
my hot anger and put you together in Jerusalem
and melt you down. 21I will put you together and
make you feel the heat of my anger. You will be
melted down inside Jerusalem. 22As silver is
melted in a furnace, you will be melted inside the
city. Then you will know that I, the LORD, have
poured out my anger on you.' "

Sins of the People

23The LORD spoke his word to me, saying:
24"Human, say to the land, 'You are a land that
has not had rain or showers when God is angry.'
25Like a roaring lion that tears the animal it has
caught, Israel's rulers make evil plans. They have
destroyed lives and have taken treasure and valuable things. They have caused many women to
become widows. 26Israel's priests do cruel things
to my teachings and do not honor my holy things.
They make no difference between holy and
unholy things, and they teach there is no difference between clean and unclean things. They do
not remember my Sabbaths, so I am dishonored
by them. 27Like wolves tearing a dead animal,
Jerusalem's leaders have killed people for profit.
28And the prophets try to cover this up by false
visions and by lying messages. They say, 'This is
what the Lord GOD says' when the LORD has not
spoken. 29The people cheat others and steal. They
hurt people who are poor and needy. They cheat
foreigners and do not treat them fairly.
30"I looked for someone to build up the walls
and to stand before me where the walls are broken to defend these people so I would not have to
destroy them. But I could not find anyone. 31So I
let them see my anger. I destroyed them with an
anger that was like fire because of all the things
they have done, says the Lord GOD."

22:7 Adoption: Malachi 3:5
22:10 Leviticus 18:19 forbids this kind of sexual activity.
22:22 Images of God: Hosea 11:1–4
22:26 Clean & Unclean: Haggai 2:11–14

Samaria and Jerusalem

23 The LORD spoke his word to me, saying: 2“Human, a woman had two daughters. 3While they were young, they went to Egypt and became prostitutes. They let men touch and hold their breasts. 4The older girl was named Oholah, and her sister was named Oholibah. They became my wives and had sons and daughters. Oholah is Samaria, and Oholibah is Jerusalem.

5“While still my wife, Samaria had sexual relations with other men. She had great sexual desire for her lovers, men from Assyria. The Assyrians were warriors and 6wore blue uniforms. They were all handsome young captains and lieutenants riding on horseback. 7Samaria became a prostitute for all the important men in Assyria and made herself unclean with all the idols of everyone she desired. 8She continued the prostitution she began in Egypt. When she was young, she had slept with men, and they touched her breasts and had sexual relations with her.

9“So I handed her over to her lovers, the Assyrians, that she wanted so badly. 10They stripped her naked and took away her sons and daughters. Then they killed her with a sword. Women everywhere began talking about how she had been punished.

11“Her sister Jerusalem saw what happened, but she became worse than her sister in her sexual desire and prostitution. 12She also desired the Assyrians, who were all soldiers in beautiful uniforms—handsome young captains and lieutenants riding horses. 13I saw that both girls were alike; both were prostitutes.

14“But Jerusalem went even further. She saw carvings of Babylonian men on a wall. They wore red 15and had belts around their waists and turbans on their heads. They all looked like chariot officers born in Babylonia. 16When she saw them, she wanted to have sexual relations with them and sent messengers to them in Babylonia. 17So these Babylonian men came and had sexual relations with her and made her unclean. After that, she became sick of them. 18But she continued her prostitution so openly that everyone knew about it. And I finally became sick of her, as I had her sister. 19But she remembered how she was a young prostitute in Egypt, so she took part in even more prostitution. 20She wanted men who behaved like animals in their sexual desire. 21In the same way you desired to do the sinful things you had done in Egypt. There men touched and held your young breasts.

God’s Judgment on Jerusalem

22“So, Jerusalem, this is what the Lord GOD says: You are tired of your lovers. So now I will make them angry with you and have them attack you from all sides. 23Men from Babylon and all Babylonia and men from Pekod, Shoa, and Koa will attack you. All the Assyrians will attack you: handsome young captains and lieutenants, all of them important men and all riding horses. 24Those men will attack with great armies and with their weapons, chariots, and wagons. They will surround you with large and small shields and with helmets. And I will give them the right to punish you, and they will give you their own kind of punishment. 25Then you will see how strong my anger can be when they punish you in their anger. They will cut off your noses and ears. They will take away your sons and daughters, and those who are left will be burned. 26They will take off your clothes and steal your jewelry. 27I will put a stop to the sinful life you began when you were in Egypt so that you will not desire it or remember Egypt anymore.

28“This is what the Lord GOD says: You became tired of your lovers, but I am going to hand you over to those men you now hate. 29They will treat you with hate and take away everything you worked for, leaving you empty and naked. Everyone will know about the sinful things you did. Your sexual sins 30have brought this on you. You have had sexual relations with the nations and made yourselves unclean by worshiping their idols. 31You did the same things your sister did, so you will get the same punishment, like a bitter cup to drink.

32“This is what the Lord GOD says:
You will drink the same cup your sister did,
  and that cup is deep and wide.
Everyone will make fun of you,
  because the cup is full.
33It will make you miserable and drunk.
  It is the cup of fear and ruin.
  It is the cup of your sister Samaria.
34You will drink everything in it,
  and then you will smash it
  and tear at your breasts.
I have spoken, says the Lord GOD.

23:4 Oholah represents the northern kingdom and Oholibah, the southern. Their names might be translated “her own tent” and “tent in her,” indicating that the northern kingdom made its own center of worship, while the southern kingdom had God’s Tent, his Temple, in Jerusalem. But this interpretation is uncertain.

23:4 *Oholah . . . Jerusalem.* Throughout this chapter Samaria is used in place of Oholah, and Jerusalem is used in place of Oholibah.

[35]"So this is what the Lord GOD says: You have
forgotten me and turned your back on me. So you
will be punished for your sexual sins."

Judgment on Samaria and Jerusalem

[36]The LORD said to me: "Human, will you judge
Samaria and Jerusalem, showing them their hateful acts? [37]They are guilty of adultery and murder.
They have taken part in adultery with their idols.
They even offered our children as sacrifices in the
fire to be food for these idols. [38]They have also
done this to me: They made my Temple unclean at
the same time they dishonored my Sabbaths.
[39]They sacrificed their children to their idols. Then
they entered my Temple at that very time to dishonor it. That is what they did inside my Temple!
[40]"They even sent for men from far away, who
came after a messenger was sent to them. The two
sisters bathed themselves for them, painted their
eyes, and put on jewelry. [41]They sat on a fine bed
with a table set before it, on which they put my
incense and my oil.
[42]"There was the noise of a reckless crowd in
the city. Common people gathered, and drunkards
were brought from the desert. They put bracelets
on the wrists of the two sisters and beautiful
crowns on their heads. [43]Then I said about the one
who was worn out by her acts of adultery, 'Let
them continue their sexual sins with her. She is
nothing but a prostitute.' [44]They kept going to her
as they would go to a prostitute. So they continued
to go to Samaria and Jerusalem, these shameful
women. [45]But men who do right will punish them
as they punish women who take part in adultery
and who murder people, because they are guilty
of adultery and murder.
[46]"This is what the Lord GOD says: Bring together a mob against Samaria and Jerusalem, and
hand them over to be frightened and robbed. [47]Let
the mob kill them by throwing stones at them,
and let them cut them down with their swords.
Let them kill their sons and daughters and burn
their houses down.
[48]"So I will put an end to sexual sins in the land.
Then all women will be warned, and they will not
do the sexual sins you have done. [49]You will be
punished for your sexual sins and the sin of worshiping idols. Then you will know that I am the
Lord GOD."

The Pot and the Meat

24 The LORD spoke his word to me in the ninth
year of our captivity, in the tenth month,
on the tenth day of the month. He said: [2]"Human,
write down today's date, this very date. The king of
Babylon has surrounded Jerusalem this very day.
[3]And tell a story to the people who refuse to obey
me. Say to them: 'This is what the Lord GOD says:
Put on the pot; put it on
and pour water in it.
[4]Put in the pieces of meat,
the best pieces—the legs and the shoulders.
Fill it with the best bones.
[5] Take the best of the flock,
and pile wood under the pot.
Boil the pieces of meat
until even the bones are cooked.
[6]" 'This is what the Lord GOD says:
How terrible it will be for the city of murderers!
How terrible it will be for the rusty pot
whose rust will not come off!
Take the meat out of it, piece by piece.
Don't choose any special piece.

[7]" 'The blood from her killings is still in the city.
She poured the blood on the bare rock.
She did not pour it on the ground
where dust would cover it.
[8]To stir up my anger and revenge,
I put the blood she spilled on the bare rock
so it will not be covered.

[9]" 'So this is what the Lord GOD says:
How terrible it will be for the city of murderers!
I myself will pile the wood high for burning.
[10]Pile up the wood
and light the fire.
Finish cooking the meat.
Mix in the spices,
and let the bones burn.
[11]Then set the empty pot on the coals
so it may become hot and its copper
sides glow.
The dirty scum stuck inside it may then melt
and its rust burn away.
[12]But efforts to clean the pot have failed.
Its heavy rust cannot be removed,
even in the fire.

[13]" 'By your sinful action you have become
unclean. I wanted to cleanse you, but you are still
unclean. You will never be cleansed from your sin
until my anger against you is carried out.
[14]" 'I, the LORD, have spoken. The time has come
for me to act. I will not hold back punishment or
feel pity or change my mind. I will judge you by
your ways and actions, says the Lord GOD.' "

23:48 Prophetic Symbolism: Ezekiel 31

23:49 Samaria: Acts 8

The Death of Ezekiel's Wife

15Then the LORD spoke his word to me, saying:
16"Human, I am going to take your wife from you,
the woman you look at with love. She will die suddenly, but you must not be sad or cry loudly for
her or shed any tears. 17Groan silently; do not cry
loudly for the dead. Tie on your turban, and put
your sandals on your feet. Do not cover your face,
and do not eat the food people eat when they are
sad about a death."
18So I spoke to the people in the morning, and
my wife died in the evening. The next morning I
did as I had been commanded.
19Then the people asked me, "Tell us, what do
the things you are doing mean for us?"
20Then I said to them, "The LORD spoke his
word to me. He said, 21'Say to the people of Israel,
This is what the Lord GOD says: I am going to dishonor my Temple. You think it gives you strength.
You are proud of it, and you look at it with love
and tenderness. But your sons and daughters that
you left behind in Jerusalem will fall dead by the
sword. 22When that happens, you are to act as
I have: you are not to cover your face, and you are
not to eat the food people eat when they are sad
about a death. 23Your turbans must stay on your
heads, and your sandals on your feet. You must
not cry loudly, but you must rot away in your sins
and groan to each other. 24So Ezekiel is to be an
example for you. You must do all the same things
he did. When all this happens, you will know that
I am the Lord GOD.'
25"And as for you, human, this is how it will be.
I will take away the Temple that gives them
strength and joy, that makes them proud. They
look at it with love, and it makes them happy. And
I will take away their sons and daughters also.
26At that time a person who escapes will come to
you with information for you to hear. 27At that
very time your mouth will be opened. You will
speak and be silent no more. So you will be a sign
for them, and they will know that I am the LORD."

Prophecy Against Ammon

25 The LORD spoke his word to me, saying:
2"Human, look toward the people of Ammon and prophesy against them. 3Say to them,
'Hear the word of the Lord GOD. This is what the
Lord GOD says: You were glad when my Temple
was dishonored, when the land of Israel was
ruined, and when the people of Judah were taken
away as captives. 4So I am going to give you to the
people of the East to be theirs. They will set up
their camps among you and make their homes
among you. They will eat your fruit and drink your
milk. 5I will make the city of Rabbah a pasture for
camels and the land of Ammon a resting place for
sheep. Then you will know that I am the LORD.
6This is what the Lord GOD says: You have clapped
your hands and stamped your feet; you have
laughed about all the insults you made against the
land of Israel. 7So I will use my power against
you. I will give you to the nations as if you were
treasures taken in war. I will wipe you out of the
lands so you will no longer be a nation, and I will
destroy you. Then you will know that I am the
LORD.'

Prophecy Against Moab and Edom

8"This is what the Lord GOD says: 'Moab and
Edom say, "The people of Judah are like all the
other nations." 9So I am going to take away the
cities that protect Moab's borders, the best cities
in that land: Beth Jeshimoth, Baal Meon, and
Kiriathaim. 10Then I will give Moab, along with
the Ammonites, to the people of the East as their
possession. Then, along with the Ammonites,
Moab will not be a nation anymore. 11So I will
punish the people of Moab, and they will know
that I am the LORD.'

Prophecy Against Edom

12"This is what the Lord GOD says: 'Edom took
revenge on the people of Judah, and the Edomites
became guilty because of it. 13So this is what the
Lord GOD says: I will use my power against Edom,
killing every human and animal in it. And I will
destroy Edom all the way from Teman to Dedan as
they die in battle. 14I will use my people Israel to
take revenge on Edom. So the Israelites will do to
Edom what my hot anger demands. Then the
Edomites will know what my revenge feels like,
says the Lord GOD.'

Prophecy Against Philistia

15"This is what the Lord GOD says: 'The Philistines have taken revenge with hateful hearts.
Because of their strong hatred, they have tried to
destroy Judah. 16So this is what the Lord GOD says:
I will use my power against the Philistines. I will
kill the Kerethites, and I will destroy those people
still alive on the coast of the Mediterranean Sea.
17I will punish them in my anger and do great acts
of revenge to them. They will know that I am the
LORD when I take revenge on them.'"

24:18 Ezekiel: See article on page 632.

24:21 Pride: Daniel 4–5

Prophecy Against Tyre

26 It was the eleventh year of our captivity, on the first day of the month. The LORD spoke his word to me, saying: 2"Human, the city of Tyre has spoken against Jerusalem: 'The city that traded with the nations is destroyed. Now we can be the trading center. Since the city of Jerusalem is ruined, we can make money.' 3So this is what the Lord GOD says: I am against you, Tyre. I will bring many nations against you, like the sea beating its waves on your island shores. 4They will destroy the walls of Tyre and pull down her towers. I will also scrape away her ruins and make her a bare rock. 5Tyre will be an island where fishermen dry their nets. I have spoken, says the Lord GOD. The nations will steal treasures from Tyre. 6Also, her villages on the shore across from the island will be destroyed by war. Then they will know that I am the LORD.

Nebuchadnezzar to Attack Tyre

7"This is what the Lord GOD says: I will bring a king from the north against Tyre. He is Nebuchadnezzar king of Babylon, the greatest king, with his horses, chariots, horsemen, and a great army. 8He will fight a battle and destroy your villages on the shore across from the island. He will set up devices to attack you. He will build a road of earth to the top of the walls. He will raise his shields against you. 9He will bring logs to pound through your city walls, and he will break down your towers with his iron bars. 10His horses will be so many that they will cover you with their dust. Your walls will shake at the noise of horsemen, wagons, and chariots. The king of Babylon will enter your city gates as men enter a city where the walls are broken through. 11The hoofs of his horses will run over your streets. He will kill your army with the sword, and your strong pillars will fall down to the ground. 12Also, his men will take away your riches and will steal the things you sell. They will break down your walls and destroy your nice houses. They will throw your stones, wood, and trash into the sea. 13So I will stop your songs; the music of your harps will not be heard anymore. 14I will make you a bare rock, and you will be a place for drying fishing nets. You will not be built again, because I, the LORD, have spoken, says the Lord GOD.

15"This is what the Lord GOD says to Tyre: The people who live along the seacoast will shake with fear when they hear about your defeat. Those of you who are injured and dying will groan. 16Then all the leaders of the seacoast will get down from their thrones, take off their beautiful needlework clothes, and show how afraid they are. They will sit on the ground and tremble all the time. When they see you, they will be shocked. 17They will begin singing a funeral song about you and will say to you:

'Tyre, you famous city, you have been
  destroyed!
 You have lost your sea power!
You and your people
 had great power on the seas.
You made everyone around you
 afraid of you.
18Now the people who live by the coast tremble,
 now that you have fallen.
The islands of the sea
 are afraid because you have been defeated.'

19"This is what the Lord GOD says: I will make you an empty city, like cities that have no people living in them. I will bring the deep ocean waters over you, and the Mediterranean Sea will cover you. 20At that time I will send you down to the place of the dead to join those who died long ago. I will make you live with the dead below the earth in places that are like old ruins. You will not come back from there or have any place in the world of the living again. 21Other people will be afraid of what happened to you, and it will be the end of you. People will look for you, but they will never find you again, says the Lord GOD."

A Funeral Song for Tyre

27 The LORD spoke his word to me, saying: 2"Human, sing a funeral song for the city of Tyre. 3Speak to Tyre, which has ports for the Mediterranean Sea and is a place for trade for the people of many lands along the seacoast. 'This is what the Lord GOD says:

Tyre, you have said,
 "I am like a beautiful ship."
4You were at home on the high seas.
 Your builders made your beauty perfect.
5They made all your boards
 of fir trees from Mount Hermon.
They took a cedar tree from Lebanon
 to make a ship's mast for you.
6They made your oars
 from oak trees from Bashan.
They made your deck
 from cypress trees from the coast of Cyprus
 and set ivory into it.
7Your sail of linen with designs sewed on it
  came from Egypt
 and became like a flag for you.

27:4 Water: Ezekiel 27:25–36

Presence of God

John 1:14

Where is God? How does he make his presence known? Where can I meet God today?

Christians know that God is with them wherever they are. God is not just in church; he is also with us as we drive, as we work, as we play. God is present everywhere and we can experience his comforting presence at any time. Of course it has always been true that God is everywhere in his creation. But God did not always choose to make his presence known to his people at just any place; rather, he chose when and where he would meet with them.

It didn't start out that way. Human beings had free and perfect fellowship with God in the Garden of Eden. However, after the fall into sin a horrible separation took place. No longer would God make his visible presence known to human beings anywhere and at any time. Sin erected a tremendous barrier between them. After Adam and Eve were removed from Eden, they and their descendants had to meet with God at specially chosen locations, and they had to offer sacrifices to acknowledge and repent for their sins.

Perhaps one of the best-known scenes where God made his presence known to his people in a special way is found in Exodus 19. The Israelites were now a large group of people and a simple altar would no longer do. God appeared on Mount Sinai, and there was smoke and fire (Exodus 19:16–19). When Moses went up on the mountain to meet with God, God revealed the plans for the building of the Holy Tent. The Holy Tent would now be the place where God would make his presence known to his people.

The Holy Tent was God's home on earth. It was the place where sinful men and women could go to meet with God after offering sacrifices for their sins. As God's home on earth, much of its symbolism had to do with heaven. The innermost curtain was a heavenly blue with designs of powerful angels woven into it. It was like standing in heaven. The Holy Tent was also placed in the middle of the camp, the place where the king would normally have his tent. God was the king of Israel, and since he was present with them, his tent, the Holy Tent, was placed in the middle.

This location explains why the Bible describes the camp of the Israelites as having rings of holiness around it. Only Israelites, not Gentiles, were allowed in the camp. And only Levites, none of the other twelve tribes, were allowed to live right around the Holy Tent. And then only the descendants of Aaron, not all the Levites, were allowed to minister in the Holy Tent itself. And only the High Priest, and only once a year, was allowed to go into the most holy part of the Holy Tent.

After a while, the Holy Tent was no longer the right type of building to represent God's presence with his people. It was appropriate while Israel was not settled in the promised land. But David completed the conquest, and then the people were settled in the land. Thus, for the next period of Israel's history the more houselike Temple was the place where God made his presence known to his people.

Unfortunately, though, the Israelites began to believe that God would be with them no matter how bad they were. After all, the Temple was in their midst; God was always with them. God had to teach them that they could not just assume he was with them even if they were evil and without faith. So God left his Temple and allowed it to be destroyed by the Babylonians.

After the Israelites repented, God allowed them to build a second Temple, less impressive than the first one, but it still represented God's presence with his people, but only temporarily. Something much better was coming in the future.

That something better is announced in John 1:14: "The Word became a human and lived among us." God made his presence known in his son Jesus Christ. When he died on the cross, the veil that separated the Holy Place of the Temple from the rest of the world was ripped in half, showing that there were now no longer any special holy places. God would meet with his people anywhere and anytime (John 4:21–24).

So today, because of Jesus, we don't need to travel to Jerusalem to meet with God. We can be in his presence anywhere. Indeed, Paul talks about how the Christian, in whom the Holy Spirit lives, is like a temple (1 Corinthians 3:16) and in another place how the church, Christians gathering together, are corporately considered the Temple (Ephesians 6:19–22).⚭

⚭**Presence of God:** For additional scriptures on this topic go to Genesis 12:7.

PETER

JOHN 1:40

How was Peter called to be a disciple of Jesus? What kind of relationship did Peter enjoy with Jesus? What role did Peter play in the early church?

Simon, (later named Peter by Christ), was from Bethsaida (John 1:44), and was the son of Jonah. He and his brother Andrew were partners with James and John, the sons of Zebedee, in the fishing business on Lake Galilee (Luke 5:10). Peter was first informed of Jesus' ministry by his brother, Andrew (John 1:42), who was a follower of John the Baptist. When John pointed Jesus out to two of his followers (John 1:35–36), Andrew went to Peter with the news that they had found the Messiah. After following Jesus for a short time, Peter apparently went back to his chosen vocation of fishing.

At one of Jesus' outdoor teaching sessions, the crowd that gathered to hear him was too large. Jesus asked Peter for the use of his fishing boat as a pulpit to give him a little distance from the crowd. After his sermon, he instructed Peter to put his boat in deeper water and let the nets out. What made this request unusual was the fact that it was not a good time for successful fishing, and Peter had already gone through the trouble of cleaning and putting away his nets after an unsuccessful night of work. A crisis moment of trust came when Peter declared, "Master, we worked hard all night trying to catch fish, and we caught nothing. But you say to put the nets in the water, so I will." There were more fish than they could put in their boats and a promise from Jesus that if they would follow him they would fish for people. From that day on, Peter followed Christ as a devoted disciple (Luke 5:1–11).

Peter quickly rose to the top as a leader among the disciples. He has the most visibility of any of the disciples in Scripture. He is named first in all the lists of disciples, a place of prominence (Matthew 10:2; Mark 3:16; Luke 6:14; Acts 1:13). He was a member of the inner circle which included James and John. This group was with Jesus at the healing of Jairus's daughter (Mark 5:37), on the mountain where Jesus was transfigured (Matthew 17:1; Mark 9:2; Luke 9:28), in intimate teaching times (Mark 13:3), and in his prayer time in the Garden of Gethsemane (Matthew 26:37; Mark 14:33).

Peter is pictured in the Bible as one who was very human. Most readers of Scripture will readily identify with him. He was quick to speak and slow to think (Matthew 17:24–27; John 13:8,9). He was incredibly impulsive, as seen in his water walk (Matthew 14:28–29), in his announcement that he was going to build tents on the mountain where Jesus was transfigured (Matthew 17:4), and in his sword play in the garden, where he was willing to take on a small army alone (Matthew 26:51). Peter was also very capable and discerning and was spokesperson for the twelve on several occasions (John 6:66–69; Matthew 17:24–27; Matthew 18:21; Matthew 19:27). The most well-known of those occasions was at Caesarea Philippi, when Jesus asked the disciples the question, "And who do you say I am?" Peter responded, "You are the Christ, the Son of the Living God" (Matthew 16:15, 16). This declaration was followed by Jesus' blessing, "you are blessed, Simon son of Jonah, because no person taught you that. My Father in Heaven showed you who I am. So I tell you, you are Peter. On this rock I will build my church, and the power of death will not be able to defeat it" (Matthew 16:17, 18). The supernatural vision of Jesus could see not only who Peter was, but who he would become.

The relationship Jesus had with Peter is a joy to behold. You can sense his great love for Peter from the moment he called him as a follower and gave him a new name. Jesus patiently bore with Peter's shortcomings and reinforced his strengths. One of the most tender moments in Scripture is when Jesus, knowing that Peter would deny him, told him that he was praying that he would not lose his faith (Luke 22:32).

Peter was also intensely loyal to Jesus. When he drew that sword in the garden, Peter was showing that he was willing to make good on his promise to die with him (Luke 22:50). Peter did as Jesus predicted and denied him three times. But Peter also discovered God's grace as he was given three opportunities to declare his love again to the risen Christ (John 21:15–23).

The Peter who emerged in the first twelve chapters of Acts was different in many ways from the one we met in the Gospels. He became the rock Jesus had seen all along. He was very active as a leader in the church: finding a replacement for Judas (Acts 1:15–26), preaching boldly (Acts 2:14–40; Acts 3:11–4:21), performing miracles of healing (Acts 3:1–10; Acts 9:33–42), courageously facing the leaders of the Temple (Acts 4:19; 5:29), ministering in Samaria (Acts 8:15), and taking the Gospel to the Gentiles (Acts 10:1–48). He was strong, decisive, courageous, and focused on the kingdom of God.

Peter: For additional scriptures on this topic go to Matthew 4:18–20.

Your cloth shades over the deck were blue
and purple
and came from the island of Cyprus.
8Men from Sidon and Arvad used oars to
row you.
Tyre, your skilled men were the sailors on
your deck.
9Workers of Byblos were with you,
putting caulk in your ship's seams.
All the ships of the sea and their sailors
came alongside to trade with you.

10" 'Men of Persia, Lydia, and Put
were warriors in your navy
and hung their shields and helmets on
your sides.
They made you look beautiful.
11Men of Arvad and Cilicia
guarded your city walls all around.
Men of Gammad
were in your watchtowers
and hung their shields around your walls.
They made your beauty perfect.

12" 'People of Tarshish became traders for you
because of your great wealth. They traded your
goods for silver, iron, tin, and lead.
13" 'People of Greece, Tubal, and Meshech became merchants for you. They traded your goods
for slaves and items of bronze.
14" 'People of Beth Togarmah traded your goods
for work horses, war horses, and mules.
15" 'People of Rhodes became merchants for
you, selling your goods on many coastlands. They
brought back ivory tusks and valuable black wood
as your payment.
16" 'People of Aram became traders for you,
because you had so many good things to sell. They
traded your goods for turquoise, purple cloth,
cloth with designs sewed on, fine linen, coral, and
rubies.
17" 'People of Judah and Israel became merchants for you. They traded your goods for wheat
from Minnith, and for honey, olive oil, and balm.
18-19" 'People of Damascus became traders for
you because you have many good things and great
wealth. They traded your goods for wine from
Helbon, wool from Zahar, and barrels of wine from
Izal. They received wrought iron, cassia, and sugar
cane in payment for your good things.
20" 'People of Dedan became merchants for you,
trading saddle blankets for riding.
21" 'People of Arabia and all the rulers of Kedar
became traders for you. They received lambs, male
sheep, and goats in payment for you.
22" 'The merchants of Sheba and Raamah became merchants for you. They traded your goods
for all the best spices, valuable gems, and gold.
23" 'People of Haran, Canneh, Eden, and the
traders of Sheba, Asshur, and Kilmad became merchants for you. 24They were paid with the best
clothes, blue cloth, cloth with designs sewed on,
carpets of many colors, and tightly wound ropes.

25" 'Trading ships
carried the things you sold.
You were like a ship full of heavy cargo
in the middle of the sea.
26The men who rowed you
brought you out into the high seas,
but the east wind broke you to pieces
in the middle of the sea.
27Your wealth, your trade, your goods,
your seamen, your sailors, your workers,
your traders, your warriors,
and everyone else on board
sank into the sea
on the day your ship was wrecked.
28The people on the shore shake with fear
when your sailors cry out.
29All the men who row
leave their ships;
the seamen and the sailors of other ships
stand on the shore.
30They cry loudly about you;
they cry very much.
They throw dust on their heads
and roll in ashes to show they are sad.
31They shave their heads for you,
and they put on rough cloth to show they
are upset.
They cry and sob for you;
they cry loudly.
32And in their loud crying
they sing a funeral song for you:
"No one was ever destroyed like Tyre,
surrounded by the sea."
33When the goods you traded went out over
the seas,
you met the needs of many nations.
With your great wealth and goods,
you made kings of the earth rich.
34But now you are broken by the sea
and have sunk to the bottom.

27:9 *caulk.* Something like tar put between the boards of a ship to make it waterproof.

27:17 *balm.* Balm is a resin that was used for treating wounds.

Your goods and all the people on board
have gone down with you.
35All those who live along the shore
are shocked by what happened to you.
Their kings are terribly afraid,
and their faces show their fear.
36The traders among the nations hiss at you.
You have come to a terrible end,
and you are gone forever.' "

Prophecy Against the King of Tyre

28 The LORD spoke his word to me, saying:
2"Human, say to the ruler of Tyre: 'This is
what the Lord GOD says:
Because you are proud,
you say, "I am a god.
I sit on the throne of a god
in the middle of the seas."
You think you are as wise as a god,
but you are a human, not a god.
3You think you are wiser than Daniel.
You think you can find out all secrets.
4Through your wisdom and understanding
you have made yourself rich.
You have gained gold and silver
and have saved it in your storerooms.
5Through your great skill in trading,
you have made your riches grow.
You are too proud
because of your riches.

6" 'So this is what the Lord GOD says:
You think you are wise
like a god,
7but I will bring foreign people against you,
the cruelest nation.
They will pull out their swords
and destroy all that your wisdom has built,
and they will dishonor your greatness.
8They will kill you;
you will die a terrible death
like those who are killed at sea.
9While they are killing you,
you will not be able to say anymore,
"I am a god."
You will be only a human, not a god,
when your murderers kill you.
10You will die like an unclean person;
foreigners will kill you.

I have spoken, says the Lord GOD.' "

11The LORD spoke his word to me, saying: 12"Human, sing a funeral song for the king of Tyre. Say
to him: 'This is what the Lord GOD says:
You were an example of what was perfect,
full of wisdom and perfect in beauty.
13You had a wonderful life,
as if you were in Eden, the garden of God.
Every valuable gem was on you:
ruby, topaz, and emerald,
yellow quartz, onyx, and jasper,
sapphire, turquoise, and chrysolite.
Your jewelry was made of gold.
It was prepared on the day you
were created.
14I appointed a living creature to guard you.
I put you on the holy mountain of God.
You walked among the gems that shined
like fire.
15Your life was right and good
from the day you were created,
until evil was found in you.
16Because you traded with countries far away,
you learned to be cruel, and you sinned.
So I threw you down in disgrace from the
mountain of God.
And the living creature who guarded you
forced you out from among the gems that
shined like fire.
17You became too proud
because of your beauty.
You ruined your wisdom
because of your greatness.
I threw you down to the ground.
Your example taught a lesson to other kings.
18You dishonored your places of worship
through your many sins and dishonest trade.
So I set on fire the place where you lived,
and the fire burned you up.
I turned you into ashes on the ground
for all those watching to see.
19All the nations who knew you
are shocked about you.
Your punishment was so terrible,
and you are gone forever.' "

Prophecy Against Sidon

20The LORD spoke his word to me, saying: 21"Human, look toward the city of Sidon and prophesy
against her. 22Say: 'This is what the Lord GOD says:
I am against you, Sidon,
and I will show my glory among you.

27:36 Water: Jonah 1–2
28:13 Garden of Eden: Ezekiel 31:8–9
28:13 The king of Tyre is described as one who lived in Eden, so great and blessed was his life.
28:19 Demon: Zechariah 3:1–2
28:19 Materialism/Possessions: Amos 2:6–8

People will know that I am the LORD
when I have punished Sidon;
I will show my holiness by defeating her.
23I will send diseases to Sidon,
and blood will flow in her streets.
Those who are wounded in Sidon will fall dead,
attacked from all sides.
Then they will know that I am the LORD.

God Will Help Israel

24" 'No more will neighboring nations be like
thorny branches or sharp stickers to hurt Israel.
Then they will know that I am the Lord GOD.
25" 'This is what the Lord GOD says: I will gather
the people of Israel from the nations where they
are scattered. I will show my holiness when the
nations see what I do for my people. Then they
will live in their own land—the land I gave to my
servant Jacob. 26They will live safely in the land
and will build houses and plant vineyards. They
will live in safety after I have punished all the
nations around who hate them. Then they will
know that I am the LORD their God.' "

Prophecy Against Egypt

29 It was the tenth year of our captivity, in the
tenth month, on the twelfth day of the
month. The LORD spoke his word to me, saying:
2"Human, look toward the king of Egypt, and
prophesy against him and all Egypt. 3Say: 'This is
what the Lord GOD says:
I am against you, king of Egypt.
You are like a great crocodile that lies in the
Nile River.
You say, "The Nile is mine;
I made it for myself."
4But I will put hooks in your jaws,
and I will make the fish of the Nile stick to
your sides.
I will pull you up out of your rivers,
with all the fish sticking to your sides.
5I will leave you in the desert,
you and all the fish from your rivers.
You will fall onto the ground;
you will not be picked up or buried.
I have given you to the wild animals
and to the birds of the sky for food.
6Then all the people who live in Egypt will know
that I am the LORD.
" 'Israel tried to lean on you for help, but you
were like a crutch made out of a weak stalk of
grass. 7When their hands grabbed you, you splintered and tore open their shoulders. When they
leaned on you, you broke and made all their backs
twist.
8" 'So this is what the Lord GOD says: I will
cause an enemy to attack you and kill your people
and animals. 9Egypt will become an empty desert.
Then they will know that I am the LORD.
" 'Because you said, "The Nile River is mine,
and I have made it," 10I am against you and your
rivers. I will destroy the land of Egypt and make it
an empty desert from Migdol in the north to
Aswan in the south, all the way to the border of
Cush. 11No person or animal will walk through it,
and no one will live in Egypt for forty years. 12I
will make the land of Egypt the most deserted country of all. Her cities will be the most deserted of
all ruined cities for forty years. I will scatter the
Egyptians among the nations, spreading them
among the countries.
13" 'This is what the Lord GOD says: After forty
years I will gather Egypt from the nations where
they have been scattered. 14I will bring back the
Egyptian captives and make them return to southern Egypt, to the land they came from. They will
become a weak kingdom there. 15It will be the
weakest kingdom, and it will never again rule
other nations. I will make it so weak it will never
again rule over the nations. 16The Israelites will
never again depend on Egypt. Instead, Egypt's
punishment will remind the Israelites of their sin
in turning to Egypt for help. Then they will know
that I am the Lord GOD.' "

Egypt Is Given to Babylon

17It was the twenty-seventh year of our captivity, in the first month, on the first day of the
month. The LORD spoke his word to me, saying:
18"Human, Nebuchadnezzar king of Babylon made
his army fight hard against Tyre. Every soldier's
head was rubbed bare, and every shoulder was
rubbed raw. But Nebuchadnezzar and his army
gained nothing from fighting Tyre. 19So this is
what the Lord GOD says: I will give the land of
Egypt to Nebuchadnezzar king of Babylon. He
will take away Egypt's people and its wealth and
its treasures as pay for his army. 20I am giving
Nebuchadnezzar the land of Egypt as a reward for
working hard for me, says the Lord GOD.
21"At that time I will make Israel grow strong
again, and I will let you, Ezekiel, speak to them.
Then they will know that I am the LORD."

29:6 *stalk of grass.* More precisely, the stalk of grass was a reed which gave the appearance of being sturdy enough to support weight, but when leaned on, it broke and threw out their shoulders and twisted their backs.

29:10 *Cush.* Cush was the area of southern Egypt and beyond to what we call the Sudan today.

Egypt Will Be Punished

30 The LORD spoke his word to me, saying:
2"Human, prophesy and say, 'This is what
the Lord GOD says:
Cry and say,
"The terrible day is coming."
3The day is near;
the LORD's day of judging is near.
It is a cloudy day
and a time when the nations will be judged.
4An enemy will attack Egypt,
and Cush will tremble with fear.
When the killing begins in Egypt,
her wealth will be taken away,
and her foundations will be torn down.

5Cush, Put, Lydia, Arabia, Libya, and some of my
people who had made an agreement with Egypt
will fall dead in war.

6" 'This is what the LORD says:
Those who fight on Egypt's side will fall.
The power she is proud of will be lost.
The people in Egypt will fall dead in war
from Migdol in the north to Aswan in
the south,
says the Lord GOD.
7They will be the most deserted lands.
Egypt's cities will be the worst of cities that
lie in ruins.
8Then they will know that I am the LORD
when I set fire to Egypt
and when all those nations on her side are
crushed.

9" 'At that time I will send messengers in
ships to frighten Cush, which now feels safe. The
people of Cush will tremble with fear when Egypt
is punished. And that time is sure to come.

10" 'This is what the Lord GOD says:
I will destroy great numbers of people in Egypt
through the power of Nebuchadnezzar king
of Babylon.
11Nebuchadnezzar and his army,
the cruelest army of any nation,
will be brought in to destroy the land.
They will pull out their swords against Egypt
and will fill the land with those they kill.
12I will make the streams of the Nile River
become dry land,
and then I will sell the land to evil people.
I will destroy the land and everything in it
through the power of foreigners.

I, the LORD, have spoken.

Egypt's Idols Are Destroyed

13" 'This is what the Lord GOD says:
I will destroy the idols
and take away the statues of gods from the
city of Memphis.
There will no longer be a leader in Egypt,
and I will spread fear through the land
of Egypt.
14I will make southern Egypt empty
and start a fire in Zoan
and punish Thebes.
15And I will pour out my anger against Pelusium,
the strong place of Egypt.
I will destroy great numbers of people
in Thebes.
16I will set fire to Egypt.
Pelusium will be in great pain.
The walls of Thebes will be broken open,
and Memphis will have troubles every day.
17The young men of Heliopolis and Bubastis
will fall dead in war,
and the people will be taken away as captives.
18In Tahpanhes the day will be dark
when I break Egypt's power.
Then she will no longer be proud of
her power.
A cloud will cover Egypt,
and her villages will be captured and
taken away.
19So I will punish Egypt,
and they will know I am the LORD.' "

Egypt Becomes Weak

20It was in the eleventh year of our captivity, in
the first month, on the seventh day of the month.
The LORD spoke his word to me, saying: 21"Human, I have broken the powerful arm of the king
of Egypt. It has not been tied up, so it will not get
well. It has not been wrapped with a bandage, so
it will not be strong enough to hold a sword in
war. 22So this is what the Lord GOD says: I am
against the king of Egypt. I will break his arms,
both the strong arm and the broken arm, and I
will make the sword fall from his hand. 23I will
scatter the Egyptians among the nations, spreading them among the countries. 24I will make the
arms of the king of Babylon strong and put my
sword in his hand. But I will break the arms of
the king of Egypt. Then when he faces the king of
Babylon, he will cry out in pain like a dying person. 25So I will make the arms of the king of
Babylon strong, but the arms of the king of Egypt
will fall. Then people will know that I am the LORD

30:3 Day of the Lord: Joel 1:15

when I put my sword into the hand of the king of
Babylon and he uses it in war against Egypt. 26Then
I will scatter the Egyptians among the nations,
spreading them among the countries. Then they
will know that I am the LORD."

A Cedar Tree

31 It was in the eleventh year of our captivity,
in the third month, on the first day of the
month. The LORD spoke his word to me, saying:
2"Human, say to the king of Egypt and his people:
'No one is like you in your greatness.
3Assyria was once like a cedar tree in Lebanon
with beautiful branches that shaded the forest.
It was very tall;
its top was among the clouds.
4Much water made the tree grow;
the deep springs made it tall.
Rivers flowed
around the bottom of the tree
and sent their streams
to all other trees in the countryside.
5So the tree was taller
than all the other trees in the countryside.
Its limbs became long and big
because of so much water.
6All the birds of the sky
made their nests in the tree's limbs.
And all the wild animals
gave birth under its branches.
All great nations
lived in the tree's shade.
7So the tree was great and beautiful,
with its long branches,
because its roots reached down to much water.
8The cedar trees in the garden of God
were not as great as it was.
The pine trees
did not have such great limbs.
The plane trees
did not have such branches.
No tree in the garden of God
was as beautiful as this tree.
9I made it beautiful
with many branches,
and all the trees of Eden in the garden of God
wanted to be like it.

10" 'So this is what the Lord GOD says: The tree
grew tall. Its top reached the clouds, and it
became proud of its height. 11So I handed it over
to a mighty ruler of the nations for him to punish
it. Because it was evil, I got rid of it. 12The cruelest
foreign nation cut it down and left it. The tree's
branches fell on the mountains and in all the valleys, and its broken limbs were in all the ravines of
the land. All the nations of the earth left the shade
of that tree. 13The birds of the sky live on the
fallen tree. The wild animals live among the tree's
fallen branches. 14So the trees that grow by the
water will not be proud to be tall; they will not put
their tops among the clouds. None of the trees
that are watered well will grow that tall, because
they all are meant to die and go under the ground.
They will be with people who have died and have
gone down to the place of the dead.

15" 'This is what the Lord GOD says: On the day
when the tree went down to the place of the dead,
I made the deep springs cry loudly. I covered them
and held back their rivers, and the great waters
stopped flowing. I dressed Lebanon in black to
show her sadness about the great tree, and all the
trees in the countryside were sad about it. 16I
made the nations shake with fear at the sound of
the tree falling when I brought it down to the
place of the dead. It went to join those who have
gone down to the grave. Then all the trees of Eden
and the best trees of Lebanon, all the well-watered
trees, were comforted in the place of the dead
below the earth. 17These trees had also gone down
with the great tree to the place of the dead. They
joined those who were killed in war and those
among the nations who had lived under the great
tree's shade.

18" 'So no tree in Eden is equal to you, Egypt, in
greatness and honor, but you will go down to join
the trees of Eden in the place below the earth. You
will lie among unclean people, with those who
were killed in war.

" 'This is about the king of Egypt and all his people, says the Lord GOD.' "

A Funeral Song

32 It was in the twelfth year of our captivity,
in the twelfth month, on the first day of
the month. The LORD spoke his word to me, saying: 2"Human, sing a funeral song about the king
of Egypt. Say to him:
'You are like a young lion among the nations.
You are like a crocodile in the seas.
You splash around in your streams
and stir up the water with your feet,
making the rivers muddy.

31:9 Garden of Eden: Ezekiel 36:35
31:15 Flood: Matthew 24:38–39
31:18 Prophetic Symbolism: Ezekiel 37

3"'This is what the Lord GOD says:
I will spread my net over you,
and I will use a large group of people
to pull you up in my net.
4Then I will throw you on the land
dropping you onto the ground.
I will let the birds of the sky rest on you
and all the animals of the earth eat you until
they are full.
5I will scatter your flesh on the mountains
and fill the valleys with what is left of you.
6I will drench the land with your flowing blood
as far as the mountains,
and the ravines will be full of your flesh.
7When I make you disappear,
I will cover the sky and make the stars dark.
I will cover the sun with a cloud,
and the moon will not shine.
8I will make all the shining lights in the sky
become dark over you;
I will bring darkness over your land,
says the Lord GOD.
9I will cause many people to be afraid
when I bring you as a captive into other
nations,
to lands you have not known.
10I will cause many people to be shocked
about you.
Their kings will tremble with fear because
of you
when I swing my sword in front of them.
They will shake every moment
on the day you fall;
each king will be afraid for his own life.

11"'So this is what the Lord GOD says:
The sword of the king of Babylon
will attack you.
12I will cause your people to fall
by the swords of mighty soldiers,
the most terrible in the world.
They will destroy the pride of Egypt
and all its people.
13I will also destroy all Egypt's cattle
which live alongside much water.
The foot of a human will not stir the water,
and the hoofs of cattle will not muddy it
anymore.
14So I will let the Egyptians' water become clear.
I will cause their rivers to run as smoothly as
olive oil,
says the Lord GOD.
15When I make the land of Egypt empty
and take everything that is in the land,
when I destroy all those who live in Egypt,
then they will know that I am the LORD.'

16"This is the funeral song people will sing for
Egypt. The women of the nations will sing it; they
will sing a funeral song for Egypt and all its people,
says the Lord GOD."

Egypt to Be Destroyed

17It was in the twelfth year of our captivity, on
the fifteenth day of the month. The LORD spoke his
word to me, saying: 18"Human, cry for the people
of Egypt. Bring down Egypt, together with the
women of the powerful nations; bring them down
to the place of the dead below the earth to join
those who go to the place of the dead. 19Say to
them: 'Are you more beautiful than others? Go lie
down in death with those who are unclean.' 20The
Egyptians will fall among those killed in war. The
sword is ready; the enemy will drag Egypt and all
her people away. 21From the place of the dead the
leaders of the mighty ones will speak about the
king of Egypt and the nations which help him: 'The
unclean, those killed in war, have come down here
and lie dead.'
22"Assyria and all its army lie dead there. The
graves of their soldiers are all around. All were
killed in war, 23and their graves were put in the
deepest parts of the place of the dead. Assyria's
army lies around its grave. When they lived on
earth, they frightened people, but now all of them
have been killed in war.
24"The nation of Elam is there with all its army
around its grave. All of them were killed in war.
They had frightened people on earth and were
unclean, so they went down to the lowest parts of
the place of the dead. They must carry their shame
with those who have gone down to the place of
the dead. 25A bed has been made for Elam with
all those killed in war. The graves of her soldiers
are all around her. All Elam's people are unclean,
killed in war. They frightened people when they
lived on earth, but now they must carry their
shame with those who have gone down to the
place of the dead. Their graves are with the rest
who were killed.
26"Meshech and Tubal are there with the graves
of all their soldiers around them. All of them are
unclean and have been killed in war. They also
frightened people when they lived on earth. 27But
they are not buried with the other soldiers who
were killed in battle long ago, those who went
with their weapons of war to the place of the dead.
These soldiers had their swords laid under their
heads and their shields on their bodies. These
mighty soldiers used to frighten people when they
lived on earth.

28“You, king of Egypt, will be broken and lie among those who are unclean, who were killed in war.

29“Edom is there also, with its kings and all its leaders. They were mighty, but now they lie in death with those killed in war, with those who are unclean, with those who have gone down to the place of the dead.

30“All the rulers of the north and all the Sidonians are there. Their strength frightened people, but they have gone down in shame with those who were killed. They are unclean, lying with those killed in war. They carry their shame with those who have gone down to the place of the dead.

31“The king of Egypt and his army will see these who have been killed in war. Then he will be comforted for all his soldiers killed in war, says the Lord GOD. 32I made people afraid of the king of Egypt while he lived on earth. But he and all his people will lie among those who are unclean, who were killed in war, says the Lord GOD.”

Ezekiel Is Watchman for Israel

33 The LORD spoke his word to me, saying: 2“Human, speak to your people and say to them: ‘Suppose I bring a war against a land. The people of the land may choose one of their men and make him their watchman. 3When he sees the enemy coming to attack the land, he will blow the trumpet and warn the people. 4If they hear the sound of the trumpet but do nothing, the enemy will come and kill them. They will be responsible for their own deaths. 5They heard the sound of the trumpet but didn’t do anything. So they are to blame for their own deaths. If they had done something, they would have saved their own lives. 6But if the watchman sees the enemy coming to attack and does not blow the trumpet, the people will not be warned. Then if the enemy comes and kills any of them, they have died because of their own sin. But I will punish the watchman for their deaths.’

7“You, human, are the one I have made a watchman for Israel. If you hear a word from my mouth, you must warn them for me. 8Suppose I say to the wicked: ‘Wicked people, you will surely die,’ but you don’t speak to warn the wicked to stop doing evil. Then they will die because they were sinners, but I will punish you for their deaths. 9But if you warn the wicked to stop doing evil and they do not stop, they will die because they were sinners. But you have saved your life.

10“So you, human, say to Israel: ‘You have said: Surely our law-breaking and sins are hurting us. They will kill us. What can we do so we will live?’ 11Say to them: ‘The Lord GOD says: As surely as I live, I do not want any who are wicked to die. I want them to stop doing evil and live. Stop! Stop your wicked ways! You don’t want to die, do you, people of Israel?’

12“Human, say to your people: ‘The goodness of those who do right will not save them when they sin. The evil of wicked people will not cause them to be punished if they stop doing it. If good people sin, they will not be able to live by the good they did earlier.’ 13If I tell good people, ‘You will surely live,’ they might think they have done enough good and then do evil. Then none of the good things they did will be remembered. They will die because of the evil they have done. 14Or, if I say to the wicked people, ‘You will surely die,’ they may stop sinning and do what is right and honest. 15For example, they may return what somebody gave them as a promise to repay a loan, or pay back what they stole. If they live by the rules that give life and do not sin, then they will surely live, and they will not die. 16They will not be punished for any of their sins. They now do what is right and fair, so they will surely live.

17“Your people say: ‘The way of the Lord is not fair.’ But it is their own ways that are not fair. 18When the good people stop doing good and do evil, they will die for their evil. 19But when the wicked stop doing evil and do what is right and fair, they will live. 20You still say: ‘The way of the Lord is not fair.’ Israel, I will judge all of you by your own ways.”

The Fall of Jerusalem Explained

21It was in the twelfth year of our captivity, on the fifth day of the tenth month. A person who had escaped from Jerusalem came to me and said, “Jerusalem has been captured.” 22Now I had felt the power of the LORD on me the evening before. He had made me able to talk again before this person came to me. I could speak; I was not without speech anymore.

23Then the LORD spoke his word to me, saying: 24“Human, people who live in the ruins in the land of Israel are saying: ‘Abraham was only one person, yet he was given the land as his own. Surely the land has been given to us, who are many, as our very own.’ 25So say to them: ‘This is what the Lord GOD says: You eat meat with the blood still in it, you ask your idols for help, and you murder people. Should you then have the land as your very own? 26You depend on your sword and do terrible things

33:25 *eat meat.* For the law against eating meat with blood in it see Leviticus 19:26.

which I hate. Each of you has sexual relations with
his neighbor's wife. So should you have the land?'
27"Say to them: 'This is what the Lord GOD says:
As surely as I live, those who are among the city
ruins in Israel will be killed in war. I will cause
those who live in the country to be eaten by wild
animals. People hiding in the strongholds and
caves will die of disease. 28I will make the land an
empty desert. The people's pride in the land's
power will end. The mountains of Israel will
become empty so that no one will pass through
them. 29They will know that I am the LORD when
I make the land an empty desert because of the
things they have done that I hate.'
30"But as for you, human, your people are talking about you by the walls and in the doorways of
houses. They say to each other: 'Come now, and
hear the message from the LORD.' 31So they come
to you in crowds as if they were really ready to listen. They sit in front of you as if they were my
people and hear your words, but they will not
obey them. With their mouths they tell me they
love me, but their hearts desire their selfish profits. 32To your people you are nothing more than a
singer who sings love songs and has a beautiful
voice and plays a musical instrument well. They
hear your words, but they will not obey them.
33"When this comes true, and it surely will happen, then the people will know that a prophet has
been among them."

The Leaders Are like Shepherds

34 The LORD spoke his word to me, saying:
2"Human, prophesy against the leaders of
Israel, who are like shepherds. Prophesy and say
to them: 'This is what the Lord GOD says: How terrible it will be for the shepherds of Israel who feed
only themselves! Why don't the shepherds feed
the flock? 3You eat the milk curds, and you clothe
yourselves with the wool. You kill the fat sheep,
but you do not feed the flock. 4You have not made
the weak strong. You have not healed the sick or
put bandages on those that were hurt. You have
not brought back those who strayed away or
searched for the lost. But you have ruled the sheep
with cruel force. 5The sheep were scattered,
because there was no shepherd, and they became
food for every wild animal. 6My flock wandered
over all the mountains and on every high hill.
They were scattered all over the face of the earth,
and no one searched or looked for them.
7" 'So, you shepherds, hear the word of the LORD.
This is what the Lord GOD says: 8As surely as I live,
my flock has been caught and eaten by all the wild
animals, because the flock has no shepherd. The
shepherds did not search for my flock. No, they
fed themselves instead of my flock. 9So, you shepherds, hear the word of the LORD. 10This is what
the Lord GOD says: I am against the shepherds. I
will blame them for what has happened to my
sheep and will not let them tend the flock anymore. Then the shepherds will stop feeding themselves, and I will take my flock from their mouths
so they will no longer be their food.
11" 'This is what the Lord GOD says: I, myself,
will search for my sheep and take care of them.
12As a shepherd takes care of his scattered flock
when it is found, I will take care of my sheep. I
will save them from all the places where they
were scattered on a cloudy and dark day. 13I will
bring them out from the nations and gather them
from the countries. I will bring them to their own
land and pasture them on the mountains of Israel,
in the ravines, and in all the places where people
live in the land. 14I will feed them in a good pasture, and they will eat grass on the high mountains of Israel. They will lie down on good ground
where they eat grass, and they will eat in rich
grassland on the mountains of Israel. 15I will feed
my flock and lead them to rest, says the Lord GOD.
16I will search for the lost, bring back those that
strayed away, put bandages on those that were
hurt, and make the weak strong. But I will destroy
those sheep that are fat and strong. I will tend the
sheep with fairness.
17" 'This is what the Lord GOD says: As for you,
my flock, I will judge between one sheep and
another, between the male sheep and the male
goats. 18Is it not enough for you to eat grass in the
good land? Must you crush the rest of the grass
with your feet? Is it not enough for you to drink
clear water? Must you make the rest of the water
muddy with your feet? 19Must my flock eat what
you crush, and must they drink what you make
muddy with your feet?
20" 'So this is what the Lord GOD says to them:
I, myself, will judge between the fat sheep and the
thin sheep. 21You push with your side and with
your shoulder, and you knock down all the weak
sheep with your horns until you have forced them
away. 22So I will save my flock; they will not be
hurt anymore. I will judge between one sheep and
another. 23Then I will put over them one shepherd, my servant David. He will feed them and
tend them and be their shepherd. 24Then I, the

34:2 *shepherds.* The shepherd was a common ancient Near Eastern image for political leaders. Here the leaders of the people of God are described as bad, evil shepherds.

34:2 Citizen: 1 Timothy 2:1–2
34:16 Mountain: Matthew 17:20
34:23 David: Zechariah 13:1

MEDIATOR

1 JOHN 2:1–2

What is a mediator?
Who can bridge the gap between God and us, his human creatures?

Deep down we know that a huge gulf separates us from God. We don't know how to find God under our own power. We need someone to show us the way. We need someone who will tell us about God and who will speak to God on our behalf. We need a mediator.

John writes of a helper or advocate who stands on our behalf in the Father's presence. This advocate role, which John says Jesus fulfills for us, is the role of mediator. A mediator is one who stands as a go-between and serves in such a way as to bring reconciliation and unity between two parties.

A mediator stands in the middle. Jesus, fully God and fully human, stands in God's presence on our behalf (Hebrews 4:14–16), and also stands in our midst as God's fullest expression of himself (John 1:18). Jesus works as the agent of our intercession with God and God's reconciliation with all humankind. Through the centuries the church has understood the nature of Christ's saving act as one in which Christ reconciles God to humankind. "God was in Christ making peace between the world and himself," we read in Paul's second letter to the Corinthians (5:19).

The role of mediator can be seen in the major characters in the Old Testament. Moses served as mediator between God and the people in the wilderness. He often spoke to God on behalf of the people. In Numbers 21:4–9, the people grumbled against God because they hated the food he gave them. In punishment, God sent poisonous snakes among them. The people then hurried to Moses to have him pray to God for them, since they knew he was the one who had God's ear. In the same way, Moses served as God's spokesperson to the people. God himself arranged it this way. God would call Moses into his presence to convey a message or direction through Moses to the people (Exodus 24:2). Moses was a true mediator.

Isaiah, as a prophet of God, mediated God's word to the people of Israel. "Whom can I send? Who will go for us?" Isaiah heard God ask (Isaiah 6:8). A prophet, in revealing God's word and work, interpreting God's actions and presence, functions as a mediating presence. When Jeremiah spoke, he would say, "This is what the Lord says" (Jeremiah 31:15) and in this way Jeremiah would mediate God's word to the people.

During the Exodus event, Aaron served as a priest for the people. (Numbers 3; Exodus 29). Aaron's role as priest was to perform the tasks that interceded or proclaimed reconciliation, such as prayers and sacrifices on behalf of the people. Aaron stood before God representing his people and stood before the people representing God's word. As a priest, Aaron mediated grace.

God established the king as a third office in the church that stood as a mediator between himself and his people. The king reflected God's rule on earth. He was to know the law and lead his people in obedience to the agreement that God had made with them (Deuteronomy 17:14–20).

In Christ, these three understandings of mediator come together. Jesus is a mediator as prophet, priest, and king. Jesus not only speaks to us on behalf of God, revealing God's word and saving work, but Jesus also reconciles people to God through performing a perfect sacrifice. He also is our king, leading us toward obedience to his father.

In the opening to Hebrews (1:1–3), we read about the old form of mediating and Christ's perfect mediation. "The Son reflects the glory of God and shows exactly what God is like. . . . When the Son made people clean from their sins, he sat down at the right side of God. . . ." At God's right hand, Jesus intercedes on our behalf with the Father. In this way, Jesus fulfills perfectly the role of mediator. He reveals the full nature of God to us. He interprets the intent and desire of God to us. He performs and becomes the sacrifice that reconciles us to God. He stands representationally in God's presence on our behalf.

What Jesus said and did, and how Jesus was and is today, stands as a mediating presence between God and humankind. In First Timothy we read, "There is one God and one way human beings can reach God. That way is through Christ Jesus, who is himself human. He gave himself as a payment to free all people" (1 Timothy 2:5–6).

John's understanding of Jesus' mediating service as helper and advocate with the Father reconciling the world to God presents the same message. Jesus, fulfilling the role of mediator, perfectly brings God and humankind into reconciliation. Through his work and word, Jesus bridges the gap.

Mediator: For additional scriptures on this topic go to Hebrews 4:14–16.

FAITH/UNBELIEF

JOHN 3:16

What is faith? Something in which to believe; or the act of believing itself? What concrete examples of faith can we find in the Bible?

Faith is the word that describes our acceptance of God's saving grace. On the one hand it is simple: Faith is saying yes to God's steadfast love. On the other hand, faith is complicated: It involves trust, commitment, obedience, hope, joy, assurance, acceptance, and love. John 3:16 illustrates two important things about faith. First, the starting point is God's love for the whole world. 1 John 4:8 tells us "God is love." Psalm 100 says "His love is forever." God loves the world so much he gave his Son to live and die for us. The second message from this passage is that our response to God's love is to believe in him. In the original language, "believe" and "faith" are two forms of the same word. To believe in Christ is the same thing as to have faith in him. Everyone who responds to God's love by faith is given eternal life, which is salvation. Those who do not believe in Christ have the opposite destination—they are lost.

Faith means deciding to belong to Christ. It is the Christian's answer to the question "Who am I?" We sometimes define ourselves by our family of birth, by our marriage, by our jobs, by the city or state in which we live, or by other affiliations. The Bible says that people who commit their lives to Christ are defined primarily in terms of their relationship to him. Christ must come first, ahead of everything else. This involves belonging to a new family—the body of Christ. It involves accepting Christ's lordship and being obedient to his will, including the commandment to love God with everything we have and to love our neighbors as we love ourselves (Matthew 22:39). Faith is often understood primarily as trusting God. He has shown himself faithful in all of his dealings with humanity, and we learn from Scripture that we can trust what he will do in the future. That gives us hope. In 1 Corinthians 13:13, faith, hope, and love are put side by side as the greatest attributes of any human being because they are so closely related to each other. The person of faith is hopeful about the future and lives a life filled with love of God and neighbor.

All of this treats faith as an attitude or aspect of an individual's life. But sometimes Scripture speaks of faith as a body of teaching, as in 1 Timothy 3:9. The word about God's love, including the offer of salvation, is a message that leads people to trust the Lord. To preach is to share this Good News with others. To witness is to communicate God's love by both our words and our deeds. When this message is really heard, God uses it to bring people to a saving relationship twith him. So faith is both a message that communicates the truth about God and us, and also the act of believing itself. Always the object of our faith is God in Christ Jesus, trusting him through his saving word in Scripture.

The Bible itself is the story of God's steadfast love and humanity's faith and unbelief. God chose Abraham to be the father of a special people. Abraham believed God, trusted his promise that he would have a son even though he was very old, and had confidence that God would fulfill his word. Genesis 15:6 says the Lord accepted Abraham's faith "and that faith made him right with God." The first of the Ten Commandments (Exodus 20:3) was a call to acknowledge the one God and refuse to believe in any other so-called gods. This was an important challenge to the people of Israel as they lived among other people who worshiped other gods. The prophets noted how many times Israel's unbelief had led to God's punishment. Yet when Isaiah (1:3) talks about how Israel had forgotten God (which is unbelief), he still announced God's love and forgiveness if the people would only repent and believe again. Hebrews 11 gives a long overview of the men and women of the Old Testament whose faith saved them.

In the New Testament, faith is given a more individual scope, because the relationship with the God of Israel is now offered not only to the chosen people but also to the Gentiles. Believing in Jesus, the Messiah of God, is the important issue. Jesus forgave the sins of the woman whose tears cleaned his feet because she believed (Luke 7:50). He healed the daughter of the centurion because of the man's faith (Mark 8:10). The Philippian jailer in Acts 16:31 believed in Jesus and was saved, along with his whole household.

Faith is the means by which we are saved. Paul states it clearly in Romans 5:1: "We have been made right with God by our faith." Ephesians 2:8 links God's grace as the beginning of our salvation, and our faith as the means by which we come to be saved. In that relationship of trust and commitment, we accept God's word as true and God's promises as trustworthy, and we willingly allow him to be the Lord of our lives.

Faith/Unbelief: For additional scriptures on this topic go to Romans 5:1.

LORD, will be their God, and my servant David will be a ruler among them. I, the LORD, have spoken.

25" 'I will make an agreement of peace with my sheep and will remove harmful animals from the land. Then the sheep will live safely in the desert and sleep in the woods. 26I will bless them and let them live around my hill. I will cause the rains to come when it is time; there will be showers to bless them. 27Also the trees in the countryside will give their fruit, and the land will give its harvest. And the sheep will be safe on their land. Then they will know that I am the LORD when I break the bars of their captivity and save them from the power of those who made them slaves. 28They will not be led captive by the nations again. The wild animals will not eat them, but they will live safely, and no one will make them afraid. 29I will give them a place famous for its good crops, so they will no longer suffer from hunger in the land. They will not suffer the insults of other nations anymore. 30Then they will know that I, the LORD their God, am with them. The nation of Israel will know that they are my people, says the Lord GOD. 31You, my human sheep, are the sheep I care for, and I am your God, says the Lord GOD.' "

Prophecy Against Edom

35 The LORD spoke his word to me, saying: 2"Human, look toward Edom and prophesy against it. 3Say to it: 'This is what the Lord GOD says: I am against you, Edom. I will stretch out my hand against you and make you an empty desert. 4I will destroy your cities, and you will become empty. Then you will know that I am the LORD.

5" 'You have always been an enemy of Israel. You let them be defeated in war when they were in trouble at the time of their final punishment. 6So the Lord GOD says, as surely as I live, I will let you be murdered. Murder will chase you. Since you did not hate murdering people, murder will chase you. 7I will make Edom an empty ruin and destroy everyone who goes in or comes out of it. 8I will fill its mountains with those who are killed. Those killed in war will fall on your hills, in your valleys, and in all your ravines. 9I will make you a ruin forever; no one will live in your cities. Then you will know that I am the LORD.

10" 'You said, "These two nations, Israel and Judah, and these two lands will be ours. We will take them for our own." But the LORD was there. 11So this is what the Lord GOD says: As surely as I live, I will treat you just as you treated them. You were angry and jealous because you hated them. So I will punish you and show the Israelites who I am. 12Then you will know that I, the LORD, have heard all your insults against the mountains of Israel. You said, "They have been ruined. They have been given to us to eat." 13You have not stopped your proud talk against me. I have heard you. 14This is what the Lord GOD says: All the earth will be happy when I make you an empty ruin. 15You were happy when the land of Israel was ruined, but I will do the same thing to you. Mount Seir and all Edom, you will become an empty ruin. Then you will know that I am the LORD.' "

Israel to Come Home

36 "Human, prophesy to the mountains of Israel and say: 'Mountains of Israel, hear the word of the LORD. 2This is what the Lord GOD says: The enemy has said about you, "Now the old places to worship gods have become ours." ' 3So prophesy and say: 'This is what the Lord GOD says: They have made you an empty ruin and have crushed you from all around. So you became a possession of the other nations. People have talked and whispered against you. 4So, mountains of Israel, hear the word of the Lord GOD. The Lord GOD speaks to the mountains, hills, ravines, and valleys, to the empty ruins and abandoned cities that have been robbed and laughed at by the other nations. 5This is what the Lord GOD says: I speak in hot anger against the other nations. I speak against the people of Edom, who took my land for themselves with joy and with hate in their hearts. They forced out the people and took their pastureland.' 6So prophesy about the land of Israel and say to the mountains, hills, ravines, and valleys: 'This is what the Lord GOD says: I speak in my jealous anger, because you have suffered the insults of the nations. 7So this is what the Lord GOD says: I promise that the nations around you will also have to suffer insults.

8" 'But you, mountains of Israel, will grow branches and fruit for my people, who will soon come home. 9I am concerned about you; I am on your side. You will be plowed, and seed will be planted in you. 10I will increase the number of people who live on you, all the people of Israel. The cities will have people living in them, and the ruins will be rebuilt. 11I will increase the number of people and animals living on you. They will grow and have many young. You will have people living on you as you did before, and I will make you

34:25 Peace: Micah 5:5
34:29 Famine: Amos 4:6–9
34:31 Blessing: Mark 10:13–16

better off than at the beginning. Then you will
know that I am the LORD. 12I will cause my people
Israel to walk on you and own you, and you will
belong to them. You will never again take their
children away from them.
13" 'This is what the Lord GOD says: People say
about you, "You eat people and take children from
your nation." 14But you will not eat people anymore or take away the children, says the Lord GOD.
15I will not make you listen to insults from the
nations anymore; you will not suffer shame from
them anymore. You will not cause your nation to
fall anymore, says the Lord GOD.' "

The Lord Acts for Himself

16The LORD spoke his word to me again, say-
ing:17"Human, when the nation of Israel was living
in their own land, they made it unclean by their
ways and the things they did. Their ways were like
a woman's uncleanness in her time of monthly
bleeding. 18So I poured out my anger against them,
because they murdered in the land and because
they made the land unclean with their idols. 19I
scattered them among the nations, and they were
spread through the countries. I punished them
for how they lived and what they did. 20They dishonored my holy name in the nations where they
went. The nations said about them: 'These are the
people of the LORD, but they had to leave the land
which he gave them.' 21But I had concern for my
holy name, which the nation of Israel had dishonored among the nations where they went.
22"So say to the people of Israel, 'This is what
the Lord GOD says: Israel, I am going to act, but not
for your sake. I will do something to help my holy
name, which you have dishonored among the
nations where you went. 23I will prove the holiness of my great name, which has been dishonored
among the nations. You have dishonored it among
these nations, but the nations will know that I am
the LORD when I prove myself holy before their
eyes, says the Lord GOD.
24" 'I will take you from the nations and gather
you out of all the lands and bring you back into
your own land. 25Then I will sprinkle clean water
on you, and you will be clean. I will cleanse you
from all your uncleanness and your idols. 26Also, I
will teach you to respect me completely, and I will
put a new way of thinking inside you. I will take
out the stubborn hearts of stone from your bodies,
and I will give you obedient hearts of flesh. 27I
will put my Spirit inside you and help you live by
my rules and carefully obey my laws. 28You will
live in the land I gave to your ancestors, and you
will be my people, and I will be your God. 29So
I will save you from all your uncleanness. I will
command the grain to come and grow; I will not
allow a time of hunger to hurt you. 30I will
increase the harvest of the field so you will never
again suffer shame among the nations because of
hunger. 31Then you will remember your evil ways
and actions that were not good, and you will hate
yourselves because of your sins and your terrible
acts that I hate. 32I want you to know that I am not
going to do this for your sake, says the Lord GOD. Be
ashamed and embarrassed about your ways, Israel.
33" 'This is what the Lord GOD says: This is
what will happen on the day I cleanse you from all
your sins: I will cause the cities to have people living in them again, and the destroyed places will be
rebuilt. 34The empty land will be plowed so it will
no longer be a ruin for everyone who passes by to
see. 35They will say, "This land was ruined, but
now it has become like the garden of Eden. The
cities were destroyed, empty, and ruined, but
now they are protected and have people living in
them." 36Then those nations still around you
will know that I, the LORD, have rebuilt what was
destroyed and have planted what was empty. I, the
LORD, have spoken, and I will do it.'
37"This is what the Lord GOD says: I will let
myself be asked by the people of Israel to do this for
them again: I will make their people grow in number like a flock. 38They will be as many as the
flocks brought to Jerusalem during her holy feasts.
Her ruined cities will be filled with flocks of people. Then they will know that I am the LORD."

The Vision of Dry Bones

37 I felt the power of the LORD on me, and he
brought me out by the Spirit of the LORD
and put me down in the middle of a valley. It was
full of bones. 2He led me around among the
bones, and I saw that there were many bones in
the valley and that they were very dry. 3Then he
asked me, "Human, can these bones live?"
I answered, "Lord GOD, only you know."
4He said to me, "Prophesy to these bones and say
to them, 'Dry bones, hear the word of the LORD.
5This is what the Lord GOD says to the bones: I will
cause breath to enter you so you will come to life.
6I will put muscles on you and flesh on you and

36:17 *unclean.* See Leviticus 18:19.
36:26 Baptism: Matthew 3:13–15
36:27 Land/Inheritance: Matthew 6:24–33
36:28 A Matter of the Heart: See article on page 409.
36:28 Spiritual Gifts: Ezekiel 37:14
36:35 Garden of Eden: See article on page 29.

cover you with skin. Then I will put breath in you so you will come to life. Then you will know that I am the LORD.' "

7So I prophesied as I was commanded. While I prophesied, there was a noise and a rattling. The bones came together, bone to bone. 8I looked and saw muscles come on the bones, and flesh grew, and skin covered the bones. But there was no breath in them.

9Then he said to me, "Prophesy to the wind. Prophesy, human, and say to the wind, 'This is what the Lord GOD says: Wind, come from the four winds, and breathe on these people who were killed so they can come back to life.' " 10So I prophesied as the LORD commanded me. And the breath came into them, and they came to life and stood on their feet, a very large army.

11Then he said to me, "Human, these bones are like all the people of Israel. They say, 'Our bones are dried up, and our hope has gone. We are destroyed.' 12So, prophesy and say to them, 'This is what the Lord GOD says: My people, I will open your graves and cause you to come up out of your graves. Then I will bring you into the land of Israel. 13My people, you will know that I am the LORD when I open your graves and cause you to come up from them. 14And I will put my Spirit inside you, and you will come to life. Then I will put you in your own land. And you will know that I, the LORD, have spoken and done it, says the LORD.' "

Judah and Israel Back Together

15The LORD spoke his word to me, saying, 16"Human, take a stick and write on it, 'For Judah and all the Israelites with him.' Then take another stick and write on it, 'The stick of Ephraim, for Joseph and all the Israelites with him.' 17Then join them together into one stick so they will be one in your hand.

18"When your people say to you, 'Explain to us what you mean by this,' 19say to them, 'This is what the Lord GOD says: I will take the stick for Joseph and the tribes of Israel with him, which is in the hand of Ephraim, and I will put it with the stick of Judah. I will make them into one stick, and they will be one in my hand.' 20Hold the sticks on which you wrote these names in your hand so the people can see them. 21Say to the people, 'This is what the Lord GOD says: I am going to take the people of Israel from among the nations where they have gone. I will gather them from all around and bring them into their own land. 22I will make them one nation in the land, on the mountains of Israel. One king will rule all of them. They will never again be two nations; they will not be divided into two kingdoms anymore. 23They will not continue to make themselves unclean by their idols, their statues of gods which I hate, or by their sins. I will save them from all the ways they sin and turn against me, and I will make them clean. Then they will be my people, and I will be their God.

24" 'My servant David will be their king, and they will all have one shepherd. They will live by my rules and obey my laws. 25They will live on the land I gave to my servant Jacob, the land in which your ancestors lived. They will all live on the land forever: they, their children, and their grandchildren. David my servant will be their king forever. 26I will make an agreement of peace with them, an agreement that continues forever. I will put them in their land and make them grow in number. Then I will put my Temple among them forever. 27The place where I live will be with them. I will be their God, and they will be my people. 28When my Temple is among them forever, the nations will know that I, the LORD, make Israel holy.' "

Prophecy Against Gog

38 The LORD spoke his word to me, saying, 2"Human, look toward Gog of the land of Magog, the chief ruler of the nations of Meshech and Tubal. Prophesy against him 3and say, 'The Lord GOD says this: I am against you, Gog, chief ruler of Meshech and Tubal. 4I will turn you around and put hooks in your jaws. And I will bring you out with all your army, horses, and horsemen, all of whom will be dressed in beautiful uniforms. They will be a large army with large and small shields and all having swords. 5Persia, Cush, and Put will be with them, all of them having shields and helmets. 6There will also be Gomer with all its troops and the nation of Togarmah from the far north with all its troops—many nations with you.

7" 'Be prepared. Be prepared, you and all the armies that have come together to make you their commander. 8After a long time you will be called for service. After those years you will come into a land that has been rebuilt from war. The people in the land will have been gathered from many nations to the mountains of Israel, which were empty for a long time. These people were brought out from the nations, and they will all be living in

37:9 *wind.* This Hebrew word could also mean "breath" or "spirit."

37:14 Spiritual Gifts: Joel 2:28–29

37:16 *a stick.* The stick is either a wooden tablet on which Ezekiel wrote or the representation of a royal scepter.

37:28 Prophetic Symbolism: Daniel 7:1–28

38:4 *put hooks in your jaws.* It was a common practice to put hooks in the nose or jaw of a captured prisoner, and then parade him through the street like an animal.

safety. 9You will come like a storm. You, all your
troops, and the many nations with you will be like
a cloud covering the land.

10" 'This is what the Lord GOD says: At that time
ideas will come into your mind, and you will think
up an evil plan. 11You will say, "I will march against
a land of towns without walls. I will attack those
who are at rest and live in safety. All of them live
without city walls or gate bars or gates. 12I will capture treasures and take loot. I will turn my power
against the rebuilt ruins that now have
people living in them. I will attack these people
who have been gathered from the nations, who
have become rich with farm animals and property,
who live at the center of the world." 13Sheba,
Dedan, and the traders of Tarshish, with all its villages, will say to you, "Did you come to capture
treasure? Did you bring your troops together to take
loot? Did you bring them to carry away silver and
gold and to take away farm animals and property?" '

14"So prophesy, human, and say to Gog, 'This is
what the Lord GOD says: Now that my people Israel
are living in safety, you will know about it. 15You
will come with many people from your place in the
far north. You will have a large group with you, a
mighty army, all riding on horses. 16You will attack
my people Israel like a cloud that covers the land.
This will happen in the days to come when I bring
you against my land. Gog, then the nations will
know me when they see me prove how holy I am
in what I do through you.

17" 'This is what the Lord GOD says: You are the
one about whom I spoke in past days. I spoke
through my servants, the prophets of Israel, who
prophesied for many years that I would bring you
against them. 18This is what will happen: On the
day Gog attacks the land of Israel, I will become
very angry, says the Lord GOD. 19With jealousy
and great anger I tell you that at that time there
will surely be a great earthquake in Israel. 20The
fish of the sea, the birds of the sky, the wild animals, everything that crawls on the ground, and
all the people on the earth will shake with fear
before me. Also the mountains will be thrown
down, the cliffs will fall, and every wall will fall to
the ground. 21Then I will call for a war against Gog
on all my mountains, says the Lord GOD. Everyone's sword will attack the soldier next to him. 22I
will punish Gog with disease and death. I will send
a heavy rain with hailstones and burning sulfur on
Gog, his army, and the many nations with him.
23Then I will show how great I am. I will show my
holiness, and I will make myself known to the
many nations that watch. Then they will know
that I am the LORD.'

The Death of Gog and His Army

39 "Human, prophesy against Gog and say,
'This is what the Lord GOD says: I am
against you, Gog, chief ruler of Meshech and Tubal.
2I will turn you around and lead you. I will bring
you from the far north and send you to attack the
mountains of Israel. 3I will knock your bow out of
your left hand and throw down your arrows from
your right hand. 4You, all your troops, and the
nations with you will fall dead on the mountains of
Israel. I will let you be food for every bird that eats
meat and for every wild animal. 5You will lie fallen
on the ground, because I have spoken, says the
Lord GOD. 6I will send fire on Magog and those
who live in safety on the coastlands. Then they will
know that I am the LORD.

7" 'I will make myself known among my people
Israel, and I will not let myself be dishonored anymore. Then the nations will know that I am the
LORD, the Holy One in Israel. 8It is coming! It will
happen, says the Lord GOD. The time I talked about
is coming.

9" 'Then those who live in the cities of Israel will
come out and make fires with the enemy's weapons. They will burn them, both large and small
shields, bows and arrows, war clubs, and spears.
They will use the weapons to burn in their fires
for seven years. 10They will not need to take wood
from the field or chop firewood from the forests,
because they will make fires with the weapons.
In this way they will take the treasures of those
who took their treasures; they will take the loot of
those who took their loot, says the Lord GOD.

11" 'At that time I will give Gog a burial place in
Israel, in the Valley of the Travelers, east of the
Dead Sea. It will block the road for travelers. Gog
and all his army will be buried there, so people
will call it The Valley of Gog's Army.

12" 'The people of Israel will be burying them for
seven months to make the land clean again. 13All
the people in the land will bury them, and they
will be honored on the day of my victory, says the
Lord GOD.

14" 'The people of Israel will choose men to
work through the land to make it clean. Along with
others, they will bury Gog's soldiers still lying dead
on the ground. After the seven months are finished, they will still search. 15As they go through
the land, anyone who sees a human bone is to put
a marker by it. The sign will stay there until the
gravediggers bury the bone in The Valley of Gog's
Army. 16A city will be there named Hamonah. So
they will make the land clean again.'

17“Human, this is what the Lord GOD says:
Speak to every kind of bird and wild animal: ‘Come
together, come! Come together from all around to
my sacrifice, a great sacrifice which I will prepare
for you on the mountains of Israel. Eat flesh and
drink blood! 18You are to eat the flesh of the mighty
and drink the blood of the rulers of the earth as if
they were fat animals from Bashan: male sheep,
lambs, goats, and bulls. 19You are to eat and drink
from my sacrifice which I have prepared for you,
eating fat until you are full and drinking blood until
you are drunk. 20At my table you are to eat until
you are full of horses and riders, mighty men and
all kinds of soldiers,’ says the Lord GOD.

21“I will show my glory among the nations. All
the nations will see my power when I punish
them. 22From that time onward the people of Israel
will know that I am the LORD their God. 23The
nations will know Israel was taken away captive
because they turned against me. So I turned away
from them and handed them over to their enemies
until all of them died in war. 24Because of their
uncleanness and their sins, I punished them and
turned away from them.

25“So this is what the Lord GOD says: Now I will
bring the people of Jacob back from captivity, and I
will have mercy on the whole nation of Israel. I will
not let them dishonor me. 26The people will forget their shame and how they rejected me when
they live again in safety on their own land with no
one to make them afraid. 27I will bring the people
back from other lands and gather them from the
lands of their enemies. So I will use my people to
show many nations that I am holy. 28Then my people will know that I am the LORD their God,
because I sent them into captivity among the
nations, but then I brought them back to their
own land, leaving no one behind. 29I will not turn
away from them anymore, because I will put my
Spirit into the people of Israel, says the Lord GOD.”

The New Temple

40 It was the twenty-fifth year of our captivity, at the beginning of the year, on the
tenth day of the month. It was in the fourteenth
year after Jerusalem was captured. On that same
day I felt the power of the LORD, and he brought me
to Jerusalem. 2In the visions of God he brought me
to the land of Israel and put me down on a very
high mountain. On the south of the mountain
there were some buildings that looked like a city.
3He took me closer to the buildings, and I saw a
man who looked as if he were made of bronze,
standing in the gateway. He had a cord made of
linen and a stick in his hand, both for measuring.
4The man said to me, “Human, look with your
eyes and hear with your ears. Pay attention to all
that I will show you, because that’s why you have
been brought here. Tell the people of Israel all
that you see.”

The East Gateway

5I saw a wall that surrounded the Temple area.
The measuring stick in the man’s hand was ten
and one-half feet long. So the man measured the
wall, which was ten and one-half feet thick and ten
and one-half feet high.

6Then the man went to the east gateway. He
went up its steps and measured the opening of the
gateway. It was ten and one-half feet deep. 7The
rooms for the guards were ten and one-half feet
long and ten and one-half feet wide. The walls that
came out between the guards’ rooms were about
nine feet thick. The opening of the gateway next
to the porch that faced the Temple was ten and
one-half feet deep.

8Then the man measured the porch of the gateway. 9It was about fourteen feet deep, and its side
walls were three and one-half feet thick. The porch
of the gateway faced the Temple.

10On each side of the east gateway were three
rooms, which measured the same on each side.
The walls between each room were the same
thickness. 11The man measured the width of the
entrance to the gateway, which was seventeen
and one-half feet wide. The width of the gate was
about twenty-three feet. 12And there was a low
wall about twenty-one inches high in front of each
room. The rooms were ten and one-half feet on
each side. 13The man measured the gateway from
the roof of one room to the roof of the opposite
room. It was about forty-four feet from one door to
the opposite door. 14The man also measured the
porch, which was about thirty-five feet wide. The
courtyard was around the porch. 15From the front
of the outer side of the gateway to the front of the
porch of the inner side of the gateway was eighty-
seven and one-half feet. 16The rooms and porch
had small windows on both sides. The windows
were narrower on the side facing the gateway.
Carvings of palm trees were on each side wall of
the rooms.

The Outer Courtyard

17Then the man brought me into the outer courtyard where I saw rooms and a pavement of stones
all around the court. Thirty rooms were along the

40:3 *a man . . . made of bronze.* As in 8:2, God sent an angel to guide him through his vision.

edge of the paved walkway. 18The pavement ran alongside the gates and was as deep as the gates were wide. This was the lower pavement. 19Then the man measured from the outer wall to the inner wall. The outer court between these two walls was one hundred seventy-five feet on the east and on the north.

The North Gateway

20The man measured the length and width of the north gateway leading to the outer courtyard. 21Its three rooms on each side, its inner walls, and its porch measured the same as the first gateway. It was eighty-seven and one-half feet long and forty-four feet wide. 22Its windows, porch, and carvings of palm trees measured the same as the east gateway. Seven steps went up to the gateway, and the gateway's porch was at the inner end. 23The inner courtyard had a gateway across from the northern gateway like the one on the east. The man measured it and found it was one hundred seventy-five feet from inner gateway to outer gateway.

The South Gateway

24Then the man led me south where I saw a gateway facing south. He measured its inner walls and its porch, and they measured the same as the other gateways. 25The gateway and its porch had windows all around like the other gateways. It was eighty-seven and one-half feet long and forty-four feet wide. 26Seven steps went up to this gateway. Its porch was at the inner end, and it had carvings of palm trees on its inner walls. 27The inner courtyard had a gateway on its south side. The man measured from gate to gate on the south side, which was one hundred seventy-five feet.

The Inner Courtyard

28Then the man brought me through the south gateway into the inner courtyard. The inner south gateway measured the same as the gateways in the outer wall. 29The inner south gateway's rooms, inner walls, and porch measured the same as the gateways in the outer wall. There were windows all around the gateway and its porch. The gateway was eighty-seven and one-half feet long and forty-four feet wide. 30Each porch of each inner gateway was about forty-four feet long and about nine feet wide. 31The inner south gateway's porch faced the outer courtyard. Carvings of palm trees were on its side walls, and its stairway had eight steps.

32The man brought me into the inner courtyard on the east side. He measured the inner east gateway, and it was the same as the other gateways. 33The inner east gateway's rooms, inside walls, and porch measured the same as the other gateways. Windows were all around the gateway and its porch. The inner east gateway was eighty-seven and one-half feet long and forty-four feet wide. 34Its porch faced the outer courtyard. Carvings of palm trees were on its inner walls on each side, and its stairway had eight steps.

35Then the man brought me to the inner north gateway. He measured it, and it was the same as the other gateways. 36Its rooms, inner walls, and porch measured the same as the other gateways. There were windows all around the gateway, which was eighty-seven and one-half feet long and forty-four feet wide. 37Its porch faced the outer courtyard. Carvings of palm trees were on its inner walls on each side, and its stairway had eight steps.

Rooms for Preparing Sacrifices

38There was a room with a door that opened onto the porch of the inner north gateway. In this room the priests washed animals for the burnt offerings. 39There were two tables on each side of the porch, on which animals for burnt offerings, sin offerings, and penalty offerings were killed. 40Outside, by each side wall of the porch, at the entrance to the north gateway, were two more tables. 41So there were four tables inside the gateway, and four tables outside. In all there were eight tables on which the priests killed animals for sacrifices. 42There were four tables made of cut stone for the burnt offering. These tables were about three feet long, three feet wide, and about two feet high. On these tables the priests put their tools which they used to kill animals for burnt offerings and the other sacrifices. 43Double shelves three inches wide were put up on all the walls. The flesh for the offering was put on the tables.

The Priests' Rooms

44There were two rooms in the inner courtyard. One was beside the north gateway and faced south. The other room was beside the south gateway and faced north. 45The man said to me, "The room which faces south is for the priests who serve in the Temple area, 46while the room that faces north is for the priests who serve at the altar. This second group of priests are descendants of Zadok, the only descendants of Levi who can come near the LORD to serve him."

47The man measured the inner courtyard. It was a square—one hundred seventy-five feet long and one hundred seventy-five feet wide. The altar was in front of the Temple.

The Temple Porch

48The man brought me to the porch of the Temple and measured each side wall of the porch. Each was about nine feet thick. The doorway was twenty-four and one-half feet wide. The side walls of the doorway were each about five feet wide. 49The porch was thirty-five feet long and twenty-one feet wide, with ten steps leading up to it. Pillars were by the side walls, one on each side of the entrance.

The Holy Place of the Temple

41 The man brought me to the Holy Place and measured its side walls, which were each ten and one-half feet thick. 2The entrance was seventeen and one-half feet wide. The walls alongside the entrance were each about nine feet wide. The man measured the Holy Place, which was seventy feet long and thirty-five feet wide.

3Then the man went inside and measured the side walls of the next doorway. Each was three and one-half feet thick. The doorway was ten and one-half feet wide, and the walls next to it were each more than twelve feet thick. 4Then the man measured the room at the end of the Holy Place. It was thirty-five feet long and thirty-five feet wide. The man said to me, "This is the Most Holy Place."

5Then the man measured the wall of the Temple, which was ten and one-half feet thick. There were side rooms seven feet wide all around the Temple. 6The side rooms were on three different stories, each above the other, with thirty rooms on each story. All around the Temple walls there were ledges for the side rooms. The upper rooms rested on the ledges but were not attached to the Temple walls. 7The side rooms around the Temple were wider on each higher story, so rooms were wider on the top story. A stairway went up from the lowest story to the highest through the middle story.

8I also saw that the Temple had a raised base all around. Its edge was the foundation for the side rooms, and it was ten and one-half feet thick. 9The outer wall of the side rooms was about nine feet thick. There was an open area between the side rooms of the Temple 10and some other rooms. It was thirty-five feet wide and went all around the Temple. 11The side rooms had doors which led to the open area around the outside of the Temple. One door faced north, and the other faced south. The open area was about nine feet wide all around.

12The building facing the private area at the west side was one hundred twenty-two and one-half feet wide. The wall around the building was about nine feet thick and one hundred fifty-seven and one-half feet long.

13Then the man measured the Temple. It was one hundred seventy-five feet long. The private area, including the building and its walls, was in all one hundred seventy-five feet long. 14Also the front of the Temple and the private area on its east side were one hundred seventy-five feet wide.

15The man measured the length of the building facing the private area on the west side, and it was one hundred seventy-five feet from one wall to the other.

The Holy Place, the Most Holy Place, and the outer porch 16had wood panels on the walls. By the doorway, the Temple had wood panels on the walls. The wood covered all the walls from the floor up to the windows, 17up to the part of the wall above the entrance.

All the walls inside the Most Holy Place and the Holy Place, and on the outside, in the porch, 18had carvings of creatures with wings and palm trees. A palm tree was between each carved creature, and every creature had two faces. 19One was a human face looking toward the palm tree on one side. The other was a lion's face looking toward the palm tree on the other side. They were carved all around the Temple walls. 20From the floor to above the entrance, palm trees and creatures with wings were carved. The walls of the Holy Place 21had square doorposts. In front of the Most Holy Place was something that looked like 22an altar of wood. It was more than five feet high and three feet wide. Its corners, base, and sides were wood. The man said to me, "This is the table that is in the presence of the LORD." 23Both the Holy Place and the Most Holy Place had double doors. 24Each of the doors had two pieces that would swing open. 25Carved on the doors of the Holy Place were palm trees and creatures with wings, like those carved on the walls. And there was a wood roof over the front Temple porch. 26There were windows and palm trees on both side walls of the porch. The side rooms of the Temple were also covered by a roof over the stairway.

The Priests' Rooms

42 Then the man led me north out into the outer courtyard and to the rooms across from the private area and the building. 2These rooms on the north side were one hundred seventy-five feet long and eighty-seven and one-half feet wide. 3There was thirty-five feet of the inner courtyard between them and the Temple. On the other side, they faced the stone pavement of the outer courtyard. The rooms were built in three

41:18 *creatures with wings.* These winged creatures were cherubim —powerful angelic beings.

stories like steps and had balconies. 4There was a
path on the north side of the rooms, which was
seventeen and one-half feet wide and one hundred seventy-five feet long. Doors led into the
rooms from this path. 5The top rooms were narrower, because the balconies took more space
from them. The rooms on the first and second stories of the building were wider. 6The rooms were
on three stories. They did not have pillars like the
pillars of the courtyards. So the top rooms were
farther back than those on the first and second
stories. 7There was a wall outside parallel to the
rooms and to the outer courtyard. It ran in front of
the rooms for eighty-seven and one-half feet. 8The
row of rooms along the outer courtyard was eighty-
seven and one-half feet long, and the rooms that
faced the Temple were about one hundred seventy-five feet long. 9The lower rooms had an
entrance on the east side so a person could enter
them from the outer courtyard, 10at the start of the
wall beside the courtyard.

There were rooms on the south side, which
were across from the private area and the building. 11These rooms had a path in front of them.
They were like the rooms on the north with the
same length and width and the same doors. 12The
doors of the south rooms were like the doors of
the north rooms. There was an entrance at the
open end of a path beside the wall, so a person
could enter at the east end.

13The man said to me, "The north and south
rooms across from the private area are holy rooms.
There the priests who go near the LORD will eat the
most holy offerings. There they will put the most
holy offerings: the grain offerings, sin offerings,
and the penalty offerings, because the place is holy.
14The priests who enter the Holy Place must leave
their serving clothes there before they go into the
outer courtyard, because these clothes are holy.
After they put on other clothes, they may go to the
part of the Temple area which is for the people."

Outside the Temple Area

15When the man finished measuring inside the
Temple area, he brought me out through the east
gateway. He measured the area all around. 16The
man measured the east side with the measuring
stick; it was eight hundred seventy-five feet by the
measuring stick. 17He measured the north side; it
was eight hundred seventy-five feet by the measuring stick. 18He measured the south side; it was
eight hundred seventy-five feet by the measuring
stick. 19He went around to the west side; it measured eight hundred seventy-five feet by the measuring stick. 20So he measured the Temple area
on all four sides. The Temple area had a wall all
around it that was eight hundred seventy-five feet
long and eight hundred seventy-five feet wide. It
separated what was holy from that which was not
holy.

The Lord Among His People

43 Then the man led me to the outer east gate
way, 2and I saw the glory of the God of
Israel coming from the east. It sounded like the
roar of rushing water, and its brightness made the
earth shine. 3The vision I saw was like the vision
I had seen when the LORD came to destroy the city
and also like the vision I had seen by the Kebar
River. I bowed facedown on the ground. 4The glory
of the LORD came into the Temple area through the
east gateway.

5Then the Spirit picked me up and brought me
into the inner courtyard. There I saw the LORD's
glory filling the Temple. 6As the man stood at my
side, I heard someone speaking to me from inside
the Temple. 7The voice from the Temple said to
me, "Human, this is my throne and the place
where my feet rest. I will live here among the
Israelites forever. The people of Israel will not make
my holy name unclean again. Neither the people
nor their kings will make it unclean with their sexual sins or with the dead bodies of their kings. 8The
kings made my name unclean by putting their
doorway next to my doorway, and their doorpost
next to my doorpost so only a wall separated me
from them. When they did their acts that I hate,
they made my holy name unclean, and so I destroyed them in my anger. 9Now let them stop their
sexual sins and take the dead bodies of their kings
far away from me. Then I will live among them forever.

10"Human, tell the people of Israel about the
Temple so they will be ashamed of their sins. Let
them think about the plan of the Temple. 11If they
are ashamed of all they have done, let them know
the design of the Temple and how it is built. Show
them its exits and entrances, all its designs, and
also all its rules and teachings. Write the rules as
they watch so they will obey all the teachings and
rules about the Temple. 12This is the teaching
about the Temple: All the area around the top of
the mountain is most holy. This is the teaching
about the Temple.

The Altar

13"These are the measurements of the altar,
using the measuring stick. The altar's gutter is
twenty-one inches high and twenty-one inches
wide, and its rim is about nine inches around its

Worship

John 4:23

What is the essential nature of worship? Why do we worship? How important is worship to the life of a Christian? How should we worship? What are some of the patterns of worship?

We are constantly told that worship is the supreme Christian activity. True, no doubt; but what is worship? The first step towards forming sound ideas of worship is to understand its nature.

The history of the word gives us our answer. The noun *worship* is a contraction of *worthship.* Used as a verb, it means "to ascribe worth" or "to acknowledge value." To worship God is to recognize his worth or worthiness—to look toward God and acknowledge in all appropriate ways his value. The Bible calls this glorifying God or giving glory to God. This is why we were made and, from one point of view, is our whole duty. "Praise the LORD for the glory of his name; worship the LORD because he is holy" (Psalm 29:2).

Worship is the response of a heart in love with the Lord. The first great commandment is: "Love the LORD your God with all your heart, all your soul, and all your strength" (Deuteronomy 6:5). Christianity is a kind of love affair with our loving Lord and Savior. The more days we turn into spiritual Valentine's Days by talking to the Lord about our relationship with him, the richer and more joyful the relationship itself will become. By expressing love, worship renews love to our Lord and to the Father, and this is the greatest joy any Christian ever knows.

People who are not Christians find the outward motions of worship tedious and boring. But to the Christian, worship is a joy. It will be so in heaven when we see our Lord; it can be so already on earth. If we know God as our Savior, then all the activities of worship will generate joy, as many of the psalms show with vividness. For worship is natural—we might even say instinctive—to those who are born again. It is the most satisfying thing one ever does. Never are Christians so fully themselves, or so happy, as when their hearts are drawn out in the worship of God.

It is already clear that worship is essentially *response*—response to God as he reveals himself to us. Worship thus assumes knowledge of God. Christian worship only takes place where there is knowledge of the biblical truths of creation and redemption and of the Jesus of the New Testament made real to us by the Holy Spirit. "The time is coming . . . and that time is here already," Jesus told the Samaritan woman, "when the true worshipers will worship the Father in *spirit and truth*" (John 4:23, emphasis mine). By this he meant that through his personal ministry as sinbearing Savior, Master, and Friend, worship was being put on a new basis and lifted to a new level.

To worship God in spirit is to worship him from the heart, "in the Spirit" (Revelation 1:10), by reaching to him in mind and will and affection. To worship God in truth is to come to him through his word and Jesus who said, "I am the way, and the truth, and the life. The only way to the Father is through me" (John 14:6).

Those who worship in spirit and truth, Christ goes on to tell the Samaritan woman, are the kind of worshipers the Father wants: "You see, the Father too is actively seeking such people to worship him" (John 4:23). God desires worship that is a true response to the truth made known in Jesus. From this it follows that what finally matters about the church's forms for worship is not whether they are new or old, but whether they follow the plans for worship that God gave us.

Worship that is Spirit-led and truth-based takes many forms but includes six basic elements:

1. Praising God for all that he is and all he has done
2. Thanking him for his gifts and goodness to us
3. Asking him to meet our own and others' needs
4. Offering him our gifts, our service, and ourselves
5. Learning of him from his word, both read and preached, and obeying his voice
6. Telling others God's "worth" by public confession and testimony to what has been done for us

Many worship patterns are found in Christian assemblies, and most of them are right and good. Minimum expectations for worship should include praise and thanksgiving to God; confession of sin and forgiveness for those who change their hearts and lives; reading and teaching of the word of God; praying for daily needs; and taking the Lord's Supper regularly. The acid test, however, is whether one's involvement in worship is wholehearted, "in spirit and truth."

Worship: For additional scriptures on this topic go to Psalm 29:2.

ANTI-SEMITISM

JOHN 5:16–18

Who are "the Jews" described as participants in the death of Jesus?
How did Nazi Germany change the world's view of the Jewish people?
How does the Good News of Jesus view the Jewish people?

Ever since Nazi Germany's abuse of the Jewish people, readers of the Bible have been jarred by racist-sounding comments using the phrase "the Jews" as a shorthand expression for "the bad guys," those who are to accept all the blame for the crucifixion of Jesus or the difficulties of the early church. One such remark is, "But no one was brave enough to talk about Jesus openly, because they were afraid of the Jews" (John 7:13). Such a comment in the hands of the Nazis was used to support a hatred of the Jewish people and to manipulate the masses to condone or overlook violence and injustice to their Jewish neighbors. This "anti-Semitism" of twentieth-century Germany has jaded our hearing of such phrases. However, authors like John probably did not use "the Jews" to mean "all Jewish people everywhere" but rather "the Jews who wanted to kill Jesus," as indicated several verses earlier in John 7:1.

Before we accept a Nazi interpretation of these passages, we must understand several things about these Bible texts, written long before their misuse and misinterpretation in Hitler's Germany. First, Jesus, many of those who reported his words, and other writers of the New Testament were Jewish. Their comments about "the Jews" are not motivated by one race against another, but are comments against the hostile religious leaders of Jesus' day. Secondly, these comments are not "anti-Semitic" (hating of the Jews for their Semitic origin), nor "anti-Jewish" (directed against all Jewish people), but reflect criticism of specific groups of Jews by other Jews who had accepted that Jesus was the Messiah. Thirdly, these authors lived in a society that had quite different sensibilities than our current climate. It was common for Jewish writers to lambaste other Jewish leaders, and for non-Jewish writers to dismiss the Jewish people as anti-social because many of them refused to participate in the idol-oriented meals common in polite society of the Roman Empire. On the other side, it must be remembered that Jewish writers also dismissed non-Jews with slurs such as "dogs."

None of these ancient practices justifies the Nazi abuse of the Jewish people, nor can we find in this ancient practice of rhetoric a pattern for Christian relationships with Jewish believers. Christians who read such texts today must hear the pain of a whole people when such words are read and must be quick to note that the comments are mainly against enemies of Jesus, and that the comments are phrased in such a way that a twentieth-century Christian would never imitate them. Rather, the apostle Paul gives a very clear directive on cultural and religious sensitivity when he outlines his own missionary principles (1 Corinthians 9:19–23), which he summarizes as,"Never do anything that might hurt others—Jews, Greeks, or God's church—just as I, also, try to please everybody in every way. I am not trying to do what is good for me but what is good for most people so they can be saved" (1 Corinthians 10:32–33). Elsewhere, Paul makes it clear that the Jewish people hold a special place in God's plan for salvaging the human race, and they themselves are able to receive this same gift of salvation (Romans 11:24–26).

The Book of John is the most harsh in its treatment of hostile religious leaders and anti-Christian Judaism. Adherents of Judaism who also oppose Jesus are simply lumped under the title "the Jews" (John 5:16–18). "The Jews" are the ones who kept the masses silent about Jesus by striking fear into their hearts (John 7:13; 19:38), using such tactics as social shunning by putting followers of Jesus out of the synagogue (John 9:22), and perhaps threatening violence such as Jesus suffered (John 20:19–20). Yet it would be inaccurate to suppose that the Book of John only characterized "the Jews" in a negative light, since there are "the Jews who believed in him" (John 8:31), and Jesus and his followers are explicitly Jewish. Nevertheless, the Book of John and several of the other New Testament writings require the modern reader to exercise a rigorous discipline of listening to these words in a way that is free from racist interpretations. It must also be remembered that it was the non-Jewish Romans who had a large part in the story of Jesus' death (John 19:1–37). The Gospel story makes it clear that all people, Jewish and non-Jewish, were responsible for this act. And all people, Jewish and non-Jewish, are invited to embrace the grace of God.

Anti-Semitism: For additional scriptures on this topic go to Matthew 27:24–25.

edge. And the altar is this tall: 14From the ground up to the lower ledge, it measures three and one-half feet. It is twenty-one inches wide. It measures seven feet from the smaller ledge to the larger ledge and is twenty-one inches wide. 15The place where the sacrifice is burned on the altar is seven feet high, with its four corners shaped like horns and reaching up above it. 16It is square, twenty-one feet long and twenty-one feet wide. 17The upper ledge is also square, twenty-four and one-half feet long and twenty-four and one-half feet wide. The rim around the altar is ten and one-half inches wide, and its gutter is twenty-one inches wide all around. Its steps are on the east side."

18Then the man said to me, "Human, this is what the Lord GOD says: These are the rules for the altar. When it is built, use these rules to offer burnt offerings and to sprinkle blood on it. 19You must give a young bull as a sin offering to the priests, the Levites who are from the family of Zadok and who come near me to serve me, says the Lord GOD. 20Take some of the bull's blood and put it on the four corners of the altar, on the four corners of the ledge, and all around the rim. This is how you will make the altar pure and ready for God's service. 21Then take the bull for the sin offering and burn it in the proper place in the Temple area, outside the Temple building.

22"On the second day offer a male goat that has nothing wrong with it for a sin offering. The priests will make the altar pure and ready for God's service as they did with the young bull. 23When you finish making the altar pure and ready, offer a young bull and a male sheep from the flock, which have nothing wrong with them. 24You must offer them in the presence of the LORD, and the priests are to throw salt on them and offer them as a burnt offering to the LORD.

25"You must prepare a goat every day for seven days as a sin offering. Also, the priests must prepare a young bull and male sheep from the flock, which have nothing wrong with them. 26For seven days the priests are to make the altar pure and ready for God's service. Then they will give the altar to God. 27After these seven days, on the eighth day, the priests must offer your burnt offerings and your fellowship offerings on the altar. Then I will accept you, says the Lord GOD."

The Outer East Gate

44 Then the man brought me back to the outer east gateway of the Temple area, but the gate was shut. 2The LORD said to me, "This gate will stay shut; it will not be opened. No one may enter through it, because the LORD God of Israel has entered through it. So it must stay shut. 3Only the ruler himself may sit in the gateway to eat a meal in the presence of the LORD. He must enter through the porch of the gateway and go out the same way."

4Then the man brought me through the outer north gate to the front of the Temple. As I looked, I saw the glory of the LORD filling the Temple of the LORD, and I bowed facedown on the ground.

5The LORD said to me, "Human, pay attention. Use your eyes to see, and your ears to hear. See and hear everything I tell you about all the rules and teachings of the Temple of the LORD. Pay attention to the entrance to the Temple and to all the exits from the Temple area. 6Then speak to those who refuse to obey. Say to the people of Israel, 'This is what the Lord GOD says: Stop doing all your acts that I hate, Israel! 7You brought foreigners into my Holy Place who were not circumcised in the flesh and had not given themselves to serving me. You dishonored my Temple when you offered me food, fat, and blood. You broke my agreement by all the things you did that I hate. 8You did not take care of my holy things yourselves but put foreigners in charge of my Temple. 9This is what the Lord GOD says: Foreigners who are not circumcised in flesh and who do not give themselves to serving me may not enter my Temple. Not even a foreigner living among the people of Israel may enter.

10" 'But the Levites who stopped obeying me when Israel left me and who followed their idols must be punished for their sin. 11These Levites are to be servants in my Holy Place. They may guard the gates of the Temple and serve in the Temple area. They may kill the animals for the burnt offering and the sacrifices for the people. They may stand before the people to serve them. 12But these Levites helped the people worship their idols and caused the people of Israel to fall, so I make this promise: They will be punished for their sin, says the Lord GOD. 13They will not come near me to serve as priests, nor will they come near any of my holy things or the most holy offerings. But they will be made ashamed of the things they did that I hate. 14I will put them in charge of taking care of the Temple area, all the work that must be done in it.

15" 'But the priests who are Levites and descendants of Zadok took care of my Holy Place when Israel left me, so they may come near to serve me. They may stand in my presence to offer me the fat and blood of the animals they sacrifice, says the

44:9 Circumcision: Acts 15

Lord GOD. 16They are the only ones who may enter
my Holy Place. Only they may come near my table
to serve me and take care of the things I gave them
to do.
17" 'When they enter the gates of the inner
courtyard, they must wear linen robes. They must
not wear wool to serve at the gates of the inner
courtyard or in the Temple. 18They will wear linen
turbans on their heads and linen underclothes.
They will not wear anything that makes them per-
spire. 19When they go out into the outer courtyard
to the people, they must take off their serving
clothes before they go. They must leave these
clothes in the holy rooms and put on other clothes.
Then they will not let their holy clothes hurt the
people.
20" 'They must not shave their heads or let their
hair grow long but must keep the hair of their heads
trimmed. 21None of the priests may drink wine
when they enter the inner courtyard. 22The priests
must not marry widows or divorced women. They
may marry only virgins from the people of Israel or
widows of priests. 23They must teach my people
the difference between what is holy and what is
not holy. They must help my people know what
is unclean and what is clean.
24" 'In court they will act as judges. When they
judge, they will follow my teachings. They must
obey my laws and my rules at all my special feasts
and keep my Sabbaths holy.
25" 'They must not go near a dead person, making themselves unclean. But they are allowed to
make themselves unclean if the dead person is
their father, mother, son, daughter, brother, or a
sister who has not married. 26After a priest has
been made clean again, he must wait seven days.
27Then he may go into the inner courtyard to serve
in the Temple, but he must offer a sin offering for
himself, says the Lord GOD.
28" 'These are the rules about the priests and
their property: They will have me instead of property. You will not give them any land to own in
Israel; I am what they will own. 29They will eat
the grain offerings, sin offerings, and penalty offerings. Everything Israel gives to me will be theirs.
30The best fruits of all the first harvests and all the
special gifts offered to me will belong to the priests.
You will also give to the priests the first part of your
grain that you grind and so bring a blessing on your
family. 31The priests must not eat any bird or animal that died a natural death or one that has been
torn by wild animals.

The Land Is Divided

45 " 'When you divide the land for the Israelite tribes by throwing lots, you must give
a part of the land to belong to the LORD. It will be
about seven miles long and about six miles wide;
all of this land will be holy. 2From this land, an area
eight hundred seventy-five feet square will be for
the Temple. There will be an open space around
the Temple that is eighty-seven and one-half feet
wide. 3In the holy area you will measure a part
about seven miles long and three miles wide, and
in it will be the Most Holy Place. 4This holy part
of the land will be for the priests who serve in the
Temple, who come near to the LORD to serve him.
It will be a place for the priests' houses and for the
Temple. 5Another area about seven miles long and
more than three miles wide will be for the Levites,
who serve in the Temple area. It will belong to
them so they will have cities in which to live.
6" 'You must give the city an area that is about
one and one-half miles wide and about seven miles
long, along the side of the holy area. It will belong
to all the people of Israel.
7" 'The ruler will have land on both sides of the
holy area and the city. On the west of the holy area,
his land will reach to the Mediterranean Sea. On
the east of the holy area, his land will reach to the
eastern border. It will be as long as the land given to
each tribe. 8Only this land will be the ruler's property in Israel. So my rulers will not be cruel to my
people anymore, but they will let each tribe in the
nation of Israel have its share of the land.
9" 'This is what the Lord GOD says: You have
gone far enough, you rulers of Israel! Stop being
cruel and hurting people, and do what is right and
fair. Stop forcing my people out of their homes,
says the Lord GOD. 10You must have honest scales,
an honest dry measurement and an honest liquid
measurement. 11The dry measure and the liquid
measure will be the same: The liquid measure
will always be a tenth of a homer, and the ephah will
always be a tenth of a homer. The measurement
they follow will be the homer. 12The shekel will
be worth twenty gerahs, and a mina will be worth
sixty shekels.

44:17 This was in keeping with the laws found in the Book of Exodus (28:42).

44:28 Earlier, when the land was given to the tribes after the Conquest, the priestly tribe of Levi did not get a portion, but were scattered throughout the land to minister to the people (Joshua 14:3; 21).

45:11 *homer.* The Hebrew word means "donkey-load." It measured about five dry bushels or one hundred seventy-five liquid quarts. So an ephah was about one-half bushel, and a bath was about eighteen quarts.

45:12 *shekel.* In Ezekiel's time a shekel weighed about two-fifths of an ounce.

Offerings and Holy Days

13“ ‘This is the gift you should offer: a sixth of an ephah from every homer of wheat, and a sixth of an ephah from every homer of barley. 14The amount of oil you are to offer is a tenth of a bath from each cor. (Ten baths make a homer and also make a cor.) 15You should give one sheep from each flock of two hundred from the watering places of Israel. All these are to be offered for the grain offerings, burnt offerings, and fellowship offerings to remove sins so you will belong to God, says the Lord GOD. 16All people in the land will give this special offering to the ruler of Israel. 17It will be the ruler's responsibility to supply the burnt offerings, grain offerings, and drink offerings. These offerings will be given at the feasts, at the New Moons, on the Sabbaths, and at all the other feasts of Israel. The ruler will supply the sin offerings, grain offerings, and fellowship offerings to pay for the sins of Israel.

18“ ‘This is what the Lord GOD says: On the first day of the first month take a young bull that has nothing wrong with it. Use it to make the Temple pure and ready for God's service. 19The priest will take some of the blood from this sin offering and put it on the doorposts of the Temple, on the four corners of the ledge of the altar, and on the posts of the gate to the inner courtyard. 20You will do the same thing on the seventh day of the month for anyone who has sinned by accident or without knowing it. This is how you make the Temple pure and ready for God's service.

Passover Feast Offerings

21“ ‘On the fourteenth day of the first month you will celebrate the Feast of Passover. It will be a feast of seven days when you eat bread made without yeast. 22On that day the ruler must offer a bull for himself and for all the people of the land as a sin offering. 23During the seven days of the feast he must offer seven bulls and seven male sheep that have nothing wrong with them. They will be burnt offerings to the LORD, which the ruler will offer every day of the seven days of the feast. He must also offer a male goat every day as a sin offering. 24The ruler must give as a grain offering one-half bushel for each bull and one-half bushel for each sheep. He must give a gallon of olive oil for each half bushel.

25“ ‘Beginning on the fifteenth day of the seventh month, when you celebrate the Feast of Shelters, the ruler will supply the same things for seven days: the sin offerings, burnt offerings, grain offerings, and the olive oil.

Rules for Worship

46 “ ‘This is what the Lord GOD says: The east gate of the inner courtyard will stay shut on the six working days, but it will be opened on the Sabbath day and on the day of the New Moon. 2The ruler will enter from outside through the porch of the gateway and stand by the gatepost, while the priests offer the ruler's burnt offering and fellowship offering. The ruler will worship at the entrance of the gateway, and then he will go out. But the gate will not be shut until evening. 3The people of the land will worship at the entrance of that gateway in the presence of the LORD on the Sabbaths and New Moons. 4This is the burnt offering the ruler will offer to the LORD on the Sabbath day: six male lambs that have nothing wrong with them and a male sheep that has nothing wrong with it. 5He must give a half-bushel grain offering with the male sheep, but he may give as much grain offering with the lambs as he pleases. He must also give a gallon of olive oil for each half bushel of grain. 6On the day of the New Moon he must offer a young bull that has nothing wrong with it. He must also offer six lambs and a male sheep that have nothing wrong with them. 7The ruler must give a half-bushel grain offering with the bull and one-half bushel with the male sheep. With the lambs, he may give as much grain as he pleases. But he must give a gallon of olive oil for each half bushel of grain. 8When the ruler enters, he must go in through the porch of the gateway, and he must go out the same way.

9“ ‘When the people of the land come into the LORD's presence at the special feasts, those who enter through the north gate to worship must go out through the south gate. Those who enter through the south gate must go out through the north gate. They must not return the same way they entered; everyone must go out the opposite way. 10The ruler will go in with the people when they go in and go out with them when they go out.

11“ ‘At the feasts and regular times of worship one-half bushel of grain must be offered with a young bull, and one-half bushel of grain must be offered with a male sheep. But with an offering of lambs, the ruler may give as much grain as he pleases. He should give a gallon of olive oil for each half bushel of grain. 12The ruler may give an offering as a special gift to the LORD; it may be a burnt offering or fellowship offering. When he gives it to the LORD, the inner east gate is to be opened for him. He must offer his burnt offering or his fellowship offering as he does on the Sabbath day. Then he will go out, and the gate will be shut after he has left.

13“ ‘Every day you will give a year-old lamb that has nothing wrong with it for a burnt offering to the LORD. Do it every morning. 14Also, you must offer a grain offering with the lamb every morning. For this you will give three and one-third quarts of grain and one and one-third quarts of olive oil, to make the fine flour moist, as a grain offering to the LORD. This is a rule that must be kept from now on. 15So you must always give the lamb, together with the grain offering and the olive oil, every morning as a burnt offering.

Rules for the Ruler

16“ ‘This is what the Lord GOD says: If the ruler gives a gift from his land to any of his sons, that land will belong to the son and then to the son's children. It is their property passed down from their family. 17But if the ruler gives a gift from his land to any of his servants, that land will belong to the servant only until the year of freedom. Then the land will go back to the ruler. Only the ruler's sons may keep a gift of land from the ruler. 18The ruler must not take any of the people's land, forcing them out of their land. He must give his sons some of his own land so my people will not be scattered out of their own land.’ ”

The Special Kitchens

19The man led me through the entrance at the side of the gateway to the priests' holy rooms that face north. There I saw a place at the west end. 20The man said to me, “This is where the priests will boil the meat of the penalty offering and sin offering and bake the grain offering. Then they will not need to bring these holy offerings into the outer courtyard, because that would hurt the people.”

21Then the man brought me out into the outer courtyard and led me to its four corners. In each corner of the courtyard was a smaller courtyard. 22Small courtyards were in the four corners of the courtyard. Each small courtyard was the same size, seventy feet long and fifty-two and one-half feet wide. 23A stone wall was around each of the four small courtyards, and places for cooking were built in each of the stone walls. 24The man said to me, “These are the kitchens where those who work in the Temple will boil the sacrifices offered by the people.”

The River from the Temple

47 The man led me back to the door of the Temple, and I saw water coming out from under the doorway and flowing east. (The Temple faced east.) The water flowed down from the south side wall of the Temple and then south of the altar. 2The man brought me out through the outer north gate and led me around outside to the outer east gate. I found the water coming out on the south side of the gate.

3The man went toward the east with a line in his hand and measured about one-third of a mile. Then he led me through water that came up to my ankles. 4The man measured about one-third of a mile again and led me through water that came up to my knees. Then he measured about one-third of a mile again and led me through water up to my waist. 5The man measured about one-third of a mile again, but it was now a river that I could not cross. The water had risen too high; it was deep enough for swimming; it was a river that no one could cross. 6The man asked me, “Human, do you see this?”

Then the man led me back to the bank of the river. 7As I went back, I saw many trees on both sides of the river. 8The man said to me, “This water will flow toward the eastern areas and go down into the Jordan Valley. When it enters the Dead Sea, it will become fresh. 9Everywhere the river goes, there will be many fish. Wherever this water goes the Dead Sea will become fresh, and so where the river goes there will be many living things. 10Fishermen will stand by the Dead Sea. From En Gedi all the way to En Eglaim there will be places to spread fishing nets. There will be many kinds of fish in the Dead Sea, as many as in the Mediterranean Sea. 11But its swamps and marshes will not become fresh; they will be left for salt. 12All kinds of fruit trees will grow on both banks of the river, and their leaves will not dry and die. The trees will have fruit every month, because the water for them comes from the Temple. The fruit from the trees will be used for food, and their leaves for medicine.”

Borders of the Land

13This is what the Lord GOD says: “These are the borders of the land to be divided among the twelve

47:1–12 The vision of Ezekiel is identical to that of John in Revelation 22:1–2. The river that flows from the Temple (verses 1, 12) is identified as the "river of the water of life" in Revelation 22:1. The trees on both sides of the river that Ezekiel saw (verse 7) are called by John the "tree of life," which also were found on each side of the river (Revelation 22:2). In both visions, the trees produce fruit every month, and their leaves are "for the healing of all the nations" (verse 12; Revelation 22:2). The hope of the Israelites in the Old Testament finds its fulfillment in the coming of the new Jerusalem, which is also the hope for those justified by faith through Jesus, in whom "there is no difference between Jew and Greek" (Galatians 3:28).

47:8 *it will become fresh.* The Dead Sea is so named because the minerals in the water are at such a high level that no living thing can survive. Part of Ezekiel's vision has to do with the change of the water of the Dead Sea, so that it can sustain life.

tribes of Israel. Joseph will have two parts of land.
14You will divide the land equally. I promised to
give it to your ancestors, so this land will belong
to you as family property.
15"This will be the border line of the land: "On
the north side it will start at the Mediterranean
Sea. It will go through Hethlon, toward Lebo
Hamath and on to the towns of Zedad, 16Berothah,
and Sibraim on the border between Damascus and
Hamath. Then it will go on to the town of Hazer
Hatticon on the border of the country of Hauran.
17So the border line will go from the Mediterranean Sea east to the town of Hazar Enan, where
the land belonging to Damascus and Hamath lies
on the north side. This will be the north side of
the land.
18"On the east side the border runs south from
a point between Hauran and Damascus. It will go
along the Jordan between Gilead and the land of
Israel and will continue to the town of Tamar on
the Dead Sea. This will be the east side of the land.
19"On the south side the border line will go east
from Tamar all the way to the waters of Meribah
Kadesh. Then it will run along the brook of Egypt
to the Mediterranean Sea. This will be the south
side of the land.
20"On the west side the Mediterranean Sea will
be the border line up to a place across from Lebo
Hamath. This will be the west side of your land.
21"You will divide this land among the tribes of
Israel. 22You will divide it as family property for
yourselves and for the foreigners who live and
have children among you. You are to treat these
foreigners the same as people born in Israel; they
are to share the land with the tribes of Israel.
23In whatever tribe the foreigner lives, you will
give him some land," says the Lord GOD.

Dividing the Land

48 "These are the areas of the tribes named
here: Dan will have one share at the northern border. It will go from the sea through Hethlon
to Lebo Hamath, all the way to Hazar Enan, where
Damascus lies to the north. It will stop there next
to Hamath. This will be Dan's northern border
from the east side to the Mediterranean Sea on
the west side.
2"South of Dan's border, Asher will have one
share. It will go from the east side to the west side.
3"South of Asher's border, Naphtali will have one
share. It will go from the east side to the west side.
4"South of Naphtali's border, Manasseh will have
one share. It will go from the east side to the west
side.
5"South of Manasseh's border, Ephraim will have
one share. It will go from the east side to the west
side.
6"South of Ephraim's border, Reuben will have
one share. It will go from the east side to the west
side.
7"South of Reuben's border, Judah will have one
share. It will go from the east side to the west side.
8"South of Judah's border will be the holy area
which you are to give. It will be about seven miles
wide and as long and wide as one of the tribes'
shares. It will run from the east side to the west
side. The Temple will be in the middle of this area.
9"The share which you will give the LORD will
be about seven miles long and three miles wide.
10The holy area will be divided among these people. The priests will have land about seven miles
long on the north and south sides, and three miles
wide on the west and east sides. The Temple of the
LORD will be in the middle of it. 11This land is for
the priests who are given the holy duty of serving
the LORD. They are the descendants of Zadok who
did my work and did not leave me when Israel and
the Levites left me. 12They will have as their share
a very holy part of the holy portion of the land. It
will be next to the land of the Levites.
13"Alongside the land for the priests, the Levites
will have a share about seven miles long and three
miles wide; its full length will be about seven miles
and its full width about three miles. 14The Levites
are not to sell or trade any of this land. They are not
to let anyone else own any of this best part of the
land, because it belongs to the LORD.

City Property

15"The rest of the area will be about one and
one-half miles wide and seven miles long. It will
not be holy but will belong to the city and be used
for homes and pastures. The city will be in the middle of it. 16These are the city's measurements: the
north side will be about one mile, the south side
about one mile, the east side about one mile, and
the west side about one mile. 17The city's land for
pastures will be about four hundred thirty-seven
feet on the north, four hundred thirty-seven feet
on the south, four hundred thirty-seven feet on
the east, and four hundred thirty-seven feet on the
west. 18Along the long side of the holy area there
will be left three miles on the east and three miles
on the west. It will be used to grow food for the
city workers. 19The city workers from all the tribes
of Israel will farm this land. 20This whole area will
be square, seven miles by seven miles. You shall

47:22 Foreigner (Alien): Matthew 25:35

give to the LORD the holy share along with the city
property.
21“Land that is left over on both sides of the holy
area and city property will belong to the ruler. That
land will extend east of the holy area to the eastern border and west of it to the Mediterranean
Sea. Both of these areas run the length of the lands
of the tribes, and they belong to the ruler. The holy
area with the Holy Place of the Temple will be in
the middle. 22The Levites' land and the city property will be in the middle of the lands belonging
to the ruler. Those lands will be between Judah's
border and Benjamin's border.

The Other Tribes' Land

23“Here is what the rest of the tribes will
receive: Benjamin will have one share. It will go
from the east side to the Mediterranean Sea on
the west side.
24“South of Benjamin's land, Simeon will have
one share. It will go from the east side to the west
side.
25“South of Simeon's land, Issachar will have one
share. It will go from the east side to the west side.
26“South of Issachar's land, Zebulun will have
one share. It will go from the east side to the west
side.
27“South of Zebulun's land, Gad will have one
share. It will go from the east side to the west side.
28“The southern border of Gad's land will go
east from Tamar on the Dead Sea to the waters of
Meribah Kadesh. Then it will run along the brook
of Egypt to the Mediterranean Sea.
29“This is the land you will divide among the
tribes of Israel to be their shares,” says the Lord
GOD.

The Gates of the City

30“These will be the outside borders of the city:
The north side will measure more than one mile.
31There will be three gates facing north: Reuben's
Gate, Judah's Gate, and Levi's Gate, named for the
tribes of Israel.
32“The east side will measure more than one
mile. There will be three gates facing east: Joseph's
Gate, Benjamin's Gate, and Dan's Gate.
33“The south side will measure more than one
mile. There will be three gates facing south: Simeon's Gate, Issachar's Gate, and Zebulun's Gate.
34“The west side will measure more than one
mile. There will be three gates facing west: Gad's
Gate, Asher's Gate, and Naphtali's Gate.
35“The city will measure about six miles around.
From then on the name of the city will be The
LORD Is There.”⚭

⚭**48:35 End Times/Last Days:** Daniel 7

BLINDNESS

JOHN 9

What does blindness represent in the Bible?
What does it mean to gain sight after having been blind?

Blindness is the absence of sight. Some people are born blind; others lose their sight later in life.The loss of sight can be a great tragedy, and being blind results in inconvenience and severe suffering. But God tells Moses that he is the one who gives sight and takes it away (Exodus 4:11). He does not do this arbitrarily, nor does he do it to punish people. Indeed, some people find great blessing and develop exceptional gifts due to their blindness. But in any case, God is in control and can overrule all obstacles in life.

The Bible frequently uses the senses of sight and sound to describe relationships with God. These metaphors graphically depict the ability and willingness of humans to acknowledge God's presence. In this sense, blindness is used in a variety of ways in the Old Testament. For instance, blindness is a quality of the fool rather than a wise person, according to the Teacher in the Book of Ecclesiastes (2:12–14). The wise person has eyes in his head so he can see. But the fool is constantly running into obstacles that he cannot see.

Blindness is often associated with unbelief. Isaiah 6:10 reveals a command by God to make the people blind so that they might receive punishment. Some are so spiritually blind that they are not able to see God's discipline and correction (Isaiah 42:18–19). The healing of blindness is a sign of God's activity and of God's chosen one (Isaiah 29:18; 35:4–5; 42:6–7, 16–17).

The New Testament writers frequently use imagery of sight and blindness in order to describe the condition of humanity. Matthew 18:9 refers to self-induced blindness as an extreme means to avoid sin. If your eye causes sin, it is better to pluck it out and be blind. This is metaphorical language, but intends to shock because the truth is so important and so overlooked. Spiritual wholeness is more important than physical wholeness. Opponents of Jesus are referred to as "blind leaders" (Matthew 15:14). They cannot lead others or themselves to God. Both the opponents and the ones they lead are bound to fall into a pit due to blindness of spirit. They are blind because they focus on the lesser rather than on the greater aspects of the law (Matthew 23:16–22).

Healing blindness is a sign that Jesus has the power of God. When asked whether he is the one sent from God, Jesus responds by making the blind see (Matthew 11:2–6; Luke 7:18–23). Luke 4:18 uses a quotation about healing blindness from Isaiah 61:1 to demonstrate that Jesus is the fulfillment of God's intentions. When Jesus is accused of having a demon in John 10:20–21, one response is that demons cannot heal blindness as Jesus has done. People wonder whether Jesus could have kept Lazarus from dying since Jesus had healed the blind (John 11:37).

In the Gospels then, blindness is generally a way of speaking about disbelief. Blindness being healed signals belief. Light and the ability to see are closely related to blindness. The Book of John uses words like light and darkness, sight and blindness as ways to talk about the relationship of Jesus to God the Father and humanity to Jesus (John 1:4–13; 3:19–21; 4:45–50; 6:26, 36; 8:12; 12:35–36, 44–46; 14:9–10; 20:8, 29). Jesus healing the physically blind reflects his ability to open the eyes of the spiritually blind.

In John 9, blindness is falsely attributed to sin. Blindness presents an opportunity for God's power to show through in a healing. Jesus proclaims that he is the light of the world, then he gives sight to the blind man. The healing provides the opportunity for the man who has been blind to be questioned about Jesus. His responses represent a person with growing faith in Jesus. His first response is that "the man named Jesus" healed him, but that he did not know where Jesus was (9:11–12). His second response is again about how he was healed (9:15). His third response is that he thought Jesus was a prophet (9:17). His fourth response restates that, while he did not know about Jesus, he himself was once blind but now can see (9:25). The fifth response suggests that the man has become a follower of Jesus (9:27). The sixth response is that Jesus truly was sent from God (9:33). The longer the man was allowed to reflect on the change from blindness to sight, the more his faith and belief became apparent. The final response is directed to Jesus. He believes that Jesus is the Son of Man and worships him (9:35–38). Gaining sight means believing, worshiping, and following Christ.

Blindness: For additional scriptures on this topic go to Ecclesiastes 2:12–13.

LEADERSHIP

JOHN 10:1–16

What is Christian leadership?
Is Christian leadership a gift or can everybody do it?
What are the qualities that Christian leaders should develop?

The importance of good leadership is well-known in all parts of society, and great attention is paid to those who would lead. When the economy is booming, the team is winning, and the business is turning a handsome profit, the president, coach, and chief executive officer reap the praise. Likewise, when the school struggles or the church faces difficulties, eyes turn to the principal and the pastor and the buck often stops at their desk. In society's terms, good leadership is "effective" and "successful," an assessment usually based on a leader's visible accomplishments. The Bible, on the other hand, identifies good leaders by how they treat people, not by how well they use people toward other ends.

Good leadership, in biblical terms, is defined by its relationship to God's leadership. God values individuals beyond all else. Though God is over all, he cares for each person and creature (Matthew 6:25–34). Care and compassion are the hallmarks of good leadership in God's eyes. This is best seen in the image of God as the good shepherd who "leads me to calm water" and leads us "on paths that are right for the good of his name" (Psalm 23:2–3). In Jesus we see that God's leadership is self-sacrificial, willing to give up all of his glory and prestige to care for and save his sheep. As Jesus says, "I am the good shepherd. The good shepherd gives his life for the sheep" (John 10:11).

Christian leadership begins with followership. The best examples of good leaders in the Bible are people who follow God's ways, who have yielded their wills to God's direction. It is no surprise then that Jesus' first words to the leaders who would found his church are "Come follow me" (Mark 1:17). The stories about Jesus' followers (called "disciples" or "learners") are stories about how God wants leaders to become humble learners of godly ways. This suggests that our natural inclinations and hunches about leadership are not necessarily the best. Those who would lead for God must first learn to follow him closely, to listen to him, to obey him, to be committed to a direction which is often against the grain.

There are some very practical questions about Christian leadership: Is Christian leadership a gift or can everybody do it? What are the qualities that Christian leaders should develop? Can Christian leaders have faults or should they be above criticism? What are the pitfalls that leaders should avoid?

Is Christian leadership a gift? Yes. The Bible makes it clear that Christian leaders are given their leadership abilities by God, and are appointed to their work by him as well (1 Kings 14:7; 16:2; 1 Chronicles 28:4; 1 Corinthians 12:27–31; Romans 13:1–2; 1 Peter 2:13–17; Acts 5:31). Leadership is a gift that God gives, yet it can be developed, and the leaders should work hard at using their gift: "Anyone who has the gift of being a leader should try hard when he leads" (Romans 12:8). This gift should be used at all times in a compassionate and patient way that cares for and up builds others (see 1 Corinthians 12:27–13:13). God gifts, appoints, and sends leaders to care for his people.

What qualities should a Christian leader emphasize? The whole teaching of the Bible is the full counsel for a Christian leader, but the key quality a leader should develop is tender and compassionate love (John 21:15–21; 1 Corinthians 13), because loving God and others is the most important moral principle in the Bible (Matthew 22:35–40). Though a loving approach is most important, the other teachings in the Bible about Christian character are essential for leaders to be effective (1 Timothy 3:1–13).

Does this mean that a leader should be faultless? On the one hand, the answer is no. The Bible makes clear that leaders have feet of clay, often recording their foibles. Moses did not want to lead. David sinned grievously against Bathsheba and her husband. Peter was impetuous, too outspoken, and denied the Lord three times. Paul was a Christian killer before becoming a Christian leader. Even afterwards he admits to great difficulties in doing what God wanted him to do.

On the other hand, the answer is a qualified yes. Since leadership is influence (see, 2 Timothy 2:16), leaders must be reputable and live in such a way as to deserve the respect of others (Deuteronomy 1:1, 15; 1 Timothy 3:2, 7, 8, 11). Furthermore, leaders set an example for other believers in how to live and believe (1 Corinthians 4:16; 11:1; Philippians 3:17; 4:9; Hebrews 13:7). Therefore, a leader should always be open to God's correction by praying, "See if there is any bad thing in me. Lead me on the road to everlasting life" (Psalm 139:24).

Leadership: For additional scriptures on this topic go to Exodus 32:34.

INTRODUCTION TO THE BOOK OF DANIEL

The Life and Visons of Daniel

WHO WROTE THIS BOOK?

Daniel, the prophet, is identified as the author of this book in various passages, such as 9:2 and 10:2.

TO WHOM WAS THIS BOOK WRITTEN?

The Book of Daniel is a message to the people of Judah in captivity in Babylon.

WHERE WAS IT WRITTEN?

The Book of Daniel was written in Babylon.

WHEN WAS IT WRITTEN?

The author probably completed this writing about 530 B.C. soon after Cyrus captured Babylon.

WHAT IS THE BOOK ABOUT?

The writings of Daniel proclaim the sovereignty of the all-powerful God of Judah, even in the harsh light of Judah's captivity.

WHY WAS THIS BOOK WRITTEN?

Like most other symbolic writings in the Bible, Daniel offers encouragement and hope to God's people during troubled times. His vision and prophecies look far into the future, to the coming of the "Anointed One," Jesus himself, who will take us home to heaven.

SO WHAT DOES THIS BOOK MEAN TO US?

The all-powerful God of Judah is also the all-powerful God of his people, Christians, today. Daniel offers hope and encouragement both to Judah and to us. Our never-changing God will guard and protect us just as he always has his people through the ages, if we remain faithful and obedient as Daniel did.

SUMMARY:

The Book of Daniel is one of the most exciting books of the Old Testament. The stories of the first six chapters tell amazing stories of faith in action. The prophecies of the second half of the book stir the imagination about God's plans for the future salvation of his people.

The book gives an account of the adventures of Daniel and his three friends in the sixth century B.C., at first a time when the people of God are living in exile in Babylon and then a time when they are dominated by the great power of Persia.

The message of the Book of Daniel is that God is all powerful. No human authority can stand in his way. He overrules and eventually will overcome all human evil. The major purpose of the Book of Daniel is to comfort those who are oppressed in the present with the knowledge that God can and will rescue them.

The book may be divided into two major sections:

I. Daniel and His Three Friends in a Foreign Land (1–6)
II. Daniel's Visions of the Future (7–12)

The vision of the Book of Daniel extends far beyond the time period of the Old Testament, indeed far into our future as well. The Book of Revelation frequently alludes to the Book of Daniel. For instance, the image of evil in the Book of Revelation as the beast that arises out of the sea (Revelation 13) reminds us of the four beasts that arise out of the sea in Daniel 7. The Book of Revelation confirms that in the Book of Daniel we have prophetically anticipated the coming of Christ who will remove all evil from the world and save his people from those who oppress them.

I. Daniel and His Three Friends in a Foreign Land (1–6)

The first six chapters of the Book of Daniel are accounts of events in the lives of Daniel and his three friends in the Babylonian court. One purpose they serve is to show how the people of God should act when they are living in a foreign land and under oppression. After the first chapter that describes Daniel's exile and his training, the remaining chapters may be divided between those that describe the faith of Daniel and his friends when they are tested by threat of death (chapters 3 and 6) and those that show that Daniel has been gifted by God with the ability to interpret visions of the future (chapters 2, 4, and 5).

II. Daniel's Visons of the Future (7–12)

The second part of the Book of Daniel contains visions of the future. Chapter 9 reports a prayer of confession and requests that God help the people of God in their present trouble.

The visions at the end of the Book of Daniel are difficult to interpret, but they are not given as a riddle that needs to be solved to find out when the end of history will come. They are visions that comfort God's people by telling them that, even though they are living in an evil time, God will defeat the forces that oppress them now and lead them to eternal life.

DANIEL

Daniel Taken to Babylon

During the third year that Jehoiakim was
king of Judah, Nebuchadnezzar king of
Babylon came to Jerusalem and surrounded it with his army. 2The Lord allowed
Nebuchadnezzar to capture Jehoiakim king of
Judah. Nebuchadnezzar also took some of the
things from the Temple of God, which he carried
to Babylonia and put in the temple of his gods.

3Then King Nebuchadnezzar ordered Ashpenaz,
his chief officer, to bring some of the Israelite men
into his palace. He wanted them to be from
important families, including the family of the
king of Judah. 4King Nebuchadnezzar wanted
only young Israelite men who had nothing wrong
with them. They were to be handsome and well
educated, capable of learning and understanding,
and able to serve in his palace. Ashpenaz was to
teach them the language and writings of the
Babylonians. 5The king gave the young men a certain amount of food and wine every day, just like
the food he ate. The young men were to be trained
for three years, and then they would become servants of the king of Babylon. 6Among those young
men were Daniel, Hananiah, Mishael, and Azariah from the people of Judah.

7Ashpenaz, the chief officer, gave them Babylonian names. Daniel's new name was Belteshazzar, Hananiah's was Shadrach, Mishael's was
Meshach, and Azariah's was Abednego.

8Daniel decided not to eat the king's food or
drink his wine because that would make him
unclean. So he asked Ashpenaz for permission not to
make himself unclean in this way.

9God made Ashpenaz, the chief officer, want to
be kind and merciful to Daniel, 10but Ashpenaz said
to Daniel, "I am afraid of my master, the king. He
ordered me to give you this food and drink. If you
begin to look worse than other young men your
age, the king will see this. Then he will cut off my
head because of you."

11Ashpenaz had ordered a guard to watch
Daniel, Hananiah, Mishael, and Azariah. 12Daniel
said to the guard, "Please give us this test for ten
days: Don't give us anything but vegetables to eat
and water to drink. 13After ten days compare how
we look with how the other young men look who
eat the king's food. See for yourself and then decide
how you want to treat us, your servants."

14So the guard agreed to test them for ten days.
15After ten days they looked healthier and better fed
than all the young men who ate the king's food.
16So the guard took away the king's special food
and wine, feeding them vegetables instead.

17God gave these four young men wisdom and
the ability to learn many things that people had
written and studied. Daniel could also understand
visions and dreams.

18At the end of the time set for them by the
king, Ashpenaz brought all the young men to
King Nebuchadnezzar. 19The king talked to them
and found that none of the young men were as
good as Daniel, Hananiah, Mishael, and Azariah.
So those four young men became the king's servants. 20Every time the king asked them about
something important, they showed much wisdom and understanding. They were ten times
better than all the fortune-tellers and magicians
in his kingdom! 21So Daniel continued to be the
king's servant until the first year Cyrus was king.

Nebuchadnezzar's Dream

2 During Nebuchadnezzar's second year as
king, he had dreams that bothered him and
kept him awake at night. 2So the king called for
his fortune-tellers, magicians, wizards, and wise
men, because he wanted them to tell him what he
had dreamed. They came in and stood in front of
the king.

3Then the king said to them, "I had a dream that
bothers me, and I want to know what it means."

4The wise men answered the king in the Aramaic language, "O king, live forever! Please tell us,
your servants, your dream. Then we will tell you
what it means."

5King Nebuchadnezzar said to them, "I meant
what I said. You must tell me the dream and what
it means. If you don't, I will have you torn apart,

1:1 *the third year that Jehoiakim was king.* The year is 605 B.C.

1:4 *young Israelite men.* The people of Babylon would take gifted young men from their captives and train them in their ways in order to make sure that the next generation would stay loyal to them.

1:7 Daniel: Daniel 1:8–21

1:8 As a member of the king's court, Daniel was required to eat from the king's table. While such delicacies were tempting, Daniel did not want to be "unclean"; that is, he did not want to break God's strict dietary laws for his people. He quietly sought his superior's permission not to eat the food, and permission was granted. Daniel could have launched a hunger strike, but it was not necessary. He achieved his objectives with minimum resistance. Where peaceful means are available, force should be avoided. This should be the path civil disobedience takes.

1:17 *understand visions and dreams.* Daniel had the type of wisdom that is learned in school as well as supernatural wisdom to interpret divine messages given through dreams. The people of Babylon, as well as the people of Israel, believed that dreams were a way that the divine communicated with humans.

1:21 Daniel: Daniel 2

and I will turn your houses into piles of stones.
6But if you tell me my dream and its meaning, I
will reward you with gifts and great honor. So tell
me the dream and what it means."

7Again the wise men said to the king, "Tell us,
your servants, the dream, and we will tell you
what it means."

8King Nebuchadnezzar answered, "I know you
are trying to get more time, because you know that
I meant what I said. 9If you don't tell me my
dream, you will be punished. You have all agreed
to tell me lies and wicked things, hoping things
will change. Now, tell me the dream so that I will
know you can tell me what it really means!"

10The wise men answered the king, saying,
"No one on earth can do what the king asks! No
great and powerful king has ever asked the fortune-tellers, magicians, or wise men to do this; 11the
king is asking something that is too hard. Only
the gods could tell the king this, but the gods do
not live among people."

12When the king heard their answer, he became
very angry. He ordered that all the wise men of
Babylon be killed. 13So King Nebuchadnezzar's
order to kill the wise men was announced, and
men were sent to look for Daniel and his friends to
kill them.

14Arioch, the commander of the king's guards,
was going to kill the wise men of Babylon. But
Daniel spoke to him with wisdom and skill, 15say-
ing, "Why did the king order such a terrible punishment?" Then Arioch explained everything to
Daniel. 16So Daniel went to King Nebuchadnezzar
and asked for an appointment so that he could tell
the king what his dream meant.

17Then Daniel went to his house and explained
the whole story to his friends Hananiah, Mishael,
and Azariah. 18Daniel asked his friends to pray that
the God of heaven would show them mercy and
help them understand this secret so he and his
friends would not be killed with the other wise
men of Babylon.

19During the night God explained the secret to
Daniel in a vision. Then Daniel praised the God of
heaven. 20Daniel said:

"Praise God forever and ever,
because he has wisdom and power.
21He changes the times and seasons of the year.
He takes away the power of kings
and gives their power to new kings.
He gives wisdom to those who are wise
and knowledge to those who understand.
22He makes known secrets that are deep
and hidden;
he knows what is hidden in darkness,
and light is all around him.
23I thank you and praise you, God of my ancestors,
because you have given me wisdom
and power.
You told me what we asked of you;
you told us about the king's dream."

The Meaning of the Dream

24Then Daniel went to Arioch, the man King
Nebuchadnezzar had chosen to kill the wise men
of Babylon. Daniel said to him, "Don't put the wise
men of Babylon to death. Take me to the king, and
I will tell him what his dream means."

25Very quickly Arioch took Daniel to the king
and said, "I have found a man among the captives
from Judah who can tell the king what his dream
means."

26The king asked Daniel, who was also called
Belteshazzar, "Are you able to tell me what I
dreamed and what it means?"

27Daniel answered, "No wise man, magician, or
fortune-teller can explain to the king the secret he
has asked about. 28But there is a God in heaven
who explains secret things, and he has shown
King Nebuchadnezzar what will happen at a later
time. This is your dream, the vision you saw while
lying on your bed: 29O king, as you were lying
there, you thought about things to come. God,
who can tell people about secret things, showed
you what is going to happen. 30God also told this
secret to me, not because I have greater wisdom
than any other living person, but so that you may
know what it means. In that way you will understand what went through your mind.

31"O king, in your dream you saw a huge, shiny,
and frightening statue in front of you. 32The head
of the statue was made of pure gold. Its chest and
arms were made of silver. Its stomach and the
upper part of its legs were made of bronze. 33The
lower part of the legs were made of iron, while its
feet were made partly of iron and partly of baked
clay. 34While you were looking at the statue, you
saw a rock cut free, but no human being touched
the rock. It hit the statue on its feet of iron and clay
and smashed them. 35Then the iron, clay, bronze,
silver, and gold broke to pieces at the same time.
They became like chaff on a threshing floor in the
summertime; the wind blew them away, and there
was nothing left. Then the rock that hit the statue
became a very large mountain that filled the whole
earth.

36"That was your dream. Now we will tell the
king what it means. 37O king, you are the greatest
king. God of heaven has given you a kingdom,
power, strength, and glory. 38Wherever people,

wild animals, and birds live, God made you ruler over them. King Nebuchadnezzar, you are the head of gold on that statue.

39“Another kingdom will come after you, but it will not be as great as yours. Next a third kingdom, the bronze part, will rule over the earth. 40Then there will be a fourth kingdom, strong as iron. In the same way that iron crushes and smashes things to pieces, the fourth kingdom will smash and crush all the other kingdoms.

41“You saw that the statue’s feet and toes were partly baked clay and partly iron. That means the fourth kingdom will be a divided kingdom. It will have some of the strength of iron in it, just as you saw iron was mixed with clay. 42The toes of the statue were partly iron and partly clay. So the fourth kingdom will be partly strong like iron and partly breakable like clay. 43You saw the iron mixed with clay, but iron and clay do not hold together. In the same way the people of the fourth kingdom will be a mixture, but they will not be united as one people.

44“During the time of those kings, the God of heaven will set up another kingdom that will never be destroyed or given to another group of people. This kingdom will crush all the other kingdoms and bring them to an end, but it will continue forever.

45“King Nebuchadnezzar, you saw a rock cut from a mountain, but no human being touched it. The rock broke the iron, bronze, clay, silver, and gold to pieces. In this way the great God showed you what will happen. The dream is true, and you can trust this explanation.”

46Then King Nebuchadnezzar fell facedown on the ground in front of Daniel. The king honored him and commanded that an offering and incense be presented to him. 47Then the king said to Daniel, “Truly I know your God is the greatest of all gods, the Lord of all the kings. He tells people about things they cannot know. I know this is true, because you were able to tell these secret things to me.”

48Then the king gave Daniel many gifts plus an important position in his kingdom. Nebuchadnezzar made him ruler over the whole area of Babylon and put him in charge of all the wise men of Babylon. 49Daniel asked the king to make Shadrach, Meshach, and Abednego leaders over the area of Babylon, so the king did as Daniel asked. Daniel himself became one of the people who stayed at the royal court.

The Gold Idol and Blazing Furnace

3 King Nebuchadnezzar made a gold statue ninety feet high and nine feet wide and set it up on the plain of Dura in the area of Babylon. 2Then he called for the leaders: the governors, assistant governors, captains of the soldiers, people who advised the king, keepers of the treasury, judges, rulers, and all other officers in his kingdom. He wanted them to come to the special service for the statue he had set up. 3So they all came for the special service and stood in front of the statue that King Nebuchadnezzar had set up. 4Then the man who made announcements for the king said in a loud voice, “People, nations, and those of every language, this is what you are commanded to do: 5When you hear the sound of the horns, flutes, lyres, zithers, harps, pipes, and all the other musical instruments, you must bow down and worship the gold statue that King Nebuchadnezzar has set up. 6Anyone who doesn’t bow down and worship will immediately be thrown into a blazing furnace.”

7Now people, nations, and those who spoke every language were there. When they heard the sound of the horns, flutes, lyres, zithers, pipes, and all the other musical instruments, they bowed down and worshiped the gold statue King Nebuchadnezzar had set up.

8Then some Babylonians came up to the king and began speaking against the men of Judah. 9They said to King Nebuchadnezzar, “O king, live forever! 10O king, you gave a command that everyone who heard the horns, lyres, zithers, harps, pipes, and all the other musical instruments would have to bow down and worship the gold statue. 11Anyone who wouldn’t do this was to be thrown into a blazing furnace. 12O king, there are some men of Judah whom you made officers in the area of Babylon that did not pay attention to your order. Their names are Shadrach, Meshach, and Abednego. They do not serve your gods and do not worship the gold statue you have set up.”

13Nebuchadnezzar became very angry and called for Shadrach, Meshach, and Abednego. When they were brought to the king, 14Nebuchadnezzar said, “Shadrach, Meshach, and Abednego, is it true that you do not serve my gods nor worship the gold statue I have set up? 15In a moment you will again hear the sound of the horns, flutes, lyres, zithers, harps, pipes, and all the other musical instruments. If you bow down and worship the statue I made, that will be good. But if you do

2:47 Dreams: Matthew 27:19
2:49 Daniel: Daniel 4

3:5 Music: Luke 15:25
3:5 *zithers.* Musical instruments with thirty to forty strings.

not worship it, you will immediately be thrown into the blazing furnace. What god will be able to save you from my power then?"

16Shadrach, Meshach, and Abednego answered the king, saying, "Nebuchadnezzar, we do not need to defend ourselves to you. 17If you throw us into the blazing furnace, the God we serve is able to save us from the furnace. He will save us from your power, O king. 18But even if God does not save us, we want you, O king, to know this: We will not serve your gods or worship the gold statue you have set up."

19Then Nebuchadnezzar was furious with Shadrach, Meshach, and Abednego, and he changed his mind. He ordered the furnace to be heated seven times hotter than usual. 20Then he commanded some of the strongest soldiers in his army to tie up Shadrach, Meshach, and Abednego and throw them into the blazing furnace.

21So Shadrach, Meshach, and Abednego were tied up and thrown into the blazing furnace while still wearing their robes, trousers, turbans, and other clothes. 22The king's command was very strict, and the furnace was made so hot that the flames killed the strong soldiers who threw Shadrach, Meshach, and Abednego into the furnace. 23Firmly tied, Shadrach, Meshach, and Abednego fell into the blazing furnace.

24Then King Nebuchadnezzar was so surprised that he jumped to his feet. He asked the men who advised him, "Didn't we tie up only three men and throw them into the fire?"

They answered, "Yes, O king."

25The king said, "Look! I see four men walking around in the fire. They are not tied up, and they are not burned. The fourth man looks like a son of the gods."

26Then Nebuchadnezzar went to the opening of the blazing furnace and shouted, "Shadrach, Meshach, and Abednego, come out! Servants of the Most High God, come here!"

So Shadrach, Meshach, and Abednego came out of the fire. 27When they came out, the governors, assistant governors, captains of the soldiers, and royal advisers crowded around them and saw that the fire had not harmed their bodies. Their hair was not burned, their robes were not burned, and they didn't even smell like smoke!

28Then Nebuchadnezzar said, "Praise the God of Shadrach, Meshach, and Abednego. Their God has sent his angel and saved his servants from the fire! These three men trusted their God and refused to obey my command. They were willing to die rather than serve or worship any god other than their own. 29So I now give this command: Anyone from any nation or language who says anything against the God of Shadrach, Meshach, and Abednego will be torn apart and have his house turned into a pile of stones. No other god can save his people like this." 30Then the king promoted Shadrach, Meshach, and Abednego in the area of Babylon.

Nebuchadnezzar's Dream of a Tree

4 King Nebuchadnezzar sent this letter to the people, nations, and those who speak every language in all the world:

I wish you peace and great wealth!

2The Most High God has done miracles and wonderful things for me that I am happy to tell you about.

3His wonderful acts are great,
and his miracles are mighty.
His kingdom goes on forever,
and his rule continues from now on.

4I, Nebuchadnezzar, was happy and successful at my palace, 5but I had a dream that made me afraid. As I was lying on my bed, I saw pictures and visions in my mind that alarmed me. 6So I ordered all the wise men of Babylon to come to me and tell me what my dream meant. 7The fortune-tellers, magicians, and wise men came, and I told them about the dream. But they could not tell me what it meant.

8Finally, Daniel came to me. (I called him Belteshazzar to honor my god, because the spirit of the holy gods is in him.) I told my dream to him. 9I said, "Belteshazzar, you are the most important of all the fortune-tellers. I know that the spirit of the holy gods is in you, so there is no secret that is too hard for you to understand. This was what I dreamed; tell me what it means. 10These are the visions I saw while I was lying in my bed: I looked, and there in front of me was a tree standing in the middle of the earth. And it was very tall. 11The tree grew large and strong. The top of the tree touched the sky and could be seen from anywhere on earth. 12The leaves

3:25 *the fourth man.* The "fourth man," as the king describes him, is either God in human form or some angelic being sent by God to help the three friends.

3:30 Martyrdom: Daniel 6:1–28

of the tree were beautiful. It had plenty of good fruit on it, enough food for everyone. The wild animals found shelter under the tree, and the birds lived in its branches. Every animal ate from it.

13“As I was looking at those things in the vision while lying on my bed, I saw an observer, a holy angel coming down from heaven. 14He spoke very loudly and said, ‘Cut down the tree and cut off its branches. Strip off its leaves and scatter its fruit. Let the animals under the tree run away, and let the birds in its branches fly away. 15But leave the stump and its roots in the ground with a band of iron and bronze around it; let it stay in the field with the grass around it.

“‘Let the man become wet with dew, and let him live among the animals and plants of the earth. 16Let him not think like a human any longer, but let him have the mind of an animal for seven years.

17“‘The observers gave this command; the holy ones declared the sentence. This is so all people may know that the Most High God rules over every kingdom on earth. God gives those kingdoms to anyone he wants, and he chooses people to rule them who are not proud.’

18“That is what I, King Nebuchadnezzar, dreamed. Now Belteshazzar, tell me what the dream means. None of the wise men in my kingdom can explain it to me, but you can, because the spirit of the holy gods is in you.”

Daniel Explains the Dream

19Then Daniel, who was called Belteshazzar, was very quiet for a while, because his understanding of the dream frightened him. So the king said, “Belteshazzar, do not let the dream or its meaning make you afraid.”

Then Belteshazzar answered, “My master, I wish the dream were about your enemies, and I wish its meaning were for those who are against you! 20You saw a tree in your dream that grew large and strong. Its top touched the sky, and it could be seen from all over the earth. 21Its leaves were beautiful, and it had plenty of fruit for everyone to eat. It was a home for the wild animals, and its branches were nesting places for the birds. 22O king, you are that tree! You have become great and powerful, like the tall tree that touched the sky. Your power reaches to the far parts of the earth.

23“O king, you saw an observer, a holy angel, coming down from heaven who said, ‘Cut down the tree and destroy it. But leave the stump and its roots in the ground with a band of iron and bronze around it; leave it in the field with the grass. Let him become wet with dew and live like a wild animal for seven years.’

24“This is the meaning of the dream, O king. The Most High God has commanded these things to happen to my master the king: 25You will be forced away from people to live among the wild animals. People will feed you grass like an ox, and dew from the sky will make you wet. Seven years will pass, and then you will learn this lesson: The Most High God is ruler over every kingdom on earth, and he gives those kingdoms to anyone he chooses.

26“Since the stump of the tree and its roots were left in the ground, your kingdom will be given back to you when you learn that one in heaven rules your kingdom. 27So, O king, please accept my advice. Stop sinning and do what is right. Stop doing wicked things and be kind to the poor. Then you might continue to be successful.”

The King’s Dream Comes True

28All these things happened to King Nebuchadnezzar. 29Twelve months later as he was walking on the roof of his palace in Babylon, 30he said, “I have built this great Babylon as my royal home. I built it by my power to show my glory and my majesty.”

31The words were still in his mouth when a voice from heaven said, “King Nebuchadnezzar, these things will happen to you: Your royal power has been taken away from you. 32You will be forced away from people. You will live with the wild animals and will be fed grass like an ox. Seven years will pass before you learn this lesson: The Most High God rules over every kingdom on earth and gives those kingdoms to anyone he chooses.”

33Immediately the words came true. Nebuchadnezzar was forced to go away from people, and he began eating grass like an ox. He became wet from dew. His hair grew long like the feathers of an eagle, and his nails grew like the claws of a bird.

4:18 *Belteshazzar.* Another name for Daniel.
4:29 *roof.* In Bible times houses were built with flat roofs. The roof was used for drying things such as flax and fruit. And it was used as an extra room, as a place for worship, and as a cool place to sleep in the summer.
4:30 Babylon: 1 Peter 5:13

34At the end of that time, I, Nebuchadnezzar, looked up toward heaven, and I could think normally again! Then I gave praise to the Most High God; I gave honor and glory to him who lives forever.

God's rule is forever,
and his kingdom continues for all time.
35People on earth
are not truly important.
God does what he wants
with the powers of heaven
and the people on earth.
No one can stop his powerful hand
or question what he does.

36At that time I could think normally again, and God gave back my great honor and power and returned the glory to my kingdom. The people who advised me and the royal family came to me for help again. I became king again and was even greater and more powerful than before. 37Now I, Nebuchadnezzar, give praise and honor and glory to the King of heaven. Everything he does is right and fair, and he is able to make proud people humble.

The Writing on the Wall

5 King Belshazzar gave a big banquet for a thousand royal guests and drank wine with them. 2As Belshazzar was drinking his wine, he gave orders to bring the gold and silver cups that his ancestor Nebuchadnezzar had taken from the Temple in Jerusalem. This was so the king, his royal guests, his wives, and his slave women could drink from those cups. 3So they brought the gold cups that had been taken from the Temple of God in Jerusalem. And the king and his royal guests, his wives, and his slave women drank from them. 4As they were drinking, they praised their gods, which were made from gold, silver, bronze, iron, wood, and stone.

5Suddenly the fingers of a person's hand appeared and began writing on the plaster of the wall, near the lampstand in the royal palace. The king watched the hand as it wrote.

6King Belshazzar was very frightened. His face turned white, his knees knocked together, and he could not stand up because his legs were too weak. 7The king called for the magicians, wise men, and wizards of Babylon and said to them, "Anyone who can read this writing and explain it will receive purple clothes fit for a king and a gold chain around his neck. And I will make that person the third highest ruler in the kingdom."

8Then all the king's wise men came in, but they could not read the writing or tell the king what it meant. 9King Belshazzar became even more afraid, and his face became even whiter. His royal guests were confused.

10Then the king's mother, who had heard the voices of the king and his royal guests, came into the banquet room. She said, "O king, live forever! Don't be afraid or let your face be white with fear! 11There is a man in your kingdom who has the spirit of the holy gods. In the days of your father, this man showed understanding, knowledge, and wisdom like the gods. Your father, King Nebuchadnezzar, put this man in charge of all the wise men, fortune-tellers, magicians, and wizards. 12The man I am talking about is named Daniel, whom the king named Belteshazzar. He was very smart and had knowledge and understanding. He could explain dreams and secrets and could answer very hard problems. Call for Daniel. He will tell you what the writing on the wall means."

13So they brought Daniel to the king, and the king asked, "Is your name Daniel? Are you one of the captives my father the king brought from Judah? 14I have heard that the spirit of the gods is in you, and that you are very smart and have knowledge and extraordinary understanding. 15The wise men and magicians were brought to me to read this writing and to explain what it means, but they could not explain it. 16I have heard that you are able to explain what things mean and can find the answers to hard problems. Read this writing on the wall and explain it to me. If you can, I will give you purple clothes fit for a king and a gold chain to wear around your neck. And you will become the third highest ruler in the kingdom."

17Then Daniel answered the king, "You may keep your gifts for yourself, or you may give those rewards to someone else. But I will read the writing on the wall for you and will explain to you what it means.

18"O king, the Most High God made your father Nebuchadnezzar a great, important, and powerful king. 19Because God made him important, all the people, nations, and those who spoke every language were very frightened of Nebuchadnezzar. If he wanted someone to die, he killed that person. If he

4:37 Daniel: Daniel 5
5:6 Alcohol: Matthew 20:22
5:16 *third highest ruler in the kingdom.* Daniel would become the third ruler in the land. We know from Babylonian historical texts that Belshazzar's father, Nabonidus, had turned over the rule of Babylon proper to his son while he went to the southern portions of his empire to assert his power there. Thus, Daniel would be third after the father and the son.

wanted someone to live, he let that person live. Those he wanted to promote, he promoted. Those he wanted to be less important, he made less important.

[20]"But Nebuchadnezzar became too proud and stubborn, so he was taken off his royal throne. His glory was taken away. [21]He was forced away from people, and his mind became like the mind of an animal. He lived with the wild donkeys and was fed grass like an ox and became wet with dew. These things happened to him until he learned his lesson: The Most High God rules over every kingdom on earth, and he sets anyone he chooses over those kingdoms.

[22]"Belshazzar, you already knew these things, because you are a descendant of Nebuchadnezzar. Still you have not been sorry for what you have done. [23]Instead, you have set yourself against the Lord of heaven. You ordered the drinking cups from the Temple of the Lord to be brought to you. Then you and your royal guests, your wives, and your slave women drank wine from them. You praised the gods of silver, gold, bronze, iron, wood, and stone that are not really gods; they cannot see or hear or understand anything. You did not honor God, who has power over your life and everything you do. [24]So God sent the hand that wrote on the wall.

[25]"These are the words that were written on the wall: 'Mene, mene, tekel, and parsin.'

[26]"This is what the words mean: Mene: God has counted the days until your kingdom will end. [27]Tekel: You have been weighed on the scales and found not good enough. [28]Parsin: Your kingdom is being divided and will be given to the Medes and the Persians."

[29]Then Belshazzar gave an order for Daniel to be dressed in purple clothes and to have a gold chain put around his neck. And it was announced that Daniel was the third highest ruler in the kingdom. [30]That very same night Belshazzar, king of the Babylonian people, was killed. [31]So Darius the Mede became the new king when he was sixty-two years old.

Daniel and the Lions

6 Darius thought it would be a good idea to choose one hundred twenty governors who would rule his kingdom. [2]He chose three men as supervisors over those governors, and Daniel was one of the supervisors. The supervisors were to ensure that the governors did not try to cheat the king. [3]Daniel showed that he could do the work better than the other supervisors and governors, so the king planned to put Daniel in charge of the whole kingdom. [4]Because of this, the other supervisors and governors tried to find reasons to accuse Daniel about his work in the government. But they could not find anything wrong with him or any reason to accuse him, because he was trustworthy and not lazy or dishonest. [5]Finally these men said, "We will never find any reason to accuse Daniel unless it is about the law of his God."

[6]So the supervisors and governors went as a group to the king and said: "King Darius, live forever! [7]The supervisors, assistant governors, governors, the people who advise you, and the captains of the soldiers have all agreed that you should make a new law for everyone to obey: For the next thirty days no one should pray to any god or human except to you, O king. Anyone who doesn't obey will be thrown into the lions' den. [8]Now, O king, make the law and sign your name to it so that it cannot be changed, because then it will be a law of the Medes and Persians and cannot be canceled." [9]So King Darius signed the law.

[10]Even though Daniel knew that the new law had been written, he went to pray in an upstairs room in his house, which had windows that opened toward Jerusalem. Three times each day Daniel would kneel down to pray and thank God, just as he always had done.

[11]Then those men went as a group and found Daniel praying and asking God for help. [12]So they went to the king and talked to him about the law he had made. They said, "Didn't you sign a law that says no one may pray to any god or human except you, O king? Doesn't it say that anyone who disobeys during the next thirty days will be thrown into the lions' den?"

The king answered, "Yes, that is the law, and the laws of the Medes and Persians cannot be canceled."

[13]Then they said to the king, "Daniel, one of the captives from Judah, is not paying attention to you, O king, or to the law you signed. Daniel still prays to his God three times every day." [14]The king became very upset when he heard this. He wanted to save Daniel, and he worked hard until sunset trying to think of a way to save him.

[15]Then those men went as a group to the king. They said, "Remember, O king, the law of the Medes and Persians says that no law or command given by the king can be changed."

[16]So King Darius gave the order, and Daniel was brought in and thrown into the lions' den. The king

5:31 Pride: Romans 15:17–19

5:31 Daniel: Daniel 6

said to Daniel, "May the God you serve all the time
save you!" 17A big stone was brought and placed
over the opening of the lions' den. Then the king
used his signet ring and the rings of his royal officers to put special seals on the rock. This ensured
that no one would move the rock and bring
Daniel out. 18Then King Darius went back to his
palace. He did not eat that night, he did not have
any entertainment brought to him, and he could
not sleep.

19The next morning King Darius got up at dawn
and hurried to the lions' den. 20As he came near
the den, he was worried. He called out to Daniel,
"Daniel, servant of the living God! Has your God
that you always worship been able to save you
from the lions?"

21Daniel answered, "O king, live forever! 22My
God sent his angel to close the lions' mouths.
They have not hurt me, because my God knows I
am innocent. I never did anything wrong to you,
O king."

23King Darius was very happy and told his servants to lift Daniel out of the lions' den. So they
lifted him out and did not find any injury on him,
because Daniel had trusted in his God.

24Then the king commanded that the men who
had accused Daniel be brought to the lions' den.
They, their wives, and their children were thrown
into the den. The lions grabbed them before they
hit the floor of the den and crushed their bones.

25Then King Darius wrote a letter to all people
and all nations, to those who spoke every language
in the world:

> I wish you great peace and wealth.
>
> 26I am making a new law for people in every
> part of my kingdom. All of you must fear and
> respect the God of Daniel.
>
> Daniel's God is the living God;
> he lives forever.
> His kingdom will never be destroyed,
> and his rule will never end.
> 27God rescues and saves people
> and does mighty miracles
> in heaven and on earth.
> He is the one who saved Daniel
> from the power of the lions.

28So Daniel was successful during the time Darius
was king and when Cyrus the Persian was king.

Daniel's Dream about Four Animals

7 In Belshazzar's first year as king of Babylon,
Daniel had a dream. He saw visions as he was
lying on his bed, and he wrote down what he had
dreamed.

2"Daniel said: "I saw my vision at night. In the
vision the wind was blowing from all four directions, which made the sea very rough. 3I saw four
huge animals come up from the sea, and each animal was different from the others.

4"The first animal looked like a lion, but had
wings like an eagle. I watched this animal until its
wings were torn off. It was lifted from the ground
so that it stood up on two feet like a human, and
it was given the mind of a human.

5"Then I saw a second animal before me that
looked like a bear. It was raised up on one of its
sides and had three ribs in its mouth between its
teeth. It was told, 'Get up and eat all the meat you
want!'

6"After that, I looked, and there before me was
another animal. This animal looked like a leopard
with four wings on its back that looked like a
bird's wings. This animal had four heads and was
given power to rule.

7"After that, in my vision at night I saw in front
of me a fourth animal that was cruel, terrible, and
very strong. It had large iron teeth. It crushed and
ate what it killed, and then it walked on whatever was left. This fourth animal was different
from any animal I had seen before, and it had ten
horns.

8"While I was thinking about the horns, another
horn grew up among them. It was a little horn with
eyes like a human's eyes. It also had a mouth, and
the mouth was bragging. The little horn pulled out
three of the other horns.

9"As I looked,
> thrones were put in their places,
> and God, who has been alive forever, sat on
> his throne.
> His clothes were white like snow,
> and the hair on his head was white like wool.
> His throne was made from fire,
> and the wheels of his throne were blazing
> with fire.

6:22 Angels: Daniel 7:10
6:28 Persecution: Matthew 5:11–12
6:28 Daniel: Daniel 7–12:13
6:28 Martyrdom: Matthew 5:10–11
7:2 *the sea.* In the Old Testament the sea is often an image of the evil forces of chaos.

7:4 *a lion, but had wings like an eagle.* The mixed nature of the beasts is a characteristic that repelled the ancient people of Israel. We know from Genesis 1–2 and the Book of Leviticus that the various types of animals were to be kept separate.
7:7 *horns.* The horn of an animal indicates its strength and power.

Mourning

JOHN 11:1–44

Why does God allow the death of his children? Does he feel pain when we mourn? Does he care when we are grieving? How do we handle the loss of a loved one?

One famous biblical God-fearing family experienced the bewilderment and pain of losing a loved one. Two sisters, Mary and Martha, mourned the loss of their brother, Lazarus, and poured out their hearts—and questions—to the one they had hoped would save their brother. In this poignant drama recorded in John 11, we catch a glimpse of how God deals with the hurts that those who grieve experience. We also gain insight into some of the reasons why he allows such pain to take place still today.

Mary and Martha offered their home to Jesus and his disciples whenever they were in the area of Judea. Apparently, Lazarus was a wealthy man, and he used his wealth to support the ministry of Christ. The fact that Mary and Martha sent for Jesus as soon as Lazarus became ill shows their faith in his power. No doubt they thought, If Jesus is willing to heal total strangers, certainly he will jump at the opportunity to heal one who has been a friend. But such was not the case: "Jesus loved Martha and her sister and Lazarus. But when he heard that Lazarus was sick, he stayed where he was for two more days" (John 11:5–6).

Humanly speaking, these verses make absolutely no sense. Obviously, Jesus loves this family; then he makes no move to relieve their suffering. I can relate to that. Whenever the bottom drops out, I go scrambling for the verses in the Bible that remind me of God's love—yet at times it seems God is unwilling to follow through with any action.

Lazarus died. When it happened, both women felt that hollow, helpless feeling that always comes with death. It was over. He was gone. Soon their thoughts turned to Jesus. Why didn't he come? How could he know what we were going through and yet stay away?

It is clear that Jesus delayed his coming to Bethany quite deliberately. He even told his disciples: "Lazarus is dead. And I am glad for your sakes I was not there so that you may believe" (John 11:14–15). Jesus was "glad"? How could he say such a thing? Two of his best friends go through emotional turmoil; another friend dies of an illness; and Jesus says he is glad? What could he have possibly been thinking? What was going through his mind?

The answer to that question is the key to unlocking the mystery of tragedy in this life. To understand what was going on in the mind of Christ in a situation like this one is to discover the universal principle that puts together and holds together all of life—both now and for eternity.

Christ had a goal in all of this, a goal so important that it was worth the emotional agony Mary and Martha had to endure. It was even worth the death of a faithful friend. Whether we can understand this easily or not, the fact remains that the Son of God allowed those he loved to suffer and die for the sake of a higher purpose.

Some individuals may think such a statement implies that we are merely pawns to be moved about and even abused at God's whims. But remember, "Jesus cried" (John 11:35). He was moved with emotion at the sight of Mary and Martha's sorrow. He was touched by the love they had for their brother. He was not "using" them. He was not emotionally isolated from their pain. He cared about these people, and he cares about us.

Through all the pain and adversity God may allow us to face, two things are always true. First, he is sensitive to what we are feeling (Hebrews 4:15). Second, whatever he is working to accomplish through our suffering will always be for our best interest (Romans 8:28). The way things work out is determined by our response. As we trust God through our adversity, when all is said and done, we will sincerely believe it was worth it all.

From the very beginning, Jesus had two specific purposes in mind. His purpose was not to cause Lazarus to die. Neither was it to cause Mary and her sister mental and emotional anguish. On the contrary, his purpose in all that happened were to bring glory to God (John 11:4) and to cause others to believe in him (John 11:15, 42). These are his purposes in every hardship we experience. When a loved one is called home to be with the Lord, we must pray for these purposes to be realized. As for our hurts, Jesus knows, he cares, and he promises never to leave us or forsake us (Hebrews 13:5).

Mourning: For additional scriptures on this topic go to Job 19:25–27.

PHARISEES & SADDUCEES

JOHN 11:43–57

Who are the Sadducees and Pharisees? What do they stand for? What role do they have in the gospel story?

Jesus was born into a society that was a powder keg of smoldering political and religious conflicts. The Jewish people, who viewed themselves as God's chosen people and the territory of Palestine as the land God had promised them, generally resented the Roman occupation forces who had seized control of their country. But within the Jewish population were various parties that disagreed about what God wanted for their nation and about how to relate to the Romans. The Pharisees and Sadducees were two such groups, and their opposing religious and political interests contributed to the volatile atmosphere in Palestine.

The Pharisees thought nothing was more important than studying the Scriptures and obeying God's laws. They believed that if the Jewish people were careful to keep God's laws and resist pagan influences, he would send them a savior, the Messiah, to overthrow the Romans and restore their independence. To ensure that the basic laws in their Scriptures would not be broken, the Pharisees also accepted a whole set of more detailed rules, called the oral tradition. The Pharisees obeyed these detailed rules themselves and urged the Jewish people to obey them so that the Messiah would come and bring the kingdom of God. The common people found it hard if not impossible to keep all the rules, but they admired the Pharisees' piety and shared their intense longing for a political and military savior. Consequently, the Pharisees were the most popular party in Palestine. Most of the teachers of the law in Jesus' time were Pharisees.

The Sadducees had very different interests. They represented the wealthy, aristocratic families in Jerusalem, and the leading priests came from this party. Being both powerful and privileged, the Sadducees naturally wanted to maintain the status quo. They were not looking for a coming savior to bring a new kingdom. They were not trying to achieve a degree of piety that would earn them life after death. They further believed that they were only required to obey the laws in the Torah, and not the rules of the oral tradition. The Sadducees were also unpopular with the common people because they cooperated closely with the Romans, knowing that the Roman forces maintained the stability in Israel that allowed them to hang onto their wealth and power.

Both Pharisees and Sadducees viewed Jesus as an enemy. The Pharisees believed he endangered the future of their nation, for Jesus did not fit their picture of the Messiah. In their eyes, he was leading the people astray. He broke the rules of the oral tradition by healing on the Sabbath and by eating with unclean people such as prostitutes and tax collectors. He took on the role of God by forgiving sins, and he assumed authority to interpret the Scriptures himself instead of adhering to the traditional interpretations of the teachers of the law. For all these reasons the Pharisees criticized Jesus and condemned his teachings.

The Sadducees apparently did not pay much attention to Jesus when he was in the villages of Galilee, but when he came to Jerusalem, they saw what an enormous threat he was. For Jesus stirred up the hopes of the oppressed common people for a Messiah and for political independence. The Sadducees feared the people would rise up and try to make Jesus king, bringing down the wrath of the Romans on the whole nation and putting an end to the comfortable, privileged life the Sadducees enjoyed.

If the Pharisees and Sadducees opposed Jesus, he also opposed them (Matthew 16:11–12; Luke 11:37–44), for they resisted the kind of salvation he offered. The kingdom Jesus brought was not one where wealth or power or social status mattered. It was not one that rewarded fanatical adherence to rules and excluded those who broke the laws. Rather, it was a kingdom where sinners from every class and nation who put their faith in a crucified savior would be forgiven and loved (Luke 15:1–7).

It is not surprising that as Jesus' ministry spread and his popularity grew, both the Pharisees and the Sadducees wanted to get rid of him. These two parties, which usually fought each other, joined forces to plot Jesus' death. In the week before his crucifixion they tried to trick him into incriminating himself (Matthew 22:15–46). When he cleverly dodged their schemes, they resorted to breaking the law themselves, using deceit and violence to bring him down. Yet throughout the Gospels, and on into the Book of Acts, it is clear the Pharisees and Sadducees, in spite of their political and religious power, were powerless to stop Jesus and the kingdom he came to establish.

Pharisees & Sadducees: For additional scriptures on this topic go to Matthew 3:1–2.

10A river of fire was flowing
from in front of him.
Many thousands of angels were serving him,
and millions of angels stood before him.
Court was ready to begin,
and the books were opened.
11“I kept on looking because the little horn was
bragging. I kept watching until finally the fourth
animal was killed. Its body was destroyed, and it
was thrown into the burning fire. 12(The power
and rule of the other animals had been taken from
them, but they were permitted to live for a certain period of time.)
13“In my vision at night I saw in front of me
someone who looked like a human being coming
on the clouds in the sky. He came near God, who
has been alive forever, and he was led to God.
14He was given authority, glory, and the strength
of a king. People of every tribe, nation, and language will serve him. His rule will last forever,
and his kingdom will never be destroyed.

The Meaning of the Dream

15“I, Daniel, was worried. The visions that went
through my mind frightened me. 16I came near one of
those standing there and asked what all this meant.
“So he told me and explained to me what these
things meant: 17‘The four great animals are four
kingdoms that will come from the earth. 18But
the holy people who belong to the Most High God
will receive the power to rule and will have the
power to rule forever, from now on.’
19“Then I wanted to know what the fourth animal meant, because it was different from all the
others. It was very terrible and had iron teeth and
bronze claws. It was the animal that crushed and
ate what it killed and then walked on whatever
was left. 20I also wanted to know about the ten
horns on its head and about the little horn that
grew there. It had pulled out three of the other
ten horns and looked greater than the others. It had
eyes and a mouth that kept bragging. 21As I
watched, the little horn began making war against
God’s holy people and was defeating them 22until
God, who has been alive forever, came. He
judged in favor of the holy people who belong to
the Most High God; then the time came for them
to receive the power to rule.
23“And he explained this to me: ‘The fourth animal is a fourth kingdom that will come on the
earth. It will be different from all the other kingdoms and will destroy people all over the world. It
will walk on and crush the whole earth. 24The ten
horns are ten kings who will come from this
fourth kingdom. After those ten kings are gone,
another king will come. He will be different from
the kings who ruled before him, and he will defeat
three of the other kings. 25This king will speak
against the Most High God, and he will hurt and
kill God’s holy people. He will try to change times
and laws that have already been set. The holy people that belong to God will be in that king’s power
for three and one-half years.
26“‘But the court will decide what should happen.
The power of the king will be taken away, and his
kingdom will be completely destroyed. 27Then the
holy people who belong to the Most High God will
have the power to rule. They will rule over all the
kingdoms under heaven with power and greatness,
and their power to rule will last forever. People from
all the other kingdoms will respect and serve them.’
28“That was the end of the dream. I, Daniel, was
very afraid. My face became white from fear, but I
kept everything to myself.”

Daniel’s Vision

8 During the third year of King Belshazzar’s
rule, I, Daniel, saw another vision, which was
like the first one. 2In this vision I saw myself in
the capital city of Susa, in the area of Elam. I was
standing by the Ulai Canal 3when I looked up and
saw a male sheep standing beside the canal. It had
two long horns, but one horn was longer and
newer than the other. 4I watched the sheep
charge to the west, the north, and the south. No
animal could stand before him, and none could save
another animal from his power. He did whatever
he wanted and became very powerful.
5While I was watching this, I saw a male goat
come from the west. This goat had one large horn
between his eyes that was easy to see. He crossed
over the whole earth so fast that his feet hardly
touched the ground.
6In his anger the goat charged the sheep with
the two horns that I had seen standing by the
canal. 7I watched the angry goat attack the sheep

7:10 Angels: Matthew 13:41–43
7:13 Holy War & Divine Warrior: Zechariah 14:3
7:13–14 Daniel’s vision of the one who “looked like a human being coming on the clouds in the sky” who will rule on God’s behalf predicts a future time when human obedience to God will be perfect and universal (Revelation 21:22–27). Christians can look forward to the return of Christ (Mark 13:26) when human disobedience will finally be overcome and eliminated.

7:14 Angels/Guardian Angels: Mark 1:13
7:14 Tongues: Acts 10:44–48
7:28 Prophetic Symbolism: Amos 8:1–3
7:28 Jesus: Mark 1:21–28
7:28 End Times/Last Days: Amos 5:18–27

and break the sheep's two horns. The sheep was
not strong enough to stop it. The goat knocked the
sheep to the ground and then walked all over him.
No one was able to save the sheep from the goat,
8so the male goat became very great. But when he
was strong, his big horn broke off and four horns
grew in place of the one big horn. Those four
horns pointed in four different directions and
were easy to see.
9Then a little horn grew from one of those four
horns, and it became very big. It grew to the south,
the east, and toward the beautiful land of Judah.
10That little horn grew until it reached to the sky.
It even threw some of the army of heaven to the
ground and walked on them! 11That little horn set
itself up as equal to God, the Commander of
heaven's armies. It stopped the daily sacrifices
that were offered to him, and the Temple, the
place where people worshiped him, was pulled
down. 12Because there was a turning away from
God, the people stopped the daily sacrifices.
Truth was thrown down to the ground, and the
horn was successful in everything it did.
13Then I heard a holy angel speaking. Another
holy angel asked the first one, "How long will the
things in this vision last—the daily sacrifices, the
turning away from God that brings destruction,
the Temple being pulled down, and the army of
heaven being walked on?"
14The angel said to me, "This will happen for
twenty-three hundred evenings and mornings.
Then the holy place will be repaired."
15I, Daniel, saw this vision and tried to understand what it meant. In it I saw someone who
looked like a man standing near me. 16And I heard
a man's voice calling from the Ulai Canal:
"Gabriel, explain the vision to this man."
17Gabriel came to where I was standing. When
he came close to me, I was very afraid and bowed
facedown on the ground. But Gabriel said to me,
"Human being, understand that this vision is about
the time of the end."
18While Gabriel was speaking, I fell into a deep
sleep with my face on the ground. Then he
touched me and lifted me to my feet. 19He said,
"Now, I will explain to you what will happen in
the time of God's anger. Your vision was about the
set time of the end.
20"You saw a male sheep with two horns, which
are the kings of Media and Persia. 21The male goat
is the king of Greece, and the big horn between its
eyes is the first king. 22The four horns that grew in
the place of the broken horn are four kingdoms.
Those four kingdoms will come from the nation of
the first king, but they will not be as strong as the
first king.
23"When the end comes near for those kingdoms, a bold and cruel king who tells lies will
come. This will happen when many people have
turned against God. 24This king will be very powerful, but his power will not come from himself. He
will cause terrible destruction and will be successful
in everything he does. He will destroy powerful
people and even God's holy people. 25This king
will succeed by using lies and force. He will think
that he is very important. He will destroy many
people without warning; he will try to fight even
the Prince of princes! But that cruel king will be
destroyed, and not by human power.
26"The vision that has been shown to you about
these evenings and mornings is true. But seal up
the vision, because those things won't happen for a
long time."
27I, Daniel, became very weak and was sick for
several days after that vision. Then I got up and
went back to work for the king, but I was very upset
about the vision. I didn't understand what it meant.

Daniel's Prayer

9 These things happened during the first year
Darius son of Xerxes was king over Babylon.
He was a descendant of the Medes. 2During
Darius' first year as king, I, Daniel, was reading the
Scriptures. I saw that the LORD told Jeremiah that
Jerusalem would be empty ruins for seventy years.
3Then I turned to the Lord God and prayed and
asked him for help. I did not eat any food. To
show my sadness, I put on rough cloth and sat in
ashes. 4I prayed to the LORD my God and told him
about all of our sins. I said, "Lord, you are a great
God who causes fear and wonder. You keep your
agreement of love with all who love you and obey
your commands.
5"But we have sinned and done wrong. We have
been wicked and turned against you, your commands, and your laws. 6We did not listen to your
servants, the prophets, who spoke for you to our
kings, our leaders, our ancestors, and all the people
of the land.
7"Lord, you are good and right, but we are full of
shame today—the people of Judah and Jerusalem,
all the people of Israel, those near and far whom
you scattered among many nations because they
were not loyal to you. 8LORD, we are all ashamed.
Our kings and leaders and our fathers are ashamed,
because we have sinned against you.

8:19 God's Anger: Amos 5:18–20

9“But, Lord our God, you show us mercy and forgive us even though we have turned against you. 10We have not obeyed the LORD our God or the teachings he gave us through his servants, the prophets. 11All the people of Israel have disobeyed your teachings and have turned away, refusing to obey you. So you brought on us the curses and promises of punishment written in the Teachings of Moses, the servant of God, because we sinned against you.

12“You said these things would happen to us and our leaders, and you made them happen; you brought on us a great disaster. Nothing has ever been done on earth like what was done to Jerusalem. 13All this disaster came to us just as it is written in the Teachings of Moses. But we have not pleaded with the LORD our God. We have not stopped sinning. We have not paid attention to your truth. 14The LORD was ready to bring the disaster on us, and he did it because the LORD our God is right in everything he does. But we still did not obey him.

15“Lord our God, you used your power and brought us out of Egypt. Because of that, your name is known even today. But we have sinned and have done wrong. 16Lord, you do what is right, but please do not be angry with Jerusalem, your city on your holy hill. Because of our sins and the evil things done by our ancestors, people all around insult and make fun of Jerusalem and your people.

17“Now, our God, hear the prayers of your servant. Listen to my prayer for help, and for your sake do good things for your holy place that is in ruins. 18My God, pay attention and hear me. Open your eyes and see all the terrible things that have happened to us. See how our lives have been ruined and what has happened to the city that is called by your name. We do not ask these things because we are good; instead, we ask because of your mercy. 19Lord, listen! Lord, forgive! Lord, hear us and do something! For your sake, don't wait, because your city and your people are called by your name.”

Gabriel's Explanation

20While I was saying these things in my prayer to the LORD, my God, confessing my sins and the sins of the people of Israel and praying for God's holy hill, 21Gabriel came to me. (I had seen him in my last vision.) He came flying quickly to me about the time of the evening sacrifice, while I was still praying. 22He taught me and said to me, “Daniel, I have come to give you wisdom and to help you understand. 23When you first started praying, an answer was given, and I came to tell you, because God loves you very much. So think about the message and understand the vision.

24“God has ordered four hundred ninety years for your people and your holy city for these reasons: to stop people from turning against God; to put an end to sin; to take away evil; to bring in goodness that continues forever; to bring about the vision and prophecy; and to appoint a most holy place.

25“Learn and understand these things. A command will come to rebuild Jerusalem. The time from this command until the appointed leader comes will be forty-nine years and four hundred thirty-four years. Jerusalem will be rebuilt with streets and a trench filled with water around it, but it will be built in times of trouble. 26After the four hundred thirty-four years the appointed leader will be killed; he will have nothing. The people of the leader who is to come will destroy the city and the holy place. The end of the city will come like a flood, and war will continue until the end. God has ordered that place to be completely destroyed. 27That leader will make firm an agreement with many people for seven years. He will stop the offerings and sacrifices after three and one-half years. A destroyer will do terrible things until the ordered end comes to the destroyed city.”

Daniel's Vision of a Man

10 During Cyrus' third year as king of Persia, Daniel, whose name was Belteshazzar, received a vision about a great war. It was a true message that Daniel understood.

2At that time I, Daniel, had been very sad for three weeks. 3I did not eat any fancy food or meat, or drink any wine, or use any perfumed oil for three weeks.

4On the twenty-fourth day of the first month, I was standing beside the great Tigris River. 5While standing there, I looked up and saw a man dressed in linen clothes with a belt of fine gold wrapped around his waist. 6His body was like shiny yellow quartz. His face was bright like lightning, and his eyes were like fire. His arms and legs were shiny like polished bronze, and his voice sounded like the roar of a crowd.

7I, Daniel, was the only person who saw the vision. The men with me did not see it, because they were so frightened that they ran away and hid. 8So I was left alone, watching this great vision. I lost my strength, my face turned white like a dead

9:18 Good Works: Matthew 20:1–16
9:19 Intercession: Acts 12:5–12
10:6 Incarnation: Matthew 11:25–27

person, and I was helpless. 9Then I heard the man in the vision speaking. As I listened, I fell into a deep sleep with my face on the ground.

10Then a hand touched me and set me on my hands and knees. I was so afraid that I was shaking. 11The man in the vision said to me, "Daniel, God loves you very much. Think carefully about the words I will speak to you, and stand up, because I have been sent to you." When he said this, I stood up, but I was still shaking.

12Then the man said to me, "Daniel, do not be afraid. Some time ago you decided to get understanding and to humble yourself before your God. Since that time God has listened to you, and I have come because of your prayers. 13But the prince of Persia has been fighting against me for twenty-one days. Then Michael, one of the most important angels, came to help me, because I had been left there with the king of Persia. 14Now I have come to explain to you what will happen to your people, because the vision is about a time in the future."

15While he was speaking to me, I bowed face-down and could not speak. 16Then one who looked like a man touched my lips, so I opened my mouth and started to speak. I said to the one standing in front of me, "Master, I am upset and afraid because of what I saw in the vision. I feel helpless. 17Master, how can I, your servant, talk with you? My strength is gone, and it is hard for me to breathe."

18The one who looked like a man touched me again and gave me strength. 19He said, "Daniel, don't be afraid. God loves you very much. Peace be with you. Be strong now; be courageous."

When he spoke to me, I became stronger and said, "Master, speak, since you have given me strength."

20Then he said, "Daniel, do you know why I have come to you? Soon I must go back to fight against the prince of Persia. When I go, the prince of Greece will come, 21but I must first tell you what is written in the Book of Truth. No one stands with me against these enemies except Michael, the angel ruling over your people.

11 In the first year that Darius the Mede was king, I stood up to support Michael in his fight against the prince of Persia.

Kingdoms of the South and North

2"Now then, Daniel, I tell you the truth: Three more kings will rule in Persia, and then a fourth king will come. He will be much richer than all the kings of Persia before him and will use his riches to get power. He will stir up everyone against the kingdom of Greece. 3Then a mighty king will come, who will rule with great power and will do anything he wants. 4After that king has come, his kingdom will be broken up and divided out toward the four parts of the world. His kingdom will not go to his descendants, and it will not have the power that he had, because his kingdom will be pulled up and given to other people.

5"The king of the South will become strong, but one of his commanders will become even stronger. He will begin to rule his own kingdom with great power. 6Then after a few years, a new friendship will develop. The daughter of the king of the South will marry the king of the North in order to bring peace. But she will not keep her power, and his family will not last. She, her husband, her child, and those who brought her to that country will be killed.

7"But a person from her family will become king of the South and will attack the armies of the king of the North. He will go into that king's strong, walled city and will fight and win. 8He will take their gods, their metal idols, and their valuable things made of silver and gold back to Egypt. Then he will not bother the king of the North for a few years. 9Next, the king of the North will attack the king of the South, but he will be beaten back to his own country.

10"The sons of the king of the North will prepare for war. They will get a large army together that will move through the land very quickly, like a powerful flood. Later, that army will come back and fight all the way to the strong, walled city of the king of the South. 11Then the king of the South will become very angry and will march out to fight against the king of the North. The king of the North will have a large army, but he will lose the battle, 12and the soldiers will be carried away. The king of the South will then be very proud and will kill thousands of soldiers from the northern army, but he will not continue to be successful. 13The king of the North will gather another army, larger than the first one. After several years he will attack with a large army and many weapons.

14"In those times many people will be against the king of the South. Some of your own people who love to fight will turn against the king of the South, thinking it is time for God's promises to come true. But they will fail. 15Then the king of the

10:13 *fighting.* The war on earth reflects a spiritual war in the heavens.

10:13 God ripped open the heavens and gave Daniel a glimpse of heavenly realities. Daniel already knew of human conflicts, but here he sees the more intense spiritual conflict that stood behind the human rulers and governments that fought on earth. The New Testament pulls the curtain back even further, so that we can see our own involvement in God's army against the spiritual powers and principalities (Ephesians 6:10–18).

North will come. He will build ramps to the tops of
the city walls and will capture a strong, walled city.
The southern army will not have the power to fight
back; even their best soldiers will not be strong
enough to stop the northern army. 16So the king of
the North will do whatever he wants; no one will
be able to stand against him. He will gain power
and control in the beautiful land of Israel and will
have the power to destroy it. 17The king of the
North will decide to use all his power to fight
against the king of the South, but he will make a
peace agreement with the king of the South. The
king of the North will give one of his daughters as
a wife to the king of the South so that he can defeat
him. But those plans will not succeed or help him.
18Then the king of the North will turn his attention
to cities along the coast of the Mediterranean Sea
and will capture them. But a commander will put
an end to the pride of the king of the North, turning his pride back on him. 19After that happens the
king of the North will go back to the strong, walled
cities of his own country, but he will lose his
power. That will be the end of him.

20"The next king of the North will send out a
tax collector so he will have plenty of money. In a
few years that ruler will be killed, although he will
not die in anger or in a battle.

21"That ruler will be followed by a very cruel
and hated man, who will not have the honor of
being from a king's family. He will attack the kingdom when the people feel safe, and he will take
power by lying to the people. 22He will sweep
away in defeat large and powerful armies and
even a prince who made an agreement. 23Many
nations will make agreements with that cruel and
hated ruler, but he will lie to them. He will gain
much power, but only a few people will support
him. 24The richest areas will feel safe, but that
cruel and hated ruler will attack them. He will
succeed where his ancestors did not. He will rob
the countries he defeats and will give those
things to his followers. He will plan to defeat and
destroy strong cities, but he will be successful for
only a short time.

25"That very cruel and hated ruler will have a
large army that he will use to stir up his strength
and courage. He will attack the king of the South.
The king of the South will gather a large and very
powerful army and prepare for war. But the people
who are against him will make secret plans, and
the king of the South will be defeated. 26People who
were supposed to be his good friends will try to
destroy him. His army will be swept away in
defeat; many of his soldiers will be killed in battle.
27Those two kings will want to hurt each other.
They will sit at the same table and lie to each
other, but it will not do either one any good,
because God has set a time for their end to come.
28The king of the North will go back to his own
country with much wealth. Then he will decide to
go against the holy agreement. He will take action
and then return to his own country.

29"At the right time the king of the North will
attack the king of the South again, but this time
he will not be successful as he was before. 30Ships
from the west will come and fight against the
king of the North, so he will be afraid. Then he
will return and show his anger against the holy
agreement. He will be good to those who have
stopped obeying the holy agreement.

31"The king of the North will send his army to
make the Temple in Jerusalem unclean. They will
stop the people from offering the daily sacrifice,
and then they will set up the destroying terror.
32The king of the North will tell lies and cause
those who have not obeyed God to be ruined. But
those who know God and obey him will be strong
and fight back.

33"Those who are wise will help the others
understand what is happening. But they will be
killed with swords, or burned, or taken captive,
or robbed of their homes and possessions. These
things will continue for many days. 34When the
wise ones are suffering, they will get a little help,
but many who join the wise ones will not help
them in their time of need. 35Some of the wise
ones will be killed. But the hard times must come
so they can be made stronger and purer and without faults until the time of the end comes. Then,
at the right time, the end will come.

The King Who Praises Himself

36"The king of the North will do whatever he
wants. He will brag about himself and praise himself and think he is even better than a god. He
will say things against the God of gods that no one
has ever heard. And he will be successful until all
the bad things have happened. Then what God has
planned to happen will happen. 37The king of the
North will not care about the gods his ancestors
worshiped or the god that women worship. He
won't care about any god. Instead, he will make
himself more important than any god. 38The king of
the North will worship power and strength,
which his ancestors did not worship. He will
honor the god of power with gold and silver,
expensive jewels and gifts. 39That king will attack
strong, walled cities with the help of a foreign
god. He will give much honor to the people who
join him, making them rulers in charge of many

other people. And he will make them pay him for the land they rule.

40“At the time of the end, the king of the South will fight a battle against the king of the North. The king of the North will attack with chariots, soldiers on horses, and many large ships. He will invade many countries and sweep through their lands like a flood. 41The king of the North will attack the beautiful land of Judah. He will defeat many countries, but Edom, Moab, and the leaders of Ammon will be saved from him. 42The king of the North will show his power in many countries; Egypt will not escape. 43The king will get treasures of gold and silver and all the riches of Egypt. The Libyan and Nubian people will obey him. 44But the king of the North will hear news from the east and the north that will make him afraid and angry. He will go to destroy completely many nations. 45He will set up his royal tents between the sea and the beautiful mountain where the holy Temple is built. But, finally, his end will come, and no one will help him.

The Time of the End

12 At that time Michael, the great prince who protects your people, will stand up. There will be a time of much trouble, the worst time since nations have been on earth, but your people will be saved. Everyone whose name is written in God’s book will be saved. 2Many people who have already died will live again. Some of them will wake up to have life forever, but some will wake up to find shame and disgrace forever. 3The wise people will shine like the brightness of the sky. Those who teach others to live right will shine like stars forever and ever.

4“But you, Daniel, close up the book and seal it. These things will happen at the time of the end. Many people will go here and there to find true knowledge.”

5Then I, Daniel, looked, and saw two other men. One was standing on my side of the river, and the other was standing on the far side. 6The man who was dressed in linen was standing over the water in the river. One of the two men spoke to him and asked, “How long will it be before these amazing things come true?”

7The man dressed in linen, who stood over the water, raised his hands toward heaven. And I heard him swear by the name of God who lives forever, “It will be for three and one-half years. The power of the holy people will finally be broken, and then all these things will come true.”

8I heard the answer, but I did not really understand, so I asked, “Master, what will happen after all these things come true?”

9He answered, “Go your way, Daniel. The message is closed up and sealed until the time of the end. 10Many people will be made clean, pure, and spotless, but the wicked will continue to be wicked. Those wicked people will not understand these things, but the wise will understand them.

11“The daily sacrifice will be stopped. Then, after 1,290 days from that time, the destroying terror will be set up. 12Those who wait for the end of the 1,335 days will be happy.

13“As for you, Daniel, go your way until the end. You will get your rest, and at the end you will rise to receive your reward.”

12:13 Numbers: Jonah 1:17

12:13 Daniel: See article on page 642.

INTRODUCTION TO THE BOOK OF

HOSEA

Israel Acts Like an Unfaithful Wife

WHO WROTE THIS BOOK?

This book was written by Hosea the prophet, who was the son of Beeri (1:1).

TO WHOM WAS THIS BOOK WRITTEN?

Hosea is the only one of the writing prophets to come from Israel's northern kingdom. These are the people to whom he wrote and prophesied.

WHERE WAS IT WRITTEN?

The Book of Hosea was probably written in Judah. This assumption is based on Hosea's comments about Judah in the book (1:7, 11; 4:15; 10:11). He also dated his ministry by Judah's kings.

WHEN WAS IT WRITTEN?

Hosea lived and prophesied during the eighth century B.C., before the fall of the northern Kingdom to Assyria in 722 B.C.

WHAT IS THE BOOK ABOUT?

The prophetic tale of Hosea is a parallel between Hosea's marriage to an unfaithful wife and God's relationship to Israel, his unfaithful people, who tried to mix the worship of the Lord with the idolatry of the surrounding nations.

WHY WAS THIS BOOK WRITTEN?

Through Hosea, God shows his people that he wants to take them back, in spite of their unfaithfulness to him, just as Hosea took Gomer back after her disloyalty to him, if only his people would repent of their religious adultery.

SO WHAT DOES THIS BOOK MEAN TO US?

God is ever-faithful to us—the ones whom he so loves—even when we fail him, even when we worship other gods in our lives, even when we don't deserve it. He is our ever-present, ever-loving, ever-forgiving God, always waiting for us to repent and come back to him.

SUMMARY:

Hosea's first three chapters, about his unusual and troubled marriage are well known, but the next eleven chapters are difficult and rarely read. Careful reading, however, yields great insight into the nature of God and his relationship with us, his people.

The book, according to Hosea 1:1, was written by the prophet Hosea. The list of kings from the northern and southern kingdoms dates his ministry to the second half of the eighth century B.C., making him the earliest of the writing prophets. His dates also coincide with important events in the history of Israel: the war between Judah, on the one hand, and Syria and the northern kingdom on the other. This war drew the attention of Assyria to the region, resulting in the overthrow of the northern kingdom in 722 B.C. and a threat to the independence of Judah in 701 B.C.

The first three chapters, though, use the life of the prophet himself to illustrate the spiritual condition of the people of God. Hosea was married to Gomer, a promiscuous woman. His marriage reflected the bad relationship between God, the faithful husband, and Israel, the wandering wife.

The overall structure of Hosea is as follows:

I. Hosea, Gomer, and Their Children (1:1–3:5)
II. First Cycle of Judgment and Restoration (4:1–11:11)
III. Second Cycle of Judgment and Restoration (11:12–14:8)

I. Hosea, Gomer, and Their Children (1:1–3:5)
The first three chapters are the best known of the book. They each speak of God's relationship with his people in the light of Hosea's marriage to his unfaithful wife Gomer. Like Gomer, Israel has wandered away from her husband in search of other lovers.

II. First Cycle of Judgment and Restoration (4:1–11:11)
Hosea lived in the period during the time that God judged Israel for their sins. Most of this section is filled with speeches that warn and anticipate that judgment, but it ends with a moving promise that God loves his people and will restore them.

III. Second Cycle of Judgment and Restoration (11:12–14:8)
As in the first cycle, Hosea begins with more blistering judgment speeches, only to conclude with a moving acknowledgment that God will once again forgive and restore them.

HOSEA

The LORD spoke his word to Hosea son of
Beeri during the time that Uzziah, Jotham,
Ahaz, and Hezekiah were kings of Judah
and Jeroboam son of Jehoash was king of Israel.

Hosea's Wife and Children

2When the LORD began speaking through Hosea,
the LORD said to him, "Go, and marry an unfaithful woman and have unfaithful children, because
the people in this country have been completely
unfaithful to the LORD." 3So Hosea married
Gomer daughter of Diblaim, and she became pregnant and gave birth to Hosea's son.

4The LORD said to Hosea, "Name him Jezreel,
because soon I will punish the family of Jehu for
the people they killed at Jezreel. In the future I will
put an end to the kingdom of Israel 5and break
the power of Israel's army in the Valley of Jezreel."

6Gomer became pregnant again and gave birth
to a daughter. The LORD said to Hosea, "Name her
Lo-Ruhamah, because I will not pity Israel anymore, nor will I forgive them. 7But I will show pity
to the people of Judah. I will save them, but not
by using bows or swords, horses or horsemen, or
weapons of war. I, the LORD their God, will save
them."

8After Gomer had stopped nursing Lo-Ruhamah,
she became pregnant again and gave birth to
another son. 9The LORD said, "Name him Lo-
Ammi, because you are not my people, and I am
not your God.

God's Promise to Israel

10"But the number of the Israelites will become
like the grains of sand of the sea, which no one can
measure or count. They were called, 'You are not
my people,' but later they will be called 'children
of the living God.' 11The people of Judah and Israel
will join together again and will choose one leader
for themselves. They will come up from the land,
because the day of Jezreel will be truly great.

2 "You are to call your brothers, 'my people,' and
your sisters, 'you have been shown pity.'

God Speaks About Israel

2"Plead with your mother.
  Accuse her, because she is no longer my wife,
  and I am no longer her husband.
Tell her to stop acting like a prostitute,
  to stop behaving like an unfaithful wife.
3If she refuses, I will strip her naked
  and leave her bare like the day she was born.
I will make her dry like a desert,
  like a land without water,
  and I will kill her with thirst.
4I will not take pity on her children,
  because they are the children of a prostitute.
5Their mother has acted like a prostitute;
  the one who became pregnant with them
    has acted disgracefully.
She said, 'I will chase after my lovers,
  who give me my food and water,
wool and flax, wine and olive oil.'
6So I will block her road with thornbushes;
  I will build a wall around her
  so she cannot find her way.
7She will run after her lovers,
  but she won't catch them.
She will look for them,
  but she won't find them.
Then she will say, 'I will go back to my
    first husband,
  because life was better then for me than
    it is now.'
8But she does not know that I was the one
  who gave her grain, new wine, and oil.

1:2 *marry an unfaithful woman.* God orders Hosea to marry an unfaithful woman. Whether she was unfaithful before the marriage or simply had leanings in that direction is unimportant to the thought of the passage, which compares the marriage of Hosea and Gomer to the relationship between God and Israel.

1:2 Celibacy: Matthew 19:10–12

1:2 Communication: John 1:18

1:6 *Lo-Ruhamah.* This name in Hebrew means "not pitied."

1:7 Weapons: Zechariah 4:6

1:7 God's message to Judah through the prophet Hosea is that he is going to save that nation (unlike the northern kingdom of Israel). But he will not save Judah by using human armies or conventional weapons. God himself is the "secret weapon" of Judah. When Jerusalem was surrounded by the Assyrian army under Sennacherib, God himself started a rumor that caused the Assyrians to lift the siege and hurry home (2 Kings 19:7, 35–37).

The Christian, according to Paul in 2 Corinthians 10:4, does not use physical weapons like swords, spears, or shields. Rather the weapons God gives us are much more powerful. They are spiritual weapons that destroy the strongholds of God's enemies. Ephesians 6:10–19 describe these weapons as faith, the Word of God, truth, right living, peace, salvation, and never giving up.

1:9 *Lo-Ammi.* This name in Hebrew means "not my people."

1:10 *You are not my people.* Paul finds the significance of these verses in the inclusion of the non-Jews in the church (Romans 9:26).

1:11 Divorce: Matthew 5:31–32

1:11 Authority: Amos

1:11 *Jezreel.* This name in Hebrew means "God plants."

2:2 *mother.* Refers to the nation of Israel here.

2:5 *lovers.* Refers to the nations surrounding Israel, who led Israel to worship false gods.

2:7 *husband.* Refers to God here.

2:8 *Baal.* Baal was the god of the people of Canaan whom the people of Israel displaced in Palestine. Baal was the god of rain, dew, and fertility, all deeply prized in the ancient Near East. Baal worship was a powerful temptation for the people of Israel.

I gave her much silver and gold,
but she used it for Baal.

9"So I will come back and take away my grain
at harvest time
and my new wine when it is ready.
I will take back my wool and linen
that covered her nakedness.
10So I will show her nakedness to her lovers,
and no one will save her from me.
11I will put an end to all her celebrations:
her yearly festivals, her New Moon festivals,
and her Sabbaths.
I will stop all of her special feasts.
12I will destroy her vines and fig trees,
which she said were her pay from her lovers.
I will turn them into a forest,
and wild animals will eat them.
13I will punish her for all the times
she burned incense to the Baals.
She put on her rings and jewelry
and went chasing after her lovers,
but she forgot me!"
says the LORD.

14"So I am going to attract her;
I will lead her into the desert
and speak tenderly to her.
15There I will give her back her vineyards,
and I will make the Valley of Trouble a door
of hope.
There she will respond as when she was young,
as when she came out of Egypt."⚭

16The LORD says, "In the future she will call me
'my husband;'
no longer will she call me 'my baal.'
17I will never let her say the names of Baal again;
people won't use their names anymore.
18At that time I will make an agreement for them
with the wild animals, the birds, and the
crawling things.
I will smash from the land
the bow and the sword and the weapons of
war,
so my people will live in safety.
19And I will make you my promised bride forever.
I will be good and fair;
I will show you my love and mercy.
20I will be true to you as my promised bride,
and you will know the LORD.

21"At that time I will speak to you," says the LORD.
"I will speak to the skies,
and they will give rain to the earth.
22The earth will produce grain, new wine, and oil;
much will grow because my people are
called Jezreel.
23I will plant my people in the land,
and I will show pity to the one I had called
'not shown pity.'
I will say, 'You are my people'
to those I had called 'not my people.'
And they will say to me, 'You are our God.'"

Hosea Buys a Wife

3 The LORD said to me again, "Go, show your
love to a woman loved by someone else, who
has been unfaithful to you. In the same way the
LORD loves the people of Israel, even though they
worship other gods and love to eat the raisin
cakes."
2So I bought her for six ounces of silver and ten
bushels of barley. 3Then I told her, "You must wait
for me for many days. You must not be a prostitute,
and you must not have sexual relations with any
other man. I will act the same way toward you."
4In the same way Israel will live many days
without a king or leader, without sacrifices or holy
stone pillars, and without the holy vest or an idol.
5After this, the people of Israel will return to the
LORD their God and follow him and the king from
David's family. In the last days they will turn in fear
to the LORD, and he will bless them.⚭

The LORD's Word Against Israel

4 People of Israel, listen to the LORD's message.
The LORD has this
against you who live in the land:
"The people are not true, not loyal to God,
nor do those who live in the land even
know him.
2Cursing, lying, killing, stealing and adultery
are everywhere.
One murder follows another.
3Because of this the land dries up,
and all its people are dying.

⚭**2:15 Exodus/New Exodus:** Matthew 3:13–17
2:15 *Valley of Trouble.* The Valley of Trouble is the name of a valley near Jericho. It was named this after the battle of Jericho and the unsuccessful battle of Ai because a man named Achan stole some of the plunder for himself (Joshua 7), thus bringing trouble on Israel. Here, though, this valley is seen to be a door of hope. Restoration will follow judgment!
2:16 *baal.* Another Hebrew word for husband, but it was the same word as the false god Baal.
2:22 *Jezreel.* This name in Hebrew means "God plants."
3:1 *raisin cakes.* This food was eaten in the feasts that honored false gods.
3:1 Though it is somewhat unclear, the best understanding of this chapter is that God wants Hosea to pursue Gomer, who has been so unfaithful to him. Thus again, Hosea's marriage is an example of the gracious and forgiving love of God toward Israel.
⚭**3:5 Last Days:** Micah 4:1

ROME

JOHN 11:48

Why was Rome so important in the time of Christ? How is the life of Jesus intertwined with the Roman government? How did the Roman way of life assist Christians in the spread of the Good News?

We cannot underestimate the importance of the Roman empire as the context in which the earliest church developed and expanded. By military prowess Rome had secured a terrifying peace throughout the Mediterranean region, and had earned a reputation for swift and brutal response to any perceived threat to this "Roman Peace." The power and brutality of Rome is behind the comments in John 11:48–50 where the leaders fear that the controversy Jesus was stirring up would be understood by the Romans as a political uprising, and they would descend with their military machine and crush Israel: "If we let him continue doing these things, everyone will believe in him. Then the Romans will come and take away our Temple and our nation." This same fear is felt when they ask Pilate to change the sign above Jesus' cross so that it wouldn't suggest that the Jewish people thought he was their king instead of the Roman emperor (John 19:19–21). Their fears were not unfounded because it had happened before. The Roman fury was unleashed against a rebellious Palestine at the time of the Maccabees in the second century before Christ, and hatred toward Rome was felt in Jewish and Jewish Christian circles (see Revelation 18). Because of the predictability of Roman governors' savagery against rebellion, a political trap was set to catch Jesus publicly speaking against paying taxes and its implied tribute to Caesar, the Roman emperor (Matthew 22:15–21). Had he fallen for it, he most certainly would have been arrested far sooner than he was.

The rule of the empire is interwoven with all the important stories of the New Testament. Jesus was born in Bethlehem because of the Roman system of census for tax purposes (Luke 2:1). Ultimately, Jesus is excuted on a Roman cross, by Roman soldiers after a Roman trial, in a typical Roman fashion (John 19:1–24). Though people in Palestine spoke Aramaic, and people throughout the empire spoke Greek, Latin remained the Roman administrative language and so the sign over Jesus' Roman cross carried the message, "Jesus of Nazareth, the King of the Jews" in the three languages (John 19:19–20). It is Jesus' status as a potential rival ruler that causes Roman concern, and Rome's jealousy of her power is a prime reason Jesus suffered a civic death on the cross (Luke 23:2; Acts 17:7).

The gospel story is also intertwined with the customs, laws, and layout of the Roman empire. The apostle Paul is a case in point. In Palestine he was known by his Jewish name "Saul" (Acts 7:58; 9:1–31), but as he began his missionary work throughout the Roman empire he was recognized by his Roman name, Paul (from Acts 13:9 on), the name he affixed to all his letters. Likewise, instead of identifying regions by their native designations, he always called them by their Roman imperial names. He himself claimed the high status designation of being a Roman citizen, granted to those who were fortunate to be born in special cities like Tarsus (Acts 22:3). Paul claimed these legal rights as a Roman citizen and, when he was wrongly punished, he used his status as a means to fulfill his desire to go to Rome to preach the gospel (Acts 19:21; 22:24–29; 23:11; 25:82; 6:32; Romans 1:15; 15:22–24). Paul's missionary calling to Rome led him to opportunistically use the situation toward the Gospel's strategic advantage, that it might be proclaimed in the capital city of the terrible empire (Acts 27:24). Along the way, Paul wrote several of his letters from Roman prisons.

Though the domination of Rome was an unshakeable social fact of the early church, Roman rule provided both stability and mobility that assisted the early Christian missionaries in spreading the gospel and the church. The Roman military outposts created a network of roads and secure travel by land and sea that was previously unknown in the ancient world, and was not experienced again until the modern era. Likewise, Roman coinage allowed trade to prosper across vast distances. Thus the missionaries were enabled to span the whole Roman empire before its end in the fifth century. For these and many other positive contributions of the Roman empire we find more than one New Testament writer extolling the God-given role of the government in the world (Romans 13:1–7; 1 Peter 2:13–17). As citizens lived under Roman rule in distant colonies, so Christians conceived of their life as living in a "colony" on earth, knowing full well that their homeland was in heaven (Philippians 3:20–21).

Rome: For additional scriptures on this topic go to Acts 19:21.

Stubbornness

John 12:37–41

How are people stubborn toward God? What does God do about it?
What does this tell us about our relationship with God?

It is one thing not to believe in God; it is another to be so set in one's unbelief that one is not even open to anything that might change one's mind. The Bible holds out God's wish that all people will turn to him (2 Peter 3:9), but it recognizes that some—the "stubborn"—never will.

Many individuals and peoples in the Bible are described as "stubborn," but three in particular stand out: (1) the king of Egypt during the Exodus; (2) the people of Israel throughout their history; and (3) the Pharisees of Jesus' day. Each, because of impenitence and hardened hearts, bitterly rejected the constant appeals from God to alter their paths.

The stubborn have always manifested the same characteristics throughout the ages. When engaged in evil, they persist in it, refusing to change. Isaiah tells of their rigidity: "Your neck was like an iron muscle and your head was like bronze" (Isaiah 48:4). Jeremiah condemns their unchangeability this way: "Can a leopard change his spots? In the same way, Jerusalem, you cannot change and do good, because you are accustomed to doing evil" (13:23). The Bible warns us against becoming "hardened" like the stubborn (Hebrews 3:8–15). The king of Egypt consistently refused to let the people of Israel go (Exodus 4:21). Even when he gave in because of the troubling plagues, he would change his mind and deny their freedom as soon the plague was lifted (Exodus 8:15, 32; 9:35; 10:20, 27). Ironically, the people of Israel, in a similar way, would routinely fall into evil once God gave them rest from their enemies (Judges 2:19). The Pharisees of Jesus' day were no different, stubbornly refusing at all costs to believe in Jesus (John 5:39–40), insisting that others disbelieve him, too (John 9:24).

The stubborn also routinely ignore the voice of God. "They tell seers, 'Don't see any more visions!' They say to the prophets, 'Don't tell us the truth! Say things that will make us feel good. . . . Stop telling us about God, the Holy One of Israel'" (Isaiah 30:10–11). They have a spiritual dullness to them: "They have eyes to see, but they do not see, and they have ears to hear, but they do not hear, because they are a people who refuse to obey" (Ezekiel 12:2; see Matthew 13:13–15). Not surprisingly, God's attempts to discipline and correct such people are fruitless (Proverbs 1:22–32; Jeremiah 17:23; Amos 4:6–11).

Amazingly, the stubborn continue in their unbelief even when confronted by displays of God's power. Miraculous signs can encourage the small in faith (Genesis 15:8–17; Judges 6:17–24), but they do nothing for the stubborn (Matthew 12:20–24). It is for this reason that Jesus refused to perform token miracles to satisfy their skepticism (Matthew 12:38; 16:4; see 27:42). The miracles of the Exodus apparently made no long-lasting impact on either the king of Egypt (Exodus 7:3; 10:1; 11:10) or the people of Israel (Nehemiah 9:16–17). The Pharisees saw the miracles that Jesus performed (John 10:25–26; 12:37), but were so committed to opposing him that they blasphemously attributed the Holy Spirit's power to Satan (Mark 3:30).

How does God respond to hardened unbelief? The Bible presents a multifaceted picture. Sometimes it emphasizes God's anger (Deuteronomy 9:7; Zechariah 7:12); sometimes his sadness and compassion (Nehemiah 9:17, 28; Romans 2:4). Interestingly, in Jesus, we see both (Matthew 12:39; Mark 3:5; Luke 13:34). Sometimes God simply allows the stubborn to take their own course (Romans 1:24; 11:32); at other times, he intervenes and renews stubborn hearts (Ezekiel 11:19; 36:26–27). Sometimes his punishment is for discipline and correction (Nehemiah 9:29–31; Proverbs 1:29–33); at other times, it is final (Psalm 95:10; 2 Kings 17:14–18; Jeremiah 19:15; Romans 2:5).

In short, God's response depends on what his purposes are. It is important to remember that, while humans are responsible and blameworthy for their own stubbornness, God is still in control of their hearts. He is able to use their unbelief for his own good purposes (Romans 9:18). God's control over human stubbornness means that we may trust that God can always bring good out of the impenitence of the stubborn. It also means we may take comfort that there is always hope, as we pray often, that God can change unyielding hearts.⚭

⚭**Stubbornness:** For additional scriptures on this topic go to Exodus 32:9–14.

Even the wild animals and the birds of the air
and the fish of the sea are dying.

God's Case Against the Priests

4"No one should accuse
or blame another person.
Don't blame the people, you priests,
when they quarrel with you.
5You will be ruined in the day,
and your prophets will be ruined with you
in the night.
I will also destroy your mother.
6My people will be destroyed,
because they have no knowledge.
You have refused to learn,
so I will refuse to let you be priests to me.
You have forgotten the teachings of your God,
so I will forget your children.
7The more priests there are,
the more they sin against me.
I will take away their honor
and give them shame.
8Since the priests live off the sin offerings of
the people,
they want the people to sin more and more.
9The priests are as wrong as the people,
and I will punish them both for what they
have done.
I will repay them for the wrong they have done.

10"They will eat
but not have enough;
they will have sexual relations with
the prostitutes,
but they will not have children,
because they have left the LORD
to give themselves to 11prostitution,
to old and new wine,
which take away their ability to understand.

God's Case Against the People

12"My people ask wooden idols for advice;
they ask those sticks of wood to advise them!
Like prostitutes, they have chased after
other gods
and have left their own God.
13They make sacrifices on the tops of
the mountains.
They burn offerings on the hills,
under oaks, poplars, and other trees,
because their shade is nice.
So your daughters become prostitutes,
and your daughters-in-law are guilty
of adultery.

14"But I will not punish your daughters
for becoming prostitutes,
nor your daughters-in-law
for their sins of adultery.
I will not punish them,
because the men have sexual relations with
prostitutes
and offer sacrifices with the temple prostitutes.
A foolish people will be ruined.

15"Israel, you act like a prostitute,
but do not be guilty toward the LORD.
Don't go to Gilgal
or go up to Beth Aven.
Don't make promises,
saying, 'As surely as the LORD lives . . .'
16The people of Israel are stubborn
like a stubborn young cow.
Now the LORD will feed them
like lambs in the open country.
17The Israelites have chosen to worship idols,
so leave them alone.
18When they finish their drinking,
they completely give themselves to being
prostitutes;
they love these disgraceful ways.
19They will be swept away as if by a whirlwind,
and their sacrifices will bring them only
shame.

God's Word Against the Leaders

5 "Listen, you priests.
Pay attention, people of Israel.
Listen, royal family,
because you will all be judged.
You have been like a trap at Mizpah
and like a net spread out at Mount Tabor.
2You have done many evil things,
so I will punish you all.
3I know all about the people of Israel;
what they have done is not hidden from me.
Now that Israel acts like a prostitute,
it has made itself unclean.

4:5 *mother.* Refers to the nation of Israel here.
4:12 *sticks of wood to advise them.* Ancient idols represented false gods, and these idols were richly decorated with gold and expensive fabrics. Underneath it all, though, they were mere wood.
4:12–14 The prophets often called Israel's worship of idols "adultery." The people who worshiped idols were unfaithful to God, with whom they had an agreement like a marriage agreement. Though God was entitled to divorce them for leaving him, he called them back to him (see Jeremiah 3:1–25). Hosea was willing to buy Gomer after she had been unfaithful to him. God, in Christ, bought his people after they were unfaithful to him. He affirms his love for his people of the agreement by accepting them and teaching them to love as he does.
4:15 *Gilgal . . . Beth Aven.* Cities in Israel where people worshiped false gods.

4“They will not give up their deeds
and return to their God.
They are determined to be unfaithful to me;
they do not know the LORD.
5Israel’s pride testifies against them.
The people of Israel will stumble because
of their sin,
and the people of Judah will stumble
with them.
6They will come to worship the LORD,
bringing their flocks and herds,
but they will not be able to find him,
because he has left them.
7They have not been true to the LORD;
they are children who do not belong to him.
So their false worship
will destroy them and their land.

8“Blow the horn in Gibeah
and the trumpet in Ramah.
Give the warning at Beth Aven,
and be first into battle,
people of Benjamin.
9Israel will be ruined
on the day of punishment.
To the tribes of Israel
I tell the truth.
10The leaders of Judah are like those
who steal other people’s land.
I will pour my punishment over them
like a flood of water.
11Israel is crushed by the punishment,
because it decided to follow idols.
12I am like a moth to Israel,
like a rot to the people of Judah.

13“When Israel saw its illness
and Judah saw its wounds,
Israel went to Assyria for help
and sent to the great king of Assyria.
But he cannot heal you
or cure your wounds.
14I will be like a lion to Israel,
like a young lion to Judah.
I will attack them
and tear them to pieces.
I will drag them off,
and no one will be able to save them.
15Then I will go back to my place
until they suffer for their guilt and turn
back to me.
In their trouble they will look for me.”

The People Are Not Faithful

6 “Come, let’s go back to the LORD.
He has hurt us, but he will heal us.
He has wounded us, but he will bandage
our wounds.
2In two days he will put new life in us;
on the third day he will raise us up
so that we may live in his presence 3and
know him.
Let’s try to learn about the LORD;
he will come to us as surely as
the dawn comes.
He will come to us like rain,
like the spring rain that waters the ground.”

4The LORD says, “Israel, what should I do with
you?
Judah, what should I do with you?
Your faithfulness is like a morning mist,
like the dew that goes away early in the day.
5I have warned you by my prophets
that I will kill you and destroy you.
My justice comes out like bright light.⚭
6I want faithful love
more than I want animal sacrifices.
I want people to know me
more than I want burnt offerings.
7But they have broken the agreement as
Adam did;
they have been unfaithful to me.⚭
8Gilead is a city of people who do evil;
their footprints are bloody.
9The priests are like robbers waiting to
attack people;
they murder people on the road
to Shechem
and do wicked things.
10I have seen horrible things in Israel.
Look at Israel’s prostitution;
Israel has become unclean.

11“Judah, I have set a harvest time for you
when I will make the lives of my people
good again.

5:10 *flood of water.* God will overwhelm them with chaos. Water often stands for disorder, confusion, and trouble. It is the opposite of creation’s order.

⚭**6:5 Repentance:** Jonah 3:1–10

6:7 Hosea addresses God’s people in Israel and Judah and tells them they have broken the agreement (or covenant) that they had with God. In this, he tells them, they are like Adam. What is particularly striking about this passage, which refers to the first sin commonly called the Fall, is that nowhere else is it described as the breach of an agreement. Indeed, it is from this passage that we learn that there was something comparable to a formal agreement between God and Adam at the time of Adam’s sin.

⚭**6:7 Agreement:** 1 Corinthians 11:25

6:9 *Shechem.* A city of safety where people could go for protection.

7 When I heal Israel,
Israel's sin will go away,
and so will Samaria's evil.

"They cheat a lot!
Thieves break into houses,
and robbers are in the streets.
2It never enters their minds
that I remember all their evil deeds.
The bad things they do are all around them;
they are right in front of me.

Israel's Evil Kings

3"They make the king happy with their
wickedness;
their rulers are glad with their lies.
4But all of them are traitors.
They are like an oven heated by a baker.
While he mixes the dough,
he does not need to stir up the fire.
5The kings get so drunk they get sick every day.
The rulers become crazy with wine;
they make agreements with those who do
not know the true God.
6They burn like an oven;
their hearts burn inside them.
All night long their anger is low,
but when morning comes, it becomes
a roaring fire.
7All these people are as hot as an oven;
they burn up their rulers.
All their kings fall,
and no one calls on me.

Israel and the Other Nations

8"Israel mixes with other nations;
he is like a pancake cooked only on one side.
9Foreign nations have eaten up his strength,
but he doesn't know it.
Israel is weak and feeble, like an old man,
but he doesn't know it.
10Israel's pride will cause their defeat;
they will not turn back to the LORD their God
or look to him for help in all this.
11Israel has become like a pigeon—
easy to fool and stupid.
First they call to Egypt for help.
Then they run to Assyria.
12When they go, I will catch them in a net,
I will bring them down like birds from the sky;
I will punish them countless times for
their evil.
13How terrible for them because they left me!
They will be destroyed, because they turned
against me.
I want to save them,
but they have spoken lies against me.
14They do not call to me from their hearts.
They just lie on their beds and cry.
They come together to ask for grain
and new wine,
but they really turn away from me.
15Though I trained them and gave them strength,
they have made evil plans against me.
16They did not turn to the Most High God.
They are like a loose bow that can't shoot.
Because their leaders brag about their strength,
they will be killed with swords,
and the people in Egypt
will laugh at them.

Israel Has Trusted Wrong Things

8 "Put the trumpet to your lips and give the
warning!
The enemy swoops down on the LORD's
people like an eagle.
The Israelites have broken my agreement
and have turned against my teachings.
2They cry out to me,
'Our God, we in Israel know you!'
3But Israel has rejected what is good,
so the enemy will chase them.
4They chose their own kings
without asking my permission.
They chose their own leaders,
people I did not know.
They made their silver and gold into idols,
and for all this they will be destroyed.
5I hate the calf-shaped idol of Israel!
I am very angry with the people.
How long will they remain unclean?
6The idol is something a craftsman made;
it is not God.
Israel's calf-shaped idol
will surely be smashed to pieces.

7"Israel's foolish plans are like planting the wind,
but they will harvest a storm.
Like a stalk with no head of grain,
it produces nothing.
Even if it produced something,
other nations would eat it.
8Israel is eaten up;
the people are mixed among the other nations
and have become useless to me.

8:5 *the calf-shaped idol.* Jeroboam I, the first ruler of the northern kingdom, introduced the worship of a calf idol (1 Kings 12:26–33). While this idol may have represented God, it was an illegitimate form of worship that had similarities to the worship of Baal.

[9]Israel is like a wild donkey all by itself.
They have run to Assyria;
They have hired other nations to protect them.
[10]Although Israel is mixed among the nations,
I will gather them together.
They will become weaker and weaker
as they suffer under the great king of Assyria.

[11]"Although Israel built more altars to remove sin,
they have become altars for sinning.
[12]I have written many teachings for them,
but they think the teachings are strange
and foreign.
[13]The Israelites offer sacrifices to me as gifts
and eat the meat,
but the LORD is not pleased with them.
He remembers the evil they have done,
and he will punish them for their sins.
They will be slaves again as they were
in Egypt.
[14]Israel has forgotten their Maker and has
built palaces;
Judah has built many strong, walled cities.
But I will send fire on their cities
and destroy their strong buildings."

Israel's Punishment

9 Israel, do not rejoice;
don't shout for joy as the other nations do.
You have been like a prostitute against
your God.
You love the pay of prostitutes on every
threshing floor.
[2]But the threshing floor and the winepress will
not feed the people,
and there won't be enough new wine.
[3]The people will not stay in the LORD's land.
Israel will return to being captives as they
were in Egypt,
and in Assyria they will eat food that they are
not allowed to eat.
[4]The Israelites will not give offerings of wine to
the LORD;
they will not give him sacrifices.
Their sacrifices will be like food that is eaten at
a funeral;
it is unclean, and everyone who eats it
becomes unclean.
Their food will only satisfy their hunger;
they cannot sacrifice it in the Temple.
[5]What will you do then on the day of feasts
and on the day of the LORD's festival?
[6]Even if the people are not destroyed,
Egypt will capture them;
Memphis will bury them.
Weeds will grow over their silver treasures,
and thorns will drive them out of their tents.
[7]The time of punishment has come,
the time to pay for sins.
Let Israel know this:
You think the prophet is a fool,
and you say the spiritual person is crazy.
You have sinned very much,
and your hatred is great.
[8]Is Israel a watchman?
Are God's people prophets?
Everywhere Israel goes, traps are set for him.
He is an enemy in God's house.
[9]The people of Israel have gone deep into sin
as the people of Gibeah did.
The Lord will remember the evil things they
have done,
and he will punish their sins.

[10]"When I found Israel,
it was like finding grapes in the desert.
Your ancestors were like
finding the first figs on the fig tree.
But when they came to Baal Peor,
they began worshiping an idol,
and they became as hateful as the thing
they worshiped.⚭
[11]Israel's glory will fly away like a bird;
there will be no more pregnancy, no more
births, no more getting pregnant.
[12]But even if the Israelites bring up children,
I will take them all away.
How terrible it will be for them
when I go away from them!
[13]I have seen Israel, like Tyre,
given a pleasant place.
But the people of Israel will soon bring out
their children to be killed."
[14]LORD, give them what they should have.
What will you give them?
Make their women unable to have children;
give them dried-up breasts that cannot feed
their babies.

[15]"The Israelites were very wicked in Gilgal,
so I have hated them there.

9:3 Leviticus 11 describes which foods were considered clean *(kosher)* and which foods were unclean. Hosea envisions a time when they will be forced to eat foods that are repulsive to them.
9:6 *Memphis.* A city in Egypt famous for its tombs.
9:9 *Gibeah.* The sins of the people of Gibeah caused a civil war. See Judges 19-21.
⚭**9:10 Wilderness (Desert):** Hosea 13:5–6
9:10 *Baal Peor.* Hosea picks out the incident at Baal Peor (Numbers 25:3) as an example of Israel's tendency to worship idols. This was an early episode occurring fairly soon after the crossing of the Red Sea.

Because of the sinful things they have done,
I will force them to leave my land.
I will no longer love them;
their leaders have turned against me.
16Israel is beaten down;
its root is dying, and it has no fruit.
If they have more children,
I will kill the children they love."

17God will reject them,
because they have not obeyed him;
they will wander among the nations.

Israel Will Pay for Sin

10 Israel is like a large vine
that produced plenty of fruit.
As the people became richer,
they built more altars for idols.
As their land became better,
they put up better stone pillars to honor gods.
2Their heart was false,
and now they must pay for their guilt.
The LORD will break down their altars;
he will destroy their holy stone pillars.

3Then they will say, "We have no king,
because we didn't honor the LORD.
As for the king,
he couldn't do anything for us."
4They make many false promises
and agreements which they don't keep.
So people sue each other in court;
they are like poisonous weeds growing in a plowed field.
5The people from Israel are worried about
the calf-shaped idol at Beth Aven.
The people will cry about it,
and the priests will cry about it.
They used to shout for joy about its glory,
6but it will be carried off to Assyria
as a gift to the great king.
Israel will be disgraced,
and the people will be ashamed for not obeying.
7Israel will be destroyed;
its king will be like a chip of wood floating on the water.
8The places of false worship will be destroyed,
the places where Israel sins.
Thorns and weeds will grow up
and cover their altars.
Then they will say to the mountains,
"Cover us!"
and to the hills, "Fall on us!"

9"Israel, you have sinned since the time of Gibeah,
and the people there have continued sinning.
But war will surely overwhelm them in Gibeah,
because of the evil they have done there.
10When I am ready,
I will come to punish them.
Nations will come together against them,
and they will be punished for their double sins.
11Israel is like a well-trained young cow
that likes to thresh grain.
I will put a yoke on her neck
and make her work hard in the field.
Israel will plow,
and Judah will break up the ground.
12I said, 'Plant goodness,
harvest the fruit of loyalty,
plow the new ground of knowledge.
Look for the LORD until he comes
and pours goodness on you like water.'
13But you have plowed evil
and harvested trouble;
you have eaten the fruit of your lies.
Because you have trusted in your own power
and your many soldiers,
14your people will hear the noise of battle,
and all your strong, walled cities will be destroyed.
It will be like the time King Shalman
destroyed Beth Arbel in battle,
when mothers and their children were bashed to death.
15The same will happen to you, people of Bethel,
because you did so much evil.
When the sun comes up,
the king of Israel will die.

God's Love for Israel

11 "When Israel was a child, I loved him,
and I called my son out of Egypt.
2But when I called the people of Israel,
they went away from me.

10:9 *Gibeah.* The sins of the people of Gibeah caused a civil war. See Judges 19-21.

10:14 *King Shalman.* The destruction of Beth Arbel under the leadership of King Shalman is not known to us from other sources either in the Bible or outside of it, but must have happened fairly close in time to the lifetime of Hosea.

11:1 *I called my son out of Egypt.* Hosea alludes to the Exodus, when God freed Israel from slavery in Egypt. Matthew 2:15 applies this verse to Jesus, the son of God, returning from Egypt after fleeing the decree of Herod. The connection is based on the fact that Jesus' life and ministry mirror the experience of Israel during the time of the Exodus, desert wandering, and conquest.

They offered sacrifices to the Baals
and burned incense to the idols.
3It was I who taught Israel to walk,
and I took them by the arms,
but they did not understand
that I had healed them.
4I led them with cords of human kindness,
with ropes of love.
I lifted the yoke from their neck
and bent down and fed them.

5"The Israelites will become captives again,
as they were in Egypt,
and Assyria will become their king,
because they refuse to turn back to God.
6War will sweep through their cities
and will destroy them
and kill them because of their wicked plans.
7My people have made up their minds
to turn away from me.
The prophets call them to turn to me,
but none of them honors me at all.

8"Israel, how can I give you up?
How can I give you away, Israel?
I don't want to make you like Admah
or treat you like Zeboiim.
My heart beats for you,
and my love for you stirs up my pity.
9I won't punish you in my anger,
and I won't destroy Israel again.
I am God and not a human;
I am the Holy One, and I am among you.
I will not come against you in anger.
10They will go after the LORD,
and he will roar like a lion.
When he roars,
his children will hurry to him from the west.
11They will come swiftly
like birds from Egypt
and like doves from Assyria.
I will settle them again in their homes,"
says the LORD.

The LORD Is Against Israel

12Israel has surrounded me with lies;
the people have made evil plans.
And Judah turns against God,
the faithful Holy One.

12 What Israel does is as useless as chasing
the wind;
he chases the east wind all day.
They tell more and more lies
and do more and more violence.
They make agreements with Assyria,
and they send a gift of olive oil to Egypt.
2The LORD also has some things against Judah.
He will punish Israel for what they have done;
he will give them what they deserve.
3Their ancestor Jacob held on to his brother's heel
while the two of them were being born.
When he grew to be a man,
he wrestled with God.
4When Jacob wrestled with the angel and won,
he cried and asked for his blessing.
Later, God met with him at Bethel
and spoke with him there.
5It was the LORD God All-Powerful;
the LORD is his great name.
6You must return to your God;
love him, do what is just,
and always trust in him as your God.

7The merchants use dishonest scales;
they like to cheat people.
8Israel said, "I am rich! I am someone
with power!"
All their money will do them no good
because of the sins they have done.

9"But I am the LORD your God,
who brought you out of Egypt.
I will make you live in tents again
as you used to do on worship days.
10I spoke to the prophets
and gave them many visions;
through them, I taught my lessons to you."

11The people of Gilead are evil,
worth nothing.
Though people sacrifice bulls at Gilgal,
their altars will become like piles of stone
in a plowed field.
12Your ancestor Jacob fled to Northwest
Mesopotamia
where he worked to get a wife;
he tended sheep to pay for her.
13Later the LORD used a prophet
to bring Jacob's descendants out of Egypt;
he used a prophet
to take care of the Israelites.
14But the Israelites made the Lord angry when
they killed other people,
and they deserve to die for their crimes.

11:4 Images of God: Matthew 18:23–27

11:8 *Admah and Zeboiim.* Admah and Zeboiim are two cities which were also destroyed at the time that Sodom and Gomorrah were wiped out by the Lord (see Deuteronomy 29:23).

12:6 Perseverance: Matthew 10:22

The Lord will make them pay
for the disgraceful things they have done.

The Final Word Against Israel

13 People used to fear the tribe of Ephraim;
they were important people in Israel.
But they sinned by worshiping Baal,
so they must die.
2But they still keep on sinning more and more.
They make idols of their silver,
idols that are cleverly made,
the work of a craftsman.
Yet the people of Israel say to each other,
"Kiss those calf idols and sacrifice to them."
3So those people will be like the morning mist;
they will disappear like the morning dew.
They will be like chaff blown from the
threshing floor,
like smoke going out a window.

4"I, the LORD, have been your God
since you were in the land of Egypt.
You should have known no other
God except me.
I am the only one who saves.
5I cared for them in the desert
where it was hot and dry.
6I gave them food, and they became full
and satisfied.
But then they became too proud and
forgot me.
7That is why I will be like a lion to them,
like a leopard waiting by the road.
8I will attack like a bear robbed of her cubs,
ripping their bodies open.
I will devour them like a lion
and tear them apart like a wild animal.

9"Israel, I will destroy you.
Who will be your helper then?
10What good is your king?
Can he save you in any of your towns?
What good are your leaders?
You said, 'Give us a king and leaders.'
11So I gave you a king, but only in anger,
and I took him away in my great anger.
12The sins of Israel are on record,
stored away, waiting for punishment.
13The pain of birth will come for him,
but he is like a foolish baby
who won't come out of its mother's womb.
14Will I save them from the place of the dead?
Will I rescue them from death?
Where is your sickness, death?
Where is your pain, place of death?
I will show them no mercy.
15Israel is doing well among the nations,
but the LORD will send a wind from the east,
coming from the desert,
that will dry up his springs and wells of water.
He will destroy from their treasure houses
everything of value.
16The nation of Israel will be ruined,
because it fought against God.
The people of Israel will die in war;
their children will be torn to pieces,
and their pregnant women will
be ripped open."

Israel Returns to God

14 Israel, return to the LORD your God,
because your sins have made you fall.
2Come back to the LORD
and say these words to him:
"Take away all our sin
and kindly receive us,
and we will keep the promises we
made to you.
3Assyria cannot save us,
nor will we trust in our horses.
We will not say again, 'Our gods,'
to the things our hands have made.
You show mercy to orphans."

4The LORD says,
"I will forgive them for leaving me
and will love them freely,
because I am not angry with them anymore.
5I will be like the dew to Israel,
and they will blossom like a lily.
Like the cedar trees in Lebanon,
their roots will be firm.
6They will be like spreading branches,
like the beautiful olive trees
and the sweet-smelling cedars in Lebanon.
7The people of Israel will again live under
my protection.
They will grow like the grain,
they will bloom like a vine,
and they will be as famous as the wine
of Lebanon.
8Israel, have nothing to do with idols.
I, the LORD, am the one who answers your
prayers and watches over you.

13:5 *in the desert.* The reference to the desert indicates the time that God took care of them during the forty years of wandering in the desert after the Exodus from Egypt.

13:6 Wilderness (Desert): Matthew 4:1–11

14:4 Guilt: Matthew 5:23–26

14:8 *green pine tree.* God is the fertile tree that provides protection and provision for his people.

I am like a green pine tree;
your blessings come from me."

9A wise person will know these things,
and an understanding person
will take them to heart.
The LORD's ways are right.
Good people live by following them,
but those who turn against God die
because of them.

SERVICE

JOHN 13

What is service? What models of good service can one find in the Bible? Are only some persons called "to serve"?

When Jesus took the towel and basin and washed the feet of the disciples in John 13, he made a dramatic statement about his own ministry. Washing the feet of one's guest was a polite and necessary courtesy in days when streets were dusty and public sewers ran outdoors. The task was reserved for the servants or slaves of household, or, in a poor house, the youngest child strong enough to do the task. If there were no servants or children, then the person in the group with the lowest status would perform the task. In Luke 22:27 Jesus asks the disciples, "Who is more important: the one sitting at the table or the one serving?" The answer to the question is self-evident: people with power are served. The servant symbolizes lack of power.

Yet in John 13 Jesus deliberately takes up the role of the servant, and then in John 13:14 applies this directly to the disciples: "If I, your Lord and Teacher, have washed your feet, you also should wash each other's feet." Jesus' act of washing the disciples' feet anticipates his sacrifice on the cross. The very heart of Jesus' mission was to come and serve by giving his life for others. And, in turn, Christians are expected to serve one another as well as any person in need.

We find this stress on service throughout the Gospels and the ministry of Jesus. In Mark 10:35–45 (and Matthew 20:20–28), James and John come seeking the promise of positions of power and authority once Jesus establishes the kingdom. Jesus tells them that the means to power and authority in the new kingdom will be quite different: "Whoever wants to be great among you must serve the rest like a servant. Whoever wants to become the first among you must serve all of you like a slave" (Mark 10:43–44). The reason for this strange reversal lies in the mission of Jesus himself! "In the same way, the Son of Man did not come to be served. He came to serve others and to give his life a ransom for many people" (Mark 10:45).

Paul also draws from the sacrifice of Jesus to encourage Christians to serve and help one another. Paul points out that Jesus left his position of heavenly glory to be "born like a man and became like a servant." Therefore Christians are urged to love each other and set aside their selfishness (Philippians 2:2–8).

Service implies humility in the servant. Jesus put on the clothes of the servant and knelt at the feet of the disciples. Likewise followers of Christ are exhorted to set aside their pride. Jesus tells the disciples, "Whoever makes himself great will be made humble. Whoever makes himself humble will be made great" (Matthew 23:12).

The first step to humility and service lies in recognizing that we need Christ to serve us. When Peter refuses to let Jesus wash his feet, the Lord rebukes Peter, "If I don't wash your feet, you are not one of my people" (John 13:8). After we have been served by the Master, no room is left for false pride. The Christian has not earned God's good gifts, but received them through Christ. Therefore, we can take no pride in what we give to others. We merely pass along what Christ has done for us.

Service also implies obedience. Jesus tells the disciples after washing their feet, "I did this as an example so that you should do as I have done for you" (John 13:15). Jesus urges the disciples in Luke 12:36–37, "Be like servants who are waiting for their master to come home from a wedding party. . . . They will be blessed when their master comes home, because he sees that they were watching for him. I tell you the truth, the master will dress himself to serve . . . and he will serve them."

What service does Jesus require? Certainly, Jesus expects the disciples to follow the law of love (John 13:34; Mark 12:30–31). Jesus further expects the disciples to be faithful witnesses to him after his death and resurrection. The parables of the servants who faithfully work while the master is away (Matthew 25:14–20; Luke 19:11–27) make this point emphatically. Beyond that, Jesus urges the disciples to care for the poor and needy (Matthew 25:31–46) and to do whatever good they can for others.

In the rest of the New Testament we find similar calls to serve. Paul urges the Philippians to continue in their obedience to God (Philippians 2:12). Peter urges believers to love and serve each other as Christ loved and served them (1 Peter 4:7–11). James sums up Christian service in this way: "Religion that God accepts as pure and without fault is this: caring for orphans or widows who need help" (James 1:27). In almost all these cases, the pattern for Christian service can be found in Christ's service for us. True power and greatness comes through giving of yourself to others in honor of Christ.

Service: For additional scriptures on this topic go to Matthew 20:20–28.

Beloved Disciple

John 13:23

Why does the Book of John speak of "the follower Jesus loved"—that is, the "beloved disciple"? Do we know who this follower of Jesus was?

The Book of John is the only New Testament book that mentions "the beloved disciple." It does so five times, but without ever identifying this follower of Jesus by name. This has led to centuries of curiosity.

For example, in light of John 11, many have thought that the beloved disciple was Lazarus, whom Jesus raised from the dead. This is because Lazarus is consistently described as one whom Jesus loves (John 11:3, 36), and he is the only one in the Book of John who is described in this way. Some have identified the beloved disciple with other followers of Jesus in the New Testament—John Mark or the apostle John, for example. Still others do not think the beloved disciple can be identified by name at all, but believe this follower of Jesus was an otherwise unknown disciple of Jesus in Jerusalem or perhaps even an unnamed woman follower of Jesus. In fact, if one is simply reading the Book of John, it is not even clear whether the beloved disciple is among the band of the twelve apostles who followed Jesus.

Another approach to the question of "the follower Jesus loved" is not only more fruitful, but also more important for Christians today. This is to ask, irrespective of *who* this disciple was, *What does the beloved disciple teach us about the nature of following Jesus?* First, even the name by which this disciple is known to us teaches us that the beloved disciple is *a close friend of Jesus*. Just as Jesus is "very close" to God (John 1:18), so this follower is close to Jesus (John 13:23–25).

This means, secondly, that he is portrayed as one through whom Jesus speaks to the other disciples. That is, just as Jesus reveals the Father, so the beloved disciple is one who reveals Jesus to others. At the last supper, Peter asks the beloved disciple for information from Jesus (John 13:23–25), and this prepares for the role of the beloved disciple following Jesus' death. In the early Christian church, he is seen as one who reveals who Jesus is to those who did not know Jesus during his earthly ministry. His role is to tell the story of Jesus so that new generations of people might come to believe in Jesus (see John 21:24–25). He apparently serves the early church as a teacher, as one who reminds other followers of Jesus about his ministry and its significance.

In a surprising way, the role of the beloved disciple is like that of the Holy Spirit who will teach people about Jesus (see John 16:4–15). It is not surprising, then, that the beloved disciple is presented by the Book of John as a *trustworthy witness*. He (and, it would seem, he alone) is present at the key events in the latter half of the book: the supper where Jesus washed the feet of his followers; the trial; the crucifixion; the examination of the empty tomb; and the appearances of Jesus to his followers following his death. As a witness, he is able to provide for the early Christian community a reliable testimony concerning the importance of these events. The beloved disciple is also known as a *faithful follower of Jesus*, a model disciple of Jesus. In fact, the Book of John says that the beloved disciple had faith even before he saw the resurrected Jesus (20:8). His faith provides a model for those, including us, who would continue to be called to believe without having had the benefit of an actual appearance of the risen Lord (see John 20:29).

Perhaps, then, it is best that we do not know exactly who the beloved disciple is. If we knew that the name of this follower was John or Lazarus or Mary, we might think of this person as a good example of discipleship. Since we know this follower only as "the beloved disciple," though, we can hear the invitation of the Word to identify ourselves as this disciple, as one who can be a friend of Jesus and even be regarded as a member of Jesus' family. In this way, we can be challenged in important ways to read ourselves into the Book of John and to be encouraged to respond with faith like a beloved disciple.

Beloved Disciple: For additional scriptures on this topic go to John 13:23.

INTRODUCTION TO THE BOOK OF

JOEL

God Will Punish Judah

WHO WROTE THIS BOOK?

Joel, son of Pethuel and prophet of God, is announced as the author of this book in verse one.

TO WHOM WAS THIS BOOK WRITTEN?

Joel brings the Lord's word to the nation of Judah.

WHERE WAS IT WRITTEN?

Based on the many references to Judah and Jerusalem, it is likely that Joel lived and wrote in that area. See 2:32; 3:1, 6, 8, 16–20.

WHEN WAS IT WRITTEN?

The Book of Joel does not reveal the time of its writing. Some controversy exists about whether Joel was written in the ninth century or sixth century B.C. But its message is not affected seriously by its date.

WHAT IS THE BOOK ABOUT?

Joel warns the people of Judah about "the overwhelming and terrible day of the LORD"—the day of the Lord's coming judgment on Judah. He also prophesies God's judgment on Israel's enemies and his eventual blessing of his own people.

WHY WAS THIS BOOK WRITTEN?

The purpose of Joel's message is to bring Judah to repentance and, ultimately, restoration to God. It promises God's new agreement with his people which will be ushered in at Pentecost (2:28, see Acts 2:16–21).

SO WHAT DOES THIS BOOK MEAN TO US?

Through the words of Joel to Judah in the Bible, we can hear our God calling us to repentance, too. We must constantly seek his forgiveness and our restoration in preparation for "the overwhelming and terrible day of the LORD"—the day of God's judgment when time is over. We also hear his beautiful promise of the new agreement, which we now enjoy.

SUMMARY:

The prophet Joel brought a prophecy of judgment against the people of God, indeed the whole world. God is holy and in control of the whole world, so sinners will pay for their deeds. As with other prophets, Joel too was sent not only to preach judgment but also restoration of the relationship between God and his people.

The book names Joel, the son of Pethuel, as the author of the book (1:1). Unfortunately, he is not named anywhere else in the book. The first verse is unusual for a prophetic book in that it does not give a date. As a result, no one is quite sure about the date of the book. Everything from the ninth century to the second century B.C. has been suggested. The evidence available suggests late sixth, early fifth centuries B.C., but we must not be dogmatic about it.

Joel has the following outline:

I. The First Locust Plague (1:1–20)
II. The Warning of a Second Locust Plague (2:1–17)
III. The Response of the Lord (2:18–3:21)

I. The First Locust Plague (1:1–20)

The prophet describes a horrible locust plague that has completely devastated the land, saddening all the people of the land.

II. The Warning of a Second Locust Plague (2:1–17)

Joel looks to the future and sees another devastating attack coming. They are described as being like a locust swarm, and some believe that a second locust plague is anticipated here. But more likely Joel describes the onslaught of God's judgment in some other form.

III. The Response of the Lord (2:18–3:21)

As the prophet looks into the future, he sees judgment and salvation. The enemies of God will be destroyed while God's people will return and be blessed.

JOEL

Locusts Destroy the Crops

The LORD spoke his word to Joel son of Pethuel:

2Older leaders, listen to this message.
Listen to me, all you who live in the land.
Nothing like this has ever happened during
your lifetime
or during your ancestors' lifetimes.
3Tell your children about these things,
let your children tell their children,
and let your grandchildren tell their children.
4What the cutting locusts have left,
the swarming locusts have eaten;
what the swarming locusts have left,
the hopping locusts have eaten,
and what the hopping locusts have left,
the destroying locusts have eaten.

5Drunks, wake up and cry!
All you people who drink wine, cry!
Cry because your wine
has been taken away from your mouths.
6A powerful nation has come into my land
with too many soldiers to count.
It has teeth like a lion,
jaws like a female lion.
7It has made my grapevine a waste
and made my fig tree a stump.
It has stripped all the bark off my trees
and left the branches white.

8Cry as a young woman cries
when the man she was going
to marry has died.
9There will be no more grain or drink offerings
to offer in the Temple of the LORD.
Because of this, the priests,
the servants of the LORD, are sad.
10The fields are ruined;
the ground is dried up.
The grain is destroyed,
the new wine is dried up,
and the olive oil runs out.
11Be sad, farmers.
Cry loudly, you who grow grapes.
Cry for the wheat and the barley.
Cry because the harvest of the field is lost.
12The vines have become dry,
and the fig trees are dried up.
The pomegranate trees, the date palm trees,
the apple trees—
all the trees in the field have died.
And the happiness of the people has died, too.
13Priests, put on your rough cloth and cry
to show your sadness.
Servants of the altar, cry out loud.
Servants of my God,
keep your rough cloth on all night to
show your sadness.
Cry because there will be no more grain
or drink offerings
to offer in the Temple of your God.
14Call for a day when no one eats food!
Tell everyone to stop work!
Bring the older leaders
and everyone who lives in the land
to the Temple of the LORD your God,
and cry out to the LORD.
15What a terrible day it will be!
The LORD's day of judging is near,
when punishment will come
like a destroying attack from the Almighty.

16Our food is taken away
while we watch.
Joy and happiness are gone
from the Temple of our God.
17Though we planted fig seeds,
they lie dry and dead in the dirt.
The barns are empty and falling down.
The storerooms for grain have
been broken down,
because the grain has dried up.
18The animals are groaning!
The herds of cattle wander around confused,
because they have no grass to eat;
even the flocks of sheep suffer.
19LORD, I am calling to you for help,
because fire has burned up the open pastures,
and flames have burned all the trees
in the field.
20Wild animals also need your help.
The streams of water have dried up,
and fire has burned up the open pastures.

1:4 *cutting . . . locusts.* These are different names for an insect like a large grasshopper. The locust can quickly destroy trees, plants, and crops, and in this destruction Joel sees a warning. God will cause this type of destruction when he punishes his people. Due to satellite surveillance and control, such destructive locust plagues are rare these days. When they do occur, the devastation which results stretches the imagination.

1:14 The call goes out for a *fast*, not eating for the purpose of special prayer and appeal to God for help.

1:15 Day of the Lord: Joel 2:1

The Coming Day of Judgment

2 Blow the trumpet in Jerusalem;
shout a warning on my holy mountain.
Let all the people who live in the land
shake with fear,
because the LORD's day of judging is coming;
it is near.
2It will be a dark, gloomy day,
cloudy and black.
Like the light at sunrise,
a great and powerful army will spread over
the mountains.
There has never been anything like it before,
and there will never be anything like it again.

3In front of them a fire destroys;
in back of them a flame burns.
The land in front of them is like the
garden of Eden;
the land behind them is like an empty desert.
Nothing will escape from them.
4They look like horses,
and they run like war horses.
5It is like the noise of chariots
rumbling over the tops of the mountains,
like the noise of a roaring fire
burning dry stalks.
They are like a powerful army lined
up for battle.
6When they see them, nations shake with fear,
and everyone's face becomes pale.

7They charge like soldiers;
they climb over the wall like warriors.
They all march straight ahead
and do not move off their path.
8They do not run into each other,
because each walks in line.
They break through all efforts to stop them
and keep coming.
9They run into the city.
They run at the wall
and climb into the houses,
entering through windows like thieves.

10Before them, earth and sky shake.
The sun and the moon become dark,
and the stars stop shining.
11The LORD shouts out orders
to his army.
His army is very large!
Those who obey him are very strong!
The LORD's day of judging
is an overwhelming and terrible day.
No one can stand up against it!

Change Your Hearts

12The LORD says, "Even now, come back to me
with all your heart.
Go without food, and cry and be sad."

13Tearing your clothes is not enough
to show you are sad;
let your heart be broken.
Come back to the LORD your God,
because he is kind and shows mercy.
He doesn't become angry quickly,
and he has great love.
He can change his mind about
doing harm.
14Who knows? Maybe he will turn
back to you
and leave behind a blessing for you.
Grain and drink offerings belong to the
LORD your God.

15Blow the trumpet in Jerusalem;
call for a day when no one eats food.
Tell everyone to stop work.
16Bring the people together
and make the meeting holy for the LORD.
Bring together the older leaders,
as well as the children,
and even babies that still feed at
their mothers' breasts.
The bridegroom should come from his room,
the bride from her bedroom.
17The priests, the LORD's servants, should cry
between the altar and the entrance
to the Temple.
They should say, "LORD, have mercy
on your people.
Don't let them be put to shame;
don't let other nations make fun of them.
Don't let people in other nations ask,
'Where is their God?'"

2:1 Day of the Lord: Joel 3:14

2:1 *the LORD's day of judging.* The LORD's day is frequently mentioned by many prophets. It is a day in the future when God will come in judgment. He will save his people and destroy his enemies.

2:1–17 Traditionally read on Ash Wednesday in liturgical churches, this passage sets the spiritual tone and parameters of a true fast—both in individual and community practice—as a penitential act. The judgment of God is at hand (verses 1–11). Repentance is required, as evidenced by a changed heart, inward prayer and fasting, and true remorse (verse 12). External sackcloth and ashes are not enough. Your heart must be broken by the things that break God's heart—injustice, corruption, exploitation, immorality, human suffering . . . The Lord is ready to forgive and bless (vv. 13–14). Therefore, blow the trumpet, proclaim a fast day, take a holiday, bring people together for prayer and worship, and let the priests and elders intercede: "Lord have mercy . . . " (vv. 15–17).

The Lord Restores the Land

18Then the LORD became concerned
about his land
and felt sorry for his people.
19He said to them:
"I will send you grain, new wine,
and olive oil,
so that you will have plenty.
No more will I shame you
among the nations.
20I will force the army from the north to
leave your land
and go into a dry, empty land.
Their soldiers in front will be forced into
the Dead Sea,
and those in the rear into the
Mediterranean Sea.
Their bodies will rot and stink.
The LORD has surely done a wonderful thing!"

21Land, don't be afraid;
be happy and full of joy,
because the LORD has done a wonderful thing.
22Wild animals, don't be afraid,
because the open pastures have grown grass.
The trees have given fruit;
the fig trees and the grapevines have
grown much fruit.
23So be happy, people of Jerusalem;
be joyful in the LORD your God.
Because he does what is right,
he has brought you rain;
he has sent the fall rain
and the spring rain for you, as before.
24And the threshing floors will be full of grain;
the barrels will overflow with new wine
and olive oil.

The Lord Speaks

25"Though I sent my great army against you—
those swarming locusts and hopping locusts,
the destroying locusts and the cutting
locusts that ate your crops—
I will pay you back
for those years of trouble.
26Then you will have plenty to eat
and be full.
You will praise the name of the
LORD your God,
who has done miracles for you.
My people will never again be shamed.
27Then you will know that I am among the
people of Israel,
that I am the LORD your God,
and there is no other God.
My people will never be shamed again.

28"After this,
I will pour out my Spirit on all kinds
of people.
Your sons and daughters will prophesy,
your old men will dream dreams,
and your young men will see visions.⚭
29At that time I will pour out my Spirit
also on male slaves and female slaves.⚭
30I will show miracles
in the sky and on the earth:
blood, fire, and thick smoke.
31The sun will become dark,
the moon red as blood,
before the overwhelming and terrible day
of the LORD comes.
32Then anyone who calls on the LORD
will be saved,
because on Mount Zion and in Jerusalem
there will be people who will be saved,
just as the LORD has said.
Those left alive after the day of punishment
are the people whom the LORD called.

Punishment for Judah's Enemies

3 "In those days and at that time,
when I will make things better for
Judah and Jerusalem,
2I will gather all the nations together
and bring them down into the Valley
Where the LORD Judges.
There I will judge them,
because those nations scattered my
own people Israel
and forced them to live in other nations.
They divided up my land
3and threw lots for my people.
They traded boys for prostitutes,
and they sold girls to buy wine to drink.

4"Tyre and Sidon and all of you regions of
Philistia! What did you have against me? Were
you punishing me for something I did, or were
you doing something to hurt me? I will very
quickly do to you what you have done to me.
5You took my silver and gold, and you put my precious treasures in your temples. 6You sold the

2:25 *swarming . . . locusts.* These are different names for an insect like a large grasshopper. The locust can quickly destroy trees, plants, and crops, and in this destruction, Joel sees a warning. God will cause this type of destruction when he punishes his people.

⚭**2:28 Vision:** Acts 10:3

⚭**2:29 Spiritual Gifts:** Micah 3:8

people of Judah and Jerusalem to the Greeks so
that you could send them far from their land.
7"You sent my people to that faraway place, but
I will get them and bring them back, and I will do
to you what you have done to them. 8I will sell
your sons and daughters to the people of Judah,
and they will sell them to the Sabean people far
away." The LORD said this.

God Judges the Nations

9Announce this among the nations:
Prepare for war!
Wake up the soldiers!
Let all the men of war come
near and attack.
10Make swords from your plows,
and make spears from your hooks
for trimming trees.
Let even the weak person say,
"I am a soldier."
11All of you nations, hurry,
and come together in that place.
LORD, send your soldiers
to gather the nations.

12"Wake up, nations,
and come to attack in the Valley
Where the LORD Judges.
There I will sit to judge
all the nations on every side.
13Swing the cutting tool,
because the harvest is ripe.
Come, walk on them as you would walk
on grapes to get their juice,
because the winepress is full
and the barrels are spilling over,
because these people are so evil!"
14There are huge numbers of people
in the Valley of Decision,
because the LORD's day of judging is near
in the Valley of Decision.
15The sun and the moon will become dark,
and the stars will stop shining.
16The LORD will roar like a lion from Jerusalem;
his loud voice will thunder from that city,
and the sky and the earth will shake.
But the LORD will be a safe place for his people,
a strong place of safety for the
people of Israel.

17"Then you will know that I, the LORD your God,
live on my holy Mount Zion.
Jerusalem will be a holy place,
and strangers will never even go
through it again.

A New Life Promised for Judah

18"On that day wine will drip from the mountains,
milk will flow from the hills,
and water will run through all the
ravines of Judah.
A fountain will flow from the Temple
of the LORD
and give water to the valley of acacia trees.
19But Egypt will become empty,
and Edom an empty desert,
because they were cruel to the people of Judah.
They killed innocent people in that land.
20But there will always be people living in Judah,
and people will live in Jerusalem
from now on.
21Egypt and Edom killed my people,
so I will definitely punish them."

The LORD lives in Jerusalem!

3:8 *Sabean people.* The Sabean people were traders who controlled the trade routes up through the sixth century B.C. in what is today known as Saudi Arabia.
3:14 *Valley of Decision.* This is like the name Valley Where the LORD Judges in 3:2 and 3:12.

3:14 Day of the Lord: Zephaniah 1:7
3:17 *Mount Zion.* Mount Zion was the location of the Temple, which symbolized God's presence among his people.
3:18 These symbols of prosperity and fertility describe a future blessed by God.

INTERCESSION

JOHN 17

What is the role of intercessory prayer in faithful living before God?
What can we learn from the intercessory efforts of key biblical characters?
How can we practice faithful intercession today?

No greater privilege exists than the privilege of praying for another person. Through prayer we have the wonderful opportunity of entering into communion and conversation on another's behalf. Intercessory prayer is a sign of our love for others, a desire for their well-being, and our confidence that God cares for them even more than we do! In a world where millions of people experience immense suffering and face formidable foes, intercessory prayer is one of the great ministries of the believer and the church.

When we begin to practice this form of prayer, we immediately confront the question: Can we actually influence the situation of others by praying for them? This is an especially troubling question when we are praying for people in ways which seem to be contrary to their own desires at the moment. For example, can we intercede for people's salvation when they actively resist the possibility? Or to put it more generally, does intercessory prayer circumvent or override another's will? The Bible does not directly answer questions like this. Rather, it shows people praying for others under all sorts of circumstances. Moses even prayed for Pharaoh in Exodus 8:9–13, and no one in the Bible had a harder heart than he! And God lifted the plague in answer to Moses' prayer.

As with prayer in general, we are dealing with mystery when we engage in intercessory prayer. We must acknowledge that. We must also acknowledge that such mystery has not kept the main figures in the Bible from engaging in sustained intercession. Abraham is a key example as he prayed for the sparing of Sodom and Gomorrah in Genesis 18:17–33. Likewise, Moses prayed for Israel in Exodus 32:32; Numbers 14:17; and Deuteronomy 9:26. Later on, David prayed for Israel in 1 Chronicles 21:17. The prophets prayed frequently and fervently for the people, and the Psalms are filled with examples of intercessory prayer. In the Old Testament people prayed for military victory, for their children, for divine guidance, for deliverance, for health, and for mercy—to name a few.

The best New Testament examples come from Jesus and Paul. While on earth, Christ prayed for others to see the reality and glory of the Father (John 11:41–42; 12:28), for his disciples (John 17:1–19), for future believers (John 17:20–23), and for the forgiveness of others (Luke 23:46). After his ascension, we are told that Christ's continuing ministry is intercession (Romans 8:34; Hebrews 7:25). Likewise, the Holy Spirit prays for us (Romans 8:26–27). And who of us is not moved and instructed as we read the many prayers of Paul for others, especially at the beginning of his letters.

Taking the biblical message as a whole, the point is that we are invited, indeed commanded (1 Timothy 2:1–3), to pray to God on behalf of others, and that we are free to ask for anything which is not contrary to the will of God as we know it. Thus intercession grants us a wide and marvelous freedom of expression. And somehow it sets in motion unseen dynamics that are beneficial to those for whom we pray. So precious is the gift of intercession that as the aged prophet, Samuel, gave his farewell speech to Israel (1 Samuel 12:23), he said, "I will surely not stop praying for you, because that would be sinning against the Lord."

Recognizing the importance of intercessory prayer, we move on to see how we can practice it effectively today. The witness of biblical characters is that we should practice it regularly in our private devotional times. The intercessory prayers of Paul at the beginning of his letters are reflections of his heartfelt intercession for the churches in his care. Using the Psalms as a guide, we learn that the entire congregation may practice intercession; indeed, intercessory prayer can be a deeply meaningful part of a congregation's worship. In this way we fulfill Isaiah's prophecy that God's house is to be a house of prayer (Isaiah 56:7), a prophecy which Christ himself repeated in Matthew 21:13, Mark 11:17, and Luke 19:46.

During these times of intercession, we are free to pray our heart's desire for others. We are not telling God what to do or forcing God to do it. But we are at full liberty to express our deepest longings for others. There is also no need to hold back our requests or our emotions in intercession. If our intentions are honorable, we can be sure that the Spirit will overlook "mistakes" and will properly interpret our prayer before the heavenly Father. In intercessory prayer, our job is not to "get it right," but rather to "get it out." God will make sense of it all and weave it together with his divine will.

Intercession: For additional scriptures on this topic go to Genesis 15:1–6.

World/Worldly

John 17

What does the Bible mean by the term "world"?
Does this denote the world as necessarily "bad"?
What does it mean that Christians live in but not of the world?

The word *world* appears throughout the Old and the New Testaments and can have a variety of definitions, depending upon its use and context. Other terms such as *this age, cosmos, creation, the inhabited world,* and *earth* are also often used with slightly different meanings and purposes.

To begin with, one sense of "the world" in the Bible is neither negative or positive, referring simply to the earth upon which we live. For example, Jesus predicted that "the Good News about God's kingdom will be preached in all the world, to every nation" (Matthew 24:14). Here the world represents our physical world, which is host to so many peoples and nations.

However, throughout the Scriptures the general term *world* refers also to the present sinful way of living by people of every nation. Jesus speaks of people who hate those who follow him, because they "don't belong to the world, just as I don't belong to the world" (John 17:14, 16). And no person is immune to these negative influences of the world, which is why Jesus does not ask that his followers be taken out of the world, but kept "safe from the Evil One" (John 17:15). Even one of Paul's missionary companions, Demas, gave up following Jesus and left the apostle because he "loved this world" (2 Timothy 4:10).

That this world of human beings is now in rebellion against God is a major theme of the Bible. And so while worldliness is not a scriptural term, it is a scriptural concept. "Jesus gave himself for our sins to free us from this evil world we live in, as God the Father planned" (Galatians 1:4). The Gospel of John tells us that Jesus has "chosen" us from out of the world, and that by this divine choosing we no longer belong to it (John 15:18–19). Later in the New Testament the apostle John commands his hearers, "Do not love the world or the things in the world. If you love the world, the love of the Father is not in you" (1 John 2:15).

And so this meaning, which we see especially in the New Testament, understands this love of the world to be an attachment to those things that, from the viewpoint of Christ's kingdom, are passing and unreal and that finally lead us away from God (see 1 John 2:16, 17; Colossians 3). Jesus says this world is worth nothing if people lose their souls to gain it (Matthew 16:26). Adopting the values of the sinful social order is the meaning of worldliness in the negative sense of the term.

In marked contrast to this evil age, however, is the world God created and loves. In the beginning, God created the world, and after a review of everything he had made declared it "very good" (Genesis 1:31). In this sense of "world" it is proper for the Christian to love the world. "God loved the world so much that he gave his one and only Son . . . ." (John 3:16). The word used here is cosmos, which refers to the human race as part of the created order. This creation is presently messed up by sin and rebellion, but it can be saved. That is why Jesus in his coming to set up the kingdom of God declared his and our commitment to the world. "God did not send his Son into the world to judge the world guilty, but to save the world through him" (John 3:17). "God was in Christ, making peace between the world and himself. In Christ, God did not hold the world guilty of its sins. And he gave us this message of peace" (2 Corinthians 5:19).

God calls us to tell the people of the world about Jesus and to "go and make followers of all people in the world" (Matthew 28:19). Even Jesus' own prayer in John 17 clearly states that he is not asking the Father to take Christians from out of the world, "but to keep them safe from the Evil One" (John 17:15). Throughout the Scriptures there is a contrast between "this world" or "this age" and the "coming age" or "heaven." Christians have a clear calling to serve God wherever we are—and for all of us, that is the world (1 Corinthians 7:17–24). It is in this sense that we live in but not of the world. "Do not change yourselves to be like the people of this world, but be changed within by a new way of thinking" (Romans 12:2).

We are therefore free in Jesus Christ to live in and love the world God created as we serve the Lord. We are as light that has come, and while this light does not belong to the world, it comes to show the Father and his love (John 14:31; 17:21, 23–24). In this way we are called to bring the Gospel to everyone "in every part of the world."

World/Worldly: For additional scriptures on this topic go to Genesis 1:31.

INTRODUCTION TO THE BOOK OF

AMOS

God Warns Israel to Stop Sinning

WHO WROTE THIS BOOK?

God chose a shepherd of Tekoa named Amos to prophesy and write the message of this book (1:1).

TO WHOM WAS THIS BOOK WRITTEN?

Amos proclaimed God's judgment to the northern kingdom of Israel.

WHERE WAS IT WRITTEN?

Bethel was where Amos probably worked and wrote, since Bethel was a worship center of the northern kingdom.

WHEN WAS IT WRITTEN?

Verse one of the book clearly dates the writing between 793–740 B.C., during the reign of Uzziah (Judah) and Jeroboam II (Israel).

WHAT IS THE BOOK ABOUT?

Amos prophesied against Israel's idol worship and the injustice of rich people's oppressing the poor.

WHY WAS THIS BOOK WRITTEN?

The Book of Amos teaches Israel to show true godliness by bringing about social justice and fairness, and by turning from the sin of pagan worship.

SO WHAT DOES THIS BOOK MEAN TO US?

As in the days of prosperous Israel, we are constantly faced with social injustice and personal sin. As Christians it is our calling from God, through the echoing message of Amos down through the ages, to be agents of change. We are prompted by God to treat all people with fairness and equility, and to live godly, upright lives.

SUMMARY:

Amos describes himself as "one of the shepherds from the town of Tekoa" (1:1). Though God uses him as a prophet, he is not a career prophet, but rather a shepherd and one who takes care of sycamore trees (7:14).

His simple profession as a shepherd contrasts with the extravagant lifestyles of the wealthy classes of his day. He prophesies in the eighth century B.C., during a time of unprecedented prosperity in Israel. Much of his message is directed toward the oppression and social crimes of the people of God and the surrounding nations.

Amos brought a message of judgment against the worship of gods and social oppression. He also looked to the future with hope after the refining judgment took place.

An outline of Amos is as follows:

I. Judgment against the Nations (Amos 1–2)
II. Judgment against Israel (Amos 3–6)
III. Amos's Visions and Final Hope (Amos 7–9)

I. Judgment against the Nations (Amos 1–2)

Amos opens with a speech naming the crimes of the nations and announces their punishments. The list includes the nations that immediately surrounded Israel and plagued them in the past. At the end, however, Judah and then Israel are included. As a matter of fact, the longest speech is reserved for Israel at the end.

II. Judgment against Israel (Amos 3–6)

Amos now focuses on Israel. He recounts their sin and the punishment that awaits them.

III. Amos's Visions and Final Hope (Amos 7–9)

God gives Amos a series of visions. These visions anticipate judgment but also an end to the punishment. Finally, the prophet ends with a picture of a restored people of God.

AMOS

These are the words of Amos, one of the shepherds from the town of Tekoa. He saw this vision about Israel two years before the earthquake. It was at the time Uzziah was king of Judah and Jeroboam son of Jehoash was king of Israel.

2Amos said,
"The LORD will roar from Jerusalem;
he will send his voice from Jerusalem.
The pastures of the shepherds will become dry,
and even the top of Mount Carmel will dry up."

Israel's Neighbors Are Punished

The People of Aram

3This is what the LORD says:
"For the many crimes of Damascus,
I will punish them.
They drove over the people of Gilead
with threshing boards that had iron teeth.
4So I will send fire upon the house of Hazael
that will destroy the strong towers
of Ben-Hadad.
5I will break down the bar of the
gate to Damascus
and destroy the king who is in the
Valley of Aven,
as well as the leader of Beth Eden.
The people of Aram will be taken captive to
the country of Kir," says the LORD.

The People of Philistia

6This is what the LORD says:
"For the many crimes of Gaza,
I will punish them.
They sold all the people of one area
as slaves to Edom.
7So I will send a fire on the walls of Gaza
that will destroy the city's strong buildings.
8I will destroy the king of the city of Ashdod,
as well as the leader of Ashkelon.
Then I will turn against the people of the
city of Ekron,
and the last of the Philistines will die,"
says the Lord GOD.

The People of Phoenicia

9This is what the LORD says:
"For the many crimes of Tyre,
I will punish them.
They sold all the people of one area
as slaves to Edom,
and they forgot the agreement among relatives they had made with Israel.
10So I will send fire on the walls of Tyre
that will destroy the city's strong buildings."

The People of Edom

11This is what the LORD says:
"For the many crimes of Edom,
I will punish them.
They hunted down their relatives, the
Israelites, with the sword,
showing them no mercy.
They were angry all the time
and kept on being very angry.
12So I will send fire on the city of Teman
that will even destroy the strong
buildings of Bozrah."

The People of Ammon

13This is what the LORD says:
"For the many crimes of Ammon,
I will punish them.
They ripped open the pregnant
women in Gilead
so they could take over that land
and make their own country larger.
14So I will send fire on the city wall of Rabbah
that will destroy its strong buildings.
It will come during a day of battle,
during a stormy day with strong winds.
15Then their king and leaders will
be taken captive;
they will all be taken away together,"
says the LORD.

The People of Moab

2 This is what the LORD says:
"For the many crimes of Moab,
I will punish them.
They burned the bones of the king of
Edom into lime.
2So I will send fire on Moab
that will destroy the strong buildings
of the city of Kerioth.
The people of Moab will die in a great noise,
in the middle of the sounds of war
and trumpets.

1:1 *the earthquake.* This earthquake, also mentioned in Zechariah 14:5, must have been huge to stand out in an area where earthquakes are common.
1:12 *Teman . . . Bozrah.* Since Teman was in northern Edom and Bozrah was in southern Edom, this means the whole country will be destroyed.
1:15 Authority: Matthew 9:2–8

3So I will bring an end to the king of Moab,
and I will kill all its leaders with him,"
says the LORD.

The People of Judah

4This is what the LORD says:
"For the many crimes of Judah,
I will punish them.
They rejected the teachings of the LORD
and did not keep his commands;
they followed the same gods
as their ancestors had followed.
5So I will send fire on Judah,
and it will destroy the strong buildings
of Jerusalem."

Israel Is Punished

6This is what the LORD says:
"For the many crimes of Israel,
I will punish them.
For silver, they sell people who have done
nothing wrong;
they sell the poor to buy a pair of sandals.
7They walk on poor people as if they were dirt,
and they refuse to be fair to those
who are suffering.
Fathers and sons have sexual relations
with the same woman,
and so they ruin my holy name.
8As they worship at their altars,
they lie down on clothes taken from the poor.
They fine people,
and with that money they buy wine to drink
in the house of their god.

9"But it was I who destroyed the Amorites
before them,
who were tall like cedar trees and
as strong as oaks—
I destroyed them completely.
10It was I who brought you from the
land of Egypt
and led you for forty years through the desert
so I could give you the land of
the Amorites.
11I made some of your children to be prophets
and some of your young people to
be Nazirites.
People of Israel, isn't this true?" says the LORD.
12"But you made the Nazirites drink wine
and told the prophets not to prophesy.
13Now I will make you get stuck,
as a wagon loaded with grain gets stuck.
14No one will escape, not even the
fastest runner.
Strong people will not be strong enough;
warriors will not be able to save themselves.
15Soldiers with bows and arrows will not stand
and fight,
and even fast runners will not get away;
soldiers on horses will not escape alive.
16At that time even the bravest warriors
will run away without their armor,"
says the LORD.

Warning to Israel

3 Listen to this word that the LORD has spoken
against you, people of Israel, against the
whole family he brought out of Egypt.
2"I have chosen only you
out of all the families of the earth,
so I will punish you
for all your sins."

3Two people will not walk together
unless they have agreed to do so.
4A lion in the forest does not roar
unless it has caught an animal;
it does not growl in its den
when it has caught nothing.
5A bird will not fall into a trap
where there is no bait;
the trap will not spring shut
if there is nothing to catch.
6When a trumpet blows a warning in a city,
the people tremble.
When trouble comes to a city,
the LORD has caused it.
7Before the Lord GOD does anything,
he tells his plans to his servants the
prophets.
8The lion has roared!
Who wouldn't be afraid?
The Lord GOD has spoken.
Who will not prophesy?

9Announce this to the strong
buildings of Ashdod
and to the strong buildings of Egypt:
"Come to the mountains of Samaria,
where you will see great confusion
and people hurting others."

2:8 Debt/Loan: Matthew 6:12
2:8 Materialism/Possessions: Amos 4:1–3
2:11 *Nazirites.* Nazirites were people who devoted themselves in a special way to the service of the Lord. They are like lay priests (Numbers 6:1–21).
2:16 Community: Amos 3:2
3:2 Community: Micah 6:8

[10]"The people don't know how to do what is
right," says the LORD.
"Their strong buildings are filled with treasures they took by force from others."

[11]So this is what the Lord GOD says:
"An enemy will take over the land
and pull down your strongholds;
he will take the treasures out of your
strong buildings."
[12]This is what the LORD says:
"A shepherd might save from a lion's mouth
only two leg bones or a scrap of an
ear of his sheep.
In the same way only a few Israelites in
Samaria will be saved—
people who now sit on their beds
and on their couches."

[13]"Listen and be witnesses against the family of Jacob," says the Lord GOD, the God All-Powerful.

[14]"When I punish Israel for their sins,
I will also destroy the altars at Bethel.
The corners of the altar will be cut off,
and they will fall to the ground.
[15]I will tear down the winter house,
together with the summer house.
The houses decorated with ivory
will be destroyed,
and the great houses will come to an end,"
says the LORD.

Israel Will Not Return

4 Listen to this message, you cows of Bashan
on the Mountain of Samaria.
You take things from the poor
and crush people who are in need.
Then you command your husbands,
"Bring us something to drink!"
[2]The Lord GOD has promised this:
"Just as surely as I am a holy God,
the time will come
when you will be taken away by hooks,
and what is left of you with fishhooks.
[3]You will go straight out of the city
through holes in the walls,
and you will be thrown on the garbage
dump," says the LORD.

[4]"Come to the city of Bethel and sin;
come to Gilgal and sin even more.
Offer your sacrifices every morning,
and bring one-tenth of your crops
every three days.
[5]Offer bread made with yeast as a sacrifice
to show your thanks,
and brag about the special offerings you bring,
because this is what you love to do,
Israelites," says the Lord GOD.

[6]"I did not give you any food in your cities,
and there was not enough to eat in any
of your towns,
but you did not come back to me,"
says the LORD.
[7]"I held back the rain from you
three months before harvest time.
Then I let it rain on one city
but not on another.
Rain fell on one field,
but another field got none and dried up.
[8]People weak from thirst went from town to
town for water,
but they could not get enough to drink.
Still you did not come back to me,"
says the LORD.
[9]"I made your crops die from disease
and mildew.
When your gardens and your
vineyards got larger,
locusts ate your fig and olive trees.
But still you did not come back to me,"
says the LORD.
[10]"I sent disasters against you,
as I did to Egypt.
I killed your young men with swords,
and your horses were taken from you.
I made you smell the stink from all
the dead bodies,

3:14 *the altars at Bethel.* These altars refer to the sacrificial sites sinfully constructed by Jeroboam I as recorded in 1 Kings 12:26–33. The corners of the altar were four projections (called "horns" in the original language) to which the sacrificial animal was tied.

3:15 *houses decorated with ivory.* Apparently the kings of Amos's day had summer and winter houses, and these were decorated with ivory, all incredibly luxurious, even by royal standards.

3:15 Election (Chosen): Amos 9:7–10

4:1 *cows of Bashan.* Bashan was a very productive, fertile area to the east of the Jordan river. The insult "cows of Bashan" refers to the overindulgence of the rich, lazy women of Samaria, in terms of sex or food or perhaps both.

4:2 *taken away by hooks.* When taken prisoner and exiled, people had hooks put through their noses or ears and were led like animals.

4:3 Materialism/Possessions: Amos 5:10–15

4:6–12 Amos interprets a series of catastrophes as God's attempt to alert the people of Israel to their sin and as an expression of his desire for them to leave their evil ways and turn back to him. Israel's refusal to respond to God's discipline (see Hebrews 12:6), manifested in drought (verse 7), destruction (verse 9), and military defeat (verse 10), shows their stubbornness.

4:9 Famine: Psalm 37:19

but still you did not come back to me,"
says the LORD.
11"I destroyed some of you
as I destroyed Sodom and Gomorrah.
You were like a burning stick pulled from a fire,
but still you did not come back to me,"
says the LORD.

12"So this is what I will do to you, Israel;
because I will do this to you,
get ready to meet your God, Israel."

13He is the one who makes the mountains
and creates the wind
and makes his thoughts known to people.
He changes the dawn into darkness
and walks over the mountains of the earth.
His name is the LORD God All-Powerful.

Israel Needs to Repent

5 Listen to this funeral song that I sing
about you, people of Israel.
2"The young girl Israel has fallen,
and she will not rise up again.
She was left alone in her own land,
and there is no one to help her up."

3This is what the Lord GOD says:
"If a thousand soldiers leave a city,
only a hundred will return;
if a hundred soldiers leave a city,
only ten will return."

4This is what the LORD says to the nation of Israel:
"Come to me and live.
5 But do not look in Bethel
or go to Gilgal,
and do not go down to Beersheba.
The people of Gilgal will be taken
away as captives,
and Bethel will become nothing."
6Come to the LORD and live,
or he will move like fire against the
descendants of Joseph.
The fire will burn Bethel,
and there will be no one to put it out.
7You turn justice upside down,
and you throw on the ground what is right.

8God is the one who made the star groups
Pleiades and Orion;
he changes darkness into the morning light,
and the day into dark night.
He calls for the waters of the sea
to pour out on the earth.
The LORD is his name.
9He destroys the protected city;
he ruins the strong, walled city.

10You hate those who speak in court against evil,
and you can't stand those who tell the truth.
11You walk on poor people,
forcing them to give you grain.
You have built fancy houses of cut stone,
but you will not live in them.
You have planted beautiful vineyards,
but you will not drink the wine from them.
12I know your many crimes,
your terrible sins.
You hurt people who do right,
you take money to do wrong,
and you keep the poor from getting
justice in court.
13In such times the wise person will keep quiet,
because it is a bad time.

14Try to do good, not evil,
so that you will live,
and the LORD God All-Powerful will be with you
just as you say he is.
15Hate evil and love good;
be fair in the courts.
Maybe the LORD God All-Powerful will be kind
to the people of Joseph who are left alive.

16This is what the Lord, the LORD God All-Powerful, says:
"People will be crying in all the streets;
they will be saying, 'Oh, no!' in the public
places.
They will call the farmers to come and weep
and will pay people to cry out loud for them.
17People will be crying in all the vineyards,
because I will pass among you to punish
you," says the LORD.

The Lord's Day of Judging

18How terrible it will be for you who want
the LORD's day of judging to come.
Why do you want that day to come?
It will bring darkness for you, not light.

4:13 Repentance: Hosea 5:15–6:5
5:12 Crime: Luke 22:37
5:15 The Remnant: Micah 4:7
5:15 Materialism/Possessions: Matthew 6:19–34
5:18 The "Lord's day of judging" (and related terms) is a common term in the Bible that describes God's future punishment either of Israel's enemies, Israel herself, or of the whole world. In the New Testament, it refers specifically to Christ's return and the believers' eager expectation of that event. Amos 5:18 refers to the complacency with which some Israelites awaited the "Lord's day of judging," thinking that they were automatically exempt from God's punishment without needing to obey him.

[19]It will be like someone who runs from a lion
and meets a bear,
or like someone who goes into his house
and puts his hand on the wall,
and then is bitten by a snake.
[20]So the LORD's day of judging will bring
darkness, not light;
it will be very dark, not light at all.

[21]The LORD says, "I completely hate your feasts;
I cannot stand your religious meetings.
[22]If you offer me burnt offerings
and grain offerings,
I won't accept them.
You bring your best fellowship offerings
of fattened cattle,
but I will ignore them.
[23]Take the noise of your songs away from me!
I won't listen to the music of your harps.
[24]But let justice flow like a river,
and let goodness flow like a stream
that never stops.

[25]"People of Israel, you did not bring me
sacrifices and offerings
while you traveled in the desert
for forty years.
[26]You have carried with you
your king, the god Sakkuth,
and Kaiwan your idol,
and the star gods you have made.
[27]So I will send you away as captives
beyond Damascus,"
says the LORD, whose name is the
God All-Powerful.

Israel Will Be Destroyed

6 How terrible it will be for those who have
an easy life in Jerusalem,
for those who feel safe living on Mount
Samaria.
You think you are the important people of the
best nation in the world;
the Israelites come to you for help.
[2]Go look at the city of Calneh,
and from there go to the great
city Hamath;
then go down to Gath of the Philistines.
You are no better than these kingdoms.
Your land is no larger than theirs.
[3]You put off the day of punishment,
but you bring near the day when you can do
evil to others.
[4]You lie on beds decorated with ivory
and stretch out on your couches.
You eat tender lambs
and fattened calves.
[5]You make up songs on your harps,
and, like David, you compose songs
on musical instruments.
[6]You drink wine by the bowlful
and use the best perfumed lotions.
But you are not sad over the ruin of Israel,
[7]so you will be some of the first ones
taken as slaves.
Your feasting and lying around will
come to an end.

[8]The Lord GOD made this promise; the LORD
God All-Powerful says:
"I hate the pride of the Israelites,
and I hate their strong buildings,
so I will let the enemy take the city
and everything in it."
[9]At that time there might be only ten people left
alive in just one house, but they will also die.
[10]When the relatives come to get the bodies to take
them outside, one of them will call to the other and
ask, "Are there any other dead bodies with you?"
That person will answer, "No."
Then the one who asked will say, "Hush! We
must not say the name of the LORD."

[11]The LORD has given the command;
the large house will be broken into pieces,
and the small house into bits.
[12]Horses do not run on rocks,
and people do not plow rocks with oxen.
But you have changed fairness into poison;
you have changed what is right
into a bitter taste.
[13]You are happy that the town of
Lo Debar was captured,
and you say, "We have taken Karnaim
by our own strength."
[14]The LORD God All-Powerful says,
"Israel, I will bring a nation against you
that will make your people suffer from Lebo
Hamath in the north
to the valley south of the Dead Sea."

5:20 God's Anger: Luke 3:7
5:24 Justice: Micah 6:8
5:26 Astrology: Zephaniah 1:5
5:26 *Sakkuth, Kaiwan.* These are two Assyrian false gods. It was the practice of ancient Near Eastern people on certain occasions to carry the statues of their gods (idols) around.
5:27 End Times/Last Days: Mark 13:24–30
6:13 *Lo Debar . . . Karnaim.* These were two not especially significant cities that the Israelites had captured in war.

The Vision of Locusts

7 This is what the Lord GOD showed me: He was forming a swarm of locusts, after the king had taken his share of the first crop and the second crop had just begun growing. 2When the locusts ate all the crops in the country, I said, "Lord GOD, forgive us. How could Israel live through this? It is too small already!"

3So the LORD changed his mind about this. "It will not happen," said the LORD.

The Vision of Fire

4This is what the Lord GOD showed me: The Lord GOD was calling for fire to come down like rain. It burned up the deep water and was going to burn up the land. 5Then I cried out, "Lord GOD, stop! How could Israel live through this? It is too small already."

6So the LORD changed his mind about this too. "It will not happen," said the Lord GOD.

The Vision of the Plumb Line

7This is what he showed me: The Lord stood by a straight wall, with a plumb line in his hand. 8The LORD said to me, "Amos, what do you see?"

I said, "A plumb line."

Then the Lord said, "See, I will put a plumb line among my people Israel to show how crooked they are. I will not look the other way any longer.

9"The places where Isaac's descendants
worship will be destroyed,
Israel's holy places will be turned into ruins,
and I will attack King Jeroboam's family
with the sword."

Amaziah Speaks Against Amos

10Amaziah, a priest at Bethel, sent this message to Jeroboam king of Israel: "Amos is making evil plans against you with the people of Israel. He has been speaking so much that this land can't hold all his words. 11This is what Amos has said:

'Jeroboam will die by the sword,
and the people of Israel will be
taken as captives
out of their own country.'"

12Then Amaziah said to Amos, "Seer, go back right now to Judah. Do your prophesying and earn your living there, 13but don't prophesy anymore here at Bethel. This is the king's holy place, and it is the nation's temple."

14Then Amos answered Amaziah, "I do not make my living as a prophet, nor am I a member of a group of prophets. I make my living as a shepherd, and I take care of sycamore trees. 15But the LORD took me away from tending the flock and said to me, 'Go, prophesy to my people Israel.' 16So listen to the LORD's word. You tell me,

'Don't prophesy against Israel,
and stop prophesying against the
descendants of Isaac.'

17"Because you have said this, the LORD says:
'Your wife will become a prostitute in the city,
and your sons and daughters will be
killed with swords.
Other people will measure your land and
divide it among themselves,
and you will die in a foreign country.
The people of Israel will definitely be taken
from their own land as captives.'"

The Vision of Ripe Fruit

8 This is what the Lord GOD showed me: a basket of summer fruit. 2He said to me, "Amos, what do you see?"

I said, "A basket of summer fruit."

Then the LORD said to me, "An end has come for my people Israel, because I will not overlook their sins anymore.

3"On that day the palace songs will become funeral songs," says the Lord GOD. "There will be dead bodies thrown everywhere! Silence!"

4Listen to me, you who walk on helpless people,
you who are trying to destroy the poor
people of this country, saying,
5"When will the New Moon festival be over
so we can sell grain?
When will the Sabbath be over
so we can bring out wheat to sell?
We can charge them more
and give them less,
and we can change the scales to
cheat the people.
6We will buy poor people for silver,
and needy people for the price of
a pair of sandals.
We will even sell the wheat that was
swept up from the floor."

7The LORD has sworn by his name, the Pride of Jacob, "I will never forget everything that these people did.

7:7 *a plumb line.* A plumb line is an instrument used to measure the straightness of a wall. Here the plumb line uncovers the crookedness of the people, the object of measurement.

8:2 *end.* The Hebrew word for "end" sounds like the Hebrew word for "summer fruit."

8:3 Prophetic Symbolism: Zechariah 1:7–21

8:4 Money: Matthew 25:31–46

8:5 Sabbath: Mark 6:2

HOLY SPIRIT

ACTS 2:1–21

How can we think of the Holy Spirit as a Person rather than an impersonal force?
What does it mean to be baptized by the Spirit, to be filled by the Spirit?
Are the gifts of the Spirit for today?

On the day of Pentecost, the Holy Spirit appeared to the apostles like "flames of fire that were separated and stood over each person there" (Acts 2:3). The church age began as the apostles were "filled with the Holy Spirit" and "began to speak different languages by the power the Holy Spirit was giving them" (Acts 2:4). Then, and now, people are dramatically changed as the Spirit enters their lives. But who is the Holy Spirit, and is the same power that came upon the apostles at Pentecost available to us today? To begin with, the Bible teaches that the Holy Spirit is a person, the third person of the Trinity: He is God—co-equal, co-existent, co-eternal with the Father and the Son. He possesses all the attributes of deity. He regenerates the believing sinner. He baptizes us into the universal body of Christ. He indwells all who have been converted. He seals us, keeping every believer securely in the family of God. He fills us, taking control of our lives as we remove any impediments and yield to him.

For us as believers, the Holy Spirit is more than a theological construct. He is the One sent to us by the Father and the Son to be our Helper (John 14:15). The Greek root from which the English word "Helper" comes is a combination of two Greek terms, *para* (alongside) and *kaleo* (to call). He is the One whom our Lord "calls alongside" for the purpose of giving us assistance in our Christian lives. He is the flame whose presence within us gives us eternal life.

In 1 Corinthians 12:13, we are told that we have been "baptized" by the Spirit into the universal body of Christ, the church. Every child of God has been identified with and made a part of the body. Romans 8:9 says the same thing in different words. If you are a Christian, you have the Spirit living within you at all times; if you are not a Christian, you do not have the Spirit.

God wants the flame of the Holy Spirit to ignite our lives. But we must fly closer to the flame to have that experience. Ephesians 5:18 contains a command that we are to be filled, and keep being filled, with the Spirit. Interestingly, in the Scriptures we are never commanded to "be baptized in the Spirit!" or "be indwelt by the Spirit!" or "be gifted!" or "be sealed!" But here in a context of various commands, we are clearly commanded to "be filled with the Spirit!" To obey this command certain conditions must be fulfilled.

I cannot be filled with the Spirit while I have known and unconfessed sin present within me. I cannot be filled with the Spirit while I am walking against God's will and depending upon myself. So the filling of the Spirit not only means our lives are totally available to God, but it also includes such things as keeping short accounts, being sensitive to whatever may have come between us and him, and walking in dependence upon him.

When we are "following the Spirit," when "the Spirit is leading" us (Galatians 5:16, 18), we are filled with the Spirit. He is then able to work through us, speak through us, use us, direct us without restraint, and empower our gifts and our efforts in ways we could never accomplish on our own. It isn't that we need more of the Spirit (an impossibility); it is that we need his power, his working, his cleansing, his freeing. And as he fills us, all that and so much more takes place.

A Christian who is baptized and filled with the Spirit is also gifted and taught by the Spirit (John 16:7–15). Some of the results of his ministry include:

- Biblical insights I would otherwise have missed.
- A sudden awareness of God's will or the presence of a danger or a sense of peace in the midst of chaos.
- A surge of bold confidence in a setting where there would otherwise have been fear and hesitation.
- A quiet, calm awareness that I am not alone, even though no one else is actually with me.
- The undeniable, surrounding awareness of evil, even the dark sinister presence of demonic forces.
- An awareness of my own sinfulness and need of repentance.
- An understanding of the gifts the Holy Spirit has imparted to me, and of the power he provides to exercise those gifts (Romans 12:6–8).

Holy Spirit: For additional scriptures on this topic go to Genesis 1:1–2.

HOPE

HEBREWS 6:17–20

What is the nature of biblical hope? On what is hope based?
How does biblical hope serve to guide faithful living in the present?

Hope can be defined as "looking forward to some desire with expectation" or as "the source of or reason for such a hope." In contemporary usage, we seem to put less emphasis on the "expectation" component of hope. "I hope it doesn't rain tomorrow — but I'm getting my umbrella and rain boots ready, just in case." "I hope the Warriors will win the championship this year — but I've been wishing that every year for the last twenty years." We still look forward to a desired end, but we don't stake our lives on whether or not it happens because the thing hoped for is uncertain at best. In fact, hope often carries the connotation of "looking forward to a desirable but remote possibility," as in "I hope I win the lottery — but I know that my chances of doing so are less than my chances of getting struck by lightning on the way to pick up the check if I do win!" Our hope tends to be feeble and desperate. Maybe this is because our reasons for hoping are so flimsy. As a society, we have become like those Paul described in Ephesians 2:12, who are separated from Christ and consequently have no hope.

But biblical hope is different. In the Bible, hope is a certainty, a confident expectation of what God will do in the future based on his past faithfulness and promises. It is certain because of who God is. God is faithful, and his Word is trustworthy; he is a reliable source/reason for our hope. It was on the basis of his own integrity and ability that God made the promise to bless Abraham and give him many descendants (Hebrews 6:13–15; compare Genesis 12:1–3, 22:16–18). Abraham and his wife Sarah were long past their childbearing years, yet his hope was not wishful thinking, but a confident trust in the One who could deliver. Biblical hope is hope in God and his promises, even though we have not yet seen the complete fulfillment of the promises; this kind of hope is solid and dependable, "an anchor for the soul, sure and strong" (Hebrews 6:19). This is a hope on which we can stake our lives.

From the beginning, God's people have been a people of hope. From the promise of a descendant of Adam and Eve who would crush the head of the serpent (Genesis 3:15), to the promise of the land of Canaan to Abraham's descendants (Genesis 12:7), to the promise of a descendant of David who would rule forever (1 Chronicles 17:11–14), to the promise of Jesus' return (1 Thessalonians 4:16; Revelation 22:7, 12, 20), the people of God have believed God and waited in hope for the day of fulfillment. Those who first received the promises rarely saw their fulfillment (Hebrews 11:39). Their willingness to walk by God's promise, not their circumstances, is an example and inspiration to us to persevere in hope (Hebrews 12:1–3).

How does any of this help us to live as faithful disciples today? To hope in God is to make God the object of our hope (Psalm 39:7)—to place our trust in his promises and his ability to fulfill them. Among other things, this would include:

- trusting God to raise us from the dead and to give us life forever (Acts 23:6; 1 Corinthians 15:19; Titus 1:2);
- trusting God to give us a share in his glory (Romans 5:1–5);
- trusting God to redeem all of creation from ruin (Romans 8:18–25).

This trust is not passive; it is demonstrated by persevering in faithful obedience to God (Hebrews 12:1–3). Trust leads to action. If we trust God, we will act on his words (Matthew 7:21–27). Our hope in him means that we take his commandments seriously.

Another aspect of hoping in God is that it causes us to adopt a long-term perspective. Hope is future-oriented; people do not hope for what they already have (Romans 8:24). The Bible makes it clear that God's promises are to be fulfilled over the course of history and even into eternity, not just in the present. Thus, hoping in God forces us to engage the present in light of the future and eternity; we cannot live only for today. Because biblical hope lengthens our perspective, it frees us from getting hung up on less significant things and allows us to focus our energy on the things that will last forever. It redirects us from a life of greed and short-term gain to a one of purity (1 John 3:3), faith, and love (Colossians 1:3–5). It allows us to face our trials with courage and joy (Romans 5:4–5; 12:12) as we wait patiently for the final, complete fulfillment of God's promises (Romans 8:25). It frees us to live by what is really true and not just by our changing circumstances (2 Corinthians 5:7). It provides an anchor for our minds, emotions, and will in the sea of constantly changing values, standards, and expectations of modern society (Hebrews 6:18–19).

Hope: For additional scriptures on this topic go to Psalm 119:49.

8The whole land will shake because of it,
and everyone who lives in the land will cry
for those who died.
The whole land will rise like the Nile;
it will be shaken, and then it will fall
like the Nile River in Egypt."

9The Lord GOD says:
"At that time I will cause the sun to go
down at noon
and make the earth dark on a bright day.
10I will change your festivals into days of crying
for the dead,
and all your songs will become
songs of sadness.
I will make all of you wear rough cloth
to show your sadness;
I will make you shave your heads as well.
I will make it like a time of crying for the
death of an only son,
and its end like the end of an awful day."

11The Lord GOD says: "The days are coming
when I will cause a time of hunger in the land.
The people will not be hungry for bread or
thirsty for water,
but they will be hungry for words
from the LORD.
12They will wander from the Mediterranean Sea
to the Dead Sea,
from the north to the east.
They will search for the word of the LORD,
but they won't find it.
13At that time the beautiful young women and
the young men
will become weak from thirst.
14They make promises by the idol in Samaria
and say, 'As surely as the god of Dan lives . . . '
and, 'As surely as the god of Beersheba lives,
we promise . . . '
So they will fall
and never get up again."

Israel Will Be Destroyed

9 I saw the Lord standing by the altar, and
he said:
"Smash the top of the pillars
so that even the bottom of the
doors will shake.
Make the pillars fall on the people's heads;
anyone left alive I will kill with a sword.
Not one person will get away;
no one will escape.
2If they dig down as deep as the
place of the dead,
I will pull them up from there.
If they climb up into heaven,
I will bring them down from there.
3If they hide at the top of Mount Carmel,
I will find them and take them away.
If they try to hide from me at the
bottom of the sea,
I will command a snake to bite them.
4If they are captured and taken away
by their enemies,
I will command the sword to kill them.
I will keep watch over them,
but I will keep watch to give them trouble,
not to do them good."

5The Lord GOD All-Powerful touches the land,
and the land shakes.
Then everyone who lives in the land cries
for the dead.
The whole land rises like the Nile River
and falls like the river of Egypt.
6The LORD builds his upper rooms
above the skies;
he sets their foundations on the earth.
He calls for the waters of the sea
and pours them out on the land.
The LORD is his name.

7The LORD says,
"Israel, you are no different to me than
the people of Cush.
I brought Israel out of the land of Egypt,
and the Philistines from Crete,
and the Arameans from Kir.
8I, the Lord GOD, am watching the
sinful kingdom Israel.
I will destroy it
from off the earth,
but I will not completely destroy
Jacob's descendants," says the LORD.
9"I am giving the command
to scatter the nation of Israel among all
nations.
It will be like someone shaking grain
through a strainer,
but not even a tiny stone falls through.

8:10 *shave your heads.* A shaved head was a sign of mourning.
8:11 The words "a time of hunger" are used here metaphorically. Amos prophesied that one day the Lord would send a famine not of bread or water but of the word of the Lord (see Micah 3:4, 7).
8:14 *Dan. . .Beersheba* Dan was the city farthest north in Israel, and Beersheba was the city farthest south. This means all the people of Israel. Both cities played a sad role in the false worship of apostate Israel.

10All the sinners among my people
will die by the sword—
those who say,
'Nothing bad will happen to us.'⚭

The Lord Promises to Restore Israel

11"The kingdom of David is like a fallen tent,
but in that day I will set it up again
and mend its broken places.
I will rebuild its ruins
as it was before.
12Then Israel will take over what is left of Edom
and the other nations that belong to me,"
says the LORD,
who will make it happen.

13The LORD says, "The time is coming when
there will be all kinds of food.
People will still be harvesting crops
when it's time to plow again.
People will still be taking the juice
from grapes
when it's time to plant again.
Wine will drip from the mountains
and pour from the hills.
14I will bring my people Israel back
from captivity;
they will build the ruined cities again,
and they will live in them.
They will plant vineyards and drink the
wine from them;
they will plant gardens and eat their fruit.
15I will plant my people on their land,
and they will not be pulled out again
from the land which I have given them,"
says the LORD your God.

⚭**9:10 Election (Chosen):** John 10:28–29

9:13 This image represents the great prosperity which God will give his restored people.

INTRODUCTION TO THE BOOK OF

OBADIAH

God Will Punish Edom

WHO WROTE THIS BOOK?

Obadiah, the prophet of God, is the author of this book. The name Obadiah, a common name of the time, means "servant of the LORD."

TO WHOM WAS THIS BOOK WRITTEN?

The Book of Obadiah is a speech of judgment against Edom—one of Israel's most hated enemies.

WHERE WAS IT WRITTEN?

It is uncertain where the Book of Obadiah was composed by the prophet.

WHEN WAS IT WRITTEN?

Obadiah probably ministered and wrote during the sixth century B.C., as a contemporary of Jeremiah.

WHAT IS THE BOOK ABOUT?

Obadiah warns Edom of God's coming judgment on them for their participation in the devastation of Israel—God's people—at the time the Babylonians overthrew Judah and Jerusalem in 586 B.C.

WHY WAS THIS BOOK WRITTEN?

Although Obadiah's message of warning is directed at Edom, indirectly it becomes a message of encouragement and victory for Israel. Edom will be destroyed, and God will cause Israel to prosper and be delivered.

SO WHAT DOES THIS BOOK MEAN TO US?

God always delivers his faithful people in the long run. So, even when we are suffering troublesome and difficult times, and it appears that our evil neighbors are prospering, we can be encouraged by remembering the message of Obadiah to Israel.

SUMMARY:

The Book of Obadiah is a prophetic judgment speech directed at Edom, one of Israel's most hated enemies. The Bible records a long history of warfare between the two neighboring nations. Indeed, Israel traced its lineage to Jacob, while Edom descended from Esau, rival sons of Isaac.

Little is known about Obadiah. He probably prophesied in the sixth century in the early part of the exile because his message reacts to the role that Edom took during that time.

Obadiah recognizes that God is the God of all nations, not just the God of Israel. God's justice will overcome the evil thoughts and actions of all people.

OBADIAH

The Lord Will Punish the Edomites

This is the vision of Obadiah.
This is what the Lord GOD says about Edom:
We have heard a message from the LORD.
A messenger has been sent among the
nations, saying,
"Attack! Let's go attack Edom!"

The Lord Speaks to the Edomites

2"Soon I will make you the smallest of nations.
You will be greatly hated by everyone.
3Your pride has fooled you,
you who live in the hollow places of the cliff.
Your home is up high,
you who say to yourself,
'No one can bring me down to the ground.'
4Even if you fly high like the eagle
and make your nest among the stars,
I will bring you down from there,"
says the LORD.
5"You will really be ruined!
If thieves came to you,
if robbers came by night,
they would steal only enough for themselves.
If workers came and picked the grapes
from your vines,
they would leave a few behind.
6But you, Edom, will really lose everything!
People will find all your hidden treasures!
7All the people who are your friends
will force you out of the land.
The people who are at peace with you
will trick you and defeat you.
Those who eat your bread with you now
are planning a trap for you,
and you will not notice it."

8The LORD says, "On that day
I will surely destroy the wise
people from Edom,
and those with understanding from the
mountains of Edom.
9Then, city of Teman, your best warriors
will be afraid,
and everyone from the mountains of
Edom will be killed.
10You did violence to your relatives, the Israelites,
so you will be covered with shame
and destroyed forever.
11You stood aside without helping
while strangers carried Israel's treasures away.
When foreigners entered Israel's city gate
and threw lots to decide what part of
Jerusalem they would take,
you were like one of them.

Commands That Edom Broke

12"Edom, do not laugh at your brother Israel in
his time of trouble
or be happy about the people of Judah when
they are destroyed.
Do not brag when cruel things are
done to them.
13Do not enter the city gate of my people
in their time of trouble
or laugh at their problems
in their time of trouble.
Do not take their treasures
in their time of trouble.
14Do not stand at the crossroads
to destroy those who are trying to escape.
Do not capture those who escape alive and
turn them over to their enemy
in their time of trouble.

The Nations Will Be Judged

15"The LORD's day of judging is coming soon
to all the nations.
The same evil things you did to other people
will happen to you;
they will come back upon your own head.⚭
16Because you drank in my Temple,
all the nations will drink on and on.
They will drink and drink
until they disappear.
17But on Mount Zion some will escape
the judgment,
and it will be a holy place.
The people of Jacob will take back their land
from those who took it from them.
18The people of Jacob will be like a fire
and the people of Joseph like a flame.
But the people of Esau will be like dry stalks.
The people of Jacob will set them on fire and
burn them up.

1:1 *Edom.* The Edomites were the people who came from Esau, Jacob's twin brother. They were enemies of the Israelites.
1:3 Edom was located in the mountains, and to them their homeland seemed defensively secure.
1:12 *do not laugh at your brother Israel.* The Edomites laughed at Israel when they were taken by Babylon. They also took advantage of them in their weakness.
⚭**1:15 Day of the Lord:** Malachi 3:2
1:18 *people of Jacob . . . Joseph.* The people who came from Jacob and Joseph, or the Israelites.
1:18 *people of Esau.* The people who came from Esau, or the Edomites.

There will be no one left of the people of Esau."
This will happen because the LORD has said it.

19Then God's people will regain southern
Judah from Edom;
they will take back the mountains of Edom.
They will take back the western hills
from the Philistines.
They will regain the lands of Ephraim
and Samaria,
and Benjamin will take over Gilead.

20People from Israel who once were forced to
leave their homes
will take the land of the Canaanites,
all the way to Zarephath.
People from Judah who once were forced to
leave Jerusalem and live in Sepharad
will take back the cities of southern Judah.
21Powerful warriors will go up on Mount Zion,
where they will rule the people living on
Edom's mountains.
And the kingdom will belong to the LORD.

The Writing Prophets & Their Times

Israel	Prophets	Judah
		885 B.C.
Omri (885–874)		Asa (910–869)
	←Obadiah?	
Ahab (874–853)		Jehoshaphat (872–848)
Ahaziah (853–852)		Jehoram (853–841)
Joram (852–841)		Ahaziah (841)
		Athaliah (841–835)
Jehu (841–814)		Joash (835–796)
	Joel→	
Jehoahaz (814–798)		
Jehoash (798–782)		Amaziah (796–767)
Jeroboam II (793–753)		
	←Jonah?	Azariah (792–740)
	←Amos	Jothan (750–735)
Zachariah (753)		
		Shallum (752)
		Ahaz (735–715)
Menahem (752–742)		
	←Hosea Micah→	
Pekah (752–732)		
		Hezekiah (715–686)
Pekahiah (742–740)	Isaiah→	
Hoshea (732–723)		Manasseh (697–642)
Captivity		Amon (642–640)
Assyria		Josiah (640–609)
722 B.C.		
	Nahum→	
	Habakkuk→	
	Zephaniah→	Jehoahaz (609)
		Jehoiakim (609–598)
	Jeremiah→	Jehoiachin (598–597)
	Ezekiel→	Zedekiah (597–586)

INTRODUCTION TO THE BOOK OF

JONAH

A Prophet Runs from God

WHO WROTE THIS BOOK?

The author of the Book of Jonah is uncertain, although tradition holds it to be the prophet himself.

TO WHOM WAS THIS BOOK WRITTEN?

The book is a message for Israel from God.

WHERE WAS IT WRITTEN?

While Jonah was from Gath Hephen in Zebulun, it is uncertain where the book was composed.

WHEN WAS IT WRITTEN?

The date of writing is uncertain, but for a variety of reasons it is most likely to be dated in the eighth century B.C.

WHAT IS THE BOOK ABOUT?

Jonah is a narrative story about a reluctant prophet of God and the way God deals with him to bring him to obedience. It is also a spiritual lesson about God's power over nature and his compassion for all peoples of the world, not just Israel.

WHY WAS THIS BOOK WRITTEN?

Through Jonah's story God shows Israel his love and concern for all people everywhere. He also shows his people their responsibility, as his chosen ones, to share his message with the world.

SO WHAT DOES THIS BOOK MEAN TO US?

Like Jonah, we are called by God to deliver his message to the world. It is our responsibility and privilege. We cannot run from our God-given task or escape from his truth—God loves all people everywhere.

SUMMARY:

Jonah was a prophet, but the book named after him is a story that contains a brief prophecy, not a prophetic book. We do not know who wrote the Book of Jonah, nor exactly when, but we do know that Jonah was a prophet who lived during the reign of Jeroboam II (786–746 B.C.) and prophesied that his reign would be prosperous (2 Kings 14:25).

The Book of Jonah is an account of a reluctant prophet. God wants him to warn the people of Nineveh of his coming judgment, and Jonah has no desire that they survive. After all, Nineveh was one of the main cities of Assyria, an empire that had harmed Israel deeply and would continue to do so. He tries to escape his divine commission, but God shows him that no place is beyond his reach (see Psalm 139). God uses even Jonah's half-hearted prophecy (Jonah 3:4) to reach the heart of the Ninevites. The city is saved, but Jonah's heart remains bitter and depressed.

Throughout the book there is a strong contrast between Jonah, the prophet, and the pagan characters. The sailors and the people of Nineveh are quick to respond to God, but Jonah seeks to escape what he knows is God's will.

The most memorable scene occurs in Jonah 1:17–2:10. Jonah tries to escape God by boat. He sends a storm that can only be stilled when Jonah is thrown into the sea. God then sends a great fish to swallow him and transport him to land. He spends three days and three nights in the belly of the fish. Jesus refers to this episode when he anticipates the three days between his death and resurrection (Matthew 12:39–41; 16:4; Luke 11:29–32).

The outline to the Book of Jonah is as follows:

I. Jonah's Commission and Flight (Jonah 1 and 2)
II. Jonah and Nineveh (Jonah 3 and 4)

I. Jonah's Commission and Flight (Jonah 1 and 2)

The book opens in Israel. Jonah is instructed by God to go to the city of Nineveh in Assyria apparently to warn them of coming judgment. Jonah wants nothing to do with these people so he goes in the opposite direction. Jonah soon learns that there is no escaping God as he uses the sea and its inhabitants, a great fish in particular, to bring him back.

II. Jonah and Nineveh (Jonah 3 and 4)

Jonah arrives in Nineveh and preaches a very short message that just announces the judgment. The Ninevites, however, are quickly convicted of their guilt and repent. God then changes his mind and allows them to live. Jonah then becomes angry and depressed, having no love for the people of Assyria. The book closes with God's dealing with Jonah.

JONAH

God Calls and Jonah Runs

The LORD spoke his word to Jonah son of Amittai: 2“Get up, go to the great city of Nineveh,
and preach against it, because I see the evil
things they do.”
3But Jonah got up to run away from the LORD by
going to Tarshish. He went to the city of Joppa,
where he found a ship that was going to the city
of Tarshish. Jonah paid for the trip and went
aboard, planning to go to Tarshish to run away
from the LORD.
4But the LORD sent a great wind on the sea,
which made the sea so stormy that the ship was
in danger of breaking apart. 5The sailors were
afraid, and each man cried to his own god. They
began throwing the cargo from the ship into the
sea to make the ship lighter.
But Jonah had gone down far inside the ship to
lie down, and he fell fast asleep. 6The captain of
the ship came and said, “Why are you sleeping?
Get up and pray to your god! Maybe your god will
pay attention to us, and we won't die!”
7Then the men said to each other, “Let's throw
lots to see who caused these troubles to happen
to us.”
When they threw lots, the lot showed that the
trouble had happened because of Jonah. 8Then
they said to him, “Tell us, who caused our trouble? What is your job? Where do you come from?
What is your country? Who are your people?”
9Then Jonah said to them, “I am a Hebrew. I
fear the LORD, the God of heaven, who made the
sea and the land.”
10The men were very afraid, and they asked
Jonah, “What terrible thing did you do?” (They
knew he was running away from the LORD
because he had told them.)
11Since the wind and the waves of the sea were
becoming much stronger, they said to him,
“What should we do to you to make the sea calm
down for us?”
12Jonah said to them, “Pick me up, and throw me
into the sea, and then it will calm down. I know it
is my fault that this great storm has come on you.”
13Instead, the men tried to row the ship back to
the land, but they could not, because the sea was
becoming more stormy.

Jonah's Punishment

14So the men cried to the LORD, “LORD, please
don't let us die because of this man's life; please
don't think we are guilty of killing an innocent
person. LORD, you have caused all this to happen;
you wanted it this way.” 15So they picked up
Jonah and threw him into the sea, and the sea
became calm. 16Then they began to fear the LORD
very much; they offered a sacrifice to the LORD
and made promises to him.
17The LORD caused a big fish to swallow Jonah,
and Jonah was inside the fish three days and
three nights.

2 While Jonah was inside the fish, he prayed to
the LORD his God and said,

2“When I was in danger,
I called to the LORD,
and he answered me.
I was about to die,
so I cried to you,
and you heard my voice.
3You threw me into the sea,
down, down into the deep sea.
The water was all around me,
and your powerful waves flowed over me.
4I said, ‘I was driven out of your presence,
but I hope to see your Holy Temple again.’
5The waters of the sea closed around my throat.
The deep sea was all around me;
seaweed was wrapped around my head.
6When I went down to where the mountains of
the sea start to rise,
I thought I was locked in this prison forever,
but you saved me from the pit of death,
LORD my God.

7“When my life had almost gone,
I remembered the LORD.
I prayed to you,
and you heard my prayers in your Holy Temple.

8“People who worship useless idols
give up their loyalty to you.
9But I will praise and thank you
while I give sacrifices to you,
and I will keep my promises to you.
Salvation comes from the LORD!”

10Then the LORD spoke to the fish, and the fish
threw up Jonah onto the dry land.

1:2 *Nineveh.* Nineveh was one of the chief cities of Assyria, the aggressive and cruel superpower of the day.
1:3 *Tarshish.* Tarshish was far away from Israel. It is thought to have been in what is called Spain today.

1:17 Numbers: Zechariah 1:18
2:10 Water: Matthew 8:23–27
2:10 The big fish vomited Jonah on the dry ground.

God Calls and Jonah Obeys

3 The LORD spoke his word to Jonah again and
said, 2“Get up, go to the great city Nineveh,
and preach to it what I tell you to say.”
3So Jonah obeyed the LORD and got up and went
to Nineveh. It was a very large city; just to walk
across it took a person three days. 4After Jonah
had entered the city and walked for one day, he
preached to the people, saying, “After forty days,
Nineveh will be destroyed!”
5The people of Nineveh believed God. They
announced that they would stop eating for a
while, and they put on rough cloth to show their
sadness. All the people in the city did this, from
the most important to the least important.
6When the king of Nineveh heard this news,
he got up from his throne, took off his robe, and
covered himself with rough cloth and sat in ashes
to show how upset he was.
7He sent this announcement through Nineveh:

By command of the king and his important
men: No person or animal, herd or flock, will
be allowed to taste anything. Do not let them
eat food or drink water. 8But every person
and animal should be covered with rough
cloth, and people should cry loudly to God.
Everyone must turn away from evil living
and stop doing harm all the time. 9Who
knows? Maybe God will change his mind.
Maybe he will stop being angry, and then we
will not die.

10When God saw what the people did, that
they stopped doing evil, he changed his mind and
did not do what he had warned. He did not punish them.⚭

God's Mercy Makes Jonah Angry

4 But this made Jonah very unhappy, and he
became angry. 2He prayed to the LORD,
“When I was still in my own country this is what
I said would happen, and that is why I quickly ran
away to Tarshish. I knew that you are a God who
is kind and shows mercy. You don't become
angry quickly, and you have great love. I knew
you would choose not to cause harm. 3So now I
ask you, LORD, please kill me. It is better for me to
die than to live.”
4Then the LORD said, “Do you think it is right
for you to be angry?”
5Jonah went out and sat down east of the city.
There he made a shelter for himself and sat in the
shade, waiting to see what would happen to the
city. 6The LORD made a plant grow quickly up over
Jonah, which gave him shade and helped him to be
more comfortable. Jonah was very pleased to have
the plant. 7But the next day when the sun rose,
God sent a worm to attack the plant so that it died.
8As the sun rose higher in the sky, God sent a
very hot east wind to blow, and the sun became
so hot on Jonah's head that he became very weak
and wished he were dead. He said, “It is better
for me to die than to live.”
9But God said to Jonah, “Do you think it is right
for you to be angry about the plant?”
Jonah answered, “It is right for me to be angry!
I am so angry I could die!”
10And the LORD said, “You are so concerned for
that plant even though you did nothing to make it
grow. It appeared one day, and the next day it
died. 11Then shouldn't I show concern for the
great city Nineveh, which has more than one hundred twenty thousand people who do not know
right from wrong, and many animals, too?”⚭

3:1–10 In a way that surprises Jonah and may surprise us, Jonah's simple message of doom leads the people in Nineveh to change their hearts and lives and God to change his mind. The people believed God; even the animals were included in their change of heart. The message of judgment became an opportunity for repentance both for the city and for God.

⚭**3:10 Fasting:** Jeremiah 36:9

⚭**3:10 Repentance:** Micah 6:8

4:1 Jonah unhappy and angry, was depressed over the events in Nineveh. This wicked city had been the cause of much suffering in Israel. God had virtually forced Jonah to preach to Nineveh a way of escape from destruction. Now that the city was safe from God's anger, Jonah sank into a listless depression.

⚭**4:11 Animals:** Matthew 6:26

LAST DAYS

ACTS 2:17

What do the "last days" refer to? Are we in the last days now or is it something in the future? How are we to live in the last days?

Much of the Bible is oriented toward the future. The biblical writers often speak of a time referred to as the "last days" (also called "later times" in 1 Timothy 4:1 and "last times" in 1 Peter 1:20).

In the Old Testament, "last days" typically refers to a future time of blessing for Israel. For example, in Isaiah 2:2 (see also Micah 4:1), the last days are a time when "the mountain on which the Lord's Temple stands" (Jerusalem) will attract people from all nations (verses 2–4). God will rule over the nations and war will be no more (verse 4). Hosea 3:5 says that this time of blessing, when the people "will turn in fear to the Lord, and he will bless them," follows a period of Israel's faithlessness and punishment.

Precisely what the Old Testament prophets had in mind when they spoke of the last days is not entirely clear. For example, did Isaiah have in mind a *political* situation that was to happen in his lifetime or shortly thereafter, or was Isaiah speaking of a far future time, even the end of the world?

The New Testament is very explicit about when the last days are to come. They refer to the period of time between Christ's first and second coming. In other words, the church has been living in the last days for nearly 2000 years. The future hope of the Old Testament prophets has been fulfilled by the coming of God to earth. As the carol says, "The hopes and fears of all the years are met in thee tonight."

We see this most clearly in Acts 2, especially verses 17–21. Peter is speaking to the people on the day of Pentecost. The disciples were "all filled with the Holy Spirit, and they began to speak different languages by the power the Holy Spirit was giving them" (2:4). Some thought they were drunk, but Peter explained it differently. This was a fulfillment of Joel's prophecy (Joel 2:28–32): "After this I will pour out my Spirit on all kinds of people." The ascension of Christ to heaven and the coming of the Holy Spirit to the church (Acts 2:1–2; the promised "Helper" spoken of in John 16:5–11) was a sign that the last days had arrived, the last days spoken of by the prophets. The long-awaited time had come.

Hebrews 1:1–2 puts it this way: "*In the past* God spoke to our ancestors through the prophets many times and in many different ways. But now *in these last days* God has spoken to us through his Son." The *past* refers to the Old Testament times; the *last days* refers to the coming of Christ. The New Testament teaches that the first coming of Christ is the great dividing point in history. Everything before that night in Bethlehem is *the past*. Everything since is the *last days*.

The church lives in the last days. The blessings hoped for by the prophets have come. Christ has come, he has been raised from the dead; and the Holy Spirit dwells in us. We see what "prophets searched carefully and tried to learn" and "things into which angels desire to look" (1 Peter 1:10–12).

But these last days are not simply a period of blessing. There are struggles, obstacles, barriers to our faith that we meet every day. Living in the last days means not only the privilege of experiencing the blessings that are in Christ. It also means the challenge of living lives worthy of this privilege. And this is a daily struggle. Second Timothy 3:1 says: "Remember this! In the last days there will be many troubles." Paul then tells Timothy of the type of people who will be living in the last days, people who pervert the Gospel (verses 2–9), warning: "Stay away from those people" (verse 5). Rather, "continue following the teachings you learned" (verse 14). First John 2:18 also speaks of the "enemies of Christ" in the last days.

The Bible warns us that living in the last days is a challenge. Yet it is precisely because we live in the last days that we, in Christ, are able to face that challenge and triumph over it. Why? Because Christ has been raised from the dead and has defeated sin and death. And not only this, but because Christ has been raised, we have also been "raised from the dead" to a new life (Romans 6:1–14; Colossians 3:1–17). Our bodies have not yet been raised (John 6:40), but becoming a Christian is, as Paul says, a spiritual resurrection from the dead. This newness of life is the great privilege of living in the last days. Part of that privilege is the responsibility to live worthy "of the life to which God called you" (Ephesians 4:1). And we are able to triumph because of the power of the risen Christ which is at work in us (Ephesians 3:20; Philippians 3:10).

Last Days: For additional scriptures on this topic go to Hosea 3:5.

FELLOWSHIP

ACTS 2:41–47

What is the nature and basis of true Christian fellowship? What responsibilities do members of a local fellowship of believers have toward one another? Can Christians have fellowship with other believers whose doctrinal convictions are not precisely the same as their own?

The church is a new community that God has chosen to signal or point to the coming kingdom. The church is no civic center, no social club or encounter group, no Sunday morning meeting place. It is a new society, the fellowship of the redeemed, created for the salvation of a lost world. It is a corporate body consisting of all those who have placed their trust in Jesus Christ as Savior and Lord, united into a fellowship of believers by the Holy Spirit who dwells within them, and uniting themselves into a local body of believers. This new community called by God is indeed a *fellowship*; its members bear one another's burdens and allow for real accountability and discipline. This fellowship is the true intimacy—and peace—available only to those united in Jesus Christ.

True fellowship was manifest in the early church when the congregation was of one heart, shared their possessions, cared for those in need, and with great power gave witness to the risen Christ. The believers enjoyed the deepest communion and truly were what they called themselves: *communio sanctorum*—or communion of saints. As the church expanded out of Jerusalem, this concept of one fellowship—one with another and with God—bound them in unity and became the very essence of the church's character and power (Acts 11:28–30).

Surveys show that the number one thing people look for in a church is fellowship. But what most modern Westerners seek is a far cry from what the Bible describes and what the early church practiced. No term in the Christian lexicon is more abused than *fellowship.* To some it means the warm, affirming, "hot tub" religion that soothes our frayed nerves and provides relief from the battering of everyday life. Often with the best of intentions Christians have turned this social notion of fellowship into an end in itself. For many, fellowship means no more than coming together for church events.

But the word for fellowship in Greek, *koinonia*, is something much richer. Literally, it means a communion, a participation of people together in God's grace. It describes a new community in which individuals willingly covenant to share in common, to be in submission to each other, to support one another.

In Scripture, this koinonia embraces both the vertical and the horizontal. "We announce to you what we have seen and heard, because we want you also to have fellowship with us. Our fellowship is with God the Father and with his Son, Jesus Christ," wrote John to the early church (1 John 1:3). It was a concept the early believers understood, because it paralleled the Old Testament concept of God's people sharing together in the covenant community in which he himself chose to dwell.

Biblical fellowship involves serious commitment by and obligations of believers to one another, based on mutual love. The early church was so committed. No wonder much of the known world came to Christ in the early centuries. They could see how believers loved one another in true fellowship. Within the community of Christ, the fellowship of believers, we are to support each other.

But fellowship is more than unconditional love that wraps its arms around someone who is hurting. It is also tough love that holds one fast to the truth and the pursuit of righteousness. For most Christians, the support side of the equation comes more easily than accountability and the subsequent discipline involved. This is one reason the behavior of Christians is often little different from the behavior of non-Christians. Maybe it's because we simply haven't taught accountability. Or maybe it's because, in today's fiercely individualistic culture, people resent being told what to do, and since we don't want to "scare them off" we succumb to cultural pressures. Too often we confuse love with permissiveness. It is not love to fail to dissuade another believer from sin any more than it is love to fail to take a drink away from an alcoholic or matches away from a baby. True fellowship out of love for one another demands *accountability.*

Harmony and oneness in spirit, true Christian fellowship, can be achieved only when Christians put aside their personal agendas and submit themselves to the authority of the Holy Spirit. For the Holy Spirit, who empowers the church, will never lead believers into disunity. The Holy Spirit produces true fellowship, even among believers of differing nonessential doctrinal convictions. Today that kind of fellowship and unity among believers would produce what it did in the early church—a mighty outpouring of God's grace.

Fellowship: For additional scriptures on this topic go to Acts 2:42.

INTRODUCTION TO THE BOOK OF

MICAH

Assyria Will Punish Israel and Judah

WHO WROTE THIS BOOK?

Micah, the prophet of God, is ascribed the authorship of this book in verse one.

TO WHOM WAS THIS BOOK WRITTEN?

Micah prophesies to God's special people—the people of Israel, addressing both the northern kingdom and Judah.

WHERE WAS IT WRITTEN?

The Book of Micah was probably written in and around where Micah live and worked.

WHEN WAS IT WRITTEN?

Micah was a contemporary of Isaiah and Hosea. He prophesied and wrote between 750 and 686 B.C.

WHAT IS THE BOOK ABOUT?

This message from God is a combination of judgment and salvation. The prophet proclaims coming restoration to glory, and prophesies the coming Messiah.

WHY WAS THIS BOOK WRITTEN?

God's message through Micah is meant to turn Israel from her rebellion, idols, and injustice and back to him.

SO WHAT DOES THIS BOOK MEAN TO US?

God's people today are like Israel in the way we are so often disloyal to him, following after other gods of our society and rebelling against his word. God's message to us is the same as his message to Israel through Micah—we must turn back to God and his precepts, repent of our rebellion, and follow his ways.

SUMMARY:

Micah of Moresheth, a village twenty-five miles southwest of Jerusalem, is named as the author of the book that bears his name. We know little about him, but the first verse of the book dates him to the second half of the eighth century B.C. and perhaps into the first few years of the next century. He is mentioned also in Jeremiah 26:17–19 as a prophet of judgment during the reign of Hezekiah.

Israel and Judah experienced great turmoil during his lifetime. The northern kingdom fell to the Assyrians in 722 B.C., who also threatened Judah's existence in 701 B.C. These events had their impact on the book.

The structure of the book is not chronological. The oracles are arranged in topical order, alternating between the warnings of judgment and the hope of restoration.

An outline of the book is as follows:

I. Judgment and Salvation, Round 1 (Micah 1–5)
II. Judgment and Salvation, Round 2 (Micah 6–7)

I. Judgment and Salvation, Round 1 (Micah 1–5)

God, through Micah, warns of coming judgment. The people have turned to other gods and have practiced evil toward one another. In 4:1 however there is an abrupt change to blessing and hope for the people of God.

II. Judgment and Salvation, Round 2 (Micah 6–7)

Once again the prophet, who speaks for God, accuses Israel of sin and rebellion. But the final word of the book is one of God's kindness and healing.

MICAH

Samaria and Israel to Be Punished

During the time that Jotham, Ahaz, and Hezekiah were kings of Judah, the word of the LORD came to Micah, who was from Moresheth. He saw these visions about Samaria and Jerusalem.

2Hear this, all you nations;
listen, earth and all you who live on it.
The Lord GOD will be a witness against you,
the Lord from his Holy Temple.
3See, the LORD is coming out of his place;
he is coming down to walk on the tops of the mountains.
4The mountains will melt under him,
and the valleys will crack open,
like wax near a fire,
like water running down a hillside.
5All this is because of Jacob's sin,
because of the sins of the nation of Israel.
What is the place of Jacob's sin?
Isn't it Samaria?
What is Judah's place of idol worship?
Isn't it Jerusalem?

The LORD Speaks

6"So I will make Samaria a pile of ruins in the open country,
a place for planting vineyards.
I will pour her stones down into the valley
and strip her down to her foundations.
7All her idols will be broken into pieces;
all the gifts to her idols will be burned with fire.
I will destroy all her idols,
and because Samaria earned her money by being unfaithful to me,
this money will be carried off by others who are not faithful to me."

Micah's Great Sadness

8I will moan and cry because of this evil,
going around barefoot and naked.
I will cry loudly like the wild dogs
and make sad sounds like the owls do,
9because Samaria's wound cannot be healed.
It will spread to Judah;
it will reach the city gate of my people,
all the way to Jerusalem.
10Don't tell it in Gath.
Don't cry in Acco.
Roll in the dust
at Beth Ophrah.
11Pass on your way, naked and ashamed,
you who live in Shaphir.
Those who live in Zaanan
won't come out.
The people in Beth Ezel will cry,
but they will not give you any support.
12Those who live in Maroth
will be anxious for good news to come,
because trouble will come from the LORD,
all the way to the gate of Jerusalem.
13You people living in Lachish,
harness the fastest horse to the chariot.
Jerusalem's sins started in you;
yes, Israel's sins were found in you.
14So you must give farewell gifts
to Moresheth in Gath.
The houses in Aczib will be false help
to the kings of Israel.
15I will bring against you people who will take your land,
you who live in Mareshah.
The glory of Israel
will go in to Adullam.
16Cut off your hair to show you are sad
for the children you love.
Make yourself bald like the eagle,
because your children will be taken away to a foreign land.

The Evil Plans of People

2 How terrible it will be for people
who plan wickedness,
who lie on their beds and make evil plans.
When the morning light comes, they do what they planned,
because they have the power to do so.

1:10 These cities were likely the ones which were overwhelmed by the Assyrian king, Sennacherib, as he made his way toward Jerusalem in 701 B.C. Each line involves a wordplay on the sound of the name of the city.
1:10 *Gath.* This name sounds like the Hebrew word for "tell."
1:10 *Acco.* This name sounds like the Hebrew word for "cry."
1:10 *Beth Ophrah.* This name means "house of dust."
1:11 *Shaphir.* This name means "beautiful."
1:11 *Zaanan.* This name sounds like the Hebrew word for "come out."
1:11 *Beth Ezel.* This name means "house by the side of another," suggesting help or support.
1:12 *Maroth.* This name sounds like the Hebrew word for "sad" or "miserable."
1:13 *Lachish.* This name sounds like the Hebrew word for "horses."
1:14 *Moresheth.* This may be a play on the word "engaged," referring to a farewell gift to a bride.
1:14 *Aczib.* This name means "lie" or "trick."
1:15 *Mareshah.* This name sounds like the Hebrew word for a person who captures other cities and lands.
1:16 *Cut off your hair.* Cutting one's hair off was a sign of mourning.

2They want fields, so they take them;
they want houses, so they take them away.
They cheat people to get their houses;
they rob them even of their property.

3That is why the LORD says:
"Look, I am planning trouble against such people,
and you won't be able to save yourselves.
You will no longer walk proudly,
because it will be a terrible time.
4At that time people will make fun of you
and sing this sad song about you:
'We are completely ruined;
the LORD has taken away my people's land.
Yes, he has taken it away from me
and divided our fields among our enemies!'"
5So you will have no one from the LORD's people
to throw lots to divide the land.

Micah Is Asked Not to Prophesy

6The prophets say, "Don't prophesy to us!
Don't prophesy about these things!
Nothing to make us feel bad will happen!"
7But I must say this, people of Jacob:
The LORD is becoming angry about what
you have done.
My words are welcome
to the person who does what is right.
8But you are fighting against my people
like an enemy.
You take the coats from people who pass by;
you rob them of their safety;
you plan war.
9You've forced the women of my people
from their nice houses;
you've taken my glory
from their children forever.
10Get up and leave.
This is not your place of rest anymore.
You have made this place unclean,
and it is doomed to destruction.
11But you people want a false prophet
who will tell you nothing but lies.
You want one who promises to prophesy
good things for you
if you give him wine and beer.
He's just the prophet for you.

The LORD Promises to Rescue His People

12"Yes, people of Jacob, I will bring all
of you together;
I will bring together all those left
alive in Israel.
I will put them together like sheep in a pen,
like a flock in its pasture;
the place will be filled with many people.
13Someone will open the way and lead
the people out.
The people will break through the gate and
leave the city where they were held captive.
Their king will go out in front of them,
and the LORD will lead them."

The Leaders of Israel Are Guilty of Evil

3 Then I said,
"Listen, leaders of the people of Jacob;
listen, you rulers of the nation of Israel.
You should know how to decide cases fairly,
2 but you hate good and love evil.
You skin my people alive
and tear the flesh off their bones.
3You eat my people's flesh
and skin them and break their bones;
you chop them up like meat for the pot,
like meat in a cooking pan.
4They will cry to the LORD,
but he won't answer them.
At that time he will hide his face from them,
because what they have done is evil."

5The LORD says this about the prophets who
teach his people the wrong way of living:
"If these prophets are given food to eat,
they shout, 'Peace!'
But if someone doesn't give them
what they ask for,
they call for a holy war against that person.⚭
6So it will become like night for them,
without visions.
It will become dark for them, without any
way to tell the future.
The sun is about to set for the prophets;
their day will become dark.
7The seers will be ashamed;
the people who see the future will
be embarrassed.
Yes, all of them will cover their mouths,
because there will be no answer from God."

Micah Is an Honest Prophet of God

8But I am filled with power,
with the Spirit of the LORD,
and with justice and strength,
to tell the people of Jacob how they have
turned against God,
and the people of Israel how
they have sinned.⚭

⚭**3:5 Leadership:** Zechariah 10:2–3

⚭**3:8 Spiritual Gifts:** 2 Samuel 23:2

[9]Leaders of Jacob and rulers of Israel,
listen to me,
you who hate fairness
and twist what is right.
[10]You build Jerusalem by murdering people;
you build it with evil.
[11]Its judges take money
to decide who wins in court.
Its priests only teach for pay,
and its prophets only look into the future
when they get paid.
But they lean on the LORD and say,
"The LORD is here with us,
so nothing bad will happen to us."
[12]Because of you,
Jerusalem will be plowed like a field.
The city will become a pile of rocks,
and the hill on which the Temple stands will
be covered with bushes.

The Mountain of the LORD

4 In the last days
the mountain on which the
LORD's Temple stands
will become the most important
of all mountains.
It will be raised above the hills,
and people from other nations will come
streaming to it.
[2]Many nations will come and say,
"Come, let us go up to the mountain
of the LORD,
to the Temple of the God of Jacob,
so that he can teach us his ways,
and we can obey his teachings."
His teachings will go out from Jerusalem,
the word of the LORD from that city.
[3]The Lord will judge many nations;
he will make decisions about strong nations
that are far away.
They will hammer their swords
into plow blades
and their spears into hooks for
trimming trees.
Nations will no longer raise swords against
other nations;
they will not train for war anymore.
[4]Everyone will sit under his own
vine and fig tree,
and no one will make them afraid,
because the LORD All-Powerful has said it.
[5]All other nations may follow their own gods,
but we will follow the LORD our God
forever and ever.

[6]The LORD says, "At that time,
I will gather the crippled;
I will bring together those who
were sent away,
those whom I caused to have trouble.
[7]I will keep alive those who were crippled,
and I will make a strong nation of those
who were sent away.
The LORD will be their king in Mount Zion
from now on and forever.
[8]And you, watchtower of the flocks,
hill of Jerusalem,
to you will come the kingdom as in the past.
Jerusalem, the right to rule will come
again to you."

Why the Israelites Must Go to Babylon

[9]Now, why do you cry so loudly?
Is your king gone?
Have you lost your helper,
so that you are in pain, like a woman trying
to give birth?
[10]People of Jerusalem, strain and be in pain.
Be like a woman trying to give birth,
because now you must leave the city
and live in the field.
You will go to Babylon,
but you will be saved from that place.
The LORD will go there
and buy you back from your enemies.
[11]But now many nations
have come to fight against you,
saying, "Let's destroy Jerusalem.
We will look at her and be glad we have
defeated her."
[12]But they don't know
what the LORD is thinking;
they don't understand his plan.
He has gathered them like bundles of grain
to the threshing floor.

[13]"Get up and beat them, people of Jerusalem.
I will make you strong as if you had
horns of iron
and hoofs of bronze.
You will beat many nations into
small pieces
and give their wealth to the LORD,
their treasure to the Lord of all the earth."

4:1 Last Days: 1 Timothy 4:1
4:2 Instruction: Luke 12:12
4:5 Names of God: Matthew 1:21

4:7 The Remnant: Micah 5:7–8
4:8 *watchtower . . . flocks.* This probably means a part of Jerusalem. The leaders would be like shepherds in a tower watching their sheep.

5 So, strong city, gather your soldiers
together,
because we are surrounded and attacked.
They will hit the leader of Israel
in the face with a club.

The Ruler to Be Born in Bethlehem

2"But you, Bethlehem Ephrathah,
though you are too small to be among the
army groups from Judah,
from you will come one who will
rule Israel for me.
He comes from very old times,
from days long ago."

3The LORD will give up his people
until the one who is having a baby gives birth;
then the rest of his relatives will return
to the people of Israel.
4At that time the ruler of Israel will stand
and take care of his people
with the LORD's strength
and with the power of the name of
the LORD his God.
The Israelites will live in safety,
because his greatness will reach all
over the earth.
5 He will bring peace.

Rescue and Punishment

Assyria will surely come into our country
and walk over our large buildings.
We will set up seven shepherds,
eight leaders of the people.⚭
6They will destroy the Assyrians
with their swords;
they will conquer the land of Assyria with
their swords drawn.
They will rescue us from the Assyrians when
they come into our land,
when they walk over our borders.

7Then the people of Jacob who are left alive
will be to other people
like dew from the LORD
or rain on the grass—
it does not wait for human beings;
it does not pause for any person.
8Those of Jacob's people who are left alive
will be scattered among many
nations and peoples.
They will be like a lion among the animals
of the forest,
like a young lion in a flock of sheep:
As it goes, it jumps on them
and tears them to pieces,
and no one can save them.⚭
9So you will raise your fist in victory
over your enemies,
and all your enemies will be destroyed.

10The LORD says, "At that time,
I will take your horses from you
and destroy your chariots.
11I will destroy the cities in your country
and tear down all your defenses.
12I will take away the magic charms you use
so you will have no more fortune-tellers.⚭
13I will destroy your statues of gods
and the stone pillars you worship
so that you will no longer worship
what your hands have made.
14I will tear down Asherah idols from you
and destroy your cities.
15In my anger and rage,
I will pay back the nations that
have not listened."

The LORD's Case

6 Now hear what the LORD says:
"Get up; plead your case in front
of the mountains;
let the hills hear your story.
2Mountains, listen to the LORD's legal case.
Foundations of the earth, listen.
The LORD has a legal case against his people,
and he will accuse Israel."

3He says, "My people, what did I do to you?
How did I make you tired of me?
Tell me.
4I brought you from the land of Egypt
and freed you from slavery;
I sent Moses, Aaron, and Miriam to you.
5My people, remember
the evil plans of Balak king of Moab
and what Balaam son of Beor told Balak.
Remember what happened from
Acacia to Gilgal
so that you will know the LORD does
what is right!"

5:2 *Bethlehem Ephrathah.* Bethlehem was a small, inconspicuous village, so it is a surprise that deliverance came from there. Of course, Bethlehem was David's hometown (1 Samuel 16), so this prophecy looks forward to a Davidic ruler. In the New Testament we learn that Jesus, the son of David, comes out of Bethlehem (Matthew 2:6).

⚭**5:5 Peace:** Matthew 5:9
⚭**5:8 The Remnant:** Micah 7:18
⚭**5:12 Magic:** Nahum 3:4

6You say, "What can I bring with me
when I come before the LORD,
when I bow before God on high?
Should I come before him with burnt offerings,
with year-old calves?
7Will the LORD be pleased with a
thousand male sheep?
Will he be pleased with ten thousand
rivers of oil?
Should I give my first child for the
evil I have done?
Should I give my very own child for my sin?"
8The LORD has told you, human, what is good;
he has told you what he wants from you:
to do what is right to other people,
love being kind to others,
and live humbly, obeying your God.⚭

9The voice of the LORD calls to the city,
and the wise person honors him.
So pay attention to the rod of punishment;
pay attention to the One who
threatens to punish.
10Are there still in the wicked house
wicked treasures
and the cursed false measure?
11Can I forgive people who cheat others
with wrong weights and scales?
12The rich people of the city
do cruel things.
Its people tell lies;
they do not tell the truth.
13As for me, I will make you sick.
I will attack you, ruining you because
of your sins.
14You will eat, but you won't become full;
you will still be hungry and empty.
You will store up, but save nothing,
and what you store up, the sword will destroy.
15You will plant,
but you won't harvest.
You will step on your olives,
but you won't get any oil from them.
You will crush the grapes,
but you will not drink the new wine.
16This is because you obey the laws of King Omri
and do all the things that Ahab's family does;
you follow their advice.
So I will let you be destroyed.
The people in your city will be laughed at,
and other nations will make fun of you.

The Evil That People Do

7 Poor me! I am like a hungry man,
and all the summer fruit has been picked—
there are no grapes left to eat,
none of the early figs I love.
2All of the faithful people are gone;
there is not one good person left
in this country.
Everyone is waiting to kill someone;
everyone is trying to trap someone else.
3With both hands they are doing evil.
Rulers ask for money,
and judges' decisions are bought for a price.
Rich people tell what they want,
and they get it.
4Even the best of them is like a thornbush;
the most honest of them is worse than a
prickly plant.
The day that your watchmen warned you
about has come.
Now they will be confused.
5Don't believe your neighbor
or trust a friend.
Don't say anything,
even to your wife.
6A son will not honor his father,
a daughter will turn against her mother,
and a daughter-in-law will be against her
mother-in-law;
a person's enemies will be members of his
own family.

The LORD's Kindness

7Israel says, "I will look to the LORD for help.
I will wait for God to save me;
my God will hear me.
8Enemy, don't laugh at me.
I have fallen, but I will get up again.
I sit in the shadow of trouble now,
but the LORD will be a light for me.
9I sinned against the LORD,
so he was angry with me,
but he will defend my case in court.
He will bring about what is right for me.

⚭**6:8 Justice:** 2 Thessalonians 1:5–7
⚭**6:8 Repentance:** Mark 1:15
6:8 Micah summarized God's ethical demands this way: "The Lord has told you, human, what is good; he has told you what he wants from you: to do what is right to other people, love being kind to others, and live humbly, obeying your God" (Micah 6:8). Micah was not naive about the evil that people do, and he was specific in his confrontation of them. But he also recalled the people to God's goodness and kindness; he held out the hope that they would return as Israel, God's people, to the land because God would be true to his people and would not stay angry forever. God "enjoys being kind" (Micah 7:18; see also Isaiah 1:17; Jeremiah 22:3–5; Hosea 6; Zechariah 7:9–14).
⚭**6:8 Community:** Micah 7:18
6:16 *King Omri.* King Omri and his son, King Ahab, were known for worshiping Baal and for their unjust business dealings.
7:4 *watchmen.* Another name for prophets. The prophets were like guards who stood on a city's wall and watched for trouble coming from far away.

Prophet & Prophecy

Acts 3:23

What is the purpose of a prophet? Are prophets only concerned about predicting the future? Was Jesus a prophet? Are there prophets today?

A prophet was a person called by God to bring his word to his people. He was the divine spokesperson, a messenger from the Lord (Exodus 6:28–7:5). Indeed, the prophet's message was often introduced by a phrase that indicated that his words were identical with the words of God himself. Two of the most common introductions to the words of the prophets are, "This is what the Lord says" and "the word of the Lord." The prophets often spoke in the first person singular, "I," on behalf of God.

The relationship between God's words and the prophet's words had an important implication for how those who heard their words should react. They should respond to the words of the prophet as if they were the very words of God. The prophet's message often, but not always, concerned the future. This characteristic of the prophet's message is so amazing and wonderful that it occasionally distorts our understanding of what a prophet did. As a matter of fact, the prophet's concern with the future usually focused on the behavior of God's people in the present. That is, the prophet often painted a picture of the future that would come true if the people did not repent. The point is that the prophets never revealed the future for the sake of the future, but in order to address the present.

Of course, the Bible also warns that people may set themselves up as prophets when they really are not. We read about false prophets like Zedekiah (1 Kings 22) and Hananiah (Jeremiah 28). God gave rules for distinguishing true prophets from false prophets. A false prophet spoke in the name of other gods. Even if his prophecy was accompanied by miracles, the people were not to believe him (Deuteronomy 13:1–5). Also, a false prophet claimed to speak for the Lord, the true God, but if his prophecy did not come true then he too was a false prophet (Deuteronomy 18:14–21).

At the heart of prophecy is the fact that the prophet was a messenger of God. But the prophet was more than a messenger.

For instance, the prophet was someone who interceded on behalf of the people. They had a divine responsibility to pray for the welfare of others. Indeed, the first mention of a prophet in the Bible is when Abraham was called a prophet in Genesis 20:7. He was called a prophet, not in the context of bringing a message from God to Abimelech, but rather because he was one who could pray that the king not die. Moses later constantly interceded for the people of Israel when God wanted to bring judgment upon them (Exodus 32:30–34). Time and time again the prophets prayed to God for others' well-being.

When kings began to rule in Israel, the prophets took on another important role. They were the king's conscience. The king himself was supposed to be an important example and encouragement to godliness (Deuteronomy 17:14–20), but more often than not the kings of Israel and Judah led people away and not to the Lord.

When this happened, it was the duty of the prophet to confront the king and, if possible, get him back on the right road. Saul was the first king, and Samuel was Saul's conscience, frequently confronting him (1 Samuel 13) and finally proclaiming God's judgment on him (1 Samuel 15).

While the prophets were mostly concerned with the present, they did reveal the future. Usually when they revealed the future, it was in the years, decades, or perhaps centuries ahead. They saw beyond the events of their own day and even beyond the time of the coming of Christ to earth. Certain prophets, like Daniel (chapters 7–12) and Zechariah (chapter 14) revealed the end of the world. These prophecies of the end of the world are often given in language that uses a lot of images. They both reveal and conceal the truth of the end times. They do not give us any indication, directly or indirectly, of when the end will come.

The purpose of these end times prophecies is to comfort God's people in the present. Living in a fallen, ungodly world, God's people often find themselves suffering in the present and looking with hope to the future. The prophets give divine comfort by saying that Christ is surely coming again in the future, and he will bring us to himself. They paint a picture of a future of joy that will make our present suffering seem like the blink of an eye (Romans 8:18–25).

Prophet & Prophecy: For additional scriptures on this topic go to Genesis 20:7.

Stephen

ACTS 6

What did it mean for Stephen to be a "Greek-speaking follower"? What kind of leadership role did Stephen play in the early church? How and why did he die?

The spirit of Hellenism is seen in much of the New Testament. Even though the roots of the early church are deep in Hebrew soil, there are branches of Greek influence that are clearly evident. It is seen in the use of Greek names for persons (Andrew, Philip, Stephen) and places (Tyre, Caesarea, Galilee), the architecture of many of the public buildings, and the widespread use of the Greek language. This influence was probably greatest in the cities.

Much of this Greek flavor was the direct result of the dispersion of the Jewish people throughout the Greek world. As they lived in the Greek environment and intermarried with those around them, they were gradually assimilated into that culture. Greek was their first language and was the one used for reading and studying Scripture. This did not mean that they abandoned their religion, but that there were elements of their culture that affected their lives.

Stephen was a Greek-speaking Jewish man (in contrast with the Hebrew-speaking Jewish people of Israel). Many of these Jewish people from other countries had been exposed to the Good News on the day of Pentecost. Stephen and six other Hellenistic Jews were chosen by the church to be deacons. The role of this group of servants does not seem to be clear. They served as a relief committee, but at least two of their number, Stephen and Philip, were also preachers.

Stephen's role as a preacher and miracle worker is how he is best remembered. His preaching was particularly objectionable to the members of the synagogue. The thing that appears to have angered them was the distinction Stephen seemed to be making between Judaism and Christianity. Up until now, the Christian faith was contained as a movement within the Jewish religion. They faithfully attended Temple services and were thoroughly orthodox. The logical end of Stephen's sermon was a Christian faith that was separate from Judaism.

When we examine the content of his sermon, the longest discourse in Acts, we find that he is claiming that the church is the true Israel and that the Jewish people have been disobedient (Acts 7:48, 51–53). He was showing that God had moved again and again outside of the nation of Israel and without the benefit of the Temple (Acts 7:2, 9, 14, 29, 45, 48). He, furthermore, accused his hearers of murdering Christ as their ancestors had the prophets (Acts 7:51). He was saying that the Christ they had rejected was the one who could bring people to God, whether they were Jewish or not (the arguments begun here are the seed that will later blossom into Gentile conversions).

The reaction of the Jewish leaders was like an explosion: "They became furious. They were so mad they were grinding their teeth at Stephen" (Acts 7:54). When Stephen saw their reaction, he described a scene in heaven where Jesus was standing as his advocate before God (Acts 7:55). What happened next can only be termed a mob scene. There was no formal sentence of death pronounced, yet Stephen was dragged outside the city and stoned to death.

A young man was present at the stoning on the side of those who carried out the death sentence. He even held their coats. This young man's name was Saul, later to be called Paul, the great apostle to the Gentiles (Acts 7:58). God would soon turn his life dramatically around.

There were many similarities between Stephen's death and that of Jesus. Both were tried before the Jewish leaders (Luke 22:66; Acts 6:12); both were falsely accused (Mark 14:56–58; Acts 6:13, 14); both were victims of a lynch-mob mentality (Luke 23:18–23; Acts 7:57–59); and both prayed for God to receive their spirit and forgive their killers (Luke 23:34, 46; Acts 7:59–60).

The immediate result of Stephen's death was the scattering of the young church before the relentless pursuit of a fervent persecution (Acts 8:1). Although the persecution was designed to cause the young fledgling movement to die, it resulted in its expansion and growth. Everywhere they went, believers proclaimed their faith in Jesus. The faith spread, just as Jesus had said, "in Jerusalem, in all of Judea, in Samaria, and in every part of the world" (Acts 1:8). Another indirect benefit of the persecution was that Saul, who had participated in the stoning of Stephen and who was committed to the destruction of this movement, found instead a new relationship with Christ and became one of the church's greatest missionaries.

Stephen: For additional scriptures on this topic go to Acts 22:20.

Then he will bring me out into the light,
and I will see him set things right.
10Then my enemies will see this,
and they will be ashamed,
those who said to me,
'Where is the LORD your God?'
I will look down on them.
They will get walked on, like mud
in the street."

Israel Will Return

11The time will come when your walls
will be built again,
when your country will grow.
12At that time your people will come back to you
from Assyria and the cities of Egypt,
and from Egypt to the Euphrates River,
and from sea to sea and mountain to mountain.
13The earth will be ruined for the
people who live in it
because of their deeds.

A Prayer to God

14So shepherd your people with your stick;
tend the flock of people who belong to you.
That flock now lives alone in the forest
in the middle of a garden land.
Let them feed in Bashan and Gilead
as in days long ago.

15"As in the days when I brought you out of Egypt,
I will show them miracles."

16When the nations see those miracles,
they will no longer brag about their power.
They will put their hands over their mouths,
refusing to listen.
17They will crawl in the dust like a snake,
like insects crawling on the ground.
They will come trembling from their holes to
the LORD our God
and will turn in fear before you.
18There is no God like you.
You forgive those who are guilty of sin;
you don't look at the sins of your people
who are left alive.
You will not stay angry forever,
because you enjoy being kind.
19You will have mercy on us again;
you will conquer our sins.
You will throw away all our sins
into the deepest part of the sea.
20You will be true to the people of Jacob,
and you will be kind to the people of Abraham
as you promised to our ancestors long ago.

7:14 *Bashan and Gilead.* Bashan and Gilead were parts of Israel's land especially known for their fertility and abundance.
7:18 The Remnant: Acts 15:17
7:18 Community: Acts 2:42–47
7:20 Abraham: Matthew 1:1

Notes:

INTRODUCTION TO THE BOOK OF

NAHUM

God Will Punish Assyria

WHO WROTE THIS BOOK?

The prophet Nahum wrote the book that bears his name, according to verse one.

TO WHOM WAS THIS BOOK WRITTEN?

Nahum wrote to the people of Judah.

WHERE WAS IT WRITTEN?

The place of writing of the Book of Nahum is uncertain though it probably was in Judah. Even Nahum's hometown of Elkosh cannot be specifically located.

WHEN WAS IT WRITTEN?

The book was probably written between 663 and 612 B.C., which makes Nahum a contemporary of Zephaniah and the young Jeremiah.

WHAT IS THE BOOK ABOUT?

The Book of Nahum centers on God's judgment of the wicked city of Nineveh. The end of the book tells of the city's destruction.

WHY WAS THIS BOOK WRITTEN?

The twofold purpose of the Book of Nahum is to pronounce judgment on the evil city of Nineveh and, at the same time, offer hope and encouragement to Judah—God's people who have been oppressed by Nineveh.

SO WHAT DOES THIS BOOK MEAN TO US?

Nahum show that God alone is in control of histories and futures. That being true, God is in control of our future, too. He is the all-powerful God of the universe—our source of hope and salvation in the presence of our enemies.

SUMMARY:

Nahum combines literary beauty with a harsh message. The book is a prophecy against Nineveh, looking forward to its destruction. Nahum, about whom we know very little, wrote after the lifetime of Jonah, and now God allowed no avenue of escape for the cruel Assyrian city. As a matter of fact, we can roughly date Nahum to the period of time between 664 and 612 B.C. In 612 the prophecy came to fulfillment when the forces of Babylon overran and destroyed Nineveh.

The Book of Nahum is filled with a variety of judgment speeches against Nineveh. While this book was bad news for that city, it was good news for Nahum's audience, the people of Judah who lived under the shadow of that superpower.

The outline of the book is as follows:

I. Opening Hymn and Prophecies against Nineveh and for Judah (1:1–2:2)
II. Visions and Images of Nineveh's End (2:3–3:18)

I. Opening Hymn and Prophecies against Nineveh and for Judah (1:1–2:2)

The book opens with a rousing hymn celebrating God as a warrior who saves his people and punishes his enemies. The prophet then applies these truths to Nineveh and Judah.

II. Visions and Images of Nineveh's End (2:3–3:18)

The prophet looks into the future and sees the destruction of Nineveh. He taunts the Assyrians, who deserve the fate that awaits them.

NAHUM

This is the message for the city of Nineveh. This is the book of the vision of Nahum, who was from the town of Elkosh.

The LORD Is Angry with Nineveh

2The LORD is a jealous God who punishes;
the LORD punishes and is filled with anger.
The LORD punishes those who are against him,
and he stays angry with his enemies.
3The LORD does not become angry quickly,
and his power is great.
The LORD will not let the guilty
go unpunished.
Where the LORD goes, there are whirlwinds
and storms,
and the clouds are the dust beneath his feet.
4He speaks to the sea and makes it dry;
he dries up all the rivers.
The areas of Bashan and Carmel dry up,
and the flowers of Lebanon dry up.
5The mountains shake in front of him,
and the hills melt.
The earth trembles when he comes;
the world and all who live in it shake
with fear.
6No one can stay alive when he is angry;
no one can survive his strong anger.
His anger is poured out like fire;
the rocks are smashed by him.⚭

7The LORD is good,
giving protection in times of trouble.
He knows who trusts in him.
8But like a rushing flood,
he will completely destroy Nineveh;
he will chase his enemies until he kills them.

9The LORD will completely destroy
anyone making plans against him.
Trouble will not come a second time.
10Those people will be like tangled thorns
or like people drunk from their wine;
they will be burned up quickly like dry weeds.

11Someone has come from Nineveh
who makes evil plans against the LORD
and gives wicked advice.

12This is what the LORD says:
"Although Assyria is strong and
has many people,
it will be defeated and brought to an end.
Although I have made you suffer, Judah,
I will make you suffer no more.
13Now I will free you from their control
and tear away your chains."

14The LORD has given you this command, Nineveh:
"You will not have descendants to
carry on your name.
I will destroy the idols and metal images
that are in the temple of your gods.
I will make a grave for you,
because you are wicked."

15Look, there on the hills,
someone is bringing good news!
He is announcing peace!
Celebrate your feasts, people of Judah,
and give your promised sacrifices to God.
The wicked will not come to attack you again;
they have been completely destroyed.

Nineveh Will Be Defeated

2 The destroyer is coming to attack you,
Nineveh.
Guard the defenses.
Watch the road.
Get ready.
Gather all your strength!
2Destroyers have destroyed God's people
and ruined their vines,
but the LORD will bring back Jacob's greatness
like Israel's greatness.

3The shields of his soldiers are red;
the army is dressed in red.
The metal on the chariots flashes like fire
when they are ready to attack;
their horses are excited.

1:1 *Nineveh.* The capital city of the country of Assyria. Nahum uses Nineveh to stand for all of Assyria.
1:1 *Elkosh.* We do not know with certainty where Elkosh was located.
1:4 *Bashan and Carmel.* Bashan and Carmel are known well for their fertility and prosperity.
⚭**1:6 Hell:** Malachi 4:1
1:11 The Book of Nahum celebrates the downfall of the evil Assyrian city of Nineveh. For years, Nineveh held sway over the world. They were known as cruel overlords. The opening of Nahum praises God, a warrior who will fight against his people's enemies. Then Nineveh is described. In this verse the core of their evil is revealed—their rebellion against the Lord himself. For this reason, according to Nahum, the city will surely fall.
2:1 *destroyer.* The Babylonians, the Scythians, and the Medes destroyed Nineveh.
2:3 *red.* We do not know whether red is the color of the army's uniforms or whether these are blood-stained uniforms. In any case, we know that this prophecy found its fulfillment when the Babylonian army attacked Nineveh in 612 B.C.

4The chariots race through the streets
and rush back and forth through
the city squares.
They look like torches;
they run like lightning.

5He calls his officers,
but they stumble on the way.
They hurry to the city wall,
and the shield is put into place.
6The river gates are thrown open,
and the palace is destroyed.
7It has been announced that the people
of Nineveh
will be captured and carried away.
The slave girls moan like doves
and beat their breasts, because
they are sad.
8Nineveh is like a pool,
and now its water is draining away.
"Stop! Stop!" the people yell,
but no one turns back.
9Take the silver!
Take the gold!
There is no end to the treasure—
piles of wealth of every kind.
10Nineveh is robbed, ruined, and destroyed.
The people lose their courage, and their
knees knock.
Stomachs ache, and everyone's
face grows pale.

11Where is the lions' den
and the place where they feed
their young?
Where did the lion, lioness, and cubs go
without being afraid?
12The lion killed enough for his cubs,
enough for his mate.
He filled his cave with the animals he caught;
he filled his den with meat he had killed.

13"I am against you, Nineveh,"
says the LORD All-Powerful.
"I will burn up your chariots in smoke,
and the sword will kill your young lions.
I will stop you from hunting down others
on the earth,
and your messengers' voices
will no longer be heard."

It Will Be Terrible for Nineveh

3 How terrible it will be for the city that has
killed so many.
It is full of lies
and goods stolen from other countries.
It is always killing somebody.
2Hear the sound of whips
and the noise of the wheels.
Hear horses galloping
and chariots bouncing along!
3Horses are charging,
swords are shining,
spears are gleaming!
Many are dead;
their bodies are piled up—
too many to count.
People stumble over the dead bodies.
4The city was like a prostitute;
she was charming and a lover of magic.
She made nations slaves with
her prostitution
and her witchcraft.⚭

5"I am against you, Nineveh," says the LORD
All-Powerful.
"I will pull your dress up over your face
and show the nations your nakedness
and the kingdoms your shame.
6I will throw filthy garbage on you
and make a fool of you.
I will make people stare at you.
7Everyone who sees you will run
away and say,
'Nineveh is in ruins. Who will cry for her?'
Nineveh, where will I find anyone
to comfort you?"

8You are no better than Thebes,
who sits by the Nile River
with water all around her.
The river was her defense;
the waters were like a wall around her.
9Cush and Egypt gave her endless strength;
Put and Libya supported her.
10But Thebes was captured
and went into captivity.
Her small children were beaten to death
at every street corner.
Lots were thrown for her important men,
and all of her leaders were put in chains.

2:5 *He.* This probably means the king of Assyria.
2:11 *lion.* We know from Assyrian records that they likened themselves to the noble and ferocious lion. Here Nahum picks up on their own language and ridicules them.
⚭**3:4 Magic:** Malachi 3:5

3:5 *pull your dress up over your face.* Nahum likens Nineveh to a prostitute. In ancient times a prostitute was punished by being publicly humiliated in this way.
3:8 *Thebes.* Assyria itself had defeated the Egyptian city of Thebes, previously thought impregnable, in 664 B.C.

11Nineveh, you will be drunk, too.
You will hide;
you will look for a place safe from the enemy.
12All your defenses are like fig trees
with ripe fruit.
When the tree is shaken, the figs fall into the
mouth of the eater.
13Look at your soldiers.
They are all women!
The gates of your land
are wide open for your enemies;
fire has burned the bars of your gates.

14Get enough water before the long war begins.
Make your defenses strong!
Get mud,
mix clay,
make bricks!
15There the fire will burn you up.
The sword will kill you;
like grasshoppers eating crops, the battle will
completely destroy you.
Grow in number like hopping locusts;
grow in number like swarming locusts!
16Your traders are more than the stars in the sky,
but like locusts, they strip the land
and then fly away.
17Your guards are like locusts.
Your officers are like swarms of locusts
that hang on the walls on a cold day.
When the sun comes up, they fly away,
and no one knows where they have gone.
18King of Assyria, your rulers are asleep;
your important men lie down to rest.
Your people have been scattered
on the mountains,
and there is no one to bring them back.
19Nothing can heal your wound;
your injury will not heal.
Everyone who hears about you applauds,
because everyone has felt your endless cruelty.

INTRODUCTION TO THE BOOK OF

HABAKKUK

Learning How to Trust God

WHO WORTE THIS BOOK?

The Book of Habakkuk was written by God's prophet of the same name.

TO WHOM WAS THIS BOOK WRITTEN?

Habakkuk writes to the people of Judah.

WHERE WAS IT WRITTEN?

Composition of this writing probably took place in Judah where Habakkuk lived and ministered.

WHEN WAS IT WRITTEN?

Habakkuk prophesied and wrote sometime during the reign of Josiah and, perhaps, Jehoiakim (640–598 B.C.).

WHAT IS THE BOOK ABOUT?

The Book of Habakkuk is a conversation between God and the prophet about the evil that is prevalent in Judah. Habakkuk is confused about God's lack of response to the sin of Judah and his use of a wicked nation (Babylon) to judge Judah. God at last reveals to the prophet his plan to judge the evildoers (both in Judah and later in Babylon).

WHY WAS THIS BOOK WRITTEN?

Through the passionate voice of Habakkuk, God speaks assuring words to the godly people of Judah who are having trouble understanding his divine ways. Finally, Habakkuk learns to wait on God and his perfect timing, and he realizes that the people who are right must live by faith (2:4).

SO WHAT DOES THIS BOOK MEAN TO US?

Even though we, as finite beings, often struggle to understand the workings of our infinite God, we must learn to rely on his superior wisdom and wait on his divine timing for our lives. We, too, must learn to live by faith (Romans 1:17).

SUMMARY:

Habakkuk is another prophet about whom we know little since he is not mentioned outside of this book. The content of his prophecy (see especially 1:6) suggests that he ministered at the end of the seventh or early sixth century B.C., thus making him a contemporary of Jeremiah, Zephaniah, Nahum, and maybe Joel.

His time was characterized by the upswing of Babylon and the fear and impending doom of Judah. He questions God's silence in the light of the evil of Judah and the power of Babylon.

The book has the following structure:

I. The Prophet's Questions and God's Response (1:1–2:20)
II. Habakkuk's Psalm (3:1–19)

I. The Prophet's Questions and God's Response (1:1–2:20)

Habakkuk does not understand what God is doing. He does not know why God allows evil people to prosper. God answers that he is using the Babylonians as the tool of his anger against them, but that he will also punish Babylon for their sins after he uses them.

III. Habakkuk's Psalm (3:1–19)

Habakkuk ends with a prayer that celebrates God as warrior. He will come and bring justice to the earth by punishing evil people and saving the good.

HABAKKUK

This is the message Habakkuk the prophet received.

Habakkuk Complains

2LORD, how long must I ask for help
and you ignore me?
I cry out to you about violence,
but you do not save us!
3Why do you make me see wrong things
and make me look at trouble?
People are destroying things and
hurting others in front of me;
they are arguing and fighting.
4So the teachings are weak,
and justice never comes.
Evil people gain while good people lose;
the judges no longer make fair decisions.

The LORD Answers

5"Look at the nations!
Watch them and be amazed and shocked.
I will do something in your lifetime
that you won't believe even when you are
told about it.
6I will use the Babylonians,
those cruel and wild people
who march across the earth
and take lands that don't belong to them.
7They scare and frighten people.
They do what they want to do
and are good only to themselves.
8Their horses are faster than leopards
and quicker than wolves at sunset.
Their horse soldiers attack quickly;
they come from places far away.
They attack quickly, like an eagle swooping
down for food.
9 They all come to fight.
Nothing can stop them.
Their prisoners are as many as
the grains of sand.
10They laugh at kings
and make fun of rulers.
They laugh at all the strong, walled cities
and build dirt piles to the top of the
walls to capture them.
11Then they leave like the wind and move on.
They are guilty of worshiping
their own strength."

Habakkuk Complains Again

12LORD, you live forever,
my God, my holy God.
We will not die.
LORD, you have chosen the Babylonians
to punish people;
our Rock, you picked them to punish.
13Your eyes are too good to look at evil;
you cannot stand to see those who do wrong.
So how can you put up with those evil people?
How can you be quiet when the wicked
swallow up people who are better
than they are?
14You treat people like fish in the sea,
like sea animals without a leader.
15The enemy brings them in with hooks.
He catches them in his net
and drags them in his fishnet.
So he rejoices and sings for joy.
16The enemy offers sacrifices to his net
and burns incense to worship it,
because it lets him live like the rich
and enjoy the best food.
17Will he keep on taking riches with his net?
Will he go on destroying people without
showing mercy?

2 I will stand like a guard to watch
and place myself at the tower.
I will wait to see what he will say to me;
I will wait to learn how God will
answer my complaint.

The LORD Answers

2The LORD answered me:
"Write down the vision;
write it clearly on clay tablets
so whoever reads it can run
to tell others.

1:6 Habakkuk complains to God concerning the treatment of the Israelites at the hand of their own leaders (1:1–4). God's response is not one that Habakkuk expected: God will send the wicked Babylonians to settle matters (1:5–11). Habakkuk, however, begins to question God's reasons for using an idolatrous nation to discipline God's chosen people (1:12–17). But God responds that Babylon's ultimate fate is not in doubt: God will come and make them drink from his "cup of anger" (2:16). Babylon ultimately represents the forces of evil that are pitted against God, and who meet their final doom in the Book of Revelation.

1:10 *build dirt piles.* One common strategy for taking a walled city was to build a dirt ramp against it so attacking troops could reach the top of the wall. Constructing such a dirt ramp, of course, was dangerous because it brought the builders within range of the defenders' weapons.

1:15 *hooks.* It was the practice of warfare during biblical times that prisoners of war have hooks put in their noses, with ropes attached, and then be dragged like animals.

2:2 *clay tablets.* In biblical times much writing was done with a reed stylus on soft clay, which would then harden.

Paul (Saul)

Acts 9

Was Paul sadistic or spiritually sincere in his participation with the death of God's servant Stephen?
Why were the Christians suspicious of Paul (Saul renamed)?
What made Paul such a great leader in the church of Christ?

When Stephen was being stoned to death for his beliefs about Jesus, Saul coldly watched the coats of those who were conspirators (Acts 7:58). Two chapters later, he himself had become a persecutor of Christians, threatening to kill or arrest any he found (Acts 9:1–2). He later tells us that his violence was motivated by religious zeal; he thought the Christian message about Jesus disgraced and threatened the Jewish religion as he had learned it (Acts 22:1–5; 26:4–12; Galatians 1:13–14; Philippians 3:5–6).

On one such trip, motivated by his aggression against Christians, Saul's life changed forever. On the road to Damascus the risen Jesus confronted Saul and made it clear that Saul's hatred of Christians was hatred of the Lord himself (Acts 9:3–6). From that encounter and ever after, Saul—better known by his Roman name, Paul (Acts 13:9)—was to become a chosen instrument for God's work among all people. The risen Jesus said of him, "I have chosen Saul for an important work. He must tell about me to those who are not Jews, to kings, and to the people of Israel. I will show him how much he must suffer for my name" (Acts 9:15). Each description in this short commission was to be fulfilled. Paul went to all people and gave his message to the great and the common, to slaves and to rulers, to Jewish people and others (Acts 13:1–28:30; Romans 1:1–15; 15:14–32). He paid a tremendous personal price, suffering greatly in the process through beatings and stonings, hunger and homelessness, thieves on the road and shipwreck at sea. His opposition came from all directions—from both religious and community leaders, from fellow Jews and those in the marketplaces (Acts 16:16–24; 27:13–44; 2 Corinthians 4:8–11; 6:4–10; 11:23).

At first the Christians were suspicious of the dramatic turnaround in Paul's life, suspecting that this was a ploy to betray them (Acts 9:26), but through the mediation of Ananias and Barnabas (Acts 9:10–19, 27) Paul was soon brought into the fellowship of Christians and began to proclaim, "Jesus is the Son of God" (Acts 9:20; Galatians 1:23). In his perhaps thirty-year career as a Christian missionary that followed, it could truly be said that Paul was a missionary of the northern region bordering the Mediterranean Sea, traveling and spreading the message about Jesus "from Jerusalem all the way around to Illyricum" (Romans 15:19), and ultimately to Rome. In his missionary travels he showed great flexibility and ingenuity, taking the message about Christ to whomever would listen.

Throughout his career Paul was quite adept at utilizing whatever resources he had at his disposal. When he was with Jewish people, he stressed his Jewish authority (1 Corinthians 9:19–23). When he was with Romans, he made use of his Roman citizenship. Having been trained in tentmaking—probably during his apprenticeship as a Pharisee under Gamaliel, a key Jewish teacher of his day (Acts 22:3)—Paul supported himself throughout his missionary work by laboring with his own hands. Not only did this provide a practical way for him to feed and clothe himself and pay for his travels, but it took him to the center of the marketplace where people were always interested to listen to craftsmen-philosophers share their latest ideas. Ultimately, his ability to support himself gave him a sure and certain defense against charges that he was in it for the money (1 Corinthians 9:1–23; 2 Corinthians 2:17; 4:2; 11:7–11; 12:13, 16; 1 Thessalonians 2:3–10). Paul endured all this because he was certain that he was sent by Christ as his "apostle" or ambassador (2 Corinthians 5:20), and he even expresses the spiritual compulsion to support himself as a sign that he was a slave of Christ, his master, a bondservant who should not receive pay for his efforts (Romans 1:1; 1 Corinthians 7:22; 9:16–19; 2 Corinthians 4:5; Galatians 1:10).

Thirteen letters in the New Testament bear Paul's name as their author. These letters are arranged from longest to shortest, beginning with letters to churches (Romans–2 Thessalonians), then letters to individuals (1 Timothy–Philemon). These letters were gathered and spread from a very early date because Christians believed they were inspired and helpful for the entire church (2 Timothy 3:10–17; 2 Peter 3:15–16). Paul's letters are written in good, ancient form, but show many signs of flexibility, creativity, and the conventions of communication and persuasion of his day. As a prolific pastor, missionary, and letter-writer Paul has left a rich legacy to the church.

Paul (Saul) For additional scriptures on this topic go to Acts 7:54–60.

Racism

Acts 10

Is racism a concept used in the Bible? By what is it motivated, and what does it look like? How does the Good News relate to racism? Can one find scriptural models for moving beyond racism?

From Jews, Egyptians, and Moabites to Samaritans and Romans, the Bible depicts a world that is full of different races and their interactions, both positive and negative. The word "racism" is a fairly modern term, but there is no lack of prejudice and tension between ethnic groups. Whether it is oppression in Egypt (Exodus 1:8–14) or tension between Jews and Romans (Mark 12:13–17), it is clear that individuals and groups often aim to gain power, security, or status by excluding or mistreating those who are ethnically and culturally different. What is also clear is God's contrasting perspective: He cares and has a redemptive purpose for all the peoples of the world.

God's care is described in Genesis 12 with the calling of Abram (renamed Abraham in Genesis 17:5). In Genesis 12:3, God promises that he will make Abram a great nation and that "all the people on earth will be blessed through [him]." God's purpose in calling together a particular group of people for himself was to bless all nations.

God's intention to bless all the people of the world did not mean that there would be no distinctives between the Jews and other nations. God commanded his chosen people to maintain some kinds of separation from the nations around them (Exodus 34:12–16; Deuteronomy 7:3–4; Joshua 23:12–13). They were to be a holy nation, set apart for God. In commanding this separation, God's concern is that the Israelites not be influenced by the religions of those around them. Too often, rather than influencing their neighbors, interactions, agreements, and marriages with non-Jews led God's people to bow down to false gods and worship idols.

While Israel was commanded to resist being influenced to worship foreign gods, they were to welcome foreigners who came into *their* midst. Exodus 12:48–49 states that a foreigner who is circumcised is to be treated like a citizen of Israel. This kindness toward strangers and foreigners was of particular importance because the Israelites were at one time foreigners in Egypt (Leviticus 19:33–34). Consequently this understanding of what it feels like to be a foreigner and be discriminated against should result in kindness toward strangers in their midst.

Jesus was a Jew and noted distinctions between Jew and non-Jew (Mark 7:24–30), but he also challenged many prejudices and assumptions prevalent in his culture. In Luke 10 Jesus tells a parable in which a Samaritan (a member of an ethnic group despised by most Jews) is the hero, contrasted to the highly esteemed priest and Levite. In John 4, Jesus spends a long time talking with a Samaritan woman. Everyone, including the woman, finds this conversation startling because "Jewish people are not friends with Samaritans" (John 4:9).

At times prejudice and racism appear as blatant mistreatment of others. At other times it is more subtle, appearing in the form of omission and exclusion. Jesus challenges people who believe that they are exclusively entitled to receive God's favor. He infuriates his own people by reminding them of their possible exclusion (due to their stubbornness) from what God is doing (Matthew 11:20–24; Luke 4:23–27).

Issues of race, primarily between Jews and non-Jews, was a critical factor in the development of the early church. With Jesus' command to "go and make followers of all people in the world" (Matthew 28:19), the church had to deal with the increasingly pressing issue of how these different groups of people would interact as they came together in their newfound faith in Christ. In a world of division and differences, the Good News of Jesus was to cut through the lines of prejudice and racism.

In the Book of Acts, Peter is persuaded by an angel to go and visit Cornelius, a Roman soldier. The vision that comes to him three times is presumably about food, but is a metaphor to prepare him for another lesson. Just as Jewish law forbids eating unclean food, "it is against . . . Jewish law for Jewish people to associate with or visit anyone who is not Jewish" (Acts 10:28). Arriving at Cornelius' home, Peter discovers the inclusive nature of the Good News and that, "to God every person is the same" (Acts 10:34). All racial distinctions are removed at the cross (Galatians 3:28; Colossians 3:11)⚭

⚭**Racism:** For additional scriptures on this topic go to Genesis 12:1–5.

[3]It is not yet time for the message to come true,
but that time is coming soon;
the message will come true.
It may seem like a long time,
but be patient and wait for it,
because it will surely come;
it will not be delayed.
[4]The evil nation is very proud of itself;
it is not living as it should.
But those who are right with God will
live by trusting in him.

[5]"Just as wine can trick a person,
those who are too proud will not last,
because their desire is like a grave's
desire for death,
and like death they always want more.
They gather other nations for themselves
and collect for themselves all the countries.
[6]But all the nations the Babylonians have hurt
will laugh at them.
They will make fun of the Babylonians
and say, 'How terrible it will be for the one
that steals many things.
How long will that nation get rich by forcing
others to pay them?'

[7]"One day the people from whom you have
taken money will turn against you.
They will realize what is happening and
make you shake with fear.
Then they will take everything you have.
[8]Because you have stolen from many nations,
those who are left will take much from you.
This is because you have killed many people,
destroying countries and cities and
everyone in them.

[9]"How terrible it will be for the nation that
becomes rich by doing wrong,
thinking they will live in a safe place
and escape harm.
[10]Because you have made plans to destroy many
people,
you have made your own houses
ashamed of you.
Because of it, you will lose your lives.
[11]The stones of the walls will cry out against you,
and the boards that support the roof will
agree that you are wrong.

[12]"How terrible it will be for the nation that kills
people to build a city,
that wrongs others to start a town.
[13]The LORD All-Powerful will send fire
to destroy what those people have built;
all the nations' work will be for nothing.
[14]Then, just as water covers the sea,
people everywhere will know the LORD's glory.

[15]"How terrible for the nation that makes
its neighbors drink,
pouring from the jug of wine until
they are drunk
so that it can look at their naked bodies.
[16]You Babylonians will be filled with disgrace,
not respect.
It's your turn to drink and fall to the ground
like a drunk person.
The cup of anger from the LORD's right
hand is coming around to you.
You will receive disgrace, not respect.
[17]You hurt many people in Lebanon,
but now you will be hurt.
You killed many animals there,
and now you must be afraid
because of what you did
to that land, those cities, and the people who
lived in them.

The Message About Idols

[18]"An idol does no good, because a
human made it;
it is only a statue that teaches lies.
The one who made it expects his own
work to help him,
but he makes idols that can't even speak!
[19]How terrible it will be for the one who says to
a wooden statue, 'Come to life!'
How terrible it will be for the one who says
to a silent stone, 'Get up!'
It cannot tell you what to do.
It is only a statue covered with gold and silver;
there is no life in it.
[20]The LORD is in his Holy Temple;
all the earth should be silent in his presence."

Habakkuk's Prayer

3 This is the prayer of Habakkuk the prophet, on shigionoth.

[2]LORD, I have heard the news about you;
I am amazed at what you have done.
LORD, do great things once again in our time;
make those things happen again
in our own days.
Even when you are angry,
remember to be kind.

3:1 *shigionoth.* The word *shigionoth* is similar to the word found in the title of Psalm 7. It remains untranslated because it is a musical term the precise meaning of which is uncertain.

3God is coming from Teman;
the Holy One comes from Mount Paran. *Selah*
His glory covers the skies,
and his praise fills the earth.
4He is like a bright light.
Rays of light shine from his hand,
and there he hides his power.
5Sickness goes before him,
and disease follows behind him.
6He stands and shakes the earth.
He looks, and the nations shake with fear.
The mountains, which stood for ages,
break into pieces;
the old hills fall down.
God has always done this.

7I saw that the tents of Cushan were in trouble
and that the tents of Midian trembled.
8LORD, were you angry at the rivers,
or were you angry at the streams?
Were you angry with the sea
when you rode your horses and
chariots of victory?
9You uncovered your bow
and commanded many arrows to
be brought to you. *Selah*
You split the earth with rivers.
10 The mountains saw you and shook with fear.
The rushing water flowed.
The sea made a loud noise,
and its waves rose high.
11The sun and moon stood still in the sky;
they stopped when they saw the flash of your
flying arrows
and the gleam of your shining spear.
12In anger you marched on the earth;
in anger you punished the nations.
13You came out to save your people,
to save your chosen one.
You crushed the leader of the wicked ones
and took everything he had, from
head to toe. *Selah*
14With the enemy's own spear you stabbed the
leader of his army.
His soldiers rushed out like a storm
to scatter us.
They were happy
as they were robbing the poor people in secret.
15But you marched through the sea
with your horses,
stirring the great waters.

16I hear these things, and my body trembles;
my lips tremble when I hear the sound.
My bones feel weak,
and my legs shake.

But I will wait patiently for the
day of disaster
that will come to the people who attack us.
17Fig trees may not grow figs,
and there may be no grapes on the vines.
There may be no olives growing
and no food growing in the fields.
There may be no sheep in the pens
and no cattle in the barns.
18But I will still be glad in the LORD;
I will rejoice in God my Savior.
19The Lord GOD is my strength.
He makes me like a deer that
does not stumble
so I can walk on the steep mountains.

For the director of music. On my stringed instruments. ⚭

3:3 *Teman and Mount Paran.* Teman and Mount Paran are locations from Israel's wilderness wandering as they moved from Mount Sinai to the Promised Land. In other words, God is seen as again coming from the direction of Mount Sinai. He came from Sinai when he rescued his people from Egypt.

3:8 *sea . . . victory.* This is probably talking about the Israelites crossing the Red Sea.

⚭**3:19 Suffering:** Matthew 5:10–11

INTRODUCTION TO THE BOOK OF

ZEPHANIAH

God Will Judge the World

WHO WROTE THIS BOOK?

As specifically identified in verse one, this book was written by the prophet Zephaniah, a direct decendant of King Hezekiah of Judah.

TO WHOM WAS THIS BOOK WRITTEN?

Zephaniah wrote his prophecy to the people of Judah.

WHERE WAS IT WRITTEN?

As a citizen of Judah, it is probable that he wrote his prophecy in and around that area.

WHEN WAS IT WRITTEN?

In 1:1 Zephaniah sets the date of his writing during the reign of King Josiah, who ruled from 640–609 B.C.

WHAT IS THE BOOK ABOUT?

Like other prophetic messengers, Zephaniah's task was to warn Judah of God's coming judgment on the nations, including Judah, and his ultimate restoration of Judah.

WHY WAS THIS BOOK WRITTEN?

Zephaniah's appointed task is to condem and console at the same time. He promises God's approaching day of judging and destroying the nations, particularly Assyria. Ironically, with the same words, he consoles Judah with the assurance of God's mercy and eventual restoration of Judah.

SO WHAT DOES THIS BOOK MEAN TO US?

We are reminded by Zephaniah that God rules the world. He will, without doubt, visit his righteous judgment on the nations of the earth. At the same moment, God will rescue his faithful people and restore us to himself for eternity.

SUMMARY:

Zephaniah, the prophet, was a descendant of Hezekiah, the king. He probably had access to the upper class of his day and could see firsthand the injustice and oppression of his society.

Zephaniah ministered during the reign of Josiah, thus at the end of the seventh century B.C. around the time of Jeremiah and Nahum.

Zephaniah's message was one of judgment for sin, and then hope for the future. He spoke of the "LORD's day for judging people," a day when God's enemies would be punished and his faithful people rescued.

The outline of the book is as follows:

I. The Judgment of Judah (1:1–2:3)
II. The Judgment of the Nations (2:4–3:8)
III. Future Hope (3:9–20)

I. The Judgment of Judah (1:1–2:3)

Zephaniah describes the coming "LORD's day for judging people" (1:7), a day of judgment against evil people in Judah.

II. The Judgment of the Nations (2:4–3:8)

God will punish the surrounding nations. At the end of this section, God returns to describe the punishment of Jerusalem.

III. Future Hope (3:9–20)

Zephaniah concludes on a joyful note. After judgment comes blessing for the people who remain.

ZEPHANIAH

This is the word of the LORD that came through
Zephaniah while Josiah son of Amon was king
of Judah. Zephaniah was the son of Cushi,
who was the son of Gedaliah. Gedaliah was the son
of Amariah, who was the son of Hezekiah.

The LORD's Judgment

2"I will sweep away everything
from the earth," says the LORD.
3"I will sweep away the people and animals;
I will destroy the birds in the air
and the fish of the sea.
I will ruin the evil people,
and I will remove human beings from the
earth," says the LORD.

The Future of Judah

4"I will punish Judah
and all the people living in Jerusalem.
I will remove from this place
all signs of Baal, the false priests, and the
other priests.
5I will destroy those who worship
the stars from the roofs,
and those who worship and make promises
by both the LORD and the god Molech,
6and those who turned away from the LORD,
and those who quit following the LORD and
praying to him for direction.
7Be silent before the Lord GOD,
because the LORD's day for judging people
is coming soon.
The LORD has prepared a sacrifice;
he has made holy his invited guests.
8On the day of the LORD's sacrifice,
I, the LORD, will punish the princes and
the king's sons
and all those who wear foreign clothes.
9On that day I will punish those who
worship Dagon,
those who hurt others and tell lies in the
temples of their gods.

10"On that day," says the LORD,
"a cry will be heard at the Fish Gate.
A wail will come from the new area of the city,
and a loud crash will echo from the hills.
11Cry, you people living in the market area,
because all the merchants will be dead;
all the silver traders will be gone.
12At that time I, the LORD, will search Jerusalem
with lamps.
I will punish those who are satisfied with
themselves,
who think, 'The LORD won't help us or
punish us.'
13Their wealth will be stolen
and their houses destroyed.
They may build houses,
but they will not live in them.
They may plant vineyards,
but they will not drink any wine from them.

The LORD's Day of Judging

14"The LORD's day of judging is coming soon;
it is near and coming fast.
The cry will be very sad on the day of the LORD;
even soldiers will cry.
15That day will be a day of anger,
a day of terror and trouble,
a day of destruction and ruin,
a day of darkness and gloom,
a day of clouds and blackness,
16a day of alarms and battle cries.
'Attack the strong, walled cities!
Attack the corner towers!'
17I will make life hard on the people;
they will walk around like the blind,
because they have sinned against the LORD.
Their blood will be poured out like dust,
and their insides will be dumped like trash.
18On the day that God will show his anger,
neither their silver nor gold will save them.
The LORD's anger will be like a fire
that will burn up the whole world;
suddenly he will bring an end, yes, an end
to everyone on earth."

The LORD Asks People to Change

2 Gather together, gather,
you unwanted people.
2Do it before it's too late,
before you are blown away like chaff,
before the LORD's terrible anger reaches you,

1:5 *roofs.* In Bible times houses were built with flat roofs. The roof was used for drying things such as flax and fruit. And it was used as an extra room, as a place for worship, and as a cool place to sleep in the summer.

1:5 *Molech.* The god Molech was an idol worshiped by the Ammonites but also by some faithless people of Israel.

1:5 Astrology: Acts 7:42–43

1:7 Day of the Lord: Zephaniah 1:14

1:9 *Dagon.* Dagon was the false god of the Philistines.

1:10 *Fish Gate.* The Fish Gate was a gate going into the city of Jerusalem. Most think it was in the wall facing north.

1:14 Day of the Lord: Zechariah 14:1

2:2 *chaff.* Chaff is dry, lifeless, and rootless vegetation.

before the day of the LORD's anger comes
to you.
3Come to the LORD, all you who are not proud,
who obey his laws.
Do what is right. Learn to be humble.
Maybe you will escape
on the day the LORD shows his anger.

Philistia Will Be Punished

4No one will be left in the city of Gaza,
and the city of Ashkelon will be destroyed.
Ashdod will be empty by noon,
and the people of Ekron will be chased away.
5How terrible it will be for you who live by the
Mediterranean Sea,
you Philistines!
The word of the LORD is against you,
Canaan, land of the Philistines.

"I will destroy you
so that no one will be left."
6The land by the Mediterranean Sea, in which
you live,
will become pastures, fields for shepherds,
and pens for sheep.
7It will belong to the descendants of Judah who
are left alive.
There they will let their sheep eat grass.
At night they will sleep
in the houses of Ashkelon.
The LORD their God will pay attention to them
and will make their life good again.

Moab and Ammon Will Be Punished

8"I have heard the insults of the country
of Moab
and the threats of the people of Ammon.
They have insulted my people
and have taken their land."
9So the LORD All-Powerful, the God of
Israel, says,
"As surely as I live,
Moab will be destroyed like Sodom,
and Ammon will be destroyed like Gomorrah—
a heap of weeds, a pit of salt,
and a ruin forever.
Those of my people who are left alive will take
whatever they want from them;
those who are left from my nation will take
their land."

10This is what Moab and Ammon get for
being proud,
because they insulted and made fun of the
people of the LORD All-Powerful.
11The LORD will frighten them,
because he will destroy all the gods of
the earth.
Then everyone in faraway places
will worship him wherever they are.

Cush and Assyria Will Be Destroyed

12"You Cushites also
will be killed by my sword."
13Then the LORD will turn against the north
and destroy Assyria.
He will make Nineveh
a ruin as dry as a desert.
14Flocks and herds will lie down there,
and all wild animals.
The owls and crows will sit
on the stone pillars.
The owl will hoot through the windows,
trash will be in the doorways,
and the wooden boards of the buildings will
be gone.
15This is the happy and safe city
that thinks there is no one else as strong
as it is.
But what a ruin it will be,
a place where wild animals live.
All those who pass by will make fun
and shake their fists.

Jerusalem Will Be Punished

3 How terrible for the wicked, stubborn city
of Jerusalem,
which hurts its own people.
2It obeys no voice;
it can't be taught to do right.
It doesn't trust the LORD;
it doesn't worship its God.
3Its officers are like roaring lions.
Its rulers are like hungry wolves that attack
in the evening,
and in the morning nothing is left of those
they attacked.
4Its prophets are proud;
they are people who cannot be trusted.
Its priests don't respect holy things;
they break God's teachings.
5But the LORD is good, and he is there in
that city.
He does no wrong.
Every morning he governs the people fairly;
every day he can be trusted.

2:4 *Gaza, Ashkelon, Ekron.* These are the chief cities of the Philistines.

2:9 *Sodom . . . Gomorrah.* Two cities God destroyed because the people were so evil.

But evil people are not ashamed of what
they do.

6"I have destroyed nations;
their towers were ruined.
I made their streets empty
so no one goes there anymore.
Their cities are ruined;
no one lives there at all.
7I said, 'Surely now Jerusalem will respect me
and will accept my teaching.'
Then the place where they lived would not
be destroyed,
and I would not have to punish them.
But they were still eager
to do evil in everything they did.
8Just wait," says the LORD.
"Some day I will stand up as a witness.
I have decided that I will gather nations
and assemble kingdoms.
I will pour out my anger on them,
all my strong anger.
My anger will be like fire
that will burn up the whole world.

A New Day for God's People

9"Then I will give the people of all nations
pure speech
so that all of them will speak the name of
the LORD
and worship me together.
10People will come from where the Nile
River begins;
my scattered people will come with gifts
for me.
11Then Jerusalem will not be ashamed
of the wrongs done against me,
because I will remove from this city
those who like to brag;
there will never be any more proud people
on my holy mountain in Jerusalem.
12But I will leave in the city
the humble and those who are not proud,
and they will trust in the LORD.
13Those who are left alive in Israel won't do
wrong or tell lies;
they won't trick people with their words.
They will eat and lie down
with no one to make them afraid."

A Happy Song

14Sing, Jerusalem.
Israel, shout for joy!
Jerusalem, be happy
and rejoice with all your heart.
15The LORD has stopped punishing you;
he has sent your enemies away.
The King of Israel, the LORD, is with you;
you will never again be afraid of being
harmed.
16On that day Jerusalem will be told,
"Don't be afraid, city of Jerusalem.
Don't give up.
17The LORD your God is with you;
the mighty One will save you.
He will rejoice over you.
You will rest in his love;
he will sing and be joyful about you."

18"I will take away the sadness planned for you,
which would have made you very ashamed.
19At that time I will punish
all those who harmed you.
I will save my people who cannot walk
and gather my people who have been
thrown out.
I will give them praise and honor
in every place where they were shamed.
20At that time I will gather you;
at that time I will bring you back home.
I will give you honor and praise
from people everywhere
when I make things go well again for you,
as you will see with your own eyes,"
says the LORD.

INTRODUCTION TO THE BOOK OF HAGGAI

The Temple Is Rebuilt

WHO WROTE THIS BOOK?

This prophecy came from God through the prophet Haggai.

TO WHOM WAS THIS BOOK WRITTEN?

Haggai is writing to his fellow Jews.

WHERE WAS IT WRITTEN?

Where Haggai was when he wrote this book is uncertain, but he may have been in Jerusalem where the Temple was to be rebuilt.

WHEN WAS IT WRITTEN?

Haggai's prophetic messages were given in 520 B.C., during the reign of King Darius of Persia.

WHAT IS THE BOOK ABOUT?

The Book of Haggai is a message to the Jews to reenergize their efforts to rebuild God's destroyed Temple. The governor, Zerubbabel, and the high priest, Joshua, are also encouraged to play their parts in completing the building of the second Temple.

WHY WAS THIS BOOK WRITTEN?

Haggai, one of the shortest books in the Old Testament, delivers a powerful message. When the people under their leader, Zerubbabel, give God first place in their lives by rebuilding his Temple, they are showered with his blessings.

SO WHAT DOES THIS BOOK MEAN TO US?

The message of Haggai holds the same promise to us as it did for God's people of old. His blessings are always available to his people who put him and his wishes in their proper position in their lives—first place.

SUMMARY:

Haggai was a prophet of the period after the return from exile. He, along with his contemporary Zechariah, was used by God to encourage those who had come back home after fifty years in Babylon. In particular, he pushed the people to rebuild the Temple. Haggai carefully dates his prophecies, so we know he preached during a four-month stretch in the year 520 B.C. The Temple was finally completed in 516 B.C.

HAGGAI

It Is Time to Build the Temple

The prophet Haggai spoke the word of the
LORD to Zerubbabel son of Shealtiel, the
governor of Judah, and to Joshua son of
Jehozadak, the high priest. This message came in
the second year that Darius was king, on the first
day of the sixth month:

2“This is what the LORD All-Powerful says: ‘The
people say the right time has not come to rebuild
the Temple of the LORD.’”

3Then Haggai the prophet spoke the word of the
LORD: 4“Is it right for you to be living in fancy
houses while the Temple is still in ruins?”

5This is what the LORD All-Powerful says: “Think
about what you have done. 6You have planted
much, but you harvest little. You eat, but you do
not become full. You drink, but you are still
thirsty. You put on clothes, but you are not warm
enough. You earn money, but then you lose it all
as if you had put it into a purse full of holes.”

7This is what the LORD All-Powerful says:
“Think about what you have done. 8Go up to the
mountains, bring back wood, and build the
Temple. Then I will be pleased with it and be
honored,” says the LORD. 9“You look for much, but
you find little. When you bring it home, I destroy
it. Why?” asks the LORD All-Powerful. “Because
you all work hard for your own houses while my
house is still in ruins! 10Because of what you have
done, the sky holds back its rain and the ground
holds back its crops. 11I have called for a time
without rain on the land, and on the mountains,
and on the grain, the new wine, the olive oil, the
plants which the earth produces, the people, the
farm animals, and all the work of your hands.”

12Zerubbabel son of Shealtiel and Joshua son of
Jehozadak, the high priest, and all the rest of the
people who were left alive obeyed the LORD their
God and the message from Haggai the prophet,
because the LORD their God had sent him. And
the people feared the LORD.

13Haggai, the LORD’s messenger, gave the LORD’s
message to the people, saying, “The LORD says, ‘I
am with you.’” 14The LORD stirred up Zerubbabel
son of Shealtiel, the governor of Judah, and
Joshua son of Jehozadak, the high priest, and all
the rest of the people who were left alive. So they
came and worked on the Temple of their God, the
LORD All-Powerful. 15They began on the twenty-
fourth day of the sixth month in the second year
Darius was king.

The Beauty of the Temple

2 On the twenty-first day of the seventh month,
the LORD spoke his word through Haggai the
prophet, saying, 2“Speak to Zerubbabel son of Shealtiel, governor of Judah, and to Joshua son of Jehozadak, the high priest, and to the rest of the people
who are left alive. Say, 3‘Do any of you remember
how great the Temple was before it was destroyed?
What does it look like now? Doesn’t it seem like
nothing to you?’ 4But the LORD says, ‘Zerubbabel,
be brave. Also, Joshua son of Jehozadak, the high
priest, be brave. And all you people who live in
the land, be brave,’ says the LORD. ‘Work, because
I am with you,’ says the LORD All-Powerful. 5‘I
made a promise to you when you came out of
Egypt, and my Spirit is still with you. So don’t be
afraid.’

6“This is what the LORD All-Powerful says: ‘In a
short time I will once again shake the heavens and
the earth, the sea and the dry land. 7I will shake all
the nations, and they will bring their wealth. Then
I will fill this Temple with glory,’ says the LORD
All-Powerful. 8‘The silver is mine, and the gold is
mine,’ says the LORD All-Powerful. 9‘The new
Temple will be greater than the one before,’ says the
LORD All-Powerful. ‘And in this place I will give
peace,’ says the LORD All-Powerful.”

10On the twenty-fourth day of the ninth month in
the second year Darius was king, the LORD spoke his
word to Haggai the prophet, saying, 11“This is what
the LORD All-Powerful says: ‘Ask the priests for a
teaching. 12Suppose a person carries in the fold of
his clothes some meat made holy for the LORD. If
that fold touches bread, cooked food, wine, olive
oil, or some other food, will that be made holy?’”

The priests answered, “No.”

13Then Haggai said, “A person who touches a
dead body will become unclean. If he touches any
of these foods, will it become unclean, too?”

The priests answered, “Yes, it would become
unclean.”

14Then Haggai answered, “The LORD says, ‘This
is also true for the people of this nation. They are
unclean, and everything they do with their hands
is unclean to me. Whatever they offer at the altar
is also unclean.

15“‘Think about this from now on! Think about
how it was before you started laying stones on top

2:14 Clean & Unclean: Matthew 15:10–20

Community

Acts 15

In the Bible, what is the role of community in ethical formation and decision-making? In what ways does this message challenge contemporary American culture?

God's call for the Israelites to become the people of God is the starting point for Old Testament ethics. God's promise, "I will make you my own people, and I will be your God" (Exodus 6:7) is also a call to form a new society, or community. Its basis is a way of life in response and gratitude to the loving and merciful God who gathers them together and protects and sustains them. While Israel is camped at Mount Sinai, God points to what he has done for them and gives them his promise that they will belong to him in a special way and will become a holy nation (Exodus 19:4–6). God's people are called into a community of the faithful to follow the holy and loving God.

Thus Old Testament history is about the history of the new community called into being and sustained by God. But the Old Testament is not sentimental or naive about human community. Sometimes people gather to make bad decisions; sometimes leaders lead people away from God into idolatry. Before Moses comes down from the mountain with God's plan for his new community, the Ten Commandments, the people become impatient and fearful. They gather together and pressure a lesser leader, Moses' brother Aaron, to "make us gods who will lead us" (Exodus 32:1). Leader and people collaborate in making an idol, the golden calf.

Early church leaders pointed to this incident as they warned the church, God's new community, about the dangers of following false leaders who are too susceptible to pressure from fearful and impatient people. Community can quickly sour and even turn violent when worship of God and reliance on his mercy is set aside. God, not the human or even the religious community, is the one worthy of worship.

Though we value the communities in which we live and the church fellowships of which we are a part, modern American Christians tend almost automatically to assume that ethics has first of all to do with personal morality. We have a very individualistic way of thinking about ethical issues, and while we tend to take personal responsibility for our actions and their consequences we also tend to excuse ourselves from responsibility for issues and problems that are too big for any individual to tackle. The biblical call to community challenges this individualistic way of thinking about ethics.

Biblical ethics is concerned not just with individual actions or thoughts but with the way a community or society lives out its life together. Social structures that do not reflect God's mercy and just ways are not pleasing to God. God is especially concerned about whether there is justice and provision for the weakest members of human communities. There is a special call for God's people to act justly and be generous—not simply as individuals, but as a believing community. God's people are to respond to this call to justice whether or not the other people around them or the nations in which they reside cooperate or agree.

The Bible is not, however, sentimental or naive about community. It warns us not to follow leaders who turn attention onto themselves (or other gods or powers) and away from the God who brings salvation in Jesus. The Bible also warns us against assuming that every religious gathering is good. People can gather into groups called "communities" to undertake projects that are essentially idolatrous.

The Bible warns us about counterfeits or substitutes for authentic community. All kinds of good human groups offer belonging and purpose on various levels—and often for good causes, but these are not to be confused with the New Community of God, the New People that Jesus is calling together in his name.

Community: For additional scriptures on this topic go to Exodus 6:7.

God's Anger

Romans 1:18–32

Does God get angry and strike out in rage as some people do? Are there evidences of God's anger already at work in the world? According to Paul, what should this show us about God's character? What is the relation between God's anger and God's mercy?

To speak of God's anger can be very misleading. To us, "anger" often means an emotion like rage, an emotional response that overrules self-control. For most of the Bible, however, God's anger is not a feeling at all. Sometimes known as "the wrath of God," God's anger is less a feeling than an action. God's anger is his judgment on sin. Were we to experience God's anger, then, we would not experience his rage against us, but rather his judgment on our sin.

The idea of God's anger is sometimes hard to grasp for us. This is because we have to use language about people to describe God. When we read about God's anger, then, it is easy for us to imagine that God is like an angry parent or friend. God's nature and actions should not be judged by our experience with human emotions, though.

How does the Bible speak of God's anger?

First, God's anger is not an uncontrollable emotion but a determined expression of God's will against sin. In Romans 1, Paul does not portray an angry God who needs to be soothed. Paul talks about God's anger as a means of emphasizing how seriously God takes sin, not in order to describe an affective quality or "feeling" on God's part. At stake in this passage is God's own integrity. Can we trust God to be righteous when he allows evil things to happen? Here is Paul's answer: God's righteousness is at work already. For people who believe in God and follow his will, God's righteousness is experienced as salvation. For those who do not believe and who act in evil ways, God's righteousness is experienced as God's anger.

In the Old Testament, God's anger is at work against human sin, too. In the story of Israel's escape from Egypt, God's anger is experienced whenever people, even Moses, try to get in the way of God's attempt to deliver his people from slavery. Afterwards, God's anger is usually mentioned when the people of Israel break the agreement they have with the Lord. Because he is their God and they are his people, they are to live in the ways that he has determined. When they disobey God's will, they experience God's anger (see, for example, Exodus 32:1–10; Deuteronomy 1:26–36).

Second, biblical writers speak of God's anger as God's activity against sin both in the present, within history, and in the future. God's anger can be immediate, such as when the people of Israel murmur against him on their journey to the land of promise (Numbers 11). Paul also speaks of God's anger now at work against "all the evil and wrong things people do" (Romans 1:18). At the same time, some Old Testament prophets also spoke of a future "day of anger" (for example, Zephaniah 1:15). John the Baptist similarly thinks in terms of a day of judgment when God's anger will be set in a final way against all evil.

Third, God's anger can be experienced by people as separation from God. Paul inherited a widespread Jewish belief that God's judgment can be understood as his giving people the very thing they sought. In Romans 1 this is illustrated in the repetition of the phrase, God "let them go their own way." God's anger is evident in allowing those who resist his way to have their own way. According to the Book of Revelation, evil leads to more evil, so that evil ends up destroying itself. This is the very opposite of what it means to have salvation, for salvation is living together with God forever (see 1 Thessalonians 5:9–10)

Finally, God's anger is not a contradiction of God's love. In fact, even though the love of God is one of God's enduring qualities, anger is not. God's anger is at work against human sin. So if there were no sin, neither would there be divine anger. On the one hand this means that when people turn from their own way to embrace the ways of God, they no longer experience his anger. Instead, they are brought into his presence to live with him forever. This means that there is now a distinction between those who follow God and those who do not, between those who experience God's righteousness as love and salvation and those who experience God's righteousness as his anger.

God's Anger: For additional scriptures on this topic go to Exodus 4:13–14.

of stones to build the Temple of the LORD. [16]A person used to come to a pile of grain expecting to find
twenty basketfuls, but there were only ten. And a
person used to come to the wine vat to take out fifty
jarfuls, but only twenty were there. [17]I destroyed
your work with diseases, mildew, and hail, but
you still did not come back to me,' says the LORD.
[18]'It is the twenty-fourth day of the ninth month,
the day in which the people finished working on
the foundation of the Temple of the LORD. From now
on, think about these things: [19]Do you have seeds
for crops still in the barn? Your vines, fig trees,
pomegranates, and olive trees have not given fruit
yet. But from now on I will bless you!'"

The LORD Makes a Promise to Zerubbabel

[20]Then the LORD spoke his word a second time
to Haggai on the twenty-fourth day of the month.
He said, [21]"Tell Zerubbabel, the governor of Judah,
'I am going to shake the heavens and the earth.
[22]I will destroy the foreign kingdoms and take
away the power of the kingdoms of the nations. I
will destroy the chariots and their riders. The
horses will fall with their riders, as people kill
each other with swords.' [23]The LORD All-Powerful
says, 'On that day I will take you, Zerubbabel son
of Shealtiel, my servant,' says the LORD, 'and I will
make you important like my signet ring, because
I have chosen you!' says the LORD All-Powerful."⚭

2:23 *signet ring.* A signet ring was a ring with a personal seal on it. When pressed into soft clay, the seal served as a signature. It is thus a symbol of endearment and intimacy, as well as importance.

⚭**2:23 Presence of God:** Matthew 24:1

Notes:

INTRODUCTION TO THE BOOK OF

ZECHARIAH

Encouraging the People

WHO WROTE THIS BOOK?

The author of this book is Zechariah, who is both priest and prophet to God's people.

TO WHOM WAS THIS BOOK WRITTEN?

Zechariah is addressing the people of Judah.

WHERE WAS IT WRITTEN?

This prophecy was probably written in and around Jerusalem where the Temple was under reconstruction.

WHEN WAS IT WRITTEN?

Zechariah is a contemporary to Haggai, who also shared his message. His ministry began around 520 B.C. and possibly continued until about 480 B.C.

WHAT IS THE BOOK ABOUT?

This book deals with the rebuilding of the Temple in Jerusalem in preparation for the Jew's being restored as the favored nation of God. It also looks ahead to the coming of the Messiah and God's presence with his people.

WHY WAS THIS BOOK WRITTEN?

The primary purpose of the Book of Zechariah is to spur the Jewish people into completing the rebuilding of the Temple of God. With the visions of the coming Messiah and his kingdom, this is a book of encouragment. The divine message delivered by Zechariah is this: If Judah will turn their hearts and lives back to God, he will turn once again to them and be their God.

SO WHAT DOES THIS BOOK MEAN TO US?

God always pursues his wayward children to bring them back to him. When we, like God's people of old, are lethargic or apathetic in our service to him, he will spur us on to repentance and greater service. He will try to keep us from drifting away into destruction. The hope of the glorious return of Christ draws us to obedience and righteous living. Then, when we turn our hearts and lives back to God, he will turn once again to us as our loving and ever-faithful God.

SUMMARY:

Zechariah, a contemporary of Haggai, returned to Judah soon after the Persian authorities allowed the exiles to come home. His genealogy hints that he may have been a priest. In any case, he, like Haggai, encouraged his generation to continue with the good work of completing the Temple. Many of his prophecies intend to encourage his generation to finish the Temple, in spite of opposition, while the last few chapters look into the future to see God's overcoming the evil of their present situation.

The message of Zechariah had a large impact on the New Testament. Quotes and allusions are found especially in passages that describe Christ's last week of life, as well as in the Book of Revelation.

An outline of Zechariah is as follows:

I. The Night Visions (Zechariah 1–8)
II. A Look into the Future (Zechariah 9–14)

I. The Night Visions (Zechariah 1–8)

The book opens with eight separate night visions. These visions focus on the judgment that non-Jewish nations deserve, the safety of Jerusalem, and the rebuilding of the Temple.

II. A Look into the Future (Zechariah 9–14)

The second part of the book is considerably more difficult to interpret than the first part. It looks to the distant future. While chapters 1–8 focus on the immediate concerns of Jerusalem and the post-exilic people of God after the exile, the last few chapters look for an even larger and more definitive salvation.

ZECHARIAH

The LORD Calls His People Back

In the eighth month of the second year Darius
was king, the LORD spoke his word to the
prophet Zechariah son of Berekiah, who
was the son of Iddo. The LORD said, 2“The LORD
was very angry with your ancestors. 3So tell the
people: This is what the LORD All-Powerful says:
‘Return to me, and I will return to you,’ says the
LORD All-Powerful. 4Don’t be like your ancestors.
In the past the prophets said to them: This is what
the LORD All-Powerful says: ‘Stop your evil ways
and evil actions.’ But they wouldn’t listen or pay
attention to me, says the LORD. 5Your ancestors are
dead, and those prophets didn’t live forever. 6I
commanded my words and laws to my servants
the prophets, and they preached to your ancestors,
who returned to me. They said, ‘The LORD All-
Powerful did as he said he would. He punished us
for the way we lived and for what we did.’”

The Vision of the Horses

7It was on the twenty-fourth day of the eleventh
month, which is the month of Shebat, in Darius’s
second year as king. The LORD spoke his word to
the prophet Zechariah son of Berekiah, who was
the son of Iddo.

8During the night I had a vision. I saw a man
riding a red horse. He was standing among some
myrtle trees in a ravine, with red, brown, and white
horses behind him.

9I asked, “What are these, sir?”

The angel who was talking with me answered,
“I’ll show you what they are.”

10Then the man standing among the myrtle trees
explained, “They are the ones the LORD sent
through all the earth.”

11Then they spoke to the LORD’s angel, who
was standing among the myrtle trees. They said,
“We have gone through all the earth, and everything is calm and quiet.”

12Then the LORD’s angel asked, “LORD All-
Powerful, how long will it be before you show
mercy to Jerusalem and the cities of Judah? You
have been angry with them for seventy years
now.” 13So the LORD answered the angel who was
talking with me, and his words were comforting
and good.

14Then the angel who was talking to me said to
me, “Announce this: This is what the LORD All-
Powerful says: ‘I have a strong love for Jerusalem.
15And I am very angry with the nations that feel
so safe. I was only a little angry at them, but they
made things worse.’

16“So this is what the LORD says: ‘I will return
to Jerusalem with mercy. My Temple will be
rebuilt,’ says the LORD All-Powerful, ‘and the
measuring line will be used to rebuild Jerusalem.’

17“Also announce: This is what the LORD All-
Powerful says: ‘My towns will be rich again. The
LORD will comfort Jerusalem again, and I will
again choose Jerusalem.’”

The Vision of the Horns

18Then I looked up and saw four animal horns.
19I asked the angel who was talking with me,
“What are these?”

He said, “These are the horns that scattered
the people of Judah, Israel, and Jerusalem.”

20Then the LORD showed me four craftsmen. 21I
asked, “What are they coming to do?”

He answered, “They have come to scare and
throw down the horns. These horns scattered the
people of Judah so that no one could even lift up
his head. These horns stand for the nations that
attacked the people of Judah and scattered them.”

The Vision of the Measuring Line

2 Then I looked up and saw a man holding a line
for measuring things. 2I asked him, “Where are
you going?”

He said to me, “I am going to measure Jerusalem,
to see how wide and how long it is.”

3Then the angel who was talking with me left,
and another angel came out to meet him. 4The second angel said to him, “Run and tell that young man,
‘Jerusalem will become a city without walls,
because there will be so many people and cattle in
it. 5I will be a wall of fire around it,’ says the LORD.
‘And I will be the glory within it.’

6“Oh no! Oh no! Run away from Babylon, because I have scattered you like the four winds of
heaven,” says the LORD.

7“Oh no, Jerusalem! Escape, you who live right
in Babylon.” 8This is what the LORD All-Powerful
says: “After he has honored me and sent me against

1:1 *eighth month of the second year Darius was king.* In terms of our modern calendar, it was October or November, 520 B.C.

1:7 *twenty-fourth day of the eleventh month.* In terms of our modern calendar, it was February, 519 B.C.

1:18 *four animal horns.* The symbol of the horn, which here clearly stands for the nations that attacked Jerusalem, derives from the horns of an animal like a bull. They symbolize power and pride.

1:18 Numbers: Zechariah 4:1–14

1:21 Prophetic Symbolism: Zechariah 4

the nations who took your possessions—because whoever touches you hurts what is precious to me— 9I will shake my hand against them so that their slaves will rob them."

Then you will know that the LORD All-Powerful sent me.

10"Shout and be glad, Jerusalem. I am coming, and I will live among you," says the LORD. 11"At that time people from many nations will join with the LORD and will become my people. Then I will live among you, and you will know that the LORD All-Powerful has sent me to you. 12The LORD will take Judah as his own part of the holy land, and Jerusalem will be his chosen city again. 13Be silent, everyone, in the presence of the LORD. He is coming out of the holy place where he lives."

The Vision of the High Priest

3 Then he showed me Joshua, the high priest, standing in front of the LORD's angel. And Satan was standing by Joshua's right side to accuse him. 2The LORD said to Satan, "The LORD says no to you, Satan! The LORD who has chosen Jerusalem says no to you! This man was like a burning stick pulled from the fire."

3Joshua was wearing dirty clothes and was standing in front of the angel. 4The angel said to those standing in front of him, "Take off those dirty clothes."

Then the angel said to Joshua, "Look, I have taken away your sin from you, and I am giving you beautiful, fine clothes."

5Then I said, "Put a clean turban on his head." So they put a clean turban on his head and dressed him while the LORD's angel stood there.

6Then the LORD's angel said to Joshua, 7"This is what the LORD All-Powerful says: 'If you do as I tell you and serve me, you will be in charge of my Temple and my courtyards. And I will let you be with these angels who are standing here.

8" 'Listen, Joshua, the high priest, and your friends who are sitting in front of you. They are symbols of what will happen. I am going to bring my servant called the Branch. 9Look, I put this stone in front of Joshua, a stone with seven sides. I will carve a message on it,' says the LORD All-Powerful. 'And in one day I will take away the sin of this land.'

10"The LORD All-Powerful says, 'In that day, each of you will invite your neighbor to sit under your own grapevine and under your own fig tree.'"

The Vision of the Lampstand

4 Then the angel who was talking with me returned and woke me up as if I had been asleep. 2He asked me, "What do you see?"

I said, "I see a solid gold lampstand with a bowl at the top. And there are seven lamps and also seven places for wicks. 3There are two olive trees by it, one on the right of the bowl and the other on the left."

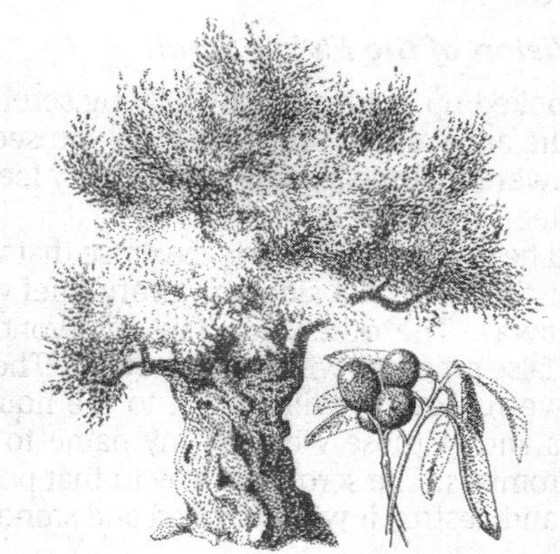

Olive tree: its fruit was used for food and oil.

4I asked the angel who talked with me, "Sir, what are these?"

5The angel said, "Don't you know what they are?"

"No, sir," I said.

6Then he told me, "This is the word of the LORD to Zerubbabel: 'You will not succeed by your own strength or power, but by my Spirit,' says the LORD All-Powerful.

7"Who are you, big mountain? In front of Zerubbabel you will become flat land, and he will bring out the topmost stone, shouting, 'It's beautiful! It's beautiful!'"

8Then the LORD spoke his word to me again, saying, 9"Zerubbabel has laid the foundation of this Temple, and he will complete it. Then you will know that the LORD All-Powerful has sent me to you.

10"The people should not think that small beginnings are unimportant. They will be happy when they see Zerubbabel with tools, building the Temple.

"(These are the seven eyes of the LORD, which look back and forth across the earth.)"

3:2 Demon: Matthew 12:22–29
3:2 Satan/Satanism: Mark 1:23–26
3:10 To sit under the grapevine or fig tree is an image of peace and prosperity.

4:2 *a solid gold lampstand with a bowl at the top.* We are probably to think of the lampstand in the Temple, also known as the Menorah.
4:6 Weapons: 2 Corinthians 6:7

11Then I asked the angel, "What are the two olive
trees on the right and left of the lampstand?"
12I also asked him, "What are the two olive
branches beside the two gold pipes, from which
the olive oil flows to the lamps?"
13He answered, "Don't you know what they are?"
"No, sir," I said.
14So he said, "They are symbols of the two who
have been appointed to serve the LORD of all the
earth."⚭

The Vision of the Flying Scroll

5 I looked up again and saw a flying scroll.
2The angel asked me, "What do you see?"
I answered, "I see a flying scroll, thirty feet long
and fifteen feet wide."
3And he said to me, "This is the curse that will go
all over the land. One side says every thief will be
taken away. The other side says everyone who
makes false promises will be taken away. 4The LORD
All-Powerful says, 'I will send it to the houses of
thieves and to those who use my name to make
false promises. The scroll will stay in that person's
house and destroy it with its wood and stones.'"⚭

The Vision of the Woman

5Then the angel who was talking with me came
forward and said to me, "Look up and see what is
going out."
6"What is it?" I asked.
He answered, "It is a measuring basket going
out." He also said, "It is a symbol of the people's
sins in all the land."
7Then the lid made of lead was raised, and
there was a woman sitting inside the basket. 8The
angel said, "The woman stands for wickedness."
Then he pushed her back into the basket and put
the lid back down.
9Then I looked up and saw two women going
out with the wind in their wings. Their wings
were like those of a stork, and they lifted up the
basket between earth and the sky.
10I asked the angel who was talking with me,
"Where are they taking the basket?"
11"They are going to Babylonia to build a temple
for it," he answered. "When the temple is ready,
they will set the basket there in its place."⚭

The Vision of the Four Chariots

6 I looked up again and saw four chariots going
out between two mountains, mountains of
bronze. 2Red horses pulled the first chariot. Black
horses pulled the second chariot. 3White horses
pulled the third chariot, and strong, spotted horses
pulled the fourth chariot. 4I asked the angel who
was talking with me, "What are these, sir?"
5He said, "These are the four spirits of heaven.
They have just come from the presence of the Lord
of the whole world. 6The chariot pulled by the
black horses will go to the land of the north. The
white horses will go to the land of the west, and
the spotted horses will go to the land of the south."
7When the powerful horses went out, they were
eager to go through all the earth. So he said, "Go
through all the earth," and they did.
8Then he called to me, "Look, the horses that
went north have caused my spirit to rest in the
land of the north."⚭

A Crown for Joshua

9The LORD spoke his word to me, saying, 10"Take
silver and gold from Heldai, Tobijah, and Jedaiah,
who were captives in Babylon. Go that same day
to the house of Josiah son of Zephaniah, who came
from Babylon. 11Make the silver and gold into a
crown, and put it on the head of Joshua son of
Jehozadak, the high priest. 12Tell him this is what
the LORD All-Powerful says: 'A man whose name
is the Branch will branch out from where he is,
and he will build the Temple of the LORD. 13One
man will build the Temple of the LORD, and the
other will receive honor. One man will sit on his
throne and rule, and the other will be a priest on
his throne. And these two men will work
together in peace.' 14The crown will be kept in
the Temple of the LORD to remind Heldai,
Tobijah, Jedaiah, and Josiah son of Zephaniah.
15People living far away will come and build the
Temple of the LORD. Then you will know the LORD
All-Powerful has sent me to you. This will happen
if you completely obey the LORD your God."⚭

The People Should Show Mercy

7 In the fourth year Darius was king, on the fourth
day of the ninth month, which is called Kislev,
the LORD spoke his word to Zechariah. 2The city of
Bethel sent Sharezer, Regem-Melech, and their
men to ask the LORD a question. 3They went to the
prophets and priests who were at the Temple of
the LORD All-Powerful. The men said, "For years in
the fifth month of each year we have shown our
sadness and gone without food. Should we continue to do this?"
4The LORD All-Powerful spoke his word to me,

⚭**4:14 Numbers:** Zechariah 6:1–8
⚭**4:14 Prophetic Symbolism:** Zechariah 5
⚭**5:4 Capital Punishment:** Matthew 5:38–42
⚭**5:11 Prophetic Symbolism:** Zechariah 6
⚭**6:8 Numbers:** Matthew 12:40
6:13 *One man.* This probably refers to Zerubbabel.
6:13 *other.* This probably refers to Joshua.
⚭**6:15 Prophetic Symbolism:** Acts 21:7–11

saying, 5“Tell the priests and the people in the land: ‘For seventy years you went without food and cried in the fifth and seventh months, but that was not really for me. 6And when you ate and drank, it was really for yourselves. 7The LORD used the earlier prophets to say the same thing, when Jerusalem and the surrounding towns were at peace and wealthy, and people lived in the southern area and the western hills.’”

8And the LORD spoke his word to Zechariah again, saying, 9“This is what the LORD All-Powerful says: ‘Do what is right and true. Be kind and merciful to each other. 10Don’t hurt widows and orphans, foreigners or the poor; don’t even think of doing evil to somebody else.’

11“But they refused to pay attention; they were stubborn and did not want to listen anymore. 12They made their hearts as hard as rock and would not listen to the teachings of the LORD All-Powerful. And they would not hear the words he sent by his Spirit through the earlier prophets. So the LORD All-Powerful became very angry.

13“‘When I called to them, they would not listen. So when they called to me, I would not listen,’ says the LORD All-Powerful. 14‘I scattered them like a hurricane to other countries they did not know. This good land was left so ruined behind them that no one could live there. They had made the desired land a ruin.’”

The LORD Will Bless Jerusalem

8 The LORD All-Powerful spoke his word, saying, 2This is what the LORD All-Powerful says: “I have a very strong love for Jerusalem. My strong love for her is like a fire burning in me.”

3This is what the LORD says: “I will return to Jerusalem and live in it. Then it will be called the City of Truth, and the mountain of the LORD All-Powerful will be called the Holy Mountain.”

4This is what the LORD All-Powerful says: “Old men and old women will again sit along Jerusalem’s streets, each carrying a cane because of age. 5And the streets will be filled with boys and girls playing.”

6This is what the LORD All-Powerful says: “Those who are left alive then may think it is too difficult to happen, but it is not too difficult for me,” says the LORD All-Powerful. 7This is what the LORD All-Powerful says: “I will save my people from countries in the east and west. 8I will bring them back, and they will live in Jerusalem. They will be my people, and I will be their good and loyal God.”

9This is what the LORD All-Powerful says: “Work hard, you who are hearing these words today. The prophets spoke these words when the foundation was laid for the house of the LORD All-Powerful, for the building of the Temple. 10Before that time there was no money to hire people or animals. People could not safely come and go because of the enemies; I had turned everyone against his neighbor. 11But I will not do to these people who are left what I did in the past,” says the LORD All-Powerful.

12“They will plant their seeds in peace, their grapevines will have fruit, the ground will give good crops, and the sky will send rain. I will give all this to the people who are left alive. 13Judah and Israel, your names have been used as curses in other nations. But I will save you, and you will become a blessing. So don’t be afraid; work hard.”

14This is what the LORD All-Powerful says: “When your ancestors made me angry, I planned to punish you. I did not change my mind,” says the LORD All-Powerful. 15“But now I will do something different. I am planning to do good to Jerusalem and Judah. So don’t be afraid. 16These are the things you should do: Tell each other the truth. In the courts judge with truth and complete fairness. 17Do not make plans to hurt your neighbors, and don’t love false promises. I hate all these things,” says the LORD.

18The LORD All-Powerful spoke his word to me again. 19This is what the LORD All-Powerful says: “The special days when you give up eating in the fourth, fifth, seventh, and tenth months will become good, joyful, happy feasts in Judah. But you must love truth and peace.”

20This is what the LORD All-Powerful says: “Many people from many cities will still come to Jerusalem. 21People from one city will go and say to those from another city, ‘We are going to pray to the LORD and to ask the LORD All-Powerful for help. Come and go with us.’ 22Many people and powerful nations will come to worship the LORD All-Powerful in Jerusalem and to pray to the LORD for help.”

23This is what the LORD All-Powerful says: “At that time, ten men from different countries will come and take hold of a Judean by his coat. They will say to him, ‘Let us go with you, because we have heard that God is with you.’”

Punishment on Israel’s Enemies

9 This message is the word of the LORD.

The message is against the land of Hadrach
and the city of Damascus.

8:3 *the Holy Mountain.* The mountain in Jerusalem is Mount Zion, the location of the Temple that symbolized God’s presence with his people.

8:23 Rahab: Matthew 1:5

The tribes of Israel and all people
belong to the LORD.
2The message is also against the city of Hamath,
on the border,
and against Tyre and Sidon, with their skill.
3Tyre has built a strong wall for herself.
She has piled up silver like dust
and gold like the mud in the streets.
4But the Lord will take away all she has
and destroy her power on the sea.
That city will be destroyed by fire.
5The city of Ashkelon will see it and be afraid.
The people of Gaza will shake with fear,
and the people of Ekron will lose hope.
No king will be left in Gaza,
and no one will live in Ashkelon anymore.
6Foreigners will live in Ashdod,
and I will destroy the pride of the Philistines.
7I will stop them from drinking blood
and from eating forbidden food.
Those left alive will belong to God.
They will be leaders in Judah,
and Ekron will become like the Jebusites.
8I will protect my Temple
from armies who would come or go.
No one will hurt my people again,
because now I am watching them.

The King Is Coming

9Rejoice greatly, people of Jerusalem!
Shout for joy, people of Jerusalem!
Your king is coming to you.
He does what is right, and he saves.
He is gentle and riding on a donkey,
on the colt of a donkey.
10I will take away the chariots from Ephraim
and the horses from Jerusalem.
The bows used in war will be broken.
The king will talk to the nations about peace.
His kingdom will go from sea to sea,
and from the Euphrates River to the ends of the earth.

11As for you, because of the blood of the agreement with you
I will set your prisoners free from the waterless pit.
12You prisoners who have hope,
return to your place of safety.
Today I am telling you
that I will give you back twice as much as before.
13I will use Judah like a bow
and Ephraim like the arrows.
Jerusalem, I will use your men
to fight the men of Greece.
I will use you like a warrior's sword.
14Then the LORD will appear above them,
and his arrows will shoot like lightning.
The Lord GOD will blow the trumpet,
and he will march in the storms of the south.
15The LORD All-Powerful will protect them;
they will destroy the enemy with slingshots.
They will drink and shout like drunk men.
They will be filled like a bowl
used for sprinkling blood at the corners of the altar.
16On that day the LORD their God will save them
as if his people were sheep.
They will shine in his land
like jewels in a crown.
17They will be so pretty and beautiful.
The young men will grow strong on the grain
and the young women on new wine.

The LORD's Promises

10 Ask the LORD for rain during the springtime rains.
The LORD is the one who makes the clouds.
He sends the showers
and gives everyone green fields.
2Idols tell lies;
fortune-tellers see false visions
and tell about false dreams.
The comfort they give is worth nothing.
So the people are like lost sheep.
They are abused, because there is no shepherd.

3The LORD says, "I am angry at my shepherds,
and I will punish the leaders.
I, the LORD All-Powerful, care
for my flock, the people of Judah.
I will make them like my proud war horses.
4From Judah will come the cornerstone,
and the tent peg,
the battle bow,
and every ruler.
5Together they will be like soldiers
marching to battle through muddy streets.
The LORD is with them,
so they will fight and defeat the horsemen.
6"I will strengthen the people of Judah
and save the people of Joseph.

9:9 This future king will ride a donkey, not a horse. The horse is a symbol of warfare and worldly power. The donkey is a sign of humility and peace. See Matthew 21:1–11.

10:3 Leadership: Matthew 4:17–22

Homosexuality

Romans 1:18–32

Does the Bible have anything to say about homosexuality? How does the Bible help us as we think about our attitudes and behavior toward homosexuality and homosexuals today?

What is homosexuality? The Bible never uses this term, though from time to time it does refer to behavior to which we now refer as homosexual. Homosexuality is the desire for and the experience of sexual behavior between members of the same sex. This way of understanding homosexuality shows the importance of consent between two adults, as Paul suggests in Romans 1:26–27.

This passage in Romans 1 is one of only a handful of passages in the Bible that directly relate to homosexuality. Homosexuality is mentioned only two or three times in all of the Old Testament. According to the Gospels, Jesus does not even talk about sex between men or of sex between women. This silence is probably a result of the common and widespread rejection of relations between people of the same sex in Israel and the church. The community of God's people, in both the Old and New Testaments, appears to have assumed that everyone would recognize that homosexual practices are not allowed by God. The Old Testament law refers to a man having sex with another man as "a hateful sin" (Leviticus 18:22), and this view of things seems to have been taken for granted throughout the Bible.

This does not mean that we receive no help from the Bible on the question of homosexuality. Questions about homosexuality must always be understood under the larger category of human sexuality as treated in the Scriptures. Like sexual practices of all kinds, sexual relations between people of the same sex do not exist as a separate category for discussion. Instead, homosexuality must be understood as one part of a much larger discussion about sexuality and marriage, and about faithfulness as God's people. According to Genesis 1–2, it is together, as *man and woman*, husband *and* wife, that people best live as God created them. Together as male and female, they reflect the image of God and are able to fulfill God's instructions to them (Genesis 1:27–28). In marriage, a man and woman are united and "become one body" (Genesis 2:24). In the same way, when Jesus speaks of marriage and divorce, he assumes the uniting of a man and a woman in marriage (see, for example, Mark 10:6–9). The Bible undoubtedly affirms sexual relations between a woman and man who are married to each other.

We should not be surprised, then, when we read biblical texts that reject sexual relations between men or between women. Desires of this kind and the sexual activities that accompany them are signs of something gone wrong in God's creation. Homosexuality results from people rebelling against God's intentions for human beings. According to Paul, homosexuality is one kind of proof that sin is active in the world (Romans 1:18–32). He even writes that those who practice homosexuality will not inherit the kingdom of God. This is true even though Paul's churches included people who had had sexual relations with people of the same sex in the past (1 Corinthians 6:9–10; see 1 Timothy 1:10).

The Bible does not make a clear distinction between people who are homosexual by orientation and people who actually engage in homosexual behavior. These are modern categories. However, the message of the Bible is actually compatible with this way of thinking. One can understand the orientation of homosexuality as a consequence of sin at work in the world. If one were to act on one's homosexual orientation through sexual activity with a person of the same sex, this would be more than a consequence of sin at work in the world. It would be to participate actively in sin. Among the biblical writers, Paul is particularly clear in his willingness to distinguish between the human condition (we are in need of God's grace already at birth) and subsequent sinful acts that separate us from God. Homosexual behavior, like all sexual relations outside of marriage, is immoral.

This does not mean that homosexuality is an especially "bad" sin, however. Paul rejects homosexuality as one of the sins that result from the rebellion of the human race against God. But he also describes as people who disobey God those who are greedy, get drunk, rob others, and so on. In fact, in Romans 1 he talks about selfish people, people who gossip, and children who disobey their parents as sinners in just the same way that women who have sex with other women or men who have sex with other men are sinners. This is a reminder that God wants all of us to be faithful to him in every part of our lives, and that no kind of sin is worse than any other in God's eyes. This is also a reminder that God's love and offer of forgiveness are not held back from those who desire and experience sexual relations with others of the same sex. Like the rest of us, homosexuals are people among whom God is at work so that we all might be members of God's family.

Homosexuality: For additional scriptures on this topic go to Genesis 2.

Thanks

ROMANS 1:21

In what way is thanks the heart of the Christian faith? What is the relationship between thanks and worship?

God calls on his human creatures to give him thanks. Indeed, Paul writes that we can describe a Christian as someone who gives thanks to God for what he has done. In Romans 1:18–32 the apostle argues that everyone knows that God exists. He has clearly revealed himself to all people by what he has made (Romans 1:20). The difference between Christians and non-Christians is not that the Christians know God and the non-Christians do not. But Christians thank God and non-Christians choose to ignore him. In the words of Romans 1:21, non-Christians "knew God, but they did not give glory to God or thank him."

Thanksgiving is thus at the heart of the Christian faith. We are to express our gratitude to God for making us, providing for us, and, most importantly, for saving us from our sins. After all, God provided for our salvation by sending his own son to die on the cross that we might live and not die. It is only proper and good that we express our gratefulness for this great sacrifice.

The Gospel of Luke recounts an event from Jesus' life that shows the importance of gratitude toward God. It also illustrates how rare it is among selfish human beings. Luke 17:11–19 describes an encounter between Jesus and ten men who had a skin disease. In the ancient world having a skin disease meant more than being physically disfigured. Such people were also rejected from regular society and were feared and hated by other people. These men had apparently heard of Jesus' power as a healer and came to him looking for help. He told them to return to the priest and show themselves to him. As they went, they were healed. Only one of the ten bothered to return to Jesus and thank him. Jesus' comment is telling. He says "Weren't ten men healed? Where are the other nine? Is this Samaritan the only one who came back to thank God?" (Luke 17:17–18).

Thanksgiving is at the heart of worship. Indeed worship is showing God our great and deep gratitude for the wonderful things he has done for us and for the wonderful person that he is. In the Old Testament one of the important sacrifices at the sanctuary was a thanksgiving offering (Leviticus 7:12; 22:29; 2 Chronicles 29:31). In response to God's great acts in an individual's life, they would give a token of their appreciation by sacrificing an animal to God. These sacrifices were accompanied by prayers to God which also expressed the worshiper's gratitude. Indeed, a large number of psalms are rightly called thanksgiving psalms. They are songs that are sung to God in response to answering an earlier request. Psalm 30 is a good example of a prayer offered to God in response to an act of grace in a person's life.

The worship of the Old Testament had as its purpose giving thanks to God, acknowledging his greatness and mercy. The purpose of the priests and Levites was to direct the Israelites "to give thanks and to praise the LORD" (1 Chronicles 25:3).

We are not surprised that thanks is also very important in New Testament worship. Christians thank Jesus Christ for the wonderful things he does in their lives (1 Timothy 1:12). As the author of Hebrews invites us, "let us be thankful, because we have a kingdom that cannot be shaken. We should worship God in a way that pleases him with respect and fear, because our God is like a fire that burns things up" (Hebrews 12:28–29).

The most sacred act of Christian worship is the celebration of communion. Here we remember the death of Christ. Jesus commanded the celebration, and he showed the thanks that our hearts should feel as we take communion: "While they were eating, Jesus took some bread and thanked God for it and broke it . . ." (Mark 14:22).

The picture of the end of time, when Christ returns again and defeats evil once and for all, is, according to the Book of Revelation, a time of thanks and praise. According to Revelation 11:17, for instance, the twenty-four elders worship God by singing,

We give thanks to you, Lord God Almighty,
  who is and who was,
because you have used your great power
  and have begun to rule! (Revelation 11:17)∞

∞**Thanks:** For additional scriptures on this topic go to Leviticus 22:29.

I will bring them back,
because I care about them.
It will be as though
I had never left them,
because I am the LORD their God,
and I will answer them.
7The people of Ephraim will be strong like
soldiers;
they will be glad as when they have
drunk wine.
Their children will see it and rejoice;
they will be happy in the LORD.
8I will call my people
and gather them together.
I will save them,
and they will grow in number as they grew
in number before.
9I have scattered them among the nations,
but in those faraway places, they will
remember me.
They and their children will live and return.
10I will bring them back from the land of Egypt
and gather them from Assyria.
I will bring them to Gilead and Lebanon
until there isn't enough room for them all.
11They will come through the sea of trouble.
The waves of the sea will be calm,
and the Nile River will dry up.
I will defeat Assyria's pride
and destroy Egypt's power over other
countries.
12I will make my people strong,
and they will live as I say," says the LORD.

11 Lebanon, open your gates
so fire may burn your cedar trees.
2Cry, pine trees, because the cedar has fallen,
because the tall trees are ruined.
Cry, oaks in Bashan,
because the mighty forest has been
cut down.
3Listen to the shepherds crying
because their rich pastures are destroyed.
Listen to the lions roaring
because the lovely land of the Jordan River
is ruined.

The Two Shepherds

4This is what the LORD my God says: "Feed the
flock that are about to be killed. 5Their buyers kill
them and are not punished. Those who sell them
say, 'Praise the LORD, I am rich.' Even the
shepherds don't feel sorry for their sheep. 6I don't
feel sorry anymore for the people of this country,"
says the LORD. "I will let everyone be under the
power of his neighbor and king. They will bring
trouble to the country, and I will not save anyone
from them."
7So I fed the flock about to be killed, particularly
the weakest ones. Then I took two sticks; I called
one Pleasant and the other Union, and I fed the
flock. 8In one month I got rid of three shepherds.
The flock did not pay attention to me, and I got
impatient with them. 9I said, "I will no longer take
care of you like a shepherd. Let those that are
dying die, and let those that are to be destroyed be
destroyed. Let those that are left eat each other."
10Then I broke the stick named Pleasant to break
the agreement God made with all the nations.
11That day it was broken. The weak ones in the
flock who were watching me knew this message
was from the LORD.
12Then I said, "If you want to pay me, pay me.
If not, then don't." So they paid me thirty pieces
of silver.∞
13The LORD said to me, "Throw the money to the
potter." That is how little they thought I was worth.
So I took the thirty pieces of silver and threw them
to the potter in the Temple of the LORD.
14Then I broke the second stick, named Union, to
break the brotherhood between Judah and Israel.
15Then the LORD said to me, "Get the things
used by a foolish shepherd again, 16because I am
going to get a new shepherd for the country. He
will not care for the dying sheep, or look for the
young ones, or heal the injured ones, or feed the
healthy. But he will eat the best sheep and tear off
their hoofs.

17"How terrible it will be for the useless
shepherd
who abandoned the flock.
A sword will strike his arm and his right eye.
His arm will lose all its strength,
and his right eye will go blind."

Jerusalem Will Be Saved

12 This message is the word of the LORD to Israel. This is what the LORD says, who stretched
out the skies, and laid the foundations of the earth,
and put the human spirit within: 2"I will make
Jerusalem like a cup of poison to the nations around
her. They will come and attack Jerusalem and

11:1 *trees.* In this poem, trees, bushes, and animals stand for leaders of countries around Judah.

∞**11:12 Judas:** Matthew 10:4

11:13 *worth.* This was a small amount. It was about the price paid for a slave.

Judah. 3One day all the nations on earth will come
together to attack Jerusalem, but I will make it
like a heavy rock; anyone who tries to move it will
get hurt. 4At that time I will confuse every horse
and cause its rider to go crazy," says the LORD. "I
will watch over Judah, but I will blind all the horses
of the enemies. 5Then the leaders of Judah will say
to themselves, 'The people of Jerusalem are strong,
because the LORD All-Powerful is their God.'

6"At that time I will make the leaders of Judah
like a fire burning a stack of wood or like a fire
burning straw. They will destroy all the people
around them left and right. But the people of
Jerusalem will remain safe.

7"The LORD will save the homes of Judah first
so that the honor given to David's family and to
the people of Jerusalem won't be greater than the
honor given to Judah. 8At that time the LORD will
protect the people in Jerusalem. Then even the
weakest of them will be strong like David. And
the family of David will be like God, like an angel
of the LORD in front of them. 9At that time I will
go to destroy all the nations that attack Jerusalem.

Crying for the One They Stabbed

10"I will pour out on David's family and the people in Jerusalem a spirit of kindness and mercy.
They will look at me, the one they have stabbed,
and they will cry like someone crying over the
death of an only child. They will be as sad as someone who has lost a firstborn son. 11At that time
there will be much crying in Jerusalem, like the
crying for Hadad Rimmon in the plain of Megiddo.
12The land will cry, each family by itself: the family of David by itself and their wives by themselves,
the family of Nathan by itself and their wives by
themselves, 13the family of Levi by itself and their
wives by themselves, the family of Shimei by itself
and their wives by themselves, 14and all the rest of
the families by themselves and their wives by
themselves.

13 "At that time a fountain will be open for
David's descendants and for the people of
Jerusalem to cleanse them of their sin and
uncleanness."

2The LORD All-Powerful says, "At that time I will
get rid of the names of the idols from the land; no
one will remember them anymore. I will also
remove the prophets and unclean spirits from the
land. 3If a person continues to prophesy, his own
father and mother, the ones who gave birth to him,
will tell him, 'You have told lies using the LORD's
name, so you must die.' When he prophesies, his
own father and mother who gave birth to him will
stab him.

4"At that time the prophets will be ashamed of
their visions and prophecies. They won't wear
the prophet's clothes made of hair to trick people.
5Each of them will say, 'I am not a prophet. I am a
farmer and have been a farmer since I was young.'
6But someone will ask, 'What are the deep cuts
on your body?' And each will answer, 'I was hurt
at my friend's house.'

The Shepherd Is Killed

7"Sword, hit the shepherd.
  Attack the man who is my friend,"
  says the LORD All-Powerful.
"Kill the shepherd,
  and the sheep will scatter,
  and I will punish the little ones."
8The LORD says, "Two-thirds of the people
  through all the land will die. They will
    be gone,
  and one-third will be left.
9The third that is left I will test with fire,
  purifying them like silver,
  testing them like gold.
Then they will call on me,
  and I will answer them.
I will say, 'You are my people,'
  and they will say, 'The LORD is our God.'"

The Day of Punishment

14 The LORD's day of judging is coming when
the wealth you have taken will be divided
among you.

2I will bring all the nations together to fight Jerusalem. They will capture the city and rob the houses
and attack the women. Half the people will be
taken away as captives, but the rest of the people
won't be taken from the city.

3Then the LORD will go to war against those
nations; he will fight as in a day of battle. 4On
that day he will stand on the Mount of Olives,
east of Jerusalem. The Mount of Olives will split
in two, forming a deep valley that runs east and
west. Half the mountain will move toward
the north, and half will move toward the south.

13:1 David: Matthew 1:1
14:1 Day of the Lord: Obadiah 15
14:3–5 The prophet describes the events surrounding the attack on Jerusalem by her enemies and centers those events on and near the Mount of Olives. Christ is pictured here as a victor standing on the Mount. There will be a massive earthquake that will split the hill apart, creating a new valley running east and west. It is to this scene that Christ returns in victory with the spirits of those already in heaven.
14:3 Holy War & Divine Warrior: Matthew 26:52–54

5 You will run through this mountain valley to the
other side, just as you ran from the earthquake
when Uzziah was king of Judah. Then the LORD
my God will come and all the holy ones with him.
6 On that day there will be no light, cold, or frost.
7 There will be no other day like it, and the LORD
knows when it will come. There will be no day or
night; even at evening it will still be light.
8 At that time fresh water will flow from Jerusalem. Half of it will flow east to the Dead Sea, and
half will flow west to the Mediterranean Sea. It will
flow summer and winter.
9 Then the LORD will be king over the whole
world. At that time there will be only one LORD,
and his name will be the only name.
10 All the land south of Jerusalem from Geba to
Rimmon will be turned into a plain. Jerusalem
will be raised up, but it will stay in the same place.
The city will reach from the Benjamin Gate and to
the First Gate to the Corner Gate, and from the
Tower of Hananel to the king's winepresses.
11 People will live there, and it will never be
destroyed again. Jerusalem will be safe.
12 But the LORD will bring a terrible disease on
the nations that fought against Jerusalem. Their
flesh will rot away while they are still standing up.
Their eyes will rot in their sockets, and their tongues
will rot in their mouths. 13 At that time the LORD will
cause panic. Everybody will grab his neighbor,
and they will attack each other. 14 The people of
Judah will fight in Jerusalem. And the wealth of
the nations around them will be collected—much
gold, silver, and clothes. 15 A similar disease will
strike the horses, mules, camels, donkeys, and all
the animals in the camps.
16 All of those left alive of the people who came
to fight Jerusalem will come back to Jerusalem
year after year to worship the King, the LORD All-
Powerful, and to celebrate the Feast of Shelters.
17 Anyone from the nations who does not go to
Jerusalem to worship the King, the LORD All-
Powerful, will not have rain fall on his land. 18 If
the Egyptians do not go to Jerusalem, they will
not have rain. Then the LORD will send them the
same terrible disease he sent the other nations
that did not celebrate the Feast of Shelters. 19 This
will be the punishment for Egypt and any nation
which does not go to celebrate the Feast of
Shelters.
20 At that time the horses' bells will have written on them: HOLY TO THE LORD. The cooking pots
in the Temple of the Lord will be like the holy
altar bowls. 21 Every pot in Jerusalem and Judah
will be holy to the LORD All-Powerful, and everyone who offers sacrifices will be able to take food
from them and cook in them. At that time there
will not be any buyers or sellers in the Temple of
the LORD All-Powerful.⚭

⚭**14:21 Holiness:** 2 Corinthians 7:1

THE JEWISH AND MODERN CALENDARS

Jewish Calendar	Our Calendar	Farm season
ABIB (NISAN) 1—New Moon 14—Passover 15—Sabbath—holy worship 16—week of unleavened bread 21—holy worship	March/April	later spring rain beginning of barley harvest
IYYAR (ZIV) 1—New Moon	April/May	barley harvest
SIVAN 1—New Moon 6–7—Feast of Weeks	May/June	wheat harvest
TAMMUZ 1—New Moon	June/July	
AB 1—New Moon	July/August	figs and olives ripen
ELUL 1—New Moon	August/September	vintage season
TISHRI (ETHANIM) 1—New Moon NEW YEAR'S DAY FEAST OF TRUMPETS 10—Day of Atonement 15–22—Feast of Tabernacles	September/October	former early rains plowing time
HESHVAN 1—New Moon	October/November	seeding time for wheat and barley
KISLEV (CHISLEV) 1—New Moon	November/December	
TEBETH	December/January	
SHEBAT	January/February	
ADAR	February/March	almond trees blossom

INTRODUCTION TO THE BOOK OF

MALACHI

God Tells Israel to Be Loyal

WHO WROTE THIS BOOK?

Malachi the prophet, whose name means "my messenger," is the author named in verse one of this book.

TO WHOM WAS THIS BOOK WRITTEN?

Malachi is writing to the people of Israel, to those who had returned after the exile.

WHERE WAS IT WRITTEN?

It is probable that Malachi lived and wrote in and around Jerusalem.

WHEN WAS IT WRITTEN?

The Book of Malachi was probably written during the fifth century B.C., probaby during the governorship of Nehemiah.

WHAT IS THE BOOK ABOUT?

The Jews who returned to Jerusalem to rebuild the Temple are becoming discouraged. Their promised restoration to glory has not yet happened, and they are beginning to doubt the love of God. Malachi rebukes their lack of faith in God and promises God's coming judgment. However, he warns Israel that God will first judge his own people before judging the other nations (3:5).

WHY WAS THIS BOOK WRITTEN?

The Book of Malachi sets the record straight between God and his people. Because he has not come to them as quickly as they had hoped, they have falsely assumed that he is not coming at all. As a result, they have stopped living by his laws and have ceased preparing for his return—a potentially fatal mistake. Malachi confirms God's earlier promise: he is coming again; be ready!

SO WHAT DOES THIS BOOK MEAN TO US?

Like Israel, many of us have decided that Christ's long physical absence from earth is an indication that his is not actually coming back at all, even though his return is promised to us (see Acts 1:11). As a result, we may have stopped following his commands and preparing for his return—an eternally fatal mistake, for "the LORD will keep all his promises" (Psalms 145:13). He *is* coming again, and we must be ready!

SUMMARY:

Malachi was likely the last prophecy of the Old Testament period. It certainly comes from the period after the exile. The Temple has been rebuilt and indeed disillusionment has set in. Thus, most people set the book's writing in the fifth century B.C.

The Temple has been rebuilt but the expected glory and joy has faded. Apparently the people of God were slipping into old sin patterns again. Malachi both warns them of the consequences of such behavior and presents a renewed and exciting vision of the future. Indeed, the book ends with the promise of the coming of Elijah, who will precede the day of the LORD's judging. Readers of the New Testament will recognize echoes of this promise immediately in the person of John the Baptist (Mark 1:2).

An outline of the book is as follows:

I. God's Love and Israel's Sin (1:1–2:16)
II. Hope for the Future (2:17–4:6)

I. God's Love and Israel's Sin (1:1–2:16)

God expresses his continuing love for Israel even though they do not follow his ways. There are sinful priests, and the men of Judah continue to marry women who worship pagan gods.

II. Hope for the Future (2:17–4:6)

MALACHI

This message is the word of the LORD given to Israel through Malachi.

God Loves Israel

[2]The LORD said, "I have loved you."

But you ask, "How have you loved us?"

The LORD said, "Esau and Jacob were brothers. I loved Jacob, [3]but I hated Esau. I destroyed his mountain country and left his land to the wild dogs of the desert."

[4]The people of Edom might say, "We were destroyed, but we will go back and rebuild the ruins."

But the LORD All-Powerful says, "If they rebuild them, I will destroy them. People will say, 'Edom is a wicked country. The LORD is always angry with the Edomites.' [5]You will see these things with your own eyes. And you will say, 'The LORD is great, even outside the borders of Israel!'"

The Priests Don't Respect God

[6]The LORD All-Powerful says, "A child honors his father, and a servant honors his master. I am a father, so why don't you honor me? I am a master, so why don't you respect me? You priests do not respect me.

"But you ask, 'How have we shown you disrespect?'

[7]"You have shown it by bringing unclean food to my altar.

"But you ask, 'What makes it unclean?'

"It is unclean because you don't respect the altar of the LORD. [8]When you bring blind animals as sacrifices, that is wrong. When you bring crippled and sick animals, that is wrong. Try giving them to your governor. Would he be pleased with you? He wouldn't accept you," says the LORD All-Powerful.

[9]"Now ask God to be kind to you, but he won't accept you with such offerings," says the LORD All-Powerful.

[10]"I wish one of you would close the Temple doors so that you would not light useless fires on my altar! I am not pleased with you and will not accept your gifts," says the LORD All-Powerful. [11]"From the east to the west I will be honored among the nations. Everywhere they will bring incense and clean offerings to me, because I will be honored among the nations," says the LORD All-Powerful.

[12]"But you don't honor me. You say about the Lord's altar, 'It is unclean, and the food has no worth.' [13]You say, 'We are tired of doing this,' and you sniff at it in disgust," says the LORD All-Powerful.

"And you bring hurt, crippled, and sick animals as gifts. You bring them as gifts, but I won't accept them from you," says the LORD. [14]"The person who cheats will be cursed. He has a male animal in his flock and promises to offer it, but then he offers to the Lord an animal that has something wrong with it. I am a great king," says the LORD All-Powerful, "and I am feared by all the nations.

Rules for Priests

2 "Priests, this command is for you. [2]Listen to me. Pay attention to what I say. Honor my name," says the LORD All-Powerful. "If you don't, I will send a curse on you and on your blessings. I have already cursed them, because you don't pay attention to what I say.

[3]"I will punish your descendants. I will smear your faces with the animal insides left from your feasts, and you will be thrown away with it. [4]Then you will know that I am giving you this command so my agreement with Levi will continue," says the LORD All-Powerful. [5]"My agreement for priests was with the tribe of Levi. I promised them life and peace so they would honor me. And they did honor me and fear me. [6]They taught the true teachings and spoke no lies. With peace and honesty they did what I said they should do, and they kept many people from sinning.

[7]"A priest should teach what he knows, and people should learn the teachings from him, because he is the messenger of the LORD All-Powerful. [8]But you priests have stopped obeying me. With your teachings you have caused many people to do wrong. You have broken the agreement with the tribe of Levi!" says the LORD All-Powerful. [9]"You have not been careful to do what I say, but instead you take sides in court cases. So I have caused you to be hated and disgraced in front of everybody."

Judah Was Not Loyal to God

[10]We all have the same father; the same God made us. So why do people break their promises to each other and show no respect for the agreement

1:6 Servant of the Lord: Matthew 10:24

1:8 Leviticus 1–7 describes the sacrifices God desires. They are the best of flock and herd, not the worst (Leviticus 22:22; Deuteronomy 15:21).

1:8 Sacrifice: 1 Corinthians 10:19

2:4 *Levi.* God chose the tribe of Levi to serve him as priests throughout the history of Israel.

2:6 Integrity: Matthew 5:37

2:7 Priesthood: Mark 14:54

our ancestors made with God? [11]The people of Judah have broken their promises. They have done something God hates in Israel and Jerusalem: The people of Judah did not respect the Temple that the LORD loves, and the men of Judah married women who worship foreign gods. [12]Whoever does this might bring offerings to the LORD All-Powerful, but the LORD will still cut that person off from the community of Israel.

[13]This is another thing you do. You cover the LORD's altar with your tears. You cry and moan, because he does not accept your offerings and is not pleased with what you bring. [14]You ask, "Why?" It is because the LORD sees how you treated the wife you married when you were young. You broke your promise to her, even though she was your partner and you had an agreement with her. [15]God made husbands and wives to become one body and one spirit for his purpose—so they would have children who are true to God.

So be careful, and do not break your promise to the wife you married when you were young.

[16]The LORD God of Israel says, "I hate divorce. And I hate people who do cruel things as easily as they put on clothes," says the LORD All-Powerful.

So be careful. And do not break your trust.

The Special Day of Judging

[17]You have tired the LORD with your words.

You ask, "How have we tired him?"

You did it by saying, "The LORD thinks anyone who does evil is good, and he is pleased with them." Or you asked, "Where is the God who is fair?"

3 The LORD All-Powerful says, "I will send my messenger, who will prepare the way for me. Suddenly, the Lord you are looking for will come to his Temple; the messenger of the agreement, whom you want, will come." [2]No one can live through that time; no one can survive when he comes. He will be like a purifying fire and like laundry soap. [3]Like someone who heats and purifies silver, he will purify the Levites and make them pure like gold and silver. Then they will bring offerings to the LORD in the right way. [4]And the LORD will accept the offerings from Judah and Jerusalem, as it was in the past. [5]The LORD All-Powerful says, "Then I will come to you and judge you. I will be quick to testify against those who take part in evil magic, adultery, and lying under oath, those who cheat workers of their pay and who cheat widows and orphans, those who are unfair to foreigners, and those who do not respect me.

Stealing from God

[6]"I the LORD do not change. So you descendants of Jacob have not been destroyed. [7]Since the time of your ancestors, you have disobeyed my rules and have not kept them. Return to me, and I will return to you," says the LORD All-Powerful.

"But you ask, 'How can we return?'

[8]"Should a person rob God? But you are robbing me.

"You ask, 'How have we robbed you?'

"You have robbed me in your offerings and the tenth of your crops. [9]So a curse is on you, because the whole nation has robbed me. [10]Bring to the storehouse a full tenth of what you earn so there will be food in my house. Test me in this," says the LORD All-Powerful. "I will open the windows of heaven for you and pour out all the blessings you need. [11]I will stop the insects so they won't eat your crops. The grapes won't fall from your vines before they are ready to pick," says the LORD All-Powerful. [12]"All the nations will call you blessed, because you will have a pleasant country," says the LORD All-Powerful.

The LORD's Promise of Mercy

[13]The LORD says, "You have said terrible things about me.

"But you ask, 'What have we said about you?'

[14]"You have said, 'It is useless to serve God. It did no good to obey his laws and to show the LORD All-Powerful that we were sorry for what we did. [15]So we say that proud people are happy. Evil people

2:16 Divorce: Hosea 1

2:16 Marriage: Matthew 22:23–33

3:2 Day of the Lord: 1 Corinthians 5:5

3:5 Adoption: John 14:18

3:5 Magic: 2 Chronicles 33:6

3:6–12 This passage on the tithe stirs controversy for at least three reasons. First, the statement, "you are robbing me" (3:8) is often used by today's preachers and has the feel of the legalism of the Pharisees. Second, the admonition to "bring to the storehouse a full tenth"(3:10) is often interpreted to mean that all the tithe should go to the local church. This is difficult for the modern Christian as it tries to control the generous impulse of the disciple, again, in a legalistic fashion. Third, "I will open the windows of heaven for you and pour out all the blessings you need" (3:10) is often related to give-to-get kind of thinking that is contrary to the Christian gospel of sacrifice. The answers to these complaints or objections are not easy. There have been as many misuses of teachings on the tithe in modern times as in the times of the Pharisees. Still, the tithe expresses a gracious guideline, given by God, for us to express our gratitude and devotion. The storehouse concept is harder to deal with. Relating an ancient Jewish community storehouse to a contemporary church is too forced. It could be likened to forcing a square peg into a round hole. The promise of "blessing" has been misused but is not inconsistent with other Scriptures. The invitation, "Test me in this" (3:10) is an exceptional opportunity. More than an invitation to riches, it is an encouragement to heighten a person's awareness of the future faithfulness of God.

3:12 Stewardship: Matthew 23:23

3:12 Tithe: Matthew 6:21

succeed. They challenge God and get away with it.'"
16Then those who honored the LORD spoke
with each other, and the LORD listened and heard
them. The names of those who honored the LORD
and respected him were written in his presence
in a book to be remembered.
17The LORD All-Powerful says, "They belong to
me; on that day they will be my very own. As a
parent shows mercy to his child who serves him,
I will show mercy to my people. 18You will again see
the difference between good and evil people,
between those who serve God and those who don't.

The Day of the LORD's Judging

4 "There is a day coming that will burn like a hot
furnace, and all the proud and evil people will
be like straw. On that day they will be completely
burned up so that not a root or branch will be left,"
says the LORD All-Powerful. 2"But for you who
honor me, goodness will shine on you like the
sun, with healing in its rays. You will jump
around, like well-fed calves. 3Then you will crush
the wicked like ashes under your feet on the day
I will do this," says the LORD All-Powerful.
4"Remember the teaching of Moses my servant, those laws and rules I gave to him on Mount
Sinai for all the Israelites.
5"But I will send you Elijah the prophet before
that great and terrifying day of the LORD's judging.
6Elijah will help parents love their children and
children love their parents. Otherwise, I will come
and put a curse on the land."

4:1–5 Malachi predicted the coming of Elijah before "that great and terrifying day of the Lord's judging" (verse 5). According to the New Testament, it was John the Baptist who is this Elijah-like prophet (Matthew 17:9–13; Mark 9:9–13; Luke 1:17). The "day of the Lord," which was to follow the coming of Elijah, will happen when Christ returns as judge (1 Corinthians 5:5).

4:1 Hell: Matthew 5:22

4:5 See Matthew 11:14; 17:10; Mark 9:11–13; and Luke 1:17 which identifies John the Baptist as the Elijah expected in this passage.

4:6 Elijah and Elisha: Matthew 11:14

4:6 John the Baptist: Matthew 11:2–6

CONSCIENCE

ROMANS 2:12–16

Is the human conscience a source of moral judgment that is self-sufficient and independent of God and his word? Can the conscience always be trusted? What is the role of the Holy Spirit in relation to conscience? Is my conscience bound by another's?

The word *conscience* (in Greek, *suneidesis*) meets us first as a technical, moral term in Greek literature, thus relatively late in history. But the reality it depicts is present from the beginning of human history. Even where the term is not expressly formulated, something corresponding to the notion of moral judgment is present in the Gentile world, although often in a more obscure sense than among the Hebrews. The natural experience of humanity, therefore, is laden with this moral phenomenon that revealed religion, particularly the Bible, ventures to interpret.

The appeal to conscience is implicit in many segments of the Old Testament. Adam hides in shame among the trees when he hears God walking in the garden (Genesis 3:8). As a result, his descendants carry within themselves a power of moral judgment and criticism.

While the term *conscience* nowhere appears in the Gospels as such, it is found thirty-one times in the New Testament. Paul is apparently the first New Testament writer to employ it, and he does so more frequently than any of the others. More than twenty times the Greek word for "conscience" appears in the Pauline letters (such as, Romans 9:1; 13:5; 1 Corinthians 8:7; 10:25, 27, 28; 2 Corinthians 1:12; 4:2; 5:11; 1 Timothy 1:5, 19; 3:9; 4:2; 2 Timothy 1:3; Titus 1:15). Twice it occurs in Acts, five times in Hebrews, three times in the Petrine epistles. Elsewhere the doctrine may be detected even where the word itself is not found.

Romans 2:12–16 is the classic location for Paul's discussion of the doctrine of conscience. Here one finds the clear recognition of a law written upon the hearts of men and women everywhere, the heathen included, and of a faculty which discerns that law and whether one obeys it or disobeys it in the sphere of conduct. The text teaches that Gentiles, while lacking the special Old Testament revelation of the law, are morally responsible because of an interior revelation of the good. It implies, therefore, that in no stage of human development and history are moral consciousness and accountability lacking, and that this recognition of the moral law, by whose authority we pass judgment upon ourselves, makes us accountable before God as surely as the revelation in the Ten Commandments.

The universality of conscience is a New Testament emphasis that connects with the biblical doctrine of humans as bearers of the image of God (the *imago Dei*). Knowledge of the good exists in human experience as a divine gift, which relates us responsibly to God's mind and will. The voice of conscience speaks with an absolute authority to human experience because of this connection with the *imago Dei.*

Scripture leaves no doubt that conscience can be debased. It may be stained by sin (1 Corinthians 8:7), seared so as to be insensitive to certain claims of the good (1 Timothy 4:2), insensitive to the pangs of reproof and remorse, and at last perverted so that it ceases almost entirely to point upward to God.

The forgiven conscience, by contrast, is marked by a growth of moral sensitivity as it matures to the implications of biblical ethics. The New Testament does not represent the conscience of the forgiven person as unerring and perfect. Rather, it indicates that the believer grows in moral judgment. For that reason, the forgiven conscience must not be regarded as self-sufficient and complete.

The Greek word for "conscience" means "to know with," and the believer's union with Christ involves the progressive shaping of the whole of life. The Christian moral consciousness must not, in any event, be elevated to a parity with Scripture as an equivalent inward means through which the Spirit speaks. For Christ and his word alone lift the claim of conscience absolutely beyond the level of human fallibility.

Under the preaching, teaching, and pervasive influence of the word, the enlightenment and education of the conscience by the Holy Spirit takes place. The one Spirit of Christ, beyond question, does not contradict himself, and speaks by one voice through the external means of Scripture and the internal voice of conscience.

There is a principle in the New Testament (1 Corinthians 10) that the conscience of the weaker brother is to be honored. Yet his conscientious objection does not in itself have final validity. Christian conscience is not infallible. It requires growth and education. It may be the conduct of the stronger (less easily offended) believer is definitely to be approved and vindicated. All are instructed to do the same thing by the Holy Spirit and Scripture. The believer's conscience is not answerable to human authority, but it is to God.

Conscience: For additional scriptures on this topic go to Genesis 3:8.

GUILT

ROMANS 3:23–24

Is guilt addressed in the Bible? Where does it appear, and how do people cope with it? Is guilt an old-fashioned idea, or is there room in today's world for talk of "guilt"?

Guilt is a major theme in both Old and New Testaments. Guilt is either implied in passages where sin is discussed, or it is directly addressed. In the Old Testament, guilt makes its appearance in Genesis 3 when Adam and Eve choose to disregard God's mandate not to eat of the tree of the knowledge of good and evil. Their guilt manifests itself dramatically as they cannot stand naked before God, and they hide from him (Genesis 3:1–7). Although failure in faithfulness to God is cited as the primary cause for guilt in Genesis, disobedience to God in relation to other people is also a reason for guilt. This well illustrates the primary reason for guilt in the Bible: sinning against God and his standard. Our goal is to be like Christ who is the perfect reflection of his heavenly Father (1 John 3:2).

It is right that people feel guilt when they sin against people as well. Adam and Eve not only hid from God, but also from each other after their sin. They could no longer stand naked and vulnerable in each other's presence, but rather they sought refuge behind clothes. This episode also illustrates the close connection between guilt and shame, the emotion we feel when our failings are publicly revealed to others.

Though it is true that we feel guilt when we hurt or fail other people, the Bible teaches that even the sins that we commit toward other people are really offenses against God. After all, the law God gave through Moses (Exodus 20:1–17) offers guidelines for the treatment of other human beings, but when we break those laws, say the law to honor our father and mother, we are ultimately offending not just our parents but God himself.

Joseph and David both show an acute awareness of the God-centeredness of our guilt. In Genesis 39 the wife of Potiphar, Joseph's master, tries to seduce him. Joseph resists, and his motives are important for our understanding of guilt. He turns to her and says, "My master trusts me with everything in his house. He has put me in charge of everything he owns. There is no one in his house greater than I. He has not kept anything from me except you, because you are his wife. How can I do such an evil thing? It is a sin against God" (Genesis 39:8–9). In other words, adultery ultimately is a slap to the face of God.

David shows the same kind of awareness. The title of Psalm 51 indicates that it is a prayer of David after he has been confronted with the sins of adultery and murder. In 2 Samuel 11, David brought Bathsheba into his bed, got her pregnant, and in order to cover up his sin, had Uriah, her husband, killed in battle.

As he was repenting of this sin, however, he strikingly shows that though sin often has devastating repercussions for other people, the real insult is directed toward God himself. In Psalm 51:3–5 he exclaims:

I know about my wrongs,
  and I can't forget my sin.
You are the only one I have sinned against;
  I have done what you say is wrong.
You are right when you speak
  and fair when you judge.
I was brought into this world in sin.
  In sin my mother gave birth to me.

The last lines of this quotation show that our human propensity is to do evil. We are sinners, rebels against God. Our guilt is not a result of our finiteness, but of our rebellion. To resolve our guilt, we have to do something far more than simply relax and come to grips with our limitations.

In the New Testament, Jesus is greatly concerned with guilt. He demonstrates compassion for those who are clearly guilty (Luke 7:36–50; John 8:1–11) and for those trapped by guilt. Jesus seems equally intent upon confronting those who judge others while vindicating themselves with their own unacknowledged guilt (Luke 7:36–50). It is clear that Jesus assumes that all human beings are guilty. Paul agrees with this (Romans 3:21–26). Guilt in both the Old and New Testaments breaks relationships with God and with other human beings. Acknowledgment of guilt and repentance repairs relationships to God and our fellow human beings (Matthew 5:23–26).

Guilt: For additional scriptures on this topic go to Genesis 3:1–13.

The New Testament

INTRODUCTION TO SECTION FOUR
MATTHEW – ACTS

THE GOSPELS AND ACTS OF APOSTLES

MATTHEW | MARK | LUKE | JOHN | ACTS

When we turn from the Old Testament to the first five books of the New Testament, we may sense that we are on familiar ground. After all, most of the Old Testament is written in narrative, telling the story of God's dealings with his people. Also, the first book of the New Testament, the Gospel of Matthew, begins with a genealogy, and this may also remind us of the Old Testament. The Gospels and Acts also relate the ongoing story of God's saving activity in conjunction with the Old Testament. The New Testament writers, sometimes called evangelists, hoped to show how the story of Jesus and the beginning of the Christian movement were rooted in the Old Testament. The New Testament story, then, begins with the promises of God in the Old Testament and continues the story begun there.

Although we call the first four books of the New Testament "Gospels," this name was given them by the church many decades after they were written. Recorded in terms that would have been familiar to the writers and hearers of the Gospels, these writings are similar to ancient biographies and historical writings. The Gospels have few of the features of modern biographies (for example, they do not even give Jesus' date of birth or speak much of his childhood), but they do focus on the one person, Jesus. They also seek to show the main features of this primary character, Jesus, by recounting incidents and sayings that show his significance. In these and other ways, the Gospels are recognized as biographies. Especially when the Gospel of Luke and the Acts of the Apostles are read as one continuous study (see Luke 1:1-4; Acts 1:1-3), they also resemble ancient history writing. Both history writing and biography share the most recognizable trait of the Gospels and Acts—namely, they present the good news of God in narrative form. This means that, above all else, the Gospels and Acts must be read as a story—a true story.

First, the Gospels and Acts should not be regarded simply as records of "what really happened." The evangelists were not interested in providing a mere chronicle of events. Instead they wanted to draw out the meaning of those events for their audiences. The evangelists were like modern-day preachers in a sense, for they wanted to explore the events of Jesus' ministry and the beginnings of the early church and to relate their significance in ways that would encourage and challenge their audiences.

Those first audiences would have been hearers of the Gospels and Acts more than *readers.* This is because not many people in the ancient world could actually read and so listened to the Gospels and Acts being read, and recited their stories by memory. This means that the modern practice of reading a bit of the Gospel of Mark here or a bit of the Gospel of John there is quite foreign to the world of the evangelists. They told the Good News in the narrative form, expecting their audiences to read and hear them all the way through, from the first sentence to the last.

In order to appreciate these narrative works, secondly, we need to read them from first to last, like we might a novel today, maybe even in one sitting. In this way we may be encouraged to develop an attachment to certain central characters in the Gospels and Acts—say Jesus, Peter, or Stephen. We may even find ourselves "living" the story as we continue to read it, wondering at some points, How would I respond to Jesus' question? or, Why do those public leaders not like Jesus and his followers? By reading the Gospels and Acts as continuous narratives, we are drawn into their worlds where our views on things might be supported or challenged.

Third, we should read each of the Gospels by itself and on its own terms. The Gospel of Matthew was written at a different time, for a different audience, than the Gospel of John. So, although they speak of the same Jesus and recount some of the same episodes, they do so from different perspectives and for different reasons. Each is trying to win a hearing for Jesus among different audiences and, by doing so, to encourage appropriate faith and behavior. So it is best first to let each one speak to us, before we compare them.

Finally, it is worth noting that the Gospels and Acts do not tell us who their writers were. They are not "signed documents." Almost a century passed between their being written and their being known formally by the names we now use for them—Matthew, Mark, Luke, and John. The Gospels were not written under false names, like some ancient literature, but under no names at all. This is almost certainly because the evangelists did not want to call attention to themselves or to suggest that the story they told was their own story. They were not "authors" in the strict sense, but, to use a phrase borrowed from Luke's Gospel, "servants of the word" (Luke 1:2). The important thing was not the identity of the writers but faith in the one about whom they wrote, Jesus of Nazareth.

In short, the Gospels tell the beautiful story of the earthly life of Jesus—the Christ, the Messiah, the Son of God. Acts continues the story by telling how Jesus established his church and how it spread throughout the world. Together, the Gospels and Acts are a storyteller's delight and a Christian's basis of faith and hope.

INTRODUCTION TO THE BOOK OF MATTHEW

Matthew Tells the Jewish People About Jesus

WHO WROTE THIS BOOK?

Church tradition, beginning with Ignatius of Antioch (about A.D. 110), attributes authorship of this book to Matthew, also called Levi, a tax collector and apostle of Jesus Christ.

TO WHOM WAS THIS BOOK WRITTEN?

Because of the large number of references to Old Testament passages fulfilled by Christ, and because of the emphasis on Jesus' identity as the promised king of Israel, it is generally believed that the primary audience was Jewish Christians.

WHERE WAS IT WRITTEN?

The place is uncertain, but it could have been written anywhere in Palestine, perhaps in Syrian Antioch.

WHEN WAS IT WRITTEN?

Opinions vary widely about its date, ranging from A.D. 50–70. Because of the Jewish nature of the content, the earlier date may be preferable.

WHAT IS THE BOOK ABOUT?

The Book of Matthew contains five major discussions. Their themes are ethics, discipleship and mission, the kingdom of heaven, the church, and end times. These discussions may be patterned after the Pentateuch (first five books of the Old Testament written by Moses). The stories of Jesus' life and ministry lead up to each of these discussions.

WHY WAS THIS BOOK WRITTEN?

Matthew was written to give Jewish Christians an appreciation for the fulfillment of Old Testament prophecies by Jesus Christ. The author wanted them to see Jesus as the promised Messiah and the coming King.

SO WHAT DOES THIS BOOK MEAN TO US?

It is important for us as Christians to see the thread of prophecies about Jesus the Messiah woven throughout the Old Testament. For those of us who are non-Jews (Gentiles), we must also realize that Jesus came as Israel's Messiah as well as the world's Savior. In other words, Jesus is "the Way" for every person in the world to come to God.

SUMMARY:

Among the four books that tell the Good News of Jesus, the Book of Matthew has the strongest Jewish flavor. For example, it begins with an Old Testament-style genealogy, rooting the family of Jesus in the history of God's people. Also, its opening chapters recount events in the birth of Jesus that, we are repeatedly told, bring to completion what was expected in the Old Testament. The Jewish focus of the Book of Matthew does not mean that this narrative was written in order to convince Jews that Jesus is the long-expected Christ, however. Instead, Matthew was written especially to Jews who followed Jesus in order to help them understand their new faith in light of the history of Israel and to encourage them to join in the mission of Jesus to the whole world.

Matthew, then, is primarily a "community document." That is, although it might be used in evangelism, it was written especially for people within the church. When we understand Matthew in this way, some of the important themes appear in sharp relief.

•Matthew is interested in showing that the life of Jesus and the development of the church is nothing less than the work of God. In Jesus and in the new community formed around Jesus, God's purposes are being fulfilled. In describing this, Matthew refers to the fulfillment of the Old Testament Scriptures, but also to the coming of the kingdom of heaven. The phrase "kingdom of heaven" is shorthand for the reality that in the words and deeds of Jesus God's purpose is being realized in history.

•Not surprisingly, then, a second major theme of Matthew concerns the identity of Jesus as the Christ. Jesus is the one who teaches with authority, who fulfills the Scriptures, and whose life, death, and resurrection bring salvation to humanity.

•Because Matthew is a community document, it is especially concerned with the appropriate behavior of Jesus' followers and with their mission in the world. True followers, Jesus says, are those who do the will of God, and much of Matthew is devoted to outlining the nature of God's will.

•However, one cannot understand Jesus' teaching on behavior without also understanding how Matthew presents world history and the coming of the end. On the one hand, the end of the world is still to come; only then will God's purpose be completed. On the other hand, Jesus asks his followers to live as though the end is already upon us. That is, he asks that the lives of his followers reflect the completion of God's purpose in the world. With the coming of Jesus, Matthew teaches, the world has dramatically changed, and we should live like it!

Clearly, then, the Good News of Matthew both continues the old story of God's activity with his people, Israel, and also opens up a new chapter in that story. Although many of the emphases of the Good News will be familiar to readers of the Old Testament, within Matthew's account those themes receive fresh significance. Old ideas and beliefs are given new life as they are understood anew within the framework of the completion of God's promises in Jesus Christ.

In Matthew 1, an angel tells Joseph that his son should be called Jesus, "because he will save his people from their sins," and Immanuel, which means "God is with us" (Matthew 1:21, 23). By the end of Matthew, we have come to realize that "his people" must mean "all people in the world," and that Jesus promises to be "with us" always, until the very end (Matthew 28:19, 20).

MATTHEW

The Family History of Jesus

This is the family history of Jesus Christ.
He came from the family of David, and David
came from the family of Abraham.
2Abraham was the father of Isaac.
Isaac was the father of Jacob.
Jacob was the father of Judah and his brothers.
3Judah was the father of Perez and Zerah.
(Their mother was Tamar.)
Perez was the father of Hezron.
Hezron was the father of Ram.
4Ram was the father of Amminadab.
Amminadab was the father of Nahshon.
Nahshon was the father of Salmon.
5Salmon was the father of Boaz.
(Boaz's mother was Rahab.)
Boaz was the father of Obed.
(Obed's mother was Ruth.)
Obed was the father of Jesse.
6Jesse was the father of King David.
David was the father of Solomon.
(Solomon's mother had been Uriah's wife.)
7Solomon was the father of Rehoboam.
Rehoboam was the father of Abijah.
Abijah was the father of Asa.
8Asa was the father of Jehoshaphat.
Jehoshaphat was the father of Jehoram.
Jehoram was the ancestor of Uzziah.
9Uzziah was the father of Jotham.
Jotham was the father of Ahaz.
Ahaz was the father of Hezekiah.
10Hezekiah was the father of Manasseh.
Manasseh was the father of Amon.
Amon was the father of Josiah.
11Josiah was the grandfather of Jehoiachin
and his brothers.
(This was at the time that the people were
taken to Babylon.)
12After they were taken to Babylon:
Jehoiachin was the father of Shealtiel.
Shealtiel was the grandfather of Zerubbabel.
13Zerubbabel was the father of Abiud.
Abiud was the father of Eliakim.
Eliakim was the father of Azor.
14Azor was the father of Zadok.
Zadok was the father of Akim.
Akim was the father of Eliud.
15Eliud was the father of Eleazar.
Eleazar was the father of Matthan.
Matthan was the father of Jacob.
16Jacob was the father of Joseph.
Joseph was the husband of Mary,
and Mary was the mother of Jesus.
Jesus is called the Christ.
17So there were fourteen generations from Abraham to David. And there were fourteen generations
from David until the people were taken to Babylon.
And there were fourteen generations from the time
when the people were taken to Babylon until Christ
was born.

The Birth of Jesus Christ

18This is how the birth of Jesus Christ came
about. His mother Mary was engaged to marry
Joseph, but before they married, she learned she
was pregnant by the power of the Holy Spirit.
19Because Mary's husband, Joseph, was a good
man, he did not want to disgrace her in public, so
he planned to divorce her secretly.
20While Joseph thought about these things, an
angel of the Lord came to him in a dream. The angel

1 Both Matthew and Luke include a family history of Jesus. Matthew highlights Jesus' connections with Abraham and David. Luke (3:23–38) starts with Joseph and goes all the way back to Adam. These birth accounts highlight Jesus' humanity and show his royal connections to the family of David (see Luke 1:32–33; Romans 1:3).

1:1 Abraham: Matthew 3:9

1:1 David: Matthew 22:41–45

1:1–16 As in Old Testament family lists, this one is important for the way it helps to establish the identity of Jesus. This one concentrates on one's relationship to one's father and, in a few instances, to one's mother. Jesus is thus identified especially as the son of Abraham and as the son of David. This gives him special status and supports his identification as the Christ through whom God's salvation would become available to all the people of the world. The inclusion of women in the genealogy, and especially of these women whose Old Testament stories are dramatic, hints at how extraordinary Jesus' birth was, and of how God uses even tragic circumstances to complete his purpose.

1:2 *father.* "Father" in Jewish lists of ancestors can sometimes mean grandfather or more distant relative.

1:5 Rahab: Acts 11:1–8

1:5 The "Great Commission" in Matthew 28:18–20 emphasizes that the Good News of salvation should be preached to all people, Jew and non-Jew alike. Matthew supports this point in his genealogy of Jesus. The inclusion of Tamar (verse 3), Rahab, Ruth (verse 5), and Uriah (verse 6) in this family history highlights the non-Jews who were Jesus' ancestors.

1:7 Solomon: Luke 12:27

1:18 *engaged.* For the Jewish people an engagement was a lasting agreement, which could only be broken by a divorce. If a bride-to-be was unfaithful, it was considered adultery, and she could be put to death.

1:18–25 After an angel told Joseph in a dream that Mary was pregnant by the power of the Holy Spirit, he commanded him to name the son who would be born *Jesus,* a Greek form of "Joshua," meaning *"Yahweh* saves." The reason for the name: "because he will save his people from their sins." Jesus is the Savior of the world.

1:20–24 God uses a dream to announce the birth of Christ to Joseph and to inaugurate the New Agreement. Numerous times throughout the Bible, God speaks through dreams or visions to reveal new information to his people. He seals his agreement with Abram through a dream (Genesis 15:9–21), he speaks to Daniel while the children of Israel are in exile (Daniel 7:1–28), and he speaks to both Peter and Paul as they begin the church age (Acts 10:9–16; 16:9).

said, "Joseph, descendant of David, don't be afraid
to take Mary as your wife, because the baby in her
is from the Holy Spirit. 21She will give birth to a son,
and you will name him Jesus, because he will save
his people from their sins."
22All this happened to bring about what the
Lord had said through the prophet: 23"The virgin
will be pregnant. She will have a son, and they
will name him Immanuel," which means "God is
with us."
24When Joseph woke up, he did what the Lord's
angel had told him to do. Joseph took Mary as his
wife, 25but he did not have sexual relations with
her until she gave birth to the son. And Joseph
named him Jesus.

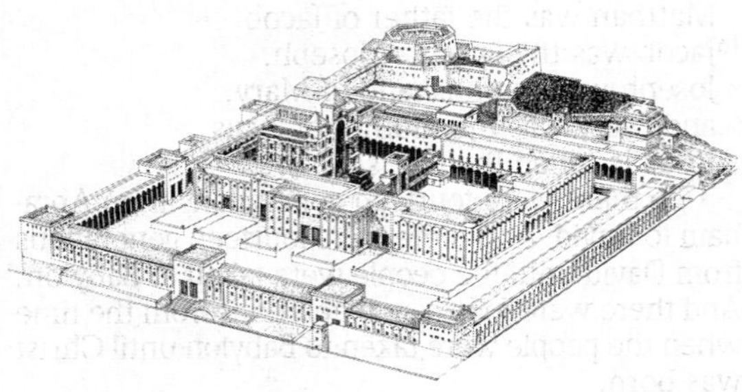

Herod's temple, surrounded by the court of the non-Jews

Wise Men Come to Visit Jesus

2 Jesus was born in the town of Bethlehem in
Judea during the time when Herod was king.
When Jesus was born, some wise men from the
east came to Jerusalem. 2They asked, "Where is
the baby who was born to be the king of the Jews?
We saw his star in the east and have come to worship him."
3When King Herod heard this, he was troubled,
as well as all the people in Jerusalem. 4Herod called
a meeting of all the leading priests and teachers of
the law and asked them where the Christ would be
born. 5They answered, "In the town of Bethlehem
in Judea. The prophet wrote about this in the
Scriptures:
6'But you, Bethlehem, in the land of Judah,
are important among the tribes of Judah.
A ruler will come from you
who will be like a shepherd for my
people Israel.'" *Micah 5:2*
7Then Herod had a secret meeting with the wise
men and learned from them the exact time they
first saw the star. 8He sent the wise men to
Bethlehem, saying, "Look carefully for the child.
When you find him, come tell me so I can worship him too."
9After the wise men heard the king, they left.
The star that they had seen in the east went before
them until it stopped above the place where the
child was. 10When the wise men saw the star, they
were filled with joy. 11They came to the house
where the child was and saw him with his mother,
Mary, and they bowed down and worshiped him.
They opened their gifts and gave him treasures of
gold, frankincense, and myrrh. 12But God warned
the wise men in a dream not to go back to Herod,
so they returned to their own country by a different way.

Jesus' Parents Take Him to Egypt

13After they left, an angel of the Lord came to
Joseph in a dream and said, "Get up! Take the
child and his mother and escape to Egypt, because
Herod is starting to look for the child so he can kill
him. Stay in Egypt until I tell you to return."
14So Joseph got up and left for Egypt during the
night with the child and his mother. 15And Joseph
stayed in Egypt until Herod died. This happened
to bring about what the Lord had said through the
prophet: "I called my son out of Egypt."

"Jesus was born in the town of Bethlehem in Judea" (2:1).

1:21 Names of God: Matthew 6:9
1:21 *Jesus.* The name Jesus means "salvation."
1:23 *"The virgin . . . Immanuel."* Quotation from Isaiah 7:14. **1:25 Family:** Matthew 2
2 Astrology was widespread in the ancient world, and Babylon was one of its strongholds. The magi who journeyed to Bethlehem to find the infant Jesus were almost certainly involved in the practice of astrology. But when they saw the baby, even they worshiped him and thereby acknowledged that his spiritual power was greater than theirs.
2:1–2 Matthew emphasizes that Jesus' birth had importance for all people by showing, first, how people from outside of Israel came to worship him and, second, how important leaders within Israel feared him even as a baby.
2:10 Moses: John 1:17
2:15 *"I called . . . Egypt."* Quotation from Hosea 11:1.

SUFFERING

ROMANS 5

Why does God allow suffering in the world? Why is so much suffering so unfair? Why do God's own children have to suffer? How should we respond to suffering?

The Bible tells us that human suffering came into the world because of the sin of the first humans, Adam and Eve (Romans 5). Genesis 3 explains that not only do we suffer death because of that first sin, but also our lives are full of frustration and hurt (vv. 17–19). God made the world in such a way that sin has consequences, and one of those consequences is suffering. God allows the suffering to happen because he *cares* about his relationship with those who are made "in his image" (Genesis 1:27; 9:6).

Sometimes suffering is the direct result of our own sin (Jeremiah 13:22). But often suffering cannot be linked to any particular sin of ours, and very often we suffer because of somebody else's sin. And sometimes we suffer for no reason that we can see at all. There is a lot of *unfair* suffering. If God is good and merciful, and he is also all-powerful, why does he allow all the unfair suffering to go on?

Some people try to solve the problem by saying that God is not all-powerful, or at least he does not use his power. They say God does not want to force his will on people. But some tragedies are not because of people. Earthquakes cause a lot of suffering to people who are no worse sinners than anyone else. Further, the Bible says that God actually plans for suffering and evil events to happen. In Exodus 4:11 God asks Moses, "Who makes someone deaf or not able to speak? Or who gives a person sight or blindness?" God says that he makes people deaf or blind! In fact, the greatest evil in history, the murder of Jesus Christ, took place because God planned it. The early disciples prayed to God in Acts 4:27–28, "[These people] Herod, Pontius Pilate, those who are not Jews, and Jewish people all came together against Jesus here in Jerusalem. . . . These people made your plan happen because of your [God's] power and will." God does not take away people's ability to choose, but he always makes things come out exactly as he intended. So suffering, even unfair suffering, must be part of God's plan.

Another way to solve the problem is to say that God is not good. But of course the Bible always understands God to be good and gives many examples of how kind and good he is.

Another way is to say that evil and suffering do not really exist. But very few people can pretend they are not hurting when they actually hurt badly. And the Bible has hardly a page that does not take for granted the reality of suffering and evil. Further, even people who think there is no such thing as death still die.

In fact, the Bible again and again, when it deals with suffering, assumes both that God is good and that he is all-powerful and uses his power. That is why all the Psalms on suffering cry out to God. The psalmists know that God is good, and that he is powerful, and they are calling out to him because they know he is the one who controls everything. Psalm 60:3 says, "You have given your people trouble. You made us unable to walk straight." The biblical writers might not have understood why they were suffering, but they never doubted that God was in control of their situation, and even *sent* the suffering for some reason.

This is why some people try to argue that if someone is suffering he must have sinned. But Jesus did not sin, and yet suffered more than anyone. Further, the entire Book of Job shows that suffering is not necessarily due to the sin of the sufferer. Job's three friends try to convince Job that he must have sinned, and Job knows that he did not. Job calls out to God to explain himself. God answers, but he does not explain why Job is suffering. He simply reminds Job of who he is. But Job's three friends are rebuked by God for saying the wrong thing. God has reasons for bringing suffering into our lives, but those reasons are often hidden from us.

However, even though the particular reasons are often hidden, the Bible does tell us some things about why Christians must suffer. "There are some things the LORD our God has kept secret, but there are some things he has let us know" (Deuteronomy 29:29).

One reason is that Christians sometimes sin and suffer the consequences (1 Corinthians 11:30). If we drink too much alcohol, we might end up suffering from liver failure. If we are sexually impure, we might get AIDS. In fact, it appears that God is more diligent in bringing home the earthly consequences of disobedience on his own children than on unbelievers, because "the Lord disciplines those he loves" (Hebrews 12:6). So suffering might be sent by the Lord to jolt us into awareness of our sin. Nehemiah 9:27 points out that God handed the disobedient Israelites over to their enemies, and their enemies treated them badly. That made them cry out to God. The Psalm writers can even rejoice that God brings suffering at certain times. Psalm 119:75 acknowledges, "it was right for you to punish me." The history of Israel in the Old Testament tells this story over and over. We are slow to learn. As C. S. Lewis pointed out in *A Grief Observed*, "God whispers in our pleasures but shouts in our pains. Pain is his megaphone to rouse a dulled world." Suffering can tenderize a hardened conscience for a believer. If we are suffering, the first thing we ought to ask is, Is there some sin I need to repent of? Even if the sin is not the direct cause of the suffering, the first thing we need to do is stop doing that sin.

Another reason God sends suffering is to help us become holy, completely focused on God. Suffering is like a trial by fire (1 Peter 1:7). Fire purifies gold, but consumes rubbish. Christians endure the fire because it burns off that part of us which is not glorious. It helps us to be patient (Romans 5:3). It also reduces our attachment to this world, and helps us focus on the future promises of God. Exodus 3:7 says that God saw the suffering of his people and delivered them. But why did he allow them to suffer in the first place? Would they have wanted to leave Egypt if they were not suffering? Why would they look to the land of Canaan (the Promised Land) if they had a nice cozy life where they already were?

Suffering also prepares us for a great glory. "We have small troubles for a while now, but they are helping us gain an eternal glory that is much greater than the troubles" (2 Corinthians 4:17). We are strengthened by troubles and hardships, so we can carry more glory, more of the image of God in Christ. "We must suffer as Christ suffered so that we will have glory as Christ has glory. The sufferings we have now are nothing compared to the great glory that will be shown to us" (Romans 8:17–18).

Finally, suffering ties the believer to Christ's suffering and death. In order to appreciate this, we have to realize how important Jesus' suffering was. First Peter 3:18 tells us, "Christ himself suffered for sins once. He was not guilty, but he suffered for those who are guilty to bring you to God." This idea of Jesus (the innocent one) suffering in place of us (the guilty ones) is based on the great prophecy of Isaiah 53. The "Servant of the Lord" is above all Jesus Christ, who "took our suffering on him, and felt our pain for us" (Isaiah 52:13–53:12). His suffering saved us. We would have had to suffer far more than we do if Jesus had not taken the just punishment for all our sins.

Jesus even "learned obedience by what he suffered" according to Hebrews 5:8. He learned what it was like to obey God in the face of hardship and suffering and pain, which is what we humans have to do. Now when we who believe in Christ suffer, we do it with him. "Be happy that you are sharing in Christ's sufferings" says Peter (1 Peter 4:13). Amazingly, Paul even tells us that "there are things that Christ must still suffer through his body, the church" (Colossians 1:24). That is, our sufferings become part of Christ's own suffering, just as his suffering death on the cross becomes our death on the cross (Romans 6:6, Galatians 2:20).

Suffering is therefore part of the Christian life. To suffer with Christ is a gift from God (Philippians 1:29). Paul told the believers in Acts 14:22 that, "we *must* suffer many things to enter God's kingdom" (italics mine). This is why the Lord's Supper is so important to believers. The Lord's Supper represents the sufferings of Christ, and when we eat the "body" and drink the "blood," we are taking on Christ's sufferings as our own, which in turn changes our own sufferings into manifestations of the suffering of Christ.

But even when we know all this, it is not easy to suffer. And the Bible makes it very clear that we are not supposed to "grin and bear it." The godly people in the Bible, even Jesus himself, cried out to God when he sent suffering (Hebrews 5:7; Matthew 27:46). The Bible even helps us cry out to God when we are in pain—God provided the whole Book of Lamentations and many Psalms that do just that. In fact *most* of the Psalms in some way either cry out to God out of need or suffering of some sort, or else praise God for meeting a need or saving the Psalm writer from suffering. See especially Psalms 13; 22; 28; 42; 43; 55; 57; 59; 60; 64; 69; 70; 74; 77; 79; 86; 88; 102; 123; 130; 137; 140; 141; 142; and 143. Again, Jesus himself in his hardest hour cried out in the words of Psalm 22, "My God, my God, why have you rejected me?" Since our suffering is with Christ, we can pray by these psalms, too. The psalmist's words become our words, and we know since they are inspired that they are prayers acceptable to God. The Lord forbids us to complain *about* him, but he wants us to complain *to* him when suffering comes. God expects us to be honest with him about our feelings when we suffer. And if we pray these complaints with the Psalms we also end up seeing what the Psalm writers saw—that God will help us through the trouble, and will rescue us in the end if we trust him.

Suffering: For additional scriptures on this topic go to Psalm 13.

Herod Kills the Baby Boys

16When Herod saw that the wise men had
tricked him, he was furious. So he gave an order to
kill all the baby boys in Bethlehem and in the surrounding area who were two years old or younger.
This was in keeping with the time he learned from
the wise men. 17So what God had said through the
prophet Jeremiah came true:
18"A voice was heard in Ramah
of painful crying and deep sadness:
Rachel crying for her children.
She refused to be comforted,
because her children are dead." *Jeremiah 31:15*

Joseph and Mary Return

19After Herod died, an angel of the Lord spoke
to Joseph in a dream while he was in Egypt. 20The
angel said, "Get up! Take the child and his mother
and go to the land of Israel, because the people
who were trying to kill the child are now dead."
21So Joseph took the child and his mother and
went to Israel. 22But he heard that Archelaus was
now king in Judea since his father Herod had died.
So Joseph was afraid to go there. After being
warned in a dream, he went to the area of Galilee,
23to a town called Nazareth, and lived there. And
so what God had said through the prophets came
true: "He will be called a Nazarene."∞

The Work of John the Baptist

3 About that time John the Baptist began
preaching in the desert area of Judea. 2John
said, "Change your hearts and lives because the
kingdom of heaven is near."∞ 3John the Baptist is
the one Isaiah the prophet was talking about when
he said:

"This is a voice of one
who calls out in the desert:
'Prepare the way for the Lord.
Make the road straight for him.'" *Isaiah 40:3*
4John's clothes were made from camel's hair, and
he wore a leather belt around his waist. For food, he

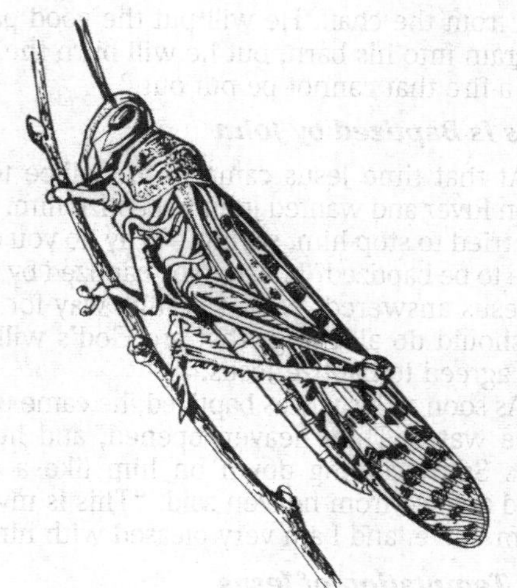

Joel used the picture of a locust plague to describe God's judgment

ate locusts and wild honey. 5Many people came
from Jerusalem and Judea and all the area around
the Jordan River to hear John. 6They confessed their
sins, and he baptized them in the Jordan River.
7Many of the Pharisees and Sadducees came to
the place where John was baptizing people. When
John saw them, he said, "You are all snakes! Who
warned you to run away from God's coming punishment? 8Do the things that show you really have
changed your hearts and lives. 9And don't think
you can say to yourselves, 'Abraham is our father.'
I tell you that God could make children for
Abraham from these rocks.∞ 10The ax is now
ready to cut down the trees, and every tree that
does not produce good fruit will be cut down and
thrown into the fire.
11"I baptize you with water to show that your
hearts and lives have changed. But there is one
coming after me who is greater than I am, whose
sandals I am not good enough to carry. He will baptize you with the Holy Spirit and fire. 12He will
come ready to clean the grain, separating the good

2:23 *Nazarene.* A person from the city of Nazareth, a name probably meaning "branch" (see Isaiah 11:1).

∞**2:23 Family:** Luke 1

3 When Jesus came to baptized, John hesitated (Matthew 3:14). He admitted to Jesus that he was the one who needed to be baptized. Why was it that Jesus came to John and submitted to baptism? Could it be that it was how Jesus identified himself with the people of this world and their sin?

3:1–6 John's ministry calling people to change their hearts is fittingly located in the wilderness (desert). It is not a call to Jerusalem, the center of religious and political power, but a call away from it to a new exodus. A new people of God will be established around the Lord who is coming. John's clothing and diet not only define him as a person of the desert; it identifies him with Elijah (2 Kings 1:8). He is the Elijah that would come to make things right for the day of the Lord (Malachi 4:5–6).

∞**3:2 Pharisees and Sadducees:** Matthew 3:7–9

3:9 Abraham was the father or patriarch of the faith of the Old Testament. The Jewish leaders of Jesus' day looked back to Abraham as the first one chosen by God. Jesus here warns them that religious belief is more than being a descendant of Abraham. Their hearts, minds, and actions need to reflect their faith.

∞**3:9 Abraham:** Matthew 8:11

∞**3:9 Pharisees and Sadducees:** Matthew 9:10–13

3:10 *The ax. . .fire.* This means that God is ready to punish his people who do not obey him.

3:12 *He will . . . out.* This means that Jesus will come to separate good people from bad people, saving the good and punishing the bad.

grain from the chaff. He will put the good part of
the grain into his barn, but he will burn the chaff
with a fire that cannot be put out."

Jesus Is Baptized by John

13At that time Jesus came from Galilee to the
Jordan River and wanted John to baptize him. 14But
John tried to stop him, saying, "Why do you come
to me to be baptized? I need to be baptized by you!"
15Jesus answered, "Let it be this way for now.
We should do all things that are God's will." So
John agreed to baptize Jesus.
16As soon as Jesus was baptized, he came up out
of the water. Then heaven opened, and he saw
God's Spirit coming down on him like a dove.
17And a voice from heaven said, "This is my Son,
whom I love, and I am very pleased with him."

The Temptation of Jesus

4 Then the Spirit led Jesus into the desert to be
tempted by the devil. 2Jesus ate nothing for
forty days and nights. After this, he was very hungry.
3The devil came to Jesus to tempt him, saying, "If
you are the Son of God, tell these rocks to become
bread."
4Jesus answered, "It is written in the Scriptures,
'A person does not live by eating only bread, but
by everything God says.'"
5Then the devil led Jesus to the holy city of
Jerusalem and put him on a high place of the
Temple. 6The devil said, "If you are the Son of God,
jump down, because it is written in the Scriptures:

'He has put his angels in charge of you.
They will catch you in their hands
so that you will not hit your foot
on a rock.'" *Psalm 91:11-12*

7Jesus answered him, "It also says in the
Scriptures, 'Do not test the Lord your God.'"
8Then the devil led Jesus to the top of a very high
mountain and showed him all the kingdoms of the
world and all their splendor. 9The devil said, "If you
will bow down and worship me, I will give you all
these things."
10Jesus said to the devil, "Go away from me,
Satan! It is written in the Scriptures, 'You must
worship the Lord your God and serve only him.'"
11So the devil left Jesus, and angels came and
took care of him.

Jesus Begins Work in Galilee

12When Jesus heard that John had been put in
prison, he went back to Galilee. 13He left Nazareth
and went to live in Capernaum, a town near Lake
Galilee, in the area near Zebulun and Naphtali.
14Jesus did this to bring about what the prophet
Isaiah had said:

15"Land of Zebulun and land of Naphtali
along the sea,
beyond the Jordan River.
This is Galilee where the
non-Jewish people live.
16These people who live in darkness
will see a great light.
They live in a place covered
with the shadows of death,
but a light will shine on them." *Isaiah 9:1-2*

Jesus Chooses Some Followers

17From that time Jesus began to preach, saying,
"Change your hearts and lives, because the kingdom of heaven is near."
18As Jesus was walking by Lake Galilee, he saw
two brothers, Simon (called Peter) and his brother
Andrew. They were throwing a net into the lake
because they were fishermen. 19Jesus said, "Come
follow me, and I will make you fish for people." 20So
Simon and Andrew immediately left their nets and
followed him.
21As Jesus continued walking by Lake Galilee, he
saw two other brothers, James and John, the sons of
Zebedee. They were in a boat with their father Zebedee, mending their nets. Jesus told them to come
with him. 22Immediately they left the boat and
their father, and they followed Jesus.

Jesus Teaches and Heals People

23Jesus went everywhere in Galilee, teaching in
the synagogues, preaching the Good News about the
kingdom of heaven, and healing all the people's
diseases and sicknesses. 24The news about Jesus
spread all over Syria, and people brought all the
sick to him. They were suffering from different
kinds of diseases. Some were in great pain, some
had demons, some were epileptics, and some were
paralyzed. Jesus healed all of them. 25Many people

3:15 Baptism: Matthew 28:16–20
3:17 Exodus/New Exodus: Hebrews 3:7–4:13
3:17 Jordan River: Luke 3
3:17 Trinity: Matthew 11:27
4:4 *'A person . . . says.'* Quotation from Deuteronomy 8:3.
4:7 *Do . . . God.'* Quotation from Deuteronomy 6:16.
4:10 *"You . . . him.'* Quotation from Deuteronomy 6:13.
4:11 Son/Child of God: Mark 12:1–12
4:11 Wilderness (Desert): Matthew 14:13–21
4:20 Peter: Matthew 10:2–4
4:22 Disciple/Discipleship/Mentoring: Matthew 5:1–2
4:22 Leadership: Matthew 20:20–28
4:22 Self-Control: Mark 6:30–44
4:23 Gospel/Good News: Matthew 9:35
4:24 *epileptics.* People with a disease that causes them sometimes to lose control of their bodies and maybe faint, shake strongly, or not be able to move.

from Galilee, the Ten Towns, Jerusalem, Judea,
and the land across the Jordan River followed him.

Jesus Teaches the People

5 When Jesus saw the crowds, he went up on a
hill and sat down. His followers came to him,
2and he began to teach them, saying:
3"Those people who know they have great
spiritual needs are happy,
because the kingdom of heaven
belongs to them.
4Those who are sad now are happy,
because God will comfort them.
5Those who are humble are happy,
because the earth will belong to them.
6Those who want to do right more than anything
else are happy,
because God will fully satisfy them.
7Those who show mercy to others are happy,
because God will show mercy to them.
8Those who are pure in their
thinking are happy,
because they will be with God.
9Those who work to bring peace are happy,
because God will call them his children.
10Those who are treated badly
for doing good are happy,
because the kingdom of
heaven belongs to them.
11"People will insult you and hurt you. They will
lie and say all kinds of evil things about you because
you follow me. But when they do, you will be
happy. 12Rejoice and be glad, because you have
a great reward waiting for you in heaven. People
did the same evil things to the prophets who lived
before you.

You Are like Salt and Light

13"You are the salt of the earth. But if the salt
loses its salty taste, it cannot be made salty again.
It is good for nothing, except to be thrown out and
walked on.
14"You are the light that gives light to the world.
A city that is built on a hill cannot be hidden.
15And people don't hide a light under a bowl. They
put it on a lampstand so the light shines for all the
people in the house. 16In the same way, you should
be a light for other people. Live so that they will
see the good things you do and will praise your
Father in heaven.

The Importance of the Law

17"Don't think that I have come to destroy the
law of Moses or the teaching of the prophets. I have
not come to destroy them but to bring about what
they said. 18I tell you the truth, nothing will disappear from the law until heaven and earth are
gone. Not even the smallest letter or the smallest
part of a letter will be lost until everything has happened. 19Whoever refuses to obey any command
and teaches other people not to obey that command
will be the least important in the kingdom of

4:25 *Ten Towns.* In Greek, called *Decapolis.* It was an area east of Lake Galilee that once had ten main towns.

5–7 Jesus giving a sermon from a hilltop on godly living is very reminiscent of Moses receiving the Law on a mountain and delivering that law to the Israelites (Exodus 19–23). Jesus even seems to contrast his new teaching to the Law (for example, Matthew 5:21, 27, 31, 38, 43). Jesus is not canceling the Law given through Moses. Rather he is giving it proper interpretation. He is the new lawgiver.

5:2 Disciple/Discipleship/Mentoring (Follow/Follower): Matthew 9:9–13

5:3 Happiness: 1 Peter 4:13–14

5:3 Jesus began his great Sermon on the Mount with a series of "beatitudes," that is blessings upon certain types of people. At the very top are those who are (translating more literally) "poor in spirit." A more dynamic translation, like the present one, captures the sense when it recognizes that the poor that Jesus is pronouncing happy are not people who lack wealth, but people who know they have no spiritual resources in themselves. Why are they happy? Because they have nowhere to turn for help except to God, and those who turn to God will gain the "kingdom of heaven."

5:4 In this verse Jesus makes this most unusual statement, because the people in view know that despite their sadness, especially over the sin, suffering, and pain of this world, God will comfort them. This is a joyful prospect which makes them truly happy, even now (Jeremiah 31:13). Also note carefully how the words of comfort given here by Jesus to those who are sad are contrasted with words of warning he gives to those who are rich (Luke 6:24).

5:4 Mourning: John 14:1–3

5:9 Peace: Luke 1:79

5:10 Grace: Luke 15

5:10 Success: Philippians 4:8–9

5:10–11 Jesus is not a masochist, valuing suffering and pain for its own sake. Rather, his teaching stands in a long line of Jewish belief that martyrdom demonstrates the highest loyalty to God, and will be rewarded in due course. The prophets and Jesus were martyred, a possibility for which the followers of Jesus should also be prepared.

5:11 Martyrdom: Matthew 10:5–42

5:11 Suffering: Acts 3:18

5:11–12 Jesus warned his followers that they would suffer persecution, that people would insult and hurt them. But he encourages them by saying that in the midst of the "evil things" people would do to them, they would be happy. He actually calls upon them to "rejoice and be glad" because suffering for Christ here means receiving a "great reward" in heaven.

5:12 Persecution: Luke 23

5:13 Salt: See article on page 279.

5:13–16 Jesus Christ calls upon believers to be the "salt of the earth" and the "light that gives light to the world." It is into this world, all the world, that Jesus sends those who believe in him (Mark 16:15). Salt may appear to be a cheap and rather common ingredient with little to contribute, but it has a preserving power and can spread through something unlike almost anything else. In the same way, the Christian community is to be a light of the world in the middle of the darkness of the present time. "The person who follows me will never live in darkness but will have the light that gives life" (John 8:12). The influence of a small body of Christians may appear no larger than a handful of salt or the flicker of a flame, but they are called upon to be the church in the world.

5:14 City: Luke 13:34–35

heaven. But whoever obeys the commands and
teaches other people to obey them will be great in
the kingdom of heaven. 20I tell you that if you are
no more obedient than the teachers of the law and
the Pharisees, you will never enter the kingdom of
heaven.

Jesus Teaches About Anger

21"You have heard that it was said to our people
long ago, 'You must not murder anyone. Anyone
who murders another will be judged.' 22But I tell
you, if you are angry with a brother or sister, you
will be judged. If you say bad things to a brother or
sister, you will be judged by the council. And if you
call someone a fool, you will be in danger of the fire
of hell.
23"So when you offer your gift to God at the altar,
and you remember that your brother or sister has
something against you, 24leave your gift there at the
altar. Go and make peace with that person, and
then come and offer your gift.
25"If your enemy is taking you to court, become
friends quickly, before you go to court. Otherwise, your enemy might turn you over to the
judge, and the judge might give you to a guard to
put you in jail. 26I tell you the truth, you will not
leave there until you have paid everything you
owe.

Jesus Teaches About Sexual Sin

27"You have heard that it was said, 'You must
not be guilty of adultery.' 28But I tell you that if anyone looks at a woman and wants to sin sexually
with her, in his mind he has already done that sin
with the woman. 29If your right eye causes you
to sin, take it out and throw it away. It is better to
lose one part of your body than to have your whole
body thrown into hell. 30If your right hand causes
you to sin, cut it off and throw it away. It is better
to lose one part of your body than for your whole
body to go into hell.

Jesus Teaches About Divorce

31"It was also said, 'Anyone who divorces his
wife must give her a written divorce paper.' 32But
I tell you that anyone who divorces his wife forces
her to be guilty of adultery. The only reason for a
man to divorce his wife is if she has sexual relations
with another man. And anyone who marries that
divorced woman is guilty of adultery.

Make Promises Carefully

33"You have heard that it was said to our people
long ago, 'Don't break your promises, but keep the
promises you make to the Lord.' 34But I tell you,
never swear an oath. Don't swear an oath using the
name of heaven, because heaven is God's throne.
35Don't swear an oath using the name of the earth,
because the earth belongs to God. Don't swear an
oath using the name of Jerusalem, because that is
the city of the great King. 36Don't even swear by
your own head, because you cannot make one hair
on your head become white or black. 37Say only
yes if you mean yes, and no if you mean no. If you
say more than yes or no, it is from the Evil One.

Don't Fight Back

38"You have heard that it was said, 'An eye for
an eye, and a tooth for a tooth.' 39But I tell you,
don't stand up against an evil person. If someone
slaps you on the right cheek, turn to him the other
cheek also. 40If someone wants to sue you in court
and take your shirt, let him have your coat also.
41If someone forces you to go with him one mile,
go with him two miles. 42If a person asks you for
something, give it to him. Don't refuse to give to
someone who wants to borrow from you.

Love All People

43"You have heard that it was said, 'Love your
neighbor and hate your enemies.' 44But I say to you,
love your enemies. Pray for those who hurt you.
45If you do this, you will be true children of your
Father in heaven. He causes the sun to rise on good

5:20 Scribes (Teachers of the Law): Matthew 7:28–29
5:21 *'You . . . anyone.'* Quotation from Exodus 20:13; Deuteronomy 5:17.
5:21–48 It is easy to think that in this long speech Jesus is rejecting the Old Testament Law. This is not true. In some cases, he is merely rejecting how people had been interpreting the Law, then acting as though their interpretations had come from God. In other cases, he is showing how the Law is not an end unto itself but a window into the character of God. The aim of Jesus' followers, he says, is not simply to obey the Law but to be like God (see 5:48).
5:22 *brother . . . sister.* Although the Greek text reads "brother" here and throughout this book, Jesus' words were meant for the entire church, including men and women.
5:22 Hell: Matthew 5:29–30
5:22 Murder: Matthew 19:18
5:26 Guilt: Mark 2:1–12
5:27 *'You . . . adultery.'* Quotation from Exodus 20:14; Deuteronomy 5:18.
5:28 Adultery: John 7:53–8:11
5:30 Hell: Matthew 18:8–9
5:30 Sin: Mark 7:1–20
5:31 *'Anyone . . . divorce paper.'* Quotation from Deuteronomy 24:1.
5:32 Divorce: Mark 10:1–12
5:33 *'Don't . . . Lord.'* This refers to Leviticus 19:12; Numbers 30:2; Deuteronomy 23:21.
5:37 Integrity: Matthew 6:1–4
5:37 Oath/Vow: Matthew 14:7–9
5:38 *'An eye . . . tooth.'* Quotation from Exodus 21:24; Leviticus 24:20; Deuteronomy 19:21.
5:42 Capital Punishment: Luke 23:40–43
5:43 *'Love your neighbor.'* Quotation from Leviticus 19:18.
5:44 Love: John 3:16

people and on evil people, and he sends rain to
those who do right and to those who do wrong. 46If
you love only the people who love you, you will get
no reward. Even the tax collectors do that. 47And if
you are nice only to your friends, you are no better
than other people. Even those who don't know
God are nice to their friends. 48So you must be
perfect, just as your Father in heaven is perfect.

Jesus Teaches About Giving

6 "Be careful! When you do good things, don't
do them in front of people to be seen by them.
If you do that, you will have no reward from your
Father in heaven.
2"When you give to the poor, don't be like the
hypocrites. They blow trumpets in the synagogues
and on the streets so that people will see them and
honor them. I tell you the truth, those hypocrites
already have their full reward. 3So when you give
to the poor, don't let anyone know what you are
doing. 4Your giving should be done in secret.
Your Father can see what is done in secret, and he
will reward you.

Jesus Teaches About Prayer

5"When you pray, don't be like the hypocrites.
They love to stand in the synagogues and on the
street corners and pray so people will see them. I
tell you the truth, they already have their full
reward. 6When you pray, you should go into your
room and close the door and pray to your Father
who cannot be seen. Your Father can see what is
done in secret, and he will reward you.
7"And when you pray, don't be like those people who don't know God. They continue saying
things that mean nothing, thinking that God will
hear them because of their many words. 8Don't be
like them, because your Father knows the things
you need before you ask him. 9So when you
pray, you should pray like this:
'Our Father in heaven,
may your name always be kept holy.
10May your kingdom come
and what you want be done,
here on earth as it is in heaven.
11Give us the food we need for each day.
12Forgive us for our sins,
just as we have forgiven those
who sinned against us.
13And do not cause us to be tempted,
but save us from the Evil One.'
14Yes, if you forgive others for their sins, your
Father in heaven will also forgive you for your sins.
15But if you don't forgive others, your Father in
heaven will not forgive your sins.

Jesus Teaches About Worship

16"When you give up eating, don't put on a sad
face like the hypocrites. They make their faces look
sad to show people they are giving up eating. I tell
you the truth, those hypocrites already have their
full reward. 17So when you give up eating, comb
your hair and wash your face. 18Then people will
not know that you are giving up eating, but your
Father, whom you cannot see, will see you. Your
Father sees what is done in secret, and he will
reward you.

God Is More Important than Money

19"Don't store treasures for yourselves here on
earth where moths and rust will destroy them and
thieves can break in and steal them. 20But store
your treasures in heaven where they cannot be
destroyed by moths or rust and where thieves cannot break in and steal them. 21Your heart will be
where your treasure is.
22"The eye is a light for the body. If your eyes are
good, your whole body will be full of light. 23But if
your eyes are evil, your whole body will be full of
darkness. And if the only light you have is really
darkness, then you have the worst darkness.
24"No one can serve two masters. The person
will hate one master and love the other, or will
follow one master and refuse to follow the other.
You cannot serve both God and worldly riches.

Don't Worry

25"So I tell you, don't worry about the food or
drink you need to live, or about the clothes you
need for your body. Life is more than food, and

6:3 Government: Luke 4:18
6:4 Integrity: Matthew 6:24
6:9 Names of God: John 17:6
6:10 Will of God: Matthew 7:21
6:12 Debt/Loan: Matthew 6:14–15
6:13 Jesus encourages his followers to pray that God would protect them from the kind of Satanic temptation that might cause them to destroy their Christian witness through some terrible sin, or get them into such a difficult situation of hardship that they might abandon their faith completely. This is the greatest temptation for the Christian.
6:13 Evil: Mark 7:21
6:13 Worship: Luke 1:46–50
6:15 Debt/Loan: Mark 12:40
6:15 Prayer: John 17:1–26
6:16 *give up eating.* This is called "fasting." The people would give up eating for a special time of prayer and worship to God. It was also done to show sadness and disappointment.
6:21 Tithe: Luke 11:42
6:23 Darkness: Mark 15:33
6:24 Integrity: Matthew 6:25–33
6:25–34 Jesus is not against industry and hard work, but rather deals with the problem of worry. Worry is mentioned five times in this

the body is more than clothes. [26]Look at the birds in the air. They don't plant or harvest or store food in barns, but your heavenly Father feeds them. And you know that you are worth much more than the birds.⚭ [27]You cannot add any time to your life by worrying about it.

[28]"And why do you worry about clothes? Look at how the lilies in the field grow. They don't work or make clothes for themselves. [29]But I tell you that even Solomon with his riches was not dressed as beautifully as one of these flowers. [30]God clothes the grass in the field, which is alive today but tomorrow is thrown into the fire. So you can be even more sure that God will clothe you. Don't have so little faith! [31]Don't worry and say, 'What will we eat?' or 'What will we drink?' or 'What will we wear?' [32]The people who don't know God keep trying to get these things, and your Father in heaven knows you need them. [33]The thing you should want most is God's kingdom and doing what God wants. Then all these other things you need will be given to you.⚭ [34]So don't worry about tomorrow, because tomorrow will have its own worries. Each day has enough trouble of its own.⚭

Be Careful About Judging Others

7 Don't judge other people, or you will be judged. [2]You will be judged in the same way that you judge others, and the amount you give to others will be given to you.

[3]"Why do you notice the little piece of dust in your friend's eye, but you don't notice the big piece of wood in your own eye? [4]How can you say to your friend, 'Let me take that little piece of dust out of your eye'? Look at yourself! You still have that big piece of wood in your own eye. [5]You hypocrite! First, take the wood out of your own eye. Then you will see clearly to take the dust out of your friend's eye.

[6]"Don't give holy things to dogs, and don't throw your pearls before pigs. Pigs will only trample on them, and dogs will turn to attack you.

Ask God for What You Need

[7]"Ask, and God will give to you. Search, and you will find. Knock, and the door will open for you. [8]Yes, everyone who asks will receive. Everyone who searches will find. And everyone who knocks will have the door opened.

[9]"If your children ask for bread, which of you would give them a stone? [10]Or if your children ask for a fish, would you give them a snake? [11]Even though you are bad, you know how to give good gifts to your children. How much more your heavenly Father will give good things to those who ask him!

The Most Important Rule

[12]"Do to others what you want them to do to you. This is the meaning of the law of Moses and the teaching of the prophets.

The Way to Heaven Is Hard

[13]"Enter through the narrow gate. The gate is wide and the road is wide that leads to hell, and many people enter through that gate. [14]But the gate is small and the road is narrow that leads to true life. Only a few people find that road.⚭

People Know You by Your Actions

[15]"Be careful of false prophets. They come to you looking gentle like sheep, but they are really dangerous like wolves. [16]You will know these people by what they do. Grapes don't come from thornbushes, and figs don't come from thorny weeds. [17]In the same way, every good tree produces good fruit, but a bad tree produces bad fruit. [18]A good tree cannot produce bad fruit, and a bad tree cannot produce good fruit. [19]Every tree that does not produce good fruit is cut down and thrown into the fire. [20]In the same way, you will know these false prophets by what they do.

[21]"Not all those who say that I am their Lord will enter the kingdom of heaven. The only people who will enter the kingdom of heaven are those who do what my Father in heaven wants.⚭ [22]On the last day many people will say to me, 'Lord, Lord, we spoke for you, and through you we forced out demons and did many miracles.' [23]Then I will tell them clearly, 'Get away from me, you who do evil. I never knew you.'

Two Kinds of People

[24]"Everyone who hears my words and obeys them is like a wise man who built his house on rock.⚭ [25]It rained hard, the floods came, and the

---

short passage, including the opening and closing verses, which show it to be the theme of these paragraphs.

⚭**6:26 Animals:** 1 Corinthians 9:9

⚭**6:33 Integrity:** Matthew 23:28

⚭**6:33 Government:** Luke 4:18

⚭**6:33 Land/Inheritance:** Matthew 28:18–20

⚭**6:34 Materialism/Possessions:** Matthew 19:16–30

⚭**7:14 Road/Way:** Acts 19:23

⚭**7:21 Will of God:** Matthew 7:24

7:21–27 Jesus ends his long sermon (5:1–7:27) by reminding people of how important it is to do more than listen to his words. It is not enough to know what Jesus says and, thus, to know what God expects of his people. Those who are faithful to God are those who demonstrate their faithfulness in their obedience to him.

⚭**7:24 Will of God:** Matthew 21:28–31

winds blew and hit that house. But it did not fall,
because it was built on rock. 26Everyone who
hears my words and does not obey them is like a
foolish man who built his house on sand. 27It
rained hard, the floods came, and the winds blew
and hit that house, and it fell with a big crash."
28When Jesus finished saying these things, the
people were amazed at his teaching, 29because he
did not teach like their teachers of the law. He
taught like a person who had authority.

Jesus Heals a Sick Man

8 When Jesus came down from the hill, great
crowds followed him. 2Then a man with a skin
disease came to Jesus. The man bowed down
before him and said, "Lord, you can heal me if
you will."
3Jesus reached out his hand and touched the
man and said, "I will. Be healed!" And immediately
the man was healed from his disease. 4Then Jesus
said to him, "Don't tell anyone about this. But go
and show yourself to the priest and offer the gift
Moses commanded for people who are made well.
This will show the people what I have done."

Jesus Heals a Soldier's Servant

5When Jesus entered the city of Capernaum, an
army officer came to him, begging for help. 6The
officer said, "Lord, my servant is at home in bed.
He can't move his body and is in much pain."
7Jesus said to the officer, "I will go and heal him."
8The officer answered, "Lord, I am not worthy
for you to come into my house. You only need to
command it, and my servant will be healed. 9I,
too, am a man under the authority of others, and I
have soldiers under my command. I tell one soldier,
'Go,' and he goes. I tell another soldier, 'Come,'
and he comes. I say to my servant, 'Do this,' and
my servant does it.
10When Jesus heard this, he was amazed. He
said to those who were following him, "I tell you
the truth, this is the greatest faith I have found,
even in Israel. 11Many people will come from
the east and from the west and will sit and eat
with Abraham, Isaac, and Jacob in the kingdom of
heaven. 12But those people who should be in
the kingdom will be thrown outside into the darkness, where people will cry and grind their teeth
with pain."
13Then Jesus said to the officer, "Go home. Your
servant will be healed just as you believed he
would." And his servant was healed that same
hour.

Jesus Heals Many People

14When Jesus went to Peter's house, he saw that
Peter's mother-in-law was sick in bed with a fever.
15Jesus touched her hand, and the fever left her.
Then she stood up and began to serve Jesus.
16That evening people brought to Jesus many
who had demons. Jesus spoke and the demons left
them, and he healed all the sick. 17He did these
things to bring about what Isaiah the prophet had
said:

"He took our suffering on him
and carried our diseases." *Isaiah 53:4*

People Want to Follow Jesus

18When Jesus saw the crowd around him, he
told his followers to go to the other side of the lake.
19Then a teacher of the law came to Jesus and said,
"Teacher, I will follow you any place you go."
20Jesus said to him, "The foxes have holes to live
in, and the birds have nests, but the Son of Man
has no place to rest his head."
21Another man, one of Jesus' followers, said to
him, "Lord, first let me go and bury my father."
22But Jesus told him, "Follow me, and let the
people who are dead bury their own dead."

Jesus Calms a Storm

23Jesus got into a boat, and his followers went
with him. 24A great storm arose on the lake so
that waves covered the boat, but Jesus was sleeping. 25His followers went to him and woke him,
saying, "Lord, save us! We will drown!"
26Jesus answered, "Why are you afraid? You
don't have enough faith." Then Jesus got up and

7:25 Obedience: John 14:15–26
7:27 Parables: Matthew 24:45–51
7:29 Spirituality/Spiritual Dryness: John 15:1–17
7:29 Scribes (Teachers of the Law): Matthew 17:10
8:1–10:10 Gathered here are several stories about Jesus showing that he has God's authority to heal physical problems, to control nature, to rid people of evil spirits, to forgive wrongdoing, and to bring back to life those who have died. These are recounted to cause us to ask, "Who is this? Even the wind and the waves obey him" (Mark 4:41)! Jesus delegates this divine authority to his followers to give credibility to the message that the kingdom of God is near (Matthew 10:7–8).
8:4 Crossing Cultural Boundaries: Matthew 15:21–28
8:4 *show . . . priest.* The Law of Moses said a priest must say when a Jewish person with a skin disease was well.
8:4 *Moses commanded.* Read about this in Leviticus 14:1-32.
8:10 Faith/Unbelief: John 11:25
8:11 Abraham: Romans 4:3
8:17 Sickness, Disease, Healing: Matthew 9:1–8
8:18–22 These words of Jesus seem harsh, as though our responsibilities to our families were unimportant. In fact, this is Jesus' point, for he wants to assert the importance of following him and participating in the new family of his followers.

gave a command to the wind and the waves, and
it became completely calm.
27The men were amazed and said, "What kind of
man is this? Even the wind and the waves obey
him!"

Jesus Heals Two Men with Demons

28When Jesus arrived at the other side of the lake
in the area of the Gadarene people, two men who
had demons in them met him. These men lived in
the burial caves and were so dangerous that people could not use the road by those caves. 29They
shouted, "What do you want with us, Son of God?
Did you come here to torture us before the right
time?"
30Near that place there was a large herd of pigs
feeding. 31The demons begged Jesus, "If you make
us leave these men, please send us into that herd
of pigs."
32Jesus said to them, "Go!" So the demons left
the men and went into the pigs. Then the whole
herd rushed down the hill into the lake and were
drowned. 33The herdsmen ran away and went
into town, where they told about all of this and
what had happened to the men who had demons.
34Then the whole town went out to see Jesus.
When they saw him, they begged him to leave
their area.

Jesus Heals a Paralyzed Man

9 Jesus got into a boat and went back across
the lake to his own town. 2Some people
brought to Jesus a man who was paralyzed and
lying on a mat. When Jesus saw the faith of these
people, he said to the paralyzed man, "Be encouraged, young man. Your sins are forgiven."
3Some of the teachers of the law said to themselves, "This man speaks as if he were God. That is
blasphemy!"
4Knowing their thoughts, Jesus said, "Why are
you thinking evil thoughts? 5Which is easier: to say,
'Your sins are forgiven,' or to tell him, 'Stand up and
walk'? 6But I will prove to you that the Son of Man
has authority on earth to forgive sins." Then Jesus
said to the paralyzed man, "Stand up, take your
mat, and go home." 7And the man stood up and
went home. 8When the people saw this, they were
amazed and praised God for giving power like this
to human beings.

Jesus Chooses Matthew

9When Jesus was leaving, he saw a man named
Matthew sitting in the tax collector's booth. Jesus
said to him, "Follow me," and he stood up and
followed Jesus.
10As Jesus was having dinner at Matthew's
house, many tax collectors and "sinners" came
and ate with Jesus and his followers. 11When the
Pharisees saw this, they asked Jesus' followers,
"Why does your teacher eat with tax collectors
and sinners?"
12When Jesus heard them, he said, "It is not the
healthy people who need a doctor, but the sick.
13Go and learn what this means: 'I want kindness
more than I want animal sacrifices.' I did not come
to invite good people but to invite sinners."

Jesus' Followers Are Criticized

14Then the followers of John came to Jesus and
said, "Why do we and the Pharisees often give up
eating for a certain time, but your followers don't?"
15Jesus answered, "The friends of the bridegroom are not sad while he is with them. But the
time will come when the bridegroom will be taken
from them, and then they will give up eating.
16"No one sews a patch of unshrunk cloth over a
hole in an old coat. If he does, the patch will shrink
and pull away from the coat, making the hole
worse. 17Also, people never pour new wine into old
leather bags. Otherwise, the bags will break, the
wine will spill, and the wine bags will be ruined.
But people always pour new wine into new wine
bags. Then both will continue to be good."

Jesus Gives Life to a Dead Girl and Heals a Sick Woman

18While Jesus was saying these things, a leader
of the synagogue came to him. He bowed down
before Jesus and said, "My daughter has just died.
But if you come and lay your hand on her, she will
live again." 19So Jesus and his followers stood up
and went with the leader.
20Then a woman who had been bleeding for
twelve years came behind Jesus and touched the

8:27 Water: Mark 6:45–51
8:28 *Gadarene.* From Gadara, an area southeast of Lake Galilee.
9:3 *blasphemy.* Saying things against God or not showing respect for God.
9:8 Authority: Matthew 20:20–28
9:8 Forgiveness: Matthew 18:21–35
9:8 Sickness, Disease, Healing: Matthew 10:7–8
9:11 Table Fellowship/Lord's Supper: Matthew 11:19
9:13 *'I want . . . sacrifices.'* Quotation from Hosea 6:6.
9:13 Disciple/Discipleship/Mentoring (Follow/Follower): Matthew 10:1–2
9:13 Hospitality: Matthew 14:13–21
9:13 Pharisees and Sadducees: Matthew 21:43–46
9:14 *John.* John the Baptist, who preached to people about Christ's coming (Matthew 3, Luke 3).
9:14 *give up . . . time.* This is called "fasting." The people would give up eating for a special time of prayer and worship to God. It was also done to show sadness and disappointment.

Sin

ROMANS 3:9–20

How does the Bible define sin? Where does sin come from and what are its effects? How is sin dealt with, both in the Bible and in the lives of Christians today?

There are few issues more important to the Christian than the issue of sin. We often come to Christ to be set free from our sinfulness, and our most intense struggles are frequently a response to Paul's command, "so do not let sin control your life here on earth" (Romans 6:12). Yet because our society avoids or misuses the term *sin*, we are confused about its meaning, in the Bible and in our lives.

The Bible uses a variety of terms to talk about sin. Some, like "breaking a command" (Romans 5:14), emphasize sin's failure to conform to God's desires. Still others, like "turning away" (Hosea 11:7), emphasize the inner attitude which sin expresses. Sin is a breach of relationship. At times this can refer to a broken relationship between individuals ("If your fellow believer sins against you . . ." Matthew 18:15), but most often the Bible speaks of sin against God.

Sin begins at the beginning of the human story. We were not created sinful; we were created good, but with the capacity for choice. God placed Adam and Eve in the garden with only one prohibition: not to eat of the fruit of the tree of the knowledge of good and evil. The account of the sin of Adam and Eve in the garden of Eden in Genesis 3 shows the combination of temptation and decision in the first sin. Paul views the sin of Adam and Eve, when they ate the forbidden fruit, as the start of an age of sinfulness (Romans 5:12–21). Adam represented all of us in the garden. We are sinners when we are born, and so we cry out with David, "I was brought into this world in sin" (Psalm 51:5).

The Old Testament talks about sin in the context of the history of the nation of Israel. Israel sinned by failing to regard the holiness of God's presence in their midst (Leviticus 20:1–9). They sinned by yielding to the temptations of security and luxury found in the surrounding nations (Isaiah 30; Hosea 7:8–16) and by unjustly treating the weak (Amos 5:10–12). Sin in the Old Testament is not living as God would want. Inwardly, it is the heart turned against God; outwardly it is the breaking of commands.

The New Testament speaks more to the sins of individuals than nations. Jesus emphasized that obedience to God's commands must go beyond mere performance of rules to changing our attitudes. Sin lies in a failure to respond positively to the revelation of God. Paul says that "they knew God, but they did not give glory to God or thank him" (Romans 1:21). New Testament sin is the human tendency against God, which says yes to evil inner impulses and says no to God.

The consequences of sin are separation and death. Because of our tendency to choose our way rather than God's way, the commands of God are not able to bring us into good relationship with God. Rather, "the law came to make sin worse" (Romans 5:20). We lack peace—with God, with ourselves, with others, and with nature. The ultimate consequence of sin is the anger of God expressed in judgment and punishment.

But the Bible teaches that God has made a way to restore relationship with him and to grow in likeness to his own ways. In the Old Testament, God provided a system of "sin offerings," animal sacrifices which would "remove the people's sins" (Leviticus 4) and bring God's favor. But sacrifices were merely the outward expression of a heart turned toward God. Hosea writes, "I want faithful love more than I want animal sacrifices" (Hosea 6:6). In the person of Jesus Christ, God himself offered for us the acceptable sacrifice for all sins. "But Christ came only once and for all time at just the right time to take away all sin by sacrificing himself" (Hebrews 9:26). Paul writes, "While we were God's enemies, he made friends with us through the death of his Son" (Romans 5:10). By trusting in the sacrifice of Christ, we are freed from the separation and penalty of sin. On earth, Jesus was found welcoming the "sinner" and forgiving sins. The risen Christ does the same for us today.

The Bible not only tells us of our rescue from the penalty of sin. It also tells of the removal of the power of sin. Paul writes, "We know that our old life died with Christ on the cross so that our sinful selves would have no power over us and we would not be slaves to sin" (Romans 6:6). "If we confess our sins, he will forgive. . . . He will cleanse us from all the wrongs we have done" (1 John 1:9). By offering the parts of our "body to God to be used in doing good" (Romans 6:13), by using "the Spirit's help to stop doing the wrong things" (Romans 8:13), looking "only to Jesus" (Hebrews 12:2), we are given a means of obtaining not only a new relationship with God, but through that, a new life in God.

Sin: For additional scriptures on this topic go to Leviticus 4.

BODY/FLESH

ROMANS 8:10

What is the body? How is it related to the soul? Is the body sinful by nature? How should I treat my body?

From the beginning, human beings are understood as a unity of body and soul whose primary identity is in relatedness to God, their creator. Genesis 2:7 describes how God made the first human being out of the dust of the ground. This dust was made alive by the "breath of life" which God breathed into his nose. God used the dust to form the material part of this new creature, but without his breath there is no life. So from the very beginning, the Bible reveals that human beings are a unity of body and soul.

This teaching stands over against two modern views of the body as an independent entity. First, it counters the view that the body, its health and beauty, is the most important asset a person can have. To be beautiful, healthy, and young is highly prized by our superficial society. Those who are not so blessed find themselves the object of neglect or abuse. The Bible stands against this view.

However, the Bible also counters a tendency in the church community to belittle the body. The body is not a temporary covering for the more important, immortal soul. This image is no more biblical than the other view. The human body is not inherently evil. Indeed, God himself says that the body is good (Genesis 1:31). Jesus Christ is God, yet he had a body. A literal rendering of Colossians 2:9 indicates that God dwells in Jesus "in bodily form." Yet the human body was certainly affected by the entrance of evil in pervasive ways (Genesis 3). The body, which was good in its entirety, has been marred in its entirety as well. As Paul tells us in 2 Corinthians 4:16, "Our physical body is becoming older and weaker." The body is subject to pain and suffering. Eventually, this body dies.

But Paul goes on in the same passage to tell us the Good News, that death is not the end of the story for the body either. He informs us that after death "this body that dies will be fully covered with life. This is what God made us for, and he has given us the Spirit to be a guarantee for this new life" (2 Corinthians 5:4–5). Paul never gives us a detailed description of this body. We are left in mystery, but we learn what is important to know. This body, as opposed to our present body, can never be destroyed.

The Bible, therefore, clearly teaches that the body is presently affected by sin. We long for that day when our weak, decaying bodies are transformed into our heavenly bodies. What is remarkable with all this, however, is that the Bible still celebrates the beauty of the human body. This is clearly seen in the Song of Solomon where the man glories in the physical beauty of the woman (Song of Solomon 4) and the woman sings the praises of the man (Song of Solomon 5:10–16). These songs are not what you might expect in the Bible. They are extremely sensual, even erotic, in their references to the human body.

Perhaps even more surprising is the Bible's teaching that we are to praise God with our bodies. Paul draws a comparison between our bodies and the holy Temple of the Old Testament. As God made his presence known in the Temple, so our bodies are filled with the Spirit. For that reason, Paul calls on us to "honor God with your bodies" (1 Corinthians 6:20) by avoiding sexual impurity. Elsewhere, he informs us that we suffer so we that "the life of Jesus can be seen in our bodies" (2 Corinthians 4:10–11).

Finally, we must make an important distinction as we explore the way the body is used in the Bible. We must distinguish the body as flesh from its use as an image of our sinful nature. In passages like Romans 8 and Galatians 5:13–26, the terms *flesh* and *body* are used to describe the whole person as sinful. Our translation of these passages rightly captures the sense of the Greek by rendering *flesh* as "sinful selves."

These important passages teach us that, with the entrance of sin and suffering, the body continues to have potential for good, and now, potential for evil. A life-long struggle between the power of sin and the power of the Holy Spirit is set in motion. Clearly, the struggle is not between the human body and spirit. Rather, the conflict is between the power of sin which leads to death and destruction, and the power of the Spirit which reclaims and makes new (see Romans 8:4–14). This reframes the idea of some that the body is either evil or unimportant by asking, 'To what power does the *whole* person yield?'

Because the body is being redeemed, there can be little question of its importance to the life of faith, individually or corporately. In Jesus himself we observe God embodied, flesh without sin. Jesus, speaking of his own death, states in John 12:24–26 the "grain of wheat must fall to the ground and die to make many seeds." He continues with a challenge to his disciples to lay down their lives [body and spirit] in order to "keep true life forever. Whoever serves me must follow me."

Body/Flesh: For additional scriptures on this topic go to Genesis 1:27.

edge of his coat. [21]She was thinking, "If I can just touch his clothes, I will be healed."

[22]Jesus turned and saw the woman and said, "Be encouraged, dear woman. You are made well because you believed." And the woman was healed from that moment on.

[23]Jesus continued along with the leader and went into his house. There he saw the funeral musicians and many people crying. [24]Jesus said, "Go away. The girl is not dead, only asleep." But the people laughed at him. [25]After the crowd had been thrown out of the house, Jesus went into the girl's room and took hold of her hand, and she stood up. [26]The news about this spread all around the area.

Jesus Heals More People

[27]When Jesus was leaving there, two blind men followed him. They cried out, "Have mercy on us, Son of David!"

[28]After Jesus went inside, the blind men went with him. He asked the men, "Do you believe that I can make you see again?"

They answered, "Yes, Lord."

[29]Then Jesus touched their eyes and said, "Because you believe I can make you see again, it will happen." [30]Then the men were able to see. But Jesus warned them strongly, saying, "Don't tell anyone about this." [31]But the blind men left and spread the news about Jesus all around that area.

[32]When the two men were leaving, some people brought another man to Jesus. This man could not talk because he had a demon in him. [33]After Jesus forced the demon to leave the man, he was able to speak. The crowd was amazed and said, "We have never seen anything like this in Israel."

[34]But the Pharisees said, "The prince of demons is the one that gives him power to force demons out."

[35]Jesus traveled through all the towns and villages, teaching in their synagogues, preaching the Good News about the kingdom, and healing all kinds of diseases and sicknesses. [36]When he saw the crowds, he felt sorry for them because they were hurting and helpless, like sheep without a shepherd. [37]Jesus said to his followers, "There are many people to harvest but only a few workers to help harvest them. [38]Pray to the Lord, who owns the harvest, that he will send more workers to gather his harvest."

The type of house owned by wealthy Jews in New Testament times

Jesus Sends Out His Apostles

10 Jesus called his twelve followers together and gave them authority to drive out evil spirits and to heal every kind of disease and sickness. [2]These are the names of the twelve apostles: Simon (also called Peter) and his brother Andrew; James son of Zebedee, and his brother John; [3]Philip and Bartholomew; Thomas and Matthew, the tax collector; James son of Alphaeus, and Thaddaeus; [4]Simon the Zealot and Judas Iscariot, who turned against Jesus.

[5]Jesus sent out these twelve men with the following order: "Don't go to the non-Jewish people or to any town where the Samaritans live. [6]But go to the people of Israel, who are like lost sheep. [7]When you go, preach this: 'The kingdom of heaven is near.' [8]Heal the sick, raise the dead to life again, heal those who have skin diseases, and force demons out of people. I give you these powers freely, so help other people freely. [9]Don't carry any money with you—gold or silver or copper. [10]Don't carry a bag or extra clothes or sandals or a walking stick. Workers should be given what they need.

[11]"When you enter a city or town, find some worthy person there and stay in that home until you leave. [12]When you enter that home, say, 'Peace be with you.' [13]If the people there welcome you, let your peace stay there. But if they don't welcome you, take back the peace you wished for them.

9:26 Death: Acts 5:1–11

9:32 Physical Handicap: Matthew 12:22

9:34 Here some of Jesus' rivals attempt to label Jesus, saying he works for the devil. If they can get others to believe this, Jesus will lose his following. Only later, in Matthew 12:24–32, does this charge come out into the open. Jesus answers that his ministry is proof that God's power is at work in the world.

9:35 Gospel/Good News: Matthew 11:5

9:37–38 *"There are . . . harvest."* As a farmer sends workers to harvest the grain, Jesus sends his followers to bring people to God.

9:38 Miracles: Luke 4

10:2 Disciple/Discipleship/Mentoring (Follow/Follower): Matthew 12:46–50

10:4 Judas: Matthew 26:14

10:4 Peter: Matthew 14:28–31

10:8 Sickness, Disease, Healing: Matthew 15:30–31

14And if a home or town refuses to welcome you or
listen to you, leave that place and shake its dust off
your feet. 15I tell you the truth, on the Judgment
Day it will be better for the towns of Sodom and
Gomorrah than for the people of that town.

Jesus Warns His Apostles

16"Listen, I am sending you out like sheep among
wolves. So be as smart as snakes and as innocent as
doves. 17Be careful of people, because they will
arrest you and take you to court and whip you in
their synagogues. 18Because of me you will be
taken to stand before governors and kings, and you
will tell them and the non-Jewish people about me.
19When you are arrested, don't worry about what
to say or how to say it. At that time you will be
given the things to say. 20It will not really be you
speaking but the Spirit of your Father speaking
through you.

21"Brothers will give their own brothers to be
killed, and fathers will give their own children to
be killed. Children will fight against their own parents and have them put to death. 22All people will
hate you because you follow me, but those people
who keep their faith until the end will be saved.
23When you are treated badly in one city, run to
another city. I tell you the truth, you will not finish
going through all the cities of Israel before the
Son of Man comes.

24"A student is not better than his teacher, and a
servant is not better than his master. 25A student
should be satisfied to become like his teacher; a
servant should be satisfied to become like his master. If the head of the family is called Beelzebul,
then the other members of the family will be called
worse names!

Fear God, Not People

26"So don't be afraid of those people, because
everything that is hidden will be shown. Everything that is secret will be made known. 27I tell
you these things in the dark, but I want you to
tell them in the light. What you hear whispered
in your ear you should shout from the housetops.
28Don't be afraid of people, who can kill the body
but cannot kill the soul. The only one you should
fear is the one who can destroy the soul and the
body in hell. 29Two sparrows cost only a
penny, but not even one of them can die without
your Father's knowing it. 30God even knows
how many hairs are on your head. 31So don't be
afraid. You are worth much more than many
sparrows.

Tell People About Your Faith

32"All those who stand before others and say
they believe in me, I will say before my Father in
heaven that they belong to me. 33But all who stand
before others and say they do not believe in me, I
will say before my Father in heaven that they do
not belong to me.

34"Don't think that I came to bring peace to the
earth. I did not come to bring peace, but a sword.
35I have come so that

'a son will be against his father,
 a daughter will be against her mother,
a daughter-in-law will be against
 her mother-in-law.
36 A person's enemies will be members of his
 own family.' *Micah 7:6*

37"Those who love their father or mother more
than they love me are not worthy to be my followers. Those who love their son or daughter more
than they love me are not worthy to be my followers. 38Whoever is not willing to carry the cross and
follow me is not worthy of me. 39Those who try to
hold on to their lives will give up true life. Those
who give up their lives for me will hold on to true
life. 40Whoever accepts you also accepts me,
and whoever accepts me also accepts the One who
sent me. 41Whoever meets a prophet and accepts
him will receive the reward of a prophet. And
whoever accepts a good person because that person is good will receive the reward of a good person.
42Those who give one of these little ones a cup of
cold water because they are my followers will
truly get their reward."

10:14 *shake . . . feet.* A warning. It showed that they had rejected these people.

10:15 *Sodom and Gomorrah.* Two cities that God destroyed because the people were so evil.

10:15 Evangelism: Mark 1:16–18

10:15 Mission: John 3:16

10:22 Perseverance: Matthew 24:13

10:24 Servant of the Lord: Matthew 24:45–47

10:28 Body/Flesh: Luke 11:33–36

10:37–39 Our God is "a jealous God" (Deuteronomy 4:24). He is ardent, passionate, and zealous in his commitment to his people, wanting the best for them, and guarding them as a father guards his children. God does not tolerate idols, infidelity, or a lukewarm relationship with him. Love of family is sacred to God and protected by the Ten Commandments, but the greatest commandment, as Jesus reminds us, is "Love the Lord your God with all your heart, all your soul, and all your mind" (Matthew 22:37).

It is from our relationship with our Father in heaven that right relationships with parents, brothers and sisters, friends, and fellow Christians will grow. Human love is prey to all the problems of the human heart, and, therefore, is at its best when that heart seeks God first.

10:39 The Crucifixion of Jesus (The Way of the Cross): Mark 8:34

10:42 Martyrdom: Matthew 14:1–12

Jesus and John the Baptist

11 After Jesus finished telling these things to his
twelve followers, he left there and went to
the towns in Galilee to teach and preach.
2John the Baptist was in prison, but he heard
about what Christ was doing. So John sent some of
his followers to Jesus. 3They asked him, "Are you
the One who is to come, or should we wait for
someone else?"
4Jesus answered them, "Go tell John what you
hear and see: 5The blind can see, the crippled can
walk, and people with skin diseases are healed.
The deaf can hear, the dead are raised to life, and
the Good News is preached to the poor. 6Those
who do not stumble in their faith because of me
are blessed."
7As John's followers were leaving, Jesus began
talking to the people about John. Jesus said, "What
did you go out into the desert to see? A reed blown
by the wind? 8What did you go out to see? A man
dressed in fine clothes? No, those who wear fine
clothes live in kings' palaces. 9So why did you go
out? To see a prophet? Yes, and I tell you, John is
more than a prophet. 10This was written about him:
'I will send my messenger ahead of you,
who will prepare the way for you.' *Malachi 3:1*
11I tell you the truth, John the Baptist is greater
than any other person ever born, but even the least
important person in the kingdom of heaven is
greater than John. 12Since the time John the Baptist
came until now, the kingdom of heaven has been
going forward in strength, and people have been
trying to take it by force. 13All the prophets and the
law of Moses told about what would happen until
the time John came. 14And if you will believe what
they said, you will believe that John is Elijah,
whom they said would come. 15You people who
can hear me, listen!
16"What can I say about the people of this time?
What are they like? They are like children sitting
in the marketplace, who call out to each other,
17'We played music for you, but you did not dance;
we sang a sad song, but you did not cry.'
18John came and did not eat or drink like other people. So people say, 'He has a demon.' 19The Son of
Man came, eating and drinking, and people say,
'Look at him! He eats too much and drinks too
much wine, and he is a friend of tax collectors and
sinners.' But wisdom is proved to be right by what
it does."

Jesus Warns Unbelievers

20Then Jesus criticized the cities where he did
most of his miracles, because the people did not
change their lives and stop sinning. 21He said,
"How terrible for you, Korazin! How terrible for
you, Bethsaida! If the same miracles I did in you
had happened in Tyre and Sidon, those people
would have changed their lives a long time ago.
They would have worn rough cloth and put ashes
on themselves to show they had changed. 22But I
tell you, on the Judgment Day it will be better for
Tyre and Sidon than for you. 23And you, Capernaum, will you be lifted up to heaven? No, you
will be thrown down to the depths. If the miracles
I did in you had happened in Sodom, its people
would have stopped sinning, and it would still be a
city today. 24But I tell you, on the Judgment Day it
will be better for Sodom than for you."

Jesus Offers Rest to People

25At that time Jesus said, "I praise you, Father,
Lord of heaven and earth, because you have hidden
these things from the people who are wise and
smart. But you have shown them to those who are
like little children. 26Yes, Father, this is what you
really wanted.

11:5 Elijah and Elisha: Matthew 11:14
11:5 Gospel/Good News: Luke 4:18–19
11:5 Poverty: Luke 6:20b-22
11:6 John the Baptist: Matthew 11:14
11:7 *reed.* It means that John was not ordinary or weak like grass blown by the wind.
11:14 Jesus informed the crowd that John the Baptist could be considered the fulfillment of the prophecy in Malachi 4:5–6 that Elijah would come back before the Messiah appeared. In saying this, Jesus clearly identified John as the promised forerunner. Jesus also, in effect, was saying that the Old Testament prophet, Elijah, was not literally and physically going to appear.
11:14 Elijah and Elisha: Matthew 17:3
11:14 John the Baptist: Matthew 14:3–11
11:14 Blindness: Matthew 20:30–34
11:19 Jesus was the friend of tax collectors and sinners—people who were widely believed to be outside of the circle of God's grace. He crossed these social and religious barriers consciously and intentionally by eating and socializing with them, while other religious leaders avoided them (Matthew 9:10–13). He also connected with non-Jews (Mark 7:24–30) in a culture where the Jews called them dogs, and talked to women (John 4, 11) in a culture where men and women did not have public dealings. Why is this significant? The Bible tells us that Jesus is not only God in the flesh (John 1:1,14), he is also the will of God in the flesh (John 5:19, 30; 8:28; 14:10). Jesus' life, as well as his words, tell us what the Father's will and values are. His example should spur us on to develop friendships and share God's love across various barriers: social and religious status, gender, and ethnicity (Galatians 3:28).
11:19 Table Fellowship/Lord's Supper: Matthew 14:13–21
11:19 Wisdom: 1 Corinthians 1:19
11:21 *Tyre and Sidon.* Towns where wicked people lived.
11:23 *Korazin.* A town by Lake Galilee where Jesus preached to the people.
11:23 *Sodom.* A city that God destroyed because the people were so evil.
11:24 Racism: Matthew 28:19
11:24 Stubbornness: Matthew 18:15–17
11:25 It is interesting here that Jesus places the wise and learned with little children. His reason for doing this is more clear in the context of

27"My Father has given me all things. No one
knows the Son, except the Father. And no one
knows the Father, except the Son and those whom
the Son chooses to tell.⚭
28"Come to me, all of you who are tired and
have heavy loads, and I will give you rest. 29Accept
my teachings and learn from me, because I am gentle and humble in spirit, and you will find rest for
your lives. 30The teaching that I ask you to accept
is easy; the load I give you to carry is light."

Jesus Is Lord of the Sabbath

12 At that time Jesus was walking through
some fields of grain on a Sabbath day. His
followers were hungry, so they began to pick the
grain and eat it. 2When the Pharisees saw this,
they said to Jesus, "Look! Your followers are doing
what is unlawful to do on the Sabbath day."
3Jesus answered, "Have you not read what David
did when he and the people with him were hungry? 4He went into God's house, and he and those
with him ate the holy bread, which was lawful only
for priests to eat. 5And have you not read in the law
of Moses that on every Sabbath day the priests in
the Temple break this law about the Sabbath day?
But the priests are not wrong for doing that. 6I tell
you that there is something here that is greater than
the Temple. 7The Scripture says, 'I want kindness
more than I want animal sacrifices.' You don't really
know what those words mean. If you understood
them, you would not judge those who have done
nothing wrong.
8"So the Son of Man is Lord of the Sabbath day."

Jesus Heals a Man's Hand

9Jesus left there and went into their synagogue,
10where there was a man with a crippled hand.
They were looking for a reason to accuse Jesus, so
they asked him, "Is it right to heal on the Sabbath
day?"
11Jesus answered, "If any of you has a sheep, and
it falls into a ditch on the Sabbath day, you will
help it out of the ditch. 12Surely a human being is
more important than a sheep. So it is lawful to do
good things on the Sabbath day."
13Then Jesus said to the man with the crippled
hand, "Hold out your hand." The man held out his
hand, and it became well again, like the other hand.
14But the Pharisees left and made plans to kill Jesus.

Jesus Is God's Chosen Servant

15Jesus knew what the Pharisees were doing, so
he left that place. Many people followed him, and
he healed all who were sick. 16But Jesus warned
the people not to tell who he was. 17He did these
things to bring about what Isaiah the prophet had
said:
18"Here is my servant whom I have chosen.
I love him, and I am pleased with him.
I will put my Spirit upon him,
and he will tell of my justice to all people.
19He will not argue or cry out;
no one will hear his voice in the streets.
20He will not break a crushed blade of grass
or put out even a weak flame
until he makes justice win the victory.
21 In him will the non-Jewish
people find hope.⚭" *Isaiah 42:1-4*

Jesus' Power Is from God

22Then some people brought to Jesus a man who
was blind and could not talk, because he had a
demon. Jesus healed the man so that he could talk
and see.⚭ 23All the people were amazed and
said, "Perhaps this man is the Son of David!"
24When the Pharisees heard this, they said,
"Jesus uses the power of Beelzebul, the ruler of
demons, to force demons out of people."
25Jesus knew what the Pharisees were thinking,
so he said to them, "Every kingdom that is divided
against itself will be destroyed. And any city or family that is divided against itself will not continue.
26And if Satan forces out himself, then Satan is
divided against himself, and his kingdom will not
continue. 27You say that I use the power of
Beelzebul to force out demons. If that is true,
then what power do your people use to force out
demons? So they will be your judges. 28But if I use
the power of God's Spirit to force out demons,
then the kingdom of God has come to you.

---

his culture than in ours. It was widely accepted that with age one gained wisdom and thus status in society. A child, then, would have little status or wisdom since they would be few in years. In this passage, Jesus questions his culture's attitude toward children by giving them status in God's eyes. God has given status to the young, as well as to the old.

⚭**11:27 Trinity:** Matthew 28:18–20

⚭**11:27 Incarnation:** Luke 10:21–22

12:1–13 By the time Jesus came the Sabbath law had become more of a burden than a blessing. Religious leaders had created detailed laws about what a person could or could not do on the Sabbath. These laws were strictly enforced. Jesus corrected this situation by teaching that the Sabbath was made for people, not people for the Sabbath. He also taught that it was lawful to do good on the Sabbath. Jesus demonstrated this as he continually taught and healed on the Sabbath day.

12:7 *'I . . . sacrifices.'* Quotation from Hosea 6:6.

12:10 *"Is it right . . . day?"* It was against Jewish Law to work on the Sabbath day.

⚭**12:21 Gentiles (Non-Jews):** Luke 2:32

⚭**12:22 Physical Handicap:** Mark 3:1–6

29“If anyone wants to enter a strong person’s house and steal his things, he must first tie up the strong person. Then he can steal the things from the house.

30“Whoever is not with me is against me. Whoever does not work with me is working against me. 31So I tell you, people can be forgiven for every sin and everything they say against God. But whoever speaks against the Holy Spirit will not be forgiven. 32Anyone who speaks against the Son of Man can be forgiven, but anyone who speaks against the Holy Spirit will not be forgiven, now or in the future.

People Know You by Your Words

33“If you want good fruit, you must make the tree good. If your tree is not good, it will have bad fruit. A tree is known by the kind of fruit it produces. 34You snakes! You are evil people, so how can you say anything good? The mouth speaks the things that are in the heart. 35Good people have good things in their hearts, and so they say good things. But evil people have evil in their hearts, so they say evil things. 36And I tell you that on the Judgment Day people will be responsible for every careless thing they have said. 37The words you have said will be used to judge you. Some of your words will prove you right, but some of your words will prove you guilty.”

The People Ask for a Miracle

38Then some of the Pharisees and teachers of the law answered Jesus, saying, “Teacher, we want to see you work a miracle as a sign.”

39Jesus answered, “Evil and sinful people are the ones who want to see a miracle for a sign. But no sign will be given to them, except the sign of the prophet Jonah. 40Jonah was in the stomach of the big fish for three days and three nights. In the same way, the Son of Man will be in the grave three days and three nights. 41On the Judgment Day the people from Nineveh will stand up with you people who live now, and they will show that you are guilty. When Jonah preached to them, they were sorry and changed their lives. And I tell you that someone greater than Jonah is here. 42On the Judgment Day, the Queen of the South will stand up with you people who live today. She will show that you are guilty, because she came from far away to listen to Solomon’s wise teaching. And I tell you that someone greater than Solomon is here.

People Today Are Full of Evil

43“When an evil spirit comes out of a person, it travels through dry places, looking for a place to rest, but it doesn’t find it. 44So the spirit says, ‘I will go back to the house I left.’ When the spirit comes back, it finds the house still empty, swept clean, and made neat. 45Then the evil spirit goes out and brings seven other spirits even more evil than it is, and they go in and live there. So the person has even more trouble than before. It is the same way with the evil people who live today.”

Jesus’ True Family

46While Jesus was talking to the people, his mother and brothers stood outside, trying to find a way to talk to him. 47Someone told Jesus, “Your mother and brothers are standing outside, and they want to talk to you.”

48He answered, “Who is my mother? Who are my brothers?” 49Then he pointed to his followers and said, “Here are my mother and my brothers. 50My true brother and sister and mother are those who do what my Father in heaven wants.”

A Story About Planting Seed

13 That same day Jesus went out of the house and sat by the lake. 2Large crowds gathered around him, so he got into a boat and sat down, while the people stood on the shore. 3Then Jesus used stories to teach them many things. He said: “A farmer went out to plant his seed. 4While he was planting, some seed fell by the road, and the birds came and ate it all up. 5Some seed fell on rocky ground, where there wasn’t much dirt. That

12:29 Demon: Mark 3:22–27

12:31 What does it mean to “speak against the Holy Spirit?” Blasphemy is a sin that takes several shapes, yet in essence, it is some word or act against God or showing disrespect toward God. The context of this passage (verses 22–32) shows that “speaking against” (that is, blaspheming) the Holy Spirit concerns attributing Jesus’ miracles to the power of Beelzebul, the devil. Many think that this particular, unforgivable blasphemy can no longer be committed today.

12:32 Rebellion: John 15:23–24

12:39–40 There are some people who have difficulty squaring the number of days and nights Jonah was in the stomach of the big fish with the number of days and nights between Jesus’ death and resurrection. The key phrase that shows Jesus was using an analogy, rather than quoting an exact number, is the phrase “In the same way, . . .” Besides, Jesus kept telling his followers he would rise on the third day (Matthew 16:21).

12:40 Numbers: Ephesians 4:1–6

12:41 *Nineveh.* The city where Jonah preached to warn the people. Read Jonah 3.

12:42 *Queen of the South.* The Queen of Sheba. She traveled a thousand miles to learn God’s wisdom from Solomon. Read 1 Kings 10:1-13.

12:50 Disciple/Discipleship/Mentoring (Follow/Follower): Matthew 28:16–20

seed grew very fast, because the ground was not
deep. 6But when the sun rose, the plants dried up,
because they did not have deep roots. 7Some other
seed fell among thorny weeds, which grew and
choked the good plants. 8Some other seed fell on
good ground where it grew and produced a crop.
Some plants made a hundred times more, some
made sixty times more, and some made thirty times
more. 9You people who can hear me, listen."

Why Jesus Used Stories to Teach

10The followers came to Jesus and asked, "Why
do you use stories to teach the people?"
11Jesus answered, "You have been chosen to
know the secrets about the kingdom of heaven, but
others cannot know these secrets. 12Those who
have understanding will be given more, and they
will have all they need. But those who do not have
understanding, even what they have will be taken
away from them. 13This is why I use stories to teach
the people: They see, but they don't really see.
They hear, but they don't really hear or understand. 14So they show that the things Isaiah said
about them are true:

'You will listen and listen,
 but you will not understand.
You will look and look, but you will not learn.
15For the minds of these
 people have become stubborn.
They do not hear with their ears,
 and they have closed their eyes.
Otherwise they might really understand
 what they see with their eyes
 and hear with their ears.
They might really understand in their minds
 and come back to me and be healed.'

Isaiah 6:9-10

16But you are blessed, because you see with your
eyes and hear with your ears. 17I tell you the truth,
many prophets and good people wanted to see the
things that you now see, but they did not see them.
And they wanted to hear the things that you now
hear, but they did not hear them.

Jesus Explains the Seed Story

18"So listen to the meaning of that story about
the farmer. 19What is the seed that fell by the road?
That seed is like the person who hears the message
about the kingdom but does not understand it. The
Evil One comes and takes away what was planted
in that person's heart. 20And what is the seed that
fell on rocky ground? That seed is like the person
who hears the teaching and quickly accepts it with
joy. 21But he does not let the teaching go deep into
his life, so he keeps it only a short time. When
trouble or persecution comes because of the teaching he accepted, he quickly gives up. 22And what is
the seed that fell among the thorny weeds? That
seed is like the person who hears the teaching but
lets worries about this life and the temptation of
wealth stop that teaching from growing. So the
teaching does not produce fruit in that person's
life. 23But what is the seed that fell on the good
ground? That seed is like the person who hears the
teaching and understands it. That person grows and
produces fruit, sometimes a hundred times more,
sometimes sixty times more, and sometimes thirty
times more."

A Story About Wheat and Weeds

24Then Jesus told them another story: "The kingdom of heaven is like a man who planted good seed
in his field.⚭ 25That night, when everyone was
asleep, his enemy came and planted weeds among
the wheat and then left. 26Later, the wheat sprouted
and the heads of grain grew, but the weeds also
grew. 27Then the man's servants came to him and
said, 'You planted good seed in your field. Where did
the weeds come from?' 28The man answered, 'An
enemy planted weeds.' The servants asked, 'Do you
want us to pull up the weeds?' 29The man answered,
'No, because when you pull up the weeds, you
might also pull up the wheat. 30Let the weeds and
the wheat grow together until the harvest time. At
harvest time I will tell the workers, "First gather the
weeds and tie them together to be burned. Then
gather the wheat and bring it to my barn."'"

Stories of Mustard Seed and Yeast

31Then Jesus told another story: "The kingdom
of heaven is like a mustard seed that a man
planted in his field.⚭ 32That seed is the smallest
of all seeds, but when it grows, it is one of the
largest garden plants. It becomes big enough for

13:10–17 The followers came to Jesus to ask why he taught the crowds using parables, natural stories that teach spiritual truths. He told them that they had been chosen by God to understand the truths of the kingdom of God, but the crowds could not understand these truths. For this reason, Jesus used parables that did not teach these truths clearly. But the followers' eyes had been opened by God so they could see and understand these truths.

13:22 *produce fruit.* To produce fruit means to have in your life the good things God wants.

⚭**13:24 Kingdom of God:** Matthew 13:31

13:24–30 Jesus knew well that there were people who were with him and those who were not. In this parable he describes the former as the wheat and the latter as the weeds, ready to be removed and destroyed. Ever since the Fall, there have been those who follow God, and those who follow the snake (who stands for the devil). The point of Jesus' parable is that, in spite of present appearances, God's people will be victorious at the end.

⚭**13:31 Kingdom of God:** Matthew 13:33

the wild birds to come and build nests in its branches."

33Then Jesus told another story: "The kingdom of heaven is like yeast that a woman took and hid in a large tub of flour until it made all the dough rise."

34Jesus used stories to tell all these things to the people; he always used stories to teach them. 35This is as the prophet said:

"I will speak using stories;
I will tell things that have been secret since
the world was made." *Psalm 78:2*

Jesus Explains About the Weeds

36Then Jesus left the crowd and went into the house. His followers came to him and said, "Explain to us the meaning of the story about the weeds in the field."

37Jesus answered, "The man who planted the good seed in the field is the Son of Man. 38The field is the world, and the good seed are all of God's children who belong to the kingdom. The weeds are those people who belong to the Evil One. 39And the enemy who planted the bad seed is the devil. The harvest time is the end of the world, and the workers who gather are God's angels.

40"Just as the weeds are pulled up and burned in the fire, so it will be at the end of the world. 41The Son of Man will send out his angels, and they will gather out of his kingdom all who cause sin and all who do evil. 42The angels will throw them into the blazing furnace, where the people will cry and grind their teeth with pain. 43Then the good people will shine like the sun in the kingdom of their Father. You people who can hear me, listen.

Stories of a Treasure and a Pearl

44"The kingdom of heaven is like a treasure hidden in a field. One day a man found the treasure, and then he hid it in the field again. He was so happy that he went and sold everything he owned to buy that field.

45"Also, the kingdom of heaven is like a man looking for fine pearls. 46When he found a very valuable pearl, he went and sold everything he had and bought it.

A Story of a Fishing Net

47"Also, the kingdom of heaven is like a net that was put into the lake and caught many different kinds of fish. 48When it was full, the fishermen pulled the net to the shore. They sat down and put all the good fish in baskets and threw away the bad fish. 49It will be this way at the end of the world. The angels will come and separate the evil people from the good people. 50The angels will throw the evil people into the blazing furnace, where people will cry and grind their teeth with pain."

51Jesus asked his followers, "Do you understand all these things?"

They answered, "Yes, we understand."

52Then Jesus said to them, "So every teacher of the law who has been taught about the kingdom of heaven is like the owner of a house. He brings out both new things and old things he has saved."

Jesus Goes to His Hometown

53When Jesus finished teaching with these stories, he left there. 54He went to his hometown and taught the people in the synagogue, and they were amazed. They said, "Where did this man get this wisdom and this power to do miracles? 55He is just the son of a carpenter. His mother is Mary, and his brothers are James, Joseph, Simon, and Judas. 56And all his sisters are here with us. Where then does this man get all these things?" 57So the people were upset with Jesus.

But Jesus said to them, "A prophet is honored everywhere except in his hometown and in his own home."

58So he did not do many miracles there because they had no faith.

How John the Baptist Was Killed

14 At that time Herod, the ruler of Galilee, heard the reports about Jesus. 2So he said to his servants, "Jesus is John the Baptist, who has risen from the dead. That is why he can work these miracles."

3Sometime before this, Herod had arrested John, tied him up, and put him into prison. Herod did this because of Herodias, who had been the wife of Philip, Herod's brother. 4John had been telling Herod, "It is not lawful for you to be married to Herodias." 5Herod wanted to kill John, but he was afraid of the people, because they believed John was a prophet.

6On Herod's birthday, the daughter of Herodias danced for Herod and his guests, and she pleased

13:33 Kingdom of God: Luke 4:18–21

13:34 Jesus speaks in parables many times in the Book of Matthew. Why? We often think Jesus used parables in order to make things clear to his audience. However, at times, not even his followers understood (see 13:10, 36). In fact, Jesus sometimes seems to use parables on purpose to puzzle his listeners. He uses parables to make people think about their own actions and attitudes toward what God is doing. We may be surprised by what we discover.

13:43 Angels: Matthew 25:41

13:52 Proverb: Luke 4:23

13:58 Doubt: Matthew 14:22–33

him. [7]So he promised with an oath to give her anything she wanted. [8]Herodias told her daughter what to ask for, so she said to Herod, "Give me the head of John the Baptist here on a platter." [9]Although King Herod was very sad, he had made a promise, and his dinner guests had heard him. So Herod ordered that what she asked for be done. [10]He sent soldiers to the prison to cut off John's head. [11]And they brought it on a platter and gave it to the girl, and she took it to her mother. [12]John's followers came and got his body and buried it. Then they went and told Jesus.

More than Five Thousand Fed

[13]When Jesus heard what had happened to John, he left in a boat and went to a lonely place by himself. But the crowds heard about it and followed him on foot from the towns. [14]When he arrived, he saw a great crowd waiting. He felt sorry for them and healed those who were sick.

[15]When it was evening, his followers came to him and said, "No one lives in this place, and it is already late. Send the people away so they can go to the towns and buy food for themselves."

[16]But Jesus answered, "They don't need to go away. You give them something to eat."

[17]They said to him, "But we have only five loaves of bread and two fish."

[18]Jesus said, "Bring the bread and the fish to me." [19]Then he told the people to sit down on the grass. He took the five loaves and the two fish and, looking to heaven, he thanked God for the food. Jesus divided the bread and gave it to his followers, who gave it to the people. [20]All the people ate and were satisfied. Then the followers filled twelve baskets with the leftover pieces of food. [21]There were about five thousand men there who ate, not counting women and children.

Jesus Walks on the Water

[22]Immediately Jesus told his followers to get into the boat and go ahead of him across the lake. He stayed there to send the people home. [23]After he had sent them away, he went by himself up into the hills to pray. It was late, and Jesus was there alone. [24]By this time, the boat was already far away from land. It was being hit by waves, because the wind was blowing against it.

[25]Between three and six o'clock in the morning, Jesus came to them, walking on the water. [26]When his followers saw him walking on the water, they were afraid. They said, "It's a ghost!" and cried out in fear.

[27]But Jesus quickly spoke to them, "Have courage! It is I. Do not be afraid."

[28]Peter said, "Lord, if it is really you, then command me to come to you on the water."

[29]Jesus said, "Come."

And Peter left the boat and walked on the water to Jesus. [30]But when Peter saw the wind and the waves, he became afraid and began to sink. He shouted, "Lord, save me!"

[31]Immediately Jesus reached out his hand and caught Peter. Jesus said, "Your faith is small. Why did you doubt?"

[32]After they got into the boat, the wind became calm. [33]Then those who were in the boat worshiped Jesus and said, "Truly you are the Son of God!"

[34]When they had crossed the lake, they came to shore at Gennesaret. [35]When the people there recognized Jesus, they told people all around there that Jesus had come, and they brought all their sick to him. [36]They begged Jesus to let them touch just the edge of his coat, and all who touched it were healed.

Obey God's Law

15 Then some Pharisees and teachers of the law came to Jesus from Jerusalem. They asked him, [2]"Why don't your followers obey the unwritten laws which have been handed down to us? They don't wash their hands before they eat."

[3]Jesus answered, "And why do you refuse to obey God's command so that you can follow your own teachings? [4]God said, 'Honor your father and your mother,' and 'Anyone who says cruel things to his father or mother must be put to death.' [5]But you say a person can tell his father or mother, 'I have something I could use to help you, but I have given it to God already.' [6]You teach that person not to honor his father or his mother. You rejected

---

14:9 Oath/Vow: Matthew 23:16–22
14:11 John the Baptist: Mark 1:2–11
14:12 Martyrdom: Matthew 16:21–28
14:21 Hospitality: Matthew 25:31–46
14:21 Table Fellowship/Lord's Supper: Matthew 26:7–13
14:21 Wilderness (Desert): Mark 6:31
14:22–33 Even Peter, a man of great faith and one of the followers Christ personally chose, is capable of doubt. The crucial point about doubt in the Bible, however, is that it not be allowed to keep one from an active life of faith. Peter, like many in Scriptures, had his moments of doubt and struggle, but he persevered in following Christ and spreading the Good News.
14:23 Loneliness: Mark 14:32–42
14:31 Peter: Matthew 16:16–19
14:33 Doubt: Matthew 21:21
15:4 *'Honor . . . mother.'* Quotation from Exodus 20:12; Deuteronomy 5:16.
15:4 *'Anyone . . . death.'* Quotation from Exodus 21:17.

FATHER

ROMANS 8:15

What does it mean to call God "Father"? Is God the Father of all or only of some? In what sense are Christians "sons" and "daughters" of God? How does our attitude toward our earthly father affect our attitude toward our heavenly Father?

What is a Christian? The question can be answered in many ways, but the richest answer I know is that a Christian is one who has God as Father. But cannot this be said of every person, Christian or not? No! The idea that all are children of God is not found in the Bible anywhere. The Old Testament shows God as the Father, not of all, but of his own people, the seed of Abraham. "Israel is my firstborn son . . . let my son go" (Exodus 4:22–23). The New Testament has a world vision, but it too shows God as the Father, not of all, but of those who, knowing themselves to be sinners, put their trust in the Lord Jesus Christ as their divine sin-bearer and master, and so become Abraham's spiritual seed. "You are all children of God through faith in Christ Jesus. . . . You are all the same in Christ Jesus. You belong to Christ, so you are Abraham's descendants" (Galatians 3:26–29). Sonship to God is not, therefore, a universal status into which everyone enters by natural birth, but a supernatural gift one receives through receiving Jesus (John 1:12).

If you want to judge how well a person understands Christianity, find out how much he makes of the thought of being God's child, and having God as his Father. If this is not the thought that prompts and controls his worship and prayers and his whole outlook on life, it means that he does not understand Christianity very well at all. For everything that Christ taught, everything that makes the New Testament new, and better than the Old, everything that is distinctively Christian as opposed to merely Jewish, is summed up in the knowledge of the Fatherhood of God. "Father" is the Christian name for God.

Father replaces *Yahweh* as God's agreement name in the New Testament—for the agreement which binds him to his people now stands revealed as a family agreement. Christians are his children, his own sons and daughters, his heirs. And the stress of the New Testament is not on the difficulty and danger of drawing near to the holy God, but on the boldness and confidence with which believers may approach him: a boldness that springs directly from faith in Christ, and from the knowledge of his saving work (Ephesians 3:12; Hebrews 10:19–22). To those who are Christ's, the holy God is a loving Father; they belong to his family; they may approach him without fear and always be sure of his fatherly concern and care.

I have heard it seriously argued that the thought of divine fatherhood can mean nothing to those whose human father was inadequate, lacking wisdom, affection, or both, nor to those many more whose misfortune it was to have a fatherless upbringing. But this is not accurate. For, in the first place, it is just not true to suggest that in the realm of personal relations positive concepts cannot be formed by contrast. The thought of our Maker becoming our perfect parent is a thought which can have meaning for everybody, whether we come to it by saying, "I had a wonderful father, and I see that God is like that, only more so," or by saying, "My father disappointed me here, and here, and here, but God, praise his name, will be very different," or even by saying, "I have never known what it is to have a father on earth, but thank God I now have one in heaven."

But in any case, God has not left us to guess what his fatherhood amounts to by drawing analogies from human fatherhood. He revealed the full meaning of this relationship once and for all through our Lord Jesus Christ, his own incarnate Son. It is from his manifested activity as "the God and Father of our Lord Jesus Christ" (Ephesians 1:3) that we learn, in this one instance which is also a universal standard, what God's fatherly relationship to us who are Christ's really means. For God intends the lives of believers to be a reflection and reproduction of Jesus' own fellowship with himself.

According to our Lord's own testimony in John's Gospel, God's fatherly relation to him implied four things. First, fatherhood implied *authority*. Jesus came to do is Father's will (John 6:38). Second, fatherhood implied *affection.* The Father loves the Son (John 5:20). Third, fatherhood implied *fellowship.* The Father is always with the Son (John 16:32). Fourth, fatherhood implied *honor.* God wills to exalt his Son (John 5:22–23). All this extends to God's adopted children. In, through, and under Jesus Christ their Lord, they are ruled, loved, companied with, and honored by their heavenly Father.

Father: For additional scriptures on this topic go to Matthew 23:9.

Authority

Romans 13

What is authority? What is the proper use of authority? What is the source of authority?

Authority is both the power of position to enforce obedience (official authority: a judge, a principal) or the influence an expert exerts on another because of his or her perceived competence (unofficial authority: a role model, an instructor). Official authority is granted by the rules, laws, or agreements of the community or nation where an elected or appointed leader holds office. Unofficial authority is held by a leader who has shown himself or herself to be competent, effective, knowledgeable, or worthy of trust in certain matters. Much authority in society, churches, and organizations is held by those who are "behind the throne," who influence the decisions and behaviors of others because of their expertise, wealth, personality, power, or any combination of these. Such unofficial authorities are not appointed or elected but hold a great deal of sway nevertheless.

All authority derives from God's authority, which he has as creator and ruler of the universe. Even governmental authority comes from God and has an appointed place in the order of things. In Romans 13:1–2, for example, we are taught, "All of you must yield to the government rulers. No one rules unless God has given him the power to rule, and no one rules now without that power from God" (see 1 Peter 2:13–17). In the family there is the God-given authority of parents, so that the fifth of the Ten Commandments tells us to honor our fathers and mothers (Exodus 20:12; see Ephesians 6:1–3). Likewise, there is authority in the church that should be respected: "The elders who lead the church well should receive double honor, especially those who work hard by speaking and teaching" (1 Timothy 5:17; 1 Corinthians 12:28). In the church, as in the family and government, there is a God-given order where leaders both exercise influence (1 Corinthians 7:6–7, 12) and enforce obedience (1 Corinthians 5:1–5; 2 Corinthians 10:1–11). All authority comes from God.

This immediately raises a difficult problem: What do we think of authority gone bad? We all know of evil governments, abusive parents, and wayward church leaders. Is God behind these too? No, yet God's authority allows disobedience for a time, but not forever (Philippians 2:11). Furthermore, the Bible offers safeguards against blind acceptance of authority. Romans 13 must be set against Revelation 13, where earthly authority is no longer the servant of God, but is opposed to God. Parents have authority to enforce the obedience of their children, but not to exasperate them (Ephesians 6:4; Colossians 3:21) nor to lead them astray (Matthew 18:6; Mark 9:42; Luke 17:2). Church leaders are constrained by the teaching they have been given (Galatians 1:1–9), and are accountable to God for the authority they exercise (James 3:1). Furthermore, God sends confrontational messengers (called prophets) to confront political, spiritual, and moral evil (see Amos 1:3–2:16; Luke 3:1–20). God must be obeyed above all human authority when that human authority has set itself against the known will of God (Acts 4:19; 5:29).

The Bible offers some very specific guidance for the Christian exercise of authority today. The clearest example is found in John 13 where it says that "Jesus knew that the Father had given him power over everything" (John 13:3; see Matthew 8:1–7; 9:1–7). What does Jesus do with this awareness of his own immense power and authority? He takes the position and role of the lowest servant in the household and washes the feet of those for whom he held the most authority (John 13:3–17). This is Christian exercise of authority: to humble oneself, to use authority to serve and build up (see also Philippians 2:1–11). Elsewhere, a negative example is given when some of Jesus' closest friends desired status, authority, and power (Matthew 20:20–28). Jesus rebukes this worldly understanding of authority and sounds an everlasting critique of the power games people play: "You know that the rulers of the non-Jewish people love to show their power over the people. And their important leaders love to use all their authority. But it should not be that way among you. Whoever wants to become great among you must serve the rest of you like a servant" (Matthew 20:25–26). "It should not be that way among you" is Jesus' clear teaching on the matter, and this is worked out by other New Testament writers in very concrete and specific ways so that the wealthy and powerful do not flaunt their status in the communal gathering (1 Corinthians 11:17–12:26; James 2:1–7). Church leaders, should not use their position to gather wealth (1 Timothy 3:3; 6:5–10). And all those who have unofficial authority because of their wealth should use that power to bless those in need (1 Timothy 6:17–19), not to show their power over the people. All those with authority should mix mercy with justice, using their authority with compassion to care for and serve others.

Authority: For additional scriptures on this topic go to Amos.

what God said for the sake of your own rules. 7You are hypocrites! Isaiah was right when he said about you:

8'These people show honor to me with words,
but their hearts are far from me.
9Their worship of me is worthless.
The things they teach are nothing but
human rules.'" *Isaiah 29:13*

10After Jesus called the crowd to him, he said, "Listen and understand what I am saying. 11It is not what people put into their mouths that makes them unclean. It is what comes out of their mouths that makes them unclean."

12Then his followers came to him and asked, "Do you know that the Pharisees are angry because of what you said?"

13Jesus answered, "Every plant that my Father in heaven has not planted himself will be pulled up by the roots. 14Stay away from the Pharisees; they are blind leaders. And if a blind person leads a blind person, both will fall into a ditch."

15Peter said, "Explain the example to us."

16Jesus said, "Do you still not understand? 17Surely you know that all the food that enters the mouth goes into the stomach and then goes out of the body. 18But what people say with their mouths comes from the way they think; these are the things that make people unclean. 19Out of the mind come evil thoughts, murder, adultery, sexual sins, stealing, lying, and speaking evil of others. 20These things make people unclean; eating with unwashed hands does not make them unclean."

Jesus Helps a Non-Jewish Woman

21Jesus left that place and went to the area of Tyre and Sidon. 22A Canaanite woman from that area came to Jesus and cried out, "Lord, Son of David, have mercy on me! My daughter has a demon, and she is suffering very much."

23But Jesus did not answer the woman. So his followers came to Jesus and begged him, "Tell the woman to go away. She is following us and shouting."

24Jesus answered, "God sent me only to the lost sheep, the people of Israel."

25Then the woman came to Jesus again and bowed before him and said, "Lord, help me!"

26Jesus answered, "It is not right to take the children's bread and give it to the dogs."

27The woman said, "Yes, Lord, but even the dogs eat the crumbs that fall from their masters' table."

28Then Jesus answered, "Woman, you have great faith! I will do what you asked." And at that moment the woman's daughter was healed.

Jesus Heals Many People

29After leaving there, Jesus went along the shore of Lake Galilee. He went up on a hill and sat there.

30Great crowds came to Jesus, bringing with them the lame, the blind, the crippled, those who could not speak, and many others. They put them at Jesus' feet, and he healed them. 31The crowd was amazed when they saw that people who could not speak before were now able to speak. The crippled were made strong. The lame could walk, and the blind could see. And they praised the God of Israel for this.

More than Four Thousand Fed

32Jesus called his followers to him and said, "I feel sorry for these people, because they have already been with me three days, and they have nothing to eat. I don't want to send them away hungry. They might faint while going home."

33His followers asked him, "How can we get enough bread to feed all these people? We are far away from any town."

34Jesus asked, "How many loaves of bread do you have?"

They answered, "Seven, and a few small fish."

35Jesus told the people to sit on the ground. 36He took the seven loaves of bread and the fish and gave thanks to God. Then he divided the food and gave it to his followers, and they gave it to the people. 37All the people ate and were satisfied. Then his followers filled seven baskets with the leftover pieces of food. 38There were about four thousand men there who ate, besides women and children. 39After sending the people home, Jesus got into the boat and went to the area of Magadan.

The Leaders Ask for a Miracle

16 The Pharisees and Sadducees came to Jesus, wanting to trick him. So they asked him to show them a miracle from God.

15:20 Clean & Unclean: Matthew 23:25–20

15:21–28 Jesus' conversation with this woman seems insensitive. In fact, to people who lived in Israel in the first century, any other response would have been strange. Indeed, that Jesus finally healed the little girl would have been astounding. This is because it was commonly believed that God's grace was especially for God's people, the people of Israel. This account shows how people who were not Jews could believe in Jesus' power to bring healing.

15:28 Crossing Cultural Boundaries: Mark 5:25–34

15:30–31 Jesus specialized in healing the handicapped. Everywhere he went, Jesus sought the lame, the blind, the crippled, those who could not speak, and many others, and he healed them. This caused the people who saw these miracles to be amazed and to praise God for what they had seen. A physical handicap should never be allowed to deter someone from coming to Jesus or serving him. What he does not heal now, he will heal at the resurrection.

15:31 Sickness, Disease, Healing: Matthew 21:14

2Jesus answered, "At sunset you say we will have good weather, because the sky is red. 3And in the morning you say that it will be a rainy day, because the sky is dark and red. You see these signs in the sky and know what they mean. In the same way, you see the things that I am doing now, but you don't know their meaning. 4Evil and sinful people ask for a miracle as a sign, but they will not be given any sign, except the sign of Jonah." Then Jesus left them and went away.

Guard Against Wrong Teachings

5Jesus' followers went across the lake, but they had forgotten to bring bread. 6Jesus said to them, "Be careful! Beware of the yeast of the Pharisees and the Sadducees."

7His followers discussed the meaning of this, saying, "He said this because we forgot to bring bread."

8Knowing what they were talking about, Jesus asked them, "Why are you talking about not having bread? Your faith is small. 9Do you still not understand? Remember the five loaves of bread that fed the five thousand? And remember that you filled many baskets with the leftovers? 10Or the seven loaves of bread that fed the four thousand and the many baskets you filled then also? 11I was not talking to you about bread. Why don't you understand that? I am telling you to beware of the yeast of the Pharisees and the Sadducees." 12Then the followers understood that Jesus was not telling them to beware of the yeast used in bread but to beware of the teaching of the Pharisees and the Sadducees.

Peter Says Jesus Is the Christ

13When Jesus came to the area of Caesarea Philippi, he asked his followers, "Who do people say the Son of Man is?"

14They answered, "Some say you are John the Baptist. Others say you are Elijah, and still others say you are Jeremiah or one of the prophets."

15Then Jesus asked them, "And who do you say I am?"

16Simon Peter answered, "You are the Christ, the Son of the living God."

17Jesus answered, "You are blessed, Simon son of Jonah, because no person taught you that. My Father in heaven showed you who I am. 18So I tell you, you are Peter. On this rock I will build my church, and the power of death will not be able to defeat it. 19I will give you the keys of the kingdom of heaven; the things you don't allow on earth will be the things that God does not allow, and the things you allow on earth will be the things that God allows." 20Then Jesus warned his followers not to tell anyone he was the Christ.

Jesus Says that He Must Die

21From that time on Jesus began telling his followers that he must go to Jerusalem, where the older leaders, the leading priests, and the teachers of the law would make him suffer many things. He told them he must be killed and then be raised from the dead on the third day.

22Peter took Jesus aside and told him not to talk like that. He said, "God save you from those things, Lord! Those things will never happen to you!"

23Then Jesus said to Peter, "Go away from me, Satan! You are not helping me! You don't care about the things of God, but only about the things people think are important."

24Then Jesus said to his followers, "If people want to follow me, they must give up the things they want. They must be willing even to give up their lives to follow me. 25Those who want to save their lives will give up true life, and those who give up their lives for me will have true life. 26It is worth nothing for them to have the whole world if they lose their souls. They could never pay enough to buy back their souls. 27The Son of Man will come again with his Father's glory and with his angels. At

16:4 *sign of Jonah.* Jonah's three days in the fish are like Jesus' three days in the tomb. The story about Jonah is in the Book of Jonah.

16:17–20 There has been a great deal of controversy concerning what Jesus meant by the words he spoke to Peter. Did he mean that Peter himself or that the truth that Peter declared concerning Jesus' deity was the rock upon which the church would be built? The teaching of Protestant scholars has historically been that the "rock" was the truth that Jesus was not merely a reincarnation of John the Baptist, or Elijah, or one of the prophets as others had supposed, but that he was the long awaited "Christ, the Son of the living God."

Jesus gave Simon the nickname "Peter," meaning "rock." The term was anything but descriptive of the impetuous fisherman, until after Pentecost. On this occasion, Jesus makes a play on words and says on this "rock" he would build his church. The Greek word for "rock" means a massive slab of stone, whereas the word "Peter" means a small stone. The "rock" (massive slab) was most likely Peter's confession, "You are the Christ, the son of the living God" (Matthew 16:16). After all, only Christ, the Rock of Ages, is the true foundation of the church.

While this is true, it is important to remember that Peter was a "rock" in the New Testament church who was used in dramatic ways, along with the other apostles, to help establish the foundation upon which the church grew (Acts 1:8; 2:14–41; 8:14–25; 10:34–48). They, in turn, were building on the foundation laid by the prophets who had gone before them (Hebrews 1:1) and Jesus, himself (Hebrews 1:3).

The keys of the kingdom which Jesus gave to Peter were utilized in the Book of Acts to open the kingdom to the Jews at Pentecost (Acts 2), the Samaritan people (Acts 8), and the non-Jewish people (Acts 10). The doors of the kingdom were opened, as Jesus said they would be, "in Jerusalem, in all of Judea, in Samaria, and in every part of the world" (Acts 1:8).

16:18 *Peter.* The Greek name *Peter,* like the Aramaic name *Cephas,* means "rock."

16:19 Peter: Matthew 16:22–23

16:23 Peter: Matthew 17:1–4

16:23 *Satan.* Name for the devil, meaning "the enemy." Jesus means that Peter was talking like Satan.

that time, he will reward them for what they have done. 28I tell you the truth, some people standing here will see the Son of Man coming with his kingdom before they die."

Jesus Talks with Moses and Elijah

17 Six days later, Jesus took Peter, James, and John, the brother of James, up on a high mountain by themselves. 2While they watched, Jesus' appearance was changed; his face became bright like the sun, and his clothes became white as light. 3Then Moses and Elijah appeared to them, talking with Jesus.

4Peter said to Jesus, "Lord, it is good that we are here. If you want, I will put up three tents here—one for you, one for Moses, and one for Elijah."

5While Peter was talking, a bright cloud covered them. A voice came from the cloud and said, "This is my Son, whom I love, and I am very pleased with him. Listen to him!"

6When his followers heard the voice, they were so frightened they fell to the ground. 7But Jesus went to them and touched them and said, "Stand up. Don't be afraid." 8When they looked up, they saw Jesus was now alone.

9As they were coming down the mountain, Jesus commanded them not to tell anyone about what they had seen until the Son of Man had risen from the dead.

10Then his followers asked him, "Why do the teachers of the law say that Elijah must come first?"

11Jesus answered, "They are right to say that Elijah is coming and that he will make everything the way it should be. 12But I tell you that Elijah has already come, and they did not recognize him. They did to him whatever they wanted to do. It will be the same with the Son of Man; those same people will make the Son of Man suffer." 13Then the followers understood that Jesus was talking about John the Baptist.

Jesus Heals a Sick Boy

14When Jesus and his followers came back to the crowd, a man came to Jesus and bowed before him. 15The man said, "Lord, have mercy on my son. He has epilepsy and is suffering very much, because he often falls into the fire or into the water. 16I brought him to your followers, but they could not cure him."

Flowers and leaves of the mustard plant

17Jesus answered, "You people have no faith, and your lives are all wrong. How long must I put up with you? How long must I continue to be patient with you? Bring the boy here." 18Jesus commanded the demon inside the boy. Then the demon came out, and the boy was healed from that time on.

19The followers came to Jesus when he was alone and asked, "Why couldn't we force the demon out?"

20Jesus answered, "Because your faith is too small. I tell you the truth, if your faith is as big as a mustard seed, you can say to this mountain, 'Move from here to there,' and it will move. All things will be possible for you." 21*

Jesus Talks About His Death

22While Jesus' followers were gathering in Galilee, he said to them, "The Son of Man will be handed over to people, 23and they will kill him. But on the third day he will be raised from the dead." And the followers were filled with sadness.

Jesus Talks About Paying Taxes

24When Jesus and his followers came to Capernaum, the men who collected the Temple tax came to Peter. They asked, "Does your teacher pay the Temple tax?"

16:28 Martyrdom: Matthew 20:17–19

17:3 *Moses and Elijah.* Two of the most important Jewish leaders. In the past God had given Moses the Law, and Elijah was an important prophet.

17:3 Elijah and Elisha: Luke 4:27

17:4 Peter: Matthew 18:21

17:10 Scribes (Teachers of the Law): Matthew 21:15

17:15 *epilepsy.* A disease that causes a person sometimes to lose control of his body and maybe faint, shake strongly, or not be able to move.

17:20 Encouragement: Mark 9:23

17:20 Mountain: Matthew 21:21

***17:21** *Verse 21.* Some Greek copies add verse 21: "That kind of spirit comes out only if you use prayer and give up eating."

25Peter answered, "Yes, Jesus pays the tax."

Peter went into the house, but before he could speak, Jesus said to him, "What do you think? The kings of the earth collect different kinds of taxes. But who pays the taxes—the king's children or others?"

26Peter answered, "Other people pay the taxes."

Jesus said to Peter, "Then the children of the king don't have to pay taxes. 27But we don't want to upset these tax collectors. So go to the lake and fish. After you catch the first fish, open its mouth and you will find a coin. Take that coin and give it to the tax collectors for you and me."

Who Is the Greatest?

18 At that time the followers came to Jesus and asked, "Who is greatest in the kingdom of heaven?"

2Jesus called a little child to him and stood the child before his followers. 3Then he said, "I tell you the truth, you must change and become like little children. Otherwise, you will never enter the kingdom of heaven. 4The greatest person in the kingdom of heaven is the one who makes himself humble like this child.

5"Whoever accepts a child in my name accepts me. 6If one of these little children believes in me, and someone causes that child to sin, it would be better for that person to have a large stone tied around the neck and be drowned in the sea. 7How terrible for the people of the world because of the things that cause them to sin. Such things will happen, but how terrible for the one who causes them to happen! 8If your hand or your foot causes you to sin, cut it off and throw it away. It is better for you to lose part of your body and live forever than to have two hands and two feet and be thrown into the fire that burns forever. 9If your eye causes you to sin, take it out and throw it away. It is better for you to have only one eye and live forever than to have two eyes and be thrown into the fire of hell.

A Lost Sheep

10"Be careful. Don't think these little children are worth nothing. I tell you that they have angels in heaven who are always with my Father in heaven. 11*

12"If a man has a hundred sheep but one of the sheep gets lost, he will leave the other ninety-nine on the hill and go to look for the lost sheep. 13I tell you the truth, he is happier about that one sheep than about the ninety-nine that were never lost. 14In the same way, your Father in heaven does not want any of these little children to be lost.

When a Person Sins Against You

15"If your fellow believer sins against you, go and tell him in private what he did wrong. If he listens to you, you have helped that person to be your brother or sister again. 16But if he refuses to listen, go to him again and take one or two other people with you. 'Every case may be proved by two or three witnesses.' 17If he refuses to listen to them, tell the church. If he refuses to listen to the church, then treat him like a person who does not believe in God or like a tax collector.

18"I tell you the truth, the things you don't allow on earth will be the things God does not allow. And the things you allow on earth will be the things that God allows.

19"Also, I tell you that if two of you on earth agree about something and pray for it, it will be done for you by my Father in heaven. 20This is true because if two or three people come together in my name, I am there with them."

An Unforgiving Servant

21Then Peter came to Jesus and asked, "Lord, when my fellow believer sins against me, how many times must I forgive him? Should I forgive him as many as seven times?"

22Jesus answered, "I tell you, you must forgive him more than seven times. You must forgive him even if he wrongs you seventy times seven.

23"The kingdom of heaven is like a king who decided to collect the money his servants owed him. 24When the king began to collect his money, a servant who owed him several million dollars was brought to him. 25But the servant did not have enough money to pay his master, the king. So the master ordered that everything the servant owned

18:1–2 People in the ancient Roman world were very concerned with the question, Who is the greatest? By anyone's reckoning, little children were the least important of all. Jesus turns this concern upside down by asking about greatness in the kingdom of heaven. Because God's purpose is being fulfilled in the ministry of Jesus, old ways of measuring greatness must be discarded. Those who are great in the kingdom are those who are least concerned with their own greatness.

18:4 Honor & Shame: Mark 10:43

18:5 Children: Matthew 19:13–15

18:9 Hell: Matthew 22:13

18:10 Jesus warns against treating little children as unimportant. They are important enough to have angels in heaven who watch over them. Angels serve God by helping "those who will receive salvation" (Hebrews 1:14).

***18:11** *Verse 11.* Some Greek copies add verse 11: "The Son of Man came to save lost people."

18:16 *'Every . . . witnesses.'* Quotation from Deuteronomy 19:15.

18:17 Conflict: Mark 7:20–22

18:17 Stubbornness: Mark 10:5

18:20 Church: Mark 2:19

18:21 Peter: Matthew 26:33–35

should be sold, even the servant's wife and children. Then the money would be used to pay the king what the servant owed.

26“But the servant fell on his knees and begged, ‘Be patient with me, and I will pay you everything I owe.’ 27The master felt sorry for his servant and told him he did not have to pay it back. Then he let the servant go free.⚭

28“Later, that same servant found another servant who owed him a few dollars. The servant grabbed him around the neck and said, ‘Pay me the money you owe me!’

29“The other servant fell on his knees and begged him, ‘Be patient with me, and I will pay you everything I owe.’

30“But the first servant refused to be patient. He threw the other servant into prison until he could pay everything he owed. 31When the other servants saw what had happened, they were very sorry. So they went and told their master all that had happened.

32“Then the master called his servant in and said, ‘You evil servant! Because you begged me to forget what you owed, I told you that you did not have to pay anything. 33You should have showed mercy to that other servant, just as I showed mercy to you.’ 34The master was very angry and put the servant in prison to be punished until he could pay everything he owed.

35“This king did what my heavenly Father will do to you if you do not forgive your brother or sister from your heart.”⚭

Jesus Teaches About Divorce

19 After Jesus said all these things, he left Galilee and went into the area of Judea on the other side of the Jordan River. 2Large crowds followed him, and he healed them there.

3Some Pharisees came to Jesus and tried to trick him. They asked, “Is it right for a man to divorce his wife for any reason he chooses?”

4Jesus answered, “Surely you have read in the Scriptures: When God made the world, ‘he made them male and female.’ 5And God said, ‘So a man will leave his father and mother and be united with his wife, and the two will become one body.’ 6So there are not two, but one. God has joined the two together, so no one should separate them.”

7The Pharisees asked, “Why then did Moses give a command for a man to divorce his wife by giving her divorce papers?”

8Jesus answered, “Moses allowed you to divorce your wives because you refused to accept God's teaching, but divorce was not allowed in the beginning. 9I tell you that anyone who divorces his wife and marries another woman is guilty of adultery. The only reason for a man to divorce his wife is if his wife has sexual relations with another man.”

10The followers said to him, “If that is the only reason a man can divorce his wife, it is better not to marry.”

11Jesus answered, “Not everyone can accept this teaching, but God has made some able to accept it. 12There are different reasons why some men cannot marry. Some men were born without the ability to become fathers. Others were made that way later in life by other people. And some men have given up marriage because of the kingdom of heaven. But the person who can marry should accept this teaching about marriage.”⚭

Jesus Welcomes Children

13Then the people brought their little children to Jesus so he could put his hands on them and pray for them. His followers told them to stop, 14but Jesus said, “Let the little children come to me. Don't stop them, because the kingdom of heaven belongs to people who are like these children.” 15After Jesus put his hands on the children, he left there.⚭

A Rich Young Man's Question

16A man came to Jesus and asked, “Teacher, what good thing must I do to have life forever?”

17Jesus answered, “Why do you ask me about what is good? Only God is good. But if you want to have life forever, obey the commands.”

18The man asked, “Which commands?”

Jesus answered, “‘You must not murder anyone; you must not be guilty of adultery; you must not steal; you must not tell lies about your neighbor;⚭

⚭**18:27 Images of God:** Luke 14:16–24
⚭**18:35 Forgiveness:** Mark 2:1–11
19:4 *‘he made . . . female.’* Quotation from Genesis 1:27 or 5:2.
19:5 *‘So . . . body.’* Quotation from Genesis 2:24.
19:10–12 In the discussion between Jesus and his followers regarding the sole basis for divorce, the question of whether a man should marry at all is raised. Jesus says there are three basic classes of individuals who cannot marry: those who are unable to be fathers for natural causes, those who are made unable to be fathers by other people, and those who choose to remain unmarried to devote themselves to God's service.
⚭**19:12 Celibacy:** 1 Corinthians 7:1–8
⚭**19:12 Women:** 1 Corinthians 7:34
19:12 *But . . . marriage.* This may also mean, “The person who can accept this teaching about not marrying should accept it.”
19:13 *put his hands on them.* Showing that Jesus gave special blessings to these children.
⚭**19:15 Children:** Mark 9:33–37
⚭**19:18 Murder:** Mark 7:21

THE MIRACLES OF JESUS

Power over nature

Turns water to wine	John 2:1–11	Cana	Jesus is God's Son
First catch of fish	Luke 5:1–11	Sea of Galilee	Shows Peter that Jesus is Lord
Stills the storm	Matthew 8:23–27 Mark 4:35–41 Luke 8:22–25	Sea of Galilee	Teach disciples to trust Jesus
Feeds 5,000	Matthew 14:15–21 Mark 6:35–44 Luke 9:12–17 John 6:5–15	near Bethsaida	Jesus cares about people in need
Walks on sea	Matthew 14:22–33 Mark 6:45–52 John 6:16–21	Sea of Galilee	Shows disciples Jesus' power
Feeds 4,000	Matthew 15:32–39 Mark 8:1–9	near Bethsaida	Jesus cares about the hungry
Money from fish	Matthew 17:24–27	Capernaum	Pay Peter's tax
Withers fig tree	Matthew 21:17–22 Mark 11:12–14; 20–25	Jerusalem	To teach faith
Second catch of fish	John 21:1–14	Sea of Tiberias	Reveal Jesus to disciples

Power over sickness

Heals nobleman's son	John 4:46–54	Cana	Faith
Cures man with harmful skin disease	Matthew 8:1–4 Mark 1:40–45 Luke 5:12–15	Galilean city	Faith, caring
Heals soldier's servant	Matthew 8:5–13 Luke 7:1–10	Capernaum	Faith
Heals Peter's mother–in–law	Matthew 8:14–17 Mark 1:29–31 Luke 4:38–39	Capernaum	Friendship
Heals paralyzed man	Matthew 9:1–8 Mark 2:1–12 Luke 5:17–26	Capernaum	Jesus has power and can forgive sins
Cures woman of bleeding	Matthew 9:20–22 Mark 5:25–34 Luke 8:43–48	Capernaum	Faith

Gives blind their sight	Matthew 9:27–31	Capernaum	Faith
Heals crippled hand	Matthew 12:9–14 Mark 3:1–6 Luke 6:6–11	Galilee	God cares for people more than for religion
Heals non–Jewish girl	Matthew 15:21–28 Mark 7:24–30	Tyre	God loves all peoples
Heals deaf man who cannot talk	Mark 7:31–37	Decapolis	Bring friends to Jesus
Heals a man at a pool	John 5:1–18	Bethesda	Faith
Gives back sight	Mark 8:22–26	Bethsaida	Bring friends to Jesus
Gives sight to man born blind	John 9:1–41	Jerusalem	God's power
Heals man with dropsy	Luke 14:1–6	Jerusalem	God loves people more than religion
Heals ten of harmful skin disease	Luke 17:11–19	Galilee	Need to be grateful
Replaces ear of high priest's servant	Luke 22:49–51 John 18:10–11	Garden of Gethsemane	Jesus' deep love for enemies
	Power over evil spirits		
Heals man who could not talk because of demon	Matthew 9:32–34	Capernaum	Jesus' power is from God
Sends evil spirit from man	Mark 1:23–27 Luke 4:33–36	Capernaum	Jesus has power over the Devil
Heals man who was blind and could not talk	Matthew 12:22 Luke 11:14	Galilee	Jesus' power is from God
Heals child with demon	Matthew 17:14–20 Mark 9:14–29	Mt. Tabor	Faith is greater than Satan
Heals woman crippled for 18 years	Luke 13:10–17	Jerusalem	God loves people, not religion
	Power over death		
Raises Jairus' daughter	Matthew 9:18–26 Mark 5:35–43 Luke 8:41–42, 49–56	Capernaum	Faith
Raises widow's only son	Luke 7:11–16	Nain	Caring
Raises Lazarus	John 11:1–45	Bethany	Jesus has power over death

19 honor your father and mother; and love your
neighbor as you love yourself.'"
20The young man said, "I have obeyed all these
things. What else do I need to do?"
21Jesus answered, "If you want to be perfect,
then go and sell your possessions and give the
money to the poor. If you do this, you will have
treasure in heaven. Then come and follow me."
22But when the young man heard this, he left
sorrowfully, because he was rich.
23Then Jesus said to his followers, "I tell you the
truth, it will be hard for a rich person to enter the
kingdom of heaven. 24Yes, I tell you that it is easier
for a camel to go through the eye of a needle than
for a rich person to enter the kingdom of God."
25When Jesus' followers heard this, they were
very surprised and asked, "Then who can be
saved?"
26Jesus looked at them and said, "This is something people cannot do, but God can do all things."
27Peter said to Jesus, "Look, we have left everything and followed you. So what will we have?"
28Jesus said to them, "I tell you the truth, when
the age to come has arrived, the Son of Man will sit
on his great throne. All of you who followed me will
also sit on twelve thrones, judging the twelve tribes
of Israel. 29And all those who have left houses,
brothers, sisters, father, mother, children, or farms
to follow me will get much more than they left, and
they will have life forever. 30Many who have the
highest place now will have the lowest place in the
future. And many who have the lowest place now
will have the highest place in the future.

A Story About Workers

20 "The kingdom of heaven is like a person
who owned some land. One morning, he
went out very early to hire some people to work
in his vineyard. 2The man agreed to pay the
workers one coin for working that day. Then he
sent them into the vineyard to work. 3About
nine o'clock the man went to the marketplace
and saw some other people standing there, doing
nothing. 4So he said to them, 'If you go and work
in my vineyard, I will pay you what your work is
worth.' 5So they went to work in the vineyard.
The man went out again about twelve o'clock and
three o'clock and did the same thing. 6About five
o'clock the man went to the marketplace again
and saw others standing there. He asked them,
'Why did you stand here all day doing nothing?'
7They answered, 'No one gave us a job.' The man
said to them, 'Then you can go and work in my
vineyard.'
8"At the end of the day, the owner of the vineyard said to the boss of all the workers, 'Call the
workers and pay them. Start with the last people
I hired and end with those I hired first.'
9"When the workers who were hired at five
o'clock came to get their pay, each received one
coin. 10When the workers who were hired first
came to get their pay, they thought they would
be paid more than the others. But each one of
them also received one coin. 11When they got
their coin, they complained to the man who
owned the land. 12They said, 'Those people were
hired last and worked only one hour. But you
paid them the same as you paid us who worked
hard all day in the hot sun.' 13But the man who
owned the vineyard said to one of those workers,
'Friend, I am being fair to you. You agreed to
work for one coin. 14So take your pay and go. I
want to give the man who was hired last the
same pay that I gave you. 15I can do what I want
with my own money. Are you jealous because I
am good to those people?'
16"So those who have the last place now will
have the first place in the future, and those who
have the first place now will have the last place in
the future."

Jesus Talks About His Own Death

17While Jesus was going to Jerusalem, he took
his twelve followers aside privately and said to
them, 18"Look, we are going to Jerusalem. The Son
of Man will be turned over to the leading priests
and the teachers of the law, and they will say that
he must die. 19They will give the Son of Man to the
non-Jewish people to laugh at him and beat him
with whips and crucify him. But on the third day,
he will be raised to life again."

19:19 *'You . . . mother.'* Quotation from Exodus 20:12-16; Deuteronomy 5:16-20.
19:19 *'love . . . yourself.'* Quotation from Leviticus 19:18.
19:19 Neighbor: Mark 12:31
19:22 Depression: 2 Corinthians 7:6
19:30 Materialism/Possessions: Mark 10:17–31
20:1–16 This parable is not about how to run a business or how to treat employees, but as the opening verse says, it is about what the kingdom of heaven is like. The story catches people's attention because of how outrageous it sounds. The emphasis is on the equal treatment received by those who have been the people of God and have labored long, and those who have recently become a part of God's people. God's generous mercy allows all people the same promise and benefit of salvation in Christ.
20:2 *coin.* A Roman denarius. One coin was the average pay for one day's work.
20:16 Good Works: Luke 18:9–14
20:16 Work: Matthew 25:14–30
20:19 Martyrdom: Matthew 23:37–39

A Mother Asks Jesus a Favor

20 Then the wife of Zebedee came to Jesus with
her sons. She bowed before him and asked him to
do something for her.
21 Jesus asked, "What do you want?"
She said, "Promise that one of my sons will sit
at your right side and the other will sit at your left
side in your kingdom."
22 But Jesus said, "You don't understand what you
are asking. Can you drink the cup that I am about to
drink?"
The sons answered, "Yes, we can."⚭
23 Jesus said to them, "You will drink from my
cup. But I cannot choose who will sit at my right or
my left; those places belong to those for whom my
Father has prepared them."
24 When the other ten followers heard this, they
were angry with the two brothers.
25 Jesus called all the followers together and said,
"You know that the rulers of the non-Jewish people love to show their power over the people. And
their important leaders love to use all their authority. 26 But it should not be that way among you.
Whoever wants to become great among you must
serve the rest of you like a servant. 27 Whoever
wants to become first among you must serve the
rest of you like a slave. 28 In the same way, the Son
of Man did not come to be served. He came to
serve others and to give his life as a ransom for
many people."⚭

Jesus Heals Two Blind Men

29 When Jesus and his followers were leaving
Jericho, a great many people followed him. 30 Two
blind men sitting by the road heard that Jesus was
going by, so they shouted, "Lord, Son of David,
have mercy on us!"
31 The people warned the blind men to be quiet,
but they shouted even more, "Lord, Son of David,
have mercy on us!"
32 Jesus stopped and said to the blind men, "What
do you want me to do for you?"
33 They answered, "Lord, we want to see."
34 Jesus felt sorry for the blind men and touched
their eyes, and at once they could see. Then they
followed Jesus.⚭

Jesus Enters Jerusalem as a King

21 As Jesus and his followers were coming
closer to Jerusalem, they stopped at Bethphage at the hill called the Mount of Olives. From
there Jesus sent two of his followers 2 and said to
them, "Go to the town you can see there. When
you enter it, you will quickly find a donkey tied
there with its colt. Untie them and bring them to
me. 3 If anyone asks you why you are taking the
donkeys, say that the Master needs them, and he
will send them at once."
4 This was to bring about what the prophet had
said:
5 "Tell the people of Jerusalem,
'Your king is coming to you.
He is gentle and riding on a donkey,
on the colt of a donkey.'" *Isaiah 62:11; Zechariah 9:9*
6 The followers went and did what Jesus told
them to do. 7 They brought the donkey and the colt
to Jesus and laid their coats on them, and Jesus sat
on them. 8 Many people spread their coats on the
road. Others cut branches from the trees and
spread them on the road. 9 The people were walking ahead of Jesus and behind him, shouting,
"Praise to the Son of David!
God bless the One who comes in the name of
the Lord! *Psalm 118:26*
Praise to God in heaven!"
10 When Jesus entered Jerusalem, all the city was
filled with excitement. The people asked, "Who is
this man?"
11 The crowd said, "This man is Jesus, the prophet
from the town of Nazareth in Galilee."

20:20–28 It seems that there are some people everywhere who seek status, authority, and power. Jesus' followers should not seek power over others, but rather should seek to serve others. Our desire should be not to control but to care, not to have our preferences but to seek the other's good. By personal example Jesus gives us a model of the kind of leaders God wants (John 13:1–17).

20:22 *drink . . . drink.* Jesus used the idea of drinking from a cup to ask if they could accept the same terrible things that would happen to him.

⚭**20:22 Alcohol:** Matthew 26:39

20:25–28 Pride is promotion of self above others (Romans 12:3; 1 Corinthians 13:4; Philippians 2:3–4). Self-promotion is also demotion of others. Both are offensive to God because they violate God's intention for how a person should gain and implement leadership. The "shepherd" (Ezekiel 34; John 10:1–18; 1 Peter 5:1–4) and the "servant" (Matthew 20:25–28) are God's models of leadership that serve the followers, even at the expense of the leader (John 10:11). Those who reverse this are warned (Matthew 20:26; Ezekiel 34:1–10). Therefore on a deeper level, when Adam and Eve tried to be like God by promoting themselves, not only were they denying the Creator/creature distinction, but they were also insulting God by saying that God is one who promotes himself at the expense of others—in reality, God is Father, Servant, Shepherd. Even when he demands praise and worship, he does everything in the best interest of his subjects. That is why he insists that his representatives on earth be servant and shepherd-type leaders, not proud tyrants who "lord it over" their subjects in order to promote themselves.

⚭**20:28 Authority:** Mark 4:36–41
⚭**20:28 Leadership:** Matthew 24:4–24
⚭**20:28 Service:** Matthew 23:12
⚭**20:34 Blindness:** Mark 10:46–52

21:9 *Praise.* Literally, *Hosanna,* a Hebrew word used at first in praying to God for help. At this time it was probably a shout of joy used in praising God or his Messiah.

Jesus Goes to the Temple

[12]Jesus went into the Temple and threw out all the people who were buying and selling there. He turned over the tables of those who were exchanging different kinds of money, and he upset the benches of those who were selling doves. [13]Jesus said to all the people there, "It is written in the Scriptures, 'My Temple will be called a house for prayer.' But you are changing it into a 'hideout for robbers.'"

[14]The blind and crippled people came to Jesus in the Temple, and he healed them. [15]The leading priests and the teachers of the law saw that Jesus was doing wonderful things and that the children were praising him in the Temple, saying, "Praise to the Son of David." All these things made the priests and the teachers of the law very angry.

[16]They asked Jesus, "Do you hear the things these children are saying?"

Jesus answered, "Yes. Haven't you read in the Scriptures, 'You have taught children and babies to sing praises'?"

[17]Then Jesus left and went out of the city to Bethany, where he spent the night.

The Power of Faith

[18]Early the next morning, as Jesus was going back to the city, he became hungry. [19]Seeing a fig tree beside the road, Jesus went to it, but there were no figs on the tree, only leaves. So Jesus said to the tree, "You will never again have fruit." The tree immediately dried up.

[20]When his followers saw this, they were amazed. They asked, "How did the fig tree dry up so quickly?"

[21]Jesus answered, "I tell you the truth, if you have faith and do not doubt, you will be able to do what I did to this tree and even more. You will be able to say to this mountain, 'Go, fall into the sea.' And if you have faith, it will happen. [22]If you believe, you will get anything you ask for in prayer."

Leaders Doubt Jesus' Authority

[23]Jesus went to the Temple, and while he was teaching there, the leading priests and the older leaders of the people came to him. They said, "What authority do you have to do these things? Who gave you this authority?"

[24]Jesus answered, "I also will ask you a question. If you answer me, then I will tell you what authority I have to do these things. [25]Tell me: When John baptized people, did that come from God or just from other people?"

They argued about Jesus' question, saying, "If we answer, 'John's baptism was from God,' Jesus will say, 'Then why didn't you believe him?' [26]But if we say, 'It was from people,' we are afraid of what the crowd will do because they all believe that John was a prophet."

[27]So they answered Jesus, "We don't know."

Jesus said to them, "Then I won't tell you what authority I have to do these things.

A Story About Two Sons

[28]"Tell me what you think about this: A man had two sons. He went to the first son and said, 'Son, go and work today in my vineyard.' [29]The son answered, 'I will not go.' But later the son changed his mind and went. [30]Then the father went to the other son and said, 'Son, go and work today in my vineyard.' The son answered, 'Yes, sir, I will go and work,' but he did not go. [31]Which of the two sons obeyed his father?"

The priests and leaders answered, "The first son."

Jesus said to them, "I tell you the truth, the tax collectors and the prostitutes will enter the kingdom of God before you do. [32]John came to show you the right way to live. You did not believe him, but the tax collectors and prostitutes believed him. Even after seeing this, you still refused to change your ways and believe him.

A Story About God's Son

[33]"Listen to this story: There was a man who owned a vineyard. He put a wall around it and dug a hole for a winepress and built a tower. Then he leased the land to some farmers and left for a trip. [34]When it was time for the grapes to be picked, he sent his servants to the farmers to get his share of the grapes. [35]But the farmers grabbed the servants, beat one, killed another, and then killed a third servant with stones. [36]So the man sent some other servants to the farmers, even more than he sent the first time. But the farmers did the same thing to the servants that they had done before. [37]So the man decided to send his son to the farmers. He said,

21:13 *'My Temple . . . prayer.'* Quotation from Isaiah 56:7.
21:13 *'hideout for robbers.'* Quotation from Jeremiah 7:11.
21:14 Sickness, Disease, Healing: Mark 5:21–43
21:15 Scribes (Teachers of the Law): Matthew 23
21:15 *Praise.* Literally, *Hosanna,* a Hebrew word used at first in praying to God for help. At this time it was probably a shout of joy used in praising God or his Messiah.
21:16 *'You . . . praises.'* Quotation from the Septuagint (Greek) version of Psalm 8:2.
21:21 Doubt: Mark 9:14–29
21:21 Mountain: Matthew 28:16–20
21:31 Will of God: Luke 22:42

CITIZEN

ROMANS 13

In what ways might God's people exercise their faith publicly as citizens?

Christians in all times and places have struggled to understand how the call to serve God might be answered in their public lives as citizens. Biblical texts suggest that citizenship involves much more than simply obeying or disobeying the laws; it involves a basic understanding of our relationship to God and to other human beings, including those in positions of authority.

For God's people citizenship is one aspect of the web of social relationships within which their lives have meaning. In Exodus 22:28 Moses tells the people of Israel, "You must not speak against God or curse a leader of your people." Moses' command is part of a long list of laws that tells how the people of Israel are to treat one another, and it emphasizes the fact that their relationship with God is reflected in their behavior toward each other and toward their leaders. This same idea is apparent in Ezra 6:10 as well.

Old Testament passages such as those mentioned above also reveal the Israelites' belief that the power held by those in authority came from God. The leaders who are chosen by Moses are told that each decision "comes from God" (Deuteronomy 1:17). When the people want to choose a king they are told "to appoint over you the king the Lord your God chooses" (Deuteronomy 17:15). If the leaders fail to govern according to the laws they have received, however, God withdraws divine favor and power, causing them to lose their authority over the people (see Isaiah 10:1; Ezekiel 34:1–2).

God's people understood that the web of social relationships within which they lived carried with it certain obligations, some of which had to do with civic responsibility. Jeremiah, writing to the exiles in Babylon, advises them to "do good things for the city where I sent you as captives" (Jeremiah 29:7). The people of Israel were forced to leave their homeland, yet Jeremiah's words indicate that they are to work for the good of the city to which they have been exiled "because if good things happen in the city, good things will happen to you also." Even in exile the people of Israel do not live in isolation; their well-being is tied to the well-being of the community in which they now must live.

Like the Israelites before them, the early followers of Jesus believed that God ordered human affairs and empowered authorities to rule. Paul writes to the Christians in Rome that they "must yield to the government rulers" because their power comes from God (Romans 13:1). This does not mean that they are to blindly submit to their rulers; rather, it is an acknowledgment of the fact that the relationship of the people to their leaders was patterned on their relationship to God.

Paul tells the Christians in Rome that they are to fulfill their civic responsibilities: "Pay everyone, then, what you owe. . . . Show respect and honor to them all" (Romans 13:7). But he is also clear that the believer must place one law above all others—the law of love—"because the person who loves others has obeyed all the law" (Romans 13:8). These statements, like those of Moses in Exodus, appear in a discussion about how believers are to behave toward one another, which again emphasizes the idea that God's people were expected to act consistently across a whole web of relationships, both public and private.

The earliest followers of Jesus lived in a world that was hostile to the message they proclaimed. They sought to overcome that hostility and to proclaim the Good News, not by promoting political insurrection or civil unrest, but by being model citizens. These Christians knew that the Good News message would not be heard or believed if they themselves did not live by the law of love about which they spoke. Thus they are to "pray for rulers" (1 Timothy 2:2), "to obey them, to be ready to do good, to speak no evil about anyone, to live in peace, and to be gentle and polite to all people" (Titus 3:1). This same idea is echoed in 1 Peter 2:16–17: "Live as servants of God. Show respect for all people: Love the brothers and sisters of God's family, respect God, honor the king."

Like all of God's people we are challenged to make our faith more than a "Sunday only" experience. The earliest followers of Jesus knew that it was not enough to *tell* about the Good News; they had to witness their belief publicly through their everyday *actions*. Each time we act as citizens—when we speak out on an issue, or vote, or even pay taxes—we have an opportunity to show others that we live by the law of love which Scripture proclaims. And each time we "look for peace and work for it" (1 Peter 3:11) we demonstrate our understanding of the fact that the lives of *all* people are woven together in God's web.

Citizen: For additional scriptures on this topic go to Exodus 22:28.

GOVERNMENT

ROMANS 13:1–7

What is the origin and purpose of the state? On what does the law rest for its judicial force? How is a community different from the state? What happens when the interests of the church are in conflict with those of the state?

The *state* was instituted by God to restrain sin and promote a just social order. One of the most common misconceptions in Western political thought is that government is decided only by the will of the people. When Pilate questioned Jesus on the eve of his execution, Christ told the governor that he would not even hold his office or political authority if it had not been granted him by God. The apostle Paul spoke of civil authority as "God's servant to punish those who do wrong" (Romans 13:4). Peter used similar language, saying that governments were set by God to "punish those who do wrong and to praise those who do right" (1 Peter 2:14).

Government began with God. It is, in one sense, God's response to the nature of the people themselves. While it cannot redeem the world or be used as a tool to establish the kingdom of God, civil government does set the boundaries for human behavior. The state is not a solution for sin, but a means to control it. Its limited task is to promote the good of the community, to protect life and property, and to keep peace and order.

When God established ancient Israel as a nation, his first order of business was the giving of law, not just for religious purposes, but for the ordering of civil life. Even before the giving of the Ten Commandments, there was great need for civil order.

The biblical text records that "Moses solved disagreements among the people, and the people stood around him from morning until night" (Exodus 18:13). (Court dockets seemed to have been clogged from the very beginning.) Moses explained that "the people come to me for God's help in solving their disagreements. When people have a disagreement, they come to me, and I decide who is right. I tell them God's laws and teachings" (Exodus 18:15–16).

Thus the Israelite involved in a dispute looked not to the whim of a judge or to an arbitrary law but rather to a ruling based on divine laws. This is the origin of the rule of law, which stands in stark contrast to modern moral relativism. Without transcendent norms, laws are either established by social elites or are merely bargains struck by competing forces in society. In the Judeo-Christian view, law is rooted in moral absolutes that do not change with public taste or the whim of fashion.

Thus rooted, government can perform not only the negative function of restraining evil, but the positive function of promoting a just social order so that people can live in harmony. The apostle Paul had this in mind when he urged his young worker Timothy to pray "for rulers and for all who have authority so that we can have quiet and peaceful lives full of worship and respect for God" (1 Timothy 2:2).

The state can protect people's voluntary efforts to shape community by granting equal protection of the law, by upholding principles of justice so the weak and powerless are not exploited, and by guaranteeing liberty and providing security. In this way the government sustains a stable environment in which people can live.

Christianity teaches, then, that the state serves a divinely appointed and divinely defined task, although it is not in itself divine. Its authority is true, though limited.

Governments, with rare exceptions, seek to expand their power beyond restraining evil, preserving order, and promoting justice. Most often they do this by venturing into religious or moral areas. The reason is twofold: the state needs religious legitimization for its policies, and an independent church is the one structure that rivals the state's claim for total allegiance.

Sometimes government interferes with the practice of religion. Encroachment upon faith in the West is usually not as dramatic as it has been in modern totalitarian states. It begins in minor ways, such as a county zoning commission barring Bible studies in homes, suppers in church basements, or religious activities on public property. And even when it appears that the state is accommodating religious viewpoints, its action may hide other motives. When government interference reaches the point of suppressing or persecuting religion, Christians may have to disobey civil government. On the one hand Scripture commands civil obedience—that individuals respect and live in subjection to governing authorities and pray for those in authority. On the other, it commands that Christians maintain their ultimate allegiance to the kingdom of God.

Government: For additional scriptures on this topic go to Exodus 18:13.

'They will respect my son.' 38But when the farmers saw the son, they said to each other, 'This son
will inherit the vineyard. If we kill him, it will be
ours!' 39Then the farmers grabbed the son, threw
him out of the vineyard, and killed him. 40So what
will the owner of the vineyard do to these farmers
when he comes?"
41The priests and leaders said, "He will surely kill
those evil men. Then he will lease the vineyard to
some other farmers who will give him his share of
the crop at harvest time."
42Jesus said to them, "Surely you have read this
in the Scriptures:

'The stone that the builders rejected
became the cornerstone.
The Lord did this,
and it is wonderful to us.' *Psalm 118:22-23*

43"So I tell you that the kingdom of God will be
taken away from you and given to people who do the
things God wants in his kingdom. 44The person who
falls on this stone will be broken, and on whomever
that stone falls, that person will be crushed."
45When the leading priests and the Pharisees
heard these stories, they knew Jesus was talking
about them. 46They wanted to arrest him, but they
were afraid of the people, because the people
believed that Jesus was a prophet.

A Story About a Wedding Feast

22 Jesus again used stories to teach the people.
He said, 2"The kingdom of heaven is like a
king who prepared a wedding feast for his son. 3The
king invited some people to the feast. When the
feast was ready, the king sent his servants to tell
the people, but they refused to come.
4"Then the king sent other servants, saying, 'Tell
those who have been invited that my feast is ready.
I have killed my best bulls and calves for the dinner,
and everything is ready. Come to the wedding feast.'
5"But the people refused to listen to the servants
and left to do other things. One went to work in his
field, and another went to his business. 6Some of the
other people grabbed the servants, beat them, and
killed them. 7The king was furious and sent his
army to kill the murderers and burn their city.
8"After that, the king said to his servants, 'The
wedding feast is ready. I invited those people, but
they were not worthy to come. 9So go to the street
corners and invite everyone you find to come to my
feast.' 10So the servants went into the streets and gathered all the people they could find, both good and bad.
And the wedding hall was filled with guests.
11"When the king came in to see the guests, he
saw a man who was not dressed for a wedding.
12The king said, 'Friend, how were you allowed
to come in here? You are not dressed for a wedding.' But the man said nothing. 13So the king told
some servants, 'Tie this man's hands and feet.
Throw him out into the darkness, where people
will cry and grind their teeth with pain.'
14"Yes, many people are invited, but only a few
are chosen."

Is It Right to Pay Taxes or Not?

15Then the Pharisees left that place and made
plans to trap Jesus in saying something wrong.
16They sent some of their own followers and some
people from the group called Herodians. They
said, "Teacher, we know that you are an honest
man and that you teach the truth about God's way.
You are not afraid of what other people think about
you, because you pay no attention to who they
are. 17So tell us what you think. Is it right to pay
taxes to Caesar or not?"
18But knowing that these leaders were trying to
trick him, Jesus said, "You hypocrites! Why are you
trying to trap me? 19Show me a coin used for paying
the tax." So the men showed him a coin. 20Then Jesus
asked, "Whose image and name are on the coin?"
21The men answered, "Caesar's."
Then Jesus said to them, "Give to Caesar the
things that are Caesar's, and give to God the things
that are God's."
22When the men heard what Jesus said, they
were amazed and left him and went away.

Some Sadducees Try to Trick Jesus

23That same day some Sadducees came to Jesus
and asked him a question. (Sadducees believed
that people would not rise from the dead.) 24They
said, "Teacher, Moses said if a married man dies
without having children, his brother must marry
the widow and have children for him. 25Once there
were seven brothers among us. The first one married and died. Since he had no children, his brother
married the widow. 26Then the second brother
also died. The same thing happened to the third

21:44 Stone: Luke 19:40
21:44 *Verse 44.* Some copies do not have verse 44.
21:46 Pharisees and Sadducees: Luke 5:17–24
22:13 Hell: Matthew 24:51
22:15–21 There are two issues to note here. First, if Jesus were to publicly oppose the paying of taxes to Caesar he would be guilty of political treason, a sure end to his career and life. Second, he probably embarrassed whoever was able to produce the coin since they would admit, by their possession of the coin, to condoning a graven image of an emperor who demanded to be worshiped as a god, which the Jewish law said was wrong (Exodus 20:3–5).
22:16 *Herodians.* A political group that followed Herod and his family.
22:19 *coin.* A Roman denarius. One coin was the average pay for one day's work.

brother and all the other brothers. 27Finally, the woman died. 28Since all seven men had married her, when people rise from the dead, whose wife will she be?"

29Jesus answered, "You don't understand, because you don't know what the Scriptures say, and you don't know about the power of God. 30When people rise from the dead, they will not marry, nor will they be given to someone to marry. They will be like the angels in heaven. 31Surely you have read what God said to you about rising from the dead. 32God said, 'I am the God of Abraham, the God of Isaac, and the God of Jacob.' God is the God of the living, not the dead."

33When the people heard this, they were amazed at Jesus' teaching.

The Most Important Command

34When the Pharisees learned that the Sadducees could not argue with Jesus' answers to them, the Pharisees met together. 35One Pharisee, who was an expert on the law of Moses, asked Jesus this question to test him: 36"Teacher, which command in the law is the most important?"

37Jesus answered, "'Love the Lord your God with all your heart, all your soul, and all your mind.' 38This is the first and most important command. 39And the second command is like the first: 'Love your neighbor as you love yourself.' 40All the law and the writings of the prophets depend on these two commands."

Jesus Questions the Pharisees

41While the Pharisees were together, Jesus asked them, 42"What do you think about the Christ? Whose son is he?"

They answered, "The Christ is the Son of David."

43Then Jesus said to them, "Then why did David call him 'Lord'? David, speaking by the power of the Holy Spirit, said,

44'The Lord said to my Lord:
  Sit by me at my right side,
  until I put your enemies under your control.'

Psalm 110:1

45David calls the Christ 'Lord,' so how can the Christ be his son?"

46None of the Pharisees could answer Jesus' question, and after that day no one was brave enough to ask him any more questions.

Jesus Accuses Some Leaders

23 Then Jesus said to the crowds and to his followers, 2"The teachers of the law and the Pharisees have the authority to tell you what the law of Moses says. 3So you should obey and follow whatever they tell you, but their lives are not good examples for you to follow. They tell you to do things, but they themselves don't do them. 4They make strict rules and try to force people to obey them, but they are unwilling to help those who struggle under the weight of their rules.

5"They do good things so that other people will see them. They make the boxes of Scriptures that they wear bigger, and they make their special prayer clothes very long. 6Those Pharisees and teachers of the law love to have the most important seats at feasts and in the synagogues. 7They love people to greet them with respect in the marketplaces, and they love to have people call them 'Teacher.'

8"But you must not be called 'Teacher,' because you have only one Teacher, and you are all brothers and sisters together. 9And don't call any person on earth 'Father,' because you have one Father,

22:30 Here we get a vague hint into the nature of heaven. The Sadducees are trying to trip up Jesus with a question about the Law. The question leads him to say something about heaven, but since the question is not about heaven, it is only a glimpse. Jesus tells us that there is no marriage in heaven; that we are like the angels. Since we do not know much about the angels, we cannot be sure exactly what this means. Many think it means that sexuality will not have a place in heaven; others think that sexuality will play a role, but a different one with our "resurrection bodies." The one thing we know for certain is that God is in heaven, and it will be a place of great happiness.

22:32 *'I am . . . Jacob.'* Quotation from Exodus 3:6.

22:33 Marriage: John 2:1–11

22:37 A Matter of the Heart: Mark 7:21–22

22:37 *'Love . . . mind.'* Quotation from Deuteronomy 6:5.

22:39 *'Love . . . yourself.'* Quotation from Leviticus 19:18.

22:45 David: Mark 11:10

23 Jesus accuses the Pharisees of being hypocrites because they proclaim their faith and observe the correct religious rituals but fail to live their lives according to God's most important teachings (23:23–24). Actions speak louder than words, and Jesus demands that his followers live their whole lives—both public and private— in accordance with God's commands.

It is important to remember that Jesus was himself a Jew, and that his form of teaching was similar to that of the Pharisees. What Matthew records here, then, is "a family feud," concerned with who best upholds the ways of God. Jesus accuses some leaders of hypocrisy. In doing so, he is not accusing them of saying one thing and doing another, as we might use the word hypocrisy, but of not understanding the ways of God. They are not deceiving people; rather, they believe they know and follow the truth when they do not.

When we read Jesus' scathing accusations against the Pharisees and the teachers of the law, we assume these people must have been terrible villains, far worse than we could ever be. We need to recognize that they were some of the most religious people in their country. They fell into the sins that "good" people are prone to—pride, judging, legalism. Probably Jesus used harsh language to try to shock them out of their self-righteousness, for unless they recognized their sinfulness and need for forgiveness, they would never enter the kingdom of God. Christians today often fall into pharisaic sins and may need the same kind of shock treatment that Jesus gave the Pharisees and teachers of the law.

23:5 *boxes.* Small leather boxes containing four important Scriptures. Some Jews tied these to their foreheads and left arms, probably to show they were very religious.

who is in heaven. 10And you should not be
called 'Master,' because you have only one Master,
the Christ. 11Whoever is your servant is the greatest among you. 12Whoever makes himself great
will be made humble. Whoever makes himself
humble will be made great.
13"How terrible for you, teachers of the law and
Pharisees! You are hypocrites! You close the door
for people to enter the kingdom of heaven. You
yourselves don't enter, and you stop others who
are trying to enter. 14*
15"How terrible for you, teachers of the law and
Pharisees! You are hypocrites! You travel across
land and sea to find one person who will change to
your ways. When you find that person, you make
him more fit for hell than you are.
16"How terrible for you! You guide the people,
but you are blind. You say, 'If people swear by
the Temple when they make a promise, that
means nothing. But if they swear by the gold that
is in the Temple, they must keep that promise.'
17You are blind fools! Which is greater: the gold
or the Temple that makes that gold holy? 18And
you say, 'If people swear by the altar when they
make a promise, that means nothing. But if they
swear by the gift on the altar, they must keep that
promise.' 19You are blind! Which is greater: the
gift or the altar that makes the gift holy? 20The
person who swears by the altar is really using the
altar and also everything on the altar. 21And the
person who swears by the Temple is really using
the Temple and also everything in the Temple.
22The person who swears by heaven is also using
God's throne and the One who sits on that
throne.
23"How terrible for you, teachers of the law and
Pharisees! You are hypocrites! You give to God one-
tenth of everything you earn—even your mint, dill,
and cumin. But you don't obey the really important teachings of the law—justice, mercy, and
being loyal. These are the things you should do,
as well as those other things. 24You guide the
people, but you are blind! You are like a person
who picks a fly out of a drink and then swallows
a camel!
25"How terrible for you, teachers of the law and
Pharisees! You are hypocrites! You wash the outside

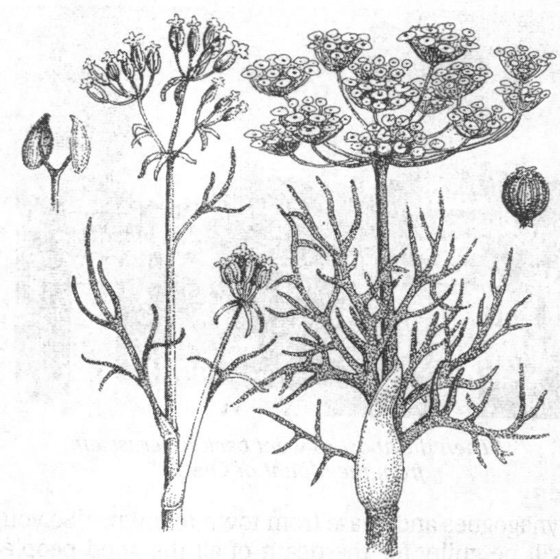
The herbs cumin and dill

of your cups and dishes, but inside they are full of
things you got by cheating others and by pleasing
only yourselves. 26Pharisees, you are blind! First
make the inside of the cup clean, and then the
outside of the cup can be truly clean.
27"How terrible for you, teachers of the law and
Pharisees! You are hypocrites! You are like tombs
that are painted white. Outside, those tombs look
fine, but inside, they are full of the bones of dead
people and all kinds of unclean things. 28It is the
same with you. People look at you and think you
are good, but on the inside you are full of hypocrisy
and evil.
29"How terrible for you, teachers of the law and
Pharisees! You are hypocrites! You build tombs for
the prophets, and you show honor to the graves of
those who lived good lives. 30You say, 'If we had
lived during the time of our ancestors, we would
not have helped them kill the prophets.' 31But you
give proof that you are children of those who murdered the prophets. 32And you will complete the
sin that your ancestors started.
33"You are snakes! A family of poisonous snakes!
How are you going to escape God's judgment? 34So
I tell you this: I am sending to you prophets and
wise men and teachers. Some of them you will kill
and crucify. Some of them you will beat in your

23:9 Father: Mark 14:36
23:12 Service: Matthew 25:14–20
***23:14** *Verse 14.* Some Greek copies add verse 14: "How terrible for you, teachers of the law and Pharisees. You are hypocrites. You take away widows' houses, and you say long prayers so that people will notice you. So you will have a worse punishment."
23:22 Oath/Vow: Acts 18:18
23:23 Stewardship: Matthew 25:14–30
23:23 *mint, dill, and cumin.* Small plants grown in gardens and used for spices. Only very religious people would be careful enough to give a tenth of these plants.
23:24 *You . . . camel!* Meaning, "You worry about the smallest mistakes but commit the biggest sin."
23:28 Integrity: Ephesians 6:5–6
23:28 Clean & Unclean: Mark 7:14–23

*"Then the apostles went back to Jerusalem
from the Mount of Olives."*

synagogues and chase from town to town. 35So you
will be guilty for the death of all the good people
who have been killed on earth—from the murder
of that good man Abel to the murder of Zechariah
son of Berakiah, whom you murdered between the
Temple and the altar. 36I tell you the truth, all of
these things will happen to you people who are
living now.

Jesus Feels Sorry for Jerusalem

37"Jerusalem, Jerusalem! You kill the prophets
and stone to death those who are sent to you. Many
times I wanted to gather your people as a hen gathers her chicks under her wings, but you did not let
me. 38Now your house will be left completely
empty. 39I tell you, you will not see me again until
that time when you will say, 'God bless the One
who comes in the name of the Lord.'"

The Temple Will Be Destroyed

24 As Jesus left the Temple and was walking
away, his followers came up to show him
the Temple's buildings. 2Jesus asked, "Do you
see all these buildings? I tell you the truth, not
one stone will be left on another. Every stone will
be thrown down to the ground."
3Later, as Jesus was sitting on the Mount of
Olives, his followers came to be alone with him.
They said, "Tell us, when will these things happen?
And what will be the sign that it is time for you to
come again and for this age to end?"
4Jesus answered, "Be careful that no one fools
you. 5Many will come in my name, saying, 'I am
the Christ,' and they will fool many people. 6You
will hear about wars and stories of wars that are
coming, but don't be afraid. These things must
happen before the end comes. 7Nations will fight
against other nations; kingdoms will fight against
other kingdoms. There will be times when there
is no food for people to eat, and there will be
earthquakes in different places. 8These things
are like the first pains when something new is
about to be born.
9"Then people will arrest you, hand you over to
be hurt, and kill you. They will hate you because
you believe in me. 10At that time, many will lose
their faith, and they will turn against each other and
hate each other. 11Many false prophets will come
and cause many people to believe lies. 12There will
be more and more evil in the world, so most people
will stop showing their love for each other. 13But
those people who keep their faith until the end will
be saved. 14The Good News about God's kingdom will be preached in all the world, to every
nation. Then the end will come.
15"Daniel the prophet spoke about 'the destroying terror.' You will see this standing in the holy
place." (You who read this should understand what
it means.) 16"At that time, the people in Judea
should run away to the mountains. 17If people are
on the roofs of their houses, they must not go down
to get anything out of their houses. 18If people are
in the fields, they must not go back to get their
coats. 19At that time, how terrible it will be for
women who are pregnant or have nursing babies!
20Pray that it will not be winter or a Sabbath day
when these things happen and you have to run
away, 21because at that time there will be much
trouble. There will be more trouble than there has
ever been since the beginning of the world until
now, and nothing as bad will ever happen again.
22God has decided to make that terrible time short.
Otherwise, no one would go on living. But God
will make that time short to help the people he has
chosen. 23At that time, someone might say to you,
'Look, there is the Christ!' Or another person might

23:35 *Abel . . . Zechariah.* In the order of the books of the Hebrew Old Testament, the first and last men to be murdered.

23:37 Jerusalem: Galatians 4:26

23:39 *'God . . . Lord.'* Quotation from Psalm 118:26.

23:39 Martyrdom: Matthew 26:1–27:56

23:39 Scribes (Teachers of the Law): Mark 1:22

24:1 Presence of God: See article on page 971.

24:7 Famine: Revelation 7:16

24:9 Hate: Luke 6:27

24:13 Perseverance: Mark 4:3–8

24:14 World/Worldly: John 3:16

24:15 *'the destroying terror.'* Mentioned in Daniel 9:27; 12:11 (see also Daniel 11:31).

24:17 *roofs.* In Bible times houses were built with flat roofs. The roof was used for drying things such as flax and fruit. And it was used as an extra room, as a place for worship, and as a cool place to sleep in the summer.

say, 'There he is!' But don't believe them. 24False
Christs and false prophets will come and perform
great wonders and miracles. They will try to fool
even the people God has chosen, if that is possible. 25Now I have warned you about this before
it happens.
26"If people tell you, 'The Christ is in the
desert,' don't go there. If they say, 'The Christ is
in the inner room,' don't believe it. 27When the
Son of Man comes, he will be seen by everyone,
like lightning flashing from the east to the west.
28Wherever the dead body is, there the vultures
will gather.
29"Soon after the trouble of those days,
'the sun will grow dark,
and the moon will not give its light.
The stars will fall from the sky.
And the powers of the heavens
will be shaken.' *Isaiah 13:10; 34:4*
30"At that time, the sign of the Son of Man will
appear in the sky. Then all the peoples of the world
will cry. They will see the Son of Man coming on
clouds in the sky with great power and glory. 31He
will use a loud trumpet to send his angels all around
the earth, and they will gather his chosen people
from every part of the world.
32"Learn a lesson from the fig tree: When its
branches become green and soft and new leaves
appear, you know summer is near. 33In the same
way, when you see all these things happening, you
will know that the time is near, ready to come. 34I
tell you the truth, all these things will happen while
the people of this time are still living. 35Earth and
sky will be destroyed, but the words I have said
will never be destroyed.

When Will Jesus Come Again?

36"No one knows when that day or time will be,
not the angels in heaven, not even the Son. Only
the Father knows. 37When the Son of Man comes,
it will be like what happened during Noah's time.
38In those days before the flood, people were eating
and drinking, marrying and giving their children to
be married, until the day Noah entered the boat.
39They knew nothing about what was happening
until the flood came and destroyed them. It will be
the same when the Son of Man comes. 40Two
men will be in the field. One will be taken, and the
other will be left. 41Two women will be grinding
grain with a mill. One will be taken, and the
other will be left.
42"So always be ready, because you don't know
the day your Lord will come. 43Remember this: If
the owner of the house knew what time of night a
thief was coming, the owner would watch and not
let the thief break in. 44So you also must be ready,
because the Son of Man will come at a time you
don't expect him.
45"Who is the wise and loyal servant that the
master trusts to give the other servants their food
at the right time? 46When the master comes and
finds the servant doing his work, the servant will
be blessed. 47I tell you the truth, the master will
choose that servant to take care of everything he
owns. 48But suppose that evil servant thinks to
himself, 'My master will not come back soon,'
49and he begins to beat the other servants and eat
and get drunk with others like him? 50The master
will come when that servant is not ready and is
not expecting him. 51Then the master will cut
him in pieces and send him away to be with the
hypocrites, where people will cry and grind their
teeth with pain.

A Story About Ten Bridesmaids

25 "At that time the kingdom of heaven will
be like ten bridesmaids who took their
lamps and went to wait for the bridegroom. 2Five
of them were foolish and five were wise. 3The five
foolish bridesmaids took their lamps, but they did
not take more oil for the lamps to burn. 4The wise
bridesmaids took their lamps and more oil in jars.
5Because the bridegroom was late, they became
sleepy and went to sleep.
6"At midnight someone cried out, 'The bridegroom is coming! Come and meet him!' 7Then all
the bridesmaids woke up and got their lamps
ready. 8But the foolish ones said to the wise,
'Give us some of your oil, because our lamps are
going out.' 9The wise bridesmaids answered, 'No,

24:24 Leadership: Mark 9:35

24:38 Jesus refers in this passage to the Flood in Genesis 6–9. From the time of God's announcement to Noah to the beginning of the rain, 120 years elapsed. During that time Noah preached a message of repentance to the people. God waited patiently for the people in Noah's time to repent, but the people refused to heed Noah's message until it was too late for deliverance. Instead, the people ate, drank, and lived as if judgment would never come. Jesus used the story of the Flood to warn the church not to be lax while waiting for his second coming. As surely as the Flood judged the wicked in the ancient world, so Christ will come back to judge the wicked in the coming age. Only those who are in God's favor ("in the ark" so to speak) will be saved. The others, like Noah's wicked neighbors, will be left behind. The Flood story is also referred to in 1 Peter 3:20 to highlight God's patience and mercy.

24:39 Flood: Luke 17:27

24:41 *mill.* Two large, round, flat rocks used for grinding grain to make flour.

24:47 Servant of the Lord: Matthew 25:21

24:51 Hell: Matthew 25:30

24:51 Parables: Matthew 25:14–46

the oil we have might not be enough for all of us.
Go to the people who sell oil and buy some for
yourselves.'
10"So while the five foolish bridesmaids went
to buy oil, the bridegroom came. The bridesmaids
who were ready went in with the bridegroom to
the wedding feast. Then the door was closed and
locked.
11"Later the others came back and said, 'Sir, sir,
open the door to let us in.' 12But the bridegroom
answered, 'I tell you the truth, I don't want to know
you.'
13"So always be ready, because you don't know
the day or the hour the Son of Man will come.⚭

A Story About Three Servants

14"The kingdom of heaven is like a man who
was going to another place for a visit. Before he
left, he called for his servants and told them to
take care of his things while he was gone. 15He
gave one servant five bags of gold, another servant two bags of gold, and a third servant one bag
of gold, to each one as much as he could handle.
Then he left. 16The servant who got five bags
went quickly to invest the money and earned
five more bags. 17In the same way, the servant
who had two bags invested them and earned two
more. 18But the servant who got one bag went
out and dug a hole in the ground and hid the
master's money.
19"After a long time the master came home
and asked the servants what they did with his
money. 20The servant who was given five bags of
gold brought five more bags to the master and
said, 'Master, you trusted me to care for five bags
of gold, so I used your five bags to earn five
more.'⚭ 21The master answered, 'You did well.
You are a good and loyal servant. Because you
were loyal with small things, I will let you care for
much greater things. Come and share my joy
with me.'⚭
22"Then the servant who had been given two
bags of gold came to the master and said, 'Master,
you gave me two bags of gold to care for, so I used
your two bags to earn two more.' 23The master
answered, 'You did well. You are a good and loyal
servant. Because you were loyal with small things, I
will let you care for much greater things. Come and
share my joy with me.'
24"Then the servant who had been given one
bag of gold came to the master and said, 'Master,
I knew that you were a hard man. You harvest
things you did not plant. You gather crops where
you did not sow any seed. 25So I was afraid and
went and hid your money in the ground. Here is
your bag of gold.' 26The master answered, 'You
are a wicked and lazy servant! You say you knew
that I harvest things I did not plant and that I
gather crops where I did not sow any seed. 27So
you should have put my gold in the bank. Then,
when I came home, I would have received my
gold back with interest.'
28"So the master told his other servants, 'Take
the bag of gold from that servant and give it to the
servant who has ten bags of gold. 29Those who
have much will get more, and they will have much
more than they need. But those who do not have
much will have everything taken away from them.'
30Then the master said, 'Throw that useless servant outside, into the darkness where people will
cry and grind their teeth with pain.'⚭

Much of Israel's wealth came from their flocks of sheep (front) and goats (back).

The King Will Judge All People

31"The Son of Man will come again in his great
glory, with all his angels. He will be King and sit
on his great throne. 32All the nations of the world
will be gathered before him, and he will separate
them into two groups as a shepherd separates the
sheep from the goats. 33The Son of Man will put
the sheep on his right and the goats on his left.
34"Then the King will say to the people on his

⚭**25:13 Hope:** Romans 5:1–5
25:14–30 Among all created things, people have the unique position of being stewards for all creation (themselves included). But, "the earth is the Lord's" (Psalm 24:1). The earth belongs to God and has been entrusted to us to use wisely. People committed to being God's stewards can do much to help care for and protect nature. Nature is ours to use but not to abuse.
⚭**25:20 Service:** Matthew 25:31–46
⚭**25:20 Stewardship:** Luke 11:42
⚭**25:21 Servant of the Lord:** Luke 1:38
⚭**25:30 Hell:** Matthew 25:46
⚭**25:30 Work:** Luke 10:38–42

right, 'Come, my Father has given you his blessing. Receive the kingdom God has prepared for you since the world was made. 35I was hungry, and you gave me food. I was thirsty, and you gave me something to drink. I was alone and away from home, and you invited me into your house. 36I was without clothes, and you gave me something to wear. I was sick, and you cared for me. I was in prison, and you visited me.'

37"Then the good people will answer, 'Lord, when did we see you hungry and give you food, or thirsty and give you something to drink? 38When did we see you alone and away from home and invite you into our house? When did we see you without clothes and give you something to wear? 39When did we see you sick or in prison and care for you?'

40"Then the King will answer, 'I tell you the truth, anything you did for even the least of my people here, you also did for me.'

41"Then the King will say to those on his left, 'Go away from me. You will be punished. Go into the fire that burns forever that was prepared for the devil and his angels. 42I was hungry, and you gave me nothing to eat. I was thirsty, and you gave me nothing to drink. 43I was alone and away from home, and you did not invite me into your house. I was without clothes, and you gave me nothing to wear. I was sick and in prison, and you did not care for me.'

44"Then those people will answer, 'Lord, when did we see you hungry or thirsty or alone and away from home or without clothes or sick or in prison? When did we see these things and not help you?'

45"Then the King will answer, 'I tell you the truth, anything you refused to do for even the least of my people here, you refused to do for me.'

46"These people will go off to be punished forever, but the good people will go to live forever."

The Plan to Kill Jesus

26 After Jesus finished saying all these things, he told his followers, 2"You know that the day after tomorrow is the day of the Passover Feast. On that day the Son of Man will be given to his enemies to be crucified."

3Then the leading priests and the older leaders had a meeting at the palace of the high priest, named Caiaphas. 4At the meeting, they planned to set a trap to arrest Jesus and kill him. 5But they said, "We must not do it during the feast, because the people might cause a riot."

Perfume for Jesus' Burial

6Jesus was in Bethany at the house of Simon, who had a skin disease. 7While Jesus was there, a woman approached him with an alabaster jar filled with expensive perfume. She poured this perfume on Jesus' head while he was eating.

8His followers were upset when they saw the woman do this. They asked, "Why waste that perfume? 9It could have been sold for a great deal of money and the money given to the poor."

10Knowing what had happened, Jesus said, "Why are you troubling this woman? She did an excellent thing for me. 11You will always have the poor with you, but you will not always have me. 12This woman poured perfume on my body to prepare me for burial. 13I tell you the truth, wherever the Good News is preached in all the world, what this woman has done will be told, and people will remember her."

Judas Becomes an Enemy of Jesus

14Then one of the twelve apostles, Judas Iscariot, went to talk to the leading priests. 15He said, "What will you pay me for giving Jesus to you?" And they gave him thirty silver coins. 16After that, Judas watched for the best time to turn Jesus in.

Jesus Eats the Passover Meal

17On the first day of the Feast of Unleavened Bread, the followers came to Jesus. They said, "Where do you want us to prepare for you to eat the Passover meal?"

18Jesus answered, "Go into the city to a certain man and tell him, 'The Teacher says: The chosen time is near. I will have the Passover with my followers at your house.'" 19The followers did what

25:35 Foreigner (Alien): Matthew 25:38
25:36 Hell: Romans 2:8–9
25:38 Foreigner (Alien): Matthew 25:43
25:40 Abortion and Crisis Pregnancy: Acts 6:1–7
25:40 Family: Genesis 22:12
25:41 Angels: Luke 20:35–36
25:43 Foreigner (Alien): Matthew 25:44
25:44 Foreigner (Alien): Ephesians 2:19–20
25:46 Hospitality: Mark 8:1–10
25:46 Money: Mark 10:17–31
25:46 Parables: Mark 4:1–20
25:46 Service: Mark 10:42–45

26:6–13 In Matthew's story of Jesus' death and resurrection, there are many people who demonstrate remarkable faith at the same time that those closest to Jesus, the followers, are noted for their failure. The name of this woman may not be remembered, but her deed is. She understood that Jesus was heading toward his death even when his followers did not.

26:13 Table Fellowship/Lord's Supper: Mark 8:1–9
26:14 Judas: Matthew 27:3
26:17 Feasts/Festivals: Mark 14:12

Jesus told them to do, and they prepared the Passover meal.

20In the evening Jesus was sitting at the table with his twelve followers. 21As they were eating, Jesus said, "I tell you the truth, one of you will turn against me."

22This made the followers very sad. Each one began to say to Jesus, "Surely, Lord, I am not the one who will turn against you, am I?"

23Jesus answered, "The man who has dipped his hand with me into the bowl is the one who will turn against me. 24The Son of Man will die, just as the Scriptures say. But how terrible it will be for the person who hands the Son of Man over to be killed. It would be better for him if he had never been born."

25Then Judas, who would give Jesus to his enemies, said to Jesus, "Teacher, surely I am not the one, am I?"

Jesus answered, "Yes, it is you."

The Lord's Supper

26While they were eating, Jesus took some bread and thanked God for it and broke it. Then he gave it to his followers and said, "Take this bread and eat it; this is my body."

27Then Jesus took a cup and thanked God for it and gave it to the followers. He said, "Every one of you drink this. 28This is my blood which is the new agreement that God makes with his people. This blood is poured out for many to forgive their sins. 29I tell you this: I will not drink of this fruit of the vine again until that day when I drink it new with you in my Father's kingdom."

30After singing a hymn, they went out to the Mount of Olives.

Jesus' Followers Will Leave Him

31Jesus told his followers, "Tonight you will all stumble in your faith on account of me, because it is written in the Scriptures:

'I will kill the shepherd,
and the sheep will scatter.' *Zechariah 13:7*

32But after I rise from the dead, I will go ahead of you into Galilee."

33Peter said, "Everyone else may stumble in their faith because of you, but I will not."

34Jesus said, "I tell you the truth, tonight before the rooster crows you will say three times that you don't know me."

35But Peter said, "I will never say that I don't know you! I will even die with you!" And all the other followers said the same thing.

Jesus Prays Alone

36Then Jesus went with his followers to a place called Gethsemane. He said to them, "Sit here while I go over there and pray." 37He took Peter and the two sons of Zebedee with him, and he began to be very sad and troubled. 38He said to them, "My heart is full of sorrow, to the point of death. Stay here and watch with me."

39After walking a little farther away from them, Jesus fell to the ground and prayed, "My Father, if it is possible, do not give me this cup of suffering. But do what you want, not what I want." 40Then Jesus went back to his followers and found them asleep. He said to Peter, "You men could not stay awake with me for one hour? 41Stay awake and pray for strength against temptation. The spirit wants to do what is right, but the body is weak."

42Then Jesus went away a second time and prayed, "My Father, if it is not possible for this painful thing to be taken from me, and if I must do it, I pray that what you want will be done."

43Then he went back to his followers, and again he found them asleep, because their eyes were heavy. 44So Jesus left them and went away and prayed a third time, saying the same thing.

45Then Jesus went back to his followers and said, "Are you still sleeping and resting? The time has come for the Son of Man to be handed over to sinful people. 46Get up, we must go. Look, here comes the man who has turned against me."

Jesus Is Arrested

47While Jesus was still speaking, Judas, one of the twelve apostles, came up. With him were many people carrying swords and clubs who had been sent from the leading priests and the older Jewish leaders of the people. 48Judas had planned to give them a signal, saying, "The man I kiss is Jesus. Arrest him." 49At once Judas went to Jesus and said, "Greetings, Teacher!" and kissed him.

50Jesus answered, "Friend, do what you came to do."

Then the people came and grabbed Jesus and arrested him. 51When that happened, one of Jesus'

26:29 *fruit of the vine.* Product of the grapevine; this may also be translated "wine."
26:30 Celebration: Mark 6:21
26:35 Peter: Matthew 26:51
26:39 Alcohol: Luke 10:34
26:39 Anger: Ephesians 4:26

26:39 *cup.* Jesus is talking about the terrible things that will happen to him. Accepting these things will be very hard, like drinking a cup of something bitter.
26:41 Test/Temptation: 1 Corinthians 3:13
26:46 Mount of Olives: Mark 14:32–42

Spirituality/ Spiritual Dryness

1 Corinthians 3:1

Does the Bible make use of the concept of spirituality? How?
What are the marks of a truly spiritual people? Is there a spirituality unique to Christian faith?
Is there such a thing as spiritual dryness? What role does it play in spiritual growth?

While the term "spirituality" does not appear in the Bible, the concept is salted through both the Old and the New Testaments. As with other themes in Scripture, there are true and false expressions of the spiritual life. The Corinthians are a prime example of Christians who were living with false notions of spirituality (see 1 Corinthians 5–8) sufficient for Paul to tell them, "I could not talk to you as I talk to spiritual people" (3:1). Likewise today we are living in a time when "spirituality" is a hot topic and a time when genuine and counterfeit expressions can be found. For that reason, it is important for us to be guided by a biblical understanding of the concept. The following terms describe the basic elements of authentic spirituality.

Essence. Spirituality is not a *part* of life; it *is* life. We do not *have* a spiritual life; we *are* spiritual beings. We are made in the image of God (Genesis 1:26–27). Through our creation, we believe that human beings are categorically distinctive from other forms of life. The psalmist echoes this perspective by writing, "You made them a little lower than the angels and crowned them with glory and honor" (8:5). To view ourselves in this way transforms spirituality from a compartment of human life to the nature of human life. This does not mean that we are gods, as some *New Age* teaching suggests. The Bible preserves the Creator-creature distinction. But it does mean that human life is spiritual in its essence; we are living souls.

Encounter. Because we are made in God's image, we have the capacity for relationship with God, others, and ourselves. We possess a hunger for *religion*, for *community*, and for *self-awareness*. Spirituality creates, sustains, and guides the human quest in each of these areas. At the deepest level, it means that we can know God and be known by God. It is God's nature to reveal; it is our nature to respond to that revelation, allowing it to shape us in all the particulars of our lives.

Enrichment. Spirituality is not a static, once-for-all quality. Just as the infant can develop into an adult, our spiritual lives can mature. Here is where terms like *spiritual formation*, *disciple-making*, the *deeper life*, and *Christian growth* come into play. We acknowledge our spirituality as the nature of our existence. We cultivate our spirituality all the days of our lives. We do so both in terms of the deepening of what we already know and the expansion of life into new areas.

When viewed in these ways, spirituality can be seen in virtually every verse in the Bible. The whole of Scripture is about establishing, maintaining, and developing our lives in God. At times we see the ways we have failed to live up to the ideal of true spirituality. At other times we are given glorious visions of what we can become by grace. Along the way we are warned, encouraged, counseled, guided, instructed, comforted, strengthened, protected, forgiven, healed, and empowered.

No verse or book gives us the complete picture. That's why the concept of spirituality grows as we become increasingly familiar with the whole of Scripture. Exposure to certain portions of the Bible will enrich our concept of spirituality in different ways. For example, Leviticus connects spirituality to the related idea of "holiness." The Psalms invite personal and corporate expression of the spiritual life in worship. The prophets describe the motifs of exile and return. First Corinthians 3:1 reveals the struggle involved in spiritual growth, and the dangers of making too many untested assumptions about our spirituality. From the whole of Scripture we can lift out key marks of true spirituality.

Character. If spirituality is rooted in our essence as human beings, then it is exemplified through dimensions of our personhood: integrity, morality, fidelity, among others. We need look no further than the fruit of the Spirit in Galatians 5:22–23 to see the qualities of character which are essential for true spirituality. These qualities include love, joy, peace, patience, kindness, goodness, faithfulness, gentleness, and self-control. As we reflect on each dimension, it is important for us to remember that the spiritual life is ultimately validated by who we are. From the bedrock of character we move to express inner qualities in outer activities.

Conduct. Behavior follows closely on the heels of personhood. The little Book of James serves us well in keeping faith and good works connected (2:14–26). James tells it like it is when he writes, "Faith that does nothing is dead" (2:26). The many activities commended in Scripture are the natural outflow of any person living in vital relationship with God. A spirituality which does not find expression in the routines and details of life is suspect at best, counterfeit at worst.

Community. True spirituality creates the desire for supportive relationships. We cannot live by ourselves or for ourselves. We need each other. Our spirituality is rounded out, developed, and expressed in relation to others. At the heart of community is our participation in the church, the Body of Christ. Unchecked, private spirituality eventually becomes no spirituality at all.

Commitment. The spiritual life is expressed in never-ending devotion. While it is possible to counterfeit the spiritual life in neurotic *perfectionism*, we are nevertheless engaged with God and others in ways which call forth our best. *Half-hearted spirituality* is a contradiction in terms. The infinite God is capable of providing us with ever-expanding attitudes and actions. Jesus taught that truly spiritual people "want to do right more than anything else" (Matthew 5:6).

Compassion. In the Old Testament the Suffering Servant stands as a dominant picture of the Messiah (Isaiah 53). As the Messiah, Jesus amplified the servant role through his life and teachings. From him we get the message that there is no authentic spirituality apart from caring for one another, especially the poor, oppressed, and those entrapped by sin. Thus, spirituality has profound social and evangelistic expressions. Across the centuries we see numerous examples of those saints who combined deep piety with notable servanthood.

It is possible to view character, conduct, community, commitment, and compassion as general marks of the spiritual life. Indeed, we can look at other major religions in the world and see these qualities manifested in one way or another. This raises the question, Is there a spirituality unique to Christian faith? The answer is decidedly yes. A look at Christian spirituality, however, begins in the key words we've just examined. Once again, the Bible shapes our understanding of the words, providing us with distinctively Christian definitions and expressions. This means that one feature of a unique Christian spirituality is that it is rooted in Scripture.

A second feature of Christian spirituality is the church. By this we mean two thousand years of tradition, coupled with contemporary expressions of Christian community. Just as we are not free to violate the Bible in our spirituality, so we are not at liberty to dissociate ourselves from the accumulated wisdom of twenty centuries or the manifestation of the Body of Christ in the world today. Vital church membership and true spirituality go hand in hand. The church is our reminder that we have no permission to "go it alone" or "make things up as we go" in the spiritual life.

Ultimately, however, the uniqueness of Christian spirituality is not in a book or a community. It is in Christ Jesus of Nazareth. Christian spirituality is inextricably connected to Christ's person, Christ's example, Christ's teaching, and Christ's presence through the Spirit. In a radically pluralistic age, this strikes some as hopelessly narrow. But because of who we believe Christ is, we believe it is marvelously revealing. Christians are *Christ-ones.* In belonging to him, we believe we can belong to God, others, and ourselves in ways we could not apart from him. Rather than restricting our spirituality, we believe Christ sets us free to experience the spiritual life in ways which cannot be paralleled or surpassed anywhere else. In Christ we experience both a centered spirituality and a creative spirituality.

Having set forth all these wonderful things about the spiritual life in general and Christian spirituality in particular, we might wonder if the saints just "float along" on ever-deepening experiences of God. A look at Scripture and tradition expands the picture of spirituality by introducing us to the idea of spiritual dryness, sometimes to the point of despair. Elijah is a burned-out prophet (1 Kings 19); Jeremiah knows deep sadness (Jeremiah 8:18–22). The psalmists cry out to God in times of doubt and frustration (6; 13; 22; 38; 42; 69; 77). Jesus knows unimaginable agony (Matthew 27:46; Luke 22:44).

Spiritual dryness has a myriad of causes. That's why we must be careful in making too quick a diagnosis in ourselves, and especially in others, when it occurs. At times it may be the result of unconfessed or hidden sin. At other times, something as natural as fatigue may be the culprit. Often, it is the result of circumstances beyond our control. Whatever the cause, spiritual dryness is not a sign of failure, so much as it is a warning light in the soul, telling us that something is happening which needs our attention. Paul put it well in describing his own experience: "This happened so we would not trust in ourselves but in God" (2 Corinthians 1:9). Whatever else it may be, spiritual dryness is an opportunity to draw close to God and to remember where the ultimate source of spirituality is. Spiritual dryness is a reminder that the spiritual life is not grounded in emotion, but in faith—faith in the one who is present in darkness as well as light.

Spirituality/Spiritual Dryness: For additional scriptures on this topic go to Leviticus 11:1–20:27.

followers reached for his sword and pulled it out. He struck the servant of the high priest and cut off his ear.

52 Jesus said to the man, "Put your sword back in its place. All who use swords will be killed with swords. 53 Surely you know I could ask my Father, and he would give me more than twelve armies of angels. 54 But it must happen this way to bring about what the Scriptures say."

55 Then Jesus said to the crowd, "You came to get me with swords and clubs as if I were a criminal. Every day I sat in the Temple teaching, and you did not arrest me there. 56 But all these things have happened so that it will come about as the prophets wrote." Then all of Jesus' followers left him and ran away.

Jesus Before the Leaders

57 Those people who arrested Jesus led him to the house of Caiaphas, the high priest, where the teachers of the law and the older leaders were gathered. 58 Peter followed far behind to the courtyard of the high priest's house, and he sat down with the guards to see what would happen to Jesus.

59 The leading priests and the whole council tried to find something false against Jesus so they could kill him. 60 Many people came and told lies about him, but the council could find no real reason to kill him. Then two people came and said, 61 "This man said, 'I can destroy the Temple of God and build it again in three days.'"

62 Then the high priest stood up and said to Jesus, "Aren't you going to answer? Don't you have something to say about their charges against you?" 63 But Jesus said nothing.

Again the high priest said to Jesus, "I command you by the power of the living God: Tell us if you are the Christ, the Son of God."

64 Jesus answered, "Those are your words. But I tell you, in the future you will see the Son of Man sitting at the right hand of God, the Powerful One, and coming on clouds in the sky."

65 When the high priest heard this, he tore his clothes and said, "This man has said things that are against God! We don't need any more witnesses; you all heard him say these things against God. 66 What do you think?"

The people answered, "He should die."

67 Then the people there spat in Jesus' face and beat him with their fists. Others slapped him. 68 They said, "Prove to us that you are a prophet, you Christ! Tell us who hit you!"

Peter Says He Doesn't Know Jesus

69 At that time, as Peter was sitting in the courtyard, a servant girl came to him and said, "You also were with Jesus of Galilee."

70 But Peter said to all the people there that he was never with Jesus. He said, "I don't know what you are talking about."

71 When he left the courtyard and was at the gate, another girl saw him. She said to the people there, "This man was with Jesus of Nazareth."

72 Again, Peter said he was never with him, saying, "I swear I don't know this man Jesus!"

73 A short time later, some people standing there went to Peter and said, "Surely you are one of those who followed Jesus. The way you talk shows it."

74 Then Peter began to place a curse on himself and swear, "I don't know the man." At once, a rooster crowed. 75 And Peter remembered what Jesus had told him: "Before the rooster crows, you will say three times that you don't know me." Then Peter went outside and cried painfully.

Jesus Is Taken to Pilate

27 Early the next morning, all the leading priests and older leaders of the people decided that Jesus should die. 2 They tied him, led him away, and turned him over to Pilate, the governor.

Judas Kills Himself

3 Judas, the one who had given Jesus to his enemies, saw that they had decided to kill Jesus. Then he was very sorry for what he had done. So he took the thirty silver coins back to the priests and the leaders, 4 saying, "I sinned; I handed over to you an innocent man."

The leaders answered, "What is that to us? That's your problem, not ours."

5 So Judas threw the money into the Temple. Then he went off and hanged himself.

6 The leading priests picked up the silver coins in the Temple and said, "Our law does not allow us to keep this money with the Temple money, because it has paid for a man's death." 7 So they decided to use the coins to buy Potter's Field as a place to bury strangers who died in Jerusalem. 8 That is why that field is still called the Field of Blood. 9 So what Jeremiah the prophet had said

26:51 Peter: Matthew 26:58–75
26:54 Holy War & Divine Warrior: Ephesians 6:10–20
26:65 Blasphemy: Acts 26:11
26:75 Peter: Mark 1:16–20

27:2 Pontius Pilate: Matthew 27:11–26
27:3 Judas: Mark 14:43
27:9–10 *"They . . . commanded me."* See Zechariah 11:12-13 and Jeremiah 32:6-9.

came true: "They took thirty silver coins. That is
how little the Israelites thought he was worth.
10They used those thirty silver coins to buy the
potter's field, as the Lord commanded me."

Pilate Questions Jesus

11Jesus stood before Pilate the governor, and
Pilate asked him, "Are you the king of the Jews?"
Jesus answered, "Those are your words."
12When the leading priests and the older leaders
accused Jesus, he said nothing.
13So Pilate said to Jesus, "Don't you hear them
accusing you of all these things?"
14But Jesus said nothing in answer to Pilate, and
Pilate was very surprised at this.

Pilate Tries to Free Jesus

15Every year at the time of Passover the governor would free one prisoner whom the people
chose. 16At that time there was a man in prison,
named Barabbas, who was known to be very bad.
17When the people gathered at Pilate's house, Pilate
said, "Whom do you want me to set free: Barabbas
or Jesus who is called the Christ?" 18Pilate knew
that the people turned Jesus in to him because they
were jealous.
19While Pilate was sitting there on the judge's
seat, his wife sent this message to him: "Don't do
anything to that man, because he is innocent.
Today I had a dream about him, and it troubled me
very much."
20But the leading priests and older leaders convinced the crowd to ask for Barabbas to be freed
and for Jesus to be killed.
21Pilate said, "I have Barabbas and Jesus. Which
do you want me to set free for you?"
The people answered, "Barabbas."
22Pilate asked, "So what should I do with Jesus,
the one called the Christ?"
They all answered, "Crucify him!"
23Pilate asked, "Why? What wrong has he done?"
But they shouted louder, "Crucify him!"
24When Pilate saw that he could do nothing
about this and that a riot was starting, he took
some water and washed his hands in front of the
crowd. Then he said, "I am not guilty of this man's
death. You are the ones who are causing it!"
25All the people answered, "We and our children
will be responsible for his death."
26Then he set Barabbas free. But Jesus was
beaten with whips and handed over to the soldiers
to be crucified.
27The governor's soldiers took Jesus into the governor's palace, and they all gathered around him.
28They took off his clothes and put a red robe on
him. 29Using thorny branches, they made a crown,
put it on his head, and put a stick in his right hand.
Then the soldiers bowed before Jesus and made
fun of him, saying, "Hail, King of the Jews!" 30They
spat on Jesus. Then they took his stick and began to
beat him on the head. 31After they finished, the soldiers took off the robe and put his own clothes on
him again. Then they led him away to be crucified.

Jesus Is Crucified

32As the soldiers were going out of the city with
Jesus, they forced a man from Cyrene, named
Simon, to carry the cross for Jesus. 33They all came
to the place called Golgotha, which means the Place
of the Skull. 34The soldiers gave Jesus wine mixed
with gall to drink. He tasted the wine but refused to
drink it. 35When the soldiers had crucified him, they
threw lots to decide who would get his clothes.
36The soldiers sat there and continued watching
him. 37They put a sign above Jesus' head with a
charge against him. It said: THIS IS JESUS, THE KING
OF THE JEWS. 38Two robbers were crucified beside
Jesus, one on the right and the other on the left.
39People walked by and insulted Jesus and shook
their heads, 40saying, "You said you could destroy
the Temple and build it again in three days. So save
yourself! Come down from that cross if you are
really the Son of God!"
41The leading priests, the teachers of the law, and
the older Jewish leaders were also making fun of
Jesus. 42They said, "He saved others, but he can't
save himself! He says he is the king of Israel! If he
is the king, let him come down now from the cross.
Then we will believe in him. 43He trusts in God, so
let God save him now, if God really wants him. He
himself said, 'I am the Son of God.'" 44And in the
same way, the robbers who were being crucified
beside Jesus also insulted him.

Jesus Dies

45At noon the whole country became dark, and
the darkness lasted for three hours. 46About three
o'clock Jesus cried out in a loud voice, "Eli, Eli,
lama sabachthani?" This means, "My God, my
God, why have you rejected me?"
47Some of the people standing there who heard
this said, "He is calling Elijah."

27:19 Dreams: Acts 16:9
27:24 *washed his hands.* He did this as a sign to show that he wanted no part in what the people did.
27:25 Anti-Semitism: John 5:16–18
27:26 Pontius Pilate: Mark 15:1–15
27:34 *gall.* Probably a drink of wine mixed with drugs to help a person feel less pain.

48Quickly one of them ran and got a sponge and
filled it with vinegar and tied it to a stick and gave
it to Jesus to drink. 49But the others said, "Don't
bother him. We want to see if Elijah will come to
save him."
50But Jesus cried out again in a loud voice and
died.
51Then the curtain in the Temple was torn into
two pieces, from the top to the bottom. Also, the
earth shook and rocks broke apart. 52The graves
opened, and many of God's people who had died
were raised from the dead. 53They came out of the
graves after Jesus was raised from the dead and
went into the holy city, where they appeared to
many people.
54When the army officer and the soldiers guarding Jesus saw this earthquake and everything else
that happened, they were very frightened and said,
"He really was the Son of God!"
55Many women who had followed Jesus from
Galilee to help him were standing at a distance
from the cross, watching. 56Mary Magdalene, and
Mary the mother of James and Joseph, and the
mother of James and John were there.

Jesus Is Buried

57That evening a rich man named Joseph, a follower of Jesus from the town of Arimathea, came
to Jerusalem. 58Joseph went to Pilate and asked to
have Jesus' body. So Pilate gave orders for the soldiers to give it to Joseph. 59Then Joseph took the
body and wrapped it in a clean linen cloth. 60He
put Jesus' body in a new tomb that he had cut out
of a wall of rock, and he rolled a very large stone to
block the entrance of the tomb. Then Joseph went
away. 61Mary Magdalene and the other woman
named Mary were sitting near the tomb.

The Tomb of Jesus Is Guarded

62The next day, the day after Preparation Day,
the leading priests and the Pharisees went to
Pilate. 63They said, "Sir, we remember that while
that liar was still alive he said, 'After three days I will
rise from the dead.' 64So give the order for the tomb
to be guarded closely till the third day. Otherwise,
his followers might come and steal the body and tell
people that he has risen from the dead. That lie
would be even worse than the first one."
65Pilate said, "Take some soldiers and go guard
the tomb the best way you know." 66So they all
went to the tomb and made it safe from thieves by
sealing the stone in the entrance and putting soldiers there to guard it.

Jesus Rises from the Dead

28 The day after the Sabbath day was the first
day of the week. At dawn on the first day,
Mary Magdalene and another woman named Mary
went to look at the tomb.
2At that time there was a strong earthquake. An
angel of the Lord came down from heaven, went to
the tomb, and rolled the stone away from the
entrance. Then he sat on the stone. 3He was shining as bright as lightning, and his clothes were
white as snow. 4The soldiers guarding the tomb
shook with fear because of the angel, and they
became like dead men.
5The angel said to the women, "Don't be afraid.
I know that you are looking for Jesus, who has been
crucified. 6He is not here. He has risen from the
dead as he said he would. Come and see the place
where his body was. 7And go quickly and tell his followers, 'Jesus has risen from the dead. He is going
into Galilee ahead of you, and you will see him
there.'" Then the angel said, "Now I have told you."
8The women left the tomb quickly. They were
afraid, but they were also very happy. They ran to
tell Jesus' followers what had happened. 9Suddenly,
Jesus met them and said, "Greetings." The women
came up to him, took hold of his feet, and worshiped him. 10Then Jesus said to them, "Don't be
afraid. Go and tell my followers to go on to Galilee,
and they will see me there."

The Soldiers Report to the Leaders

11While the women went to tell Jesus' followers,
some of the soldiers who had been guarding the
tomb went into the city to tell the leading priests
everything that had happened. 12Then the priests
met with the older leaders and made a plan. They
paid the soldiers a large amount of money 13and
said to them, "Tell the people that Jesus' followers
came during the night and stole the body while you
were asleep. 14If the governor hears about this, we
will satisfy him and save you from trouble." 15So the
soldiers kept the money and did as they were told.
And that story is still spread among the people
even today.

Jesus Talks to His Followers

16The eleven followers went to Galilee to the
mountain where Jesus had told them to go. 17On
the mountain they saw Jesus and worshiped
him, but some of them did not believe it was
really Jesus. 18Then Jesus came to them and said,
"All power in heaven and on earth is given to me.

27:51 *curtain in the Temple.* A curtain divided the Most Holy Place from the other part of the Temple. That was the special building in Jerusalem where God commanded the Jewish people to worship him.

27:56 Martyrdom: Mark 6:14–29

19So go and make followers of all people in the
world. Baptize them in the name of the Father
and the Son and the Holy Spirit. 20Teach them
to obey everything that I have taught you, and I
will be with you always, even until the end of
this age."

28:19 Racism: Mark 12:13–17

28:20 Jesus is the master teacher. Throughout his earthly life, he taught his followers about the ways of the Lord. The Gospels are full of the lessons he taught (Sermon on the Mount, parables). After Jesus' ascension into heaven, it became the church's job to continue teaching Christ's followers. The church can meet this task, since she is the Body of Christ, and the spirit of Christ dwells in her (Romans 8:9-ll).

28:20 Stress: John 14:27

28:20 Baptism: Mark 1:4–11

28:20 Disciple/Discipleship/Mentoring (Follow/Follower): Mark 1:16–20

28:20 Land/Inheritance: Mark 1:14–15

28:20 Mountain: Mark 13:14

28:20 Trinity: John 1:1–18

INTRODUCTION TO THE BOOK OF MARK

Mark Tells About the Power of Jesus

WHO WROTE THIS BOOK?

Church tradition is unanimous in naming Mark as the author of this book. He is also called John Mark in the New Testament.

TO WHOM WAS THIS BOOK WRITTEN?

Mark was most likely writing to a non-Jewish audience, perhaps to the church at Rome. This is based on the book's translation of Aramaic words, explanations of Jewish customs, and external commentators.

WHERE WAS IT WRITTEN?

Because Mark worked with Peter in ministry, this book may have been written in Rome where Peter was near the end of his ministry.

WHEN WAS IT WRITTEN?

The book could have been authored anywhere from A.D. 50 to 70. If it was written near the end of Peter's life, its date would be in the A.D. 60s when Nero's persecution of the church began in earnest.

WHAT IS THE BOOK ABOUT?

The major thrust of Mark's account of the Good News is the ministry, death, and resurrection of Jesus. It begins with the baptism of Jesus and moves briskly to Jesus' public ministry in Galilee and the surrounding regions. It concludes with his final trip to Jerusalem and the events of his crucifixion. Mark emphasizes Jesus' role as Teacher, and particularly his teachings about suffering and discipleship.

WHY WAS THIS BOOK WRITTEN?

The Book of Mark was written to show non-Jews (Gentiles) how Jesus, as a true Israelite, submitted himself to the word of God. It shows that he is both the Son of God and the Son of Man. Mark stresses Jesus' power over sickness and death, as well as his teaching about suffering to encourage a persecuted church.

SO WHAT DOES THIS BOOK MEAN TO US?

Jesus was the suffering servant of God. He took upon himself our sins, and he accepted the cruel penalty that rightly belongs to each of us. Jesus set an example of self-sacrifice, humility, and submission to the will of God that we, as his followers, need to imitate daily. If we follow his beautiful example well, non-Christians around us will be drawn to the Savior through us.

SUMMARY:

The Book of Mark was probably the first account of the Good News to be written. Like the other three accounts of the life of Christ, Mark tells the story of Jesus' ministry in story form intending it primarily for a Christian audience. Its main purpose is to interpret and proclaim the significance of Jesus for followers struggling with the pressures of faithful living in the midst of trials and suffering.

How does Mark address these important issues? The Book of Mark has two main storylines that thread their way through the entire narrative. The first storyline has to do with the identity of Jesus. At the outset Mark presents Jesus as the Christ, Son of God. He roots Jesus' identity and mission in the good news promised in the Old Testament book of Isaiah. Following this, he portrays Jesus as God's agent who brings the kingdom of God, as shown in Jesus' miracles and teaching.

Although the first half of the Book of Mark is especially concerned with the power of Jesus—his miracles and authority—one also reads numerous and regular allusions to his coming suffering and death. Similarly, although the second half of Mark is concerned above all with the anticipations and events of Jesus' suffering and death, one also finds continuing references to power and authority. This shows that Jesus is the one whose authoritative teaching and powerful miracles lead to his death on the cross. The cross of Christ, then, is not a contradiction of Jesus' status as God's Son, but it is the natural conclusion to a life lived in utter obedience to God in the midst of a world that resists God's purpose.

The second storyline in the Book of Mark focuses on how Jesus' special followers (apostles) respond to their Teacher. Although they join his band of followers easily enough, they prove to be slow learners and often respond to Jesus as though they were his enemies. Although all four accounts of the Good News record how one of Jesus' special followers betrayed him and another denied him, these occurrences have special significance in Mark since they come at the end of a long narrative of the failure of the apostles.

The followers do not understand who Jesus is. In spite of his repeated teaching about his own identity and their need to embrace serving rather than greatness, they continue to struggle over these very issues. There are flashes of insight, such as when Peter affirms that Jesus is the Christ. But even in this instance Peter seems to think of Jesus in terms of his power and glory, rather than in terms of the necessity of his suffering and death.

Mark weaves together these two storylines for two reasons. First, Mark's narrative invites us to reflect more deeply on the significance of the story of Jesus. If the followers, who are so close to Jesus and continually hear him teach, do not understand fully what God is doing in Jesus, should Mark's readers not be challenged to think even more carefully on the meaning of these events? Second, Mark wants to show that suffering, and even death, are not incompatible with service to God. Following closely the ways of God does not guarantee that one will escape pain. Just as God is opposed, just as Jesus' ministry attracted conflict, so those who follow Jesus may anticipate hostility and resistance.

The Book of Mark continues the Old Testament story of promise and salvation. But it is also especially concerned with the new chapter in that story signaled by the arrival of Jesus. With his coming, the time of anticipation has come to an end, and people are both challenged and empowered to live new lives in the service of God's kingdom.

MARK

John Prepares for Jesus

This is the beginning of the Good News about
Jesus Christ, the Son of God, 2as the prophet
Isaiah wrote:

"I will send my messenger ahead of you,
who will prepare your way." *Malachi 3:1*

3"This is a voice of one
who calls out in the desert:
'Prepare the way for the Lord.
Make the road straight
for him.'" *Isaiah 40:3*

4John was baptizing people in the desert and
preaching a baptism of changed hearts and lives
for the forgiveness of sins. 5All the people from
Judea and Jerusalem were going out to him. They
confessed their sins and were baptized by him in
the Jordan River. 6John wore clothes made from
camel's hair, had a leather belt around his waist,
and ate locusts and wild honey. 7This is what John
preached to the people: "There is one coming after
me who is greater than I; I am not good enough
even to kneel down and untie his sandals. 8I baptize you with water, but he will baptize you with
the Holy Spirit."

Jesus Is Baptized

9At that time Jesus came from the town of
Nazareth in Galilee and was baptized by John in
the Jordan River. 10Immediately, as Jesus was
coming up out of the water, he saw heaven open.
The Holy Spirit came down on him like a dove,
11and a voice came from heaven: "You are my
Son, whom I love, and I am very pleased with
you."

12Then the Spirit sent Jesus into the desert. 13He
was in the desert forty days and was tempted by
Satan. He was with the wild animals, and the angels
came and took care of him.

Jesus Chooses Some Followers

14After John was put in prison, Jesus went into
Galilee, preaching the Good News from God. 15He
said, "The right time has come. The kingdom of
God is near. Change your hearts and lives and
believe the Good News!"

A fisherman casting his net into the sea

16When Jesus was walking by Lake Galilee, he
saw Simon and his brother Andrew throwing a net
into the lake because they were fishermen. 17Jesus
said to them, "Come follow me, and I will make
you fish for people." 18So Simon and Andrew
immediately left their nets and followed him.

19Going a little farther, Jesus saw two more
brothers, James and John, the sons of Zebedee.
They were in a boat, mending their nets. 20Jesus
immediately called them, and they left their father
in the boat with the hired workers and followed
Jesus.

Jesus Forces Out an Evil Spirit

21Jesus and his followers went to Capernaum.
On the Sabbath day He went to the synagogue

1:1 *the Son of God.* Some Greek copies omit these words.

1:3 This introduction to the Good News of Jesus Christ quotes from Isaiah 40:3. It reminds us that God's salvation was not completed when he saved Israel from Egypt under Moses, nor when he allowed Israel to return to Israel after their Babylonian captivity. These were just pale reflections of the fulfillment of salvation, Jesus Christ. He is the One who will truly lead God's people to salvation.

1:11 Baptism: Luke 3:16

1:11 John the Baptist: Luke 1:5–25

1:13 Angels/Guardian Angels: Mark 13:26

1:13 Fasting: Acts 13:2–3

1:15 When Jesus starts his preaching, he announces that the kingdom of God has come. Everyone should respond by changing their hearts and lives and believing in God. From the earliest days of his ministry Christ stressed that faith in God is the only way to participate in the kingdom.

1:15 Repentance: Luke 15:11–32

1:15 Land/Inheritance: Luke 6:23

1:16 *Simon.* Simon's other name was Peter.

1:16–20 Having announced the arrival of God's kingdom in Jesus' ministry, Mark now illustrates what it means to have new hearts and new lives (see 1:14). Followers are called upon to embrace new loyalties and to join the new family of those who follow Jesus and obey God (see Mark 3:31–35).

1:18 Evangelism: Luke 2:29–32

1:20 Disciple/Discipleship/Mentoring (Follow/Follower): Mark 10:42–45

1:20 Peter: Mark 3:13–19

and began to teach. 22The people were amazed at his teaching, because he taught like a person who had authority, not like their teachers of the law. 23Just then, a man was there in the synagogue who had an evil spirit in him. He shouted, 24"Jesus of Nazareth! What do you want with us? Did you come to destroy us? I know who you are—God's Holy One!"

25Jesus commanded the evil spirit, "Be quiet! Come out of the man!" 26The evil spirit shook the man violently, gave a loud cry, and then came out of him.

27The people were so amazed they asked each other, "What is happening here? This man is teaching something new, and with authority. He even gives commands to evil spirits, and they obey him." 28And the news about Jesus spread quickly everywhere in the area of Galilee.

Jesus Heals Many People

29As soon as Jesus and his followers left the synagogue, they went with James and John to the home of Simon and Andrew. 30Simon's mother-in-law was sick in bed with a fever, and the people told Jesus about her. 31So Jesus went to her bed, took her hand, and helped her up. The fever left her, and she began serving them.

32That evening, after the sun went down, the people brought to Jesus all who were sick and had demons in them. 33The whole town gathered at the door. 34Jesus healed many who had different kinds of sicknesses, and he forced many demons to leave people. But he would not allow the demons to speak, because they knew who he was.

35Early the next morning, while it was still dark, Jesus woke and left the house. He went to a lonely place, where he prayed. 36Simon and his friends went to look for Jesus. 37When they found him, they said, "Everyone is looking for you!"

38Jesus answered, "We should go to other towns around here so I can preach there too. That is the reason I came." 39So he went everywhere in Galilee, preaching in the synagogues and forcing out demons.

Jesus Heals a Sick Man

40A man with a skin disease came to Jesus. He fell to his knees and begged Jesus, "You can heal me if you will."

41Jesus felt sorry for the man, so he reached out his hand and touched him and said, "I will. Be healed!" 42Immediately the disease left the man, and he was healed.

43Jesus told the man to go away at once, but he warned him strongly, 44"Don't tell anyone about this. But go and show yourself to the priest. And offer the gift Moses commanded for people who are made well. This will show the people what I have done." 45The man left there, but he began to tell everyone that Jesus had healed him, and so he spread the news about Jesus. As a result, Jesus could not enter a town if people saw him. He stayed in places where nobody lived, but people came to him from everywhere.

Jesus Heals a Paralyzed Man

2 A few days later, when Jesus came back to Capernaum, the news spread that he was at home. 2Many people gathered together so that there was no room in the house, not even outside the door. And Jesus was teaching them God's message. 3Four people came, carrying a paralyzed man. 4Since they could not get to Jesus because of the crowd, they dug a hole in the roof right above where he was speaking. When they got through, they lowered the mat with the paralyzed man on it. 5When Jesus saw the faith of these people, he said to the paralyzed man, "Young man, your sins are forgiven."

6Some of the teachers of the law were sitting there, thinking to themselves, 7"Why does this man say things like that? He is speaking as if he were God. Only God can forgive sins."

8Jesus knew immediately what these teachers of the law were thinking. So he said to them, "Why are you thinking these things? 9Which is easier: to tell this paralyzed man, 'Your sins are forgiven,' or to tell him, 'Stand up. Take your mat and walk'? 10But I will prove to you that the Son of Man has authority on earth to forgive sins." So Jesus said to the paralyzed man, 11"I tell you, stand up, take your mat, and go home." 12Immediately the paralyzed man stood up, took his mat, and walked out while everyone was watching him.

The people were amazed and praised God. They said, "We have never seen anything like this!"

13Jesus went to the lake again. The whole crowd

1:22 Even before Jesus opened his mouth in Capernaum, people were ready to listen. Why? Because his reputation as an authoritative teacher preceded him. He was different from other teachers of the Law; his life backed it up. In this way, he gained a hearing.

1:22 Scribes (Teachers of the Law): Mark 2:6–7

1:26 Satan/Satanism: Mark 3:23

1:28 Jesus: Mark 2:1–12

1:29 *Simon.* Simon's other name was Peter.

1:44 *Moses . . . well.* Read about this in Leviticus 14:1-32.

2:7 Scribes (Teachers of the Law): Mark 7:5–8

2:11 Forgiveness: Luke 5:17–20

2:12 Guilt: Luke 20:45–47

2:12 Jesus: Mark 13:32

2:13 The Books of Matthew, Mark, Luke and John tell us about a core of twelve followers called by Jesus into a special relationship with

STEWARDSHIP

1 CORINTHIANS 4:1

What is a steward? Is stewardship more than what a person does with money or possessions? Is stewardship more than giving to the church budget?

A steward in the Bible is a person who has the responsibility to manage all that God has entrusted to him or her. Good stewardship is the proper management of all that God has trusted into our care. It is true that the actual words steward and stewardship are not used in this translation. In their place, we will find such words as "servant" and "manager" and such phrases as "those chosen to care," "chief servant," "servant in charge," and "God's manager."

All humans are stewards. We have no choice in the matter. God has put the whole world in our hands as well as much more of spiritual value. The big question is, What kind of steward will you be? Will your service or management help to promote the purposes of God, or be for nothing?

The beginning point for good stewardship is to recognize that God is the owner and that we are servant-managers of what God has trusted into our care. King David demonstrates the proper attitude in 1 Chronicles 29. David had purchased and gathered all the material with which to build the Temple. In this prayer of dedication, he praises God saying: "Everything in heaven and on earth belongs to you. The kingdom belongs to you, LORD; you are the ruler over everything. . . . These things did not really come from me and my people. Everything comes from you; we have given you back what you gave us" (verses 11, 14).

Faithful stewards accept responsibility for what God has trusted to their care. What has God trusted to our care? A steward has been entrusted with the responsible care of God's creation. Since the sixth day of creation, human beings have been given charge of all life on earth (Genesis 1:26–31). Psalm 8:6 says of God: "You put them in charge of everything you made. You put all things under their control."

A steward has been entrusted with gifts for service to God and others. Good stewards manage their time to use these gifts as God intended. This teaching is more commonly found in the New Testament (1 Peter 4:10; Ephesians 4:11–12). While there is no teaching on gifts in the Old Testament, there are many stories of God equipping leaders and regular people to accomplish his purposes and serve others.

In addition, a steward has been entrusted with relationships. Christian stewards are charged to encourage those within the church as well as to be winsome to those outside the church.

Faithful stewards care for their own bodies. Even a person's own body is entrusted to them by God. A Christian's body is the home to the Holy Spirit that dwells in them as well. This is additional motivation for what Christians do with the body that God has given them (1 Corinthians 6:19).

A steward has been entrusted with the management of money and possessions. Nearly half of the parables of Jesus deal with the topic of money and possessions. The struggle with the proper attitude and management of money and possessions is a subject frequently addressed in the New Testament. Stewards are taught that all we have is given to us by God. Both the Old and New Testaments clearly teach that giving generously to both God and others is critical to good stewardship. Our generosity should be accompanied by joy as we recognize that our money and possessions come to us as a gift that was given for a purpose.

Both Testaments teach that proper stewardship involves giving in proportion to what a person has received. One name for proportionate giving is tithing. Tithing is the practice of giving one-tenth to God (Genesis 14:20; 28:22; Malachi 3:6–12). Jesus affirms the practice (Matthew 23:23; Luke 11:42) and the apostle Paul teaches it as proportionate giving (1 Corinthians 16:1–2).

As Christian stewards, we have been entrusted with the very secrets of Christ (1 Corinthians 4:1). These secrets are the Good News that leads to salvation and life in Christ. As stewards we are responsible to receive, study, follow, and proclaim this revelation that has come to us.

Stewardship is being responsible for all that God has put in our care and under our management. We will be held accountable for how faithful we are. This is the point of the two of Jesus' parables that contrast good with bad stewards (Matthew 25:14–30; Luke 12:42–48). Good stewards not only take care of what God has given them, but multiply its value. In the Matthew parable, the steward given five bags of gold returned ten and the one who was given two bags returned four. They were both rewarded. As for the last steward, he was given one bag, which he buried and simply returned to his master. The master was not at all pleased and took even the one bag and gave it to the more productive servants.⚭

⚭**Stewardship:** For additional scriptures on this topic go to Genesis 14:20.

SELF-CONTROL

1 CORINTHIANS 9

What does the Bible mean by "self-control"?
How are we to live our lives according to the biblical call to exercise self-control?

The exercise of self-control in human conduct has a privileged place in the moral traditions of the Hebrews, Greeks, and Christians. Paul, imprisoned in Caesarea, discussed self-control with Roman governor Felix and his Jewish wife Drusilla (Acts 24:25). By the Middle Ages the seven deadly sins were contrasted with the seven virtues, and temperance (or self-control) was one of the four cardinal virtues of the Greeks to which Christians added the three theological virtues of faith, hope, and love. The word *temperance*, fallen into disuse today, means "the willful control of one's desires, inclinations to passionate action, and response to provocation." Like tempered steel, the temperate response is emotion mixed with the strengthening and qualifying alloy of consideration.

In a series of similes concerning practical wisdom, Proverbs 25:28 cautions that, "like a city breached, without walls, is one who lacks self-control." Such a person fails to restrain his or her spirit and so is subject to its whims and responses to outside forces. The biblical texts that first come to mind regarding self-control are Paul's advice on sexual continence in 1 Corinthians 7, and in 1 Corinthians 9 his explanation of his severe physical disciplining of his appetites for food, drink, marriage, and rest from labor for the sake of his witness. Like an athlete suffering deprivation in order to achieve excellence, so Paul "enslaves" his body and contains his energies for the sake of serving God and God's people.

Many stories in the Bible illustrate the virtue of self-control—the negative examples of David with Bathsheba (2 Samuel 11); Peter denying Jesus (Luke 22:56–62); the positive examples of Jesus' resistance to temptations in the wilderness (Matthew 4:1–11); and Abraham's obedience in the wrenching assignment to sacrifice Isaac (Genesis 22). Other stories show that the theological virtues of faith, hope, and love may move us beyond the cardinal virtues of self-control, prudence, courage, and justice. Joseph, moved by love, loses control, weeps, and reveals his identity to his brothers (Genesis 45:1); Ruth violates custom and reason to accompany the mother-in-law she loves, and then takes seemingly foolish risks to ensure her physical and social survival; when called by Jesus, Peter, Andrew, James, and John "immediately" abandon work and families (Matthew 4:18–22).

The challenge today, as always, is one of discernment. Do our efforts at self-control protect us from God, faith, hope, and love, or do they preserve ourselves for service to God and his people as with Paul in 1 Corinthians 9? Certainly, self-control may be a tool for ambition as well as sanctification. Conversely, we must ask when surrendering self-control: are we weakening or becoming foolish for the sake of Christ (as in 1 Corinthians 4:10), or for some unrighteousness? In Bethany before their final Passover with Jesus, the disciples were horrified that a woman poured costly ointment on Jesus' head. They saw it as an intemperate act and scolded her. Jesus said, "She did an excellent thing for me" (Mark 14:6). Jesus did not enter into the disciples' economic calculations about wastefulness versus the benevolent distribution of resources; rather, he commended the woman's act of kindness.

Our industrialized world is dominated by the poles of rational and sensual ends. Industry is driven by ideals of efficiency, productivity, and profitability and is dependent on appealing to consumers' desires for comfort, pleasure, and status. Any contemporary reflection on self-control is liable to respond to these two poles of significance. What biblical reflection on self-control yields is an alternative view in which the rightness or wrongness of any particular exercise of self-control must refer to Jesus and his call to love God and our neighbor. Self-control for the sake of efficiency pales next to that exerted for the sake of love; likewise, self-control abandoned for the sake of comfort bears little resemblance to the movement of a heart touched by love.

Discerning motivation in ourselves is exceedingly difficult, and the ease with which we presume to discern it in others is illusory. Scripture reminds us that our only hope for righteous living with respect to self-control, courage, justice, or any other ideal, is to trust in the Lord. The Lord's words to Jeremiah describe the kind of self-control that pervades the life of one who trusts him: "He will be strong, like a tree planted near water, that sends its roots by a stream. It is not afraid when the days are hot; its leaves are always green. It does not worry in a year when no rain comes; it always produces fruit" (Jeremiah 17:8). Self-control arising out of trust in God is steady, reliable, and deep as well as lively, fruitful, and responsive.

Self-Control: For additional scriptures on this topic go to Genesis 45:1.

followed him there, and he taught them. 14While
he was walking along, he saw a man named Levi
son of Alphaeus, sitting in the tax collector's booth.
Jesus said to him, "Follow me," and he stood up
and followed Jesus.
15Later, as Jesus was having dinner at Levi's
house, many tax collectors and "sinners" were eating there with Jesus and his followers. Many people
like this followed Jesus. 16When the teachers of the
law who were Pharisees saw Jesus eating with
the tax collectors and "sinners," they asked his
followers, "Why does he eat with tax collectors
and sinners?"
17Jesus heard this and said to them, "It is not
the healthy people who need a doctor, but the sick.
I did not come to invite good people but to invite
sinners."

Jesus' Followers Are Criticized

18Now the followers of John and the Pharisees
often gave up eating for a certain time. Some people
came to Jesus and said, "Why do John's followers
and the followers of the Pharisees often give up
eating, but your followers don't?"
19Jesus answered, "The friends of the bridegroom do not give up eating while the bridegroom
is still with them. As long as the bridegroom is
with them, they cannot give up eating.⚭ 20But the
time will come when the bridegroom will be taken
from them, and then they will give up eating.
21"No one sews a patch of unshrunk cloth over
a hole in an old coat. Otherwise, the patch will
shrink and pull away—the new patch will pull
away from the old coat. Then the hole will be
worse. 22Also, no one ever pours new wine into
old leather bags. Otherwise, the new wine will
break the bags, and the wine will be ruined along
with the bags. But new wine should be put into
new leather bags."

Jesus Is Lord of the Sabbath

23One Sabbath day, as Jesus was walking through
some fields of grain, his followers began to pick
some grain to eat. 24The Pharisees said to Jesus,
"Why are your followers doing what is not lawful
on the Sabbath day?"
25Jesus answered, "Have you never read what
David did when he and those with him were hungry
and needed food? 26During the time of Abiathar the
high priest, David went into God's house and ate
the holy bread, which is lawful only for priests to
eat. And David also gave some of the bread to those
who were with him."
27Then Jesus said to the Pharisees, "The Sabbath
day was made to help people; they were not made
to be ruled by the Sabbath day. 28So then, the Son
of Man is Lord even of the Sabbath day."

Jesus Heals a Man's Hand

3 Another time when Jesus went into a synagogue, a man with a crippled hand was there.
2Some people watched Jesus closely to see if he
would heal the man on the Sabbath day so they
could accuse him.
3Jesus said to the man with the crippled hand,
"Stand up here in the middle of everyone."
4Then Jesus asked the people, "Which is lawful
on the Sabbath day: to do good or to do evil, to save a
life or to kill?" But they said nothing to answer him.
5Jesus was angry as he looked at the people, and
he felt very sad because they were stubborn. Then
he said to the man, "Hold out your hand." The
man held out his hand and it was healed.⚭ 6Then
the Pharisees left and began making plans with the
Herodians about a way to kill Jesus.⚭

Many People Follow Jesus

7Jesus left with his followers for the lake, and a
large crowd from Galilee followed him. 8Also many
people came from Judea, from Jerusalem, from Idumea, from the lands across the Jordan River, and
from the area of Tyre and Sidon. When they heard
what Jesus was doing, many people came to him.
9When Jesus saw the crowds, he told his followers
to get a boat ready for him to keep people from
crowding against him. 10He had healed many people, so all the sick were pushing toward him to
touch him. 11When evil spirits saw Jesus, they fell
down before him and shouted, "You are the Son of
God!" 12But Jesus strongly warned them not to tell
who he was.

Jesus Chooses His Twelve Apostles

13Then Jesus went up on a mountain and called
to him the men he wanted, and they came to him.
14Jesus chose twelve men and called them apostles.

him. Jesus chose the Twelve from among the larger number of followers and then named them as *apostles* (Matthew 10:2–4; Luke 6:13–16). The Twelve were first called to become followers of Jesus, (or disciples); then they were chosen and named as *apostles* (Matthew 4:18–22; Mark 1:16–20; 2:13). The circumstances of the lives of these Twelve were quite different from other followers, because they were called to follow Jesus around, join him in the missionary outreach to Israel, and be trained for their special role in the future church.

2:18 *John.* John the Baptist, who preached to the Jewish people about Christ's coming (Mark 1:4-8).

2:18 *gave . . . time.* This is called "fasting." The people would give up eating for a special time of prayer and worship to God. It was also done to show sadness and disappointment.

⚭**2:19 Church:** Acts 2:42–47

⚭**3:5 Conscience:** Romans 9:1

3:6 *Herodians.* A political group that followed Herod and his family.

⚭**3:6 Physical Handicap:** Luke 4:31–35

He wanted them to be with him, and he wanted
to send them out to preach 15and to have the
authority to force demons out of people. 16These
are the twelve men he chose: Simon (Jesus named
him Peter), 17James and John, the sons of Zebedee
(Jesus named them Boanerges, which means "Sons
of Thunder"), 18Andrew, Philip, Bartholomew,
Matthew, Thomas, James the son of Alphaeus,
Thaddaeus, Simon the Zealot, 19and Judas Iscariot,
who later turned against Jesus.

Some People Say Jesus Has a Devil

20Then Jesus went home, but again a crowd
gathered. There were so many people that Jesus
and his followers could not eat. 21When his family heard this, they went to get him because they
thought he was out of his mind. 22But the teachers
of the law from Jerusalem were saying, "Beelzebul
is living inside him! He uses power from the ruler
of demons to force demons out of people."

23So Jesus called the people together and taught
them with stories. He said, "Satan will not force
himself out of people. 24A kingdom that is divided cannot continue, 25and a family that is divided cannot continue. 26And if Satan is against
himself and fights against his own people, he cannot continue; that is the end of Satan. 27No one
can enter a strong person's house and steal his
things unless he first ties up the strong person.
Then he can steal things from the house. 28I tell
you the truth, all sins that people do and all the
things people say against God can be forgiven.
29But anyone who speaks against the Holy Spirit
will never be forgiven; he is guilty of a sin that
continues forever."

30Jesus said this because the teachers of the law
said that he had an evil spirit inside him.

Jesus' True Family

31Then Jesus' mother and brothers arrived.
Standing outside, they sent someone in to tell him
to come out. 32Many people were sitting around
Jesus, and they said to him, "Your mother and
brothers are waiting for you outside."

33Jesus asked, "Who are my mother and my
brothers?" 34Then he looked at those sitting around
him and said, "Here are my mother and my brothers! 35My true brother and sister and mother are
those who do what God wants."

A Story About Planting Seed

4 Again Jesus began teaching by the lake. A great
crowd gathered around him, so he sat down in
a boat near the shore. All the people stayed on the
shore close to the water. 2Jesus taught them many
things, using stories. He said, 3"Listen! A farmer
went out to plant his seed. 4While he was planting, some seed fell by the road, and the birds came
and ate it up. 5Some seed fell on rocky ground
where there wasn't much dirt. That seed grew
very fast, because the ground was not deep. 6But
when the sun rose, the plants dried up because
they did not have deep roots. 7Some other seed
fell among thorny weeds, which grew and choked
the good plants. So those plants did not produce a
crop. 8Some other seed fell on good ground and
began to grow. It got taller and produced a crop.
Some plants made thirty times more, some made
sixty times more, and some made a hundred times
more."

9Then Jesus said, "You people who can hear me,
listen!"

Jesus Tells Why He Used Stories

10Later, when Jesus was alone, the twelve apostles and others around him asked him about the
stories.

11Jesus said, "You can know the secret about
the kingdom of God. But to other people I tell
everything by using stories 12so that:

'They will look and look, but they will
not learn.
They will listen and listen, but they
will not understand.
If they did learn and understand,
they would come back to me and
be forgiven.'" *Isaiah 6:9-10*

Jesus Explains the Seed Story

13Then Jesus said to his followers, "Don't you
understand this story? If you don't, how will
you understand any story? 14The farmer is like a
person who plants God's message in people.
15Sometimes the teaching falls on the road. This is
like the people who hear the teaching of God, but
Satan quickly comes and takes away the teaching
that was planted in them. 16Others are like the
seed planted on rocky ground. They hear the

3:14 Career/Careerism: John 5:36

3:14 Jesus called the twelve apostles, first, to be with him, and only then to be sent out. Those who would continue his ministry of teaching and healing must first become like him in relationship with him.

3:19 Peter: Mark 5:37

3:22 Family: Luke 2:41–51

3:23 Satan/Satanism: Mark 3:26

3:26 Satan/Satanism: Mark 5:1–20

3:27 Demon: Mark 5:1–19

4:8 Perseverance: John 8:31

teaching and quickly accept it with joy. 17But
since they don't allow the teaching to go deep into
their lives, they keep it only a short time. When
trouble or persecution comes because of the
teaching they accepted, they quickly give up.
18Others are like the seed planted among the
thorny weeds. They hear the teaching, 19but the
worries of this life, the temptation of wealth, and
many other evil desires keep the teaching from
growing and producing fruit in their lives.
20Others are like the seed planted in the good
ground. They hear the teaching and accept it.
Then they grow and produce fruit—sometimes
thirty times more, sometimes sixty times more,
and sometimes a hundred times more."

Use What You Have

21Then Jesus said to them, "Do you hide a lamp
under a bowl or under a bed? No! You put the lamp
on a lampstand. 22Everything that is hidden will be
made clear and every secret thing will be made
known. 23You people who can hear me, listen!
24"Think carefully about what you hear. The
way you give to others is the way God will give to
you, but God will give you even more. 25Those
who have understanding will be given more. But
those who do not have understanding, even what
they have will be taken away from them."

Jesus Uses a Story About Seed

26Then Jesus said, "The kingdom of God is like
someone who plants seed in the ground. 27Night
and day, whether the person is asleep or awake, the
seed still grows, but the person does not know how
it grows. 28By itself the earth produces grain. First
the plant grows, then the head, and then all the
grain in the head. 29When the grain is ready, the
farmer cuts it, because this is the harvest time."

A Story About Mustard Seed

30Then Jesus said, "How can I show you what
the kingdom of God is like? What story can I use to
explain it? 31The kingdom of God is like a mustard
seed, the smallest seed you plant in the ground.
32But when planted, this seed grows and becomes
the largest of all garden plants. It produces large
branches, and the wild birds can make nests in its
shade."
33Jesus used many stories like these to teach the
crowd God's message—as much as they could
understand. 34He always used stories to teach them.
But when he and his followers were alone, Jesus
explained everything to them.

Jesus Calms a Storm

35That evening, Jesus said to his followers, "Let's
go across the lake." 36Leaving the crowd behind,
they took him in the boat just as he was. There
were also other boats with them. 37A very strong
wind came up on the lake. The waves came over
the sides and into the boat so that it was already
full of water. 38Jesus was at the back of the boat,
sleeping with his head on a cushion. His followers
woke him and said, "Teacher, don't you care that
we are drowning!"
39Jesus stood up and commanded the wind and
said to the waves, "Quiet! Be still!" Then the wind
stopped, and it became completely calm.
40Jesus said to his followers, "Why are you afraid?
Do you still have no faith?"
41The followers were very afraid and asked each
other, "Who is this? Even the wind and the waves
obey him!"

A Man with Demons Inside Him

5 Jesus and his followers went to the other side
of the lake to the area of the Gerasene people.
2When Jesus got out of the boat, instantly a man
with an evil spirit came to him from the burial
caves. 3This man lived in the caves, and no one
could tie him up, not even with a chain. 4Many
times people had used chains to tie the man's hands
and feet, but he always broke them off. No one
was strong enough to control him. 5Day and night
he would wander around the burial caves and on
the hills, screaming and cutting himself with
stones. 6While Jesus was still far away, the man saw
him, ran to him, and fell down before him.

4:19 *producing fruit.* To produce fruit means to have in your life the good things God wants.

4:20 Parables: Mark 12:1–12

4:26–29 The Book of Mark begins, "The kingdom of God is near" (Mark 1:15). The parable of the seed illustrates this understanding of the advent of the kingdom and pushes us to see it as a *process.* As we go through the routines of daily living, the kingdom of God is slowly at work in the hearts and minds of all believers and will be harvested in its fullness at the second coming of Christ.

4:26–32 Even though Jesus announced the arrival of God's kingdom (see Mark 1:15), the truth is that it did not look as though God had broken into the world to set things right at all. Evil was still at work in the world. Jesus explains (1) that we must develop new eyes to see how God is at work—sometimes in small ways, sometimes in quite unexpected ways, and (2) that the grandeur of God's kingdom is visible in its small beginnings.

4:41 Authority: Luke 3:1–20

5:1–19 In this encounter between Jesus and a man with demons, Christ not only casts out the demons that harass this man, but restores him to his community. The work of demons seeks to undo the life-giving power of God. Christ's work of redemption is seen in this encounter with demons; he brings this man back to the wholeness of mind and community that God offers.

7The man shouted in a loud voice, "What do you want with me, Jesus, Son of the Most High God? I command you in God's name not to torture me!" 8He said this because Jesus was saying to him, "You evil spirit, come out of the man."

9Then Jesus asked him, "What is your name?"

He answered, "My name is Legion, because we are many spirits." 10He begged Jesus again and again not to send them out of that area.

11A large herd of pigs was feeding on a hill near there. 12The demons begged Jesus, "Send us into the pigs; let us go into them." 13So Jesus allowed them to do this. The evil spirits left the man and went into the pigs. Then the herd of pigs—about two thousand of them—rushed down the hill into the lake and were drowned.

14The herdsmen ran away and went to the town and to the countryside, telling everyone about this. So people went out to see what had happened. 15They came to Jesus and saw the man who used to have the many evil spirits, sitting, clothed, and in his right mind. And they were frightened. 16The people who saw this told the others what had happened to the man who had the demons living in him, and they told about the pigs. 17Then the people began to beg Jesus to leave their area.

18As Jesus was getting back into the boat, the man who was freed from the demons begged to go with him.

19But Jesus would not let him. He said, "Go home to your family and tell them how much the Lord has done for you and how he has had mercy on you." 20So the man left and began to tell the people in the Ten Towns about what Jesus had done for him. And everyone was amazed.

Jesus Gives Life to a Dead Girl and Heals a Sick Woman

21When Jesus went in the boat back to the other side of the lake, a large crowd gathered around him there. 22A leader of the synagogue, named Jairus, came there, saw Jesus, and fell at his feet. 23He begged Jesus, saying again and again, "My daughter is dying. Please come and put your hands on her so she will be healed and will live." 24So Jesus went with him.

A large crowd followed Jesus and pushed very close around him. 25Among them was a woman who had been bleeding for twelve years. 26She had suffered very much from many doctors and had spent all the money she had, but instead of improving, she was getting worse. 27When the woman heard about Jesus, she came up behind him in the crowd and touched his coat. 28She thought, "If I can just touch his clothes, I will be healed." 29Instantly her bleeding stopped, and she felt in her body that she was healed from her disease.

30At once Jesus felt power go out from him. So he turned around in the crowd and asked, "Who touched my clothes?"

31His followers said, "Look at how many people are pushing against you! And you ask, 'Who touched me?'"

32But Jesus continued looking around to see who had touched him. 33The woman, knowing that she was healed, came and fell at Jesus' feet. Shaking with fear, she told him the whole truth. 34Jesus said to her, "Dear woman, you are made well because you believed. Go in peace; be healed of your disease."

35While Jesus was still speaking, some people came from the house of the synagogue leader. They said, "Your daughter is dead. There is no need to bother the teacher anymore."

36But Jesus paid no attention to what they said. He told the synagogue leader, "Don't be afraid; just believe."

37Jesus let only Peter, James, and John the brother of James go with him. 38When they came to the house of the synagogue leader, Jesus found many people there making lots of noise and crying loudly. 39Jesus entered the house and said to them, "Why are you crying and making so much noise? The child is not dead, only asleep." 40But they laughed at him. So, after throwing them out of the house, Jesus took the child's father and mother and his three followers into the room where the child was. 41Taking hold of the girl's hand, he said to her, "Talitha, koum!" (This means, "Young girl, I tell you to stand up!") 42At once the girl stood right up and began walking. (She was twelve years old.) Everyone was completely amazed. 43Jesus gave them strict orders not to tell people about this. Then he told them to give the girl something to eat.

5:9 *Legion.* Means very many. A legion was about five thousand men in the Roman army.

5:19 Demon: Mark 6:13

5:19–20 In the Book of Mark, Jesus typically tells people to be quiet about his miracles and healing because his growing popularity only gets in the way of the effectiveness of his ministry. Here, though, he sends the man who had been delivered of an evil spirit home to tell what the Lord had done for him. In this way, this man is restored to his own circle of family and friends and becomes an evangelist for Jesus.

5:20 *Ten Towns.* In Greek, called *Decapolis.* It was an area east of Lake Galilee that once had ten main towns.

5:20 Satan/Satanism: Luke 4:13

5:34 Crossing Cultural Boundaries: Mark 12:28–35

5:37 Peter: Mark 8:29–33

5:43 Sickness, Disease, Healing: Luke 5:17

Jesus Goes to His Hometown

6 Jesus left there and went to his hometown, and his followers went with him. 2On the Sabbath day he taught in the synagogue. Many people heard him and were amazed, saying, "Where did this man get these teachings? What is this wisdom that has been given to him? And where did he get the power to do miracles? 3He is just the carpenter, the son of Mary and the brother of James, Joseph, Judas, and Simon. And his sisters are here with us." So the people were upset with Jesus.

4Jesus said to them, "A prophet is honored everywhere except in his hometown and with his own people and in his own home." 5So Jesus was not able to work any miracles there except to heal a few sick people by putting his hands on them. 6He was amazed at how many people had no faith.

Then Jesus went to other villages in that area and taught. 7He called his twelve followers together and got ready to send them out two by two and gave them authority over evil spirits. 8This is what Jesus commanded them: "Take nothing for your trip except a walking stick. Take no bread, no bag, and no money in your pockets. 9Wear sandals, but take only the clothes you are wearing. 10When you enter a house, stay there until you leave that town. 11If the people in a certain place refuse to welcome you or listen to you, leave that place. Shake its dust off your feet as a warning to them."

12So the followers went out and preached that people should change their hearts and lives. 13They forced many demons out and put olive oil on many sick people and healed them.

How John the Baptist Was Killed

14King Herod heard about Jesus, because he was now well known. Some people said, "He is John the Baptist, who has risen from the dead. That is why he can work these miracles."

15Others said, "He is Elijah."

Other people said, "Jesus is a prophet, like the prophets who lived long ago."

16When Herod heard this, he said, "I killed John by cutting off his head. Now he has risen from the dead!"

17Herod himself had ordered his soldiers to arrest John and put him in prison in order to please his wife, Herodias. She had been the wife of Philip, Herod's brother, but then Herod had married her. 18John had been telling Herod, "It is not lawful for you to be married to your brother's wife." 19So Herodias hated John and wanted to kill him. But she couldn't, 20because Herod was afraid of John and protected him. He knew John was a good and holy man. Also, though John's preaching always bothered him, he enjoyed listening to John.

21Then the perfect time came for Herodias to cause John's death. On Herod's birthday, he gave a dinner party for the most important government leaders, the commanders of his army, and the most important people in Galilee. 22When the daughter of Herodias came in and danced, she pleased Herod and the people eating with him.

So King Herod said to the girl, "Ask me for anything you want, and I will give it to you." 23He promised her, "Anything you ask for I will give to you—up to half of my kingdom."

24The girl went to her mother and asked, "What should I ask for?"

Her mother answered, "Ask for the head of John the Baptist."

25At once the girl went back to the king and said to him, "I want the head of John the Baptist right now on a platter."

26Although the king was very sad, he had made a promise, and his dinner guests had heard it. So he did not want to refuse what she asked. 27Immediately the king sent a soldier to bring John's head. The soldier went and cut off John's head in the prison 28and brought it back on a platter. He gave it to the girl, and the girl gave it to her mother. 29When John's followers heard this, they came and got John's body and put it in a tomb.

More than Five Thousand Fed

30The apostles gathered around Jesus and told him about all the things they had done and taught. 31Crowds of people were coming and going so that Jesus and his followers did not even have time to eat. He said to them, "Come away by yourselves, and we will go to a lonely place to get some rest."

32So they went in a boat by themselves to a lonely place. 33But many people saw them leave

6:2 Sabbath: Mark 6:31
6:11 *Shake . . . feet.* A warning. It showed that they were rejecting these people.
6:13 Demon: Luke 4:33
6:15 *Elijah.* A great prophet who spoke for God and who lived hundreds of years before Christ. See 1 Kings 17.
6:21 Celebration: John 2:1–10
6:29 Martyrdom: Mark 9:30–32
6:31 Sabbath: Luke 4:16

6:31 Wilderness (Desert): Luke 8:26–39
6:31 At a crucial time in Jesus' ministry when he and his followers were being besieged by the needs of people, he said, "Come away by yourselves, and we will go to a lonely place to get some rest" (Mark 6:31). The words actually mean, "Come away *for* yourselves and rest a while." The Lord wants us to love ourselves as we are loved by him and give ourselves the gift of time each day for stress-reducing communion with him. We can talk to him about the difficulties and delights of life. He helps us to overcome our times of suffering and truly enjoy our times of praise (James 5:13).

and recognized them. So from all the towns they ran to the place where Jesus was going, and they got there before him. 34When he arrived, he saw a great crowd waiting. He felt sorry for them, because they were like sheep without a shepherd. So he began to teach them many things.

35When it was late in the day, his followers came to him and said, "No one lives in this place, and it is already very late. 36Send the people away so they can go to the countryside and towns around here to buy themselves something to eat."

37But Jesus answered, "You give them something to eat."

They said to him, "We would all have to work a month to earn enough money to buy that much bread!"

38Jesus asked them, "How many loaves of bread do you have? Go and see."

When they found out, they said, "Five loaves and two fish."

39Then Jesus told his followers to have the people sit in groups on the green grass. 40So they sat in groups of fifty or a hundred. 41Jesus took the five loaves and two fish and, looking up to heaven, he thanked God for the food. He divided the bread and gave it to his followers for them to give to the people. Then he divided the two fish among them all. 42All the people ate and were satisfied. 43The followers filled twelve baskets with the leftover pieces of bread and fish. 44There were five thousand men who ate.

Jesus Walks on the Water

45Immediately Jesus told his followers to get into the boat and go ahead of him to Bethsaida across the lake. He stayed there to send the people home. 46After sending them away, he went into the hills to pray.

47That night, the boat was in the middle of the lake, and Jesus was alone on the land. 48He saw his followers struggling hard to row the boat, because the wind was blowing against them. Between three and six o'clock in the morning, Jesus came to them, walking on the water, and he wanted to walk past the boat. 49But when they saw him walking on the water, they thought he was a ghost and cried out. 50They all saw him and were afraid. But quickly Jesus spoke to them and said, "Have courage! It is I. Do not be afraid." 51Then he got into the boat with them, and the wind became calm. The followers were greatly amazed. 52They did not understand about the miracle of the five loaves, because their minds were closed.

53When they had crossed the lake, they came to shore at Gennesaret and tied the boat there. 54When they got out of the boat, people immediately recognized Jesus. 55They ran everywhere in that area and began to bring sick people on mats wherever they heard he was. 56And everywhere he went—into towns, cities, or countryside—the people brought the sick to the marketplaces. They begged him to let them touch just the edge of his coat, and all who touched it were healed.

Obey God's Law

7 When some Pharisees and some teachers of the law came from Jerusalem, they gathered around Jesus. 2They saw that some of Jesus' followers ate food with hands that were not clean, that is, they hadn't washed them. 3(The Pharisees and all the Jews never eat before washing their hands in a special way according to their unwritten laws. 4And when they buy something in the market, they never eat it until they wash themselves in a special way. They also follow many other unwritten laws, such as the washing of cups, pitchers, and pots.)

5The Pharisees and the teachers of the law said to Jesus, "Why don't your followers obey the unwritten laws which have been handed down to us? Why do your followers eat their food with hands that are not clean?"

6Jesus answered, "Isaiah was right when he spoke about you hypocrites. He wrote,

'These people show honor to me with words,
but their hearts are far from me.
7Their worship of me is worthless.
The things they teach are nothing but
human rules.' *Isaiah 29:13*

8You have stopped following the commands of God, and you follow only human teachings."

6:39–44 In the ancient world, Jewish people were often very careful about what they ate and with whom they ate. This was one way they could show their concern to be faithful to God in a world full of compromise (see Daniel 1:8–16). But this also separated Jewish people from the rest of the world, so that many people were not able to hear about God's love for all people. In this account, Jesus not only used a few loaves and fish to feed a huge crowd, but also broke down the barriers that separated people from each other. (This idea is developed further in Mark 7:1–23.)

6:44 Self-Control: Mark 14:6

6:51 Water: John 4:5–14

7:1–23 In this encounter between Jesus and some Pharisees and teachers of the Law, we see one of the principal sources of conflict between them. The Pharisees stress the importance of obeying all the detailed requirements of the oral tradition—"The unwritten laws which have been handed down to us" (v 5). Many of these laws concerned outward cleanness of hands, cups, etc. But Jesus tells them that in focusing on the letter of the Law, they have missed the spirit of God's teaching in Scripture. It is inward cleanness and goodness that God really cares about. When Jesus says that keeping the laws of outward cleanness is not important, he is striking at the heart of the Pharisees' teachings. When he suggests that their minds and hearts are full of uncleanness, he is attacking their assumed piety.

9Then Jesus said to them, "You cleverly ignore the commands of God so you can follow your own teachings. 10Moses said, 'Honor your father and your mother,' and 'Anyone who says cruel things to his father or mother must be put to death.' 11But you say a person can tell his father or mother, 'I have something I could use to help you, but it is Corban—a gift to God.' 12You no longer let that person use that money for his father or his mother. 13By your own rules, which you teach people, you are rejecting what God said. And you do many things like that."⚭

14After Jesus called the crowd to him again, he said, "Every person should listen to me and understand what I am saying. 15There is nothing people put into their bodies that makes them unclean. People are made unclean by the things that come out of them."16*

17When Jesus left the people and went into the house, his followers asked him about this story. 18Jesus said, "Do you still not understand? Surely you know that nothing that enters someone from the outside can make that person unclean. 19It does not go into the mind, but into the stomach. Then it goes out of the body." (When Jesus said this, he meant that no longer was any food unclean for people to eat.)

20And Jesus said, "The things that come out of people are the things that make them unclean.⚭ 21All these evil things begin inside people, in the mind: evil thoughts, sexual sins, stealing, murder, adultery,⚭ 22greed, evil actions, lying, doing sinful things, jealousy, speaking evil of others, pride, and foolish living.⚭ 23All these evil things come from inside and make people unclean."⚭

Jesus Helps a Non-Jewish Woman

24Jesus left that place and went to the area around Tyre. When he went into a house, he did not want anyone to know he was there, but he could not stay hidden. 25A woman whose daughter had an evil spirit in her heard that he was there. So she quickly came to Jesus and fell at his feet. 26She was Greek, born in Phoenicia, in Syria. She begged Jesus to force the demon out of her daughter.

27Jesus told the woman, "It is not right to take the children's bread and give it to the dogs. First let the children eat all they want."

28But she answered, "Yes, Lord, but even the dogs under the table can eat the children's crumbs."

29Then Jesus said, "Because of your answer, you may go. The demon has left your daughter."

30The woman went home and found her daughter lying in bed; the demon was gone.

Jesus Heals a Deaf Man

31Then Jesus left the area around Tyre and went through Sidon to Lake Galilee, to the area of the Ten Towns. 32While he was there, some people brought a man to him who was deaf and could not talk plainly. The people begged Jesus to put his hand on the man to heal him.

33Jesus led the man away from the crowd, by himself. He put his fingers in the man's ears and then spit and touched the man's tongue. 34Looking up to heaven, he sighed and said to the man, "Ephphatha!" (This means, "Be opened.") 35Instantly the man was able to hear and to use his tongue so that he spoke clearly.

36Jesus commanded the people not to tell anyone about what happened. But the more he commanded them, the more they told about it. 37They were completely amazed and said, "Jesus does everything well. He makes the deaf hear! And those who can't talk he makes able to speak."

More than Four Thousand People Fed

8 Another time there was a great crowd with Jesus that had nothing to eat. So Jesus called his followers and said, 2"I feel sorry for these people, because they have already been with me for three days, and they have nothing to eat. 3If I send

⚭**7:8 Family:** Mark 7:13

⚭**7:8 Scribes (Teachers of the Law):** Mark 11:15–19

7:10 *'Anyone . . . death.'* Quotation from Exodus 21:17.

7:10 *'Honor . . . mother'.* Quotation from Exodus 20:12; Deuteronomy 5:16.

⚭**7:13 Family:** Matthew 25:35–40

***7:16** *Verse 16.* Some Greek copies add verse 16: "You people who can hear me, listen!"

7:18 Jesus switches the focus concerning what makes a person unclean. Instead of emphasizing external washings (verses 1–4) or what a person eats, Jesus understands the problem of uncleanness to be rooted in the human heart. Although the Old Testament regulations on not eating unclean food (Leviticus 11) had taught the people about holiness, those regulations are no longer binding on the people of God with the coming of Jesus Christ.

⚭**7:20 Sin:** Luke 5:27–32

⚭**7:21 Evil:** Romans 7:14–24

⚭**7:21 Murder:** Luke 18:20

⚭**7:22 A Matter of the Heart:** Psalm 139:23

⚭**7:22 Conflict:** Romans 5:1–5

⚭**7:23 Clean & Unclean:** Luke 11:39–41

⚭**7:23 Greed:** Luke 11:39

7:24–30 The Greek woman in this story demonstrates two admirable qualities. She is persistent, even in the face of what appears to be a direct affront on Jesus' part. Rather than being dissuaded by Jesus' comment that children's bread should not go to dogs, the woman shows her understanding that around Jesus there is an abundance of the "bread" she seeks. This is something that his own followers have had trouble grasping.

7:31 *Ten Towns.* In Greek, called *Decapolis.* It was an area east of Lake Galilee that once had ten main towns.

them home hungry, they will faint on the way.
Some of them live a long way from here."∞
4Jesus' followers answered, "How can we get
enough bread to feed all these people? We are far
away from any town."
5Jesus asked, "How many loaves of bread do you
have?"
They answered, "Seven."
6Jesus told the people to sit on the ground. Then
he took the seven loaves, gave thanks to God, and
divided the bread. He gave the pieces to his followers to give to the people, and they did so. 7The
followers also had a few small fish. After Jesus
gave thanks for the fish, he told his followers to
give them to the people also. 8All the people ate
and were satisfied. Then his followers filled seven
baskets with the leftover pieces of food. 9There
were about four thousand people who ate. After
they had eaten, Jesus sent them home.∞ 10Then
right away he got into a boat with his followers
and went to the area of Dalmanutha.∞

The Leaders Ask for a Miracle

11The Pharisees came to Jesus and began to ask
him questions. Hoping to trap him, they asked
Jesus for a miracle from God. 12Jesus sighed deeply
and said, "Why do you people ask for a miracle as
a sign? I tell you the truth, no sign will be given to
you." 13Then Jesus left the Pharisees and went in
the boat to the other side of the lake.

Guard Against Wrong Teachings

14His followers had only one loaf of bread with
them in the boat; they had forgotten to bring more.
15Jesus warned them, "Be careful! Beware of the
yeast of the Pharisees and the yeast of Herod."
16His followers discussed the meaning of this,
saying, "He said this because we have no bread."
17Knowing what they were talking about, Jesus
asked them, "Why are you talking about not having bread? Do you still not see or understand? Are
your minds closed? 18You have eyes, but you don't
really see. You have ears, but you don't really listen. Remember when 19I divided five loaves of
bread for the five thousand? How many baskets
did you fill with leftover pieces of food?"
They answered, "Twelve."
20"And when I divided seven loaves of bread for
the four thousand, how many baskets did you fill
with leftover pieces of food?"
They answered, "Seven."
21Then Jesus said to them, "Don't you understand yet?"

Jesus Heals a Blind Man

22Jesus and his followers came to Bethsaida.
There some people brought a blind man to Jesus
and begged him to touch the man. 23So Jesus took
the blind man's hand and led him out of the village. Then he spit on the man's eyes and put his
hands on the man and asked, "Can you see now?"
24The man looked up and said, "Yes, I see people,
but they look like trees walking around."
25Again Jesus put his hands on the man's eyes.
Then the man opened his eyes wide and they were
healed, and he was able to see everything clearly.
26Jesus told him to go home, saying, "Don't go into
the town."

Peter Says Jesus Is the Christ

27Jesus and his followers went to the towns
around Caesarea Philippi. While they were traveling, Jesus asked them, "Who do people say I am?"
28They answered, "Some say you are John the
Baptist. Others say you are Elijah, and others say
you are one of the prophets."
29Then Jesus asked, "But who do you say I am?"
Peter answered, "You are the Christ."
30Jesus warned his followers not to tell anyone
who he was.
31Then Jesus began to teach them that the Son
of Man must suffer many things and that he would
be rejected by the older Jewish leaders, the leading
priests, and the teachers of the law. He told them
that the Son of Man must be killed and then rise
from the dead after three days. 32Jesus told them
plainly what would happen. Then Peter took Jesus
aside and began to tell him not to talk like that.
33But Jesus turned and looked at his followers.
Then he told Peter not to talk that way. He said,

∞**8:3 Healing:** John 11:1–44
∞**8:9 Table Fellowship/Lord's Supper:** Mark 15:12–26
∞**8:10 Hospitality:** Luke 5:27–30

8:22–26 The two-stage healing of a blind man in 8:22–26 parallels the followers' gradual change from unbelief to belief. Peter rightly declares that Jesus is the Christ, but he refuses to believe that suffering and death are to be part of God's purpose for Jesus or the followers (8:27–33). Jesus uses this as an opportunity to teach that following him requires a single-minded focus that overcomes even suffering (8:34–38). Blindness is not only about unbelief, but also unwillingness to accept suffering. The healing of blind Bartimaeus in Mark 10:46–52 is an important link to this passage. Healing and believing are tied together (10:52). The man is then able to follow Jesus, not just because he can physically see, but because he believes.

8:27–33 At first glance, it looks as though Peter understands exactly who Jesus is, the Christ (see Mark 1:1). But when Jesus announces that he must suffer many things, Peter shows that he understands very little after all. Peter believes Jesus is powerful and should not suffer. Jesus knows that God's power is expressed in his suffering; Peter, then, does not yet understand the ways of God. Interestingly, Jesus notes that those who follow the Christ who must suffer, will also undergo suffering (see Mark 8:34).

8:28 *Elijah.* A man who spoke for God and who lived hundreds of years before Christ. See 1 Kings 17.

TABLE FELLOWSHIP/LORD'S SUPPER

1 CORINTHIANS 11

Why is table fellowship so important in the life of Israel and the ministry of Jesus?
How is table fellowship important in Jesus' message of goodness and in the life of the early church?
What is the relationship between table fellowship and the Lord's Supper?

Students of the Bible and Bible times sometimes use the term "table fellowship" instead of "meal" or "gathering" to highlight some important features of life among biblical peoples. Meals for them were never simply about eating food and quenching thirst; at meals biblical people displayed kinship and friendship, and the fellowship they enjoyed around tables strengthened their social bonds. They felt it was especially important to maintain harmony at meals, and among God's chosen people table fellowship was a way of enjoying God's presence and provision.

Early in Israel's history God demonstrated his love and care for his people by providing food for them on their way to the Promised Land. The memories of God's provision—of manna, water, quail—were deeply embedded in the people's understanding of their utter reliance on God and of God's trustworthiness and nearness (Exodus 16–17). Special meals were held to celebrate the acceptance of covenants (agreements) between rulers or between a ruler and some subjects. A cycle of feasts and ceremonial meals developed as important parts of Israel's worship life.

God's presence was also often expected or hoped for at ordinary meals. Since God is holy, rules and customs were developed to help insure the peoples' readiness to be in God's presence at mealtimes. The kosher (or Kashruth) laws about handling food had to do with this desire for readiness to be in God's presence. Tables, then, and the fellowship meals shared around them, became places where God's goodness (his provision, protection and, presence) was invited and celebrated.

The hope of heaven and future fulfillment of God's *shalom* and justice was expressed in the picture of a heavenly banquet, the ultimate table fellowship, at which people from all nations would share the blessing of God's immediate presence and endless bounty (Isaiah 25:6–8; see also Joel 3:18; Matthew 8:11; Mark 14:25; Luke 13:24, 29; 22:18, 30; Revelation 3:20; 19:9, 17–18; 22:17).

Table fellowship is an important part of Jesus' ministry. He taught and healed and demonstrated his deity in the context of ordinary meals (Matthew 26:6–13; Luke 5:29–32; 7:36–50; 14:1–24). His presence had a way of transforming an ordinary meal into an extraordinary moment—like when the tax collector, Zacchaeus, declares that he is going to change his whole way of life after Jesus has invited himself into his home (Luke 19:1–10). Jesus also displayed his kingdom/Good News message in miraculous show-and-tell meals. The psalmist had raised a rhetorical question: "Can God prepare food in the desert?" (Psalm 78:19). Jesus answered it with actions that declared the presence of the same God who provided manna in the wilderness. He provided plenty of food for thousands of people at a time (Luke 9:10–17; Matthew 14:13–21; 15:32–39; Mark 6:32–43; 8:1–9; John 6:5–13).

Table fellowship was also a main part of life in the early church. Luke tells us that "breaking of bread" (the fellowship enjoyed at meals) was a habit of the believers: "They ate together in their homes, happy to share their food with joyful hearts" (Acts 2: 42, 46; see also 6:1; 20:7; 27:33–38).

The Lord's Supper is a special kind of table fellowship for Jesus' friends. In it the believers remember Jesus, his life and death, remember God's faithful provision for his people throughout salvation history, and celebrate the sealing of the New Agreement. Like the meals in which Jesus enjoyed fellowship with his friends and with sinners, the Lord's Supper is for the unholy. Jesus himself supplies the holiness required for God to be fully present among us. Only sinners who have become Jesus' friends and understand him to be Lord share this supper.

Paul says that in the Lord's Supper, "you (believers) are telling others about the Lord's death until he comes." The Lord's Supper looks back in time, proclaiming the historical reality of Jesus' death, and forward to the end of time, expressing the hope that Jesus will come again. The Lord's Supper anticipates the Wedding Meal of the Lamb (Revelation 19:9). By sharing it, believers proclaim their hope and trust that they will share that meal with Jesus—and all of his other friends.

Table Fellowship/Lord's Supper: For additional scriptures on this topic go to Genesis 18:1–16.

Spiritual Gifts

1 Corinthians 12

What are "spiritual gifts"?
Do all Christians have spiritual gifts? For what purposes are gifts given?

The concept of "spiritual gifts" comes primarily from lists of such gifts found in the letters of Paul (Romans 12:6–8; 1 Corinthians 12:4–11, 28–31; Ephesians 4:11, but see also 1 Peter 4:10–11). Paul's term for these gifts in Greek is *charisma,* which comes from the basic Greek root *charis*, which means "grace." The "gifts" of God are extensions of God's basic gift of grace to believers. In particular, the gifts enable the believer to participate in the ongoing ministry of God through his or her function in the church.

The gifts are called "spiritual gifts" because they are given through the agency of the Holy Spirit. In the Old Testament people recognized that certain individuals were given extraordinary roles and power through the Holy Spirit. In Exodus 31:3 the Lord tells Moses that "I have filled Bezalel with the Spirit of God." This meant that God had given this man the ability and the skill required for craftwork to build the Meeting Tent. Similarly, the Spirit empowered the rulers of Israel to perform their leadership function (Numbers 12:6–8; Judges 3:10), and moved the prophets to speak the words and warnings of God (Micah 3:8; 2 Samuel 23:2).

However, these references emphasize that the Spirit is given only rarely to select individuals in order to equip these people to serve God in special ways. The prophets looked forward to a time when all people could experience the presence of the Spirit and more faithfully serve God and follow the Lord's will (Ezekiel 36:26–28; 37:14; Joel 2:28–29; Isaiah 44:3).

In Acts 2 the Spirit falls on the disciples, enabling them to proclaim Christ in the languages of the crowd in the streets of Jerusalem. Peter interprets this miracle as the fulfillment of the Old Testament promise that the Spirit would be poured out on all (see especially Joel 2:28).

Paul relates the gifts of the Spirit to the anatomy of the human body (1 Corinthians 12:12–22; Romans 12:3–5). As a body is one unit, but has many parts, so the one Spirit gives Christians different gifts (1 Corinthians 12:12–22). Each part of the body has a function, and every part is needed for the body to work. In the same way, there is one Spirit but many gifts of the Spirit—each needed for the church to do the work of Christ. No one person has all the gifts (1 Corinthians 12:28), but each person can expect the Spirit to give them some gift and a role to play in the body of Christ. The key emphasis for Paul seems to be that the Spirit decides who gets which gift (1 Corinthians 12:11) and that all gifts are equally valuable and important (1 Corinthians 12:12–25; Romans 12:6).

Paul is responding in these verses in 1 Corinthians 12–14 to the controversy over spiritual gifts that seems to have focused in Corinth over the use of the gifts in worship (1 Corinthians 14). Paul is well aware that all the gifts can be misused, but he does not deny the validity of the gifts. Instead, Paul seeks to guide the use of spiritual gifts in these verses. He stresses first that a spiritual gift is given to an individual for the encouragement of that person and the encouragement of the whole church (1 Corinthians 14:4–6). He tells the Corinthians that a Christian has control over the use of a spiritual gift. Rightly used, the spiritual gift helps educate and direct the church (1 Corinthians 14:26).

It is worth noting that not one of Paul's three lists of the gifts of the Spirit agrees with the others. None of the lists seem to intend to give us an exhaustive list of the gifts, and in fact, all of them together may not cover the whole realm of the gifts of the Spirit.

Only the gift of prophecy appears in all four lists. The role of the prophet seems to be a person (male or female, see Acts 21:9; 1 Corinthians 11:5) who speaks under inspiration of God to warn, exhort, comfort or correct the church.

Other gifts are more difficult to define and understand. Paul talks of two gifts involving speaking "with wisdom" and speaking "with knowledge" (1 Corinthians 12:8) without defining the difference between the two. Not all the gifts seem to relate to offices—the gift of tongues appears primarily as a means of encouraging the individual believer, and only with some hesitation and restrictions will Paul allow tongues in a worship service (1 Corinthians 14:6–19). All the gifts were given to help the believer function positively in the church. The Spirit gifts some people to be helpful followers, insightful friends, and creative givers of their resources. The gifts are not possessions about which the believer is to boast, but gifts of grace to help us serve and follow Christ better, particularly in the life of the church.

Spiritual Gifts: For additional scriptures on this topic go to Numbers 12:2.

"Go away from me, Satan! You don't care about
the things of God, but only about things people
think are important."
34Then Jesus called the crowd to him, along
with his followers. He said, "If people want to follow me, they must give up the things they want.
They must be willing even to give up their lives to
follow me. 35Those who want to save their lives
will give up true life. But those who give up their
lives for me and for the Good News will have true
life. 36It is worth nothing for them to have the
whole world if they lose their souls. 37They could
never pay enough to buy back their souls. 38The
people who live now are living in a sinful and evil
time. If people are ashamed of me and my teaching, the Son of Man will be ashamed of them
when he comes with his Father's glory and with
the holy angels."
9 Then Jesus said to the people, "I tell you the
truth, some people standing here will see the
kingdom of God come with power before they die."

Jesus Talks with Moses and Elijah

2Six days later, Jesus took Peter, James, and John
up on a high mountain by themselves. While they
watched, Jesus' appearance was changed. 3His
clothes became shining white, whiter than any
person could make them. 4Then Elijah and Moses
appeared to them, talking with Jesus.
5Peter said to Jesus, "Teacher, it is good that we
are here. Let us make three tents—one for you,
one for Moses, and one for Elijah." 6Peter did not
know what to say, because he and the others were
so frightened.
7Then a cloud came and covered them, and a
voice came from the cloud, saying, "This is my Son,
whom I love. Listen to him!"
8Suddenly Peter, James, and John looked around,
but they saw only Jesus there alone with them.
9As they were coming down the mountain, Jesus
commanded them not to tell anyone about what
they had seen until the Son of Man had risen from
the dead.
10So the followers obeyed Jesus, but they discussed what he meant about rising from the dead.
11Then they asked Jesus, "Why do the teachers
of the law say that Elijah must come first?"
12Jesus answered, "They are right to say that Elijah must come first and make everything the way
it should be. But why does the Scripture say that
the Son of Man will suffer much and that people
will treat him as if he were nothing? 13I tell you
that Elijah has already come. And people did to
him whatever they wanted to do, just as the Scriptures said it would happen."

Jesus Heals a Sick Boy

14When Jesus, Peter, James, and John came back
to the other followers, they saw a great crowd
around them and the teachers of the law arguing
with them. 15But as soon as the crowd saw Jesus,
the people were surprised and ran to welcome
him.
16Jesus asked, "What are you arguing about?"
17A man answered, "Teacher, I brought my son
to you. He has an evil spirit in him that stops him
from talking. 18When the spirit attacks him, it
throws him on the ground. Then my son foams at
the mouth, grinds his teeth, and becomes very stiff.
I asked your followers to force the evil spirit out, but
they couldn't."
19Jesus answered, "You people have no faith.
How long must I stay with you? How long must I
put up with you? Bring the boy to me."
20So the followers brought him to Jesus. As soon
as the evil spirit saw Jesus, it made the boy lose
control of himself, and he fell down and rolled on
the ground, foaming at the mouth.
21Jesus asked the boy's father, "How long has this
been happening?"
The father answered, "Since he was very young.
22The spirit often throws him into a fire or into
water to kill him. If you can do anything for him,
please have pity on us and help us."
23Jesus said to the father, "You said, 'If you can!'
All things are possible for the one who believes."
24Immediately the father cried out, "I do believe!
Help me to believe more!"
25When Jesus saw that a crowd was quickly gathering, he ordered the evil spirit, saying, "You spirit
that makes people unable to hear or speak, I command you to come out of this boy and never enter
him again!"
26The evil spirit screamed and caused the boy to
fall on the ground again. Then the spirit came out.
The boy looked as if he were dead, and many people said, "He is dead!" 27But Jesus took hold of the
boy's hand and helped him to stand up.

8:33 *Satan.* Name for the devil meaning "the enemy." Jesus means that Peter was talking like Satan.

8:33 Peter: Mark 9:2–6

8:34 Lordship: Acts 2:36

8:34 The Crucifixion of Jesus (The Way of the Cross): Luke 23:20–38

9:4 *Elijah and Moses.* Two of the most important Jewish leaders in the past. God had given Moses the Law, and Elijah was an important prophet.

9:6 Peter: Mark 14:29–31

9:23 Encouragement: John 16:33

28When Jesus went into the house, his followers
began asking him privately, "Why couldn't we force
that evil spirit out?"
29Jesus answered, "That kind of spirit can only be
forced out by prayer."

Jesus Talks About His Death

30Then Jesus and his followers left that place
and went through Galilee. He didn't want anyone
to know where he was, 31because he was teaching
his followers. He said to them, "The Son of Man
will be handed over to people, and they will kill
him. After three days, he will rise from the dead."
32But the followers did not understand what Jesus
meant, and they were afraid to ask him.

Who Is the Greatest?

33Jesus and his followers went to Capernaum.
When they went into a house there, he asked
them, "What were you arguing about on the road?"
34But the followers did not answer, because their
argument on the road was about which one of them
was the greatest.
35Jesus sat down and called the twelve apostles
to him. He said, "Whoever wants to be the most
important must be last of all and servant of all."
36Then Jesus took a small child and had him
stand among them. Taking the child in his arms,
he said, 37"Whoever accepts a child like this in my
name accepts me. And whoever accepts me accepts
the One who sent me."

Anyone Not Against Us Is for Us

38Then John said, "Teacher, we saw someone
using your name to force demons out of a person.
We told him to stop, because he does not belong
to our group."
39But Jesus said, "Don't stop him, because anyone who uses my name to do powerful things will
not easily say evil things about me. 40Whoever is
not against us is with us. 41I tell you the truth, whoever gives you a drink of water because you belong
to the Christ will truly get his reward.
42"If one of these little children believes in me,
and someone causes that child to sin, it would be
better for that person to have a large stone tied
around his neck and be drowned in the sea. 43If
your hand causes you to sin, cut it off. It is better
for you to lose part of your body and live forever
than to have two hands and go to hell, where the
fire never goes out. 44* 45If your foot causes you to
sin, cut it off. It is better for you to lose part of your
body and to live forever than to have two feet and
be thrown into hell. 46* 47If your eye causes you
to sin, take it out. It is better for you to enter the
kingdom of God with only one eye than to have
two eyes and be thrown into hell. 48In hell the
worm does not die; the fire is never put out.
49Every person will be salted with fire.
50"Salt is good, but if the salt loses its salty taste,
you cannot make it salty again. So, be full of salt,
and have peace with each other."

Jesus Teaches About Divorce

10 Then Jesus left that place and went into the
area of Judea and across the Jordan River.
Again, crowds came to him, and he taught them
as he usually did.
2Some Pharisees came to Jesus and tried to trick
him. They asked, "Is it right for a man to divorce
his wife?"
3Jesus answered, "What did Moses command
you to do?"
4They said, "Moses allowed a man to write out
divorce papers and send her away."
5Jesus said, "Moses wrote that command for you
because you were stubborn. 6But when God
made the world, 'he made them male and female.'
7'So a man will leave his father and mother and be
united with his wife, 8and the two will become
one body.' So there are not two, but one. 9God has
joined the two together, so no one should separate them."
10Later, in the house, his followers asked Jesus
again about the question of divorce. 11He answered,
"Anyone who divorces his wife and marries another
woman is guilty of adultery against her. 12And the
woman who divorces her husband and marries
another man is also guilty of adultery."

9:29 Doubt: Luke 24:36–39
9:32 Martyrdom: Mark 10:32–34
9:35 Leadership: Luke 22:26
9:37 Children: Mark 10:13–16
***9:44** *Verse 44.* Some Greek copies of Mark add verse 44, which is the same as verse 48.
***9:46** *Verse 46.* Some Greek copies of Mark add verse 46, which is the same as verse 48.
9:49–50 Jesus says that "every person will be salted with fire" (Mark 9:49). Verse 49 most likely should be understood to refer to the preceding verses (Mark 9:43–48) rather than verse 50. It means that all people who are in hell are cursed and will be punished until they are like barren, salty lands . . . like Sodom and Gomorrah (Genesis 19:24–28).
10:4 *"Moses . . . away."* Quotation from Deuteronomy 24:1.
10:5 Stubbornness: Acts 7:51
10:6 *'he made . . . female.'* Quotation from Genesis 1:27.
10:7–8 *'So . . . body.'* Quotation from Genesis 2:24.
10:12 Divorce: Luke 16:18

Jesus Accepts Children

[13]Some people brought their little children to Jesus so he could touch them, but his followers told them to stop. [14]When Jesus saw this, he was upset and said to them, "Let the little children come to me. Don't stop them, because the kingdom of God belongs to people who are like these children. [15]I tell you the truth, you must accept the kingdom of God as if you were a little child, or you will never enter it." [16]Then Jesus took the children in his arms, put his hands on them, and blessed them.

A Rich Young Man's Question

[17]As Jesus started to leave, a man ran to him and fell on his knees before Jesus. The man asked, "Good teacher, what must I do to have life forever?"

[18]Jesus answered, "Why do you call me good? Only God is good. [19]You know the commands: 'You must not murder anyone. You must not be guilty of adultery. You must not steal. You must not tell lies about your neighbor. You must not cheat. Honor your father and mother.'"

[20]The man said, "Teacher, I have obeyed all these things since I was a boy."

[21]Jesus, looking at the man, loved him and said, "There is one more thing you need to do. Go and sell everything you have, and give the money to the poor, and you will have treasure in heaven. Then come and follow me."

[22]He was very sad to hear Jesus say this, and he left sorrowfully, because he was rich.

[23]Then Jesus looked at his followers and said, "How hard it will be for the rich to enter the kingdom of God!"

[24]The followers were amazed at what Jesus said. But he said again, "My children, it is very hard to enter the kingdom of God! [25]It is easier for a camel to go through the eye of a needle than for a rich person to enter the kingdom of God."

[26]The followers were even more surprised and said to each other, "Then who can be saved?"

[27]Jesus looked at them and said, "This is something people cannot do, but God can. God can do all things."

[28]Peter said to Jesus, "Look, we have left everything and followed you."

[29]Jesus said, "I tell you the truth, all those who have left houses, brothers, sisters, mother, father, children, or farms for me and for the Good News [30]will get more than they left. Here in this world they will have a hundred times more homes, brothers, sisters, mothers, children, and fields. And with those things, they will also suffer for their belief. But in the age that is coming they will have life forever. [31]Many who have the highest place now will have the lowest place in the future. And many who have the lowest place now will have the highest place in the future."

Jesus Talks About His Death

[32]As Jesus and the people with him were on the road to Jerusalem, he was leading the way. His followers were amazed, but others in the crowd who followed were afraid. Again Jesus took the twelve apostles aside and began to tell them what was about to happen in Jerusalem. [33]He said, "Look, we are going to Jerusalem. The Son of Man will be turned over to the leading priests and the teachers of the law. They will say that he must die, and they will turn him over to the non-Jewish people, [34]who will laugh at him and spit on him. They will beat him with whips and crucify him. But on the third day, he will rise to life again."

Two Followers Ask Jesus a Favor

[35]Then James and John, sons of Zebedee, came to Jesus and said, "Teacher, we want to ask you to do something for us."

10:13–16 In rebuking his own followers' attitudes about children, Jesus illustrates his anger at society's treatment of children. In this account, Jesus places children foremost in importance precisely because they are considered the least. Jesus redefines what it means to be important for his audience. God honors the wisdom of old age but does not want us to despise the young.

This passage is sometimes taken to refer to the baptism or dedication of children, but it has a more simple and prophetic sense. Here Jesus publicly values children in a society that devalued them, making a radical statement of how God's kingdom turns upside down worldly values, placing greatest worth on the least, the last, and the lost.

10:16 Blessing: John 17:11

10:16 Children: Luke 1–2

10:19 *'You . . . mother.'* Quotation from Exodus 20:12-16; Deuteronomy 5:16-20.

10:28–30 When Peter pointed out the level of the followers' commitment to Jesus, as evidenced by what they had given up to follow him, the Lord's response was that our commitment to him never means loss ultimately, either in this life or the life to come, but a gain in every area of our lives. We have multiplied blessings, even in suffering, when our lives are committed to Christ.

10:29–31 "Fathers" are among those people one leaves, but not among those one receives back. This is consistent with Jesus' earlier remark that his family of brothers, sisters, and mothers are those who do what God wants (see Mark 3:33–35). In fact, throughout the Book of Mark Jesus calls into question a way of relating to others that resembled the way "fathers" treated their extended families in the Roman world. "Fathers" were widely know for their abuses of authority, their claims to greatness, their lack of compassion, and for the control they exercised over others. Such behavior has no place in the Christian family.

10:30 House/Home: Luke 10:5–11

10:31 Materialism/Possessions: Mark 14:3–9

10:31 Money: Luke 20:45–21:4

10:34 Martyrdom: Mark 14:1–15:41

36Jesus asked, "What do you want me to do for
you?"
37They answered, "Let one of us sit at your right
side and one of us sit at your left side in your glory
in your kingdom."
38Jesus said, "You don't understand what you are
asking. Can you drink the cup that I must drink?
And can you be baptized with the same kind of
baptism that I must go through?"
39They answered, "Yes, we can."
Jesus said to them, "You will drink the same cup
that I will drink, and you will be baptized with the
same baptism that I must go through. 40But I cannot choose who will sit at my right or my left;
those places belong to those for whom they have
been prepared."
41When the other ten followers heard this, they
began to be angry with James and John.
42Jesus called them together and said, "The other
nations have rulers. You know that those rulers
love to show their power over the people, and
their important leaders love to use all their authority. 43But it should not be that way among you.
Whoever wants to become great among you must
serve the rest of you like a servant. 44Whoever
wants to become the first among you must serve
all of you like a slave. 45In the same way, the Son
of Man did not come to be served. He came to
serve others and to give his life as a ransom for
many people."

Jesus Heals a Blind Man

46Then they came to the town of Jericho. As Jesus
was leaving there with his followers and a great
many people, a blind beggar named Bartimaeus son
of Timaeus was sitting by the road. 47When he heard
that Jesus from Nazareth was walking by, he began
to shout, "Jesus, Son of David, have mercy on me!"
48Many people warned the blind man to be
quiet, but he shouted even more, "Son of David,
have mercy on me!"
49Jesus stopped and said, "Tell the man to come
here."
So they called the blind man, saying, "Cheer up!
Get to your feet. Jesus is calling you." 50The blind
man jumped up, left his coat there, and went to
Jesus.
51Jesus asked him, "What do you want me to do
for you?"
The blind man answered, "Teacher, I want to
see."
52Jesus said, "Go, you are healed because you
believed." At once the man could see, and he followed Jesus on the road.

Jesus Enters Jerusalem as a King

11 As Jesus and his followers were coming closer
to Jerusalem, they came to the towns of
Bethphage and Bethany near the Mount of Olives.
From there Jesus sent two of his followers 2and
said to them, "Go to the town you can see there.
When you enter it, you will quickly find a colt tied,
which no one has ever ridden. Untie it and bring it
here to me. 3If anyone asks you why you are doing
this, tell him its Master needs the colt, and he will
send it at once."
4The followers went into the town, found a colt
tied in the street near the door of a house, and
untied it. 5Some people were standing there
and asked, "What are you doing? Why are you
untying that colt?" 6The followers answered the
way Jesus told them to answer, and the people let
them take the colt.
7They brought the colt to Jesus and put their
coats on it, and Jesus sat on it. 8Many people spread
their coats on the road. Others cut branches in
the fields and spread them on the road. 9The people were walking ahead of Jesus and behind him,
shouting,
"Praise God!
God bless the One who comes in the name
of the Lord! *Psalm 118:26*
10God bless the kingdom of our father David!
That kingdom is coming!
Praise to God in heaven!"
11Jesus entered Jerusalem and went into the
Temple. After he had looked at everything, since it
was already late, he went out to Bethany with the
twelve apostles.
12The next day as Jesus was leaving Bethany, he
became hungry. 13Seeing a fig tree in leaf from far
away, he went to see if it had any figs on it. But he
found no figs, only leaves, because it was not the
right season for figs. 14So Jesus said to the tree,
"May no one ever eat fruit from you again." And
Jesus' followers heard him say this.

Jesus Goes to the Temple

15When Jesus returned to Jerusalem, he went into
the Temple and began to throw out those who were

10:38 *Can you . . . through?* Jesus was asking if they could suffer the same terrible things that would happen to him.

10:43 Honor & Shame: Luke 22:6

10:45 Disciple/Discipleship/Mentoring (Follow/Follower): Luke 9:57–62

10:45 Service: Mark 12:30–31

10:52 Blindness: Luke 7:18–23

11:9 *Praise.* Literally, *Hosanna,* a Hebrew word used at first in praying to God for help, but at this time it was probably a shout of joy used in praising God or his Messiah.

11:10 David: Luke 1:32

buying and selling there. He turned over the tables
of those who were exchanging different kinds of
money, and he upset the benches of those who
were selling doves. 16Jesus refused to allow anyone
to carry goods through the Temple courts. 17Then
he taught the people, saying, "It is written in the
Scriptures, 'My Temple will be called a house for
prayer for people from all nations.' But you are
changing God's house into a 'hideout for robbers.'"
18The leading priests and the teachers of the law
heard all this and began trying to find a way to kill
Jesus. They were afraid of him, because all the people were amazed at his teaching. 19That evening,
Jesus and his followers left the city.

The Power of Faith

20The next morning as Jesus was passing by with
his followers, they saw the fig tree dry and dead,
even to the roots. 21Peter remembered the tree
and said to Jesus, "Teacher, look! The fig tree you
cursed is dry and dead!"
22Jesus answered, "Have faith in God. 23I tell you
the truth, you can say to this mountain, 'Go, fall
into the sea.' And if you have no doubts in your
mind and believe that what you say will happen,
God will do it for you. 24So I tell you to believe that
you have received the things you ask for in prayer,
and God will give them to you. 25When you are
praying, if you are angry with someone, forgive
him so that your Father in heaven will also forgive
your sins." 26*

Leaders Doubt Jesus' Authority

27Jesus and his followers went again to Jerusalem. As Jesus was walking in the Temple, the
leading priests, the teachers of the law, and
the older leaders came to him. 28They said to
him, "What authority do you have to do these
things? Who gave you this authority?"
29Jesus answered, "I will ask you one question. If
you answer me, I will tell you what authority I have
to do these things. 30Tell me: When John baptized
people, was that authority from God or just from
other people?"
31They argued about Jesus' question, saying, "If
we answer, 'John's baptism was from God,' Jesus
will say, 'Then why didn't you believe him?' 32But
if we say, 'It was from other people,' the crowd will
be against us." (These leaders were afraid of the
people, because all the people believed that John
was a prophet.)
33So they answered Jesus, "We don't know."
Jesus said to them, "Then I won't tell you what
authority I have to do these things."

A Story About God's Son

12 Jesus began to use stories to teach the people. He said, "A man planted a vineyard. He
put a wall around it and dug a hole for a winepress
and built a tower. Then he leased the land to some
farmers and left for a trip. 2When it was time for
the grapes to be picked, he sent a servant to the
farmers to get his share of the grapes. 3But
the farmers grabbed the servant and beat him and
sent him away empty-handed. 4Then the man sent
another servant. They hit him on the head and
showed no respect for him. 5So the man sent
another servant, whom they killed. The man
sent many other servants; the farmers beat some
of them and killed others.
6"The man had one person left to send, his son
whom he loved. He sent him last of all, saying,
'They will respect my son.'
7"But the farmers said to each other, 'This son
will inherit the vineyard. If we kill him, it will be
ours.' 8So they took the son, killed him, and threw
him out of the vineyard.
9"So what will the owner of the vineyard do? He
will come and kill those farmers and will give the
vineyard to other farmers. 10Surely you have read
this Scripture:

'The stone that the builders rejected
became the cornerstone.
11The Lord did this,
and it is wonderful to us.'" *Psalm 118:22-23*

12The Jewish leaders knew that the story was
about them. So they wanted to find a way to arrest
Jesus, but they were afraid of the people. So the
leaders left him and went away.

Is It Right to Pay Taxes or Not?

13Later, the Jewish leaders sent some Pharisees
and Herodians to Jesus to trap him in saying something wrong. 14They came to him and said, "Teacher, we know that you are an honest man. You are
not afraid of what other people think about you,
because you pay no attention to who they are.
And you teach the truth about God's way. Tell us:
Is it right to pay taxes to Caesar or not? 15Should
we pay them, or not?"
But knowing what these men were really trying
to do, Jesus said to them, "Why are you trying to

11:17 *'My Temple . . . nations.'* Quotation from Isaiah 56:7.
11:17 *'hideout for robbers.'* Quotation from Jeremiah 7:11.
11:19 Scribes (Teachers of the Law): Mark 12:28–34
***11:26** *Verse 26.* Some early Greek copies add verse 26: "But if you don't forgive other people, then your Father in heaven will not forgive your sins."
12:12 Jesus: Mark 13:32
12:12 Parables: Luke 10:25–37
12:12 Son/Child of God: Luke 3:21–4:13
12:13 *Herodians.* A political group that followed Herod and his family.

trap me? Bring me a coin to look at." 16They gave
Jesus a coin, and he asked, "Whose image and
name are on the coin?"
They answered, "Caesar's."
17Then Jesus said to them, "Give to Caesar the
things that are Caesar's, and give to God the things
that are God's." The men were amazed at what
Jesus said.

Some Sadducees Try to Trick Jesus

18Then some Sadducees came to Jesus and asked
him a question. (Sadducees believed that people
would not rise from the dead.) 19They said,
"Teacher, Moses wrote that if a man's brother
dies, leaving a wife but no children, then that man
must marry the widow and have children for his
brother. 20Once there were seven brothers. The
first brother married and died, leaving no children. 21So the second brother married the widow,
but he also died and had no children. The same
thing happened with the third brother. 22All
seven brothers married her and died, and none of
the brothers had any children. Finally the woman
died too. 23Since all seven brothers had married
her, when people rise from the dead, whose wife
will she be?"
24Jesus answered, "Why don't you understand?
Don't you know what the Scriptures say, and
don't you know about the power of God? 25When
people rise from the dead, they will not marry, nor
will they be given to someone to marry. They will
be like the angels in heaven. 26Surely you have
read what God said about people rising from the
dead. In the book in which Moses wrote about
the burning bush, it says that God told Moses, 'I
am the God of Abraham, the God of Isaac, and the
God of Jacob.' 27God is the God of the living, not
the dead. You Sadducees are wrong!"

The Most Important Command

28One of the teachers of the law came and heard
Jesus arguing with the Sadducees. Seeing that Jesus
gave good answers to their questions, he asked
Jesus, "Which of the commands is most important?"
29Jesus answered, "The most important command is this: 'Listen, people of Israel! The Lord our
God is the only Lord. 30Love the Lord your God
with all your heart, all your soul, all your mind,
and all your strength.' 31The second command is
this: 'Love your neighbor as you love yourself.'
There are no commands more important than
these."
32The man answered, "That was a good answer,
Teacher. You were right when you said God is the
only Lord and there is no other God besides him.
33One must love God with all his heart, all his
mind, and all his strength. And one must love
his neighbor as he loves himself. These commands
are more important than all the animals and sacrifices we offer to God."
34When Jesus saw that the man answered him
wisely, Jesus said to him, "You are close to the kingdom of God." And after that, no one was brave
enough to ask Jesus any more questions.
35As Jesus was teaching in the Temple, he asked,
"Why do the teachers of the law say that the Christ
is the son of David? 36David himself, speaking by
the Holy Spirit, said:

'The Lord said to my Lord:
Sit by me at my right side,
until I put your enemies under your control.'
Psalm 110:1

37David himself calls the Christ 'Lord,' so how can
the Christ be his son?" The large crowd listened to
Jesus with pleasure.
38Jesus continued teaching and said, "Beware of
the teachers of the law. They like to walk around
wearing fancy clothes, and they love for people to
greet them with respect in the marketplaces.
39They love to have the most important seats in the
synagogues and at feasts. 40But they cheat widows
and steal their houses and then try to make themselves look good by saying long prayers. They will
receive a greater punishment."

True Giving

41Jesus sat near the Temple money box and
watched the people put in their money. Many rich
people gave large sums of money. 42Then a poor
widow came and put in two small copper coins,
which were only worth a few cents.
43Calling his followers to him, Jesus said, "I tell
you the truth, this poor widow gave more than all
those rich people. 44They gave only what they did
not need. This woman is very poor, but she gave
all she had; she gave all she had to live on."

12:17 Racism: Luke 4:23–27
12:26 *burning bush.* Read Exodus 3:1-12 in the Old Testament.
12:26 *'I am . . . Jacob.'* Quotation from Exodus 3:6.
12:29–30 *'Listen . . . strength.'* Quotation from Deuteronomy 6:4-5.
12:31 *'Love . . . yourself.'* Quotation from Leviticus 19:18.
12:31 Neighbor: Mark 12:33
12:31 Service: Luke 19:11–27
12:33 Neighbor: Luke 10:27
12:34 Scribes (Teachers of the Law): Luke 14:1–6
12:35 Crossing Cultural Boundaries: Luke 9:37–43
12:40 Debt/Loan: Luke 6:34–36

The Temple Will Be Destroyed

13 As Jesus was leaving the Temple, one of his followers said to him, "Look, Teacher! How beautiful the buildings are! How big the stones are!"

2Jesus said, "Do you see all these great buildings? Not one stone will be left on another. Every stone will be thrown down to the ground."

3Later, as Jesus was sitting on the Mount of Olives, opposite the Temple, he was alone with Peter, James, John, and Andrew. They asked Jesus, 4"Tell us, when will these things happen? And what will be the sign that they are going to happen?"

5Jesus began to answer them, "Be careful that no one fools you. 6Many people will come in my name, saying, 'I am the One,' and they will fool many people. 7When you hear about wars and stories of wars that are coming, don't be afraid. These things must happen before the end comes. 8Nations will fight against other nations, and kingdoms against other kingdoms. There will be earthquakes in different places, and there will be times when there is no food for people to eat. These things are like the first pains when something new is about to be born.

9"You must be careful. People will arrest you and take you to court and beat you in their synagogues. You will be forced to stand before kings and governors, to tell them about me. This will happen to you because you follow me. 10But before these things happen, the Good News must be told to all people. 11When you are arrested and judged, don't worry ahead of time about what you should say. Say whatever is given you to say at that time, because it will not really be you speaking; it will be the Holy Spirit.

12"Brothers will give their own brothers to be killed, and fathers will give their own children to be killed. Children will fight against their own parents and cause them to be put to death. 13All people will hate you because you follow me, but those people who keep their faith until the end will be saved.

14"You will see 'the destroying terror' standing where it should not be." (You who read this should understand what it means.) "At that time, the people in Judea should run away to the mountains.∞ 15If people are on the roofs of their houses, they must not go down or go inside to get anything out of their houses. 16If people are in the fields, they must not go back to get their coats. 17At that time, how terrible it will be for women who are pregnant or have nursing babies! 18Pray that these things will not happen in winter, 19because those days will be full of trouble. There will be more trouble than there has ever been since the beginning, when God made the world, until now, and nothing as bad will ever happen again. 20God has decided to make that terrible time short. Otherwise, no one would go on living. But God will make that time short to help the people he has chosen. 21At that time, someone might say to you, 'Look, there is the Christ!' Or another person might say, 'There he is!' But don't believe them. 22False Christs and false prophets will come and perform great wonders and miracles. They will try to fool even the people God has chosen, if that is possible. 23So be careful. I have warned you about all this before it happens.

24"During the days after this trouble comes,

'the sun will grow dark,
    and the moon will not give its light.
25The stars will fall from the sky.
    And the powers of the heavens will
        be shaken.' *Isaiah 13:10; 34:4*

26"Then people will see the Son of Man coming in clouds with great power and glory.∞ 27Then he will send his angels all around the earth to gather his chosen people from every part of the earth and from every part of heaven.

28"Learn a lesson from the fig tree: When its branches become green and soft and new leaves appear, you know summer is near. 29In the same way, when you see these things happening, you will know that the time is near, ready to come. 30I tell you the truth, all these things will happen while the people of this time are still living.∞ 31Earth and sky will be destroyed, but the words I have said will never be destroyed.

32"No one knows when that day or time will be, not the angels in heaven, not even the Son. Only the Father knows.∞ 33Be careful! Always be ready,

---

13:1–37 In Mark 13, Jesus outlines the difficulties that Christians will suffer in the time before the end of the world. Then, in Mark 14–15, we read how Jesus himself suffers in many of these ways. They will be delivered to the authorities, just as he is (Mark 13:9–13; 14:41, 42; 15:1); they will be betrayed by families and friends, just as he is (Mark 13:12, 13; 14:10, 20, 43); and so on. This means that the end has already begun; in his suffering and death, Jesus inaugurated the coming of the new world. Faithful suffering is not without purpose but draws meaning from the great work of God by which he is ushering in that day when there will be no more suffering.

13:14 *'the destroying terror.'* Mentioned in Daniel 9:27; 12:11 (cf. Daniel 11:31).

∞**13:14 Mountain:** Revelation 6:14–16

13:15 *roofs.* In Bible times houses were built with flat roofs. The roof was used for drying things such as flax and fruit. And it was used as an extra room, as a place for worship, and as a cool place to sleep in the summer.

∞**13:26 Angels/Guardian Angels:** Mark 14:62

∞**13:30 End Times/Last Days:** Luke 10:12

∞**13:32 Jesus:** Mark 14:36

because you don't know when that time will be. [34]It is like a man who goes on a trip. He leaves his house and lets his servants take care of it, giving each one a special job to do. The man tells the servant guarding the door always to be watchful. [35]So always be ready, because you don't know when the owner of the house will come back. It might be in the evening, or at midnight, or in the morning while it is still dark, or when the sun rises. [36]Always be ready. Otherwise he might come back suddenly and find you sleeping. [37]I tell you this, and I say this to everyone: 'Be ready!'"

The Plan to Kill Jesus

14 It was now only two days before the Passover and the Feast of Unleavened Bread. The leading priests and teachers of the law were trying to find a trick to arrest Jesus and kill him. [2]But they said, "We must not do it during the feast, because the people might cause a riot."

A Woman with Perfume for Jesus

[3]Jesus was in Bethany at the house of Simon, who had a skin disease. While Jesus was eating there, a woman approached him with an alabaster jar filled with very expensive perfume, made of pure nard. She opened the jar and poured the perfume on Jesus' head.

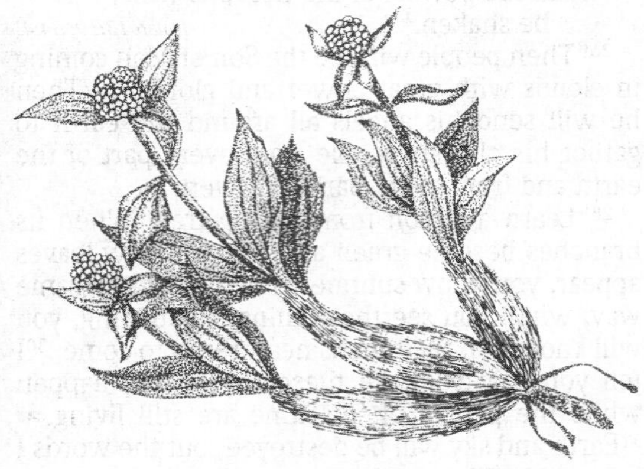

The fragrant nard (spikenard) plant

[4]Some who were there became upset and said to each other, "Why waste that perfume? [5]It was worth a full year's work. It could have been sold and the money given to the poor." And they got very angry with the woman.

[6]Jesus said, "Leave her alone. Why are you troubling her? She did an excellent thing for me. [7]You will always have the poor with you, and you can help them anytime you want. But you will not always have me. [8]This woman did the only thing she could do for me; she poured perfume on my body to prepare me for burial. [9]I tell you the truth, wherever the Good News is preached in all the world, what this woman has done will be told, and people will remember her."

Judas Becomes an Enemy of Jesus

[10]One of the twelve apostles, Judas Iscariot, went to talk to the leading priests to offer to hand Jesus over to them. [11]These priests were pleased about this and promised to pay Judas money. So he watched for the best time to turn Jesus in.

Jesus Eats the Passover Meal

[12]It was now the first day of the Feast of Unleavened Bread when the Passover lamb was sacrificed. Jesus' followers said to him, "Where do you want us to go and prepare for you to eat the Passover meal?"

[13]Jesus sent two of his followers and said to them, "Go into the city and a man carrying a jar of water will meet you. Follow him. [14]When he goes into a house, tell the owner of the house, 'The Teacher says: Where is my guest room in which I can eat the Passover meal with my followers?' [15]The owner will show you a large room upstairs that is furnished and ready. Prepare the food for us there."

[16]So the followers left and went into the city. Everything happened as Jesus had said, so they prepared the Passover meal.

[17]In the evening, Jesus went to that house with the twelve. [18]While they were all eating, Jesus said, "I tell you the truth, one of you will turn against me—one of you eating with me now."

[19]The followers were very sad to hear this. Each one began to say to Jesus, "I am not the one, am I?"

[20]Jesus answered, "It is one of the twelve—the one who dips his bread into the bowl with me. [21]The Son of Man will die, just as the Scriptures say. But how terrible it will be for the person who hands the Son of Man over to be killed. It would be better for him if he had never been born."

The Lord's Supper

[22]While they were eating, Jesus took some bread and thanked God for it and broke it. Then he gave it to his followers and said, "Take it; this is my body."

14:6 Self-Control: Luke 43–48
14:9 Materialism/Possessions: Luke 19:1–19
14:12 Feasts/Festivals: Luke 14:13
14:22 Thanks: Hebrews 12:28–29

Body of Christ

1 Corinthians 12

What does it mean that we are members of the body of Christ?
How does that affect our relationship with each other and Christ's relationship with us?

There are several references, by Jesus or others, to his physical body (John 19:38; Acts 2:31; 1 Corinthians 11:24; 1 Timothy 3:16; 1 Peter 3:18). Once Jesus compared his body to the "temple," presumably because it was God's special dwelling place while he was on earth (John 2:19–21). The bread at the Lord's Supper is also portrayed as Christ's body.

As well, the image of Christ's "body" is Paul's favorite way of talking about the people of God. It appears several times and receives extended treatment in four of his letters. In the earlier passages he focuses upon believers' relationship with one another in Christ; in the later passages on the relationship of the church as a whole with Christ.

Referring to a group of people as a body was not new. Several ancient writers pictured their society this way. Paul borrowed this image from the surrounding culture, but used it in a more novel fashion. He was the first to apply it to a smaller group within society, the local church, and the first to use it of people's personal rather than civic responsibilities. He saw believers joined both to Christ (1 Corinthians 6:15) and to one another (1 Corinthians 10:17). This was accomplished by the Spirit the moment they were baptized (1 Corinthians 12:13). Membership in a church was not something you signed up for, nor was it in an institution. It was to Christ, and to a specific group of people, that you were joined when you became a believer.

In his earlier letters to the Corinthians and to the Romans, Paul's description of the church as a body has several features:

1. A church is the body—that is, the full expression—of Christ in a particular place (1 Corinthians 12:27), not just part, or a partial expression of, some wider denominational body of Christ. Though belonging to a network of churches is part of Paul's vision, he does not use body language to describe this.
2. Since it is made up of people of different genders, races, and classes, the local church is quite diverse. Yet, just as the different organs in the body make up a unity, so it is with the church (1 Corinthians 12:12–13).
3. As they come to eat the Lord's Supper together, believers are to express their unity by welcoming and serving one another. Otherwise it is not the giving of Christ's body they are celebrating and receiving in the meal (1 Corinthians 10:17; 11:29).
4. The Spirit distributes a diverse range of gifts to individual members of the body to share with one another (1 Corinthians 12:4–11). None of these should be disregarded or overvalued in the church's meetings. Only when all gifts are present is the church made fully whole (Romans 12:4–6; 1 Corinthians 12:14–21).
5. Each member of the church should have a realistic understanding of the gifts they do and do not possess (Romans 12:3), otherwise they misunderstand their function in the body. Also, they should only exercise gifts to the degree they have been given them (Romans 12:3, 6–8).
6. It is often the least prominent contributors to the life of the congregation who should be given greatest respect. Just as many of the body's most important parts are hidden, so are many of the most significant functions in the church (1 Corinthians 12:22–25).
7. So close is the link between members that what affects one necessarily affects all. It is as if each local body of believers had a common nerve placed in them by and connected with Christ (1 Corinthians 12:26).

In these early uses of the image of the local church as a body, Christ appears to be present in and through the whole body (Romans 12:5; 1 Corinthians 12:12). In the later passages in Ephesians and Colossians Paul's vision expands and Christ is represented as the head of the body (Ephesians 1:22–23; Colossians 1:18, 24; 2:19–20; 3:15), which is a heavenly entity made up of all believers, alive and dead. Such an idea is difficult for us to grasp. We have to think of our living in two dimensions—here on earth inhabited by the Spirit who draws us into a concrete Christian community, and at the same time in heaven with Christ along with all the saints. As Paul says: "[God] raised us up with Christ and gave us a seat with him in the heavens" (Ephesians 2:6).

Body of Christ: For additional scriptures on this topic go to 1 Corinthians 6:15.

LORDSHIP

2 CORINTHIANS 4:5

What does it mean to say Jesus is our Lord as well as our Savior? Is belief in, and submission to, the lordship of Jesus Christ necessary for salvation? Since sanctification is a process that is never complete in this life, how does this relate to Christ's total lordship?

How shall we tell others about the (Good News) gospel? Do we present Jesus to unbelievers as Lord, or as Savior only? What are the essential truths of the gospel message? What does it mean to be *saved*? Surrender to Jesus' lordship is not a last-minute addition to the biblical terms of salvation; submission is at the heart of the gospel invitation throughout Scripture: "If you use your mouth to say, 'Jesus is Lord,' and if you believe in your heart that God raised Jesus from the dead, you will be saved" (Romans 10:9).

The lordship controversy is a disagreement over the nature of true faith. Those who want to remove Christ's lordship from the gospel see faith as simple trust in a set of truths about Christ (that he died for our sins and rose again for us). Faith, as they describe it, is merely believing the promise of eternal life granted on the basis of these truths about Christ.

True saving faith in Christ *always* involves submitting to him as Lord. Those who have saving faith will love Christ (Romans 8:28; 1 Corinthians 16:22; 1 John 4:19). They will therefore want to obey him. How could someone who truly believes in Christ continue to deny his authority and pursue what he hates? In this sense, then, the crucial issue for lordship salvation is not merely authority and submission, but the feelings of the heart. Jesus as Lord is far more than just an authority figure; he's also our highest treasure and most precious companion. We obey him out of sheer delight.

Lordship salvation does *not* teach that true Christians are perfect or sinless. Wholehearted commitment to Christ does not mean that we never disobey or that we live perfect lives. But commitment to Christ *does* mean that obedience, rather than disobedience, will be our lifestyle. God will deal with the sin in our lives, and we will respond to his loving guidance by becoming more holy (Hebrews 12:5–11).

One cannot believe in Jesus as Savior and Lord without first repenting of sin. The whole sense of saving faith is that we trust Christ to free us from the power and penalty of sin. Therefore sinners cannot come to sincere faith apart from a complete change of heart, a turnaround of the mind and feelings and will. That is repentance. It is not a supplement to the gospel invitation any more than submitting to the lordship of Christ is; it is precisely what the gospel demands. Our Lord himself described his primary mission as that of calling sinners to repent (Matthew 9:13). Though it is not itself a "work" the sinner performs any more than faith is, true repentance will certainly produce good works as its fruit (Matthew 3:8).

One turns away from all past sin at the initial point of salvation, when God makes us right by giving his goodness to us (Romans 4:5–6). One repents of all current sins after the initial point of salvation by confessing and turning away from them (1 John 1:9) and then living right. The latter is the life-long process of growth in holiness. One cannot separate owning Jesus Christ as Savior from living in obedience to him as Lord.

Note this crucial distinction: When we repent, we give up the *principle* of sin and self-rule. As we grow in the Christian life, we give up the *practice* of specific sins. Total surrender to Christ's lordship means that when we trust Christ for salvation, we settle the issue of who is in charge. At salvation we surrender to Christ in principle, but as Christians we will surrender in practice again and again. The Christian life is a process that begins at conversion, continues throughout this life, and is completed in the life to come.

Jesus is Lord, and those who refuse him as Lord cannot use him as Savior. Everyone who receives him must surrender to his authority, for to say we receive Christ when in fact we reject his right to reign over us is false. It is a useless attempt to hold onto sin with one hand and take Jesus with the other. Jesus must be Lord of all, and at all times, or he is not Lord at all.

Lordship: For additional scriptures on this topic go to Mark 8:34.

23Then Jesus took a cup and thanked God for it
and gave it to the followers, and they all drank from
the cup.
24Then Jesus said, "This is my blood which is the
new agreement that God makes with his people.
This blood is poured out for many. 25I tell you the
truth, I will not drink of this fruit of the vine again
until that day when I drink it new in the kingdom
of God."
26After singing a hymn, they went out to the
Mount of Olives.

Jesus' Followers Will Leave Him

27Then Jesus told the followers, "You will all
stumble in your faith, because it is written in the
Scriptures:
'I will kill the shepherd,
and the sheep will scatter.' *Zechariah 13:7*
28But after I rise from the dead, I will go ahead of
you into Galilee."
29Peter said, "Everyone else may stumble in their
faith, but I will not."
30Jesus answered, "I tell you the truth, tonight
before the rooster crows twice you will say three
times you don't know me."
31But Peter insisted, "I will never say that I don't
know you! I will even die with you!" And all the
other followers said the same thing.

Jesus Prays Alone

32Jesus and his followers went to a place called
Gethsemane. He said to them, "Sit here while I
pray." 33Jesus took Peter, James, and John with
him, and he began to be very sad and troubled.
34He said to them, "My heart is full of sorrow, to
the point of death. Stay here and watch."
35After walking a little farther away from them,
Jesus fell to the ground and prayed that, if possible, he would not have this time of suffering. 36He
prayed, "Abba, Father! You can do all things. Take
away this cup of suffering. But do what you want,
not what I want."
37Then Jesus went back to his followers and found
them asleep. He said to Peter, "Simon, are you
sleeping? Couldn't you stay awake with me for one
hour? 38Stay awake and pray for strength against
temptation. The spirit wants to do what is right,
but the body is weak."
39Again Jesus went away and prayed the same
thing. 40Then he went back to his followers, and
again he found them asleep, because their eyes
were very heavy. And they did not know what to
say to him.
41After Jesus prayed a third time, he went back
to his followers and said to them, "Are you still
sleeping and resting? That's enough. The time has
come for the Son of Man to be handed over to sinful people. 42Get up, we must go. Look, here comes
the man who has turned against me."

Jesus Is Arrested

43At once, while Jesus was still speaking, Judas,
one of the twelve apostles, came up. With him
were many people carrying swords and clubs who
had been sent from the leading priests, the teachers of the law, and the older Jewish leaders.
44Judas had planned a signal for them, saying,
"The man I kiss is Jesus. Arrest him and guard him
while you lead him away." 45So Judas went straight
to Jesus and said, "Teacher!" and kissed him. 46Then
the people grabbed Jesus and arrested him. 47One
of his followers standing nearby pulled out his
sword and struck the servant of the high priest and
cut off his ear.
48Then Jesus said, "You came to get me with
swords and clubs as if I were a criminal. 49Every
day I was with you teaching in the Temple, and
you did not arrest me there. But all these things
have happened to make the Scriptures come true."
50Then all of Jesus' followers left him and ran away.
51A young man, wearing only a linen cloth, was
following Jesus, and the people also grabbed him.
52But the cloth he was wearing came off, and he ran
away naked.

Jesus Before the Leaders

53The people who arrested Jesus led him to the
house of the high priest, where all the leading
priests, the older leaders, and the teachers of the
law were gathered. 54Peter followed far behind and
entered the courtyard of the high priest's house.

14:24 Jesus tells the followers that the wine they are drinking symbolizes his blood, which is the new agreement between God and them. This new agreement was anticipated in Jeremiah 31 and fulfills the agreements with Noah, Abraham, Moses, and David.
14:25 *fruit of the vine.* Product of the grapevine; this may also be translated "wine."
14:26 Table Fellowship/Lord's Supper: Mark 16:14
14:31 Peter: Mark 14:47
14:36 Father: Luke 11:2
14:36 Jesus: Luke 4:18–19
14:36 *Abba.* Name that a Jewish child called his father.
14:36 *cup.* Jesus is talking about the terrible things that will happen to him. Accepting these things will be very hard, like drinking a cup of something bitter.
14:42 Loneliness: Luke 1:26–38
14:42 Mount of Olives: John 12:27–29
14:43 Judas: John 6:70
14:47 Peter: Mark 14:54–72

There he sat with the guards, warming himself by
the fire.
55The leading priests and the whole council tried
to find something that Jesus had done wrong so
they could kill him. But the council could find no
proof of anything. 56Many people came and told
false things about him, but all said different
things—none of them agreed.
57Then some people stood up and lied about
Jesus, saying, 58"We heard this man say, 'I will
destroy this Temple that people made. And three
days later, I will build another Temple not made by
people.'" 59But even the things these people said
did not agree.
60Then the high priest stood before them and
asked Jesus, "Aren't you going to answer? Don't
you have something to say about their charges
against you?" 61But Jesus said nothing; he did not
answer.
The high priest asked Jesus another question:
"Are you the Christ, the Son of the blessed God?"
62Jesus answered, "I am. And in the future you
will see the Son of Man sitting at the right hand of
God, the Powerful One, and coming on clouds in
the sky."
63When the high priest heard this, he tore his
clothes and said, "We don't need any more witnesses! 64You all heard him say these things against
God. What do you think?"
They all said that Jesus was guilty and should die.
65Some of the people there began to spit at Jesus.
They blindfolded him and beat him with their fists
and said, "Prove you are a prophet!" Then the
guards led Jesus away and beat him.

Peter Says He Doesn't Know Jesus

66While Peter was in the courtyard, a servant
girl of the high priest came there. 67She saw Peter
warming himself at the fire and looked closely at
him.
Then she said, "You also were with Jesus, that
man from Nazareth."
68But Peter said that he was never with Jesus. He
said, "I don't know or understand what you are
talking about." Then Peter left and went toward the
entrance of the courtyard. And the rooster crowed.
69The servant girl saw Peter there, and again
she said to the people who were standing nearby,
"This man is one of those who followed Jesus."
70Again Peter said that it was not true.
A short time later, some people were standing
near Peter saying, "Surely you are one of those
who followed Jesus, because you are from
Galilee, too."
71Then Peter began to place a curse on himself
and swear, "I don't know this man you're talking
about!"
72At once, the rooster crowed the second time.
Then Peter remembered what Jesus had told him:
"Before the rooster crows twice, you will say three
times that you don't know me." Then Peter lost
control of himself and began to cry.

Pilate Questions Jesus

15 Very early in the morning, the leading priests,
the older leaders, the teachers of the law,
and all the Jewish council decided what to do with
Jesus. They tied him, led him away, and turned
him over to Pilate, the governor.
2Pilate asked Jesus, "Are you the king of the Jews?"
Jesus answered, "Those are your words."
3The leading priests accused Jesus of many
things. 4So Pilate asked Jesus another question,
"You can see that they are accusing you of many
things. Aren't you going to answer?"
5But Jesus still said nothing, so Pilate was very
surprised.

Pilate Tries to Free Jesus

6Every year at the time of the Passover the governor would free one prisoner whom the people
chose. 7At that time, there was a man named
Barabbas in prison who was a rebel and had committed murder during a riot. 8The crowd came to
Pilate and began to ask him to free a prisoner as he
always did.
9So Pilate asked them, "Do you want me to free
the king of the Jews?" 10Pilate knew that the leading priests had turned Jesus in to him because they
were jealous. 11But the leading priests had persuaded the people to ask Pilate to free Barabbas,
not Jesus.
12Then Pilate asked the crowd again, "So what
should I do with this man you call the king of the
Jews?"
13They shouted, "Crucify him!"
14Pilate asked, "Why? What wrong has he done?"
But they shouted even louder, "Crucify him!"
15Pilate wanted to please the crowd, so he freed
Barabbas for them. After having Jesus beaten with
whips, he handed Jesus over to the soldiers to be
crucified.

14:54 Priesthood: Hebrews 2:17
14:62 Angels/Guardian Angels: Luke 1–2
14:68 *And . . . crowed.* A few, early Greek copies leave out this phrase.
14:72 Peter: Luke 5:1–11
15:15 Pontius Pilate: Luke 13:1

16The soldiers took Jesus into the governor's
palace (called the Praetorium) and called all the
other soldiers together. 17They put a purple robe
on Jesus and used thorny branches to make a
crown for his head. 18They began to call out to
him, "Hail, King of the Jews!" 19The soldiers beat
Jesus on the head many times with a stick. They
spit on him and made fun of him by bowing on
their knees and worshiping him. 20After they finished, the soldiers took off the purple robe and put
his own clothes on him again. Then they led him
out of the palace to be crucified.

Jesus Is Crucified

21A man named Simon from Cyrene, the father
of Alexander and Rufus, was coming from the
fields to the city. The soldiers forced Simon to carry
the cross for Jesus. 22They led Jesus to the place
called Golgotha, which means the Place of the
Skull. 23The soldiers tried to give Jesus wine mixed
with myrrh to drink, but he refused. 24The soldiers
crucified Jesus and divided his clothes among themselves, throwing lots to decide what each soldier
would get.

25It was nine o'clock in the morning when they
crucified Jesus. 26There was a sign with this charge
against Jesus written on it: THE KING OF THE JEWS.
27They also put two robbers on crosses beside
Jesus, one on the right, and the other on the left. 28*
29People walked by and insulted Jesus and shook
their heads, saying, "You said you could destroy
the Temple and build it again in three days. 30So
save yourself! Come down from that cross!"

31The leading priests and the teachers of the law
were also making fun of Jesus. They said to each
other, "He saved other people, but he can't save
himself. 32If he is really the Christ, the king of
Israel, let him come down now from the cross.
When we see this, we will believe in him." The
robbers who were being crucified beside Jesus also
insulted him.

Jesus Dies

33At noon the whole country became dark, and
the darkness lasted for three hours. 34At three
o'clock Jesus cried in a loud voice, "Eloi, Eloi, lama
sabachthani." This means, "My God, my God, why
have you rejected me?"

35When some of the people standing there heard
this, they said, "Listen! He is calling Elijah."

36Someone there ran and got a sponge, filled it
with vinegar, tied it to a stick, and gave it to Jesus
to drink. He said, "We want to see if Elijah will
come to take him down from the cross."

37Then Jesus cried in a loud voice and died.

38The curtain in the Temple was torn into two
pieces, from the top to the bottom. 39When the
army officer who was standing in front of the cross
saw what happened when Jesus died, he said, "This
man really was the Son of God!"

40Some women were standing at a distance from
the cross, watching; among them were Mary Magdalene, Salome, and Mary the mother of James
and Joseph. (James was her youngest son.) 41These
women had followed Jesus in Galilee and helped
him. Many other women were also there who had
come with Jesus to Jerusalem.

Jesus Is Buried

42This was Preparation Day. (That means the day
before the Sabbath day.) That evening, 43Joseph
from Arimathea was brave enough to go to Pilate
and ask for Jesus' body. Joseph, an important member of the Jewish council, was one of the people
who was waiting for the kingdom of God to come.
44Pilate was amazed that Jesus would have already
died, so he called the army officer who had
guarded Jesus and asked him if Jesus had already
died. 45The officer told Pilate that he was dead, so
Pilate told Joseph he could have the body. 46Joseph
bought some linen cloth, took the body down from
the cross, and wrapped it in the linen. He put the
body in a tomb that was cut out of a wall of rock.
Then he rolled a very large stone to block the
entrance of the tomb. 47And Mary Magdalene and
Mary the mother of Joseph saw the place where
Jesus was laid.

Jesus Rises from the Dead

16 The day after the Sabbath day, Mary Magdalene, Mary the mother of James, and Salome bought some sweet-smelling spices to put on
Jesus' body. 2Very early on that day, the first day of
the week, soon after sunrise, the women were on
their way to the tomb. 3They said to each other,
"Who will roll away for us the stone that covers the
entrance of the tomb?"

4Then the women looked and saw that the stone
had already been rolled away, even though it was
very large. 5The women entered the tomb and saw
a young man wearing a white robe and sitting on
the right side, and they were afraid.

***15:28** *Verse 28.* Some Greek copies add verse 28: "And the Scripture came true that says, 'They put him with criminals.' "

15:33 Darkness: Luke 11:34

15:34 Complaint/Lament/Protest: See article on page 631.

15:38 *curtain in the Temple.* A curtain divided the Most Holy Place from the other part of the Temple, the special building in Jerusalem where God commanded the Jewish people to worship him.

15:41 Martyrdom: Luke 9:44–45

[6]But the man said, "Don't be afraid. You are looking for Jesus from Nazareth, who has been crucified. He has risen from the dead; he is not here. Look, here is the place they laid him. [7]Now go and tell his followers and Peter, 'Jesus is going into Galilee ahead of you, and you will see him there as he told you before.'"

[8]The women were confused and shaking with fear, so they left the tomb and ran away. They did not tell anyone about what happened, because they were afraid.

Verses 9-20 are not included in two of the best and oldest Greek manuscripts of Mark.

Some Followers See Jesus

[[9]After Jesus rose from the dead early on the first day of the week, he showed himself first to Mary Magdalene. One time in the past, he had forced seven demons out of her. [10]After Mary saw Jesus, she went and told his followers, who were very sad and were crying. [11]But Mary told them that Jesus was alive. She said that she had seen him, but the followers did not believe her.

[12]Later, Jesus showed himself to two of his followers while they were walking in the country, but he did not look the same as before. [13]These followers went back to the others and told them what had happened, but again, the followers did not believe them.

Jesus Talks to the Apostles

[14]Later Jesus showed himself to the eleven apostles while they were eating, and he criticized them because they had no faith. They were stubborn and refused to believe those who had seen him after he had risen from the dead.⚭

[15]Jesus said to his followers, "Go everywhere in the world, and tell the Good News to everyone. [16]Anyone who believes and is baptized will be saved, but anyone who does not believe will be punished. [17]And those who believe will be able to do these things as proof: They will use my name to force out demons. They will speak in new languages. [18]They will pick up snakes and drink poison without being hurt. They will touch the sick, and the sick will be healed."

[19]After the Lord Jesus said these things to his followers, he was carried up into heaven, and he sat at the right side of God. [20]The followers went everywhere in the world and told the Good News to people, and the Lord helped them. The Lord proved that the Good News they told was true by giving them power to work miracles.]

16:8 Most scholars agree that the Book of Mark ended with 16:8, with other endings added by later scribes who thought the account of the Good News was incomplete without the story of Jesus' appearance to the followers after his resurrection. In fact, the ending at 16:8 does make sense, especially in light of the larger theme of the failure of the followers in Mark. We come to the end of the book wondering if the followers ever came to understand who Jesus is and whether they ever came to participate fully in his ministry. Mark ends, in a sense, with a question, not about those first followers but about followers in every generation who read this book: Have we understood the significance of Jesus' mission? Do we believe; and are we participating in the mission to which Jesus called his followers?

⚭**16:14 Table Fellowship/Lord's Supper:** Luke 5:29–32

16:17 *languages.* This can also be translated "tongues."

INTRODUCTION TO THE BOOK OF

LUKE

Luke Tells the Non-Jewish People About Jesus

WHO WROTE THIS BOOK?

Church tradition names Luke, the non-Jewish physician, as the author of this account of the Good News of Jesus.

TO WHOM WAS THIS BOOK WRITTEN?

Theophilus, a highly respected individual, is specifically named as the recipient of the Book of Luke in 1:3. However, Luke is clearly writing to both Jewish and non-Jewish Christians.

WHERE WAS IT WRITTEN?

The Book of Luke was most likely written in Rome, since Luke accompanied Paul there.

WHEN WAS IT WRITTEN?

The Book of Acts, which continues Luke's accounts in this book, ends with Paul's house arrest in Rome. So the most likely date for the writing of Luke is A.D. 62 to 63.

WHAT IS THE BOOK ABOUT?

Luke provides us the most orderly of all the accounts of the life, ministry, death, resurrection, and ascension of Jesus Christ. He is the only writer to record the amazing events surrounding Jesus' birth and other events. He most likely learned these facts by interviewing Jesus' mother, Mary, and others. Luke emphasizes such issues as salvation, Jesus as the Son of Man, Jesus' concern for largely ignored segments of society (women, children, and the poor), prayer, and the Holy Spirit.

WHY WAS THIS BOOK WRITTEN?

Luke wrote his account of the Good News to give a complete record of Jesus' life and ministry. This account would help ground the faith of his readers, based on the facts he had learned from eye-witnesses. Led by the Holy Spirit, Luke also brings out certain events and teachings that the other writers of the Good News had not stressed.

SO WHAT DOES THIS BOOK MEAN TO US?

Like the early Christians of Luke's day, we still struggle with such issues as the role of women, children, families, the poor, and salvation through the sacrifice of Jesus and his resurrection. Answers to these and other important spiritual questions, provided to us by God via his servant Luke, are available and highly relevant to us today in this book. Reading Luke will ground our faith in the truth of God's word, just as it did our first-century counterparts.

SUMMARY:

Among the four accounts of the Good News, the Book of Luke is unique because it continues the story of Jesus into the story of the early church. That is, the Book of Luke is the first of a two-volume series, with Acts serving as the second volume (see Acts 1:1–3). This means that Luke sees a direct connection between Jesus and the early church, especially around the activity of the Holy Spirit, the foundation of the new story in the Old Testament, and the realization of the plan of God in the mission of Jesus and his followers.

Luke is primarily concerned with the theme of salvation, and this book tells the story of God's purpose to bring salvation in all of its fullness to all people. Salvation for Luke has many faces: It is deliverance from enemies, forgiveness of sins, renewal of health, and more. The Book of Luke does separate segments of life—for example, spiritual versus political, social versus private—that we sometimes take for granted. Salvation reaches every aspect of life.

The mission of Jesus to bring salvation comes to its most complete expression in his sermon at Nazareth in Luke 4:16–30. A number of motifs surface in this passage that are developed more fully in the narrative as a whole:

•Behind the mission of Jesus is (1) the purpose of God expressed above all in the Old Testament and (2) the empowering presence of the Holy Spirit.

•Jesus' mission is especially to set people free. Liberty or release can be expressed in several ways in the Book of Luke—as forgiveness of (release from) sins, as freedom from the shackles of the devil and the bonds of all sorts of diseases, and as liberty from those who abuse others through their misuse of power.

•Who receives this ministry of freedom? Jesus speaks of good news to the poor. Within the ancient world in general and within the Book of Luke in particular, "the poor" refer not only to those who are poor economically, but also to others who are regarded as outsiders in society. In Jesus' ministry in Luke, this would include people with skin diseases and who are under the power of evil spirits, children and women, people from Samaria, and all people who were not normally regarded as members of God's family.

Some of Luke's best-known and loved stories, stories not found in the other Good News accounts, develop these ideas. The stories of the Good Samaritan (Luke 10:25–37) and of the Lost Son (Luke 15:11–32), for example, demonstrate the sort of love that knows no limitations, but goes even to those who seem least to deserve it.

The Book of Luke is clear that the story of Jesus is not a *new* story. Instead, it is the continuation of the old story of God's love for Israel and of his purpose for all humanity. Luke portrays the story of Jesus, and then of the early church, as the opening of the next and final chapter in God's story, in which God's plan comes to completion.

LUKE

Luke Writes About Jesus' Life

Many have tried to report on the things that happened among us. 2They have written the same things that we learned from others—the people who saw those things from the beginning and served God by telling people his message. 3Since I myself have studied everything carefully from the beginning, most excellent Theophilus, it seemed good for me to write it out for you. I arranged it in order 4to help you know that what you have been taught is true.

Zechariah and Elizabeth

5During the time Herod ruled Judea, there was a priest named Zechariah who belonged to Abijah's group. Zechariah's wife, Elizabeth, came from the family of Aaron. 6Zechariah and Elizabeth truly did what God said was good. They did everything the Lord commanded and were without fault in keeping his law. 7But they had no children, because Elizabeth could not have a baby, and both of them were very old.

8One day Zechariah was serving as a priest before God, because his group was on duty. 9According to the custom of the priests, he was chosen by lot to go into the Temple of the Lord and burn incense. 10There were a great many people outside praying at the time the incense was offered. 11Then an angel of the Lord appeared to Zechariah, standing on the right side of the incense table. 12When he saw the angel, Zechariah was startled and frightened. 13But the angel said to him, "Zechariah, don't be afraid. God has heard your prayer. Your wife, Elizabeth, will give birth to a son, and you will name him John. 14He will bring you joy and gladness, and many people will be happy because of his birth. 15John will be a great man for the Lord. He will never drink wine or beer, and even from birth, he will be filled with the Holy Spirit. 16He will help many people of Israel return to the Lord their God. 17He will go before the Lord in spirit and power like Elijah. He will make peace between parents and their children and will bring those who are not obeying God back to the right way of thinking, to make a people ready for the coming of the Lord."

18Zechariah said to the angel, "How can I know that what you say is true? I am an old man, and my wife is old, too."

19The angel answered him, "I am Gabriel. I stand before God, who sent me to talk to you and to tell you this good news. 20Now, listen! You will not be able to speak until the day these things happen, because you did not believe what I told you. But they will really happen."

21Outside, the people were still waiting for Zechariah and were surprised that he was staying so long in the Temple. 22When Zechariah came outside, he could not speak to them, and they knew he had seen a vision in the Temple. He could only make signs to them and remained unable to speak. 23When his time of service at the Temple was finished, he went home.

24Later, Zechariah's wife, Elizabeth, became pregnant and did not go out of her house for five months. Elizabeth said, 25"Look what the Lord has done for me! My people were ashamed of me, but now the Lord has taken away that shame."

An Angel Appears to Mary

26During Elizabeth's sixth month of pregnancy, God sent the angel Gabriel to Nazareth, a town in Galilee, 27to a virgin. She was engaged to marry a man named Joseph from the family of David. Her name was Mary. 28The angel came to her and said, "Greetings! The Lord has blessed you and is with you."

29But Mary was very startled by what the angel said and wondered what this greeting might mean.

30The angel said to her, "Don't be afraid, Mary; God has shown you his grace. 31Listen! You will become pregnant and give birth to a son, and you

---

1:3 *excellent.* This word was used to show respect to an important person like a king or ruler.

1:4 Luke: Acts 1:13

1:5 *Abijah's group.* The Jewish priests were divided into twenty-four groups. See 1 Chronicles 24.

1:25 *ashamed.* The Jewish people thought it was a disgrace for women not to have children.

1:25 John the Baptist: Luke 1:57–80

1:26–28 In the ancient world, people were often introduced and known in relationship to their families. This was the case with Zechariah and Elizabeth (Luke 1:5–6) and Joseph (1:27), but not with Mary. She is engaged to be married to Joseph, but is not yet a member of his family; her own family is not mentioned at all. This is because the relationship that defines her identity is her relationship with God. When she claims that she is the Lord's servant in Luke 1:38, she claims membership in the household of God. This is her real claim to fame.

1:26–38 The story of the angel Gabriel coming to Mary is one of the most remarkable in all of Scripture. When the angel related the message that she would be the mother of the Messiah, Mary's only question had to do with how such a thing was possible, given the fact that she was engaged to Joseph and was still a virgin. The angel's answer made it clear that God himself, through the Holy Spirit, would cause the pregnancy to occur, and so proved that the Messiah would be the Son of God. Mary was entirely submissive to what God wanted, making her an example for all womankind.

will name him Jesus. 32He will be great and will
be called the Son of the Most High. The Lord God
will give him the throne of King David, his ancestor. 33He will rule over the people of Jacob forever, and his kingdom will never end."
34Mary said to the angel, "How will this happen since I am a virgin?"
35The angel said to Mary, "The Holy Spirit will
come upon you, and the power of the Most High
will cover you. For this reason the baby will be
holy and will be called the Son of God. 36Now
Elizabeth, your relative, is also pregnant with a
son though she is very old. Everyone thought she
could not have a baby, but she has been pregnant
for six months. 37God can do anything!"
38Mary said, "I am the servant of the Lord. Let
this happen to me as you say!" Then the angel
went away.

Mary Visits Elizabeth

39Mary got up and went quickly to a town in
the hills of Judea. 40She came to Zechariah's house
and greeted Elizabeth. 41When Elizabeth heard
Mary's greeting, the unborn baby inside her
jumped, and Elizabeth was filled with the Holy
Spirit. 42She cried out in a loud voice, "God has
blessed you more than any other woman, and he
has blessed the baby to which you will give birth.
43Why has this good thing happened to me, that
the mother of my Lord comes to me? 44When I
heard your voice, the baby inside me jumped with
joy. 45You are blessed because you believed that
what the Lord said to you would really happen."

Mary Praises God

46Then Mary said,
"My soul praises the Lord;
47 my heart rejoices in God my Savior,
48because he has shown his concern for his
humble servant girl.
From now on, all people will say that
I am blessed,
49 because the Powerful One has done
great things for me.
His name is holy.
50God will show his mercy forever and ever
to those who worship and serve him.
51He has done mighty deeds by his power.
He has scattered the people who are proud
and think great things about themselves.
52He has brought down rulers from their thrones
and raised up the humble.
53He has filled the hungry with good things
and sent the rich away with nothing.
54He has helped his servant, the people of Israel,
remembering to show them mercy
55as he promised to our ancestors,
to Abraham and to his children forever."
56Mary stayed with Elizabeth for about three
months and then returned home.

The Birth of John

57When it was time for Elizabeth to give birth,
she had a boy. 58Her neighbors and relatives heard
how good the Lord was to her, and they rejoiced
with her.
59When the baby was eight days old, they came
to circumcise him. They wanted to name him Zechariah because this was his father's name, 60but his
mother said, "No! He will be named John."
61The people said to Elizabeth, "But no one in
your family has this name." 62Then they made
signs to his father to find out what he would like
to name him.
63Zechariah asked for a writing tablet and
wrote, "His name is John," and everyone was surprised. 64Immediately Zechariah could talk again,
and he began praising God. 65All their neighbors
became alarmed, and in all the mountains of
Judea people continued talking about all these
things. 66The people who heard about them wondered, saying, "What will this child be?" because
the Lord was with him.

Zechariah Praises God

67Then Zechariah, John's father, was filled with
the Holy Spirit and prophesied:
68"Let us praise the Lord, the God of Israel,
because he has come to help his people and
has given them freedom.
69He has given us a powerful Savior
from the family of God's servant David.
70He said that he would do this
through his holy prophets who lived long ago:
71He promised he would save us from our enemies
and from the power of all those who hate us.
72He said he would give mercy to our fathers
and that he would remember
his holy promise.

1:32 David: Luke 2:4
1:38 Loneliness: Luke 10:39–42
1:38 Servant of the Lord: John 12:26
1:38 In the ancient world, the status of slaves, whether male or female, was determined by the status of their master. Within the Book of Luke thus far, Mary has not been presented as a member of anybody's household, though she is preparing to join Joseph's family as his wife. Calling herself "the servant of the Lord," she not only confirms her submission to the will of God but also claims membership and status in the family of God.
1:50 Worship: Hebrews 13:15

Love

1 Corinthians 13:4–8

How is love a precept, a principle, and a person? What is the difference between love that is self-centered, condition-centered, and other-centered? What are the marks of mature love, especially in a marriage relationship?

An accomplished rabbi once posed a question to Jesus that many rabbis before him had debated. "Teacher," he said, "which command in the law is the most important?" "'Love the Lord your God,'" Jesus answered, "' with all your heart, all your soul, and all your mind.' This is the first and most important command. And the second command is like the first: 'Love your neighbor as you love yourself'" (Matthew 22:36–39).

The greatest precept in the law, according to Jesus, is the command to love. He even went so far as to say, "Love your enemies. Pray for those who hurt you. If you do this, you will be true children of your Father in heaven" (Matthew 5:44–45). The precept is clear: love—for God, for our spouses, for our neighbors, even for our enemies—is commanded. "This is the teaching you have heard from the beginning," according to the apostle John. "We must love each other" (1 John 3:11).

Like all precepts, these commands point to a principle: love for God and love for others. The principle is larger than the precept. We might dodge or circumvent the precept by clever maneuvering, the way we might take advantage of a loophole in the tax law, but we cannot avoid the principle. Regardless of whether a specific precept addresses a certain decision or behavior, the principle of love for God and others dictates whether our actions are right or wrong, because love is a principle of values.

Ultimately, of course, love is a virtue not simply because it is commanded, nor even because it is a principle God values, but because God is like that. The precept and the principle both point to the person of God himself. "God is love" (1 John 4:16b). He loves us "with a love that will last forever" (Jeremiah 31:3). He loves us so much that he gave his Son to die for us (John 3:16). He loves us so much that, while we were still sinners—displaying enmity toward God—Christ died for us (Romans 5:8). He is the kind of God who loves even those who curse him, because love is his nature. It is not something he does, it is something he is.

First Corinthians 13:4–8 is perhaps the best known text on love in the Bible. It is certainly the greatest description of love ever penned. But it is not a definition of love. The only real definition of love—the kind of love God is—found in the Bible is that of Christ's death on the cross. Christ did not die for us because of what he could get, but because of what he could give. True love is spelled G-I-V-E.

Our model of mature love is Jesus Christ. His love was willing to sacrifice. He was a living example of his teachings on love: "The greatest love a person can show is to die for his friends" (John 15:13). In Ephesians 5:1–2, Paul emphasized our need "to be like him. Live a life of love just as Christ loved us and gave himself to us as a sweet-smelling offering and sacrifice to God."

First Corinthians 13:4–8 is a description of how a mature love, the kind modeled by Jesus Christ in his sacrificial death on our behalf, behaves in relation to others. Mature love is not self-centered, or condition-centered, but condition-less and other-person centered. With this kind of love, we will stop demanding to have everything our way. We will put no conditions on our love and put the interests and desires of the loved person before our own, just as Jesus did for us.

In self-centered love, our purpose is to gain something in exchange for our love. In condition-centered love, our love is contingent upon or based upon something the other person is or has. In the first case, love lasts only as long as I get something out of it. In the second case, it lasts only as long as you have the qualities that attracted me to you in the first place.

I'm happy to say there is still another kind of love. It is love without conditions, or condition-less love. This love says, "I love you in spite of what you may be like deep down inside. I love you no matter what may change about you. I love you, PERIOD!" The reason I like to call this third type of love condition-less rather than unconditional is that each of us is restrained and limited by our nature, which is selfish. Only God through Jesus Christ has demonstrated a total unconditional love.

First Corinthians 13 is not the final word on love; God's love is shown in countless ways throughout the Bible. However, I challenge you to take the qualities of mature love found in this passage and make an effort to implement them in your life and in your relationships with others.

Love: For additional scriptures on this topic go to Deuteronomy 7:7–8.

TONGUES

1 CORINTHIANS 14

When the Bible talks of speaking in "tongues," or "other languages," what does it mean? What value do tongues have for believers in Scripture and today?

The Book of Genesis tells a story about the beginnings of the world's languages. As the people were building a tower, the Lord confused their language so that they were "not able to understand each other" (Genesis 11:7). From this point people began to spread out over the earth, speaking different languages. People who speak different languages are mentioned as enemies of God's people (Jeremiah 5:15). But God's promise was that one day all the different peoples of the world would worship the LORD All-Powerful (Zechariah 8:23).

The New Testament tells of the fulfillment of this promise of worship in different languages. In Acts 2 we read that some of Jesus' followers were gathered in a room a few weeks after his resurrection. The Scriptures say that "they were all filled with the Holy Spirit, and they began to speak different languages by the power the Holy Spirit was giving them" (Acts 2:4). When visitors from different countries gathered to see what was going on, they heard praises to God in their own languages. Peter, one of Jesus' followers, explained to them that this gift of languages was the fulfillment of God's promise of a new relationship with his people.

The Book of Acts tells of two other times when the Holy Spirit visited God's people and they spoke in different languages, or "tongues." In the first, Peter had gone to speak to a family about Jesus. As Peter spoke, "the Holy Spirit came down on all those who were listening." The Jewish believers who had come with Peter knew that the Holy Spirit had come down, for they and Peter "heard them speaking in different languages and praising God" (Acts 10:44, 46). In the second, the apostle Paul helped some people to believe in Jesus and baptized them. He "laid his hands on them and the Holy Spirit came upon them. They began speaking different languages and prophesying" (Acts 19:6). Acts also describes receiving the Holy Spirit without mentioning tongues (Acts 4:31; Acts 8:17). It is likely that the first apostles saw speaking in different languages, or "speaking in tongues," as one visible sign of the Lord's powerful presence and ministry in the lives of those to whom they spoke.

The Holy Spirit continued to bring the presence of God to the Christian believers as they settled into local churches, and their experience of God's presence included the experience of speaking in tongues. The apostle Paul instructed the church of Corinth that this experience was a gift from God, but must be understood and practiced in such a way that everybody would be helped. "The Spirit gives one person the ability to speak in different kinds of languages and to another the ability to interpret those languages," Paul says (1 Corinthians 12:10). "Not all speak in different languages. Not all interpret those languages" (1 Corinthians 12:30). The story of the gift of languages in Acts 2 indicated that those who heard also understood Jesus' followers speaking in their own native languages. Paul's words to the believers at Corinth show that the languages God gives are often not understandable to others; they express a close communication between believers and God (1 Corinthians 14:2). Paul writes elsewhere about the Holy Spirit's praying with "deep feelings that words cannot explain" (Romans 8:26). Therefore, tongues are valuable for personal prayer, but less helpful in a church gathering. Paul writes, "I thank God that I speak in different kinds of languages more than all of you. But in the church meetings I would rather speak five words I understand in order to teach others than thousands of words in a different language" (1 Corinthians 14:18–19). Paul encourages those who have the gift of tongues to "pray for the gift to interpret what is spoken" (1 Corinthians 14:13). Paul concludes his comments about the use of tongues in church by saying, "Do not stop people from using the gift of speaking in different kinds of languages. But let everything be done in a right and orderly way" (1 Corinthians 14:39–40).

Our special abilities or experiences given by God must never become a source of pride. Rather, love must be the enduring sign of the true believer. Paul writes, "I may speak in different languages of people or even angels. But if I do not have love, I am only a noisy bell or a clashing cymbal" (1 Corinthians 13:1). Tongues are only a temporary way in which we relate to God, either alone or in church. Love expresses the very eternal nature of God himself. Again Paul writes, "Love never ends. . . . There are gifts of speaking in different languages, but those gifts will stop" (1 Corinthians 13:8). Some may have the gift of tongues, but everybody should have love.

Tongues: For additional scriptures on this topic go to Genesis 11:1–9.

73God promised Abraham, our father,
74 that he would save us from the power
of our enemies
so we could serve him without fear,
75being holy and good before God as long
as we live.

76"Now you, child, will be called a prophet of
the Most High God.
You will go before the Lord to
prepare his way.
77You will make his people know that they
will be saved
by having their sins forgiven.
78With the loving mercy of our God,
a new day from heaven will dawn upon us.
79It will shine on those who live in darkness,
in the shadow of death.
It will guide us into the path of peace."

80And so the child grew up and became strong
in spirit. John lived in the desert until the time
when he came out to preach to Israel.

Statue of Emperor Augustus Caesar

The Birth of Jesus

2 At that time, Augustus Caesar sent an order
that all people in the countries under Roman
rule must list their names in a register. 2This was
the first registration; it was taken while Quirinius
was governor of Syria. 3And all went to their own
towns to be registered.

4So Joseph left Nazareth, a town in Galilee, and
went to the town of Bethlehem in Judea, known
as the town of David. Joseph went there because
he was from the family of David. 5Joseph registered with Mary, to whom he was engaged and
who was now pregnant. 6While they were in
Bethlehem, the time came for Mary to have the
baby, 7and she gave birth to her first son. Because
there were no rooms left in the inn, she wrapped
the baby with pieces of cloth and laid him in a
box where animals are fed.

Shepherds Hear About Jesus

8That night, some shepherds were in the fields
nearby watching their sheep. 9Then an angel of
the Lord stood before them. The glory of the Lord
was shining around them, and they became very
frightened. 10The angel said to them, "Do not be
afraid. I am bringing you good news that will be a
great joy to all the people. 11Today your Savior
was born in the town of David. He is Christ, the
Lord. 12This is how you will know him: You will
find a baby wrapped in pieces of cloth and lying
in a feeding box."

13Then a very large group of angels from heav-
en joined the first angel, praising God and saying:
14"Give glory to God in heaven,
and on earth let there be peace among the
people who please God."

15When the angels left them and went back to
heaven, the shepherds said to each other, "Let's
go to Bethlehem. Let's see this thing that has happened which the Lord has told us about."

16So the shepherds went quickly and found Mary
and Joseph and the baby, who was lying in a feeding box. 17 When they had seen him, they told what
the angels had said about this child. 18Everyone was
amazed at what the shepherds said to them. 19But
Mary treasured these things and continued to
think about them. 20Then the shepherds went
back to their sheep, praising God and thanking
him for everything they had seen and heard. It
had been just as the angel had told them.

1:79 Peace: John 14:27
1:80 John the Baptist: John 3:22–33
1:80 Family: Luke 2
2:2 *registration.* Census. A counting of all the people and the things they own.
2:4 David: Acts 2:34
2:5 *engaged.* For the Jewish people, an engagement was a lasting agreement. It could only be broken by divorce.

21When the baby was eight days old, he was circumcised and was named Jesus, the name given by
the angel before the baby began to grow inside Mary.

Jesus Is Presented in the Temple

22When the time came for Mary and Joseph to
do what the law of Moses taught about being
made pure, they took Jesus to Jerusalem to present him to the Lord. 23(It is written in the law of
the Lord: "Every firstborn male shall be given to
the Lord.") 24Mary and Joseph also went to offer a
sacrifice, as the law of the Lord says: "You must
sacrifice two doves or two young pigeons."

Simeon Sees Jesus

25In Jerusalem lived a man named Simeon who
was a good man and godly. He was waiting for the
time when God would take away Israel's sorrow,
and the Holy Spirit was in him. 26Simeon had been
told by the Holy Spirit that he would not die before
he saw the Christ promised by the Lord. 27The
Spirit led Simeon to the Temple. When Mary and
Joseph brought the baby Jesus to the Temple to
do what the law said they must do, 28Simeon took
the baby in his arms and thanked God:

29"Now, Lord, you can let me, your servant,
die in peace as you said.
30With my own eyes I have seen your salvation,
31 which you prepared before all people.
32It is a light for the non-Jewish people to see
and an honor for your people, the Israelites."

33Jesus' father and mother were amazed at
what Simeon had said about him. 34Then Simeon
blessed them and said to Mary, "God has chosen
this child to cause the fall and rise of many in
Israel. He will be a sign from God that many people will not accept 35so that the thoughts of many
will be made known. And the things that will
happen will make your heart sad, too."

Anna Sees Jesus

36There was a prophetess, Anna, from the family of Phanuel in the tribe of Asher. Anna was
very old. She had once been married for seven
years. 37Then her husband died, and she was a
widow for eighty-four years. Anna never left the
Temple but worshiped God, going without food
and praying day and night. 38Standing there at
that time, she thanked God and spoke about Jesus
to all who were waiting for God to free Jerusalem.

Joseph and Mary Return Home

39When Joseph and Mary had done everything
the law of the Lord commanded, they went home
to Nazareth, their own town in Galilee. 40The little child grew and became strong. He was filled
with wisdom, and God's goodness was upon him.

Jesus As a Boy

41Every year Jesus' parents went to Jerusalem
for the Passover Feast. 42When he was twelve years
old, they went to the feast as they always did.
43After the feast days were over, they started home.
The boy Jesus stayed behind in Jerusalem, but his
parents did not know it. 44Thinking that Jesus was
with them in the group, they traveled for a whole
day. Then they began to look for him among their
family and friends. 45When they did not find him,
they went back to Jerusalem to look for him there.
46After three days they found Jesus sitting in the
Temple with the teachers, listening to them and
asking them questions. 47All who heard him were
amazed at his understanding and answers. 48When
Jesus' parents saw him, they were astonished. His
mother said to him, "Son, why did you do this to
us? Your father and I were very worried about you
and have been looking for you."

49Jesus said to them, "Why were you looking for
me? Didn't you know that I must be in my Father's
house?" 50But they did not understand the meaning of what he said.

51Jesus went with them to Nazareth and was
obedient to them. But his mother kept in her mind
all that had happened. 52Jesus became wiser and
grew physically. People liked him, and he pleased
God.

2:22 *pure.* The Law of Moses said that forty days after a Jewish woman gave birth to a son, she must be cleansed by a ceremony at the Temple. Read Leviticus 12:2-8.

2:23 *"Every . . . Lord."* Quotation from Exodus 13:2.

2:24 *"You . . . pigeons."* Quotation from Leviticus 12:8.

2:32 Gentiles (Non-Jews): Acts 22:21

2:32 Evangelism: Luke 24:46–49

2:34–35 Simeon blessed Joseph and Mary and then spoke prophetically to Mary about the pivotal role Jesus would play in the future of the people of that nation. He told her that many would not accept Jesus, but because of him the way would be opened for all people to know God personally. The price for Mary would be the pain she would experience at seeing him crucified.

2:40–52 The Bible tells us almost nothing about Jesus from the time of his birth to the time of his adult ministry. In this episode, Jesus is presented as only twelve years old, and yet having enough wisdom to talk with the important teachers in the Temple of Jerusalem. This emphasizes the importance of Jesus' growth in a home that honors God, and also shows how Jesus is different from other children. His father is not Joseph, but God!

2:51 Family: John 2:1–12

2:52 Luke tells us that as Jesus was growing up, he was filled with wisdom. As a boy, Jesus went with his parents to visit the Temple. While he was there, he amazed the learned teachers. From the very beginning of his life, Jesus showed that he was wise. Indeed, as God himself, he was the source of wisdom.

2:52 Angels/Guardian Angels: Luke 15:10

2:52 Children: See article on page 399.

2:52 Family: John 19:26–27

The Preaching of John

3 It was the fifteenth year of the rule of Tiberius Caesar. These men were under Caesar: Pontius Pilate, the ruler of Judea; Herod, the ruler of Galilee; Philip, Herod's brother, the ruler of Iturea and Traconitis; and Lysanias, the ruler of Abilene. 2Annas and Caiaphas were the high priests. At this time, the word of God came to John son of Zechariah in the desert. 3He went all over the area around the Jordan River preaching a baptism of changed hearts and lives for the forgiveness of sins. 4As it is written in the book of Isaiah the prophet:

"This is a voice of one
  who calls out in the desert:
'Prepare the way for the Lord.
  Make the road straight for him.
5Every valley should be filled in,
  and every mountain and hill should
    be made flat.
Roads with turns should be made straight,
  and rough roads should be made smooth.
6And all people will know about the
    salvation of God!'" *Isaiah 40:3-5*

7To the crowds of people who came to be baptized by John, he said, "You are all snakes! Who warned you to run away from God's coming punishment? 8Do the things that show you really have changed your hearts and lives. Don't begin to say to yourselves, 'Abraham is our father.' I tell you that God could make children for Abraham from these rocks. 9The ax is now ready to cut down the trees, and every tree that does not produce good fruit will be cut down and thrown into the fire."

10The people asked John, "Then what should we do?"

11John answered, "If you have two shirts, share with the person who does not have one. If you have food, share that also."

12Even tax collectors came to John to be baptized. They said to him, "Teacher, what should we do?"

13John said to them, "Don't take more taxes from people than you have been ordered to take."

14The soldiers asked John, "What about us? What should we do?"

John said to them, "Don't force people to give you money, and don't lie about them. Be satisfied with the pay you get."

15Since the people were hoping for the Christ to come, they wondered if John might be the one.

16John answered everyone, "I baptize you with water, but there is one coming who is greater than I am. I am not good enough to untie his sandals. He will baptize you with the Holy Spirit and fire. 17He will come ready to clean the grain, separating the good grain from the chaff. He will put the good part of the grain into his barn, but he will burn the chaff with a fire that cannot be put out." 18And John continued to preach the Good News, saying many other things to encourage the people.

19But John spoke against Herod, the governor, because of his sin with Herodias, the wife of Herod's brother, and because of the many other evil things Herod did. 20So Herod did something even worse: He put John in prison.

Jesus Is Baptized by John

21When all the people were being baptized by John, Jesus also was baptized. While Jesus was praying, heaven opened 22and the Holy Spirit came down on him in the form of a dove. Then a voice came from heaven, saying, "You are my Son, whom I love, and I am very pleased with you."

The Family History of Jesus

23When Jesus began his ministry, he was about thirty years old. People thought that Jesus was Joseph's son.

Joseph was the son of Heli.
24Heli was the son of Matthat.
Matthat was the son of Levi.
Levi was the son of Melki.
Melki was the son of Jannai.
Jannai was the son of Joseph.
25Joseph was the son of Mattathias.
Mattathias was the son of Amos.
Amos was the son of Nahum.
Nahum was the son of Esli.

3:7 God's Anger: John 3:36

3:9 *The ax . . . fire.* This means that God is ready to punish his people who do not obey him.

3:16 Baptism: Acts 8:12–13

3:17 *He will . . . out.* This means that Jesus will come to separate good people from bad people, saving the good and punishing the bad.

3:20 Authority: John 13

3:23–28 *son.* "Son" in Jewish lists of ancestors can sometimes mean grandson or a more distant relative.

Genealogies in the Bible usually serve to show a person's importance in the story of God's activity with his people. This one does so in a strange way. It does not emphasize the importance of fathers, but instead focuses on one's identity as a "son." Jesus' family is traced all the way back to Adam, who is "son of God." This ties in with God's pronouncement of Jesus' status as his Son at his baptism (Luke 3:22) and with the story of Jesus' temptation as the Son of God (4:1–13). In short, Jesus is God's Son, even though people would think that he was Joseph's son (3:23).

Luke's genealogy of Jesus differs somewhat from Matthew's because Matthew probably traces the kingly inheritance rather than the physical descent of Jesus (see note at Matthew 1:2).

Esli was the son of Naggai.
26Naggai was the son of Maath.
Maath was the son of Mattathias.
Mattathias was the son of Semein.
Semein was the son of Josech.
Josech was the son of Joda.
27Joda was the son of Joanan.
Joanan was the son of Rhesa.
Rhesa was the son of Zerubbabel.
Zerubbabel was the grandson of Shealtiel.
Shealtiel was the son of Neri.
28Neri was the son of Melki.
Melki was the son of Addi.
Addi was the son of Cosam.
Cosam was the son of Elmadam.
Elmadam was the son of Er.
29Er was the son of Joshua.
Joshua was the son of Eliezer.
Eliezer was the son of Jorim.
Jorim was the son of Matthat.
Matthat was the son of Levi.
30Levi was the son of Simeon.
Simeon was the son of Judah.
Judah was the son of Joseph.
Joseph was the son of Jonam.
Jonam was the son of Eliakim.
31Eliakim was the son of Melea.
Melea was the son of Menna.
Menna was the son of Mattatha.
Mattatha was the son of Nathan.
Nathan was the son of David.
32David was the son of Jesse.
Jesse was the son of Obed.
Obed was the son of Boaz.
Boaz was the son of Salmon.
Salmon was the son of Nahshon.
33Nahshon was the son of Amminadab.
Amminadab was the son of Admin.
Admin was the son of Arni.
Arni was the son of Hezron.
Hezron was the son of Perez.
Perez was the son of Judah.
34Judah was the son of Jacob.
Jacob was the son of Isaac.
Isaac was the son of Abraham.
Abraham was the son of Terah.
Terah was the son of Nahor.
35Nahor was the son of Serug.
Serug was the son of Reu.
Reu was the son of Peleg.
Peleg was the son of Eber.
Eber was the son of Shelah.
36Shelah was the son of Cainan.
Cainan was the son of Arphaxad.
Arphaxad was the son of Shem.
Shem was the son of Noah.
Noah was the son of Lamech.
37Lamech was the son of Methuselah.
Methuselah was the son of Enoch.
Enoch was the son of Jared.
Jared was the son of Mahalalel.
Mahalalel was the son of Kenan.
38Kenan was the son of Enosh.
Enosh was the son of Seth.
Seth was the son of Adam.
Adam was the son of God.

Jesus Is Tempted by the Devil

4 Jesus, filled with the Holy Spirit, returned
from the Jordan River. The Spirit led Jesus
into the desert 2where the devil tempted Jesus for
forty days. Jesus ate nothing during that time, and
when those days were ended, he was very hungry.
3The devil said to Jesus, "If you are the Son of
God, tell this rock to become bread."
4Jesus answered, "It is written in the Scriptures:
'A person does not live by eating only bread.'"
5Then the devil took Jesus and showed him all
the kingdoms of the world in an instant. 6The
devil said to Jesus, "I will give you all these kingdoms and all their power and glory. It has all been
given to me, and I can give it to anyone I wish. 7If
you worship me, then it will all be yours."
8Jesus answered, "It is written in the Scriptures:
'You must worship the Lord your God and serve
only him.'"
9Then the devil led Jesus to Jerusalem and put
him on a high place of the Temple. He said to
Jesus, "If you are the Son of God, jump down. 10It
is written in the Scriptures:

'He has put his angels in charge of you
to watch over you.' *Psalm 91:11*

11It is also written:

'They will catch you in their hands
so that you will not hit your foot
on a rock.'" *Psalm 91:12*

12Jesus answered, "But it also says in the
Scriptures: 'Do not test the Lord your God.'"
13After the devil had tempted Jesus in every
way, he left him to wait until a better time.

Jesus Teaches the People

14Jesus returned to Galilee in the power of the

3:38 Adam: 1 Corinthians 15:22
3:38 Births: Galatians 3:29
3:38 Jordan River: Acts 18:25
4:4 *'A person . . . bread.'* Quotation from Deuteronomy 8:3.
4:8 *'You . . . him.'* Quotation from Deuteronomy 6:13.
4:12 *'Do . . . God.'* Quotation from Deuteronomy 6:16.
4:13 Satan/Satanism: Luke 10:18
4:13 Son/Child of God: John 20:31–32

Holy Spirit, and stories about him spread all through the area. 15He began to teach in their synagogues, and everyone praised him.

16Jesus traveled to Nazareth, where he had grown up. On the Sabbath day he went to the synagogue, as he always did, and stood up to read. 17The book of Isaiah the prophet was given to him. He opened the book and found the place where this is written:

18"The Lord has put his Spirit in me,
because he appointed me to tell the Good News to the poor.
He has sent me to tell the captives they are free
and to tell the blind that they can see again. *Isaiah 61:1*
God sent me to free those who have been treated unfairly *Isaiah 58:6*
19 and to announce the time when the Lord will show his kindness." *Isaiah 61:2*

20Jesus closed the book, gave it back to the assistant, and sat down. Everyone in the synagogue was watching Jesus closely. 21He began to say to them, "While you heard these words just now, they were coming true!"

22All the people spoke well of Jesus and were amazed at the words of grace he spoke. They asked, "Isn't this Joseph's son?"

23Jesus said to them, "I know that you will tell me the old saying: 'Doctor, heal yourself.' You want to say, 'We heard about the things you did in Capernaum. Do those things here in your own town!'" 24Then Jesus said, "I tell you the truth, a prophet is not accepted in his hometown. 25But I tell you the truth, there were many widows in Israel during the time of Elijah. It did not rain in Israel for three and one-half years, and there was no food anywhere in the whole country. 26But Elijah was sent to none of those widows, only to a widow in Zarephath, a town in Sidon. 27And there were many with skin diseases living in Israel during the time of the prophet Elisha. But none of them were healed, only Naaman, who was from the country of Syria."

28When all the people in the synagogue heard these things, they became very angry. 29They got up, forced Jesus out of town, and took him to the edge of the cliff on which the town was built. They planned to throw him off the edge, 30but Jesus walked through the crowd and went on his way.

Jesus Forces Out an Evil Spirit

31Jesus went to Capernaum, a city in Galilee, and on the Sabbath day, he taught the people. 32They were amazed at his teaching, because he spoke with authority. 33In the synagogue a man who had within him an evil spirit shouted in a loud voice, 34"Jesus of Nazareth! What do you want with us? Did you come to destroy us? I know who you are—God's Holy One!"

35Jesus commanded the evil spirit, "Be quiet! Come out of the man!" The evil spirit threw the man down to the ground before all the people and then left the man without hurting him.

36The people were amazed and said to each other, "What does this mean? With authority and power he commands evil spirits, and they come out." 37And so the news about Jesus spread to every place in the whole area.

Jesus Heals Many People

38Jesus left the synagogue and went to the home of Simon. Simon's mother-in-law was sick with a high fever, and they asked Jesus to help her. 39He came to her side and commanded the fever to leave. It left her, and immediately she got up and began serving them.

40When the sun went down, the people brought those who were sick to Jesus. Putting his hands on each sick person, he healed every one of them. 41Demons came out of many people, shouting, "You are the Son of God." But Jesus commanded the demons and would not allow them to speak, because they knew Jesus was the Christ.

42At daybreak, Jesus went to a lonely place, but the people looked for him. When they found him, they tried to keep him from leaving. 43But Jesus said to them, "I must preach about God's kingdom to other towns, too. This is why I was sent."

4:16 Sabbath: Acts 13:14
4:18 Government: Acts 5:29
4:19 Gospel/Good News: Luke 7:22
4:19 Jesus: Luke 7:36–50
4:19 Slavery: 1 Corinthians 7:21–24
4:21 Freedom: John 8:31–38
4:21 Kingdom of God: See article on page 811.
4:22 If Jesus is Joseph's son, then wouldn't the Good News he was announcing be for Joseph's family and friends, and for the whole town of Nazareth? But, we have already learned (Luke 3:23), Jesus only *seemed* to be Joseph's son. He is really the son of God. The people at first welcomed Jesus' ministry, but when they saw that the Good News was given to those in other cities and other nations, they grew angry and wanted to kill him.
4:23 Proverb: See article on page 574.
4:23 Jesus taught in parables, which are extended proverbs that use an ordinary situation to teach a spiritual truth. Here he recognizes the shorter version of a parable called a "proverb," or "old saying." The proverb he cited was a familiar old saying that Jesus says "Practice on yourself what you have practiced on others," "Do in Nazareth what you have done in Capernaum."
4:27 Elijah and Elisha: John 1:21
4:27 Racism: John 10:14–16
4:33 Demon: Luke 10:18
4:35 Physical Handicap: Luke 6:1–51
4:38 *Simon.* Simon's other name was Peter.

44Then he kept on preaching in the synagogues
of Judea.

Jesus' First Followers

5 One day while Jesus was standing beside Lake
Galilee, many people were pressing all around
him to hear the word of God. 2Jesus saw two
boats at the shore of the lake. The fishermen had
left them and were washing their nets. 3Jesus got
into one of the boats, the one that belonged to
Simon, and asked him to push off a little from the
land. Then Jesus sat down and continued to teach
the people from the boat.

4When Jesus had finished speaking, he said to
Simon, "Take the boat into deep water, and put
your nets in the water to catch some fish."

5Simon answered, "Master, we worked hard all
night trying to catch fish, and we caught nothing.
But you say to put the nets in the water, so I will."
6When the fishermen did as Jesus told them, they
caught so many fish that the nets began to break.
7They called to their partners in the other boat to
come and help them. They came and filled both
boats so full that they were almost sinking.

8When Simon Peter saw what had happened,
he bowed down before Jesus and said, "Go away
from me, Lord. I am a sinful man!" 9He and the
other fishermen were amazed at the many fish
they caught, as were 10James and John, the sons
of Zebedee, Simon's partners.

Jesus said to Simon, "Don't be afraid. From now
on you will fish for people." 11When the men
brought their boats to the shore, they left everything and followed Jesus.

Jesus Heals a Sick Man

12When Jesus was in one of the towns, there
was a man covered with a skin disease. When he
saw Jesus, he bowed before him and begged him,
"Lord, you can heal me if you will."

13Jesus reached out his hand and touched the
man and said, "I will. Be healed!" Immediately
the disease disappeared. 14Then Jesus said, "Don't
tell anyone about this, but go and show yourself
to the priest and offer a gift for your healing, as
Moses commanded. This will show the people
what I have done."

15But the news about Jesus spread even more.
Many people came to hear Jesus and to be healed
of their sicknesses, 16but Jesus often slipped away
to be alone so he could pray.

Jesus Heals a Paralyzed Man

17One day as Jesus was teaching the people, the
Pharisees and teachers of the law from every
town in Galilee and Judea and from Jerusalem
were there. The Lord was giving Jesus the power
to heal people. 18Just then, some men were carrying on a mat a man who was paralyzed. They
tried to bring him in and put him down before
Jesus. 19But because there were so many people
there, they could not find a way in. So they went
up on the roof and lowered the man on his mat
through the ceiling into the middle of the crowd
right before Jesus. 20Seeing their faith, Jesus said,
"Friend, your sins are forgiven."

21The Jewish teachers of the law and the
Pharisees thought to themselves, "Who is this man
who is speaking as if he were God? Only God can
forgive sins."

22But Jesus knew what they were thinking and
said, "Why are you thinking these things? 23Which
is easier: to say, 'Your sins are forgiven,' or to say,
'Stand up and walk'? 24But I will prove to you that
the Son of Man has authority on earth to forgive
sins." So Jesus said to the paralyzed man, "I tell
you, stand up, take your mat, and go home."

25At once the man stood up before them,
picked up his mat, and went home, praising God.
26All the people were fully amazed and began to
praise God. They were filled with much respect
and said, "Today we have seen amazing things!"

Levi Follows Jesus

27After this, Jesus went out and saw a tax collector named Levi sitting in the tax collector's
booth. Jesus said to him, "Follow me!" 28So Levi
got up, left everything, and followed him.

29Then Levi gave a big dinner for Jesus at his
house. Many tax collectors and other people were
eating there, too. 30But the Pharisees and the men
who taught the law for the Pharisees began to
complain to Jesus' followers, "Why do you eat and
drink with tax collectors and sinners?"

31Jesus answered them, "It is not the healthy
people who need a doctor, but the sick. 32I have
not come to invite good people but sinners to
change their hearts and lives."

4:44 Miracles: Luke 11:20
5:3 *Simon.* Simon's other name was Peter.
5:10 Physical Handicap: Luke 6
5:11 Peter: Luke 6:12–16
5:14 *show . . . priest.* The Law of Moses said a priest must say when a Jewish person with a skin disease was well.
5:14 *Moses commanded.* Read about this in Leviticus 14:1-32.
5:17 Sickness, Disease, Healing: Luke 6:17–19
5:20 Forgiveness: Luke 6:37
5:24 Pharisees and Sadducees: Luke 6:6–11
5:30 Hospitality: Luke 7:36–50
5:32 Sin: Romans 7–8
5:32 Table Fellowship/Lord's Supper: Luke 7:36–50

Jesus Answers a Question

33They said to Jesus, "John's followers often give
up eating for a certain time and pray, just as the
Pharisees do. But your followers eat and drink all
the time."

34Jesus said to them, "You cannot make the
friends of the bridegroom give up eating while he
is still with them. 35But the time will come when
the bridegroom will be taken away from them,
and then they will give up eating."

36Jesus told them this story: "No one takes
cloth off a new coat to cover a hole in an old coat.
Otherwise, he ruins the new coat, and the cloth
from the new coat will not be the same as the old
cloth. 37Also, no one ever pours new wine into
old leather bags. Otherwise, the new wine will
break the bags, the wine will spill out, and the
leather bags will be ruined. 38New wine must be
put into new leather bags. 39No one after drinking
old wine wants new wine, because he says, 'The
old wine is better.'"

Jesus Is Lord over the Sabbath

6 One Sabbath day Jesus was walking through
some fields of grain. His followers picked the
heads of grain, rubbed them in their hands, and
ate them. 2Some Pharisees said, "Why do you do
what is not lawful on the Sabbath day?"

3Jesus answered, "Have you not read what David
did when he and those with him were hungry? 4He
went into God's house and took and ate the holy
bread, which is lawful only for priests to eat. And
he gave some to the people who were with him."
5Then Jesus said to the Pharisees, "The Son of
Man is Lord of the Sabbath day."

Jesus Heals a Man's Hand

6On another Sabbath day Jesus went into the
synagogue and was teaching, and a man with a
crippled right hand was there. 7The teachers of
the law and the Pharisees were watching closely
to see if Jesus would heal on the Sabbath day so
they could accuse him. 8But he knew what they
were thinking, and he said to the man with the
crippled hand, "Stand up here in the middle of
everyone." The man got up and stood there.
9Then Jesus said to them, "I ask you, which is lawful on the Sabbath day: to do good or to do evil, to
save a life or to destroy it?" 10Jesus looked around
at all of them and said to the man, "Hold out your
hand." The man held out his hand, and it was
healed.

11But the Pharisees and the teachers of the law
were very angry and discussed with each other
what they could do to Jesus.

Jesus Chooses His Apostles

12At that time Jesus went off to a mountain to
pray, and he spent the night praying to God.
13The next morning, Jesus called his followers to
him and chose twelve of them, whom he named
apostles: 14Simon (Jesus named him Peter), his
brother Andrew, James, John, Philip, Bartholomew, 15Matthew, Thomas, James son of
Alphaeus, Simon (called the Zealot), 16Judas son
of James, and Judas Iscariot, who later turned
Jesus over to his enemies.

Jesus Teaches and Heals

17Jesus and the apostles came down from the
mountain, and he stood on level ground. A large
group of his followers was there, as well as many
people from all around Judea, Jerusalem, and the
seacoast cities of Tyre and Sidon. 18They all came
to hear Jesus teach and to be healed of their sicknesses, and he healed those who were troubled
by evil spirits. 19All the people were trying to
touch Jesus, because power was coming from
him and healing them all.

20Jesus looked at his followers and said,

"You people who are poor are happy,
    because the kingdom of God belongs to you.
21You people who are now hungry are happy,
    because you will be satisfied.
You people who are now crying are happy,
    because you will laugh with joy.

22"People will hate you, shut you out, insult
you, and say you are evil because you follow the
Son of Man. But when they do, you will be
happy. 23Be full of joy at that time, because you
have a great reward waiting for you in heaven.

5:33 *give up eating.* This is called "fasting." The people would give up eating for a special time of prayer and worship to God. It was also done to show sadness and disappointment.

6:11 Pharisees and Sadducees: Luke 7:30

6:16 Peter: Luke 8:51

6:17 Luke's beatitudes contrast two different kinds of people and their very different future expectations. Those who are presently suffering because of their faithfulness to Christ (6:20–23), who are poor and hungry and crying now will find happiness in the fulfillment of God's kingdom. Their present misery reflects the fact that these people have not benefited from the culture and society which rejects Christ. Oppositely, those who are now rich and well fed and laughing (6:24–26) can only expect misery in the future. They are warned that, if their present good life comes from friendship with those who hate Christ, they can only expect judgment in the future. This type of contrast between the good and those who compromise their faith is a frequent feature in wisdom literature. The passage contrasts the costs of faith and benefits of faithfulness with the long-term dangers of spiritual compromise.

6:19 Sickness, Disease, Healing: Luke 13:10–17

6:22 Poverty: Luke 7:21–23

Their ancestors did the same things to the
prophets.
24“But how terrible it will be for you who are rich,
because you have had your easy life.
25How terrible it will be for you who are full now,
because you will be hungry.
How terrible it will be for you who
are laughing now,
because you will be sad and cry.

26“How terrible when everyone says only good
things about you, because their ancestors said the
same things about the false prophets.

Love Your Enemies

27“But I say to you who are listening, love your
enemies. Do good to those who hate you, 28bless
those who curse you, pray for those who are cruel
to you. 29If anyone slaps you on one cheek, offer
him the other cheek, too. If someone takes your
coat, do not stop him from taking your shirt. 30Give
to everyone who asks you, and when someone
takes something that is yours, don’t ask for it back.
31Do to others what you would want them to do to
you. 32If you love only the people who love you,
what praise should you get? Even sinners love the
people who love them. 33If you do good only to
those who do good to you, what praise should you
get? Even sinners do that! 34If you lend things to
people, always hoping to get something back, what
praise should you get? Even sinners lend to other
sinners so that they can get back the same amount!
35But love your enemies, do good to them, and
lend to them without hoping to get anything back.
Then you will have a great reward, and you will be
children of the Most High God, because he is kind
even to people who are ungrateful and full of sin.
36Show mercy, just as your Father shows mercy.

Look at Yourselves

37“Don’t judge other people, and you will not
be judged. Don’t accuse others of being guilty, and
you will not be accused of being guilty. Forgive,
and you will be forgiven. 38Give, and you will
receive. You will be given much. Pressed down,
shaken together, and running over, it will spill
into your lap. The way you give to others is the
way God will give to you.”

39Jesus told them this story: “Can a blind person lead another blind person? No! Both of them
will fall into a ditch. 40A student is not better than
the teacher, but the student who has been fully
trained will be like the teacher.

41“Why do you notice the little piece of dust in
your friend’s eye, but you don’t notice the big
piece of wood in your own eye? 42How can you
say to your friend, ‘Friend, let me take that little
piece of dust out of your eye’ when you cannot
see that big piece of wood in your own eye! You
hypocrite! First, take the wood out of your own
eye. Then you will see clearly to take the dust out
of your friend’s eye.

Two Kinds of Fruit

43“A good tree does not produce bad fruit, nor
does a bad tree produce good fruit. 44Each tree is
known by its own fruit. People don’t gather figs
from thornbushes, and they don’t get grapes
from bushes. 45Good people bring good things
out of the good they stored in their hearts. But
evil people bring evil things out of the evil they
stored in their hearts. People speak the things
that are in their hearts.

Two Kinds of People

46“Why do you call me, ‘Lord, Lord,’ but do not
do what I say? 47I will show you what everyone is
like who comes to me and hears my words and
obeys. 48That person is like a man building a
house who dug deep and laid the foundation on
rock. When the floods came, the water tried to
wash the house away, but it could not shake it,
because the house was built well. 49But the one
who hears my words and does not obey is like a
man who built his house on the ground without a
foundation. When the floods came, the house
quickly fell and was completely destroyed.”

Jesus Heals a Soldier’s Servant

7 When Jesus finished saying all these things to
the people, he went to Capernaum. 2There
was an army officer who had a servant who was
very important to him. The servant was so sick he

6:23 Land/Inheritance: Luke 12:22–31
6:27 Hate: John 3:20
6:27–36 People in the ancient world generally lived in a careful balance: If I do something for you, then you owe me, and vice versa. Within one’s family, and among one’s closest friends, though, it was appropriate to give to one another freely, without expectation of return. Jesus undercuts the normal way of behaving toward one another in the world by insisting that people treat each other, and especially those in need, as though they were one’s close kin or friends.
6:36 Debt/Loan: Luke 7:36–50
6:37 Forgiveness: Luke 11:4

6:40 Jesus declares that to be a follower is to become like the Master (Matthew 10:24–25; Luke 6:40). Becoming like Jesus includes going out with the same message, ministry, and compassion (Matthew 10:5–15), practicing the same religious and social traditions (Matthew 12:1–8; Mark 2:18–22), belonging to the same family of obedience (Matthew 12:46–49), exercising the same servanthood (Mark 10:42–45), experiencing the same suffering (Matthew 10:16–25), doing all as he did. The true follower is to know Jesus so well, is to follow him so closely, that he or she will become like him. The ultimate goal is to be conformed to his image (see Luke 6:40; Romans 8:28–29).
6:49 Physical Handicap: See article on page 912.

Body/Resurrection

1 Corinthians 15

What sort of body did Jesus have after the resurrection?
What do we know about our resurrection body?

Perhaps it's incomprehensible to think that Jesus' close companions who had spent most of three years with him wouldn't recognize him when he returned. But that is what the Scriptures tell us. While two of Jesus' followers "were talking and discussing, Jesus himself came near and began walking with them, but they were kept from recognizing him" (Luke 24:14–16). This picture of seeing him, yet not knowing him is repeated twice in Luke 24 and twice in John 20 & 21. Only when their eyes were opened or when he called them by name could they see him or recognize him. Yet the Scripture also says that Jesus was present bodily, walking and talking with them, showing them his hands and feet, inviting them to touch and see, and at least on two occasions ate fish in their presence.

From this account we learn that Jesus was knowable in his physical resurrection body, though human eyes alone seem not to understand until helped with supernatural sight. This implies his new body was changed in some way, though not wholly unlike his previous body. In addition, as the disciples heard him speak and act they seemed to connect with past situations where he had spoken or acted in a very similar manner. (Compare John 21:6, 7 with Luke 5:4–8; Luke 24:30 with Matthew 14:19, and Mark 14:22). The account in Acts 1:1–11 records Jesus appearing to a larger group of his followers with one difference noted. Here there is an absence of questioning, "Is this Jesus?" and no mention of a delayed recognition.

These accounts seem consistent with Paul's encounter on the road to Damascus where he both sees a bright light and hears a voice. It is unknown whether Paul had previously seen Jesus in person or not. Whichever, he has to ask "Who are you, Lord?" (Acts 9:1–7). Later, in Acts 22:9, Paul says, "Those who were with me did not hear the voice, but they saw the light." Again, Jesus in his resurrected body is discernable in part, but not in whole, by the human eye.

Paul in his letter to the Corinthians gives the most complete description of resurrection for Christ and his followers. Before discussing what kind of body Christ's followers will have, Paul declares with certainty, "In Adam all of us die [a physical bodily death]. In the same way, in Christ all of us will be made alive again [bodily]" (1 Corinthians 15:22). He then uses the analogy of the seed, a bare kernel, to illustrate the limits of human understanding concerning the resurrection, and how the earthly and heavenly will be connected. Interestingly enough, this is the same analogy Jesus used when talking about his own death (John 12:23–26). Jesus teaches the pattern of bodily death and bodily resurrection.

Paul is clear, with no room for doubt: both the earthly seed and the plant which is to come have bodies, though they be different. "When you sow a seed, it must die in the ground before it can live and grow. And when you sow it, it does not have the same 'body' it will have later. . . . But God gives it a body that he has planned for it, and God gives each kind of seed its own body" (1 Corinthians 15:36–38). With this established, Paul introduces the language of physical body and spiritual body. This does not negate that both this side and the other side of the resurrection we will have bodies. Rather, we are limited in being able to understand what a spiritual body will be like.

So Paul describes the physical body that we can fully understand and the spiritual body that is beyond our understanding. The body that is "planted" is a physical body, which will decay. It is without honor, weak, and limited to the physical realm. The spiritual body is this same body transformed by resurrection power, so that it can no longer be destroyed. It is powerful and glorious. (See 1 Corinthians 15:42–47). Paul then continues, "People who belong to the earth are like the first man of earth. But those people who belong to heaven are like the man of heaven. Just as we were made like the man of earth [Adam], so we will also be made like the man of heaven [Jesus]" (1 Corinthians 15:48–49).

Paul continues by emphasizing the mystery of the resurrection. Surely Jesus' disciples stood in awe of being with Jesus, yet not recognizing him. Seconds later they were enabled to see and touch and know and sense "It is the Lord!" (John 21:7). When this body dies and is clothed with that which can never die, we then can recognize bodily who it is that has loved us, dealt mercifully with us, and called us to himself. And just as we can then recognize him, we will recognize many others in the throng of those who surround him in their transformed bodies.

Body/Resurrection: For additional scriptures on this topic go to Luke 24.

IMMORTALITY

1 CORINTHIANS 15:50–57

Are human beings immortal? What happens when we die? Do our souls keep living on even after our bodies are dead?

One of the clearest messages of Scripture is that God alone is immortal (1 Timothy 6:16). To speak of immortality is to speak of an existence that never suffers decay, that never dies, that lives on from eternity to eternity. In biblical thought, this is not a characteristic we humans share with God.

To affirm that God alone is immortal, however, raises questions about the nature of the eternal life promised to those who believe in Christ (as in John 3:16). The Gospel of John, along with other New Testament writings, can affirm that life with God begins now for those who believe in Christ without assuming that human beings are immortal, however. Paul, writing in 1 Corinthians 15, is the most clear on this subject. In 1 Corinthians 15:38–58, he affirms the following: (1) There is a profound continuity between present life in this world and life everlasting with God. For human beings, this continuity has to do with bodily existence. That is, Paul (unlike the Greek philosopher Plato, but very much in contact with Old Testament thought) cannot think in terms of a free-floating soul separate from a body. (2) Present human existence, however, is marked by frailty, deterioration, and weakness, and is unsuited for eternal life. Therefore, in order for Christian believers to share in eternal life, their bodies must be transformed. Paul, then, does not think of "immortality of the soul." Neither does he proclaim a resuscitation of dead bodies that might serve as receptacles for souls that had escaped the body in death. Instead, he sets before his audience the promise of the transformation of bodies into glorified bodies (compare Philippians 3:21).

(3) Paul's ideas are, in part, rooted in images from the natural world and, in part, related to the resurrection of Jesus Christ. As it was with Christ's body, Paul insists, so it will be with ours: the same, yet not the same; transformed for the new conditions of life with God forever. (4) Paul teaches that this change will take place when Christ returns. At that moment, both the living and the dead will be transformed. (5) For Paul, this has important meaning for the nature of Christian life in the present. For example, this message underscores the significance of life in this world—a fact that many Christians at Corinth had not been taking seriously. We should not imagine that our bodies are unimportant, then, or that what we do to our bodies or with our bodies is somehow unrelated to eternal life. The idea of eternal life is not "escapism." Rather, it provides the Christian both with hope as well as with a vision of what is important to God; as a result, we may look forward to the future while also allowing this vision of the future to help determine the nature of our lives in the present.

Although the Old Testament knows nothing of human immortality, the picture is complicated somewhat in some parts of the New Testament. This is because the New Testament was written in the first century AD, following three hundred years of influence from Greek ways of thinking. The great philosopher Plato, for example, spoke of the "immortality of the soul," and many Greeks and Romans took special precautions to ensure that nothing hindered the soul following death. For example, because it was believed that leaving a corpse unburied had unpleasant consequences for the fate of the departed soul, Romans were known to join "funeral clubs," whose primary function was to ensure the burial of their deceased members. The separate existence of the soul, as though it were already alive, ready to be placed in a body at birth, is reflected in the question asked about a man born blind in John 9:2. In his response, Jesus does not embrace this idea of the pre-existence of the soul, but relates the man's blindness to God's larger purpose.

Denial of human immortality is one of the important biblical affirmations that separate Christianity from those world religions and New Age religious beliefs that teach reincarnation today. The idea of reincarnation assumes that our essence as humans is separable from our bodies. This essence leaves the body at death so that it might enter a new physical "shell," whether human or non-human, where it continues its life. Against this view, Christian faith affirms the unity of human existence, the inseparability of body and soul. For Christians, death does not mark the departure of an immortal soul, as though this alone marked our identity as humans. Ongoing life does not depend on the soul's ability to take up residence in a new physical frame, but on God's power to transform our existence altogether. In this way, we obtain a form of life that is well-suited to eternity.

Immortality: For additional scriptures on this topic go to John 3:16.

A Roman centurion: a military officer, who commanded one hundred men

was nearly dead. 3When the officer heard about Jesus, he sent some older Jewish leaders to him to ask Jesus to come and heal his servant. 4The men went to Jesus and begged him, saying, "This officer is worthy of your help. 5He loves our people, and he built us a synagogue."

6So Jesus went with the men. He was getting near the officer's house when the officer sent friends to say, "Lord, don't trouble yourself, because I am not worthy to have you come into my house. 7That is why I did not come to you myself. But you only need to command it, and my servant will be healed. 8I, too, am a man under the authority of others, and I have soldiers under my command. I tell one soldier, 'Go,' and he goes. I tell another soldier, 'Come,' and he comes. I say to my servant, 'Do this,' and my servant does it."

9When Jesus heard this, he was amazed. Turning to the crowd that was following him, he said, "I tell you, this is the greatest faith I have found anywhere, even in Israel."

10Those who had been sent to Jesus went back to the house where they found the servant in good health.

Jesus Brings a Man Back to Life

11Soon afterwards Jesus went to a town called Nain, and his followers and a large crowd traveled with him. 12When he came near the town gate, he saw a funeral. A mother, who was a widow, had lost her only son. A large crowd from the town was with the mother while her son was being carried out. 13When the Lord saw her, he felt very sorry for her and said, "Don't cry." 14He went up and touched the coffin, and the people who were carrying it stopped. Jesus said, "Young man, I tell you, get up!" 15And the son sat up and began to talk. Then Jesus gave him back to his mother.

16All the people were amazed and began praising God, saying, "A great prophet has come to us! God has come to help his people."

17This news about Jesus spread through all Judea and into all the places around there.

John Asks a Question

18John's followers told him about all these things. He called for two of his followers 19and sent them to the Lord to ask, "Are you the One who is to come, or should we wait for someone else?"

20When the men came to Jesus, they said, "John the Baptist sent us to you with this question: 'Are you the One who is to come, or should we wait for someone else?'"

21At that time, Jesus healed many people of their sicknesses, diseases, and evil spirits, and he gave sight to many blind people. 22Then Jesus answered John's followers, "Go tell John what you saw and heard here. The blind can see, the crippled can walk, and people with skin diseases are healed. The deaf can hear, the dead are raised to life, and the Good News is preached to the poor. 23Those who do not stumble in their faith because of me are blessed!"

24When John's followers left, Jesus began talking to the people about John: "What did you go out into the desert to see? A reed blown by the wind? 25What did you go out to see? A man

7:11–15 The focus of this story is the needs of this woman, who has lost her only means of economic and social support. Jesus addresses her needs by bringing her dead son back to life and giving him to her. Time after time, Jesus' healing ministry has as much to do with the restoration of family and community as with the curing of physical diseases.

7:22 Gospel/Good News: Luke 9:6
7:23 Blindness: See article on page 999.
7:23 Poverty: Acts 3:6–9
7:24 *reed.* It means that John was not ordinary or weak like grass blown by the wind.

dressed in fine clothes? No, people who have fine
clothes and much wealth live in kings' palaces.
26But what did you go out to see? A prophet? Yes,
and I tell you, John is more than a prophet. 27This
was written about him:

'I will send my messenger ahead of you,
who will prepare the way
for you.' *Malachi 3:1*

28I tell you, John is greater than any other person
ever born, but even the least important person in
the kingdom of God is greater than John."

29(When the people, including the tax collectors, heard this, they all agreed that God's teaching was good, because they had been baptized by
John. 30But the Pharisees and experts on the law
refused to accept God's plan for themselves; they
did not let John baptize them.)⚭

31Then Jesus said, "What shall I say about the
people of this time? What are they like? 32They
are like children sitting in the marketplace, calling to one another and saying,

'We played music for you, but you
did not dance;
we sang a sad song, but you did not cry.'

33John the Baptist came and did not eat bread or
drink wine, and you say, 'He has a demon in
him.' 34The Son of Man came eating and drinking, and you say, 'Look at him! He eats too much
and drinks too much wine, and he is a friend of
tax collectors and sinners!' 35But wisdom is
proved to be right by what it does."

A Woman Washes Jesus' Feet

36One of the Pharisees asked Jesus to eat with
him, so Jesus went into the Pharisee's house and
sat at the table. 37A sinful woman in the town
learned that Jesus was eating at the Pharisee's
house. So she brought an alabaster jar of perfume
38and stood behind Jesus at his feet, crying. She
began to wash his feet with her tears, and she
dried them with her hair, kissing them many times
and rubbing them with the perfume. 39When the
Pharisee who asked Jesus to come to his house
saw this, he thought to himself, "If Jesus were a
prophet, he would know that the woman touching him is a sinner!"

40Jesus said to the Pharisee, "Simon, I have something to say to you."

Simon said, "Teacher, tell me."

41Jesus said, "Two people owed money to the
same banker. One owed five hundred coins and
the other owed fifty. 42They had no money to pay
what they owed, but the banker told both of them
they did not have to pay him. Which person will
love the banker more?"

43Simon, the Pharisee, answered, "I think it
would be the one who owed him the most money."

Jesus said to Simon, "You are right." 44Then
Jesus turned toward the woman and said to
Simon, "Do you see this woman? When I came
into your house, you gave me no water for my
feet, but she washed my feet with her tears and
dried them with her hair. 45You gave me no kiss
of greeting, but she has been kissing my feet
since I came in. 46You did not put oil on my head,
but she poured perfume on my feet. 47I tell you
that her many sins are forgiven, so she showed
great love. But the person who is forgiven only a
little will love only a little."⚭

48Then Jesus said to her, "Your sins are forgiven."

49The people sitting at the table began to say
among themselves, "Who is this who even forgives sins?"

50Jesus said to the woman, "Because you believed,
you are saved from your sins. Go in peace."⚭

⚭**7:30 Pharisees and Sadducees:** Luke 18:9–14

7:36–50 Jesus frequently emphasizes both human need for God's forgiveness and our need to forgive one another. Although there are many examples of each emphasis in Matthew, Mark, Luke, and John, no one passage includes both understandings of forgiveness. In the first text listed above (Luke 7:36–50), Jesus focuses on human need for God's forgiveness, and we find a pair of opposites. Jesus both forgives a woman who recognizes her sinfulness, and he also confronts a man with his need for forgiveness who is blind to his own sinfulness. The second text (Luke 6:37) places together another pair of opposites: our willingness to forgive others as it is tied to God's willingness to forgive us.

Jesus demonstrates that all human beings are both guilty and potentially forgiven. A woman attracted by the hope in Jesus' message extends hospitality to him. Jesus tenderly receives her. A Pharisee, protected from guilt by his own religious deeds, offers Jesus no hospitality and judges the woman. Jesus confronts him with his own guilt, offering him a chance to be forgiven and be reunited with God and other people.

7:36–50 Simon is a Pharisee, someone who is very careful to follow kosher meal customs and who is also expecting the Messiah. While he must have invited Jesus to the meal, he neglects to perform the customary actions that would have signified his acceptance of Jesus as an honored guest; perhaps he is afraid of rejection by his associates if he honors Jesus. The woman he labels "a sinner" does honor Jesus. So a main idea of Luke is shown: "I have not come to invite good people but sinners to change their hearts and lives" (Luke 5:32).

7:41 *coins.* Roman denarii. One coin was the average pay for one day's work.

⚭**7:47 Forgiveness:** Luke 11:4

7:50 The woman who washed Jesus' feet with her tears was saved from her sins because of her faith. While salvation is offered to everyone, to some it has more meaning because they have been forgiven for so much. Forgiveness of sins and acceptance by Jesus were important parts of her salvation.

⚭**7:50 Debt/Loan:** See article on page 752.

⚭**7:50 Hospitality:** Luke 13:22–30

⚭**7:50 Jesus:** Luke 17:19

⚭**7:50 Table Fellowship/Lord's Supper:** Luke 14:1–24

The Group with Jesus

8 After this, while Jesus was traveling through
some cities and small towns, he preached
and told the Good News about God's kingdom.
The twelve apostles were with him, 2and also
some women who had been healed of sicknesses and evil spirits: Mary, called Magdalene,
from whom seven demons had gone out; 3Joanna,
the wife of Cuza (the manager of Herod's
house); Susanna; and many others. These women
used their own money to help Jesus and his
apostles.

A Story About Planting Seed

4When a great crowd was gathered, and people
were coming to Jesus from every town, he told
them this story:
5"A farmer went out to plant his seed. While he
was planting, some seed fell by the road. People
walked on the seed, and the birds ate it up.
6Some seed fell on rock, and when it began to
grow, it died because it had no water. 7Some seed
fell among thorny weeds, but the weeds grew up
with it and choked the good plants. 8And some
seed fell on good ground and grew and made a
hundred times more."
As Jesus finished the story, he called out, "You
people who can hear me, listen!"
9Jesus' followers asked him what this story
meant.
10Jesus said, "You have been chosen to know
the secrets about the kingdom of God. But I use
stories to speak to other people so that:
'They will look, but they may not see.
They will listen, but they may
not understand.' *Isaiah 6:9*
11"This is what the story means: The seed is
God's message. 12The seed that fell beside the
road is like the people who hear God's teaching,
but the devil comes and takes it away from them
so they cannot believe it and be saved. 13The seed
that fell on rock is like those who hear God's
teaching and accept it gladly, but they don't allow
the teaching to go deep into their lives. They
believe for a while, but when trouble comes, they
give up. 14The seed that fell among the thorny
weeds is like those who hear God's teaching, but
they let the worries, riches, and pleasures of this
life keep them from growing and producing good
fruit. 15And the seed that fell on the good ground
is like those who hear God's teaching with good,
honest hearts and obey it and patiently produce
good fruit.

Use What You Have

16"No one after lighting a lamp covers it with a
bowl or hides it under a bed. Instead, the person
puts it on a lampstand so those who come in will
see the light. 17Everything that is hidden will
become clear, and every secret thing will be made
known. 18So be careful how you listen. Those who
have understanding will be given more. But those
who do not have understanding, even what they
think they have will be taken away from them."

Jesus' True Family

19Jesus' mother and brothers came to see him,
but there was such a crowd they could not get to
him. 20Someone said to Jesus, "Your mother and
your brothers are standing outside, wanting to
see you."
21Jesus answered them, "My mother and my
brothers are those who listen to God's teaching
and obey it!"

Jesus Calms a Storm

22One day Jesus and his followers got into a boat,
and he said to them, "Let's go across the lake." And
so they started across. 23While they were sailing,
Jesus fell asleep. A very strong wind blew up on
the lake, causing the boat to fill with water, and
they were in danger.
24The followers went to Jesus and woke him,
saying, "Master! Master! We will drown!"
Jesus got up and gave a command to the wind
and the waves. They stopped, and it became calm.
25Jesus said to his followers, "Where is your faith?"
The followers were afraid and amazed and said
to each other, "Who is this that commands even
the wind and the water, and they obey him?"

A Man with Demons Inside Him

26Jesus and his followers sailed across the lake
from Galilee to the area of the Gerasene people.
27When Jesus got out on the land, a man from the
town who had demons inside him came to Jesus.
For a long time he had worn no clothes and had
lived in the burial caves, not in a house. 28When
he saw Jesus, he cried out and fell down before
him. He said with a loud voice, "What do you
want with me, Jesus, Son of the Most High God?
I beg you, don't torture me!" 29He said this because
Jesus was commanding the evil spirit to come out
of the man. Many times it had taken hold of him.
Though he had been kept under guard and
chained hand and foot, he had broken his chains
and had been forced by the demon out into a
lonely place.

30 Jesus asked him, "What is your name?"

He answered, "Legion," because many demons were in him. 31 The demons begged Jesus not to send them into eternal darkness. 32 A large herd of pigs was feeding on a hill, and the demons begged Jesus to allow them to go into the pigs. So Jesus allowed them to do this. 33 When the demons came out of the man, they went into the pigs, and the herd ran down the hill into the lake and was drowned.

34 When the herdsmen saw what had happened, they ran away and told about this in the town and the countryside. 35 And people went to see what had happened. When they came to Jesus, they found the man sitting at Jesus' feet, clothed and in his right mind, because the demons were gone. But the people were frightened. 36 The people who saw this happen told the others how Jesus had made the man well. 37 All the people of the Gerasene country asked Jesus to leave, because they were all very afraid. So Jesus got into the boat and went back to Galilee.

38 The man whom Jesus had healed begged to go with him, but Jesus sent him away, saying, 39 "Go back home and tell people how much God has done for you." So the man went all over town telling how much Jesus had done for him.

Jesus Gives Life to a Dead Girl and Heals a Sick Woman

40 When Jesus got back to Galilee, a crowd welcomed him, because everyone was waiting for him. 41 A man named Jairus, a leader of the synagogue, came to Jesus and fell at his feet, begging him to come to his house. 42 Jairus' only daughter, about twelve years old, was dying.

While Jesus was on his way to Jairus' house, the people were crowding all around him. 43 A woman was in the crowd who had been bleeding for twelve years, but no one was able to heal her. 44 She came up behind Jesus and touched the edge of his coat, and instantly her bleeding stopped. 45 Then Jesus said, "Who touched me?"

When all the people said they had not touched him, Peter said, "Master, the people are all around you and are pushing against you."

46 But Jesus said, "Someone did touch me, because I felt power go out from me." 47 When the woman saw she could not hide, she came forward, shaking, and fell down before Jesus. While all the people listened, she told why she had touched him and how she had been instantly healed. 48 Jesus said to her, "Dear woman, you are made well because you believed. Go in peace."

49 While Jesus was still speaking, someone came from the house of the synagogue leader and said to him, "Your daughter is dead. Don't bother the teacher anymore."

50 When Jesus heard this, he said to Jairus, "Don't be afraid. Just believe, and your daughter will be well."

51 When Jesus went to the house, he let only Peter, John, James, and the girl's father and mother go inside with him. 52 All the people were crying and feeling sad because the girl was dead, but Jesus said, "Stop crying. She is not dead, only asleep."

53 The people laughed at Jesus because they knew the girl was dead. 54 But Jesus took hold of her hand and called to her, "My child, stand up!" 55 Her spirit came back into her, and she stood up at once. Then Jesus ordered that she be given something to eat. 56 The girl's parents were amazed, but Jesus told them not to tell anyone what had happened.

Jesus Sends Out the Apostles

9 Jesus called the twelve apostles together and gave them power and authority over all demons and the ability to heal sicknesses. 2 He sent the apostles out to tell about God's kingdom and to heal the sick. 3 He said to them, "Take nothing for your trip, neither a walking stick, bag, bread, money, or extra clothes. 4 When you enter a house, stay there until it is time to leave. 5 If people do not welcome you, shake the dust off of your feet as you leave the town, as a warning to them."

6 So the apostles went out and traveled through all the towns, preaching the Good News and healing people everywhere.

Herod Is Confused About Jesus

7 Herod, the governor, heard about all the things that were happening and was confused, because some people said, "John the Baptist has risen from the dead." 8 Others said, "Elijah has come to us." And still others said, "One of the prophets who lived long ago has risen from the dead." 9 Herod said, "I cut off John's head, so who is this man I hear such things about?" And Herod kept trying to see Jesus.

8:30 *"Legion."* Means very many. A legion was about five thousand men in the Roman army.

8:31 *eternal darkness.* Literally, "the abyss," something like a pit or a hole that has no end.

8:39 Wilderness (Desert): Revelation 12:6

8:48 Self-Control: Acts 24:25

8:51 Peter: Luke 9:20

9:5 *shake . . . feet.* A warning. It showed that they had rejected these people.

9:6 Gospel/Good News: John 3:16–21

More than Five Thousand Fed

10When the apostles returned, they told Jesus
everything they had done. Then Jesus took them
with him to a town called Bethsaida where they
could be alone together. 11But the people learned
where Jesus went and followed him. He welcomed
them and talked with them about God's kingdom
and healed those who needed to be healed.
12Late in the afternoon, the twelve apostles came
to Jesus and said, "Send the people away. They
need to go to the towns and countryside around
here and find places to sleep and something to eat,
because no one lives in this place."
13But Jesus said to them, "You give them something to eat."
They said, "We have only five loaves of bread
and two fish, unless we go buy food for all these
people." 14(There were about five thousand men
there.)
Jesus said to his followers, "Tell the people to
sit in groups of about fifty people."
15So the followers did this, and all the people sat
down. 16Then Jesus took the five loaves of bread
and two fish, and looking up to heaven, he thanked
God for the food. Then he divided the food and
gave it to the followers to give to the people.
17They all ate and were satisfied, and what was left
over was gathered up, filling twelve baskets.

Jesus Is the Christ

18One time when Jesus was praying alone, his
followers were with him, and he asked them,
"Who do the people say I am?"
19They answered, "Some say you are John the
Baptist. Others say you are Elijah. And others say
you are one of the prophets from long ago who
has come back to life."
20Then Jesus asked, "But who do you say I am?"
Peter answered, "You are the Christ from God."
21Jesus warned them not to tell anyone, saying,
22"The Son of Man must suffer many things. He
will be rejected by the older Jewish leaders, the
leading priests, and the teachers of the law. He
will be killed and after three days will be raised
from the dead."
23Jesus said to all of them, "If people want to
follow me, they must give up the things they want.
They must be willing to give up their lives daily to
follow me. 24Those who want to save their lives
will give up true life. But those who give up their
lives for me will have true life. 25It is worth nothing for them to have the whole world if they
themselves are destroyed or lost. 26If people are
ashamed of me and my teaching, then the Son of
Man will be ashamed of them when he comes in
his glory and with the glory of the Father and the
holy angels. 27I tell you the truth, some people
standing here will see the kingdom of God before
they die."

Jesus Talks with Moses and Elijah

28About eight days after Jesus said these things,
he took Peter, John, and James and went up on a
mountain to pray. 29While Jesus was praying, the
appearance of his face changed, and his clothes
became shining white. 30Then two men, Moses
and Elijah, were talking with Jesus. 31They
appeared in heavenly glory, talking about his
departure which he would soon bring about in
Jerusalem. 32Peter and the others were very
sleepy, but when they awoke fully, they saw the
glory of Jesus and the two men standing with
him. 33When Moses and Elijah were about to
leave, Peter said to Jesus, "Master, it is good that
we are here. Let us make three tents—one for
you, one for Moses, and one for Elijah." (Peter did
not know what he was talking about.)
34While he was saying these things, a cloud
came and covered them, and they became afraid
as the cloud covered them. 35A voice came from
the cloud, saying, "This is my Son, whom I have
chosen. Listen to him!"
36When the voice finished speaking, only Jesus
was there. Peter, John, and James said nothing
and told no one at that time what they had seen.

Jesus Heals a Sick Boy

37The next day, when they came down from
the mountain, a large crowd met Jesus. 38A man
in the crowd shouted to him, "Teacher, please
come and look at my son, because he is my only
child. 39An evil spirit seizes my son, and suddenly
he screams. It causes him to lose control of himself and foam at the mouth. The evil spirit keeps

9:19 *Elijah.* A man who spoke for God and who lived hundreds of years before Christ. See 1 Kings 17.

9:20 Peter: Luke 9:28–33

9:23–25 Lest anyone make the mistake of thinking the Good News is just a "feel good" message, Jesus clarifies his offer. Those who would follow him must give up their desires and even their own lives every day for Jesus' sake. This Good News costs the follower his or her whole life, but promises to give the only true life in return.

9:28–36 Even though Jesus had said that John the Baptist had fulfilled the prophecy concerning Elijah (Matthew 11:14), it is striking that Elijah himself did put in an appearance in his glorified state on the Mount of Transfiguration. By so doing, Elijah did return before Christ was glorified, but his appearance was not public and was limited to the inner circle of Jesus' followers.

9:30 *Moses and Elijah.* Two of the most important Jewish leaders in the past. God had given Moses the Law, and Elijah was an important prophet.

9:33 Peter: Luke 22:8

on hurting him and almost never leaves him. 40I
begged your followers to force the evil spirit out,
but they could not do it."

41Jesus answered, "You people have no faith, and
your lives are all wrong. How long must I stay with
you and put up with you? Bring your son here."

42While the boy was coming, the demon threw
him on the ground and made him lose control of
himself. But Jesus gave a strong command to the
evil spirit and healed the boy and gave him back
to his father. 43All the people were amazed at the
great power of God.

Jesus Talks About His Death

While everyone was wondering about all that
Jesus did, he said to his followers, 44"Don't forget what I tell you now: The Son of Man will be
handed over to people." 45But the followers did
not understand what this meant; the meaning
was hidden from them so they could not understand. But they were afraid to ask Jesus about it.

Who Is the Greatest?

46Jesus' followers began to have an argument
about which one of them was the greatest. 47Jesus
knew what they were thinking, so he took a little
child and stood the child beside him. 48Then
Jesus said, "Whoever accepts this little child in
my name accepts me. And whoever accepts me
accepts the One who sent me, because whoever
is least among you all is really the greatest."

Anyone Not Against Us Is for Us

49John answered, "Master, we saw someone
using your name to force demons out of people.
We told him to stop, because he does not belong
to our group."

50But Jesus said to him, "Don't stop him,
because whoever is not against you is for you."

A Town Rejects Jesus

51When the time was coming near for Jesus to
depart, he was determined to go to Jerusalem.
52He sent some men ahead of him, who went
into a town in Samaria to make everything ready
for him. 53But the people there would not welcome him, because he was set on going to
Jerusalem. 54When James and John, followers of
Jesus, saw this, they said, "Lord, do you want us
to call fire down from heaven and destroy those
people?"*

55But Jesus turned and scolded them. 56Then
they went to another town.

Following Jesus

57As they were going along the road, someone
said to Jesus, "I will follow you any place you go."

58Jesus said to them, "The foxes have holes to
live in, and the birds have nests, but the Son of
Man has no place to rest his head."

59Jesus said to another man, "Follow me!"

But he said, "Lord, first let me go and bury my
father."

60But Jesus said to him, "Let the people who
are dead bury their own dead. You must go and
tell about the kingdom of God."

61Another man said, "I will follow you, Lord,
but first let me go and say good-bye to my family."

62Jesus said, "Anyone who begins to plow a
field but keeps looking back is of no use in the
kingdom of God."

A farmer using a simple plow: a wooden stake with a metal tip at the bottom

---

9:43 Crossing Cultural Boundaries: Luke 10:38–42

9:43–48 Arguing about who is the greatest, the followers are normal people concerned about issues of power and position. They even want to control who can and cannot work for Jesus. Jesus tries to teach them a new way of behaving by using the example of a little child. "To accept" little children would mean to treat them as special guests in one's home, as though they were the most important members of the community. In order to do this, Jesus' followers would have to stop thinking of themselves as so important. By commanding his followers to welcome a child, he asks them to risk lowering themselves to a child's status. It is humility and not greatness that Jesus expects from his followers.

9:45 Martyrdom: Luke 12:8–12

9:50 Unity: John 17

***9:54** *Verse 54.* Here, some Greek copies add: ". . . as Elijah did."

9:55-56 *Verse 55-56.* Some copies read: "But Jesus turned and scolded them. And Jesus said, 'You don't know what kind of spirit you belong to. 56The Son of Man did not come to destroy the souls of people but to save them.' Then. . . ."

9:57–62 Jesus' words seem harsh, and they are. He is beginning a journey with great determination (Luke 9:51, 53), knowing that at the journey's end he will be crucified (see Luke 9:21–22, 44). Those who join him in this journey, on which they will learn what is required to follow him, must share his single-mindedness (see Luke 9:23–24).

9:62 Disciple/Discipleship/Mentoring (Follow/Follower): John 1:35

Jesus Sends Out the Seventy-Two

10 After this, the Lord chose seventy-two others and sent them out in pairs ahead of him into every town and place where he planned to go. 2He said to them, "There are a great many people to harvest, but there are only a few workers. So pray to God, who owns the harvest, that he will send more workers to help gather his harvest. 3Go now, but listen! I am sending you out like sheep among wolves. 4Don't carry a purse, a bag, or sandals, and don't waste time talking with people on the road. 5Before you go into a house, say, 'Peace be with this house.' 6If peaceful people live there, your blessing of peace will stay with them, but if not, then your blessing will come back to you. 7Stay in the peaceful house, eating and drinking what the people there give you. A worker should be given his pay. Don't move from house to house. 8If you go into a town and the people welcome you, eat what they give you. 9Heal the sick who live there, and tell them, 'The kingdom of God is near you.' 10But if you go into a town, and the people don't welcome you, then go into the streets and say, 11'Even the dirt from your town that sticks to our feet we wipe off against you. But remember that the kingdom of God is near.' 12I tell you, on the Judgment Day it will be better for the people of Sodom than for the people of that town.

Jesus Warns Unbelievers

13"How terrible for you, Korazin! How terrible for you, Bethsaida! If the miracles I did in you had happened in Tyre and Sidon, those people would have changed their lives long ago. They would have worn rough cloth and put ashes on themselves to show they had changed. 14But on the Judgment Day it will be better for Tyre and Sidon than for you. 15And you, Capernaum, will you be lifted up to heaven? No! You will be thrown down to the depths!

16"Whoever listens to you listens to me, and whoever refuses to accept you refuses to accept me. And whoever refuses to accept me refuses to accept the One who sent me."

Satan Falls

17When the seventy-two came back, they were very happy and said, "Lord, even the demons obeyed us when we used your name!"

18Jesus said, "I saw Satan fall like lightning from heaven. 19Listen, I have given you power to walk on snakes and scorpions, power that is greater than the enemy has. So nothing will hurt you. 20But you should not be happy because the spirits obey you but because your names are written in heaven."

Jesus Prays to the Father

21Then Jesus rejoiced in the Holy Spirit and said, "I praise you, Father, Lord of heaven and earth, because you have hidden these things from the people who are wise and smart. But you have shown them to those who are like little children. Yes, Father, this is what you really wanted.

22"My Father has given me all things. No one knows who the Son is, except the Father. And no one knows who the Father is, except the Son and those whom the Son chooses to tell."

23Then Jesus turned to his followers and said privately, "You are blessed to see what you now see. 24I tell you, many prophets and kings wanted to see what you now see, but they did not, and they wanted to hear what you now hear, but they did not."

The Good Samaritan

25Then an expert on the law stood up to test Jesus, saying, "Teacher, what must I do to get life forever?"

10:1 *seventy-two.* Many Greek copies read seventy. When Jesus sent out the seventy-two, he told them it would not be easy. But they were to heal the sick and announce the coming of God's kingdom. Those early missionaries saw great signs of power done by God through their bold ministry.

10:1–16 As Jesus sends out seventy-two of his followers he tells them to pray that God would provide more workers to go into the harvest of people. In doing so, he highlights that the entire process belongs to God. As they go forth to spread the Good News, they are to exhibit their reliance on God. He tells them not to carry a purse, bag, or sandals. They are not to worry about those who do not respond to their message. Because they are sent out as Jesus' representatives, when people reject them, Jesus is the one who is really rejected.

10:11 *dirt . . . you.* A warning. It showed that they had rejected these people.

10:11 House/Home: Acts 20:7–12

10:12 End Times/Last Days: Revelation 21

10:12 *Sodom.* City that God destroyed because the people were so evil.

10:13 *Tyre and Sidon.* Towns where wicked people lived.

10:13, 15 *Korazin, Bethsaida, Capernaum.* Towns by Lake Galilee where Jesus preached to the people.

10:17 *seventy-two.* Many Greek copies read seventy.

10:18 Demon: John 12:31

10:18 Satan/Satanism: Luke 13:16

10:22 Incarnation: John 1:1

10:25–37 Jesus uses this conversation with the expert on the Law to discuss the meaning of life. The expert answers correctly that the Old Testament Law can be summed up in the commands to love God and neighbor. By using the Samaritan as an example of faithfulness, Jesus turns the lawyer's question, Who is my neighbor? around. A "neighbor" is not defined as one group to the exclusion of another group. Instead, neighbors are those to whom a person extends kindness and compassion. Instead of asking, Who is my neighbor? one should perhaps ask the question, To whom can *I be* a neighbor?

10:25–37 Though both Jewish people and Samaritans originally came from the twelve tribes of Israel, a split in the kingdom shortly after King Solomon's death led to battles and subsequent rivalry between them.

[26]Jesus said, "What is written in the law? What do you read there?"

[27]The man answered, "Love the Lord your God with all your heart, all your soul, all your strength, and all your mind." Also, "Love your neighbor as you love yourself."

[28]Jesus said to him, "Your answer is right. Do this and you will live."

[29]But the man, wanting to show the importance of his question, said to Jesus, "And who is my neighbor?"

[30]Jesus answered, "As a man was going down from Jerusalem to Jericho, some robbers attacked him. They tore off his clothes, beat him, and left him lying there, almost dead. [31]It happened that a priest was going down that road. When he saw the man, he walked by on the other side. [32]Next, a Levite came there, and after he went over and looked at the man, he walked by on the other side of the road. [33]Then a Samaritan traveling down the road came to where the hurt man was. When he saw the man, he felt very sorry for him. [34]The Samaritan went to him, poured olive oil and wine on his wounds, and bandaged them. Then he put the hurt man on his own donkey and took him to an inn where he cared for him. [35]The next day, the Samaritan brought out two coins, gave them to the innkeeper, and said, 'Take care of this man. If you spend more money on him, I will pay it back to you when I come again.'"

[36]Then Jesus said, "Which one of these three men do you think was a neighbor to the man who was attacked by the robbers?"

[37]The expert on the law answered, "The one who showed him mercy."

Jesus said to him, "Then go and do what he did."

Mary and Martha

[38]While Jesus and his followers were traveling, Jesus went into a town. A woman named Martha let Jesus stay at her house. [39]Martha had a sister named Mary, who was sitting at Jesus' feet and listening to him teach. [40]But Martha was busy with all the work to be done. She went in and said, "Lord, don't you care that my sister has left me alone to do all the work? Tell her to help me."

[41]But the Lord answered her, "Martha, Martha, you are worried and upset about many things. [42]Only one thing is important. Mary has chosen the better thing, and it will never be taken away from her."

Jesus Teaches About Prayer

11 One time Jesus was praying in a certain place. When he finished, one of his followers said to him, "Lord, teach us to pray as John taught his followers."

[2]Jesus said to them, "When you pray, say:
'Father, may your name always be kept holy.
May your kingdom come.
[3]Give us the food we need for each day.
[4]Forgive us for our sins,
because we forgive everyone who has done wrong to us.
And do not cause us to be tempted.'"

Continue to Ask

[5]Then Jesus said to them, "Suppose one of you went to your friend's house at midnight and said to him, 'Friend, loan me three loaves of bread. [6]A friend of mine has come into town to visit me, but I have nothing for him to eat.' [7]Your friend inside the house answers, 'Don't bother me! The door is already locked, and my children and I are in bed. I cannot get up and give you anything.' [8]I tell you, if friendship is not enough to make him

10:27 *"Love . . . mind."* Quotation from Deuteronomy 6:5.
10:27 *"Love . . . yourself."* Quotation from Leviticus 19:18.
10:27 Neighbor: Romans 13:9
10:32 *Levite.* Levites were members of the tribe of Levi who helped the Jewish priests with their work in the Temple. Read 1 Chronicles 23:24-32.
10:33 *Samaritan.* Samaritans were people from Samaria. These people were part Jewish, but the Jews did not accept them as true Jews. Samaritans and Jews disliked each other.
10:34 *olive oil and wine.* Oil and wine were used like medicine to soften and clean wounds.
10:35 *coins.* Roman denarii. One coin was the average pay for one day's work.
10:34 Alcohol: Luke 12:45
10:36–37 Jesus changed the question from Who is my neighbor? to What does it mean to be a neighbor? The question of "neighbor" is not so much a noun as it is a verb. It has more to do with actions and doing than with legalistic definitions by telling the inquirer, "Then go and do what he did."
10:37 Abortion and Crisis Pregnancy: Matthew 25:34–40
10:37 Parables: Luke 15
10:38–42 This brief episode between Jesus, Mary, and Martha should not be mistaken as a put down of work and industry. Rather, Jesus deals with Martha's attitude of worrying about many things (verse 41; Matthew 6:25–34).
10:42 Crossing Cultural Boundaries: Luke 13:29
10:42 Loneliness: See article on page 30.
10:42 Work: Luke 12:41–48
11:2 Father: John 5:19–23
11:4 Forgiveness: Luke 17:4
11:5–8 Often in the Book of Luke, Jesus draws on everyday experience to make his point. Often, too, he does so without asking us to identify one of the characters as God, one as Jesus, and so on. In this case, he paints a scenario with which his audience would agree, then goes on to draw a comparison, using an argument whose structure is "if this, how much more that": If we will help persistent friends, even if they come at inconvenient times, how much more will God, who loves us far more than our friends do, help us in our need? Because God is faithful, he will hear and act (see also Luke 18:1–8).

COMFORT

2 CORINTHIANS 1:3

What is the difference between worldly and Christian comfort?
What is the source of true comfort for us?

During times of adversity, there is nothing we need more than to be comforted. The people who lived in Bible times were no different. They also experienced difficult times in such forms as physical and emotional suffering (Job 42:11), the loss of a loved one (2 Samuel 12:24), national crisis (Lamentations), the guilt of sin (2 Corinthians 2:7), and the general hardships of life brought about by the curse that sin brings (Genesis 5:29).

During such periods of crisis it is very natural for loved ones (Genesis 37:35; Job 42:11) and friends (Job 2:11; John 11:19) to come alongside to help ease the grief and pain of the sufferer. Yet there may be times when we feel all alone, comforted by no one (Psalm 69:20; Ecclesiastes 4:1; 1 Timothy 4:16). Or perhaps our grief is so intense that the comfort of humans is simply insufficient (Genesis 37:35; Psalm 77:2)

Unfortunately, a sufferer may also seek comfort from worldly sources. Some people seek comfort in false religion. For example, in Bible times it was thought that idols could bring comfort (Zechariah 10:2), but such comfort was worthless, since idols were the creations of human hands (Habakkuk 2:18) and thus could not help (Jeremiah 14:22). In another case people believed the words of false prophets and were misled into a false comfort and security at the hands of those who told them no judgment was coming (Jeremiah 6:14). In still other cases mediums and fortune-tellers were sought out for help (Isaiah 8:19; Zechariah 10:2). All of these are denounced in the Bible as worthless.

Another very dangerous source of comfort is material wealth, which tends to give people a false sense of security and deceives people into thinking that they have no other needs. Jesus issues a very serious warning that to be rich and comfortable in this life is no guarantee of comfort in the next (Luke 6:24), a warning dramatically portrayed for us in the story of the rich man and Lazarus (Luke 16:25). Finally, people may look for revenge as a sort of comfort when others have wronged them, as in the case of Esau, who plotted the murder of his brother Jacob (Genesis 27:42).

Tragically, when the people of God forget the Lord as both their creator and comforter (Isaiah 51:12–13), they will be plagued by other fears. When we try to find comfort from a source other than the Lord, that comfort will not last, for it lacks the accompanying inner peace that only God can give. When we forsake the Lord, ultimately there is no one else who can bring comfort (Isaiah 51:19).

Therefore, the Bible emphasizes over and over again that true and lasting comfort comes ultimately from God himself (Psalm 71:21). In fact, all three persons of the Trinity are described as bringing comfort—the Father (2 Corinthians 1:3), the Son (Isaiah 61:1), and the Holy Spirit (John 14:16–18, where "helper" may also be understood as "comforter"). Quite frequently in the Psalms the writer pours out his heart before God, crying out to him for help (Psalm 102:1; 130:1) and receiving God's comfort (Psalm 94:19), for there is nothing more comforting than God's love (Psalm 119:76; Philippians 2:1). Like a loving parent to his child, the Lord brings comfort to his people after he has disciplined them for their sins (Isaiah 12:1; 40:12).

One specific means the Lord uses to bring comfort to his people is through the word of God, such as the promises of God (Psalm 119:50), the laws of God (119:52), and the preaching ministry of the word (1 Corinthians 14:3).

In 2 Corinthians 1:3–7 Paul offers praise to the Father for his ministry of comfort while he and his companions underwent extremely distressing circumstances in Asia. Through these experiences Paul had come to appreciate the mercy and compassion of God in a deeper way. Yet Paul shows that God's comfort was not intended just to benefit him. Rather, he was to be a channel of God's comfort to others in affliction. Paul suffered because he was actively involved in the ministry of Christ, but the more he experienced suffering, the greater comfort he received from God. In addition, the more comfort he received, the more of it he was able to pass on to his brothers and sisters in Christ. He recognized that his experience was not isolated from the rest of the Christian community. In fact, the New Testament expects the people of God to comfort and encourage one another by virtue of their common membership within the body of Christ, so that when "one part of the body suffers, all the other parts suffer with it" (1 Corinthians 12:26).

Believers can experience great joy even now over the glorious prospect that awaits them when they will experience eternal comfort, for God "will wipe away every tear from their eyes" (Revelation 7:17).

Comfort: For additional scriptures on this topic go to Genesis 37:35.

PERSEVERANCE

2 CORINTHIANS 5

Against what must God's people persevere? What is the outcome of perseverance? On what resources might we draw?

There are several notable Old Testament examples of perseverance. In Genesis 32 is the story of Jacob and his wrestling match with the angel of God. When the angel told Jacob to let him go, Jacob's response was, "I will let you go if you will bless me" (Genesis 32:26). In the story of Joshua and Caleb and their spy mission into the Promised Land, after the twelve men returned from looking things over, ten of them declared, "We can't attack those people; they are stronger than we are" (Numbers 13:31). Joshua and Caleb said, "Don't be afraid of the people in that land! We will chew them up. They have no protection, but the Lord is with us. So don't be afraid of them" (Numbers 14:9). Job went from great health, great family, and great riches to nothing. In the midst of all he declared, "Even if God kills me, I have hope in him" (Job 13:15).

In each case we see the conscious choice made to persevere in the face of great odds and we find that those who persevered were rewarded:

- Jacob was given a new name. "Your name will no longer be Jacob. Your name will now be Israel, because you have wrestled with God and with people, and you have won" (Genesis 32:28).
- Caleb and Joshua found favor with God. "Not one of you will enter the land where I promised you would live; only Caleb son of Jephunneh and Joshua son of Nun will go in" (Numbers 14:30).
- Job's riches and family were restored to him: ". . . the Lord gave him success again" (Job 42:10).

Much of the New Testament is a record of the growth of the church in the midst of great opposition and struggle. Because of that, much of the writing of the New Testament sounds like that of a cheerleader, rather than a theologian: ". . . we do not give up. Our physical body is becoming older and weaker, but our spirit inside us is made new every day" (2 Corinthians 4: 16).

Jesus taught that ". . . those people who keep their faith until the end will be saved" (Matthew 24:13; Mark 13:13). He taught that Christians are "born again" in a spiritual birth that gives them "eternal life" (John 3). He called them to walk in obedience to his commands (John 8:31), and he promised to be the source of the strength we need to walk in that obedience (John 15:4–9). Finally, he promised that no one would be able to take away our salvation (John 10:28–29). This is the perseverance of the saints.

The theme of perseverance is also found in Acts and the epistles. In all the preaching and writing, the desire seems to be to teach the church about the kingdom of God, and to encourage and equip the believers to stay in it and tell others how they can be part of it. Some of the motivations used were:

- *Reward*—". . . God will have a house for us. It will not be a house made by human hands; instead, it will be a home in heaven that will last forever" (2 Corinthians 5:1). This theme of eternity is a reminder that all that happens here is temporary.
- *Punishment*—"God will reward or punish every person for what that person has done" (Romans 2:6). ". . . we must all stand before Christ to be judged" (2 Corinthians 5:10). The judgment of God was declared alongside his love.
- *God's love for us and our response to that love*—"But in all these things we have full victory through God who showed his love for us" (Romans 8:37). "Christ died for all so that those who live would not continue to live for themselves. He died for them and was raised from the dead so that they would live for him" (2 Corinthians 5:15). The sacrament of communion was designed to be a regular reminder to the church of this sacrifice.
- *God's partnership and protection*—"Keep on working to complete your salvation with fear and trembling, because God is working in you to help you want to do and be able to do what pleases him" (Philippians 2:12b–13). "That is why you need to put on God's full armor. Then on the day of evil you will be able to stand strong"(Ephesians 6:13). God has chosen to involve himself in helping us become what he has called us to be. And he will complete the work he has begun in us (Philippians 1:6).
- *The expected soon return of Jesus*—"You know very well that the day the Lord comes again will be a surprise, like a thief that comes in the night. . . . So we should not be like other people who are sleeping, but we should be alert and have self-control" (1 Thessalonians 5:2, 6). These Christians lived their lives fully expecting that the trumpet of the Lord could sound at any moment and Christ would take his church home to live with him for eternity.

Perseverance: For additional scriptures on this topic go to Genesis 32:24–26.

get up to give you the bread, your boldness will
make him get up and give you whatever you need.
9So I tell you, ask, and God will give to you. Search,
and you will find. Knock, and the door will open
for you. 10Yes, everyone who asks will receive. The
one who searches will find. And everyone who
knocks will have the door opened. 11If your children ask for a fish, which of you would give them
a snake instead? 12Or, if your children ask for an
egg, would you give them a scorpion? 13Even
though you are bad, you know how to give good
things to your children. How much more your
heavenly Father will give the Holy Spirit to those
who ask him!"

Jesus' Power Is from God

14One time Jesus was sending out a demon that
could not talk. When the demon came out, the
man who had been unable to speak, then spoke.
The people were amazed. 15But some of them
said, "Jesus uses the power of Beelzebul, the ruler
of demons, to force demons out of people."

16Other people, wanting to test Jesus, asked
him to give them a sign from heaven. 17But knowing their thoughts, he said to them, "Every kingdom that is divided against itself will be
destroyed. And a family that is divided against
itself will not continue. 18So if Satan is divided
against himself, his kingdom will not continue.
You say that I use the power of Beelzebul to force
out demons. 19But if I use the power of Beelzebul
to force out demons, what power do your people
use to force demons out? So they will be your
judges. 20But if I use the power of God to force
out demons, then the kingdom of God has come
to you.

21"When a strong person with many weapons
guards his own house, his possessions are safe.
22But when someone stronger comes and defeats
him, the stronger one will take away the weapons
the first man trusted and will give away the possessions.

23"Anyone who is not with me is against me,
and anyone who does not work with me is working against me.

The Empty Person

24"When an evil spirit comes out of a person, it
travels through dry places, looking for a place to
rest. But when it finds no place, it says, 'I will go
back to the house I left.' 25And when it comes back,
it finds that house swept clean and made neat.
26Then the evil spirit goes out and brings seven
other spirits more evil than it is, and they go in
and live there. So the person has even more trouble than before."

People Who Are Truly Happy

27As Jesus was saying these things, a woman in
the crowd called out to Jesus, "Happy is the
mother who gave birth to you and nursed you."
28But Jesus said, "No, happy are those who
hear the teaching of God and obey it."

The People Want a Miracle

29As the crowd grew larger, Jesus said, "The
people who live today are evil. They want to see a
miracle for a sign, but no sign will be given them,
except the sign of Jonah. 30As Jonah was a sign for
those people who lived in Nineveh, the Son of
Man will be a sign for the people of this time. 31On
the Judgment Day the Queen of the South will
stand up with the people who live now. She will
show they are guilty, because she came from far
away to listen to Solomon's wise teaching. And I
tell you that someone greater than Solomon is
here. 32On the Judgment Day the people of
Nineveh will stand up with the people who live
now, and they will show that you are guilty. When
Jonah preached to them, they were sorry and
changed their lives. And I tell you that someone
greater than Jonah is here.

Be a Light for the World

33"No one lights a lamp and puts it in a secret
place or under a bowl, but on a lampstand so the
people who come in can see. 34Your eye is a light
for the body. When your eyes are good, your
whole body will be full of light. But when your
eyes are evil, your whole body will be full of darkness. 35So be careful not to let the light in you
become darkness. 36If your whole body is full of
light, and none of it is dark, then you will shine
bright, as when a lamp shines on you."

Jesus Accuses the Pharisees

37After Jesus had finished speaking, a Pharisee
asked Jesus to eat with him. So Jesus went in and
sat at the table. 38But the Pharisee was surprised

11:20 Miracles: John 2

11:29 *sign of Jonah.* Jonah's three days in the fish are like Jesus' three days in the tomb. See Matthew 12:40.

11:31 *Queen of the South.* The Queen of Sheba. She traveled a thousand miles to learn God's wisdom from Solomon. Read 1 Kings 10:1-3.

11:34 Darkness: John 1:5

11:36 Body/Flesh: John 12:24–26

11:38 *wash his hands.* This was a Jewish religious custom that the Pharisees thought was very important.

when he saw that Jesus did not wash his hands before the meal. 39The Lord said to him, "You Pharisees clean the outside of the cup and the dish, but inside you are full of greed and evil.⚭ 40You foolish people! The same one who made what is outside also made what is inside. 41So give what is in your dishes to the poor, and then you will be fully clean.⚭ 42How terrible for you Pharisees! You give God one-tenth of even your mint, your rue, and every other plant in your garden. But you fail to be fair to others and to love God. These are the things you should do while continuing to do those other things.⚭ 43How terrible for you Pharisees, because you love to have the most important seats in the synagogues, and you love to be greeted with respect in the marketplaces. 44How terrible for you, because you are like hidden graves, which people walk on without knowing."

Jesus Talks to Experts on the Law

45One of the experts on the law said to Jesus, "Teacher, when you say these things, you are insulting us, too."

46Jesus answered, "How terrible for you, you experts on the law! You make strict rules that are very hard for people to obey, but you yourselves don't even try to follow those rules. 47How terrible for you, because you build tombs for the prophets whom your ancestors killed! 48And now you show that you approve of what your ancestors did. They killed the prophets, and you build tombs for them! 49This is why in his wisdom God said, 'I will send prophets and apostles to them. They will kill some, and they will treat others cruelly.' 50So you who live now will be punished for the deaths of all the prophets who were killed since the beginning of the world— 51from the killing of Abel to the killing of Zechariah, who died between the altar and the Temple. Yes, I tell you that you who are alive now will be punished for them all.

52"How terrible for you, you experts on the law. You have taken away the key to learning about God. You yourselves would not learn, and you stopped others from learning, too."

53When Jesus left, the teachers of the law and the Pharisees began to give him trouble, asking him questions about many things, 54trying to catch him saying something wrong.

Don't Be Like the Pharisees

12 So many thousands of people had gathered that they were stepping on each other. Jesus spoke first to his followers, saying, "Beware of the yeast of the Pharisees, because they are hypocrites. 2Everything that is hidden will be shown, and everything that is secret will be made known. 3What you have said in the dark will be heard in the light, and what you have whispered in an inner room will be shouted from the housetops.

4"I tell you, my friends, don't be afraid of people who can kill the body but after that can do nothing more to hurt you. 5I will show you the one to fear. Fear the one who has the power to kill you and also to throw you into hell. Yes, this is the one you should fear.

6"Five sparrows are sold for only two pennies, and God does not forget any of them. 7But God even knows how many hairs you have on your head. Don't be afraid. You are worth much more than many sparrows.

Don't Be Ashamed of Jesus

8"I tell you, all those who stand before others and say they believe in me, I, the Son of Man, will say before the angels of God that they belong to me. 9But all who stand before others and say they do not believe in me, I will say before the angels of God that they do not belong to me.

10"Anyone who speaks against the Son of Man can be forgiven, but anyone who speaks against the Holy Spirit will not be forgiven.

11"When you are brought into the synagogues before the leaders and other powerful people, don't worry about how to defend yourself or what to say. 12At that time the Holy Spirit will teach you what you must say."⚭

Jesus Warns Against Selfishness

13Someone in the crowd said to Jesus, "Teacher, tell my brother to divide with me the property our father left us."

14But Jesus said to him, "Who said I should judge

⚭**11:39 Greed:** Luke 16:14
⚭**11:41 Clean & Unclean:** 2 Corinthians 7:1
⚭**11:42 Stewardship:** Luke 12:42–48
⚭**11:42 Tithe:** 1 Corinthians 16:12
11:51 *Abel . . . Zechariah.* In the Hebrew Old Testament, the first and last men to be murdered.
⚭**12:12 Instruction:** John 14:26
⚭**12:12 Martyrdom:** Luke 13:31–35
12:13–21 This man comes to Jesus looking for help in obtaining property he thinks is rightfully his. Instead, Jesus tells a parable that attacks the assumption that a greater abundance of goods means greater abundance of life. It also reveals that possessions do not deserve the amount of trust we put in them.

In today's world, one's measure of worth or self-esteem is often based on the quantity of one's possessions or wealth. Jesus denies this concept and says that life is measured not by how much one owns but by how much one is "rich toward God" (v. 21). (Note that in v. 13 we are not told exactly what was the nature of the misunderstanding. The person may only have been asking for that which was rightfully his, or he may have been greedily asking for more than he should have, or he may have simply been going against the principle of Psalm 133:1.)

or decide between you?" [15]Then Jesus said to them,
"Be careful and guard against all kinds of greed. Life
is not measured by how much one owns."

[16]Then Jesus told this story: "There was a rich
man who had some land, which grew a good crop.
[17]He thought to himself, 'What will I do? I have no
place to keep all my crops.' [18]Then he said, 'This
is what I will do: I will tear down my barns and
build bigger ones, and there I will store all my
grain and other goods. [19]Then I can say to myself,
"I have enough good things stored to last for many
years. Rest, eat, drink, and enjoy life!"'

[20]"But God said to him, 'Foolish man! Tonight
your life will be taken from you. So who will get
those things you have prepared for yourself?'

[21]"This is how it will be for those who store up
things for themselves and are not rich toward
God."

Don't Worry

[22]Jesus said to his followers, "So I tell you, don't
worry about the food you need to live, or about
the clothes you need for your body. [23]Life is more
than food, and the body is more than clothes.
[24]Look at the birds. They don't plant or harvest,
they don't have storerooms or barns, but God
feeds them. And you are worth much more than
birds. [25]You cannot add any time to your life by
worrying about it. [26]If you cannot do even the little things, then why worry about the big things?
[27]Consider how the lilies grow; they don't work
or make clothes for themselves. But I tell you that
even Solomon with his riches was not dressed as
beautifully as one of these flowers. [28]God
clothes the grass in the field, which is alive today
but tomorrow is thrown into the fire. So how
much more will God clothe you? Don't have so
little faith! [29]Don't always think about what you
will eat or what you will drink, and don't keep
worrying. [30]All the people in the world are trying
to get these things, and your Father knows you
need them. [31]But seek God's kingdom, and all the
other things you need will be given to you.

Don't Trust in Money

[32]"Don't fear, little flock, because your Father
wants to give you the kingdom. [33]Sell your possessions and give to the poor. Get for yourselves
purses that will not wear out, the treasure in
heaven that never runs out, where thieves can't
steal and moths can't destroy. [34]Your heart will
be where your treasure is.

Always Be Ready

[35]"Be dressed, ready for service, and have your
lamps shining. [36]Be like servants who are waiting
for their master to come home from a wedding
party. When he comes and knocks, the servants
immediately open the door for him. [37]They will be
blessed when their master comes home, because
he sees that they were watching for him. I tell you
the truth, the master will dress himself to serve
and tell the servants to sit at the table, and he will
serve them. [38]Those servants will be happy when
he comes in and finds them still waiting, even if it
is midnight or later.

[39]"Remember this: If the owner of the house
knew what time a thief was coming, he would
not allow the thief to enter his house. [40]So you
also must be ready, because the Son of Man will
come at a time when you don't expect him!"

Who Is the Trusted Servant?

[41]Peter said, "Lord, did you tell this story to us
or to all people?"

[42]The Lord said, "Who is the wise and trusted
servant that the master trusts to give the other
servants their food at the right time? [43]When
the master comes and finds the servant doing
his work, the servant will be blessed. [44]I tell you
the truth, the master will choose that servant to
take care of everything he owns. [45]But suppose
the servant thinks to himself, 'My master will
not come back soon,' and he begins to beat the
other servants, men and women, and to eat and
drink and get drunk. [46]The master will come
when that servant is not ready and is not expecting him. Then the master will cut him in pieces
and send him away to be with the others who
don't obey.

[47]"The servant who knows what his master
wants but is not ready, or who does not do what
the master wants, will be beaten with many
blows! [48]But the servant who does not know what
his master wants and does things that should be
punished will be beaten with few blows. From
everyone who has been given much, much will be
demanded. And from the one trusted with much,

12:21 Pleasure: Romans 12:2
12:27 Solomon: Acts 7:47
12:31 Land/Inheritance: Acts 1:8
12:42–48 This parable emphasizes the need for good stewards to always be diligent and at work for the master, because he might return at any time and ask for an account of gifts he has entrusted to the steward. Jesus is the Master who has left his stewards charged with a number of important responsibilities. When Jesus comes again, he will ask for an accounting of the steward's activities.
12:45 Alcohol: Luke 21:34
12:48 Stewardship: 1 Corinthians 6:19–20
12:48 Work: John 13:1–17

much more will be expected.

Jesus Causes Division

49"I came to set fire to the world, and I wish it were already burning! 50I have a baptism to suffer through, and I feel very troubled until it is over. 51Do you think I came to give peace to the earth? No, I tell you, I came to divide it. 52From now on, a family with five people will be divided, three against two, and two against three. 53They will be divided: father against son and son against father, mother against daughter and daughter against mother, mother-in-law against daughter-in-law and daughter-in-law against mother-in-law."

Understanding the Times

54Then Jesus said to the people, "When you see clouds coming up in the west, you say, 'It's going to rain,' and it happens. 55When you feel the wind begin to blow from the south, you say, 'It will be a hot day,' and it happens. 56Hypocrites! You know how to understand the appearance of the earth and sky. Why don't you understand what is happening now?

Settle Your Problems

57"Why can't you decide for yourselves what is right? 58If your enemy is taking you to court, try hard to settle it on the way. If you don't, your enemy might take you to the judge, and the judge might turn you over to the officer, and the officer might throw you into jail. 59I tell you, you will not get out of there until you have paid everything you owe."

Change Your Hearts

13 At that time some people were there who told Jesus that Pilate had killed some people from Galilee while they were worshiping. He mixed their blood with the blood of the animals they were sacrificing to God. 2Jesus answered, "Do you think this happened to them because they were more sinful than all others from Galilee? 3No, I tell you. But unless you change your hearts and lives, you will be destroyed as they were! 4What about those eighteen people who died when the tower of Siloam fell on them? Do you think they were more sinful than all the others who live in Jerusalem? 5No, I tell you. But unless you change your hearts and lives, you will all be destroyed too!"

The Useless Tree

6Jesus told this story: "A man had a fig tree planted in his vineyard. He came looking for some fruit on the tree, but he found none. 7So the man said to his gardener, 'I have been looking for fruit on this tree for three years, but I never find any. Cut it down. Why should it waste the ground?' 8But the servant answered, 'Master, let the tree have one more year to produce fruit. Let me dig up the dirt around it and put on some fertilizer. 9If the tree produces fruit next year, good. But if not, you can cut it down.'"

Jesus Heals on the Sabbath

10Jesus was teaching in one of the synagogues on the Sabbath day. 11A woman was there who, for eighteen years, had an evil spirit in her that made her crippled. Her back was always bent; she could not stand up straight. 12When Jesus saw her, he called her over and said, "Woman, you are free from your sickness." 13Jesus put his hands on her, and immediately she was able to stand up straight and began praising God.

14The synagogue leader was angry because Jesus healed on the Sabbath day. He said to the people, "There are six days when one has to work. So come to be healed on one of those days, and not on the Sabbath day."

15The Lord answered, "You hypocrites! Doesn't each of you untie your work animals and lead them to drink water every day—even on the Sabbath day? 16This woman that I healed, a daughter of Abraham, has been held by Satan for eighteen years. Surely it is not wrong for her to be freed from her sickness on a Sabbath day!" 17When Jesus said this, all of those who were criticizing him were ashamed, but the entire crowd rejoiced at all the wonderful things Jesus was doing.

Stories of Mustard Seed and Yeast

18Then Jesus said, "What is God's kingdom like? What can I compare it with? 19It is like a mustard seed that a man plants in his garden. The seed grows and becomes a tree, and the wild

---

12:49 *I . . . baptism.* Jesus was talking about the suffering he would soon go through.

13:1 Pontius Pilate: Luke 23:1–5

13:1 *Pilate.* Pontius Pilate was the Roman governor of Judea from A.D. 26 to A.D. 36.

13:1–3 Even before he met the Roman governor, Pontius Pilate, Jesus knew of his reputation for cruelty which, along with Pilate's insensitivity to Jewish religious scruples, had caused him to be recalled to Rome. Both failings of Pilate were reported to Jesus on this occasion. Pilate showed no respect for the fact that the Galileans he massacred were in the act of presenting their sacrificial offerings. Pilate had his soldiers slaughter them at the altar, causing their blood to mingle with the blood of their sacrificial animals.

13:16 Satan/Satanism: John 16:11

13:17 Sickness, Disease, Healing: Luke 14:1–6

birds build nests in its branches."

[20]Jesus said again, "What can I compare God's kingdom with? [21]It is like yeast that a woman took and hid in a large tub of flour until it made all the dough rise."

The Narrow Door

[22]Jesus was teaching in every town and village as he traveled toward Jerusalem. [23]Someone said to Jesus, "Lord, will only a few people be saved?"

Jesus said, [24]"Try hard to enter through the narrow door, because many people will try to enter there, but they will not be able. [25]When the owner of the house gets up and closes the door, you can stand outside and knock on the door and say, 'Sir, open the door for us.' But he will answer, 'I don't know you or where you come from.' [26]Then you will say, 'We ate and drank with you, and you taught in the streets of our town.' [27]But he will say to you, 'I don't know you or where you come from. Go away from me, all you who do evil!' [28]You will cry and grind your teeth with pain when you see Abraham, Isaac, Jacob, and all the prophets in God's kingdom, but you yourselves thrown outside. [29]People will come from the east, west, north, and south and will sit down at the table in the kingdom of God.⚭ [30]There are those who have the lowest place in life now who will have the highest place in the future. And there are those who have the highest place now who will have the lowest place in the future."⚭

Jesus Will Die in Jerusalem

[31]At that time some Pharisees came to Jesus and said, "Go away from here! Herod wants to kill you!"

[32]Jesus said to them, "Go tell that fox Herod, 'Today and tomorrow I am forcing demons out and healing people. Then, on the third day, I will reach my goal.' [33]Yet I must be on my way today and tomorrow and the next day. Surely it cannot be right for a prophet to be killed anywhere except in Jerusalem.

[34]"Jerusalem, Jerusalem! You kill the prophets and stone to death those who are sent to you. Many times I wanted to gather your people as a hen gathers her chicks under her wings, but you would not let me. [35]Now your house is left completely empty. I tell you, you will not see me until that time when you will say, 'God bless the One who comes in the name of the Lord.'"⚭

Healing on the Sabbath

14 On a Sabbath day, when Jesus went to eat at the home of a leading Pharisee, the people were watching Jesus very closely. [2]And in front of him was a man with dropsy. [3]Jesus said to the Pharisees and experts on the law, "Is it right or wrong to heal on the Sabbath day?" [4]But they would not answer his question. So Jesus took the man, healed him, and sent him away. [5]Jesus said to the Pharisees and teachers of the law, "If your child or ox falls into a well on the Sabbath day, will you not pull him out quickly?" [6]And they could not answer him.⚭

Don't Make Yourself Important

[7]When Jesus noticed that some of the guests were choosing the best places to sit, he told this story: [8]"When someone invites you to a wedding feast, don't take the most important seat, because someone more important than you may have been invited. [9]The host, who invited both of you, will come to you and say, 'Give this person your seat.' Then you will be embarrassed and will have to move to the last place. [10]So when you are invited, go sit in a seat that is not important. When the host comes to you, he may say, 'Friend, move up here to a more important place.' Then all the other guests will respect you. [11]All who make themselves great will be made humble, but those who make themselves humble will be made great."

You Will Be Rewarded

[12]Then Jesus said to the man who had invited him, "When you give a lunch or a dinner, don't invite only your friends, your family, your other relatives, and your rich neighbors. At another time they will invite you to eat with them, and you will

---

⚭**13:29 Crossing Cultural Boundaries:** Acts 10

⚭**13:30 Hospitality:** Luke 14:1–24

13:31 According to Luke, no one is outside the grace of God. Because God has initiated salvation through his Son, Jesus, all have the capacity to respond through changing their hearts and lives and embracing God's purpose. Often throughout the Book of Luke, groups of Pharisees are portrayed as Jesus' enemies, but here a group of Pharisees tries to help Jesus.

13:35 *'God . . . Lord.'* Quotation from Psalm 118:26.

⚭**13:35 City:** Revelation 22

⚭**13:35 Martyrdom:** Luke 22:47–23:49

14 Table fellowship was governed by important social rules, some Jewish, others Roman and Greek. In the ancient world people ate only with their families and close friends, but even among friends there could be conflict over who got to sit in the choice seats. Both in his choice of table companions and in his teaching at the table, Jesus insists that those who are normally excluded from one's circle of friends should be included as table guests. And table practices that determined who among the guests was the most important ought to be abandoned. Jesus thus struck at the heart of the boundary-making practices of the people of his world. His teaching must have been tough meat for his audiences!

14:2 *dropsy.* A sickness that causes the body to swell larger and larger.

⚭**14:6 Scribes (Teachers of the Law):** Luke 20:39

⚭**14:6 Sickness, Disease, Healing:** John 9:1–7

⚭**14:13 Feasts/Festivals:** John 2:13

be repaid. 13Instead, when you give a feast, invite the poor, the crippled, the lame, and the blind. 14Then you will be blessed, because they have nothing and cannot pay you back. But you will be repaid when the good people rise from the dead."

A Story About a Big Banquet

15One of those at the table with Jesus heard these things and said to him, "Happy are the people who will share in the meal in God's kingdom."

16Jesus said to him, "A man gave a big banquet and invited many people. 17When it was time to eat, the man sent his servant to tell the guests, 'Come. Everything is ready.'

18"But all the guests made excuses. The first one said, 'I have just bought a field, and I must go look at it. Please excuse me.' 19Another said, 'I have just bought five pairs of oxen; I must go and try them. Please excuse me.' 20A third person said, 'I just got married; I can't come.' 21So the servant returned and told his master what had happened. Then the master became angry and said, 'Go at once into the streets and alleys of the town, and bring in the poor, the crippled, the blind, and the lame.' 22Later the servant said to him, 'Master, I did what you commanded, but we still have room.' 23The master said to the servant, 'Go out to the roads and country lanes, and urge the people there to come so my house will be full. 24I tell you, none of those whom I invited first will eat with me.'"

The Cost of Being Jesus' Follower

25Large crowds were traveling with Jesus, and he turned and said to them, 26"If anyone comes to me but loves his father, mother, wife, children, brothers, or sisters—or even life—more than me, he cannot be my follower. 27Whoever is not willing to carry the cross and follow me cannot be my follower. 28If you want to build a tower, you first sit down and decide how much it will cost, to see if you have enough money to finish the job. 29If you don't, you might lay the foundation, but you would not be able to finish. Then all who would see it would make fun of you, 30saying, 'This person began to build but was not able to finish.'

31"If a king is going to fight another king, first he will sit down and plan. He will decide if he and his ten thousand soldiers can defeat the other king who has twenty thousand soldiers. 32If he can't, then while the other king is still far away, he will send some people to speak to him and ask for peace. 33In the same way, you must give up everything you have to be my follower.

Don't Lose Your Influence

34"Salt is good, but if it loses its salty taste, you cannot make it salty again. 35It is no good for the soil or for manure; it is thrown away.

"You people who can hear me, listen."

A Lost Sheep, a Lost Coin

15 The tax collectors and sinners all came to listen to Jesus. 2But the Pharisees and the teachers of the law began to complain: "Look, this man welcomes sinners and even eats with them."

3Then Jesus told them this story: 4"Suppose one of you has a hundred sheep but loses one of them. Then he will leave the other ninety-nine sheep in the open field and go out and look for the lost sheep until he finds it. 5And when he finds it, he happily puts it on his shoulders 6and goes home. He calls to his friends and neighbors and says, 'Be happy with me because I found my lost sheep.' 7In the same way, I tell you there is more joy in heaven over one sinner who changes his heart and life, than over ninety-nine good people who don't need to change.

8"Suppose a woman has ten silver coins, but loses one. She will light a lamp, sweep the house, and look carefully for the coin until she finds it. 9And when she finds it, she will call her friends and neighbors and say, 'Be happy with me because I have found the coin that I lost.' 10In the same way, there is joy in the presence of the angels of God when one sinner changes his heart and life."

The Son Who Left Home

11Then Jesus said, "A man had two sons. 12The younger son said to his father, 'Give me my share of the property.' So the father divided the property between his two sons. 13Then the younger son gathered up all that was his and traveled far away to another country. There he wasted his money in foolish living. 14After he had spent everything, a time came when there was no food anywhere in the country, and the son was poor and hungry.

14:24 Hospitality: Luke 15:1–2
14:24 Images of God: Hebrews 12:6–9
14:24 Table Fellowship/Lord's Supper: Luke 15:2
14:25–33 Jesus' gracious call to follow him is accompanied by an intense demand to count the cost of doing so (see Luke 9:57–62; 14:25–33). Jesus recognizes that various securities in this life can be a substitute for allegiance to him. The demand to count the cost of following him means exchanging the securities of this world for salvation and security in him. The call to be a follower in Jesus' lifetime meant to count the cost of full allegiance to him.
15:2 Table Fellowship/Lord's Supper: Luke 19:1–10
15:2 Hospitality: Luke 19:1–10
15:8 *silver coins.* Roman denarii. One coin was the average pay for one day's work.
15:10 Angels/Guardian Angels: Acts 5:19–20

[15]So he got a job with one of the citizens there who sent the son into the fields to feed pigs. [16]The son was so hungry that he wanted to eat the pods the pigs were eating, but no one gave him anything. [17] When he realized what he was doing, he thought, 'All of my father's servants have plenty of food. But I am here, almost dying with hunger. [18]I will leave and return to my father and say to him, "Father, I have sinned against God and have done wrong to you. [19]I am no longer worthy to be called your son, but let me be like one of your servants."' [20]So the son left and went to his father.

"While the son was still a long way off, his father saw him and felt sorry for his son. So the father ran to him and hugged and kissed him. [21]The son said, 'Father, I have sinned against God and have done wrong to you. I am no longer worthy to be called your son.' [22]But the father said to his servants, 'Hurry! Bring the best clothes and put them on him. Also, put a ring on his finger and sandals on his feet. [23]And get our fat calf and kill it so we can have a feast and celebrate. [24]My son was dead, but now he is alive again! He was lost, but now he is found!' So they began to celebrate.

[25]"The older son was in the field, and as he came closer to the house, he heard the sound of music and dancing. [26]So he called to one of the servants and asked what all this meant. [27]The servant said, 'Your brother has come back, and your father killed the fat calf, because your brother came home safely.' [28]The older son was angry and would not go in to the feast. So his father went out and begged him to come in. [29]But the older son said to his father, 'I have served you like a slave for many years and have always obeyed your commands. But you never gave me even a young goat to have at a feast with my friends. [30]But your other son, who wasted all your money on prostitutes, comes home, and you kill the fat calf for him!' [31]The father said to him, 'Son, you are always with me, and all that I have is yours. [32]We had to celebrate and be happy because your brother was dead, but now he is alive. He was lost, but now he is found.'"

True Wealth

16 Jesus also said to his followers, "Once there was a rich man who had a manager to take care of his business. This manager was accused of cheating him. [2]So he called the manager in and said to him, 'What is this I hear about you? Give me a report of what you have done with my money, because you can't be my manager any longer.' [3]The manager thought to himself, 'What will I do since my master is taking my job away from me? I am not strong enough to dig ditches, and I am ashamed to beg. [4]I know what I'll do so that when I lose my job people will welcome me into their homes.'

[5]"So the manager called in everyone who owed the master any money. He asked the first one, 'How much do you owe?' [6]He answered, 'Eight hundred gallons of olive oil.' The manager said to him, 'Take your bill, sit down quickly, and write four hundred gallons.' [7]Then the manager asked another one, 'How much do you owe?' He answered, 'One thousand bushels of wheat.' Then the manager said to him, 'Take your bill and write eight hundred bushels.' [8]So, the master praised the dishonest manager for being smart. Yes, worldly people are smarter with their own kind than spiritual people are.

[9]"I tell you, make friends for yourselves using worldly riches so that when those riches are gone, you will be welcomed in those homes that continue forever. [10]Whoever can be trusted with a little can also be trusted with a lot, and whoever is dishonest with a little is dishonest with a lot. [11]If you cannot be trusted with worldly riches, then who will trust you with true riches? [12]And if you cannot be trusted with things that belong to someone else, who will give you things of your own?

[13]"No servant can serve two masters. The servant will hate one master and love the other, or will follow one master and refuse to follow the other. You cannot serve both God and worldly riches."

God's Law Cannot Be Changed

[14]The Pharisees, who loved money, were listening to all these things and made fun of Jesus. [15]He said to them, "You make yourselves look good in front of people, but God knows what is really in your hearts. What is important to people is hateful in God's sight.

[16]"The law of Moses and the writings of the prophets were preached until John came. Since

15:17 Conversion: Acts 8:2–39
15:25 Music: Ephesians 5:19
15:32 Grace: John 1:14–17
15:32 Parables: Luke 16:9–31
15:32 Repentance: Luke 17:3–4

16:8 In this story, the Lord is not commending the manager for his dishonest practices, but for his wisdom in planning ahead and using the resources at his disposal to enable him to live securely once he lost his job. Then the Lord makes the spiritual application, namely, that as stewards, we are wisely and intelligently to use our God-given resources for the salvation of the lost so that we will be welcomed by those we have reached by our ministry when we enter heaven.

16:14 Greed: 1 Corinthians 5:10–11
16:15 A Matter of the Heart: Ezekiel 36:24–28

16:16 *John.* John the Baptist, who preached to people about Christ's coming (Matthew 3, Luke 3).

then the Good News about the kingdom of God is being told, and everyone tries to enter it by force. 17It would be easier for heaven and earth to pass away than for the smallest part of a letter in the law to be changed.

Divorce and Remarriage

18"If a man divorces his wife and marries another woman, he is guilty of adultery, and the man who marries a divorced woman is also guilty of adultery."

The Rich Man and Lazarus

19Jesus said, "There was a rich man who always dressed in the finest clothes and lived in luxury every day. 20And a very poor man named Lazarus, whose body was covered with sores, was laid at the rich man's gate. 21He wanted to eat only the small pieces of food that fell from the rich man's table. And the dogs would come and lick his sores. 22Later, Lazarus died, and the angels carried him to the arms of Abraham. The rich man died, too, and was buried. 23In the place of the dead, he was in much pain. The rich man saw Abraham far away with Lazarus at his side. 24He called, 'Father Abraham, have mercy on me! Send Lazarus to dip his finger in water and cool my tongue, because I am suffering in this fire!' 25But Abraham said, 'Child, remember when you were alive you had the good things in life, but bad things happened to Lazarus. Now he is comforted here, and you are suffering. 26Besides, there is a big pit between you and us, so no one can cross over to you, and no one can leave there and come here.' 27The rich man said, 'Father, then please send Lazarus to my father's house. 28I have five brothers, and Lazarus could warn them so that they will not come to this place of pain.' 29But Abraham said, 'They have the law of Moses and the writings of the prophets; let them learn from them.' 30The rich man said, 'No, father Abraham! If someone goes to them from the dead, they would believe and change their hearts and lives.' 31But Abraham said to him, 'If they will not listen to Moses and the prophets, they will not listen to someone who comes back from the dead.'"

Sin and Forgiveness

17 Jesus said to his followers, "Things that cause people to sin will happen, but how terrible for the person who causes them to happen! 2It would be better for you to be thrown into the sea with a large stone around your neck than to cause one of these little ones to sin. 3So be careful!

"If another follower sins, warn him, and if he is sorry and stops sinning, forgive him. 4If he sins against you seven times in one day and says that he is sorry each time, forgive him."

How Big Is Your Faith?

5The apostles said to the Lord, "Give us more faith!"

6The Lord said, "If your faith were the size of a mustard seed, you could say to this mulberry tree, 'Dig yourself up and plant yourself in the sea,' and it would obey you.

Be Good Servants

7"Suppose one of you has a servant who has been plowing the ground or caring for the sheep. When the servant comes in from working in the field, would you say, 'Come in and sit down to eat'? 8No, you would say to him, 'Prepare something for me to eat. Then get yourself ready and serve me. After I finish eating and drinking, you can eat.' 9The servant does not get any special thanks for doing what his master commanded. 10It is the same with you. When you have done everything you are told to do, you should say, 'We are unworthy servants; we have only done the work we should do.'"

Be Thankful

11While Jesus was on his way to Jerusalem, he was going through the area between Samaria and Galilee. 12As he came into a small town, ten men who had a skin disease met him there. They did not come close to Jesus 13but called to him, "Jesus! Master! Have mercy on us!"

14When Jesus saw the men, he said, "Go and show yourselves to the priests."

As the ten men were going, they were healed. 15When one of them saw that he was healed, he went back to Jesus, praising God in a loud voice. 16Then he bowed down at Jesus' feet and thanked him. (And this man was a Samaritan.) 17Jesus said, "Weren't ten men healed? Where are the other nine? 18Is this Samaritan the only one who came back to thank God?" 19Then Jesus said to him, "Stand up and go on your way. You were healed because you believed."

16:18 Divorce: 1 Corinthians 7:10–24
16:31 Parables: See article on page 891.
17:4 Forgiveness: Luke 19:1–10
17:4 Repentance: Acts 2:38
17:7–10 Much of the Book of Luke is devoted to Jesus' teaching about the human tendency to desire greatness and to lord it over others. He knows that some people might take pride in their obedience to God and in their servant-like behavior.
17:14 *show . . . priests.* The Law of Moses said a priest must say when a person with a skin disease became well.
17:18 Thanks: 1 Timothy 1:12
17:19 Jesus: See article on page 681.

Reconciliation

2 Corinthians 5

Why do we need reconciliation? Why are we fragmented from ourselves, other people, from God? How is reconciliation achieved?

Reconciliation, in the first place, is the act of making peace between God and people. It is overcoming something that has alienated persons from God and bringing peace in its place. It is a new relationship where a broken friendship has been restored. This new relationship was made possible through the life, death, and resurrection of Jesus Christ.

The need for reconciliation was established in the story of the rebellion of Adam and Eve in the book of Genesis. Adam became the first in a long line of sinners who were distanced from God by sin and sentenced to die.

Yet God was not content to let his creation stay in this condition of separation. The Old Testament is filled with the promise and hope of restoration. It is a story of God constantly reaching out to humankind and offering them a unique relationship. Because of the holiness of God and the sin of the people of the world, the judgment of God was deserved, but he chose to be merciful.

From the beginning, God had a plan that would draw humanity back into relationship with himself. This plan was hinted at in the Old Testament system of sacrifices where sins of the covenant community were atoned for through the death of an innocent animal (Exodus 24:8; 30:10; Leviticus 5:9). The sacrifice showed that sin was taken seriously by God and that it carried a penalty.

The Old Testament prophets pointed to a day when God would send a Messiah to establish a new reign of God on this earth. Isaiah declared, "A child has been born to us; God has given a son to us. He will be responsible for leading the people. His name will be Wonderful Counselor, Powerful God, Father Who Lives Forever, Prince of Peace" (Isaiah 9:6). Isaiah also referred to the Messiah in the language of sacrifice. "But he was wounded for the wrong we did; he was crushed for the evil we did. The punishment, which made us well, was given to him, and we are healed because of his wounds" (Isaiah 53:5). In these verses we find God offering to make peace with his people, but his holiness still demanded that sin be judged.

Jesus Christ is the answer to this great dilemma of sin (Romans 5:9). Through his death we can now have peace with God. Jesus is the new "Adam" who makes people right with God (Romans 5:19). Jesus became our "merciful and faithful high priest," and at the same time, the sacrifice for our sin (Hebrews 2:17). Paul says it best in these verses from his letter to the Colossians. "At one time you were separated from God. You were his enemies in your minds, and the evil things you did were against God. But now God has made you his friends again. He did this through Christ's death in the body so that he might bring you into God's presence as people who are holy, with no wrong, and with nothing of which God can judge you guilty" (Colossians 1:21–22).

This new relationship has been made available for all the world through what Christ has done. He has ended the separation that sin caused between God and his creation. He has removed the guilt of sin and with it the reason for judgment. Peace with God becomes reality for people when they recognize the separation caused by sin (Romans 3:9); change their hearts and lives by turning away from sin (Acts 2:37–39); and receive this new relationship by faith (Romans 5:1). Faith is trusting or depending on God to be who he says he is and to do what he says he will do. It is more than a mental exercise; it is the act of choosing to trust God. "God loved the world so much that he gave his one and only Son so that whoever believes in him may not be lost, but have eternal life" (John 3:16).

Once God's people have been restored to a place of friendship and peace, they are given the task of helping others to find that same peace. "God was in Christ, making peace between the world and himself. In Christ, God did not hold the world guilty of its sins. And he gave us this message of peace" (2 Corinthians 5:19). This is because God's ultimate plan is "to bring all things back to himself again" (Colossians 1:20). "His goal was to carry out his plan, when the right time came, that all things in heaven and on earth would be joined together in Christ as the head" (Ephesians 1:10). Jesus is the "firstborn of many brothers" (Romans 8:29). The exciting task of the church is to bring many more into God's family and let them know his peace.

The marvelous byproduct of our reconciliation with God is that we begin the process of reconciliation with one another. Racial, ethnic, and gender divisions immediately begin to break down (Galatians 3:28). Jesus calls his followers to mirror our oneness by living with each other in unity (John 17:12–17).

Reconciliation: For additional scriptures on this topic go to Exodus 24:8.

Creation/New Creation

2 Corinthians 5:17

What does "new creation" mean? How does the new creation relate to the creation in Genesis? What does the creation/new creation theme teach us about salvation?

"In the beginning God created the sky and the earth." These are the famous words that begin the Book of Genesis and the Bible. The Bible begins with the story of how God created the world and everything in it. He divided the water from the land; he created the heavenly bodies and set them in their place; he created all plant life and animal life. The culmination of God's work was the creation of beings in his "image and likeness" (1:27). And at each step, God pronounced that what he had created was "good." Indeed, the creation of human beings he pronounced "very good" (1:31).

The creation story, however, does not simply end with the opening chapters of Genesis, nor does the beauty of God's creation remain unmarred. The result of Adam and Eve's giving in to the serpent's temptation brought about a fundamental change to the world that God had pronounced "good." The natural order was deeply disturbed, no longer the garden that Adam and Eve were used to.

The remainder of the Bible sets out to tell how God takes it upon himself to restore that intimacy and bring his people back to paradise. To put it another way, we see throughout the Bible that this restoration is described as a "new creation," a reestablishing of God's creation. The Bible does this by describing God's various acts of salvation in "creation-like" language. We see this happening from Genesis all the way to Revelation.

With the story of Noah and the Flood (Genesis 6–9), God was so displeased with his creation that he decided to destroy the whole world and everything in it (6:5–7). This is a "reversal" of creation: God destroys what he had created; he is displeased with what he had once pronounced "good"; the waters that had been safely divided from the land now come crashing down to drown the inhabitants. Yet saving Noah and his family is a "new creation": after the Flood, the waters recede *once again* from the land; Noah and his family begin the human race *anew* (second "Adams and Eves" so to speak).

The story of the Exodus, especially chapters 1–14, is also expressed in creation-like language. The Israelites arrive in Egypt and, like Adam and Eve and Noah before them, fulfill the creation mandate: They have many children, grow very strong, and fill the land (Exodus 1:7). The plagues, God's punishments against the oppressive Egyptians, are reversals of creation: water is affected (1st plague); darkness returns where there had once been light (9th plague); animals and other creatures suffer (for example, 5th plague); even humans die (10th plague). But how does God deliver his people? First of all, the Israelites are immune from this "creation reversal" (as was Noah in the safety of the ark). Second, the Egyptians are destroyed by water. Once again, the waters that God had once tamed at creation are unleashed.

A final Old Testament example is found throughout the latter half of Isaiah. It concerns the release of the Israelites from their captivity in Babylon. Isaiah describes the salvation of God's people as both an act of new creation as well a new exodus (for example, Isaiah 43:14–21; 45:1–25). The result is a biblical pattern like the following: creation—exodus (which is like a new creation)—release from Babylon (which is like a new exodus/new creation).

Each of these three acts of salvation is patterned after God's act of creation; each is a new creation. Taken together, they form a pattern that spans the bulk of the time period of the Old Testament. With the coming of Christ, however, this pattern comes to its fullest expression.

It is not mere coincidence that the beginning of John's book (1:1–5) is similar to the opening of Genesis: "*In the beginning* there was the Word" (verse 1). Specific references to creation are clear: "All things were made by him" (verse 3); "in him there was life" (verse 4); "the Light shines in the darkness" (verse 5). The coming of Christ to earth signals a new creation.

Indeed, when someone accepts Jesus Christ as their Lord and Savior, they are born anew in the spirit (John 3:1–21). This in effect is a "new creation" (2 Corinthians 5:17; Galations 6:15; 2 Peter 3:13; Revelation 21:1).

The Bible ends by describing the final and complete new creation. According to Revelation 21:1, there is "a new heaven and a new earth" (21:1). The end of history will give birth to a return to paradise, a new garden where "[God] will wipe away every tear from their eyes, and there will be no more death, sadness, crying, or pain, because all the old ways are gone" (21:4).

Creation/New Creation: For additional scriptures on this topic go to Genesis 9:1.

God's Kingdom Is Within You

20Some of the Pharisees asked Jesus, "When will the kingdom of God come?"

Jesus answered, "God's kingdom is coming, but not in a way that you will be able to see with your eyes. 21People will not say, 'Look, here it is!' or, 'There it is!' because God's kingdom is within you."

22Then Jesus said to his followers, "The time will come when you will want very much to see one of the days of the Son of Man. But you will not see it. 23People will say to you, 'Look, there he is!' or, 'Look, here he is!' Stay where you are; don't go away and search.

When Jesus Comes Again

24"When the Son of Man comes again, he will shine like lightning, which flashes across the sky and lights it up from one side to the other. 25But first he must suffer many things and be rejected by the people of this time. 26When the Son of Man comes again, it will be as it was when Noah lived. 27People were eating, drinking, marrying, and giving their children to be married until the day Noah entered the boat. Then the flood came and killed them all. 28It will be the same as during the time of Lot. People were eating, drinking, buying, selling, planting, and building. 29But the day Lot left Sodom, fire and sulfur rained down from the sky and killed them all. 30This is how it will be when the Son of Man comes again.

31"On that day, a person who is on the roof and whose belongings are in the house should not go inside to get them. A person who is in the field should not go back home. 32Remember Lot's wife. 33Those who try to keep their lives will lose them. But those who give up their lives will save them. 34I tell you, on that night two people will be sleeping in one bed; one will be taken and the other will be left. 35There will be two women grinding grain together; one will be taken, and the other will be left." 36*

37The followers asked Jesus, "Where will this be, Lord?"

Jesus answered, "Where there is a dead body, there the vultures will gather."

God Will Answer His People

18 Then Jesus used this story to teach his followers that they should always pray and never lose hope. 2"In a certain town there was a judge who did not respect God or care about people. 3In that same town there was a widow who kept coming to this judge, saying, 'Give me my rights against my enemy.' 4For a while the judge refused to help her. But afterwards, he thought to himself, 'Even though I don't respect God or care about people, 5I will see that she gets her rights. Otherwise she will continue to bother me until I am worn out.'"

6The Lord said, "Listen to what the unfair judge said. 7God will always give what is right to his people who cry to him night and day, and he will not be slow to answer them. 8I tell you, God will help his people quickly. But when the Son of Man comes again, will he find those on earth who believe in him?"

Being Right with God

9Jesus told this story to some people who thought they were very good and looked down on everyone else: 10"A Pharisee and a tax collector both went to the Temple to pray. 11The Pharisee stood alone and prayed, 'God, I thank you that I am not like other people who steal, cheat, or take part in adultery, or even like this tax collector. 12I give up eating twice a week, and I give one-tenth of everything I get!'

13"The tax collector, standing at a distance, would not even look up to heaven. But he beat on his chest because he was so sad. He said, 'God, have mercy on me, a sinner.' 14I tell you, when this man went home, he was right with God, but the Pharisee was not. All who make themselves great will be made humble, but all who make themselves humble will be made great."

Who Will Enter God's Kingdom?

15Some people brought even their babies to Jesus so he could touch them. When the followers saw this, they told them to stop. 16But Jesus called for the children, saying, "Let the little children come to me. Don't stop them, because the kingdom of God belongs to people who are like these children. 17I tell you the truth, you must accept the kingdom of God as if you were a child, or you will never enter it."

A Rich Man's Question

18A certain leader asked Jesus, "Good Teacher, what must I do to have life forever?"

17:21 *within.* Or "among."

17:27 Flood: 2 Peter 2:5

17:28 *Sodom.* City that God destroyed because the people were so evil.

17:32 *Lot's wife.* A story about what happened to Lot's wife is found in Genesis 19:15-17, 26.

***17:36** *Verse 36.* A few Greek copies add verse 36: "Two people will be in the field. One will be taken, and the other will be left."

18:12 *give up eating.* This is called "fasting." The people would give up eating for a special time of prayer and worship to God. It was also done to show sadness and disappointment.

18:14 Good Works: Romans 2–4

18:14 Pharisees and Sadducees: John 7:31–32

[19]Jesus said to him, "Why do you call me good? Only God is good. [20]You know the commands: 'You must not be guilty of adultery. You must not murder anyone. You must not steal. You must not tell lies about your neighbor. Honor your father and mother.'"

[21]But the leader said, "I have obeyed all these commands since I was a boy."

[22]When Jesus heard this, he said to him, "There is still one more thing you need to do. Sell everything you have and give it to the poor, and you will have treasure in heaven. Then come and follow me." [23]But when the man heard this, he became very sad, because he was very rich.

[24]Jesus looked at him and said, "It is very hard for rich people to enter the kingdom of God. [25]It is easier for a camel to go through the eye of a needle than for a rich person to enter the kingdom of God."

Who Can Be Saved?

[26]When the people heard this, they asked, "Then who can be saved?"

[27]Jesus answered, "God can do things that are not possible for people to do."

[28]Peter said, "Look, we have left everything and followed you."

[29]Jesus said, "I tell you the truth, all those who have left houses, wives, brothers, parents, or children for the kingdom of God [30]will get much more in this life. And in the age that is coming, they will have life forever."

Jesus Will Rise from the Dead

[31]Then Jesus took the twelve apostles aside and said to them, "We are going to Jerusalem. Everything the prophets wrote about the Son of Man will happen. [32]He will be turned over to those who are evil. They will laugh at him, insult him, spit on him, [33]beat him with whips, and kill him. But on the third day, he will rise to life again." [34]The apostles did not understand this; the meaning was hidden from them, and they did not realize what was said.

Jesus Heals a Blind Man

[35]As Jesus came near the city of Jericho, a blind man was sitting beside the road, begging. [36]When he heard the people coming down the road, he asked, "What is happening?"

[37]They told him, "Jesus, from Nazareth, is going by."

[38]The blind man cried out, "Jesus, Son of David, have mercy on me!"

[39]The people leading the group warned the blind man to be quiet. But the blind man shouted even more, "Son of David, have mercy on me!"

[40]Jesus stopped and ordered the blind man to be brought to him. When he came near, Jesus asked him, [41]"What do you want me to do for you?"

He said, "Lord, I want to see."

[42]Jesus said to him, "Then see. You are healed because you believed."

[43]At once the man was able to see, and he followed Jesus, thanking God. All the people who saw this praised God.

Zacchaeus Meets Jesus

19 Jesus was going through the city of Jericho. [2]A man was there named Zacchaeus, who was a very important tax collector, and he was wealthy. [3]He wanted to see who Jesus was, but he was not able because he was too short to see above the crowd. [4]He ran ahead to a place where Jesus would come, and he climbed a sycamore tree so he could see him. [5]When Jesus came to that place, he looked up and said to him, "Zacchaeus, hurry and come down! I must stay at your house today."

[6]Zacchaeus came down quickly and welcomed him gladly. [7]All the people saw this and began to complain, "Jesus is staying with a sinner!"

[8]But Zacchaeus stood and said to the Lord, "I will give half of my possessions to the poor. And if I have cheated anyone, I will pay back four times more."

[9]Jesus said to him, "Salvation has come to this house today, because this man also belongs to the family of Abraham. [10]The Son of Man came to find lost people and save them."

A Story About Three Servants

[11]As the people were listening to this, Jesus told them a story because he was near Jerusalem and they thought God's kingdom would appear

18:20 *'You . . . mother.'* Quotation from Exodus 20:12-16; Deuteronomy 5:16-20.

18:20 Murder: Romans 1:29

18:43 Salvation: Acts 2:21

19 The story of Zacchaeus, the wealthy tax collector, helps to define Jesus' mission to the poor. In Luke 4:18, Jesus says he intends to preach Good News to the poor. Though Zacchaeus is wealthy in riches, he is poor in social status and in spirit. This is evidenced by the fact that he had to climb a tree in order to see Jesus (a sign that the crowd would not part for him).

Jesus chooses to go to Zacchaeus's house despite the grumbling of the people around him. It may seem inappropriate for a revered teacher such as Jesus to go to stay at the house of a hated tax collector. But because Jesus goes to his house, Zacchaeus's life is changed. Zacchaeus's transformation is evidenced in his declaration to make restitution for the ways that he has cheated people through his tax collecting. In declaring that Zacchaeus has a part in the inheritance of God's people, Jesus reiterates the crux of his Good News: "The Son of Man came to find lost people and save them" (verse 10).

19:10 Forgiveness: John 8:3–11

19:10 Hospitality: Acts 16:13–15

19:10 Table Fellowship/Lord's Supper: Luke 22:7–30

immediately. 12He said: "A very important man went to a country far away to be made a king and then to return home. 13So he called ten of his servants and gave a coin to each servant. He said, 'Do business with this money until I get back.' 14But the people in the kingdom hated the man. So they sent a group to follow him and say, 'We don't want this man to be our king.'

15"But the man became king. When he returned home, he said, 'Call those servants who have my money so I can know how much they earned with it.'

16"The first servant came and said, 'Sir, I earned ten coins with the one you gave me.' 17The king said to the servant, 'Excellent! You are a good servant. Since I can trust you with small things, I will let you rule over ten of my cities.'

18"The second servant said, 'Sir, I earned five coins with your one.' 19The king said to this servant, 'You can rule over five cities.'⚭

20"Then another servant came in and said to the king, 'Sir, here is your coin which I wrapped in a piece of cloth and hid. 21I was afraid of you, because you are a hard man. You even take money that you didn't earn and gather food that you didn't plant.' 22Then the king said to the servant, 'I will condemn you by your own words, you evil servant. You knew that I am a hard man, taking money that I didn't earn and gathering food that I didn't plant. 23Why then didn't you put my money in the bank? Then when I came back, my money would have earned some interest.'

24"The king said to the men who were standing by, 'Take the coin away from this servant and give it to the servant who earned ten coins.' 25They said, 'But sir, that servant already has ten coins.' 26The king said, 'Those who have will be given more, but those who do not have anything will have everything taken away from them. 27Now where are my enemies who didn't want me to be king? Bring them here and kill them before me.'"⚭

Jesus Enters Jerusalem as a King

28After Jesus said this, he went on toward Jerusalem. 29As Jesus came near Bethphage and Bethany, towns near the hill called the Mount of Olives, he sent out two of his followers. 30He said, "Go to the town you can see there. When you enter it, you will find a colt tied there, which no one has ever ridden. Untie it and bring it here to me. 31If anyone asks you why you are untying it, say that the Master needs it."

32The two followers went into town and found the colt just as Jesus had told them. 33As they were untying it, its owners came out and asked the followers, "Why are you untying our colt?"

34The followers answered, "The Master needs it." 35So they brought it to Jesus, threw their coats on the colt's back, and put Jesus on it. 36As Jesus rode toward Jerusalem, others spread their coats on the road before him.

37As he was coming close to Jerusalem, on the way down the Mount of Olives, the whole crowd of followers began joyfully shouting praise to God for all the miracles they had seen. 38They said,

"God bless the king who comes in the name
of the Lord! *Psalm 118:26*

There is peace in heaven and glory to God!"

39Some of the Pharisees in the crowd said to Jesus, "Teacher, tell your followers not to say these things."

40But Jesus answered, "I tell you, if my followers didn't say these things, then the stones would cry out."⚭

Jesus Cries for Jerusalem

41As Jesus came near Jerusalem, he saw the city and cried for it, 42saying, "I wish you knew today what would bring you peace. But now it is hidden from you. 43The time is coming when your enemies will build a wall around you and will hold you in on all sides. 44They will destroy you and all your people, and not one stone will be left on another. All this will happen because you did not recognize the time when God came to save you."

Jesus Goes to the Temple

45Jesus went into the Temple and began to throw out the people who were selling things there. 46He said, "It is written in the Scriptures, 'My Temple will be a house for prayer.' But you have changed it into a 'hideout for robbers'!"

47Jesus taught in the Temple every day. The leading priests, the experts on the law, and some of the leaders of the people wanted to kill Jesus. 48But they did not know how they could do it,

19:13 *coin.* A Greek "mina." One mina was enough money to pay a person for working three months.

⚭**19:19 Materialism/Possessions:** Acts 2:41–47

⚭**19:27 Service:** John 12:26

⚭**19:40 Stone:** Revelation 21:19

19:46 Christ echoes Isaiah's words (56:7), declaring God's desire for the Temple to be a house of prayer for all the nations; that is, a place dedicated to intercession. We can do nothing finer than to make our churches similar places today.

19:46 *'My Temple . . . prayer.'* Quotation from Isaiah 56:7.

19:46 *'hideout for robbers'*. Quotation from Jeremiah 7:11.

19:47–48 The scribes saw Jesus as a threat to national security because of the popular excitement caused by his radical ministry (Mark 11:15–19). This was not just a threat to the professional pride of the scribes, but was a threat to the entire scribal system that had developed during the second Temple period. It was such a threat to the religious establishment that those scribes who were members of the Sanhedrin shared the guilt of turning Jesus over to the Roman authorities to be crucified.

because all the people were listening closely to him.

Jewish Leaders Question Jesus

20 One day Jesus was in the Temple, teaching the people and telling them the Good News. The leading priests, teachers of the law, and older leaders came up to talk with him, [2]saying, "Tell us what authority you have to do these things? Who gave you this authority?"

[3]Jesus answered, "I will also ask you a question. Tell me: [4]When John baptized people, was that authority from God or just from other people?"

[5]They argued about this, saying, "If we answer, 'John's baptism was from God,' Jesus will say, 'Then why did you not believe him?' [6]But if we say, 'It was from other people,' all the people will stone us to death, because they believe John was a prophet." [7]So they answered that they didn't know where it came from.

[8]Jesus said to them, "Then I won't tell you what authority I have to do these things."

A Story About God's Son

[9]Then Jesus told the people this story: "A man planted a vineyard and leased it to some farmers. Then he went away for a long time. [10]When it was time for the grapes to be picked, he sent a servant to the farmers to get some of the grapes. But they beat the servant and sent him away empty-handed. [11]Then he sent another servant. They beat this servant also, and showed no respect for him, and sent him away empty-handed. [12]So the man sent a third servant. The farmers wounded him and threw him out. [13]The owner of the vineyard said, 'What will I do now? I will send my son whom I love. Maybe they will respect him.' [14]But when the farmers saw the son, they said to each other, 'This son will inherit the vineyard. If we kill him, it will be ours.' [15]So the farmers threw the son out of the vineyard and killed him.

"What will the owner of this vineyard do to them? [16]He will come and kill those farmers and will give the vineyard to other farmers."

When the people heard this story, they said, "Let this never happen!"

[17]But Jesus looked at them and said, "Then what does this verse mean:

'The stone that the builders rejected
became the cornerstone'? *Psalm 118:22*

[18]Everyone who falls on that stone will be broken, and the person on whom it falls, that person will be crushed!"

[19]The teachers of the law and the leading priests wanted to arrest Jesus at once, because they knew the story was about them. But they were afraid of what the people would do.

Is It Right to Pay Taxes or Not?

[20]So they watched Jesus and sent some spies who acted as if they were sincere. They wanted to trap Jesus in saying something wrong so they could hand him over to the authority and power of the governor. [21]So the spies asked Jesus, "Teacher, we know that what you say and teach is true. You pay no attention to who people are, and you always teach the truth about God's way. [22]Tell us, is it right for us to pay taxes to Caesar or not?"

[23]But Jesus, knowing they were trying to trick him, said, [24]"Show me a coin. Whose image and name are on it?"

They said, "Caesar's."

[25]Jesus said to them, "Then give to Caesar the things that are Caesar's, and give to God the things that are God's."

[26]So they were not able to trap Jesus in anything he said in the presence of the people. And being amazed at his answer, they became silent.

Some Sadducees Try to Trick Jesus

[27]Some Sadducees, who believed people would not rise from the dead, came to Jesus. [28]They asked, "Teacher, Moses wrote that if a man's brother dies and leaves a wife but no children, then that man must marry the widow and have children for his brother. [29]Once there were seven brothers. The first brother married and died, but had no children. [30]Then the second brother married the widow, and he died. [31]And the third brother married the widow, and he died. The same thing happened with all seven brothers; they died and had no children. [32]Finally, the woman died also. [33]Since all seven brothers had married her, whose wife will she be when people rise from the dead?"

[34]Jesus said to them, "On earth, people marry and are given to someone to marry. [35]But those who will be worthy to be raised from the dead and live again will not marry, nor will they be given to someone to marry. [36]In that life they are like angels and cannot die. They are children of God, because they have been raised from the dead. [37]Even Moses clearly showed that the dead are raised to life. When he wrote about the burning bush, he said that the Lord is 'the God of Abraham, the God of Isaac, and the God of Jacob.' [38]God is the God of the living, not the dead, because all people are alive to him."

20:36 Angels: 2 Thessalonians 1:7
20:37 *burning bush.* Read Exodus 3:1-12 in the Old Testament.
20:37 *'the God of . . . Jacob'.* These words are taken from Exodus 3:6.
20:38 Samuel: Ephesians 1:18–23

39Some of the teachers of the law said, "Teacher, your answer was good." 40No one was brave enough to ask him another question.

Is the Christ the Son of David?

41Then Jesus said, "Why do people say that the Christ is the Son of David? 42In the book of Psalms, David himself says:

'The Lord said to my Lord:
Sit by me at my right side,
43 until I put your enemies under
your control.' *Psalm 110:1*

44David calls the Christ 'Lord,' so how can the Christ be his son?"

Jesus Accuses Some Leaders

45While all the people were listening, Jesus said to his followers, 46"Beware of the teachers of the law. They like to walk around wearing fancy clothes, and they love for people to greet them with respect in the marketplaces. They love to have the most important seats in the synagogues and at feasts. 47But they cheat widows and steal their houses and then try to make themselves look good by saying long prayers. They will receive a greater punishment."

True Giving

21 As Jesus looked up, he saw some rich people putting their gifts into the Temple money box. 2Then he saw a poor widow putting two small copper coins into the box. 3He said, "I tell you the truth, this poor widow gave more than all those rich people. 4They gave only what they did not need. This woman is very poor, but she gave all she had to live on."

The Temple Will Be Destroyed

5Some people were talking about the Temple and how it was decorated with beautiful stones and gifts offered to God.

But Jesus said, 6"As for these things you are looking at, the time will come when not one stone will be left on another. Every stone will be thrown down."

7They asked Jesus, "Teacher, when will these things happen? What will be the sign that they are about to take place?"

8Jesus said, "Be careful so you are not fooled. Many people will come in my name, saying, 'I am the One' and, 'The time has come!' But don't follow them. 9When you hear about wars and riots, don't be afraid, because these things must happen first, but the end will come later."

10Then he said to them, "Nations will fight against other nations, and kingdoms against other kingdoms. 11In various places there will be great earthquakes, sicknesses, and a lack of food. Fearful events and great signs will come from heaven.

12"But before all these things happen, people will arrest you and treat you cruelly. They will judge you in their synagogues and put you in jail and force you to stand before kings and governors, because you follow me. 13But this will give you an opportunity to tell about me. 14Make up your minds not to worry ahead of time about what you will say. 15I will give you the wisdom to say things that none of your enemies will be able to stand against or prove wrong. 16Even your parents, brothers, relatives, and friends will turn against you, and they will kill some of you. 17All people will hate you because you follow me. 18But none of these things can really harm you. 19By continuing to have faith you will save your lives.

Jerusalem Will Be Destroyed

20"When you see armies all around Jerusalem, you will know it will soon be destroyed. 21At that time, the people in Judea should run away to the mountains. The people in Jerusalem must get out, and those who are near the city should not go in. 22These are the days of punishment to bring about all that is written in the Scriptures. 23How terrible it will be for women who are pregnant or have nursing babies! Great trouble will come upon this land, and God will be angry with these people. 24They will be killed by the sword and taken as prisoners to all nations. Jerusalem will be crushed by non-Jewish people until their time is over.

Don't Fear

25"There will be signs in the sun, moon, and stars. On earth, nations will be afraid and confused because of the roar and fury of the sea. 26People

---

20:39 Scribes (Teachers of the Law): Acts 5:34

20:43 *until . . . control.* Literally, "until I make your enemies a footstool for your feet."

20:45–21:4 It is unfortunate that these two stories are separated by a chapter break, since they are concerned with the same problem: some people like to think they are special, but their behaviors end up hurting poor people, like the widows mentioned in Luke 20:47; 21:3–4. Although Jesus is impressed by this widow's willingness to give everything, he is more concerned about those who run the Temple. They do not give everything they have, but instead want others to give them both respect and money.

20:47 Guilt: Romans 8:1–4

21:1 *money box.* A special box in the Jewish place of worship where people put their gifts to God.

21:4 Money: Acts 2:44–47

21:20–24 Jesus prophesied the destruction of Jerusalem and warned his hearers to flee when they saw Jerusalem surrounded by armies (see also Matthew 24, Mark 13). In the year AD 70, under the Roman emperor Titus, the Romans destroyed Jerusalem and the Temple.

will be so afraid they will faint, wondering what is happening to the world, because the powers of the heavens will be shaken. 27Then people will see the Son of Man coming in a cloud with power and great glory. 28When these things begin to happen, look up and hold your heads high, because the time when God will free you is near!"

Jesus' Words Will Live Forever

29Then Jesus told this story: "Look at the fig tree and all the other trees. 30When their leaves appear, you know that summer is near. 31In the same way, when you see these things happening, you will know that God's kingdom is near.

32"I tell you the truth, all these things will happen while the people of this time are still living. 33Earth and sky will be destroyed, but the words I have spoken will never be destroyed.

Be Ready All the Time

34"Be careful not to spend your time feasting, drinking, or worrying about worldly things. If you do, that day might come on you suddenly,⚭ 35like a trap on all people on earth. 36So be ready all the time. Pray that you will be strong enough to escape all these things that will happen and that you will be able to stand before the Son of Man."

37During the day, Jesus taught the people in the Temple, and at night he went out of the city and stayed on the Mount of Olives. 38Every morning all the people got up early to go to the Temple to listen to him.

Judas Becomes an Enemy of Jesus

22 It was almost time for the Feast of Unleavened Bread, called the Passover Feast. 2The leading priests and teachers of the law were trying to find a way to kill Jesus, because they were afraid of the people.

3Satan entered Judas Iscariot, one of Jesus' twelve apostles. 4Judas went to the leading priests and some of the soldiers who guarded the Temple and talked to them about a way to hand Jesus over to them. 5They were pleased and agreed to give Judas money. 6He agreed and watched for the best time to hand Jesus over to them when he was away from the crowd.⚭

Jesus Eats the Passover Meal

7The Day of Unleavened Bread came when the Passover lambs had to be sacrificed. 8Jesus said to Peter and John, "Go and prepare the Passover meal for us to eat."⚭

9They asked, "Where do you want us to prepare it?" 10Jesus said to them, "After you go into the city, a man carrying a jar of water will meet you. Follow him into the house that he enters, 11and tell the owner of the house, 'The Teacher says: Where is the guest room in which I may eat the Passover meal with my followers?' 12Then he will show you a large, furnished room upstairs. Prepare the Passover meal there."

13So Peter and John left and found everything as Jesus had said. And they prepared the Passover meal.

The Lord's Supper

14When the time came, Jesus and the apostles were sitting at the table. 15He said to them, "I wanted very much to eat this Passover meal with you before I suffer. 16I will not eat another Passover meal until it is given its true meaning in the kingdom of God."

17Then Jesus took a cup, gave thanks, and said, "Take this cup and share it among yourselves. 18I will not drink again from the fruit of the vine[n] until God's kingdom comes."

19Then Jesus took some bread, gave thanks, broke it, and gave it to the apostles, saying, "This is my body, which I am giving for you. Do this to remember me." 20In the same way, after supper, Jesus took the cup and said, "This cup is the new agreement that God makes with his people. This new agreement begins with my blood which is poured out for you.

Who Will Turn Against Jesus?

21"But one of you will turn against me, and his hand is with mine on the table. 22What God has planned for the Son of Man will happen, but how terrible it will be for that one who turns against the Son of Man."

23Then the apostles asked each other which one of them would do that.

Be Like a Servant

24The apostles also began to argue about which one of them was the most important. 25But Jesus said to them, "The kings of the non-Jewish people rule over them, and those who have authority over others like to be called 'friends of the people.' 26But you must not be like that. Instead, the greatest among you should be like the youngest, and the leader should be like the servant.⚭

⚭**21:34 Alcohol:** Acts 2:13
⚭**22:6 Honor & Shame:** Philippians 3:4–6
⚭**22:8 Peter:** Luke 22:31–46

22:18 *fruit of the vine.* Product of the grapevine; this may also be translated "wine."

⚭**22:26 Leadership:** John 10:1–16

27 Who is more important: the one sitting at the table
or the one serving? You think the one at the table is
more important, but I am like a servant among you.
28 "You have stayed with me through my struggles. 29 Just as my Father has given me a kingdom,
I also give you a kingdom 30 so you may eat and
drink at my table in my kingdom. And you will sit
on thrones, judging the twelve tribes of Israel.∞

Don't Lose Your Faith!

31 "Simon, Simon, Satan has asked to test all of
you as a farmer sifts his wheat. 32 I have prayed
that you will not lose your faith! Help your brothers be stronger when you come back to me."
33 But Peter said to Jesus, "Lord, I am ready to
go with you to prison and even to die with you!"
34 But Jesus said, "Peter, before the rooster
crows this day, you will say three times that you
don't know me."

Be Ready for Trouble

35 Then Jesus said to the apostles, "When I sent
you out without a purse, a bag, or sandals, did you
need anything?"
They said, "No."
36 He said to them, "But now if you have a purse
or a bag, carry that with you. If you don't have a
sword, sell your coat and buy one. 37 The Scripture
says, 'He was treated like a criminal,' and I tell you
this scripture must have its full meaning. It was
written about me, and it is happening now."∞
38 His followers said, "Look, Lord, here are two
swords."
He said to them, "That is enough."

Jesus Prays Alone

39 Jesus left the city and went to the Mount of
Olives, as he often did, and his followers went
with him. 40 When he reached the place, he said
to them, "Pray for strength against temptation."
41 Then Jesus went about a stone's throw away
from them. He kneeled down and prayed, 42 "Father,
if you are willing, take away this cup of suffering.
But do what you want, not what I want."∞ 43 Then
an angel from heaven appeared to him to
strengthen him. 44 Being full of pain, Jesus prayed
even harder. His sweat was like drops of blood
falling to the ground.∞ 45 When he finished praying, he went to his followers and found them
asleep because of their sadness. 46 Jesus said to
them, "Why are you sleeping? Get up and pray
for strength against temptation."∞

Jesus Is Arrested

47 While Jesus was speaking, a crowd came up,
and Judas, one of the twelve apostles, was leading
them. He came close to Jesus so he could kiss him.
48 But Jesus said to him, "Judas, are you using
the kiss to give the Son of Man to his enemies?"
49 When those who were standing around him
saw what was happening, they said, "Lord, should

22:27 In the midst of the Last Supper the followers begin to argue about who among them was the most important. Jesus quickly moves to contrast "power" in the coming Kingdom of God with men's ideas of status and authority. For those who follow Jesus, true power comes with humility and the desire to serve and help others.

22:27–30 He assured his followers of the hope of heaven and the kingdom coming in its fullness by indicating that he would enjoy table fellowship with them there. Heaven and the future kingdom are thus not abstract concepts or wishful images; Jesus promises his followers that the fellowship and festivity there will be tangible, real.

∞**22:30 Table Fellowship/Lord's Supper:** Luke 24:30–32

22:31 Jesus was fully aware of what was about to happen to him. He knew that his arrest, trial, and crucifixion could be used by Satan to get the frightened followers to abandon their faith completely. Simon Peter did deny the Lord (Matthew 26:57–75), but was brought back to Jesus (John 2). Judas, however, betrayed the Lord (Matthew 26:20–25; 27:3–10) and then killed himself (27:3–10). In contrast to God's testing, which is good, Satan's testing is destructive.

22:35–38 In the past, Jesus' followers could depend on the hospitality of others as they shared the Good News from place to place. If people will crucify their master, though, will his followers not also meet hostility? His words about buying a sword are a sign for their need to prepare for conflict and division. When his followers misunderstand him, thinking he actually wants them to carry swords, he dismisses such thoughts with "That is enough!"

22:37 Although Jesus was innocent of any wrongdoing, he was treated like a criminal after the Pharisees and Sadducees falsely accused him before the Roman governor, Pilate. The mistreatment Jesus received at the hands of his accusers fulfilled Isaiah 53:12, which foretold of the suffering Jesus would endure in bearing the penalty for human sin.

22:37 *'He . . . criminal.'* Quotation from Isaiah 53:12.

∞**22:37 Crime:** Luke 22:52

22:40–46 Luke draws a dramatic picture of Jesus' coping with loneliness while facing a terrible decision. Jesus reveals his torment to his closest friends and requests prayer support. They can't cope with his distress; they fall asleep. Luke does not mention God's nurturing presence with Jesus at this time, and we know that God does not rescue him. Jesus must act on his best understanding of God's will and trust God to use his actions. In this way he moves from loneliness to an ability to be and act alone. Like Jesus, we experience times of intense loneliness when friends and family offer no support and when God seems distant. We also are called to act with the information we have, and trust God to use our actions.

∞**22:42 Will of God:** John 5:30

22:42 *cup.* Jesus is talking about the painful things that will happen to him. Accepting these things will be hard, like drinking a cup of something bitter.

22:43–44 Luke portrays Jesus' struggle in prayer almost as an athletic contest. Will Jesus align himself with God's will? As he pushes himself to the limits, seeking to submit fully to the will of his Father, Jesus is not alone. God hears his prayers and sends help in the form of a heavenly messenger to strengthen Jesus.

∞**22:44 Fear:** See article on page 552.

∞**22:46 Peter:** Luke 22:55–62

22:47–53 Judas shows himself to be an apostate at this point. He illustrates the principles behind Hebrews 6:4–6. He was in the innermost circle. He heard Jesus teach and perform miracles. He enjoyed the fellowship of those who also had an intimate relationship with the Lord, yet he turned against the Lord. He denied the truth to which he was exposed, showing at his core a rebellious heart.

we strike them with our swords?" 50And one of
them struck the servant of the high priest and cut
off his right ear.

51Jesus said, "Stop! No more of this." Then he
touched the servant's ear and healed him.

52Those who came to arrest Jesus were the leading priests, the soldiers who guarded the Temple,
and the older leaders. Jesus said to them, "You
came out here with swords and clubs as though I
were a criminal. 53I was with you every day in
the Temple, and you didn't arrest me there. But
this is your time—the time when darkness rules."

Peter Says He Doesn't Know Jesus

54They arrested Jesus, and led him away, and
brought him into the house of the high priest.
Peter followed far behind them. 55After the soldiers started a fire in the middle of the courtyard
and sat together, Peter sat with them. 56A servant
girl saw Peter sitting there in the firelight, and
looking closely at him, she said, "This man was
also with him."

57But Peter said this was not true; he said,
"Woman, I don't know him."

58A short time later, another person saw Peter
and said, "You are also one of them."

But Peter said, "Man, I am not!"

59About an hour later, another man insisted,
"Certainly this man was with him, because he is
from Galilee, too."

60But Peter said, "Man, I don't know what you
are talking about!"

At once, while Peter was still speaking, a rooster
crowed. 61Then the Lord turned and looked straight
at Peter. And Peter remembered what the Lord
had said: "Before the rooster crows this day, you
will say three times that you don't know me."
62Then Peter went outside and cried painfully.

The People Make Fun of Jesus

63The men who were guarding Jesus began
making fun of him and beating him.

64They blindfolded him and said, "Prove that
you are a prophet, and tell us who hit you." 65They
said many cruel things to Jesus.

Jesus Before the Leaders

66When day came, the council of the older leaders of the people, both the leading priests and the
teachers of the law, came together and led Jesus
to their highest court. 67They said, "If you are the
Christ, tell us."

Jesus said to them, "If I tell you, you will not
believe me. 68And if I ask you, you will not
answer. 69But from now on, the Son of Man will
sit at the right hand of the powerful God."

70They all said, "Then are you the Son of God?"

Jesus said to them, "You say that I am."

71They said, "Why do we need witnesses now?
We ourselves heard him say this."

Pilate Questions Jesus

23 Then the whole group stood up and led
Jesus to Pilate. 2They began to accuse Jesus,
saying, "We caught this man telling things that
mislead our people. He says that we should not pay
taxes to Caesar, and he calls himself the Christ, a
king."

3Pilate asked Jesus, "Are you the king of the
Jews?"

Jesus answered, "Those are your words."

4Pilate said to the leading priests and the people, "I find nothing against this man."

5They were insisting, saying, "But Jesus makes
trouble with the people, teaching all around Judea.
He began in Galilee, and now he is here."

Pilate Sends Jesus to Herod

6Pilate heard this and asked if Jesus was from
Galilee. 7Since Jesus was under Herod's authority,
Pilate sent Jesus to Herod, who was in Jerusalem at
that time. 8When Herod saw Jesus, he was very
glad, because he had heard about Jesus and had
wanted to meet him for a long time. He was hoping to see Jesus work a miracle. 9Herod asked Jesus
many questions, but Jesus said nothing. 10The leading priests and teachers of the law were standing
there, strongly accusing Jesus. 11After Herod and
his soldiers had made fun of Jesus, they dressed
him in a kingly robe and sent him back to Pilate.
12In the past, Pilate and Herod had always been
enemies, but on that day they became friends.

Jesus Must Die

13Pilate called the people together with the leading priests and the rulers. 14He said to them, "You
brought this man to me, saying he makes trouble
among the people. But I have questioned him
before you all, and I have not found him guilty of
what you say. 15Also, Herod found nothing wrong
with him; he sent him back to us. Look, he has
done nothing for which he should die. 16So, after I
punish him, I will let him go free." 17*

22:52 Crime: Luke 23:40

22:62 Peter: Luke 24:12

23:1 *Pilate.* Pontius Pilate was the Roman governor of Judea from AD 26 to AD 36.

23:5 Pontius Pilate: Luke 23:13–25

***23:17** *Verse 17.* A few Greek copies add verse 17: "Every year at the Passover Feast, Pilate had to release one prisoner to the people."

PEACE

2 CORINTHIANS 5:18

What does the Bible mean when it talks about peace? Where can we find peace?

Jesus told us, "Those who work to bring peace are happy, because God will call them his children." (Matthew 5:9). This is a great promise, and it inevitably raises the question of what Jesus means about working to bring peace. The answer contains some surprises.

The Hebrew word for peace (*shalom*) used in the Old Testament basically means "well-being." In some cases it is used like our English word "peace" to mean tranquillity (Job 3:26) or the absence of hostility (Deuteronomy 20:10, 12). More often it refers to security or safety from threats of harm (Leviticus 26:6; Psalm 4:8; Isaiah 54:13), a meaning that we do not usually associate with the English word "peace." The traditional Israelite farewell, "Go in peace" (1 Samuel 25:35) means, "May everything go well with you." Another difference between peace in the Old Testament and the meaning of peace in modern English is that in the Old Testament peace refers primarily not to a calm, restful state of mind, but to calm, safe, and favorable circumstances. One exception is Proverbs 14:30, "Peace of mind means a healthy body," but that passage does not use the usual Hebrew word for peace.

In the troubled days of the Hebrew kings, the people of Israel often lacked peace. This was a consequence of their sins. As Isaiah told them, "There is no peace for evil people" (Isaiah 48:22). God's prophets warned the people not to listen to false prophets who said, "It's all right, it's all right," when the sins of the people made peace impossible (Jeremiah 6:14; 8:11). God also promised that someday he would give peace to his people again. In Isaiah 32:15–20 God promises to send his Spirit and create justice and fairness in Israel. Then Israel will have peace. In Isaiah 54:9–10, God promises not to be angry with his people anymore, but instead to love them and give them peace forever. In Isaiah 57:14–19 God promises that he will heal sinful people who are humble and heartbroken and give them peace.

God tells his people that the king he promised is the one who will bring peace. Isaiah calls the coming king "Prince of Peace" (Isaiah 9:6). Ezekiel connects God's promised peace with the king like David that God will set up to rule his people (Ezekiel 34:23–25; 37:24–26).

Since Jesus is the promised king, it is no surprise that the New Testament tells us Jesus brings peace. Paul tells us in Ephesians 2:14, "Christ himself is our peace." The New Testament authors build on the Old Testament teaching about peace to show that having the peace that Jesus brings changes every one of a person's relationships. Christ brings the believer peace with God (2 Corinthians 5:18–20). Christ brings peace between Jews and Gentiles by making the Gentiles part of God's people (Ephesians 2:11–18). Christ brings peace between people in the church (Colossians 3:15). Christ brings safety and well-being to the believer (John 14:27). The New Testament writers also introduce the aspect of peace rarely found in the Old Testament: peace of mind. Jesus Christ calms the inner turmoil of anxiety and fear (Philippians 4:7), and wrong desires (James 3:16–18).

People obtain peace by trusting God (Isaiah 26:3). Peace with God comes by faith in Christ (Romans 5:1). Being filled with the Holy Spirit brings inner peace, since peace is part of his work in the Christian (Galatians 5:22). Thankful prayer brings inner peace, because we know our needs are securely in God's hands (Philippians 4:7). Obeying God in difficult circumstances also brings peace (Hebrews 12:11). The peace of security comes to those who love God's word (Psalm 119:165). Following Jesus's example of humility, forgiveness, patience, and love maintains peace between Christians (Ephesians 4:2–3).

Jesus clearly teaches, however, that in one sense he did not bring peace. He says in Matthew 10:34–36 that his coming will divide families. He goes on to explain that people who believe in him will be persecuted by those who don't believe, even by members of their own families. It is in this context that one should understand the saying of Jesus in Matthew 5:9. Christians are to love their enemies and pray for those who hurt them (Matthew 5:44). They must seek to live peacefully with all people (Romans 12:18). In other words, Christians attempt to make peace with people who are against them. In the long run, the only way this peace will be made is if people believe the Good News. Christians work to bring peace by persuading others to believe the Good News about Christ (2 Corinthians 5:20). When God blesses their efforts, the peace he promised in his kingdom comes into people's lives (Romans 14:17).

Peace: For additional scriptures on this topic go to Leviticus 26:6.

Commitment

GALATIANS 3:15–17

What does it mean to commit ourselves to someone, a cause, or to God? What is the relationship between commitment and promise? Between commitment and agreement?

In the Old and New Testaments, the concept of commitment is most spoken about within the context of an agreement between God and humans. It begins with a declaration by God, "I will make an agreement with you . . ." (Genesis 6:18). From the beginning, God is committed to his people unconditionally, and promises to be ever faithful to this commitment. In fact, when the rainbow appears in the clouds, he sees it and remembers "the agreement that continues forever between me and every living thing on the earth" (Genesis 9:16). All God requires of his promise of commitment to each person and to the church as a whole is that we freely respond in faith. And that opportunity for people is through the person and work of Jesus Christ.

Commitment is the binding agent for the whole of life and is at the core of a meaningful relationship with God and with our fellow human beings. In its original Hebrew context it means a "duty to serve another person." "God made promises both to Abraham and to his descendant" (Galatians 3:16). Not just Abraham, but the generations who follow, will benefit from the commitment. At its core, commitment is a covenant freely made between God and an individual, or between two persons, and is "firm." "After that agreement is accepted by both people, no one can stop it or add anything to it" (Galatians 3:15). It is a firm promise for the future. Perhaps the nature of commitment in the Scriptures is best summarized by the promise "I will walk with you and be your God, and you will be my people" (Leviticus 26:12).

And so as God has modeled commitment to us from the beginning, and supremely through Jesus Christ, it is just as important a concept between two people, binding and obliging them to each other, for the benefit of each party.

What are the elements that define the nature of commitment between God and human persons, or between people? At the basis of any commitment is love. The act of commitment is ultimately a promise of love freely given. "God loved the world so much that he gave his one and only Son . . ." (John 3:16). On the human level, in the Old Testament is the story of David and Jonathan, where it is recorded that "Jonathan made an agreement with David, because he loved David as much as himself" (1 Samuel 18:3). We make commitments out of love and loyalty, and ultimately because God first loved us.

Commitments are rooted in a promise, and are maintained forever on that basis. "God had an agreement with Abraham and promised to keep it," and neither the law or anything else can change that agreement and so destroy God's promise to Abraham (Genesis 13:17). God's promise to the nation of Israel is that he will make them "a great nation, and I will bless you" (Genesis 12:2). Through Jesus Christ, Christians are brought into an agreement with God through Christ our Savior, "as he promised" (Acts 13:23).

Commitment in this context has a permanent and unalterable character to it, whether that be to a person, a cause, or to God. Commitment involves a certain cost. As part of our commitments we surrender individual control over our destiny. We make commitments in marriage, to our children, to our church, and ultimately to Jesus Christ that become binding for the rest of our lives. Like the people he called as his disciples, Jesus calls each of us to follow him, the essence of commitment (see Mark 2:14). This is the "new agreement from God to his people" spoken about in Hebrews (see Hebrews 9:15–17). Indeed, whatever firm agreements we make today have positive consequences for the generations who follow, just as they did for Abraham. Ultimately, it is the love-motivated promise at the root of commitment, whether between God and humans, or between people, that is our only hope and guarantee for the future.

Commitment: For additional scriptures on this topic go to Genesis 6:18.

18But the people shouted together, "Take this man away! Let Barabbas go free!" 19(Barabbas was a man who was in prison for his part in a riot in the city and for murder.)

20Pilate wanted to let Jesus go free and told this to the crowd. 21But they shouted again, "Crucify him! Crucify him!"

22A third time Pilate said to them, "Why? What wrong has he done? I can find no reason to kill him. So I will have him punished and set him free."

23But they continued to shout, demanding that Jesus be crucified. Their yelling became so loud that 24Pilate decided to give them what they wanted. 25He set free the man who was in jail for rioting and murder, and he handed Jesus over to them to do with him as they wished.

Jesus Is Crucified

26As they led Jesus away, Simon, a man from Cyrene, was coming in from the fields. They forced him to carry Jesus' cross and to walk behind him.

27A large crowd of people was following Jesus, including some women who were sad and crying for him. 28But Jesus turned and said to them, "Women of Jerusalem, don't cry for me. Cry for yourselves and for your children. 29The time is coming when people will say, 'Happy are the women who cannot have children and who have no babies to nurse.' 30Then people will say to the mountains, 'Fall on us!' And they will say to the hills, 'Cover us!' 31If they act like this now when life is good, what will happen when bad times come?"

32There were also two criminals led out with Jesus to be put to death. 33When they came to a place called the Skull, the soldiers crucified Jesus and the criminals—one on his right and the other on his left. 34Jesus said, "Father, forgive them, because they don't know what they are doing."*

The soldiers threw lots to decide who would get his clothes. 35The people stood there watching. And the leaders made fun of Jesus, saying, "He saved others. Let him save himself if he is God's Chosen One, the Christ."

36The soldiers also made fun of him, coming to Jesus and offering him some vinegar. 37They said, "If you are the king of the Jews, save yourself!" 38At the top of the cross these words were written: THIS IS THE KING OF THE JEWS.

39One of the criminals on a cross began to shout insults at Jesus: "Aren't you the Christ? Then save yourself and us."

40But the other criminal stopped him and said, "You should fear God! You are getting the same punishment he is. 41We are punished justly, getting what we deserve for what we did. But this man has done nothing wrong." 42Then he said, "Jesus, remember me when you come into your kingdom."

43Jesus said to him, "I tell you the truth, today you will be with me in paradise."

Jesus Dies

44It was about noon, and the whole land became dark until three o'clock in the afternoon, 45because the sun did not shine. The curtain in the Temple was torn in two. 46Jesus cried out in a loud voice, "Father, I give you my life." After Jesus said this, he died.

47When the army officer there saw what happened, he praised God, saying, "Surely this was a good man!"

48When all the people who had gathered there to watch saw what happened, they returned home, beating their chests because they were so sad. 49But those who were close friends of Jesus, including the women who had followed him from Galilee, stood at a distance and watched.

Joseph Takes Jesus' Body

50There was a good and religious man named Joseph who was a member of the council. 51But he had not agreed to the other leaders' plans and actions against Jesus. He was from the town of Arimathea and was waiting for the kingdom of God to come. 52Joseph went to Pilate to ask for the body of Jesus. 53He took the body down from the cross, wrapped it in cloth, and put it in a tomb that was cut out of a wall of rock. This tomb had never been used before. 54This was late on Preparation Day, and when the sun went down, the Sabbath day would begin.

55The women who had come from Galilee with Jesus followed Joseph and saw the tomb and how Jesus' body was laid. 56Then the women left to prepare spices and perfumes.

On the Sabbath day they rested, as the law of Moses commanded.

23:25 Pontius Pilate: John 18:28–19:15

23:31 *If . . . come?* Literally, "If they do these things in the green tree, what will happen in the dry?"

***23:34** *Verse 34.* Some early Greek copies do not have this first part of the verse.

23:38 The Crucifixion of Jesus (The Way of the Cross): John 19:16–23

23:40 Crime: Acts 18:14

23:42 Memory: Romans 1:9

23:43 Capital Punishment: Acts 12:23

23:43 *paradise.* Another word for heaven.

23:45 *curtain in the Temple.* A curtain divided the Most Holy Place from the other part of the Temple, the special building in Jerusalem where God commanded the Jewish people to worship him.

23:49 Martyrdom: John 15:18–27

23:56 Persecution: John 15:20

Jesus "is not here; he has risen from the dead" (24:6).

Jesus Rises from the Dead

24 Very early on the first day of the week, at dawn, the women came to the tomb, bringing the spices they had prepared. 2They found the stone rolled away from the entrance of the tomb, 3but when they went in, they did not find the body of the Lord Jesus. 4While they were wondering about this, two men in shining clothes suddenly stood beside them. 5The women were very afraid and bowed their heads to the ground. The men said to them, "Why are you looking for a living person in this place for the dead? 6He is not here; he has risen from the dead. Do you remember what he told you in Galilee? 7He said the Son of Man must be handed over to sinful people, be crucified, and rise from the dead on the third day." 8Then the women remembered what Jesus had said.

9The women left the tomb and told all these things to the eleven apostles and the other followers. 10It was Mary Magdalene, Joanna, Mary the mother of James, and some other women who told the apostles everything that had happened at the tomb. 11But they did not believe the women, because it sounded like nonsense. 12But Peter got up and ran to the tomb. Bending down and looking in, he saw only the cloth that Jesus' body had been wrapped in. Peter went away to his home, wondering about what had happened.

Jesus on the Road to Emmaus

13That same day two of Jesus' followers were going to a town named Emmaus, about seven miles from Jerusalem. 14They were talking about everything that had happened. 15While they were talking and discussing, Jesus himself came near and began walking with them, 16but they were kept from recognizing him. 17Then he said, "What are these things you are talking about while you walk?"

The two followers stopped, looking very sad. 18The one named Cleopas answered, "Are you the only visitor in Jerusalem who does not know what just happened there?"

19Jesus said to them, "What are you talking about?"

They said, "About Jesus of Nazareth. He was a prophet who said and did many powerful things before God and all the people. 20Our leaders and the leading priests handed him over to be sentenced to death, and they crucified him. 21But we were hoping that he would free Israel. Besides this, it is now the third day since this happened. 22And today some women among us amazed us. Early this morning they went to the tomb, 23but they did not find his body there. They came and told us that they had seen a vision of angels who said that Jesus was alive! 24So some of our group went to the tomb, too. They found it just as the women said, but they did not see Jesus."

25Then Jesus said to them, "You are foolish and slow to believe everything the prophets said. 26They said that the Christ must suffer these things before he enters his glory." 27Then starting with what Moses and all the prophets had said about him, Jesus began to explain everything that had been written about himself in the Scriptures.

28They came near the town of Emmaus, and Jesus acted as if he were going farther. 29But they begged him, "Stay with us, because it is late; it is almost night." So he went in to stay with them.

30When Jesus was at the table with them, he took some bread, gave thanks, divided it, and gave it to them. 31And then, they were allowed to recognize Jesus. But when they saw who he was, he disappeared. 32They said to each other, "It felt like a fire burning in us when Jesus talked to us on the road and explained the Scriptures to us."

33So the two followers got up at once and went back to Jerusalem. There they found the eleven apostles and others gathered. 34They were saying, "The Lord really has risen from the dead! He showed himself to Simon."

24 One of the ways Jesus revealed his identity after the resurrection was to eat with his followers (Mark 16:14; Luke 24:30–32, 35, 41–43; John 21:9–14). Eating and drinking with them was one of the ways he had welcomed them into his new family; perhaps the particular way in which he broke the bread helped them recognize him as well.

24:12 Peter: Luke 24:34

24:19 Samuel: Luke 20:38

24:32 Table Fellowship/Lord's Supper: Luke 24:35

24:34 Peter: John 1:42

35Then the two followers told what had happened on the road and how they recognized Jesus
when he divided the bread.

Jesus Appears to His Followers

36While the two followers were telling this,
Jesus himself stood right in the middle of them
and said, "Peace be with you."
37They were fearful and terrified and thought
they were seeing a ghost. 38But Jesus said, "Why
are you troubled? Why do you doubt what you
see? 39Look at my hands and my feet. It is I
myself! Touch me and see, because a ghost does
not have a living body as you see I have."
40After Jesus said this, he showed them his
hands and feet. 41While they still could not believe
it because they were amazed and happy, Jesus said
to them, "Do you have any food here?" 42They
gave him a piece of broiled fish. 43While the followers watched, Jesus took the fish and ate it.
44He said to them, "Remember when I was with
you before? I said that everything written about me
must happen—everything in the law of Moses, the
books of the prophets, and the Psalms."
45Then Jesus opened their minds so they could
understand the Scriptures. 46He said to them, "It
is written that the Christ would suffer and rise
from the dead on the third day 47and that a
change of hearts and lives and forgiveness of sins
would be preached in his name to all nations,
starting at Jerusalem. 48You are witnesses of these
things. 49I will send you what my Father has
promised, but you must stay in Jerusalem until
you have received that power from heaven."

Jesus Goes Back to Heaven

50Jesus led his followers as far as Bethany, and
he raised his hands and blessed them. 51While he
was blessing them, he was separated from them
and carried into heaven. 52They worshiped him and
returned to Jerusalem very happy. 53They stayed in
the Temple all the time, praising God.

24:35 Table Fellowship/Lord's Supper: Luke 24:41–43
24:39 Doubt: John 14:15
24:43 Table Fellowship/Lord's Supper: John 21:9–14
24:49 Evangelism: John 1:35–51
24:53 Body/Resurrection: John 20

JESUS' LAST WEEK ON EARTH

		Matthew	Mark	Luke	John
Jesus enters Jerusalem on donkey	Sunday	21:1–17	11:1–11	19:29–44	
Jesus drives sellers from the Temple	Monday	21:12–13	11:15–18	19:45–46	
Jesus teaches in the Temple	Tuesday	22:23–24:14	11:27–12:12	20:41–44	
Judas agrees to betray Jesus	Wednesday	26:14–16	14:10–11	22:3–6	
Jesus shares last supper with his disciples	Thursday	26:17–25	14:12–26	22:7–30	13:1–30
Jesus gives last teaching to his disciples	Thursday night				14–16
Jesus prays in Gethsemane garden	Thursday night	26:30–46	14:26–42	22:39–46	18:1
Jesus arrested and tried by Sanhedrin	Friday (before dawn)	26:47–27:1	14:43–15:1	22:47–71	18:2–27
Jesus judged to die by Pilate	Friday (morning)	27:11–26	15:1–5	23:1–25	18:28–19:16
Jesus is killed on a cross	Friday	27:31–56	15:20–46	23:26–49	19:17–30
Jesus is buried	Friday to Sunday	27:57–66	15:42–47	23:50–56	19:31–42
Jesus' tomb found empty	Sunday	28:1–10	16:1–8	24:1–12	20:1–10
Jesus seen by Mary	Sunday		16:9–11		20:11–18
Jesus seen on Emmaus Road by two believers	Sunday		16:12–13	24:13–35	
Jesus comes to his disciples	Sunday		16:14	24:36–43	20:19–25

Jesus seen by many in the next 40 days!

INTRODUCTION TO THE BOOK OF

JOHN

John Tells About Jesus, the Son of God

WHO WROTE THIS BOOK?

Although he is not identified by name, but simply as "the follower Jesus loved" (13:23), John the apostle is the most likely author of this book. He is the only major apostle not named, and he clearly was an eyewitness to many of the major events of Jesus' ministry.

TO WHOM WAS THIS BOOK WRITTEN?

John uses some abstract concepts in his book (e.g., Jesus is called "the Word" in 1:1). This writing style makes some scholars believe the book was written for Greeks. But Jewish customs and feasts are also mentioned often, which argues for a Jewish readership. The author clearly had an evangelistic purpose (see 20:31), and the book speaks to both Jews and non-Jews.

WHERE WAS IT WRITTEN?

If the book was written late in the John's life, Ephesus would be the most likely place of its writing. If written earlier, it could have been written anywhere in Palestine.

WHEN WAS IT WRITTEN?

Latest evidence, including the Dead Sea Scrolls, indicate John likely wrote this book between A.D. 50 and 70.

WHAT IS THE BOOK ABOUT?

John wrote his account of the Good News of Jesus to present evidence that would lead people to believe that Jesus is the Christ, the Son of God (20:31). It begins with an exalted view of Christ as the eternal Word, the Creator of the universe (1:3). It contrasts his deity with the humanity of John the Baptist. John also presents several of Jesus' miracles and a number of startling claims about Jesus. He verifies Jesus' humanity (1:14).

WHY WAS THIS BOOK WRITTEN?

John's purpose was to produce faith in people that Jesus is the God-man anointed to be the Savior of the world. It presents Jesus' deity clearly and teaches more about the Holy Spirit than the other three accounts of the Good News.

SO WHAT DOES THIS BOOK MEAN TO US?

For us to have eternal life, we must see Jesus as he is. We must believe that he is the Son of God, sent down from heaven to lay down his life as the Son of Man so that we can be forgiven and saved. Because Jesus took our punishment for our sins, we should not expect to be punished again for those sins. We have eternal life because he died in our place.

SUMMARY:

Readers turning from the Books of Matthew, Mark, and Luke to the fourth account of the Good News will find themselves on less familiar territory. The first three accounts share a common outline and many common stories. But John presents extensive narrative material and sayings of Jesus not found in the other books. From earliest days, the Book of John was prized by those who discovered therein greater reflection on the significance of the story of Jesus for the whole world.

The purpose of the Book of John is stated openly in 20:31: "These are written so that you may believe that Jesus is the Christ, the Son of God. Then, by believing, you may have life through his name." When this is read within the larger narrative of the book, it becomes clear that John wrote especially for people who had come to follow Jesus in the several decades following the ministry of Jesus. These people had no firsthand interaction with the wonderful things Jesus had done during his earthly activity. John wants to encourage these people in their faith, as well as to clarify for them the ongoing significance of Jesus' work as the Messiah and Son of God.

One of the most striking features of the Book of John is its opening statements about the identity of Jesus. He is the "Word" who was "in the beginning." This is striking not only because it provides us with such a majestic view of Jesus but also because, in the chapters that follow, Jesus is never again called the "Word." This is part of John's strategy. He wants people to understand that Jesus is God's son, but he is aware that different people might understand Jesus' relationship to God as son in different ways. Therefore, he begins by using language that would have been more familiar, identifying Jesus as the Word—God's self-expression to humanity, in creation and in his coming to live with humans (1:14), Then, John identifies the Word as the Son of God (1:18) and uses the title Son of God to identify Jesus throughout the book.

John identifies Jesus in other ways, too. For example, John reports that Jesus used a series of "I am" sayings to describe his importance. Sometimes, Jesus is simply "I am"—that is, he uses a name for himself that reminds us of God's own name (see Exodus 3:14). At other times, Jesus is the way, the truth, and the life; the light of the world; the resurrection and the life; and so on. These are distinctive ways in which Jesus presents himself as the one who brings salvation to human beings.

What sort of salvation does Jesus bring? Salvation, according to John, is summarized in the words "eternal life." This is life with God. It begins now, as one comes to him through faith in Jesus, and continues forever. One does not have to wait for salvation, but begins to experience it now, in this world and at this time.

This suggests an additional emphasis. For John, salvation is very personal, but never focused simply on the individual. Individuals might come to faith in God through Jesus, but life is lived above all within the community of followers. This community is known for its unity and its selfless love. It is also known for its particular stance toward the world. The community of Jesus' followers lives in the world, but their lives together are not determined by the values of the world. What is more, just as the world-at-large is hostile toward God's truth, so it will be hostile toward God's people.

The Good News of John begins by taking God's story back to the beginning, even before the making of the world. The Word, John says, existed even before the world was created. However, the same Word that was active in the making of the universe is active now, to bring life to those who will believe.

JOHN

Christ Comes to the World

In the beginning there was the Word. The Word
was with God, and the Word was God.⚭
2He was with God in the beginning. 3All things
were made by him, and nothing was made without
him. 4In him there was life, and that life was the light
of all people.⚭ 5The Light shines in the darkness,
and the darkness has not overpowered it.⚭
6There was a man named John who was sent by
God. 7He came to tell people the truth about the
Light so that through him all people could hear
about the Light and believe.⚭ 8John was not the
Light, but he came to tell people the truth about
the Light. 9The true Light that gives light to all was
coming into the world!
10The Word was in the world, and the world
was made by him, but the world did not know
him. 11He came to the world that was his own,
but his own people did not accept him. 12But to
all who did accept him and believe in him he
gave the right to become children of God. 13They
did not become his children in any human way—
by any human parents or human desire. They were
born of God.
14The Word became a human and lived among
us. We saw his glory—the glory that belongs to the
only Son of the Father—and he was full of grace
and truth.⚭ 15John tells the truth about him and
cries out, saying, "This is the One I told you about:
'The One who comes after me is greater than I
am, because he was living before me.'"
16Because he was full of grace and truth, from
him we all received one gift after another. 17The
law was given through Moses, but grace and truth
came through Jesus Christ.⚭ 18No one has ever
seen God. But God the only Son is very close to the
Father, and he has shown us what God is like.⚭

John Tells People About Jesus

19Here is the truth John told when the leaders in
Jerusalem sent priests and Levites to ask him,
"Who are you?"
20John spoke freely and did not refuse to
answer. He said, "I am not the Christ."
21So they asked him, "Then who are you? Are
you Elijah?"⚭
He answered, "No, I am not."
"Are you the Prophet?" they asked.
He answered, "No."
22Then they said, "Who are you? Give us an
answer to tell those who sent us. What do you say
about yourself?"
23John told them in the words of the prophet
Isaiah:

"I am the voice of one
calling out in the desert:
'Make the road straight for the Lord.'" *Isaiah 40:3*

24Some Pharisees who had been sent asked John:
25"If you are not the Christ or Elijah or the Prophet,
why do you baptize people?"
26John answered, "I baptize with water, but there
is one here with you that you don't know about.
27He is the One who comes after me. I am not good
enough to untie the strings of his sandals."
28This all happened at Bethany on the other
side of the Jordan River, where John was baptizing people.
29The next day John saw Jesus coming toward
him. John said, "Look, the Lamb of God, who takes
away the sin of the world! 30This is the One I was
talking about when I said, 'A man will come after
me, but he is greater than I am, because he was
living before me.' 31Even I did not know who he

1:1 *Word.* The Greek word is *logos*, meaning any kind of communication; it could be translated "message." Here, it means Christ, because Christ was the way God told people about himself.

1:1 The coming of Christ to earth is described in terms very similar to the opening words of Genesis: *"In the beginning* God created the sky and the earth." With Jesus, there is a new beginning. This is in keeping with a theme that runs throughout the Old and New Testaments: God's salvation is a new creation.

⚭**1:1 Family:** Acts 2:17

⚭**1:1 Incarnation:** John 5:19

⚭**1:4 Luke:** Acts 1:1–3

⚭**1:5 Darkness:** John 3:19

1:6, 19 *John.* John the Baptist, who preached to people about Christ's coming (Matthew 3, Luke 3).

⚭**1:7 Blood:** Revelation 5:9

1:12–13 In the Book of John the first evangelical blessing to be named is adoption (1:12), and the climax of the first resurrection appearance is Jesus' statement that he was ascending to "my Father and your Father, to my God and your God" (20:17). Our sonship and God's fatherhood are not rooted in our being creatures of God. Rather, they result from our being spiritually "born of God." (See John 3:3–7.)

⚭**1:14 Glory:** 1 Peter 1:7

⚭**1:17 Grace:** John 8:1–11

⚭**1:17 Moses:** See article on page 209.

⚭**1:18 Communication:** Acts 2

⚭**1:18 Mediator:** John 14:6

⚭**1:18 Trinity:** John 10:30

1:18 *But . . . Father.* This could be translated, "But the only God is very close to the Father." Also, some Greek copies say, "But the only Son is very close to the Father."

1:21 *Elijah.* A prophet who spoke for God. He lived hundreds of years before Christ and was expected to return before Christ (Malachi 4:5-6).

1:21 *Prophet.* They probably meant the prophet that God told Moses he would send (Deuteronomy 18:15-19).

⚭**1:21 Elijah and Elisha:** James 5:17

1:29 *Lamb of God.* Name for Jesus. Jesus is like the lambs that were offered for a sacrifice to God.

was, although I came baptizing with water so that the people of Israel would know who he is."

32-33Then John said, "I saw the Spirit come down from heaven in the form of a dove and rest on him. Until then I did not know who the Christ was. But the God who sent me to baptize with water told me, 'You will see the Spirit come down and rest on a man; he is the One who will baptize with the Holy Spirit.' 34I have seen this happen, and I tell you the truth: This man is the Son of God."

The First Followers of Jesus

35The next day John was there again with two of his followers. 36When he saw Jesus walking by, he said, "Look, the Lamb of God!"[n]

37The two followers heard John say this, so they followed Jesus. 38When Jesus turned and saw them following him, he asked, "What are you looking for?"

They said, "Rabbi, where are you staying?" ("Rabbi" means "Teacher.")

39He answered, "Come and see." So the two men went with Jesus and saw where he was staying and stayed there with him that day. It was about four o'clock in the afternoon.

40One of the two men who followed Jesus after they heard John speak about him was Andrew, Simon Peter's brother. 41The first thing Andrew did was to find his brother Simon and say to him, "We have found the Messiah." ("Messiah" means "Christ.")

42Then Andrew took Simon to Jesus. Jesus looked at him and said, "You are Simon son of John. You will be called Cephas." ("Cephas" means "Peter.")

43The next day Jesus decided to go to Galilee. He found Philip and said to him, "Follow me."

44Philip was from the town of Bethsaida, where Andrew and Peter lived. 45Philip found Nathanael and told him, "We have found the man that Moses wrote about in the law, and the prophets also wrote about him. He is Jesus, the son of Joseph, from Nazareth."

46But Nathanael said to Philip, "Can anything good come from Nazareth?"

Philip answered, "Come and see."

47As Jesus saw Nathanael coming toward him, he said, "Here is truly an Israelite. There is nothing false in him."

48Nathanael asked, "How do you know me?"

Jesus answered, "I saw you when you were under the fig tree, before Philip told you about me."

49Then Nathanael said to Jesus, "Teacher, you are the Son of God; you are the King of Israel."

50Jesus said to Nathanael, "Do you believe simply because I told you I saw you under the fig tree? You will see greater things than that." 51And Jesus said to them, "I tell you the truth, you will all see heaven open and 'angels of God going up and coming down' on the Son of Man."

Traditional style houses in the town of Nazareth

The Wedding at Cana

2 Two days later there was a wedding in the town of Cana in Galilee. Jesus' mother was there, 2and Jesus and his followers were also invited to the wedding. 3When all the wine was gone, Jesus' mother said to him, "They have no more wine."

4Jesus answered, "Dear woman, why come to me? My time has not yet come."

5His mother said to the servants, "Do whatever he tells you to do."

6In that place there were six stone water jars that the Jews used in their washing ceremony. Each jar held about twenty or thirty gallons.

1:35 *John.* John the Baptist, who preached to people about Christ's coming (Matthew 3, Luke 3).

1:35 Disciple/Discipleship/Mentoring (Follow/Follower): John 8:31–32

1:35–40 We are not told that one of the two followers of John the Baptist, who followed after Jesus, was the apostle John (the other one's name, Andrew, is mentioned). But it is a reasonable assumption since it is clear that the author of this book and the reporter of this incident was an eyewitness. Of Jesus' early followers, the only one whose name is not explicitly mentioned is John, leaving "the beloved follower" as the most likely candidate.

1:42 *Peter.* The Greek name *Peter,* like the Aramaic name *Cephas,* means "rock."

1:42 Peter: John 6:68–69

1:51 *'angels . . . down.'* These words are from Genesis 28:12.

1:51 Evangelism: Acts 1:7–9

2:1–11 The exchange between Jesus and Mary at the wedding feast in Cana reveals the close relationship between the two, and the intuitive understanding Mary had of Jesus. This comes out most clearly when Mary gives instructions to the servants at the feast, "Do whatever he tells you to do." She had presented the problem; he had in effect asked her if she knew what she was asking; and then Mary simply leaves the matter in his hands.

2:4–5 An important theme in the Book of John concerns the proper "time," when the purpose for Jesus' coming will become clear.

2:5 Deborah: John 20:11–18

2:6 *washing ceremony.* The Jewish people washed themselves in special ways before eating, before worshiping in the Temple, and at other special times.

FREEDOM

GALATIANS 5

From a biblical viewpoint, what is freedom? How is freedom achieved? Who or what is the source of true freedom?

The Bible places great importance on freedom, or liberty, in the life of God's people. However, the biblical understanding of freedom is often very different from that of the world around us. In the world we think of freedom as personal liberty, that is, the ability to do whatever we choose without interference from others. Yet the Bible shows us that true freedom is possible only through a right relationship with God, and this gives us the liberty to live as we should. The apostle Paul makes this clear in his letter to the Galatians, where he reminds us that "Jesus gave himself for our sins to free us from this evil world we live in, as God the Father planned" (Galatians 1:4).

Although we often think of freedom as our "right," in the Bible it is a gift from God. This is clear throughout Scripture, in both the Old and New Testaments. In the Old Testament Book of Exodus, we see how God brought freedom to his people Israel. Out of love for his people and faithfulness to his promise, the Lord brought Israel out of slavery and into freedom (Deuteronomy 7:8-11). In the New Testament there is an emphasis on spiritual slavery, which is slavery to sin (John 8:34–36). Like the Israelites, we cannot free ourselves from our slavery, but must look to God for our release.

Our spiritual freedom in God is not "free": it was bought with a price. The apostle Paul tells us that "Christ took away the curse the law put on us [for not obeying God's law]. He changed places with us and put himself under that curse" (Galatians 3:13). The freedom we enjoy in God was bought with the death of Christ. On the cross "Jesus died so that by our believing we could receive the Spirit that God promised" (Galatians 3:14).

Having accepted this blessing, we can say to one another, "Let us come near to God with a sincere heart and a sure faith, because we have been made free from a guilty conscience, and our bodies have been washed with a pure water" (Hebrews 10:22).

True human freedom comes only from God through the gift of Jesus Christ and his death on the cross. Paul in Ephesians tells us that "In Christ we are set free by the blood of his death, and so we have forgiveness of sins. How rich is God's grace, which he has given to us so fully and freely" (Ephesians 1:7–8). Through faith in Christ Jesus we are released from our captivity to sin and into new life in the Spirit. Through the power of the Lord we are free, for "The Lord is the Spirit, and where the Spirit of the Lord is, there is freedom" (2 Corinthians 3:17). Yet as we know, the Bible teaches us that freedom requires obedience. In the Gospel of John, Jesus says, "If you continue to obey my teaching, you are truly my followers. Then you will know the truth, and the truth will make you free" (John 8:31–32).

The biblical principle that freedom leads to obedience conflicts with the view of personal liberty that we find in the world around us. Yet Christians are called to a new liberty, a new realm of freedom where we are no longer controlled by the power of evil thoughts, motives, and actions. Through the goodness of God we are set free from the rule of sin and death in our lives. In this new liberty we must exercise a thoughtful responsibility over our lives in order to keep a right relationship with him. This is why Paul says to the Galatians, "My brothers and sisters, God called you to be free, but do not use your freedom as an excuse to do what pleases your sinful self" (Galatians 5:13). In the same way, First Peter reminds us, "Now that you are obedient children of God do not live as you did in the past. You did not understand, so you did the evil things you wanted. But be holy in all you do, just as God, the One who called you, is holy" (1 Peter 1:14–15).

This gift of freedom in Christ brings with it a responsibility for others. For this reason Scripture cautions us, "But be careful that your freedom does not cause those who are weak in faith to fall into sin" (1 Corinthians 8:9). This means that we as Christians should be careful how we use our freedom in Christ, because we must not let our choices cause others to lose their freedom through sin.

Put another way, biblical freedom is the freedom to love God and to love our neighbors as ourselves (Matthew 22:36–40). In this way, free Christian believers fulfill the law even though we are no longer under bondage to it. We are freed by Christ to live in the Spirit with joy, love, and courage each day of our lives (Romans 8:3–4; Galatians 5:13–26). This is because we have a sure hope in God, who has promised that some day "everything God made would be set free from ruin to have the freedom and glory that belong to God's children" (Romans 8:21).

Freedom: For additional scriptures on this topic go to Exodus 3:4–15.

GRACE

EPHESIANS 2

What is grace? What can we do to receive God's grace?

The word *grace* is a common and important word in the New Testament. Sometimes it simply means "thanks," but there is a much more profound usage of the term that is sometimes translated as "free gift" (Romans 4:16). Grace is God's gift of love, forgiveness, strength, and mercy. God's grace fills the pages of the New Testament and is evident in places where the word itself does not appear.

In Luke 15, the description Jesus gave of God's love describes God's grace. The chapter opens with religious leaders complaining about Jesus' eating with "tax collectors and sinners," associations not religiously acceptable (Luke 15:1–2). In reply, Jesus told three famous stories about God's grace: the lost sheep, the lost coin, and the lost son. God is like the persistent shepherd who leaves behind ninety-nine sheep, risking their safety to find the one lost sheep, looking until it is found (15:3–7). God is like the woman who loses one of her dowry coins and searches the whole house until it is found (15:8–10). God is like the generous father, who gives his son freedom to waste his life and inheritance, and then accepts him back with open arms (15:11–32). God rejoices "over one sinner who changes his heart and life" (15:7, 10), and is like the father who threw a huge celebration at the event (15:22–24). God is generous and persistent and patient in his willingness to forgive and accept those who have fallen short of his standards, when they repent and return to him.

God's grace is forgiving and merciful and mystifies those who think themselves to be morally good. In John 8:1–11, Jesus demonstrated God's forgiving grace toward a woman who "was caught having sexual relations with a man who is not her husband" (John 8:4). The religious leaders expected Jesus to condemn her, but instead by his actions he showed that God is merciful rather than condemnatory. In Jesus' punch line we find a simple summary of grace: "I also don't judge you guilty. You may go now, but don't sin anymore" (8:11). In this last sentence grace has a moral demand (as in Luke 15:7, 10, 21): God's grace, though abounding, creates and demands a change in our lives. By God's grace we are forgiven—by God's gift of grace we are enabled to stop sinning (see Romans 5:12–6:2; Titus 2:11–14; 1 Peter 1:13–16).

God's grace is found in Jesus Christ, and Christ is God's gift of mercy. "The law was given through Moses, but grace and truth came through Jesus Christ" (John 1:17; see 2 Timothy 2:1). We can never hope to earn God's gift of forgiveness, which is found only by knowing Jesus Christ as Lord (Philippians 3:3–11; 2 Peter 3:18). Those who know God's salvation from sin and its punishment know that it is based on God's kindness in Christ: "by God's grace, he died for everyone" (Hebrews 2:9). It is no coincidence that the Bible ends with this rich blessing, "The grace of the Lord Jesus be with all. Amen" (Revelation 22:21).

Paul used *grace* more than any other New Testament writer (100 of the 155 times it is used). In Ephesians 2:4–10 he made explicit what has been said above: "God's mercy is great, and he loved us very much" (2:4). "You have been saved by God's grace" (2:5). "I mean that you have been saved by grace through believing. You did not save yourselves; it was a gift from God" (2:8). Grace means that God's blessing in our lives is his initiative rather than ours, that God's mercy and love are bountiful, and that forgiveness and being saved from sin and its punishment are God's free gift. In Ephesians 2:9 it says that God's gift of forgiveness "was not the result of your own efforts, so you cannot brag about it." Grace, by definition, is not deserved or earned but given.

There is something about our human pride toward God that causes us to misinterpret God's gift of grace as the natural result of our own efforts and abilities (James 4:6). We see this in the story of the lost son in Luke 15, where the older brother represents the rational resistance we feel to God's forgiving love. The whole story shocks us to an awareness of God's amazing grace. Paul notes this same attitude in Ephesians 2:8–9 and Philippians 3:4–7, and describes a personal lesson he learned through a "painful physical problem" (2 Corinthians 12:7). It is in our helplessness that we often learn God's gracious gift of love, strength, and mercy. Those who want God's strength find it best in their own humility, by reaching out to God, by admitting need. It took a clear and persistent weakness for Paul to realize this important lesson about God's grace—then the Lord said to him, "My grace is sufficient for you. When you are weak, my power is made perfect in you" (2 Corinthians 12:9).

Grace: For additional scriptures on this topic go to Matthew 5:3–10.

7Jesus said to the servants, "Fill the jars with
water." So they filled the jars to the top.
8Then he said to them, "Now take some out and
give it to the master of the feast."
So they took the water to the master. 9When he
tasted it, the water had become wine. He did not
know where the wine came from, but the servants
who had brought the water knew. The master of
the wedding called the bridegroom 10and said to
him, "People always serve the best wine first.
Later, after the guests have been drinking awhile,
they serve the cheaper wine. But you have saved
the best wine till now."
11So in Cana of Galilee Jesus did his first miracle. There he showed his glory, and his followers
believed in him.

Jesus in the Temple

12After this, Jesus went to the town of Capernaum
with his mother, brothers, and followers. They
stayed there for just a few days. 13When it was
almost time for the Jewish Passover Feast, Jesus
went to Jerusalem. 14In the Temple he found
people selling cattle, sheep, and doves. He saw
others sitting at tables, exchanging different
kinds of money. 15Jesus made a whip out of cords
and forced all of them, both the sheep and cattle,
to leave the Temple. He turned over the tables and
scattered the money of those who were exchanging
it. 16Then he said to those who were selling pigeons,
"Take these things out of here! Don't make my
Father's house a place for buying and selling!"
17When this happened, the followers remembered
what was written in the Scriptures: "My strong love
for your Temple completely controls me."
18Some of his people said to Jesus, "Show us a
miracle to prove you have the right to do these
things."
19Jesus answered them, "Destroy this temple,
and I will build it again in three days."
20They answered, "It took forty-six years to build
this Temple! Do you really believe you can build it
again in three days?"
21(But the temple Jesus meant was his own body.
22After Jesus was raised from the dead, his followers
remembered that Jesus had said this. Then they
believed the Scripture and the words Jesus had said.)
23When Jesus was in Jerusalem for the Passover
Feast, many people believed in him because they
saw the miracles he did. 24But Jesus did not trust
himself to them because he knew them all. 25He
did not need anyone to tell him about people,
because he knew what was in people's minds.

Nicodemus Comes to Jesus

3 There was a man named Nicodemus who was
one of the Pharisees and an important Jewish
leader. 2One night Nicodemus came to Jesus and
said, "Teacher, we know you are a teacher sent
from God, because no one can do the miracles you
do unless God is with him."
3Jesus answered, "I tell you the truth, unless one
is born again, he cannot be in God's kingdom."
4Nicodemus said, "But if a person is already old,
how can he be born again? He cannot enter his
mother's body again. So how can a person be born
a second time?"
5But Jesus answered, "I tell you the truth, unless
one is born from water and the Spirit, he cannot
enter God's kingdom. 6Human life comes from
human parents, but spiritual life comes from the
Spirit. 7Don't be surprised when I tell you, 'You
must all be born again.' 8The wind blows where it
wants to and you hear the sound of it, but you don't
know where the wind comes from or where it is
going. It is the same with every person who is born
from the Spirit."
9Nicodemus asked, "How can this happen?"
10Jesus said, "You are an important teacher in
Israel, and you don't understand these things? 11I
tell you the truth, we talk about what we know,
and we tell about what we have seen, but you don't
accept what we tell you. 12I have told you about
things here on earth, and you do not believe me.
So you will not believe me if I tell you about things
of heaven. 13The only one who has ever gone up to
heaven is the One who came down from heaven—
the Son of Man.

2:10 Celebration: John 7:37–38

2:11 Marriage: 1 Corinthians 7:1–40

2:12 Family: Mark 7:8

2:13 Feasts/Festivals: John 6:4

2:17 *"My . . . me."* Quotation from Psalm 69:9.

2:19–21 Jesus here refers to his body as the temple. The Temple was the building in which God caused his glory to dwell and symbolized his presence with his people in the land. Jesus' body is the temple in that he is God dwelling among humankind (John 1:14). He here anticipates his crucifixion and resurrection, though his hearers do not immediately understand the reference.

2:25 Miracles: John 9

3:3 When Jesus told Nicodemus that "unless one is born again, he cannot be in God's kingdom," he was talking about the change that is sometimes called conversion. The Greek word can mean either "again" or "from above," which indicates that people who accept and obey Jesus as Lord and Savior take on a new identity and become new persons through him.

3:3–4 Jesus uses a play on words that Nicodemus does not understand. To be "born again" is to be born "from above." With this phrase Jesus refers to the necessity of the new work of the Holy Spirit through which one enters new life with God.

3:8 Holy Spirit: John 14:15–17

14“Just as Moses lifted up the snake in the desert,
the Son of Man must also be lifted up. 15So that everyone who believes can have eternal life in him.
16“God loved the world so much that he gave
his one and only Son so that whoever believes in
him may not be lost, but have eternal life. 17God
did not send his Son into the world to judge the
world guilty, but to save the world through him.
18People who believe in God’s Son are not judged
guilty. Those who do not believe have already been
judged guilty, because they have not believed in
God’s one and only Son. 19They are judged by this
fact: The Light has come into the world, but they did
not want light. They wanted darkness, because they
were doing evil things. 20All who do evil hate the
light and will not come to the light, because it will
show all the evil things they do. 21But those who
follow the true way come to the light, and it shows
that the things they do were done through God.”

Jesus and John the Baptist

22After this, Jesus and his followers went into the
area of Judea, where he stayed with his followers
and baptized people. 23John was also baptizing in
Aenon, near Salim, because there was plenty of
water there. People were going there to be baptized.
24(This was before John was put into prison.)
25Some of John’s followers had an argument with
a Jew about religious washing. 26So they came to
John and said, “Teacher, remember the man who
was with you on the other side of the Jordan
River, the one you spoke about so much? He is
baptizing, and everyone is going to him.”
27John answered, “A man can get only what God
gives him. 28You yourselves heard me say, ‘I am
not the Christ, but I am the one sent to prepare
the way for him.’ 29The bride belongs only to the
bridegroom. But the friend who helps the bridegroom stands by and listens to him. He is thrilled
that he gets to hear the bridegroom’s voice. In the
same way, I am really happy. 30He must become
greater, and I must become less important.

The One Who Comes from Heaven

31“The One who comes from above is greater
than all. The one who is from the earth belongs to
the earth and talks about things on the earth. But the
One who comes from heaven is greater than all.
32He tells what he has seen and heard, but no one
accepts what he says. 33Whoever accepts what he
says has proven that God is true. 34The One
whom God sent speaks the words of God, because
God gives him the Spirit fully. 35The Father loves
the Son and has given him power over everything.
36Those who believe in the Son have eternal life,
but those who do not obey the Son will never have
life. God’s anger stays on them.”

Jesus and a Samaritan Woman

4 The Pharisees heard that Jesus was making and
baptizing more followers than John, 2although
Jesus himself did not baptize people, but his followers did. 3Jesus knew that the Pharisees had
heard about him, so he left Judea and went back
to Galilee. 4But on the way he had to go through
the country of Samaria.
5In Samaria Jesus came to the town called
Sychar, which is near the field Jacob gave to his
son Joseph. 6Jacob’s well was there. Jesus was tired
from his long trip, so he sat down beside the well.
It was about twelve o’clock noon. 7When a Samaritan woman came to the well to get some water,

3:14 *Moses . . . desert.* When the Israelites were dying from snake bites, God told Moses to put a brass snake on a pole. The people who looked at the snake were healed (Numbers 21:4-9).

3:16 Immortality: John 9:2

3:16 Love: John 13:34–35

3:16 Mission: Acts 15:1–35

3:16 Reconciliation: Acts 2:37–39

3:16 World/Worldly: John 17:15

3:19 Darkness: John 12:35

3:20 Hate: John 15:23–25

3:21 Gospel/Good News: Romans 1:16

3:22–36 There can be little doubt, in view of John 3–4, that Jesus’ followers, some of whom had originally been John’s followers, took John’s baptism in earnest as their own practice, not least because Jesus’ acceptance of baptism at the hands of John showed Jesus approved of it. There continued to be, well into the first century AD, a certain overlap of the followers of John and of Jesus (cf. Acts 18:25, 19:3–4), and John’s baptism continued to be practiced. As such it reminded one and all that cleansing and passing over from the unholy to the holy had always been God’s call first to the Israelites as they left Egypt and crossed Jordan into the Promised Land, and then to all people. The Jordan was and remains a symbol of the cleansing, holiness and new life God can give, and a symbol that God indeed fulfills the Old Testament promises of life, land, and descendants that were first promised to the forefather of all believers—Abraham.

3:25 *religious washing.* The Jewish people washed themselves in special ways before eating, before worshiping in the Temple, and at other special times.

3:33 John the Baptist: Acts 19:1–7

3:36 God’s wrath is directed against sin. That is, he cannot permit sin to go unpunished, so he chose in love to provide a substitute who would experience his wrath against sin. He chose his own Son to be the sin-bearer for all mankind. If human beings reject his son as their savior, then God’s wrath will be directed at them on the day of judgment.

3:36 God’s Anger: Ephesians 5:1–7

4 Jesus’ conversation with this woman is astounding, not only because of the rigid cultural boundary between men and women, but also because she is a Samaritan. Jesus’ own followers are stumped as to what Jesus might be doing with this woman (4:27–27). But they, unlike the woman, are timid about approaching Jesus with their questions. By crossing the cultural gulf between them, Jesus finds an inquisitive and spiritually astute woman who becomes a means by which many others from her town come to faith in him (4:39–42).

Jesus said to her, "Please give me a drink." 8(This happened while Jesus' followers were in town buying some food.)

9The woman said, "I am surprised that you ask me for a drink, since you are a Jewish man and I am a Samaritan woman." (Jewish people are not friends with Samaritans.)

10Jesus said, "If you only knew the free gift of God and who it is that is asking you for water, you would have asked him, and he would have given you living water."

11The woman said, "Sir, where will you get this living water? The well is very deep, and you have nothing to get water with. 12Are you greater than Jacob, our father, who gave us this well and drank from it himself along with his sons and flocks?"

13Jesus answered, "Everyone who drinks this water will be thirsty again, 14but whoever drinks the water I give will never be thirsty. The water I give will become a spring of water gushing up inside that person, giving eternal life."

15The woman said to him, "Sir, give me this water so I will never be thirsty again and will not have to come back here to get more water."

16Jesus told her, "Go get your husband and come back here."

17The woman answered, "I have no husband."

Jesus said to her, "You are right to say you have no husband. 18Really you have had five husbands, and the man you live with now is not your husband. You told the truth."

19The woman said, "Sir, I can see that you are a prophet. 20Our ancestors worshiped on this mountain, but you say that Jerusalem is the place where people must worship."

21Jesus said, "Believe me, woman. The time is coming when neither in Jerusalem nor on this mountain will you actually worship the Father. 22You Samaritans worship something you don't understand. We understand what we worship, because salvation comes from the Jews. 23The time is coming when the true worshipers will worship the Father in spirit and truth, and that time is here already. You see, the Father too is actively seeking such people to worship him. 24God is spirit, and those who worship him must worship in spirit and truth."

25The woman said, "I know that the Messiah is coming." (Messiah is the One called Christ.) "When the Messiah comes, he will explain everything to us."

26Then Jesus said, "I am he—I, the one talking to you."

27Just then his followers came back from town and were surprised to see him talking with a woman. But none of them asked, "What do you want?" or "Why are you talking with her?"

28Then the woman left her water jar and went back to town. She said to the people, 29"Come and see a man who told me everything I ever did. Do you think he might be the Christ?" 30So the people left the town and went to see Jesus.

31Meanwhile, his followers were begging him, "Teacher, eat something."

32But Jesus answered, "I have food to eat that you know nothing about."

33So the followers asked themselves, "Did somebody already bring him food?"

34Jesus said, "My food is to do what the One who sent me wants me to do and to finish his work. 35You have a saying, 'Four more months till harvest.' But I tell you, open your eyes and look at the fields ready for harvest now. 36Already, the one who harvests is being paid and is gathering crops for eternal life. So the one who plants and the one who harvests celebrate at the same time. 37Here the saying is true, 'One person plants, and another harvests.' 38I sent you to harvest a crop that you did not work on. Others did the work, and you get to finish up their work."

39Many of the Samaritans in that town believed in Jesus because of what the woman said: "He told me everything I ever did." 40When the Samaritans came to Jesus, they begged him to stay with them, so he stayed there two more days. 41And many more believed because of the things he said.

4:9 *Jewish people . . . Samaritans.* This can also be translated "Jewish people don't use things that Samaritans have used." Jewish people and Samaritans have a long history of disagreements leading back to the time of King Solomon. Though the two kingdoms were united during his reign, after his death they promptly split into the northern kingdom, which was centered in a city called Samaria, and a southern kingdom, which was centered in a city called Jerusalem. Later in its history, the Samaritans worshiped on a mountain called Gerezim, while the southern kingdom worshiped on a mountain called Zion. Samaria's pursuit of false gods led to its final destruction and to the disbursement of the Israelites.

4:14 Water: See article on page 499.

4:21–24 Jesus' words to the Samaritan woman are nothing short of revolutionary. During the Old Testament period God revealed himself only under special circumstances to his people at certain locations. Most often God made his presence known at the sanctuary—first the Holy Tent and then the Temple. There was a disagreement between Samaritans and Judeans over the proper location to worship God. The former thought that God was present on Mount Gerezim near Shechem, while the latter felt God was present on Mount Zion in Jerusalem. Jesus looks to the future where God, who is spirit, will make his presence felt everywhere. Jesus himself is the presence of God, and when he died the curtain of the Temple was torn in half (Matthew 27:51), showing that there was no longer any special holy place. We can now meet God anywhere.

4:34 Ambition: Acts 10:28–29

4:38 *I . . . their work.* As a farmer sends workers to harvest grain, Jesus sends his followers out to bring people to God.

42They said to the woman, "First we believed in Jesus because of your speech, but now we believe because we heard him ourselves. We know that this man really is the Savior of the world."

Jesus Heals an Officer's Son

43Two days later, Jesus left and went to Galilee. 44(Jesus had said before that a prophet is not respected in his own country.) 45When Jesus arrived in Galilee, the people there welcomed him. They had seen all the things he did at the Passover Feast in Jerusalem, because they had been there, too.

46Jesus went again to visit Cana in Galilee where he had changed the water into wine. One of the king's important officers lived in the city of Capernaum, and his son was sick. 47When he heard that Jesus had come from Judea to Galilee, he went to Jesus and begged him to come to Capernaum and heal his son, because his son was almost dead. 48Jesus said to him, "You people must see signs and miracles before you will believe in me."

49The officer said, "Sir, come before my child dies."

50Jesus answered, "Go. Your son will live."

The man believed what Jesus told him and went home. 51On the way the man's servants came and met him and told him, "Your son is alive."

52The man asked, "What time did my son begin to get well?"

They answered, "Yesterday at one o'clock the fever left him."

53The father knew that one o'clock was the exact time that Jesus had said, "Your son will live." So the man and all the people who lived in his house believed in Jesus.

54That was the second miracle Jesus did after coming from Judea to Galilee.

Jesus Heals a Man at a Pool

5 Later Jesus went to Jerusalem for a special feast. 2In Jerusalem there is a pool with five covered porches, which is called Bethzatha in the Hebrew language. This pool is near the Sheep Gate. 3Many sick people were lying on the porches beside the pool. Some were blind, some were crippled, and some were paralyzed.* 5A man was lying there who had been sick for thirty-eight years. 6When Jesus saw the man and knew that he had been sick for such a long time, Jesus asked him, "Do you want to be well?"

7The sick man answered, "Sir, there is no one to help me get into the pool when the water starts moving. While I am coming to the water, someone else always gets in before me."

8Then Jesus said, "Stand up. Pick up your mat and walk." 9And immediately the man was well; he picked up his mat and began to walk.

The day this happened was a Sabbath day. 10So the Jews said to the man who had been healed, "Today is the Sabbath. It is against our law for you to carry your mat on the Sabbath day."

11But he answered, "The man who made me well told me, 'Pick up your mat and walk.'"

12Then they asked him, "Who is the man who told you to pick up your mat and walk?"

13But the man who had been healed did not know who it was, because there were many people in that place, and Jesus had left.

14Later, Jesus found the man at the Temple and said to him, "See, you are well now. Stop sinning so that something worse does not happen to you."

15Then the man left and told his people that Jesus was the one who had made him well.

16Because Jesus was doing this on the Sabbath day, some evil people began to persecute him. 17But Jesus said to them, "My Father never stops working, and so I keep working, too."

18This made them try still harder to kill him. They said, "First Jesus was breaking the law about the Sabbath day. Now he says that God is his own Father, making himself equal with God!"

Jesus Has God's Authority

19But Jesus said, "I tell you the truth, the Son can do nothing alone. The Son does only what he sees the Father doing, because the Son does whatever the Father does. 20The Father loves the Son and shows the Son all the things he himself does. But

5:1 The organization of the Book of John reflects a high degree of sensitivity to the festivals of Judaism. John 5:1 probably refers to Feast of Weeks, or Pentecost. Passover is referred to in 2:13 and 6:4; the Feast of Shelters, or Tabernacles, in 7:1–2 and following, and Hanukkuh, or the Feast of Dedication, in 10:22. Jesus' claims for himself often take up and exploit the concepts of these festivals. In John 7:38 Jesus picks up on the ritual of the Feast of Shelters where the priest pours out a drink of water on the altar and says that "rivers of living water" shall flow from those who believe in him. In John 6 Jesus takes the idea of "bread" from Passover and Exodus narratives and claims to be the "Bread from Heaven." Jesus walks in the Temple during the festival that celebrates the rededication of the Temple (10:22) and challenges his hearers to believe that he is one with the Father (10:30). The concepts and ideas behind the Jewish feasts are continually applied to Jesus in John with the suggestion that Jesus fulfills the meaning and the hope of these festivals.

5:2 *Bethzatha.* Also called Bethsaida or Bethesda, it is a pool of water north of the Temple in Jerusalem.

5:2 *Hebrew language.* Hebrew, or Aramaic, the languages of many people in this region in the first century.

***5:3** *Verse 3.* Some Greek copies add "and they waited for the water to move." A few later copies add verse 4: "Sometimes an angel of the Lord came down to the pool and stirred up the water. After the angel did this, the first person to go into the pool was healed from any sickness he had."

5:18 Anti-Semitism: John 7:13

5:19 Incarnation: John 10:30

the Father will show the Son even greater things
than this so that you can all be amazed. 21Just as
the Father raises the dead and gives them life, so
also the Son gives life to those he wants to. 22In
fact, the Father judges no one, but he has given
the Son power to do all the judging 23so that all
people will honor the Son as much as they honor
the Father. Anyone who does not honor the Son
does not honor the Father who sent him.

24"I tell you the truth, whoever hears what I say
and believes in the One who sent me has eternal life.
That person will not be judged guilty but has already
left death and entered life. 25I tell you the truth, the
time is coming and is already here when the dead
will hear the voice of the Son of God, and those who
hear will have life. 26Life comes from the Father himself, and he has allowed the Son to have life in himself as well. 27And the Father has given the Son the
power to judge, because he is the Son of Man.
28Don't be surprised at this: A time is coming when
all who are dead and in their graves will hear his
voice. 29Then they will come out of their graves.
Those who did good will rise and have life forever,
but those who did evil will rise to be judged guilty.

Jesus Is God's Son

30"I can do nothing alone. I judge only the way
I am told, so my judgment is fair. I don't try to
please myself, but I try to please the One who
sent me.

31"If only I tell people about myself, what I say is
not true. 32But there is another who tells about me,
and I know that the things he says about me are true.

33"You have sent people to John, and he has told
you the truth. 34It is not that I accept such human
telling; I tell you this so you can be saved. 35John
was like a burning and shining lamp, and you
were happy to enjoy his light for a while.

36"But I have a proof about myself that is greater
than that of John. The things I do, which are the
things my Father gave me to do, prove that the
Father sent me. 37And the Father himself who
sent me has given proof about me. You have never
heard his voice or seen what he looks like. 38His
teaching does not live in you, because you don't
believe in the One the Father sent. 39You carefully
study the Scriptures because you think they give
you eternal life. They do in fact tell about me,
40but you refuse to come to me to have that life.

41"I don't need praise from people. 42But I know
you—I know that you don't have God's love in you.
43I have come from my Father and speak for him,
but you don't accept me. But when another person
comes, speaking only for himself, you will accept
him. 44You try to get praise from each other, but
you do not try to get the praise that comes from the
only God. So how can you believe? 45Don't think
that I will stand before the Father and say you are
wrong. The one who says you are wrong is Moses,
the one you hoped would save you. 46If you really
believed Moses, you would believe me, because
Moses wrote about me. 47But if you don't believe
what Moses wrote, how can you believe what I say?"

More than Five Thousand Fed

6 After this, Jesus went across Lake Galilee (or,
Lake Tiberias). 2Many people followed him
because they saw the miracles he did to heal the
sick. 3Jesus went up on a hill and sat down there
with his followers. 4It was almost the time for the
Jewish Passover Feast.

5When Jesus looked up and saw a large crowd
coming toward him, he said to Philip, "Where can
we buy enough bread for all these people to eat?"
6(Jesus asked Philip this question to test him, because
Jesus already knew what he planned to do.)

7Philip answered, "We would all have to work
a month to buy enough bread for each person to
have only a little piece."

8Another one of his followers, Andrew, Simon
Peter's brother, said, 9"Here is a boy with five
loaves of barley bread and two little fish, but that
is not enough for so many people."

10Jesus said, "Tell the people to sit down." This
was a very grassy place, and about five thousand
men sat down there. 11Then Jesus took the loaves of
bread, thanked God for them, and gave them to the
people who were sitting there. He did the same
with the fish, giving as much as the people wanted.

12When they had all had enough to eat, Jesus
said to his followers, "Gather the leftover pieces of
fish and bread so that nothing is wasted." 13So they
gathered up the pieces and filled twelve baskets
with the pieces left from the five barley loaves.

14When the people saw this miracle that Jesus
did, they said, "He must truly be the Prophet who
is coming into the world."

15Jesus knew that the people planned to come
and take him by force and make him their king,
so he left and went into the hills alone.

5:23 Father: John 20:17

5:28–29 John tells us that it will be Jesus' voice that raises the dead to life again and gives them resurrection bodies. Both the saved and the lost will be raised, the former to enjoy the blessings of the eternal kingdom of Christ, but the latter to face a judgment of condemnation for their sins. Whether eternal life or eternal judgment, both will be spent in resurrection bodies.

5:30 Will of God: John 6:38

5:36 Career/Careerism: John 9:4

6:4 Feasts/Festivals: John 7:2

6:14 *Prophet.* They probably meant the prophet that God told Moses he would send (Deuteronomy 18:15-19).

Jesus Walks on the Water

16That evening Jesus' followers went down to
Lake Galilee. 17It was dark now, and Jesus had not
yet come to them. The followers got into a boat
and started across the lake to Capernaum. 18By
now a strong wind was blowing, and the waves
on the lake were getting bigger. 19When they had
rowed the boat about three or four miles, they saw
Jesus walking on the water, coming toward the
boat. The followers were afraid, 20but Jesus said to
them, "It is I. Do not be afraid." 21Then they were
glad to take him into the boat. At once the boat came
to land at the place where they wanted to go.

The People Seek Jesus

22The next day the people who had stayed on
the other side of the lake knew that Jesus had not
gone in the boat with his followers but that they
had left without him. And they knew that only
one boat had been there. 23But then some boats
came from Tiberias and landed near the place where
the people had eaten the bread after the Lord had
given thanks. 24When the people saw that Jesus
and his followers were not there now, they got into
boats and went to Capernaum to find Jesus.

Jesus, the Bread of Life

25When the people found Jesus on the other side
of the lake, they asked him, "Teacher, when did
you come here?"
26Jesus answered, "I tell you the truth, you aren't
looking for me because you saw me do miracles.
You are looking for me because you ate the bread
and were satisfied. 27Don't work for the food that
spoils. Work for the food that stays good always
and gives eternal life. The Son of Man will give you
this food, because on him God the Father has put
his power."
28The people asked Jesus, "What are the things
God wants us to do?"
29Jesus answered, "The work God wants you to
do is this: Believe the One he sent."
30So the people asked, "What miracle will you
do? If we see a miracle, we will believe you. What
will you do? 31Our fathers ate the manna in the
desert. This is written in the Scriptures: 'He gave
them bread from heaven to eat.'"
32Jesus said, "I tell you the truth, it was not Moses
who gave you bread from heaven; it is my Father
who is giving you the true bread from heaven.
33God's bread is the One who comes down from
heaven and gives life to the world."
34The people said, "Sir, give us this bread
always."
35Then Jesus said, "I am the bread that gives life.
Whoever comes to me will never be hungry, and
whoever believes in me will never be thirsty. 36But
as I told you before, you have seen me and still don't
believe. 37The Father gives me my people. Every
one of them will come to me, and I will always
accept them. 38I came down from heaven to do what
God wants me to do, not what I want to do.
39Here is what the One who sent me wants me to
do: I must not lose even one whom God gave me,
but I must raise them all on the last day. 40Those
who see the Son and believe in him have eternal
life, and I will raise them on the last day. This is
what my Father wants."
41Some people began to complain about Jesus
because he said, "I am the bread that comes down
from heaven." 42They said, "This is Jesus, the son
of Joseph. We know his father and mother. How
can he say, 'I came down from heaven'?"
43But Jesus answered, "Stop complaining to
each other. 44The Father is the One who sent me.
No one can come to me unless the Father draws
him to me, and I will raise that person up on the
last day. 45It is written in the prophets, 'They will
all be taught by God.' Everyone who listens to the
Father and learns from him comes to me. 46No
one has seen the Father except the One who is
from God; only he has seen the Father. 47I tell you
the truth, whoever believes has eternal life. 48I
am the bread that gives life. 49Your ancestors ate
the manna in the desert, but still they died.
50Here is the bread that comes down from
heaven. Anyone who eats this bread will never
die. 51I am the living bread that came down from
heaven. Anyone who eats this bread will live forever. This bread is my flesh, which I will give up
so that the world may have life."
52Then the evil people began to argue among
themselves, saying, "How can this man give us his
flesh to eat?"
53Jesus said, "I tell you the truth, you must eat the
flesh of the Son of Man and drink his blood. Otherwise, you won't have real life in you. 54Those who
eat my flesh and drink my blood have eternal life,

6:16–21 *Lake.* According to some Old Testament passages, the lake (or "sea") was occupied by an evil power and represented chaos; one of the Old Testament pictures of God concerns his mastery of the sea, his overcoming of evil (see, for example, Psalms 65:7; 74:13–14; 89:9; 104:4–9; 106:9; 107:25–30). In this scene, Jesus both walks on water and speaks words that remind us of God's own name, "It is I" (see Exodus 3:14). In relating this story, then, John shows us that God's power is at work in Jesus in a unique way.

6:31 *'He gave . . . eat.'* Quotation from Psalm 78:24.

6:38 Will of God: John 7:17–18

6:45 *'They . . . God.'* Quotation from Isaiah 54:13.

and I will raise them up on the last day. 55My flesh is true food, and my blood is true drink. 56Those who eat my flesh and drink my blood live in me, and I live in them. 57The living Father sent me, and I live because of the Father. So whoever eats me will live because of me. 58I am not like the bread your ancestors ate. They ate that bread and still died. I am the bread that came down from heaven, and whoever eats this bread will live forever." 59Jesus said all these things while he was teaching in the synagogue in Capernaum.

The Words of Eternal Life

60When the followers of Jesus heard this, many of them said, "This teaching is hard. Who can accept it?"

61Knowing that his followers were complaining about this, Jesus said, "Does this teaching bother you? 62Then will it also bother you to see the Son of Man going back to the place where he came from? 63It is the Spirit that gives life. The flesh doesn't give life. The words I told you are spirit, and they give life. 64But some of you don't believe." (Jesus knew from the beginning who did not believe and who would turn against him.) 65Jesus said, "That is the reason I said, 'If the Father does not bring a person to me, that one cannot come.'"

66After Jesus said this, many of his followers left him and stopped following him.

67Jesus asked the twelve followers, "Do you want to leave, too?"

68Simon Peter answered him, "Lord, where would we go? You have the words that give eternal life. 69We believe and know that you are the Holy One from God."

70Then Jesus answered, "I chose all twelve of you, but one of you is a devil."

71Jesus was talking about Judas, the son of Simon Iscariot. Judas was one of the twelve, but later he was going to turn against Jesus.

Jesus' Brothers Don't Believe

7 After this, Jesus traveled around Galilee. He did not want to travel in Judea, because some evil people there wanted to kill him. 2It was time for the Feast of Shelters. 3So Jesus' brothers said to him, "You should leave here and go to Judea so your followers there can see the miracles you do. 4Anyone who wants to be well known does not hide what he does. If you are doing these things, show yourself to the world." 5(Even Jesus' brothers did not believe in him.)

6Jesus said to his brothers, "The right time for me has not yet come, but any time is right for you. 7The world cannot hate you, but it hates me, because I tell it the evil things it does. 8So you go to the feast. I will not go yet to this feast, because the right time for me has not yet come." 9After saying this, Jesus stayed in Galilee.

10But after Jesus' brothers had gone to the feast, Jesus went also. But he did not let people see him. 11At the feast some people were looking for him and saying, "Where is that man?"

12Within the large crowd there, many people were whispering to each other about Jesus. Some said, "He is a good man."

Others said, "No, he fools the people." 13But no one was brave enough to talk about Jesus openly, because they were afraid of the older leaders.

Jesus Teaches at the Feast

14When the feast was about half over, Jesus went to the Temple and began to teach. 15The people were amazed and said, "This man has never studied in school. How did he learn so much?"

16Jesus answered, "The things I teach are not my own, but they come from him who sent me. 17If people choose to do what God wants, they will know that my teaching comes from God and not from me. 18Those who teach their own ideas are trying to get honor for themselves. But those who try to bring honor to the one who sent him speak the truth, and there is nothing false in them. 19Moses gave you the law, but none of you obeys that law. Why are you trying to kill me?"

20The people answered, "A demon has come into you. We are not trying to kill you."

21Jesus said to them, "I did one miracle, and you are all amazed. 22Moses gave you the law about circumcision. (But really Moses did not give you

---

6:60–66 During the beginning stages of Jesus' ministry, a large, radical group of followers attached themselves to him. Some, apparently thinking that he was merely a revolutionary prophet, left Jesus when he disappointed their expectations (John 6:60–66). They seemed to be looking for a leader to overthrow the Romans and restore the rule to Israel. Many of them left their homes and jobs to follow Jesus; some were even ready to die for their cause. When Jesus didn't do things their way, they left him.

6:60–71 It seems clear that Judas was among the followers who were disillusioned when Jesus refused to allow the crowd to make him king after the feeding of the five thousand, and when Jesus taught the "hard teaching" about the need for them to eat his flesh and drink his blood in order to live. John comments immediately after Jesus told his followers, "But some of you don't believe," that "Jesus knew from the beginning . . . who would turn against him."

6:69 Peter: John 13:6–11

6:70 Judas: John 12:4

7:2 Feasts/Festivals: John 10:22

7:13 Anti-Semitism: John 8:39–44

7:18 Will of God: Romans 12:2

7:19 *law.* Moses gave God's people the Law that God gave him on Mount Sinai (Exodus 34:29-32).

circumcision; it came from our ancestors.) And yet you circumcise a baby on a Sabbath day. 23If a baby can be circumcised on a Sabbath day to obey the law of Moses, why are you angry at me for healing a person's whole body on the Sabbath day? 24Stop judging by the way things look, but judge by what is really right."

Is Jesus the Christ?

25Then some of the people who lived in Jerusalem said, "This is the man they are trying to kill. 26But he is teaching where everyone can see and hear him, and no one is trying to stop him. Maybe the leaders have decided he really is the Christ. 27But we know where this man is from. And when the real Christ comes, no one will know where he comes from."

28Jesus, teaching in the Temple, cried out, "Yes, you know me, and you know where I am from. But I have not come by my own authority. I was sent by the One who is true, whom you don't know. 29But I know him, because I am from him, and he sent me."

30When Jesus said this, the people tried to take him. But no one was able to touch him, because it was not yet the right time. 31But many of the people believed in Jesus. They said, "When the Christ comes, will he do more miracles than this man has done?"

The Leaders Try to Arrest Jesus

32The Pharisees heard the crowd whispering these things about Jesus. So the leading priests and the Pharisees sent some Temple guards to arrest him. 33Jesus said, "I will be with you a little while longer. Then I will go back to the One who sent me. 34You will look for me, but you will not find me. And you cannot come where I am."

35Some people said to each other, "Where will this man go so we cannot find him? Will he go to the Greek cities where our people live and teach the Greek people there? 36What did he mean when he said, 'You will look for me, but you will not find me,' and 'You cannot come where I am'?"

Jesus Talks About the Spirit

37On the last and most important day of the feast Jesus stood up and said in a loud voice, "Let anyone who is thirsty come to me and drink. 38If anyone believes in me, rivers of living water will flow out from that person's heart, as the Scripture says." 39Jesus was talking about the Holy Spirit. The Spirit had not yet been given, because Jesus had not yet been raised to glory. But later, those who believed in Jesus would receive the Spirit.

The People Argue About Jesus

40When the people heard Jesus' words, some of them said, "This man really is the Prophet."

41Others said, "He is the Christ."

Still others said, "The Christ will not come from Galilee. 42The Scripture says that the Christ will come from David's family and from Bethlehem, the town where David lived." 43So the people did not agree with each other about Jesus. 44Some of them wanted to arrest him, but no one was able to touch him.

Some Leaders Won't Believe

45The Temple guards went back to the leading priests and the Pharisees, who asked, "Why didn't you bring Jesus?"

46The guards answered, "The words he says are greater than the words of any other person who has ever spoken!"

47The Pharisees answered, "So Jesus has fooled you also! 48Have any of the leaders or the Pharisees believed in him? No! 49But these people, who know nothing about the law, are under God's curse."

50Nicodemus, who had gone to see Jesus before, was in that group. He said, 51"Our law does not judge a man without hearing him and knowing what he has done."

52They answered, "Are you from Galilee, too? Study the Scriptures, and you will learn that no prophet comes from Galilee."

Some early Greek manuscripts do not contain 7:53–8:11.

[53And everyone left and went home.

The Woman Caught in Adultery

8 Jesus went to the Mount of Olives. 2But early in the morning he went back to the Temple, and all the people came to him, and he sat and taught them. 3The teachers of the law and the Pharisees brought a woman who had been caught in adultery. They forced her to stand before the people. 4They said to Jesus, "Teacher, this woman was caught having sexual relations with a man who is

---

7:32 Pharisees and Sadducees: John 7:43–49
7:38 Celebration: Acts 2
7:40 *Prophet.* They probably meant the prophet God told Moses he would send (Deuteronomy 18:15–19).

7:49 Pharisees and Sadducees: John 9:13–16
7:50 *Nicodemus . . . group.* The story about Nicodemus going and talking to Jesus is in John 3:1–21.

GOOD WORKS

EPHESIANS 2:18–10

What is the relationship between believing and doing for the Christian?
How is our faith expressed in good works?

The Bible teaches us two important truths about the relationship between human good works and Christian faith. On the one hand, "You did not save yourselves. . . . It was not a result of your own efforts, so you cannot brag about it" (Ephesians 2:8,9). On the other hand, "In Christ Jesus, God made us to do good works" (Ephesians 2:10). How do these two things, saving faith and good works, fit together in the Christian life?

Holy Scripture teaches us that we are not saved by being good, by our good work, or anything good in us. Even as early as Deuteronomy, we learn that we are chosen because of God's great love for us, and not through anything that we ourselves have done. "You are a holy people who belong to the Lord your God.... The Lord did not care for you and choose you because there were many of you—you are the smallest nation of all. But the Lord chose you because he loved you, and he kept his promise to your ancestors" (Deuteronomy 7:6–8). Likewise, Daniel concluded his prayer with: "We do not ask these things because we are good; instead, we ask because of your mercy" (Daniel 9:18). We learn a similar thing from Jesus' parable about the Pharisee and the tax collector. Here we see that being good is not what makes us right with God. We are right with God when we have acknowledged our sin and asked for forgiveness (Luke 18:9–14; see also Matthew 20:1–16). The Bible clearly teaches that "All have sinned and are not good enough for God's glory, and all need to be made right with God by his grace, which is a free gift" (Romans 3:23, 24). God's love is a free gift, not based upon our good works.

So we are saved by our faith, not by our being good. As the apostle Paul tells us, "God makes people right with himself through their faith in Jesus Christ" (Romans 3:22). Our salvation is a gift; it is not something we earn by being good or righteous. Salvation is by faith. At the same time, good works have an important place in the Christian life of faith. According to the Bible, belief or faith has three elements: a feeling of trust (believing "in" someone—Romans 4:4; Hebrews 10:23); accepting an idea as true (believing "that" something is true—Hebrews 11:1); and finally an action or good work that is based upon our trust and belief (Romans 3:31; James 2:14, 22, 26). All these are important biblical elements of faith. What this means is summed up by James: "Faith that does nothing is dead" (James 2:26).

But what exactly is a good work? Can a nonbeliever do good works? On one level, the answer seems to be yes. One can think of many examples of people who sacrifice themselves for the well-being of others. A prominent example would be Albert Schweitzer, whose work in the jungles of Africa is so well-known that he is a legendary doer of good deeds. However, one must look behind the deed itself to see the motivation for the act. Does someone do the good deed for his or her own reputation or out of guilt? That should not minimize the value of the work, but we must realize that truly good works have only one motivation, and that is the glory not of the self, but of God himself. Schweitzer is also known for his work as a New Testament scholar where he argued that Jesus was not God, but a disillusioned man. So, perhaps this legendary doer of good deeds did not glorify God in his actions, but rather himself. From a biblical perspective, we would have to say that Schweitzer's deeds were not truly and ultimately good.

Our good works should be a result of our faith in Christ. They do not earn our salvation, but they do display our love for Jesus and our trust (belief) in him. That is why Paul says, "So brothers and sisters, since God has shown us great mercy, I beg you to offer your lives as a living sacrifice to him" (Romans 12:1). What is the essence of this sacrifice that faith demands? It is a life of good works, that is, a life of love and justice (or righteousness) lived out in faith and hope in God. The letter to the Hebrews tells us, "Live the right way so that you will be saved and your weakness will not cause you to be lost," and "Keep on loving each other as brothers and sisters" (Hebrews 12:13; 13:1). In the same way, the apostle John wrote: "This is how we can be sure we are living in God: Whoever says that he lives in God must live as Jesus lived," and that means "We must love each other" (1 John 2:5, 6; 3:11).

Good Works: For additional scriptures on this topic go to Deuteronomy 6:1–7:12.

SALVATION

EPHESIANS 2:8–10

What is salvation? Is it from something, or for something? Is it spiritual? Social? Psychological? To whom is salvation offered? What are some of the various metaphors with which the Bible speaks of salvation?

Salvation is the way of life where persons are freed from the past effects of sin and freed for the love and power of God in their lives. It is a present reality, because the Bible talks about salvation as something available in this life. But it also has a future aspect, since the saved belong to God and will be cared for by God in life after death, just as they are now.

Salvation is *from* sin. The Bible teaches that sin is the fundamental human problem. Adam and Eve wanted to be like God, and their disobedience resulted in death and separation from the Lord. To be saved means that we are forgiven for our sins and accepted by God, despite our wrong thoughts, words, and actions. When we deserve punishment, God chooses to pardon us and accept us as his sons and daughters because of Christ's death on the cross. We are also freed from the power of sin in our lives. Anyone who has wrestled directly with a significant problem knows how hard it is to overcome it quickly. In the same way, God's love helps us overcome the continuing power of sin by helping us to grow and become more loving and holy persons as we grow in our relationship to him.

Salvation is *for* a life of joy and peace and abundant living. When we become God's children, all sorts of good things are in store for us. We share in God's love and the blessings he offers his people. We participate in a church family where the Spirit ministers to us. We often gain as much personally from serving others as we are able to give to them. The abundant life we experience here is only a foretaste of the heavenly banquet prepared for all of God's people after death.

Salvation is thus a relationship with God that has spiritual, social, and psychological dimensions. Spiritually, we become new persons in Christ. Socially, we take on a new set of relationships. We participate in the body of believers called the church, and we carry Christ's message of love and forgiveness out into the world. Psychologically, we find a peace that the world cannot give (John 14:27). Although God rejoices over finding every one of his lost sheep, the salvation of an individual is not only for that person's benefit. God wants to use that saved person as part of his overall plan to unite all things to himself and to bring all human beings into the kingdom.

Salvation is offered to every human being. God's love for the world is so great that anyone who believes in Christ is given the blessings of salvation. No one is excluded because of their race, nationality, ethnic background, or any other reason. All that is necessary is faith in Christ. But it is true that not everyone accepts this salvation. Without Christ, there is no salvation, and it is important that Christians share the Good News that has so changed their lives and destinies with others. As Paul says, "As the Scripture says, 'Anyone who calls on the Lord will be saved.' But before people can ask the Lord for help, they must believe in him, and before they can believe in him, they must hear about him; and for them to hear about the Lord, someone must tell them" (Romans 10:13–14).

While God is the One who saves, human beings must respond with faith. The book of Hebrews records that "without faith no one can please God" (Hebrews 11:6). As a matter of fact, the Bible clearly teaches that no one can be right with God without having faith in Jesus Christ (Galatians 3:2). As we think of faith, we must come to grips with two facts that are seemingly in tension with one another. The first is that faith is an act of our own will. We must choose to have faith in God through Christ (John 14:1; Acts 16:31). But as Ephesians 2:8 indicates, our ability to exercise faith is a result of a gift from God. We are made right with God through faith in Christ.

Still, the act of salvation is not yet fully described because it includes our life with God. After all, we do not become automatically perfect when we become Christians. Sin still remains in our heart. Thus we must pursue holiness in our lives. This part of our salvation, like all the other parts, both demands action on our part as well as recognition that our success in growing more like Christ is the result of a gift of God. We should pursue a holy life (Hebrews 12:14), while noting that it is a work of God in our hearts.

The end result of the process is that God will bring us to glory. We were created in the image of God, reflecting God's perfect character. When he brings us to himself at the end of time, we will once again be restored to our original sinless state, and we will live in eternal bliss with him.

Salvation: For additional scriptures on this topic go to Psalm 44:7

not her husband. 5The law of Moses commands that we stone to death every woman who does this. What do you say we should do?" 6They were asking this to trick Jesus so that they could have some charge against him.

But Jesus bent over and started writing on the ground with his finger. 7When they continued to ask Jesus their question, he raised up and said, "Anyone here who has never sinned can throw the first stone at her." 8Then Jesus bent over again and wrote on the ground.

9Those who heard Jesus began to leave one by one, first the older men and then the others. Jesus was left there alone with the woman standing before him. 10Jesus raised up again and asked her, "Woman, where are they? Has no one judged you guilty?"

11She answered, "No one, sir."

Then Jesus said, "I also don't judge you guilty. You may go now, but don't sin anymore."]⚭

Jesus Is the Light of the World

12Later, Jesus talked to the people again, saying, "I am the light of the world. The person who follows me will never live in darkness but will have the light that gives life."

13The Pharisees said to Jesus, "When you talk about yourself, you are the only one to say these things are true. We cannot accept what you say."

14Jesus answered, "Yes, I am saying these things about myself, but they are true. I know where I came from and where I am going. But you don't know where I came from or where I am going. 15You judge by human standards. I am not judging anyone. 16But when I do judge, my judging is true, because I am not alone. The Father who sent me is with me. 17Your own law says that when two witnesses say the same thing, you must accept what they say. 18I am one of the witnesses who speaks about myself, and the Father who sent me is the other witness."

19They asked, "Where is your father?"

Jesus answered, "You don't know me or my Father. If you knew me, you would know my Father, too." 20Jesus said these things while he was teaching in the Temple, near where the money is kept. But no one arrested him, because the right time for him had not yet come.

The People Misunderstand Jesus

21Again, Jesus said to the people, "I will leave you, and you will look for me, but you will die in your sins. You cannot come where I am going."

22So the Jews asked, "Will Jesus kill himself? Is that why he said, 'You cannot come where I am going'?"

23Jesus said, "You people are from here below, but I am from above. You belong to this world, but I don't belong to this world. 24So I told you that you would die in your sins. Yes, you will die in your sins if you don't believe that I am he."

25They asked, "Then who are you?"

Jesus answered, "I am what I have told you from the beginning. 26I have many things to say and decide about you. But I tell people only the things I have heard from the One who sent me, and he speaks the truth."

27The people did not understand that he was talking to them about the Father. 28So Jesus said to them, "When you lift up the Son of Man, you will know that I am he. You will know that these things I do are not by my own authority but that I say only what the Father has taught me. 29The One who sent me is with me. I always do what is pleasing to him, so he has not left me alone." 30While Jesus was saying these things, many people believed in him.

Freedom from Sin

31So Jesus said to the Jews who believed in him, "If you continue to obey my teaching, you are truly my followers.⚭ 32Then you will know the truth, and the truth will make you free."⚭

33They answered, "We are Abraham's children, and we have never been anyone's slaves. So why do you say we will be free?"

34Jesus answered, "I tell you the truth, everyone who lives in sin is a slave to sin. 35A slave does not stay with a family forever, but a son belongs to the family forever. 36So if the Son makes you free, you will be truly free. 37I know you are Abraham's children, but you want to kill me because you don't accept my teaching. 38I am telling you what my Father has shown me, but you do what your father has told you."⚭

39They answered, "Our father is Abraham."

Jesus said, "If you were really Abraham's children,

⚭**8:11 Adultery:** See article on page 251.

⚭**8:11 Forgiveness:** See article on page 881.

⚭**8:11 Grace:** Romans 5:1–2

⚭**8:31 Perseverance:** John 10:28

⚭**8:32 Disciple/Discipleship/Mentoring (Follow/Follower):** John 13:34–35

⚭**8:38 Freedom:** Romans 8

8:39–44 Jesus here speaks rather harshly as a Jewish person to others in the Jewish community who believed in him (John 8:31) about an issue that was held very dear in Judaism: they believed they were "children of Abraham." Jesus confronts them with the claim that if they are really children of Abraham then they would accept him and not oppose his message.

you would do the things Abraham did. 40I am a man who has told you the truth which I heard from God, but you are trying to kill me. Abraham did nothing like that. 41So you are doing the things your own father did."

But they said, "We are not like children who never knew who their father was. God is our Father; he is the only Father we have."

42Jesus said to them, "If God were really your Father, you would love me, because I came from God and now I am here. I did not come by my own authority; God sent me. 43You don't understand what I say, because you cannot accept my teaching. 44You belong to your father the devil, and you want to do what he wants. He was a murderer from the beginning and was against the truth, because there is no truth in him. When he tells a lie, he shows what he is really like, because he is a liar and the father of lies.⚭ 45But because I speak the truth, you don't believe me. 46Can any of you prove that I am guilty of sin? If I am telling the truth, why don't you believe me? 47The person who belongs to God accepts what God says. But you don't accept what God says, because you don't belong to God."

Jesus Is Greater than Abraham

48They answered, "We say you are a Samaritan and have a demon in you. Are we not right?"

49Jesus answered, "I have no demon in me. I give honor to my Father, but you dishonor me. 50I am not trying to get honor for myself. There is One who wants this honor for me, and he is the judge. 51I tell you the truth, whoever obeys my teaching will never die."

52They said to Jesus, "Now we know that you have a demon in you! Even Abraham and the prophets died. But you say, 'Whoever obeys my teaching will never die.' 53Do you think you are greater than our father Abraham, who died? And the prophets died, too. Who do you think you are?"

54Jesus answered, "If I give honor to myself, that honor is worth nothing. The One who gives me honor is my Father, and you say he is your God. 55You don't really know him, but I know him. If I said I did not know him, I would be a liar like you. But I do know him, and I obey what he says. 56Your father Abraham was very happy that he would see my day. He saw that day and was glad."

57They said to him, "You have never seen Abraham! You are not even fifty years old."

58Jesus answered, "I tell you the truth, before Abraham was even born, I am!" 59When Jesus said this, the people picked up stones to throw at him. But Jesus hid himself, and then he left the Temple.

Jesus Heals a Man Born Blind

9 As Jesus was walking along, he saw a man who had been born blind. 2His followers asked him, "Teacher, whose sin caused this man to be born blind—his own sin or his parents' sin?"⚭

3Jesus answered, "It is not this man's sin or his parents' sin that made him be blind. This man was born blind so that God's power could be shown in him. 4While it is daytime, we must continue doing the work of the One who sent me. Night is coming, when no one can work.⚭ 5While I am in the world, I am the light of the world."

6After Jesus said this, he spit on the ground and made some mud with it and put the mud on the man's eyes. 7Then he told the man, "Go and wash in the Pool of Siloam." (Siloam means Sent.) So the man went, washed, and came back seeing.⚭

8The neighbors and some people who had earlier seen this man begging said, "Isn't this the same man who used to sit and beg?"

9Some said, "He is the one," but others said,

8:39–47 Jesus' words here make it clear that the Pharisees' rejection of him is indicative of the rebellious relationship they have with God the Father (John 15:23–24). Jesus teaches that he speaks God's words (John 8:40) and was sent by God (v.42). The world's hateful response to God's messenger (Hebrews 12:3; Matthew 21:38–40, 45) is a sign that it loves the evil it does and does not want it exposed (John 3:20; 7:7).

⚭**8:44 Anti-Semitism:** John 9:22

9 When Jesus heals someone he does not do it just to eliminate the person's physical handicap, but to eliminate a greater cause of suffering. People who had a physical handicap were not treated like a full member of the community, because it was thought their handicap was a punishment from God. Jesus heals the blind and others with limitations to teach the people that physical handicaps are not a punishment for a person's sin. In John 9 when Jesus and his followers meet a blind man, they ask him if the man is blind because of his sin or his parents' sin. Jesus says, "It is not this man's sin or his parents' sin that made him be blind. This man was born blind so that God's power could be shown in him." John describes how the man is treated after Jesus heals him. The Pharisees do not believe he is healed because they thought he was being punished by God for his sin. They insist that Jesus must be a sinner also for associating with this man that God had punished (John 9:24–25). Jesus explains that it is not this man's sin that has caused his blindness, but the Pharisees sin has caused them to be *spiritually* blind. They cannot see that the community of God is open to everyone (John 9:40–41).

9:1–2 The connection between sin and tragedy was debated in the ancient world, just as it is now. Jesus does not address this question here, but instead uses this opportunity to show that he has come to bring light to the world. Throughout John 9, then, we see how a blind person has been enabled to see—not only physically, but also spiritually; while others who can see physically are actually blind spiritually.

⚭**9:2 Immortality:** 1 Corinthians 15:38–58

⚭**9:4 Career/Careerism:** John 21:19

⚭**9:7 Sickness, Disease, Healing:** Acts 3:1–10

"No, he only looks like him."

The man himself said, "I am the man."

10They asked, "How did you get your sight?"

11He answered, "The man named Jesus made some mud and put it on my eyes. Then he told me to go to Siloam and wash. So I went and washed, and then I could see."

12They asked him, "Where is this man?"

"I don't know," he answered.

Pharisees Question the Healing

13Then the people took to the Pharisees the man who had been blind. 14The day Jesus had made mud and healed his eyes was a Sabbath day. 15So now the Pharisees asked the man, "How did you get your sight?"

He answered, "He put mud on my eyes, I washed, and now I see."

16So some of the Pharisees were saying, "This man does not keep the Sabbath day, so he is not from God."

But others said, "A man who is a sinner can't do miracles like these." So they could not agree with each other.

17They asked the man again, "What do you say about him since it was your eyes he opened?"

The man answered, "He is a prophet."

18These leaders did not believe that he had been blind and could now see again. So they sent for the man's parents 19and asked them, "Is this your son who you say was born blind? Then how does he now see?"

20His parents answered, "We know that this is our son and that he was born blind. 21But we don't know how he can now see. We don't know who opened his eyes. Ask him. He is old enough to speak for himself." 22His parents said this because they were afraid of the older leaders, who had already decided that anyone who said Jesus was the Christ would be avoided. 23That is why his parents said, "He is old enough. Ask him."

24So for the second time, they called the man who had been blind. They said, "You should give God the glory by telling the truth. We know that this man is a sinner."

25He answered, "I don't know if he is a sinner. One thing I do know: I was blind, and now I see."

26They asked, "What did he do to you? How did he make you see again?"

27He answered, "I already told you, and you didn't listen. Why do you want to hear it again? Do you want to become his followers, too?"

28Then they insulted him and said, "You are his follower, but we are followers of Moses. 29We know that God spoke to Moses, but we don't even know where this man comes from."

30The man answered, "This is a very strange thing. You don't know where he comes from, and yet he opened my eyes. 31We all know that God does not listen to sinners, but he listens to anyone who worships and obeys him. 32Nobody has ever heard of anyone giving sight to a man born blind. 33If this man were not from God, he could do nothing."

34They answered, "You were born full of sin! Are you trying to teach us?" And they threw him out.

Spiritual Blindness

35When Jesus heard that they had thrown him out, Jesus found him and said, "Do you believe in the Son of Man?"

36He asked, "Who is the Son of Man, sir, so that I can believe in him?"

37Jesus said to him, "You have seen him. The Son of Man is the one talking with you."

38He said, "Lord, I believe!" Then the man worshiped Jesus.

39Jesus said, "I came into this world so that the world could be judged. I came so that the blind would see and so that those who see will become blind."

40Some of the Pharisees who were nearby heard Jesus say this and asked, "Are you saying we are blind, too?"

41Jesus said, "If you were blind, you would not be guilty of sin. But since you keep saying you see, your guilt remains."

The Shepherd and His Sheep

10 Jesus said, "I tell you the truth, the person who does not enter the sheepfold by the door, but climbs in some other way, is a thief and a robber. 2The one who enters by the door is the shepherd of the sheep. 3The one who guards the door opens it for him. And the sheep listen to the voice of the shepherd. He calls his own sheep by name and leads them out. 4When he brings all his sheep out, he goes ahead of them, and they follow him because they know his voice. 5But they will never follow a stranger. They will run away from him because they don't know his voice." 6Jesus told the people this story, but they did not understand what it meant.

9:16 Pharisees and Sadducees: Acts 4:1–2

9:22 Anti-Semitism: John 19:38

6:39 *blind.* Jesus is talking about people who are spiritually blind, not physically blind.

9:41 Miracles: John 11

Jesus Is the Good Shepherd

7So Jesus said again, "I tell you the truth, I am the door for the sheep. 8All the people who came before me were thieves and robbers. The sheep did not listen to them. 9I am the door, and the person who enters through me will be saved and will be able to come in and go out and find pasture. 10A thief comes to steal and kill and destroy, but I came to give life—life in all its fullness.

11"I am the good shepherd. The good shepherd gives his life for the sheep. 12The worker who is paid to keep the sheep is different from the shepherd who owns them. When the worker sees a wolf coming, he runs away and leaves the sheep alone. Then the wolf attacks the sheep and scatters them. 13The man runs away because he is only a paid worker and does not really care about the sheep.

14-15"I am the good shepherd. I know my sheep, as the Father knows me. And my sheep know me, as I know the Father. I give my life for the sheep. 16I have other sheep that are not in this flock, and I must bring them also. They will listen to my voice, and there will be one flock and one shepherd. 17The Father loves me because I give my life so that I can take it back again. 18No one takes it away from me; I give my own life freely. I have the right to give my life, and I have the right to take it back. This is what my Father commanded me to do."

19Again the leaders did not agree with each other because of these words of Jesus. 20Many of them said, "A demon has come into him and made him crazy. Why listen to him?"

21But others said, "A man who is crazy with a demon does not say things like this. Can a demon open the eyes of the blind?"

Jesus Is Rejected

22The time came for the Feast of Dedication at Jerusalem. It was winter, 23and Jesus was walking in the Temple in Solomon's Porch. 24Some people gathered around him and said, "How long will you make us wonder about you? If you are the Christ, tell us plainly."

25Jesus answered, "I told you already, but you did not believe. The miracles I do in my Father's name show who I am. 26But you don't believe, because you are not my sheep. 27My sheep listen to my voice; I know them, and they follow me. 28I give them eternal life, and they will never die, and no one can steal them out of my hand. 29My Father gave my sheep to me. He is greater than all, and no person can steal my sheep out of my Father's hand. 30The Father and I are one."

31Again some of the people picked up stones to kill Jesus. 32But he said to them, "I have done many good works from the Father. Which of these good works are you killing me for?"

33They answered, "We are not killing you because of any good work you did, but because you speak against God. You are only a human, but you say you are the same as God!"

34Jesus answered, "It is written in your law that God said, 'I said, you are gods.' 35This Scripture called those people gods who received God's message, and Scripture is always true. 36So why do you say that I speak against God because I said, 'I am God's Son'? I am the one God chose and sent into the world. 37If I don't do what my Father does, then don't believe me. 38But if I do what my Father does, even though you don't believe in me, believe what I do. Then you will know and understand that the Father is in me and I am in the Father."

39They tried to take Jesus again, but he escaped from them.

40Then he went back across the Jordan River to the place where John had first baptized. Jesus stayed there, 41and many people came to him and said, "John never did a miracle, but everything John said about this man is true." 42And in that place many believed in Jesus.

The Death of Lazarus

11 A man named Lazarus was sick. He lived in the town of Bethany, where Mary and her sister Martha lived. 2Mary was the woman who later put perfume on the Lord and wiped his feet with her hair. Mary's brother was Lazarus, the man who was now sick. 3So Mary and Martha sent someone to tell Jesus, "Lord, the one you love is sick."

4When Jesus heard this, he said, "This sickness will not end in death. It is for the glory of God, to bring glory to the Son of God." 5Jesus loved Martha

10:10 The essence of spirituality is "life." The spiritual life is not a component, it is life itself—life in all its fullness, as promised and made available by Christ. Christ serves as both the example and enabler of true spirituality.

10:16 Leadership: John 13:1–17

10:16 Racism: Acts 11:1–18

10:22 The Feast of Dedication was a feast to celebrate the dedication of the Temple after it had been defiled by Antiochus Epiphanies in the second century B.C. The Maccabean family led a revolt when they were ordered to sacrifice pigs on the altar in violation of Old Testament regulations.

10:22 Feasts/Festivals: Acts 2:1

10:28 Perseverance: John 15:4–9

10:29 Election (Chosen): Romans 9–11

10:30 Incarnation: John 10:38

10:30 Trinity: John 14:25–26

10:34 *'I . . . gods.'* Quotation from Psalm 82:6.

10:38 Incarnation: John 14:1

and her sister and Lazarus. 6But when he heard that Lazarus was sick, he stayed where he was for two more days. 7Then Jesus said to his followers, "Let's go back to Judea."

8The followers said, "But Teacher, some people there tried to stone you to death only a short time ago. Now you want to go back there?"

9Jesus answered, "Are there not twelve hours in the day? If anyone walks in the daylight, he will not stumble, because he can see by this world's light. 10But if anyone walks at night, he stumbles because there is no light to help him see."

11After Jesus said this, he added, "Our friend Lazarus has fallen asleep, but I am going there to wake him."

12The followers said, "But Lord, if he is only asleep, he will be all right."

13Jesus meant that Lazarus was dead, but his followers thought he meant Lazarus was really sleeping. 14So then Jesus said plainly, "Lazarus is dead. 15And I am glad for your sakes I was not there so that you may believe. But let's go to him now."

16Then Thomas (the one called Didymus) said to the other followers, "Let us also go so that we can die with him."

Jesus in Bethany

17When Jesus arrived, he learned that Lazarus had already been dead and in the tomb for four days. 18Bethany was about two miles from Jerusalem. 19Many of the Jews had come there to comfort Martha and Mary about their brother.

20When Martha heard that Jesus was coming, she went out to meet him, but Mary stayed home. 21Martha said to Jesus, "Lord, if you had been here, my brother would not have died. 22But I know that even now God will give you anything you ask."

23Jesus said, "Your brother will rise and live again."

24Martha answered, "I know that he will rise and live again in the resurrection on the last day."

25Jesus said to her, "I am the resurrection and the life. Those who believe in me will have life even if they die.⚭ 26And everyone who lives and believes in me will never die. Martha, do you believe this?"

27Martha answered, "Yes, Lord. I believe that you are the Christ, the Son of God, the One coming to the world."

Jesus Cries

28After Martha said this, she went back and talked to her sister Mary alone. Martha said, "The Teacher is here and he is asking for you." 29When Mary heard this, she got up quickly and went to Jesus. 30Jesus had not yet come into the town but was still at the place where Martha had met him. 31The Jews were with Mary in the house, comforting her. When they saw her stand and leave quickly, they followed her, thinking she was going to the tomb to cry there.

32But Mary went to the place where Jesus was. When she saw him, she fell at his feet and said, "Lord, if you had been here, my brother would not have died."

33When Jesus saw Mary crying and the Jews who came with her also crying, he was upset and was deeply troubled. 34He asked, "Where did you bury him?"

"Come and see, Lord," they said.

35Jesus cried.

36So the Jews said, "See how much he loved him."

37But some of them said, "If Jesus opened the eyes of the blind man, why couldn't he keep Lazarus from dying?"

Jesus Raises Lazarus

38Again feeling very upset, Jesus came to the tomb. It was a cave with a large stone covering the entrance. 39Jesus said, "Move the stone away."

Martha, the sister of the dead man, said, "But, Lord, it has been four days since he died. There will be a bad smell."

40Then Jesus said to her, "Didn't I tell you that if you believed you would see the glory of God?"

41So they moved the stone away from the entrance. Then Jesus looked up and said, "Father, I thank you that you heard me. 42I know that you always hear me, but I said these things because of the people here around me. I want them to believe that you sent me." 43After Jesus said this, he cried out in a loud voice, "Lazarus, come out!" 44The dead man came out, his hands and feet wrapped with pieces of cloth, and a cloth around his face.

Jesus said to them, "Take the cloth off of him and let him go."⚭

11:17–44 This passage validates the mixed emotions that Christians have about death. We know that Jesus has conquered death, and we can trust that those who believe in him will share in his resurrection and eternal life. Nevertheless, when those we love die, their passing is a cruel loss for us who remain behind in this world. Jesus joined Mary in weeping for their dead friend and brother, Lazarus. So Christians view death as both triumph and tragedy. This tension we feel is inevitable because we are living in the time between Christ's first and second comings. He has already defeated death, but has not yet destroyed it (1 Corinthians 15:23–26).

11:24 *resurrection.* Being raised from the dead to live again.

⚭**11:25 Faith/Unbelief:** John 20:31

⚭**11:44 Healing:** Acts 14:1–10

The Plan to Kill Jesus

45Many of the people, who had come to visit
Mary and saw what Jesus did, believed in him.
46But some of them went to the Pharisees and
told them what Jesus had done. 47Then the leading priests and Pharisees called a meeting of the
council. They asked, "What should we do? This
man is doing many miracles. 48If we let him continue doing these things, everyone will believe in
him. Then the Romans will come and take away
our Temple and our nation."
49One of the men there was Caiaphas, the high
priest that year. He said, "You people know nothing! 50You don't realize that it is better for one man
to die for the people than for the whole nation to be
destroyed."
51Caiaphas did not think of this himself. As high
priest that year, he was really prophesying that
Jesus would die for their nation 52and for God's
scattered children to bring them all together and
make them one.
53That day they started planning to kill Jesus.
54So Jesus no longer traveled openly among the
people. He left there and went to a place near the
desert, to a town called Ephraim and stayed there
with his followers.
55It was almost time for the Passover Feast. Many
from the country went up to Jerusalem before the
Passover to do the special things to make themselves pure. 56The people looked for Jesus and
stood in the Temple asking each other, "Is he
coming to the Feast? What do you think?" 57But
the leading priests and the Pharisees had given
orders that if anyone knew where Jesus was, he
must tell them. Then they could arrest him.⚭

Jesus with Friends in Bethany

12 Six days before the Passover Feast, Jesus
went to Bethany, where Lazarus lived. (Lazarus is the man Jesus raised from the dead.) 2There
they had a dinner for Jesus. Martha served the food,
and Lazarus was one of the people eating with
Jesus. 3Mary brought in a pint of very expensive
perfume made from pure nard. She poured the
perfume on Jesus' feet, and then she wiped his
feet with her hair. And the sweet smell from the
perfume filled the whole house.
4Judas Iscariot, one of Jesus' followers who would
later turn against him, was there. Judas said,⚭
5"This perfume was worth three hundred coins.
Why wasn't it sold and the money given to the
poor?" 6But Judas did not really care about the poor;
he said this because he was a thief. He was the one
who kept the money box, and he often stole from it.
7Jesus answered, "Leave her alone. It was right for
her to save this perfume for today, the day for me to
be prepared for burial. 8You will always have the
poor with you, but you will not always have me."

The Plot Against Lazarus

9A large crowd of people heard that Jesus was
in Bethany. So they went there to see not only
Jesus but Lazarus, whom Jesus raised from the
dead. 10So the leading priests made plans to kill
Lazarus, too. 11Because of Lazarus many of the
Jews were leaving them and believing in Jesus.

Jesus Enters Jerusalem

12The next day a great crowd who had come to
Jerusalem for the Passover Feast heard that Jesus
was coming there. 13So they took branches of palm
trees and went out to meet Jesus, shouting,

"Praise God!
God bless the One who comes in the
name of the Lord!
God bless the King of Israel!" *Psalm 118:25-26*

14Jesus found a colt and sat on it. This was as the
Scripture says,
15"Don't be afraid, people of Jerusalem!
Your king is coming,
sitting on the colt of a donkey." *Zechariah 9:9*
16The followers of Jesus did not understand this
at first. But after Jesus was raised to glory, they
remembered that this had been written about
him and that they had done these things to him.

11:48 John provides us with an important insight into the problem Jesus created for the Jewish leaders in Jerusalem. Although Jesus' teaching and miracles were troublesome, it did not pose a serious threat. Rather, the problem is that Jesus' ministry was drawing a large crowd, some who really wanted to follow him, all who were curious about him. His ministry was disturbing the peace, and this the Jewish leadership could not allow, for this might cause the Roman authorities to take drastic action.

⚭**11:57 Miracles:** Galatians 4:13–15

⚭**12:4 Judas:** John 13:26

12:4-7 John, by allowing us to see the character of Judas, is the one who gives us the most insight into his actions. In Judas was a secret sin which became the seed of his betrayal. No one knew that he was stealing and putting on a front of concern for the poor (John 12:4–6). Sin, when left unrepented and unconfessed, becomes a snare that can destroy us (James 1:14–15). One of the uncomfortable things we find in the story of Judas is the possibility for betrayal that is in the best of us. The followers feared that Jesus could be talking about them when he mentioned betrayal (John 13:21f). Each follower of Christ has the potential of betraying Jesus by selling out to baser passions. First Corinthians 10:12 warns us against being too sure of ourselves. An exciting promise follows that warning: "But you can trust God, who will not permit you to be tempted more than you can stand. But when you are tempted, he will also give you a way to escape so that you will be able to stand it." It is the individual follower's task to choose that way of escape.

12:5 *coins.* One coin, a denarius, was the average pay for one day's work.

12:12 *Praise.* Literally, *Hosanna,* a Hebrew word used at first in praying to God for help, but at this time it was probably a shout of joy used in praising God or his Messiah.

People Tell About Jesus

17There had been many people with Jesus when he raised Lazarus from the dead and told him to come out of the tomb. Now they were telling others about what Jesus did. 18Many people went out to meet Jesus, because they had heard about this miracle. 19So the Pharisees said to each other, "You can see that nothing is going right for us. Look! The whole world is following him."

Jesus Talks About His Death

20There were some Greek people, too, who came to Jerusalem to worship at the Passover Feast. 21They went to Philip, who was from Bethsaida in Galilee, and said, "Sir, we would like to see Jesus." 22Philip told Andrew, and then Andrew and Philip told Jesus.

23Jesus said to them, "The time has come for the Son of Man to receive his glory. 24I tell you the truth, a grain of wheat must fall to the ground and die to make many seeds. But if it never dies, it remains only a single seed. 25Those who love their lives will lose them, but those who hate their lives in this world will keep true life forever. 26Whoever serves me must follow me. Then my servant will be with me everywhere I am. My Father will honor anyone who serves me.∞

27"Now I am very troubled. Should I say, 'Father, save me from this time'? No, I came to this time so I could suffer. 28Father, bring glory to your name!"

Then a voice came from heaven, "I have brought glory to it, and I will do it again."

29The crowd standing there, who heard the voice, said it was thunder.∞

But others said, "An angel has spoken to him."

30Jesus said, "That voice was for your sake, not mine. 31Now is the time for the world to be judged; now the ruler of this world will be thrown down.∞ 32If I am lifted up from the earth, I will draw all people toward me." 33Jesus said this to show how he would die.

34The crowd said, "We have heard from the law that the Christ will live forever. So why do you say, 'The Son of Man must be lifted up'? Who is this 'Son of Man'?"

35Then Jesus said, "The light will be with you for a little longer, so walk while you have the light. Then the darkness will not catch you. If you walk in the darkness, you will not know where you are going.∞ 36Believe in the light while you still have it so that you will become children of light." When Jesus had said this, he left and hid himself from them.

Some People Won't Believe in Jesus

37Though Jesus had done many miracles in front of the people, they still did not believe in him. 38This was to bring about what Isaiah the prophet had said:

"Lord, who believed what we told them?
  Who saw the Lord's power in this?" *Isaiah 53:1*

39This is why the people could not believe: Isaiah also had said,

40"He has blinded their eyes,
  and he has closed their minds.
Otherwise they would see with their eyes
  and understand in their minds
  and come back to me and
    be healed." *Isaiah 6:10*

41Isaiah said this because he saw Jesus' glory and spoke about him.

42But many believed in Jesus, even many of the leaders. But because of the Pharisees, they did not say they believed in him for fear they would be put out of the synagogue. 43They loved praise from people more than praise from God.

44Then Jesus cried out, "Whoever believes in me is really believing in the One who sent me. 45Whoever sees me sees the One who sent me. 46I have come as light into the world so that whoever believes in me would not stay in darkness.

47"Anyone who hears my words and does not obey them, I do not judge, because I did not come to judge the world, but to save the world. 48There is a judge for those who refuse to believe in me and do not accept my words. The word I have taught will be their judge on the last day. 49The things I taught were not from myself. The Father who sent me told me what to say and what to teach. 50And I know that eternal life comes from what the Father commands. So whatever I say is what the Father told me to say."

Jesus Washes His Followers' Feet

13 It was almost time for the Passover Feast. Jesus knew that it was time for him to leave this world and go back to the Father. He had always loved those who were his own in the world, and he loved them all the way to the end.

∞**12:26 Servant of the Lord:** Acts 2:18
∞**12:26 Service:** John 13:34
∞**12:26 Body/Flesh:** Romans 12:1–5
∞**12:29 Mount of Olives:** Acts 1:9–12
∞**12:31 Demon:** John 14:30
∞**12:35 Darkness:** 1 Corinthians 4:5

13:1–15 The long-awaited time has finally come, and Jesus reveals his purpose for coming into the world. This purpose, simply put, is service. Though he is Teacher and Lord, Jesus performs this ultimate act of service, foot washing, for his followers. In doing so, he shows that his death is an act of service that will allow them to have life (see John 15:13). He also shows his followers how they ought to act toward one another.

2Jesus and his followers were at the evening meal. The devil had already persuaded Judas Iscariot, the son of Simon, to turn against Jesus. 3Jesus knew that the Father had given him power over everything and that he had come from God and was going back to God. 4So during the meal Jesus stood up and took off his outer clothing. Taking a towel, he wrapped it around his waist. 5Then he poured water into a bowl and began to wash the followers' feet, drying them with the towel that was wrapped around him.

6Jesus came to Simon Peter, who said to him, "Lord, are you going to wash my feet?"

7Jesus answered, "You don't understand now what I am doing, but you will understand later."

8Peter said, "No, you will never wash my feet."

Jesus answered, "If I don't wash your feet, you are not one of my people."

9Simon Peter answered, "Lord, then wash not only my feet, but wash my hands and my head, too!"

10Jesus said, "After a person has had a bath, his whole body is clean. He needs only to wash his feet. And you men are clean, but not all of you." 11Jesus knew who would turn against him, and that is why he said, "Not all of you are clean."

12When he had finished washing their feet, he put on his clothes and sat down again. He asked, "Do you understand what I have just done for you? 13You call me 'Teacher' and 'Lord,' and you are right, because that is what I am. 14If I, your Lord and Teacher, have washed your feet, you also should wash each other's feet. 15I did this as an example so that you should do as I have done for you. 16I tell you the truth, a servant is not greater than his master. A messenger is not greater than the one who sent him. 17If you know these things, you will be happy if you do them.

18"I am not talking about all of you. I know those I have chosen. But this is to bring about what the Scripture said: 'The man who ate at my table has turned against me.' 19I am telling you this now before it happens so that when it happens, you will believe that I am he. 20I tell you the truth, whoever accepts anyone I send also accepts me. And whoever accepts me also accepts the One who sent me."

Jesus Talks About His Death

21After Jesus said this, he was very troubled. He said openly, "I tell you the truth, one of you will turn against me."

22The followers all looked at each other, because they did not know whom Jesus was talking about. 23One of the followers sitting next to Jesus was the follower Jesus loved. 24Simon Peter motioned to him to ask Jesus whom he was talking about.

25That follower leaned closer to Jesus and asked, "Lord, who is it?"

26Jesus answered, "I will dip this bread into the dish. The man I give it to is the man who will turn against me." So Jesus took a piece of bread, dipped it, and gave it to Judas Iscariot, the son of Simon. 27As soon as Judas took the bread, Satan entered him. Jesus said to him, "The thing that you will do—do it quickly." 28No one at the table understood why Jesus said this to Judas. 29Since he was the one who kept the money box, some of the followers thought Jesus was telling him to buy what was needed for the feast or to give something to the poor.

30Judas took the bread Jesus gave him and immediately went out. It was night.

31When Judas was gone, Jesus said, "Now the Son of Man receives his glory, and God receives glory through him. 32If God receives glory through him, then God will give glory to the Son through himself. And God will give him glory quickly."

33Jesus said, "My children, I will be with you only a little longer. You will look for me, and what I told the Jews, I tell you now: Where I am going you cannot come.

34"I give you a new command: Love each other. You must love each other as I have loved you. 35All people will know that you are my followers if you love each other."

Peter Will Say He Doesn't Know Jesus

36Simon Peter asked Jesus, "Lord, where are you going?"

Jesus answered, "Where I am going you cannot follow now, but you will follow later."

37Peter asked, "Lord, why can't I follow you now? I am ready to die for you!"

38Jesus answered, "Are you ready to die for me?

13:11 Peter: John 13:36–38
13:17 Friend: Galatians 3:26–28
13:17 Leadership: John 21:15–19
13:17 Work: John 21:1–19
13:18 *'The man . . . me.'* Quotation from Psalm 41:9.
13:23 *sitting.* Literally, "lying." The people of that time ate lying down and leaning on one arm.
13:23 Beloved Disciple: John 19:26–27
13:26 Judas: John 13:30
13:30 Judas: Acts 1:16
13:34 Service: Acts 20:35
13:35 Disciple/Discipleship/Mentoring (Follow/Follower): John 15:7–8
13:35 Love: Galatians 5:13

UNITY

EPHESIANS 4:5

How much unity can we expect to experience? Why are there so many denominations if Jesus prayed for unity? Are all differences between Christians the result of sin?

One of the oldest confessions that Christians inherited from their Jewish roots is a belief in one God. A logical consequence of this belief is that God's people will be one. Here Paul draws together the existence of one God with the one faith of God's people, symbolized by one baptism.

The unity of the people of Israel is rooted in the common ancestry in Adam (Genesis 2), spiritual lineage through Abraham (Genesis 12), and most importantly, their common liberation from Pharaoh's oppression through Moses (Exodus 1–15). Later David united the twelve tribes of Israel under his one kingship. And yet, the unity of God's people, Israel, was difficult to maintain. By the time of Jesus, there were several different strains in Judaism, including the Pharisees and the Sadducees, the Zealots, and the separatist Essenes.

In the Gospels, the disciples show early on a tendency to fight one another. For example, in Luke 9:46–48, they argue over who will be the greatest in Jesus' kingdom. (Compare with a similar discussion in Matthew 20:20–28.) Their fighting reveals that the desire for power causes disagreements. It is no wonder then that in Jesus' prayer just before his crucifixion in John 17:11 and 21, he asks for the unity of his followers. Acts 15 records both a serious doctrinal disagreement over circumcision (verses 1–29; compare Galatians 2:11–14), as well as a serious dispute between Paul and Barnabas over including John Mark in missionary work (verses 36–41), perhaps because of differences in personality.

Some of Paul's strongest ethical teaching underlines the importance of Christian unity. Galatians 3:28 says that a common faith in Christ overcomes national differences. His description of Christian love in 1 Corinthians 13 is placed between his discussion of spiritual gifts in chapters 12 and 14 to demonstrate that love binds the Christian community together, especially when the use of gifts might threaten to tear it apart. His discussion of the church as the "body of Christ" emphasizes that the entire Christian community, though possessing different gifts, is to be one in purpose (1 Corinthians 12:12–31). Still, differences in gifts, genders, and nationality are reasons that the Christian community goes different directions. Paul's solution is that the body of Christ is to be united under the common head, Christ himself (Ephesians 1:22; 4:15; 5:23). Spiritually speaking, all believers are in fact members of his body (Ephesians 5:30).

In addition to baptism, the Lord's Supper is a symbol of Christian unity. Paul writes of the unity that should be echoed in communion (but which was not among the Corinthian Christians): "Because there is one loaf of bread, we who are many are one body, because we all share that one loaf" (1 Corinthians 10:17).

Unity has always been difficult for Christians, and this problem should help believers today see that the early church was not perfect. In 1 Corinthians 1:10, Paul writes, "I beg you, brothers and sisters, by the name of our Lord Jesus Christ that all of you agree with each other and not be split into groups." He goes on to describe Christian communities that are disagreeing with one another based on who they say they are following. Here the cause of disunity is that most identify with one of the prominent Christian leaders, whether Paul, Apollos, or Peter, while some identify themselves directly with Christ (1 Corinthians 1:11–13). In this light, one of the works of the flesh, according to Galatians 5:20, is "causing divisions among people."

Today the church's unity is doubtful not only by its split into three major branches (Roman Catholic, Eastern Orthodox, and Protestant), but by the variety and number of Protestant denominations. There are historical and cultural reasons for these splits. In the United States, for example, some reasons are that we place importance on being part of a group by choice. We also stress personal religious freedom and individualism.

Since there are so many Christian churches, the main question is if unity is important, will it be based on organization or teaching (doctrine)? Those who seek organizational unity either choose levels of authority or go along with a broad acceptance of doctrinal difference. Those who like doctrinal unity often reject other people who confess Christ. The degree to which one believes the unity of the Christian church is possible before the return of Christ can be described as a matter of deciding between these options. Certainly, at any rate, Christ's followers are to pray and work for unity.

Unity: For additional scriptures on this topic go to Luke 9:46–50.

TONGUE

EPHESIANS 4:29

What kind of power does the tongue have? What are the sins of the tongue? How can the tongue be used for God?

From the beginning to the end the Bible places an enormous emphasis upon the power of our speech for either good or evil. On the personal level, who among us has not been either deeply hurt or wonderfully healed by words spoken to us by another? On a much larger level, the destiny of nations has been affected by the speeches its leaders have given. A verse in Proverbs says it best: "What you say can mean life or death" (18:21). When the tongue is used in a life-giving way it blesses both the one who speaks and the one who hears, and it pleases the Lord (Proverbs 15:26). Good words are like a fountain of water (Proverbs 10:11), a tree which gives fruit (Proverbs 15:4), pure silver (Proverbs 10:20), and a honeycomb (Proverbs 16:24). As such, they protect an individual's life (Proverbs 13:3), prevent trouble (Proverbs 21:23), stop civil war (Judges 8:1–3), calm anger (Proverbs 15:1), save lives (Proverbs 14:25), provide encouragement (Proverbs 12:25), give happiness (Proverbs 16:24), promote healing (Proverbs 12:18), spread knowledge (Proverbs 15:7), and help many people (Proverbs 10:21), just to name a few of the many positive results of good speech.

On the other hand, when the tongue is used in a deadly way, it brings vast destruction, like a forest fire (James 3:5), making the speaker evil (James 3:6) and those who listen. It is hated by God (Proverbs 12:22). Evil words are like snake poison (James 3:8; Psalm 140:30), a sharp razor (Psalm 52:2), deadly swords and arrows (Psalm 64:3), and a fire (James 3:6). As such, they crush the spirit (Proverbs 15:4), cause even more anger (Proverbs 15:1), break up friendships (Proverbs 17:9), start quarrels (Proverbs 18:6), lead to ruin (Proverbs 13:3), cause trouble (Proverbs 17:20), entrap a person (Proverbs 18:6), and do many other harmful things. What one says reveals his or her true character as being either evil or good (Matthew 12:35). In other words, "what people say with their mouths comes from the way they think" (Matthew 15:18). One of the most sobering thoughts in all of Scripture is the truth that "people will be responsible for every careless thing they have said" (Matthew 12:36). The words they have used will determine their guilt or innocence when they stand before God on the day of judgment (Matthew 12:27). One's eternal destiny is greatly affected by the tongue, either for salvation (Romans 10:9) or damnation (1 Corinthians 6:10—those who lie about others; Revelation 21:8, 27—note that those who tell lies are mentioned two times as being shut out of God's eternal kingdom). No wonder James tells us that "if people never said anything wrong, they would be perfect" (James 3:2)!

There are very few sins that people commit in which the tongue is not involved. Three of the seven things God hates involve the misuse of the tongue (Proverbs 6:16–19). Sins of the tongue are a characteristic of those who are evil (Psalm 64:2–5), which have their source in Satan who is the master of lies and deceptive words (John 8:44). The sins of the tongue described in the Bible are many, but we will list some of the most commonly mentioned: lying (Leviticus 19:11), cursing God (Leviticus 24:11, 15), swearing falsely or misusing God's name (Exodus 20:7; Matthew 5:33–37, which in the Bible means to make a promise in God's name that you do not plan to keep or to make a serious statement in God's name that is not true), evil jokes (Ephesians 5:4), profanity or evil words (Colossians 3:8), slander (Leviticus 19:16, which means to tell false stories about another person that would damage their character), gossip (Proverbs 11:13, which means to spread around private stories told in trust), making fun of God's ways or his people (Psalm 73:8; Proverbs 14:6), complaining (James 5:9), quarreling (1 Corinthians 3:3), and bragging (Psalm 10:3).

However the tongue can also be used to glorify God and help others. The Lord Jesus Christ is our perfect example of the use of good words, who was himself the truth (John 14:6) and who spoke the truth (John 8:45) using words of grace (Luke 4:22) and encouragement (John 16:33). There were many ways we used the tongue sinfully before our new life in Christ. Now there are many ways we can use the tongue that will be a blessing, including (to name just a few): praising God (Psalm 145:1–3), giving thanks to God (Psalm 136:1–3), confessing our sins (1 John 1:9), praying (1 Thessalonians 5:17), singing (Ephesians 5:19), telling others the Good News (Acts 8:4), teaching others (Colossians 3:16), encouraging (1 Thessalonians 5:14), telling the truth in a loving manner (Ephesians 4:15, 25), warning those who are doing or speaking wrongly (2 Timothy 2:14), and saying the right thing at the right time (Proverbs 15:23). We should let Psalm 141:3 and Ephesians 4:29 be our motto every day!

Tongue: For additional scriptures on this topic go to Psalm 12.

I tell you the truth, before the rooster crows, you
will say three times that you don't know me."

Jesus Comforts His Followers

14 Jesus said, "Don't let your hearts be troubled.
Trust in God, and trust in me. 2There are
many rooms in my Father's house; I would not
tell you this if it were not true. I am going there to
prepare a place for you. 3After I go and prepare a
place for you, I will come back and take you to be
with me so that you may be where I am. 4You
know the way to the place where I am going."

5Thomas said to Jesus, "Lord, we don't know
where you are going. So how can we know the
way?"

6Jesus answered, "I am the way, and the truth,
and the life. The only way to the Father is through
me. 7If you really knew me, you would know my
Father, too. But now you do know him, and you
have seen him."

8Philip said to him, "Lord, show us the Father.
That is all we need."

9Jesus answered, "I have been with you a long
time now. Do you still not know me, Philip?
Whoever has seen me has seen the Father. So
why do you say, 'Show us the Father'? 10Don't
you believe that I am in the Father and the Father
is in me? The words I say to you don't come from
me, but the Father lives in me and does his own
work. 11Believe me when I say that I am in the
Father and the Father is in me. Or believe
because of the miracles I have done. 12I tell you
the truth, whoever believes in me will do the
same things that I do. Those who believe will do
even greater things than these, because I am
going to the Father. 13And if you ask for anything
in my name, I will do it for you so that the
Father's glory will be shown through the Son. 14If
you ask me for anything in my name, I will do it.

The Promise of the Holy Spirit

15"If you love me, you will obey my commands.
16I will ask the Father, and he will give you another
Helper to be with you forever— 17the Spirit of
truth. The world cannot accept him, because it
does not see him or know him. But you know him,
because he lives with you and he will be in you.

18"I will not leave you all alone like orphans; I
will come back to you. 19In a little while the
world will not see me anymore, but you will see
me. Because I live, you will live, too. 20On that
day you will know that I am in my Father, and
that you are in me and I am in you. 21Those who
know my commands and obey them are the ones
who love me, and my Father will love those who
love me. I will love them and will show myself to
them."

22Then Judas (not Judas Iscariot) said, "But,
Lord, why do you plan to show yourself to us and
not to the rest of the world?"

23Jesus answered, "If people love me, they will
obey my teaching. My Father will love them, and
we will come to them and make our home with
them. 24Those who do not love me do not obey
my teaching. This teaching that you hear is not
really mine; it is from my Father, who sent me.

25"I have told you all these things while I am
with you. 26But the Helper will teach you everything and will cause you to remember all that I
told you. This Helper is the Holy Spirit whom the
Father will send in my name.

27"I leave you peace; my peace I give you. I do
not give it to you as the world does. So don't let
your hearts be troubled or afraid. 28You heard me
say to you, 'I am going, but I am coming back to
you.' If you loved me, you should be happy that I
am going back to the Father, because he is greater
than I am. 29I have told you this now, before it

13:38 Authority: Acts 4:19
13:38 Peter: John 18:15–27
14:1 Incarnation: John 17:3
14:3 Mourning: John 14:27

14:6 Life is a journey, and the Bible uses that image to describe the adventure of the time from our birth to our death. We are walking the road of life and have a tendency to get off it. Jesus here is telling his followers that he is the only one who knows the right direction to the Father. *In fact, he is the only way to the Father.*

14:6 Mediator: Acts 4:12

14:15–18 Jesus comforted his followers who were already grieving and feeling lonely in anticipation of his being taken away from them. He gave them two words of assurance: the Holy Spirit would come to live inside them on a permanent basis, and Jesus himself would come back to them. Of course, Jesus did spend time with them after the resurrection, and at Pentecost the Holy Spirit did take up permanent residence within them. We are never alone as believers.

14:15 Doubt: John 20:24–29

14:16 *Helper.* "Counselor" or "Comforter." Jesus is talking about the Holy Spirit.

14:17 Holy Spirit: John 14:25–26

14:18 After the initial shock has subsided and we have shed tears of release, after the funeral is over and everyone has gone home, we may begin to feel intense loneliness and even depression. Jesus knew his own followers would have such feelings and so reassured them of his continuing presence with them. Jesus himself lives in our hearts through the person of the Holy Spirit, and he will never leave us (Matthew 28:20b). We need to practice the presence of the Lord during times of loneliness, and he will make himself real to us.

14:18 Adoption: Romans 8:14–23
14:26 Instruction: 1 Corinthians 12:28
14:26 Holy Spirit: John 16:7–15
14:26 Obedience: Acts 5:29
14:26 Trinity: John 15:26–27
14:27 Mourning: Romans 8:28
14:27 Peace: Romans 5:1
14:27 Stress: Romans 8:38–39

happens, so that when it happens, you will believe.
30I will not talk with you much longer, because
the ruler of this world is coming. He has no power
over me,∞ 31but the world must know that I love
the Father, so I do exactly what the Father told me
to do.
"Come now, let us go.

Jesus Is Like a Vine

15 "I am the true vine; my Father is the gardener. 2He cuts off every branch of mine that
does not produce fruit. And he trims and cleans
every branch that produces fruit so that it will
produce even more fruit. 3You are already clean
because of the words I have spoken to you.
4Remain in me, and I will remain in you. A
branch cannot produce fruit alone but must
remain in the vine. In the same way, you cannot
produce fruit alone but must remain in me.
5"I am the vine, and you are the branches. If
any remain in me and I remain in them, they produce much fruit. But without me they can do
nothing. 6If any do not remain in me, they are like

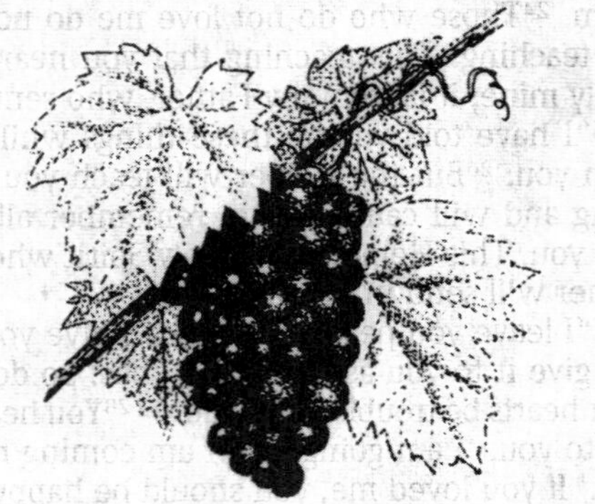

"I am the vine, and you are the branches" (15:5).

a branch that is thrown away and then dies. People
pick up dead branches, throw them into the fire,
and burn them. 7If you remain in me and follow
my teachings, you can ask anything you want,
and it will be given to you. 8You should produce
much fruit and show that you are my followers,
which brings glory to my Father.∞ 9I loved you as
the Father loved me. Now remain in my love.∞
10I have obeyed my Father's commands, and I
remain in his love. In the same way, if you obey
my commands, you will remain in my love. 11I
have told you these things so that you can have
the same joy I have and so that your joy will be the
fullest possible joy.
12"This is my command: Love each other as I
have loved you. 13The greatest love a person can
show is to die for his friends. 14You are my friends
if you do what I command you. 15I no longer call
you servants, because a servant does not know
what his master is doing. But I call you friends,
because I have made known to you everything I
heard from my Father. 16You did not choose me;
I chose you. And I gave you this work: to go and
produce fruit, fruit that will last. Then the Father
will give you anything you ask for in my name.
17This is my command: Love each other.∞

Jesus Warns His Followers

18"If the world hates you, remember that it hated
me first. 19If you belonged to the world, it would
love you as it loves its own. But I have chosen you
out of the world, so you don't belong to it. That is
why the world hates you.∞ 20Remember what I
told you: A servant is not greater than his master.
If people did wrong to me, they will do wrong to
you, too. And if they obeyed my teaching, they
will obey yours, too.∞ 21They will do all this to
you on account of me, because they do not know

∞**14:30 Demon:** John 16:11

∞**15:8 Disciple/Discipleship/Mentoring (Follow/Follower):** Acts 6:2

∞**15:9 Perseverance:** Acts 14:22

15:12–17 In this passage, Jesus does a remarkable thing. He tells the followers that he does not want to relate to them fundamentally as their master, but as their friend. This still involves obedience to his commands (15:14), but there is more. Not only is Jesus about to die for them (15:13), he is making them partners in his mission; he shares with them all that God has told him (15:15), and they will be sent to carry out the mission, even as the Father sent him (20:21). This is our inheritance as believers: the friendship of God and partnership in his mission.

15:13 Jesus himself defined what mature love really is. In an allusion to his forthcoming death on the cross, Jesus said, "The greatest love a person can show is to die for his friends." This statement is sandwiched between his command that we love each other as he has loved us (John 15:12), and his definition of what it means to be his friends: "you are my friends if you do what I command you" (John 15:14). The clear implication is that self-sacrificial love for others is not an option for the believers, but a command we must obey.

∞**15:17 Spirituality/Spiritual Dryness:** Romans 12:1–21

15:18–20 Jesus, the perfect servant of God, was hated, misunderstood, rejected, and ultimately killed. It was not because of any sin on his part, nor was it due to any character flaw. He suffered because he brought the truth and light of God to a sinful people, exposing their guilt. Wicked people prefer the darkness! Faithful servants of God in every generation have experienced similar treatment. If sinners despised the Master, how will they treat his servants?

While committed to a world that God loves, there will still always be a sense in which the world hates the Christian person. "If the world hates you, remember that it hated me first" (v. 18). Because the world hated Jesus first, it should therefore not be surprising that his followers will also be hated. However, while the world may be known by its hatred, Jesus calls upon his followers to be known by their love. "This is my command: Love each other as I have loved you" (John 15:12).

∞**15:19 World/Worldly:** Romans 12:2

∞**15:20 Persecution:** Acts 4:18–31

the One who sent me. 22If I had not come and
spoken to them, they would not be guilty of sin,
but now they have no excuse for their sin.
23Whoever hates me also hates my Father. 24I did
works among them that no one else has ever done.
If I had not done these works, they would not be
guilty of sin. But now they have seen what I have
done, and yet they have hated both me and my
Father. 25But this happened so that what is written in their law would be true: 'They hated me for
no reason.'

26"I will send you the Helper from the Father;
he is the Spirit of truth who comes from the Father.
When he comes, he will tell about me, 27and you
also must tell people about me, because you have
been with me from the beginning.

16 "I have told you these things to keep you
from giving up. 2People will put you out of
their synagogues. Yes, the time is coming when
those who kill you will think they are offering service to God. 3They will do this because they have
not known the Father and they have not known me.
4I have told you these things now so that when the
time comes you will remember that I warned you.

The Work of the Holy Spirit

"I did not tell you these things at the beginning,
because I was with you then. 5Now I am going
back to the One who sent me. But none of you
asks me, 'Where are you going?' 6Your hearts are
filled with sadness because I have told you these
things. 7But I tell you the truth, it is better for you
that I go away. When I go away, I will send the
Helper to you. If I do not go away, the Helper will
not come. 8When the Helper comes, he will prove
to the people of the world the truth about sin, about
being right with God, and about judgment. 9He will
prove to them that sin is not believing in me. 10He
will prove to them that being right with God comes
from my going to the Father and not being seen
anymore. 11And the Helper will prove to them that
judgment happened when the ruler of this world
was judged.

12"I have many more things to say to you, but
they are too much for you now. 13But when the
Spirit of truth comes, he will lead you into all
truth. He will not speak his own words, but he
will speak only what he hears, and he will tell you
what is to come. 14The Spirit of truth will bring
glory to me, because he will take what I have to
say and tell it to you. 15All that the Father has is
mine. That is why I said that the Spirit will take
what I have to say and tell it to you.

Sadness Will Become Happiness

16"After a little while you will not see me, and then
after a little while you will see me again."

17Some of the followers said to each other, "What
does Jesus mean when he says, 'After a little while
you will not see me, and then after a little while you
will see me again'? And what does he mean when
he says, 'Because I am going to the Father'?" 18They
also asked, "What does he mean by 'a little
while'? We don't understand what he is saying."

19Jesus saw that the followers wanted to ask him
about this, so he said to them, "Are you asking
each other what I meant when I said, 'After a little while you will not see me, and then after a little
while you will see me again'? 20I tell you the truth,
you will cry and be sad, but the world will be
happy. You will be sad, but your sadness will
become joy. 21When a woman gives birth to a baby,
she has pain, because her time has come. But when
her baby is born, she forgets the pain, because
she is so happy that a child has been born into the
world. 22It is the same with you. Now you are sad,
but I will see you again and you will be happy, and
no one will take away your joy. 23In that day you
will not ask me for anything. I tell you the truth,
my Father will give you anything you ask for in my
name. 24Until now you have not asked for anything
in my name. Ask and you will receive, so that
your joy will be the fullest possible joy.

Victory over the World

25"I have told you these things, using stories
that hide the meaning. But the time will come when

15:24 Rebellion: Jude 12

15:25 *'They . . . reason.'* These words could be from Psalm 35:19 or Psalm 69:4.

15:25 Hate: Romans 12:9

15:26; 16:7 *Helper.* "Counselor" or "Comforter." Jesus is talking about the Holy Spirit.

15:27 Martyrdom: John 18:1–19:37

15:27 Trinity: John 20:28

16:8–11 Even the unbelieving world under the dominion and influence of Satan has a conscience that stands condemned because of its rejection of Christ. It stands convicted by the Spirit of the sinfulness of its unbelief, of the holy righteousness of Christ whom it rejects, and of its service to the prince of this world who is already under sentence. If the Holy Spirit convicts the conscience of unbelievers, how much more the conscience of believers in whom he dwells?

16:11 Demon: Romans 8:9–17

16:11 Satan/Satanism: 1 Corinthians 15:20–28

16:15 Holy Spirit: Acts 7:57–60

16:25–30 Jesus sometimes deliberately obscured what he was saying by using parables because his time to be delivered into the hands of those who would kill him had not yet come. And sometimes even the followers did not understand Jesus' sayings and stories. Jesus did, on occasion, plainly say he came from the Father and was returning to the Father (John 16:28), to which the followers replied that now he was "speaking clearly" and "not using stories that are hard to understand" (John 16:29).

I will not use stories like that to tell you things; I will
speak to you in plain words about the Father. 26In
that day you will ask the Father for things in my
name. I mean, I will not need to ask the Father for
you. 27The Father himself loves you. He loves you
because you loved me and believed that I came from
God. 28I came from the Father into the world. Now I
am leaving the world and going back to the Father."

29Then the followers of Jesus said, "You are
speaking clearly to us now and are not using stories that are hard to understand. 30We can see now
that you know all things. You can answer a person's question even before it is asked. This makes
us believe you came from God."

31Jesus answered, "So now you believe? 32Listen
to me; a time is coming when you will be scattered,
each to his own home. That time is now here. You
will leave me alone, but I am never really alone,
because the Father is with me.

33"I told you these things so that you can have
peace in me. In this world you will have trouble,
but be brave! I have defeated the world."∞

Jesus Prays for His Followers

17 After Jesus said these things, he looked
toward heaven and prayed, "Father, the time
has come. Give glory to your Son so that the Son
can give glory to you. 2You gave the Son power
over all people so that the Son could give eternal
life to all those you gave him. 3And this is eternal life: that people know you, the only true God,
and that they know Jesus Christ, the One you
sent.∞ 4Having finished the work you gave me to
do, I brought you glory on earth.∞ 5And now,
Father, give me glory with you; give me the glory
I had with you before the world was made.

6"I showed what you are like to those you gave
me from the world. They belonged to you, and you
gave them to me, and they have obeyed your teaching.∞ 7Now they know that everything you gave
me comes from you. 8I gave them the teachings you
gave me, and they accepted them. They knew that
I truly came from you, and they believed that you
sent me. 9I am praying for them. I am not praying for
people in the world but for those you gave me,
because they are yours. 10All I have is yours, and all
you have is mine. And my glory is shown through
them. 11I am coming to you; I will not stay in the
world any longer. But they are still in the world.
Holy Father, keep them safe by the power of your
name, the name you gave me, so that they will be
one, just as you and I are one.∞ 12While I was with
them, I kept them safe by the power of your name,
the name you gave me. I protected them, and
only one of them, the one worthy of destruction,
was lost so that the Scripture would come true.

13"I am coming to you now. But I pray these things
while I am still in the world so that these followers
can have all of my joy in them. 14I have given them
your teaching. And the world has hated them,
because they don't belong to the world, just as I
don't belong to the world. 15I am not asking you to
take them out of the world but to keep them safe
from the Evil One.∞ 16They don't belong to the
world, just as I don't belong to the world. 17Make
them ready for your service through your truth; your
teaching is truth. 18I have sent them into the world,
just as you sent me into the world. 19For their
sake, I am making myself ready to serve so that
they can be ready for their service of the truth.

20"I pray for these followers, but I am also praying for all those who will believe in me because of
their teaching. 21Father, I pray that they can be
one. As you are in me and I am in you, I pray that
they can also be one in us. Then the world will
believe that you sent me. 22I have given these
people the glory that you gave me so that they can
be one, just as you and I are one.∞ 23I will be in
them and you will be in me so that they will be
completely one. Then the world will know that
you sent me and that you loved them just as
much as you loved me.

24"Father, I want these people that you gave
me to be with me where I am. I want them to see
my glory, which you gave me because you loved
me before the world was made.∞ 25Father, you are

∞**16:33 Encouragement:** Romans 5:3–5
∞**17:3 Incarnation:** John 17:11
∞**17:4 Earth:** Romans 1:20
∞**17:6 Names of God:** John 17:26
∞**17:6 Reputation:** John 17:26

17:11 The unity of the church is clearly presented in the New Testament as God's intention. Here Jesus prays for this unity. Somehow the unity of Jesus and the Father are to be modeled by the Christian community: a unity that apparently is not sameness, since here Jesus and the Father are distinct. (This is a basic feature of the Trinity.) The fact that Jesus prayed for this unity and that it is not yet a feature of the worldwide church means that we ought also to pray to this end.

∞**17:11 Blessing:** John 17:24
∞**17:11 Incarnation:** John 17:22
∞**17:15 World/Worldly:** John 15:18–19
∞**17:22 Incarnation:** 1 Corinthians 1:2

17:24 The concept of God's glory is somewhat elusive. It is meant to be that way, indicating that God is far above our ability to comprehend him totally. We get glimpses of his nature, his character, and we see that he is a powerful and unique being. His glory is so overwhelming that people in the Old Testament had to take special precautions not to be destroyed by exposure to God. The wonderful news of the New Testament is that Jesus, who is God himself, reveals God's glory to us. We can learn about God through looking at Jesus, who prays here that God allows us to see his glory.

∞**17:24 Blessing:** Ephesians 1:3–6

the One who is good. The world does not know
you, but I know you, and these people know you
sent me. 26I showed them what you are like, and
I will show them again. Then they will have the
same love that you have for me, and I will live in
them."

Jesus Is Arrested

18 When Jesus finished praying, he went with
his followers across the Kidron Valley. On
the other side there was a garden, and Jesus and
his followers went into it.

2Judas knew where this place was, because Jesus
met there often with his followers. Judas was the
one who turned against Jesus. 3So Judas came there
with a group of soldiers and some guards from the
leading priests and the Pharisees. They were carrying
torches, lanterns, and weapons.

4Knowing everything that would happen to him,
Jesus went out and asked, "Who is it you are looking for?"

5They answered, "Jesus from Nazareth."

"I am he," Jesus said. (Judas, the one who turned
against Jesus, was standing there with them.)
6When Jesus said, "I am he," they moved back and
fell to the ground.

7Jesus asked them again, "Who is it you are
looking for?"

They said, "Jesus of Nazareth."

8"I told you that I am he," Jesus said. "So if you
are looking for me, let the others go." 9This happened so that the words Jesus said before would
come true: "I have not lost any of the ones you
gave me."

10Simon Peter, who had a sword, pulled it out
and struck the servant of the high priest, cutting off
his right ear. (The servant's name was Malchus.)
11Jesus said to Peter, "Put your sword back.
Shouldn't I drink the cup the Father gave me?"

Jesus Is Brought Before Annas

12Then the soldiers with their commander and
the guards arrested Jesus. They tied him 13and led
him first to Annas, the father-in-law of Caiaphas,
the high priest that year. 14Caiaphas was the one
who told the Jews that it would be better if one man
died for all the people.

Peter Says He Doesn't Know Jesus

15Simon Peter and another one of Jesus' followers went along after Jesus. This follower knew the
high priest, so he went with Jesus into the high
priest's courtyard. 16But Peter waited outside near
the door. The follower who knew the high priest
came back outside, spoke to the girl at the door,
and brought Peter inside. 17The girl at the door
said to Peter, "Aren't you also one of that man's
followers?"

Peter answered, "No, I am not!"

18It was cold, so the servants and guards had built
a fire and were standing around it, warming themselves. Peter also was standing with them, warming himself.

The High Priest Questions Jesus

19The high priest asked Jesus questions about
his followers and his teaching. 20Jesus answered,
"I have spoken openly to everyone. I have always
taught in synagogues and in the Temple, where
all the Jews come together. I never said anything in
secret. 21So why do you question me? Ask the
people who heard my teaching. They know what
I said."

22When Jesus said this, one of the guards standing there hit him. The guard said, "Is that the way
you answer the high priest?"

23Jesus answered him, "If I said something wrong,
then show what it was. But if what I said is true,
why do you hit me?"

24Then Annas sent Jesus, who was still tied, to
Caiaphas the high priest.

Peter Says Again He Doesn't Know Jesus

25As Simon Peter was standing and warming himself, they said to him, "Aren't you one of that man's
followers?"

Peter said it was not true; he said, "No, I am not."

26One of the servants of the high priest was there.
This servant was a relative of the man whose ear
Peter had cut off. The servant said, "Didn't I see
you with him in the garden?"

27Again Peter said it wasn't true. At once a
rooster crowed.

Jesus Is Brought Before Pilate

28Early in the morning they led Jesus from
Caiaphas's house to the Roman governor's palace.
They would not go inside the palace, because they
did not want to make themselves unclean; they
wanted to eat the Passover meal. 29So Pilate went
outside to them and asked, "What charges do you
bring against this man?"

17:26 Names of God: Philippians 2:9–10
17:26 Prayer: Romans 8:26–27
17:26 Reputation: 2 Corinthians 6:6–7
17:26 Unity: Acts 15
18:11 *cup.* Jesus is talking about the painful things that will happen to him. Accepting these things will be very hard, like drinking a cup of something bitter.
18:27 Peter: John 20:2–6
18:28 *unclean.* Going into the Roman palace would make them unfit to eat the Passover Feast, according to their Law.

30They answered, "If he were not a criminal, we
wouldn't have brought him to you."
31Pilate said to them, "Take him yourselves and
judge him by your own law."
"But we are not allowed to put anyone to death,"
the Jews answered. 32(This happened so that what
Jesus said about how he would die would come
true.)
33Then Pilate went back inside the palace and
called Jesus to him and asked, "Are you the king
of the Jews?"
34Jesus said, "Is that your own question, or did
others tell you about me?"
35Pilate answered, "I am not one of you. It was
your own people and their leading priests who
handed you over to me. What have you done
wrong?"
36Jesus answered, "My kingdom does not belong
to this world. If it belonged to this world, my servants would fight so that I would not be given over
to the Jews. But my kingdom is from another place."
37Pilate said, "So you are a king!"
Jesus answered, "You are the one saying I am a
king. This is why I was born and came into the
world: to tell people the truth. And everyone who
belongs to the truth listens to me."
38Pilate said, "What is truth?" After he said this,
he went out to the crowd again and said to them,
"I find nothing against this man. 39But it is your
custom that I free one prisoner to you at Passover
time. Do you want me to free the 'king of the
Jews'?"
40They shouted back, "No, not him! Let
Barabbas go free!" (Barabbas was a robber.)

19 Then Pilate ordered that Jesus be taken away
and whipped. 2The soldiers made a crown
from some thorny branches and put it on Jesus'
head and put a purple robe around him. 3Then they
came to him many times and said, "Hail, King of
the Jews!" and hit him in the face.
4Again Pilate came out and said to them,
"Look, I am bringing Jesus out to you. I want you
to know that I find nothing against him." 5So Jesus
came out, wearing the crown of thorns and the
purple robe. Pilate said to them, "Here is the man!"
6When the leading priests and the guards saw
Jesus, they shouted, "Crucify him! Crucify him!"
But Pilate answered, "Crucify him yourselves,
because I find nothing against him."
7The leaders answered, "We have a law that
says he should die, because he said he is the Son
of God."
8When Pilate heard this, he was even more
afraid. 9He went back inside the palace and asked
Jesus, "Where do you come from?" But Jesus did
not answer him. 10Pilate said, "You refuse to speak
to me? Don't you know I have power to set you
free and power to have you crucified?"
11Jesus answered, "The only power you have over
me is the power given to you by God. The man who
turned me in to you is guilty of a greater sin."
12After this, Pilate tried to let Jesus go. But some
in the crowd cried out, "Anyone who makes himself king is against Caesar. If you let this man go,
you are no friend of Caesar."
13When Pilate heard what they were saying, he
brought Jesus out and sat down on the judge's seat
at the place called The Stone Pavement. (In the
Hebrew language the name is Gabbatha.) 14It was
about noon on Preparation Day of Passover week.
Pilate said to the crowd, "Here is your king!"
15They shouted, "Take him away! Take him
away! Crucify him!"
Pilate asked them, "Do you want me to crucify
your king?"
The leading priests answered, "The only king
we have is Caesar."
16So Pilate handed Jesus over to them to be crucified.

Jesus Is Crucified

The soldiers took charge of Jesus. 17Carrying
his own cross, Jesus went out to a place called
The Place of the Skull, which in the Jewish language is called Golgotha. 18There they crucified
Jesus. They also crucified two other men, one on
each side, with Jesus in the middle. 19Pilate wrote
a sign and put it on the cross. It read: JESUS OF
NAZARETH, THE KING OF THE JEWS. 20The sign was
written in Hebrew, in Latin, and in Greek. Many
of the people read the sign, because the place
where Jesus was crucified was near the city.
21The leading priests said to Pilate, "Don't write,
'The King of the Jews.' But write, 'This man said,
"I am the King of the Jews."' "
22Pilate answered, "What I have written, I have
written."
23After the soldiers crucified Jesus, they took his
clothes and divided them into four parts, with each

18:36 When Jesus said to Pilate, "My kingdom does not belong to this world," Pilate may have breathed a sigh of relief. He should have reconsidered. Which is more threatening to a ruler—an external foe with mighty but visible armies or an eternal king who rules the very souls of men and women? The latter can command the will and affections, demand absolute obedience, give unlimited power to his subjects, and radically change their values and their lives. His followers fear no earthly power, and his Kingdom has no end. In the face of such a ruler, any mere political leader must shudder.

19:13 *Hebrew language.* Hebrew, or Aramaic, the languages of many people in this region in the first century.

19:15 Pontius Pilate: 1 Timothy 6:13–15

soldier getting one part. They also took his long
shirt, which was all one piece of cloth, woven from
top to bottom.∞ 24So the soldiers said to each other,
"We should not tear this into parts. Let's throw
lots to see who will get it." This happened so that
this Scripture would come true:

"They divided my clothes among them,
and they threw lots for
my clothing." *Psalm 22:18*

So the soldiers did this.
25Standing near his cross were Jesus' mother,
his mother's sister, Mary the wife of Clopas, and
Mary Magdalene. 26When Jesus saw his mother
and the follower he loved standing nearby, he said
to his mother, "Dear woman, here is your son."
27Then he said to the follower, "Here is your
mother." From that time on, the follower took
her to live in his home.∞

Jesus Dies

28After this, Jesus knew that everything had been
done. So that the Scripture would come true, he
said, "I am thirsty." 29There was a jar full of vinegar there, so the soldiers soaked a sponge in it,
put the sponge on a branch of a hyssop plant, and
lifted it to Jesus' mouth. 30When Jesus tasted the
vinegar, he said, "It is finished." Then he bowed
his head and died.
31This day was Preparation Day, and the next
day was a special Sabbath day. Since the religious
leaders did not want the bodies to stay on the cross
on the Sabbath day, they asked Pilate to order that
the legs of the men be broken and the bodies be
taken away. 32So the soldiers came and broke the
legs of the first man on the cross beside Jesus.
Then they broke the legs of the man on the other
cross beside Jesus. 33But when the soldiers came
to Jesus and saw that he was already dead, they
did not break his legs. 34But one of the soldiers
stuck his spear into Jesus' side, and at once blood
and water came out. 35(The one who saw this
happen is the one who told us this, and whatever

A sprig of hyssop (marjoram)

he says is true. And he knows that he tells the
truth, and he tells it so that you might believe.)
36These things happened to make the Scripture
come true: "Not one of his bones will be broken."
37And another Scripture says, "They will look at
the one they stabbed."∞

Jesus Is Buried

38Later, Joseph from Arimathea asked Pilate if
he could take the body of Jesus. (Joseph was a secret
follower of Jesus, because he was afraid of some of
the leaders.) Pilate gave his permission, so Joseph
came and took Jesus' body away.∞ 39Nicodemus,
who earlier had come to Jesus at night, went with
Joseph. He brought about seventy-five pounds of
myrrh and aloes. 40These two men took Jesus'
body and wrapped it with the spices in pieces of
linen cloth, which is how they bury the dead. 41In
the place where Jesus was crucified, there was a
garden. In the garden was a new tomb that had
never been used before. 42The men laid Jesus in
that tomb because it was nearby, and they were
preparing to start their Sabbath day.

Jesus' Tomb Is Empty

20 Early on the first day of the week, Mary
Magdalene went to the tomb while it was
still dark. When she saw that the large stone had

∞**19:23 The Crucifixion of Jesus (The Way of the Cross):** 1 Corinthians 1:24

19:25–27 One of the most touching scenes in all the Bible is that moment on the cross when Jesus made provision for the welfare of his earthly mother. As Mary stood next to the apostle John at the foot of the cross, Jesus tenderly consigned her to the care of John: "Dear woman, here is your son." In so doing, he forever hallowed family commitment and family responsibility.

∞**19:27 Beloved Disciple:** John 19:34–37

∞**19:27 Family:** Revelation 21:7

19:28 *"I am thirsty."* Read Psalms 22:15; 69:21.

19:30 No finer one-sentence definition of success can be found than this: to accomplish what God has put you on the earth to do. Anyone is successful who can come down to the end of life and say, "It is finished! I have lived as I was supposed to have lived, and I have done what I was supposed to do."

19:31, 36 *broken.* The breaking of their bones would make them die sooner.

19:36 *"Not one . . . broken."* Quotation from Psalm 34:20. The idea is from Exodus 12:46; Numbers 9:12.

19:37 *"They . . . stabbed."* Quotation from Zechariah 12:10.

∞**19:37 Martyrdom:** Acts 7:1–8:4

∞**19:37 Beloved Disciple:** John 20:1–10

∞**19:38 Anti-Semitism:** John 20:19

20:1–10 The other follower to whom Mary Magdalene told her experience is not mentioned by name, but the description "the follower whom Jesus loved," shows it was probably the apostle John. The fact that he went with Peter to the tomb suggests this because John is reported by Luke to be a companion of Peter's (see Acts 3:1ff, 4:1ff), and by Paul to be one of the three leaders of the Jerusalem church (Galatians 2:9).

Parables of Jesus

Parable	*Passage*	*Subject*	*Lesson*
New winebags	Matthew 9:16-17	Jesus' message	Jesus has a new message from God
Farmer and the seed	Matthew 13:1-8 Mark 4:3–8 Luke 8:5-8	God's word	We must hear and obey God's word
Weeds	Matthew 13:24-30	God's people	The good and bad will be separated
Mustard seed	Matthew 13:31-32 Mark 4:30–32 Luke 13:18-19	God's people	Small beginnings can lead to big things
Yeast	Matthew 13:33 Luke 13:20-21	God's people	Small beginnings can lead to big things
Hidden treasure	Matthew 13:44	God's people	Choose what is truly valuable in life
Very valuable pearl	Matthew 13:45-46	God's people	Choose what is truly valuable in life
Fishing net	Matthew 13:47-50	God's people	The good and bad will be separated
Lost sheep	Matthew 18:12-14 Luke 15:3-7	God's love	God loves each person deeply
Servant who would not forgive	Matthew 18:23-25	God's people	We forgive because God forgave us
Workers in a vineyard	Matthew 20:1-16	Service	God rewards us generously
Two sons	Matthew 21:28-32	God's love	God welcomes the sinner who comes to him
Evil renters	Matthew 21:33-46 Mark 12:1-12	Punishment	People who hate God's Son will be punished
Wedding dinner	Matthew 22:1-14	Punishment	People who do not accept God's invitation will be punished
Ten virgins	Matthew 25:1-13	Jesus' return	We must be ready when he comes back
Talents	Matthew 25:14-30	Service	We must use our abilities to serve God
Wise and evil servants	Matthew 24:45-51 Luke 12:42-48	Service	We are to serve God and others as we wait for Jesus to return
Two men who owed money	Luke 7:41-43	God's people	We love God more when we realize we are sinners
Good Samaritan	Luke 10:30-37	Service	Do good to all in need
Friend at midnight	Luke 11:5-8	God's love	God is always willing to help
Unimportant seat at party	Luke 14:7-11	Humility	Don't be proud: let God reward
Lost coin	Luke 15:8-10	God's love	Each one is important to God

Son who left home	Luke 15:11-32	God's love	God forgives all who change their hearts and minds and return to him
Clever manager	Luke 16:1-10	God's people	We are to use money to do good and prepare for the future
Rich man and Lazarus	Luke 16:19-31	Punishment	People who love money more than God are foolish
Unworthy servants	Luke 17:7-10	Service	Serve God because we are thankful
Unfair judge	Luke 18:1-8	God's love	God will answer our prayers if we ask him
Pharisee and tax collector	Luke 18:9-14	God's love	Anyone who changes his heart and life can be forgiven
Bags of money	Luke 19:11-27	Service	Use our talents to serve God

been moved away from the tomb, 2she ran to
Simon Peter and the follower whom Jesus loved.
Mary said, "They have taken the Lord out of the
tomb, and we don't know where they have put
him."
3So Peter and the other follower started for the
tomb. 4They were both running, but the other follower ran faster than Peter and reached the tomb
first. 5He bent down and looked in and saw the
strips of linen cloth lying there, but he did not go
in. 6Then following him, Simon Peter arrived and
went into the tomb and saw the strips of linen lying
there. 7He also saw the cloth that had been
around Jesus' head, which was folded up and laid
in a different place from the strips of linen. 8Then
the other follower, who had reached the tomb
first, also went in. He saw and believed. 9(They
did not yet understand from the Scriptures that
Jesus must rise from the dead.)

Jesus Appears to Mary Magdalene

10Then the followers went back home. 11But
Mary stood outside the tomb, crying. As she was
crying, she bent down and looked inside the
tomb. 12She saw two angels dressed in white, sitting where Jesus' body had been, one at the head
and one at the feet.
13They asked her, "Woman, why are you crying?"
She answered, "They have taken away my Lord,
and I don't know where they have put him." 14When
Mary said this, she turned around and saw Jesus
standing there, but she did not know it was Jesus.
15Jesus asked her, "Woman, why are you crying? Whom are you looking for?"
Thinking he was the gardener, she said to him,
"Did you take him away, sir? Tell me where you
put him, and I will get him."
16Jesus said to her, "Mary."
Mary turned toward Jesus and said in Hebrew,
"Rabboni." (This means Teacher.)
17Jesus said to her, "Don't hold on to me,
because I have not yet gone up to the Father. But
go to my brothers and tell them, 'I am going back
to my Father and your Father, to my God and your
God.'"
18Mary Magdalene went and said to the followers, "I saw the Lord!" And she told them what
Jesus had said to her.

Jesus Appears to His Followers

19When it was evening on the first day of the
week, the followers were together. The doors
were locked, because they were afraid of the
older leaders. Then Jesus came and stood right in
the middle of them and said, "Peace be with
you." 20After he said this, he showed them his
hands and his side. The followers were thrilled
when they saw the Lord.
21Then Jesus said again, "Peace be with you. As
the Father sent me, I now send you." 22After he
said this, he breathed on them and said, "Receive
the Holy Spirit. 23If you forgive anyone his sins,
they are forgiven. If you don't forgive them, they
are not forgiven."

Jesus Appears to Thomas

24Thomas (called Didymus), who was one of
the twelve, was not with them when Jesus came.
25The other followers kept telling Thomas, "We
saw the Lord."
But Thomas said, "I will not believe it until I see the
nail marks in his hands and put my finger where
the nails were and put my hand into his side."
26A week later the followers were in the house
again, and Thomas was with them. The doors were
locked, but Jesus came in and stood right in the
middle of them. He said, "Peace be with you."
27Then he said to Thomas, "Put your finger here,
and look at my hands. Put your hand here in my
side. Stop being an unbeliever and believe."
28Thomas said to him, "My Lord and my God!"
29Then Jesus told him, "You believe because
you see me. Those who believe without seeing me
will be truly happy."

Why John Wrote This Book

30Jesus did many other miracles in the presence
of his followers that are not written in this book.
31But these are written so that you may believe

20:6 Peter: John 21:1–23
20:10 Beloved Disciple: John 21:7
20:16 *Hebrew language.* Hebrew, or Aramaic, the languages of many people in this region in the first century.
20:17 Father: Romans 8:15
20:18 Deborah: Acts 16:14–15
20:19 Anti-Semitism: Acts 2:36
20:24–29 Thomas is, unfairly, the most famous doubter of all time, though the Bible never calls him "doubting Thomas." His life illustrates that having doubts and questions need not keep one from active and courageous faith. Thomas is also the follower who expresses his willingness to die with Jesus (John 11:16), and church tradition indicates Thomas took the Good News all the way to India where he died a martyr.

The story of Thomas speaks of the many followers of Jesus who would live in the years following Jesus's death and resurrection. They have not "seen" the physical Jesus, yet Jesus calls them to have faith anyway. John's Book is written especially for these people, that through this narrative of Jesus' teaching and signs they will be encouraged in their faith.
20:28 Trinity: 1 Corinthians 13:14
20:29 Doubt: Hebrews 11:6

The Powers

EPHESIANS 6:10–18

Who or what are "the powers" to which Paul refers? How are we to respond to the powers? Is there an appropriate use of power?

Paul never explained who or what the rulers and powers were. He wrote as if those reading his letters already knew. How would Paul's readers have thought about these powers? Paul's readers would have understood "rulers and powers" to refer to heavenly beings that controlled and/or lived in earthly rulers or governments. Some who read Paul's words today think only of earthly institutions. Others think only of evil spiritual beings harassing individual Christians. Paul would probably challenge both of these views as too limited. Since he did not seek to correct the common first-century understanding of the powers, we can assume that he too would see a greater blending between the intangible and tangible and between the corporate and individual than either of these two interpretations.

Although Paul is vague on what the powers are, he states clearly what they do. They enslave and seek to separate humans from God. Paul presents the powers as giving life and autonomy to institutions and structures. Humans are controlled by objects which would not normally possess them. In Galatians and Colossians, Paul describes religious rules as a power (Galatians 4:3–11; Colossians 2:20–23). This provides us a concrete example of Paul's concept of a power. Religious rules themselves are apparently powerless and without life. Most of us would assume a human could decide to stop following those rules at any time. Paul presents them, however, as an enslaving power to which we yield control.

Although Paul does not describe it explicitly as a power, money is another example of what Paul means by a power. Jesus recognized that money is more than just metal or paper we can use to buy things when he called it mammon, or riches (Matthew 6:24). We can see this is our lives. There is a spirit of money—something more than just the physical paper. It drives us to accumulate more money and promises us security. It leads us to measure people's value by how much money they have. Money as a simple paper object would be controlled by humans. Money becomes the power that controls us.

We see similar happenings with governments and institutions. Perhaps we could say the powers are at work when the total impact is greater than the sum of the pieces. We can take a number of individuals who on their own, for their own benefit, would not commit injustices or kill. Yet put together within an institution, for the benefit of the institution, they often do things they would consider wrong in another setting. The institution appears to have an independent spirit that controls them.

Paul does not specifically link demons, as we know them in the Gospels, with the powers. Since, however, Paul's concept of the powers is broad and general, it would be appropriate to include demons within our concept of the powers. If, however, we limit our concept of the powers to include only demonic spirits that possess individuals, we will miss much of the significance of Paul's writing for our lives today.

The whole of Paul's writing on the powers communicates two truths of vital importance. First, although the powers act as gods, at the cross God stripped them of this false status and returned them to their appropriate position of created things (Colossians 1:16; 2:13–15). This victory has already been achieved, but we await their total submission at Christ's Second Coming. Therefore, the second truth is that we are clearly still in a battle. The powers continue to live out the lie of their usurped position.

We must be on guard and be aware of the forces seeking to control us, but we can respond to them knowing the truth. They do not have the authority to control. Mammon actually is just money—a thing. Paul clearly states in Colossians that religious rules are just human-made things (2:22). We show the spirit of mammon does not control us when we give money to the Lord's work. We do not have to fear and obey the powers indwelling institutions. We know that these powers cannot separate us from the love of God.

What does all of this mean about our own use of power? First, we should not follow the coercive model of the powers. Paul calls us to take up the armor of God, not their weapons. The victory over these powers occurred at the cross. The victor is a surprising figure—not a mighty warrior, but a crucified God-man (1 Corinthians 1:18–31; Philippians 2:6–11; Colossians 2:11–15). We must base our redefinition of acceptable use of power on the model of our Savior on the cross.

Powers, The: For additional scriptures on this topic go to Romans 8:38.

WEAPONS

EPHESIANS 67:10–18

What kind of weapons can God's people use to fight the battles of life? What are spiritual weapons?

The Bible has many stories of conflict and warfare. Fights begin immediately after the account of the fall into sin. In Genesis 4 we read of the first murder when Cain kills his brother Abel. No specific weapon is described, but this episode begins a long tale of violence that stretches from Genesis to Revelation.

The Old Testament describes many different types of weapons and their use in warfare and other violence. They mention offensive (fighting) weapons like swords, spears, axes, javelins, knives, clubs, slings, and bows and arrows. They also mention defensive (protective) weapons including walls, various types of shields, helmets, and other kinds of armor.

One of the interesting themes of the Old Testament is that God does not depend on how good the weapons of his people are to win his battles. It is true that they must fight, but it is important to God that his people go into battle outnumbered and with fewer weapons than their enemy.

A number of biblical stories illustrate the principle that it is not the weapons that win the battle, but rather God (see Hosea 1:7; Zechariah 4:6). During the conquest of the land of Canaan (the Promised Land), Joshua's first battle was against Jericho, the oldest city in the area and the first to have walls. God caused these walls to crumble without the use of any human weapons. In his campaign against the Canaanite kingdoms, Joshua used weapons of war, but as the biblical writer states: "More people were killed by the hailstones than by the Israelites' swords" (Joshua 10:11).

But perhaps the most well–known example is the encounter between David and Goliath. Goliath was a trained and experienced soldier. He was also an imposing figure, standing nine feet and four inches tall. The passage also describes Goliath's weapons in great detail. It says he came into the camp with "a bronze helmet on his head and a coat of bronze armor that weighed about one hundred twenty-five pounds. He wore bronze protectors on his legs, and he had a bronze spear on his back. The wooden part of his larger spear was like a weaver's rod, and its blade weighed about fifteen pounds. The officer who carried his shield walked in front of him" (1 Samuel 17:5–7).

In contrast David could not fit into Saul's armor, so he entered the battle without it, armed only with a slingshot. His statement to Goliath sums it all up: "You come to me using a sword and two spears. But I come to you in the name of the LORD All-Powerful" (1 Samuel 17:45). The outcome was never in doubt. Goliath fell dead, and David cut off his head.

To draw the meanings of these stories out clearly, it is not human intelligence or skill that wins the battles; it is God himself. For this reason, humans cannot boast or feel pride in their victories, because they would have been defeated if God had not come to their help.

By seeing this idea in the Old Testament we are prepared for the change in the New Testament. Jesus signals the change at the time he is arrested. The angry mob confronts him and the always impetuous Peter responds by pulling his sword and cutting off the ear of the servant of the high priest. Jesus turns to him with these words, "Put your sword back in its place. All who use swords will be killed with swords. Surely you know I could ask my Father, and he would give me more than twelve armies of angels" (Matthew 26:52–53).

This statement fits in with the pattern that we find throughout the New Testament—physical warfare is replaced by spiritual warfare. The Christian does not use physical weapons in their struggle in the present world but rather spiritual ones. These weapons are listed in Ephesians 6. The weapons that are described are both defensive (for protection) and offensive (for fighting). The apostle tells us to "stand strong, with the belt of truth tied around your waist and the protection of right living on your chest. On your feet wear the Good News of peace to help you stand strong. And also use the shield of faith with which you can stop all the burning arrows of the Evil One. Accept God's salvation as your helmet, and take the sword of the Spirit, which is the word of God" (Ephesians 6:14–17). These are the weapons the Christian uses: faith, the word of God, prayer, the Gospel, salvation, and hope. These are the things that will bring Satan's kingdom down. Indeed, Jesus already won the victory over Satan not by killing him with physical weapons but by defeating him by means of his death upon the cross (Colossians 2:15).

Weapons: For additional scriptures on this topic go to 2 Samuel 22:3

that Jesus is the Christ, the Son of God. Then, by believing, you may have life through his name.

Jesus Appears to Seven Followers

21 Later, Jesus showed himself to his followers again—this time at Lake Galilee. This is how he showed himself: 2Some of the followers were together: Simon Peter, Thomas (called Didymus), Nathanael from Cana in Galilee, the two sons of Zebedee, and two other followers. 3Simon Peter said, "I am going out to fish."

The others said, "We will go with you." So they went out and got into the boat. They fished that night but caught nothing.

4Early the next morning Jesus stood on the shore, but the followers did not know it was Jesus. 5Then he said to them, "Friends, did you catch any fish?"

They answered, "No."

6He said, "Throw your net on the right side of the boat, and you will find some." So they did, and they caught so many fish they could not pull the net back into the boat.

7The follower whom Jesus loved said to Peter, "It is the Lord!" When Peter heard him say this, he wrapped his coat around himself. (Peter had taken his clothes off.) Then he jumped into the water. 8The other followers went to shore in the boat, dragging the net full of fish. They were not very far from shore, only about a hundred yards. 9When the followers stepped out of the boat and onto the shore, they saw a fire of hot coals. There were fish on the fire, and there was bread.

10Then Jesus said, "Bring some of the fish you just caught."

11Simon Peter went into the boat and pulled the net to the shore. It was full of big fish, one hundred fifty-three in all, but even though there were so many, the net did not tear. 12Jesus said to them, "Come and eat." None of the followers dared ask him, "Who are you?" because they knew it was the Lord. 13Jesus came and took the bread and gave it to them, along with the fish.

14This was now the third time Jesus showed himself to his followers after he was raised from the dead.

Jesus Talks to Peter

15When they finished eating, Jesus said to Simon Peter, "Simon son of John do you love me more than these?"

He answered, "Yes, Lord, you know that I love you."

Jesus said, "Feed my lambs."

16Again Jesus said, "Simon son of John do you love me?"

He answered, "Yes, Lord, you know that I love you."

Jesus said, "Take care of my sheep."

17A third time he said, "Simon son of John do you love me?"

Peter was hurt because Jesus asked him the third time, "Do you love me?" Peter said, "Lord, you know everything; you know that I love you!"

He said to him, "Feed my sheep. 18I tell you the truth, when you were younger, you tied your own belt and went where you wanted. But when you are old, you will put out your hands and someone else will tie you and take you where you don't want to go." 19(Jesus said this to show how Peter would die to give glory to God.) Then Jesus said to Peter, "Follow me!"

20Peter turned and saw that the follower Jesus loved was walking behind them. (This was the follower who had leaned against Jesus at the supper and had said, "Lord, who will turn against you?") 21When Peter saw him behind them, he asked Jesus, "Lord, what about him?"

22Jesus answered, "If I want him to live until I come back, that is not your business. You follow me."

23So a story spread among the followers that this one would not die. But Jesus did not say he would not die. He only said, "If I want him to live until I come back, that is not your business."

24That follower is the one who is telling these

20:31 Body/Resurrection: John 21

20:31 Faith/Unbelief: See article on page 982.

20:31 Son/Child of God: Romans 8:1–4

21:1 *Lake Galilee.* Literally, "Sea of Tiberias."

21:7 Beloved Disciple: John 21:20–23

21:14 Table Fellowship/Lord's Supper: Acts 2:42

21:15–22 All of us can take some comfort in the stumbling of Peter. He made many mistakes, including denying Jesus at the very time in which he swore he would maintain faithfulness. After Jesus had been raised from the dead, he appeared to Peter in John 21 and questioned him three times saying, "Simon son of John do you love me?" Peter replied in the affirmative each time. Then after Jesus commanded Peter to feed his sheep, he said to him: "Follow me" (John 21:19)!

As sinful human beings we have each made many mistakes. Our fallen humanity, of course, spills over into our careers causing us all to have less than godly motives within our areas of work. But Jesus is patient and loving with us. In his amazing love he took a rough fisherman named Peter and used him to help start the very church that we are a part of today. With that same love, Jesus comes to each of us today and asks, "Do you love me?" If we truly love him and give our lives to him, then we will obediently respond to his second command, "Follow me!" And then our careers will become a lifelong response of love expressed in true vocational fidelity to Christ.

21:19 Career/Careerism: Philippians 1:22

21:19 Leadership: Acts 5:31

21:19 Work: Romans 12:6–11

21:23 Beloved Disciple: See article on page 1034.

21:23 Peter: Acts 1:13–22

things and who has now written them down. We know that what he says is true.
[25]There are many other things Jesus did. If every one of them were written down, I suppose the whole world would not be big enough for all the books that would be written.

21:25 Body/Resurrection: Acts 1:1–11

INTRODUCTION TO THE BOOK OF

ACTS

The Good News of Jesus Spreads

WHO WROTE THIS BOOK?

The same witnesses who identify Luke as the author of the Book of Luke also name him as the author of Acts.

TO WHOM WAS THIS BOOK WRITTEN?

Acts 1:1 addresses this book to the same person—Theophilus—as was addressed in the beginning of the Book of Luke (see Luke 1:3). The ultimate audience is both Jews and non-Jews of the last third of the first century.

WHERE WAS IT WRITTEN?

Assuming that Luke was with the apostle Paul in Rome during his first imprisonment, which is the point at which the Book of Acts ends, it is likely that this book was written at Rome.

WHEN WAS IT WRITTEN?

Since no reference is made to events after A.D. 63, this is the probable date of its writing.

WHAT IS THE BOOK ABOUT?

As Acts 1:8 suggests, this book is about Jesus' followers fulfilling his command for them to carry the Good News about him from Jerusalem to the entire world. It is the story of the birth of the church at Pentecost. And it tells the story of how the apostles and other followers accomplished their task in only thirty years. The ministries of the apostles Peter and Paul are highlighted in the book, along with the first deacons and James. Acts, true to its name, is a book of exciting *actions* and happenings of the church in the first century.

WHY WAS THIS BOOK WRITTEN?

The Book of Acts was written as a bridge between the four accounts of the Good News (Matthew, Mark, Luke, and John) and the letters of the apostles (Romans–Jude). It was written to show the ministry of the Holy Spirit in establishing the earthly church and carrying out the ministry of Christ in this world. It teaches us a history of the spread of the Good News to the world. And it guides us in the proper establishment of local churches and carrying out missionary activities.

SO WHAT DOES THIS BOOK MEAN TO US?

Christ's commission to his followers has not changed; it has not been repealed. We, as Christians, are still responsible for taking the Good News of Jesus with us into the whole world—to every people, to every nation, to every nook and cranny of the earth. At the same time, Jesus' promise to be with us as we go is also still in effect. The Holy Spirit, who empowered and directed the first-century Christians, still empowers and directs us today as we go into our world for the Lord.

SUMMARY:

As the second volume of Luke's two-part series (see Luke 1:1–4; Acts 1:1–3), The Book of Acts continues the story of the spread of the Good News following Jesus' resurrection. In our New Testament, Acts comes between the four accounts of the Good News and a lengthy section of letters to specific churches. Acts thus provides a bridge from the ministry of Jesus to the concrete problems faced by followers of Jesus as they formed small house churches throughout the Roman world. Acts also demonstrates the success of Jesus' vision, as his ministry in the region of Palestine (known as Galilee) is expanded so that it embraces the whole world.

Like the Book of Luke, Acts is primarily about salvation: God's purpose to bring salvation in all of its fullness to all people. A number of themes are developed under this general heading.

The primary force in the spread of the Good News is the Holy Spirit. The Spirit empowers and directs those who are involved in the mission. In fact, every time the mission has a fresh beginning or new twist, it is because of the activity of the Holy Spirit leading the church into new frontiers of mission. Moreover, the Holy Spirit indwells believers, making them one people and proving to those who doubt that even non-Jews are to be counted among the family of God.

Throughout the Book of Acts, the church struggles to catch up with God. In spite of the teaching of Jesus that had formed their early days as followers, these vagabond followers of Jesus seem continually to be surprised by the new things God is doing. Through references to the Old Testament, through visions and dreams, through the voice of prophets, and through other means, God repeatedly works to teach those early Christians how he is bringing his purpose to completion in sometimes surprising ways.

The vision for the mission is clear: from Jerusalem to Judea to Samaria and to every part of the world (Acts 1:8). Jewish thinking about the end time often focused on the coming of all the nations to worship God in Jerusalem. In his parting words to his followers, Jesus turns this idea around, insisting that God's grace has gone out from Jerusalem to the rest of the world, and God's people must do the same. Every boundary must be crossed as people are challenged with the Good News of salvation.

Salvation in Acts has both personal and social implications. Above all else, salvation means membership in the new community of those who serve the will of God. Baptism and the gift of the Holy Spirit are both related to membership in this growing family of believers. Salvation in Acts is also presented as the forgiveness of sins; forgiveness means both restored relationship with God, and also admission or readmission into the group of those who follow Jesus.

Early in Acts, we learn that the early community participated in the sharing of their money and other possessions. This was not a requirement for membership in the community, but a demonstration of the unity of the church, as though its members shared life together as a family.

Finally, Acts repeatedly tells the story of how Christians encountered difficulty in their dealings with the authorities. Paul is brought before public hearings again and again, just as Peter and John had been brought up on charges before him. As Acts tells the story, Christians should not necessarily expect trouble from authorities; instead, Christians are encouraged to maintain complete allegiance to God even when human authorities oppose them.

ACTS

Luke Writes Another Book

To Theophilus.

The first book I wrote was about everything Jesus began to do and teach 2until the day he was taken up into heaven. Before this, with the help of the Holy Spirit, Jesus told the apostles he had chosen what they should do. 3After his death, he showed himself to them and proved in many ways that he was alive. The apostles saw Jesus during the forty days after he was raised from the dead, and he spoke to them about the kingdom of God. 4Once when he was eating with them, he told them not to leave Jerusalem. He said, "Wait here to receive the promise from the Father which I told you about. 5John baptized people with water, but in a few days you will be baptized with the Holy Spirit."

Jesus Is Taken Up Into Heaven

6When the apostles were all together, they asked Jesus, "Lord, are you now going to give the kingdom back to Israel?"

7Jesus said to them, "The Father is the only One who has the authority to decide dates and times. These things are not for you to know. 8But when the Holy Spirit comes to you, you will receive power. You will be my witnesses—in Jerusalem, in all of Judea, in Samaria, and in every part of the world."

9After he said this, as they were watching, he was lifted up, and a cloud hid him from their sight. 10As he was going, they were looking into the sky. Suddenly, two men wearing white clothes stood beside them. 11They said, "Men of Galilee, why are you standing here looking into the sky? Jesus, whom you saw taken up from you into heaven, will come back in the same way you saw him go."

A New Apostle Is Chosen

12Then they went back to Jerusalem from the Mount of Olives. (This mountain is about half a mile from Jerusalem.) 13When they entered the city, they went to the upstairs room where they were staying. Peter, John, James, Andrew, Philip, Thomas, Bartholomew, Matthew, James son of Alphaeus, Simon (known as the Zealot), and Judas son of James were there. 14They all continued praying together with some women, including Mary the mother of Jesus, and Jesus' brothers.

15During this time there was a meeting of the believers (about one hundred twenty of them). Peter stood up and said, 16-17"Brothers and sisters, in the Scriptures the Holy Spirit said through David something that must happen involving Judas. He was one of our own group and served together with us. He led those who arrested Jesus." 18(Judas bought a field with the money he got for his evil act. But he fell to his death, his body burst open, and all his intestines poured out. 19Everyone in Jerusalem learned about this so they named this place Akeldama. In their language Akeldama means "Field of Blood.") 20"In the Book of Psalms," Peter said, "this is written:

'May his place be empty;
leave no one to live in it.' *Psalm 69:25*

And it is also written:

'Let another man replace him
as leader.' *Psalm 109:8*

21-22"So now a man must become a witness with us of Jesus' being raised from the dead. He must be one of the men who were part of our group during all the time the Lord Jesus was among us—from the time John was baptizing people until the day Jesus was taken up from us to heaven."

23They put the names of two men before the group. One was Joseph Barsabbas, who was also called Justus. The other was Matthias. 24-25The apostles prayed, "Lord, you know the thoughts of everyone. Show us which one of these two you have chosen to do this work. Show us who should

1:3 Luke: Acts 16:10–17

1:8 This is more than a list of places on a map. Jerusalem was known as the center of the world for the Jewish people. Samaria was not far away on the map, but in terms of religious commitments, people who lived in Samaria were separated from the Jews. Jesus is instructing his followers to ignore divisions between people and to take the Good News to all.

The kingdom of God was announced through the earthly ministry of Jesus to Jewish people, centering on Jerusalem. But by God's plan it spread to all of Judea, then to Samaria, and then to the whole world. We are in the final phase of that process, where everyone is invited to accept Christ. That's our mission!

1:8 Land/Inheritance: Acts 4:34–37

1:9 Evangelism: Acts 2:14–42

1:9–12 The Mount of Olives plays a significant role in the major events near the end of Jesus' life on earth. It was here Jesus told his disciples the signs of the end times, he was arrested in the Garden of Gethsemane, he ascended from the earth, and he will return one day. Even today, visitors to this hill overlooking Jerusalem are thrilled by the panorama of the city.

1:11 Body/Resurrection: Acts 9:1–19

1:12 Mount of Olives: Hebrews 5:7

1:16 *Brothers and sisters.* Although the Greek text says "Brothers" here and throughout this book, the words of the speakers were meant for the entire church, including men and women.

1:16 Judas: See article on page 778.

1:22 Peter: Acts 2:14–40

be an apostle in place of Judas, who turned away
and went where he belongs." [26]Then they used
lots to choose between them, and the lots showed
that Matthias was the one. So he became an apostle
with the other eleven.

The Coming of the Holy Spirit

2 When the day of Pentecost came, they were
all together in one place. [2]Suddenly a noise
like a strong, blowing wind came from heaven
and filled the whole house where they were sitting. [3]They saw something like flames of fire that
were separated and stood over each person there.
[4]They were all filled with the Holy Spirit, and
they began to speak different languages by the
power the Holy Spirit was giving them.

"You will be my witnesses . . . in every part of the world" (1:8).

[5]There were some religious Jews staying in
Jerusalem who were from every country in the
world. [6]When they heard this noise, a crowd came
together. They were all surprised, because each one
heard them speaking in his own language. [7]They
were completely amazed at this. They said, "Look!
Aren't all these people that we hear speaking from
Galilee? [8]Then how is it possible that we each hear
them in our own languages? We are from different
places: [9]Parthia, Media, Elam, Mesopotamia, Judea,
Cappadocia, Pontus, Asia, [10]Phrygia, Pamphylia,
Egypt, the areas of Libya near Cyrene, Rome [11](both
Jews and those who had become Jews), Crete, and
Arabia. But we hear them telling in our own languages about the great things God has done!"
[12]They were all amazed and confused, asking each
other, "What does this mean?"
[13]But others were making fun of them, saying,
"They have had too much wine."

Peter Speaks to the People

[14]But Peter stood up with the eleven apostles,
and in a loud voice he spoke to the crowd: "My fellow Jews, and all of you who are in Jerusalem, listen
to me. Pay attention to what I have to say. [15]These
people are not drunk, as you think; it is only nine
o'clock in the morning! [16]But Joel the prophet
wrote about what is happening here today:

[17]'God says: In the last days
I will pour out my Spirit on all kinds of people.
Your sons and daughters will prophesy.
Your young men will see visions,
and your old men will dream dreams.
[18]At that time I will pour out my Spirit
also on my male slaves and female slaves,
and they will prophesy.
[19]I will show miracles
in the sky and on the earth:
blood, fire, and thick smoke.
[20]The sun will become dark,
the moon red as blood,
before the overwhelming and glorious day
of the Lord will come.

2 This passage tells the story of God's first gift of "tongues," or different languages, to the church. A few weeks after Jesus had died and risen from the dead, his followers were together in a room in Jerusalem and experienced a powerful work of God's Spirit, including being able to speak in different languages. The outpouring of the Spirit in this way signals the fulfillment of Joel 2:28 and the promise that all people could receive the Holy Spirit.

The effects of God's Spirit drew a crowd and provided the setting for the preaching of the Good News of Jesus' resurrection. The passage stresses that these different languages were God's gift, for "they were all filled with the Holy Spirit, and they began to speak different languages by the power the Holy Spirit was giving them" (Acts 2:4). This story also mentions the miracle of what the visitors from many countries heard as they said, "we hear them telling in our own languages about the great things God has done" (Acts 2:11). This is the only reference in the Bible to a gift of languages which mentions that the languages were naturally understood. Peter, one of Jesus' followers, explained to the onlookers that what they were seeing and hearing was the result of God's promise to pour out his Spirit on his people, and give them abilities to speak about God. The experience of God's people speaking in new languages of the greatness of God was a sign that God was beginning a new way of relating to his people, the way of the Holy Spirit.

The phrase "speaking in different languages" also occurs in Acts 10:46; 19:6 and 1 Corinthians 14 (where it is listed as a specific spiritual gift). It is not clear in these passages that the gift relates to communicating the Good News to others as it does in Acts 2 (in fact in 1 Corinthians 14 Paul wants to guide the use of gift precisely because it does not help the communication of the Good News). Pentecost in some ways appears unique among the biblical references to tongues, but there is no real systematic examination of this experience in the biblical texts.

2:1 Feasts/Festivals: 1 Corinthians 5:6–8

2:6 *languages.* This can also be translated "tongues."

2:13 Alcohol: 1 Corinthians 6:10

2:17 Family: Genesis 3:20

2:18 Servant of the Lord: Acts 3:13

21 Then anyone who calls on the Lord
will be saved.' *Joel 2:28-32*

22 "People of Israel, listen to these words: Jesus
from Nazareth was a very special man. God clearly
showed this to you by the miracles, wonders, and
signs he did through Jesus. You all know this,
because it happened right here among you. 23 Jesus
was given to you, and with the help of those who
don't know the law, you put him to death by nailing him to a cross. But this was God's plan which
he had made long ago; he knew all this would
happen. 24 God raised Jesus from the dead and set
him free from the pain of death, because death
could not hold him. 25 For David said this about
him:

'I keep the Lord before me always.
Because he is close by my side,
I will not be hurt.
26 So I am glad, and I rejoice.
Even my body has hope,
27 because you will not leave me in the grave.
You will not let your Holy One rot.
28 You will teach me how to live a holy life.
Being with you will fill me with joy.' *Psalm 16:8-11*

29 "Brothers and sisters, I can tell you truly that
David, our ancestor, died and was buried. His
grave is still here with us today. 30 He was a
prophet and knew God had promised him that he
would make a person from David's family a king
just as he was. 31 Knowing this before it happened,
David talked about the Christ rising from the dead.
He said:

'He was not left in the grave.
His body did not rot.'

32 So Jesus is the One whom God raised from the
dead. And we are all witnesses to this. 33 Jesus
was lifted up to heaven and is now at God's right
side. The Father has given the Holy Spirit to Jesus
as he promised. So Jesus has poured out that
Spirit, and this is what you now see and hear.
34 David was not the one who was lifted up to
heaven, but he said:

'The Lord said to my Lord,
"Sit by me at my right side,
35 until I put your enemies under
your control."' *Psalm 110:1*

36 "So, all the people of Israel should know this
truly: God has made Jesus—the man you nailed
to the cross—both Lord and Christ."

37 When the people heard this, they felt guilty
and asked Peter and the other apostles, "What
shall we do?"

38 Peter said to them, "Change your hearts and
lives and be baptized, each one of you, in the
name of Jesus Christ for the forgiveness of your
sins. And you will receive the gift of the Holy
Spirit. 39 This promise is for you, for your children, and for all who are far away. It is for everyone the Lord our God calls to himself."

40 Peter warned them with many other words.
He begged them, "Save yourselves from the evil
of today's people!" 41 Then those people who
accepted what Peter said were baptized. About
three thousand people were added to the number
of believers that day. 42 They spent their time
learning the apostles' teaching, sharing, breaking
bread, and praying together.

The Believers Share

43 The apostles were doing many miracles and
signs, and everyone felt great respect for God.
44 All the believers were together and shared
everything. 45 They would sell their land and the
things they owned and then divide the money
and give it to anyone who needed it. 46 The believers met together in the Temple every day. They
ate together in their homes, happy to share their
food with joyful hearts. 47 They praised God and
were liked by all the people. Every day the Lord
added those who were being saved to the group
of believers.

2:21 Salvation: Romans 12:1–2
2:30 *God . . . was.* See 2 Samuel 7:13; Psalm 132:11.
2:34 David: Acts 13:34
2:35 *until . . . control.* Literally, "until I make your enemies a footstool for your feet."
2:36 Anti-Semitism: Romans 11:7–12
2:36 Lordship: Acts 10:36
2:38 Repentance: Acts 3:19
2:39 Reconciliation: 2 Corinthians 5:19
2:40 Peter: Acts 3:1–26
2:42 Fellowship: 1 Corinthians 1:9
2:42 Table Fellowship/Lord's Supper: Acts 2:46
2:42 Evangelism: Acts 5:12–16
2:42 *breaking bread.* This may mean a meal as in verse 46, or the Lord's Supper, the special meal Jesus told his followers to eat to remember him (Luke 22:14-20).
2:43–47 Luke, the writer of Acts, often stops the action of the narrative in order to provide a summary statement like this one. This gives us an idea of what was typical for those first Christians. Twice he mentions that the believers ate together. This reminds us of Jesus' table fellowship, and suggests that the believers have learned to treat each other as family gathered around a common meal.
2:46 Table Fellowship/Lord's Supper: 1 Corinthians 10:14–22
2:47 Church: Acts 9:31
2:47 Community: Acts 4:32–36
2:47 Materialism/Possessions: Acts 4:32–5:11
2:47 Money: Acts 4:32–37
2:47 Celebration: 1 Corinthians 11:23–26
2:47 Communication: Acts 9:15

Peter Heals a Crippled Man

3 One day Peter and John went to the Temple at three o'clock, the time set each day for the afternoon prayer service. 2There, at the Temple gate called Beautiful Gate, was a man who had been crippled all his life. Every day he was carried to this gate to beg for money from the people going into the Temple. 3The man saw Peter and John going into the Temple and asked them for money. 4Peter and John looked straight at him and said, "Look at us!" 5The man looked at them, thinking they were going to give him some money. 6But Peter said, "I don't have any silver or gold, but I do have something else I can give you. By the power of Jesus Christ from Nazareth, stand up and walk!" 7Then Peter took the man's right hand and lifted him up. Immediately the man's feet and ankles became strong. 8He jumped up, stood on his feet, and began to walk. He went into the Temple with them, walking and jumping and praising God. 9-10All the people recognized him as the crippled man who always sat by the Beautiful Gate begging for money. Now they saw this same man walking and praising God, and they were amazed. They wondered how this could happen.

Peter Speaks to the People

11While the man was holding on to Peter and John, all the people were amazed and ran to them at Solomon's Porch. 12When Peter saw this, he said to them, "People of Israel, why are you surprised? You are looking at us as if it were our own power or goodness that made this man walk. 13The God of Abraham, Isaac, and Jacob, the God of our ancestors, gave glory to Jesus, his servant. But you handed him over to be killed. Pilate decided to let him go free, but you told Pilate you did not want Jesus. 14You did not want the One who is holy and good but asked Pilate to give you a murderer instead. 15And so you killed the One who gives life, but God raised him from the dead. We are witnesses to this. 16It was faith in Jesus that made this crippled man well. You can see this man, and you know him. He was made completely well because of trust in Jesus, and you all saw it happen!

17"Brothers and sisters, I know you did those things to Jesus because neither you nor your leaders understood what you were doing. 18God said through the prophets that his Christ would suffer and die. And now God has made these things come true in this way. 19So you must change your hearts and lives! Come back to God, and he will forgive your sins. Then the Lord will send the time of rest. 20And he will send Jesus, the One he chose to be the Christ. 21But Jesus must stay in heaven until the time comes when all things will be made right again. God told about this time long ago when he spoke through his holy prophets. 22Moses said, 'The Lord your God will give you a prophet like me, who is one of your own people. You must listen to everything he tells you. 23Anyone who does not listen to that prophet will die, cut off from God's people.' 24Samuel, and all the other prophets who spoke for God after Samuel, told about this time now. 25You are descendants of the prophets. You have received the agreement God made with your ancestors. He said to your father Abraham, 'Through your descendants all the nations on the earth will be blessed.' 26God has raised up his servant Jesus and sent him to you first to bless you by turning each of you away from doing evil."

Peter and John at the Council

4 While Peter and John were speaking to the people, priests, the captain of the soldiers that guarded the Temple, and Sadducees came up to them. 2They were upset because the two apostles were teaching the people and were preaching that people will rise from the dead through the power of Jesus. 3The older leaders grabbed Peter

---

3:9 Poverty: See article on page 872.
3:10 Sickness, Disease, Healing: Acts 4:30
3:13 In Peter's address to the people after the healing of the lame man at the Beautiful Gate, he accused them of handing Jesus over to the Roman governor, Pontius Pilate. He said they were responsible for Jesus being killed by the Romans (Acts 3:15). Peter adds that they did this despite the fact that Pilate had "decided to let him go free." Actually, Pilate tried to release Jesus not once but three times (John 18:38; 19:4, 6).
3:13 Servant of the Lord: Acts 26:16
3:14 *murderer.* Barabbas, the man the crowd asked Pilate to set free instead of Jesus (Luke 23:18).
3:18 Suffering: Acts 17:3
3:18–24 In Peter's sermon, after healing the lame man at the Beautiful Gate, he refers to the prophecy concerning a prophet who would arise like Moses and attributes that prophecy to Jesus. Jesus is the "Prophet," the Messiah who is to come that everyone must listen to or risk being cut off from the people of God. He fulfills all the prophecies about the Messiah.

Samuel and all the Old Testament prophets were living examples of what Jesus would do as the great prophet Moses spoke of in Deuteronomy 18. Samuel was a unique prophet because he was also a priest and a judge (kingly role). His three-fold office looked forward to Jesus who is a greater prophet, priest, and king. The story of Samuel's life is found in 1 Samuel 1–25.
3:19 Repentance: Revelation 2:1–7
3:22–23 *'The Lord . . . people.'* Quotation from Deuteronomy 18:15, 19.
3:25 *'Through . . . blessed.'* Quotation from Genesis 22:18; 26:4.
3:26 Peter: Acts 4:1–23
3:26 Promise: Romans 4:20–21
4:2 Pharisees and Sadducees: Acts 5:12–18

FRIENDSHIP

PHILIPPIANS 1

What is the meaning of friendship in Israel and in the world of the New Testament? In what way did New Testament writers use cultural notions of friendship to communicate something of the challenge of Christian relations? In what ways do these understandings shed light on or challenge contemporary experiences of friendship?

From the beginning, the Bible recognizes that human beings are social creatures who need one another. God said in Genesis 2:18, "It is not good for the man to be alone," and from that time forward, there is a recognition that part of what it means to be fully human is to be in relationship with other people.

A great example of friendship in the Old Testament is the relationship between Jonathan and David. Jonathan had many reasons to avoid relationship with David, not the least of which was that David has been anointed to be the next king (1 Samuel 16:1–13), a position that by birthright should have belonged to Jonathan (1 Samuel 20:30–31). But Jonathan loved David as much as he loved himself (1 Samuel 18:3) and proved it by contending with his father, Saul, over his treatment of David (1 Samuel 19:1–7).

Friendship is also a very important topic in the thoughts and writings of the Greek and Roman philosophers, who considered true friendship the most valuable of relationships and taught that apart from friendship, life was not really worth living.

Paul used this friendship vocabulary in his letter to the Philippians: "I thank God for the help you gave me while I preached the Good News" (1:5); "all of you share in God's grace with me" (1:7); "standing strong with one purpose . . . work together as one for the faith of the Good News" (1:27); "do we share together in the spirit?" (2:1); "make me very happy by having the same thoughts, sharing the same love, and having one mind and purpose" (2:2); "do not be interested only in your own life, but be interested in the lives of others" (2:4). Given the importance of true friendship in the Greek world, it is significant that Paul thought of his relationship with them in friendship terms and called them to this kind of relationship with one another.

But something else was going on here. The Greek friendship ideal was between two good men, alike in integrity and thought. But Paul commanded that type of friendship be between all believers. Moreover, Paul insisted that the unity of friendship be preserved, even though the participants were not always alike. Paul and the Philippians were different in many ways: he was a Jew, while they were Greeks; he was a man and some of them were women (4:2–3); he was an apostle, and they were his converts. How could their friendships cross the ethnic, gender, and status barriers? Where was their commonality, their sameness? Paul taught that their relationships must be rooted in the Good News (1:5), in the fact that they all shared God's grace (1:7) and his Spirit (2:1). Thus the common bond they shared did not originate in themselves, but in God. Another difference between Greek friendship and what we find in Philippians is that their relationships were to go beyond equality to serving one another (2:3–4, 5–11). As Jesus himself taught, they were not to show their power over one another, but to serve each other (Mark 10:42–45). Finally, their relationships were not just for their own enjoyment; they were to work together for the Good News (1:27–30). It was friendship with a purpose.

What does this mean for us today? As believers, we are called not only to God, but to one another, in love, unity, and service. Relating to other Christians is a command, not an option. In particular, this means making a special effort to reach out to those who are different than we are. Friendship with those who are like us is much easier, and it is certainly more comfortable. But we are to have friendship—not just friendly feelings—with people across social status, ethnic, and gender boundaries, rooted in God's grace toward us all; Jesus himself modeled this lifestyle (see note on Matthew 11:19). By sharing God's love across these barriers (barriers which are mostly uncrossed today, both inside and outside of the church), we demonstrate the transforming power of God's Good News in our lives, for the believing community, and ultimately, for our unbelieving society.∞

∞**Friendship:** For additional scriptures on this topic go to 1 Samuel 18:1–4.

LUKE

COLOSSIANS 4:14

Who was Luke? How does he help us to understand better the Christian faith?

Luke is only mentioned by name in the New Testament three times. This is surprising, given his popularity among Christians who often refer to him as "Luke the physician." It is also surprising because of his importance as a New Testament author.

The third gospel in the New Testament bears the name, "The Gospel of Luke." Of course, like all of the New Testament Gospels, the third gospel was an anonymous narrative. None of the Gospels contain within the narratives themselves the name of their authors. Instead, their names were added as headings to the gospel writings in the second century. No doubt, this was to ensure that no one missed the central importance of Jesus to those narratives. The writers of the Gospels told the story of Jesus in order to draw attention to him and to declare his significance, not to say something about themselves!

Nevertheless, only a few decades after this book was written, it was maintained that Luke wrote the third gospel. Because of the similarity between Luke 1:1–4 and Acts 1:1–3, most believe that Luke was the author of the Acts of the Apostles too. This means that he is responsible for writing more than one-fourth of the New Testament, having written even more pages in the New Testament than Paul.

According to Paul, Luke was a physician and sometime fellow-worker (Philemon 24; Colossians 4:14). It is true that physicians in the first century could have bad reputations as money-grabbing quacks (see Mark 5:26), but they usually enjoyed great respect in the Roman world. They were even known as "saviors" in the language of the day. Physicians were not only concerned with healing physical ailments, but added to their medical skills their reputations as philosophers. Since human beings were not usually thought of as consisting of bodies separate from souls, illnesses needed to be addressed at more than a physical level. People, and not only their bodies, were sick. Because of this background, it is not surprising to see how Luke presents the work of Jesus in his gospel. Luke emphasizes more than any other New Testament writer that Jesus is the Savior who heals the sick (see Luke 4:43; 5:21). He has many stories of healing; in them, it is typical to find Jesus restoring persons to physical, social, and spiritual health, all at once (see Luke 7:11–17; 8:26–56).

Luke was almost certainly a Gentile, and this gives him a distinctive way of looking at the message of Jesus. In fact, it is fair to say that he has written both the Gospel of Luke and the Acts of the Apostles from the point of view of one who is attempting to show the importance of Jesus especially for the wider world. For example, he locates the birth of Jesus on the stage of world history (see Luke 2:1–2) and reports how Peter came to the realization that Jesus was "Lord of all," and not only of the Jewish people (Acts 10:36; see Acts 10:1–11:18). At the same time, though, Luke's two volumes highlight for an increasingly Gentile Christian church the roots of Christianity in Judaism and the Old Testament. It is as if he wants to tell the story of the church from its beginnings in the promises of Abraham in the Old Testament, straight through to Jesus and into the early church (see Acts 13:16–26). He writes in order to show that those who believe in Jesus are the people of God, and to encourage them to respond to the grace of God by embracing his purpose for them fully and faithfully.

To Luke belongs the honor of being the first Christian historian. He alone among the New Testament writers tells the story of the early church. The other writers of the Gospels end their narratives with the resurrection of Jesus and his commission to his followers. Luke continues the story into the first decades of the church. On the one hand, this provides us with a great deal of information we would not otherwise have about the growing church, including the missionary journeys of Paul. On the other, Luke is able to show how the grace of God at work in the ministry of Jesus was also at work through the apostles and other messengers on whom the Holy Spirit had fallen; they continue the ministry he had begun. The result is not only an informative history, but an exciting story of the power of God at work.

Luke is able to tell this story because he experienced part of it himself. It is true that he did some research, collecting material about Jesus and his disciples from other witnesses (see Luke 1:1–4). At several points in the story, Luke himself seems to have been present. He travels with Paul during parts of his mission, even experiencing with Paul the shipwreck on the way to Paul's imprisonment in Rome (see Acts 16:10–17; 27:1–28:16). Luke, then, is a second- or third-generation Christian who includes himself with the "us" among whom God has acted to bring to fulfillment his saving purpose for the whole world (Luke 1:1–2).

Luke: For additional scriptures on this topic go to Luke 1:1–4.

and John and put them in jail. Since it was
already night, they kept them in jail until the
next day. 4But many of those who had heard
Peter and John preach believed the things they
said. There were now about five thousand in the
group of believers.
5The next day the rulers, the older leaders, and
the teachers of the law met in Jerusalem. 6Annas
the high priest, Caiaphas, John, and Alexander
were there, as well as everyone from the high
priest's family. 7They made Peter and John stand
before them and then asked them, "By what
power or authority did you do this?"
8Then Peter, filled with the Holy Spirit, said to
them, "Rulers of the people and you older leaders, 9are you questioning us about a good thing
that was done to a crippled man? Are you asking
us who made him well? 10We want all of you and
all the people to know that this man was made
well by the power of Jesus Christ from Nazareth.
You crucified him, but God raised him from the
dead. This man was crippled, but he is now well
and able to stand here before you because of the
power of Jesus. 11Jesus is

'the stone that you builders rejected,
which has become the cornerstone.'

Psalm 118:22

12Jesus is the only One who can save people. His
name is the only power in the world that has been
given to save people. We must be saved through
him."
13The leaders saw that Peter and John were
not afraid to speak, and they understood that
these men had no special training or education.
So they were amazed. Then they realized that
Peter and John had been with Jesus. 14Because
they saw the healed man standing there beside
the two apostles, they could say nothing against
them. 15After the leaders ordered them to leave
the meeting, they began to talk to each other.
16They said, "What shall we do with these men?
Everyone in Jerusalem knows they have done a
great miracle, and we cannot say it is not true.
17But to keep it from spreading among the people, we must warn them not to talk to people
anymore using that name."
18So they called Peter and John in again and
told them not to speak or to teach at all in the
name of Jesus. 19But Peter and John answered
them, "You decide what God would want. Should
we obey you or God? 20We cannot keep quiet.
We must speak about what we have seen and
heard." 21The leaders warned the apostles again
and let them go free. They could not find a way to
punish them, because all the people were praising God for what had been done. 22The man who
received the miracle of healing was more than
forty years old.

The Believers Pray

23After Peter and John left the meeting of leaders, they went to their own group and told them
everything the leading priests and the older leaders
had said to them. 24When the believers heard
this, they prayed to God together, "Lord, you are
the One who made the sky, the earth, the sea,
and everything in them. 25By the Holy Spirit,
through our father David your servant, you said:

'Why are the nations so angry?
Why are the people making useless plans?
26The kings of the earth prepare to fight,
and their leaders make plans together
against the Lord
and his Christ.'

Psalm 2:1-2

27These things really happened when Herod,
Pontius Pilate, and some of the people all came
together against Jesus here in Jerusalem. Jesus is
your holy servant, the One you made to be the
Christ. 28These people made your plan happen
because of your power and your will. 29And now,
Lord, listen to their threats. Lord, help us, your
servants, to speak your word without fear. 30Help
us to be brave by showing us your power to heal.
Give proofs and make miracles happen by the
power of Jesus, your holy servant."
31After they had prayed, the place where they
were meeting was shaken. They were all filled
with the Holy Spirit, and they spoke God's word
without fear.

The Believers Share

32The group of believers were united in their
hearts and spirit. All those in the group acted as
though their private property belonged to everyone in the group. In fact, they shared everything.
33With great power the apostles were telling people that the Lord Jesus was truly raised from the
dead. And God blessed all the believers very
much. 34No one in the group needed anything.
From time to time those who owned fields or
houses sold them, brought the money, 35and gave
it to the apostles. Then the money was given to
anyone who needed it.

4:11 *stone.* A symbol meaning Jesus.
4:12 Mediator: 1 Corinthians 8:6
4:19 Authority: Acts 5:29
4:23 Peter: Acts 5:1–11
4:30 Sickness, Disease, Healing: Acts 8:5–8
4:31 Persecution: Romans 12:14

36One of the believers was named Joseph, a Levite born in Cyprus. The apostles called him Barnabas (which means "one who encourages"). 37Joseph owned a field, sold it, brought the money, and gave it to the apostles.

Ananias and Sapphira Die

5 But a man named Ananias and his wife Sapphira sold some land. 2He kept back part of the money for himself; his wife knew about this and agreed to it. But he brought the rest of the money and gave it to the apostles. 3Peter said, "Ananias, why did you let Satan rule your thoughts to lie to the Holy Spirit and to keep for yourself part of the money you received for the land? 4Before you sold the land, it belonged to you. And even after you sold it, you could have used the money any way you wanted. Why did you think of doing this? You lied to God, not to us!" 5-6When Ananias heard this, he fell down and died. Some young men came in, wrapped up his body, carried it out, and buried it. And everyone who heard about this was filled with fear.

7About three hours later his wife came in, but she did not know what had happened. 8Peter said to her, "Tell me, was the money you got for your field this much?"

Sapphira answered, "Yes, that was the price."

9Peter said to her, "Why did you and your husband agree to test the Spirit of the Lord? Look! The men who buried your husband are at the door, and they will carry you out." 10At that moment Sapphira fell down by his feet and died. When the young men came in and saw that she was dead, they carried her out and buried her beside her husband. 11The whole church and all the others who heard about these things were filled with fear.

The Apostles Heal Many

12The apostles did many signs and miracles among the people. And they would all meet together on Solomon's Porch. 13None of the others dared to join them, but all the people respected them. 14More and more men and women believed in the Lord and were added to the group of believers. 15The people placed their sick on beds and mats in the streets, hoping that when Peter passed by at least his shadow might fall on them. 16Crowds came from all the towns around Jerusalem, bringing their sick and those who were bothered by evil spirits, and all of them were healed.

Leaders Try to Stop the Apostles

17The high priest and all his friends (a group called the Sadducees) became very jealous. 18They took the apostles and put them in jail. 19But during the night, an angel of the Lord opened the doors of the jail and led the apostles outside. The angel said, 20"Go stand in the Temple and tell the people everything about this new life." 21When the apostles heard this, they obeyed and went into the Temple early in the morning and continued teaching.

When the high priest and his friends arrived, they called a meeting of the leaders and all the important older men. They sent some men to the jail to bring the apostles to them. 22But, upon arriving, the officers could not find the apostles. So they went back and reported to the leaders. 23They said, "The jail was closed and locked, and the guards were standing at the doors. But when we opened the doors, the jail was empty!" 24Hearing this, the captain of the Temple guards and the leading priests were confused and wondered what was happening.

25Then someone came and told them, "Listen! The men you put in jail are standing in the Temple teaching the people." 26Then the captain and his men went out and brought the apostles back. But the soldiers did not use force, because they were afraid the people would stone them to death.

27The soldiers brought the apostles to the meeting and made them stand before the leaders. The high priest questioned them, 28saying, "We gave you strict orders not to continue teaching in that name. But look, you have filled Jerusalem with your teaching and are trying to make us responsible for this man's death."

4:36 Community: Acts 6:1–7
4:37 Land/Inheritance: Romans 4:6–7
4:37 Money: 2 Corinthians 8–9

5 God's people are always citizens of the divine community first, and citizens of human communities second. It is God to whom ultimate obedience is owed, and all human laws must be judged by their conformity with divine commands. When human laws violate that which God has commanded, people of faith are called to act in accordance with God's law, even when those actions lead to conflict with human authorities (5:29).

5:1–11 Luke has just portrayed the early church as a close-knit group of friends and family who share everything (Acts 4:32–35). Barnabas is a good example of those who share their possessions with those in need (Acts 4:36–37). Ananias and Sapphira apparently want to participate in this close-knit group but are unwilling to share their possessions freely. They want to present themselves as a companion like Barnabas, but their actions show that, in their public presentation, they are liars.

5:11 Materialism/Possessions: 2 Corinthians 8–9
5:11 Death: Romans 5:6–10
5:11 Peter: Acts 5:17–42
5:16 Evangelism: Acts 17:16–34
5:17 Jealousy: 1 Corinthians 3:3
5:18 Pharisees and Sadducees: Philippians 3:2–9
5:20 Angels/Guardian Angels: Acts 10:1–6

29Peter and the other apostles answered, "We
must obey God, not human authority!∞ 30You
killed Jesus by hanging him on a cross. But God,
the God of our ancestors, raised Jesus up from the
dead! 31Jesus is the One whom God raised to be
on his right side, as Leader and Savior. Through
him, all people could change their hearts and
lives and have their sins forgiven.∞ 32We saw all
these things happen. The Holy Spirit, whom God
has given to all who obey him, also proves these
things are true."
33When the leaders heard this, they became
angry and wanted to kill them. 34But a Pharisee
named Gamaliel stood up in the meeting. He was
a teacher of the law, and all the people respected
him. He ordered the apostles to leave the meeting
for a little while.∞ 35Then he said, "People of Israel,
be careful what you are planning to do to these men.
36Remember when Theudas appeared? He said he
was a great man, and about four hundred men
joined him. But he was killed, and all his followers were scattered; they were able to do nothing.
37Later, a man named Judas came from Galilee at
the time of the registration. He also led a group of
followers and was killed, and all his followers were
scattered. 38And so now I tell you: Stay away from
these men, and leave them alone. If their plan
comes from human authority, it will fail. 39But if
it is from God, you will not be able to stop them.
You might even be fighting against God himself!"
The leaders agreed with what Gamaliel said.
40They called the apostles in, beat them, and told
them not to speak in the name of Jesus again.
Then they let them go free. 41The apostles left the
meeting full of joy because they were given the
honor of suffering disgrace for Jesus. 42Every day
in the Temple and in people's homes they continued teaching the people and telling the Good
News—that Jesus is the Christ.∞

Seven Leaders Are Chosen

6 The number of followers was growing. But
during this same time, the Greek-speaking
followers had an argument with the other followers. The Greek-speaking widows were not getting
their share of the food that was given out every
day. 2The twelve apostles called the whole group
of followers together and said, "It is not right for
us to stop our work of teaching God's word in
order to serve tables.∞ 3So, brothers and sisters,
choose seven of your own men who are good, full
of the Spirit and full of wisdom. We will put them
in charge of this work. 4Then we can continue to
pray and to teach the word of God."
5The whole group liked the idea, so they chose
these seven men: Stephen (a man with great faith
and full of the Holy Spirit), Philip, Procorus, Nicanor,
Timon, Parmenas, and Nicolas (a man from Antioch
who had become a follower of the Jewish religion).
6Then they put these men before the apostles, who
prayed and laid their hands on them.
7The word of God was continuing to spread.
The group of followers in Jerusalem increased,
and a great number of the Jewish priests believed
and obeyed.∞

Stephen Is Accused

8Stephen was richly blessed by God who gave
him the power to do great miracles and signs

∞**5:29 Authority:** 1 Corinthians 5:1–5
∞**5:29 Government:** 1 Timothy 2:2
∞**5:29 Obedience:** Romans 6:16–18
∞**5:31 Leadership:** Romans 12:8
∞**5:34 Scribes (Teachers of the Law):** Acts 23:9
5:37 *registration.* Census. A counting of all the people and the things they own.
5:41 Here we see the paradox of the gospel. The apostles had witnessed to the great deeds of Jesus and the officials had imprisoned them, disgraced them publicly. However, this made the apostles glad because by being so disgraced in the eyes of their society, they were following in the path of their beloved Lord, Jesus, and, therefore, were actually given honor.
∞**5:42 Peter:** Acts 8:14–25
6:1–7 The problem the church faces is more than a practical problem; rather, it shows how prejudice against outsiders was still a part of the early Christian community. Those who spoke Greek, even though they were also Jewish Christians, were not being treated as well as those Jewish Christians who spoke the language of Palestine, Aramaic. These practices actually challenged the unity of all believers through their common faith and the gift of the Spirit. The solution the church comes to is important: They add representatives of the Greek-speaking Jewish Christians to the leadership of the whole community. (Note the Greek and Roman names in the list of 6:5–6.)
∞**6:2 Disciple/Discipleship/Mentoring (Follow/Follower):** Acts 11:26
6:5 *Philip.* Not the apostle named Philip.
6:5 The appointment of these servants shows that there was genuine concern in the early church for the physical, as well as the spiritual, needs of its members. In doing this, they reflected the loving heart of God. It is the same spirit we find in Jesus in the Gospels: "When he saw the crowds, he felt sorry for them because they were hurting and helpless, like sheep without a shepherd" (Matthew 9:36). "When he arrived, he saw a great crowd waiting. He felt sorry for them and healed those who were sick" (Matthew 14:14). When Jesus saw people who were hurting, he first *felt* something for them, then he *did* something about it.
This is still the pattern for the church. We need to open our eyes to recognize the needs of people and then do something to help. James 1:27 says, "Religion that God accepts as pure and without fault is this: caring for orphans or widows who need help, and keeping yourself free from the world's evil influence." What these seven men did was more than just form a relief committee; they became the hands and feet of Jesus reaching out to those who were most in need.
6:6 *laid their hands.* The laying on of hands had many purposes, including the giving of a blessing, power, or authority.
∞**6:7 Abortion and Crisis Pregnancy:** James 1:27
∞**6:7 Community:** Acts 7

among the people. 9But some people were against him. They belonged to the synagogue of Free Men (as it was called), which included people from Cyrene, Alexandria, Cilicia, and Asia. They all came and argued with Stephen.

10But the Spirit was helping him to speak with wisdom, and his words were so strong that they could not argue with him. 11So they secretly urged some men to say, "We heard Stephen speak against Moses and against God."

12This upset the people, the older leaders, and the teachers of the law. They came and grabbed Stephen and brought him to a meeting of the leaders. 13They brought in some people to tell lies about Stephen, saying, "This man is always speaking against this holy place and the law of Moses. 14We heard him say that Jesus from Nazareth will destroy this place and that Jesus will change the customs Moses gave us." 15All the people in the meeting were watching Stephen closely and saw that his face looked like the face of an angel.

Stephen's Speech

7 The high priest said to Stephen, "Are these things true?"

2Stephen answered, "Brothers and fathers, listen to me. Our glorious God appeared to Abraham, our ancestor, in Mesopotamia before he lived in Haran. 3God said to Abraham, 'Leave your country and your relatives, and go to the land I will show you.' 4So Abraham left the country of Chaldea and went to live in Haran. After Abraham's father died, God sent him to this place where you now live. 5God did not give Abraham any of this land, not even a foot of it. But God promised that he would give this land to him and his descendants, even before Abraham had a child. 6This is what God said to him: 'Your descendants will be strangers in a land they don't own. The people there will make them slaves and will mistreat them for four hundred years. 7But I will punish the nation where they are slaves. Then your descendants will leave that land and will worship me in this place.' 8God made an agreement with Abraham, the sign of which was circumcision. And so when Abraham had his son Isaac, Abraham circumcised him when he was eight days old. Isaac also circumcised his son Jacob, and Jacob did the same for his sons, the twelve ancestors of our people.

9"Jacob's sons became jealous of Joseph and sold him to be a slave in Egypt. But God was with him 10and saved him from all his troubles. The king of Egypt liked Joseph and respected him because of the wisdom God gave him. The king made him governor of Egypt and put him in charge of all the people in his palace.

11"Then all the land of Egypt and Canaan became so dry that nothing would grow, and the people suffered very much. Jacob's sons, our ancestors, could not find anything to eat. 12But when Jacob heard there was grain in Egypt, he sent his sons there. This was their first trip to Egypt. 13When they went there a second time, Joseph told his brothers who he was, and the king learned about Joseph's family. 14Then Joseph sent messengers to invite Jacob, his father, to come to Egypt along with all his relatives (seventy-five persons altogether). 15So Jacob went down to Egypt, where he and his sons died. 16Later their bodies were moved to Shechem and put in a grave there. (It was the same grave Abraham had bought for a sum of money from the sons of Hamor in Shechem.)

17"The promise God made to Abraham was soon to come true, and the number of people in Egypt grew large. 18Then a new king, who did not know who Joseph was, began to rule Egypt. 19This king tricked our people and was cruel to our ancestors, forcing them to leave their babies outside to die. 20At this time Moses was born, and he was very beautiful. For three months Moses was cared for in his father's house. 21When they put Moses outside, the king's daughter adopted him and raised him as if he were her own son. 22The Egyptians taught Moses everything they knew, and he was a powerful man in what he said and did.

23"When Moses was about forty years old, he thought it would be good to visit his own people, the people of Israel. 24Moses saw an Egyptian mistreating one of his people, so he defended the Israelite and punished the Egyptian by killing him. 25Moses thought his own people would understand that God was using him to save them, but they did not. 26The next day when Moses saw two men of Israel fighting, he tried to make peace between them. He said, 'Men, you are brothers. Why are you hurting each other?' 27The man who was hurting the other pushed Moses away and said, 'Who made you our ruler and judge? 28Are

6:9 *Free Men.* Jewish people who had been slaves or whose fathers had been slaves, but were now free.
7:3 *'Leave . . . you.'* Quotation from Genesis 12:1.
7:7 *'Your descendants . . . place.'* Quotation from Genesis 15:13-14 and Exodus 3:12.
7:8 *twelve ancestors.* Important ancestors of the people of Israel; the leaders of the twelve tribes of Israel.
7:10 Joseph: Hebrews 11:22

you going to kill me as you killed the Egyptian
yesterday?' [29]When Moses heard him say this, he
left Egypt and went to live in the land of Midian
where he was a stranger. While Moses lived in
Midian, he had two sons.
[30]"Forty years later an angel appeared to Moses
in the flames of a burning bush as he was in the
desert near Mount Sinai. [31]When Moses saw this,
he was amazed and went near to look closer. Moses
heard the Lord's voice say, [32]'I am the God of your
ancestors, the God of Abraham, Isaac, and Jacob.'
Moses began to shake with fear and was afraid to
look. [33]The Lord said to him, 'Take off your sandals,
because you are standing on holy ground. [34]I have
seen the troubles my people have suffered in Egypt.
I have heard their cries and have come down to
save them. And now, Moses, I am sending you back
to Egypt.'
[35]"This Moses was the same man the two men
of Israel rejected, saying, 'Who made you a ruler
and judge?' Moses is the same man God sent to
be a ruler and savior, with the help of the angel that
Moses saw in the burning bush. [36]So Moses led the
people out of Egypt. He worked miracles and signs
in Egypt, at the Red Sea, and then in the desert for
forty years. [37]This is the same Moses that said to
the people of Israel, 'God will give you a prophet
like me, who is one of your own people.' [38]This is
the Moses who was with the gathering of the
Israelites in the desert. He was with the angel that
spoke to him at Mount Sinai, and he was with our
ancestors. He received commands from God that
give life, and he gave those commands to us.
[39]"But our ancestors did not want to obey Moses.
They rejected him and wanted to go back to Egypt.
[40]They said to Aaron, 'Make us gods who will lead
us. Moses led us out of Egypt, but we don't know
what has happened to him.' [41]So the people made
an idol that looked like a calf. Then they brought
sacrifices to it and were proud of what they had
made with their own hands. [42]But God turned
against them and did not try to stop them from
worshiping the sun, moon, and stars. This is what
is written in the book of the prophets: God says,

'People of Israel, you did not bring me
sacrifices and offerings
while you traveled in the desert for forty years.
[43]You have carried with you
the tent to worship Molech
and the idols of the star god Rephan that you
made to worship.
So I will send you away beyond
Babylon.' *Amos 5:25-27*

[44]"The Holy Tent where God spoke to our ancestors was with them in the desert. God told Moses
how to make this Tent, and he made it like the plan
God showed him. [45]Later, Joshua led our ancestors
to capture the lands of the other nations. Our people
went in, and God forced the other people out.
When our people went into this new land, they
took with them this same Tent they had received
from their ancestors. They kept it until the time of
David, [46]who pleased God and asked God to let
him build a house for him, the God of Jacob. [47]But
Solomon was the one who built the Temple.
[48]"But the Most High does not live in houses that
people build with their hands. As the prophet says:

[49]'Heaven is my throne,
and the earth is my footstool.
So do you think you can build a house for me?
says the Lord.
Do I need a place to rest?
[50]Remember, my hand made all
these things!'" *Isaiah 66:1-2*

[51]Stephen continued speaking: "You stubborn
people! You have not given your hearts to God,
nor will you listen to him! You are always against
what the Holy Spirit is trying to tell you, just as
your ancestors were. [52]Your ancestors tried to
hurt every prophet who ever lived. Those prophets said long ago that the One who is good would
come, but your ancestors killed them. And now
you have turned against and killed the One who
is good. [53]You received the law of Moses, which
God gave you through his angels, but you haven't
obeyed it."

Stephen Is Killed

[54]When the leaders heard this, they became furious. They were so mad they were grinding their
teeth at Stephen. [55]But Stephen was full of the Holy
Spirit. He looked up to heaven and saw the glory of
God and Jesus standing at God's right side. [56]He
said, "Look! I see heaven open and the Son of Man
standing at God's right side."

7:28 *'Who . . . yesterday?'* Quotation from Exodus 2:14.
7:32 *'I am . . . Jacob.'* Quotation from Exodus 3:6.
7:33–34 *'Take . . . Egypt.'* Quotation from Exodus 3:5–10.
7:35 *'Who . . . judge?'* Quotation from Exodus 2:14.
7:37 *'God . . . people.'* Quotation from Deuteronomy 18:15.
7:40 *'Make . . . him.'* Quotation from Exodus 32:1.
7:43 Astrology: Colossians 1:15–20
7:45 Joshua: Hebrews 4:8
7:47 Solomon: See article on page 419.
7:51 Stubbornness: Romans 2:5
7:55 *"But Stephen was full of the Holy Spirit."* Why would Luke suddenly insert that comment? Because that was the unseen source of Stephen's strength. That was the reason behind his invincibility and perseverance. With death's hot breath blowing against the back of his neck, Stephen literally saw that ageless, penetrating light of God's glory pouring out of heaven. Full of the Spirit, he saw what no other eyes could see.

57Then they shouted loudly and covered their ears and all ran at Stephen. 58They took him out of the city and began to throw stones at him to kill him. And those who told lies against Stephen left their coats with a young man named Saul. 59While they were throwing stones, Stephen prayed, "Lord Jesus, receive my spirit." 60He fell on his knees and cried in a loud voice, "Lord, do not hold this sin against them." After Stephen said this, he died.

8 Saul agreed that the killing of Stephen was good.

Troubles for the Believers

On that day the church of Jerusalem began to be persecuted, and all the believers, except the apostles, were scattered throughout Judea and Samaria. 2And some religious people buried Stephen and cried loudly for him. 3Saul was also trying to destroy the church, going from house to house, dragging out men and women and putting them in jail. 4And wherever they were scattered, they told people the Good News.

Philip Preaches in Samaria

5Philip went to the city of Samaria and preached about the Christ. 6When the people there heard Philip and saw the miracles he was doing, they all listened carefully to what he said. 7Many of these people had evil spirits in them, but Philip made the evil spirits leave. The spirits made a loud noise when they came out. Philip also healed many weak and crippled people there. 8So the people in that city were very happy.

9But there was a man named Simon in that city. Before Philip came there, Simon had practiced magic and amazed all the people of Samaria. He bragged and called himself a great man. 10All the people—the least important and the most important—paid attention to Simon, saying, "This man has the power of God, called 'the Great Power'!" 11Simon had amazed them with his magic so long that the people became his followers. 12But when Philip told them the Good News about the kingdom of God and the power of Jesus Christ, men and women believed Philip and were baptized. 13Simon himself believed, and after he was baptized, he stayed very close to Philip. When he saw the miracles and the powerful things Philip did, Simon was amazed.

14When the apostles who were still in Jerusalem heard that the people of Samaria had accepted the word of God, they sent Peter and John to them. 15When Peter and John arrived, they prayed that the Samaritan believers might receive the Holy Spirit. 16These people had been baptized in the name of the Lord Jesus, but the Holy Spirit had not yet come upon any of them. 17Then, when the two apostles began laying their hands on the people, they received the Holy Spirit.

18Simon saw that the Spirit was given to people when the apostles laid their hands on them. So he offered the apostles money, 19saying, "Give me also this power so that anyone on whom I lay my hands will receive the Holy Spirit."

20Peter said to him, "You and your money should both be destroyed, because you thought you could buy God's gift with money. 21You cannot share with us in this work since your heart is not right before God. 22Change your heart! Turn away from this evil thing you have done, and pray to the Lord. Maybe he will forgive you for thinking this. 23I see that you are full of bitter jealousy and ruled by sin."

24Simon answered, "Both of you pray for me to the Lord so the things you have said will not happen to me."

7:60 Community: 1 Corinthians 10:1–13

7:60 Holy Spirit: Acts 20:22–24

7:60 Paul (Saul): Acts 9:1–31

8:1 Even though Jesus had instructed his followers to go to Judea and Samaria with the Good News, thus far they had remained in Jerusalem. Ironically, the killing of Stephen, as terrible as it was, had as one of its results the scattering of Christians to the very places Jesus had told them to go: Judea and Samaria (see 1:8).

8:1 Jesus was not only persecuted when he lived in Israel, he was also persecuted after his resurrection through the persecution of his followers, the church. Christians in the New Testament times were often persecuted for telling others about the Good News of Jesus' resurrection by being put in jail or killed. After the Jewish leaders put Stephen, a servant of Jesus, to death, "the church of Jerusalem began to be persecuted." Acts says that, "Saul was also trying to destroy the church, going from house to house, dragging out men and women and putting them in jail" (Acts 8:1–3). As Saul was traveling to arrest believers, a bright light flashed around him and he heard a voice saying to him, "Saul, Saul! Why are you persecuting me?" Saul asked who the voice was and the voice answered, "I am Jesus, whom you are persecuting" (Acts 9:3–5). Saul had been persecuting Jesus by sending Christians to jail. After this, he became a Christian himself, changing his name to Paul, but the memories of his earlier persecution of the church often made him sad (1 Corinthians 15:9; 1 Timothy 1:13). Paul himself experienced mistreatment from others as he traveled preaching the Good News of Jesus. God had said of Paul at his conversion, "I will show him how much he must suffer for my name" (Acts 9:16). He became a marked man, experiencing insult, imprisonment, and beatings for the sake of Christ.

8:2–4 The word *church* here refers to the group of people who have gathered in the name of the risen Jesus to continue to preach his Good News. Originally, *church* simply meant a gathering of people for a common purpose and did not refer to a distinct, ongoing organization. At first, the religious people of Israel did not see the "church" of Christ as a new or rival religion, but as a gathering of Jewish people around a powerful Jewish teacher. As the teaching of Jesus and the strong community that formed after his death began to challenge the religious leaders, they sought to destroy the new movement. As the church grew and its message was accepted by many non-Jewish people, it came to be understood as separate from the religious organization of Israel.

8:4 Martyrdom: Acts 12:1–19

8:8 Sickness, Disease, Healing: Acts 28:7–9

8:13 Baptism: Acts 16:15

8:24 Magic: Acts 13:6–12

25After Peter and John told the people what they had seen Jesus do and after they had spoken the message of the Lord, they went back to Jerusalem. On the way, they went through many Samaritan towns and preached the Good News to the people.⚭

Philip Teaches an Ethiopian

26An angel of the Lord said to Philip, "Get ready and go south to the road that leads down to Gaza from Jerusalem—the desert road." 27So Philip got ready and went. On the road he saw a man from Ethiopia, a eunuch. He was an important officer in the service of Candace, the queen of the Ethiopians; he was responsible for taking care of all her money. He had gone to Jerusalem to worship. 28Now, as he was on his way home, he was sitting in his chariot reading from the Book of Isaiah, the prophet. 29The Spirit said to Philip, "Go to that chariot and stay near it."

30So when Philip ran toward the chariot, he heard the man reading from Isaiah the prophet. Philip asked, "Do you understand what you are reading?"

31He answered, "How can I understand unless someone explains it to me?" Then he invited Philip to climb in and sit with him. 32The portion of Scripture he was reading was this:

"He was like a sheep being led to be killed.
  He was quiet, as a lamb is quiet while its
    wool is being cut;
  he never opened his mouth.
33 He was shamed and was treated unfairly.
  He died without children to continue his family.
    His life on earth has ended." *Isaiah 53:7-8*

34The officer said to Philip, "Please tell me, who is the prophet talking about—himself or someone else?" 35Philip began to speak, and starting with this same Scripture, he told the man the Good News about Jesus.

36While they were traveling down the road, they came to some water. The officer said, "Look, here is water. What is stopping me from being baptized?" 37* 38Then the officer commanded the chariot to stop. Both Philip and the officer went down into the water, and Philip baptized him. 39When they came up out of the water, the Spirit of the Lord took Philip away; the officer never saw him again. And the officer continued on his way home, full of joy.⚭ 40But Philip appeared in a city called Azotus and preached the Good News in all the towns on the way from Azotus to Caesarea.⚭

Saul Is Converted

9 In Jerusalem Saul was still threatening the followers of the Lord by saying he would kill them. So he went to the high priest⚭ 2and asked him to write letters to the synagogues in the city of Damascus. Then if Saul found any followers of Christ's Way, men or women, he would arrest them and bring them back to Jerusalem.

3So Saul headed toward Damascus. As he came near the city, a bright light from heaven suddenly flashed around him. 4Saul fell to the ground and heard a voice saying to him, "Saul, Saul! Why are you persecuting me?"

5Saul said, "Who are you, Lord?"

The voice answered, "I am Jesus, whom you are persecuting. 6Get up now and go into the city. Someone there will tell you what you must do."

7The people traveling with Saul stood there but said nothing. They heard the voice, but they saw no one. 8Saul got up from the ground and opened his eyes, but he could not see. So those with Saul took his hand and led him into Damascus. 9For three days Saul could not see and did not eat or drink.

10There was a follower of Jesus in Damascus named Ananias. The Lord spoke to Ananias in a vision, "Ananias!"

Ananias answered, "Here I am, Lord."

11The Lord said to him, "Get up and go to Straight Street. Find the house of Judas, and ask for a man named Saul from the city of Tarsus. He is there now, praying. 12Saul has seen a vision in which a man named Ananias comes to him and lays his hands on him. Then he is able to see again."

13But Ananias answered, "Lord, many people have told me about this man and the terrible things he did to your holy people in Jerusalem. 14Now he has come here to Damascus, and the leading priests have given him the power to arrest everyone who worships you."

15But the Lord said to Ananias, "Go! I have chosen Saul for an important work. He must tell about me to those who are not Jews, to kings, and to the people of Israel.⚭ 16I will show him how much he must suffer for my name."

⚭**8:25 Peter:** Acts 9:32–43

***8:37** *Verse 37.* Some late copies of Acts add verse 37: "Philip answered, 'If you believe with all your heart, you can.' The officer said, 'I believe that Jesus Christ is the Son of God.'"

⚭**8:39 Conversion:** Acts 9:1

⚭**8:40 Samaria:** See article on page 429.

⚭**9:1 Conversion:** Romans 12:1–2

9:3 Some conversions are sudden, others gradual. Paul was knocked to the ground by a special revelation from the risen Lord. He was blinded for three days and then healed. This was the turning point where the persecutor of Christians became their friend and leader. There are persons today who have also made dramatic turns toward the Lord. For others, conversion is more like growing and affirming what they have always known. But just as Paul had to choose to follow the Lord's direction and trust Ananias, so everyone must make the choice to accept God's saving grace through faith.

9:11 *Judas.* This is not either of the apostles named Judas.

⚭**9:15 Communication:** Galatians 1:11–12

17So Ananias went to the house of Judas. He laid his hands on Saul and said, "Brother Saul, the Lord Jesus sent me. He is the one you saw on the road on your way here. He sent me so that you can see again and be filled with the Holy Spirit." 18Immediately, something that looked like fish scales fell from Saul's eyes, and he was able to see again! Then Saul got up and was baptized. 19After he ate some food, his strength returned.⚭

Saul Preaches in Damascus

Saul stayed with the followers of Jesus in Damascus for a few days. 20Soon he began to preach about Jesus in the synagogues, saying, "Jesus is the Son of God."

21All the people who heard him were amazed. They said, "This is the man who was in Jerusalem trying to destroy those who trust in this name! He came here to arrest the followers of Jesus and take them back to the leading priests."

22But Saul grew more powerful. His proofs that Jesus is the Christ were so strong that his own people in Damascus could not argue with him.

23After many days, they made plans to kill Saul. 24They were watching the city gates day and night, but Saul learned about their plan. 25One night some followers of Saul helped him leave the city by lowering him in a basket through an opening in the city wall.

Saul Preaches in Jerusalem

26When Saul went to Jerusalem, he tried to join the group of followers, but they were all afraid of him. They did not believe he was really a follower. 27But Barnabas accepted Saul and took him to the apostles. Barnabas explained to them that Saul had seen the Lord on the road and the Lord had spoken to Saul. Then he told them how boldly Saul had preached in the name of Jesus in Damascus.

28And so Saul stayed with the followers, going everywhere in Jerusalem, preaching boldly in the name of the Lord. 29He would often talk and argue with the Jewish people who spoke Greek, but they were trying to kill him. 30When the followers learned about this, they took Saul to Caesarea and from there sent him to Tarsus.

31The church everywhere in Judea, Galilee, and Samaria had a time of peace and became stronger. Respecting the Lord by the way they lived, and being encouraged by the Holy Spirit, the group of believers continued to grow.⚭

Peter Heals Aeneas

32As Peter was traveling through all the area, he visited God's people who lived in Lydda. 33There he met a man named Aeneas, who was paralyzed and had not been able to leave his bed for the past eight years. 34Peter said to him, "Aeneas, Jesus Christ heals you. Stand up and make your bed." Aeneas stood up immediately. 35All the people living in Lydda and on the Plain of Sharon saw him and turned to the Lord.

Peter Heals Tabitha

36In the city of Joppa there was a follower named Tabitha (whose Greek name was Dorcas). She was always doing good deeds and kind acts. 37While Peter was in Lydda, Tabitha became sick and died. Her body was washed and put in a room upstairs. 38Since Lydda is near Joppa and the followers in Joppa heard that Peter was in Lydda, they sent two messengers to Peter. They begged him, "Hurry, please come to us!" 39So Peter got ready and went with them. When he arrived, they took him to the upstairs room where all the widows stood around Peter, crying. They showed him the shirts and coats Tabitha had made when she was still alive. 40Peter sent everyone out of the room and kneeled and prayed. Then he turned to the body and said, "Tabitha, stand up." She opened her eyes, and when she saw Peter, she sat up. 41He gave her his hand and helped her up. Then he called the saints and the widows into the room and showed them that Tabitha was alive. 42People everywhere in Joppa learned about this, and many believed in the Lord. 43Peter stayed in Joppa for many days with a man named Simon who was a tanner.⚭

Peter Teaches Cornelius

10 At Caesarea there was a man named Cornelius, an officer in the Italian group of the Roman army. 2Cornelius was a religious man. He and all the other people who lived in his house worshiped the true God. He gave much of his money to the poor and prayed to God often. 3One afternoon about three o'clock, Cornelius clearly saw a vision. An angel of God came to him and said, "Cornelius!"⚭

⚭**9:19 Body/Resurrection:** Acts 22:6–16
⚭**9:31 Church:** 1 Thessalonians 1:1
⚭**9:31 Paul (Saul):** Acts 13:1–28:30
⚭**9:43 Peter:** Acts 10:1–48

10:1–16 As Peter himself will remark (10:28), it was unusual for Jews, even Jewish Christians, to associate with non-Jews. This is what makes these two visions so important. Cornelius, a non-Jew who is religious but has not converted either to Judaism or to Christianity, receives instructions from an angel, while Peter has a vision about unclean food. As the story develops, we see how God has planned this whole encounter so that Peter can learn that Jesus is Lord even of the other nations and so that Cornelius and his family can hear the Good News and receive the Holy Spirit.

⚭**10:3 Vision:** Revelation 9:17

SLAVERY

PHILEMON

Does the Bible allow or condone human slavery?

The institution of slavery, in which one person owns another person as a piece of property, was widely practiced in Bible times. Slavery in the ancient world, and especially in the Greek and Roman world of the New Testament, must be distinguished from the forms of slavery known to people in the Americas in the seventeenth, eighteenth, and nineteenth centuries. Although we can find only a few indirect attempts to reject owning and using other people like property in the Bible, neither does the Bible condone human slavery.

One of the most commonplace ways of obtaining a slave in the ancient world was through "debt slavery." This was the process by which a person borrowed money from the wealthy and, when he was unable to repay the loan, sold himself into slavery. In the Old Testament, an Israelite who became a slave because of economic need could be held as a slave for only six years, after which he would be set free (Exodus 21:2). In a sense, then, selling oneself into slavery did not lead to actual (permanent) slavery. This was not the case with non-Israelites; if they sold themselves into slavery, they could live forever as slaves unless payment was made for their release.

Within Israel, slaves were never regarded only as property, however. Regulations under Israelite law protected slaves as human beings and not only as the property of their owners. Male slaves were to be circumcised like any Israelite male and were to share in such religious celebrations as the Passover.

Slavery was an everyday reality in the Roman world of the early church. This ancient form of slavery contrasts sharply with slavery as we think of it in the modern period. For example, Roman slaves were often better educated than their masters, many slaves carried high-level positions in businesses and in the government, slaves could own property and even have their own slaves, and slaves, at times, exercised more power than free persons. Moreover, slavery was not related to class or racial issues in the Roman world.

Without a doubt, many early Christians had slaves, as the Letter to Philemon makes clear. This is not the whole story, however. According to the prayer Jesus taught his followers to pray (Luke 11:4), we are to forgive everyone who owes us anything (literally, "we forgive everyone who has done wrong to us"). When it is recalled that slavery was often the result of selling oneself for one's debts, the message of Jesus has a surprisingly direct focus. If they take Jesus' words seriously, the people of God would not be able to take people into slavery on account of financial debts.

In other instances, Paul instructs his readers to practice compassion and fairness toward one another. In particular, masters and slaves are both charged to act toward one another as Christians ought to act. Masters should be good and fair to their slaves, remembering that "you have a Master in heaven," while slaves should serve out of respect for the Lord (Colossians 3:22–4:1; see also Ephesians 6:5–9). Paul goes so far as to affirm that, from the perspective of life determined by the Lord Jesus, there is no distinction between slaves and free people (Galatians 3:28). Similarly, in 1 Corinthians 7:21–24, Paul encourages slaves to embrace their freedom before the Lord and to live with the knowledge that their true master or lord was Christ.

Paul's instructions to Philemon are not always easy to follow since we know so little about why Philemon's slave, Onesimus, is no longer living in Philemon's house. What we do know is that Paul is asking Philemon to change the way he views Onesimus. Because of previous circumstances, Philemon might be angry with Onesimus. Paul asks Philemon to look upon his slave no longer as a slave, but as a new brother in Christ. Since both are now Christians, their social relationship must be transformed. Most likely, this means that Philemon should give Onesimus a new status before the law—no longer as slave but as a free person.

Ancient Israel could be called the "servant of the Lord" because Israel was delivered from bondage in Egypt in order to serve the Lord. At times, New Testament writers can build on this use of "slavery" or "service" as a symbol for their relationship to the Lord. This highlights their having been purchased by the Lord (see 1 Corinthians 6:19–20), their allegiance and submission to him, and their status as members of the Lord's family.

Slavery: For additional scriptures on this topic go to Leviticus 25.

PRIESTHOOD

HEBREWS 4:14

What do priests do? What is the relationship between Old Testament priests and contemporary church leaders? Who are priests today?

Priests appear frequently in the Old Testament, but rarely in the New. Most Protestant churches are led by ministers or pastors; Catholic, Episcopal, and a few other Protestant churches do have priests, but what is their relationship to the Old Testament priests? These and other questions lead us back to the Bible to find out what the priesthood is all about.

Priesthood involves being set apart for special service to God. In a broad sense, it can be said that all Israelites are priests, since they are set aside for a special relationship with God (Exodus 19:6). But in a narrow sense, priesthood in Israel began when Aaron, Moses' brother, was set apart along with his family for special service to God. The service that made Aaron and his sons priests took place during the wandering in the wilderness and in connection with the building of the tabernacle, the Holy Tent (Exodus 28; Leviticus 8).

To understand the role of priests until the time of Jesus, we need to know something about the way God made his presence known to his people during the Old Testament period (for the fuller story see Presence of God). God revealed himself in special places like the Holy Tent and later the Temple, and these places became holy ground. This meant that only certain people under certain conditions can approach God. The priests were set apart in a special way so they could be near God while taking care of the needs of the holy place and guiding other people in the proper way of approaching God.

The priests wore special clothes that were ornate and extremely expensive. Indeed, the clothes were made of the same material as the Holy Tent itself and indicated that the priests were part and parcel of the holy space dedicated to the presence of God (Exodus 28:6–43). The same point is made when Moses sprinkled special oil both on the Holy Tent as well as the heads of Aaron and his sons (Leviticus 8:10–13).

Because of their special position as priests before God, they could live and work in the area of the Holy Tent and then later the Temple. But not all priests were equal. The whole family group of Levites, for instance, were only priests in the general sense. Because of their special concern for the holiness of God (Exodus 32:29; Leviticus 3), the tribe was set apart for service in the holy places of God. They assisted the priestly family of Aaron, but the immediate descendants of Aaron could get closer to the most Holy Place, the innermost part of the sanctuary, and only the high priest, and he only once a year (see Leviticus 16), could actually go into the most Holy Place. The sons of Aaron were clearly in charge of the family group of Levites (Numbers 18:1–7).

The priests and their Levitical assistants actually performed many tasks in ancient Israel. In the first place, the priests were guardians of God's holiness. They protected and maintained the areas that were specially set apart for the worship of the Lord, places like the Holy Tent and the Temple. They lived around these areas and would stop people who were not spiritually prepared from entering the area and thus offending God. They also served as mediators between God and his people. A rough distinction can be made between a prophet and a priest, in that the prophet brings God's Word to his people and the priest brings the people to God.

The specific duties of priests and Levites are mentioned in Moses' blessing on the priestly family group of Levi (Deuteronomy 33:8–11). Perhaps the most well-known task of the priests is offering sacrifices on behalf of the people's sins. In this way, they serve as mediators of the people in God's presence as well as guardians of God's holiness. After all, the sacrifices atone for the sins of the people as they approach God's holy place. Without sacrifices, sin would keep men and women from approaching God.

The priests and Levites were also charged with teaching the people the law of God (Jeremiah 18:18; Malachi 2:7). In this way, the people would know how to obey in a way that would please the Lord and would keep them from sinning and thus again offending his holiness.

When we turn to the New Testament we learn the wonderful news that Jesus Christ is our great high priest (Hebrews 4:14–5:10). He is not a high priest like Aaron. He does not have to offer sacrifices for his own sins as well as the sins of other people, because he does not sin. He is also a priest who offers only one sacrifice for the sins of everyone who believes in him and that sacrifice is himself (Hebrews 9:23–10:18).

Also, in the New Testament we learn that after Jesus there is a change that takes place in the spiritual leadership of the church. Now all Christians are priests. We are all able to enter into the very presence of God and offer him our thanks and praise (1 Peter 2:1–10).

Priesthood: For additional scriptures on this topic go to Genesis 14:18.

4Cornelius stared at the angel. He became afraid
and said, "What do you want, Lord?"
The angel said, "God has heard your prayers. He
has seen that you give to the poor, and he remembers you. 5Send some men now to Joppa to bring
back a man named Simon who is also called Peter.
6He is staying with a man, also named Simon, who
is a tanner and has a house beside the sea." 7When
the angel who spoke to Cornelius left, Cornelius
called two of his servants and a soldier, a religious
man who worked for him. 8Cornelius explained
everything to them and sent them to Joppa.
9About noon the next day as they came near
Joppa, Peter was going up to the roof to pray. 10He
was hungry and wanted to eat, but while the food
was being prepared, he had a vision. 11He saw
heaven opened and something coming down that
looked like a big sheet being lowered to earth by
its four corners. 12In it were all kinds of animals,
reptiles, and birds. 13Then a voice said to Peter,
"Get up, Peter; kill and eat."
14But Peter said, "No, Lord! I have never eaten
food that is unholy or unclean."
15But the voice said to him again, "God has made
these things clean so don't call them 'unholy'!"
16This happened three times, and at once the sheet
was taken back to heaven.
17While Peter was wondering what this vision
meant, the men Cornelius sent had found Simon's
house and were standing at the gate. 18They asked,
"Is Simon Peter staying here?"
19While Peter was still thinking about the
vision, the Spirit said to him, "Listen, three men
are looking for you. 20Get up and go downstairs.
Go with them without doubting, because I have
sent them to you."
21So Peter went down to the men and said, "I am
the one you are looking for. Why did you come here?"
22They said, "A holy angel spoke to Cornelius,
an army officer and a good man; he worships God.
All the people respect him. The angel told
Cornelius to ask you to come to his house so that
he can hear what you have to say." 23So Peter
asked the men to come in and spend the night.
The next day Peter got ready and went with
them, and some of the followers from Joppa joined
him. 24On the following day they came to Caesarea.
Cornelius was waiting for them and had called
together his relatives and close friends. 25When
Peter entered, Cornelius met him, fell at his feet,
and worshiped him. 26But Peter helped him up,
saying, "Stand up. I too am only a human." 27As he
talked with Cornelius, Peter went inside where he
saw many people gathered. 28He said, "You people
understand that it is against our law for Jewish people to associate with or visit anyone who is not
Jewish. But God has shown me that I should not
call any person 'unholy' or 'unclean.' 29That is why
I did not argue when I was asked to come here.
Now, please tell me why you sent for me."
30Cornelius said, "Four days ago, I was praying
in my house at this same time—three o'clock in
the afternoon. Suddenly, there was a man standing before me wearing shining clothes. 31He said,
'Cornelius, God has heard your prayer and has
seen that you give to the poor and remembers
you. 32So send some men to Joppa and ask Simon
Peter to come. Peter is staying in the house of a
man, also named Simon, who is a tanner and has
a house beside the sea.' 33So I sent for you immediately, and it was very good of you to come. Now
we are all here before God to hear everything the
Lord has commanded you to tell us."
34Peter began to speak: "I really understand
now that to God every person is the same. 35In
every country God accepts anyone who worships
him and does what is right. 36You know the message that God has sent to the people of Israel is
the Good News that peace has come through
Jesus Christ. Jesus is the Lord of all people!

10:5 Angels/Guardian Angels: Acts 12:6–11

10:10–16 The difficulty of early Jewish believers to set aside some of the Old Testament regulations is clearly brought out in Peter's vision. When Peter is told to eat unclean food from a sheet lowered from heaven he is appalled because he has never eaten anything unclean (Leviticus 11). However, God is preparing Peter to see the implications of what taking the Good News to the non-Jews means: the issue is faith in Christ and not the regulations of the Mosaic Law (see also Galatians 2:11–16).

10:9 *roof.* In Bible times houses were built with flat roofs. The roof was used for drying things such as flax and fruit. And it was used as an extra room, as a place for worship, and as a cool place to sleep in the summer.

10:9–48 In Peter's vision, he was commanded to eat animals that the Jews had earlier been forbidden to eat (see Leviticus 11). These dietary restrictions were part of what made Israel distinct from other nations that did not worship and serve the true God. God's command to Peter to eat unclean animals demonstrated that just as the distinction between clean and unclean animals has been eliminated, Peter should no longer consider those who weren't Jews unclean. The Good News of Jesus Christ is not limited by nationality, but rather God accepts those in any country who worship and serve him.

10:29 Ambition: 2 Corinthians 2:14

10:34–35 Paul was the apostle to the non-Jews. But it was Peter who first opened the door of ministry to the non-Jews. He obeyed the vision he received from God and went to the house of the Roman centurion, Cornelius, to proclaim the Good News of forgiveness of sins through Jesus Christ. Peter began his message by saying that he now understood that God sees every person as the same, as on the same footing before God.

10:36 Throughout the Book of Acts Jesus' total lordship occurs often. When Peter opened the Good News ministry to non-Jews at the house of Cornelius, he again declared, "Jesus is the Lord of all people!" In the Book of Acts alone, the title "Lord" is used of Jesus fifty times as often as "Savior." The truth of his lordship was the key to the apostles' preaching. Christ's lordship is the Good News according the apostles.

10:36 Lordship: Acts 16:31

[37]You know what has happened all over Judea, beginning in Galilee after John preached to the people about baptism. [38]You know about Jesus from Nazareth, that God gave him the Holy Spirit and power. You know how Jesus went everywhere doing good and healing those who were ruled by the devil, because God was with him. [39]We saw what Jesus did in Judea and in Jerusalem, but the Jews in Jerusalem killed him by hanging him on a cross. [40]Yet, on the third day, God raised Jesus to life and caused him to be seen, [41]not by all the people, but only by the witnesses God had already chosen. And we are those witnesses who ate and drank with him after he was raised from the dead. [42]He told us to preach to the people and to tell them that he is the one whom God chose to be the judge of the living and the dead. [43]All the prophets say it is true that all who believe in Jesus will be forgiven of their sins through Jesus' name."

[44]While Peter was still saying this, the Holy Spirit came down on all those who were listening. [45]The Jewish believers who came with Peter were amazed that the gift of the Holy Spirit had been given even to the nations. [46]These believers heard them speaking in different languages and praising God. Then Peter said, [47]"Can anyone keep these people from being baptized with water? They have received the Holy Spirit just as we did!" [48]So Peter ordered that they be baptized in the name of Jesus Christ. Then they asked Peter to stay with them for a few days.

Peter Returns to Jerusalem

11 The apostles and the believers in Judea heard that some who were not Jewish had accepted God's teaching too. [2]But when Peter came to Jerusalem, some people argued with him. [3]They said, "You went into the homes of people who are not circumcised and ate with them!"

[4]So Peter explained the whole story to them. [5]He said, "I was in the city of Joppa, and while I was praying, I had a vision. I saw something that looked like a big sheet being lowered from heaven by its four corners. It came very close to me. [6]I looked inside it and saw animals, wild beasts, reptiles, and birds. [7]I heard a voice say to me, 'Get up, Peter. Kill and eat.' [8]But I said, 'No, Lord! I have never eaten anything that is unholy or unclean.' [9]But the voice from heaven spoke again, 'God has made these things clean, so don't call them unholy.' [10]This happened three times. Then the whole thing was taken back to heaven. [11]Right then three men who were sent to me from Caesarea came to the house where I was staying. [12]The Spirit told me to go with them without doubting. These six believers here also went with me, and we entered the house of Cornelius. [13]He told us about the angel he saw standing in his house. The angel said to him, 'Send some men to Joppa and invite Simon Peter to come. [14]By the words he will say to you, you and all your family will be saved.' [15]When I began my speech, the Holy Spirit came on them just as he came on us at the beginning. [16]Then I remembered the words of the Lord. He said, 'John baptized with water, but you will be baptized with the Holy Spirit.' [17]Since God gave them the same gift he gave us who believed in the Lord Jesus Christ, how could I stop the work of God?"

[18]When the believers heard this, they stopped arguing. They praised God and said, "So God is allowing even other nations to turn to him and live."

The Good News Comes to Antioch

[19]Many of the believers were scattered when they were persecuted after Stephen was killed. Some of them went as far as Phoenicia, Cyprus, and Antioch telling the message to others, but only to Jews. [20]Some of these believers were people from Cyprus and Cyrene. When they came to Antioch, they spoke also to Greeks, telling them the Good News about the Lord Jesus. [21]The Lord was helping the believers, and a large group of people believed and turned to the Lord.

[22]The church in Jerusalem heard about all of this, so they sent Barnabas to Antioch. [23-24]Barnabas was a good man, full of the Holy Spirit and full of faith. When he reached Antioch and saw how God had blessed the people, he was glad. He encouraged all the believers in Antioch always to obey the Lord with all their hearts, and many people became followers of the Lord.

10:37 *John.* John the Baptist, who preached to people about Christ's coming (Luke 3).

10:44–48 After Peter preached to the Roman centurion, Cornelius, and his household, the Holy Spirit came to them, and they began to speak in different languages. On the basis of this evidence of true faith, Peter asked the Jewish believers who were with him if they could keep these new non-Jewish believers from being baptized. This event was retold by Peter later at the Jerusalem council when the issue of making the non-Jews observe the Law was raised (Acts 15:7–11).

10:46 *languages.* This can also be translated "tongues."

10:46 Spiritual Gifts: Acts 19:6
10:48 Crossing Cultural Boundaries: Acts 11:1–18
10:48 Peter: Acts 11:1–18
10:48 Tongues: Romans 8:26
11:8 Rahab: Hebrews 11:31
11:18 Crossing Cultural Boundaries: Acts 15:1–35
11:18 Peter: Acts 12:3–19
11:18 Racism: Acts 15:1–35

25Then Barnabas went to the city of Tarsus to look for Saul, 26and when he found Saul, he brought him to Antioch. For a whole year Saul and Barnabas met with the church and taught many people there. In Antioch the followers were called Christians for the first time.

27About that time some prophets came from Jerusalem to Antioch. 28One of them, named Agabus, stood up and spoke with the help of the Holy Spirit. He said, "A very hard time is coming to the whole world. There will be no food to eat." (This happened when Claudius ruled.) 29The believers all decided to help the followers who lived in Judea, as much as each one could. 30They gathered the money and gave it to Barnabas and Saul, who brought it to the elders in Judea.

Herod Agrippa Hurts the Church

12 During that same time King Herod began to mistreat some who belonged to the church. 2He ordered James, the brother of John, to be killed by the sword. 3Herod saw that some of the people liked this, so he decided to arrest Peter, too. (This happened during the time of the Feast of Unleavened Bread.)

4After Herod arrested Peter, he put him in jail and handed him over to be guarded by sixteen soldiers. Herod planned to bring Peter before the people for trial after the Passover Feast. 5So Peter was kept in jail, but the church prayed earnestly to God for him.

Peter Leaves the Jail

6The night before Herod was to bring him to trial, Peter was sleeping between two soldiers, bound with two chains. Other soldiers were guarding the door of the jail. 7Suddenly, an angel of the Lord stood there, and a light shined in the cell. The angel struck Peter on the side and woke him up. "Hurry! Get up!" the angel said. And the chains fell off Peter's hands. 8Then the angel told him, "Get dressed and put on your sandals." And Peter did. Then the angel said, "Put on your coat and follow me." 9So Peter followed him out, but he did not know if what the angel was doing was real; he thought he might be seeing a vision. 10They

The Emperor Claudius

went past the first and second guards and came to the iron gate that separated them from the city. The gate opened by itself for them, and they went through it. When they had walked down one street, the angel suddenly left him.

11Then Peter realized what had happened. He thought, "Now I know that the Lord really sent his angel to me. He rescued me from Herod and from all the things the people thought would happen."

12When he considered this, he went to the home of Mary, the mother of John Mark. Many people were gathered there, praying. 13Peter knocked on the outside door, and a servant girl named Rhoda came to answer it. 14When she recognized Peter's voice, she was so happy she forgot to open the door. Instead, she ran inside and told the group, "Peter is at the door!"

15They said to her, "You are crazy!" But she kept on saying it was true, so they said, "It must be Peter's angel."

16Peter continued to knock, and when they opened the door, they saw him and were amazed.

11:26 Disciple/Discipleship/Mentoring (Follow/Follower): See article on page 821.

11:28 *no food to eat.* In the Old Testament, famine often meant discipline from God towards his people (Leviticus 26:14–20; Deuteronomy 28:15–24; 32:24; 1 Kings 8:35–40; Amos 4:6; Haggai 1:10). Here, however, famine was opportunity for believers to help one another (Galatians 6:10).

11:28–30 One of the clearest marks of Christian fellowship, the unity and love of believers for one another, is their response to needs within the Body. The immediate response of the church at Antioch to the news of impending famine was spontaneous decision to send relief aid to the disciples in Judea. There was a generous spirit among the believers at Antioch who determined to help their brothers in Judea "as much as each one could." And they became personally involved in the relief effort, sending Barnabas and Saul, as well as their money, to Judea.

12:11 Angels/Guardian Angels: Acts 12:15

12:12 Intercession: Ephesians 3:14–21

12:15 Angels/Guardian Angels: Colossians 2:18

17Peter made a sign with his hand to tell them to be quiet. He explained how the Lord led him out of the jail, and he said, "Tell James and the other believers what happened." Then he left to go to another place.

18The next day the soldiers were very upset and wondered what had happened to Peter. 19Herod looked everywhere for him but could not find him. So he questioned the guards and ordered that they be killed.⚭

The Death of Herod Agrippa

Later Herod moved from Judea and went to the city of Caesarea, where he stayed. 20Herod was very angry with the people of Tyre and Sidon, but the people of those cities all came in a group to him. After convincing Blastus, the king's personal servant, to be on their side, they asked Herod for peace, because their country got its food from his country.

21On a chosen day Herod put on his royal robes, sat on his throne, and made a speech to the people. 22They shouted, "This is the voice of a god, not a human!" 23Because Herod did not give the glory to God, an angel of the Lord immediately caused him to become sick, and he was eaten by worms and died.⚭

24God's message continued to spread and reach people.

25After Barnabas and Saul finished their task in Jerusalem, they returned to Antioch, taking John Mark with them.

Barnabas and Saul Are Chosen

13 In the church at Antioch there were these prophets and teachers: Barnabas, Simeon (also called Niger), Lucius (from the city of Cyrene), Manaen (who had grown up with Herod, the ruler), and Saul. 2They were all worshiping the Lord and giving up eating for a certain time. During this time the Holy Spirit said to them, "Set apart for me Barnabas and Saul to do a special work for which I have chosen them."

3So after they gave up eating and prayed, they laid their hands on Barnabas and Saul and sent them out.⚭

Barnabas and Saul in Cyprus

4Barnabas and Saul, sent out by the Holy Spirit, went to the city of Seleucia. From there they sailed to the island of Cyprus. 5When they came to Salamis, they preached the Good News of God in the synagogues. John Mark was with them to help.

6They went across the whole island to Paphos where they met a magician named Bar-Jesus. He was a false prophet 7who always stayed close to Sergius Paulus, the governor and a smart man. He asked Barnabas and Saul to come to him, because he wanted to hear the message of God. 8But Elymas, the magician, was against them. (Elymas is the name for Bar-Jesus in the Greek language.) He tried to stop the governor from believing in Jesus. 9But Saul, who was also called Paul, was filled with the Holy Spirit. He looked straight at Elymas 10and said, "You son of the devil! You are an enemy of everything that is right! You are full of evil tricks and lies, always trying to change the Lord's truths into lies. 11Now the Lord will touch you, and you will be blind. For a time you will not be able to see anything—not even the light from the sun."

Then everything became dark for Elymas, and he walked around, trying to find someone to lead him by the hand. 12When the governor saw this, he believed because he was amazed at the teaching about the Lord.

Paul and Barnabas Leave Cyprus

13Paul and those with him sailed from Paphos and came to Perga, in Pamphylia. There John Mark left them to return to Jerusalem. 14They continued their trip from Perga and went to Antioch, a city in Pisidia. On the Sabbath day they went into the synagogue and sat down.⚭ 15After the law of Moses and the writings of the prophets were read, the leaders of the synagogue sent a message to Paul and Barnabas: "Brothers, if you have any message that will encourage the people, please speak."

16Paul stood up, raised his hand, and said, "You Israelites and you who worship God, please listen! 17The God of the Israelites chose our ancestors. He made the people great during the time they lived

---

⚭**12:19 Martyrdom:** Acts 16:16–40

⚭**12:19 Peter:** Acts 15:7–11

12:21–23 Throughout the Book of Acts, Jesus' followers are very careful to inform people that they are acting on behalf of God, and that they are not gods themselves (see 14:15). This is because (1) in the larger Roman world the gods might appear in various forms and (2) Jesus' followers perform great miracles. Herod, on the other hand, allows people to think of him as more than a human, as a god. The result is his death.

⚭**12:23 Capital Punishment:** See article on page 121.

13:2–3 *giving up . . . time.* This is called "fasting." The people would give up eating for a special time of prayer and worship to God. It was also sometimes done to show sadness and disappointment.

The Lord is able to communicate his will more easily and more clearly when he has our full attention. We are so easily distracted, and the practice of fasting, or "giving up eating," helps to focus our attention on him. The early church adopted the practice of fasting when important decisions or selections of church leaders were about to be made, as in this case.

⚭**13:3 Fasting:** Acts 14:23

13:3 *laid their hands on.* The laying on of hands had many purposes, including the giving of a blessing, power, or authority.

⚭**13:12 Magic:** Acts 19:13–19

⚭**13:14 Sabbath:** Acts 13:27

in Egypt, and he brought them out of that country
with great power. 18And he was patient with them
for forty years in the desert. 19God destroyed seven
nations in the land of Canaan and gave the land to
his people. 20All this happened in about four hundred fifty years.

"After this, God gave them judges until the time
of Samuel the prophet. 21Then the people asked for
a king, so God gave them Saul son of Kish. Saul was
from the tribe of Benjamin and was king for forty
years. 22After God took him away, God made
David their king. God said about him: 'I have found
in David son of Jesse the kind of man I want. He
will do all I want him to do.' 23So God has brought
Jesus, one of David's descendants, to Israel to be its
Savior, as he promised. 24Before Jesus came, John
preached to all the people of Israel about a baptism
of changed hearts and lives. 25When he was finishing his work, he said, 'Who do you think I am?
I am not the Christ. He is coming later, and I am
not worthy to untie his sandals.'

26"Brothers, sons of the family of Abraham, and
others who worship God, listen! The news about
this salvation has been sent to us. 27Those who
live in Jerusalem and their leaders did not realize
that Jesus was the Savior. They did not understand the words that the prophets wrote, which
are read every Sabbath day. But they made them
come true when they said Jesus was guilty.
28They could not find any real reason for Jesus to
be put to death, but they asked Pilate to have him
killed. 29When they had done to him all that the
Scriptures had said, they took him down from the
cross and laid him in a tomb. 30But God raised
him up from the dead! 31After this, for many days,
those who had gone with Jesus from Galilee to
Jerusalem saw him. They are now his witnesses
to the people. 32We tell you the Good News about
the promise God made to our ancestors. 33God
has made this promise come true for us, his children, by raising Jesus from the dead. We read
about this also in Psalm 2:

'You are my Son.
Today I have become your Father.' *Psalm 2:7*

34God raised Jesus from the dead, and he will
never go back to the grave and become dust. So
God said:

'I will give you the holy and sure blessings
that I promised to David.' *Isaiah 55:3*

35But in another place God says:

'You will not let your Holy One rot.' *Psalm 16:10*

36David did God's will during his lifetime. Then he
died and was buried beside his ancestors, and his
body did rot in the grave. 37But the One God raised
from the dead did not rot in the grave. 38-39Brothers,
understand what we are telling you: You can have
forgiveness of your sins through Jesus. The law of
Moses could not free you from your sins. But
through Jesus everyone who believes is free from
all sins. 40Be careful! Don't let what the prophets
said happen to you:

41'Listen, you people who doubt!
You can wonder, and then die.
I will do something in your lifetime
that you won't believe even when you are
told about it!'" *Habakkuk 1:5*

42While Paul and Barnabas were leaving the
synagogue, the people asked them to tell them
more about these things on the next Sabbath.
43When the meeting was over, many people with
those who had changed to worship God followed
Paul and Barnabas from that place. Paul and
Barnabas were persuading them to continue
trusting in God's grace.

44On the next Sabbath day, almost everyone in
the city came to hear the word of the Lord.
45Seeing the crowd, the Jewish people became
very jealous and said insulting things and argued
against what Paul said. 46But Paul and Barnabas
spoke very boldly, saying, "We must speak the
message of God to you first. But you refuse to listen. You are judging yourselves not worthy of
having eternal life! So we will now go to the people of other nations. 47This is what the Lord told
us to do, saying:

'I have made you a light for the nations;
you will show people all over the world the
way to be saved.'" *Isaiah 49:6*

48When those who were not Jewish heard Paul
say this, they were happy and gave honor to the
message of the Lord. And the people who were
chosen to have life forever believed the message.

49So the message of the Lord was spreading
through the whole country. 50But the Jewish people stirred up some of the important religious
women and the leaders of the city. They started
trouble against Paul and Barnabas and forced
them out of their area. 51So Paul and Barnabas
shook the dust off their feet and went to Iconium.
52But the followers were filled with joy and the
Holy Spirit.

13:24 *John.* John the Baptist, who preached to people about Christ's coming (Luke 3).
13:27 Sabbath: Acts 13:42–44
13:34 David: 2 Timothy 2:8
13:44 Sabbath: Hebrews 4:1–16
13:51 *shook . . . feet.* A warning. It showed that they had rejected these people.

Paul and Barnabas in Iconium

14 In Iconium, Paul and Barnabas went as usual to the synagogue. They spoke so well that a great many Jews and Greeks believed. 2But some people who did not believe excited the others and turned them against the believers. 3Paul and Barnabas stayed in Iconium a long time and spoke bravely for the Lord. He showed that their message about his grace was true by giving them the power to work miracles and signs. 4But the city was divided. Some of the people agreed with the Jews, and others believed the apostles.

5Some who were not Jews, some Jews, and some of their rulers wanted to mistreat Paul and Barnabas and to stone them to death. 6When Paul and Barnabas learned about this, they ran away to Lystra and Derbe, cities in Lycaonia, and to the areas around those cities. 7They announced the Good News there, too.

Paul in Lystra and Derbe

8In Lystra there sat a man who had been born crippled; he had never walked. 9As this man was listening to Paul speak, Paul looked straight at him and saw that he believed God could heal him. 10So he cried out, "Stand up on your feet!" The man jumped up and began walking around. 11When the crowds saw what Paul did, they shouted in the Lycaonian language, "The gods have become like humans and have come down to us!" 12Then the people began to call Barnabas "Zeus" and Paul "Hermes," because he was the main speaker. 13The priest in the temple of Zeus, which was near the city, brought some bulls and flowers to the city gates. He and the people wanted to offer a sacrifice to Paul and Barnabas. 14But when the apostles, Barnabas and Paul, heard about it, they tore their clothes. They ran in among the people, shouting, 15"Friends, why are you doing these things? We are only human beings like you. We are bringing you the Good News and are telling you to turn away from these worthless things and turn to the living God. He is the One who made the sky, the earth, the sea, and everything in them. 16In the past, God let all the nations do what they wanted. 17Yet he proved he is real by showing kindness, by giving you rain from heaven and crops at the right times, by giving you food and filling your hearts with joy." 18Even with these words, they were barely able to keep the crowd from offering sacrifices to them.

19Then some evil people came from Antioch and Iconium and persuaded the people to turn against Paul. So they threw stones at him and dragged him out of town, thinking they had killed him. 20But the followers gathered around him, and he got up and went back into the town. The next day he and Barnabas left and went to the city of Derbe.

The Return to Antioch in Syria

21Paul and Barnabas told the Good News in Derbe, and many became followers. Paul and Barnabas returned to Lystra, Iconium, and Antioch, 22making the followers of Jesus stronger and helping them stay in the faith. They said, "We must suffer many things to enter God's kingdom." 23They chose elders for each church, by praying and giving up eating for a certain time. These elders had trusted the Lord, so Paul and Barnabas put them in the Lord's care.

24Then they went through Pisidia and came to Pamphylia. 25When they had preached the message in Perga, they went down to Attalia. 26And from there they sailed away to Antioch where the believers had put them into God's care and had sent them out to do this work. Now they had finished.

27When they arrived in Antioch, Paul and Barnabas gathered the church together. They told the church all about what God had done with them and how God had made it possible for those who were not Jewish to believe. 28And they stayed there a long time with the followers.

The Meeting at Jerusalem

15 Then some people came to Antioch from Judea and began teaching the non-Jewish believers: "You cannot be saved if you are not circumcised as Moses taught us." 2Paul and Barnabas were against this teaching and argued with them about it. So the church decided to send Paul, Barnabas, and some others to Jerusalem where they could talk more about this with the apostles and elders.

14:10 Healing: 1 Corinthians 12:9

14:12 *"Zeus."* The Greeks believed in many false gods, of whom Zeus was most important.

14:12 *"Hermes."* The Greeks believed he was a messenger for the other gods.

14:15–17 These followers of Jesus do not have a set sermon they preach in every town. In Antioch, for example, they tell the story of Israel, citing the Old Testament (Acts 13:16–41). But when they preach here in Lystra, they do not even mention the Old Testament. In fact, they do not even mention Jesus yet. This is because their audience is made up of people who are not familiar with the God of Israel. This leads Paul to talk about "the living God" in terms that his audience will understand.

14:22 Perseverance: Romans 8:30–39

14:23 Fasting: See article on page 721.

14:23 *giving . . . time.* This is called "fasting." The people would give up eating for a special time of prayer and worship to God. It was also done sometimes to show sadness and disappointment.

[3]The church helped them leave on the trip, and they went through the countries of Phoenicia and Samaria, telling all about how the other nations had turned to God. This made all the believers very happy. [4]When they arrived in Jerusalem, they were welcomed by the apostles, the elders, and the church. Paul, Barnabas, and the others told about everything God had done with them. [5]But some of the believers who belonged to the Pharisee group came forward and said, "The non-Jewish believers must be circumcised. They must be told to obey the law of Moses."

[6]The apostles and the elders gathered to consider this problem. [7]After a long debate, Peter stood up and said to them, "Brothers, you know that in the early days God chose me from among you to preach the Good News to the nations. They heard the Good News from me, and they believed. [8]God, who knows the thoughts of everyone, accepted them. He showed this to us by giving them the Holy Spirit, just as he did to us. [9]To God, those people are not different from us. When they believed, he made their hearts pure. [10]So now why are you testing God by putting a heavy load around the necks of the non-Jewish believers? It is a load that neither we nor our ancestors were able to carry. [11]But we believe that we and they too will be saved by the grace of the Lord Jesus."⚭

[12]Then the whole group became quiet. They listened to Paul and Barnabas tell about all the miracles and signs that God did through them among the people. [13]After they finished speaking, James said, "Brothers, listen to me. [14]Simon has told us how God showed his love for those people. For the first time he is accepting from among them a people to be his own. [15]The words of the prophets agree with this too:

[16]'After these things I will return.
The kingdom of David is like a fallen tent.
But I will rebuild its ruins,
and I will set it up.
[17]Then those people who are left alive may ask
the Lord for help,
and the other nations that belong to me,
says the Lord,
who will make it happen.⚭
[18] And these things have been known
for a long time.' *Amos 9:11-12*

[19]"So I think we should not bother the other people who are turning to God. [20]Instead, we should write a letter to them telling them these things: Stay away from food that has been offered to idols (which makes it unclean), any kind of sexual sin, eating animals that have been strangled, and blood. [21]They should do these things, because for a long time in every city the law of Moses has been taught. And it is still read in the synagogue every Sabbath day."

Letter to Non-Jewish Believers

[22]The apostles, the elders, and the whole church decided to send some of their men with Paul and Barnabas to Antioch. They chose Judas Barsabbas and Silas, who were respected by the believers. [23]They sent the following letter with them:

From the apostles and elders, your brothers.
To all the non-Jewish believers in Antioch, Syria, and Cilicia:
Greetings!

[24]We have heard that some of our group have come to you and said things that trouble and upset you. But we did not tell them to do this. [25]We have all agreed to choose some messengers and send them to you with our dear friends Barnabas and Paul— [26]people who have given their lives to serve our Lord Jesus Christ. [27]So we are sending Judas and Silas, who will tell you the same things. [28]It has pleased the Holy Spirit that you should not have a heavy load to carry, and we agree. You need to do only these things: [29]Stay away from any food that has been offered to idols, eating any animals that have been strangled, and blood, and any kind of sexual sin. If you stay away from these things, you will do well.

Good-bye.

[30]So they left Jerusalem and went to Antioch where they gathered the church and gave them the letter. [31]When they read it, they were very happy because of the encouraging message. [32]Judas and Silas, who were also prophets, said many things to encourage the believers and make them stronger. [33]After some time Judas and Silas were sent off in peace by the believers, and they went back to those who had sent them. [34]*

⚭**15:11 Peter:** 1 Corinthians 15:5

15:13–18 Here we see that James's position to accept non-Jews as recipients of God's salvation and not to require them to be circumcised is based on God's promise in Amos 9:11–12. When God reestablishes Israel ("the kingdom of David") as the church ("I will rebuild its ruins"), non-Jews who belong to him will seek him out. James indicates that God's promise to include non-Jews among his chosen people (Genesis 12:4; Isaiah 49:6; Romans 15:9–12) has been known for a long time.

⚭**15:17 The Remnant:** See article on page 671.

***15:34** *Verse 34.* Some Greek copies add verse 34: ". . . but Silas decided to remain there."

35But Paul and Barnabas stayed in Antioch and,
along with many others, preached the Good News
and taught the people the message of the Lord.

Paul and Barnabas Separate

36After some time, Paul said to Barnabas, "We
should go back to all those towns where we preached
the message of the Lord. Let's visit the believers
and see how they are doing."
37Barnabas wanted to take John Mark with them,
38but he had left them at Pamphylia; he did not continue with them in the work. So Paul did not think
it was a good idea to take him. 39Paul and Barnabas
had such a serious argument about this that they
separated and went different ways. Barnabas took
Mark and sailed to Cyprus, 40but Paul chose Silas
and left. The believers in Antioch put Paul into the
Lord's care, 41and he went through Syria and Cilicia, giving strength to the churches.

Timothy Goes with Paul

16 Paul came to Derbe and Lystra, where a
follower named Timothy lived. Timothy's
mother was Jewish and a believer, but his father
was a Greek.
2The believers in Lystra and Iconium respected
Timothy and said good things about him. 3Paul
wanted Timothy to travel with him, but all the people living in that area knew that Timothy's father
was Greek. So Paul circumcised Timothy to please
his mother's people. 4Paul and those with him
traveled from town to town and gave the decisions
made by the apostles and elders in Jerusalem for
the people to obey. 5So the churches became
stronger in the faith and grew larger every day.

Paul Is Called Out of Asia

6Paul and those with him went through the
areas of Phrygia and Galatia since the Holy Spirit
did not let them preach the Good News in the
country of Asia. 7When they came near the country of Mysia, they tried to go into Bithynia, but the
Spirit of Jesus did not let them. 8So they passed by
Mysia and went to Troas. 9That night Paul saw in a
vision a man from Macedonia. The man stood and
begged, "Come over to Macedonia and help us."
10After Paul had seen the vision, we immediately
prepared to leave for Macedonia, understanding
that God had called us to tell the Good News to
those people.

Lydia Becomes a Christian

11We left Troas and sailed straight to the island of
Samothrace. The next day we sailed to Neapolis.
12Then we went by land to Philippi, a Roman colony
and the leading city in that part of Macedonia. We
stayed there for several days.
13On the Sabbath day we went outside the city
gate to the river where we thought we would find
a special place for prayer. Some women had gathered there, so we sat down and talked with them.
14One of the listeners was a woman named Lydia
from the city of Thyatira whose job was selling
purple cloth. She worshiped God, and he opened
her mind to pay attention to what Paul was saying. 15She and all the people in her house were
baptized. Then she invited us to her home, saying, "If you think I am truly a believer in the Lord,
then come stay in my house." And she persuaded
us to stay with her.

Paul and Silas in Jail

16Once, while we were going to the place for
prayer, a servant girl met us. She had a special
spirit in her, and she earned a lot of money for her
owners by telling fortunes. 17This girl followed Paul

15:35 Circumcision: Romans 2:29
15:35 Crossing Cultural Boundaries: Galatians 2:11–16
15:35 Mission: Romans 10:14–15
15:35 Racism: Romans 4:18
15:35 Unity: 1 Corinthians 1:10–13

16 Magical practices are condemned throughout the Bible. Not only are they spiritually harmful in themselves, but they can lead to social and economic exploitation. When Paul and Silas saw the plight of the girl in Philippi, whose spiritual powers were being used to make money for other people, they had no hesitation invoking the greater power of Jesus Christ to deliver her.

16:3 Paul circumcised Timothy as a practical matter so that no unnecessary barrier might exist for ministry among the Jewish people. Paul and the early church, however, clearly believed that circumcision was no longer necessary for the Christian believer as it had been for the Jewish people (Galatians 5:6; 6:15; Acts 15). In Galatians 2:3 the apostles had recognized the validity of Paul's message to the non-Jews as evidenced by the fact that they did not require Paul's non-Jewish companion, Titus, to be circumcised.

16:9 Dreams: See article on page 159.

16:10–17 The pronouns used to describe the events of the Book of Acts change from the third person ("he" and "they") to the first person ("we" and "us"), indicating that Luke, the author of Acts, met Paul in Troas and accompanied him on his missionary journey at the time he received his Macedonian vision. Some people even speculate that Luke was from Philippi, accounting for their going there first.

16:11 *Neapolis.* City in Macedonia. It was the first city Paul visited on the continent of Europe.

16:12 *Roman colony.* A town begun by Romans with Roman laws, customs, and privileges.

16:15 As a whole, women in the Roman world were not highly regarded. However, there are many examples of successful women, like Lydia. Lydia has her own home and business, and when she becomes a believer, she makes her home available to Paul and his companions. Like others in the early church (see 4:32–33), she no longer regards her money and possessions as her own, but shares them with her new family of believers.

16:15 Baptism: Romans 6:1–14
16:15 Deborah: Acts 16:40
16:15 Hospitality: Romans 16:3–16

16:16 *spirit.* This was a spirit from the devil, which caused her to say she had special knowledge.

Apostasy

Hebrews 10:19–39

What does the Bible say about apostasy?
Should Christians be concerned about the possibility of apostasy?

Many Christians have been driven by the fear that they might fall away from Christ and lose their salvation. The warning that "if we decide to go on sinning after we have learned the truth, there is no longer any sacrifice for sins" (Hebrews 10:26), can be a terrifying prospect.

The concern with humanity's ability to fall away from God is rooted in the Old Testament. Moses, and later the prophets, struggled to keep the Israelites faithful to God. For example, in Exodus 15:22–17:7, after God saved Israel from Egypt, they complained bitterly, then turned away. Many were destroyed even after the agreement was established (Exodus 32–33). Rebellions are condemned and guilty persons are destroyed (Numbers 14; 16). In the New Testament, the refusal of the people to heed God's call ended in judgment (Matthew 23:37–39). However, there are also many attempts to call the people back to faithfulness even after they turned from God (for example, Jeremiah 3:14; Daniel 9:9; Hosea). In the New Testament, Peter denied Christ, yet he became a leading figure in the early church.

The word *apostasy* is used as a verb in the New Testament, meaning "to draw away from" or "to fall away." It is an accusation made against Paul in Acts 21:21. Some people accused the apostle of apostasy, or falling away from the Law of Moses. In 1 Timothy 4:1 it is part of a warning that in later times some will depart from the faith. People will turn against Jesus. Such a betrayal of Jesus is the heart of apostasy.

In the New Testament, "apostasy" may be applied to all those who once lived in relationship with Christ and the church but who now live as enemies of the cross of Christ (Philippians 3:18). False prophets may include those who were formerly part of the church or who pretend to be part of it (2 Peter 2; 2 Timothy 3:1–9). Those who apostatize are characterized by how they live. They love themselves and money, brag, are proud, say evil things against others, do not obey their parents, are not thankful, do not love others, refuse to forgive, gossip, do not control themselves, hate what is good, turn against friends, are conceited, love pleasure instead of God, act as if they serve God but do not have his power (2 Timothy 3:1–9; 2 Peter 2:10–21). They work to draw others away from Christ and to exploit them (2 Peter 2:1–3).

In the New Testament, the purpose of talking about apostasy was to use it as a means to exhort one another to greater faithfulness. The threat of the possibility of apostasy acts as a strong warning. However, it is never used in the New Testament to accuse someone of having lost their salvation. The threat of punishment is used in 2 Peter 2:15–21 and Jude 5–6 to warn about the serious consequences of failing to remain faithful. Hebrews 3:12 warns about an evil and unbelieving heart that leads astray. Paul urges Timothy to correct others with care, hoping that they will repent (2 Timothy 2:25–26). Hebrews 10:19–39 is an encouragement to keep exhorting one another to greater faithfulness. Warning about apostasy includes the confidence that it is possible to remain faithful.

Hebrews 6:4–6 is a hard-hitting and frightening passage that warns of the dangers of apostasy. It seems to say that those who "were once in God's light" and then fell away are not able to repent and return to the faith. The author puts it this way: "It is impossible to bring them back to a changed life again, because they are nailing the Son of God to a cross again and are shaming him in front of others." This passage strikes fear in the hearts of those who are Christians but sin. It leads them to wonder whether they have gone so far as to not be able to return to Christ.

At first, the difficulty with this passage is heightened when it is compared with the seemingly contradictory 1 John 2:19: "These enemies of Christ were in our fellowship, but they left us. They never really belonged to us; if they had been a part of us, they would have stayed with us. But they left, and this shows that none of them really belonged to us."

Reading these and other passages together lead to the following understanding. Just because someone is a church-going, apparently devout Christian does not necessarily mean they are one in actuality. They may even deceive themselves. But if they leave the faith, they are not showing that God has taken away the gift of salvation. They are rather showing, as John states, that they were really never Christians to begin with.

Christians should not fear that specific sins take them out of the realm of the faith and make it impossible for them to repent and get grace. The Scriptures are too full of examples of those, like David, who sinned horribly, but repented and came back to the faith.

Apostasy: For additional scriptures on this topic go to Exodus 15:22–17:7.

HELL

REVELATION 20:7–15

What is so bad about hell?

If there are so many people in hell, then I can tolerate it, too. If my relatives and friends are in hell, then I would rather spend my eternity there with them.

These are some of the comments we often hear about hell. It is difficult for us to conceptualize hell because it is a realm we cannot truly comprehend while we are still living in the present world. For this reason, people often correlate their experience on earth with hell; for example, since most people enjoy the presence of relatives and friends, some believe such enjoyment also exists in hell.

However, the Book of Revelation denies such belief. A major theme of that book is that a day will come when the world as we know it now will be replaced by two types of existence: one within the walls of the new Jerusalem and one outside. Revelation 21:27 points to the factor which will determine our final destiny: "Only those whose names are written in the Lamb's book of life will enter the city." Anyone whose name is not found in that book belongs in the existence outside of new Jerusalem, which is hell, and that existence is not a continuation of our experience on earth.

Although the Bible does not provide every detail concerning hell, it is clear that hell is not, at the very least, a place where we want to go. First, Revelation 20:7–10 tells us that hell is prepared for Satan and his followers. This dampens the hope of finding any goodness in hell. Second, hell is depicted as a "lake of burning sulfur" (20:10) and a "lake of fire" (20:14). Whether we interpret them literally or figuratively, there is only suffering in hell; no trace of joy can ever be found. Amos described the Lord's day of judging as a day of "darkness" (Amos 5:18, 20) and as an encounter with a lion, a bear, and the bite of a snake (5:19). Jesus depicted hell as a place of darkness where "people will cry and grind their teeth with pain" (Matthew 24:51; 25:30).

The picture of hell in the Bible is so appalling because it is the opposite of heaven. Since heaven is where God lives with his people (Revelation 21:3) with all of his blessings, then hell is a place where only God's wrath and condemnation can be found. At the present time, God is patient with this sinful world and still "causes the sun to rise on good people and on evil people, and he sends rain to those who do right and to those who do wrong" (Matthew 5:45). God is the source of "every perfect gift" (James 1:17) we find on earth. But those in hell "will be kept away from the Lord and from his great power" (2 Thessalonians 1:8–9).

Such expulsion from God's presence is seen throughout the Bible for those who are against God. When Adam and Eve disobeyed God, he forced them out of the garden. This meant more than leaving a particular location on earth, it symbolized their separation from God along with his favor. The curse on the original creation order (Genesis 3:16–19) is inevitable due to that alienation.

Since then, the estrangement from God is deemed as the ultimate curse, because it meant the loss of God's favor. When God was angered by the worship of a gold calf at Mount Sinai, he declared that he would not go with them to the Promised Land, though the Israelites would enter it (Exodus 33:3). However, Moses would rather not enter the land because he understood the absence of God meant the loss of his favor (Exodus 33:15–16); what good would the promised land be without God's presence with them? The removal of the Israelites from the Promised Land was a curse in the Mosaic agreements, because they would be separated from God and unable to worship him (Deuteronomy 4:27–28). Later, when Judah was devastated by the Babylonians, the Israelites grieved over not only the destruction of their nation, but also the rejection of God (Jeremiah 2:37). The Israelites became *Lo-Ruhamah*, not pitied by God, and *Lo-Ammi*, not God's people (Hosea 1:6, 9). God's presence departed from the Temple in the midst of the rebellious Israelites (Ezekiel 10).

This notion of separation from God as the horrible nature of punishment for sin continues in the New Testament. According to Paul, the unsaved sinners are "separated from God" (Colossians 1:21) and separated from the "life that God gives" (Ephesians 4:18). And in Revelation 20, we find the ultimate reality of this separation in the existence of hell.

We may have many questions concerning hell due to our curiosity, but the most important fact that we should know is what God wants to tell us through the Bible. Hell is a place where unsaved sinners will be kept away from God, who is the Source of all goodness and blessings. The only way to enjoy the blessed presence of God is to have a personal relationship with him through Jesus Christ, who, when he cried, "My God, my God, why have you rejected me?" (Matthew 27:46) on the cross, was separated from God the Father on the behalf of his people so that they may come into God's presence.

Hell: For additional scriptures on this topic go to Isaiah 51:17–23.

and us, shouting, "These men are servants of the Most High God. They are telling you how you can be saved."

[18]She kept this up for many days. This bothered Paul, so he turned and said to the spirit, "By the power of Jesus Christ, I command you to come out of her!" Immediately, the spirit came out.

[19]When the owners of the servant girl saw this, they knew that now they could not use her to make money. So they grabbed Paul and Silas and dragged them before the city rulers in the marketplace. [20]They brought Paul and Silas to the Roman rulers and said, "These men are Jews and are making trouble in our city. [21]They are teaching things that are not right for us as Romans to do."

[22]The crowd joined the attack against them. The Roman officers tore the clothes of Paul and Silas and had them beaten with rods. [23]Then Paul and Silas were thrown into jail, and the jailer was ordered to guard them carefully. [24]When he heard this order, he put them far inside the jail and pinned their feet down between large blocks of wood.

[25]About midnight Paul and Silas were praying and singing songs to God as the other prisoners listened. [26]Suddenly, there was a strong earthquake that shook the foundation of the jail. Then all the doors of the jail broke open, and all the prisoners were freed from their chains. [27]The jailer woke up and saw that the jail doors were open. Thinking that the prisoners had already escaped, he got his sword and was about to kill himself. [28]But Paul shouted, "Don't hurt yourself! We are all here."

[29]The jailer told someone to bring a light. Then he ran inside and, shaking with fear, fell down before Paul and Silas. [30]He brought them outside and said, "Men, what must I do to be saved?"

[31]They said to him, "Believe in the Lord Jesus and you will be saved—you and all the people in your house." [32]So Paul and Silas told the message of the Lord to the jailer and all the people in his house. [33]At that hour of the night the jailer took Paul and Silas and washed their wounds. Then he and all his people were baptized immediately. [34]After this the jailer took Paul and Silas home and gave them food. He and his family were very happy because they now believed in God.

[35]The next morning, the Roman officers sent the police to tell the jailer, "Let these men go free."

[36]The jailer said to Paul, "The officers have sent an order to let you go free. You can leave now. Go in peace."

[37]But Paul said to the police, "They beat us in public without a trial, even though we are Roman citizens. And they threw us in jail. Now they want to make us go away quietly. No! Let them come themselves and bring us out."

[38]The police told the Roman officers what Paul said. When the officers heard that Paul and Silas were Roman citizens, they were afraid. [39]So they came and told Paul and Silas they were sorry and took them out of jail and asked them to leave the city. [40]So when they came out of the jail, they went to Lydia's house where they saw some of the believers and encouraged them. Then they left.

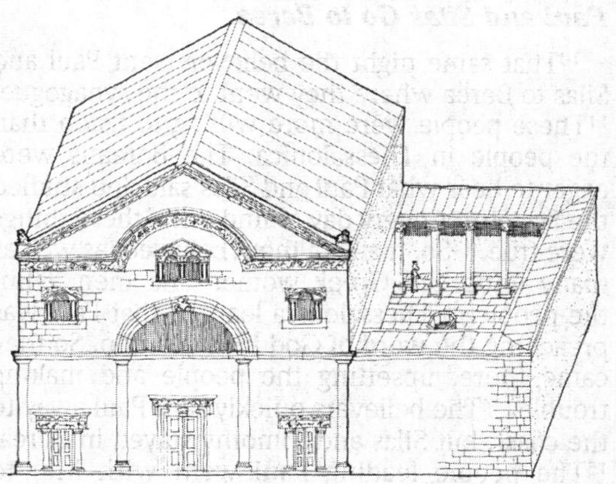

A model of the third-century A.D. synagogue at Capernaum

Paul and Silas in Thessalonica

17 Paul and Silas traveled through Amphipolis and Apollonia and came to Thessalonica where there was a synagogue. [2]Paul went into the synagogue as he always did, and on each Sabbath day for three weeks, he talked with his fellow Jews about the Scriptures. [3]He explained and proved that the Christ must die and then rise from the dead. He said, "This Jesus I am telling you about is the Christ." [4]Some of them were convinced and joined Paul and Silas, along with many of the Greeks who worshiped God and many of the important women.

16:17 Luke: Acts 20:5–15

16:27 *kill himself.* He thought the leaders would kill him for letting the prisoners escape.

16:31 Lordship: Romans 10:9–10

16:37 *Roman citizens.* Roman law said that Roman citizens must not be beaten before they had a trial.

16:40 Deborah: See article on page 379.

16:40 Martyrdom: Acts 21:30–28:31

17:3 Suffering: Romans 5:3

5But some others became jealous. So they got some evil men from the marketplace, formed a mob, and started a riot. They ran to Jason's house, looking for Paul and Silas, wanting to bring them out to the people. 6But when they did not find them, they dragged Jason and some other believers to the leaders of the city. The people were yelling, "These people have made trouble everywhere in the world, and now they have come here too! 7Jason is keeping them in his house. All of them do things against the laws of Caesar, saying there is another king, called Jesus."

8When the people and the leaders of the city heard these things, they became very upset. 9They made Jason and the others put up a sum of money. Then they let the believers go free.

Paul and Silas Go to Berea

10That same night the believers sent Paul and Silas to Berea where they went to the synagogue. 11These people were more willing to listen than the people in Thessalonica. The Bereans were eager to hear what Paul and Silas said and studied the Scriptures every day to find out if these things were true. 12So, many of them believed, as well as many important Greek women and men. 13But the people in Thessalonica learned that Paul was preaching the word of God in Berea, too. So they came there, upsetting the people and making trouble. 14The believers quickly sent Paul away to the coast, but Silas and Timothy stayed in Berea. 15The people leading Paul went with him to Athens. Then they carried a message from Paul back to Silas and Timothy for them to come to him as soon as they could.

Paul Preaches in Athens

16While Paul was waiting for Silas and Timothy in Athens, he was troubled because he saw that the city was full of idols. 17In the synagogue, he talked with the Jews and the Greeks who worshiped God. He also talked every day with people in the marketplace.

18Some of the Epicurean and Stoic philosophers argued with him, saying, "This man doesn't know what he is talking about. What is he trying to say?" Others said, "He seems to be telling us about some other gods," because Paul was telling them about Jesus and his rising from the dead. 19They got Paul and took him to a meeting of the Areopagus, where they said, "Please explain to us this new idea you have been teaching. 20The things you are saying are new to us, and we want to know what this teaching means." 21(All the people of Athens and those from other countries who lived there always used their time to talk about the newest ideas.)

22Then Paul stood before the meeting of the Areopagus and said, "People of Athens, I can see you are very religious in all things. 23As I was going through your city, I saw the objects you worship. I found an altar that had these words written on it: TO A GOD WHO IS NOT KNOWN. You worship a god that you don't know, and this is the God I am telling you about! 24The God who made the whole world and everything in it is the Lord of the land and the sky. He does not live in temples built by human hands. 25This God is the One who gives life, breath, and everything else to people. He does not need any help from them; he has everything he needs. 26God began by making one person, and from him came all the different people who live everywhere in the world. God decided exactly when and where they must live. 27God wanted them to look for him and perhaps search all around for him and find him, though he is not far from any of us: 28'We live in him. We walk in him. We are in him.' Some of your own poets have said: 'For we are his children.' 29Since we are God's children, you must not think that God is like something that people imagine or make from gold, silver, or rock.∞ 30In the past, people did not understand God, and he ignored this. But now, God tells all people in the world to change their hearts and lives. 31God has set a day

17:6–7 An enraged mob in Thessalonica threatened Paul and Silas, shouting, "These people have made trouble everywhere in the world, and now they have come here too! . . . All of them do things against the laws of Caesar, saying there is another king, called Jesus." During the early centuries Christians were killed not for religious reasons—Rome, after all, was a land of many gods—but because they refused to worship the emperor. Because they would not say, offering incense before the statue of the emperor, "We have no king but Caesar," the Roman government saw them as political enemies.

17:16–34 Paul takes advantage of the Athenians' love for discussing new ideas to introduce them to Jesus. He notes an idol with the inscription, *To an unknown god*, and uses it to assert that Jesus Christ made God knowable and understandable. He uses aspects of the Athenian culture (the idol, poetry) as a platform for discussion about God's purposes toward humanity. He also tailors his speech to meet his audience, focusing on God's unlimited power compared to the limitation of stone idols. In fact, he only mentions Jesus at the very end of his speech, and then not even by name. Some call this pre-evangelism. Of course, the reason he had been invited to speak on Mars Hill was because he had been preaching Jesus and the resurrection in the marketplace (verse 18).

17:18 *Epicurean and Stoic philosophers.* Philosophers were those who searched for truth. Epicureans believed that pleasure, especially pleasures of the mind, were the goal of life. Stoics believed that life should be without feelings of joy or grief.

17:19 *Areopagus.* A council or group of important leaders in Athens. They were like judges.

∞**17:29 Idolatry:** Galatians 4:8–9

that he will judge all the world with fairness, by the
man he chose long ago. And God has proved this to
everyone by raising that man from the dead!"
32When the people heard about Jesus being
raised from the dead, some of them laughed. But
others said, "We will hear more about this from
you later." 33So Paul went away from them. 34But
some of the people believed Paul and joined him.
Among those who believed was Dionysius, a member of the Areopagus, a woman named Damaris,
and some others.

Paul in Corinth

18 Later Paul left Athens and went to Corinth.
2Here he met a Jew named Aquila who had
been born in the country of Pontus. But Aquila
and his wife, Priscilla, had recently moved to
Corinth from Italy, because Claudius commanded
that all Jews must leave Rome. Paul went to visit
Aquila and Priscilla. 3Because they were tentmakers, just as he was, he stayed with them and worked
with them. 4Every Sabbath day he talked with the
Jews and Greeks in the synagogue, trying to persuade them to believe in Jesus.
5Silas and Timothy came from Macedonia and
joined Paul in Corinth. After this, Paul spent all
his time telling people the Good News, showing
them that Jesus is the Christ. 6But they would not
accept Paul's teaching and said some evil things.
So he shook off the dust from his clothes and said
to them, "If you are not saved, it will be your own
fault! I have done all I can do! After this, I will go
only to other nations." 7Paul left the synagogue
and moved into the home of Titius Justus, next to
the synagogue. This man worshiped God. 8Crispus
was the leader of that synagogue, and he and all
the people living in his house believed in the Lord.
Many others in Corinth also listened to Paul and
believed and were baptized.
9During the night, the Lord told Paul in a vision:
"Don't be afraid. Continue talking to people and
don't be quiet. 10I am with you, and no one will
hurt you because many of my people are in this
city." 11Paul stayed there for a year and a half, teaching God's word to the people.

Paul Is Brought Before Gallio

12When Gallio was the governor of the country
of Southern Greece, some people came together
against Paul and took him to the court. 13They
said, "This man is teaching people to worship
God in a way that is against our law."
14Paul was about to say something, but Gallio
spoke, saying, "I would listen to you if you were
complaining about a crime or some wrong. 15But
the things you are saying are only questions about
words and names—arguments about your own
law. So you must solve this problem yourselves. I
don't want to be a judge of these things." 16And
Gallio made them leave the court.
17Then they all grabbed Sosthenes, the leader
of the synagogue, and beat him there before the
court. But this did not bother Gallio.

Paul Returns to Antioch

18Paul stayed with the believers for many more
days. Then he left and sailed for Syria, with
Priscilla and Aquila. At Cenchrea Paul cut off his
hair, because he had made a promise to God.
19Then they went to Ephesus, where Paul left
Priscilla and Aquila. While Paul was there, he went
into the synagogue and talked with the people.
20When they asked him to stay with them longer,
he refused. 21But as he left, he said, "I will come
back to you again if God wants me to." And so he
sailed away from Ephesus.
22When Paul landed at Caesarea, he went and
gave greetings to the church in Jerusalem. After
that, Paul went to Antioch. 23He stayed there for a
while and then left and went through the regions of
Galatia and Phrygia. He traveled from town to town
in these regions, giving strength to all the followers.

Apollos in Ephesus and Corinth

24A Jew named Apollos came to Ephesus. He was
born in the city of Alexandria and was a good
speaker who knew the Scriptures well. 25He had
been taught about the way of the Lord and was
always very excited when he spoke and taught the
truth about Jesus. But the only baptism Apollos
knew about was the baptism that John taught.

17:34 Evangelism: 1 Corinthians 15:3–4

18:1–3 Paul's missionary strategy, as it is related here, makes good sense. When he arrives in a new town, he finds people who are very much like himself and begins his work there. Aquila and Priscilla are, like him, well-traveled, Jewish, and tentmakers.

18:2 *Claudius.* The emperor (ruler) of Rome, A.D. 41–54.

18:6 *shook . . . clothes.* This was a warning to show that Paul was finished talking to the people in that city.

18:14 Crime: Acts 25:16

18:18 *cut . . . hair.* Jews did this to show that the time of a special promise to God was finished.

18:18 Oath/Vow: Hebrews 6:16

18:24–28 John's influence continued to be felt beyond his lifetime. We get a glimpse of this when Apollos comes on the scene at the end of Acts 18. This man met Aquila and Priscilla in the city of Ephesus, where they told him about Jesus. Up to this point, "the only baptism that Apollos knew about was the baptism that John taught" (Acts 18:25). Apollos became a Christian after hearing Aquila and Priscilla and then went on to become a powerful missionary.

18:25 Jordan River: Acts 19:3–4

18:25 *John.* John the Baptist, who preached to people about Christ's coming (Luke 3).

[26]Apollos began to speak very boldly in the synagogue, and when Priscilla and Aquila heard him,
they took him to their home and helped him better understand the way of God. [27]Now Apollos
wanted to go to the country of Southern Greece.
So the believers helped him and wrote a letter to
the followers there, asking them to accept him.
These followers had believed in Jesus because of
God's grace, and when Apollos arrived, he helped
them very much. [28]He argued very strongly with
the Jews before all the people, clearly proving
with the Scriptures that Jesus is the Christ.

Paul in Ephesus

19 While Apollos was in Corinth, Paul was visiting some places on the way to Ephesus.
There he found some followers [2]and asked them,
"Did you receive the Holy Spirit when you
believed?"

They said, "We have never even heard of a Holy
Spirit."

[3]So he asked, "What kind of baptism did you
have?"

They said, "It was the baptism that John taught."

[4]Paul said, "John's baptism was a baptism of
changed hearts and lives. He told people to believe
in the one who would come after him, and that one
is Jesus."∞

[5]When they heard this, they were baptized in the
name of the Lord Jesus. [6]Then Paul laid his hands on
them, and the Holy Spirit came upon them. They
began speaking different languages and prophesying.∞ [7]There were about twelve people in this
group.∞

[8]Paul went into the synagogue and spoke out
boldly for three months. He talked with the people
and persuaded them to accept the things he said
about the kingdom of God. [9]But some of them
became stubborn. They refused to believe and said
evil things about the Way of Jesus before all the
people. So Paul left them, and taking the followers
with him, he went to the school of a man named
Tyrannus. There Paul talked with people every day
[10]for two years. Because of his work, every Jew
and Greek in the country of Asia heard the word
of the Lord.

The Sons of Sceva

[11]God used Paul to do some very special miracles.
[12]Some people took handkerchiefs and clothes that
Paul had used and put them on the sick. When they
did this, the sick were healed and evil spirits left
them.

[13]But some people also were traveling around
and making evil spirits go out of people. They tried
to use the name of the Lord Jesus to force the evil
spirits out. They would say, "By the same Jesus that
Paul talks about, I order you to come out!" [14]Seven
sons of Sceva, a leading priest, were doing this.

[15]But one time an evil spirit said to them, "I know
Jesus, and I know about Paul, but who are you?"

[16]Then the man who had the evil spirit jumped
on them. Because he was so much stronger than all
of them, they ran away from the house naked and
hurt. [17]All the people in Ephesus—Jews and
Greeks— learned about this and were filled with
fear and gave great honor to the Lord Jesus. [18]Many
of the believers began to confess openly and tell
all the evil things they had done. [19]Some of them
who had used magic brought their magic books and
burned them before everyone. Those books were
worth about fifty thousand silver coins.∞

[20]So in a powerful way the word of the Lord
kept spreading and growing.

[21]After these things, Paul decided to go to Jeru-
salem, planning to go through the countries of
Macedonia and Southern Greece and then on to
Jerusalem. He said, "After I have been to Jerusalem,
I must also visit Rome."∞ [22]Paul sent Timothy and
Erastus, two of his helpers, ahead to Macedonia,
but he himself stayed in Asia for a while.

Trouble in Ephesus

[23]And during that time, there was some serious
trouble in Ephesus about the Way of Jesus.∞ [24]A
man named Demetrius, who worked with silver,
made little silver models that looked like the temple of the goddess Artemis. Those who did this
work made much money. [25]Demetrius had a
meeting with them and some others who did the
same kind of work. He told them, "Men, you
know that we make a lot of money from our business. [26]But look at what this man Paul is doing.
He has convinced and turned away many people
in Ephesus and in almost all of Asia! He says the
gods made by human hands are not real. [27]There

∞**19:4 Jordan River:** Hebrews 3:17–19
∞**19:6 Spiritual Gifts:** 1 Peter 4:11
19:6 *laid his hands on them.* The laying on of hands had many purposes, including the giving of a blessing, power, or authority.
19:6 *languages.* This can also be translated "tongues."
∞**19:7 John the Baptist:** See article on page 852.
∞**19:7 Tongues:** Romans 8:26
∞**19:19 Magic:** See article on page 354.
19:19 *fifty thousand silver coins.* Probably drachmas. One coin was enough to pay a worker for one day's labor.
∞**19:21 Rome:** Acts 22:24–29
∞**19:23 Road/Way:** Acts 22:14
19:24 *Artemis.* A Greek goddess that the people of Asia Minor worshiped.

is a danger that our business will lose its good name, but there is also another danger: People will begin to think that the temple of the great goddess Artemis is not important. Her greatness will be destroyed, and Artemis is the goddess that everyone in Asia and the whole world worships."

28When the others heard this, they became very angry and shouted, "Artemis, the goddess of Ephesus, is great!" 29The whole city became confused. The people grabbed Gaius and Aristarchus, who were from Macedonia and were traveling with Paul, and ran to the theater. 30Paul wanted to go in and talk to the crowd, but the followers did not let him. 31Also, some leaders of Asia who were friends of Paul sent him a message, begging him not to go into the theater. 32Some people were shouting one thing, and some were shouting another. The meeting was completely confused; most of them did not know why they had come together. 33They put a man named Alexander in front of the people, and some of them told him what to do. Alexander waved his hand so he could explain things to the people. 34But when they saw that Alexander was a Jew, they all shouted the same thing for two hours: "Great is Artemis of Ephesus!"

35Then the city clerk made the crowd be quiet. He said, "People of Ephesus, everyone knows that Ephesus is the city that keeps the temple of the great goddess Artemis and her holy stone that fell from heaven. 36Since no one can say this is not true, you should be quiet. Stop and think before you do anything. 37You brought these men here, but they have not said anything evil against our goddess or stolen anything from her temple. 38If Demetrius and those who work with him have a charge against anyone they should go to the courts and judges where they can argue with each other. 39If there is something else you want to talk about, it can be decided at the regular town meeting of the people. 40I say this because some people might see this trouble today and say that we are rioting. We could not explain this, because there is no real reason for this meeting." 41After the city clerk said these things, he told the people to go home.

Paul In Macedonia and Greece

20 When the trouble stopped, Paul sent for the followers to come to him. After he encouraged them and then told them good-bye, he left and went to the country of Macedonia. 2He said many things to strengthen the followers in the different places on his way through Macedonia. Then he went to Greece, 3where he stayed for three months. He was ready to sail for Syria, but some evil people were planning something against him. So Paul decided to go back through Macedonia to Syria. 4The men who went with him were Sopater son of Pyrrhus, from the city of Berea; Aristarchus and Secundus, from the city of Thessalonica; Gaius, from Derbe; Timothy; and Tychicus and Trophimus, two men from the country of Asia. 5These men went on ahead and waited for us at Troas. 6We sailed from Philippi after the Feast of Unleavened Bread. Five days later we met them in Troas, where we stayed for seven days.

Paul's Last Visit to Troas

7On the first day of the week, we all met together to break bread, and Paul spoke to the group. Because he was planning to leave the next day, he kept on talking until midnight. 8We were all together in a room upstairs, and there were many lamps in the room. 9A young man named Eutychus was sitting in the window. As Paul continued talking, Eutychus was falling into a deep sleep. Finally, he went sound asleep and fell to the ground from the third floor. When they picked him up, he was dead. 10Paul went down to Eutychus, knelt down, and put his arms around him. He said, "Don't worry. He is alive now." 11Then Paul went upstairs again, broke bread, and ate. He spoke to them a long time, until it was early morning, and then he left. 12They took the young man home alive and were greatly comforted.

The Trip from Troas to Miletus

13We went on ahead of Paul and sailed for the city of Assos, where he wanted to join us on the ship. Paul planned it this way because he wanted to go to Assos by land. 14When he met us there, we took him aboard and went to Mitylene. 15We sailed from Mitylene and the next day came to a place near Kios. The following day we sailed to Samos, and the next day we reached Miletus. 16Paul had already decided not to stop at Ephesus, because he did not want to stay too long in the country of Asia. He was hurrying to be in Jerusalem on the day of Pentecost, if that were possible.

19:35 *holy stone.* Probably a meteorite or stone that the people thought looked like Artemis.
20:7 *first day of the week.* Sunday, which for Jews began at sunset on our Saturday. But if in this part of Asia a different system of time was used, then the meeting was on our Sunday night.
20:7 *break bread.* Probably the Lord's Supper, the special meal that Jesus told his followers to eat to remember him (Luke 22:14–20).
20:12 House/Home: Romans 16:3–5
20:15 Luke: Acts 21:1–18

The Elders from Ephesus

17Now from Miletus Paul sent to Ephesus and
called for the elders of the church. 18When they
came to him, he said, "You know about my life
from the first day I came to Asia. You know the
way I lived all the time I was with you.⚭ 19The
evil people made plans against me, which troubled
me very much. But you know I always served the
Lord unselfishly, and I often cried. 20You know I
preached to you and did not hold back anything
that would help you. You know that I taught you
in public and in your homes. 21I warned both Jews
and Greeks to change their lives and turn to God
and believe in our Lord Jesus. 22But now I must
obey the Holy Spirit and go to Jerusalem. I don't
know what will happen to me there. 23I know only
that in every city the Holy Spirit tells me that troubles and even jail wait for me. 24I don't care about
my own life. The most important thing is that I
complete my mission, the work that the Lord Jesus
gave me—to tell people the Good News about
God's grace.⚭
25"And now, I know that none of you among
whom I was preaching the kingdom of God will
ever see me again. 26So today I tell you that if any of
you should be lost, I am not responsible, 27because
I have told you everything God wants you to know.
28Be careful for yourselves and for all the people the
Holy Spirit has given to you to care for. You must
be like shepherds to the church of God, which he
bought with the death of his own son. 29I know
that after I leave, some people will come like wild
wolves and try to destroy the flock. 30Also, some
from your own group will rise up and twist the
truth and will lead away followers after them. 31So
be careful! Always remember that for three years,
day and night, I never stopped warning each of you,
and I often cried over you.
32"Now I am putting you in the care of God and
the message about his grace. It is able to give you
strength, and it will give you the blessings God
has for all his holy people. 33When I was with
you, I never wanted anyone's money or fine
clothes. 34You know I always worked to take care
of my own needs and the needs of those who
were with me. 35I showed you in all things that
you should work as I did and help the weak. I
taught you to remember the words Jesus said: 'It
is more blessed to give than to receive.'"⚭
36When Paul had said this, he knelt down with
all of them and prayed. 37-38And they all cried
because Paul had said they would never see him
again. They put their arms around him and kissed
him. Then they went with him to the ship.

Paul Goes to Jerusalem

21 After we all said good-bye to them, we sailed
straight to the island of Cos. The next day
we reached Rhodes, and from there we went to
Patara. 2There we found a ship going to Phoenicia,
so we went aboard and sailed away. 3We sailed
near the island of Cyprus, seeing it to the north,
but we sailed on to Syria. We stopped at Tyre
because the ship needed to unload its cargo there.
4We found some followers in Tyre and stayed with
them for seven days. Through the Holy Spirit they
warned Paul not to go to Jerusalem. 5When we finished our visit, we left and continued our trip. All
the followers, even the women and children, came
outside the city with us. After we all knelt on the
beach and prayed, 6we said good-bye and got on
the ship, and the followers went back home.
7We continued our trip from Tyre and arrived
at Ptolemais, where we greeted the believers and
stayed with them for a day. 8The next day we left
Ptolemais and went to the city of Caesarea. There
we went into the home of Philip the preacher, one
of the seven helpers, and stayed with him. 9He
had four unmarried daughters who had the gift of
prophesying. 10After we had been there for some
time, a prophet named Agabus arrived from Judea.
11He came to us and borrowed Paul's belt and
used it to tie his own hands and feet. He said,
"The Holy Spirit says, 'This is how evil people in
Jerusalem will tie up the man who wears this belt.
Then they will give him to the older leaders.'"⚭
12When we all heard this, we and the people
there begged Paul not to go to Jerusalem. 13But he
said, "Why are you crying and making me so sad?
I am not only ready to be tied up in Jerusalem, I
am ready to die for the Lord Jesus!"

20:17–21 Paul gathered the elders of Ephesus together for a farewell address. He recounted his ministry among them and emphasized the common message he preached to both Jews and non-Jews—the message of repentance and faith in the Lord Jesus. Repentance is a change of mind, heart, and life that must take place if one is to receive forgiveness of sins. In essence, it is an acknowledgment of one's sin and a turning from it by the power of God.

⚭**20:18 Luke:** Luke 27:1–28:16

⚭**20:24 Holy Spirit:** Romans 8:2–11

20:28 *of God.* Some Greek copies say, "of the Lord."

⚭**20:35 Service:** Romans 1:1

21:7–11 The gift of prophecy continued to be exercised during the time of the New Testament church. On this occasion, Agabus used prophetic symbolism to communicate God's message to Paul. The tying of his hands and feet with Paul's belt symbolized Paul's arrest in Jerusalem and his being put into the hands of "those who are not Jews," i.e., the Romans.

21:8 *helpers.* The seven men chosen for a special work described in Acts 6:1–6. Sometimes they are called "deacons."

⚭**21:11 Prophetic Symbolism:** Revelation 22:10–11

[14]We could not persuade him to stay away from Jerusalem. So we stopped begging him and said, "We pray that what the Lord wants will be done."

[15]After this, we got ready and started on our way to Jerusalem. [16]Some of the followers from Caesarea went with us and took us to the home of Mnason, where we would stay. He was from Cyprus and was one of the first followers.

Paul Visits James

[17]In Jerusalem the believers were glad to see us. [18]The next day Paul went with us to visit James, and all the elders were there.∞ [19]Paul greeted them and told them everything God had done among the other nations through him. [20]When they heard this, they praised God. Then they said to Paul, "Brother, you can see that many thousands of our people have become believers. And they think it is very important to obey the law of Moses. [21]They have heard about your teaching, that you tell our people who live among the nations to leave the law of Moses. They have heard that you tell them not to circumcise their children and not to obey customs. [22]What should we do? They will learn that you have come. [23]So we will tell you what to do: Four of our men have made a promise to God. [24]Take these men with you and share in their cleansing ceremony. Pay their expenses so they can shave their heads. Then it will prove to everyone that what they have heard about you is not true and that you follow the law of Moses in your own life. [25]We have already sent a letter to the non-Jewish believers. The letter said: 'Do not eat food that has been offered to idols, or blood, or animals that have been strangled. Do not take part in sexual sin.'"

[26]The next day Paul took the four men and shared in the cleansing ceremony with them. Then he went to the Temple and announced the time when the days of the cleansing ceremony would be finished. On the last day an offering would be given for each of the men.

[27]When the seven days were almost over, some of his people from Asia saw Paul at the Temple. They caused all the people to be upset and grabbed Paul. [28]They shouted, "People of Israel, help us! This is the man who goes everywhere teaching against the law of Moses, against our people, and against this Temple. Now he has brought some Greeks into the Temple and has made this holy place unclean!" [29](They said this because they had seen Trophimus, a man from Ephesus, with Paul in Jerusalem. They thought that Paul had brought him into the Temple.)

[30]All the people in Jerusalem became upset. Together they ran, took Paul, and dragged him out of the Temple. The Temple doors were closed immediately. [31]While they were trying to kill Paul, the commander of the Roman army in Jerusalem learned that there was trouble in the whole city. [32]Immediately he took some officers and soldiers and ran to the place where the crowd was gathered. When the people saw them, they stopped beating Paul. [33]The commander went to Paul and arrested him. He told his soldiers to tie Paul with two chains. Then he asked who he was and what he had done wrong. [34]Some in the crowd were yelling one thing, and some were yelling another. Because of all this confusion and shouting, the commander could not learn what had happened. So he ordered the soldiers to take Paul to the army building. [35]When Paul came to the steps, the soldiers had to carry him because the people were ready to hurt him. [36]The whole mob was following them, shouting, "Kill him!"

[37]As the soldiers were about to take Paul into the army building, he spoke to the commander, "May I say something to you?"

The commander said, "Do you speak Greek? [38]I thought you were the Egyptian who started some trouble against the government not long ago and led four thousand killers out to the desert."

[39]Paul said, "No, I am a Jew from Tarsus in the country of Cilicia. I am a citizen of that important city. Please, let me speak to the people."

[40]The commander gave permission, so Paul stood on the steps and waved his hand to quiet the people. When there was silence, he spoke to them in the Hebrew language.

Paul Speaks to the People

22 Paul said, "Friends, fellow Jews, listen to my defense to you." [2]When they heard him speaking the Hebrew language, they became very quiet. Paul said, [3]"I am a Jew, born in Tarsus in the country of Cilicia, but I grew up in this city. I was a student of Gamaliel, who carefully taught me everything about the law of our ancestors. I was very serious about serving God, just as are all of

---

∞**21:18 Luke:** Acts 27:1–28:16

21:24 *shave their heads.* Jews did this to show that their promise was finished.

21:24 *cleansing ceremony.* The special things Jews did to end the Nazirite promise.

21:38 Records show that many Jewish people tried to start revolutions against the Romans in the first century (see also 5:36–37). Because of the mob surrounding Paul, he is mistaken for one of these leaders. This shows the carefully balanced relationship the Jews had with Rome during this time, and how easily that balance could be upset.

22:2 *Hebrew language.* Hebrew, or Aramaic, the languages of many people in this region in the first century.

22:3 *Gamaliel.* A very important teacher of the Pharisees, a Jewish religious group (Acts 5:34).

you here today. 4I persecuted the people who followed the Way of Jesus, and some of them were even killed. I arrested men and women and put them in jail. 5The high priest and the whole council of older leaders can tell you this is true. They gave me letters to the brothers in Damascus. So I was going there to arrest these people and bring them back to Jerusalem to be punished.

6"About noon when I came near Damascus, a bright light from heaven suddenly flashed all around me. 7I fell to the ground and heard a voice saying, 'Saul, Saul, why are you persecuting me?' 8I asked, 'Who are you, Lord?' The voice said, 'I am Jesus from Nazareth whom you are persecuting.' 9Those who were with me did not hear the voice, but they saw the light. 10I said, 'What shall I do, Lord?' The Lord answered, 'Get up and go to Damascus. There you will be told about all the things I have planned for you to do.' 11I could not see, because the bright light had made me blind. So my companions led me into Damascus.

12"There a man named Ananias came to me. He was a religious man; he obeyed the law of Moses, and all the Jews who lived there respected him. 13He stood by me and said, 'Brother Saul, see again!' Immediately I was able to see him. 14He said, 'The God of our ancestors chose you long ago to know his plan, to see the Righteous One, and to hear words from him.⚭ 15You will be his witness to all people, telling them about what you have seen and heard. 16Now, why wait any longer? Get up, be baptized, and wash your sins away, trusting in him to save you.'⚭

17"Later, when I returned to Jerusalem, I was praying in the Temple, and I saw a vision. 18I saw the Lord saying to me, 'Hurry! Leave Jerusalem now! The people here will not accept the truth about me.' 19But I said, 'Lord, they know that in every synagogue I put the believers in jail and beat them. 20They also know I was there when Stephen, your witness, was killed. I stood there agreeing and holding the coats of those who were killing him!'⚭ 21But the Lord said to me, 'Leave now. I will send you far away to the other nations.'"⚭

22The crowd listened to Paul until he said this. Then they began shouting, "Kill him! Get him out of the world! He should not be allowed to live!" 23They shouted, threw off their coats, and threw dust into the air.

24Then the commander ordered the soldiers to take Paul into the army building and beat him. He wanted to make Paul tell why the people were shouting against him like this. 25But as the soldiers were tying him up, preparing to beat him, Paul said to an officer nearby, "Do you have the right to beat a Roman citizen who has not been proven guilty?"

26When the officer heard this, he went to the commander and reported it. The officer said, "Do you know what you are doing? This man is a Roman citizen."

27The commander came to Paul and said, "Tell me, are you really a Roman citizen?"

He answered, "Yes."

28The commander said, "I paid a lot of money to become a Roman citizen."

But Paul said, "I was born a citizen."

29The men who were preparing to question Paul moved away from him immediately. The commander was frightened because he had already tied Paul, and Paul was a Roman citizen.⚭

Paul Speaks to Leaders

30The next day the commander decided to learn why the Jews were accusing Paul. So he ordered the leading priests and the council to meet. The commander took Paul's chains off. Then he brought Paul out and stood him before their meeting.

23 Paul looked at the council and said, "Brothers, I have lived my life without guilt feelings before God up to this day." 2Ananias, the high priest, heard this and told the men who were standing near Paul to hit him on the mouth. 3Paul said to Ananias, "God will hit you, too! You are like a wall that has been painted white. You sit there and judge me, using the law of Moses, but you are telling them to hit me, and that is against the law."

4The men standing near Paul said to him, "You cannot insult God's high priest like that!"

⚭**22:14 Road/Way:** Acts 24:22

⚭**22:16 Body/Resurrection:** See article on page 1213.

22:17–21 The story of Paul's encounter with Jesus on the Damascus Road is told three times in Acts (9:1–19; 22:1–21; 26:12–23). In this one, Paul adds that he had a vision in the Temple. This is significant since the Temple was regarded as the dwelling place of God; not only was it a holy place, then, but it was also a place where God might reveal his ways to people. According to Paul, then, God told him in the Temple to take the Good News to those who were not Jews. Paul's audience reacts with anger, because they know that Paul is saying what they believe God could never say: that the place to meet God would no longer be the Temple.

22:20 Paul now tells the Jerusalem crowd the story of his conversion. God had dealt with him quite dramatically. He took him from being at the center of the persecution of the church (he even held the coats of those who stoned Stephen [Acts 7:58]) and made him a great missionary to the non-Jewish people.

⚭**22:20 Stephen:** See article on page 1072.

⚭**22:21 Gentiles (Non-Jews):** Romans 1:14–16

22:23 *threw off their coats.* This showed that the people were very angry with Paul.

22:23 *threw dust into the air.* This showed even greater anger.

22:25 *Roman citizen.* Roman law said that Roman citizens must not be beaten before they had a trial.

⚭**22:29 Rome:** Acts 23:11

23:2 *Ananias.* This is not the same man named Ananias in Acts 22:12.

STRESS

JAMES 1:2–8

What makes some of us experience the stress of certain kinds of people and situations? What are the unresolved conflicts that make us incapable of handling the pressures of life?

The word *stress* has become a catchall synonym for the pace, pressure, and problems of life. We talk about being under stress, facing stressful situations, and dealing with stress-producing people. We have a general understanding of what causes stress, but too little knowledge of how to live with it. The word for stress in Latin its *strictus,* "to be drawn tight." In Old French it is *estresse*, meaning narrowness or tightness. In English a clear definition of stress is complicated by its many different uses. However, in the worlds of physics and mechanics it is used both for the forces which cause external pressure and for the internal strength to balance them.

It is interesting to note that stress capacity on metals is measured by what is called yield point or failure point. Yield point is the point at which the stress on the material actually makes it stronger; the failure point is the point at which the strain exceeds the load-bearing capacity of the material. The same is true of human beings. External stress can strengthen our internal coping system, but extreme stress will bring us to the failure or breaking point.

Medical science also has its special definition of stress. In response to external stress, the nervous system provides the needed energy to meet the responsibilities, pressures, crises, and alarms of life. Unless controlled, it also sets us up for a breakdown of critical bodily functions.

When we are hit with either the dangers or difficulties of life, our brain cortex, the center of many of our conscious functions, goes into "red alert." Body systems kick in to provide the hormonal level required to meet the external demands of life. Unfortunately, many of us live in a constant state of "red alert" because of the pressures or problems we face. And added to the external causes that prompt a "red alert" are the memory and imagination resident within the brain. This means that we keep our bodies in a state of emergency long after the crisis has passed.

The physical reaction triggered by these successions of stress alerts puts us into a dangerous continuing state of physiologic overdrive. The blood hormone levels remain abnormal, blood pressure stays high; fat metabolism (cholesterol production) and clotting elements that have been triggered to meet the high state of stress persist. Consequently, we become susceptible to a variety of health problems, including high blood pressure, stroke, and heart attacks.

To solve the problems of stress, the brain must become a computer that consciously sorts out the stresses of life and controls the degree of response from the body. It is imperative that we discover a way to control our reactions to the threats and trials of life so that we do not keep our bodies in a constant state of tension. Having God's Word in our hearts helps us.

Here is the good news—you can manage stress! The Lord has endowed you and me with a stress management mechanism that gives us an immense capacity for coping with the pressures and problems of life. We do not have to be the helpless victims of stress-producing situations, people, or circumstances. We have been given an inner ability to handle the external pressures of life.

In the first chapter of James, we read a rather mind-boggling statement about how to react to "troubles"—and that could well be translated "stresses:" "When you have many kinds of troubles, you should be full of joy" (James 1:2). From this amazing word, we discover that the first secret of stress management is to think about stress as a reason to rejoice!

Joy is the result of grace. When Christ's mind, which becomes ours upon conversion (1 Corinthians 2:16), controls us, we know that we are loved regardless of what happens to us or around us. The stresses of life are the negatives that release the positives. They can be either the occasion of deeper trust, with the release of fresh grace (2 Corinthians 12:9–10), or the source of frustration. When we consciously surrender our stresses to Christ, giving them all to him (1 Peter 5:7), he uses them for our growth and his glory. We know that he will not leave or forsake us. Joy springs forth.

We can turn stress into a stepping stone! It all depends on how we think about it. We must invite Christ to dwell in our minds.∞

∞**Stress:** For additional scriptures on this topic go to Psalm 9:9–10.

DOUBT

JAMES 1:5–8

How can I honestly say I am a Christian or act in faith when I have so many doubts?

Doubt in the Bible is depicted as fatal when it signifies disbelief, and as an understandable reaction to the difficulty and pain of life when it reflects questioning. It is found in the lives of many people of faith in the Bible and in church history, but it should never be the defining characteristic of people of faith or keep them from action.

The Bible recognizes different kinds and consequences of doubt. The two most basic categories of doubt are mentioned in Hebrews 11:6: doubts about God's existence and doubts about his provision and protection. Scripture only passingly acknowledges the fundamental modern doubt about whether God exists. It is taken as so obvious that the Bible only rarely argues the question (Romans 1:20). Even the psalmist's condemnation of the fool who says there is no God (Psalms 14:1; 53:1) refers more to people who think God does not punish evil than to atheists.

The more common doubt in the Bible, especially in the Old Testament, is that God actually keeps all his promises (Job; Psalm 89:38–47). Given the suffering, injustice, and seeming triumph of evil in the world, it often seems God is either not in control or does not really care about his own. This feeling is all the more pointed for those who have been faithful to God and feel that faithfulness has not been rewarded (Job; Psalms 10; 13; 22; 43; 60; 74; 88; 102).

In the New Testament we find doubt about whether Jesus is, in fact, the Messiah, and about claims that he is uniquely the Son of God (Matthew 16:13–18; 28:17; Mark 8:27–30; Luke 9:18–21). John the Baptist proclaimed the beginning of Jesus' ministry when baptizing him in the Jordan (Matthew 3; Mark 1; Luke 3), but even John the Baptist later sent messengers to Jesus to ask whether he is, in fact, the Messiah (Luke 7:17–22). Even when seeing Christ after the Resurrection, some of the disciples closest to Jesus doubted what they were seeing (Luke 24:36–39).

It is important to understand that doubt is not the same as disbelief. Disbelief is turning away from God, whereas doubt can be a form of questioning. Disbelief is incompatible with a life of faith, but doubt is not, or at least does not have to be. What is crucial is not so much the existence of doubt as its consequence.

The kind of doubt which the Bible condemns most clearly and often is the doubt that results in paralysis, passivity, and inaction. Such doubt is an obstacle to God's working in the world (Matthew 13:58; 21:21). The Bible is less concerned with a psychological state of belief (even the demons are said to believe in Christ—James 2:19) than with a life marked by actions which testify to the presence of faith (John 14:15; James 2:14).

There are many examples throughout the Bible of people of faith who have hard questions for God, even doubts about his faithfulness, who nevertheless continue to act in faith and who are rewarded for doing so. One such person was the man who brought his son to Jesus for healing (Mark 9:14–29). The man asked Jesus to help, "If you can do anything for him." Jesus mildly rebukes him for his doubting "if," saying, "All things are possible for the one who believes." The man gives the very human and honest response, "I do believe! Help me to believe more!" Significantly, Jesus does not reject the man for his doubts. Rather, he rewards the man's action even in the midst of his struggle, and heals his son.

The Psalms are filled with doubts that God is listening, or being fair, or punishing evil, or protecting and rewarding the righteous. The apostle Peter combines a moment of great faith when he walks on the water to meet Jesus with a moment of doubt when he takes his eyes off Jesus and sinks (Matthew 14:22–33). Another disciple, Thomas, proclaims his refusal to believe in the resurrection until he has physical proof (John 20:24–29). In each case, the doubts are expressed by people of faith who, despite their moments of doubt, continue to live out that faith to the best of their ability.

In the Book of James, doubters are described as "thinking two different things at the same time, and they cannot decide about anything they do" (James 1:5–8) This sobering description should warn against taking doubt too lightly or trying to explain it away. At the same time, it is a description not of every believer who has questions and doubts, but of a person whose life is defined by those doubts. That is, doubters in this sense are those whose lives are characterized by lack of commitment, wishy-washiness, and paralysis.

Doubt is never depicted as desirable or pleasing to God in the Bible. One the other hand, it is not seen as incompatible with faith. Believers are told to be merciful to doubters (Jude 1:22), not to ostracize them.

Doubt: For additional scriptures on this topic go to Psalm 10.

5Paul said, "Brothers, I did not know this man was the high priest. It is written in the Scriptures, 'You must not curse a leader of your people.'"

6Some of the men in the meeting were Sadducees, and others were Pharisees. Knowing this, Paul shouted to them, "My brothers, I am a Pharisee, and my father was a Pharisee. I am on trial here because I believe that people will rise from the dead."

7When Paul said this, there was an argument between the Pharisees and the Sadducees, and the group was divided. 8(The Sadducees do not believe in angels or spirits or that people will rise from the dead. But the Pharisees believe in them all.) 9So there was a great uproar. Some of the teachers of the law, who were Pharisees, stood up and argued, "We find nothing wrong with this man. Maybe an angel or a spirit did speak to him."∞

10The argument was beginning to turn into such a fight that the commander was afraid some evil people would tear Paul to pieces. So he told the soldiers to go down and take Paul away and put him in the army building.

11The next night the Lord came and stood by Paul. He said, "Be brave! You have told people in Jerusalem about me. You must do the same in Rome."∞

12In the morning some evil people made a plan to kill Paul, and they took an oath not to eat or drink anything until they had killed him. 13There were more than forty men who made this plan. 14They went to the leading priests and the older leaders and said, "We have taken an oath not to eat or drink until we have killed Paul. 15So this is what we want you to do: Send a message to the commander to bring Paul out to you as though you want to ask him more questions. We will be waiting to kill him while he is on the way here."

16But Paul's nephew heard about this plan and went to the army building and told Paul. 17Then Paul called one of the officers and said, "Take this young man to the commander. He has a message for him."

18So the officer brought Paul's nephew to the commander and said, "The prisoner, Paul, asked me to bring this young man to you. He wants to tell you something."

19The commander took the young man's hand and led him to a place where they could be alone. He asked, "What do you want to tell me?"

20The young man said, "The Jews have decided to ask you to bring Paul down to their council meeting tomorrow. They want you to think they are going to ask him more questions. 21But don't believe them! More than forty men are hiding and waiting to kill Paul. They have all taken an oath not to eat or drink until they have killed him. Now they are waiting for you to agree."

22The commander sent the young man away, ordering him, "Don't tell anyone that you have told me about their plan."

Paul Is Sent to Caesarea

23Then the commander called two officers and said, "I need some men to go to Caesarea. Get two hundred soldiers, seventy horsemen, and two hundred men with spears ready to leave at nine o'clock tonight. 24Get some horses for Paul to ride so he can be taken to Governor Felix safely." 25And he wrote a letter that said:

> 26From Claudius Lysias.
> To the Most Excellent Governor Felix:
> Greetings.
>
> 27Some of the Jews had taken this man and planned to kill him. But I learned that he is a Roman citizen, so I went with my soldiers and saved him. 28I wanted to know why they were accusing him, so I brought him before their council meeting. 29I learned that these people said Paul did some things that were wrong by their own laws, but no charge was worthy of jail or death. 30When I was told that some of them were planning to kill Paul, I sent him to you at once. I also told them to tell you what they have against him.

31So the soldiers did what they were told and took Paul and brought him to the city of Antipatris that night. 32The next day the horsemen went with Paul to Caesarea, but the other soldiers went back to the army building in Jerusalem. 33When the horsemen came to Caesarea and gave the letter to the governor, they turned Paul over to him. 34The governor read the letter and asked Paul, "What area are you from?" When he learned that Paul was from Cilicia, 35he said, "I will hear your case when those who are against you come here, too." Then the governor gave orders for Paul to be kept under guard in Herod's palace.

Paul Is Accused

24 Five days later Ananias, the high priest, went to the city of Caesarea with some of

23:5 *'You . . . people.'* Quotation from Exodus 22:28.

∞**23:9 Scribes (Teachers of the Law):** See article on page 722.

23:10 The high priest's unjust action shows Paul that he has no hope of being treated fairly by the Jewish council, and Paul already knows that his Christian faith is unacceptable to both the Pharisees and the Sadducees. So he cleverly shifts the focus of the hearing, claiming that the real issue is his belief that people will rise from the dead. This sets the Pharisees (who believe in resurrection from the dead) and the Sadducees (who do not) fighting among themselves over their different religious beliefs. The argument gets so heated that the soldiers take Paul away to protect him.

∞**23:11 Rome:** Acts 25:82–6:32

the older leaders and a lawyer named Tertullus. They had come to make charges against Paul before the governor. [2]Paul was called into the meeting, and Tertullus began to accuse him, saying, "Most Excellent Felix! Our people enjoy much peace because of you, and many wrong things in our country are being made right through your wise help. [3]We accept these things always and in every place, and we are thankful for them. [4]But not wanting to take any more of your time, I beg you to be kind and listen to our few words. [5]We have found this man to be a troublemaker, stirring up his people everywhere in the world. He is a leader of the Nazarene group. [6]Also, he was trying to make the Temple unclean, but we stopped him.* [8]By asking him questions yourself, you can decide if all these things are true." [9]The others agreed and said that all of this was true.

[10]When the governor made a sign for Paul to speak, Paul said, "Governor Felix, I know you have been a judge over this nation for a long time. So I am happy to defend myself before you. [11]You can learn for yourself that I went to worship in Jerusalem only twelve days ago. [12]Those who are accusing me did not find me arguing with anyone in the Temple or stirring up the people in the synagogues or in the city. [13]They cannot prove the things they are saying against me now. [14]But I will tell you this: I worship the God of our ancestors as a follower of the Way of Jesus. The others say that the Way of Jesus is not the right way. But I believe everything that is taught in the law of Moses and that is written in the books of the Prophets. [15]I have the same hope in God that they have—the hope that all people, good and bad, will surely be raised from the dead. [16]This is why I always try to do what I believe is right before God and people.

[17]"After being away from Jerusalem for several years, I went back to bring money to my people and to offer sacrifices. [18]I was doing this when they found me in the Temple. I had finished the cleansing ceremony and had not made any trouble; no people were gathering around me. [19]But there were some people from the country of Asia who should be here, standing before you. If I have really done anything wrong, they are the ones who should accuse me. [20]Or ask these people here if they found any wrong in me when I stood before the council in Jerusalem. [21]But I did shout one thing when I stood before them: 'You are judging me today because I believe that people will rise from the dead!'"

[22]Felix already understood much about the Way of Jesus. He stopped the trial and said, "When commander Lysias comes here, I will decide your case." [23]Felix told the officer to keep Paul guarded but to give him some freedom and to let his friends bring what he needed.

Paul Speaks to Felix and His Wife

[24]After some days Felix came with his wife, Drusilla, who was Jewish, and asked for Paul to be brought to him. He listened to Paul talk about believing in Christ Jesus. [25]But Felix became afraid when Paul spoke about living right, self-control, and the time when God will judge the world. He said, "Go away now. When I have more time, I will call for you." [26]At the same time Felix hoped that Paul would give him some money, so he often sent for Paul and talked with him.

[27]But after two years, Felix was replaced by Porcius Festus as governor. But Felix had left Paul in prison to please the Jews.

Paul Asks to See Caesar

25 Three days after Festus became governor, he went from Caesarea to Jerusalem. [2]There the leading priests and the important leaders made charges against Paul before Festus. [3]They asked Festus to do them a favor. They wanted him to send Paul back to Jerusalem, because they had a plan to kill him on the way. [4]But Festus answered that Paul would be kept in Caesarea and that he himself was returning there soon. [5]He said, "Some of your leaders should go with me. They can accuse the man there in Caesarea, if he has really done something wrong."

[6]Festus stayed in Jerusalem another eight or ten days and then went back to Caesarea. The next day he told the soldiers to bring Paul before him. Festus was seated on the judge's seat [7]when Paul came into the room. The people who had come from

***24:6** *Verse 6.* Some Greek copies add 6b–8a: "And we wanted to judge him by our own law. [7]But the officer Lysias came and used much force to take him from us. [8]And Lysias commanded those who wanted to accuse Paul to come to you."

24:14 In his defense before the Roman governor, Felix, Paul identified his personal faith as "the Way of Jesus." Christians were known as followers of "the Way," a phrase connected with Jesus' words in John 14:6, "I am the way." The Good News says there is only one road or way to God, and that is by faith in Jesus Christ. Paul argues here that "the Way" is consistent with what is written in the Law and the Prophets.

24:22 Road/Way: See article on page 470.

24:25 Self-Control: 1 Corinthians 4:10

24:27 This is only one of many points at which Luke, as author of Acts, shows that the Roman government was not on the side of the Christians. Sometimes Roman officials want to do favors for the Jews so they will keep Jewish support; at other times, according to Acts, Roman officials are open to being bribed. In any case, it is evident that Christians cannot depend on Rome or on any other human authority and must give their allegiance only to God.

Jerusalem stood around him, making serious charges against him, which they could not prove. [8]This is what Paul said to defend himself: "I have done nothing wrong against the law, against the Temple, or against Caesar."

[9]But Festus wanted to please the people. So he asked Paul, "Do you want to go to Jerusalem for me to judge you there on these charges?"

[10]Paul said, "I am standing at Caesar's judgment seat now, where I should be judged. I have done nothing wrong to them; you know this is true. [11]If I have done something wrong and the law says I must die, I do not ask to be saved from death. But if these charges are not true, then no one can give me to them. I want Caesar to hear my case!"

[12]Festus talked about this with his advisers. Then he said, "You have asked to see Caesar, so you will go to Caesar!"

Paul Before King Agrippa

[13]A few days later King Agrippa and Bernice came to Caesarea to visit Festus. [14]They stayed there for some time, and Festus told the king about Paul's case. Festus said, "There is a man that Felix left in prison. [15]When I went to Jerusalem, the leading priests and the older leaders there made charges against him, asking me to sentence him to death. [16]But I answered, 'When a man is accused of a crime, Romans do not hand him over until he has been allowed to face his accusers and defend himself against their charges.'∞ [17]So when these people came here to Caesarea for the trial, I did not waste time. The next day I sat on the judge's seat and commanded that the man be brought in. [18]They stood up and accused him, but not of any serious crime as I thought they would. [19]The things they said were about their own religion and about a man named Jesus who died. But Paul said that he is still alive. [20]Not knowing how to find out about these questions, I asked Paul, 'Do you want to go to Jerusalem and be judged there?' [21]But he asked to be kept in Caesarea. He wants a decision from the emperor. So I ordered that he be held until I could send him to Caesar."

[22]Agrippa said to Festus, "I would also like to hear this man myself."

Festus said, "Tomorrow you will hear him."

[23]The next day Agrippa and Bernice appeared with great show, acting like very important people. They went into the judgment room with the army leaders and the important men of Caesarea. Then Festus ordered the soldiers to bring Paul in. [24]Festus said, "King Agrippa and all who are gathered here with us, you see this man. All the people, here and in Jerusalem, have complained to me about him, shouting that he should not live any longer. [25]When I judged him, I found no reason to order his death. But since he asked to be judged by Caesar, I decided to send him. [26]But I have nothing definite to write the emperor about him. So I have brought him before all of you—especially you, King Agrippa. I hope you can question him and give me something to write. [27]I think it is foolish to send a prisoner to Caesar without telling what charges are against him."

Paul Defends Himself

26 Agrippa said to Paul, "You may now speak to defend yourself."

Then Paul raised his hand and began to speak. [2]He said, "King Agrippa, I am very happy to stand before you and will answer all the charges the evil people make against me. [3]You know so much about all the customs and the things they argue about, so please listen to me patiently.

[4]"All my people know about my whole life, how I lived from the beginning in my own country and later in Jerusalem. [5]They have known me for a long time. If they want to, they can tell you that I was a good Pharisee. And the Pharisees obey the laws of my tradition more carefully than any other group. [6]Now I am on trial because I hope for the promise that God made to our ancestors. [7]This is the promise that the twelve tribes of our people hope to receive as they serve God day and night. My king, they have accused me because I hope for this same promise! [8]Why do any of you people think it is impossible for God to raise people from the dead?

[9]"I, too, thought I ought to do many things against Jesus from Nazareth. [10]And that is what I did in Jerusalem. The leading priests gave me the power to put many of God's people in jail, and when they were being killed, I agreed it was a good thing. [11]In every synagogue, I often punished them and tried to make them speak against Jesus. I was so angry against them I even went to other cities to find them and punish them.∞

[12]"One time the leading priests gave me permission and the power to go to Damascus. [13]On the way there, at noon, I saw a light from heaven. It was brighter than the sun and flashed all around me and those who were traveling with me. [14]We

∞**25:16 Crime:** Romans 13:1–5

25:21 *emperor.* The ruler of the Roman Empire, which was almost all the known world.

∞**26:11 Blasphemy:** Revelation 13:1

all fell to the ground. Then I heard a voice speaking to me in the Jewish language, saying, 'Saul, Saul, why are you persecuting me? You are only hurting yourself by fighting me.' 15I said, 'Who are you, Lord?' The Lord said, 'I am Jesus, the one you are persecuting. 16Stand up! I have chosen you to be my servant and my witness—you will tell people the things that you have seen and the things that I will show you. This is why I have come to you today. 17I will keep you safe from your own people and also from the others. I am sending you to them 18to open their eyes so that they may turn away from darkness to the light, away from the power of Satan and to God. Then their sins can be forgiven, and they can have a place with those people who have been made holy by believing in me.'

19"King Agrippa, after I had this vision from heaven, I obeyed it. 20I began telling people that they should change their hearts and lives and turn to God and do things to show they really had changed. I told this first to those in Damascus, then in Jerusalem, and in every part of Judea, and also to the other people. 21This is why the Jews took me and were trying to kill me in the Temple. 22But God has helped me, and so I stand here today, telling all people, small and great, what I have seen. But I am saying only what Moses and the prophets said would happen— 23that the Christ would die, and as the first to rise from the dead, he would bring light to all people."

Paul Tries to Persuade Agrippa

24While Paul was saying these things to defend himself, Festus said loudly, "Paul, you are out of your mind! Too much study has driven you crazy!"

25Paul said, "Most excellent Festus, I am not crazy. My words are true and sensible. 26King Agrippa knows about these things, and I can speak freely to him. I know he has heard about all of these things, because they did not happen off in a corner. 27King Agrippa, do you believe what the prophets wrote? I know you believe."

28King Agrippa said to Paul, "Do you think you can persuade me to become a Christian in such a short time?"

29Paul said, "Whether it is a short or a long time, I pray to God that not only you but every person listening to me today would be saved and be like me—except for these chains I have."

A Roman merchant ship built to carry large grain cargoes

30Then King Agrippa, Governor Festus, Bernice, and all the people sitting with them stood up 31and left the room. Talking to each other, they said, "There is no reason why this man should die or be put in jail." 32And Agrippa said to Festus, "We could let this man go free, but he has asked Caesar to hear his case."

Paul Sails for Rome

27 It was decided that we would sail for Italy. An officer named Julius, who served in the emperor's army, guarded Paul and some other prisoners. 2We got on a ship that was from the city of Adramyttium and was about to sail to different ports in the country of Asia. Aristarchus, a man from the city of Thessalonica in Macedonia, went with us. 3The next day we came to Sidon. Julius was very good to Paul and gave him freedom to go visit his friends, who took care of his needs. 4We left Sidon and sailed close to the island of Cyprus, because the wind was blowing against us. 5We went across the sea by Cilicia and Pamphylia and landed at the city of Myra, in Lycia. 6There the officer found a ship from Alexandria that was going to Italy, so he put us on it.

7We sailed slowly for many days. We had a hard time reaching Cnidus because the wind was

26:14 *Hebrew language.* Hebrew, or Aramaic, the languages of many people in the region in the first century.

26:15–20 At the center of Paul's defense of himself and his ministry before King Agrippa was his retelling of his vision of the Lord at his conversion on the Damascus Road. Visions are to be obeyed says Paul, so he "began telling people that they should change their hearts and lives and turn to God and do things to show they had really changed" (Acts 26:19–20). With this statement was the call to repent and to turn to God, and nothing is more solid evidence of true change than the good works of a changed person. Visions are provided to elected people in the Christian community, such as Paul, because the Lord wants to reveal what he wants known about his desires.

26:16 Servant of the Lord: Romans 14:4

26:32 Rome: Acts 27:24

27:1 *emperor.* The ruler of the Roman Empire, which was almost all the known world.

blowing against us, and we could not go any farther. So we sailed by the south side of the island of Crete near Salmone. [8]Sailing past it was hard. Then we came to a place called Fair Havens, near the city of Lasea.

[9]We had lost much time, and it was now dangerous to sail, because it was already after the Day of Cleansing. So Paul warned them, [10]"Men, I can see there will be a lot of trouble on this trip. The ship, the cargo, and even our lives may be lost." [11]But the captain and the owner of the ship did not agree with Paul, and the officer believed what the captain and owner of the ship said. [12]Since that harbor was not a good place for the ship to stay for the winter, most of the men decided that the ship should leave. They hoped we could go to Phoenix and stay there for the winter. Phoenix, a city on the island of Crete, had a harbor which faced southwest and northwest.

The Storm

[13]When a good wind began to blow from the south, the men on the ship thought, "This is the wind we wanted, and now we have it." So they pulled up the anchor, and we sailed very close to the island of Crete. [14]But then a very strong wind named the "northeaster" came from the island. [15]The ship was caught in it and could not sail against it. So we stopped trying and let the wind carry us. [16]When we went below a small island named Cauda, we were barely able to bring in the lifeboat. [17]After the men took the lifeboat in, they tied ropes around the ship to hold it together. The men were afraid that the ship would hit the sandbanks of Syrtis, so they lowered the sail and let the wind carry the ship. [18]The next day the storm was blowing us so hard that the men threw out some of the cargo. [19]A day later with their own hands they threw out the ship's equipment. [20]When we could not see the sun or the stars for many days, and the storm was very bad, we lost all hope of being saved.

[21]After the men had gone without food for a long time, Paul stood up before them and said, "Men, you should have listened to me. You should not have sailed from Crete. Then you would not have all this trouble and loss. [22]But now I tell you to cheer up because none of you will die. Only the ship will be lost. [23]Last night an angel came to me from the God I belong to and worship. [24]The angel said, 'Paul, do not be afraid. You must stand before Caesar. And God has promised you that he will save the lives of everyone sailing with you.' [25]So men, have courage. I trust in God that everything will happen as his angel told me. [26]But we will crash on an island."

[27]On the fourteenth night we were still being carried around in the Adriatic Sea. About midnight the sailors thought we were close to land, [28]so they lowered a rope with a weight on the end of it into the water. They found that the water was one hundred twenty feet deep. They went a little farther and lowered the rope again. It was ninety feet deep. [29]The sailors were afraid that we would hit the rocks, so they threw four anchors into the water and prayed for daylight to come. [30]Some of the sailors wanted to leave the ship, and they lowered the lifeboat, pretending they were throwing more anchors from the front of the ship. [31]But Paul told the officer and the other soldiers, "If these men do not stay in the ship, your lives cannot be saved." [32]So the soldiers cut the ropes and let the lifeboat fall into the water.

[33]Just before dawn Paul began persuading all the people to eat something. He said, "For the past fourteen days you have been waiting and watching and not eating. [34]Now I beg you to eat something. You need it to stay alive. None of you will lose even one hair off your heads." [35]After he said this, Paul took some bread and thanked God for it before all of them. He broke off a piece and began eating. [36]They all felt better and started eating, too. [37]There were two hundred seventy-six people on the ship. [38]When they had eaten all they wanted, they began making the ship lighter by throwing the grain into the sea.

The Ship Is Destroyed

[39]When daylight came, the sailors saw land. They did not know what land it was, but they saw a bay with a beach and wanted to sail the ship to the beach if they could. [40]So they cut the ropes to the anchors and left the anchors in the sea. At the same time, they untied the ropes that were holding the rudders. Then they raised the front sail into the wind and sailed toward the beach. [41]But the ship hit a sandbank. The front of the ship stuck there and could not move, but the back of the ship began to break up from the big waves.

[42]The soldiers decided to kill the prisoners so none of them could swim away and escape. [43]But Julius, the officer, wanted to let Paul live and did not allow the soldiers to kill the prisoners. Instead he ordered everyone who could swim to jump into the water first and swim to land. [44]The rest were to

27:9 *Day of Cleansing.* An important Jewish holy day in the fall of the year. This was the time of year that bad storms arose on the sea.

27:17 *Syrtis.* Shallow area in the sea near the Libyan coast.

27:24 Rome: Acts 28:14

27:27 *Adriatic Sea.* The sea between Greece and Italy, including the central Mediterranean.

follow using wooden boards or pieces of the ship.
And this is how all the people made it safely to land.

Paul on the Island of Malta

28 When we were safe on land, we learned
that the island was called Malta. 2The
people who lived there were very good to us.
Because it was raining and very cold, they made a
fire and welcomed all of us. 3Paul gathered a pile
of sticks and was putting them on the fire when a
poisonous snake came out because of the heat
and bit him on the hand. 4The people living on
the island saw the snake hanging from Paul's
hand and said to each other, "This man must be a
murderer! He did not die in the sea, but Justice
does not want him to live." 5But Paul shook the
snake off into the fire and was not hurt. 6The people thought that Paul would swell up or fall down
dead. They waited and watched him for a long
time, but nothing bad happened to him. So they
changed their minds and said, "He is a god!"

The Roman Forum: political and business center of ancient Rome

7There were some fields around there owned
by Publius, an important man on the island. He
welcomed us into his home and was very good to
us for three days. 8Publius' father was sick with a
fever and dysentery. Paul went to him, prayed,
and put his hands on the man and healed him.
9After this, all the other sick people on the island
came to Paul, and he healed them, too. 10-11The
people on the island gave us many honors. When
we were ready to leave, three months later, they
gave us the things we needed.

Paul Goes to Rome

We got on a ship from Alexandria that had
stayed on the island during the winter. On the
front of the ship was the sign of the twin gods.
12We stopped at Syracuse for three days. 13From
there we sailed to Rhegium. The next day a wind
began to blow from the south, and a day later we
came to Puteoli. 14We found some believers there
who asked us to stay with them for a week. Finally,
we came to Rome. 15The believers in Rome heard
that we were there and came out as far as the
Market of Appius and the Three Inns to meet us.
When Paul saw them, he was encouraged and
thanked God.

Paul in Rome

16When we arrived at Rome, Paul was allowed
to live alone, with the soldier who guarded him.
17Three days later Paul sent for the leaders there.
When they came together, he said, "Brothers, I
have done nothing against our people or the customs of our ancestors. But I was arrested in
Jerusalem and given to the Romans. 18After they
asked me many questions, they could find no reason why I should be killed. They wanted to let me
go free, 19but the evil people there argued against
that. So I had to ask to come to Rome to have my
trial before Caesar. But I have no charge to bring
against my own people. 20That is why I wanted
to see you and talk with you. I am bound with this
chain because I believe in the hope of Israel."
21They answered Paul, "We have received no letters from Judea about you. None of our Jewish brothers who have come from there brought news or told

28:4 *Justice.* The people thought there was a god named Justice who would punish bad people.
28:8 *dysentery.* A sickness like diarrhea.
28:9 Sickness, Disease, Healing: 1 Corinthians 12:9
28:11 *twin gods.* Statues of Castor and Pollux, gods in old Greek tales.
28:14 Rome: Acts 28:16–19
28:15 *Market of Appius.* A town about twenty-seven miles from Rome.
28:15 *Three Inns.* A town about thirty miles from Rome.
28:16 Luke: Colossians 4:14
28:17–20 From first to last, Paul, like other Christians in Acts, asserts that he has done nothing against the Jewish people or against the Jewish religion. Throughout, the writer of Acts, Luke, insists that the Christian movement is only the continuation of the story of God's activity on behalf of Israel as told in the Old Testament. Christianity, Luke insists, is nothing but the best of Israel's faith, brought to completion in the work of Jesus. Those Jews who reject Jesus are only rejecting the true expression of their own faith in God.
28:19 Rome: Romans 1:7

us anything bad about you. 22But we want to hear
your ideas, because we know that people everywhere are speaking against this religious group."
23Paul and the people chose a day for a meeting
and on that day many more of the Jews met with
Paul at the place he was staying. He spoke to
them all day long. Using the law of Moses and the
prophets' writings, he explained the kingdom of
God, and he tried to persuade them to believe
these things about Jesus. 24Some believed what
Paul said, but others did not. 25So they argued and
began leaving after Paul said one more thing to
them: "The Holy Spirit spoke the truth to your
ancestors through Isaiah the prophet, saying,
26'Go to this people and say:
You will listen and listen, but you
will not understand.
You will look and look, but you will not learn,
27because these people have become stubborn.
They don't hear with their ears,
and they have closed their eyes.
Otherwise, they might really understand
what they see with their eyes
and hear with their ears.
They might really understand in their minds
and come back to me and
be healed.' *Isaiah 6:9-10*
28"I want you to know that God has also sent his
salvation to all nations, and they will listen!" 29*
30Paul stayed two full years in his own rented
house and welcomed all people who came to visit
him.⚭ 31He boldly preached about the kingdom
of God and taught about the Lord Jesus Christ, and
no one tried to stop him.⚭

28:23–24 As Paul used the phrase "the kingdom of God," he was making it synonymous with the Good News of Jesus Christ. Even in prison, he tried to persuade the Jewish leaders at Rome through the Old Testament that Jesus was the promised Messiah, the one who would restore the kingdom to Israel upon his return. As is always the case with the preaching of the Good News, "some believed . . . but others did not."

***28:29** *Verse 29.* Some late Greek copies add verse 29: "After Paul said this, the Jews left. They were arguing very much with each other."

⚭**28:30 Paul (Saul):** Romans 1:1–15
⚭**28:31 Martyrdom:** Romans 8:35–39

Paul's Missionary Journeys

Acts and New Testament Letters

Crucifixion of Jesus	A.D. 30
Pentecost (Acts 2)	A.D. 30
Stephen martyred (Acts 7)	early A.D. 35
Paul converted	summer A.D. 35
Paul in Damascus (Acts 9)	A.D. 35–37
Paul to Jerusalem (Acts 9)	summer A.D. 37
Paul in Tarsus	A.D. 37–43
Paul in Antioch	A.D. 43–48
Paul's first missionary journey	A.D. 48–49
Galatians written	A.D. 49
Jerusalem Council (Acts 15)	A.D. 49
Paul's second missionary journey	A.D. 50–52
1 Thessalonians written	A.D. 51
2 Thessalonians written	A.D. 51
Paul's third missionary journey	A.D. 53–57
1 Corinthians written	A.D. 56
2 Corinthians written	A.D. 56
Romans written	A.D. 57
Paul's visit to Jerusalem (Acts 21)	A.D. 57
Paul's arrest (Acts 21–24)	A.D. 57
Paul in prison	A.D. 57–59
Paul's sea voyage to Rome	A.D. 59–60
Paul's first Roman imprisonment	A.D. 60–62
Ephesians written	A.D. 60
Colossians written	A.D. 61
Philemon written	A.D. 61
Philippians written	A.D. 62
Paul released and traveling	A.D. 62–64
1 Timothy written	A.D. 62
Paul travels to Spain	A.D. 64–66
Titus written	A.D. 66
Paul in Greece	A.D. 67
Paul arrested and taken to Rome	A.D. 67
2 Timothy written	A.D. 67
Paul put to death in Rome	A.D. 68
City of Jerusalem destroyed	A.D. 70

INTRODUCTION TO SECTION FIVE
ROMANS – JUDE

THE PASTORAL LETTERS

ROMANS	1 THESSALONIANS	JAMES
1 CORINTHIANS	2 THESSALONIANS	1 PETER
2 CORINTHIANS	1 TIMOTHY	2 PETER
GALATIANS	2 TIMOTHY	1 JOHN
EPHESIANS	TITUS	2 JOHN
PHILIPPIANS	PHILEMON	3 JOHN
COLOSSIANS	HEBREWS	JUDE

The New Testament is made up of three basic kinds of literature: narrative (the Gospels and Acts), revelatory literature (Revelation), and letters (the remaining books), which often look like ancient letters. Paul's brief note to Philemon is one of the best examples of letters in the New Testament. Here is the typical format:

- Opening Greetings: the writer identifies himself, those to whom the letter was written, and extends initial greetings. The particularly Christian flavor of these greetings is evident in Paul's letters, where he identifies himself and his audience in relationship to God in Christ, and where he wishes his audience grace and peace.

- Introductory Thanksgiving or Blessing: the writer expresses gratitude to God for what God has accomplished in the lives of the audience. In Paul's letters, the thanksgiving generally includes hints of the subject of the letter to follow.

- Body of the Letter: the writer addresses the issue or issues motivating the writing of the letter in the first place.

- Closing: the writer includes closing greetings, sometimes mentioning particular persons by name, and pronounces a benediction.

Most characteristic of these letters is their "occasional" nature and their "pastoral" function. By occasional nature, we mean that they were written for a specific occasion—at particular times to particular people for particular reasons. By "pastoral" we mean that they are written for the purpose of correcting and encouraging other Christians in the midst of particular struggles or questions, just as a pastor or leader would correct or encourage people.

From the standpoint of reading these New Testament books, a few tips are especially important. First, we should remember that Paul, James, John, and others wrote these letters to be read from beginning to end in church meetings. They did not write in numbered verses as the Bible is now formatted, but penned them as letters or complete documents, which we now call books. As a result, readers today will want to read these letters straight through. In addition, we should remember that these letter writers were not writing to people in the third, the fifteenth, or twentieth centuries. They were writing to people, many of whom they knew, who were caught up in the midst of the real struggles of living as Christians. As we read through these letters, then, we want to hear in them the problems that writers like John or James were addressing, and not assume that their problems were precisely our own. How did Paul, for example, encourage those believers in that situation? How might he communicate that message to us today?

Some New Testament books that are sometimes called letters actually do not resemble letters very much at all. Hebrews, for example, looks like an "exposition"—a message written to encourage (Hebrews 13:22)—while 1 John looks more like an "essay." Even though these books do not look like letters, it is still appropriate to read them as if they were. This is because, like the New Testament letters, these books are both "occasional" and "pastoral." They address specific people regarding specific issues at specific times.

Why are the pastoral letters important today? In many ways the old adage from Ecclesiastes 1:9 applies here: All things continue the way they have been since the beginning. What has happened will happen again; there is nothing new here on earth. Many of the problems and struggles addressed by the New Testament letter writers are still prevalent today. The church still suffers occasional disunity; couples still must cope with marriage difficulties; individual Christians continue to face the same sins as our first century counterparts.

So answers to these unchanging problems, given by God through inspiration to the writers of these letters, are still valid and valuable today. The entire Bible is, in fact, a long love letter from God to his beloved children—you and me.

INTRODUCTION TO THE BOOK OF

ROMANS

God's Plan to Save Us

Who wrote this book?

According to the first verse, this book, or letter, was written by the apostle Paul.

To whom was this book written?

This letter was written to the church at Rome, a church not established by Paul but one he intended to visit on his way to Spain (15:23–24). It was predominantly a non-Jewish (Gentile) church, with a Jewish minority.

Where was it written?

The most likely place of its writing was Corinth or nearby Cenchrea.

When was it written?

Most scholars believe Paul wrote the letter to the Romans in the early spring of A.D. 57.

What is the book about?

The Book of Romans is about the basic Good News of salvation. It presents the grace of God through faith, based on the work of Christ, as the basis of our salvation. It argues for the sinfulness of all people. It claims their justification, or right standing before God, based on faith. It also claims sanctification, or growth in holy living, based on obedience and a Spirit-filled life. Romans makes clear the plan God has for both the Jews and non-Jews.

Why was this book written?

This letter was written to acquaint the Christians at Rome with the Good News of God's grace, which Paul had preached everywhere and wanted them to know as well. It was also written to prepare this church for Paul's planned visit once he delivered the offering for the poor sent by the non-Jewish churches to the church at Jerusalem.

So what does this book mean to us?

The message Paul wrote to Rome is a message that we also need today. We are lost sinners, unable to save ourselves. But God, in his kindness, grants us the faith to trust in the finished work of Jesus Christ as the sacrifice acceptable to God for our sins. Paul encourages us to live for Christ, in the power of the Holy Spirit, day by day, growing to be more and more like him.

Summary:

Paul's letter to the Romans is often regarded as his most developed and mature statement of the Christian message. It is also unusual among his letters, since when he wrote this letter Paul had never actually been to Rome and, therefore, he was not writing to a church he had himself founded. Why, then, did Paul write this letter? Paul needed to set out the nature of the Good News, why he preached it, and how this message should take root in the daily lives and community of those who were committed to it.

In setting out the nature of the Good News to the Christians at Rome, Paul is most concerned with the nature of God. Apparently, the unity of Jew and non-Jew had raised doubts about God's faithfulness to some. After all, how can the God of Israel include in his purpose those outside of Israel? And how can God be faithful to Israel when he is allowing people from outside Israel to be full members of the family of God? For some, God's activity seemed to suggest that God was changing his mind, or that God was soft on sin.

Paul addresses these issues by weaving together important themes:

•According to Romans, at an important level, there is no difference between those who are Jewish and those who are not. All are created by God, all have rejected God's purpose, and all are in need of God's grace.

•God's faithfulness is evident, first, in his anger. This is not God's emotional outburst at human sin. Rather, it is what people experience when they reject God's purpose for them. If people choose a life apart from God, then their punishment is a life apart from God.

•God's faithfulness is evident, second, in the faithful obedience of Jesus and in Jesus' death. The faithfulness of Jesus, in life and death, restores to relationship with God all who believe. This is true for Jews as well as for those who are not Jews.

•Because of Jesus' faithfulness, and because of the faithfulness of God, those who have faith are enabled and called to live new lives. The law, which once set Jews apart from non-Jews, now has as its primary role the call to love.

The importance of Paul's letter to the Romans is matched by its difficulty. Paul's writing here is tightly packed. As with all of the New Testament letters, it is best to read Romans straight through, from beginning to end. In doing so, you may be helped by reading Romans a section at a time:

Romans 1:1–3:20 Introduction. The Nature of Humanity
Romans 3:21–5:21 The Good News
Romans 6:1–8:39 The Ongoing Problem of Sin, Death, and the Law
Romans 9:1–11:36 The Place of Israel in God's Purpose
Romans 12:1–16:27 Christian Living. Closing

ROMANS

From Paul, a servant of Christ Jesus. God called me to be an apostle and chose me to tell the Good News.

2God promised this Good News long ago through his prophets, as it is written in the Holy Scriptures. 3-4The Good News is about God's Son, Jesus Christ our Lord. As a man, he was born from the family of David. But through the Spirit of holiness he was appointed to be God's Son with great power by rising from the dead. 5Through Christ, God gave me the special work of an apostle, which was to lead people of all nations to believe and obey. I do this work for him. 6And you who are in Rome are also called to belong to Jesus Christ.

7To all of you in Rome whom God loves and has called to be his holy people:

Grace and peace to you from God our Father and the Lord Jesus Christ.

A Prayer of Thanks

8First I want to say that I thank my God through Jesus Christ for all of you, because people everywhere in the world are talking about your faith. 9God, whom I serve with my whole heart by telling the Good News about his Son, knows that I always mention you 10every time I pray. I pray that I will be allowed to come to you, and this will happen if God wants it. 11I want very much to see you, to give you some spiritual gift to make you strong. 12I mean that I want us to help each other with the faith we have. Your faith will help me, and my faith will help you. 13Brothers and sisters, I want you to know that I planned many times to come to you, but this has not been possible. I wanted to come so that I could help you grow spiritually as I have helped the other non-Jewish people.

14I have a duty to all people—Greeks and those who are not Greeks, the wise and the foolish.

A Roman husband and wife in typical Roman dress

15That is why I want so much to preach the Good News to you in Rome.

16I am proud of the Good News, because it is the power God uses to save everyone who believes—to save the Jews first, and also to save those who are not Jews. 17The Good News shows how God makes people right with himself—that it begins and ends with faith. As the Scripture says, "But those who are right with God will live by trusting in him."

All People Have Done Wrong

18God's anger is shown from heaven against all the evil and wrong things people do. By their own evil lives they hide the truth. 19God shows his anger because some knowledge of him has been made clear to them. Yes, God has shown himself to them. 20There are things about him that people cannot see—his eternal power and all the things that make him God. But since the beginning of the world those things have been easy to understand by what

1:1 Service: 1 Corinthians 4:1

1:3 Jesus Christ was a descendant of King David (Matthew 1). David was told that he would have a king on the throne forever (2 Samuel 7), and the New Testament often, as here, reveals that that promise comes to its final and ultimate fulfillment in Jesus Christ.

1:3–4 Paul here hints at Jesus' dual nature as man, but more than man. He is a son of David, a literal descendant of that king. Thus, he fulfills all the expectations of a royal Messiah from the Old Testament. But he is more than David's son; he is also God's Son. His resurrection demonstrates the latter.

1:7 Rome: Romans 1:15

1:9 Memory: 2 Timothy 2:8

1:13 *Brothers and sisters.* Although the Greek text says "Brothers" here and throughout this book, Paul's words were meant for the entire church, including men and women.

1:15 Rome: Romans 13:1–7

1:15 Paul (Saul): Romans 7:7–25

1:16 The Good News of Jesus Christ is not for *either* Jewish or non-Jewish people; it is for both. The Good News is that in Jesus Christ all who believe can be saved regardless of their race, color, or gender. Jesus himself announced that this Good News would go out from Jerusalem to all the peoples of the world (Acts 1:8).

1:16 Gospel/Good News: 1 Corinthians 15:1–4

1:16 Gentiles (Non-Jews): Romans 11:11–12

1:17 *"But those . . . him."* Quotation from Habakkuk 2:4.

1:18–32 People have no excuse for worshiping idols. Since the beginning, God has shown his greatness and goodness through the things he has made. When people worship anything other than God, he judges them by letting them have their own way. God gave humans his rules for their own protection. When people disobey God by following their own ways, they end up hurting themselves.

God has made. So people have no excuse for the
bad things they do. 21They knew God, but they
did not give glory to God or thank him. Their
thinking became useless. Their foolish minds were
filled with darkness. 22They said they were wise,
but they became fools. 23They traded the glory of
God who lives forever for the worship of idols
made to look like earthly people, birds, animals,
and snakes.

24Because they did these things, God left them
and let them go their sinful way, wanting only to
do evil. As a result, they became full of sexual sin,
using their bodies wrongly with each other. 25They
traded the truth of God for a lie. They worshiped
and served what had been created instead of the
God who created those things, who should be
praised forever. Amen.

26Because people did those things, God left them
and let them do the shameful things they wanted
to do. Women stopped having natural sex and
started having sex with other women. 27In the
same way, men stopped having natural sex and
began wanting each other. Men did shameful
things with other men, and in their bodies they
received the punishment for those wrongs.

28People did not think it was important to have a
true knowledge of God. So God left them and
allowed them to have their own worthless thinking and to do things they should not do. 29They are
filled with every kind of sin, evil, selfishness, and
hatred. They are full of jealousy, murder, fighting,
lying, and thinking the worst about each other.
They gossip 30and say evil things about each
other. They hate God. They are rude and conceited
and brag about themselves. They invent ways of
doing evil. They do not obey their parents. 31They
are foolish, they do not keep their promises, and they
show no kindness or mercy to others. 32They know
God's law says that those who live like this should
die. But they themselves not only continue to do
these evil things, they applaud others who do them.

You People Also Are Sinful

2 If you think you can judge others, you are
wrong. When you judge them, you are really
judging yourself guilty, because you do the same
things they do. 2God judges those who do wrong
things, and we know that his judging is right. 3You
judge those who do wrong, but you do wrong yourselves. Do you think you will be able to escape the
judgment of God? 4He has been very kind and
patient, waiting for you to change, but you think
nothing of his kindness. Perhaps you do not understand that God is kind to you so you will change
your hearts and lives. 5But you are stubborn and
refuse to change, so you are making your own punishment even greater on the day he shows his
anger. On that day everyone will see God's right
judgments. 6God will reward or punish every
person for what that person has done. 7Some people, by always continuing to do good, live for God's
glory, for honor, and for life that has no end. God
will give them life forever. 8But other people are
selfish. They refuse to follow truth and, instead, follow evil. God will give them his punishment and
anger. 9He will give trouble and suffering to everyone who does evil—to the Jews first and also to
those who are not Jews. 10But he will give glory,
honor, and peace to everyone who does good—to
the Jews first and also to those who are not Jews.
11For God judges all people in the same way.

12People who do not have the law and who are
sinners will be lost, although they do not have the
law. And, in the same way, those who have the law
and are sinners will be judged by the law. 13Hearing
the law does not make people right with God. It is
those who obey the law who will be right with
him. 14(Those who are not Jews do not have the
law, but when they freely do what the law commands, they are the law for themselves. This is
true even though they do not have the law. 15They
show that in their hearts they know what is right
and wrong, just as the law commands. And they
show this by their consciences. Sometimes their
thoughts tell them they did wrong, and sometimes
their thoughts tell them they did right.) 16All these
things will happen on the day when God, through
Christ Jesus, will judge people's secret thoughts.
The Good News that I preach says this.

The Jews and the Law

17What about you? You call yourself a Jew. You
trust in the law of Moses and brag that you are close
to God. 18You know what he wants you to do and
what is important, because you have learned the
law. 19You think you are a guide for the blind and

1:20 Earth: Romans 8:20
1:23 Human: Romans 1:25
1:25 Human: Colossians 2:9
1:29 Murder: Romans 13:9
1:30 Tongue: Romans 3:13
2:5 Stubbornness: Romans 11:32
2:7 *life forever:* "Immortality" literally means "deathlessness," or "life that has no end." The original Greek word in the text suggest a life that does not suffer decay. It is the life we will enjoy in our resurrection bodies after Christ raises us up or transforms us when he returns. Our immortal bodies will be like his body and will never be capable of dying or experiencing decay. Immortality in this sense is not something we have now, even though in our spirits we already have eternal life as believers.
2:9 Hell: Philippians 3:18–19

a light for those who are in darkness. 20You think
you can show foolish people what is right and teach
those who know nothing. You have the law; so you
think you know everything and have all truth.
21You teach others, so why don't you teach yourself? You tell others not to steal, but you steal. 22You
say that others must not take part in adultery, but
you are guilty of that sin. You hate idols, but you
steal from temples. 23You brag about having God's
law, but you bring shame to God by breaking his
law, 24just as the Scriptures say: "Those who are not
Jews speak against God's name because of you."

25If you follow the law, your circumcision has
meaning. But if you break the law, it is as if you
were never circumcised. 26People who are not Jews
are not circumcised, but if they do what the law
says, it is as if they were circumcised. 27You Jews
have the written law and circumcision, but you
break the law. So those who are not circumcised in
their bodies, but still obey the law, will show that
you are guilty. 28They can do this because a person
is not a true Jew if he is only a Jew in his physical
body; true circumcision is not only on the outside
of the body. 29A person is a Jew only if he is a Jew
inside; true circumcision is done in the heart by
the Spirit, not by the written law. Such a person
gets praise from God rather than from people.

3 So, do Jews have anything that other people
do not have? Is there anything special about
being circumcised? 2Yes, of course, there is in every
way. The most important thing is this: God trusted
the Jews with his teachings. 3If some Jews were
not faithful to him, will that stop God from doing
what he promised? 4No! God will continue to be
true even when every person is false. As the
Scriptures say:

"So you will be shown to be right
when you speak,
and you will win your case." *Psalm 51:4*

5When we do wrong, that shows more clearly
that God is right. So can we say that God is wrong
to punish us? (I am talking as people might talk.)
6No! If God could not punish us, he could not judge
the world.

7A person might say, "When I lie, it really gives
him glory, because my lie shows God's truth. So
why am I judged a sinner?" 8It would be the same
to say, "We should do evil so that good will come."
Some people find fault with us and say we teach
this, but they are wrong and deserve the punishment they will receive.

All People Are Guilty

9So are we Jews better than others? No! We
have already said that Jews and those who are not
Jews are all guilty of sin. 10As the Scriptures say:

"There is no one who always does what is right,
not even one.
11 There is no one who understands.
There is no one who looks to God for help.
12All have turned away.
Together, everyone has become useless.
There is no one who does anything good;
there is not even one." *Psalm 14:1-3*
13"Their throats are like open graves;
they use their tongues for telling lies." *Psalm 5:9*
"Their words are like snake poison." *Psalm 140:3*
14 "Their mouths are full of cursing and hate." *Psalm 10:7*
15"They are always ready to kill people.
16 Everywhere they go they cause ruin and misery.
17They don't know how to live in peace." *Isaiah 59:7-8*
18 "They have no fear of God." *Psalm 36:1*

19We know that the law's commands are for
those who have the law. This stops all excuses and
brings the whole world under God's judgment,
20because no one can be made right with God by
following the law. The law only shows us our sin.

How God Makes People Right

21But God has a way to make people right with
him without the law, and he has now shown us
that way which the law and the prophets told us
about. 22God makes people right with himself
through their faith in Jesus Christ. This is true for
all who believe in Christ, because all people are
the same: 23All have sinned and are not good
enough for God's glory, 24and all need to be made
right with God by his grace, which is a free gift.
They need to be made free from sin through Jesus
Christ. 25God gave him as a way to forgive sin
through faith in the blood of Jesus' death. This
showed that God always does what is right and
fair, as in the past when he was patient and did
not punish people for their sins. 26And God gave

2:24 *"Those . . . you."* Quotation from Isaiah 52:5; Ezekiel 36:20.

2:29 Circumcision: Romans 4:11

3:13 Tongue: Ephesians 5:4

3:21 Law does not make one right with God. Only God's grace through Christ can do this. Yet, as Paul writes here, such an understanding of the Law is precisely what the Law itself teaches. In this sense, Paul's view of the Law is in harmony with Jesus' words in Matthew 5:17–20.

3:21–27 When Paul speaks of "making people right," he is thinking especially in terms of relationship. Jesus' death opens the door so that those who have faith can have a good relationship with God and with God's people. This also means that those who have faith will show in their lives that they are in relationship with God.

Jesus to show today that he does what is right. God
did this so he could judge rightly and so he could
make right any person who has faith in Jesus.
27So do we have a reason to brag about ourselves?
No! And why not? It is the way of faith that stops all
bragging, not the way of trying to obey the law. 28A
person is made right with God through faith, not
through obeying the law. 29Is God only the God of
the Jews? Is he not also the God of those who are
not Jews? 30Of course he is, because there is only
one God. He will make Jews right with him by
their faith, and he will also make those who are not
Jews right with him through their faith. 31So do we
destroy the law by following the way of faith? No!
Faith causes us to be what the law truly wants.

The Example of Abraham

4 So what can we say that Abraham, the father
of our people, learned about faith? 2If Abraham
was made right by the things he did, he had a reason to brag. But this is not God's view, 3because
the Scripture says, "Abraham believed God, and
God accepted Abraham's faith, and that faith made
him right with God."
4When people work, their pay is not given as a
gift, but as something earned. 5But people cannot
do any work that will make them right with God.
So they must trust in him, who makes even evil
people right in his sight. Then God accepts their
faith, and that makes them right with him. 6David
said the same thing. He said that people are truly
blessed when God, without paying attention to
good deeds, makes people right with himself.

7"Happy are they
whose sins are forgiven,
whose wrongs are pardoned.
8Happy is the person
whom the Lord does not consider guilty."
Psalm 32:1-2

9Is this blessing only for those who are circumcised
or also for those who are not circumcised? We have
already said that God accepted Abraham's faith and
that faith made him right with God. 10So how did
this happen? Did God accept Abraham before or
after he was circumcised? It was before his circumcision. 11Abraham was circumcised to show that he
was right with God through faith before he was
circumcised. So Abraham is the father of all those
who believe but are not circumcised; he is the
father of all believers who are accepted as being
right with God. 12And Abraham is also the father
of those who have been circumcised and who live
following the faith that our father Abraham had
before he was circumcised.

God Keeps His Promise

13Abraham and his descendants received the
promise that they would get the whole world. He
did not receive that promise through the law, but
through being right with God by his faith. 14If people could receive what God promised by following the law, then faith is worthless. And God's
promise to Abraham is worthless, 15because the
law can only bring God's anger. But if there is no
law, there is nothing to disobey.
16So people receive God's promise by having
faith. This happens so the promise can be a free
gift. Then all of Abraham's children can have that
promise. It is not only for those who live under the
law of Moses but for anyone who lives with faith
like that of Abraham, who is the father of us all.
17As it is written in the Scriptures: "I am making
you a father of many nations." This is true before
God, the God Abraham believed, the God who
gives life to the dead and who creates something
out of nothing.
18There was no hope that Abraham would have
children. But Abraham believed God and continued
hoping, and so he became the father of many
nations. As God told him, "Your descendants also
will be too many to count." 19Abraham was
almost a hundred years old, much past the age for
having children, and Sarah could not have children. Abraham thought about all this, but his faith
in God did not become weak. 20He never doubted
that God would keep his promise, and he never
stopped believing. He grew stronger in his faith
and gave praise to God. 21Abraham felt sure that
God was able to do what he had promised. 22So,
"God accepted Abraham's faith, and that faith
made him right with God." 23Those words ("God
accepted Abraham's faith") were written not only
for Abraham 24but also for us. God will accept us
also because we believe in the One who raised

4:1 *Abraham.* Most respected ancestor of the Jews. Every Jew hoped to see Abraham.
4:3 *"Abraham . . . God."* Quotation from Genesis 15:6.
4:3 Abraham: Galatians 3:6
4:7 Land/Inheritance: Romans 8:23
4:11 Circumcision: 1 Corinthians 7:19
4:13 *Abraham.* See 4:1.
4:17 *"I . . . nations."* Quotation from Genesis 17:5.
4:18 *"Your . . . count."* Quotation from Genesis 15:5.
4:18 Racism: Romans 10:12
4:19 Abraham's trust in God's promise to raise up a son was nothing less than trust in God's power to overcome the deadness of Abraham's own body and the deadness of Sarah's womb. Christians are like Abraham because they trust in the fact that God's power raised Christ from the dead and will one day raise us from spiritual death (Romans 4:23, 24).
4:21 Promise: Galatians 3:14–29
4:22 *"God . . . God."* Quotation from Genesis 15:6.

Jesus our Lord from the dead. 25Jesus was given to
die for our sins, and he was raised from the dead
to make us right with God.

Right with God

5 Since we have been made right with God by
our faith, we have peace with God. This happened through our Lord Jesus Christ, 2who has
brought us into that blessing of God's grace that we
now enjoy. And we are happy because of the hope
we have of sharing God's glory. 3We also have joy
with our troubles, because we know that these
troubles produce patience. 4And patience produces character, and character produces hope.
5And this hope will never disappoint us, because
God has poured out his love to fill our hearts. He
gave us his love through the Holy Spirit, whom
God has given to us.

6When we were unable to help ourselves, at the
moment of our need, Christ died for us, although
we were living against God. 7Very few people will
die to save the life of someone else. Although
perhaps for a good person someone might possibly die. 8But God shows his great love for us in
this way: Christ died for us while we were still
sinners.

9So through Christ we will surely be saved
from God's anger, because we have been made
right with God by the blood of Christ's death.
10While we were God's enemies, he made friends
with us through the death of his Son. Surely, now
that we are his friends, he will save us through
his Son's life. 11And not only that, but now we
are also very happy in God through our Lord Jesus
Christ. Through him we are now God's friends
again.

Adam and Christ Compared

12Sin came into the world because of what one
man did, and with sin came death. This is why
everyone must die—because everyone sinned.
13Sin was in the world before the law of Moses, but
sin is not counted against us as breaking a command when there is no law. 14But from the time of
Adam to the time of Moses, everyone had to die,
even those who had not sinned by breaking a command, as Adam had.

Adam was like the One who was coming in the
future. 15But God's free gift is not like Adam's sin.
Many people died because of the sin of that one
man. But the grace from God was much greater;
many people received God's gift of life by the grace
of the one man, Jesus Christ. 16After Adam sinned
once, he was judged guilty. But the gift of God is different. God's free gift came after many sins, and it
makes people right with God. 17One man sinned,
and so death ruled all people because of that one
man. But now those people who accept God's full
grace and the great gift of being made right with
him will surely have true life and rule through the
one man, Jesus Christ.

18So as one sin of Adam brought the punishment
of death to all people, one good act that Christ did
makes all people right with God. And that brings
true life for all. 19One man disobeyed God, and
many became sinners. In the same way, one man
obeyed God, and many will be made right. 20The
law came to make sin worse. But when sin grew
worse, God's grace increased. 21Sin once used
death to rule us, but God gave people more of his
grace so that grace could rule by making people
right with him. And this brings life forever through
Jesus Christ our Lord.

4:25 Good Works: Galatians 3

5:1 Faith/Unbelief: Ephesians 2:8

5:1 Peace: Ephesians 2:11–18

5:1 One part of salvation is being made right with God. It comes by faith and brings us peace with him. Through this step we are adopted as God's sons and daughters. We take on a new family, the Body of Christ. All of this comes because of God's grace, and we are thus saved by grace through our faith (Ephesians 2:8).

5:2 Grace: Romans 5:12–6:2

5:3 Suffering: Romans 8:17–18

5:5 Conflict: Romans 5:9–11

5:5 Encouragement: 2 Corinthians 4:8–9

5:5 Hope: Romans 8:8–15

5:8 The best evidence that God's love for us is unconditional is the fact that Jesus died for us before we became his friends. In fact, "Christ died for us while we were still sinners." That is, while we were in a state of disobedience and rebellion against him, God sent his Son to redeem us. We were his enemies and "unable to help ourselves" (Romans 5:6). There was nothing that we could do or offer to save ourselves. In that helpless condition, God's love reached out to rescue us.

5:9 Blood: 1 Corinthians 11:23–26

5:9–11 These verses display the biblical balance of God's love and his justice. God would not have been true to his character if he had declared that the penalty for sin is death and then simply ignored our rebellion. He also would have belied who he is had he simply destroyed us without compassion. Instead, he sent his own Son to die in our place, that we might have the opportunity to be restored into a right relationship with him.

5:10 Death: 1 Corinthians 15:20–26

5:11 Conflict: Romans 8:18–25

5:12–21 The first sin, sometimes referred to as the Fall, brought guilt and the punishment of death to all people. Jesus is the "second Adam." Adam's disobedience in the garden resulted in breaking the relationship between him and God. The results of this fracture were passed on to his offspring, which is all humanity. A proper relationship between God and humanity could only be brought about by "starting over," so to speak. Jesus is the "second Adam" and fully restores our relationship to God. As Adam's disobedience brought alienation from God, and was passed on to all humanity, Jesus' obedience restored intimacy, and is passed on to all who follow him.

5:21 Creation/New Creation: Romans 8:22

Dead to Sin but Alive in Christ

6 So do you think we should continue sinning so that God will give us even more grace? 2No! We died to our old sinful lives, so how can we continue living with sin? 3Did you forget that all of us became part of Christ when we were baptized? We shared his death in our baptism. 4When we were baptized, we were buried with Christ and shared his death. So, just as Christ was raised from the dead by the wonderful power of the Father, we also can live a new life.

5Christ died, and we have been joined with him by dying too. So we will also be joined with him by rising from the dead as he did. 6We know that our old life died with Christ on the cross so that our sinful selves would have no power over us and we would not be slaves to sin. 7Anyone who has died is made free from sin's control.

8If we died with Christ, we know we will also live with him. 9Christ was raised from the dead, and we know that he cannot die again. Death has no power over him now. 10Yes, when Christ died, he died to defeat the power of sin one time—enough for all time. He now has a new life, and his new life is with God. 11In the same way, you should see yourselves as being dead to the power of sin and alive with God through Christ Jesus.

12So, do not let sin control your life here on earth so that you do what your sinful self wants to do. 13Do not offer the parts of your body to serve sin, as things to be used in doing evil. Instead, offer yourselves to God as people who have died and now live. Offer the parts of your body to God to be used in doing good. 14Sin will not be your master, because you are not under law but under God's grace.

Be Slaves of Righteousness

15So what should we do? Should we sin because we are under grace and not under law? No! 16Surely you know that when you give yourselves like slaves to obey someone, then you are really slaves of that person. The person you obey is your master. You can follow sin, which brings spiritual death, or you can obey God, which makes you right with him. 17In the past you were slaves to sin—sin controlled you. But thank God, you fully obeyed the things that you were taught. 18You were made free from sin, and now you are slaves to goodness. 19I use this example because this is hard for you to understand. In the past you offered the parts of your body to be slaves to sin and evil; you lived only for evil. In the same way now you must give yourselves to be slaves of goodness. Then you will live only for God.

20In the past you were slaves to sin, and goodness did not control you. 21You did evil things, and now you are ashamed of them. Those things only bring death. 22But now you are free from sin and have become slaves of God. This brings you a life that is only for God, and this gives you life forever. 23When people sin, they earn what sin pays—death. But God gives us a free gift—life forever in Christ Jesus our Lord.

An Example from Marriage

7 Brothers and sisters, all of you understand the law of Moses. So surely you know that the law rules over people only while they are alive. 2For example, a woman must stay married to her husband as long as he is alive. But if her husband dies, she is free from the law of marriage. 3But if she marries another man while her husband is still alive, the law says she is guilty of adultery. But if her husband dies, she is free from the law of marriage. Then if she marries another man, she is not guilty of adultery.

4In the same way, my brothers and sisters, your old selves died, and you became free from the law through the body of Christ. This happened so that you might belong to someone else—the One who was raised from the dead—and so that we might be used in service to God. 5In the past, we were ruled by our sinful selves. The law made us want to do sinful things that controlled our bodies, so the things we did were bringing us death. 6In the past, the law held us like prisoners, but our old selves died, and we were made free from the law. So now we serve God in a new way with the Spirit, and not in the old way with written rules.

Our Fight Against Sin

7You might think I am saying that sin and the law are the same thing. That is not true. But the

---

6:2 Grace: 2 Corinthians 12:7–10

6:3–4 Paul is concerned that some will think that being made right with God means that they can now do as they please. The opposite is much more the case. Paul speaks not so much of baptism as an experience for Christians in the past as an entry into a whole new way of life.

6:10–14 This passage makes it clear that the body should not automatically be identified with the evil of sin. Paul encourages his readers to give their bodies to God and not give in to the temptations of sin. The body can be offered to God and used for doing good, not evil.

6:14 Baptism: 1 Corinthians 1:13–17

6:17 The Fall: 1 Corinthians 15:22

6:18 Obedience: 2 Corinthians 10:4–6

7:7–25 It is difficult to know if Paul is speaking here of his life before or after becoming a Christian, or if he weaves together aspects of both in order to lead up to his climactic statement about the liberating power of Jesus: "I thank God for saving me through Jesus Christ our Lord" (Romans 7:25)! Paul uses "I" in several places in his

law was the only way I could learn what sin meant. I would never have known what it means to want to take something belonging to someone else if the law had not said, "You must not want to take your neighbor's things." [8]And sin found a way to use that command and cause me to want all kinds of things I should not want. But without the law, sin has no power. [9]I was alive before I knew the law. But when the law's command came to me, then sin began to live, [10]and I died. The command was meant to bring life, but for me it brought death. [11]Sin found a way to fool me by using the command to make me die.

[12]So the law is holy, and the command is holy and right and good. [13]Does this mean that something that is good brought death to me? No! Sin used something that is good to bring death to me. This happened so that I could see what sin is really like; the command was used to show that sin is very evil.

The War Within Us

[14]We know that the law is spiritual, but I am not spiritual since sin rules me as if I were its slave. [15]I do not understand the things I do. I do not do what I want to do, and I do the things I hate. [16]And if I do not want to do the hated things I do, that means I agree that the law is good. [17]But I am not really the one who is doing these hated things; it is sin living in me that does them. [18]Yes, I know that nothing good lives in me—I mean nothing good lives in the part of me that is earthly and sinful. I want to do the things that are good, but I do not do them. [19]I do not do the good things I want to do, but I do the bad things I do not want to do. [20]So if I do things I do not want to do, then I am not the one doing them. It is sin living in me that does those things.

[21]So I have learned this rule: When I want to do good, evil is there with me. [22]In my mind, I am happy with God's law. [23]But I see another law working in my body, which makes war against the law that my mind accepts. That other law working in my body is the law of sin, and it makes me its prisoner. [24]What a miserable man I am! Who will save me from this body that brings me death? [25]I thank God for saving me through Jesus Christ our Lord!

So in my mind I am a slave to God's law, but in my sinful self I am a slave to the law of sin.

Be Ruled by the Spirit

8 So now, those who are in Christ Jesus are not judged guilty. [2]Through Christ Jesus the law of the Spirit that brings life made me free from the law that brings sin and death. [3]The law was without power, because the law was made weak by our sinful selves. But God did what the law could not do. He sent his own Son to earth with the same human life that others use for sin. By sending his Son to be an offering for sin, God used a human life to destroy sin. [4]He did this so that we could be the kind of people the law correctly wants us to be. Now we do not live following our sinful selves, but we live following the Spirit.

[5]Those who live following their sinful selves think only about things that their sinful selves want. But those who live following the Spirit are thinking about the things the Spirit wants them to do. [6]If people's thinking is controlled by the sinful self, there is death. But if their thinking is controlled by the Spirit, there is life and peace. [7]When people's thinking is controlled by the sinful self, they are against God, because they refuse to obey God's law and really are not even able to obey God's law. [8]Those people who are ruled by their sinful selves cannot please God.

[9]But you are not ruled by your sinful selves. You are ruled by the Spirit, if that Spirit of God really lives in you. But the person who does not have the Spirit of Christ does not belong to Christ. [10]Your body will always be dead because of sin. But if Christ is in you, then the Spirit gives you life, because Christ made you right with God. [11]God raised Jesus from the dead, and if God's Spirit is living in you, he will also give life to your bodies that die. God is the One who raised Christ from the dead, and he will give life through his Spirit that lives in you.

[12]So, my brothers and sisters, we must not be ruled by our sinful selves or live the way our sinful selves want. [13]If you use your lives to do the wrong things your sinful selves want, you will die

letters for argumentative effect, that are not to be taken in a straightforward way. This is not as obvious in this translation of the Bible because sometimes "I" is translated as "we" or the English construction is changed for readability and cloaks Paul's use of "I" (Romans 3:7; 1 Corinthians 5:12; 6:12; 8:13; 10:31–33; 13:1–13; Galatians 2:15–21).

7:7 *"You . . . things."* Quotation from Exodus 20:17.

7:24 Evil: Romans 8:28–30

7:25 Paul (Saul): Romans 11:1

8 The Fall so corrupted our natural selves that we were unable to do anything but live according to our own sinful thinking. Those who respond in faith to God's graciously offered payment for our sin, Jesus Christ, are given the Holy Spirit so that they are now able to do those things that please God.

8:4 Son/Child of God: See article on page 961.

8:11 Holy Spirit: 1 Corinthians 2:2–5

spiritually. But if you use the Spirit's help to stop
doing the wrong things you do with your body,
you will have true life.
14The true children of God are those who let
God's Spirit lead them. 15The Spirit we
received does not make us slaves again to fear; it
makes us children of God. With that Spirit we cry
out, "Father." 16And the Spirit himself joins with
our spirits to say we are God's children. 17If we
are God's children, we will receive blessings from
God together with Christ. But we must suffer as
Christ suffered so that we will have glory as
Christ has glory.

Our Future Glory

18The sufferings we have now are nothing compared to the great glory that will be shown to
us. 19Everything God made is waiting with
excitement for God to show his children's glory
completely. 20Everything God made was changed
to become useless, not by its own wish but
because God wanted it and because all along
there was this hope: 21that everything God
made would be set free from ruin to have the
freedom and glory that belong to God's children.
22We know that everything God made has been
waiting until now in pain, like a woman ready to
give birth. 23Not only the world, but we also
have been waiting with pain inside us. We have
the Spirit as the first part of God's promise. So we
are waiting for God to finish making us his own children, which means our bodies will be made free.
24We were saved, and we have this hope. If we see
what we are waiting for, that is not really hope.
People do not hope for something they already
have. 25But we are hoping for something we do not
have yet, and we are waiting for it patiently.
26Also, the Spirit helps us with our weakness.
We do not know how to pray as we should. But the
Spirit himself speaks to God for us, even begs God
for us with deep feelings that words cannot
explain. 27God can see what is in people's hearts.
And he knows what is in the mind of the Spirit,
because the Spirit speaks to God for his people in
the way God wants.
28We know that in everything God works for the
good of those who love him. They are the people he
called, because that was his plan. 29God knew
them before he made the world, and he decided
that they would be like his Son so that Jesus would
be the firstborn of many brothers. 30God planned
for them to be like his Son; and those he planned to
be like his Son, he also called; and those he
called, he also made right with him; and those he
made right, he also glorified.

God's Love in Christ Jesus

31So what should we say about this? If God is
with us, no one can defeat us. 32He did not spare his
own Son but gave him for us all. So with Jesus, God
will surely give us all things. 33Who can accuse the
people God has chosen? No one, because God is
the One who makes them right. 34Who can say
God's people are guilty? No one, because Christ
Jesus died, but he was also raised from the dead,
and now he is on God's right side, begging God for

8:14 Guilt: See article on page 1112.

8:14–16 Unlike other creatures who operate their lives out of instinct, we are equipped with sufficient "internal machinery" to connect with the living God. In fact, when we become children of God through faith in his Son, that connection with him takes on a whole new dimension. Look closely at the concluding comment. God's Spirit literally communicates with our inner beings, called here "our spirits." In other words, an entire system of inner communication is established at the time of salvation, making it possible for us to receive whatever it is the Spirit wishes to communicate!

8:15 *Father.* Literally, "Abba, Father." Jewish children called their fathers "Abba."Just as Jesus had prayed to God as "Father" (for example, Mark 14:36), Paul now teaches followers of Jesus to address God in the same way. Sent by God, Jesus the Son of God (Romans 8:3) has opened the way for people to become the children of God.

8:15 Father: 1 Corinthians 8:6
8:15 Hope: Romans 12:12
8:16 The People of God: Hebrews 11
8:17 Demon: Ephesians 6:10–18
8:18 Suffering: 2 Corinthians 1:3–7
8:20 Earth: Revelation 21:1
8:22 Creation/New Creation: 1 Corinthians 15:22
8:23 Land/Inheritance: 2 Corinthians 1:22
8:23 Adoption: Romans 9:4
8:25 Conflict: Galatians 6:1–2
8:25 Heaven: Hebrews 11:10
8:26 Tongues: 1 Corinthians 12:1–11

8:26–27 This passage relieves us of undue pressure to make sure our prayers are "correct" in every way. Sometimes we simply do not know how to pray. Words fail to convey our deepest longings. At such times, prayer is validated by our intentions, not by our language. We are free to pray the best we can, trusting the Spirit to sort it all out and to properly represent us before our Heavenly Father.

8:27 Prayer: 1 Thessalonians 5:17

8:28 God is almighty and in complete control over all his creation. Nevertheless, making decisions is part of our everyday lives. We are to make these decisions, confident that God will ultimately make everything— every decision we make, whether good or bad—work for the good for those who love him.

8:28 Esther: See article on page 440.
8:28 Mourning: 2 Corinthians 5:6
8:29 Circumcision: Romans 4:11

8:29 *firstborn.* Here this probably means that Christ was the first in God's family to share God's glory.

8:30 Evil: Romans 12:17

8:31–39 Here Paul assures Christians that God does not lose anyone whom he saves. The danger of apostasy, turning our backs on God, is real. But if a person whom we thought was a Christian clearly and definitively rejects Christ, we understand it is not that a Christian is lost but that an imposter is exposed (1 John 2:17).

8:34 At the present time, Jesus is seated at the right hand of God as our high priest. He is interceding on our behalf with the Father.

PRIDE

JAMES 4:1–10

What is pride? Why is it sometimes called the source of all sin?
How should we live in order to avoid pride?

Pride is the exaltation of one's self. Pride means that we think that we are better than anyone else. One important aspect of pride is not making room for God in our life. As Psalm 10:4 puts it, "The wicked people are too proud. They do not look for God; there is no room for God in their thoughts." Some people do this by saying there is no God, while others admit that there might be a God, but he does not have any right to run their lives. Both deny that God is the Creator and people are his creatures. He has made us, after all, "from scratch," and therefore we belong to him. That is the message of Genesis 1 and 2. God created people, and to deny this is the very source of all sin. Pride is the refusal to obey, depend on, or worship God. Instead, we depend on and worship ourselves, other people, or "the world."

As we look at James 4:1–10, an important passage concerning pride, we can see that it can be organized into three separate parts. This text teaches us first about the sinfulness of not depending on God alone. Second, it informs us of the sinfulness of not loving God alone; and lastly it tells us of the grace of God that removes our sin. It is in verse 10 that James identifies that sin as pride.

In the Garden of Eden, Adam and Eve gave in to the temptation of doubting God's care for them, and they thought that they could get along better by being independent of God's direction (Genesis 2:15–17; 3:1–6). They rejected God's right, as their Creator, to direct them. They said, in effect, "I will not submit! I will not be ruled by you!" Because of their pride they did not want to admit that God was worthy of praise. They set themselves up as gods in their own eyes, and sought security in themselves. And so they fell: "Pride will destroy a person; a proud attitude leads to ruin" (Proverbs 16:18), as Satan had fallen before them.

The Bible makes frequent reference to the ideal relationship between God and humanity: "I will be your God and you will be my people" (Jeremiah 23:7; 24:7; 31:33; Ezekiel 11:20; 36:28; 37:23, 27; Hebrews 8:10). We have chosen the way of pride, but God constantly calls us back to the way of humility (Matthew 5:5).

It is bad to look for salvation in one's own strength, but it is equally bad to seek it in some other human leader or institution (Jeremiah 17:5–8). Daniel 5:20 points out that when King Nebuchadnezzar became too proud God deposed him. Verse 3 in Obadiah mentions the nation of Edom, who thought themselves secure because of their fortresses in the rocky cliff and canyons. But they didn't reckon with the fact that they had become enemies of the Lord All-Powerful, who would surely defeat them. Even the nation of Israel, God's chosen people, would be defeated because they had pride in themselves instead of trusting in God (Hosea 7:10). Jeremiah 13:9 is like Ezekiel 24:21, where the people took pride in, and trusted in, the city of Jerusalem where the Temple is. But our salvation does not come from political leaders and nations, or even religious leaders and buildings. It comes only from God.

Since it is our pride that keeps us from seeking God, it is a gracious thing for God to undermine the basis of our pride. He wants us to come to repentance, and to save our eternal souls. Thus, Job 33:16–17 says, "He speaks in their ears and frightens them with warnings to turn them away from doing wrong and to keep them from being proud" (see also Proverbs 16:18; 29:23). God is also jealous of anybody or anything that is praised instead of him. He protects the unique sacredness of his reputation. Isaiah 2:11 says, "Proud people will be made humble, and they will bow low with shame. At that time only the LORD will still be praised" (see Zephaniah 3:11–13). The sin of pride is that a person directs love and praise to himself or others, instead of to God. Amos 8:7 says that one of the names of God is "the Pride of Jacob." This means that people should take pride in God, and in God alone. If people are going to boast about anything, it should be about God and what he has done (Jeremiah 9:23–24; Romans 15:17–19; 2 Corinthians 1:12–14; 5:12).

To avoid pride in our lives we must recognize who we are and who God is. God is our Creator and Sustainer, and as such is worthy of our praise and worship. We are his creatures, and totally dependent upon him, whether or not we acknowledge it. We must not be proud of the country we live in apart from what God is doing in it. We must not depend on our church or its leaders. We must ultimately acknowledge our total reliance on God's grace. If we do not acknowledge it, we are proud, and we set ourselves up as rivals—enemies—of God ("God is against the proud"). But God is also the loving Father who delights to provide for his children who call upon him in humility ("he gives grace to the humble").

Pride: For additional scriptures on this topic go to Genesis 2:15–3:19.

Stone

1 Peter 2:4

What were stones used for in the Bible? Why is Jesus called a "living Stone"? What does it mean for Christians to be "living stones"?

Stone was plentiful in Palestine, and therefore large stones were used for a variety of purposes where permanence was desired, including construction of buildings (Leviticus 14:45), especially the foundations, marking boundaries (Proverbs 22:28), closing up tombs (Matthew 27:60) and wells (Genesis 29:2–3), and commemorating special events or places. This last purpose is the most frequent use mentioned in the Bible. Stones could be pagan cult symbols (Leviticus 26:1–2; Kings 3:2, 10:26–27; Hosea 3:4), but were also used in relation to the true God. Altars to God had to be built with uncut stones (Exodus 20:25; Deuteronomy 27:6; Joshua 8:31). They were to be unhewn because God ultimately provides the altar for himself.

Agreements (covenants/treaties) were also marked by stones. In Genesis 31:45–54 Laban and Jacob make a treaty and set up stones as a reminder. In Joshua 24:26–27 Joshua set up a witness stone to remind the people of their covenant with God. The Ten Commandments were inscribed on stone (Deuteronomy 5:22).

In particular, promises and visitations from God were remembered by stones. In Joshua 4:3–9 the crossing into the promised land is marked by removing twelve stones from the river, one for each of the twelve tribes. Jacob set up stones to mark where God had spoken to him (Genesis 28:18; 35:14). When God delivered Israel from the Philistines, Samuel marked the event with a stone (1 Samuel 7:12), naming God the "stone of help" (Ebenezer).

Precious stones were also used as symbols. In Exodus 28:15–21, twelve different precious stones were placed in the high priest's breastplate to represent the twelve tribes. And Isaiah 54:11–12 depicts the future restored people of God as a whole new Jerusalem built with precious stones. Perhaps the most significant use of the word *stone* in the Bible is as a symbol of the coming reign of God. Daniel 2:44–45 interprets the "rock cut from a mountain, but no human being touched it" as being the new kingdom of God that would crush all the human kingdoms. Since it represented the kingdom of God, it also represents the anointed King himself. Psalm 118:22 depicts a "Cornerstone" rejected by builders but chosen by God. This probably originally depicted David, whom the leaders of Israel thought unlikely as a king, but whom God had chosen.

Finally, Isaiah 28:16 prophesies a precious or choice stone: and "everything will be built on this important and precious rock." This cornerstone is also proven (tested). And "anyone who trusts in it [him] will never be disappointed." This, too, is a stone that marks the end of Israel's agreement with death (verse 18).

It is not surprising that the New Testament understands these passages as speaking about Jesus Christ. Actually Jesus himself started this. In Matthew 21:42 Jesus quotes Psalm 118:22–23 and relates it to himself. Peter also understands Jesus as this stone, both in his sermon in Acts (4:11) and in his first letter (1 Peter 2:7). Just as David was not at first recognized by the leaders of Israel, so Jesus was rejected by the Jewish leaders of his day. And yet God had chosen him to be the foundation for his kingdom.

This provides the starting point for understanding the other stone prophecies as prophecies of Christ. In Isaiah 8:14, the stone of stumbling for Israel is perhaps already hinted at by Jesus in Matthew 21:44 when he says, "The person who falls on this stone will be broken." Peter directly understands the stone of stumbling to be Christ (1 Peter 2:7–8). Peter also understands Isaiah 28:16, the precious cornerstone, to be Christ. The only time a *precious* (costly) stone was used as a cornerstone was in the foundation for Solomon's Temple (1 Kings 5:17). Jesus is the precious chosen cornerstone for God's temple, the church.

Paul combines Isaiah 8:14 and 28:16 in Romans 9:32–33, and applies them to the doctrine of justification by faith alone. If "anyone who trusts in him will never be disappointed," then those who do not trust in him *will* be disappointed. Those who reject a righteousness through Christ alone, also reject Christ.

Peter also says that believers are stones which was the name given to him by Jesus in Matthew 16:18. As Jesus is a living stone (1 Peter 2:4), believers are also "like living stones" which are being used "to build a spiritual temple" (verse 5). Instead of using literal stones to build a building which can be destroyed, God is using Christians to make a spiritual building as his home.

The fact that Isaiah prophesied that *precious* , or costly, stones would be used in building the new Temple of God (Isaiah 28:16; 54:11–12) is picked up again in Revelation 21:19, where precious stones are used in the foundation of the walls of the whole heavenly city of Jerusalem. Believers, like Jesus the foundation stone, are precious in God's sight, and together will become the eternal dwelling place of God himself.

Stone: For additional scriptures on this topic go to Genesis 28:18.

us. 35Can anything separate us from the love Christ has for us? Can troubles or problems or sufferings or hunger or nakedness or danger or violent death? 36As it is written in the Scriptures:

"For you we are in danger of death all the time.
People think we are worth no more than
sheep to be killed." *Psalm 44:22*

37But in all these things we have full victory through God who showed his love for us. 38Yes, I am sure that neither death, nor life, nor angels, nor ruling spirits, nothing now, nothing in the future, no powers, 39nothing above us, nothing below us, nor anything else in the whole world will ever be able to separate us from the love of God that is in Christ Jesus our Lord.

God and the Jewish People

9 I am in Christ, and I am telling you the truth; I do not lie. My conscience is ruled by the Holy Spirit, and it tells me I am not lying. 2I have great sorrow and always feel much sadness. 3I wish I could help my Jewish brothers and sisters, my people. I would even wish that I were cursed and cut off from Christ if that would help them. 4They are the people of Israel, God's chosen children. They have seen the glory of God, and they have the agreements that God made between himself and his people. God gave them the law of Moses and the right way of worship and his promises. 5They are the descendants of our great ancestors, and they are the earthly family into which Christ was born, who is God over all. Praise him forever! Amen.

6It is not that God failed to keep his promise to them. But only some of the people of Israel are truly God's people, 7and only some of Abraham's descendants are true children of Abraham. But God said to Abraham: "The descendants I promised you will be from Isaac." 8This means that not all of Abraham's descendants are God's true children. Abraham's true children are those who become God's children because of the promise God made to Abraham. 9God's promise to Abraham was this: "At the right time I will return, and Sarah will have a son." 10And that is not all. Rebekah's sons had the same father, our father Isaac. 11-12But before the two boys were born, God told Rebekah, "The older will serve the younger." This was before the boys had done anything good or bad. God said this so that the one chosen would be chosen because of God's own plan. He was chosen because he was the one God wanted to call, not because of anything he did. 13As the Scripture says, "I loved Jacob, but I hated Esau."

14So what should we say about this? Is God unfair? In no way. 15God said to Moses, "I will show kindness to anyone to whom I want to show kindness, and I will show mercy to anyone to whom I want to show mercy." 16So God will choose the one to whom he decides to show mercy; his choice does not depend on what people want or try to do. 17The Scripture says to the king of Egypt: "I made you king for this reason: to show my power in you so that my name will be talked about in all the earth." 18So God shows mercy where he wants to show mercy, and he makes stubborn the people he wants to make stubborn.

19So one of you will ask me: "Then why does God blame us for our sins? Who can fight his will?" 20You are only human, and human beings have no right to question God. An object should not ask the person who made it, "Why did you make me like this?" 21The potter can make anything he wants to make. He can use the same clay to make one thing for special use and another thing for daily use.

22It is the same way with God. He wanted to show his anger and to let people see his power. But he patiently stayed with those people he was angry with—people who were made ready to be

---

According to the writer of Hebrews, this is one of the reasons our salvation is secure (Hebrews 7:25). We need no other mediator, and there is only "one way human beings can reach God" (1 Timothy 2:5), and that is through Jesus Christ.

∞**8:35 Famine:** Matthew 24:7
∞**8:39 Freedom:** 1 Corinthians 8
∞**8:38 The Powers:** 1 Corinthians 1:18–31
∞**8:39 Martyrdom:** 1 Corinthians 4:9–13
∞**8:39 Perseverance:** 1 Corinthians 1:8
∞**8:39 Sin:** Hebrews 9–10
∞**8:39 Stress:** Philippians 4:6–7
∞**9:1 Conscience:** 1 Corinthians 10:25
∞**9:4 Adoption:** Galatians 3:29

9:5 *born . . . forever!* This can also mean, "born. May God, who rules over all things, be praised forever!"

9:6 *God's people.* Literally, "Israel," the people God chose to bring his blessings to the world.

9:7 *Abraham.* Most respected ancestor of the Jews. Every Jew hoped to see Abraham.

9:7 *"The descendants . . . Isaac."* Quotation from Genesis 21:12.

9:9 *"At . . . son."* Quotation from Genesis 18:10, 14.

9:11 *"The older . . . younger."* Quotation from Genesis 25:23.

9:13 *"I . . . Esau."* Quotation from Malachi 1:2-3.

9:13 "To hate" in this sense means to have a strong preference of one over another. It is not to be understood in the human sense of malice or ill-will, but is expressive of the freedom of God as the Ruler of the Universe to make choices that are in keeping with his wise and wonderful purpose of blessing the entire world through Jacob and his descendants. A careful study of the life of Esau and his descendants reveals that God was also kind to them (Genesis 33:9; Deuteronomy 2:5; 2:22) and regarded them as important in biblical history (Genesis 36).

9:14 Here and elsewhere in Romans, Paul makes use of a form of argument called a "diatribe." That is, he discusses the Good News with an imaginary conversation partner. This allows him to state in a positive way the nature of the Christian message, while at the same time protecting the message from bad interpretations.

9:15 *"I . . . mercy."* Quotation from Exodus 33:19.

9:17 *"I . . . earth."* Quotation from Exodus 9:16.

destroyed. 23He waited with patience so that he
could make known his rich glory to the people who
receive his mercy. He has prepared these people to
have his glory, 24and we are those people whom
God called. He called us not from the Jews only but
also from those who are not Jews. 25As the Scripture says in Hosea:

"I will say, 'You are my people'
 to those I had called 'not my people.'
And I will show my love
 to those people I did not love." *Hosea 2:1, 23*

26"They were called,
 'You are not my people,'
but later they will be called
 'children of the living God.'" *Hosea 1:10*

27And Isaiah cries out about Israel:

"The people of Israel are many,
 like the grains of sand by the sea.
But only a few of them will be saved,
28 because the Lord will quickly and completely
  punish the people on the earth."
Isaiah 10:22-23

29It is as Isaiah said:

"The Lord All-Powerful
 allowed a few of our descendants to live.
Otherwise we would have been
  completely destroyed
 like the cities of Sodom and Gomorrah."
Isaiah 1:9

30So what does all this mean? Those who are not
Jews were not trying to make themselves right with
God, but they were made right with God because of
their faith. 31The people of Israel tried to follow a
law to make themselves right with God. But they
did not succeed, 32because they tried to make themselves right by the things they did instead of trusting in God to make them right. They stumbled
over the stone that causes people to stumble. 33As
it is written in the Scripture:

"I will put in Jerusalem a stone that causes
  people to stumble,
 a rock that makes them fall.
Anyone who trusts in him will never
  be disappointed." *Isaiah 8:14; 28:16*

10 Brothers and sisters, the thing I want most
is for all the Jews to be saved. That is my
prayer to God. 2I can say this about them: They
really try to follow God, but they do not know the
right way. 3Because they did not know the way that
God makes people right with him, they tried to
make themselves right in their own way. So they
did not accept God's way of making people right.
4Christ ended the law so that everyone who
believes in him may be right with God.

5Moses writes about being made right by following the law. He says, "A person who obeys
these things will live because of them." 6But this
is what the Scripture says about being made right
through faith: "Don't say to yourself, 'Who will
go up into heaven?'" (That means, "Who will go
up to heaven and bring Christ down to earth?")
7"And do not say, 'Who will go down into the
world below?'" (That means, "Who will go down
and bring Christ up from the dead?") 8This is
what the Scripture says: "The word is near you;
it is in your mouth and in your heart." That is the
teaching of faith that we are telling. 9If you use
your mouth to say, "Jesus is Lord," and if you
believe in your heart that God raised Jesus from
the dead, you will be saved. 10We believe with our
hearts, and so we are made right with God. And
we use our mouths to say that we believe, and so
we are saved.∞ 11As the Scripture says, "Anyone
who trusts in him will never be disappointed."
12That Scripture says "anyone" because there is
no difference between those who are Jews and
those who are not. The same Lord is the Lord of all
and gives many blessings to all who trust in him,∞
13as the Scripture says, "Anyone who calls on the
Lord will be saved."

14But before people can ask the Lord for help,
they must believe in him; and before they can
believe in him, they must hear about him; and
for them to hear about the Lord, someone must
tell them; 15and before someone can go and tell
them, that person must be sent. It is written,
"How beautiful is the person who comes to
bring good news."∞ 16But not all the Jews
accepted the good news. Isaiah said, "Lord, who
believed what we told them?" 17So faith comes
from hearing the Good News, and people hear
the Good News when someone tells them about
Christ.

9:29 *Sodom and Gomorrah.* Two cities that God destroyed because the people were so evil.

9:33 Paul is combining two "stone" prophecies found in Isaiah 8:14 and 28:16. Jesus is both the stone in whom people trust and are never disappointed, and he is also the "stone that causes people to stumble." Since to deny justification by faith in Christ alone is to deny Christ himself, those who cannot accept the righteousness, which is by faith, are stumbling over Christ himself.

10:5 *"A person . . . them."* Quotation from Leviticus 18:5.

10:8 *Verses 6–8.* Quotations from Deuteronomy 9:4; 30:12–14; Psalm 107:26.

∞**10:10 Lordship:** 1 Corinthians 1:2

10:11 *"Anyone . . . disappointed."* Quotation from Isaiah 28:16.

∞**10:12 Racism:** 1 Corinthians 12:13

10:13 *"Anyone . . . saved."* Quotation from Joel 2:32.

∞**10:15 Mission:** James 2:15–16

10:15 *"How . . . news."* Quotation from Isaiah 52:7.

10:16 *"Lord, . . . them?"* Quotation from Isaiah 53:1.

18 But I ask: Didn't people hear the Good News?
Yes, they heard—as the Scripture says:

"Their message went out through all the world;
their words go everywhere on earth."

Psalm 19:4

19 Again I ask: Didn't the people of Israel understand? Yes, they did understand. First, Moses says:

"I will use those who are not a nation to make
you jealous.
I will use a nation that does not understand
to make you angry." *Deuteronomy 32:21*

20 Then Isaiah is bold enough to say:

"I was found by those who were not asking me
for help.
I made myself known to people who were
not looking for me." *Isaiah 65:1*

21 But about Israel God says,

"All day long I stood ready to accept
people who disobey and are stubborn."

Isaiah 65:2

God Shows Mercy to All People

11 So I ask: Did God throw out his people? No!
I myself am an Israelite from the family of
Abraham, from the tribe of Benjamin.∞ 2 God
chose the Israelites to be his people before they
were born, and he has not thrown his people out.
Surely you know what the Scripture says about
Elijah, how he prayed to God against the people of
Israel. 3 "Lord," he said, "they have killed your
prophets, and they have destroyed your altars. I
am the only prophet left, and now they are trying
to kill me, too." 4 But what answer did God give
Elijah? He said, "But I have left seven thousand
people in Israel who have never bowed down
before Baal." 5 It is the same now. There are a few
people that God has chosen by his grace. 6 And if he
chose them by grace, it is not for the things they have
done. If they could be made God's people by what
they did, God's gift of grace would not really be a gift.

7 So this is what has happened: Although the
Israelites tried to be right with God, they did not
succeed, but the ones God chose did become right
with him. The others were made stubborn and
refused to listen to God. 8 As it is written in the
Scriptures:

"God gave the people a dull mind so they
could not understand."

Isaiah 29:10

"He closed their eyes so they could not see
and their ears so they could not hear.
This continues until today."

Deuteronomy 29:4

9 And David says:

"Let their own feasts trap them
and cause their ruin;
let their feasts cause them to
stumble and be paid back.
10 Let their eyes be closed so they cannot see
and their backs be forever
weak from troubles." *Psalm 69:22-23*

11 So I ask: When the Jews fell, did that fall destroy
them? No! But their mistake brought salvation to
those who are not Jews, in order to make the Jews
jealous. 12 The Jews' mistake brought rich blessings
for the world, and the Jews' loss brought rich blessings for the non-Jewish people. So surely the world
will receive much richer blessings when enough
Jews become the kind of people God wants.∞

13 Now I am speaking to you who are not Jews.
I am an apostle to those who are not Jews, and
since I have that work, I will make the most of it.
14 I hope I can make my own people jealous and,
in that way, help some of them to be saved.∞
15 When God turned away from the Jews, he
became friends with other people in the world. So
when God accepts the Jews, surely that will bring
them life after death.

16 If the first piece of bread is offered to God, then
the whole loaf is made holy. If the roots of a tree
are holy, then the tree's branches are holy too.

17 It is as if some of the branches from an olive
tree have been broken off. You non-Jewish people
are like the branch of a wild olive tree that has
been joined to that first tree. You now share the
strength and life of the first tree, the Jews. 18 So do
not brag about those branches that were broken
off. If you brag, remember that you do not support
the root, but the root supports you. 19 You will say,
"Branches were broken off so that I could be joined
to their tree." 20 That is true. But those branches
were broken off because they did not believe, and
you continue to be part of the tree only because

∞**11:1 Paul (Saul):** Romans 11:13–14
11:3 *"They . . . too."* Quotation from 1 Kings 19:10, 14.
11:4 *"But . . . Baal."* Quotation from 1 Kings 19:18.
11:5 Paul makes a case for God's choice of a "remnant," or "a few" Jewish believers who would come to believe in Jesus as the Messiah. He reminds his readers that God had told Elijah how he had left seven thousand people who remained faithful to him. Paul argues that God has chosen "a few" of the nation of Israel at the present time to believe in Christ on the basis of his grace.

∞**11:12 Anti-Semitism:** 1 Thessalonians 1:14–16
∞**11:12 Gentiles (Non-Jews):** Galatians 3:28
∞**11:14 Paul (Saul):** Romans 15:14–32
11:19–21 Note that pride is contrasted with fear of the punishment of God. This is because pride is belief or confidence in oneself, other people, or the world, which brings God's punishment because we should instead recognize him as our Creator and Sustainer. Proud self-confidence interferes with one's daily reliance on the grace of God (James 4:13–16).

you believe. Do not be proud, but be afraid. 21If
God did not let the natural branches of that tree
stay, then he will not let you stay if you don't
believe.
22So you see that God is kind and also very strict.
He punishes those who stop following him. But
God is kind to you, if you continue following in his
kindness. If you do not, you will be cut off from the
tree. 23And if the Jews will believe in God again, he
will accept them back. God is able to put them
back where they were. 24It is not natural for a wild
branch to be part of a good tree. And you who are
not Jews are like a branch cut from a wild olive tree
and joined to a good olive tree. But since those Jews
are like a branch that grew from the good tree, surely they can be joined to their own tree again.
25I want you to understand this secret, brothers
and sisters, so you will understand that you do not
know everything: Part of Israel has been made stubborn, but that will change when many who are not
Jews have come to God. 26And that is how all
Israel will be saved. It is written in the Scriptures:

"The Savior will come from Jerusalem;
he will take away all evil from
the family of Jacob.
27And I will make this agreement
with those people
when I take away their sins."

Isaiah 59:20-21; 27:9

28The Jews refuse to accept the Good News, so
they are God's enemies. This has happened to help
you who are not Jews. But the Jews are still God's
chosen people, and he loves them very much
because of the promises he made to their ancestors.
29God never changes his mind about the people he
calls and the things he gives them. 30At one time
you refused to obey God. But now you have
received mercy, because those people refused to
obey. 31And now the Jews refuse to obey, because
God showed mercy to you. But this happened so
that they also can receive mercy from him. 32God
has given all people over to their stubborn ways so
that he can show mercy to all.

Praise to God

33Yes, God's riches are very great, and his wisdom and knowledge have no end! No one can
explain the things God decides or understand his
ways. 34As the Scripture says,

"Who has known the mind of the Lord,
or who has been able to give him advice?"

Isaiah 40:13

35"No one has ever given God anything
that he must pay back." *Job 41:11*

36Yes, God made all things, and everything continues through him and for him. To him be the
glory forever! Amen.

Give Your Lives to God

12 So brothers and sisters, since God has
shown us great mercy, I beg you to offer
your lives as a living sacrifice to him. Your offering must be only for God and pleasing to him,
which is the spiritual way for you to worship.
2Do not change yourselves to be like the people
of this world, but be changed within by a new
way of thinking. Then you will be able to decide
what God wants for you; you will know what is
good and pleasing to him and what is perfect.
3Because God has given me a special gift, I have
something to say to everyone among you. Do not
think you are better than you are. You must
decide what you really are by the amount of faith
God has given you. 4Each one of us has a body
with many parts, and these parts all have different
uses. 5In the same way, we are many, but in Christ
we are all one body. Each one is a part of that body,
and each part belongs to all the other parts.

11:26 Paul struggles in Romans 9–11 with the election of Israel in the Scriptures and the election of the Gentiles through Jesus. This is a difficult and debated passage that does not leave every question answered. Nevertheless, Paul affirms that salvation is assured in Christ (Romans 10:9–11) and at the same time, "all Israel will be saved" because God is faithful and loves Israel (Romans 11:28–29). Finally he says that election is part of the mystery of God and leads him to praise God (Romans 11:33–36).

11:26 *Jacob.* Father of the twelve family groups of Israel, the people God chose to be his people.

11:32 Stubbornness: Ephesians 4:18

11:36 Election (Chosen): Ephesians 1:3–10

12:1 *living sacrifice.* In the past God asked for animal sacrifices. Today God wants a living sacrifice from the Christian in the form of faithful service. Like the sacrifices in Bible times, this sacrifice is to be holy and acceptable to God.

12:2 Christians continue in the process of becoming more and more like Christ. In this way, what we want, desire, think, plan, and decide come to look more and more like what God wants, rather than what we would want apart from God.

12:2 Pleasure: Romans 15:1–3

12:2 Will of God: Ephesians 1:11

12:2 World/Worldly: 1 Corinthians 7:17–24

12:2 Conversion: 1 Peter 1:22

12:2 Salvation: Romans 13:11

12:4–5 Paul compares the unity of the parts of a physical body to the spiritual unity we share as parts of "one body," the church. We automatically become "a part of that body" when we become Christians. We also are immediately related to one another by being in the Body of Christ so that "each part belongs to all the other parts."

12:5 Body/Flesh: 1 Corinthians 6:13–20

6We all have different gifts, each of which came
because of the grace God gave us. The person who
has the gift of prophecy should use that gift in
agreement with the faith. 7Anyone who has the gift
of serving should serve. Anyone who has the gift of
teaching should teach. 8Whoever has the gift of
encouraging others should encourage. Whoever
has the gift of giving to others should give freely.
Anyone who has the gift of being a leader should
try hard when he leads. Whoever has the gift of
showing mercy to others should do so with joy.∞
9Your love must be real. Hate what is evil, and
hold on to what is good.∞ 10Love each other like
brothers and sisters. Give each other more honor
than you want for yourselves. 11Do not be lazy but
work hard, serving the Lord with all your heart.∞
12Be joyful because you have hope. Be patient when
trouble comes, and pray at all times.∞ 13Share with
God's people who need help. Bring strangers in
need into your homes.
14Wish good for those who harm you; wish them
well and do not curse them.∞ 15Be happy with
those who are happy, and be sad with those who
are sad. 16Live in peace with each other. Do not
be proud, but make friends with those who seem
unimportant. Do not think how smart you are.
17If someone does wrong to you, do not pay him
back by doing wrong to him. Try to do what everyone thinks is right.∞ 18Do your best to live in
peace with everyone. 19My friends, do not try to
punish others when they wrong you, but wait for
God to punish them with his anger. It is written:
"I will punish those who do wrong; I will repay
them," says the Lord. 20But you should do this:

"If your enemy is hungry, feed him;
if he is thirsty, give him a drink.
Doing this will be like pouring burning coals
on his head." *Proverbs 25:21-22*

21Do not let evil defeat you, but defeat evil by doing
good.∞

Christians Should Obey the Law

13 All of you must yield to the government
rulers. No one rules unless God has given
him the power to rule, and no one rules now without that power from God. 2So those who are against
the government are really against what God has
commanded. And they will bring punishment on
themselves.∞ 3Those who do right do not have to
fear the rulers; only those who do wrong fear them.
Do you want to be unafraid of the rulers? Then do
what is right, and they will praise you. 4The ruler is
God's servant to help you. But if you do wrong,
then be afraid. He has the power to punish; he is
God's servant to punish those who do wrong. 5So
you must yield to the government, not only because
you might be punished, but because you know it
is right.∞
6This is also why you pay taxes. Rulers are working for God and give their time to their work. 7Pay
everyone, then, what you owe. If you owe any
kind of tax, pay it. Show respect and honor to
them all.

Loving Others

8Do not owe people anything, except always owe
love to each other, because the person who loves
others has obeyed all the law. 9The law says, "You
must not be guilty of adultery. You must not murder
anyone. You must not steal. You must not want to
take your neighbor's things." All these commands

12:6–8 The list of seven "gifts of the Spirit" in Romans 12 differs somewhat from the parallel lists in 1 Corinthians 12 and Ephesians 4. Paul tells the Romans that the differences among Christians in terms of inclination and grace are given by God. Paul encourages Christians to work hard at using their own gift(s) as best they can, and to avoid comparisons with others. No gift is higher or better than another. All are needed if the full work of Christ is to be done.

∞**12:8 Leadership:** Romans 13:1–2

∞**12:9 Hate:** 1 John 3:15

∞**12:11 Work:** 1 Corinthians 3:5–15

∞**12:12 Hope:** Colossians 1:3–8

∞**12:14 Persecution:** 2 Corinthians 11:23–29

∞**12:17 Evil:** Ephesians 5:16

12:19 *"I . . . them."* Quotation from Deuteronomy 32:35.

∞**12:21 Spirituality/Spiritual Dryness:** 1 Corinthians 12:1–13:13

13 Even ungodly rulers have received their authority from God in order to punish criminals. Although we may sometimes disagree with laws given by ungodly authorities, the Bible instructs us to honor these rulers as God's servants. Only those who commit crimes should fear the authorities.

13:1–7 The Bible clearly teaches that God instituted capital punishment for certain crimes. God gave the authority to apply and carry out capital punishment to those in authority (Exodus 21:23). God's institution of capital punishment for murder is special because it was given after the Flood. God told Noah, "Whoever kills a human being will be killed by a human being" (Genesis 9:6). This is what Paul means when he tells us that the government does not bear the sword in vain. The Old Testament is very clear in describing what wrongdoing was to be punished by death. God wanted to protect the lives and well-being of people by ordaining a punishment that would be certain to put an end to the evil doer and warn others not to follow evil practices. The Bible also teaches that capital punishment is not to be executed for personal revenge. Only certain people, civil authorities, may determine when the death penalty is required according to God's law, and no person was to be put to death on the testimony of only one witness. The consistent purpose of capital punishment in the Bible is thus to preserve life.

∞**13:2 Leadership:** 1 Corinthians 1:12

∞**13:5 Crime:** 1 Peter 4:15

∞**13:7 Rome:** Romans 15:22–32

13:8 In the ancient world, to owe people things was to come under their authority. Debts were often paid back in the form of the sort of loyalty and respect one should reserve only for God. Hence, Paul warns believers not to get involved in relationships where they owe other people anything except the debt of love.

13:9 *"You . . . things."* Quotation from Exodus 20:13–15, 17.

and all others are really only one rule: "Love your neighbor as you love yourself." [10]Love never hurts a neighbor, so loving is obeying all the law.

[11]Do this because we live in an important time. It is now time for you to wake up from your sleep, because our salvation is nearer now than when we first believed. [12]The "night" is almost finished, and the "day" is almost here. So we should stop doing things that belong to darkness and take up the weapons used for fighting in the light. [13]Let us live in a right way, like people who belong to the day. We should not have wild parties or get drunk. There should be no sexual sins of any kind, no fighting or jealousy. [14]But clothe yourselves with the Lord Jesus Christ and forget about satisfying your sinful self.

Do Not Criticize Other People

14 Accept into your group someone who is weak in faith, and do not argue about opinions. [2]One person believes it is right to eat all kinds of food. But another, who is weak, believes it is right to eat only vegetables. [3]The one who knows that it is right to eat any kind of food must not reject the one who eats only vegetables. And the person who eats only vegetables must not think that the one who eats all foods is wrong, because God has accepted that person. [4]You cannot judge another person's servant. The master decides if the servant is doing well or not. And the Lord's servant will do well because the Lord helps him do well.

[5]Some think that one day is more important than another, and others think that every day is the same. Let all be sure in their own mind. [6]Those who think one day is more important than other days are doing that for the Lord. And those who eat all kinds of food are doing that for the Lord, and they give thanks to God. Others who refuse to eat some foods do that for the Lord, and they give thanks to God. [7]We do not live or die for ourselves. [8]If we live, we are living for the Lord, and if we die, we are dying for the Lord. So living or dying, we belong to the Lord.

[9]The reason Christ died and rose from the dead to live again was so he would be Lord over both the dead and the living. [10]So why do you judge your brothers or sisters in Christ? And why do you think you are better than they are? We will all stand before God to be judged, [11]because it is written in the Scriptures:

"'As surely as I live,' says the Lord,
'Everyone will bow before me;
everyone will say that I am God.'" *Isaiah 45:23*

[12]So each of us will have to answer to God.

Do Not Cause Others to Sin

[13]For that reason we should stop judging each other. We must make up our minds not to do anything that will make another Christian sin. [14]I am in the Lord Jesus, and I know that there is no food that is wrong to eat. But if a person believes something is wrong, that thing is wrong for him. [15]If you hurt your brother's or sister's faith because of something you eat, you are not really following the way of love. Do not destroy someone's faith by eating food he thinks is wrong, because Christ died for him. [16]Do not allow what you think is good to become what others say is evil. [17]In the kingdom of God, eating and drinking are not important. The important things are living right with God, peace, and joy in the Holy Spirit. [18]Anyone who serves Christ by living this way is pleasing God and will be accepted by other people.

[19]So let us try to do what makes peace and helps one another. [20]Do not let the eating of food destroy the work of God. All foods are all right to eat, but it is wrong to eat food that causes someone else to sin. [21]It is better not to eat meat or drink wine or do anything that will cause your brother or sister to sin.

[22]Your beliefs about these things should be kept secret between you and God. People are happy if they can do what they think is right without feeling guilty. [23]But those who eat something without being sure it is right are wrong because they did not believe it was right. Anything that is done without believing it is right is a sin.

15 We who are strong in faith should help the weak with their weaknesses, and not please only ourselves. [2]Let each of us please our neighbors for their good, to help them be stronger in faith. [3]Even Christ did not live to please himself. It was as the Scriptures said: "When people insult you, it hurts me." [4]Everything that was written in the past was written to teach us. The Scriptures give us

13:9 *"Love . . . yourself."* Quotation from Leviticus 19:18.
13:9 Murder: 1 Timothy 1:9
13:9 Neighbor: Galatians 5:14
13:10 Neighbor: Romans 15:2
13:10 Law: Galatians 3:11
13:11 Salvation: 1 Corinthians 5:5
13:12 *"night."* This is used as a symbol of the sinful world we live in. This world will soon end.
13:12 *"day."* This is used as a symbol of the good time that is coming, when we will be with God.
14:2 *all . . . food.* The Jewish law said there were some foods Jews should not eat. When Jews became Christians, some of them did not understand they could now eat all foods.
14:4 Servant of the Lord: 1 Corinthians 3:5
15:2 Neighbor: James 2:8
15:3 *"When . . . me."* Quotation from Psalm 69:9.
15:3 Pleasure: Romans 16:18

patience and encouragement so that we can have
hope. 5Patience and encouragement come from
God. And I pray that God will help you all agree
with each other the way Christ Jesus wants. 6Then
you will all be joined together, and you will give
glory to God the Father of our Lord Jesus Christ.
7Christ accepted you, so you should accept each
other, which will bring glory to God. 8I tell you that
Christ became a servant of the Jews to show that
God's promises to the Jewish ancestors are true.
9And he also did this so that those who are not Jews
could give glory to God for the mercy he gives to
them. It is written in the Scriptures:

"So I will praise you among the
non-Jewish people.
I will sing praises to your name." *Psalm 18:49*

10The Scripture also says,

"Be happy, you who are not Jews, together
with his people." *Deuteronomy 32:43*

11Again the Scripture says,

"All you who are not Jews, praise the Lord.
All you people, sing praises to him." *Psalm 117:1*

12And Isaiah says,

"A new king will come from the family of Jesse.
He will come to rule over the
non-Jewish people,
and they will have hope because of him." *Isaiah 11:10*

13I pray that the God who gives hope will fill you
with much joy and peace while you trust in him.
Then your hope will overflow by the power of the
Holy Spirit.

Paul Talks About His Work

14My brothers and sisters, I am sure that you
are full of goodness. I know that you have all the
knowledge you need and that you are able to teach
each other. 15But I have written to you very openly
about some things I wanted you to remember. I did
this because God gave me this special gift: 16to be a
minister of Christ Jesus to those who are not Jews.
I served God by teaching his Good News, so that
the non-Jewish people could be an offering that
God would accept—an offering made holy by the
Holy Spirit.

17So I am proud of what I have done for God in
Christ Jesus. 18I will not talk about anything except
what Christ has done through me in leading those
who are not Jews to obey God. They have obeyed
God because of what I have said and done,
19because of the power of miracles and the great
things they saw, and because of the power of the
Holy Spirit. I preached the Good News from
Jerusalem all the way around to Illyricum, and so I
have finished that part of my work.∞ 20I always
want to preach the Good News in places where
people have never heard of Christ, because I do
not want to build on the work someone else has
already started. 21But it is written in the Scriptures:

"Those who were not told about him will see,
and those who have not heard about him
will understand." *Isaiah 52:15*

Paul's Plan to Visit Rome

22This is the reason I was stopped many times
from coming to you. 23Now I have finished my
work here. Since for many years I have wanted to
come to you, 24I hope to visit you on my way to
Spain. After I enjoy being with you for a while, I
hope you can help me on my trip. 25Now I am going
to Jerusalem to help God's people. 26The believers
in Macedonia and Southern Greece were happy
to give their money to help the poor among God's
people at Jerusalem. 27They were happy to do this,
and really they owe it to them. These who are not
Jews have shared in the Jews' spiritual blessings,
so they should use their material possessions to
help the Jews. 28After I am sure the poor in
Jerusalem get the money that has been given for
them, I will leave for Spain and stop and visit you.
29I know that when I come to you I will bring
Christ's full blessing.

30Brothers and sisters, I beg you to help me in
my work by praying to God for me. Do this because
of our Lord Jesus and the love that the Holy Spirit
gives us. 31Pray that I will be saved from the nonbelievers in Judea and that this help I bring to Jerusalem will please God's people there. 32Then, if God
wants me to, I will come to you with joy, and
together you and I will have a time of rest.∞ 33The
God who gives peace be with you all. Amen.

Greetings to the Christians

16 I recommend to you our sister Phoebe,
who is a helper in the church in Cenchrea.
2I ask you to accept her in the Lord in the way
God's people should. Help her with anything she

15:12 *Jesse.* Jesse was the father of David, king of Israel. Jesus was from their family.

∞**15:19 Pride:** See article on page 1347.

15:20–21 Paul's ambition was to be a pioneer missionary, to preach the Good News where the name of Christ had never been heard. He did not want to build on top of someone else's ministry but to open up new fields. Even his projected visit to Rome, where a church already existed, was intended as a staging area for a trip to Spain (Romans 15:24, 28).

∞**15:32 Paul (Saul):** 1 Corinthians 1:17–2:5

∞**15:32 Rome:** Philippians 1:13–14

16:1 *helper.* Literally, "deaconess." This might mean the same as one of the special women helpers in 1 Timothy 3:11.

needs, because she has helped me and many other
people also.
3Give my greetings to Priscilla and Aquila, who
work together with me in Christ Jesus 4and who
risked their own lives to save my life. I am thankful
to them, and all the non-Jewish churches are thankful as well. 5Also, greet for me the church that
meets at their house.

Greetings to my dear friend Epenetus, who was
the first person in the country of Asia to follow
Christ. 6Greetings to Mary, who worked very hard
for you. 7Greetings to Andronicus and Junia, my relatives, who were in prison with me. They are very
important apostles. They were believers in Christ
before I was. 8Greetings to Ampliatus, my dear
friend in the Lord. 9Greetings to Urbanus, a worker
together with me for Christ. And greetings to my
dear friend Stachys. 10Greetings to Apelles, who
was tested and proved that he truly loves Christ.
Greetings to all those who are in the family of
Aristobulus. 11Greetings to Herodion, my fellow
citizen. Greetings to all those in the family of
Narcissus who belong to the Lord. 12Greetings to
Tryphena and Tryphosa, women who work very
hard for the Lord. Greetings to my dear friend
Persis, who also has worked very hard for the
Lord. 13Greetings to Rufus, who is a special person
in the Lord, and to his mother, who has been like
a mother to me also. 14Greetings to Asyncritus,
Phlegon, Hermes, Patrobas, Hermas, and all the
brothers who are with them. 15Greetings to Philologus
and Julia, Nereus and his sister, and Olympas, and to
all God's people with them. 16Greet each other
with a holy kiss. All of Christ's churches send
greetings to you.

17Brothers and sisters, I ask you to look out for
those who cause people to be against each other
and who upset other people's faith. They are
against the true teaching you learned, so stay away
from them. 18Such people are not serving our Lord
Christ but are only doing what pleases themselves. They use fancy talk and fine words to fool
the minds of those who do not know about evil.
19All the believers have heard that you obey, so I
am very happy because of you. But I want you to
be wise in what is good and innocent in what is
evil.

20The God who brings peace will soon defeat
Satan and give you power over him.

The grace of our Lord Jesus be with you.

21Timothy, a worker together with me, sends
greetings, as well as Lucius, Jason, and Sosipater,
my relatives.

22I am Tertius, and I am writing this letter from
Paul. I send greetings to you in the Lord.

23Gaius is letting me and the whole church here
use his home. He also sends greetings to you, as
do Erastus, the city treasurer, and our brother
Quartus. 24*

25Glory to God who can make you strong in faith
by the Good News that I tell people and by the message about Jesus Christ. The message about Christ is
the secret that was hidden for long ages past but
is now made known. 26It has been made clear
through the writings of the prophets. And by the
command of the eternal God it is made known to
all nations that they might believe and obey.

27To the only wise God be glory forever through
Jesus Christ! Amen.

16:5 House/Home: 2 Corinthians 5:1–10

16:16 Kissing was practiced by family and friends. Paul wants Christians to forget the walls that separate people in the wider world, especially racial-ethnic walls, and to act as though the church were a group of family and friends. The holy kiss, then, is a powerful symbol of Christian unity.

16:16 Hospitality: 1 Corinthians 10–11

16:18 Pleasure: Galatians 6:7–8

16:22 Paul often used secretaries to help him write his letters, in this case Tertius. In other letters we know he did the same thing because he signed his name at the end (1 Corinthians 16:21; Colossians 4:18; 2 Thessalonians 3:17; Galatians 6:11).

***16:24** *Verse 24.* Some Greek copies add verse 24: "The grace of our Lord Jesus Christ be with all of you. Amen."

INTRODUCTION TO THE BOOK OF

1 CORINTHIANS

Help for a Church with Problems

WHO WROTE THIS BOOK?

Scholars agree that the apostle Paul wrote this letter. This is verified by Clement of Rome as early as A.D. 96.

TO WHOM WAS THIS BOOK WRITTEN?

This book was written to the church in the Greek city of Corinth.

WHERE WAS IT WRITTEN?

It is most likely that Paul wrote this letter during the three years that he lived in Ephesus.

WHEN WAS IT WRITTEN?

The Book of 1 Corinthians was written about A.D. 55.

WHAT IS THE BOOK ABOUT?

Paul wrote this letter to address problems in the church at Corinth, as well as to answer questions raised by members of the church there. These problems and questions included such concepts as these: factions in the church; moral problems; lawsuits between Christians; marriage and divorce; abuse of the Lord's Supper; intolerance of the supposedly less-mature by the more-mature Christians; spiritual gifts; faulty views of the resurrection; and handling offerings for the poverty stricken believers in Jerusalem.

WHY WAS THIS BOOK WRITTEN?

First Corinthians was written to correct numerous problems in the church at Corinth. These problems arose out of immaturity and worldliness in a church where Paul had spent eighteen months himself and felt he had reason to expect more.

SO WHAT DOES THIS BOOK MEAN TO US?

People and their problems change little through the centuries. Christians in Corinth and Christians today share the problems of factions in the church, moral problems, lawsuits between Christians, marriage and divorce, intolerance of each other, and other human issues. Because the church is made up of people, and people are imperfect, we can expect these kinds of problems in the church. The church was not established for perfect people but for sinners. We must not, then, be surprised to see sinners and their shortcomings in the church. Rather, we should rejoice that Christ gave us the church where we can help each other through our weaknesses and failures. We must demonstrate the love of Christ to one another (see chapter 13) and not condemn each other as we seek the truth of God's word together as brothers and sisters.

SUMMARY:

According to Acts 18, Paul spent some eighteen months in Corinth where he founded the church. Within only a couple of years—that is, around A.D. 54 or 55—he wrote 1 Corinthians. It was an attempt to deal with wayward behavior among the Corinthians, which was itself rooted in a misunderstanding of the Christian message.

According to 1 Corinthians 1:10; 16:17, Paul had received information about the Corinthians from members of the Corinthian church. They reported to him that the Corinthian Christians were dividing up into groups or cliques. In addition, in 1 Corinthians 7:1 we read that the Corinthians had sent a letter to Paul, seeking advice on a number of issues, including sex and marriage, eating and worship practices, and spiritual gifts. Throughout the letter, we can peer through the window into a host of ethical problems at Corinth. No doubt, these grew out of struggles to understand how to live the Good News in a city known in the ancient world for its wealth, immorality, and lack of traditional roots.

Although Paul must deal with many issues, several are more central to his attempt to get the Corinthian Christians back on track in their faith and their lives together:

•Throughout the letter, Paul explores with the Corinthians the importance of the body, and he does so in what might have been surprising ways. As the physical body is the "home" for the human spirit, he says, so the church as a "body" is the "home" for the Spirit of God. This means that what believers do as individuals affects both their own spiritual lives, and also the lives of all other believers; they are joined together by the one Spirit of God. So the Corinthians should take more seriously the sexual problems of some Christians among them.

•Closely related is Paul's concern with the lack of unity among the believers at Corinth. Their divisions and hostility between different cliques, he insists, is actually a denial of the truth of the Good News. This becomes most evident in the way they share in church meals (1 Corinthians 11:17–34). Their meals do not honor the Lord because these Christians are not caring for one another. In fact, they are embarrassing the poor among them. Paul's response is simple: The actions of those who follow Jesus ought to be like the actions of Jesus, who did not think of himself but of others when he gave up his life on the cross.

•Finally, in 1 Corinthians 15, the real problem among the Corinthians comes to the surface. Paul recognizes that these believers want to act as though the end of time has already come. They believe the time of resurrection has already come, so they can now live as they please. Not so, Paul insists. This is not the time to live as though salvation had come in its fullness. Instead, our lives in the present should be shaped by the example of Jesus on the cross. We await his return, and in the meantime we allow his selflessness, his fundamental concern for others, to shape how we live with each other.

First Corinthians, then, is largely a call to follow Christ, who was crucified. This is why Paul insists that the Good News is really about Jesus Christ and his death on the cross (1 Corinthians 2:2). It is also why he devotes such a long section of the letter to love (1 Corinthians 13).

1 CORINTHIANS

From Paul. God called me to be an apostle of
Christ Jesus because that is what God
wanted. Also from Sosthenes, our brother
in Christ.
2To the church of God in Corinth, to you who
have been made holy in Christ Jesus. You were
called to be God's holy people with all people everywhere who pray in the name of the Lord Jesus
Christ—their Lord and ours:
3Grace and peace to you from God our Father
and the Lord Jesus Christ.

Paul Gives Thanks to God

4I always thank my God for you because of the
grace God has given you in Christ Jesus. 5I thank
God because in Christ you have been made rich
in every way, in all your speaking and in all your
knowledge. 6Just as our witness about Christ has
been guaranteed to you, 7so you have every gift
from God while you wait for our Lord Jesus Christ
to come again. 8Jesus will keep you strong until
the end so that there will be no wrong in you on the
day our Lord Jesus Christ comes again. 9God, who
has called you to share everything with his Son,
Jesus Christ our Lord, is faithful.

Problems in the Church

10I beg you, brothers and sisters, by the name
of our Lord Jesus Christ that all of you agree with
each other and not be split into groups. I beg that
you be completely joined together by having the
same kind of thinking and the same purpose. 11My
brothers and sisters, some people from Chloe's
family have told me quite plainly that there are
quarrels among you. 12This is what I mean: One of
you says, "I follow Paul"; another says, "I follow
Apollos"; another says, "I follow Peter"; and

Ruins of the city of Corinth

another says, "I follow Christ." 13Christ has been
divided up into different groups! Did Paul die on
the cross for you? No! Were you baptized in the
name of Paul? No! 14I thank God I did not baptize
any of you except Crispus and Gaius 15so that
now no one can say you were baptized in my
name. 16(I also baptized the family of Stephanas,
but I do not remember that I baptized anyone
else.) 17Christ did not send me to baptize people
but to preach the Good News. And he sent me to
preach the Good News without using words of
human wisdom so that the cross of Christ would
not lose its power.

Christ Is God's Power and Wisdom

18The teaching about the cross is foolishness to
those who are being lost, but to us who are being
saved it is the power of God. 19It is written in the
Scriptures:

"I will cause the wise men to lose their wisdom;
I will make the wise men unable to
understand." *Isaiah 29:14*

20Where is the wise person? Where is the educated person? Where is the skilled talker of this
world? God has made the wisdom of the world foolish. 21In the wisdom of God the world did not know
God through its own wisdom. So God chose to
use the message that sounds foolish to save those
who believe. 22The Jews ask for miracles, and the
Greeks want wisdom. 23But we preach a crucified

1:2 Incarnation: 1 Corinthians 1:24
1:2 Lordship: 1 Corinthians 8:5–6
1:7–8 It is customary for Paul to use the thanksgiving section of his letters to introduce topics that will be important in the letter as a whole. In light of the letter as a whole, it is almost humorous to read Paul's positive comments about gifts from God or about how the Corinthians are waiting for Jesus to come again. In fact, the Corinthians are having a hard time with spiritual gifts (see 1 Corinthians 12–14), and they are not doing very well at waiting for Jesus to return (see 1 Corinthians 15).
1:8 Perseverance: 1 Corinthians 15:2
1:9 Fellowship: 1 Corinthians 10:20–21
1:10 *brothers and sisters.* Although the Greek text says "brothers" here and throughout this book, Paul's words were meant for the entire church, including men and women.
1:12 Leadership: 1 Corinthians 3:1–23
1:13 Unity: 1 Corinthians 10:17
1:12–17 Paul is not attacking the practice of baptism, but the specific Corinthian problem of factions dividing over church leadership.
1:17 *cross.* Paul uses the cross as a picture of the Good News, the story of Christ's death and rising from the dead for people's sins. The cross, or Christ's death, was God's way to save people.
1:17 Baptism: 1 Corinthians 12:13
1:19 Wisdom: Colossians 2:3
1:22–24 Paul here refers to two cultures with which he is personally very familiar. He came from a Jewish background (Philippians 3:3–6) and traveled extensively throughout the Greek-speaking world, writing his letters in Greek. From his familiarity he notes some main reasons ancient persons did not accept Christ: Some wanted to see miracles to prove the message was true, and others thought this message about Christ's death and resurrection sounded foolish. Yet Paul is adamant that this crucified Christ is the heart of the message that the earliest Christians believed and taught (1 Corinthians 1:30).

Christ. This is a big problem to the Jews, and it is foolishness to those who are not Jews. 24But Christ is the power of God and the wisdom of God to those people God has called—Jews and Greeks.∞ 25Even the foolishness of God is wiser than human wisdom, and the weakness of God is stronger than human strength.

26Brothers and sisters, look at what you were when God called you. Not many of you were wise in the way the world judges wisdom. Not many of you had great influence. Not many of you came from important families. 27But God chose the foolish things of the world to shame the wise, and he chose the weak things of the world to shame the strong. 28He chose what the world thinks is unimportant and what the world looks down on and thinks is nothing in order to destroy what the world thinks is important. 29God did this so that no one can brag in his presence. 30Because of God you are in Christ Jesus, who has become for us wisdom from God. In Christ we are put right with God, and have been made holy, and have been set free from sin. 31So, as the Scripture says, "If someone wants to brag, he should brag only about the Lord."∞

The Message of Christ's Death

2 Dear brothers and sisters, when I came to you, I did not come preaching God's secret with fancy words or a show of human wisdom. 2I decided that while I was with you I would forget about everything except Jesus Christ and his death on the cross. 3So when I came to you, I was weak and fearful and trembling. 4My teaching and preaching were not with words of human wisdom that persuade people but with proof of the power that the Spirit gives. 5This was so that your faith would be in God's power and not in human wisdom.∞

God's Wisdom

6However, I speak a wisdom to those who are mature. But this wisdom is not from this world or from the rulers of this world, who are losing their power. 7I speak God's secret wisdom, which he has kept hidden. Before the world began, God planned this wisdom for our glory. 8None of the rulers of this world understood it. If they had, they would not have crucified the Lord of glory.∞ 9But as it is written in the Scriptures:

"No one has ever seen this,
 and no one has ever heard about it.
No one has ever imagined
 what God has prepared for those
 who love him." *Isaiah 64:4*

10But God has shown us these things through the Spirit.

The Spirit searches out all things, even the deep secrets of God.∞ 11Who knows the thoughts that another person has? Only a person's spirit that lives within him knows his thoughts. It is the same with God. No one knows the thoughts of God except the Spirit of God. 12Now we did not receive the spirit of the world, but we received the Spirit that is from God so that we can know all that God has given us. 13And we speak about these things, not with words taught us by human wisdom but with words taught us by the Spirit. And so we explain spiritual truths to spiritual people. 14A person who does not have the Spirit does not accept the truths that come from the Spirit of God. That person thinks they are foolish and cannot understand them, because they can only be judged to be true by the Spirit. 15The spiritual person is able to judge all things, but no one can judge him. The Scripture says:

16"Who has known the mind of the Lord?
 Who has been able to teach him?" *Isaiah 40:13*
But we have the mind of Christ.

1:23 Jesus Christ is the source of all wisdom (Colossians 2:3), but it is not a wisdom recognized by the world. The Good News of a Savior who is fully God as well as fully human hanging on the cross to save people from their sins sounded bizarre to the non believers of Paul's world as well as our own. But this foolishness, Paul tells us, is wisdom from above.

The significance of this verse is often a puzzle for the modern-day believer because we have lost an understanding of the scandal associated with the cross of Christ.

In Deuteronomy 21:22–23, if someone died by hanging on a cross or a tree, they were cursed by God. This indeed was a big problem to Jewish people. How could the Messiah die cursed by God? To all other people it was foolishness that God incarnate would die. Throughout the New Testament, the writers had to interpret the death of Christ (John 1:29; Romans 3:25; 5:8; 1 Corinthians 15:3; Galatians 3:13–14; Ephesians 1:7; 5:2; Colossians 1:14; Hebrews 9:6–15; 1 Peter 2:21, 24; 4:13; Revelation 5:9). Through these interpretations, the New Testament writers directly addressed the "big problem" of Christ crucified.

∞**1:24 Incarnation:** 1 Corinthians 8:6

∞**1:24 The Crucifixion of Jesus (The Way of the Cross):** 1 Peter 1:6–7

∞**1:31 The Powers:** 1 Corinthians 2:6–8

1:31 *"If . . . Lord."* Quotation from Jeremiah 9:24.

∞**2:5 Paul (Saul):** 1 Corinthians 4:9–13

∞**2:5 Holy Spirit:** 1 Corinthians 2:6–10

∞**2:8 The Powers:** 1 Corinthians 15:24

∞**2:10 Holy Spirit:** Ephesians 5:18

2:12–15 First, we received "the Spirit that is from God" that we might "know" God's thoughts and "speak" those thoughts using words "taught us by the Spirit." The inexpressible becomes expressible because God's Spirit enables us to verbalize God's thoughts! And second, we received the Spirit that we might "judge all things." To judge means "to sift, to discern." By being filled with the Spirit, we are given a discernment that filters incidentals from essentials, truth from error. In other words, Christians are provided with an inner filtering system.

Following People Is Wrong

3 Brothers and sisters, in the past I could not talk to you as I talk to spiritual people. I had to talk to you as I would to people without the Spirit—babies in Christ. 2The teaching I gave you was like milk, not solid food, because you were not able to take solid food. And even now you are not ready. 3You are still not spiritual, because there is jealousy and quarreling among you, and this shows that you are not spiritual. You are acting like people of the world. 4One of you says, "I belong to Paul," and another says, "I belong to Apollos." When you say things like this, you are acting like people of the world.

5Is Apollos important? No! Is Paul important? No! We are only servants of God who helped you believe. Each one of us did the work God gave us to do. 6I planted the seed, and Apollos watered it. But God is the One who made it grow. 7So the one who plants is not important, and the one who waters is not important. Only God, who makes things grow, is important. 8The one who plants and the one who waters have the same purpose, and each will be rewarded for his own work. 9We are God's workers, working together; you are like God's farm, God's house.

10Using the gift God gave me, I laid the foundation of that house like an expert builder. Others are building on that foundation, but all people should be careful how they build on it. 11The foundation that has already been laid is Jesus Christ, and no one can lay down any other foundation. 12But if people build on that foundation, using gold, silver, jewels, wood, grass, or straw, 13their work will be clearly seen, because the Day of Judgment will make it visible. That Day will appear with fire, and the fire will test everyone's work to show what sort of work it was. 14If the building that has been put on the foundation still stands, the builder will get a reward. 15But if the building is burned up, the builder will suffer loss. The builder will be saved, but it will be as one who escaped from a fire.

16Don't you know that you are God's temple and that God's Spirit lives in you? 17If anyone destroys God's temple, God will destroy that person, because God's temple is holy and you are that temple.

18Do not fool yourselves. If you think you are wise in this world, you should become a fool so that you can become truly wise, 19because the wisdom of this world is foolishness with God. It is written in the Scriptures, "He catches those who are wise in their own clever traps." 20It is also written in the Scriptures, "The Lord knows what wise people think. He knows their thoughts are just a puff of wind." 21So you should not brag about human leaders. All things belong to you: 22Paul, Apollos, and Peter; the world, life, death, the present, and the future—all these belong to you. 23And you belong to Christ, and Christ belongs to God.

Apostles Are Servants of Christ

4 People should think of us as servants of Christ, the ones God has trusted with his secrets. 2Now in this way those who are trusted with something valuable must show they are worthy of that trust. 3As for myself, I do not care if I am judged by you or by any human court. I do not even judge myself. 4I know of no wrong I have done, but this does not make me right before the Lord. The Lord is the One who judges me. 5So do not judge before the right time; wait until the Lord comes. He will bring to light things that are now hidden in darkness, and will make known the secret purposes of people's hearts. Then God will praise each one of them.

6Brothers and sisters, I have used Apollos and myself as examples so you could learn through us the meaning of the saying, "Follow only what is written in the Scriptures." Then you will not be more proud of one person than another. 7Who says you are better than others? What do you have that was not given to you? And if it was given to you, why do you brag as if you did not receive it as a gift?

8You think you already have everything you need. You think you are rich. You think you have become kings without us. I wish you really were kings so we could be kings together with you. 9But

3:3 Jealousy: Galatians 5:20
3:5 Servant of the Lord: 2 Corinthians 6:4–10
3:13 *Day of Judgment.* The day Christ will come to judge all people and take his people home to live with him.
3:13 Test/Temptation: 2 Corinthians 13:5–8
3:15 Work: 1 Corinthians 4:12
3:16–17 God's special presence had been reserved for the holy of holies in the Temple. Now his presence can be found inside every believer through the indwelling of the Holy Spirit. The Temple built with hands was considered holy. Our bodies must also be kept holy since God's Spirit lives in our bodies, making our bodies the temple of the Holy Spirit.
3:19 *"He . . . traps."* Quotation from Job 5:13.
3:20 *"The Lord . . . wind."* Quotation from Psalm 94:11.
3:23 Leadership: 1 Corinthians 4:16
4:1 Service: 1 Corinthians 10:24
4:1 Faithfulness is a key ingredient in the fulfillment of a steward's responsibilities. Both the Old and New Testaments require the steward to be faithful to God and his Word in both action and attitude. A faithful steward will remember that he is the manager and that God is the owner and provider. The faithful steward can only succeed as a co-worker with God, being faithful to his instructions.
4:3 Anti-Christ (Enemy of Christ): 2 John 7
4:5 Darkness: 1 Thessalonians 5:4

it seems to me that God has put us apostles in last place, like those sentenced to die. We are like a show for the whole world to see—angels and people. 10We are fools for Christ's sake, but you are very wise in Christ. We are weak, but you are strong. You receive honor, but we are shamed. 11Even to this very hour we do not have enough to eat or drink or to wear. We are often beaten, and we have no homes in which to live. 12We work hard with our own hands for our food. When people curse us, we bless them. When they hurt us, we put up with it. 13When they tell evil lies about us, we speak nice words about them. Even today, we are treated as though we were the garbage of the world—the filth of the earth.

14I am not trying to make you feel ashamed. I am writing this to give you a warning as my own dear children. 15For though you may have ten thousand teachers in Christ, you do not have many fathers. Through the Good News I became your father in Christ Jesus, 16so I beg you, please follow my example. 17That is why I am sending to you Timothy, my son in the Lord. I love Timothy, and he is faithful. He will help you remember my way of life in Christ Jesus, just as I teach it in all the churches everywhere.

18Some of you have become proud, thinking that I will not come to you again. 19But I will come to you very soon if the Lord wishes. Then I will know what the proud ones do, not what they say, 20because the kingdom of God is present not in talk but in power. 21Which do you want: that I come to you with punishment or with love and gentleness?

Wickedness in the Church

5 It is actually being said that there is sexual sin among you. And it is a kind that does not happen even among people who do not know God. A man there has his father's wife. 2And you are proud! You should have been filled with sadness so that the man who did this should be put out of your group. 3I am not there with you in person, but I am with you in spirit. And I have already judged the man who did that sin as if I were really there. 4When you meet together in the name of our Lord Jesus, and I meet with you in spirit with the power of our Lord Jesus, 5then hand this man over to Satan. So his sinful self will be destroyed, and his spirit will be saved on the day of the Lord.

6Your bragging is not good. You know the saying, "Just a little yeast makes the whole batch of dough rise." 7Take out all the old yeast so that you will be a new batch of dough without yeast, which you really are. For Christ, our Passover lamb, has been sacrificed. 8So let us celebrate this feast, but not with the bread that has the old yeast—the yeast of sin and wickedness. Let us celebrate this feast with the bread that has no yeast—the bread of goodness and truth.

9I wrote you in my earlier letter not to associate with those who sin sexually. 10But I did not mean you should not associate with those of this world who sin sexually, or with the greedy, or robbers, or those who worship idols. To get away from them you would have to leave this world. 11I am writing to tell you that you must not associate with those who call themselves believers in Christ but who sin sexually, or are greedy, or worship idols, or abuse others with words, or get drunk, or cheat people. Do not even eat with people like that.

12-13It is not my business to judge those who are not part of the church. God will judge them. But you must judge the people who are part of the church. The Scripture says, "You must get rid of the evil person among you."

Judging Problems Among Christians

6 When you have something against another Christian, how can you bring yourself to go before judges who are not right with God? Why do you not let God's people decide who is right? 2Surely you know that God's people will judge the world. So if you are to judge the world, are you not able to judge small cases as well? 3You know that in the future we will judge angels, so surely we can judge the ordinary things of this life. 4If you have ordinary cases that must be judged, are you going to appoint people as judges who mean nothing to the church? 5I say this to shame you. Surely there is someone among you wise enough to judge a complaint between believers. 6But now one believer goes to court against another believer—and you do this in front of unbelievers!

4:10 Self-Control: 1 Corinthians 7
4:12 Curse: Galatians 3:10
4:12 Work: 1 Corinthians 9
4:13 Martyrdom: 1 Corinthians 13:3
4:13 Paul (Saul): 1 Corinthians 7:7–8
4:16 Leadership: 1 Corinthians 11:1
5:5 Authority: 1 Corinthians 7:6–7
5:5 Day of the Lord: 2 Peter 3:10
5:5 Salvation: Galatians 5:1
5:5 *sinful self.* Literally, "flesh." This could also mean his body.

5:8 Feasts/Festivals: See article on page 220.
5:11 Greed: 1 Corinthians 6:9–10

6:1–8 We live in a society where people are quick to take each other to court, but Christians should not take other Christians to court because it is a bad testimony to unbelievers. Since Christians will one day judge angels, they should be able to find someone among them who is wise enough to judge a complaint between believers. Christians should be able to resolve conflict more successfully than unbelievers.

6:13 *"You . . . you."* Quotation from Deuteronomy 17:7; 19:19; 22:21, 24; 24:7.

7The fact that you have lawsuits against each other shows that you are already defeated. Why not let yourselves be wronged? Why not let yourselves be cheated? 8But you yourselves do wrong and cheat, and you do this to other believers!

9-10Surely you know that the people who do wrong will not inherit God's kingdom. Do not be fooled. Those who sin sexually, worship idols, take part in adultery, those who are male prostitutes, or men who have sexual relations with other men, those who steal, are greedy, get drunk, lie about others, or rob—these people will not inherit God's kingdom. 11In the past, some of you were like that, but you were washed clean. You were made holy, and you were made right with God in the name of the Lord Jesus Christ and in the Spirit of our God.

Use Your Bodies for God's Glory

12"I am allowed to do all things," but all things are not good for me to do. "I am allowed to do all things," but I will not let anything make me its slave. 13"Food is for the stomach, and the stomach for food," but God will destroy them both. The body is not for sexual sin but for the Lord, and the Lord is for the body. 14By his power God has raised the Lord from the dead and will also raise us from the dead. 15Surely you know that your bodies are parts of Christ himself. So I must never take the parts of Christ and join them to a prostitute! 16It is written in the Scriptures, "The two will become one body." So you should know that anyone who joins with a prostitute becomes one body with the prostitute. 17But the one who joins with the Lord is one spirit with the Lord.

18So run away from sexual sin. Every other sin people do is outside their bodies, but those who sin sexually sin against their own bodies. 19You should know that your body is a temple for the Holy Spirit who is in you. You have received the Holy Spirit from God. So you do not belong to yourselves, 20because you were bought by God for a price. So honor God with your bodies.

About Marriage

7 Now I will discuss the things you wrote me about. It is good for a man not to have sexual relations with a woman. 2But because sexual sin is a danger, each man should have his own wife, and each woman should have her own husband. 3The husband should give his wife all that he owes her as his wife. And the wife should give her husband all that she owes him as her husband. 4The wife does not have full rights over her own body; her husband shares them. And the husband does not have full rights over his own body; his wife shares them. 5Do not refuse to give your bodies to each other, unless you both agree to stay away from sexual relations for a time so you can give your time to prayer. Then come together again so Satan cannot tempt you because of a lack of self-control. 6I say this to give you permission to stay away from sexual relations for a time. It is not a command to do so. 7I wish that everyone were like me, but each person has his own gift from God. One has one gift, another has another gift.

8Now for those who are not married and for the widows I say this: It is good for them to stay unmarried as I am. 9But if they cannot control themselves, they should marry. It is better to marry than to burn with sexual desire.

10Now I give this command for the married people. (The command is not from me; it is from the Lord.) A wife should not leave her husband. 11But if she does leave, she must not marry again, or she should make up with her husband. Also the husband should not divorce his wife.

6:9 Adultery is a sin that is mentioned frequently in both the New Testament and the Old Testament. It refers to sexual intimacy apart from your spouse. It never concerns only those people actually involved, but other family members and, most importantly, God himself. Adultery is ultimately a sin against God.

6:10 Alcohol: 1 Timothy 5:23

6:10 Greed: Ephesians 5:3

6:10 Homosexuality: 1 Timothy 1:10

6:12 Since the physical world is morally neutral, it can be used for good or evil. The conscience of the believer is under no prior legislative bondage as he approaches this world. But what is permitted generally may not be permitted in the life of a particular believer in a particular situation. Whatever disrupts his communion with God or weakens his appetite for the Bible or dulls his concern for others must be set aside. The spiritual health and well-being of the person takes its place alongside the glory of God as a major consideration in Christian ethics.

6:15 Body of Christ: 1 Corinthians 10:17

6:16 *"The two . . . body."* Quotation from Genesis 2:24.

6:19 Paul is concerned because the Corinthians are not taking the sins of their individual members seriously, but it is not easy to capture the sense of Paul's words here. His explanation actually refers to "you all" (plural) rather than to "you" (singular). It is not, then, that each Christian is the temple of the Spirit, but that Christians as a body of believers make up the temple of the Holy Spirit. This means that the sin committed by one believer affects them all; the sin of one believer could make the whole church an unsuitable home for the Holy Spirit.

6:20 Body/Flesh: 1 Corinthians 15:35–54

6:20 Stewardship: 1 Corinthians 16:1–2

7:1 The idea that a man should not have sexual relations with a woman is not Paul's. Rather, Paul is taking up the issues raised by the Corinthians: It is they (or at least some of them) who want to forbid sexual relations. Paul replies by agreeing that celibacy is a good thing (1 Corinthians 7:7, 32–35), but also noting that within marriage sexual relations are perfectly appropriate.

7:7 Authority: See article on page 1142.

7:8 Celibacy: 1 Corinthians 7:25–26

7:8 Paul (Saul): 1 Corinthians 9:1–27

12 For all the others I say this (I am saying this, not
the Lord): If a Christian man has a wife who is not
a believer, and she is happy to live with him, he
must not divorce her. 13 And if a Christian woman
has a husband who is not a believer, and he is
happy to live with her, she must not divorce him.
14 The husband who is not a believer is made holy
through his believing wife. And the wife who is not
a believer is made holy through her believing husband. If this were not true, your children would not
be clean, but now your children are holy.
15 But if those who are not believers decide to
leave, let them leave. When this happens, the
Christian man or woman is free. But God called us
to live in peace. 16 Wife, you don't know; maybe you
will save your husband. And husband, you don't
know; maybe you will save your wife.

Live as God Called You

17 But in any case each one of you should continue to live the way God has given you to live—
the way you were when God called you. This is a
rule I make in all the churches. 18 If a man was
already circumcised when he was called, he should
not undo his circumcision. If a man was without
circumcision when he was called, he should not be
circumcised. 19 It is not important if a man is circumcised or not. The important thing is obeying
God's commands.⚭ 20 Each one of you should stay
the way you were when God called you. 21 If you
were a slave when God called you, do not let that
bother you. But if you can be free, then make good
use of your freedom. 22 Those who were slaves when
the Lord called them are free persons who belong
to the Lord. In the same way, those who were free
when they were called are now Christ's slaves.
23 You all were bought at a great price, so do not
become slaves of people. 24 Brothers and sisters,
each of you should stay as you were when you were
called, and stay there with God.⚭

Questions About Getting Married

25 Now I write about people who are not married.
I have no command from the Lord about this; I give
my opinion. But I can be trusted, because the Lord
has shown me mercy. 26 The present time is a time
of trouble, so I think it is good for you to stay the
way you are.⚭ 27 If you have a wife, do not try to
become free from her. If you are not married, do
not try to find a wife. 28 But if you decide to marry,
you have not sinned. And if a girl who has never
married decides to marry, she has not sinned. But
those who marry will have trouble in this life, and
I want you to be free from trouble.
29 Brothers and sisters, this is what I mean: We
do not have much time left. So starting now, those
who have wives should live as if they had no wives.
30 Those who are crying should live as if they were
not crying. Those who are happy should live as if
they were not happy. Those who buy things should
live as if they own nothing. 31 Those who use the
things of the world should live as if they were not
using them, because this world in its present form
will soon be gone.
32 I want you to be free from worry. A man who
is not married is busy with the Lord's work, trying
to please the Lord. 33 But a man who is married is
busy with things of the world, trying to please his
wife. 34 He must think about two things—pleasing
his wife and pleasing the Lord. A woman who is
not married or a girl who has never married is busy
with the Lord's work. She wants to be holy in body
and spirit. But a married woman is busy with
things of the world, as to how she can please her
husband.⚭ 35 I am saying this to help you, not to limit
you. But I want you to live in the right way, to give
yourselves fully to the Lord without concern for
other things.
36 If a man thinks he is not doing the right thing
with the girl he is engaged to, if she is almost past
the best age to marry and he feels he should marry
her, he should do what he wants. They should get
married. It is no sin. 37 But if a man is sure in his
mind that there is no need for marriage, and has
his own desires under control, and has decided not
to marry the one to whom he is engaged, he is
doing the right thing. 38 So the man who marries
his girl does right, but the man who does not
marry will do better.
39 A woman must stay with her husband as long
as he lives. But if her husband dies, she is free to
marry any man she wants, but she must marry in
the Lord. 40 The woman is happier if she does not
marry again. This is my opinion, but I believe I also
have God's Spirit.⚭

About Food Offered to Idols

8 Now I will write about meat that is sacrificed
to idols. We know that "we all have knowledge." Knowledge puffs you up with pride, but love
builds up. 2 If you think you know something, you

⚭**7:19 Circumcision:** Galatians 5:6
⚭**7:24 Divorce:** See article on page 761
⚭**7:24 Slavery:** Galatians 3:28
⚭**7:24 World/Worldly:** 2 Corinthians 5:19
⚭**7:26 Celibacy:** 1 Corinthians 7:32–40
⚭**7:34 Women:** 1 Corinthians 11:11–12
⚭**7:40 Celibacy:** 1 Corinthians 9:5
⚭**7:40 Marriage:** 1 Timothy 4:3
⚭**7:40 Self-Control:** See article on page 1174.
⚭**7:40 Sexuality:** Ephesians 5:25–33

do not yet know anything as you should. 3But if any
person loves God, that person is known by God.
4So this is what I say about eating meat sacrificed
to idols: We know that an idol is really nothing in
the world, and we know there is only one God.
5Even though there are things called gods, in
heaven or on earth (and there are many "gods"
and "lords"), 6for us there is only one God—our
Father. All things came from him, and we live for
him. And there is only one Lord—Jesus Christ. All
things were made through him, and we also were
made through him.
7But not all people know this. Some people are
still so used to idols that when they eat meat,
they still think of it as being sacrificed to an idol.
Because their conscience is weak, when they eat it,
they feel guilty. 8But food will not bring us closer to
God. Refusing to eat does not make us less pleasing
to God, and eating does not make us better in
God's sight.
9But be careful that your freedom does not
cause those who are weak in faith to fall into sin.
10You have "knowledge," so you eat in an idol's
temple. But someone who is weak in faith might
see you eating there and be encouraged to eat
meat sacrificed to idols while thinking it is
wrong to do so. 11This weak believer for whom
Christ died is ruined because of your "knowledge." 12When you sin against your brothers and
sisters in Christ like this and cause them to do
what they feel is wrong, you are also sinning
against Christ. 13So if the food I eat causes them to
fall into sin, I will never eat meat again so that I will
not cause any of them to sin.

Paul Is like the Other Apostles

9 I am a free man. I am an apostle. I have seen
Jesus our Lord. You people are all an example
of my work in the Lord. 2If others do not accept me
as an apostle, surely you do, because you are proof
that I am an apostle in the Lord.
3This is the answer I give people who want to
judge me:4Do we not have the right to eat and
drink? 5Do we not have the right to bring a believing wife with us when we travel as do the other
apostles and the Lord's brothers and Peter? 6Are
Barnabas and I the only ones who must work to
earn our living? 7No soldier ever serves in the
army and pays his own salary. No one ever plants
a vineyard without eating some of the grapes. No
person takes care of a flock without drinking some
of the milk.
8I do not say this by human authority; God's law
also says the same thing. 9It is written in the law of
Moses: "When an ox is working in the grain, do
not cover its mouth to keep it from eating." When
God said this, was he thinking only about oxen?
No. 10He was really talking about us. Yes, that
Scripture was written for us, because it goes on to
say: "The one who plows and the one who works
in the grain should hope to get some of the grain
for their work." 11Since we planted spiritual seed
among you, is it too much if we should harvest
from you some things for this life? 12If others have
the right to get something from you, surely we have
this right, too. But we do not use it. No, we put up
with everything ourselves so that we will not keep
anyone from believing the Good News of Christ.
13Surely you know that those who work at the
Temple get their food from the Temple, and those
who serve at the altar get part of what is offered at
the altar. 14In the same way, the Lord has commanded that those who tell the Good News should
get their living from this work.
15But I have not used any of these rights. And I
am not writing this now to get anything from you.
I would rather die than to have my reason for bragging taken away. 16Telling the Good News does not
give me any reason for bragging. Telling the Good
News is my duty—something I must do. And how
terrible it will be for me if I do not tell the Good
News. 17If I preach because it is my own choice, I
have a reward. But if I preach and it is not my
choice to do so, I am only doing the duty that was
given to me. 18So what reward do I get? This is my
reward: that when I tell the Good News I can offer
it freely. I do not use my full rights in my work of
preaching the Good News.
19I am free and belong to no one. But I make
myself a slave to all people to win as many as I can.
20To the Jews I became like a Jew to win the Jews.
I myself am not ruled by the law. But to those
who are ruled by the law I became like a person who
is ruled by the law. I did this to win those who are
ruled by the law. 21To those who are without the
law I became like a person who is without the law.
I did this to win those people who are without the
law. (But really, I am not without God's law—I
am ruled by Christ's law.) 22To those who are weak,
I became weak so I could win the weak. I have

8:6 Father: 2 Corinthians 6:18
8:6 Incarnation: 2 Corinthians 5:19
8:6 Mediator: 2 Corinthians 5:19
8:6 Lordship: 1 Corinthians 12:3
8:10 *idol's temple.* Building where a god is worshiped.
8:13 Freedom: 2 Corinthians 3:12–18
9:5 Celibacy: 1 Timothy 4:1–3
9:9 Animals: See article on page 9.
9:9 *"When an ox . . . eating."* Quotation from Deuteronomy 25:4.

become all things to all people so I could save some of them in any way possible. [23]I do all this because of the Good News and so I can share in its blessings.

[24]You know that in a race all the runners run, but only one gets the prize. So run to win! [25]All those who compete in the games use self-control so they can win a crown. That crown is an earthly thing that lasts only a short time, but our crown will never be destroyed. [26]So I do not run without a goal. I fight like a boxer who is hitting something—not just the air. [27]I treat my body hard and make it my slave so that I myself will not be disqualified after I have preached to others.

Warnings from Israel's Past

10 Brothers and sisters, I want you to know what happened to our ancestors who followed Moses. They were all under the cloud and all went through the sea. [2]They were all baptized as followers of Moses in the cloud and in the sea. [3]They all ate the same spiritual food, [4]and all drank the same spiritual drink. They drank from that spiritual rock that followed them, and that rock was Christ. [5]But God was not pleased with most of them, so they died in the desert.

[6]And these things happened as examples for us, to stop us from wanting evil things as those people did. [7]Do not worship idols, as some of them did. Just as it is written in the Scriptures: "They sat down to eat and drink, and then they got up and sinned sexually." [8]We must not take part in sexual sins, as some of them did. In one day twenty-three thousand of them died because of their sins. [9]We must not test Christ as some of them did; they were killed by snakes. [10]Do not complain as some of them did; they were killed by the angel that destroys.

[11]The things that happened to those people are examples. They were written down to teach us, because we live in a time when all these things of the past have reached their goal. [12]If you think you are strong, you should be careful not to fall. [13]The only temptation that has come to you is that which everyone has. But you can trust God, who will not permit you to be tempted more than you can stand. But when you are tempted, he will also give you a way to escape so that you will be able to stand it.

[14]So, my dear friends, run away from the worship of idols. [15]I am speaking to you as to intelligent people; judge for yourselves what I say. [16]We give thanks for the cup of blessing, which is a sharing in the blood of Christ. And the bread that we break is a sharing in the body of Christ. [17]Because there is one loaf of bread, we who are many are one body, because we all share that one loaf.

[18]Think about the Israelites: Do not those who eat the sacrifices share in the altar? [19]I do not mean that the food sacrificed to an idol is important. I do not mean that an idol is anything at all. [20]But I say that what is sacrificed to idols is offered to demons, not to God. And I do not want you to share anything with demons. [21]You cannot drink the cup of the Lord and the cup of demons also. You cannot share in the Lord's table and the table of demons. [22]Are we trying to make the Lord jealous? We are not stronger than he is, are we?

How to Use Christian Freedom

[23]"We are allowed to do all things," but all things are not good for us to do. "We are allowed to do all things," but not all things help others grow stronger. [24]Do not look out only for yourselves. Look out for the good of others also.

[25]Eat any meat that is sold in the meat market. Do not ask questions to see if it is meat you think is wrong to eat. [26]You may eat it, "because the earth belongs to the Lord, and everything in it."

[27]Those who are not believers may invite you to eat with them. If you want to go, eat anything that is put before you. Do not ask questions to see if you think it might be wrong to eat. [28]But if anyone says to you, "That food was offered to idols," do not eat it. Do not eat it because of that person who told you and because eating it might be thought to be wrong. [29]I don't mean you think it is wrong, but the other person might. But why, you ask, should my freedom be judged by someone else's conscience? [30]If I eat the meal with

9:27 Paul (Saul): 1 Corinthians 14:18–19
9:27 Work: 1 Corinthians 12
10:1–22 Apparently some Corinthians thought that if they were baptized and if they shared in the Lord's Supper, then they were free from sin. Paul uses the story of Israel's past to tell them that such thinking is wrong. We must share in Christ, not only in baptism and the Lord's Supper, but also in new ways of living in the world and with each other.
10:3 Community: James 2:1–16
10:7 *"They . . . sexually."* Quotation from Exodus 32:6.
10:16 *cup of blessing.* The cup of the fruit of the vine that Christians thank God for and drink at the Lord's Supper.
10:17 Body of Christ: 1 Corinthians 11:29
10:17 Unity: 1 Corinthians 12:4–26
10:19 Sacrifice: Philippians 2:17
10:21 Fellowship: 2 Corinthians 6:14
10:22 Table Fellowship/Lord's Supper: 1 Corinthians 10:31–33
10:24 Service: Galatians 6:2
10:25 Conscience: 1 Corinthians 10:27–28
10:26 *"because . . . it."* Quotation from Psalms 24:1; 50:12; 89:11.
10:28 Conscience: 2 Corinthians 1:12

THE PEOPLE OF GOD

1 PETER 2:9–10

Who are the people of God? What makes someone a part of God's people?
Is there a difference between the people of God in the New Testament and the Old Testament?

Peter heaps up descriptions of his readers' identity as the people of God to give them a sense of value and to encourage them in a time of persecution. They are a chosen people, priests, a holy nation.

Because of our distance from the events of the Bible, we may not fully realize the significance of being God's people. What does it *really* mean to be part of God's people?

The Beginning of God's People

Adam and Eve were the first people with whom God had a special relationship. The Lord God, after all, had made Adam and Eve in his own image and likeness (Genesis 1:27) and placed them in the Garden of Eden with the charge to bear children and rule over the created order.

But this special relationship between God and Adam and Eve was broken when the human pair broke God's commandment and ate from the tree that gives the knowledge of good and evil (Genesis 2). God could not leave their sin unpunished. After all, he is holy and righteous. Thus, Adam and Eve's disobedience resulted in a curse on all humanity. The glorious image of God in human beings was marred by sin. People became evil and desired sin more than they desired relationship with God (Genesis 6:5; Romans 1).

However, even in the midst of their sin, God brought grace to Adam and Eve and gave them the first glimpse of the Good News: "I will make you [the snake] and the woman enemies to each other. Your descendants and her descendants will be enemies. One of her descendants will crush your head, and you will bite his heel" (Genesis 3:15).

Those who follow in the way of the snake will oppose the descendants of the woman, and a descendant of the woman will be caught up in a mighty struggle with the snake. The woman's descendant will be wounded but will ultimately defeat the serpent. This look into the future points to the work of Jesus, who is a descendant of Eve, who defeated Satan on the cross (Romans 16:20; Hebrews 2:14). That is why we can consider Genesis 3:15 to be a promise of redemption and grace to sinners. Adam and Eve continue to be God's people because of the grace he has given them.

The People of God Receive an Agreement through Abraham

In Genesis 1–11, the Bible follows the story of the whole world through a vast amount of time. When we come to Genesis 12, we see the story slow down and focus on one man out of whom God is going to create a people for himself. That one man is Abraham, whom God called to be the father of a great nation. God promises Abraham descendants and land, and further he told him that all peoples would be blessed through him (Genesis 12:1–3; 15:5; 17:3–8). God also promised Abraham that "I will be your God and the God of all your descendants" (Genesis 17:7). Abraham responded to God in faith. "Abram believed the Lord. And the Lord accepted Abram's faith, and that faith made him right with God" (Genesis 15:6).

Abraham serves as an example of several things involved in becoming part of God's people: God's choice, personal faith, and covenant relationship. First, God freely chose Abraham to bless him and make him part of his people. God always chooses those who belong to him. Second, Abraham responded to God's call in faith. To be part of God's people, the person called must respond with faith. Without faith, it is impossible to please God, according to Hebrews 11:6. Third, God bound himself to his people with an agreement (covenant) and promised blessings for his people.

God Brings Salvation to his People: Moses and the Exodus

In the last part of the Book of Genesis, famine strikes the land of Canaan, and a small group of Abraham's descendants, the sons of Jacob his grandson, moved to Egypt. While in Egypt, the population of this group increased dramatically in size, and the Egyptian government used them for slave labor.

God, though, heard the suffering cries of his people: "I have seen the troubles my people have suffered in Egypt, and I have heard their cries when the Egyptian slave masters hurt them. I am concerned about their pain, and I have come down to save them from the Egyptians" (Exodus 3:7–8).

God showed his people just how completely committed he was to them because of the agreement he had made with Abraham (Exodus 2:24–25). Israel's deliverance from Egypt is the most important act of salvation in the Old Testament. In the events surrounding the Exodus, God revealed himself as someone who cares deeply for his people and fights battles to deliver them from distress.

The Law Gives Instructions about How to Relate to God

The relationship between God and his people developed further when God gave his people laws at Mount Sinai. These laws are an important part of the agreement between God and Israel.

By giving his people the Ten Commandments (Exodus 20) and other laws (Exodus 21–31), God provided his people with a framework for how sinful people can relate to a holy God. The law was just one part of God's plan to restore people to a right relationship with him.

The Effects of Sin on a Relationship with God

After God settled Israel in the land he promised to Abraham, he gave the nation a king after his own heart—King David. The Lord made a special agreement with King David that his descendants would automatically rule after him. David's descendants had the responsibility to follow God's ways; when they sinned, they would be punished (2 Samuel 7:12–14). Obedience has always been an important aspect of being part of God's family. God wants his people to enjoy fellowship with him, but the fellowship between God and people is continually broken by sin. Adam and Eve had a command to obey, and Abraham's faith was tested when God asked him to offer his son Isaac as a sacrifice (Genesis 22). The people of Israel were saved from slavery in Egypt so that they would be a holy nation and royal priesthood for God (Exodus 19:3–6). But in spite of warnings from God's prophets, his people did not remain true to him. Eventually God wiped out both the northern and southern kingdoms of Israel and Judah because their sin became too great (2 Kings 17:7–18; 2 Chronicles 36:15–21).

Hope for God's People who Remain

Throughout history, there are always those who will love and obey the true God. After the destruction of the Israelite kingdoms, God promised to restore the faithful few who remained. The prophets spoke about the Lord leading his followers back to their homeland (Isaiah 40:10–11; 43:16–21; Jeremiah 31:3–4).

Those who remained faithful to God received a marvelous promise: Look, the time is coming, says the Lord, when I will make a new agreement with the people of Israel and the people of Judah. It will not be like the agreement I made with their ancestors when I took them by the hand to bring them out of Egypt. I was a husband to them, but they broke that agreement, says the Lord. This is the agreement I will make with the people of Israel at that time, says the Lord: I will put my teachings in their minds and write them on their hearts. I will be their God, and they will be my people" (Jeremiah 31:31–33).

Jesus Christ began the new agreement through his death and resurrection. He spoke of this new covenant when he initiated the Lord's Supper. When Jesus gave the disciples the cup, he said, "This is my blood which is the new agreement that God makes with his people. This blood is poured out for many to forgive their sins" (Matthew 26:28). This new agreement is God's final answer to the problem of sin which separates people from God.

The salvation brought by Jesus was not only for the Israelite people, but for every people on the earth. The apostle John explains how men and women become part of God's people: "He [Jesus] came to the world that was his own, but his own people did not accept him. But to all who did accept him and believe in him, he gave the right to become children of God. They did not become his children in any human way—by any human parents or human desire. They were born of God" (John 1:11–13).

People who accept Christ are reborn spiritually; they are new creations (John 3:16; 2 Corinthians 5:17). The new agreement is given by the Holy Spirit, who dwells in believers and is continually changing people into the glorious image of God, which was marred by the fall of Adam and Eve (2 Corinthians 3:18).

The New Testament clarifies the importance of personal faith as a requirement for belonging to the people of God. In the Old Testament, God primarily identified himself with the Israelite people. Many Israelites misunderstood their relationship with God. They thought that simply being a descendant of Abraham would mean that they had salvation (John 8:32). These people did not surrender their hearts to God and respond to his promises in belief. But in the New Testament, it is clear that only the men and women who respond to God's call in faith belong to God's family. Paul told the church in Galatia: "So you should know that the true children of Abraham are those who have faith. You belong to Christ, so you are Abraham's descendants. You will inherit all of God's blessings because of the promise God made to Abraham" (Galatians 3:7, 29).

The people of God in the Old and New Testaments are essentially the same people. They are men and women called by God who have responded in faith and who live in a covenant relationship with him.

The people of God have a rich heritage. Understanding our history as God's family can lead to a greater appreciation for our salvation. All the believers throughout time will one day stand before God's throne and worship him together (Revelation 19:6–8).⚭

⚭**The People of God:** For additional scriptures on this topic go to Exodus 15:1–18.

thankfulness, why am I criticized because of
something for which I thank God?
31The answer is, if you eat or drink, or if you do
anything, do it all for the glory of God. 32Never
do anything that might hurt others—Jews, Greeks,
or God's church— 33just as I, also, try to please
everybody in every way. I am not trying to do what
is good for me but what is good for most people so
they can be saved.⚭

11 Follow my example, as I follow the example
of Christ.⚭

Being Under Authority

2I praise you because you remember me in everything, and you follow closely the teachings just as I
gave them to you. 3But I want you to understand
this: The head of every man is Christ, the head of
a woman is the man, and the head of Christ is God.
4Every man who prays or prophesies with his head
covered brings shame to his head. 5But every
woman who prays or prophesies with her head
uncovered brings shame to her head. She is the
same as a woman who has her head shaved. 6If a
woman does not cover her head, she should have
her hair cut off. But since it is shameful for a woman
to cut off her hair or to shave her head, she should
cover her head. 7But a man should not cover his
head, because he is the likeness and glory of God.
But woman is man's glory.⚭ 8Man did not come
from woman, but woman came from man. 9And
man was not made for woman, but woman was
made for man. 10So that is why a woman should
have a symbol of authority on her head, because of
the angels.
11But in the Lord women are not independent
of men, and men are not independent of women.
12This is true because woman came from man, but
also man is born from woman. But everything
comes from God.⚭ 13Decide this for yourselves: Is
it right for a woman to pray to God with her head
uncovered? 14Even nature itself teaches you that
wearing long hair is shameful for a man. 15But long
hair is a woman's glory. Long hair is given to her as
a covering. 16Some people may still want to argue
about this, but I would add that neither we nor the
churches of God have any other practice.

Unleavened bread and wine, shared by Christians at the Lord's Supper

The Lord's Supper

17In the things I tell you now I do not praise you,
because when you come together you do more
harm than good. 18First, I hear that when you meet
together as a church you are divided, and I believe
some of this. 19(It is necessary to have differences
among you so that it may be clear which of you
really have God's approval.) 20When you come
together, you are not really eating the Lord's
Supper. 21This is because when you eat, each person eats without waiting for the others. Some people do not get enough to eat, while others have too
much to drink. 22You can eat and drink in your own
homes! You seem to think God's church is not
important, and you embarrass those who are poor.
What should I tell you? Should I praise you? I do not
praise you for doing this.
23The teaching I gave you is the same teaching
I received from the Lord: On the night when the
Lord Jesus was handed over to be killed, he took
bread 24and gave thanks for it. Then he broke
the bread and said, "This is my body; it is for
you. Do this to remember me." 25In the same way,

⚭**10:33 Table Fellowship/Lord's Supper:** 1 Corinthians 11:17–34
⚭**11:1 Leadership:** 1 Corinthians 12:22–31
11:3 *the man.* This could also mean "her husband."
⚭**11:7 Human:** 1 Corinthians 15:49
⚭**11:12 Women:** 1 Corinthians 14:34–36
11:20 *Lord's Supper.* The meal Jesus told his followers to eat to remember him (Luke 22:14-20).
11:23–29 Each person, in friendship with other Christians, shares in Jesus' sacrifice on the cross. This is pictured by the bread (his body) and wine (his blood). During this time, Christians are to look at their relationship with Christ while they think about his great sacrifice on the cross. The celebration of the Lord's Supper, like Passover, is a remembrance and a witness. Both are feasts, or celebrations, that remember the Lord's deliverance and provide a public witness to others of how God uses the blood of a lamb to cover, or protect, his people from judgment. When we celebrate communion together, we show we are individual members of Christ's one body. By doing this act we demonstrate our faith in Christ and also our unity in him.

after they ate, Jesus took the cup. He said, "This cup is the new agreement that is sealed with the blood of my death. When you drink this, do it to remember me." 26Every time you eat this bread and drink this cup you are telling others about the Lord's death until he comes.

27So a person who eats the bread or drinks the cup of the Lord in a way that is not worthy of it will be guilty of sinning against the body and the blood of the Lord. 28Look into your own hearts before you eat the bread and drink the cup, 29because all who eat the bread and drink the cup without recognizing the body eat and drink judgment against themselves. 30That is why many in your group are sick and weak, and many have died. 31But if we judged ourselves in the right way, God would not judge us. 32But when the Lord judges us, he punishes us so that we will not be destroyed along with the world.

33So my brothers and sisters, when you come together to eat, wait for each other. 34Anyone who is too hungry should eat at home so that in meeting together you will not bring God's judgment on yourselves. I will tell you what to do about the other things when I come.

Gifts from the Holy Spirit

12 Now, brothers and sisters, I want you to understand about spiritual gifts. 2You know the way you lived before you were believers. You let yourselves be influenced and led away to worship idols—things that could not speak. 3So I want you to understand that no one who is speaking with the help of God's Spirit says, "Jesus be cursed." And no one can say, "Jesus is Lord," without the help of the Holy Spirit.

4There are different kinds of gifts, but they are all from the same Spirit. 5There are different ways to serve but the same Lord to serve. 6And there are different ways that God works through people but the same God. God works in all of us in everything we do. 7Something from the Spirit can be seen in each person, for the common good. 8The Spirit gives one person the ability to speak with wisdom, and the same Spirit gives another the ability to speak with knowledge. 9The same Spirit gives faith to one person. And, to another, that one Spirit gives gifts of healing. 10The Spirit gives to another person the power to do miracles, to another the ability to prophesy. And he gives to another the ability to know the difference between good and evil spirits. The Spirit gives one person the ability to speak in different kinds of languages and to another the ability to interpret those languages. 11One Spirit, the same Spirit, does all these things, and the Spirit decides what to give each person.

The Body of Christ Works Together

12A person's body is only one thing, but it has many parts. Though there are many parts to a body, all those parts make only one body. Christ is like that also. 13Some of us are Jews, and some are Greeks. Some of us are slaves, and some are free. But we were all baptized into one body through one Spirit. And we were all made to share in the one Spirit.

14The human body has many parts. 15The foot might say, "Because I am not a hand, I am not part of the body." But saying this would not stop the foot from being a part of the body. 16The ear might say, "Because I am not an eye, I am not part of the body." But saying this would not stop the ear from being a part of the body. 17If the whole body were an eye, it would not be able to hear. If the whole body were an ear, it would not be able to smell. 18-19If each part of the body were the same part, there would be no body. But truly God put all the parts, each one of them, in the body as he wanted them. 20So then there are many parts, but only one body.

21The eye cannot say to the hand, "I don't need you!" And the head cannot say to the foot, "I don't need you!" 22No! Those parts of the body that seem to be the weaker are really necessary. 23And the parts of the body we think are less deserving are

11:25 Agreement: Hebrews 7:22
11:26 Blood: Hebrews 9
11:26 Celebration: Revelation 19:6–11
11:27–30 Paul's concern in this larger section (11:17–34) is not with the sins of individuals but with the behavior of the whole church when they come together to share in a meal. Hence, eating or drinking "in a manner that is not worthy" has to do with the hostile relations within the church that destroy the unity of the church and pay no attention to the example of Jesus who gave his life "for us." The sickness and death about which Paul speaks in 1 Corinthians 11:30, is not due to the sins of particular individuals, but is a symptom of the cancer at work in the church as a whole! The only solution is to recognize the nature of the Body of Christ and act accordingly.
11:29 Body of Christ: Ephesians 1:22–23
11:34 Hospitality: 1 Timothy 3:2
11:34 Table Fellowship/Lord's Supper: Revelation 3:20
12:3 Lordship: 2 Corinthians 4:5
12:3 Antichrist (Enemy of Christ): 2 Thessalonians 2:3–4
12:9 Healing: 1 Corinthians 12:28
12:9 Sickness, Disease, Healing: Revelation 22:1–2
12:10 *languages.* This can also be translated "tongues."
12:11 Prophet & Prophecy: 1 Corinthians 14
12:11 Tongues: 1 Corinthians 12:27–31
12:12–31 Here the people of God are described as a body, each person having different gifts. These different gifts contribute to the good and growth of the whole body. We are not to be jealous of other people's gifts, nor are we to look down on anyone's particular role among the people of God.
12:13 Baptism: 1 Corinthians 15:29
12:13 Racism: Galatians 2:11–16

the parts to which we give the most honor. We give special respect to the parts we want to hide. [24]The more respectable parts of our body need no special care. But God put the body together and gave more honor to the parts that need it [25]so our body would not be divided. God wanted the different parts to care the same for each other. [26]If one part of the body suffers, all the other parts suffer with it. Or if one part of our body is honored, all the other parts share its honor.

[27]Together you are the body of Christ, and each one of you is a part of that body. [28]In the church God has given a place first to apostles, second to prophets, and third to teachers. Then God has given a place to those who do miracles, those who have gifts of healing, those who can help others, those who are able to govern, and those who can speak in different languages. [29]Not all are apostles. Not all are prophets. Not all are teachers. Not all do miracles. [30]Not all have gifts of healing. Not all speak in different languages. Not all interpret those languages. [31]But you should truly want to have the greater gifts.

Love Is the Greatest Gift

And now I will show you the best way of all.

13 I may speak in different languages of people or even angels. But if I do not have love, I am only a noisy bell or a crashing cymbal. [2]I may have the gift of prophecy. I may understand all the secret things of God and have all knowledge, and I may have faith so great I can move mountains. But even with all these things, if I do not have love, then I am nothing. [3]I may give away everything I have, and I may even give my body as an offering to be burned. But I gain nothing if I do not have love.

[4]Love is patient and kind. Love is not jealous, it does not brag, and it is not proud. [5]Love is not rude, is not selfish, and does not get upset with others. Love does not count up wrongs that have been done. [6]Love is not happy with evil but is happy with the truth. [7]Love patiently accepts all things. It always trusts, always hopes, and always remains strong.

[8]Love never ends. There are gifts of prophecy, but they will be ended. There are gifts of speaking in different languages, but those gifts will stop. There is the gift of knowledge, but it will come to an end. [9]The reason is that our knowledge and our ability to prophesy are not perfect. [10]But when perfection comes, the things that are not perfect will end. [11]When I was a child, I talked like a child, I thought like a child, I reasoned like a child. When I became a man, I stopped those childish ways. [12]It is the same with us. Now we see a dim reflection, as if we were looking into a mirror, but then we shall see clearly. Now I know only a part, but then I will know fully, as God has known me. [13]So these three things continue forever: faith, hope, and love. And the greatest of these is love.

Desire Spiritual Gifts

14 You should seek after love, and you should truly want to have the spiritual gifts, especially the gift of prophecy. [2]I will explain why. Those who have the gift of speaking in different languages are not speaking to people; they are speaking to God. No one understands them; they are speaking secret things through the Spirit. [3]But those who prophesy are speaking to people to give them strength, encouragement, and comfort. [4]The ones who speak in different languages are helping only themselves, but those who prophesy are helping the whole church. [5]I wish all of you had the gift of speaking in different kinds of languages, but more, I wish you would prophesy. Those who prophesy are greater than those who can only speak in different languages—unless someone is there who can explain what is said so that the whole church can be helped.

[6]Brothers and sisters, will it help you if I come to you speaking in different languages? No! It will help you only if I bring you a new truth or some new knowledge, or prophecy, or teaching. [7]It is the same as with lifeless things that make sounds—like a flute or a harp. If they do not make clear musical notes, you will not know what is being played. [8]And in a war, if the trumpet does not give a clear sound, who will prepare for battle? [9]It is the same

12:28; 13:1; 14:2 *languages.* This can also be translated "tongues."
12:26 Unity: 1 Corinthians 13
12:28 Healing: James 5:14–16
12:28 Instruction: See article on page 329.
12:31 Leadership: 1 Corinthians 14:34–35
12:31 Tongues: 1 Corinthians 13:1–10
12:31 Work: 1 Corinthians 14:1–25
13:3 *Verse 3.* Other Greek copies read: "hand over my body in order that I may brag."
13:3 Martyrdom: 2 Corinthians 4:7–18
13:10 Tongues: See article on page 1204.
13:11 Growing Old: 1 Timothy 5:1
13:12 Family: Psalm 27:10
13:13 Spirituality/Spiritual Dryness: Galatians 5:22–23
13:13 Unity: Galatians 2:11–14
14:9–12 Paul provides important principles of communication in these verses. He is discussing prophecy and the use of unknown languages to communicate to the church. If the church is to be helped by preaching (one meaning of "prophecy"), it must be clear and its meaning understood. Otherwise, it would be as if the preacher were speaking a foreign language, which helps no one.

with you. Unless you speak clearly with your tongue, no one can understand what you are saying. You will be talking into the air! 10It may be true that there are all kinds of sounds in the world, and none is without meaning. 11But unless I understand the meaning of what someone says to me, I will be a foreigner to him, and he will be a foreigner to me. 12It is the same with you. Since you want spiritual gifts very much, seek most of all to have the gifts that help the church grow stronger.

13The one who has the gift of speaking in a different language should pray for the gift to interpret what is spoken. 14If I pray in a different language, my spirit is praying, but my mind does nothing. 15So what should I do? I will pray with my spirit, but I will also pray with my mind. I will sing with my spirit, but I will also sing with my mind. 16If you praise God with your spirit, those persons there without understanding cannot say amen to your prayer of thanks, because they do not know what you are saying. 17You may be thanking God in a good way, but the other person is not helped.

18I thank God that I speak in different kinds of languages more than all of you. 19But in the church meetings I would rather speak five words I understand in order to teach others than thousands of words in a different language.∞

20Brothers and sisters, do not think like children. In evil things be like babies, but in your thinking you should be like adults. 21It is written in the Scriptures:

"With people who use strange words
 and foreign languages
I will speak to these people.
But even then they will not listen to me,"

Isaiah 28:11-12

says the Lord.

22So the gift of speaking in different kinds of languages is a proof for those who do not believe, not for those who do believe. And prophecy is for people who believe, not for those who do not believe. 23Suppose the whole church meets together and everyone speaks in different languages. If some people come in who do not understand or do not believe, they will say you are crazy. 24But suppose everyone is prophesying and some people come in who do not believe or do not understand. If everyone is prophesying, their sin will be shown to them, and they will be judged by all that they hear. 25The secret things in their hearts will be made known. So they will bow down and worship God saying, "Truly, God is with you."∞

Meetings Should Help the Church

26So, brothers and sisters, what should you do? When you meet together, one person has a song, and another has a teaching. Another has a new truth from God. Another speaks in a different language, and another person interprets that language. The purpose of all these things should be to help the church grow strong. 27When you meet together, if anyone speaks in a different language, it should be only two, or not more than three, who speak. They should speak one after the other, and someone else should interpret. 28But if there is no interpreter, then those who speak in a different language should be quiet in the church meeting. They should speak only to themselves and to God.

29Only two or three prophets should speak, and the others should judge what they say. 30If a message from God comes to another person who is sitting, the first speaker should stop. 31You can all prophesy one after the other. In this way all the people can be taught and encouraged. 32The spirits of prophets are under the control of the prophets themselves. 33God is not a God of confusion but a God of peace.

As is true in all the churches of God's people, 34women should keep quiet in the church meetings. They are not allowed to speak, but they must yield to this rule as the law says. 35If they want to learn something, they should ask their own husbands at home. It is shameful for a woman to speak in the church meeting.∞ 36Did God's teaching come from you? Or are you the only ones to whom it has come?∞

37Those who think they are prophets or spiritual persons should understand that what I am writing to you is the Lord's command. 38Those who ignore this will be ignored by God.

39So my brothers and sisters, you should truly want to prophesy. But do not stop people from using the gift of speaking in different kinds of languages. 40But let everything be done in a right and orderly way.∞

14:16 *amen.* To say amen means to agree with the things that were said.

∞**14:19 Paul (Saul):** 1 Corinthians 15:8–11

∞**14:25 Work:** Ephesians 4:7–13

14:26 *language.* This can also be translated "tongue."

14:33 Paul contrasts confusion, not with order, but peace. God is not primarily concerned that worship follow a set of rules. Rule-bound worship can be just as bad as confusion, if the Holy Spirit does not have control of the worshipers. God is concerned for the well-being and good relations of his people. Disorderly worship deprives people of the benefits of worship and gives occasion for pride, ambition, and jealousy to take the place of devotion to God in the hearts of the worshipers. Paul's point is that the Holy Spirit, who is given by the God of peace, would never lead worshipers to create chaos.

∞**14:35 Leadership:** 2 Corinthians 2:14

∞**14:36 Women:** Galatians 3:28

∞**14:40 Prophet & Prophecy:** Revelation 1:1–3

The Good News About Christ

15 Now, brothers and sisters, I want you to remember the Good News I brought to you. You received this Good News and continue strong in it. [2]And you are being saved by it if you continue believing what I told you. If you do not, then you believed for nothing.

[3]I passed on to you what I received, of which this was most important: that Christ died for our sins, as the Scriptures say; [4]that he was buried and was raised to life on the third day as the Scriptures say; [5]and that he was seen by Peter and then by the twelve apostles. [6]After that, Jesus was seen by more than five hundred of the believers at the same time. Most of them are still living today, but some have died. [7]Then he was seen by James and later by all the apostles. [8]Last of all he was seen by me—as by a person not born at the normal time. [9]All the other apostles are greater than I am. I am not even good enough to be called an apostle, because I persecuted the church of God. [10]But God's grace has made me what I am, and his grace to me was not wasted. I worked harder than all the other apostles. (But it was not I really; it was God's grace that was with me.) [11]So if I preached to you or the other apostles preached to you, we all preach the same thing, and this is what you believed.

We Will Be Raised from the Dead

[12]Now since we preached that Christ was raised from the dead, why do some of you say that people will not be raised from the dead? [13]If no one is ever raised from the dead, then Christ has not been raised. [14]And if Christ has not been raised, then our preaching is worth nothing, and your faith is worth nothing. [15]And also, we are guilty of lying about God, because we testified of him that he raised Christ from the dead. But if people are not raised from the dead, then God never raised Christ. [16]If the dead are not raised, Christ has not been raised either. [17]And if Christ has not been raised, then your faith has nothing to it; you are still guilty of your sins. [18]And those in Christ who have already died are lost. [19]If our hope in Christ is for this life only, we should be pitied more than anyone else in the world.

[20]But Christ has truly been raised from the dead—the first one and proof that those who sleep in death will also be raised. [21]Death has come because of what one man did, but the rising from death also comes because of one man. [22]In Adam all of us die. In the same way, in Christ all of us will be made alive again. [23]But everyone will be raised to life in the right order. Christ was first to be raised. When Christ comes again, those who belong to him will be raised to life, [24]and then the end will come. At that time Christ will destroy all rulers, authorities, and powers, and he will hand over the kingdom to God the Father. [25]Christ must rule until he puts all enemies under his control. [26]The last enemy to be destroyed will be death. [27]The Scripture says that God put all things under his control. When it says "all things" are under him, it is clear this does not include God himself. God is the One who put everything under his control. [28]After everything has been put under the Son, then he will put himself under God, who had put all things under him. Then God will be the complete ruler over everything.

[29]If the dead are never raised, what will people do who are being baptized for the dead? If the dead are not raised at all, why are people being baptized for them?

[30]And what about us? Why do we put ourselves in danger every hour? [31]I die every day. That is true, brothers and sisters, just as it is true that I brag about you in Christ Jesus our Lord. [32]If I fought wild animals in Ephesus only with human hopes, I have gained nothing. If the dead are not raised, "Let us eat and drink, because tomorrow we will die."

[33]Do not be fooled: "Bad friends will ruin good habits." [34]Come back to your right way of thinking and stop sinning. Some of you do not know God—I say this to shame you.

15:2 Perseverance: 2 Corinthians 1:21
15:3–5 Here Paul summarizes the heart of the Good News in a short form that tells what the "faith" is which leads people to trust the Lord. This is the message about the death and resurrection of Christ and the forgiveness of sins it brings. It is also called the Gospel.
15:4 Evangelism: 2 Timothy 4:5
15:4 Gospel/Good News: 1 Peter 4:17
15:5 Peter: 2 Peter 1:17–18
15:11 Paul (Saul): 1 Corinthians 15:30–32
15:22 Adam: Jude 14
15:22 Creation/New Creation: See article on page 1234.
15:22 The Fall: 1 Corinthians 15:45–49
15:24 The Powers: Ephesians 1:21
15:26 Death: 2 Corinthians 5:1–5
15:27 *God put . . . control.* From Psalm 8:6.
15:28 Satan/Satanism: 2 Corinthians 4:4
15:29 This is a very difficult verse to understand, but one of two possibilities makes the most sense. Most likely, the Corinthians had a practice of baptism for the dead that Paul neither approves nor disapproves of here, but he uses their practice to support his teaching about resurrection from the dead. Another possibility is that Paul uses "dead" in a symbolic way to refer to those who are "dead in their sins" (see Colossians 2:13).
15:29 Baptism: Galatians 3:26–28
15:32 Paul (Saul): 1 Corinthians 16:1–9
15:32 *"Let us . . . die."* Quotation from Isaiah 22:13; 56:12.

What Kind of Body Will We Have?

[35]But someone may ask, "How are the dead raised? What kind of body will they have?" [36]Foolish person! When you sow a seed, it must die in the ground before it can live and grow. [37]And when you sow it, it does not have the same "body" it will have later. What you sow is only a bare seed, maybe wheat or something else. [38]But God gives it a body that he has planned for it, and God gives each kind of seed its own body. [39]All things made of flesh are not the same: People have one kind of flesh, animals have another, birds have another, and fish have another. [40]Also there are heavenly bodies and earthly bodies. But the beauty of the heavenly bodies is one kind, and the beauty of the earthly bodies is another. [41]The sun has one kind of beauty, the moon has another beauty, and the stars have another. And each star is different in its beauty.

[42]It is the same with the dead who are raised to life. The body that is "planted" will ruin and decay, but it is raised to a life that cannot be destroyed. [43]When the body is "planted," it is without honor, but it is raised in glory. When the body is "planted," it is weak, but when it is raised, it is powerful. [44]The body that is "planted" is a physical body. When it is raised, it is a spiritual body.

There is a physical body, and there is also a spiritual body. [45]It is written in the Scriptures: "The first man, Adam, became a living person." But the last Adam became a spirit that gives life. [46]The spiritual did not come first, but the physical and then the spiritual. [47]The first man came from the dust of the earth. The second man came from heaven. [48]People who belong to the earth are like the first man of earth. But those people who belong to heaven are like the man of heaven. [49]Just as we were made like the man of earth, so we will also be made like the man of heaven.

[50]I tell you this, brothers and sisters: Flesh and blood cannot have a part in the kingdom of God. Something that will ruin cannot have a part in something that never ruins. [51]But look! I tell you this secret: We will not all sleep in death, but we will all be changed. [52]It will take only a second—as quickly as an eye blinks—when the last trumpet sounds. The trumpet will sound, and those who have died will be raised to live forever, and we will all be changed. [53]This body that can be destroyed must clothe itself with something that can never be destroyed. And this body that dies must clothe itself with something that can never die. [54]So this body that can be destroyed will clothe itself with that which can never be destroyed, and this body that dies will clothe itself with that which can never die. When this happens, this Scripture will be made true:

"Death is destroyed forever in victory."

Isaiah 25:8

[55]"Death, where is your victory?
Death, where is your pain?"

Hosea 13:14

[56]Death's power to hurt is sin, and the power of sin is the law. [57]But we thank God! He gives us the victory through our Lord Jesus Christ.

[58]So my dear brothers and sisters, stand strong. Do not let anything change you. Always give yourselves fully to the work of the Lord, because you know that your work in the Lord is never wasted.

The Gift for Other Believers

16 Now I will write about the collection of money for God's people. Do the same thing I told the Galatian churches to do: [2]On the first day of every week, each one of you should put aside money as you have been blessed. Save it up so you will not have to collect money after I come. [3]When I arrive, I will send whomever you approve to take your gift to Jerusalem. I will send them with letters of introduction, [4]and if it seems good for me to go also, they will go along with me.

Paul's Plans

[5]I plan to go through Macedonia, so I will come to you after I go through there. [6]Perhaps I will stay with you for a time or even all winter. Then you can help me on my trip, wherever I go. [7]I do not want to see you now just in passing. I hope to stay a longer time with you if the Lord allows it. [8]But I will stay at Ephesus until Pentecost, [9]because a

15:45 *"The first . . . person."* Quotation from Genesis 2:7.
15:49 At present, the bodies of humans are natural bodies like that of the first man, Adam, who was made from the dust of the earth. In the resurrection, the bodies of Christians will be turned into heaven-like bodies like that of the second Adam, Jesus.
15:49 Human: 2 Corinthians 4:4
15:49 The Fall: 1 Timothy 2:12–14
15:54 Body/Flesh: 2 Corinthians 4:10–12
15:58 Leisure: See article on page 892.
15:58 Immortality: 1 Thessalonians 4
16:1 Throughout his letters, Paul encourages the church to participate in this "collection." Remember that these churches are made up primarily of non-Jewish believers. And the collection was for churches in Palestine made up primarily of Jewish believers. So we see why the collection was so important. The collection has become for Paul a visible symbol of the unity of people in Christ, even of people who are normally separated in the larger world.
16:2 Stewardship: Ephesians 4:11–12

good opportunity for a great and growing work has
been given to me now. And there are many people
working against me.
10If Timothy comes to you, see to it that he has
nothing to fear with you, because he is working for
the Lord just as I am. 11So none of you should treat
Timothy as unimportant, but help him on his trip in
peace so that he can come back to me. I am expecting him to come with the brothers.
12Now about our brother Apollos: I strongly
encouraged him to visit you with the other brothers. He did not at all want to come now; he will
come when he has the opportunity.

Paul Ends His Letter

13Be alert. Continue strong in the faith. Have
courage, and be strong. 14Do everything in love.
15You know that the family of Stephanas were
the first believers in Southern Greece and that they
have given themselves to the service of God's
people. I ask you, brothers and sisters, 16to follow
the leading of people like these and anyone else
who works and serves with them.
17I am happy that Stephanas, Fortunatus, and
Achaicus have come. You are not here, but they
have filled your place. 18They have refreshed my
spirit and yours. You should recognize the value
of people like these.
19The churches in the country of Asia send
greetings to you. Aquila and Priscilla greet you in
the Lord, as does the church that meets in their
house. 20All the brothers and sisters here send
greetings. Give each other a holy kiss when you
meet.
21I, Paul, am writing this greeting with my own
hand.
22If anyone does not love the Lord, let him be
separated from God—lost forever!
Come, O Lord!
23The grace of the Lord Jesus be with you.
24My love be with all of you in Christ Jesus.

16:9 Paul (Saul): 1 Corinthians 16:21
16:9 Time: Ephesians 5:15–17
16:12 Tithe: See article on page 353.
16:21 Paul (Saul): 2 Corinthians 1–13

Notes:

INTRODUCTION TO THE BOOK OF 2 CORINTHIANS

Paul Answers Those Who Accuse Him

WHO WROTE THIS BOOK?

The author of this letter is the apostle Paul.

TO WHOM WAS THIS BOOK WRITTEN?

The Book of 2 Corinthians was addressed to the Corinthian believers in particular, but its message included all believers in Greece (Achaia).

WHERE WAS IT WRITTEN?

Based on internal evidence, it is likely that 2 Corinthians was written in Macedonia.

WHEN WAS IT WRITTEN?

It appears that 2 Corinthians was written later in the same year as 1 Corinthians—A.D. 55.

WHAT IS THIS BOOK ABOUT?

A note of thanksgiving for a report from Titus about the change of heart and behavior among Christians in Corinth opens this letter. It then offers an explanation for Paul's delayed visit and praise to God for his comfort and encouragement in the midst of Paul's suffering. Paul defends his personal integrity and authority as an apostle and encourages the Corinthians to complete the collection for the poor in Jerusalem. Finally, he gives warnings to the false teachers that he is going to exercise his authority as an apostle when he comes.

WHY WAS THIS BOOK WRITTEN?

Second Corinthians was written by Paul to encourage the Corinthians in the changes they had made in their lives. He also wrote to exhort them to carry out their pledge and to defend his authority as an apostle.

SO WHAT DOES THIS BOOK MEAN TO US?

Like the Corinthian Christians, each of us also have areas in our lives that need improvement. Reading Second Corinthians gives us encouragement to continue on that path of personal improvement and spiritual growth. Likewise, we need to be sympathetic and encouraging to our fellow Christians who are trying to make positive changes in their lives as well. In addition, we need to exhibit a Christlike concern and understanding of the sacrifices that God's servants make in their work for Christ and his church. Elders of the church, especially, deserve our respect for their God-given authority and leadership. In truth, all Christians using their special gifts and talents from the Lord should be encouraged to continue praising him in their unique ways so that, as Paul says in his first letter, we can "save some of them [the lost] in any way possible" (1 Corinthians 9:22).

SUMMARY:

Following the delivery of Paul's first letter to the Corinthians, Paul has encountered a new set of extremely difficult problems with these Christians. Most importantly, they have come to doubt his care for them, wonder if he is even an apostle, and question whether the message he preached to them was genuine. In 2 Corinthians, then, Paul is very much on the defensive, and we gain important insight into his understanding of himself and the message he proclaimed.

The tension between Paul and the Corinthians is related, first, to his change in travel plans—an issue he takes up in the opening chapters of this letter. More to the point, between the writing of 1 Corinthians and of this letter, perhaps a year later, other missionaries have come to Corinth and caused trouble for Paul. Although they are Christians, they do not share with Paul all of the same ideas about the Christian message. In 2 Corinthians, then, we are allowed to listen in on one side of the conversation as early Christian leaders struggle to understand as fully as they can the nature of the Good News.

Paul takes these outsiders, these intruders, to task for a variety of reasons. They "sell the word of God for a profit" (2:17), for example. And they look too much on outside appearances and not enough on what God is doing on the inside of his people. Most importantly, Paul believes they preach "a different Jesus" (11:4). As he demonstrates throughout the letter, these intruders identify with Jesus only in their showy signs, their powerful works, their extraordinary spiritual experiences. Even though Paul could talk about these same kinds of experiences, he does not do so. Instead, he insists that the true way to prove you follow Jesus is to identify with Jesus in his suffering and rejection. For this reason, Paul provides lists of his own suffering (for example, 6:3–10; 23–33).

In other words, in 2 Corinthians Paul is contending with Christians who would like to think that the Christian life is about success, power, and fame. Because Paul has suffered so much, because he has been rejected by many local Jewish groups, been thrown in prison, whipped, and so on, these Christians doubt whether he really is a Christian leader. Paul's position is that those who serve Jesus can and should expect the same treatment he received: misunderstanding, rejection, suffering.

2 Corinthians

From Paul, an apostle of Christ Jesus. I am an apostle because that is what God wanted. Also from Timothy our brother in Christ.

To the church of God in Corinth, and to all of God's people everywhere in Southern Greece:

[2]Grace and peace to you from God our Father and the Lord Jesus Christ.

Paul Gives Thanks to God

[3]Praise be to the God and Father of our Lord Jesus Christ. God is the Father who is full of mercy and all comfort. [4]He comforts us every time we have trouble, so when others have trouble, we can comfort them with the same comfort God gives us. [5]We share in the many sufferings of Christ. In the same way, much comfort comes to us through Christ. [6]If we have troubles, it is for your comfort and salvation, and if we have comfort, you also have comfort. This helps you to accept patiently the same sufferings we have. [7]Our hope for you is strong, knowing that you share in our sufferings and also in the comfort we receive.

[8]Brothers and sisters, we want you to know about the trouble we suffered in Asia. We had great burdens there that were beyond our own strength. We even gave up hope of living. [9]Truly, in our own hearts we believed we would die. But this happened so we would not trust in ourselves but in God, who raises people from the dead. [10]God saved us from these great dangers of death, and he will continue to save us. We have put our hope in him, and he will save us again. [11]And you can help us with your prayers. Then many people will give thanks for us—that God blessed us because of their many prayers.

The Change in Paul's Plans

[12]This is what we are proud of, and I can say it with a clear conscience: In everything we have done in the world, and especially with you, we have had an honest and sincere heart from God. We did this by God's grace, not by the kind of wisdom the world has. [13-14]We write to you only what you can read and understand. And I hope that as you have understood some things about us, you may come to know everything about us. Then you can be proud of us, as we will be proud of you on the day our Lord Jesus Christ comes again.

[15]I was so sure of all this that I made plans to visit you first so you could be blessed twice. [16]I planned to visit you on my way to Macedonia and again on my way back. I wanted to get help from you for my trip to Judea. [17]Do you think that I made these plans without really meaning it? Or maybe you think I make plans as the world does, so that I say yes, yes and at the same time no, no.

[18]But if you can believe God, you can believe that what we tell you is never both yes and no. [19]The Son of God, Jesus Christ, that Silas and Timothy and I preached to you, was not yes and no. In Christ it has always been yes. [20]The yes to all of God's promises is in Christ, and through Christ we say yes to the glory of God. [21]Remember, God is the One who makes you and us strong in Christ. God made us his chosen people. [22]He put his mark on us to show that we are his, and he put his Spirit in our hearts to be a guarantee for all he has promised.

[23]I tell you this, and I ask God to be my witness that this is true: The reason I did not come back to Corinth was to keep you from being punished or hurt. [24]We are not trying to control your faith. You are strong in faith. But we are workers with you for your own joy.

2 So I decided that my next visit to you would not be another one to make you sad. [2]If I make you sad, who will make me glad? Only you can make me glad—particularly the person whom I made sad. [3]I wrote you a letter for this reason: that when I came to you I would not be made sad by the people who should make me happy. I felt sure of all of you, that you would share my joy. [4]When I wrote to you before, I was very troubled and unhappy in my heart, and I wrote with many tears. I did not write to make you sad, but to let you know how much I love you.

Forgive the Sinner

[5]Someone there among you has caused sadness, not to me, but to all of you. I mean he caused sadness to all in some way. (I do not want to make it sound worse than it really is.) [6]The punishment that

1:3–4 If we have lost a loved one and found the Lord to be faithful in our time of grief, we can share the comfort we have received with others. Each of us who has been brought through the valley of the shadow of death, who has been held up and lifted up by the grace of God, can put an understanding arm around a grieving brother and sister. We can weep with them, share God's Word and our experience with them, and encourage them to trust the Lord. We have been there, and he has taken us through.

1:7 Suffering: 2 Corinthians 4:17

1:8 *Brothers and sisters.* Although the Greek text says "Brothers" here and throughout this book, Paul's words were meant for the entire church, including men and women.

1:12 Conscience: 2 Corinthians 4:2

1:21 Perseverance: Galatians 6:9

1:22 Land/Inheritance: Galatians 5:22–25

most of you gave him is enough for him. 7But now you should forgive him and comfort him to keep him from having too much sadness and giving up completely. 8So I beg you to show that you love him. 9I wrote you to test you and to see if you obey in everything. 10If you forgive someone, I also forgive him. And what I have forgiven—if I had anything to forgive—I forgave it for you, as if Christ were with me. 11I did this so that Satan would not win anything from us, because we know very well what Satan's plans are.

Paul's Concern in Troas

12When I came to Troas to preach the Good News of Christ, the Lord gave me a good opportunity there. 13But I had no peace, because I did not find my brother Titus. So I said good-bye to them at Troas and went to Macedonia.

Victory Through Christ

14But thanks be to God, who always leads us in victory through Christ. God uses us to spread his knowledge everywhere like a sweet-smelling perfume. 15Our offering to God is this: We are the sweet smell of Christ among those who are being saved and among those who are being lost. 16To those who are lost, we are the smell of death that brings death, but to those who are being saved, we are the smell of life that brings life. So who is able to do this work? 17We do not sell the word of God for a profit as many other people do. But in Christ we speak the truth before God, as messengers of God.

Servants of the New Agreement

3 Are we starting to brag about ourselves again? Do we need letters of introduction to you or from you, like some other people? 2You yourselves are our letter, written on our hearts, known and read by everyone. 3You show that you are a letter from Christ sent through us. This letter is not written with ink but with the Spirit of the living God. It is not written on stone tablets but on human hearts.

4We can say this, because through Christ we feel certain before God. 5We are not saying that we can do this work ourselves. It is God who makes us able to do all that we do. 6He made us able to be servants of a new agreement from himself to his people. This new agreement is not a written law, but it is of the Spirit. The written law brings death, but the Spirit gives life.

7The law that brought death was written in words on stone. It came with God's glory, which made Moses' face so bright that the Israelites could not continue to look at it. But that glory later disappeared. 8So surely the new way that brings the Spirit has even more glory. 9If the law that judged people guilty of sin had glory, surely the new way that makes people right with God has much greater glory. 10That old law had glory, but it really loses its glory when it is compared to the much greater glory of this new way. 11If that law which disappeared came with glory, then this new way which continues forever has much greater glory.

12We have this hope, so we are very bold. 13We are not like Moses, who put a covering over his face so the Israelites would not see it. The glory was disappearing, and Moses did not want them to see it end. 14But their minds were closed, and even today that same covering hides the meaning when they read the old agreement. That covering is taken away only through Christ. 15Even today, when they read the law of Moses, there is a covering over their minds. 16But when a person changes and follows the Lord, that covering is taken away. 17The Lord is the Spirit, and where the Spirit of the Lord is, there is freedom. 18Our faces, then, are not covered. We all show the Lord's glory, and we are being changed to be like him. This change in us brings ever greater glory, which comes from the Lord, who is the Spirit.

Preaching the Good News

4 God, with his mercy, gave us this work to do, so we don't give up. 2But we have turned away from secret and shameful ways. We use no trickery, and we do not change the teaching of God. We teach the truth plainly, showing everyone who we are. Then they can know in their hearts what kind of people we are in God's sight. 3If the Good News that we preach is hidden, it is hidden only to those

2:14 Ambition: Philippians 2:3–8
2:14 Leadership: 2 Corinthians 12:7–10
3:3 *stone tablets.* Meaning the Law of Moses that was written on stone tablets (Exodus 24:12; 25:16).
3:16–18 Paul makes reference to Moses, one of the most important figures in the Jewish religion. Paul was very familiar with the Jewish religion as a trained Jewish scholar (Acts 22:3), but as a Christian he held the view that Christ had more fully revealed God's plan and purpose and will. In this passage Paul explains how Christ reveals God's plan in a way that is superior to Moses, and it may be that there were opponents in the background using this same story to undermine Paul's teaching about Christ.
3:17–18 Just as the Book of John says in many places that Jesus is God, so Paul tells the Corinthians that the Holy Spirit is God. Twice in two verses he says, "The Lord is the Spirit" and that our transformation is into the Spirit's likeness and comes "from the Lord, who is the Spirit." "Lord" is a title reserved for God. Further, since Paul says elsewhere that we are being changed into the likeness of Christ, that makes Christ and the Holy Spirit equal persons in the Trinity (see Romans 8:29).
3:18 Freedom: Galatians 3
4:2 Conscience: 2 Corinthians 5:11

who are lost. 4The devil who rules this world has blinded the minds of those who do not believe. They cannot see the light of the Good News—the Good News about the glory of Christ, who is exactly like God. 5We do not preach about ourselves, but we preach that Jesus Christ is Lord and that we are your servants for Jesus. 6God once said, "Let the light shine out of the darkness!" This is the same God who made his light shine in our hearts by letting us know the glory of God that is in the face of Christ.

Spiritual Treasure in Clay Jars

7We have this treasure from God, but we are like clay jars that hold the treasure. This shows that the great power is from God, not from us. 8We have troubles all around us, but we are not defeated. We do not know what to do, but we do not give up the hope of living. 9We are persecuted, but God does not leave us. We are hurt sometimes, but we are not destroyed. 10We carry the death of Jesus in our own bodies so that the life of Jesus can also be seen in our bodies. 11We are alive, but for Jesus we are always in danger of death so that the life of Jesus can be seen in our bodies that die. 12So death is working in us, but life is working in you.

13It is written in the Scriptures, "I believed, so I spoke." Our faith is like this, too. We believe, and so we speak. 14God raised the Lord Jesus from the dead, and we know that God will also raise us with Jesus. God will bring us together with you, and we will stand before him. 15All these things are for you. And so the grace of God that is being given to more and more people will bring increasing thanks to God for his glory.

Living by Faith

16So we do not give up. Our physical body is becoming older and weaker, but our spirit inside us is made new every day. 17We have small troubles for a while now, but they are helping us gain an eternal glory that is much greater than the troubles. 18We set our eyes not on what we see but on what we cannot see. What we see will last only a short time, but what we cannot see will last forever.

5 We know that our body—the tent we live in here on earth—will be destroyed. But when that happens, God will have a house for us. It will not be a house made by human hands; instead, it will be a home in heaven that will last forever. 2But now we groan in this tent. We want God to give us our heavenly home, 3because it will clothe us so we will not be naked. 4While we live in this body, we have burdens, and we groan. We do not want to be naked, but we want to be clothed with our heavenly home. Then this body that dies will be fully covered with life. 5This is what God made us for, and he has given us the Spirit to be a guarantee for this new life.

6So we always have courage. We know that while we live in this body, we are away from the Lord. 7We live by what we believe, not by what we can see. 8So I say that we have courage. We really want to be away from this body and be at home with the Lord. 9Our only goal is to please God whether we live here or there, 10because we must all stand before Christ to be judged. Each of us will receive what we should get—good or bad—for the things we did in the earthly body.

Becoming Friends with God

11Since we know what it means to fear the Lord, we try to help people accept the truth about us. God knows what we really are, and I hope that in your hearts you know, too. 12We are not trying to prove ourselves to you again, but we are telling you about ourselves so you will be proud of us. Then you will have an answer for those who are proud about things that can be seen rather than what is in the heart. 13If we are out of our minds, it is for God. If we have our right minds, it is for you. 14The love of Christ controls us, because we know that One died for all, so all have died. 15Christ died for all so that those who live would not continue to live for themselves. He died for them and was raised from the dead so that they would live for him.

16From this time on we do not think of anyone as the world does. In the past we thought of Christ as the world thinks, but we no longer think of him in that way. 17If anyone belongs to Christ, there is a new creation. The old things have gone; everything is made new! 18All this is from God. Through

---

4:4 Human: James 3:9
4:4 Satan/Satanism: Ephesians 6:10–18
4:5 Lordship: 2 Corinthians 5:17
4:5 God's justice will not be mocked. On the final day, Christ will return to give judgment upon those who have disobeyed God's commands. The integrity of God's justice will be demonstrated in the punishment of offenders and the salvation of believers.
4:9 Encouragement: Philippians 4:13
4:12 Body/Flesh: 2 Corinthians 5:1–10
4:13 *"I . . . spoke."* Quotation from Psalm 116:10.
4:17 Suffering: Philippians 1:29
4:18 Martyrdom: 2 Corinthians 6:4–10
5:5 Death: 2 Corinthians 5:14–15
5:6 Mourning: 2 Corinthians 5:8
5:8 Mourning: Philippians 1:23
5:10 Body/Flesh: 2 Corinthians 7:1
5:10 House/Home: 1 Timothy 3:4–5
5:11 Conscience: 1 Timothy 1:5
5:15 Death: See article on page 460.
5:17 Lordship: Ephesians 4:5

Christ, God made peace between us and himself,
and God gave us the work of telling everyone
about the peace we can have with him. 19God was
in Christ, making peace between the world and
himself. In Christ, God did not hold the world guilty
of its sins. And he gave us this message of peace.
20So we have been sent to speak for Christ. It is as
if God is calling to you through us. We speak for
Christ when we beg you to be at peace with God.
21Christ had no sin, but God made him become sin
so that in Christ we could become right with God.

6 We are workers together with God, so we beg
you: Do not let the grace that you received
from God be for nothing. 2God says,

"At the right time I heard your prayers.
On the day of salvation I helped you."

Isaiah 49:8

I tell you that the "right time" is now, and the "day
of salvation" is now.
3We do not want anyone to find fault with our
work, so nothing we do will be a problem for anyone. 4But in every way we show we are servants of
God: in accepting many hard things, in troubles, in
difficulties, and in great problems. 5We are beaten
and thrown into prison. We meet those who become upset with us and start riots. We work hard,
and sometimes we get no sleep or food. 6We
show we are servants of God by our pure lives, our
understanding, patience, and kindness, by the Holy
Spirit, by true love, 7by speaking the truth, and by
God's power. We use our right living to defend ourselves against everything. 8Some people honor
us, but others blame us. Some people say evil things
about us, but others say good things. Some people
say we are liars, but we speak the truth. 9We are
not known, but we are well known. We seem to be
dying, but we continue to live. We are punished,
but we are not killed. 10We have much sadness, but
we are always rejoicing. We are poor, but we are
making many people rich in faith. We have nothing, but really we have everything.
11We have spoken freely to you in Corinth and
have opened our hearts to you. 12Our feelings of
love for you have not stopped, but you have stopped
your feelings of love for us. 13I speak to you as if you
were my children. Do to us as we have done—open
your hearts to us.

Warning About Non-Christians

14You are not the same as those who do not
believe. So do not join yourselves to them. Good
and bad do not belong together. Light and darkness
cannot share together. 15How can Christ and
Belial, the devil, have any agreement? What can a
believer have together with a nonbeliever? 16The
temple of God cannot have any agreement with
idols, and we are the temple of the living God. As
God said: "I will live with them and walk with
them. And I will be their God, and they will be my
people."

17"Leave those people,
and be separate, says the Lord.
Touch nothing that is unclean,
and I will accept you."

Isaiah 52:11; Ezekiel 20:34, 41

18"I will be your father,
and you will be my sons and daughters,
says the Lord Almighty." *2 Samuel 7:14; 7:8*

7 Dear friends, we have these promises from
God, so we should make ourselves pure—free
from anything that makes body or soul unclean.
We should try to become holy in the way we live,
because we respect God.

Paul's Joy

2Open your hearts to us. We have not done wrong
to anyone, we have not ruined the faith of anyone,
and we have not cheated anyone. 3I do not say this
to blame you. I told you before that we love you so
much we would live or die with you. 4I feel very

5:19 Incarnation: Philippians 2:6
5:19 Mediator: Numbers 21:6
5:19 Reconciliation: Galatians 3:28
5:19 World/Worldly: 2 Timothy 4:10

6:4–13 Paul listed troubles and difficulties he and the other servants of God had suffered. Other similar lists of suffering occur in 1 Corinthians 4:8–13 and 2 Corinthians 11:16–12:10. The Corinthians appeared to want to avoid any suffering or trials. They may have believed that Christians were not to have any troubles, difficulties, or suffering. Paul identified with the cross of Christ through the sufferings he endured. In these lists of sufferings, it was explained to the Corinthians that as followers of Christ, they could expect suffering and trials. Paul described a life of radical discipleship in the first century as a servant of Jesus; the way of the cross.

6:7 Weapons: Revelation 1:16
6:7 Reputation: 1 Thessalonians 4:12
6:10 Martyrdom: 2 Corinthians 11:23–25
6:10 Servant of the Lord: Galatians 1:10
6:14 Fellowship: 2 Corinthians 8:4

6:14 Although it has a wider application to other relationships, this verse prohibits believers from marrying non-believers. This is the New Testament counterpart to the Old Testament prohibition against marriages between Israelites and Gentiles (see Exodus 34:16; Deuteronomy 7:3, 4; Ezra 9:2, 10–12; Nehemiah 10:30; 13:23–27).

6:16 *"I . . . people."* Quotation from Leviticus 26:11-12; Jeremiah 32:38; Ezekiel 37:27.

6:18 Father: Ephesians 4:6
7:1 Body/Flesh: Galatians 5:16–25
7:1 Clean & Unclean: Ephesians 5:25–27
7:1 Holiness: Colossians 1:22

sure of you and am very proud of you. You give me much comfort, and in all of our troubles I have great joy.

[5]When we came into Macedonia, we had no rest. We found trouble all around us. We had fighting on the outside and fear on the inside. [6]But God, who comforts those who are troubled, comforted us when Titus came. [7]We were comforted, not only by his coming but also by the comfort you gave him. Titus told us about your wish to see me and that you are very sorry for what you did. He also told me about your great care for me, and when I heard this, I was much happier.

[8]Even if my letter made you sad, I am not sorry I wrote it. At first I was sorry, because it made you sad, but you were sad only for a short time. [9]Now I am happy, not because you were made sad, but because your sorrow made you change your lives. You became sad in the way God wanted you to, so you were not hurt by us in any way. [10]The kind of sorrow God wants makes people change their hearts and lives. This leads to salvation, and you cannot be sorry for that. But the kind of sorrow the world has brings death. [11]See what this sorrow—the sorrow God wanted you to have—has done to you: It has made you very serious. It made you want to prove you were not wrong. It made you angry and afraid. It made you want to see me. It made you care. It made you want the right thing to be done. You proved you were innocent in the problem. [12]I wrote that letter, not because of the one who did the wrong or because of the person who was hurt. I wrote the letter so you could see, before God, the great care you have for us. [13]That is why we were comforted.

Not only were we very comforted, we were even happier to see that Titus was so happy. All of you made him feel much better. [14]I bragged to Titus about you, and you showed that I was right. Everything we said to you was true, and you have proved that what we bragged about to Titus is true. [15]And his love for you is stronger when he remembers that you were all ready to obey. You welcomed him with respect and fear. [16]I am very happy that I can trust you fully.

Christian Giving

8 And now, brothers and sisters, we want you to know about the grace God gave the churches in Macedonia. [2]They have been tested by great troubles, and they are very poor. But they gave much because of their great joy. [3]I can tell you that they gave as much as they were able and even more than they could afford. No one told them to do it. [4]But they begged and pleaded with us to let them share in this service for God's people. [5]And they gave in a way we did not expect: They first gave themselves to the Lord and to us. This is what God wants. [6]So we asked Titus to help you finish this special work of grace since he is the one who started it. [7]You are rich in everything—in faith, in speaking, in knowledge, in truly wanting to help, and in the love you learned from us. In the same way, be strong also in the grace of giving.

[8]I am not commanding you to give. But I want to see if your love is true by comparing you with others that really want to help. [9]You know the grace of our Lord Jesus Christ. You know that Christ was rich, but for you he became poor so that by his becoming poor you might become rich.

[10]This is what I think you should do: Last year you were the first to want to give, and you were the first who gave. [11]So now finish the work you started. Then your "doing" will be equal to your "wanting to do." Give from what you have. [12]If you want to give, your gift will be accepted. It will be judged by what you have, not by what you do not have. [13]We do not want you to have troubles while other people are at ease, but we want everything to be equal. [14]At this time you have plenty. What you have can help others who are in need. Then later, when they have plenty, they can help you when you are in need, and all will be equal. [15]As it is written in the Scriptures, "The person who gathered more did not have too much, nor did the person who gathered less have too little."

Titus and His Companions Help

[16]I thank God because he gave Titus the same love for you that I have. [17]Titus accepted what we asked him to do. He wanted very much to go to you, and this was his own idea. [18]We are sending with him the brother who is praised by all the churches because of his service in preaching the Good News. [19]Also, this brother was chosen by the churches to go with us when we deliver this gift of money. We are doing this service to bring glory to the Lord and to show that we really want to help.

[20]We are being careful so that no one will criticize us for the way we are handling this large gift.

7:5–7 Titus must have been an encourager to Paul because Paul reports on one occasion that he was discouraged when he could not find Titus (even with an open door for ministry, 2 Corinthians 2:12–13). Here we see Paul's spirit being uplifted in the midst of a difficult ministry situation just because Titus showed up. As a result, Paul's depression turned to joy. People make a difference.

7:6 Depression: See article on page 490.

8:4 Fellowship: 2 Corinthians 13:14

8:7–9 Paul motivates the Corinthians to be charitable by reminding them of the sacrifice that Jesus made on their behalf. They, in turn, should be willing to make a sacrifice for their brothers and sisters. They cannot say that they are too poor to give, because, as he tells them, they are rich in spiritual blessings.

8:15 *"The person . . . little."* Quotation from Exodus 16:18.

21We are trying hard to do what the Lord accepts as right and also what people think is right.

22Also, we are sending with them our brother, who is always ready to help. He has proved this to us in many ways, and he wants to help even more now, because he has much faith in you.

23Now about Titus—he is my partner who is working with me to help you. And about the other brothers—they are sent from the churches, and they bring glory to Christ. 24So show these men the proof of your love and the reason we are proud of you. Then all the churches can see it.

Help for Fellow Christians

9 I really do not need to write you about this help for God's people. 2I know you want to help. I have been bragging about this to the people in Macedonia, telling them that you in Southern Greece have been ready to give since last year. And your desire to give has made most of them ready to give also. 3But I am sending the brothers to you so that our bragging about you in this will not be empty words. I want you to be ready, as I said you would be. 4If any of the people from Macedonia come with me and find that you are not ready, we will be ashamed that we were so sure of you. (And you will be ashamed, too!) 5So I thought I should ask these brothers to go to you before we do. They will finish getting in order the generous gift you promised so it will be ready when we come. And it will be a generous gift—not one that you did not want to give.

6Remember this: The person who plants a little will have a small harvest, but the person who plants a lot will have a big harvest. 7Each one should give as you have decided in your heart to give. You should not be sad when you give, and you should not give because you feel forced to give. God loves the person who gives happily. 8And God can give you more blessings than you need. Then you will always have plenty of everything—enough to give to every good work. 9It is written in the Scriptures:

"He gives freely to the poor.
The things he does are right and will
continue forever." *Psalm 112:9*

10God is the One who gives seed to the farmer and bread for food. He will give you all the seed you need and make it grow so there will be a great harvest from your goodness. 11He will make you rich in every way so that you can always give freely. And your giving through us will cause many to give thanks to God. 12This service you do not only helps the needs of God's people, it also brings many more thanks to God. 13It is a proof of your faith. Many people will praise God because you obey the Good News of Christ—the gospel you say you believe—and because you freely share with them and with all others. 14And when they pray, they will wish they could be with you because of the great grace that God has given you. 15Thanks be to God for his gift that is too wonderful for words.

Paul Defends His Ministry

10 I, Paul, am begging you with the gentleness and the kindness of Christ. Some people say that I am easy on you when I am with you and bold when I am away. 2They think we live in a worldly way, and I plan to be very bold with them when I come. I beg you that when I come I will not need to use that same boldness with you. 3We do live in the world, but we do not fight in the same way the world fights. 4We fight with weapons that are different from those the world uses. Our weapons have power from God that can destroy the enemy's strong places. We destroy people's arguments 5and every proud thing that raises itself against the knowledge of God. We capture every thought and make it give up and obey Christ. 6We are ready to punish anyone there who does not obey, but first we want you to obey fully.

7You must look at the facts before you. If you feel sure that you belong to Christ, you must remember that we belong to Christ just as you do. 8It is true that we brag freely about the authority the Lord gave us. But this authority is to build you up, not to tear you down. So I will not be ashamed. 9I do not want you to think I am trying to scare you with my letters. 10Some people say, "Paul's letters are powerful and sound important, but when he is with us, he is weak. And his speaking is nothing."

9:15 Materialism/Possessions: 1 Timothy 6:3–10

9:15 Money: James 2:1–7

10:3–6 Paul here describes warfare in spiritual terms. We fight not with swords or guns, but rather with spiritual weapons (see Ephesians 6:10–20) like faith, hope, and love, which are powerful and destroy the strongholds of God's enemies. Here we see that even our thought life is the scene of spiritual battle. Our minds are the scene of struggle as our Christian view of the world comes into conflict with secular thinking. Fortunately, just as in Israel's wars against the Canaanites in the Old Testament, it is God's power, not our own, that wins the victory. We are not the ones to humble the proud (Job 40:12). But since we have been sent by God (2 Corinthians 5:20), we use "power from God" to show the weaknesses in the arguments people use in support of their proud rebellion against God.

10:6 Obedience: James 1:22–25

10:10–11 Paul's letters were effective, and were often accompanied by one of his many coworkers to interpret them (1 Corinthians 4:17). In a Greek area like Corinth, there was a high expectation that public communicators employ the established rules of language. Apparently,

11They should know this: We are not there with you now, so we say these things in letters. But when we are there with you, we will show the same authority that we show in our letters.

12We do not dare to compare ourselves with those who think they are very important. They use themselves to measure themselves, and they judge themselves by what they themselves are. This shows that they know nothing. 13But we will not brag about things outside the work that was given us to do. We will limit our bragging to the work that God gave us, and this includes our work with you. 14We are not bragging too much, as we would be if we had not already come to you. But we have come to you with the Good News of Christ. 15We limit our bragging to the work that is ours, not what others have done. We hope that as your faith continues to grow, you will help our work to grow much larger. 16We want to tell the Good News in the areas beyond your city. We do not want to brag about work that has already been done in another person's area. 17But, "If someone wants to brag, he should brag only about the Lord." 18It is not those who say they are good who are accepted but those who the Lord thinks are good.

Paul and the False Apostles

11 I wish you would be patient with me even when I am a little foolish, but you are already doing that. 2I am jealous over you with a jealousy that comes from God. I promised to give you to Christ, as your only husband. I want to give you as his pure bride. 3But I am afraid that your minds will be led away from your true and pure following of Christ just as Eve was tricked by the snake with his evil ways. 4You are very patient with anyone who comes to you and preaches a different Jesus from the one we preached. You are very willing to accept a spirit or gospel that is different from the Spirit and Good News you received from us.

5I do not think that those "great apostles" are any better than I am. 6I may not be a trained speaker, but I do have knowledge. We have shown this to you clearly in every way.

7I preached God's Good News to you without pay. I made myself unimportant to make you important. Do you think that was wrong? 8I accepted pay from other churches, taking their money so I could serve you. 9If I needed something when I was with you, I did not trouble any of you. The brothers who came from Macedonia gave me all that I needed. I did not allow myself to depend on you in any way, and I will never depend on you. 10No one in Southern Greece will stop me from bragging about that. I say this with the truth of Christ in me. 11And why do I not depend on you? Do you think it is because I do not love you? God knows that I love you.

12And I will continue doing what I am doing now, because I want to stop those people from having a reason to brag. They would like to say that the work they brag about is the same as ours. 13Such men are not true apostles but are workers who lie. They change themselves to look like apostles of Christ. 14This does not surprise us. Even Satan changes himself to look like an angel of light. 15So it does not surprise us if Satan's servants also make themselves look like servants who work for what is right. But in the end they will be punished for what they do.

Paul Tells About His Sufferings

16I tell you again: No one should think I am a fool. But if you think so, accept me as you would accept a fool. Then I can brag a little, too. 17When I brag because I feel sure of myself, I am not talking as the Lord would talk but as a fool. 18Many people are bragging about their lives in the world. So I will brag too. 19You are wise, so you will gladly be patient with fools! 20You are even patient with those who order you around, or use you, or trick you, or think they are better than you, or hit you in the face. 21It is shameful to me to say this, but we were too "weak" to do those things to you!

But if anyone else is brave enough to brag, then I also will be brave and brag. (I am talking as a fool.) 22Are they Hebrews? So am I. Are they Israelites? So am I. Are they from Abraham's family? So am I. 23Are they serving Christ? I am serving him more. (I am crazy to talk like this.) I have worked much

Paul was able to do this in his letters but not in person. This may be accounted for by the fact that he had assistance in writing his letters (Romans 16:22; 1 Corinthians 16:21; Colossians 4:18; 2 Thessalonians 3:17; Galatians 6:11). Part and parcel of training to write letters in the Roman world was training in the rules of language, and thus Paul's secretaries provided him with essential help to communicate effectively.

10:17 *"If . . . Lord."* Quotation from Jeremiah 9:24.

11:3 Eve's seduction by Satan is used as a warning to the Christians in Corinth not to be deceived themselves by the subtlety of Satan and turn aside from their single-minded devotion to Christ. Just as Eve's willingness to talk with the serpent created an opportunity to be lured into sin, so the Corinthians' willingness to listen to the false teachers put them in danger of apostasy.

11:4 Cults: Galatians 1:6–7

11:14 *angel of light.* Messenger from God. The devil fools people so that they think he is from God.

11:22 *Hebrews.* A name for the Jews that some Jews were very proud of.

harder than they. I have been in prison more often. I have been hurt more in beatings. I have been near death many times. 24Five times the Jews have given me their punishment of thirty-nine lashes with a whip. 25Three different times I was beaten with rods. One time I was almost stoned to death. Three times I was in ships that wrecked, and one of those times I spent a night and a day in the sea. 26I have gone on many travels and have been in danger from rivers, thieves, my own people, the Jews, and those who are not Jews. I have been in danger in cities, in places where no one lives, and on the sea. And I have been in danger with false Christians. 27I have done hard and tiring work, and many times I did not sleep. I have been hungry and thirsty, and many times I have been without food. I have been cold and without clothes. 28Besides all this, there is on me every day the load of my concern for all the churches. 29I feel weak every time someone is weak, and I feel upset every time someone is led into sin.

30If I must brag, I will brag about the things that show I am weak. 31God knows I am not lying. He is the God and Father of the Lord Jesus Christ, and he is to be praised forever. 32When I was in Damascus, the governor under King Aretas wanted to arrest me, so he put guards around the city. 33But my friends lowered me in a basket through a hole in the city wall. So I escaped from the governor.

A Special Blessing in Paul's Life

12 I must continue to brag. It will do no good, but I will talk now about visions and revelations from the Lord. 2I know a man in Christ who was taken up to the third heaven fourteen years ago. I do not know whether the man was in his body or out of his body, but God knows. 3-4And I know that this man was taken up to paradise. I don't know if he was in his body or away from his body, but God knows. He heard things he is not able to explain, things that no human is allowed to tell. 5I will brag about a man like that, but I will not brag about myself, except about my weaknesses. 6But if I wanted to brag about myself, I would not be a fool, because I would be telling the truth. But I will not brag about myself. I do not want people to think more of me than what they see me do or hear me say.

7So that I would not become too proud of the wonderful things that were shown to me, a painful physical problem was given to me. This problem was a messenger from Satan, sent to beat me and keep me from being too proud. 8I begged the Lord three times to take this problem away from me. 9But he said to me, "My grace is enough for you. When you are weak, my power is made perfect in you." So I am very happy to brag about my weaknesses. Then Christ's power can live in me. 10For this reason I am happy when I have weaknesses, insults, hard times, sufferings, and all kinds of troubles for Christ. Because when I am weak, then I am truly strong.

Paul's Love for the Christians

11I have been talking like a fool, but you made me do it. You are the ones who should say good things about me. I am worth nothing, but those "great apostles" are not worth any more than I am! 12When I was with you, I patiently did the things that prove I am an apostle—signs, wonders, and miracles. 13So you received everything that the other churches have received. Only one thing was different: I was not a burden to you. Forgive me for this!

14I am now ready to visit you the third time, and I will not be a burden to you. I want nothing from you, except you. Children should not have to save up to give to their parents. Parents should save to

---

11:25 Martyrdom: Philippians 1:12–26

11:29 Persecution: 1 Peter 2:18–25

12:1 *revelations.* Revelation is making known a truth that was hidden.

12:3 *paradise.* Another word for heaven.

12:7 *painful physical problem.* Literally, "thorn in the flesh."

12:7 Demon: See article on page 742.

12:7 Paul's thorn in the flesh has spawned a great deal of conjecture. What is important to note is that the Greek text suggests that Paul is referring to some kind of painful physical problem that causes suffering—it is a thorn in the flesh, not a mental or emotional or spiritual problem. In this case, it was not God's will to miraculously heal Paul. Perhaps the most probable explanation of his malady is that Paul had problems with his eyes which caused him to appear to be weak to some (2 Corinthians 10:10; Galatians 4:13–15, especially verse 15), a problem perhaps caused by the blinding revelations Paul received first on the Damascus road, then again during this time in Arabia.

12:7–9 This experience is our best reminder in Scripture that the ultimate value of prayer is not whether we "get answers," but the realization that it is through prayer that we "receive grace." God's grace is the ultimate answer to any prayer, and it is sufficient to carry us through the good and bad experiences of life, concluding that "when I am weak, then I am truly strong" (2 Corinthians 12:10).

Tough times never last, but tough people do. Tough people stick it out. They have learned to choose the most positive reaction in managing problems. For in spite of all of our possibility thinking, there are after all some problems that defy solutions. I have seen people face the most catastrophic problems with a positive mental attitude, turning their problems into creative experiences. They turned their scars into stars.

God's grace is his undeserved kindness in bringing us salvation by sending his Son into the world. It is also the strength and power we receive from the indwelling Holy Spirit in order to carry out his will and persevere in the midst of trials.

12:10 Grace: Ephesians 2:4–10

12:10 Leadership: Philippians 3:17

give to their children. [15]So I am happy to give everything I have for you, even myself. If I love you more, will you love me less?

[16]It is clear I was not a burden to you, but you think I was tricky and lied to catch you. [17]Did I cheat you by using any of the messengers I sent to you? No, you know I did not. [18]I asked Titus to go to you, and I sent our brother with him. Titus did not cheat you, did he? No, you know that Titus and I did the same thing and with the same spirit.

[19]Do you think we have been defending ourselves to you all this time? We have been speaking in Christ and before God. You are our dear friends, and everything we do is to make you stronger. [20]I am afraid that when I come, you will not be what I want you to be, and I will not be what you want me to be. I am afraid that among you there may be arguing, jealousy, anger, selfish fighting, evil talk, gossip, pride, and confusion. [21]I am afraid that when I come to you again, my God will make me ashamed before you. I may be saddened by many of those who have sinned because they have not changed their hearts or turned from their sexual sins and the shameful things they have done.

Final Warnings and Greetings

13 I will come to you for the third time. "Every case must be proved by two or three witnesses." [2]When I was with you the second time, I gave a warning to those who had sinned. Now I am away from you, and I give a warning to all the others. When I come to you again, I will not be easy with them. [3]You want proof that Christ is speaking through me. My proof is that he is not weak among you, but he is powerful. [4]It is true that he was weak when he was killed on the cross, but he lives now by God's power. It is true that we are weak in Christ, but for you we will be alive in Christ by God's power.

[5]Look closely at yourselves. Test yourselves to see if you are living in the faith. You know that Jesus Christ is in you—unless you fail the test. [6]But I hope you will see that we ourselves have not failed the test. [7]We pray to God that you will not do anything wrong. It is not important to see that we have passed the test, but it is important that you do what is right, even if it seems we have failed. [8]We cannot do anything against the truth, but only for the truth. [9]We are happy to be weak, if you are strong, and we pray that you will become complete. [10]I am writing this while I am away from you so that when I come I will not have to be harsh in my use of authority. The Lord gave me this authority to build you up, not to tear you down.

[11]Now, brothers and sisters, I say good-bye. Try to be complete. Do what I have asked you to do. Agree with each other, and live in peace. Then the God of love and peace will be with you.

[12]Greet each other with a holy kiss. [13]All of God's holy people send greetings to you.

[14]The grace of the Lord Jesus Christ, the love of God, and the fellowship of the Holy Spirit be with you all.

13:1 *"Every . . . witnesses."* Quotation from Deuteronomy 19:15.

13:8 Test/Temptation: Galatians 6:1

13:14 Fellowship: Galatians 2:9

13:14 Trinity: Ephesians 4:4–6

13:14 The Trinity is based on the Bible's description of the one God in three persons, as in this famous letter ending from Paul. The worship of one God is central to the ancient Jews: "You must not have any other gods except me" (Exodus 20:3). In the New Testament, this one God is revealed in three persons—the Father, the Son, and the Holy Spirit. (See Ephesians 4:4–6; John 1:1–18.) Paul's blessing is thus in the name of the One who offers grace in his life, death, and resurrection (Jesus Christ), who loves us everlastingly (the Father), and who binds together the Christian community (the Holy Spirit).

13:14 Paul (Saul): Galatians 1:1–2

Notes:

INTRODUCTION TO THE BOOK OF
GALATIANS

Christians Are Saved by Grace

WHO WROTE THIS BOOK?

The apostle Paul wrote Galatians (1:1).

TO WHOM WAS THIS BOOK WRITTEN?

There are two theories about the intended destination of Paul's letter to the Galatians. The North Galatian Theory says that the letter was meant for the territory north of the Roman province of Galatia that Paul visited on his missionary journeys. The South Galatian Theory says that he meant the letter for the churches he established in Antioch, Iconium, Lystra, and Derbe. Because no reference is made to the Jerusalem Council, which dealt with the issues raised in Galatians, the South Galatian Theory is preferable.

WHERE WAS IT WRITTEN?

If the North Galatian Theory is correct, the Book of Galatians was probably written from Ephesus or Macedonia after Paul passed through there on his third missionary journey (see Acts 18:23). If the South Galatian Theory is correct, the letter was likely written in Syrian Antioch shortly after Paul's first missionary journey and before the Jerusalem Council.

WHEN WAS IT WRITTEN?

If the North Galatian Theory is correct, the Book of Galatians was written about A.D. 54 or 55. This was about the same time as the writing of the Book of Romans, which contains similar, but more developed, content. If the South Galatian Theory is correct, the letter was written as early as A.D. 49 or as late as A.D. 53. This would make it the oldest of Paul's letters.

WHAT IS THE BOOK ABOUT?

The Book of Galatians is Paul's defense of the Good News about grace and justification by faith. A group of false teachers, who have been called "the Judaizers," opposed Paul's teaching and sought to bring the new non-Jewish (Gentile) Christians under the authority of the old Law. They specifically wanted the non-Jewish Christians to be circumcised, among other things. Paul scolds the Galatians for allowing these false teachers to move them backward from liberty in Christ to the bondage of the Law.

WHY WAS THIS BOOK WRITTEN?

Paul's purpose in writing Galatians was to combat legalistic corrupters of the simple Good News of salvation by grace through faith, based on Christ's work on the cross. The letter was also written to correct the opposite problem of the Galatians—taking their Christian liberty to excess.

SO WHAT DOES THIS BOOK MEAN TO US?

Paul's message of salvation by grace through faith is as vital today as it was to the Galatians. It is a simple message, it is a pure message, a message of love from God to us as his dearly loved children. The message is this: Christ did all the work necessary to save us on the cross. What God wants from us is not more work, but our complete faith in the work already done by his precious Son and our Savior, Jesus Christ, the Lamb of God sacrificed for us. We must resist false teachers who present any other form of the Good News. Salvation is the free gift of God, available to each person who faithfully follows the Savior. At the same time, we must not use our liberty in Christ as a license to sin, but rather as a reason to praise God with holy living for his amazing gift of grace.

SUMMARY:

Acts 13–14 recounts the mission of Paul during which he established the churches in Galatia. Since his initial work in those churches, some troublemakers have come and confused the Galatian Christians (see 1:7; 5:10). Paul is writing this letter to persuade the Christians in the Galatian churches to remain true to the message of God he had taught them, and to resist those who want to change the Good News.

Paul establishes the central message of his letter in his opening words, which focus, first, on his identity as an apostle and, secondly, on the importance of Jesus' death (1:1–4). Clearly, those who oppose Paul's understanding of the Good News also oppose his identity as an apostle. This is why so much of the Book of Galatians is concerned with Paul's talking about himself and how his authority as an apostle comes from God.

The troublemakers in Galatia taught people that the way to prove to others that you were Christians was to keep the Law. This meant that non-Jewish people who believed in Jesus should also be circumcised, practice Jewish food laws, and in other ways behave as though they were Jews. Paul, on the other hand, taught people that the only way to prove to others that you were Christians was to be faithful to God as Jesus was when he died on the cross. Christians can do this, he says, because the Holy Spirit is at work in the lives of those who believe.

Freedom and unity, therefore, are central themes of Paul's letter to the Galatians. Those troublemakers are trying to change the Good News, and this divides people. According to Paul, because of Jesus' death on the cross, those who are led by the Spirit live together in harmony. Those troublemakers want Christians not only to believe in Jesus but also to live in ways that prove they are Jews. Paul insists that Jesus' death on the cross means that people no longer must prove they are God's people by keeping the Jewish Law; instead, the Holy Spirit teaches them to be faithful to God.

GALATIANS

From Paul, an apostle. I was not chosen to be
an apostle by human beings, nor was I sent
from human beings. I was made an apostle
through Jesus Christ and God the Father who raised
Jesus from the dead. 2This letter is also from all
those of God's family who are with me.
To the churches in Galatia:⚭
3Grace and peace to you from God our Father
and the Lord Jesus Christ. 4Jesus gave himself for
our sins to free us from this evil world we live in,
as God the Father planned. 5The glory belongs to
God forever and ever. Amen.

The Only Good News

6God, by his grace through Christ, called you to
become his people. So I am amazed that you are
turning away so quickly and believing something
different than the Good News. 7Really, there is no
other Good News. But some people are confusing
you; they want to change the Good News of
Christ.⚭ 8We preached to you the Good News. So
if we ourselves, or even an angel from heaven,
should preach to you something different, we
should be judged guilty! 9I said this before, and
now I say it again: You have already accepted the
Good News. If anyone is preaching something different to you, he should be judged guilty!
10Do you think I am trying to make people accept
me? No, God is the One I am trying to please. Am I
trying to please people? If I still wanted to please
people, I would not be a servant of Christ.⚭

Paul's Authority Is from God

11Brothers and sisters, I want you to know that
the Good News I preached to you was not made up
by human beings. 12I did not get it from humans,
nor did anyone teach it to me, but Jesus Christ
showed it to me.⚭
13You have heard about my past life in the Jewish
religion. I attacked the church of God and tried to
destroy it. 14I was becoming a leader in the Jewish
religion, doing better than most other Jews of my

One-humped Arabian camels

age. I tried harder than anyone else to follow the
teachings handed down by our ancestors.
15But God had special plans for me and set me
apart for his work even before I was born. He called
me through his grace⚭ 16and showed his son to me
so that I might tell the Good News about him to
those who are not Jewish. When God called me, I
did not get advice or help from any person. 17I did
not go to Jerusalem to see those who were apostles
before I was. But, without waiting, I went away to
Arabia and later went back to Damascus.
18After three years I went to Jerusalem to meet
Peter and stayed with him for fifteen days. 19I met
no other apostles, except James, the brother of the
Lord. 20God knows that these things I write are not
lies. 21Later, I went to the areas of Syria and Cilicia.
22In Judea the churches in Christ had never met
me. 23They had only heard it said, "This man who
was attacking us is now preaching the same faith
that he once tried to destroy." 24And these believers praised God because of me.

Other Apostles Accepted Paul

2 After fourteen years I went to Jerusalem again,
this time with Barnabas. I also took Titus with
me. 2I went because God showed me I should go.
I met with the believers there, and in private I told
their leaders the Good News that I preach to the
non-Jewish people. I did not want my past work
and the work I am now doing to be wasted. 3Titus
was with me, but he was not forced to be circumcised, even though he was a Greek. 4We talked

1:2 *those . . . family.* The Greek text says "brothers."
1:2 *Galatia.* Probably the same country where Paul preached and began churches on his first missionary trip. Read the Book of Acts, chapters 13 and 14.
1:11 *Brothers and sisters.* Although the Greek text says "Brothers" here and throughout this book, Paul's words were meant for the entire church, including men and women.
⚭**1:2 Paul (Saul):** Galatians 1:10–2:21
1:6–9 Normally, Paul begins his letters with an introduction that leads into a thanksgiving. Here, though, the thanksgiving is missing. This shows how distressed Paul is as he writes this letter.
⚭**1:7 Cults:** 2 Peter 1:12–2:22
⚭**1:10 Servant of the Lord:** Philippians 2:5–11
⚭**1:12 Communication:** Exodus 4:17
⚭**1:15 Abortion and Crisis Pregnancy:** Jeremiah 1:5
1:15 The same God who set Paul apart for the ministry from his mother's womb later called him into his apostolic mission on the road to Damascus. God's purpose for us even precedes our conception, making it clear that he views us as persons even from the moment of conception.

about this problem because some false believers had come into our group secretly. They came in like spies to overturn the freedom we have in Christ Jesus. They wanted to make us slaves. 5But we did not give in to those false believers for a minute. We wanted the truth of the Good News to continue for you.

6Those leaders who seemed to be important did not change the Good News that I preach. (It doesn't matter to me if they were "important" or not. To God everyone is the same.) 7But these leaders saw that I had been given the work of telling the Good News to those who are not Jewish, just as Peter had the work of telling the Jews. 8God gave Peter the power to work as an apostle for the Jewish people. But he also gave me the power to work as an apostle for those who are not Jews. 9James, Peter, and John, who seemed to be the leaders, understood that God had given me this special grace, so they accepted Barnabas and me. They agreed that they would go to the Jewish people and that we should go to those who are not Jewish. 10The only thing they asked us was to remember to help the poor—something I really wanted to do.

Paul Shows that Peter Was Wrong

11When Peter came to Antioch, I challenged him to his face, because he was wrong. 12Peter ate with the non-Jewish people until some Jewish people sent from James came to Antioch. When they arrived, Peter stopped eating with those who weren't Jewish, and he separated himself from them. He was afraid of the Jews. 13So Peter was a hypocrite, as were the other Jewish believers who joined with him. Even Barnabas was influenced by what these Jewish believers did. 14When I saw they were not following the truth of the Good News, I spoke to Peter in front of them all. I said, "Peter, you are a Jew, but you are not living like a Jew. You are living like those who are not Jewish. So why do you now try to force those who are not Jewish to live like Jews?"

15We were not born as non-Jewish "sinners," but as Jews. 16Yet we know that a person is made right with God not by following the law, but by trusting in Jesus Christ. So we, too, have put our faith in Christ Jesus, that we might be made right with God because we trusted in Christ. It is not because we followed the law, because no one can be made right with God by following the law.

17We Jews came to Christ, trying to be made right with God, and it became clear that we are sinners, too. Does this mean that Christ encourages sin? No! 18But I would really be wrong to begin teaching again those things that I gave up. 19It was the law that put me to death, and I died to the law so that I can now live for God. 20I was put to death on the cross with Christ, and I do not live anymore—it is Christ who lives in me. I still live in my body, but I live by faith in the Son of God who loved me and gave himself to save me. 21By saying these things I am not going against God's grace. Just the opposite, if the law could make us right with God, then Christ's death would be useless.

Blessing Comes Through Faith

3 You people in Galatia were told very clearly about the death of Jesus Christ on the cross. But you were foolish; you let someone trick you. 2Tell me this one thing: How did you receive the Holy Spirit? Did you receive the Spirit by following the law? No, you received the Spirit because you heard the Good News and believed it. 3You began your life in Christ by the Spirit. Now are you trying to make it complete by your own power? That is foolish. 4Were all your experiences wasted? I hope not! 5Does God give you the Spirit and work miracles among you because you follow the law? No, he does these things because you heard the Good News and believed it.

6The Scriptures say the same thing about Abraham: "Abraham believed God, and God accepted Abraham's faith, and that faith made him right with God." 7So you should know that the true children of Abraham are those who have faith. 8The Scriptures, telling what would happen in the future, said that God would make the non-Jewish people right through their faith. This Good News was told to Abraham beforehand, as the Scripture says: "All nations will be blessed through you." 9So all who believe as Abraham believed are blessed just as Abraham was. 10But those who depend on following the law to make them right are under a curse, because the Scriptures say, "Anyone will be cursed

2:9 Fellowship: Philippians 1:5
2:14 Unity: Galatians 3:26–29
2:16 Crossing Cultural Boundaries: Ephesians 2:13–14
2:16 Racism: Galatians 3:8
2:21 Paul (Saul): Galatians 4:11–20
3:6 Abraham: Hebrews 7:1
3:6 *"Abraham . . . God."* Quotation from Genesis 15:6.
3:6–14 Here Paul shows how the Good News of Jesus Christ can be traced back to God's promise to Abraham. God intended that through Abraham and his descendants all the people of the earth would be blessed (Genesis 12:3). Now it is through the true children of Abraham, those who have faith, that the Good News will be brought to all the non-Jewish people.
3:8 *"All . . . you."* Quotation from Genesis 12:3 and 18:18.
3:8 Racism: Galatians 3:28

who does not always obey what is written in the Book of the Law." 11Now it is clear that no one can be made right with God by the law, because the Scriptures say, "Those who are right with God will live by trusting in him." 12The law is not based on faith. It says, "A person who obeys these things will live because of them." 13Christ took away the curse the law put on us. He changed places with us and put himself under that curse. It is written in the Scriptures, "Anyone whose body is displayed on a tree is cursed." 14Christ did this so that God's blessing promised to Abraham might come through Jesus Christ to those who are not Jews. Jesus died so that by our believing we could receive the Spirit that God promised.

The Law and the Promise

15Brothers and sisters, let us think in human terms: Even an agreement made between two persons is firm. After that agreement is accepted by both people, no one can stop it or add anything to it. 16God made promises both to Abraham and to his descendant. God did not say, "and to your descendants." That would mean many people. But God said, "and to your descendant." That means only one person; that person is Christ. 17This is what I mean: God had an agreement with Abraham and promised to keep it. The law, which came four hundred thirty years later, cannot change that agreement and so destroy God's promise to Abraham. 18If the law could give us Abraham's blessing, then the promise would not be necessary. But that is not possible, because God freely gave his blessings to Abraham through the promise he had made.

19So what was the law for? It was given to show that the wrong things people do are against God's will. And it continued until the special descendant, who had been promised, came. The law was given through angels who used Moses for a mediator to give the law to people. 20But a mediator is not needed when there is only one side, and God is only one.

The Purpose of the Law of Moses

21Does this mean that the law is against God's promises? Never! That would be true only if the law could make us right. But God did not give a law that can bring life. 22Instead, the Scriptures showed that the whole world is bound by sin. This was so the promise would be given through faith to people who believe in Jesus Christ.

23Before this faith came, we were all held prisoners by the law. We had no freedom until God showed us the way of faith that was coming. 24In other words, the law was our guardian leading us to Christ so that we could be made right with God through faith. 25Now the way of faith has come, and we no longer live under a guardian.

26-27You were all baptized into Christ, and so you were all clothed with Christ. This means that you are all children of God through faith in Christ Jesus. 28In Christ, there is no difference between Jew and Greek, slave and free person, male and female. You are all the same in Christ Jesus. 29You belong to Christ, so you are Abraham's descendants. You will inherit all of God's blessings because of the promise God made to Abraham.

4 I want to tell you this: While those who will inherit their fathers' property are still children, they are no different from slaves. It does not matter that the children own everything. 2While they are children, they must obey those who are

3:10 Curse: Galatians 3:13
3:10 The laws which God gave to Moses contained blessings for obedience and curses for disobedience. Because no one, except Jesus, has kept the whole Law, all are under the curse of death. By keeping the whole Law on our behalf, Jesus was able to take the curse upon himself with his death on a cross. We may become right with God and be delivered from the curse by trusting in Christ.
3:10 *"Anyone . . . Law."* Quotation from Deuteronomy 27:26.
3:11 *"Those . . . him."* Quotation from Habakkuk 2:4.
3:11 Law: 1 Timothy 1:8
3:12 *"A person . . . them."* Quotation from Leviticus 18:5.
3:13 *displayed on a tree.* Deuteronomy 21:22–23 says that when a person was killed for doing wrong, the body was hung on a tree to show shame. Paul means that the cross of Jesus was like that.
3:13 Curse: See article on page 150.
3:19 *mediator.* A person who helps one person talk to or give something to another person. A go-between.
3:28 Through his one sacrifice on behalf of both Jewish and non-Jewish people, Christ has broken down the barriers which once separated them so that all who have faith in Christ, including the non-Jews, may be called children of Abraham.
3:28 Gentiles (Non-Jews): Revelation 5:9
3:28 Racism: Ephesians 2:11–18
3:28 Reconciliation: Colossians 1:21–22
3:28 Slavery: See article on page 1305.
3:28 Women: Ephesians 5:22–24
3:28 Baptism: Ephesians 4:4–6
3:28 Friend: Ephesians 2:11–22
3:29 Adoption: Galatians 4:5
3:29 Births: See article on page 89.
3:29 Freedom: Galatians 5
3:29 Good Works: Galatians 5
3:29 Promise: Galatians 4:21–31
3:29 Unity: Ephesians 1:22–23
4:1–7 The presence of the Holy Spirit in the heart of a believer establishes his or her adoption as a child of God and prompts him or her to call God "Father." Adoption is a *family* idea, conceived in terms of *love,* and viewing God as *father.* In adoption, God takes us out of slavery to sin and into his family and fellowship—he establishes us as his children and heirs. Closeness, affection, and generosity are at the heart of the relationship. To be right with God the Judge is a great thing, but to be loved and cared for by God the Father is greater.
4:1–11 The Galatians are under pressure to follow Jewish laws and traditions. Paul equates pagan gods with Jewish rules (4:9). It is not a

chosen to care for them. But when the children
reach the age set by their fathers, they are free. 3It
is the same for us. We were once like children,
slaves to the useless rules of this world. 4But when
the right time came, God sent his Son who was
born of a woman and lived under the law. 5God
did this so he could buy freedom for those who
were under the law and so we could become his
children.∞
6Since you are God's children, God sent the Spirit
of his Son into your hearts, and the Spirit cries out,
"Father." 7So now you are not a slave; you are
God's child, and God will give you the blessing he
promised, because you are his child.

Paul's Love for the Christians

8In the past you did not know God. You were
slaves to gods that were not real. 9But now you
know the true God. Really, it is God who knows
you. So why do you turn back to those weak and
useless rules you followed before? Do you want to
be slaves to those things again?∞ 10You still follow
teachings about special days, months, seasons, and
years. 11I am afraid for you, that my work for you
has been wasted.
12Brothers and sisters, I became like you, so I
beg you to become like me. You were very good to
me before. 13You remember that it was because of
an illness that I came to you the first time, preaching the Good News. 14Though my sickness was a
trouble for you, you did not hate me or make me
leave. But you welcomed me as an angel from God,
as if I were Jesus Christ himself! 15You were very
happy then, but where is that joy now? I am ready
to testify that you would have taken out your eyes
and given them to me if that were possible.∞
16Now am I your enemy because I tell you the
truth?
17Those people are working hard to persuade
you, but this is not good for you. They want to persuade you to turn against us and follow only them.
18It is good for people to show interest in you, but
only if their purpose is good. This is always true,
not just when I am with you. 19My little children,
again I feel the pain of childbirth for you until you
truly become like Christ. 20I wish I could be with
you now and could change the way I am talking
to you, because I do not know what to think
about you.∞

The Example of Hagar and Sarah

21Some of you still want to be under the law. Tell
me, do you know what the law says? 22The Scriptures say that Abraham had two sons. The mother
of one son was a slave woman, and the mother of
the other son was a free woman. 23Abraham's son
from the slave woman was born in the normal
human way. But the son from the free woman
was born because of the promise God made to
Abraham.
24This story teaches something else: The two
women are like the two agreements between God
and his people. One agreement is the law that
God made on Mount Sinai, and the people who are
under this agreement are like slaves. The mother
named Hagar is like that agreement. 25She is like
Mount Sinai in Arabia and is a picture of the
earthly Jewish city of Jerusalem. This city and its
people, the Jews, are slaves to the law. 26But the
heavenly Jerusalem, which is above, is like the free
woman. She is our mother.∞ 27It is written in the
Scriptures:

"Be happy, Jerusalem.
You are like a woman who never gave
birth to children.
Start singing and shout for joy.
You never felt the pain of giving birth,
but you will have more children
than the woman who has
a husband." *Isaiah 54:1*

28My brothers and sisters, you are God's children because of his promise, as Isaac was then.
29The son who was born in the normal way treated
the other son badly. It is the same today. 30But

question of a correct and incorrect set of rules. In fact, the word Paul uses for "rules" in verses 3 and 9 refers not just to standards, but to an enslaving power (Colossians 2). Paul maintains that the Good News frees us from this power, which uses rules to enslave people and divide communities.

∞**4:5 Adoption:** Ephesians 1:5

4:6 *"Father."* Literally, "Abba, Father." Jewish children called their fathers "Abba."

∞**4:9 Idolatry:** 1 Thessalonians 1:9

4:15 Paul had some kind of recurrent physical trouble that he carried with him (2 Corinthians 12:7–10). This verse is suggestive that it may have been eye trouble, scars that were visible to all who met him (Galatians 6:17). It is possible to translate Galatians 6:17 as "the scars which come from Jesus" and make a connection with Paul's conversion on the Damascus road where he was blinded by his encounter with Jesus (Acts 9:8–9, 17–18). After the what "looked like fish scales" fell from his eyes, there may have remained some sort of ongoing eye trouble that made the Galatians want to tear out their eyes and give them to Paul.

∞**4:15 Miracles:** See article on page 731.

4:17 *Those people.* They are the false teachers who were bothering the believers in Galatia (Galatians 1:7).

∞**4:20 Paul (Saul):** Galatians 6:11–18

4:21–31 Sarah, the "free woman," is contrasted to Hagar her slave. This is a picture of the contrast between the freedom of life under the New Agreement and the slavery to the Law which characterized life under the Old Agreement.

4:24 *Mount Sinai.* Mountain in Arabia where God gave his Law to Moses (Exodus 19 and 20).

∞**4:26 Jerusalem:** Hebrews 12:22

what does the Scripture say? "Throw out the slave woman and her son. The son of the slave woman should not inherit anything. The son of the free woman should receive it all." 31So, my brothers and sisters, we are not children of the slave woman, but of the free woman.

Keep Your Freedom

5 We have freedom now, because Christ made us free. So stand strong. Do not change and go back into the slavery of the law. 2Listen, I Paul tell you that if you go back to the law by being circumcised, Christ does you no good. 3Again, I warn every man: If you allow yourselves to be circumcised, you must follow all the law. 4If you try to be made right with God through the law, your life with Christ is over—you have left God's grace. 5But we have the true hope that comes from being made right with God, and by the Spirit we wait eagerly for this hope. 6When we are in Christ Jesus, it is not important if we are circumcised or not. The important thing is faith—the kind of faith that works through love.

7You were running a good race. Who stopped you from following the true way? 8This change did not come from the One who chose you. 9Be careful! "Just a little yeast makes the whole batch of dough rise." 10But I trust in the Lord that you will not believe those different ideas. Whoever is confusing you with such ideas will be punished.

11My brothers and sisters, I do not teach that a man must be circumcised. If I teach circumcision, why am I still being attacked? If I still taught circumcision, my preaching about the cross would not be a problem. 12I wish the people who are bothering you would castrate themselves!

13My brothers and sisters, God called you to be free, but do not use your freedom as an excuse to do what pleases your sinful self. Serve each other with love. 14The whole law is made complete in this one command: "Love your neighbor as you love yourself." 15If you go on hurting each other and tearing each other apart, be careful, or you will completely destroy each other.

The Spirit and Human Nature

16So I tell you: Live by following the Spirit. Then you will not do what your sinful selves want. 17Our sinful selves want what is against the Spirit, and the Spirit wants what is against our sinful selves. The two are against each other, so you cannot do just what you please. 18But if the Spirit is leading you, you are not under the law.

19The wrong things the sinful self does are clear: being sexually unfaithful, not being pure, taking part in sexual sins, 20worshiping gods, doing witchcraft, hating, making trouble, being jealous, being angry, being selfish, making people angry with each other, causing divisions among people, 21feeling envy, being drunk, having wild and wasteful parties, and doing other things like these. I warn you now as I warned you before: Those who do these things will not inherit God's kingdom. 22But the Spirit produces the fruit of love, joy, peace, patience, kindness, goodness, faithfulness, 23gentleness, self-control. There is no law that says these things are wrong. 24Those who belong to Christ Jesus have crucified their own sinful selves. They have given up their old selfish feelings and the evil things they wanted to do. 25We get our new life from the Spirit, so we should follow the Spirit. 26We must not be proud or make trouble with each other or be jealous of each other.

Help Each Other

6 Brothers and sisters, if someone in your group does something wrong, you who are spiritual

---

4:30 *"Throw . . . all."* Quotation from Genesis 21:10.
4:31 Promise: Hebrews 6:13–18
5:1 Salvation: 1 Timothy 1:1
5:6 Circumcision: Galatians 6:15
5:12 *castrate.* To cut off part of the male sex organ. Paul uses this word because it is similar to "circumcision." Paul wanted to show that he is very upset with the false teachers.
5:13 Love: Ephesians 5:2
5:14 Neighbor: Romans 13:10
5:14 *"Love . . . yourself."* Quotation from Leviticus 19:18.
5:16–26 Paul tells the Galatian believers to "live by following the Spirit. Then you will not do what your sinful selves want" (Galatians 5:16). Improper ambition that seeks to elevate the self above others or that seeks to make personal gain an end in itself, is to be crucified with Christ. In all areas of our lives—including our goals and ambitions—we are to draw our energy and direction from the Holy Spirit.
5:20 Jealousy: See article on page 601.
5:20 Magic: Acts 8:9–24
5:22–23 In Paul's list of nine aspects of the fruit of the Spirit, the ninth is self-control. Like the others, self-control is a result of the Spirit's control in our lives. That is why the filling of the Spirit is contrasted with drunkenness, which produces a *loss* of self-control Ephesians 5:18). Again, like the other aspects, self-control is a characteristic of Jesus Christ we are to incorporate into our lives.
5:23 Spirituality/Spiritual Dryness: 1 Peter 1:13–2:10
5:25 Body/Flesh: Hebrews 10:5
5:25 Land/Inheritance: Ephesians 1:13–14
5:26 Conflict: Ephesians 2:11–22
5:26 Freedom: See article on page 1253.
5:26 Good Works: Philippians 2:12–13
6:1–2 Christian fellowship is more than social activities or lending a helping hand in time of trouble. It is taking responsibility for the spiritual growth and welfare of fellow believers in the Body of Christ. Here Paul urges the Galatian community to exercise church discipline in the case of someone caught in sin. Such discipline is to be carried out by mature believers who are on guard lest they be tempted as well. In so doing, they show Christian love as Paul tells them: "You truly obey the law of Christ."

should go to that person and gently help make him
right again. But be careful, because you might be
tempted to sin, too. 2By helping each other with
your troubles, you truly obey the law of Christ.
3If anyone thinks he is important when he really is
not, he is only fooling himself. 4Each person should
judge his own actions and not compare himself
with others. Then he can be proud for what he
himself has done. 5Each person must be responsible for himself.

6Anyone who is learning the teaching of God
should share all the good things he has with his
teacher.

Life Is like Planting a Field

7Do not be fooled: You cannot cheat God. People
harvest only what they plant. 8If they plant to satisfy their sinful selves, their sinful selves will bring
them ruin. But if they plant to please the Spirit,
they will receive eternal life from the Spirit.
9We must not become tired of doing good. We
will receive our harvest of eternal life at the right
time if we do not give up. 10When we have the
opportunity to help anyone, we should do it. But
we should give special attention to those who are
in the family of believers.

Paul Ends His Letter

11See what large letters I use to write this myself.
12Some people are trying to force you to be circumcised so the Jews will accept them. They are
afraid they will be attacked if they follow only the
cross of Christ. 13Those who are circumcised do
not obey the law themselves, but they want you to
be circumcised so they can brag about what they
forced you to do. 14I hope I will never brag about
things like that. The cross of our Lord Jesus Christ
is my only reason for bragging. Through the cross
of Jesus my world was crucified, and I died to the
world. 15It is not important if a man is circumcised
or uncircumcised. The important thing is being
the new people God has made. 16Peace and
mercy to those who follow this rule—and to all of
God's people.

17So do not give me any more trouble. I have
scars on my body that show I belong to Christ Jesus.

18My brothers and sisters, the grace of our Lord
Jesus Christ be with your spirit. Amen.

6:1 Test/Temptation: Ephesians 6:10–20
6:2 Service: Philippians 2:3–4
6:2 Conflict: Galatians 5:16–26
6:8 Pleasure: Hebrews 11:6
6:9 Perseverance: Philippians 1:6
6:12–17 In these closing sentences, Paul moves back and forth from circumcision to the cross of Jesus Christ. Here is the nature of Paul's conflict with the Galatians at its starkest. They are being told that they must identify themselves as believers by keeping the Jewish law. He maintains that they will identify themselves as Christ's followers by a new life, a life modelled on the faithfulness Jesus showed even in his death.

6:12 *cross of Christ.* Paul uses the cross as a picture of the Good News, the story of Christ's death and rising from the dead to pay for our sins. The cross, or Christ's death, was God's way to save us.
6:15 Circumcision: Philippians 3:3
6:17 *that show.* Many times Paul was beaten and whipped by people who were against him because he was teaching about Christ. The scars were from these beatings.
6:18 Paul (Saul): Ephesians 3:1–13

INTRODUCTION TO THE BOOK OF

EPHESIANS

God Unites His People

Who wrote this book?

The author of the Book of Ephesians is the apostle Paul (1:1).

To whom was this book written?

Although this letter does not bear the name of the Ephesians in some ancient biblical manuscripts, scholars regard this as a circular letter sent to Ephesus and then on to other cities of Asia Minor.

Where was it written?

It is most likely that this letter was written in Rome, during Paul's first prison term.

When was it written?

Paul was under house arrest from about A.D. 60 to 62. So, it is probable that the letter was written during that period, perhaps immediately after he wrote the Book of Colossians. Ephesians and Colossians share a number of themes.

What is the book about?

The Book of Ephesians does not address any particular theological or practical problem. It seeks to build up the Ephesians in their faith. Themes of the book include salvation by grace through faith, the sovereignty of God, unity of all believers, and Christ as head of the Body (the church). The church is portrayed as the glorious bride of Christ and, as such, should remain pure and holy, ready for his return.

Why was this book written?

Paul wrote to the Ephesians to instruct them, and others, in the Good News of their salvation. He wanted to build an awareness of their being connected to each other and to the church universal. He also taught them the principles of living the Spirit-filled life and waging spiritual warfare against their enemy, the devil.

So what does this book mean to us?

Like the Ephesian Christians, we often feel isolated in our faith. Paul's letter to them also reminds us that we are universally connected to other Christians like us, who are in mortal combat with our common enemy, Satan. It is vitally important that we stay in close fellowship with other Christians so that we can be encouraged and gain the spiritual strength to resist the devil, who "goes around like a roaring lion looking for someone to eat" (1 Peter 5:8). Alone, we are weak and vulnerable to him; together, we "have full victory through God who showed his love for us" (Romans 8:37).

Summary:

Like other letters in the New Testament, Ephesians will have been directed toward particular issues being faced within a particular setting. In comparison with other New Testament letters, though, Ephesians is notable for its lack of urgency and direct argument. It seems rather to have been written for a church in need of a solid grounding in the Good News that emphasized the unity of all believers in Christ. Central aspects of the Christian message thus come in for discussion in this letter, including the great love of God, the suffering and exalted Christ, and the present relationship believers have with God through Christ. It is also in Ephesians that we find one of the strongest statements about the unity of all people, Jew and non-Jew, in the one Body of Christ (see 2:12–18).

Many Christians at Ephesus came from pagan backgrounds, or from religious backgrounds where evil spirits and cosmic powers were emphasized. So, an explanation of the Good News for Ephesian Christians quite naturally focuses on issues raised within this context. Ephesians deals with the question of hostile spirits, primarily by emphasizing the superiority of God and of Christ. Christians need not fear those evil powers because they have access to an even greater power, the power of God. Moreover, in the last half of the letter, we read specific guidance designed to help those who were formally pagans to know what behavior was appropriate, given their new relationship to Christ.

EPHESIANS

Remains of the theater in the Hellenistic city of Ephesus

From Paul, an apostle of Christ Jesus. I am an apostle because that is what God wanted.

To God's holy people living in Ephesus, believers in Christ Jesus:

2Grace and peace to you from God our Father and the Lord Jesus Christ.

Spiritual Blessings in Christ

3Praise be to the God and Father of our Lord Jesus Christ. In Christ, God has given us every spiritual blessing in the heavenly world. 4That is, in Christ, he chose us before the world was made so that we would be his holy people—people without blame before him. 5Because of his love, God had already decided to make us his own children through Jesus Christ. That was what he wanted and what pleased him, 6and it brings praise to God because of his wonderful grace. God gave that grace to us freely, in Christ, the One he loves. 7In Christ we are set free by the blood of his death, and so we have forgiveness of sins. How rich is God's grace, 8which he has given to us so fully and freely. God, with full wisdom and understanding, 9let us know his secret purpose. This was what God wanted, and he planned to do it through Christ. 10His goal was to carry out his plan, when the right time came, that all things in heaven and on earth would be joined together in Christ as the head.

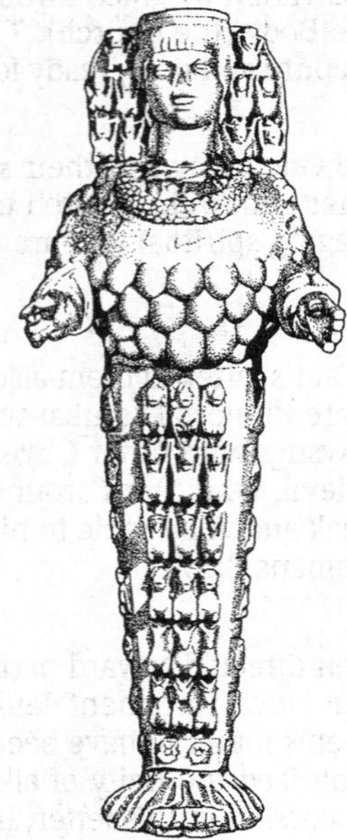

A statue of the false goddess Diana, found at Ephesus

11In Christ we were chosen to be God's people, because from the very beginning God had decided this in keeping with his plan. And he is the One who makes everything agree with what he decides and wants. 12We are the first people who hoped in Christ, and we were chosen so that we would bring praise to God's glory. 13So it is with you. When you heard the true teaching—the Good News about your salvation—you believed in Christ. And in Christ, God put his special mark of ownership on you by giving you the Holy Spirit that he had promised. 14That Holy Spirit is the guarantee that we will receive what God promised for his people until God gives full freedom to those who are his—to bring praise to God's glory.

Paul's Prayer

15That is why since I heard about your faith in the Lord Jesus and your love for all God's people, 16I have not stopped giving thanks to God for you. I always remember you in my prayers, 17asking the God of our Lord Jesus Christ, the glorious Father, to give you a spirit of wisdom and revelation so that you will know him better. 18I pray also that you will have

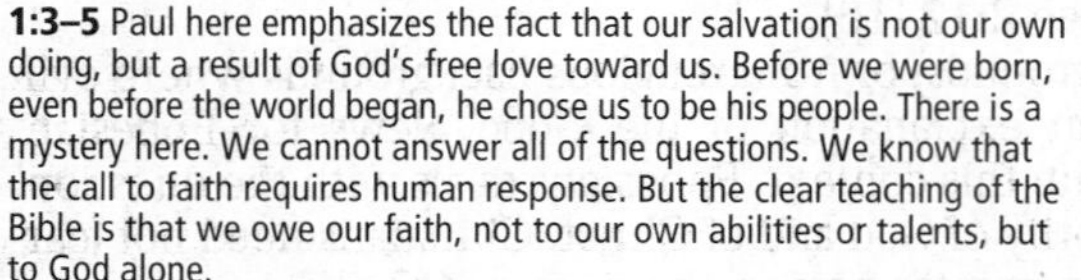

1:3–5 Paul here emphasizes the fact that our salvation is not our own doing, but a result of God's free love toward us. Before we were born, even before the world began, he chose us to be his people. There is a mystery here. We cannot answer all of the questions. We know that the call to faith requires human response. But the clear teaching of the Bible is that we owe our faith, not to our own abilities or talents, but to God alone.

1:5 By God's grace, we have been made his own children. This is like an adoption in which a new parent takes the initiative and provides everything needed to make an orphan fully part of a family. That new son or daughter is guaranteed a full inheritance (Ephesians 3:6). All of the initiative is God's. The adopted child's role is to be receptive and responsive.

1:5 Adoption: Ephesians 3:6
1:6 Blessing: 2 Thessalonians 2:16–17
1:10 Election (Chosen): 2 Peter 1:10
1:11 Will of God: Ephesians 5:17
1:14 Land/Inheritance: Hebrews 9:15

greater understanding in your heart so you will know the hope to which he has called us and that you will know how rich and glorious are the blessings God has promised his holy people. 19And you will know that God's power is very great for us who believe. That power is the same as the great strength 20God used to raise Christ from the dead and put him at his right side in the heavenly world. 21God has put Christ over all rulers, authorities, powers, and kings, not only in this world but also in the next. 22God put everything under his power and made him the head over everything for the church, 23which is Christ's body. The church is filled with Christ, and Christ fills everything in every way.

We Now Have Life

2 In the past you were spiritually dead because of your sins and the things you did against God. 2Yes, in the past you lived the way the world lives, following the ruler of the evil powers that are above the earth. That same spirit is now working in those who refuse to obey God. 3In the past all of us lived like them, trying to please our sinful selves and doing all the things our bodies and minds wanted. We should have suffered God's anger because of the way we were. We were the same as all other people.

4But God's mercy is great, and he loved us very much. 5Though we were spiritually dead because of the things we did against God, he gave us new life with Christ. You have been saved by God's grace. 6And he raised us up with Christ and gave us a seat with him in the heavens. He did this for those in Christ Jesus 7so that for all future time he could show the very great riches of his grace by being kind to us in Christ Jesus. 8I mean that you have been saved by grace through believing. You did not save yourselves; it was a gift from God. 9It was not the result of your own efforts, so you cannot brag about it. 10God has made us what we are. In Christ Jesus, God made us to do good works, which God planned in advance for us to live our lives doing.

One in Christ

11You were not born Jewish. You are the people the Jews call "uncircumcised." Those who call you "uncircumcised" call themselves "circumcised." (Their circumcision is only something they themselves do on their bodies.) 12Remember that in the past you were without Christ. You were not citizens of Israel, and you had no part in the agreements with the promise that God made to his people. You had no hope, and you did not know God. 13But now in Christ Jesus, you who were far away from God are brought near through the blood of Christ's death. 14Christ himself is our peace. He made both Jewish people and those who are not Jews one people. They were separated as if there were a wall between them, but Christ broke down that wall of hate by giving his own body. 15The Jewish law had many commands and rules, but Christ ended that law. His purpose was to make the two groups of people become one new people in him and in this way make peace. 16It was also Christ's purpose to end the hatred between the two groups, to make them into one body, and to bring them back to God. Christ did all this with his death on the cross. 17Christ came and preached peace to you who were far away from God, and to those who were near to God. 18Yes, it is through Christ we all have the right to come to the Father in one Spirit.

19Now you who are not Jewish are not foreigners or strangers any longer, but are citizens together

1:21 The Powers: Colossians 1:15–20

1:22–23 The church is God's people. They are the Body of Christ. Christ is found in their midst. Christ is over the entire church. While a simple equation cannot be drawn between the church of the New Testament and the institutional church, the latter is a visible manifestation of the people of God. The institutional church is only faithful when it remembers who is really at the top. It is Jesus, and Jesus alone.

1:23 Body of Christ: Ephesians 2:6

1:23 Samuel: Hebrews 2:14–18

1:23 Unity: Ephesians 4:4–6

2:6 Body of Christ: Ephesians 4:12–16

2:8 Faith/Unbelief: Matthew 8:10

2:8–10 Submitting to Christ's lordship, living righteous lives in obedience to his commands, shows true salvation. It cannot be overemphasized that works play no role in gaining salvation. But good works have everything to do with living out salvation. No good works can earn salvation, but many good works result from genuine salvation. Good works are not necessary to become a disciple, but good works are the necessary marks of all true disciples. God has, after all, said that we "were made . . . to do good works."

2:10 Grace: Ephesians 3:1–13

2:11 *uncircumcised.* People not having the mark of circumcision as the Jews had.

2:11–14 Paul is comparing the agreement God made with the people of Israel to the new agreement God made with all people through Christ. God made an agreement with Abraham that he would be the God of his descendants and would always be near to the great nation that they would become (Genesis 12:1–3). God sealed this agreement he made with Israel's patriarchs by commanding Moses to sacrifice an animal and sprinkle its blood on the people (Exodus 24:8). The Israelites were required to continue to make blood sacrifices as part of the agreement for the forgiveness of their sins (see Leviticus 4). In saying, "You who were far away from God are brought near through the blood of Christ's death" (Ephesians 2:13), Paul makes it clear that the Lord is God no longer of just the Israelites, but of all people. The new agreement is not sealed through the blood of animals, nor does it require ongoing sacrifices. Paul uses the image of Christ's blood to communicate that Jesus' death and resurrection seal the new agreement and bring the forgiveness of sin to all people in one divine and definitive act.

2:13 Commitment: Hebrews 6:16–17

2:14 Crossing Cultural Boundaries: James 2:1–4

2:18 Peace: Philippians 4:7

2:18 Racism: Colossians 3:11

with God's holy people. You belong to God's family. 20You are like a building that was built on the
foundation of the apostles and prophets. Christ
Jesus himself is the most important stone in that
building,∞ 21and that whole building is joined
together in Christ. He makes it grow and become a
holy temple in the Lord. 22And in Christ you, too,
are being built together with the Jews into a place
where God lives through the Spirit.∞

Paul's Work in Telling the Good News

3 So I, Paul, am a prisoner of Christ Jesus for
you who are not Jews. 2Surely you have heard
that God gave me this work through his grace to
help you. 3He let me know his secret by showing it
to me. I have already written a little about this. 4If
you read what I wrote then, you can see that I truly
understand the secret about the Christ. 5People
who lived in other times were not told that secret.
But now, through the Spirit, God has shown that
secret to his holy apostles and prophets. 6This is
that secret: that through the Good News those
who are not Jews will share with the Jews in God's
blessing. They belong to the same body, and they
share together in the promise that God made in
Christ Jesus.∞
7By God's special gift of grace given to me
through his power, I became a servant to tell that
Good News. 8I am the least important of all God's
people, but God gave me this gift—to tell those
who are not Jews the Good News about the riches
of Christ, which are too great to understand fully.
9And God gave me the work of telling all people
about the plan for his secret, which has been hidden in him since the beginning of time. He is the
One who created everything. 10His purpose was
that through the church all the rulers and powers
in the heavenly world will now know God's wisdom, which has so many forms. 11This agrees with
the purpose God had since the beginning of time,
and he carried out his plan through Christ Jesus
our Lord. 12In Christ we can come before God
with freedom and without fear. We can do this
through faith in Christ. 13So I ask you not to become
discouraged because of the sufferings I am having
for you. My sufferings are for your glory.∞

The Love of Christ

14So I bow in prayer before the Father 15from
whom every family in heaven and on earth gets its
true name. 16I ask the Father in his great glory to
give you the power to be strong inwardly through
his Spirit. 17I pray that Christ will live in your hearts
by faith and that your life will be strong in love and
be built on love. 18And I pray that you and all God's
holy people will have the power to understand the
greatness of Christ's love—how wide and how long
and how high and how deep that love is. 19Christ's
love is greater than anyone can ever know, but I
pray that you will be able to know that love. Then
you can be filled with the fullness of God.
20With God's power working in us, God can do
much, much more than anything we can ask or
imagine. 21To him be glory in the church and in
Christ Jesus for all time, forever and ever. Amen.∞

The Unity of the Body

4 I am in prison because I belong to the Lord.
God chose you to be his people, so I urge you
now to live the life to which God called you. 2Always
be humble, gentle, and patient, accepting each other
in love. 3You are joined together with peace through
the Spirit, so make every effort to continue together
in this way. 4There is one body and one Spirit,
and God called you to have one hope. 5There is
one Lord, one faith, and one baptism.∞ 6There
is one God and Father of everything. He rules everything and is everywhere and is in everything.∞
7Christ gave each one of us the special gift of
grace, showing how generous he is. 8That is why
it says in the Scriptures,

"When he went up to the heights,
he led a parade of captives,
and he gave gifts to people." *Psalm 68:18*

9When it says, "He went up," what does it mean?
It means that he first came down to the earth. 10So
Jesus came down, and he is the same One who
went up above all the heaven. Christ did that to fill

∞**2:20 Foreigner (Alien):** See article on page 1410.
2:20 *most important stone.* Literally, "cornerstone." The first and most important stone in a building.
∞**2:22 Conflict:** Ephesians 6
∞**2:22 Friend:** See article on page 1295.
∞**3:6 Adoption:** James 1:27
∞**3:13 Grace:** Philippians 3:3–11
∞**3:13 Paul (Saul):** Philippians 1:12–26
3:14–17 In this passage, two different notions of a "house" or "home" are presented. In verse 14, the term "family" is applied to every related being, human or angelic, created in the image of God. In verse 17, our hearts are described as Christ's "home" when we invite him to live there by faith.
∞**3:21 Intercession:** See article on page 1041.
4:1 This verse marks an important transition in the letter. In the first three chapters, the Letter to the Ephesians focuses especially on the nature of the Good News. Now it will draw out the implications of the Good News for everyday life.
∞**4:5 Lordship:** Philippians 2:9–11
∞**4:6 Father:** 1 Peter 1:17
∞**4:6 Baptism:** Colossians 2:11–14
∞**4:6 Numbers:** See article on page 561.
∞**4:6 Trinity:** Colossians 2:9
∞**4:6 Unity:** Ephesians 4:15

everything with his presence. 11And Christ gave
gifts to people—he made some to be apostles, some
to be prophets, some to go and tell the Good News,
and some to have the work of caring for and teaching God's people. 12Christ gave those gifts to prepare God's holy people for the work of serving, to
make the body of Christ stronger.⚭ 13This work
must continue until we are all joined together in
the same faith and in the same knowledge of the
Son of God. We must become like a mature person,
growing until we become like Christ and have his
perfection.⚭

14Then we will no longer be babies. We will not
be tossed about like a ship that the waves carry one
way and then another. We will not be influenced
by every new teaching we hear from people who
are trying to fool us. They make plans and try any
kind of trick to fool people into following the wrong
path. 15No! Speaking the truth with love, we will
grow up in every way into Christ, who is the head.⚭
16The whole body depends on Christ, and all the
parts of the body are joined and held together.
Each part does its own work to make the whole
body grow and be strong with love.⚭

The Way You Should Live

17In the Lord's name, I tell you this. Do not continue living like those who do not believe. Their
thoughts are worth nothing. 18They do not understand, and they know nothing, because they refuse
to listen. So they cannot have the life that God
gives.⚭ 19They have lost all feeling of shame, and
they use their lives for doing evil. They continually
want to do all kinds of evil. 20But what you learned
in Christ was not like this. 21I know that you heard
about him, and you are in him, so you were taught
the truth that is in Jesus. 22You were taught to
leave your old self—to stop living the evil way you
lived before. That old self becomes worse, because
people are fooled by the evil things they want to
do. 23But you were taught to be made new in your
hearts, 24to become a new person. That new person is made to be like God—made to be truly good
and holy.

25So you must stop telling lies. Tell each other the
truth, because we all belong to each other in the same
body. 26When you are angry, do not sin, and be sure
to stop being angry before the end of the day.⚭
27Do not give the devil a way to defeat you.
28Those who are stealing must stop stealing and
start working. They should earn an honest living
for themselves. Then they will have something to
share with those who are poor.

29When you talk, do not say harmful things, but
say what people need—words that will help others become stronger. Then what you say will do
good to those who listen to you. 30And do not
make the Holy Spirit sad. The Spirit is God's proof
that you belong to him. God gave you the Spirit
to show that God will make you free when the
final day comes. 31Do not be bitter or angry or
mad. Never shout angrily or say things to hurt
others. Never do anything evil. 32Be kind and loving to each other, and forgive each other just as
God forgave you in Christ.

Living in the Light

5 You are God's children whom he loves, so try
to be like him. 2Live a life of love just as Christ
loved us and gave himself for us as a sweet-smelling
offering and sacrifice to God.⚭

3But there must be no sexual sin among you, or
any kind of evil or greed. Those things are not right
for God's holy people.⚭ 4Also, there must be no
evil talk among you, and you must not speak foolishly or tell evil jokes. These things are not right for
you. Instead, you should be giving thanks to God.⚭
5You can be sure of this: No one will have a place in
the kingdom of Christ and of God who sins sexually, or does evil things, or is greedy. Anyone who is
greedy is serving a false god.⚭

6Do not let anyone fool you by telling you things
that are not true, because these things will bring
God's anger on those who do not obey him. 7So

4:11 The list of gifts in Ephesians 4:11 emphasizes the functions needed in the church to lead the church. The church needs founders (apostles), people who provide correction and keep us true to God's call (prophets), people who go out and tell the Good News to nonbelievers (evangelists) and people who lead the teaching of and caring for the church (pastors-teachers). The spiritual gifts do not enable some people to do all the work of the church but are intended to help all Christians grow and work together in the service of Christ.

4:12 We are not saved by works, but after we are saved, we show that we truly believe by doing good works. According to this verse, even our good works are a gift from God. He prepares us for "works of service" by giving us the ability we need to do them.

⚭**4:12 Stewardship:** Philippians 2:2–5
⚭**4:13 Work:** Colossians 3:17
⚭**4:15 Lying/Dishonesty:** Ephesians 6:14
⚭**4:15 Unity:** Ephesians 5:30
⚭**4:16 Body of Christ:** Ephesians 6:22–23
⚭**4:18 Stubbornness:** Hebrews 3:7–15

4:25 *Tell . . . body.* This is a quotation of Zechariah 8:16 and emphasizes that believers, whether of the Old Testament or the New, are all members of the same community and "neighbors" in this sense (Deuteronomy 5:20–21; Exodus 20:16–17).

⚭**4:26 Anger:** James 1:19–20
⚭**5:2 Love:** Colossians 3:14
⚭**5:3 Greed:** Ephesians 5:5
⚭**5:4 Tongue:** Philippians 2:14
⚭**5:5 Greed:** Colossians 3:5

have nothing to do with them.⚭ 8In the past you were full of darkness, but now you are full of light in the Lord. So live like children who belong to the light. 9Light brings every kind of goodness, right living, and truth. 10Try to learn what pleases the Lord. 11Have nothing to do with the things done in darkness, which are not worth anything. But show that they are wrong. 12It is shameful even to talk about what those people do in secret. 13But the light makes all things easy to see, 14and everything that is made easy to see can become light. This is why it is said:

"Wake up, sleeper!
Rise from death,
and Christ will shine on you."

15So be very careful how you live. Do not live like those who are not wise, but live wisely. 16Use every chance you have for doing good, because these are evil times.⚭ 17So do not be foolish but learn what the Lord wants you to do.⚭ 18Do not be drunk with wine, which will ruin you, but be filled with the Spirit.⚭ 19Speak to each other with psalms, hymns, and spiritual songs, singing and making music in your hearts to the Lord.⚭ 20Always give thanks to God the Father for everything, in the name of our Lord Jesus Christ.

Wives and Husbands

21Yield to obey each other because you respect Christ.

22Wives, yield to your husbands, as you do to the Lord, 23because the husband is the head of the wife, as Christ is the head of the church. And he is the Savior of the body, which is the church. 24As the church yields to Christ, so you wives should yield to your husbands in everything.⚭

25Husbands, love your wives as Christ loved the church and gave himself for it 26to make it belong to God. Christ used the word to make the church clean by washing it with water. 27He died so that he could give the church to himself like a bride in all her beauty. He died so that the church could be pure and without fault, with no evil or sin or any other wrong thing in it.⚭ 28In the same way, husbands should love their wives as they love their own bodies. The man who loves his wife loves himself. 29No one ever hates his own body, but feeds and takes care of it. And that is what Christ does for the church, 30because we are parts of his body.⚭ 31The Scripture says, "So a man will leave his father and mother and be united with his wife, and the two will become one body." 32That secret is very important—I am talking about Christ and the church. 33But each one of you must love his wife as he loves himself, and a wife must respect her husband.⚭

Children and Parents

6 Children, obey your parents as the Lord wants, because this is the right thing to do.

⚭**5:7 God's Anger:** 1 Thessalonians 5:9–10

5:15–20 We must be careful how we spend the time God has given us. Whether at work or during our leisure time, we should not try to find satisfaction in the pleasures offered by the world. Rather, we should seek to be filled with the Spirit so that we will be able to use every chance we have for doing good. Then we will know the real joy and pleasure that comes from fellowship with God (Psalm 16:11; John 15:11).

⚭**5:16 Evil:** Hebrews 3:12

⚭**5:17 Will of God:** Hebrews 13:20–21

⚭**5:17 Time:** Colossians 2:16–17

5:18 Here is a direct command prohibiting drunkenness because alcohol is a depressant that lowers our self-control and opens us up to shameful behavior. Interestingly, it is contrasted in the same verse with the command to be continuously filled with the Spirit, who raises our self-control to the maximum.

⚭**5:18 Holy Spirit:** Titus 3:5–6

⚭**5:19 Music:** Colossians 3:16

⚭**5:24 Women:** Ephesians 5:33

5:25 The standard of love God holds up to husbands is very high indeed. Husbands are to be willing to sacrifice their own wishes, and even themselves if need be, for their wives. This is what Christ did for the church. Even beyond sacrificing their lives, husbands are to dedicate themselves to promoting the welfare and spiritual growth of their wives. Christ died "so that the church could be pure and without fault" (Ephesians 5:27). Husbands should live so their wives will be all God intended them to be.

Paul likens the marriage relationship to the relationship Christians enjoy with Jesus Christ. These two relationships share an intimacy and exclusiveness that can be found in no other relationship. Our love for our spouse reflects the love that Christ has for his people.

⚭**5:27 Clean & Unclean:** 1 John 1:7–9

⚭**5:30 Unity:** Revelation 15:1–4

5:31 *"So . . . body."* Quotation from Genesis 2:24.

⚭**5:33 Women:** Colossians 3:18

⚭**5:33 Sexuality:** See article on page 602.

6 Here, as in many of Paul's writings, there is a flurry of last chapter instruction and encouragement given to the reader. In verses 10–18, he returns to a favorite comparison of the Christian life to a battle. He reminds them of the nature of the enemy (verse 12), the need for adequate protection (verse 13), the makeup of the armor (verses 14–18) and the importance of preparation, persistence, and prayer (verse 18). While writing from prison, he challenged young Timothy to, "Fight the good fight of faith, grabbing hold of the life that continues forever. You were called to have that life when you confessed the good confession before many witnesses" (1 Timothy 6:12). And just before his martyrdom, he reminded Timothy, "I have fought the good fight, I have finished the race, I have kept the faith" (2 Timothy 4:7). These action analogies show that Paul did not believe the Christian life was designed for the weak at heart.

Jesus did not ever say that following would be easy. His invitations were never easy to respond to. His hearers must have shuddered when he said, "If people want to follow me, they must give up the things they want. They must be willing even to give up their lives to follow me" (Mark 8:34). His statement to the rich young man caused him to walk away: "If you want to be perfect, then go and sell your possessions and give the money to the poor. If you do this, you will have treasure in heaven. Then come and follow me" (Matthew 19:21). People are quick to point out the unfairness of asking the man to sell everything. What this overlooks is Jesus' promise that he would have treasure in heaven. In the end, he had everything to gain and nothing to lose.

2The command says, "Honor your father and mother." This is the first command that has a promise with it— 3"Then everything will be well with you, and you will have a long life on the earth."

4Fathers, do not make your children angry, but raise them with the training and teaching of the Lord.

Slaves and Masters

5Slaves, obey your masters here on earth with fear and respect and from a sincere heart, just as you obey Christ. 6You must do this not only while they are watching you, to please them. With all your heart you must do what God wants as people who are obeying Christ. 7Do your work with enthusiasm. Work as if you were serving the Lord, not as if you were serving only men and women. 8Remember that the Lord will give a reward to everyone, slave or free, for doing good.

9Masters, in the same way, be good to your slaves. Do not threaten them. Remember that the One who is your Master and their Master is in heaven, and he treats everyone alike.

Wear the Full Armor of God

10Finally, be strong in the Lord and in his great power. 11Put on the full armor of God so that you can fight against the devil's evil tricks. 12Our fight is not against people on earth but against the rulers and authorities and the powers of this world's darkness, against the spiritual powers of evil in the heavenly world. 13That is why you need to put on God's full armor. Then on the day of evil you will be able to stand strong. And when you have finished the whole fight, you will still be standing. 14So stand strong, with the belt of truth tied around your waist and the protection of right living on your chest. 15On your feet wear the Good News of peace to help you stand strong. 16And also use the shield of faith with which you can stop all the burning arrows of the Evil One. 17Accept God's salvation as your helmet, and take the sword of the Spirit, which is the word of God. 18Pray in the Spirit at all times with all kinds of prayers, asking for everything you need. To do this you must always be ready and never give up. Always pray for all God's people.

19Also pray for me that when I speak, God will give me words so that I can tell the secret of the Good News without fear. 20I have been sent to preach this Good News, and I am doing that now, here in prison. Pray that when I preach the Good News I will speak without fear, as I should.

Final Greetings

21I am sending to you Tychicus, our brother whom we love and a faithful servant of the Lord's work. He will tell you everything that is happening with me. Then you will know how I am and what I am doing. 22I am sending him to you for this reason—so that you will know how we are, and he can encourage you.

23Peace and love with faith to you from God the Father and the Lord Jesus Christ. 24Grace to all of you who love our Lord Jesus Christ with love that never ends.

6:2 *"Honor . . . mother."* Quotation from Exodus 20:12; Deuteronomy 5:16.
6:3 *"Then . . . earth."* Quotation from Exodus 20:12; Deuteronomy 5:16.
6:4 This verse is addressed to fathers because they are considered ultimately responsible for the training of their children, not because Paul has a low opinion of the mother's role in child-rearing. The word "angry" refers to a child's frustration with excessively harsh or inconsistent discipline, or parental inattention and indecision. Parents are to be actively involved in training their children to know, love, and serve Jesus Christ.

6:6 Integrity: James 1:6–8
6:14 Lying/Dishonesty: Philippians 4:8
6:18 Demon: 2 Corinthians 12:7
6:18 Satan/Satanism: Colossians 1:21–23
6:20 Holy War & Divine Warrior: Revelation 19:11–21
6:20 Test/Temptation: 1 Thessalonians 2:4
6:23 Body of Christ: Colossians 1:18
6:23 Conflict: Hebrews 9:14

Notes:

INTRODUCTION TO THE BOOK OF PHILIPPIANS

Serve Others with Joy

WHO WROTE THIS BOOK?

The apostle Paul is the author of the Book of Philippians (1:1).

TO WHOM WAS THIS BOOK WRITTEN?

This letter is written to the first church Paul established in Europe—Philippi, a Roman colony in Macedonia. The Philippine church was largely non-Jewish.

WHERE WAS IT WRITTEN?

Some scholars think this book was written during an unrecorded imprisonment of Paul at Ephesus. Others says Paul wrote the book during his brief prison term at Caesarea. However, the consensus of church tradition is that the letter was written during Paul's house arrest in Rome.

WHEN WAS IT WRITTEN?

From the book's internal evidence, it is clear that Philippians was written in the middle of Paul's first prison term at Rome, which would have been about A.D. 61.

WHAT IS THE BOOK ABOUT?

The Book of Philippians deals with several important themes: joy, the three-person God, the example of Christ's humility, justification (being made right with God) through faith, and the Christian life. Paul encourages the members of the church to maintain their unity. And he commends his fellow workers, Timothy and Epaphroditus, to the Philippians. Paul also expresses his own contentment, no matter what his circumstances.

WHY WAS THIS BOOK WRITTEN?

This letter was written to express Paul's gratitude to the Philippians for the gifts they had sent to him while he was under house arrest in Rome. It was also written to encourage a church he loved dearly to maintain harmony and unity in the face of impending persecution. Finally, it was written out of a full heart of joy and praise to God, and he exhorts the Philippians to rejoice as well, no matter what happens.

SO WHAT DOES THIS BOOK MEAN TO US?

All people need to be lifted up when they are down. That's what the Philippians did for Paul and what he tried to do for them in return. Because of the amazing gift of God's Son, Jesus Christ, we can rejoice with Paul, no matter what our circumstances may be. Our overflowing joy is always possible because we know that God will use his wonderful riches in Christ Jesus to give us everything we need (4:19). As Paul says it so beautifully, and as we can echo with confidence, "I have learned the secret of being happy at any time in everything that happens . . . I can do all things through Christ because he gives me strength" (4:12–13).

SUMMARY:

Paul wrote this letter from prison (see 1:13–14), yet it is full of joy. In fact, the word *joy* is mentioned more than fifteen times. Also important in this letter is the notion of partnership. Paul sees the Christians at Philippi as his partners in the Good News.

At one level, the letter to the Philippians is an extended "thank you" letter, since Paul is writing to thank the Philippians for their support in his missionary efforts. At another level, though, Paul wants the Philippians to take a further step in their own growth as Christians. In particular, he is concerned that they learn the lesson that comes through humility and through serving others.

PHILIPPIANS

From Paul and Timothy, servants of Christ Jesus.

To all of God's holy people in Christ Jesus who live in Philippi, including your elders and deacons:

[2]Grace and peace to you from God our Father and the Lord Jesus Christ.

Paul's Prayer

[3]I thank my God every time I remember you, [4]always praying with joy for all of you. [5]I thank God for the help you gave me while I preached the Good News—help you gave from the first day you believed until now. [6]God began doing a good work in you, and I am sure he will continue it until it is finished when Jesus Christ comes again.

[7]And I know that I am right to think like this about all of you, because I have you in my heart. All of you share in God's grace with me while I am in prison and while I am defending and proving the truth of the Good News. [8]God knows that I want to see you very much, because I love all of you with the love of Christ Jesus.

[9]This is my prayer for you: that your love will grow more and more; that you will have knowledge and understanding with your love; [10]that you will see the difference between good and bad and will choose the good; that you will be pure and without wrong for the coming of Christ; [11]that you will do many good things with the help of Christ to bring glory and praise to God.

Paul's Troubles Help the Work

[12]I want you brothers and sisters to know that what has happened to me has helped to spread the Good News. [13]All the palace guards and everyone else knows that I am in prison because I am a believer in Christ. [14]Because I am in prison, most of the believers have become more bold in Christ and are not afraid to speak the word of God.

[15]It is true that some preach about Christ because they are jealous and ambitious, but others preach about Christ because they want to help. [16]They preach because they have love, and they know that God gave me the work of defending the Good News. [17]But the others preach about Christ for selfish and wrong reasons, wanting to make trouble for me in prison.

[18]But it doesn't matter. The important thing is that in every way, whether for right or wrong reasons, they are preaching about Christ. So I am happy, and I will continue to be happy. [19]Because you are praying for me and the Spirit of Jesus Christ is helping me, I know this trouble will bring my freedom. [20]I expect and hope that I will not fail Christ in anything but that I will have the courage now, as always, to show the greatness of Christ in my life here on earth, whether I live or die. [21]To me the only important thing about living is Christ, and dying would be profit for me. [22]If I continue living in my body, I will be able to work for the Lord. I do not know what to choose—living or dying. [23]It is hard to choose between the two. I want to leave this life and be with Christ, which is much better, [24]but you need me here in my body. [25]Since I am sure of this, I know I will stay with you to help you grow and have joy in your faith. [26]You will be very happy in Christ Jesus when I am with you again.

[27]Only one thing concerns me: Be sure that you live in a way that brings honor to the Good News of Christ. Then whether I come and visit you or am away from you, I will hear that you are standing strong with one purpose, that you work together as one for the faith of the Good News, [28]and that you are not afraid of those who are against you. All of this is proof that your enemies will be destroyed but that you will be saved by God. [29]God gave you the honor not only of believing in Christ but also of

---

1:1 According to widespread ways of thinking, leadership might be exercised either "in the service of the people" or "by dominating people." Paul and Timothy portray themselves as servants of Christ Jesus, affirming their supreme loyalty to Christ, as well as disclosing the nature of their leadership among the Philippians. They are servants, not bosses.

1:5 Fellowship: Philippians 2:1
1:6 Perseverance: 2 Thessalonians 3:13

1:12 *brothers and sisters.* Although the Greek text says "brothers" here and throughout this book, Paul's words were meant for the entire church, including men and women.

1:13–14 The "palace guards" could refer to one of several groups—either those who guarded the Roman emperor's or Roman governor's residences, or elite guards stationed in the metropolis of Rome, or senatorial guards stationed in the provincial capitals of Ephesus, Caesarea, or Corinth.

1:14 Rome: Philippians 3:20–21
1:22 Career/Careerism: See article on page 140.
1:23 Mourning: Philippians 4:6–7
1:26 Martyrdom: Philippians 2:6–8
1:26 Paul (Saul): Philippians 2:19–3:14

1:27–2:4 As believers, we are to live our lives in a way that brings honor to the Good News. In particular, we should have more than an individual relationship with God, but also a life together with other believers, which is marked by a shared purpose: working together for the faith of the Good News (1:27). In this shared mission, we are to expect opposition and suffering, and to face them in unity, with courage and faith (1:28–30). In addition, we are to work hard to come to agreement, so that unity will be real and not in word only (2:1–2). And we are to look out for the honor and needs of others, not just ourselves (2:3–4).

1:29 Paul addresses the struggles the Christians of Philippi were undergoing in an unusual way. Naturally speaking, no one wants to suffer, and suffering is considered by most people to be a punishment. But for believers undergoing persecution for the sake of Christ, suffering is to be regarded as an honor given by God. Our testimony in the midst of such suffering brings glory to God, just as our faith does.

suffering for him, both of which bring glory to
Christ. 30When I was with you, you saw the
struggles I had, and you hear about the struggles I
am having now. You yourselves are having the
same kind of struggles.

2 Does your life in Christ give you strength?
Does his love comfort you? Do we share
together in the spirit? Do you have mercy and kindness? 2If so, make me very happy by having the
same thoughts, sharing the same love, and having
one mind and purpose. 3When you do things, do
not let selfishness or pride be your guide. Instead,
be humble and give more honor to others than to
yourselves. 4Do not be interested only in your
own life, but be interested in the lives of others.

Be Unselfish Like Christ

5In your lives you must think and act like Christ
Jesus.

6Christ himself was like God in everything.
But he did not think that being equal with
God was something to be used for his
own benefit.
7But he gave up his place with God and made
himself nothing.
He was born to be a man
and became like a servant.
8And when he was living as a man,
he humbled himself and was
fully obedient to God,
even when that caused his death—
death on a cross.
9So God raised him to the highest place.
God made his name greater
than every other name
10so that every knee will bow to
the name of Jesus—
everyone in heaven, on earth,
and under the earth.
11And everyone will confess
that Jesus Christ is Lord
and bring glory to God the Father.

Be the People God Wants You to Be

12My dear friends, you have always obeyed God
when I was with you. It is even more important
that you obey now while I am away from you.
Keep on working to complete your salvation with
fear and trembling, 13because God is working in
you to help you want to do and be able to do what
pleases him.
14Do everything without complaining or arguing. 15Then you will be innocent and without any
wrong. You will be God's children without fault.
But you are living with crooked and mean people all
around you, among whom you shine like stars in
the dark world. 16You offer the teaching that gives
life. So when Christ comes again, I can be happy
because my work was not wasted. I ran the race
and won.
17Your faith makes you offer your lives as a sacrifice in serving God. If I have to offer my own blood
with your sacrifice, I will be happy and full of joy with
all of you. 18You also should be happy and full of
joy with me.

Timothy and Epaphroditus

19I hope in the Lord Jesus to send Timothy to
you soon. I will be happy to learn how you are. 20I

1:29 Suffering: Philippians 3:10
2 says the name of "Jesus" is above all names and is one day to be acknowledged as "Lord," which is the name of God, which Jesus claims is rightfully his (John 13:13). The earliest Christian confession was that the one born Jesus of Nazareth was now the risen and exalted Lord in heaven.
2:1 Comfort: Colossians 4:11
2:1 Fellowship: Philippians 3:10
2:4 Service: James 1:27
2:5 Paul wants to provide specific illustrations for the kind of life he has called upon the Philippians to live in 1:27–2:4. His first illustration is this poem about Jesus Christ, the supreme example of one who acted unselfishly, and who was honored by God. He goes on to add his own example (2:17–18), and the examples of Timothy (2:19–24) and Epaphroditus (2:25–30).
2:5 Stewardship: 1 Peter 4:10
2:5–11 Some scholars believe this passage to be a song that was sung by the first Christians. Its words contain the basic facts about Jesus that all Christians should know. The first Christians sang such songs in their worship and in their daily lives.
2:6 Incarnation: Colossians 1:15
2:6–11 In describing Christ as being "like God in everything" and saying that Christ was "born a man," these verses attribute both a divine and human nature to Christ. This idea is closely related to what we find in Colossians 1:15–20 where Christ is said to be "exactly like God" and John 1:1–5 where Christ is called "the Word." We cannot see or know through human senses the true God or Father of the universe, but that God is revealed first in the divine figure (who is "like God in everything") and then in human existence in Jesus Christ. Jesus is not simply a good man or even an inspired prophet, but fully God.
2:8 Ambition: Titus 2:14
2:8 Martyrdom: Philippians 3:10–11
2:10 Names of God: 1 Timothy 6:15
2:11 Lordship: 1 Timothy 6:15
2:11 Servant of the Lord: 2 Timothy 2:24
2:12–13 This passage well expresses the interaction between divine initiative and human response in our faith before God. Paul does this while still maintaining a sense of mystery about the relationship between divine initiative and human response. First, Paul encourages his readers to work hard at their salvation. This indicates that they need to exercise their whole person toward godliness. In the next verse, he just as clearly expresses that it is God who works in our lives; our growth toward God is a result of grace.

The meaning of Paul's writing in the original Greek language is not easy to give in English. Paul calls on the many (plural) to work for the one salvation (singular). That is, the "salvation" he has in mind is concerned with the life of the church and not only with its individuals. Salvation, in this sense, means living as people who take seriously the example of Jesus (2:5–11).
2:13 Good Works: Titus 3:5–8
2:14 Tongue: Colossians 4:6
2:17 Sacrifice: Philippians 4:18

have no one else like Timothy, who truly cares for you. 21Other people are interested only in their own lives, not in the work of Jesus Christ. 22You know the kind of person Timothy is. You know he has served with me in telling the Good News, as a son serves his father. 23I plan to send him to you quickly when I know what will happen to me. 24I am sure that the Lord will help me to come to you soon.

25Epaphroditus, my brother in Christ, works and serves with me in the army of Christ. When I needed help, you sent him to me. I think now that I must send him back to you, 26because he wants very much to see all of you. He is worried because you heard that he was sick. 27Yes, he was sick, and nearly died, but God had mercy on him and me too so that I would not have more sadness. 28I want very much to send him to you so that when you see him you can be happy, and I can stop worrying about you. 29Welcome him in the Lord with much joy. Give honor to people like him, 30because he almost died for the work of Christ. He risked his life to give me the help you could not give in your service to me.

The Importance of Christ

3 My brothers and sisters, be full of joy in the Lord. It is no trouble for me to write the same things to you again, and it will help you to be more ready. 2Watch out for those who do evil, who are like dogs, who demand to cut the body. 3We are the ones who are truly circumcised. We worship God through his Spirit, and our pride is in Christ Jesus. We do not put trust in ourselves or anything we can do,⚭ 4although I might be able to put trust in myself. If anyone thinks he has a reason to trust in himself, he should know that I have greater reason for trusting in myself. 5I was circumcised eight days after my birth. I am from the people of Israel and the tribe of Benjamin. I am a Hebrew, and my parents were Hebrews. I had a strict view of the law, which is why I became a Pharisee. 6I was so enthusiastic I tried to hurt the church. No one could find fault with the way I obeyed the law of Moses.⚭ 7Those things were important to me, but now I think they are worth nothing because of Christ. 8Not only those things, but I think that all things are worth nothing compared with the greatness of knowing Christ Jesus my Lord. Because of him, I have lost all those things, and now I know they are worthless trash. This allows me to have Christ 9and to belong to him. Now I am right with God, not because I followed the law, but because I believed in Christ. God uses my faith to make me right with him.⚭ 10I want to know Christ and the power that raised him from the dead. I want to share in his sufferings and become like him in his death.⚭ 11Then I have hope that I myself will be raised from the dead.⚭

Continuing Toward Our Goal

12I do not mean that I am already as God wants me to be. I have not yet reached that goal, but I continue trying to reach it and to make it mine. Christ wants me to do that, which is the reason he made me his. 13Brothers and sisters, I know that I have not yet reached that goal, but there is one thing I always do. Forgetting the past and straining toward what is ahead, 14I keep trying to reach the goal and get the prize for which God called me through Christ to the life above.⚭

15All of us who are spiritually mature should think this way, too. And if there are things you do not agree with, God will make them clear to you. 16But we should continue following the truth we already have.

17Brothers and sisters, all of you should try to follow my example and to copy those who live the way we showed you.⚭ 18Many people live like enemies of the cross of Christ. I have often told you about them, and it makes me cry to tell you about them now.⚭ 19In the end, they will be destroyed. They do whatever their bodies want, they are proud of their shameful acts, and they think only about earthly things.⚭ 20But our homeland is in heaven, and we are waiting for our Savior, the Lord

3:1–11 To those who have no relationship with God, the idea of serving him seems like drudgery, as if he just wants to steal all our fun. But to those who have seen the ugliness of sin and the beauty of the Lord, serving and worshiping him is the highest calling and the most wonderful delight. Whatever we sacrifice in the process of doing his will is just "worthless trash."

3:2 *cut.* The word in Greek is like the word "circumcise," but it means "to cut completely off."

⚭3:3 Circumcision: Colossians 2:11

3:4–7 Genealogies were important to the Jews in both the Old and New Testaments. They established the genuineness of someone's claim to be a descendant of one of the twelve tribes and an heir of God's promises to Israel. Paul makes it clear that while his own genealogical record was impeccable, it meant nothing to him in comparison with his relationship to Christ.

⚭3:6 Honor & Shame: Hebrews 6:6

⚭3:9 Pharisees and Sadducees: See article on page 1012.

⚭3:10 Fellowship: See article on page 1064.

⚭3:10 Suffering: Colossians 1:24

⚭3:11 Grace: Titus 2:11–14

⚭3:11 Martyrdom: Colossians 1:24–29

⚭3:14 Paul (Saul): Philippians 4:10–23

⚭3:17 Leadership: Philippians 4:9

⚭3:18 Apostasy: 1 Timothy 4:1

⚭3:19 Hell: 2 Thessalonians 1:7–9

CITY

REVELATION 21

Why does God care, and why should Christians be concerned, about the city? In what ways does the Bible address urban life? Why is Jerusalem called the City of God?

Today, most of the world's population live in urban centers. It is true that the Bible introduces city life in a predominantly negative way. After all, the first city was built by Cain after he killed his brother Abel. He named that city after his son Enoch. An early story of city building is recounted in Genesis 11:1–9, an episode that we know as the "Tower of Babel." In both cases, the building of a city was an act of rebellion against God. Sometimes cities are just that, an attempt to accumulate human power that is sometimes used for wonderful projects and at other times for horrible evil.

Does that mean that Christians should be afraid of cities and seek refuge in the countryside? No. While it is true that the biblical story of cities begins with Cain and Babylon, it ends with another city, the new Jerusalem, which is "coming down out of heaven from God" (Revelation 21:2). As they await that final day, Christians are to seek the peace and welfare of "the city where you are living, because if good things happen in the city, good things will happen to you also" (Jeremiah 29:4–7).

The Bible is an urban book in many ways. The Hebrew and Greek words for *city* occur approximately 1200 times in the Bible in reference to over one hundred different cities. In the West, the distinction is often made between a city and the people who live there. In the Bible, there is no such distinction—the city herself is the focus of God's concern. (Observe how Jesus weeps over Jerusalem in Luke 13:34–35). Every city has a unique personality, resources and needs, and citizens who are precious in God's sight. (See the story of Jonah and Nineveh, for example, in the Book of Jonah).

Cities in Scripture are sacred in that they are established by God and permeated with his presence through his representatives who dwell there. "The earth belongs to the Lord, and everything in it—the world and all its people" (Psalms 24:1). That includes every city, every zip code, both cattle and lands, people and trees, rocks that cry out, and all the rest of creation that "waits in pain" for its redemption (Romans 8:22).

Tokyo is the world's largest urban center, followed closely by Mexico City. In the 21st century, Sao Paulo is predicted to surpass Tokyo. New York is only the fourth largest metropolitan area. These four cities each have over twenty million citizens! Many Christians are anti-urban, avoiding the city at all cost. But God cares supremely about the city, where most of the world population lives, and calls many of us to live there as salt and light.

God's heart has always been in the city with the people he cares so much about. The first city in biblical history emerged in the land of Babylonia. In their pride, arrogance, and desire to become famous, the people began to build a great tower for themselves, whose top would reach into the heavens. The Lord considered it a direct affront, came down and confounded their language. Construction ceased, the city destroyed, the people were scattered. The place became known as Babel (Genesis 11:1–9). Centuries later, the city of Babylon arose as a great rival power to Israel. King Nebuchadnezzer attacked the city of Jerusalem three times, eventually destroying it, killing many Jews and carrying others off into captivity. The prophet Jeremiah interpreted the exile into Babylon, as tragic as it was, as part of God's permissive will: "This is what the LORD All-Powerful, the God of Israel says to all those people I sent away from Jerusalem as captives to Babylon . . ." Since it was God who ultimately sent them into exile, the Jewish people were to understand that what Nebuchadnezzer meant for evil, God meant for good (Jeremiah 29:4).

In God's providence, we are sent to live where God wants us to go and live. "God began by making one person, and from him came all the different people who live everywhere in the world. God decided exactly when and where they must live" (Acts 17:26). If God has sent you to live in a difficult and challenging city, as he did some of his people displaced from Jerusalem to Babylon, how should we then live? According to Jeremiah in the passage quoted above (29:4–6), we should work hard in the city to establish our homes, raise our families, and pray for the city's prosperity.

The new Jerusalem is called the holy city because it is God's prototype of urban life. The prophetic vision of this city is found in Isaiah 65:17–22, its fulfillment in Revelation 21. History began in the garden but ends in the city that comes down out of heaven from God. As God's people embrace their cities and the city that is to come, God can work to make all things new.

City: For additional scriptures on this topic go to Numbers 35.

Foreigner (Alien)

1 Peter 2:11

Why is the Bible concerned about foreigners, aliens, and strangers?
Why are believers sometimes called "foreigners"?

The Bible has a number of words to refer to outsiders: *foreigners*, *visitors*, and *strangers*. The words refer to people who are away from their homeland, who are not citizens of the country they live in. Such people usually have certain disadvantages in life, because they do not have family and friends to help them, and frequently cannot own property.

The word *stranger* is sometimes used in a bad sense, meaning "enemy" (for example, Isaiah 1:7). A stranger could be a threat to Israel, either by war (Lamentations 5:2; Obadiah 11), or by getting the people of God to worship false gods (Jeremiah 3:13). But the word *stranger* and the other words for outsiders usually refer to people who have lost certain rights. God has a special interest in these people.

There are three major concerns: First, Israel was to have one law for both Israelites and non-Israelites; second, Israelites had certain obligations toward foreigners and strangers; third, foreigners had a different religious status, but they also had certain religious rights and obligations similar to those of Israelites.

There is to be one law for both native and foreigner (Exodus 12:49; Leviticus 24:22; Numbers 15:15–16; 15:29–30). God demands equal justice. The foreigner is protected by law, and also must keep the law. Foreigners as well as natives must be equally punished for violating the law. Even religious laws such as blasphemy (Leviticus 24:16), eating blood (Leviticus 17:10–13), and offering children to Molech (Leviticus 20:2) apply equally to Israelites and foreigners. They are also to be equally protected (Deuteronomy 1:16). They enjoy both the privilege and obligation of sharing in the Sabbath rest (Exodus 20:10; 23:12).

Not only that, but Israelites had an obligation to the foreigners, just as to other poor in Israel. Farmers must leave the edges of the field for foreigners (Leviticus 19:10; 23:22; Deuteronomy 24:19–21), and people must even give them some of the tithe (Deuteronomy 14:29; 26:12). Taking advantage of foreigners is frequently condemned in very harsh tones (Deuteronomy 27:19: "Anyone will be cursed who is unfair to foreigners." See also Exodus 22:21; 23:9, Leviticus 19:13; Deuteronomy 24:14–17; Jeremiah 7:6; 22:3; Ezekiel 22:7, 29; Zechariah 7:10; Malachi 3:5). In fact, the Israelites were to *love* the foreigner (Leviticus 19:34) because God himself does (Deuteronomy 10:18–19), something that the Pharisees of Jesus' day seem to have forgotten (Luke 10:25–37). This was because God cares in a special way for the foreigner, just as for orphans and widows (Psalm 146:9), and because the Israelites themselves were once foreigners. (Exodus 23:9: "You must not mistreat a foreigner. You know how it feels to be a foreigner, because you were foreigners in Egypt.")

The one area where foreigners were to be treated differently was in religious practices. Foreigners could not fully participate in worship (Leviticus 22:10). They could participate in the Passover only if they were dwelling with an Israelite and were circumcised (Exodus 12:45–48). However, all foreigners were encouraged to hear the Word of God (Deuteronomy 31:12) and were permitted to bring offerings (Numbers 15:14). God's plan had always been to bless all the people on earth through Abraham's descendants (Genesis 12:3), and foreigners by turning to God in prayer could enjoy the blessings of God (1 Kings 8:41).

These concerns are echoed in the New Testament briefly; Christians are to welcome and show hospitality to strangers (Hebrews 13:2; 3 John 5). Jesus even says that love shown to a stranger is love shown to him (Matthew 25:35–44). But most New Testament references use the terms for "outsider" in a figurative sense.

The roots of this idea are also found in the Old Testament. The patriarchs wandered in Canaan, the land symbolic of God's promises, as foreigners and visitors (Genesis 23:4; see Hebrews 11:13). Even after Israel was situated in Canaan, they were still to think of themselves as "temporary guests" in the land (Leviticus 25:23; Psalms 39:12; 119:19). David knew that this life, for all its blessings, was only a shadow and not our true home (1 Chronicles 29:15). God's chosen ones are "away from their homes and are scattered" in various places (1 Peter 1:1). This is because they are like "foreigners and strangers in this world" (1 Peter 2:11). People who believe in Jesus are not really at home in this world (John 14:19). This means that believers do not put too much hope in this world's politics, and it also means that as foreigners they do not participate in the sinful activities of the world's natives (1 Peter 1:17; 2:11–12).

Believers live like foreigners in this world because they are citizens of a different world. Jesus said his kingdom is not of this world (John 18:36). Believers are full citizens in Jesus' kingdom.

Foreigner (Alien): For additional scriptures on this topic go to Genesis 23:4.

Jesus Christ, to come from heaven. [21]By his power to rule all things, he will change our simple bodies and make them like his own glorious body.

What the Christians Are to Do

4 My dear brothers and sisters, I love you and want to see you. You bring me joy and make me proud of you, so stand strong in the Lord as I have told you.

[2]I ask Euodia and Syntyche to agree in the Lord. [3]And I ask you, my faithful friend, to help these women. They served with me in telling the Good News, together with Clement and others who worked with me, whose names are written in the book of life.

[4]Be full of joy in the Lord always. I will say again, be full of joy.

[5]Let everyone see that you are gentle and kind. The Lord is coming soon. [6]Do not worry about anything, but pray and ask God for everything you need, always giving thanks. [7]And God's peace, which is so great we cannot understand it, will keep your hearts and minds in Christ Jesus.

[8]Brothers and sisters, think about the things that are good and worthy of praise. Think about the things that are true and honorable and right and pure and beautiful and respected. [9]Do what you learned and received from me, what I told you, and what you saw me do. And the God who gives peace will be with you.

Paul Thanks the Christians

[10]I am very happy in the Lord that you have shown your care for me again. You continued to care about me, but there was no way for you to show it. [11]I am not telling you this because I need anything. I have learned to be satisfied with the things I have and with everything that happens. [12]I know how to live when I am poor, and I know how to live when I have plenty. I have learned the secret of being happy at any time in everything that happens, when I have enough to eat and when I go hungry, when I have more than I need and when I do not have enough. [13]I can do all things through Christ, because he gives me strength.

[14]But it was good that you helped me when I needed it. [15]You Philippians remember when I first preached the Good News there. When I left Macedonia, you were the only church that gave me help. [16]Several times you sent me things I needed when I was in Thessalonica. [17]Really, it is not that I want to receive gifts from you, but I want you to have the good that comes from giving. [18]And now I have everything, and more. I have all I need, because Epaphroditus brought your gift to me. It is like a sweet-smelling sacrifice offered to God, who accepts that sacrifice and is pleased with it. [19]My God will use his wonderful riches in Christ Jesus to give you everything you need. [20]Glory to our God and Father forever and ever! Amen.

[21]Greet each of God's people in Christ. Those who are with me send greetings to you. [22]All of God's people greet you, particularly those from the palace of Caesar.

[23]The grace of the Lord Jesus Christ be with you all.

3:21 Rome: 2 Timothy 1:17
4:3 *book of life.* God's book that has the names of all God's chosen people (Revelation 3:5; 21:27).
4:7 Peace: Colossians 3:15
4:7 Mourning: 1 Thessalonians 4:13
4:7 Stress: 2 Timothy 1:7
4:8 Lying/Dishonesty: 1 John 1:6
4:8 Meditation: Colossians 3:1–4
4:8 The process of renewing our minds as believers includes meditation. The habit of meditation, of pondering God's revelation, must be matched by appropriate content of meditation. What we think about is as important as the thinking itself. And so Paul exhorts us to include in our reflective thinking every possible positive subject matter, knowing this will bring us joy and peace.
4:9 Leadership: 1 Thessalonians 5:11–13
4:9 Success: See article on page 479.
4:10–13 Paul tells the Philippians he can do all things through Christ—even live with plenty! Our society might agree that it is a challenge to learn to live with a little, but would probably assume that the more one has, the easier life would be. Paul's words make us aware that having plenty brings challenges Christians must be aware of.
4:13 Encouragement: Colossians 3:23–24
4:18 Sacrifice: Hebrews 9:12
4:23 Paul (Saul): Colossians 1:24–2:5

Notes:

INTRODUCTION TO THE BOOK OF

COLOSSIANS

Only Christ Can Save People

WHO WROTE THIS BOOK?

The apostle Paul wrote the letter to the Colossians (1:1).

TO WHOM WAS THIS BOOK WRITTEN?

The letter is written to the Christians at Colossae, a city in the Lycus Valley some one hundred miles east of Ephesus in south central Asia Minor.

WHERE WAS IT WRITTEN?

Like Ephesians, with which it shares a number of points in common, Colossians was written during Paul's first imprisonment at Rome.

WHEN WAS IT WRITTEN?

It was written during Paul's two-year house arrest between A.D. 60 and 62.

WHAT IS THE BOOK ABOUT?

The Book of Colossians deals with a Jewish religious philosophy that had led the believers in Colossae to consider their faith in Christ lacking. Paul points out the "fullness," the completeness of Christ, and holds him up as the one in whom all the treasures of wisdom and knowledge are contained. They needed nothing in addition to Christ, who is the fullness of God in bodily form. Paul also reminds them of the Christian virtues they are to develop and gives special instructions for their major relationships.

WHY WAS THIS BOOK WRITTEN?

This letter was written to correct false teaching that drew the Colossian believers away from exclusive devotion to Christ. It seduced them into believing and participating in a Jewish mystical philosophy that praised angels and practiced Jewish customs. It was written to paint a picture of Christ as the supreme and only head of the church. He alone is worthy of worship and is all they needed to be accepted by God.

SO WHAT DOES THIS BOOK MEAN TO US?

False teaching is as prevalent today as it was in Colossae. The New Age philosophy similarly tempts people today to worship supernatural beings, like the angels praised by the false teachers at Colossae. We are still urged to engage in mystical practices as a substitute for faith in Christ. So, like the Colossians, we also need to see the painting of Christ as the supreme and only one worthy to be worshipped. This book can help us see him clearly.

SUMMARY:

Paul had not actually started the church in Colossae, but, according to Acts 19:10, his message had reached people throughout Asia. A man named Epaphrus was probably the one who started the church at Colossae, and Paul regarded him as a partner in ministry (1:7; 4:12). It was apparently from Epaphrus that Paul heard about the life of the Colossian church.

Epaphrus told Paul good news about the Colossians (1:8; 2:5), but also about a big problem. An attractive, but false, teaching had been heard at Colossae, and some were accepting it. Paul knew that if this teaching continued, it could undermine the Christian message. It was to oppose this false teaching that Paul wrote the letter to the Colossians.

It is not easy to say exactly what this false teaching was. It seems to have been related to an ancient philosophy that denied that the body, or anything else that is physical or material, was good. What was important, then, was the spiritual world, and Christians who followed this teaching might find themselves trying to please cosmic spirits and powers. In addition, they would find themselves not worrying about how they lived in this world, as though things done in this world really don't matter.

Paul opposes this false teaching, first, by asserting the supremacy of Christ (1:15–20). Second, he insists that those who believe in Jesus need not please any other power, since Jesus is the sole mediator between God and humanity. Third, he writes that life in this world is very important, since the present world is the arena in which we work out what it means to be faithful to God.

COLOSSIANS

From Paul, an apostle of Christ Jesus. I am an apostle because that is what God wanted. Also from Timothy, our brother.

2To the holy and faithful brothers and sisters in Christ that live in Colossae:

Grace and peace to you from God our Father.

3In our prayers for you we always thank God, the Father of our Lord Jesus Christ, 4because we have heard about the faith you have in Christ Jesus and the love you have for all of God's people. 5You have this faith and love because of your hope, and what you hope for is kept safe for you in heaven. You learned about this hope when you heard the message about the truth, the Good News 6that was told to you. Everywhere in the world that Good News is bringing blessings and is growing. This has happened with you, too, since you heard the Good News and understood the truth about the grace of God. 7You learned about God's grace from Epaphras, whom we love. He works together with us and is a faithful servant of Christ for us. 8He also told us about the love you have from the Holy Spirit.∞

9Because of this, since the day we heard about you, we have continued praying for you, asking God that you will know fully what he wants. We pray that you will also have great wisdom and understanding in spiritual things 10so that you will live the kind of life that honors and pleases the Lord in every way. You will produce fruit in every good work and grow in the knowledge of God. 11God will strengthen you with his own great power so that you will not give up when troubles come, but you will be patient. 12And you will joyfully give thanks to the Father who has made you able to have a share in all that he has prepared for his people in the kingdom of light. 13God has freed us from the power of darkness, and he brought us into the kingdom of his dear Son. 14The Son paid for our sins, and in him we have forgiveness.

The Importance of Christ

15No one can see God, but Jesus Christ is exactly like him. He ranks higher than everything that has been made.∞ 16Through his power all things were made—things in heaven and on earth, things seen and unseen, all powers, authorities, lords, and rulers. All things were made through Christ and for Christ. 17He was there before anything was made, and all things continue because of him. 18He is the head of the body, which is the church. Everything comes from him. He is the first one who was raised from the dead. So in all things Jesus has first place.∞ 19God was pleased for all of himself to live in Christ. 20And through Christ, God has brought all things back to himself again—things on earth and things in heaven. God made peace through the blood of Christ's death on the cross.∞

21At one time you were separated from God. You were his enemies in your minds, and the evil things you did were against God. 22But now God has made you his friends again. He did this through Christ's death in the body so that he might bring you into God's presence as people who are holy, with no wrong, and with nothing of which God can judge you guilty.∞ 23This will happen if you continue strong and sure in your faith. You must not be moved away from the hope brought to you by the Good News that you heard. That same Good News has been told to everyone in the world, and I, Paul, help in preaching that Good News.∞

---

1 Many people in the ancient world believed their destiny was controlled by spiritual forces related to the stars and the planets. It appears that in Colossae some were identifying these with angels and were even giving them reverence as if they were divine. In response, Paul emphasized that Christ is the only one with true spiritual power, and to rely on the guidance of other celestial bodies would undermine true faith.

1:2 *brothers and sisters.* Although the Greek text says "brothers" here and throughout this book, Paul's words were meant for the entire church, including men and women.

∞**1:8 Hope:** Titus 2:11–14

1:9–14 In Colossians 1, Paul prays for the Christians in Colossae to "have great wisdom and understanding in spiritual things so that you will live the kind of life that honors and pleases the Lord in every way" (vv. 9–10). This was a prayer for them and for us today to live a spiritually centered life of faith in Christ that opens our hearts to receive knowledge about what God wants for our lives. We have been placed on the earth for one purpose: to do what God wants.

When we please God, we "will produce fruit in every good work," (Colossians 1:10), and we will be strengthened, "with his own great power" (v. 11). And in all things the Lord's name will be praised.

1:15 Colossians 1:15 could also be translated, "He is the image of the invisible God," where "image" brings to mind the divine image that God impressed on human beings in creation, according to Genesis 1:26–28. Bearing God's image gives human beings the special privilege of relating to God and to be God's representative governing creation. Here the importance for the incarnation of Christ is revealed: because human beings bear the image of God, God can come to earth in human form. Thus Christ is the perfect union of the human and the divine. He is fully God and fully human.

∞**1:15 Incarnation:** 2 Thessalonians 1:12

∞**1:18 Body of Christ:** Colossians 2:19

∞**1:20 Astrology:** Colossians 2:16–19

∞**1:20 The Powers:** Colossians 2:8–23

∞**1:22 Holiness:** 1 Thessalonians 4:7

∞**1:22 Reconciliation:** Hebrews 2:17

∞**1:23 Satan/Satanism:** 2 Thessalonians 2:1–12

Paul's Work for the Church

24I am happy in my sufferings for you. There are things that Christ must still suffer through his body, the church. I am accepting, in my body, my part of these things that must be suffered. 25I became a servant of the church because God gave me a special work to do that helps you, and that work is to tell fully the message of God. 26This message is the secret that was hidden from everyone since the beginning of time, but now it is made known to God's holy people. 27God decided to let his people know this rich and glorious secret which he has for all people. This secret is Christ himself, who is in you. He is our only hope for glory. 28So we continue to preach Christ to each person, using all wisdom to warn and to teach everyone, in order to bring each one into God's presence as a mature person in Christ. 29To do this, I work and struggle, using Christ's great strength that works so powerfully in me.

2 I want you to know how hard I work for you, those in Laodicea, and others who have never seen me. 2I want them to be strengthened and joined together with love so that they may be rich in their understanding. This leads to their knowing fully God's secret, that is, Christ himself. 3In him all the treasures of wisdom and knowledge are safely kept.

4I say this so that no one can fool you by arguments that seem good, but are false. 5Though I am absent from you in my body, my heart is with you, and I am happy to see your good lives and your strong faith in Christ.

Continue to Live in Christ

6As you received Christ Jesus the Lord, so continue to live in him. 7Keep your roots deep in him and have your lives built on him. Be strong in the faith, just as you were taught, and always be thankful.

8Be sure that no one leads you away with false and empty teaching that is only human, which comes from the ruling spirits of this world, and not from Christ. 9All of God lives in Christ fully (even when Christ was on earth), 10and you have a full and true life in Christ, who is ruler over all rulers and powers.

11Also in Christ you had a different kind of circumcision, a circumcision not done by hands. It was through Christ's circumcision, that is, his death, that you were made free from the power of your sinful self. 12When you were baptized, you were buried with Christ, and you were raised up with him through your faith in God's power that was shown when he raised Christ from the dead. 13When you were spiritually dead because of your sins and because you were not free from the power of your sinful self, God made you alive with Christ, and he forgave all our sins. 14He canceled the debt, which listed all the rules we failed to follow. He took away that record with its rules and nailed it to the cross. 15God stripped the spiritual rulers and powers of their authority. With the cross, he won the victory and showed the world that they were powerless.

Don't Follow People's Rules

16So do not let anyone make rules for you about eating and drinking or about a religious feast, a New Moon Festival, or a Sabbath day. 17These things were like a shadow of what was to come. But what is true and real has come and is found in Christ.

1:24 Suffering: 2 Thessalonians 1:3–10

1:24 Here Paul talks about the significance of his life of suffering. In some mysterious way, he sees that it bears analogy to the suffering of Christ himself. What is interesting is that he sees his suffering, and the suffering of the church, as related to the suffering of Christ. After all, the church is the Body of Christ. This reference to the church refers to the whole body of believers wherever they live in the world.

1:29 Martyrdom: 1 Thessalonians 1:6–8

2:3 Folly/Foolishness: See article on page 541.

2:3 Wisdom: James 3:13–18

2:5 Paul (Saul): Colossians 4:18

2:6–10 Paul's advice to the Colossians, who were being misled by cultic teachers who ranked angels above Jesus, was to center their faith in Christ, who created angels and everything else (Colossians 1:16). Paul warns them in this passage to "be sure that no one leads you away with false and empty teaching that is only human" (Colossians 2:80), a good description of the unscriptural man-centered teachings of the cults.

2:9 Human: Colossians 3:10

2:9 Trinity: Jude 20–21

2:11 Circumcision: See article on page 160.

2:11–12 Sometimes this passage is taken as support for comparing infant baptism with Israelite circumcision. Instead, we must be aware that there were many in the earliest churches who taught that baptism was not enough for a non-Jewish adult convert to Christianity, and that they must be circumcised also (see Galatians and Philippians 3). Here the message seems to be that baptism has replaced the need for circumcision of adult converts to Christianity.

2:14 Baptism: 1 Peter 3:21

2:15 The culmination of God's war against Satan and his forces, both spiritual and human, takes place on the cross. Here the crucifixion is described as a great military victory and has as its background the holy wars of the Old Testament.

These rulers and powers were created lower than Christ (1:15–18), but they have acted as if they were equal or superior to him. Christ has defeated them—exposing this illusion. Their defeat, however, was not through a triumph of greater military-like power. It came in an unexpected way through the cross. They have been disrobed of their assumed authority and returned to their appropriate position.

2:16 Jesus fulfilled the Sabbath. He is the reality of the Old Testament shadow. He is the one who provides rest for his people. For this reason, no one is to judge other Christians in respect to their practice in keeping the Sabbath day.

2:17 Time: James 4:13–17

18Do not let anyone disqualify you by making you humiliate yourself and worship angels. Such people enter into visions, which fill them with foolish pride because of their human way of thinking. 19They do not hold tightly to Christ, the head. It is from him that all the parts of the body are cared for and held together. So it grows in the way God wants it to grow.

20Since you died with Christ and were made free from the ruling spirits of the world, why do you act as if you still belong to this world by following rules like these: 21"Don't eat this," "Don't taste that," "Don't even touch that thing"? 22These rules refer to earthly things that are gone as soon as they are used. They are only man-made commands and teachings. 23They seem to be wise, but they are only part of a man-made religion. They make people pretend not to be proud and make them punish their bodies, but they do not really control the evil desires of the sinful self.

Your New Life in Christ

3 Since you were raised from the dead with Christ, aim at what is in heaven, where Christ is sitting at the right hand of God. 2Think only about the things in heaven, not the things on earth. 3Your old sinful self has died, and your new life is kept with Christ in God. 4Christ is our life, and when he comes again, you will share in his glory.

5So put all evil things out of your life: sexual sinning, doing evil, letting evil thoughts control you, wanting things that are evil, and greed. This is really serving a false god. 6These things make God angry. 7In your past, evil life you also did these things.

8But now also put these things out of your life: anger, bad temper, doing or saying things to hurt others, and using evil words when you talk. 9Do not lie to each other. You have left your old sinful life and the things you did before. 10You have begun to live the new life, in which you are being made new and are becoming like the One who made you. This new life brings you the true knowledge of God. 11In the new life there is no difference between Greeks and Jews, those who are circumcised and those who are not circumcised, or people who are foreigners, or Scythians. There is no difference between slaves and free people. But Christ is in all believers, and Christ is all that is important.

12God has chosen you and made you his holy people. He loves you. So always do these things: Show mercy to others, be kind, humble, gentle, and patient. 13Get along with each other, and forgive each other. If someone does wrong to you, forgive that person because the Lord forgave you. 14Do all these things; but most important, love each other. Love is what holds you all together in perfect unity. 15Let the peace that Christ gives control your thinking, because you were all called together in one body to have peace. Always be thankful. 16Let the teaching of Christ live in you richly. Use all wisdom to teach and instruct each other by singing psalms, hymns, and spiritual songs with thankfulness in your hearts to God. 17Everything you do or say should be done to obey Jesus your Lord. And in all you do, give thanks to God the Father through Jesus.

Your New Life with Other People

18Wives, yield to the authority of your husbands, because this is the right thing to do in the Lord.

19Husbands, love your wives and be gentle with them.

20Children, obey your parents in all things, because this pleases the Lord.

21Fathers, do not nag your children. If you are too hard to please, they may want to stop trying.

22Slaves, obey your masters in all things. Do not obey just when they are watching you, to gain their favor, but serve them honestly, because you respect the Lord. 23In all the work you are doing, work the best you can. Work as if you were doing it for the Lord, not for people. 24Remember that you will receive your reward from the Lord, which he promised to his people. You are serving the Lord

2:18 Angels/Guardian Angels: See article on page 652.
2:19 Body of Christ: Colossians 3:15
2:19 Astrology: See article on page 662.
2:23 The Powers: See article on page 1285.
3:4 Meditation: Hebrews 12:1–4
3:5 Greed: 1 Timothy 3:8
3:6 *These . . . angry.* Some Greek copies add "against the people who do not obey God."
3:10 Human: 1 Corinthians 11:7
3:11 Racism: See article on page 1082.
3:11 *Scythians.* The Scythians were known as very wild and cruel people.
3:11 The barrier wall between Jews and non-Jews was broken down at the cross where Jesus died for all. All the old prejudices, including racial prejudices, have been removed by Christ. If we continue to entertain them or engage in racist practices, we fail to understand the Good News. Jesus does not teach tolerance for people of other races, but love—the same love he showed all of us on the cross.
3:14 Love: 1 John 3:14
3:15 Body of Christ: See article on page 1193.
3:15 Peace: See article on page 1243.
3:15 *body.* The spiritual body of Christ, meaning the church or his people.
3:16 Music: Revelation 5:8–14
3:17 Work: 1 Thessalonians 2:8–10
3:18 Women: Titus 2:3–5
3:21 Parenting: Hebrews 12:4–11
3:24 Encouragement: James 1:5–6

Christ. 25But remember that anyone who does
wrong will be punished for that wrong, and the
Lord treats everyone the same.

4 Masters, give what is good and fair to your
slaves. Remember that you have a Master in
heaven.

What the Christians Are to Do

2Continue praying, keeping alert, and always
thanking God. 3Also pray for us that God will give
us an opportunity to tell people his message. Pray
that we can preach the secret that God has made
known about Christ. This is why I am in prison.
4Pray that I can speak in a way that will make it
clear, as I should.

5Be wise in the way you act with people who
are not believers, making the most of every opportunity. 6When you talk, you should always be kind
and pleasant so you will be able to answer everyone in the way you should.

News About the People with Paul

7Tychicus is my dear brother in Christ and a
faithful minister and servant with me in the Lord.
He will tell you all the things that are happening
to me. 8This is why I am sending him: so you may
know how we are and he may encourage you. 9I
send him with Onesimus, a faithful and dear
brother in Christ, and one of your group. They will
tell you all that has happened here.

10Aristarchus, a prisoner with me, and Mark,
the cousin of Barnabas, greet you. (I have already
told you what to do about Mark. If he comes, welcome him.) 11Jesus, who is called Justus, also greets
you. These are the only Jewish believers who work
with me for the kingdom of God, and they have
been a comfort to me.

12Epaphras, a servant of Jesus Christ, from your
group, also greets you. He always prays for you that
you will grow to be spiritually mature and have
everything God wants for you. 13I know he has
worked hard for you and the people in Laodicea
and in Hierapolis. 14Demas and our dear friend
Luke, the doctor, greet you.

15Greet the brothers in Laodicea. And greet
Nympha and the church that meets in her house.
16After this letter is read to you, be sure it is also
read to the church in Laodicea. And you read the
letter that I wrote to Laodicea. 17Tell Archippus,
"Be sure to finish the work the Lord gave you."

18I, Paul, greet you and write this with my own
hand. Remember me in prison. Grace be with you.

4:6 Tongue: 2 Timothy 2:24–25
4:11 Comfort: See article on page 1223.
4:14 Luke: Philemon 24
4:16 Although Paul's letters were written to specific churches, they were also "circular letters," since they were shared with churches in other cities too. Paul refers to an additional letter, written to Laodicea, that we do not have.
4:18 Paul (Saul): 1 Thessalonians 2:1–20

Notes:

INTRODUCTION TO THE BOOK OF
1 THESSALONIANS
Paul Encourages New Christians

WHO WROTE THIS BOOK?

The apostle Paul is named as the author of 1 Thessalonians in 1:1. Church tradition also says Paul is the writer.

TO WHOM WAS THIS BOOK WRITTEN?

This letter is written to the believers in Thessalonica, which was the provincial capital of Macedonia. Paul had established a church there on his second missionary journey.

WHERE WAS IT WRITTEN?

It is likely that this letter was written by Paul at Corinth.

WHEN WAS IT WRITTEN?

First Thessalonians was probably written about A.D. 51 to 52, which makes it the oldest of Paul's letters, with the possible exception of Galatians.

WHAT IS THE BOOK ABOUT?

Every chapter of 1 Thessalonians ends with a reference to the second coming of Christ. Chapter four especially stresses this theme (4:13–18). The deity of Christ is taught in all of Paul's references to him. He refers to him as Lord and describes his close relationship with the Father.

WHY WAS THIS BOOK WRITTEN?

Paul's purposes for writing this book were several. He wrote to encourage the young believers of Thessalonica through their trials. He wanted to instruct them in godly living and to urge some of them not to stop working as they waited for Christ's return. He also wanted to assure them about the future of believers who die before Christ comes again.

SO WHAT DOES THIS BOOK MEAN TO US?

Many people today, like the Thessalonians, believe we are living in the last days before Christ returns to claim his own people and take them home to heaven. As Paul told the Christians in Thessalonians, the timetable is not for us to know. We must be about the business of normal living, telling others about Christ Jesus at every opportunity. We need to stay ready with holy lives so we will not be ashamed to meet him when he does appear, which could, in fact, be at any moment or any millennium.

SUMMARY:

The story of Paul's early mission at Thessalonica is told in Acts 17:1–10. Having founded the Thessalonian church, Paul now writes this letter in order to encourage these Christians in their suffering and in faithful living. He especially addresses issues that have been raised about the second coming of Jesus.

Paul's earliest message to the Thessalonians had apparently emphasized the end times and especially the Lord's return. Since the founding of the church, this emphasis of his had apparently become the focal point of their understanding of the Good News. Believing that Jesus' return would be very soon, for example, they wondered whether those members of the church who had died would be included in the triumph of Jesus' appearing.

Paul's response is not to deny the coming of Jesus, but to assert that the return of Jesus calls for faithful living now. Thus, he can encourage them to be ready for the Lord's return, for example, by abstaining from sexual sin, continuing to work, constant prayer, self-control, and so on.

1 Thessalonians

From Paul, Silas, and Timothy.

To the church in Thessalonica, the church in God the Father and the Lord Jesus Christ:

Grace and peace to you.

The Faith of the Thessalonians

2We always thank God for all of you and mention you when we pray. 3We continually recall before God our Father the things you have done because of your faith and the work you have done because of your love. And we thank him that you continue to be strong because of your hope in our Lord Jesus Christ.

4Brothers and sisters, God loves you, and we know he has chosen you, 5because the Good News we brought to you came not only with words, but with power, with the Holy Spirit, and with sure knowledge that it is true. Also you know how we lived when we were with you in order to help you. 6And you became like us and like the Lord. You suffered much, but still you accepted the teaching with the joy that comes from the Holy Spirit. 7So you became an example to all the believers in Macedonia and Southern Greece. 8And the Lord's teaching spread from you not only into Macedonia and Southern Greece, but now your faith in God has become known everywhere. So we do not need to say anything about it. 9People everywhere are telling about the way you accepted us when we were there with you. They tell how you stopped worshiping idols and began serving the living and true God. 10And you wait for God's Son, whom God raised from the dead, to come from heaven. He is Jesus, who saves us from God's angry judgment that is sure to come.

Paul's Work in Thessalonica

2 Brothers and sisters, you know our visit to you was not a failure. 2Before we came to you, we suffered in Philippi. People there insulted us, as you know, and many people were against us. But our God helped us to be brave and to tell you his Good News. 3Our appeal does not come from lies or wrong reasons, nor were we trying to trick you. 4But we speak the Good News because God tested us and trusted us to do it. When we speak, we are not trying to please people, but God, who tests our hearts. 5You know that we never tried to influence you by saying nice things about you. We were not trying to get your money; we had no selfishness to hide from you. God knows that this is true. 6We were not looking for human praise, from you or anyone else, 7even though as apostles of Christ we could have used our authority over you.

But we were very gentle with you, like a mother caring for her little children. 8Because we loved you, we were happy to share not only God's Good News with you, but even our own lives. You had become so dear to us! 9Brothers and sisters, I know you remember our hard work and difficulties. We worked night and day so we would not burden any of you while we preached God's Good News to you.

10When we were with you, we lived in a holy and honest way, without fault. You know this is true, and so does God. 11You know that we treated each of you as a father treats his own children. 12We encouraged you, we urged you, and we insisted that you live good lives for God, who calls you to his glorious kingdom.

13Also, we always thank God because when you heard his message from us, you accepted it as the word of God, not the words of humans. And it really is God's message which works in you who believe. 14Brothers and sisters, your experiences have been like those of God's churches in Christ that are in Judea. You suffered from the people of your own country, as they suffered from the Jews, 15who killed both the Lord Jesus and the prophets and forced us to leave that country. They do not please God and are against all people. 16They try to stop us from teaching those who are not Jews so they may be saved. By doing this, they are increasing their sins to the limit. The anger of God has come to them at last.

Paul Wants to Visit Them Again

17Brothers and sisters, though we were separated from you for a short time, our thoughts were still with you. We wanted very much to see you and tried hard to do so. 18We wanted to come to you. I, Paul, tried to come more than once, but Satan stopped us. 19You are our hope, our joy, and the crown we will take pride in when our Lord Jesus Christ comes. 20Truly you are our glory and our joy.

1:1 Church: Hebrews 10:25

1:4 *Brothers and sisters.* Although the Greek text says "Brothers" here and throughout this book, Paul's words were meant for the entire church, including men and women.

1:6 Suffering was not a hindrance for the witness of these believers. Rather, it was through their suffering that they became like the apostles and the Lord, who also suffered because of their faithfulness.

1:8 Martyrdom: 1 Thessalonians 2:14–16

1:9 Idolatry: 1 Peter 4:3

2:4 Test/Temptation: 1 Timothy 6:9

2:10 Work: 2 Thessalonians 3:6–15

2:14 *Judea.* The Jewish land where Jesus lived and taught and where the church first began.

2:16 Anti-Semitism: Titus 1:10–11

2:16 Martyrdom: Hebrews 11:24–28

2:20 Paul (Saul): 2 Thessalonians 3:17

3 When we could not wait any longer, we decided it was best to stay in Athens alone 2and send Timothy to you. Timothy, our brother, works with us for God and helps us tell people the Good News about Christ. We sent him to strengthen and encourage you in your faith 3so none of you would be upset by these troubles. You yourselves know that we must face these troubles. 4Even when we were with you, we told you we all would have to suffer, and you know it has happened. 5Because of this, when I could wait no longer, I sent Timothy to you so I could learn about your faith. I was afraid the devil had tempted you, and then our hard work would have been wasted.

6But Timothy now has come back to us from you and has brought us good news about your faith and love. He told us that you always remember us in a good way and that you want to see us just as much as we want to see you. 7So, brothers and sisters, while we have much trouble and suffering, we are encouraged about you because of your faith. 8Our life is really full if you stand strong in the Lord. 9We have so much joy before our God because of you. We cannot thank him enough for all the joy we feel. 10Night and day we continue praying with all our heart that we can see you again and give you all the things you need to make your faith strong.

11Now may our God and Father himself and our Lord Jesus prepare the way for us to come to you. 12May the Lord make your love grow more and multiply for each other and for all people so that you will love others as we love you. 13May your hearts be made strong so that you will be holy and without fault before our God and Father when our Lord Jesus comes with all his holy ones.

A Life that Pleases God

4 Brothers and sisters, we taught you how to live in a way that will please God, and you are living that way. Now we ask and encourage you in the Lord Jesus to live that way even more. 2You know what we told you to do by the authority of the Lord Jesus. 3God wants you to be holy and to stay away from sexual sins. 4He wants each of you to learn to control your own body in a way that is holy and honorable. 5Don't use your body for sexual sin like the people who do not know God. 6Also, do not wrong or cheat another Christian in this way. The Lord will punish people who do those things as we have already told you and warned you. 7God called us to be holy and does not want us to live in sin. 8So the person who refuses to obey this teaching is disobeying God, not simply a human teaching. And God is the One who gives us his Holy Spirit.

9We do not need to write you about having love for your Christian family, because God has already taught you to love each other. 10And truly you do love the Christians in all of Macedonia. Brothers and sisters, now we encourage you to love them even more.

11Do all you can to live a peaceful life. Take care of your own business, and do your own work as we have already told you. 12If you do, then people who are not believers will respect you, and you will not have to depend on others for what you need.

The Lord's Coming

13Brothers and sisters, we want you to know about those Christians who have died so you will not be sad, as others who have no hope. 14We believe that Jesus died and that he rose again. So, because of him, God will raise with Jesus those who have died. 15What we tell you now is the Lord's own message. We who are living when the Lord comes again will not go before those who have already died. 16The Lord himself will come down from heaven with a loud command, with the voice of the archangel, and with the trumpet call of God. And those who have died believing in Christ will rise first. 17After that, we who are still alive will be gathered up with them in the clouds to meet the Lord in the air. And we will be with the Lord forever. 18So encourage each other with these words.

4:4 *learn . . . body.* This might also mean "learn to live with your own wife."

4:7 Holiness: 1 Peter 1:15–16

4:12 Reputation: 1 Timothy 3:2

4:13 The Thessalonian Christians are concerned that death will disqualify some of their church members from being with Jesus when he returns. Paul comforts them by noting that those Christians who have died, far from being left out, will actually have a prominent place when Christ returns.

4:13 Mourning: See article on page 1011.

4:15–17 In this passage, Paul shows how we will receive our resurrection bodies. First, it will occur when Christ returns in glory. Second, the dead in Christ will receive their resurrection bodies first. Third, those who are alive when Christ returns will then have their bodies instantly transformed into resurrection bodies and be caught up into the air to join the Lord and the resurrected dead.

4:16 *archangel.* The leader among God's angels or messengers.

4:17 Paul's description of the rapture is believed by some to be an event that precedes the "great distress" (Revelation 7:14). By others, it is viewed as synonymous with the final triumph associated with Christ's return, with judgment and the eternal kingdom immediately following. Still others see this as occurring after the "great distress." Whichever view of end times one takes, the advice to believers of all times is to "be ready."

4:18 Immortality: 1 Timothy 6:11–16

Be Ready for the Lord's Coming

5 Now, brothers and sisters, we do not need to
write you about times and dates. 2You know
very well that the day the Lord comes again will
be a surprise, like a thief that comes in the night.
3While people are saying, "We have peace and
we are safe," they will be destroyed quickly. It
is like pains that come quickly to a woman having a baby. Those people will not escape. 4But
you, brothers and sisters, are not living in darkness, and so that day will not surprise you like a
thief. 5You are all people who belong to the
light and to the day. We do not belong to the
night or to darkness. 6So we should not be like
other people who are sleeping, but we should
be alert and have self-control. 7Those who
sleep, sleep at night. Those who get drunk, get
drunk at night. 8But we belong to the day, so
we should control ourselves. We should wear
faith and love to protect us, and the hope of salvation should be our helmet. 9God did not
choose us to suffer his anger but to have salvation through our Lord Jesus Christ. 10Jesus died
for us so that we can live together with him,
whether we are alive or dead when he comes.
11So encourage each other and give each other
strength, just as you are doing now.

Final Instructions and Greetings

12Now, brothers and sisters, we ask you to appreciate those who work hard among you, who lead
you in the Lord and teach you. 13Respect them with
a very special love because of the work they do.
Live in peace with each other. 14We ask you,
brothers and sisters, to warn those who do not
work. Encourage the people who are afraid. Help
those who are weak. Be patient with everyone.
15Be sure that no one pays back wrong for wrong,
but always try to do what is good for each other
and for all people.
16Always be joyful. 17Pray continually, 18and
give thanks whatever happens. That is what God
wants for you in Christ Jesus.
19Do not hold back the work of the Holy Spirit.
20Do not treat prophecy as if it were unimportant.
21But test everything. Keep what is good, 22and
stay away from everything that is evil.
23Now may God himself, the God of peace, make
you pure, belonging only to him. May your whole
self—spirit, soul, and body—be kept safe and without fault when our Lord Jesus Christ comes. 24You
can trust the One who calls you to do that for you.
25Brothers and sisters, pray for us.
26Give each other a holy kiss when you meet.
27I tell you by the authority of the Lord to read
this letter to all the believers.
28The grace of our Lord Jesus Christ be with you.

5:1–8 Paul encourages the Thessalonians to be joyful, to pray continually, and to "give thanks whatever happens." When things are going well, it is relatively easy to give thanks. But when we are going through trials, it is far more difficult to express gratitude to God. Yet it is exactly what God wants us to do. As believers in Christ Jesus and beneficiaries of the grace of God, we are always to be thankful.

5:4 Darkness: See article on page 692.

5:10 God's Anger: Revelation 16

5:12 The Bible clearly teaches that we are not made right with God through our works. But that does not mean good works are unimportant to God. Here Paul tells the Thessalonians that they should especially honor and respect people who work hard among them. Paul goes on and warns those who do not work. Hard work is a part of the Christian life, though we know from other Bible passages (Ephesians 4:12) that even our ability to work well and hard is a gift from God.

5:13 Leadership: 1 Timothy 3:1–13

5:17 Prayer: Revelation 5:8

INTRODUCTION TO THE BOOK OF

2 THESSALONIANS

The Problems of New Christians

WHO WROTE THIS BOOK?

It is clear, from various sources, including 1:1 of this book, that it was written by the apostle Paul.

TO WHOM WAS THIS BOOK WRITTEN?

Like his first letter, Paul wrote this book to the believers in Thessalonica, the provincial capital of Macedonia, where Paul had established a church on his second missionary journey.

WHERE WAS IT WRITTEN?

This letter, too, was probably written at Corinth.

WHEN WAS IT WRITTEN?

Second Thessalonians was written several months after First Thessalonians, about A.D. 51 to 52.

WHAT IS THE BOOK ABOUT?

This letter was written perhaps six months after the first one because the issue of the first letter—Christ's second coming—had not been resolved. A misunderstanding arose over whether Christ had already returned. Paul made it clear that Christ's return was impossible at that time because the "Man of Evil" had not yet appeared. He also reinforced the need for people to earn a living and not be idle just because they think the second coming could happen at any moment.

WHY WAS THIS BOOK WRITTEN?

The problems in the Thessalonian church have not resolved themselves. So, Paul writes to them again with much the same purpose as 1 Thessalonians. See introduction to 1 Thessalonians.

SO WHAT DOES THIS BOOK MEAN TO US?

As believers today, we naturally anticipate Christ's soon return. Whatever our view of the end times, it is clear that Satan will mount a vicious assault before Jesus comes back. But Christians need not fear because our victory has already been won by Christ Jesus when he rose from the dead. Our responsibility—our great joy—like the wise young bridesmaids in Jesus' parable (Matthew 25:1–13), is to be prepared and waiting with holy lives when he comes to take his bride, the church, to the mansion he has adorned for her, and us, in heaven.

SUMMARY:

In spite of his earlier letter to the Thessalonians, their situation had not changed much. In fact, it may have worsened, since some had apparently come to believe that Jesus had already returned (2:2).

Paul addresses the Thessalonians with much the same message as before. He encourages them in their suffering and instructs them about the second coming of Jesus. He also devotes time to the problem that some Thessalonians were refusing to work (perhaps because they expected the Lord to return so quickly).

2 Thessalonians

From Paul, Silas, and Timothy.

To the church in Thessalonica in God our Father and the Lord Jesus Christ:

2Grace and peace to you from God the Father and the Lord Jesus Christ.

Paul Talks About God's Judgment

3We must always thank God for you, brothers and sisters. This is only right, because your faith is growing more and more, and the love that every one of you has for each other is increasing. 4So we brag about you to the other churches of God. We tell them about the way you continue to be strong and have faith even though you are being treated badly and are suffering many troubles.

5This is proof that God is right in his judgment. He wants you to be counted worthy of his kingdom for which you are suffering. 6God will do what is right. He will give trouble to those who trouble you. 7And he will give rest to you who are troubled and to us also when the Lord Jesus appears with burning fire from heaven with his powerful angels. 8Then he will punish those who do not know God and who do not obey the Good News about our Lord Jesus Christ. 9Those people will be punished with a destruction that continues forever. They will be kept away from the Lord and from his great power. 10This will happen on the day when the Lord Jesus comes to receive glory because of his holy people. And all the people who have believed will be amazed at Jesus. You will be in that group, because you believed what we told you.

11That is why we always pray for you, asking our God to help you live the kind of life he called you to live. We pray that with his power God will help you do the good things you want and perform the works that come from your faith. 12We pray all this so that the name of our Lord Jesus Christ will have glory in you, and you will have glory in him. That glory comes from the grace of our God and the Lord Jesus Christ.

Evil Things Will Happen

2 Brothers and sisters, we have something to say about the coming of our Lord Jesus Christ and the time when we will meet together with him. 2Do not become easily upset in your thinking or afraid if you hear that the day of the Lord has already come. Someone may say this in a prophecy or in a message or in a letter as if it came from us. 3Do not let anyone fool you in any way. That day of the Lord will not come until the turning away from God happens and the Man of Evil, who is on his way to hell, appears. 4He will be against and put himself above anything called God or anything that people worship. And that Man of Evil will even go into God's Temple and sit there and say that he is God.

5I told you when I was with you that all this would happen. Do you not remember? 6And now you know what is stopping that Man of Evil so he will appear at the right time. 7The secret power of evil is already working in the world, but there is one who is stopping that power. And he will continue to stop it until he is taken out of the way. 8Then that Man of Evil will appear, and the Lord Jesus will kill him with the breath that comes from his mouth and will destroy him with the glory of his coming. 9The Man of Evil will come by the power of Satan. He will have great power, and he will do many different false miracles, signs, and wonders. 10He will use every kind of evil to trick those who are lost. They will die, because they refused to love the truth. (If they loved the truth, they would be saved.) 11For this reason God sends them something powerful that leads them away from the truth so they will believe a lie. 12So all those will be judged guilty who did not believe the truth, but enjoyed doing evil.

You Are Chosen for Salvation

13Brothers and sisters, whom the Lord loves, God chose you from the beginning to be saved. So

1:3 *brothers and sisters.* Although the Greek text says "brothers" here and throughout this book, Paul's words were meant for the entire church, including men and women.

1:7 Angels: Hebrews 1:14

1:7 Justice: See article on page 459.

1:9 Hell: Hebrews 10:27

1:10 Suffering: Hebrews 2:10

1:12 Incarnation: 1 Peter 3:22

2:2 The return of Christ is described in the New Testament as the "day of the Lord" (see also the related terms "coming of Christ" [Philippians 1:10; 2:16], "the day the Lord comes again", 1 Thessalonians 5:2], "the day" [Romans 2:16], and "the Day of Judgment "[1 Corinthians 3:13]). The term picks up on the popular Old Testament theme, which uses the term to describe God's impending punishment of Israel's enemies, rebellious Israel herself, and the entire world.

2:3 *turning away.* Or "the rebellion."

2:3–4 The Bible predicts a final worldwide rebellion that will come near the time of Christ's return. It will be marked by the false worship of an "anti-christ" figure who, through the power of Satan, will lead the world astray with lies (2:9–11; Revelation 13:8). He will be swiftly destroyed, however, by Jesus Christ (2:8; Revelation 20:10).

2:4 Antichrist (Enemy of Christ): 1 John 2:18–20

2:12 Satan/Satanism: 1 Peter 5:8

we must always thank God for you. You are saved
by the Spirit that makes you holy and by your
faith in the truth. 14God used the Good News that
we preached to call you to be saved so you can
share in the glory of our Lord Jesus Christ. 15So,
brothers and sisters, stand strong and continue to
believe the teachings we gave you in our speaking
and in our letter.

16-17May our Lord Jesus Christ himself and God
our Father encourage you and strengthen you in
every good thing you do and say. God loved us,
and through his grace he gave us a good hope and
encouragement that continues forever.

Pray for Us

3 And now, brothers and sisters, pray for us that
the Lord's teaching will continue to spread
quickly and that people will give honor to that
teaching, just as happened with you. 2And pray
that we will be protected from stubborn and evil
people, because not all people believe.

3But the Lord is faithful and will give you
strength and will protect you from the Evil One.
4The Lord makes us feel sure that you are doing
and will continue to do the things we told you.
5May the Lord lead your hearts into God's love and
Christ's patience.

The Duty to Work

6Brothers and sisters, by the authority of our
Lord Jesus Christ we command you to stay away
from any believer who refuses to work and does
not follow the teaching we gave you. 7You yourselves know that you should live as we live. We
were not lazy when we were with you. 8And
when we ate another person's food, we always
paid for it. We worked very hard night and day so
we would not be an expense to any of you. 9We
had the right to ask you to help us, but we worked
to take care of ourselves so we would be an example for you to follow. 10When we were with you,
we gave you this rule: "Anyone who refuses to
work should not eat."

11We hear that some people in your group refuse
to work. They do nothing but busy themselves in
other people's lives. 12We command those people
and beg them in the Lord Jesus Christ to work quietly and earn their own food. 13But you, brothers
and sisters, never become tired of doing good.

14If some people do not obey what we tell you
in this letter, then take note of them. Have nothing to do with them so they will feel ashamed.
15But do not treat them as enemies. Warn them as
fellow believers.

Final Words

16Now may the Lord of peace give you peace at
all times and in every way. The Lord be with all
of you.

17I, Paul, end this letter now in my own hand-
writing. All my letters have this to show they are
from me. This is the way I write.

18The grace of our Lord Jesus Christ be with
you all.

2:17 Blessing: See article on page 179.

3:8 In order to encourage others to work, Paul refers to how he worked even while he served as a missionary among them. This shows the high value Paul placed on work and how he refused to allow his needs to be a drain on others.

3:13 Perseverance: Hebrews 4:14

3:15 Work: James 2:14–26

3:17 Paul (Saul): 1 Timothy 1:12–14

Notes:

INTRODUCTION TO THE BOOK OF

1 TIMOTHY

Advice to a Young Preacher

WHO WROTE THIS BOOK?

Early church tradition and verse 1:1 ascribe this book to the apostle Paul.

TO WHOM WAS THIS BOOK WRITTEN?

This letter is written to a young preacher and Paul's protégé, Timothy. He was a young convert to Christianity from Lystra in Galatia, and he became Paul's co-worker in the faith. Timothy had a Jewish Christian mother and a non-Jewish father (see Acts 16:1).

WHERE WAS IT WRITTEN?

Based on references within the letter, Paul wrote this letter while in Macedonia (1:3).

WHEN WAS IT WRITTEN?

Because the itinerary and references in 1 and 2 Timothy and Titus do not match the journeys described in Acts, it has been proposed that Paul wrote this letter on a fourth missionary journey, sometime after his release from house arrest, perhaps between A.D. 62 and 64.

WHAT IS THE BOOK ABOUT?

The Book of 1 Timothy was written to encourage Timothy, both personally and as Paul's representative in Ephesus. It deals with false teaching that has become prevalent in Ephesus. And it provides instructions to Timothy on the proper conduct of worship in the church, as well as qualifications for elders and deacons. In addition, Paul gives special guidance on the correct treatment of different groups within the church, such as widows, elders, and slaves.

WHY WAS THIS BOOK WRITTEN?

Paul wrote this letter to his young co-worker in the ministry. Timothy was, perhaps, not very assertive and had difficulty exercising authority because of his youth. Paul gives him encouragement and detailed guidelines for overseeing the life and work of the church. He also warned young Timothy against the false teachers who were misleading many of the Christians.

SO WHAT DOES THIS BOOK MEAN TO US?

It matters to God how the work of his church is conducted and who carries it out. First Timothy provides guidelines and criteria that are still as valid today as they were in Ephesus. Just as Paul had done with the Corinthians, he encourages both the Ephesians and Christians today in the use of the spiritual gifts received from God, but he is concerned that "everything be done in a right and orderly way" (1 Corinthians 14:40). The Book of 1 Timothy is our handbook from God via Paul for accomplishing those parallel goals.

SUMMARY:

1 Timothy was written primarily to deal with problems of false teaching in Ephesus. First Timothy, then, like the rest of the letters in the New Testament, provides specific teaching in a particular setting. Unlike most other letters, though, this one is written to an individual, Timothy, who represents the apostolic mission in Ephesus, and not primarily to the church itself.

The message of 1 Timothy focuses first, on addressing the false teaching that has found a foothold in Ephesus. Although the Ephesian church was generally mature, some within the church seem to be moving away from the truth. Responsibilities within one's family are being neglected, some are claiming special knowledge, and still others are practicing world-denying behavior and calling it the Good News.

This letter is also concerned about the qualifications for church leaders. These qualities are important above all because this church must have leadership that is committed to the truth and that does not participate in the false teaching that has begun to grow in this Christian community.

1 Timothy

From Paul, an apostle of Christ Jesus, by the command of God our Savior and Christ Jesus our hope. 2To Timothy, a true child to me because you believe: Grace, mercy, and peace from God the Father and Christ Jesus our Lord.

Warning Against False Teaching

3I asked you to stay longer in Ephesus when I went into Macedonia so you could command some people there to stop teaching false things. 4Tell them not to spend their time on stories that are not true and on long lists of names in family histories. These things only bring arguments; they do not help God's work, which is done in faith. 5The purpose of this command is for people to have love, a love that comes from a pure heart and a good conscience and a true faith. 6Some people have missed these things and turned to useless talk. 7They want to be teachers of the law, but they do not understand either what they are talking about or what they are sure about.

8But we know that the law is good if someone uses it lawfully. 9We also know that the law is not made for good people but for those who are against the law and for those who refuse to follow it. It is for people who are against God and are sinful, who are not holy and have no religion, who kill their fathers and mothers, who murder, 10who take part in sexual sins, who have sexual relations with people of the same sex, who sell slaves, who tell lies, who speak falsely, and who do anything against the true teaching of God. 11That teaching is part of the Good News of the blessed God that he gave me to tell.

Thanks for God's Mercy

12I thank Christ Jesus our Lord, who gave me strength, because he trusted me and gave me this work of serving him. 13In the past I spoke against Christ and persecuted him and did all kinds of things to hurt him. But God showed me mercy, because I did not know what I was doing. I did not believe. 14But the grace of our Lord was fully given to me, and with that grace came the faith and love that are in Christ Jesus.

15What I say is true, and you should fully accept it: Christ Jesus came into the world to save sinners, of whom I am the worst. 16But I was given mercy so that in me, the worst of all sinners, Christ Jesus could show that he has patience without limit. His patience with me made me an example for those who would believe in him and have life forever. 17To the King that rules forever, who will never die, who cannot be seen, the only God, be honor and glory forever and ever. Amen.

18Timothy, my child, I am giving you a command that agrees with the prophecies that were given about you in the past. I tell you this so you can follow them and fight the good fight. 19Continue to have faith and do what you know is right. Some people have rejected this, and their faith has been shipwrecked. 20Hymenaeus and Alexander have done that, and I have given them to Satan so they will learn not to speak against God.

Some Rules for Men and Women

2 First, I tell you to pray for all people, asking God for what they need and being thankful to him. 2Pray for rulers and for all who have authority so that we can have quiet and peaceful lives full of worship and respect for God. 3This is good, and it pleases God our Savior, 4who wants all people to be saved and to know the truth. 5There is one God and one way human beings can reach God. That way is through Christ Jesus, who is himself human. 6He gave himself as a payment to free all people. He is proof that came at the right time. 7That is why I was chosen to tell the Good News and to be an apostle. (I am telling the truth; I am not lying.) I was chosen to teach those who are not Jews to believe and to know the truth.

8So, I want the men everywhere to pray, lifting up their hands in a holy manner, without anger and arguments.

9Also, women should wear proper clothes that show respect and self-control, not using braided hair or gold or pearls or expensive clothes. 10Instead,

1:1 Salvation: Hebrews 9:28
1:5 Conscience: 1 Timothy 1:19
1:8 Law: See article on page 702.
1:9 Murder: James 2:11
1:10 Homosexuality: See article on page 1101.
1:12 Thanks: Revelation 11:17
1:13, 20 Speaking against Christ (verse 13) or rejecting the teaching of the Gospel (verse 20) is blasphemy. Blasphemy is not simply claiming to be God, but rejecting him and working against his message.
1:14 Paul (Saul): 2 Timothy 3:10–13
1:19 Conscience: 1 Timothy 3:9
2:2 Government: 1 Peter 2:14
2:2 Citizen: Titus 3:1–2
2:5–6 Today, we would like to think there are many ways to God. We would like to believe that we can take our choice of mediators to the divine. But the New Testament clearly teaches that this is not true. There is only one person who can speak to us on God's behalf and that is Jesus Christ. He is God and man. He can speak to us with divine authority and bring our needs before his Father.

they should do good deeds, which is right for women who say they worship God.

11Let a woman learn by listening quietly and being ready to cooperate in everything. 12But I do not allow a woman to teach or to have authority over a man, but to listen quietly, 13because Adam was formed first and then Eve. 14And Adam was not tricked, but the woman was tricked and became a sinner. 15But she will be saved through having children if they continue in faith, love, and holiness, with self-control.

Elders in the Church

3 What I say is true: Anyone wanting to become an elder desires a good work. 2An elder must not give people a reason to criticize him, and he must have only one wife. He must be self-controlled, wise, respected by others, ready to welcome guests, and able to teach. 3He must not drink too much wine or like to fight, but rather be gentle and peaceable, not loving money. 4He must be a good family leader, having children who cooperate with full respect. 5(If someone does not know how to lead the family, how can that person take care of God's church?) 6But an elder must not be a new believer, or he might be too proud of himself and be judged guilty just as the devil was. 7An elder must also have the respect of people who are not in the church so he will not be criticized by others and caught in the devil's trap.

Deacons in the Church

8In the same way, deacons must be respected by others, not saying things they do not mean. They must not drink too much wine or try to get rich by cheating others. 9With a clear conscience they must follow the secret of the faith that God made known to us. 10Test them first. Then let them serve as deacons if you find nothing wrong in them. 11In the same way, women must be respected by others. They must not speak evil of others. They must be self-controlled and trustworthy in everything. 12Deacons must have only one wife and be good leaders of their children and their own families. 13Those who serve well as deacons are making an honorable place for themselves, and they will be very bold in their faith in Christ Jesus.

The Secret of Our Life

14Although I hope I can come to you soon, I am writing these things to you now. 15Then, even if I am delayed, you will know how to live in the family of God. That family is the church of the living God, the support and foundation of the truth. 16Without doubt, the secret of our life of worship is great:

He was shown to us in a human body,
  proved right in spirit,
and seen by angels.
  He was preached to those who are not Jews,
believed in by the world,
  and taken up in glory.

A Warning About False Teachers

4 Now the Holy Spirit clearly says that in the later times some people will stop believing the faith. They will follow spirits that lie and teachings of demons. 2Such teachings come from the false words of liars whose consciences are destroyed as if by a hot iron. 3They forbid people to marry and tell them not to eat certain foods which God created to be eaten with thanks by people who believe and know the truth.

2:11–14 In a male-led society it is not surprising the church reflects its culture. As elsewhere there are comments supportive of slavery, so here there are comments that are against women in leadership. Again it should be noted that Paul's churches were used to women leaders (Romans 16:1–15; 1 Corinthians 1:11), and Paul's statement in Galatians 3:28 may set the stage for an equality that wasn't yet worked out in his own day. For these reasons, many scholars think that this passage in 1 Timothy must be addressed to a specific situation that Timothy was facing, and is not to be taken as counsel for the entire church in all places.

Paul uses Eve as an illustration to back up his own policy of not allowing women to assume positions of authority in the church. Essentially, he argues on the basis of chronology (Adam was formed before Eve) and the history of the fall (Eve was tricked first). This does not make a woman inferior to a man, but recognizes the order ordained by God.

In Paul's teachings about orderly worship within the church, he connects the teaching authority of the husband to the order of creation and to the fact that the woman was the first to give in to Satan's tricks. This does not make man superior to the woman in the sight of God, since they both gave in to temptation the first time it was presented. But it does give responsibility for spiritual leadership to the man. It also gives promised blessing to the woman for following his leadership.

2:14 Eve: See article on page 49.
2:14 The Fall: See article on page 60.
3:2 Hospitality: 1 Timothy 5:10
3:2 Reputation: 1 Timothy 6:12
3:3 Greed: 1 Timothy 6:10
3:5 House/Home: 1 Timothy 3:12
3:8 Greed: 1 Timothy 3:3

3:8–13 Here the office of deacon is described. This office began at the time of Stephen the martyr in response to the physical needs of the widows of Hellenistic Christians in Jerusalem.

3:9 Conscience: 1 Timothy 4:2

3:11 *women.* This might mean the wives of the deacons, or it might mean women who serve in the same way as deacons.

3:12 House/Home: 2 Timothy 2:20–21
3:13 Leadership: 2 Timothy 2:16
4:1 Apostasy: 2 Peter 2:1
4:1 Last Days: 1 Peter 1:20
4:2 Conscience: 2 Timothy 1:3
4:3 Marriage: Revelation 19:6–10
4:3 Celibacy: See article on page 622.

4Everything God made is good, and nothing
should be refused if it is accepted with thanks,
5because it is made holy by what God has said
and by prayer.

Be a Good Servant of Christ

6By telling these things to the brothers and sisters, you will be a good servant of Christ Jesus. You
will be made strong by the words of the faith and
the good teaching which you have been following.
7But do not follow foolish stories that disagree with
God's truth, but train yourself to serve God.
8Training your body helps you in some ways, but
serving God helps you in every way by bringing
you blessings in this life and in the future life, too.
9What I say is true, and you should fully accept it.
10This is why we work and struggle: We hope in
the living God who is the Savior of all people, especially of those who believe.

11Command and teach these things. 12Do not let
anyone treat you as if you are unimportant because
you are young. Instead, be an example to the believers with your words, your actions, your love, your
faith, and your pure life. 13Until I come, continue to
read the Scriptures to the people, strengthen them,
and teach them. 14Use the gift you have, which
was given to you through prophecy when the
group of elders laid their hands on you. 15Continue
to do those things; give your life to doing them so
your progress may be seen by everyone. 16Be careful in your life and in your teaching. If you continue to live and teach rightly, you will save both
yourself and those who listen to you.

Rules for Living with Others

5 Do not speak angrily to an older man, but
plead with him as if he were your father. Treat
younger men like brothers, 2older women like
mothers, and younger women like sisters. Always
treat them in a pure way.

3Take care of widows who are truly widows. 4But
if a widow has children or grandchildren, let them
first learn to do their duty to their own family and
to repay their parents or grandparents. That pleases
God. 5The true widow, who is all alone, puts her
hope in God and continues to pray night and day
for God's help. 6But the widow who uses her life
to please herself is really dead while she is alive.
7Tell the believers to do these things so that no
one can criticize them. 8Whoever does not care for
his own relatives, especially his own family members, has turned against the faith and is worse than
someone who does not believe in God.

9To be on the list of widows, a woman must be
at least sixty years old. She must have been faithful
to her husband. 10She must be known for her good
works—works such as raising her children, welcoming strangers, washing the feet of God's people,
helping those in trouble, and giving her life to do
all kinds of good deeds.

11But do not put younger widows on that list.
After they give themselves to Christ, they are pulled
away from him by their physical needs, and then
they want to marry again. 12They will be judged for
not doing what they first promised to do. 13Besides
that, they learn to waste their time, going from
house to house. And they not only waste their time
but also begin to gossip and busy themselves with
other people's lives, saying things they should not
say. 14So I want the younger widows to marry, have
children, and manage their homes. Then no enemy
will have any reason to criticize them. 15But some
have already turned away to follow Satan.

16If any woman who is a believer has widows in
her family, she should care for them herself. The
church should not have to care for them. Then it
will be able to take care of those who are truly
widows.

17The elders who lead the church well should
receive double honor, especially those who work
hard by speaking and teaching, 18because the
Scripture says: "When an ox is working in the
grain, do not cover its mouth to keep it from eating," and "A worker should be given his pay."

4:4 Environment: See article on page 10.

4:6 *brothers and sisters.* Although the Greek text says "brothers" here and throughout this book, Paul's words refer to the entire church, including men and women.

4:13 The Bible is clear in expressing God's intent that people marry and bear children. Genesis 1:28, 2:17, and 9:1 state that it is not good for man to be alone. Rather, each person should have a spouse, be fruitful, and multiply. In the New Testament Jesus' disciples asked him if it would not be better for a person to remain single (Matthew 19:10–12). Jesus responded that it would be better, but only if a person were given that ability by God. In 1 Corinthians 7:1ff Paul warns that people ought to be married if they are not able to remain celibate. Paul also defends his right to take a wife in 1 Corinthians 9:5. In Paul's first letter to Timothy he condemns the teaching that forbids marriage as the doctrine of demons.

On the other hand, the New Testament encourages people to be celibate if they are given this ability by God. Celibacy allows a person to focus more attention on service to God and others with less distraction (1Corinthians 7:32–40). The Bible never requires celibacy, it only commends it to those who are able to remain this way, for the sake of service to God.

4:14 *laid their hands on.* The laying on of hands had many purposes, including the giving of a blessing, power, or authority.

5:1 Growing Old: 2 Timothy 2:22

5:5–6 Paul is contrasting two kinds of widows in this passage. The first widow places her complete trust in God to satisfy all her needs and desires. The second widow is described as one who lives just for self-pleasure in a self-indulgent lifestyle. Such a person is described as being already dead—spiritually.

5:10 Hospitality: Titus 1:8

5:18 *"When . . . eating,"* Quotation from Deuteronomy 25:4.

5:18 *"A worker . . . pay."* Quotation from Luke 10:7.

19Do not listen to someone who accuses an
elder, without two or three witnesses. 20Tell those
who continue sinning that they are wrong. Do this
in front of the whole church so that the others will
have a warning.
21Before God and Christ Jesus and the chosen
angels, I command you to do these things without
showing favor of any kind to anyone.
22Think carefully before you lay your hands on
anyone, and don't share in the sins of others. Keep
yourself pure.
23Stop drinking only water, but drink a little
wine to help your stomach and your frequent
sicknesses.
24The sins of some people are easy to see even
before they are judged, but the sins of others are
seen only later. 25So also good deeds are easy to
see, but even those that are not easily seen cannot stay hidden.

6 All who are slaves under a yoke should show
full respect to their masters so no one will speak
against God's name and our teaching. 2The slaves
whose masters are believers should not show their
masters any less respect because they are believers.
They should serve their masters even better,
because they are helping believers they love.
You must teach and preach these things.

False Teaching and True Riches

3Anyone who has a different teaching does not
agree with the true teaching of our Lord Jesus
Christ and the teaching that shows the true way to
serve God. 4This person is full of pride and understands nothing, but is sick with a love for arguing
and fighting about words. This brings jealousy,
fighting, speaking against others, evil mistrust,
5and constant quarrels from those who have evil
minds and have lost the truth. They think that
serving God is a way to get rich.
6Serving God does make us very rich, if we are
satisfied with what we have. 7We brought nothing
into the world, so we can take nothing out. 8But, if
we have food and clothes, we will be satisfied with
that. 9Those who want to become rich bring temptation to themselves and are caught in a trap. They
want many foolish and harmful things that ruin and
destroy people. 10The love of money causes all
kinds of evil. Some people have left the faith,
because they wanted to get more money, but they
have caused themselves much sorrow.

Some Things to Remember

11But you, man of God, run away from all those
things. Instead, live in the right way, serve God,
have faith, love, patience, and gentleness. 12Fight
the good fight of faith, grabbing hold of the life
that continues forever. You were called to have
that life when you confessed the good confession
before many witnesses. 13In the sight of God,
who gives life to everything, and of Christ Jesus, I
give you a command. Christ Jesus made the good
confession when he stood before Pontius Pilate.
14Do what you were commanded to do without
wrong or blame until our Lord Jesus Christ comes
again. 15God will make that happen at the right
time. He is the blessed and only Ruler, the King of
all kings and the Lord of all lords. 16He is the only
One who never dies. He lives in light so bright no
one can go near it. No one has ever seen God, or
can see him. May honor and power belong to God
forever. Amen.
17Command those who are rich with things of
this world not to be proud. Tell them to hope in
God, not in their uncertain riches. God richly gives
us everything to enjoy. 18Tell the rich people to do
good, to be rich in doing good deeds, to be generous
and ready to share. 19By doing that, they will be saving a treasure for themselves as a strong foundation
for the future. Then they will be able to have the
life that is true life.
20Timothy, guard what God has trusted to you.
Stay away from foolish, useless talk and from the
arguments of what is falsely called "knowledge."
21By saying they have that "knowledge," some
have missed the true faith.
Grace be with you.

5:22 *lay your hands on.* The laying on of hands had many purposes, including the giving of a blessing, power, or authority.

5:23 Alcohol: Revelation 14:8

6:9 Test/Temptation: 1 Peter 4:12–13

6:9–10 God can use money as a tool to accomplish his purposes in the world and in our lives. But our attitude toward money makes all the difference in how it affects us. If we want money and wealth for the material benefits they bring, we open ourselves to many temptations. The love of money and what money can buy can tempt us to do all kinds of harmful and sinful things to get it.

6:10 Greed: 2 Timothy 3:2

6:10 Materialism/Possessions: 1 Timothy 6:17–19

6:12 Reputation: 1 Peter 3:1–6

6:15 Lordship: 2 Peter 1:2–3

6:15 Names of God: Hebrews 12:9

6:15 Pontius Pilate: See article on page 785.

6:16 Paul clearly teaches that God is the only one who has immortality in himself, by virtue of who he is: "He is the only one who never dies." Not only does he not die, but he cannot die. He is the only eternal being in the universe who has no beginning and will have no end. The kind of "life that has no end" that Christ has becomes ours spiritually when we believe in Christ and physically when Christ raises up our bodies at the end of the age (see 1 Corinthians 15:53).

6:16 Immortality: See article on page 1214.

6:19 Materialism/Possessions: James 2:1–7

Notes:

INTRODUCTION TO THE BOOK OF

2 TIMOTHY

Paul Encourages Timothy

WHO WROTE THIS BOOK?

Paul, the author of 1 Timothy, also wrote 2 Timothy.

TO WHOM WAS THIS BOOK WRITTEN?

As in the first letter to Timothy, this letter is also addressed to Paul's young protégé, Timothy.

WHERE WAS IT WRITTEN?

Based on evidence within the letter itself, scholars agree that Paul probably wrote this book during his second imprisonment in Rome.

WHEN WAS IT WRITTEN?

The Book of 2 Timothy would most likely have been written betwen A.D. 64 and 68, or perhaps about A.D. 66 and 67.

WHAT IS THE BOOK ABOUT?

In this letter to his young friend and co-worker, Paul expresses his concern for the teaching of sound doctrine. He teaches about the grace of God and the faithfulness of Christ. He also explains the nature, function, and inspiration of Scripture. Paul goes on to share how most of his friends had deserted him during his first hearing. Then he admits that the end of his ministry and life are at hand. Finally, he claims confidence in his eternal salvation.

WHY WAS THIS BOOK WRITTEN?

The Book of 2 Timothy was written as Paul's final word of encouragement to Timothy and as a plea for Timothy to join him before he died. It is, in a real sense, Paul's last will and testament and his final wishes. It is also his final instructions to help Timothy carry on the ministry.

SO WHAT DOES THIS BOOK MEAN TO US?

When we near the ends of our lives, there are final words we will want to share with those nearest and dearest to us. If possible, we will want our loved ones by our sides for mutual comfort as we pass through the door from life to eternal life. As believers, we will be able to express the same confidence Paul did in the faithfulness of our Lord, and we will be able to claim the same precious promises that he did.

SUMMARY:

Although, like 1 Timothy, 2 Timothy has in view the influence of false teachers, this letter is more personal in its focus on Timothy. Second Timothy is written to encourage Timothy in his ongoing ministry in a least two ways.

First, throughout the letter Paul is presented as a model for Timothy; Paul is the steadfast teacher who continues to serve faithfully in spite of suffering. Second, this letter draws a contrast between the attitudes and actions of false teachers and the attitudes and actions that are to characterize Timothy's life.

2 TIMOTHY

From Paul, an apostle of Christ Jesus by the
will of God. God sent me to tell about the
promise of life that is in Christ Jesus.
2To Timothy, a dear child to me:
Grace, mercy, and peace to you from God the
Father and Christ Jesus our Lord.

Encouragement for Timothy

3I thank God as I always mention you in my
prayers, day and night. I serve him, doing what I
know is right as my ancestors did. 4Remem-
bering that you cried for me, I want very much to
see you so I can be filled with joy. 5I remember
your true faith. That faith first lived in your grandmother Lois and in your mother Eunice, and I
know you now have that same faith. 6This is why
I remind you to keep using the gift God gave you
when I laid my hands on you. Now let it grow, as
a small flame grows into a fire. 7God did not give us
a spirit that makes us afraid but a spirit of power
and love and self-control.
8So do not be ashamed to tell people about our
Lord Jesus, and do not be ashamed of me, in
prison for the Lord. But suffer with me for the
Good News. God, who gives us the strength to do
that, 9saved us and made us his holy people. That
was not because of anything we did ourselves but
because of God's purpose and grace. That grace
was given to us through Christ Jesus before time
began, 10but it is now shown to us by the coming
of our Savior Christ Jesus. He destroyed death,
and through the Good News he showed us the
way to have life that cannot be destroyed. 11I was
chosen to tell that Good News and to be an apostle and a teacher. 12I am suffering now because I
tell the Good News, but I am not ashamed,
because I know Jesus, the One in whom I have
believed. And I am sure he is able to protect what
he has trusted me with until that day. 13Follow
the pattern of true teachings that you heard from
me in faith and love, which are in Christ Jesus.
14Protect the truth that you were given; protect it
with the help of the Holy Spirit who lives in us.
15You know that everyone in the country of
Asia has left me, even Phygelus and Hermogenes.
16May the Lord show mercy to the family of
Onesiphorus, who has often helped me and was
not ashamed that I was in prison. 17When he came
to Rome, he looked eagerly for me until he found
me. 18May the Lord allow him to find mercy
from the Lord on that day. You know how many
ways he helped me in Ephesus.

A Loyal Soldier of Christ Jesus

2 You then, Timothy, my child, be strong in the
grace we have in Christ Jesus. 2You should

Greek discus thrower

1:3 Conscience: Titus 1:15

1:5 Timothy was a third-generation Christian. It is clear that he had "known the Holy Scriptures" from childhood (2 Timothy 3:15). When children are raised in a Christian family, it is hoped they learn the Bible just as Timothy did. For such young people, conversion is different than it is for persons who come to know Jesus for the first time as adults. Becoming a Christian after participating in a church all one's life is a natural extension of everything one has always known and valued. But conversion is still necessary, for everyone must make a choice for or against Christ.

1:6 *laid my hands on.* The laying on of hands had many purposes, including the giving of a blessing, power, or authority.

1:7 If you have many fears, all you have to do is rid yourself of one fear, and that's the fear of failure. This will help: "I'd rather attempt something great and fail than attempt nothing and succeed." Even if you fail, you win because you have overcome your fear of failure by trying something. Remember, success is never certain, and failure is never final.

1:7 Stress: See article on page 1325.

1:12 *day.* The day Christ will come to judge all people and take his people to live with him.

1:17 Rome: 1 Peter 2:13–17

teach people whom you can trust the things you and many others have heard me say. Then they will be able to teach others. 3Share in the troubles we have like a good soldier of Christ Jesus. 4A soldier wants to please the enlisting officer, so no one serving in the army wastes time with everyday matters. 5Also an athlete who takes part in a contest must obey all the rules in order to win. 6The farmer who works hard should be the first person to get some of the food that was grown. 7Think about what I am saying, because the Lord will give you the ability to understand everything.

8Remember Jesus Christ, who was raised from the dead, who is from the family of David. This is the Good News I preach, 9and I am suffering because of it to the point of being bound with chains like a criminal. But God's teaching is not in chains. 10So I patiently accept all these troubles so that those whom God has chosen can have the salvation that is in Christ Jesus. With that salvation comes glory that never ends.

11This teaching is true:

If we died with him, we will also live with him.
12 If we accept suffering, we will also
rule with him.
If we refuse to accept him, he will refuse to
accept us.
13 If we are not faithful, he will still be faithful,
because he cannot be false to himself.

A Worker Pleasing to God

14Continue teaching these things, warning people in God's presence not to argue about words. It does not help anyone, and it ruins those who listen. 15Make every effort to give yourself to God as the kind of person he will accept. Be a worker who is not ashamed and who uses the true teaching in the right way. 16Stay away from foolish, useless talk, because that will lead people further away from God. 17Their evil teaching will spread like a sickness inside the body. Hymenaeus and Philetus are like that. 18They have left the true teaching, saying that the rising from the dead has already taken place, and so they are destroying the faith of some people. 19But God's strong foundation continues to stand. These words are written on the seal: "The Lord knows those who belong to him," and "Everyone who wants to belong to the Lord must stop doing wrong."

20In a large house there are not only things made of gold and silver, but also things made of wood and clay. Some things are used for special purposes, and others are made for ordinary jobs. 21All who make themselves clean from evil will be used for special purposes. They will be made holy, useful to the Master, ready to do any good work.

22But run away from the evil young people like to do. Try hard to live right and to have faith, love, and peace, together with those who trust in the Lord from pure hearts. 23Stay away from foolish and stupid arguments, because you know they grow into quarrels. 24And a servant of the Lord must not quarrel but must be kind to everyone, a good teacher, and patient. 25The Lord's servant must gently teach those who disagree. Then maybe God will let them change their minds so they can accept the truth. 26And they may wake up and escape from the trap of the devil, who catches them to do what he wants.

The Last Days

3 Remember this! In the last days there will be many troubles, 2because people will love themselves, love money, brag, and be proud. They will say evil things against others and will not obey their parents or be thankful or be the kind of people God wants. 3They will not love others, will refuse to forgive, will gossip, and will not control themselves. They will be cruel, will hate what is good, 4will turn against their friends, and will do foolish things without thinking. They will be conceited, will love pleasure instead of God, 5and will act as if they serve God but will not have his power. Stay away from those people. 6Some of them go into homes and get control of silly women who are full of sin and are led by many evil desires. 7These women are always learning new teachings, but they are never able to understand the truth fully. 8Just as Jannes and Jambres were against Moses, these people are

2:8 David: Revelation 22:16
2:8 Memory: See article on page 510.
2:16 Leadership: Hebrews 13:7
2:19 *"The Lord . . . him."* Quotation from Numbers 16:5.
2:21 House/Home: See article on page 109.
2:22 Growing Old: Hebrews 5:14
2:24 Servant of the Lord: 1 Peter 2:16
2:25 Tongue: James 1:19
3 Paul warns Timothy about the troubles he can expect "in the last days" from those who have fallen away from the Lord. After a lengthy description of their actions and character in 2 Timothy 3:2–8, he offers the encouragement that those who fall away and who try to draw others away with them will not be successful.

In contrast to those who fall away from the Lord and lead immoral and unethical lives, those who remain faithful will be able to do every good work. Paul's concern is not with losing one's salvation. He is concerned with living a life pleasing to God.

Although the last days is a time of great blessing, living in these last days also calls for responsible, moral living in the midst of opposition to the Gospel.

3:2 Greed: Hebrews 13:5
3:4 Leisure: Titus 3:3–8

against the truth. Their thinking has been ruined, and they have failed in trying to follow the faith. 9But they will not be successful in what they do, because as with Jannes and Jambres, everyone will see that they are foolish.

Obey the Teachings

10But you have followed what I teach, the way I live, my goal, faith, patience, and love. You know I never give up. 11You know how I have been hurt and have suffered, as in Antioch, Iconium, and Lystra. I have suffered, but the Lord saved me from all those troubles. 12Everyone who wants to live as God desires, in Christ Jesus, will be hurt. 13But people who are evil and cheat others will go from bad to worse. They will fool others, but they will also be fooling themselves.

14But you should continue following the teachings you learned. You know they are true, because you trust those who taught you. 15Since you were a child you have known the Holy Scriptures which are able to make you wise. And that wisdom leads to salvation through faith in Christ Jesus. 16All Scripture is given by God and is useful for teaching, for showing people what is wrong in their lives, for correcting faults, and for teaching how to live right. 17Using the Scriptures, the person who serves God will be capable, having all that is needed to do every good work.

4 I give you a command in the presence of God and Christ Jesus, the One who will judge the living and the dead, and by his coming and his kingdom: 2Preach the Good News. Be ready at all times, and tell people what they need to do. Tell them when they are wrong. Encourage them with great patience and careful teaching, 3because the time will come when people will not listen to the true teaching but will find many more teachers who please them by saying the things they want to hear. 4They will stop listening to the truth and will begin to follow false stories. 5But you should control yourself at all times, accept troubles, do the work of telling the Good News, and complete all the duties of a servant of God.

6My life is being given as an offering to God, and the time has come for me to leave this life. 7I have fought the good fight, I have finished the race, I have kept the faith. 8Now, a crown is being held for me—a crown for being right with God. The Lord, the judge who judges rightly, will give the crown to me on that day—not only to me but to all those who have waited with love for him to come again.

A court secretary copying a Bible manuscript about A.D. 1340

Personal Words

9Do your best to come to me as soon as you can, 10because Demas, who loved this world, left me and went to Thessalonica. Crescens went to Galatia, and Titus went to Dalmatia. 11Luke is the only one still with me. Get Mark and bring him with you when you come, because he can help me in my work here. 12I sent Tychicus to Ephesus. 13When I was in Troas, I left my coat there with Carpus. So when you come, bring it to me, along with my books, particularly the ones written on parchment. 14Alexander the metalworker did many harmful things against me. The Lord will punish him for what he did. 15You also should be careful that he does not hurt you, because he fought strongly against our teaching.

16The first time I defended myself, no one helped me; everyone left me. May they be forgiven. 17But the Lord stayed with me and gave me strength so I could fully tell the Good News

3:13 Paul (Saul): 2 Timothy 4:9–18
3:16 Conversion: See article on page 953.
4:5 Evangelism: See article on page 793.
4:8 *day.* The day Christ will come to judge all people and take his people to live with him.
4:10 World/Worldly: 1 John 2:15–17
4:11 Luke: See article on page 1296.

4:11 Paul's account of how everyone deserted him during his first trial, except for the Lord (2 Timothy 4:16–17), is relieved by his reference to Luke as the only one still with him. The beloved physician ministered to Paul's needs to the very end. His faithfulness shines as a beacon light in Scripture and challenges us not to quit when the going gets rough.
4:13 *parchment.* A writing paper made from the skins of sheep.

to all those who are not Jews. So I was saved
from the lion's mouth. [18]The Lord will save me
when anyone tries to hurt me, and he will bring
me safely to his heavenly kingdom. Glory forever
and ever be the Lord's. Amen.⚭

Final Greetings

[19]Greet Priscilla and Aquila and the family of
Onesiphorus. [20]Erastus stayed in Corinth, and I
left Trophimus sick in Miletus. [21]Try as hard as
you can to come to me before winter.

Eubulus sends greetings to you. Also Pudens, Linus, Claudia, and all the brothers and sisters in Christ greet you.

[22]The Lord be with your spirit. Grace be with
you.

⚭**4:18 Paul (Saul):** Titus 1:1–3

Notes:

INTRODUCTION TO THE BOOK OF TITUS

Paul Instructs Titus

WHO WROTE THIS BOOK?

The apostle Paul is the author of the Book of Titus (1:1).

TO WHOM WAS THIS BOOK WRITTEN?

This letter was written to Titus, a co-worker of Paul's, who Paul had probably converted (1:4).

WHERE WAS IT WRITTEN?

Like 1 Timothy, which it parallels in many ways, the Titus was written in Madeconia during Paul's possible fourth missionary journey.

WHEN WAS IT WRITTEN?

Again, like 1 Timothy, Titus was written after Paul's release from his first imprisonment in Rome about A.D. 62 to 64.

WHAT IS THE BOOK ABOUT?

Paul gives instructions to Titus regarding the church in Crete as he had to Timothy regarding the church in Ephesus. In both instances, Paul states the requirements for elders (bishops). And in both cases, he warns against false teachers. He encourages Titus to maintain sound doctrine. One of the clearest descriptions of salvation through God's regenerating work in the life of a sinner is given in this letter (3:5, 7). Instructions for different ages and genders in the church are also given, as well as for the proper behavior of believers in civil society.

WHY WAS THIS BOOK WRITTEN?

Paul wanted to provide guidelines to help Titus in his development of the church in Crete. From other references to Titus in Scripture, it is clear that Paul regarded him as a troubleshooter and had sent him to difficult places, such as Corinth. Crete was notorious for the violent, untrustworthy nature of its people (1:12).

SO WHAT DOES THIS BOOK MEAN TO US?

We may be called upon to serve God in some difficult situations, too. But God never calls us to any place without preparing us and preparing the way. God's word always provides guidelines for Christian living and service. We are not alone, as we remember the promise of Jesus in Matthew 28:20 to "be with you (us) always" to the end.

SUMMARY:

When Paul tells Titus to "finish doing the things that still needed to be done" (1:5), he clearly has in mind straightening out some difficult problems among the Christians on Crete. These problems had more to do with the affect of the Good News in the larger world—that is, in one's own household and larger community—and only to a lesser degree in the church itself. This letter's dual emphasis on doing good deeds (1:16; 2:7, 14; 3:1, 8, 14) and on the nature of the Good News (2:11–14; 3:4–7) indicate how closely tied together these two are, right faith and right actions.

TITUS

From Paul, a servant of God and an apostle of Jesus Christ. I was sent to help the faith of God's chosen people and to help them know the truth that shows people how to serve God. 2That faith and that knowledge come from the hope for life forever, which God promised to us before time began. And God cannot lie. 3At the right time God let the world know about that life through preaching. He trusted me with that work, and I preached by the command of God our Savior.

4To Titus, my true child in the faith we share:

Grace and peace from God the Father and Christ Jesus our Savior.

Titus' Work in Crete

5I left you in Crete so you could finish doing the things that still needed to be done and so you could appoint elders in every town, as I directed you. 6An elder must not be guilty of doing wrong, must have only one wife, and must have believing children. They must not be known as children who are wild and do not cooperate. 7As God's manager, an elder must not be guilty of doing wrong, being selfish, or becoming angry quickly. He must not drink too much wine, like to fight, or try to get rich by cheating others. 8An elder must be ready to welcome guests, love what is good, be wise, live right, and be holy and self-controlled. 9By holding on to the trustworthy word just as we teach it, an elder can help people by using true teaching, and he can show those who are against the true teaching that they are wrong.

10There are many people who refuse to cooperate, who talk about worthless things and lead others into the wrong way—mainly those who say all who are not Jews must be circumcised. 11These people must be stopped, because they are upsetting whole families by teaching things they should not teach, which they do to get rich by cheating people. 12Even one of their own prophets said, "Cretans are always liars, evil animals, and lazy people who do nothing but eat." 13The words that prophet said are true. So firmly tell those people they are wrong so they may become strong in the faith, 14not accepting Jewish false stories and the commands of people who reject the truth. 15To those who are pure, all things are pure, but to those who are full of sin and do not believe, nothing is pure. Both their minds and their consciences have been ruined. 16They say they know God, but their actions show they do not accept him. They are hateful people, they refuse to obey, and they are useless for doing anything good.

Following the True Teaching

2 But you must tell everyone what to do to follow the true teaching. 2Teach older men to be self-controlled, serious, wise, strong in faith, in love, and in patience.

3In the same way, teach older women to be holy in their behavior, not speaking against others or enslaved to too much wine, but teaching what is good. 4Then they can teach the young women to love their husbands, to love their children, 5to be wise and pure, to be good workers at home, to be kind, and to yield to their husbands. Then no one will be able to criticize the teaching God gave us.

6In the same way, encourage young men to be wise. 7In every way be an example of doing good deeds. When you teach, do it with honesty and seriousness. 8Speak the truth so that you cannot be criticized. Then those who are against you will be ashamed because there is nothing bad to say about us.

9Slaves should yield to their own masters at all times, trying to please them and not arguing with them. 10They should not steal from them but should show their masters they can be fully trusted so that in everything they do they will make the teaching of God our Savior attractive.

11That is the way we should live, because God's grace that can save everyone has come. 12It teaches us not to live against God nor to do the evil things the world wants to do. Instead, that grace teaches us to live now in a wise and right way and in a way that shows we serve God. 13We should live like that while we wait for our great hope and the coming of the glory of our great God and Savior Jesus Christ. 14He gave himself for us so he might pay the price to free us from all evil and to make us pure people who belong only to him—people who are always wanting to do good deeds.

15Say these things and encourage the people and tell them what is wrong in their lives, with all authority. Do not let anyone treat you as if you were unimportant.

1:3 Paul (Saul): Philemon 9
1:8 Hospitality: 1 Peter 4:9
1:11 Anti-Semitism: Revelation 2:9
1:15 Conscience: See article on page 1111.
2:5 Women: 1 Peter 3:1–6
2:14 Ambition: See article on page 832.
2:14 Grace: Hebrews 2:9
2:14 Hope: Hebrews 7:19

The Right Way to Live

3 Remind the believers to yield to the authority of rulers and government leaders, to obey them, to be ready to do good, 2 to speak no evil about anyone, to live in peace, and to be gentle and polite to all people.

3 In the past we also were foolish. We did not obey, we were wrong, and we were slaves to many things our bodies wanted and enjoyed. We spent our lives doing evil and being jealous. People hated us, and we hated each other. 4 But when the kindness and love of God our Savior was shown, 5 he saved us because of his mercy. It was not because of good deeds we did to be right with him. He saved us through the washing that made us new people through the Holy Spirit. 6 God poured out richly upon us that Holy Spirit through Jesus Christ our Savior. 7 Being made right with God by his grace, we could have the hope of receiving the life that never ends.

8 This teaching is true, and I want you to be sure the people understand these things. Then those who believe in God will be careful to use their lives for doing good. These things are good and will help everyone.

9 But stay away from those who have foolish arguments and talk about useless family histories and argue and quarrel about the law. Those things are worth nothing and will not help anyone. 10 After a first and second warning, avoid someone who causes arguments. 11 You can know that such people are evil and sinful; their own sins prove them wrong.

Some Things to Remember

12 When I send Artemas or Tychicus to you, make every effort to come to me at Nicopolis, because I have decided to stay there this winter. 13 Do all you can to help Zenas the lawyer and Apollos on their journey so that they have everything they need. 14 Our people must learn to use their lives for doing good deeds to provide what is necessary so that their lives will not be useless.

15 All who are with me greet you. Greet those who love us in the faith.

Grace be with you all.

3:2 Citizen: 1 Peter 2:13–17
3:6 Holy Spirit: See article on page 1051.
3:8 Good Works: James 2:8–26
3:8 Leisure: 1 Corinthians 15:58

Notes:

INTRODUCTION TO THE BOOK OF

PHILEMON

A Slave Becomes a Christian

WHO WROTE THIS BOOK?

The apostle Paul wrote this brief letter (verse 1).

TO WHOM WAS THIS BOOK WRITTEN?

Paul wrote this very personal letter to a respected friend and Christian slave owner, Philemon, who lived in Colossae.

WHERE WAS IT WRITTEN?

Like Colossians, this letter was written from Rome during Paul's first imprisonment.

WHEN WAS IT WRITTEN?

It was written during the two-year house arrest Paul underwent between A.D. 60 and 62.

WHAT IS THE BOOK ABOUT?

This little letter relates to a runaway slave, Onesimus, who had left Philemon and gone to Rome only to be encountered and led to Christ by Paul. Paul does not ask for Onesmus's freedom directly, but asks Philemon to treat Onesimus no longer as a slave but as a brother (verse 16). In seeking Philemon's forgiveness of, and reconciliation with Onesimus, Paul pleads Onesimus's case, appealing to the spiritual debt Philemon owed Paul. Paul goes beyond this to offer to pay for any loss Philemon may have incurred because Onesimus ran away.

WHY WAS THIS BOOK WRITTEN?

The Book of Philemon was written to bring two men together—a slave owner and a runaway slave. Both men were believers. Philemon had been one of Paul's earlier converts, just as Onesimus was one of his later ones. Paul does not deal with the topic of slavery as such, but he lays the foundation for the emancipation of one slave.

SO WHAT DOES THIS BOOK MEAN TO US?

We face many difficult social problems today, too, and it would be a healing step if opposing factions could be brought together in the name of Christ. This applies to such tensions as labor versus management, the disadvantaged versus the advantaged, races versus each other, and on it goes. Christ calls for a unity of all believers, no matter what their backgrounds, social standings, races, or political preferences. We are "all one in Christ Jesus."

SUMMARY:

This is the most personal of Paul's letters. Although it is written to a member of a house church, and thus, clearly, to that church as a whole, it concerns the relationship between Philemon and his slave, Onesimus. It is not completely clear what Paul wants Philemon to do about Onesimus' status as a slave, though it is clear that he wants Philemon to accept his slave now as a brother in Christ. Here is a great drama of grace, as the church struggles with the implications of the Good News in all of life, including slavery.

PHILEMON

From Paul, a prisoner of Christ Jesus, and
from Timothy, our brother.

To Philemon, our dear friend and worker with us;
2to Apphia, our sister; to Archippus, a worker with
us; and to the church that meets in your home:
3Grace and peace to you from God our Father
and the Lord Jesus Christ.

Philemon's Love and Faith

4I always thank my God when I mention you in
my prayers, 5because I hear about the love you have
for all God's holy people and the faith you have in
the Lord Jesus. 6I pray that the faith you share may
make you understand every blessing we have in
Christ. 7I have great joy and comfort, my brother,
because the love you have shown to God's people
has refreshed them.

Accept Onesimus as a Brother

8So, in Christ, I could be bold and order you to
do what is right. 9But because I love you, I am
pleading with you instead. I, Paul, an old man
now and also a prisoner for Christ Jesus, 10am
pleading with you for my child Onesimus, who
became my child while I was in prison. 11In the
past he was useless to you, but now he has
become useful for both you and me.
12I am sending him back to you, and with him
I am sending my own heart. 13I wanted to keep
him with me so that in your place he might help
me while I am in prison for the Good News. 14But
I did not want to do anything without asking you
first so that any good you do for me will be because
you want to do it, not because I forced you.
15Maybe Onesimus was separated from you for a
short time so you could have him back forever—
16no longer as a slave, but better than a slave, as a
loved brother. I love him very much, but you will
love him even more, both as a person and as a
believer in the Lord.
17So if you consider me your partner, welcome
Onesimus as you would welcome me. 18If he has
done anything wrong to you or if he owes you
anything, charge that to me. 19I, Paul, am writing
this with my own hand. I will pay it back, and I
will say nothing about what you owe me for your
own life. 20So, my brother, I ask that you do this
for me in the Lord: Refresh my heart in Christ.
21I write this letter, knowing that you will do what
I ask you and even more.
22One more thing—prepare a room for me in
which to stay, because I hope God will answer
your prayers and I will be able to come to you.

This Roman slave badge reads, "Seize me if I should try to escape and send me back to my master."

Final Greetings

23Epaphras, a prisoner with me for Christ Jesus,
sends greetings to you. 24And also Mark,
Aristarchus, Demas, and Luke, workers together
with me, send greetings.
25The grace of our Lord Jesus Christ be with
your spirit.

1:9 Paul (Saul): 2 Peter 3:15–16

1:24 Luke: 2 Timothy 4:11

INTRODUCTION TO THE BOOK OF

HEBREWS

A Better Life Through Christ

WHO WROTE THIS BOOK?

No one is certain about who wrote the Book of Hebrews. Different possibilities have been suggested, including Paul, Barnabas, Apollos, and others. Still, it is safest just to refer to the author as "the writer of Hebrews."

TO WHOM WAS THIS BOOK WRITTEN?

The likely recipients of this letter were Jewish Christians outside of Palestine who were being tempted by "the Judaizers" to become another Jewish sect (like the Essenes).

WHERE WAS IT WRITTEN?

Because of a reference to Italy (13:24), it is quite possible that this book was written in Rome or somewhere in Italy.

WHEN WAS IT WRITTEN?

Since it appears the Temple was still standing and the sacrificial system was still in use (10:2, 3, 11), the Hebrew letter was probably written before A.D. 70. It may have been composed during the time of Emperor Nero's persecution of Christians about A.D. 64, with the suffering mentioned in 10:32–34 being caused by the edict of Claudius in A.D. 49.

WHAT IS THE BOOK ABOUT?

Hebrews shows Jesus' fulfillment of the sanctuary, sacrifices, and priesthood established in the Law of Moses. The writer of Hebrews quotes extensively from the Greek Old Testament to show the limitations of the Law and its sacrificial system. He also shows how the Law points to a new high priest—Jesus Christ. He says Christ is better than the mediators, sanctuary, and sacrifices under the Law. He is worthy of "more honor" than Moses (3:3). The way of the Law has been superseded by the way of faith in Christ (chapter 11), and there is no turning back from the superior to the inferior.

WHY WAS THIS BOOK WRITTEN?

This letter was written to encourage and exhort scattered Jewish Christians to persevere in their faith, in spite of persecution. It warns them not to retreat into a displaced and inferior Jewish legal and sacrificial system. It argues passionately for the superiority of Christ over the old system, pointing out how he accomplished once for all people and all time what the fulfilled older system could never do.

SO WHAT DOES THIS BOOK MEAN TO US?

Each of us has come out of some older outlook on life when we came to believe and obey Christ. There may be times, especially when the going gets rough, when we may be tempted to give up and go back to what is familiar, even though it's inferior by far to life in Christ. The writer of Hebrews has a word for us, too: "Never, never, never go back!" Life in Christ and, eventually eternal life through him, are worth the struggle and worth the wait. Remain faithful!

SUMMARY:

Although Hebrews is often called a "letter," only its closing resembles this form of communication. It is better to think of Hebrews as an "essay" or "treatise" that develops its argument point by point. At the same time, its closing does remind us of the closing verses of Paul's letters; this observation urges us to read Hebrews, like the other New Testament materials, as a document written to address particular people facing particular issues at a particular time.

What were those issues? In terms of content, the primary focus of Hebrews is the absolute supremacy of Christ as the one who shows and provides the grace of God to humanity. The way God has spoken to us in Christ is superior to every form through which God has spoken in the past (1:1–4). He is superior to the angels (1:5–2:18), greater than Moses (3:1–4:13), and greater than the priests

(4:14–7:28). Hence, the new agreement he has made through his death is better than the old one (8:1–10:39), since through his death we have forgiveness of sins.

Why does Hebrews emphasize the relative greatness of Christ? Hebrews was written to Jewish people who had become Christians. These believers were thinking of going back to their old ways; would they continue the journey of being followers? Hebrews is written to them, to encourage them to persist in their faith. This is why even those first ten chapters that emphasize the superiority of Christ also urge people to follow as they were taught (2:1–2) and not to turn away from God (3:12). Hebrews 11, then, provides a long list of people who continued in their faith; these people are examples to us, and the witness of their lives ought to encourage us to live faithfully too (Hebrews 12).

Because of the length of this book, and because of the nature of its argument, it is probably best to read Hebrews section by section:

Hebrews 1:1–4:13 The Superiority of Christ, Part One
Hebrews 4:14–10:39 The Superiority of Christ, Part Two
Hebrews 11:1–13:25 Continuing in the Faith. Closing Remarks.

HEBREWS

God Spoke Through His Son

In the past God spoke to our ancestors
through the prophets many times and in
many different ways. 2But now in these last
days God has spoken to us through his Son. God
has chosen his Son to own all things, and through
him he made the world. 3The Son reflects the
glory of God and shows exactly what God is like.
He holds everything together with his powerful
word. When the Son made people clean from
their sins, he sat down at the right side of God,
the Great One in heaven. 4The Son became much
greater than the angels, and God gave him a
name that is much greater than theirs.

5This is because God never said to any of the
angels,

"You are my Son.
Today I have become your Father." *Psalm 2:7*

Nor did God say of any angel,

"I will be his Father,
and he will be my Son." *2 Samuel 7:14*

6And when God brings his firstborn Son into the
world, he says,

"Let all God's angels worship him." *Psalm 97:7*

7This is what God said about the angels:

"God makes his angels become like winds.
He makes his servants become
like flames of fire." *Psalm 104:4*

8But God said this about his Son:

"God, your throne will last forever and ever.
You will rule your kingdom with fairness.
9You love right and hate evil,
so God has chosen you from
among your friends;
he has set you apart with
much joy." *Psalm 45:6-7*

10God also says,

"Lord, in the beginning you made the earth,
and your hands made the skies.
11They will be destroyed, but you will remain.
They will all wear out like clothes.
12You will fold them like a coat.
And, like clothes, you will change them.
But you never change,
and your life will never end." *Psalm 102:25-27*

13And God never said this to an angel:

"Sit by me at my right side
until I put your enemies under
your control." *Psalm 110:1*

14All the angels are spirits who serve God and
are sent to help those who will receive salvation.

Our Salvation Is Great

2 So we must be more careful to follow what
we were taught. Then we will not stray away
from the truth. 2The teaching God spoke through
angels was shown to be true, and anyone who did
not follow it or obey it received the punishment
that was earned. 3So surely we also will be punished if we ignore this great salvation. The Lord
himself first told about this salvation, and it was
proven true to us by those who heard him. 4God
also proved it by using wonders, great signs,
many kinds of miracles, and by giving people gifts
through the Holy Spirit, just as he wanted.

Christ Became like Humans

5God did not choose angels to be the rulers of the
new world that was coming, which is what we have
been talking about. 6It is written in the Scriptures,

"Why are people important to you?
Why do you take care of human beings?
7You made them a little lower than the angels
and crowned them with glory and honor.
8You put all things under
their control." *Psalm 8:4-6*

When God put everything under their control,
there was nothing left that they did not rule. Still,
we do not yet see them ruling over everything.
9But we see Jesus, who for a short time was made
lower than the angels. And now he is wearing a
crown of glory and honor because he suffered and
died. And by God's grace, he died for everyone.

1:1–2 The first coming of Christ is the great dividing point in history. Everything before is *the past.* Everything after is *these last days.* The last days began in the manger in Bethlehem and continue until the second coming.

1:1–2 After the Fall into sin, there was a huge gap between God and his human creations. We needed someone who could speak on our behalf to God and who could speak to us the words of God. In the Old Testament, God used prophets, priests, and kings in this capacity. But now, we have something much better than human beings. God himself became a man in Jesus Christ. Jesus is the perfect mediator, since he is both God and man.

1:3 In the Old Testament we read that human beings cannot see God, but they can see the reflection of the glory of God—the light that comes from God's being and character (Exodus 33:18–23). Hebrews 1 claims that Jesus expresses as a human being the essence of God's character and will. In this sense, Jesus Christ is "much greater than the angels" (Hebrews 1:4) and fit to serve as the true high priest for humanity, the Lord who will sit at God's right hand and reign over us (8:1; 12:2).

1:6 *"Let . . . him."* These words are found in Deuteronomy 32:43 in the Septuagint, the Greek version of the Old Testament, and in a Hebrew copy among the Dead Sea Scrolls.

1:13 *until . . . control.* Literally, "until I make your enemies a footstool for your feet."

1:14 Angels: Hebrews 13:2

2:9 Grace: James 4.6

10God is the One who made all things, and all
things are for his glory. He wanted to have many
children share his glory, so he made the One who
leads people to salvation perfect through suffering.
11Jesus, who makes people holy, and those who
are made holy are from the same family. So he is
not ashamed to call them his brothers and sisters.
12He says,

"Then, I will tell my fellow Israelites
about you;
I will praise you in the
public meeting." *Psalm 22:22*

13He also says,

"I will trust in God." *Isaiah 8:17*

And he also says,

"I am here, and with me are the children God
has given me." *Isaiah 8:18*

14Since these children are people with physical
bodies, Jesus himself became like them. He did
this so that, by dying, he could destroy the one who
has the power of death—the devil— 15and free those
who were like slaves all their lives because of their
fear of death. 16Clearly, it is not angels that Jesus
helps, but the people who are from Abraham. 17For
this reason Jesus had to be made like his brothers
in every way so he could be their merciful and
faithful high priest in service to God. Then Jesus
could bring forgiveness for their sins. 18And now
he can help those who are tempted, because he
himself suffered and was tempted.

Jesus Is Greater than Moses

3 So all of you holy brothers and sisters, who
were called by God, think about Jesus, who was
sent to us and is the high priest of our faith. 2Jesus
was faithful to God as Moses was in God's family.
3Jesus has more honor than Moses, just as the
builder of a house has more honor than the house
itself. 4Every house is built by someone, but the
builder of everything is God himself. 5Moses was
faithful in God's family as a servant, and he told
what God would say in the future. 6But Christ is
faithful as a Son over God's house. And we are
God's house if we keep on being very sure about
our great hope.

We Must Continue to Follow God

7So it is as the Holy Spirit says:

"Today listen to what he says.
8Do not be stubborn as in the past
when you turned against God,
when you tested God in the desert.
9There your ancestors tried me and tested me
and saw the things I did for forty years.
10I was angry with them.
I said, 'They are not loyal to me
and have not understood my ways.'
11I was angry and made a promise,
'They will never enter my rest.'" *Psalm 95:7-11*

12So brothers and sisters, be careful that none
of you has an evil, unbelieving heart that will turn
you away from the living God. 13But encourage
each other every day while it is "today." Help each
other so none of you will become hardened
because sin has tricked you. 14We all share in
Christ if we keep till the end the sure faith we had
in the beginning. 15This is what the Scripture says:

"Today listen to what he says.
Do not be stubborn as in the past
when you turned against God." *Psalm 95:7-8*

16Who heard God's voice and was against him?
It was all those people Moses led out of Egypt.
17And with whom was God angry for forty
years? He was angry with those who sinned,
who died in the desert. 18And to whom was God
talking when he promised that they would
never enter his rest? He was talking to those
who did not obey him. 19So we see they were
not allowed to enter and have God's rest,
because they did not believe.

2:10 Suffering: Hebrews 13:12–14

2:11 *brothers and sisters.* Although the Greek text says "brothers" here and throughout this book, the writer's words were meant for the entire church, including men and women.

2:16 *Abraham.* Most respected ancestor of the Jews. Every Jew hoped to see Abraham.

2:17 Priesthood: Hebrews 7:1

2:17 Reconciliation: See article on page 1233.

2:18 Samuel: Hebrews 9:15–26

3:3 Throughout Hebrews, 3:1–6 in particular and up to 4:13, Jesus is compared and contrasted to Moses. He is like Moses, yet he is far better than Moses. Jesus is like Moses in that he has brought his church out of their Egypt (bondage to sin). The church is presently wandering through its forty years in the desert (3:7–19) and awaits entrance into the promised land (heaven, 4:8–11). Jesus is unlike Moses in that he is the final deliverer. No one will come after him.

3:11 *rest.* A place of rest God promised to give his people.

3:12 Evil: James 1:13

3:12–15 From time to time in this essay, the writer indicates that he is talking about the greatness of Christ in order to encourage people to stay true to Christ.

3:13 *"today."* This word is taken from verse 7. It means that it is important to do these things now.

3:15 Stubbornness: See article on page 1024.

3:15–19 The author of Hebrews exhorts his readers to persevere through persecution (10:32–34) and not to leave the Christian faith. He uses as a negative example the rebellion of the stubborn Israelites in the desert, recounted in Psalm 95. Just as they were never allowed to rest in the Promised Land, so also the Hebrew Christians were at risk of not receiving the heavenly rest that lay before them if they did not persevere.

3:19 Jordan River: See article on page 370.

4 Now, since God has left us the promise that
we may enter his rest, let us be very careful
so none of you will fail to enter. 2The Good News
was preached to us just as it was to them. But the
teaching they heard did not help them, because
they heard it but did not accept it with faith. 3We
who have believed are able to enter and have
God's rest. As God has said,

"I was angry and made a promise,
'They will never enter my rest.'" *Psalm 95:11*

But God's work was finished from the time he
made the world. 4In the Scriptures he talked
about the seventh day of the week: "And on the
seventh day God rested from all his works." 5And
again in the Scripture God said, "They will never
enter my rest."

6It is still true that some people will enter God's
rest, but those who first heard the way to be
saved did not enter, because they did not obey.
7So God planned another day, called "today." He
spoke about that day through David a long time
later in the same Scripture used before:

"Today listen to what he says.
Do not be stubborn." *Psalm 95:7-8*

8We know that Joshua did not lead the people
into that rest, because God spoke later about
another day.⚭ 9This shows that the rest for
God's people is still coming. 10Anyone who
enters God's rest will rest from his work as God
did. 11Let us try as hard as we can to enter God's
rest so that no one will fail by following the example of those who refused to obey.

12God's word is alive and working and is
sharper than a double-edged sword. It cuts all the
way into us, where the soul and the spirit are
joined, to the center of our joints and bones. And
it judges the thoughts and feelings in our hearts.
13Nothing in all the world can be hidden from
God. Everything is clear and lies open before
him, and to him we must explain the way we
have lived.⚭

Jesus Is Our High Priest

14Since we have a great high priest, Jesus the
Son of God, who has gone into heaven, let us hold
on to the faith we have.⚭ 15For our high priest is
able to understand our weaknesses. When he
lived on earth, he was tempted in every way that
we are, but he did not sin. 16Let us, then, feel
very sure that we can come before God's throne
where there is grace. There we can receive
mercy and grace to help us when we need it.⚭

5 Every high priest is chosen from among
other people. He is given the work of going
before God for them to offer gifts and sacrifices
for sins. 2Since he himself is weak, he is able to
be gentle with those who do not understand and
who are doing wrong things. 3Because he is
weak, the high priest must offer sacrifices for his
own sins and also for the sins of the people.

4To be a high priest is an honor, but no one
chooses himself for this work. He must be called
by God as Aaron was. 5So also Christ did not
choose himself to have the honor of being a high
priest, but God chose him. God said to him,

"You are my Son.
Today I have become your Father." *Psalm 2:7*

6And in another Scripture God says,

"You are a priest forever,
a priest like Melchizedek." *Psalm 110:4*

7While Jesus lived on earth, he prayed to God and
asked God for help. He prayed with loud cries and
tears to the One who could save him from death,
and his prayer was heard because he trusted God.⚭
8Even though Jesus was the Son of God, he learned
obedience by what he suffered. 9And because his obedience was perfect, he was able to give eternal salvation to all who obey him. 10In this way God made
Jesus a high priest, a priest like Melchizedek.

Warning Against Falling Away

11We have much to say about this, but it is hard
to explain because you are so slow to understand.

4:4 *"And . . . works."* Quotation from Genesis 2:2.

4:8 *Joshua.* After Moses died, Joshua became leader of the Jewish people and led them into the land that God promised to give them.

⚭**4:8 Joshua:** See article on page 362.

4:9 *rest.* Literally, "sabbath rest," meaning a sharing in the rest that God began after he created the world.

⚭**4:13 Exodus/New Exodus:** Exodus 12:31–51

⚭**4:14 Perseverance:** Hebrews 6:12

4:15 We appreciate the kind words and deeds of others at a time of loss, but we yearn for someone to come alongside who really understands what we are going through. As human beings, we long for empathy from the God of heaven. We know he cares for us, but can he feel our pain and sorrow? Because the eternal Son of God became a human being like us, it is possible to affirm God's understanding of our human condition. Jesus can feel our deepest pain, and he can take our pain away and replace it with his peace.

⚭**4:16 Mediator:** John 1:18

⚭**4:16 Sabbath:** Revelation 6:11

5:4 *Aaron.* Aaron was Moses' brother and the first Jewish high priest.

5:6 *Melchizedek.* A priest and king who lived in the time of Abraham. (Read Genesis 14:17–24.)

⚭**5:7 Mount of Olives:** See article on page 954.

5:7–9 The Book of Hebrews focuses not only on the sinlessness of Jesus (Hebrews 4:15; 7:26–27), but also on his obedience to the will of God in going to the cross (12:2–3; Philippians 2:6–8). Here the point is made that Jesus' willingness to obey God was necessary to make us right with God (Romans 5:18–19) and to make our obedience possible (1 Corinthians 15:45–49).

5:11–12 The writer indicates his concern for his audience. They should be further along in the faith, but they have failed to mature as they should have. He is concerned that they might give up on the journey of being followers.

12 By now you should be teachers, but you need
someone to teach you again the first lessons of
God's message. You still need the teaching that is
like milk. You are not ready for solid food.
13 Anyone who lives on milk is still a baby and
knows nothing about right teaching. 14 But solid
food is for those who are grown up. They have
practiced in order to know the difference between
good and evil.

6 So let us go on to grown-up teaching. Let us
not go back over the beginning lessons we
learned about Christ. We should not again start
teaching about faith in God and about turning
away from those acts that lead to death. 2 We
should not return to the teaching about baptisms,
about laying on of hands, about the raising of the
dead and eternal judgment. 3 And we will go on to
grown-up teaching if God allows.

4 Some people cannot be brought back again
to a changed life. They were once in God's
light, and enjoyed heaven's gift, and shared in
the Holy Spirit. 5 They found out how good
God's word is, and they received the powers of
his new world. 6 But they fell away from Christ.
It is impossible to bring them back to a changed
life again, because they are nailing the Son of
God to a cross again and are shaming him in
front of others.

7 Some people are like land that gets plenty of
rain. The land produces a good crop for those
who work it, and it receives God's blessings.
8 Other people are like land that grows thorns and
weeds and is worthless. It is in danger of being
cursed by God and will be destroyed by fire.

9 Dear friends, we are saying this to you, but we
really expect better things from you that will lead
to your salvation. 10 God is fair; he will not forget
the work you did and the love you showed for
him by helping his people. And he will remember
that you are still helping them. 11 We want each of
you to go on with the same hard work all your
lives so you will surely get what you hope for.
12 We do not want you to become lazy. Be like
those who through faith and patience will receive
what God has promised.

13 God made a promise to Abraham. And as
there is no one greater than God, he used himself
when he swore to Abraham, 14 saying, "I will
surely bless you and give you many descendants."
15 Abraham waited patiently for this to happen,
and he received what God promised.

16 People always use the name of someone greater
than themselves when they swear. The oath proves
that what they say is true, and this ends all arguing. 17 God wanted to prove that his promise
was true to those who would get what he
promised. And he wanted them to understand
clearly that his purposes never change, so he
made an oath. 18 These two things cannot
change: God cannot lie when he makes a
promise, and he cannot lie when he makes an
oath. These things encourage us who came to
God for safety. They give us strength to hold on to
the hope we have been given. 19 We have this
hope as an anchor for the soul, sure and strong. It
enters behind the curtain in the Most Holy Place
in heaven, 20 where Jesus has gone ahead of us
and for us. He has become the high priest forever,
a priest like Melchizedek.

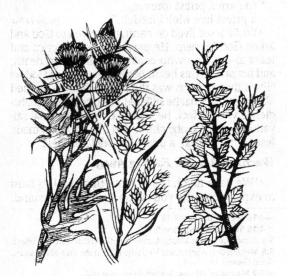

A thistle or weed (left) and thorns (right)

The Priest Melchizedek

7 Melchizedek was the king of Salem and a
priest for God Most High. He met Abraham
when Abraham was coming back after defeating

5:14 Growing Old: 1 Peter 5:5

6:2 *baptisms.* The word here may refer to Christian baptism, or it may refer to the Jewish ceremonial washings.

6:2 *laying on of hands.* The laying on of hands had many purposes, including the giving of a blessing, power, or authority.

6:6 Honor & Shame: See article on page 945.

6:12 Perseverance: Hebrews 10:23

6:14 *"I . . . descendants."* Quotation from Genesis 22:17.

6:16 Oath/Vow: James 5:12

6:17 Commitment: Hebrews 9:15–17

6:18 Promise: Hebrews 10:35–36

6:20 *Melchizedek.* A priest and king who lived in the time of Abraham. (Read Genesis 14:17–24.)

the kings. When they met, Melchizedek blessed Abraham, 2and Abraham gave him a tenth of everything he had brought back from the battle. First, Melchizedek's name means "king of goodness," and he is king of Salem, which means "king of peace." 3No one knows who Melchizedek's father or mother was, where he came from, when he was born, or when he died. Melchizedek is like the Son of God; he continues being a priest forever.

4You can see how great Melchizedek was. Abraham, the great father, gave him a tenth of everything that he won in battle. 5Now the law says that those in the tribe of Levi who become priests must collect a tenth from the people—their own people—even though the priests and the people are from the family of Abraham. 6Melchizedek was not from the tribe of Levi, but he collected a tenth from Abraham. And he blessed Abraham, the man who had God's promises. 7Now everyone knows that the more important person blesses the less important person. 8Priests receive a tenth, even though they are only men who live and then die. But Melchizedek, who received a tenth from Abraham, continues living, as the Scripture says. 9We might even say that Levi, who receives a tenth, also paid it when Abraham paid Melchizedek a tenth. 10Levi was not yet born, but he was in the body of his ancestor when Melchizedek met Abraham.

11The people were given the law based on a system of priests from the tribe of Levi, but they could not be made perfect through that system. So there was a need for another priest to come, a priest like Melchizedek, not Aaron. 12And when a different kind of priest comes, the law must be changed, too. 13We are saying these things about Christ, who belonged to a different tribe. No one from that tribe ever served as a priest at the altar. 14It is clear that our Lord came from the tribe of Judah, and Moses said nothing about priests belonging to that tribe.

Jesus Is like Melchizedek

15And this becomes even more clear when we see that another priest comes who is like Melchizedek. 16He was not made a priest by human rules and laws but through the power of his life, which continues forever. 17It is said about him,

"You are a priest forever,
a priest like Melchizedek." *Psalm 110:4*

18The old rule is now set aside, because it was weak and useless. 19The law of Moses could not make anything perfect. But now a better hope has been given to us, and with this hope we can come near to God. 20It is important that God did this with an oath. Others became priests without an oath, 21but Christ became a priest with God's oath. God said:

"The Lord has made a promise
and will not change his mind.
'You are a priest forever.'" *Psalm 110:4*

22This means that Jesus is the guarantee of a better agreement from God to his people.

23When one of the other priests died, he could not continue being a priest. So there were many priests. 24But because Jesus lives forever, he will never stop serving as priest. 25So he is able always to save those who come to God through him because he always lives, asking God to help them.

26Jesus is the kind of high priest we need. He is holy, sinless, pure, not influenced by sinners, and he is raised above the heavens. 27He is not like the other priests who had to offer sacrifices every day, first for their own sins, and then for the sins of the people. Christ offered his sacrifice only once and for all time when he offered himself. 28The law chooses high priests who are people with weaknesses, but the word of God's oath came later than the law. It made God's Son to be the high priest, and that Son has been made perfect forever.

Jesus Is Our High Priest

8 Here is the point of what we are saying: We have a high priest who sits on the right side of God's throne in heaven. 2Our high priest serves in the Most Holy Place, the true place of worship that was made by God, not by humans.

3Every high priest has the work of offering gifts and sacrifices to God. So our high priest must also offer something to God. 4If our high priest were now living on earth, he would not be a priest, because there are already priests here who follow the law by offering gifts to God. 5The work they do as priests is only a copy and a shadow of what

7:1 Abraham: James 2:23
7:1 Priesthood: Hebrews 13:11
7:3 *No . . . was.* Literally, "Melchizedek was without father, without mother, without genealogy."
7:11 *The . . . law.* This refers to the people of Israel who were given the Law of Moses.
7:15 *Melchizedek.* A priest and king who lived in the time of Abraham. (Read Genesis 14:17–24.)
7:19 Hope: See article on page 1052.
7:22 Agreement: Hebrews 8:13
7:22 *agreement.* God gives a contract or agreement to his people. For the Jews, this agreement was the Law of Moses. But now God has given a better agreement to his people through Christ.
8–10 The "unclear picture" provided by the holy priests, sacrifices, and Temple of the Old Testament is made clear by the coming of Jesus Christ. He is our high priest (Hebrews 8), who offers the perfect sacrifice of himself in our behalf (Hebrews 9:12). We are now free from the power of sin so that we may serve the living God (Hebrews 9:14) and enter into his holy presence without fear (Hebrews 10:19–22).
8:5 *"Be . . . mountain."* Quotation from Exodus 25:40.

is in heaven. This is why God warned Moses when he was ready to build the Holy Tent: "Be very careful to make everything by the plan I showed you on the mountain." [6]But the priestly work that has been given to Jesus is much greater than the work that was given to the other priests. In the same way, the new agreement that Jesus brought from God to his people is much greater than the old one. And the new agreement is based on promises of better things.

[7]If there had been nothing wrong with the first agreement, there would have been no need for a second agreement. [8]But God found something wrong with his people. He says:

"Look, the time is coming, says the Lord,
 when I will make a new agreement
with the people of Israel
 and the people of Judah.
[9]It will not be like the agreement
 I made with their ancestors
when I took them by the hand
 to bring them out of Egypt.
But they broke that agreement,
 and I turned away from them, says the Lord.
[10]This is the agreement I will make
 with the people of Israel at that time,
  says the Lord.
I will put my teachings in their minds
 and write them on their hearts.
I will be their God,
 and they will be my people.
[11]People will no longer have to teach their
  neighbors and relatives
 to know the Lord,
because all people will know me,
 from the least to the most important.
[12]I will forgive them for the wicked
  things they did,
 and I will not remember their
  sins anymore." *Jeremiah 31:31-34*

[13]God called this a new agreement, so he has made the first agreement old. And anything that is old and worn out is ready to disappear.⚭

The Old Agreement

9 The first agreement had rules for worship and a man-made place for worship. [2]The Holy Tent was set up for this. The first area in the Tent was called the Holy Place. In it were the lamp and the table with the bread that was made holy for God. [3]Behind the second curtain was a room called the Most Holy Place. [4]In it was a golden altar for burning incense and the Ark covered with gold that held the old agreement. Inside this Ark was a golden jar of manna, Aaron's rod that once grew leaves, and the stone tablets of the old agreement. [5]Above the Ark were the creatures that showed God's glory, whose wings reached over the lid. But we cannot tell everything about these things now.⚭

[6]When everything in the Tent was made ready in this way, the priests went into the first room every day to worship. [7]But only the high priest could go into the second room, and he did that only once a year. He could never enter the inner room without taking blood with him, which he offered to God for himself and for sins the people did without knowing they did them. [8]The Holy Spirit uses this to show that the way into the Most Holy Place was not open while the system of the old Holy Tent was still being used. [9]This is an example for the present time. It shows that the gifts and sacrifices offered cannot make the conscience of the worshiper perfect. [10]These gifts and sacrifices were only about food and drink and special washings. They were rules for the body, to be followed until the time of God's new way.

The New Agreement

[11]But when Christ came as the high priest of the good things we now have, he entered the greater and more perfect tent. It is not made by humans and does not belong to this world. [12]Christ entered the Most Holy Place only once—and for all time. He did not take with him the blood of goats and calves. His sacrifice was his own blood, and by it he set us free from sin forever.⚭ [13]The blood of goats and bulls and the ashes of a cow are sprinkled on the people who are unclean, and this makes their bodies clean again. [14]How much more is done by the blood of Christ. He offered himself through the eternal Spirit as a perfect sacrifice to God. His blood will make our consciences pure from useless acts so we may serve the living God.⚭

[15]For this reason Christ brings a new agreement from God to his people. Those who are called by God can now receive the blessings he has promised, blessings that will last forever. They can have those things because Christ died so that the people who lived under the first agreement could be set free from sin.⚭

8:7 *first agreement.* The contract God gave the Jewish people when he gave them the Law of Moses.

⚭**8:13 Agreement:** Jeremiah 31:31

9:1 *first agreement.* See 8:7.

⚭**9:5 Ark of the Agreement:** See article on page 259.

⚭**9:12 Sacrifice:** Hebrews 10:1

9:14 *Spirit.* This refers to the Holy Spirit, to Christ's own spirit, or to the spiritual and eternal nature of his sacrifice.

⚭**9:14 Conflict:** Hebrews 9:26

⚭**9:15 Land/Inheritance:** See article on page 149.

Persecution

1 Peter 2:18–25

When the Bible speaks of God's people being "persecuted," what does it mean? Is persecution always physical and violent? How should Christians respond to persecution?

Those of us who are followers of God can expect, at some time, to be mistreated, attacked, hurt—in short, to be persecuted. People are persecuted when they are intentionally hurt by another person or group because of their beliefs. This mistreatment of believers, or persecution, comes in a variety of types. The Bible prepares Christians for these various kinds of mistreatment by warning us to expect persecution, by telling of the blessings that come with persecution, and by teaching us how to respond.

God's people have a long history of being mistreated by foreign countries and wicked leaders. While the Israelites were in Egypt, the Egyptians "made their lives bitter," forcing them into slavery and killing their baby sons (Exodus 1:11–18). Much later the Israelites themselves rejected God's commands, persecuting the messengers of God who warned them of God's anger. The prophet Jeremiah cried to God, "Make those who are hurting me be ashamed" (Jeremiah 17:18). Jesus' life attracted not only the admiration of many followers, but also the concern of many religious leaders. He would heal others when their rules said that he ought not. He spoke as if he were equal with God. "Because Jesus was doing this on the Sabbath," John writes, "the Jews began to persecute him" (John 5:16–18). Their persecution was completed as Jesus stood before Pilate in Jerusalem and heard the people cry, "Crucify him" (Luke 23:20).

After Jesus death, it was his followers who received mistreatment. Acts 8:1 says that after Stephen died for his faith, "the church of Jerusalem began to be persecuted." The believers were thrown in jail, beaten, and put to death for their faith in Christ. The apostle Paul wrote of his experience, "We are persecuted, but God does not leave us. We are hurt sometimes, but we are not destroyed" (2 Corinthians 4:9). The persecution of Christian believers has continued throughout history and shall only end when the evil world, symbolized in Revelation by "the woman drunk . . . with the blood of those who were killed because of their faith in Jesus" (Revelation 17:6), is put to death (Revelation 20:4–6).

Persecution comes in a variety of forms. Often the mistreatment is less violent than murder. Paul speaks of the apostles' being treated as "the garbage of the world." He mentions people cursing, hurting, and telling lies about them (1 Corinthians 4:11–13). Peter encourages believers that "when people insult you because you follow Christ, you are blessed" (1 Peter 4:14). The wicked mistreat the godly poor in Psalms 10 by unjust use of money and legal systems. We experience persecution in uncomfortable relationships, lies or gossip, laws or social situations which intentionally favor the unbeliever, insults, rejection from family and friends, and violence.

The Bible teaches that Christians can expect persecution. Jesus says in John 15:20, "If people did wrong to me, they will do wrong to you, too." Likewise Paul says, "Everyone who wants to live as God desires, in Christ Jesus, will be hurt." This "hurt" cannot be avoided, for it is an expression of the world's resistance to Christ. It is especially to be expected near the end of this age, when even "brothers will give their own brothers to be killed, and fathers will give their own children to be killed" (Mark 13:12). However, the Bible also teaches that with the persecutions come blessings. Peter says, "But be happy that you are sharing in Christ's sufferings so that you will be happy and full of joy when Christ comes again in glory" (1 Peter 4:13).

The Bible also instructs us how to respond to persecution when it comes. First, we are to be careful that the persecution we are experiencing is a response to our life in Christ, and not because of our poor behavior. Peter says, "Keep a clear conscience so that those who speak evil of your good life in Christ will be made ashamed. It is better to suffer for doing good than for doing wrong" (1 Peter 3:16–17; 1 Peter 2:18–21). Second, we are to treat our persecutors with kindness, rather than with bitterness. Jesus says, "Love your enemies, pray for those who hurt you" (Matthew 5:44). Paul tells the believers in Rome to "Wish good for those who harm you; wish them well and do not curse them" (Romans 12:14). Third, we are to persevere in our faithful walk with the Lord. Paul, after telling Timothy that followers of Jesus will be hurt, encourages Timothy to "continue following the teachings you learned" (2 Timothy 3:14). Jesus says of the last days that, "all people will hate you because you follow me, but those people who keep their faith until the end will be saved" (Mark 13:13).

Persecution can be as violent as being killed, or as subtle as gossip. Believers in all ages have experienced persecution, and if we follow the life of Jesus, we, too, will experience it. This need not burden us. Instead we have cause to rejoice, for those who are persecuted can expect a great reward. Those who suffer persecution should take care that it is for good that they are suffering. They should bless, and not curse, those who hurt them. The ones who keep the faith through the pain of persecution will experience the salvation of God.

Persecution: For additional scriptures on this topic go to Exodus 1:1–18.

PROMISE

2 PETER 1:3–4

What are God's promises to us? How do they function in the Bible?

The Bible teaches not only that God is in control of the future, but also that we must guide our daily living in the light of this assurance. We do this by learning God's promises and by trusting that he will keep them (2 Peter 3:9).

This is what the people in the Old Testament were called to do when they first received word of God's loving intention to save humankind from its sin. Interestingly, God did not reveal this plan all at once; he unfolded it progressively. He did not allow his people to see the entire picture, but required that they trust only in the portion they received. At each stage, God made a new promise, or, as some say, continued his single promise, of what he would do to restore humankind's broken relationship with him.

God began his blueprint with a general promise of blessing to Abraham. In response to the sin that entered the world (Genesis 3:6; 6:5; 11:4), God said: "I will make you a great nation, and I will bless you . . . . And all the people on earth will be blessed through you" (Genesis 12:2–3). Although Abraham did not live to see the full benefits of this promise (Hebrews 11:13, 39), he was called simply to trust that God would do as he said (Genesis 15:6; Romans 4:20–21; Galatians 3:6).

In the next stage, God looked to the nation inheriting this promised salvation. He raised up the people of Israel (Deuteronomy 29:12–13; Acts 7:17) and called them also to order their lives around his promises: "See, today I am letting you choose a blessing or a curse. You will be blessed if you obey the commands of the LORD . . . . You will be cursed if you disobey" (Deuteronomy 11:26–28). Later prophetic calls to return to God's laws reminded the people to take seriously his promises of prosperity and destruction (Jeremiah 7:22–29).

Once the nation of Isreal was established, God focused more on the king through whose family this promised salvation would come. He pledged to David an eternal kingdom: "Also I will choose a place for my people Israel . . . They will not be bothered anymore. . . . But your family and your kingdom will continue always before me. Your throne will last forever" (2 Samuel 7:10, 16). For later generations, especially after the kingship was eliminated, faith in God meant clinging through great sorrow to God's promise to David (Ezekiel 37:24–28).

Finally, God attended to the people's enablement for his promised salvation. He joyfully announced a new agreement with humankind, unlike the old one set up through Moses: "I will put my teachings in their minds and write them on their hearts" (Jeremiah 31:33).

God dramatically brought his saving plan to fulfillment by sending his Son. (Acts 13:23, 32–33). Paul writes, "The yes to all of God's promises is in Christ" (2 Corinthians 1:20). The Bible proclaims that belief in Jesus Christ is the way one receives the full benefits of the promise to Abraham (Galatians 3:22, 29).

Jesus is also the king who will reign forever (1 Corinthians 15:23–25) promised to David (Luke 1:32; Romans 1:3–4). Jesus brought the promised new agreement when he said, "This new agreement begins with my blood which is poured out for you" (Luke 22:20; cf. Hebrews 9:15). The Holy Spirit, whom Jesus brought, is part of the fulfillment of God's Word made long ago (Acts 2:33–39).

In other words, salvation is, and always has been, carried by God's promises. It is promised to those who trust in Jesus Christ, "that whoever believes in him may not be lost, but have eternal life" (John 3:16; 1 John 2:25). Those who search for him can be assured that they will find him (John 6:37; Matthew 7:7–8). Our rightness with God, therefore, comes not by our own efforts at obedience, but by having confidence that God will save us through Christ as he says he will (Romans 3:21–22).

The promises of God, however, cover more than just his plan of salvation. Many of them have to do with daily, godly living. They help guide our decisions and conduct by providing assurances in the middle of life's uncertainties. An effective prayer life, for example, relies on many of God's promises. The Bible teaches that we may pray and expect God to answer if we pray within God's will (1 John 5:14–15), in faith (Mark 11:24), in repentance (James 5:16), in obedience (1 John 3:21–22), with right motives (James 4:3), with persistence (Luke 11:9), and with a forgiving heart (Matthew 6:14–15).

Other promises guide us during difficult periods. The Bible assures us that God will keep us from overpowering temptation (1 Corinthians 10:13), forgive us when we confess our sins (1 John 1:9), make up losses we suffer for following Christ (Luke 18:29, 30), provide for our needs (Philippians 4:19), and work all things for good (Romans 8:28).

Promise: For additional scriptures on this topic go to Genesis 17:1–8.

16When there is a will, it must be proven that
the one who wrote that will is dead. 17A will
means nothing while the person is alive; it can be
used only after the person dies. 18This is why
even the first agreement could not begin without
blood to show death. 19First, Moses told all the
people every command in the law. Next he took
the blood of calves and mixed it with water. Then
he used red wool and a branch of the hyssop plant
to sprinkle it on the book of the law and on all the
people. 20He said, "This is the blood that begins
the Agreement that God commanded you to
obey." 21In the same way, Moses sprinkled the
blood on the Holy Tent and over all the things
used in worship. 22The law says that almost
everything must be made clean by blood, and sins
cannot be forgiven without blood to show death.

Christ's Death Takes Away Sins

23So the copies of the real things in heaven had
to be made clean by animal sacrifices. But the real
things in heaven need much better sacrifices.
24Christ did not go into the Most Holy Place made
by humans, which is only a copy of the real one.
He went into heaven itself and is there now
before God to help us. 25The high priest enters the
Most Holy Place once every year with blood that is
not his own. But Christ did not offer himself
many times. 26Then he would have had to suffer
many times since the world was made. But
Christ came only once and for all time at just the
right time to take away all sin by sacrificing himself. 27Just as everyone must die once and be
judged, 28so Christ was offered as a sacrifice one
time to take away the sins of many people. And
he will come a second time, not to offer himself
for sin, but to bring salvation to those who are
waiting for him.

10 The law is only an unclear picture of the
good things coming in the future; it is not
the real thing. The people under the law offer the
same sacrifices every year, but these sacrifices can
never make perfect those who come near to worship God. 2If the law could make them perfect,
the sacrifices would have already stopped. The
worshipers would be made clean, and they would
no longer have a sense of sin. 3But these sacrifices
remind them of their sins every year, 4because it
is impossible for the blood of bulls and goats to
take away sins.

5So when Christ came into the world, he said:

"You do not want sacrifices and offerings,
but you have prepared a body for me.
6You do not ask for burnt offerings
and offerings to take away sins.
7Then I said, 'Look, I have come.
It is written about me in the book.
God, I have come to do what
you want.'" *Psalm 40:6-8*

8In this Scripture he first said, "You do not want
sacrifices and offerings. You do not ask for burnt
offerings and offerings to take away sins." (These
are all sacrifices that the law commands.) 9Then he
said, "Look, I have come to do what you want."
God ends the first system of sacrifices so he can set
up the new system. 10And because of this, we are
made holy through the sacrifice Christ made in his
body once and for all time.

11Every day the priests stand and do their religious service, often offering the same sacrifices.
Those sacrifices can never take away sins. 12But
after Christ offered one sacrifice for sins, forever,
he sat down at the right side of God. 13And now
Christ waits there for his enemies to be put under
his power. 14With one sacrifice he made perfect
forever those who are being made holy.

15The Holy Spirit also tells us about this. First
he says:

16"This is the agreement I will make
with them at that time, says the Lord.
I will put my teachings in their hearts
and write them on
their minds." *Jeremiah 31:33*

17Then he says:

"Their sins and the evil things they do—
I will not remember anymore." *Jeremiah 31:34*

18Now when these have been forgiven, there is
no more need for a sacrifice for sins.

9:16 *will.* A legal document that shows how a person's money and property are to be distributed at the time of death. This is the same word in Greek as "agreement" in verse 15.

9:17 Commitment: See article on page 1244.

9:20 *"This . . . obey."* Quotation from Exodus 24:8.

9:26 Conflict: James 4:1–3

9:26 Samuel: See article on page 390.

9:28 Blood: John 1:7

9:28 Salvation: 1 Peter 1:15

10 The Old Testament sacrifices provided "an unclear picture" of the coming of the perfect sacrifice of Jesus Christ. Unlike the outer, temporary cleansing provided by the sacrifice of animals, the cleansing provided by the blood of Christ cleanses our consciences from the guilt of sin once and for all time. We are now free to enter into God the Father's presence without fear because we have been made perfectly clean by the sacrifice of God the Son.

10:1 Sacrifice: 1 Peter 2:5

10:5 Body/Flesh: See article on page 1132.

10:16 *agreement.* God gives a contract or agreement to his people. For the Jews, this agreement was the Law of Moses. But now God has given a better agreement to his people through Christ.

Continue to Trust God

19So, brothers and sisters, we are completely free to enter the Most Holy Place without fear because of the blood of Jesus' death. 20We can enter through a new and living way that Jesus opened for us. It leads through the curtain—Christ's body. 21And since we have a great priest over God's house, 22let us come near to God with a sincere heart and a sure faith, because we have been made free from a guilty conscience, and our bodies have been washed with pure water. 23Let us hold firmly to the hope that we have confessed, because we can trust God to do what he promised.

24Let us think about each other and help each other to show love and do good deeds. 25You should not stay away from the church meetings, as some are doing, but you should meet together and encourage each other. Do this even more as you see the day coming.

26If we decide to go on sinning after we have learned the truth, there is no longer any sacrifice for sins. 27There is nothing but fear in waiting for the judgment and the terrible fire that will destroy all those who live against God. 28Anyone who refused to obey the law of Moses was found guilty from the proof given by two or three witnesses. He was put to death without mercy. 29So what do you think should be done to those who do not respect the Son of God, who look at the blood of the agreement that made them holy as no different from others' blood, who insult the Spirit of God's grace? Surely they should have a much worse punishment. 30We know that God said, "I will punish those who do wrong; I will repay them." And he also said, "The Lord will judge his people." 31It is a terrible thing to fall into the hands of the living God.

32Remember those days in the past when you first learned the truth. You had a hard struggle with many sufferings, but you continued strong. 33Sometimes you were hurt and attacked before crowds of people, and sometimes you shared with those who were being treated that way. 34You helped the prisoners. You even had joy when all that you owned was taken from you, because you knew you had something better and more lasting.

35So do not lose the courage you had in the past, which has a great reward. 36You must hold on, so you can do what God wants and receive what he has promised. 37For in a very short time,

"The One who is coming will come
and will not be delayed.
38The person who is right with me
will live by trusting in me.
But if he turns back with fear,
I will not be pleased with him." *Habakkuk 2:3-4*

39But we are not those who turn back and are lost. We are people who have faith and are saved.

What Is Faith?

11 Faith means being sure of the things we hope for and knowing that something is real even if we do not see it. 2Faith is the reason we remember great people who lived in the past.

3It is by faith we understand that the whole world was made by God's command so what we see was made by something that cannot be seen.

4It was by faith that Abel offered God a better sacrifice than Cain did. God said he was pleased with the gifts Abel offered and called Abel a good man because of his faith. Abel died, but through his faith he is still speaking.

5It was by faith that Enoch was taken to heaven so he would not die. He could not be found, because God had taken him away. Before he was taken, the Scripture says that he was a man who truly pleased God. 6Without faith no one can please God. Anyone who comes to God must believe that he is real and

---

10:19–23 The Most Holy Place in both the Meeting Tent and in the Temple symbolizes the presence of God, which is evident by the presence of the Ark (Exodus 26:33–34; 1 Kings 6:19; 8:6, 9) and the two creatures above the lid of the Ark, which "showed God's glory" (Hebrews 9:5). Numbers 7:89 specifically says that the Lord spoke with Moses "from between the two gold creatures with wings that were above the lid of the Ark of the Agreement. In this way the Lord spoke with him."

Just as the creatures guarded the way to Eden, the Most Holy Place was also inaccessible with the exception of the high priest, who must make offerings before entering. However, Jesus opened a "new and living way" (Hebrews 10:20) and to "come near to God" (Hebrews 10:22). This points to the new Jerusalem, or heaven, in which believers will enjoy the blessed presence of God (Revelation 21:3).

10:23 Perseverance: Hebrews 10:35

10:25 *day.* The day Christ will come to judge all people and take his people to live with him.

10:25 Church: See article on page 751.

10:26–31 The writer of Hebrews is so concerned about the possibility of some Christians not continuing in the faith that he provides this stern warning. Jesus Christ, the Son of God, has done his part by giving himself as a sacrifice once and for all. Believers cannot take advantage of this by knowingly continuing to sin, but must continue to grow in their faith and obedience.

10:27 Hell: Jude 13

10:30 *"I . . . them."* Quotation from Deuteronomy 32:35.

10:30 *"The Lord . . . people."* Quotation from Deuteronomy 32:36; Psalm 135:14.

10:35 Perseverance: Hebrews 12:1–3

10:36 Promise: 2 Peter 3:9

10:39 Sin: James 5:16

11:1 This clear definition of "faith" talks about it as being sure of what God will do despite our being unable to touch or feel or see it directly. It is the conviction that God is in charge and that we belong to him which guides our lives and leads us to follow Jesus.

11:4 Abel's faith is here identified as the reason his sacrifice was acceptable. Cain's sacrifice was not acceptable because his heart attitude was wrong. Since it is only possible to please God by faith (verse 6), Cain's offering was rejected because it was done in unbelief. The what and how of Cain's offering failed to please God solely because they revealed a sinful heart commitment.

that he rewards those who truly want to find him.

7It was by faith that Noah heard God's warnings about things he could not yet see. He obeyed God and built a large boat to save his family. By his faith, Noah showed that the world was wrong, and he became one of those who are made right with God through faith.

8It was by faith Abraham obeyed God's call to go to another place God promised to give him. He left his own country, not knowing where he was to go. 9It was by faith that he lived like a foreigner in the country God promised to give him. He lived in tents with Isaac and Jacob, who had received that same promise from God. 10Abraham was waiting for the city that has real foundations—the city planned and built by God.

11He was too old to have children, and Sarah could not have children. It was by faith that Abraham was made able to become a father, because he trusted God to do what he had promised. 12This man was so old he was almost dead, but from him came as many descendants as there are stars in the sky. Like the sand on the seashore, they could not be counted.

13All these great people died in faith. They did not get the things that God promised his people, but they saw them coming far in the future and were glad. They said they were like visitors and strangers on earth. 14When people say such things, they show they are looking for a country that will be their own. 15If they had been thinking about the country they had left, they could have gone back. 16But they were waiting for a better country—a heavenly country. So God is not ashamed to be called their God, because he has prepared a city for them.

17It was by faith that Abraham, when God tested him, offered his son Isaac as a sacrifice. God made the promises to Abraham, but Abraham was ready to offer his own son as a sacrifice. 18God had said, "The descendants I promised you will be from Isaac." 19Abraham believed that God could raise the dead, and really, it was as if Abraham got Isaac back from death.

20It was by faith that Isaac blessed the future of Jacob and Esau. 21It was by faith that Jacob, as he was dying, blessed each one of Joseph's sons. Then he worshiped as he leaned on the top of his walking stick.

22It was by faith that Joseph, while he was dying, spoke about the Israelites leaving Egypt and gave instructions about what to do with his body.

23It was by faith that Moses' parents hid him for three months after he was born. They saw that Moses was a beautiful baby, and they were not afraid to disobey the king's order.

24It was by faith that Moses, when he grew up, refused to be called the son of the king of Egypt's daughter. 25He chose to suffer with God's people instead of enjoying sin for a short time. 26He thought it was better to suffer for the Christ than to have all the treasures of Egypt, because he was looking for God's reward. 27It was by faith that Moses left Egypt and was not afraid of the king's anger. Moses continued strong as if he could see the God that no one can see. 28It was by faith that Moses prepared the Passover and spread the blood on the doors so the one who brings death would not kill the firstborn sons of Israel.

29It was by faith that the people crossed the Red Sea as if it were dry land. But when the Egyptians tried it, they were drowned.

30It was by faith that the walls of Jericho fell after the people had marched around them for seven days.

31It was by faith that Rahab, the prostitute, welcomed the spies and was not killed with those who refused to obey God.

32Do I need to give more examples? I do not

11:6 Doubt: James 1:5-8

11:6 Pleasure: James 5:1-5

11:7 Noah: 2 Peter 2:5

11:10 *city.* The spiritual "city" where God's people live with him. Also called "the heavenly Jerusalem." (See Hebrews 12:22.)

11:10 Heaven: 2 Peter 3:13

11:11 Sarah: See article on page 169.

11:13 Abraham called himself a "stranger and a foreigner" when he bought the cave to bury his wife in (Genesis 23:4). He bought that cave because he believed God was going to fulfill his promises and give Canaan to his descendants one day. According to Hebrews, he also believed he was a stranger here on earth, because God was promising a country even better than Canaan — a heavenly country (Hebrews 11:16).

11:18 *"The descendants . . . Isaac."* Quotation from Genesis 21:12.

11:19 Abraham's life was a journey in faith. God gave him certain promises, most notably the promise of numerous children. But when he was still old, he and Sarah had not yet had a child. Though he had moments of serious doubt, Abraham continued to believe God and finally Isaac was born, but the challenge to faith only grew stronger. God then told Abraham to take Isaac to Mount Moriah to sacrifice him. By this time, Abraham so believed God that he was willing even to do this. Once he arrived at the site, God provided a substitute for Isaac.

11:22 Joseph: See article on page 197.

11:22 The writer of Hebrews refers to Joseph's faith when he was dying and looked ahead to the day when the descendants of Jacob would leave Egypt. Joseph's request that his body be taken back to the Promised Land when the Israelites left Egypt was clear evidence that he believed the Exodus would take place. Moses later carried out Joseph's request (Exodus 13:19).

11:28 Martyrdom: Hebrews 11:32–40

11:31 Rahab: James 2:25

11:32 Samson is listed among the heroes of the faith by the author of Hebrews, but this citation raises an immediate question. After all, when we read about Samson in Judges, he appears never to act from selfless motives. The story of Samson teaches us that God can use us even when we are rebellious. He can overrule the evil and incompetence of his servants. At the end, when he pulled down the temple of Dagon, though he did it to revenge himself, he did pray to God for strength (Judges 16:28). Samson's story also turns us to Christ, the perfect, sinless deliverer who saves us eternally from the greatest enemy of all, sin and death.

11:32 Here Samuel is listed with many other Old Testament characters as an example of faith and what it can accomplish. We can read about Samuel in 1 Samuel 1–25.

have time to tell you about Gideon, Barak, Samson, Jephthah, David, Samuel, and the prophets. 33Through their faith they defeated kingdoms. They did what was right, received God's promises, and shut the mouths of lions. 34They stopped great fires and were saved from being killed with swords. They were weak, and yet were made strong. They were powerful in battle and defeated other armies. 35Women received their dead relatives raised back to life. Others were tortured and refused to accept their freedom so they could be raised from the dead to a better life. 36Some were laughed at and beaten. Others were put in chains and thrown into prison. 37They were stoned to death, they were cut in half, and they were killed with swords. Some wore the skins of sheep and goats. They were poor, abused, and treated badly. 38The world was not good enough for them! They wandered in deserts and mountains, living in caves and holes in the earth.

39All these people are known for their faith, but none of them received what God had promised. 40God planned to give us something better so that they would be made perfect, but only together with us.

Follow Jesus' Example

12 We have around us many people whose lives tell us what faith means. So let us run the race that is before us and never give up. We should remove from our lives anything that would get in the way and the sin that so easily holds us back. 2Let us look only to Jesus, the One who began our faith and who makes it perfect. He suffered death on the cross. But he accepted the shame as if it were nothing because of the joy that God put before him. And now he is sitting at the right side of God's throne. 3Think about Jesus' example. He held on while wicked people were doing evil things to him. So do not get tired and stop trying.

God Is like a Father

4You are struggling against sin, but your struggles have not yet caused you to be killed. 5You have forgotten the encouraging words that call you his children:

"My child, don't think the Lord's discipline is
worth nothing,
and don't stop trying when he corrects you.
6The Lord disciplines those he loves,
and he punishes everyone he accepts
as his child." *Proverbs 3:11-12*

7So hold on through your sufferings, because they are like a father's discipline. God is treating you as children. All children are disciplined by their fathers. 8If you are never disciplined (and every child must be disciplined), you are not true children. 9We have all had fathers here on earth who disciplined us, and we respected them. So it is even more important that we accept discipline from the Father of our spirits so we will have life. 10Our fathers on earth disciplined us for a short time in the way they thought was best. But God disciplines us to help us, so we can become holy as he is. 11We do not enjoy being disciplined. It is painful, but later, after we have learned from it, we have peace, because we start living in the right way.

Be Careful How You Live

12You have become weak, so make yourselves strong again. 13Live in the right way so that you will be saved and your weakness will not cause you to be lost.

14Try to live in peace with all people, and try to live free from sin. Anyone whose life is not holy will never see the Lord. 15Be careful that no one fails to receive God's grace and begins to cause trouble among you. A person like that can ruin many of you. 16Be careful that no one takes part in sexual sin or is like Esau and never thinks about God. As the oldest son, Esau would have received everything from his father, but he sold all that for a single meal. 17You remember that after Esau did this, he wanted to get his father's blessing, but his father refused. Esau could find no way to change what he had done, even though he wanted the blessing so much that he cried.

18You have not come to a mountain that can be touched and that is burning with fire. You have not come to darkness, sadness, and storms. 19You have not come to the noise of a trumpet or to the sound of a voice like the one the people of Israel heard and begged not to hear another word. 20They did not want to hear the command: "If anything, even an animal, touches the mountain, it must be put to death with stones." 21What they saw was so terrible that Moses said, "I am shaking with fear."

11:40 Martyrdom: Hebrews 12:3-4
11:40 The People of God: Hebrews 12:1
12:1 The People of God: 1 John 5:1
12:3 Perseverance: Hebrews 12:7
12:4 Martyrdom: 1 Peter 4:12-19
12:4 Meditation: See article on page 531.
12:7 Perseverance: James 1:25
12:9 Names of God: James 1:17
12:9 Images of God: See article on page 260.
12:11 Parenting: See article on page 551.
12:20 *"If . . . stones."* Quotation from Exodus 19:12–13.
12:21 *"I . . . fear."* Quotation from Deuteronomy 9:19.

[22]But you have come to Mount Zion, to the city of the living God, the heavenly Jerusalem. You have come to thousands of angels gathered together with joy. [23]You have come to the meeting of God's firstborn children whose names are written in heaven. You have come to God, the judge of all people, and to the spirits of good people who have been made perfect. [24]You have come to Jesus, the One who brought the new agreement from God to his people, and you have come to the sprinkled blood that has a better message than the blood of Abel.

[25]So be careful and do not refuse to listen when God speaks. Others refused to listen to him when he warned them on earth, and they did not escape. So it will be worse for us if we refuse to listen to God who warns us from heaven. [26]When he spoke before, his voice shook the earth, but now he has promised, "Once again I will shake not only the earth but also the heavens." [27]The words "once again" clearly show us that everything that was made—things that can be shaken—will be destroyed. Only the things that cannot be shaken will remain.

[28]So let us be thankful, because we have a kingdom that cannot be shaken. We should worship God in a way that pleases him with respect and fear, [29]because our God is like a fire that burns things up.

13

Keep on loving each other as brothers and sisters. [2]Remember to welcome strangers, because some who have done this have welcomed angels without knowing it. [3]Remember those who are in prison as if you were in prison with them. Remember those who are suffering as if you were suffering with them.

[4]Marriage should be honored by everyone, and husband and wife should keep their marriage pure. God will judge as guilty those who take part in sexual sins. [5]Keep your lives free from the love of money, and be satisfied with what you have. God has said,

"I will never leave you;
I will never forget you." *Deuteronomy 31:6*

[6]So we can be sure when we say,

"I will not be afraid, because the Lord
is my helper.
People can't do anything to me." *Psalm 118:6*

[7]Remember your leaders who taught God's message to you. Remember how they lived and died, and copy their faith. [8]Jesus Christ is the same yesterday, today, and forever.

[9]Do not let all kinds of strange teachings lead you into the wrong way. Your hearts should be strengthened by God's grace, not by obeying rules about foods, which do not help those who obey them.

[10]We have a sacrifice, but the priests who serve in the Holy Tent cannot eat from it. [11]The high priest carries the blood of animals into the Most Holy Place where he offers this blood for sins. But the bodies of the animals are burned outside the camp. [12]So Jesus also suffered outside the city to make his people holy with his own blood. [13]So let us go to Jesus outside the camp, holding on as he did when we are abused.

[14]Here on earth we do not have a city that lasts forever, but we are looking for the city that we will have in the future. [15]So through Jesus let us always offer to God our sacrifice of praise, coming from lips that speak his name. [16]Do not forget to do good to others, and share with them, because such sacrifices please God.

[17]Obey your leaders and act under their authority. They are watching over you, because they are responsible for your souls. Obey them so that they will do this work with joy, not sadness. It will not help you to make their work hard.

[18]Pray for us. We are sure that we have a clear conscience, because we always want to do the right thing. [19]I especially beg you to pray so that God will send me back to you soon.

[20-21]I pray that the God of peace will give you every good thing you need so you can do what he wants. God raised from the dead our Lord Jesus, the Great Shepherd of the sheep, because of the blood of his death. His blood began the eternal agreement that God made with his people. I pray that God will do in us what pleases him, through Jesus Christ, and to him be glory forever and ever. Amen.

12:22 *Mount Zion.* Another name for Jerusalem, here meaning the spiritual city of God's people.

12:22 Jerusalem: See article on page 410.

12:23 *firstborn.* The first son born in a Jewish family was given the most important place in the family and received special blessings. All of God's children are like that.

12:24 *sprinkled blood.* The blood of Jesus' death.

12:24 *Abel.* The son of Adam and Eve, who was killed by his brother Cain (Genesis 4:8).

12:26 *"Once . . . heavens."* Quotation from Haggai 2:6, 21.

12:29 Thanks: Luke 17:17–18

13:2 Angels: Revelation 12:7

13:4 The Bible makes it clear that sexual relations are reserved for marriage alone. God honors the institution of marriage and so should we. Husbands and wives are to keep the marriage bed pure, knowing that God will judge all forms of sexual immorality. The modern world places feelings above commitment, but God subordinates feelings to commitment.

13:5 Greed: 1 Peter 5:2

13:7 Leadership: Hebrews 13:17

13:11 Priesthood: 1 Peter 2:5

13:14 Suffering: 1 Peter 2:19–25

13:15 Worship: See article on page 991.

13:17 Leadership: 1 Peter 2:13-17

13:21 Will of God: 1 John 5:3

22My brothers and sisters, I beg you to listen
patiently to this message I have written to encourage
you, because it is not very long. 23I want you to know
that our brother Timothy has been let out of prison.
If he arrives soon, we will both come to see you.
24Greet all your leaders and all of God's people.
Those from Italy send greetings to you.
25Grace be with you all.

INTRODUCTION TO THE BOOK OF

JAMES

How to Live as a Christian

WHO WROTE THIS BOOK?

James the half brother of the Lord, is the author of this book (1:1).

TO WHOM IS THIS BOOK WRITTEN?

The Book of James was written to Jewish Christians scattered from Judea because of the persecution that arose after the stoning of Stephen (Acts 8:1).

WHERE WAS IT WRITTEN?

It is likely that, since James was the leader of the church in Jerusalem, this book was written from there.

WHEN WAS IT WRITTEN?

Since no mention is made of the circumstances that led to the Council of Jerusalem, the Book of James was probably written between A.D. 44 and 49, making it the oldest New Testament letter, with the possible exception of Galatians.

WHAT IS THE BOOK ABOUT?

James wrote highly practical book dealing with faulty teaching and faulty behavior. It exhorts the scattered Jewish believers to live consistent lives. Opening with a discussion of trials and temptations, James proceeds to a strong case for a faith that exhibits good works. Other topics covered in this book include favoritism and the misuse of the tongue, earthly versus heavenly wisdom, quarrels and slanders, and others.

WHY WAS THIS BOOK WRITTEN?

The Book of James was written to encourage persecuted Jewish Christians to live as Jesus taught. There are many parallels in this book to Jesus' Sermon on the Mount (Matthew 3). James offers practical advice for Christian living, with special attention given to class divisions in the church and the abuse of the tongue. Prayer is held out as the only way to receive wisdom, the meeting of needs, or healing.

SO WHAT DOES THIS BOOK MEAN TO US?

While salvation comes by God's grace through our faith, we must not misunderstand that fact to mean that it does not matter how we live as long as we believe. Sloppy or sinful lifestyles that do not take seriously the disciplines of the faith, including self-control and obedience, are not acceptable to the Lord and will not stand up under God's scrutiny. Constant prayer is necessary to help us continually change our hearts and lives to conform to the example of Jesus and, thus, bring joy to the heart of God.

SUMMARY:

The letter of James was probably written by James, the brother of Jesus (see Matthew 13:55; Acts 15). It is like the Jewish form of literature known as "wisdom literature" (see Proverbs), but it is also a letter. This means that James was not simply providing common sense teaching about the Christian life, but he was writing to address specific issues in the lives of some believers.

James weaves together three primary themes. First, James has a great deal to say about wealth and poverty, and especially about the importance of caring for those who are poor. Second, James is concerned with violence—especially with the violence people can do to each other with their words, and the violence the rich can do to the poor through dishonesty. What ties these two themes together is a third: the necessity of not only *hearing* God's teaching, but also doing it! Faith, James insists, must lead to action. Christians should not commit acts of violence on behalf of the poor—this is not the sort of action James supports. Instead, Christians should wait for God to bring justice into the world and, while they are waiting, they should care for the poor around them.

JAMES

From James, a servant of God and of the Lord Jesus Christ.

To all of God's people who are scattered everywhere in the world:

Greetings.

Faith and Wisdom

2My brothers and sisters, when you have many kinds of troubles, you should be full of joy, 3because you know that these troubles test your faith, and this will give you patience. 4Let your patience show itself perfectly in what you do. Then you will be perfect and complete and will have everything you need. 5But if any of you needs wisdom, you should ask God for it. He is generous and enjoys giving to all people, so he will give you wisdom. 6But when you ask God, you must believe and not doubt. Anyone who doubts is like a wave in the sea, blown up and down by the wind. 7-8Such doubters are thinking two different things at the same time, and they cannot decide about anything they do. They should not think they will receive anything from the Lord.

True Riches

9Believers who are poor should be proud, because God has made them spiritually rich. 10Those who are rich should be proud, because God has shown them that they are spiritually poor. The rich will die like a wild flower in the grass. 11The sun rises with burning heat and dries up the plants. The flower falls off, and its beauty is gone. In the same way the rich will die while they are still taking care of business.

Temptation Is Not from God

12When people are tempted and still continue strong, they should be happy. After they have proved their faith, God will reward them with life forever. God promised this to all those who love him. 13When people are tempted, they should not say, "God is tempting me." Evil cannot tempt God, and God himself does not tempt anyone. 14But people are tempted when their own evil desire leads them away and traps them. 15This desire leads to sin, and then the sin grows and brings death.

16My dear brothers and sisters, do not be fooled about this. 17Every good action and every perfect gift is from God. These good gifts come down from the Creator of the sun, moon, and stars, who does not change like their shifting shadows. 18God decided to give us life through the word of truth so we might be the most important of all the things he made.

Listening and Obeying

19My dear brothers and sisters, always be willing to listen and slow to speak. Do not become angry easily, 20because anger will not help you live the right kind of life God wants. 21So put out of your life every evil thing and every kind of wrong. Then in gentleness accept God's teaching that is planted in your hearts, which can save you.

22Do what God's teaching says; when you only listen and do nothing, you are fooling yourselves. 23Those who hear God's teaching and do nothing are like people who look at themselves in a mirror. 24They see their faces and then go away and quickly forget what they looked like. 25But the truly happy people are those who carefully study God's perfect law that makes people free, and they continue to study it. They do not forget what they heard, but they obey what God's teaching says. Those who do this will be made happy.

1:2 The Protestant reformers talked about "the perseverance of the saints," that God enables his own to "continue strong" even though they undergo various trials and temptations. Here James says there is a blessing that comes with the experience of enduring such tests. In fact, there's a reward for such endurance that God has promised to all who love him.

1:2 *brothers and sisters.* Although the Greek text says "brothers" here and throughout this book, James' words were meant for the entire church, including men and women.

1:6 Encouragement: See article on page 611.

1:8 Doubt: James 2:14

1:8 Integrity: 1 Peter 2:1–2

1:13 Evil: 1 Peter 2:16

1:17 Names of God: James 5:4

1:19 Tongue: James 1:26

1:19–20 Uncalled for attacks of anger, or, as the original word for "wrath" in these verses suggests, a slow burning resentment against someone, indicate a lack of control. Since self-control is part of the fruit of the Spirit, it is clear that a lack of control demonstrated by anger is fleshly.

1:20 Anger: See article on page 272.

1:22 When James says, "Do what God's teaching says," he is not merely challenging his readers to do the Word; he is telling them that real Christians are doers of the Word. He is describing characteristic behavior, not occasional activity. "Doers of the word" describes the basic disposition and lifestyle of those who believe unto salvation. James tells those who think they can believe in Christ without obeying his teaching, i.e., without submitting to him as Lord, that they are "fooling" themselves.

1:25 James pronounces God's blessing on those who not only hear God's Word, but obey it. They are the ones who find true happiness, not those who hear it and then forget it.

1:25 Perseverance: James 5:10–11

1:25 Obedience: 1 John 2:3–6

The True Way to Worship God

[26]People who think they are religious but say things they should not say are just fooling themselves. Their "religion" is worth nothing. [27]Religion that God accepts as pure and without fault is this: caring for orphans or widows who need help, and keeping yourself free from the world's evil influence.

Love All People

2 My dear brothers and sisters, as believers in our glorious Lord Jesus Christ, never think some people are more important than others. [2]Suppose someone comes into your church meeting wearing nice clothes and a gold ring. At the same time a poor person comes in wearing old, dirty clothes. [3]You show special attention to the one wearing nice clothes and say, "Please, sit here in this good seat." But you say to the poor person, "Stand over there," or, "Sit on the floor by my feet." [4]What are you doing? You are making some people more important than others, and with evil thoughts you are deciding that one person is better.

[5]Listen, my dear brothers and sisters! God chose the poor in the world to be rich with faith and to receive the kingdom God promised to those who love him. [6]But you show no respect to the poor. The rich are always trying to control your lives. They are the ones who take you to court. [7]And they are the ones who speak against Jesus, who owns you.

[8]This royal law is found in the Scriptures: "Love your neighbor as you love yourself." If you obey this law, you are doing right. [9]But if you treat one person as being more important than another, you are sinning. You are guilty of breaking God's law. [10]A person who follows all of God's law but fails to obey even one command is guilty of breaking all the commands in that law. [11]The same God who said, "You must not be guilty of adultery," also said, "You must not murder anyone." So if you do not take part in adultery but you murder someone, you are guilty of breaking all of God's law. [12]In everything you say and do, remember that you will be judged by the law that makes people free. [13]So you must show mercy to others, or God will not show mercy to you when he judges you. But the person who shows mercy can stand without fear at the judgment.

Faith and Good Works

[14]My brothers and sisters, if people say they have faith, but do nothing, their faith is worth nothing. Can faith like that save them? [15]A brother or sister in Christ might need clothes or food. [16]If you say to that person, "God be with you! I hope you stay warm and get plenty to eat," but you do not give what that person needs, your words are worth nothing. [17]In the same way, faith that is alone—that does nothing—is dead.

[18]Someone might say, "You have faith, but I have deeds." Show me your faith without doing anything, and I will show you my faith by what I do. [19]You believe there is one God. Good! But the demons believe that, too, and they tremble with fear.

1:26 Tongue: 1 Peter 3:9

1:27 The Old Testament frequently calls upon God's people, especially their rulers, to care for orphans. Without parents to care for them, they are vulnerable and in great danger. James makes it clear that this responsibility carries over to the church as well. Christians have a responsibility to take care of parentless children.

1:27 Abortion and Crisis Pregnancy: Deuteronomy 24:17

1:27 Adoption: See article on page 198.

1:27 Service: See article on page 1033.

1:27 The Widow: See article on page 361.

2 Was Abraham made right with God by faith and not by good works, as Paul wrote (Romans 4); or was he made right with God by his works, as James taught? Who is right? From the point of view of the whole Bible, the answer is clear: both are right. Paul insisted that Abraham was not made right with God because of any prior good deeds or works of the law. Rather, "Abraham believed the Lord . . . and that faith made him right with God" (Genesis 15:6, cited at Romans 4:3 and James 2:23). James would not deny this fact. He, too, quotes this verse from Genesis. But James equally insisted that faith must result in good works if it is real faith. "Faith that does nothing is dead," he wrote (James 2:26). Notice carefully what is actually said about Abraham's faith and works: "Abraham's faith and the things he did worked together. His faith was made perfect by what he did" (James 2:22). This does not deny that Abraham was made right by faith; rather, it teaches that Abraham's faith was of the right kind. The right kind of faith is made perfect, that is shown to be genuine, in what we do in obedience to God. So James and Paul both teach important truths for the Christian life from the example of Abraham.

2:4 Crossing Cultural Boundaries: See article on page 831.

2:7 Materialism/Possessions: James 5:1–7

2:7 Money: James 4:13–5:6

2:8 Neighbor: James 4:12

2:8 *"Love . . . yourself."* Quotation from Leviticus 19:18.

2:11 *"You . . . adultery."* Quotation from Exodus 20:14 and Deuteronomy 5:18.

2:11 *"You . . . anyone."* Quotation from Exodus 20:13 and Deuteronomy 5:17.

2:11 Murder: 1 Peter 4:15

2:14 Doubt: James 2:17

2:16 Community: 1 Peter 2:4–12

2:16 Mission: 1 Peter 3:15

2:17 Doubt: Jude 22

2:18 James explains that faith is always active, not simply words of the mouth. Real faith will be seen in its deeds of service to God and neighbor.

2:19 James begins to quote the central affirmation of faith used in Israel, found in Deuteronomy 6:4–5: "The Lord our God is the only Lord" (or "The Lord our God is one Lord"). Making this confession is not enough, even though it is important; it must also lead to faithful actions.

20 You foolish person! Must you be shown that faith that does nothing is worth nothing? 21 Abraham, our ancestor, was made right with God by what he did when he offered his son Isaac on the altar. 22 So you see that Abraham's faith and the things he did worked together. His faith was made perfect by what he did. 23 This shows the full meaning of the Scripture that says: "Abraham believed God, and God accepted Abraham's faith, and that faith made him right with God." And Abraham was called God's friend. 24 So you see that people are made right with God by what they do, not by faith only.

25 Another example is Rahab, a prostitute, who was made right with God by something she did. She welcomed the spies into her home and helped them escape by a different road.

26 Just as a person's body that does not have a spirit is dead, so faith that does nothing is dead!

Controlling the Things We Say

3 My brothers and sisters, not many of you should become teachers, because you know that we who teach will be judged more strictly. 2 We all make many mistakes. If people never said anything wrong, they would be perfect and able to control their entire selves, too. 3 When we put bits into the mouths of horses to make them obey us, we can control their whole bodies. 4 Also a ship is very big, and it is pushed by strong winds. But a very small rudder controls that big ship, making it go wherever the pilot wants. 5 It is the same with the tongue. It is a small part of the body, but it brags about great things.

A big forest fire can be started with only a little flame. 6 And the tongue is like a fire. It is a whole world of evil among the parts of our bodies. The tongue spreads its evil through the whole body. The tongue is set on fire by hell, and it starts a fire that influences all of life. 7 People can tame every kind of wild animal, bird, reptile, and fish, and they have tamed them, 8 but no one can tame the tongue. It is wild and evil and full of deadly poison. 9 We use our tongues to praise our Lord and Father, but then we curse people, whom God made like himself. 10 Praises and curses come from the same mouth! My brothers and sisters, this should not happen. 11 Do good and bad water flow from the same spring? 12 My brothers and sisters, can a fig tree make olives, or can a grapevine make figs? No! And a well full of salty water cannot give good water.

True Wisdom

13 Are there those among you who are truly wise and understanding? Then they should show it by living right and doing good things with a gentleness that comes from wisdom. 14 But if you are selfish and have bitter jealousy in your hearts, do not brag. Your bragging is a lie that hides the truth. 15 That kind of "wisdom" does not come from God but from the world. It is not spiritual; it is from the devil. 16 Where jealousy and selfishness are, there will be confusion and every kind of evil. 17 But the wisdom that comes from God is first of all pure, then peaceful, gentle, and easy to please. This wisdom is always ready to help those who are troubled and to do good for others. It is always fair and honest. 18 People who work for peace in a peaceful way plant a good crop of right-living.

Give Yourselves to God

4 Do you know where your fights and arguments come from? They come from the selfish desires that war within you. 2 You want things, but you do not have them. So you are ready to kill and are jealous of other people, but you still cannot get what you want. So you argue and fight. You do not

2:23 Abraham: 1 Peter 3:6
2:23 *"Abraham . . . God."* Quotation from Genesis 15:6.
2:23 *God's friend.* These words about Abraham are found in 2 Chronicles 20:7 and Isaiah 41:8.
2:25 Rahab was a Canaanite woman from Jericho who gave up her pagan ways in order to follow the God of Israel. Her faith in God was demonstrated by saving the lives of two Israelite spies who came to spy out the city (Joshua 2). After the destruction of Jericho, she became part of the Israelite community and one of Jesus' ancestors (Matthew 1:5).
2:25 Rahab: See article on page 369.
2:26 Good Works: 1 John 2:7–3:24
2:26 Work: See article on page 69.
3:1 Teaching and instruction is a common theme found throughout the Bible. God's people are said to be instructed in remembering God's mighty acts of deliverance (Exodus 10:2). They are also instructed in how to live godly lives (Proverbs 23:12). In the Old Testament, God also teaches his people (Deuteronomy 6:1) as does Jesus in the New Testament (John 13:14). In this light, James' warning is not surprising. Teaching is a high calling and bears with it a high responsibility.
3:1–12 This passage shows us that the tongue, when it is controlled, can be very helpful, just like the horse's bit or ship's rudder (3:3–4). However, when the tongue is uncontrolled, it can bring vast destruction, like a forest fire (3:5). But what is especially terrible is to use the tongue for both good and evil, sometimes in the same breath (3:9–10). How tragic when a Christian praises God on Sunday and then on Monday curses a fellow worker or family member.
3:9 Human: 1 John 3:2
3:11–12 Water that was unfit for drinking was a major problem in biblical times and in more remote areas of the world even today. A water source provides life to people, animals, and crops. If salt water ruins the well, the people who depended upon the well had to leave the area and go live in another place. This passage means that a person who claims to be a Christian but whose speech is evil is like a well full of salty water. He is supposed to be filled with life but instead is filled with death.
3:18 Wisdom: See article on page 542.

get what you want, because you do not ask God. [3]Or when you ask, you do not receive because the reason you ask is wrong. You want things so you can use them for your own pleasures.

[4]So, you are not loyal to God! You should know that loving the world is the same as hating God. Anyone who wants to be a friend of the world becomes God's enemy. [5]Do you think the Scripture means nothing that says, "The Spirit that God made to live in us wants us for himself alone?" [6]But God gives us even more grace, as the Scripture says,

"God is against the proud,
but he gives grace to the humble."

Proverbs 3:34

[7]So give yourselves completely to God. Stand against the devil, and the devil will run from you. [8]Come near to God, and God will come near to you. You sinners, clean sin out of your lives. You who are trying to follow God and the world at the same time, make your thinking pure. [9]Be sad, cry, and weep! Change your laughter into crying and your joy into sadness. [10]Don't be too proud in the Lord's presence, and he will make you great.

You Are Not the Judge

[11]Brothers and sisters, do not tell evil lies about each other. If you speak against your fellow believers or judge them, you are judging and speaking against the law they follow. And when you are judging the law, you are no longer a follower of the law. You have become a judge. [12]God is the only Lawmaker and Judge. He is the only One who can save and destroy. So it is not right for you to judge your neighbor.

Let God Plan Your Life

[13]Some of you say, "Today or tomorrow we will go to some city. We will stay there a year, do business, and make money." [14]But you do not know what will happen tomorrow! Your life is like a mist. You can see it for a short time, but then it goes away. [15]So you should say, "If the Lord wants, we will live and do this or that." [16]But now you are proud and you brag. All of this bragging is wrong. [17]Anyone who knows the right thing to do, but does not do it, is sinning.

A Warning to the Rich

5 You rich people, listen! Cry and be very sad because of the troubles that are coming to you. [2]Your riches have rotted, and your clothes have been eaten by moths. [3]Your gold and silver have rusted, and that rust will be a proof that you were wrong. It will eat your bodies like fire. You saved your treasure for the last days. [4]The pay you did not give the workers who mowed your fields cries out against you, and the cries of the workers have been heard by the Lord All-Powerful. [5]Your life on earth was full of rich living and pleasing yourselves with everything you wanted. You made yourselves fat, like an animal ready to be killed. [6]You have judged guilty and then murdered innocent people, who were not against you.

Be Patient

[7]Brothers and sisters, be patient until the Lord comes again. A farmer patiently waits for his valuable crop to grow from the earth and for it to receive the autumn and spring rains. [8]You, too, must be patient. Do not give up hope, because the Lord is coming soon. [9]Brothers and sisters, do not complain against each other or you will be judged guilty. And the Judge is ready to come! [10]Brothers and sisters, follow the example of the prophets who spoke for the Lord. They suffered many hard things, but they were patient. [11]We say they are happy because they did not give up. You have heard about Job's patience, and you know the Lord's purpose for him in the end. You know the Lord is full of mercy and is kind.

Be Careful What You Say

[12]My brothers and sisters, above all, do not use an oath when you make a promise. Don't use the name of heaven, earth, or anything else to prove what you say. When you mean yes, say only yes,

---

4:3 Conflict: 1 John 1:9

4:5 *"The Spirit . . . alone."* These words may be from Exodus 20:5.

4:6 Grace: 1 Peter 1:13

4:12 Neighbor: See article on page 901.

4:14–15 Throughout James, we can hear echoes of the teaching of Jesus, which has been incorporated into this letter. Here, the words of James remind us of the story Jesus told in Luke 12:13–21.

4:17 Time: Revelation 22:20

5:1 James is not judging these people because they are rich, but because they have misused their wealth. These people have lived soft, easy lives of luxury at the expense of others, taking advantage of them and treating them cruelly, completely unaware of the swift and terrible judgment about to fall upon them if they do not repent.

5:4 Names of God: See article on page 219.

5:5 Pleasure: 1 John 2:15–17

5:6 Money: Revelation 18

5:7 Materialism/Possessions: Revelation 18

5:11 This verse has led to the proverbial expression about the "patience of Job." This reference has confused readers of the Book of Job, because often Job seems far more confused and angry than patient. The Greek word here translated "patience" may better be translated "perserverance." Patience is a passive attitude toward adversity, whereas perserverance allows for the type of active and dogged pursuit of God that Job illustrates so well.

5:11 Perseverance: 1 Peter 1:4–8

and when you mean no, say only no so you will
not be judged guilty.

The Power of Prayer

13Anyone who is having troubles should pray.
Anyone who is happy should sing praises.
14Anyone who is sick should call the church's
elders. They should pray for and pour oil on the
person in the name of the Lord. 15And the prayer
that is said with faith will make the sick person
well; the Lord will heal that person. And if the
person has sinned, the sins will be forgiven.
16Confess your sins to each other and pray for each
other so God can heal you. When a believing person
prays, great things happen. 17Elijah was a human
being just like us. He prayed that it would not
rain, and it did not rain on the land for three and
a half years! 18Then Elijah prayed again, and the
rain came down from the sky, and the land produced crops again.

Saving a Soul

19My brothers and sisters, if one of you wanders
away from the truth, and someone helps that person come back, 20remember this: Anyone who
brings a sinner back from the wrong way will save
that sinner's soul from death and will cause many
sins to be forgiven.

5:12 Oath/Vow: See article on page 180.

5:14 *pour oil on the person.* Oil was used in the name of the Lord as a sign that the person was now set apart for God's special attention and care.

5:16 Sin: See article on page 1131.

5:16 Healing: See article on page 732.

5:17 Elijah and Elisha: See article on page 420.

INTRODUCTION TO THE BOOK OF

1 PETER

Encouragement for Suffering Christians

WHO WROTE THIS BOOK?

From internal evidence (1:1) and attestation by early church tradition, there is universal agreement that Peter is the author of this book.

TO WHOM WAS THIS BOOK WRITTEN?

Some references suggest Peter is writing to dispersed Jewish Christians (quotations from the Greek Old Testament), while other statements point to a non-Jewish audience (references to pagan behavior). It is a general letter addressed to churches in various regions of Asia Minor (1:1).

WHERE WAS IT WRITTEN?

Peter's reference to "Babylon," together with his reference to Mark (5:13), who was known to be in Rome with Paul, suggests that "Babylon" is a code name for Rome, from where the book was written.

WHEN WAS IT WRITTEN?

Church tradition places Peter in Rome near the end of his life. And Peter shows he is acquainted with letters written by Paul while the latter was under house arrest. So, this letter was likely written between A.D. 60 and 68.

WHAT IS THE BOOK ABOUT?

Writing to Christians facing persecution, Peter encourages them with thoughts of the joys and glories of their eternal inheritance. And he instructs them about proper Christian behavior in the midst of unjust suffering. Peter's advice is to trust God and do what is right (4:19). He gives instruction for living as Christian citizens and as Christian family members. He urges mutual submission in the church and humbling themselves under the providential hand of God. Peter says he has been writing to them about the "true grace of God" and to "stand strong in that grace" (5:12), all the while controlling themselves and staying on the alert against Satan (5:8).

WHY WAS THIS BOOK WRITTEN?

Peter wrote to churches in Asia Minor that were undergoing persecution to encourage them to persevere and maintain hope in the face of suffering. He assured them that "God, who gives all grace, will make everything right . . . and keep you from falling" (5:10).

SO WHAT DOES THIS BOOK MEAN TO US?

We may find ourselves suffering persecution in one form or another just because we are Christians. In fact, Jesus told us we would face persecution in the world but that he has "defeated the world" (John 16:33). When we do suffer unjustly, we can take comfort from the knowledge that God will give us the grace we need to go through such times of testing.

SUMMARY:

The primary purpose of 1 Peter is noted already in the letter's opening, where Peter addresses God's people who are "away from their homes." They are, then, strangers in the world. However, their alien condition does not consist in their location in the world. Instead, wherever they live, they are "away from their homes" for their lives are defined by their relationship to God. Even if they live in the world, they do not follow its ways nor allow themselves to grow comfortable with its patterns.

Their stance toward the world, though, is not a popular one. As a result, even though they have the blessing of God, in the world they are insulted, and people speak evil of them. Peter writes that those who suffer because they are Christians should not see their suffering as a contradiction of their relationship with God. After all, they follow Christ who also suffered; just as Jesus did not insult those who insulted him, so his followers should learn not to repay evil with more evil.

Much of 1 Peter, then, is concerned with relationships in the world. Peter, writing in the first century, knows that Christians will make up the minority in the larger world, in cities and towns, often even in larger families. So he gives them counsel about how to live as "strangers."

1 PETER

From Peter, an apostle of Jesus Christ.
To God's chosen people who are away from
their homes and are scattered all around the
countries of Pontus, Galatia, Cappadocia, Asia, and
Bithynia. 2God planned long ago to choose you by
making you his holy people, which is the Spirit's
work. God wanted you to obey him and to be made
clean by the blood of the death of Jesus Christ.
Grace and peace be yours more and more.

We Have a Living Hope

3Praise be to the God and Father of our Lord
Jesus Christ. In God's great mercy he has caused us
to be born again into a living hope, because Jesus
Christ rose from the dead. 4Now we hope for the
blessings God has for his children. These blessings, which cannot be destroyed or be spoiled or
lose their beauty, are kept in heaven for you.
5God's power protects you through your faith until
salvation is shown to you at the end of time. 6This
makes you very happy, even though now for a
short time different kinds of troubles may make
you sad. 7These troubles come to prove that your
faith is pure. This purity of faith is worth more
than gold, which can be proved to be pure by fire
but will ruin. But the purity of your faith will bring
you praise and glory and honor when Jesus Christ
is shown to you. 8You have not seen Christ, but
still you love him. You cannot see him now, but
you believe in him. So you are filled with a joy
that cannot be explained, a joy full of glory.
9And you are receiving the goal of your faith—the
salvation of your souls.

10The prophets searched carefully and tried to
learn about this salvation. They prophesied about
the grace that was coming to you. 11The Spirit of
Christ was in the prophets, telling in advance about
the sufferings of Christ and about the glory that
would follow those sufferings. The prophets tried
to learn about what the Spirit was showing them,
when those things would happen, and what the
world would be like at that time. 12It was shown
them that their service was not for themselves but
for you, when they told about the truths you have
now heard. Those who preached the Good News to
you told you those things with the help of the Holy
Spirit who was sent from heaven—things into
which angels desire to look.

A Call to Holy Living

13So prepare your minds for service and have
self-control. All your hope should be for the gift of
grace that will be yours when Jesus Christ is shown
to you. 14Now that you are obedient children of
God do not live as you did in the past. You did not
understand, so you did the evil things you wanted.
15But be holy in all you do, just as God, the One
who called you, is holy. 16It is written in the
Scriptures: "You must be holy, because I am
holy."

17You pray to God and call him Father, and he
judges each person's work equally. So while you
are here on earth, you should live with respect for
God. 18You know that in the past you were living
in a worthless way, a way passed down from the
people who lived before you. But you were saved
from that useless life. You were bought, not with
something that ruins like gold or silver, 19but
with the precious blood of Christ, who was like a
pure and perfect lamb. 20Christ was chosen before
the world was made, but he was shown to the
world in these last times for your sake.
21Through Christ you believe in God, who raised
Christ from the dead and gave him glory. So your
faith and your hope are in God.

22Now that you have made your souls pure by
obeying the truth, you can have true love for your
Christian brothers and sisters. So love each other
deeply with all your heart. 23You have been
born again, and this new life did not come from
something that dies, but from something that cannot die. You were born again through God's living
message that continues forever. 24The Scripture says,

1:3–16 *living hope.* A Christian's hope is a living hope (1:3). It is based on a historical reality — that Jesus physically rose from the dead—and it produces real change in the believer's life. It allows us to face trials and suffering with confidence that God is in control and blessing us in the midst of (and sometimes through) the hard times (1:4–9). This hope sets us free from our pasts to live lives that honor God by reflecting his holiness (1:13–16).

1:7 Glory: Revelation 21:23

1:7 The Crucifixion of Jesus (The Way of the Cross): 1 Peter 2:20–21

1:8 Perseverance: 2 Peter 3:17–18

1:13 In the New Testament *grace* is usually referred to as a current gift we possess in Christ. Here the author draws attention to the future gift of grace that awaits us at the return of Christ.

1:13 Grace: 2 Peter 3:18

1:15 Salvation: See article on page 1264.

1:16 *"You must be . . . holy."* Quotation from Leviticus 11:45; 19:2; 20:7.

1:16 Holiness: 2 Peter 3:11

1:17 Father: See article on page 1141.

1:20 Last Days: 1 John 2:18

1:22 *brothers and sisters.* Although the Greek text says "brothers" here and throughout this book, Peter's words were meant for the entire church, including men and women.

1:22 Conversion: 2 Timothy 3:1–16

"All people are like the grass,
and all their glory is like the
flowers of the field.
The grass dies and the flowers fall,
25but the word of the Lord will live forever."
Isaiah 40:6-8

And this is the word that was preached to you.

Jesus Is the Living Stone

2 So then, rid yourselves of all evil, all lying,
hypocrisy, jealousy, and evil speech. 2As newborn babies want milk, you should want the pure
and simple teaching. By it you can grow up and be
saved, 3because you have already examined and
seen how good the Lord is.
4Come to the Lord Jesus, the "stone" that lives.
The people of the world did not want this stone, but
he was the stone God chose, and he was precious.
5You also are like living stones, so let yourselves be
used to build a spiritual temple—to be holy priests
who offer spiritual sacrifices to God. He will accept
those sacrifices through Jesus Christ. 6The
Scripture says:

"I will put a stone in the ground in Jerusalem.
Everything will be built on this important
and precious rock.
Anyone who trusts in him
will never be disappointed." *Isaiah 28:16*

7This stone is worth much to you who believe.
But to the people who do not believe,
"the stone that the builders rejected
has become the cornerstone." *Psalm 118:22*
8Also, he is
"a stone that causes people to stumble,
a rock that makes them fall." *Isaiah 8:14*
They stumble because they do not obey what God
says, which is what God planned to happen to
them.
9But you are a chosen people, royal priests, a holy
nation, a people for God's own possession. You
were chosen to tell about the wonderful acts of
God, who called you out of darkness into his wonderful light. 10At one time you were not a people,
but now you are God's people. In the past you had
never received mercy, but now you have received
God's mercy.

Live for God

11Dear friends, you are like foreigners and
strangers in this world. I beg you to avoid the evil
things your bodies want to do that fight against
your soul. 12People who do not believe are living
all around you and might say that you are doing
wrong. Live such good lives that they will see the
good things you do and will give glory to God on
the day when Christ comes again.

Yield to Every Human Authority

13For the Lord's sake, yield to the people who
have authority in this world: the king, who is the
highest authority, 14and the leaders who are sent
by him to punish those who do wrong and to
praise those who do right. 15It is God's desire
that by doing good you should stop foolish people
from saying stupid things about you. 16Live as free
people, but do not use your freedom as an excuse
to do evil. Live as servants of God. 17Show
respect for all people: Love the brothers and sisters
of God's family, respect God, honor the king.

Follow Christ's Example

18Slaves, yield to the authority of your masters
with all respect, not only those who are good and

2:2 Integrity: See article on page 469.

2:4–8 *"stone."* The most important stone in God's spiritual temple or house (his people). Peter weaves together these Old Testament texts that talk about "stones." He does so in order to compare Christians with the Lord Jesus. Just as Jesus was God's chosen and precious stone, even though people rejected him, so Christians are God's chosen and precious stones, even when they are rejected by others.

2:5 Priesthood: See article on page 1306.

2:5 Sacrifice: See article on page 280.

2:5, 9 In the Old Testament, God's presence among his people was associated with the holy Temple. Because God has now made us a holy nation by the sacrifice of Jesus Christ (1 Peter 2:9; Colossians 1:22), he can now live within us as his spiritual temple (1 Peter 1:5; 1 Corinthians 3:16). Just as the priests offered sacrifices to God in the Old Testament, believers today are called holy priests because they offer the spiritual sacrifice of their lives in service to God (Romans 12:1; 1 Peter 2:5).

The New Testament sees the church as a people saved to serve who regard prayer and praise as the basic form of Christian service. Believers, says Peter, have become by grace "holy priests who offer spiritual sacrifices to God . . . chosen to tell about the wonderful acts of God, who called you out of darkness into his wonderful light" (1 Peter 2:5, 9). The main thing in view is the pouring out of praise before God, and then about God to others.

The priests of the Old Testament were special people set apart for service to God. They were the only ones who were able to come close to God. They served as mediators between God and the people. The wonderful truth of the New Testament is that all believers are priests. All of us are special servants of God and all of us are invited into close relationship with God.

2:10 Spirituality/Spiritual Dryness: See article on page 1163.

2:12 Community: See article on page 1091.

2:13–17 Governmental authority comes from God's authority. Respect and honor for human authorities is a way of respecting and honoring God's authority. However, sometimes God sends a messenger to challenge human authority (see Luke 3:1–19); even so, that messenger must submit to the power of the current authorities (Matthew 14:1–12; Luke 3:20).

2:14 Government: See article on page 1153.

2:16 Evil: 1 Peter 2:18–25

2:16 Servant of the Lord: Revelation 22:3

2:17 Citizen: 1 Peter 3:11

2:17 Leadership: See article on page 1000.

2:17 Rome: See article on page 1023.

kind, but also those who are dishonest. 19A person might have to suffer even when it is unfair, but if he thinks of God and stands the pain, God is pleased. 20If you are beaten for doing wrong, there is no reason to praise you for being patient in your punishment. But if you suffer for doing good, and you are patient, then God is pleased. 21This is what you were called to do, because Christ suffered for you and gave you an example to follow. So you should do as he did.

22"He had never sinned,
and he had never lied." *Isaiah 53:9*

23People insulted Christ, but he did not insult them in return. Christ suffered, but he did not threaten. He let God, the One who judges rightly, take care of him. 24Christ carried our sins in his body on the cross so we would stop living for sin and start living for what is right. And you are healed because of his wounds. 25You were like sheep that wandered away, but now you have come back to the Shepherd and Protector of your souls.

Wives and Husbands

3 In the same way, you wives should yield to your husbands. Then, if some husbands do not obey God's teaching, they will be persuaded to believe without anyone's saying a word to them. They will be persuaded by the way their wives live. 2Your husbands will see the pure lives you live with your respect for God. 3It is not fancy hair, gold jewelry, or fine clothes that should make you beautiful. 4No, your beauty should come from within you—the beauty of a gentle and quiet spirit that will never be destroyed and is very precious to God. 5In this same way the holy women who lived long ago and followed God made themselves beautiful, yielding to their own husbands. 6Sarah obeyed Abraham, her husband, and called him her master. And you women are true children of Sarah if you always do what is right and are not afraid.

7In the same way, you husbands should live with your wives in an understanding way, since they are weaker than you. But show them respect, because God gives them the same blessing he gives you—the grace that gives true life. Do this so that nothing will stop your prayers.

Suffering for Doing Right

8Finally, all of you should be in agreement, understanding each other, loving each other as family, being kind and humble. 9Do not do wrong to repay a wrong, and do not insult to repay an insult. But repay with a blessing, because you yourselves were called to do this so that you might receive a blessing. 10The Scripture says,

"A person must do these things
to enjoy life and have many happy days.
He must not say evil things,
and he must not tell lies.
11He must stop doing evil and do good.
He must look for peace and work for it.
12The Lord sees the good people
and listens to their prayers.
But the Lord is against
those who do evil." *Psalm 34:12-16*

13If you are trying hard to do good, no one can really hurt you. 14But even if you suffer for doing right, you are blessed.

"Don't be afraid of what they fear;
do not dread those things." *Isaiah 8:12-13*

15But respect Christ as the holy Lord in your hearts. Always be ready to answer everyone who asks you to explain about the hope you have, 16but answer in a gentle way and with respect. Keep a clear conscience so that those who speak evil of your good life in Christ will be made ashamed. 17It is better to suffer for doing good than for doing wrong if that is what God wants. 18Christ himself suffered for sins once. He was not guilty, but he suffered for those who are guilty to bring you to God. His body was killed, but he was made alive in the spirit. 19And in the spirit he went and preached to the spirits in prison 20who refused to obey God long ago in the time of Noah. God was waiting patiently for them while Noah was building the boat. Only a few people—eight in all—were saved

2:21 The Crucifixion of Jesus (The Way of the Cross): 1 Peter 4:13
2:25 Evil: 3 John 11
2:25 Persecution: 1 Peter 3:8–18
2:25 Suffering: 1 Peter 3:14–18
3:1 Unbelieving husbands are won by their wives' reputations, not just their words. Peter reminds his readers that a life of beauty will lure unbelievers to faith.
3:5–6 Despite Sarah's physical beauty (Genesis 12:11,14), Peter focuses on the fact that she called Abraham "master" (Genesis 18:12) as the proof that her true beauty came from her attitude rather than her appearance.
3:6 Abraham: See article on page 139.
3:6 Reputation: See article on page 573.
3:6 Women: See article on page 40.
3:9 Tongue: Revelation 16:21
3:11 Citizen: See article on page 1153.
3:14 Living a joyous Christian life does not include running from suffering and sadness. In fact, Peter reminds his readers that throughout history righteous people have suffered injustice at the hands of evil people. This suffering, however, is not the ultimate issue. Holiness and righteous living is what is required for a happy, blessed life. When Christians suffer, they should remember to suffer for doing good, never for imitating the ones who do evil.
3:15 Mission: See article on page 794.
3:18 Persecution: 1 Peter 4:1–6
3:18 Suffering: 1 Peter 4:1
3:20–21 Salvation in Christ, Peter writes, is similar to God's

by water.⚭ [21]And that water is like baptism that now saves you—not the washing of dirt from the body, but the promise made to God from a good conscience. And this is because Jesus Christ was raised from the dead.⚭ [22]Now Jesus has gone into heaven and is at God's right side ruling over angels, authorities, and powers.⚭

Change Your Lives

4 Since Christ suffered while he was in his body, strengthen yourselves with the same way of thinking Christ had. The person who has suffered in the body is finished with sin.⚭ [2]Strengthen yourselves so that you will live here on earth doing what God wants, not the evil things people want. [3]In the past you wasted too much time doing what nonbelievers enjoy. You were guilty of sexual sins, evil desires, drunkenness, wild and drunken parties, and hateful idol worship.⚭ [4]Nonbelievers think it is strange that you do not do the many wild and wasteful things they do, so they insult you. [5]But they will have to explain this to God, who is ready to judge the living and the dead. [6]For this reason the Good News was preached to those who are now dead. Even though they were judged like all people, the Good News was preached to them so they could live in the spirit as God lives.⚭

Use God's Gifts Wisely

[7]The time is near when all things will end. So think clearly and control yourselves so you will be able to pray. [8]Most importantly, love each other deeply, because love will cause many sins to be forgiven. [9]Open your homes to each other, without complaining.⚭ [10]Each of you has received a gift to use to serve others. Be good servants of God's various gifts of grace.⚭ [11]Anyone who speaks should speak words from God. Anyone who serves should serve with the strength God gives so that in everything God will be praised through Jesus Christ. Power and glory belong to him forever and ever. Amen.⚭

Suffering as a Christian

[12]My friends, do not be surprised at the terrible trouble which now comes to test you. Do not think that something strange is happening to you. [13]But be happy that you are sharing in Christ's sufferings so that you will be happy and full of joy when Christ comes again in glory.⚭ [14]When people insult you because you follow Christ, you are blessed, because the glorious Spirit, the Spirit of God, is with you.⚭ [15]Do not suffer for murder, theft, or any other crime, nor because you trouble other people.⚭ [16]But if you suffer because you are a Christian, do not be ashamed. Praise God because you wear that name. [17]It is time for judgment to begin with God's family. And if that judging begins with us, what will happen to those people who do not obey the Good News of God?⚭

[18]"If it is very hard for a good person to be saved,
the wicked person and the sinner will surely
be lost!"

[19]So those who suffer as God wants should trust their souls to the faithful Creator as they continue to do what is right.⚭

The Flock of God

5 Now I have something to say to the elders in your group. I also am an elder. I have seen Christ's sufferings, and I will share in the glory that

---

deliverance of Noah in the Flood. The water of the Flood is a symbol pointing forward to the water of Christian baptism. Here, baptism itself symbolizes the work of Christ, his death and resurrection. Both the Flood and this baptism represent judgment to those who do not believe, yet salvation to those who do. Another similarity between Noah and salvation in Christ is the agreement God makes with his people. God promises to be faithful to his people. For Noah, this meant God's promise never to bring another flood to the whole earth (Genesis 6:18; 9:8–17). For Christians, it is the new agreement God makes with his people, in Christ, for eternity (Luke 22:20).

⚭**3:20 Noah's Ark:** See article on page 100.

⚭**3:21 Baptism:** See article on page 682.

⚭**3:22 Incarnation:** Revelation 1:13

4:1 "The person who has suffered in the body is finished with sin" does not mean that a person who has suffered no longer commits any sin. Peter is talking about suffering *with* Christ and *like* Christ. The believer who suffers for the sake of Christ is focused on God and not on this world, so he puts his sinful desires behind him; he is "finished" with sin.

⚭**4:1 Suffering:** 1 Peter 4:12–5:1

⚭**4:3 Idolatry:** See article on page 131.

⚭**4:6 Persecution:** 1 Peter 4:12–19

4:7–11 Service is described in these verses in terms of the basic Christian virtues: love, forgiveness, hospitality. As people who have been given the grace of God, Christians in turn are called to love and serve and help others.

⚭**4:9 Hospitality:** 3 John 5–10

⚭**4:10 Stewardship:** See article on page 1173.

⚭**4:11 Spiritual Gifts:** See article on page 1184.

⚭**4:13 The Crucifixion of Jesus (The Way of the Cross):** See article on page 786.

⚭**4:13 Test/Temptation:** 1 Peter 5:8–9

⚭**4:14 Happiness:** See article on page 562.

⚭**4:15 Crime:** See article on page 509.

⚭**4:15 Murder:** 1 John 3:12

4:16 Peter is not thinking of a worldwide persecution of Christians in the first century. Instead, he is concerned with the suffering Christians undergo in their local communities, even homes, because they are faithful to God. He advises these believers to follow the example of Christ.

⚭**4:17 Gospel/Good News:** See article on page 802.

4:18 *"If . . . lost!"* Quotation from Proverbs 11:31 in the Septuagint, the Greek version of the Old Testament.

⚭**4:19 Martyrdom:** Revelation 2:8–13

⚭**4:19 Persecution:** 1 Peter 5:10–11

will be shown to us. I beg you to 2shepherd
God's flock, for whom you are responsible. Watch
over them because you want to, not because you
are forced. That is how God wants it. Do it because
you are happy to serve, not because you want
money. 3Do not be like a ruler over people you
are responsible for, but be good examples to them.
4Then when Christ, the Chief Shepherd, comes,
you will get a glorious crown that will never lose
its beauty.

5In the same way, younger people should be willing to be under older people. And all of you should
be very humble with each other.

"God is against the proud,
but he gives grace to
the humble." *Proverbs 3:34*

6Be humble under God's powerful hand so he
will lift you up when the right time comes. 7Give all
your worries to him, because he cares about you.

8Control yourselves and be careful! The devil,
your enemy, goes around like a roaring lion looking
for someone to eat. 9Refuse to give in to him, by
standing strong in your faith. You know that your
Christian family all over the world is having the
same kinds of suffering.

10And after you suffer for a short time, God,
who gives all grace, will make everything right.
He will make you strong and support you and
keep you from falling. He called you to share in his
glory in Christ, a glory that will continue forever.
11All power is his forever and ever. Amen.

Final Greetings

12I wrote this short letter with the help of Silas,
who I know is a faithful brother in Christ. I wrote
to encourage you and to tell you that this is the
true grace of God. Stand strong in that grace.

13The church in Babylon, who was chosen like
you, sends you greetings. Mark, my son in Christ,
also greets you. 14Give each other a kiss of
Christian love when you meet.

Peace to all of you who are in Christ.

5:1 Suffering: Revelation 1:9

5:2 Greed: 2 Peter 2:3

5:5 Growing Old: See article on page 210.

5:7 The secret to managing stress is to hand it over to the Lord for him to carry. That requires humbling ourselves in difficult circumstances and allowing the Lord to carry us (1 Peter 5:6). In commanding us to "give all your worries to him," Peter is literally telling us to throw our stresses on to the Lord. Instead of holding on to our troubles, we are to offload them onto our loving Lord "because he cares about you" (1 Peter 5:7).

5:8 Satan/Satanism: See article on page 452.

5:9 Test/Temptation: 1 John 4:1

5:11 Persecution: Revelation 13:5–10

5:13 Babylon: Revelation 16:19

INTRODUCTION TO THE BOOK OF

2 PETER

Correcting False Teachings

WHO WROTE THIS BOOK?

Based on internal evidence (1:1) and the witness of the later church leaders (Athanasius, Cyril of Jerusalem, Ambrose, and Augustine), Peter came to be regarded as the author of 2 Peter.

TO WHOM WAS THIS BOOK WRITTEN?

Since the letter of 1 Peter is alluded to, the recipients of 1 Peter (the persecuted churches of Asia Minor) are the likely recipients of 2 Peter.

WHERE WAS IT WRITTEN?

Based on Peter's reference to the imminence of his death (2 Peter 1:14) and church tradition that he was martyred in Rome, it is likely that 2 Peter was written in Rome.

WHEN WAS IT WRITTEN?

Since it was written later than 1 Peter and before Peter's death, 2 Peter was likely written between A.D. 65 and 68.

WHAT IS THE BOOK ABOUT?

First Peter addresses persecution of the church from without, while 2 Peter warns against false teachers from within (2:1). Appealing to the authority of Scripture, Peter provides some of the strongest statements in the Bible regarding the inspiration and truthfulness of Scripture (2 Peter 1:16, 20, 21). This is to counter the false teachers' claims to "knowledge" as well as their licentious lifestyle. The false teachers were using Christian liberty as a license to sin (2:14), thereby denying the Lord (2:1), despising authority and slandering spirit beings (2:10), and mocking the second coming of Christ (3:3, 4). Peter describes the fiery end of the world (3:7, 10), the certainty of the Lord's coming, and the motive this should provide for holy living (3:14).

WHY WAS THIS BOOK WRITTEN?

Second Peter was written: to stimulate Christian growth (chapter 1), to combat false teaching (chapter 2), and to encourage watchfulness in view of the Lord's certain return (chapter 3).

SO WHAT DOES THIS BOOK MEAN TO US?

As believers, we should have a sense of expectancy regarding the Lord's next coming. The Lord promised to return, and he always keeps his promises. That should motivate us to holy living so we will be ready to meet him in the air (1Thessalonians 4:17) when he appears. We should also be on guard against false teaching, appealing to the authority of Scripture to expose error, so that we are not distracted from the truth. Our days should be filled with anticipation, looking forward to his coming, while we make the most of every day here on earth to tell others about him.

SUMMARY:

Second Peter has the form and feel of a farewell speech, as though it contained Peter's last instructions to those who would remain following his death. Two primary issues are discussed. First, the threat of false teaching and false teachers is taken up. Second, 2 Peter discusses the second coming of Jesus. This short letter uses these two issues for the same purpose: to encourage believers to continue to grow in their relationship to God.

2 PETER

From Simon Peter, a servant and apostle of Jesus Christ.

To you who have received a faith as valuable as ours, because our God and Savior Jesus Christ does what is right.

[2]Grace and peace be given to you more and more, because you truly know God and Jesus our Lord.

God Has Given Us Blessings

[3]Jesus has the power of God, by which he has given us everything we need to live and to serve God. We have these things because we know him. Jesus called us by his glory and goodness. [4]Through these he gave us the very great and precious promises. With these gifts you can share in being like God, and the world will not ruin you with its evil desires.

[5]Because you have these blessings, do your best to add these things to your lives: to your faith, add goodness; and to your goodness, add knowledge; [6]and to your knowledge, add self-control; and to your self-control, add patience; and to your patience, add service for God; [7]and to your service for God, add kindness for your brothers and sisters in Christ; and to this kindness, add love. [8]If all these things are in you and are growing, they will help you to be useful and productive in your knowledge of our Lord Jesus Christ. [9]But anyone who does not have these things cannot see clearly. He is blind and has forgotten that he was made clean from his past sins.

[10]My brothers and sisters, try hard to be certain that you really are called and chosen by God. If you do all these things, you will never fall. [11]And you will be given a very great welcome into the eternal kingdom of our Lord and Savior Jesus Christ.

[12]You know these things, and you are very strong in the truth, but I will always help you remember them. [13]I think it is right for me to help you remember as long as I am in this body. [14]I know I must soon leave this body, as our Lord Jesus Christ has shown me. [15]I will try my best so that you may be able to remember these things even after I am gone.

We Saw Christ's Glory

[16]When we told you about the powerful coming of our Lord Jesus Christ, we were not telling just smart stories that someone invented. But we saw the greatness of Jesus with our own eyes. [17]Jesus heard the voice of God, the Greatest Glory, when he received honor and glory from God the Father. The voice said, "This is my Son, whom I love, and I am very pleased with him." [18]We heard that voice from heaven while we were with Jesus on the holy mountain.

[19]This makes us more sure about the message the prophets gave. It is good for you to follow closely what they said as you would follow a light shining in a dark place, until the day begins and the morning star rises in your hearts. [20]Most of all, you must understand this: No prophecy in the Scriptures ever comes from the prophet's own interpretation. [21]No prophecy ever came from what a person wanted to say, but people led by the Holy Spirit spoke words from God.

False Teachers

2 There used to be false prophets among God's people, just as you will have some false teachers in your group. They will secretly teach things that are wrong—teachings that will cause people to be lost. They will even refuse to accept the Master, Jesus, who bought their freedom. So they will bring quick ruin on themselves. [2]Many will follow their evil ways and say evil things about the way of truth. [3]Those false teachers only want your money, so they will use you by telling you lies. Their judgment spoken against them long ago is still coming, and their ruin is certain.

[4]When angels sinned, God did not let them go free without punishment. He sent them to hell and put them in caves of darkness where they are being held for judgment. [5]And God punished the

---

1:3 Lordship: 1 John 2:3–4

1:10 Election (Chosen): See article on page 345.

1:10 *brothers and sisters.* Although the Greek text reads "brothers" here and throughout this book, Peter's words were meant for the entire church, including men and women.

1:13 The body is an integral part of human beings, but when they die, it decays. Peter here anticipates his death as a departure from the body. However, we are not to think of heavenly life as bodiless. In 1 Corinthians 15:35–58, Paul teaches us that our physical bodies will be replaced by heavenly ones that can never be destroyed!

1:18 Peter: See article on page 972.

2:1 Apostasy: 2 Peter 2:15–21

2:3 Greed: 2 Peter 2:14

2:5 Peter uses a story from the past to guarantee the future. At the time Peter wrote this letter, the words and doubts of several false prophets appeared to be more sure and true than God's promises about the future. These false prophets preached that Jesus was not coming back, and that his failure to return by then should be proof enough of this. But Peter comforts and encourages the recipients of his letter with the Flood story. This story, as seen in light of other passages, teaches two essential truths about God and his promises: (1) he is patient (Matthew 24:38; 1 Peter 3:20) so that his delay in coming is a result of his abundant mercy, and (2) his punishment is sure (Genesis 6; Revelation 12:15–16). The Flood reminds the reader that false prophets will be judged in the future.

world long ago when he brought a flood to the world that was full of people who were against him. But God saved Noah, who preached about being right with God, and seven other people with him. 6And God also destroyed the evil cities of Sodom and Gomorrah by burning them until they were ashes. He made those cities an example of what will happen to those who are against God. 7But he saved Lot from those cities. Lot, a good man, was troubled because of the filthy lives of evil people. 8(Lot was a good man, but because he lived with evil people every day, his good heart was hurt by the evil things he saw and heard.) 9So the Lord knows how to save those who serve him when troubles come. He will hold evil people and punish them, while waiting for the Judgment Day. 10That punishment is especially for those who live by doing the evil things their sinful selves want and who hate authority.

These false teachers are bold and do anything they want. They are not afraid to speak against the angels. 11But even the angels, who are much stronger and more powerful than false teachers, do not accuse them with insults before the Lord. 12But these people speak against things they do not understand. They are like animals that act without thinking, animals born to be caught and killed. And, like animals, these false teachers will be destroyed. 13They have caused many people to suffer, so they themselves will suffer. That is their pay for what they have done. They take pleasure in openly doing evil, so they are like dirty spots and stains among you. They delight in trickery while eating meals with you. 14Every time they look at a woman they want her, and their desire for sin is never satisfied. They lead weak people into the trap of sin, and they have taught their hearts to be greedy. God will punish them! 15These false teachers left the right road and lost their way, following the way Balaam went. Balaam was the son of Beor, who loved being paid for doing wrong. 16But a donkey, which cannot talk, told Balaam he was sinning. It spoke with a man's voice and stopped the prophet's crazy thinking.

17Those false teachers are like springs without water and clouds blown by a storm. A place in the blackest darkness has been kept for them. 18They brag with words that mean nothing. By their evil desires they lead people into the trap of sin—people who are just beginning to escape from others who live in error. 19They promise them freedom, but they themselves are not free. They are slaves of things that will be destroyed. For people are slaves of anything that controls them. 20They were made free from the evil in the world by knowing our Lord and Savior Jesus Christ. But if they return to evil things and those things control them, then it is worse for them than it was before. 21Yes, it would be better for them to have never known the right way than to know it and to turn away from the holy teaching that was given to them. 22What they did is like this true saying: "A dog goes back to what it has thrown up," and, "After a pig is washed, it goes back and rolls in the mud."

Jesus Will Come Again

3 My friends, this is the second letter I have written you to help your honest minds remember. 2I want you to think about the words the holy prophets spoke in the past, and remember the command our Lord and Savior gave us through your apostles. 3It is most important for you to understand what will happen in the last days. People will laugh at you. They will live doing the evil things they want to do. 4They will say, "Jesus promised to come again. Where is he? Our fathers have died, but the world continues the way it has been since it was made." 5But they do not want to remember what happened long ago. By the word of God heaven was made, and the earth was made from water and with water. 6Then the world was flooded and destroyed with water. 7And that same word of God is keeping heaven and earth that we now have in order to be destroyed by fire. They are being kept for the Judgment Day and the destruction of all who are against God.

8But do not forget this one thing, dear friends: To the Lord one day is as a thousand years, and a thousand years is as one day. 9The Lord is not slow in doing what he promised—the way some people understand slowness. But God is being patient with you. He does not want anyone to be lost, but he wants all people to change their hearts and lives.

10But the day of the Lord will come like a thief. The skies will disappear with a loud noise.

2:5 Flood: Revelation 12:15

2:5 Noah: See article on page 99.

2:6 *Sodom and Gomorrah.* Two cities God destroyed because the people were so evil.

2:14 Greed: See article on page 911.

2:21 Apostasy: See article on page 1315.

2:22 Cults: 1 John 2:3–6

2:22 *"A dog . . . up."* Quotation from Proverbs 26:11.

3:9 Promise: Revelation 21:1–4

3:10–13 What is the purpose for this presentation of the horrible things that will come at the end of time? It is not to cause people to think about when the end will be. Instead, as Peter says clearly, it is to encourage Christians to lives of holiness and service.

Everything in them will be destroyed by fire, and
the earth and everything in it will be burned
up.⚭ 11In that way everything will be destroyed.
So what kind of people should you be? You should
live holy lives and serve God,⚭ 12as you wait for
and look forward to the coming of the day of God.
When that day comes, the skies will be destroyed
with fire, and everything in them will melt with
heat. 13But God made a promise to us, and we are
waiting for a new heaven and a new earth where
goodness lives.⚭

14Dear friends, since you are waiting for this to
happen, do your best to be without sin and without
fault. Try to be at peace with God. 15Remember
that we are saved because our Lord is patient.
Our dear brother Paul told you the same thing
when he wrote to you with the wisdom that God
gave him. 16He writes about this in all his letters.
Some things in Paul's letters are hard to understand, and people who are ignorant and weak in
faith explain these things falsely. They also falsely
explain the other Scriptures, but they are destroying themselves by doing this.⚭

17Dear friends, since you already know about
this, be careful. Do not let those evil people lead
you away by the wrong they do. Be careful so you
will not fall from your strong faith. 18But grow in the
grace and knowledge of our Lord and Savior Jesus
Christ. Glory be to him now and forever! Amen.⚭

⚭**3:10 Day of the Lord:** Revelation 16:14
3:10 *will be burned up.* Many Greek copies say, "will be found." One copy says, "will disappear."
⚭**3:11 Holiness:** Revelation 4:8
3:13 It is important that we know about and look forward to God's promise of a new earth. This promise is a source of hope for the Christian. The bad things which we suffer in this world under the curse will someday be traded for good things.
⚭**3:13 Heaven:** See article on page 1516.
⚭**3:16 Paul (Saul):** See article on page 1081.
⚭**3:18 Grace:** Revelation 22:21
⚭**3:18 Perseverance:** Revelation 2:7

INTRODUCTION TO THE BOOK OF

1 JOHN

Love One Another

WHO WROTE THIS BOOK?

From the internal evidence of 1 John (its language, style, and subject matter), as well as the witness of the church leaders (Irenaeus, Clement of Alexandria, Tertullian, and Origen), the author of this letter is the apostle John.

TO WHOM WAS THIS BOOK WRITTEN?

By inference from the fact that John spent the last thirty years of his life in Ephesus, it is reasonable to assume that this was a circular letter that went to churches in Asia Minor.

WHERE WAS IT WRITTEN?

It is probable that 1 John was written in Ephesus.

WHEN WAS IT WRITTEN?

Given the fact that 1 John was written after the Book of John, and that book was written later in John's life, it is likely that 1 John was written between A.D. 85 and 95.

WHAT IS THE BOOK ABOUT?

This book is about the appearance in the flesh of the Word, Jesus Christ, and the marks of a true believer. First a true believer will walk in the light, keeping God's commandments. The first commandment is to love one another. It is also about the enemies of Christ who deny that he has come in the flesh. John points out that anyone who lives in Christ does not continue to sin but shows love to fellow Christians by meeting their needs. The presence of the Holy Spirit within is a necessary fact about true believers and leads them to confess that Christ came to earth as a human. Another fact about true believers is that they love one another. True believers also confess that Jesus is the eternal Son of God. To become a true believer, one must have the Son of God living within through the Holy Spirit. We who have the Son of God living within can know we have eternal life, and can pray with confidence that God hears us.

WHY WAS THIS BOOK WRITTEN?

John wrote this book to expose certain false teachers, who denied the truth that Jesus is the eternal Son of God who became a human being. It is also to teach the marks of a true believer: love for fellow believers, obedience to Christ's commandments, and confession that Christ became a human being. Finally, it is to encourage holy living and a discerning of false teachers.

SO WHAT DOES THIS BOOK MEAN TO ME?

Many today think it does not matter what we believe about God as long as we live ethically. John says we cannot love God and still deny the truth about who Jesus Christ is or fail to love our fellow believers. In addition, we cannot love God and fail to keep his commandments.

SUMMARY:

Although usually called a letter, 1 John is more like a written sermon or tract. It is a kind of "family book" in that it outlines who are genuinely members of the family of God. Clearly, John is writing at a time when there are many opposing claims about what it means to be a true follower of Jesus. He wants people to know whether they have eternal life (5:16), so he provides three important measures of faithfulness. First, he says, true believers will distinguish themselves by their obedience to God (see 2:3–6, 17, 29; 3:4–10). Second, true believers are known by their love for one another (see 3:10, 16–20; 4:12, 21). Third, those who are Jesus' true followers experience the witness of the Spirit (3:24–4:3; 4:13–16a). Throughout the letter, then, John emphasizes the necessary relationship between what one believes and how one lives.

1 JOHN

We write you now about what has always existed, which we have heard, we have seen with our own eyes, we have looked at, and we have touched with our hands. We write to you about the Word that gives life. 2He who gives life was shown to us. We saw him and can give proof about it. And now we announce to you that he has life that continues forever. He was with God the Father and was shown to us. 3We announce to you what we have seen and heard, because we want you also to have fellowship with us. Our fellowship is with God the Father and with his Son, Jesus Christ. 4We write this to you so you can be full of joy with us.

God Forgives Our Sins

5Here is the message we have heard from Christ and now announce to you: God is light, and in him there is no darkness at all. 6So if we say we have fellowship with God, but we continue living in darkness, we are liars and do not follow the truth. 7But if we live in the light, as God is in the light, we can share fellowship with each other. Then the blood of Jesus, God's Son, cleanses us from every sin.

8If we say we have no sin, we are fooling ourselves, and the truth is not in us. 9But if we confess our sins, he will forgive our sins, because we can trust God to do what is right. He will cleanse us from all the wrongs we have done. 10If we say we have not sinned, we make God a liar, and we do not accept God's teaching.

Jesus Is Our Helper

2 My dear children, I write this letter to you so you will not sin. But if anyone does sin, we have a helper in the presence of the Father—Jesus Christ, the One who does what is right. 2He is the way our sins are taken away, and not only our sins but the sins of all people.

3We can be sure that we know God if we obey his commands. 4Anyone who says, "I know God," but does not obey God's commands is a liar, and the truth is not in that person. 5But if someone obeys God's teaching, then in that person God's love has truly reached its goal. This is how we can be sure we are living in God: 6Whoever says that he lives in God must live as Jesus lived.

The Command to Love Others

7My dear friends, I am not writing a new command to you but an old command you have had from the beginning. It is the teaching you have already heard. 8But also I am writing a new command to you, and you can see its truth in Jesus and in you, because the darkness is passing away, and the true light is already shining.

9Anyone who says, "I am in the light," but hates a brother or sister, is still in the darkness. 10Whoever loves a brother or sister lives in the light and will not cause anyone to stumble in his faith. 11But whoever hates a brother or sister is in darkness, lives in darkness, and does not know where to go, because the darkness has made that person blind.

12I write to you, dear children,
because your sins are forgiven through Christ.

1:1 *Word.* The Greek word is *logos,* meaning any kind of communication. Here, it means Christ, who was the way God told people about himself.

1:3–9 Christian fellowship has both a vertical and a horizontal dimension. The presence of the Holy Spirit within our hearts gives us new life in Christ and makes us members of God's family. We become sons and daughters of God and brothers and sisters of one another. The Holy Spirit enters when we repent of our sins, and thereafter sin in the life of a believer breaks the fellowship he or she enjoys with God and with fellow believers. But if a believer confesses and forsakes his or her sin, fellowship is restored with God and with other believers.

1:5–7 Darkness is used throughout the Bible as a symbol of not knowing God and the life-changing message of Jesus Christ. In 1 John, the writer used darkness as a symbol of the behavior that results from not knowing God. When he wrote that, "God is light and in God there is no darkness," he was emphasizing the righteousness of God and the absence of any sin. So if we say we know God and continue to behave like we have not seen Jesus' example of how to live, we do not understand his life-changing message. In 1 John we are encouraged to fully understand Christ's message and to follow his example in the way we live our lives. Living in the darkness is ignoring the knowledge of God's call to love others the way God loves us. Living in the light is living with the full understanding of God's forgiveness. Living in the dark is willfully sinning. Living in the light is living righteously.

1:6 Lying/Dishonesty: 1 John 2:21

1:7 Blood: Revelation 5:9

1:9 Conflict: See article on page 59.

1:9 Clean & Unclean: Revelation 21:27

1:9 For the believer, there is a daily need to examine one's heart and life to discern whether in thought, word, or action one has broken God's commandments. The Holy Spirit applies the Scripture to our lives and shows us where we have willfully fallen short. When we become aware of sin, we can and should immediately confess it, knowing God will always forgive us and empower us to eliminate it from our lives.

2:3 John uses the word "know" more than forty times in this short letter. Some Christians claimed that they had secret "knowledge" about God and God's purpose; on this basis they claimed to be genuine Christians and rejected those who did not have this knowledge. John combats this way of thinking by making it clear how one can *know* that they know God.

2:4 Lordship: See article on page 1194.

2:6 Cults: 1 John 3:16–20

2:6 Obedience: Revelation 21:22–27

2:9 *light.* Here, this word is used as a symbol of God's goodness or truth.

2:9 *brother or sister.* Although the Greek text says "brother" here and throughout this book, the writer's words were meant for the entire church, including men and women.

13I write to you, parents,
because you know the One who existed
from the beginning.
I write to you, young people,
because you have defeated the Evil One.
14I write to you, children,
because you know the Father.
I write to you, parents,
because you know the One who existed
from the beginning.
I write to you, young people,
because you are strong;
the teaching of God lives in you,
and you have defeated the Evil One.

15Do not love the world or the things in the world. If you love the world, the love of the Father is not in you. 16These are the ways of the world: wanting to please our sinful selves, wanting the sinful things we see, and being too proud of what we have. None of these come from the Father, but all of them come from the world. 17The world and everything that people want in it are passing away, but the person who does what God wants lives forever.

Reject the Enemies of Christ

18My dear children, these are the last days. You have heard that the enemy of Christ is coming, and now many enemies of Christ are already here. This is how we know that these are the last days. 19These enemies of Christ were in our fellowship, but they left us. They never really belonged to us; if they had been a part of us, they would have stayed with us. But they left, and this shows that none of them really belonged to us.

20You have the gift that the Holy One gave you, so you all know the truth. 21I do not write to you because you do not know the truth but because you do know the truth. And you know that no lie comes from the truth.

22Who is the liar? It is the person who does not accept Jesus as the Christ. This is the enemy of Christ: the person who does not accept the Father and his Son. 23Whoever does not accept the Son does not have the Father. But whoever confesses the Son has the Father, too.

24Be sure you continue to follow the teaching you heard from the beginning. If you continue to follow what you heard from the beginning, you will stay in the Son and in the Father. 25And this is what the Son promised to us—life forever.

26I am writing this letter about those people who are trying to lead you the wrong way. 27Christ gave you a special gift that is still in you, so you do not need any other teacher. His gift teaches you about everything, and it is true, not false. So continue to live in Christ, as his gift taught you.

28Yes, my dear children, live in him so that when Christ comes back, we can be without fear and not be ashamed in his presence. 29If you know that Christ is all that is right, you know that all who do right are God's children.

We Are God's Children

3 The Father has loved us so much that we are called children of God. And we really are his children. The reason the people in the world do not know us is that they have not known him. 2Dear friends, now we are children of God, and we have not yet been shown what we will be in the future. But we know that when Christ comes again, we will be like him, because we will see him as he really is. 3Christ is pure, and all who have this hope in Christ keep themselves pure like Christ.

2:15–17 Love for the Father is the natural response of the child of God to the one who has first loved him (see 4:19). If we love someone, we want to please him or her. Formerly, we loved ourselves and were always "wanting to please our sinful selves" (v. 16). Now we love the Father and want to please him. Pleasing him is obeying him (see 5:3). Put simply, the one who loves the Father is "the person who does what God wants" (v. 17). One day when we stand before Jesus to have our lives inspected, he will say concerning those things that have pleased him: "You did well. You are a good and loyal servant" (Matthew 25:21).

2:17 Pleasure: See article on page 489.

2:17 World/Worldly: See article on page 1042.

2:18 Last Days: See article on page 1063.

2:20 Antichrist (Enemy of Christ): 1 John 22

2:20 *gift.* This might mean the Holy Spirit, or it might mean teaching or truth as in verse 24.

2:21 Lying/Dishonesty: See article on page 320.

2:22 Antichrist (Enemy of Christ): 1 John 4:1–3

3 The children of God look like their Father. That is the point of this chapter. But in this context John does not mean we are perfect. After all, he has already stated that, "If we say we have no sin, we are fooling ourselves" (1:8). When we sin, we confess; and "if we confess our sins, he will forgive our sins" (1:9). The knowledge that we have a forgiving God keeps us from unwarranted anxiety concerning sin in our lives.

But this letter is also careful to urge that our status as "God's children" not be an excuse for impure living. "Christ is pure, and all who have this hope in Christ keep themselves pure like Christ. . . . Those who are God's children do not continue sinning, because the new life from God remains in them" (1 John 3:3, 9). This letter encourages us, as children of God, both to run to our Father when we fall, and to do our best to live like the Father so we don't fall.

3:1–3 It's hard for many Christians to believe that God has made us his children (3:1–2). This is due, at least in part, to the fact that it is often painfully obvious that we are not yet all that we should be as God's children. But the Bible clearly teaches that we are already the children of God and that rather than being discouraged by our shortcomings in character and action, our hope in Christ's coming again — and in our being like him when he does — should spur us on to a lifestyle of Christlike holiness and purity (3:3).

3:2 Human: See article on page 19.

4The person who sins breaks God's law. Yes, sin is living against God's law. 5You know that Christ came to take away sins and that there is no sin in Christ. 6So anyone who lives in Christ does not go on sinning. Anyone who goes on sinning has never really understood Christ and has never known him.

7Dear children, do not let anyone lead you the wrong way. Christ is all that is right. So to be like Christ a person must do what is right. 8The devil has been sinning since the beginning, so anyone who continues to sin belongs to the devil. The Son of God came for this purpose: to destroy the devil's work.

9Those who are God's children do not continue sinning, because the new life from God remains in them. They are not able to go on sinning, because they have become children of God. 10So we can see who God's children are and who the devil's children are: Those who do not do what is right are not God's children, and those who do not love their brothers and sisters are not God's children.

We Must Love Each Other

11This is the teaching you have heard from the beginning: We must love each other. 12Do not be like Cain who belonged to the Evil One and killed his brother. And why did he kill him? Because the things Cain did were evil, and the things his brother did were good.

13Brothers and sisters, do not be surprised when the people of the world hate you. 14We know we have left death and have come into life because we love each other. Whoever does not love is still dead. 15Everyone who hates a brother or sister is a murderer, and you know that no murderers have eternal life in them. 16This is how we know what real love is: Jesus gave his life for us. So we should give our lives for our brothers and sisters. 17Suppose someone has enough to live and sees a brother or sister in need, but does not help. Then God's love is not living in that person. 18My children, we should love people not only with words and talk, but by our actions and true caring.

19-20This is the way we know that we belong to the way of truth. When our hearts make us feel guilty, we can still have peace before God. God is greater than our hearts, and he knows everything. 21My dear friends, if our hearts do not make us feel guilty, we can come without fear into God's presence. 22And God gives us what we ask for because we obey God's commands and do what pleases him. 23This is what God commands: that we believe in his Son, Jesus Christ, and that we love each other, just as he commanded. 24The people who obey God's commands live in God, and God lives in them. We know that God lives in us because of the Spirit God gave us.

Warning Against False Teachers

4 My dear friends, many false prophets have gone out into the world. So do not believe every spirit, but test the spirits to see if they are from God. 2This is how you can know God's Spirit: Every spirit who confesses that Jesus Christ came to earth as a human is from God. 3And every spirit who refuses to say this about Jesus is not from God. It is the spirit of the enemy of Christ, which you have heard is coming, and now he is already in the world.

4My dear children, you belong to God and have defeated them; because God's Spirit, who is in you, is greater than the devil, who is in the world. 5And they belong to the world, so what they say is from the world, and the world listens to them. 6But we belong to God, and those who know God listen to us. But those who are not from God do not listen to us. That is how we know the Spirit that is true and the spirit that is false.

3:12 Cain's act of murdering his brother is a striking illustration of the jealous hatred the world has for God's children. Cain's actions prove that he was under the influence of the devil and could not tolerate his brother's righteousness. In contrast, the child of God is identified by his love for others.

3:12 Murder: 1 John 3:15

3:12–15 The author is faithfully interpreting the teaching of Jesus in Matthew 5:21–22. Hatred violates the spirit of the law against murder, by violating the law of love of others made in God's image.

3:14 Love: See article on page 1203.

3:15 *Everyone . . . murderer.* If one person hates a brother or sister, then in the heart that person has killed that brother or sister. Jesus taught about this sin to his followers (Matthew 5:21-26).

3:15 Hate: See article on page 189.

3:15 Murder: Revelation 9:21

3:20 Cults: 1 John 4:1–6

3:24 Good Works: See article on page 1263.

4:1 Test/Temptation: See article on page 691.

4:1–3 John warns against the spirit of the enemy of Christ—the antichrist. The enemy of Christ at the end of the age will lead a rebellion against Christ, but John already sees the evidence of the enemy's presence in the world. He points to the denial of Jesus as the Christ come in the flesh as the chief evidence of the spirit of the Antichrist.

4:1–6 John provides one test for identifying cults that is crucial; it always minimizes or denies the deity of Christ and the incarnation of Christ. It denies that the eternal Son of God took on a second human nature without ceasing to be the Son of God. Cults always criticize and reject evangelical Christianity. As John says, "Those who are not from God do not listen to us" (4:6).

4:2 The problem of false prophets and antichrists (enemies of Christ) is an old one that is addressed throughout the Bible. John is especially concerned with people who deny that Jesus Christ was a human being. Since Jesus was only a spiritual being, they would say, what we do in this physical life is unimportant. Not so, John insists. When Jesus Christ became a human being, he underscored how important life in this world is. It is here that we learn to be faithful to God and to act lovingly toward each other.

4:3 Antichrist: 2 John 7

4:4 Many people are afraid of the devil and the demons who follow him. After providing a basis for discerning demonic influence (which includes a denial of Jesus as both God and man), the apostle John encourages believers to claim the victory over Satan won by Jesus on the cross, and to realize that Satan's power does not begin to compare to that of the indwelling Holy Spirit.

4:6 Cults: 2 John

Love Comes from God

[7]Dear friends, we should love each other, because love comes from God. Everyone who loves has become God's child and knows God. [8]Whoever does not love does not know God, because God is love. [9]This is how God showed his love to us: He sent his one and only Son into the world so that we could have life through him. [10]This is what real love is: It is not our love for God; it is God's love for us in sending his Son to be the way to take away our sins.

[11]Dear friends, if God loved us that much we also should love each other. [12]No one has ever seen God, but if we love each other, God lives in us, and his love is made perfect in us.

[13]We know that we live in God and he lives in us, because he gave us his Spirit. [14]We have seen and can testify that the Father sent his Son to be the Savior of the world. [15]Whoever confesses that Jesus is the Son of God has God living inside, and that person lives in God. [16]And so we know the love that God has for us, and we trust that love.

God is love. Those who live in love live in God, and God lives in them. [17]This is how love is made perfect in us: that we can be without fear on the day God judges us, because in this world we are like him. [18]Where God's love is, there is no fear, because God's perfect love drives out fear. It is punishment that makes a person fear, so love is not made perfect in the person who fears.

[19]We love because God first loved us. [20]If people say, "I love God," but hate their brothers or sisters, they are liars. Those who do not love their brothers and sisters, whom they have seen, cannot love God, whom they have never seen. [21]And God gave us this command: Those who love God must also love their brothers and sisters.

Faith in the Son of God

5 Everyone who believes that Jesus is the Christ is God's child, and whoever loves the Father also loves the Father's children. [2]This is how we know we love God's children: when we love God and obey his commands. [3]Loving God means obeying his commands. And God's commands are not too hard for us, [4]because everyone who is a child of God conquers the world. And this is the victory that conquers the world—our faith. [5]So the one who wins against the world is the person who believes that Jesus is the Son of God.

[6]Jesus Christ is the One who came by water and blood. He did not come by water only, but by water and blood. And the Spirit says that this is true, because the Spirit is the truth. [7]So there are three witnesses that tell us about Jesus: [8]the Spirit, the water, and the blood; and these three witnesses agree. [9]We believe people when they say something is true. But what God says is more important, and he has told us the truth about his own Son. [10]Anyone who believes in the Son of God has the truth that God told us. Anyone who does not believe makes God a liar, because that person does not believe what God told us about his Son. [11]This is what God told us: God has given us eternal life, and this life is in his Son. [12]Whoever has the Son has life, but whoever does not have the Son of God does not have life.

We Have Eternal Life Now

[13]I write this letter to you who believe in the Son of God so you will know you have eternal life. [14]And this is the boldness we have in God's presence: that if we ask God for anything that agrees with what he wants, he hears us. [15]If we know he hears us every time we ask him, we know we have what we ask from him.

[16]If anyone sees a brother or sister sinning (sin that does not lead to eternal death), that person should pray, and God will give the sinner life. I am talking about people whose sin does not lead to eternal death. There is sin that leads to death. I do not mean that a person should pray about that sin. [17]Doing wrong is always sin, but there is sin that does not lead to eternal death.

[18]We know that those who are God's children do not continue to sin. The Son of God keeps them safe, and the Evil One cannot touch them. [19]We know that we belong to God, but the Evil One controls the whole world. [20]We also know that the Son of God has come and has given us understanding so that we can know the True One. And our lives are in the True One and in his Son, Jesus Christ. He is the true God and the eternal life.

[21]So, dear children, keep yourselves away from gods.

4:8 Family: John 1:1

5:1 The People of God: See article on page 1367.

5:3 Will of God: See article on page 711.

5:6 *water.* This probably means the water of Jesus' baptism.

5:6 *blood.* This probably means the blood of Jesus' death.

5:14–15 One of the great promises of Scripture is that God will answer prayers in accordance with his revealed will. In fact, we have a guarantee that we already have what we ask for in such cases. That is why Jesus taught us to pray, "May your kingdom come and what you want be done, here on earth as it is in heaven" (Matthew 6:10).

Notes:

INTRODUCTION TO THE BOOK OF

2 JOHN

Do Not Help False Teachers

WHO WROTE THIS BOOK?

Based on internal evidence (language, grammar, and style), the author of 2 John is the same as the author of 1 John, John, the apostle.

TO WHOM WAS THIS BOOK WRITTEN?

This book, unlike 1 John, is in letter form and is written to a Christian lady and her family.

WHERE WAS IT WRITTEN?

Like 1 John, it was most likely written in Ephesus.

WHEN WAS IT WRITTEN?

Again like 1 John, it was probably written between A.D. 85 and 95.

WHAT IS THE BOOK ABOUT?

The letter repeats the same warning as in 1 John against false teachers who deny that Christ has come in the flesh. If a person does not believe the correct doctrine about Christ, that person does not know God.

WHY WAS THIS BOOK WRITTEN?

This letter was written to encourage a Christian lady and her family to walk in the truth and to warn them against the false teachers who deny that Christ came to earth as a human being.

SO WHAT DOES THIS BOOK MEAN TO US?

We may hesitate to confront individuals about their faulty doctrine; but if we love them, we will. If they fail to believe the right things about Christ, they will not go to heaven. It is both our responsibility and our joy to help them learn the truth, but we must approach them in a spirit of concern and love.

SUMMARY:

Probably written to a church in Asia ("the chosen lady"—verse 1) and its members ("her children"), 2 John addresses the problem of false teaching. In particular, 2 John is concerned that Christians be careful about the ministries they support. In the ancient world, it was common to help missionaries by giving them hospitality and food. This is a good practice, unless the missionary is a false teacher; in this case, a family would be supporting the spread of an enemy of Christ.

2 JOHN

From the Elder.
To the chosen lady and her children:
I love all of you in the truth, and all those
who know the truth love you. 2We love you
because of the truth that lives in us and will be
with us forever.
3Grace, mercy, and peace from God the Father
and his Son, Jesus Christ, will be with us in
truth and love.
4I was very happy to learn that some of your children are following the way of truth, as the Father
commanded us. 5And now, dear lady, this is not a
new command but is the same command we
have had from the beginning. I ask you that we all
love each other. 6And love means living the way
God commanded us to live. As you have heard
from the beginning, his command is this: Live a
life of love.
7Many false teachers are in the world now who
do not confess that Jesus Christ came to earth as a
human. Anyone who does not confess this is a false
teacher and an enemy of Christ. 8Be careful yourselves that you do not lose everything you have
worked for, but that you receive your full reward.
9Anyone who goes beyond Christ's teaching and
does not continue to follow only his teaching does
not have God. But whoever continues to follow the
teaching of Christ has both the Father and the Son.
10If someone comes to you and does not bring
this teaching, do not welcome or accept that person into your house. 11If you welcome such a person, you share in the evil work.
12I have many things to write to you, but I do not
want to use paper and ink. Instead, I hope to come
to you and talk face to face so we can be full of joy.
13The children of your chosen sister greet you.

1:1 *Elder.* "Elder" means an older person. It can also mean a special leader in the church (as in Titus 1:5).

1:1 *lady.* This might mean a woman, or in this letter it might mean a church. If it is a church, then "her children" would be the people of the church.

1:1 *truth.* The truth or "Good News" about Jesus Christ that joins all believers together.

1:7 Antichrist (Enemy of Christ): See article on page 851.

1:13 *sister.* Sister of the "lady" in verse 1. This might be another woman or another church.

1:13 Cults: 3 John

INTRODUCTION TO THE BOOK OF

3 JOHN

Help Christians Who Teach Truth

WHO WROTE THIS BOOK?

Based on the same internal evidence as 2 John, the author of 3 John is the apostle John.

TO WHOM WAS THIS BOOK WRITTEN?

This letter was written to Gaius, a friend of John.

WHERE WAS IT WRITTEN?

Most likely, this letter was written in Ephesus.

WHEN WAS IT WRITTEN?

Because it does not deal with the false teaching about Christ, it may have been written earlier than 1 John or 2 John, perhaps in the early A.D. 80s.

WHAT IS THE BOOK ABOUT?

The book is about hospitality. John commends Gaius for entertaining traveling believers and criticizes Diotrephes for his lack of hospitality and outright hostility to God's people. John also commends Demetrius for his good reputation.

WHY WAS THIS BOOK WRITTEN?

This book was written to encourage Gaius for showing hospitality to fellow believers and to call Diotrephes to task for failing to do so. Almost as an afterthought, John also commends Demetrius.

SO WHAT DOES THIS BOOK MEAN TO US?

We should take the trouble to encourage or confront fellow believers about spiritual matters, as the case may be, so they will receive what they need to persist or to change their hearts and lives. This is a way of showing we love our fellow believers and care about their spiritual welfare.

SUMMARY:

In the ancient world, it was common to help missionaries by giving them hospitality and food. A man named Diotrephes, however, in trying to take over the leadership of a church, has denied hospitality to some of the teachers sent out by John. So, John writes this letter to commend John's teachers to Gaius and to tell Diotrephes that his actions are wrong.

3 JOHN

From the Elder.
To my dear friend Gaius, whom I love in
the truth:
[2]My dear friend, I know your soul is doing fine,
and I pray that you are doing well in every way and
that your health is good. [3]I was very happy when
some brothers and sisters came and told me about
the truth in your life and how you are following the
way of truth. [4]Nothing gives me greater joy than to
hear that my children are following the way of truth.
[5]My dear friend, it is good that you help the
brothers and sisters, even those you do not know.
[6]They told the church about your love. Please help
them to continue their trip in a way worthy of God.
[7]They started out in service to Christ, and they
have been accepting nothing from nonbelievers.
[8]So we should help such people; when we do, we
share in their work for the truth.
[9]I wrote something to the church, but Diotrephes,
who loves to be their leader, will not listen to us.
[10]So if I come, I will talk about what Diotrephes is
doing, about how he lies and says evil things about
us. But more than that, he refuses to accept the
other brothers and sisters; he even stops those
who do want to accept them and puts them out of
the church.
[11]My dear friend, do not follow what is bad; follow what is good. The one who does good belongs
to God. But the one who does evil has never known
God.
[12]Everyone says good things about Demetrius,
and the truth agrees with what they say. We also
speak well of him, and you know what we say is
true.
[13]I have many things I want to write you, but I
do not want to use pen and ink. [14]I hope to see you
soon and talk face to face. [15]Peace to you. The
friends here greet you. Please greet each friend
there by name.

1 *Elder.* "Elder" means an older person. It can also mean a special leader in the church (as Titus 1:5).

1 *truth.* The truth or "Good News" about Jesus Christ that joins all believers together.

3 *brothers and sisters.* Although the Greek text says "brothers," here and throughout this book, the writer's words were meant for the entire church, including men and women.

10 Hospitality: See article on page 921.

11 Evil: Revelation 21:1–4

15 Cults: See article on page 1509.

INTRODUCTION TO THE BOOK OF

JUDE

Warnings About False Teachers

WHO WROTE THIS BOOK?

Based on internal evidence (verse 1), Jude, the brother of James and half brother of Jesus, wrote this book.

TO WHOM WAS THIS BOOK WRITTEN?

It is not clear to whom this circular letter was written, although Jude's use of references from the Old Testament and the Apocrypha (historical books not usually considered inspired that fall chronologically between the Old and New Testaments) suggests a Jewish Christian audience.

WHERE WAS IT WRITTEN?

It is not clear where Jude wrote his letter.

WHEN WAS IT WRITTEN?

Because 2 Peter makes use of several verses in Jude, this suggests Jude must have written his letter between A.D. 65 and 67.

WHAT IS THE BOOK ABOUT?

Like 2 Peter, Jude warns against false teachers whose lives are loose and who show disrespect for spirit beings. Jude reminds his readers that the apostles had warned them about mockers who would appear in the last days living according to their own rules and causing divisions in the church. Jude urges his readers to grow in their faith and to exercise discernment in the case of mockers, showing patience toward some and using drastic measures in the case of others.

WHY WAS THIS BOOK WRITTEN?

Jude was written as an exhortation to believers to grow in their own spiritual lives. It is also a warning against those who show disrespect for spiritual things and whose lives show no evidence of a relationship with God.

SO WHAT DOES THIS BOOK MEAN TO US?

We have to "read" the unbelieving people around us carefully to know which ones to deal with gently and which ones to confront boldly regarding their sin. The goal in both cases is to see them saved, to take them out of the fire of final judgment.

SUMMARY:

Although Jude wanted to write to his audience about salvation, he felt it necessary to warn them about false teaching and false teachers that have come their way. The false teachers he has in mind are evil people, just the sort of people Jesus warned would be coming. The work of such people divides Christ's church, and their presence is a reminder of the need for renewed faithfulness and trust in God.

JUDE

From Jude, a servant of Jesus Christ and a brother of James.

To all who have been called by God. God the Father loves you, and you have been kept safe in Jesus Christ:

2Mercy, peace, and love be yours richly.

God Will Punish Sinners

3Dear friends, I wanted very much to write you about the salvation we all share. But I felt the need to write you about something else: I want to encourage you to fight hard for the faith that was given the holy people of God once and for all time. 4Some people have secretly entered your group. Long ago the prophets wrote about these people who will be judged guilty. They are against God and have changed the grace of our God into a reason for sexual sin. They also refuse to accept Jesus Christ, our only Master and Lord.

5I want to remind you of some things you already know: Remember that the Lord saved his people by bringing them out of the land of Egypt. But later he destroyed all those who did not believe. 6And remember the angels who did not keep their place of power but left their proper home. The Lord has kept these angels in darkness, bound with everlasting chains, to be judged on the great day. 7Also remember the cities of Sodom and Gomorrah and the other towns around them. In the same way they were full of sexual sin and people who desired sexual relations that God does not allow. They suffer the punishment of eternal fire, as an example for all to see.

8It is the same with these people who have entered your group. They are guided by dreams and make themselves filthy with sin. They reject God's authority and speak against the angels. 9Not even the archangel Michael, when he argued with the devil about who would have the body of Moses, dared to judge the devil guilty. Instead, he said, "The Lord punish you." 10But these people speak against things they do not understand. And what they do know, by feeling, as dumb animals know things, are the very things that destroy them. 11It will be terrible for them. They have followed the way of Cain, and for money they have given themselves to doing the wrong that Balaam did. They have fought against God as Korah did, and like Korah, they surely will be destroyed. 12They are like dirty spots in your special Christian meals you share. They eat with you and have no fear, caring only for themselves. They are clouds without rain, which the wind blows around. They are autumn trees without fruit that are pulled out of the ground. So they are twice dead. 13They are like wild waves of the sea, tossing up their own shameful actions like foam. They are like stars that wander in the sky. A place in the blackest darkness has been kept for them forever.

14Enoch, the seventh descendant from Adam, said about these people: "Look, the Lord is coming with many thousands of his holy angels to 15judge every person. He is coming to punish all who are against God for all the evil they have done against him. And he will punish the sinners who are against God for all the evil they have said against him."

16These people complain and blame others, doing the evil things they want to do. They brag about themselves, and they flatter others to get what they want.

A Warning and Things to Do

17Dear friends, remember what the apostles of our Lord Jesus Christ said before. 18They said to you, "In the last times there will be people who laugh about God, following their own evil desires which are against God." 19These are the people who divide you, people whose thoughts are only of this world, who do not have the Spirit.

20But dear friends, use your most holy faith to build yourselves up, praying in the Holy Spirit. 21Keep yourselves in God's love as you wait for the Lord Jesus Christ with his mercy to give you life forever.

22Show mercy to some people who have doubts. 23Take others out of the fire, and save them. Show mercy mixed with fear to others, hating even their clothes which are dirty from sin.

---

7 *Sodom and Gomorrah.* Two cities God destroyed because they were so evil.

9 *archangel.* The leader among God's angels or messengers.

11 Cain: See article on page 80.

12 Rebellion: See article on page 319.

13 Hell: Revelation 21:8

14 Adam: See article on page 39.

14–15 Jude pictures the coming of judgment as the coming of the heavenly army of the Divine Warrior. Although the ultimate source for this idea is Zechariah 14:5, Jude cites an early Jewish text not found in our Bible, known as *1 Enoch.* In Jude, the Divine Warrior is Jesus; he, together with his heavenly army, will come to bring judgment especially against the false teachers with whom this short letter is concerned.

21 Trinity: See article on page 801.

22 Doubt: See article on page 1326.

23 This passage underscores the well-known saying, "loving the

Praise God

24God is strong and can help you not to fall. He can bring you before his glory without any wrong in you and can give you great joy. 25He is the only God, the One who saves us. To him be glory, greatness, power, and authority through Jesus Christ our Lord for all time past, now, and forever. Amen.

sinner, hating the sin." On the one hand, believers are to show *mercy* to the false teachers who are about to fall into the precipice of judgment. On the other hand, believers should approach this with both *fear*—lest they themselves become polluted by the filth, and *hate*—for the evil character and practice of the false teachers are vividly described as clothes that are "dirty from sin" (Zechariah 3:2–3).

Notes:

INTRODUCTION TO SECTION SIX
REVELATION

REVELATORY LITERATURE

REVELATION

Apart from the Old Testament Book of Daniel and small portions of other biblical books, the Book of Revelation is unique as a form of biblical writing. It presents a dramatic narrative with elaborate descriptions of fantastic journeys, visions, and figures very much at home in the ancient form of literature known as "apocalyptic" (revelatory literature). As challenging as Revelation is for contemporary readers, it is well to remember that this book, written by John (Revelation 1:4, 9), was understandable to his first-century audience. Books like Revelation grew out of particular social contexts, among people who lived on the margins of society, who were experiencing direct or indirect social rejection as a result of their Christian stance toward the world.

Revelation presents itself as a "letter" (1:4-5), a "prophecy" (1:3; 22:7), and as "apocalyptic" (1:1 "revelation"). By presenting his book as a letter, John communicated his concern for the Christians in a number of towns in modern-day Turkey (see the list in Revelation 1:11; 2—3). We expect him to address specific problems they are experiencing. As prophecy, Revelation will be concerned first and foremost with "speaking on God's behalf," giving God's perspective on current events. As a prophet, John calls his readers to faithful response in light of God's work in the world. Finally, as apocalyptic, John's book places the crisis his audience was facing in the context of God's over-arching plan. *John wants to show his audience how God is at work right now, in these difficult times, even when God's presence is not always evident.*

Like the Book of Daniel, Revelation is best read as a drama. As is often the case with Jesus' parables, the overall picture, the images we see with our imaginations, is more central to a faithful reading of Revelation than are the details of its symbolism.

In many cases, clues to the interpretation of John's symbolism appear in the text itself—such as the identity of the dragon of 12:18 in 12:9 and 20:2; or the identity of the beast with the woman who sits on seven mountains (17:9, 18; that is, Rome, widely known as "the city on seven hills"). Like other parts of the Bible, Revelation tends to use numbers in a symbolic way. References to "seven eyes" or "ten horns" should not be taken literally, but refer to universal sight and absolute power, respectively. Readers unfamiliar with this type of symbolism may first want to read an article on numbers or numerology in a Bible dictionary.

Like revelatory literature in general, Revelation makes extensive use of the Old Testament. For example, a comparison of Revelation 13:2 with Daniel 7:1-6 suggests that the beast is a political power of some sort. *One caution:* John not only alludes to Old Testament passages, he also interprets them. In the end, then, it is not enough to say, "This passage refers to that Old Testament text." One must ask, "What does John mean by this?"

What Does Revelation Mean Today?

The Book of Revelation was written to address first-century crises, but this does not mean that its relevance is now lost. Its message continues to have profound meaning, especially for Christians in the midst of suffering or who find themselves in oppressive social conditions.

The primary message of the book is eternal victory. The Christ of God and our Savior has already defeated the beast, who is Satan, when Jesus rose triumphant over death. To us as his followers, Christians, Jesus makes this promise in the Revelation to John: "Be faithful, even if you have to die, and I will give you the crown of Life" (2:10). The victory is won! We are saved. Our task is but to remain faithful to the Victor until he comes again to take us home to heaven for all eternity.

God's servants will worship him. . .
There will never be night again.
They will not need the light of a lamp
or the light of the sun, because the
Lord God will give them light.
And they will rule as kings forever and ever.

REVELATION 22:5

INTRODUCTION TO THE BOOK OF REVELATION

Christ Will Win over Evil

WHO WROTE THIS BOOK?

John, the apostle, is the author of Revelation (1:1).

TO WHOM IS THIS BOOK WRITTEN?

Revelation is addressed to seven churches in Asia Minor.

WHERE WAS IT WRITTEN?

Most likely, Revelation was written in Ephesus.

WHEN WAS IT WRITTEN?

This book was written near the end of John's life, around A.D. 95.

WHAT IS THE BOOK ABOUT?

It begins with a majestic vision of Jesus Christ in his glorified state. Christ addresses the special needs of the seven churches to which Revelation is sent. John receives a series of visions to open Christians' eyes to the kingship and majesty of God, the nature of spiritual warfare, God's judgments on evil, and the outcome of the conflict. God wins the final battle. Satan and his angels and those who follow them are judged and punished forever. Those whose names are written in the Lamb's Book of Life are judged according to how they lived their lives and enter into a state of bliss. John invites Jesus to come quickly.

WHY WAS THIS BOOK WRITTEN?

This book was written as an encouragement to those undergoing persecution, to assure them of the final victory by Christ over all his enemies. It was written so believers would purify their lives in anticipation of Christ's Second Coming. It shows the justice, as well as the mercy, of God. And it shows that God is sovereign over history.

SO WHAT DOES THIS BOOK MEAN TO US?

Reading the Revelation of John is like watching a rerun of a war movie. We know who the forces are, and we're watching the battles, but we already know who has won. In the spiritual world described in Revelation, the forces are Jesus Christ and his heavenly armies versus Satan and his demonic armies. But here's the Good News: Jesus Christ has already won the war! When he rose victorious over death, he defeated Satan forever. Now, we Christians can do battle on a daily basis with Satan knowing that ultimately the war has been won. We are saved! And Jesus, our Savior and Lord of Heaven's Armies, will return to take us home someday to eternal life if we remain faithful (2:10).

SUMMARY:

The Book of Revelation may be the most difficult book in the New Testament to understand. For us, it is certainly the strangest. This is largely because our normal reading fare today does not include books like this. It is important to remember, then, that when Revelation was written, it was one of a number of similar books. Even if we have a hard time with it, we can be confident that its readers in the first century would have been able to understand its message.

The Book of Revelation was written probably at the end of the first century A.D., by a Christian prophet whose name was John (1:4, 9). John was a travelling prophet who had been banished from his work in Asia Minor to a small island west of modern-day Turkey named Patmos. He had been forced to live on Patmos because of his witness as a Christian (1:9).

John wrote to a group of seven churches, each mentioned in chapters 2–3. His purpose was to alert Christians to the crisis coming upon them. Disaster awaited them, he wrote, because the way of God was so directly opposed by the government of Rome. Christians must stay alert so that they will not be surprised by the evil growing around them like a cancer.

John also wanted Christians to know that God was bigger than any evil that could stand against God and God's people. In fact, one of the chief pictures that John presents in the Book of Revelation is the picture of God on the throne (see chapter 4). Another image of God emphasizes God's timelessness: God has always been and always will be (see 1:8). Even when times look bad, John insists, God is on the throne, and God will always be God!

A very important part of the good news John presents centers on the work of Jesus. Jesus is presented as the "lamb" (see chapter 5) who won salvation. As the Lamb, Jesus also shows Christ's followers how to fight in the war against evil—not with weapons and violence but through faithfulness. Jesus is also the One who is coming to defeat evil once and for all!

The Book of Revelation is also difficult to read because it is not easy at first to follow the story it is trying to tell. This is because Revelation is a series of visions that tell and re-tell the story of God's work throughout all of history. Remember: John wants to put the difficult times Christians are facing and will face in perspective. He wants to remind them of how everything fits into God's overview plan. John does this by a series of visions of the future, of pictures of the present, and of flashbacks to the past. For this reason, it is probably best to read the Book of Revelation a few chapters at a time:

Revelation 1–3: Introduction: Jesus and the Churches
Revelation 4–5: God and the Lamb
Revelation 6–8:5: The Seven Seals
Revelation 8:6–11:19: The Seven Trumpets
Revelation 12–14: The Dragon, the Beasts, and the Faithful
Revelation 15–16: The Seven Bowls
Revelation 17–19: 10:The Vision of Babylon
Revelation 19:11–22:21: Judgment and the Final Victory

REVELATION

John Tells About This Book

This is the revelation of Jesus Christ, which God gave to him, to show his servants what must soon happen. And Jesus sent his angel to show it to his servant John, 2who has told everything he has seen. It is the word of God; it is the message from Jesus Christ. 3Happy is the one who reads the words of God's message, and happy are the people who hear this message and do what is written in it. The time is near when all of this will happen.

Jesus' Message to the Churches

4From John.

To the seven churches in the country of Asia:

Grace and peace to you from the One who is and was and is coming, and from the seven spirits before his throne, 5and from Jesus Christ. Jesus is the faithful witness, the first among those raised from the dead. He is the ruler of the kings of the earth.

He is the One who loves us, who made us free from our sins with the blood of his death. 6He made us to be a kingdom of priests who serve God his Father. To Jesus Christ be glory and power forever and ever! Amen.

7Look, Jesus is coming with the clouds, and everyone will see him, even those who stabbed him. And all peoples of the earth will cry loudly because of him. Yes, this will happen! Amen.

8The Lord God says, "I am the Alpha and the Omega. I am the One who is and was and is coming. I am the Almighty."

9I, John, am your brother. All of us share with Christ in suffering, in the kingdom, and in patience to continue. I was on the island of Patmos, because I had preached the word of God and the message about Jesus. 10On the Lord's day I was in the Spirit, and I heard a loud voice behind me that sounded like a trumpet. 11The voice said, "Write what you see in a book and send it to the seven churches: to Ephesus, Smyrna, Pergamum, Thyatira, Sardis, Philadelphia, and Laodicea."

12I turned to see who was talking to me. When I turned, I saw seven golden lampstands 13and someone among the lampstands who was "like a Son of Man." He was dressed in a long robe and had a gold band around his chest. 14His head and hair were white like wool, as white as snow, and his eyes were like flames of fire. 15His feet were like bronze that glows hot in a furnace, and his voice was like the noise of flooding water. 16He held seven stars in his right hand, and a sharp double-edged sword came out of his mouth. He looked like the sun shining at its brightest time.

17When I saw him, I fell down at his feet like a dead man. He put his right hand on me and said, "Do not be afraid. I am the First and the Last. 18I am the One who lives; I was dead, but look, I am alive forever and ever! And I hold the keys to death and to the place of the dead. 19So write the things you see, what is now and what will happen later. 20Here is the secret of the seven stars that you saw in my right hand and the seven golden lampstands: The seven lampstands are the seven churches, and the seven stars are the angels of the seven churches.

To the Church in Ephesus

2 "Write this to the angel of the church in Ephesus:

"The One who holds the seven stars in his right hand and walks among the seven golden lampstands says this: 2I know what you do, how you work hard and never give up. I know you do not put up with the false teachings of evil people. You have tested those who say they are apostles but really are not, and you found they are liars. 3You

1:1 *revelation.* Making known truth that has been hidden.

1:3 This book opens with an inviting promise. Those who read and obey the book will be happy. After all, the book's message is that Jesus is coming again to take away all suffering and evil and is establishing his own kingdom where everyone who follows him will enjoy total peace and happiness.

1:3 Prophet & Prophecy: See article on page 1071.

1:4–6 The beginning of the Book of Revelation looks like a letter, even though its content is more like a long story. (Compare the beginnings of other letters in the New Testament.) In this way John shows his concern as a shepherd for his first-century readers.

1:8 *Alpha and the Omega.* The first and last letters of the Greek alphabet. This means "the beginning and the end."

1:9 *Patmos.* A small island in the Aegean Sea, near the coast of Asia Minor (modern Turkey).

1:9 Suffering: See article on page 1121.

1:13 *"like . . . Man."* "Son of Man" is a name Jesus called himself.

1:13 Incarnation: Revelation 19:13

1:16 Weapons: Revelation 19:15

2–3 Among those who call themselves "the church," most have soiled their garments. Five out of the seven churches Jesus addressed here were strongly rebuked. They lost their purity, or their devotion had grown cold, or they introduced heretical teachings, or their lives were unclean. Yet there was a remnant—a few who remained faithful.

Jesus commended two out of the seven congregations (Smyrna and Philadelphia) without offering any correction at all, and even among the churches he chastised, there were individuals who did not compromise their faith or their conduct: "You have a few there in Sardis," a church soundly rebuked by the Lord, "who have kept their clothes unstained, so they will walk with me and wear white clothes, because they are worthy" (Revelation 3:4).

have patience and have suffered troubles for my
name and have not given up.
4“But I have this against you: You have left the
love you had in the beginning. 5So remember
where you were before you fell. Change your hearts
and do what you did at first. If you do not change,
I will come to you and will take away your lampstand from its place. 6But there is something you
do that is right: You hate what the Nicolaitans do,
as much as I.
7“Every person who has ears should listen to
what the Spirit says to the churches. To those who
win the victory I will give the right to eat the fruit
from the tree of life, which is in the garden of
God.

To the Church in Smyrna

8“Write this to the angel of the church in Smyrna:
“The One who is the First and the Last, who
died and came to life again, says this: 9I know your
troubles and that you are poor, but really you are
rich! I know the bad things some people say about
you. They say they are Jews, but they are not true
Jews. They are a synagogue that belongs to Satan.
10Do not be afraid of what you are about to suffer.
I tell you, the devil will put some of you in prison
to test you, and you will suffer for ten days. But be
faithful, even if you have to die, and I will give you
the crown of life.
11“Everyone who has ears should listen to what
the Spirit says to the churches. Those who win the
victory will not be hurt by the second death.

To the Church in Pergamum

12“Write this to the angel of the church in
Pergamum:
“The One who has the sharp, double-edged
sword says this: 13I know where you live. It is where
Satan has his throne. But you are true to me. You
did not refuse to tell about your faith in me even
during the time of Antipas, my faithful witness who
was killed in your city, where Satan lives.
14“But I have a few things against you: You have
some there who follow the teaching of Balaam.
He taught Balak how to cause the people of Israel
to sin by eating food offered to idols and by taking
part in sexual sins. 15You also have some who follow the teaching of the Nicolaitans. 16So change
your hearts and lives. If you do not, I will come to
you quickly and fight against them with the sword
that comes out of my mouth.
17“Everyone who has ears should listen to what
the Spirit says to the churches.
“I will give some of the hidden manna to everyone who wins the victory. I will also give to each
one who wins the victory a white stone with a new
name written on it. No one knows this new name
except the one who receives it.

To the Church in Thyatira

18“Write this to the angel of the church in
Thyatira:
“The Son of God, who has eyes that blaze like
fire and feet like shining bronze, says this: 19I know
what you do. I know about your love, your faith,
your service, and your patience. I know that you
are doing more now than you did at first.
20“But I have this against you: You let that
woman Jezebel spread false teachings. She says
she is a prophetess, but by her teaching she leads
my people to take part in sexual sins and to eat
food that is offered to idols. 21I have given her
time to change her heart and turn away from her
sin, but she does not want to change. 22So I will
throw her on a bed of suffering. And all those
who take part in adultery with her will suffer
greatly if they do not turn away from the wrongs
she does. 23I will also kill her followers. Then all
the churches will know I am the One who
searches hearts and minds, and I will repay each
of you for what you have done.
24“But others of you in Thyatira have not followed her teaching and have not learned what
some call Satan's deep secrets. I say to you that I
will not put any other load on you. 25Only continue
in your loyalty until I come.
26“I will give power over the nations to everyone

2:6, 15 *Nicolaitans.* This is the name of a religious group that followed false beliefs and ideas.

2:7 Perseverance: Revelation 2:10–11

2:7 Repentance: See article on page 871.

2:9 Anti-Semitism: Revelation 3:9

2:11 Perseverance: Revelation 2:17

2:13 In a long tradition stemming from Samson and Daniel in the Old Testament, and Jesus, John the Baptist, and Stephen in the New Testament, Antipas gave his life as a "faithful witness." His death demonstrated his loyalty to Christ, but also witnessed to others in an upsetting way the truth of the message about Christ. The martyrs were willing to face death because of their confidence that they would receive "the crown of life" (2:10).

2:13 Martyrdom: Revelation 5:9–12

2:14–17 Here and throughout Revelation, John counsels his readers to separate themselves from the larger society. During times like this when God's people are under attack, they must be even more determined to reject the ways of the world. This may mean that they will suffer, but God will provide for them, just as he provided manna for the Israelites in the Exodus.

2:17 Perseverance: Revelation 2:26

2:20–23 Jesus condemns the church in Thyatira for its tolerance of an immoral woman whom he calls "Jezebel." Like her namesake in the Old Testament, this woman was a stumbling block to the church because she lead people into immorality and the worship of idols. She claimed to be a prophetess, but she was really a tool of Satan to undermine the life and witness of that church.

who wins the victory and continues to be obedient to me until the end.

27'You will rule over them with an iron rod,
as when pottery is broken into pieces.'
Psalm 2:9

28This is the same power I received from my Father. I will also give him the morning star. 29Everyone who has ears should listen to what the Spirit says to the churches.

To the Church in Sardis

3 "Write this to the angel of the church in Sardis: "The One who has the seven spirits and the seven stars says this: I know what you do. People say that you are alive, but really you are dead. 2Wake up! Make yourselves stronger before what you have left dies completely. I have found that what you are doing is less than what my God wants. 3So do not forget what you have received and heard. Obey it, and change your hearts and lives. So you must wake up, or I will come like a thief, and you will not know when I will come to you. 4But you have a few there in Sardis who have kept their clothes unstained, so they will walk with me and will wear white clothes, because they are worthy. 5Those who win the victory will be dressed in white clothes like them. And I will not erase their names from the book of life, but I will say they belong to me before my Father and before his angels. 6Everyone who has ears should listen to what the Spirit says to the churches.

To the Church in Philadelphia

7"Write this to the angel of the church in Philadelphia:

"This is what the One who is holy and true, who holds the key of David, says. When he opens a door, no one can close it. And when he closes it, no one can open it. 8I know what you do. I have put an open door before you, which no one can close. I know you have a little strength, but you have obeyed my teaching and were not afraid to speak my name. 9Those in the synagogue that belongs to Satan say they are Jews, but they are not true Jews; they are liars. I will make them come before you and bow at your feet, and they will know that I have loved you. 10You have obeyed my teaching about not giving up your faith. So I will keep you from the time of trouble that will come to the whole world to test those who live on earth.

11"I am coming soon. Continue strong in your faith so no one will take away your crown. 12I will make those who win the victory pillars in the temple of my God, and they will never have to leave it. I will write on them the name of my God and the name of the city of my God, the new Jerusalem, that comes down out of heaven from my God. I will also write on them my new name. 13Everyone who has ears should listen to what the Spirit says to the churches.

To the Church in Laodicea

14"Write this to the angel of the church in Laodicea:

"The Amen, the faithful and true witness, the beginning of all God has made, says this: 15I know what you do, that you are not hot or cold. I wish that you were hot or cold! 16But because you are lukewarm—neither hot, nor cold—I am ready to spit you out of my mouth. 17You say, 'I am rich, and I have become wealthy and do not need anything.' But you do not know that you are really miserable, pitiful, poor, blind, and naked. 18I advise you to buy from me gold made pure in fire so you can be truly rich. Buy from me white clothes so you can be clothed and so you can cover your shameful nakedness. Buy from me medicine to put on your eyes so you can truly see.

19"I correct and punish those whom I love. So be eager to do right, and change your hearts and lives. 20Here I am! I stand at the door and knock. If you hear my voice and open the door, I will come in and eat with you, and you will eat with me.

21"Those who win the victory will sit with me on my throne in the same way that I won the victory and sat down with my Father on his throne. 22Everyone who has ears should listen to what the Spirit says to the churches."

John Sees Heaven

4 After the vision of these things I looked, and there before me was an open door in heaven. And the same voice that spoke to me before, that sounded like a trumpet, said, "Come up here, and

2:26 Perseverance: Revelation 3:5
3:5 Perseverance: Revelation 3:11–12
3:9 Anti-Semitism: See article on page 992.
3:9 At the end of the first century A.D., Christians had become separated from Judaism and were no longer welcome in Jewish synagogues. John teaches that those who remain faithful to Jesus are the true Jews (see 2:9); they are the ones who are really God's people.
3:12 Perseverance: Revelation 3:21
3:12 *Jerusalem.* This name is used to mean the spiritual city God built for his people. See Revelation 21-22.
3:14 *Amen.* Used here as a name for Jesus; it means to agree fully that something is true.
3:20 Table Fellowship/Lord's Supper: Revelation 19:9
3:21 Perseverance: Revelation 21:7

I will show you what must happen after this." 2Immediately I was in the Spirit, and before me was a throne in heaven, and someone was sitting on it. 3The One who sat on the throne looked like precious stones, like jasper and carnelian. All around the throne was a rainbow the color of an emerald. 4Around the throne there were twenty-four other thrones with twenty-four elders sitting on them. They were dressed in white and had golden crowns on their heads. 5Lightning flashes and noises and thundering came from the throne. Before the throne seven lamps were burning, which are the seven spirits of God. 6Also before the throne there was something that looked like a sea of glass, clear like crystal.

In the center and around the throne were four living creatures with eyes all over them, in front and in back. 7The first living creature was like a lion. The second was like a calf. The third had a face like a man. The fourth was like a flying eagle. 8Each of these four living creatures had six wings and was covered all over with eyes, inside and out. Day and night they never stop saying:

"Holy, holy, holy is the Lord God Almighty.
He was, he is, and he is coming."

9These living creatures give glory, honor, and thanks to the One who sits on the throne, who lives forever and ever. 10Then the twenty-four elders bow down before the One who sits on the throne, and they worship him who lives forever and ever. They put their crowns down before the throne and say:

11"You are worthy, our Lord and God,
to receive glory and honor and power,
because you made all things.
Everything existed and was made,
because you wanted it."

5 Then I saw a scroll in the right hand of the One sitting on the throne. The scroll had writing on both sides and was kept closed with seven seals. 2And I saw a powerful angel calling in a loud voice, "Who is worthy to break the seals and open the scroll?" 3But there was no one in heaven or on earth or under the earth who could open the scroll or look inside it. 4I cried hard because there was no one who was worthy to open the scroll or look inside. 5But one of the elders said to me, "Do not cry! The Lion from the tribe of Judah, David's descendant, has won the victory so that he is able to open the scroll and its seven seals."

6Then I saw a Lamb standing in the center of the throne and in the middle of the four living creatures and the elders. The Lamb looked as if he had been killed. He had seven horns and seven eyes, which are the seven spirits of God that were sent into all the world. 7The Lamb came and took the scroll from the right hand of the One sitting on the throne. 8When he took the scroll, the four living creatures and the twenty-four elders bowed down before the Lamb. Each one of them had a harp and golden bowls full of incense, which are the prayers of God's holy people. 9And they all sang a new song to the Lamb:

"You are worthy to take the scroll
and to open its seals,
because you were killed,
and with the blood of your death you bought
people for God
from every tribe, language, people,
and nation.
10You made them to be a kingdom of
priests for our God,
and they will rule on the earth."

11Then I looked, and I heard the voices of many angels around the throne, and the four living creatures, and the elders. There were thousands and thousands of angels, 12saying in a loud voice:

"The Lamb who was killed is worthy
to receive power, wealth, wisdom,
and strength,
honor, glory, and praise!"

13Then I heard all creatures in heaven and on earth and under the earth and in the sea saying:

"To the One who sits on the throne
and to the Lamb
be praise and honor and glory and power
forever and ever."

14The four living creatures said, "Amen," and the elders bowed down and worshiped.

4:8 Holiness: See article on page 301.

4:11 In Revelation 4, twenty-four elders (probably representing the whole company of believers of Old and New Testament times, the company headed by the twelve patriarchs and twelve apostles) worship God, acknowledging his worthiness "to receive glory and honor and power, because you made all things . . . " (Revelation 4:11). And in the next chapter they sing, "The Lamb who was killed is worthy" (Revelation 5:12). The substance of Christian worship is the declaration of the worth of God and the Lamb, the glory of creation, and the greater glory of the cross.

5:5 *Lion.* Here refers to Christ.

5:5–6 This is an important fusion of images: the Lion from the tribe of Judah is the Lamb that looked as if he had been killed. Some Jews thought of the coming Savior as a mighty warrior-lamb, but in the Book of John Jesus is presented as the Lamb who dies that people can be forgiven (John 1:29). John's lamb combines both of these ideas. It is by dying in order that people might be forgiven that Jesus (the Lamb) fights against evil as the Warrior-Lamb.

5:8 Prayer: See article on page 902.

5:9 Blood: See article on page 777.

5:9 Gentiles (Non-Jews): See article on page 330.

5:12 Martyrdom: Revelation 16:6

5:14 Music: See article on page 430.

Communication

1 John 1:1–4

The New Testament proposes a worldwide sharing of the Good News of Jesus. Does the Bible also indicate how the Good News might be translated to others and by what means this might happen? On what biblical principles might we draw as we think about interpersonal communication today?

When we communicate, we share ideas, thoughts, and feelings with others. Each act of communication can never be seen as an isolated event, for the means of communication and the understanding of a message are dependent upon the context in which we live. How we speak, the words we use and the meaning we give to those words, which actions or expressions we use to express ourselves, and what key events and their significance we allude to are all part of the complex process of communication. The cross, an instrument of cruel execution, takes on new meaning to a Christian. It becomes a symbol of grace.

Communication is symbolic by nature. Every sound, action, event, or movement has a meaning attached to it by human beings. Words themselves are merely sounds and symbols which are meaningless unless given meaning. In communication, people explain their meaning by the varied use of symbols. Word sounds, gestures, tones, and facial expressions as well as actions convey meaning. For example, while we might use the word *heart* to mean the center of our feelings, another culture might use a sound that roughly translated into our language means *throat* or *eyes*. The meaning is still true even though the symbol is quite different. Communication is achieved not when the symbol is shared, but when the meaning is conveyed.

The Bible uses many means to convey meaning. Words, translated from the Hebrew, Greek, and Aramaic languages and cultures spanning some 1,200 years, convey a message through recalling significant events, stories, sayings, songs, laws, and dialogues. One could truly say that communication is a primary theme in the Bible.

God expresses himself to Moses out of a burning bush and then directs Moses to communicate this message to others (Exodus 3). The prophets receive God's Word (meaning) in dreams, events, visions (Isaiah 6), and voices in the night (1 Samuel 3:4). Each sets about conveying this message to the culture in which they live. Jeremiah bought a field in the center of a ruined town to convey the message of hope in God's faithfulness (Jeremiah 32). Hosea married an unfaithful woman and stayed with her to express God's faithfulness to a prostitute people (Hosea 1:2; 2:2). Throughout the Bible, God's meaning took different expression in varied context to communicate.

The birth of Jesus is God's most personal communication to us of his personal nature. "No one has ever seen God. But God the only Son is very close to the Father, and he has shown us what God is like" (John 1:18). Through Jesus' life, teachings (words), deeds, healings, sufferings, death, and resurrection, God has "shown us what God is like" (John 1:18). God has communicated with us.

Pentecost demonstrates the church's place in God's passion to communicate (Acts 2). Paul's encounter on the road to Damascus with a risen Lord (Acts 9:15) becomes a charge to him to become a communicator to the world of God's message. Not only did Paul teach, but it is his letters that communicate with us today the meaning he found in Christ. This meaning, he asserts, did not come from men or from himself, but from God (Galatians 1:11–12). Paul's charge is to communicate God's meaning, not his own.

As John's first letter opens, we can note how seriously he considers the nature of communication. What he has received is what he wants to pass on to others. That "which we have heard, we have seen with our own eyes, we have looked at," or beheld and understood, "and we have touched with our hands" is what John is about to share with his readers (1 John 1:1–4). "We announce to you what we have seen and heard." Good communication is faithful to the intended meaning. This is important because John desired that his readers come to understand what he is communicating, and come to share in that understanding. For communication to happen, there needs to be a response. "We want you also to have fellowship with us. Our fellowship is with God the Father and with his Son, Jesus Christ" (1 John 1:3). Communication is the basis for fellowship because it not only shares a message, but it creates the opportunity for a common ground and a common reference. In this case, the common reference is Jesus Christ and what God means to convey to us through him. Good News is the term used for this message when it is understood. We are to communicate what God means by *Good News*.

Communication: For additional scriptures on this topic go to Exodus 3.

Jezebel

Revelation 2

Is Jezebel a real person or just a character type? What is the fate of today's "Jezebels"?

Few names are as notorious as the name Jezebel. The name connotes "an ambitious, conniving adulteress, intent on ruining the reputation of all innocent young men." But just where this reputation came from is not always clear.

The Books of Kings tell of a historical person by the name of Jezebel who was zealous for her native religion. She is introduced in 1 Kings 16:31 as the new wife of King Ahab. Being the daughter of the king of Sidon, of course she would worship the God of Sidon, Baal, and not the God of Israel, Yahweh. Perhaps this is why the text says, "[Ahab] did even worse things. He married Jezebel" (1 Kings 16:31). Being the king of Israel, one might hope that Ahab would marry a worshiper of Yahweh. That not being the case, one might have wished Jezebel to take on the faith of her new homeland. The move from Sidon to Israel, however, did not impact Jezebel's commitment. She continued to pursue her worship of Baal and Asherah with zeal. She entertained the prophets of these two gods in her own home (1 Kings 18:19). She used her position to lead others to worship false gods (1 Kings 18:19–21; 21:25) and to kill (1 Kings 18:4, 13; 2 Kings 9:7) those who continued to prophesy for Yahweh.

In another story about Queen Jezebel, we are shown the tactics she used to obtain her wishes. By deceiving King Ahab and the officials of Jezreel, Jezebel was able to obtain Naboth's vineyard for her husband's vegetable garden (1 Kings 21). Naboth was unwilling to hand over his family's land to King Ahab when asked. Jezebel, therefore, using Ahab's name, had Naboth stoned to death. Instead of telling her husband *how* Naboth had died, she said simply, "Naboth of Jezreel is dead. Now you may go and take for yourself the vineyard he would not sell to you" (1 Kings 21:15). Shortly thereafter, Ahab was confronted by a prophet from Yahweh who accused him of leading Israel astray and continually doing what Yahweh says is wrong (1 Kings 21:20). Ultimately, Ahab's habit of wrong choices was blamed on Jezebel because she "influenced him to do evil" (1 Kings 21:25).

In the end, Jezebel is killed by a newly appointed king for Israel. She tried to dissuade her assailant with eye makeup and words of flattery, saying, "Have you come in peace, you [king]?" (2 Kings 9:31). This was to no avail, as she was immediately thrown from the window and trampled by horses. This is the end of the information we are given concerning the historical person of Jezebel and her influences in Israel.

Revelation describes a more sexually explicit character named Jezebel who, in addition to leading people astray spiritually (Revelation 2:20, 24), also leads people to commit sexual sins (Revelation 2:20, 22). She is blamed for "the evil things of the earth" (Revelation 17:5). This Jezebel is not far from the factual character in the books of Kings, however. Revelation 2:22 says, "I will throw her on a bed of suffering." Could this be a reference to the street "bed" that Jezebel was thrown to from her window (2 Kings 9:33–37)? And Revelation 2:23 refers to the death of her followers. This could refer to the death of Jezebel's 850 prophets in 1 Kings 18:40.

The woman of Revelation 2 is given a name, whereas the woman in Revelation 17 is not, but the two portraits are really very similar, and we can assume that they refer to the same "type" of character. In addition, we need not assume that there is a factual woman at work in these kinds of ways. Since cities are often referred to as feminine (Revelation 17:5; 18:2), we can imagine that the problem may encompass something far greater than one person could carry out on his or her own. The name Jezebel comes to symbolize some greater evil. In Revelation 18, the writer has given up referring to a woman altogether and now describes Babylon, yet the images used to describe the evils of Babylon are identical to those used to describe the woman in Revelation 17. In addition, Revelation 18:6 refers to the woman being "drunk with . . . the blood of those who were killed because of their faith in Jesus." This echoes Jezebel's murderous rampage against the prophets of Yahweh in 1 Kings 18.

Therefore, when we consider the contemporary connotations behind the word *Jezebel*, we must look beyond "adulterous." The Jezebel of Kings teaches us that it is not our religious vigor that is important, but rather our sole commitment to Yahweh. Like Jezebel, we, too, can be led astray or lead others astray when we follow our own gods and not the One True God. Her story then, leaves us with a warning and promise. Those who refuse to honor the Lord their God will not go unpunished.

Jezebel: For additional scriptures on this topic go to 1 Kings 16:31.

6 Then I watched while the Lamb opened the first of the seven seals. I heard one of the four living creatures say with a voice like thunder, "Come!" [2]I looked, and there before me was a white horse. The rider on the horse held a bow, and he was given a crown, and he rode out, determined to win the victory.

[3]When the Lamb opened the second seal, I heard the second living creature say, "Come!" [4]Then another horse came out, a red one. Its rider was given power to take away peace from the earth and to make people kill each other, and he was given a big sword.

[5]When the Lamb opened the third seal, I heard the third living creature say, "Come!" I looked, and there before me was a black horse, and its rider held a pair of scales in his hand. [6]Then I heard something that sounded like a voice coming from the middle of the four living creatures. The voice said, "A quart of wheat for a day's pay, and three quarts of barley for a day's pay, and do not damage the olive oil and wine!"

[7]When the Lamb opened the fourth seal, I heard the voice of the fourth living creature say, "Come!" [8]I looked, and there before me was a pale horse. Its rider was named death, and Hades was following close behind him. They were given power over a fourth of the earth to kill people by war, by starvation, by disease, and by the wild animals of the earth.

[9]When the Lamb opened the fifth seal, I saw under the altar the souls of those who had been killed because they were faithful to the word of God and to the message they had received. [10]These souls shouted in a loud voice, "Holy and true Lord, how long until you judge the people of the earth and punish them for killing us?" [11]Then each one of them was given a white robe and was told to wait a short time longer. There were still some of their fellow servants and brothers and sisters in the service of Christ who must be killed as they were. They had to wait until all of this was finished.

[12]Then I watched while the Lamb opened the sixth seal, and there was a great earthquake. The sun became black like rough black cloth, and the whole moon became red like blood. [13]And the stars in the sky fell to the earth like figs falling from a fig tree when the wind blows. [14]The sky disappeared as a scroll when it is rolled up, and every mountain and island was moved from its place.

[15]Then the kings of the earth, the rulers, the generals, the rich people, the powerful people, the slaves, and the free people hid themselves in caves and in the rocks on the mountains. [16]They called to the mountains and the rocks, "Fall on us. Hide us from the face of the One who sits on the throne and from the anger of the Lamb! [17]The great day for their anger has come, and who can stand against it?"

The 144,000 People of Israel

7 After the vision of these things I saw four angels standing at the four corners of the earth. The angels were holding the four winds of the earth to keep them from blowing on the land or on the sea or on any tree. [2]Then I saw another angel coming up from the east who had the seal of the living God. And he called out in a loud voice to the four angels to whom God had given power to harm the earth and the sea. [3]He said to them, "Do not harm the land or the sea or the trees until we mark with a sign the foreheads of the people who serve our God." [4]Then I heard how many people were marked with the sign. There were one hundred forty-four thousand from every tribe of the people of Israel.

[5]From the tribe of Judah twelve thousand were marked with the sign,
from the tribe of Reuben twelve thousand,
from the tribe of Gad twelve thousand,
[6]from the tribe of Asher twelve thousand,
from the tribe of Naphtali twelve thousand,
from the tribe of Manasseh twelve thousand,
[7]from the tribe of Simeon twelve thousand,
from the tribe of Levi twelve thousand,
from the tribe of Issachar twelve thousand,
[8]from the tribe of Zebulun twelve thousand,
from the tribe of Joseph twelve thousand,
and from the tribe of Benjamin twelve thousand were marked with the sign.

6:8 *Hades.* The unseen world of the dead.

6:11 *brothers and sisters.* Although the Greek text says "brothers" here and throughout this book, both men and women would have been included.

6:11 Sabbath: Revelation 14:13

6:16 Mountain: Revelation 16:17–21

7:4–9 John uses the number 144,000 in a symbolic way to draw attention to the faithful people from old Israel. To this number he immediately adds a countless group of people (7:9) from *every* nation, tribe, and so on. His vision, then, is of all God's people—whether Jewish or non-Jewish, from every culture, every language, every color—worshiping God together.

The Great Crowd Worships God

9After the vision of these things I looked, and there was a great number of people, so many that no one could count them. They were from every nation, tribe, people, and language of the earth. They were all standing before the throne and before the Lamb, wearing white robes and holding palm branches in their hands. 10They were shouting in a loud voice, "Salvation belongs to our God, who sits on the throne, and to the Lamb." 11All the angels were standing around the throne and the elders and the four living creatures. They all bowed down on their faces before the throne and worshiped God, 12saying, "Amen! Praise, glory, wisdom, thanks, honor, power, and strength belong to our God forever and ever. Amen!"

13Then one of the elders asked me, "Who are these people dressed in white robes? Where did they come from?"

14I answered, "You know, sir."

And the elder said to me, "These are the people who have come out of the great distress. They have washed their robes and made them white in the blood of the Lamb. 15Because of this, they are before the throne of God. They worship him day and night in his temple. And the One who sits on the throne will be present with them. 16Those people will never be hungry again, and they will never be thirsty again. The sun will not hurt them, and no heat will burn them, 17because the Lamb at the center of the throne will be their shepherd. He will lead them to springs of water that give life. And God will wipe away every tear from their eyes."

The Seventh Seal

8 When the Lamb opened the seventh seal, there was silence in heaven for about half an hour. 2And I saw the seven angels who stand before God and to whom were given seven trumpets.

3Another angel came and stood at the altar, holding a golden pan for incense. He was given much incense to offer with the prayers of all God's holy people. The angel put this offering on the golden altar before the throne. 4The smoke from the incense went up from the angel's hand to God with the prayers of God's people. 5Then the angel filled the incense pan with fire from the altar and threw it on the earth, and there were flashes of lightning, thunder and loud noises, and an earthquake.

The Seven Angels and Trumpets

6Then the seven angels who had the seven trumpets prepared to blow them.

7The first angel blew his trumpet, and hail and fire mixed with blood were poured down on the earth. And a third of the earth, and all the green grass, and a third of the trees were burned up.

8Then the second angel blew his trumpet, and something that looked like a big mountain, burning with fire, was thrown into the sea. And a third of the sea became blood, 9a third of the living things in the sea died, and a third of the ships were destroyed.

10Then the third angel blew his trumpet, and a large star, burning like a torch, fell from the sky. It fell on a third of the rivers and on the springs of water. 11The name of the star is Wormwood. And a third of all the water became bitter, and many people died from drinking the water that was bitter.

12Then the fourth angel blew his trumpet, and a third of the sun, and a third of the moon, and a third of the stars were struck. So a third of them became dark, and a third of the day was without light, and also the night.

13While I watched, I heard an eagle that was flying high in the air cry out in a loud voice, "Trouble! Trouble! Trouble for those who live on the earth because of the remaining sounds of the trumpets that the other three angels are about to blow!"

9 Then the fifth angel blew his trumpet, and I saw a star fall from the sky to the earth. The star was given the key to the deep hole that leads to the bottomless pit. 2Then it opened up the hole that leads to the bottomless pit, and smoke came up from the hole like smoke from a big furnace. Then the sun and sky became dark because of the smoke from the hole. 3Then locusts came down to the earth out of the smoke, and they were given the power to sting like scorpions. 4They were told not to harm the grass on the earth or any plant or tree. They could harm only the people who did not have the sign of God on their foreheads. 5These locusts were not given the power to kill anyone, but to cause pain to the people for five months. And the pain they felt was like the pain a scorpion gives when it stings someone. 6During those days people will look for a way to die, but they will not find it. They will want to die, but death will run away from them.

7The locusts looked like horses prepared for

7:14 *washed their robes.* This means they believed in Jesus so that their sins could be forgiven by Christ's blood.

7:16 Famine: Revelation 18:8

8:11 *Wormwood.* Name of a very bitter plant; used here to give the idea of bitter sorrow.

9:3 *scorpions.* A scorpion is an insect that stings with a bad poison.

9:4 Here and throughout Revelation, John emphasizes the question, To whom do you belong? The seal of God, or sign on the forehead, is a symbol of loyalty or faithfulness to God.

battle. On their heads they wore what looked like crowns of gold, and their faces looked like human faces. 8 Their hair was like women's hair, and their teeth were like lions' teeth. 9 Their chests looked like iron breastplates, and the sound of their wings was like the noise of many horses and chariots hurrying into battle. 10 The locusts had tails with stingers like scorpions, and in their tails was their power to hurt people for five months. 11 The locusts had a king who was the angel of the bottomless pit. His name in the Hebrew language is Abaddon and in the Greek language is Apollyon.

12 The first trouble is past; there are still two other troubles that will come.

13 Then the sixth angel blew his trumpet, and I heard a voice coming from the horns on the golden altar that is before God. 14 The voice said to the sixth angel who had the trumpet, "Free the four angels who are tied at the great river Euphrates." 15 And they let loose the four angels who had been kept ready for this hour and day and month and year so they could kill a third of all people on the earth. 16 I heard how many troops on horses were in their army—two hundred million.

17 The horses and their riders I saw in the vision looked like this: They had breastplates that were fiery red, dark blue, and yellow like sulfur. The heads of the horses looked like heads of lions, with fire, smoke, and sulfur coming out of their mouths. 18 A third of all the people on earth were killed by these three terrible disasters coming out of the horses' mouths: the fire, the smoke, and the sulfur. 19 The horses' power was in their mouths and in their tails; their tails were like snakes with heads, and with them they hurt people.

20 The other people who were not killed by these terrible disasters still did not change their hearts and turn away from what they had made with their own hands. They did not stop worshiping demons and idols made of gold, silver, bronze, stone, and wood—things that cannot see or hear or walk. 21 These people did not change their hearts and turn away from murder or evil magic, from their sexual sins or stealing.

The Angel and the Small Scroll

10 Then I saw another powerful angel coming down from heaven dressed in a cloud with a rainbow over his head. His face was like the sun, and his legs were like pillars of fire. 2 The angel was holding a small scroll open in his hand. He put his right foot on the sea and his left foot on the land. 3 Then he shouted loudly like the roaring of a lion. And when he shouted, the voices of seven thunders spoke. 4 When the seven thunders spoke, I started to write. But I heard a voice from heaven say, "Keep hidden what the seven thunders said, and do not write them down."

5 Then the angel I saw standing on the sea and on the land raised his right hand to heaven, 6 and he made a promise by the power of the One who lives forever and ever. He is the One who made the skies and all that is in them, the earth and all that is in it, and the sea and all that is in it. The angel promised, "There will be no more waiting! 7 In the days when the seventh angel is ready to blow his trumpet, God's secret will be finished. This secret is the Good News God told to his servants, the prophets."

8 Then I heard the same voice from heaven again, saying to me: "Go and take the open scroll that is in the hand of the angel that is standing on the sea and on the land."

9 So I went to the angel and told him to give me the small scroll. And he said to me, "Take the scroll and eat it. It will be sour in your stomach, but in your mouth it will be sweet as honey." 10 So I took the small scroll from the angel's hand and ate it. In my mouth it tasted sweet as honey, but after I ate it, it was sour in my stomach. 11 Then I was told, "You must prophesy again about many peoples, nations, languages, and kings."

The Two Witnesses

11 I was given a measuring stick like a rod, and I was told, "Go and measure the temple of God and the altar, and count the people worshiping there. 2 But do not measure the yard outside the temple. Leave it alone, because it has been given to those who are not God's people. And they will trample on the holy city for forty-two months. 3 And I will give power to my two witnesses to prophesy for one thousand two hundred sixty days, and they will be dressed in rough cloth to show their sadness."

4 These two witnesses are the two olive trees and the two lampstands that stand before the Lord of the earth. 5 And if anyone tries to hurt them, fire comes from their mouths and kills their enemies. And if anyone tries to hurt them in whatever way, in that same way that person will die. 6 These witnesses have the power to stop the sky from raining during the time they are prophesying. And they have power to make the waters become blood, and

9:11 *Abaddon, Apollyon.* Both names mean "Destroyer."
9:17 Vision: See article on page 309.
9:21 Murder: Revelation 21:8

they have power to send every kind of trouble to
the earth as many times as they want.
7When the two witnesses have finished telling
their message, the beast that comes up from the
bottomless pit will fight a war against them. He
will defeat them and kill them. 8The bodies of the
two witnesses will lie in the street of the great city
where the Lord was killed. This city is named
Sodom and Egypt, which has a spiritual meaning.
9Those from every race of people, tribe, language,
and nation will look at the bodies of the two witnesses for three and one-half days, and they will
refuse to bury them. 10People who live on the earth
will rejoice and be happy because these two are
dead. They will send each other gifts, because these
two prophets brought much suffering to those who
live on the earth.
11But after three and one-half days, God put the
breath of life into the two prophets again. They
stood on their feet, and everyone who saw them
became very afraid. 12Then the two prophets heard
a loud voice from heaven saying, "Come up here!"
And they went up into heaven in a cloud as their
enemies watched.
13In the same hour there was a great earthquake,
and a tenth of the city was destroyed. Seven thousand people were killed in the earthquake, and
those who did not die were very afraid and gave
glory to the God of heaven.
14The second trouble is finished. Pay attention:
The third trouble is coming soon.

The Seventh Trumpet

15Then the seventh angel blew his trumpet. And
there were loud voices in heaven, saying:
"The power to rule the world
now belongs to our Lord and his Christ,
and he will rule forever and ever."
16Then the twenty-four elders, who sit on their
thrones before God, bowed down on their faces
and worshiped God. 17They said:
"We give thanks to you, Lord God Almighty,
who is and who was,
because you have used your great power
and have begun to rule!
18The people of the world were angry,
but your anger has come.
The time has come to judge the dead,
and to reward your servants the prophets
and your holy people,
all who respect you, great and small.
The time has come to destroy those who
destroy the earth!"
19Then God's temple in heaven was opened.
The Ark that holds the agreement God gave to his
people could be seen in his temple. Then there
were flashes of lightning, noises, thunder, an
earthquake, and a great hailstorm.

The Woman and the Dragon

12 And then a great wonder appeared in heav-
en: A woman was clothed with the sun,
and the moon was under her feet, and a crown of
twelve stars was on her head. 2She was pregnant
and cried out with pain, because she was about to
give birth. 3Then another wonder appeared in
heaven: There was a giant red dragon with seven
heads and seven crowns on each head. He also
had ten horns. 4His tail swept a third of the stars
out of the sky and threw them down to the earth.
He stood in front of the woman who was ready to
give birth so he could eat her baby as soon as it was
born. 5Then the woman gave birth to a son who
will rule all the nations with an iron rod. And her
child was taken up to God and to his throne. 6The
woman ran away into the desert to a place God
prepared for her where she would be taken care of
for one thousand two hundred sixty days.
7Then there was a war in heaven. Michael and
his angels fought against the dragon, and the dragon
and his angels fought back. 8But the dragon was
not strong enough, and he and his angels lost their
place in heaven. 9The giant dragon was thrown
down out of heaven. (He is that old snake called the
devil or Satan, who tricks the whole world.) The
dragon with his angels was thrown down to the
earth.
10Then I heard a loud voice in heaven saying:
"The salvation and the power and the kingdom
of our God
and the authority of his Christ have now come.
The accuser of our brothers and sisters,
who accused them day and night
before our God,
has been thrown down.
11And our brothers and sisters defeated him

11:8 *Sodom.* City that God destroyed because the people were so evil.

11:7–11 That the evil beast only now makes his first appearance in Revelation indicates John's special interest in images of victory over evil. Nevertheless, evil must be reckoned with, and here evil apparently wins over the two witnesses, who probably represent the whole people of God. Their defeat is emphasized by the fact that they are denied burial, a great dishonor in the ancient world. But by "breath of life" (11:11), John means "resurrection."

11:17 Thanks: See article on page 1102.

11:18 Praise: Revelation 12:10–12

12:6 Wilderness (Desert): Revelation 12:14

12:7 Angels: See article on page 519.

12:7 *Michael.* The archangel—leader among God's angels or messengers (Jude 9).

by the blood of the Lamb's death
and by the message they preached.
They did not love their lives so much
that they were afraid of death.
12So rejoice, you heavens
and all who live there!
But it will be terrible for the earth and the sea,
because the devil has come down to you!
He is filled with anger,
because he knows he does not
have much time."

13When the dragon saw he had been thrown
down to the earth, he hunted for the woman who
had given birth to the son. 14But the woman was
given the two wings of a great eagle so she could fly
to the place prepared for her in the desert. There
she would be taken care of for three and one-half
years, away from the snake. 15Then the snake
poured water out of its mouth like a river toward
the woman so the flood would carry her away.
16But the earth helped the woman by opening its
mouth and swallowing the river that came from
the mouth of the dragon. 17Then the dragon was
very angry at the woman, and he went off to make
war against all her other children—those who
obey God's commands and who have the message
Jesus taught.

18And the dragon stood on the seashore.

The Two Beasts

13 Then I saw a beast coming up out of the sea.
It had ten horns and seven heads, and
there was a crown on each horn. A name against
God was written on each head. 2This beast
looked like a leopard, with feet like a bear's feet
and a mouth like a lion's mouth. And the dragon
gave the beast all of his power and his throne and
great authority. 3One of the heads of the beast
looked as if it had been killed by a wound, but
this death wound was healed. Then the whole
world was amazed and followed the beast.
4People worshiped the dragon because he had
given his power to the beast. And they also worshiped the beast, asking, "Who is like the beast?
Who can make war against it?"

5The beast was allowed to say proud words and
words against God, and it was allowed to use its
power for forty-two months. 6It used its mouth to
speak against God, against God's name, against the
place where God lives, and against all those who
live in heaven. 7It was given power to make war
against God's holy people and to defeat them. It was
given power over every tribe, people, language, and
nation. 8And all who live on earth will worship the
beast—all the people since the beginning of the
world whose names are not written in the Lamb's
book of life. The Lamb is the One who was killed.

9Anyone who has ears should listen:
10If you are to be a prisoner,
then you will be a prisoner.
If you are to be killed with the sword,
then you will be killed with the sword.
This means that God's holy people must have
patience and faith.

11Then I saw another beast coming up out of the
earth. It had two horns like a lamb, but it spoke
like a dragon. 12This beast stands before the first
beast and uses the same power the first beast has.
By this power it makes everyone living on earth
worship the first beast, who had the death wound
that was healed. 13And the second beast does great
miracles so that it even makes fire come down
from heaven to earth while people are watching.
14It fools those who live on earth by the miracles it
has been given the power to do. It does these miracles to serve the first beast. The second beast
orders people to make an idol to honor the first
beast, the one that was wounded by the deadly
sword but sprang to life again. 15The second beast
was given power to give life to the idol of the first
one so that the idol could speak. And the second
beast was given power to command all who will
not worship the image of the beast to be killed.
16The second beast also forced all people, small
and great, rich and poor, free and slave, to have
a mark on their right hand or on their forehead.
17No one could buy or sell without this mark,
which is the name of the beast or the number of
its name. 18This takes wisdom. Let the one who
has understanding find the meaning of the number, which is the number of a person. Its number
is six hundred sixty-six.

12:12 Praise: Revelation 15:3–4
12:14 Wilderness (Desert): Revelation 17:3
12:15 Flood: See article on page 90.
13 The Book of Revelation never uses the term "antichrist," or "enemy of Christ" but the beast from the sea is clearly portrayed in this role. He has crowns, like Jesus (13:1; 19:12), and ungodly names in opposition to Jesus' honorable names (13:1; 19:11–13, 16). He exercises the power of Satan (13:2), just as Jesus exercises God's power (12:5, 10). He causes people to worship Satan, just as Jesus directs people to worship God (1:6). Just as Jesus died and was raised to life, so the beast of the sea has a death-wound from which it has been healed (13:3). The beast claims to exercise absolute power and so requires that people honor him.
13:1 Blasphemy: See article on page 741.
13:10 Persecution: Revelation 17:1–6
13:11–16 John portrays Rome as the beast from the earth (see 17:9; Rome was known as "the city on seven hills"). The beast from the earth, then, probably represents the temples and worship set up to worship the Roman emperor and the goddess of Rome, *Roma*.
13:18 Many have tried to work out the meaning of this number 666.

The Song of the Saved

14 Then I looked, and there before me was the
Lamb standing on Mount Zion. With him
were one hundred forty-four thousand people who
had his name and his Father's name written on
their foreheads. 2And I heard a sound from heaven
like the noise of flooding water and like the sound
of loud thunder. The sound I heard was like people
playing harps. 3And they sang a new song before
the throne and before the four living creatures and
the elders. No one could learn the new song except
the one hundred forty-four thousand who had been
bought from the earth. 4These are the ones who did
not do sinful things with women, because they kept
themselves pure. They follow the Lamb every place
he goes. These one hundred forty-four thousand
were bought from among the people of the earth as
people to be offered to God and the Lamb. 5They
were not guilty of telling lies; they are without fault.

The Three Angels

6Then I saw another angel flying high in the air.
He had the eternal Good News to preach to those
who live on earth—to every nation, tribe, language,
and people. 7He preached in a loud voice, "Fear
God and give him praise, because the time has
come for God to judge all people. So worship God
who made the heavens, and the earth, and the sea,
and the springs of water."

8Then the second angel followed the first angel
and said, "Ruined, ruined is the great city of
Babylon! She made all the nations drink the wine
of the anger of her adultery."

9Then a third angel followed the first two angels,
saying in a loud voice: "If anyone worships the
beast and his idol and gets the beast's mark on the
forehead or on the hand, 10that one also will drink
the wine of God's anger, which is prepared with
all its strength in the cup of his anger. And that person will be put in pain with burning sulfur before
the holy angels and the Lamb. 11And the smoke
from their burning pain will rise forever and ever.
There will be no rest, day or night, for those who
worship the beast and his idol or who get the mark
of his name." 12This means God's holy people must
be patient. They must obey God's commands and
keep their faith in Jesus.

13Then I heard a voice from heaven saying,
"Write this: Happy are the dead who die from now
on in the Lord."

The Spirit says, "Yes, they will rest from their
hard work, and the reward of all they have done
stays with them."

The Earth Is Harvested

14Then I looked, and there before me was a
white cloud, and sitting on the white cloud was
One who looked like a Son of Man. He had a gold
crown on his head and a sharp sickle in his hand.
15Then another angel came out of the temple and
called out in a loud voice to the One who was sitting on the cloud, "Take your sickle and harvest
from the earth, because the time to harvest has
come, and the fruit of the earth is ripe." 16So the
One who was sitting on the cloud swung his sickle
over the earth, and the earth was harvested.

17Then another angel came out of the temple in
heaven, and he also had a sharp sickle. 18And
then another angel, who has power over the fire,
came from the altar. This angel called to the angel
with the sharp sickle, saying, "Take your sharp
sickle and gather the bunches of grapes from the
earth's vine, because its grapes are ripe." 19Then
the angel swung his sickle over the earth. He
gathered the earth's grapes and threw them into
the great winepress of God's anger. 20They were

The number 666 is also the name of the beast according to verse 17. Accordingly the letters of many names have been added up over the centuries to determine who was meant. (Both Greek and Hebrew speaking people used the letters of their alphabets as a numbering system, much as Roman numerals are sometimes used on clocks or in movie credits.) The Roman Caesar Nero is probably the most famous of these "guesses." But this passage should probably be read in connection with Revelation 19:11–16. Here, Jesus has written on his robe and upper leg "KING OF KINGS AND LORD OF LORDS" for which the numerical value of the letters may be interpreted to be 777. It should not be of great concern that the meaning of 666 is disputed. One should remember that in chapter 13 a *clue* is given, 666. In chapter 19 the *answer* is given, "KING OF KINGS AND LORD OF LORDS."

14:1 *Mount Zion.* Another name for Jerusalem; here meaning the spiritual city of God's people.

14:8 Alcohol: Revelation 14:10

14:9–11 This passage contains some important facts about hell. First, the people who deserve divine anger and punishment are those who worship the beast (14:9), who receives power and authority from Satan (13:2). As followers of Satan in rebellion against God, they receive the "beast's mark on the forehead or on the hand" (14:9). Second, their fate is to drink the "wine of God's anger, which is prepared with all its strength in the cup of his anger" (14:10). In the Old Testament, the cup of God's anger was reserved for the rebellious Israelites (Isaiah 51:17–23) and for the nations which were against God's people (Jeremiah 25:15–29). This same cup is described here as a punishment for those who belong to the beast. Third, the severity of this punishment goes beyond our imagination. It is painful because it is described as being put into "burning sulfur" (14:10). Fourth, this punishment is not instant death, or annihilation; the burning pain will "rise forever and ever. There will be no rest, day or night, for those who worship the beast and his idol or who get the mark of his name" (14:11).

14:10 Alcohol: Revelation 17:1–2

14:13 Beatitudes: See article on page 701.

14:13 Sabbath: See article on page 244.

14:14 *Son of Man.* "Son of Man" is a name Jesus called himself. See dictionary.

14:14 *sickle.* A farming tool with a curved blade. It was used to harvest grain.

trampled in the winepress outside the city, and
blood flowed out of the winepress as high as
horses' bridles for a distance of about one hundred eighty miles.

The Last Troubles

15 Then I saw another wonder in heaven that
was great and amazing. There were seven
angels bringing seven disasters. These are the last
disasters, because after them, God's anger is
finished.
2I saw what looked like a sea of glass mixed with
fire. All of those who had won the victory over the
beast and his idol and over the number of his name
were standing by the sea of glass. They had harps
that God had given them. 3They sang the song of
Moses, the servant of God, and the song of the
Lamb:

"You do great and wonderful things, *Psalm 111:2*
  Lord God Almighty. *Amos 3:13*
Everything the Lord does is right and true, *Psalm 145:17*
  King of the nations.
4Everyone will respect you, Lord, *Jeremiah 10:7*
  and will honor you.
Only you are holy.
All the nations will come
  and worship you, *Psalm 86:9-10*
because the right things you have done
  are now made known." *Deuteronomy 32:4*

5After this I saw that the temple (the Tent of
the Agreement) in heaven was opened. 6And the
seven angels bringing the seven disasters came
out of the temple. They were dressed in clean,
shining linen and wore golden bands tied around
their chests. 7Then one of the four living creatures gave to the seven angels seven golden
bowls filled with the anger of God, who lives forever and ever. 8The temple was filled with smoke
from the glory and the power of God, and no one
could enter the temple until the seven disasters of
the seven angels were finished.

The Bowls of God's Anger

16 Then I heard a loud voice from the temple
saying to the seven angels, "Go and pour
out the seven bowls of God's anger on the earth."
2The first angel left and poured out his bowl on
the land. Then ugly and painful sores came upon
all those who had the mark of the beast and who
worshiped his idol.
3The second angel poured out his bowl on the
sea, and it became blood like that of a dead man,
and every living thing in the sea died.
4The third angel poured out his bowl on the
rivers and the springs of water, and they became
blood. 5Then I heard the angel of the waters saying:

"Holy One, you are the One who
  is and who was.
You are right to decide to punish
  these evil people.
6They have poured out the blood of your holy
  people and your prophets.
So now you have given them blood to drink
  as they deserve."

7And I heard a voice coming from the altar saying:

"Yes, Lord God Almighty,
  the way you punish evil people is
  right and fair."

8The fourth angel poured out his bowl on the
sun, and he was given power to burn the people
with fire. 9They were burned by the great heat,
and they cursed the name of God, who had control
over these disasters. But the people refused to
change their hearts and lives and give glory to God.
10The fifth angel poured out his bowl on the
throne of the beast, and darkness covered its
kingdom. People gnawed their tongues because
of the pain. 11They also cursed the God of heaven
because of their pain and the sores they had, but
they refused to change their hearts and turn away
from the evil things they did.
12The sixth angel poured out his bowl on the
great river Euphrates so that the water in the river
was dried up to prepare the way for the kings from
the east to come. 13Then I saw three evil spirits
that looked like frogs coming out of the mouth of
the dragon, out of the mouth of the beast, and out
of the mouth of the false prophet. 14These evil
spirits are the spirits of demons, which have
power to do miracles. They go out to the kings of
the whole world to gather them together for the
battle on the great day of God Almighty.
15"Listen! I will come as a thief comes! Happy
are those who stay awake and keep their clothes
on so that they will not walk around naked and
have people see their shame."
16Then the evil spirits gathered the kings
together to the place that is called Armageddon in
the Hebrew language.
17The seventh angel poured out his bowl into the
air. Then a loud voice came out of the temple from
the throne, saying, "It is finished!" 18Then there
were flashes of lightning, noises, thunder, and a big

15:4 Praise: See article on page 500.
15:4 Unity: See article on page 1273.
16:6 Martyrdom: Revelation 17:6
16:14 Day of the Lord: See article on page 661.

earthquake—the worst earthquake that has ever
happened since people have been on earth. 19The
great city split into three parts, and the cities of the
nations were destroyed. And God remembered the
sins of Babylon the Great, so he gave that city the
cup filled with the wine of his terrible anger.
20Then every island ran away, and mountains disappeared. 21Giant hailstones, each weighing about
a hundred pounds, fell from the sky upon people.
People cursed God for the disaster of the hail,
because this disaster was so terrible.

The Woman on the Animal

17 Then one of the seven angels who had the
seven bowls came and spoke to me. He said,
"Come, and I will show you the punishment that
will be given to the great prostitute, the one sitting
over many waters. 2The kings of the earth sinned
sexually with her, and the people of the earth
became drunk from the wine of her sexual sin."

3Then the angel carried me away by the Spirit
to the desert. There I saw a woman sitting on a red
beast. It was covered with names against God written on it, and it had seven heads and ten horns.
4The woman was dressed in purple and red and
was shining with the gold, precious jewels, and
pearls she was wearing. She had a golden cup in
her hand, a cup filled with evil things and the
uncleanness of her sexual sin. 5On her forehead a
title was written that was secret. This is what was
written:

THE GREAT BABYLON
MOTHER OF PROSTITUTES
AND OF THE EVIL THINGS OF THE EARTH

6Then I saw that the woman was drunk with the
blood of God's holy people and with the blood of
those who were killed because of their faith in
Jesus.

When I saw the woman, I was very amazed.
7Then the angel said to me, "Why are you amazed?
I will tell you the secret of this woman and the
beast she rides—the one with seven heads and ten
horns. 8The beast you saw was once alive but is not
alive now. But soon it will come up out of the bottomless pit and go away to be destroyed. There are
people who live on earth whose names have not
been written in the book of life since the beginning
of the world. They will be amazed when they see
the beast, because he was once alive, is not alive
now, but will come again.

9"You need a wise mind to understand this. The
seven heads on the beast are seven mountains where
the woman sits. 10And they are seven kings. Five
of the kings have already been destroyed, one of
the kings lives now, and another has not yet come.
When he comes, he must stay a short time. 11The
beast that was once alive, but is not alive now, is
also an eighth king. He belongs to the first seven
kings, and he will go away to be destroyed.

12"The ten horns you saw are ten kings who have
not yet begun to rule, but they will receive power to
rule with the beast for one hour. 13All ten of these
kings have the same purpose, and they will give
their power and authority to the beast. 14They will
make war against the Lamb, but the Lamb will
defeat them, because he is Lord of lords and King
of kings. He will defeat them with his called, chosen, and faithful followers."

15Then the angel said to me, "The waters that
you saw, where the prostitute sits, are peoples,
races, nations, and languages. 16The ten horns and
the beast you saw will hate the prostitute. They will
take everything she has and leave her naked. They
will eat her body and burn her with fire. 17God
made the ten horns want to carry out his purpose
by agreeing to give the beast their power to rule,
until what God has said comes about. 18The
woman you saw is the great city that rules over the
kings of the earth."

Babylon Is Destroyed

18 After the vision of these things, I saw
another angel coming down from heaven.
This angel had great power, and his glory made
the earth bright. 2He shouted in a powerful voice:

"Ruined, ruined is the great city of Babylon!
She has become a home for demons
and a prison for every evil spirit,
and a prison for every unclean bird and
unclean beast.
3She has been ruined, because all the
peoples of the earth
have drunk the wine of the desire of
her sexual sin.

16:19 Babylon: Revelation 17:5
16:21 God's Anger: See article on page 1092.
16:21 Mountain: Revelation 17:9
16:21 Tongue: See article on page 1274.
17:2 Alcohol: See article on page 520.
17:3 Wilderness (Desert): See article on page 812.
17:5 Babylon: Revelation 18:2
17:6 Martyrdom: Revelation 20:4–6
17:6 Persecution: Revelation 20:4–6
17:9 Mountain: See article on page 346.
17:18 Jezebel: See article on page 1500.

18:2 God has appointed a day to destroy everything that competes with him for first place in people's lives. The city Babylon was the capital of idolatry in the Old Testament world. It also serves as a symbol for every kind of idol. The destruction of Babylon symbolizes the removal of all idolatry when God sets up his kingdom on the new earth.

18:2 Babylon: Revelation 18:10

Cults

Revelation 9:20

New religious movements seem to be springing up all around us; how do we know whether they really represent the truth? What does the Bible have to say about cults?

Whether we are walking through airports, relaxing at home on Saturday morning, or watching the evening news, the chances are good that, from time to time, people and ideas from various cults will intersect our lives. Sometimes this seems rather harmless, such as when we are asked for a donation or invited to discuss religion on our doorsteps. At other times—one has only to recall those news items of recent decades focusing on people like David Koresh or Jim Jones—the activity of cults takes on a more sinister look.

During much of Israel's early life, the lure of cults was not a significant matter. To be sure, Israel had constantly to be reminded to stay true to its God and not to pursue the ways of their neighbors and their gods (see, for example, Deuteronomy 13, 18). But here the problem is following after a false religion, after false gods, not distinguishing the message of a cult from the message of genuine faith. In fact, one of the most distressing dilemmas presented by cults today lies here, in the reality that they are not easily perceived as false religion. Instead, these new religious movements typically build on traditional faith. Contemporary cults usually have deep roots in biblical faith, often refer to the Bible, and may even speak well of Jesus. As a consequence, they are not easily recognized as false religions; indeed, newer religious movements—whether one is thinking of Mormonism, the Jehovah Witnesses, or smaller and more recent groups—often present themselves as representatives of authentic Christianity.

Even more importantly, cults seem to meet needs in genuinely Christian ways. For example, many new religious movements are fundamentally experience-based; this means that many of their members are able to bear witness to their faith: "When I joined this group," they might say, "My needs were met!" In addition, new religious movements may foster values that seem well-grounded in Christianity, such as the importance of family; or they may emphasize prayer, meditation, and similar practices that Christians will also support. Cults also place a high emphasis on finding one's identity in the group, making a clear separation between "us" (who belong) and "them" (outsiders, who do not understand the truth). People seeking close-knit relationships and a heightened sense of belonging—again, hallmarks of genuinely Christian fellowship—might be drawn to new religious groups. Still further, cults often provide well-formulated answers to the many religious questions with which people struggle today. On intellectual, spiritual, and social grounds, then, these new religious movements seem to have much to offer; they seem to provide a genuine experience of God.

Just because in its earliest days Israel had to be concerned more with distinguishing itself from neighboring religions than with counterfeit versions of its own faith does not mean that this would always be the case. Israel's prophets were often called upon to speak against other prophets—that is, against people claiming to speak for the Lord God, but whose message was not genuine (see Amos or Micah). Among the variety of ways Jewish people experienced faith in God in the first century, Christianity itself must have seemed what we today call a "cult" or "new religious movement" to some (see Acts 24:14).

More to the point, as the Christian faith developed in the first century it saw the development of offshoots that we today might regard as cultic in nature. This is evident especially in 1 John, which asks, Who are the genuine Christians? What is authentic Christian faith?

It is in the context of such questions, both in Acts and 1 John, that one begins to see clearly how to differentiate true Christianity from its forgeries. This can be summarized by drawing attention to three emphases. First, Luke highlights throughout the Book of Acts how important it is for one's faith to be grounded in the purpose of God as this is revealed in the Scriptures. Those who spoke for the truth of Christian faith did so in part by showing that God had not suddenly changed his mind. Instead, the Scriptures as a whole point to their realization in Christ and in those who serve him. Second, both Luke and John underscore the importance of holding at the center of one's faith Jesus Christ. For the Book of Acts, this is often related to the necessity of his death and the significance of his resurrection, while in 1 John, Jesus' incarnation (the coming of God as a real human being) is stressed. New religious movements often distinguish themselves from biblical Christianity by their de-emphasis on the centrality of Jesus to God's plan of salvation. Third, 1 John in particular places a heavy emphasis on love for one another and obedience to God—that is, on being Christlike in our relationships toward God and toward one another.

Cults: For additional scriptures on this topic go to Deuteronomy 13.

BABYLON

REVELATION 14:8

What is Babylon? How does Babylon behave in the Bible? Does "Babylon" have any significance in the Bible beyond merely being the name of a nation?

Babylon was certainly one of the biggest and most important cities of the ancient biblical world. In the Old Testament, Babylon (along with Assyria and Egypt) is depicted as Israel's archenemy. At times, however, Babylon is used by the Lord to punish the Israelites when they are unfaithful. When taken as a whole, and especially in light of the Book of Revelation, Babylon seems to represent the forces that are opposed to God.

Babylon is first mentioned in Genesis 10:10 as one of the four cities founded by a certain Nimrod, "a great hunter before the Lord" (10:9). Nimrod was a descendent of Ham, one of Noah's three sons. This mention of Babylon sets the stage for the famous Tower of Babel story (Genesis 11:1–9). All the peoples of the world gathered in Babylonia (also called Babel) and decided to build a high tower. God thwarts their plans, and punishes them by confusing their language "so they will not be able to understand each other" (verse 7). We can see already in this first mention of Babylon how it represents more than just a nation, but forces that are opposed to God.

Babylon, however, becomes a major player in the Bible only later on. During Isaiah's day Babylon begins to pose a threat to Israel. Babylon is seen as a mighty invader bent on destroying Israel. Two of Isaiah's messages are directed against Babylon and predict her eventual destruction (Isaiah 13:1–113;14:1–8; 21:1–16). Isaiah 13:19 and 21:9 speak of Babylon's impending destruction this way: "Babylon has fallen. It has fallen!" This is precisely the language used in Revelation 14:8 and 18:2, but there it most likely refers not to literal Babylon but to the forces of Satan.

Babylon becomes most prominent in the Old Testament during the time of the Babylonian Captivity (597–539 B.C.). During the period in Israel's history when kings ruled (beginning with Saul and David and lasting over 300 years), the Israelites fell further away from trusting God and obeying his commandments. They even turned their backs on God and worshiped the gods of the nations that surrounded them. The fitting punishment for God's disobedient people was to send them into exile under idolatrous Babylon.

The utter dismay the Israelites felt at being banished from Israel, is seen in Psalm 137: "By the rivers of Babylon we sat and cried when we remembered Jerusalem" (verse 1). "We cannot sing songs about the Lord while we are in this foreign country" (verse 4). The intensity of the hatred the Israelites felt toward their archenemy is expressed in graphic and even disturbing terms in verses 8 and 9: "People of Babylon, you will be destroyed. The people who pay you back for what you did to us will be happy. They will grab your babies and throw them against the rocks."

With such intense feelings toward Babylon, we can see why the prophet Habakkuk would want to question why God would use the Babylonians, of all people, to punish the Israelites. In Habakkuk 1:1–4, the prophet calls upon God to step in and put an end to the oppression the Israelites are experiencing at the hand of their own leaders. God responds in verses 5–11 that he would punish the Israelites by bringing upon them "the Babylonians, those cruel and wild people" (verse 6). Habakkuk responds in utter disbelief: How can God allow "the wicked swallow up people who are better than they" (verse 13)? The Lord responds in chapters 2 and 3 that Babylon's triumph will be short lived: "The cup of anger from the Lord's right hand is coming around to you. You will receive disgrace, not respect" (2:16).

Although God used the Babylonians to punish his disobedient people, the fate of the Babylonians is nevertheless firmly in God's hand. Their ultimate destiny is never in doubt. We see this not only in Habakkuk and Isaiah, but in Jeremiah as well (chapters 50 and 51). Although Jeremiah has much to say against other nations, the bulk of his words is directed against Babylon and her impending destruction.

The only significant mention of Babylon in the New Testament is in the Book of Revelation (14:8; 16:19; 17:5; 18:2, 10, 21). The Lord's ultimate victory over evil is depicted as the defeat of Babylon. Once again, Israel's archenemy meets her end, but here the nation itself is not in view, but all the forces, led by Satan, that pit themselves against the power of the Lord. This is the "Babylon" that God's people have had to contend with for all time, but whose ultimate destruction has been just as sure as that of the nation spoken of by the Old Testament prophets. The risen Christ holds the scepter of power and Babylon is defeated. "Ruined, ruined is the great city of Babylon" (Revelation 18:2).⚭

⚭**Babylon:** For additional scriptures on this topic go to Genesis 10:10.

She has been ruined also because the
kings of the earth
have sinned sexually with her,
and the merchants of the earth
have grown rich from the great
wealth of her luxury."

4Then I heard another voice from heaven saying:
"Come out of that city, my people,
so that you will not share in her sins,
so that you will not receive the disasters that
will come to her.
5Her sins have piled up as high as the sky,
and God has not forgotten the wrongs
she has done.
6Give that city the same as she gave to others.
Pay her back twice as much as she did.
Prepare wine for her that is twice as strong
as the wine she prepared for others.
7She gave herself much glory and rich living.
Give her that much suffering and sadness.
She says to herself, 'I am a queen sitting
on my throne.
I am not a widow; I will never be sad.'
8So these disasters will come to her in one day:
death, and crying, and great hunger,
and she will be destroyed by fire,
because the Lord God who judges her
is powerful."⚭

9The kings of the earth who sinned sexually with
her and shared her wealth will see the smoke from
her burning. Then they will cry and be sad because
of her death. 10They will be afraid of her suffering
and stand far away and say:
"Terrible! How terrible for you, great city,
powerful city of Babylon,
because your punishment has come
in one hour!"⚭

11And the merchants of the earth will cry and be
sad about her, because now there is no one to buy
their cargoes— 12cargoes of gold, silver, jewels,
pearls, fine linen, purple cloth, silk, red cloth; all
kinds of citron wood and all kinds of things made
from ivory, expensive wood, bronze, iron, and
marble; 13cinnamon, spice, incense, myrrh, frankincense, wine, olive oil, fine flour, wheat, cattle,
sheep, horses, carriages, slaves, and human lives.
14The merchants will say,
"Babylon, the good things you wanted are
gone from you.
All your rich and fancy things have disappeared.
You will never have them again."
15The merchants who became rich from selling to
her will be afraid of her suffering and will stand
far away. They will cry and be sad 16and say:
"Terrible! How terrible for the great city!
She was dressed in fine linen, purple
and red cloth,
and she was shining with gold, precious
jewels, and pearls!
17All these riches have been destroyed
in one hour!"

Every sea captain, every passenger, the sailors,
and all those who earn their living from the sea
stood far away from Babylon. 18As they saw the
smoke from her burning, they cried out loudly,
"There was never a city like this great city!" 19And
they threw dust on their heads and cried out,
weeping and being sad. They said:
"Terrible! How terrible for the great city!
All the people who had ships on the sea
became rich because of her wealth!
But she has been destroyed in one hour!
20Be happy because of this, heaven!
Be happy, God's holy people and apostles
and prophets!
God has punished her because of what she did
to you."

21Then a powerful angel picked up a large stone,
like one used for grinding grain, and threw it into
the sea. He said:
"In the same way, the great city of Babylon
will be thrown down,
and it will never be found again.⚭
22The music of people playing harps and other
instruments, flutes, and trumpets,
will never be heard in you again.
No workman doing any job
will ever be found in you again.
The sound of grinding grain
will never be heard in you again.
23The light of a lamp
will never shine in you again,
and the voices of a bridegroom and bride
will never be heard in you again.
Your merchants were the world's great people,
and all the nations were tricked by your magic.
24You are guilty of the death of the prophets and
God's holy people
and all who have been killed on earth."⚭

18:3 Rome controlled the seas and the buying and selling of goods. John is calling attention to the misuse of wealth and power by Rome. One ancient historian wrote, "When Rome creates a desert, they call it peace."

⚭**18:8 Famine:** See article on page 190.

⚭**18:10 Babylon:** Revelation 18:21

⚭**18:21 Babylon:** See article on page 1510.

⚭**18:24 Materialism/Possessions:** See article on page 946.

⚭**18:24 Money:** See article on page 933.

People in Heaven Praise God

19 After this vision and announcement I heard
what sounded like a great many people in
heaven saying:

"Hallelujah!
Salvation, glory, and power belong to our God,
2 because his judgments are true and right.
He has punished the prostitute
who made the earth evil with
her sexual sin.
He has paid her back for the death of
his servants."

3 Again they said:

"Hallelujah!
She is burning, and her smoke will rise
forever and ever."

4 Then the twenty-four elders and the four living
creatures bowed down and worshiped God, who
sits on the throne. They said:

"Amen, Hallelujah!"

5 Then a voice came from the throne, saying:

"Praise our God, all you who serve him
and all you who honor him,
both small and great!"

6 Then I heard what sounded like a great many
people, like the noise of flooding water, and like
the noise of loud thunder. The people were
saying:

"Hallelujah!
Our Lord God, the Almighty, rules.
7 Let us rejoice and be happy
and give God glory,
because the wedding of the Lamb has come,
and the Lamb's bride has made herself ready.
8 Fine linen, bright and clean, was given to her
to wear."

(The fine linen means the good things done by
God's holy people.)

9 And the angel said to me, "Write this: Happy
are those who have been invited to the wedding
meal of the Lamb!" And the angel said, "These are
the true words of God."

10 Then I bowed down at the angel's feet to worship him, but he said to me, "Do not worship me!
I am a servant like you and your brothers and sisters who have the message of Jesus. Worship God,
because the message about Jesus is the spirit that
gives all prophecy."

The Rider on the White Horse

11 Then I saw heaven opened, and there before
me was a white horse. The rider on the horse is
called Faithful and True, and he is right when he
judges and makes war. 12 His eyes are like burning fire, and on his head are many crowns. He has
a name written on him, which no one but himself
knows. 13 He is dressed in a robe dipped in blood,
and his name is the Word of God. 14 The armies
of heaven, dressed in fine linen, white and clean,
were following him on white horses. 15 Out of the
rider's mouth comes a sharp sword that he will use
to defeat the nations, and he will rule them with a
rod of iron. He will crush out the wine in the winepress of the terrible anger of God the Almighty.
16 On his robe and on his upper leg was written
this name: KING OF KINGS AND LORD OF LORDS.

17 Then I saw an angel standing in the sun, and
he called with a loud voice to all the birds flying in
the sky: "Come and gather together for the great
feast of God 18 so that you can eat the bodies of
kings, generals, mighty people, horses and their riders, and the bodies of all people—free, slave, small,
and great."

19 Then I saw the beast and the kings of the
earth. Their armies were gathered together to
make war against the rider on the horse and his
army. 20 But the beast was captured and with him
the false prophet who did the miracles for the
beast. The false prophet had used these miracles to
trick those who had the mark of the beast and worshiped his idol. The false prophet and the beast
were thrown alive into the lake of fire that burns
with sulfur. 21 And their armies were killed with
the sword that came out of the mouth of the rider
on the horse, and all the birds ate the bodies until
they were full.

The Thousand Years

20 I saw an angel coming down from heaven.
He had the key to the bottomless pit and a
large chain in his hand. 2 The angel grabbed the
dragon, that old snake who is the devil and Satan,

19:1 *Hallelujah.* This means "praise God!"

19:7–8 The church is the bride of the Lamb, who is Christ. The best earthly picture of the intimacy that God's people share with him, both now and especially in eternity, is the intimacy of husband and wife. Like a faithful wife, the church is to be adorned in fine white linen. So husbands and wives are to be faithful to one another.

19:9 The kingdom of God was often portrayed as a great banquet (see Luke 14). With this image, people looked ahead to the celebration of God's provision for his people, the passing of times of sorrow, and friendship with God and one another.

19:9 Table Fellowship/Lord's Supper: Revelation 19:17–18
19:10 Marriage: See article on page 50.
19:11 Celebration: See article on page 290.
19:13 Incarnation: See article on page 962.
19:15 Weapons: See article on page 1286.
19:18 Table Fellowship/Lord's Supper: Revelation 22:17
19:21 Holy War & Divine Warrior: See article on page 230.

20 Careful study of the Book of Revelation reveals that John the Seer

and tied him up for a thousand years. 3Then he
threw him into the bottomless pit, closed it, and
locked it over him. The angel did this so he could
not trick the people of the earth anymore until the
thousand years were ended. After a thousand years
he must be set free for a short time.
4Then I saw some thrones and people sitting on
them who had been given the power to judge.
And I saw the souls of those who had been killed
because they were faithful to the message of Jesus
and the message from God. They had not worshiped the beast or his idol, and they had not
received the mark of the beast on their foreheads
or on their hands. They came back to life and
ruled with Christ for a thousand years. 5(The others that were dead did not live again until the thousand years were ended.) This is the first raising of
the dead. 6Happy and holy are those who share in
this first raising of the dead. The second death has
no power over them. They will be priests for God
and for Christ and will rule with him for a thousand years.
7When the thousand years are over, Satan will
be set free from his prison. 8Then he will go out to
trick the nations in all the earth—Gog and
Magog—to gather them for battle. There are so
many people they will be like sand on the
seashore. 9And Satan's army marched across the
earth and gathered around the camp of God's people and the city God loves. But fire came down
from heaven and burned them up. 10And Satan,
who tricked them, was thrown into the lake of
burning sulfur with the beast and the false
prophet. There they will be punished day and
night forever and ever.

People of the World Are Judged

11Then I saw a great white throne and the One
who was sitting on it. Earth and sky ran away from
him and disappeared. 12And I saw the dead, great
and small, standing before the throne. Then books
were opened, and the book of life was opened. The
dead were judged by what they had done, which
was written in the books. 13The sea gave up the
dead who were in it, and Death and Hades gave up
the dead who were in them. Each person was
judged by what he had done. 14And Death and
Hades were thrown into the lake of fire. The lake
of fire is the second death. 15And anyone whose
name was not found written in the book of life was
thrown into the lake of fire.

The New Jerusalem

21 Then I saw a new heaven and a new earth.
The first heaven and the first earth had disappeared, and there was no sea anymore. 2And I
saw the holy city, the new Jerusalem, coming down
out of heaven from God. It was prepared like a
bride dressed for her husband. 3And I heard a
loud voice from the throne, saying, "Now God's
presence is with people, and he will live with

drew on images from all over the prophetic books in the Old Testament to paint a portrait of the end times. Sometimes the images are quite close to what we find in Ezekiel or Daniel; sometimes they are very different, showing that John did not take these images literally (see Ezra 1 and Revelation 4) as they are the products of dreams and visions. It would be a mistake, however, to assume that John is simply dealing in myths that have no space-time reference points. Rather he is drawing on Old Testament symbols to portray the importance and magnitude of end time events that he believes are happening and will happen. John's visions are not flights of fantasy from the real historical world, but rather ways of peeling back the tapestry of time in order to show how heaven and earth, things human and things divine, interact to work out history as it moves toward its end.

20:6 Martyrdom: See article on page 651.

20:6 Persecution: See article on page 1453.

20:10 Much debate surrounds the interpretation of the details of this passage, but one thing is agreed upon by all. That is, the Bible teaches that Satan will be defeated and totally destroyed by God. Thanks to the defeat of Satan on the cross (Colossians 2:15), there is no doubt as to the outcome of the struggle that began ages ago between God and Satan. God is the victory in Jesus Christ!

20:10 The New Testament constantly points us to a "time" in the future when God will bring history to a magnificent close, and we will once again live in his presence.

20:13 *Hades.* The place of the dead.

21:1 This is the climax of a theme that runs through the entire Bible, beginning with Genesis itself. Adam and Eve's rebellion against God corrupted all of creation. And since then, God's salvation of his people has had as its ultimate goal the restoration of creation. This is why Jesus came to earth as a second Adam (Romans 5:14–21). With the new heaven and new earth in Revelation 21:1, the goal has been reached. God's people are back in paradise.

21:1 Earth: See article on page 20.

21:1 God gives John a vision of the end of history. Only God knows what will finally happen, and he has chosen to draw back the curtains a bit and give us a look at that future in order to comfort us while we live in an evil present. God will do away with evil, and we will once again live in his presence.

21:1–4 The hope of the Bible is that one day God will remake the world and take away all evil and suffering. This hope is based on the promise of God's character and faithfulness. At times this hope has been used by Christians to avoid dealing with the problems of everyday life; instead, it should offer a vision for what life can be like when it is lived in full agreement with God's will. Jesus taught his disciples to pray that God's will would be realized here on earth, as it already is in heaven (Matthew 6:10).

21:2 Why is there no longer any sea? The sea sometimes symbolizes hostility, untamed violence, evil (see Job 38:8–11; Psalm 89:9; Isaiah 57:20). In the new creation there is no room for this!

21:2 *new Jerusalem.* The spiritual city where God's people live with him.

21:2 Nehemiah: Revelation 21:12–14

21:3 The new Jerusalem is the place where the new heaven will meet the new earth. John says that God will make his home there among his people. The old agreement with Israel established a place where God would choose to be worshiped, the old Jerusalem. The new agreement must have a place to worship God that reflects the changes God has made in the redemption of his people. This requires the new city, Jerusalem.

them, and they will be his people. God himself will
be with them and will be their God. 4He will wipe
away every tear from their eyes, and there will be
no more death, sadness, crying, or pain, because
all the old ways are gone."

5The One who was sitting on the throne said,
"Look! I am making everything new!" Then he
said, "Write this, because these words are true
and can be trusted."

6The One on the throne said to me, "It is finished. I am the Alpha and the Omega, the
Beginning and the End. I will give free water from
the spring of the water of life to anyone who is
thirsty. 7Those who win the victory will receive
this, and I will be their God, and they will be my
children. 8But cowards, those who refuse to
believe, who do evil things, who kill, who sin sexually, who do evil magic, who worship idols, and
who tell lies—all these will have a place in the lake
of burning sulfur. This is the second death."

9Then one of the seven angels who had the
seven bowls full of the seven last troubles came to
me, saying, "Come with me, and I will show you
the bride, the wife of the Lamb." 10And the angel
carried me away by the Spirit to a very large and
high mountain. He showed me the holy city,
Jerusalem, coming down out of heaven from
God. 11It was shining with the glory of God and
was bright like a very expensive jewel, like a
jasper, clear as crystal. 12The city had a great high
wall with twelve gates with twelve angels at the
gates, and on each gate was written the name of
one of the twelve tribes of Israel. 13There were
three gates on the east, three on the north, three
on the south, and three on the west. 14The walls
of the city were built on twelve foundation
stones, and on the stones were written the names
of the twelve apostles of the Lamb.

15The angel who talked with me had a measuring rod made of gold to measure the city, its gates,
and its wall. 16The city was built in a square, and its
length was equal to its width. The angel measured
the city with the rod. The city was twelve thousand stadia long, twelve thousand stadia wide, and
twelve thousand stadia high. 17The angel also measured the wall. It was one hundred forty-four cubits
high, by human measurements, which the angel
was using. 18The wall was made of jasper, and the
city was made of pure gold, as pure as glass. 19The
foundation stones of the city walls were decorated
with every kind of jewel. The first foundation was
jasper, the second was sapphire, the third was
chalcedony, the fourth was emerald, 20the fifth
was onyx, the sixth was carnelian, the seventh was
chrysolite, the eighth was beryl, the ninth was
topaz, the tenth was chrysoprase, the eleventh was
jacinth, and the twelfth was amethyst. 21The
twelve gates were twelve pearls, each gate having
been made from a single pearl. And the street of
the city was made of pure gold as clear as glass.

22I did not see a temple in the city, because the
Lord God Almighty and the Lamb are the city's temple. 23The city does not need the sun or the moon
to shine on it, because the glory of God is its light,
and the Lamb is the city's lamp. 24By its light the
people of the world will walk, and the kings of the
earth will bring their glory into it. 25The city's gates
will never be shut on any day, because there is no
night there. 26The glory and the honor of the nations
will be brought into it. 27Nothing unclean and no
one who does shameful things or tells lies will ever
go into it. Only those whose names are written in
the Lamb's book of life will enter the city.

22 Then the angel showed me the river of the
water of life. It was shining like crystal and
was flowing from the throne of God and of the
Lamb 2down the middle of the street of the city.
The tree of life was on each side of the river. It
produces fruit twelve times a year, once each
month. The leaves of the tree are for the healing

21:4 Evil: See article on page 592.
21:4 Promise: See article on page 1454.
21:6 *Alpha and the Omega.* The first and last letters of the Greek alphabet. This means "the beginning and the end."
21:7 Family: Revelation 21:9–10
21:7 Perseverance: See article on page 1224.
21:8 Hell: See article on page 1316.
21:8 Murder: Revelation 22:15
21:10 Family: 1 John 4:8
21:10–22:7 On a very large and high mountain, John receives the last vision of the Book of Revelation: the vision of the holy city, Jerusalem. In the vision, the Lord himself and the Lamb are revealed as the Temple of the new city. The setting of this vision keeps continuity with the biblical function of mountains as places where God appeared and the revelation of God's purposes.
21:14 Nehemiah: See article on page 439.
21:16 *stadia.* One stadion was a distance of about two hundred yards; about one-eighth of a Roman mile.
21:17 *cubits.* A cubit is about half a yard, the length from the elbow to the tip of the little finger.
21:19 Stone: See article on page 1348.
21:23 Glory: See article on page 271.
21:27 Clean & Unclean: See article on page 289.
21:27 End Times/Last Days: See article on page 762.
21:27 Obedience: See article on page 170.
22:2 This is a casual reference back to Genesis, which speaks of the Garden of Eden and the tree of life in its center (Genesis 2:9). Whereas the tree of knowledge of good and evil brought death to all nations in the Genesis story, the tree of life in Revelation brings life to all nations who share its leaves. Humanity was cut off from the tree of life when sin entered the world, but now in the new Jerusalem, humanity will eat from the tree of life once again. These images symbolize God's redemption of fallen humanity and the reversal of the curse in Genesis 3.

"Then the angel showed me the river of the water of life" (22:1).

of all the nations.⚭ 3Nothing that God judges
guilty will be in that city. The throne of God and
of the Lamb will be there, and God's servants will
worship him.⚭ 4They will see his face, and his
name will be written on their foreheads. 5There
will never be night again. They will not need the
light of a lamp or the light of the sun, because
the Lord God will give them light. And they will
rule as kings forever and ever.

6The angel said to me, "These words can be
trusted and are true." The Lord, the God of the
spirits of the prophets, sent his angel to show his
servants the things that must happen soon.

7"Listen! I am coming soon! Happy is the one
who obeys the words of prophecy in this book."

8I, John, am the one who heard and saw these
things. When I heard and saw them, I bowed
down to worship at the feet of the angel who
showed these things to me. 9But the angel said to
me, "Do not worship me! I am a servant like you,
your brothers the prophets, and all those who
obey the words in this book. Worship God!"

10Then the angel told me, "Do not keep secret
the words of prophecy in this book, because the
time is near for all this to happen. 11Let whoever
is doing evil continue to do evil. Let whoever is
unclean continue to be unclean. Let whoever
is doing right continue to do right. Let whoever is
holy continue to be holy."⚭

12"Listen! I am coming soon! I will bring my
reward with me, and I will repay each one of you
for what you have done. 13I am the Alpha and the
Omega, the First and the Last, the Beginning and
the End.

14"Happy are those who wash their robes so
that they will receive the right to eat the fruit
from the tree of life and may go through the gates
into the city. 15Outside the city are the evil people, those who do evil magic, who sin sexually,
who murder, who worship idols, and who love
lies and tell lies.⚭

16"I, Jesus, have sent my angel to tell you these
things for the churches. I am the descendant from
the family of David, and I am the bright morning
star."⚭

17The Spirit and the bride say, "Come!" Let the
one who hears this say, "Come!" Let whoever is
thirsty come; whoever wishes may have the water
of life as a free gift.⚭

18I warn everyone who hears the words of the
prophecy of this book: If anyone adds anything to
these words, God will add to that person the disasters written about in this book. 19And if anyone
takes away from the words of this book of prophecy,
God will take away that one's share of the tree of
life and of the holy city, which are written about in
this book.

20Jesus, the One who says these things are true,
says, "Yes, I am coming soon."

Amen. Come, Lord Jesus!⚭

21The grace of the Lord Jesus be with all.
Amen.⚭

⚭**22:2 Sickness, Disease, Healing:** See article on page 243.
⚭**22:3 Servant of the Lord:** See article on page 612.
⚭**22:11 Prophetic Symbolism:** See article on page 641.

22:13 *Alpha and the Omega.* The first and last letters of the Greek alphabet. This means "the beginning and the end."

22:14 *wash their robes.* This means they believed and obeyed Jesus so that their sins could be forgiven by Christ's blood. The "washing" may refer to baptism (Acts 22:16).

⚭**22:15 Murder:** See article on page 79.
⚭**22:16 David:** See article on page 400.
⚭**22:17 Table Fellowship/Lord's Supper:** See article on page 1183.
⚭**22:20 Time:** See article on page 581.
⚭**22:21 City:** See article on page 1409.
⚭**22:21 Grace:** See article on page 1254.

HEAVEN

REVELATION 21–22

Where is heaven? What will we look like in heaven? What will we do there?

These are questions that we often hear concerning heaven. As we search for answers, we find that the Bible provides us with relatively few details. Although we may want to know what heaven is like to satisfy our curiosity, let us not forget that our primary goal is to learn what God wants us to know about heaven in the Bible.

God brought some people into heaven for a glimpse of heavenly reality. For instance, the prophet Isaiah appears to be in heaven when he sees God seated on a throne (Isaiah 6). God gave Stephen a glimpse of heaven just before he was killed as a martyr of the faith (Acts 7:55–56), and Paul, too, was brought into heaven (2 Corinthians 12:2). These were special events at crucial moments in these men's lives. We do not learn much about heaven from these descriptions, except that God is in heaven and it is a marvelous place.

John tells us what the most important fact about heaven is—God is present there: "God's presence is with people, and he will live with them, and they will be his people. God himself will be with them and will be their God" (Revelation 21:3). In heaven, believers will enjoy the climactic presence of God, an experience that has not been available to humankind since the fall of Adam and Eve.

In the Garden of Eden, Adam and Eve had a perfect relationship with God. It was there that we see the presence of Immanuel, "God is with us," for the first time. Ezekiel called it the "garden of God" (Ezekiel 28:13). That came to an end when Adam and Eve gave in to temptation. God forced them out of the garden and "placed angels and a sword of fire that flashed around in every direction on its eastern border" (Genesis 3:24); anyone who wishes to return to God's presence must pass through the judgment of the sword of fire.

Although the presence of God found in Eden no longer exists, we, as God's people, can still experience the closeness of God on earth, however fractional that may be. All the longing for the presence of God with his people came to its fullest realization on earth in the incarnation of the Lord Jesus. Isaiah prophesied the coming of Jesus, whose name was Immanuel, which means, "God is with us" (Isaiah 7:14; Matthew 1:23). Jesus was the Word who became a human and lived, or made his tent, among people on earth (John 1:14). Since Solomon's Temple was a shadow of Jesus, in whom the presence of God was found, Jesus spoke of his body as the Temple (John 2:19). The apostle John made this clear when he wrote, "No one has ever seen God. But God the only Son . . . has shown us what God is like" (John 1:18). The incarnation of Jesus manifested the ultimate form of God's presence with his people on earth.

During his incarnation, Jesus went through the judgment of the sword of fire on the cross so that believers may be "completely free to enter the Most Holy Place without fear" and to "come near to God" (Hebrews 10:19, 22). Through the redemption of Jesus, God made his dwelling place in believers through the Holy Spirit; Paul says each believer is a "temple for the Holy Spirit" (1 Corinthians 6:19).

Throughout biblical history, God appeared to humankind in various forms through which they might enjoy the blessings of his presence. But these are only partial fulfillments of the experience that believers will have in heaven; therefore, Paul refers to the experience on earth as *away from the Lord* (2 Corinthians 5:6). Heaven, on the other hand, is the place where God lives with his people in the fullest manner. The abundance of blessings that God's people find in heaven even exceeds those in Eden. John reveals in Revelation 21 and 22 that, in heaven, there is more than one tree of life, and they produce fruits twelve times a year. It is there that the Lamb is on his throne.

This, then, is the clearest truth about heaven. God is there. As a result, "God will wipe away every tear from their eyes" (Revelation 7:17). We get hints only of other activities in heaven.

In the first place, we will have bodies, though they will be different than the bodies that we presently have. Paul calls them "heavenly bodies" (1 Corinthians 15:35–58) and Jesus' resurrection appearances may give us an idea of what they are like (Luke 24).

We learn that there will be no marriage in heaven (Matthew 22:30). Paul tells us that we will judge the world, even angels (1 Corinthians 6:2).

So we do get brief glimpses into the activity and nature of heaven, but the most important truth is that we will enjoy eternal fellowship with Jesus Christ and one another.

Heaven: For additional scriptures on this topic go to Isaiah 25:6–8.

DICTIONARY WITH TOPICAL CONCORDANCE

Dictionary with Topical Concordance

A

Aaron (AIR-ohn) *older brother of Moses.*
- before the king of Egypt, Exodus 4:14–16; 5:1–5; 7:1–2
- death of, Numbers 20:22–29

Abba (AB-uh) *word for "father" in Aramaic.*
- Jesus called God "Abba," Mark 14:36
- we can call God "Abba," Romans 8:15; Galatians 4:6

Abednego (a-BED-nee-go) *one of the three friends of Daniel whom God protected from the fiery furnace.*
- refused the king of Babylon's food, Daniel 1:3–17
- thrown into the fiery furnace, Daniel 3

Abel (AY-bul) *the second son of Adam and Eve.*
- born to Adam and Eve, Genesis 4:2
- approved by God, Genesis 4:3–4; Hebrews 11:4
- murdered by Cain, Genesis 4:8; 1 John 3:12

Abib (ah-BEEB) *first month of the Jewish calendar, about the time of year as our March or April; also called "Nisan"; means "young ears of grain."*
- the time the Israelites left Egypt, Exodus 13:3–4
- the time for the Feast of Unleavened Bread, Exodus 23:15; 34:18

Abigail, sister of David (AB-eh-gale) 1 Chronicles 2:13–17

Abigail, wife of Nabal
- brought food to David, 1 Samuel 25:14–35
- became David's wife, 1 Samuel 25:36–42

Abijah, king of Judah (a-BY-jah) 1 Kings 15:1–8; 2 Chronicles 13:1–14:1

Abijah, son of Jeroboam
- death of, 1 Kings 14:1–18

Abijah, son of Samuel, 1 Samuel 8:1–3

ability
- given by God, 2 Corinthians 3:5–6
- through Christ, Philippians 4:13
- differing abilities, 1 Corinthians 12:7–11

Abimelech, king of Gerar (a-BIM-eh-lek)
- tried to take Sarah as his wife, Genesis 20

Abimelech, king of the Philistines
- tried to take Rebekah as his wife, Genesis 26:6–11

Abimelech, son of Gideon
- birth of, Judges 8:29–31
- murdered his brothers, Judges 9:1–6
- defeated the people of Shechem, Judges 9:22–45
- burned the Tower of Shechem, Judges 9:46–49
- death of, Judges 9:50–55

Abishai (a-BISH-eye) *nephew of King David.*
- served in David's army, 2 Samuel 23:18–19; 1 Chronicles 18:12–13
- saved David's life, 2 Samuel 21:15–17

Abner (AB-nur) *commander of Saul's army.*
- at Goliath's defeat, 1 Samuel 17:55–57
- made Ish-Bosheth king of Israel, 2 Samuel 2:8–10
- later loyal to David, 2 Samuel 3:6–21
- killed by Joab, 2 Samuel 3:22–27

abortion, See article on page 252.
- injuring a pregnant woman, Exodus 21:22
- chosen in the womb, Jeremiah 1:5
- formed in mother, Psalm 139:13–16

Abraham (AY-bra-ham) *father of the Jewish nation.*
- called from Ur by God, Genesis 12:1–4
- lied about Sarai, Genesis 12:10–20
- separated from Lot, Genesis 13
- God's agreement with, Genesis 15; 17
- name changed, Genesis 17:3–6
- father of Isaac, Genesis 21:1–7
- offered Isaac as a sacrifice, Genesis 22:1–19
- father of the faithful, Romans 4
- God's friend, James 2:23

Absalom (AB-sah-lum) *one of David's sons.*
- turned against David, 2 Samuel 15:1–18:8
- killed by Joab, 2 Samuel 18:9–15

abstain (ab-STAIN) *to keep from doing something.*
- from food offered to idols, Acts 15:20
- from evil, 1 Thessalonians 5:22
- from lust, 1 Peter 2:11

abyss (uh-BISS) See "bottomless pit."

accept
- a prophet not accepted, Luke 4:24
- accepted by God, Acts 10:35; 15:7–8; Romans 14:3
- each other, Romans 14:1; 15:7
- Jesus, John 12:48

accuse
- Jesus accused by the Jews, Matthew 27:12–13; Mark 15:3; Luke 6:7
- Paul accused by the Jews, Acts 23:27–29; 26:7
- the Devil as the accuser, Revelation 12:10

Achaia (a-KA-yuh) See "Greece."

Achan (AY-can) *an Israelite who disobeyed God during the battle of Jericho,* Joshua 7

Achish (AY-kish) *king of the Philistine city of Gath.*
- David pretends to be insane, 1 Samuel 21:10–15
- David in his army, 1 Samuel 27; 29

actions
- judged by, Proverbs 20:11; Matthew 11:19; Galatians 6:4
- of love, 1 John 3:18
- of goodness, Matthew 5:16

Adam (AD-um) *the first man.*
- created by God, Genesis 1:26–2:25
- disobeyed God, Genesis 3
- compared to Christ, 1 Corinthians 15:21–22, 45–49

adder, *a poisonous snake.* See "snake."

Adonijah (ad-oh-NY-jah) *David's fourth son.*
- son of Haggith, 2 Samuel 3:4
- tried to become king, 1 Kings 1
- killed by Solomon, 1 Kings 2:12–25

Adoni-Zedek (a-DOH-ny-ZEE-dek) *an Amorite king of Jerusalem.*
- defeated by Joshua, Joshua 10:1–28

adoption, See article on page 198.
- of Moses, Exodus 2
- God's children, Romans 8:16; Ephesians 1:5

Adullam (a-DOO-lum) *a city about thirteen miles from Bethlehem.*
- David hid in a cave there, 2 Samuel 23:13

adultery (ah-DUL-ter-ee) *breaking a marriage promise by having sexual relations with someone other than your husband or wife.*
- "You must not be guilty of adultery," Exodus 20:14
- Christ teaches about, Matthew 5:27–32; Luke 16:18
- woman caught in adultery, John 8:1–11

advice
- given by Ahithophel, 2 Samuel 15:30–17:23
- given to Rehoboam, 1 Kings 12:1–15
- teachings about, Proverbs 11:14; 12:5, 15; 19:20

Agabus (AG-uh-bus) *a Christian prophet.*
- warned the people, Acts 11:27–30
- warned Paul about going to Jerusalem, Acts 21:10–11

Agag (AY-gag) *king of the Amalekites.*
- captured by Saul, 1 Samuel 15

agreement *a contract, promise, or covenant.*
- with Noah, Genesis 9:1–17
- with Abraham, Genesis 15; 17:1–14
- Ark of the Agreement, Exodus 25:10–22; 1 Samuel 4–5; 2 Samuel 6:1–15
- with the Israelites, Exodus 19:3–8, 24; Deuteronomy 29
- new agreement, 2 Corinthians 2:12–3:18
- difference between the old and new agreements, Hebrews 8–10

aging, See article on page 210.
- Moses's humility, Exodus 4
- respect for the aging, Leviticus 19:32.

Agrippa (uh-GRIP-pah) See "Herod Agrippa."

Ahab (AY-hab) *evil king of Israel who was married to Jezebel.*
- worshiped Baal, 1 Kings 16:29–33
- had Naboth killed, 1 Kings 21
- death of, 1 Kings 22:1–40

Ahasuerus (ah-HAZ-oo-EE-rus) *Hebrew word for the Greek name Xerxes.* See "Xerxes."

Ahaz, *twelfth king of Judah,* 2 Kings 16; 2 Chronicles 28

Ahaziah, king of Judah (ay-ha-ZY-uh) 2 Chronicles 22:1–9

Ahaziah, son of Ahab
- king of Israel, 1 Kings 22:40–53

Ahijah, great-grandson of Eli (a-HY-jah) 1 Samuel 14:1–23

Ahijah, the prophet
- told Jeroboam the kingdom would be divided, 1 Kings 11:29–39
- told that Jeroboam's son would die, 1 Kings 14:1–18

Ahimelech, the high priest (a-HIM-eh-lek)
- helped David, 1 Samuel 21:1–9

Ahimelech, the Hittite warrior, 1 Samuel 26:6

Ahithophel (a-HITH-oh-fel) *gave advice to King David.*
- helped Absalom rebel against David, 1 Samuel 15:31; 16:15–17:23

Ai (AY-eye) *a city completely destroyed by the Israelites,* Joshua 7:1–8:28

Akeldama (a-KEL-dah-mah) *field bought with the money Judas received for betraying Jesus,* Matthew 27:3–10; Acts 1:18–19

alabaster (AL-a-bass-ter) *light-colored stone with streaks or stripes through it,* Matthew 26:7; Mark 14:3; Luke 7:37

alamoth (AL-a-moth) *a musical word, which may mean "like a flute" or "high-pitched,"* Psalm 46

alcohol, See article on page 520.
- given by God, Psalm 104:15
- effects of, Proverbs 23:29–35
- drunkards will not inherit, 1 Corinthians 6:9–10

alien, See "foreigner."

All-Powerful, *a name for God,* 1 Chronicles 11:9; Psalm 24:10; Isaiah 6:3–5; Malachi 3:1–17

Almighty, *a name for God.*
- "I am God Almighty," Genesis 17:1
- "I appeared to Abraham . . . by the name, God Almighty," Exodus 6:3
- "Holy, holy, holy is the Lord God Almighty," Revelation 4:8

almond
- design of the lampstands in Holy Tent, Exodus 25:31–36
- Aaron's stick produced, Numbers 17:8

aloes (AL-ohs) *oils from sweet-smelling sap of certain trees; used to make perfume and medicine and to prepare bodies for burial,* Psalm 45:8; Proverbs 7:17
- used to prepare Jesus' body for burial, John 19:39

Alpha and Omega (AL-fah and oh-MAY-guh) *the first and last letters of the Greek alphabet, like our A and Z.*
- used to describe Jesus, Revelation 1:8; 21:6; 22:13

altar (ALL-ter) *a place where sacrifices, gifts, or prayers were offered to a god.*
- built by Noah, Genesis 8:20
- built by Abraham, Genesis 22:9
- for burnt offerings, Exodus 27:1–8
- for incense, Exodus 30:1–10
- corners of, Exodus 27:2; 30:10; 1 Kings 1:50
- for the Temple, 2 Chronicles 4:1

Amalekites (AM-a-lah-kites) *fierce, fighting people who descended from Esau; they were enemies of Israel and were finally wiped out during the time of Hezekiah.*

- enemies of Israel, Exodus 17:8–16; 1 Samuel 15
- destroyed by King Hezekiah, 1 Chronicles 4:43

Amasa (AM-a-sa) *leader of Absalom's army when he rebelled against David,* 2 Samuel 17:25
- made leader of David's army, 2 Samuel 19:13
- killed by Joab, 2 Samuel 20:1–10

Amaziah (am-ah-ZY-uh) *the ninth king of Judah,* 2 Kings 14; 2 Chronicles 25

ambition, See article on page 832.
- of the disciples, Mark 9:33–37
- interest in other lives, Philippians 2:3–4
- to do good, Titus 2:14

amen (AY-MEN or AH-MEN) *Hebrew word for "that is right,"* 1 Chronicles 16:36; Psalm 106:48; 1 Corinthians 14:16
- "Amen. Come, Lord Jesus!" Revelation 22:20

Ammonites (AM-on-ites) *descendants of Lot's son, Ben-Ammi,* Genesis 19:36–38
- enemies of Israel, Judges 10:6–11:33; 1 Samuel 11; 2 Samuel 10:1–14
- worshiped Molech, 1 Kings 11:5

Amon (AM-on) *the fifteenth king of Judah,* 2 Kings 21:18–26; 2 Chronicles 33:20–25
- an ancestor of Jesus, Matthew 1:10

Amorites (AM-or-ites) *a group of wicked people who worshiped false gods and lived in Canaan when the Israelites arrived.*
- defeated by Israel, Numbers 21:21–32; Joshua 10:1–11:14

Amos (AY-mos) *a prophet who warned Israel of God's punishment for disobedience.*
- a shepherd from Tekoa, Amos 1:1
- his visions, Amos 7:1–9:10

Anak/Anakites (A-nak/AN-uh-kites) *a group of large, fighting people who lived in Canaan when the Israelites arrived.*
- feared by the twelve spies, Numbers 13:22, 28, 33; Deuteronomy 1:26–28
- defeated by Joshua, Joshua 11:21–23

Ananias, husband of Sapphira (an-uh-NY-us)
- killed for lying to the Holy Spirit, Acts 5:1–6

Ananias, a Christian in Damascus
- helped Saul of Tarsus, Acts 9:10–19; 22:12–16

Ananias, the high priest
- at Paul's trial, Acts 23:1–5

Andrew, *a fisherman and brother of the apostle Peter.*
- chosen by Jesus to be an apostle, Mark 1:16–18; 3:13–19
- brought Peter to Jesus, John 1:40–42
- waited with the apostles in Jerusalem, Acts 1:13

angel (AIN-jel) *a heavenly being.*
- rescued Lot from Sodom, Genesis 19:1–22
- led Israel to Canaan, Exodus 23:20–23; 32:34
- announced Jesus' birth, Matthew 1:20–21; Luke 1:26–37; 2:8–15
- helped Jesus, Matthew 4:11; Luke 22:43
- helped the apostles, Acts 5:19–20; 12:6–10
- will bring judgment, Matthew 13:24–50; 24:31
- archangel, 1 Thessalonians 4:16; Jude 9
- less than Christ, Hebrews 1:4–14; 1 Peter 3:22
- rebellious angels, 2 Peter 2:4; Jude 6
- serving in heaven, Revelation 7–10

anger, *wrath.*
- of God toward people, John 3:36; Romans 1:18; 2:5–6; Colossians 3:5–6
- saved from God's anger by Christ, Romans 5:9; 1 Thessalonians 1:10; 5:9
- warnings against, Matthew 5:21–22; Ephesians 4:26, 31; James 1:19–20

animal
- created by God, Genesis 1:20–25
- to be ruled by people, Genesis 1:26
- named by Adam, Genesis 2:19–20
- saved by Noah, Genesis 6:19–20
- clean, Leviticus 11:1–3, 9; Deuteronomy 14:3–6
- unclean, Leviticus 11:4–8, 10–12, 26–44; Deuteronomy 14:7–8

Annas (AN-us) *a high priest of the Jews during Jesus' lifetime,* Luke 3:2; John 18:13
- questioned Peter and John, Acts 4:5–22

anoint (uh-NOINT) *to pour oil on.*
- to appoint a priest, Exodus 28:41; 40:13
- to appoint a king, 1 Samuel 10:1; 16:12–13; 2 Kings 9:6
- the Holy Tent, Numbers 7:1
- to heal sickness, Mark 6:13; James 5:14

Antichrist (AN-tee KRYST) See "enemy of Christ."

Antioch in Pisidia (AN-tee-ahk) *a small city in the country of Pisidia.*
- Paul preached there, Acts 13:14–15

Antioch in Syria, *third largest city in the Roman Empire.*
- Saul and Barnabus preached there, Acts 11:19–26
- followers first called "Christians" there, Acts 11:26
- Peter in Antioch, Galatians 2:11–12
- Paul preaches there, Acts 13:14–15

anti-Semitism, See article on page 992.
- Jews persecuting Jesus, John 5:16–18
- Jews' special place with God, Romans 11:24–26
- Children of Abraham, John 8:39–44

Apollos (uh-POL-us) *an educated Jew from Alexandria.*
- taught by Aquila and Priscilla, Acts 18:24–28
- preached to the Corinthians, 1 Corinthians 1:12; 3:4–6
- friend of Paul, Titus 3:13

apostasy, See article on page 1315.
- continued sinning, Hebrews 10:19–39
- "come back to me, . . . children," Jeremiah 3:14
- of Judas, Luke 22:47–53

apostle (uh-POS-'l) *someone who is sent off. Jesus chose these twelve special followers and sent them to tell the Good News about him to the whole world.*
- twelve chosen by Jesus, Mark 3:14–19
- Matthias chosen, Acts 1:12–26
- Paul chosen, 1 Corinthians 15:3–11; 2 Corinthians 12:11–12

- duties and powers of, Luke 9:1–6; Acts 5:12–16; 8:18
- leaders of the church, Acts 15; 16:4; 1 Corinthians 12:28
- false apostles, 2 Corinthians 11:13; Revelation 2:2

appearance
- not to judge by, 1 Samuel 16:7; John 7:24
- deceiving, Matthew 23:27–28
- of Jesus, Isaiah 53:2; Philippians 2:7

Aquila (AK-wi-lah) *a Jewish Christian from Rome.*
- friend of Paul, Acts 18:2–3; Romans 16:3–5
- taught Apollos, Acts 18:24–28

Arabah (AIR-uh-bah) *the Hebrew word for the Jordan Valley.* See "Jordan Valley."

Arabah, Sea of, See "Dead Sea."

Aram (AIR-um) *a country northeast of Israel,* 1 Kings 11:25; 15:18; 2 Kings 5:1; Isaiah 7:1
- known as "Syria" in the New Testament, Matthew 4:24; Acts 15:23

Aramaic (AIR-uh-MAY-ik) *the language of the people in the nation of Aram.*
- common language of the Jews, 2 Kings 18:26; John 19:13, 17, 20; Acts 21:40

Ararat (AIR-uh-rat) *a group of mountains located in what is now Turkey and the Soviet Union.*
- Noah's boat landed there, Genesis 8:14

Araunah (a-RAW-nah) *a Jebusite who was also called Ornan.*
- sold his threshing floor to King David, 2 Samuel 24:15–25; 1 Chronicles 21:18–28

archangel (ark-AIN-jel) *the leader of God's angels,* 1 Thessalonians 4:16; Jude 9

Areopagus (AIR-ee-OP-uh-gus) *a council or group of important leaders in Athens.*
- Paul spoke there, Acts 17:16–34

argue
- the apostles argued, Mark 9:33–37; Luke 9:46–48
- avoid arguments, Philippians 2:14; 2 Timothy 2:23–26; Titus 3:9
- Michael argued with the devil, Jude 9

Aristarchus (air-i-STAR-kus) *a man from Thessalonica who often traveled with Paul,* Acts 27:2; Colossians 4:10; Philemon 24

ark, Noah's, *the huge boat that Noah built to save his family from the flood God sent to cover the earth.* See "boat."

Ark of the Agreement, *a special box made of acacia wood and gold. Inside were the stone tablets on which the Ten Commandments were written. Later, a pot of manna and Aaron's walking stick were also put into the Ark. It was to remind the people of Israel of God's promise to be with them.*
- building of, Exodus 25:10–22; 37:1–9
- crossing the Jordan River, Joshua 3:1–17
- captured by the Philistines, 1 Samuel 4:1–7:1
- touched by Uzzah, 2 Samuel 6:1–8; 1 Chronicles 13
- placed in the Temple, 2 Chronicles 5:2–10
- contents of, Hebrews 9:4–5

Ark of the Covenant, See "Ark of the Agreement."

armor
- of Saul, 1 Samuel 17:38–39; 31:9–10
- of God, Ephesians 6:10–17

arrest
- John the Baptist arrested, Matthew 14:3; Mark 6:17
- Jesus arrested, Matthew 26:50–57; Mark 14:44–50; John 18:1–14
- Peter arrested, Acts 12:1–4
- Paul arrested, Acts 28:17–20

Artaxerxes (ar-tah-ZERK-sees) *the title or name of Persian kings,* Ezra 4:7; Nehemiah 2:1
- his letter to Ezra, Ezra 7:11–26

Artemis (AR-tuh-mis) *a goddess that many Greeks worshiped,* Acts 19:23–41

Asa (AY-sah) *the third king of Judah,* 1 Kings 15:9–24; 2 Chronicles 14–16

Asaph (AY-saf) *a leader of singers when David was king,* 1 Chronicles 16:5, 7; 25:1–2; 2 Chronicles 5:12
- songs of, Psalms 73–83

ascension (uh-SIN-shun) *lifted up; used to describe Jesus' return to heaven,* Acts 1:2–11; 2:32–33

ashamed
- of Jesus, Mark 8:38; Luke 9:26; 2 Timothy 1:8
- for suffering as a Christian, 1 Peter 4:16

Ashdod (ASH-dahd) *one of the five strong, walled cities of the Philistines; called Azotus in the New Testament.*
- Ark of the Agreement there, 1 Samuel 5:1–8
- later called "Azotus," Acts 8:40

Asherah (ah-SHIR-ah) *a Canaanite goddess thought to be the wife of the god Baal.*
- worshiped by Israelites, 1 Kings 14:14–15, 22–23; 15:13
- worship forbidden, Exodus 34:13–14; Deuteronomy 16:21–22

Ashkelon (ASH-keh-lon) *one of the five important cities of the Philistines,* Judges 1:18; Zephaniah 2:4, 7
- thirty of its men killed by Samson, Judges 14:19

Ashtoreth (ASH-toh-reth) *a goddess of the people of Assyria and Canaan. At times the Israelites forgot God and built idols to worship her.* Judges 2:13; 1 Samuel 7:3–4; 12:10
- worshiped by Solomon, 1 Kings 11:5, 33

Asia (AY-zhuh) *the western part of the country now called "Turkey."*
- Paul preached there, Acts 19:10, 26
- seven churches of, Revelation 1:4

assembly (a-SEM-blee) *a meeting; a group of people gathered for a purpose.*
- of the church, Hebrews 10:24–25
- conduct in, James 2:1–4

assurance (uh-SHURE-ans) *with confidence; without doubts.*
- about the gospel, 1 Thessalonians 1:5
- before God, Hebrews 10:22–23; 1 John 5:14–15
- faith as, Hebrews 11:1

Assyria (uh-SEER-ee-uh) *a powerful nation north and east of Israel.*
- enemy of Israel, 2 Kings 15:19–20; 17:3–6
- enemy of Judah, 2 Kings 18:13–19:36; Isaiah 36:1–37:37

Astarte (ah-STAR-tay) *another name for the goddess Ashtoreth.* See "Ashtoreth."

astrology, See article on page 662.
- God warns star-worshipers, Zephaniah 1:5
- God created the stars, Genesis 1:16
- sun stands still, Joshua 10:12–13

Athaliah (ath-uh-LY-uh) *the only woman who ruled over Judah,* 2 Kings 11; 2 Chronicles 22:10–23:21

Athens (ATH-enz) *the leading city of the country of Greece.*
- Paul preached there, Acts 17:16–34

atonement (uh-TONE-ment) *to remove or forgive sins.*
- through animal sacrifices, Exodus 30:10; Leviticus 17:11; Numbers 25:13
- through faith in the blood of Jesus' death, Romans 3:25; Hebrews 2:17; 9:22; 10:11–12

Atonement, Day of, See "Cleansing, Day of."

Augustus Caesar (aw-GUS-tus SEE-zer) *or Caesar Augustus, the first Roman emperor,* Luke 2:1

authority (uh-THAR-uh-tee) *power or right to control.*
- proper use of, Matthew 20:25–26; Luke 22:24–30; Titus 2:15
- respect for, Luke 20:20–26; Romans 13:1–7; 1 Timothy 2:2; 1 Peter 2:13–17; Hebrews 13:17
- Jesus' authority, Matthew 7:29; 9:6; Mark 11:27–33; Luke 5:24; John 5:19–29

B

Baal (BAY-el) *a god of the Canaanites; "Baal" was the common word for "master, lord." He was known as the son of Dagon, or the son of El, who was known as the father of the false gods.*
- worshiped by Israelites, Judges 2:10–11; Jeremiah 11:13
- Elijah defeated prophets of Baal, 1 Kings 18:1–40
- Baal worship destroyed by Jehu, 2 Kings 10:18–28

Baal-Zebub, See "Beelzebul."

Baasha (BAY-ah-shah) *the third king of Israel,* 1 Kings 15:27–16:7; 2 Chronicles 16:1–6; Jeremiah 41:9

Babel (BAY-bel) *a tower built to reach the sky,* Genesis 11:1–9

baby
- Moses as, Exodus 2:1–10
- Solomon determined mother of, 1 Kings 3:16–28
- Elizabeth's, Luke 1:39–44
- Jesus as, Luke 2:6–21
- as a symbol of new Christians, 1 Peter 2:2

Babylon (BAB-uh-lun) *city on the Euphrates River; capital of Babylonia.*
- captives in Babylon, Psalm 137:1; Jeremiah 29:10
- destruction predicted, Jeremiah 51:36–37
- as a symbol of evil, Revelation 14:8; 17:5

Babylonians (bab-e-LONE-e-unz) *people of the country Babylonia. Also called "Chaldeans."*
- capture warned by Jeremiah, Jeremiah 21; 25
- captured the people of Judah, 2 Kings 20:12–18; 24–25; Jeremiah 39:1–10
- Daniel in Babylon, Daniel 1–4
- released Israelite captives, Ezra 2

Balaam (BAY-lum) *a prophet from Midian.*
- asked by Balak to prophesy, Numbers 22–24; 2 Peter 2:15–16; Revelation 2:14
- death of, Numbers 31:8

balm, *oil from a plant used as medicine,* Genesis 37:25; Jeremiah 8:22; 51:8; Ezekiel 27:17

Baptist, John the (BAP-tist) *someone who baptizes. John, a relative of Jesus, was called this because he baptized many people.* Matthew 3:1–6
- condemned Pharisees and Sadducees, Matthew 3:7–10
- preached about Jesus, Matthew 3:11–12
- baptized Jesus, Matthew 3:13–17
- in prison, Matthew 11:1–6; Luke 7:18–23
- described by Jesus, Matthew 11:7–12; 17:10–13; Luke 7:24–28
- death of, Matthew 14:1–12; Mark 6:14–29
- baptism of, Matthew 21:25–26; Acts 10:37; 18:25; 19:3–4
- Jesus mistaken for, Matthew 16:13–14; Mark 8:27–28; Luke 9:18–19

baptism (BAP-tiz-em) *dipping or immersing.*
- by John, Matthew 3:6; Mark 1:4; Luke 3; Acts 19:3
- of Jesus, Matthew 3:13–17
- examples of, Acts 2:38–41; 8:36–38; 16:15, 33
- with fire, Matthew 3:11; Luke 3:16
- with the Holy Spirit, Mark 1:8; Acts 1:5; 11:16

Barabbas (bah-RAB-us) *a robber who had murdered someone in Jerusalem. He was freed instead of Jesus.* Matthew 27:15–26; Mark 15:6–11

Barak (BAY-rak) *a leader of Israel's army when Deborah was judge,* Judges 4–5

Bar-Jesus, See "Elymas."

barley (BAR-lee) *a type of grain.*
- harvest of, Ruth 1:22; 2:17, 23; 2 Samuel 21:9
- loaves of, John 6:9–13

barn
- storing in, Matthew 6:26
- rich man's, Luke 12:16–20

Barnabas (BAR-nah-bus) *an encourager who helped the apostles,* Acts 4:36; 11:23
- worked with Paul, Acts 11:26; 13–15
- influenced by hypocrites, Galatians 2:13

barrenness, See "infertility."

Bartholomew (bar-THOL-oh-mew) *one of the twelve apostles of Jesus,* Matthew 10:3; Mark 3:18; Luke 6:14; Acts 1:13

Bartimaeus (bar-teh-MAY-us) *a blind man who was healed by Jesus,* Mark 10:46–52

Baruch (BAH-rook) *a friend of the prophet Jeremiah,* Jeremiah 36

Bathsheba (bath-SHE-buh) *the mother of Solomon and wife of David,* 2 Samuel 11:1–12:25; 1 Kings 1–2; 22

beatitude (bee-A-ti-tyood) *blessed or happy; often used for Jesus' teaching in Matthew 5:3–12; Luke 6:20–22.*

Beelzebul (bee-EL-ze-bull) *false god of the Philistines; in the New Testament it often refers to the devil.*
- name for Satan, Matthew 12:24; Mark 3:22; Luke 11:15

Beersheba (beer-SHE-buh) *the town farthest south in the land of Judah,* 2 Samuel 3:10; 2 Chronicles 30:5
- Abraham made an agreement there, Genesis 21:14–34

beg
- Jesus begged by demons, Matthew 8:28–34; Mark 5:1–13; Luke 8:26–33
- Jesus begged by people, Matthew 14:36; Mark 7:24–26, 32; 8:22

beggar
- Bartimaeus, Mark 10:46–52
- Lazarus, Luke 16:19–31
- at Beautiful Gate, Acts 3:1–10
- man born blind, John 9:1–12

Bel, *a false god of the Babylonians,* Jeremiah 50:2; 51:44

believe
- in God, Acts 16:34; Romans 4:24
- in Jesus, Matthew 18:6; John 12:44; 14:11–12; 1 John 5:10
- in the Good News, Mark 1:15; 11:24; Acts 15:7
- rewards of believing, Matthew 21:22; John 20:31; 1 Thessalonians 2:13
- a lie, 2 Thessalonians 2:11

believers (be-LEE-vers) *the followers of Jesus,* John 3:16; Acts 4:32; 5:14; Galatians 6:10

beloved disciple, the, See article on page 1034.
- sitting next to Jesus, John 13:23
- writing the Book of John, John 21:20–24
- at the crucifixion, John 19:26

Belshazzar (bell-SHAZ-er) *a ruler of Babylon,* Daniel 5

Belteshazzar (BELL-teh-SHAZ-er) *the Babylonian name that Nebuchadnezzar gave to Daniel,* Daniel 4:8; 5:12

Benaiah (bee-NAY-uh) *the captain of David's bodyguard,* 2 Samuel 23:20–23
- commander of Solomon's army, 1 Kings 2:34–35

Ben-Hadad (ben-HAY-dad) *name of two or three Syrian kings who often fought against Israel,* 1 Kings 20:1–34; 2 Kings 6:24–8:15

Benjamin (BEN-jah-min) *the youngest son of Jacob and Rachel.*
- birth of, Genesis 35:16–20
- reunited with Joseph, Genesis 42–45

Bernice (bur-NY-see) *the oldest daughter of Herod Agrippa I,* Acts 25:13–26:32

Bethany (BETH-uh-nee) *a small town about two miles from Jerusalem.*
- home of Mary, Martha, and Lazarus, John 11:1; 12:1
- home of Simon, Mark 14:3

Bethel (BETH-el) *a town about twelve miles north of Jerusalem.*
- named by Jacob, Genesis 28:10–19
- Jeroboam built idols there, 1 Kings 12:26–33

Bethesda (be-THES-da) See "Bethzatha, pool of."

Bethlehem (BETH-le-hem) *a small town five miles from Jerusalem.*
- hometown of King David, 1 Samuel 16:1, 13
- birthplace of Jesus, Matthew 2:1; Luke 2:15–17

Bethsaida (beth-SAY-ih-duh) *a city in Galilee and home of Peter, Andrew, and Philip,* John 1:44; 12:21
- rejected Jesus, Matthew 11:20–21; Luke 10:13

Bethzatha, pool of (beth-ZAY-tha) *a pool in Jerusalem near the Sheep Gate.*
- Jesus healed a man there, John 5:1–18

betray (be-TRAY) *to turn against.*
- families against each other, Mark 13:12–13
- Jesus betrayed, Matthew 26:20–25; Mark 14:18–46; John 13:2–30

birds
- created by God, Genesis 1:20–21
- saved by Noah, Genesis 6:19–20; 7:1–3
- unclean, Leviticus 11:13–19
- cared for by God, Matthew 6:25–27; Luke 12:24

birth
- spiritual birth, John 1:13; 3:3–8; 1 Peter 1:23

bishop, See "elder."

bitter
- water, Exodus 15:22–25; Numbers 5:18–27; Revelation 8:11
- herbs, Exodus 12:8

bitterness (BIT-er-nes) *sorrow or pain; anger or hatred.*
- warning against, Acts 8:23; Ephesians 4:31; James 3:14

blasphemy (BLAS-feh-mee) *saying things against God or not showing respect for God.*
- examples of, 1 Timothy 1:13; Revelation 13:6
- warnings against, Matthew 12:31–32; Mark 3:28–29
- Jesus accused of, Matthew 9:3; 26:65; Mark 2:6–7; John 10:36

blessing (BLES-ing) *a gift from God; asking God's favor on.*
- promised to Abraham, Genesis 12:1–3
- Isaac blessed Jacob, Genesis 27:1–41
- from God, Acts 3:25; Romans 10:12; 15:27; Hebrews 6:7
- by Jesus, Mark 10:16; Luke 24:50; John 1:16
- by each other, Luke 6:28; 1 Corinthians 4:12; 1 Peter 3:9

blind
- the blind healed, Matthew 9:27–31; 15:30; Mark 8:22–26; John 9
- Saul struck blind, Acts 9:8–9
- spiritually blind, Matthew 23:16–26; John 9:35–41; 2 Peter 1:5–9

blood, *sometimes used to mean "death."*

Caesarea (SES-uh-REE-uh) *a city on the Mediterranean Sea,* Acts 10:1; 21:8; 23:32

Caesarea Philippi (SES-uh-REE-uh fih-LIP-eye) *a city at the base of Mount Hermon,* Matthew 16:13; Mark 8:27

Caiaphas (KAY-uh-fus) *the Jewish high priest from A.D. 18 to 36.*
- plotted to kill Jesus, Matthew 26:3–5; John 11:45–54
- father-in-law to Annas, John 18:13
- at Jesus' trial, Matthew 26:57–67
- questioned Peter and John, Acts 4:5–22

Cain, *the first son of Adam and Eve.*
- killed his brother Abel, Genesis 4:1–24; 1 John 3:12

Caleb (KAY-leb) *one of the twelve men Moses sent to spy out Canaan.*
- explored Canaan, Numbers 13–14
- given the city of Hebron, Joshua 14:6–15

calf
- gold idol, Exodus 32:1–20; 1 Kings 12:26–30; 2 Kings 10:28–29
- fatted, Luke 15:23, 27, 30

camel, Genesis 37:25; 1 Samuel 30:17; 1 Kings 10:2
- Rebekah watered Abraham's camels, Genesis 24:10–20
- "easier for a camel to go through the eye of a needle," Matthew 19:24; Mark 10:25; Luke 18:25
- "swallows a camel," Matthew 23:24

Cana (KAY-nah) *a small town near the city of Nazareth in Galilee.*
- place of Jesus' first miracle, John 2:1–11

Canaan (KAY-nun) *land God promised to the Israelites,* Leviticus 25:38; Numbers 13:2; 33:51; Psalm 105:11

Capernaum (kay-PUR-nay-um) *a city on the western shore of Lake Galilee.*
- Jesus lived there, Matthew 4:12–13
- Jesus healed there, Matthew 8:5–13; Luke 4:31–41
- rejected Jesus, Matthew 11:23–24

capital, *the top of a pillar, usually decorated with beautiful carvings.*
- in the Temple, 1 Kings 7:16–20; 2 Kings 25:17

capital punishment, See article on page 121.
- punishment for killing, Genesis 9:6
- God kills Herod, Acts 12:23
- death by sword, Matthew 26:52

captive
- Israelites as captives, Deuteronomy 28:41; 2 Kings 25:21; Jeremiah 30:3

career/careerism, See article on page 140.
- Abraham's task, Genesis 12
- doing the Lord's work, John 9:4

cassia (CASH-ah) *a pleasant-smelling powder. Its odor is like the bark of the cinnamon plant.* Exodus 30:23–24; Psalm 45:8

celebration, See article on page 290.
- Feast of the Harvest, Leviticus 23:9–14
- the ark returns, 2 Samuel 6:12–23
- Feast of Purim, Esther 9:18–32

celibacy, See article on page 622.
- Jeremiah remains single, Jeremiah 16:2
- of Daniel, Daniel 1:1–21
- versus marriage, 1 Corinthians 7:1–7

census (SIN-sus) *a count of the number of people who live in an area.*
- the Israelites counted, Numbers 1:2; 26:2
- ordered by David, 1 Chronicles 21:1–2
- ordered by Augustus Caesar, Luke 2:1–3

centurion (sin-TUR-ree-un) *a Roman army officer who commanded a hundred soldiers.*
- centurion's servant healed by Jesus, Matthew 8:5–13; Luke 7:1–10
- at Jesus' death, Matthew 27:54; Mark 15:39; Luke 23:47
- Cornelius, Acts 10

Cephas (SEE-fuss) *the Aramaic word for "rock"; in Greek, "Peter." Jesus gave this name to the apostle Simon.* John 1:42

chaff (CHAF) *the husk of a head of grain. Farmers would toss the grain and chaff into the air. Since the chaff is lighter, the wind would blow it away, and the good grain would fall back to the threshing floor.*
- sinners to be destroyed like chaff, Psalms 1:4; 35:5; Matthew 3:12; Luke 3:17

Chaldeans, See "Babylonians."

change of heart and life, *repentance.*
- commanded, Matthew 3:2; Mark 1:15; Luke 13:3; Acts 3:19; 17:30
- causes of, Romans 2:4; 2 Corinthians 7:9–10
- examples of, Matthew 12:41; Luke 11:32

chariot
- Egyptians' chariots destroyed, Exodus 14:5–28
- of fire, 2 Kings 2:11; 6:17
- Ethiopian taught in a chariot, Acts 8:27–31

Chemosh (KEE-mosh) *a god of the Moabites,* Jeremiah 48:13
- worshiped by Solomon, 1 Kings 11:7

cherubim (CHAIR-uh-bim) *heavenly beings with wings and the faces of men and animals.*
- guarded the garden of Eden, Genesis 3:24
- on the Ark of the Agreement, Exodus 25:18–22; 1 Kings 6:23–28
- seen by Ezekiel, Ezekiel 10:1–20

childlessness, See "infertility."

children
- of God, John 1:12; Romans 8:14; 1 Peter 1:14; 1 John 3:1–10
- training of, Ephesians 6:4; Colossians 3:21
- obedience of, Ephesians 6:1; Colossians 3:20; 1 Timothy 3:4
- become like, Matthew 18:3–4
- "Let the little children come to me," Matthew 19:14; Mark 10:14; Luke 18:16

chosen
- Israelites chosen by God, Deuteronomy 7:7–8; 9:4–5; Isaiah 44:1

- people chosen by God, Romans 8:33; Ephesians 1:4–5; 2 Timothy 2:10; 1 Peter 1:2; 2:9
- Jesus chosen by God, Hebrews 1:2; 1 Peter 2:4

Christ (KRYST) *anointed (or chosen) one. Jesus is the Christ, chosen by God to save people from their sins.*
- active in creation, John 1:1–3; Colossians 1:15–17; Hebrews 1:2, 10
- equal with God, John 5:23; 10:30; Philippians 2:6; Colossians 2:9; Hebrews 1:3
- purpose of his death, Romans 5:6; 14:9; Hebrews 9:28; 1 Peter 3:18
- gives life, John 5:21; 6:35; 10:28; 11:25; 14:6
- as Savior, Matthew 1:21; John 12:47
- as judge, Matthew 10:32–33; 25:31–46; John 5:22; Acts 17:31
- living in Christians, John 17:23; Romans 8:10; 2 Corinthians 1:21; Ephesians 3:17
- his return, Acts 1:11; 1 Thessalonians 5:1–11; Hebrews 9:28; 2 Peter 3:10
- enemy of, 1 John 2:18, 22; 4:3; 2 John 7

Christians (KRIS-chuns) *Christ's followers,* Acts 11:26; 26:28; 1 Peter 4:16

church
- established by Christ, Matthew 16:18
- Christ as its head, Ephesians 1:22; 5:23; Colossians 1:18
- Christ died for, Ephesians 5:25
- activities of, Acts 12:5; 1 Corinthians 14:26–40; 1 Timothy 5:16; Hebrews 10:24–25

circumcision (SIR-kum-SIH-zhun) *the cutting off of the foreskin of the male sex organ; each Jewish boy was circumcised on the eighth day after he was born; this was done as a sign of the agreement God had made with his people, the Jews.*
- commanded by God, Genesis 17; Leviticus 12:1–3
- spiritual circumcision, Philippians 3:3; Colossians 2:11

citizen See article on page 1153
- yielding to the government, Romans 13
- God is over human authority, Acts 5:29
- pray for the rulers, 1 Timothy 2:2

city, See article on page 1409.
- the New Jerusalem, Revelation 21
- pray for Babylon, Jeremiah 29:4–7

city of refuge, See "safety, city of."

Claudius (CLAW-dee-us) *the fourth Roman emperor. He ruled from A.D. 41 to 54.* Acts 11:28; 17:7; 18:2

clean, *the state of a person, animal, or action that is pleasing to God. Under the Teachings of Moses, unclean animals could not be eaten. People who were considered clean could live and serve God normally.*
- clean and unclean animals, Deuteronomy 14:1–21; Mark 7:19; Acts 10
- clean and unclean people, Leviticus 13
- spiritually clean, Ephesians 5:26; Hebrews 9:14; 2 Peter 1:9

Cleansing, Day of, *the Day of Atonement; the most special day of the year for the Israelites when the high priest could go into the Most Holy Place. Animals were sacrificed for the sins of the people as a sign that people were cleansed of their sins for a year.*
- rules about, Leviticus 23:26–32; 25:9

cloud
- Israel led by pillar of cloud, Exodus 13:21
- cloud as small as a fist, 1 Kings 18:44
- Jesus leaves and will return in clouds, Luke 21:27; Acts 1:9; 1 Thessalonians 4:17; Revelation 1:7

Colossae (koh-LAH-see) *a city in the country of Turkey,* Colossians 1:1–2

comfort, *to help ease someone's pain, grief, or trouble.*
- bad comforters, Job 16:2
- by shepherd's rod, Psalm 23:4
- from God, Isaiah 49:13; Matthew 5:4; 2 Corinthians 1:3–4
- from the Holy Spirit, John 14:16–18

commands
- to be taught, Deuteronomy 6:1–7; Matthew 5:19
- to be obeyed, Deuteronomy 8:6; Proverbs 19:16; John 15:10
- a new command, John 13:34
- to love, Galatians 5:14; 1 Timothy 1:5; 2 John 6

commitment, See article on page 1244.
- God promises Abraham, Galatians 3:15–17
- agreement between two people, Galatians 3:15
- agreement between kings, Ezekiel 17:11–19

communication, See article on page 1499.
- why John writes, 1 John 1:1–4
- God helps Moses speak, Exodus 4:15

communion (kuh-MYU-nyun) See "Lord's Supper."

community, See article on page 1091.
- in the council of churches, Acts 15
- of the early church, Acts 2:42–47
- sins with a gold calf, Exodus 32

complain
- Pharisees complained, Luke 5:30
- disciples complained, John 6:61
- warnings against, Philippians 2:14

concubine (KON-kyu-bine) See "slave woman."

condemn (kun-DIM) *to judge someone guilty of doing wrong,* John 3:16–18; Romans 2:1; 8:1

coney, See "rock badger."

confess
- admitting sin, Psalm 32:5; Proverbs 28:13; James 5:16; 1 John 1:9
- admitting Christ is Lord, Romans 10:9–10; Philippians 2:11; 1 Timothy 6:12; 1 John 4:2–3

confidence (KON-fuh-dens) *a feeling of assurance; trust.*
- from the Lord, 2 Thessalonians 3:4; 2 Timothy 1:7
- in Christ, Philippians 4:13
- before God, 1 John 3:21

conflict, See article on page 59.
- at Eden, Genesis 3
- between Jews and non-Jews, Ephesians 2:14
- resolving, Matthew 18:15–17

conscience (KON-shunts) *a person's belief about what is right and wrong.*
- Paul's good conscience, Acts 23:1
- commanded to have a good conscience, 1 Timothy 3:9; Hebrews 9:14
- a troubled conscience, Hebrews 10:22; 1 John 3:20
- a corrupt conscience, 1 Timothy 4:2; Titus 1:15

contentment, *satisfaction.*
- Paul learned, Philippians 4:11
- with possessions, Luke 3:14; 1 Timothy 6:6; Hebrews 13:5

conversion (kon-VER-zhun) *a person's turning toward God and becoming a Christian.*
- examples of, Acts 9:1–22; 11:19–21; 1 Thessalonians 1:9

coral (KOR-al) *a type of limestone that forms in the ocean,* Job 28:18; Ezekiel 27:16

Corinth (KOR-inth) *a large seaport in the country of Greece.*
- Paul preached there, Acts 18:1–11
- Paul's letters to the church there, 1 and 2 Corinthians

Cornelius (kor-NEEL-yus) *a Roman army officer in charge of a hundred soldiers,* Acts 10

cornerstone, *the most important stone at the corner of the base of a building; Jesus is called the cornerstone of the new law.*
- Christ as the cornerstone, Ephesians 2:20; 1 Peter 2:4–8

council (KOWN-s'l) *or meeting; the highest Jewish court in the days of Jesus.*
- Jesus before the council, Matthew 26:57–68; Mark 14:53–65
- apostles before the council, Acts 4:1–22; 22:30–23:10
- Stephen before the council, Acts 6:18–7

courage
- need for, Joshua 1:6–9; Psalm 27:14; 1 Corinthians 16:13; Philippians 1:20
- examples of, Acts 4:13; 5:17–32; 20:22–24

court, courtyard, *part of a building that has walls, but no roof. The Temple had four courts:*
- the Court of the Non-Jews (Gentiles), a large open area just inside the walls of Herod's Temple, Mark 11:15–17; John 10:23; Acts 3:11
- the Court of Women, the next area, where both men and women were allowed, Mark 12:41–44
- the Court of Israel, the inner area of the Temple, where only Jewish men were allowed
- the Court of the Priests, the innermost court in the Temple, where only priests were allowed, Matthew 23:35

covenant (KUV-eh-nant) See "agreement."

covet (KUV-et) *to want strongly something that belongs to someone else.*
- forbidden by God, Exodus 20:17; Romans 13:9; Hebrews 13:5

creation
- of the world, Genesis 1–2; Job 38–41; Psalm 8; Isaiah 40:21–26; John 1:1–3; Hebrews 11:3

creation/new creation, See article on page 1234.
- belongs to Christ, 2 Corinthians 5:17
- new heaven and earth, Revelation 21:1

creator, *one who makes something out of nothing.*
- God as our Maker, Deuteronomy 32:6
- "Remember your Creator," Ecclesiastes 12:1

Crete (KREET) *an island in the Mediterranean Sea.*
- Paul visited there, Acts 27:7; Titus 1:5

cross, *two rough beams of wood nailed together; criminals were killed on crosses.*
- Jesus died on a cross, Matthew 27:31–50; Mark 15:20–37; Luke 23:26–46; John 19:16–30
- importance of, 1 Corinthians 1:18; 2:2; Galatians 6:14; Ephesians 2:16; Colossians 2:13–14
- as a symbol of death to oneself, Matthew 10:38; Luke 9:23; Romans 6:6; Galatians 5:24

crown, *a special band worn around the head.*
- a king's crown, Psalm 21:2–3; Song of Solomon 3:11; Revelation 12:3
- of thorns, Matthew 27:29; Mark 15:17; John 19:2
- of victory, 1 Corinthians 9:25; 2 Timothy 4:8; 1 Peter 5:4

crucifixion (kroo-suh-FIK-shun) *to be killed on a cross.* See "cross."

cubit (KU-bit) *a measurement in Bible times; about eighteen inches,* Revelation 21:17

cud, *an animal's food that is chewed slightly, swallowed, brought up, then chewed more completely a second time,* Leviticus 11; Deuteronomy 14

cults, See article on page 1509.
- people turning to, Revelation 9:20
- testing authenticity of, 1 John 2:3–6
- preaching a different Jesus, Galatians 1:6–7

cultural boundaries, See article on page 831.
- defied by Jesus, Mark 2:14–17
- Ruth goes beyond, Ruth 2:11–12
- between Jew and non-Jew, Galatians 2:11–16

cup
- of the king of Egypt, Genesis 40:11
- of Joseph, Genesis 44:1–17
- of Lord's Supper, Matthew 26:27–29; Mark 14:22–25; Luke 22:17–20; 1 Corinthians 11:25–29
- of anger, Isaiah 51:17–23
- of water, Matthew 10:42; Mark 9:41

cupbearer, *the officer who tasted and served the king his wine.*
- to the king of Egypt, Genesis 40
- Nehemiah, cupbearer to Artaxerxes, Nehemiah 1:11

curse
- from God, Deuteronomy 11:26–29; John 7:49; Galatians 3:10–13
- forbidden to people, Matthew 15:4; Romans 12:14; James 3:9–10
- response to, Luke 6:28; 1 Corinthians 4:12

curtain
- of the Holy Tent, Exodus 26:1–2; 36:9
- of the Temple, Matthew 27:51; Mark 15:38; Luke 23:45

Cush, *a country in Africa,* Genesis 2:13; Psalm 68:31; Isaiah 18; 20
Cush, grandson of Noah, Genesis 10
Cyprus (SY-prus) *an island in the Mediterranean Sea,* Acts 11:19–20; 13:4; 15:39
Cyrene (sy-REE-nee) *a city in North Africa,* Acts 2:10; 6:9
- Simon of, Matthew 27:32; Mark 15:21; Luke 23:26

Cyrus (SY-rus) *a king of Persia,* Daniel 1:21
- sent captives home, Ezra 1; 6
- chosen by God, Isaiah 44:28–45:13

D

Dagon (DAY-gon) *a false god of the Philistines,* Judges 16:23; 1 Samuel 5:2–7; 1 Chronicles 10:10
Damascus (duh-MAS-kus) *a city forty miles east of Lake Galilee.*
- a chief city of Syria, 1 Kings 15:18; 2 Chronicles 24:23
- condemned by Amos, Amos 1:3, 5
- Paul converted there, Acts 9:1–22

Dan, a city
- Israel's most northern city, Judges 20:1; 2 Samuel 16:11

Dan, son of Jacob, Genesis 30:6; 49:16–17; Joshua 19:40–48
Daniel (DAN-yel) *a Hebrew captive taken to Babylon as a young man.*
- taken to Babylon, Daniel 1:1–6
- became king's servant, Daniel 1:7–21
- explained Nebuchadnezzar's dreams, Daniel 2; 4
- read the writing on the wall, Daniel 5
- thrown into lions' den, Daniel 6
- his visions, Daniel 7; 8; 10
- a prophet, Matthew 24:15

Darius Hystaspes (dah-RYE-us his-TAHS-peez) *a ruler of Persia who allowed the Jews to finish rebuilding the Temple,* Ezra 5–6
Darius the Mede, *the king of Persia who made Daniel an important ruler under him,* Daniel 5:31–6:28; Haggai 1:1; Zechariah 1:1
darkness, *having no light; a symbol of evil.*
- before creation, Genesis 1:2
- as a plague, Exodus 10:21–23
- at Jesus' death, Matthew 27:45; Mark 15:33; Luke 23:44–45
- spiritual, John 1:5; Romans 13:12; Colossians 1:13
- as punishment, Matthew 8:12; 2 Peter 2:17; Jude 6; 13

David (DAY-vid) *Israel's greatest king.*
- son of Jesse, 1 Samuel 16:13–23
- played harp for Saul, 1 Samuel 16:14–23
- killed Goliath, 1 Samuel 17
- friend of Jonathan, 1 Samuel 18:1–4; 19:1–7; 20
- chased by Saul, 1 Samuel 18–19; 23:7–29
- protected Saul, 1 Samuel 24; 26
- became king, 2 Samuel 2:1–7; 5:1–14
- married Bathsheba, 2 Samuel 11:1–12:25
- reign of, 2 Samuel 5–1 Kings 1
- not allowed to build the Temple, 2 Samuel 7:1–17
- death of, 1 Kings 2:1–11
- Jesus as son of David, Matthew 22:42–45; Luke 1:27; 20:41–44

Day of the Lord, See article on page 661.
- sun will become dark, Joel 2:31
- the Lord warns about, Zechariah 14
- return of Christ, 2 Thessalonians 2:2

deacon (DEE-kun) *a person chosen to serve the church in special ways,* Philippians 1:1; 1 Timothy 3:8–13
Dead Sea, *large lake at the south end of the Jordan River. Several small streams flow into it, but it has no outlet. It is so salty that nothing lives in it. It is also called the "Sea of Arabah," the "Salt Sea," and the "Eastern Sea."* Genesis 14:3; Numbers 34:3, 12; Joshua 3:16
deaf, *unable or unwilling to hear.*
- healed, Matthew 11:5; Luke 7:22
- and dumb spirit, Mark 9:25

death
- a result of sin, Genesis 2:16–17; Romans 5:12; 6:23; 1 Corinthians 15:21
- Christ's victory over, 1 Corinthians 15:24–26, 54–57; 2 Timothy 1:10; Hebrews 2:14; Revelation 1:18
- spiritual death, Ephesians 2:1; Colossians 2:13

Deborah (DEB-oh-rah) *the only woman judge over Israel,* Judges 4–5
debt, See article on page 752.
- parable of unforgiving servant, Matthew 18:21–35
- don't guarantee another's, Proverbs 22:26–27
- forgiving another's, Matthew 6:12

Decapolis (dee-KAP-oh-lis) *ten towns in an area southeast of Lake Galilee,* Matthew 4:25; Mark 5:20; 7:31
decision making/plan, See article on page 621.
- life is not yours, Jeremiah 10:23
- depends on God, Proverbs 19:21
- God controls the nations, Isaiah 40:15

Delilah (dee-LYE-luh) *an evil Philistine woman whom Samson loved,* Judges 16:4–20
Demas (DEE-mus) *a Christian who helped the apostle Paul when Paul was in prison.*
- worked with Paul, Colossians 4:14; Philemon 24
- left Paul, 2 Timothy 4:10

Demetrius (deh-MEE-tree-us) *a silver worker in Ephesus,* Acts 19:23–27, 38
demon, *an evil spirit from the devil. Sometimes demons lived in people, but Jesus could make them come out.*
- people possessed by, Matthew 8:28–32; 9:32–33; Mark 7:24–30; 9:17–29
- Jesus accused of demon possession, Mark 3:22; John 7:20; 8:48; 10:20–21
- demons recognized Jesus, Mark 1:23–26; 3:11–12; 5:7–8; Acts 19:15; James 2:19

deny (di-NY) *refusing to believe the truth.*
- denying Christ, Matthew 10:32–33; 2 Timothy 2:12; 1 John 2:22–23
- Peter denied Christ, Matthew 26:34–35, 69–75

depression, See article on page 490.
- lamenting to God about, Psalm 42
- of Elijah, 1 Kings 19
- from goals unfulfilled, Proverbs 13:12

descendants (de-SIN-dants) *family members who are born to a person or his children: grandchildren, great-grandchildren, great-great-grandchildren and so on,* Genesis 13:14–16; 15:12–16

devil (DEV-'l) *Satan; a spirit and the enemy of God and humans.*
- Jesus tempted by, Matthew 4:1–11; Luke 4:1–13
- children of, John 8:41–44; Acts 13:10; 1 John 3:7–10
- people to oppose, Ephesians 4:27; 6:11; James 4:7

Didymus (DID-ee-mus) *another name for Thomas, one of Jesus' apostles,* John 11:16; 20:24; 21:2

disciple (dih-SYE-p'l) See "follower."

disease
- a result of sin, Exodus 15:26; Deuteronomy 7:15; 28:60–61
- healed by Jesus, Matthew 4:23–24; 15:30–31; 21:14; Luke 7:21
- healed by apostles, Acts 5:12–16; 9:32–35; 14:8–10; 19:11–12; 28:8–9

dishonesty, See "lying."

disobedience
- brought sin, Romans 5:19
- to be punished, 2 Corinthians 10:6; Hebrews 4:11

divide
- heavens and earth, Genesis 1:6–8
- Red Sea, Exodus 14:16, 21
- family against itself, Matthew 12:25; Mark 3:25; Luke 11:17

divorce
- teachings about, Deuteronomy 22:13–19, 28–29; 24:1–4; Matthew 5:31–32; 19:1–12; 1 Corinthians 7:10–16

dog
- drinking water like a dog, Judges 7:5–6
- returns to its vomit, Proverbs 26:11; 2 Peter 2:22
- licked Ahab's blood, 1 Kings 22:38
- licked Lazarus's sores, Luke 16:20–21

door
- Jesus as the door, John 10:1
- "Knock, and the door will open," Luke 11:9–10
- "I stand at the door and knock." Revelation 3:20

donkey
- Balaam's, Numbers 22:21–30
- jawbone of, Judges 15:15–17
- ridden by Jesus, Matthew 21:1–7

Dorcas (DOR-kus) *Tabitha; a Christian woman known for helping the poor.*
- raised from the dead, Acts 9:36–43

doubt, See article on page 1326.
- doubters will not receive, James 1:5–8
- only fools, Psalm 14:1
- Thomas doubts, John 20:24–29

dove, *a small bird similar to a pigeon; often a symbol for love, peace, and the Holy Spirit.*
- sent out by Noah, Genesis 8:8–12
- form taken by the Spirit of God, Matthew 3:16; Mark 1:10
- sellers of, John 2:14–16

dreams
- Joseph's, Genesis 37:1–11
- the king of Egypt's, Genesis 41:1–36
- Nebuchadnezzar's, Daniel 2; 4
- angel appeared to Joseph, Matthew 1:20–21; 2:13,19
- "your old men will dream dreams," Acts 2:17

drunkenness
- Noah became drunk, Genesis 9:20–23
- warnings against, Romans 13:13; 1 Corinthians 6:10; Ephesians 5:18; 1 Peter 4:3

E

eagle
- to "rise up as an eagle," Isaiah 40:31

earth
- creation of, Genesis 1:9–10; Jeremiah 51:15
- belongs to God, Exodus 19:5; Psalm 24:1

earthquake
- experienced by Elijah, 1 Kings 19:11–12
- at the death of Jesus, Matthew 27:51–54
- at Jesus' resurrection, Matthew 28:2
- experienced by Paul and Silas, Acts 16:25–26

Ebal (EE-buhl) *a mountain in Samaria next to Mount Gerizim.*
- place to announce curses, Deuteronomy 11:29; 27:12–13; Joshua 8:30–35

Eden, garden of (EE-den) *the home God created for Adam and Eve,* Genesis 2:8–3:24; Ezekiel 36:35; Joel 2:3

Edom (EE-dum) *Esau; the land where Esau's descendants lived.*
- the land of Esau, Genesis 36:8–9
- refused to let Israelites pass through, Numbers 20:14–21; Judges 11:17–18
- broke away from Judah, 2 Kings 8:20–22
- to be punished, Jeremiah 49:7–22; Ezekiel 25:12–14; Obadiah

education
- of Moses, Acts 7:22
- of children, Deuteronomy 6:1–7
- brings wisdom, Proverbs 8:33; 22:6

Eglon (EGG-lon) *a king of Moab,* Judges 3:12–25

Egypt (EE-jipt) *a country in the northeast part of Africa.*
- Joseph there, Genesis 39–50
- Israelites there, Genesis 46:5–34; Exodus 1; Acts 7:9–38
- Israelites left, Exodus 12:31–51
- Jesus there, Matthew 2:13–15

Ehud (EE-hud) *the second judge of Israel,* Judges 3:12–30

elder (EL-der) *older men who led God's people; appointed leaders in the church.*
- leaders of the Jews, Numbers 11:16–25; Deuteronomy 19:11–12; Matthew 21:23; Acts 4:5–7
- leaders of the church, Acts 11:30; 14:23; 15:2; 16:4
- duties and qualities, Acts 20:28; 1 Timothy 3:1–7; Titus 1:6–9; 1 Peter 5:1–3

Eleazar (el-ee-A-zar) *son of Aaron.*
- birth of, Exodus 6:23–25
- Moses became angry with, Leviticus 10:16–20
- a high priest, Numbers 3:32
- divided the promised land, Numbers 34:17

election, *process of selecting.* **See "chosen."**

Eli (EE-lye) *a priest and the next-to-last judge of Israel.*
- trained Samuel, 1 Samuel 1:9–28; 2:11; 3
- didn't discipline his sons, 1 Samuel 2:12–36
- death of, 1 Samuel 4:1–18

Elihu (ee-LYE-hew) *the fourth of Job's friends to try to explain Job's troubles,* Job 32–37

Elijah (ee-LIE-juh) *a prophet who spoke for God.*
- fed by ravens, 1 Kings 17:1–6
- brought boy to life, 1 Kings 17:7–24
- against prophets of Baal, 1 Kings 18:1–40
- condemned Ahab, 1 Kings 21:17–29
- taken to heaven, 2 Kings 2:1–12
- appeared with Jesus, Matthew 17:1–13; Mark 9:2–13; Luke 9:28–36

Elisha (ee-LYE-shuh) *the prophet who took Elijah's place as God's messenger.*
- received Elijah's spirit, 2 Kings 2:9–14
- helped a Shunammite woman, 2 Kings 4:1–36
- miracles of, 2 Kings 2:19–22; 4:38–44; 6:1–7
- healed Naaman, 2 Kings 5
- death of, 2 Kings 13:14–20

Elizabeth (ee-LIZ-uh-beth) *the wife of Zechariah, a priest.*
- mother of John the Baptist, Luke 1:5–25, 57–66
- visited by Mary, Luke 1:39–45

Elkanah (el-KAY-nuh) *the father of Samuel,* 1 Samuel 1:1–2:11

Elymas (EL-ih-mus) *Bar-Jesus; a magician in the city of Paphos in Cyprus,* Acts 13:4–12

Emmaus (ee-MAY-us) *a town seven miles from Jerusalem.*
- Jesus appeared to disciples near there, Luke 24:13–39

encourage
- encouragement from God, Romans 15:4–5
- Christians to encourage each other, 1 Thessalonians 5:14; 2 Timothy 4:2; Hebrews 3:13; 10:24–25
- examples of encouragement, Acts 11:23; 13:15; 15:31–32

end times/last days, See article on page 762.
- Jesus discusses, Matthew 24
- John describes, Revelation 20

endurance, See "patience."

enemy
- attitude toward, Exodus 23:4–5; Matthew 5:43–48; Luke 6:27–36; Romans 12:20
- God's enemies, Romans 5:10; Philippians 3:18–19; James 4:4

enemy of Christ, *the anti-Christ,* 1 John 2:18, 22; 4:3; 2 John 7

Enoch (E-nuk) *a man who walked with God,* Genesis 5:21–24; Hebrews 11:5

enrollment, See "census."

environment, See article on page 10.
- created by God, Genesis 1:9–25
- stewardship over, Matthew 25:14–30
- making land unclean, Jeremiah 2:7

envy, See "jealousy."

Epaphras (EP-ah-fruhs) *a Christian who started the church at Colossae,* Colossians 1:7–8; 4:12–13; Philemon 23

Epaphroditus (ee-PAF-ro-DYE-tus) *a Christian in the church at Philippi,* Philippians 2:25–30; 4:18

ephah (EE-fah) *a common measurement for dry materials, about twenty quarts,* Exodus 16:36

Ephesus (EF-eh-sus) *the capital city in the Roman state of Asia.*
- Paul's work there, Acts 18:18–20; 1 Corinthians 16:8–9
- church there, Ephesians 1:1; Revelation 2:1–7

ephod (EF-ahd) See "vest, holy."

Ephraim (EE-frah-im) *Joseph's younger son,* Genesis 41:50–52; 48:8–20
- descendants of, Numbers 26:35; Joshua 16:5–10

equality (ee-KWAHL-eh-tee) *being identical in value.*
- in death, Ecclesiastes 3:19–20
- of Jewish and non-Jewish people, Romans 10:12
- in Christ, Galatians 3:26–28

Esau (EE-saw) See "Edom."

Esther (ES-ter) *a Jewish girl who became the wife of Ahasuerus, king of Persia,* Esther 1–10
- became queen, Esther 1:1–2:18
- learned of the plan to kill the Jews, Esther 3–4
- saved the Jews, Esther 5–8

eternal, See "forever."

eternal life, *the new kind of life promised to those who follow Jesus.*
- conditions for, Mark 10:17–31; John 3:14–15; 12:25; 17:3; Galatians 6:7–8
- source of, John 6:27–29; 10:28; Titus 1:2; 1 John 5:11–12

Ethiopia, earlier called "Cush." See "Cush."

eunuch (YOU-nuk) *a man who cannot have sexual relations. In Bible times, eunuchs were often high officers in royal palaces or armies.* 2 Kings 9:32; Esther 2:3; Isaiah 56:3–5; Acts 8:26–40

Euphrates (you-FRAY-teez) *a long, important river in Bible lands.*
- in the garden of Eden, Genesis 2:10–14
- a boundary, Genesis 15:18; 1 Kings 4:21; 2 Kings 24:7

Eutychus (YOU-ti-cus) *a young man in the city of Troas who was brought back to life,* Acts 20:7–12

evangelism, See article on page 793.
- the Great Commission, Matthew 28:16–20
- Jesus sends out seventy-two, Luke 10:1–16
- Paul preaches to the Greeks, Acts 17:16–34

evangelist (ee-VAN-juh-list) *someone who tells the Good News.*
- Philip, the evangelist, Acts 21:8
- as a gift from Christ, Ephesians 4:11

Eve (EEV) *the first woman.*
- created by God, Genesis 2:18–25
- tricked by Satan, Genesis 3; 2 Corinthians 11:3; 1 Timothy 2:13–14

everlasting, *living forever; eternal.*
- God, Genesis 21:33; Nehemiah 9:5; Isaiah 40:28
- Christ, Isaiah 9:6
- kingdom, Daniel 4:3; 2 Peter 1:11
- fire, Matthew 18:8, 25, 41
- gospel, Revelation 14:6

evil
- warnings against, Amos 5:15; Romans 12:9; 1 Thessalonians 5:22
- to be punished, Proverbs 24:20; Isaiah 13:11

evil spirit, See "demon."

Exodus, The
- out of Egypt, Exodus 12:31–51
- praising God for, Psalm 77:16–20

Exodus, New Exodus, See article on page 229.
- Isaiah's prophecy, Isaiah 40:3–5
- Christians are wanderers, Hebrews 3:7–4:13

eye
- "eye for eye," Exodus 21:23–24; Matthew 5:38
- wood in, Matthew 7:3–5; Luke 6:41–42

eyewitness, *one who sees an occurrence and reports on it.*
- of Jesus' life, Luke 1:2; 2 Peter 1:16; 1 John 1:1

Ezekiel (ee-ZEEK-yel) *a prophet during the time the Jews were captured by the Babylonians,* Ezekiel 1:3
- his vision of dry bones, Ezekiel 37:1–14

Ezra (EZ-ra) *the leader of a group of Israelites who were allowed to return to Jerusalem from Babylon,* Ezra 7–10; Nehemiah 8

F

faith (FAYTH) *belief and trust.*
- definition of, Hebrews 11:1
- sources of, Romans 1:20; 10:17
- examples of, Matthew 8:5–10; 15:21–28; Hebrews 11
- power of, Matthew 17:20–21; Ephesians 6:16
- made right with God by, Romans 4:3; 5:1; Philippians 3:9
- salvation by, Mark 16:15–16; John 5:24; 20:31; Romans 10:9; Galatians 2:16
- blessings by, Galatians 3:1–14; Ephesians 3:12; 1 Peter 1:5
- continue in, 2 Corinthians 13:5; Colossians 1:23; 1 Timothy 1:19; 2 Timothy 2:22
- lack of, Matthew 8:26; 14:31; 16:8

faithful (FAYTH-ful) *honest, loyal, true.*
- God is faithful, Deuteronomy 32:3–4; Isaiah 49:7; 2 Timothy 2:13; Hebrews 3:6; Revelation 19:11
- God's people must be faithful, Matthew 25:21; Revelation 2:10; 14:12; 17:14

fall, *sometimes used to describe the first sin.*
- Adam and Eve sinned, Genesis 3

false
- gods, Exodus 20:3; Deuteronomy 4:28; 1 Chronicles 16:26
- prophets, Deuteronomy 13:1–11; 18:22; Jeremiah 14:13–16; Matthew 7:15
- Christs, Matthew 24:24; Mark 13:22
- apostles, 2 Corinthians 11:13
- brothers, Galatians 2:4
- teachers, 2 Peter 2:1

family
- of believers, Galatians 6:10; Hebrews 2:11; 1 Peter 4:17

famine (FAM-un) *a time of hunger when there is very little food.*
- in Egypt, Genesis 41:30–31, 53–57
- in Moab, Ruth 1:1
- in Israel, 1 Kings 17:1
- in Jerusalem during Claudius's rule, Acts 11:27–28

fasting (FAST-ing) *giving up food for a while.*
- to show sorrow, 1 Samuel 1:11–12; 2 Samuel 12:15–22
- of Jesus, Matthew 4:1–2
- how to fast, Matthew 6:16–18
- combined with prayer, Ezra 8:23; Luke 5:33; Acts 13:1–3

father
- to be honored, Exodus 20:12; Ephesians 6:2
- commands to, Colossians 3:21
- God as Father, Matthew 6:9; 23:9; 2 Corinthians 6:18; Galatians 4:6; Hebrews 12:4–11

fear, *a feeling of being afraid, or one of deep respect.*
- of God, Matthew 10:26–31; Luke 23:40
- overcoming, 2 Timothy 1:7; Hebrews 13:6; 1 John 4:18
- "your salvation . . . with fear and trembling," Philippians 2:12

feast (FEEST) *a special meal and celebration for a certain purpose.*
- Feast of Dedication, an eight-day celebration for the Jews that showed they were thankful that the Temple had been cleansed again, John 10:22
- Feast of Harvest, see "Feast of Weeks."

- Feast of Purim (PURE-rim) reminded the Israelites of how they were saved from death during the time of Queen Esther, Esther 9:18–32
- Feast of Shelters, "Feast of Booths" or "Feast of Tents"; reminded the Israelites of how God had taken care of them when they left Egypt and lived in tents in the wilderness, Exodus 23:16; Deuteronomy 16:13–17
- Feast of Unleavened Bread, or "Passover"; reminded the Israelites how God brought them out of Egyptian slavery, Exodus 12:1–30; Numbers 28:16–25; Deuteronomy 16:1–8
- Feast of Weeks, or "Pentecost," the "Feast of Harvest," or the "Day of Firstfruits"; a feast of thanksgiving for the summer harvest, Exodus 34:22; Leviticus 23:15–22; Numbers 28:26–31

Felix (FEE-lix) *the Roman governor of Judea from A.D. 52 to 54.*
- put Paul on trial, Acts 23:23–24; 24

fellowship (FEL-o-ship) *sharing friendship and love with others.*
- with Christ, Matthew 18:20; 1 Corinthians 1:9; 1 John 1:3
- with the Holy Spirit, 2 Corinthians 13:14; Philippians 2:1
- with believers, Acts 2:42; 1 John 1:7

festivals, See "feasts."

Festus (FES-tus) *governor of Judea after Felix.*
- put Paul on trial, Acts 25–26

fighting
- against evil, 2 Corinthians 10:3–6; Ephesians 6:12
- "fight the good fight," 1 Timothy 1:18
- "I have fought the good fight." 2 Timothy 4:7

fire, *used by God as a sign of his presence and power.*
- the burning bush, Exodus 3:1–6
- pillar of, Exodus 13:21–22
- chariot of, 2 Kings 2:11
- wrong kind of, Numbers 26:61
- fiery furnace, Daniel 3:25
- baptism of, Matthew 3:11
- of punishment, Matthew 5:22; 13:41–42; Mark 9:43; 2 Thessalonians 1:8; Hebrews 10:27
- everything destroyed by fire, 2 Peter 3:10
- evidence of the Holy Spirit, Acts 2:3

firstborn (FIRST-born) *the oldest child in a family; the firstborn son in a Jewish family received a double share of his father's wealth and became the leader of the family when his father died.*
- Esau sold his rights, Genesis 25:27–34
- Israelites as God's firstborn, Exodus 4:22; Jeremiah 31:9
- death of, Exodus 11:1–8
- given to God, Exodus 13:1–16

firstfruits (FIRST-fruits) *the first and best crops and animals the Israelites raised and gave to God at harvest time,* Exodus 34:26; Numbers 28:26; Deuteronomy 18:3–4

fish
- clean and unclean, Deuteronomy 14:9–10
- used in miracles, Matthew 14:17; Luke 5:1–7; John 21:1–13

flax (FLAKS) *a plant used to make clothing and ropes,* Exodus 9:31; Isaiah 19:9
- used by Rahab, Joshua 2:6

flood, Genesis 6:9–8; Matthew 24:37–39; 2 Peter 3:5–6

follower (FAHL-o-wer) *a person who is learning from someone else; a "disciple."*
- of John, Matthew 9:14; 11:2; Mark 2:18
- of Christ, Matthew 11:1; 28:18–20; John 19:38; Acts 6:1–7; 11:26

folly, See "fool"

fool, *someone who is not wise,* Proverbs 10:8–23; 17:7–28; 26:1–12
- examples of, Matthew 7:24–27; 25:1–13
- rejects God, Psalms 14:1; 53:1; Romans 1:20–23

footwashing, *done as an act of hospitality in Bible times because people wore sandals.*
- examples of, 1 Samuel 25:41; Luke 7:44; John 13:1–17

foreigner (alien), See article on page 1410.
- believers in this world, 1 Peter 2:11; Hebrews 11:13
- being unfair to, Deuteronomy 24:14–17

forever
- God's love continues forever, 1 Chronicles 16:34; Psalm 136
- praise God forever, Psalm 44:8; Romans 9:5
- be with God forever, 1 Thessalonians 4:17; 1 John 2:17
- Jesus lives forever, Hebrews 7:24
- "word of the Lord will live forever," 1 Peter 1:25

forgiveness
- of others, Matthew 6:14–15; 18:21–35; Mark 11:25; Luke 17:3–4
- by God, Luke 24:47–48; Acts 10:43; Ephesians 1:7; 1 John 1:9
- not given, Matthew 12:31–32; Mark 3:28–29; Luke 12:10; John 20:19–23
- "Father, forgive them," Luke 23:34

fornication (for-ni-KAY-shun) *having sexual relations with someone to whom you are not married.* See "adultery."

fountain, Proverbs 10:11; 13:14; 14:27; 16:22

frankincense (FRANK-in-senz) *a very expensive, sweet-smelling perfume,* Exodus 30:34; Revelation 18:13
- given to Jesus, Matthew 2:11

freedom, *having liberty; not being a slave.*
- given to Jesus, Matthew 2:11
- in Christ, 2 Corinthians 3:17; Galatians 5:1; Hebrews 2:15
- from sin, Romans 6; 8:2; Hebrews 9:15
- to be used wisely, 1 Corinthians 8:9; Galatians 5:13; 1 Peter 2:16
- "truth will make you free," John 8:32

friend
- characteristics of, Proverbs 17:17; 18:24
- of Jesus, John 15:13–15
- Abraham, as a friend of God, James 2:23

frontlet, See "box of Scriptures."

fruit, *often used to mean "result."*
- spiritual, Matthew 7:15–20; John 15:1–17; Colossians 1:10
- of the Spirit, Galatians 5:22

fulfill (full-FILL) *to give the full meaning or to cause something to come true.*
- prophecy fulfilled, Matthew 2:14–15, 17–18; Luke 4:16–21; 24:44–46; John 19:24

furnace
- Shadrach, Meshach, and Abednego thrown into, Daniel 3
- hell compared to, Matthew 13:42

G

Gabriel (GAY-bree-el) *an angel of God.*
- seen in a vision, Daniel 8:16; 9:21–27
- announced Jesus' birth, Luke 1:8–20, 26–38

Gad, a prophet
- David's seer, 1 Samuel 22:5; 2 Samuel 24:11–19

Gad, son of Jacob
- birth of, Genesis 30:9–11
- land of, Deuteronomy 33:20–21; Joshua 22:1–4
- tribe of, Numbers 26:15

Gadarenes (gad-uh-REENZ) *people who lived in Gadara, southeast of Lake Galilee,* Matthew 8:28–34

Galatia (guh-LAY-shuh) *a district of Asia,* Acts 16:6; 18:23; Galatians 1:2; 1 Corinthians 16:1

Galilee (GAL-i-lee) *the country between the Jordan River and the Mediterranean Sea,* 2 Kings 15:29; Matthew 4:23; 21:11; John 7:1

Galilee, Lake (GAL-i-lee) *or "Sea of Galilee," "Sea of Kinnereth," "Lake of Gennesaret," "Sea of Tiberias"; a lake thirteen miles long and eight miles wide.*
- Jesus preached there, Matthew 4:12–22; 8:23–27; John 6:1–2, 16–21

Gallio (GAL-ee-oh) *a Roman governor in the country of Achaia.*
- refused to punish Paul, Acts 18:12–17

Gamaliel (guh-MAY-lee-el) *a Pharisee and Jewish teacher of the Law of Moses.*
- prevented deaths of Peter and John, Acts 5:17–40
- Paul's teacher, Acts 22:1–3

gate
- Samson removed, Judges 16:3
- narrow, Matthew 7:13–14
- of heaven, Revelation 21:21

Gath, *one of the Philistines' five strong cities,* Joshua 13:3; 1 Samuel 21:10–12
- captured Ark taken there, 1 Samuel 5:1–10
- home of Goliath, 1 Samuel 17:4

Gaza (GAY-zuh) *one of the Philistines' five strong cities,* Joshua 13:3; Acts 8:26
- Samson in prison there, Judges 16

gazelle (gah-ZEL) *an animal of the antelope family; known for its beauty and speed,* Deuteronomy 12:15; 1 Chronicles 12:8

Gedaliah (ged-uh-LYE-uh) *made governor of Judah by Nebuchadnezzar after capturing Jerusalem,* 2 Kings 25:22–26; Jeremiah 39:14–41:18

Gehazi (geh-HAY-zye) *a servant of the prophet Elisha.*
- and the Shunammite woman, 2 Kings 4:8–37
- and Naaman, 2 Kings 5:1–27

Gehenna, See "Hinnom."

genealogy (jee-nee-AHL-o-jee) *a list of the descendants in a family.*
- of Jesus, Matthew 1:1–17; Luke 3:23–38

generosity (jen-uh-RAHS-et-ee) *unselfishness.*
- shown to Ruth, Ruth 2:14–16
- to the needy, Nehemiah 8:10
- rewarded, Proverbs 11:25; Matthew 7:11

Gennesaret, Lake of, See "Galilee, Lake."

Gentiles (JEN-tiles) *anyone not Jewish.*
- received the Good News, Acts 10:44–45; 11:18; Romans 11:11–15; Ephesians 3:6–8
- conflict with the Jews, Acts 15:5–11; Galatians 2:11–14

Gerasenes (GER-un-seenz) *or "Gadarenes."* See "Gadarenes."

Gerizim (GER-i-zim) *a mountain next to Mount Ebal about thirty miles north of Jerusalem.*
- blessings announced from there, Deuteronomy 11:29; 27:12; Joshua 8:33

Gethsemane (geth-SEM-uh-nee) *a garden of olive trees just outside Jerusalem.*
- Jesus arrested there, Matthew 26:36–56; Mark 14:32–50

Gibeah (GIB-ee-uh) *a city about three miles north of Jerusalem,* Judges 19:12–20:43; 1 Samuel 10:26

Gibeon (GIB-ee-uhn) *a town about six miles northwest of Jerusalem.*
- Joshua defeated Amorites there, Joshua 9–10

Gideon (GID-ee-uhn) *the judge who led Israel to defeat the Midianites,* Judges 6:1–8:35
- angel appeared to, Judges 6:11–24
- destroyed Baal idol, Judges 6:25–32
- defeated Midianites, Judges 6:33–8:21
- the sign of the fleece, Judges 6:36–40
- built an idol, Judges 8:22–27
- death of, Judges 8:28–32
- hero of faith, Hebrews 11:32–34

gifts, *talents or abilities.*
- spiritual, Romans 12:6–8; 1 Corinthians 7:7; 12; 14:1–25; Ephesians 4:7

Gihon (GYE-hohn) *a spring outside the walls of Jerusalem,* 1 Kings 1:38–39; 2 Chronicles 32:30; 33:14

Gilead (GIL-ee-ad) *the area that Israel owned east of the Jordan River,* Numbers 32; Deuteronomy 3:10–16

Gilgal (GIL-gal) *the first place the Israelites camped after entering the promised land,* Joshua 4:19–5:12

gittith (GIT-tith) *probably a musical word and a musical instrument,* Psalms 8; 81; 84

giving
- examples of generous giving, Mark 12:43; Acts 10:2; 11:29–30; 2 Corinthians 8:3–5
- proper attitude toward, Matthew 6:3–4; Romans 12:8; 1 Corinthians 13:3; 2 Corinthians 9:7

gleaning (GLEEN-ing) *to gather grain left in the field after harvest,* Ruth 2

glory, *visible sign of God's greatness.*
- appeared in a cloud, Exodus 16:10; 24:16–17
- seen by Moses, Exodus 33:18–23
- "The heavens tell the glory of God," Psalm 19:1
- seen by Ezekiel, Ezekiel 1:26–28; 3:23; 8:4
- at Jesus' birth, Luke 2:8–14
- of Jesus, Luke 9:28–32
- seen by Stephen, Acts 7:55
- in the temple in heaven, Revelation 15:8

gluttony (GLUH-tun-ee) *eating too much.*
- warnings against, Deuteronomy 21:20; Proverbs 23:20–21
- Jesus accused of, Matthew 11:19; Luke 7:34

goat
- for a sin offering, Leviticus 9:3
- divided from sheep, Matthew 25:32–33
- blood of, Hebrews 9:12–13; 10:4

God, *the One who made the world and everything in it.* See also "glory."
- the creator, Genesis 1; Acts 17:24; Romans 1:25
- nearness of, Acts 17:27–28; James 4:8
- goodness of, Matthew 19:17; Acts 14:17; Romans 2:4; 1 John 4:7–11
- eternal nature of, Psalm 102:24–28; 1 Timothy 1:17; 6:16
- images of, Exodus 33:18–23; 2 Samuel 22:7–20; Psalm 50:1–7
- names of, Exodus 3:13–14; Exodus 6:23; 1 Timothy 6:15; Hebrews 12:9; James 1:17; 5:4
- power of, Job 9:4–19; Isaiah 40:12–31; Matthew 19:26
- presence of, John 1:14; John 4:21–24
- mercy of, Exodus 20:6; Numbers 14:18; Ephesians 2:4
- justice of, Psalm 67:4; Acts 17:31; Romans 2:2
- will of, Matthew 6:10; Colossians 1:9–14; Proverbs 3:5–7

golden calf, *an idol made to worship false gods.*
- made by Aaron, Exodus 32:1–24
- made by Jeroboam, 1 Kings 12:26–33

golden rule, *a name often used for Jesus' command: "Do to others what you want them to do to you,"* Matthew 7:12; Luke 6:31

Golgotha (GOL-guh-thuh) *Calvary; the hill where Jesus was crucified,* Matthew 27:33; Mark 15:22; John 19:17

Goliath (go-LYE-eth) *the giant from Gath whom David killed,* 1 Samuel 17

Gomorrah (goh-MOR-ruh) *an evil city near Sodom.*
- destroyed by God, Genesis 18:17–19:29; Matthew 10:11–15; 2 Peter 2:6

Good News, *also called the "gospel." Jesus died on the cross, was buried, and came back to life so people can be saved.* Mark 1:1; Acts 5:42; 13:26–39
- power of, Romans 1:16–17; Colossians 1:5–6; 1 Corinthians 15:2
- preached by the apostles, Luke 9:6; Acts 8:25; Philippians 1:5, 12–14

good works, See article on page 1263.
- made by God to do, Ephesians 2:8–10
- faith without action, James 2:14–26
- blessing comes from faith, Galatians 3

Goshen (GO-shen) *an area in the Nile delta of Egypt.*
- home for Joseph's family, Genesis 45:9–10; 47:1–6, 27

gospel (GOS-p'l) *"good news." The first four books of the New Testament are called the Gospels because they tell the good news of what Jesus has done for us.* See "Good News."

gossip
- to be avoided, Romans 1:28–32; 2 Corinthians 12:20; 1 Timothy 5:13

government (GUV-er-ment) *group of people in charge of managing and making laws for people in a country, state, or city.*
- to be obeyed, Matthew 22:15–21; Romans 13:1–7; Titus 3:1; 1 Peter 2:13–17

governor
- Joseph, governor of Egypt, Genesis 42:6
- Nehemiah, governor of Judah, Nehemiah 5:14
- Pilate, governor of Judea, Matthew 27:2
- Felix, governor of Judea, Acts 23:26

grace, *God's kindness and love shown to us, even though we do not deserve them.*
- source of, Ephesians 3:7; Hebrews 4:14–16
- saved by, Acts 15:11; Romans 3:24; Ephesians 2:5–8; 2 Timothy 1:9
- misuse of, Romans 6; Galatians 5:4; Jude 4

grandchildren
- a blessing, Ruth 4:15; Proverbs 17:6
- inherit grandparents' wealth, Proverbs 13:22

grave, See "tomb."

Great Sea, See "Mediterranean Sea."

Greece, *once the most powerful nation in southeast Europe. Northern Greece was called "Macedonia." Southern Greece was called "Achaia."*
- Paul preached there, Acts 16:11–12; 20:1–6

greed, *selfish desire for more than one's share of something.*
- never satisfied, Proverbs 27:20
- beware of, Luke 12:15
- love of money, 1 Timothy 6:10

Greek
- the language of Greece, John 19:20; Acts 21:37; Revelation 9:11
- the people from Greece, Acts 14:1; 16:1; Colossians 3:11

grief
- of David for Absalom, 2 Samuel 18:33
- of the disciples, Matthew 17:23; John 16:6

growing old, See article on page 210.
- Moses' humility, Exodus 4
- respect for the aging, Leviticus 19:32

guidance (GYD-ns) *direction.*
- by God, Exodus 13:21
- of the humble, Psalm 25:9
- of the Holy Spirit, John 16:15

guilt, *fact of having done wrong; regret, shame.*
- for improper worship, 1 Corinthians 11:27
- for breaking the Law, James 2:10
- cleansed of, Job 33:9; Isaiah 6:7; Hebrews 10:22

H

Habakkuk (ha-BAK-uk) *a prophet who wrote about the same time as Jeremiah,* Habakkuk 1–3

Hades (HAY-deez) *the world of the dead,* Revelation 6:8; 20:13–14

Hagar (HAY-gar) *Sarah's slave girl.*
- gave birth to Ishmael, Genesis 16
- sent away by Sarah, Genesis 21:8–21

Haggai (HAG-ay-eye) *a prophet in Jerusalem when the Israelites came back from Babylon,* Ezra 5:1; 6:14; Haggai 1–2

half-tribe, *one of the two parts of the tribe of Manasseh. One half-tribe settled east of the Jordan and the other settled west of the Jordan.* Joshua 1:12–15; 13:8–9; 22

Ham, *the son of Noah,* Genesis 6:10; 9:18–19; 10:6

Haman (HAY-man) *the chief officer under Ahasuerus, king of Persia.*
- planned to kill the Jews, Esther 3–6
- hanged, Esther 7

handicap, physical, See article on page 912.
- feast without debts, Luke 14:7–11
- blind man healed, John 9
- care for the handicapped, Leviticus 19:14

hands, laying on, *a ceremony where a person places his hands upon another.*
- for healing, Mark 5:23; 6:5; Luke 4:40
- to receive the Holy Spirit, Acts 8:17–19; 19:6
- for blessing, Mark 10:16; Acts 13:3

Hannah (HAN-uh) *the mother of Samuel,* 1 Samuel 1–2:21

happiness
- of the people of God, Psalms 144:15; 146:5; Proverbs 16:20; Matthew 5:3–12
- comes from wisdom, Proverbs 3:13

Haran (HAY-ran)
- Abraham's brother, Genesis 11:26–31
- home of Abraham, Genesis 11:31–12:5

harlot, See "prostitute."

harp, *the favorite musical instrument of the Jews.*
- first played, Genesis 4:21
- played by David, 1 Samuel 16:23; 18:10–11
- to praise God, Psalms 33:2; 71:22; 150:3

harvest
- of the poor, Ruth 2
- as a symbol, Matthew 9:37–38; 13:24–30, 39; Revelation 14:14–16

hate
- seven things God hates, Proverbs 6:16–19
- a time to, Ecclesiastes 3:8
- of the world toward Jesus, John 15:18
- equal to murder, 1 John 3:15
- commands against, Galatians 5:19–21; 1 John 4:19–21

head
- a part of the body, Genesis 3:15; Psalm 23:5; Matthew 8:20; 1 Corinthians 12:21; Revelation 14:14
- a leader, Ephesians 1:22; 5:23; Colossians 1:18

heal
- a time to, Ecclesiastes 3:3
- by faith, Matthew 9:21–22; James 5:15
- "Doctor, heal yourself." Luke 4:23

heart, *the mind or feelings; not the physical heart that pumps blood,* Deuteronomy 6:5; Matthew 22:37

heaven
- the home of God, Matthew 5:34; Mark 16:19; John 3:13; Revelation 4
- angel spoke from, Genesis 21:17; 22:11
- opened, Matthew 3:16; Acts 7:56; 10:11
- fire from, 2 Kings 1:10–14; 1 Chronicles 21:26
- third heaven, 2 Corinthians 12:2
- the new heaven, Revelation 21:1–4
- kingdom of, Matthew 3:2; 5:3, 19–20

Hebrews (HEE-brooz) *another name for the Jewish people,* Exodus 7:16; 2 Corinthians 11:22; Philippians 3:5

Hebron (HEE-bron) *a city about twenty miles southwest of Jerusalem,* Genesis 13:18; Numbers 13:22; 2 Samuel 2:1–11

heir (AIR) *the person who inherits what belongs to a relative. Because through Christ we can be adopted children of God, Christians are heirs to God's riches.*
- Abraham's heir, Genesis 15:3–4
- heir of God, Romans 8:17; Galatians 4:7

hell
- home of the devil and his angels, 2 Peter 2:4
- future home of sinners, Matthew 10:28; 23:33; Revelation 21:8
- descriptions of, Matthew 13:42; Mark 9:47–48; James 3:6; Revelation 14:11

helmet
- worn in battle, 1 Samuel 17:5; Ezekiel 23:24
- a symbol of salvation, Isaiah 59:17; Ephesians 6:17; 1 Thessalonians 5:8

help
- the stone of help, 1 Samuel 7:12
- the Holy Spirit as helper, Romans 8:26; Philippians 1:19
- from God, Psalms 46:1; 121:1–2; Isaiah 41:10
- commanded, 1 Thessalonians 5:14; Hebrews 6:10

Herod I (HEH-rud) *"Herod the Great"; king of Palestine from 40 to 4 B.C.,* Matthew 2:1; Luke 1:5

Herod Agrippa I (uh-GRIP-a) *king of Palestine from AD 41 to 44,* Acts 12:1

Herod Agrippa II, *king of Palestine from AD 52 to 70,* Acts 25:13–26:32

Herod Antipas (AN-ti-pus) *king of Palestine from 4 B.C. to about AD 39,* Matthew 14:1; Mark 6:14; Luke 23:7

Herodias (heh-ROW-dee-us) *the granddaughter of Herod I.*
- asked for John's head, Matthew 14:3–12; Mark 6:17–28; Luke 3:19

Hezekiah (hez-eh-KY-uh) *one of the good kings of Judah.*
- destroyed idols, 2 Kings 18:1–8; 2 Chronicles 29–31
- attacked by Assyria, 2 Kings 18:9–19:37; 2 Chronicles 32:1–23; Isaiah 36–37
- life extended by God, 2 Kings 20:1–11; Isaiah 38
- death of, 2 Kings 20:12–21; 2 Chronicles 32:24–33

higgaion (hig-GI-on) *probably a time to think quietly during a song,* Psalm 9:16

high place, *a place to worship gods,* 1 Kings 14:23; 2 Chronicles 31:1; 33:3

high priest, *the most important religious leader of the Jewish people.*
- rules for, Leviticus 21:10–15
- of the Jews, Exodus 29:30; Numbers 35:25; Matthew 26:3; Acts 23:2
- Jesus as, Hebrews 2:17; 3:1; 4:14–5:10; 8:1–6

Hilkiah (hil-KY-ah) *high priest when Josiah was king,* 2 Kings 22–23; 2 Chronicles 34

Hinnom, Valley of (HIN-num) *an area where trash was burned just outside of Jerusalem; also called "Gehenna,"* Joshua 15:8; 18:16; Nehemiah 11:30

Hiram (HY-rum) *king of Tyre when David and Solomon were kings over Israel.*
- supplied trees for Solomon's Temple, 2 Samuel 5:11; 1 Kings 5:1–18; 9:11–27; 10:22

Hittites (HIT-tites) *people who lived in what is now Turkey,* Genesis 23:1–16; Exodus 3:8; Joshua 1:4; 1 Samuel 11:3

holy (HO-lee) *pure, belonging to and willing to serve God.*
- holiness of God, Leviticus 11:45; Isaiah 6:3; Hebrews 12:10; Revelation 4:8
- holy kiss, Romans 16:16
- people to be holy, Ephesians 1:4; Colossians 1:22–23; 3:2; 1 Peter 1:15–16

Holy of Holies, See "Most Holy Place."

Holy Place, *a room in the Holy Tent and the Temple,* Exodus 26:31–35; 28:29; Leviticus 6:30; 1 Kings 8:10–11

Holy Spirit (HO-lee SPIH-rit) *one of the three persons of God. The Holy Spirit helped the apostles do miracles and led men to write God's word; he lives in Christians today.*
- in creation, Genesis 1:2
- living in Christians, John 14:15–17; 1 Corinthians 6:19; Galatians 4:6
- as a helper, John 14:25–26; 16:7–15; Romans 8:1–27; Galatians 5:22–25
- filled with, Luke 1:15; Acts 2:4; 7:55; 11:23–24
- sin against, Matthew 12:31; Acts 5:3; 1 Thessalonians 5:19; Hebrews 10:29

Holy Tent, See "Meeting Tent."

Holy War & Divine Warrior, See article on page 230.
- God as a warrior, Exodus 15:3
- laws for war, Deuteronomy 20
- spiritual battles, 2 Corinthians 10:3–6

home, See "house."

homosexuality, See article on page 1101.
- Paul condemns, Romans 1:26–27
- "a hateful sin," Leviticus 18:22
- Sodom and Gomorrah, Genesis 19:1–29

honest
- heart, Luke 8:15
- people, 2 Kings 12:15
- answer, Proverbs 24:26
- commanded, Mark 10:19; Philippians 4:8

honor
- for the old, Leviticus 19:32
- from God, 1 Samuel 2:30
- comes from humility, Proverbs 15:33
- to the deserving, Romans 13:7
- shown to parents, Exodus 20:12; Matthew 15:4
- shown to God, Proverbs 3:9; John 5:23; Revelation 4:9
- not shown to a prophet in his own town, Matthew 13:57

hope, *looking forward to something you really expect to happen.*
- reason for, Romans 5:3–5; 15:4; 2 Thessalonians 2:16; 1 Peter 1:13
- nature of, Romans 8:24–25
- results of, Colossians 1:5; Hebrews 6:18

Hophni (HOF-nee) *an evil son of Eli the priest,* 1 Samuel 2:12–34; 3:11–4:18

Horeb, Mount, See "Sinai."

horses, Exodus 14:9; 1 Kings 10:26–29; Psalm 33:16–17; James 3:3

Hosanna (ho-ZAN-ah) *a shout of joy in praising God,* Matthew 21:9, 15; Mark 11:9; John 12:13

Hosea (ho-SEE-uh) *a prophet who lived about seven hundred years before Christ.*
- his unfaithful wife, Hosea 1
- his warnings to Israel, Hosea 2; 4–14

hospitality
- of Abraham, Genesis 18:1–16
- teachings about, Romans 12:13; 1 Timothy 3:2; 5:9–10; 1 Peter 4:9

hosts, *armies; God is called the "Lord of hosts."* See "Lord of hosts."

house/home, See article on page 109.
- Abram moves, Genesis 12:1
- parable of foundations, Matthew 7:24–27
- Christians as household items, 2 Timothy 2:20–21

Huldah (HUL-duh) *a woman prophet,* 2 Kings 22:14–20; 2 Chronicles 34:22–28

human, See article on page 19.
- created in God's image, Genesis 1:26–28
- "whom God made like himself," James 3:9–10

humble (HUM-bul) *not bragging or calling attention to yourself.*
- Moses as example of, Numbers 12:3
- humility commanded, Luke 14:7–11; 22:24–27; Ephesians 4:2; Philippians 2:3
- Jesus' humility, Philippians 2:5–8

hunger
- feeding the hungry, Matthew 25:34–35; Romans 12:20
- spiritual, John 6:35; 1 Peter 2:2

husband
- responsibilities of, 1 Corinthians 7:3–5; Ephesians 5:25–33; Colossians 3:19; 1 Peter 3:7

hymn (HIM) *a song that teaches us about God or praises him,* Matthew 26:30; Ephesians 5:19; Colossians 3:16
- Jesus and apostles sang, Matthew 26:30; Mark 14:26
- teachings about, Ephesians 5:19; Colossians 3:16

hypocrisy (hi-POK-ri-see) acting as if one is good when that is not true, Matthew 23:28; 1 Peter 2:1

hypocrite (HIP-oh-krit) *a person who acts as if he is good but isn't.*
- warnings about, Matthew 6:2, 5, 16; 7:3–5; Luke 13:15–17
- Pharisees as hypocrites, Matthew 15:1–9; 23:13–32

hyssop (HIS-op) *a small bushy plant; marjoram,* Exodus 12:22; Leviticus 14:4, 6; John 19:29

I

Iconium (eye-KOH-nee-um) *a city in Galatia where Paul preached,* Acts 14:1–7, 19–23

idol (EYE-d'l) *a statue of a false god.* See also "Baal," "Chemosh," "Molech."
- worship of, 2 Kings 17:12–17; Acts 17:16–23; 19:24; Romans 1:25
- warnings against worship of, Leviticus 19:4; Deuteronomy 6:14–15; 1 Corinthians 5:10–11; 6:9–10
- Baal, 1 Kings 18:17–40
- Chemosh, Numbers 21:29
- Molech, Jeremiah 32:35

ignorance (IG-nur-rance) *a lack of knowledge.*
- not an excuse, Leviticus 5:17

image, *likeness.*
- God's, Genesis 1:26–27
- Caesar's, Luke 20:24
- the Lord's, 2 Corinthians 3:18
- Jesus in God's image, Hebrews 1:3

immorality (IM-mor-RAL-i-tee) *evil; sinfulness.* See also "sin."
- warnings against, 1 Corinthians 5:9–11; 6:9–10; Galatians 5:19–21; Ephesians 5:5

immortality (IM-mor-TAL-i-tee) *life after death,* Job 14:1–14; Daniel 12:1–2; 1 Corinthians 15:12–58; 2 Timothy 1:10. See also "eternal life."

impossible
- people cannot do, Matthew 19:26
- for God to lie, Hebrews 6:18
- without faith to please God, Hebrews 11:6

incarnation, See article on page 962.
- "the Word became human," John 1:14
- became like a servant, Philippians 2:7
- "exactly like God," 2 Corinthians 4:4

incense (IN-sents) *a spice burned to make a sweet smell.*
- altar of, Exodus 30:1–10, 34–38; Revelation 8:3–5
- used in worship, Psalm 141:2
- as a gift, Matthew 2:11

infertility (childlessness/barrenness), See article on page 862.
- Elizabeth was childless, Luke 1:7
- Hannah desires a child, 1 Samuel 1:11

inheritance (in-HEH-ri-tence) *something valuable that is handed down within a family.* See "land."
- of land, Numbers 36:8; Deuteronomy 3:28; Psalm 25:13

iniquity, See "sin."

inn, *a place for travelers to spend the night,* Luke 2:7; 10:34

innocence (IN-uh-sens) *not guilty of sin.*
- of Adam and Eve, Genesis 2:25
- declared by Job, Job 34:5
- declared by Pilate, Matthew 27:24

inspiration (IN-spi-RAY-shun) *"God-breathed." It is used to mean that the Bible writers wrote what God wanted them to write.* 2 Timothy 3:16; 2 Peter 1:20–21

instruction, See article on page 329.
- to Israel, Deuteronomy 6:4–9
- for children, Proverbs 22:6
- "become teachers," James 3:1

integrity, See article on page 469.
- of Job, Job 2:1–10
- guides good people, Proverbs 11:3
- of Joseph, Genesis 39:7–23

intercession, See article on page 1041.
- for Jesus' followers, John 17; Romans 8:34
- Jeremiah prays for Judah, Jeremiah 42:1–6

Isaac (EYE-zak) *the son of Abraham and Sarah.*
- birth of, Genesis 21:1–4
- offered as a sacrifice, Genesis 22:1–19
- married Rebekah, Genesis 24
- tricked by Jacob, Genesis 27
- hero of faith, Hebrews 11:20

Isaiah (eye-ZAY-uh) *prophet who lived about seven hundred years before Christ.*
- became a prophet, Isaiah 6:1–8
- prophesied to Hezekiah, 2 Kings 19–20
- prophecies fulfilled, Matthew 3:3; 4:14; 13:14–15

Ish-Bosheth (ish-BOW-sheth) *son of Saul,* 2 Samuel 2:8–4

Ishmael (ISH-may-el) *son of Abraham and Hagar.*
- birth of, Genesis 16:2–16
- sent away from Abraham's camp, Genesis 21:8–21

Israel, kingdom of (IZ-rah-el) *the northern kingdom which had ten tribes.*
- beginning of, 1 Kings 11:27–12
- fall of, 2 Kings 17:1–18
- rulers of, 1 Kings 15:25–16; 22:51–53; 2 Kings 13; 14:23–17:6

Israel, son of Isaac, *Hebrew for "he who wrestles with God." Jacob's name was changed to Israel when he struggled with an angel at Bethel.* Genesis 32:22–28; 35:9–10. See also "Jacob."
- name given to Jacob's descendants, Genesis 49:28; Exodus 4:22; Psalm 22:23; Romans 9:3–5

Issachar (IS-uh-car) *a son of Jacob and Leah,* Genesis 30:18
- his descendants, Numbers 1:28–29; 26:23

ivory (EYE-voh-ree) *a creamy white bone that comes from elephant tusks,* 1 Kings 10:18; 22:39; Psalm 45:8; Ezekiel 27:15

J

Jabbok River (JAB-ok) *a stream about fifty miles long that runs into the Jordan River,* Numbers 21:24; Joshua 12:2; Judges 11:13

Jabesh Gilead (JAY-besh GIL-ee-ad) *a small town on the east side of the Jordan River,* Judges 21:6–14; 2 Samuel 2:4–7

Jabin, king of Hazor (JAY-bin) *led a group of kings against the Israelites,* Joshua 11:1–11

Jabin, king of Canaan, *defeated by Israel when Deborah was judge,* Judges 4

Jacob (JAY-cub) *one of the sons of Isaac.*
- cheated Esau, Genesis 25:29–34
- tricked Isaac, Genesis 27:1–29
- his dream of a ladder to heaven, Genesis 28:10–22
- tricked by his sons, Genesis 37:10–22
- moved to Egypt, Genesis 45:25–47:12
- hero of faith, Hebrews 11:20–21

Jacob's Portion (JAY-cubs POR-shun) *a name for God, meaning he cares for Jacob's people,* Jeremiah 10:16; 51:19

jailer, *a keeper of a jail.*
- of Paul and Silas, Acts 16:23

Jairus (jay-EYE-rus) *a ruler of the synagogue.*
- Jesus brought his daughter back to life, Matthew 9:18–26; Mark 5:21–43; Luke 8:40–56

James, brother of Jesus, Matthew 13:55; Acts 12:17; 21:18
- later an apostle, Galatians 1:19

James, son of Alphaeus, *an apostle,* Matthew 10:3; Mark 3:18; Luke 6:15; Acts 1:13

James, son of Zebedee, *an apostle of Jesus and a brother of the apostle John,* Matthew 10:2; Mark 10:35; Acts 12:2

Japheth (JAY-fith) *one of Noah's three sons,* Genesis 5:32; 7:13; 9:18–27; 10:1–5

Jashar, Book of, *a book mentioned in the Bible, but not part of it,* Joshua 10:12–13; 2 Samuel 1:17–27

Jason (JAY-son) *a Christian in Thessalonica,* Acts 17:5–9

jealousy
- to describe God, Exodus 20:5; 34:14; Deuteronomy 5:9
- examples of, Genesis 37:11; 1 Samuel 18:19; Matthew 27:18; Acts 5:17
- warnings against, Romans 13:13; 1 Corinthians 13:4; 1 Timothy 6:4; 1 Peter 2:1

Jebusites (JEB-you-sites) *people who lived around Jerusalem before the time of David,* Joshua 15:63; Judges 19:10–11; 2 Samuel 4:6–8

Jehoahaz, son of Jehu (jeh-HO-uh-haz) *king of Israel who lived about eight hundred years before Christ,* 2 Kings 13:1–9

Jehoahaz, son of Josiah, *king of Judah for only three months,* 2 Kings 23:31–34; 2 Chronicles 36:1–4

Jehoash (jeh-HO-ash) *a king of Israel,* 2 Kings 13:10–14:16

Jehoiachin (jeh-HO-uh-kin) *the next-to-last king of Judah.*
- surrendered to Babylon, 2 Kings 24:8–17
- in Babylon, 2 Kings 25:27–30

Jehoiada (jeh-HO-yah-duh) *the chief priest in Jerusalem during Joash's rule,* 2 Kings 11–12; 2 Chronicles 22:11–24

Jehoiakim (jeh-HO-uh-kim) *king of Judah about 600 B.C.,* 2 Kings 23:34–24:6
- tried to kill Jeremiah, Jeremiah 26:1–23
- burned Jeremiah's scroll, Jeremiah 36:1–23

Jehoram (jeh-HOR-am) *or "Joram"; the fifth king of Judah,* 2 Kings 8:16–29; 2 Chronicles 21:4–20

Jehoshaphat (jeh-HOSH-uh-fat) *one of the good kings of Judah.*
- faithful to God, 2 Chronicles 17:1–9
- appointed judges, 2 Chronicles 19:4–11
- defeated Moab and Ammon, 2 Chronicles 20

Jehovah (jeh-HOVE-uh) *a name for God; also translated "LORD,"* Exodus 3:15; 6:3; Deuteronomy 28:58; Psalm 83:18

Jehu (JEE-hew) *an army captain who became king of Israel.*
- appointed as king, 2 Kings 9:1–13
- killed Joram and Ahaziah, 2 Kings 9:14–29
- stopped Baal worship, 2 Kings 10:18–35

Jephthah (JEF-thuh) *one of the judges of Israel.*
- fought the Ammonites, Judges 11:1–29, 32–33
- his vow, Judges 11:30–31, 34–39
- fought the people of Ephraim, Judges 12:2–7

Jeremiah (jer-eh-MY-ah) *a prophet who warned the people of Judah,* Jeremiah 1–52
- became a prophet, Jeremiah 1:1–10
- songs of, 2 Chronicles 35:25
- his prophecies fulfilled, 2 Chronicles 36:21–22; Matthew 2:17; 27:9
- wrote a scroll, Jeremiah 36

Jericho (JEHR-ih-ko) *probably the oldest city in the world,* Mark 10:46; Luke 10:30; 19:1
- fall of, Joshua 2–6
- rebuilt, 1 Kings 16:34

Jeroboam, son of Jehoash (jeh-ro-BO-am) *a king of Israel,* 2 Kings 14:23–29; Amos 7:7–17

Jeroboam, son of Nebat, *first ruler of the northern kingdom of Israel.*
- given ten tribes by God, 1 Kings 11:26–40
- built idols, 1 Kings 12:26–33
- warned by God, 1 Kings 13:1–34
- death of his son, 1 Kings 14:1–20

Jerusalem (jeh-ROO-suh-lem) *"Zion" or "City of David"; the greatest city of Palestine.*
- the City of David, 2 Samuel 5:6–7
- captured by Babylonians, 2 Chronicles 36:15–23
- Jews returned to, Ezra 1–2
- the new Jerusalem, Galatians 4:26; Hebrews 12:22; Revelation 3:12; 21–22

Jesse (JEH-see) *father of King David,* 1 Samuel 16–17; 1 Chronicles 2:13–15; Luke 3:32; Romans 15:12

Jesus (JEE-zus) *"Savior"; the son of God.* See also "Christ," "Son of David," "Son of Man."
- birth and childhood of, Matthew 1–2; Luke 1–2
- temptation of, Matthew 4:1–11; Mark 1:12–13; Luke 4:1–13
- miracles of, Matthew 8–9; Mark 6:30–56; Luke 17:11; 22:50–51; John 2:1; 11
- appeared with Moses and Elijah, Matthew 17:1–13; Mark 9:2–13; Luke 9:28–36
- forced men from the Temple, Matthew 21:12–13; John 2:13–17
- the Last Supper, Matthew 26:17–30; Luke 22:1–20; John 13
- trial and death of, Matthew 26:57–27:66; Mark 15; Luke 22:66–23:56; John 18–19
- appearances after resurrection, Matthew 28; Mark 16; Luke 24; John 20–21; 1 Corinthians 15:5–8
- Son of God, Matthew 3:16–17; 26:63–64; John 1:14

Jethro (JETH-row) *father of Moses' wife,* Exodus 2:16–21
- advised Moses, Exodus 18

Jews (JOOZ) *first, the tribe of Judah; later, any of the twelve tribes,* Ezra 4:12; Esther 3–10; Acts 2:5
- against Jesus, John 5:16–18; 7:1, 32–36; 10:25–42
- Jesus, king of, Matthew 2:2; 27:11–14, 29; John 19:17–22
- and non-Jewish people, 1 Corinthians 12:13; Galatians 3:28; Colossians 3:11

Jezebel (JEZ-eh-bell) *the evil wife of King Ahab.*
- married Ahab, 1 Kings 16:31
- killed the Lord's prophets, 1 Kings 18:4–14
- killed Naboth, 1 Kings 21:1–23
- death of, 2 Kings 9:30–37

Jezreel (JEZ-reel) *the name of a town and a valley near the Jordan River,* Judges 6:33; 1 Kings 21:1; 2 Kings 8:29

Joab (JO-ab) *the commander of King David's army,* 2 Samuel 2:12–3; 10–11; 14; 18–20; 24; 1 Kings 1–2

Joanna (jo-ANN-uh) *a woman Jesus healed,* Luke 8:2–3; 23:55–24:11

Joash, Gideon's father (JO-ash)
- protected Gideon, Judges 6:28–32

Joash, son of Ahaziah, *became king of Judah when he was seven,* 2 Kings 11–12; 2 Chronicles 22:10–24

Job (JOBE) *a wealthy man who honored God.*
- ruined by Satan, Job 1:1–2:10
- wealth restored, Job 42:7
- example of patience, James 5:11

Joel (JO-el) *a prophet who wrote the Book of Joel,* Joel 1–3; Acts 2:16

Johanan (jo-HAY-nan) *a Jewish army captain,* Jeremiah 40:8–43

John, the apostle, *one of the sons of Zebedee.*
- called by Jesus, Mark 1:19–20
- at Jesus' transfiguration, Mark 9:2
- with Jesus in Gethsemane, Mark 14:33–42
- in the early church, Acts 3–4
- writer of Revelation, Revelation 1:1–4, 9

John the Baptist, *Jesus' relative and the son of Elizabeth and Zechariah the priest.*
- birth of, Luke 1:5–25, 57–80
- preached at the Jordan River, Matthew 3:1–12
- baptized Jesus, Matthew 3:13–17
- killed by Herod, Matthew 14:1–12

John Mark, See "Mark."

Jonah (JO-nah) *a prophet whom God told to preach to the city of Nineveh.*
- ran from God, Jonah 1:1–3
- swallowed by a fish, Jonah 1:4–2:10
- went to Nineveh, Jonah 3
- complained to God, Jonah 4
- the sign of, Matthew 12:38–41; 16:4; Luke 11:29–32

Jonathan (JAH-nah-thun) *the oldest son of King Saul.*
- David's friend, 1 Samuel 18:1–4
- saved David's life, 1 Samuel 19:1–7; 20
- death of, 1 Samuel 31:2

Joppa (JOP-uh) *a city on the coast of Palestine,* Jonah 1:3
- Peter preached there, Acts 9:36–42; 10:9–36

Joram (JO-ram) *son of Ahab; also a king of Israel,* 2 Kings 3:1–3; 8:29; 9:14–29

Jordan (JOR-d'n) *the only large river in Palestine.*
- Israelites crossed, Joshua 3
- Jesus baptized in, Matthew 3:13–17; Mark 1:9–11

Jordan Valley, *the valley along the Jordan River,* Deuteronomy 1:1; 3:17; Joshua 11:2

Joseph of Arimathea (JOZ-uf) *took the body of Jesus down from the cross and buried it in a tomb Joseph had dug for himself,* Matthew 27:57–60; Mark 15:42–46; Luke 23:50–54

Joseph of Nazareth, *husband of Mary, Jesus' mother.*
- angel appeared to, Matthew 1:18–24
- went to register in Bethlehem, Luke 2:4–7
- took Jesus to the Temple, Luke 2:21–52

Joseph, son of Jacob, *one of the twelve sons of Israel.*
- sold into slavery, Genesis 37
- put into prison, Genesis 39
- interpreted dreams, Genesis 40–41
- reunited with family, Genesis 42–50

Joshua (JAH-shoo-ah) *leader of the Israelites into the promised land.*
- spied out Canaan, Numbers 13
- chosen to replace Moses, Numbers 27:12–23; Deuteronomy 34:9–10
- conquered Canaan, Joshua 1; 3–12
- death of, Joshua 23–24

Josiah (jo-SY-uh) *king of Judah about 640 to 609 B.C.*
- became king, 2 Kings 22:1–2
- found the lost laws of God, 2 Kings 22:3–20
- gave the law to the people, 2 Kings 23:1–30

Jotham, youngest son of Gideon (JO-tham) Judges 9:1–21, 57

Jotham, son of Uzziah, *a king of Judah,* 2 Kings 15:32–38; 2 Chronicles 27

joy, Psalm 43:4; John 15:11; 17:13; 1 Thessalonians 1:6
- a fruit of the Holy Spirit, Galatians 5:22
- God as the source, Psalms 43:4; 45:7; Romans 15:13
- joy from the Holy Spirit, Luke 10:21; Romans 14:17; Galatians 5:22; 1 Thessalonians 1:6

Jubilee (JOO-bih-lee) *a Jewish celebration that took place once every fifty years. Israelites were to let the soil rest, to free their slaves, and to return land and houses to their first owners or their descendants.* Leviticus 25; 27:17–24; Numbers 36:4

Judah, son of Jacob (JOO-duh) Genesis 29:35
- saved Joseph, Genesis 37:26–27
- deceived by Tamar, Genesis 38
- reunited with Joseph, Genesis 43–44
- tribe of, Numbers 1:26–27; 26:20–22; Joshua 15
- Jesus, a descendant of, Matthew 1:2–3; Luke 3:33–34; Revelation 5:5

Judah, kingdom of, *the southern kingdom when Israel split in two.*
- beginning of, 1 Kings 11:27–12:20
- rulers of, 1 Kings 14:21–15:24; 22:41–50; 2 Kings 8:16–29; 11–12; 14–16; 18–24
- fall of, 2 Kings 24:18–25:22

Judas Iscariot (JOO-dus is-CARE-ee-ut) *apostle who handed Jesus over to be killed.*
- chosen by Jesus, Matthew 10:4; Mark 3:19
- apostles' treasurer, John 12:4–6; 13:27–29
- betrayed Jesus, Matthew 26:14–16, 47–50; Luke 22:1–6; John 6:70–71; 13:2, 21–30
- death of, Matthew 27:3–5

Judas, brother of Jesus, Matthew 13:55; Mark 6:3

Judas, son of James
- an apostle, Luke 6:16; Acts 1:13

Jude (JOOD) *brother of James,* Jude 1

Judea (joo-DEE-uh) *the land of the Jews,* Matthew 2:1; 3:1; Luke 1:5; 3:1; Acts 1:8

judges (JUJ-es) *leaders of Israel prior to the kings,* Judges 2:16–19; 3:7–4; 10–12; 1 Samuel 8:1–5

judging
- warnings against, Matthew 7:1–5; 1 Corinthians 4:5; James 4:11–12
- good kinds of judging, 1 Corinthians 5:12; 6:2; 10:15
- God's judging of people, Matthew 11:22; Acts 17:31; 2 Peter 2:9; 3:7

Judgment Day (JUJ-ment) *the day Christ will judge all people,* Matthew 11:20–24; 12:33–37; 2 Peter 2:9–10; 3:7–13

Julius (JOOL-yus) *a Roman soldier in charge of Paul while Paul was taken to Rome,* Acts 27:1–3

justice, See article on page 459.
- God discusses with Job, Job 40:8
- not found on Earth, Ecclesiastes 5:8
- proof of God's, 2 Thessalonians 1:5–7

justify (JUS-teh-fy) *to make someone right with God,* Romans 3:24; 5:1; Galatians 2:16; Titus 3:7

K

Kadesh/Kadesh Barnea (KAY-desh BAR-nee-uh) *a town in the Desert of Zin,* Numbers 20:1–21; Joshua 10:41

Kenites (KEE-nites) *a tribe of early metal workers,* Genesis 15:19; Judges 1:16; 4:11; 1 Samuel 27:10

Kerethites (KAIR-uh-thites) *King David's bodyguards,* 2 Samuel 8:18; 1 Kings 1:38

Keturah (keh-TOO-ruh) *Abraham's second wife,* Genesis 25:1–4; 1 Chronicles 1:32–33

key, *something that solves or explains.*
- to God's kingdom, Matthew 16:19
- to death, Revelation 1:18

Kidron Valley (KEH-dron) *a valley between Jerusalem and the Mount of Olives,* 2 Samuel 15:23; John 18:1
- idols burned there, 1 Kings 15:13; 2 Kings 23:4

kill
- Cain killed, Genesis 4:10–11
- laws against, Exodus 20:13
- of baby boys, Exodus 1:16; Matthew 2:16
- Jesus killed, Matthew 27:31–50; Mark 15:20–37; Luke 23:25–46; John 19:16–30

kindness
- of God, Exodus 34:6–7; Jeremiah 9:24; Romans 2:4; Ephesians 2:4–7
- commanded, 2 Corinthians 6:6; Ephesians 4:32; Colossians 3:12; 2 Peter 1:5–7

king
- King of kings, 1 Timothy 6:15; Revelation 17:14

kingdom (KING-d'm) *the kingdom of heaven is God ruling in the lives of his people.*
- the nature of, Matthew 5:19–20; 19:14; Luke 17:20–21; Romans 14:17
- parables of, Matthew 13:24–52; 18:23–35; 20:1–16; 25:1–30; Mark 4:30–33; Luke 13:18–21
- belongs to, Matthew 5:3, 10; 19:14

Kiriath Jearim (KEER-yath JEE-ah-rim) *a town in the hills about twelve miles west of Jerusalem,* 1 Samuel 6:20–7:20; 1 Chronicles 13:5–6; 2 Chronicles 1:4

Kish, *father of Saul,* 1 Samuel 9:1–2

Kishon (KY-shon) *the name of a valley and a stream,* Judges 4:13; 5:21; 1 Kings 18:40

kiss, *a greeting of friendship, love, or respect.*
- of Judas, Matthew 26:48–49; Mark 14:44–45; Luke 22:47–48
- holy kiss, Romans 16:16; 1 Corinthians 16:20; 1 Peter 5:14

Kittim (KEH-tim) *the island of Cyprus,* Genesis 10:4; Numbers 24:24; 1 Chronicles 1:7; Isaiah 23:1, 12

kneel
- Solomon kneeled before God, 1 Kings 8:54
- Daniel kneeled before God, Daniel 6:10
- everyone to kneel before Jesus, Philippians 2:10

knock
- "knock, and the door will open," Matthew 7:7
- at the door, Luke 13:25
- Peter knocked, Acts 12:13, 16
- Jesus knocks, Revelation 3:20

knowledge
- tree of, Genesis 2:9, 17
- value of, Proverbs 1:7; 8:10; 18:15; 24:5; 2 Peter 1:5–6
- lack of, Hosea 4:6; Romans 1:28
- limitations of, 1 Corinthians 8:1–2; 13:2, 8–10

Kohath (KO-hath) *a son of Levi,* Exodus 6:16–20; Numbers 3:17–19

Kohathites (KO-hath-ites) *descendants of Kohath.*
- worked in the Holy Tent and Temple, Numbers 3:27–31; 4:1–20; 1 Chronicles 9:17–32

Korah (KO-ruh) *the musician,* Psalms 42; 44–49; 84

Korah, *son of Izhar, rebelled against Moses,* Numbers 16:1–40

L

Laban (LAY-ban) *father of Leah and Rachel.*
- Jacob worked for, Genesis 29:13–30
- divided his flocks with Jacob, Genesis 30:29–43
- chased Jacob, Genesis 31:19–55

Lachish (LAY-kish) *a city about thirty miles southwest of Jerusalem.*
- Joshua defeated, Joshua 10

lake
- of Galilee, Luke 5:1–2; 8:22–23, 33
- of fire, Revelation 19:20
- of sulfur, Revelation 20:10; 21:8

lamb (LAM) *an animal that the Jews often offered as a gift to God.*
- as sacrifice, Genesis 4:4; Exodus 12:3–10; Leviticus 3:6–11; 4:32–35; 5:6; 14:24–25
- Jesus, the lamb of God, John 1:29, 36; 1 Corinthians 5:7; 1 Peter 1:19; Revelation 5–7

Lamech, *a descendant of Cain* (LAY-mek) Genesis 4:18–24

Lamech, *son of Methuselah, the father of Noah,* Genesis 5:28–31

lament, See "complain."

lamp, *a small bowl which held a wick and burned olive oil, thus giving light,* Matthew 25:1–13; Luke 8:16–18
- "Your word is like a lamp for my feet," Psalm 119:105

lampstand, *a holder for a lamp.*
- in the Holy Tent, Exodus 25:31–40; Numbers 8:1–4
- in the Temple, 1 Kings 7:49
- symbol of the church, Revelation 1:12–13, 20

land, See article on page 149.
- Promised Land, Genesis 12:1–3

language
- world spoke only one, Genesis 11:1, 6
- confused at Babel, Genesis 11:7, 9
- Aramaic, 2 Kings 18:26; Ezra 4:7; John 19:20
- Latin, John 19:20
- Greek, John 19:20; Acts 21:37

Laodicea (lay-ah-deh-SEE-uh) *a town in what is now Turkey,* Colossians 4:13–16; Revelation 3:14–22

Last Days, See article on page 1063.
- "pour out my Spirit," Acts 2:17
- Israel will turn to God, Hosea 3:5
- "these are the last days," 1 John 2:18

Last Supper, *the meal Jesus ate with his followers the night before his death,* Matthew 26:17–30; Mark 14:12–26; Luke 22:7–20; 1 Corinthians 11:23–26

Latin (LAT-in) *the language spoken by the Romans during New Testament times,* John 19:20

laughter
- Sarah laughed, Genesis 18:12
- mouths filled with, Psalm 126:2
- sorrow better than, Ecclesiastes 7:3
- changed into crying, James 4:9

law
- as rules, Romans 4:15; 6:14–15; Galatians 5:18
- as God's rules or teachings, Psalm 119; Romans 7:22; 8:7; James 1:25; 1 John 3:4

Law of Moses, See "Teachings of Moses."

laying on of hands, See "hands, laying on."

Lazarus of Bethany (LAZ-uh-rus) *a brother to Mary and Martha and a friend of Jesus,* John 11:1–45; 12:1–11

Lazarus, the beggar, Luke 16:19–31

laziness
- brings poverty, Proverbs 10:4
- not to be fed, 2 Thessalonians 3:10

leadership
- blind, Matthew 15:14
- of own family, 1 Timothy 3:5
- elders worthy of honor, 1 Timothy 5:17

Leah (LEE-uh) *a wife of Jacob,* Genesis 29:15–35; 30:9–21; 49:31

leather, Leviticus 13:47–59; Matthew 3:4

leaven, See "yeast."

Lebanon (LEH-beh-nun) *a country north of Israel.*
- cedars of, 1 Kings 5:1–11; Ezra 3:7
- prophecy of Lebanon's fall, Isaiah 10:34

Legion (LEE-jun) *a man who had many evil spirits in him,* Mark 5:9; Luke 8:30

leisure, See article on page 892.
- like seed among thorns, Luke 8:14
- the uselessness of, Ecclesiastes 2:1–2
- care in living, Ephesians 5:15–20

lend
- money, Exodus 22:25
- borrower, a servant to lender, Proverbs 22:7
- sinners to sinners, Luke 6:34
- to enemies, Luke 6:35

leprosy (LEH-prah-see) *bad skin disease. A person with leprosy was called a leper and had to live outside the city.* Leviticus 13:45–46
- disease of Naaman, 2 Kings 5:1–27
- healed by Jesus, Matthew 8:2–3; Luke 7:11–19

Leviathan (lee-VI-ah-than) *a sea monster; possibly a crocodile,* Job 3:8; 41:1; Psalm 74:14; Isaiah 27:1

Levites (LEE-vites) *descendants of Levi, one of Jacob's sons.*
- served as priests, Numbers 1:47–53; 8:5–26; Deuteronomy 10:8–9; 18:1–8
- towns assigned to, Joshua 21

liar
- better to be poor, Proverbs 19:22
- Satan as a, John 8:44
- Cretans as, Titus 1:12
- to be punished, Revelation 21:8

lid on the Ark of the Agreement, *the mercy seat; the gold lid on the Ark of the Agreement,* Exodus 25:17–22; Hebrews 9:5

life
- breath of, Genesis 2:7
- book of, Philippians 4:3; Revelation 3:5; 21:27
- in the blood, Leviticus 17:14
- length of, Psalm 90:10
- true life, John 12:25
- "I am the . . . life." John 14:6
- eternal, John 5:24–29; 6:35–51

light
- creation of, Genesis 1:3–4
- of the world, Matthew 5:14
- God is, 1 Timothy 6:16; 1 John 1:5
- Jesus is, John 1:4–9; 3:19–20; 8:12; 12:46
- God's word is light, Psalm 119:105
- symbol of God's presence, 2 Corinthians 4:6; Ephesians 5:8–9; 1 Peter 2:9

linen (LEH-nin) *a type of cloth made from the flax plant.*
- used for priests' clothes, Exodus 28:39–42; Leviticus 6:10
- used for royal clothes, Esther 8:15
- Jesus' body wrapped in, Matthew 27:59

lion
- killed by Samson, Judges 14:5–18
- killed by David, 1 Samuel 17:34–37
- devil like a lion, 1 Peter 5:8

lips
- touched by hot coal, Isaiah 6:5–7

loan, See "debt."

loaves
- used to feed five thousand, Matthew 14:17–19
- used to feed four thousand, Matthew 15:34–38

locust (LO-cust) *an insect that looks like a grasshopper. Locusts travel in large groups and can destroy crops.*
- as a plague, Exodus 10:3–19; Deuteronomy 28:38–42; Joel 1:1–4; Nahum 3:15–17
- food for John the Baptist, Matthew 3:4; Mark 1:6

loneliness, See article on page 30.
- of Adam, Genesis 2:18
- of Jesus, Matthew 27:46
- psalm of loneliness, Psalm 22

Lord, *master or one who is in control; ruler of all the world and universe.*
- God as Lord, Exodus 3:15; 7:16; Psalms 31:5; 106:48
- Jesus as Lord, Acts 2:36; 1 Corinthians 8:6; Philippians 2:11; 1 Peter 3:15
- Holy Spirit as Lord, 2 Corinthians 3:18

Lord of hosts, *one of the names used for God; also called "Lord All-Powerful" and "Lord Sabaoth,"* 1 Chronicles 11:9; Psalm 24:10; Isaiah 6:3–5; Malachi 3:1–17

Lord's day
- the first day of the week, Acts 20:7; Revelation 1:10
- as the Judgment Day, 1 Corinthians 5:5; 2 Corinthians 1:14; 1 Thessalonians 5:2; 2 Peter 3:10

Lord's Prayer, *the name often given to the model prayer Jesus taught his followers,* Matthew 6:9–13; Luke 11:1–4

Lord's Supper, *the meal Jesus' followers eat to remember how he died for them; also called "communion."*
- beginning of, Matthew 26:26–29; Mark 14:22–25; Luke 22:14–20
- examples of, Acts 20:7; 1 Corinthians 10:16; 11:17–34

Lot, *Abraham's nephew,* Genesis 11:27–30
- divided land with Abram, Genesis 13
- captured, Genesis 14:1–16

- escaped destruction of Sodom, Genesis 19:1–29
- death of wife, Genesis 19:15–26

lots, *sticks, stones, or pieces of bone thrown like dice to decide something. Often God controlled the result of the lots to let people know what he wanted them to do.*
- Canaan divided by, Numbers 26:55–56
- Jonah found guilty by, Jonah 1:7
- Jesus' clothes divided by, Luke 23:34
- Matthias chosen by, Acts 1:26

love, *a strong feeling of affection, loyalty, and concern for someone.*
- love of God commanded, Deuteronomy 6:5; 11:1; Matthew 22:36–38
- of God for people, Psalm 36; John 3:16; Romans 5:8; 8:39; Ephesians 1:4; 1 John 4:10–11
- of people for God, 1 Corinthians 8:3; 1 John 5:3
- of Christ for people, John 13:1; 15:9; Romans 8:35; Galatians 2:20; 1 John 3:16
- of people for Christ, Matthew 10:37; 1 Corinthians 16:22; 1 Peter 1:8
- of people for each other, Leviticus 19:18; Luke 6:27–35; John 13:34–35; 1 Corinthians 13; 1 John 4:7

Luke, *a non-Jewish doctor who often traveled with the apostle Paul,* Colossians 4:14; 2 Timothy 4:11

lust, *wanting something evil.*
- to be avoided, Proverbs 6:25; Matthew 5:28; Colossians 3:5; 1 Thessalonians 4:5
- typical of the ungodly, Romans 1:26; 1 Peter 4:3

Lydia (LID-ee-uh) *a woman from the city of Thyatira who sold purple cloth,* Acts 16:13–15, 40

lying
- warnings against, Ephesians 4:25; Colossians 3:9; Revelation 21:8
- devil as a liar, John 8:44
- to the Holy Spirit, Acts 5:1–6

lyre (LIRE) *a musical instrument with strings, similar to a harp,* 1 Chronicles 15:16; Psalms 33:2; 81:2

Lystra (LIS-tra) *a city of Lycaonia.*
- Paul preached there, Acts 14:6–20; 16:1; 2 Timothy 3:11

M

Macedonia (mas-eh-DOH-nee-uh) *the northern part of Greece.*
- Paul preached there, Acts 16:6–10; 20:1–6; 1 Corinthians 16:5–9; Philippians 4:15

Machpelah (mack-PEE-luh) *the land Abraham bought from Ephron, the Hittite.*
- Sarah buried there, Genesis 23:7–19
- Abraham buried there, Genesis 25:7–10
- Jacob buried there, Genesis 49:29–33; 50:12–13

magic (MAJ-ik) *trying to use the power of evil spirits to make unnatural things happen.*
- magicians of Egypt, Genesis 41:8; Exodus 7:11–12
- condemned, Leviticus 19:26; 20:27; Deuteronomy 18:10–12
- Simon the magician, Acts 8:9–24
- Elymas the magician, Acts 13:6–11
- Ephesian magicians burn their books, Acts 19:17–19

mahalath (mah-HAY-lath) *probably a musical word; may be the name of a tune or may mean to dance and shout,* Psalms 53; 88

Malachi (MAL-uh-ky) *a prophet who lived about the time of Nehemiah. He wrote the last book of the Old Testament.* Malachi 1:1

man, *humankind; a male.*
- created by God, Genesis 1:26–27; 2:7–23
- born of woman, Job 14:1
- important to God, Psalm 8:4–8
- woman created for, 1 Corinthians 11:9

Manasseh, son of Hezekiah (mah-NASS-uh) *a king of Judah for fifty-five years,* 2 Kings 21:1–17; 2 Chronicles 33:1–20

Manasseh, son of Joseph, *older brother of Ephraim. His descendants were the tribe of Manasseh.* Genesis 41:51; 46:20; 48:1–20
- descendants of, Numbers 1:34; 26:29–34; Joshua 13:8–13; 17
- eastern half-tribe, Joshua 1:12–17; 22
- western half-tribe, Joshua 21:5, 25; 22:7

manger (MAIN-jur) *a box where animals are fed,* Luke 2:6–17

manna (MAN-ah) *the white, sweet-tasting food God gave the people of Israel in the wilderness. It appeared on the ground during the night so they could gather it in the morning.*
- God sent to Israel, Exodus 16:11–36; Joshua 5:10–12
- kept in the Ark, Exodus 16:31–34; Hebrews 9:1–4

Manoah (mah-NO-uh) *the father of Samson,* Judges 13

Marduk (MAR-dook) *a god of the Babylonians. The Babylonians believed that people were evil because Marduk had created them from the blood of an evil god.* Jeremiah 50:2

Mark, *John Mark; a cousin to Barnabas; traveled with Paul and Barnabas and wrote the Gospel of Mark,* Acts 12:12, 25; 13:5; Colossians 4:10; 2 Timothy 4:11
- left Paul, Acts 13:13
- traveled with Barnabas, Acts 15:36–41

marketplace, *usually a large open area inside a city where people came to buy and sell goods,* Matthew 20:3; Mark 7:4; 12:38; Luke 7:32; Acts 16:19

marriage
- teachings about, Mark 10:6–9; 1 Corinthians 7:1–16; Hebrews 13:4; 1 Timothy 5:14
- authority in, Ephesians 5:21; Colossians 3:18

Mars Hill, See "Areopagus."

Martha (MAR-thuh) *the sister of Mary and Lazarus who lived in Bethany.*
- criticized Mary, Luke 10:38–42
- at death of Lazarus, John 11:17–44

martyr (MAR-ter) *"witness"; one who knows about something. Later, martyr came to mean a person who was killed for being a witness.*
- Stephen, first Christian martyr, Acts 7:54–60
- James killed, Acts 12:2
- heroes of faith killed, Hebrews 11:32–37

Mary Magdalene (MAG-duh-lun) *a follower of Jesus from the town of Magdala; the first person to see Jesus after he came back to life.*
- at Jesus' death, Matthew 27:55–56, 61
- saw Jesus after his resurrection, Matthew 28:1–10; Mark 16:1–11; John 20:10–18

Mary, mother of Jesus
- engaged to marry Joseph, Matthew 1:18–25; Luke 2:4–5
- angel appeared to, Luke 1:26–45
- birth of Jesus, Luke 2:6–21
- with Jesus in Jerusalem, Luke 2:41–52
- at wedding in Cana, John 2:1–10
- at Jesus' death, John 19:25–27
- with the apostles, Acts 1:14

Mary of Bethany, *sister of Martha and Lazarus, and a friend of Jesus.*
- sat at Jesus' feet, Luke 10:38–42
- at death of Lazarus, John 11:1–45
- poured oil on Jesus' feet, John 12:1–8

maskil (MAS-kil) *probably a description of the kind of song that some of the Psalms were,* Psalms 32, 42, 44, 45

master, *lord; ruler.*
- "No one can serve two masters." Matthew 6:24
- not to be called, Matthew 23:10
- to be obeyed, Ephesians 6:5
- how to treat slaves, Ephesians 6:9
- in heaven, Ephesians 6:9; Colossians 4:1
- Jesus as, Luke 5:5; 8:24; 17:13

materialism/possessions, See article on page 946.
- the rich leader, Luke 18:18–30
- satisfaction despite wealth, Philippians 4:10–13
- Jesus discusses selfishness, Luke 12:13–21

Matthew (MATH-you) *also called Levi; a tax collector; wrote the Gospel of Matthew,* Matthew 9:9–10; 10:3; Acts 1:13

Matthias (muh-THY-us) *chosen to be an apostle after Judas Iscariot killed himself,* Acts 1:15–26

meat
- given by God in the wilderness, Exodus 16:1–15; Numbers 11:4–34; Psalm 78:27
- eating meat sacrificed to idols, Acts 15:20; 1 Corinthians 8; 10:25–32

Medes (MEEDS) *the people who lived in Media, which is called "Iran" today,* 2 Kings 17:6; Ezra 6:2; Esther 1:3–19; Daniel 5:28; 6:8–15

mediator (MEE-dee-a-ter) *a go-between.*
- Jesus as, 1 Timothy 2:5

medicine
- happy heart as, Proverbs 17:22

meditation, See article on page 531.
- on God's rules, Psalm 119:99
- Paul's exhortation on, Philippians 4:8
- think about things in heaven, Colossians 3:1–4

Mediterranean Sea (med-ih-teh-RANE-ih-an) *a large sea west of Canaan; also called the "Great Sea" or the "Western Sea,"* Numbers 34:6–7; Joshua 1:4

medium (MEED-ee-um) *a person who tries to help living people talk to the spirits of the dead.*
- condemned, Leviticus 19:31; Deuteronomy 18:11–13; Isaiah 8:19–20
- of Endor, 1 Samuel 28
- Josiah destroyed mediums, 2 Kings 23:24

Meeting Tent, *"Tabernacle" or "Holy Tent"; a special tent where the Israelites worshiped God. It was used from the time they left Egypt until Solomon built the Temple in Jerusalem.*
- description of, Exodus 25–27
- set up, Exodus 39:32–40:36

Megiddo (meh-GID-oh) *important town in northern Israel where many battles were fought. The Book of Revelation tells about a great battle between good and evil at "Armageddon," which means "the hill of Megiddo."* Joshua 12:8–21; 2 Kings 23:29–30; Revelation 16:16

Melchizedek (mel-KIZ-ih-dek) *priest and king who worshiped God in the time of Abraham,* Genesis 14:17–24
- Christ compared to, Hebrews 5:4–10; 7

memory, See article on page 510.
- psalm of remembrance, Psalm 77
- monument to God's faithfulness, Joshua 4:7
- remember Christ, 2 Timothy 2:8

Mene, mene, tekel, parsin (MEE-nee, TEE-kul, PAR-sun) *the words written on the wall by a mysterious hand at Belshazzar's feast,* Daniel 5

mentoring, See "follower."

Mephibosheth (me-FIB-o-sheth) *crippled son of Jonathan,* 2 Samuel 4:4
- David's agreement with, 2 Samuel 9
- tricked by Ziba, 2 Samuel 16:1–4; 19:24–30

Merab (MEE-rab) *daughter of King Saul,* 1 Samuel 14:49; 18:17–19

Merarites (mee-RAY-rites) *descendants of Merari, a son of Levi; they were responsible for caring for the frame of the Holy Tent,* Numbers 3:17, 33–37; 4:29–33

mercy (MUR-see) *kindness and forgiveness.*
- God's mercy to people, Exodus 34:6; Deuteronomy 4:31; Luke 1:50; Ephesians 2:4
- people's mercy to each other, Matthew 5:7; James 2:13

mercy seat, See "lid on the Ark of the Agreement."

Mesha (MEE-shuh) *an evil king of Moab,* 2 Kings 3:4–27

Meshach (MEE-shack) *friend of Daniel who was put in the fiery furnace,* Daniel 1–3

messenger, 1 Samuel 23:27; 1 Kings 19:2
- John the Baptist as, Matthew 11:10; Mark 1:2; Luke 7:27
- of Satan, 2 Corinthians 12:7

Messiah (muh-SYE-uh) *"anointed one"; the Greek word for Messiah is "Christ." Christians believe that Jesus is the Messiah or the Christ.* John 1:40–41; 4:25–26

Methuselah (meh-THOO-zeh-lah) *lived 969 years, longer than anyone else in the Bible; the son of Enoch and the grandfather of Noah,* Genesis 5:21–27

Micah (MY-cuh) *a prophet who told the people of Israel and Judah about their sins,* Micah 1–7

Micaiah (mi-KAY-uh) *a prophet of God,* 1 Kings 22:8–28; 2 Chronicles 18

Michael (MY-kul) *the archangel of God,* Jude 9; Revelation 12:7

Michal (MY-kul) *a daughter of Saul and wife of David,* 1 Samuel 18:20–29; 19:11–17; 2 Samuel 3:13–16
- criticized David, 2 Samuel 6:16–23

Michmash (MIK-mash) *a hilly area about seven miles northeast of Jerusalem,* 1 Samuel 13:23–14:23; Isaiah 10:28

Midian (MID-ee-un) *a son of Abraham; his descendants were called "Midianites,"* Genesis 25:1–6
- Joseph sold to, Genesis 37:18–36
- Jethro, a descendant of, Exodus 2:15–21
- enemy of Israel, Judges 6–7

midnight
- when the firstborn of Egypt died, Exodus 12:29
- Paul and Silas freed from jail, Acts 16:25–26
- Paul preached until, Acts 20:7

miktam (MIK-tam) *a kind of song that may describe some of the Psalms. It may mean that it is a sad song or a song about danger.* Psalms 16; 56–60

mildew (MIL-doo) *a growth that appears on things that have been damp for a long time,* Leviticus 13:47–59; 14:33–54

milk, 1 Peter 2:2

millstones, *huge stones used for grinding grain into flour or meal,* Deuteronomy 24:6; Matthew 18:6; Luke 17:1–2
- used to kill Abimelech, Judges 9:53; 2 Samuel 11:21

minister (MIN-i-ster) *servant; one who lives serving God and others,* Romans 15:15–16; Colossians 4:7

miracle (MEER-ih-k'l) *"wonderful thing"; a great event which can be done only by God's help. Miracles are special signs to show God's power.*
- purpose of, Exodus 10:1–2; Mark 2:8–12; John 2:11; Acts 3:1–10
- over nature, Exodus 14:21–22; Joshua 10:12–13; Matthew 8:23–27; 14:22–32; 21:18–22
- of healing, Matthew 8:14–17; 9:27–31; Mark 7:31–37; Acts 14:3
- of bringing people back to life, Mark 5:21–43; John 11:1–44; Acts 9:36–43

Miriam (MEER-ee-um) *the sister of Moses and Aaron.*
- watched over Moses, Exodus 2:1–8
- song of, Exodus 15:19–21
- punished, Numbers 12:1–15
- death of, Numbers 20:1

mission, See article on page 794.
- the Great Commission, Matthew 28:16–20
- Jesus sends out the seventy-two, Luke 10:1

mistress (MISS-tres) *a female head of the household,* Proverbs 30:21–23
- Hagar as, Genesis 16:4–9

Mizpah (MIZ-pah) *the place where Jacob and Laban made a pile of stones to remind them of their agreement not to be angry with each other,* Genesis 31:44–49

Mizpah, *the city, a few miles north of Jerusalem,* Judges 11:29–34; 1 Samuel 7:5–16; 2 Kings 25:23

Moab (MO-ab) *the country on the east side of the Dead Sea.*
- fought with Israel, Numbers 22:1–25:9; Judges 3:12–30
- home of Ruth, Ruth 1:2, 4
- rebelled against Israel, 2 Kings 3:4–27

mob
- against Paul, Acts 17:5; 21:30–36

Molech (MO-lek) *a god of the Canaanite people. Those who worshiped Molech often sacrificed their own children to him by burning them on altars.* Leviticus 18:21; 20:1–5; 2 Kings 23:10; Jeremiah 32:35

money, *Many kinds of money were used in Bible days—gold, silver, and copper.*
- proper attitudes toward, Luke 16:13; Hebrews 13:5; 1 Timothy 3:3; 6:10

moneychangers, *people who traded money from other countries for Jewish money.*
- of the Temple, Matthew 21:12–13; Mark 11:15–17; Luke 19:45–46; John 2:13–16

Mordecai (MOR-deh-kye) *a man who helped Esther to save the Jews from death.*
- discovered a plot, Esther 2:19–23
- asked Esther to help, Esther 4
- honored by the king, Esther 6

Moriah (moh-RYE-uh) *the land where Abraham went to sacrifice Isaac,* Genesis 22:2
- site of the Temple, 2 Chronicles 3:1

mortar (MORE-tar) *a stone bowl where grain is ground into flour by pounding; also, the sticky material that holds bricks together,* Genesis 11:3; Exodus 1:14

Moses (MO-zez) *the man who led God's people out of the land of Egypt; the author of the first five books of the Old Testament.*
- birth of, Exodus 2:1–10
- in Midian, Exodus 2:11–4:17
- led Israel out of Egypt, Exodus 4:18–12:51; 13:17–31
- received the law, Exodus 20–31

- struck the rock, Numbers 20:1–13
- death of, Deuteronomy 31:14–34:12

Most Holy Place, *the inner and most special room in the Holy Tent and the Temple.*
- rules about, Leviticus 16:2–20
- in the Temple, 1 Kings 6:16–35
- entered by Christ, Hebrews 9:3–25

mother-in-law
- law about, Deuteronomy 27:23
- of Ruth, Ruth 1:3–4
- Peter's, Matthew 8:14–15; Luke 4:38–39
- family against, Matthew 10:35; Luke 12:53

mothers
- treatment of, Exodus 20:12; 21:15, 17; Proverbs 1:8; Matthew 15:4; 1 Timothy 5:2, 4

Mount of Olives, *a hill covered with olive trees near Jerusalem; site of the garden of Gethsemane,* Matthew 21:1; 24:3; John 8:1
- David cried there, 2 Samuel 15:30
- Jesus prayed there, Luke 22:39–53
- Jesus ascended from there, Acts 1:6–12

Mount Sinai (SYE-nye) *a mountain in the Sinai Peninsula.*
- Lord spoke with Moses there, Exodus 24:16; Acts 7:30, 38
- law given on, Exodus 31:18

Mount Zion (ZI-on) *one of the hills on which Jerusalem was built; later, it became another name for the whole city of Jerusalem; also a name for heaven.*
- hill of Jerusalem, 2 Kings 19:31; Psalm 48:2, 11; Isaiah 24:23
- as heaven, Hebrews 12:22; Revelation 14:1

mountain, See article on page 346.
- announce the Lord's blessings, Deuteronomy 11:29–30
- Israel gathers, 1 Kings 18:2–40
- vision from God, Revelation 21:10–22:7

mourning (MORN-ing) *showing sadness, especially when someone has died.*
- examples of, Genesis 50:3; Deuteronomy 34:8; 1 Samuel 31:11–13

murder
- laws against, Exodus 20:13; Deuteronomy 5:17; Matthew 5:21
- committed by Barabbas, Mark 15:7
- devil as a murderer, John 8:44
- full of, Romans 1:29

music
- to the Lord, Judges 5:3; Ephesians 5:19
- in the Temple, 1 Chronicles 25:6–7

myrrh (MUR) *sweet-smelling liquid taken from certain trees and shrubs; used as a perfume and a painkiller,* Genesis 37:25; 43:11; Proverbs 7:17
- given to Jesus, Matthew 2:11; Mark 15:23
- used in Jesus' burial, John 19:39–40

mystery (MIH-ster-ee) *a secret.*
- revealed by God, Daniel 2:28
- of the message of Christ, Romans 16:25–26; Colossians 2:2; 4:3
- of Gentiles also being saved, Ephesians 3:1–6; Colossians 1:25–27
- of life after death, 1 Corinthians 15:51

N

Naaman (NAY-uh-mun) *a commander of the Aramean army; healed by Elisha of a skin disease,* 2 Kings 5; Luke 4:27

Nabal (NAY-bal) *husband of Abigail.*
- refused to help David, 1 Samuel 25:2–13
- saved by Abigail, 1 Samuel 25:14–35
- death of, 1 Samuel 25:36–38

Naboth (NAY-both) *killed by Jezebel so she could steal his vineyard,* 1 Kings 21

Nadab (NAY-dab) *son of Aaron.*
- saw God, Exodus 24:1–11
- death of, Leviticus 10:1; Numbers 3:4; 26:61

Nahum (NAY-hum) *a prophet of God; wrote the book of Nahum,* Nahum 1–3

naked
- Adam and Eve, Genesis 2:25
- realization of nakedness, Genesis 3:7–10
- born, Job 1:21

Naomi (nay-OH-me) *mother-in-law of Ruth,* Ruth 1:1–5
- returned to Bethlehem, Ruth 1:6–22
- encouraged Ruth, Ruth 2:19–3:4
- became a grandmother, Ruth 4:13–17

Naphtali (NAF-tuh-lye) *the sixth son of Jacob; his descendants were the tribe of Naphtali,* Genesis 30:7–8; Numbers 26:48–50; Joshua 19:32–39

nard, *an expensive perfume which was imported from India,* Song of Solomon 4:13; Mark 14:3; John 12:3

Nathan (NAY-thun) *a prophet during the time of David and Solomon,* 1 Kings 1
- told David not to build the Temple, 2 Samuel 7:1–17
- told David the parable of the lamb, 2 Samuel 12:1–25

Nathanael (nuh-THAN-yul) *one of Jesus' twelve apostles; probably called "Bartholomew,"* John 1:43–51

nation
- formed and spread, Genesis 10:32
- against nation, Mark 13:8
- Good News preached to every one, Revelation 14:6

Nazarene (NAZ-uh-reen) *a person from the town of Nazareth. Jesus was called a Nazarene, so his followers sometimes were also called Nazarenes.* Matthew 2:21–23; Acts 24:5

Nazareth (NAZ-uh-reth) *the city in Galilee where Jesus grew up,* Matthew 2:21–23; Luke 4:16–30; John 1:45–46

Nazirite (NAZ-e-rite) *one who makes a special promise to God, which had rules about eating certain foods and cutting the hair.*
- rules for, Numbers 6:1–21
- made by Samson, Judges 13:2–7; 16:17

Nebo, god of the Babylonians (NEE-boh) Isaiah 46:1

Nebo, the mountain
- Moses died there, Deuteronomy 34:1–5

Nebuchadnezzar (neb-you-kud-NEZ-zur) *a Babylonian king.*
- conquered Jerusalem, 2 Kings 24–25; 2 Chronicles 36
- his dreams, Daniel 2; 4
- and fiery furnace, Daniel 3

Nebuzaradan (NEB-you-ZAR-ah-dan) *the commander of Nebuchadnezzar's army.*
- captured Jerusalem, 2 Kings 25:8–12; Jeremiah 39:8–14; 40:1–6

Neco (NECK-o) *king of Egypt from 609 to 594 B.C.*
- killed King Josiah, 2 Kings 23:29–37; 2 Chronicles 35:20–27
- captured Jehoahaz, 2 Chronicles 36:1–4
- defeated by Nebuchadnezzar, Jeremiah 46:2

Nehemiah (NEE-uh-MY-uh) *led the first group of Israelites back to Jerusalem from Babylon.*
- sent to Jerusalem, Nehemiah 2
- rebuilt walls of Jerusalem, Nehemiah 3–4; 6
- as governor, Nehemiah 8:9; 10:1

neighbor
- teachings about, Exodus 20:16–17; Leviticus 19:13–18; Proverbs 3:27–29; Matthew 19:19; Luke 10:25–37

Nephilim (NEF-eh-lim) *people who were famous for being large and strong. The ten spies who were afraid to enter Canaan had seen the Nephilim who lived there,* Genesis 6:4; Numbers 13:30–33

Ner (NUR) *father of Kish,* 1 Chronicles 8:33; 9:36, 39

net
- fishing with, Matthew 4:18; Luke 5:5, 6; John 21:6–11
- kingdom of heaven like, Matthew 13:47

new
- a new song, Psalms 40:3; 98:1
- a new name, Isaiah 62:2; Revelation 2:17
- new mercies every morning, Lamentations 3:22–23
- a new heart, Ezekiel 18:31; 36:26
- a new life, Romans 6:4; Ephesians 4:23–24; Colossians 3:10; 1 Peter 1:3
- a new agreement, Jeremiah 31:31; 1 Corinthians 11:25; Hebrews 8:8; 9:15; 12:24
- a new heaven and earth, 2 Peter 3:13; Revelation 21:1

New Moon, *a Jewish feast held on the first day of the month. It was celebrated with animal sacrifices and the blowing of trumpets. It was to dedicate the month to the Lord,* Numbers 10:10; 2 Chronicles 2:4; 8:13; Psalm 81:3; Isaiah 1:11–17

Nicodemus (nick-uh-DEE-mus) *an important Jewish ruler and teacher. Jesus taught him about spiritual life,* John 3:1–21; 7:45–53; 19:38–42

night, *can refer to ordinary darkness or be a symbol of distress, judgment, or evil.*
- created by God, Genesis 1:5; Psalm 19:1–2
- time of distress, Psalms 30:5; 42:8; 77:6
- time of judgment, John 9:4
- symbol of evil, 1 Thessalonians 5:5
- no night in heaven, Revelation 21:25

Nile River, *a river in Africa more than twenty-five hundred miles long.*
- baby Moses placed there, Exodus 2:1–10
- turned to blood, Exodus 7:14–25
- produced plague of frogs, Exodus 8:1–15

Nineveh (NIN-eh-vuh) *one of the oldest and most important cities in the world. For many years it was the capital of Assyria.* Genesis 10:8–11
- Jonah preached there, Jonah 1:1–2; 3–4; Matthew 12:41
- Nahum prophesied against, Nahum 1–3

Noah (NO-uh) *saved his family and the animals from the flood.*
- built the boat, Genesis 6:8–22
- saved from the flood, Genesis 7–8
- agreement with God, Genesis 9:1–17

Nob, *a town where priests lived during the days of King Saul,* 1 Samuel 21:1

noise
- joyful, Psalm 66:1
- of many people, Isaiah 17:12
- skies will disappear with, 2 Peter 3:10

noon
- sun to go down at, Amos 8:9
- bright light at, Acts 22:6

numbers, See article on page 561.
- seven things God hates, Proverbs 6:16–19
- the number 666, Revelation 13:18

O

oath, *a promise or vow.*
- rules about, Matthew 5:33–37; 23:16–22; James 5:12
- God's oath, Hebrews 6:16–18
- examples of, 1 Samuel 14:24–28; 1 Kings 1:29–30; Psalm 132:1–12

Obadiah (oh-buh-DYE-uh) *a prophet of God who warned the Edomites they would be punished,* Obadiah 1–21

obedience
- to God, Leviticus 25:18; Deuteronomy 27:10; Acts 5:29
- to parents, Ephesians 6:1; Colossians 3:20
- to government, Romans 13:1–7; Titus 3:1–2; Matthew 22:17–21
- punishment for disobedience, Ephesians 5:6; 2 Thessalonians 1:8; 1 Timothy 1:9

offering (AW-fer-ing) *a gift or sacrifice.* See "sacrifice."
- brought by Cain, Genesis 4:3–5
- of non-Jewish people, Romans 15:16
- of Christ, Hebrews 10:5–18

Og (AHG) *the king of Bashan who was defeated by the Israelites,* Numbers 21:33–35; Deuteronomy 3:1–11

oil, *in Bible times usually means olive oil; used for cooking, medicine, burning in lamps, and anointing.* See "anoint."
- for lamps, Exodus 25:5–6; Matthew 25:1–10
- as medicine, Luke 10:34
- in offerings, Leviticus 2; 14:12–31
- in cooking, 1 Kings 17:10–16

ointment, See "perfume."

olive (OL-iv) *a small fruit; its oil was used in anointing ceremonies and as medicine.* See "oil."
- leaf, Genesis 8:11
- trees, Deuteronomy 6:11; 1 Samuel 8:14; Habakkuk 3:17; John 18:1

Omega, See "Alpha and Omega."

Omri (AHM-rih) *a strong, evil king of Israel,* 1 Kings 16:15–28

Onesimus (oh-NES-ih-mus) *the slave of a Christian named Philemon,* Colossians 4:9; Philemon

Onesiphorus (OH-nih-SIF-uh-russ) *a Christian friend of Paul who lived in Ephesus,* 2 Timothy 1:16–18; 4:19

onyx (AHN-ix) *a precious stone with layers of black and white running through it,* Genesis 2:12; Job 28:16
- used in the holy vest, Exodus 25:7; 28:9–14; 39:6–7, 13

Orpah (OR-pah) *the sister-in-law of Ruth,* Ruth 1:3–14

Ophir (OH-fur) *a land known for its gold and beautiful trees. Its location is uncertain.* Psalm 45:9; Isaiah 13:12
- Solomon traded with Ophir, 1 Kings 9:28; 10:11; 1 Chronicles 29:4

oven, *fire was built in the bottom of a clay barrel to bake bread,* Exodus 8:3; Leviticus 2:4; Hosea 7:4

oxen
- not to be coveted, Exodus 20:17
- as offering, Numbers 7:12–83
- not to be denied food, Deuteronomy 25:4; 1 Corinthians 9:9
- Elisha plowed with, 1 Kings 19:19–21
- pulled the cart containing the Ark, 1 Chronicles 13:9

P

pain
- of a woman in childbirth, Genesis 3:16; Isaiah 13:8; Romans 8:22; Galatians 4:19, 27
- not found in the new Jerusalem, Revelation 21:4

palace
- of David, 2 Samuel 5:11–12
- of Solomon, 1 Kings 7:1–12

palm tree, *a tall tree with long, fan-shaped branches growing out of the top; gives dates for food and wood for building,* Exodus 15:27; Nehemiah 8:15
- Jericho, city of, Deuteronomy 34:3; Judges 1:16; 3:13
- branches spread before Jesus, John 12:12–13

papyrus (puh-PY-rus) *a tall reed that grows in swampy places; used to make paper,* Job 8:11; 9:26

parable (PARE-uh-b'l) *a story that teaches a lesson by comparing two things.*
- of the kingdom of God, Matthew 13; 20:1–16
- of the lost sheep, coin, and son, Luke 15:1–31
- of the Judgment Day, Matthew 25

Paradise (PARE-uh-dice) *another word for heaven,* Luke 23:43; 2 Corinthians 12:3–4

Paran (PAY-ran) *a desert area between Egypt and Canaan,* Genesis 21:20; Numbers 10:12; 12:16; 13:1–26

parchment (PARCH-ment) *a kind of writing material; made from the skin of sheep or goats,* 2 Timothy 4:13

parents
- responsibilities of, Ephesians 6:4; Colossians 3:21

Passover Feast (PASS-o-ver FEEST) *an important holy day for the Jews in the spring of each year. They ate a special meal on this day to remind them that God had freed them from being slaves in Egypt.*
- first Passover, Exodus 12:1–30
- commanded, Numbers 9:1–14
- celebrated by Jesus, Matthew 26:2, 17–19

patience (PAY-shentz) *to handle pain or difficult times calmly and without complaining.*
- of God, Romans 2:4; 2 Peter 3:9
- teachings about, 1 Corinthians 13:4, 7; Hebrews 6:12
- comes from the Holy Spirit, Galatians 5:22
- commanded, Romans 12:12; Ephesians 4:2; 1 Thessalonians 5:14; James 5:7–8

Patmos (PAT-mus) *a small, rocky island in the Aegean Sea between Greece and Turkey,* Revelation 1:9

Paul, *the Roman name for "Saul." Saul was a Jew, born in the city of Tarsus. He became an apostle and a great servant of God.*
- conversion of, Acts 9:1–22
- name changed from "Saul," Acts 13:9
- healings by, Acts 14:8–10; 19:11–12; 20:7–12; 28:1–11
- imprisoned, Acts 23:35–28:31
- death of, 2 Timothy 4:6–8

peace
- from God, Psalm 29:11; John 14:27; Romans 5:1
- commanded, Romans 12:18; 14:17–19; Colossians 3:15
- Prince of Peace, Isaiah 9:6
- from the Holy Spirit, Galatians 5:22

pearl (PURL), Matthew 7:6; 1 Timothy 2:9; Revelation 21:21
- parable of, Matthew 13:45–46

Pekah (PEE-kuh) *an evil king of Israel,* 2 Kings 15:25–16:9; Isaiah 7:1–10

Pekahiah (peck-uh-HI-uh) *an evil king of Israel,* 2 Kings 15:22–26

Pelethites (PELL-eh-thites) *King David's bodyguards,* 2 Samuel 15:18; 20:6–7, 23

Peninnah (pe-NIN-uh) *a wife of Elkanah,* 1 Samuel 1:2–6

people of god, the, See article on page 1367.
- a chosen people, 1 Peter 2:9–10
- God's children, 1 John 5:1–2
- defended by God, Deuteronomy 32:36–40

Pentecost (PEN-tee-cost) *a Jewish feast day celebrating the summer harvest. The apostles began telling the Good News on Pentecost after Jesus died.* Acts 2:1–41; 20:16; 1 Corinthians 16:8

perfect
- describing Jesus, Hebrews 2:10; 5:9; 7:28
- describing God, Psalm 18:30; Matthew 5:48
- God's perfect law, James 1:25
- will of God, Romans 12:2
- love, 1 John 4:18
- people made perfect, 2 Corinthians 13:11; Hebrews 10:1–14; 11:40; 12:23

perfume
- used in idol worship, Isaiah 57:9
- poured on Jesus' feet, Mark 14:3–9; Luke 7:36–39; John 12:3

Pergamum (PER-guh-mum) *a town in the Roman province of Asia in what is now Turkey,* Revelation 2:12–17

persecution (PUR-seh-CUE-shun) *trying to hurt people. Christians in the New Testament times were often persecuted by being put in jail or killed.*
- blessings with, Matthew 5:11–12; 1 Peter 3:8–17
- examples of, Acts 8:1–4; 1 Peter 3:13–15
- response to, Matthew 5:44; Romans 12:14; 1 Corinthians 4:12; 2 Corinthians 12:2
- of Christians, Matthew 13:21; 2 Timothy 3:12

perseverance, See article on page 1224.
- for a heavenly reward, 2 Corinthians 5:1–5
- Israel punished for lack of, Numbers 14:26–38
- salvation for, Matthew 24:13

Persia (PUR-zhuh) *a powerful country during the last years of the Old Testament; now called "Iran."*
- defeated Babylon, 2 Chronicles 36:20–23
- let captives return to Jerusalem, Ezra 1:1–11

Peter, *a fisherman; he and his brother, Andrew, were the first two apostles Jesus chose. First called "Simon" or "Peter," Jesus changed his name to "Cephas," which means "rock."*
- called to follow Jesus, Matthew 4:18–20
- walked on water, Matthew 14:22–33
- at the Last Supper, John 13:1–11
- defended Jesus, John 18:10–11
- denied Jesus, Mark 14:66–72; Luke 22:54–62
- preached the Good News, Acts 2:14–40
- an elder in the church, 1 Peter 5:1

pharaoh (FAY-row) *the title given to the kings of Egypt.*
- made Joseph ruler of Egypt, Genesis 40–47
- made Israelites slaves, Exodus 1–14

Pharisees (FARE-ih-seez) *"the separate people"; they followed the Jewish religious laws and customs very strictly. Jesus often spoke against them for their religious teachings and traditions.*
- practices of, Matthew 9:14; 15:1–9; Mark 7:1–13; Luke 7:30
- against Jesus, Matthew 12:14; 22:15; John 8:1–6
- criticized by Jesus, Matthew 5:20; 23

Philadelphia (fill-uh-DEL-fee-uh) *a city in the country now called "Turkey,"* Revelation 3:7–13

Philemon (fih-LEE-mun) *a Christian in the city of Colossae,* Philemon 1–25

Philip, the apostle (FIL-ip) *friend of Peter and Andrew.*
- called by Jesus, John 1:43
- brought Nathanael to Jesus, John 1:44–50
- brought Greeks to Jesus, John 12:21–22

Philip, the evangelist, *a Greek-speaking Jew chosen to serve in the church in Jerusalem.*
- preached in Samaria, Acts 8:5–13
- preached to the Ethiopian, Acts 8:26–39
- his daughters prophesied, Acts 21:8–9

Philip, *the tetrarch, son of Herod I and Cleopatra.*
- ruler of Iturea and Trachonitis, Luke 3:1

Philippi (fih-LIP-eye) *a city in northeastern Greece,* Philippians 1:1; 4:15
- Paul in jail there, Acts 16:11–40

Philistines (FIL-ih-steens) *people who were Israel's enemy for many years; worshiped false gods.*
- Samson defeated, Judges 15–16
- captured the Ark of the Agreement, 1 Samuel 4–6
- David defeated, 1 Samuel 17–18; 2 Samuel 5:17–25; 21:15–22

Phinehas, son of Eleazar (FIN-ee-us) *a priest and grandson of Aaron,* Numbers 25:1–13

Phinehas, son of Eli, *an evil priest,* 1 Samuel 1:3; 2:34; 4:4–11

Phoebe (FEE-beh) *a woman in the church in Cenchrea,* Romans 16:1

Phoenicia (foh-NEE-shuh) *an early name for the land on the east coast of the Mediterranean Sea; called "Lebanon" today,* Mark 7:26; Acts 11:19; 15:3

phylactery (fil-LAK-tur-ee) See "box of Scriptures."

pigs
- considered unclean, Leviticus 11:7
- snout of, Proverbs 11:22
- "don't throw your pearls before pigs," Matthew 7:6
- demons sent into, Matthew 8:30–33; Mark 5:11–13; Luke 8:32–33
- fed by prodigal son, Luke 15:15–16

Pilate, Pontius (PIE-lut, PON-shus) *the Roman governor of Judea from A.D. 26 to 36,* Luke 3:1; 13:1
- handed Jesus over to be killed, Matthew 27; Mark 15; Luke 23; John 18:28–19:38

pillar (PILL-ur) *a large stone that is set upright; also a tall column of stone that supports the roof of a building.*
- of Jacob, Genesis 28:18–22
- to worship false gods, 2 Kings 17:9–12
- in the Temple, 1 Kings 7:6, 15–22
- of cloud and fire, Exodus 13:21–22; 14:19–24; 33:8–10

Pisgah, Mount (PIS-guh) *one of the high spots on Mount Nebo where Moses stood to see into the promised land,* Numbers 23:14; Deuteronomy 3:27; 34:1

plague (PLAYG) *a disaster. God sent ten plagues on the land of Egypt so the Egyptians would set the Israelites free.*
- on the Egyptians, Exodus 7–11
- on the Israelites, Exodus 32:35; Numbers 11:31–33; 16:41–50; 25:1–9

plan, See "decision making."

pleasure, See article on page 489.
- found in the Lord, Psalm 16:11
- abuse of wealth for, James 5:1–6
- self-indulging widow, 1 Timothy 5:5–6

plumb line (PLUM LINE) *a string with a rock or other weight on one end. People used it to see if a wall was straight.*
- symbol for God's judging, 2 Kings 21:10–13; Amos 7:7–8

pomegranate (PAHM-gran-it) *a reddish fruit about the size of an apple,* Numbers 13:23; Joel 1:12
- design on priests' clothing, Exodus 28:33–34
- design of Temple decorations, 1 Kings 7:18–20

poor
- God's care for, Psalm 140:12; Proverbs 22:22–23; Matthew 11:5; James 2:5
- treatment of, Leviticus 19:9–10; Matthew 25:34–36; Luke 14:12–14

possessions
- promised land given to Israelites, Genesis 17:8; Numbers 32:22; Joshua 1:11
- proper attitudes toward, Ecclesiastes 5:10–6:6; Luke 12:13–21; Acts 2:45; 1 John 3:17
- danger of, Matthew 19:22
- sold by Christians, Acts 2:45

Potiphar (POT-ih-fur) *an officer for the king of Egypt. He put Joseph in charge of his household.* Genesis 39

pottage (POT-edge) *a thick vegetable soup or stew,* Genesis 25:29–34; 2 Kings 4:38–41

potter (POT-ur) *a person who makes pots and dishes out of clay.*
- as a symbol of God, Jeremiah 18:1–6

poverty, See "poor."

power
- of Jesus, Matthew 24:30; 28:18; Luke 6:19
- of the Spirit, Luke 4:14; Acts 1:8; Romans 15:19
- of Satan, Acts 26:18
- of the apostles, Luke 9:1; Acts 4:33

praetorium (pray-TORE-ee-um) *the governor's palace in New Testament times,* Matthew 27:27; Acts 23:35

praise (PRAYZ) *to say good things about someone or something. God's people can praise him by singing, praying, and by living the way he tells us to live.* 1 Chronicles 16:4–7; Psalms 103; 104; 145–150

prayer
- teachings about, Matthew 5:44–45; 21:18–22; Philippians 4:6; James 5:15–16
- Jesus' model prayer, Matthew 6:5–15

preach, *to give a talk on a religious subject; to tell the Good News.*
- Jonah preached to Nineveh, Jonah 3:2–4
- John preached, Matthew 3:1; Mark 1:4; Luke 3:3
- Jesus preached, Matthew 4:17; Mark 2:2; Luke 4:43–44
- Good News preached, Acts 8:25, 40; Galatians 2:7; 1 Thessalonians 2:9
- preaching commanded, 2 Timothy 4:2

pregnancy, crisis, See "abortion."

Preparation Day (prep-a-RAY-shun DAY) *the day before the Sabbath day. On that day the Jews prepared for the Sabbath.* Luke 23:54; John 19:14, 31

pride
- warnings against, Romans 12:3; 1 Corinthians 13:4; Philippians 2:3; James 4:6

priest (PREEST) *in the Old Testament, a servant of God who worked in the Holy Tent or Temple.* See also "high priest."
- clothes for, Exodus 28
- appointing of, Exodus 29:1–37
- rules for, Leviticus 21:1–22:16

Priscilla (prih-SIL-uh) *a friend of Paul,* Acts 18:1–4, 18–19; Romans 16:3–4
- taught Apollos, Acts 18:24–26

prison
- Joseph in prison, Genesis 39:20–41:40
- Peter in prison, Acts 5:17–20
- Paul in prison, Acts 16:23–34

prodigal (PRAH-dih-gul) *careless and wasteful.*
- the prodigal son, Luke 15:11–32

promise
- from God, Joshua 1:3; 1 Kings 8:20; Galatians 3:14; Ephesians 3:6
- first commandment with, Ephesians 6:2
- Lord is not slow in keeping, 2 Peter 2:9

prophecy (PRAH-feh-see) *a message; God speaking through chosen people called "prophets,"* Ezekiel 14:9; 1 Thessalonians 5:20; 2 Peter 1:20–21

prophesy (PRAH-fes-sy) *to speak a prophecy,* Acts 2:17–18. See "prophecy."
- a spiritual gift, 1 Corinthians 14:1–5

prophet (PRAH-fet) *a messenger; one who is able, with God's help, to tell God's message correctly. Sometimes prophets told what would happen in the future.* Matthew 11:13–14
- how to judge, Deuteronomy 13:1–5; 18:21–22
- examples of, Ezra 5:1; Jeremiah 1:1–9; Matthew 3:3
- false prophets, Deuteronomy 13:1–5

prophetess (PRAH-feh-tess) *a female prophet,* Exodus 15:20; Judges 4:4; 2 Kings 22:14; Luke 2:36. See "prophet."

prophetic symbolism, See article on page 641.
- city images from Ezekiel, Ezekiel 4
- war images from Isaiah, Isaiah 5:26–30
- belt symbol for Paul, Acts 21:11

prostitute (PRAH-sti-toot) *a person who sells his or her body for sex.*
- warnings against, 1 Corinthians 6:15
- examples of, Genesis 38:15–16; Jeremiah 3:1–3; Hosea 3:2–3; Matthew 21:32

protest, See "complain."

proverbs (PRAH-verbs) *wise sayings. The Book of Proverbs contains many wise sayings that tell how to live a good and happy life.* 1 Kings 4:32; Proverbs

psalm (SAHM) *a song. The Book of Psalms is like a songbook.* Ephesians 5:19; Colossians 3:16

publican (PUB-leh-kun) See "tax collector."

Publius (POOB-lih-us) *an important man of the island of Malta,* Acts 28:7–8

Pul, See "Tiglath-Pileser."

punishment
- of Cain, Genesis 4:13
- everlasting, Matthew 25:46; 2 Thessalonians 1:8–9
- for rejecting Jesus, Hebrews 10:29
- by government, Romans 13:4; 1 Peter 2:14

pure
- gold, Exodus 25:11–39; 37; 1 Kings 6:20–21
- heart, Psalm 51:10; Matthew 5:8
- describing Jesus, Hebrews 7:26
- describing people, Job 4:17; 15:14; Philippians 1:10; Titus 1:15
- water, Hebrews 10:22

Purim, See "Feast of Purim."

purple, *a color that, in Bible times, was worn by kings, queens, and other rich people. Purple cloth was expensive because the purple dye came from special shellfish.* Exodus 25:1–4; Judges 8:26; Mark 15:17; Acts 16:14

Q

quail (KWALE) *a brownish-white bird.*
- given by God to Israel, Exodus 16:11–13; Numbers 11:31–34; Psalm 105:40

quarrel
- Israelites quarreled with Moses, Exodus 17:1–7

Queen Goddess, *Ishtar; a goddess of the Babylonians,* Jeremiah 7:18; 44:15–29

Queen of Heaven, See "Queen Goddess."

queen of Sheba, See "Sheba, queen of."

question
- Solomon questioned by queen of Sheba, 1 Kings 10:1–3
- Jesus questioned, Mark 8:11; Luke 23:9; John 8:6
- asked by Jesus, Matthew 21:24
- apostles questioned by Jews, Acts 4:7; 5:27

quiet
- words, Ecclesiastes 9:17
- riot quieted, Acts 19:35–36
- life, 1 Thessalonians 4:11; 1 Timothy 2:2

Quirinius (kwy-RIN-ee-us) *the Roman governor of Syria when Jesus was born,* Luke 2:1–3

quiver (KWIH-vur) *a bag to hold arrows,* Psalm 127:5; Isaiah 49:2

R

Rabbah (RAB-uh) *the capital city of the Ammonites,* 2 Samuel 11:1; 12:26–29; Ezekiel 25:5

rabbi/rabboni (RAB-eye/rah-BONE-eye) *teacher. Jesus' followers often called him "rabbi" as a sign of respect.* John 1:38; 20:16

Rachel (RAY-chel) *a wife of Jacob and the mother of Benjamin and Joseph.*
- married Jacob, Genesis 29:1–30
- gave birth to Joseph, Genesis 30:22–24
- stole Laban's idols, Genesis 31:19–35
- death of, Genesis 35:16–20

racism, See article on page 1082.
- Peter rejects the "unclean," Acts 10
- Jesus helps a Greek woman, Mark 7:24–30
- church council on non-Jews, Acts 15

Rahab, the dragon (RAY-hab) *In a well-known story, Rahab was defeated. Egypt was sometimes called Rahab to show that it would be defeated.* Job 9:13; Isaiah 30:7

Rahab, the prostitute, *a woman in Jericho. She hid the Israelite spies and helped them escape.*
- hid the spies, Joshua 2:1–21
- rescued from Jericho, Joshua 6:16–25
- an example of faith, Hebrews 11:31; James 2:25

rainbow
- a sign of God's agreement with people, Genesis 9:8–17

raisin, 1 Samuel 25:18; 30:12; 1 Chronicles 12:40

ram, *a male sheep.*
- offered instead of Isaac, Genesis 22:13
- used for burnt offerings, Exodus 29; Leviticus 8:18–29; Numbers 28:11–29:37
- with two horns, Daniel 8:3–22

Ramah (RAY-muh) *a town about five miles north of Jerusalem,* Jeremiah 31:15; Matthew 2:18

Rameses (RAM-eh-seez) *one of the cities built by the Israelites when they were slaves in Egypt,* Exodus 1:11; 12:37; Numbers 33:3

Ramoth Gilead (RAY-moth GIL-ee-ad) *one of the cities of safety on the east side of the Jordan River,* Joshua 20:8; 1 Kings 4:13; 2 Kings 8:28–9:14

ransom, *a payment that frees a captive.*
- Jesus as a ransom for sins, Matthew 20:28; 1 Timothy 2:6; Hebrews 9:15

Rapha (RAY-fa) *a leader of a group of people in Canaan who may have been giants. The descendants of Rapha are called "Rephaites."* 2 Samuel 21:15–22; Joshua 13:12

raven, *a large black bird similar to a crow that eats dead things.*
- sent out by Noah, Genesis 8:7
- fed Elijah, 1 Kings 17:4–6

read
- the Book of the Teachings, Joshua 8:34–35; Nehemiah 8:2–9
- reading the teachings commanded, Deuteronomy 17:18–19; 31:9–13
- brings happiness, Revelation 1:3

Rebekah (ree-BEK-uh) *the wife of Isaac and the mother of Jacob and Esau.*
- married Isaac, Genesis 24
- gave birth to Jacob and Esau, Genesis 25:19–26
- helped deceive Isaac, Genesis 27
- buried at Machpelah, Genesis 49:31

rebellion, See article on page 319.
- of the people of Israel, Numbers 14
- Pharisees' rebellion, John 8:34–47
- Samuel warns against, 1 Samuel 12:14–15

reconciliation, See article on page 1233.
- by Christ, 2 Corinthians 5:18
- now a friend of God, Romans 5:9–11
- healed by his wounds, Isaiah 53:5

redeem (ree-DEEM) *to buy something back or to buy a slave's freedom.*
- property, Leviticus 25:23–34; Ruth 4:3–6
- slave, Leviticus 25:47–49
- redeemed by God, 1 Corinthians 6:20; Galatians 4:5; Titus 2:14

Red Sea, *Sea of Reeds; a large body of water between Africa and Arabia.*
- Israelites crossed, Exodus 13:17–14:31

refuge, *a place of safety or protection.*
- God as our refuge, Deuteronomy 33:27; 2 Samuel 22:3; Psalms 18:2; 31:2; 71:3; 91:2
- city of, Numbers 35:6–34; Joshua 20

Rehoboam (ree-ho-BO-um) *son of Solomon who took his place as king.*
- became king, 1 Kings 11:41–43
- Israel rebelled against, 1 Kings 12:1–24
- strengthened Judah, 2 Chronicles 11:5–17
- disobeyed God, 2 Chronicles 12

rejoice
- commanded to, Matthew 5:11–12; Romans 12:15; Philippians 4:4; 1 Peter 4:13
- examples of, 1 Samuel 6:13; Nehemiah 12:43

remission (rih-MISH-un) See "forgiveness."

remnant (REM-nant) *a small part that is left; a name used for the Jews who were left alive after their captivity in Babylon.*
- of Israelites who returned to Jerusalem, Ezra 9:15; Nehemiah 1:2; Isaiah 10:20–22

repent (ree-PENT) *being sorry for doing something wrong and not continuing to do that wrong.* See "change of heart and life."

Rephaites, See "Rapha."

reputation, See article on page 573.
- greater than wealth, Proverbs 22:1
- wives' reputations and husbands, 1 Peter 3:1
- Solomon's, 1 Kings 10:1–13

respect
- to parents, Leviticus 19:3; 1 Timothy 3:4
- between husbands and wives, Ephesians 5:33; 1 Peter 3:7
- to all people, 1 Peter 2:17; 3:16

rest
- on the seventh day, Genesis 2:2; Exodus 31:15; Hebrews 4:4
- given by the Lord, Psalm 95:11; Jeremiah 6:16; Matthew 11:28
- heaven as a place of rest, Revelation 14:13

resurrection (REZ-uh-REK-shun) *a dead person's coming back to life.*
- of Jesus, Matthew 28:1–10; Mark 16; Luke 24; John 20–21; Acts 2:24–32; Romans 1:4
- of God's people, John 6:39; Acts 24:15; 1 Corinthians 15; Philippians 3:10–11; Hebrews 11:35

Reuben (ROO-ben) *oldest of Jacob's twelve sons.*
- birth of, Genesis 29:32
- tried to save Joseph, Genesis 37:18–29
- descendants of, Exodus 6:14; Numbers 1:20; Joshua 13:15–23

revelation (rev-uh-LAY-shun) *showing plainly something that has been hidden,* 2 Corinthians 12:1; Revelation 1:1–3

revenge
- warnings against, Leviticus 19:18; Romans 12:19; 1 Thessalonians 5:15; 1 Peter 3:9

reward
- in heaven, Matthew 5:12
- for obedience, Psalm 19:11
- for what a person does, Matthew 6:1–18; 10:42; 16:27; Colossians 3:24
- children as a reward, Psalm 127:3

Rhoda (ROAD-uh) *a servant girl in the home of John Mark's mother,* Acts 12:6–17

righteousness (RY-chuss-ness) *being right with God and doing what is right.*
- explained, Romans 3:19–26; 2 Corinthians 5:21; 6:4–7; Philippians 3:8–9
- Abraham as an example of, Romans 4:3
- right living, 2 Corinthians 6:7; Ephesians 5:9; 1 Timothy 6:11; 1 Peter 2:24

road, See "way."

robber

- Temple as a hideout for, Jeremiah 7:11; Matthew 21:13
- attacked man on road to Jericho, Luke 10:30
- killed with Jesus, Matthew 27:38–44; John 18:40

Rock, *often used as a name for God. As a large rock is strong and provides a hiding place, so God is strong and protects us from our enemies.* Genesis 49:24; 2 Samuel 22:32–49; Psalm 19:14

rock badger (ROK BAD-jur) *a coney; a small, tailless animal like a rabbit that hides among the mountain gorges and rocky areas of Arabia,* Psalm 104:18; Proverbs 30:26

Rome, *the capital city of the Roman Empire at the time of Christ,* Acts 2:10; 18:2; Romans 1:7

- Paul sent there, Acts 23:11; 28:14–15

roof

- spies hid there, Joshua 2:6
- David saw Bathsheba from there, 2 Samuel 11:2
- built room for Elisha there, 2 Kings 4:8–10
- man lowered through, Mark 2:3–4
- Peter prayed there, Acts 10:9

Ruth (ROOTH) *a widow from Moab.*

- moved to Judah, Ruth 1
- worked in Boaz's field, Ruth 2
- married Boaz, Ruth 3–4
- birth of Obed, Ruth 4:13–22

S

Sabbath (SAB-uth) *means "rest"; the seventh day of the Jewish week; the Jews' day to worship God. They were not allowed to work on this day.*

- commands about, Exodus 20:8–11; 31:12–17
- Jesus is Lord of, Matthew 12:1–13; Mark 2:23–28; Luke 6:1–11

sackcloth (SAK-cloth) *a type of clothing made from rough cloth; worn by people to show their sadness,* Genesis 37:33–35; Esther 4:1; Matthew 11:21

sacrifice (SAK-rih-fice) *to give something valuable to God.*

- burnt sacrifices, Leviticus 6:8–13
- drink sacrifices, Leviticus 23:13; Numbers 15:5; 28:7
- penalty sacrifices, Leviticus 7:1–10
- fellowship sacrifices, Leviticus 3; 7:11–27
- sin sacrifices, Leviticus 4
- limits of, Hebrews 9; 10
- living sacrifice, Romans 12:1

Sadducees (SAD-you-seez) *a Jewish religious group that didn't believe in angels or resurrection; they believed only the first five books of the Old Testament were true.*

- challenged Jesus, Matthew 22:23–33
- arrested Peter and John, Acts 4:1–3
- arrested the apostles, Acts 5:17–42
- Paul spoke to the council, Acts 23:1–9

safety, city of, *city of refuge. In Bible times, someone who had accidentally killed another person could go to a city of safety for protection. As long as he was there, the dead person's relative could not punish him.*

- rules about, Numbers 35:6–34; Joshua 20

saffron (SAF-ron) *a purple flower; parts of it are used as a spice,* Song of Solomon 4:14

saint, *holy person; another word for "Christian,"* Acts 9:41; Romans 1:7; 1 Corinthians 14:33

Salem (SAY-lem) *means "peace"; an old name for Jerusalem.*

- home of Melchizedek, Genesis 14:18; Hebrews 7:1–2

Salome, daughter of Herodias (sah-LO-mee)

- had John the Baptist killed, Matthew 14:3–12; Mark 6:17–29

Salome, wife of Zebedee, *the mother of the apostles James and John,* Mark 15:40; 16:1

salt

- used to preserve foods, Job 6:6; Mark 9:50
- Lot's wife turned into salt, Genesis 19:15–26
- "You are the salt of the earth," Matthew 5:13

Salt Sea, See "Dead Sea."

salvation (sal-VAY-shun) *being rescued from danger; being saved from sin and its punishment.*

- as God's gift, John 3:16; Ephesians 2:8; Titus 2:11
- through Christ, Acts 4:12; 1 Thessalonians 5:9; 1 Timothy 1:15; Hebrews 5:7–9
- as a helmet, Ephesians 6:17; 1 Thessalonians 5:8
- urgency of, 2 Corinthians 6:2; Hebrews 2:3
- rejoice in, Psalms 9:14; 13:5; 51:12; Isaiah 25:9

Samaritan (sah-MEHR-ih-ton) *a person from the area of Samaria in Palestine. These people were only partly Jewish, so the Jews hated them.* John 4:9

- Jesus taught a Samaritan woman, John 4:1–42
- story of the good Samaritan, Luke 10:25–37

Samson (SAM-son) *one of Israel's judges; he was famous for his great strength.*

- birth of, Judges 13
- married a Philistine, Judges 14–15
- tricked by Delilah, Judges 16:4–22
- death of, Judges 16:23–31
- hero of faith, Hebrews 11:32

Samuel (SAM-u-el) *the last judge in Israel.*

- birth of, 1 Samuel 1:1–20
- worked in the Temple, 1 Samuel 1:21–2:26
- became a prophet, 1 Samuel 3
- appointed Saul as king, 1 Samuel 10
- appointed David as king, 1 Samuel 16:1–13
- death of, 1 Samuel 25:1

Sanballat (san-BAL-lat) *governor of Samaria who tried to stop Nehemiah from rebuilding the walls of Jerusalem,* Nehemiah 4–6

sanctify (SANK-teh-fy) *to make holy or ready for service to God,* John 17:17–19; 1 Corinthians 6:11; 1 Peter 1:2

sanctuary (SANK-choo-air-ee) See "Holy Place."

sand
- Abraham's descendants as numerous as, Genesis 22:17; 32:12
- Job's days as numerous as, Job 29:18
- house built on, Matthew 7:26–27

Sanhedrin (san-HEE-drin) See "council."

Sapphira (sah-FY-ruh) *wife of Ananias.*
- lied to the Holy Spirit, Acts 5:1–11

Sarah (SAIR-uh) *wife of Abraham,* Genesis 11:29–30
- gave Hagar to Abraham, Genesis 16:1–6
- name changed from "Sarai," Genesis 17:15–16
- gave birth to Isaac, Genesis 21:1–7
- death of, Genesis 23

Satan (SAY-ton) *means "enemy"; the devil; the enemy of God and man.*
- encouraged David to sin, 1 Chronicles 21:1
- tested Job, Job 1:6–12; 2:1–7
- tempted Jesus, Luke 4:1–13
- a fallen angel, Luke 10:18–19
- to be thrown into lake of fire, Revelation 20:10

Satanism, See "Satan."

Saul, king of Israel
- appointed king, 1 Samuel 9–10
- disobeyed God, 1 Samuel 15
- tried to kill David, 1 Samuel 19; 23:7–29
- death of, 1 Samuel 31

Saul of Tarsus, Acts 13:9. See "Paul."

savior
- God as Savior, Psalm 25:5; Isaiah 45:21; Luke 1:47; 1 Timothy 1:1
- Christ as Savior, Luke 2:11; John 4:42; Ephesians 5:23; Titus 2:13

scarlet (SCAR-let) *a bright red color,* Exodus 26:1; Joshua 2:18; Isaiah 1:18; Matthew 27:28

scepter (SEP-tur) *a wand or a rod that the king holds; a sign of his power,* Esther 4:11; Psalm 60:7

scourge (SKURJ) *to beat someone with a whip or stick,* 1 Kings 12:11
- Jesus scourged, Matthew 27:26; Mark 15:15
- Paul scourged, Acts 21:32; 2 Corinthians 11:24

scribe, *to write, to count, and to put in order. In New Testament times scribes were men who wrote copies of the Scriptures.*
- Ezra as scribe, Nehemiah 8:1
- against Jesus, Matthew 15:1–9
- condemned by Jesus, Matthew 23:13–36

Scriptures (SCRIP-churs) *special writings of God's word for people. When the word Scriptures is used in the New Testament, it usually means the Old Testament. Later, it came to mean the whole Bible.*
- fulfilled, Matthew 26:52–54; John 19:24, 28, 36
- given by God, 2 Timothy 3:16

scroll, *a long roll of paper used for writing,* Deuteronomy 17:18; Jeremiah 36; Revelation 5:1–5

Scythians (SITH-ee-unz) *a group of wandering people who lived near the Black Sea,* Colossians 3:11

Sea of Galilee, See "Galilee, Lake."

Sea of Reeds, See "Red Sea."

seal, *a tool with a design or picture carved on it. Kings pressed this seal into wax and used it like a signature. Sometimes these seals were worn as rings.*
- examples of, 1 Kings 21:8; Esther 8:8

seed
- created by God, Genesis 1:11, 12, 29
- parables of, Matthew 13:1–43

seer, *another name for prophet.* See "prophet."

Selah (SEE-lah) *probably a musical direction; used in the Psalms. It may mean to pause. The word was not intended to be spoken when reading the psalm.* Psalms 3:2, 4, 8; 89:4, 37, 45, 48

self-control, See article on page 1174.
- in Paul's ministry, 1 Corinthians 9:19–27
- broken walls, Proverbs 25:28
- addressed to Felix, Acts 24:25

Sennacherib (sen-AK-ur-ib) *king of Assyria from 705 to 681 B.C.*
- attacked Jerusalem, 2 Kings 18:13–19; 2 Chronicles 32:1–23; Isaiah 36–37

Sermon on the Mount, *a sermon Jesus preached as he was sitting on the side of a mountain near Lake Galilee,* Matthew 5–7

serpent, See "snake."

servant
- of the Lord, Deuteronomy 34:5; Joshua 2:8; 1 Kings 11:32; Luke 1:38
- Jesus as a, Philippians 2:7
- parable of, Matthew 25:14–30
- Jesus' followers to be, Matthew 20:25–27

service, See article on page 1033.
- washing feet in, John 13:14
- importance of servant, Luke 22:27
- with the strength of God, 1 Peter 4:11

Seth, *the third son of Adam and Eve,* Genesis 4:25–26; 5:6–8; Luke 3:38

sexuality, See article on page 602.
- Solomon's love song, Song of Solomon 1
- in marriage, 1 Corinthians 7
- created by God, Genesis 1:27

Shadrach (SHAYD-rak) *a friend of Daniel.*
- taken into captivity, Daniel 1
- became a leader, Daniel 2:49
- saved from the furnace, Daniel 3

Shallum, king of Israel (SHAL-um) *ruled for only one month in 752 B.C.,* 2 Kings 15:10–15

Shalmaneser (shal-mah-NEE-zer) *a king of Assyria,* 2 Kings 17:1–6; 18:9

shame, See "honor."

Shaphan (SHAY-fan) *an assistant to King Josiah,* 2 Kings 22:3–14; 2 Chronicles 34:8–21

sharing
- commanded, Luke 3:11; Romans 12:13; 1 Timothy 6:18
- examples of, Acts 2:42–47; 4:32; 2 Corinthians 8:1–4

Sharon (SHAIR-un) *the plain in Palestine along the coast of the Mediterranean Sea,* 1 Chronicles 5:16; 27:29; Song of Solomon 2:1; Isaiah 33:9

sheaf (SHEEF) *a bundle of grain stalks that have been cut and tied together,* Genesis 37:7; Leviticus 23:10; Job 24:10

Sheba, queen of (SHE-buh) *a queen who came to visit Solomon and see his wealth,* 1 Kings 10:1–13

Shebna (SHEB-nuh) *the manager of the palace for King Hezekiah,* 2 Kings 18:17–19:4; Isaiah 36:1–37:4

sheep
- God's people compared to, Ezekiel 34; John 10:1–18; 1 Peter 2:25
- parable of, Luke 15:1–7

Shem, *Noah's oldest son,* Genesis 6:10; 7:13; 10:21–31

sheminith (SHEM-ih-nith) *a musical term in the Psalms that means an octave (eight notes); may mean to use an instrument with eight strings,* Psalms 6; 12

shepherd
- David as, 1 Samuel 17:15, 34–36
- Lord as, Psalm 23
- Jesus, the good shepherd, John 10:1–18
- elders as, 1 Peter 5:1–4

Sheshbazzar (shesh-BAZ-ur) *governor of the Jews in 538 B.C.,* Ezra 1:7–11; 5:13–16

shiggaion (shi-GY-on) *probably a musical term; used in the Psalms; may mean that the psalm is a sad song,* Psalm 7

shigionoth (shi-GY-o-noth) *probably a musical term,* Habakkuk 3:1

Shiloh (SHY-lo) *a town north of Jerusalem.*
- location of the Holy Tent, Joshua 18:1, 8; Judges 18:31; Jeremiah 7:12

Shimei (SHIM-ee-i) *a relative of King Saul.*
- cursed David, 2 Samuel 16:5–14
- asked forgiveness, 2 Samuel 19:16–23
- death of, 1 Kings 2:36–46

ship, 1 Kings 9:26–28; 22:48; Acts 27

Shishak (SHY-shak) *king of Egypt during the time of Solomon and Rehoboam.*
- attacked Jerusalem, 1 Kings 14:25–28; 2 Chronicles 12:1–9

showbread, See "bread that shows we are in God's presence."

Shunammite (SHOO-nah-mite) *a person from Shunem, a town in northern Israel.*
- Shunammite woman took care of Elisha, 2 Kings 4:8–17
- her son raised from the dead, 2 Kings 4:18–37
- given back her land, 2 Kings 8:1–6

sickle (SICK-ul) *a tool for cutting grain,* Revelation 14:14–19

sickness, See "healing."

Sidon (SY-don) *a Phoenician city on the coast of the Mediterranean Sea,* Genesis 10:19; Matthew 11:21–22; Mark 7:31; Acts 27:3–4

siege mound (SEEJ) *dirt piled against a city wall to make it easier for attackers to climb up and attack the city,* 2 Samuel 20:15; Isaiah 37:33; Jeremiah 6:6

signet ring (SIG-net RING) *a ring worn by a king or other important person. It had his seal on it.* Genesis 41:42; Esther 3:10; 8:2–10; Daniel 6:17. See "seal."

Sihon (SY-hon) *a king of the Amorites when the Israelites came out of Egypt.*
- refused to let Israelites pass, Numbers 21:21–31; Deuteronomy 2:24–37

Silas (SY-lus) *also "Silvanus"; a teacher in the church in Jerusalem who often traveled with Paul.*
- sent to the Gentiles, Acts 15:22–23; 17:16
- joined Paul in Corinth, Acts 18:5
- helped with Peter's letter, 1 Peter 5:12

Siloam, pool of (sy-LO-um) *a pool of water in Jerusalem,* John 9:1–12

Silvanus (sil-VAY-nus) See "Silas."

Simeon of Jerusalem (SIM-ee-un) *a godly man who saw baby Jesus in the Temple,* Luke 2:25–35

Simeon, son of Israel, *one of the twelve sons of Israel,* Genesis 29:33; 42:23–36
- descendants of, Numbers 1:22–23; 26:12–14

Simon, brother of Jesus (SY-mun) Matthew 13:55

Simon of Cyrene (sy-REE-ni) *carried the cross of Jesus,* Matthew 27:32; Mark 15:21; Luke 23:26

Simon Peter, See "Peter."

Simon the magician, *tried to buy the power of the Holy Spirit,* Acts 8:9–24

Simon the Zealot, *an apostle of Jesus,* Matthew 10:4; Mark 3:18; Luke 6:15; Acts 1:13

sin, *a word, thought, or act against the law of God.*
- offering for, Leviticus 4; 6:24–30; Hebrews 7:27; 10:4–12
- committed by everyone, Romans 3:23; 1 John 1:8–10
- Christ died for, Romans 4:25; 1 Corinthians 15:3; 1 Peter 2:24; 1 John 2:2; 3:5
- results of, Isaiah 59:2; Romans 6:23; Ephesians 2:1; Hebrews 12:1

Sinai (SY-ny) *a mountain in the desert between Egypt and Canaan.*
- Moses received the Ten Commandments there, Exodus 19–20

singing, *a way of praising God and teaching each other,* Judges 5:3; Psalm 30:4; Ephesians 5:19; Colossians 3:16

Sisera (SIS-er-uh) *captain of a Canaanite army,* Judges 4

slave
- rules about, Exodus 21:1–11, 16, 26–32; Ephesians 6:5–9; 1 Timothy 6:1–2

slave woman, *concubine; she bore children for her master but was not considered equal to a wife.*
- Hagar as, Genesis 16:1–3
- of Solomon, 1 Kings 11:2–3

sleep
- God never sleeps, Psalm 121:4
- danger of, Proverbs 6:10–11
- Eutychus fell asleep, Acts 20:9
- to awake from, Romans 13:11
- a gift from the Lord, Psalm 127:2

sling, *a weapon for throwing rocks,* Judges 20:16; 1 Samuel 17:39–50; 2 Kings 3:24–25

slothful (SLAWTH-ful) *lazy and undependable,* Proverbs 6:6–11; 13:4; Matthew 25:26; Hebrews 6:12

sluggard, See "slothful."

snake
- sticks became snakes, Exodus 7:8–13
- bronze snake made by Moses, Numbers 21:4–9; John 3:14
- Paul bitten by, Acts 28:1–6

Sodom (SOD-um) *a town known for its evil people.*
- destroyed, Genesis 18:17–19:29
- symbol of evil, Matthew 10:11–15; 11:20–24; Revelation 11:8

soldier
- arrested Jesus, John 18:12–13
- made fun of Jesus, Matthew 27:27–31; Luke 23:11
- at Jesus' death, Matthew 27:32–37; Luke 23:26–38, 47; John 19:1–3,16–24, 28–35
- lied about Jesus' resurrection, Matthew 28:11–15
- Cornelius, Acts 10:1
- guarded Peter, Acts 12:6
- Christian compared to, 2 Timothy 2:3–4

Solomon (SOL-o-mon) *a son of David; famous for his wisdom.*
- became king, 1 Kings 1:28–53
- wisdom of, 1 Kings 3:1–15; 4:29–34
- made a wise decision, 1 Kings 3:16–28
- built the Temple, 1 Kings 6; 7:13–51
- visited by the queen of Sheba, 1 Kings 10:1–13; Matthew 12:42
- married many women, 1 Kings 11:1–8
- death of, 1 Kings 11:40–41

Solomon's Porch (SOL-o-mon's PORCH) *a covered courtyard on the east side of the Temple,* 1 Kings 7:6; John 10:23; Acts 3:11; 5:12

Son of David, *a name the Jews used for the Christ because the Savior was to come from the family of King David,* Matthew 1:1; 9:27; 15:22; 21:9

Son of Man, *a name Jesus called himself. It showed that he was God's Son, but he was also a human being.* Matthew 24:30; Mark 13:26; Luke 21:27; 22:69–70

son/child of God, See article on page 961.
- "the Son of the Father," John 1:14
- Israel the firstborn, Exodus 4:21–23
- a believer as, Romans 8:14–17

sorcery (SOR-sir-ee) *trying to put magical spells on people or harming them by magic,* Acts 8:9–25; 19:18–19
- warnings against, Leviticus 19:26; Deuteronomy 18:14–15; 2 Kings 17:17

soul (SOLE) *what makes a person alive. Sometimes the Bible writers used words like "heart" and "soul" to mean a person's whole being or the person himself.*
- "destroy the soul and the body," Matthew 10:28
- losing, Matthew 16:26
- "all your heart and all your soul," Matthew 22:37
- joined with the spirit, Hebrews 4:12

sower, *someone who plants seeds to grow into crops,* Matthew 13:1–43; 2 Corinthians 9:6

Spirit (SPIH-rit) See "Holy Spirit."

spirit, *the part of humans that was made to be like God because God is spirit. The New Testament also talks about evil spirits.* Isaiah 26:9; 1 Thessalonians 5:23; James 2:26
- evil spirit, Matthew 12:43; Mark 1:23; 5:2; Luke 4:33

spiritual dryness, See "spirituality."

spiritual gifts, *special talents or abilities that God gives his people,* Romans 12:6–8; 1 Corinthians 12:1–11; 14; Ephesians 4:7–13

spirituality, See article on page 1163.
- spiritual growth, 1 Corinthians 3:1
- living sacrifices to God, Romans 12:1–21

spring, *a natural fountain,* Genesis 7:11; Exodus 15:27

staff, *a shepherd's walking stick,* Exodus 4:1–5; 7:8–12; Numbers 20:6–11; Psalm 23:4

steal, See also "robber."
- commands against, Exodus 20:15; Matthew 19:18; Romans 13:9; Ephesians 4:28

Stephen (STEE-ven) *one of the seven men chosen to serve the church in Jerusalem; the first martyr for Christ.*
- chosen to serve the church, Acts 6:5–6
- killed by the Jews, Acts 6:8–7:60

stewardship, See article on page 1173.
- of God's secrets, 1 Corinthians 4:1
- over the earth, Genesis 1:26–28
- servants of God, Luke 12:42–48

stone, See article on page 1348.
- the living "stone," 1 Peter 2:4
- "would cry out," Luke 19:40
- at Jacob and Laban's agreement, Genesis 31:43–53

stoning, *a way of killing someone by throwing rocks at him.*
- commanded, Deuteronomy 17:2–7
- Naboth stoned, 1 Kings 21:13
- Stephen stoned, Acts 7:54–60
- Paul stoned, Acts 14:19

strength
- love God with all your strength, Deuteronomy 6:5; Mark 12:30
- God as the source, Psalms 18:1; 73:26; Philippians 4:13; 1 Peter 4:11

stress, See article on page 1325.
- opportunity for God's glory, James 1:2–8
- give worries to God, 1 Peter 5:7
- peace from the Lord, Matthew 14:27

stronghold, *a fortress, a well protected place,* 1 Samuel 22:4; 2 Samuel 5:17

stubbornness, See article on page 1024.
- despite Jesus' miracles, John 12:37–41
- in Pharaoh, Exodus 4:21; 7:3; 10:1, 20, 27
- in Israel's continuing sin, Amos 4:6–12

success, See article on page 479.
- of God's people, Psalm 1:3
- driven by jealousy, Ecclesiastes 4:4
- Christ teaches on, Matthew 5:1–10

suffering
- proper attitude toward, 2 Corinthians 1:3–7; James 5:10
- value of, Romans 8:17–18; 1 Peter 3:8–17
- of Jesus, Isaiah 53:3–10; Luke 24:26, 46; Philippians 3:10; Hebrews 2:18

swaddling clothes, *pieces of cloth that were wrapped around a newborn baby in Jesus' time,* Luke 2:7–12

sword
- of fire, Genesis 3:24
- a weapon, Joshua 5:13; 1 Samuel 17:45; Matthew 26:51–52
- the word of God, Ephesians 6:17; Hebrews 4:12

Sychar (SY-kar) *a small town in Samaria near Jacob's well,* John 4:5–6

synagogue (SIN-uh-gog) *"a meeting." By the first century, the Jews met in synagogues to read and study the Scriptures. The building was also used as the Jewish court and as a school.*
- Jesus taught in, Matthew 4:23; Mark 1:21; Luke 4:16–17
- Paul spoke there, Acts 17:1, 10

Syria (SEER-ee-uh) *an area north of Galilee and east of the Mediterranean Sea; called "Aram" in Old Testament times.* See "Aram."
- enemy of Israel, 1 Kings 11:25; 20:1–34; 2 Kings 13:22–25
- learned about Jesus, Matthew 4:24

T

tabernacle (TAB-er-NAK-'l) See "Meeting Tent."

table fellowship, See "Lord's Supper."

tablets of the agreement, *two flat stones on which God wrote the Ten Commandments.*
- given to Moses, Exodus 19–20; 24:12–18
- broken by Moses, Exodus 32:15–19
- the second tablets, Exodus 34:1–4
- in the Most Holy Place, Hebrews 9:4

Tabitha (TAB-eh-thuh) See "Dorcas."

Tabor, Mount (TAY-bur) *in the Valley of Jezreel about twelve miles from Lake Galilee,* Judges 4:6–16; Psalm 89:12

tambourine (tam-bah-REEN) *a musical instrument that is beaten to keep rhythm,* Exodus 15:20; 1 Samuel 18:6; Psalm 81:2

Tarshish (TAR-shish) *a city somewhere on the western side of the Mediterranean Sea,* Jonah 1:3; 4:2

Tarsus (TAR-sus) *the most important city in Cilicia, which is now the country of Turkey,* Acts 9:30; 11:25–26
- home of Paul, Acts 9:11; 21:39; 22:3

tax collector, *a Jew hired by the Romans to collect taxes,* Matthew 9:10–11
- Matthew, Matthew 10:3; Luke 5:27
- Zacchaeus, Luke 19:1–10

teacher
- Jesus called a, Matthew 8:19; Mark 10:17; John 1:38; 3:2
- in the church, Romans 12:7; Ephesians 4:11; 1 Timothy 4:13
- false, 1 Timothy 4:1–5; 2 Peter 2:1
- to be judged more strictly, James 3:1

teaching
- commanded, Deuteronomy 6:1–7; Matthew 28:20; 2 Timothy 2:2, 14–15; Titus 2

Teachings of Moses, *or the "Law of Moses,"* Deuteronomy 31:24–26; Joshua 23:6; Nehemiah 8
- purpose of, Romans 3:20; 5:20; Galatians 3:21–25
- limitations of, Romans 8:3; Galatians 2:19; Hebrews 10:1

temple (TEM-p'l) *a building where people worship. God told the Jewish people to worship him at the Temple in Jerusalem.*
- Solomon's Temple, 1 Kings 6–8; 2 Chronicles 2–7
- the Temple rebuilt, Ezra 3
- the body as a temple, John 2:19–22; 1 Corinthians 3:16–17; 6:19–20; 2 Corinthians 6:16

temptation (temp-TAY-shun) *the devil's attempt to get us to do something wrong.*
- Jesus tempted, Matthew 4:1–11; Luke 4:1–13; Hebrews 4:15–16
- a way of escape from, 1 Corinthians 10:13
- source of, James 1:13–15

Ten Commandments, *the rules God gave Moses on Mount Sinai,* Exodus 20:1–20; 31:18; 34:1–28; Deuteronomy 5:1–22

tent
- Abram's tents, Genesis 13:18
- peg, Judges 4:21–22
- makers of, Acts 18:3

Tent, See "Meeting Tent."

test, See "temptation."

Thaddaeus (THAD-ee-us) *one of the twelve apostles,* Matthew 10:3; Mark 3:18

thankfulness, Psalm 107:1; 1 Thessalonians 5:8; Hebrews 12:28

Theophilus (thee-AHF-ih-lus) *the person to whom the books of Luke and Acts were written,* Luke 1:1–4; Acts 1:1

Thessalonica (THES-ah-lah-NY-kah) *the capital of the country of Macedonia, which is now northern Greece,* 1 Thessalonians 1:1; 2 Thessalonians 1:1
- Paul preached there, Acts 17:1–9

Thomas (TOM-us) *Didymus; one of the twelve apostles,* Matthew 10:2–3
- questioned Jesus, John 14:5–7
- saw Jesus after resurrection, John 20:24–29; 21:2

thorn, *sharp points on a branch or stem of a plant.*
- as a curse on Adam, Genesis 3:17–18
- crown of, Matthew 27:29; Mark 15:17; John 19:2–5

threshing floor, *a place where farmers separated grain from chaff. This was done by beating the stalks on the hard ground, throwing them in the air, and letting the wind blow the chaff away.*
- angel visited Gideon there, Judges 6:11
- David bought, 2 Samuel 24:16–25

throne
- king's throne, 1 Kings 10:18–19
- God's throne, Matthew 5:34; Hebrews 4:16; Revelation 3:21; 4

Thummim (THUM-im) *the Urim and Thummim may have been gems. They were attached to the holy vest of the high priest and were used to learn God's will.* Exodus 28:29–30; Leviticus 8:8; Deuteronomy 33:8

Thyatira (THY-ah-TY-rah) *an important city in Asia famous for its purple cloth,* Acts 16:13–14; Revelation 1:11; 2:18–29

Tiberius Caesar (tie-BEER-ee-us SEE-zur) *Roman emperor during the last half of Jesus' life,* Luke 3:1

Tiglath-Pileser (TIG-lath-peh-LEE-zur) *king of Assyria who helped Ahaz; also called "Pul."*
- attacked Israel, 2 Kings 15:19–20
- rescued Ahaz, 2 Kings 16:7–10

Tigris (TY-gris) *a great river in the eastern part of the Bible lands,* Genesis 2:14; Daniel 10:4

time, See article on page 581.
- "a time for everything," Ecclesiastes 3:1–8
- for rest, Exodus 20:8–11
- wise use of, Ephesians 5:15–17

Timothy (TIM-oh-thee) *close friend and helper of the apostle Paul.*
- helped Paul, Acts 16:1–3; 17:13–16; 1 Corinthians 4:17
- instructed by Paul, 1 and 2 Timothy

tithe (TIETH) *"tenth." The Jews were told to give one-tenth of what they earned to God.* Leviticus 27:30–32; Deuteronomy 12:1–6; Luke 11:42; 18:12

Titus (TIE-tus) *trusted friend and helper of the apostle Paul.*
- helped Corinthians, 2 Corinthians 7:6–7, 13–15; 8:6, 16, 23
- appointed elders, Titus 1:4–5
- Paul's instructions to, Titus 1–3

Tobiah (toe-BY-uh) *tried to keep Nehemiah from rebuilding the walls of Jerusalem,* Nehemiah 2:10–20; 6:10–19; 13:4–9

tomb
- of Lazarus, John 11:38–44
- of Jesus, Matthew 27:57–28:15; Mark 15:42–16:30; Luke 23:50–24:12; John 19:38–20:9

tongue
- lying tongue hated by God, Proverbs 6:16–17
- cannot be tamed, James 3:2–12

tongues, speaking in, See Article on Page 1204.
- as a spiritual gift, 1 Corinthians 14
- Pentecost, Acts 2
- non-Jews, Acts 10:44–48

tower of Babel, See "Babel."

transfiguration (tranz-fig-you-RAY-shun) *"to change." Jesus was transfigured in front of Peter, James, and John when his face and clothes began to shine brightly.* Matthew 17:1–9; Mark 9:2–9; Luke 9:28–36

tree
- of knowledge of good and evil, Genesis 2:9; 3:3
- of life, Genesis 2:9; Revelation 2:7; 22:2, 14
- people compared to, Psalms 1:3; 92:12; Jeremiah 17:8; Matthew 3:10; 12:33
- cross described as a tree, Galatians 3:13

trespass, See "sin."

tribe, *all descendants of a certain person. The twelve tribes of Israel were descendants of the twelve sons of Jacob, who was later named "Israel."* Numbers 1–2
- Canaan divided among, Joshua 13:7–33; 15–19

trinity, See article on page 801.
- baptizing in the name of, Matthew 28:18–20
- in Paul's salutation, 2 Corinthians 13:14
- the unity of, Ephesians 4:3–6

triumphal entry (tri-UMF-ul) *the time Jesus entered Jerusalem just before his death,* Matthew 21:1–11; Mark 11:1–19; Luke 19:28–44; John 12:12–15

Troas (TRO-az) *one of the most important cities in northwest Asia,* Acts 16:8–10; 20:5–12; 2 Corinthians 2:12

Trophimus (TROF-eh-mus) *non-Jewish Christian who traveled with Paul,* Acts 20:3–4; 21:27–29; 2 Timothy 4:20

trumpet (TRUM-pet) *in Bible times it was made from animal horns; used to call an army together or announce something important,* Numbers 10:2–10; Joshua 6:4–20; 1 Corinthians 15:52

trust
- a duty, Luke 16:11; 1 Corinthians 4:2; Titus 2:10
- in God, Psalm 20:7; Proverbs 3:5; 16:20; Romans 4:5; 10:11; 1 Peter 2:6
- in lesser things, Psalms 49:13–14; 118:9; Proverbs 11:28; Isaiah 2:22

truth
- speaking honestly, Psalm 15:2; Proverbs 16:13
- God's message, John 17:17; Romans 1:25; Ephesians 1:13; 1 John 1:6

tunic (TOO-nik) *a kind of coat,* Exodus 28:39–40; John 19:23

Tychicus (TIK-ih-kus) *Christian from Asia who did important jobs for Paul,* Acts 20:4; Ephesians 6:21–22; Colossians 4:7–9

Tyre (TIRE) *large, important city in Phoenicia, which is now part of the country of Lebanon,* Mark 7:24–31; Acts 12:20
- Hiram, king of, 2 Samuel 5:11; 1 Kings 9:10–14; 2 Chronicles 2
- a wicked city, Matthew 11:21–22; Luke 10:13–14

U

unbelief, See "faith."
uncircumcised, See "circumcision."
unclean, *the state of a person, animal, or action that was not pleasing to God. In the Old Testament God said certain animals were unclean and were not to be eaten. If a person disobeyed the rules about being clean, he was called unclean and could not serve God until he was made clean again.* See "clean."
- unclean animals, Leviticus 11; Acts 10:9–15
- unclean people, Leviticus 12–15
- God declared everyone to be clean, Acts 10

unity, See Article on Page 1273.
- one faith, Ephesians 4:5
- of God and Christ, John 17:11, 21
- "be completely joined together," 1 Corinthians 1:10–13

unleavened bread (un-LEV-'nd BREAD) *bread made without yeast.*
- used in the Passover Feast, Exodus 12:20; Deuteronomy 16:1–4

Unleavened Bread, Day of, *the first day of the Feast of Unleavened Bread or Passover,* Matthew 26:17; Luke 22:7
upper room, *upstairs room in a house.*
- Jesus and his followers met there, Mark 14:14–15; Luke 22:9–12

Ur, *a great city thousands of years ago; today in the country of Iraq.*
- home of Abram, Genesis 11:28–31

Uriah (you-RY-uh) *a soldier in King David's army.*
- killed by David, 2 Samuel 11

Urim (YOUR-im) See "Thummim."
Uzzah (UZ-uh) *touched the Ark of the Agreement and died,* 2 Samuel 6:1–8; 1 Chronicles 13:1–14
Uzziah (uh-ZY-uh) *a king of Judah,* 2 Kings 15:13–15; 2 Chronicles 26; Isaiah 6:1

V

Vashti (VASH-ty) *the wife of Ahasuerus, king of Persia,* Esther 1:1–20
veil (VALE) *a head covering usually worn by women; also, a curtain in the Temple.*
- worn by women, Genesis 24:65; Song of Solomon 4:1; Isaiah 3:19
- the Temple veil, Matthew 27:51; Mark 15:38; Luke 23:45

vest, holy, *"ephod"; a special type of clothing for the priests in the Old Testament. The holy vest for the high priest had gold and gems on it.*
- description of, Exodus 25:7; 28:6–14; 39:2–7
- one made by Micah, Judges 17:1–5; 18:14–20
- worn by David, 2 Samuel 6:14

vine
- fruit of the, Matthew 26:29; Mark 14:25; Luke 22:18
- Jesus as the, John 15:1–11

vineyard
- Naboth's, 1 Kings 21
- parables of, Matthew 20:1–16; 21:28–46; Mark 12:1–12; Luke 20:9–19

virgin (VUR-jin) *person who has not had sexual relations,* Deuteronomy 22:13–29; Isaiah 7:14; Matthew 1:23; Luke 1:34
vision (VIZ-zhun) *like a dream. God often spoke to his people in visions.*
- of Abram, Genesis 15:1
- of Daniel, Daniel 2:19
- of Peter and Cornelius, Acts 10:1–16
- of Paul, Acts 16:9

vow, *a special and serious promise often made to God.*
- rules about, Numbers 30; Deuteronomy 23:21–23
- the Nazirite, Numbers 6:1–21
- of Jephthah, Judges 11:29–40
- of Paul, Acts 18:18

W

war
- rumors of, Matthew 24:6–7; Mark 13:7–8; Luke 21:9–10
- spiritual, 2 Corinthians 10:3–4
- will end, Micah 4:1–3

warrior, divine, See "Holy War."
watchman
- examples of, 2 Samuel 18:24–27; Psalm 130:6
- prophets as watchmen, Ezekiel 3:17; Micah 7:4

water
- in creation, Genesis 1:1–2, 6–10
- bitter, Exodus 15:22–27
- from a rock, Exodus 17:1–7
- for David, 2 Samuel 23:15–17
- drink of, Matthew 10:42; Mark 9:41
- Jesus walked on, Matthew 14:22–36
- turned to wine, John 2:1–11
- living water, John 4:1–15

way, See article on page 470.
- two ways to live, Psalm 1
- Christ as the way, John 14:6
- the Way of Jesus, Acts 19:23; Acts 24:22

"Way, the," *one of the earliest names given to Christians. Jesus said he was "the way" to reach God.* Acts 9:1–2; 19:9, 23; 22:4; 24:14, 22
weapons, See article on page 1286.
- the armor of God, Ephesians 6:10–18
- not of this world, 2 Corinthians 10:4
- "killed with swords," Matthew 26:52

wedding, Matthew 22:1–14; Luke 14:8; John 2:1–11
Western Sea, See "Mediterranean Sea."

widow
- examples of, Ruth 4:10; 1 Kings 17:8–24; Luke 21:2–4
- care for, Deuteronomy 24:17–22; 1 Timothy 5:3–16; James 1:27

wife
- man united with, Genesis 2:24
- the good wife, Proverbs 31:10–31
- teachings about, 1 Corinthians 7:1–16
- responsibility of, Ephesians 5:21–24, 33; Colossians 3:18; 1 Peter 3:1

wilderness, *a desert area,* See article on page 812.
- John baptizes in, Mark 1:1–8; Matthew 3:1–6,13–17
- Israel in, Deuteronomy 8:1–5; 32:10
- will blossom, Isaiah 35

wine
- danger of, Proverbs 20:1; Ephesians 5:18
- at wedding in Cana, John 2:1–11
- for the stomach, 1 Timothy 5:23

winepress, *a pit where grapes were mashed to get the juice out. The winepress is sometimes used to describe how enemy armies will defeat people as if they were grapes crushed in a winepress.*
- examples of, Judges 6:11; Matthew 21:33
- as a symbol of punishment, Lamentations 1:15; Revelation 14:19–20; 19:15

wisdom (WIZ-d'm) *understanding what is really important in life. This wisdom comes from God.* Proverbs 1:1–2, 7; 2; 4
- Solomon asked for, 1 Kings 4:29–34
- source of, James 1:5
- a parable about, Matthew 25:1–13

wise men, *"magi"; men who studied the stars,* Genesis 41:8; Exodus 7:11; Matthew 2:1–12

witchcraft, *using the power of the devil to do magic.*
- warnings against, Deuteronomy 18:10–12; Galatians 5:19–21
- examples of, 2 Kings 9:22; 2 Chronicles 33:6

witness, Acts 1:8, 22; 2:32; 22:14–15

woman
- created by God, Genesis 2:22–23
- how to treat a, 1 Timothy 5:2, 14

word, *in the Bible often means God's message to us in the Scriptures. Jesus is called the "Word" because he shows us what God is like.*
- like a lamp, Psalm 119:105
- like a sword, Hebrews 4:12
- living in God's people, John 15:7; Colossians 3:16; 1 John 2:14
- lasts forever, Matthew 24:35; 1 Peter 1:25
- people's words, Proverbs 12:25; 25:11; Matthew 12:36–37
- as a message, 1 Peter 1:24–25; 1 John 2:14
- Jesus as the "Word," John 1:1–5, 14; 1 John 1:1–2

work, See article on page 69.
- those who won't, 2 Thessalonians 3:6–13
- of the vineyard workers, Matthew 20:1–16
- laziness, Proverbs 26:14–16

world, *the planet Earth; also the people on this earth who follow Satan.*
- as the Earth, 2 Samuel 22:16; Psalm 18:15
- as a symbol of wickedness, Romans 12:2; Ephesians 2:2

worship, *to praise and serve God.*
- commanded, Exodus 34:14; Luke 4:8; John 4:20–24

X

Xerxes (ZERK-sees) *a king of Persia; also called "Ahasuerus,"* Esther 1–10

Y

yeast (YEEST) *an ingredient used to make breads and cakes rise; used in the New Testament to stand for a person's influence over others.* See also "unleavened bread."
- as a symbol for influence, Mark 8:15; Luke 13:21

yoke, *a wooden frame that fits on the necks of animals to hold them together while working.*
- examples of, Deuteronomy 21:3; 1 Kings 19:19–21

youth
- "Remember your Creator," Ecclesiastes 12:1
- teachings about, 1 Timothy 4:12

Z

Zacchaeus (za-KEE-us) *Jewish tax collector in the city of Jericho,* Luke 19:1–8

Zadok (ZAY-dok) *priest who helped King David,* 2 Samuel 15:24–36; 17:15–21; 1 Kings 1:18–45

Zarephath (ZAIR-eh-fath) *a Canaanite town where Elijah helped a widow,* 1 Kings 17:8–24; Luke 4:25–26

Zealots (ZEL-ots) *a group of Jewish men also called "Enthusiasts." They hated the Romans for controlling their home country, and they planned to force the Romans out.*
- Simon the Zealot, Luke 6:15; Acts 1:13

Zebedee (ZEB-uh-dee) *a fisherman on Lake Galilee,* Matthew 4:21–22; Mark 1:19–20

Zechariah, father of John the Baptist, (ZEK-uh-RY-uh) *a Jewish priest,* Luke 1:5–25, 57–80

Zechariah, king of Israel, *ruled for only six months; killed by Shallum,* 2 Kings 14:29; 15:8–11

Zechariah, son of Berekiah, *a prophet who wrote the next-to-the-last book in the Old Testament,* Ezra 5:1; Zechariah 1–14

Zechariah, son of Jehoiada, *a priest who taught the people to serve God,* 2 Chronicles 24:20–25

Zedekiah, son of Josiah, (zed-ee-KY-uh) *the last king of Judah,* 2 Kings 24:16–25:7

Zedekiah, son of Kenaanah, *a false prophet during the time of King Ahab,* 1 Kings 22:1–24

Zedekiah, son of Maaseiah, *a false prophet in Babylon during the time of Jeremiah,* Jeremiah 29:21–23

Zephaniah (zef-uh-NY-uh) *a prophet who lived when Josiah was king of Judah; wrote the short book of Zephaniah,* Zephaniah 1:1

Zerubbabel (zeh-RUB-uh-bull) *governor of Jerusalem after the Jews had been in captivity in Babylon for seventy years.*
- returned from exile, Ezra 2:2
- built the altar of God, Ezra 3:1–6
- rebuilt the Temple, Ezra 3:7–10; 5:2

Ziba (ZY-buh) *a servant of Saul,* 2 Samuel 9:1–11; 16:1–4; 19:24–30

Zimri (ZIM-rye) *a king of Israel,* 1 Kings 16:11–20

Zion (ZY-on) *a hill inside the city of Jerusalem.* See "Mount Zion."

Ziph (ZIF) *a city about twenty-five miles south of Jerusalem,* 1 Samuel 23:14–28; 26:1–25

Zipporah (zih-PO-ruh) *the wife of Moses,* Exodus 2:15–22; 4:24–26; 18:1–3

zither (ZITH-ur) *a type of musical instrument that had about forty strings on it,* Ezekiel 3:5, 7, 10, 15

Additional Study Tools

Index of Thematic Articles &
One-Year Daily Bible Study Plan

Money of Bible Times

Table of Weights and Measures

Maps of Bible Lands

Index of Thematic Articles & One-Year Daily Bible Study Plan

To enhance your personal Bible study and meditation time, may we suggest that you choose a topic that interests you from the alphabetical list below for each day of the week (Monday–Friday). Turn to the page number listed beside the topic, and you will find a Thematic Article on the topic.

As you read the article carefully, refer to the text of the *New Century Version* included in this book as scriptures are mentioned. When you have completed the article, follow the helpful chain of additional scriptures indicated by the small chain icon ⚭ at the end of the article. The icon will appear again at the bottom of the page and lead you from scripture to scripture dealing with the theme you have chosen to study for that day. At each turn of the page you will find new insights and valuable information on the theme you are studying. Eventually, the chain will lead you back to the article where you began. End your study time with a prayer asking God to show you how to apply to your life what you have learned.

At the end of one year, you will have successfully covered the two hundred sixty most important topics and ideas in the Bible, lead by highly qualified Bible scholars and teachers. Your Bible knowledge and understanding will expand greatly in that time, and you will come away spiritually enriched and empowered from an exciting journey into the mind and heart of God.

Index to Charts, Illustrations, and Maps

Charts:

Illustrations:

Maps:

MONEY OF BIBLE TIMES

Denarius of Tiberius
16¢

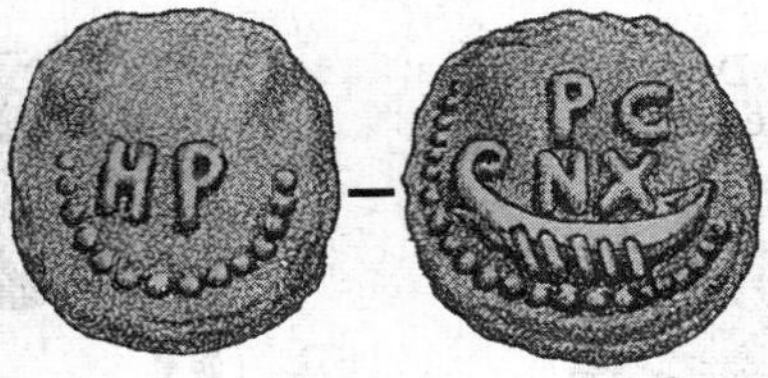

A Mite = 1/8¢

A Silver
Tetradrachm

Coin of
Herod Philip

Denarius of Augustus Caesar
16¢

Coin by
Pontius Pilate

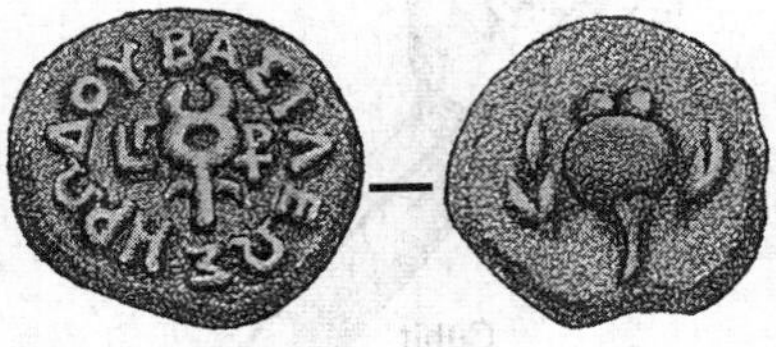

Copper Coin of
Herod the Great

Coin of
Herod Antipas

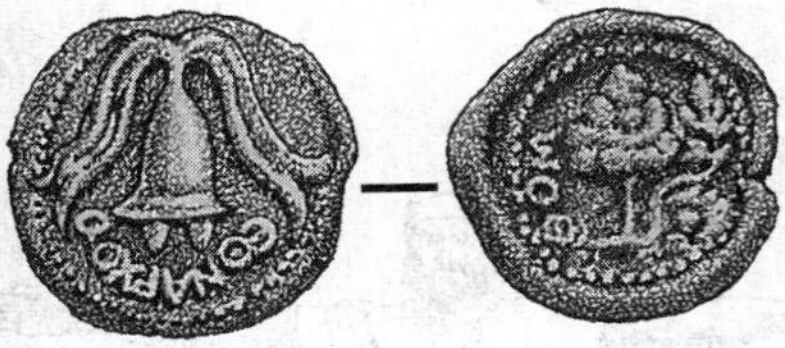

Coin of
Herod Archelaus

Mite of Coponius
1/8¢

Shekel of AD 2
64¢

Ancient Greek
Coin

Macedonian
Coin

TABLE OF WEIGHTS AND MEASURES

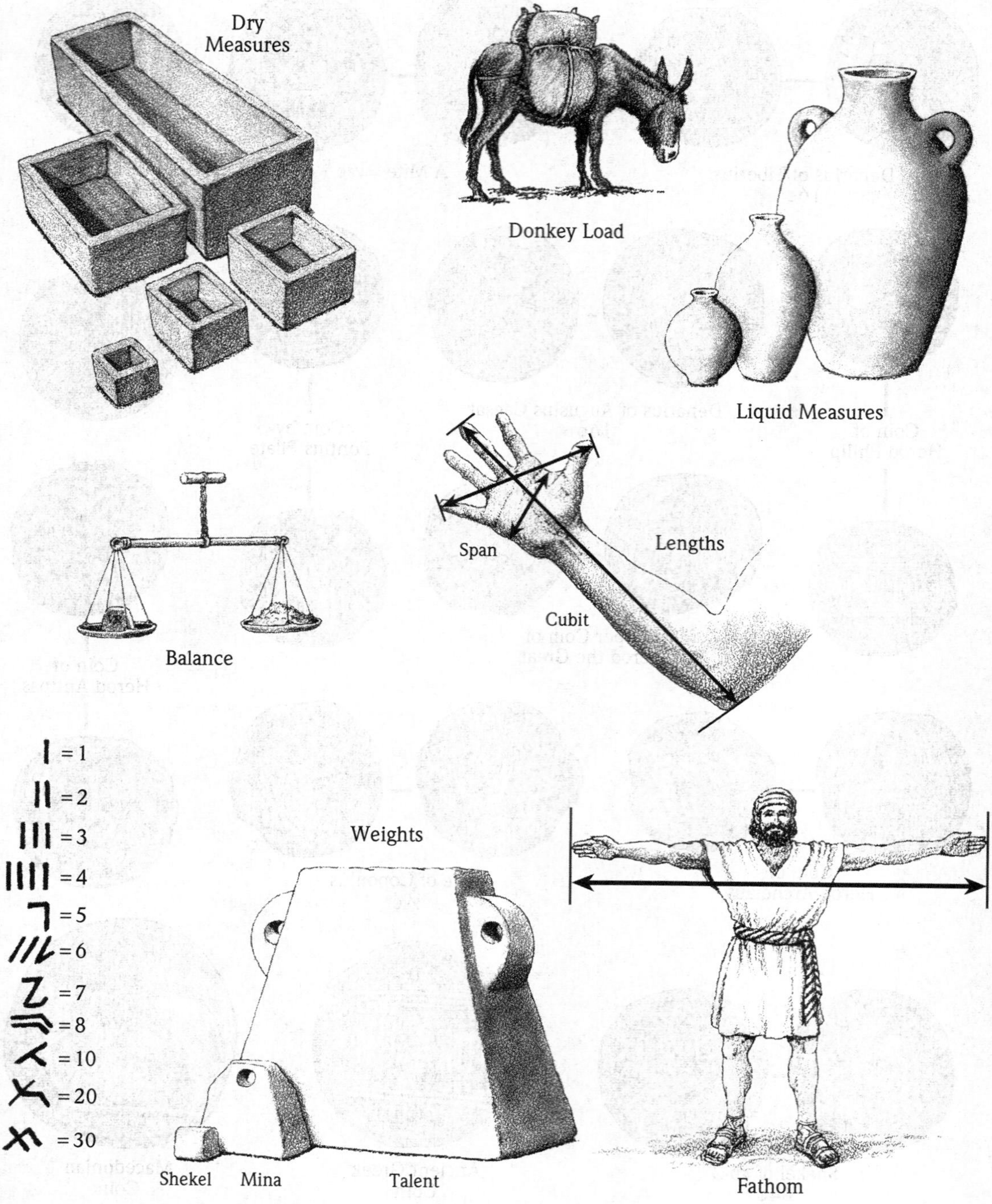

Dry Measures

Donkey Load

Liquid Measures

Balance

Span

Lengths

Cubit

= 1
= 2
= 3
= 4
= 5
= 6
= 7
= 8
= 10
= 20
= 30

Weights

Shekel Mina Talent

Fathom

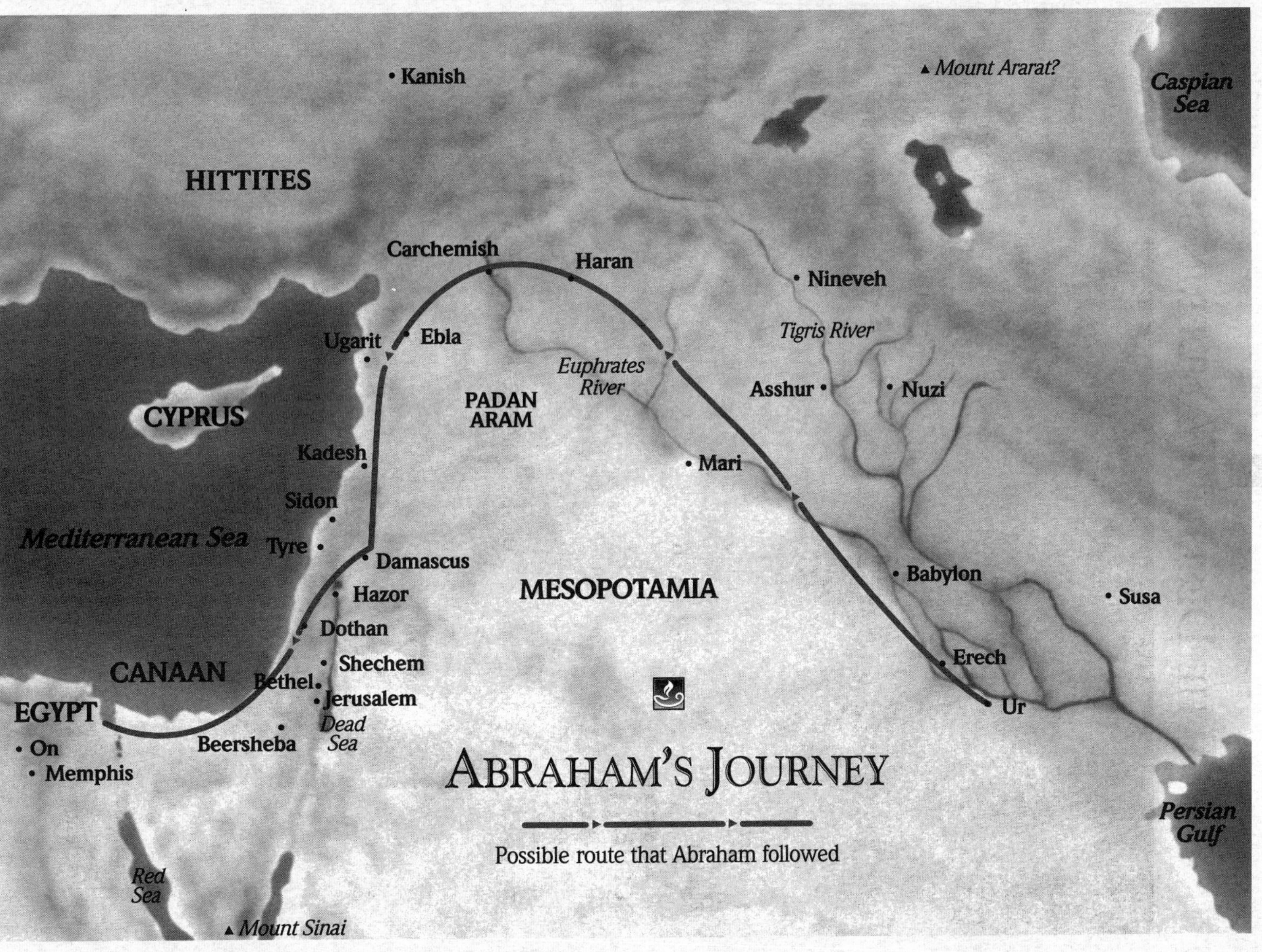

Kanish
Mount Ararat?
Caspian Sea
HITTITES
Carchemish
Haran
Nineveh
Ugarit
Ebla
Tigris River
Euphrates River
Asshur
Nuzi
PADAN ARAM
CYPRUS
Kadesh
Mari
Sidon
Mediterranean Sea
Tyre
Damascus
Babylon
Hazor
MESOPOTAMIA
Susa
Dothan
Erech
Shechem
CANAAN
Bethel
Jerusalem
Ur
EGYPT
Beersheba
Dead Sea
On
Memphis
ABRAHAM'S JOURNEY
Persian Gulf
Possible route that Abraham followed
Red Sea
Mount Sinai

The Desert Wanderings

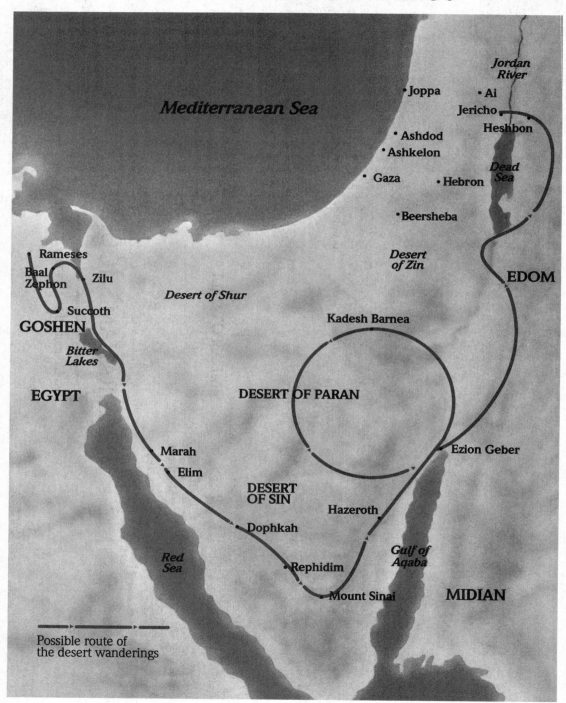

Mediterranean Sea
Jordan River
Joppa
Ai
Jericho
Heshbon
Ashdod
Ashkelon
Dead Sea
Gaza
Hebron
Beersheba
Desert of Zin
Rameses
Baal Zephon
Zilu
Desert of Shur
EDOM
Succoth
GOSHEN
Kadesh Barnea
Bitter Lakes
EGYPT
DESERT OF PARAN
Marah
Ezion Geber
Elim
DESERT OF SIN
Hazeroth
Dophkah
Gulf of Aqaba
Red Sea
Rephidim
Mount Sinai
MIDIAN

Possible route of the desert wanderings

The Twelve Tribes During the Judges

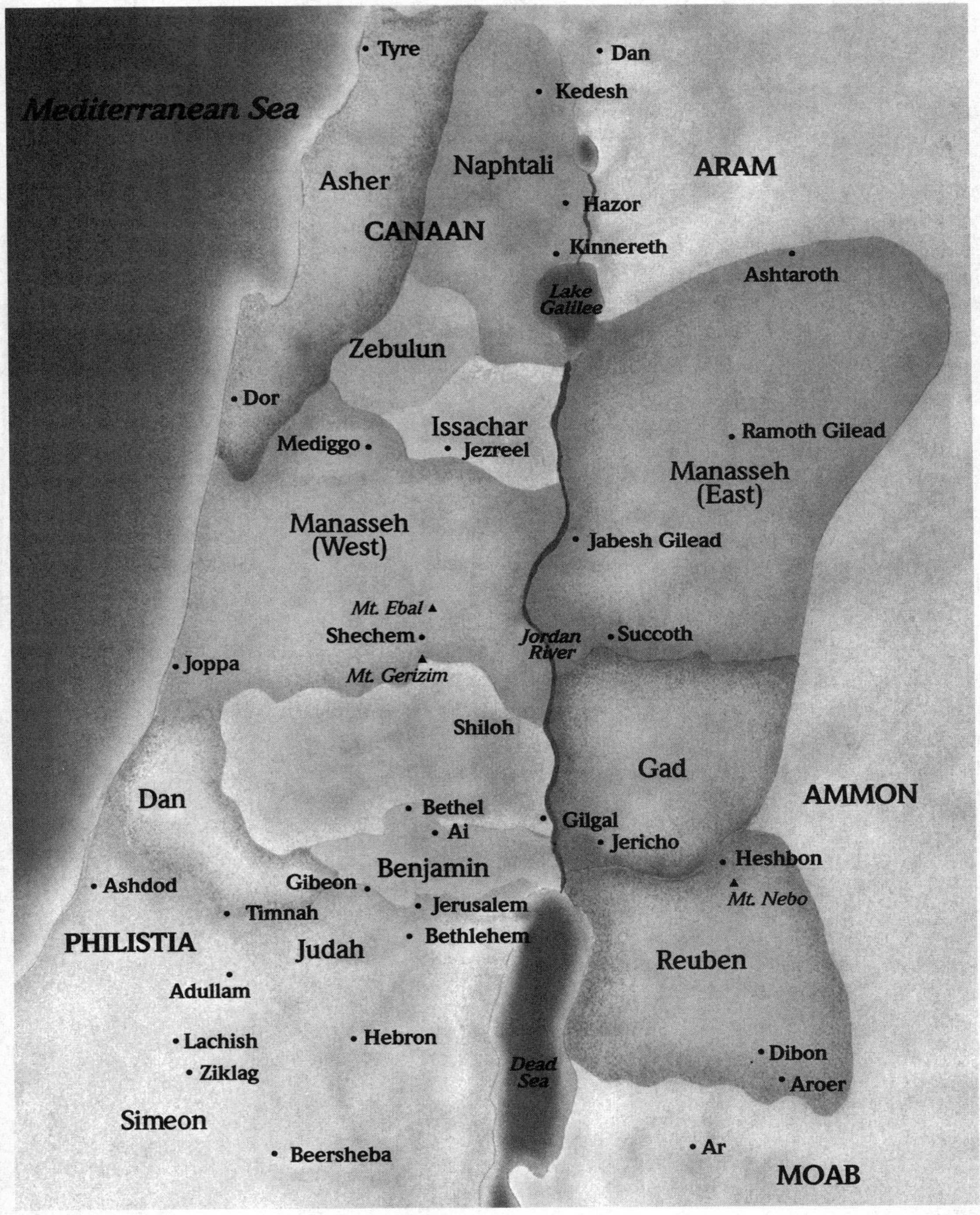
Tyre
Dan
Kedesh
Mediterranean Sea
Asher
Naphtali
ARAM
Hazor
CANAAN
Kinnereth
Ashtaroth
Lake Galilee
Zebulun
Dor
Issachar
Mediggo
Jezreel
Ramoth Gilead
Manasseh (East)
Manasseh (West)
Jabesh Gilead
Mt. Ebal
Shechem
Jordan River
Succoth
Joppa
Mt. Gerizim
Shiloh
Gad
Dan
AMMON
Bethel
Gilgal
Ai
Jericho
Heshbon
Benjamin
Ashdod
Gibeon
Mt. Nebo
Jerusalem
Timnah
PHILISTIA
Bethlehem
Judah
Reuben
Adullam
Lachish
Hebron
Dibon
Dead Sea
Ziklag
Aroer
Simeon
Ar
Beersheba
MOAB

The Kingdoms of Judah and Israel

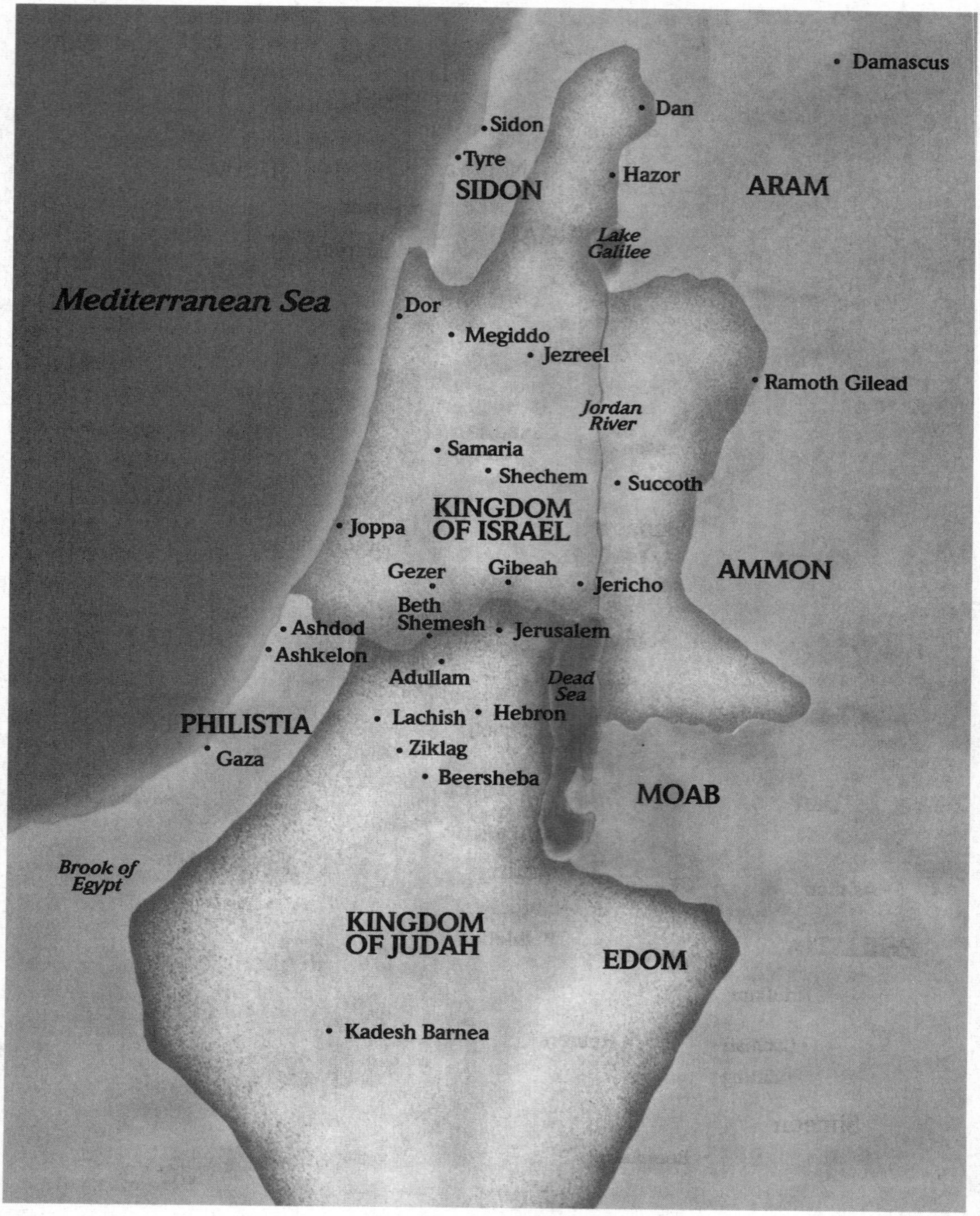

PALESTINE IN JESUS' LIFE

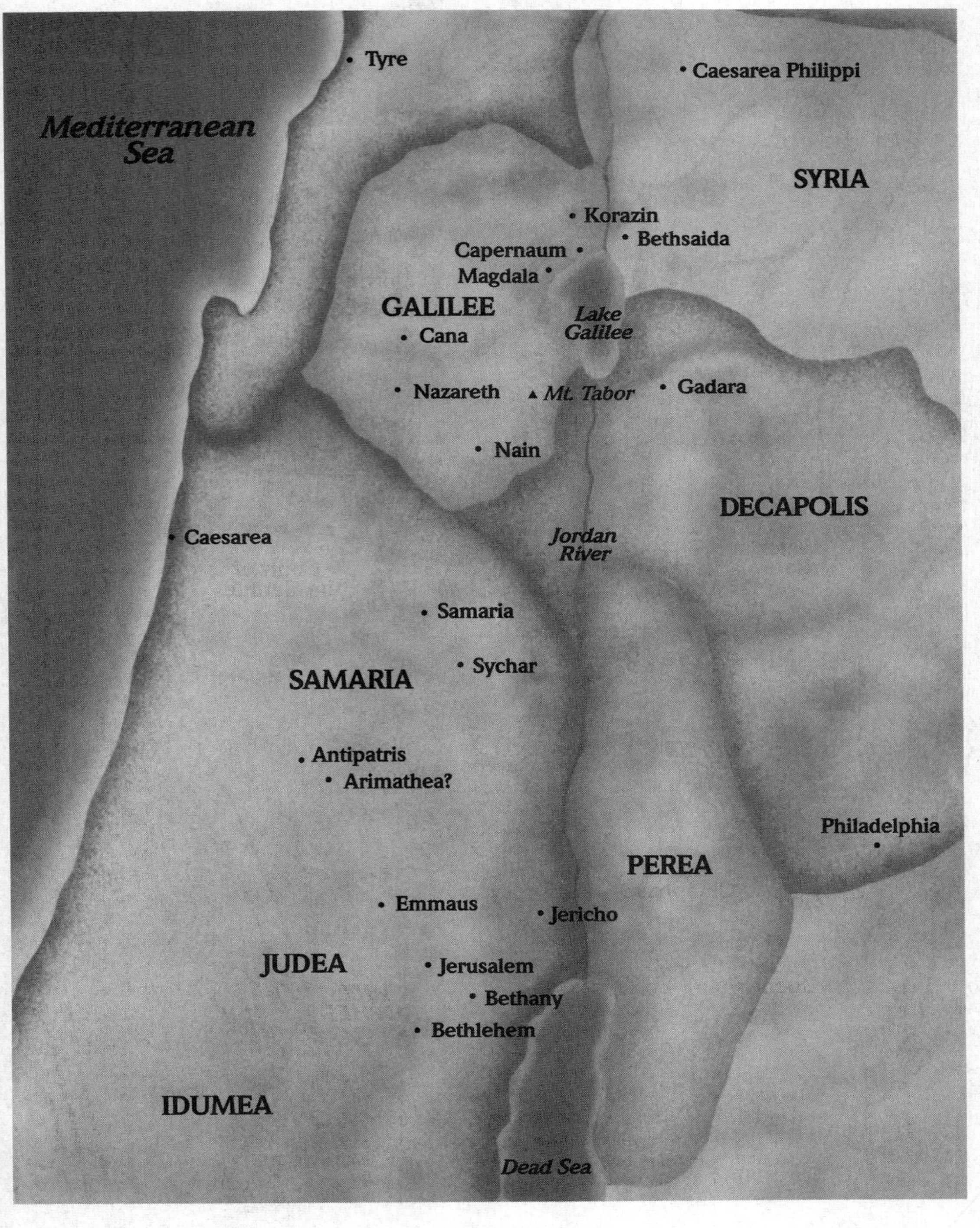

Tyre
Caesarea Philippi
Mediterranean Sea
SYRIA
Korazin
Bethsaida
Capernaum
Magdala
GALILEE
Lake Galilee
Cana
Nazareth
Mt. Tabor
Gadara
Nain
DECAPOLIS
Caesarea
Jordan River
Samaria
Sychar
SAMARIA
Antipatris
Arimathea?
Philadelphia
PEREA
Emmaus
Jericho
JUDEA
Jerusalem
Bethany
Bethlehem
IDUMEA
Dead Sea

JESUS' LAST WEEK IN JERUSALEM

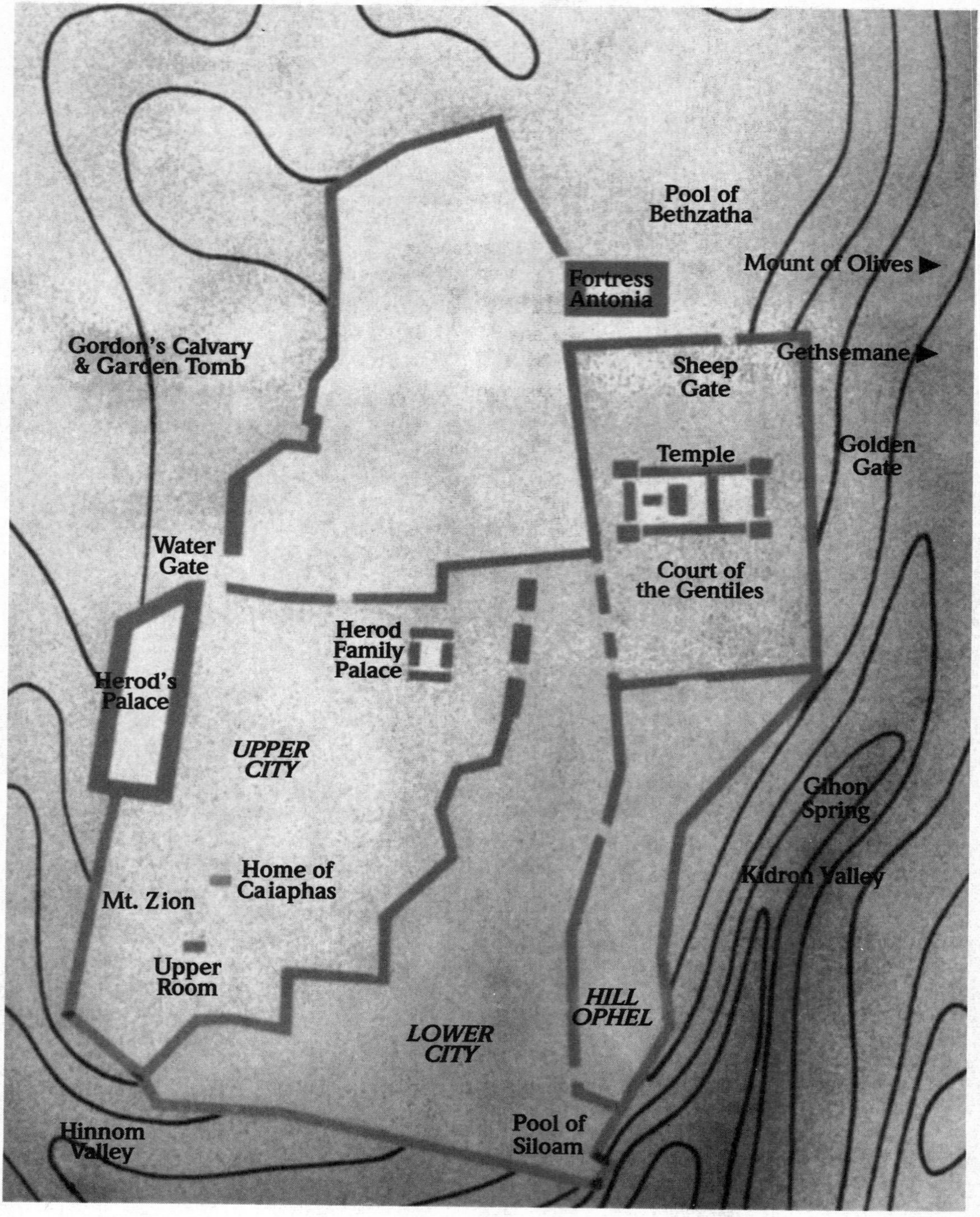

Pool of Bethzatha

Fortress Antonia

Mount of Olives ▶

Gordon's Calvary & Garden Tomb

Sheep Gate

Gethsemane ▶

Temple

Golden Gate

Water Gate

Court of the Gentiles

Herod Family Palace

Herod's Palace

UPPER CITY

Gihon Spring

Home of Caiaphas

Kidron Valley

Mt. Zion

Upper Room

HILL OPHEL

LOWER CITY

Pool of Siloam

Hinnom Valley

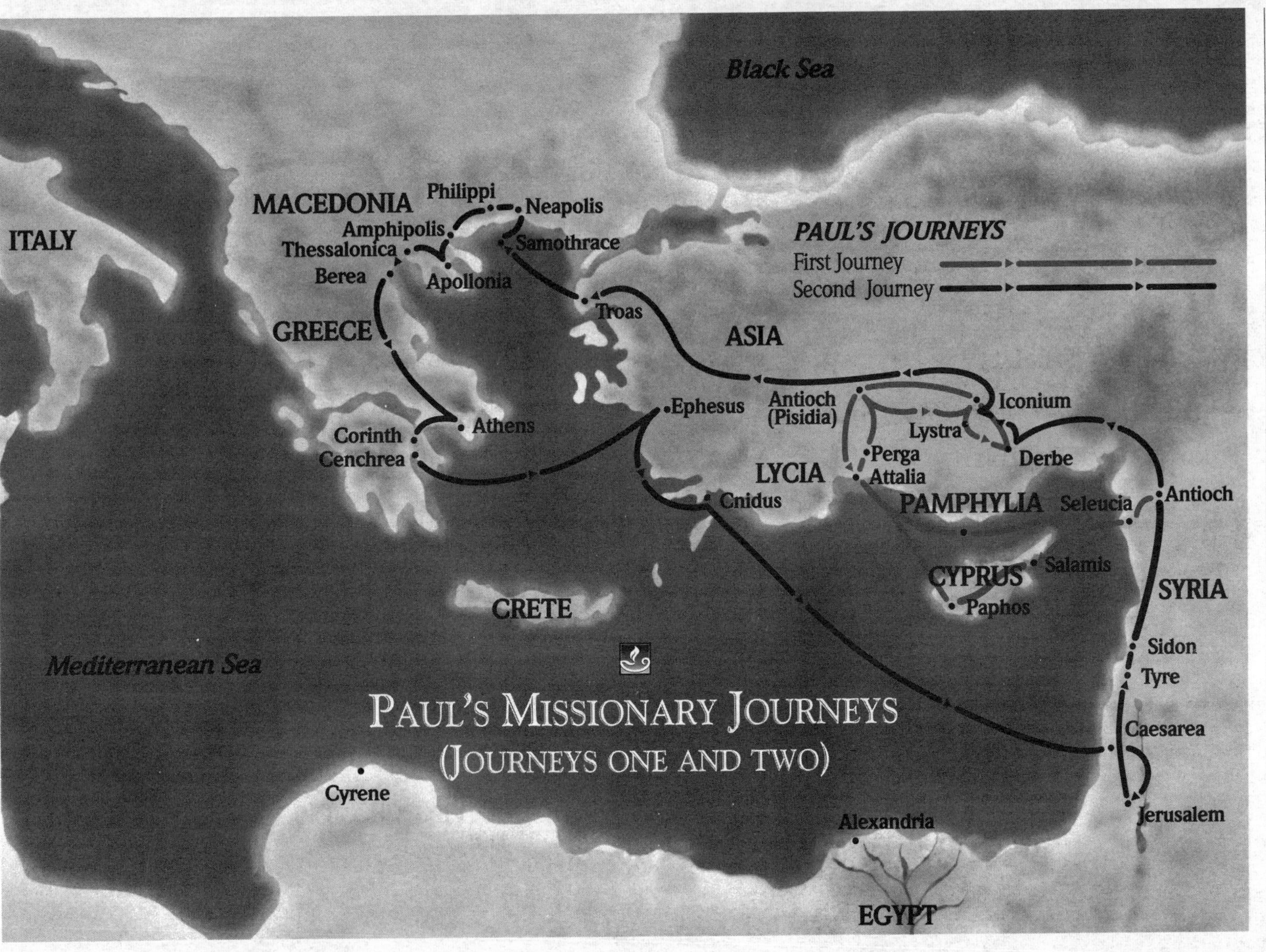
Black Sea
ITALY
MACEDONIA
Philippi
Neapolis
Amphipolis
Samothrace
Thessalonica
Berea
Apollonia
PAUL'S JOURNEYS
First Journey
Second Journey
Troas
GREECE
ASIA
Ephesus
Antioch (Pisidia)
Iconium
Lystra
Athens
Corinth
Cenchrea
Perga
Attalia
Derbe
LYCIA
Cnidus
PAMPHYLIA
Seleucia
Antioch
Salamis
CYPRUS
Paphos
SYRIA
CRETE
Sidon
Mediterranean Sea
Tyre
PAUL'S MISSIONARY JOURNEYS
(JOURNEYS ONE AND TWO)
Caesarea
Cyrene
Jerusalem
Alexandria
EGYPT

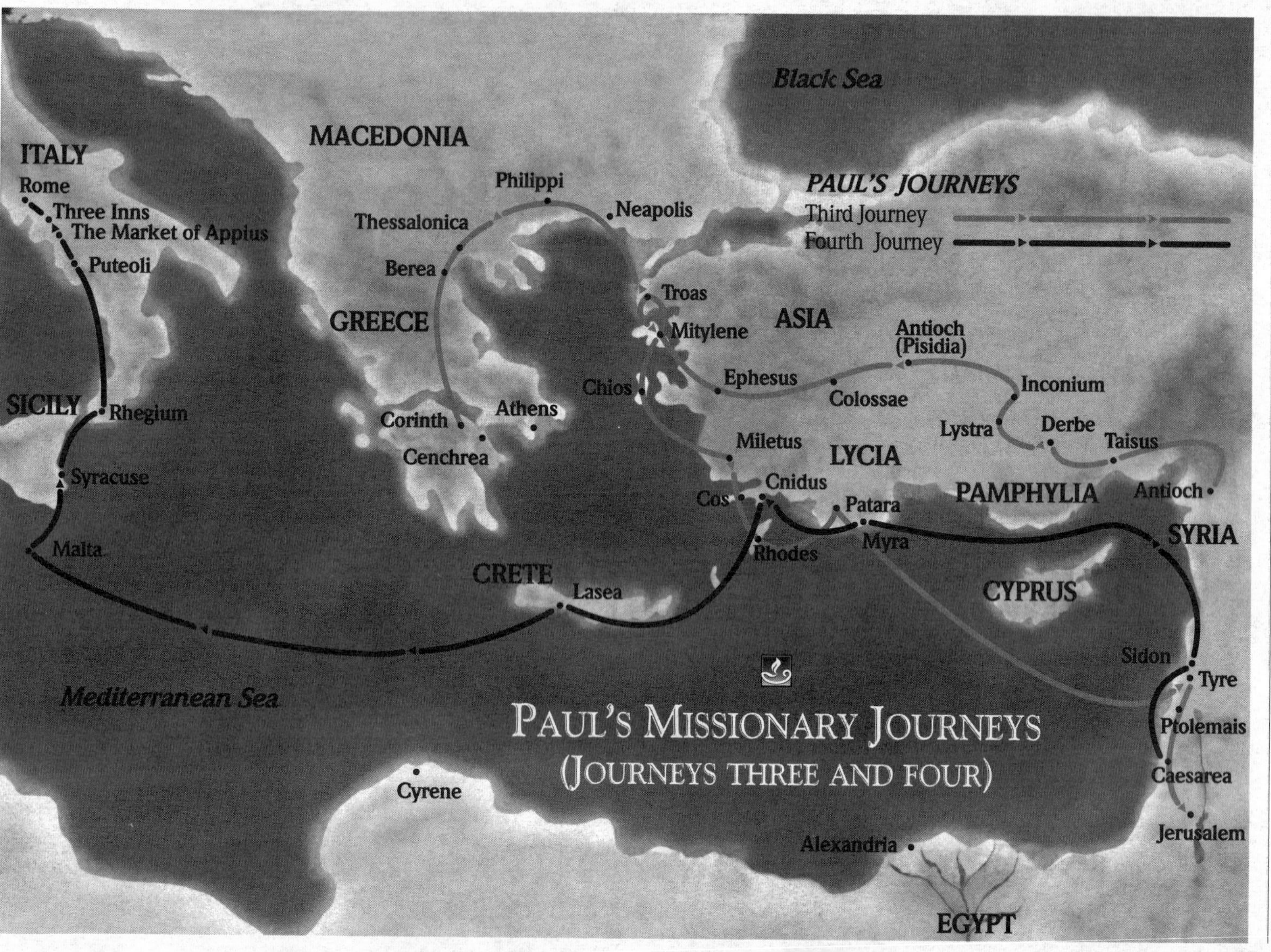

Black Sea
MACEDONIA
ITALY
Rome
Three Inns
The Market of Appius
Puteoli
Philippi
Neapolis
Thessalonica
Berea
PAUL'S JOURNEYS
Third Journey
Fourth Journey
Troas
Mitylene
ASIA
GREECE
Antioch
(Pisidia)
Ephesus
Colossae
Inconium
Chios
SICILY
Rhegium
Corinth
Athens
Cenchrea
Lystra
Derbe
Taisus
Miletus
LYCIA
Syracuse
Cnidus
Cos
Patara
PAMPHYLIA
Antioch
Myra
Rhodes
SYRIA
Malta
CRETE
Lasea
CYPRUS
Sidon
Tyre
Mediterranean Sea
Paul's Missionary Journeys
(Journeys Three and Four)
Ptolemais
Caesarea
Cyrene
Jerusalem
Alexandria
EGYPT